THE YEAR'S WORK 2015

# The Year's Work in English Studies
# Volume 96

Covering work published in 2015

Edited by
## WILLIAM BAKER
and
## KENNETH WOMACK

with associate editors

OLGA FISCHER
A. S. G. EDWARDS
RICHARD WOOD
KIRSTIE BLAIR
KATIE HALSEY
MATTHEW CREASY
THERESA SAXON
JAMES GIFFORD
MARK WILLIAMS

Published for
THE ENGLISH ASSOCIATION

by

## OXFORD
UNIVERSITY PRESS

# OXFORD

Great Clarendon Street, Oxford OX2 6DP, UK

Oxford University Press is a department of the University of Oxford.
It furthers the University's objective of excellence in research, scholarship,
and education by publishing worldwide in

Oxford New York

Athens Auckland Bangkok Bogotá Buenos Aires Cape Town
Chennai Dar es Salaam Delhi Florence Hong Kong Istanbul Karachi
Kolkata Kuala Lumpur Madrid Melbourne Mexico City Mumbai Nairobi
Paris São Paulo Shanghai Taipei Tokyo Toronto Warsaw

Oxford is a registered trade mark of Oxford University Press
in the UK and in certain other countries

British Library Cataloguing in Publication Data
Data available
ISSN 0084-4144
ISBN 9780198820963
1 3 5 7 9 10 8 6 4 2
Typeset by Cenveo publisher services, Bangalore, India
Printed in Great Britain by Bell & Bain, Glasgow

# The English Association

The object of The English Association is to promote the knowledge and appreciation of English language and its literatures.

The Association pursues these aims by creating opportunities of co-operation among all those interested in English; by furthering the recognition of English as essential in education; by discussing methods of English teaching; by holding lectures, conferences, and other meetings; by publishing several journals, books, and leaflets; and by forming local branches overseas and at home. English Association Fellowships recognize distinction and achievement in the field of English worldwide.

## Publications

*The Year's Work in English Studies.* An annual narrative bibliography which aims to cover all work of quality in English studies published in a given year. Published by Oxford University Press.

*The Year's Work in Critical and Cultural Theory.* An annual narrative bibliography which aims to provide comprehensive cover of all work of quality in critical and cultural theory published in a given year. Published by Oxford University Press.

*Essays and Studies.* A well-established series of annual themed volumes edited each year by a distinguished academic.

*English.* This internationally-known journal of the Association is aimed at teachers of English in universities and colleges, with articles on all aspects of literature and critical theory, an extensive reviews section and original poetry. Four issues per year. Published by Oxford University Press.

*Use of English.* The longest-standing journal for English teachers in schools and colleges. Three issues per year.

*English 4–11.* Designed and developed by primary English specialists to give practical help to primary and middle school teachers. Three issues per year.

*English Association Studies.* A monograph series published in association with Liverpool University Press.

*Issues in English.* Occasional pamphlet series.

## Membership

Membership information can be found at http://www.le.ac.uk/engassoc or please write to The English Association, University of Leicester, University Road, Leicester LE1 7RH, UK or email: engassoc@le.ac.uk.

# The Year's Work in English Studies

## Subscriptions for Volume 96

*Institutional* (combined rate to both *The Year's Work in English Studies* and *The Year's Work in Critical and Cultural Theory*) print and online: £487.00/$916.00/ €731.00. *Institutional* (*The Year's Work in English Studies* only) print and online: £337.00/$631.00/€507.00.

Please note: £/€ rates apply in Europe, US$ elsewhere. All prices include postage, and for subscribers outside the UK delivery is by Standard Air. There may be other subscription rates available. For a complete listing, please visit https://academic.oup.com/ywes/oup_journals/ywes/access_purchase/price_list.html.

### Online Access

For details please email Oxford University Press Journals Customer Services on: jnls.cust.serv@oup.com.

### Order Information

Full prepayment, in the correct currency, is required for all orders. Orders are regarded as firm and payments are not refundable. Subscriptions are accepted and entered on a complete volume basis. Claims cannot be considered more than FOUR months after publication or date of order, whichever is later. All subscriptions in Canada are subject to GST. Subscriptions in the EU may be subject to European VAT. If registered, please supply details to avoid unnecessary charges. For subscriptions that include online versions, a proportion of the subscription price may be subject to UK VAT.

*Methods of payment.* (i) Cheque (payable to Oxford University Press, Cashiers Office, Great Clarendon Street, Oxford OX2 6DP, UK) in GB£ Sterling (drawn on a UK bank), US$ Dollars (drawn on a US bank), or EU€ Euros. (ii) Bank transfer to Barclays Bank Plc, Oxford Group Office, Oxford (bank sort code 20-65-18) (UK), overseas only Swift code BARC GB 22 (GB£ Sterling to account no. 70299332, IBAN GB89BARC20651870299332; US$ Dollars to account no. 66014600, IBAN GB27BARC20651866014600; EU€ Euros to account no. 78923655, IBAN GB16BARC20651878923655). (iii) Credit card (Mastercard, Visa, Switch or American Express).

### Back Issues

The current volume plus two back volumes are available from Oxford University Press. Previous volumes can be obtained from the Periodicals Service Company, 11 Main Street, Germantown, NY 12526, USA. Email: psc@periodicals.com; tel: +1 (518) 537 4700; fax: +1 (518) 537 5899.

*Further information.* Journals Customer Service Department, Oxford University Press, Great Clarendon Street, Oxford OX2 6DP, UK. Email: jnls.cust.serv@oup.com; tel (and answerphone outside normal working hours): +44 (0) 1865 353907; fax: +44 (0) 1865 353485. *In the US, please contact:* Journals Customer Service Department, Oxford University Press, 2001 Evans Road, Cary, NC 27513, USA. Email: jnlorders@oup.com; tel (and answerphone outside normal working hours): 800 852 7323 (toll-free in USA/Canada); fax: 919 677 1714. *In Japan, please contact:* Journals Customer Services, Oxford Journals, Oxford University Press, Tokyo, 4-5-10-8F Shiba, Minato-ku, Tokyo 108-8386, Japan. Email: custserv.jp@oup.com; Tel: +81 3 5444 5858; Fax: +81 3 3454 2929.

*The Year's Work in English Studies* (ISSN 0084 4144) is published annually by Oxford University Press, Oxford, UK. Annual subscription price is £337.00/$631.00/ €507.00. *The Year's Work in English Studies* is distributed in the USA by Central Mailing Services c/o UKP Worldwide, 1637 Stelton Road B2, Piscataway, NJ 08854.

US Postmaster: send address changes to *The Year's Work in English Studies*, Oxford University Press, Central Mailing Services c/o UKP Worldwide, 1637 Stelton Road B1-2, Piscataway, NJ 08854.

The Table of Contents email alerting service allows anyone who registers their email address to be notified via email when new content goes online. Details are available at https://academic.oup.com/ywes/cgi/alerts/etoc.

## Permissions

For permissions requests, please visit https://academic.oup.com/permissions.

## Advertising

Inquiries about advertising should be sent to Oxford Journals Advertising, Oxford University Press, Great Clarendon Street, Oxford, OX2 6DP, UK. Email: jnlsadvertising@oup.com; tel: +44 (0) 1865 354767; fax: +44 (0) 1865 353774.

## Disclaimer

Statements of fact and opinion in the articles in *The Year's Work in English Studies* are those of the respective authors and contributors and not of the English Association or Oxford University Press. Neither Oxford University Press nor the English Association make any representation, express or implied, in respect of the accuracy of the material in this journal and cannot accept any legal responsibility or liability for any errors or omissions that may be made.

JYWES.J1701M

# Contents

# Abbreviations

## 1. Journals, Series and Reference Works

| | |
|---|---|
| *19* | *Interdisciplinary Studies in the Long Nineteenth Century* |
| *AAR* | *African American Review* |
| *AAS* | *Australian Aboriginal Studies* |
| *ABäG* | *Amsterdamer Beiträge zur Älteren Germanistik* |
| *ABELL* | *Annual Bibliography of English Language and Literature* |
| *ABSt* | *A/B: Auto/Biography Studies* |
| *ABD* | *African and Black Diaspora: An International Journal* |
| *AC* | *Archeologia Classica* |
| *AcadSF* | *Academia Scientiarum Fennica* |
| *ACar* | *Analecta Cartusiana* |
| *Accessus* | *Accessus: A Journal of Premodern Literature and New Media* |
| *ACH* | *Australian Cultural History* |
| *ACM* | *Aligarh Critical Miscellany* |
| *ACR* | *Australasian Catholic Record* |
| *ACS* | *Australian-Canadian Studies: A Journal for the Humanities and Social Sciences* |
| *ActaS* | *Acta Scieniarum: Language and Culture* |
| *ActR* | *Action Research* |
| *AdI* | *Annali d'Italianistica* |
| *AdLLS* | *Advances in Language and Literary Studies* |
| *ADS* | *Australasian Drama Studies* |
| *AEnglishes* | *Asian Englishes* |
| *AES* | *Asian English Studies* |
| *AF* | *Anglistische Forschungen* |
| *Affirmations* | *Affirmations: Of The Modern* |
| *AfId* | *African Identities* |
| *AfricanA* | *African Affairs* |
| *AfrSR* | *African Studies Review* |
| *AfT* | *African Theatre* |
| *AgeJ* | *Age of Johnson: A Scholarly Annual* |
| *AGON* | *AGON: Rivista Internazionale di Studi Culturali, Linguistici e Letterari* |
| *AH* | *Art History* |
| *AHR* | *American Historical Review* |
| *AI* | *American Imago* |
| *AIQ* | *American Indian Quarterly* |
| *AJ* | *Art Journal* |
| *AJFS* | *Australian Journal of French Studies* |
| *AJHSS* | *American Journal of Humanities and Social Sciences* |
| *AJIS* | *Australian Journal of Irish Studies* |
| *AJL* | *Australian Journal of Linguistics* |
| *AJP* | *American Journal of Psychoanalysis* |
| *AJPH* | *Australian Journal of Politics and History* |

| | |
|---|---|
| *AJS* | *American Journal of Semiotics* |
| *AL* | *American Literature* |
| *ALA* | *African Literature Association Annuals* |
| *ALASH* | *Acta Linguistica Academiae Scientiarum Hungaricae* |
| *ALJ* | *The Australian Library Journal* |
| *AlexS* | *Alexander Shakespeare* |
| *ALH* | *Acta Linguistica Hafniensia; International Journal of Linguistics* |
| *Alif* | *Journal of Comparative Poetics* (Cairo, Egypt) |
| *ALN* | *American Literary Nationalism Newsletter* |
| *ALR* | *American Literary Realism, 1870–1910* |
| *ALS* | *Australian Literary Studies* |
| *ALT* | *African Literature Today* |
| *AltMo* | *Altre Modernita* |
| *AltT* | *alt.theatre:cultural diversity and the stage* |
| *AmasJ* | *Amerasian Journal* |
| *AmDram* | *American Drama* |
| *AmerP* | *American Poetry* |
| *AmerS* | *American Studies* |
| *AmLH* | *American Literary History* |
| *AmLS* | *American Literary Scholarship: An Annual* |
| *AMon* | *Atlantic Monthly* |
| *AmPer* | *American Periodicals* |
| *Amst* | *Amerikastudien/American Studies* |
| *AN* | *Acta Neophilologica* |
| *AnBol* | *Analecta Bollandiana* |
| *ANCH* | *American Nineteenth Century History* |
| *ANF* | *Arkiv för Nordisk Filologi* |
| *Angermion* | *Angermion: Yearbook for Anglo-German Literary Criticism, Intellectual History and Cultural Transfers* |
| *Anglia* | *Anglia: Zeitschrift für Englische Philologie* |
| *Anglica* | *Anglica: An International Journal of English Studies* |
| *Anglistik* | *Anglistik: Mitteilungen des Verbandes Deutscher Anglisten* |
| *AnH* | *Analecta Husserliana* |
| *AnL* | *Anthropological Linguistics* |
| *AnM* | *Annuale Mediaevale* |
| *Ann* | *Annales: Économies, Sociétés, Civilisations* |
| *ANQ* | *ANQ: A Quarterly Journal of Short Articles, Notes and Reviews* |
| *AnT* | *Anthropology Today* |
| *AntColl* | *Antique Collector* |
| *Anthurium* | *Anthurium: A Caribbean Studies Journal* |
| *AntigR* | *Antigonish Review* |
| *Antipodes* | *Antipodes: A North American Journal of Australian Literature* |
| *ANStu* | *Anglo-Norman Studies* |
| *ANZSC* | *Australian and New Zealand Studies in Canada* |
| *ANZTR* | *Australian and New Zealand Theatre Record* |
| *APBR* | *Atlantic Provinces Book Review* |
| *APJLE* | *Asia Pacific Journal of Education* |
| *APL* | *Antwerp Papers in Linguistics* |
| *AppLing* | *Applied Linguistics* |
| *AppLiRev* | *Applied Linguistics Review* |
| *AppPsycholing* | *Applied Psycholinguistics* |
| *APR* | *American Poetry Review* |
| *AQ* | *American Quarterly* |

| | |
|---|---|
| *AR* | *Antioch Review* |
| *ArAA* | *Arbeiten aus Anglistik und Amerikanistik* |
| *ARAL* | *Annual Review of Applied Linguistics* |
| *Arcadia* | *Arcadia: Internationale Zeitschrift für Literaturwissenschaft* |
| *Archiv* | *Archiv für das Stadium der Neueren Sprachen und Literaturen* |
| *ARCS* | *American Review of Canadian Studies* |
| *Area* | *Area: Journal of the Royal Geographical Society* |
| *ArielE* | *Ariel: A Review of International English Literature* |
| *Arion* | *Arion: A Journal of the Humanities and the Classics* |
| *ArkQ* | *Arkansas Quarterly: A Journal of Criticism* |
| *ArkR* | *Arkansas Review: A Journal of Criticism* |
| *ArQ* | *Arizona Quarterly* |
| *ARS* | *Augustan Reprint Society* |
| *Ars&H* | *Ars & Humanitas* |
| *ARSR* | *Australian Religion Studies Review* |
| *ArtB* | *Art Bulletin* |
| *Arth* | *Arthuriana* |
| *ArthI* | *Arthurian Interpretations* |
| *ArthL* | *Arthurian Literature* |
| *Arv* | *Arv: Nordic Yearbook of Folklore* |
| *AS* | *American Speech* |
| *ASch* | *American Scholar* |
| *ASE* | *Anglo-Saxon England* |
| *Asiatic* | *Asiatic: An International Journal of Asian Literatures, Cultures and Englishes* |
| *ASInt* | *American Studies International* |
| *ASoc* | *Arts in Society* |
| *Aspects* | *Aspects: Journal of the Language Society* (University of Essex) |
| *AspectsAF* | *Aspects of Australian Fiction* |
| *Asp* | *Anglais de spécialité* |
| *ASR* | *Asian Studies Review* |
| *Assaph* | *Assaph: Studies in the Arts (Theatre Studies)* |
| *ATJ* | *Asian Theatre Journal* |
| *Atlantis* | *Atlantis: A Journal of the Spanish Association for Anglo-American Studies* |
| *ATR* | *Anglican Theological Review* |
| *AtS* | *Atlantic Studies* |
| *AuBR* | *Australian Book Review* |
| *AuFolk* | *Australian Folklore* |
| *AuFS* | *Australian Feminist Studies* |
| *AuHR* | *Australian Humanities Review* |
| *AuJL* | *Australian Journal of Linguistics* |
| *Aurealis* | *Australian Fantasy and Science Fiction Magazine* |
| *AuS* | *Australian Studies* |
| *AuSA* | *Australian Studies* (Australia) |
| *AusCan* | *Australian-Canadian Studies* |
| *AusPl* | *Australian Playwrights* |
| *AustrianS* | *Austrian Studies* |
| *AuWBR* | *Australian Women's Book Review* |
| *AVSJ* | *Australasian Journal of Victorian Studies* |
| *AY* | *Arthurian Yearbook* |
| *BAF1900* | *British and American Fiction to 1900* |
| *BakhtinN* | *Bakhtin Newsletter* |

| | |
|---|---|
| BALF | Black American Literature Forum |
| B&A | Brain and Language |
| BAReview | British Academy Review |
| BARS Bulletin | British Association for Romantic Studies Bulletin & Review |
| BAS | British and American Studies |
| BASAM | BASA Magazine |
| BaylorJ | Baylor Journal of Theatre and Performance |
| BBCS | Bulletin of the Board of Celtic Studies |
| BBCSh | BBC Shakespeare |
| BBN | British Book News |
| BBSIA | Bulletin Bibliographique de la Société Internationale Arthurienne |
| BC | Book Collector |
| BCan | Books in Canada |
| BCS | B.C. Studies |
| BCT | The Bible and Critical Theory |
| Bell | Belgian Essays on Language and Literature |
| BEPIF | Bulletin des Itudes Portugaises et Brésiliennes |
| BFLS | Bulletin de la Faculté des Lettres de Strasbourg |
| BH | Book History |
| BHI | British Humanities Index |
| BHL | Bibliotheca Hagiographica Latina Antiquae et Mediae Aetatis |
| BHM | Bulletin of the History of Medicine |
| BHR | Bibliothèque d'Humanisme et Renaissance |
| BHS | Bulletin of Hispanic Studies |
| BI | Books at Iowa |
| Bibliotheck | Bibliotheck: A Scottish Journal of Bibliography and Allied Topics |
| Big Muddy | Big Muddy: A Journal of the Mississippi River |
| Biography | Biography: An Interdisciplinary Quarterly |
| BioL | Biolinguistics |
| BJA | British Journal of Aesthetics |
| BJCS | British Journal of Canadian Studies |
| BJDC | British Journal of Disorders of Communication |
| BJECS | British Journal for Eighteenth-Century Studies |
| BJHP | British Journal for the History of Philosophy |
| BJHS | British Journal for the History of Science |
| BJJ | Ben Jonson Journal |
| BJL | Belgian Journal of Linguistics |
| BJPS | British Journal for the Philosophy of Science |
| BJRL | Bulletin of the John Rylands (University Library of Manchester) |
| BJS | British Journal of Sociology |
| Blake | Blake: An Illustrated Quarterly |
| BLC | Bilingualism: Language and Cognition |
| BLE | Bulletin de Littérature Ecclésiastique |
| BLJ | British Library Journal |
| BLR | Bodleian Library Record |
| BN | Beiträge zur Namenforschung |
| BNB | British National Bibliography |
| BoH | Book History |
| Bookbird | Bookbird: A Journal of International Children's Literature |
| Boundary | Boundary 2: A Journal of Postmodern Literature and Culture |
| BP | Banasthali Patrika |
| BPMA | Bulletin of Philadelphia Museum of Art |
| BPN | Barbara Pym Newsletter |

| | |
|---|---|
| *BrAJ* | *British Art Journal Branch Branch: Britain, Representation, and Nineteenth-Century History* |
| *BRASE* | *Basic Readings in Anglo-Saxon England* |
| *BRH* | *Bulletin of Research in the Humanities* |
| *Brick* | *Brick: A Journal of Reviews* |
| *BRMMLA* | *Bulletin of the Rocky Mountain Modern Language Association* |
| *BRN* | *Black Renaissance Noire* |
| *BS* | *Bronte Studies* |
| *BSE* | *Brno Studies in English* |
| *BSJ* | *Baker Street Journal: An Irregular Quarterly of Sherlockiana* |
| *BSLP* | *Bulletin de la Société de Linguistique de Paris* |
| *BSNotes* | *Browning Society Notes* |
| *BSRS* | *Bulletin of the Society for Renaissance Studies* |
| *BSSA* | *Bulletin de la Société de Stylistique Anglaise* |
| *BST* | *Brontë Society Transactions* |
| *BSUF* | *Ball State University Forum* |
| *BTHGNewsl* | *Book Trade History Group Newsletter* |
| *BTLV* | *Bijdragen tot de Taal-, Land- en Volkenhunde* |
| *Bul* | *Bulletin* (Australia) |
| *BunyanS* | *Bunyan Studies* |
| *BuR* | *Bucknell Review* |
| *BurlM* | *Burlington Magazine* |
| *BurnsC* | *Burns Chronicle* |
| *BWPLL* | *Belfast Working Papers in Language and Linguistics* |
| *ByronJ* | *Byron Journal* |
| *CABS* | *Contemporary Authors Bibliographical Series* |
| *CahiersE* | *Cahiers Élisabéthains* |
| *CahiersRMH* | *Cahiers de recherches médiévales et humanistes* |
| *CAIEF* | *Cahiers de l'Association Internationale des Études Françaises* |
| *CalR* | *Calcutta Review* |
| *CamObsc* | *Camera Obscura: A Journal of Feminism and Film Theory* |
| *CamR* | *Cambridge Review* |
| *CanD* | *Canadian Drama/L'Art Dramatique Canadienne* |
| *CanJL* | *Canadian Journal of Linguistics* |
| *C&L* | *Christianity and Literature* |
| *C&Lang* | *Communication and Languages* |
| *C&M* | *Classica et Medievalia* |
| *CanL* | *Canadian Literature* |
| *CanPo* | *Canadian Poetry* |
| *CapR* | *Capilano Review* |
| *CARA* | *Centre Aixois de Recherches Anglaises* |
| *CaribW* | *Caribbean Writer* |
| *CarQ* | *Caribbean Quarterly* |
| *CarR* | *Caribbean Review* |
| *CASE* | *Cambridge Studies in Anglo-Saxon England* |
| *CathHR* | *Catholic Historical Review* |
| *CatR* | *Catalan Review* |
| *CBEL* | *Cambridge Bibliography of English Literature* |
| *CC* | *Chimurenga Chronic* |
| *CCL* | *Canadian Children's Literature* |
| *CCompCon* | *College Composition and Communication* |
| *CCor* | *Cardiff Corvey: Reading the Romantic Text* |
| *CCRes* | *Cross-Cultural Research* |

| | |
|---|---|
| CCRev | Comparative Civilizations Review |
| CCS | Comparative Critical Studies |
| CCrit | Comparative Criticism: An Annual Journal |
| CCW | Critical and Creative Wings |
| CD | Comparative Drama |
| CDALB | Concise Dictionary of American Literary Biography |
| CDCP | Comparative Drama Conference Papers |
| CDIL | Cahiers de l'Institut de Linguistique de Louvain |
| CdL | Cahiers de Lexicologie |
| CDS | Critical Discourse Studies |
| CE | College English |
| CEA | CEA Critic |
| CEAfr | Cahiers d'Études Africaines |
| CE&S | Commonwealth Essays and Studies |
| CEch | Caietele Echinox |
| CentR | Centennial Review |
| Centro | Centro: Journal for the Centre for Puerto Rican Studies |
| CF | Crime Factory |
| CFM | Canadian Fiction Magazine |
| CH | Computers and the Humanities |
| ChauR | Chaucer Review |
| ChauY | Chaucer Yearbook |
| ChE | Changing English |
| ChildL | Children's Literature: Journal of Children's Literature Studies |
| ChiR | Chicago Review |
| ChLB | Charles Lamb Bulletin |
| CHR | Camden History Review |
| ChRC | Church History and Religious Culture |
| CHum | Computers and the Humanities |
| CI | Critical Idiom |
| CinJ | Cinema Journal |
| CIQ | Colby Quarterly |
| CISh | Contemporary Interpretations of Shakespeare |
| CJ | Classical Journal |
| CJE | Cambridge Journal of Education |
| CJH | Canadian Journal of History |
| CJL | Canadian Journal of Linguistics |
| CJPLI | The Cambridge Journal of Postcolonial Literary Inquiry |
| CJR | Christian–Jewish Relations |
| CK | Common Knowledge |
| CL | Comparative Literature (Eugene, OR) |
| CLAJ | CLA Journal |
| ClassRJ | Classical Receptions Journal |
| ClassW | Classical World |
| CLC | Columbia Library Columns |
| CLCWeb | Comparative Literature and Culture (online) |
| CLE | Children's Literature in Education |
| CLet | Confronto Letterario |
| CLetras | Cadernos de Letras (Faculdade de Letras–UFRJ) |
| CLIN | Cuadernos de Literatura |
| CLLT | Corpus Linguistics and Linguistic Theory |
| CLS | Comparative Literature Studies |
| Clues | Clues: A Journal of Detection |

| | |
|---|---|
| CMCS | Cambridge Medieval Celtic Studies |
| CML | Classical and Modern Literature |
| CN | Chaucer Newsletter |
| CNIE | Commonwealth Novel in English |
| CogAH | Cogent Arts & Humanities |
| CogLing | Cognitive Linguistics |
| Cog&Em | Cognition and Emotion |
| CogSem | Journal of Cognitive Studies |
| ColB | Coleridge Bulletin |
| ColF | Columbia Forum |
| CollG | Colloquia Germanica |
| CollL | College Literature |
| Colloquy | Colloquy: Text Theory Critique |
| Com | Commonwealth |
| Comitatus | Comitatus: A Journal of Medieval and Renaissance Studies |
| Comparatist | Comparatist: Journal of the Southern Comparative Literature Association |
| ComparativeCS | Comparative Critical Studies |
| CompAS | Comparative American Studies |
| CompD | Comparative Drama |
| CompLit | Comparative Literature |
| ComS | Commentary |
| Concentric | Concentric: Literary and Cultural Studies |
| ConL | Contemporary Literature |
| ConLing | Contemporary Linguistics |
| Connotations | Connotations: A Journal for Critical Debate |
| ConnR | Connecticut Review |
| ContempR | Contemporary Review |
| ConTR | Contemporary Theatre Review |
| COPAS | Current Objectives of Postgraduate American Studies |
| Cordite | Cordite Poetry Review |
| Corp | Corpora |
| Costume | Journal of the Costume Society |
| CP | Concerning Poetry |
| CQ | Cambridge Quarterly |
| CR | Critical Review |
| CRCL | Canadian Review of Comparative Literature |
| CRev | Chesterton Review |
| CRevAS | Canadian Review of American Studies |
| Crit | Critique: Studies in Contemporary Fiction |
| CritE | The Critical Endeavour |
| Criterion | The Criterion |
| CritI | Critical Inquiry |
| Criticism | Criticism: A Quarterly for Literature and the Arts |
| CritQ | Critical Quarterly |
| CritSTV | Critical Studies in Television |
| CritT | Critical Texts: A Review of Theory and Criticism |
| CrM | Critical Mass |
| CRJ | Classical Receptions Journal |
| CS | Critical Survey |
| CSA | Carlyle Studies Annual |
| CSASE | Cambridge Studies in Anglo-Saxon England |
| CSCC | Case Studies in Contemporary Criticism |

| | |
|---|---|
| *CSELT* | *Cambridge Studies in Eighteenth-Century Literature and Thought* |
| *CSLT* | *Cultural Studies and Literary Theory* |
| *CSMC* | *Critical Studies in Media Communication* |
| *CSML* | *Cambridge Studies in Medieval Literature* |
| *CSNCLC* | *Cambridge Studies in Nineteenth-Century Literature and Culture* |
| *CSPC* | *Cambridge Studies in Paleography and Codicology* |
| *CSR* | *Cambridge Studies in Romanticism* |
| *CSRev* | *Christian Scholar's Review* |
| *CSSAM* | *Comparative Studies of South Asia, Africa and the Middle East* |
| *CStA* | *Carlyle Studies Annual* (previously *CAnn*) |
| *CTR* | *Canadian Theatre Review* |
| *Cuadernos* | *Cuadernos de Literatura Infantil y Juvenil* |
| *CuadHisp* | *Cuadernos Hispanoamericanos* |
| *CulA* | *Cultural Anthropology* |
| *CulC* | *Cultural Critique* |
| *CulS* | *Cultural Studies* |
| *CulSR* | *Cultural Studies Review* |
| *CultSoc* | *Cultural Sociology* |
| *Current Writing* | *Current Writing: Text and Reception in Southern Africa* |
| *CV2* | *Contemporary Verse 2* |
| *CVE* | *Cahiers Victoriens et Edouardiens* |
| *CW* | *Current Writing: Text and Perception in Southern Africa* |
| *CWS* | *Canadian Woman Studies* |
| *CWW* | *Contemporary Women's Writing* |
| *DA* | *Dictionary of Americanisms* |
| *DAE* | *Dictionary of American English* |
| *DAEM* | *Deutsches Archiv für Erforschung des Mittelalters* |
| *DAI* | *Dissertation Abstracts International* |
| *DAL* | *Descriptive and Applied Linguistics* |
| *D&C* | *Discourse and Communication* |
| *D&S* | *Discourse and Society* |
| *Daphnis* | *Daphnis: Zeitschrift für Mittlere Deutsche Literatur* |
| *DC* | *Dickens Companions* |
| *DC&M* | *Discourse, Content & Media* |
| *DetG* | *Dialectologia et Geolinguistica* |
| *DHLR* | *D.H. Lawrence Review* |
| *DHS* | *Dix-huitième Siècle* |
| *Diac* | *Diacritics* |
| *Dialogue* | *Dialogue: Canadian Philosophical Review* |
| *DiaS* | *Diaspora Studies* |
| *DickensM* | *Dickens Magazine* |
| *DicS* | *Dickinson Studies* |
| *Dictionaries* | *Dictionaries: Journal of the Dictionary Society of North America* |
| *DisS* | *Discourse Studies* |
| *DJDSNA* | *Dictionaries: Journal of the Dictionary of North America* |
| *DJJJ* | *Dublin James Joyce Journal* |
| *DLB* | *Dictionary of Literary Biography* |
| *DLS* | *Doris Lessing Studies* |
| *DM* | *Dublin Magazine* |
| *DMT* | *Durham Medieval Texts* |
| *DNB* | *Dictionary of National Biography* |
| *DOE* | *Dictionary of Old English* |
| *DOST* | *Dictionary of the Older Scottish Tongue* |

| | |
|---|---|
| DownR | Downside Review |
| DPhil | Digital Philology |
| DPr | Discourse Processes |
| DQ | Denver Quarterly |
| DQR | Dutch Quarterly Review of Anglo-American Letters |
| DQu | Dickens Quarterly |
| DR | Dalhousie Review |
| Drama | Drama: The Quarterly Theatre Review |
| DrS | Dreiser Studies |
| DS | Deep South |
| DSA | Dickens Studies Annual |
| DSCP | Discourse: Studies in the Cultual Politics of Education |
| DSH | Digital Scholarship in the Humanities |
| DSNA | DSNA Newsletter |
| DSQ | Disability Quarterly |
| EA | Études Anglaises |
| EAf | English in Africa |
| EAL | Early American Literature |
| E&D | Enlightenment and Dissent |
| E&S | Essays and Studies |
| E&Soc | Economy and Society |
| EALCS | Eastern African Literary and Cultural Studies |
| EARev | English Academy Review |
| EarT | Early Theatre |
| EAS | Early American Studies |
| EASt | Englisch Amerikanische Studien |
| eBLJ | Electronic British Library Journal |
| EBST | Edinburgh Bibliographical Society Transactions |
| EC | Études Celtiques |
| ECan | Études Canadiennes/Canadian Studies |
| ECCB | Eighteenth Century: A Current Bibliography |
| ECent | Eighteenth Century: Theory and Interpretation |
| ECF | Eighteenth-Century Fiction |
| ECI | Eighteenth-Century Ireland |
| ECIntell | Eighteenth-Century Intelligencer |
| ECLife | Eighteenth-Century Life |
| ECM | Eighteenth-Century Music |
| ECN | Eighteenth-Century Novel |
| ECon | L'Époque Conradienne |
| ECr | L'Esprit Créateur |
| ECS | Eighteenth-Century Studies |
| ECW | Essays on Canadian Writing |
| EDAMR | Early Drama, Art, and Music Review |
| EDJ | The Emily Dickinson Journal |
| EdL | Études de Lettres |
| EDSL | Encyclopedic Dictionary of the Sciences of Language |
| EES | Early English Studies |
| EF | Études Francaises |
| EHL | English Historical Linguistics |
| EHR | English Historical Review |
| EI | Études Irlandaises (Lille) |
| EIC | Essays in Criticism |
| Eiha | Eighth Lamp–Ruskin Studies Today |

| | |
|---|---|
| *EinA* | *English in Africa* |
| *EiP* | *Essays in Poetics* |
| *EiR* | *Essays in Romanticism* |
| *EIRC* | *Explorations in Renaissance Culture* |
| *Éire* | *Éire-Ireland* |
| *EJ* | *English Journal* |
| *EJAL* | *European Journal of Applied Linguistics* |
| *EJCSt* | *European Journal of Cultural Studies* |
| *EJES* | *European Journal of English Studies* |
| *EJLP* | *European Journal of Language Policy* |
| *EJP* | *European Journal of Philosophy* |
| *EL* | *Études lawrenciennes* |
| *ELA* | *Études Littéraires Africaines* |
| *ELet* | *Esperienze Letterarie: Rivista Trimestrale di Critica e Cultura* |
| *ELF* | *English Language and Literary Forum* |
| *ELH* | *English Literary History* |
| *ELing* | *English Linguistics* |
| *ELL* | *English Language and Linguistics* |
| *ELN* | *English Language Notes* |
| *ELR* | *English Literary Renaissance* |
| *ELS* | *English Literary Studies* |
| *ELT* | *English Literature in Transition* |
| *Embl* | *Emblematica: An Interdisciplinary Journal of English Studies* |
| *EMD* | *European Medieval Drama* |
| *EME* | *Early Modern Europe* |
| *EMedE* | *Early Medieval Europe* (online) |
| *EMLS* | *Early Modern Literary Studies* (online) |
| *EMMS* | *Early Modern Manuscript Studies* |
| *EMS* | *English Manuscript Studies, 1100–1700* |
| *EMu* | *Early Music* |
| *EMW* | *Early Modern Women* |
| *Encult* | *Enculturation: Cultural Theories and Rhetorics* |
| *EnginP* | *Englishes in Practice* |
| *English* | *English: The Journal of the English Association* |
| *EnLT* | *English Language Training* |
| *EnT* | *English Today: The International Review of the English Language* |
| *EONR* | *Eugene O'Neill Review* |
| *EPD* | *English Pronouncing Dictionary* |
| *ER* | *English Review* |
| *ERLM* | *Europe-Revue Littéraire Mensuelle* |
| *ERP* | *Education Research and Perspectives* |
| *ERR* | *European Romantic Review* |
| *ERS* | *Ethnic and Racial Studies* |
| *ES* | *English Studies* |
| *ESA* | *English Studies in Africa* |
| *ESC* | *English Studies in Canada* |
| *ESLAYb* | *EUROSLA Yearbook* |
| *Espéculo* | *Espéculo: Revista de Estudios Literarios* |
| *ESPJ* | *English for Specific Purposes* |
| *ESQ* | *ESQ: A Journal of the American Renaissance* |
| *ESRS* | *Emporia State Research Studies* |
| *EssaysMedSt* | *Essays in Medieval Studies* |

| | |
|---|---|
| EST | Eureka Street |
| Estudios Ingleses | Estudios Ingleses de la Universidad Complutense |
| ET | Elizabethan Theatre |
| ETC | English Text Construction |
| EtudesE | Études écossaises |
| EuLeg | European Legacy |
| EWhR | Edith Wharton Review |
| EWN | Evelyn Waugh Newsletter |
| EWPAL | Edinburgh Working Papers in Applied Linguistics |
| EWW | English World-Wide |
| Exemplaria | Exemplaria: A Journal of Theory in Medieval and Renaissance Studies |
| Expl | Explicator |
| Extrapolation | Extrapolation: A Journal Science Fiction and Fantasy |
| FC | Feminist Collections: A Quarterly of Women's Studies Resources |
| FCS | Fifteenth-Century Studies |
| FDT | Fountainwell Drama Texts |
| FemF | Feminist Formations |
| FeministMS | Feminist Media Studies |
| FemR | Feminist Review |
| FemSEL | Feminist Studies in English Literature |
| FemT | Feminist Theory |
| FFW | Food and Foodways |
| FG | Fourth Genre: Explorations in Non-Fiction |
| FH | Die Neue Gesellschaft/Frankfurter Hefte |
| FilmJ | Film Journal |
| FilmQ | Film Quarterly |
| FilmS | Film Studies |
| FLH | Folia Linguistica Historica |
| Florilegium | Florilegium: Journal of the Canadian Society of Medievalists |
| FLS | Foreign Literature Studies / Wai Guo Wen Xue Yan Jie (online) |
| FMLS | Forum for Modern Language Studies |
| FoLi | Folia Linguistica |
| FourthG | Fourth Genre: Explorations in Nonfiction |
| FranS | Franciscan Studies |
| FreeA | Free Associations |
| FrontenacR | Revue Frontenac |
| Frontiers | Frontiers: A Journal of Women's Studies |
| FS | French Studies |
| FSFR | The F. Scott Fitzgerald Review |
| FSt | Feminist Studies |
| FT | Fashion Theory |
| FU | Facta Universitatis |
| FuL | Functions of Language |
| FWLS | Forum for World Literature Studies |
| GAG | Göppinger Arbeiten zur Germanistik |
| G&E | Gender & Education |
| G&H | Gender & History |
| G&L | Gender & Language |
| GaR | Georgia Review |
| GBB | George Borrow Bulletin |
| GBK | Gengo Bunka Kenkyu: Studies in Language and Culture |
| GEGHLS | George Eliot–George Henry Lewes Studies |

| | |
|---|---|
| *GeM* | *Genealogists Magazine* |
| *GER* | *George Eliot Review* |
| *Gestus* | *Gestus: A Quarterly Journal of Brechtian Studies* |
| *GF* | *Gender Forum: An Internet Journal for Gender Studies* |
| *GHJ* | *George Herbert Journal* |
| *GhJL* | *Ghana Journal of Linguistics* |
| *GissingJ* | *Gissing Journal* |
| *GJ* | *Gutenberg-Jahrbuch* |
| *GJS* | *Genetic Joyce Studies* |
| *GL* | *General Linguistics* |
| *GL&L* | *German Life and Letters* |
| *GlasR* | *Glasgow Review* |
| *GlobRev* | *Global Review: A Biannual Special Topics Journal* |
| *GLobS* | *Global South* |
| *Glossa* | *Glossa: An International Journal of Linguistics* |
| *Glossator* | *Glossator: Practice and Theory of the Commentary* |
| *GLS* | *Grazer Linguistische Studien* |
| *GPQ* | *Great Plains Quarterly* |
| *GR* | *Germanic Review* |
| *Gramma* | *Gramma: Journal of Theory and Criticism* |
| *GrandS* | *Grand Street* |
| *GreenL* | *Green Letters: Studies in Ecocriticism* |
| *Greyfriar* | *Greyfriar Siena Studies in Literature* |
| *GriffithR* | *Griffith Review* |
| *GRM* | *Germanisch-Romanische Monatsschrift* |
| *Grove* | *The Grove: Working Papers on English Studies* |
| *GS* | *Gothic Studies* |
| *GSE* | *Gothenberg Studies in English* |
| *GSJ* | *Gaskell Society Journal* |
| *GSN* | *Gaskell Society Newsletter* |
| *HA* | *History Australia* |
| *HamS* | *Hamlet Studies* |
| *H&T* | *History and Theory* |
| *HardyR* | *Hardy Review* |
| *Harvard Law Review* | *Harvard Law Review* |
| *HatcherR* | *Hatcher Review* |
| *HazlittR* | *The Hazlitt Review* |
| *HC* | *Hollins Critic* |
| *HE* | *History of Education* |
| *Hecate* | *Hecate: An Interdisciplinary Journal of Women's Liberation* |
| *HEdQ* | *History of Education Quarterly* |
| *HEI* | *History of European Ideas* |
| *HEL* | *Histoire Épistémologie Language* |
| *HEng* | *History of the English Language* |
| *Hermathena* | *Hermathena: A Trinity College Dublin Review* |
| *Hermes* | *Hermes–Journal of Language and Communication in Business* |
| *HeroicA* | *Heroic Age: A Journal of Early Medieval Northwestern Europe* |
| *HES* | *Helsinki English Studies* (online) |
| *HeyJ* | *Heythrop Journal* |
| *HFR* | *Hayden Ferry Review* |
| *HistJ* | *Historical Journal* |
| *History* | *History: The Journal of the Historical Association* |
| *HistR* | *Historical Research* |

| | |
|---|---|
| *HJEAS* | *Hungarian Journal of English and American Studies* |
| *HJRev* | *Henry James Review* |
| *HL* | *Historiographia Linguistica* |
| *HLB* | *Harvard Library Bulletin* |
| *HLQ* | *Huntingdon Library Quarterly* |
| *HLSL* | *Harvard Law School Library* (online) |
| *HMAS* | *Journal of the History of Medicine and Allied Sciences* |
| *HMJ* | *Hypermedia Joyce Studies* |
| *HNR* | *Harvester New Readings* |
| *HomeCult* | *Home Cultures* |
| *HOPE* | *History of Political Economy* |
| *HopRev* | *Hopkins Review* |
| *HPT* | *History of Political Thought* |
| *HQ* | *Hopkins Quarterly* |
| *HR* | *Harvard Review* |
| *HRB* | *Hopkins Research Bulletin* |
| *HSci* | *History of Science* |
| *HSE* | *Hungarian Studies in English* |
| *HSJ* | *Housman Society Journal* |
| *HSL* | *University of Hartford Studies in Literature* |
| *HSN* | *Hawthorne Society Newsletter* |
| *HSSh* | *Hungarian Studies in Shakespeare* |
| *HSSN* | *Henry Sweet Society Newsletter* |
| *HT* | *History Today* |
| *HTR* | *Harvard Theological Review* |
| *HudR* | *Hudson Review* |
| *HumeS* | *Hume Studies* |
| *Humor* | *Humor: International Journal of Humor Research* |
| *HUSL* | *Hebrew University Studies in Literature and the Arts* |
| *HWJ* | *History Workshop* |
| *HWS* | *History Workshop Series* |
| *IACLALS* | *Indian Association for Commonwealth Language and Literature Studies* |
| *IACS* | *Inter-Asia Cultural Studies* |
| *IAFM* | *Image: Art, Faith, Mystery* |
| *IAL* | *Issues in Applied Linguistics* |
| *IAN* | *Izvestiia Akademii Nauk SSSR* (Moscow) |
| *I&C* | *Ideology and Consciousness* |
| *I&M* | *Immigrants and Minorities* |
| *I&P* | *Ideas and Production* |
| *IbéricaR* | *Ibérica: Revista de la Asociación Europea de Lenguas para Fines Específicos* |
| *IbsenSt* | *Ibsen Studies* |
| *ICAME* | *International Computer Archive of Modern and Medieval English* |
| *ICS* | *Illinois Classical Studies* |
| *IF* | *Indogermanische Forschungen* |
| *IFR* | *International Fiction Review* |
| *IGK* | *Irland: Gesellschaft and Kultur* |
| *IH* | *Interdisciplinarity Humanities* |
| *IHR* | *Intellectual History Review* |
| *IJAES* | *International Journal of Arabic-English Studies* |
| *IJAL* | *International Journal of Applied Linguistics* |
| *IJB* | *International Journal of Bilingualism* |
| *IJBC* | *International Journal of Business Communication* |

| | |
|---|---|
| *IJBEB* | *International Journal of Bilingual Education & Bilingualism* |
| *IJCL* | *International Journal of Corpus Linguistics* |
| *IJCP* | *International Journal of Critical Pedagogy* |
| *IJCS* | *International Journal of Canadian Studies* |
| *IJCT* | *International Journal of the Classical Tradition* |
| *IJECS* | *Indian Journal for Eighteenth-Century Studies* |
| *IJEL* | *International Journal of English Linguistics* |
| *IJES* | *Indian Journal of English Studies* |
| *IJH* | *The International Journal of the Humanities* |
| *IJHSS* | *International Journal of Humanities and Social Science* |
| *IJL* | *International Journal of Lexicography* |
| *IJM* | *International Journal of Multilingualism* |
| *IJMES* | *International Journal of Middle East Studies* |
| *IJPR* | *International Journal for Philosophy of Religion* |
| *IJSL* | *International Journal of the Sociology of Language* |
| *IJSS* | *Indian Journal of Shakespeare Studies* |
| *IJWS* | *International Journal of Women's Studies* |
| *IlhaD* | *Ilha do Desterro: A Journal of Language and Literature* |
| *ILLT* | *Innovation in Language Learning and Teaching* |
| *ILR* | *Indian Literary Review* |
| *ILS* | *Irish Literary Supplement* |
| *ILStud* | *Interdisciplinary Literary Studies: A Journal of Criticism and Theory* |
| *Imago* | *Imago: New Writing* |
| *IMB* | *International Medieval Bibliography* |
| *IndH* | *Indian Horizons* |
| *IndL* | *Indian Literature* |
| *Information & Culture* | *Information & Culture: A Journal of History* |
| *InG* | *In Geardagum: Essays on Old and Middle English Language and Literature* |
| *Inklings* | *Inklings: Jahrbuch für Literatur and Ästhetik* |
| *InnR* | *Innes Review* |
| *Inquiry* | *Inquiry: An Interdisciplinary Journal of Philosophy* |
| *Interactions* | *Interactions: Ege Journal of British and American Studies / Ege İngiliz ve Amerikan İncelemeleri Dergisi* |
| *Interlit* | *Interlitteraria* |
| *Interventions* | *Interventions: The International Journal of Postcolonial Studies* |
| *IntJEL* | *International Journal of English and Literature* |
| *IntJSL* | *International Journal of Scottish Literature* |
| *IoJCS* | *Iowa Journal of Cultural Studies* |
| *IPrag* | *Intercultural Pragmatics* |
| *IRAL* | *IRAL: International Review of Applied Linguistics in Language Teaching* |
| *IRCL* | *International Research in Children's Literature* |
| *IRE* | *International Review of Education* |
| *Iris* | *Iris: A Journal of Theory on Image and Sound* |
| *IRP* | *International Review of Pragmatics* |
| *IRWLE* | *Indian Review of World Literature in English* |
| *IS* | *Italian Studies* |
| *ISh* | *Independent Shavian* |
| *Island* | *Island Magazine* |
| *Isle* | *Interdisciplinary Studies in Literature and Environment* |

| | |
|---|---|
| *ISR* | *Irish Studies Review* |
| *ITSK* | *Interpreting and Translation Studies (Korea)* |
| *ITT* | *The Interpreter and Translator Trainer* |
| *IUR* | *Irish University Review: A Journal of Irish Studies* |
| *JAAC* | *Journal of Aesthetics and Art Criticism* |
| *JAAR* | *Journal of the American Academy of Religion* |
| *JAAS* | *Journal of Asian American Studies* |
| *JACS* | *Journal of African Cultural Studies* |
| *JADT* | *Journal of American Drama and Theatre* |
| *JAF* | *Journal of American Folklore* |
| *JafM* | *Journal of African Marxists* |
| *JAFP* | *Journal of Adaptation in Film & Performance* |
| *JAIS* | *Journal of Anglo-Italian Studies* |
| *JAL* | *Journal of Australian Literature* |
| *JALA* | *Journal of the African Literature Association* |
| *JamC* | *Journal of American Culture* |
| *JAmH* | *Journal of American History* |
| *JAmS* | *Journal of American Studies* |
| *JAP* | *Journal of Analytical Psychology* |
| *JAPC* | *Journal of Asian Pacific Communication* |
| *JAR* | *Journal of Anthropological Research* |
| *JArabL* | *Journal of Arabic Literature* |
| *JAS* | *Journal of Australian Studies* |
| *JASAL* | *Journal of the Association for the Study of Australian Literature* |
| *JAStT* | *Journal of American Studies of Turkey* |
| *JAW* | *Journal of Academic Writing* |
| *JBC* | *Journal of Business Communication* |
| *JBeckS* | *Journal of Beckett Studies* |
| *JBGU* | *Journal of Bunkgo Gakuin University* |
| *JBIIP* | *Journal of British and Irish Innovative Poetry* |
| *JBrowS* | *Journal of Browning Studies* |
| *JBS* | *Journal of British Studies* |
| *JBTC* | *Journal of Business and Technical Communication* |
| *JBuchJ* | *John Buchan Journal* |
| *JCanL* | *Journal of Canadian Literature* |
| *JCarL* | *Journal of Caribbean Literatures* |
| *JCC* | *Journal of Canadian Culture* |
| *JCDE* | *Journal of Contemporary Drama in English* |
| *JCERL* | *Journal of Classic and English Renaissance Literature* |
| *JCF* | *Journal of Canadian Fiction* |
| *JCGL* | *Journal of Comparative Germanic Linguistics* |
| *JChL* | *Journal of Child Language* |
| *JChLS* | *Journal of Children's Literature Studies* |
| *JCL* | *Journal of Commonwealth Literature* |
| *JCLA* | *Journal of Comparative Literature and Aesthetics* |
| *JCP* | *Journal of Canadian Poetry* |
| *JCPCS* | *Journal of Commonwealth and Postcolonial Studies* |
| *JCSJ* | *John Clare Society Journal* |
| *JCSR* | *Journal of Canadian Studies/Revue d'Études Canadiennes* |
| *JCSt* | *Journal of Caribbean Studies* |
| *JCT* | *Journal for Contemporary Thought* |
| *JDHLS* | *Journal of D.H. Lawrence Studies* |
| *JDJ* | *John Donne Journal* |

| | |
|---|---|
| JDN | *James Dickey Newsletter* |
| JDS | *Journal of Dracula Studies* |
| JDTC | *Journal of Dramatic Theory and Criticism* |
| JEAfS | *Journal of Eastern African Studies* |
| JEAP | *Journal of English for Academic Purposes* |
| JEASA | *Journal of the European Association for the Study of Australian Literature* |
| JEBS | *Journal of the Early Book Society* |
| JECS | *Journal of Eighteenth-Century British Studies* |
| JEdBS | *Journal of the Edinburgh Bibliographical Society* |
| JEH | *Journal of Ecclesiastical History* |
| JELF | *Journal of English as a Lingua Franca* |
| JELL | *Journal of English Language and Literature* |
| JEMCS | *Journal for Early Modern Cultural Studies* |
| JEMS | *Journal of Early Modern Studies* |
| JEn | *Journal of English* (Sana'a University) |
| JEngL | *Journal of English Linguistics* |
| JENS | *Journal of the Eighteen Nineties Society* |
| JEP | *Journal of Evolutionary Psychology* |
| JEPNS | *Journal of the English Place-Name Society* |
| JES | *Journal of European Studies* |
| JESCL | *Journal of English Studies and Comparative Literature* |
| JESR | *Journal of Educational and Social Research* |
| JETS | *Journal of the Evangelical Theological Society* |
| JFL | *Journal of Faculty of Letters/Edebiyat Fakültesi Dergisi* |
| JFR | *Journal of Folklore Research* |
| JGE | *Journal of General Education* |
| JGenS | *Journal of Gender Studies* |
| JGH | *Journal of Garden History* |
| JGL | *Journal of Germanic Linguistics* |
| JGN | *John Gower Newsletter* |
| JGSL | *Journal of the Graduate School of Letters* |
| JH | *Journal of Homosexuality* |
| JHI | *Journal of the History of Ideas* |
| JHLP | *Journal of Historical Linguistics and Philology* |
| JHP | *Journal of the History of Philosophy* |
| JHPrag | *Journal of Historical Pragmatics* |
| JHSex | *Journal of the History of Sexuality* |
| JHSL | *Journal of Historical Sociolinguistics* |
| JHu | *Journal of Humanities* |
| JHuP | *Journal of Humanistic Psychology* |
| JIAS | *Journal of the International Arthurian Society* |
| JICH | *Journal of Imperial and Commonwealth History* |
| JIEP | *Journal of Indo-European Perspectives* |
| JIES | *Journal of Indo-European Studies* |
| JIH | *Journal of Interdisciplinary History* |
| JIL | *Journal of Irish Literature* |
| JIPA | *Journal of the International Phonetic Association* |
| JISR | *Journal of International Social Research* |
| JIWE | *Journal of Indian Writing in English* |
| JIWS | *Journal of International Women's Studies* |
| JJ | *Jamaica Journal* |
| JJA | *James Joyce Annual* |

| | |
|---|---|
| JJB | James Joyce Broadsheet |
| JJLS | James Joyce Literary Supplement |
| JJQ | James Joyce Quarterly |
| JKS | Journal of Kentucky Studies |
| JL | Journal of Linguistics |
| JLAE | Journal of Leadership, Accountability & Ethics |
| JLA&C | Journal of Language Aggression and Conflict |
| JLAS | Journal of Literature and Art Studies |
| JLCDS | Journal of Literary and Cultural Disability Studies |
| JLG | Journal of Linguistic Geography |
| JLitSc | Journal of Literature and Science |
| JLLC | Journal of Language, Literature and Culture (previously AUMLA) |
| JLLE | Journal of Language and Literature Education |
| JLLI | Journal of Logic, Language and Information |
| JLP | Journal of Linguistics and Politics |
| JLS | Journal of Literary Semanitcs |
| JLST | Journal of Literary Studies/Tydskrif vir Literatuurwetenskap |
| JLSP | Journal of Language and Social Psychology |
| JLVSG | Journal of the Longborough Victorian Studies Group |
| JMBRAS | Journal of the Malaysian Branch of the Royal Asiatic Society |
| JMD | Journal of Multicultural Discourses |
| JMED | Journal of Modern English Drama |
| JMedH | Journal of Medical Humanities |
| JMedL | Journal of Medieval Latin |
| JMemL | Journal of Memory and Language |
| JMEMS | Journal of Medieval and Early Modern Studies |
| JMennS | Journal of Mennonite Studies |
| JMGS | Journal of Modern Greek Studies |
| JMH | Journal of Medieval History |
| JMJS | Journal of Modern Jewish Studies |
| JML | Journal of Modern Literature |
| JMLang | Journal of Modern Languages |
| JMMD | Journal of Multilingual and Multicultural Development |
| JMMLA | Journal of the Midwest Modern Language Association |
| JModH | Journal of Modern History |
| JModPerS | Journal of Modern Periodical Studies |
| JMRC | Journal of Medieval Religious Cultures (formerly MysticsQ) |
| JMRS | Journal of Medieval and Renaissance Studies |
| JMS | Journal of Men's Studies |
| JMTP | Journal of Marketing Theory and Practice |
| JNLH | Journal of Narrative and Life History |
| JNPH | Journal of Newspaper and Periodical History |
| JNR | Journal of the Northern Renaissance |
| JNT | Journal of Narrative Theory (formerly Technique) |
| JNZL | Journal of New Zealand Literature |
| JNZS | Journal of New Zealand Studies |
| Journeys | Journeys: The International Journal of Travel and Travel Writing |
| Jouvert | Jouvert: A Journal of Postcolonial Studies |
| JoyceSA | Joyce Studies Annual |
| JP | Journal of Philosophy |
| JPC | Journal of Popular Culture |
| JPCL | Journal of Pidgin and Creole Languages |
| JPhon | Journal of Phonetics |

| | |
|---|---|
| *JPJ* | *Journal of Psychology and Judaism* |
| *JPolR* | *Journal of Politeness Research: Language, Behavior, and Culture* |
| *JPP* | *Journal of Poetry and Poetics* |
| *JPrag* | *Journal of Pragmatics* |
| *JPRAS* | *Journal of Pre-Raphaelite and Aesthetic Studies* |
| *JPRS* | *Journal of Pre-Raphaelite Studies* |
| *JPS* | *Journal of Postcolonial Studies* |
| *JPW* | *Journal of Postcolonial Writing* |
| *JQ* | *Journalism Quarterly* |
| *JR* | *Journal of Religion* |
| *JRH* | *Journal of Religious History* |
| *JRMA* | *Journal of the Royal Musical Association* |
| *JRSA* | *Journal of the Royal Society of Arts* |
| *JRT* | *Journal of Religion and Theatre* |
| *JRUL* | *Journal of the Rutgers University Libraries* |
| *JSA* | *Journal of the Society of Archivists* |
| *JSAS* | *Journal of Southern African Studies* |
| *JScholP* | *Journal of Scholarly Publishing* |
| *JSem* | *Journal of Semantics* |
| *JSLHR* | *Journal of Speech, Language and Hearing Research* |
| *JSoc* | *Journal of Sociolinguistics* |
| *JSP* | *Journal of Scottish Philosophy* |
| *JSSE* | *Journal of the Short Story in English* |
| *JTAS* | *Journal of Transnational American Studies* |
| *JTheoS* | *Journal of Theological Studies* |
| *JVC* | *Journal of Victorian Culture* |
| *JW&CS* | *Journal of War & Culture Studies* |
| *JWCI* | *Journal of the Warburg and Courtauld Institutes* |
| *JWCP* | *Journal of Writing in Creative Practice* |
| *JWH* | *Journal of Women's History* |
| *JWIL* | *Journal of West Indian Literature* |
| *JWMS* | *Journal of the William Morris Society* |
| *JWSL* | *Journal of Women's Studies in Literature* |
| *KanE* | *Kansas English* |
| *KanQ* | *Kansas Quarterly* |
| *KB* | *Kavya Bharati* |
| *KCLMS* | *King's College London Medieval Series* |
| *KCS* | *Kobe College Studies* (Japan) |
| *KDNews* | *Kernerman Dictionary News* |
| *KK* | *Kritika Kultura* |
| *KJ* | *Kipling Journal* |
| *KN* | *Kwartalnik Neoflologiczny* (Warsaw) |
| *KompH* | *Komparatistische Hefte* |
| *Kotare* | *Kotare: New Zealand Notes and Queries* |
| *KPR* | *Kentucky Philological Review* |
| *KR* | *Kenyon Review* |
| *KS* | *Književna Smotra* |
| *KSJ* | *Keats-Shelley Journal* |
| *KSMB* | *Keats-Shelley Memorial Bulletin* |
| *KSR* | *Keats-Shelley Review* |
| *KWS* | *Key-Word Studies in Chaucer* |
| *KYD* | *Kill Your Darlings* |
| *LAB* | *Linguistic Approaches to Bilinguilism* |

| | |
|---|---|
| *LabPhon* | *Laboratory Phonology* |
| *L&A* | *Literature and Aesthetics* |
| *L&B* | *Literature and Belief* |
| *L&C* | *Language and Communication* |
| *L&D* | *Language & Dialogue* |
| *L&E* | *Linguistics and Education: An International Research Journal* |
| *Landfall* | *Landfall: A New Zealand Quarterly* |
| *L&H* | *Literature and History* |
| *L&IC* | *Language & Intercultural Communication* |
| *L&L* | *Language and Literature* |
| *L&LC* | *Literary and Linguistic Computing* |
| *L&M* | *Literature and Medicine* |
| *L&P* | *Literature and Psychology* |
| *L&S* | *Language and Speech* |
| *L&T* | *Literature and Theology: An Interdisciplinary Journal of Theory and Criticism* |
| *L&U* | *Lion and the Unicorn: A Critical Journal of Children's Literature* |
| *LangAcq* | *Language Acquisition* |
| *Lang&Edu* | *Language and Education* |
| *Lang&H* | *Language and History* |
| *Lang&S* | *Language and Style* |
| *LangAw* | *Language Awareness* |
| *LangCog* | *Language and Cognition* |
| *LangF* | *Language Forum* |
| *LangLearn* | *Language Learning: A Journal of Research in Language Studies* |
| *LangM* | *Language Matters* |
| *LangQ* | *USF Language Quarterly* |
| *LangR* | *Language Research* |
| *LangS* | *Language Sciences* |
| *Language* | *Language* (Linguistic Society of America) |
| *LAQ* | *Language Assessment Quarterly* |
| *LASB* | *Leeds African Studies Bulletin* |
| *Latchkey* | *The Latchkey: Journal of New Women Studies* |
| *LATR* | *Latin American Theatre Review* |
| *LaTrobe* | *La Trobe Journal* |
| *LawL* | *Law and Literature* |
| *LawLi* | *Law and the Literary Imagination* |
| *LB* | *Leuvense Bijdragen* |
| *LBR* | *Luso-Brazilian Review* |
| *LC&C* | *Language, Culture and Curriculum* |
| *LCrit* | *Literary Criterion* (Mysore, India) |
| *LCSAW* | *Learner Corpus Studies in Asia and the World* |
| *LCUT* | *Library Chronicle* (University of Texas at Austin) |
| *LDOCE* | *Longman Dictionary of Contemporary English* |
| *LeedsSE* | *Leeds Studies in English* |
| *LeF* | *Linguistica e Filologia* |
| *Legacy* | *Legacy: A Journal of Nineteenth-Century American Women Writers* |
| *L'EpC* | *L'Epoque Conradienne* |
| *LeSim* | *Le Simplegadi* |
| *LeS* | *Lingua e Stile* |
| *LexAsia* | *Lexicography: The Journal of AsiaLex* |
| *Lexicographica* | *Lexicographica: International Annual for Lexicography* |

| | |
|---|---|
| *Lexikos* | *Lexikos, Journal of the African Association for Lexicography* |
| *LFQ* | *Literature/Film Quarterly* |
| *LH* | *Library History* |
| *LHY* | *Literary Half-Yearly* |
| *LI* | *Studies in the Literary Imagination* |
| *Library* | *The Library* |
| *LibrQ* | *Library Quarterly* |
| *Likhaan* | *Likhaan: The Journal of Contemporary World Literature* |
| *LIN* | *Linguistics in the Netherlands* |
| *LinC* | *Languages in Contrast* |
| *LingA* | *Linguistic Analysis* |
| *Ling&P* | *Linguistics and Philosophy* |
| *Ling&Philol* | *Linguistics and Philology* |
| *LingAnth* | *Linguistic Anthropology* |
| *LingB* | *Linguistische Berichte* |
| *LingI* | *Linguistic Inquiry* |
| *LingInv* | *Lingvisticæ Investigationes* |
| *LingP* | *Linguistica Pragensia* |
| *LingRev* | *Linguistic Review* |
| *Lingua* | *Lingua: International Review of General Linguistics* |
| *LinguistikO* | *Lingusitik Online* |
| *Linguistique* | *La Linguistique* |
| *LingV* | *Linguistic Variation* |
| *LiNQ* | *Literature in Northern Queensland* |
| *LIT* | *LIT: Literature, Interpretation, Theory* |
| *LitComp* | *Literature Compass* (previously *LiteratureC*) |
| *LitH* | *Literary Horizons* |
| *LitI* | *Literary Imagination: The Review of the Association of Literary Scholars and Critics* |
| *LitLon* | *Literary London* |
| *LitR* | *Literary Review: An International Journal of Contemporary Writing* |
| *LittPrag* | *Litteraria Pragensia: Studies in Literature and Culture* |
| *LLR* | *Liverpool Law Review* |
| *LJCS* | *London Journal of Canadian Studies* |
| *LJHum* | *Lamar Journal of the Humanities* |
| *LLJ* | *Language Learning Journal* |
| *LMag* | *London Magazine* |
| *LockeN* | *Locke Newsletter* |
| *LocusF* | *Locus Focus* |
| *Logos* | *Logos: A Journal of Catholic Thought and Culture* |
| *LP* | *Lingua Posnaniensis* |
| *LPI* | *Linguistic and Philosophical Investigations* |
| *LPLD* | *Liverpool Papers in Language and Discourse* |
| *LPLP* | *Language Problems and Language Planning* |
| *LPol* | *Language Policy* |
| *LR* | *Les Lettres Romanes* |
| *LRB* | *London Review of Books* |
| *LSE* | *Lund Studies in English* |
| *LSoc* | *Language in Society* |
| *LSp* | *Language and Speech* |
| *LST* | *Longman Study Texts* |
| *LTeach* | *Language Teaching* |
| *LTM* | *Leeds Texts and Monographs* |

| | |
|---|---|
| *LTP* | *LTP: Journal of Literature Teaching Politics* |
| *LTR* | *London Theatre Record* |
| *LuK* | *Literatur und Kritik* |
| *LVC* | *Language Variation and Change* |
| *LW* | *Life Writing* |
| *LWU* | *Literatur in Wissenschaft und Unterricht* |
| *M&Lang* | *Mind and Language* |
| *MÆ* | *Medium Ævum* |
| *MAEL* | *Macmillan Anthologies of English Literature* |
| *Magistra* | *Magistra: A Women's Spirituality in History* |
| *MagL* | *Magazine Littéraire* |
| *MAS* | *Modern Asian Studies* |
| *M&H* | *Medievalia et Humanistica* |
| *M&L* | *Music and Letters* |
| *M&SW* | *Metaphor and the Social World* |
| *M&Sym* | *Metaphor and Symbol* (also *Met&Sym*) |
| *M&T* | *Marvels & Tales* |
| *MAR* | *Mid-American Review* |
| *Marang* | *Marang: Journal of Language and Literature* |
| *Margin* | *Margin: Life and Letters in Early Australia* |
| *MarkhamR* | *Markham Review* |
| *Matatu* | *Matatu: Journal for African Culture and Society* |
| *MBL* | *Modern British Literature* |
| *MC&S* | *Media, Culture and Society* |
| *MCI* | *Modern Critical Interpretations* |
| *MCJNews* | *Milton Centre of Japan News* |
| *McNR* | *McNeese Review* |
| *MCV* | *Modern Critical Views* |
| *MD* | *Modern Drama* |
| *MdLSBC* | *Mémoires du Livre / Studies in Book Culture* (online) |
| *ME* | *Medieval Encounters* |
| *MED* | *Middle English Dictionary* |
| *MedFor* | *Medieval Forum* (online) |
| *MedHis* | *Media History* |
| *MedJ* | *The Medieval Journal* |
| *MedPers* | *Medieval Perspectives* |
| *Meridians* | *Meridians: Feminsims, Race, Transnationalism* |
| *MES* | *Medieval and Early Modern English Studies* |
| *MESN* | *Mediaeval English Studies Newsletter* |
| *MET* | *Middle English Texts* |
| *METh* | *Medieval English Theatre* |
| *MFF* | *Medieval Feminist Forum* |
| *MFRT* | *Meridiens: Feminism, Race, Transnationalism* |
| *MFS* | *Modern Fiction Studies* |
| *MH* | *Malahat Review* |
| *MHJ* | *Melbourne Historical Journal* |
| *MHL* | *Macmillan History of Literature* |
| *MHLS* | *Mid-Hudson Language Studies* |
| *MichA* | *Michigan Academician* |
| *MiltonQ* | *Milton Quarterly* |
| *MiltonS* | *Milton Studies* |
| *MinnR* | *Minnesota Review* |

| | |
|---|---|
| *Miranda* | *Miranda: Multidisciplinary Peer-Reviewed Journal on the English-Speaking World* |
| *MissQ* | *Mississippi Quarterly* |
| *MissR* | *Missouri Review* |
| *MJLF* | *Midwestern Journal of Language and Folklore* |
| *ML* | *Music and Letters* |
| *MLAIB* | *Modern Language Association International Bibliography* |
| *MLing* | *Modèles Linguistiques* |
| *MLJ* | *Modern Language Journal* |
| *MLQ* | *Modern Language Quarterly* |
| *MLR* | *Modern Language Review* |
| *MLRev* | *Malcolm Lowry Review* |
| *MLS* | *Modern Language Studies* |
| *MMG* | *Macmillan Master Guides* |
| *MMisc* | *Midwestern Miscellany* |
| *MOCS* | *Magazine of Cultural Studies* |
| *ModA* | *Modern Age: A Quarterly Review* |
| *ModCult* | *Modernist Cultures* |
| *ModET* | *Modern English Teacher* |
| *ModM* | *Modern Masters* |
| *ModSp* | *Moderne Sprachen* |
| *Mo/Mo* | *Modernism/Modernity* (previously *M/M*) |
| *MonSP* | *Monash Swift Papers* |
| *Month* | *Month: A Review of Christian Thought and World Affairs* |
| *MOR* | *Mount Olive Review* |
| *Mosaic* | *Mosaic: A Journal for the Interdisciplinary Study of Literature* |
| *MoyA* | *Moyen Age* |
| *MP* | *Modern Philology* |
| *MPR* | *Mervyn Peake Review* |
| *MPsych* | *Media Psychology* |
| *MQ* | *Midwest Quarterly* |
| *MQR* | *Michigan Quarterly Review* |
| *MR* | *Massachusetts Review* |
| *MRDE* | *Medieval and Renaissance Drama in England* |
| *MRTS* | *Medieval and Renaissance Texts and Studies* |
| *MS* | *Mediaeval Studies* |
| *MSC* | *Malone Society Collections* |
| *MSE* | *Massachusetts Studies in English* |
| *MSEx* | *Melville Society Extracts* |
| *MSh* | *Macmillan Shakespeare* |
| *MSNH* | *Mémoires de la Société Néophilologique de Helsinki* |
| *MSpr* | *Moderna Språk* |
| *MSR* | *Malone Society Reprints* |
| *MSSN* | *Medieval Sermon Studies Newsletter* |
| *MT* | *Musical Times* |
| *MTJ* | *Mark Twain Journal* |
| *Multilingua* | *Multilingua: Journal of Cross-Cultural and Interlanguage Communication* |
| *MultSh* | *Multicultural Shakespeare* |
| *MusR* | *Music Review* |
| *MW* | *Muslim World* (Hartford, CT) |
| *MWQ* | *Mid-West Quarterly* |
| *NA* | *Nuova Antologia* |

| | |
|---|---|
| *Names* | *Names: Journal of the American Name Society* |
| *NAmR* | *North American Review* |
| *N&Q* | *Notes and Queries* |
| *Narrative* | *Narrative: Journal of the International Society for the Study of Narrative* |
| *NatIds* | *National Identities* |
| *NCaS* | *New Cambridge Shakespeare* |
| *NCBEL* | *New Cambridge Bibliography of English Literature* |
| *NCC* | *Nineteenth-Century Contexts* |
| *NCE* | *Norton Critical Editions* |
| *NCentR* | *The New Centennial Review* |
| *NCFiction* | *Nineteenth-Century Fiction* |
| *NCFS* | *Nineteenth-Century French Studies* |
| *NCGS* | *Nineteenth Century Gender Studies* |
| *NCI* | *New Critical Idiom* |
| *NCL* | *Nineteenth-Century Literature* |
| *NCLE* | *Nineteenth-Century Literature in English* |
| *NConL* | *Notes on Contemporary Literature* |
| *NCP* | *Nineteenth-Century Prose* |
| *NCS* | *New Clarendon Shakespeare* |
| *NCSR* | *New Chaucer Society Readings* |
| *NCSTC* | *Nineteenth-Century Short Title Catalogue* |
| *NCStud* | *Nineteenth-Century Studies* |
| *NCT* | *Nineteenth-Century Theatre* |
| *NCTFilm* | *Nineteenth-Century Theatre and Film* |
| *NDQ* | *North Dakota Quarterly* |
| *NegroD* | *Negro Digest* |
| *NELS* | *North Eastern Linguistic Society* |
| *Neoh* | *Neohelicon* |
| *Neophil* | *Neophilologus* |
| *NEQ* | *New England Quarterly* |
| *NERMS* | *New England Review* |
| *NewA* | *New African* |
| *NewBR* | *New Beacon Review* |
| *NewC* | *New Criterion* |
| *New Casebooks* | *New Casebooks: Contemporary Critical Essays* |
| *NewF* | *New Formations* |
| *NewHibR* | *New Hibernian Review* |
| *NewHR* | *New Historical Review* |
| *NewR* | *New Republic* |
| *NewSt* | *Newfoundland Studies* |
| *Nexus* | *The International Henry Miller Journal* |
| *NF* | *Neiophilologica Fennica* |
| *NfN* | *News from Nowhere* |
| *NF&LS* | *Newfoundland and Labrador Studies* |
| *NFS* | *Nottingham French Studies* |
| *NGC* | *New German Critique* |
| *NGS* | *New German Studies* |
| *NH* | *Northern History* |
| *NHR* | *Nathaniel Hawthorne Review* |
| *NILR* | *Northern Illinois Law Review* |
| *NIS* | *Nordic Irish Studies* |
| *NJES* | *Nordic Journal of English Studies* |

| | |
|---|---|
| *NJL* | *Nordic Journal of Linguistics* |
| *NL* | *Nouvelles Littéraires* |
| *NLAN* | *National Library of Australia News* |
| *NL&LT* | *Natural Language and Linguistic Theory* |
| *NLH* | *New Literary History: A Journal of Theory and Interpretation* |
| *NLitsR* | *New Literatures Review* |
| *NLR* | *New Left Review* |
| *NLS* | *Natural Language Semantics* |
| *NLWJ* | *National Library of Wales Journal* |
| *NM* | *Neuphilologische Mitteilungen* |
| *NMAL* | *NMAL: Notes on Modern American Literature* |
| *NMIL* | *Notes on Modern Irish Literature* |
| *NML* | *New Medieval Literatures* |
| *NMS* | *Nottingham Medieval Studies* |
| *NMW* | *Notes on Mississippi Writers* |
| *NN* | *Nordiska Namenstudier* |
| *NNER* | *Northern New England Review* |
| *NoH* | *Northern History* |
| *NoP* | *Northern Perspective* |
| *NOR* | *New Orleans Review* |
| *Nordlit* | *Nordlit: Arbeidstidsskrift i litteratur og kultur* |
| *NorfolkA* | *Norfolk Archaeology* |
| *NortonCE* | *Norton Critical Edition* |
| *Novel* | *Novel: A Forum on Fiction* |
| *NOWELE* | *North-Western European Language Evolution* |
| *NPEC* | *New Perspectives on the Eighteenth Century* |
| *NPS* | *New Penguin Shakespeare* |
| *NR* | *Nassau Review* |
| *NRF* | *La Nouvelle Revue Française* |
| *NRRS* | *Notes and Records of the Royal Society of London* |
| *NS* | *Die neuren Sprachen* |
| *NSS* | *New Swan Shakespeare* |
| *NTQ* | *New Theatre Quarterly* |
| *NTU* | *NTU: Studies in Language and Literature* (also *NTUSLL*) |
| *NVS* | *Neo-Victorian Studies* |
| *NW* | *New Writing: The International Journal for the Practice and Theory of Creative Writing* |
| *NwJ* | *Northward Journal* |
| *NWR* | *Northwest Review* |
| *NWRev* | *New Welsh Review* |
| *NYH* | *New York History* |
| *NYLF* | *New York Literary Forum* |
| *NYRB* | *New York Review of Books* |
| *NYT* | *New York Times* |
| *NYTBR* | *New York Times Book Review* |
| *NZB* | *New Zealand Books* |
| *NZJAS* | *New Zealand Journal of Asian Studies* |
| *OA* | *Oxford Authors* |
| *OB* | *Ord och Bild* |
| *Obsidian* | *Obsidian II: Black Literature in Review* |
| *OED* | *Oxford English Dictionary* |
| *OEDNews* | *Oxford English Dictionary News* |

| | |
|---|---|
| *OENews* | *Old English Newsletter* |
| *OELH* | *Oxford English Literary History* |
| *OET* | *Oxford English Texts* |
| *OH* | *Over Here: An American Studies Journal* |
| *OHEL* | *Oxford History of English Literature* |
| *OhR* | *Ohio Review* |
| *OJEP* | *Ostrava Journal of English Philology* |
| *OLR* | *Oxford Literary Review* |
| *OnCan* | *Onomastica Canadiana* |
| *OPBS* | *Occasional Papers of the Bibliographical Society* |
| *OpenGL* | *Open Guides to Literature* |
| *OpL* | *Open Letter* |
| *OPL* | *Oxford Poetry Library* |
| *OPSL* | *Occasional Papers in Systemic Linguistics* |
| *OralT* | *Oral Tradition* |
| *OrbisLit* | *Orbis Litterarum* |
| *OresEng* | *Oxford Research in English* |
| *OS* | *Oxford Shakespeare* |
| *OSci* | *Organization Science* |
| *OSE* | *Otago Studies in English* |
| *OSS* | *Oxford Shakespeare Studies* |
| *OT* | *Oral Tradition* |
| *PA* | *Présence Africaine* |
| *PacStud* | *Pacific Studies* |
| *PAJ* | *Performing Art Journal* |
| *P&C* | *Pragmatics and Cognition* |
| *P&CT* | *Psychoanalysis and Contemporary Thought* |
| *P&L* | *Philosophy and Literature* |
| *P&P* | *Past and Present* |
| *P&R* | *Philosophy and Rhetoric* |
| *P&S* | *Pragmatics and Society* |
| *P&SC* | *Philosophy and Social Criticism* |
| *PAns* | *Partial Answers* |
| *PAPA* | *Publications of the Arkansas Philological Association* |
| *Papers* | *Papers: Explorations into Children's Literature* |
| *PAPS* | *Proceedings of the American Philosophical Society* |
| *PAR* | *Performing Arts Resources* |
| *Parabola* | *Parabola: The Magazine of Myth and Tradition* |
| *Paragraph* | *Paragraph: The Journal of the Modern Critical Theory Group* |
| *ParisR* | *Paris Review* |
| *Parnassus* | *Parnassus: Poetry in Review* |
| *PastM* | *Past Masters* |
| *PaterN* | *Pater Newsletter* |
| *PAus* | *Poetry Australia* |
| *PBerLS* | *Proceedings of the Berkeley Linguistics Society* |
| *PBSA* | *Papers of the Bibliographical Society of America* |
| *PBSC* | *Papers of the Biographical Society of Canada* |
| *PCL* | *Perspectives on Contemporary Literature* |
| *PCP* | *Pacific Coast Philology* |
| *PCRev* | *Popular Culture Review* |
| *PCS* | *Penguin Critical Studies* |
| *PEAN* | *Proceedings of the English Association North* |

| | |
|---|---|
| *Pedagogy* | *Pedagogy: Critical Approaches to Teaching Literarature, Language and Culture* |
| *PEGS* | *Publications of the English Goethe Society* |
| *PELL* | *Papers on English Language and Literature* (Japan) |
| *PennHist* | *Pennsylvania History: A Journal of Mid-Atlantic Studies* |
| *PerfR* | *Performance Review* |
| *Peritia* | *Peritia: Journal of the Medieval Academy of Ireland* |
| *Perspectives* | *Perspectives: Studies in Translatology* |
| *Persuasions* | *Persuasions: Journal of the Jane Austen Society of North America* |
| *Persuasions On-Line* | *The Jane Austen Journal On-Line* |
| *Pertanika* | *Pertanika: Journal of Social Sciences and Humanities* |
| *Philament* | *Philament: Online Journal of the Arts and Culture Phonology* |
| *PhilRev* | *Philosophical Review: A Quarterly Journal* |
| *PhiN* | *Philologie im Netz* |
| *PHist* | *Printing History* |
| *Phonetica* | *Phonetica: International Journal of Speech Science* |
| *Phonology* | *Phonology* |
| *PHOS* | *Publishing History Occasional Series* |
| *PhRA* | *Philosophical Research Archives* |
| *PhT* | *Philosophy Today* |
| *PiL* | *Papers in Linguistics* |
| *PIMA* | *Proceedings of the Illinois Medieval Association* |
| *PIMS* | *Pontifical Institute of Mediaeval Studies* |
| *PinterR* | *Pinter Review* |
| *Pismo* | *Pismo: Journal for Linguistics and Literary Studies* |
| *PJCL* | *Prairie Journal of Canadian Literature* |
| *PJSS* | *Pakistan Journal of Social Sciences* |
| *PJSSH* | *Pertanika Journal of Social Sciences & Humanities* |
| *Plat* | *Platform* |
| *PLL* | *Papers on Language and Literature* |
| *PLoS ONE* | *PLoS ONE* |
| *PM* | *Penguin Masterstudies* |
| *PMHB* | *Pennsylvania Magazine of History and Biography* |
| *PMPA* | *Proceedings of the Missouri Philological Association* |
| *PNotes* | *Pynchon Notes* |
| *PNR* | *Poetry and Nation Review* |
| *PocoS* | *Postcolonial Studies* |
| *PocoT* | *Postcolonial Text* (online) |
| *PoeS* | *Poe Studies* |
| *Poetica* | *Poetica: An International Journal of Linguistic-Literary Studies* |
| *Poetics* | *Poetics: International Review for the Theory of Literature* |
| *Poétique* | *Poétique: Revue de Théorie et d'Analyse Littéraires* |
| *Poetry* | *Poetry* (Chicago) |
| *PoetryCR* | *Poetry Canada Review* |
| *PoetryNZ* | *Poetry New Zealand* |
| *PoetryR* | *Poetry Review* |
| *PoetryW* | *Poetry Wales* |
| *POMA* | *Proceedings of Meetings on Acoustics* |
| *POMPA* | *Publications of the Mississippi Philological Association* |
| *Positions* | *positions: asia critique* |
| *PostEng* | *Postgraduate English* |
| *Postmed* | *Postmedieval: A Journal of Medieval Cultural Studies* |

| | |
|---|---|
| PostS | Past Script: Essays in Film and the Humanities |
| PoT | Poetics Today |
| PP | Penguin Passnotes |
| PP | Philologica Pragensia |
| PPA | Philosophical Perspectives Annual |
| PPR | Philosophy and Phenomenological Research |
| PQ | Philological Quarterly |
| PR | Partisan Review |
| Pragmatics | Pragmatics: Quarterly Publication of the International Pragmatics Association |
| PrairieF | Prairie Fire |
| Praxis | Praxis: A Journal of Cultural Criticism |
| Prépub | (Pré)publications |
| PRev | Powys Review |
| PRIA | Proceedings of the Royal Irish Academy |
| Procedia | Procedia –Social and Behavioral Sciences |
| ProfileITP | Profile: Issues in Teachers' Professional Development |
| Prospects | Prospects: An Annual Journal of American Cultural Studies |
| Proteus | Proteus: A Journal of Ideas |
| PRR | Public Relations Review |
| PrS | Prairie Schooner |
| PRSt | Philip Roth Studies |
| PSiCL | Poznań Studies in Contemporary Linguistics |
| PSP | Population, Space and Place |
| PSt | Prose Studies |
| PsyArt | Psychological Study of the Arts (hyperlink journal) |
| PsychR | Psychological Reports |
| PTBI | Publications of the Sir Thomas Browne Institute |
| PubH | Publishing History |
| PULC | Princeton University Library Chronicle |
| PVR | Platte Valley Review |
| PWC | Pickering's Women's Classics |
| PY | Phonology Yearbook |
| QE | Quarterly Essay |
| QI | Quaderni d'Italianistica |
| QJS | Quarterly Journal of Speech |
| QLing | Quantitative Linguistics |
| QQ | Queen's Quarterly |
| QR | Queensland Review |
| QRFV | Quarterly Review of Film and Video |
| QS | Quebec Studies |
| Quadrant | Quadrant (Sydney) |
| Quest | The Quest |
| RadP | Radical Philosophy |
| RAL | Research in African Literatures |
| RALS | Resources for American Literary Study |
| Ramus | Ramus: Critical Studies in Greek and Roman Literature |
| Ranam | Recherches anglaises et nord-américaines |
| R&C | Race and Class |
| R&L | Religion and Literature |
| Raritan | Raritan: A Quarterly Review |
| Rask | Rask: International tidsskrift for sprog og kommunikation |
| RaVoN | Romanticism and Victorianism on the Net |

| | |
|---|---|
| *RB* | *Revue Bénédictine* |
| *RBPH* | *Revue Belge de Philologie et d'Histoire* |
| *RBR* | *Rare Book Review* (formerly *ABR*) |
| *RCEI* | *Revista Canaria de Estudios Ingleses* |
| *RCF* | *Review of Contemporary Fiction* |
| *RCPS* | *Romantic Circles Praxis Series* |
| *RDE* | *Research in Drama Education* |
| *RDN* | *Renaissance Drama Newsletter* |
| *RE* | *Revue d'Esthétique* |
| *Reader* | *Reader: Essays in Reader-Oriented Theory, Criticism, and Pedagogy* |
| *ReAL* | *Re: Artes Liberales* |
| *ReAr* | *Religion and the Arts* |
| *RecL* | *Recovery Literature* |
| *RECTR* | *Restoration and Eighteenth-Century Theatre Research* |
| *RedL* | *Red Letters: A Journal of Cultural Politics* |
| *REED* | *Records of Early English Drama* |
| *REEDN* | *Records of Early English Drama Newsletter* |
| *ReFr* | *Revue Française* |
| *REL* | *Review of English Literature* (Kyoto) |
| *Ren&R* | *Renaissance and Reformation* |
| *Renascence* | *Renascence: Essays on Values in Literature* |
| *RenD* | *Renaissance Drama* |
| *Renfor* | *Renaissance Forum* (online) |
| *RenP* | *Renaissance Papers* |
| *RenQ* | *Renaissance Quarterly* |
| *Rep* | *Representations* |
| *RES* | *Review of English Studies* |
| *Restoration* | *Restoration: Studies in English Literary Culture, 1660–1700* |
| *REurSt* | *Review of European Studies* |
| *RevAli* | *Revista Alicantina de Estudios Ingleses* |
| *Revels* | *Revels Plays* |
| *RevelsCL* | *Revels Plays Companion Library* |
| *RevelsSE* | *Revels Student Editions* |
| *RevR* | *Revolution and Romanticism, 1789–1834* |
| *Revue/Lisa* | *Revue/Lisa* (e-journal) |
| *RFEA* | *Revue Française d'Études Américaines* |
| *RFR* | *Robert Frost Review* |
| *RG* | *Revue Générale* |
| *RH* | *Recusant History* |
| *Rhetorica* | *Rhetorica: A Journal of the History of Rhetoric* |
| *Rhetorik* | *Rhetorik: Ein Internationales Jahrbuch* |
| *RhetR* | *Rhetoric Review* |
| *RHist* | *Rural History* |
| *RHL* | *Revue d'Histoire Littéraire de la France* |
| *RHT* | *Revue d'Histoire du Théâtre* |
| *RIB* | *Revista Interamericana de Bibliografia: Inter-American Reviews of Bibliography* |
| *Ricardian* | *Ricardian: Journal of the Richard III Society* |
| *RJ* | *Richard Jefferies Society Newsletter* |
| *RJES* | *Romanian Journal of English Studies* |
| *RL* | *Rereading Literature* |
| *RLAn* | *Romance Languages Annual* |

| | |
|---|---|
| RLC | Revue de Littérature Comparée |
| RL&C | Research on Language and Computation |
| RLing | Rivista di Linguistica |
| RLit | Russian Literature |
| RLMC | Rivista di Letterature Moderne e Comparate |
| RLT | Russian Literature Triquarterly |
| RM | Rethinking Marxism |
| RMR | Rocky Mountain Review of Language and Literature |
| RM | Renaissance and Modern Studies |
| RMNews | Retrospective Methods Newsletter |
| RMSt | Reading Medieval Studies |
| ROA | Rutgers Optimality Archive |
| RoCL | Review of Cognitive Linguistics |
| RomN | Romance Notes |
| RomS | Romance Studies |
| RoN | Romanticism and Victorianism on the Net |
| ROO | Room of One's Own: A Feminist Journal of Literature and Criticism |
| RORD | Research Opportunities in Renaissance Drama |
| RPh | Respectus Philologicus |
| RPT | Russian Poetics in Translation |
| RQ | Riverside Quarterly |
| RR | Romanic Review |
| RRDS | Regents Renaissance Drama Series |
| RRestDS | Regents Restoration Drama Series |
| RS | Renaissance Studies |
| RSQ | Rhetoric Society Quarterly |
| RSV | Rivista di Studi Vittoriani |
| RUO | Revue de l'Université d'Ottawa |
| RUSEng | Rajasthan University Studies in English |
| RuskN | Ruskin Newsletter |
| RUUL | Reports from the Uppsala University Department of Linguistics |
| R/WT | Readerly/Writerly Texts |
| SA | South Asia: Journal of Asian Studies |
| SAC | Studies in the Age of Chaucer |
| SATJ | South African Theatre Journal |
| SBA | Studies in Bible & Antiquity |
| SAD | Studies in American Drama, 1945–Present |
| SAF | Studies in American Fiction |
| Saga-Book | Saga-Book (Viking Society for Northern Research) |
| SAIL | Studies in American Indian Literatures: The Journal of the Association for the Study of American Indian Literatures |
| SAJL | Studies in American Jewish Literature |
| SAJMRS | South African Journal of Medieval and Renaissance Studies |
| Sal | Salmagundi: A Quarterly of the Humanities and Social Sciences |
| SALALS | Southern African Linguistics and Applied language Studies |
| S&CG | Social and Cultural Geography |
| S&P | Script and Print |
| S&Prag | Semantics and Pragmatics |
| S&S | Sight and Sound |
| Sanglap | Sanglap: Journal of Literary and Critical Inquiry |
| SAntS | Studia Anthroponymica Scandinavica |
| Salt | Salt: An International Journal of Poetry and Poetics |

| | |
|---|---|
| SAP | Studia Anglica Posnaniensia |
| SAQ | South Atlantic Quarterly |
| SAR | Studies in the American Renaissance |
| SARB | South African Review of Books |
| SARE | South Asian Review |
| SAsD | South Asia Diaspora |
| SASLC | Studies in Anglo-Saxon Literature and Culture |
| SatR | Saturday Review |
| SB | Studies in Bibliography |
| SC | Seventeenth Century |
| Scan | Scandinavica: An International Journal of Scandinavian Studies |
| ScanS | Scandinavian Studies |
| SCel | Studia Celtica |
| SCER | Society for Critical Exchange Report |
| Scintilla | Scintilla: Annual Journal of Vaughan Studies and New Poetry |
| SCJ | Sixteenth Century Journal |
| SCL | Studies in Canadian Literature |
| SCLOP | Society for Caribbean Linguistics Occasional Papers |
| SCN | Seventeenth-Century News |
| ScotL | Scottish Language |
| ScotLR | Scottish Literary Review |
| ScottN | Scott Newsletter |
| SCR | South Carolina Review |
| Screen | Screen (London) |
| SCRev | South Central Review |
| Scripsi | Scripsi |
| Scriptorium | Scriptorium: International Review of Manuscript Studies |
| SCRLL | Scottish Cultural Review of Language and Literature |
| Scru2 | Scrutiny 2 |
| ScTh | Scottish Journal of Theology |
| SD | Social Dynamics |
| SDR | South Dakota Review |
| SECC | Studies in Eighteenth-Century Culture |
| SECOLR | SECOL Review: Southeastern Conference on Linguistics |
| SED | Survey of English Dialects |
| SEEJ | Slavic and East European Journal |
| SEL | Studies in English Literature, 1500–1900 (Rice University) |
| SELing | Studies in English Linguistics (Tokyo) |
| SELit | Studies in English Literature (Tokyo) |
| SELL | Studies in English Language and Literature |
| Sem | Semiotica: Journal of the International Association for Semiotic Studies |
| SEMC | Studies in Early Medieval Coinage |
| Semiosis | Semiosis: Internationale Zeitschrift für Semiotik und Ästhetik |
| SER | Studien zur Englischen Romantik |
| Seven | Seven: An Anglo-American Literary Review |
| SF&R | Scholars' Facsimiles and Reprints |
| SFic | Science Fiction: A Review of Speculative Literature |
| SFNL | Shakespeare on Film Newsletter |
| SFQ | Southern Folklore Quarterly |
| SFR | Stanford French Review |
| SFS | Science-Fiction Studies |
| SH | Studia Hibernica (Dublin) |

| | |
|---|---|
| *ShakB* | *Shakespeare Bulletin* |
| *ShakS* | *Shakespeare Studies* (New York) |
| *Sh&Sch* | *Shakespeare and Schools* |
| *ShawR* | *Shaw: The Annual of Bernard Shaw Studies* |
| *SherHR* | *Sherlock Holmes Review* |
| *ShFTP* | *Short Fiction in Theory & Practise* |
| *ShIntY* | *Shakespeare International Yearbook* |
| *ShJE* | *Shakespeare Jahrbuch* (Weimar) |
| *ShLR* | *Shoin Literary Review* |
| *ShN* | *Shakespeare Newsletter* |
| *Shofar* | *Shofar: An Interdisciplinary Journal of Jewish Studies* |
| *SHPS* | *Studies in the History and Philosophy of Science* |
| *SHR* | *Southern Humanities Review* |
| *ShS* | *Shakespeare Survey* |
| *ShSA* | *Shakespeare in Southern Africa* |
| *ShStud* | *Shakespeare Studies* (Tokyo) |
| *SHW* | *Studies in Hogg and his World* |
| *ShY* | *Shakespeare Yearbook* |
| *SI* | *Social Identities: Journal for the Study of Race, Nation and Culture* |
| *SiAF* | *Studies in American Fiction* |
| *SiCS* | *Sino-Christian Studies: An International Journal of the Bible, Theology, and Philosophy* |
| *SIcon* | *Studies in Iconography* |
| *SidJ* | *Sidney Journal* |
| *SidN* | *Sidney Newsletter and Journal* |
| *Signa* | *Signa: Revista de la Asociación Española de Semiótica* |
| *Signs* | *Signs: Journal of Women in Culture and Society* |
| *SiHoLS* | *Studies in the History of the Language Sciences* |
| *SIL* | *Studies in Literature* |
| *SiMed* | *Studies in Medievalism* |
| *SIM* | *Studies in Music* |
| *SiP* | *Shakespeare in Performance* |
| *SiPr* | *Shakespeare in Production* |
| *SiR* | *Studies in Romanticism* |
| *SJL* | *Southwest Journal of Linguistics* |
| *SL* | *Studia Linguistica* |
| *SLang* | *Studies in Language* |
| *SLCS* | *Studies in Language Companion Series* |
| *SLI* | *Studies in the Literary Imagination* |
| *SLJ* | *Southern Literary Journal* |
| *SLJH* | *Sri Lanka Journal of the Humanities* |
| *SLL* | *Studies in Literature and Language* |
| *SLR* | *Second Language Research* |
| *SLRev* | *Stanford Literature Review* |
| *SLSc* | *Studies in the Linguistic Sciences* |
| *SMART* | *Studies in Medieval and Renaissance Teaching* |
| *SmAx* | *Small Axe: A Caribbean Journal of Criticism* |
| *SMC* | *Studies in Medieval Culture* |
| *SMed* | *Studi Medievali* |
| *SMELL* | *Studies in Medieval English Language and Literature* |
| *SMLit* | *Studies in Mystical Literature* (Taiwan) |
| *SMP* | *Studia Metrica et Poetica* |

| | |
|---|---|
| SMRH | Studies in Medieval and Renaissance History |
| SMRT | Studies in Medieval and Renaissance Teaching |
| SMS | Studier i Modern Språkvetenskap |
| SMy | Studia Mystica |
| SN | Studia Neophilologica |
| SNNTS | Studies in the Novel (North Texas State University) |
| SO | Shakespeare Originals |
| SOA | Sydsvenska Ortnamnssällskapets Årsskrift |
| SoAR | South Atlantic Review |
| SoC | Senses of Cinema (online) |
| Societies | Societies, an open access sociology journal |
| Sociocrit | Sociocriticism |
| Socioling | Sociolinguistica |
| SociolingS | Sociolinguistic Studies |
| SocN | Sociolinguistics |
| SocSem | Social Semiotics |
| SocT | Social Text |
| SohoB | Soho Bibliographies |
| SoQ | Southern Quarterly |
| SoR | Southern Review (Baton Rouge, LA) |
| SoRA | Southern Review (Adelaide) |
| SoSt | Southern Studies: An Interdisciplinary Journal of the South |
| Soundings | Soundings: An Interdisciplinary Journal |
| Southerly | Southerly: A Review of Australian Literature |
| SoutherlyLP | Southerly Long Paddock |
| SovL | Soviet Literature |
| SP | Studies in Philology |
| SPAN | SPAN: Newsletter of the South Pacific Association for Commonwealth Literature and Language Studies |
| SPAS | Studies in Puritan American Spirituality |
| SPC | Studies in Popular Culture |
| Speculum | Speculum: A Journal of Medieval Studies |
| SPELL | Swiss Papers in English Language and Literature |
| Spiritus | Spiritus: A Journal of Christian Spirituality |
| SpM | Spicilegio Moderno |
| SpNL | Spenser Newsletter |
| Sprachwiss | Sprachwissenschalt |
| SpringE | Spring: The Journal of the e.e. cummings Society |
| SPub | Studies in Publishing |
| SQ | Shakespeare Quarterly |
| SR | Sewanee Review |
| SRen | Studies in the Renaissance |
| SSEL | Stockholm Studies in English |
| SSEng | Sydney Studies in English |
| SSF | Studies in Short Fiction |
| SSL | Studies in Scottish Literature |
| SSLA | Studies in Second Language Acquisition |
| SSLLT | Studies in Second Language Learning and Teaching |
| SSOL | Scientific Study of Literature |
| SPap | Sydney Papers |
| SSR | Scottish Studies Review |
| SSt | Spenser Studies |
| SStud | Swift Studies: The Annual of the Ehrenpreis Center |

| | |
|---|---|
| *Staffrider* | *Staffrider* |
| *StaffordS* | *Staffordshire Studies* |
| *STAH* | *Strange Things Are Happening* |
| *StAPos* | *Studia Anglicana Posnaniensa* |
| *StCH* | *Studies in Church History* |
| *STDR* | *Sigma Tau Delta Review* (International English Honor Society) |
| *STE* | *Studying Teacher Education* |
| *SteinbeckSt* | *Steinbeck Studies* |
| *STGM* | *Studien und Texte zur Geistegeschichte des Mittelalters* |
| *StHR* | *Stanford Historical Review* |
| *StHum* | *Studies in the Humanities* |
| *StIn* | *Studi Inglesi* |
| *StLF* | *Studi di Letteratura Francese* |
| *STP* | *Studies in Theatre and Performance* |
| *StQ* | *Steinbeck Quarterly* |
| *StrR* | *Structuralist Review* |
| *StTCL* | *Studies in Twentieth-Century Literature* |
| *StTW* | *Studies in Travel Writing* |
| *STUF* | *Sprachtypologie und Universalienforschung* |
| *Style* | *Style* (De Kalb, IL) |
| *SUAS* | *Stratford-upon-Avon Studies* |
| *SubStance* | *SubStance: A Review of Theory and Literary Criticism* |
| *SUS* | *Susquehanna University Studies* |
| *Suvannabhumi* | *Suvannabhumi: Multi-disciplinary Journal of Southeast Asian Studies* |
| *SVEC* | *Studies on Voltaire and the Eighteenth Century* |
| *SWPLL* | *Sheffield Working Papers in Language and Linguistics* |
| *SWR* | *Southwest Review* |
| *SwR* | *Swansea Review: A Journal of Criticism* |
| *Symbolism* | *Symbolism: An International Journal of Critical Aesthetics* |
| *Symploke* | *Symploke: Theoretical, Cultural and Literary Scholarship* |
| *Synthese* | *Synthese, an International Journal for Epistemology, Methodology, and Philosophy of Science* |
| *TA* | *Theatre Annual* |
| *Tabu* | *Bulletin voor Taalwetenschap, Groningen* |
| *TC* | *Textual Cultures: Texts, Contexts, Interpretation* |
| *T&C* | *Text and Context* |
| *T&L* | *Translation and Literature* |
| *T&P* | *Text and Performance* |
| *T&S* | *Theology and Sexuality* |
| *T&T* | *Text & Talk* |
| *TAnt* | *Transforming Anthropology* |
| *TAPS* | *Transactions of the American Philosophical Society* |
| *Target* | *Target: International Journal on Translation Studies* |
| *TCBH* | *Twentieth-Century British History* |
| *TCBS* | *Transactions of the Cambridge Bibliographical Society* |
| *TCE* | *Texas College English* |
| *TCL* | *Twentieth-Century Literature* |
| *TCQ* | *Technical Communication Quarterly* |
| *TD* | *Themes in Drama* |
| *TDR* | *Drama Review* |
| *TEAMS* | *Consortium for the Teaching of the Middle Ages* |
| *Telos* | *Telos: A Quarterly Journal of Post-Critical Thought* |
| *TennEJ* | *Tennessee English Journal* |

| | |
|---|---|
| *TennQ* | *Tennessee Quarterly* |
| *TennSL* | *Tennessee Studies in Literature* |
| *TeReo* | *Te Reo: Journal of the Linguistic Society of New Zealand* |
| *TesolQ* | *TESOL Quarterly* |
| *Text* | *Text: Transactions of the Society for Textual Scholarship* |
| *TextJW* | *Text: Journal of Writing and Writing Courses* |
| *TextM* | *Text Matters: A Journal of Literature, Theory and Culture* |
| *Textus* | *Textus, English Studies in Italy* |
| *TF* | *TheatreForum* |
| *TH* | *Texas Humanist* |
| *THA* | *Thomas Hardy Annual* |
| *Thalia* | *Thalia: Studies in Literary Humor* |
| *Th&Event* | *Theory and Event* (online) |
| *Th&Text* | *Theory and Text* (online) |
| *ThC* | *Theatre Crafts* |
| *TheatreS* | *Theatre Studies* |
| *Theatre Symposium* | *Theatre Symposium* |
| *THEPES* | *Theory and Practice in English Studies* |
| *THES* | *Times Higher Education Supplement* |
| *Thesis* | *Thesis Eleven* |
| *The Victorian* | *The Victorian* |
| *THIC* | *Theatre History in Canada* |
| *THJ* | *Thomas Hardy Journal* |
| *ThN* | *Thackeray Newsletter* |
| *Thought* | *Thought: A Review of Culture and Ideas* |
| *ThreR* | *Threepenny Review* |
| *ThS* | *Theatre Survey: The American Journal of Theatre History* |
| *THSJ* | *Thomas Hardy Society Journal* |
| *THSLC* | *Transactions of the Historic Society of Lancashire and Cheshire* |
| *THStud* | *Theatre History Studies* |
| *ThTop* | *Theatre Topics* |
| *THY* | *Thomas Hardy Yearbook* |
| *TiLSM* | *Trends in Linguistics: Studies and Monographs* |
| *Tip* | *Theory in Practice* |
| *TIR* | *The Irish Review* |
| *TIS* | *Translation and Interpreting Studies* |
| *TJ* | *Theatre Journal* |
| *TJS* | *Transactions* (Johnson Society) |
| *TkR* | *Tamkang Review* |
| *TL* | *Theoretical Linguistics* |
| *TLJ* | *The Linguistics Journal* |
| *TLR* | *Linguistic Review* |
| *TLS* | *Times Literary Supplement* |
| *TM* | *Tout Moun: Caribbean Journal of Cultural Studies* |
| *TMLT* | *Toronto Medieval Latin Texts* |
| *TN* | *Theatre Notebook* |
| *TP* | *Terzo Programma* |
| *TPLL* | *Tilbury Papers in Language and Literature* |
| *TPLS* | *Theory and Practice in Language Studies* |
| *TPQ* | *Text and Performance Quarterly* |
| *TPr* | *Textual Practice* |
| *TPS* | *Transactions of the Philological Society* |
| *TR* | *Theatre Record* |

| | |
|---|---|
| *Traditio* | *Traditio: Studies in Ancient and Medieval History, Thought, and Religion* |
| *TransL* | *Transnational Literature* |
| *TransS* | *Translation Studies* |
| *TRB* | *Tennyson Research Bulletin* |
| *TRHS* | *Transactions of the Royal Historical Society* |
| *TRI* | *Theatre Research International* |
| *TriQ* | *TriQuarterly* |
| *Troll* | *Trollopiana* |
| *TRT* | *The Reading Teacher* |
| *TSAR* | *Toronto South Asian Review* |
| *TSB* | *Thoreau Society Bulletin* |
| *TSLang* | *Typological Studies in Language* |
| *TSLL* | *Texas Studies in Literature and Language* |
| *TStud* | *Tolkien Studies* |
| *TSWL* | *Tulsa Studies in Women's Literature* |
| *TTR* | *Trinidad and Tobago Review* |
| *TUSAS* | *Twayne's United States Authors Series* |
| *TvL* | *Tydskrif vir Letterkunde* |
| *TWAS* | *Twayne's World Authors Series* |
| *TWBR* | *Third World Book Review* |
| *TWQ* | *Third World Quarterly* |
| *TWR* | *Thomas Wolfe Review* |
| *Txt* | *Text: An Interdisciplinary Annual of Textual Studies* |
| *Typophiles* | *Typophiles* (New York) |
| *UCrow* | *Upstart Crow* |
| *UCTSE* | *University of Cape Town Studies in English* |
| *UCWPL* | *UCL Working Papers in Linguistics* |
| *UDR* | *University of Drayton Review* |
| *UE* | *Use of English* |
| *UEAPL* | *UEA Papers in Linguistics* |
| *UES* | *Unisa English Studies* |
| *Ufahamu* | *Ufahamu: African Studies Journal* |
| *ULR* | *University of Leeds Review* |
| *UMSE* | *University of Mississippi Studies in English* |
| *UOQ* | *University of Ottawa Quarterly* |
| *Upstart* | *Upstart: A Journal of English Renaissance Studies* |
| *USSE* | *University of Saga Studies in English* |
| *UtopST* | *Utopian Studies* |
| *UTQ* | *University of Toronto Quarterly* |
| *UWR* | *University of Windsor Review* |
| *Var* | *Varianta* |
| *VCT* | *Les Voies de la Création Théâtrale* |
| *VEAW* | *Varieties of English around the World* |
| *Verbatim* | *Verbatim: The Language Quarterly* |
| *Viator* | *Viator: Medieval and Renaissance Studies* |
| *VicNet* | *Victorian Network* |
| *Victo* | *Victoriographies* |
| *Views* | *Viennese English Working Papers* |
| *VIJ* | *Victorians Institute Journal* |
| *VisCom* | *Visual Communication* |
| *VJCL* | *Victorian Journal of Culture and Literature* |
| *VLC* | *Victorian Literature and Culture* |

| | |
|---|---|
| *VN* | *Victorian Newsletter* |
| *VP* | *Victorian Poetry* |
| *VPR* | *Victorian Periodicals Review* |
| *VQR* | *Virginia Quarterly Review* |
| *VR* | *Victorian Review* |
| *VS* | *Victorian Studies* |
| *VSB* | *Victorian Studies Bulletin* |
| *VWB* | *Virginia Woolf Bulletin* |
| *VWM* | *Virginia Woolf Miscellany* |
| *WAJ* | *Women's Art Journal* |
| *WAL* | *Western American Literature* |
| *WAM* | *Western American Literature* |
| *W&I* | *Word and Image* |
| *W&L* | *Women and Literature* |
| *W&Lang* | *Women and Language* |
| *WarL&A* | *War, Literature and the Arts* |
| *Wasafiri* | *Wasafiri* |
| *WascanaR* | *Wascana Review* |
| *WBEP* | *Wiener Beiträge zur Englischen Philologie* |
| *WC* | *World's Classics* |
| *WC* | *Wordsworth Circle* |
| *WCJ* | *Wilkie Collins Society Newsletter* |
| *WCR* | *West Coast Review* |
| *WCWR* | *William Carlos Williams Review* |
| *Wellsian* | *Wellsian: The Journal of the H.G. Wells Society* |
| *WEn* | *World Englishes* |
| *Westerly* | *Westerly: An Annual Review* |
| *WF* | *Western Folklore* |
| *WFE* | *Writing from the Edge* |
| *WHASN* | *W.H. Auden Society Newsletter* |
| *WHR* | *Western Humanities Review* |
| *WI* | *Word and Image* |
| *WLA* | *Wyndham Lewis Annual* |
| *WLT* | *World Literature Today* |
| *WLWE* | *World Literature Written in English* |
| *WMQ* | *William and Mary Quarterly* |
| *WoHR* | *Women's History Review* |
| *Women* | *Women: A Cultural Review* |
| *WomGY* | *Women in German Yearbook* |
| *WomHR* | *Women's History Review* |
| *WORD* | *WORD: Journal of the International Linguistic Association* |
| *WPEL* | *Working papers in Educational Linguistics* |
| *WPULL* | *Working Papers in Urban Language & Literacy* |
| *WPW* | *Working Papers on the Web* |
| *WQ* | *Wilson Quarterly* |
| *WRB* | *Women's Review of Books* |
| *WS* | *Women's Studies: An Interdisciplinary Journal* |
| *WSIF* | *Women's Studies: International Forum* |
| *WSJour* | *Wallace Stevens Journal* |
| *Wstr* | *Word Structure* |
| *WSR* | *Wicazo Sa Review* |
| *WstA* | *Woolf Studies Annual* |
| *WTW* | *Writers and their Work* |

| WUSA | Working USA |
|------|-----------|
| WVUPP | West Virginia University Philological Papers |
| WW | Women's Writing |
| WWPiELF | Waseda Working Papers in ELF |
| WWR | Walt Whitman Quarterly Review |
| XR | Xavier Review |
| YCC | Yearbook of Comparative Criticism |
| YeA | Yeats Annual |
| YER | Yeats Eliot Review |
| YES | Yearbook of English Studies |
| YEuS | Yearbook of European Studies/Annuaire d'Études Européennes |
| YFS | Yale French Studies |
| Yiddish | Yiddish/Modern Jewish Studies |
| YJC | Yale Journal of Criticism: Interpretation in the Humanities |
| YJLH | Yale Journal of Law and the Humanities |
| YLS | Yearbook of Langland Studies |
| YM | Yearbook of Morphology |
| YNS | York Note Series |
| YPL | York Papers in Linguistics |
| YR | Yale Review |
| YREAL | The Yearbook of Research in English and American Literature |
| YULG | Yale University Library Gazette |
| YWES | Year's Work in English Studies |
| ZAA | Zeitschrift für Anglistik und Amerikanistik |

Volume numbers are supplied in the text, as are individual issue numbers for journals that are not continuously paginated through the year.

## 2. Publishers

| A&UA | Allen & Unwin, Sydney, NSW, Australia |
|------|-----------|
| AarhusUP | Århus UP, Århus, Denmark |
| Abbeville | Abbeville Press, New York, NY |
| AberdeenUP | Aberdeen UP, Aberdeen |
| Abhinav | Abhinav Publications, New Delhi, India |
| ABL | Armstrong Browning Library, Waco, TX |
| Ablex | Ablex Publishing, Norwood, NJ |
| Åbo | Åbo Akademi, Åbo, Finland |
| Abrams | Harry N. Abrams, New York, NY |
| AC | Ayebia Clark, UK |
| Academia | Academia Press, Melbourne, VIC, Australia |
| Academic | Academic Press, London and Orlando |
| Academica | Academica Press, Palo Alta, CA |
| Academy | Academy Press, Dublin, Eire |
| AcademyC | Academy Chicago Publishers, Chicago, IL |
| AcademyE | Academy Editions, London |
| Acadiensis | Acadiensis Press, Fredericton, NB, Canada |
| ACarS | Association for Caribbean Studies, Coral Gables, FL |
| ACC | Antique Collectors' Club, Woodbridge, Suffolk |
| ACCO | ACCO, Leuven, Belgium |
| ACMRS | Arizona Center for Medieval and Renaissance Studies |
| ACP | Another Chicago Press, Chicago, IL |
| ACS | Association for Canadian Studies, Ottawa, ON, Canada |
| Adam Hart | Adam Hart Publishers, London |

| | |
|---|---|
| Adam Matthew | Adam Matthew, Suffolk |
| Addison-Wesley | Addison-Wesley, Wokingham, Berkshire |
| Adhyayan | Adhyayan Publishers & Distributors, New Delhi, India |
| Adosa | Adosa, Clermont-Ferrand, France |
| AEMS | American Early Medieval Studies |
| AF | Akademisk Forlag, Copenhagen, Denmark |
| Affiliated | Affiliated East–West Press, New Delhi, India |
| AfHP | African Heritage Books, London |
| AFP | Associated Faculty Press, New York, NY |
| AFWP | Africa World Press, Lawrenceville, NJ |
| Africana | Africana Publications, New York, NY |
| Agate | Agate Publishing, Evanston, IL |
| A–H | Amold-Heinemann, New Delhi, India |
| Ahriman | Ahriman-Verlag, Freiburg im Breisgau, Germany |
| Ajanta | Ajanta Publications, Delhi, India |
| AK | Akadémiai Kiadó, Budapest, Hungary |
| AKP | AK Press, Edinburgh |
| ALA | ALA Editions, Chicago, IL |
| Al&Ba | Allen & Bacon, Boston, MA |
| Albatross | Albatross Books, Sutherland, NSW, Australia |
| Albion | Albion, Appalachian State University, Boone, NC |
| Alderman | Alderman Press, London |
| Aldwych | Aldwych Press, London |
| AligarhMU | Aligarh Muslim University, Uttar Pradesh, India |
| Alioth | Alioth Press, Beaverton, OR |
| Allen | W.H. Allen, London |
| Allied Publishers | Allied Indian Publishers, Lahore and New Delhi, India |
| Alma | Alma Books, London |
| Almond | Almond Press, Sheffield |
| AM | Aubier Montaigne, Paris, France |
| AmberL | Amber Lane, Oxford |
| Amistad | Amistad Press, New York, NY |
| AMP | Aurora Metro Press, London |
| AMS | AMS Press, New York, NY |
| AMU | Adam Mickiewicz University, Posnan, Poland |
| Anansi | Anansi Press, Toronto, ON, Canada |
| Anderson-Lovelace | Anderson-Lovelace, Los Altos Hills, CA |
| Annick | Annick Press, Toronto, Canada |
| Anthem | Anthem Press, London, New York, Delhi |
| Antipodes | Antipodes Press, Plimmerton, New Zealand |
| ANUP | ANU (Australia National University) Press, Canberra, Australia |
| Anvil | Anvil Press Poetry, London |
| APA | APA, Maarssen, The Netherlands |
| APH | Associated Publishing House, New Delhi, India |
| API | API Network, Perth, WA, Australia |
| APL | American Poetry and Literature Press, Philadelphia, PA |
| APP | Australian Professional Publications, Mosman, NSW, Australia |
| Applause | Applause Theatre Book Publishers |
| APS | American Philosophical Society, Philadelphia, PA |
| Aquarian | Aquarian Press, Wellingborough, Northants |
| Arbeiter | Arbeiter Ring Publishing, Winnipeg, ON, Canada |
| ArborH | Arbor House Publishing, New York, NY |
| Arcade | Arcade Publishing, New York, NY |

| | |
|---|---|
| Archon | Archon Books, Hamden, CT |
| ArchP | Architectural Press Books, Guildford, Surrey |
| ArdenS&Theory | Arden Shakespeare and Theory |
| Ardis | Ardis Publishers, Ann Arbor, MI |
| Ariel | Ariel Press, London |
| Aristotle | Aristotle University, Thessaloniki, Greece |
| Ark | Ark Paperbacks, London |
| Arkona | Arkona Forlaget, Aarhus, Denmark |
| Arlington | Arlington Books, London |
| Arnold | Edward Arnold, London |
| ARP | Australian Reference Publications, North Balwyn, VIC, Australia |
| Arrow | Arrow Books, London |
| Artmoves | Artmoves, Parkdale, VIC, Australia |
| ASchP | Australian Scholarly Publishing, Melbourne, VIC, Australia |
| Ashfield | Ashfield Press, London |
| Ashgate | Ashgate, Brookfield, VT |
| ASLS | Association for Scottish Literary Studies, Aberdeen |
| ASP | Australian Scholarly Publishing |
| AStP | Aboriginal Studies Press, Canberra, ACT, Australia |
| ASU | Arizona State University, Tempe, AZ |
| Atheneum | Atheneum Publishers, New York, NY |
| Athlone | Athlone Press, London |
| Atlantic | Atlantic Publishers, Darya Ganj, New Delhi, India |
| Atlas | Atlas Press, London |
| Attic | Attic Press, Dublin, Eire |
| Atuanui | Atuanui Press, Waikato, New Zealand |
| AuBC | Australian Book Collector |
| AucklandUP | Auckland UP, Auckland, New Zealand |
| AUC Press | American University Press in Cairo, Egypt |
| AUG | Acta Universitatis Gothoburgensis, Sweden |
| AUP | Associated University Presses, London and Toronto |
| AUPG | Academic & University Publishers, London |
| Aurum | Aurum Press, London |
| Auslib | Auslib Press, Adelaide, SA, Australia |
| Austin Macauley | Austin Macauley Publishers Ltd, London |
| AUU | Acta Universitatis Umensis, Umeå, Sweden |
| AUUp | Acta Universitatis Upsaliensis, Uppsala, Sweden |
| Avebury | Avebury Publishing, Aldershot |
| Avero | Avero Publications, Newcastle upon Tyne |
| A-V Verlag | A-V Verlag, Franz Fischer, Augsburg, Germany |
| Axeltree | Axletree Books, New York |
| BA | British Academy, London |
| Bagel | August Bagel Verlag, Dusseldorf, Germany |
| Bahri | Bahri Publications, New Delhi, India |
| Bamberger | Bamberger Books, Flint, MI |
| B&B | Boydell & Brewer, Woodbridge, Suffolk |
| B&J | Barrie & Jenkins, London |
| B&N | Barnes & Noble, Totowa, NJ |
| B&O | Burns & Oates, Tunbridge Wells, Kent |
| Banff | Banff Centre Press, Banff, Canada |
| BAR | British Archaelogical Reports, Oxford |
| BarbarianP | Barbarian Press, Mission, BC, Canada |
| Barn Owl | Barn Owl Books, Taunton |

| | |
|---|---|
| Barnes | A.S. Barnes, San Diego, CA |
| Basic Books | Basic Books, New York |
| Bath UP | Bath UP, Bath |
| BaylorUP | Baylor University Press, Waco, TX |
| Bayreuth | Bayreuth African Studies, University of Bayreuth, Germany |
| BBC | BBC Publications, London |
| BCP | Bristol Classical Press, Bristol |
| Beacon | Beacon Press, Boston, MA |
| Beck | Verlag C.H. Beck oHG, Munich, Germany |
| Becket | Becket Publications, London |
| Beckford Society | Beckford Society, UK |
| Belin | Éditions Belin, Paris, France |
| Belknap | Belknap Press, Cambridge, MA |
| Belles Lettres | Société d'Édition les Belles Lettres, Paris, France |
| Bellew | Bellew Publishing, London |
| Bellflower | Belflower Press, Case University, Cleveland, OH |
| Benjamins | John Benjamins, Amsterdam, The Netherlands |
| BenjaminsNA | John Benjamins North America, Philadelphia, PA |
| BennC | Bennington College, Bennington, VT |
| Berg | Berg Publishers, Oxford |
| Berghahn | Berghahn Books, Oxford and New York, NY |
| BFI | British Film Institute, London |
| BibS | Bibliographical Society, London |
| BilinguaGA | Bilingua GA Editions |
| Bilingual | Bilingual Press, Arizona State University, Tempe, AZ |
| Binnacle | Binnacle Press, London |
| Biografia | Biografia Publishers, London |
| Birkbeck | Birkbeck College, University of London |
| Bishopsgate | Bishopsgate Press, Tonbridge, Kent |
| BL | British Library, London |
| Black | Adam & Charles Black, London |
| Black Cat | Black Cat Press, Blackrock, Eire |
| Black Dog | Black Dog Publishing, London |
| Blackie | Blackie & Son, Glasgow |
| Black Swan | Black Swan, Curtin, UT |
| Blackwell | Basil Blackwell, Oxford |
| BlackwellR | Blackwell Reference, Oxford |
| Blackwood | Blackwood, Pillans & Wilson, Edinburgh |
| Blaue Eule | Verlag die Blaue Eule, Essen, Germany |
| BlazeVOX Books | BlazeVOX Books, Buffalo, NY |
| Bloodaxe | Bloodaxe Books, Newcastle upon Tyne |
| Bloomsbury | Bloomsbury Publishing, London |
| BM | Bobbs-Merrill, New York, NY |
| BMP | British Museum Publications, London |
| Bodleian | Bodleian Library, Oxford |
| Bodley | Bodley Head, London |
| Bogle | Bogle L'Ouverture Publications, London |
| Böhlau | Böhlau Verlag, Vienna, Austria |
| BoiseSUP | Boise State UP, Boise, ID |
| Bookcraft | Bookcraft, Ibadan, Nigeria |
| Book Enclave | Book Enclave, Shanti Nagar, Jaipur, India |
| Book Guild | Book Guild, Lewes |
| BookplateS | Bookplate Society, Birmingham |

| | |
|---|---|
| Booksplus | Booksplus Nigeria Limited, Lagos, Nigeria |
| Boombana | Boombana Press, Brisbane, QLD, Australia |
| Borealis | Borealis Press, Ottawa, ON, Canada |
| Borgo | Borgo Press, San Bernardino, CA |
| BostonAL | Boston Athenaeum Library, Boston, MA |
| Bowker | R.R. Bowker, New Providence, NJ |
| Boyars | Marion Boyars, London and Boston, MA |
| Boydell | Boydell Press, Woodbridge, Suffolk |
| Boyes | Megan Boyes, Allestree, Derbyshire |
| Bradwell | Books Bradwell Books, Sheffield |
| Braumüller | Wilhelm Braumüller, Vienna, Austria |
| Breakwater | Breakwater Books, St John's, NL, Canada |
| Brentham | Brentham Press, St Albans, Hertfordshire |
| Brepols | Brepols, Turnhout, Belgium |
| Brewer | D.S. Brewer, Woodbridge, Suffolk |
| Brewin | Brewin Books, Studley, Warwicks |
| Bridge | Bridge Publishing, S. Plainfield, NJ |
| Brill | E.J. Brill, Leiden, Belgium |
| BrillA | Brill Academic Publishers |
| Brilliance | Brilliance Books, London |
| Broadview | Broadview, London, ON and Lewiston, NY |
| Brookside | Brookside Press, London |
| Browne | Sinclair Browne, London |
| Brownstone | Brownstone Books, Madison, IN |
| BrownUP | Brown UP, Providence, RI |
| Brynmill | Brynmill Press, Harleston, Norfolk |
| BSA | Bibliographical Society of America |
| BSP | Black Sparrow Press, Santa Barbara, CA |
| BSU | Ball State University, Muncie, IN |
| BuckUP | Bucknell UP, Lewisburg, PA |
| BUP | Birmingham UP, Birmingham |
| Burnett | Burnett Books, London |
| Buske | Helmut Buske, Hamburg, Germany |
| Butterfly | Butterfly Books, San Antonio, TX |
| CA | Creative Arts Book, Berkeley, CA |
| Cadmus | Cadmus Editions, Tiburon, CA |
| Cairns | Francis Cairns, University of Leeds |
| Calaloux | Calaloux Publications, Ithaca, NY |
| Calder | John Calder, London |
| CALLS | Centre for Australian Language and Literature Studies, University of New England, NSW, Australia |
| Cambria | Cambria Press, Amherst, NY |
| CambridgeSP | Cambridge Scholars Publishing, Newcastle upon Tyne |
| Camden | Camden Press, London |
| CamdenH | Camden House, Rochester, NY |
| C&W | Chatto & Windus, London |
| Canongate | Canongate Publishing, Edinburgh |
| Canterbury | Canterbury Press, Norwich |
| Canterbury UP | Canterbury University Press, Christchurch, New Zealand |
| Cape | Jonathan Cape, London |
| Capra | Capra Press, Santa Barbara, CA |
| Carcanet | Carcanet New Press, Manchester, Lancashire |
| CaribB | Caribbean Books, Parkersburg, IA |

| | |
|---|---|
| CarletonUP | Carleton UP, Ottawa, ON, Canada |
| Carucci | Carucci, Rome, Italy |
| Cascadilla | Cascadilla Press, Somerville, MA |
| Cass | Frank Cass, London |
| Cassell | Cassell, London |
| Cavaliere Azzurro | Cavaliere Azzurro, Bologna, Italy |
| Cave | Godfrey Cave Associates, London |
| CBS | Cambridge Bibliographical Society, Cambridge |
| CCCP | Critical, Cultural and Communications Press, Nottingham |
| CDSH | Centre de Documentation Sciences Humaines, Paris, France |
| CENS | Centre for English Name Studies, University of Nottingham |
| Century | Century Publishing, London |
| C–H | Chadwyck–Healey, Cambridge |
| Chambers | W. & R. Chambers, Edinburgh |
| Champion | Librairie Honoré Champion, Paris, France |
| Chand | S. Chand, Madras, India |
| Chaucer | Chaucer Press |
| Checkmark Books | Checkmark Books, New York, NY |
| ChiR | Chicago Review Press, Chicago, IL |
| Christendom | Christendom Publications, Front Royal, VA |
| Chronicle | Chronicle Books, London |
| ChuoUL | Chuo University Library, Tokyo, Japan |
| Churchman | Churchman Publishing, Worthing, W. Sussex |
| Cistercian | Cistercian Publications, Kalamazoo, MI |
| CL | City Lights Books, San Francisco, CA |
| CLA | Canadian Library Association, Ottawa, ON, Canada |
| Clarendon | Clarendon Press, Oxford |
| Claridge | Claridge, St Albans, Hertfordshire |
| Clarion | Clarion State College, Clarion, PA |
| Clark | T. & T. Clark, Edinburgh |
| Clarke | James Clarke, Cambridge |
| Classical | Classical Publishing, New Delhi, India |
| ClemsonUP | Clemson University Press, Clemson, SC |
| CMST | Centre for Medieval Studies, University of Toronto, ON, Canada |
| Coach House | Coach House Press, Toronto, ON, Canada |
| Codesria | Codesria, Senegal, Africa |
| Colleagues | Colleagues Press, East Lansing, MI |
| Collector | Collector, London |
| College-Hill | College-Hill Press, San Diego, CA |
| Collins | William Collins, London |
| CollinsA | William Collins (Australia), Sydney, NSW, Australia |
| Collins & Brown | Collins & Brown, London |
| ColUP | Columbia UP, New York, NY |
| Comedia | Comedia Publishing, London |
| Comet | Comet Books, London |
| Connell Guides | Connell Guides, London |
| Constable | Constable, London |
| Contemporary | Contemporary Books, Chicago, IL |
| Continuum | Continuum Publishing, New York, NY |
| ContinuumL | Continuum, London |
| Copp | Copp Clark Pitman, Mississauga, ON, Canada |
| Corgi | Corgi Books, London |
| CorkUP | Cork UP, Eire |

| | |
|---|---|
| Cornford | Cornford Press, Launceston, TAS, Australia |
| CornUP | Cornell UP, Ithaca, NY |
| Cornwallis | Cornwallis Press, Hastings, E. Sussex |
| Coronado | Coronado Press, Lawrence, KS |
| Cosmo | Cosmo Publications, New Delhi, India |
| Coteau | Coteau Books, Regina, SK, Canada |
| Counterpoint Press | Counterpoint Press, Berkeley, CA |
| Cowfeather | Cowfeather Press, Middleton, WI |
| Cowley | Cowley Publications, Cambridge, MA |
| Cowper | Cowper House, Pacific Grove, CA |
| CPP | Canadian Poetry Press, London, Ontario, ON, Canada |
| CQUP | Central Queensland UP, Rockhampton, QLD, Australia |
| Craftsman House | Craftsman House, The Netherlands |
| Craig Pottoon | Craig Pottoon Publishing, New Zealand |
| Crawford | Crawford House Publishing, Hindmarsh, SA |
| Creag Darach | Creag Durach Publications, Stirling |
| CreativeB | Creative Books, New Delhi, India |
| CreateSpace | CreateSpace Independent Publishing Platform |
| Cresset | Cresset Library, London |
| Crossing | Crossing Press, Freedom, CA |
| Crossroad | Crossroad Publishing, New York, NY |
| Crown | Crown Publishers, New York, NY |
| Crowood | Crowood Press, Marlborough, Wiltshire |
| CSP | Canadian Scholars' Press, Toronto, ON, Canada |
| CSU | Cleveland State University, Cleveland, OH |
| CULouvain | Catholic University of Louvain, Louvain-la-Neuve, Belgium |
| CULublin | Catholic University of Lublin, Poland |
| CUP | Cambridge UP, Cambridge, New York, and Melbourne |
| Currency | Currency Press, Paddington, NSW, Australia |
| Currey | James Currey, London |
| Cushing | Cushing Memorial Library & Archives |
| CV | Cherry Valley Edition, Rochester, NY |
| CVK | Cornelson-Velhagen & Klasing, Berlin, Germany |
| CWU | Carl Winter Universitätsverlag, Heidelberg, Germany |
| Da Capo | Da Capo Press, New York |
| Daisy | Daisy Books, Peterborough, Cambridgeshire |
| D&H | Duncker & Humblot, Berlin, Germany |
| D&M | Douglas & McIntyre, Vancouver, BC, Canada |
| D&S | Duffy and Snellgrove, Polts Point, NSW, Australia |
| Dangaroo | Dangaroo Press, Mundelstrup, Denmark |
| Daniel | Daniel & Daniel Publishers Inc., McKinleyville, CA |
| Dawson | Dawson Publishing, Folkestone, Kent |
| DawsonsPM | Dawsons Pall Mall |
| DBAP | Daphne Brasell Associates Press |
| DBP | Drama Book Publishers, New York, NY |
| Deakin UP | Deakin UP, Geelong, VIC, Australia |
| De Boeck | De Boeck-Wesmael, Brussels, Belgium |
| Dee | Ivan R. Dee Publishers, Chicago, IL |
| De Graaf | De Graaf, Nierwkoup, The Netherlands |
| Denoël | Denoël S.A.R.L., Paris, France |
| Dent | J.M. Dent, London |
| DentA | Dent, Ferntree Gully, VIC, Australia |
| Depanee | Depanee Printers and Publishers, Nugegoda, Sri Lanka |

| | |
|---|---|
| Deutsch | André Deutsch, London |
| Didier | Éditions Didier, Paris, France |
| Diesterweg | Verlag Moritz Diesterweg, Frankfurt am Main, Germany |
| DLSUP | De La Salle University UP, Manila, Philippines |
| Doaba | Doaba House, Delhi, India |
| Dobby | Eric Dobby Publishing, St Albans |
| Dobson | Dobson Books, Durham |
| Dolmen | Dolmen Press, Portlaoise, Eire |
| Donald | John Donald, Edinburgh |
| Doubleday | Doubleday, London and New York |
| Dove | Dove, Sydney, NSW, Australia |
| Dovecote | Dovecote Press, Wimborne, Dorset |
| Dovehouse | Dovehouse Editions, Canada |
| Dover | Dover Publications, New York, NY |
| Drew | Richard Drew, Edinburgh |
| Droste | Droste Verlag, Düsseldorf, Germany |
| Droz | Librairie Droz SA, Geneva, Switzerland |
| DublinUP | Dublin UP, Dublin, Eire |
| Duckworth | Gerald Duckworth, London |
| Duculot | J. Duculot, Gembloux, Belgium |
| DukeUP | Duke UP, Durham, NC |
| Dundurn | Dundurn Press, Toronto and London, ON, Canada |
| Duquesne | Duquesne UP, Pittsburgh, PA |
| Dutton | E.P. Dutton, New York, NY |
| EA | English Association, London |
| EAS | English Association Sydney Incorporated |
| Eason | Eason & Son, Dublin, Eire |
| East Bay | East Bay Books, Berkeley, CA |
| Ebony | Ebony Books, Melbourne, SA, Australia |
| Ecco | Ecco Press, New York, NY |
| ECW | ECW Press, Downsview, Ontario, ON, Canada |
| Eden | Eden Press, Montreal and St Albans, VT |
| EdinUP | Edinburgh UP, Edinburgh |
| Editoriale Anicia | Editoriale Anicia, Rome, Italy |
| Educare | Educare, Burnwood, VIC, Australia |
| Edward Elgar | Edward Elgar, Cheltenham |
| EEM | East European Monographs, Boulder, CO |
| Eerdmans | William Eerdmans, Grand Rapids, MI |
| EETS | Early English Text Society, c/o Exeter College, Oxford |
| Eihosha | Eihosha, Tokyo, Japan |
| Elephas | Elephas Books, Kewdale, WA, Australia |
| Elibank | Elibank Press, Wellington, New Zealand |
| Elm Tree | Elm Tree Books, London |
| ELS | ELS Editions, Victoria, BC, Canada |
| Ember | Ember Press, Brixham, South Devon |
| Emerald | Emerald Group Publishing, Bingley, Yorkshire |
| EMSH | Editions de la Maison des Sciences de l'Homme, Paris, France |
| Enitharmon | Enitharmon Press, London |
| Enzyklopädie | Enzyklopädie, Leipzig, Germany |
| EONF | Eugene O'Neill Foundation, Danville, CA |
| EPNS | English Place-Name Society, Beeston, Nottingham |
| epubli | e-book branch of Holzbrinck, Stuttgart, Germany |
| EPURE | Editions et Presses universitaires de Reims, France |

| | |
|---|---|
| Epworth | Epworth Press, Manchester |
| Equinox | Equinox Publishing, Sheffield |
| Eriksson | Paul Eriksson, Middlebury, VT |
| Erlbaum | Erlbaum Associates, NJ |
| Erskine | Erskine Press, Harleston, Norfolk |
| ESI | Edizioni Scientifiche Italiane, Naples, Italy |
| ESL | Edizioni di Storia e Letteratura, Rome, Italy |
| EUFS | Editions Universitaires Fribourg Suisse, Switzerland |
| EUL | Edinburgh University Library, Edinburgh |
| Europa | Europa Publishers, London |
| Evans | M. Evans, New York, NY |
| Exact Change | Exact Change, Boston, MA |
| Exeter UP | Exeter UP, Devon |
| Exile | Exile Editions, Toronto, ON, Canada |
| Eyre | Eyre Methuen, London |
| FAB | Free Association Books, London |
| Faber | Faber & Faber, London |
| FAC | Federation d'Activites Culturelles, Paris, France |
| FACP | Fremantle Arts Centre Press, Fremantle, WA, Australia |
| Fahrenheit | Fahrenheit Publishing, Capetown, South Africa |
| Falcon Books | Falcon Books, Eastbourne |
| F&F | Fels & Firn Press, San Anselmo, CA |
| F&S | Feffer & Simons, Amsterdam, The Netherlands |
| Fantagraphics | Fantagraphics, Seattle, WA |
| Farrand | Farrand Press, London |
| Fay | Barbara Fay, Stuttgart, Germany |
| F–B | Ford–Brown, Houston, TX |
| FCP | Four Courts Press, Dublin, Eire |
| FDUP | Fairleigh Dickinson UP, Madison, NJ |
| FE | Fourth Estate, London |
| Feminist | Feminist Press, New York, NY |
| Fence | Fence Books, Albany, NY |
| Field Day | Field Day, Derry |
| Fifth House | Fifth House Publications, Saskatoon, Saskatchewan |
| Fine | Donald Fine, New York, NY |
| Fink | Fink Verlag, Munich, Germany |
| Five Leaves | Five Leaves Publications, Nottingham |
| Flamingo | Flamingo Publishing, Newark, NJ |
| Flammarion | Flammarion, Paris, France |
| Flood | Flood Editions, Chicago, IL |
| Floris | Floris Books, Edinburgh |
| FlorSU | Florida State University, Tallahassee, FL |
| FOF | Facts on File, New York, NY |
| Folger | Folger Shakespeare Library, Washington, DC |
| Folio | Folio Press, London |
| Fontana | Fontana Press, London |
| Footprint | Footprint Press, Colchester, Essex |
| FordUP | Fordham UP, New York, NY |
| Foris | Foris Publications, Dordrecht, The Netherlands |
| Forsten | Egbert Forsten Publishing, Groningen, The Netherlands |
| Fortress | Fortress Press, Philadelphia, PA |
| ForItal | Forum Italicum, Stony Brook University, New York, NY |
| Francis Boutle | Francis Boutle Publishers, London |

| | |
|---|---|
| Francke | Francke Verlag, Berne, Switzerland |
| Frank & Timme | Frank & Timme, Berlin, Germany |
| Franklin | Burt Franklin, New York, NY |
| FreedomP | Freedom Press, London |
| FreeP | Free Press, New York, NY |
| FreeUP | Free UP, Amsterdam, The Netherlands |
| Freundlich | Freundlich Books, New York, NY |
| FS&G | Farrar, Straus & Giroux |
| FSP | Five Seasons Press, Madley, Hereford |
| FW | Fragments West/Valentine Press, Long Beach, CA |
| FWA | Fiji Writers' Association, Suva, Fiji |
| FWP | Falling Wall Press, Bristol |
| Gale | Gale Research, Detroit, MI |
| Galilée | Galilée, Paris, France |
| Gallimard | Gallimard, Paris, France |
| G&G | Grevatt & Grevatt, Newcastle upon Tyne |
| G&M | Gill & Macmillan, Dublin, Eire |
| Garland | Garland Publishing, New York, NY |
| Gasson | Roy Gasson Associates, Wimbourne, Dorset |
| Gateway | Gateway Editions, Washington, DC |
| GE | Greenwich Exchange, UK |
| Getty | Getty Publications, New York, NY |
| GIA | GIA Publications, USA |
| Gininderra | Gininderra Press, Canberra, Australia |
| Girasole | Edizioni del Girasole, Ravenna, Austria |
| GlasgowDL | Glasgow District Libraries, Glasgow |
| Gleerup | Gleerupska, Lund, Sweden |
| GMSmith | Gibbs M. Smith, Layton, UT |
| Golden Dog | Golden Dog, Ottawa, ON, Canada |
| Gollancz | Victor Gollancz, London |
| Gomer | Gomer Press, Llandysul, Dyfed |
| GothU | Gothenburg University, Gothenburg, Sweden |
| Gower | Gower Publishing, Aldershot, Hants |
| GRAAT | Groupe de Recherches Anglo-Américaines de Tours |
| Grafton | Grafton Books, London |
| GranB | Granary Books, New York, NY |
| Granta | Granta Publications, London |
| Granville | Granville Publishing, London |
| Grasset | Grasset & Fasquelle, Paris, France |
| Grassroots | Grassroots, London |
| Graywolf | Graywolf Press, St Paul, MI |
| Greenhalgh | M.J. Greenhalgh, London |
| Greenhill | Greenhill Books, London |
| Greenwood | Greenwood Press, Westport, CT |
| Gregg | Gregg Publishing, Surrey |
| Greville | Greville Press, Warwick |
| Greymitre | Greymitre Books, London |
| GroC | Grolier Club, New York, NY |
| Groos | Julius Groos Verlag, Heidelberg, Switzerland |
| Grove | Grove Press, New York, NY |
| GRP | Greenfield Review Press, New York, NY |
| Grüner | B.R. Grüner, Amsterdam, The Netherlands |
| Gruyter | Walter de Gruyter, Berlin, Germany |

| | |
|---|---|
| Guernica | Guernica Editions, Montreal, QC, Canada |
| Guilford | Guilford, New York, NY |
| Gulmohar | Gulmohar Press, Islamabad, Pakistan |
| Hackett | Hackett Publishing Company, Indianapolis, IN |
| Haggerston | Haggerston Press, London |
| Hale | Robert Hale, London |
| Hall | G.K. Hall, Boston, MA |
| Halstead | Halstead Press, Rushcutters Bay, NSW, Australia |
| HalsteadP | Halstead Press, c/o J. Wiley & Sons, Chichester, W. Sussex |
| Hambledon | Hambledon Press, London |
| HamptonP | Hampton Press, New York, NY |
| Handel | Handel Books, Nigeria |
| H&I | Hale & Iremonger, Sydney, NSW, Australia |
| H&L | Hambledon and London |
| H&M | Holmes & Meier, London and New York |
| H&S | Hodder & Stoughton, London |
| H&SNZ | Hodder & Stoughton, Auckland, New Zealand |
| H&W | Hill & Wang, New York, NY |
| Hansib | Hansib Publishing, London |
| Harbour | Harbour Publishing, Madeira Park, BC |
| Harman | Harman Publishing House, New Delhi, India |
| Harper | Harper & Row, New York, NY |
| Harrap | Harrap, Edinburgh |
| Hart | Hart Publishing |
| HarvardUP | Harvard UP, Cambridge, MA |
| Harvill Secker | Harvill Secker, London |
| Harwood | Harwood Academic Publishers, Langhorne, PA |
| Haytee | Haytee Press and Publishing, Ilorin, Nigeria |
| HBJ | Harcourt Brace Jovanovich, New York and London |
| HC | HarperCollins, London |
| HCAus | HarperCollins Australia, Pymble, NSW, Australia |
| Headline | Headline Book Publishing, London |
| Heath | D.C. Heath, Lexington, MS |
| HebrewUMP | Hebrew University Magnes Press |
| HeidelbergUP | Heidelberg University Press, Germany |
| Heinemann | William Heinemann, London |
| HeinemannA | William Heinemann, St Kilda, VIC, Australia |
| HeinemannC | Heinemann Educational Books, Kingston, Jamaica |
| HeinemannK | Heinemann Kenya Ltd |
| HeinemannNg | Heinemann Educational Books, Nigeria |
| HeinemannNZ | Heinemann Publishers, Auckland (now Heinemann Reed) |
| HeinemannR | Heinemann Reed, Auckland, New Zealand |
| Helm | Christopher Helm, London |
| Herbert | Herbert Press, London |
| Hermitage | Hermitage Antiquarian Bookshop, Denver, CO |
| Henry Southeran | Henry Southeran Ltd, London |
| Hern | Nick Hern Books, London |
| Hertfordshire | Hertfordshire Publications |
| Hesperus | Hesperus Press, London |
| Heyday | Heyday Books, Berkeley, CA |
| HH | Hamish Hamilton, London |
| Hilger | Adam Hilger, Bristol |
| Hippocampus | Hippocampus Press, New York, NY |

| | |
|---|---|
| History Press | History Press, Stroud |
| HM | Harvey Miller, London |
| HMSO | HMSO, London |
| Hodge | A. Hodge, Penzance, Cornwall |
| Hogarth | Hogarth Press, London |
| Holmby | Holmby Press, Flyinge, Sweden |
| HongKongUP | Hong Kong UP, Hong Kong |
| Horsdal & Schubart | Horsdal & Schubart, Victoria, BC, Canada |
| Horwood | Ellis Horwood, Hemel Hempstead, Hertfordshire |
| HoughtonM | Houghton Mifflin, Boston, MA |
| House of Breathings | House of Breathings, Lansing, MI |
| Howard | Howard UP, Washington, DC |
| HRW | Holt, Reinhart & Winston, New York, NY |
| Hudson | Hudson Hills Press, New York, NY |
| Hueber | Max Hueber, Ismaning, Germany |
| HUL | Hutchinson University Library, London |
| HullUP | Hull UP, University of Hull |
| Human & Rousseau | Human & Rousseau, Cape Town, South Africa |
| Humanities | Humanities Press, Atlantic Highlands, NJ |
| Humming Earth | Kilkerran, Scotland |
| Huntington | Huntington Library, San Marino, CA |
| Hurst | C. Hurst, Covent Garden, London |
| Hutchinson | Hutchinson Books, London |
| HW | Harvester Wheatsheaf, Hemel Hempstead, Hertfordshire |
| Hyland House | Hyland House Publishing, VIC, Australia |
| HyphenP | Hyphen Press, London |
| IAAS | Indian Institute of Advanced Studies, Lahore and New Delhi |
| Ian Henry | Ian Henry Publications, Hornchurch, Essex |
| IAP | Irish Academic Press, Dublin |
| Ibadan | Ibadan University Press, Ibadan, Nigeria |
| ICA | Institute of Contemporary Arts, London |
| Icon | Icon Books, London |
| IHA | International Hopkins Association, Waterloo, ON, Canada |
| IJamaica | Institute of Jamaica Publications, Kingston, Jamaica |
| Imago | Imago Imprint, New York, NY |
| Imperial CollegeP | Imperial College Press, London |
| IN | Impressions Nouvelles, Brussels, Belgium |
| Indigo | Indigo Dreams Publishing |
| IndUP | Indiana UP, Bloomington, IN |
| Inkblot | Inkblot Publications, Berkeley, CA |
| InstEducP | Institute of Education Press, University of London, London |
| Intellect | Intellect Books, Bristol, and Wilmington, NC |
| IntUP | International Universities Press, New York, NY |
| Inventions | Inventions Press, London |
| IonaC | Iona College, New Rochelle, NY |
| IowaSUP | Iowa State UP, Ames, IA |
| Ipswich | Ipswich Press, Ipswich, MA |
| IrishAP | Irish Academic Press, Dublin, Eire |
| ISE | Internet Shakespeare Editions |
| ISEAS | Institute of Southeast Asian Studies, Singapore |
| ISI | ISI Press, Philadelphia, PA |
| Italica | Italica Press, New York, NY |
| IULC | Indiana University Linguistics Club, Bloomington, IN |

| | |
|---|---|
| IUP | Indiana University of Pennsylvania Press, Indiana, PA |
| Ivon | Ivon Publishing House, Bombay, India |
| Jacana | Jacana Media, Johannesburg, South Africa |
| Jacaranda | Jacaranda Wiley, Milton, QLD, Australia |
| JadavpurU | Jadavpur University, Calcutta, India |
| Jesperson | Jesperson Press, St John's, NL, Canada |
| JHall | James Hall, Leamington Spa, Warwickshire |
| JHUP | Johns Hopkins UP, Baltimore, MD |
| JIWE | JIWE Publications, University of Gulbarga, India |
| JLRC | Jack London Research Center, Glen Ellen, CA |
| Jonas | Jonas Verlag, Marburg, Germany |
| Joseph | Michael Joseph, London |
| JPGM | J. Paul Getty Museum |
| JT | James Thin, Edinburgh |
| Junction | Junction Books, London |
| Junius-Vaughan | Junius-Vaughan Press, Fairview, NJ |
| Jupiter | Jupiter Press, Lake Bluff, IL |
| Juvenilia | Juvenilia Press, Sydney, NSW, Australia |
| JyväskyläU | Jyväskylä University, Jyväskylä, Finland |
| Kaibunsha | Kaibunsha, Tokyo, Japan |
| K&N | Königshausen & Neumann, Würzburg, Germany |
| K&W | Kaye & Ward, London |
| Kanishka | Kaniksha Publishers & Distributors, Delhi, India |
| Kansai | Kansai University of Foreign Studies, Osaka, Japan |
| Kardo | Kardo, Coatbridge, Scotland |
| Kardoorair | Kardoorair Press, Adelaide, SA, Australia |
| Karia | Karia Press, London |
| Karnac | Karnac Books, London |
| Karnak | Karnak House, London |
| Karoma | Karoma Publishers, Ann Arbor, MI |
| Katha | Katha, New Delhi, India |
| KC | Kyle Cathie, London |
| KCL | King's College London |
| KeeleUP | Keele University Press |
| Kegan Paul | Kegan Paul International, London |
| Kenkyu | Kenkyu-Sha, Tokyo, Japan |
| Kennikat | Kennikat Press, Port Washington, NY |
| KentSUP | Kent State University Press, Kent, OH |
| KenyaLB | Kenya Literature Bureau, Nairobi, Kenya |
| Kerosina | Kerosina Publications, Worcester Park, Surrey |
| Kerr | Charles H. Kerr, Chicago, IL |
| Kestrel | Viking Kestrel, London |
| K/H | Kendall/Hunt Publishing, Dubuque, IA |
| Kingsley | J. Kingsley Publishers, London |
| Kingston | Kingston Publishers, Kingston, Jamaica |
| Kinseido | Kinseido, Tokyo, Japan |
| KITLV | KITLV Press, Leiden, The Netherlands |
| Klostermann | Vittorio Klostermann, Frankfurt am Main, Germany |
| Kluwer | Kluwer Academic Publications, Dordrecht, The Netherlands |
| Knopf | Alfred A. Knopf, New York, NY |
| Knowledge | Knowledge Industry Publications, White Plains, NY |
| Köppe | Rüdiger Köppe Verlag, Cologne, Germany |
| Kraft | Kraft Books, Ibadan, Nigeria |

| | |
|---|---|
| Kraus | Kraus International Publications, White Plains, NY |
| KSUP | Kent State UP, Kent OH |
| LA | Library Association, London |
| Lake View | Lake View Press, Chicago, IL |
| LAm | Library of America, New York, NY |
| Lancelot | Lancelot Press, Hantsport, NS |
| Landesman | Jay Landesman, London |
| Lane | Allen Lane, London |
| Lang | Peter D. Lang, Frankfurt, Berne, New York, London |
| Langaa | Langaa Research and Publishing, Bamenda, Cameroon |
| LauU | Laurentian University, Greater Sudbury, Ontario, Canada |
| Lavengro Press | Lavengro Press, Wallingford |
| Learning Media | Learning Media Ltd, Wellington, New Zealand |
| Legacy | The Legacy Press, Ann Arbor, MI |
| Legenda | Legenda, London |
| LehighUP | Lehigh University Press, Bethlehem, PA |
| LeicAE | University of Leicester, Department of Adult Education |
| LeicUP | Leicester UP, Leicester |
| LeidenUP | Leiden UP, Leiden, The Netherlands |
| Leopard's Head | Leopard's Head Press, Oxford |
| Letao | Letao Press, Albury, NSW, Australia |
| LeuvenUP | Leuven UP, Leuven, Belgium |
| Levante | Levante editori, Bari, Italy |
| Lexik | Lexik House, Cold Spring, NY |
| Lexington | Lexington Publishers |
| LF | LiberFörlag, Stockholm, Sweden |
| LH | Lund Humphries Publishers, London |
| Liberty | Liberty Classics, Indianapolis, IN |
| Libris | Libris, London |
| LibrU | Libraries Unlimited, Englewood, CO |
| Liffey | Liffey Press, Dublin, Eire |
| Liguori | Liguori, Naples, Italy |
| Limelight | Limelight Editions, New York, NY |
| Lime Tree | Lime Tree Press, Octopus Publishing, London |
| LincolnUP | Lincoln University Press, NB, Canada |
| LINCOM | LINCOM Europa, Munich, Germany |
| LIT | Lit Verlag |
| LITIR | LITIR Database, University of Alberta, AB, Canada |
| LittleH | Little Hills Press, Burwood, NSW, Australia |
| LittPrag | Litteraria Pragensia, Prague, Czech Republic |
| Liveright | Liveright Publishing, New York, NY |
| LiverUP | Liverpool UP, Liverpool |
| Livre de Poche | Le Livre de Poche, Paris, France |
| Llanerch | Llanerch Enterprises, Lampeter, Dyfed |
| Locust Hill | Locust Hill Press, West Cornwall, CT |
| Loewenthal | Loewenthal Press, New York, NY |
| Longman | Pearson Longman Wesley, Harlow, Essex |
| LongmanC | Longman Caribbean, Harlow, Essex |
| LongmanF | Longman, France |
| LongmanNZ | Longman, Auckland, New Zealand |
| Longspoon | Longspoon Press, University of Alberta, Edmonton, AB, Canada |
| Lovell | David Lovell Publishing, Brunswick, VIC, Australia |
| Lowell | Lowell Press, Kansas City, MS |

| | |
|---|---|
| Lowry | Lowry Publishers, Johannesburg, South Africa |
| LPB | Litteraria Pragensia.Prague, Czech Republic |
| LSUP | Louisiana State UP, Baton Rouge, LA |
| LundU | Lund University, Lund, Sweden |
| LUP | Loyola UP, Chicago, IL |
| Lymes | Lymes Press, Newcastle, Staffordshire |
| Lythrum | Lythrum Press, Adelaide, SA, Australia |
| MAA | Medieval Academy of America, Cambridge, MA |
| Macleay | Macleay Press, Paddington, NSW, Australia |
| Macmillan | Macmillan Publishers, London |
| MacmillanC | Macmillan Caribbean |
| Madison | Madison Books, Lanham, MD |
| Madurai | Madurai University, Madurai, India |
| Maecenas | Maecenas Press, Iowa City, IA |
| Magabala | Magabala Books, Broome, WA |
| Magnes | Magnes Press, The Hebrew University, Jerusalem, Israel |
| Mainstream | Mainstream Publishing, Edinburgh |
| Maisonneuve | Maisonneuve Press, Washington, DC |
| Malone | Malone Society, c/o King's College, London |
| Mambo | Mambo Press, Gweru, Zimbabwe |
| M&E | Macdonald & Evans, Estover, Plymouth, Devon |
| M&S | McClelland & Stewart, Toronto, ON, Canada |
| Maney | W.S. Maney & Sons, Leeds |
| Mango | Mango Publishing, London, United Kingdom |
| Manohar | Manohar Publishers, Darya Gan, New Delhi |
| Mansell | Mansell Publishing, London |
| Mantra | Mantra Books, New Delhi, India |
| Manufacture | La Manufacture, Lyons, France |
| ManUP | Manchester UP, Manchester |
| Mariner | Mariner Books, Boston, MA |
| MarquetteUP | Marquette UP, Milwaukee, WI |
| Marvell | Marvell Press, Calstock, Cornwall |
| MB | Mitchell Beazley, London |
| McDougall, Littel | McDougall, Littel, Evanston, IL |
| McFarland | McFarland, Jefferson, NC |
| McG-QUP | McGill-Queen's UP, Montreal, QC, Canada |
| McGraw-Hill | McGraw-Hill, New York, NY |
| McIndoe | John McIndoe, Dunedin, New Zealand |
| McPheeG | McPhee Gribble Publishers, Fitzroy, VIC, Australia |
| McPherson | McPherson, Kingston, NY |
| MCSU | Maria Curie Skłodowska University, Lublin, Poland |
| ME | M. Evans, New York, NY |
| Meany | P.D. Meany Publishing, Port Credit, ON, Canada |
| Meckler | Meckler Publishing, Westport, CT |
| MelbourneUP | Melbourne UP, Carlton South, VIC, Australia |
| Melville | Melville House, New York, NY |
| Mellen | Edwin Mellen Press, Lewiston, NY |
| MellenR | Mellen Research UP |
| Menzies | Menzies Centre for Australian Studies |
| MercerUP | Mercer UP, Macon, GA |
| Mercury | Mercury Press, Stratford, ON, Canada |
| Merlin | Merlin Press, London |
| Methuen | Methuen, London |

| | |
|---|---|
| MethuenA | Methuen Australia, North Ryde, NSW, Australia |
| MethuenC | Methuen, Toronto, ON, Canada |
| Metro | Metro Publishing, Auckland, New Zealand |
| Metzler | Metzler, Stuttgart, Germany |
| MGruyter | Mouton de Gruyter, Berlin, New York, and Amsterdam |
| MH | Michael Haag, London |
| MHRA | Modern Humanities Research Association, London |
| MHS | Missouri Historical Society, St Louis, MO |
| MI | Microforms International, Pergamon Press, Oxford |
| Micah | Micah Publications, Marblehead, MA |
| MichSUP | Michigan State UP, East Lansing, MI |
| Milestone | Milestone Publications, Horndean, Hampshire |
| Millennium | Millennium Books, E.J. Dwyer, Newtown, Australia |
| Millstream | Millstream Books, Bath |
| Milner | Milner, London |
| MIMBr | Multilingual Matters, Bristol |
| Minuit | Éditions de Minuit, Paris, France |
| MIP | Medieval Institute Publications, Western Michigan University, Kalamazoo, MI |
| MITP | Massachusetts Institute of Technology Press, Cambridge, MA |
| MLA | Modern Language Association of America, New York, NY |
| MIM | Multilingual Matters, Clevedon, Avon |
| MLP | Manchester Literary and Philosophical Society, Manchester |
| MnaN | Mkuki na Nyota Publishers, Dar es Salaam, Tanzania |
| Modern Library | Modern Library (Random House), New York, NY |
| Mohr-Siebeck | Mohr-Siebeck GmbH & Co., Tubingen, Germany |
| Monarch | Monarch Publications, Sussex |
| MonashUP | Monash University Publishing, Clayton, VIC, Australia |
| Moonraker | Moonraker Press, Bradford-on-Avon, Wiltshire |
| Moorland | Moorland Publishing, Ashbourne, Derby |
| Moreana | Moreana, Angers, France |
| MorganSU | Morgan State University, Baltimore, MD |
| Morrow | William Morrow, New York, NY |
| Mosaic | Mosaic Press, Oakville, ON, Canada |
| Motley | Motley Press, Romsey, Hampshire |
| Mountain | Mountain Press, Cambridge |
| Mouton | Mouton Publishers, New York and Paris |
| Mowbray | A.R. Mowbray, Oxford |
| MR | Martin Robertson, Oxford |
| MRTS | MRTS, Binghamton, NY |
| MSUP | Memphis State UP, Memphis, TN |
| MtAllisonU | Mount Allison University, Sackville, NB, Canada |
| MTP | Museum Tusculanum Press, University of Copenhagen, Denmark |
| Mulini | Mulini Press, ACT, Australia |
| Muller | Frederick Muller, London |
| MULP | McMaster University Library Press |
| Murray | John Murray, London |
| MuseIndia | MuseIndia, Vikrampuri, India |
| MVP | Modernist Versions Project, Victorial, BC, Canada |
| NAL | New American Library, New York, NY |
| Narr | Gunter Narr Verlag, Tübingen, Germany |
| Nathan | Fernand Nathan, Paris, France |
| NBB | New Beacon Books, London |

| | |
|---|---|
| NBCAus | National Book Council of Australia, Melbourne, VIC, Australia |
| NCP | New Century Press, Durham |
| ND | New Directions, New York, NY |
| NDT | Nottingham Drama Texts, c/o University of Nottingham |
| NEL | New English Library, London |
| NELM | National English Literary Museum, Grahamstown, S. Africa |
| Nelson | Nelson Publishers, Melbourne, VIC, Australia |
| NelsonT | Thomas Nelson, London |
| New Endeavour | New Endeavour Press |
| NeWest | NeWest Press, Edmonton, AB, Canada |
| New Horn | New Horn Press, Ibadan, Nigeria |
| New Island | New Island Press |
| NewIssuesP | New Issues Press, Western Michigan University, MI |
| NH | New Horizon Press, Far Hills, NJ |
| N-H | Nelson-Hall, Chicago, IL |
| NHPC | North Holland Publishing, Amsterdam and New York |
| NIACE | National Institute of Adult Continuing Education |
| NicV | Nicolaische Verlagsbuchhandlung, Berlin, Germany |
| NIE | La Nuova Italia Editrice, Florence, Italy |
| Niemeyer | Max Niemeyer, Tübingen, Germany |
| Nightwood | Nightwood Editions, Toronto, ON, Canada |
| NIP | Naval Institute Press, San Diego, CA |
| NIUP | Northern Illinois UP, De Kalb, IL |
| NLA | National Library of Australia |
| NLB | New Left Books, London |
| NLC | National Library of Canada, Ottawa, ON, Canada |
| NLP | New London Press, Dallas, TX |
| NLS | National Library of Scotland, Edinburgh |
| NLW | National Library of Wales, Aberystwyth, Dyfed |
| Nodus | Nodus Publikationen, Münster, Germany |
| Northcote | Northcote House Publishers, Plymouth |
| NortheastemU | Northeastern University, Boston, MA |
| NorthwesternUP | Norhwestem UP, Evanston, IL |
| Norton | W.W. Norton, New York and London |
| NorUP | Norwegian University Press, Oslo, Norway |
| Novus | Novus Press, Oslo, Norway |
| NPF | National Poetry Foundation, Orono, ME |
| NPG | National Portrait Gallery, London |
| NPP | North Point Press, Berkeley, CA |
| NSP | New Statesman Publishing, New Delhi, India |
| NSU Press | Northern States Universities Press |
| NSWUP | New South Wales UP, Kensington, NSW, Australia |
| NT | National Textbook, Lincolnwood, IL |
| NUC | Nipissing University College, North Bay, ON, Canada |
| NUP | National University Publications, Millwood, NY |
| NUSam | National University of Samoa |
| NUU | New University of Ulster, Coleraine |
| NWAP | North Waterloo Academic Press, Waterloo, ON, Canada |
| NWP | New World Perspectives, Montreal, QC, Canada |
| NYUP | New York UP, New York, NY |
| OakK | Oak Knoll Press, New Castle, DE |
| O&B | Oliver & Boyd, Harlow, Essex |
| Oasis | Oasis Books, London |

| | |
|---|---|
| OBAC | Organization of Black American Culture, Chicago, IL |
| OberlinCP | Oberlin College Press, Oberlin, OH |
| Oberon | Oberon Books, London |
| O'Brien | O'Brien Press, Dublin, Eire |
| OBS | Oxford Bibliographical Society, Bodleian Library, Oxford |
| OccP | Occasional Papers, London |
| Octopus | Octopus Books, London |
| OdenseUP | Odense UP, Odense, Denmark |
| OE | Officina Edizioni, Rome, Italy |
| OEColl | Old English Colloquium, Berkeley, CA |
| Offord | John Offord Publications, Eastbourne, E. Sussex |
| OhioUP | Ohio UP, Athens, OH |
| Oldcastle | Oldcastle Books, Harpenden, Hertfordshire |
| Olms | Georg Ohms, Hildesheim, Germany |
| Olschki | Leo S. Olschki, Florence, Italy |
| O'Mara | Michael O'Mara Books, London |
| Omnigraphics | Omnigraphics, Detroit, MI |
| Open Books | Open Books Publishing, Wells, Somerset |
| Open Court | Open Court Publishing, IL |
| OpenUP | Open UP, Buckingham and Philadelphia |
| OPP | Oxford Polytechnic Press, Oxford |
| Orbis | Orbis Books, London |
| OregonSUP | Oregon State UP, Corvallis, OR |
| Oriel | Oriel Press, Stocksfield, Northumberland |
| Orient Longman | Orient Longman, India |
| OrientUP | Oriental UP, London |
| OriginalNZ | Original Books, Wellington, New Zealand |
| ORP | Ontario Review Press, Princeton, NJ |
| Ortnamnsarkivet | Ortnamnsarkivet i Uppsala, Sweden |
| Orwell | Orwell Press, Southwold, Suffolk |
| Oryx | Oryx Press, Phoenix, AR |
| OSUP | Ohio State UP, Columbus, OH |
| Other | Otherland, Kingsbury, VIC, Australia |
| OTP | Oak Tree Press, London |
| OUCA | Oxford University Committee for Archaeology, Oxford |
| QUP | Oxford UP, Oxford |
| OUPAm | Oxford UP, New York, NY |
| OUPAus | Oxford UP, Melbourne, VIC, Australia |
| OUPC | Oxford UP, Toronto, ON, Canada |
| OUPI | Oxford UP, New Delhi, India |
| OUPNZ | Oxford UP, Auckland, New Zealand |
| OUPSA | Oxford UP Southern Africa, Cape Town, South Africa |
| Outlet | Outlet Book, New York, NY |
| Outskirts | Outskirts Press, Parker, CO |
| Overlook | Overlook Press, New York, NY |
| Owen | Peter Owen, London |
| OWS | Oscar Wilde Society, London |
| Pace UP | Pace University Press, New York, NY |
| Pacifica | Press Pacifica, Kailua, Hawaii, HI |
| PAJ | PAJ Publications, New York, NY |
| Paladin | Paladin Books, London |
| Palgrave | Palgrave, NY |
| Pan | Pan Books, London |

| | |
|---|---|
| PalMac | Palgrave Macmillan, Hampshire, UK |
| PanAmU | Pan American University, Edinburgh, TX |
| P&C | Pickering & Chatto, London |
| Pandanus | Pandanus Press, Canberra, ACT, Australia |
| Pandion | Pandion Press, Capitola, CA |
| Pandora | Pandora Press, London |
| Pan Macmillan | Pan Macmillan Australia, South Yarra, VIC, Australia |
| Pantheon | Pantheon Books, New York, NY |
| Paradigm | Paradigm Publishers, Boulder, CO |
| ParagonH | Paragon House Publishers, New York, NY |
| Paris | Paris Press Books, Paris, France |
| Parnassus | Parnassus Imprints, Hyannis, MA |
| Paternoster | Paternoster Press, Carlisle, Cumbria |
| Patten | Patten Press, Penzance |
| Paulist | Paulist Press, Ramsey, NJ |
| Paupers | Paupers' Press, Nottingham |
| Pavilion | Pavilion Books, London |
| PBFA | Provincial Booksellers' Fairs Association, Cambridge |
| PCP | Playwrights Canada Press, ON, Canada |
| Peachtree | Peachtree Publishers, Atlanta, GA |
| Pearson | David Pearson, Huntingdon, Cambridge |
| Peepal Tree | Peepal Tree Books, Leeds |
| Peeters | Peeters Publishers and Booksellers, Leuven, Belgium |
| Pelham | Pelham Books, London |
| Pembridge | Pembridge Press, London |
| Pemmican | Pemmican Publications, Winnipeg, MB, Canada |
| PencraftI | Pencraft International, Ashok Vihar II, Delhi, India |
| Penguin | Penguin Books, Harmondsworth, Middlesex |
| PenguinA | Penguin Books, Ringwood, VIC, Australia |
| PenguinNZ | Penguin Books, Auckland, New Zealand |
| Penkevill | Penkevill Publishing, Greenwood, FL |
| Pentland | Pentland Press, Ely, Cambridge |
| Penumbra | Penumbra Press, Moonbeam, Ontario, ON, Canada |
| People's | People's Publications, London |
| Pergamon | Pergamon Press, Oxford |
| Permanent | Permanent Press, Sag Harbor, NY |
| Permanent Black | Permanent Black, Delhi, India |
| Perpetua | Perpetua Press, Oxford |
| Petton | Petton Books, Oxford |
| Pevensey | Pevensey Press, Newton Abbot, Devon |
| PH | Prentice-Hall, Englewood Cliffs, NJ |
| Phaidon | Phaidon Press, London |
| PHI | Prentice-Hall International, Hemel Hempstead, Hertfordshire |
| PhilL | Philosophical Library, New York, NY |
| Phillimore | Phillimore, Chichester |
| Piatkus | Piatkus Books, London |
| PicadorAf | Picador Africa, Johannesburg, South Africa |
| Pickwick | Pickwick Publications, Allison Park, PA |
| Pilgrim | Pilgrim Books, Norman, OK |
| PIMS | Pontifical Institute of Mediaeval Studies |
| Pinter | Frances Pinter Publishers, London |
| PLA | Private Libraries Association |
| Plains | Plains Books, Carlisle |

| | |
|---|---|
| Plenum | Plenum Publishing, London and New York |
| Plexus | Plexus Publishing, London |
| Pliegos | Editorial Pliegos, Madrid, Spain |
| Ploughshares | Ploughshares Books, Watertown, MA |
| PlovdivUP | Plovdiv University Press, Bulgaria |
| PML | Pierpont Morgan Library, New York, NY |
| Polity | Polity Press, Cambridge |
| Polygon | Polygon, Edinburgh |
| Polymath | Polymath Press, TAS, Australia |
| Poolbeg | Poolbeg Press, Swords, Dublin, Eire |
| Porcepic | Press Porcepic, Victoria, BC, Canada |
| Porcupine | Porcupine's Quill, ON, Canada |
| PortN | Port Nicholson Press, Wellington, NZ |
| Potter | Clarkson N. Potter, New York, NY |
| Power | Power Publications, University of Sydney, NSW, Australia |
| PPUBarcelona | Promociones y Publicaciones Universitarias, Barcelona, Spain |
| Praeger | Praeger, New York, NY |
| Prakash | Prakash Books, India |
| Prestel | Prestel Verlag, Germany |
| PrestigeB | Prestige Books, New Delhi, India |
| Primavera | Edizioni Primavera, Gunti Publishing, Florence, Italy |
| Primrose | Primrose Press, Alhambra, CA |
| PrincetonAP | Princeton Architectural Press, Princeton, NJ |
| PrincetonUL | Princeton University Library, Princeton, NJ |
| PrincetonUP | Princeton UP, Princeton, NJ |
| Printwell | Printwell Publishers, Jaipur, India |
| Prism | Prism Press, Bridport, Dorset |
| PRO | Public Record Office, London |
| Profile | Profile Books, Ascot, Berks |
| ProgP | Progressive Publishers, Calcutta, India |
| PSUP | Pennsylvania State UP, University Park, PA |
| PsychP | Psychology Press (Routledge), New York, NY |
| PublishNation | PublishNation, London |
| PUF | Presses Universitaires de France, Paris, France |
| PULM | Presses Universitaires de la Méditérrannée, Montpellier, France |
| Punctum | Punctum Books, Brooklyn, New York, NY |
| PUPOuest | Presses Universitaires de Paris Ouest, Paris, France |
| PUPV | Publications de l'université Paul-Valéry, Montpellier 3, France |
| PurdueUP | Purdue UP, Lafayette, IN |
| Pushcart | Pushcart Press, Wainscott, NY |
| Pustet | Friedrich Pustet, Regensburg, Germany |
| Putnam | Putnam Publishing, New York, NY |
| QED | QED Press, Ann Arbor, MI |
| Quaritch | Bernard Quaritch Ltd, London |
| Quarry | Quarry Press, Kingston, ON, Canada |
| Quartet | Quartet Books, London |
| QUT | Queensland University of Technology, QLD, Australia |
| RA | Royal Academy of Arts, London |
| Rainforest | Rainforest Publishing, Faxground, NSW, Australia |
| R&B | Rosenklide & Bagger, Copenhagen, Denmark |
| R&L | Rowman & Littlefield, Totowa, NJ |
| Randle | Ian Randle, Kingston, Jamaica |
| RandomH | Random House, London and New York |

| | |
|---|---|
| RandomHAus | Random House Australia, VIC, Australia |
| RandomHNZ | Random House New Zealand Limited, Auckland, New Zealand |
| Ravan | Ravan Press, Johannesburg, South Africa |
| Ravette | Ravette, London |
| Ravi Dayal | Ravi Dayal Publishers, New Delhi, India |
| Rawat | Rawat Publishing, Jaipur and New Delhi, India |
| Readworthy | Readworthy Publications, New Delhi, India |
| Reaktion | Reaktion Books, London |
| Rebel | Rebel Press, London |
| Red Kite | Red Kite Press, Guelph, ON, Canada |
| Red Rooster | Red Rooster Press, Hotham Hill, VIC, Australia |
| Red Sea | Red Sea Press, NJ |
| Reed | Reed Books, Port Melbourne, VIC, Australia |
| Reed NZ | Reed Publishing NZ Ltd., Auckland, New Zealand |
| Reference | Reference Press, Toronto, ON, Canada |
| Regents | Regents Press of Kansas, Lawrence, KS |
| Reichenberger | Roswitha Reichenberger, Kessel, Germany |
| Reinhardt | Max Reinhardt, London |
| Remak | Remak, Alblasserdam, The Netherlands |
| RenI | Renaissance Institute, Sophia University, Tokyo, Japan |
| Research | Research Publications, Reading |
| ReScript | ReScript Books, Hastings, Sussex |
| RETS | Renaissance English Text Society, Chicago, IL |
| RH | Ramsay Head Press, Edinburgh |
| RHS | Royal Historical Society, London |
| RIA | Royal Irish Academy, Dublin, Eire |
| RiceUP | Rice UP, Houston, TX |
| Richarz | Hans Richarz, St Augustin, Germany |
| RITP | Rochester Institute of Technology Press, Rochester, NY |
| Rivers Oram | Rivers Oram Press, London |
| Rizzoli | Rizzoli International Publications, New York, NY |
| Robinson | Robinson Publishing, London |
| Robson | Robson Books, London |
| Rockport | Rockport Publishers, Rockport, MA |
| Rodopi | Rodopi, Amsterdam, The Netherlands |
| Roebuck | Stuart Roebuck, Suffolk |
| RoehamptonI | Roehampton Institute London |
| Ronsdale | Ronsdale Press |
| Routledge | Routledge, London and New York |
| Royce | Robert Royce, London |
| RS | Royal Society, London |
| RSC | Royal Shakespeare Company, London |
| RSL | Royal Society of Literature, London |
| RSVP | Research Society for Victorian Periodicals, University of Leicester |
| RT | RT Publications, London |
| Running | Running Press, Philadelphia, PA |
| Russell | Michael Russell, Norwich |
| RutgersUP | Rutgers UP, New Brunswick, NJ |
| Ryan | Ryan Publishing, London |
| SA | Sahitya Akademi, New Delhi, India |
| Sage | Sage Publications, London |
| SageIn | SAGE Publications India, New Delhi, India |
| Sagittaire | Éditions du Sagittaire, Paris |

| | |
|---|---|
| SAI | Sociological Abstracts, San Diego, CA |
| Salamander | Salamander Books, London |
| Salem | Salem Press, Englewood Cliffs, NJ |
| S&A | Shukayr and Akasheh, Amman, Jordan |
| S&D | Stein & Day, Briarcliff Manor, NJ |
| S&J | Sidgwick & Jackson, London |
| S&M | Sun & Moon Press, Los Angeles, CA |
| S&P | Simon & Piere, Toronto, ON, Canada |
| S&S | Simon & Schuster, New York and London |
| S&W | Secker & Warburg, London |
| Sangam | Sangam Books, London |
| Sangsters | Sangsters Book Stores, Kingston, Jamaica |
| SAP | Scottish Academic Press, Edinburgh |
| Saros | Saros International Publishers |
| Sarup | Sarup & Sons, New Delhi, India |
| Saur | Bowker-Saur, Sevenoaks, Kent |
| Savacou | Savacou Publications, Kingston, Jamaica |
| S-B | Schwann-Bagel, Düsseldorf, Germany |
| ScanUP | Scandinavian University Presses, Oslo, Norway |
| Scarecrow | Scarecrow Press, Metuchen, NJ |
| Schäuble | Schäuble Verlag, Rheinfelden, Germany |
| Schmidt | Erich Schmidt Verlag, Berlin, Germany |
| Schneider | Lambert Schneider, Heidelberg, Germany |
| Schocken | Schocken Books, New York, NY |
| Scholarly | Scholarly Press, St Clair Shores, MI |
| ScholarsG | Scholars Press, GA |
| Schöningh | Ferdinand Schöningh, Paderborn, Germany |
| Schwinn | Michael Schwinn, Neustadt, Germany |
| SCJP | Sixteenth-Century Journal Publications |
| Scolar | Scolar Press, Aldershot, Hampshire |
| ScotLitInt | Scottish Literature International, Glasgow |
| SCP | Second Chance Press, Sag Harbor, NY |
| Scribe | Scribe Publishing, Colchester |
| Scribner | Charles Scribner, New York, NY |
| SDSU | Department of English, South Dakota State University, SD |
| Seafarer | Seafarer Books, London |
| Seaver | Seaver Books, New York, NY |
| Segue | Segue, New York, NY |
| Semiotext(e) | Semiotext(e), Columbia University, New York, NY |
| Sensations Press | Sensations Press, UK |
| SePA | Self-Publishing Association |
| Sequart | Sequart Research & Literary Organization |
| Seren Books | Seren Books, Bridgend |
| Serpent's Tail | Serpent's Tail Publishing, London |
| Sessions | William Sessions, York |
| Seuil | Éditions du Seuil, Paris, France |
| 7:84 Pubns | 7:84 Publications, Glasgow |
| SH | Somerset House, Teaneck, NJ |
| Shalabh | Shalabh Book House, Meerut, India |
| Shanghai JiaotongUP | Shanghai Jiaotong University Press, Shanghai |
| ShAP | Sheffield Academic Press, Sheffield |
| Shaun Tyas | Paul Watkins Publishing, Donington, Lincolnshire |

| | |
|---|---|
| Shearsman | Shearsman Books, Exeter |
| Shearwater | Shearwater Press, Lenah Valley, TAS, Australia |
| Sheba | Sheba Feminist Publishers, London |
| Sheed&Ward | Sheed & Ward, London |
| Sheila Markham | Sheila Markham Rare Books |
| Sheldon | Sheldon Press, London |
| Shinozaki | Shinozaki Shorin, Tokyo, Japan |
| Shinshindo | Shinshindo Publishing, Tokyo, Japan |
| Shire | Shire Publications, Princes Risborough, Buckinghamshire |
| Shoal Bay Press | Shoal Bay Press, New Zealand |
| Shoe String | Shoe String Press, Hamden, CT |
| SIAS | Scandinavian Institute of African Studies, Uppsala, Sweden |
| SIL | Summer Institute of Linguistics, Academic Publications, Dallas, TX |
| SIUP | Southern Illinois University Press, IL |
| Simon King | Simon King Press, Milnthorpe, Cumbria |
| Sinclair-Stevenson | Sinclair-Stevenson, London |
| SingaporeUP | Singapore UP, Singapore |
| SIUP | Southern Illinois UP, Carbondale, IL |
| SJSU | San Jose State University, San Jose, CA |
| Skilton | Charles Skilton, London |
| Slatkine | Éditions Slatkine, Paris, France |
| Slavica | Slavica Publishers, Columbus, OH |
| Sleepy Hollow | Sleepy Hollow Press, Tarrytown, NY |
| Smith Settle | Smith Settle, W. Yorkshire |
| SMUP | Southern Methodist UP, Dallas, TX |
| Smythe | Colin Smythe, Gerrards Cross, Buckinghamshire |
| SNH | Société Néophilologique de Helsinki, Finland |
| SNLS | Society for New Language Study, Denver, CO |
| SNTA | Society of Nigerian Theatre Artistes, Lagos, Nigeria |
| SOA | Society of Authors, London |
| Soho | Soho Book, London |
| SohoP | Soho Press, New York, NY |
| Solaris | Solaris Press, Rochester, MI |
| SonoNis | Sono Nis Press, Victoria, BC |
| Sorbonne | Publications de la Sorbonne, Paris, France |
| Souvenir | Souvenir Press, London |
| Spaniel | Spaniel Books, Paddington, NSW, Australia |
| SPCK | SPCK, London |
| Spectrum | Spectrum Books, Ibadan, Nigeria |
| Split Pea | Split Pea Press, Edinburgh |
| Spokesman | Spokesman Books, Nottingham |
| Spoon River | Spoon River Poetry Press, Granite Falls, MN |
| Springer | Springer Verlag, Berlin, Germany |
| SRI | Steinbeck Research Institute, Ball State University, Muncie, IN |
| SriA | Sri Aurobindo, Pondicherry, India |
| Sri Satguru | Sri Satguru Publications, Delhi, India |
| SSA | John Steinbeck Society of America, Muncie, IN |
| SSAB | Sprakförlaget Skriptor AB, Stockholm, Sweden |
| SSNS | Scottish Society for Northern Studies, Edinburgh |
| Stämpfli | Stämpfli Verlag, Bern, Switzerland |
| StanfordUP | Stanford UP, Stanford, CA |
| Staple | Staple, Matlock, Derbyshire |

| | |
|---|---|
| Starmont | Starmont House, Mercer Island, WA |
| Station Hill | Station Hill, Barrytown, NY |
| Stauffenburg | Stauffenburg Verlag, Tübingen, Germany |
| StDL | St Deiniol's Library, Hawarden, Clwyd |
| Steel Rail | Steel Rail Publishing, Ottawa, ON, Canada |
| Steele Roberts | Steele Roberts Publishing Ltd, Wellington, New Zealand |
| Steiner | Franz Steiner, Wiesbaden, Germany |
| Sterling | Sterling Publishing, New York, NY |
| SterlingND | Sterling Publishers, New Delhi, India |
| Stichting | Stichtig Neerlandistiek, Amsterdam, The Netherlands |
| St James | St James Press, Andover, Hampshire |
| St Martin's | St Martin's Press, New York, NY |
| Stockwell | Arthur H. Stockwell, Ilfracombe, Devon |
| Stoddart | Stoddart Publishing, Don Mills, ON, Canada |
| StPB | St Paul's Bibliographies, Winchester, Hampshire |
| STR | Society for Theatre Research, London |
| Strauch | R.O.U. Strauch, Ludwigsburg, Germany |
| Streamline | Streamline Creative, Auckland, New Zealand |
| Stree | Stree/Bhatkal, Kolkata, India |
| Studio | Studio Editions, London |
| Stump Cross | Stump Cross Books, Stump Cross, Essex |
| Sud | Sud, Marseilles, France |
| Suhrkamp | Suhrkamp Verlag, Frankfurt am Main, Germany |
| Summa | Summa Publications, Birmingham, AL |
| SUNYP | State University of New York Press, Albany, NY |
| SUP | Sydney University Press, NSW, Australia |
| Surtees | R.S. Surtees Society, Frome, Somerset |
| SusquehannaUP | Susquehanna UP, Selinsgrove, PA |
| SussexAP | Sussex Academic Press, Sydney, NSW, Australia |
| SussexUP | Sussex UP, University of Sussex, Brighton |
| Sutton | Alan Sutton, Stroud, Gloucester |
| Swallow | Swallow Press, Athens, OH |
| SWG | Saskatchewan Writers Guild, Regina, SK, Canada |
| Sybylla | Sybylla Feminist Press |
| SydneyUP | Sydney UP, Sydney, NSW, Australia |
| SyracuseUP | Syracuse UP, Syracuse, NY |
| Tabb | Tabb House, Padstow, Cornwall |
| Taishukan | Taishukan Publishing, Tokyo, Japan |
| Talonbooks | Talonbooks, Vancouver, BC, Canada |
| TamilU | Tamil University, Thanjavur, India |
| T&F | Taylor & Francis Books |
| T&H | Thames & Hudson, London |
| Tantivy | Tantivy Press, London |
| Tarcher | Jeremy P. Tarcher, Los Angeles, CA |
| Tartarus | Tartarus Press |
| Tate | Tate Gallery Publications, London |
| Tavistock | Tavistock Publications, London |
| Taylor | Taylor Publishing, Bellingham, WA |
| TaylorCo | Taylor Publishing, Dallas, TX |
| TCG | Theatre Communications Group, New York, NY |
| TCP | Three Continents Press, Washington, DC |
| TCUP | Texas Christian UP, Fort Worth, TX |
| TEC | Third Eye Centre, Glasgow |

| | |
|---|---|
| Tecumseh | Tecumseh Press, Ottawa, ON, Canada |
| Telos | Telos Press, St Louis, MO |
| TempleUP | Temple UP, Philadelphia, PA |
| Teneo | Teneo Press, Amherst, NY |
| TennS | Tennyson Society, Lincoln |
| TexA&MUP | Texas A&MUP, College Station, TX |
| Text | Text Publishing, Melbourne, VIC, Australia |
| TextileB | Textile Bridge Press, Clarence Center, NY |
| The Smith | The Smith, New York, NY |
| Third Millennium | Third Millennium Publishing, London |
| Thoemmes | Thoemmes Press, Bristol |
| Thornes | Stanley Thornes, Cheltenham |
| Thorpe | D.W. Thorpe, Port Melbourne, VIC, Australia |
| Thorsons | Thorsons Publishers, London |
| Times | Times of Gloucester Press, Gloucester, ON, Canada |
| Totem | Totem Books, Don Mills, ON, Canada |
| Toucan | Toucan Press, St Peter Port, Guernsey |
| Touzot | Jean Touzot, Paris, France |
| Tragara | Tragara Press, Edinburgh |
| Transaction | Transaction Publishers, New Brunswick, NJ |
| Transcendental | Transcendental Books, Hartford, CT |
| Transcript | Transcript Verlag, Bielefeld, Germany |
| Transworld | Transworld, London |
| TrinityUP | Trinity UP, San Antonio, TX |
| Troubador | Troubador Publishing, Kibworth Beauchamp, Leicestershire |
| TRP | Texas Review Press, Huntsville, TX |
| TTUP | Texas Technical University Press, Lubbock, TX |
| TulaneUP | Tulane UP, New Orleans, LA |
| Tunué | Tunué, Rome, Italy |
| TurkuU | Turku University, Turku, Finland |
| Turnstone | Turnstone Press, Winnipeg, MB, Canada |
| UAB | University of Aston, Birmingham |
| UAdelaide | University of Adelaide, Australia |
| UAkronP | University of Akron Press, Akron, OH |
| UAlaP | University of Alabama Press, Tuscaloosa, AL |
| UAlbertaP | University of Alberta Press, Edmonton, AB, Canada |
| UAntwerp | University of Antwerp, The Netherlands |
| UArizP | University of Arizona Press, Tucson, AZ |
| UArkP | University of Arkansas Press, Fayetteville, AR |
| UAthens | University of Athens, Greece |
| UBarcelona | University of Barcelona, Spain |
| UBCP | University of British Columbia Press, Vancouver, BC, Canada |
| UBergen | University of Bergen, Norway |
| UBrno | J.E. Purkyne University of Brno, Czechoslovakia |
| UBrussels | University of Brussels, Belgium |
| UBuckP | University of Buckingham Press, Buckingham |
| UCalgaryP | University of Calgary Press, AB, Canada |
| UCalP | University of California Press, Berkeley, CA |
| UCAP | University of Central Arkansas Press, Conway, AR |
| UCapeT | University of Cape Town Press, South Africa |
| UChicP | University of Chicago Press, IL |
| UChesterP | University of Chester Press, Chester. Cheshire |
| UCDubP | University College Dublin Press, Eire |

| | |
|---|---|
| UCL | University College London Press |
| UCopenP | University of Copenhagen Press, Denmark |
| UDelP | University of Delaware Press, Newark, DE |
| UDijon | University of Dijon, France |
| UDur | University of Durham, Durham, UK |
| UEA | University of East Anglia, Norwich |
| UErlangen-N | University of Erlangen-Nuremberg, Germany |
| UEssex | University of Essex, Colchester |
| UExe | University of Exeter, Devon |
| UFlorence | University of Florence, Italy |
| UFlorP | University of Florida Press, FL |
| UFR | Université François Rabelais, Tours, France |
| UGal | University College, Galway, Eire |
| UGeoP | University of Georgia Press, Athens, GA |
| UGhent | University of Ghent, Belgium |
| UGlasP | University of Glasgow Press |
| UHawaiiP | University of Hawaii Press, Honolulu, HI |
| UHertP | University of Hertfordshire Press |
| UHuelva | Universidad de Huelva Publicaciones, Spain |
| UIfeP | University of Ife Press, Ile-Ife, Nigeria |
| UIllp | University of Illinois Press, Champaign, IL |
| UInnsbruck | University of Innsbruck, Austria |
| UIowaP | University of Iowa Press, Iowa City, IA |
| UKanP | University of Kansas Press, Lawrence, KS |
| UKL | University of Kentucky Libraries, Lexington, KY |
| UKwaZulu-NatalP | University of KwaZulu-Natal Press, Scottsville, South Africa |
| ULavalP | Les Presses de l'Université Laval, Quebec, QC, Canada |
| ULiège | University of Liège, Belgium |
| ULilleP | Presses Universitaires de Lille, France |
| ULondon | University of London |
| Ulster | University of Ulster, Coleraine |
| UMalta | University of Malta, Msida, Malta |
| UManitobaP | University of Manitoba Press, Winnipeg, MB, Canada |
| UMassP | University of Massachusetts Press, Amherst, MA |
| Umeå | Umeå Universitetsbibliotek, Umeå, Sweden |
| UMichP | University of Michigan Press, Ann Arbor, MI |
| UMinnP | University of Minnesota Press, Minneapolis, MN |
| UMirail-ToulouseP | University of Mirail-Toulouse Press, France |
| UMIRes | UMI Research Press, Ann Arbor, MI |
| UMissP | University of Missouri Press, Columbia, MO |
| UMontP | Montpellier University Press, France |
| UMP | University of Mississippi Press, Lafayette, MS |
| Umuzi | Umuzi, Cape Town, South Africa |
| UMysore | University of Mysore, India |
| UNancyP | Presses Universitaires de Nancy, France |
| UNCP | University of North Carolina Press, Chapel Hill, NC |
| Undena | Undena Publications, Malibu, CA |
| UNDP | University of Notre Dame Press, Notre Dame, IN |
| UNebP | University of Nebraska Press, Lincoln, NE |
| UNethAnt | University of The Netherlands, Antilles |
| UNevP | University of Nevada Press, Reno, NV |
| UNewE | University of New England, Armidale, NSW, Australia |
| UNewH | University of New Hampshire Press, Durham, NH |

| | |
|---|---|
| UNGP | University Press of North Georgia, Dahlonega, GA |
| Unicopli | Edizioni Unicopli, Milan, Italy |
| UnisaP | University of South Africa Press, Muckleneuk, South Africa |
| Unity | Unity Press, Hull |
| UnityP | Unity Press Woollahra, NSW, Australia |
| Universa | Uilgeverij Universa, Wetteren, Belgium |
| UNMP | University of New Mexico Press, Albuquerque, NM |
| UNorthTP | University of North Texas Press, TX |
| UNott | University of Nottingham |
| UNSW | University of New South Wales, NSW, Australia |
| Unwin | Unwin Paperbacks, London |
| Unwin Hyman | Unwin Hyman, London |
| UOklaP | University of Oklahoma Press, Norman, OK |
| UOslo | University of Oslo, Norway |
| UOtagoP | University of Otago Press, Dunedin, New Zealand |
| UOttawaP | University of Ottawa Press, ON, Canada |
| UPA | UP of America, Lanham, MD |
| UParis | University of Paris, France |
| UPColorado | UP of Colorado, Niwot, CO |
| UPennP | University of Pennsylvania Press, Philadelphia, PA |
| UPFlorida | University Press of Florida, FL |
| UPhilP | University of the Philippines Press, Quezon City, Philippines |
| UPittP | University of Pittsburgh Press, Pittsburgh, PA |
| UPKen | University Press of Kentucky, Lexington, KY |
| UPMissip | UP of Mississippi, Jackson, MS |
| UPN | Université de Paris Nord, Paris, France |
| UPNE | UP of New England, Hanover, NH |
| Uppsala | Uppsala University, Uppsala, Sweden |
| UProvence | University of Provence, Aix-en-Provence, France |
| UPSouth | University Press of the South, NO |
| UPSouthDen | University Press of Southern Denmark |
| UPValéry | University Paul Valéry, Montpellier, France |
| UPVirginia | UP of Virginia, Charlottesville, VA |
| UQP | University of Queensland Press, St Lucia, QLD, Australia |
| URegP | University of Regina Press, Regina, SK, Canada |
| URouen | University of Rouen, Mont St Aignan, France |
| URP | University of Rochester Press |
| USalz | Institut für Anglistik and Amerikanstik, University of Salzburg, Austria |
| USantiago | University of Santiago, Spain |
| USCP | University of South Carolina Press, Columbia, SC |
| USFlorP | University of South Florida Press, Florida, FL |
| USheff | University of Sheffield |
| Usher | La Casa Usher, Florence, Italy |
| UST | University of Santo Tomas Publishing House, Manila |
| USydP | University of Sydney Press, Sydney, NSW, Australia |
| USzeged | University of Szeged, Hungary |
| UtahSUP | Utah State UP, Logan, UT |
| UTampereP | University of Tampere Press, Knoxville, TN |
| UTas | University of Tasmania, Hobart, TAS, Australia |
| UTennP | University of Tennessee Press, Knoxville, TN |
| UTexP | University of Texas Press, Austin, TX |
| UTorP | University of Toronto Press, Toronto, ON, Canada |

| | |
|---|---|
| UTours | Université de Tours, France |
| UVerm | University of Vermont, Burlington, VT |
| UVict | University of Victoria, Victoria, BC |
| UWalesP | University of Wales Press, Cardiff |
| UWAP | University of Western Australia Press, Nedlands, WA, Australia |
| UWarwick | University of Warwick, Coventry |
| UWashP | University of Washington Press, Seattle, WA |
| UWaterlooP | University of Waterloo Press, Waterloo, ON, Canada |
| UWI | University of the West Indies, St Augustine, Trinidad |
| UWIndiesP | University of West Indies Press, Mona, Jamaica |
| UWiscM | University of Wisconsin, Milwaukee, WI |
| UWiscP | University of Wisconsin Press, Madison, WI |
| UWoll | University of Wollongong, NSW, Australia |
| UYork | University of York, York |
| Valentine | Valentine Publishing and Drama, Rhinebeck, NY |
| V&A | Victoria and Albert Museum, London |
| VanderbiltUP | Vanderbilt UP, Nashville, TE |
| V&R | Vandenhoeck & Ruprecht, Göttingen, Germany |
| Van Riebeeck | Van Riebeeck Society, Cape Town, South Africa |
| Vantage | Vantage Press, New York, NY |
| Variorum | Variorum, Ashgate Publishing, Hampshire |
| Vehicule | Vehicule Press, Montreal, QC, Canada |
| Verdant | Verdant Publications, Chichester |
| Verso | Verso Editions, London |
| VictUP | Victoria UP, Victoria University of Wellington, New Zealand |
| Vieweg | Vieweg Braunschweig, Wiesbaden, Germany |
| Viking | Viking Press, New York, NY |
| VikingNZ | Viking, Auckland, New Zealand |
| Virago | Virago Press, London |
| Vision | Vision Press, London |
| VLB | VLB Éditeur, Montreal, QC, Canada |
| Voltaire | Voltaire Foundation, Oxford |
| VP | Vulgar Press, Carlton North, VIC, Australia |
| VR | Variorum Reprints, London |
| Vrin | J. Vrin, Paris, France |
| VUP | Victoria University Press, Wellington, New Zealand |
| VUUP | Vrije Universiteit UP, Amsterdam, The Netherlands |
| VWSGB | Virginia Woolf Society of Great Britain |
| Wadsworth | Wadsworth Cengage Learning, Boston, MA |
| Wakefield | Wakefield Press |
| Walker | Walker & Co., New York, NY |
| W&B | Whiting & Birch, London |
| W&N | Weidenfeld & Nicolson, London |
| Water Row | Water Row Press, Sudbury, MA |
| Watkins | Paul Watkins, Stanford, Lincsolnshire |
| WB | Wissenschaftliche Buchgesellschaft, Darmstadt, Germany |
| W/B | Woomer/Brotherson, Revere, PA |
| Weaver | Weaver Press |
| Webb&Bower | Webb & Bower, Exeter |
| Wedgestone | Wedgestone Press, Winfield, KS |
| Wedgetail | Wedgetail Press, Earlwood, NSW, Australia |
| WesleyanUP | Wesleyan UP, Middletown, CT |
| West | West Publishing, St Paul, MN |

| | |
|---|---|
| WestviewP | Westview Press, Boulder, CO |
| WHA | William Heinemann Australia, Port Melbourne, VIC, Australia |
| Wheatsheaf | Wheatsheaf Books, Brighton |
| Whiteknights | Whiteknights Press, University of Reading, Berkshire |
| White Lion | White Lion Books, Cambridge |
| Whitston | Whitston Publishing, Troy, NY |
| Whittington | Whittington Press, Herefordshire |
| WHP | Warren House Press, Sale, Cheshire |
| Wiener | Wiener Publishing, New York, NY |
| Wildwood | Wildwood House, Aldershot, Hampshire |
| Wiley | (or Wiley-Blackwell) John Wiley, Chichester, New York and Brisbane |
| Wilmington | Wilmington Square Books, London |
| Wilson | Philip Wilson, London |
| Winter | Carl Winter Universitätsverlag, Heidelberg, Germany |
| Wits | Witwatersrand University Press, Johannesburg, South Africa |
| WIU | Western Illinois University, Macomb, IL |
| WL | Ward Lock, London |
| WLUP | Wilfrid Laurier UP, Waterloo, ON, Canada |
| WMP | World Microfilms Publications, London |
| WMU | Western Michigan University, Kalamazoo, MI |
| Wolfhound | Wolfhound Press, Dublin, Eire |
| Wombat | Wombat Press, Wolfville, NS |
| Woolf | Cecil Woolf, London |
| Word Power | Word Power Books, Edinburgh |
| Words | Words, Framfield, E. Sussex |
| Worldview | Worldview Publishers, New Delhi and Kolkata, India |
| WP | Women's Press, London |
| WPC | Women's Press of Canada, Toronto, ON, Canada |
| WSUP | Wayne State UP, Detroit, MI |
| WUO | Wydawnictwo Uniwersytetu Opolskiego, Warsaw, Poland |
| WUS | Wydawnictwo Uniwersytetu Slaskiego, Katowice, Poland |
| WVT | Wissenschaftlicher Verlag Trier, Germany |
| WVUP | West Virginia UP, Morgantown, WV |
| W-W | Williams-Wallace, Toronto, ON, Canada |
| WWU | Western Washington University, Bellingham, WA |
| Xanadu | Xanadu Publications, London |
| XLibris | XLibris Corporation |
| YaleUL | Yale University Library Publications, New Haven, CT |
| YaleUP | Yale UP, New Haven, CO and London |
| Yamaguchi | Yamaguchi Shoten, Kyoto, Japan |
| YMP | York Medieval Press |
| YorkP | York Press, Fredericton, NB, Canada |
| Zed | Zed Books, London |

## 3. Acronyms

| | |
|---|---|
| AAVE | African-American Vernacular English |
| AmE | American English |
| AusE | Australian English |
| BELF | English as a Lingua Franca in Business |
| BrE | British English |

| | |
|---|---|
| DP | Determiner Phrase |
| ECP | Empty Category Principle |
| EFL | English as a Foreign Language |
| EIL | English as an International Language |
| ELFA | English as a Lingua Franca in Academic Settings |
| ELT | English Language Teaching |
| ʼeModE | early Modern English |
| ENL | English as a Native Language |
| EPNS | English Place-Name Society |
| ESL | English as a Second Language |
| ESP | English for Special Purposes |
| HPSG | Head-driven Phrase Structure Grammar |
| LF | Logical Form |
| LFG | Lexical Functional Grammar |
| ME | Middle English |
| MED | Middle English Dictionary |
| MICASE | Michigan Corpus of Academic Spoken English |
| NZE | New Zealand English |
| ODan | Old Danish |
| OE | Old English |
| OED | Oxford English Dictionary |
| OF | Old French |
| ON | Old Norse |
| OT | Optimality Theory |
| PDE | Present-Day English |
| PF | Phonological Form |
| PhilE | Philippine English |
| PP | Prepositional Phrase |
| RP | Received Pronunciation |
| SABE | South African Black English |
| SAE | South African English |
| SingE | Singapore English |
| TESOL | Teaching English to Speakers of other Languages |
| TMA | Tense, Mood and Aspect |
| UG | Universal Grammar |
| VOICE | Vienna-Oxford International Corpus of English |
| WE | World Englishes |

# Preface

*The Year's Work in English Studies* is a narrative bibliography that records and evaluates scholarly writing on English language and on literatures written in English. It is published by Oxford University Press on behalf of the English Association.

The Editors and the English Association are pleased to announce that this year's Beatrice White Prize has been awarded to Annie Sutherland, *English Psalms in the Middle Ages, 1300-1450* (2015), published by Oxford University Press.

The authors of *YWES* attempt to cover all significant contributions to English studies. Writers of articles can assist this process by sending offprints to the journal, and editors of journals that are not readily available in the UK are urged to join the many who send us complete sets of current and back issues. These materials should be addressed to The Editors, *YWES*, The English Association, The University of Leicester, University Road, Leicester LEI 7RH, UK.

The views expressed in *YWES* are those of its individual contributors and are not necessarily shared by the Editors, Associate Editors, the English Association, or Oxford University Press.

This issue marks a farewell to James Ogden, who contributed the Dryden section for many decades and surpassed the record of our previously longest serving contributor, the redoubtable Edith Julia Morley, the first female Professor of English in a British university. Professor Ogden contributed to volumes 54 through 96, an incredible run of excellence and professionalism. Additionally, we must bid a fond farewell to Helen Lucas, the Executive Administrator of the English Association who is retiring after many years of service. Her guidance, her wisdom, her common sense, and her high standards of excellence have been very much appreciated. The English Association is truly in her debt.

The Editors

*The Year's Work in English Studies, Volume 96 (2017)* © *The Author 2017. Published by Oxford University Press on behalf of the English Association. All rights reserved.*
*For Permissions, please email: journals.permissions@oup.com*
doi:10.1093/ywes/max004

# I

# English Language

ROBERT CLOUTIER, ANITA AUER,
RADOSŁAW ŚWIĘCIŃSKI, PHILLIP WALLAGE,
GEA DRESCHLER, BEÁTA GYURIS, KATHRYN ALLAN,
LIESELOTTE ANDERWALD, ALEXANDER KAUTZSCH,
TIHANA KRAŠ, ALESSIA COGO, TIAN GAN, IDA PARISE,
CHARLOTTE TAYLOR, AND AGNES MARSZALEK

This chapter has thirteen sections: 1. General; 2. History of English Linguistics; 3. Phonetics and Phonology; 4. Morphology; 5. Syntax; 6. Semantics; 7. Lexicography, Lexicology and Lexical Semantics; 8. Dialectology and Sociolinguistics; 9. New Englishes and Creolistics; 10. Second Language Acquisition. 11. English as a Lingua Franca; 12. Pragmatics and Discourse Analysis; 13. Stylistics. Section 1 is by Robert A. Cloutier; section 2 is by Anita Auer; section 3 is by Radosław Święciński; sections 4 and 5 are by Phillip Wallage and Gea Dreschler; section 6 is by Beáta Gyuris; section 7 is by Kathryn Allan; section 8 is by Lieselotte Anderwald; section 9 is by Alexander Kautzsch; section 10 is by Tihana Kraš; section 11 is by Alessia Cogo, Tian Gan, and Ida Parise; section 12 is by Charlotte Taylor; section 13 is by Agnes Marszalek.

## 1. General

The four books discussed in this section can be broadly divided into two groups: two introductory texts on using statistics for linguistic research and two books focused on theory.

Both *Statistics for Linguists: A Step-by-Step Guide for Novices* by David Eddington and *How to do Linguistics with R: Data Exploration and Statistical Analysis* by Natalia Levshina offer an introduction to statistics and, more specifically, how it can be applied to linguistic research. Covering the same basic statistical concepts and tests and including hands-on exercises with answer keys, the textbooks differ primarily in two respects: the choice of statistical software package (with subsequent differences reflecting this choice)

*The Year's Work in English Studies, Volume 96 (2017)* © *The Author 2017. Published by Oxford University Press on behalf of the English Association. All rights reserved.*
*For Permissions, please email: journals.permissions@oup.com*
doi:10.1093/ywes/max019

and the scope of statistical tests and methods that each covers. Whereas Eddington's text is based on widely used but costly SPSS and focuses on the most common statistical tests, Levshina's text makes use of open-source software R and includes additional methods, such as Semantic Vector Spaces and making maps, which are not yet mainstream.

In his introduction to *Statistics for Linguists*, Eddington explains he chose SPSS over R because of its graphical user interface, though he acknowledges that 'in comparison to SPSS, R is more powerful, produces better graphics, and is free' (p. xvi). This text is therefore more appropriate for researchers and students who are more comfortable with point-and-click computer programs and/or do not have time to learn to manoeuvre the command-line interface of R. Eddington's book also has the goal of being 'a truly basic introduction—not just in title, but in essence' (p. xvi) and thus focuses on the most mainstream statistical tools available for linguistic analysis. This is reflected in the length of the book, which is divided into nine chapters: the first ('Getting to Know SPSS') introduces the reader to the basics of SPSS, the second ('Descriptive and Inferential Statistics') contains some of the basic concepts of statistics-based research, and the last seven chapters each focus on a particular statistical test (chapter 3, 'Pearson Correlation'; chapter 4, 'Chi-square'; chapter 5, 'T-Test'; chapter 6, 'ANOVA (Analysis of Variance)'; chapter 7, 'Multiple Linear Regression'; chapter 8, 'Mixed-Effects Models'; chapter 9, 'Mixed-Effects Logistic Regression'). A number of hands-on exercises are included for practice, and readers are referred to the author's website for answer keys and data sets for some of the exercises; it is odd, though, that these documents are not made available through the publisher's website. Moreover, the webpage itself is quite basic, with a simple alphabetical list of the documents, which are not named for the relevant chapter, but it is still easy enough to access the necessary documents. Two nice features of the text are how chapters 3 to 9 start and end. Each chapter starts by clearly stating what kinds of questions the test can be used to answer and what kind of data is appropriate for the test—this makes it easy to use the book as a quick statistical reference. Moreover, near the end of each chapter, the author provides a 'recipe' for the statistical test—a step-by-step guide to the application of the statistical test. The layout of the text, however, is plain and at times a bit difficult to follow.

Levshina's *How To Do Linguistics with R* not only offers an introduction to the more common statistical tests but also includes more specific linguistic approaches such as the measure of associations between words and constructions. It is divided into nineteen chapters that can be broadly divided into four parts. The preparatory section of the book includes chapter 1, which introduces statistics in research as well as some basic statistical concepts, and chapter 2, which provides a clear and gentle introduction to R, whose command-line interface might initially intimidate those with no or only a limited background in programming. The next two chapters continue with basic statistical concepts, including the first descriptive analysis of quantitative (chapter 3) and qualitative (chapter 4) variables. Chapters 5 to 14 explain the main statistical tests and analytical statistics: *t*-test (chapter 5), correlational analysis (chapter 6), linear regression (chapter 7), different types of ANOVA (chapter 8), various association measures (chapters 9–11), logistic regressions (chapters 12–13), and conditional inference trees and random forests (chapter 14). The final chapters focus on various exploratory multivariate methods: distributional approaches to semantics (chapters 15 and 16), Multidimensional Scaling (chapter 17), Principal Components Analysis and Factor Analysis (chapter 18), and Simple and Multiple Correspondence Analysis (chapter 19). All of the study questions and hands-on exercises with keys are available on a dedicated webpage through the publisher that is easy to access and navigate. Some useful features of the text are its layout and formatting (it includes blue textboxes with useful additional information that can be skipped, if necessary) and its description of how to report the various statistical tests in research— the information you should include for each test and a template for reporting the data.

Evelien Keizer's *A Functional Discourse Grammar for English* is the first textbook on Functional Discourse Grammar (FDG), a typologically based theory of language structure and the recent incarnation of and elaboration on Simon Dik's Functional Grammar. Clearly and accessibly written, the book focuses on outlining FDG and showing how it can be used to analyse the most important grammatical features of PDE while also including several examples from various languages so as not to lose sight of FDG's typological orientation. Keizer presents the theory in a detailed and structured way over seven chapters. Chapter 1 ('Why Functional Discourse Grammar?') introduces the basics of linguistic theory in general, contrasting functional and formal approaches, before going into more detail about FDG specifically, including the relevance of each of the components of the name to the theory and its underlying assumptions. Chapter 2 ('The General Architecture of FDG') briefly outlines the basic concepts of FDG and its hierarchical structure. The four levels of representation are fleshed out in the following chapters 3 to 6: 'The Interpersonal Level', 'The Representational Level', 'The Morphosyntactic Level', and 'The Phonological Level'. Three concrete and elaborated applications of the theory to analyses of sentences in English are demonstrated in chapter 7, 'Sample Representations'. Each chapter includes short questions throughout that engage the student while reading and ends with exercises that challenge students to apply the theory to new data.

Edited by Jonathan J. Webster, *The Bloomsbury Companion to M.A.K. Halliday* is a collection of essays exploring the life, influences, and theory of Halliday, the founder of Systemic Functional Linguistics (SFL). Aimed at a professional audience, this comprehensive volume contains nineteen contributions divided into four sections representing different periods in Halliday's life and the development of his theory of language. The single essay in Part I ('Halliday's Life') by Jonathan J. Webster begins the entire collection by succinctly outlining Halliday's life in a brief biography. Part II ('Halliday: The Making of a Mind') includes five chapters, each of which deals with a particular influence that shaped Halliday and his ideas about language, ranging from politics ('The Influence of Marxism' by M.A.K. Halliday), to general trends in science ('The "History of Ideas" and Halliday's Natural Science of Meaning' by David G. Butt), to more specific linguistic influences ('Halliday in China: Legacies and Advances from LUO, WANG and Beyond' by Peng Xuanwei; ' "Socially Realistic Linguistics": The Firthian Tradition' by Braj B. Kachru; 'Systemic Functional Linguistics: Halliday and the Evolution of a Social Semiotic' by Ruqaiya Hasan).

The eight chapters in Part III ('Halliday: Ideas about Language') examine in more detail various phenomena that Halliday has explored through the lens of his theory, reinforcing how strongly grounded in language use his theory is. The two chapters by Christian M.I.M. Matthiessen, 'Halliday on Language' and 'Halliday's Conception of Language as a Probabilistic System', lay down the basics of SFL and elaborate more fully on Halliday's idea of language as a probabilistic system. 'Language Development in Early Childhood: Learning How to Mean' by Jane Torr outlines Halliday's research into child language development, primarily based on a detailed analysis of his son Nigel's linguistic transition. J.R. Martin offers an introduction to Halliday's view on grammar from a pedagogical perspective in 'Halliday the Grammarian: Axial Foundations'. In 'Intonation', Bradley A. Smith and William S. Greaves provide an account of Halliday's description of intonation: what it is, how to study it, and how it is used in English grammar. Focusing on Halliday's call for descriptions of texts, Jonathan J. Webster discusses the notion of 'text' and its importance within SFL in 'Text Linguistics'. 'Halliday as an International Educator' by Geoff Williams presents some of the key educational concepts Halliday has introduced and how they have influenced educational practice. Related in subject matter to the chapter 'Text Linguistics', Annabelle Lukin explores Halliday's approach to language in literature in 'A Linguistics of Style: Halliday on Literature'; she advocates using the same method to analyse literary texts as any other text, though acknowledging that grammar can be used as an aesthetic resource.

Part IV ('Directions of Development from Halliday)' brings together five contributions that demonstrate the breadth and versatility of Halliday's ideas through its extension to other fields both inside and outside linguistics. These include music and painting ('Halliday's Three Functions and Their Interaction in the Interpretation of Painting and Music' by Michael O'Toole), multimodal analysis ('Multimodal Semiosis and Semiotics' by Kay L. O'Halloran, Marissa K.L.E., and Sabine Tan), translation ('Halliday's Contributions to a Theory of Translation' by Erich Steiner), typological studies ('Halliday in Relation to Language Comparison and Typology' by Kazuhiro Teruya and Christian M.I.M. Matthiessen), and computational linguistics ('Computational Linguistics: The Halliday Connection' by John Bateman and Mick O'Donnell).

## 2. History of English Linguistics

The history of English linguistics received a fair amount of attention in 2015. In the monograph *Grammar, Rhetoric and Usage in English: Preposition Placement 1500–1900*, which is based on her Ph.D. thesis, Nuria Yáñez-Bouza describes in great detail the precept and the usage of the competing linguistic features called preposition stranding and pied piping in the ModE period. The monograph consists of six chapters and a conclusion. The introduction spells out the linguistic features in some detail and outlines the theoretical framework in which the study is couched, notably that of language standardization and normative linguistics. Chapter 2, 'Methodology', describes the two corpora that serve as the basis of the investigation, i.e. (a) a precept corpus that consists of grammar books, as well as other works that include grammar sections such as letter-writing manuals and dictionaries, and (b) a usage corpus, which are two standard diachronic multi-genre corpora, namely the Helsinki Corpus (HC) and A Representative Corpus of Historical English Registers (ARCHER). Chapter 3 is dedicated to the precept corpus and in particular the attitudes expressed towards the linguistic features throughout the eighteenth century; this allows the author to determine the development of prescriptive and proscriptive comments. Chapter 4 focuses on the actual usage development of the two competing linguistic features. A thorough analysis of syntactic and genre variation reveals that preposition stranding was already around at the beginning of the period investigated, i.e. around 1500, and that the feature declined in the late eighteenth century. The latter development thus indicates that the stigmatization of the feature in precept works is unlikely to have developed during the same time period. The issue of stigmatization is then the main focus of chapter 5, 'Grammar, Rhetoric and Style', where Yáñez-Bouza determines the beginnings of the stigmatization by discussing grammatical correctness in early English grammars and their Latin models. Chapter 6, 'Latent Awareness', is concerned with the role of John Dryden and other individuals in relation to the emergence and development of language norms. Finally, in the conclusion, all major findings are revisited and links to present-day and contemporary attitudes on preposition stranding are made. All in all, this thorough and well-researched monograph makes a significant contribution to the history of English linguistics as well as related fields such as historical sociolinguistics.

The volume *Letter Writing and Language Change*, edited by Anita Auer, Daniel Schreier, and Richard J. Watts, also contains a few contributions that are of relevance for the linguistic history of English. Notably, the chapters by Tony Fairman on 'Language in Print and Handwriting' (pp. 53–71) and Anita Auer on 'Stylistic Variation' (pp. 133–55) briefly mention the role that grammars play—or do not play—in relation to schooling of different social layers of society. More attention to the normative role of grammars is given in Stefan Dollinger's contribution, 'Emerging Standards in the Colonies: Variation and the Canadian Letter Writer' (pp. 101–13). He focuses on early grammars in Canada and, in particular, on the precept of first-person *shall* and *will* in those works. This precept is then viewed in comparison to actual letter-writing data. Based on this investigation, Dollinger concludes that 'grammar books in widespread circulation in Ontario at the time offered no clues for the heterogeneous practice in early Canadian letters' (p. 112).

Transatlantic views on grammar writing are also presented in the volume *Transatlantic Perspectives of Late Modern English*, edited by Marina Dossena, which is based on talks given at the fifth Late Modern English conference (University of Bergamo, 2013). The volume consists of an introduction by the editor and ten chapters written by different scholars, of which several contribute new findings to the history of English linguistics. For instance, Carol Percy's 'Political Perspectives on Linguistic Innovation in Independent

America. Learning from the Libraries of Thomas Jefferson (1743–1826)' (pp. 37–53) sheds light on the linguistic views of the politician and scholar Thomas Jefferson by way of scrutinizing book catalogues of his libraries as well as related correspondence. On a linguistic level, Percy focuses particularly on American neologisms in order to determine the relationship between the 'linguistic tradition in Britain and . . . political affiliations in America' (p. 37). In fact, she finds that Jefferson supported neither the imposition of new linguistic standards nor the founding of an academy. Ingrid Tieken-Boon van Ostade's 'Five Hundred Mistakes Corrected: An Early American English Usage Guide' (pp. 55–71) takes a close look at the usage guide *Five Hundred Mistakes Corrected* [1856] by an anonymous author. She focuses particularly on the content of the work and possible sources of the discussed mistakes. A comparison with British usage guides makes Tieken-Boon van Ostade conclude that early usage guides had different functions in Britain and America, that is, they were of use for the socially mobile at the time of the Industrial Revolution in Britain while they served as useful books for immigrants from Europe in mid-nineteenth-century America. Usage guides are also the focus of Ulrich Busse's contribution, 'Transatlantic Perspectives on Late Nineteenth-Century English Usage. Alford (1864) Compared to White (1871)' (pp. 73–97). While Alford's *The Queen's English* [1864] has been published in Britain, White's *Words and Their Uses* [1871] is an American usage guide. Busse argues that both handbooks can be seen as 'early specimens of prescriptive guides' (p. 73). The comparison of both usage guides in terms of content and ideological approach reveals that while both authors seem to be concerned with similar uses, White is clearly more conservative in his views in that he opposes innovation. Both authors see language use and morality as closely linked. The chapter ' "Provincial in England, but in common use with us": John R. Bartlett's Dictionary of Americanisms and the *English Dialect Dictionary*' by Javier Ruano-García, Maria F. Garcia-Bermejo Giner, and Pilar Sánchez-García (pp. 99–116) is concerned with the adoption and inclusion of American words in Joseph Wright's *English Dialect Dictionary* [1898–1905]. While Wright relied on several American sources, John R. Bartlett's *Dictionary of Americanisms* [1848] served as a particularly important source. The authors 'determine the proportion of terms taken from this source' (p. 99) as well as Wright's application of usage labels, comments, and quotations.

A special issue on the sense of place in the history of English (*ELL* 19:ii[2015]), edited by Karen P. Corrigan and Chris Montgomery, which celebrates the work of Professor Emeritus Joan Beal, also contains a few contributions that are concerned with the history of English linguistics. Nuria Yáñez-Bouza and David Denison discuss 'Which Comes First in the Double Object Construction?' (*ELL* 19[2015] 247–68) or, more precisely, in the pronominal pattern of the double object construction as in *Jim gave it him*, particularly in relation to the indirect object before direct object construction as in *Jim gave the driver £5*. This study is based on a range of contemporary and historical corpora and databases such as the Penn-Helsinki parsed corpora, the Salamanca Corpus, and the Corpus of Late 18th-Century Prose. Apart from investigating the double object constructions in usage corpora, the authors also shed light on the construction's development as a regional and social marker, as reflected in early normative grammars. They show, for instance, that the V-O$_d$-O$_i$ *give it me* has not been marginalized by prescriptive works in the ModE period, but appears to be on its way to becoming enregistered in specific areas, notably the north of England, at present (more on this in Section 5). A comparison between usage and precept approach is also taken in Ingrid Tieken-Boon van Ostade and Viktorija Kostadinova's contribution, 'Have Went—An American Usage Problem' (*ELL* 19[2015] 293–312). The authors based their investigation on a usage-guide corpus, attitude studies (questionnaire and face-to-face interviews), as well as British and American corpus data, both diachronic and synchronic. Their findings show that *have went* is considered a usage problem in AmE while being perceived as a non-standard dialectal feature in BrE. Most importantly, the authors report that the forms *have went* and *have gone* are seen as differing in meaning by North Americans with different socio-demographic backgrounds.

Another study published in 2015 is Ute Tintemann's 'The Traditions of Grammar Writing in Karl Philipp Moritz's (1756–93) Grammars of English (1784) and Italian (1791)' (*HL* 42[2015] 39–62). As the title indicates, the author is concerned with grammar-writing traditions of the English and Italian vernaculars and, in particular, the influence that the Latin model had on these traditions. The study reveals that the author relied extensively on the work of other authors that he translates from, for example James Greenwood's *Royal English Grammar* [1737] for his English work and Benedetto Rogacci's *Pratica, e compendiosa istruzione circa l'uso emendato, ed elegante della Lingua Italiana* [1711] for his Italian grammar. 'Senses of "Grammar" in the Eighteenth-Century English Tradition' (*ES* 96[2015] 913–43) is the focus of one of Nuria Yáñez-Bouza's article, in which she tries to determine the meaning of the term 'grammar' in eighteenth-century England. To this end, she bases herself on Ian Michael's seminal work on English grammar-writing and the so-called ECEG (Eighteenth-Century English Grammars) database. More precisely, she critically examines divisions into primary constituents such as orthography, etymology, and syntax. 'and the subsidiary content that accompanies the main parts of grammar' (p. 913) as, for instance, punctuation and irregular verbs. Her investigation reveals that the primary parts appear to be fairly uniform, while the additional content is extremely varied. Thomas Godard, in 'A New Grammar by Joseph Priestley (1733–1804)' (*Lang&H* 58[2015] 1–23), applies approaches from attribution studies in order to determine that the grammar Joseph Priestley wrote is the anonymous grammar that is prefixed to the *Vocabulary, or Pocket Dictionary* [1765]. In order to do so, he bases himself on biographical evidence, on the one hand, and on plagiarism software for grammar content comparisons on the other. Apart from being able to show that great parts of the 1765 grammar 'anticipated word for word the second edition of Priestley's *Rudiments of English Grammar* (1768)' (p. 1), Godard also shows that some of the most important innovations of the latter grammar, such as the definitions of parts of speech as well as the use of sourced examples, can already be found in the hitherto anonymous prefixed grammar.

## 3. Phonetics and Phonology

The publication of *The Handbook of English Pronunciation* edited by Marnie Reed and John M. Levis seems to be the major event of 2015 when it comes to books on English phonetics and phonology. The volume is a comprehensive source of reference for language researchers and teachers alike, covering a wide array of issues related to English pronunciation. Part I, presenting the subject matter from a historical perspective, is devoted to such issues as phonological changes that occurred in the language, the emergence and role of accent as a social symbol, as well as the history of teaching English pronunciation. The next section of the work focuses on the description of PDE segmentals and prosodic features, such as syllables, stress, rhythm, and intonation. The relation between discourse and pronunciation constitutes the centre of discussion in the third part of the book. Here readers can find information about connected speech phenomena in English, and the effect that discourse has on intonation and other prosodic features of the language. Another part of the handbook provides material about pronunciation features of the major varieties of the language, including North American, British, Australian, New Zealand, South African, and Indian English (see also Section 10 below for more research on the phonetics and the phonology of other Englishes). Part V of the book focuses on the acquisition of English pronunciation both in L1 and L2. The concluding and longest section of the volume contains an extensive discussion related to pronunciation teaching. A wide selection of the presented topics makes *The Handbook of English Pronunciation* a valuable source of information and an interesting read.

Voice onset time (VOT) does not cease to arouse interest among phoneticians and phonologists. Measurements of this parameter in spontaneous Scottish English speech provided an array of observations to Jane Stuart-Smith, Morgan Sonderegger, Tamara Rathcke, and Rachel Macdonald in 'The Private Life of Stops: VOT in a Real-Time Corpus of Spontaneous Glaswegian' (*LabPhon* 6[2015] 505–49). The authors provide a thorough overview of previous studies on VOT, which constitutes a solid background to the research questions asked in the paper. The investigators set out to discover the factors that influence the values of positive VOT in stressed syllable-initial stops (e.g. in *people*, *ten*). Additionally, the study is a search for evidence that positive VOT values changed over time in Scottish English. The results show that the stop's place of articulation exerts a significant effect on voice onset time. Similarly, it was attested that increasing local speaking rate results in the shortening of VOT in stops. Moreover, phrase-initial position of the plosive in comparison to phrase-medial one was found to be linked to a slight but significant increase in VOT. Trends related to the influence of the word's frequency and the height of the following vowel were also noticed. Regarding the change of VOT values in Glaswegian over time, the findings suggest that VOT in both voiced and voiceless stops became longer in the twentieth century.

New insights into the relation between voice onset time, onset fundamental frequency, and phonological voicing categories were delivered by Olga Dmitrieva, Fernando Llanos, Amanda A. Shultz, and Alexander L. Francis in 'Phonological Status, Not Voice Onset Time, Determines the Acoustic Realization of Onset *f*0 as a Secondary Voicing Cue in Spanish and English' (*JPhon* 49[2015] 77–95). Their experiments showed that English stops belonging to different phonological voice categories displayed dissimilar onset *f*0 values. In the case of phonologically voiceless stops, the onset value of the fundamental frequency was significantly higher than in stops with the phonological feature [+voice]. Moreover, phonetic voicing did not seem to affect the value of onset *f*0 in English stops that belonged to the same phonological voice category, even though their VOT characteristics differed (short lag VOT and lead voicing VOT). On the grounds of these observations, the authors postulate that the covariation between VOT and onset *f*0 values aims at enhancing phonological distinctiveness and aiding auditory perception of the consonants.

Uriel Priva, in his thorough article 'Informativity Affects Consonant Duration and Deletion Rates' (*LabPhon* 6[2015] 243–78), answers the question why some consonants become reduced or deleted while others do not. In a corpus study of AmE, the author considers such information theoretic properties of segments as frequency, probability, predictability, and informativity. The presented analysis indicates that low average (rather than local) segment predictability, contributing to its high informativity, is related to longer consonant duration and reduced likelihood to delete, which explains, for example, the existence of the process of /d/-deletion in words, such as *order* or *sudden*.

The pronunciation of Australian children's /l/ was scrutinized by Susan Lin and Katherine Demuth and presented in 'Children's Acquisition of English Onset and Coda /l/: Articulatory Evidence' (*JSLHR* 58[2015] 13–27). Examination of ultrasound images confirmed previous findings that /l/ is acquired later in the coda position than in the onset. Moreover, perceptual judgements of the lateral in syllable-initial positions did not always match articulatory data because the majority of highly variable /l/ productions were judged perceptually as adult-like. Based on this finding, the authors stipulate that articulatory norms should be formulated in conjunction with perceptual norms.

American children did not escape attention in 2015, either. In the article titled 'Development of Phonetic Variants (Allophones) in 2-Year-Olds Learning American English: A Study of Alveolar Stop /t, d/ Codas' (*JPhon* 52[2015] 152–69), Jae Yung Song, Stefanie Shattuck-Hufnagel, and Katherine Demuth examined whether children learn to produce canonical variants of phonemes first and then discover how to produce their allophones, or whether they begin by articulating the phonetic variants of sounds in specific contexts and grasp that these variants are realizations of the same phoneme only later. Acoustic and perceptual analyses of alveolar plosives revealed that children were more likely to articulate the consonants in the canonical manner rather than in the form of unreleased, flapped, or glottalized variants, as their mothers did. The text ends with a detailed discussion about the implications of these results for early phonological representations in children.

Georgia Zellou and Rebecca Scarborough, in 'Lexically Conditioned Phonetic Variation in Motherese: Age-of-Acquisition and Other Word-

Specific Factors on Infant- and Adult-Directed speech' (*LabPhon* 6[2015] 305–36), argue that the speakers of English are by no means self-centred. Their corpus analysis of utterances directed towards infants and adults indicates that interlocutors articulate certain words in a way that enhances the perceptibility of the speech signal. It appeared that mothers talking to their infants were likely to hyper-articulate vowels and increase the amount of co-articulatory nasalization (features that facilitate better perception) in lexical items that are characterized by lower frequency of occurrence or are reported to be acquired by children at later stages than earlier-learned and more frequent words. When communicating with adults, vowel hyper-articulation and greater nasality were attested in words with low frequency and high phonological neighbourhood density (words that are phonologically similar to many other lexical items). On the basis of these findings, the authors assert that speakers assess word difficulty and take the type of interlocutor into consideration and adjust their articulation accordingly.

The subject of the relevance of phonological neighbourhood density in English was challenged by Susanne Gahl, who reveals in 'Lexical Competition in Vowel Articulation Revisited: Vowel Dispersion in the Easy/Hard Database' (*JPhon* 49[2015] 96–116) that the increased dispersion of vowels in words with greater recognition difficulty does not necessarily result from the drive to ensure intelligibility. Having examined vowels and their consonantal context in a previously described dataset, Gahl points out that the more peripheral vowel productions may be attributed to co-articulatory effects exerted by flanking consonants.

The question whether phonotactic constraints help users of BrE discover word boundaries was raised by Katrin Skoruppa, Andrew Nevins, Adam Gillard, and Stuart Rosen in 'The Role of Vowel Phonotactics in Native Speech Segmentation' (*JPhon* 49[2015] 67–76). Their experiments involving the segmentation of nonsense syllable sequences revealed that vowel phonotactics exert an influence on English listeners' segmentation of speech. Specifically, it was shown that the constraint on the appearance of lax vowels syllable-finally displayed a small but robust effect on the participants' segmentation of nonsense words.

Margaret E. Renwick and Caitlin N. Cassidy revisited the phenomenon of palatalization in BrE in 'Detecting Palatalization in Spontaneous Spoken English' (*POMA* 23[2015] 1–10). Their study of word-final /s/ in pre-/j/ contexts, as in *miss you*, consisted in analysing acoustically spontaneous speech recordings gathered from the Audio BNC Corpus. The results showed that [s], in the examined context and dataset, does not acquire the acoustic properties of the post-alveolar fricative <sh>. The measurements of the spectral centre of gravity revealed that the fricative segment before the palatal glide [j] was intermediate between <s> and <sh>. Moreover, Renwick and Cassidy confirmed previous conclusions that the strength of palatalization is related to lexical frequency of word pairs involved in the process and observed that the /s/ in low-frequency word pairs was realized in a longer manner with [s]-like characteristics, while the examined consonants in high-frequency tokens were shorter and displayed spectral properties more similar to those of <sh>. The outcomes of this analysis compel the authors to assert that palatalization in BrE is best classified as a process of gestural overlap, which becomes stronger in word pairs of high frequency, in fast or casual word conditions.

## 4. Morphology

Two articles explored the semantics of derivational affixes in PDE. Marion Schulte's 'Polysemy and Synonymy in Derivational Affixation—A Case Study of the English Suffixes -*age* and -*ery*' (*Morphology* 25[2015] 371–90) investigates the semantics of the two suffixes in the title based on corpus data from the BNC. Proposing a new version of the semantic map method, Schulte shows that although there is an overlap in the range of semantic readings of the derivatives of these suffixes, -*age* and -*ery* are not entirely synonymous, as previously proposed. The second article is Marios Andreou's 'Lexical Negation in Lexical Semantics: The Prefixes *in*- and *dis*-' (*Morphology* 25[2015] 391–410). Andreou investigates the semantics of the negative prefixes *in*- and *dis*-. He describes the range of meanings for both, specifically the different types of negativity they express (e.g. contrary, as in the pair *clear–unclear*, or contradictory, as in the pair *animate–inanimate*) in combination with different types of bases (nouns, adjectives, and verbs). He then proposes an analysis in terms of Lieber's framework of lexical semantics.

Chris P. Palmer, in 'Measuring Productivity Diachronically: Nominal Suffixes in English Letters, 1400–1600' (*ELL* 19[2015] 107–29), addresses the problem of determining the productivity of suffixes in earlier periods of English and argues that this can only be done using a combination of different measures, rather than just one (such as new occurrences only, or hapaxes). He analyses five suffixes (native -*ness* and borrowed -*ity*, -*cion*, -*age* and -*ment*) in the Corpus of Early English Correspondence, looking at absolute frequencies, new combinations per subperiod, transparency, and hybrid formations, and then presents a ranking of these five suffixes in terms of their productivity.

## 5. Syntax

*(a) Modern English*
In *The Syntax of Yes and No*, Anders Holmberg explores a hitherto largely neglected area, the syntax of the response particles YES and NO. Holmberg argues that far from being syntactically inert adverbial fragments, YES and NO represent the initial element of full clauses, with IP-ellipsis. He argues that this explains the distribution of various types of response across a range of languages. The basic insight is that different types of question elicit different types of response. The outline of Holmberg's main argument is as follows: he argues that bare YES is felicitous in response to neutral questions, because the polarity of the question and the response do not differ. In such cases, according to the author, the IP in the response is syntactically identical to its

antecedent in the interrogative and can therefore be ellipted. However, he distinguishes two types of negative yes/no question, each of which elicits different responses. Holmberg claims that inner-negation questions such as *Is John not here?*, in which the negation scopes within the proposition ('is it the case that John is not here'), can be answered YES. In these, YES affirms the negative proposition. These responses are full clauses with ellipsis of the IP under identity with the IP in the interrogative antecedent ('Yes, John is not here'). On the other hand, in outer-negation questions where negation scopes over the proposition ('Is it not the case that John is here?'), Holmberg claims that a simple YES answer is insufficient, arguing that ellipsis is not possible in response to these questions because the IP in the response and the antecedent question are not identical; one is positive, the other negative. Instead, responses to these questions in PDE take the form of a clause in which the IP is spelled out and only the vP is ellipted. These clauses may optionally be introduced by YES (Q: *Isn't John coming?*—A: *(Yes), he is*). Other languages exhibit a similar distinction; Holmberg discusses Finnish in detail as an example of this. Cross-linguistically, the availability of inner- and outer-negation questions correlates with the position of negation in the clause. English is somewhat unusual, in having both inner- and outer-negation questions, and their two distinct responses. Throughout, the monograph exhibits very careful and detailed scholarship, linking a formal syntactic analysis of responses to their semantics. The resulting account boasts wide empirical reach, explaining cross-linguistic differences in response systems in a database of 132 languages, not solely European languages. The analysis presents interesting implications not only for the syntax of responses but the syntax of clauses more generally, providing strong arguments in favour of a polarity operator within the CP layer of all clauses. Without this, Holmberg's findings are difficult to explain.

Several new undergraduate textbooks on English linguistics appeared, either for the first time or in revised editions, in 2015. Roger Berry's *From Words to Grammar: Discovering English Usage* takes a novel approach to English grammar by discussing individual words from a usage-based perspective. The words chosen are some of the most frequently occurring in English corpus data, those which are deemed representative of a word class, or that exhibit interesting grammatical properties. The grammatical description is bottom-up, based on data drawn from English corpora, primarily the BNC and COCA. The analysis is data-driven: through data and exercises students are encouraged to make linguistic generalizations on the basis of the data presented. The kind of words chosen introduce students to issues around categorization and subcategorization, determiners and reference, modification, verbal argument structure and phrasal verbs, auxiliaries and modals. The data and exercise format used throughout makes students participants in doing linguistics—discovering grammatical patterns and generalizations which the author then explains. While this works well, the pedagogical value of the book could be enhanced by exercises directing students to gather and analyse their own examples from linguistic corpora. The data and exercise format works well, and while this book might not be a first choice for an introduction to grammatical structure, given its lack of syntactic formalism, it provides a useful set of exercises to test students' knowledge of key concepts around categorization, complementation, argument structure, and the like. More importantly, it engages students with the process of doing corpus linguistics in a way which makes them more active participants in learning grammar than with many more traditional textbooks. To those of us who teach introductory grammar, it provides a clear demonstration of how a corpus-based approach to teaching grammar can work.

Ingo Plag, Sabine Arndt-Lappe, Maria Braun, and Mareile Schram's *Introduction to English Linguistics* is a new edition of a book first published in 2009. It provides an overview of phonetics, phonology, morphology, syntax, semantics, and pragmatics appropriate for a first-year undergraduate module. It has breadth rather than depth on any of these individual topics, but provides a clear explanation of the key foundational concepts in each of these linguistic domains, for example phonemes and allophones, morphological structure, constituency and X'-theoretic phrase structure. Useful exercises and bibliographies are provided for each chapter. While the discussions of phonology and morphology succeed in conveying the basic concepts well, the discussion of semantics (chapter 5) is very brief, raising more questions about word and sentence meaning than it in fact answers. With the exception of chapter 6, which discusses pragmatics, the book focuses on the formal structural aspects of language, rather than on language use. Chapter 7 acknowledges issues of language variation and change, but does little more than outline issues for further study. As such, the book does not provide a comprehensive introduction to linguistics, and additional materials will be required to introduce students to core concepts and issues in sociolinguistics (such as the sociolinguistic variable), and in historical linguistics. However, the book is clearly structured, systematic in its approach, and written in a way that addresses the reader directly, raising questions on the basis of linguistic data. The discussion of these data is very detailed: for example the discussion of phonemes and allophones in chapter 2 is extensive. The authors state in the introduction that the book may be used for undirected study. While the book will prove easy for most students to follow independently, some direction may be required, particularly to understand the phonetics and phonology sections. The second edition of this book continues to provide a highly detailed, data- and issue-driven exposition of key linguistic concepts, and as such remains a useful teaching tool.

This year also saw the fourth edition of Sidney Greenbaum and Gerald Nelson's *Introduction to English Grammar*. This book takes a somewhat different approach to English grammar. Its focus is less on formal syntactic theory, more on a functional description. As in previous editions, it contains a particularly detailed discussion of word classes and sentences, without overwhelming students with syntactic theory. One particular advantage is the discussion of what the authors call 'usage problems' (chapter 6)—in fact aspects of language variation or change in PDE. The fourth edition expands this chapter, including data from the survey of English usage and its associated corpora (the Diachronic Corpus of Present-Day Spoken English). A discussion of register variation is presented in chapter 8, and it is good to see that this now includes discussion of various recent forms of computer-mediated communication. This is an area of interest to many students. Teaching grammar through these aspects of variation in English usage, the book remains a useful source of detailed linguistic data and description.

Louise Mullany and Peter Stockwell's *Introducing English Language: A Resource Book for Students*, now in its second edition, provides an introduction to English linguistics that is much wider in scope than Plag et al. or Greenbaum and Nelson. The book assumes readers have no knowledge of linguistics, beginning at a very basic level, but provides less detailed discussion of linguistic data than Plag et al. The discussion of concepts also comes across as rather fragmented, for example a rather cursory description of phonetics is followed by a rather cursory description of morphology in chapter 3. The brevity with which key concepts are described is particularly problematic for the discussion of grammatical constituents and phrases—phrase structure tree diagrams are introduced with little explanation. As a consequence, it is difficult to see how this book could be adopted as a course book on an introductory linguistics course, although it would offer very useful additional reading, provided students are directed to relevant sections. The way the book is organized into introductory, intermediate, and advanced material lends itself to this kind of use. The most valuable aspect of the book is section D, which collects together several key papers on a number of linguistic topics. These expose students to a number of different issues and, more importantly, methodological approaches to linguistics.

*The Verb Phrase in English: Investigating Recent Language Change with Corpora*, a volume edited by Bas Aarts, Joanne Close, Geoffrey Leech, and Sean Wallis, already appeared as a hardcover edition in 2013, but because it was not featured here before, we discuss the 2015 paperback version. In chapter 1, 'Introduction' (pp. 1–13), the editors describe the 'recent language change' from the title as an 'exciting emerging research area', which involves investigating changes 'over decades rather than centuries' (p. 1). The fourteen remaining chapters in the book all deal with changes related to the VP in contemporary English. All studies are based on corpus analyses, and methodological issues receive ample consideration. Bas Aarts, Joanne Close, and Sean Willis, in 'Choices Over Time: Methodological Issues in Investigating Current Change' (pp. 14–45), argue that corpus linguists should carefully establish those cases where there is true variation between alternative options, and eliminate as many other factors as possible that may also influence the choice, such as what they call 'knock-out' contexts. To support this methodological point, they explore two case studies in a corpus of spoken English between 1960 and 1990: the use of the progressive and variation between *shall* and *will*. In 'Recent Shifts with Three Nonfinite Verbal Complements in English: Data from the 100 Million Word TIME Corpus (1920s–2000s)' (pp. 46–67), Mark Davies comments on the tradition in English linguistics to use relatively small corpora, and highlights the advantages of larger-scale corpora with his analysis of three cases of verbal complementation in the *Time Magazine* corpus: *We [talked] Bill into staying, He started [to walk/ walking] down the street*, and *I'd really like (for) them to leave now*. For these three cases, the corpus provides many examples which, Davies shows, challenge existing views on the development of these complementation patterns. The authors of 'Verb Structures in Twentieth-Century British English' (pp. 68–98), Nicholas Smith and Geoffrey Leech, use one of these 'smaller' corpora for their research, the so-called Brown family. They make a case for these corpora providing more reliable results—at least for the more frequent constructions—because more of the annotation has been checked manually and the corpora have been compiled to represent English as a whole rather than focusing on one genre. They present data which provide more details on the development of *not*-contractions, modal verbs, the progressive, and the passive between 1931 and 2006. Douglas Biber and Bethany Grey, in 'Nominalizing the Verb Phrase in Academic Research Writing' (pp. 99–132), investigate a corpus of various types of informational writing between 1700 and 2005, with a particular focus on science research writing in the twentieth century. Their data confirms earlier assumptions that there is a large increase in nominal structures, but they also show that there is only a small decrease in verbal structures, for which they provide a further analysis in terms of the phrases that have replaced these verbs. Sali Tagliamonte's 'The Verb Phrase in Contemporary Canadian English' (pp. 133–54), focuses on changes in the VP in CanE, based on the Toronto English Archive, the compilation of which, based on fieldwork, is described in detail in the chapter. She investigates the increase of *have to* over *must* and *have got* to express deontic modality, the increase in *have* over *have got* for stative possession, the use of *be going to* over *will*, and the increase in the use of *be like* for quotatives. For each of these, she provides frequencies differentiated for sex and age, providing an interesting insight into changes that are currently under way, some of which seem to be taking place at great speed. In 'Recent Change and Grammaticalization' (pp. 155–86), Manfred Krug and Ole Schützler argue that the construction *the idea is*, followed by a clausal complement, is going through a grammaticalization process and becoming an intention marker, similar to *want to* or *be going to*. Based on data from the *Time* magazine corpus and phonological factors, they show that there are several signs of grammaticalization, such as syntagmatic fixation and phonological specialization. Magnus Levin's 'The Progressive Verb in Modern American English' (pp. 187–216), analyses progressive verbs in the *Time* corpus, focusing on the 1920s, 1960s, and 2000s, compared with multi-genre contemporary corpora of AmE. He especially focuses on the increase in the use of two forms: *be being* [adjective] (*I was being facetious*) and the progressive with private verbs (*believe*, *wonder*). He explains this increase with reference to concepts commonly used to explain changes in the twentieth century such as democratization and subjectification. Meike Pfaff, Alexander Bergs and Thomas Hoffmann, in '*I Was Just Reading this Article*—On the Expression of Recentness and the English Past Progressive' (pp. 217–38), continue with the topic of the progressive but focus on one specific form, the past progressive. Based on data from the BNC and COCA, they propose that the past progressive was commonly used to mark the introduction of a new discourse topic, but is being reanalysed as a marker of recent past time because of the high frequency of recent past with these topic introductions, a change they refer to as 'context-induced reinterpretation'. Marcus Callies's 'Bare Infinitival Complements in Present-Day English' (pp. 239–55), presents corpus data from the BNC and COCA on the occurrence of bare infinitives after a range of verbs (*help them make* vs. *help them to make*), showing that they are more common than previously thought and occur with more verbs. He discusses various factors that may be involved in their use such as analogy and complexity, and suggests that this 'erosion' is part of larger trend of deletion of function words, especially in AmE. The contribution by José Ramón Varela Pérez, 'Operator and Negative Contraction in Spoken British English: A Change in Progress' (pp. 256–85), examines full forms of *not* against operator contraction (*you're not*) and negation contraction (*you aren't*) in two spoken corpora of BrE between 1950 and 1990. The data show that *be* behaves differently in all periods in preferring operator contraction, while *have, will*, and *would* move towards a pattern where they almost exclusively appear with negative contraction, like other auxiliaries. Gunther Kaltenböck, in 'The Development of Comment Clauses' (pp. 286–317), investigates comment clauses, focusing on *I think* when used as a type of epistemic marker. Based on data of spoken English between 1960 and 1990, he discusses signs of further grammaticalization, an increase in some related forms (e.g. *I'm thinking*), and finally proposes a construction grammar analysis in an attempt to explain their formal and functional characteristics. Jill Bowie, Sean Wallis, and Bas Aarts also investigate spoken English in the second half of the twentieth century in 'The Perfect in Spoken British English' (pp. 318–52). Using a variety of frequency measures, during which they discuss many methodological issues, they question an initially observed increase in the present perfect and show there is a decrease in infinitival perfects (*may have seen*) and the past perfect (*had seen*), for which they suggest several factors, such as American influence and simplification. Christopher Williams, in 'Changes in the Verb Phrase in Legal English' (pp. 353–71), analyses three corpora of legal documents between 1970 and 2010, one UK, one Australian, and one UK corpus, and shows that even though legal texts are generally seen as conservative, there is a great change in the use of *shall*, largely due to the influence of prescriptive rules (the plain language movement). The short and final contribution to this volume, 'Modals and Semi-modals of Obligation in American English' (pp. 372–80) is a written-out version of the presentation by the late Stig Johannson at the symposium on which the book builds. He investigates *must, have to*, *have got to*, and *need to* in the COCA, and shows how in recent years the decrease in *must* continues and the previously found increase in *have to* stabilizes. He ends with a cautionary note on the risks of basing every linguistic investigation on corpus research only.

Continuing with the theme of verbal syntax, Johanna Gerwin, in *Ditransitives in British English Dialects* [2014], examines dialectal variation in patterns of dative alternation (*John gave a book to Mary—John gave Mary a book*). The dative alternation is subject to several linguistic constraints and Gerwin, in this published version of her doctoral thesis, argues that patterns of dialect variation in dative alternation are more complex and subtle than hitherto supposed, and that diatopic variation interacts with linguistic constraints. The level of detail provided offers a new diachronic and diatopic perspective on dative alternation. The study demonstrates how new data from the Freiburg English Dialect corpus (FRED) inform our understanding of dialectal variation in morphosyntax. Chapters 5 and 6 present the FRED data in great detail. It is particularly welcome to see Gerwin discuss synchronic variation in the context of patterns of diachronic change in chapter 6. Overall, Gerwin argues that dative alternation varies according to the particular ditransitive verb. Data from FRED involving pronouns, as in *She gave it him*, are typically associated with varieties of BrE from the Midlands, whereas northern varieties tend to employ canonical double-object constructions (*She gave him it*) and southern varieties prepositional constructions (*She gave it to him*). The book explores a number of independent variable constraints on dative alternation and it clearly presents a very thorough analysis of new corpus data. However, the quantitative analysis is limited to distributional analysis of individual variable constraints. The obvious question is how linguistic and extra-linguistic constraints interact, and whether linguistic constraints pattern the same way in all dialects. While some of the datasets are small, some regression analysis of the dialect data might have at least begun to address this question. Similarly, regression analysis would have enabled Gerwin to examine patterns of change in greater detail, perhaps even change in individual constraints.

*(b) Earlier English*

Several individual papers also address ditransitive verbs but from a diachronic perspective. Ludovic De Cuypere's 'The Old English *to*-Dative Construction' (*ELL* 19[2015] 1–26) investigates frequency and ordering effects of the *to*-dative (e.g. *gave the books to Mary*) in OE. He finds that the *to*-dative, compared to the double object construction (*gave Mary the books*), is not rare, as previously claimed. He also finds that in the variation between the two orders with *to* (*gave the books to Mary* vs. *gave to Mary the books*) similar factors determine the order as in PDE (such as length and definiteness). Finally, he argues that the development of *to* from a Goal to Recipient marker has its origins in OE. Another article investigating ditransitive verbs is Nuria Yáñez-Bouza and David Denison's 'Which Comes First in the Double Object Construction?' (*ELL* 19[2015] 247–68). They investigate variation in ditransitive verbs from ME to late ModE, focusing on the less frequent pattern of the double object construction (*gave it him*), compared against the prepositional variants (*gave the book to him, gave him the book*). Their analysis concentrates on pronominal variants, as these particularly allow the *gave it him* order, which they finally account for in terms of a CxG version of prefabs, i.e. 'ready-made multi-word strings' (see also Section 2 above).

On the topic of OE and ME word order, there is Øystein Heggelund's 'On the Use of Data in Historical Linguistics: Word Order in Early English Subordinate Clauses' (*ELL* 19[2015] 83–106). He re-examines evidence from the literature which was used by David Lightfoot as support for his degree-0 theory of language acquisition, which built on the lack of evidence for SV/VO orders in subordinate clauses as evidence that children use data from main clauses to acquire word order, and he also presents his own data of OE and ME clauses. He concludes that there is more evidence for VO order in subordinate clauses than previously assumed, that the changes are more gradual than previously indicated, and that the development of main and subordinate clauses is in fact quite similar (although the numbers differ). Also dealing with issues of syntax on the transition from OE to ME, in 'The Expression of Impersonals in Middle English' (*ELL* 19[2015] 227–45), Caitlin Light and Joel Wallenberg investigate a hypothesis previously proposed in the literature that the English uses passives more extensively due to the loss of V2. They use sixteenth-century Bible translations to compare English with Icelandic and German, and use translations of the *Rule of St Benedict* to investigate English at different stages and from different regions. They suggest that varying rates of passivization are not linked to the presence or absence of V2, but rather to the presence or absence of alternative impersonalization strategies, most notably *man*.

Investigating early ME syntax, Nynke de Haas and Ans van Kemenade address 'The Origin of the Northern Subject Rule' (NSR), concentrating on 'Subject Positions and Verbal Morphosyntax in Older English' (*ELL* 19[2015] 49–81). Based on a detailed corpus study, the authors identify a core area for the NSR around Yorkshire in early ME, where both the subject type and adjacency of verb and subject determines the ending on the verb (*they sing* vs. *birds sings* and *they always sings*). In other northern and northern Midlands areas, the adjacency condition was weaker. They then provide an account for the rise of the NSR based on an analysis of multiple subject positions, for which they find new evidence in the northern ME data.

Moving to studies of eModE syntax, there is an article by Hendrik De Smet and Evelyn Vancayzeele, 'Like a Rolling Stone: The Changing Use of English Premodifying Present Participles' (*ELL* 19[2015] 131–56). They investigate premodifying present participles (as in *a rolling stone*) and propose a classification of functions of these participles in PDE. Based on an analysis of eModE corpus data (mostly fiction), they then show that there is a decrease in identifying uses (*the following evening*) and type-oriented uses (*a talking dog*), while there is an increase in situation-oriented uses (*a passing car*). They propose that this change is an example of 'clausalization', which can be described as those participles relating more to the event described in the main clause than the actual noun they premodify.

Functional perspectives on grammaticalization continue to be a fertile area for new work, particularly exploring the notions of subjectification and intersubjectification. Two books from last year deal with the topic of intersubjectification: Lobke Ghesquière, *The Directionality of (Inter)Subjectification in the English Noun Phrase* [2014], and Lieselotte Brems, Lobke Ghesquière, and Freek Van de Velde, eds., *Intersubjectivity and Intersubjectification in Grammar and Discourse* [2014].

Ghesquière focuses on change within a functional-cognitive model of the English NP, in which changes in the syntactic distribution of modifying elements within the NP correlate with changes in their interpretation. She argues that a structural model in which there is a linear progression from objective to subjective meanings is too simple to account for the different developments that individual pre-modifiers undergo. She puts forward the idea of textually intersubjective meanings in which linguistic elements direct the interpretation by the hearer/reader. Chapter 5 examines pathways by which nominal premodifiers of completeness such as *complete, total* and *whole* become intensifiers, with (inter)subjective meanings, expressing (inter)-speaker judgements or evaluations. Chapter 6 extends the argument to the specificity modifiers *specific* and *particular*. Chapter 7 is devoted to intensifier uses of *such* and *what*. Throughout, Ghesquière presents carefully analysed data from diachronic corpora to test different models of change. She identifies two prevalent pathways of change: from description to noun intensification, and from identification to noun intensification, and identifies both the triggering contexts for, and the cognitive mechanisms involved within these two types of (inter)subjectification. The book is both empirically detailed and well grounded in cognitive linguistic theory. It advances our understanding of the development of the English NP. More importantly though, it provides detailed evidence of what (inter)subjectification is, and clear empirical evidence to determine its role in language change.

Brems et al. is a collection of papers that was first published as a special issue of the journal *English Text Construction* in 2012. In 'Intersubjectification and the Clausal Periphery' (pp. 7–28) Elizabeth Traugott seeks to define and operationalize intersubjectification in such a way that it is distinct from subjectification and identifiable in written historical corpus data, where we do not have access to native speaker construal of the text or to paralinguistic cues for interpretation. She demonstrates, using as case studies the development of English *no doubt* and *surely*, that subjective and intersubjective meanings can be distinguished. She concludes that subjective and intersubjective meanings are not always encoded in different positions within clausal structure: *no doubt* is subjective at both the right and left periphery, whereas *surely* is intersubjective in both these domains. In 'Beyond Intersubjectification' (pp. 29–52), Heiko Narrog shows that there is a shift in English modal constructions from subjective through intersubjective to textual meanings, which focus on marking relationships between propositions within the text or discourse. Narrog argues that concessive *may* is one such element in PDE, and that the diachronic appearance of these textual meanings is subsequent to the development of more generalized intersubjective meanings in the earlier history of English. He then adduces further evidence for a similar development in Japanese concessives, arguing that the development of textual meanings represents the end point of a change from descriptive > subjective > intersubjective > textual meanings. In 'Notions of (Inter)Subjectivity' (pp. 53–76), Jan Nuyts usefully summarizes different definitions of intersubjectivity, arguing that these definitions in fact describe different processes, and therefore should be regarded as distinct. He concludes that Traugott's and Langacker's definitions of intersubjectivity are not mutually exclusive and that they often do not describe the same phenomenon. In 'Intersubjectivity in Newspaper Editorials' (pp. 77–100) Geoff Thompson applies notions of intersubjectivity to the analysis of the relationship between newspaper editorials and their intended audiences. Through an analysis of two British newspapers, he argues that different newspapers use intersubjectification strategies such as modality to construe their audiences in different ways that reflect the different demographics of their readerships. Similarly, in '"What I want you to remember is...": Audience Orientation in Monologic Academic

Discourse' (pp. 101–28), Annelie Ädel examines the way academic and pedagogical texts construe their audience and manage audience orientation. The paper presents a detailed corpus study of English for Academic Purposes textbooks, focusing on uses of the second person, *you*, in the texts. By identifying audience orientation strategies, her work shows how better audience orientation and interaction could be achieved in academic discourse. The final paper, by the editors themselves, 'Intersubjectivity and Intersubjectification: Typology and Operationalisation' (pp. 129–54), highlights the volume's contribution to the literature on (inter)subjectivity in three noteworthy areas: first, by addressing some of the issues as to how intersubjectivity is defined, in particular how different and apparently competing definitions relate to each other; second, by showing how to operationalize subjectivity and identify it in written (particularly historical) corpus data; and third, by emphasizing the diachronic relationship between subjectivity, intersubjectivity, and textual meanings in processes of change. The book succeeds, particularly in the first two areas, but more work remains to be done concerning change.

Continuing the theme of usage-based approaches to morphosyntactic variation and change, Yuri Yerastov, in his article 'A Construction Grammar Analysis of the Transitive *be* Perfect in Present-Day Canadian English' (*ELL* 19[2015] 157–78), analyses the use of *be* with a perfect meaning such as in *I am finished my homework*, examples which occur with the verbs *do*, *finish*, and *start* only, in several L1 varieties of English, including CanE. He reviews the properties of this perfect in comparison to related construction and then presents a CxG analysis of this phenomenon, which contains a lexical component (some more details on this can be found in Section 9 below).

Another development of interest to diachronic linguists is the spread of the study of recent and ongoing morphosyntactic change from BrE and AmE into the varieties of New English, as found in the volume *Grammatical Change in English World-Wide*, edited by Peter Collins. Most contributions here focus on changes that have already been identified in BrE or AmE, for example the replacement of modals by semi-modals, extension of the progressive into punctual contexts. The papers build up a broader picture of these changes across several varieties and facilitate cross-variety comparison, allowing us to pose the question of why a change may take different forms across varieties, or why it may happen in one variety and not another, while at the same time they inform our understanding of earlier periods of English as well. For example, in the same way that those interested in typology and language phylogeny adduce common ancestors for related languages on the basis of perceived similarities between them, patterns of variation or change that are common to several English varieties might suggest that these patterns of variation and change are already established in earlier periods of English. This extends our understanding variation and change, particularly in spoken varieties, for which corpus evidence is lacking until the mid-twentieth century. The papers in this volume take great care to situate patterns of variation and change in this historical context. The volume thus adds to our understanding of early English grammar and change within it. (A full discussion of the individual papers included in the volume can be found in Section 8 below.)

This year saw the publication of several new textbooks, including two particularly good works on historical linguistics and language change. In *Language Change*, Joan Bybee provides a very comprehensive account of functionalist theories of language change, suitable for an advanced undergraduate audience. Her scope is ambitiously wide: unlike many books on language diachrony, which focus on the histories of particular languages, Bybee is more concerned with principles, theories, and mechanisms of language change, and their place within a usage-based theory of linguistics. Bybee's case studies and examples come from a wide range of different languages, with English contributing many case studies. While the book is clearly written and argued throughout, it assumes good knowledge of phonology, morphology, and syntax on the part of the reader. The book divides into three sections—sound change, grammaticalization, and syntactic change—although it also addresses how these different types of change intersect. The discussions of sound change and grammaticalization are particularly thorough, presenting an impressive number of case studies, although these case studies are often treated rather briefly (for instance, discussion of the English Great Vowel Shift receives three pages). Unsurprisingly, given her research paradigm, Bybee's approach is largely usage-based. Her explanations of changes often appeal to functional factors and semantic change. This approach lends itself particularly well to the description of grammaticalization in chapters 6 and 7. The discussion here integrates a large number of case studies, though it seems odd that negation (the Jespersen Cycle) is not among them. Bybee highlights the need for a book presenting grammaticalization research to an undergraduate audience as one of her reasons for writing. This volume presents one of the most comprehensive and up-to-date summaries of grammaticalization research since Hopper and Traugott [2nd edn. 2003], at least from a usage-based perspective. Chapter 8 discusses syntactic change. Here, it is important to bear in mind that Bybee's approach to syntax is construction-based rather than generative; hence generative theories of syntactic change are addressed only very briefly. Chapters 9–11 describe lexical change, typology and historical reconstruction, and causes of change. These chapters are less detailed, and while it is important to discuss these topics within a comprehensive account of language change, they do not receive such detailed or comprehensive treatment as either sound change or grammaticalization do here. Overall, though, this is a very impressive textbook, one that will be extremely useful particularly to those teaching sound change or grammaticalization to advanced-level undergraduates. Challenging concepts are presented clearly, and incrementally, with suggestions for further reading on each topic clearly made throughout. The reference list itself represents a hugely useful directory of recent research. However, certain sections of the book may be more useful than others. The sections on sound change and, particularly, on grammaticalization constitute excellent surveys of recent research in these areas, and as such fill a gap in the existing pedagogical literature on language change.

Bettelou Los's *A Historical Syntax of English* is mostly aimed at advanced students—it presupposes quite a bit of knowledge of linguistic topics (although not necessarily on the history of English)—containing a wealth of detail about all the important syntactic changes in the history of English. In chapter 1, Los discusses three parameters that represent sources for syntactic change, which provide a structuring principle for the remainder of the book. The first parameter, explored in chapters 2 to 4, is the variation between syntactic and morphological expression of functional information. Chapter 2 explores changes in this parameter in a number of specific cases in the nominal domain, which in the history of English mostly amount to losses of morphological marking, such as loss of gender and loss of case endings. Chapter 3 is the first of two chapters looking at verbal categories, specifically the increase in use of *be* and *have* auxiliaries. After an explanation of general notions of tense, aspect and mood, with a focus on aspect, and alternative ways of expressing aspect (e.g. prefixes and particles), Los looks in detail at the development of the perfect, progressive, and passive. Chapter 4 addresses the topic of the modal auxiliaries. It explains the NICE properties in detail, including their historical development, addressing issues like the loss of V-to-I movement for lexical verbs, the rise of *do*-support, and the grammaticalization process of modals from verb to auxiliary. The second parameter of change is the expression of arguments of the verb, which is addressed in chapter 5. Here, Los focuses on complementation patterns involving verbal complements, such as the question why *set* is followed by an *-ing*-gerund (*The examples here should set you thinking*) but *made* is followed by a bare infinitive *It made Euphrasia think* (p. 125). She then discusses the origins and spread of the gerund, the present participles and the *to*-infinitive as complementation options in detail, providing the historical stages and causes of each of these developments. The third parameter is word order, which is addressed in chapters 6 and 7. Chapter 6 explores issues of word order in subordinate clauses, focusing on the change from O–V to V–O order, and includes a discussion of the role information structure plays. Chapter 7 zooms in on main clauses, addressing the V2 system in OE and tracing its decline from ME onwards, including a treatment of all factors involved in this development, again with an important role for information-structural principles. The book ends with a chapter that explores the expression of discourse functions (i.e. foregrounding, back-grounding, and episode boundaries), providing a more functional perspective on syntactic structures. Each chapter ends with a 'Summary of Points', a set of exercises, and suggestions for further reading.

In *Syntax in Three Dimensions*, Carola Trips attempts to link the history of grammatical thought with both synchronic comparative syntax and diachronic syntax. The first part of the book (chapters 1–6) provides a detailed history of grammatical analysis from Aristotle and Quintillian to Chomsky's minimalist architecture. This is clearly not a textbook of the kind used on introductory undergraduate syntax courses. It assumes basic grammatical knowledge, and thus is more suitable for intermediate students who are ready to apply basic syntactic concepts to more advanced issues of grammar and to the study of languages other than PDE. The second part, on comparative syntax, provides a useful, broader perspective than the earlier narrow focus on English, elucidating concepts such as movement with the help of cross-linguistic data. However, the chapter on syntactic variation (chapter 10) is less successful. It is rather brief in its treatment of complex concepts and case studies (for example double modal constructions), touching on variationist sociolinguistics, but without really establishing clearly the notion of a syntactic parameter within syntactic theory. The third part provides a good overview of the syntax of OE and ME for intermediate-level undergraduate students, highlighting issues in morphosyntactic change such as grammatical reanalysis and competition between grammars. This section is by no means comprehensive—for example it has little to say about grammaticalization, and the section on negation does not really address the Jespersen Cycle—but it provides a good introduction for students in conjunction with other introductory texts. A diachronic perspective is a welcome addition to an introductory textbook, given that an understanding of earlier English is useful to interpret some of the quirks of PDE syntax. While the individual sections on the history of grammatical thought and on the syntax of early English are thorough and detailed, it is difficult to see how they fit together coherently. However, this textbook may be a useful one to add to reading lists on intermediate-level syntax courses, as additional reading to extend the curriculum and stretch students who are highly engaged and curious about the foundations of grammatical thought, or about issues of syntactic variation or syntactic change.

## 6. Semantics

The second edition of *The Handbook of Contemporary Semantic Theory*, co-edited by Shalom Lappin, sole editor of the first edition, and Chris Fox, is the result of such a radical restructuring and revision of the previous edition that it can be considered a new book. The integration of new approaches and achievements did not only take place on the level of the individual chapters, but sometimes required the introduction of entirely new sections. This applies especially to computational approaches to semantics, which were summarized in one chapter in the first edition, but are devoted a whole section consisting of seven chapters in the current one, some of which are concerned with foundational topics in this area such as rich-type theories and proof-theoretical approaches for natural language. Another new direction of research given particular attention in the new edition concerns probabilistic theories of semantics. Somewhat surprisingly, considering traditional assumptions about the semantics/pragmatics division, there is also a chapter devoted to presuppositions and implicatures, which indicates that the editors—probably following recent developments—do not consider these phenomena to be located entirely within pragmatics. In addition to the range of new topics, the volume distinguishes itself from the previous one in that in the discussion of more established topics, a special effort is made to substantiate theoretical claims with the help of data from controlled experiments and corpus research. The collection consists of five parts. Part I, 'Quantifiers, Scope, Plurals, and Ellipsis', consists of chapters discussing 'Generalized Quantifiers in Natural Language Semantics (pp. 9–39) by Dag Westerståhl, 'Scope' (pp. 40–76) by Chris Barker, 'Plurals' (pp. 77–113) by Yoad Winter and Remko Scha, and 'Ellipsis' (pp. 114–40) by Ruth Kempson, Ronnie Cann, Arash Eshghi, Eleni Gregoromichelaki, and Matthew Purwer.

Part II, 'Modification, Presupposition, Tense, and Modality', features chapters on 'Adjectival Modification and Gradation' (pp. 143–67) by Daniel Lassiter, 'Presupposition and Implicature' (pp. 168–202) by Christopher Potts, 'The Semantics of Tense and Aspect: A Finite-State Perspective' (pp. 203–36) by Tim Fernando, and 'Conditionals and Modality' (pp. 237–70) by Magdalena and Stefan Kaufmann. Part III, 'Nondeclaratives', contains a chapter on the 'Semantics of Questions' (pp. 273–313) by Andrzej Wiśniewski, and one on 'the Semantics of Imperatives' (pp. 314–41) by Chris Fox. Part IV, 'Type Theory and Computational Semantics', consists of the following chapters: 'Constructive Type Theory' (pp. 343–74) by Aarne Ranta, 'Type Theory with Records for Natural Language Semantics' (pp. 375–407) by Robin Cooper and Jonathan Ginzburg, 'Curry Typing, Polymorphism, and Fine-Grained Intensionality' (pp. 408–28) by Shalom Lappin, 'Semantic Complexity in Natural Language' (pp. 429–54) by Ian Pratt-Hartmann, 'Implementing Semantic Theories' (pp. 455–92) by Jan van Eijck, 'Vector Space Models of Lexical Meaning' (pp. 493–522) by Stephen Clark, and 'Recognizing Textual Entailment' (pp. 523–57) by Mark Sammons. The final Part V, 'Interfaces', includes a discussion of 'Natural Logic' (pp. 561–92) by Lawrence S. Moss, 'The Syntax–Semantics Interface: Semantic Roles and Syntactic Arguments' (pp. 593–624) by Malka Rappaport Hovav and Beth Levin, 'Reference in Discourse' (pp. 625–54) by Andrew Kehler, 'Probabilistic Semantics and Pragmatics: Uncertainty in Language and Thought' (pp. 655–86) by Noah D. Goodman and Daniel Lassiter, 'Semantics and Dialogue' (pp. 687–713) by David Schlangen, and 'Semantics and Language Acquisition' (pp. 714–33) by Eve V. Clark.

Staying with reference works with a more general scope, the advanced textbook *English Historical Semantics* by Christian Kay and Kathryn Allan aims to familiarize readers with basic distinctions relevant to the study of lexical semantics (sense relations, questions of reference, componential analysis, prototypes, frames), general tendencies in the historical development of the lexicon of English, and the meaning change certain selected lexical items have gone through (including the whole domain of English colour terms discussed in a separate chapter authored by C.P. Biggam). Further sections of the book discuss the ways word meaning can change and how it can be studied, emphasizing the role of metaphor and metonymy as triggers for change, as well as the interconnections between language and culture. Practical sections on the structure and use of dictionaries and thesauruses, as well as a glossary of key terms, enhance the utility of the volume for its intended readership (more on this in Section 7).

An exceptionally large proportion of publications on English and general semantics was devoted in 2015 to theoretical or empirical studies on the semantic interpretation of quantificational and numerical expressions. In *Constraints on Numerical Expressions*, Chris Cummins argues that the most straightforward approaches to the use of number, which work with semantic analyses based on set-theoretic principles in the spirit of Montague grammar (Richard Montague [1970]), do not adequately explain how numbers are used and understood in language. He proposes instead an analysis in which the use of numerical expressions is modelled in terms of multiple constraint satisfaction. According to the author, the set of constraints that affect the choice of numerically quantified expressions, which are both 'implicated in the speaker's choice of utterance' and 'reflected in the hearer's interpretation of utterances' (p. 18), include the informativeness constraint, which requires that the utterance 'convey the strongest numerical information available to the speaker about the topic' (p. 22). Further constraints have to do with the criterion of using 'the appropriate level of granularity' determined by the context, or of using 'the simplest quantifier possible' (p. 30). Other additional constraints require that the numeral used be 'intrinsically salient' (p. 35), and that if a numeral or quantifier is 'primed in the preceding context, it must be used in the utterance' (p. 40). After motivating the constraints by experimental evidence from the literature or from his own work, the author models their interactions in determining the choice of numerically quantified expressions in a particular context within the formalism of classical OT and its variants. Given the nature of the constraints, the author predicts within-speaker variability across different kinds of prior context. Two chapters are devoted to illustrating the application of the model to comparative and superlative quantifiers, which the author considers to fundamentally differ in complexity due to the fact that they convey the $\leq$ and $\geq$ vs. the $<$ and $>$ relations, respectively. He argues that the origin of the modal meaning Bart Geurts and Rick Nouwen [2007] associate with superlative quantifiers has a semantic and not pragmatic origin. A further case study derives a novel prediction concerning the ability of comparative quantifiers to give rise to scalar implicature, which are then shown to be confirmed experimentally. Finally, it is shown that 'corpus-testable' predictions derived from the model, involving quantifier simplicity and numeral salience, are also borne out by data from the British National Corpus. In 'Modified Numerals: The Epistemic Effect' (in Alonso-Ovalle and Menéndez-Benito, eds., *Epistemic Indefinites: Exploring Modality beyond the Verbal Domain*, pp. 244–66), Rick Nouwen revisits the issue of the origin of the modal component of *at least n*, but argues that it should be considered an implicature (without postulating that it is equivalent to a disjunction), which arises due to the pragmatic competition of the *at least n* expression with alternatives of the form *exactly n, exactly n + 1*, and also *at least n + 1, at least n + 2*, etc.

'What Do Quantifier Particles Do?' (*Ling&P* 38[2015] 159–204) by Anna Szabolcsi argues that the fact that the same particles that form quantifier words are used as connectives, additive and scalar particles, question markers, or roots of existential verbs across languages motivates a unified seman- tic approach, which is formulated in the paper in terms of inquisitive semantics. Nicholas Fleischer, 'Comparative Quantifiers and Negation: Implications for Scope Economy' (*JSem* 32[2014] 139–71), proposes a new account—synthetizing the proposals of Shoichi Takahashi [2006] and Clemens Mayr and Benjamin Spector [2012]—of the scope-taking properties of comparative quantifier phrases [CQP] such as *more than three books* and *fewer than five students*, which explains why they can undergo scopal inversion in object position with negation but not in subject position, unless they occur in an embedded clause selected by a downward-entailing or non-monotone operator. Christopher Kennedy puts forth 'A "De-Fregean" Semantics (and Neo-Gricean Pragmatics) for Modified and Unmodified Numerals' (*S&Prag* 8[2015] 1–44), which treats both superlative-modified numerals and comparative-modified numerals as generalized quantifiers over degrees, and accounts for why the former systematically give rise to ignorance implications about exact quantity but the latter do not.

The contributions to the collection *Quantifiers, Quantifiers and Quantifiers: Themes in Logic, Metaphysics and Language*, edited by Alessandro Torza, cover five topic areas: the study of quantifiers as logical constants, the relevance of quantification theory to the semantics of natural language, Carnap's and Quine's legacy on quantification theory, the role quantification theory has played in reshaping ontology (or more generally, metaphysics), and issues in quantification theory within specific logical systems. Among the papers in the second group, special attention should be paid to 'Quantification with Intentional and with Intensional Verbs' by Friederike Moltmann (pp. 141–68), which argues that the compositional analysis of constructions involving 'intentional verbs' such as *think of*, *describe*, and *imagine* rely on positing intentional, non-existent objects, which are strictly dependent on intentional acts. This approach to the semantics of intentional verbs, which is fundamentally different from that normally assumed for intensional transitive verbs, such as *need*, *look for*, and *owe*, is justified by the author on the basis of differences in the semantic properties of their quantificational complements. Ken Akiba's paper on 'Conjunctive, Disjunctive, Negative Objects and Generalized Quantification' (in Torza ed., pp. 73–95) provides a uniform compositional derivation of the truth conditions of sentences containing proper names and quantificational NPs in the same syntactic position such as *Socrates is Athenian* vs. *Somebody is Athenian*. Instead of lifting names to the type of quantifiers, as done in Montague grammar, the theory proposes to lower quantifiers to the type of names and consider them to denote individuals. Nissim Francez and Glad Ben-Avi propose a 'Proof-Theoretic Reconstruction of Generalized Quantifiers' (*JSem* 32[2015] 313–71), which has the advantage over the traditional model-theoretic analysis that it is able to prove the conservativity property of determiners, instead of only postulating it and corroborating it empirically. 'The Interaction of Compositional Semantics and Event Semantics' (*Ling&P* 38[2015] 31–66) by Lucas Champollion presents a new system, 'quantificational event semantics', which makes it possible to integrate the findings of compositional semantic theories on quantification, negation and conjunction into Neo-Davidsonian event semantics. Dylan Bumford's 'Incremental Quantification and the Dynamics of Pair-List Phenomena' (*S&Prag* 8[2015] 1–70) offers an account of distributive universals that derives their interpretation directly from sentential conjunction, which can explain why matrix interrogatives containing them accept pair-list answers; why indefinites and disjunctions in their scope may assume arbitrary functional readings; and why they permit sentence-internal interpretations of comparative adjectives, like *new* and *different*.

Turning now to experimental studies on quantifier interpretation, first Adrian Brasoveanu and Jakub Dotlačil's paper 'Strategies for Scope Taking' (*NLS* 23[2015] 1–19) deserves mention, which investigates the distinct scopal properties of *each* and *every*. Hadas Kotek, Yasutada Sudo, and Martin Hackl, 'Experimental Investigations of Ambiguity: The Case of *Most*' (*NLS* 23[2015] 119–56), discuss new evidence supporting a decompositional analysis of *most* in the spirit of Hackl [2011], which considers it a superlative construction built from a gradable predicate *many* or *much* and the superlative operator *-est*. Paul Egré and Florian Cova are concerned with 'Moral Asymmetries and the Semantics of *Many*' (*S&Prag* 8[2015] 1–45). Four experiments that were used to find out how speakers evaluate sentences containing *many* indicated sensitivity of the speakers to moral expectations (desirability of an outcome) as opposed to pure estimates of chances.

Adjectives of quantity, such as *many*, *few*, *much*, and *little*, are also the topic of Stephanie Solt's 'Q-Adjectives and the Semantics of Quantity' (*JSem* 32[2015] 221–73); she takes them to be gradable predicates of sets of degrees or (equivalently) gradable quantifiers over degrees. In 'Measurement Scales in Natural Language' (*L&LC* 9[2015] 14–32), the same author provides an accessible overview of the ontology of scales, the range of scalar categories in languages, and the results of research on the linguistically relevant structural properties of scales. In 'Degrees as Kinds' (*NL&LT* 33[2015] 791–828) Curt Anderson and Marcin Morzycki explore the possibility of viewing degrees as kinds of states (and, following previous work, manners as kinds of events) to explain a fundamental connection between kinds, manners, and degrees cross-linguistically. Jessica Rett's monograph *The Semantics of Evaluativity* proposes a novel approach to the semantics of evaluative constructions that makes 'reference to a degree which exceeds a contextually valued standard' (p. 1), such as the so-called 'positive construction' containing an unmodified or unbound gradable adjective, as in *Adam is tall*. As opposed to previous compositional approaches, including the author's own, presented in Rett [2007, 2008] that assume a null morpheme (POS or EVAL) to introduce the evaluativity component into the compositional semantics, the current theory treats evaluativity as a conversational implicature, based on parallels between evaluativity and other types of implicature. In addition to the clarity of the exposition, we should acknowledge the usefulness of the well-written 'tutorials' on the history of the treatment of evaluativity, of degree semantics, and implicatures.

Several papers address issues in the semantics of comparison. In 'Measure Phrase Equatives and Modified Numerals' (*JSem* 32[2015] 425–75), Jessica Rett proposes a unified approach to the equative morpheme that can account for distributional and semantic differences between 'measure phrase equatives' such as *John can dive as deep as 500m*, which prefer an 'at most' interpretation, and clausal equatives, such as *John can dive as deep as Sue can*, with a default 'at least' interpretation. Alexis Wellwood, 'On the Semantics of Comparison' (*Ling&P* 38[2015] 67–101), argues for the presence of a single morpheme in all comparative sentences, nominal, verbal, and adjectival, which contributes a structure-preserving map from entities, events, or states to their measures along various dimensions. In 'Same but Different' (*Ling&P* 38[2015] 289–314) Daniel Hardt and Line Mikkelsen suggest for the first time that the adjective *same* is fundamentally different from *different*, since it imposes a discourse condition on eventualities, while *different* compares individuals. The proposal can also account for the contribution of the definite article that is obligatorily associated with *same*. 'Sentence Internal *Same* and Its Quantificational Licensors: A New Window into the Processing of Inverse Scope (*S&Prag* 8[2015] 1–52) by Adrian Brasoveanu and Jakub Dotlačil describes the results of self-paced reading studies that tested the interpretation of sentence-internal *same* with four licensors (*all*, *each*, *every*, and *the*); they found no general effect of surface vs. inverse scope.

Rachel Szekely's monograph *Truth without Predication: The Role of Placing in the Existential* There-*Sentence* proposes a new philosophical and linguistic analysis of the construction type in the title, which takes as its inspiration Peter F. Strawson's suggestion in his monograph *Individuals* [1959] that *there*-sentences lack predication, given that they do 'not contain any expressions that refer to or presuppose, the existence of individuals' (p. 1), but merely 'place' a 'feature'. One chapter is concerned with the importance of Strawson's concept of feature-placing in the context of the quest by analytic philosophers for 'basic' forms of language, and with the relation of the thetic–categorical distinction to the analysis of *there*-sentences. Three chapters are devoted next to the question of how the interpretation of particular constituents in the *there*-construction can be captured in the feature-placing account. The author proposes a new interpretation for postverbal NPs: they stand for a feature, which is a universal, something that is 'instantiated in ("present in") individuals, but cannot be predicated of individuals', thus, 'it has a location only in virtue of being instantiated in an item' (p. 60). The reason why cardinal quantifiers but not strong quantifiers are allowed as postverbal NPs is claimed to be that the former involves the counting of successful placings of a feature-universal, while strong quantifiers require more than counting. A further chapter is devoted to the locative prepositional phrases and similar expressions that are possible in the 'coda', following the NP, which thus seem to be correctly described by the term 'placer'. The role of the verbal element is looked at in a further chapter, where the difference between *there*-sentences with *exist* and *be* as the main verb is discussed. Finally, the role of negation in *there*-sentences is addressed, which are taken to be expressions of cardinality zero rather than expressions containing a negative operator.

*Epistemic Indefinites*, edited by Luis Alonso-Ovalle and Paula Menéndez-Benito, is a valuable addition to the rapidly growing body of work on non-verbal modality. In their informative introduction ('Epistemic Indefinites: An Overview', pp. 1–27), the editors define epistemic indefinites as 'indefinite determiners or indefinite pronouns that signal ignorance on the part of the speaker, conveying information about her epistemic state' (p. 2), and provide a concise summary of relevant empirical findings and theoretical proposals in the field. 'A Short History of English Epistemic Indefinites' (pp. 100–13) by Benjamin Slade offers a synchronic and diachronic comparison of English *some* and *some or other*. It is suggested that the former indicates that the speaker is unable to identify the individual in certain ways but he may be able to identify it in other ways, while the latter signals that the speaker is unable to identify the relevant individual by ostension or name (but he may be able to identify it by description). Lisa Matthewson, 'Evidential Restrictions on Epistemic Modals' (pp. 142–60), provides data supporting the claim made by

Kai von Fintel and Anthony Gillies [2010] that English *must* and *might* make an evidential contribution. She argues that these expressions require that 'the set of propositions representing the speaker's trustworthy evidence must not contain any single proposition which entails the prejacent' (p. 159), and provides arguments for extending the proposal that epistemic modals quantify over words compatible with types of evidence to all languages. 'Certain Properties of Certain Indefinites: An Experimental Perspective' (pp. 183–210) by Tania Ionin looks at experimental evidence concerning the extent to which the indefinites *a certain* and *a* give rise to functional and non-functional intermediate readings. Kyle Rawlins, 'Indifference and Scalar Inferences in Free Relatives' (pp. 267–88), and Cleo Condoravdi, 'Ignorance, Indifference, and Individuation with *Wh-ever* (pp. 213–43), both deal with the modal aspect of the meaning of English *-ever* free relatives. Rawlins's paper is concerned with the agent indifference readings of sentences like *Alfonso grabbed whatever tool was handy*, arguing that they arise because the hearer compares the description given with other alternative ways of describing the referent. Condoravdi looks both at agent indifference (indiscriminacy) and speaker ignorance readings, as in *Whoever entered the house first saw what happened*, arguing that both interpretations of *wh-ever*-free relatives make reference to alternative descriptions of the individual in question that are more specific than the one provided by the *wh-ever* phrase.

Still on indefinites, Edgar Onea, 'Why Indefinites Can Escape Scope Islands' (*Ling&P* 38[2015] 237–67), aims to account for the exceptional scope-taking behaviour of these expressions, illustrated by the fact that the NP *some professor* is able to take widest, intermediate, and narrowest scope in *Exactly five boys read most books that were recommended by some professor*. He suggests that they should be considered referential expressions, similar to definites, and not plain existential quantifiers. Sela Mador-Haim and Yoad Winter, 'Far from Obvious: The Semantics of Locative Indefinites' (*Ling&P* 38[2015] 437–76), look at quantificational variability effects in locative sentences containing indefinites with the *a* article, as in *Michael is far from a gas station* vs. *Michael is close to a gas station*, and propose a theory in which indefinites denote properties and are assigned locations similarly to other spatial descriptions.

Further publications relevant to the study of modality include Sarah Moss's paper 'On the Semantics and Pragmatics of Epistemic Vocabulary' (*S&Prag* 8[2015] 1–81), which defends a novel semantics for possibility and necessity modals and indicative conditionals, according to which the semantic values of sentences consist of sets of probability measures (instead of sets of words, as assumed in truth-conditional theories). 'Neg-Raising and Positive Polarity: The View from Modals' (*S&Prag* 8[2015] 1–88) by Vincent Homer argues that the reason why the deontic modals *must*, *should*, and *supposed to* take scope over clausemate negation—as opposed to *have to* and *required to*, for example—is that the former are ('mobile') Positive Polarity Items. 'The Syntax of Modality and the Actuality Entailment' (in Guéron, ed., *Sentence and Discourse*, pp. 121–39) by Jacqueline Guéron argues for a predicative analysis of modal verbs that derives aspectual constraints on the modals' propositional argument from assumptions about the affinity of goal-directedness to open time intervals.

Turning now to studies on verbal aspect, Bridget Copley and Heidi Harley, 'A Force-Theoretic Framework for Event Structure' (*Ling&P* 38[2015] 103–58), propose a new account of dynamic predicates, which views them as forces, 'functions from an initial situation to a final situation that occurs *ceteris paribus*' (p. 103). The theory enables a new analysis of non-culminating accomplishment predicates, expressed in English with the progressive (*Mary was painting the dresser black, but she didn't finish*), offers strictly compositional denotations for the substructures of change-of-state verbs, incremental theme verbs, manner verbs, resultatives, activity and semelfactive predicates, and accounts for certain differences between dynamic and stative predicates in terms of adverbial selection and coercion. Nicholas Asher and Jacqueline Guéron, 'Perfect Puzzles in Discourse' (in Guéron, ed., pp. 162–77) address certain puzzles concerning the combinability of English perfect and pluperfect tenses with certain temporal adverbs (as in \**We met John last night. He had arrived yesterday.*) arguing for the instrumental role of information and discourse structure in constraining the explanatorily crucial interaction of causal links and discourse relations.

In a target article of *Theoretical Linguistics*, 'Stratified Reference: The Common Core of Distributivity, Aspect, and Measurement' (*TL* 41[2015] 109–49), Lucas Champollion proposes an integrated approach to aspect, measurement, and distributivity in terms of the unifying framework of algebraic event semantics. The author argues that '[s]ingular, telic, and collective predicates are delimited or bounded in ways that plural, mass, atelic, and distributive predicates are not' (p. 110), which can be accounted for by attributing a second-order property to all the latter categories. This property, 'stratified reference', applies to a predicate that holds of a certain entity or event if it also 'hold[s] of its parts along a certain dimension and down to a certain level of granularity' (pp. 110–11).

In a special issue of *Synthese* on logical analyses of questions, Ivano Ciardelli, Jeroen Groenendijk, and Floris Roelofsen, 'On the Semantics and Logic of Declaratives and Interrogatives' (*Synthese* 192[2015] 1689–1728), argue that whereas inquisitive semantics, as a general approach to meaning, does not require a clear-cut syntactic distinction between declaratives and interrogatives (cf. Groenendijk and Roelofsen [2009]; Ciardelli [2009]; Ciardelli and Roelofsen [2011]), it is compatible with such a distinction, and provide a complete axionatization of the associated logic. In the same issue, Benjamin Spector and Paul Egré, 'A Uniform Semantics for Embedded Interrogatives: *An* Answer, Not Necessarily *the* Answer' (*Synthese* 192[2015] 1729–84), investigate the semantics of attitude verbs that embed both questions and declaratives (referred to as 'responsive predicates' by Utpal Lahiri [2002]), arguing that the meaning of a verb of the above kind plus its interrogative complement is to be characterized as being in the relation expressed by the former to some potential complete answer to the latter. Still on the topic of question semantics, mention has to be made of María Biezma and Kyle Rawlins's overview article, which summarizes recent results on 'Alternative Questions' (*L&LC* 9[2015] 450–68). Finally, Andreea C. Nicolae looks at 'Questions with NPIs' (*NLS* 23[2015] 21–76) and proposes an account of the distribution of NPIs that relates it to the strength of exhaustivity in questions, which is encoded 'internal to the question nucleus rather than in different answer-hood operators' (p. 21).

Staying with polarity items, in 'A Fresh Look at the Compatibility between *Any* and Veridical Contexts: The Quality of Indefiniteness is Not Strained' (*Lingua* 158[2015] 35–53) Patrick J. Duffley and Pierre Larrivée conduct a corpus study on the polarity item *any*. Their findings contradict Anastasia Giannakidou and Josep Quer's [2013] assumptions, according to which *any* is restricted to nonveridical contexts, since Duffley and Larrivée found this expression also in the context of episodic past perfectives, progressives, affirmative existentials, and predicates expressing epistemic attitudes, where emphasis is placed on indiscriminacy of reference,

Two questions about infinitival complements are addressed in *Control and Restructuring* by Thomas Grano: what determines the reference of their subject, and under what circumstances can they be integrated into their matrix to form a monoclausal unit? One part of the answer given is that syntactic restructuring correlates with exhaustive control as opposed to partial control. What is more, restructuring predicates are shown to correspond semantically to those functions that are represented by functional heads in the scope of tense in the syntactic hierarchy developed by Guglielmo Cinque [1999, 2004]. Among these belong volitionals, root modalities, and aspectuals. By contrast, 'higher' functions related to speech acts, evaluations, knowledge, and evidence outscope tense, which goes along with a ban on restructuring for the associated control predicates. Grano implements this dichotomy in terms of the status of restructuring vs. non-restructuring predicates as functional vs. lexical heads. In addition, syntactic movement of the subject plus obligatory variable binding is taken to guarantee exhaustive control in the former case. The analysis is further tested against a variety of criteria such as the possibility of substituting the infinitival structure by a finite clause and the flexibility of temporal construal for control infinitives. An entire chapter is devoted to peculiarities of the predicate *want*, whose apparently non-uniform behaviour is accounted for in terms of postulating absence vs. presence of an abstract predicate *have*. Considerable additional space is devoted to enriching and verifying the approach cross-linguistically.

*Use-Conditional Meaning: Studies in Multidimensional Semantics* by Daniel Gutzmann deals with conventional meaning aspects of expressions that cannot be reduced to truth conditions. Among these belong expressive (primarily pejorative) connotations of lexical units, specifications of social speaker–hearer relations conveyed by (pronominal) forms of address, and illocution- and discourse-governing contributions by sentence moods and modal particles. Generalizing earlier work by Christopher Potts [2005], the approach pursued here is based on a 'multidimensional' logic of types that systematically interrelates the level of truth conditions and a level of use conditions. Use-conditional propositions are evaluated with respect to their contextual felicity. An important part of the study consists in a classification of varieties of use-conditional items (UCIs) recognizing (i) ±2-dimensional UCIs according to whether or not both truth- and use-conditional content is

contributed, (ii) ±functional UCIs according to whether or not argument-taking is involved, and, among the functional UCIs, (iii) ±resource-sensitive UCIs according to whether or not the content of an argument is shifted over to the use-conditional level. One of the major strengths of this work lies in the careful and didactic development of the formal compositional machinery supported by numerous tables and graphs as expository devices. In addition to comprehensive case studies of sentence moods and modal particles, a brief final chapter ventures into speculations concerning use-conditionality, language change, and cross-linguistic typology.

A book-length study of free indirect discourse (FID) is undertaken by Regine Eckardt in *The Semantics of Free Indirect Discourse: How Texts Allow Us to Mind-Read and Eavesdrop*. The characteristic 'two voices' of FID, that is, the narrator's and the protagonist's, are formally captured in terms of the manipulation of two contexts of the kind familiar from the work by David Kaplan. Substantial efforts are made to provide fully explicit rules for the interaction of these contexts, with tense and aspect, discourse particles, and sentence moods such as the exclamative. Likewise, care is taken to account for non-interactions, that is, the ban on vocatives and imperatives from FID. The formalism is further embedded in a framework that carefully distinguishes between (ordinary) information and common ground update, on the one hand, and narration and story update on the other. Also, the author devotes an entire chapter to the discussion of predecessors and alternatives such as the influential approaches by Ann Banfield [1982] and Philippe Schlenker [2004].

The collection *Bayesian Natural Language Semantics and Pragmatics*, edited by Henk Zeevat and Hans-Christian Schmitz, is the first one to apply Bayesian interpretation, a technique in signal processing, to natural language. The underlying assumption is based on Bayes' theorem: the most probable interpretation $H$ of a signal $S$ can be calculated from the prior probability of $H$, the production probability of $S$, and the likelihood of the signal given the interpretation. Zeevat's chapter ('Perspectives on Bayesian Natural Language Semantics and Pragmatics', pp. 1–24) provides a general introduction to Bayesian natural language interpretation; Anton Benz's study ('Causal Bayesian Frameworks, Signalling Games and Implicature of '*More Than n*', pp. 25–42) shows the application of the framework in explaining data on implicatures arising for *more than n*; Jacques Jayez's 'Orthogonality and Presuppositions: A Bayesian Perspective' (pp. 145–78) aims to account for differences between various presupposition triggers in allowing presupposition suspension, and Grégoire Winterstein's study applies the Bayesian approach to exclusive particles like *only* ('Layered Meanings and Bayesian Argumentation: The Case of Exclusives', pp. 179–200).

The collection *Experimental Perspectives on Presuppositions*, edited by Florian Schwarz, addresses the general question of how the different aspects of natural language meaning that supplement truth conditions, the assumed core of linguistic meaning, can be characterized, by looking at presuppositions from an experimental perspective. The contributions address one or more of three issues prominent in the theoretical literature. The first one concerns the way presuppositional content becomes available in online processing, addressed, for example, in 'Presuppositions vs. Asserted Content in Online Processing', by Florian Schwarz (pp. 89–108) and in 'Presupposition Satisfaction, Locality and Discourse Constituency' (pp. 109–34), by Christina S. Kim, as well as potential differences between different classes of presupposition triggers, studied in 'A Cross-Linguistic Study on the Non-Issueness of Exhaustive Inferences' (pp. 135–56), by Emilie Destruel, Daniel Velleman, Edgar Onea, Dylan Bumford, Jingyang Xue, and David Beaver. The second key question concerns ways of modelling projection, that is, 'the phenomenon that presuppositions introduced in many embedding environments are interpreted outside of that environment' (p. 18). Florian Schwarz's second study, 'Symmetry and Incrementality in Conditionals (pp. 195–213), looks at presuppositions introduced in the antecedents of conditionals in this connection. The third general question concerns the relation of presuppositions to other types of meaning. Jacopo Romoli and Florian Schwarz ('An Experimental Comparison between Presuppositions and Indirect Scalar Implicatures', pp. 215–40) compare the processing properties of the presuppositional trigger *stop* and the strong scalar item *always* under negation.

Staying with empirical studies on interpretation, Katy Carlson's 'Clefting, Parallelism, and Focus in Ellipsis Sentences (in Frazier and Gibson, eds., *Explicit and Implicit Prosody in Sentence Processing*, pp. 63–83) investigates whether the different indicators of semantic focus (i.e. the constituent introducing alternatives, in the sense of Mats Rooth [1992]), such as clefts or pitch accents, introduce different effects in the course of processing ambiguous ellipsis sentences in cases where the resolution is sensitive to focus. The results suggest that the effect of different focus indicators is similar, but also that they function additively. 'Epistemic Parenthetical Verb Phrases: C-Command, Semantic Scope and Prosodic Phrasing' (in Schneider, Glikman, and Avanzi, eds., *Parenthetical Verbs*, pp. 225–56), by Nancy Hedberg and Noureddine Elouazizi, reports on corpus findings supporting a transparent scope-prosody mapping for parenthetically used expressions like *I believe* and *I guess*. This consists in joint prosodic phrasing and results in an operation (i.e. mitigation), affecting the focused material scoped over. In 'Experimental Evidence for the Truth Conditional Contribution and Shifting Information Status of Appositives' (*JSem* 32[2015] 525–77) Kristen Syrett and Fedor Koev propose that sentence-final appositive relative clauses can become 'at issue', based on the fact that they do become the target of a direct rejection and that whenever an appositive is false, participants judge the entire sentence false. The authors argue for a unidimensional semantics which treats appositives as dynamic conjuncts. 'Constraints on Donkey Pronouns' (*JSem* 32[2015] 619–48), by Patrick G. Grosz, Pritty Patel-Grosz, Evelina Fedorenko, and Edward Gibson, studies the interpretation of so-called donkey pronouns, and argues that they generally prefer an overt NP antecedent that is not part of another word to be present, but an antecedent that is part of another word is potentially also acceptable, depending on salience.

## 7. Lexicography, Lexicology, and Lexical Semantics

This section begins with a discussion of publications in the field of lexicography, and goes on to look at work in lexicology and lexical semantics. In each part, the more general publications related to each sub-field will be discussed first, followed by more specialized publications. Research on current synchronic topics will precede historical studies.

Stefan J. Schierholz's survey of 'Methods in Lexicography and Dictionary Research' (*Lexikos* 25[2015] 323–52) describes the procedures and decisions involved in the creation of dictionaries by detailing lexicographical methods and their theoretical underpinnings. At the same time, it outlines practical considerations such as the staffing and management of dictionary projects and the ongoing maintenance of data, and sets out the various fields of meta-lexicography. Several other papers look at specific elements of lexicographical methodology. In 'From Print to Digital: Implications for Dictionary Policy and Lexicographic Conventions' (*Lexikos* 25[2015] 301–22), Michael Rundell examines long-established editorial policies, and asks how relevant these are for digital dictionaries and what alternatives might replace them. The paper particularly considers inclusion criteria, definitions, and example sentences, and concludes that although promising innovations have been introduced in some digital resources, the amount of outdated material that is still included by online dictionaries is problematic. Xiqin Liu also considers the possibilities offered by the digital format in 'Multimodal Definition: The Multiplication of Meaning in Electronic Dictionaries' (*Lexikos* 25[2015] 210–32), and notes that it is problematic for online dictionaries to think of themselves simply as another incarnation of print dictionaries. Rather, entries which use a number of interacting modes (including, for example, pictures and diagrams and audio material) can overcome some of the problems of verbal definitions, but more research into this area is needed. In 'The Design of Morphological/Linguistic Data in L1 and L2 Monolingual, Explanatory Dictionaries: A Functional and/ or Linguistic Approach?' (*Lexikos* 25[2015] 353–86), P.H. Swanepoel critically discusses a 2013 article by Henning Bergenholtz and Rufus Gouws which favours a functional theoretical approach over a linguistic approach to lexicography. Swanepoel concludes that, in the presentation of morphological data and more generally, 'what lexicography needs now is a truly multidisciplinary approach' (p. 383) rather than an over-simplified version of one theoretical stance. Also worth mentioning here is the publication in paperback of Howard Jackson's excellent edited volume *The Bloomsbury Companion to Lexicography*, reviewed last year.

Rufus Gouws discusses the role and usefulness of simple and complex collocations, comparing dictionaries of languages including English, in 'The Presentation and Treatment of Collocations as Secondary Guiding Elements in Dictionaries' (*Lexikos* 25[2015] 170–90). He argues that the importance and frequency of collocations in everyday language mean that their status needs to be elevated in dictionaries, so that they are presented with more prominence and explained more fully. Geoffrey Williams considers how collocational networks, collocational resonance, and lexicographical prototypes can help to make sense of uses of the proper noun *Europe* in 'Many Shades of Europe' (in Karpova and Kartashkova, eds., *Life Beyond Dictionaries*, pp. 6–25), and uses data from a range of dictionaries and corpora; the study is part of a project on European identity. Elsabé Taljard's 'Collocations and Grammatical Patterns in a Multilingual Online Term Bank' (*Lexikos* 25[2015] 387–402) discusses the nature of collocation and the value of collocational information for English learners. Taljard explores the difference between empirical collocation, which relates to semantic prosody, and grammatical collocation, and recommends providing explicit information on collocations and listing multiword expressions so that users can access these directly.

In 'Using an Online Dictionary for Identifying the Meanings of Verb Phrases by Chinese EFL Learners' (*Lexikos* 25[2015] 191–209), Lingling Li and Hai Xu focus on the *Macmillan English Dictionary Online* in a study involving thirty-two students. Like many earlier studies, the paper concludes that training in dictionary skills would help learners to use online dictionaries more effectively, but in some cases information in dictionaries is deficient and could be improved. Mari Carmen Campoy-Cubillo's paper 'Assessing Dictionary Skills' (*LexAsia* 2[2015] 119–41) similarly considers the role of dictionary skills in language learning. The paper sets out the relationship between language proficiency levels and learner dictionary skills, the role of educational and cultural context, and the different stages in the process of dictionary use, and finally proposes a framework for dictionary skills proficiency levels. The paper 'A Course in Dictionary Use for Korean EFL teachers', by Susanna Bae (*LexAsia* 2[2015] 45–69), reports on a twelve-hour course delivered to eighty-five school teachers (in several groups), during which participants were surveyed about perceived training needs. Findings from these courses indicate that even experienced dictionary users benefit from explicit training, since this enables them to discover features that they may not otherwise know about. Also related to learners' dictionaries, Shin'ichiro Ishikawa considers 'The Contribution of Learner Corpus Studies for Dictionary Making: Identification of Deviant L2 Vocabulary Use by Asian Learners' (in Karpova and Kartashkova, eds., pp. 174–84); by 'deviant vocabulary use' Ishikawa means the over- and under-use of particular words by comparison with native speakers, and he suggests that dictionaries could incorporate tailor-made usage information for different learner groups on the basis of studies of this kind.

Carolin Ostermann uses monolingual learners' dictionaries to inform a study which argues for an integration of cognitive semantic theory and lexicographical practice, in *Cognitive Lexicography: A New Approach to Lexicography Making Use of Cognitive Semantics*. The volume focuses on three elements of dictionary content—example sentences, definitions, and the microstructure of entries—and suggests a new cognitive lexicographical way of handling these. The purpose of the volume is set out in a short introduction, and followed by a history of learner lexicography in chapter 2, and description of its principles in chapter 3. Like Anna Wierzbicka, Ostermann criticizes 'the status of lexicography as a craft lacking theory' (p. 21), but goes on to note that some of the principles of cognitive linguistics, particularly the perspective it offers on categorization, appear to underlie traditional lexicography. Despite animosity between the disciplines, an emphasis on cognitive processes can better describe the way users process language. Chapter 4 compares cognitive accounts of semantic structure, which emphasize the prototypical nature of category membership, with dictionary entries for entities in the same category, using terms for birds as an example. The core of the volume shows 'what cognitive lexicography looks like in particular' (p. 67), by examining three lexical categories: person-denoting nouns are presented with attention to the theory of frame semantics in chapter 5; abstract nouns associated with emotion are related to conceptual metaphor and metonymy theory in chapter 6; and particles are the subject of chapter 7, viewed in light of the principled polysemy approach. In chapters 5 and 6, user studies which require subjects to match headwords and definitions show that the resulting entries are more successful than entries from established dictionaries, and this is persuasive evidence that cognitive lexicography can produce dictionaries that users can better understand, Ostermann's claim in the final chapters of the volume, which also suggest future directions.

Labels are the focus of Marjeta Vrbinc and Alenka Vrbinc's 'Diasystematic Information in the "Big Five": A Comparison of Print Dictionaries, CD-ROMS/ DVD-ROMS and Online Dictionaries' (*Lexikos* 25[2015] 424–45), which compares the information in monolingual learners' dictionaries and interrogates its intelligibility for users. Vrbinc and Vrbinc argue that the labelling in online dictionaries is deficient in comparison with that of print dictionaries, and learners of English would benefit from more detailed information about what labels mean. 'Phases and Steps in the Access to Data in Information Tools', by Henning Bergenholtz, Theo Bothma, and Rufus Gouws (*Lexikos* 25[2015] 1–30), considers how those encountering unknown words (or other kinds of symbols) access information on their meaning; there is no single source which integrates linguistic and encyclopedic information and which is tailored to a specific user's needs, and the authors argue that lexicographers can be instrumental in working towards such a source. Tatyana Taganova focuses on the way that modern dictionaries handle neologisms, with particular attention to the way that professional lexicography interacts with contemporary users and volunteer contributors, in 'Lexicographic Description of New Realia of Culture' (in Karpova and Kartashkova, eds., pp. 143–54).

Sandro Nielsen examines the treatment of specialized terms in general dictionaries, comparing four corpus-based monolingual English dictionaries, in 'Legal Terms in General Dictionaries of English: The Civil Procedure Mystery' (*Lexikos* 25[2015] 246–61). Nielsen questions the exclusion of relatively recent but well-established legal terms, and argues that lexicographers need better electronic corpora if they are to reduce the time lag in the incorporation of useful specialized headwords. Sven Tarp's paper 'On the Disciplinary and Functional Status of Economic Lexicography' (*IbéricaR* 29[2015] 179–200) considers specialized dictionaries of various languages including English. After surveying their history, Tarp discusses their contributors and the way in which their design and content meet the needs of their users, and finally he makes a number of recommendations for the future which encourage innovation for authors. Marina Solnyshkina looks at 'Pragmatic Information in LSP Dictionaries and Professional Discourse' (in Karpova and Kartashkova, eds., pp. 65–75), using entries in a range of dictionaries as the starting point for an analysis of the way fixed phrases are defined in a specialized corpus of low-register professional discourse.

A cluster of papers look specifically at the treatment of trademarks in lexicography, and conversely at the use of dictionary evidence in trademark litigation. In 'Trademarks and the Lexicographer in the Digital Age' (*DJDSNA* 36[2015] 88–99), Orin Hargraves looks at the way trademarks have been recorded in dictionaries from the mid-nineteenth century onwards, and describes different approaches to genericized trademarks, arguing that these should be treated as ordinary lexemes to reflect their usage. The late Adam Kilgarriff considers the role of 'Corpus Linguistics in Trademark Cases' (*DJDSNA* 36[2015] 100–14), and describes several legal cases in which he served as an expert witness. In each case, corpus evidence was used to determine whether trademarks registered by one company were 'ordinary words', so that their use by another company could not be considered theft; Kilgarriff details how this evidence can be found and evaluated. Ronald Buttars's 'Using Lexicographical Methodology in Trademark Litigation: Analyzing Similatives' (*DJDSNA* 36[2015] 115–30) considers how helpful dictionaries can be in establishing whether a firm can assert trademark rights to a noun–adjective compound particularly associated with a commercial product or company. The paper examines the evidence for *whisper-quiet*, concluding that dictionaries themselves cannot answer this kind of question, though lexicographical methods may be promising.

Among this year's work on bilingual dictionaries of English and other languages is Sven Tarp's account of the plan for a new English–Spanish dictionary, 'Preparing an Online Dictionary of Business Communication: From Idea to Design' (*Lexikos* 25[2015] 403–23). This work sits somewhere between general and specialized, with a heterogeneous user group. Unlike existing dictionaries it will be composed of two monolingual dictionaries which sit alongside one another, and will therefore offer more detailed entries. Wenge Chen adopts a CDA perspective in 'Bilingual Lexicography as Recontextualization: A Case Study of Illustrative Examples in *A New English–Chinese Dictionary*' (*AuJL* 35[2015] 311–33). A comparison of different editions focuses on the changing frequency of keywords in quotations, and shows a shift from politically charged terms like *socialism* and *revolution* and their Chinese equivalents to the more neutral vocabulary of science and technology; Chen argues that this reflects different constructions of social reality. Joanna Szerszunowicz's paper 'Lacunarity, Lexicography and Beyond: Integration of the Introduction of a Linguo-Cultural Concept and the Development of L2 Learners' Dictionary Skills' (*LexAsia* 2[2015] 108–18) examines lacunae, linguistic and referential gaps that are found when comparing Polish and English. Szerszunowicz argues that although lacunae are generally a minor topic for foreign language learners, they have great potential as a means to bridge theory-orientated and practice-focused teaching, and can help students improve their use of bilingual dictionaries alongside their linguistic and cultural knowledge. In 'Developing a Dictionary Culture through Integrated Dictionary Pedagogy in the Outer Texts of South African School Dictionaries: The Case of *Oxford Bilingual School Dictionary:*

*IsiXhosa and English*' (*LexAsia* 2[2015] 71–99), Dion Nkomo notes the growing number of South African school dictionaries that are being produced despite a 'patchy dictionary culture' (p. 72). This context makes it particularly important that dictionaries incorporate outside matter, material additional to the central word list which integrates dictionary pedagogy into the work, but this should be complemented by explicit teaching of the kinds detailed in the article. Toshiko Koyama focuses on another group of learners who have received training on an online Japanese–English bilingual dictionary, in 'The Impact of E-Dictionary Strategy Training on EFL Class' (*LexAsia* 2[2015] 35–44). After an eighteen-week course informed by earlier research, students were found to have benefited, with better reading comprehension, although Koyama notes that some findings were unexpected, and further research is needed. A paper with related interests is Jun Ding's 'A Study of English Majors in a Chinese University as Dictionary Users' (*LexAsia* 2[2015] 5–34), based on a questionnaire completed by thirty-seven first-year students. The results show a predictable preference for digital rather than print dictionaries, but also 'highly complex and individual' look-up patterns (p. 14) often involving multiple dictionaries. Despite this, many informants over-rely on L1 translations, and struggle to identify the appropriate sub-entries for words in context.

The field of historical lexicography sees a particularly important publication this year in Lynda Mugglestone's monograph *Samuel Johnson and the Journey into Words*. Mugglestone explores the context and content of the *Dictionary*, connecting up Johnson's lexicography with his many other roles and his attitudes towards both linguistic and extra-linguistic matters, in a critical and nuanced way. The introduction explains the theme and axis of the book. Johnson commented that in writing the *Dictionary* he 'sailed a long and painful journey around the world of the English Language' (quoted on p. 2); this metaphor has implications for the way he conceived of and treated many different aspects of the work. Chapter 2 chronicles the beginning of Johnson's lexicographical life, and his intentions for the *Dictionary* in a working 'Scheme' written before his 1747 *Plan*. In 'Excursions into Books' (chapter 3) Mugglestone documents the process of collection Johnson undertook to exemplify his entries: though his methods were selective, and unsystematic by modern standards, annotated books show his thorough engagement with his materials. His ongoing attempts to 'order' his work, and his complicated and evolving ideas about prescription, are explored in chapter 4, and picked up again in a discussion of his approach to sense discrimination and labelling in chapter 5, titled 'Meaning, Governance, and the "Colours of Words"'. Chapter 6, 'Defending the Citadel, Patrolling the Borders', goes on to interrogate Johnson's role in determining his word list, and his approach to French loanwords. His at times 'strikingly neutral' attitude to language innovation and change (p. 171), and the way in which the *Dictionary* engages with the history of English, are the focus of chapter 7, and the final chapter documents the reception of the work. This is a fascinating read which answers many of the questions that are often asked of the *Dictionary*, and a welcome addition to existing scholarship.

Elizabeth Knowles focuses on quotations from the eighteenth century and their legacy in 'Guarding Even Our Enemies and the Triumph of Evil: Actual and Supposed Eighteenth-Century Voices in Twentieth-Century Politics' (*DJDSNA* 36[2015] 1–16). Using quotations attributed to Edmund Burke and Thomas Paine, the paper asks how best quotation dictionaries can present examples which do not appear to be verbatim and cannot be dated, but which are well established in later (in this case political) discourse. A pair of papers by David-Antoine Williams considers the ways in which T.S. Eliot and *OED* quote one another. 'The "Oxford Dictionary" and T.S. Eliot' (*N&Q* 62[2015] 293–6) shows that Eliot frequently talked about and quoted the 'Oxford Dictionary', but in practice he confused the *Concise Oxford Dictionary*, *Shorter OED*, and *OED*, and did not appear to understand their differences. The companion paper by the same author, 'T.S. Eliot in the *Oxford English Dictionary*' (*N&Q* 62[2015] 296–301), looks at the use of quotations from Eliot in Robert Burchfield's supplement to the first edition and the second edition. Eliot is one of the most frequently quoted authors of his period in the supplement, including quotations in some dubious cases. The contribution of volunteer readers to *OED* is the focus of Peter Gilliver's paper 'The Quotation Collectors: A Conspectus of Readers for the *Oxford English Dictionary*' (*DJDSNA* 36[2015] 47–71). Readers were recruited even before the Philological Society formally began the dictionary project, and brief but fascinating biographies of a few are detailed along with the attestations they supplied. Philip Durkin also focuses on *OED* in investigating '*Mackems*, *Geordies* and *Ram-Raiders*: Documenting Regional Variation in Historical Dictionaries' (*ELL* 19[2015] 313–26). The paper describes the difficulties of indicating the regional distribution of lexemes, forms, or senses, not least a lack of systematic information, then presents case studies of three dialect forms from the north-east to show how these difficulties might best be handled (for some more detail on this, see Section 9 below). Moving away from *OED*, 'Language Ideologies and *The American Heritage Dictionary of the English Language*: Evidence from Motive, Structure, and Design' (*DJDSNA* 36[2015] 17–46), by Michael Adams, examines a dictionary apparently conceived as a prescriptive reaction to more descriptive works of the period. Adams describes the aims and practices of the first edition, and argues that it showed some descriptive tendencies in its design; later editions show some ideological evolution, although they are still normative in many respects.

Several papers from one volume focus on the connection between the lexicography and culture of English, some looking particularly at specific varieties. Susan Rennie opens up '*A Kist of Ferlies*: Scottish Culture in Jamieson and the Later Dictionaries of Scots' (in Karpova and Kartashkova, eds., pp. 32–41). She argues that Jamieson's work 'refocused the lens of Scottish lexicography' (p. 39) by moving from glossaries of Scotticisms to a work that took account of cultural vocabulary in a new way, and his work was an important precursor to the *SND*. Valentyna Skybina's 'Australian Diachronic Dictionaries: A Cultural Portrait of Australia' (in Karpova and Kartashkova, eds., pp. 42–53) begins with a survey of eighteen dictionaries, from the single work published in the nineteenth century to six between 2000 and 2005; it goes on to look at entries for distinctively Australian words, including *bush* and its derivatives, in the *Australian National Dictionary*. Nataliya Bytko looks at the role of *Hobson-Jobson* in the development of IndE in 'Indian Culture in the Indian English Dictionary' (in Karpova and Kartashkova, eds., pp. 54–64), and presents a selection of words that were considered 'exoticisms' at its time of publication, in lexico-thematic groups. Olga Melentyeva sets out the case for 'Old Words in Chaucer Dictionaries as the Linguistic Heritage of Great Britain' (in Karpova and Kartashkova, eds., pp. 76–90), starting from the claim that author dictionaries offer a rare window onto the culture of a particular place and period. The main part of the paper describes and compares past and present Chaucer glossaries and dictionaries. Olga Karpova writes on 'Dictionaries of National Heritage and Culture (with Special Reference to the Dictionary Project *Florence in the Works of World Famous People*' (in Karpova and Kartashkova, eds., pp. 92–104), giving a brief account of this branch of lexicography and then a more lengthy description of the content of this collaborative work. 'Cultural Dictionaries' by Olga Uzhova (in Karpova and Kartashkova eds., pp. 165–71) looks particularly at a dictionary compiled specifically for Russian learners of English, and gives examples of the entries for words that refer to aspects of English history.

One of several short papers on etymology, by Ben Parsons, looks at ' "Pet" Names in *OED3*' (*N&Q* 62[2015] 370–4). This offers antedatings of terms including *billy goat*, *Grimalkin*, and *polly*, with a discussion of the evidence in each case. Kathryn Walls discusses '*OED* Add, *v*.1.b. "To add faith to": A Problematic Citation' (*N&Q* 62[2015] 22–3), and concludes that a citation from Thomas Becon's 'Sick Man's Salve' does not attest the appropriate sense. John-Wilhelm Flattun finds an antedating for an *OED* entry in 'A Note on Backswords in Thomas Middleton' (*N&Q* 62[2015] 533), and Eric Weiskott discusses 'A Postdating of *Throw* "Time" in *Twelfth Night*' (*N&Q* 62[2015] 421–2), showing that this example of *throw* has been misunderstood by some scholars. Fourteenth-century evidence for 'Middle English *\*Gannoken* "To Regrate" ' is examined by Keith Briggs, Rosemary Hoppitt, and John Ridgard (*N&Q* 62[2015] 531–2), and Alfred Bammesberger considers 'The Meaning of Old English *Ambyrne Wind* and the Adverb *Amberlice*' (*N&Q* 62[2015] 179–80), suggesting 'appropriate wind' and 'appropriately', respectively.

A substantial and hugely useful resource in the field of lexicology and lexical semantics that appeared this year is John Taylor's edited volume *The Oxford Handbook of the Word*. This is a collection which is wide-ranging in its interests, with some papers focused more on English than others. Forty-two papers plus an introduction are presented in eight sections as follows: Part I, 'Words: General Aspects', covers topics such as the size of the lexicon, word frequency and length, and collocation; Part II, 'Words and Linguistic Theory', relates mainly to morphology, syntax, and phonology; Part III looks at 'Meanings, Referents, and Concepts'; Part IV, 'Words in Time and Space', has a historical dimension; Part V, 'Words in the Mind', explores topics in psycholinguistics; Part VI is titled 'Words in Acquisition and Learning'; Part VII is devoted to 'Names'; and finally Part VIII, 'Fun with Words', comprises two papers on verbal humour and word puzzles, and is followed by a separate 'Final Word' on the nature of the word. Of interest here are papers that cross over into lexicography, including contributions on thesauri and etymology, and on other topics as diverse as multi-word units, taboo words, borrowing and lexical change; these will be described briefly, but the remainder of the volume, which relates to other disciplines, will not be covered here. Following Taylor's introductory chapter, David Crystal begins with some thoughts on 'The Lure of Words' (pp. 23–8), which introduces some of the issues that will be addressed in a more technical way by the following papers. 'How Many Words Are There?' is discussed by the late Adam Kilgarriff (pp. 29–36) mainly in relation to English; no definitive answer can be provided, but rather further questions necessarily follow, relating to issues such as the difference between general and specialist lexis and how to count borrowed words and formal variants. Marc Alexander surveys the relationship between 'Words and Dictionaries' (pp. 37–52), with attention to the history of lexicography and the nature and roles of different dictionaries, and includes a particularly interesting section on the tension involved in giving an artificial account of naturally occurring language (pp. 49–51). The late Christian Kay's paper 'Words and Thesauri' (pp. 53–67) similarly gives an account of the history of the thesaurus, and explores the nature of synonymy and the necessity of real-world knowledge in classifying semantically related words. Kay refers to *Historical Thesaurus of the OED* (*HTOED*), and the paper is a reminder of the legacy she leaves; her various publications in this section show how active she was until her death in 2016 and what a sad loss to the community she is. Joseph Sorell explains statistical techniques for measuring 'Word Frequencies' (pp. 68–88), detailing the contribution of George Kingsley Zipf and others whose work followed his, and examining data from different corpora and the network structure of the World Wide Web. In 'Multi-Word Items' (pp. 120–40) Rosamund Moon looks at more and less fixed strings that can be considered lexical items, and surveys different approaches to their description and study. She discusses particular types, including idioms, proverbs and bi- and trinomials, and argues that these 'point towards phraseological modes for the lexicon rather than atomistic ones' (p. 139). Michael Hoey discusses the semantic and grammatical relationships between collocates in a small *Guardian* corpus and a Web-derived mini-corpus in 'Words and Their Neighbours' (pp. 140–53), taking the expression *crude forgeries* as a starting point. The dynamic nature of 'Taboo Words' and their effects are examined by Kate Burridge, who includes sections on strategies for avoiding taboo words, and the taboo nature of names in some cultures. Part III of the volume begins with Nick Riemer's account of 'Word Meanings' (pp. 305–19). Riemer considers the nature of definitions, internalist and externalist approaches to meaning, and the difference between meaning and reference; he goes on to offer a cognitive perspective on concepts and multiple meanings. Barbara Malt's paper 'Words as Names for Objects, Actions, Relations, and Properties' (pp. 320–33) explores the different options available to speakers and what informs the choices they make, showing convincingly that multiple factors interact to determine the names that are used in any specific context. 'Terminologies and Taxonomies', by Marie-Claude L'Homme (pp. 334–49), looks more specifically at naming conventions in specialized subject fields including zoology, and the difficulties of standardizing these across languages.

Christiane Fellbaum describes the nature and range of 'Lexical Relations' (pp. 350–63), including lexical relations such as synonymy and antonymy and relations that might more properly be called conceptual-semantic, such as meronymy and hyponymy. Part of her paper outlines one attempt to organize the lexicon via these relations, WordNet. Two papers take a cross-linguistic approach to meaning: first, Asifa Majid writes on 'Comparing Lexicons Cross-Linguistically' (pp. 364–79), drawing examples from colour terms and body-part terms; second, Cliff Goddard argues for 'Words as Carriers of Cultural Meaning' (pp. 380–98), exploring the notions of semantic primes and cultural keywords, and going on to discuss other culturally important words including terms of address. The final section of the volume that will be reviewed here adopts a historical perspective, starting with Philip Durkin's chapter on 'Etymology' (pp. 401–15). Concentrating on English words, Durkin describes the core methods of etymology, and considers difficult cases such as lexical mergers and splits where word histories show 'messiness' (p. 411). Dirk Geeraerts discusses onomasiological and semasiological mechanisms for lexical change, as well as addressing the question of why words and meanings disappear, in 'How Words and Vocabularies Change' (pp. 416–30). The paper ends by stressing the frequent and typical interaction between mechanisms of change. Anthony Grant's chapter, 'Borrowing' (pp. 431–44), looks across languages to consider mechanisms and motivations, and distinguishes different types of borrowing that do or do not involve replacement of existing terms. He goes on to review particularly influential studies that use the Swadesh list to measure the extent to which different areas of lexis borrow. The diachronic and synchronic effects of borrowing are also considered in Margaret Winters's chapter, 'Lexical Layers' (pp. 445–61), which concludes this section of the volume by examining different kinds of language contact and their consequences for English and other languages. Philip Durkin's influential work *Borrowed Words: A History of Loanwords in English*, which is published in paperback this year (and was reviewed in this section last year) gives a more detailed account of this topic.

Daphné Kerremans's monograph *A Web of New Words: A Corpus-Based Study of the Conventionalization Process of English Neologisms* is a highly significant publication that tracks the earliest appearances of neologisms and their subsequent linguistic 'careers'. Using an innovative software tool to identify and collect new formations on the Web, Kerremans examines their nature and meanings over a two-year period, and uses this data to suggest a conventionalization process with four stages, and to examine the emergence of 'syntagmatic lexical relations', or networks of collocates. After an introduction that explains the aims of the study, the volume begins with a detailed survey of neolinguistics, the study of neologisms, detailing tensions in terminology and established accounts of conventionalization (chapter 2). Kerremans goes on to discuss the theoretical difficulties and practical problems with using the Web as a corpus, in chapter 3. Despite these, the Web offers a source of more immediate neologisms, and a much larger amount of data, than any corpus; and the development of the NeoCrawler allows better data collection than other Web crawlers. The study focuses on particular types of Web source, including interactive platforms like blogs and discussion forums, which are particularly interesting in the insight they give into speech communities. Chapter 4 gives an account of the process of conventionalization, which Kerremans argues should be seen as a continuum, using data from the study, and considering the effect of potential constraints such as blocking. An important factor which influences this process is the presence of collocations, and this is the focus of chapter 5. Finally, the conclusion in chapter 6 summarizes the findings of the study, comparing the effects of different factors on conventionalization and arguing for the importance of a model that recognizes both social and cognitive factors. This is a beautifully written, highly sophisticated volume which shows great attention to detail and offers new insights into lexical innovation and change.

Another major work is *The Routledge Handbook of Semantics*, edited by Nick Riemer. This covers a range of approaches and perspectives; as Riemer says in the introduction (pp. 1–10), 'comprehensive' readers 'will hardly fail to be struck by the major contrast between approaches to meaning rooted in formal logic and those rooted in cognitive hypotheses about meaning as mental representation' (p. 8), and some papers in the collection, including the introduction, work hard to show the relationship between these different areas of the discipline. For example, Keith Allan's chapter 3, 'A History of Semantics' (pp. 48–68), gives a very helpful account which contextualizes developments in lexical and historical semantics. Chapter 5, 'Cognitive Semantics' by Maarten Lemmens (pp. 90–105), similarly incorporates a survey of relevant work on lexical semantics in a cognitivist context, with sections on conceptual networks and metaphor and metonymy; Michael Stubbs's account of 'Corpus Semantics' in chapter 6 (pp. 106–21) includes material on phraseology, collocation, and colligation that will also be of interest to some readers; and Nick Riemer's summary of decompositional approaches to lexical content in chapter 12, 'Lexical Decomposition' (pp. 213–32), gives helpful introductions to componential analysis and the theory of natural semantic metalanguage. Only a relatively small number of papers are more directly relevant to this section, though, and these will be outlined here. In the excellent chapter 13, Dirk Geeraerts discusses 'Sense Individuation' (pp. 233–47), explaining the difference between polysemy and vagueness, and between utterance and systemic meaning, and considering how these might be distinguished in practice. He goes on to report recent theoretical and methodological approaches to these aspects of meaning, and sets out some questions that need to be explored further. In chapter 14, Petra Storjohann explores 'Sense Relations' (pp. 248–65), detailing traditional classifications but focusing on more empirically informed and cognitively grounded approaches, specifically to antonymy and synonymy. Finally, John Newman surveys 'Semantic Shift' in chapter 15 (pp. 266–80), concentrating on shifts 'in very ordinary kinds of language activity as happens in our lived experience' (p. 266) and considering different methods of accounting for this kind of change. Like the rest of the book, this is an interesting and thought-provoking piece, but the whole thing is very little informed by a historical perspective, and this seems like a missed opportunity.

Alishova Ramila Bebir examines verbs denoting life and death in 'The Scopes of Word Semantics' (*IJEL* 5:vi[2015] 169–75), and considers the relationship between words and concepts, and different theories of meaning; she concludes that the word is a problematic unit for semantic analysis. In 'Semasiology and Onomasiology: Empirical Questions between Meaning, Naming and Context' (in Daems, Zenner, Heylen, Speelman, and Cuyckens, eds., *Change of Paradigms—New Paradoxes: Recontextualizing Language and Linguistics*, pp. 47–79), Dylan Glynn interrogates a distinction which is theoretically helpful but analytically problematic, via a corpus-based study of the meanings of *over*. He argues that meaning variation results from the interaction between linguistic forms and the contexts in which they occur, so that there is a correlation between contexts of use and semasiological structure. M. Lynne Murphy, Steven Jones, and Anu Koskela analyse 'Signals of Contrastiveness: *But*, Oppositeness, and Formal Similarity in Parallel Contexts' (*JEngL* 43[2015] 227–49), focusing particularly on the role of ancillary antonymy, 'the use of an established antonym pair to help support and/or accentuate contrast between a less established pair' (p. 227), in novel lexical contrasts. They use evidence from a range of corpora to measure and compare the contribution of different contrast markers.

Mark Wyatt and Glenn Hadikin's paper, '"They parked two buses": A Corpus Study of a Football Expression' (*EnT* 31[2015] 34–41), presents evidence from a number of corpora for a metaphor that has become a cliché within football discourse but is relatively unknown for other speakers. Brian Poole considers a claim by the writer Kenneth Tynan in 1974 that reports of a murder suspect's absence had a class bias, in 'Lord Lucan: "Missing" or "On the Run"?' (*EnT* 31[2015] 10–15) , and uses this as a starting point for a discussion of the relationship between lexical choice and social class. In '*A Little Bit About*: Differences in Native and Non-Native Speakers' Use of Formulaic Language' (*AuJL* 35[2015] 297–310), Hadi Kashiha and Swee Heng Chan compare the frequency with which English and Malaysian speakers use four-word lexical bundles. They find that native speakers use more, and more varied, formulae of this kind, but classifying these by discourse functions reveals more fine-grained differences between the groups. María Luisa Carrió-Pastor and Rut Muñiz Calderón discuss the 'Identification and Causes of Lexical Variation in Chinese Business English' (*EnT* 31[2015] 10–15), comparing the frequency of lexical features including calques and abbreviations in an email corpus of speakers from China and Hong Kong. They find that Chinese speakers use more non-standard and more informal English, though point out that their data is limited.

Dilin Liu and Hongwei Zhan present a study which marries synchronic and diachronic perspectives by using both COCA and COHA in 'The Use of the -*Free* Compound and *Free of* and *Free from* Phrasal Constructions: A Diachronic and Synchronic Study' (*JEngL* 43[2015] 201–26). In the period which is their focus, -*free* and *free of* increase in use, while *free from* decreases in frequency, and the paper considers the semantic and structural functions of each. In 'Corpus Linguistic Analysis of the Connotative Meaning of Some Terms Used in the Context of "The War on Terror"' (*IJEL* 5:i[2015] 113–34), Alaa Ghazi Rababah examines the frequency and use of eight terms (and variants) in COCA including *terrorist/terrorism* and *fundamentalist/fundamentalism*, comparing the decade leading up to and the decade following 9/11. The paper shows that the collocation of many of these terms has changed, indicating shifts in connotation towards more clearly negative meanings.

Turning to work with a longer diachronic perspective, *English Historical Semantics*, by Christian Kay and Kathryn Allan, is a textbook aimed at advanced undergraduates and postgraduates which mainly focuses on structuralist and cognitivist approaches to lexical semantics. After a brief introduction which introduces key terms, the book begins with an outline of the history of the English lexicon, divided into periods, and goes on to consider categories of meaning. In chapter 4, the authors give a detailed explanation of the information presented in *OED* and what it means; for example, they caution against treating first dates of attestation uncritically. An account of 'How and Why Words Change Meaning' engages with the complications of semantic change, and illustrates different tendencies with detailed examples. A relatively unusual inclusion is a chapter on *HTOED*, which balances a description of the history and nature of thesauruses with a guide to using the resource. Carole Biggam is a guest author for a chapter on 'English Colour Terms', which is an excellent introduction to the field and is followed by a broader consideration of the relationship between language and culture, which considers areas of the lexicon such as kinship terms and ways of expressing time. The penultimate chapter focuses on metaphor and metonymy, and finally a short chapter brings together the preceding material in a discussion of the history and recent meanings of *green*. The book aims to be both practical and accessible; each chapter is accompanied by exercises and further reading, and the glossary should also be a helpful resource.

In 'Testing the Dynamic Model: The Evolution of the Hong Kong English Lexicon (1858–2012)' (*JEngL* 43[2015] 175–200), Stephen Evans traces the developmental cycle of an Outer Circle variety, using a 91-million word corpus of Legislative Council proceedings to represent spoken HKE. He concludes that the milestones used by Schneider to divide the evolutionary cycle of the variety into periods are not significant in terms of its lexis, and the 1990s seem more important (see also Section 9). Susan Fitzmaurice discusses 'Ideology, Race and Place in Historical Constructions of Belonging: The Case of Zimbabwe' (*ELL* 19[2015] 327–54), in a paper which sits at the intersection between lexical semantics, pragmatics and sociolinguistics. Fitzmaurice examines the importance of key terms in the construction of identity, and concludes that the meanings of these terms are highly unstable, changing with different users and in different periods and contexts. Further back in time, Adam Mearns writes on 'This, That and the Other: Locating the Supernatural Enemy in Old English' (*ELL* 19[2015] 213–26), using prototype semantics as a framework: despite the lexical gap in OE for the meaning 'supernatural', he argues that there is a conceptual category which accommodates monsters and devils and associates them with other alien beings such as foreigners and criminals.

*Mapping English Metaphor through Time*, edited by Wendy Anderson, Ellen Bramwell, and Carole Hough, grew out of interest in metaphor facilitated by the Mapping Metaphor with the Historical Thesaurus of English project at Glasgow, a spin-off from the project published on paper in 2009 as *HTOED*. The collection of papers explores different areas of the lexicon across the history of English, many of them using data from these sister projects; like *HTOED*, the collection is structured in three sections, and papers in each will be outlined briefly here. Andrew Prescott's introduction, subtitled 'The Pursuit of Metaphors' (pp. 1–12), explains the motivation for the Mapping Metaphor project and includes images of the revealing and beautiful metaphor maps that can be generated on the project website. Part I, 'The External World', includes six papers on data from the corresponding *HTOED* section, beginning with Carole Hough's paper 'The Metaphorical Landscape' (pp. 13–31). This presents several metaphors, with LANDSCAPE as either the source or target, identified by polysemous words that appear in this category and another in the Mapping Metaphor data; these include the widely recognized LANDSCAPE IS A BODY metaphor, but also other less studied mappings such as the more specific LANDSCAPE IS A CLOTHED BODY and PEOPLE ARE LANDSCAPE, and illustrate the variety of metaphors associated with a single concept. Judith Paterson compares the metaphorical links to horses and pigs in 'Metaphorical Beasts in the History of English' (pp. 32–46). Though both animals have a long history of domestication, the concepts which they map onto provide fascinating evidence of their different relationships to humans, with more, and far more positive, connections to equines. Carole Biggam's 'Plants as Metaphorical Headgear in English' (pp. 47–65) examines a perhaps unexpected link between categories: Biggam details plant names featuring *crown*, *hat*, and *cap*, including *Crown of the Field* 'Corncockle', *Fairy Hat* 'Foxglove', and *Gentleman's Cap and Frills* 'Lesser Celandine'. Generally these are motivated by the appearance of flowers, and many are PART FOR WHOLE metonymies used to refer to the whole plant. The late Christian Kay focuses on one of the categories that shows the most connections to other Mapping Metaphor categories in 'Food as a Fruitful Source of Metaphor' (pp. 66–78), and notes a particular interest in the hierarchical level at which metaphorical targets appear in the *HTOED* classification. Beth Ralston's paper 'Morbid Curiosity and Metaphors of Death in the History of English' (pp. 79–89) shows the euphemistic nature of metaphors with the target DEATH, but also gives a sketch of DEATH as a source domain, used to talk about targets including EMOTIONS and COMPETITION. In Part II the volume moves to concepts associated with 'The Mental World'. 'The Metaphorical Qualities of Cool, Clear, and Clashing Colours' are considered by Rachael Hamilton (pp. 97–114), who outlines connections between colour and concepts including ill health, sound, and morality, most of which are entrenched to the extent that speakers of ModE probably consider polysemous terms to be non-metaphorical. Wendy Anderson looks at a prototypical but relatively little-studied emotion in 'Waves of Excitement, Waves of Metaphor' (pp. 115–36); though she is hesitant about accepting Gabriela-Alina Sauciuc's claim that 'non-metaphorical conceptualizations may not be possible for emotion concepts' (quoted on p. 134), she notes that there are very few non-metaphorical items in the *HTOED* category 'Excitement', and the Mapping Metaphor data shows a significant number of mappings. In 'Metaphors of Religious Anxiety in Early Modern England' (pp. 137–51), Kenneth Austin examines metaphors of fear in a historical context, drawing from texts in Early English Books Online (EEBO), and argues for the value of interdisciplinary research that marries linguistic evidence with close textual analysis. Ellen Bramwell's 'Madness, Sanity, and Metaphor' (pp. 152–64) looks at the large number of links between mental health and categories in the three *HTOED* sections, which show mappings in both directions, and observes the patterns that characterize some of the these mappings. A convincing and thought-provoking paper by Antonette diPaolo Healey, 'The Importance of Old English *Head*' (pp. 165–84), begins by making the case for a lexicography informed by modern theories of linguistics, and particularly cognitive semantics, and goes on to give a nuanced picture of the mapping A HEAD IS IMPORTANCE, drawing from a range of sources represented in *DOE*. Finally, the third section of the volume, 'The Social World', begins with 'The Metaphorical Understanding of Power and Authority' (pp. 191–207), in which Marc Alexander examines Mapping Metaphor data which falls into seven clusters including *Large/strong*, *Sight*, and *Game*. Each of these is illustrated by textual examples from a semantically tagged version of EEBO and, for the more modern period, the *Hansard Corpus* 1803–2005, supplemented by other recent texts including the scripts of the TV sitcom *Yes Minister*. Fraser Dallachy's 'The Dehumanized Thief' (pp. 208–20) considers data that shows the 'cultural tendency to conceptualize criminals and societal outsiders as in some way less than human' (p. 208), specifically in metaphors with animals as their sources, and Dallachy notes the surprisingly small number of specific animals and birds that are involved in these mappings. Daria Izdebska presents 'Metaphors of Weapons and Armour through Time' (pp. 221–42), and shows that from OE to the present day these metaphors are prevalent; viewing them diachronically also provides evidence of technological and scientific developments in this field. In 'Silent Reading' (pp. 243–59), Jane Roberts looks at the target concept READING, and notes the different conceptions of the activity across the history of English, for example from 'wise person' to 'scholar'. Lastly, Irma Taavitsainen considers 'The Case of Address Terms' as metaphorical sources (pp. 260–80), detailing the sociolinguistic parameters encoded in different address terms and the ways in which these motivate mappings. In a separate publication, Kathryn Allan gives an overview of 'Education in the *Historical Thesaurus of the Oxford English Dictionary*' (in Daems et al., eds., pp. 81–95), comparing the relatively late-attested noun *education* with partially synonymous competitors across the history of English, and arguing for the inseparability of semasiological and onomasiological approaches to lexical change.

At the popular end of the market, 2015 saw a number of relevant publications. David Crystal's *The Disappearing Dictionary: A Treasury of Lost English Dialect Words* is perhaps the most scholarly of these: he presents a simplified selection from Joseph Wright's *English Dialect Dictionary* with updated etymologies, together with an introduction to Wright's work and the maps he included. Amanda Laugesen of the *Australian National Dictionary* examines the use of slang words by Australian soldiers in the First World War, and relates these to different aspects of their experiences, in *Furphies and Whizz-Bangs: Anzac Slang from the Great War*. Caroline Taggart's *New Words for Old: Recycling Our Language for the Modern World* is a less academic collection of short notes on 'very common words' (p. 8) ranging from *train* to *emoji*, grouped together under headings such as 'Sex'n'Drugs'n'Rock'n'Roll' and 'A Splash of Colour'. Finally, Graeme Donald gives a similar account of words which are etymologically related in *Words of a Feather: An Etymological Exploration of Astonishing Word Pairs*, including *aftermath* and *mow* and *Alcatraz* and *albatross*.

## 8. Dialectology and Sociolinguistics

In the field of dialectology and sociolinguistics, for the first time in recent history we have no new textbooks to report on, and only one new edition of an old favourite, Annabelle Mooney and Betsy E. Evans's excellent textbook *Language, Society & Power: An Introduction*, now in its fourth edition (the first edition was from 1999, the third edition from 2011). This new edition now has an added chapter on 'Linguistic Landscapes' (pp. 86–107), which also looks at online 'landscapes' (on YouTube and Twitter), and a chapter on 'Global Englishes' (pp. 198–219), perhaps relevant for the next section. This expands the scope of the book to ten chapters plus one on 'Projects' (pp. 220–32), which should still be well in the scope of a usual university course. Talking of projects, Miriam Meyerhoff, Erik Schleef, and Laurel MacKenzie will be teaching your students about *Doing Sociolinguistics: A Practical Guide to Data Collection and Analysis*, a book which complements Meyerhoff's *Introducing Sociolinguistics* (with its second edition from 2011), and Meyerhoff and Schleef's complementary *Reader* (from 2010). This hands-on guide takes students (and junior researchers) through 'Data Collection' (Part I), i.e. how to find a topic, how to design a sample and define the envelope of variation, through questions of ethics and archiving; the authors discuss sampling techniques, how to conduct interviews or record spontaneous speech, how to use corpora or written surveys, and how to study perceptions and attitudes. The second part is devoted to 'Data Analysis', i.e. how to design your transcription, code and summarize data, to the actual analysis (including some statistics), presenting data (graphically, clearly, honestly), some multivariate analysis, qualitative analysis, up to writing up your research. This short book is replete with actual data and very, very sensible advice, and just as a by-product you get a good sense of the work sociolinguists do, and the methods they use. Staying with methodologies, Eric Friginal and Jack A. Hardy introduce the reader to *Corpus-Based Sociolinguistics: A Guide for Students* [2014], and as in every introductory book on this matter the question is, what is regarded as sociolinguistics? In this case, the authors report on corpus studies that have investigated regional variation (unfortunately, also including large-scale comparisons of (standard) AmE and BrE here, which are not really sociolinguistic in outlook or method), studies of gender, sexuality, and age (not going much beyond the claim that 17-year-old high-school students use more pronouns in blogs than older men), the study of politeness, and workplace discourse. The section on 'Studying Temporal Change' proposes as a basis for study screenplays, or presidential inaugural addresses. In other words, what is advocated is not a sophisticated concept of sociolinguistics, and the student population might be better served by looking at Meyerhoff et al.'s short chapter on the same topic (pp. 64–70).

It probably has to be said that this was the year of handbooks. The first one to be mentioned here is *The Oxford Handbook of Historical Phonology*, edited by Patrick Honeybone and Joseph Salmons, which has a section on 'Sociolinguistic and Exogenous Factors in Historical Phonology' (Part VI), where Alexandra D'Arcy shows the implications of Labov's model of 'Variation, Transmission, Incrementation' (pp. 583–602). She distinguishes men and women in their contributions to language change, and discusses at length the initially unexpected peak in apparent time (typically in late adolescence); rather than an 'oddity' (p. 597), she argues that it is in fact a 'general requirement' (p. 591) of changes in progress. Continuing on from D'Arcy, David Bowie and Malcah Yaeger-Dror challenge the old axiom of the critical period for learning languages in 'Phonological Change in Real Time' (pp. 603–18) and summarize the mounting sociolinguistic evidence of speakers changing their language beyond adolescence. Another factor (besides age) influencing language change is mobility, and based on lexical information drawn from census data from the 1940s R. Urbatsch, in 'Movers as Early Adopters of Linguistic Innovation' (*JSoc* 19[2015] 372–90), finds that long-distance migrants in the United States are much more likely to adopt innovative linguistic features, too—presumably because they tend to be people with an 'openness to trying out new things' (p. 372). In Urbatsch's study, the 'new thing' is the innovative term *mortician* or *funeral director* over the traditional *undertaker*, but surely the point is a more general one.

Also in quite a general vein, Alexandra D'Arcy and Sali A. Tagliamonte claim that grammar is 'Not Always Variable: Probing the Vernacular Grammar' (*LVC* 27[2015] 255–85). Thus, there are phenomena in English that are consistently variable in writing (the genitive, the dative alternation, the comparative, or relative pronouns), but in the vernacular a different situation obtains. As the authors claim, 'for each variable there is at least one grammatical factor that splits the system' (p. 267), e.g. animacy and possessor relation for the genitive, syllable length for the comparative, or syntactic function for relatives, making them highly atypical variables in sociolinguistics—presumably due to their status as changes from above.

Another handbook with a section on sociolinguistics is *The Routledge Handbook of Language and Culture*, edited by Farzad Sharifian. Here, Meredith Marra reports on 'Language and Culture in Sociolinguistics' (pp. 373–85), including in particular John Gumperz's work and the newer approach of Communities of Practice. However, it has to be said that even at the end of her article, Marra remains quite vague about what concept of 'culture' she refers to ('exactly what does and does not count is still hard to pinpoint', p. 382—perhaps indicative of Sharifian's approach more generally), ultimately relying on a rather nebulous notion of culture as something participants are aware of. (In contrast, proper cultural studies have taken a firmer stand in linguistics this year, see Burkette's work reviewed below.)

As already indicated by Meyerhoff et al.'s overview of what to study in sociolinguistics more generally, perceptual dialectology is an integral part of the field these days, and many individual contributions this year testify to that status. In a general vein, Dennis R. Preston asks (rhetorically) 'Does Language Regard Vary?' (in Prikhodkine and Preston, eds., *Responses to Language*

*Varieties: Variability, Processes and Outcomes*, pp. 3–36), 'language regard' being his cover term for language attitudes, metalinguistic beliefs, and language ideologies. And indeed a summary of (his and others') studies of perceptual dialectology shows that language regard varies, and interferes with perception and production of speech data, and Preston argues that studies of regard features 'can enhance the understanding of the social embedding of language change' (p. 32). In the same collection, Brandon C. Loudermilk shows experimentally that 'Implicit Attitudes and the Perception of Sociolinguistic Variation' (pp. 137–56) do indeed influence real-time language processing: speakers with strong stereotypes (about variation) actually perceive less variation. Erez Levon and Isabelle Buchstaller in 'Perception, Cognition, and Linguistic Structure: The Effect of Linguistic Modularity and Cognitive Style on Sociolinguistic Processing' (*LVC* 27[2015] 319–48) show experimentally that not only phonetic variation (e.g. TH-fronting), but also 'higher-level', i.e. morphosyntactic, variation (like the Northern Subject Rule) elicits perceptual reactions and is 'subject to social evaluation' (p. 336) (*pace* Labov's interface principle)—although there may be differences in salience between the two types of phenomena. (For more studies in perceptual dialectology see the regional sections below.)

Finally, Walt Wolfram makes the general point that, as sociolinguists, researchers incur debts to the communities they investigate, and proposes 'Sociolinguistic Engagement in Community Perspective' (in Picone and Davies, eds., *New Perspectives on Language Variety in the South: Historical and Contemporary Approaches*, pp. 731–47) as a remedy. He reports on various projects he and his team have so far undertaken, such as video documentaries, community exhibits, or curricular language materials for use in the school-room, but also cautions fellow researchers that their 'specialized language expertise sets up an asymmetrical relationship of authority with respect to language matters' (p. 742)—something that may be quite difficult to overcome, especially when it comes to conflicting beliefs about language (and language varieties).

Moving to more specific contributions to the field, we will first look at an important new(-ish) field in sociolinguistics: historical sociolinguistics. This area now has its own specialized journal devoted to it, the *Journal of Historical Sociolinguistics* (*JHSL*). In its first volume, J. Camilo Conde-Silvestre and Javier Calle-Martín investigate the rise of 'Zero *That*-Clauses in the History of English: A Historical Sociolinguistic Approach (1424–1681)' (*JHSL* 1[2015] 57–86). Based on the Corpus of Early English Correspondence, they find that zero *that*-clauses rose especially in speech-based text types and became the majority option in the sixteenth and seventeenth centuries, and that this change was 'led by members of the urban non-gentry' (p. 78), quite possibly making it a change from below. Most regional varieties now also have studies devoted to earlier stages of the dialect, and more historical studies will therefore be discussed below.

We will start the regional overview with studies of IrE. Here, the publication of Carolina P. Amador-Moreno, Kevin McCafferty, and Elaine Vaughan, eds., *Pragmatic Markers in Irish English*, has to be mentioned. In it, Raymond Hickey gives an overview of 'The Pragmatics of Irish English and Irish' (pp. 17–36), more specifically of the Irish English discourse markers (DMs) *sure, though, so, then, just,* focusing *like,* hedging *now,* approving *grand,* and the attention-capturing *lookit.* He also points out that while originally the influence may have been from Irish on English, today it is actually Irish that is changing, and adopting English DMs. Karen P. Corrigan also takes a wider view, but of Northern IrE, in ' "I always think of people here, you know, saying 'like' after every sentence": The Dynamics of Discourse-Pragmatic Markers in Northern Irish English' (pp. 37–64), where she looks at initial *och* (not mentioned by Hickey) final *like,* and final *but,* although based on a relatively small sample of speakers. However, there are some interesting developments, such that younger speakers seem to be the main users of initial *ach/och,* female speakers use final *like* more, and both genders use final *but* in quite a similar manner. Corrigan also notes that some DMs that have been described for IrE are absent (such as Irish *arrah, musha, mar-yah*) or less frequent (such as *so*) in her Northern Irish sample. *Like* and *sure* are taken up by Bróna Murphy in 'A Corpus-Based Investigation of Pragmatic Markers and Sociolinguistic Variation in Irish English' (pp. 65–88), albeit again based on a very small corpus, but one of casual conversations. Like Corrigan, Murphy finds that discourse *like* is used the most by young females (this includes uses as approximator, exemplifier, emphasizer, hedge, focus marker, but also quotative BE LIKE), whereas *sure* shows no age or gender differences, and a smaller range of functions (as emphasizer or hedge). For both DMs, the hedging function is the dominant one. For *sure,* Carolina P. Amador-Moreno and Kevin McCafferty investigate the historical development in ' "[B]ut *sure* its only a penny after all": Irish English Discourse Marker *Sure*' (in Dossena, ed., *Transatlantic Perspectives on Late Modern English,* pp. 179–97). Based on several corpora, including emigrants' letters and drama, they find that this DM (used as an appeal for consensus, or a hedge, or a mitigator) rose in frequency until the mid-nineteenth century—a fact they link to the enregisterment of this feature as a marker of IrE. In quite a similar matter, both authors combine the historical trajectory for *like* with *sure* in ' "Sure this is a great country for drink and rowing at elections": Discourse Markers in the *Corpus of Irish English Correspondence,* 1750–1940' (in Amador-Moreno et al., eds., pp. 270–91). Their results suggest that final *like* was already present in IrE in the nineteenth century, and that it was actually exported to North America. *Sure* is attested even longer (since the 1760s), and its use as a DM seems to set IrE apart from other varieties (as in the title)—in fact *sure* became a linguistic stereotype of IrE speech by the nineteenth century, as they pointed out above. Continuing with *like* for the present day, Mario Serrano-Losada investigates a subset of its functions based on ICE-Ireland in 'Element-Final *Like* in Irish English: Notes on Its Pervasiveness, Incidence and Distribution' (in Suárez-Gómez and Seoane, eds., *Englishes Today: Multiple Varieties, Multiple Perspectives,* pp. 9–31). He finds this discourse marker (as in *he used to race bikes, like*) well established in IrE, in particular in informal speech, but also occasionally 'crossing into more formal settings' (p. 26). Since it can co-occur with other discourse markers like *you know* or *so* (as also in Corrigan's quotation above), Serrano-Losada proposes a subjective (rather than intersubjective) meaning for clause-final *like*. Still on *like*, Martin Schweinberger conducts 'A Comparative Study of the Pragmatic Marker *Like* in Irish English and in South-Eastern Varieties of British English' (in Amador-Moreno et al., eds., pp. 114–34) and finds that *like* overall is much more frequent in IrE than in BrE, actually in all positions, but of course especially in clause-final position, the hallmark of this IrE DM. Since his analysis is also based on ICE-Ireland, it is perhaps not surprising that he also finds a striking peak in the use of *like* by female speakers in their late twenties, whereas in Britain hardly anyone over 26 uses *like*; instead it is 'associated specifically with teenage speakers' (p. 130). Still on discourse markers, John M. Kirk examines '*Kind of* and *Sort of*: Pragmatic Discourse Markers in the SPICE-Ireland Corpus' (in Amador-Moreno et al., eds., pp. 89–113), also as to their prosody. For both DMs, the evidential function dominates (downtoning an infelicitous expression, engendering vagueness, or mitigating uncertainty), but the affective function is also present (negotiating face). It is interesting that Kirk finds a clear geopolitical difference, and *sort of* is by far the dominant DM in Northern Ireland, whereas *kind of* is used much more in the Republic. Jeffrey L. Kallen investigates ' "Actually, it's unfair to say that I was throwing stones": Comparative Perspectives on Uses of *Actually* in ICE-Ireland' (in Amador-Moreno et al., eds., pp. 135–55), comparing this DM to other ICE corpora. *Actually* occurs at the phrase level (*you were actually a Reid Professor*) and at the clause level (*that's quite a nice meal actually*), but in the shift to clause-marginal uses IrE seems to lag behind other national varieties (although it has to be said that this study only considers synchronic data, and diachronic trends can thus only be speculation).

Away from DMs as such, Michael McCarthy sighs, ' "'Tis mad, yeah": Turn Openers in Irish and British English' (in Amador-Moreno et al., eds., pp. 156–75), where this is actually quite a distinctive IrE construction. Other differences are the use of *Jesus/Christ/God* as interjections and in continuing turns, reflecting 'the Roman Catholic culture of Ireland' (p. 165), and specific adjectives like *grand* in the same slot as *mad* above that also give turn-openers a distinctive Irish flavour. Anne Barron finds in ' "And your wedding is the twenty-second <.> of June is it?" Tag Questions in Irish English' (in Amador-Moreno et al., eds., pp. 203–28) that what is specific to IrE when it comes to tag questions is the use of *sure* tags (as in *it doesn't get easier—sure it doesn't*), a use of invariant *is it* (as in the title), as well as a higher proportion of positive polarity tags compared to BrE.

Moving away from pragmatics altogether, Lukas Pietsch links 'Archaism and Dialect in Irish Emigrant Letters' (in Auer et al., eds., pp. 223–39), in particular archaisms in formulae that were (presumably) handed down by family tradition and thus kept alive 'for decades or even centuries after the demise of their original models' (p. 225). His example is periphrastic *do*, which does not match the dialect distribution of this form (i.e. as a present-tense habitual marker), and which disappeared from written English in the seventeenth century, but is regularly encountered in his Irish emigrant letters from the nineteenth century in quasi-formulaic expressions like *I do assure you* or *she does request*. Marije Van Hattum compares '*May* and *Might* in Nineteenth Century Irish English and English English' (in Collins, ed., pp. 221–46) and finds that for subjective possibility, in both varieties '*might* lost its ability to signal past time reference throughout the 19th and 20th centuries' (p. 241), perhaps linked to the grammaticalization of the perfect. However, overall *might* is used more frequently in IrE.

For present-day IrE, Patricia Ronan and Gerold Schneider are 'Determining Light Verb Constructions in Contemporary British and Irish English' (*IJCL* 20[2015] 326–54) automatically—quite a feat, and they find that 'ICE-GB favours fewer high frequency light verbs while ICE-IRE contains more diverse lower frequency light verbs and more passives' (p. 326). Typical Irish light-verb constructions are to *ask (a) question, give advice, do work, give (a) view*, and *make (a) decision* (whereas you would *take* a decision in BrE).

John M. Kirk asks, 'The Progressive in Irish English: Looking Both Ways?' (in Collins, ed., pp. 87–118). As is well known, in the Celtic Englishes the progressive is used more frequently than in other British varieties, and Kirk offers an extension of functions as an explanation, since the IrE progressive incorporates 'functions transferred from Irish . . . and also functions shared with British English' (p. 87). Some functions are only found in IrE, such as the 'extended-*now* progressive' (*two girls are missing since Saturday*), the 'single-occasion repetitive progressive' (*at the moment I'm thinking about it a lot*), or the well-known habitual progressive with DO BE or *bees*. Other constructions are more frequent than in BrE, such as the progressive with modals (*he may be looking for it*), and the 'WILL as a matter of course progressive' (*I will be thinking of travelling north*), presumably through reinforcement from Irish source constructions.

Göran Wolf asks, 'Does Present-Day Written Ulster Scots Abandon Tradition?' (in Suárez-Gómez and Seoane, eds., pp. 51–78). During the current 'renaissance' of Ulster Scots, Wolf observes a 'notable growth in literary output in the variety' (p. 53) which differs self-consciously from older dialect literature, and also extends into new domains (such as Internet chats, websites, or periodicals), a development Wolf calls 'deliberate detraditionalization' (p. 62), or, in Ulster Scots, 'sell-defineition agin the Erse leid' (p. 62).

This already moves us to Scots in Scotland, where Jennifer Bann and John Corbett report on *Spelling Scots: The Orthography of Literary Scots, 1700–2000*. Despite the title, they also include discussions of older Scots consonants and vowels, and their discussion of graphemes found since the 1400s is actually a good introduction to the historical evolution of Scottish sounds as distinct from English, as shown by their discussion of the Great Vowel Shift, the Scottish Vowel Length Rule, etc. They then trace the evolution of Modern Scots orthography, especially linked to the 'Eighteenth-Century Vernacular Revival' of Scots (pp. 61–75) across books, broadsides, magazines, journals, and newspapers. They also include an overview of orthoepy and activism (chapter 5), that is, the movement of 'spelling reform with a view to raising the status of Scots and extending its domains of use beyond the literary' (p. 91) that continues today. Overall, the spelling system of Scots is characterized by much more flexibility (and thus variability) than English English, and in order to investigate the consistency of authors and their overall comparability, Bann and Corbett also provide cluster analyses (relating to vowel representation, consonant representation, and lexical items)

of Scots poetry and prose that document this variability. They do not conclude
with a new suggestion for a unified orthography of Scots, but point out that
this would probably 'be undesirable for writers of Modern Scots' (p. 139).
Nevertheless, the careful analyses could be taken as a pointer in the direction
of consensus spellings, as indicating the 'relations between language, identity
and power' (p. 139). On the other hand, James Costa asks, 'Can Schools
Dispense with Standard Language? Some Unintended Consequences of
Introducing Scots in a Scottish Primary School' (*LingAnth* 25[2015] 25–42).
Because Scots is not standardized, as Bann and Corbett above have clearly
shown (and apparently there is no consensus about what Scots is, and what it
isn't), Costa argues, pupils make the indexical link that Scots serves purposes
of 'amusement, lack of seriousness', pupils as speakers of Scots are othered,
and they are 'locked' (p. 25) in a non-standard identity. In fact, as Costa
criticizes, the Scots language movement 'leaves little room for learning...since
there is no clear definition of what is to be learned' (p. 38).

If you want to look up specific Scotticisms, you may be happy to hear that
James A.C. Stevenson and Iseabail Macleod's *Scoor-Oot: A Dictionary of
Scots Words and Phrases in Current Use* from 1989 has just been reprinted.
Although essentially in dictionary form, entries are ordered thematically in
fifteen sections (people, including parts of the body, human attributes and
behaviour, health and dress, eating and drinking, communication, movement
(including violence), law and administration, education/religion/the supernatural, festivals and local customs, sports and games, countryside, farming and
industry, construction and household, and 'grammar words') and these
sections make for some interesting sociocultural reading as well. If you were
wondering about the title, *scoor-oot* is 'the custom...of scattering coins at or
after a wedding to be scrambled for by children' (p. 131), but you will also find
information on Burns Night, tossing the caber, the rules of curling, the history
of golf, and how to plant a 'lazy bed' (p. 174), should you be so interested. The
question remains, however, how widely used these 'most widely used words
and expressions' (foreword) still are, more than twenty-five years on.

Moving to the few individual regional studies on Scotland this year, Peter
Sundkvist and Man Gao take 'A Regional Survey of the Relationship between
Vowel and Consonant Duration in Shetland Scots' (*FoLi* 49[2015] 57–83).
These two features are related in Shetland Scots, since typically stressed
syllables contain 'a long vowel followed by a short consonant...or a short
vowel followed by a long consonant' (p. 57)—a pattern that can be traced back
to Norn. Perhaps not surprisingly, therefore, this correlation is strongest in the
northern part of the Shetlands, where Norn survived the longest. Back on the
mainland, Sydney Kingstone provides a perceptual dialectology survey of
'"Scottish", "English" or "Foreign": Mapping Scottish Dialect Perceptions'
(*EWW* 36[2015] 315–47), based on fifty-one informants from Buckie (north-
east Scotland). She found the 'clearest example of urban Scots stigma' (p. 338)
for Glasgow (which is seen as the least pleasant, and the least correct), whereas
Edinburgh was considered 'posh' or 'proper', but not very Scottish. The
Borders region was (falsely) perceived as being influenced by English, whereas
Inverness was very positively associated, also with correctness, and Kingstone
suggests that these northern speakers 'might be looking...to the neighbouring

Highlands for a speech model' (p. 27). Speaking of Glasgow, Jane Stuart-Smith, Tamara Rathcke, Morgan Sonderegger, and Rachel Macdonald conduct 'A Real-Time Study of Plosives in Glaswegian Using an Automatic Measurement Algorithm: Change or Age-Grading?' (in Torgersen, Hårstad, Mæhlum, and Røyneland, eds., *Language Variation: European Perspectives V*, pp. 225–37). What the authors investigate is the voice onset time (VOT) of plosives in data from the 1970s and the 2000s, since ScE is reported to have shorter aspiration phases than English English. They find that 'a change in the phonetic realization of the stops may have been in progress since the middle of the twentieth century, specifically a lengthening of aspiration for /p/ and /t/, and a trend to a longer release in their voiced counterparts' (p. 225), which may be due to the spread of SSE into Scots, and shorter VOTs today probably index more vernacular speech.

Warren Maguire characterizes Scotland as 'The North above the North: Scotland and Northern English' (in Hickey, ed., *Researching Northern English*, pp. 437–57) and investigates the complex relationship between these northern varieties through time. While historically, northern English dialects (above the Humber–Ribble line) and Scots were grouped together by a bundle of traditional features, 'most of the traditional dialect isoglosses ... are now irrelevant to speakers of English in Scotland and Northern England in the late twentieth and early twenty-first centuries' (p. 449). Instead, due to supra-regionalization and the increasing importance of the political border, Scottish StE has become significantly different from northern England accents, which in turn have come to resemble Midlands and southern English dialects more.

This already moves our focus to the north of England, an area that is very well documented this year, mainly due to contributions in Raymond Hickey, ed., *Researching Northern English*, a collection that represents the state of the art in regional dialect studies in that it contains synchronic as well as diachronic studies, on the phonology and lexis as well as dialect grammar, ranging from perception and enregisterment to smaller-scale regional descriptions. The first part, 'The North of England: Language and Culture', sets the scene rather broadly, and Joan C. Beal and Paul Cooper trace 'The Enregisterment of Northern English' (pp. 27–49) to the Late Modern English period, although an awareness of northern speech as 'other' is documented earlier (but this is not linked to specific linguistic features yet). Also on a historical note, Hilary Prichard discusses 'The Great Vowel Shift in the North of England' (pp. 51–70), based on the SED data, and finds 'regular patterns that aid our understanding of the structure and chronology of the shift' (p. 52). In particular, she argues that diphthongized outcomes of ME /u:/ are due to secondary diffusion of southern forms (rather than independent, spontaneous developments) to an area north of the Lune–Humber line, where /o:/ was fronted (preventing the regular shifting of /u:/). In addition, she also documents ME /i:/ developing beyond /ai/ to backed variants and even monophthong /a:/ in some places. Isabelle Buchstaller and Karen P. Corrigan, in a much less convincing contribution, give an overview of 'Morphosyntactic Features of Northern English' (pp. 71–98), where they lament the 'dearth of knowledge' on morphosyntactic features and their regional distribution. However, their proposed surveys of acceptability judgements are highly unlikely to really remedy the situation, and this overview chapter does not really add to the sources (and methods) we are already familiar with. Julia Fernández Cuesta by contrast can offer some new insights into 'The History of Present Indicative Morphosyntax from a Northern Perspective' (pp. 99–130). She shows how the northern 3sg < s > competed with the supra-regional < th > and proceeded through the paradigms, interacting with the Northern Subject Rule (NSR), a phenomenon the author calls 'one of the most resilient features of Northern English' (p. 110), which also spread considerably beyond the north (for more on the NSR from a diachronic point of view, see Section 5(b) above). Javier Ruano-García, Pilar Sánchez-García, and María F. García-Bermejo Giner report on 'Northern English: Historical Lexis and Spelling' (in Hickey, ed., pp. 131–57), in a way harking back to Beal and Cooper above, since they trace the literary representation of the north from 1500 to 1900. There they find the representation of features such as lack of rounding, or /o:/-fronting, but also lexemes like LAD, LASS, GANG ('go'), NOWT ('nothing'), or BAIRN ('child').

The second part of Hickey's collection describes a wide range of 'Locations within the North: Variation and Change', including some that have not been described comprehensively before. Contributions provide some sociohistorical and geographical background, report on the linguistic investigations conducted so far, and then give an overview of the phonology and sometimes dialect grammar, and even discourse features; these contributions alone would already have made for a valuable collection. Thus Adam Mearns reports on 'Tyneside' (pp. 161–81), pointing out for phonetics, morphosyntax, and lexis as well as discourse features that traditional features (such as unshifted ME /u:/ or /i:/ in HOUSE or NIGHT, the NURSE-NORTH merger, or *divn't* for *don't* and *wor* for *our*) are becoming more tied to working-class, male speakers, whereas other, supra-regional features are spreading, such as /e:/ and /o:/ for FACE and GOAT, or T-glottaling. Tyneside is also the subject of a number of other studies, all by Carol Fehringer and Karen Corrigan. They look at three morphosyntactic features in more detail: modals, GOING-TO future, and stative HAVE. Thus they claim that ' "You've got to sort of eh hoy the Geordie out": Modals of Obligation and Necessity in Fifty Years of Tyneside English' (*ELL* 19[2015] 355–81), the example in the title illustrating that semi-modal HAVE GOT TO (but also HAVE TO and NEED TO) has been replacing MUST. However, it has to (!) be said that even in their materials from the 1960s, MUST was already a minority variant used in less than 10 per cent of all cases. In all periods, HAVE GOT TO and HAVE TO dominate the field of obligation, but NEED TO seems to be gaining ground. In a second contribution, Fehringer and Corrigan report on 'The Rise of the *Going to* Future in Tyneside English: Evidence for Further Grammaticalisation' (*EWW* 36[2015] 198–227), 'further' relating to internal constraints (clause type, subject type, verb type, imminence of event) that have been proposed as distinguishing GOING TO from WILL. Even though in their data WILL is still the majority variant (if only by a sliver for the most recent period), GOING TO 'has steadily increased from the 1960s... to the 2010 sub-corpus' (p. 214), probably due to being generalized to distal time reference, non-animate subjects, and motion verbs, and thus becoming a true equivalent of WILL. Finally, Fehringer and Corrigan claim that ' "The Geordie accent has a bit of a bad reputation": Internal and External Constraints on Stative Possession in the Tyneside English of the 21st Century' (*EnT* 31[2015] 38–50).

In their data, HAVE GOT is used in the majority of cases, but strangely its dominance seems to be decreasing, in favour of the older variant (stative HAVE, as in the title), which seems to be gaining ground again, but there is no link to a difference in prestige the authors could discover—perhaps a development to look out for in other dialect areas too.

Isabelle Buchstaller looks at the use of BE LIKE in Newcastle, in 'Exploring Linguistic Malleability Across the Life Span: Age-Specific Patterns in Quotative Use' (*LSoc* 44[2015] 457–96), which has increased in overall quotative use from 6 per cent to over 20 per cent in the 2010s. There seem to be two conflicting trends: the more general trend sees speakers 'move away from this ongoing community-wide trend as they leave adolescence behind' (p. 464), and actually reduce their use of BE LIKE, since clearly it is still frowned upon in academic and professional contexts. However, her data from six speakers in their sixties show some occurrences of BE LIKE too, especially in working-class speakers and in one speaker with a lot of contact with young people, indicating that some small-scale change over the lifetime of speakers is going on here, too.

The dialect area closest to Newcastle (and often amalgamated with it by outsiders, much to the chagrin of its inhabitants), is Sunderland, and Lourdes Burbano-Elizondo describes the rivalry between the two areas (and of course football club supporters) in her contribution on 'Sunderland' (we are now back in Hickey, ed., pp. 183–204). Especially after the county reform in 1974, the local identity of Sunderlanders changed, and Burbano-Elizondo traces this in a number of phonetic variants that distinguish the 'Mackems' from the 'Geordies'. ('Mackem' comes from 'make 'em' and illustrates the distinctive /a/-vowel in FACE lexemes, where Geordie speakers would have /e/). Speaking of these terms, Philip Durkin's paper in *English Language and Linguistics* is relevant, since he reports on '*Mackems*, *Geordies* and *Ram-Raiders*: Documenting Regional Variation in Historical Dictionaries' (*ELL* 19[2015] 313–26). Tying in quite well with Burbano-Elizondo above, Durkin's paper shows that these three lexical items (plus *pet*) have different status(es): *Mackem* has been current only since the 1980s, signalling Sunderland or Wearside identity, and is only used within the north-east, especially to contrast supporters of Sunderland FC with their Newcastle counterparts; *Geordie* is widely known (and used), also to designate north-easterners more widely (as Burbano-Elizondo also stressed), *pet* (a term of endearment) does not even originate in the north-east, but 'its use can act as a highly compressed index of such an identity both within the region and beyond' (p. 315), whereas *ram-raid* (also current since the 1980s), despite being a local term, has no regional salience whatsoever (and in case you were wondering: it means to 'use a car to ram a window, door, or wall as part of a smash-and-grab robbery' p. 322). A bit further south, Carmen Llamas investigates voiceless stops in 'Middlesbrough' (again in Hickey, ed., pp. 251–70), specifically whether the glottalized Newcastle variants have had any recent influence. She finds that especially glottal (t) has become almost categorical for young speakers, which can be linked to the 'shifting identity of Middlesbrough' (p. 265), that is, from belonging to Yorkshire to being 'Middlesbrough' since the county reform of 1974.

Over in the north-west, Sandra Jansen reports on an area rarely investigated so far, 'Carlisle and Cumbria' (in Hickey, ed., pp. 205–25). Perhaps it is not surprising that the only urban variety, Carlisle, 'has lost many of the traditional features of Cumbrian English' (p. 214), such as unshifted /u:/ in MOUTH, traditional /iə/ in FACE, or aspirated /ʍ/. One traditional feature, the lack of H-dropping, is coming back, but presumably this has to do with the fact that it is also the StE variant. In a different collection, Jansen in addition provides a more detailed study on 'A Century of Change in Prevocalic (r) in Carlisle English: Internal Constraints in a Levelling Process' (in Torgersen et al., eds., pp. 129–43). She finds that the local form (tapped ʀ) is being replaced by the supra-regional prestige form [ɹ]. Although only three young female speakers in her sample use it, the innovative labiodental approximant [ʋ] is also documented, surely something to keep track of in future studies.

A bit further south, Katie Finnegan introduces readers to 'Sheffield' English (in Hickey, ed., pp. 227–50), more specifically to middle-class variants of FACE and GOAT. While her speakers use the traditional local variants less and less, converging (perhaps like Jansen's speakers in Carlisle for H) on the StE diphthongs, Finnegan can also document the emergence of one new variant, fronted [ɵ] in GOAT, which seems to be led by young females and seems to index for them a modern Yorkshire identity. Another vowel feature is discussed by Sam Kirkham in 'Intersectionality and the Social Meanings of Variation: Class, Ethnicity, and Social Practice' (*LSoc* 44[2015] 629–52). Kirkham looks at the HAPPY-vowel in Sheffield English, which varies between a (more working-class) hyper-lax and a (more middle-class) tense realization. As Kirkham points out, these sociolinguistic categories often erase ethnicity, in that 'ethnically White people [are] typically defined in terms of social class, and minority ethnic people typically . . . in terms of ethnic heritage' (p. 632). In his investigation of four adolescent communities of practice, he finds that there is (of course) interaction of these categories; some Pakistani and Somali adolescents use a hyper-tense HAPPY-vowel, presumably to distance themselves from the associations of the very lax realization with being 'common', 'chav', or 'anti-school'. On the other hand, some other girls use lax HAPPY as 'part of an urban-oriented street style' (p. 644).

William Barras summarizes research on 'Lancashire' (in Hickey, ed., pp. 271–92) and shows how the traditional feature of rhoticity is receding rapidly, but still exists in an island around Accrington and Rossendale. Overall, the differences between urban and rural Lancashire seem to be increasing, and Barras notes that 'it could well be the case that parts of the rural north of Lancashire have more in common with southern parts of Cumbria than with the predominantly urban southern half of Lancashire' (p. 286), where speakers are more oriented towards Manchester (more on which below). Based on historical data from Bolton, Ivor Timmis investigates 'Pronouns and Identity: A Case Study from a 1930s Working-Class Community' (*ICAME* 39[2015] 111–34). In transcripts of a sociological study from the 1930s Timmis discovers several instances of homophoric *they*, relating to 'the remote and authoritative other', 'obstructive officials', and 'controllers and manipulators of information', probably a sign of the war-torn times, and the close community ties that allowed reference assignment nevertheless. Staying in Lancashire, Helen Faye West examines 'Language Attitudes and Divergence on the Merseyside/Lancashire Border' (in Hickey, ed., pp. 317–41), in particular in relation to the NURSE-SQUARE merger, which is stereotypically a front merger in Liverpool. In neighbouring Lancashire, 'more positive attitudes and more frequent contact with Liverpool...ha[ve] encouraged the fronting of NURSE' (p. 338) in some localities. Also, a centralized SQUARE vowel is not perceptually as salient as a fronted NURSE vowel, although both involve a merger (something that Kevin Watson and Lynn Clark pointed out two years ago, cf. *YWES* 94[2015] 49). Speaking of Liverpool, Amanda Cardoso investigates 'Variation in Nasal-Obstruent Clusters and Its Influence on PRICE and MOUTH in Scouse' (*ELL* 19[2015] 505–32), where she observes 'a Canadian-Raising-type pattern' for PRICE, but more monophthongization for MOUTH. This is interesting because generally, voiceless obstruents cause raising, and nasals cause monophthongization. Here, the two elements of these clusters seem to act differently on the two diphthongs. Liverpool, one of the most 'recognizable varieties of English' (p. 52), also features in Kevin Watson and Lynn Clark's examination of 'Exploring Listeners' Real-Time Reactions to Regional Accents' (*LangAw* 24[2015] 38–59), 'real time' here relating to constant evaluation during the speech event. In their comparison of reactions to five regional varieties of BrE (Cambridge, Cardiff, Dublin, Liverpool, and Newcastle), there are significant differences in evaluation strategies, and Liverpool has the earliest reactions, Cardiff the latest, and especially highly salient markers like affricated /k/ for Liverpool seem to have been the 'tipping point' for evaluating the social status of speakers (negatively).

As we have noted before, another city that has only recently come to dialectologists' attention is Manchester, but a couple of contributions this year do deal with this important new area. 'Manchester English' is presented by Maciej Baranowski and Danielle Turton (in Hickey, ed., pp. 293–316). They give a useful overview of Mancunian as 'essentially a Northern dialect of English' (p. 295) before they look at how new and vigorous changes like T-glottaling and TH-fronting proceed. In contrast to H-dropping, a case of stable variation, TH-fronting is led by younger speakers, cementing its status as 'an urban youth norm' (p. 303). Like TH-fronting, T-glottaling (especially in intervocalic position) is led by working-class men, but unlike TH-fronting it is highly sensitive to style-shifting, attesting to the different status of these variables. Manchester is also the focus of two other studies: Erik Schleef, Nicholas Flynn, and Michael Ramsammy report on the 'Production and Perception of (ing) in Manchester English' (in Torgersen et al., eds., pp. 197–209). This is interesting because a third variant (besides /ɪŋ/ and /ɪn/) still exists here (at least marginally), the so-called velar nasal plus (i.e. /ɪŋg/). The social meaning of the two more widespread variants seems to be similar to US studies (*pace* Levon and Fox, cf. *YWES* 95[2016] 67, who found less stigmatization of /ɪn/ in Britain), such that '/ɪŋ/ is heard as more articulate, educated and less casual' (p. 197). The local variant /ɪŋg/, by contrast, is 'often considered a local prestige form' (p. 203) and has connotations of correctness, more specifically 'of an uptight, non-dynamic formalness' (p. 207), surely quite unusual for a rare, traditional dialect feature. Continuing with the topic, Erik

Schleef and Nicholas Flynn find that this evaluation of /ɪŋg/ varies with age in 'Ageing Meanings of (ing): Age and Indexicality in Manchester, England' (*EWW* 36[2015] 48–90); especially younger (i.e. adolescent and young adult) speakers see the traditional dialect variant /ɪŋg/ as 'more reliable and posher sounding' (p. 48) than /ɪŋ/, presumably due to its (perceived) closeness to the spelling.

Chris Montgomery summarizes expert and lay people's 'Borders and Boundaries in the North of England' (in Hickey, ed., pp. 345–68), and shows that lay people's perception of the boundary of 'the north' also depends on their own location (the closer they are to this imaginary boundary, the more strictly it is defined). The striking common feature, however, is the perception that 'the area of most agreement about the location of the North-South dividing line is the Wash' (p. 365), placing a much larger area in 'the north' than is commonly accepted in dialectology, since in fact it would include much of the Midlands as well.

And indeed, since by some the English Midlands are included in the northern area, Hickey's collection does contain a contribution on 'The West Midlands' (pp. 393–16) by Esther Asprey. However, the author claims that 'these varieties do not sit comfortably with the varieties of the North' (p. 393). Phonologically they show features of both the north (no FOOT-STRUT split, the NURSE-SQUARE merger, T-to-R) and the south (PRICE-CHOICE merger, some TRAP-BATH split), and new supra-local changes (T-glottaling and TH-fronting) are spreading rapidly. Morphosyntactically, some older Midland features are preserved, such as the 3sg feminine pronoun /ɜː/, a plural form of BE *bin*, or the use of ablaut for negative contracted forms, making the West Midlands quite distinctive. Natalie Braber and Nicholas Flynn present 'The East Midlands' (in Hickey, ed., pp. 369–91) as a separate dialect area, pointing out that 'the dialect lacks the frequently lowered monophthongal realizations of FACE and GOAT that typify a northern accent, while retaining the northern BATH vowel and, to some extent merged STRUT and FOOT' (p. 388), with the same current changes being documented as elsewhere, such as TH-fronting, T-glottaling and L-vocalization. However, as Natalie Braber shows in 'Language Perception in the East Midlands in England' (*EnT* 31[2015] 16–26), East Midlands speakers themselves are 'not able to distinguish different dialects within the East Midlands' (p. 23), not even to identify their own ; also they do not mention the East Midlands as a separate dialect area and hold rather negative attitudes towards their own dialect, perhaps indicating that for lay persons this dialect is indeed not enregistered with any social meaning (yet).

But even the East Anglian Fenland is situated 'Between North and South: The Fenland', according to David Britain (in Hickey, ed., pp. 417–35), because, as he points out, 'the Fenland area straddles two of the most iconic isoglosses in English dialectology—the FOOT-STRUT boundary and the TRAP-BATH boundary' (p. 417), and perhaps it is thus not surprising that Britain attests that this area has a 'transitional status' between northern and southern dialects (p. 432), with some interdialectal forms (e.g. a fudged STRUT vowel) and even some phonological redistribution, such as the reallocation of the PRICE vowel, depending on phonetic context (although see Cardoso above, who also documents this feature in Liverpool).

Over in the (upper) south-west, Laura Wright uncovers 'Some More on the History of Present-Tense -*s*, *Do* and Zero: West Oxfordshire, 1837' (*JHSL* 1[2015] 111–30). Although this study is based on the diary of just one informant, this is interesting because it provides access to a clearly working-class speaker, a West Oxfordshire 'footman who had been schooled enough to write, but not enough for a complete grasp of Standard English' (p. 112). In his diary, *do* only occurs under emphasis, but zero forms at a 'surprisingly high rate of 21%' (p. 111), presumably because the system was still in flux. Wright hypothesizes that we are witnessing the transition from periphrastic *do*, to zero, to generalized -*s* (documented for West Oxfordshire since the end of the nineteenth century), and that this speaker is caught in the middle of this transition with 'a temporarily heightened, short-lived, amount of indicative zeroes' (p. 127).

For London, Ignacio Palacios Martínez investigates 'Variation, Development and Pragmatic Uses of *Innit* in the Language of British Adults and Teenagers' (*ELL* 19[2015] 383–405) across corpora from the 1990s and 2004. Palacios Martínez finds that *innit* continues to be used by teenagers (but is infrequent in the speech of adults), and may be developing from an invariant tag to a discourse marker, since it can now also be used in other than final positions, serving as an emphasizer and discourse organizer ('*you're the man of the house.' 'Yeah. Innit'*).

Out at sea, Emma Moore and Paul Carter discuss 'Dialect Contact and Distinctiveness: The Social Meaning of Language Variation in an Island Community' (*JSoc* 19[2015] 3–36), more specifically on the Isles of Scilly off the coast of Cornwall (they have a population of just over 2,000). This variety has to our knowledge not featured in this section ever before, and indeed it is generally reported to be like StE and thus of little dialectological interest. However, the authors can show that the TRAP and BATH vowels (which are distinguished only by length in mainland Cornish English, but by length *and* quality in StE) are used atypically of speakers' educational status, and speakers exploit the multidimensional meanings of linguistic variants to reflect and construct local practices and alignments (p. 3).

Quite a lot further south, David Levey presents the sociohistorical background as well as the pronunciation and some lexical peculiarities of 'Gibraltar English' (in Williams, Schneider, Trudgill, and Schreier, eds., *Further Studies in the Lesser-Known Varieties of English*, pp. 51–69), not surprisingly showing much Spanish influence (such as no distinction between KIT and FLEECE vowels, no distinction between TRAP and STRUT, /b/∼/v/ merger, no use of weak vowels, or a distinct syllable timing), although his remarks on younger speakers make it clear that the system is changing, and perhaps Gibraltar English is becoming more of a distinct, focused variety.

Across the Atlantic, James A. Walker introduces readers to *Canadian English: A Sociolinguistic Perspective*. This rather short, accessible book is really an up-to-date summary of other linguists' empirical studies of CanE, plus a brief introduction to linguistic terms and methods. It looks at 'The Origins and Development of Canadian English' (chapter 3), describing eighteenth- and nineteenth-century Canada as a 'tabula rasa situation' (p. 57) in terms of new dialect formation, and stressing the mixed (AmE and

BrE) heritage of CanE, as well as its internal homogeneity, perhaps with the exception of newer ethnic groups. Walker then gives an overview of what has so far been studied, in particular 'Lexical Variation' (chapter 4), where at least for some items, CanE emerges as distinct from AmE, but where we also find regional variation within Canada (mostly due to French influence, e.g. *parking garage* vs. *parkade*, *corner store* vs. *dépanneur*). 'Phonetic and Phonological Variation' (chapter 5) contains the obligatory explanations of the COT-CAUGHT merger, Canadian Raising, and the Canadian Shift but also a description of regional variants, especially in the Maritimes (somewhat belying Walker's earlier claim of general homogeneity). In 'Grammatical Variation' (chapter 6) he notes that CanE 'is not greatly differentiated from other varieties of English through its grammatical features' (p. 99)—nor does he find internal variation, with the exception of Newfoundland. The final chapter, on 'The Present and the Future of Canadian English', summarizes real-time and apparent-time studies for the features noted above, and Walker finds massive increases in AmE lexical variants (*couch* instead of *chesterfield*, *gutters* instead of *eavestroughs*, *zee* instead of *zed*), increased lowering and retraction in the CS, and increases in grammatical variants such as deontic HAVE TO, possessive HAVE (more on which below), and of course the new quotative BE LIKE.

In more detail, Stefan Dollinger argues for the validity of employing *The Written Questionnaire in Social Dialectology: History, Theory, Practice*. As the subtitle shows, he gives an overview of historical and present-day question-naire studies that have been conducted and introduces the theoretical variables that can sensibly be included. Since modern written questionnaire studies have mainly been conducted in Canada, from our point of view the most interesting chapter is chapter 4, 'Types of Traditional WQ Variables', where Dollinger summarizes the results of those studies pertaining to CanE (adding some corpus-based studies where necessary). In particular, he can document (like Walker above) that some Canadianisms are dropping out of use (e.g. *chesterfield* for *sofa*), some remain distinctive (e.g. *tap* for *faucet*), but there are also some new forms (e.g. *take up* meaning *discuss*). Some other variants (like *snuck* for *sneaked*) seem to be spreading beyond North America, but Dollinger also reports on some phonemic variants, which—with some clever questionnaire design—can be investigated profitably too, such as YOD-retention (e.g. in *avenue*), which seems to pattern along an urban vs. rural dimension. Dollinger also includes (in the second part, 'Practice') hands-on tutorials for using spreadsheet software, graphics programmes, and statistics. This includes many screenshots and actual examples, but unfortu-nately this means that this part of the book will date rather quickly.

Moving to individual analyses, Yuri Yerastov provides us with 'A Construction Grammar Analysis of the Transitive *Be* Perfect in Present-Day Canadian English' (*ELL* 19[2015] 157–78), a form not mentioned by either Walker or Dollinger above, as in *I am done dinner*, *I am finished my homework*, or *I am started this project*—a construction Yerastov says is quite different from neighbouring constructions (*I am done working*, *I am done with work*, *or I have done my work*), and has its own specific constraints: it prefers animate subjects, the verbs are restricted to *done*, *finished*, and *started*, the direct object tends to be definite, comes from the semantic fields of education and household, and resists low-frequency nouns. By contrast, Josef Fruehwald and Neil Myler argue, in 'I'm Done My Homework—Case Assignment in a Stative Passive' (*LingV* 15[2015] 141–68) that this construction (synchronically) is not a perfect at all, but (as the title says) a stative (adjectival) passive. In their analysis, case assignment comes from 'an exceptional Case-assigning little-*a* head' (p. 144), similar to *worth* in *(not) worth the worry*, and thus is a case of micro-parametric variation caused by the formal properties of this individual functional head. Of course this analysis leaves open the question of where this construction may have come from, or whether it may have evolved from (ScE, IrE, or historical remnants of) the BE-perfect proper.

Sandra Clarke takes up 'The Continuing Story of Verbal -*s*: Revisiting the Northern Subject Rule as a Diagnostic of Historical Relationship' (in Torres Cacoullos, Dion, and Lapierre, eds., *Linguistic Variation: Confronting Fact and Theory*, pp. 74–95) and argues against a simple diffusion of this feature; instead, she writes, Newfoundland English patterns like (historically attested) southern BrE, where 'verbal -*s* constituted a (variable) present-tense lexical verb marker, for all subject types' (p. 90). The present-day status of verbal -*s* in Newfoundland is also discussed by Gerard Van Herk and Becky Childs in 'Active Retirees: The Persistence of Obsolescent Features' (in Torres Cacoullos et al., eds., pp. 193–207), because this non-standard -*s* (there regarded as a rural feature) is used especially by well-educated, female speakers 'for (sometimes ironic) identity performance' (p. 196) in a small number of constructions, with a small number of lexical items (especially *loves*, *hates*, *wants*, *needs*, *thinks*, or *knows*).

Further west, Nicole Rosen and Crystal Skriver look at the 'Vowel Patterning of Mormons in Southern Alberta, Canada' (*L&C* 41[2015] 104–15). In southern Alberta generally, '/æ/ is significantly raised before /g/' (p. 104) (in an exception to the more general trend of /æ/-lowering as part of the Canadian Shift), but Mormons do not participate as much in this raising, presumably due to their strong network ties within their community, which even has features of 'a potential linguistic enclave: a shared immigration history, a strong sense of identity, and a dense and multiplex network of ongoing interactions' (p. 106). It is interesting that young Mormon women are particularly conservative (their raising of *bag* only results in the same vowel as /ɛ/, whereas their non-Mormon counterparts raise *bag* to /ɪ/), possibly resulting from their particularly close-knit social (church) networks. In British Columbia, Alexandra D'Arcy stands 'At the Crossroads of Change: Possession, Periphrasis, and Prescriptivism in Victoria English' (in Collins, ed., pp. 43–63). Contrary to other varieties of English (but see Fehringer and Corrigan on Newcastle above), North American varieties have come to favour full verb HAVE again (over HAVE GOT, as already noted by Walker above), but require full DO-support with HAVE. In D'Arcy's analysis of the Victoria (BC) newspaper *The British Colonist* since 1850 HAVE GOT is indeed strikingly infrequent, a feature D'Arcy links to the strong prescriptive stance against HAVE GOT, but which may also have system-internal reasons; as she claims, '*do* blocks *have got*, ultimately marginalising it within the system' (p. 60).

Moving south of the 49th parallel, Susan Tamasi and Lamont Antieau have written a great introductory book on *Language and Linguistic Diversity in the*

*US.* They familiarize students with some basic tenets of linguistics ('language is governed by rules', 'all languages are created equal', 'language changes', and 'language varies'), discuss prescriptive grammar and the standard language ideology, as well as language attitudes, before they come to chapters on 'Colonial American English' (chapter 4), where they provide a brief overview of lexical and grammatical differences between British and American Englishes, regional and social varieties (chapters 5 and 6), and a separate chapter on 'African American English' (chapter 7). The remainder of the book (eight chapters) is devoted to multilingualism, and the other main languages (Spanish, native American languages, pidgins and creoles, sign language) in use in the United States. Although chapters are short (typically around twenty pages), they are full of linguistic detail, extra information in boxes, activities, and suggestions for discussion and research. Each chapter starts with guiding questions, and some common myths that the following text then seeks to dispel (e.g. *y'all* is only used by Southerners, Appalachians speak Elizabethan English, or text messaging does not follow the rules of grammar). In addition, readers are referred to the companion website for extra information, videos, and other resources. All in all, a valuable addition for the very beginner, with a host of materials that might also come in handy for seasoned instructors.

On quite a general note, William A. Kretzschmar Jr. discusses the importance of keeping in mind 'Complex Systems in the History of American English' (in Taavitsainen, Kytö, Claridge, and Smith, eds., *Developments in English: Expanding Electronic Evidence*, pp. 251–64). Kretzschmar proposes that in the evolution of AmE, 'particular linguistic features came to prevail . . . different features could become more common in different areas' through 'random interaction of complex systems between speakers of different input varieties of British English' (p. 251). Instead of a unified, national *koiné*, Kretzschmar claims that there must have been locally different varieties from the beginning, and that also present-day variation (intra- and inter-speaker) is better served by being described in terms of complex systems, rather than as homogeneous sociolinguistic patterns.

On Twitter, Jacob Eisenstein discovers 'Systematic Patterning in Phonologically Motivated Orthographic Variation' (*JSoc* 19[2015] 161–88), especially of (-ing) and T/D-deletion. In particular, he claims, 'reduction of the *-ing* suffix depends on the word's syntactic category, and reduction of the *-t, -d* suffix depends on the succeeding phonological context' (p. 161), and both pattern according to formality and ethnicity—that is, they follow the same constraints as in spoken language (although it has to be said that, strictly speaking in the phonology, /in/ for /iŋ/ does not involve a reduction of anything). Nevertheless, Eisenstein concludes that in both phenomena, 'we . . . see echoes of the system of socially linked variation from spoken language' (p. 181). (For more studies using Twitter as a data source, see below.)

Cynthia G. Clopper and Rajka Smiljanic examine 'Regional Variation in Temporal Organization in American English' (*JPhon* 49[2015] 1–15), by which they mean variation in the speaking rate (measured by articulation rate, pause frequency, pause duration, vowel and consonant duration)—see also Tyler Kendall's study from 2013 (*YWES* 94[2015] 52–3). Similar to Kendall, although their material comes from read passages and not more naturalistic interview data, Clopper and Smiljanic find that the 'the Southern dialect is characterized by a slow overall speaking rate, long pauses, and highly variable vowel durations [probably heard as the 'Southern drawl']. The New England dialect is characterized by a fast overall speaking rate, short pauses, and relatively high variability in consonant durations' (p. 11), supporting popular stereotypes quite well. However, 'patterns for the other dialects [i.e. Northern, Mid-Atlantic, Midland, and Western] are quite mixed' (p. 1), and the Midland dialect overall is more similar to Southern varieties.

Daniel R. McCloy, Richard A. Wright, and Pamela E. Souza contrast 'Talker versus Dialect Effects on Speech Intelligibility: A Symmetrical Study' (*L&S* 58[2015] 371–86), using speakers (and listeners) from the Pacific Northwest and northern cities. They find 'no systematic difference in intelligibility attributable to talker-listener dialect difference' (p. 382), but a small advantage in intelligibility for speakers from the Pacific Northwest.

Suzanne Evans Wagner, Ashley Hesson, Kali Bybel, and Heidi Little use a new method for 'Quantifying the Referential Function of General Extenders [GE] in North American English' (*LSoc* 44[2015] 705–31), that is, phrases like *and stuff like that, or whatever, and all that kind of thing* when they are clearly used for reference (disregarding their non-referential interpersonal functions, e.g. for closing social distance). As the main criterion they use lists because 'the speaker must show evidence of listing behaviour in order to pragmatically convey that the list is incomplete or otherwise extendable' (p. 712). Their comparison of data from young women in Toronto, Philadelphia, and Pennsylvania shows that the syntagmatic length of GEs interacts with their referentiality in all locales, probably due to the grammaticalization of GEs as they develop intersubjective meanings (and become shorter).

Allison Burkette moves our attention to 'necrogeography' (work out the meaning of this compound) in 'The Burial Ground: A Bridge between Language and Culture' (*JLG* 3[2015] 60–71), showing how 'colonial influence, cultural changes, and physical locations contribute to linguistic variation' (p. 60). Data from LANE and LAMSAS show that the most frequent responses (*cemetery, graveyard*, and *burying ground*) make up over 80 per cent of the data, although more than sixty other variants are also mentioned, and are worth analysing. For New England, Burkette finds in these terms reflections of the Puritan tradition of burying members in open, public spaces in the centre of town, rather than near churches (reflected in *burying ground, burial ground, burying place, boneyard*), whereas in the South, burials occurred in either the churchyard or in family graveyards (giving rise to terms like *family burying ground, family graveyard, family plot, private graveyard*). The more opaque (and euphemistic) *cemetery* is a nineteenth-century innovation linked to the rise in landscape architecture and could include lakes, paths, and winding roads (thus *lawn cemetery, park cemetery*).

Moving to regionally more specific studies, we start with the US East Coast. Maeve Eberhardt and Corinne Downs want to know ' "(r) you saying yes to the dress?": Rhoticity on a Bridal Reality Television Show' (*JEngL* 43[2015] 118–42), which is set in Manhattan, in a nice twist on Labov's department-store study taking 'the brides' budgets as a proxy for social status' (p. 118).

And indeed, they find in their analysis of seventy-eight episodes that
'consultants design their speech with their audience in mind, shifting towards
more rhoticity/standard speech when their client is willing to spend more
money' (p. 121), resulting in 57 per cent rhoticity in the high-budget category,
in contrast to just 43 per cent in the low-budget one. Renée Blake, Cara
Shousterman, and Luiza Newlin Lukowicz investigate 'African American
Language in New York City' (in Lanehart, ed., *The Oxford Handbook of
African American Language*, pp. 280–98), more specifically the language of
two quite different ethnic groups, AAE speakers and second-generation West
Indian Americans (SGWAs). They look at R-vocalization, which is used
slightly more rarely by SGWA speakers, the distinctive New York BOUGHT-
raising, where SGWA speakers show even 'more dramatic formant changes'
(p. 290) than speakers of AAE, and the realization of BOAT, where all speakers
have an upglide (as opposed to a more general Caribbean monophthong, or
basilectal /uo/), although SGWAs show some evidence of monophthongization, in sum presenting themselves as 'I'm a Black New Yorker who is
somewhere in between African American and West Indian' (p. 292). Similar
results are found by Patrick-André Mather in 'The (Non-) Acquisition of New
York City Vowels by Two Generations of Caribbean Immigrants' (*LangS*
48[2015] 48–61). Even though his Puerto Rican and Dominican immigrants
have a Spanish, not an English (creole) background, they also raise the
BOUGHT-vowel but do not consistently follow the (extremely complex) NY
short-*a* split, perhaps because it is disappearing even in white NY speech.
Instead (like AAE speakers, and like most other American dialects) they show
raising before nasals. Down the Atlantic seaboard, but staying with short-*a*,
William Labov and Sabriya Fisher investigate 'African American Phonology
in a Philadelphia Community' (also in Lanehart ed., pp. 256–79). Even though
overall they discover 'a measurable influence of the surrounding White dialect
on the phonetic parameters of African American speech' (p. 258), this does not
extend to the intricate phonological constraints e.g. of the Philadelphian short-
*a* split, where even 'moderate levels of cross-racial contact [lead] to only a
limited importation of the traditional Philadelphia short-*a* system' (p. 277).
Moving inland from Philadelphia, Jennifer Bloomquist and Shelmoe Gooden
report on 'African American Language in Pittsburgh and the Lower
Susquehanna Valley [LSV]' (in Lanehart ed., pp. 236–55). Although
Pittsburghese is generally equated with 'sounding white', AAE speakers are
also reported to have /ai/- and /au/-monophthongization, as well as the *cot-
caught* merger, if at different frequencies from whites. AAE speakers from the
LSV, by contrast, are often heard as 'country' or 'white' by outsiders,
indicating that they use similar local features, but at the same time they
distinguish themselves, for example by not using particular lexical items, such
as the Scots-derived *redd up* 'tidy up' or German-derived *outen the light*.
Talking of German(ic) substrate influence, Brent Allen and Joseph C. Salmons
discover the remains of 'Heritage Language Obstruent Phonetics and
Phonology: American Norwegian and Norwegian-American English'
(in Johannessen and Salmons, eds., *Germanic Heritage Languages in North
America: Acquisition, Attrition and Change*, pp. 97–116) in the Upper Midwest.
Contrary to received opinion, they find little evidence for sonorant devoicing

or absence of /z/. However, they do find a subtle Norwegian influence in their speakers' realizations of final laryngeal contrasts, where they 'rely less on vowel length than is otherwise reported for English' (p. 111).

Kathryn Campbell-Kibler and M. Kathryn Bauer report on 'Competing Reflexive Models of Regional Speech in Northern Ohio' (*JEngL* 43[2015] 95–117), because in contrast to central Ohioan speakers investigated before, northern Ohioans are split in their responses over the perceptual dialectology of Ohio: some 'classify themselves as divergent . . . [others] classify themselves as normative' (p. 112). On the other hand, all Ohioans share the conceptualization of a north–south orientation of Ohioan dialects, of a rural–urban distinction (with urbanity linked to young/black/slang speakers, but only for northerners also linked to more standard speech). This may indicate that northerners may have 'a stake in avoiding the notion of accent as applied to their own speech' (p. 114).

This already brings us to the American South, definitely the region that is covered best this year. This is mainly due to the collection of papers in Michael D. Picone and Catherine Evans Davies, eds., *New Perspectives on Language Variety in the South: Historical and Contemporary Approaches*, actually going beyond just English. Thus the collection, thankfully, also includes five chapters on indigenous languages, two chapters on earlier French, and two on Louisiana French. Earlier English, early AAE, present-day AAE, language change, and questions of identity are all covered in this excellent state-of-the-art collection. Those contributions that are relevant for our section will be presented in some more detail, starting with Michael B. Montgomery, who claims that the period from 1750 to 1850 was 'The Crucial Century for English in the American South' (pp. 97–117), and his investigation of three white letter-writers shows that linguistic patterns 'coalesce . . . towards more regional homogeneity' (p. 105) during that period, for example for *was*/*were*-levelling. He also looks at prescriptive Southern textbooks, and finds interesting evidence for local features such as the Southern drawl, or perfective *done*, in some cases pushing back dates of first attestation. Also on a historical note, but for phonology, William Labov speculates on 'The Beginnings of the Southern Shift' (in Torres Cacoullos et al., eds., pp. 284–96), based on (later generations of) expatriate Southern States speakers in Brazil, and concludes (very tentatively) that by the end of the Civil War, stage 1 (monophthongization of /ai/) was probably already in place, but stage 2 (lowering of /ei/) was not. For the traditional dialects, John Nerbonne conducts 'Various Variation Aggregates in the LAMSAS South' (in Picone and Davies, eds., 369–82), and his dialectometric approach (over vowels in LAMSAS) confirms that 'the major break is indeed the North-South area' (p. 377), and especially the Piedmont comes out as a subcluster of the South: vowels are indeed responsible for a great deal of the dialectal differences in the South. However, Nerbonne does not take into account that LANE and LAMSAS also contain social information. By contrast, Robert Shackleton puts 'Southern American English in Perspective: A Quantitative Comparison with Other English and American Dialects' (in Picone and Davies, eds., pp. 118–48), making use also of the social information in LANE and LAMSAS. His careful quantitative comparison with (phonetic) dialect data from England confirms that 'American speech is a relatively uniform amalgam of variants largely brought from the south of England, with a predominance of features from the southeast' (p. 132). His social analysis for the Southern states is even more interesting, since he finds a fascinating split, such that American social differences ('folk' speakers vs. 'cultivated' ones in the atlas projects) correlate with English regional differences (Southwest vs. Southeast features), leading Shackelton to speculate that 'speech features of West Country indentured servants acquired lower prestige in some social circles in the South but also became markers of local or regional identity in others' (p. 133). Edgar W. Schneider looks at 'Earlier Southern Englishes in Black and White: Corpus-Based Approaches' (in Picone and Davies, eds., p. 182–99), and finds that verbal -s was once much more widespread in the South. He can also document a 'missing link' construction in his corpus of blues lyrics, a three-verb pattern with *done* (e.g. *the cook is done gone mad*), which links AAE perfective *done* with constructions attested in British dialects.

For grammar, Jan Tillery observes 'Some Developments in Southern English Grammar' (in Picone and Davies, eds., pp. 149–65), such that many traditional dialect features are disappearing, either in both black and white speech (e.g. *liketa*, perfective *done*, verbal -s with plural, *a*-prefixing, or a number of non-standard past- tense forms), or only in white speech (e.g. zero copula, or invariant BE). Finally, some innovative forms are expanding, such as *y'all, fixin to*, or past tense *dove*, overall leading to 'a striking change in the fundamental character of SAE' (p. 162) due to fundamental demographic, economic, and social changes in the South. These demographic changes are investigated in much detail by Guy Bailey in 'Demography as Destiny? Population Change and the Future of Southern American English' (in Picone and Davies, eds., pp. 327–49). On the basis of US census figures, Bailey sees rapid population growth, foreign and domestic migration, ethnic diversification, and metropolitanization as processes where the South will catch up with the rest of the United States, in the process presumably changing its cultural and linguistic uniqueness. If you are ever in need of detailed figures on immigration, out-migration, and re-migration to or from the South, this is definitely the chapter to return to.

Dennis R. Preston claims that, in public perception, 'The South [Is] Still Different' (in Picone and Davies, eds., pp. 311–26). In particular, the South still seems to be the most salient speech area; it is regarded as 'incorrect' but also as quite pleasant (casual, friendly, down-to-earth, polite). Preston also gives an overview of which individual features have been studied in terms of perceptual salience (lexemes, perfective *done*, /z/-stopping, the *pen-pin* merger, /ai/-monophthongization, drawling before /r/, YOD-dropping, /i/-lowering), and in particular /ai/-monophthongization seems to be indexical of Southern speech. J. Daniel Hasty looks at the perception of a syntactic Southern feature, double modals, in 'Well, He May Could Have Sounded Nicer: Perceptions of the Double Modal in Doctor-Patient Interactions' (*AS* 90[2015] 347–68). Hasty finds that the use of this non-standard feature (as in *we may can always add the Pulmicort*) does not have a downgrading effect on the (perceived) competence of the doctor; instead the speaker was rated as being more polite. Jim Wood, Laurence Horn, Raffaella Zanuttini, and Luke Lindemann discover another little-studied syntactic construction typical of the South, 'The Southern Dative Presentative Meets Mechanical Turk' (*AS* 90[2015] 291–320) (the Mechanical Turk is a crowdsourcing platform by Amazon used for studying acceptability judgements here, and actually in quite a number of other contributions this year). The dative presentative (not to be confused with the benefactive dative), as in *here's you some money*, or *here's me a good pair of jeans*, is 'widely accepted in the South, and quite generally rejected in the North' (p. 301), according to their results.

Jon Forrest reports on 'Community Rules and Speaker Behavior: Individual Adherence to Group Constraints on (ING)' (*LVC* 27[2015] 377–406) in speakers from Raleigh, North Carolina, and finds (perhaps like Eisenstein above) a 'lexical category constraint hierarchy for the community' (p. 377), consisting of progressive > participle > gerund > pronoun > noun > adjective (favouring /ɪŋ/ for the more nominal categories). These constraints remain in place, even though there seems to be a community-wide change away from /in/, towards the supra-regional prestige form.

Moving to specific regions in the South, Melina L. Richards diagnoses *Appalachian English: Another Endangered Dialect* (this is her dissertation, originally from 2001, but not published until this year). She looks at eight vowels in ten families of three generations in upper East Tennessee: BOIL (with a raised variant, a reduced offglide, or even the archaic /bɑɪl/), diphthong smoothing in FIRE (to /ɑːr/ or /aːr/), rhoticized /ɛ/ (which tends to be lowered to /ɑ/), the realization of final unstressed –*o* as /ɚ/, unstressed schwa (with a tensed variant), stressed /ɪ/ with a tensed variant (as in /fiʃ/), diphthongized and raised /æ/, and stressed /ir/ as in HERE (which is lowered). Richards finds generational differences, especially between the oldest generation and the others, for the three rhoticized vowels (FIRE, rhoticized /ɛ/, and stressed /ir/), but also for /ɪ/ and schwa, such that the oldest and the youngest generations showed the greatest number of differences, but the middle generation and the younger generation did not pattern significantly differently. For Richards, this suggests a change in progress towards more general Southern AmE that presumably started in the middle of the twentieth century, which 'may have been a watershed time for linguistic change' (p. 46), bringing improved infrastructure, accessibility and tourism, and thus leading to the decline of this isolated dialect. Speakers also for the most part exhibited style-shifting in the predicted direction (towards more general Southern English in more formal tasks), but the younger two generations shifted back towards Appalachian English (AppE) for /æ/ and /ɪ/ (especially before /l/, making *pill* and *peel* homonymous)—an interesting development that Richards unfortunately does not examine further beyond discussing the phonetic contexts of these shifts. A hint of what might be involved can be gleaned from the article by Kirk Hazen, Jacqueline Kinnaman, Lily Holz, Madeline Vendevender, and Kevin Walden, who look at 'The Interplay of Morphological, Phonological, and Social Constraints for *Ain't* in Appalachia' (in Donaher and Katz, eds., *Ain'thology: The History and Life of a Taboo Word*, pp. 178–95), an expression they call 'an iconic stereotype for rural speakers in the US' (p. 178), and it is this iconicity (or perhaps better indexicality) they trace through three phases: in the nineteenth century *ain't* would have been a form used by everyone. With

increasing education in the twentieth century, it became a shibboleth of
uneducated speech. After the 1980s, using *ain't* became 'a choice of social
identity' (p. 191), and today it can index the 'good old times . . . where modern
progress had not intruded upon a supposed idyllic West Virginia life' (p. 191).
Christine Mallinson and Becky Childs remind us that Appalachia is not only
white (or male, or working-class) as they investigate 'The Language of Black
Women in the Smoky Mountain Region of Appalachia' (in Picone and Davies,
eds., pp. 475–91), in particular in two quite different communities of practice
of middle-aged and older women. The 'church ladies', oriented towards
traditional community life, show a much higher use of some regional AppE
variables (e.g. 3pl. -*s*, regional vowels), whereas the group of 'porch sitters' are
more oriented towards wider urban norms, and have more AAE features in
their speech (e.g. 3sg zero, copula absence, AAE vowels). One of these vowel
features is of course /ai/-monophthongization; this feature is investigated
in more detail by Bridget L. Anderson in 'A Quantitative Acoustic Approach
to /ai/ Glide-Weakening among Detroit African American and Appalachian
White Southern Migrants' (in Picone and Davies, eds., pp. 536–50).
Monophthongization before voiced consonants (*died, tide*) is described as
the traditional (presumably older) pattern in the plantation South and in
AAE, whereas the extension to voiceless contexts (*right, sight*) seems to be
more recent, and has been attested in AppE and progressive Southern white
speech. Anderson shows that 'glide-weakening in prevoiceless contexts is not
restricted to Southern white varieties' (p. 536), as it is in fact attested in her
younger AAE participants, and in all her AppE speakers (as Feagin points out
below, there may also be internal social differentiations for this feature). For
her Detroit informants, Anderson claims that 'it is likely that glide-weakening
of /ai/ in the prevoiceless context is a result of dialect contact' (p. 547) of
Detroit AAE speakers with AppE migrants following migration, and that it
indexes cultural loyalty to the South, and a contrastive identity with white
Midwesterners.

For Georgia, Lisa D. McNair reports on 'Negotiating Linguistic Capital in
Economic Decline: Dialect Change in Mill Villager and Farmer Speech'
(in Picone and Davies, eds., pp. 591–608). In the small mill town of Griffin,
these two groups of white speakers (differing in regional origin, network scores,
and linguistic features) represent an important cultural distinction locally,
and McNair shows that individual 'speakers disassemble and recreate
another communal dialect, formed by idiolectal choices from the new and
expanded feature pool' (p. 606). This feature pool contains traditional features
of Southern speech (non-rhoticity, *pen-pin* merger), more recent developments (like the *cot-caught* merger), and of course the Southern Shift, and
overall the tight-knit mill workers maintain their traditional variants (rhoticity,
/ai/-monophthongization, *pen-pin* merger) more strongly. William A.
Kretzschmar Jr. listens to 'African American Voices in Atlanta' (in Lanehart
ed., pp. 219–35) and, perhaps not surprisingly, discovers that reality is more
complex than previously assumed. He finds some evidence that AAE speakers
do participate in (parts of) the Southern Shift, and are not categorically
different from white communities (some of whom obviously do not participate
in the Southern Shift either). Overall, he documents 'scale-free patterns in vowel

usage that vary in frequency, not categorically' (p. 234), which still leaves the possibility that frequency differences will be heard as significant. Moving west, Crawford Feagin reports on 'A Century of Sound Change in Alabama' (in Picone and Davies, eds., pp. 353–68), more specifically in the white community in Anniston. In her informants, R-lessness (traditionally a feature of the older upper class) 'is a feature on its way out' in all speakers (p. 355), /ai/-monophthongization has an unchanged stable pattern and differentiates the classes sharply especially before voiceless consonants (where the upper class has diphthongs, but the working class has a monophthong, as in the shibboleth *nice white rice*); diphthongization of lax front vowels ('drawling') 'is in the process of becoming... a working-class phenomenon' (p. 359), whereas traditionally it seems to have indexed femininity; the *cot-caught* merger is progressing in younger speakers, and so is YOD-deletion, such that the traditional pronunciation of *tune, duke*, or *news* (with /j/) is also becoming 'an emerging feature of working-class speech' (p. 361). As a result, 'younger working-class speakers are now much more local in their speech than their counterparts on the other side of town' (p. 363), who are oriented more towards supra-local norms.

Slightly up north from Alabama, in Memphis, Tennessee, Valerie Fridland and Kathryn Bartlett study 'What We Hear and What It Expresses: The Perception and Meaning of Vowel Differences among Dialects' (in Picone and Davies, eds., pp. 523–35), combining production studies, perception studies, and perceptual dialectology. They find that Memphians rank 'more Southern shifted vowel variants as less educated and less pleasant' (p. 532), perhaps because they link them with more rural speech (and thus less prestige), and there seem to be very few ethnic differences—overall making 'Southern speech... not an ethnic marker but a cultural one' (p. 533). Valerie Fridland also looks at 'The Spread of the *cot/caught* Merger in the Speech of Memphians: An Ethnolinguistic Marker?' (in Picone and Davies, eds., pp. 551–64). The South is traditionally characterized by maintaining the distinction between *cot* and *caught*, but merged forms seem to be making inroads in white speech, as several authors have already pointed out. However, Fridland finds that 'there is little evidence that any Memphians are moving toward a fully merged low-back vowel system' (p. 562), even though the strategies to maintain distinct *cot* and *caught* vowels differ, such that African Americans have more rounded glide segments and a more unrounded *caught* vowel, overlapping with the *cot* space.

Patricia Cukor-Avila and Guy Bailey characterize 'Rural Texas African American Vernacular English' (in Lanehart, ed., pp. 181–200) by 'obsolescence, continuity, and innovation' (p. 183) caused by the demographic changes this Southern state has undergone since the colonial period, in particular the Great Migration and more recently the Reversal of the Great Migration (cf. also Bailey above). It seems to be the morphosyntactic features shared with white Southern speech that are obsolescent today (such as non-3sg -s, *for to*-infinitives, a-prefixing, or invariant BE), whereas a whole range of other features have become more frequent (*y'all, fixin to*, multiple modals, and inceptive *get to*, but also habitual *be*, or *had* + past).

Further south-west, in Louisiana, Sylvie Dubois and Barbara Horvath document 'The Persistence of Dialect Features' (in Picone and Davies, eds., pp. 383–96) in their comparison of (originally French-speaking) white Cajuns and black African American creole speakers. In the older generation, the two ethnic groups are virtually indistinguishable linguistically, and are characterized by the absence of vowel glides, T/D-deletion, and absence of *are* (especially in the progressive, and with *gonna*). The younger generations differ, however, because whereas for the creole speakers, older dialect forms persist, young Cajun speakers have revived their grandparents' features in the wake of the Cajun revival, taking 'pride in their Cajunness and . . . returning to local speech forms as a badge of their pride' (p. 393).

Rose Wilkerson studies 'African American English in the Mississippi Delta: A Case Study of Copula Absence and r-Lessness in the Speech of African American Women in Coahoma County' (in Lanehart ed., pp. 201–18), for which she claims 'linguistic uniqueness' (p. 201): in contrast to other present-day varieties of AAE (urban or rural), Coahoma County speakers have patterns of copula absence that are more similar to Caribbean creoles and older AAE, and copula absence (as well as non-rhoticity) are actually favoured by college-level speakers: 'the higher the educational level of the subject, the higher the occurrence of copula absence and r-lessness' (p. 211).

For the US West, Lamont D. Antieau exclaims '"You ain't seen nothing yet": The Distribution of *Ain't* in *The Linguistic Atlas of the Middle Rockies*' (in Donaher and Katz, eds., pp. 156–77). In fact, speakers in these rural communities use *ain't* in quite a restricted manner, and in particular in idiomatic expressions (as in the title). It is used most by the less educated, and by men, and typically co-occurs with other markers of non-standardness (such as multiple negation, again as in the title).

Wendy Baker-Smemoe and David Bowie link 'Linguistic Behavior and Religious Activity' (*L&C* 41[2015] 116–24) in another study of Mormon speakers (see Nicole Rosen and Crystal Skriver, 'Vowel Patterning of Mormons in Southern Alberta, Canada' (*L&C* 41[2015] 104–15), above, for the Mormon expats in Canada), but this time in Utah County, Utah. They compare peripheral (inactive) Mormon speakers with more central, active ones as well as with non-Mormons and find 'linguistic differences among Mormons based on their level of activity within that religious tradition' (p. 122)—presumably because participation in church is time-consuming. It even looks as if speakers who consciously choose to become less active 'choose to mark themselves linguistically as being different from that in-group . . . possibly even overshooting the difference' (p. 123), at least in some of the vowel features the authors investigate.

Another area where relatively little work has been done so far is the Pacific Northwest, but this year Alicia Beckford Wassink reports on 'Sociolinguistic Patterns in Seattle English' (*LVC* 27[2015] 31–58). In her twenty-five speakers she documents the *cot-caught* merger and investigates other vowel phonemes, also finding 'a tendency for . . . speakers to monophthongize /eː/ *bake* and to raise prevelar /æ/ *bag* and /ɛ/ *beg* toward /eː/' (p. 31) in a near-merger. As to the California Vowel Shift (CVS), young Seattleites (yes, that is the adjective) show only extreme (uw)-fronting, but no (ow)-fronting—quite possibly a feature by which to distinguish Oregon and California. Speaking of which, Robert J. Podesva, Annette D'Onofrio, Janneke Van Hofwegen, and Seung Kyung Kim uncover 'Country Ideology and the California Vowel Shift' (*LVC* 27[2015] 157–86) away from the buzzing metropolises. They can show that the CVS has progressed through the rural, inland hinterland, though there it is 'not as robust as in urban, coastal areas' (p. 157), making the CVS a marker of Californian-ness. However, there also seems to be an internal differentiation, and features of the shift 'index town, as opposed to country, orientation' (p. 162) more strongly. Annette D'Onofrio claims that 'Persona-Based Information Shapes Linguistic Perception: Valley Girls and California Vowels' (*JSoc* 19[2015] 241–56). In her investigation of just one vowel of the CVS, the backing of TRAP, both the information that the speaker is from California and the claim that the speaker is a 'Valley Girl' causes hearers to expect TRAP-backing—the persona-based social meaning is thus as strong as more macro-sociological categories. Speaking of the Valley Girl, Ashley Hesson and Madeline Shellgren follow the development of 'Discourse Marker *Like* in Real Time: Characterizing the Time-Course of Sociolinguistic Impression Formation' (*AS* 90[2015] 154–86). Even a single use of discourse marker *like* (*Like, what do you mean?*) results in the perception of the speaker as less friendly and less intelligent (clearly linked to the persona of the Valley Girl). As the authors find out in their real-time study of continuous assessment over the course of the samples played to the informants, 'the "unfriendly" perception is relatively transient [and is perhaps a 'knee-jerk reaction' to societal stigma], the "unintelligent" evaluation persists and intensifies over time' (p. 154). Finally, Joseph C. Tyler is 'Expanding and Mapping the Indexical Field: Rising Pitch, the Uptalk Stereotype, and Perceptual Variation' (*JEngL* 43[2015] 284–310). In various perception tests, Tyler finds that utterances with final rises ('uptalk') are linked with youth, with speaking clearly, being happy, certain, confident, intelligent, and with paying attention, but they are also perceived as annoying. They are still heard as Californian most (and as Southern the least), clearly due to the perceptual link with the Valley Girl stereotype.

John R. Rickford looks back on studies of 'African American Vernacular English in California: Over Four Decades of Vibrant Variationist Research' (in Lanehart ed., pp. 299–315), which he says have been characterized by ethnographic methods and a careful investigation of stylistic and identity factors. Rickford also points out that some new features of AAE were first reported in California, such as future perfective *be done*, aspectual *steady*, indignant *come*, preterite *had*, and invariant *be₃* (as in *the Clovers be the baddest ones around here*; see also below), and that California is also the site where the use of AAE features by other ethnicities has been studied best.

Moving to ethnicity, we note here the publication of Jean-Jacques Weber's interesting short book *Language Racism*. In it, he first takes the perspective of (Wilhelm Reich's 1930s) 'Little Man', entering his stream of consciousness to demonstrate very impressively how racism can become part of 'common sense', before then debunking these myths by looking at the link of nation and language, language purism, standard language ideology (including prejudice against non-standard varieties), and multilingualism. Instead of these myths,

Weber proposes a social-constructivist perspective on the role of language and identity (or rather identities), language and culture, and language and education. Weber identifies four steps of racism, or a 'cline from verbal to physical racism' (p. 103): going from 'covert' to 'overt' racism, to the dehumanization of 'Others', culminating in physical violence against these dehumanized Others, with psychological mechanisms that reinforce each other. In the final short chapter, Weber sets up his 'Great Woman' as an antidote to the Little Man from the beginning, and tries to characterize her way of thinking: she's not afraid of multilingualism, sees identity as a process, links integration to social justice, supports flexible multilingual education, and thus tries to 'break down the walls of prejudice and racism' (p. 118). This book is well worth reading, and may serve as an eye-opener for many students too. In a way continuing on from Weber, John D. Foster studies *White Race Discourse* (actually from 2013, our apologies for the delayed report) ethnographically, based on in-depth interviews with white college students in the United States. Although on the surface the dominant discourse is one of colour-blindness, i.e. that racism in the US is a matter of the past, underlying fears and attitudes paint a different picture. If race discourse is not avoided altogether (the most common strategy), these college students show (presumably representative of larger trends) that whites think 'race' is something other people have, making 'whiteness' invisible, natural, or the norm. Particular strategies of 'Defending White Supremacy' (the title of chapter 5) are selective consciousness (not being able to recall specific incidents involving racism), majority/minority games (constructing their own, white, status as a minority), leading to the idea that 'whiteness is under attack' (p. 40) and thus constructing whites as the victims, or using constructivism to preserve whiteness (if race is a social construction, there is no further need to analyse it). Segregation is typically rationalized, and the 'White Racial Frame' (p. 80) is validated. Overall, though, these privileged white college kids 'generally wish to hear less from racial minorities, and allow whites to maintain their privileged positions in society' (p. 155), although they have learned to express these sentiments indirectly, or, as Foster calls it, as 'racism with a smile' (p. 155). As one specific strategy of overt racism, Adam M. Croom looks at 'Slurs, Stereotypes, and In-Equality: A Critical Review of "How Epithets and Stereotypes are Racially Unequal"' (*LangS* 52[2015] 139–54), taking issue with the proposal that slurs and racial stereotypes are 'necessarily considered as negative or derogatory' (p. 139), and that they apply to non-whites exclusively. Instead, Croom proposes a more differentiated view, showing that there are also slurs that apply to whites, that all slurs are generally restricted to applying to non-prototypical group members, and that they always affect someone's life chances. Finally, slurs can also serve important in-group functions (e.g. of solidarity). Unpleasant—to say the least—as they may seem, slurs feature quite heavily this year, due to a special issue of *Language Sciences* (52[2015]) devoted to the topic. Continuing on from Croom, Conor J. O'Dea, Stuart S. Miller, Emma B. Andres, Madelyn H. Ray, Derrick F. Till, and Donald A. Saucier are 'Out of Bounds: Factors Affecting the Perceived Offensiveness of Racial Slurs' (*LangS* 52[2015] 155–64). Manipulating contexts, they find that the use of the N-word from a white to a black was perceived as less offensive if this exchange took place between friends (as opposed to strangers), that *nigga* was perceived as less offensive than *nigger*, and that there were also individual differences relating to individuals' 'beliefs about the appropriateness of expressing prejudice' (p. 163). And Onoso Imoagene discovers 'Broken Bridges: An Exchange of Slurs between African Americans and Second Generation Nigerians and the Impact on Identity Formation among the Second Generation' (*LangS* 52[2015] 176–86). Imoagene finds that in the fraught relationship between black communities since the 1970s, characterized by 'teasing, ridicule, and social ostracism' (p. 180), 'the Nigerian/African second generation are targets of an ethnic slur used by African Americans and also appropriate the slur they use against African Americans as a socialization message in their Nigerian community' (p. 177), again promoting solidarity of their own group by this in-group use.

Overall, though, the most detailed (and up-to-date) discussion of AAE this year happens in the monumental *Oxford Handbook of African American Language*, edited by Sonja Lanehart, encompassing over 900 pages. Where relevant, individual parts and their contributions will be presented below; regional varieties of AAE have already been discussed above. The first part of this handbook is devoted to 'Origins and Historical Perspective', and creolist vs. anglicist, monogenetic vs. polygenetic, but also hybrid positions are represented in seven contributions. Gerard Van Herk defends 'The English Origins Hypothesis' (pp. 23–34) on the basis of features like verb morphology, auxiliary inversion in questions, negation patterns, and relative markers, noting that these morphosyntactic features are indeed the most likely to be transferred from the input dialects. By contrast, John R. Rickford in 'The Creole Origins Hypothesis' (pp. 35–56) points out that 'whatever distinctive grammatical features of AAVE might have come from British dialects...copula absence is not likely to have been one of them' (p. 41), which would thus be a potential indicator of persistent African language influence. Salikoko S. Mufwene finds neither position convincing. He asks, 'The Emergence of African American English: Monogenetic or Polygenetic? With or Without "Decreolization"? Under How Much Substrate Influence?' (pp. 57–84), and claims that 'the development of plantations from homesteads...did not favour prior pidginization' (p. 75); instead, substrate and dialectal English features must have been recombined. Mufwene makes the underlying point more forcefully in 'Race, Racialism, and the Study of Language Evolution in America' (in Picone and Davies, eds., 449–74) when he claims that most linguists do not treat 'race' as a social construct but take it as a fixed characteristic, an attitude he calls 'racialism' and which he traces to nineteenth-century imperialism. This attitude, he claims, shows especially in the debate on creole exceptionalism, which treats creoles (and, by implication, AAE) as a different type of language than non-creole languages. Back in the *Handbook*, Donald Winford provides some more information on the socio-historical contexts of 'The Origins of African American Vernacular English: Beginnings' (in Lanehart, ed., pp. 85–104) (i.e. in the seventeenth and eighteenth centuries), also claiming that 'the demographic evidence provides little support for the view that an English-lexicon creole language was in general use among the Black population of the South during the colonial era'

(p. 99). One exception may have been the areas where Gullah was spoken; the sociohistorical circumstances as well as the different theories of its origin are summarized by Tracey L. Weldon and Simanique Moody in 'The Place of Gullah in the African American Linguistic Continuum' (in Lanehart, ed., pp. 163–80). Overall, the most likely scenario seems to be that AAE 'preceded Gullah in its emergence, rather than descending from it' (p. 172). Certainly, through long-standing contact the two varieties today can be situated on a continuum. To clarify the history of AAE, John Victor Singler looks at 'African American English over Yonder: The Language of the Liberian Settler Community' (pp. 105–24), as typically expatriate communities are investigated in order to reconstruct earlier forms of AAE. However, these former slaves started coming to Liberia in 1822—nearly two hundred years ago, so that a comparison of present-day Liberian English can hardly be taken as indicative of early nineteenth-century AAE. Edgar W. Schneider, in 'Documenting the History of African American Vernacular English: A Survey and Assessment of Sources and Results' (pp. 125–39), notes that more and more hybrid positions are held by scholars, and that the discussion on the origin of AAE 'is no longer as heated as it once was' (p. 125).

More detailed studies on the history of AAE have also appeared outside the *Handbook* based on actual historical data. Thus, Lucia Siebers presents a corpus of AAE letters from the 1760s to 1910, which may be able to shed light on earlier AAE (in Auer et al., eds., pp. 240–63). In data from the end of the nineteenth century, she diagnoses in particular *was*-levelling (used in the second person singular and the first person plural), and verbal plural-*s* on BE and HAVE in the third person plural, essentially following the NSR, but possibly only indirectly transmitted from Scots-Irish settlers. Also based on historical letters (this time by Liberian settlers), Gerard Van Herk tries to investigate 'Regional Variation in Nineteenth-Century African American English' (in Picone and Davies, eds., pp. 219–31). These ex-slaves from the middle and the deep South also show NSR-like constraints in their use of verbal -*s*, and they use traditional past tense forms like *come*, *run*, and *give*, which is more consistent in the middle South than in the deep South, because in the middle South landholdings were smaller and the ratio of black to white population was lower, 'favouring uninterrupted transmission from dialects to AAE' (pp. 227–8). By contrast, David Sutcliffe provides 'Prima Facie Evidence for the Persistence of Creole Features in African American English and Evidence for Residual Creole' (also in Picone and Davies, eds., pp. 233–53), listing non-inversion in questions, perfective *done*, invariant verb morphology, possessive juxtaposition, associative plural, unmarked past-tense forms, and the expression *what make* 'why' as evidence that situates AAE 'in terms of linguistic space, between mainstream English and the Atlantic Creoles' (p. 234).

Back in the *Handbook*, Walt Wolfram and Mary E. Kohn remind us, in 'Regionality in the Development of African American English' (in Lanehart, ed., pp. 140–59), that it is rather unlikely that AAE developed uniformly everywhere (as Weldon and Moody already showed convincingly for Gullah)—in fact, this 'homogeneity myth' has racialized overtones ('all black folks talk the same way') and may well have resulted from 'biased sampling...authoritative entextualization by sociolinguists, and interpretive ethnocentrism' (p. 141),—quite a harsh criticism of early sociolinguists' work, including Wolfram himself. By contrast, Wolfram and Kohn's data on regional AAE show different developments in the twentieth century: in some cases a reduction of regional features combined with intensification of AAE; in others, a reduction of AAE features with the maintenance of regional dialect forms, or a curvilinear pattern of black and white speech becoming more similar during the phase of integration, and since then diverging again. Walt Wolfram takes up his point again in 'The Sociolinguistic Construction of African American Language' (pp. 338–52), where he notes self-critically that 'scholars have unwittingly participated in the creation of a type of sociolinguistic folklore about the nature of AAL' (p. 339). These entrenched positions include the definition of AAE (as confined to male, working-class, urban youth), the reduction to an invariant structure (ignoring its overall systematicity), questions of change, and intra- and inter-speaker variation. Luckily, some of these *monenda* are addressed by other contributions, which takes us to the most important theme in AAE studies this year: the study of internal variation, including regional varieties. In the *Handbook*, ten shorter contributions deal with 'Lects and Variation', ranging from Atlanta, Texas, and Mississippi via New York, Philadelphia, and Pittsburgh to California. Because of their regional focus, they have already been presented above. As an innovative method, it may be appropriate here to report on Taylor Jones's (successful) attempt, 'Toward a Description of African American Vernacular English Dialect Regions Using "Black Twitter"' (*AS* 90[2015] 403–40). Based on non-standard orthography indicating distinct lexical and phonological features in Twitter (and using its geotagging), Jones discovers AAE dialect regions that are 'not coterminous with traditional North American dialect regions; rather, they align with patterns of movement during the Great Migrations' (p. 403): a general AAVE area, including all cities and regions (also on the West Coast) where AAVE is spoken, a Southern area (the area of origin of AAVE), a Northeast corridor from Washington DC to New York City (the megalopolis that also includes Baltimore and Philadelphia), and a 'Great Migration Region', consisting of a 'vertical band from former slave states to the Northern cities Chicago, Detroit, and Cleveland' (p. 426), but excluding the Northeast. Moreover, Jones also finds varying intensities of new orthographies and can demonstrate the influence of cities inside these dialect areas radiating outwards, such as Atlanta for *yeen* (*you ain't*) and *talmbout* (*talking about*), or St Louis for *sholl* (*sure*). There are also other interesting findings, such as an almost categorical use of *nuffin* in Philadelphia and Washington, vs. *nuttin* in New York City—a treasure trove of interesting data, and possibly a method for future investigations to come. In addition to regional variation, social and stylistic variation is also dealt with in the *Handbook* in the final section, on 'Language and Identity' (Part VII). The contributions here pick out areas that are often neglected by other studies, such as the notion of an African American Standard English (by Arthur Spears, see below), social variation in AAE (by Erica Britt and Tracey L. Weldon, see below), or the intersection with gender (by Marcyliena Morgan or David E. Kirkland, see also below). The *Handbook* also has extensive covering of 'Child Language Acquisition and Development' (Part IV) and the role of AAE in 'Education' (Part V), as well as the use of AAE in other domains (such as church, literature, comedy, poetry, or animated films), which we will not report on in detail here.

Janneke Van Hofwegen reports on a 'Dyadic Analysis: Factors Affecting African American English Usage and Accommodation in Adolescent Peer Dyads' (*L&C* 41[2015] 28–45). In her analysis of forty-one morphosyntactic and three phonological variables in 201 dyadic interactions between black adolescents, she finds that the number of AAE features is more similar within dyads than between dyads, and thus there is significant accommodation between adolescents. Boys are overall less accommodative, especially to strangers, perhaps related to social skills, or to a willingness to accommodate (or not). Jeannie Waller in 'African American English and Code Switching in School' (in Seawright, ed., *Going Global: Transnational Perspectives on Globalization, Language, and Education* [2014], pp. 98–112) points out that demanding code-switching of black children is fraught with difficulties, and may send the wrong message (there is an acceptable way to communicate, and your way isn't)—ultimately silencing students, and reinforcing a self-fulfilling prophecy of academic failure.

Contributions to a structural description of AAE are also prominent this year, again mainly because of Lanehart's *Handbook*, starting with Erik R. Thomas and Guy Bailey, who give an overview of studies on the 'Segmental Phonology of African American English' (pp. 403–19), overall much less studied than, say, morphosyntactic features. They note, perhaps somewhat frustratedly, that 'as more research is conducted on AAE, consensus becomes more elusive' (p. 416), but they actually do a very good job of summarizing the various constraints and tendencies that have been uncovered so far, relating to consonant and vowel features. Many features also occur in white vernaculars, if at differing frequencies; nevertheless, the authors note consonant cluster reduction, R-lessness (including intervocalic R-deletion, as in [sɒ.i] 'sorry'), TH-stopping, TH-fronting, L-vocalization, and some consonant shifts as distinctive. The picture for vowels is complicated by the complex situation of white vernaculars, but recurrent features (also carried outside the South by AAE speakers) are /ai/-monophthongization, the *pen-pin* merger, the lack of fronting of back vowels (e.g. as opposed to the Southern Shift), and resistance to the *cot-caught* merger. One historical consonant feature is discussed in more detail by Rudolph C. Troike, 'Creole /l/ → /r/ in African American English/ Gullah: Historical Fact and Fiction' (*AS* 90[2015] 6–83). The use of /r/ for /l/ (*bress, prease, grad*), according to Troike, is found in literature from colonial times to the mid-twentieth century, but also in non-literary sources, and can be considered 'an iconic stereotype, fuelled in part by the minstrel show tradition' (p. 6). Rather than being wholly invented, according to Troike it can be traced back to various creoles, and thus perhaps ultimately to African language phonologies. However, this feature has died out, and is not part of current AAE anymore. Possibly even less studied than features of segmental phonology, though clearly one of the most salient features for listeners, are 'Prosodic Features of African American English' (in Lanehart, ed., pp. 420–35), as Erik R. Thomas points out in what may very well be one of the best contributions to the study of AAE this year. This elusive subject has only been studied in fragments, but Thomas manages to convey a coherent overall picture of the prosodic distinctiveness of AAE. This comes from 'forestressing' (placing primary stress on the first syllable of words), the impression of differences in the overall speech rate (at least the ex-slave narratives were more syllable-timed), the AAE use of a wider pitch range and falsetto voice, especially in the context of 'competitive speech acts' (p. 424), and differences in intonation—particularly difficult to describe because they seem to vary with style, social class, and possibly region (and they may carry remnants of a tonal system). Continuing on from this, Erik R. Thomas and Jeffrey Reaser also conduct 'An Experiment on Cues Used for Identification of Voices as African American or European American' (in Picone and Davies, eds., pp. 507–22). Their surprising result is that 'listeners focus... on different cues for male and female voices' (p. 516), namely on fronting/backing of /o/ and /u/ for female speakers, but breathiness for male speakers. In particular, 'backed /u/ marks African American speech... fronted /o/ glides mark European American speech' (p. 518), as do low /æ/ tokens. James A. Walker reports 'On the Syntax-Prosody Interface in African American English' (in Lanehart, ed., pp. 387–402), and finds that prosody does condition copula contraction/deletion, but has no effect on verbal -s—presumably due to the different morphological status of these features (clitic vs. inflection).

Usually more prominent in studies of AAE are lists of morphosyntactic features. Despite this prominence, Lisa J. Green and Walter Sistrunk argue that 'Syntax and Semantics in African American English' (in Lanehart, ed., pp. 355–70) is still an under-studied area, but what they regard as missing is a formal discussion of semantic and syntactic properties, for example of tense/aspect markers, or of complex sentences (i.e. meaning associated with morphosyntactic surface constructions, syntactic placement of markers, combination with other markers, predicate selection, or co-occurrence restrictions). Charles E. Debose also takes a more structuralist view of 'The Systematic Marking of Tense, Modality, and Aspect in African American Language' (in Lanehart, ed., pp. 371–86), claiming that the TMA system of AAE is what is 'most distinctive about the grammar' (p. 371). In fact, he attempts to provide 'a description of the variety in terms of its internal structure without reference to other language varieties' (p. 376) along Green's criteria. His analysis proposes, for example, that verbal -s is not a person inflectional marker, but overtly marks a verb, and 'applies to all lexical items thusly marked' (p. 384). Similarly, stressed BIN differs from unstressed been, and can appear with a wide range of predicate types; this has evolved quite dramatically from its (presumed) origin as an anterior marker. In fact, Tim Beyer, Karlyn A. Edwards, and Caitlin C. Fuller uncover 'Misinterpretation of African American African American English bin by Adult Speakers of Standard American English' (L&C 45[2015] 59–69), because stressed BIN (the remote past marker) is what they call a 'false cognate', or what Spears has called a 'camouflaged' form: a form with a surface similarity, but different in meaning or syntactic behaviour, which typically goes unnoticed, 'resulting in unresolved structural conflict' (p. 59). In their experiment, StE speakers heard stressed BIN as referring to the recent past (like been), even though they claimed they were familiar with AAE, showing that 'mere exposure to the other variety does not appear to be enough to learn false cognates' (p. 67). Arthur K. Spears himself expands on this in 'African American Standard English' (AASE) (in Lanehart, ed., pp. 786–99), a variety which has 'distinctively Black grammatical features, but none that are stigmatized or considered nonstandard... no one but an AAE specialist could detect [them] because they are grammatically camouflaged' (p. 786). More specifically, these features correspond segmentally to StE (although the meaning may be very different), such as the disapproval marker *come* (*He came coming in my room* 'He had the nerve to come in my room'), or the stressed BIN mentioned by the other authors above. As Spears points out, historically AASE was 'an object of desire... a fetish... an index of social status... a form of cultural capital unhinged from financial capital and thus almost served as a substitute for it' (pp. 796–7), and camouflaged constructions infused these externally imposed norms with (at least some) blackness. A similar point is made by Erica Britt and Tracey L. Weldon, who summarize the little there is on 'African American English in the Middle Class' (in Lanehart, ed., pp. 800–16), and the push and pull between external norms (to assimilate to StE) and signalling one's ethnic identity (by not sounding white).

Moving into gender variation, Marcyliena Morgan claims that 'African American Women's Language' (in Lanehart, ed., pp. 817–33) has traditionally been neglected in sociolinguistic studies. Studies have found that their language is characterized by 'an elaborate system of indirectness' (p. 824), including signifying, extended *he said/she said*-events in conflicts that involve investigating, interrogating, and clearing friends, the instigator and/or offending parties, and conflict resolution, and instances of *reading dialect*, where AAE features and StE are contrasted and analysed. The distinctiveness has not pervaded public discourse yet, though, and black women are still compared to middle-class white women in terms of behaviour, look, and language. Indeed, the use of AAE is stereotypically linked to masculinity, not femininity, as David E. Kirkland points out in 'Black Masculine Language' (BML) (in Lanehart, ed., pp. 834–49). BML is still seen as 'the basis of legitimate language prejudice... as [a symbol] of menace and threat', but also as the language of 'noble warriors' (p. 837). On the other hand, for example in jazz, BML also became a language of innovation and subversion, and BML can be a language of resistance (e.g. to mainstream norms), as demonstrated in the extension of invariant *be* to non-habitual contexts in hip-hop language (*I be the king supreme*), according to Kirkland, to 'reconfigure the language with brazenly masculine undertones... machismo and braggadocio' (p. 841). H. Samy Alim continues on from this in his contribution on 'Hip Hop Nation Language [HHNL]: Localization and Globalization' (in Lanehart, ed., pp. 850–62)—HHNL (which is not coterminous with AAE) is used to 'articulate the shifting terms of Black marginality in the United States' (p. 852), in the process developing local identities for hip-hop youth (e.g. Bay Area *mane* for 'man', or St Louis *hurr* for 'here'), which in turn might be taken up by other communities, and thus become more global again. But of course hip hop reaches much further, and Cecelia Cutler and Unn Royneland ask (excuse the expletive), 'Where the Fuck Am I From? Hip-Hop Youth and the

(Re-)Negotiation of Language and Identity in Norway and the US' (in Nortier and Svendsen, eds., *Language, Youth and Identity in the 21st Century: Linguistic Practices across Urban Spaces*, pp. 139–63). They argue that multi-ethnic linguistic practices in both countries are mediated via hip-hop music (and culture) because hip hop is symbolic of opposition and is associated with 'non-standard, multi-ethnolectal and heteroglossic language practices' that work as a 'means for hip-hop youth to differentiate themselves from others and express pride in their identity' (p. 140).

Patricia Irwin discovers 'Expressive Meaning in an AAE Attributive Construction' (*LangS* 50[2015] 12–29), namely in what she calls the discourse-*ass* construction (as in *get that ugly-ass junk out of here*). Irwin argues that this is an expressive, marking the utterance as direct speech and uncensored. Syntactically, -*ass* behaves like a bound affix, not a compound. Although *ass* is semantically bleached (e.g. it can refer to inanimate objects like *junk*), it retains its force as a swearword. Incidentally, this construction also appears in Marcin Widawski's collection *African American Slang: A Linguistic Description*. This is really two books in one, since Widawski introduces his collection by defining what he considers specific AAE slang, analysing it formally, semantically, and functionally. Morphosyntactically, there are compounds, affixes, some rhymed forms like *rusty-dusty*, or alliterative forms (*beat box*, *main man*), phrases, shortenings (*hood*, *box*, *dis*), but also initialisms, conversions, blends (*sexcellent*, *bootylicious*), some instances of coinage, onomatopoeia (*bling*), and of course respellings (*madd*, *flava*, *dawg*). Semantically, Widawski catalogues metaphors, metonymy, figuration, especially based on body parts (*big eyes* 'desire, craving', *man with paper ass* 'insignificant man') and animals (*alligators*, *fox*, *roaches*), pejoration, amelioration, and maybe the most famous category, complete reversals (antiphrasis), as in *baddest, mean, sick*, or *vicious* (all meaning 'admirable, excellent'). Common themes running through the collection are of course sexuality, the body, alcohol, drugs, violence, and racism, but also entertainment and, especially, music. As to its specific functions, slang identifies AAE speakers as in-group members, serves functions of secrecy and rebellion, especially historically, expresses emotions, humour, and toughness, informality, and of course is used in wordplay and word battle. If you are puzzled by individual expressions, refer to the alphabetical glossary in the second part of this book, where Widawski also gives a host of attestations, often from films, TV series, and songs, making this the collection to keep on your bookshelf as you listen to your favourite hip-hop artists. Speaking of which, Maeve Eberhardt and Kara Freeman say: ' "First things first, I'm the realest": Linguistic Appropriation, White Privilege, and the Hip-Hop Persona of Iggy Azalea' (*JSoc* 19[2015] 303–27), investigating a white Australian hip-hopper who uses copula absence to an extremely high degree (the authors call it 'overzealous', p. 303), and the authors show how this is another case of a white 'co-opting' and profiting from black cultural forms, a kind of appropriation that is 'at its core not different from the linguistic minstrelsy and mock language that reflect whites' ongoing participation in and upholding of the status quo racist structure' (pp. 304–5).

Moving briefly to a few studies of other ethnic groups, Sarah Bunin Benor tells the story of 'How Synagogues Became *Shuls*: The Boomerang Effect in Yiddish-Influenced English' (in Johannessen and Salmons, eds., pp. 217–33), the 'boomerang effect' relating to the pattern in which substrate features that were previously on the wane may resurge in younger speakers. Even though (or perhaps because?) these speakers may not be fluent in Yiddish, they use more and more loanwords, such as *shul* (for 'synagogue'), *leyn* ('chant Torah'), *daven* ('pray'), or *chutzpah* ('nerve, gall'), a pattern that has also been called 'postvernacular'. Benor claims that the social meaning of using Yiddish terms has changed and is now indexing 'young, hip, ironic, urban Jewishness' (p. 227)—or 'Heebster' culture. Cynthia Bernstein collects 'Lexical Features of Jewish English in the Southern United States' (in Picone and Davies, eds., pp. 607–24), documenting the merging of the two cultures (as in the emblematic greeting *shalom y'all*). Bernstein finds Jewish lexemes of different status: 'some remain largely within the Jewish community [such as *chutzpah*, *schlep*, *tchotchke*, or *kvetch*], while some spread . . . into more general usage' (p. 621) (such as *glitch*, *maven*, *schmooze*, *schlock*, or *nebbish*). Overall, since the number of Jews in the South has been increasing, it is possible that this variety will play a larger part in the future.

Moving to another ethnic group, Adam M. Croom has also collected 'Slurs and Stereotypes for Italian Americans: A Context-Sensitive Account of Derogation and Appropriation' (*JPrag* 81[2015] 36–51)—expressions like *guido*, *guinea*, or *wop* that 'pack some of the nastiest punches natural language has to offer' (p. 36), but, as Croom also notes, that can in some contexts also be used non-derogatorily 'to convey affiliation among in-group members' (p. 37), something that seems to have happened to *guido* in particular, which now apparently can also be used to refer to a particular (urban, clubby, fashionable) lifestyle. Elizabeth L. Coggshall reports on 'American Indian English' (in Williams et al., eds., pp. 99–127), surely one of the most under-studied groups of ethnic varieties. With the extinction of most indigenous languages, Coggshall points out that 'separate varieties of English . . . replaced heritage languages as a locus for speakers to express American Indian identity' (p. 105). Besides community-specific features, there are also features common to all (or many) American IndE varieties, such as a more syllable-timed rhythm and the use of glottal stops, as well as some morphosyntactic features that may indicate an earlier creole, such as copula deletion, uninflected BE, non-punctual *-ing*, lack of inflections, some pro-drop, and a freer word order. Perhaps one of the most striking features is the avoidance of asking direct questions, and the use of silence, 'to the point that [speakers] may seem baffling or even rude' (p. 119) to outsiders.

Going back to the UK briefly, but staying with the topic of ethnic groups, Ben Rampton's important monograph on *Crossing: Language and Ethnicity Among Adolescents* [2014] appeared last year in a second edition. The main text is only expanded by a fuller historical background in the introductory chapter, but otherwise remains unchanged. In addition, in the preface, Rampton locates his study (originally published in 2005) in the research context of the time. Otherwise it is very useful to be able to refer to this study still. Rampton also investigates what happens when speakers of what he now calls 'Contemporary Urban Vernaculars' grow older (in Nortier and Svendsen, eds., pp. 24–44). His 40-year-old informant of Panjabi descent still uses a mix of creole features, Panjabi, and traditional London vernacular ('a style forged in his youth', p. 31) in conversation with friends, and Rampton thus describes this style as a 'socially embedded and relatively stable resource in the everyday interactional practice of middle-aged' speakers (p. 25), which has 'affectively powerful connotations of peer-group familiarity' (p. 31). Partly based on the same materials, Devyani Sharma and Ben Rampton report on 'Lectal Focusing in Interaction: A New Methodology for the Study of Style Variation' (*JEngL* 43[2015] 3–35). 'Lectal focusing' measures how much speakers shift between StE, London English, and IndE, and Sharma and Rampton find in their study of Southall, a lower-middle-class Asian suburb of London, that although overall frequencies of non-standard features are actually similar across the community, older Asian men use shifts strategically more than younger men, 'shifting dramatically at times to achieve subtly strategic, interactionally tuned ends' (p. 3) in their use of the realization of /t/, /l/, the FACE and GOAT vowels, interdental fricatives, and the realization of -*ing* (as well as individual features like specific lexemes). Sharma and Rampton link the generational differences back to the sociocultural climate at the time of the speakers' growing up, which was more hostile for older men, forcing them to be able to adapt linguistically, while younger men grew up in an Asian-majority community, and thus developed a more unified (rather than bicultural) Asian English identity. By contrast, Michelle Braña-Straw documents (lack of) 'Language Change in a Post-Creole, British Contact Setting: Non-Standard *Ain't* Negation' (in Donaher and Katz, eds., pp. 227–48), more specifically in a community of Barbadians in Suffolk. She finds that ethnic differences persist, and Barbadian-descent speakers use *ain't* in different linguistic contexts than their Anglo peers, and they also use invariant *innit*.

Next, in this section we will look at more studies relating to gender. Rolf Kreyer is ' "Funky fresh dressed to impress": A Corpus-Linguistic View on Gender Roles in Pop Songs' (*IJCL* 20[2015] 174–204), but finds, perhaps rather depressingly, that the depiction of women (both by male and female artists) 'might contribute to the consolidation of unfavourable roles for women' (p. 174). He discovers taboo expressions especially in rap and hip hop, women singing more about romance (but also independence) than men, and men more about violence, substance abuse, and impoliteness—painting a picture of men as 'more violent, more aggressive, and more domineering' (p. 196). However, Kreyer does not take into account genre, which might be an important influence, as the various contributions on hip hop above have already shown. Ann Weatherall looks at male–female differences from a different perspective in 'Sexism in Language and Talk-in-Interaction' (*JSLP* 34[2915] 410–26), and diagnoses 'the derogation of women and participants' orientations to gender inclusiveness' (p. 410) in about fifty instances of conversations involving 'gender trouble', including the negative use of female references (*he sounds like a girl, you old moaning wife*), and the subsequent references of gender-neutral terms, often 'driven by common sense' (p. 423), which is of course already ideological.

If you have ever asked yourself, 'Why Are Males Inclined to Use Strong Swear Words More than Females? An Evolutionary Explanation Based on Male Intergroup Aggressiveness' (*LangS* 50[2015] 133–9), Emre Güvendir provides that explanation. There seems to be a biological difference such that women 'have larger volumes of orbital frontal cortex that modulates anger and aggressiveness created by the amygdala' (p. 133), and in so far as strong swearing is intended to hurt someone, it can be classified as aggressive behaviour. The question then is, which environmental or social pressures could have led to this biological difference evolutionarily? According to studies, 'lower levels of aggression in the female reflect an adaptive behavior motivated by the importance of her survival' (e.g. as a mother) (p. 136). Perhaps swearing can be compared to animals growling, relieving anger or frustration, but also warning the environment of impending battle. Staying with masculine aggression, Donald A. Saucier, Derrick F. Till, Stuart S. Miller, Conor J. O'Dea, and Emma Andres present 'Slurs Against Masculinity: Masculine Honor Beliefs and Men's Reactions to Slurs' (*LangS* 52[2015] 108–20)—perhaps not surprisingly, one of those reactions (at least based on the self-reports of men) is physical violence. The slurs they collected were homophobic (*faggot, queer*), feminine (*bitch, pussy*, see also the use of *girl* or *wife* in Weatherall's study above), intelligence-related (*dumbass, retard*), on general personality (*douchebag*), and, to only a small degree, bravery-related (*coward*), physical (*fatass, ugly*), and ethnic (for examples of which see above). Although general personality slurs are the biggest category, homophobic and feminine slurs actually evince the most violent reactions. The authors also show that 'men's masculine honor beliefs are associated with their perceptions of slurs as offensive' (p. 108), especially values like 'pride in manhood', 'virtue' ('you would praise a man who reacted aggressively to an insult'), and 'provocation' ('if a man is insulted, his manhood is insulted').

Erik C. Tracy, Sierra A. Bainter, and Nicholas P. Satariano use 'Judgments of Self-Identified Gay and Heterosexual Male Speakers: Which Phonemes Are Most Salient in Determining Sexual Orientation?' (*JPhon* 52[2015] 13–25) and find that word-length stimuli are long enough for quite an accurate identification of the speakers' sexual orientation in AmE. This is due to the quality of the vowels, and (to a lesser degree) consonants, especially /s/ (as demonstrated by earlier studies), but also /l/ and /n/, not investigated before. Staying with perception, Adrienne B. Hancock, Holly Wilder Stutts, and Annie Bass report on 'Perceptions of Gender and Femininity Based on Language: Implications for Transgender Communication Therapy' (*L&S* 58[2015] 315–33). On the basis of the transcripts of narratives (rather than voice recordings), the authors find that the gender of speakers cannot be clearly identified (only about 50 per cent of the speakers were correctly identified—a chance result), and there was no clear correlation with any of the linguistic variables noted in the literature, so that overall, these 'studies do not provide strong evidence for language differences between males and females' (p. 325), which also calls into question specific 'femininity' training for male-to-female transgender individuals. Similarly, Adrienne B. Hancock and Benjamin A. Rubin find little 'Influence of Communication Partner's Gender on Language' (*JLSP* 34[2015] 46–64). Dependent clauses, fillers, tag questions, intensifying adverbs, negation, hedges, personal pronouns, self-references, justifiers, and interruptions show 'no significant changes based on speaker gender' (p. 46). However, speakers did (slightly) change their behaviour towards stereotypical 'female' features when talking to a woman, perhaps indicating that speakers' perceptions, or their 'internal female-language schema' (p. 55) might be quite influential.

Returning to gay men, Christopher Hajek investigates 'Gay Men in Early Midlife: Intergenerational Accommodation for Approval, Reclaimed Status, and Distinctiveness' (*L&C* 41[2015] 46–56); early midlife in this study ranging from the ages of 40 to 53. These midlife gay men accommodated verbally and non-verbally to younger gay men, in order to gain 'compensatory social and psychological experiences, including younger men's approval, a reclaiming of a "younger" social status' (p. 54), including physical attractiveness, but there was also some divergence establishing their own, older identity. And with this we conclude our year's review of publications in dialectology and sociolinguistics.

## 9. New Englishes and Creolistics

This section presents this year's publications in the fields of New Englishes and creolistics. The subsection on New Englishes will proceed from supra-regional contributions to country- and variety-specific studies and from general accounts in book format to articles. In continuation of the surveys for 2013 and 2014, non-postcolonial Englishes are also included, since they have come to represent one of the most prolific areas of World Englishes (WE) research. The section on creolistics will first treat books then articles.

Beginning with publications on New Englishes, we start with one edited volume which covers several varieties, *Further Studies in the Lesser-Known Varieties of English* by Jeffrey P. Williams, Edgar W. Schneider, Peter Trudgill, and Daniel Schreier. In addition to the introduction (pp. 1–7) by the editors, the volume contains thirteen further accounts of 'lesser known varieties' (in addition to the first volume *The Lesser-Known Varieties of English: An Introduction* [2010] by the same editors in reverse order). Part I encompasses three varieties from Europe: 'Maltese English' (pp. 11–50) by Manfred Krug, 'Gibraltar English' (pp. 51–69) by David Levey, and 'Irish Traveller English' (pp. 70–96) by Maria Rieder. The second part, 'The Americas', provides accounts of 'American Indian English' (pp. 99–127) by Elizabeth L. Coggshall, 'Bequia English' (pp. 128–43) by James A. Walker and Miriam Meyerhoff, 'Saban English' (pp. 144–64) by Jeffrey P. Williams and Caroline Myrick, 'St. Eustatius English' (pp. 165–98) by Michael Aceto, 'The English of Gustavia, St. Barthélemy' (pp. 198–218) by Ken Decker, 'Anglo-Paraguayan English' (pp. 219–35) by Danae M. Perez-Inofuentes, and 'Gullah West: Texas Afro-Seminole Creole' (pp. 236–64) by Ian Hancock. In the final Part III, 'Asia and the Pacific', Rachel Hendery reports on 'Palmerston Island English' (pp. 267–87), Donna Starks, Andy Gibson, and Allan Bell inform us about 'Pasifika Englishes in New Zealand' (pp. 288–304), and David Britain and Kazuko Matsumoto describe 'Palauan English' (pp. 305–43). Taken together, the papers in this volume do not follow a common pattern of description, which might have been helpful in establishing systematic similarities among the less well-known varieties. But this might not have been the editors' intention (especially since it seems that the only feature all these varieties share is that they are 'lesser known'). Instead, the contributions provide rich and welcome documentation of the global spread of English to many different places and of the resulting varieties under very diverse contact conditions.

Moving on to general articles and articles on more than one variety, we begin with Salikoko S. Mufwene's 'Colonization, Indigenization, and the Differential Evolution of English: Some Ecological Perspectives' (*WEn* 34[2015] 6–21). Here the author builds on his earlier work and argues that the processes behind the development of pidgins and creoles are in principle very similar to those involved in the emergence of indigenized Englishes. In a similar vein, Gaëtanelle Gilquin compares indigenized Englishes and learner Englishes in 'At the Interface of Contact Linguistics and Second Language Acquisition Research: New Englishes and Learner Englishes Compared' (*EWW* 36[2015] 91–124). Based on corpus data, she investigates four phenomena on different levels of linguistic description and argues that due to similarities between the two types of Englishes a uniform account might be justified.

Next, we turn to publications by region, starting with Oceania/Australia. The only book-length examination in this part of the world is Carolin Biewer's *South Pacific Englishes: A Sociolinguistic and Morphosyntactic Profile of Fiji English, Samoan English and Cook Islands English*. The introduction underlines the necessity to study Englishes in the Pacific, a largely neglected area, surveys earlier research in the region and makes a case for not examining L2 varieties as deviant from L1 Englishes. In chapter 2, Biewer gives a historical overview of 'The Language Situation in Fiji, Samoa and the Cook Islands'. The next chapter describes 'The Theoretical Framework' of 'South Pacific Englishes'. It provides the theoretical background discusses the (non-)applicability of earlier models of WE to the context under scrutiny and introduces the author's expanded version of Mufwene's feature pool (p. 114). Chapter 4 lays out the 'Methodology and Database', showing that the analysis will be grounded in a framework of variationist sociolinguistics and based on a corpus of annotated speech data and questionnaires. In chapters 5 and 6, Biewer turns to linguistic description, giving 'An Overview' of 'The Morphosyntax of South Pacific Englishes' and an account of past-tense reference ('Talking about the Past in South Pacific Englishes'). Chapter 7 discusses the notion of 'New Zealand English as a Potential Epicentre in the South Pacific', and chapter 8 draws a reasonable 'Conclusion'. All in all, this book is a rich and welcome addition to WE research, not least thanks to its broad coverage and its theoretical contribution to the emergence of L2 varieties.

Turning to articles in journals in this region, we start with 'Attitudes in Fiji towards Varieties of English' (*WEn* 34[2015] 688–707) by Marianne Hundt, Lena Zipp, and André Huber. The authors investigate to which variety young people in Fiji aspire and conclude that, while BrE and AmE are still highly regarded, it is difficult to draw a clear distinction between endo- and exonormative orientation. Minna Korhonen's 'Spelling the Extra Letter? The Case of Australian English' (*EnT* 31:i[2015] 5–9) examines spelling changes in words with potential digraphs like *medi(a)eval* or *(a)esthetic* and with a potential <e> in front of the endings *-able* and *-ment* and concludes that the 'extra letter' is still firmly in place in AusE.

Moving to South Asia, this year's only monograph on a variety in this region is Tobias Bernaisch's corpus-based study *The Lexis and Lexicogrammar of Sri Lankan English*. Chapter 1 introduces 'Sri Lankan English and Sri Lankan Englishes [SLE]', while chapter 2, 'The Development of Sri Lankan English', provides a historical perspective. Chapter 3 surveys the 'Methodology'. In chapters 4 and 5, Bernaisch gives detailed quantitative accounts of 'Sri Lankan English Lexis' and 'Sri Lankan English Lexicogrammar'. The author ultimately shows that the structural, that is, lexical and lexico-grammatical, profile of SLE is clearly distinct from other varieties of English. In order to arrive at an explanation for this, he concludes by proposing 'A Model of (the Emergence of) Distinctive Structural Profiles of Semiautonomous Varieties of English'. Here he suggests that the development of semiautonomous Englishes like SLE is shaped by four layers: '(a) forces on semiautonomous variety, (b) paths of structural nativization, (c) nativization indicators and (d) the distinctive structural profile of the semiautonomous variety' (p. 215).

In addition to this book on Sri Lanka, two articles deal with English in India. The first is Raphaél Domange's 'A Language Contact Perspective on Indian English Phonology' (*WEn* 34[2015] 533–56). Here the author takes a diachronic perspective and traces the origins of some present-day pronunciation features of IndE to British dialect input from outside the south of England, proposing that these features are continuations of British dialects rather than deviations from a British standard. In the second, Sujata S. Kathpalia and Kenneth Keng Wee Ong investigate 'The Use of Code-Mixing in Indian Billboard Advertising' (*WEn* 34[2015] 557–75) and show how advertisers appeal to bilingual Hindi–English speakers by using code-mixing.

English in Southeast Asia is examined in two books and three articles. The two books are on SingE. The first is Zhiming Bao's very inspiring *The Making of Vernacular Singapore English: System, Transfer, and Filter*. In his introduction the author gives a brief account of SingE and New Englishes and then provides an overview of the book's aims, with an integration of the study of New Englishes and creolistics at the core of his 'contact-theoretic approach' (p. 2). Chapter 2, 'The Ecology of Singapore English', summarizes the socio-historical and linguistic set-up of Singapore, also including sub-chapters on education and language shift and maintenance in the region. Bao's ultimate aim is to establish his own framework of language contact by showing that substrate influence on the lexifier comes in two shapes: 'substratum transfer, when the contact language appropriates a grammatical feature from the linguistic substratum, and convergence-to-substratum, when a construction of the lexifier acquires the lexical or grammatical meanings of a semantically similar construction in the substratum' (p. 187). This is built up step by step in the following chapters by focusing on 'Grammatical System and Substratum Transfer' (chapter 3), using the aspectual system of SingE as a case in point, by analysing 'Topic Prominence, Empty Categories, and the Bare Conditional' (chapter 4), by examining 'Substratum, Lexifier, and Typological Universals' (chapter 5), and by looking into 'Frequency, Usage, and the Circumscriptive Role of the Lexifier' (chapter 6). Chapter 7 then introduces the notion of 'Convergence-to-Substratum' and a final 'Epilogue' summarizes the relevant claims.

In the second monograph, which is based on the author's Ph.D. thesis, Jakob R.E. Leimgruber presents an account of *Singapore English: Structure, Variation, and Usage*. In chapter 1, a historical introduction to SingE is accompanied by a survey of Singapore's linguistic diversity and of earlier approaches to this variability. Chapter 2 goes into the details of modelling variation in SingE. While chapter 3 is a slim account of SingE phonology and lexis, chapter 4 covers grammar, semantics, and pragmatics in more detail and demonstrates graphically how the study's subjects switch between H(igh) and L(ow) speech styles. This takes the author to the theoretical core of his book in chapter 5, where he elaborates on his indexicality model, which he claims to be appropriate for an account of the regular switches between H and L in SingE. In chapter 6, Leimgruber concludes by locating variation in SingE in a wider scenario of variation in Southeast Asia and beyond.

The first of two articles on SingE is Yin-Ying Tan's '"Native" and "Non-Native" Perception of Stress in Singapore English' (*WEn* 34[2015] 355–69). Here the author shows that speakers of different varieties of English (AmE, BrE, AusE, SingE) perceive the stress patterns of SingE in different ways, with Inner Circle speakers identifying stressed syllables even in positions not licensed by acoustic analyses. In the second article, Mie Hiramoto studies 'Sentence-Final Adverbs in Singapore English and Hong Kong English' (*WEn* 34[2015] 636–53) by comparing SingE and HKE to BrE and CanE. She finds that in the Asian Englishes, because of substrate influences, 'modifying' adverbs like *already* or *only* occur more frequently in clause-final position.

Moving to East Asia, there has been a plethora of articles on English in China, Hong Kong, Taiwan, and Japan. Comparing three regions, Yonghou Liu and Ye Zhao investigate 'English Spelling Variation and Change in Newspapers in Mainland China, Hong Kong and Taiwan' (*EnT* 31:iv[2015] 5–14) and conclude that AmE spelling is on the rise there, reflecting the increasing prestige of AmE world-wide. Next are two contributions by Stephen Evans on Hong Kong. The first paper aims at 'Modelling the Development of English in Hong Kong' (*WEn* 34[2015] 389–410) and analyses the authorship of letters to the editor in a diachronic corpus of Hong Kong newspapers to trace the history of bilingualism among speakers of Chinese. The second article, 'Testing the Dynamic Model: The Evolution of the Hong Kong English Lexicon (1858–2012)' (*JEngL* 43[2015] 175–200), examines the occurrences of new HKE words in a diachronic corpus of Legislative Council proceedings. In both papers, Evans's goal, inspired by Schneider's Dynamic Model, is to delimit the phases of the evolution of HKE based on historical data. In his contribution on Taiwan: 'The Ownership of English in Taiwan' (*WEn* 34[2015] 370–88), Mark F. Seilhamer reports on six young women's attitudes towards English with respect to prevalent usage, affective belonging, and legitimate knowledge, concluding that the study of the ownership of English requires a multi-dimensional approach. In the first of two contributions on English in Japan, Keith Barrs examines 'Errors in the Use of English in the Japanese Linguistic Landscape' (*EnT* 31:iv[2015] 30–3). In view of the social importance of English in Japan, he calls for more careful proofreading when using English words in the public domain. In the second, Mayuko Inagawa looks into 'Creative and Innovative Uses of English in Contemporary Japan' (*EnT* 31:iii[2015] 11–16) and documents some English/Japanese puns on Japanese 'manner posters'.

Turning to articles on English in China, this year's second issue of *World Englishes* 34 was a special one on 'English in Contemporary China' edited by Kingsley Bolton and Werner Botha. The editors' introduction, 'Researching English in Contemporary China' (*WEn* 34[2015] 169–74), first discusses the status of English in China and then briefly outlines the remaining eight articles. In the first, 'Surveying the English Language Across China' (*WEn* 34[2015] 175–89), Rining Wei and Jinzhi Su analyse the use of English in seven major Chinese cities based on the national survey of 2000. In 'English in China's Universities: Past and Present' (*WEn* 34[2015] 190–210), Kingsley Bolton and Werner Botha give diachronic and synchronic accounts of language policies and sociolinguistic realities in Chinese higher education. Two papers study English on the Chinese Internet: Haiyang Ai and Xiaoye You examine 'The Grammatical Features of English in a Chinese Internet Discussion Forum' (*WEn* 34[2015] 211–30) and present corpus analyses of new ditransitive verbs, verb-complementation patterns, and collocations, while Wei Zhang's 'Multilingual Creativity on China's Internet' (*WEn* 34[2015] 231–46) gives an account of code-mixing in weather messages on an official microblog in Shanghai. Joseph J. Alvaro's 'Analysing China's English-Language Media' (*WEn* 34[2015] 260–77) shows how the English in Chinese media is ideologically loaded, exhibiting a variety of carefully crafted terms and fixed expressions. Two of the contributions—Fan Dai's 'Teaching Creative Writing in English in the Chinese Context' (*WEn* 34[2015] 247–59) and Lijia Zhang's 'Writing in English in China: An Autobiographical Essay' (*WEn* 34[2015] 278–81)—focus on writing in English and are thus only mentioned here for the sake of completeness. The special issue is rounded up by Kingsley Bolton, Werner Botha, and Wei Zhang's 'English in China: A Contemporary Bibliography' (*WEn* 34[2015] 282–92), which lists relevant literature on the topic as published between 2003 and 2015, both with major international publishers and in major Chinese journals. In addition to this special issue, Maria Luisa Carrió-Pastor and Rut Muñiz Calderón examine 'Identification and Causes of Lexical Variation in Chinese Business English' (*EnT* 31:i[2015] 10–15). Based on a corpus of business e-mails by Chinese and Hong Kong users of English, the authors demonstrate that the Chinese writers use more non-standard forms than the writers from Hong Kong.

Moving on to another region in which English is neither used natively nor as a second official language, two contributions this year deal with English in the Middle East (Saudi Arabia and Kuwait). Manal A. Ismail investigates 'The Sociolinguistic Dimensions of Code-Switching between Arabic and English by Saudis' (*IJEL* 5[2015] 100–9). Based on recorded conversations of six male and six female L1 Arabic / L2 English communicative bilinguals, the author documents that code-switching to English is much more frequent in female speakers and that in mixed-sex conversations male and female interlocutors do not follow the other speaker's switch to English. This is interpreted as an indicator of sticking to the conversational norms of Saudi society, where a distance between women and men prevails. Abdulmohsen Dashti gives an account of 'The Role and Status of the English Language in Kuwait' (*EnT* 31:iii[2015] 28–33). He gives a variety of examples how English has been making inroads in the Kuwaiti educational system, in interpersonal contexts and in creative writing, highlighting its high prestige as a language 'of glamour' (p. 33).

Next, we turn to English in sub-Saharan Africa. The first article is Eyamba G. Bokamba's 'African Englishes and Creative Writing' (*WEn* 34[2015] 315–35). Here the author uses a selection of fictional works by renowned African writers to demonstrate how and where African languages and cultures influence the use of English. Next are two studies on South Africa. In the first, Rajend Mesthrie, Alilda Chevalier, and Timothy Dunne present 'A Regional and Social Dialectology of the BATH Vowel in South African English' (*LVC* 27[2015] 1–30). They investigate potential sociolinguistic and regional variation of this vowel in five South African cities and uncover some relevant differences with respect to gender, region, and ethnicity. The second article, Sabine Zerbian's 'Syntactic and Prosodic Focus Marking in Contact Varieties of South African English' (*EWW* 36[2015] 228–58), compares a newly emerging middle-class variety of BlSAfrE to BlSAfrE and GenSAfrE and concludes that it shares prosodic features with the former and syntactic features with the latter. Two further articles take us to Nigeria. Akin Adetunji, 'English in a Nigerian Linguistic Landscape' (*WEn* 34[2015] 654–68), gives an account of layering on public signs in the city of Ibadan. Rotimi O. Oladipupo presents 'A Comparative Study of Connected Speech Features in Nigerian English and Received Pronunciation' (*EnT* 31:iv[2015] 21–9), concluding that in NigE assimilation and elision are clearly less frequent phenomena than in RP. The article by Ameyo S. Awuku looks into 'French Influence on English in Togo' (*EnT* 31:iii[2015] 22–7). Here the author claims that the gender marking of Togo's official language (i.e. French) prevents speakers of English in Togo from using gender-neutral reference and they continue, for example, to employ masculine singular reference in generic contexts. Dunlop Ochieng reports on 'The Revival of the Status of English in Tanzania' (*EnT* 31:ii[2015] 25–31) and demands that language planners should stop promoting Kiswahili and instead provide wider access to English. The final contribution relating to Africa investigates 'Diasporic Second Language Englishes in the African Communities of Germany's Ruhr Area' (*IJEL* 5[2015] 1–13). Here, Christiane Meierkord, Bridget Fonkeu, and Eva Zumhasch argue, with a focus on a group of speakers of Cameroon (pidgin) English in the German diaspora, that such cases are important to expand this line of research to current linguistic and societal realities.

Moving on to the Caribbean, one article each on Jamaica and the Bahamas will be reported on; for contributions with a greater focus on pidgins and creoles in this region see the second part of this section. Michael Westphal examines 'Attitudes toward Accents of Standard English in Jamaican Radio Newscasting' (*JEngL* 43[2015] 311–33). He shows that endonormative stabilization, that is, the acceptance of standard JamE or Jamaican Creole as norms and exonormative orientation towards BrE or AmE, strongly depends on the context in which they are used. Stephanie Hackert's contribution, 'Pseudotitles in Bahamian English: A Case of Americanization?' (*JEngL* 43[2015] 143–67), investigates how in BahE usages like 'linguist Allan Bell' (p. 143) could serve as an indicator for increasing Americanization. Based on a diachronic corpus of news reports she finds that even during British colonial times, Bahamian authors used this type of Americanism.

Three journal articles this year deal with English in Slavic-speaking Europe. In the first, Elena Salakhyan studies 'The Attitude of Slavic Speakers toward English(es)' (*EnT* 31:iii[2015] 34–9) by using a small sample of fifteen interviews with speakers from various Slavic countries (Ukraine, Slovak Republic, Russia, and Poland). She finds that AmE is preferred over BrE, while non-native Englishes do not play a role as models at all. Alexandra Rivlina investigates 'Bilingual Creativity in Russia: English–Russian Language Play' (*WEn* 34[2015] 436–55) and concludes that the aim of the creative use of English can either be to entertain or to express reservations regarding the 'Englishization of Russian society' (p. 436). In their paper 'Evolving and Adapting to Global Changes Regarding English: English Language Teaching in the Siberian City of Irkutsk' (*EnT* 31:ii[2015] 5–10), Valerie Sartor and Svetlana Bogdanova give anecdotal insight into how English is and used to be taught in the Eurasian Linguistic Institute in Irkutsk. Finally, the last paper on New Englishes comes from South America. Here Francia Martinez examines 'English in Advertising in Colombia' (*WEn* 34[2015] 600–19) and concludes that the use of English in these contexts has a mainly ornamental, sometimes humorous, function to increase the marketing value of a certain product.

Turning to the section on creolistics now, we begin with five books. The first is Viveka Velupillai's *Pidgins, Creoles and Mixed Languages: An Introduction*. Here the author presents a new up-to-date textbook with fifteen chapters, including rich sociohistorical and linguistic information on three languages per chapter in what are called 'snapshots'. After the 'General Introduction', chapters 1 to 3 are very readable introductions to the three types of contact language mentioned in the book's title. Chapter 4 illustrates the sociohistorical contexts of their formation, development, and diffusion. Chapters 5 and 6 present the controversial theoretical approaches that have developed about the formation of pidgins and creoles. Chapter 7 investigates variation and change, the former with reference to continua, implicational scales, and diglossia, the latter with an eye on depidginization and decreolization. Sociological issues and the status of pidgins, creoles, and mixed languages in society and their use in the media and in educational systems are examined in chapter 8. In the second part of the book, Velupillai turns to levels of linguistic description. Here chapters 9 to 15 deal with 'Phonology', 'Morphology', 'Noun Phrases', 'Verb Phrases and Predication', 'Simple Sentences', 'Complex Sentences', and the 'Pragmatics' of pidgin, creole, and mixed language, respectively. These chapters all start by presenting generalizations that have been made and then discuss the chosen features with respect to the three types of contact language. Velupillai explicitly states that she would like to 'remain theory-neutral' but invites 'the reader to apply these figures [i.e. the empirical data presented] to various theories on the possible typological uniqueness of pidgin and creole languages' (p. 285).

Next, Lisa Lim and Umberto Ansaldo's book, which, strictly speaking, could also have been discussed in the section on New Englishes since it focuses both on pidgins/creoles and on (mostly) Asian Englishes, takes a sociolinguistic perspective on *Languages in Contact*. It is subdivided into eight chapters that treat relevant issues in turn. Chapter 1, 'Perspectives in Contact', gives an overview of contact linguistics, claims that language contact is highly relevant for a theory of language, and summarizes the crucial effects of contact in language evolution. Chapter 2 focuses on 'code choice' in multilingual settings. Based on a variety of case studies from Asia, Lim and Ansaldo show that multilingualism is the norm rather than an exception and also discuss the related concepts of diglossia, hybrid competence, code-switching, and code-mixing. The next chapter surveys the central concepts of pidgin and creole studies, providing accounts of the major frameworks of creole genesis, of the superstratist and substratist approaches, and of language transfer in creole and ordinary acquisition contexts. Chapter 4 contrasts in more detail the differences between two theories of transmission, that is, John McWhorter's Creole Prototype as opposed to 'uniformitarian transmission', and then resorts to highlighting the differences between contact and non-contact languages. Chapter 5 exemplarily investigates the relationship between 'Contact and Ecology' on the basis of tone and particle use in Asian Englishes, and the authors claim that, in an analysis of substrate features, demographic information is as crucial as typological information about the substrates. Taking an Asian perspective again in chapter 6, Lim and Ansaldo turn their focus to language shift, explaining essential notions and relevant factors in language endangerment. Chapter 7 then is centred around globalization and its influence on language contact. With the global economy shifting from West to East and Asia having the highest number of English speakers world-wide, the authors take a look at new contact phenomena in, among others, computer-mediated communication, the globalized economy, and pop music. Chapter 8 finally serves as a summary of the book, as an account of current research trends and of shortcomings in the field, and as an outlook on future research.

Next, Andrea Moll's study, *Jamaican Creole Goes Web: Sociolinguistic Styling and Authenticity in a Digital 'Yaad'*, investigates the social and structural changes in Jamaican Creole in diaspora communities as reflected in a Web discussion forum. In the first chapter, the author gives an account of how globalization has led to the creation of diasporas and how this can be connected to linguistic changes. Chapter 2 is a brief description of Moll's 17-million-word Corpus of Cyber Jamaican. An outline of the various methods applied is presented in chapter 3. Here Moll focuses on how to describe and account for communities of practice in cyberspace, for virtual identity, and for how authenticity is negotiated. Chapters 4 to 6, then, provide qualitative and quantitative analyses of the linguistic characteristics of Jamaican Creole as represented in this forum. Here Moll examines orthographical practices, finding that the spelling conventions in this medium 'establish a socially meaningful, visual contrast with the norms of StE orthography' (p. 250); tackles the notion of a 'digital ethnolinguistic repertoire' (p. 127), which shows that the morphosyntactic peculiarities in her corpus do not follow the rules of the creole continuum, with basilectal forms being over-represented; and follows up on how the posts in the forum are seen as authentic by Jamaicans and how this authenticity is negotiated online. In the final chapter 7, Moll pulls together the relevant results and provides an outlook on future research.

In her edited volume, *Language Issues in Saint Vincent and the Grenadines*, Paula Prescod presents six articles giving a comprehensive account of the English spoken in this part of the Caribbean, with the introduction setting the stage for the volume. In 'Sociohistorical and Linguistic Account of St Vincent and the Grenadines' (pp. 1–44), Paula Prescod and Adrian Fraser aim at correlating settlement history with the linguistic outcomes in the region but concede that, as a result of the limited amount of information available, a description of the situation needs to remain sketchy. The two chapters to follow deal with the linguistics of the small island of Bequia. Agata Daleszynska examines 'The Fate of the Local in Light of the Global: Analysis of Variation in the Use of Preverbal Markers in Bequia Creole' (pp. 45–66). Her data from two villages suggest that creole-like preverbal markers tend to decrease in more heterogeneous locations, while they are used as identity markers in more homogeneous communities. Miriam Meyerhof and James A. Walker study 'Subject and Object Pronoun Use in Bequia (St Vincent and the Grenadines)' (pp. 67–86) in three villages. They find that, although speakers claim to be able to identify speakers from other villages linguistically, the individual speaker is the strongest predictor for choosing a variant. Next, in ' "A she gi me words; well me gi she back de change": The Reframing of Stigmatized Talk by Everyday Women-of-Words in St Vincent' (pp. 87–112), Elizabeth Fortenbery investigates how communicatively strong women in three villages reframe stigmatized performance strategies and thus retain a respectable image. In the next article, Andrei A. Avram's 'The Distribution of Diagnostic Features in English-Lexified Contact Languages: Vincentian' (pp. 113–40) takes a diachronic perspective. Based on first attestations and comparisons with other contact languages in the region, he shows that this creole is more closely related to Antiguan, Bajan, and Kittitian than to Surinamese and Jamaican varieties. Then Paula Prescod investigates 'Creole Reflexes of *Do*: Zeroing in on Tense, Aspect and Modality in Vincentian Creole' (pp. 141–64). She surveys the system of the variants of *do* and establishes a split in the use of *done* sensitive to verb type. The volume is rounded off by Donna E. Cromer's 'Languages in St Vincent & the Grenadines: An Annotated Bibliography' (pp. 165–80).

This year's last fully original book in creolistics is Enoch Oladé Aboh's *The Emergence of Hybrid Grammars: Language Contact and Change*. With his focus on Haitian Creole and Saramaccan, the author aims at providing a theory of creolization and language change in situations of language contact. The core idea of his theory is that 'monolithic theories that account for creole genesis exclusively by invoking inheritance from the superstrate, substrate influence, language universals, or fossilization of some early interlanguage stage are untenable' (p. 304). Aboh's claim is that the recombination of linguistic features from various sources is responsible for the creation of hybrid linguistic forms, i.e. creole languages. The book is structured as follows. After an introduction, chapter 2 surveys 'The Agents of Creole Formation: Geopolitics and Cultural Aspects of the Slave Coast', while chapter 3, 'The Emergence of Creoles: A Review of Some Current Hypotheses', sets the scene for the author's own model by criticizing earlier ones. Chapter 4 on 'Competition and Selection', which is at times not easy to read for non-generativists, details Aboh's approach, which combines Mufwene's idea of a feature pool with the Minimalist Program. Chapters 5 ('The Role of Vulnerable Interfaces in Language Change: The Case of the D-System'), 6 ('The Emergence of the Clause Left Periphery'), and 7 ('The Emergence of Serial Verb Constructions') are case studies on how the grammars of Haitian Creole and Saramaccan diverge from the grammars of their donor languages. The final chapter, 'Conclusions: Some Final Remarks on Hybrid Grammars, the Creole Prototype, and Language Acquisition and Change', summarizes the results.

Brief mention also needs to be made of Claire Lefebvre's edited volume *Functional Categories in Three Atlantic Creoles: Saramaccan, Haitian and Papiamentu*. After the introduction (pp. 1–16), seven chapters are reprints of previously published papers on these three Atlantic creoles by the editor, in five cases co-authored by her associates. The only original chapter (chapter 9, 'The Properties of Functional Categories in the Three Creoles') and a 'Conclusion' pull together the results of the earlier papers and present, once more, Lefebvre's relabelling-based account of creole genesis.

In addition to these books, 2015 has seen the publication of seven articles relating to English-lexifier pidgins or creoles. In his guest column 'Creoles, Creole Studies and Sign Languages' (*JPCL* 30[2015] 357–69), Peter Bakker gives an account of how a comparison of creoles and sign languages can shed light on creole typology and the 'creation of languages in challenging environments' (p. 367). Next we see, very much in line with polemic debates on pidgins and creoles published in *JPCL* on a regular basis, two articles by Salikoko S. Mufwene and Peter Mühlhäusler, in which the former, 'Creoles and Pidgins Don't Have Inadequate Lexica: A Response to Peter Mühlhäusler' (*JPCL* 30[2015] 142–58), comments on an article by the latter, 'Language Form and Language Substance' (*JPCL* 26[2011] 341–62); and then the latter replies in 'Language and the World: A Response to Mufwene' (*JPCL* 30[2015] 159–66) to the response of the former. The debate centres around Mühlhäusler's claim that an ecolinguistic approach to creoles with a focus on vocabulary ('substance') and its denotations offers a more relevant account of these varieties than a mere focus on structural properties. As in many debates of such a categorical nature, the truth clearly lies somewhere in between, and readers are recommended to read the originals to form their own opinions. In a large-scale sociolinguistic survey in French Guyana and Surname, Bettina Migge and Isabelle Léglise, 'Assessing the Sociolinguistic Situation of the Maroon Creoles' (*JPCL* 30[2015] 63–115), show that, contrary to common assumptions, 'migration, urbanization and increased participation in the urban multi-ethnic and multilingual contexts has not led to language attrition among Maroons' (p. 109). Stéphanie Durrlemann, 'Nominal Architecture in

Jamaican Creole' (*JPCL* 30[2015] 265–306), takes a generative approach to Jamaican Creole syntax and shows that the intricate set-up of the extended nominal projection in Jamaican Creole suggests parallels to the structure of bare sentences. On the basis of data from a Nigerian Web forum, Theresa Heyd examines 'The Metacommunicative Lexicon of Nigerian Pidgin' (*WEn* 34[2015] 669–87). She argues that her analysis of verbs referring to speaking and of labels for varieties offers a way to understand how speakers of Nigerian Pidgin place themselves in the Nigerian linguistic ecology. In the final article reported on this year, Vincent A. Tanda makes an attempt at 'Rationalizing the Attitude-Acquisition Conundrum in Cameroon Pidgin English' (*EnT* 31:iii[2015] 17–21), and concludes that negative attitudes towards Cameroon Pidgin fail to acknowledge the fact that the pidgin is a carrier of identity among the anglophone minority in Cameroon and will be difficult to eradicate.

## 10. Second Language Acquisition

Work devoted to English as ESL or EFL has continued to feature prominently in the field of SLA in 2015. All components of interlanguage grammar and all language skills have continued to be studied, and research into L2 processing, individual learner differences, and different learning contexts has been extensively conducted. L1 transfer has remained one of the most explored research topics. A broad range of theoretical frameworks and research methodologies has been adopted, and establishing links between theory, research, and classroom practice has been gaining in importance. In the first part of this review, I provide an overview of work focused on L2 English, and in the second part I present work of general relevance to SLA, which has also been abundant in 2015. When presenting work on different components of interlanguage grammar in the first part of the review, I place particular emphasis on phonology, but I also review work on morphosyntax, vocabulary, discourse, and pragmatics (in that order).

Starting with work on L2 English, in the domain of phonology, Fred R. Eckman, Gregory K. Iverson, and Jae Yung Song explore a 'Covert Contrast in the Acquisition of Second Language Phonology' (in Farris-Trimble and Barlow, eds., *Perspectives on Phonological Theory and Development: In Honor of Daniel A. Dinnsen* [2014], pp. 25–48) focusing on the acquisition of the English /s/–/z/ phonemic contrast by native Spanish speakers. The term 'covert contrast' refers to a phenomenon, typically observed in L1 acquisition, in which children produce a statistically reliable sound distinction that is not perceived by adults. A group of fourteen Spanish-speaking L2 learners of English, in whose L1 [s] and [z] are allophones of the phoneme /s/, produced English words containing /s/ or /z/ in word-initial, word-medial, and inter-morphemic position. Their audio recordings were submitted to statistical analysis and transcribed by phonetically trained research assistants. The results of the acoustic analysis revealed that four participants produced a contrast between [s] and [z] that was not perceived by the transcribers. This is interpreted as evidence for the existence of an intermediate stage of covert contrast in the acquisition of L2 phonology, which, according to the authors, has not yet been reported. In 'Setting Segmental Priorities for English Learners: Evidence from a Longitudinal Study' (*IRAL* 53[2015] 39–60) Murray J. Munro, Tracey M. Derwing, and Ron I. Thomson examine the production of consonants and consonant clusters in Mandarin- and Slavic-speaking adult English L2 learners. The participants took part in a delayed repetition task on four occasions over a two-year period. They were at the beginner proficiency level at the start of their study. A range of sounds—stops, liquids, nasals, and fricatives—was included in the task, in onset and coda positions. Target intelligibility was evaluated by two expert judges. Considerable variability in performance both between and within the two groups was revealed, on the basis of which the authors argue for an individualized rather than common or L1-based pronunciation instruction for L2 learners. Kazuya Saito also deals with instruction in 'Communicative Focus on Second Language Phonetic Form: Teaching Japanese Learners to Perceive and Produce English /ɹ/ without Explicit Instruction' (*AppPsycholing* 36[2015] 377–409). He looks into the effects of form-focused instruction on the L2 speech perception and production of /ɹ/ by Japanese-speaking adult L2 learners of English. Two experimental groups received form-focused instruction—one with and the other without corrective feedback in the form of recasts—on the target pronunciation features of /ɹ/, while the control group received comparable communicative language instruction without focus on phonetic form. During the pre-test and the post-test the participants' perception, controlled production, and spontaneous production of /ɹ/ was assessed with trained and untrained items. The two experimental groups outperformed the control group, but they did not significantly differ from one another. This suggests that form-focused instruction itself can facilitate the development of speech perception and production of /ɹ/, while corrective feedback does not seem to increase the size of instructional gain.

Two papers are concerned with L2 ortography. Reem Alsadoon and Trude Heift look into 'Textual Input Enhancement for Vowel Blindness' in 'A Study with Arabic ESL Learners' (*MLJ* 99[2015] 57–79). The phenomenon of vowel blindness refers to 'Arabic learners' difficulty in the textual decoding and encoding of English vowels' (p. 57), well documented in SLA literature. A study with beginner learners was conducted, in which the experimental group received vowel training in the form of textual input enhancement. An eye tracker recorded the participants' eye movements during the training. The participants' knowledge of word form (i.e. their orthographic vowel knowledge of the word) and word meaning was tested in an online multiple-choice recognition task, administered in the pre-test, the immediate post-test, and the delayed post-test phase. The experimental group's orthographic vowel knowledge of the test items was significantly improved, possibly as a result of longer eye-fixation durations on the target words during the training phase. This confirms the effectiveness of textual input enhancement in reducing vowel blindness. Bene Bassetti and Nathan Atkinson investigate the 'Effects of Orthographic Forms on Pronunciation in Experienced Instructed Second Language Learners' (*AppPsycholing* 36[2015] 67–91). They conducted four studies with Italian-speaking instructed L2 learners who had been learning

English for an average of 11.2 years and whose native language (Italian) uses a phonologically transparent writing system. Various orthographic effects on the pronunciation of L2 English segments, morphemes, and words were examined: the effects of 'silent letters' (i.e. letters with a zero phonetic correspondence, e.g. in <lamb> or <l> in <walk>) by means of a word-reading task and a word-repetition task in Study 1, the effects of vowel spelling on vowel duration by means of a reading-aloud task in Study 2, the effects of the morphemic spelling of the past tense marker <ed> by means of a verb paradigm-production task in Study 3, and the effects of spelling in homophonic words by means of a reading-aloud task and a word-repetition task in Study 4. The participants' speech production was affected by orthographic forms in all sub-studies, especially in reading-aloud tasks, suggesting that L2 speech production is affected by orthography.

Five papers deal with spontaneous L2 speech production focusing on accentedness and/or comprehensibility. Kazuya Saito looks into 'Experience Effects on the Development of Late Second Language Learners' Oral Proficiency' (*LangLearn* 65[2015] 563–95), with L2 experience being operationalized as length of residence (LOR). Data was collected from three groups of adult Japanese-speaking L2 learners of English who had been living in Canada for different lengths of time (the shortest period being eight months), a baseline group of adult Japanese-speaking L2 learners who had just arrived in Canada, and a baseline group of native English speakers in a picture-description task. Speech samples were rated for accentedness and comprehensibility (ease of understanding) by native-speaking English raters and then submitted to pronunciation, fluency, vocabulary, and grammar analyses. LOR proved to be a good predictor of improved comprehensibility but not of reduced accentedness. Improved comprehensibility was associated with good prosody, optimal speech rate, and proper lexico-grammar usage, and less accented speech with refined segmental accuracy, vocabulary richness, and grammatical complexity. The results show that L2 experience affects comprehensibility and accentedness of L2 speech in a different way. The author also conducted a study into 'The Role of Age of Acquisition in Late Second Language Oral Proficiency Attainment' with Japanese-speaking L2 learners of English focusing on comprehensibility and accentedness of their speech (*SSLA* 37[2015] 713–74). In 'Second Language Comprehensibility Revisited: Investigating the Effects of Learner Background' Dustin Crowther, Pavel Trofimovich, Kazuya Saito, and Talia Isaacs (*TesolQ* 49[2015] 814–37) explore the effect of speakers' L1 on listener judgement of L2 comprehensibility and accentedness. Chinese-, Hindi/Urdu- and Farsi-speaking L2 learners of English performed a picture narrative task. Audio-recorded samples of their L2 speech (or written transcripts of it) were evaluated for comprehensibility, accentedness, and ten linguistic categories from the domains of pronunciation, fluency, lexis, grammar, and discourse by native English speakers by means of continuous sliding scales. The analysis showed that comprehensibility was linked to linguistic categories (namely segmentals, prosody, fluency, lexis, grammar), while accentedness was primarily associated with pronunciation categories (namely segmentals, word stress, intonation). The strength of the relationship between linguistic variables and speech ratings depended on the speakers' L1, especially for comprehensibility. Comprehensibility was most strongly linked to pronunciation for Chinese speakers and to lexico-grammar for Hindi/Urdu speakers, not being strongly associated with any linguistic variable for Farsi speakers. Results suggest that listener judgements of L2 comprehensibility are affected by speakers' L1, especially as far as linguistic influences on comprehensibility are concerned. The same authors (but in a slightly different order) address a question: 'Does a Speaking Task Affect Second Language Comprehensibility?' (*MLJ* 99[2015] 80–95) in a study based on the data from the same corpus as the study described above. A different portion of the data was used in the present study: audio recordings of Chinese, Hindi/Urdu-, Farsi- and Romance-speaking L2 learners of English during their performance in the IELTS long-turn speaking task and the TOEFL iBT integrated listening/reading and speaking task. The same native English speakers rated the audio recordings by means of continuous sliding scales for comprehensibility and ten linguistic categories. The analysis revealed that comprehensibility was associated with different variables in the two tasks: in the IELTS task, it was linked only to pronunciation and fluency variables (namely segmentals, word stress, rhythm, and speech rate) for all groups apart from the Farsi group, while in the cognitively more demanding TOEFL iBT integrated task, it was also additionally associated with several categories from the domains of grammar, lexicon, and discourse for all groups. In addition, L1 effects were observed in the relative strength of obtained associations between linguistic variables and speech ratings. The results suggest that speaking task, in addition to speakers' L1, does indeed affect listener judgements of L2 comprehensibility. Francisco Gallardo del Puerto, María Luisa García Lecumberri, and Esther Gómez Lacabex deal with 'The Assessment of Foreign Accent and Its Communicative Effects by Naïve Native Judges vs. Experienced Non-Native Judges' (*IJAL* 25[2015] 202–24) in order to explore the non-native evaluators' ability to perform foreign accent judgements. Two groups of judges—a group of linguistically trained non-native judges who were teachers of EFL and were familiar with the learners' L1s and a group of naive native judges unfamiliar with the students' L1s—rated speech samples of L2 learners of English who were bilingual in Spanish and Basque. The learners were divided into a group of less experienced learners and a group of more experienced learners. The learners' samples were obtained in a story-telling task and were evaluated for the degree of foreign accent, comprehensibility, and irritation. The two groups of judges assessed the degree of foreign accent and irritation similarly, as well as the samples of more and less experienced learners, differing in their judgements of comprehensibility: the non-native judges rated the samples as more comprehensible than the native judges, probably as a result of their familiarity with the learners' L1s and their foreign accent. Results suggest that non-native listeners can be as reliable foreign accent evaluators as native listeners.

An overview of L2 speech research, together with guidelines for conducting this research, is provided by Laura Colantoni, Jeffrey Steele, and Paola Escudero in *Second Language Speech: Theory and Practice*. The book is divided into four parts: the first part is devoted to theoretical issues in L2 speech research, the second to research methodology used in the field, and the third to previous experimental studies on L2 English, French, and Spanish phonetics and phonology. Directions for future research are also given in the third part. Each chapter includes review questions, with chapters in the third part also including practical tutorials and lab exercises. Answers to the review questions, tutorials, and lab exercises are provided on a companion website, which also includes supplementary materials. More pedagogically oriented is a monograph dedicated to L2 pronunciation research and instruction, *Pronunciation Fundamentals: Evidence-Based Perspectives for L2 Teaching and Research* by Tracey M. Derwing and Murray J. Munro. The book focuses on L2 English, but is relevant for other languages as well. After the chapters explaining key concepts and providing a historical overview of pronunciation teaching, chapters devoted to L2 phonetic acquisition, pronunciation errors, pronunciation instruction research, pronunciation assessment, the role of technology in L2 pronunciation instruction, social aspects of foreign accent, and ethical issues involved in L2 accent reduction follow. A volume devoted to *Teaching and Researching the Pronunciation of English: Studies in Honour of Włodzimierz Sobkowiak*, edited by Ewa Waniek-Klimczak and Mirosław Pawlak, contains pedagogically oriented studies into L2 English pronunciation, some of which are primarily focused on pronunciation instruction. Studies in this group address issues such as learners' beliefs, the application of new technologies in pronunciation teaching, and different types of educational resources. Some of the less practically oriented studies deal with Polish-speaking L2 learners' English pronunciation errors and areas of difficulty in English vowel learning, the importance of the larynx in the study of English pronunciation, the use of L2 accent imitation in the L1 in L2 speech research, and the use of imitation and repair methods in L2 pronunciation teaching.

Moving on to morphosyntax, a broad range of topics and phenomena has been explored in journal articles. Elma Blom and Johanne Paradis look into 'Sources of Individual Differences in the Acquisition of Tense Inflection by English Second Language Learners with and without Specific Language Impairment' (*AppPsycholing* 36[2015] 953–76). Focusing on six morphosyntactic phenomena (subject–verb agreement with copula verb *be*, subject–verb agreement with full verbs, genitive *-s*, negation, plural marker *-s*, canonical verb order) in L2 English of French L1 speakers, Aafke Buyl and Alex Housen examine 'Developmental Stages in Receptive Grammar Acquisition' using 'A Processability Theory Account' (*SLR* 31[2015] 523–50). Søren W. Eskildsen asks 'What Counts as a Developmental Sequence?' and demonstrates 'Exemplar-Based L2 Learning of English Questions' (*LangLearn* 65[2015] 33–62) in a study with Spanish-speaking L2 learners. Nikolay Slavkov investigates 'Long-Distance Wh-Movement and Long-Distance Wh-Movement Avoidance in L2 English' providing 'Evidence from French and Bulgarian Speakers' (*SLR* 31[2015] 179–210). 'Prenominal Adjective Order Preferences in Chinese and German L2 English' are studied by Stefanie Wulff and Stefan Th. Gries in 'A Multifactorial Corpus Study' (*LAB* 5[2015] 122–50). The 'Acquisition of English Verb Transitivity by Native Speakers of Japanese' is explored by Tomonori Nagano (*LAB* 5[2015] 322–55). Jingyu Zhang studies 'Animacy Hierarchy Effects on the Second Language Acquisition of Attributive Psych Adjectives' (*AppPsycholing* 36[2015] 275–98) in English by Chinese-speaking L2 learners. Anna Ewert and Weronika Krzebietke investigate 'Manner and Path of Motion in Descriptions of Motion Trajectories by Polish L2 Users of English' (*ESLAYb* 15[2015] 95–113). Analysing the production of the definite article *the* and plural marking -*s* by Thai-speaking L2 learners of English, Gavin Austin, Nattama Pongpairoj, and Danijela Trenkic provide evidence for 'Structural Competition in Second Language Production' pointing 'Towards a Constraint-Satisfaction Model' (*LangLearn* 65[2015] 689–722) of L2 production/processing. Focusing on 'Clause Linking in L2 English' of Dutch-speaking learners Manon Buysse explores 'The Interaction between Syntax and Semantics' (*ESLAYb* 15[2015] 41–68). Roumyana Slabakova examines 'The Effect of Construction Frequency and Native Transfer on Second Language Knowledge of the Syntax–Discourse Interface' (*AppPsycholing* 36[2015] 671–99) by looking at the acquisition of English topicalization and fronted focus construction by Spanish-speaking L2 learners.

In the area of vocabulary, a volume addressing *Lexical Issues in L2 Writing* has been edited by Päivi Pietilä, Katalin Doró, and Renata Pípalová. The volume is a collection of eight corpus-based studies looking into various lexical aspects of writing in L2 English (or, in one case, L3 French) from different perspectives and using different methodologies. All studies deal with academic writing; the genres considered include free composition, essays, portfolios, BA and MA theses, and monographs; both expository and argumentative prose is included, as well as topics concerning both literature and linguistics. The writers in the studies differ in their L1 backgrounds (L1s being Czech, Danish, Finnish, Hungarian, and Swedish), age, L2 proficiency level, and education. The lexical phenomena considered in the studies include lexical frequency, lexical density, lexical distribution, lexical richness, lexical variation, lexical diversity, lexical sophistication, and lexical errors. Different types of vocabulary are analysed, including academic vocabulary, hedges, reporting verbs, collocations, and lexical bundles. The volume consists of nine chapters. The first, by Katalin Doró and Päivi Pietilä, reviews dominant trends in 'Researching Vocabulary in L2 Writing' focusing on 'Methodological Issues and Pedagogical Implications' (pp. 11–26). The remaining eight chapters, containing empirical studies, belong to one of the three parts of the volume: the first part deals with external influences on L2 vocabulary knowledge, the second focuses on the differences between writing in linguistics and literature, while the third explores syntagmatic relationships in lexis focusing on collocations and lexical bundles.

Quite a number of journal articles have also appeared on the topic of vocabulary. Bastien De Clercq tackles 'The Development of Lexical Complexity in Second Language Acquisition' in 'A Cross-Linguistic Study of L2 French and English' (*ESLAYb* 15[2015] 69–94). 'Nativelike Expression in the Speech of Long-Residency L2 Users' is explored by Britt Erman, Annika Denke, Lars Fant, and Fanny Forsberg Lundell in 'A Study of Multiword Structures in L2 English, French and Spanish' (*IJAL* 25[2015] 160–82) with Swedish-speaking learners. Xian Zhang and Xiaofei Lu conducted a study with Chinese-speaking L2 learners of English into 'The Relationship between Vocabulary Learning Strategies and Breadth and Depth of

Vocabulary Knowledge' (*MLJ* 99[2015] 740–53). Tatsuya Nakata deals with the 'Effects of Expanding and Equal Spacing on Second Language Vocabulary Learning' in a study with Japanese-speaking L2 learners of English, which addresses the following question: 'Does Gradually Increasing Spacing Increase Vocabulary Learning?' (*SSLA* 37[2015] 677–711). Jin Kyoung Hwang, Joshua F. Lawrence, Elaine Mo, and Catherine E. Snow examine 'Differential Effects of a Systematic Vocabulary Intervention on Adolescent Language Minority Students with Varying Levels of English Proficiency' (*IJB* 19[2015] 314–32). In a study with Chinese-speaking L2 learners of English, Stuart Webb and Anna C.-S. Chang tackle the following question: 'How Does Prior Word Knowledge Affect Vocabulary Learning Progress in an Extensive Reading Program?' (*SSLA* 37[2015] 651–75). Yi-chen Chen and Huei-ling Lai look into 'Developing EFL Learners' Metaphoric Competence through Cognitive-Oriented Methods' (*IRAL* 53[2015] 415–38) in a study with Chinese native speakers. Soren W. Eskildsen and Johannes Wagner investigate 'Embodied L2 Construction Learning' (*LangLearn* 65[2015] 268–97), focusing on the learning of English prepositions *under* and *across* by a Spanish native speaker. 'The Effects of Vocabulary Breadth and Depth on English Reading' (*AppLing* 36[2015] 611–34) are explored by Miao Li and John R. Kirby in a study with Chinese-speaking L2 learners of English. Based on the data from a corpus of L2 English, Scott A. Crossley, Tom Salsbury, and Danielle S. McNamara deal with 'Assessing Lexical Proficiency Using Analytic Ratings', making 'A Case for Collocation Accuracy' (*AppLing* 36[2015] 570–90).

Among studies devoted to discourse, Mary Grantham O'Brien and Caroline Féry deal with the acquisition of information structure in an L2 in 'Dynamic Localization in Second Language English and German' (*BLC* 18[2015] 400–18). More specifically, they investigate the marking of newness and givenness by means of morphosyntactic and phonological cues in L2 English and German, namely articles, word order, and pitch accents. Intermediate and advanced German-speaking L2 learners of English and English-speaking L2 learners of German described constellations of pictures in a dynamic localization task, first in their L2 and two weeks later in their L1. In each picture a new or reintroduced toy animal changed position relative to other (given) toy animals in a constellation. The results showed that English and German native speakers use the same repertoire of morphosyntactic and prosodic cues to mark newness and givenness in their L1 differently, and that they both exhibit non-native-like behaviour when they use this repertoire to mark newness and givenness in each other's language as the L2. According to the authors, their non-native-like behaviour might be due to underspecification, L1 transfer, or processing limitations, and it indicates that acquiring properties at the interface of morphosyntax, phonology, and discourse poses a challenge for L2 learners. Sandrine Zufferey, Willem Mak, Liesbeth Degand, and Ted Sanders look into 'Advanced Learners' Comprehension of Discourse Connectives' focusing on 'The Role of L1 Transfer across On-Line and Off-Line Tasks' (*SLR* 31[2015] 389–411). Advanced Dutch-speaking L2 learners of English, advanced French-speaking L2 learners of English, and native English speakers participated in an offline grammaticality judgement task and an online reading experiment using eye-tracking, in which their ability to detect non-native-like semantic uses of the connectives *when* and *if* in English, often produced by L2 learners as a result of transfer from French and Dutch, was tested. The learners performed in a fully native-like way in the online task, but not in the offline task, in which they proved less able than the native speakers to identify incorrect uses of connectives which corresponded to licensed uses in their L1. Such results point to a discrepancy between the learners' implicit and explicit knowledge of connectives and the operation of L1 transfer in their comprehension of connectives.

Moving on to pragmatics, Wei Ren deals with *L2 Pragmatic Development in Study Abroad Contexts*. This monograph reports on a longitudinal study on the effect of study abroad on L2 learners' productive and receptive pragmatic competence and their cognitive processes during speech-act production. Two groups of Chinese-speaking L2 learners of English took part in a study: a group of MA students studying at a university in the UK and a control group of MA students studying at a university in China. Data was collected by means of the multimedia elicitation task, the appropriateness judgement task, and the retrospective verbal reports over a one-year period. The results showed that some aspects of L2 pragmatic competence developed to a greater degree in the study abroad context, while other aspects developed to a similar degree in the two learning contexts. The relationship between adult speakers' communication strategic competence and their language proficiency is explored by Chihsia Tang in 'Applications of Stalling Mechanisms in Chinese–English Bilinguals' L1 and L2 Spoken Discourse' (*IJB* 19[2015] 92–114). The term 'stalling mechanism' is used in the paper to refer to the communication strategy of hesitation. Chinese-speaking L2 learners of English took part in a non-interactive story-retelling activity and an interactive question-answering activity. The same types of stalling strategy were observed in their L1 and L2 utterances, namely unfilled pause, umming and ah-ing, sound prolongation, lexicalized filler, self-repetition, and other-repetition. However, the participants were found to use a greater variety of Chinese than English lexicalized fillers, which is partly explained by their insufficient exposure to authentic English communications. In addition, the frequency of the stalling strategies in the participants' L2 discourse was about twice that in their L1 discourse, suggesting, according to the author, that L2 processing is less automatic than L1 processing. A valuable contribution to the field of L2 pragmatics (and beyond) is *Sociolinguistics and Second Language Acquisition: Learning to Use Language in Context* [2014] by Kimberly L. Geeslin and Avizia Yim Long, which bridges the gap between sociolinguistics and SLA. This textbook deals with social factors in L2 acquisition and with the development of L2 sociolinguistic competence, defined as 'a learner's ability to interpret an utterance for its social meaning' (p. 5) and viewed as part of communicative competence. The book reviews basic concepts and issues in the study of sociolinguistic variation, provides an overview of the social approaches to L2 acquisition as well as of the cognitive and variationist approaches to the development of L2 sociolinguistic competence, reviews empirical research into the acquisition of L2 sociolinguistic competence, and discusses the application of sociolinguistics to L2 instruction. It includes examples from different languages as well as summary tables, lists of additional readings, discussion questions, and application activities.

As far as work into L2 processing is concerned, Yoonsang Song looks at 'L2 Processing of Plural Inflection in English' by Korean-speaking learners (*LangLearn* 65[2015] 233–67). Jung Hyun Lim and Kiel Christianson explore 'Second Language Sensitivity to Agreement Errors', providing 'Evidence from Eye Movements during Comprehension and Translation' (*AppPsycholing* 36[2015] 1283–315) of Korean-speaking L2 learners of English. 'Referential Context Effects in Non-Native Relative Clause Ambiguity Resolution' (*IJB* 19[2015] 298–313) are examined by Hui-Yu Pan, Sarah Schimke, and Claudia Felser in a study with German- and Chinese-speaking L2 learners of English. Also focusing on relative clauses, Koji Suda investigates 'The Influences of Proficiency Levels and Working Memory Capacities on Sentence Comprehension by Japanese Learners of English' (*ESLAYb* 15[2015] 143–63). Looking at the processing of object relatives in English by Dutch-speaking L2 learners, Edith Kaan, Jocelyn C. Ballantyne, and Frank Wijnen tackle 'Effects of Reading Speed on Second-Language Sentence Processing' (*AppPsycholing* 36[2015] 799–830). Holger Hopp studies 'Individual Differences in the Second Language Processing of Object–Subject Ambiguities' (*AppPsycholing* 36[2015] 129–73) on the part of German-speaking learners of English. 'The Role of Island Constraints in Second Language Sentence Processing' (*LangAcq* 22[2015] 384–416) is explored by Eunah Kim, Soondo Baek, and Annie Tremblay in a study on the processing of English *wh*-questions by Spanish- and Korean-speaking L2 learners. Focusing on definite articles, Vasiliki Chondrogianni, Nada Vasić, Theodoros Marinis, and Elma Blom look into 'Production and On-Line Comprehension of Definiteness in English and Dutch by Monolingual and Sequential Bilingual Children' (*SLR* 31[2015] 309–41). Eunah Kim, Silvina Montrul, and James Yoon investigate 'The On-Line Processing of Binding Principles in Second Language Acquisition' providing 'Evidence from Eye Tracking' (*AppPsycholing* 36[2015] 1317–74) coming from Korean-speaking L2 learners of English during their processing of reflexives and pronouns. In 'Fatal Mistake, Awful Mistake, or Extreme Mistake?' Suhad Sonbul examines 'Frequency Effects on Off-Line/On-Line Collocational Processing' (*BLC* 18[2015] 419–37) in a study with English L2 learners coming from a variety of L1 backgrounds. Brent Wolter and Junko Yamashita also deal with 'Processing Collocations in a Second Language' by testing Japanese-speaking L2 learners of English and ask whether this is 'A Case of First Language Activation?' (*AppPsycholing* 36[2015] 1193–221). Finally, Ewa Tomczak and Anna Ewert explore 'Real and Fictive Motion Processing in Polish L2 Users of English and Monolinguals', providing 'Evidence for Different Conceptual Representations' (*MLJ* 99[2015] 49–65).

Among studies on the development of language skills, Mirosław Pawlak and Ewa Waniek-Klimczak address (as editors) *Issues in Teaching, Learning and Testing Speaking in a Second Language*. This collection of sixteen papers explores linguistic, cognitive, and affective factors in the development of speaking in the L2 and contains proposals for teaching and assessing this complex skill. The majority of the papers report on empirical studies, mostly on L2 English. The book is divided into three parts. The first part consists of five papers aiming to establish connections between theory, research, and classroom practice in relation to issues such as developing spontaneity in conversation, intercultural communication, and the use of hedging devices. Six papers in the second part focus on the factors that influence speaking skills, such as willingness to communicate, anxiety, communication strategies, and the role of silence. The third part includes five papers concerned with teaching and assessing speaking skills, tackling issues such as the use of videoconferencing and storybooks as teaching devices, business meetings as a genre, and self-assessment.

Bringing many strands of research together is a monograph *Investigating Linguistic Knowledge of a Second Language* by Runhan Zhang. It reports on an experimental study on the development of linguistic knowledge (both implicit and explicit) in L2 English and its relationship to general language proficiency and individual learner differences in the classroom context. Participants in the study were Chinese-speaking advanced L2 learners of English, studying English at university. The book consists of three parts. The first part (chapters 2 to 4) introduces the concepts of implicit and explicit knowledge, reviews previous empirical studies that explore ways of measuring implicit and explicit L2 knowledge, and presents the study results which concern the participants' implicit and explicit knowledge. The second part (chapters 5 to 7) presents a model of general L2 proficiency, reviews previous empirical studies on the relationship between implicit/explicit knowledge and general L2 proficiency, and reports on the study results addressing this issue. The third part (chapters 8 and 9) describes four individual difference variables, namely language analytic ability, motivation, foreign language anxiety, and learner beliefs, reports on the study results relating to the role of individual difference variables in the participants' linguistic knowledge, summarizes the results of the whole study, discusses its theoretical contributions, pedagogical implications, and limitations, and provides suggestions for future research. A related study on 'Measuring University-Level L2 Learners' Implicit and Explicit Linguistic Knowledge' (*SSLA* 37[2015] 457–86) has also been conducted by Runhan Zhang.

In the area of individual learner differences, Keita Kikuchi examines *Demotivation in Second Language Acquisition* providing *Insights from Japan*. The monograph reports on four empirical studies on demotivators in Japanese-speaking instructed L2 learners of English—two quantitative, one qualitative, and one mixed-methods study. The quantitative studies address the topic from cognitive and individual difference perspectives while the other two studies deal with it from social and environmental perspectives. Before presenting the four studies in chapters 4 to 7, the author explains the concept of demotivation in relation to the concept of motivation, reviews previous studies on demotivators, demotivation, and strategies for dealing with learner demotivation, and contextualizes the study of demotivation within the field of SLA in chapters 1 to 3. Chapters 8 to 10 contain a summary of the findings of the four empirical studies, a discussion of how teachers can deal with learner demotivation using motivational strategies, and suggestions for future research. Masuko Miyahara deals with *Emerging Self-Identities and Emotion in Foreign Language Learning* adopting *A Narrative-Oriented Approach*. The monograph reports on a qualitative longitudinal study, based on data from narrative interviews, on identity construction and development of Japanese-speaking classroom L2 learners of English. Combining psychological and sociological perspectives, the study explores how the learners' past English-learning experiences, their relationship and orientation to English, and their views of themselves as English users influence their identity as learners. The introductory chapter presents research questions and describes the context of the study; chapter 2 provides the theoretical framework(s) within which the study is conducted; chapter 3 describes the narrative approach in identity studies; chapter 4 details the research design of the study; chapters 5 to 7 present individual data from the six study participants; chapter 8 connects the data of all the participants and puts it in relation to the research questions; the final chapter discusses the pedagogical implications of the study, acknowledges its limitations, and proposes directions for future research. Identity construction is also addressed by Yan Zhao in *Second Language Creative Writers: Identities and Writing Processes*. The monograph presents an interview and think-aloud protocol-based study investigating how L2 creative writers construct their autobiographical identity in their retrospective accounts of their literacy, linguistic, educational, and professional experience. Participants in the study were fifteen L2 creative writers who were all advanced adult L2 learners of English and whose native languages included Chinese, Malay, French, German, Spanish, Catalan, Russian, Latvian, Farsi, and Hindi. The study is intended as an integration of two fields of L2 studies: L2 creative writing research and L2 writer identity research. It is based on the assumption that 'L2 creative writing is simultaneously a cognitive construct and a social phenomenon and these two are mutually exclusive' (p. 45). The book consists of eight chapters. Following the introduction, chapter 2 explains the theoretical background of the study; chapter 3 describes its methodology; chapters 4 and 5 present the results of the quantitative data analyses; chapters 6 and 7 describe the results of the qualitative data analyses; the final chapter summarizes the findings of the study, discusses its implications for the two fields of L2 studies involved, points to some limitations of the study, and proposes a creative approach to L2 disciplinary writing. Largely belonging to the field of individual learner differences is a volume edited by Ewa Piechurska-Kuciel and Magdalena Szyszka, *The Ecosystem of the Foreign Language Learner: Selected Issues*. Applying the metaphor of the ecosystem to the foreign language learning process, the volume explores how the internal or personal ecosystem of the learner, in which the learner's affective states and cognitive processes are at work, interacts with other personal ecosystems (e.g. those of parents and teachers) and culture. In other words, the volume examines the interaction of internal (affective and cognitive) and external (social and cultural) forces with the ecosystem of the foreign language learner. This is reflected in the volume's structure: six chapters in the first part look at the influence of internal factors/processes on language learning, namely dreaming, attitudes, willingness to communicate, personality, cognitive load, and cognitive associations, while six chapters in the second part deal with the influence of external factors/forces, such as teachers' level of emotional intelligence, teachers' foreign language speaking anxiety, parents' level of foreign language knowledge and the use of rhetoric as a teaching tool, and the culture component in L2–L1 translation. Most of the chapters are empirical studies involving L2 learners of English; the learners' native language is Polish, with the exception of Spanish and Arabic in two studies.

Dealing with L2 acquisition in naturalistic settings, Fanny Forsberg Lundell and Inge Bartning have edited a collection that explores the phenomenon of *Cultural Migrants and Optimal Language Acquisition*. The volume introduces a concept of 'cultural migrant' to refer to 'individuals who migrate from one country to another for cultural purposes' (p. 5) and examines the influence of cultural migration, a factor that has received little attention so far, on L2 ultimate attainment. The studies are highly original in linking SLA research and migration studies. In addition to the introductory and concluding chapters, there are seven empirical studies looking into linguistic, psycholinguistic, sociolinguistic, and pragmatic aspects of L2 acquisition with Italian, French, Spanish, and English as L2s. Studies dealing with L2 English investigate vocabulary development in Swedish migrants in London ('L2 English Vocabulary in a Long-Residency Swedish Group Compared to a Group of English Native Speakers' by Britt Erman and Margareta Lewis, pp. 115–34), the use of discourse-pragmatic markers by Polish and Chinese migrants in Dublin ('Migratory Experience and Second Language Acquisition among Polish and Chinese Migrants in Dublin, Ireland' by Chloé Diskin and Vera Regan, pp. 137–77), and the sociolinguistic, temporal and socio-biographical aspects of L2 attainment in Polish migrants in the UK ('Acculturation as the Key to the Ultimate Attainment? The Case of Polish–English Bilinguals in the UK' by Kate Hammer and Jean-Marc Dewaele, pp. 178–202). In the concluding chapter the editors relate the findings of the studies to the notion of nativelikeness, discuss their implications for Schumann's acculturation model (J.H. Schumann 'Research on the Acculturation Model for Second Language Acquisition' in *JMMD* 6[1986] 379–92), and give some directions for future research on cultural migrants.

Focusing on L2 acquisition in instructed contexts, Jelena Mihaljević Djigunović and Marta Medved Krajnović have edited a volume on *Early Learning and Teaching of English* examining *New Dynamics of Primary English*, a collection of nine empirical studies, together with an introduction and afterword, reporting on some of the results of the five-year 'Learning English from an Early Age: Analysis of Learner Language' research project conducted within a Croatian socio-educational context. Adopting a variety of theoretical frameworks and using a variety of methodologies, the studies look into different aspects of learning EFL by Croatian-speaking young learners. Issues addressed include: the relationship between individual learner differences (in particular motivation, attitudes and self-concept), age, and language proficiency ('Individual Differences among Young EFL Learners: Age- or Proficiency-Related? A Look from the Affective Learner Factors Perspective' by Jelena Mihaljević Djigunović, pp. 10–36), the development of pronunciation ('Croatian Primary School Pupils and English Pronunciation in Light of the Emergence of English as a Lingua Franca' by Višnja Josipović Smojver, pp. 37–65), the acquisition of markers of definiteness and indefiniteness ('Acquisition of Markers of Definiteness and Indefiniteness in Early EFL' by

Lovorka Zergollern-Miletić, pp. 66–79), the acquisition of the present ('Present Tense Development in 11- to 13-Year-Old EFL Learners' by Marta Medved Krajnović and Irena Kocijan Pevec, pp. 80–109), the 'Associat[ion of] Temporal Meanings with Past and Present Verb Forms' by Smiljana Narančić Kovač and Ivana Milković, pp. 110–48), learners' lexicon networks ('What Vocabulary Networks Reveal about Young Learners' Language' by Renata Geld, pp. 149–73), the development of listening and reading skills ('Receptive Skills in the Linguistic and Non-Linguistic Context of EFL Learning' by Renata Šamo, pp. 174–90), and the development of oral proficiency ('Early EFL Development from a Dynamic Systems Perspective' by Stela Letica Krevelj and Marta Medved Krajnović, pp. 191–213). A model of EFL learning with implications for EFL teaching is offered in the afterword.

Among work on ELT relevant to SLA, Anne Swan, Pamela Aboshiha, and Adrian Holliday deal (in the role of editors) with *(En)Countering Native-Speakerism* from *Global Perspectives*. The volume addresses the concept of native-speakerism, that is, native-speaker dominance and the belief in their superiority, in ELT. Twelve chapters in the volume written by ELT professionals from several continents contain critical reflections on native-speakerism based on authors' observations and past experiences. The issues discussed include cultural disbelief characteristic of some native-speaking teachers, the role of native-speakerism in the construction of professional identity, and the type of research methodology suitable for investigating the impact of native-speakerism.

Turning to work of general relevance to SLA, 2015 has seen the publication of the second edition of Rod Ellis's acclaimed textbook *Understanding Second Language Acquisition*, which provides an overview of key topics and research findings in SLA. Compared to the first edition, published in 1985, the new edition has retained some thematic areas and omitted others, adding new ones as well. Among the areas that have been retained, there is the role of age in L2 acquisition, individual differences in L2 acquisition, the order and sequence of L2 acquisition, variability in learner language, the role of the L1 in L2 acquisition and the interactionist perspective on L2 acquisition. The treatment of these areas has been fully updated in the new edition. A separate chapter devoted to learning strategies has been omitted, as well as the treatment of linguistic universals and UG. The chapter dealing with theories of L2 acquisition has been replaced by two new chapters, addressing cognitive and sociolinguistic approaches to L2 acquisition. Finally, a single chapter considering the role of formal instruction in L2 acquisition has been replaced by two chapters, on explicit and implicit instruction. The concluding chapter contains some general statements about L2 acquisition and a discussion about the relevance of SLA for language pedagogy. *Key Terms in Second Language Acquisition* by Bill VanPatten and Alessandro G. Benati, first published in 2010, has also been republished. This reference book contains a concise overview of key questions, key theories/frameworks, and key terms in SLA, as well as a list of key readings in SLA. Each of these thematic areas receives a chapter of its own. The additional, introductory, chapter covers a definition of SLA, a brief history of the field, and a brief discussion of the relationship between SLA and language teaching. The chapter on key questions contains nine of the essential questions in SLA and a summary of the findings on them. The chapters on key terms and key readings do not aim to be exhaustive, but are meant to provide basic information to suit the beginner in the field. The book content has been updated for the new edition.

Yet another second edition published in 2015 is to be found among works devoted to SLA theories, namely *Theories in Second Language Acquisition: An Introduction*, edited by Bill VanPatten and Jessica Williams. The volume contains a survey of the major linguistic, psycholinguistic, and cognitive theories in SLA. Compared to the first edition of 2007, two new theories have been added—the declarative/procedural model and the complexity theory—and one theory has been omitted—the autonomous induction theory. The introductory chapter, written by the editors, contains a discussion of the terms 'theory', 'model', 'hypothesis', and 'constructs', a list of ten observations that need to be explained by SLA theories, as well as a short discussion of the debate concerning the roles of explicit and implicit learning and knowledge in L2 acquisition. The subsequent eleven chapters are devoted to individual theories, and each is written by some of their main proponents (the exception is the chapter devoted to early theories, which covers more than one theory and is written by the editors). They are structured around the following topics: the theory and its constructs, what counts as evidence for the theory, common misunderstandings, an exemplary study, how the theory addresses the observable phenomena of SLA, and the explicit/implicit debate; they all close with discussion questions and suggested further reading. The final chapter, written by Lourdes Ortega, compares the theories included in the book with the ten observed phenomena presented in the introductory chapter. A glossary of key terms can be found at the end of the book. Four of the theories included in the volume have also received book-length treatment in 2015. Aspects of the input-processing theory relating to input processing at lexical levels are developed by Joe Barcroft in *Lexical Input Processing and Vocabulary Learning*. The monograph is intended as a synthesis of theory and research in the area of lexical input processing, clarifying how future research in this area can promote our understanding of L2 vocabulary learning and L2 acquisition in general. *Theoretical and Methodological Developments in Processability Theory* are explored in a volume edited by Kristof Baten, Aafke Buyl, Katja Lochtman, and Mieke Van Herreweghe. Contributions explore the interface between morphosyntax and other linguistic domains (pragmatics, semantics, and discourse), constraints on productive and receptive processing, and practical applications of processability theory in instructed settings, which is reflected in the tripartite organization of the volume. Each part of the volume also contains a response paper, in which theoretical issues raised and empirical findings presented in the preceding chapters are discussed. Aspects of the interactionist theory are explored by Hossein Nassaji in *The Interactional Feedback Dimension in Instructed Second Language Learning: Linking Theory, Research, and Practice*. The monograph provides a comprehensive account of the theoretical, empirical, and pedagogical issues concerning the role of interactional feedback in L2 acquisition. It addresses the question of how interactional feedback is provided, used, and processed and how it promotes L2 acquisition. Empirical studies reviewed in the book include those involving child and adult L2 learners and those conducted in classroom and laboratory settings. The book consists of nine chapters, each of which has a list of objectives at the beginning and a list of discussion questions at the end. The first chapter contains a review of key terms and concepts. The remaining nine chapters belong to one of the four parts of the book; the first part provides a theoretical framework for the subsequent parts, Part II contains a review of empirical studies, the third part deals with various factors affecting interactional feedback, while Part IV discusses the pedagogical implications of the issues tackled in the book and contains recommendations for classroom practice. From the perspective of sociocultural theory, Rémi A. van Compernolle provides an account of the role of interaction in L2 development in *Interaction and Second Language Development: A Vygotskian Perspective.* After the introduction, the book's second chapter presents key concepts and theoretical issues in sociocultural theory, while the remaining seven chapters examine different domains of research within this theory, such as communicative interaction, negotiation for meaning, the role of L1 interaction in L2 classroom contexts, participation and active reception, dynamic assessment, and interactional competence. Excerpts from authentic conversations are dispersed throughout the book to illustrate the points discussed. Each chapter ends with pedagogical implications, a data set (in the form of a transcript of classroom interaction) with instructions for analysis, and discussion questions. Links for accessing videos for the data sets for analysis are also provided.

The notion of language proficiency has been extensively covered by Jan H. Hulstijn in *Language Proficiency in Native and Non-Native Speakers: Theory and Research.* The monograph presents a theory of language proficiency, referred to as the theory of basic and higher language cognition (the BLC-HLC theory). The book consists of ten chapters falling into two groups, the first dealing with theoretical and the second with empirical issues. The BLC-HLC theory is presented in chapters 3 to 5 against the theoretical background provided in chapters 1 and 2. Chapters 6 to 8 present a critical review of empirical studies on language proficiency in native speakers, language proficiency in non-native speakers, and the relationship between L1 and L2 literacy respectively. Chapter 9 discusses conceptual and methodological issues related to measuring language proficiency (not for educational purposes) in SLA and bilingualism studies, also providing a list of methodological recommendations. Chapter 10 critically assesses the concept of L2 proficiency levels in scales of educational assessment, such as the CEFR, and proposes solutions to some of the problems identified in this regard. The notion of language proficiency is related to the notion of *Implicit and Explicit Learning of Languages,* explored in a volume edited by Patrick Rebuschat. The volume comprises eighteen chapters (plus an introduction) written by linguists, cognitive psychologists, developmental psychologists, educationalists, and computer scientists, approaching the topic from a variety of theoretical perspectives and by means of different methodologies. The volume consists of three parts: ten chapters in the first part examine different theoretical issues in the study of implicit and explicit learning, five chapters in Part II review research paradigms and methods used in this type of research (e.g. artificial grammar learning, eye tracking, event-related potentials), while three chapters in the third part discuss practical applications of research into implicit and explicit learning in instructed L2 acquisition.

In the area of language processing, *The Cambridge Handbook of Bilingual Processing*, edited by John W. Schwieter, provides a comprehensive overview of current theoretical thinking and empirical findings in bilingual processing. Considering L2 acquisition as a form of bilingualism, the volume's thirty chapters are organized into six thematic areas: theories and methodologies, acquisition and development, comprehension and representation, production, control, and consequences of bilingualism. The handbook thus considers in detail how a bilingual mind acquires, comprehends, produces, and controls multiple languages and what the cognitive and neuro-cognitive consequences of being bilingual are. An overview of research into *Bilingual Figurative Language Processing* is provided in a volume edited by Roberto R. Heredia and Anna B. Cieślicka, connecting two complex topics in the field of language processing: figurative language and bilingualism. Contributions deal with the acquisition, comprehension, production, and processing of non-literal language in bilinguals from psycholinguistic and neurolinguistic perspectives, touching upon metaphors, idioms, phrasal verbs, humour, and irony. The volume is divided into four parts: the first focuses on theoretical, the second on methodological, and the fourth on cross-linguistic and pedagogical issues, while the third part presents some of the existing models of bilingual figurative language processing. Each chapter ends with a list of keywords, thought questions, suggested student research projects, related Internet sites, and suggested further reading, making the volume a good platform for further explorations of the topic.

Formulaic language is in the focus of interest of David Wood's *Fundamentals of Formulaic Language: An Introduction*, the fifth chapter of which, 'Formulaic Language and Acquisition—First and Second' (pp. 67–80), provides a short overview of research into L2 (and L1) acquisition of formulaic language. The author stresses that work on L2 acquisition of formulaic language has been relatively scarce and that examining the links between use of formulaic language and SLA theories might be a most promising area of study.

In the field of individual learner differences, *The Psychology of the Language Learner Revisited* by Zoltán Dörnyei and Stephen Ryan presents an up-to-date overview of theory and research on individual learner differences. The book is based on Zoltán Dörnyei's *The Psychology of the Language Learner: Individual Differences in Second Language Acquisition*, published in 2005, but in addition to updating the empirical basis of the original text, it also enters into dialogue with it in order to take into account reconceptualization that several individual difference constructs have undergone in the meantime. The book retains the structure of the original: after the introductory chapter containing a general discussion of the field, six chapters dedicated to personality, language aptitude, motivation, learning styles and cognitive styles, learning strategies, and other learner characteristics (creativity, anxiety, willingness to communicate, self-esteem, learner beliefs) follow; the concluding chapter discusses the theoretical changes that the field of individual differences is presently undergoing. Working memory is sometimes considered as an individual difference variable. The role of *Working Memory in Second Language Acquisition and Processing* is examined in a collection of papers edited by Zhisheng (Edward) Wen, Mailce Borges Mota, and Arthur McNeill. The volume addresses the foremost theoretical and methodological issues related to this topic and contains contributions from cognitive psychologists and cognitively oriented SLA researchers, with the aim of bridging the gap between cognitive psychology and SLA in the study of working memory. The volume's nine empirical and seven commentary chapters are organized into four sections: the first addresses theoretical perspectives and models, the second the role of working memory in L2 processing, the third the role of working memory in L2 interaction and performance, and the fourth the role of working memory in L2 instruction and development. The final chapter is a commentary by John Williams ('Working Memory in SLA Research: Challenges and Prospects', pp. 301–7) that identifies potential challenges and advocates a top-down approach to the study of the role of working memory in SLA. The role of age as an individual difference factor in classroom L2 learning is examined by Amelia Lambelet and Raphael Berthele in *Age and Foreign Language Learning in School*. The monograph reviews the main theoretical issues and empirical findings relating to the question of how age of first exposure influences the rate and the outcome of foreign language learning at school. It consists of four chapters in addition to an introduction and a conclusion: chapter 1 introduces the key terms, concepts, and methods in the study of the age factor; chapter 2 presents the main theories, hypotheses, and studies pertaining to the influence of age on L1 acquisition and L2 acquisition in naturalistic contexts; chapter 3 contains an overview of studies on age effects on L2 acquisition in classroom settings, also discussing the role of attitudes, motivation, and learner strategies in relation to age; chapter 4 examines how age of first exposure interacts with factors related to instruction and curriculum (e.g. contact hours, type of instruction, L2 exposure outside school) and factors related to the students themselves (e.g. motivation and attitudes, learning difficulties, individual bilingualism) in the foreign language learning setting; the concluding chapter identifies a number of gaps that need to be filled by future research.

Among studies on classroom L2 acquisition, *Domains and Directions in the Development of TBLT: A Decade of Plenaries from the International Conference*, edited by Martin Bygate, is a collection of papers based on plenary addresses from the International Conference on Task-Based Language Teaching in the period from 2005 to 2013. Task-based language teaching is an approach to language education which 'places tasks at the centre of the teaching and learning enterprise' (p. xvi). The papers explore key topics in TBLT. Most of these are rather pedagogically oriented; more theoretically oriented topics include: the effect of ensuring different types of focus on form on task performance ('TBLT: Building the Road as We Travel' by Mike Long, pp. 10–26), the effect of varying the aspects of task design and sequencing on task performance ('The Cognition Hypothesis, Second Language Task Demands, and the SSARC Model of Pedagogic Task Sequencing' by Peter Robinson, pp. 87–122), the effect of varying on-task conditions on task performance ('Limited Attention Capacity and

Cognition: Two Hypotheses Regarding Second Language Performance on Tasks' by Peter Skehan, pp. 123–56), and the use of tasks with the purpose of engaging learners in different types of discourse ('Tasks, Experiential Learning, and Meaning Making Activities: A Functional Approach' by Bernard A. Mohan, Tammy Slater, Gulbahar H. Beckett, and Esther Tong, pp. 157–92). *Subtitles and Language Learning: Principles, Strategies and Practical Experiences*, edited by Yves Gambier, Annamaria Caimi, and Cristina Mariotti, is another collection of papers originally presented at an international conference. It aims to provide an overview of research on the use of subtitles and audiovisuals in formal and informal foreign language learning contexts. The papers can be divided into four groups: the first group contains two review papers addressing the relationship between subtitles and language learning based on empirical findings accumulated over the past thirty years, the second group consists of four papers discussing aspects and/or reporting on the results or practical implementations of an EU research project into subtitles and language learning, while the third and the fourth parts present four papers each reporting on experimental and classroom-based studies respectively on the role of subtitles in language learning.

Spanning corpus linguistics and SLA, *The Cambridge Handbook of Learner Corpus Research*, edited by Sylviane Granger, Gaëtanelle Gilquin, and Fanny Meunier, aims to provide a comprehensive overview of the rapidly growing field of learner corpus research, within which work on L2 English has always occupied an important position. The handbook is divided into five parts, devoted to learner corpus design and methodology, analysis of learner language, learner corpus research and SLA, learners corpus research and language teaching, and learner corpus research and natural language processing. The six chapters addressing learner corpus research and SLA focus on SLA theory, L1 transfer, formulaic language, developmental patterns, variability, and learning context. All chapters in the volume have the same layout and contain an introduction to the topic, a discussion of core issues, a description of two to four representative studies, critical assessment of the core issues with an outline of future directions, and an annotated list of key readings. An interesting feature of the volume is that, in addition to author and subject indexes, it also includes a corpus and a software (tools) index. A survey of learner corpus research is also provided in a chapter entitled 'Learner Language' by Gaëtanelle Gilquin and Sylviane Granger (in Biber and Reppen, eds., *The Cambridge Handbook of English Corpus Linguistics*, pp. 418–35). It contains a critical discussion of previous work in learner corpus research and a presentation of an empirical case study. Those more oriented towards teaching practice will find the chapters on 'Classroom Applications of Corpus Analysis' by Thomas Cobb and Alex Boulton (pp. 478–97) and on 'Corpus versus Non-Corpus-Informed Pedagogical Materials: Grammar as the Focus' by Fanny Meunier and Randi Reppen (pp. 498–514) of interest.

Of general relevance to SLA are also two books devoted to research methodology in applied linguistics. Wide in scope is a volume edited by Brian Paltridge and Aek Phakiti, *Research Methods in Applied Linguistics: A*

*Practical Resource*. The volume is divided into two parts: the first concerns research methods and approaches, and the second different research areas. The methods/approaches and areas included are those most relevant to language learning and teaching. Of particular relevance for SLA are, for example, quantitative, qualitative, and mixed methods research, experimental research, case studies, research synthesis, ethics, speaking, listening, reading, writing, grammar, vocabulary, pragmatics, motivation, language learner strategies, and young learners. The first part of the book contains fifteen chapters, most of which are structured in such a way as to address the assumptions underlying and the methodology pertaining to a particular approach, issues of validity and reliability, techniques and instruments used in the approach, a sample study, and resources for further reading. The last chapter in this part discusses the development of a research project. Sixteen chapters contained in the second part of the book include a synthesis of current thinking and research as well as a summary of the research strategies and techniques pertaining to a particular area of study, a sample study (or sample studies), and resources for further reading. The book also contains a glossary of key research terms. Published in 2014, a highly practical source is *Writing about Quantitative Research in Applied Linguistics* by Lindy Woodrow. The book opens with a glossary of key terms. This is followed by an introduction and fifteen chapters belonging to three thematic areas: general issues concerning writing about quantitative research (e.g. writing about research design and participants, issues of reliability, validity, and ethics, presenting descriptive statistics), writing about the most common statistical procedures in applied linguistics (e.g. *t*-tests, ANOVA, regression, correlation, factor analysis, non-parametric tests), and practical issues relating to publishing quantitative research in applied linguistics (in journal articles, book chapters, and books). The book closes with a list of useful resources for conducting and writing about quantitative research in applied linguistics.

Of related interest to SLA is work on *Multilingualism*, where Anat Stavans and Charlotte Hoffmann explore societal and individual multilingualism, using this term to refer to the use of more than two languages. In the part of the book in which they focus on individual multilingualism, they in fact deal with the phenomenon of trilingualism. The topics discussed in this part of the book include multilingual competence, multilingual language processing, multilingual language use (including trilingual language mixing and code-switching), language choice, negotiation of identities, multilingual education, and multilingual literacies. The topic of cross-linguistic influence in L3 acquisition is addressed in nine empirical studies collected in *Crosslinguistic Influence and Crosslinguistic Interaction in Multilingual Language Learning*, edited by Gessica De Angelis, Ulrike Jessner, and Marijana Kresić. Languages dealt with include English, Italian, Scottish Gaelic, Dutch, Finnish, Spanish, Catalan, and German. The volume testifies to the vibrancy of L3 acquisition, a relatively young field of enquiry.

## 11. English as a Lingua Franca

With its twenty years of investigation, ELF has produced a substantial body of research, ranging from studies dealing with different levels of linguistic analysis to investigations on different applied linguistic contexts and domains. It has also shown a considerable increase in the number of researchers involved in investigating this phenomenon and in the range of publication outlets too (see AILA ELF ReN for a list of research publications at english-lingua-franca.org). Some of these are journals dedicated to the field, such as the *Journal of English as a Lingua Franca* (*JELF*), edited by Barbara Seidlhofer, the open-access journal *Englishes in Practice* (*EngiP*), edited by Robert Baird, and *Waseda Working Papers in ELF* (*WWPiELF*), edited by Kumiko Murata. Research monographs find space in the book series Developments of English as a Lingua Franca (DELF), published by de Gruyter and edited by Jennifer Jenkins and Will Baker, and many other papers, Ph.D. theses, and MA dissertations have contributed to important discussion and understanding of the field, and its interdisciplinary implications and applications for other areas.

In the research carried out so far, ELF has been investigated in a number of domains, such as business, academic and touristic settings, but more recent research—Maria Grazia Guido, 'ELF Authentication and Accommodation Strategies in Crosscultural Immigration Encounters' (*JELF* 1[2012] 219–40); Nora Dorn, Martina Rienzner, Brigitta Busch and Anita Santner-Wolfartsberger, ' "Here I find myself to be judged": ELF/Plurilingual Perspectives on Language Analysis for the Determination of Origin' (*JELF* 3[2014] 409–24)—has emphasized the importance of the role ELF can play in gate-keeping domains or encounters, such as the ones involving asylum seekers, where both migrants and immigration officials use ELF extensively as a means of communication. Barbara Seidlhofer, 'The Global Significance of ELF' (*WWPiELF* 4[2015] 28–36), reflects on the contribution of ELF research to such social issues and includes a discussion of international publishing and teaching as thorny and gate-keeping issues for academics from diverse backgrounds and for learners/teachers in different pedagogical contexts. The pedagogical aspect is also crucially related to critical language testing, an area addressed by Elana Shohamy in relation to ELF research in 'Critical Language Testing and English as a Lingua Franca: How Can One Help the Other?' (*WWPiELF* 4[2015] 37–51). Shohamy critically reviews current testing practices and shows how measuring methods and proficiency definitions on which these are based do not reflect the increasingly multilingual world and classes, nor have they adapted to an ELF approach to language. She suggests that when making tests, language varieties, and especially language variation in the case of ELF, should be addressed, replacing the current tendency towards a monolingual orientation in international tests. She then illustrates the very different reality of language use with examples of linguistic landscape and multilingual/multimodal data. These sociopolitical and pedagogical aspects emphasize the global significance of ELF and, although they are still at the beginning of being investigated, they will, no doubt, develop in future years and more work on these will find space in future *YWES* reviews.

This review will first concentrate on the nature of the phenomenon of ELF. In the past two decades research in ELF has consolidated some important findings in this respect, and there has also been some discussion and debate, which has helped to refine the concept and clarify aspects of the investigation even further. Among these are the 'Topic & Comment' feature by Sabine Fiedler, 'ELF and the Alternatives: Comments on Ian MacKenzie's "Topic & Comment"' (*JELF* 4[2015] 333–7) and Ian MacKenzie, 'Response to Sabine Fiedler' (*JELF* 4[2014] 339–40), which considers alternatives to the use of ELF, in particular Esperanto, and the related tension between the notions of error and creativity; the response by Antje Wilton, '"It's all Greek to me!" or "Am I speaking Chinese?"' (*JELF* 3[2015] 387–93) to Peter Trudgill's 'Before ELF: GLF from Samarkand to Sfakia' (*JELF* 3[2014] 387–93), commenting on the decline of English as the world's lingua franca and supporting a multiplicity of international lingua francas in future; and, finally, the debate between Will Baker/Jennifer Jenkins, 'Criticizing ELF' (*JELF* 4[2015] 191–8) and John O'Regan, 'English as a Lingua Franca: An Immanent Critique' (*AppLing* 35[2014] 533–52), dealing with the criticism of ELF as 'undertheorized' and 'reified', to which Baker/Jenkins reply by referring to the copious empirical research and theoretical discussion confirming the richness of ELF research and the fluidity and complexity of its nature, and reminding critics of the field that criticism should be informed by in-depth reading of the research that is being criticized and supported by academic rigour (cf. Tomokatsu Ishikawa's 'Academic Rigour in Criticising English as a Lingua Franca' (*EngiP* 2[2015] 39–48)).

Despite these debates, researchers are now in agreement that ELF is not a single variety because of its fluid, variable, and contingent nature which does not allow for conventional codification. The question of whether ELF is a variety was a particularly thorny issue at the beginning of research in this field, but as more descriptive and theoretical research appeared, agreement has now been reached on the nature of the phenomenon. Henry Widdowson, 'ELF and the Pragmatics of Language Variation' (*JELF* 4[2015] 359–72), reflects on the distinctive nature of ELF as relying not on the sociolinguistics of variety but on the pragmatics of variation. He indicates how this perspective relates to current ELF research and its possible development in the future, and suggests its implications for pedagogy in terms of a genuinely learner-centred approach to English language teaching (pedagogical aspects are discussed at the end of this section).

Another aspect on which researchers have agreed so far is that ELF is essentially a multilingual phenomenon where English interacts with other languages in a lingua franca mode. Jenkins, 'Repositioning English and Multilingualism in English as a Lingua Franca' (*EngiP* 2[2015] 49–85), reflects on the conceptualizations of English and multilingualism in ELF and argues that ELF is in need of further theorization in respect of its essentially multilingual nature: a nature that has always been present in ELF theory and empirical work, but which, she believes, has not so far been sufficiently foregrounded. Through three phases of evolution—'ELF 1', focused on forms; 'ELF 2', focused on its variability and pragmatic processes as ELF's defining features; 'ELF 3', conceptualizing it within a framework of multilingualism—Jenkins attempts to redress the balance by taking ELF theorization a small step further in its evolution. Turning to studies on communication in ELF, today's ELF communication largely takes place as a global and de-territorialized phenomenon, which when it is used or constructed can take forms that depart from StE and the typical NS usage. The corpus research carried out in the past ten years in this area has contributed to describing these forms and, perhaps more importantly, has provided the empirical data needed to analyse the processes that underlie and support ELF communication. Anna Mauranen, 'What Is Going On in Academic ELF? Findings and Implications' (in Vettorel, ed., *New Frontiers in Teaching and Learning English*, pp. 31–52), examines some of these underlying processes and provides examples of academic ELF from the ELFA corpus. She explores how processes of simplification and complexification work simultaneously in ELFA, with the former involving regularization and approximation and the latter concerning increased flexibility of forms. She foregrounds the importance of multi-word units for ensuring clarity and understanding. For example, an expression like 'to put the end on it' (p. 43) is easily understood in the ELFA corpus because the multi-word unit contains the same key vocabulary and the same order as the equivalent NS expression 'to put an end to it', while function words such as prepositions and articles can change. Mauranen also explores the effectiveness of clarity-boosting strategies such as rephrasing and reformulation in ensuring intelligibility, which reveals that successful interaction is an outcome of collaborative efforts that speakers put into securing shared understanding through skilful deployment of various strategies. Working on aspects of conceptualization, Svetlana Vetchinnikova, 'Usage-Based Recycling or Creative Exploitation of the Shared Code? The Case of Phraseological Patterning' (*JELF* 4[2015] 223–52), argues that there are two distinct explanations of the differences between NS and ELF usage in ELF research, which she exemplifies using examples of phraseological patterning to illustrate different paradigms of linguistic scholarship: classical Saussurean and usage-based. The first one, exemplified by the work of Barbara Seidlhofer and Henry Widdowson, maintains that ELF users draw on the virtual language to create new forms, while according to the second, usage-based explanation, exemplified by the work of Anna Mauranen, language emerges from usage rather than that existing independently of it. She argues that the issues of whether native-like phraseological patterning in ELF is a result of creation or approximation, the first or the second approach, and of whether on the whole ELF speakers predominantly operate on the open-choice or on the idiom principle, have far-reaching implications for our understanding of the properties of L2 processing and use.

Concerning the area of pronunciation, research has shown how intelligibility is not directly related to accuracy and does not depend on approximation to native speaker pronunciation, but is strictly related to accommodation skills instead. George O'Neal's study on 'Segmental Repair and Interactional Intelligibility: The Relationship between Consonant Deletion, Consonant Insertion, and Pronunciation Intelligibility in English as a Lingua Franca in Japan' (*JPrag* 85[2015] 122–34) provides empirical evidence of the importance of accommodation for intelligibility. The study concerns pronunciation in Japanese contexts and the issue of intelligibility in relation to segmental repair, i.e. the modification of segmental phonemes to address the source of a failure of understanding caused by unintelligible pronunciation. It carries out a conversation-analytic exploration of ELF interactions among university students, which were recorded as part of their English conversation homework assignments. The findings show that problems of mutual intelligibility are not caused by non-standard pronunciation, while examples of standard pronunciation could create intelligibility problems. The study demonstrates that consonant deletion can harm mutual intelligibility and that consonant insertion can help restore it. In another paper, 'ELF Intelligibility: The Vowel Quality Factor' (*JELF* 4[2015] 347–58), O'Neal investigates the negotiation of intelligibility in segmental repair sequences within which vowel quality is oriented to as unintelligible and then modified into a more intelligible variant. He analyses extracts from ELF interaction among Japanese undergraduate students and non-Japanese exchange students at a large public university in Japan. The examples show that maintaining mutual intelligibility can be a collaborative process among ELF speakers, who use segmental repair as an effective communication strategy to overcome miscommunication.

In terms of what is acceptable or non-acceptable in ELF communication, researchers agree that the aspects of ELF communication that do not conform to ENL models are considered acceptable if intelligible in the context of communication and if they do not create problems with understanding. This is valid at all levels of linguistic analysis, that is, pronunciation, lexico-grammar, and discourse. Ishamina Athirah and David Deterding analyse the relationship between lexico-grammatical use and understanding in 'The Role of Noun Phrases in Misunderstandings in Brunei English in ELF settings' (*JELF* 4[2015] 283–308) in a study of NPs in English conversations between Bruneians and people from elsewhere. Through the analysis of ten recordings of elicited semi-structured interviews, their aim is to investigate the extent to which grammatical adjustments involving NPs influence mutual understanding. Despite the constructed nature of the methodological approach, which is untypical of ELF empirical research (normally based on naturally occurring data), the authors find limited evidence of problematicity in ELF communication among speakers of Brunei English. In terms of vocabulary research, Leah Gilner investigates ELF speakers' vocabulary preferences in terms of general service vocabulary in 'A Consideration of the Methodological Underpinnings in the Elicitation of ELF Speakers' Vocabulary Preferences' (*WWPiELF* 4[2015] 168–83). She explores the preference for this vocabulary in the VOICE and ELFA corpora and finds that speakers tend to use the same general vocabulary listed in the general service lists of ENL corpora.

Apart from pronunciation and lexico-grammar, discourse and interactional aspects have also been important areas of ELF research. Mayu Konakahara carries out a conversation analysis of overlapping questions that request the turn space in elicited casual ELF interactions in 'An Analysis Overlapping Questions in Casual ELF Conversation: Cooperative or Competitive Contribution' (*JPrag* 84[2015] 37–53). This examines how overseas students at UK universities use and respond to overlapping questions to develop ongoing communication in informal contexts. The findings indicate that speakers regard overlapping questions as neither interruptive nor competitive, demonstrating their interactional competence in smoothly resolving the overlap and collaboratively moving the talk forward. The appropriate use of overlapping questions signals the interactants' understanding of and interest in the interlocutor's preceding utterance and also encourages clarification of previous ambiguous points, which, consequently, helps to facilitate ELF-effective exchanges. Also from a conversation analytic (CA) perspective, Anita Santner-Wolfartsberger, 'Parties, Persons, and One-at-a-Time: Conversation Analysis and ELF' (*JELF* 2[2015] 253–82), deals with the characteristics and complexities of turn-taking in interactions involving three or more participants. She relies on the key CA model of a party, which posits that turn-taking does not take place between individual speakers, but between parties (hence the term multi-party conversation) potentially consisting of several speakers (cf. Emanuel Schegloff [1995] 32–3). Scrutinizing the applicability of the turn-taking model for group interactions, the present paper offers a preliminary account of this aspect of turn-taking in multi-participant interaction by discussing data extracts from an ELF workplace meeting of seven speakers and suggests possible avenues for further research on the phenomenon.

Moving to the role of culture in ELF, researchers often refer to ELF as an area of investigation that concerns the use of English in *intercultural* contexts where people from different lingua-*cultural* backgrounds use English as their common means of communication. They also point out that ELF is not a neutral medium of communication, and though 'ELF speakers do not share a cultural background or a first language' (Mauranen [2012] 5), they also do not refer to the 'culture' of English NSs or of English native-speaking countries of the Inner Circle. Instead, they do share and co-construct cultural references from the situation, contexts, and practices they have in common. Therefore, NSs' cultural conventions may be rather inappropriate in an ELF context, but also a combination of national or 'target' cultures may be totally irrelevant and unsuited. ELF communication is intercultural, but it highlights the complexity and fluidity of culture, rather than the national, fixed, and limited notion of 'culture' (see A. Suresh Canagarajah, *Translingual Practice: Global Englishes and Cosmopolitan Relations* [2013]).

In this area, a substantial body of work this year is provided by Will Baker's contribution on cultural aspects of ELF, *Culture and Identity through English as a Lingua Franca. Rethinking Concepts and Goals in Intercultural Communication*. Baker argues that ELF research has some major implications for our conception of the relationships between communication, language, identity, and culture. He provides relevant evidence of the substantial body of knowledge documenting how cultures and identities are constructed and enacted in intercultural communication within ELF practices to reconsider how we approach English language teaching (ELT) and teaching intercultural communication. These concerns are summarized in four main arguments. Firstly, Baker considers the points of convergence and divergence between ELF and intercultural communication research. He remarks that ELF is a form of intercultural communication by definition since it involves interlocutors who have different linguistic and cultural backgrounds. Both intercultural communication and ELF studies have focused on the aspects of communication that contribute to effective intercultural interaction, and this typically goes beyond linguistic features and positions issues of pragmatics, power, and identity as equally important. Secondly, Baker argues for the influence provided by studies of intercultural communication through ELF on our understanding of the relationship between culture, identity, and language. He argues that new cultural practices and references emerging from interaction should be seen through the lens of complexity theory because it allows us to examine culture as a constantly changing and evolving whole. He argues that the work on interculturality provides a productive framework for investigating identity construction and negotiation in a manner that avoids predetermined assumptions about participants' cultural identity. Thirdly, Baker considers how participants successfully manage the diversity and variety of communicative practices in intercultural communication through ELF. He outlines how intercultural awareness (ICA) is specifically engaged with the more fluid notions of culture and communication. ICA also contains a high degree of reflexivity and criticality since participants in intercultural communication through ELF often need or desire to challenge and reinterpret communicative practices, and related cultural references, in ways that are appropriate to the communicative situations in which they find themselves. Finally, he gives reasons for the impact of ELF and ICA research on ELT. Moving away from prescriptive approaches to teaching, Baker suggests a recognition of L2 learning and use as an intercultural process of adaptation and negotiation of communicative practices for successful intercultural communication. According to him, ICA offers a model and a set of pedagogical goals for the knowledge, skills, and attitudes needed for intercultural communication through ELF as well as how these can be put into practice in intercultural communication. Baker outlines five general themes for the development of ICA in the classroom. He adds a case study of a course on intercultural communication, intercultural awareness, and Global Englishes implemented at a Thai university as an example of an alternative teaching praxis to normative applications of a narrow range of linguistic structures, Anglocentric perspectives on communication and culture, and a restricted notion of communicative competence.

In another paper on this topic, 'Research into Practice: Cultural and Intercultural Awareness' (*LTeach* 48[2015] 130–41), Baker reflects on the gap between 'what research has suggested' and 'what practitioners actually do in terms of policy and teaching' with regard to the role of cultural awareness and intercultural awareness in the English-language classroom. Drawing on his own teaching experiences in the UK and Thailand, Baker emphasizes how English-language learners are still poorly equipped for the flexibility of linguistic forms and the diversity of communication they will encounter in intercultural interactions. Nonetheless, Baker demonstrates the recognition of the significance of culture in language learning by prevailing language policy and the feasibility of adopting an intercultural awareness-fostering approach in the classroom. Baker also notes that cultural comparisons should be handled carefully as they could produce stereotypes and thus impede successful intercultural communication. In another contribution, 'Culture and Complexity through English as a Lingua Franca: Rethinking Competences and Pedagogy in ELT' (*JELF* 4[2015] 9–30), Baker discusses how complexity theory offers a framework for understanding culture as a constantly changing but nonetheless meaningful category in ELF research, while avoiding essentialism and reductionism. Moreover, he critically questions simplistic and essentialist cultural characterizations of intercultural competence offered in language pedagogy. He concludes by giving some suggestions and examples for how such complex understandings of culture and language through ELF can be meaningfully incorporated into pedagogical practice.

The focus on the role of culture in ELF, therefore, has been mainly on intercultural awareness, emphasizing the role of attitudes, knowledge, and skills in relation to ELF communication, but interculturality, as the ability to construct and negotiate aspects of cultural identity in actual interactions, is another important aspect of this research. Interculturality is a key aspect of Zhu Hua's work who, in 'Negotiation as the Way of Engagement in Intercultural and Lingua Franca Communication: Frames of Reference and Interculturality' (*JELF* 4[2015] 63–90), focuses on how the concept of interculturality can shed light on cultural aspects of ELF. Zhu highlights the essential role that negotiation plays in intercultural and ELF interactions, where speakers tend to bring in differing cultural schemata and identities. She draws on the VOICE corpus to exemplify how cultural frames of reference could be revised as well as how the degree of alignment between self-preferred identities and assumed-by-interactants identities is signalled through negotiation. Accordingly, attention should be placed on how negotiation can provide opportunities for intercultural learning and also illustrate the role of culture in intercultural and ELF talk.

Aspects of interculturality and intercultural awareness are also strongly connected with issues of identity. Previous research on identity focused mainly on ELT professionals (Jennifer Jenkins, *English as a Lingua Franca: Attitude and Identity* [2007]) and explored identity in relation to attitudes to ELF. However, the notion of identity for L2 speakers is another aspect of particular interest. Chit Cheung Matthew Sung's contribution, 'Exploring Second Language Speakers' Linguistic Identities in ELF Communication: A Hong Kong Study' (*JELF* 2[2015] 309–32), aims to shed light on the complexity of identity construction in ELF settings within an Asian context. The paper reports on a qualitative study of a group of Hong Kong university students' perceptions of their linguistic identity. The participants consider their 'nonnativeness' as an empowering force in ELF interactions, validating their identity as multilingual, multicompetent, and translingual speakers of English. Relying upon a diverse set of multilingual resources, the participants define their linguistic identity by constructing and negotiating it in relation to the perceived linguistic competence of other ELF speakers, especially L2 speakers from other cultural/national backgrounds.

Possibly the domain of expertise that ELF is mostly associated with is business. This area has also produced a considerable amount of research since its beginnings; the findings show that ELF is today considered the language of international business and that business English as a lingua franca (BELF) communication is generally considered content-oriented rather than form-focused (usually in terms of ENL forms). In international business contexts, especially multinational corporations, the use of English as a 'corporate language' has become common practice, if not given official recognition in the company's language policy. BELF is now a requirement in globalized business and, even more, an essential aspect of business knowledge. In a special issue of *JELF* focusing on 'Teaching ELF, BELF, and/or Intercultural Communication?' (*JELF* 4:i[2015]), the editors Susanne Ehrenreich and Marie-Luise Pitzl embark on the ambitious attempt of bringing together ELF, intercultural communication, and BELF, and the more application-oriented dimension of teaching. The papers included in the issue range from conceptualizations of BELF and conceptualizations of culture to the inclusion of intercultural competence in curricula, and analysis of the CEFR.

Anne Kankaanranta, Leena Louhiala-Salminen, and Päivi Karhunen, in 'English as Corporate Language: Implications for Teaching "English" at an International Business School' (*JELF* 4[2015] 125–48), explore the role of English as a shared 'corporate language' in multinational corporations. The article concentrates on three research streams—applied linguistics, international management, and corporate communication—to explore how this research informs the teaching of English for business professionals, and how this can impact on international business schools' teaching programmes and course design. They explore BELF research and introduce the notion of global communicative competence, constituted by three intertwined layers, multicultural competence, competence in BELF, and business know-how. The authors also discuss a continuum between 'official' English and 'working language BELF' which is critically reviewed in the response paper by Alessia Cogo, 'Complexity, Negotiability and Ideologies: A Response to Zhu, Pitzl, and Kankaanranta et al.' (*JELF* 4[2015] 149–55). In this paper Cogo offers a response to three papers in the special issue and highlights how the papers converge on at least two aspects, the fluid conceptualization of 'English'/ 'language', and the complexity of ELF communication. She clarifies that a reconceptualization has occurred in some related disciplines, such as applied linguistics and language teaching, which have shifted towards more fluid and emergent conceptualizations. However, in international management and corporate communication a unified model still persists, which is reflected in Kankaanranta et al.'s contribution. Another paper in the collection explores the integration of intercultural competence into curricula designed for students studying business administration and economics in higher education. Patricia Pullin, in 'Culture, Curriculum Design, Syllabus and Course Development in the Light of BELF' (*JELF* 4[2015] 31–53), chooses a research-based approach to curriculum development, in the light of BELF research findings, to focus in particular on the interface between language and culture, drawing on pragmatics, and the need to raise awareness of the impact of cultural differences in business communication. The final aim of the article is to consider ways in which educators can draw on BELF findings to integrate more authentic interaction into the classroom, notably in relation to intercultural awareness and communication. This paper is also reviewed in a response article by Anita Santner-Wolfartsberger, 'Intercultural Awareness, (B)ELF, and Bridging the Gap between Theory and Practice: A Response to Baker and Pullin' (*JELF* 4[2015] 55–61), which relates to both Baker's (reviewed above) and Pullin's contributions. She stresses the procedural nature of culture as a concept, highlighting that culture is not something static but dynamic, negotiated, and emergent. From this comparison of ideas, Santner-Wolfartsberger is able to conclude that, although Pullin's paper is probably of greater relevance for day-to-day pedagogical practice, Baker's conceptualization of culture as a complex, emergent social system covers much of the conceptual groundwork that is needed for ELF research to build on. In her conclusion she evaluates these two papers as important, starting points for reconsidering assumptions we hold regarding best practices of teaching language and culture. The last paper in the special issue explores a completely different topic, 'Understanding and Misunderstanding in the Common European Framework of Reference: What We Can Learn from Research on BELF and Intercultural Communication' (*JELF* 4[2015] 91–124). The author, Marie-Luise Pitzl, discusses the concepts of 'understanding' and 'misunderstanding' as they are discursively constructed in CEFR (Council of Europe [2001]). Pitzl critically reviews the general aim of CEFR 'to develop a plurilingual competence' where the native speaker is 'no longer the ultimate model', and the inconsistencies between this aim and the tables of descriptors for the different levels of competence, which refer to the native speaker model. The CEFR is responsible for creating an unreal, imagined, and unachievable picture of successful communication, as communication where miscommunication does not occur. Also the CEFR creates imagined scenarios of communication as happening only with native speakers, and puts the responsibility of achieving understanding exclusively on the non-native speakers/learners-users. Pitzl demonstrates that the CEFR uses a wide range of terms to describe instances of miscommunication, but fails to provide satisfactory definitions and coherent theoretical argumentation to support its premises in terms of international development of intercultural competence and skills for intercultural communication.

Another interesting area of BELF research concerns the analysis of actual business communication, as for example in naturally occurring business exchanges. Owing to difficulties in data collection, papers exploring this kind of empirical data are generally more difficult to find, but two appeared in 2015. The first, by Jane Lockwood, 'Virtual Team Management: What is Causing Communication Breakdown?' (*L&IC* 15[2015] 125–40), addresses the root causes of a virtual team communication failure within a globalized workplace. The researcher carries out a 'training needs analysis' for this particular programme of communicating in a virtual team. The causes of interactive breakdown are examined through reviews of corporate documentation, surveys, and interviews with managers and team members and observation of meetings. The findings note the inadequacy of both technology quality and meeting strategies, and the differences in language use and culture as surface symptoms, revealing the issue of disempowerment and distrust over offshoring members as the fundamental cause of unsuccessful virtual team interaction. The second paper is by Akiko Otsu, 'Beyond "Nice to Meet You": Small Talk in ELF for Initial Business Communication' (*WWPiELF* 4[2015] 55–69) , and is a CA exploration of a business encounter between a Japanese architect and a Malaysian taxi driver who takes the architect from his hotel to work at their first meeting. Otsu focuses on the use of repetitions in building rapport and securing understanding in their small talk. She demonstrates how the participants, despite their limited English proficiency, manage to communicate by using all the resources available to them, including paying attention to face and enjoying the exchange. The paper further confirms the need to view ELF communication as 'successful' and 'proficient' in terms of the communication itself and the purposes it is put to. Finally, Catherine Nickerson, in 'The Death of the Non-Native Speaker? English as a Lingua Franca in Business Communication: A Research Agenda' (*LTeach* 48[2015] 390–404), outlines a research agenda for ELF in business communication of relevance to scholars and language-teaching practitioners. An understanding of both the production and reception of BELF will further develop English in business theory and how this impacts on language teaching, including the role played by NSs of English in the co-construction of business. Furthermore, an understanding of the increasingly advanced levels of proficiency, and of what constitutes professional communicative competence in business, in addition to both the production and reception of BELF, internationally used, will be instrumental in determining pedagogy and teaching material.

Probably the second biggest domain of investigation at the moment is the use and conceptualization of ELF in academic settings. Universities around the world are increasing their number of international students and are becoming common settings of ELF exchanges concerning academic subjects. Research in this area has focused both on descriptions of academic communication and reflections on the role and consequences of 'English' in the 'international' university. The nature of ELF academic exchange has become the subject of empirical analysis thanks to the creation of corpora, such as the aforementioned ELFA and the latest addition, WrELFA, or Written ELFA, a collection of academic texts written in ELF including evaluative reports (examiners' and peer reviewers' reports) and academic/ research blogs (see http://www.helsinki.fi/englanti/elfa/index.html).

Apart from Mauranen's contribution (in Vettorel, ed.) concerning the nature of ELFA more generally, empirical research into exchanges in academic settings has also focused on pragmatic speech acts. Mayu Konakahara's 'How ELF Users Negotiate Face During Complaining' (*WWPiELF* 4[2015] 128–48) is a multimodal CA exploration of ELF interactions among international students at a UK university focusing on third-party complaints. The author pays attention to complaint sequences in relation to eye movement, facial expression, hand gestures, and postures which become relevant in her analytic approach. The author skilfully describes how ELF speakers manage a very sensitive and face-threatening act such as complaining about an absent third party by using both non-verbal communication and skilled communication strategies.

From actual communication we now turn to the very topical area of English as a medium of instruction (EMI) in international university courses. As seen in Jennifer Jenkins's research (*English as a Lingua Franca in the International University* [2014]) universities are increasing the number of programmes in English and present themselves as 'international', although their English language policies and practices do not necessarily reflect this. While some studies have addressed the implications of this development, others have started evaluating the effectiveness of English instruction. Hassan Belhiah and Maha Elhami, in 'English as a Medium of Instruction in the Gulf: When Students and Teachers Speak' (*LPol* 14[2015] 3–23) examine the effectiveness of EMI in the Gulf according to solicited perceptions from both students and instructors. Five hundred students and 100 teachers from six UAE universities were involved in the survey questionnaire and structured email interview. The findings show a general consensus among participants that EMI enhanced students' English proficiency. However, it is also reported that the exclusive use of English was an impediment to learning for many students; accordingly, a preference for a bilingual curriculum is expressed by a majority of informants. This paper advocates a move towards bilingualism in education policy-making.

Three other papers on EMI focus on the Japanese context, where, as Kumiko Murata maintains, 'the Japanese government is currently very eager to promote EMI to develop more globally-minded human resources although the connection between "global" and "English" is not necessarily well defined': 'Furthering ELF Research in Academic and Business Contexts' (*WWPiELF* 4[2015] 9) . Based on his experience in conducting EMI classes in Japan, Nobuyuki Hino suggests incorporating ELF into content and language integrated learning (CLIL) and provides the conditions for implementing CELFIL in his paper 'Towards the Development of CELFIL [Content and ELF Integrated Learning] for EMI classes in Higher Education in Japan' (*WWPiELF* 4[2015] 187–98). The second paper, by Masaki Oda, 'University English Language Programs in Transition: EFL to ELF, and Then?' (*WWPiELF* 4[2015] 199–208), discusses the challenges and rationale of a Japanese private institution, Tamagawa University (Tokyo), in shifting its mainly English as a foreign language programme to an ELF one. The author also offers a discussion of the innovative recruitment policy, which, unlike other similar policies that require lecturers to be NSs of English, specifies the need for lecturers to be bi- or multi-lingual with TESOL qualifications. The third paper, by James D'Angelo, 'Nurturing EMI in Broad-Based Japanese Higher Education: The Case of Chukyo University' (*WWPiELF* 4[2015] 219–28), discusses the successes and challenges of implementing EMI in a Japanese university at the interfaces between World Englishes and ELF paradigms.

Similarly to Japan, Chinese institutions are also developing 'getting on the international track': Ying Wang, 'A Case Study of the Role of English in a Chinese University' (*WWPiELF* 4[2015] 209), reports on a qualitative study of one university, China Three Gorges University, where she analysed language-policy documents and media communication (website, advertisements, bulletins, etc.), and conducted interviews and classroom observations. She observes a mismatch between policies and classroom practices: whereas Chinese is the preferred language in education policies, English is actually used and expected in university practice. She also notices a lack of engagement with what 'English' is and a lack of ELF awareness in the pedagogical and classroom contexts.

Turning now to ELF and pedagogy, since the beginning of research in this field questions have been raised about how research findings could be applied for pedagogical purposes, but ELF researchers were initially reluctant to engage with this topic. However, since descriptive research of how English is used in lingua franca settings has started to consolidate, pedagogical suggestions have also started to appear. This was possibly the strongest year so far in terms of publications concerning pedagogy and a turning point for applications of ELF research, not only for the considerable number of publications that address this area, but also for the coverage of topics and for the depth of engagement with them. The publications reviewed in this section, however, show rather different approaches to ELF and pedagogy, which vary from referring to 'features of ELF' to suggestions of teaching 'for ELF communication' rather than teaching ELF itself, to ELF-aware pedagogy and transformative pedagogy. There were three edited books that engaged with this area and which included chapters from most ELF researchers: Yasemin Bayyurt and Sumru Akcan, eds., *Current Perspectives on Pedagogy for English as a Lingua Franca*; Hugo Bowles and Alessia Cogo, eds., *International Perspectives on English as a Lingua Franca*; and Paola Vettorel, ed., *New Frontiers in Teaching and Learning English*. Together they offer a wide range of papers covering a multiplicity of aspects.

ELF research has shown that effective communication is not directly proportional to grammatical accuracy in NS terms, but rather requires engagement in accommodation and pragmatic strategies which put into question the relationship between 'complexity', 'fluency', and 'accuracy'. Barbara Seidlhofer, 'ELF-Informed Pedagogy: From Code-Fixation towards Communicative Awareness' (in Vettorel, ed., pp. 19–30), particularly elaborates on this matter. The mismatch between ELT and the changed reality of English at a time of globalization requires practitioners to re-evaluate the relation between accuracy, fluency, and complexity, encouraging users to move away from how to achieve native-like competence and turn to 'how they language' (p. 28), that is, how English users strategically exploit the potential of language. An ELF-informed pedagogy would inspire teachers to approach textbooks in a different manner and meanwhile encourage students to reflect on the language, the rationale for learning it, and the relationship between being accurate and being communicative, fostering language and communication awareness. Pedagogical emphasis should be placed on 'how language is learned' (p. 30) rather than 'how much of it is picked up' (p. 32). Similarly, Henry Widdowson reflects on the pragmatics of language variation in 'English and the Pragmatics of Language Variation' (*JELF* 4[2015] 359–72) and maintains that ELF can offer a genuinely learner-centred approach to ELT, but also a particularly challenging one. According to Widdowson, 'Frontiers of English and the Challenge of Change' (in Vettorel, ed., pp. 227–32), 'new ways of thinking are of their nature disruptive and disturbing. They call into question the validity of the established order and create uncertainty and insecurity' (p. 230). Perhaps not surprisingly then, some of the papers in this area relate the challenges that teachers, students, and stakeholders experience in introducing an ELF-oriented pedagogy. Patrick NG Chin Leong and Patrick Shaou-Whea Dodge, in 'Situating English as a Lingua Franca in Context: Narratives from Japanese and Chinese Classrooms' (*Journal of Intercultural Communication Studies* 24:iii[2015] 50–63), for instance, explore two teachers' statements about their teaching philosophies, their immediate linguistic environment, and the obstacles they encountered in introducing ELF in two university classrooms in Japan and China. The authors also explain what tactics the teachers employed to encourage a positive attitude towards ELF-oriented pedagogy among students. The article accentuates that certain contextual elements, namely, the sociolinguistic circumstances in which English is studied, the classroom culture, and students' perceptions of English learning, need to be considered while practising ELF in institutions.

The challenges to an ELF-oriented pedagogy are also explored in the first part of Yasemin Bayyurt and Sumru Akcan's edited book, *Current Perspectives on Pedagogy for English as a Lingua Franca*, which examines the implications of ELF at virtually every educational level, specifically, from elementary schools in Italy (Lucilla Lopriore, 'ELF and Early Language Learning: Multiliteracies, Language Policies and Teacher Education', pp. 69–86) and secondary schools in Germany (Kurt Kohn, 'A Pedagogical Space for ELF in the English Classroom', pp. 51–67) to universities in Hong Kong (Lynne Flowerdew, 'Adjusting Pedagogically to an ELF World: An ESP Perspective', pp. 13–34) and Japan (Nobuyuki Hino and Setsuko Oda, 'Integrated Practice in Teaching English as an International Language (IPTEIL): A Classroom ELF Pedagogy in Japan', pp. 35–50). These four chapters emphasize the need to integrate ELF concepts into ELT/English for specific purposes, calling for a transformation of the practitioners' and learners' mindsets with regard to the ownership of English and the awareness of content overriding form. The researchers emphasize, in particular, the importance of accommodation and meaning-negotiation in both spoken and written English, but also acknowledge the challenges of practising such communicative strategies in the traditional classroom environment. In this regard, several suggestions have been put forward to maximize students' exposure to and participation in real-life intercultural communication, for example, the English Café programme and programmes enabling trans-national experience like Global Challenge (both Hino and Oda), and introducing online learning platforms (Kohn), among others. Another challenge faced by teachers and educators is the increasing number of diverse classrooms, including learners from different linguistic/cultural back-grounds. Lucilla Lopriore points out that primary classes in Europe have become increasingly multilingual with English serving as their lingua franca. In 'Young Learners in ELF Classrooms: A Shift in Perspective' (in Vettorel, ed., pp. 159–77), Lopriore explores spoken communication in primary English-language classrooms in Italy. She observes diversity in the classroom, together with learners' exposure to English outside the classroom, and the strength of their desire to communicate using all available strategies (including the use of multilingual resources). She then argues that primary-teacher education should include awareness-raising of the ways in which such ELF practices emerge in their classrooms and how they can be capitalized on in their teaching. A further challenge identified by various researchers in the field concerns assessment and its role in driving norms of language learning and teaching. David Newbold maintains, in 'Assessing ELF in European Universities: The Challenges Ahead' (in Vettorel, ed., pp. 205–26) that European university entry tests should include more appropriate and ELF-oriented tasks. He discusses a project on oral production, where an ELF-oriented listening test was designed by a group of researchers and then taken by a group of students at an Italian university, and also explores proposals for a speaking test that involves using students as ELF informants. He concludes by observing that, although developing tests to assess ELF interaction and writing is recommended, the task presents major challenges, which are related both to the validity issue and the washback effect, that is, the way such tests would lead to more ELF-aware teaching and learning.

Martin Dewey's 'Time to Wake Up Some Dogs! Shifting the Culture of Language in ELT' (in Bayyurt and Akcan, eds., pp. 121–34) reflects on current practices in ELT, which continue to foster a norm-based approach to language, and criticizes the persistence of supposedly 'global' textbooks in referring to NS standard Englishes, such as BrE and AmE. He suggests refocusing teachers' priorities and argues for an approach to language and communication that would be 'less concerned with language as an abstracted system and more in line with a notion of language as "local practice"' (p. 133).

A considerable part of research on pedagogy focuses on materials for the classroom. Researchers tend to promote awareness of the diversity of English and an ELF orientation in coursebooks, classroom materials, and material development. What researchers also emphasize is that the ELF approach to materials is not about abandoning or replacing current NS-oriented materials; instead practitioners are encouraged to add to current materials by shifting the perspective towards more intercultural, situated, and fluid orientations to language and linguistic practices.

In 'Promoting Awareness of Englishes and ELF in the English Language Classroom' (in Bowles and Cogo, eds., pp. 13–34), Lucilla Lopriore and Paola Vettorel engage with the two distinct paradigms of ELF and World Englishes and promote awareness-raising of their differences in classroom teaching materials and text books. The chapter contains a number of practical suggestions for raising awareness and attempts at clarifying the confusion that still exists between the two phenomena, i.e. the relatively bounded and describable World English varieties, and the fluid and variable use of ELF.

In 'Developing Critical Classroom Practice for ELF Communication: A Taiwanese Case Study of ELT Materials Evaluation' (in Bowles and Cogo eds., pp. 35–54), Huiyen Melissa Yu presents a case study of two Taiwanese teachers reflecting on classroom material and promotes an ELF approach for evaluating material and developing resources for ELF-oriented teaching. The author also touches upon how these aspects can be incorporated into teacher-education programmes.

Telma Gimenez, Luciana Cabrini Simões Calvo, and Michele Salles El Kadri, 'Beyond Madonna: Teaching Materials as Windows into Pre-Service Teachers' Understandings of ELF' (in Bayyurt and Akcan, eds., pp. 225–38), analyse teaching materials produced by prospective English teachers in Brazil which aimed at moving away from a strict EFL perspective and the typical celebrity-oriented coursebook units. Despite the short teacher-training course the initiative proved successful, but the authors suggest further development towards a more in-depth discussion of English as a practice (rather than a system) and a more context-sensitive pedagogy. The paper by Domingos Sávio Pimentel Siqueira, 'English as a Lingua Franca and ELT Materials: Is the "Plastic World" Really Melting?' (in Bayyurt and Akcan, eds., pp. 239–57) explores ELT textbooks, which are found to place heavy emphasis on English as a native language, and concludes that more work is needed to translate ELF into the classroom.

Some of the studies in this area attempt to suggest classroom-related activities that implement an ELF-oriented pedagogy. Enrico Grazzi's contribution, 'Linking ELF and ELT in Secondary School through Web-Mediation: The Case of Fan Fiction' (in Bowles and Cogo, eds., pp. 55–71), is a pilot study of creative writing and fan fiction in Italian secondary schools. Students engaged in Web-based collaborative writing tasks, and the author analyses some interesting examples of creative use of idiomatic expressions. The project questionnaires, instead, show that ELF is still controversial (and poorly understood) and that standard native English is preferred. The author emphasizes the importance of classroom ELF awareness-raising, especially in same-L1 student groups, and the development of training programmes that integrate an ELF approach. Another project concerning online communication and applications for the classroom is developed by Grazzi, 'ELF and the Development of Intercultural Communicative Competence: An Italian–American Telecollaboration Project' (in Vettorel, ed., pp. 179–204). Unlike the previous one, this project aims to develop intercultural competence among Italian and US university students through telecollaboration. Iris Schaller-Schwaner's contribution, 'ELF Oral Presentations in a Multilingual Context: Intelligibility, Familiarity and Agency' (in Bowles and Cogo, eds., pp. 72–95), carries out an ethnographic study of academic presentations in a higher education institution in Switzerland; the author argues in favour of prioritizing intelligibility, particularly in respect of pronunciation, and of the importance of promoting familiarity and multilingual awareness in this respect. Other examples of classroom engagement with ELF communication concern the use of naturally occurring data extracts of conversations with the aim of developing awareness of language variation and diversity. One such study is Luciana Pedrazzini's 'Raising Trainee Teachers' Awareness of Language Variation through Data-Based Tasks' (in Vettorel, ed., pp. 77–101). Trainee teachers were asked to engage in data-based tasks exemplifying ELF communication. These tasks were audio-recorded samples of different accents and written transcripts of spoken data taken from research, and teachers were asked to express their opinions in relation to the different accents, their perceptions of ELF and their awareness of language variation. Although her findings confirmed 'conservative' orientations towards language variation, Pedrazzini concludes that this kind of work opens trainees' minds to the kind of variation found in ELF communication, even though they might eventually opt for the 'safety' of established native varieties in their teaching. Luisa Bozzo's paper, 'Which English(es) to Teach? Empowering EFL Trainee

Teachers to Make Their Choices' (in Vettorel, ed., pp. 103–27), also focuses on trainee teachers in the Italian context and which English variety or varieties is/ are most suited to them. She concludes that learners should be taught about World Englishes and ELF and then embarks on a detailed description of teacher-education curricula that would include such an approach.

Most researchers agree that for change towards an ELF-perspective to happen researchers need to engage with the attitudes and perceptions of teachers and learners. Research on attitudes towards ELF and perceptions of English variation and change has been particularly fruitful in pedagogical contexts. Paola Vettorel's 'Primary School Teachers' Perceptions: Englishes, ELF and Classroom Practices—Between "Correctness" and "Communicative Effectiveness" ' (in Vettorel, ed., pp. 129–55) describes a follow-up phase of a project involving primary school-experienced teachers from Italy. She argues, by means of a questionnaire survey, a focus group, and individual interviews, that the EFL primary teachers are aware of the lingua franca role that English increasingly plays in their pupils' lives outside their school environment. Although teachers are aware of the importance of communicative effectiveness over correctness, they seem to experience tension between this awareness and the idea of a 'pure' standard model experienced in formal education, as well as in their teacher training. The author reflects on the implications of these aspects to promote ELF-informed pedagogical practices that should involve realistic opportunities to communicate with both native and non-native speakers in connection to the global spread of English and its international lingua franca role. Ying Wang explores 'Language Awareness and ELF Perceptions of Chinese University Students' (in Bowles and Cogo, eds., pp. 96–116) and demonstrates that explicit knowledge and awareness of ELF can lead to a change in students' attitudes towards English. She suggests useful ways of raising students' consciousness of ELF, and ends by asking readers (in her 'Engagement Priorities' section) to consider whether her findings could apply to their own context.

Veronika Quinn Novotná and Jiřina Dunková's 'Teaching through ELF at International Post-Secondary Institutions: A Case Study at United World Colleges' (in Bowles and Cogo, eds., pp. 159–75) focuses on the attitudes of teachers and students in international schools towards ELF usage in relation to CLIL (content and language integrated learning). Teachers reported a focus on English-only communication in the schools despite the multilingual background of the students, a general focus on content rather than language form, linguistically a tendency to focus on subject-specific vocabulary, and an awareness of the importance of accommodation strategies. Although the implications of their work connect more with CLIL than ELF per se, the authors make suggestions that contribute to ELF, such as the importance of exposure not only to the use of ELF inside the classroom but also to 'social' ELF, i.e. outside it, and to the recommendation to teachers to exploit multilingual resources and teaching practices. The authors also suggest in-class reflective activities on ELF and World Englishes for language-awareness training.

ELF researchers and practitioners have made a strong case for the importance of ELF-aware teacher education. This research has focused mainly on pre- or in-service teacher-education programmes, and has covered different countries and institutions. For instance, Dilek İnal and Esra Özdemir's 'Re/Considering the English Language Teacher Education Programs in Turkey from an ELF Standpoint: What Do the Academia, Pre-Service and In-Service Teachers Think? (in Bayyurt and Akcan, eds., pp. 135–52) shows that awareness-raising of ELF increased participants' favourable attitudes towards ELF. And Areti-Maria Sougari and Roxani Faltzi, in 'Drawing upon Greek Pre-Service Teachers' Beliefs about ELF-Related Issues' (in Bayyurt and Akcan, eds., pp. 153–69), conclude that the participants with intercultural experience considered they were more likely to use English with NNSs of the language than those who did not have such experience, but that such experience may not lead to more ELF-aware perceptions concerning the teaching of English in Greece. In general, these contributions are important in shedding light on the current situation of teacher education in different countries and in providing suggestions for further action. Other contributions also point to possible obstacles to introducing ELF in teacher education. The findings of Luísa Azuaga and Lili Cavalheiro's 'Bringing New ELT Policies and ELF to Teacher Training Courses' (in Bayyurt and Akcan, eds., pp. 103–20) imply a tendency for teachers in Portugal to be influenced by NS models, which then prompts the authors to call for a reconsideration of the appropriateness of the NS model and English native language cultural content in English teaching, as well as for a critical analysis of cultural content to increase intercultural awareness. In Austria, Elisabeth Weber's paper 'Can We Change the Subject, Please? A Pedagogic Perspective of ELF' (in Bayyurt and Akcan, eds., pp. 171–89) criticizes the current foreign-language assistant system, where nativeness is the only criterion required from an assistant. The problem is that in this system simply being a native speaker of a particular language may be valued more highly than language-pedagogical knowledge and experience. Weber suggests that in order to provide learners of English with a realistic reference point, schools would do well to hire multilingual assistants who have experience of using English as a lingua franca and who are also interested in the teaching profession, rather than (monolingual) native English speakers simply for being NSs.

Yasemin Bayyurt and Nicos C. Sifakis write on 'Developing an ELF-Aware Pedagogy: Insights from a Self-Education Programme' (in Vettorel, ed., pp. 55–76), where they describe their ELF-teacher education distance-learning project, which aims to develop the idea of ELF awareness-raising for teacher education. In their study, teachers engage with ELF research and develop awareness in relation to the decentring of the native speaker in ELT, a critical view of the ownership of English, and empowerment as non-native teachers. However, the study also shows that some teachers resist ELF-aware pedagogy because of the influence of other stakeholders (institutional constraints, parents, and so on). The same authors focus more on the transformative aspect of teacher education in 'ELF-Aware In-Service Teacher Education: A Transformative Perspective' (in Bowles and Cogo, eds., 117–35), presenting the findings of their joint Greek–Turkish pilot study in which they provided teachers with readings and questions to enable them to reflect on the relevance of ELF for their own classrooms. They concentrated on the transformative stage of teachers' development and found that the teachers underwent change during the course of the study, particularly in relation to becoming aware that English is an international language for a vast number of non-native English speakers, and as a result, the change concerned their perceptions of themselves as non-native English teachers. However, the study also emphasizes the lack of available ELF-aware teaching materials, and to help fill this gap their chapter ends with suggested activities that teachers and teacher trainers could use 'when engaging in ELF-aware teaching and teacher education' (p. 132). Development of language awareness, and especially awareness of ELF, is a key aspect of an ELF-aware pedagogy and the first step in the development of change. Martin Dewey's 'ELF, Teacher Knowledge and Professional Development' (in Bowles and Cogo, eds., pp. 176–93) considers two popular and international teacher-training courses/awards in order to explore the extent to which ELF is introduced at this stage of professional development. His study is based on a questionnaire that he administered to a group of trainee teachers on one of these courses, which shows that the trainee teachers were familiar with StE, but had little knowledge of ELF, since this is not part of the courses' curricula. Dewey therefore argues for the early introduction of ELF in teacher training. In an article entitled 'The Pedagogical Implications of ELF in a Domestic Migrant Workplace' (in Bowles and Cogo, eds., pp. 136–58), Kellie Gonçalves builds on a growing and increasingly important line of investigation, that is, mobile, migrant workers in multilingual workplace settings, in this case Portuguese- and Spanish-speakers working in the United States. The study explores the communicative practices of these workers in relation to English and other languages and suggests possible pedagogical implications. Migrant domestic workers from Portuguese- and Spanish-speaking backgrounds do not normally use English in their private lives but use English as an additional language of wider communication. Their lack of exposure to English/ELF outside the workplace and the negative perceptions of their own English have a considerable impact on their confidence in using English and affect their investment and motivation. Working on these premises, Gonçalves develops useful suggestions for the teacher's approach, such as the inclusion of 'translanguaging' in classes for migrant workers (translanguaging being a key part of the 'more multilingual turn' in ELF research, see above), and for appropriate materials development.

## 12. Pragmatics and Discourse Analysis

Following on from the publication of two new readers for discourse studies in 2014, we have yet another in 2015. The second edition of *The Handbook of Discourse Analysis* (edited by Deborah Tannen, Heidi Hamilton and Deborah Schiffrin) has been extensively revised since the 2003 edition, with twenty new chapters and nineteen chapters omitted. The audience for the volume is still both scholars within discourse studies as well as those from other disciplines which may draw on discourse analysis, such as education, law, and medicine.

The deleted chapters are often those which applied more traditional linguistic methods to discourse, such as variationist approaches, typology, linguistic structure, and semantics. The new chapters reflect new trends within discourse analysis, such as the increased attention to sexuality ('Queer Linguistics'), the attempt to account for text beyond the word ('Gesture in Discourse', 'Multimodality'), and the focus on space in relation to discourse (also seen this year in the special issue of *Critical Discourse Studies* on 'Space, Time and Evaluation in Ideological Discourse', edited by Laura Filardo-Llamas, Christopher Hart, and Bertie Kaal).

The emergence of new textbooks seems to have been led by Routledge in 2015. In pragmatics, we see the third edition of the successful introductory textbook *Pragmatics: A Resource Book for Students*, by Joan Cutting. Like the second edition, the volume follows the series format of being divided into four sections ('Introduction', 'Development', 'Exploration', 'Extension') with themes cutting across these. Also as in previous editions, a real strength is the large number of exercises which will help students engage with the new ideas. The main title, however, is different; it used to be *Pragmatics and Discourse* Given this change in name, it is rather unexpected to find a section on CDA. While there are clear areas of overlap between pragmatics and discourse analysis at many levels, it is difficult to do justice to one within an undergraduate module largely dedicated to the other. The second change is that the book now has eight chapters; it includes additions examining intercultural pragmatics, pragmatics, and language learning, and introducing students to the use of corpus linguistics. All of these are likely to be of interest and useful to students.

In discourse work, *Discourse and Digital Practice: Doing Discourse Analysis in the Digital Age*, edited by Rodney Jones, Alice Chik, and Christoph Hafner, is described as being designed for advanced students studying courses on digital literacies or language and digital practices. The editors position the volume as a response to the challenges posed by digital practices to traditional ways of doing discourse analysis. While many of the practices they discuss pre-date online interactions, including multimodal texts, multiparty inter-actions, interactive writing, remixing, and curating texts, such practices have undoubtedly become more visible and therefore less easy to brush away in favour of more amenable mono-logic, mono-authored, prepared texts. One way in which the contributions start to build on existing tools is through triangulation with other approaches, including the use of interviews and focus groups. This volume thus presents a welcome push at the boundaries of discourse analysis as it stands, as well as recognition of the value of discourse-analytic tools for understanding language practices. It is likely to be of interest beyond the non-specialist intended student audience.

A welcome trend to be noted in the work of 2015 across both pragmatics and discourse is a move away from treating language communicated via technology as a homogeneous or discrete entity. The boundaries between computer-mediated and non- computer-mediated communication are increas-ingly blurred. (Is a phone call to be treated differently if it is occurs via a hand-held computer or a desktop one? Is a newspaper article to be classified differently if it is read in paper format or on a tablet?) Furthermore, as the use of technology is no longer novel (we have a whole generation who grew up with the Internet) such integration is part of natural language behaviour, which needs to be reflected in the analytic approaches. The collection *Participation in Public and Social Media Interactions*, edited by Marta Dynel and Jan Chovanec, brings together, as the title suggests, studies on public and social media in recognition of the similarities they share. Refreshingly, the contents are not organized by discourse type but on the basis of their theoretical orientation to participation ('Reconsidering Participation Frameworks', 'Participation and Interpersonal Pragmatics', 'Forms of Participation'). Indeed, the notion of participation is kept at the centre of the collection and the editors note how this volume helps us to move away from traditional models of one-way or dyadic communication, to a much more comprehensive understanding of the complexity of participation roles. Another strength is the way in which they set out to include works which test participation frameworks on new modes of communication, rather than assume that any new mode requires an entirely new method of analysis. Just as participants adapt their existing repertoire of communicative strategies, so we can assume that researchers should be able to adapt robust models of analysis.

In *The Pragmatics of Quoting Now and Then*, the editors, Jenny Arendholz, Wolfram Bublitz, and Monika Kirner-Ludwig, address the use of quotations as 'a ubiquitous meta-communicative act' (p. 1) and also integrate work examining both online and offline data. They have collated a unique set of chapters covering a truly impressive range of contexts, which stretch across period, genre, mode and participation type (from ME dialogues to contemporary online news articles). As the editors state, 'integrating what other people said or meant (and even how they said it) into one's own discourse seems to be a universal feature of all natural languages and, what is more, one of the more prevalent joys of ordinary life' (p. 1). Thus, quoting is positioned as a feature which can be tracked across a broad range of text types. The chapters operationalize the *Now and Then* 'by adopting a synchronic or diachronic perspective, on the one hand, and by investigating media-induced developments on the other' (p. 15), and this structure is reflected in the division of the book into two sections ('Quoting Then' and 'Quoting Now'). Importantly, this means that time and mode elements are not conflated, and the range can be fully recognized. The collection is also wide-reaching in the types of quoting that are dealt with, including direct quotes (which constitute the main focus), indirect quotes, mixed quotes, and scare quotes. The chapters selected for this volume also fall in with another continuing trend, as discussed below, which is the increase in the use of corpora in discourse studies.

This kind of integrated approach, is also evident in another collection: *The Dynamics of Political Discourse: Forms and Functions of Follow-Ups*, edited by Anita Fetzer, Elda Weizman, and Lawrence Berlin. The ten chapters (which follow an accessible introduction) all investigate follow-ups, which are 'conceptualised as communicative acts, in and through which a prior communicate act is accepted, challenged, or otherwise negotiated by third parties' (p. 2). The editors frame the collection as a response to the increasingly dynamic nature of political discourse, which is driven by changes in society, 'especially considering our mediatized society and the so-called new media' (p.

1). Thus, in the second part, 'Follow-Ups across Genres', we see contributions examining election debates, online political discussion on social media, 'social TV', and reception of a political speech on blogs and forums. The move to include reception is an important one, and the theoretical chapters in this volume will be of great use to researchers in the area. The special issue of *Pragmatics* (25:i[2015]), edited by Miriam Locher, Brook Bolander, and Nicole Höhn, on 'Relational Work in Facebook and Discussion Boards/Fora in Pragmatics' also takes a more nuanced approach to online discourse, by focusing on the interpersonal aspect of language within similar kinds of interactional spaces: two papers examine discussion boards, and two focus on the social network of Facebook. Where variation is addressed, it is not from a simplistic perspective, but rather prioritizes the pragmatic variables, recognizing that 'interactants play with different possibilities of expressing themselves in order to achieve interpersonal effects and to use language creatively in identity performance' (p. 5). The special edition of *Discourse, Context & Media* (*DC&M* 9[2015]), dedicated to 'Communicating Time and Place on Digital Media' (edited by Alexandra Georgakopoulou) also addresses online discourses. In this case there is less unity in the kinds of interactional spaces that are considered (from Tinder to Second Life to online reviews) although they do all share a public element. The coherence of the collection comes principally from the theme of examining time and place, bringing deixis once more to the fore in pragmatics research.

In 2015 we also welcomed two substantial volumes whose primary goal is to contribute to teaching practice. In *Researching Sociopragmatic Variability: Perspectives from Variational, Interlanguage and Contrastive Pragmatics*, the editors Kate Beeching and Helen Woodfield pick up the challenge that (scholars in) the areas of sociolinguistics and pragmatics have perhaps not been as well acquainted as might be desirable, collating studies on variational pragmatics, interlanguage pragmatics, contrastive pragmatics, and sociopragmatic competence in a volume that 'aims to present research on sociopragmatic variability which can inform teaching' (p. 2). The eleven chapters draw on a wide range of methods, from traditional discourse-completion tasks to corpus analysis; they will prove especially useful to researchers just coming to this new field and looking for tools they can replicate or adapt. The collection is also rich in the number of languages covered and the range of contexts. *Teaching and Learning (Im)Politeness*, edited by Barbara Pizziconi and Miriam Locher, similarly wishes to connect teachers, researchers, and research topics, in this case by bringing together researchers from the fields of im/politeness, language pedagogy, and language learning 'in an endeavour to enrich the outlook of teachers as well as researchers, and to further engender a useful dialogue between (im)politeness theorists, language teachers and Second Language Acquisition (SLA) researchers' (p. 1). The strands of 'learning' and 'teaching' are interpreted in both narrow and broad senses (hence the use of inverted commas when they are discussed in the framing of the book). The first part of the volume, '(Im)Politeness in L2 Instructional Contexts', contains four chapters examining im/politeness in language classrooms, while the second part, ' "Teaching" and "Learning" (about) (Im)Politeness in L1 and L2', opens up with three chapters that examine acculturation in wider contexts (for instance, the relationship between (spoken) BrE and British Sign Language or the development of communication skills in British medical degree students). The volume is wrapped up with a closing epilogue by Juliane House, which both provides reflections on the themes emerging and notes a significant absent theme: work on teaching and learning *im*politeness. It is hoped that in highlighting this lacuna, we may look forward to a future collection dedicated to teaching and learning impoliteness.

The continued rise of impoliteness or verbal aggression as an important research area is noticeable across a range of publications but perhaps most prominently in the journal dedicated to this topic *Journal of Language Aggression and Conflict*. In 2015, this included a special issue (*JLA&C* 3/1[2015]) on the topic of 'Contemporary Discourses of Hate and Radicalism across Space and Genres', which brought together nine articles covering sadly topical issues including homophobia, anti-migrant discourse, and Holocaust denial. This responsiveness to social events is once again prominent across publications in discourse studies and is a real strength in this area. A noticeable theme relates to hate targets of populist discourses. In 'Satire, Racist Humour and the Power of (Un)Laughter: On the Restrained Nature of Swedish Online Racist Discourse Targeting EU-Migrants Begging for Money' (*D&S* 26([2015] 733–53), Karl Malmqvist challenges assumptions about the nature of online discourse and shows how, far from being consistently explicit, racism is also expressed in more subtle (and therefore less easily detectable) ways. This is significant in two ways, first in showing similarities and continuity across online/offline discourses, and second in highlighting the role of irony, satire, and humour in communicating racist views. 'The American Dream? Anti-Immigrant Discourse Bubbling Up from the Coca-Cola "It's Beautiful' Advertisement"' by Mikaela L. Marlow (*D&C* 9[2015] 625–41) also examines online comments, in this case responses to a multilingual advert which was screened in the United States. The analysis develops the 'Model of Normalized Hate Speech' in order to structure and promote more research in the area of hate speech. A revealing feature from this paper is the identification of how xenophobic postings align with the US English-Only movement. Language ideologies are similarly invoked in Heike Wiese's study ' "This migrants' babble is not a German dialect!": The Interaction of Standard Language Ideology and "Us"/"Them" Dichotomies in the Public Discourse on a Multiethnolect' (*LSoc* 44[2015] 341–68), in which language ideologies are also employed to communicate and express racism by proxy. Melani Schröter's '80,000,000 HOOLIGANS: Discourse of Resistance to Racism and Xenophobia in German Punk Lyrics 1991–1994' (*CDS* 12/4[2015] 398–425) also examines the German context, but rather than documenting racist discourses turns its attention to discourses of resistance. While anti-racism has a substantial history in sociology, in language studies it has perhaps been overlooked to some extent. Thus this is a very welcome addition which, we hope, will lead to more consideration of how discourse studies can be employed not only to document and identify (non-obvious) racist discourses but also to consider how they may be challenged.

The topicality of subjects treated within discourse studies may also be seen in three highly relevant contributions published by Benjamins. In *Discourse, Identity and Legitimacy: Self and Other in Representations of Iran's Nuclear Programme*, Majid KhosraviNik tackles the British and Iranian news reporting on Iran's nuclear programme. In so doing, he not only casts light on the case in hand but also illustrates how the tools of the discourse-historical approach may be systematically employed in this kind of study to uncover and understand the operationalization of ideologies in media texts. As such, it will be of great use to students and researchers from a theoretical-methodological perspective. Two collections, *Discourse, Politics and Women as Global Leaders*, edited by Diana Boxer and John Wilson, and *Singing, Speaking and Writing Politics: South African Political Discourses*, edited by Mirjana N. Dedaić, also respond to ongoing social issues. The first feels particularly relevant in a year which saw a female US presidential candidate repeatedly criticized for being female. In the concluding chapter, the editors state that there is no 'discursive "magic bullet"' and the 'media continue to contribute significantly more so than any other factor to the sustained institution of dominant masculine political identities, identities which women political leaders either have to relegate, replicate or trump in public perception in order to be viewed as equally credible and legitimate holders of leadership positions' (p. 345). By bringing together papers treating the discourse around female leaders across different countries, the volume is able to show how culturally specific the expectations are. The second collection covers a range of important and topical social issues, including representations of gender, sexuality, race, and xenophobia in the context of South Africa. As with the other volumes, this is also a welcome move away from a British/US focus, which can only enrich the field.

As in previous years, we may also note a trend towards increased integration of corpus linguistics in our field . In 2015 this was more evident in discourse studies than in pragmatics. A special issue of *D&C* (9:ii[2015]), edited by Paul Baker, brings together five research papers all of which employ innovative methods within corpus-assisted (critical) discourse analysis. As argued in the introduction, corpus methods are well suited to the analysis of media discourse for two reasons. First, by providing a way of handling (the increasingly) vast amount of data which may be generated for any given topic. Articles within the volume help to show how this may done (in particular those by Amanda Potts, Monika Bednarek, and Helen Caple, 'How can computer-based methods help researchers to investigate news values in large datasets? A corpus linguistic study of the construction of newsworthiness in the reporting on Hurricane Katrina', (*D&C* 9 [2015] 149–72) and by Paul Baker and Erez Levon, 'Picking the right cherries? A comparison of corpus-based and qualitative analyses of news articles about masculinity' (*D&C* 9 [2015] 221–36)). Second, by reducing researcher bias through bringing different aspects of the data to their attention. As the introduction suggests, 'for example, a list of corpus-derived keywords can stubbornly occupy the analyst's screen, quietly demanding that those words which were not expected to be statistically salient be concordanced and explained, driving the analysis in unexpected directions' (p. 144). The monograph *Representation of the British Suffrage Movement* by

Kat Gupta comes in the Research in Corpus and Discourse series (series editors Wolfgang Teubert and Michaela Mahlberg). Alongside the rewarding Routledge Advances in Corpus Linguistics series (editors Tony McEnery and Michael Hoey), this is an important source of studies offering exciting applications of corpus and discourse studies. As in the special *D&C* issue just mentioned, Gupta's book also examines media discourse, but in this case from a historical perspective as it examines the *Times* in the UK from 1908 to 1914. As the UK approaches the centenary celebrations of the Representation of the People Act 1918, which gave some women the vote for the first time, looking back at how those involved were represented seems particularly timely. The volume will provide fascinating food for thought both for those interested in the topic and for its methodology.

## 13. Stylistics

A useful starting point for the review of the year's work in stylistics is a volume which provides a broad overview of some of the main theoretical approaches, methods of analysis, and current areas of research within the discipline: *The Bloomsbury Companion to Stylistics*, edited by Violeta Sotirova. The book begins with an introduction to the key theoretical directions in the area, showing how stylisticians are able to draw on such fields as pragmatics (Siobhan Chapman's 'Pragmatics and Stylistics', pp. 78–91), discourse analysis (Marina Lambrou's 'Discourse Stylistics', pp. 92–108), and corpus linguistics (Michaela Mahlberg's 'Corpus Stylistics, pp. 139–57), among others. This overview of the various perspectives and methods is followed by chapters which outline a number of areas of research within stylistics, where such classic topics as foregrounding, point of view, and metaphor are discussed and illustrated by examples from a range of texts, such as neurological illness autobiographies (Catherine Emmott and Marc Alexander's 'Defamiliarization and Foregrounding: Representing Experiences of Change of State and Perception in Neurological Illness Narratives', pp. 289–307), email novels (Joe Bray's 'Narrative Point of View', pp. 341–55), and love poems (Gerard Steen's 'Metaphor: Metaphor and Style through Genre, with Illustrations from Carol Ann Duffy's *Rapture*', pp. 308–24). Steen's discussion of metaphor in literary texts focuses on the notion of genre—a topic which is expanded in the final section of the volume, and which extends from considerations of style in OE literary compositions (Sara M. Pons-Sanz's 'Old English Style', pp. 569–82), to the language of contemporary popular novels, specifically horror fiction dealing with vampiric themes (Rocío Montoro, 'Style in Popular Literature', pp. 671–7).

Whether it is horror fiction novels or illness memoirs, narratives continue to be one of the key areas of study within stylistics and narratology. *Narrative: The Basics* by Bronwen Thomas is a concise, accessible overview of some of the basic concepts and questions in the study of narrative. Rather than providing a comprehensive summary of narrative theory, this short book aims to offer a jargon-free beginner's guide to many of the terms and theories used by narratologists, and to show how these can be applied in discussions of various types of narrative, such as fairy tales, news stories, advertising campaigns, and tweets. Popular films and television series are used in particular to illustrate theoretical concepts, with Thomas discussing Propp's idea of 'spheres of action' in relation to the characters in *Fight Club* [1999], explaining the distinction between story and discourse with regard to the ordering of events in *Memento* [2000], and showing how point-of-view shots in *Peep Show* (Channel 4 [2003–16]) relate to the concept of focalization. Following brief introductions to such essential narratological topics as point of view, types of narration, and speech and thought representation, Thomas discusses the intersections of narrative and genre, readership, ideology, and finally, the changing nature of the narrative in the digital age. This last chapter particularly, as well as the range of examples from different media used throughout, allow Thomas to address one of her primary goals, that is, to explore 'the specific ways in which narratives continue to enthral, move and unsettle us in an age when the boundaries between different forms and media, between authors and readers and even between fiction and reality are becoming more and more blurred' (p. 8).

While Thomas addresses narrative theory as a whole, Henrik Skov Nielsen, James Phelan, and Richard Walsh's 'Ten Theses about Fictionality' (*Narrative* 23[2015] 61–73) focuses on one particular issue in the study of narrative, namely fictionality, understood as 'the intentional use of invented stories and scenarios' such as spoofs, what-if projections, if-only regrets, thought experiments, and hypotheses (p. 61)—a mode or quality of discourse rather than a set of genres. The topic of fictionality is further explored by Paul Dawson in 'Ten Theses against Fictionality' (*Narrative* 23[2015] 74–100), which focuses on non-fictional narratives and their treatment in narratology. Meir Sternberg and Tamar Yacobi tackle another complex issue relevant to narratology: unreliability. Their '(Un)Reliability in Narrative Discourse: A Comprehensive Overview' (*PoT* 36[2015] 327–498) presents a thorough outline of the various aspects of reliability/unreliability in narrative texts (taking Wayne Booth's work on unreliable narration as a starting point), exploring, among other issues, concepts such as 'narrator', 'author', and 'implied author', and their role in affecting reliability judgements. These subjects are further discussed in Tamar Yacobi's 'Narrative and Normative Pattern: On Interpreting Fiction, with Special Regard to (Un)Reliability' (*PoT* 36[2015] 499–528), which explores how the type of mediation between the interpreter and the implied author shapes the interpretation of different texts. Another topic of interest to narratologists is time. Eyal Segal's 'Time Travel Stories as a Challenge to Narratology: The Case of *The Time Traveler's Wife*' (*PoT* 36[2015] 529–60) examines the story-world (including its chronology and its order of presentation) and the different time perspectives in Audrey Niffenegger's novel, suggesting that the way in which time-travel stories play with the temporality of the story-world is of interest to narratology. Time and place are also discussed in Alistair Brown's 'Communication Technology and Narrative: Letters, Instant Messaging, and Mobile Phones in Three Romantic Novels' (*PoT* 36[2015] 33–58), in which the author considers how communicative devices (letters, emails, phone calls) connect fictional characters in different times and places, helping novelists structure plots, create characters and present narrative voice. These communicative devices are explored in the context of three romantic novels from different periods, with a focus on how they allow romance to develop in various ways. Plot development is also one of the topics in Dan Shen's 'Dual Textual Dynamics and Dual Readerly Dynamics: Double Narrative Movements in Mansfield's "Psychology"' (*Style* 49[2015] 411–38), which discusses the hidden narrative movements that lie behind the plot development in fictional narratives. This kind of covert textual progression, according to Shen, can be described as 'a powerful dynamic that runs, at a deeper level, throughout the text' (p. 411). The double narrative movements constitute dual textual dynamics—these, in turn, encourage dual readerly dynamics, inviting complex responses from readers.

The ways in which different types of narrative can invite particular reader responses have also been the focus of research in stylistics. In 'Language Varieties and Youthful Involvement in Indonesian Fiction' (*L&L* 24[2015] 108–28), Dwi Noverini Djenar and Michael C. Ewing explore how the interplay between standard and colloquial varieties can encourage young readers' involvement with Indonesian teen fiction and comics, focusing on those techniques that help to shift narrators' and characters' perspectives, building empathy and involvement in the story-world. Leah Anderst's 'Feeling with Real Others: Narrative Empathy in the Autobiographies of Doris Lessing and Alison Bechdel' (*Narrative* 23[2015] 271–90) addresses the issue of narrative empathy by discussing the empathetic responses to 'real' people, representing characters in autobiographical writing. Finally, Louise Brix Jacobsen's 'Vitafiction as a Mode of Self-Fashioning: The Case of Michael J. Fox in *Curb Your Enthusiasm*' (*Narrative* 23[2015] 252–70) examines the construction and perception of unsympathetic behaviour in an audio-visual narrative which seems 'simultaneously fictional and non-fictional' (p. 252)—a mode which Jacobsen terms 'vitafiction'.

While the studies outlined above focus on narratives, poetry has also been the subject of stylistic investigation. For example, Eva María Gómez-Jiménez's '"Oride Lesgo Eckshun": Spelling Foregrounding in the Experimental Poetry of e.e. cummings' (*L&L* 24[2015] 307–21) examines the use of misspelling in e.e. cummings's poetry. In a sample of sixty-six poems, she identifies and classifies techniques used by cummings in spelling foregrounding, and discusses the functions, effects, and meanings of those spelling choices in his poetry. Wit Pietrzak's 'Survivals: The Yeatsian Element in Paul Muldoon's "At the Sign of the Black Horse, September 1999"' (*ETC* 8[2015] 177–93) considers intertextuality in Muldoon's poem, suggesting how an examination of the references to Yeats's work present in the poem show Muldoon challenging Yeats's ideology and aesthetic. Another poet who has received considerable scholarly attention this year has been Emily Dickinson. In 'Overcoming Oneself as Subject in Dickinson's Poetry: Adorno and Heidegger' (*Style* 49[2015] 334–54), Colleen Shu-Ching Wu applies Adorno's and Heidegger's work in an analysis of Dickinson's poems, showing how the philosophical ideas are challenged by the 'lyric self' in her poetry. Matthias Bauer, Nadine Bade, Sigrid Beck, Carmen Dörge, Burkhard von Eckartsberg, Janina Niefer, Saskia Ottschofski, and Angelika Zirker's 'Emily Dickinson's

"My Life Had Stood a Loaded Gun"—An Interdisciplinary Analysis' (*JLS* 44[2015] 115–40) shows a very different methodological approach: the authors identify the possible interpretations of Dickinson's poem by combining two analytical methods: first, by carrying out linguistic text analysis (involving grammar and compositional semantics), and second, by undertaking a more 'subjective' literary analysis, which involves considering the wider external context of the poem. These two methods, the authors suggest, complement each other in helping to uncover the interpretative process. Finally, Richard Cureton, in 'A Reading in Temporal Poetics: Emily Dickinson's "I Taste a Liquor Never Brewed"' (*Style* 49[2015] 354–62), discusses the relationship between rhythm and form in poetry, using Dickinson's poem to explore the idea that poems are mixtures of temporalities—these mixtures are said to give poems their unique sensibility, or '"inner" form'. Rhythm in poetry is also the subject of Tatiana Nikitina and Boris Maslov's 'Verse Structure and Literary Tradition: The Interaction between Rhyme and Stress in the Onegin Stanza' (*Style* 49[2015] 439–69), which explores the relationship between rhyme and rhythm (stress within the line) in syllabo-accented verse, with an aim of showing how these effects correlate. Their statistical analysis of Pushkin's *Eugene Onegin* suggests that rhythm of individual lines can mimic rhyming structures within the stanza.

Rhythm is also a recurring topic in 'Free Verse Rhythms', a special issue of *Style*, which addresses, amongst other topics, the role of prosodic features in the performance of free verse poems. Roi Tartakovsky's 'The Case for Pace' (*Style* 49[2015] 65–77), for example, focuses on pace as a way of discussing rhythm in both metrical and non-metrical verse, outlining punctuation, stress, and other pacing devices that can cause the reader to increase and decrease speed in the course of reading. In 'Intonation and the Conventions of Free Verse' (*Style* 49[2015] 8–34), Natalie Gerber argues for the crucial role of intonation in prosodic criticism, suggesting that an analysis of free verse must consider the relationship between line, syntax, and intonation—where intonation is seen as a prosodic measure with its own structure. Reuven Tsur's 'Free Verse, Enjambment, Irony: A Case Study' (*Style* 49[2015] 35–45) examines the role that blank verses play in the perception of free verse poems, discussing the vocal strategies used by a performer during the reading of Yehuda Amichai's 'Rain in the Battlefield', and the relationship between the perception of blank verse and irony. Clive Scott's 'The Rhythms of Free Verse and the Rhythms of Translation' (*Style* 49[2015] 46–64) explores the affinities between free verse and translation, suggesting that both place an emphasis on performance, that is 'the translation of the linguistic toward the paralinguistic' (p. 46). Richard Cureton, finally, also focuses on rhythm (as well as theme, time, and form) in 'Rhythm, Temporality, and "Inner Form"' (*Style* 49[2015] 78–109).

Listeners' perceptions of the performer's prosodic features in the reading of poems have also been the subject of empirical research. Chen Gafni and Reuven Tsur's '"Softened" Voice Quality in Poetry Reading and Listener Response' (*SSOL* 5[2015] 49–83) investigates listeners' perceptions of a 'softened' voice quality by eliciting open-ended descriptions and ratings on scales, and confirm that listeners are sensitive to this 'emotional' style of delivery. Also on the subject of reader response to poetry, David I. Hanauer's 'Beauty Judgements of Non-Professional Poetry: Regression Analyses of Authorial Attribution, Emotional Response and Perceived Writing Quality' (*SSOL* 5[2015] 183–99) explores the responses to poems written by non-professional writers, suggesting that 'the decision that a poem is written by a published poet predicted the quality of writing' (p. 183). Readers' predictions (but in the context of fictional narratives) are also the topic of an article by Peter Dixon, Marisa Bortolussi, and Blaine Mullins, 'Judging a Book by Its Cover' (*SSOL* 5[2015] 23–48), which investigates how those readers who identify as either science-fiction or mystery fans apply their knowledge in using the visual information on book covers to determine the genre of the text. The authors conclude that for experienced readers of particular genres book covers do provide a source of valuable information. Massimo Salgaro's 'How Literary Can Literariness Be? Methodological Problems in the Study of Foregrounding' (*SSOL* 5[2015] 229–49) recounts two experiments in which his team investigated the role of genre expectations (literary texts vs. newspaper articles) in the processing of literary language—specifically, rhetorical devices associated with foregrounding. The fact that the studies did not produce analogous results, Salgaro suggests, points to the 'limitations of an exclusive focus on foregrounding' (p. 229) without giving consideration to background-ing elements. While the studies above relied on self-report as methods of measuring reader response, Gareth Carrol, Kathy Conklin, Josephine Guy, and Rebekah Scott, in 'Processing Punctuation and Word Changes in Different Editions of Prose Fiction' (*SSOL* 5[2015] 200–28), discuss the results of an eye-tracking experiment in which readers' attention to minor lexical and punctuation changes in various editions of prose extracts was compared, allowing the authors to consider the implications of adopting such methodology in the study of text processing. Various methodologies for such 'scientific' studies of literature are compared in Arthur M. Jacobs's 'The Scientific Study of Literary Experience: Sampling the State of the Art' (*SSOL* 5[2015] 139–70), which reviews four recent empirical studies of literary experience (from fields such as phenomenology and cognitive neuroscience) and outlines various theoretical and methodological issues involved in the scientific study of literature.

A unique approach to the study of reader response is outlined in *The Discourse of Reading Groups: Integrating Cognitive and Sociocultural Perspectives* by David Peplow, Joan Swann, Paola Trimarco, and Sara Whiteley, in which the authors explore reading as a collaborative activity, investigating the talk produced when readers interact with each other in reading groups. By focusing specifically on the discussion taking place in these groups, the authors further develop the already established 'discursive approach' to the study of reading groups (e.g. Swann and Allington [2009], Allington [2011], Peplow [2011])—an approach which draws on sociocultural work in literacy studies and sociology of reading but which relies on the analytical tools from discourse analysis (primarily interactional sociolinguis-tics and conversation analysis). One of this book's contributions is that it adds a new, *cognitive* perspective to the existing sociocultural frameworks, resulting in what the authors refer to as a 'sociocognitive' perspective on reading-group discourse; one which, as the authors suggest, can be applied more broadly to other fields that investigate the practice of reading. While this cognitive focus is particularly evident in chapter 2, which draws on text-world theory, chapters 3 and 4 offer a more sociocultural approach to individual and group readings (respectively). The remainder of the book explores the significance of settings for reading-group interaction—from institutional settings (the authors discuss groups at the University of the Third Age, a university medical department and primary/secondary schools) to reading and writing in online contexts (specifically, in blogs, online genre groups, and social networking sites). By bringing together a selection of discursive studies of reading groups which the authors have carried out over the last seven years, Peplow et al. illustrate the nature, functions, and complexity of everyday literary discussions in a way which not only aids our understanding of readers' interpretative activity and the behaviour of interpretative communities but also points to 'the value of stylistic and discourse analysis that looks for common ground between cognitive and sociocultural perspectives' (p. 194).

The way cognitive perspectives can help to shed light on readers' interpretation of texts continues to be investigated in stylistics, as is evident in Kathryn S. McCarthy's 'Reading Beyond the Lines: A Critical Review of Cognitive Approaches to Literary Interpretation and Comprehension' (SSOL 5[2015] 99–128), which reviews existing work in literary theory, empirical approaches to literature, and cognitive work on text comprehension to explore what is known about the psychological mechanisms involved in literary interpretation. Elżbieta Chrzanowska-Kluczewska's 'Textual Indeterminacy Revisited: From Roman Ingarden Onwards' (JLS 44[2015] 1–21) focuses on the work of the Polish philosopher Roman Ingarden (in the period between the 1930s and 1960s), whose model of textual 'indeterminacy' is, as Chrzanowska-Kluczewska suggests, still of relevance to those approaches to aesthetic response which connect phenomenology, cognitive studies, and neuroscience. Alexandra Berlina (PoT 36[2015] 151–74) revisits another classic text that has had an impact on the development of cognitive stylistics, and offers a retranslation of Victor Shklovsky's essay 'Art, as Device' (first published in Poetika in 1919), which she precedes with a discussion of Shklovsky's key term, 'ostranenie', translated variously as 'defamiliarization', 'estrangement', and 'enstrangement'. While Shklovsky's text does not focus on cognition in itself, it has nevertheless been instrumental in providing a key theoretical direction to those working in cognitive stylistics and the empirical study of literature, including a number of the studies mentioned in this review (see Emmott and Alexander, and Salgaro, discussed above).

A study that directly addresses the relationship between cognition and our engagement with literature—specifically narratives—is Yanna B. Popova's Stories, Meaning, and Experience: Narrativity and Enaction, which argues for the centrality of storytelling in human lives and the crucial role stories play in organizing our knowledge and experience. 'The study of narrative', the author suggests, 'presents a unique way to approach the study of the human mind'— her book, consequently, is 'a view of the mind through narrative' (p. 3). Based on the embodied/enactive view of cognitive science, Popova proposes to study narrative as an aspect of social cognition, with a focus on the interaction between the represented world and the reader's perception of it. The first part of the monograph outlines a theory of narrativity that is based on the notions of causality, enaction, and metaphor. These issues are subsequently analysed in detail in reference to works by Gabriel García Márquez, Kazuo Ishiguro, and Henry James. Even though considerable attention is devoted to literary narratives, such an enactive approach to narrativity and cognition can, as Popova suggests, be applied to any story we tell each other.

*Refiguring Minds in Narrative Media* by David Ciccoricco, also drawing on narratology to explore cognition in relation to literary reading, is interested in the treatment and representation of minds, cognition, and consciousness in different kinds of narrative media: print novels, digital fiction, and video games. Ciccoricco not only explores how we understand the minds presented in digital narratives but also provides suggestions as to how we comprehend the multimodal and computational elements in these texts more generally. By discussing the notions of attention and perception (Part I of the book) and memory and emotion (Part II) with reference to digital narratives, Ciccoricco extends insights from the existing cognitive-oriented literary studies framework (typically applied to print texts) to a wider range of narrative media, with a view to 'placing these narrative media in dialogue' (p. 237). This is a contribution which is likely to be of relevance to those narrative and literary scholars with an interest in media studies (particularly digital art and culture), game studies, and digital humanities more broadly.

Like Ciccoricco's book, much of the work in cognitive stylistics (and cognitive approaches to literary study generally) has focused on the issue of representing and attributing minds to characters in fiction. Louise Nuttall's 'Attributing Minds to Vampires in Richard Matheson's *I Am Legend*' (*L&L* 24[2015] 23–39) draws on cognitive grammar and psychological research on 'mind attribution' to explore the construction of vampire characters in Matheson's [1954] science fiction/horror novel. She points to the linguistic choices that shape readers' perceptions of these characters, supporting her analysis with a discussion of the readers' online responses to the text. Sandrine Sorlin, in 'Person Deixis and Impersonation in Iain Banks's *Complicity*' (*L&L* 24[2015] 40–53), combines linguistic, stylistic, cognitive, and psychological approaches to suggest how personal pronouns (specifically, first- and second-person) can be used to create different mindstyles, and how readers construct mental representations to comprehend ambiguities in literary style. In 'When Narrative Takes Over: The Representation of Embedded Mindstates in Shakespeare's *Othello*' (*L&L* 24[2015] 148–66), Max J. van Duijn, Ineke Sluiter, and Arie Verhagen discuss readers' ability to process 'embedded mindstates' (e.g. 'A believes that B thinks that C intends')—a cognitive task, which, as the authors suggest, increases in difficulty with every level of embedding added. Based on an analysis of *Othello*, the article outlines a number of 'expository strategies' which are used in the text of the play to help readers make sense of the various level of embedding. Finally, Jonas Grethlein's 'Is Narrative "The Description of Fictional Mental Functioning"? Heliodorus against Palmer, Zunshine & Co' (*Style* 49[2015] 257–99), perhaps controversially, challenges the idea that our reading of narratives relies primarily on our ability to apply our theory of mind mechanism to 'read the minds' of characters. While Grethlein agrees that the concept of mind-reading can be relevant to readers' engagement with modern novels, his discussion of Heliodorus's ancient novel *Ethiopica* aims to show that in narratives that do not focus on the presentation of characters' consciousness, a theory-of-mind approach is insufficient as it downplays the role of the temporal dynamics of narrative and its experiential features such as suspense and curiosity.

Minds in narratives are also the topic of a special issue of *Narrative*, 'Social Minds'. In this issue, editors Maximilian Alders and Eva von Contzen bring together a range of contributions which address the issue of the representation of a collective, shared experience in textual narratives—the formation of *social*, rather than individual, minds (the idea based on Alan Palmer's *Social Minds in the Novel* [2010]). This investigation of social minds in literature is done diachronically and includes discussions of the writers of ancient Greece, in Jonas Grethlein's 'Social Minds and Narrative Time: Collective Experience in Thucydides and Heliodorus' (*Narrative* 23[2015] 123–39), medieval literature, in Eva von Contzen's 'Why Medieval Literature Does Not Need the Concept of Social Minds: Exemplarity and Collective Experience' (*Narrative* 23[2015] 140–53), and Shakespearean drama, in Miranda Anderson's 'Fission-Fusion Cognition in Shakespearean Drama: The Case for *Julius Caesar*' (*Narrative* 23[2015] 154–68). Twentieth-century narratives are discussed in the last two articles: Brian Richardson's 'Representing Social Minds: "We" and "They" Narratives, Natural and Unnatural' (*Narrative* 23[2015] 200–12) and Jan Alber's 'The Social Minds in Factual and Fictional We-Narratives of the Twentieth Century' (*Narrative* 23[2015] 213–25), both of which focus on the use of personal pronouns in the construction of social minds.

Another topic explored by those interested in cognitive approaches to stylistic analysis is the cognitive linguistic notion of metaphor. María D. López Maestre's '"Man the Hunter": A Critical Reading of Hunt-Based Conceptual Metaphors of Love and Sexual Desire' (*JLS* 44[2015] 89–113) combines cognitive linguistics and CDA to explore metaphorical expressions relating to love and sexual desire involving the source domain of the hunt (specifically: male hunters and female prey), and considers the ideological implications of such a portrayal of men and women. Metaphor is also one of the topics discussed by Leona Toker, whose 'Hypallage and the Literalization of Metaphors in a Dickens Text' (*Style* 49[2015] 113–25) explores the uses and effects of hypallage in Dickens's *A Tale of Two Cities*. Like metaphor, metonymy, personification, and enthymeme, hypallage is seen as 'epithet transfer' which, amongst other functions, serves as a conceptual blend in the narrative.

Aside from being analysed qualitatively, as in the studies above, metaphors in fiction and other texts have also been studied using corpus methods. Aletta G. Dorst, in 'More or Different Metaphors in Fiction? A Quantitative Cross-Register Comparison' (*L&L* 24[2015] 3–22), compares the frequency and types of metaphors in prose fiction, news texts, academic discourse, and conversation. The metaphors are identified using the MIPVU method (Gerard Steen et al. [2010], an extension from the 'Metaphor Identification Procedure', Pragglejaz Group [2007]). The analysis shows that, while fiction is not (contrary to expectations) the register with the highest number of metaphors,

metaphors in fiction can exhibit characteristics that set them apart from those in other text types. Another corpus-based comparison of language use in different corpora is Rolf Kreyer's '"Funky fresh dressed to impress": A Corpus-Linguistic View on Gender Roles in Pop Songs' (*IJCL* 20[2015] 174–204), which explores the representation of men and women in the lyrics of pop songs by analysing two corpora of contemporary songs by male and female artists. While the analysis points to similarities in the corpora, it is suggested that the portrayal of women and their roles can be considered damaging. A rather different genre is analysed by Sean Murphy in '*I Will Proclaim Myself What I Am*: Corpus Stylistics and the Language of Shakespeare's Soliloquies' (*L&L* 24[2015] 338–54), which uses WordSmith Tools to compare the language of soliloquies with that of dialogue in thirty-seven Shakespeare plays with a view to identifying key language forms in soliloquies and testing those interpretations of the forms that have been proposed within literary criticism. Murphy additionally compares the linguistic features of comedy, tragedy, and history soliloquies, and discusses the functions of particular language forms in Shakespeare's works. Another study testing qualitative hypotheses with quantitative methods is 'REMEMBER and FORGET in Dan Brown's *Angels and Demons*: A Corpus-Informed Account' (*L&L* 24[2015] 292–306), in which Ernestine Lahey uses corpus tools (specifically, WordSmith) to examine the frequency and function of the verbs 'remember' and 'forget' in Brown's *Angels and Demons* [2000]. The corpus-informed investigation is used to test hypotheses generated through a qualitative analysis of the novel—while these are partly validated, some results are contradictory to expectations.

While Dorst's metaphor study outlined above focuses on the intersection of cognitive linguistics and corpus linguistics, a mixed corpus and cognitive *stylistic* approach is used in Peter Stockwell and Michaela Mahlberg's 'Mind-Modelling with Corpus Stylistics in *David Copperfield*' (*L&L* 24[2015] 129–47), which applies corpus linguistic methods to explore the cognitive stylistic notion of mind-modelling in literary characterization (mind-modelling is a concept related to the representation of fictional minds, discussed above with regard to cognitive stylistics). The authors use the CLiC (Corpus Linguistics in Cheshire) tool to analyse the textual information around the character of Mr Dick from Dickens's *David Copperfield*—this is done in order to identify the linguistic patterns in the text that act as triggers of character information. Stockwell and Mahlberg's study seems very much in line with the approach Dan McIntyre proposes in 'Towards an Integrated Corpus Stylistics' (*TL* 16[2015] 59–68). McIntyre points to a number of problems with the term 'corpus stylistics': its potentially narrow definition as the corpus linguistics of literary language (somewhat misleading because stylistics is, of course, not restricted to the study of literary texts), as well as the assumption that traditional, non-corpus stylistics somehow lacks academic rigour. McIntyre argues for a more integrated view of corpus stylistics, one that aims to 'incorporate theories, models and methods from qualitative stylistic analysis to augment computational techniques' (p. 60). He adds that a particularly productive link can be made between the disciplines of corpus stylistics and cognitive stylistics; these should be used to complement each other, rather than in isolation.

A discipline making use of both corpus and cognitive approaches to stylistics is translation studies. In 'Translation Meets Cognitive Science: The Imprint of Translation on Cognitive Processing' (*Multilingua* 34[2015] 721–46), Ana Rojo reviews the current work in translation studies focusing on the cognitive aspects of translation, drawing from disciplines such as cognitive linguistics, psycholinguistics, and neurology. Applying cognitive science in the study of translation has potential implications, according to the author, not only for understanding the translation process but also for the research on language processing generally. Anna Čermáková's 'Repetition in John Irving's Novel *A Widow for One Year*: A Corpus Stylistics Approach to Literary Translation' (*IJCL* 20[2015] 355–77), on the other hand, uses corpus methods (cluster and keyword analysis) to examine the repetition in Irving's book and its translations into Czech and Finnish. By identifying repetitive textual features in the texts, Čermáková shows that while repetition is central to the original novel, it has been avoided by translators—this suggests that corpus analysis may bring to light certain stylistic features in literary texts, allowing translators to keep their translations consistent with the original.

A study which, like Čermáková's, combines stylistics, corpus linguistics, and translation studies is Libo Huang's *Style in Translation: A Corpus-Based Perspective*. The author investigates Mona Baker's [2000] notion of the 'style of the literary translator', which is understood as the translator's 'thumbprint' evident in the target text—a concept said to mark a shift of perspective from the interest in the source text and the original author to the linguistic patterning in the work of the translator. Huang approaches the translator's style statistically through a corpus-based translation studies (CTS, Mona Baker [1993]) framework applied to Chinese prose and its translations into English, based on an analysis of the Chinese–English Parallel Corpus of Modern and Contemporary Chinese Novels (built by Huang). Following a review of some stylistic notions relevant to translation (chapter 2) and an outline of the design of the corpus (chapter 3), Huang uses corpus tools—such as standardized type–token ratio, mean sentence length, frequencies of reporting verbs—to compare the literary styles of two translators, Howard Goldblatt and Gladys Yang (chapter 4); the analysis points to common features in the style of these translators, something that Huang links to 'translational style' or 'translation universals' rather than the translator's own way of writing. The remainder of the book focuses on corpus statistical comparisons of such issues as speech and thought representation, direct and inverse translation, and readability in a range of translations of Chinese narrative fiction. Even though the corpus analysis is sometimes found to be insufficient (especially when it comes to defining the concept of 'style'), Huang believes that, by enabling a comparison of a large number of texts, the computational method makes the study 'more scientific and objective' (p. 113).

A different, cognitive-based approach to applying stylistics in translation is *Translation and Linguistic Hybridity: Constructing World-View* by Suzanne Klinger. Klinger analyses linguistic hybridity in cross-cultural writing (e.g. migrant, travel, postcolonial writing), focusing on anglophone Nigerian narrative prose and its translations into German. Drawing on concepts from narratology and (cognitive) stylistics, the author proposes a typology of linguistic hybridity—a typology which subsequently allows her to investigate 'whether and how linguistic hybridity potentially has an impact on the mental representations the reader constructs when interacting with the text and, hence, whether and how TT [target text] shifts in linguistic hybridity can affect the text's meaning potential' (p. 2). The three main aspects of this discussed in the book are the perspective from which readers perceive narrative events (chapter 3), narrator's identification or allegiance with the narrated cultures (chapter 4), and characters' cultural identity and world-views (chapter 5). By using concepts such as focalization, mind-style, text-world theory and schema theory, Klinger demonstrates how existing work on cross-cultural writing (as well as translation studies more generally) can be enriched by extending its conceptual apparatus to include those narratological and cognitive stylistic notions which focus on voice, perspective, and ideology.

Aside from translation, another area that can be enhanced by the application of stylistics is teaching, particularly teaching English as a foreign language. *Literature and Language Learning in the EFL Classroom*, edited by Masayuki Teranishi, Yoshifumi Saito, and Katie Wales, explores how literary texts can be used in English-language teaching. The volume first describes the current approaches to using literature in EFL/ESL contexts (Part I), and then presents a number of case studies illustrating how the theories can be applied in teaching and learning settings (Part II). The collection begins with Geoff Hall's 'Recent Developments in Uses of Literature in Language Teaching' (pp. 13–25), which provides an overview of some of the trends, such as the use of new technologies, creative writing, and translation in English-teaching classes. While creative writing in the classroom is also the topic of Yoshifumi Saito's 'From Reading to Writing: Creative Stylistics as a Methodology for Bridging the Gap between Literary Appreciation and Creative Writing in ELT' (pp. 61–74), Soichiro Oku explores the use of new media ('A Stylistic Approach to Digital Texts: Teaching Literary Texts through New Media', pp. 131–50), and Kiyo Sakamoto's 'Translation of Japanese Poems into English: Literature in the First Language as a Motive to Communicate in a Second Language' (pp. 197–211) provides a case study of using translation to motivate learners in a Japanese college class. Whereas many of the chapters in the collection are concerned with current trends in English-language teaching in Japan, others explore stylistics in EFL/ESL teaching and learning generally—for example, Marina Lambrou in 'Pedagogical Stylistics in an ELT Teacher Training Setting' (pp. 298–315) recounts her experience as a stylistician teaching a postgraduate module for students (primarily non-native speakers of English) training to become language teachers. In 'Unpacking and Evaluating Properties in Conceptual Metaphor Domain Mapping: Cognitive Stylistics as a Language Learning Tool' (pp. 75–93), Michael Burke proposes blending stylistics with cognitive linguistics by 'asking learners to consider the nature of underlying conceptual metaphor in literature and other creative texts' (p. 91). The range of topics and contributors means that while this book may be of particular interest to those teaching in Japan, it will also be relevant to teachers wishing to incorporate literature (and pedagogical stylistics) into EFL classrooms more widely.

Stylistics in language teaching is also the topic of Gary G. Fogal's 'Pedagogical Stylistics in Multiple Foreign Language and Second Language Contexts: A Synthesis of Empirical Research' (L&L 24[2015] 54–72), which considers the ability of pedagogical stylistics to assist in foreign- and second-language teaching, synthesizing a number of studies that investigate the adoption of stylistic techniques into language classrooms. While the synthesis points to the role of stylistics in improving L2 performance, language awareness, and developing academic skills, Fogal outlines under-reporting and under-collecting of data as a reason for the weak representation of stylistics as a tool in language teaching. Kieran O'Halloran provides a different perspective on using stylistics in the classroom. In 'Creating a Film Poem with Stylistic Analysis: A Pedagogical Approach' (L&L 24[2015] 83–107), he outlines an activity which can be used in stylistics teaching, one where students 'draw on their cinematic literacy to dramatise a poem imaginatively' (p. 83), creating film images connected to the poem's stylistic detail. Explicitly connecting the image and stylistic layer of the poem is argued to enhance the creativity of the film, setting it apart from others in the film poem genre.

The relationship between style and film discourse is also the topic of Marc Raymond's 'Two-Shots and Group Shots: Hong Sang-soo's Mannerist and Classical Mise-en-scène' (Style 49[2015] 196–217). The article explores the style of the South Korean film director Hong Sang-soo using two methodological approaches—mise-en-scène criticism and statistical style analysis—with an aim to develop and enhance both approaches to the analysis of cinematic staging. In 'Back to Owl Creek Bridge: Robert Enrico's Adaptation Reconsidered' (Style 49[2015] 181–95), Toru Sasaki examines the visual and auditory devices in the filmic discourse of Enrico's The Occurrence at Owl Creek Bridge, focusing on the dramatic irony created in the text. Alan Palmer and Andrew Salway's 'Audio Description on the Thought–Action Continuum' (Style 49[2015] 126–48), finally, focuses on 'audio description' in film soundtracks, suggesting how it may convey information about characters' mental states. The authors use a narratological approach combined with corpus-linguistic analysis to create a classification of how these states are conveyed by audio describers.

Another aspect of film and television discourse relevant to stylistics is the study of dialogue. Simon Statham, in ' "A guy in my position is a government target . . . you got to be extra, extra careful": Participation and Strategies in Crime Talk in The Sopranos' (L&L 24[2015] 322–37), analyses dialogue extracts from the HBO drama The Sopranos, applying Erving Goffman's [1981] participation framework and Paul Grice's [1975] conversational maxims to investigate the conversational caution strategies used by characters engaged in 'crime talk'. Laura Dorigato, Gill Philip, Ramona Bongelli, and Andrzej Zuczkowski study utterances of characters in written narrative fiction. In 'Knowing, Unknowing, Believing Stances and Characters' Dialogic Identities in the Harry Potter Books' (L&D 5[2015] 62–89), they consider the dialogues in the seven books in J.K. Rowling's saga to explore the construction and development of the identities of Harry Potter and Lord Voldemort and their epistemic roles in the dialogues, with the additional aim of comparing linguistic and literary analyses. Bálint Péter Furkó's 'From Mediatized Political Discourse to *The Hobbit*: The Role of Pragmatic Markers in the Construction of Dialogues, Stereotypes and Literary Style' (*L&D* 5[2015] 264–82) points to the common ground between literary pragmatics, dialogue analysis, and pragmatic markers research, proposing the analysis of pragmatic markers as a tool for studying the interactional dynamics of naturally occurring, scripted, and literary dialogues. Another application of pragmatics to the study of literary language is Andreas H. Jucker's 'Pragmatics of Fiction: Literary Uses of *uh* and *um*' (*JPrag* 86[2015] 63–7), which considers the use of the planners 'uh' and 'um' in Douglas Adams's *The Hitchhiker's Guide to the Galaxy* as part of a more general discussion of the potential of fictional language (particularly the language of literature) as a legitimate source of data for pragmatic analysis. Neal R. Norrick's 'Narrative Illocutionary Acts Direct and Indirect' (*JPrag* 86[2015] 94–9), finally, develops the pragmatics of narrative by analysing the stories which people tell each other in interaction. He considers the illocutionary forces (e.g. confessing, apologizing, warning—directly or indirectly) evident in short conversational stories, suggesting that stories can fulfil speech-act functions, rather than simply entertain or illustrate points.

The study of spoken language may also enhance stylistic analysis in other ways, as can be seen in 'Code-Switching in Literature: Expanding the Paradigm', a special issue of *Language and Literature*. Guest editors Penelope Gardner-Chloros and Daniel Weston discuss the relationship between spoken and written code-switching, pointing to a partial overlap between the functions of the two, in 'Code-Switching and Multilingualism in Literature' (*L&L* 24[2015] 182–93). They also argue, in 'Mind the Gap: What Code-Switching in Literature Can Teach Us about Code-Switching' (*L&L* 24[2015] 194–212) that the study of literary code-switching is highly relevant to the sociolinguistic study of code-switching in spontaneous speech, as it provides information on the patterns of speech modes and language choices, multicultural identities, and tensions in various communities. Alex Mullen's ' "In both our languages": Greek–Latin Code-Switching in Roman Literature' (*L&L* 24[2015] 213–32) explores the historical dimensions of the topic by considering code-switching in ancient Roman letter-writing. A historical perspective is also adopted by Herbert Schendl, whose 'Code-Switching in Early English Literature' (*L&L* 24[2015] 233–48) investigates the functions of code-switching in medieval literature, focusing on the uses (and different status of) of Latin, French, and English in early poetry and drama. The two final articles deal with more contemporary texts, with Katharina B. Müller, in 'Code-Switching in Italo-Brazilian Literature from Rio Grande do Sul and São Paulo: A Sociolinguistic Analysis of the Forms and Functions of Literary Code-Switching' (*L&L* 24[2015] 249–63), discussing how the switching between Brazilian Portuguese and Italian in Italo-Brazilian prose texts represents the roles of code-switching in multilingual immigrants' communities, and Cecilia Montes-Alcalá, in 'Code-Switching in US Latino Literature: The Role of Biculturalism' (*L&L* 24[2015] 264–81), analysing a range of Spanish–English literary texts written by Mexican American, Nuyorican, and Cuban American authors, and exploring the socio-pragmatic and cultural aspects of code-switching in their works.

While the work discussed so far has been relevant primarily to literary, film, and television discourse, the remainder of the review will concentrate on stylistic approaches to other text types. *The Stylistics of Professional Discourse* by Martin Solly, for example, shows how stylistic methods of analysis can be applied to the study of the language of professional communities—focusing primarily on healthcare, legal, and educational discourse. Solly's interest is in 'stylistic distinctiveness' as a feature of the discourse of particular communities of practice (p. 4), i.e. the linguistic choices made by practitioners to express their meaning and construct their identity. The book begins with a concise introduction to style, stylistics, and approaches within linguistics (e.g. CDA, conversation analysis, narrative and corpus analysis) that form part of the practice of stylistics. The author applies a range of these methods in an analysis of extracts from blogs, speeches, statutes and job advertisements (among others) in order to outline some of the linguistic trends and strategies in healthcare communication (chapter 3), legal texts (chapter 4), and educational discourse (chapter 5). He additionally provides a discussion of how technological developments can affect the language use of professional communities, and devotes a chapter to an exploration of the relationship between pedagogy and stylistics, suggesting how a stylistic approach can benefit students of professional discourse. As Solly reiterates throughout the book, his interest is largely pedagogical—hoping not only to allow new participants of the professional groups to become aware of the modes of communication within their domains, but also to help members of these communities to communicate effectively both with those in their field and with outsiders. In line with this pedagogical focus, each chapter provides a number of activities which can be used in learning and teaching professional discourse, both in English and in other languages.

Another book using stylistic methods of analysis to explore the patterns of language use in non-literary texts is *Crime and Corpus: The Linguistic Representation of Crime in the Press*, in which Ulrike Tabbert considers the intersection of language and ideology by investigating the way crime is reported in the British and German media. On the basis of her experience as a prosecutor and her training as a linguist, Tabbert investigates the language used to construct the representation of victims, offenders, and crimes in the press and discusses the relationship between these portrayals and the underlying ideologies that can be said to inform the discourse surrounding the issues. The approach in this study is primarily corpus-linguistic: two corpora containing representative articles from German and British national newspapers were compiled and subsequently analysed with WordSmith in order to identify the most significant linguistic devices used to represent crime. A new method for identifying the keywords in a specialized corpus and the issues encountered in an analysis of data in two different languages are outlined in chapter 5. The results of the corpus analysis are subsequently discussed in relation to the critical stylistics framework (Lesley Jeffries [2010]), with a focus on the naming, representation of processes and states, and contrasting (among others) devices that are most commonly used to construct victims and offenders in both British and German news crime reports. The volume thus provides a mixed, corpus-linguistic and critical-stylistic approach to media discourse—an approach which, additionally, broadens our understanding of the ideologies that inform our perceptions of crime.

This kind of mixed approach is also used by Matthew Evans and Lesley Jeffries in 'The Rise of Choice as an Absolute "Good": A Study of British Manifestos (1900–2010)' (*JLP* 14[2015] 751–77), which combines quantitative and qualitative methods of analysis to explore the use of the word *choice* by the Conservative, Labour, and Liberal parties in their General Election manifestos between 1900 and 2010. The authors map the changing frequency of the lexical item throughout the years (suggesting that the term is going out of fashion), as well as outlining how *choice* has taken on a range of meanings in political language. Lesley Jeffries's critical-stylistic framework is also used by Matthew Evans and Simone Schuller in 'Representing "Terrorism": The Radicalisation of the May 2013 Woolwich Attack in British Press Reportage' (*JLA&C* 3[2015] 128–50), in which the authors use critical stylistics to investigate the application of the term *terrorism* in the British press—specifically, how a number of the newspaper articles covering the 2013 attack in Woolwich justify the use of this label in their reporting of the incident, and how their use compares with the academic definitions of the term.

Another key application of stylistics, next to broadening our understanding of the language of the press, political discourse, and communication within different communities of practice, is the analysis of texts relating to our experiences of health and illness. *Narrative Matters in Medical Contexts across Disciplines*, edited by Franziska Gygax and Miriam A. Locher, brings together work in literary and cultural studies, linguistics, psychology, and medicine to explore the concept of 'narrative' in medical contexts. Focusing specifically on 'illness narratives' (stories patients tell about their illness), this volume provides an interdisciplinary account of a range of texts, from autobiographies and first-person reports (Part I) to transcripts of sessions, interviews with patients, and computer-mediated communication (Part II). In 'Autism and the American Dream: Progress and Recovery in the American Autie-Biography' (pp. 17–31), for example, Annette Kern-Stähler and Anna Thieman investigate a selection of US American life narratives of people with autism and their carers, discussing how issues of disability, gender, class, and race are negotiated in relation to the master-narrative of the American Dream and the notions of progress, autonomy, and self-reliance. Also in Part I, Franziska Gygax's '"Woundable, around the bounds": Life (beyond) Writing and Terminal Illness' (pp. 33–45) and Dominique Brancher's 'Pox Pain and Redeeming Narratives in Renaissance Europe' (pp. 47–69) offer literary discussions of life-writing, focusing, respectively, on the representation of death in contemporary autobiographical novels dealing with terminal illness and the description of pain in fifteenth-century accounts of sufferers from pox. Part II moves from medical life-writing to interactions in healthcare contexts that contain narratives. Brigitte Booth investigates 'Illness Narratives in the Psychotherapeutic Session' (pp. 74–98), focusing on the role of the narrator in transcripts of narrative sequences in patient–psychotherapist interaction.

Gabriele Lucius-Hoene, Sandra Adami, and Janka Koschack, in 'Narratives that Matter: Illness Stories in the "Third Space" of Qualitative Interviewing' (pp. 99–116), explore positioning and contextualization strategies (among other issues) in narrative interviews with patients. Cynthia Gordon's '"I would suggest you tell this ^^^ to your doctor": Online Narrative Problem-Solving Regarding Face-to-Face Doctor–Patient Interaction about Body Weight' (pp. 118–40) applies computer-mediated discourse analysis (Susan C. Herring [2004]) and the concept of 'small stories' (e.g. Michael Bamberg [2004], Alexandra Georgakopolou [2007]) in the analysis of the discourse of an online support forum. In the last chapter in this section, 'A Genre Analysis of Reflective Writing Texts by English Medical Students: What Role Does Narrative Play?', Miriam A. Locher, Regula Koening, and Janine Meier (pp. 141–64) broaden the definition of 'illness narrative' to analyse medical students' narratives that reflect on their encounters with patients.

Another study exploring the intersection of language and illness is Zsófia Demjén's *Sylvia Plath and the Language of Affective States: Written Discourse and the Experience of Depression*, in which Demjén investigates what the language of Sylvia Plath's Smith Journal can tell us about the poet's emotional life—particularly, what it suggests about her experience of depression. In order to explore the linguistic patterns in Plath's writing, Demjén combines qualitative and quantitative methods, beginning with a corpus analysis (parts of speech and semantic category frequencies, using Paul Rayson's [2009] Wmatrix), which outlines the main linguistic characteristics of the whole text, before pursuing a more detailed, intensive qualitative stylistic analysis of a selection of extracts. Comparing the Journal to the autobiography section of the Speech, Writing and Thought Presentation corpus (Elena Semino and Mick Short [2004]) allows Demjén to make general observations about the unusual level of description and pronoun use in Plath's text; these characteristics are subsequently analysed in more detail with reference to, for example, concepts such as metaphor and second-person narration. While the mixed methodological approach to stylistic analysis is a particular strength of the monograph, the book is likely to be relevant not only to stylisticians, but also to those interested in how linguistic choices can provide clues about affective states. By discussing her findings with reference to research in psychology and psychopathology, the author suggests the specific ways in which Plath's linguistic choices reveal the poet's negative self-image, insecurity, and self-doubt, outlining patterns consistent with theories of depression, but which 'add to the clinical descriptions by highlighting aspects of the experience that might otherwise be backgrounded' (p. 214).

Zsófia Demjén's joint work with Elena Semino is also of particular interest here: 'Henry's Voices: The Representation of Auditory Verbal Hallucinations in an Autobiographical Narrative' (*MedH* 41[2015] 57–62) investigates the linguistic representation of auditory verbal hallucinations (voice-hearing) in the autobiographical narrative *Henry's Demons: Living with Schizophrenia: A Father and Son's Story* by Henry and Patrick Cockburn. Henry's hallucinations, or 'voices', are classified according to their type (based, primarily, on who uttered them and which speech-acts are involved), and subsequently analysed with regard to the speech-presentation strategies adopted to recount them (e.g. direct vs. indirect speech), as well as other distinctive linguistic features appearing in them (such as sensory verbs or expressions which indicate uncertainty). The linguistic analysis of the different types of voice provides insight into the experience of voice-hearing that offers potential implications for healthcare practitioners. Both linguists and medical professionals are also the target readership for 'The Online Use of Violence and Journey Metaphors by Patients with Cancer, as Compared with Health Professionals: A Mixed Methods Study' by Elena Semino, Zsófia Demjén, Jane Demmen, Veronika Koller, Sheila Payne, Andrew Hardie, and Paul Rayson (*BMJ Supportive and Palliative Care* [2015] 1–7), in which the authors analyse two corpora of online writing to investigate the way patients and health professionals use metaphorical language to talk about cancer. In view of recent UK policy documents promoting the notion of cancer as a 'journey' rather than a 'war', the authors consider the frequency and, crucially, functions of the 'journey' and 'violence' metaphors in an online forum for cancer patients and a website for health professionals. They conclude that neither metaphor is wholly positive or negative—in fact, patients are found to be using each of these in both empowering and disempowering ways to describe their experience of cancer. The same authors, but in a slightly different order of appearance, investigate 'violence' metaphors for cancer in 'A Computer-Assisted Study of the Use of Violence Metaphors for Cancer and End of Life by Patients, Family Carers and Health Professionals' (*IJCL* 20[2015] 205–31). They compare the way the metaphor is used by three different groups: patients, healthcare professionals, and family carers. As in their other study, the authors combine quantitative corpus methods with qualitative analysis to analyse a corpus of online data, showing the wide, varied range of 'violence' metaphors used by the different stakeholder groups in the treatment of cancer.

Moving from studies with direct applications in healthcare, education, and translation to those developing classic theoretical frameworks or outlining new methodological directions, the best stylistics research of 2015 has, as always, focused on the study of the *text*, investigating what Lesley Jeffries refers to as 'textual meaning' ('Textual Meaning and Its Place in a Theory of Language' (*TL* 15[2015] n.p.)). By placing the text at the heart of linguistic enquiry and concentrating on the purely text-based layer of meaning separate from the linguistic or interpersonal meaning associated with the context, Jeffries argues, stylisticians are able to situate their work within other rigorous approaches to the study of language.

**Books Reviewed**

Aarts, Bas, Joanne Close, Geoffrey Leech, and Sean Wallis, eds. *The Verb Phrase in English: Investigating Recent Language Change with Corpora.*

CUP. [2013] pp. xxviii + 445. hb £72 ISBN 9 7811 0701 6354, pb [2015] £28.99 ISBN 9 7811 0755 8502.

Aboh, Enoch Oladé. *The Emergence of Hybrid Grammars: Language Contact and Change. Cambridge Approaches to Language Contact.* CUP. [2015] pp. xviii + 348. £69.99 ISBN 9 7805 2176 9983.

Alonso-Ovalle, Luis, and Paula Menéndez-Benito, eds. *Epistemic Indefinites: Exploring Modality beyond the Verbal Domain.* OUP. [2015] pp. xi + 309. £65 ISBN 9 7801 9966 5297.

Amador-Moreno, Carolina P., Kevin McCafferty, and Elaine Vaughan, eds. *Pragmatic Markers in Irish English.* Benjamins. [2015] pp. vi + 443. €99 ISBN 9 7890 2725 6638.

Anderson, Wendy, Ellen Bramwell, and Carole Hough, eds. *Mapping English Metaphor through Time.* OUP. [2015] pp. xii + 321. £65 ISBN 9 7801 9874 4573.

Arendholz, Jenny, Wolfram Bublitz, and Monika Kirner-Ludwig, eds. *The Pragmatics of Quoting Now and Then.* MGruyter. [2015] pp. v + 428. £89.99 ISBN 9 7831 1043 1759.

Auer, Anita, Daniel Schreier, and Richard J. Watts, eds. *Letter Writing and Language Change.* CUP. [2015] pp. xiii + 352. £67 ISBN 9 7811 0701 8648, e-book £51 ISBN 9 7811 3998 9725.

Baker, Will. *Culture and Identity through English as a Lingua Franca: Rethinking Concepts and Goals in Intercultural Communication.* MGruyter. [2015] pp. xii + 296. £74.99 ISBN 9 7815 0150 2149.

Bann, Jennifer, and John Corbett. *Spelling Scots: The Orthography of Literary Scots, 1700–2000.* EdinUP. [2015] pp. v + 162. £70 ISBN 9 7807 4864 3059.

Bao, Zhiming. *The Making of Vernacular Singapore English: System, Transfer, and Filter. Cambridge Approaches to Language Contact.* CUP. [2015] pp. xvi + 216. £69.99 ISBN 9 7811 0702 2089.

Barcroft, Joe. *Lexical Input Processing and Vocabulary Learning.* Benjamins. [2015] pp. viii + 213. hb €95 ISBN 9 7890 2721 3280, pb €33 ISBN 9 7890 2721 3297.

Baten, Kristof, Aafke Buyl, Katja Lochtman, and Mieke Van Herreweghe, eds. *Theoretical and Methodological Developments in Processability Theory.* Benjamins. [2015] pp. vi + 273. €99 ISBN 9 7890 2720 3045.

Bayyurt, Yasemin, and Sumru Akcan, eds. *Current Perspectives on Pedagogy for English as a Lingua Franca.* MGruyter. [2015] pp. ix + 260. € 99.95 ISBN 9 7831 1033 5965.

Beeching, Kate, and Helen Woodfield, eds. *Perspectives from Variational, Interlanguage and Contrastive Pragmatics.* PalMac. [2015] pp. xi + 305. £65 ISBN 9 7811 3737 3946.

Bernaisch, Tobias. *The Lexis and Lexicogrammar of Sri Lankan English. Varieties of English Around the World 54.* Benjamins. [2015] pp. xiv + 248. €99 ISBN 9 7890 2724 9142.

Berry, Roger. *From Words to Grammar: Discovering English Usage.* Routledge. [2015]. pp. 190. hb £90 ISBN 9 7804 1571 3757, pb £26 ISBN 9 7804 1571 3764.

Biber, Douglas, and Randi Reppen, eds. *The Cambridge Handbook of English Corpus Linguistics.* CUP. [2015] pp. xviii + 623. £98 ISBN 9 7811 0703 7380.

Biewer, Carolin. *South Pacific Englishes: A Sociolinguistic and Morphosyntactic Profile of Fiji English, Samoan English and Cook Islands English. Varieties of English Around the World 52.* Benjamins. [2015] pp. xvi + 35. €99 ISBN 9 7890 2724 9128.

Bowles, Hugo, and Alessia Cogo, eds. *International Perspectives on English as a Lingua Franca Pedagogical Insights.* PalMac. [2015] pp. 212. hb $95 ISBN 9 7811 3739 8079, pb $32 ISBN 9 7811 3739 8093.

Boxer, Diana, and John Wilson, eds. *Discourse, Politics and Women as Global Leaders.* Benjamins. [2015] pp. 366. €99 ISBN 9 7890 2726 7979.

Brems, Lieselotte, Lobke Ghesquière, and Freek Van de Velde, eds. *Intersubjectivity and Intersubjectification in Grammar and Discourse.* Benjamins. [2014] pp. 161. €85 ISBN 9 7890 2724 2532.

Bybee, Joan. *Language Change.* CUP. [2015] pp. xvii + 292. hb £65 ISBN 9 7811 0702 0160, pb £20 ISBN 9 7811 0765 5829.

Bygate, Martin, ed. *Domains and Directions in the Development of TBLT: A Decade of Plenaries from the International Conference.* Benjamins. [2015] pp. xxiv + 325. hb €99 ISBN 9 7890 2720 7319, pb €33 ISBN 9 7890 2720 7326.

Ciccoricco, David. *Refiguring Minds in Narrative Media.* UNebP. [2015] pp. ix + 317. $55 ISBN 9 7808 0324 8373.

Colantoni, Laura, Jeffrey Steele, and Paola Escudero. *Second Language Speech: Theory and Practice.* CUP. [2015] pp. xxii + 407. hb £64.99 ISBN 9 7811 0701 8341, pb £25.99 ISBN 9 7811 0765 5751.

Collins, Peter, ed. *Grammatical Change in English World-Wide.* Benjamins. [2015] pp. vi + 488. €105 ISBN 9 7890 2720 3755.

Crystal, David. *The Disappearing Dictionary: A Treasury of Lost English Dialect Words.* Macmillan. [2015] pp. xx + 224. £12.99 ISBN 9 7814 4728 2808.

Cummins, Chris. *Constraints on Numerical Expressions.* OUP. [2015] pp. 210. hb £65 ISBN 9 7801 9968 7909, pb £30 ISBN 9 7801 9968 7916.

Cutting, Joan. *Pragmatics: A Resource Book for Students.* 3rd edn. Routledge. [2015] pp. 298. hb £85 ISBN 9 7804 1553 4376, pb £28.99 ISBN 9 7804 1553 4369.

Daems, Jocelyne, Eline Zenner, Kris Heylen, Dirk Speelman, and Hubert Cuyckens, eds. *Change of Paradigms—New Paradoxes: Recontextualizing Language and Linguistics.* MGruyter. [2015] pp. x + 387. £74.99 ISBN 9 7831 1043 5597.

De Angelis, Gessica, Ulrike Jessner, and Marijana Kresić, eds. *Crosslinguistic Influence and Crosslinguistic Interaction in Multilingual Language Learning.* Bloomsbury. [2015] pp. xii + 260. hb £95 ISBN 9 7814 7423 5853, pb £26.09 ISBN 9 7813 5003 6482.

Dedaić, Mirjana N., ed. *Singing, Speaking and Writing Politics: South African Political Discourses.* Benjamins. [2015] pp. vii + 250. €99 ISBN 9 7890 2720 6565.

Demjén, Zsófia. *Sylvia Plath and the Language of Affective States: Written Discourse and the Experience of Depression.* Bloomsbury. [2015] pp. xiv + 256. hb £95 ISBN 9 7814 7421 2663, pb £24.99 ISBN 9 7813 5002 4250.

Derwing, Tracey M., and Murray J. Munro. *Pronunciation Fundamentals: Evidence-Based Perspectives for L2 Teaching and Research.* Benjamins.

[2015] pp. xiii + 208. hb €95 ISBN 9 7890 2721 3266, pb €33 ISBN 9 7890 2721 3273.

Dollinger, Stefan. *The Written Questionnaire in Social Dialectology: History, Theory, Practice*. Benjamins. [2015] pp. xxvi + 397. hb €105 ISBN 9 7890 2725 8311, pb €36 ISBN 9 7890 2725 8328.

Donaher, Patricia, and Seth Katz, eds. *Ain'thology: The History and Life of a Taboo Word*. CambridgeSP. [2015] pp. x + 366. £52.99 ISBN 9 7814 4387 4502.

Donald, Graeme. *Words of a Feather: An Etymological Exploration of Astonishing Word Pairs*. Metro. [2015] pp. viii + 231. £9.99 ISBN 9 7817 8418 8146.

Dörnyei, Zoltán, and Stephen Ryan. *The Psychology of the Language Learner Revisited*. Routledge/T&F. [2015] pp. xiv + 259. hb £100 ISBN 9 7811 3801 8730, pb £40.99 ISBN 9 7811 3801 8747.

Dossena, Marina, ed. *Transatlantic Perspectives of Late Modern English. Advances in Historical Sociolinguistics 4*. Benjamins. [2015] pp. vii + 221. €95 ($143) ISBN 9 7890 2720 0839, e-book €95 ($143) ISBN 9 7890 2726 8877.

Durkin, Philip. *Borrowed Words: A History of Loanwords in English*. OUP. [2015] pp. xix + 491. pb £18.99 ISBN 9 7801 9873 6493.

Dynel, Marta, and Jan Chovanec, eds. *Participation in Public and Social Media Interactions*. Benjamins. [2015] pp. 285. hb €95 ISBN 9 7890 2725 6614.

Eckardt, Regine. *The Semantics of Free Indirect Discourse: How Texts Allow Us to Mind-Read and Eavesdrop*. Brill. [2015] pp. xi + 283. €115 ISBN 9 7890 0426 6728.

Eddington, David. *Statistics for Linguists: A Step-by-Step Guide for Novices*. CambridgeSP. [2015] pp. xvi + 170. pb £41.99 ISBN 9 7814 4387 6384.

Ellis, Rod. *Understanding Second Language Acquisition*. 2nd edn. OUP. [2015] pp. x + 365. pb £42.20 ISBN 9 7801 9442 2048.

Farris-Trimble, Ashley W., and Jessica A. Barlow, eds. *Perspectives on Phonological Theory and Development: In Honor of Daniel A. Dinnsen*. Benjamins. [2014] pp. viii + 256. €95 ISBN 9 7890 2725 3187.

Fetzer, Anita, Elda Weizman, and Lawrence N. Berlin, eds. *The Dynamics of Political Discourse: Forms and Functions of Follow-Ups*. Benjamins. [2015] pp. 278. €95 ISBN 9 7890 2725 6645.

Forsberg Lundell, Fanny, and Inge Bartning, eds. *Cultural Migrants and Optimal Language Acquisition*. MlM. [2015] pp. x + 230. hb £99.95 ISBN 9 7817 8309 4035, pb £29.95 ISBN 9 7817 8309 4028.

Foster, John D. *White Race Discourse*. Lexington. [2013] pp. xiii + 207. £24.95 ISBN 9 7814 9851 5559.

Frazier, Lyn, and Edward Gibson, eds. *Explicit and Implicit Prosody in Sentence Processing: Studies in Honor of Janet Dean Fodor*. Springer. [2015] pp. x + 307. $179 ISBN 9 7833 1912 9600.

Friginal, Eric, and Jack A. Hardy. *Corpus-Based Sociolinguistics: A Guide for Students*. Routledge. [2014] pp. xvi + 312. hb £95 ISBN 9 7803 1552 9556, pb £34.99 ISBN 9 7804 1552 9463.

Gambier, Yves, Annamaria Caimi, and Cristina Mariotti, eds. *Subtitles and Language Learning: Principles, Strategies and Practical Experiences.* Lang. [2015] pp. 351. pb £65 ISBN 9 7830 3431 5296.

Geeslin, Kimberly L., and Avizia Yim Long. *Sociolinguistics and Second Language Acquisition: Learning to Use Language in Context.* Routledge/ T&F. [2014] pp. xxiv + 320. hb £95 ISBN 9 7804 1552 9471, pb £34.99 ISBN 9 7804 1552 9488.

Gerwin, Johanna. *Ditransitives in British English Dialects.* MGruyter. [2014] pp. xiv + 238. €110 ISBN 9 7831 1035 2320.

Ghesquière, Lobke. *The Directionality of (Inter)Subjectification in the English Noun Phrase.* MGruyter. [2014] pp. xiv + 310. €110 ISBN 9 7831 1031 8579.

Granger, Sylviane, Gaëtanelle Gilquin, and Fanny Meunier, eds. *The Cambridge Handbook of Learner Corpus Research.* CUP. [2015] pp. xiii + 748. £98 ISBN 9 7811 0704 1196.

Grano, Thomas. *Control and Restructuring.* OUP. [2015] pp. xi + 244. hb £65 ISBN 9 7801 9870 3921, pb £24.99 ISBN 9 7801 9870 3938.

Greenbaum, Sidney, and Gerald Nelson. *Introduction to English Grammar.* 4th edn. Routledge. [2015] pp. xiii + 337. hb £89 ISBN 9 7811 3885 5458, pb £26 ISBN 9 7811 3885 5496.

Guéron, Jacqueline, ed. *Sentence and Discourse.* OUP. [2015] pp. xix + 310. hb £65 ISBN 9 7801 9873 9418, pb £29.99 ISBN 9 7801 9873 9425.

Gupta, Kat. *Representation of the British Suffrage Movement.* Bloomsbury. [2015] pp. 270. £85 ISBN 9 7814 7257 0895.

Gutzmann, Daniel. *Use-Conditional Meaning: Studies in Multidimensional Semantics.* OUP. [2015] pp. xvii + 304. £65 ISBN 9 7801 9872 3820, pb £29.99 ISBN 9 7801 9872 3837.

Gygax, Franziska, and Miriam A. Locher, eds. *Narrative Matters in Medical Contexts across Disciplines.* Benjamins. [2015] pp. vii + 217. €90 ISBN 9 7890 2722 6600.

Heredia, Roberto R., and Anna B. Cieślicka, eds. *Bilingual Figurative Language Processing.* CUP. [2015] pp. xxiii + 418. hb £67 ISBN 9 7811 0702 9545, pb £30.99 ISBN 9 7811 0760 9501.

Hickey, Raymond, ed. *Researching Northern English.* Benjamins. [2015] pp. x + 483. €99 ISBN 9 7890 2724 9159.

Holmberg, Anders. *The Syntax of Yes and No.* OUP. [2015] pp. xi + 250. £60 ISBN 9 7801 9870 1859.

Honeybone, Patrick, and Joseph Salmons, eds. *The Oxford Handbook of Historical Phonology.* OUP. [2015] pp. xv + 792. £95 ISBN 9 7801 9923 2819.

Huang, Libo. *Style in Translation: A Corpus-Based Perspective.* Springer. [2015] pp. v + 161. $129 ISBN 9 7836 6245 5654.

Hulstijn, Jan H. *Language Proficiency in Native and Non-Native Speakers: Theory and Research.* Benjamins. [2015] pp. xi + 195. hb €95 ISBN 9 7890 2721 3242, pb €33 ISBN 9 7890 2721 3259.

Jackson, Howard, ed. *The Bloomsbury Companion to Lexicography.* Bloomsbury. [2015] pp. xiii + 420. pb £28.99 ISBN 9 7814 7423 7376.

Jenkins, Jennifer. *English as a Lingua Franca: Attitude and Identity.* OUP. [2007] pp 296. £40.10 ISBN 9 7801 9442 2376.

Jenkins, Jennifer. *English as a Lingua Franca in the International University: The Politics of Academic English Language Policy.* Routledge. [2014] pp. 248. hb £30.99 ISBN 9 7804 1568 4644, pb £105 ISBN 9 7804 1568 4637.

Johannessen, Janne Bondi, and Joseph C. Salmons, eds. *Germanic Heritage Languages in North America: Acquisition, Attrition and Change.* Benjamins. [2015] pp. vi + 418. €105 ISBN 9 7890 2723 4988.

Jones, Rodney H, Alice Chik, and Christoph Hafner, eds. *Discourse and Digital Practice: Doing Discourse Analysis in the Digital Age.* Routledge. [2015] pp. xii + 262. hb £95 ISBN 9 7811 3802 2324, pb £26.99 ISBN 9 7811 3802 2324.

Karpova, Olga, and Faina Kartashkova, eds. *Life beyond Dictionaries.* CambridgeSP. [2015] pp. vii + 214. £47.99 ISBN 9 7814 4388 1470.

Kay, Christian, and Kathryn Allan. *English Historical Semantics.* EdinUP. [2015] pp. xi + 206. hb £70 ISBN 9 7807 4864 4780, pb £19.99 ISBN 9 7807 4864 4773.

Keizer, Evelien. *A Functional Discourse Grammar for English.* OUP. [2015] pp. xviii + 336. hb £65 ISBN 9 7801 9957 1864, pb £24.99 ISBN 9 7801 9957 1871.

Kerremans, Daphné. *A Web of New Words: A Corpus-Based Study of the Conventionalization Process of English Neologisms.* Lang. [2015] pp. 278. £59.37 ISBN 9 7836 3165 5788.

KhosraviNik, Majid. *Discourse, Identity and Legitimacy: Self and Other in Representations of Iran's Nuclear Programme.* Benjamins. [2015] pp. 304. €99 ISBN 9 7890 2720 6534.

Kikuchi, Keita. *Demotivation in Second Language Acquisition: Insights from Japan.* MlM. [2015] pp. xii + 161. £79.95 ISBN 9 7817 8309 3946.

Klinger, Suzanne. *Translation and Linguistic Hybridity: Constructing World-View.* Routledge. [2015] pp. vii +195. £95 ISBN 9 7811 3880 1592.

Lambelet, Amelia, and Raphael Berthele. *Age and Foreign Language Learning in School.* PalMac. [2015] pp. xvii + 106. hb £45 ISBN 9 7811 3752 5895, pb £45 ISBN 9 7813 4950 6743.

Lanehart, Sonja L., ed. *The Oxford Handbook of African American Language.* OUP. [2015] pp. xxxvii + 903. £115 ISBN 9 7801 9979 5390.

Lappin, Shalom, and Chris Fox, eds. *The Handbook of Contemporary Semantic Theory.* 2nd edn. Wiley-Blackwell. [2015] pp. xv + 755. £120 ISBN 9 7804 7067 0736.

Laugesen, Amanda. *Furphies and Whizz-Bangs: Anzac Slang from the Great War.* OUP. [2015] pp. 250. pb £23.99 ISBN 9 7801 9559 7356.

Lefebvre, Claire, ed. *Functional Categories in Three Atlantic Creoles: Saramaccan, Haitian and Papiamentu.* Creole Language Library 50. Benjamins. [2015] pp. xvii + 368. €105 ISBN 9 7890 2725 2746.

Leimgruber, Jakob R.E. *Singapore English: Structure, Variation, and Usage.* Studies in English Language. CUP. [2015] pp. xvi + 152. £24.99 ISBN 9 7811 0755 8731.

Levshina, Natalia. *How To Do Linguistics with R: Data Exploration and Statistical Analysis.* Benjamins. [2015] pp. xii + 443. hb €105 ISBN 9 7890 2721 2245, pb €36 ISBN 9 7890 2721 2252.

Lim, Lisa, and Umberto Ansaldo. *Languages in Contact. Key Topics in Sociolinguistics.* CUP. [2015] pp. xiv + 237. £21.99 ISBN 9 7805 2114 9259.

Los, Bettelou. *A Historical Syntax of English.* EdinUP. [2015] pp. xx + 284. hb £70 ISBN 9 7807 4864 1444, pb £19.99 ISBN 9 7807 4864 1437.

Meyerhoff, Miriam, Erik Schleef, and Laurel MacKenzie. *Doing Sociolinguistics: A Practical Guide to Data Collection and Analysis.* Routledge. [2015] pp. xxii + 190. hb £70 ISBN 9 7804 1569 8214, pb £20.99 ISBN 9 7804 1569 8207.

Mihaljević Djigunović, Jelena, and Marta Medved Krajnović, eds. *Early Learning and Teaching of English: New Dynamics of Primary English.* MlM. [2015] pp. xii + 228. hb £99.95 ISBN 9 7817 8309 3380, pb £29.95 ISBN 9 7817 8309 3373.

Miyahara, Masuko. *Emerging Self-Identities and Emotion in Foreign Language Learning: A Narrative-Oriented Approach.* MlM. [2015] pp. xii + 200. £89.95 ISBN 9 7817 8309 3816.

Moll, Andrea. *Jamaican Creole Goes Web: Sociolinguistic Styling and Authenticity in a Digital 'Yaad'. Creole Language Library 49.* Benjamins. [2015] pp. viii + 294. €105 ISBN 9 7890 2725 2739.

Mooney, Annabelle, and Betsy E. Evans. *Language, Society & Power: An Introduction.* 4th edn. Routledge. [2015] pp. xxvi + 262. hb £78.99 ISBN 9 7804 1573 9993, pb £22.99 ISBN 9 7804 1574 0005.

Mugglestone, Lynda. *Samuel Johnson and the Journey into Words.* OUP. [2015] pp. xi + 290. £25 ISBN 9 7801 9967 9904.

Mullany, Louise, and Peter Stockwell. *Introducing English Language: A Resource Book for Students.* 2nd edn. Routledge. [2015] pp. xii + 310. hb £85 ISBN 9 7811 3801 6187, pb £26 ISBN 9 7811 3801 6194.

Nassaji, Hossein. *The Interactional Feedback Dimension in Instructed Second Language Learning: Linking Theory, Research, and Practice.* Bloomsbury. [2015] pp. xi + 246. hb £95 ISBN 9 7814 7251 0143, pb £28.99 ISBN 9 7813 5000 9899.

Nortier, Jacomine, and Bente A. Svendsen, eds. *Language, Youth and Identity in the 21st Century: Linguistic Practices across Urban Spaces.* CUP. [2015] pp. xviii + 348. £65 ISBN 9 7811 0701 6989.

Ostermann, Carolin. *Cognitive Lexicography: A New Approach to Lexicography Making Use of Cognitive Semantics.* MGruyter. [2015] pp. xii + 380. £74.99 ISBN 9 7831 1042 7448.

Paltridge, Brian, and Aek Phakiti, eds. *Research Methods in Applied Linguistics: A Practical Resource.* Bloomsbury. [2015] pp. xv + 590. hb £95 ISBN 9 7814 7252 4560, pb £28.99 ISBN 9 7814 7252 5017.

Pawlak, Mirosław, and Ewa Waniek-Klimczak, eds. *Issues in Teaching, Learning and Testing Speaking in a Second Language.* Springer. [2015] pp. xiv + 265. €99.99 ISBN 9 7836 4238 3380.

Peplow, David, Joan Swann, Paola Trimarco, and Sara Whiteley. *The Discourse of Reading Groups: Integrating Cognitive and Sociocultural Perspectives.* Routledge. [2015] pp. vii + 197. £100 ISBN 9 7804 1572 9697.

Picone, Michael D., and Catherine Evans Davies, eds. *New Perspectives on Language Variety in the South: Historical and Contemporary Approaches.* UAlaP. [2015] pp. viii + 813. £54.50 ISBN 9 7808 1731 8154.

Piechurska-Kuciel, Ewa, and Magdalena Szyszka, eds. *The Ecosystem of the Foreign Language Learner: Selected Issues*. Springer. [2015] pp. xv + 200. €103.99 ISBN 9 7833 1914 3330.

Pietilä, Päivi, Katalin Doró, and Renata Pípalová, eds. *Lexical Issues in L2 Writing*. CambridgeSP. [2015] pp. 237. £47 ISBN 9 7814 4388 0220.

Pizziconi, Barbara, and Miriam A. Locher, eds. *Teaching and Learning (Im)Politeness*. MGruyter. [2015] pp. v + 272. £74.99 ISBN 9 7815 0150 8424.

Plag, Ingo, Sabine Arndt-Lappe, Maria Braum, and Mareile Schramm. *Introduction to English Linguistics*. 2nd edn. MGruyter. [2015] pp. xii + 290. pb €25 ISBN 9 7831 1037 6180.

Popova, Yanna B. *Stories, Meaning, and Experience: Narrativity and Enaction*. Routledge. [2015] pp. ix + 195. £95 ISBN 9 7804 1571 5881.

Prescod, Paula, ed. *Language Issues in Saint Vincent and the Grenadines. Varieties of English Around the World 51*. Benjamins. [2015] pp. xv + 191. €95 ISBN 9 7890 2724 9111.

Prikhodkine, Alexei, and Dennis R. Preston. *Responses to Language Varieties: Variability, Processes and Outcomes*. Benjamins. [2015] pp. xiv + 249. €95 ISBN 9 7890 2725 8304.

Rampton, Ben. *Crossing: Language and Ethnicity Among Adolescents*. Routledge. [2014] pp. 180. hb £90 ISBN 9 8811 3814 8949, pb £26.99 ISBN 9 7819 0065 0779.

Rebuschat, Patrick, ed. *Implicit and Explicit Learning of Languages*. Benjamins. [2015] pp. xxii + 489. hb €105 ISBN 9 7890 2724 1894, pb €36 ISBN 9 7890 2724 1900.

Reed, Marine, and J.M. Levis, eds. *The Handbook of English Pronunciation*. Wiley. [2015] pp. 552. £156 ISBN 9 7811 1831 4470.

Ren, Wei. *L2 Pragmatic Development in Study Abroad Contexts*. Lang. [2015] pp. viii + 256. pb £53 ISBN 9 7830 3431 3582.

Rett, Jessica. *The Semantics of Evaluativity*. OUP. [2015] pp. 195. hb £60 ISBN 9 7801 9960 2476, pb £24.99 ISBN 9 7801 9960 2483.

Richards, Melinda L. *Appalachian English: Another Endangered Dialect*. Lambert/Omniscriptum. [2015] pp. xiii + 222. €38.90 ISBN 9 7836 5956 6691.

Riemer, Nick, ed. *The Routledge Handbook of Semantics*. Routledge. [2015] pp. xvi + 533. £158 ISBN 9 7804 1566 1737.

Schneider, Stefan, Julie Glikman, and Mathieu Avanzi, eds. *Parenthetical Verbs*. Mouton. [2015] pp. vii + 357. €99.95 ISBN 9 7831 1037 6036.

Schwarz, Florian, ed. *Experimental Perspectives on Presuppositions*. Springer. [2015] pp. viii + 262. $179 ISBN 9 7833 1907 9790.

Schwieter, John W., ed. *The Cambridge Handbook of Bilingual Processing*. CUP. [2015] pp. xviii + 841. £98 ISBN 9 7811 0706 0586.

Seawright, Leslie, ed. *Going Global: Transnational Perspectives on Globalization, Language, and Education*. CambridgeSP. [2014] pp. xiv + 223. £58.76 ISBN 9 7814 4386 3339.

Sharifian, Farzad, ed. *The Routledge Handbook of Language and Culture*. Routledge. [2015] pp. xv + 522. £158 ISBN 9 7804 1552 7019.

Solly, Martin. *The Stylistics of Professional Discourse*. EdinUP. [2015] pp. vi + 168. £70 ISBN 9 7807 4869 1692.

Sotirova, Violeta, ed. *The Bloomsbury Companion to Stylistics*. Bloomsbury. [2015] pp. vii + 744. £130 ISBN 9 7814 4116 0058.

Stavans, Anat, and Charlotte Hoffmann, *Multilingualism*. CUP. [2015] pp. xii + 308. hb £62 ISBN 9 7811 0709 2990, pb £20.99 ISBN 9 7811 0747 1481.

Stevenson, James A.C., and Iseabail Macleod. *Scoor-Oot: A Dictionary of Scots Words and Phrases in Current Use*. Bloomsbury. [2015] pp. xiii + 256. £59.99 ISBN 9 7814 7424 7191.

Suárez-Gómez, Cristina, and Elena Seoane, eds. *Englishes Today: Multiple Varieties, Multiple Perspectives*. CambridgeSP. [2015] pp. viii + 194. £47.99 ISBN 9 7814 4388 3863.

Swan, Anne, Pamela Aboshiha, and Adrian Holliday, eds. *(En)Countering Native-Speakerism: Global Perspectives*. PalMac. [2015] pp. xiv + 212. £63 ISBN 9 7811 3746 3494.

Szekely, Rachel. *Truth without Predication: The Role of Placing in the Existential There-Sentence*. Palgrave. [2015] pp. viii + 169. $95 ISBN 9 7800 3748 3287.

Taavitsainen, Irma, Merja Kytö, Claudia Claridge, and Jeremy Smith, eds. *Developments in English: Expanding Electronic Evidence*. CUP. [2015] pp. xxiii + 299. £80.66 ISBN 9 7811 0703 8509.

Tabbert, Ulrike. *Crime and Corpus: The Linguistic Representation of Crime in the Press*. Benjamins. [2015] xvii + 181. €95 ISBN 9 7890 2723 4094.

Taggart, Caroline. *New Words for Old: Recycling Our Language for the Modern World*. O'Mara. [2015] pp. 191. £9.99 ISBN 9 7817 8243 4726.

Tamasi, Susan, and Lamont Antieau. *Language and Linguistic Diversity in the US: An Introduction*. Routledge. [2015] pp. xix + 380. hb £95 ISBN 9 7804 1580 6671, pb £37.99 ISBN 9 7804 1580 6688.

Tannen, Deborah, Heidi E. Hamilton, and Deborah Schiffrin, eds. *The Handbook of Discourse Analysis*. 2nd edn. Wiley. [2015] pp. xix + 992. £316 ISBN 9 7804 7067 0743.

Taylor, John, ed. *The Oxford Handbook of the Word*. OUP. [2015] pp. xviii + 864. £110 ISBN 9 7801 9964 1604.

Teranishi, Masayuki, Yoshifumi Saito, and Katie Wales, eds. *Literature and Language Learning in the EFL Classroom*. PalMac. [2015] pp. xxi + 329. $105 ISBN 9 7811 3744 3656.

Thomas, Bronwen. *Narrative: The Basics*. Routledge. [2015] pp. viii + 149. hb £70 ISBN 9 7804 1583 2649, pb £14.99 ISBN 9 7804 1583 2656.

Torgersen, Eivind, Stian Hårstad, Brit Mæhlum, and Unn Røyneland, eds. *Language Variation: European Perspectives V*. Benjamins. [2015] pp. xiii + 240. €105 ISBN 9 7890 2723 4971.

Torres Cacoullos, Rena, Nathalie Dion, and André Lapierre, eds. *Linguistic Variation: Confronting Fact and Theory*. Routledge. [2015] pp. xv + 356. hb £95 ISBN 9 8811 3802 4540, pb £39.99 ISBN 9 7811 3802 4557.

Torza, Alessandro, ed. *Quantifiers, Quantifiers and Quantifiers: Themes in Logic, Metaphysics and Language*. Springer. [2015] pp. viii + 526. $249 ISBN 9 7833 1918 3619.

Trips, Carola. *Syntax in Three Dimensions*. MGruyter. [2015] pp. xiv + 240. pb €30 ISBN 9 7831 1028 9848.

van Compernolle, Rémi A. *Interaction and Second Language Development: A Vygotskian Perspective*. Benjamins. [2015] pp. viii + 213. hb €95 ISBN 9 7890 2721 3303, pb €33 ISBN 9 7890 2721 3310.

VanPatten, Bill, and Alessandro G. Benati. *Key Terms in Second Language Acquisition*. 2nd edn. Bloomsbury. [2015] pp. 219. hb £85 ISBN 9 7814 7422 7513, pb £21.99 ISBN 9 7814 7422 7506.

VanPatten, Bill, and Jessica Williams, eds. *Theories in Second Language Acquisition: An Introduction*. 2nd edn. Routledge/T&F. [2015] pp. x + 293. hb £100 ISBN 9 7804 1582 4200, pb £37.99 ISBN 9 7804 1582 4217.

Velupillai, Viveka. *Pidgins, Creoles and Mixed Languages: An Introduction*. *Creole Language Library 48*. Benjamins. [2015] pp. xxvii + 599. €99 ISBN 9 7890 2725 2715.

Vettorel, Paola, ed. *New Frontiers in Teaching and Learning English*. CambridgeSP. [2015] pp. xi + 290. hb £47.99 ISBN 9 7814 4387 4588.

Walker, James A. *Canadian English: A Sociolinguistic Perspective*. Routledge. [2015] pp. xiv + 147. hb £95 ISBN 9 7804 1553 5366, pb £25.99 ISBN 9 7804 1553 5373.

Waniek-Klimczak, Ewa, and Mirosław Pawlak, eds. *Teaching and Researching the Pronunciation of English: Studies in Honour of Włodzimierz Sobkowiak*. Springer. [2015] pp. xv + 247. €129.99 ISBN 9 7833 1911 0912.

Weber, Jean-Jacques. *Language Racism*. PalMac. [2015] pp. vii + 130. hb €64.19 ISBN 9 7811 3753 1063.

Webster, Jonathan J., ed. *The Bloomsbury Companion to M.A.K. Halliday*. Bloomsbury. [2015] pp. xiv +512. hb $190 ISBN 9 7814 4117 2754.

Wen, Zhisheng (Edward), Mailce Borges Mota, and Arthur McNeill, eds. *Working Memory in Second Language Acquisition and Processing*. MlM. [2015] pp. xxiv + 314. hb £109.95 ISBN 9 7817 8309 3588, pb £34.95 ISBN 9 7817 8309 3571.

Widawski, Maciej. *African American Slang: A Linguistic Description*. CUP. [2015] pp. xv + 296. £70 ISBN 9 7811 0707 4170.

Williams, Jeffrey P., Edgar W. Schneider, Peter Trudgill, and Daniel Schreier, eds. *Further Studies in the Lesser-Known Varieties of English*. CUP. [2015] pp. xvi + 345. £65 ISBN 9 7811 0702 1204.

Wilson, John, and Diana Boxer, eds. *Discourse, Politics and Women as Global Leaders*. Benjamins. [2015] pp. 360. €99 ISBN 9 7890 2720 6541.

Wood, David. *Fundamentals of Formulaic Language: An Introduction*. Bloomsbury. [2015] pp. vii + 198. hb £95 ISBN 9 7805 6718 6416, pb £28.99 ISBN 9 7805 6727 8982.

Woodrow, Lindy. *Writing about Quantitative Research in Applied Linguistics*. PalMac. [2014] pp. xx + 199. hb £66 ISBN 9 7802 3036 9962, pb £25 ISBN 9 7802 3036 9979.

Yáñez-Bouza, Nuria. *Grammar, Rhetoric and Usage in English: Preposition Placement 1500–1900*. CUP. [2015] pp. xviii + 392. £67 ISBN 9 7811 0700 0797, e-book £51 ISBN 9 7813 1623 5874.

Zeevat, Henk, and Hans-Christian Schmitz, eds. *Bayesian Natural Language Semantics and Pragmatics*. Springer. [2015] pp. xi + 246. €103.99 ISBN 9 7833 1917 0640.

Zhang, Runhan. *Investigating Linguistic Knowledge of a Second Language*. Lang. [2015] pp. 210. pb £44 ISBN 9 7830 3431 3308.

Zhao, Yan. *Second Language Creative Writers: Identities and Writing Processes*. MlM. [2015] pp. xiii + 200. hb £89.95 ISBN 9 7817 8309 3007, pb £24.95 ISBN 9 7817 8309 2994.

# II

# Old English

ERIC LACEY, VICTORIA SYMONS, AND SIMON THOMSON

This chapter has eleven sections: 1. Bibliography; 2. Manuscript Studies, Palaeography, and Facsimiles; 3. Social, Cultural, and Intellectual Contexts: 4. Literature: General; 5. The Poems of the Exeter Book; 6. The Poems of the Vercelli Book; 7. The Poems of the Junius Manuscript; 8. *Beowulf* and the *Beowulf* Manuscript; 9. Other Poems; 10. Prose; 11. Reception. Sections 1, 2, 7, and 8 are by Simon Thomson; sections 3, 4, 10, and 11 are by Eric Lacey; sections 5, 6, and 9 are by Victoria Symons.

## 1. Bibliography

Issue 45:ii of the *Old English Newsletter*, due to appear in 2014, was published in January this year. The issue covers 2010 for the *Year's Work in Old English*, and includes sections on 'Anglo-Saxon Literature' and 'Manuscripts, Illuminations, Charters', amongst others. Issue 45:iv, the annual bibliography, was published in late 2015. The website includes a searchable database of annual bibliographies 1973–2009, free to all users who register.

## 2. Manuscript Studies, Palaeography, and Facsimiles

Several studies of individual texts have considered them explicitly in their manuscript context, each reviewed in the relevant section below. These are Benjamin D. Weber's 'A Harmony of Contrasts: The Guthlac Poems of the Exeter Book' (in Section 5), Kazutomo Karasawa's 'The *Menologium* and *Maxims II* in the Manuscript Context', and Eric Stanley's 'The *Gnomes* of Cotton Manuscript Tiberius B.i' (both in Section 9).

Tracey-Anne Cooper has published an exhaustive study of ninety-six different texts in *Monk-Bishops and the English Benedictine Reform Movement: Reading London BL, Cotton Tiberius A.iii in its Manuscript Context*. In chapter 2, Cooper's fresh analysis of the Benedictine Reform, and especially its manifestation in the mid eleventh century, is vividly presented with a strong sense of individuals, their relationships, and their influences. In particular,

*The Year's Work in English Studies, Volume 96 (2017)* © *The Author 2017. Published by Oxford University Press on behalf of the English Association. All rights reserved.*
*For Permissions, please email: journals.permissions@oup.com*
doi:10.1093/ywes/max002

chapter 4's consideration of the attitude of churchmen towards the laity and the desire to form a full 'Holy Society' is significant. The claim is that the Reform was a 'broad-based and long-lasting movement' (p. 72) and it is this that Cooper presents as the background to the production and use of Tiberius A.iii. In a rigorous, occasionally overwhelming, display of scholarship, each significant text's editorial history is given, often with interrogation of the genre to which it is usually assigned. The text is then discussed in relation to the context established in chapter 2, including consideration of other roughly contemporary presentations of the same text. All of these elements are brought together to establish what the text is doing in this particular manuscript, and how its meanings are modified or developed by the group in which it has been placed. The volume is important for any future engagement with the texts considered, and makes some important claims about the fluidity of textual genre in the period, with utility (of which Cooper has an impressively strong vision) more important than category. There is less consideration of the actual process of producing the book than there could have been—how, for instance, were the decisions Cooper identifies signalled to the scribes? But this is a fine model for study of a single manuscript.

Another method of identifying manuscripts for close attention is taken by Alun J. Ford in his *Marvel and Artefact: The 'Wonders of the East' in its Manuscript Contexts*. This has, of course, significance for students of the currently popular *Wonders of the East* (one version of which is included in the *Beowulf* manuscript), but is included in this section as it is focused on questions of manuscript presentation, and particularly art-historical issues. As his title implies, Ford is consciously focused on materiality, though his theoretical discussions are perhaps not as productive or useful as his close discussion of London, British Library, Cotton MS Vitellius A. xv (part 2) and London, British Library, Cotton MS Tiberius B. v (part 1). Ford summarizes the complex scholarship very well—with some interesting discussion of the dating of script in the early eleventh century—but probably his most significant proposal is the similarity of some illustrative techniques to the Icelandic Physiologus manuscript: Reykjavik, Stofnun Árna Magnússonar í íslenskum fræðum, MS 673 a, 4° (formerly Copenhagen, Den Arnamagnæanske Samling, MS 673 a ɪ + ɪɪ, 4°). His sense of the potential significance of Tiberius B. v in the Canterbury community devastated by Viking raids is intriguing, proposing its production as 'a symbolic re-engagement with an idealized Anglo-Saxon past' (p. 83). Ford's capacity to use multidisciplinary approaches to specific issues is impressive, but some forays are inevitably more successful than others. Given the relative slightness of the *Wonders* text, it is also perhaps inevitable that each chapter says rather more about its individual manuscript as an overall production than about that text itself; the collective contribution to studies of the *Wonders* text is perhaps a little slighter than one might have expected. On the whole, though, this is a very stimulating monograph with superb observation of manuscript detail, and Ford marshals complex arguments with considerable skill.

The impact of manuscript context on textual meaning is the concern of Helen Foxhall Forbes's 'Affective Piety and the Practice of Penance in Late-Eleventh-Century Worcester: The Address to the Penitent in Oxford, Bodleian

Library, Junius 121' (*ASE* 44[2015] 309–45). Forbes's convincing argument—which can be usefully compared with Cooper's analysis of Tiberius A.iii discussed above—is that what has been assumed to be a Lenten homily should be understood in its penitential context. Forbes's discussion is wide-ranging, taking in St Wulfstan of Worcester, the legacy of Wulfstan of York, late eleventh-century theology and the role of penitence therein, and of course the compilation and use of manuscripts. Given their close relationship, the argument here takes in and has implications for Oxford, Bodleian Library, Hatton MS 113 + 114. Forbes's proposals about the purposes of rubrication and crosses for a reader's use also have wider significance.

There have been a number of formal analyses of individual manuscripts in *Anglia* this year. In 'Tracking the Moving Ratio of þ to ð in Anglo-Saxon Texts: A New Method, and Evidence for a Lost Old English Version of the *Song of the Three Youths*' (*Anglia* 133[2015] 278–319), Michael Drout and Elie Chauvet revisit an old technique for analysing scribal activity. Their formula is $\theta=þ/(þ/ð)$, so identifying the frequency of þ in proportion to the total use of both graphemes. By calculating $\theta$ and representing it as a 'continuous multi-line rolling ratio' (p. 290) across a text, they claim to be able to extract sections that seem to have undergone separate transmission at some point. As the title implies, their immediate finding is that a short section of *Daniel* (lines 362–408) may have transmitted separately at some point; as they observe, it is intriguing that the first two lines of this section correspond to John Hines's discovery of a short inscription on a silver artefact (the 'Honington Clip'), published in the preceding article and reviewed in Section 9 below: 'The *Benedicite* Canticle in Old English Verse: An Early Runic Witness from Southern Lincolnshire'. Usefully, Drout and Chauvet also give some discussion of the challenges in using any such methodology and of the variability in scribal practice which makes this kind of identification so uncertain. Given the widely differing sample sizes they rely on, it would be useful to have some significance tests applied to their findings; the majority of their readers probably do not have a working knowledge of statistical analysis, and so may well ascribe more significance to this particular finding than it perhaps deserves, though the methodology is clearly significant and exciting.

Also in this volume of *Anglia* is another study of scribal habits: Sanne J.F. van der Schee's 'Breaking of /æ_rC/ in Early Old English: Personal Names and Place-Names in Latin Charters and Manuscripts of Bede's *Historia Ecclesiastica Gentis Anglorum*' (*Anglia* 133[2015] 225–56). Primarily concerned with considering orthographic development—and hence primarily of linguistic interest—there is nonetheless some useful summary discussion of the dating and localizing of the earliest manuscripts of the *Historia Ecclesiastica* as well as interesting consideration of whose language scribes are recording. Both could be productively read alongside Leonard Neidorf's 'Cain, Cam, Jutes, Giants, and the Textual Criticism of *Beowulf*' (*SP* 112 [2015] 599–632), discussed in Section 8 below.

Finally, there are more general essays of at least tangential interest to Anglo-Saxonists. There is a superb volume of collected essays on *Textus Roffensis: Law, Language, and Libraries in Early Medieval England*, edited by Bruce O'Brien and Barbara Bombi. The longest section, with seven essays on the legal codes in the manuscript, is important for historians, with some useful comment on language (most notably in Carole Hough's 'The Earliest English Texts? The Language of the Kentish Laws Reconsidered', pp. 137–56) and some texts of interest to students of literature (most notably Tracey-Anne Cooper's 'Episcopal Power and Performance: The Fugitive-Thief Rite in *Textus Roffensis* (also Known as the Cattle-Theft Charm)', pp. 193–214). Most immediately relevant here, however, are the four essays in the first section: 'The Book'. Mary P. Richards's 'The *Textus Roffensis*: Keystone of the Medieval Library at Rochester' (pp. 19–48) supplements Bruce O'Brien's introduction (pp. 1–16) with an overview of the manuscript and careful consideration of its construction. Richards has a fine sense of the place of this book and its maker in Norman Rochester. Nicholas Karn's '*Textus Roffensis* and its Uses' (pp. 49–67) is a productive consideration of the use of manuscripts as ritual artefacts, with significant implications for the continuity of Anglo-Saxon customs and culture in the twelfth century. Thomas Gobbitt uses the *Textus Roffensis* to give a close study of scribal practice in 'The Other Book: Cambridge, Corpus Christi College, MS 383 in Relation to the *Textus Roffensis*' (pp. 69–82). Finally, Stefan Jurasinski's 'Scribal Malpractice and the Study of Anglo-Saxon Law in the Twelfth Century' (pp. 83–101) perceptively analyses the understanding and use of Anglo-Saxon legislation in the early Norman period through the eyes of the *Textus* scribe.

Stewart Brookes, Peter Stokes, Matilda Watson, and Débora Marques de Matos's chapter in Aidan Conti, Orietta Da Rold, and Philip Shaw's edited collection *Writing Europe, 500–1450: Texts and Contexts*, 'The DigiPal Project for European Scripts and Decorations', is a contemplation of the potential of digital tools. It introduces the DigiPal project and its capabilities (pp. 27–36), and then applies its functionality to English vernacular minuscule (pp. 36–42). The resulting study is inconclusive, but it demonstrates the rapidity and ease with which large sets of palaeographic data can be compared, and suggests that we might look beyond identifying scribal hands to students of *scriptoria*.

Simon Thomson's 'Scribes, Sources and Readers: Using a Digital Edition to Develop Understanding of the Beowulf Manuscript' is discussed below, in Section 8.

## 3. Social, Cultural, and Intellectual Contexts

The social, cultural, and intellectual contexts of a specific part of Anglo-Saxon England form the focus of Stephen E. Harding, David Griffith, and Elizabeth Royles's edited volume *In Search of Vikings: Interdisciplinary Approaches to the Scandinavian Heritage of North-West England*, which offers a comprehensive overview of the main sources and methods used in researching Viking presence in north-west Anglo-Saxon England, spanning archaeological, material, linguistic, historical, literary, and genetic approaches. Of most relevance here are the contributions by Judith Jesch, Christina Lee, John Quanrud, and Paul Cavill; the contributions by Quanrud and Cavill are discussed below in Sections 9 and 10 respectively. Judith Jesch's 'Speaking like a Viking: Language and Cultural Interaction in the Irish Sea Region' (pp. 51–60) examines the Viking settlements in England as diasporas, and provides general commentary on how this was realized linguistically in the place names and inscriptions of these areas, with a minor discussion on their role in promulgating the Sigurd/Fafnir stories. Christina Lee's 'Viking Age Women' (pp. 61–70) mostly discusses textiles and Viking women, but like Jesch's chapter adduces place-name evidence for the prominent position of women in some areas. Both chapters articulate the importance of not assuming that names, clothing, or language indicate ethnicity.

Most of the essays in Clemens Gantner, Rosamund McKitterick, and Sven Meeder's edited volume, *The Resources of the Past in Early Medieval Europe* focus heavily on Continental material and reception. While oriented towards Carolingian history, many of the sources discussed here (such as Orosius' *Historiae adversus paganos*) are immediate sources for Anglo-Saxon texts. Marianne Pollheimer surveys the reception of one text in particular—the *Instituta regularia divinae legis* (*The Handbook of the Basic Principles of Divine Law*) by Junillus Africanus—in 'Divine Law and Imperial Rule: The Carolingian Reception of Junillus Africanus' (pp. 118–34), and she briefly describes the text's manuscript history and usage in England, where the first Junillus manuscript probably originates. The most clearly relevant for Old English studies must be Ian Wood's 'Who Are the Philistines? Bede's Readings of Old Testament Peoples' (pp. 172–87). Focusing on the parallels between the peoples of the Old Testament and those contemporary to Bede (such as the Britons, the Irish, and the Anglo-Saxons themselves), Wood studies the literal and non-literal interpretations of the Bible and of biblical genealogy in Bede's writings, paying particular attention to how people are grouped together according to the context and argument. Wood's argument resonates with the scepticism regarding the concept of ethnicity seen elsewhere this year, such as in Harding, Griffith, and Royles's *In Search of Vikings*, as he sees faith and faithfulness as the key criteria in Bede's grouping of peoples.

Jesse Keskiaho's *Dreams and Visions in the Early Middle Ages: The Reception and Use of Patristic Ideas, 400–900* examines the dreams and visions in Bede's *Historia*, the Whitby *Vita Gregorii Magni*, and the outputs of the Canterbury school. This is a valuable examination of how the ideas in Gregory's and Augustine's work were selectively interpreted and recombined to be used for a range of differing purposes, and his attention to the manuscripts and their annotations is tremendously useful. An appendix listing the manuscript witnesses of the main texts he discusses, in complete, excerpted, and epitomed form, is symptomatic of this (pp. 223–47).

Maijastina Kahlos's chapter, 'The Early Church' (in Collins, ed., *The Cambridge History of Magic and Witchcraft in the West: From Antiquity to the Present*, pp. 148–82), outlines some fundamentals of magic in the early medieval period. It discusses magic from two perspectives: first, as a designator for non-Christian practices; second, as a term applied to Christian practices which are today termed magical. The rhetorical strategy of the former is a familiar sight in Old English; the latter encompasses both saintly performative miracles and the use of their relics apotropaically and remedially.

There are two studies of the influence of the Irish on Anglo-Saxon intellectual culture. Conor O'Brien's 'The Cleansing of the Temple in Early Medieval Northumbria' (*ASE* 44[2015] 201–20) examines Bede and Stephen of Ripon, and argues for a culturally pervasive identification of churches with the Jewish temple grounded in liturgical language, Irish attitudes to sacred space, the writings of Gregory the Great, and Anglo-Saxon fascination with stone buildings. A similar case for Irish influence on Anglo-Saxon intellectual culture is put forward by Máirín Mac Carron in 'Bede, Irish *Computistica*, and *Annus Mundi*' (*EMedE* 23[2015] 290–307), who argues that Bede's decision to move towards the Vulgate *Annus Mundi* mode of reckoning time was indebted to Irish *computistica*.

Not all Irish influence can be so certainly detected, however. Annina Seiler's chapter 'Writing the Germanic Languages: The Early History of the Digraphs < th >, < ch > and < uu >' (in Conti, Da Rold, and Shaw, eds., pp. 101–21) is an eminently readable assessment of the cultural contact lying behind three innocuous spelling conventions in Old English (and some other Germanic languages): the use of the spelling < th > for the sound /þ/, < ch > for /χ/, and < uu > for /w/. Seiler evaluates arguments that < th > and < ch > demonstrate the influence of Irish orthographic traditions on English and finds that they are generally inadequate, though she is reluctant to rule out Irish influence altogether. Seiler convincingly argues that the most probable source of these spelling innovations, however, was Merovingian influence (and that this was unquestionably the case for < uu >), and that this common source informed both Old High German and Old English spelling conventions.

Jane Hawkes's '"Hail the Conquering Hero': Coming and Going at Ruthwell: *Adventus* and Transition' (in Boulton and Hawkes with Herman, eds., *The Art, Literature and Material Culture of the Medieval World. Transition, Transformation and Taxonomy*, pp. 80–96) discusses an ambiguous panel on the Ruthwell cross which has variously been interpreted as either depicting the flight to Egypt or the return from Egypt. In a lavishly illustrated survey of theology and comparable art, and with clear implications for the study of *The Dream of the Rood*, Hawkes argues that the image is intentionally ambiguous in order to evoke all the 'comings' of Christ—his Incarnation, his Second Coming, and his triumph over death in the *Adventus Christii* topos. Also concerned with salvation is Diarmuid Scully's 'Ends of Empire and the Earth: Themes of Transition and the Orkney Island from Antiquity to Bede' (pp. 125–37), which contributes to our understanding of the spiritual and geographical learning of the early medieval period, particularly as found in Bede's *Historia Ecclesiastica*. He demonstrates that Orkney is given such prominence because it emphasizes narratives of salvation by extending Christianity to a conventional marker of the edge of the world.

Eric Lacey's 'When Is a *Hroc* Not a *Hroc*? When It Is a *Crawe* or *Hrefn*! A Case-Study in Recovering Old English Folk-Taxonomies' (pp. 138–52 in the same volume) is an examination of the issues of transitioning between Anglo-Saxon and present-day categorization and semantics, and the implications this has for perception of the natural world. Semantic enquiry is also at the heart of Michael D.J. Bintley's 'Settlements in Transition: Where Are the *Wīc*s in Old English Poetry?' (pp. 153–63), though his subject is the semantic range of *wīc*.

He examines the usage of the word in the poetic corpus, focusing particularly on *Maxims I*, *Exodus*, and *The Whale*, and compares this with *wīcs* in settlement archaeology.

The final three essays in O'Brien and Bombi's *Textus Roffensis* look behind the documents therein to think about the contexts which produced them. Simon Keynes's 'King Æthelred the Unready and the Church of Rochester' (pp. 315–62) is a detailed examination of the politics, both at the micro-level of the bishops and the macro-level of the kings Edgar and Æthelred, lying behind the Rochester charters preserved in the *Textus Roffensis*. Richard Sharpe is similarly concerned with the politics behind the document in his 'Doing Business with William Rufus: The Haddenham Narrative' (pp. 363–85), where he takes us behind the scenes of royal negotiation and demonstrates that the witness list was a roll-call of participants in the process. Sally Vaughn's 'Gundulf of Rochester and the Influence of the School of Bec at Rochester' (pp. 387–402) argues that Gundulf of Rochester was more likely to be the compiler of the *Textus Roffensis* than his successor Ernulf, and at least 'its architect in concept, if not in deed ' (p. 404).

The poetic art of Aldhelm can now be appreciated by a much wider audience thanks to A.M. Juster's translation of all one hundred Enigmata in *Saint Aldhelm's Riddles*. The crisp and idiomatic translations face the Latin original. The solutions are not listed with the texts but are given in a key at the end. There are eighty-five pages of textual commentary (pp. 73–158) articulating textual difficulties and spelling-out difficulties in the Latin.

## 4. Literature, General

Carolyne Larrington's *Brothers and Sisters in Medieval European Literature* ranges over Latin, Old Norse, Old and Middle English, Middle High German, and more in this psychologically grounded examination of siblings. It begins with their place in medieval history and culture before examining siblings along more thematic dimensions: brotherly love (chapter 2), sister–brother relations (chapter 3), brotherly hate (chapter 4), sisterly hate (chapter 5), incest (chapters 6 and 7), and socially constructed siblinghood (such as foster-brothers, chapter 8). The broad scope is more advantageous than detrimental, as it draws attention to the relative universality of fraternal and sororal practices (being defined by similar socio-cultural environments) and gives an empirical basis on which to reckon truly exceptional behaviour. Old English texts discussed include *Guthlac B*, *Maxims I*, and *Beowulf*.

The chapters in Michael Bintley and Tom Williams's *Representing Beasts in Early Medieval England and Scandinavia* collectively offer a great deal of information on the perception and representation of animals in the early medieval period. Bintley and Williams's introduction contains a brief survey of the critical and theoretical modes which have hitherto been applied in medieval scholarship's examination of man, beast, and the boundaries between them, but explicitly leaves any engagement with these modes to the ensuing contributions. Several are not discussed here because they do not explicitly deal with literary contexts, but the volume as a whole provides useful material on the iconography beasts in early medieval England. The study of the superstitious and naturalistic presentation of ravens in Old English is the subject of Marijane Osborn's chapter, 'The Ravens on the Lejre Throne: Avian Identifiers, Odin at Home, Farm Ravens' (pp. 94–112), which argues for the presence of domestic 'home ravens' underlying some portrayals of the bird in Old English.

László Sándor Chardonnens, in 'Do Anglo-Saxons Dream of Exotic Sheep?' (pp. 131–50), ponders how the Anglo-Saxons would have imagined those beasts with which they had no familiarity, such as camels, phoenixes, and lions, but who nonetheless populate texts such as prognostics. Chardonnens examines how translators of prognostic texts handled their sources in this respect, and argues that literal comprehension of these animals was less important than the associative understanding of them, which Anglo-Saxons would have encountered elsewhere (such as in the Bible). Especially useful here is the index cataloguing the various associations of animals in the prognostics (pp. 146–7); while it provides a good overview, the lack of cross-referencing is a shame. Richard North's 'The Pig in a Villa in Vandalic North Africa, and Boar Cults in Old Germanic Heathendom' (pp. 151–75) also begins by pondering far-off animals—in this case a pig in a Latin epigram by the Vandal poet Luxorius. In a wide-ranging essay, North argues for resonances of ancient Germanic boar cults in Luxorius' poem, and highlights correspondences between Old Norse and Old English texts—including *Beowulf*, *Elene*, and the *Rune Poem*—as part of his case for the shared inheritance of the boar's fertile and martial aspects. The martial theme is continued in Thomas J.T. Williams, ' "For the Sake of Bravado in the Wilderness": Confronting the Bestial in Anglo-Saxon Warfare' (pp. 176–204). Williams's multidisciplinary approach brings together literature, history, archaeology, and topography to interrogate the cultural and experiential realities underlying the conception of warfare, warriors, and battle-sites as bestial, and he makes an important argument for the Anglo-Saxon conceptions of monstrous places in the literary record being identical to early historical locations of conflict. Particular attention should be drawn to Williams's useful chart of all battles mentioned in the *Anglo-Saxon Chronicle* and Bede's *Historia* between 429 and 860 (pp. 182–7), listing the battles' names, locations, topographical features, and their attestations. Michael Bintley's 'Where the Wild Things Are in Old English Poetry' (pp. 205–28) also considers the relationship between the bestial, the human, and place, and in an argument that ranges over most of the poetic corpus he demonstrates that the monstrousness of a location is determined by the actions of its occupants. In doing so, and drawing attention to the environmental consequences of peoples' actions, Bintley also demonstrates the ease with which the line between bestial and human can be crossed. The last two chapters, by John Baker and Della Hooke, are discussed in Section 10 below.

Animals also form part of the focus of Joshua Davies, 'The Landscapes of Thanet and the Legend of St Mildrith: Human and Nonhuman Voices, Agencies and Histories' (*ES* 96[2015] 487–506), which surveys the legends of St Mildrith in both Latin and Old English and provides an ecologically and ecocritically minded reading of them. Davies compares the localized interactions Mildrith has with agentive nature (such as animals) with non-agentive nature (such as stones) on Thanet to illustrate the interdependence of human, natural, and spiritual.

As glossed material fits no other section particularly well, it may as well be discussed here. Brandon Hawk's 'Psalm 151 in Anglo-Saxon England' (*RES* 66[2015] 805–21) is the first study to focus on the apocryphal Psalm 151, which exists in two places in Old English (in the glosses of the Vespasian and Eadwine psalters). He gives a tantalizing glimpse into the earliest scholarship on the psalm, which seems to originate in the schools of medieval Britain and Ireland, drawing on sources in both Old English and Old Irish, but does not pursue this too far to avoid excessive speculation. He then traces the transmission of the psalm into England and compares and contrasts the translational strategies of the Eadwine and Vespasian translations. Particularly noteworthy is that Hawk comes to the startling conclusion that the Vespasian glosses preserve a hitherto unidentified poem.

Glosses also lie at the heart of Damian Fleming's '*Sundorhalgan*, Winchester, and Ælfric' (*RES* 66[2015] 822–42), which similarly looks at strategies of translation. Fleming observes that only a few texts use *Sundorhalgan* in place of simply co-opting the Latin *Pharisees*, and notes that its peculiar semantics ('separate holy ones') suggests a single point of origin. He demonstrates that it only occurs in the works of Ælfric and some other works—such as the West Saxon gospel—associated with Winchester, and argues that it derives from a single inventive writer's reading of Isidore—who may well be Ælfric. Ciaran Arthur's 'Three Marginal Notes in London, British Library, MS Cotton Caligula A. vii' (*N&Q* 62[2015] 211–17) examines three comments—two tenth-century Latin and one eleventh-century Old English—on the Old Saxon *Heliand*, and suggests that the first two, concerned with martial occupation, reflect anxieties after Cnut's coronation, while the last, concerned with fertility, might have been by the scribe of the *æcerbot* charm.

This year has seen a surge of publications concerned with the semantics of Old English words and the assumptions often found accompanying them. Megan Cavell's 'Formulaic *Friþuwebban*: Reexamining Peace-Weaving in Light of Old English Poetics' (*JEGP* 114[2015] 355–72) demonstrates that scholarship has unnecessarily gendered the role of peace-weaver in Old English, where both masculine and feminine *friþuwebba/e* are found. Drawing on *Widsið*, *Elene*, and *Beowulf*, Cavell draws attention to the qualities of status, moral superiority, and leadership as defining *friþuwebban*, rather than masculinity or femininity. Filip Missuno's 'Glowing Paradoxes and Glimmers of Doom: A Re-evaluation of the Meaning of Old English *Fāh* in Poetic Contexts' (*Neophil* 99[2015] 125–42) is a philologically rigorous but literarily sensitive exploration of the semantics of *fāh*, arguing convincingly that its central meaning was 'gleaming', but that its poetic employment invariably involved gloomier connotations such as death. Bernard Mees's 'Of Ettins and Ents' (*ES* 96:vi[2015] 611–18) evaluates the etymologies and meanings of three Old English 'monster' words: *þyrs*, *eoten*, and *ent*. He reluctantly accepts a connection between *eoten* and 'eat' (*etan*), but cautions against over-interpreting the connection given that it can have positive interpretations. *Pyrs* is clearly linked with the semantics of 'wounding', while *ent* is etymologically unclear—Mees suggests a loan from Latin, possibly mediated by Old High German.

Hate and hostility have also proven quite popular this year. Rolf H. Bremmer Jr.'s 'Looking Back at Anger: Wrath in Anglo-Saxon England' (*RES* 66[2015] 423–48) is a culturally attentive examination of anger. He begins by examining the words used for anger and their semantic fields, but then situates . this in a wider—not just literary—context by looking at depictions of anger iconographically and textually (indeed, he points out that there is more of the former than the latter!). He concludes that anger was a typically male emotion associated particularly with irascibility, but that it was a more positive trait in heroic poetry and, with the exception of curses, considered inappropriate in Christian contexts. David R. Wilton's '*Fæhða Gemyndig*: Hostile Acts Versus Enmity' (*Neophil* 99 [2015] 647–66) looks at the performance of wrath and anger. He queries the traditional definition of *fæhþ* as 'feud' in a wide-ranging survey of its uses in the law-codes, in heroic poetry, and in religious literature, and argues that while 'feud' is appropriate sometimes, it could, especially in poetic contexts, more profitably be understood to mean 'hostile act'. John D. Niles's 'The Myth of the Feud in Anglo-Saxon England' (*JEGP* 114[2015] 163–200) also interrogates the semantics of *fæhþ*, though his case is a much broader-reaching one. In a powerful polemic, Niles argues that the term 'feud' has no place either as the translation of *fæhþ* or in the scholarship and general understanding of Anglo-Saxon culture. Part of Niles's argument is concerned with the historiography of 'the feud', and he draws attention to how it 'came into the English language with a primitivist aura about it from the start' (p. 172). He also demonstrates that the word 'feud' never works in translations of OE *fæhþ*, which is better rendered by '[illegitimate] violence', generally, or 'sanctioned vengeance', or, along much the same lines as Wilton, by 'general state of hostility of enmity'. He rounds off his paper with a defence of his sweeping claim that 'no feuds worthy of that name are depicted in either the historical or literary records', using *Beowulf*, the *Anglo-Saxon Chronicle*, *The Husband's Message*, *The Wife's Lament*, *The Battle of Maldon*, and even the tumultuous eleventh century, the subject of Richard Fletcher's *Bloodfeud*.

Eric Stanley's 'Colours, Hues, Shades and Tints: How Subtle Were the Anglo-Saxons When They Recorded What They Saw?' (*Poetica* 83[2015] 1–18) is a series of notes on passages in verse and prose concerned with colour.

Alexandra Bolintineanu's 'Beyond the Sun's Setting: Webs of Unknowing in Old English' (*DigPhil* 4[2015] 160–89) is a methodologically innovative attempt to bring digital tools, traditional semantic study, and Old English literature together. It broadly surveys Old English literature to explore how unknowing is declared, articulated, and expressed, and seeks to map this into a conceptual network marking out connections and their frequency. Her data— some fifteen passages—is collated in a handy table (pp. 179–85), but real highlights are her graphic networks showing the interrelating terms and concepts used for unknowing. She finds that these expressions almost always concern the wondrous, but that the metaphors and expressions used also form distinct semantic clusters which would benefit from further research.

In addition to the articles by Weiskott, Pascual, and Neidorf, discussed in Sections 5 and 8, this year sees two methodological contributions to the study of Old English metre. Ian Cornelius's 'The Accentual Paradigm in Early English Metrics' (*JEGP* 114[2015] 459–81) is a teasingly provocative appraisal of the implications of Nicolay Yakovlov's work on Old and Middle English metre for accentual metrics. It is not written with a non-specialist in mind. More accessible is Megan Hartman's 'A New Justification for an Old Analysis of the Hypermetric Onset' (*N&Q* 62[2015] 513–16), which argues that hypermetric onsets can usefully be categorized into 'light' and 'heavy' variants.

## 5. The Poems of the Exeter Book

The premise of Mercedes Salvador-Bello's *Isidorean Perceptions of Order: The Exeter Book of Riddles and Medieval Latin Enigmata* is deceptively straightforward. Through a comparative study of various early medieval literary collections, starting with Isidore of Seville's *Etymologiae*, moving through the Latin *enigmata* of Symphosius, Aldhelm, Tatwine, Eusebius, and others, and finishing with the Old English riddles of the Exeter Book, Salvador-Bello argues for a common structuring principle based on four key thematic groupings: cosmology, zoology, instruments, and prodigies. This principle is extended in the riddle collections through their further subdivision into pairs and triplets, employing the technique of analogy and difference often favoured by Isidore in the *Etymologiae*.

This approach allows Salvador-Bello to make some quite detailed claims about the composition and—more specifically—the compilation of the Exeter Book riddle collection. She identifies Riddles 1–40 as a 'source collection', delineated by an envelope of cosmological riddles that begin and end this Group 1. To this initial group were added further riddles in two movements: Group 2 (Riddles 41–59), and Group 3 (Riddles 61–95), with an eye to meeting the 'traditional requirements of the canonical hundred' (p. 445). This division accounts for such oddities as the 'rather awkward' (p. 444) juxtaposition of Riddle 40 ('Creation') with the sexual riddle series that follows shortly thereafter in Group 2, or the increasing resort to extremely brief and occasionally scatological riddles towards the end of Group 3.

It is impossible to convey in a summary way the detail and nuance that Salvador-Bello brings to her discussion of these groups and subgroups (and sub-subgroups). In a pleasing echo of its own argument, this is a book that is remarkably structured. Chapters are devoted to particular literary collections, and are further subdivided along the same lines as the divisions in the primary texts. Tables make a frequent appearance. This rigorously methodical approach is complemented by no fewer than ten appendices, each of which gives a welcome summary of the structural divisions of individual collections discussed, an extensive bibliography, and an impressively lengthy index. The density of the scholarship on offer here is offset against the eminently readable prose: this is not a forbidding tome. The enduring popularity of the Exeter Book riddles means their Latin analogues are all too often relegated to the sidelines, particularly in the field of English literature. Mercedes Salvador-Bello makes a firm case for the intellectual milieu that unites these various compositions in a study that is surely destined to become a cornerstone of the field.

There are various chapters and articles on the Exeter Book riddles, mainly concerned with the analysis and fine-tuning of established readings. Robert Stanton's chapter 'Mimicry, Subjectivity, and the Embodied Voice in Anglo-Saxon Bird Riddles' (in Kleiman, ed., *Voice and Voicelessness in Medieval Europe*, pp. 29–43) presents the riddles of the Anglo-Saxon period as 'a rich field in which to explore the nature, operation, and function of voice as a fundamental of language' (p. 29). This chapter draws together two currently lively fields of academic study (animals and communication). Stanton's impressive survey situates 'riddlic birds' from both the Anglo-Latin and Old English riddle collections in the context of classical philosophical approaches to sound and the voice. Several of the Exeter Book riddles, Stanton argues, show clear engagement with this classical learning.

Peter Orton's 'The Exeter Books *Riddles*: Authorship and Transmission' (*ASE* 44[2015] 131–62) treats the collection in two blocks (Riddles 1–59 and 61–95), arguing that the composition of many riddles in the latter group was influenced by a reading of the former. The argument develops over various points of consideration (opening formulas challenged), with a particular emphasis on repeated solutions as grounds for comparison. This stylistic comparison suggests a further division of the first riddle block (Riddles 1–27 and 28–59). Orton also argues, with close textual analysis to support the argument, that the later riddles were influenced by their preceding counterparts.

In 'Of Water and the Spirit: Metaphorical Focus in Exeter Book Riddle 74' (*RES* 66[2015] 1–19) Thomas Klein assesses the function of metaphor in a riddle whose proposed solutions have ranged from sea-eagle to pen, to oak or boat. Klein's favoured interpretation, is 'water', with a strong hint of the Holy Spirit mixed in. Klein suggests that the Holy Spirit functions as a focusing metaphor to direct the reader's attention to the properties of water. Through this web of metaphor and allusion, the reader is challenged to grasp why the solution is 'water' and not 'the Holy Spirit', while recognizing the similarities that bind the two together.

In a second article, 'The Metaphorical Cloak of Exeter Riddle 83, "Ore/Gold/Metal"' (*ANQ* 28[2015] 11–14), Klein argues that the speaker of the riddle, 'ore' or perhaps 'gold', is personified not as the obscure biblical smith Tubalcain but as a fallen angel. This allows for a more provocative, and in places more poignant, reading of the poem as a meditation on the allure of evil and the extent to which its power is granted by those it afflicts.

Medieval beekeeping practices form the starting position taken in Helen Price's 'A Hive of Activity: Realigning the Figure of the Bee in the Mead-Making Network of *Exeter Book* Riddle 27' (*Postmed* 6[2015]). Price combines theoretical approaches (drawing in particular on the increasingly popular field of literary ecocriticism) with a wide-ranging discussion of archaeological and historical sources. Not all of this is directly relevant to Riddle 27, but it makes for an impressive survey of Anglo-Saxon beekeeping practices. Price's argument is that the figure of the bee, overtly absent for most of the riddle, is in fact continually evoked through a network of interactions between various human and non-human entities. Those interested in bees, medieval or otherwise, may also enjoy the more academically relaxed discussion in Felix Hausleitner's 'Anglo-Saxon Riddle Hints at the Making of a Medieval Honey Bee Skep Hive' (*Bee World* 92[2015] 87–9). Hausleitner argues that a hint towards the solution 'beehive' is to be found in each sentence of Riddle 17; the brief sentence-by-sentence analysis of the poem is complemented by a reproduced photograph of a skep-maker at work in 1950s Yorkshire.

Several poems of the Exeter Book are discussed, some at length, in P.S. Langeslag's *Seasons in the Literatures of the Medieval North*. These include *Christ II*, *The Husband's Message*, *Maxims I*, *Phoenix*, *The Ruin*, *The Seafarer*, *Soul and Body I*, *The Wanderer*, and *The Wife's Lament*. The elegies, as may be expected, receive particular attention in this work; the landscapes of the poems, their use of architecture and setting, and the seascapes of *The Wanderer* and *The Seafarer* are discussed in detail as part of a broader consideration of 'winter mindscapes' and an argument that winter settings in Old English literature are commonly evoked 'for reasons of contrast with society' as a means of delineating 'who belongs where in the landscape' (p. 63).

Langeslag's book ranges widely, covering a hefty selection of prose and poetry in Old English, Middle English, Old Norse, and Latin. Looking beyond the Exeter Book, his study includes extended discussions of *Andreas*, *Genesis B*, *Menologium*, and, of course, *Beowulf*. It is this last poem that most substantially informs Langeslag's examination of the seasons—particularly the winter season—in Old English literature. He identifies in the poem a 'triad of water, winter, and monsters' (p. 90), one that rests on a figurative understanding of cold as not simply a measure of temperature but, particularly when associated with water, also of danger and hostility. This, Langeslag argues, allows authors of Old English (and Old Norse) literature to invoke elements of winter for certain associative effects, rather than to establish a literal chronological setting. Other Old English works discussed, more briefly, include *The Battle of Maldon*, the Blickling Homilies, *Death of Edward*, *Exodus*, *Genesis A*, *Maxims II*, *Metres of Boethius*, and *Solomon and Saturn II*.

Langeslag begins with an engaging introduction that sets medieval literature in the context of contemporary experiences, and understandings, of time, the seasons, and the yearly cycle. The discussion that follows is structured by themes rather than by texts. Four chapters divide the study into 'Myth and Ritual', covering seasonal celebrations both pre- and post-conversion, 'Winter Mindscapes', which focuses on literary tropes and themes associated with winter, 'Winter Institutions', which builds on the preceding chapter by examining the use to which those tropes are put, and finally 'Summer Adventure', which closes the study in the romance landscapes of Middle English literature. This is a carefully researched and impeccably presented book that offers an up-to-date consideration of a topic centrally important to so many medieval literary works.

The *Guthlac* poems are assessed in Benjamin D. Weber's 'A Harmony of Contrasts: The *Guthlac* Poems of the Exeter Book' (*JEGP* 114[2015] 201–18). Weber seeks to demonstrate that, in spite of their significant differences, continuity can be found between *Guthlac A* and *B* through their 'complementary explorations of two different ideals of spiritual perfection' (p. 201). This, interestingly, is one of several articles this year that seeks to find unity in or between various of the Exeter Book's poems. Weber characterizes *Guthlac A* as concerned with solitary spiritual growth leading to the possibility of bliss on earth, while *Guthlac B* is a meditation on the role of teachers in a world beset by suffering. Putting aside issues of dating, which are often contentious, Weber instead considers the reception of the poems in the only context we can talk about with certainty: the Exeter Book itself. He argues that the pairing of the two in this manuscript, against a backdrop of the Benedictine Reform, would have spoken compellingly to the evolving role of monks in later Anglo-Saxon society.

In '*Guthlac A* and the Temptation of the Barrow' (*SN* 87[2015] 48–72), Stephanie Clark tackles the meaning of OE *beorg* and potential influence from Felix's *Vita sancti Guthlaci*. Clark identifies a tendency towards translating *beorg*—whether as 'barrow' or as 'hill'—in a way that chimes with pre-existing assumptions about the poem. The titular 'temptation of the barrow' is argued to be just that, with Clark favouring 'hill' as an interpretation that, though more prosaic to modern ears, fits better with the poem's concerns and carries its own web of suggestive connotations. As to overlap between *Guthlac A* and the Latin *Vita*, Clark dismisses the possibility. Such conflation, she suggests, is another form of temptation, allowing modern readers to construct a text suited to modern tastes.

*The Order of the World* is the starting point for Alexandra Bolintineanu's study of 'declarations of unknowing' in Old English, 'Beyond the Sun's Setting: Webs of Unknowing in Old English' (*DigPhil* 4[2015] 160–89). The movement of the sun, presented in the poem as an unfathomable mystery, was actually 'fairly well-fathomed' in Anglo-Saxon England (p. 161); the assertion is rather a motif intended to function as a marker of wonder at the supernatural. Bolintineanu constructs a network of such declarations using the *Dictionary of Old English Web Corpus*, complemented by close readings of the *Advent Lyrics*, *The Order of the World*, and Wulfstan's *Incipiunt sermones Lupi episcopi*. *The Order of the World* also forms the basis for Jacob Riyeff's exploration of the nature and function of Old English poetry in '*Homo Contemplans*: *The Order of the World*, Gregorian Contemplative Anthropology, and Old English Poetics' (*Viator* 46[2015] 1–20). This composition is chosen not least for its singular description, within the surviving Old English corpus, of poetry itself as an 'aid to contemplation' (p. 2). Riyeff's analysis is informed by the writing both of Gregory the Great and modern monastics, and argues for the poem's engagement with Gregorian models of language and contemplation.

Eric Stanley's '*The Gifts of Men*: A Favourable Appraisal, with Some New Understandings' (*Anglia* 133[2015] 330–77) presents a new edition and translation of the poem, with extensive commentary to boot. The edition is divided into sections (ll. 1–29, 30–90, 91–6, and 97–113), allowing for discussion to immediately follow the lines in question. Particularly noteworthy are Stanley's study of compound words in the poem, his detailed analysis of the *sum*-catalogue ('no mindless anaphoric listing' here), and the intriguing suggestion that the poem draws to a close with a reflection on the talents of its own poet. *The Gifts of Men*, Stanley argues, is a religious poem far removed from the world of *Beowulf*, but no less excellent for that. Stanley returns with '*The Descent into Hell*: A Poem in the Exeter Book' (*N&Q* 62[2015] 6–12), offering a varied defence of a work that has historically 'had few friends' (p. 6). Points for discussion include the meaning of OE *reþe*, translation of ll. 33–43 and 107–14, a catalogue of the poem's epithets for Christ (46 in total: a 'Cædmonian' density, pp. 10–11) and, finally, a consideration of the poem's end as a 'well-constructed thanksgiving' (p. 11).

The dating of *Widsith* provided lively debate between a pair of articles both published this year. The first, Eric Weiskott's 'The Meter of *Widsith* and the Distant Past' (*Neophil* 99[2015] 143–50), is a response to a previous article in the same journal (Leonard Neidorf, 'The Dating of *Widsið* and the Study of Germanic Antiquity', *Neophil* 97[2013] 165–83), which argued for an early, in some places very early, dating of the poem. Weiskott briskly addresses several of Neidorf's arguments, before settling into a weighty technical analysis of both Old English and hypothesized pre-Old English metre, and their implications for dating. *Widsith*, he concludes, 'is not an ancient poem from a pan-Germanic distant past' but rather an Old English composition that 'turns inherited vocabulary to its own rhetorical purposes' (p. 149). Broader paradigmatic issues are raised throughout this discussion, most notably the problems of prioritizing a hypothesized 'text' over its recorded form.

Neidorf's response to Weiskott's response was also, remarkably, published this year. Neidorf takes the dispute over the dating of *Widsith*, summarized above, as the starting point for a forceful evaluation of methodological approaches, in 'On the Epistemology of Old English Scholarship' (*Neophil* 99[2015] 631–46). The first part of the article focuses on the minutiae of *Widsith* itself, while the second presents a broader assessment of the field. Admirable as this aim may be, there is no great room for nuance in an approach that characterizes all such disagreement as a struggle between the 'rational scholar' and the 'obscurantist'.

A case for the textual unity of *Resignation*—often taken to be fragments of two separate poems—is made by Helena W. Sobol in 'In Defence of the Textual Integrity of the Old English Poem *Resignation*' (*SAP* 50[2015] 71–93). Codicological issues are briefly discussed, followed by a lengthier examination of spelling and phonology. The greater part of the article focuses on literary analysis of the poem as a coherent text, considered in the context of Old English elegies and devotional literature, with the argument that such a reading is possible 'without forcing any unnatural interpretation' upon the poem (p. 78). Sobol concludes that, although some elegiac motifs do appear towards the end of *Resignation*, it is confessional prayer that provides the prevailing mode of the poem as a whole.

Alfred Bammesberger's 'The Old English Poem *Deor*: Its Structural Units and the Grammatical Analysis of its Refrain' (*Anglia* 133[2015] 320–9) tackles the question of whether the separation of lines 28–34 from the following lines 35–42—an editorial commonplace—is justified on the basis of the poem's grammar, content, and manuscript presentation. He argues that these lines should in fact be taken as a single structural unit, comparable to the five that precede it. His grammatical analysis of the notoriously tricky refrain, and its evolving relationship to the structural units it follows, is of particular interest.

In 'Vikings and Victories: Sea-Stories from "The Seafarer" to *Skyfall* and the Future of British Maritime Culture' (*Journal for Maritime Research* 17[2015] 1–15), Marion Gibson seeks to establish the literary representation of seafarers as an indicator of contemporary attitudes towards the maritime. Old English is treated rather briefly, with the greater part of the article focusing on historiography and literary trends from the 1790s through to the present day. Nevertheless, a literature review that begins with *The Seafarer* and ends with the television series *Deadliest Catch* ('"manly men can fish"', p. 9) makes an appealing, if unusual, case for the lasting cultural relevance of Old English poetry. The Exeter Book elegies (or lyrics) are also the topic of discussion in Daniel Anlezark's 'From Lyric to Elegy: Changing Emotion in Early English Poetry' (in Michael Champion and Andrew Lynch, eds., *Understanding Emotions in Early Europe*). This book was not available for review.

## 6. The Poems of the Vercelli Book

There are three articles discussing *Andreas*. In an argument that could be read alongside Vickrey's volume on *Genesis B* (reviewed in Section 7 below) is Megan Cavell's 'The Binding of Religious Heroes in *Andreas* and the *Hêliand*' (*ES* 96[2015] 507–24), which argues that more connections should be drawn between the Old Saxon and Old English corpora. Specifically, she sees binding and bondage as a probable influence from the *Hêliand* to *Andreas*. The linguistic arguments here are strong: a surprisingly unusual collocation of *hand* and *bindan* (only in *Andreas* and *Genesis B*); OE *leoðubend* / OS *liðobend* being shared only by *Andreas* and *Hêliand*. The observation that the two texts 'share a great deal of formulaic language with *Beowulf*, which was also likely known in Alfred's court' (p. 519) is interesting. The conclusions to such an engaging and provocative piece are perhaps a little light, and one hopes that there will be rather more work on this textual group, as well as on the literary links between Saxony and England in the period.

Helen Appleton has written about 'The Book of Isaiah as an Influence on *Andreas*' (*N&Q* 62[2015] 1–6). Like Cavell, Appleton thinks that our understanding of the poet's borrowing from *Beowulf* has not been adequately extended to consider what other sources he drew on. She identifies five different echoes of Isaiah, some more convincing than others, each one 'a correspondence of idea ... rather than an exact verbal parallel' (p. 4). This naturally limits how convincing each proposal is, but there is no doubt that Appleton's reading of Isaiah alongside the poem is productive. The suggestion that the unusual conversion of Mermedonia into an island could be an echo of Isaiah 49 is particularly intriguing.

In 'Baptism, Conversion, and Selfhood in the Old English *Andreas*' (*SP* 112[2015] 1–23), Amity Reading argues that the Vercelli Book as a whole is 'a codex about death' (p. 1). A proposal that has implications for many discussions of the intertextuality of Anglo-Saxon manuscripts is that the first text in a volume 'sets its tone' (p. 3). Reading shows an elegant sense of the difference between the poet's and Ælfric's handling of Andrew. Close readings and structural analysis show the poem as deeply concerned with the ties between baptism, conversion, death, and judgement, and there is a useful review of the complex Anglo-Saxon attitude towards Jews as 'both the source of Christianity and its doppelgänger, the threatening "other"' (p. 7).

Michael D.J. Bintley's 'Where the Wild Things Are in Old English Poetry' (in Bintley and Williams, eds., pp. 205–28) discusses *Andreas* alongside several other Old English poems (pp. 218–21), showing how conversion results in the transformation of a bestial and horrific people.

Finally, Jacob Riyeff is interested in 'Dualism in Old English Literature: The Body-and-Soul Theme and Vercelli Homily IV' (*SP* 112[2015] 453–68). Comparing Vercelli Homily IV with *Soul and Body I*, he finds a contrast between their treatment of the dualism of the soul and the body. The well-known loathing the poetic soul has for its body is convincingly contrasted with the homily's sense of complementarity. The homilist's use of Christ as a voice for unity is effectively demonstrated, and Riyeff's sense of the text as an active working out of the problem of dualism is engaging. There could be more consideration of what the texts do to one another when in the same manuscript.

## 7. The Poems of the Junius Manuscript

The most significant publication on Junius 11 this year is John Vickrey's monograph on *Genesis B and the Comedic Imperative*. It is fluently and confidently written, with a comprehensive overview of scholarship on the major aspects of the poem. Vickrey firmly rejects the school of thought that Adam and Eve are exonerated by the poet and seeks to reinstate the text as clearly orthodox, and gives a strong defence of philological analysis. He gives the many critics with whom he disagrees a fair hearing, and the book thus forms a strong, if sometimes dense, introduction to the text. Moving with consummate ease between narrative, allegorical, and tropological levels of the text, the book constructs a clear sense of the poet's wit and interest and has some superb close readings of both characters' emotions and theological import. Key to the rejection of an exonerative reading is the meaning of *tacen*: is Adam shown as demanding and receiving a sign of truth from Satan's messenger or is he not? Vickrey's argument proposes exoneration as a modern misreading of the poet's intention as the result of a shift in emphasis (from *tacen* to *ænig* in line 541) when the text was translated from Old Saxon into Old English. Vickrey's interest is in the Saxon poet, but he does not always clarify how he is reading the poet's thinking through the late tenth-century copy of a translated and multiply reproduced text. Seeing the poem as coming to England as a gift on the occasion of Æthelwulf's marriage to Charles the Bald's daughter Judith, Vickrey sees both Old Saxon and Old English poems as arguing for obedience, penitence, and the Christianization of ties of loyalty.

Daniel Anlezark clarifies the meaning of 'Old English *Exodus* 487 *Werbeamas*' (*N&Q* 62[2015] 497–508). A clear review of previous interpretations is quite heavily critical of Peter Lucas's reading of the hapax legomenon. The key line of argument is that *wer* meaning 'weir' or 'dam' is used in compounds in charters. That the semantically equivalent *torr* is compounded in *Exodus* and *Genesis A* shows that this kind of place marker can be poetic; Anlezark therefore proposes 'beam of a dam' as the most likely translation, which makes sense in both cultural and poetic contexts.

## 8. *Beowulf* and the *Beowulf* Manuscript

The *Wonders of the East* in British Library Cotton Vitellius A. xv is discussed above (Section 2) in Alun Ford's monograph on *Marvel and Artefact*. Asa Simon Mittman's latest contribution to the discussion of *Wonders* is the challenging 'Are the "Monstrous Races" Races?' (*Postmed* 6[2015] 36–51). Mittman's proposal of the text as 'a catalog of difference' (p. 46) is convincing and so, broadly, is her assertion that our use of the term 'race' for each of the wondrous beings is anachronistic, artificial, and even pernicious in its privileging of the (thereby constructed as) dominant and central white, European, Christian 'race'. Mittman's willingness to interrogate her own work is particularly welcome given a recent trend towards vituperative scholarship.

Several chapters in Bintley and Williams' *Representing Beasts* volume, mentioned above in sections 4 and 6, engage with the texts of the *Beowulf* manuscript. Lászlo Sándor Chardonnens, in 'Do Anglo-Saxons Dream of Exotic Sheep?' (pp. 131–50), has interesting implications for the reading of *Wonders of the East*, finding a reference to the section on using camels to steal gold in Oxford, Bodleian Library, Hatton MS 115's sunshine prognostications. Bintley's own 'Where the Wild Things Are in Old English Poetry' (pp. 205–28) considers the wild places in *Beowulf*, particularly the Grendelkin's Mere, arguing that its potential for cleansing shows that nature is not intrinsically evil. Eric Lacey discusses the difficulty of '*Beowulf*'s Blithe-Hearted Raven' (pp. 113–30). Making an important argument that a text like *Beowulf* should be primarily encountered linearly, Lacey argues that subsequent ravens in the text cannot renegotiate the meaning of the first to appear. Showing that the poet could have clarified the ambiguous *blaca* (which could be a form of *blac* 'bright', or *blæc* 'black') by using the strong form, Lacey's proposal that the adjective is intended to be ambiguous is convincing, as is his parallel point that the iridescence of ravens is a naturalistic detail widely deployed in the literature. The observation that every raven in the text is unambiguously associated with dawn moves the discussion on; this raven, like the others, heralds the coming day. The 'multivalent and unstable' properties of the raven image are shown to be carefully exploited and modified by the poet (p. 130). Finally, Victoria Symons shows the close ties between dragons and runes in and beyond *Beowulf* in '*Wreopenhilt ond Wyrmfah*: Confronting Serpents in *Beowulf* and Beyond' (pp. 73–93). Demonstrating that dragons and runes are conceptually opposed in a number of different contexts, Symons explores the idea that dragons connote concealment while runes bring revelation. Given that both are also associated with treasure, a clever argument sets the Icelandic and Old English *Rune Poems* against one another. In the Old English text, where dragons do not appear, wealth is positive; the contrast between the texts demonstrates that when dragons (and the secrecy with which they are associated) come into contact with treasure, the wealth itself becomes negative. A much wider cultural argument is smoothly brought into sharp focus on Hrothgar's engagement with the hilt from Grendel's mother's cave with its 'interplay between the revealing runic letters and the concealing serpents' (p. 91).

Paul S. Langeslag has produced a comprehensive overview of the use of 'Monstrous Landscape in *Beowulf*' (*ES* 96[2015] 119–38). Arguing that 'the poet associates his monsters with their habitats to such a degree that landscape becomes a part of their very identities' (p. 120), Langeslag covers some well-travelled ground on the humidity of the Grendelkin's home. Identifying the dry cave beneath a mere as a clever sleight of hand enabling humanoid creatures to survive the flood, their very existence but also their consistent association with both the dark and the wet are tied in to folk-tales and 'popular convention' (p. 131). More analogues may have been useful here, but the broad point is strong. Langeslag goes on to discuss the liminality of the monsters through their placement in this hostile landscape, proposing that 'geographic distancing serves in part the ethical delineation of the self' (p. 131), with the human/not-human nature of the Grendelkin placing them at the margins of civilization and thus most threatening to it. Their presence, then, demands that the poet and his world identify what distinguishes the human from the monstrous, ultimately focusing on social rituals and religious practice. But it simultaneously requires a hero who is (or who can be) equally liminal in order to overcome them.

Holly Wendt also discusses Beowulf's possibly marginal positioning, in '"Breme Beowulf" and "Inclite Pelagi": Colonizing the Comitatus' (*CEA* 77[2015] 39–57). With a broad conception of the *comitatus* ethic being predicated on the rejection of those outside it, Grendel is argued to be 'the essentialized view of such an outsider' (p. 46). The proposal that, by rejecting weapons in his fight against Grendel, Beowulf 'takes on the disadvantaged mantle as a way to exert supreme agency over his situation and demonstrate his inclusion status' is interesting (p. 48), as is the comparison between his suicidal mission against the Dragon and a martyr's interest in glorious death. But details are cherry-picked from the poem: it is true to say that 'Beowulf has no close community' when fighting the Dragon (p. 51), but in the terms of the earlier discussion of the Grendel fight it is surely more true to say that he tries to bring the weapons and strength of a community with him, but that both fail. In general, ideas about the expansion of Christianity by utilizing and incorporating Germanic ideas are handled too broadly, and the comparison with Hrotsvit of Gandersheim's late tenth-century *Passio Sancti Pelagii* is strained to the point of irrelevance.

In 'The Swedish Wars in *Beowulf*' (*JEGP* 114[2015] 32–60), James W. Earl revisits the poet's presentation of the wars. Earl's focus on the phenomenology of the text, on his personal experience of it as a reader, produces the suggestion that *Beowulf* is structured as a sequence of surprises with, for instance, Wiglaf's Wægmunding affiliation being pointed out at line 2602 but only becoming significant when revealed to be connected with Beowulf's own family 200 lines later. In a discussion crucial for any teacher of the text, Earl identifies twelve points of uncertainty about the course of the Swedish–Geatish wars as presented by the poet, and finds that 'the poet seems to have gone out of his way to make this part of the poem difficult to follow' (p. 35). In a fine conclusion, he discusses the possible purposes and effects of this design, ultimately tying it into our ongoing experience of historical events as an incoherent muddle, and our immediate apprehension of histories as a jumbled accumulation of pastnesses, of which random elements are evoked by immediate experiences. Earl produces a refreshing and exciting '*Beowulf* of reversed tendencies, unprecedented surprises, and constantly disorienting shifts in the terms of the story' (p. 56).

In 'On the Epithet *Freca Scyldinga* for Beowulf, a Geat (*Beowulf*, line 1563b)' (*N&Q* 62[2015] 185–8), Alexandra Reider points out that, other than in this verse, Beowulf is always connected with his own tribe and not with the Danes. Thus *freca* is not likely to have the narrow sense 'man' or 'warrior', but is easier to comprehend if it can have the more specific meaning 'champion [of the Scyldings]'. Evidence from compounds in *Exodus* and *Andreas* supports the principle that *freca* has connotations of military service, and there's an engaging survey of mostly old translations which engage with this issue more than modern editions of the poem do, representing Beowulf here as the Scyldings' champion, helper, or friend.

In a return to a thorny issue, Leonard Neidorf discusses 'Cain, Cam, Jutes, Giants, and the Textual Criticism of *Beowulf*' (*SP* 112[2015] 599–632). As noted in Section 2 above, this has a lot to say about scribal practice and our reading of it in this and other manuscripts, but is discussed here as its primary focus is on the text of *Beowulf*. In a fine discussion of the scribal correction at line 107a changing *cames* to *caines*, Neidorf points out that everything is confusion—we aren't even sure who we think was confused between the scribe(s), the poet, textual tradition, exegesis, or some combination of them all. In a convincing metrical argument, Neidorf sees *cames* as the likely original form here, with an interesting suggestion (though not one strictly necessary to his wider argument), based on the pattern of his other changes to Scribe A's work, that the alteration may have been made by Scribe B. There is a lovely, if fragile, suggestion that the probable original use of *cam* in the first position may have resulted in an alert intervening scribe altering *cain* (almost certainly the original reading on metrical grounds) to *cam* at line 1261b, with the current manuscript's Scribe A then turning *cam* into the current manuscript reading *camp* (though this requires Scribe A to accurately copy *cam* in the first instance but not in the second; it is also a little circular to then adduce this as additional evidence for 107a being initially *cam*). This gives us a poet who refers to Cam at 107a and Cain at 1261b. Neidorf reminds us at length that Cam and Cain were very closely related in the period, with an uncharacteristically impish suggestion that the *Beowulf*-poet may have been part of the same circles that were discussing their closeness in eighth-century Northumbria. Moving on to considering the manuscript *eotenas* which might represent either Jutes or giants, Neidorf is convinced by analogues that there is little reason not to see the Jutes, and he deals confidently with the counter-arguments. Neidorf's observation that *cyn* is rarely used in *Beowulf* with reference to specific human ethnic groups is of interest in relation to Mittman's musings on definitions of race in the period, discussed above. On scribal practice, Neidorf's broad argument is that manuscript readings are rarely random nonsense, but mostly produced as a result of immediate lexical concerns without consideration of wider semantic context (although he creates an exception to this when it comes to line 1261b, as above). It is, perhaps, a little unhelpful to call all of these scribal attempts to correct 'conscious corruptions' (p. 622), as he does, but the broader reading of scribal activity is useful. As is inevitable in a discussion ranging across so many fields, some assertions can be challenged: on who changed *cames*, for instance, it may be coincidental but it is certainly not a 'remarkable coincidence' that the alteration is just below a known Scribe B intervention (p. 605). A cursory look at the manuscript shows that on the same side Scribe A makes a correction at line 19 and, in fact, of all of Scribe B's accepted alterations to Scribe A's text, only one (on 144 (BL146)r.5) is not on the same side as a correction by Scribe A; this single point, then, does not make it significantly more likely that the erasure is Scribe B's, as Neidorf claims it does. The claim, then, that any counter-argument to any part of Neidorf's interpretation flies in the face of evidence is itself rather fragile. Indeed, this would be a somewhat stronger piece if it were less aggressively certain of its own rectitude, a characteristic most evident as it works towards its close. The final third seeks to contribute to the ongoing discussion of the value of scribal interventions when editing poetic texts. It is no surprise that Neidorf is firmly on the side of editors seeking to reconstruct 'authorial' forms (an argument countered this year by Eric Weiskott's 'The Meter of *Widsith* and the Distant Past', discussed in Section 5 above), but his argument is weakened somewhat by rhetorically overblown claims, such as that any other approach represents an unethical lack of respect for the poet and for the medieval period itself.

Another believer that any argument against his own position must be based on 'remarkable coincidence' (p. 172) is Rafael J. Pascual in 'On a Crux in *Beowulf*: The Alliteration of Finite Verbs and the Scribal Understanding of Metre' (*SN* 87[2015] 171–85). Like Neidorf, Pascual argues that 'the practice of the *Beowulf* poet is so regular that a scribal deviation from the poet's norm can be detected and emended regardless of what its origin might have been' (p. 172). The interest of this essay is why *fela* has been introduced in line 1379a. As discussed in the literature Pascual reviews, most likely a scribe at some point assumed that 1379a formed a pair with 1378b, with *fela* thereby inserted to form a properly alliterating line. The implications of this, however, have not been fully discussed before. To make such a mistake, Pascual argues, the scribe most likely did not recognize that *sec* could carry alliteration; finite verbs usually do not—and did not in prosody—but conditions exist in verse where they can. The body of this essay, then, is a clear and useful explanation of the assignation and (to some extent) the function of alliteration and stress in Old English verse, with a focus on the principle drawn out here that 'a finite verb that occurs at the head of the off-verse, not preceded by any stress word, is non-ictic unless its chief syllable may participate in the alliteration of the on-verse, in which case it invariably receives ictus' (p. 178). This new rule is significant for metrical studies, but also interesting in how it engages with the process of receiving Old English verse along the same lines as Lacey and Earl (discussed above). Pascual's point is that at the start of an off-verse you cannot have ornamental alliteration because we already know the line's alliterative scheme: the first alliterating word in an off-verse fulfils the metre and is significant. But at the start of an on-verse (at the beginning of a line), the alliterative scheme for that line is yet to be received. Like Lacey's blithe-hearted raven, a usually non-ictic word at the start of a line can be revealed to have more significance by being drawn into the alliterative pattern. Whichever scribe made this insertion did not understand this principle, and therefore did not fully understand the four-position rule upon which it is based. The rules of metre, in this case, are not related at all to the rules of the spoken language—supporting Pascual (and Neidorf) in their general industry of emendation on metrical grounds.

In 'Beowulf's Address to Hrothgar: Textual Notes on *Beowulf*, lines 442–448' (*N&Q* 62[2015] 508–11), Alfred Bammesberger seeks to establish whether the intended compound in Beowulf's speech at line 445a (a hapax either way) is *mægenhreð* or *hreðman*. Running through the possibilities, he finds them all quite unlikely and ultimately suggests that there is no compounded noun; that this is an instance of asyndetic parataxis where two grammatically identical nouns are juxtaposed without a conjunction. The verse then means something like 'the strength, the glory, of men' or (with *hreðman* functioning as a compound) 'the strength, which is the glory of men'. This all works, but gives less attention than it might to the quite reasonable reading of *mægenhreð* as 'great glory' or similar. Further, Bammesberger suggests that *unforhte* in line 444a is unlikely to act as an adverb describing Grendel's imagined consumption of the Geats and is thereby more likely to be a plural adjective for the Geats themselves. Again, this is not unreasonable, but is based almost entirely on the principle that Grendel has no need to be eating fearfully so it is redundant to imagine him eating without fear. This is a fragile line of argument, with technically redundant description a not infrequent appearance in the text and other readings available (such as an ironizing of Grendel's fearless cannibalism while mocking the likelihood of Beowulf's own death).

Eric Weiskott problematizes '*Beowulf* 2910a "leofes ond laðes"' (*N&Q* 62[2015] 188–90). Conventionally, these are applied to the respective corpses of Beowulf and the Dragon, over both of which Wiglaf keeps watch. However, if *hygemeðe* ('weary of mind' i.e. 'dead'), as Weiskott shows, probably means Beowulf, then Wiglaf has a dative relationship with one object of his watch, but a genitive one with two others. This does not seem likely—a probability only intensified by the strong argument that *heafodweard* is not likely to have taken a genitive in any case. The uniting of the corpses in the verse also forces Wiglaf to give them equally ceremonial guard, which seems unlikely, even given the rhetorically opposed emotions. While it is a little disappointing to lose the unity of the two corpses, Weiskott's discussion is convincing, and his neat solution is to make them the different things that Wiglaf is guarding the corpse of Beowulf against: *leofes ond laðes* becoming 'all of human experience'.

Simon Thomson, in 'Scribes, Sources and Readers: Using a Digital Edition to Develop Understanding of the Beowulf Manuscript' (*Poetica* 83[2015] 59–77), discusses the potential of digital facsimiles to enable modern readers 'to engage with and analyze scribal negotiations' (p. 69) particularly as these relate to the *Beowulf* manuscript.

## 9. Other Poems

The publication of greatest note in this section this year is Kazutomo Karasawa's *The Old English Metrical Calendar (Menologium)*, a study and critical edition. This text has not gathered much scholarly attention: as a piece of poetry, it is rather thin on narrative and action; as a calendar, its usefulness is marred by its convoluted poetic form; as a historical text it is near-unanalysable because of its uncertain function. Karasawa interrogates the *Menologium* on two fronts: its immediate manuscript context and its relationship to analogous texts. He argues that it is placed as preface to the C-text of the *Anglo-Saxon Chronicle* in Cotton Tiberius B.i, where other *Chronicle* texts have laws, because it enshrined, poetically, the natural laws of time which govern the world, and that it also mediated translating the reckoning of time between traditional and classical/Latinate modes of dating. He also convincingly argues that it is misleading to read the *Menologium* as of a piece with the poetic calendrical texts we find elsewhere. The *Menologium* is a mnemonic device which provides a rough framework for anticipating feast-days rather than a computus-text for calculating them, and in this sense it has popular currency by comparison with its analogues. His comprehensive introduction (linguistically, stylistically, palaeographically, historically, and literarily) outlines the text's editorial history, manuscript context, potential sources, and analogues, the poem's structure and use of feast-days, its relationship with the prose *Menologium*, and its language, prosody, and possible dates and places of composition. Following the edited text, which is accompanied by facing-page translation, there is a full commentary and glossary and nine appendices, including a catalogue of Anglo-Saxon calendars, and a very useful essay on the use of Latin and Old English month-names in Old English literature.

Alongside this edition, Karasawa has published two articles on the *Menologium*. The first deals with the poem's literary analogues: 'Irish Influence upon the Old English Poem *Menologium* Reconsidered' (*Anglia* 133[2015] 706–34). In spite of the long-standing and influential assertion that Old Irish calendar poems, in particular *Félire Adamnáin* and *Énlaith betha*, are 'obvious' counterparts to the Old English *Menologium*, Karasawa finds it difficult to detect 'any major affinity' between the works (p. 353). What similarities can be drawn are purely superficial, he argues, while a closer consideration of the structure and style of the poems brings their very different natures to the fore. The precision and computistical learning of the *Menologium* stand in contrast to the naturalistic, impressionistic, and, above all, devotional tone adopted in the Old Irish examples.

In 'The *Menologium* and *Maxims II* in the Manuscript Context' (*N&Q* 62[2015] 353–6), Karasawa posits that these two poems, often taken as preliminaries to the C-text of the *Anglo-Saxon Chronicle*, in fact relate equally to the *Orosius* that precedes them. The purpose of both poems, Karasawa suggests, is to bridge the perspectival shift from the foreign, non-Christian affairs of the *Orosius* to the Christian, domestic world of the *Chronicle*. Discussion of *Maxims II*, also with reference to its manuscript context, continues in Eric Stanley's 'The *Gnomes* of Cotton Manuscript Tiberius B.i'

(*N&Q* 62[2015] 190–9). In emulation of the poem itself, perhaps, Stanley presents his readings as a series of individual observations, on matters ranging from the definition of 'gnome', to the poet's 'adjectival inventiveness' (p. 194), the various meanings of *sceal*, and the poem's political undertones.

Megan Hartman's chapter, 'Style and Politics in *The Battle of Brunanburh* and *The Battle of Maldon*' (in Adams, Brinton, and Fulk, eds., *Studies in the History of the English Language VI: Evidence and Method in Histories of English*, pp. 201–17), discusses two other poems often studied in tandem. She argues, through close linguistic analysis and comparison with *Beowulf*, that the style of the *Brunanburh*-poet is notably conservative, in contrast with the more contemporary syntax of the *Maldon* poet. The traditional features exhibited by *Brunanburh* would create a 'distinctive sound' and a connection with the past (p. 208), whereas a recitation of *Maldon* would echo the 'cadence and features of contemporary language' (p. 215). Those interested in *The Battle of Brunanburh* may also wish to read Paul Cavill's chapter '*Battle of Brunanburh* in 937: Battlefield Despatches' (in Harding et al., eds., pp. 95–108), which lays out the case for locating the battle-site at Bromborough on the Wirral.

The *Solomon and Saturn* poems continue to draw scholarly attention. *Solomon and Saturn I*'s repeated description of the Pater Noster as a *palmtreow* that is *gepalmtwigede* is a long-standing puzzle, one that Tiffany Beechy seeks to demystify in 'The "Palmtwigede" Pater Noster Revisited: An Associative Network in Old English' (*Neophil* 99[2015] 301–13). The associative network of the title is traced through uses of *palmtwig* and the less well attested *palmtreow* in the Old English corpus. In most contexts, Beechy finds, these terms denote branches, trees, or vines, either literally or metaphorically, in a manner quite different from their use in *Solomon and Saturn I*. A few examples, however, suggest that the palm did convey a kind of importance, as 'an object of reverence in its own right' (p. 306) and, in the Blickling Homilies repeatedly, as a stand-in for Christ (p. 310). This latter characteristic is particularly pertinent to *Solomon and Saturn I*. Beechy concludes that the poem specifically plays on the overlap between palm trees and the Pater Noster as metonyms for Christ.

James Paz combines ecocritical approaches with an eye for performative detail in 'Magic That Works: Performing *Scientia* in the Old English Metrical Charms and Poetic Dialogues of Solomon and Saturn' (*JMEMS* 45[2015] 219–43). Paz argues for the breakdown of perceived barriers between such (modern) oppositions as oral and literate, mental and physical, abstract and practical. Chief among them is the division of literature and science; texts that combine the two tend to be overlooked by scholars of both. One opposition that remains largely unaddressed, however, is that of prose and poetry. Paz's apt observation that the metrical charms 'are not metrical by accident' (p. 225) raises the legitimacy of dividing these poetic compositions from their vastly more numerous prose analogues in the first place, and leaves one to wonder what the prose charms could deliver if placed under comparably close scrutiny.

A newly discovered Old English inscription in runes, found to be verse, whose lines can be related to not one but two extant manuscript poems is, as John Hines aptly puts it, 'extraordinarily important' (p. 257): 'The *Benedicite* Canticle in Old English Verse: An Early Runic Witness from Southern

Lincolnshire' (*Anglia* 133[2015] 257–77). The Honington clip is a 'gripping instrument' of some kind, made of base silver, and found in 2011 in the vicinity of Honington, Lincolnshire. The inscription, which includes one rare and one otherwise unattested rune form, is identified by Hines as Anglian, produced *circa* 750–800. This inscription is shown to be a verse paraphrase of Daniel 3:57–61, bearing a marked similarity to lines 362–4 of *Daniel* and lines 73–5 of *Azarias*. Hines's discussion of the relationship between these three texts is made with close reference to Drout and Chauvet's article in the same volume, reviewed in Section 2 above.

Several other poems are also discussed in P.S. Langeslag's *Seasons in the Literatures of the Medieval North*, albeit sometimes briefly; these include *The Battle of Maldon*, *The Death of Edward*, *Maxims II*, and *Solomon and Saturn II*.

The Franks Casket features in two publications this year. The first is Katherine Cross's 'The Mediterranean Scenes on the Franks Casket: Narrative and Exegesis' (*JWCI* 78[2015] 1–40). This study places the iconography of the casket alongside Continental analogues, with a focus on the three scenes drawn from Mediterranean tradition. Although the literary aspects of the casket are treated only briefly, Cross's article will be a fascinating read for anyone with an interest in this intriguing and enigmatic artefact. Also published this year was Victoria Symons, 'The Aesthetics of Transition on the Franks Casket' (in Boulton et al., eds., pp. 164–78).

## 10. Prose

There has been a considerable amount of work published on prose in 2015. Charters have proven most popular this year, with legal codes and homiletic texts faring reasonably well, too, and a gamut of obscure prose texts receiving a modicum of attention. The single most important contribution to the study of Old English prose this year must be the integrated study of the contents of *Textus Roffensis* in O'Brien and Bombi's edited volume *Textus Roffensis: Law, Language and Libraries in Early Medieval England*. Various essays from this collection are discussed in Sections 2 and 3 above.

Nicholas Brooks's 'The Laws of King Æthelberht of Kent: Preservation, Content, and Composition' (in O'Brien and Bombi, eds., pp. 105–36), like the two chapters that follow, highlights the archaic nature and features of the law-code; Brooks particularly stresses the dearth of apparent Christian influence outside the first five clauses of the code. A major line of enquiry here is why it was written in English, and, rather startlingly, Brooks suggests it might have originally been written in runes before being consigned to parchment. He also considers the antiquity of the language, a topic taken up in more detail in Carole Hough's 'The Earliest English Texts? The Language of the Kentish Laws Reconsidered' (pp. 137–56). Rather than focus on the archaic features, however, Hough seeks to assess whether the law-code represents an example of Kentish (with its implications of authenticity), and does this on phonological, lexical, and grammatical grounds. She discusses the problems of identifying the Kentish dialect more generally, as well as the complexities that arise from stringently applying dialectological analysis to stylistically rigid legal texts. Daniela Fruscione's '*Drihtinbeag* and the Question of the Beginnings of Punishment' (pp. 157–74) continues this linguistic theme, though the object of focus here is a *hapax legomenon* which occurs only in the early Kentish law-code. Her accessible and lucid philological analysis convincingly demonstrates the antiquity of the word, which, as the only non-literary attestation of *drihtin* describing a secular lord, appears to be a hangover from migration-era *comitatus*-oriented society.

The less often discussed *Geþyncðu* group, cattle-theft charm, and *Wergeld*, respectively, are the focus of the next three studies in the collection. Andrew Rabin's 'Archbishop Wulfstan's "Compilation on Status" in the *Textus Roffensis*' (pp. 175–92) examines the Wulfstanian compilation known as the *Geþyncðu* group or the 'Compilation on Status' and argues that the *Textus Roffensis* recension marks the development of an ideology in Wulfstan's work, illustrated rather more clearly in his *Institutes of Polity*, aspiring to 'a legal polity that fulfils his vision for a holy society' (p. 189). Tracy-Anne Cooper's 'Episcopal Power and Performance: The Fugitive-Thief Rite in *Textus Roffensis* (also known as The Cattle-Theft Charm)' (pp. 193–214), like Pelteret's chapter, is interested in the public rituals that accompany texts. Cooper re-evaluates the so-called 'cattle-theft charm' and its curious presence in the manuscript through a fourfold examination of the language used to analyse it (she objects to 'charm' and prefers 'rite'), the Christian allusions of the rite, its *mise-en-page* and its placement in the manuscript, and an articulation of the episcopal links between the *Textus Roffensis* and other manuscripts containing the rite. Julie Mumby's 'Fathers or Uncles? A Problem in the Old English Tract Known as *Wergeld*' (pp. 215–30) scrutinizes the problematic word *fæderan* in the text called *Wergeld*. The stakes for this are relatively high, given that this is the only pre-Conquest text to clearly state who should receive a slain man's *healsfang*, among whom the *fæderan* numbers. Mumby surveys the four extant interpretations ('father's brother', 'father's brothers', 'fathers', and 'parents') and offers a new interpretation: 'father'.

The discussion of legal texts is rounded off by Lisi Oliver's 'Who Wrote Alfred's Laws?' (pp. 231–54). In a combination of close and comparative reading of Alfred's law-code and its preface, she persuasively argues for the text being apportioned out between different specialists well versed in penitentials, in English law, and in Frisian law.

Ben Snook's *The Anglo-Saxon Chancery: The History, Language and Production of Anglo-Saxon Charters from Alfred to Edgar* is not actually concerned with the thorny problem of the Anglo-Saxon chancery, but chiefly with the literary nature of the Latin used in charter documents issued between the reigns of Alfred and Edgar, which he examines chronologically. Snook argues for Aldhelmian influence on the draftsman known as 'Æthelstan A', though he sees Aldhelm R behind the Latinity of all the charters surveyed. Although there is very little attention to the Old English, there is much to commend here in terms of cultural background: Snook's highly readable account of the development, use, and re-use of literary formulae and techniques and their interplay with local politics raises interesting questions about Latin teaching and learning, and his arguments for reading charters as literary texts are convincing. There are some rather puzzling choices, however, which might impinge on the book's general usefulness. While the introduction, which outlines the history of the charter and the key methodological issues and debates (such as authenticity and editing), and gives a summary of scholarly approaches to charters, seems to be targeted at non-specialists of the diplomatic, there are no discussions of the technical terminology of charter analysis (for example, proem, disposition, and so on). Nor are the longest excerpts and lists of Latin terms translated.

Two chapters in O'Brien and Bombi's *Textus Roffensis* also concern charters. Ben Snook's 'Who Introduced Charters into England? The Case for Theodore and Hadrian' (pp. 257–89) demarcates the main positions in this debate before arguing for Theodore's agency on the grounds of timing, the religious formulaic phrases prevalent in early charters, the dependency upon Roman diplomatic procedure, and the correspondences between Theodore's reforms and the inherent charter concerns for protecting church property from secular encroachment. Unlike everyone else in the volume, Snook does not provide translations of his primary sources. David A.E. Pelteret's 'The Religious Elements in the *Textus Roffensis* Charters' (pp. 291–311) goes beyond the 'template criticism' which he sees as characterizing so much charter scholarship, and queries why the form of the Anglo-Saxon charter was so rigidly maintained. Focusing on just two charters in some detail (S 33 and S 893), but situating them dynamically in the context of other historical documents and the politics of their periods, Pelteret advances an erudite—and ultimately convincing—argument that the religious elements of the documents preserve elements of public ceremony that once accompanied them. Pelteret's consistent translation (and references to both translations and primary source editions), and the way in which he situates charters within broader cultural practice in Anglo-Saxon England, make this chapter both an accessible starting point to researching these documents and a rousing call to arms to think more about the ceremony and liturgy that intertwined these texts with both secular and ecclesiastical practice.

The final two chapters of Bintley and Williams's *Representing Beasts* also engage with charters, though they are less concerned with reconstructing their politics and performance and more interested in their value as repositories for place names and broader environmental knowledge. John Baker's 'Entomological Etymologies: Creepy-Crawlies in English Place-Names' (pp. 229–52) is a splendid examination of the motivations for naming places after insects. Its usefulness is fourfold, and of interest to onomasts and non-onomasts alike: it provides a useful introduction to the problems and possibilities of place-name analysis; it provides useful semantic discussions of some insect names in Old English (e.g. *ceafor*, nominally 'beetle', *wibba*, nominally 'weevil'); it explores the ways in which insect place names were useful in Anglo-Saxon everyday life (for example to indicate a resource, such as bees, or to indicate pests); and, related to the last point, it presents the ways in which place names are useful sources for landscape perception and usage. Della Hooke's 'Beasts, Birds and Other Creatures in Pre-Conquest Charters and Place-Names in England' (pp. 253–82) is a very broad overview of some of the creatures—mythological and otherwise—which populate the place names of Anglo-Saxon England. Like Baker, Hooke is also interested in the motivation behind these names: at times they are rather pedestrian (for example indicating sites for grazing pigs); at times they are rather more exciting (for example *drakehord*, representing a barrow filled with treasure!). Both these chapters illustrate the usefulness—and importance—of place names in the articulation of cultural values and practicality that underpinned the Anglo-Saxon perception of animals.

Malasree Home's *The Peterborough Version of the Anglo-Saxon Chronicle* seeks to read the *Peterborough Chronicle* as the immediate product of twelfth-century Peterborough. The chronological scope of the book runs from the early twelfth-century composition of the proto-text of the *Chronicle* to its thirteenth-century afterlife. The first chapter, 'Textualising the Past', examines the interpolations inserted into the proto-text after its arrival at Peterborough in the early twelfth century, and argues that the use of local charters, as well as the interpolations' imitation of the extant style and structure, appropriate the older material into a distinctly local text, expressing local concerns and clearly demarcating a local sense of history and identity. The second, 'Continuing the *Chronicle*', examines the two continuations made to the *Chronicle* in much the same vein, and argues that the first was made by the same author/scribe as the interpolations. 'Making the *Chronicle*: Form, Genre, Identity' is a bold attempt to reconstruct the compilation process of the *Chronicle*; using a fourfold method of examining other scribal activity at Peterborough, exploring the influence Canterbury and its scribal activity may have had over Peterborough, surveying the relationship between the *Peterborough Chronicle* and contemporary Latin historiography, and interrogating the generic presentation of the *Chronicle* itself (particularly its straddling of history and diplomatic). The book closes with 'Beyond the *Chronicle*', which moves away from looking closely at the Peterborough text and considers why it stands at a point of decline in vernacular writing.

John Quanrud's chapter, 'Taking Sides: North-West England Vikings at the Battle of Tettenhall, AD 910' (in Harding et al., eds., pp. 71–93), offers a new interpretation of the *Anglo-Saxon Chronicle*'s account of the battle (*c*.909 and 910) through a combination of rereading the entries alongside other sources (both non-English pre-Conquest and English post-Conquest) and close linguistic attentiveness to the semantic ambiguity of *Denisc*, *norðhere*, and *Norðanhymbre* (nominally 'Danish', 'north army', and 'Northumbrian'). His argument that these terms may indeed refer to north-western Irish/English Vikings holds significant implications historically, and however this is received, his de-tangling of nationality, ethnicity, and regional identity (*pace* the other chapters in the collection) is noteworthy in and of itself.

Ælfric receives critical attention. Fleming's '*Sundorhalgan*, Winchester, and Ælfric' is discussed above, in Section 4. A similar lexical investigation is Sandra M. Hordis's '*Neorxnawang*: Aelfric's Flawed Anglo-Saxon Paradise' (*HeroicA* [2015]). Hordis draws attention to the confounding employment of the unusual word *neorxnawang* in Ælfric's work, and its relationship with Latin *Paradisum*. Hugh Magennis's 'ælfric's Apostles' (*ASE* 44[2015] 181–99) is a consideration of Ælfric's portrayal of the apostles, arguing that, as a hagiographer, Ælfric idealizes them, but that as an exegete he draws attention to the apostle's shortcomings and extrapolates moral lessons. However, to do the latter he draws upon the 'generic tools of scriptural exegesis'; Ælfric has no interest in portraying their human dimensions out of concern not to undermine his glorification of their saintly nature. Katherine A. Lowe's 'Filling the Silence: Shared Content in Four Related Manuscripts of Ælfric's *Catholic Homilies*' (*DigPhil* 4[2015] 190–224) examines the collocation of Ælfrician and non-ælfrician homiletic material in four manuscripts, and demonstrates that, despite Ælfric's concern for the preservation of his work, at least two of these mixed-content manuscripts were compiled during Ælfric's lifetime, and that all of the homilies in all the manuscripts were copied together as carefully as each other. The implications of this, she argues, are that editing Ælfric's material separately from its accompanying pieces 'risks skewing our understanding of how medievals themselves viewed and transmitted these texts' (p. 205).

This year has also seen an increased interest in the perception of Jews in Anglo-Saxon homilies. Mo Pareles's 'Men as Meat: Exploiting Jewish Law in Ælfric's Translation of Maccabees' (*Exemplaria* 27[2015] 185–204) argues for Ælfric appropriating Jewish dietary law as a rhetorical and conceptual means for differentiating Christian from non-Christian, and saved from unsaved. George Younge's chapter, 'The New Heathens: Anti-Jewish Hostility in Early English Literature' (in Conti et al., eds., pp. 123–45), enquires into how and why the term 'heathen' came to be so prevalently applied to the Jews in the twelfth century. He notes that there are no instances of this before the Norman Conquest, and that earlier Old English texts carefully denote *hæðen* in opposition to Jewishness as well as Christianity. Younge identifies a key shift in the meaning of OE *hæðen* in the eleventh century, when Wulfstan of York used the term for degencrate Christians, and he argues that this, along with the acquisition of anti-Jewish scholastic texts by monastic cathedrals in the twelfth century, may have provided the appropriate intellectual backdrop for the pejorative expansion of *hæðen* to the Jews.

Wulfstan has not fared quite as well as his predecessor this year. In addition to Younge's chapter, he is the focus of only one article, Jay Paul Gates's 'Preaching, Politics, and Episcopal Reform in Wulfstan's Early Writings' (*EMedE* 23[2015] 93–116). Gates compares Wulfstan's homilies with his earliest legal texts (the *Canons of Edgar* and the so-called *Peace of Edward and Guthrum*) in order to argue that Wulfstan, looking back at a perceived golden age associated with Alfred, Edgar, and the Benedictine Reform, sought to depict bishops as the land's primary authority—even over the king—in line with his views of a legal framework that prioritized promoting moral Christian behaviour.

Thijs Porck's 'Treasures in a Sooty Bag? A Note on *Durham Proverb* 7' (*N&Q* 62[2015] 203–6) examines the pairing of the Latin proverb *Sepe in [u]ile sacculo fulget aurum* ('Often gold shines in a cheap purse') with the Old English *Oft on sotigum bylige searowa licgað* ('Often there is cunning in a sooty bag' [i.e. 'someone who sits by the fire all day']) in the *Durham Proverbs*. Porck evaluates claims that one is a (bad) translation of the other and finds them all unsatisfactory. His charmingly simple suggestion seems best: they are independent proverbs in each language which were placed together for their similar meaning. Stephen Pelle's 'The Devil's Name in the Vernon *Lyff of Adam and Eue* and the Old English *Prose Solomon and Saturn Pater Noster Dialogue*' (*N&Q* 62[2015] 360–4) notes that a curious name for the Devil in the Middle English Vernon *Lyff* is actually a witness, along with the *Prose Solomon and Saturn*, of long-lasting medieval knowledge of the demon-name 'Sathael', known to Byrtferth of Ramsay. Adrian Papahagi's '*Wið his Wyrd* in the Old English *Monasteriales Indicia*' (*N&Q* 62[2015] 511–13) argues that a single unusual use of *wyrd* in the Old English monastic sign language treatise should be emended to *weard*, and that it indicates the direction of the gesture rather than 'fate' or 'destiny'. Finally, Alfred Bammesberger's 'The Corrupt Reading *Ealle Omo* (Manuscript Cotton Vespasian D.xx)' (*N&Q* 62[2015] 206–7) discusses the line *mid eagan 7 earan 7 ealle omo* in a little-known penitential prayer in Vespasian D.xx, and argues that *ealle omo* is a corruption of an original *ealle leomo*, rendering the passage 'with eyes and ears and all limbs'. The prose *Menologium* in Karasawa's monograph, *The Old English Metrical Calendar*, is discussed above in Section 9.

Both the Old English Bede and the elusive *West Saxon Genealogical Regnal List* are discussed in Greg Waites's 'The Preface to the Old English Bede: Authorship, Transmission, and Connection with the *West Saxon Genealogical Regnal List*' (*ASE* 44[2015] 31–93), which is an intriguing foray into forensic palaeography. Waite deduces that the *West Saxon Genealogical Regnal List* was at one time attached to the *Preface* to the Old English translation of Bede's *Historia*, and argues that the *Preface* itself was a later addition to the main text, and by a different, probably early tenth-century, author, on stylistic and linguistic grounds. Waites suggests that the *Regnal List* may have been introduced at the same time or later than the *Preface*, though he concedes that the *Regnal List* may have accompanied the *Historia* translation before the *Preface* was appended. The article ends with an edition of both the *Preface* and the *Regnal List*.

Stefan Jurasinski's *The Old English Penitentials and Anglo-Saxon Law* was not available for review.

## 11. Reception

There is a range of studies that explore the Old English literary and cultural heritage. John D. Niles's *The Idea of Anglo-Saxon England 1066–1901: Remembering, Forgetting, Deciphering and Renewing the Past*, is interested in the reception of the idea of the Anglo-Saxon. His chronological scope, rather neatly, runs from the rule of King Alfred the Great (who was already recycling a sense of Anglo-Saxon history) to the Victorian celebration of the Alfred Millenary in 1901. The book proceeds chronologically, with the first few chapters forming a history of Anglo-Saxon medievalism up to 1800: at this point the chapters divide into a more thematic narrative: on the Romantics (chapter 6), on the rise of the discipline of philology (chapter 7); on its use in the British empire (chapter 9). Particularly interesting—innovative in its scope—is chapter 8, which narrates the rise of Old English studies in North America.

Two other books this year consider the reception of Anglo-Saxons and their ideas, though they focus specifically on saints, and discuss them in the contexts of their cults. The first is Cynthia Turner Camp's *Anglo-Saxon Saints' Lives as History Writing in Late Medieval England*. It has comparatively little to offer in terms of analysis of Old English texts per se, being concerned with late medieval (particularly Middle English) reception of the characters and the didactics of their narrative episodes (rather than the reception of particular Anglo-Saxon texts on these characters). What is valuable for the Anglo-Saxonist here, however, is the interest in medieval historiography, which 'deploy[s] historical discourse to assert a stable social identity despite clear evidence of political, ethical and religious difference ... [s]eeking to establish rather than deny continuities' (p. 11); Camp's central argument is that 'Middle English writers go to great formal lengths to affirm temporal continuity and spiritual homogeneity' between late medieval audiences and these Anglo-Saxon saints (p. 21). Using Mikhail Bakhtin's theory of the literary chronotope (the sum total of literary conventions and commonplaces viewed as characteristic of a period), Camp argues that the Anglo-Saxon era was enshrined as a Christian golden age whose spiritual purity was concretely preserved in—and accessed via—the incorruptible bodies of their saints. Each of the book's five chapters examines a different Anglo-Saxon saint: Edith of Wilton (OE Eadgyth, d.984), Audrey of Ely (OE Æthelthryth, d.679), Werburgh of Chester (OE Wærburg, d.699), Edward the Confessor (d.1066), and Edmund the Martyr (d.869). Brief summaries are provided of what is known about the historical figures as well as of their historiography; the three female saints are discussed in more detail than the male ones in this respect due to the relative obscurity of the former. There are no detailed discussions of the pre-fourteenth-century sources, but Camp's articulation of the late medieval moralizing representation of the past fits tidily with the study of Anglo-Saxon medievalism in later periods of English history.

In contrast to Camp's wide-ranging and holistic approach to Anglo-Saxon saints is Rebecca Pinner's *The Cult of St Edmund in Medieval East Anglia*, a diachronic study of the origins and development of devotion to St Edmund from its origins in the ninth century through to the Reformation, drawing primarily on literary and iconographic data. It is structured thematically: it starts by surveying the development of the Edmund legend, beginning with the Latin lives of Edmund by Abbo of Fleury, through eleventh-century works by the likes of Herman the Archdeacon and Osbert de Clare, as well as the now intertwining *vitae* and *miraculae*, to the vernacularization of the legend into French and English in the thirteenth and fourteenth centuries; the second section explores the history of the relics, shrines, and pilgrimages of Edmund at Bury, beginning in 1043 with Edward the Confessor's visit to Bury St Edmunds; the third section examines the subsequent diffusion of his cult through East Anglia. The interdisciplinarity of this is commendable: French, Latin, English, palaeography, art history, archaeology are all seamlessly woven into each other in Pinner's broadly chronological examination, and her reading of legend and history alike shows the best aspects of the methods of historian and literary critic. It is rather disappointing, then, that the *Anglo-Saxon Chronicle* account of Edmund's death is not submitted to particular critical scrutiny or reading, and that all discussion of Ælfric's *Life of Edmund* is relegated to a footnote to Abbo's text.

In a similar vein is Philippa Turner's 'St Everilda: Evidence for a Saint's Cult in Transition' (in Boulton et al., eds., pp. 97–10). Turner is also concerned with the later medieval reception of an elusive, possibly seventh-century West Saxon saint by the name of Everilda, and she examines how such a figure rises to such prominence in York.

An innovative contribution to the study of medieval literature is the revised and updated edition of Stuart Lee and Elizabeth Solopova's *The Keys of Middle Earth: Discovering Medieval Literature through the Fiction of J.R.R. Tolkien*. The basic premise is stated in the title: it is not a source-book for Tolkien's lore, but an introduction to medieval literature mediated through events and narratives in Tolkien's canon. The organizing principle of the book is to select episodes or themes from Tolkien's work and to use this platform to introduce mirroring episodes and themes in medieval literature. Thus the fight against insurmountable odds at Balin's Tomb in *The Fellowship of The Ring* is a springboard to *The Fight at Finnsburg* and the 'Cyneheard and Cynewulf' episode in the *Anglo-Saxon Chronicle* (*c*.755) (pp. 220–39), and Bilbo and Gollum's riddling contest in *The Hobbit* funnels into *Solomon and Saturn II*, Exeter Riddle 1 ('Storm'), and Exeter Riddle 47 ('Moth', pp. 136–77). The focus is very much on the medieval literature: the Tolkien material is introduced very briefly (perhaps too briefly—there is an assumption that the reader is already familiar with it) and the Old English broadly contextualized in the space of a page or so. The original faces a parallel translation, and there are endnotes articulating points of interest (usually these are textual cruces, but they are sometimes points of linguistic difficulty or of literary significance, such as the presence of a prevalent motif or topos) and suggestions for further reading. As an undergraduate-level introduction there is much to commend here: none of the discussions of medieval literature assume prior knowledge and the notes and introductions strike a neat balance between the rudimentary and the interesting, between catholic and contentious. It is also particularly useful for an introduction to Old English: almost all the texts surveyed are in Old English (*Christ I*, *Solomon and Saturn II*, Exeter Riddles 1 and 47, *Beowulf*, *The Ruin*, *The Fight at Finnsburg*, 'Cynewulf and Cyneheard', *Maxims II*, *The Wanderer*, *The Battle of Maldon*, Ælfric's homily *On the Maccabees*, and *The Seafarer*); *Christ I* is completely new to this edition.

Carolyne Larrington brings us what must be the most entertaining book on medievalism this year: *Winter is Coming: The Medieval World of Game of Thrones*. Here she sets the Starks and the Lannisters alongside historically analogous counterparts, and their obstacles, goals, and grisly ends alongside legends like Weland and texts like *Beowulf* and *The Wonders of the East*.

Of interest to students of *Beowulf* is Patrick J. Murphy and Fred Porcheddu's 'Lay of a Last Survivor: *Beowulf*, Great War Memorials, and M.R. James's Ghost Story "A Warning to the Curious"' (*RES* 66[2015] 205–22). This analysis of James's medievalism in his personal, historical, and critical context finds James working to remake *Beowulf* in an English landscape, and to emulate its achievement in transcending 'the generic cheapness of monster stories in this literary memorial of the dead' (p. 220).

Peter Buchanan's 'Cædmon and the Gift of Song in Black Mountain Poetry' (*Postmed* 6[2015] 165–73) has no great amount to say about Cædmon himself, and even less about *Cædmon's Hymn*, but this should not deter anyone with an interest in the poem or the modern reception of medieval verse. Buchanan focuses his attention on the use of the Cædmon story by two modern poets: Robert Duncan and Denise Levertov. He provides detailed and informed close readings of both writers' work, and in so doing characterizes the story of Cædmon as a 'perennial beginning for poetic inspiration' (p. 166).

**Books Reviewed**

Adams, Michael, Laurel J. Brinton, and R.D. Fulk, eds. *Studies in the History of the English Language VI: Evidence and Method in Histories of English.* Gruyter. [2015] pp. vi + 337. £82.99 ISBN 9 7831 1034 5957.

Bintley, Michael D.J., and Thomas J.T. Williams, eds. *Representing Beasts in Early Medieval England and Scandinavia.* Anglo-Saxon Studies 29. Boydell. [2015] pp. 312. £60 ISBN 9 7817 8204 4925.

Boulton, Meg, and Jane Hawkes, with Melissa Herman, eds. *The Art, Literature and Material Culture of the Medieval World. Transition, Transformation and Taxonomy.* FCP. [2015] pp. x + 334. £65 ISBN 9 7818 4682 5613.

Camp, Cynthia Turner. *Anglo-Saxon Saints' Lives as History Writing in Late Medieval England.* Brewer. [2015] pp. xiii + 246. £60 ISBN 9 7818 4384 4020.

Collins, David J., ed. *The Cambridge History of Magic and Witchcraft in the West: From Antiquity to the Present.* CUP. [2015] pp. xi + 798. £98 ISBN 9 7805 2119 4181.

Conti, Aidan, Orietta Da Rold, and Philip Shaw, eds. *Writing Europe, 500–1450: Texts and Contexts.* Brewer [2015] pp. xv + 198. £30 ISBN 9 7818 4384 4150.

Cooper, Tracey-Anne. *Monk-Bishops and the English Benedictine Reform Movement: Reading London BL, Cotton Tiberius A.iii in its Manuscript Context.* PIMS. [2015] pp. xviii + 368. £80 ISBN 9 7808 8844 1935.

Ford, A.J. *Marvel and Artefact: The 'Wonders of the East' in its Manuscript Contexts.* Library of the Written Word—The Manuscript World 45. Brill. [2015]. pp. xvi + 178. £100 ISBN 9 7890 0430 1382.

Gantner, Clemens, Rosamund McKitterick, and Sven Meeder, eds. *The Resources of the Past in Early Medieval Europe.* CUP. [2015] pp. xvi + 354. £67 ISBN 9 7811 0709 1719.

Harding, Stephen E., David Griffiths, and Elizabeth Royles, eds., *In Search of Vikings: Interdisciplinary Approaches to the Scandinavian Heritage of North-West England.* CRC Press. [2015] pp. 204. £33.99 ISBN 9 7814 8220 7576.

Home, Malasree. *The Peterborough Version of the Anglo-Saxon Chronicle: Rewriting Post-Conquest History.* Anglo-Saxon Studies 27. Boydell. [2015] pp. ix + 184. £60 ISBN 9 7817 8327 0019.

Juster, A.M. *Saint Aldhelm's Riddles.* UTorP. [2015] pp. xi + 173. $29.95 ISBN 9 7814 4262 8922.

Karasawa, Katzutomo. *The Old English Metrical Calendar (Menologium).* Anglo-Saxon Texts 12. Brewer. [2015] pp. xvi + 228. £60 ISBN 9 7818 4384 4099.

Keskiaho, Jesse. *Dreams and Visions in the Early Middle Ages: The Reception and Use of Patristic Ideas, 400–900.* Cambridge Studies in Medieval Life and Thought: Fourth Series, 99. CUP. [2015] pp. ix + 329. £65 ISBN 9 7811 0708 2137.

Kleiman, Irit Ruth, ed. *Voice and Voicelessness in Medieval Europe.* Palgrave. [2015] pp. xvii + 264. £62.50 ISBN 9 7811 3739 7058.

Langeslag, P.G. *Seasons in the Literatures of the Medieval North.* Brewer. [2015] pp. 258. £60 ISBN 9 7818 4384 4259.

Larrington, Carolyne. *Brothers and Sisters in Medieval European Literature.* YMP. [2015] pp. ix + 275. £60 ISBN 9 7819 0315 3628.

Larrington, Carolyne. *Winter is Coming: The Medieval World of Game of Thrones.* I.B. Tauris. [2015] pp. xii + 252. £12.99 ISBN 9 7817 8453 2567.

Lee, Stuart, and Elizabeth Solopova. *The Keys of Middle Earth: Discovering Medieval Literature through the Fiction of J.R.R. Tolkien.* 2nd edn. PalMac. [2015] pp. xv + 380. £67 ISBN 9 7811 3745 4683.

Niles, John D. *The Idea of Anglo-Saxon England, 1066–1901: Remembering, Forgetting, Deciphering and Renewing the Past.* Wiley Blackwell. [2015] pp. 448. £60 ISBN 9 7811 1894 3328.

O'Brien, Bruce, and Barbara Bombi, eds. *Textus Roffensis: Law, Languages, and Libraries in Early Medieval England.* Studies in the Early Middles Ages 30. Brepols. [2015] pp. xiv + 415. £100 ISBN 9 7825 0354 2331.

Pinner, Rebecca. *The Cult of St Edmund in Medieval East Anglia.* Boydell. [2015] pp. xi + 276. £60 ISBN 9 7817 8327 0354.

Salvador-Bello, Mercedes. *Isidorean Perceptions of Order: The Exeter Book of Riddles and Medieval Latin Enigmata.* WVUP. [2015] pp. 512. $44.99 ISBN 9 7819 3597 8510.

Snook, Ben. *The Anglo-Saxon Chancery: The History, Language and Production of Anglo-Saxon Charters from Alfred to Edgar.* Anglo-Saxon Studies 28. Boydell [2015] pp. xvi + 234. £60 ISBN 9 7817 8327 0064.

Vickrey, John F. *Genesis B and the Comedic Imperative.* LehighUP. [2015] ISBN 9 7816 1146 1671.

# III

# Middle English

KATE ASH-IRISARRI, TAMARA ATKIN,
ANNE BADEN-DAINTREE, ALASTAIR BENNETT,
DAISY BLACK, ANNA DOW, MARY C. FLANNERY,
CARRIE GRIFFIN, GARETH GRIFFITH, HARRIET HOWES,
YOSHIKO KOBAYASHI, MICHAEL MADRINKIAN,
THERESA O'BYRNE, NIAMH PATTWELL,
WILLIAM ROGERS, AND KATIE WALTER

This chapter has fifteen sections: 1. General; 2. Theory; 3. Manuscript and Textual Studies; 4. Early Middle English; 5. Secular Verse; 6. Religious Verse; 7. Secular Prose; 8. Religious Prose; 9. *Piers Plowman*; 10. *Sir Gawain and the Green Knight, Pearl, Patience, Cleanness*; 11. Romance: Metrical, Alliterative, Prose; 12. Gower; 13. Hoccleve and Lydgate; 14. Older Scots; 15. Drama. Sections 1 and 6 are by Anne Baden-Daintree; section 2 is by Katie Walter; section 3 is by Carrie Griffin; section 4 is by Alastair Bennett; section 5 is by Harriet Howes; section 7 is by Theresa O'Byrne; section 8 is by Niamh Pattwell; section 9 is by William Rogers; section 10 is by Michael Madrinkian; section 11 is by Gareth Griffith and Anna Dow; section 12 is by Yoshiko Kobayashi; section 13 is by Mary C. Flannery; section 14 is by Kate Ash-Irisarri; section 15 is by Daisy Black and Tamara Atkin.

## 1. General

Douglas Gray's *Simple Forms: Essays on Medieval English Popular Literature* examines the large body of oral or folk literature that survives in many medieval literary texts, and at the same time provides an introduction to many forms of 'popular literature' in written form. Gray's interpretation of popular literature is broad, including the expected categories of romance, fable, song, folk tale, and ballad, but also encompassing proverb and riddle, drama, and satire. The book is largely organized around these genre categories, with a chapter on each preceded by three introductory chapters. There is an extended attempt to explain what constitutes popular literature, and some reflections on

*The Year's Work in English Studies, Volume 96 (2017)* © *The Author 2017. Published by Oxford University Press on behalf of the English Association. All rights reserved.*
*For Permissions, please email: journals.permissions@oup.com*
doi:10.1093/ywes/max006

popular culture, before Gray moves into the main body of his study, with an exploration of the narrative forms of the oral tradition. He defines categories 'loosely and simply in a way that would shock a determined and rigorous theorist'. The introductory chapters provide a range of evidence for the coexistence of oral and written literary cultures, and the implications of increasing levels of literacy for the survival of oral forms of transmission. The various forms of public and communal reading practices attested throughout the Middle Ages form, suggests Gray, a bridge between the two cultures, and he then provides a series of snapshots of the social and cultural contexts in which such texts were produced and disseminated. The interaction between popular and literary is more complex than is sometimes assumed, and, as Gray demonstrates, in some cases 'it is difficult, if not impossible, to decide which came first, the popular motif or the literary one'. There is clearly much overlap between the survey of narrative forms undertaken here and the interpretative work of *Truth and Tales*, discussed below. Throughout *Simple Forms* there is a necessary emphasis on uncovering source material; this serves to remind scholars and students focusing on various theoretical approaches that such work detailing the 'building blocks' of canonical literary texts is not yet complete, and Gray both invites and lays foundations for further scholarship in this field.

*Learning to Die in London, 1380–1540* by Amy Appleford examines death cultures in London during the fifteenth century, in terms of the circulation and reading cultures surrounding various *artes moriendi*, together with the associated practices and social and civic relationships. The first chapter focuses on the widely circulated fourteenth-century version of *The Visitation of the Sick*, which was employed as a text for both lay and clerical deathbed attendants. Appleford shows how this text supported the development of the deathbed in the domestic household as a site for a model of Christian community where the sacraments were no longer necessarily at the centre of the death rite; instead, the process of dying needed to be supported and managed in terms of a form of spiritual self-governance. Chapter 2 shows how John Carpenter employed the financial legacy of Richard Whittington to fund a series of commemorative building projects rather than funding annual obits and masses. Appleford analyses the commissioned wall painting *The Daunce of Poulys*, based on a version of Lydgate's *Dance of Death*, as representing the transience of human life alongside the importance of self-governance in ensuring the endurance of the city. She summarizes: 'Dying well secures the future of the city and all its generations.' Chapter 3 moves away from the communal realms of household and city to the individual, considering a range of texts including the *Pety Job*, the *Seven Points of True Love*, and Hoccleve's *Series*, in an examination of the individual responsibility for preparation for death. Chapter 4 turns to the late fifteenth-century *Book of the Craft of Dying* and examines its Latin origins in terms of the theological implications of its intended audience as being both lay and monastic readers. The final chapter moves on to the death culture of the 1530s, the first decade of the English Reformation, and explores the various attempts to alleviate anxieties about appropriate preparation for death which are attributed largely to the prescriptive nature of the fifteenth-century death manuals discussed earlier in this study. The new *artes moriendi* position the conquering of fear as central to the process of dying a good death, particularly in a troubled political climate where death becomes, in many cases, a public act. The focus of this informative study on the particular geographical location of London and a relatively brief time period enables a strong understanding of manuscript circulation and readership of texts which gain their significance as much in their practical application and context as in their literary qualities.

Alistair Minnis's *From Eden to Eternity: Creations of Paradise in the Later Middle Ages* is an important study which explores the ways in which biblical accounts provided an imaginative space for medieval writers and artists to debate and explore a detailed understanding and representation of Eden and paradise. Minnis draws on a wide range of source material, from early medieval scholastic sources to early modern poetry, opening up a largely new field of scholarship. This book clarifies the interrelationship between scholastic debate and more popular forms of culture, including both text and visual art (altarpieces and manuscript illustration), demonstrating the degree to which such complex debate was reflected and commented on in lay and secular contexts. It draws on textual sources for much of its evidence, and also places such literature in its cultural and theological contexts. As well as much Latin theological material, Minnis includes close study of several Middle English texts, including *Mandeville's Travels*, *Pearl*, and the *Prick of Conscience*, while also considering texts and authors as diverse as Chaucer, Milton, the *Roman de la Rose*, and Middle English purgatory poems. After introducing the idea of the creation of Eden, and the various questions that it raised for medieval theologians, Minnis addresses such debates in detail, organizing the material thematically in chapters examining the body in Eden, the distribution of power in paradise, and finally the relationship between death and the life beyond. This third chapter is particularly compelling in its account of the way in which poets as well as theologians represented the enhanced experience of the senses, affect, and intellect in the afterlife. Minnis finishes with a brief coda which considers how and why such questions about what happens in Eden and paradise were justified; he summarizes the kinds of understanding that medieval theologians reached for, and the curious focus on insignificant detail alongside major theological issues, together with a necessary consideration of the sensory pleasures implied by paradise, and the way that such concerns have sometimes been sidelined in studies of medieval religion. The achievement of this book is not just the opening up of new areas of scholarship, but the presentation of a mass of complex material in an engaging and, at times, conversational style, effortlessly weaving together detail from seemingly disparate sources, and this is enhanced by the inclusion of a substantial quantity of visual material and accompanying discussion of this medieval art and manuscript illumination which completes the range of representations of paradise.

Ellen Rentz's study *Imagining the Parish in Late Medieval England* draws on a wide range of literary texts, together with sermons, liturgical texts, spiritual handbooks, church wall paintings, and stained glass as evidence of the perception of the parish as a model of spiritual community in late medieval England. This focus on the parish and the range of devotional experiences it

encompasses reinforces Eamon Duffy's perspective that individual ownership
of liturgical texts encouraged participation in the ritual life of the parish; here
we see individual salvation being accomplished through active engagement
with the communal practices of the parish church. Rentz considers the idea of
the medieval English parish as, simultaneously, a community of worshippers
and residents, a physical location, and an ideology reflecting 'the eternal
community of heaven'. She argues that vernacular theology promotes the
importance of the 'ritual life of the parish' as essential to salvation. This
understanding of the practices of collective worship as shaping the relationships between Church, individual, and community is largely developed
through close readings of *Piers Plowman, Handlyng Synne*, and *The Prick of
Conscience*, but also draws on sermons and liturgical texts, and the material
culture of the parish church, particularly stained glass and wall paintings. The
texts are employed as a means of exploring both religious metaphor and
religious practice, moving through the font and the grave, to penitential
practice and the move towards a more collective concept of confession, then to
the use of walking and manual labour as metaphors for the work of achieving
salvation, before finally considering how an individual parish used visual and
verbal reference to *The Prick of Conscience* in collective worship. See Sections
6 and 9 below for further discussion of individual chapters of this book.

The Gnostic Paradigm: Forms of Knowing in English Literature of the Late
Middle Ages, by Natanela Elias, examines the influence of Gnosticism on later
medieval thought and writing. It provides a detailed overview and contextual
understanding of the principles of Gnosticism, and considers the traces and
'residues' of Gnostic influence which continued in literary texts centuries after
Gnosticism as a belief system had ceased to exist, explaining that the dream
vision genre is particularly appropriate for exploring such ideas. Elias suggests
that the underlying Christian framework of various medieval literary texts
contains 'heretical elements of the ancient Gnostic tradition drawn along the
lines of duality and the processes of gnosis, or the attainment of certain,
salvific knowledge'. She examines evidence of instances of successful and
unsuccessful Gnostic 'Passing' in her close readings of *Piers Plowman,
Confessio Amantis, Pearl, Patience*, and *Cleanness*, examining both the process
of acquiring knowledge and the language used to effect this, in an analysis
which challenges the accepted orthodoxy of these works.

Elaine Treharne's *Medieval Literature: A Very Short Introduction* is aimed a
broad and non-specialist audience and seeks to offer a general account of the
nature of the field and the significant figures in it.

The collection of essays edited by Naoë Kukita Yoshikawa, *Medicine,
Religion and Gender in Medieval Culture*, is an important contribution to the
field of medical humanities. It demonstrates, from various perspectives, the
interrelationship between physical and spiritual health in the writings and
practices of the European Middle Ages, with a wide range of contributions
strongly weighted towards literary and religious texts, and female experience.
The various chapters emphasize the interactions between medical metaphor
and medical roles or practice in a religious context, as well as drawing
attention to the literary qualities of medical and religious writings. Yoshikawa
introduces the collection by providing an overview of some significant recent

scholarship in this and related fields, together with a summary of some of the important cultural contexts (and concepts) for the convergence of medical and religious discourse in the Middle Ages. While the focus on gender results in a strong selection of women writers and accounts of women's experience, male health and illness could perhaps have received more focused attention. In 'Mary the Physician: Women, Religion and Medicine in the Middle Ages' (pp. 27–44) Diane Watt considers the model of the Virgin Mary as physician, or *Maria medica*, in late medieval England, a role extended beyond that of intercessory healer and her association with childbirth through an examination of the Virgin's medical interventions in *The Life of Christina of Markyate* and, less directly, in *The Book of Margery Kempe*, where Margery herself adopts the role of *Maria medica* in assisting another woman in her post-partum suffering. Watt then turns to the evidence of the Paston Letters to show that the continuation of the role of women as healers has an enduring association with female Marian devotion into the fifteenth century. Roberta Magnani, in 'Chaucer's Physicians: Raising Questions of Authority' (pp. 45–64), also considers the depiction of the Virgin Mary as physician, but with a focus on Chaucer's portrayal of the Virgin, beginning with the descriptive language employed in the *ABC* and the prologue to the *Prioress's Tale*. Magnani then explores the way in which some of these associations work their way through the language of the *Physician's Tale*, particularly in terms of the implicit associations between Virginia, Nature, and the Virgin Mary. Part II of this collection, 'Female Mysticism and Metaphors of Sickness', opens with 'Heavenly Vision and Psychosomatic Healing: Medical Discourse in Mechtild of Hackeborn's *The Book of Gostlye Grace*' (pp. 67–84), Naoë Kukita Yoshikawa's account of the Middle English translation of Mechtild of Hackeborn's Latin text, *Liber specialis gratiae*. Arguing that Mechtild had medical knowledge which underpins her use of medical imagery, Yoshikawa shows how Mechtild combines medical and spiritual discourses, including the employment of common tropes such as Christ as physician, effecting both spiritual and physical healing. The visions work towards an exploration of mystical union as spiritual health, with a strong emphasis on the therapeutic use of sensory experience. Yoshikawa demonstrates that the bodily senses are experienced by Mechtild as a means of healing and maintaining physical, spiritual, and psychological health, and spiritual experience is described by means of sensory metaphor, so that the 'revelations emerge as a psychosomatic healing process from suffering to eternal bliss in her pursuit of mystical union with God'. Liz Herbert McAvoy discusses the practice of blood-letting alongside the idea of confession as spiritual medicine, in 'Bathing in Blood: The Medicinal Cures of Anchoritic Devotion' (pp. 85–102). Examining various anchoritic texts, including the *Ancrene Wisse* and the writings of Julian of Norwich, McAvoy explores the patterns of suffering and healing, and the relationships between physical and spiritual health, including the actual and figurative use of medical practices including blood-letting and bathing in blood, at times employed in a distinctive form of *imitatio Christi*. Juliette Vuille's important evaluation of scholarly perspectives on female mystical experience and mental illness, '"Maybe I'm Crazy?": Diagnosis and Contextualisation of Medieval Female Mystics' (pp. 103–20), considers the evidence for the social construction of mental illness, and advises against the anachronistic application of psychiatric diagnoses to mystics such as Julian of Norwich and Margery Kempe. Vuille outlines the multidisciplinary approach that is needed to fully contextualize the understanding of episodes of 'madness' as portrayed in the writings of both women, demonstrating the degree to which the relationship between physical illness and mental illness, together with the differences in perception of the initial episode described in each text to subsequent events, render such analyses inappropriate. The representations of visions and other spiritual experiences are entirely in accord with the conventions of the literary genres on which both women draw, and it is this context, argues Vuille, which most usefully illuminates the processes of imitation and validation that underpin their texts; the occasional episodes of 'divine insanity' only serve to authenticate the appearance of madness as a genuine and legitimate spiritual experience. Part III of this collection, 'Fifteenth-Century Poetry and Theological Prose', considers the relationship between physical and spiritual health in the works of John Audelay and Reginald Pecock. Takami Matsuda's essay, 'Purgatory and Spiritual Healing in John Audelay's Poems' (pp. 123–37; discussed further in Section 6 below), examines the positive effects of bodily illness for spiritual well-being. Louise Bishop, in 'Reginald Pecock's Reading Heart and the Health of Body and Soul' (pp. 139–58), provides a detailed and informative account of the physiological nature and function of the heart in terms of medieval medicine alongside the heart's metaphorical implications, particularly the way in which the heart's 'porosity' allows vernacular reading to leave its imprint. The heart becomes, therefore, a site for conflict, and a target for appropriation by politically threatening vernacular theology. Bishop centres her analysis on the fifteenth-century Middle English translation of *De doctrina cordis* (*The Doctrine of the Hert*) with respect to its popularity, in contrast to the condemnation of Pecock's writings, accused of 'imprinting men's hearts by secret and unheard means'. Part IV of this collection has less of a literary focus, with chapters by medical historians. An afterword by Denis Renevey (pp. 237–48) places this important collection of essays in its scholarly context, in this flourishing (and rapidly developing) area of scholarship.

*The Art of Vision: Ekphrasis in Medieval Literature and Culture*, edited by Andrew James Johnston, Ethan Knapp, and Margitta Rouse, is a stimulating collection of essays which builds on a recent growth of interest in the relationship between the visual and the literary in Middle English literary studies. Rather than offering their own prescriptive definition of ekphrasis, the editors instead present the varying theoretical perspectives, including both contemporary literary criticism and a historical perspective, which allows the essays in the volume the freedom to explore the complex and dynamic operation of ekphrasis in a range of medieval texts. The authors of individual chapters employ a number of different approaches: the essays in the first section of the book, 'Ekphrasis and the Object', consider various ways in which ekphrasis engages with material objects, including the representation of visual art, but extends beyond this to other forms of textual-material representation, including inventory. Part II, 'The Desire of Ekphrasis', considers the affective and psychological potential of ekphrastic writing.

Part III, 'The Epistemology of Ekphrasis', demonstrates the ways in which the interactions of the allegorical or didactic with the ekphrastic in early modern texts provide a connection with medieval uses of the device. Part IV, 'The Borders of Ekphrasis', considers the interactions between poetic tradition and mimesis. There is a strong focus on Chaucer and the *Gawain*-poet throughout the collection, with essays on Chaucer's lyric 'The Former Age' (Sarah Stanbury), the historical context of Lollardy in the representation of pagan and classical images in dream vision and the *Knight's Tale* (John M. Bowers) and the *Merchant's Tale* (Hans Jürgen Scheuer), and two chapters on *Pearl* (Anke Bernau and Larry Scanlon); see Chapter IV in this volume and Section 10 below. Ethan Knapp's chapter is wider-ranging in its choice of literary texts (spanning Chaucer, Gower, and Hoccleve), but narrows in perspective to examine representations of the human face. Other chapters move further afield, with essays on Middle Scots (Johnston and Rouse on Gavin Douglas, discussed below), medieval Latin, Middle High German, and Old French texts, as well as later authors (Spenser and Shakespeare). One of the strengths of this collection is its repeated willingness to extend the definition of ekphrasis beyond the narrower focus of studies of post-medieval texts as, in James Heffernan's terms, 'the verbal representation of visual representation', which effectively means writing descriptively about works of visual art. This is complicated not only by the way in which such writing engages with the perception of the artwork, but in late medieval terms by the problematic issues raised by the visual qualities of Lollard writing in the face of professed iconophobia. In engaging with this complex and politicized landscape, the editors invite a wide range of scholarship addressing a specifically pre-modern notion of ekphrasis which acknowledges the range of religious and secular contexts 'where all manner of discourses are refracted through the complex lens of verbalized visuality'.

*Truth and Tales: Cultural Mobility and Medieval Media*, edited by Fiona Somerset and Nicholas Watson, challenges the ideas of separation of oral and literate cultures, and of learned and popular forms of discourse, in a series of fourteen essays which represent something of the complexity of the interactions between these different cultures, and the range of cultural networks that inform and intermingle with medieval literary culture. The first section, containing a single chapter by Richard Firth Green, '"The Vanishing Leper" and "The Murmuring Monk": Two Medieval Urban Legends' (pp. 19–37), explores the circulation of stories in both oral and written form, demonstrating that the process of validating 'truth' is reinforced by personal association regardless of context. In other words, the social bonds which confer a connection with the event are as significant as direct witness in providing authority. The movement of popular or folkloric tales in and out of the more learned context where they might be used as exempla also encourages a rethinking of the boundaries between forms of discourse. Part II of this collection, 'Repetition and Continuity: The Claims of History', focuses on the social relationships that are formed and reinforced by the transactions of storytelling. Thomas Hahn's chapter, 'Don't Cry for Me, Augustinus: Dido and the Dangers of Empathy' (pp. 41–59), considers Chaucer's portrayal of Dido in *The House of Fame* and *The Legend of Good Women* in terms of the connections made between writing and affect in these texts, suggesting that the complexity of his textual processes validates what might otherwise be seen as an inappropriate object for emotional engagement. Drawing connections with the language employed by Julian of Norwich, Hahn argues that Chaucer's 'fixation on Dido as a pre-Christian martyr of love' enables the rechannelling of 'emotions associated with religious feeling or devotional affect' into a secular poetic context. In 'The New Plow and the Old: Law, Orality, and the Figure of Piers the Plowman in B 19' (pp. 60–78), Stephen Yeager also reflects on textual engagement with the past, but here considers the degree to which Piers adopts the language of Anglo-Saxon legal documents, reinforcing through this sense of continuity with the past that it is an earlier model of political order which is presented, rather than a new model for society. 'The Exegesis of Tears in Lambeth Homily 17' (pp. 79–95), by M.J. Toswell, examines the complexity of interactions between oral and written cultures in twelfth-century England, and, through the examination of two overlapping homily collections, demonstrates that there is no straightforward answer to questions of continuity in England between the Anglo-Saxon and Anglo-Norman learned cultures. Fiona Somerset assesses the continuities across time in Laȝamon's *Brut* in her chapter, 'Mingling with the English in Layamon's *Brut*' (pp. 96–113), where the processes of intermingling of ethnicities and languages form part of the larger narrative of British history, through processes of migration and invasion. Part III, 'Cultural Divides and their Common Ground', contains four wide-ranging essays connected by their representation of 'surprising convergences' in the face of disparate concerns or interests. In 'Unquiet Graves: *Pearl* and the Hope of Reunion' (pp. 117–34), Alistair Minnis explores the popular hope for the continuation of family ties beyond death in relation to the rejection of such comforting imaginative reconstruction of family life by the *Pearl*-maiden. Minnis demonstrates, however, that while *Pearl* may offer a perspective which does not follow popular example (such as the *Vision of Tundale*) in privileging family values and relationships in terms of the rewards and status in the afterlife, it is instead consistent with scholastic theology. The poet, suggests Minnis, offers an alternative which, although not allowing the 'exclusive intimacy' of earthly relationships instead allows for a 'far superior' version, in accordance with standard resurrection theology, where the possibility of reunion is clearly within a transformed and 'more substantial' heavenly form. Michael Johnston's 'Mercantile Gentry in Cambridge, University Library MS Ff.2.38' (pp. 135–50) analyses a moral exemplum surviving in a single late fifteenth-century manuscript, 'A Good Matter of the Merchant and his Son', which tells the story of a wealthy franklin, who succeeds by dishonest acts, and his son, who rejects his father's values in favour of becoming a merchant, eventually sacrificing his own freedom in order to pay off his father's purgatorial debts. This poem reconsiders contemporary concerns about ethics and social class, and the compilation of the manuscript for an urban mercantile readership makes sense of the transfer of the qualities of gentility away from the landed gentry and onto the merchant classes of the son and his guild-master. Examination of other texts by Chaucer and Langland, and the alliterative *Mum and the Sothsegger*, shows that franklins were positioned 'at the margins of landed society' and so provide a particularly apt focus for the social anxieties of the merchant classes; and in fact, 'A Good Matter' in the end collapses the boundaries between urban and rural, and merchant and landed gentry. Lisa J. Kiser examines the kinds of truth that underlie beast fables in 'The Literary Ecology of Medieval Mice' (pp. 151–67), suggesting that these tales imply more than simply images of animals representing the human in their preoccupation with the natural order, but are underpinned by an engagement with folk knowledge of the workings of the natural world. 'Toward the Common Good: Punishing Fraud among the Victualers of Medieval London' (pp. 168–84), by Barbara A. Hanawalt, examines the potential for fraudulent transactions and deficiencies in food supply in medieval London, and the associated popular anxieties and public punishments. Hanawalt includes a glance at literary comment by poets such as Chaucer, Langland, and Lydgate, alongside a wide range of documentary evidence of the written, visual, and oral sources for the moral and legal framework of such behaviour. Part IV, 'New Media and the Literate Laity', is based on the potentialities of increasing lay literacy for the development of new forms, genres, and media in the fifteenth century. Nicholas Watson's chapter, 'The Ignorance of the Laity: *Twelve Tracts on Bible Translation*' (pp. 187–205), is concerned with this development in literacy which undermined the divide between clergy and laity, particularly in terms of the increasingly problematic process of providing spiritual instruction to laymen. The twelve tracts under discussion here, rather than providing a prescriptive single model, instead attempt to characterize a range of models of lay learning across different media.

Robyn Malo's 'York Merchants at Prayer: The Confessional Formula of the Bolton Hours' (pp. 206–22) examines a lay-authored devotional text written into the outer folios of a Book of Hours which appears to be aimed at the mercantile classes. It provides a model for approaching the process of confession by, unusually, suggesting the kinds of sin that might be committed in terms of each of the commandments in turn. This tailoring of the 'truth' of a universal spiritual process provides compelling evidence for greater religious literacy amongst the laity in this period. 'A London Legal Miscellany, Popular Law, and Medieval Print Culture' (pp. 223–37), by Kathleen E. Kennedy, demonstrates the degree to which the urban laity were also becoming increasingly literate in law. Kennedy suggests that a household miscellany manuscript, 'Arnold's Book', was, unusually, transferred into a print edition because of the popularity of the legal texts within its contents. Michael Van Dussen, in 'Tourists and *Tabulae* in Late-Medieval England' (pp. 238–54), discusses an aspect of lay literacy whose influence has often been overlooked: the written tablets providing description or commemoration related to a specific location at which the *tabula* was displayed. Van Dussen provides examples of the various ways in which the contents of such tablets were adopted as source material and incorporated into a range of other media. Andrew Taylor's 'Oral Performance and the Force of the Law: Taillefer at Hastings and Antgulilibix in Smithers' (pp. 257–74), concludes the book with powerful evidence (from the eleventh and twentieth centuries) of the interactions between oral and written cultures, and the ways in which audiences determine what 'truth-value' to place on different media and forms of representation. In both examples, it is the narrative accounts of oral performance (specifically, song) which effect historical change, raising ethical questions about how truth is determined, and how different cultures privilege different media according to context.

Serina Patterson's edited collection *Games and Gaming in Medieval Literature* explores the tensions between the world of games and the 'real' world. It considers the ways in which games functioned to shape social categories and identities, as well as examining the act of playing games in a variety of social and literary contexts: this collection contains essays on the employment of games and gaming in a range of late medieval texts, in French, Spanish and English, in settings including court, church and household. 'Gaming' is interpreted widely to include 'textual games' in Spanish *cancionero* poetry, and reading games in *Somer Soneday*, but the focus is mainly on board games such as chess and tables, and the social context of gaming. Nicholas Orme, in 'Games and Education in Medieval England' (pp. 45–60), explores the consequences of classical models of education based on strict discipline as a means of enforcing adult values and attributes, for the role of games and play in English education. Serina Patterson considers the social role of gaming, in 'Sexy, Naughty, and Lucky in Love: Playing *Ragemon le Bon* in English Gentry Households' (pp. 79–102), with reference to the circulation of what she describes as 'game-texts': games which 'manifested as literature in medieval manuscripts'. Nora Corrigan's reading of the *Canterbury Tales*, 'The Knight's Earnest Game in Chaucer's *Canterbury Tales*' (pp. 147–68), reflects on the balance between 'ernest' and 'game' in relation to the Knight. Kimberly Bell, in '"Rounes to rede": Ludic Reading Games in the Alliterative Wheel of Fortune Poem *Somer Soneday*' (pp. 169–86), interprets the alliterative poem *Somer Soneday* in terms of its dual-game structure (of the hunt and the Wheel of Fortune), suggesting that the author is playing an interpretative literary game with his readers, based on an underestimation of the serious dimension of games. There are also chapters on the use of games in motets (Tamsyn Rose-Steel), French literature (Daniel O'Sullivan), Spanish poetry (Juan Escourido), and the Middle Dutch *Walawein* (Jenny Adams), reflecting the wider cultural and European perspective of the collection. An afterword by Betsy McCormick, 'Medieval Ludens' (pp. 209–22), places the various chapters in their wider theoretical context, exploring the history of cultural game theory and its origins in medieval culture, while also showing how the expanding interdisciplinary field of game studies has a bearing on medieval practices, particularly with regard to the idea of the 'ludic function'.

*Medieval Robots: Mechanism, Magic, Nature, and Art*, by E.R. Truitt, is a study of science and technology in medieval literature and culture, specifically in terms of the development of mechanical automata, incorporating varied forms, from mechanical clocks with animal and human figures, to oracular metal statues, to the artificial maintenance of human life. Truitt draws on a wide range of sources, including texts in Arabic, Greek, and Latin, as well as medieval literary texts from Spain, France, and England, across many of the major literary genres, including history, romance, chronicle, and travel writing. Many objects described in these texts first appeared as gifts from foreign courts, raising anxieties about the origins of such new forms of knowledge. While little in the way of mechanical objects survives, there are many accounts in fiction, and archival materials detailing their construction. Much of the literary material is French, but this book also details some significant examples in Middle English. This includes an account of the descriptions of mechanical birds and animals in *The Travels of Sir John Mandeville*, comparing these with Mandeville's sources; the story of Grosseteste's construction of an oracular brass head in Gower's *Confessio Amantis*; and the detailed account of the medical and mechanical preservation of Hector's corpse in Lydgate's *Troy Book*. In each case the embellishment or variation of source material is examined in respect of the differing concerns and priorities of the English writers from their sources. Also relevant to the study of many medieval literary texts is Truitt's discussion of the development of pictorial representations of Fortune's Wheel, with its increasing reflection of the processes of mechanization.

*Seeing Sodomy in the Middle Ages*, by Robert Mills, uses both literary and visual source material to consider representations of gender and sexuality, particularly in terms of sodomy and motifs of vision and visibility. But the study is wide-ranging in its consideration of fluidity in terms of gender categorization and sexual identity and practices. Mills draws on a number of Middle English texts, including the *Canterbury Tales* and the *House of Fame*, *Confessio Amantis*, *Sir Orfeo*, and *Ancrene Wisse*, but this book never pauses for long on a single text or visual source, and also moves rapidly across genres and languages, from classical texts, to many Old French literary sources, to manuscript illustrations (particularly those in illuminated bibles). Mills presents a convincing case for the visibility of the practice of sodomy in the Middle Ages, but the dazzling array of source material in this book also pulls in many other directions, involving complex argument which adopts knowingly anachronistic theoretical perspectives in its connections between diverse source materials.

Dannie Leigh Chalk examines the representation of the midwife in literary, medical, and religious texts in 'Savior, Witness, and Comic Relief: The Midwife in English Texts of the Fifteenth and Sixteenth Centuries' (*SP* 112[2015] 93–113). Chalk explores the range of positive images in medieval medical or religious sources (where the midwife might be seen as having legal authority and considerable medical skills, and perform important administrative functions within the church) and negative literary stereotypes (as an ignorant, ill-tempered old woman), also tracing a development of the midwife's religious role, from one which encompassed the performance of infant baptisms to a more regulatory role by the mid-sixteenth century, 'rooting out any traditions in the birth room that might bear a "Catholic" connotation'. Through the many scattered references in late medieval texts including the *Legenda Aurea*, the N-Town plays, the Chester Cycle, and works by Lydgate and John Mirk, the midwife can clearly be seen, argues Chalk, as having an important role as medical practitioner, comforter, and witness (of a woman's sexual status in legal situations, but also of miraculous events occurring in the private space of the birth room). However, as Chalk demonstrates, the later literary portrayals of midwives turn more to their comic potential, drawing on those negative stereotypes of ignorant, drunken, and foolish gossips, which arose partly from shifts in medicine towards male-dominated practice and authority.

In '"What shalt thou do when thou hast an English to make into Latin?"': The Proverb Collection of Cambridge, St John's College, MS F.26' (*SP* 112[2015] 68–92), Joanna Bellis and Venetia Bridges consider the transfer of oral, vernacular folk material (which gains authority precisely from its universality and anonymity) to other, more literary, contexts: specifically the use of English proverbs as schoolroom translation exercises, but also the incorporation of the same proverbs elsewhere into poetry. The oral 'power' of proverbs might be lost when translated into Latin, but the recontextualization as written text alongside other more authoritative texts transforms them into 'learned wisdom'. The process of translation also, suggest the authors, complicates the simple binaries of English/Latin, oral/written, and the associated values ascribed to material in the different languages and forms. Suggestions are made as to why particular proverbs might have been selected for translation (including bawdier examples to lighten the process in some cases, rather than providing moral instruction alongside grammatical instruction through the more serious content). The transfer of some of the same material into a separate poetic context then imparts a different layer of authority to this simple material, and Bellis and Bridges offer some direct comparisons where the attribution to a named speaker and the immediate poetic context serve to encourage a more prescriptive and didactic reading of practical advice.

## 2. Theory

This section treats work falling broadly into two categories: scholarship on Middle English literary theory, and publications that bring contemporary theoretical approaches to Middle English texts. The year 2015 saw a particular emphasis, among other areas, on genre and the medical humanities, as well as continued interest in medieval theories of translation, authorship, and reading.

A special issue of *Exemplaria* on medieval genre makes substantial contributions to both medieval and modern genre theory, with a large number of essays in the issue concentrating specifically on Middle English texts. Ingrid Nelson and Shannon Gayk, 'Introduction: Genre as Form-of-Life' (*Exemplaria* 27[2015] 3–17), take up Giorgio Agamben's discussion of two related ideas, the 'rule' (which he founds on a discussion of medieval monastic life) and 'form-of-life', as a means of pushing against Derrida's use of 'law' in thinking about genre theory. They explore this in case studies from *Piers Plowman*, Richard Rolle's prologue to the *English Psalter*, and Osbern Bokenham's prologue to *Legendys of Hooly Wummen*. Jennifer Jahner, 'Reading for the End: Prescriptive Writing and the Practice of Genre' (*Exemplaria* 27[2015] 18–34), focuses on one manuscript miscellany (San Marino, Huntington Library, HM 144) and its 'didactic' texts ('less a genre . . . [than] an incursion into other generic structures', p. 20). Engaging a range of theory—from Derrida to Jauss, Kant, and Paul de Man—Jahner explores the claims of genre to shaping conduct and social consensus in HM 144's Middle English items, including John Lydgate's *Horse, Sheep, and Goose* and Chaucer's *Melibee*. Matthew Giancarlo utilizes Fredric Jameson's notion of 'sedimentation' (the 'over-laying of genres in history whereby one mode builds from and supplements a pre-existing one without totally supplanting it', p. 39) and Agamben's dissection of sovereignty, in 'Mirror, Mirror: Princely Hermeneutics, Practical Constitutionalism, and the Genres of the English *Fürstenspiegel*' (*Exemplaria* 27[2015] 35–54), to explore the 'insistent ways the *Fürstenspiegel* makes specifically hermeneutic demands on how sovereignty is constituted in the figure of the prince' (p. 37). With Hoccleve's *Regiment of Princes* providing a key example, Giancarlo argues that generic expectations are implicated in a 'right' reading of 'what constitutes a proper exercise of authority' (p. 37). Nancy Mason Bradbury, 'The Proverb as Embedded Microgenre in Chaucer and *The Dialogue of Solomon and Marcolf*' (*Exemplaria* 27[2015] 55–72), resists current theory's emphasis on the fluidity of genre boundaries and categories by looking to the discrete, short, fixed form of the proverb (its 'finalized wholeness', p. 63) and its use within the Middle English *Dialogue of Solomon and Marcolf*, as well as the poetry of Chaucer. Bradbury does so with the provocation of Bakhtin's 'The Problem of Speech Genres', which provides a means of thinking about the incorporation of a 'smaller' genre, such as the proverb, into 'a longer and more complex work' (p. 56). The Middle English *Alexander and Dindimus* provides a central example in Jane Gilbert's 'Genus and Genre: The Old French Verse *Roman d'Alexandre*, *Alexander and Dindimus*, and MS Bodl. 264' (*Exemplaria* 27[2015] 110–28). Gilbert proposes the usefulness of Agamben's discussion of the biological term *genus* (emphasizing the distinction between human and animal) as 'a tool of poetic analysis' (p. 111) alongside Derrida's consideration of the law of genre. Gilbert highlights the way genre (along with form and theme) operates in works like *Alexander and Dindimus* to propose '"openness" as the principal test of humanity, specifically in an "open" relationship to law' (p. 113). Emily Steiner, 'Compendious Genres: Higden, Trevisa, and the Medieval Encyclopaedia' (*Exemplaria* 27[2015] 73–92), focuses on John Trevisa's English translation of Ranulph Higden's *Polychronicon* to show the ways in which 'compendiousness in this period was not only an indicator of genre but also a pretext for genre thinking' (p. 73), as well as for generating other literary forms such as lyric. In 'Towards a Material Allegory: Allegory and Urban Space in Hoccleve, Langland and Gower' (*Exemplaria* 27[2015] 93–109), Ethan Knapp demonstrates the importance of the city and the crowd to the genre of allegory as it is worked out in Hoccleve's *La Male Regle*, Langland's *Piers Plowman*, and the *visio* of Gower's *Vox Clamantis*. Bringing a materialist bent to his reading, Knapp uses Walter Benjamin's work, and the idea of the *flâneur*, to foreground the ways allegory makes (in the terms of Benjamin's argument) an 'obsessive return to a narrow collection of signifying and objects and spaces' (p. 94). Seeta Chaganti, 'Dance in a Haunted Space: Genre, Form, and the Middle English Carol' (*Exemplaria* 27[2015] 129–49), proposes a 'model of medieval genre as a spatial and kinetic phenomenon' (p. 129). Chaganti does so through putting the spatiality of medieval ghosts— simulating both material presence and absence—into conversation with Wai

Chee Dimock's conception of the virtuality of genre in a selection of Middle English carols found in British Library MS Sloane 2593. In 'Horrific Visions of the Host: A Meditation on Genre' (*Exemplaria* 27[2015] 150–66), Eleanor Johnson offers a way of categorizing two Middle English texts in contrasting forms, *Cleanness* and the Croxton Play of the Sacrament, on the basis of their capacity to evoke horror. In centring on 'the idea of transubstantiation, Eucharistic devotion, and host desecration' (p. 150), these texts suggest a genre of medieval horror that shapes readerly communities. Finally, Ardis Butterfield, 'Afterwords: Forms of Death' (*Exemplaria* 27[2015] 167–82), closes the issue by taking up Derrida on 'living on' and Bakhtin on speech genre to reflect on medieval genre and our response to it in terms of truisms, clichés, and dead metaphors (p. 167). While focusing mainly on Anglo-French and French poetry, Butterfield also includes some discussion of fifteenth-century Middle English poetry, as well as Chaucer's *Troilus and Criseyde*.

A number of essays appeared in 2015 that contribute to scholarship on Middle English theories of authorship, reading, and translation, as well as narrativity. Rory Critten's 'Imagining the Author in Late Medieval England and France: The Transmission and Reception of Christine de Pizan's *Epistre au dieu d'Amours* and Thomas Hoccleve's *Letter of Cupid*' (*SP* 112[2015] 680–97) furthers understandings of medieval ideas of authorship. Critten suggests the *Letter* marks an attempt by Hoccleve to take up the French model provided by Christine of self-publication and its attendant scope for authorial control. Critten understands this as an innovative but ultimately failed project, since 'the idea that an English-language author could stand as the guarantor of both the textual and codicological nature of his book had yet to be established' (p. 695). Daniel McCann, 'Medicine of Words: Purgative Reading in Richard Rolle's *Meditations on the Passion*' (*MedJ* 5[2015] 53–83), adds to our understanding of medicalized theories of literature and of reading by highlighting the purgative effects (for both body and soul) of the affective states aroused through the use of rhetorical techniques (such as *enargeia* and interjections) and different literary forms (such as the lyric). Focusing on a wide range of Rolle's English works, but principally the *Meditations on the Passion*, McCann demonstrates Rolle's use of a medieval theory of poetry that 'has the power to combine purgation with praise, rhythm with reality—to move and medicate us in mysterious ways' (p. 80).

Annie Sutherland's monograph, *English Psalms in the Middle Ages, 1300–1450*, offers useful additions to scholarship on medieval theories of translation and of reading. Chapter 2 ('Theorizing Translation') appraises the models of translation (especially Ciceronian and Hieronymian)—faithful imitation, deference or contestation, rhetorical invention or commentary—available to vernacular Bible translators. She suggests that many Middle English psalm translations recognize 'that accurate translation can legitimately depart from verbatim reproduction of the source ... [and acknowledge] the provisionality of any language, including Latin, as a vehicle for truth' (p. 81). Chapter 4 ('Reading the English Psalms') foregrounds medieval literary theoretical concerns arising out of exegetical and reading practices. Drawing on the prologues and commentaries to translations of the psalms by John Lydgate, Richard Rolle, Eleanor of Hull, Thomas Brampton, and Richard Maidstone, as well as in the *Prose* and *Metrical Psalter*, the chapter situates the vernacular psalm tradition within medieval reading practices that require active reading and forms of work that 'effect change in the user and his environment' (p. 208).

A.C. Spearing, 'What Is a Narrator? Narrator Theory and Medieval Narratives' (*DPhil* 4[2015] 59–105), urges medievalists to bring a more theoretical approach to narrative, and narratologists to bring medieval examples into their purview. Three Middle English case studies, of Malory's *Morte Darthur*, Chaucer's *Physician's Tale*, and the anonymous *Pearl*, as well as evidence from marginal annotations in Middle English manuscripts, are used to reassess the extent to which current narrative theory of the 'narrator' (as a 'necessary figure *internal* to a narrative', p. 60) accounts for and properly represents medieval understandings of the narrator.

Work bringing contemporary critical theory to readings of Middle English continues to abound, with notable contributions on trauma, psychoanalysis, anthropological and feminist understandings of time and space, and metrical theory. An issue of *Literature and Medicine* includes a cluster of essays on 'Pain and Trauma in Middle English Literature', several of which offer readings of Middle English works through the lens of contemporary theory. Erin Felicia Labbie's introduction, 'Pain, Trauma, and *Philia* in Middle English Literature' (*L&M* 33[2015] 235–57), suggests that Aristotelian understandings of *philia*, which she reads partly through Derrida's *Politics of Friendship*, can help 'produce a new understanding of the articulation of pain and trauma in Middle English' (p. 242). Labbie further employs Lacan and Freud in her close reading of *Sir Gawain and Green Knight*, concluding: 'the question of *surviving* is at the core of both pain and *philia*, of presence and mourning in a temporal conflux of moments' (p. 249). Patricia A. DeMarco, in 'Cultural Trauma and Christian Identity in the Late Medieval Epic, *The Siege of Jerusalem*' (*L&M* 33[2015] 279–301), examines the particular way medieval genres depict violent events, such as the Passion of Christ (for example, in 'The Privity of the Passion') and the Vengeance of Our Lord, as traumatizing. Utilizing a range of trauma theory, DeMarco gives substantial space to drawing out Freud's reading of Tasso's *Gerusalemme Liberata*—for him, 'an instructive portrait of trauma' (p. 292)—in order to provide a comparative reading of trauma in *The Siege of Jerusalem*. R.D. Perry argues, in an essay on 'Lydgate's *Danse Macabre* and the Trauma of the Hundred Years' War' (*L&M* 33[2015] 326–47), that the *Danse*, through its mix of genres (tragedy, estates satire, and *Fürstenspiegel*), 'allows Lydgate to present an overview of the trauma caused by warfare as a critique of the nobility' (p. 328). The essentiality of repetition to trauma, identified by Freud and developed by trauma theorists such as Cathy Caruth and Eva Hoffman, provides Perry with the means to read the poem's repeated enactment of death in terms of trauma.

Mark Miller's essay, 'Sin and Structure in *Piers Plowman*: On the Medieval Split Subject' (*MLQ* 76[2015] 201–24), is concerned with 'the problematic relation between structural necessity and agency' (p. 201) in *Piers Plowman*. Lacan here provides a parallel for understanding Langland: both, according to Miller, view 'the subject's embeddedness in and division by social and political structures as a function of a fundamental ontological split that conditions human being' (p. 202). First privileging a close reading of the split subject in *Piers Plowman*, Miller suggests Langland's 'formal experimentation' in the dream vision genre sheds light on Langland's understanding of inevitability, and so, in turn, of the inevitability of sin.

In 'Gendered Strategies of Time and Memory in the Writing of Julian of Norwich and the Recluse of Winchester' (in Cox, McAvoy, and Magnani, eds., *Reconsidering Gender, Time and Memory in Medieval Culture*, pp. 95–110), Liz Herbert McAvoy takes up Henri Lefebvre (on the notion of 'the woman as an embodiment of a dwelling-space', p. 96) and Luce Irigaray (on *espacement*) as lenses through which to think about female enclosure. Interpreting the anchorhold in Julian of Norwich's writings and in *A Revelation of Purgatory* as, in Foucauldian terms, heterotopic (characterized as space that 'combines the here-and-now and the transcendent', p. 101), enclosure provides a space in 'which women do … gain access' to the transcendent (p. 110). Robert Allen Rouse, 'Emplaced Reading, or Towards a Spatial Hermeneutic for Medieval Romance' (in Perkins, ed., *Medieval Romance and Material Culture*, pp. 41–57), adopts Michel de Certeau's concept of 'culturally constructed space' (p. 42) and Pierre Nora's notion of *lieux de mémoire* to advocate the reading of Middle English texts 'in place'. 'Emplaced' readings of *St Erkenwald*, *The Siege of Jerusalem*, and *Titus and Vespasian* shed particular light on London as 'a complex site of identity negotiation within the developing national fantasy of Englishness' (p. 41).

Eric Weiskott, 'Alliterative Metre and the Textual Criticism of the *Gawain* Group' (*YLS* 29[2015] 151–75), reflects on how current metrical theory might be used in the editing of Middle English texts. It is discussed in Section 10 below.

## 3. Manuscript and Textual Studies

Several editions of Middle English texts appeared in 2015. Jesús Romero-Barranco, *The Late Middle English Version of Constantinus Africanus' Venerabilis Anatomia in London, Wellcome Library, MS 290 (ff. 1r–41v)* is a semi-diplomatic edition of the *Anatomia*, keeping editorial interventions to a minimum in order to facilitate research into linguistics and the history of medicine. The edition pays close attention to the manuscript and to matters such as scribal hand, corrections, contraction, punctuation, and language, but does not directly discuss the text itself (though a glossary is supplied). John H. Chandler edited the poem *The King of Tars*, which can be dated to *c*.1330, for TEAMS Middle English Texts in 2015. An early version of the Constance story, in 1,241 lines it combines elements of hagiography, romance, miracle tale, and political drama; the editor discusses its generic challenges at length. *Tars* survives in three important medieval manuscript witnesses—the Auchinleck, Vernon, and Simeon manuscripts—and although the Auchinleck is the oldest of the three, its version is incomplete and variant. Nonetheless Chandler chooses it as his base text, stating that the variants present in the other two manuscripts are inferior and that they 'reflect a variety of scribal changes, from simple dialectical [*sic*] differences and scribal errors to large-scale textual revision' (p. 16), and noting too that there is very little missing when compared to the Vernon and Simeon versions. This edition has a comprehensive introduction, which discusses the work from a literary perspective, and the editor offers a detailed discussion of the choice of base-text manuscript and of the approaches taken by previous editors. The text itself is presented with marginal glosses, and has explanatory and textual notes as well as a full glossary and bibliography.

Peter Larkin's edition of *Richard Coer de Lyon* was also published by TEAMS Middle English Texts in 2015. This is a one of a few Crusade poems to survive in Middle English. This lengthy work (over 7,000 lines) is extant in seven manuscripts and two early prints.

TEAMS Middle English Texts also published *John Hardyng, Chronicle*, edited from British Library MS Lansdowne 204 (volume 1), edited by James Simpson and Sarah Peverley. John Hardyng composed this version of his 18,782-line verse *Chronicle* in the 1440s and 1450s; the prologue states that it was completed in 1457 when Hardyng was a corrodiary at the Augustinian priory of South Kyme. The work was probably presented to Henry VI that same year. Hardyng went on to write a second version for Richard, duke of York, promoting his claim to the throne, and it is this second, unfinished, version that enjoyed great popularity: it survives in twelve manuscripts and in two printed editions. Simpson and Peverley edit for the first time the complete version from British Library, MS Lansdowne 204, which they argue is Hardyng's presentation copy. Volume 1 contains Books I to III as well as a detailed introduction.

For the Middle English Texts series Janet Cowen edits the unique Middle English anonymous part-translation of Boccaccio's *De mulieribus claris* in London, British Library, MS Additional 10304, the first edition for over ninety years. It consists of nearly 2,000 lines of rhyme royal, and contains mentions of Lydgate's *Fall of Princes*. The manuscript, which can be dated to c.1440–60, is described in detail here, as is the source, the translation and versification, and—since the translator demonstrates an affinity—the allusions to and comparisons with Lydgate's work. Cowen's edition includes a particularly detailed commentary and glossary.

Also for Middle English Texts, Joanna Bellis published John Page's *Siege of Rouen*. This verse narrative, edited from London, British Library, MS Egerton 1995, is an eyewitness account of the siege laid by Henry V to Rouen in 1418–19 and, as Bellis notes, 'is unique ... in providing a first-hand narrative of a significant event in contemporary warfare' (p. xiii). It is partly preserved in some versions of the prose *Brut* chronicle. Bellis argues for both its literary value and its reliability as a historical source. The poem was probably written before the death of Henry in August 1422 and it is extant in fourteen manuscripts, only two of which are complete versions: Egerton 1995 and Oxford, Balliol College MS 354. Bellis supplies detailed descriptions of all manuscripts, as well as a discussion of the relationships between them. The edition has detailed variants and a glossary, textual commentary, and a list of names and places mentioned.

The Early English Text Society published *A Mirror to Devout People (Speculum Devotorum)*, edited by Paul J. Patterson. The text is a fifteenth-century Middle English life of Christ in the tradition of the pseudo-Bonaventuran *Meditationes Vitae Christi*, and is extant in two manuscripts: Notre Dame, University of Notre Dame, Hesburgh Library, cod. Eng. d. I (*olim* MS 67) and Cambridge University Library, MS Gg.1.6; a colophon in Latin in both manuscripts suggests that the text originated at the House of Jesus of Bethlehem at Sheen. Patterson suggests that an anonymous monk at Sheen probably wrote the text for a nun at the neighbouring Birgittine Syon Abbey. The editor also notes that the two extant manuscripts indicate a wider audience for the text outside the monastic setting; the Scrope family owned the Notre Dame manuscript in the Middle Ages. The editor also asserts that variations between the two manuscripts confirm that they were copied with two different audiences in mind. The edition uses the version found in the Cambridge manuscript as its copy text.

Also published in 2015 was *The Complete Harley 2253 Manuscript*, volumes 1 and 3, edited and translated by Susanna Fein, with David Raybin and Jan Ziolkowski, and completing the three-volume edition and translation of the entire manuscript. Volume 1 contains texts from booklets 1 and 2, together with explanatory and textual notes, an appendix of the full contents, an index of first lines, manuscripts cited, and proper names, and a bibliography. The first two booklets were copied by an older scribe (not Ludlow) and contain religious works in Anglo-French. Volume 3 focuses on the works in booklets 5–7, booklet 5 being the longest and most complex of the sections in Harley 2253 which contains the English lyrics, as well as the romance *King Horn*. Booklet 6 contains the largest collection of Anglo-Norman fabliaux found in England; booklet 7 is written in Latin and French and is a 'handbook of popular religion' (p. 17).

Finally, Oxford World's Classics published two new translations of Middle English prose texts in 2015, both sure to be widely used by students: *The Book of Margery Kempe*, edited by Anthony Bale, and *Julian of Norwich: Revelations of Divine Love*, edited by Barry Windeatt. The latter includes both the long and short versions of Julian's texts. Both translations are prefaced by introductions that pay attention to sources and issues of authorship.

Two editions were unavailable for review: Daniel M. Myers, *Recipes from the Wagstaff Miscellany: A Transcription of Beinecke MS 163* (Blackspoon Press) and John Adams and Stuart Forbes, eds., *The Syon Abbey Herbal: The Last Monastic Herbal in England c. AD 1517: From St. John's College, Cambridge Manuscript 109 (E.6)* (AMCD Publishers).

An important publication in 2015 was *Insular Books: Vernacular Manuscript Miscellanies in Late Medieval Britain*, edited by Margaret Connolly and Raluca Radulescu. Connolly and Radulescu's introduction (pp. 1–29) is a comprehensive survey of scholarly attitudes to 'multi-text' manuscripts as well as a consideration of some of the ways in which we might better appreciate the cultural significance and complex issues that such manuscripts embody. Marianne Ailes and Phillipa Hardman, in 'Texts in Conversation: Charlemagne Epics and Romances in Insular Plural-Text Codices' (pp. 31–47), examine both French and Middle English manuscripts of the insular Charlemagne texts, arguing that contexts that might initially seem to be miscellaneous in fact display certain unifying features that can be said to comment on the Matter of France material. Keith Busby's chapter, 'Multilingualism, the Harley Scribe, and Johannes Jacobi' (pp. 49–60), argues that although the term 'miscellany' is set to remain contentious, and although there is often no way of being certain about scribal authority, we question why certain texts are ordered and coexist in miscellany volumes. He considers the 'ramifications of multilingualism' in the work of the Harley scribe and in other insular manuscripts, comparing them to the work of a thirteenth-century Italian copyist. Multilingual miscellanies are also the chief concern in Ad Putter's contribution, 'The Organisation of Multilingual Miscellanies: The Contrasting Fortunes of Middle English Lyrics and Romances' (pp. 81–100). He asks why some miscellanies from the later Middle Ages that contain English texts are multilingual while others are not, noting that 'multi-text collections of miscellaneous content' are the main context for the dissemination of medieval English lyrics and romances.

In 'Literary Scribes: The Harley Scribe and Robert Thornton as Case Studies' (pp. 61–79), Susanna Fein argues for a category of agents operating in the later medieval period who fall into the space between an author and a copyist, who are 'scribes of a compiling and editorial bent who possess well-defined oeuvres, documentable locales, traceable affiliations, and observable habits and mindsets' (p. 62). The following three essays focus on particular manuscript miscellanies. Wendy Scase, in 'John Northwood's Miscellany Revisited' (pp. 101–20), examines London, British Library, Add. MS 37787, questioning the associations traditionally made between this volume and Cistercian involvement in literary production in the West Midlands. Raluca Radulescu, in 'Vying for Attention: The Contents of Dublin, Trinity College, MS 432' (pp. 121–42), assesses the effect of modern editorial practices on this manuscript, showing how the choice and presentation of texts have an influence on modern attitudes and interpretations. Andrew Taylor's essay, 'The Chivalric Miscellany: Classifying John Paston's "Grete Booke"' (pp. 143–56), revisits London, British Library, Lansdowne MS 285, finds analogies between the contemporary fanbook and the fifteenth-century miscellany. Carol M. Meale examines MSS Bodleian Tanner 407 and New Haven, Beinecke 365 in 'Amateur Book Production and the Miscellany in Medieval East Anglia' (pp. 157–73). She notes that these volumes have been categorized as commonplace books by editors, and argues that they are better understood as 'personal compilations' that can offer much evidence about the interplay between a compiler and their material.

William Marx's essay, 'Aberystwyth, National Library of Wales, MS Peniarth 12: The Development of a Bilingual Miscellany—Welsh and English' (pp. 247–62), traces the content, structure, and provenance of a manuscript that contains texts in Middle English and Latin but that privileges the Welsh language. Emily Wingfield's chapter, '*Lancelot of the Laik* and the Literary Manuscript Miscellany in 15th- and 16th-Century Scotland' (pp. 209–30), offers a summary of the main features of Scottish miscellanies from the period 1400–1600 before an examination of Cambridge University Library MS Kk.1.5. Oxford, Bodleian Library, MS Rawlinson C.813 is the subject of Deborah Youngs's contribution; in 'Entertainment Networks, Reading

Communities, and the Early Tudor Anthology' (pp. 231–46) she argues that, though the manuscript can be attributed to Humfrey Welles, we should not lose sight of the social and literary networks that influenced the production of the volume.

In 'Towards a Taxonomy of Middle English Manuscript Assemblages' (pp. 263–79), Julia Boffey and A.S.G. Edwards identify factors other than presentation, annotation, and choice of texts in miscellanies that may have significance for the shaping of a manuscript. They focus on miscellanies containing 'literary' material, and specifically on what we can learn about the production and classification of a manuscript, by looking at processes of assemblage. Finally Margaret Connolly's piece, 'The Whole Books and the Whole Picture: Editions and Facsimiles of Medieval Miscellanies and Their Influence' (pp. 281–99), provides an overview and discussion of the ways in which editors and scholars have chosen to present studies of manuscripts, catalogues, and digital editions and, importantly, how those decisions have shaped our scholarly perceptions. Ardis Butterfield supplies a brief afterword, bringing the discussion into the territory of Continental book production (pp. 301–5)

Michael Johnston and Michael van Dussen, in their introduction to *The Medieval Manuscript Book: Cultural Approaches* (pp. 1–13), state that the purpose of their collection is to move towards an appreciation of the medieval manuscript in the context of the literary and cultural history of medieval Europe. Seth Lerer, in 'Toward a History of the Premodern Book' (pp. 17–33), attempts to understand the book in the medieval and early modern periods as a kind of exploration of what it represented, not driven by technological advances but by social attitudes. In 'What Is a Manuscript Culture? Technologies of the Manuscript Matrix' (pp. 34–59), Stephen G. Nichols thinks through some of the issues involved in the role that medieval manuscripts played in shaping the culture of their time. In 'Decoding the Material Book: Cultural Residue in Medieval Manuscripts' (pp. 60–76), Erik Kwakkel considers how both readers and scribes left traces of their preferences, cultural milieux, intentions, and attitudes on the material book, factors that all contribute to its production and which in part can be recovered. Jeffrey Todd Knight, in 'Organizing Manuscript and Print: From *Compilatio* to Compilation' (pp. 77–95), addresses the 'space of indistinction between scribal and printed, personal and published, medieval and modern in the storehouse of English writing' (p. 79).

Siân Echard's 'Containing the Book: Institutional Afterlives of Medieval Manuscripts' (pp. 96–118) considers that practices of cataloguing and classifying manuscripts contain value judgements about the hierarchy of manuscript and text. She illustrates her point with manuscripts associated with the sixteenth-century collector Archbishop Matthew Parker. Martin K. Foys's 'Medieval Manuscripts: Media Archaeology and the Digital Incunable' (pp. 119–39) examines, through the eleventh-century London, British Library, Cotton Tiberius B.v, how the digitization of a manuscript alters the identity and meaning of a work by 'extending its media history into a new technological incarnation, a process that builds upon earlier remediations of the work in print and photography' (p. 119). In 'The Circulation of Texts in

Manuscript Culture' (pp. 140–59), Pascale Bourgain examines the movement and diffusion of text, establishing that at times copying did not ensure circulation or success, and examining the various processes that a text went through on its way to becoming firmly established in a textual tradition. Lucie Doležalová examines 'Multilingualism and Late Medieval Manuscript Culture' (pp. 160–80), noting similarities between medieval England and medieval Bohemia with respect to manuscripts that communicate in three languages, often reflecting 'contentious realities' even in limited geographical locations (p. 60). Arthur Bahr, in 'Miscellaneity and Variance in the Medieval Book' (pp. 181–98), emphasizes the temporal and conceptual gap that produces terms like 'miscellaneity' and 'variance', commonly used to describe medieval manuscripts. His work uses that 'gap' to produce new readings of them, advocating a blended approach that reflects variety and embraces a hybrid way of understanding medieval books.

In 'Vernacular Authorship and the Control of Manuscript Production' (pp. 199–214), Andrew Taylor considers the relationship authors in medieval Europe had with material texts. Kathryn Kerby-Fulton's 'Afterword: Social History of the Book and Beyond *Originalia*, Medieval Literary Theory, and the Aesthetics of Palaeography' (pp. 243–54) reviews the role that palaeography and codicology might have in the delivery of a social history of the manuscript and their influence on the recovery of a vocabulary of medieval literary theory.

Laura Esteban-Segura, in 'The Middle English *Circa Instans*: A Pharmacopoeia from Glasgow, University Library, MS Hunter 307 (U.7.1)' (*Manuscripta* 59:i[2015] 29–60), edits a previously unedited version of a glossary of botanical and pharmaceutical terms.

J.S. Adams has made his study of the books and manuscripts used at Syon Abbey, *Syon Abbey: Its Herbal, Medical Books and Care of the Sick: Healthcare in a Mixed Mediaeval Monastery* freely available online at < https://syonabbeysociety.files.wordpress.com/2012/09/syon-abbey-healthcare-and-medical-books-8-jan-2016.pdf >. The work is particularly focused on Thomas Betson, the last recorded librarian of Syon, and his notebook (including his herbal), and library catalogue.

Aisling Byrne and Victoria Flood, in 'The Romance of the Stanleys: Regional and National Imaginings in the Percy Folio' (*Viator* 46:i[2015] 327–52), link the manuscript with the construction of a local identity and dynastic mythology for the Stanley family.

Anthony McGrath explores 'Using Religious Art as Pictorial Evidence for Medieval Book History' (*BH* 18[2015] 22–47) to show how images of saints holding books in paintings, from the thirteenth century onwards, can help scholars learn more about the form and appearance of medieval book bindings from medieval western Europe.

Peter Murray Jones and Lea T. Olsan draw heavily on manuscript material in Middle English to analyse the rituals and performances that are associated with maternity and that are found in charms, prayers, and amulets before the 1500s. 'Performative Rituals for Conception and Childbirth in England, 900–1500' (*BHM* 89:iii[2015] 406–33) seeks to 'reveal medieval people in various roles involved in performing or providing rituals for conception and birth, and to bring attention to those who communicated rituals for purposes other than direct performance' (p. 408). A significant part of the paper looks at 'making rituals textual', and at the ways in which these performed pieces may have been recorded and were preserved and transmitted, referring to several late medieval English manuscripts in examples.

Rory G. Critten, in 'Bourgeois Ethics Again: The Conduct Texts and the Romances in Oxford, Bodleian Library MS Ashmole 61' (*ChauR* 50:i–11[2015] 108–33), focuses on shared ideas around comportment and behaviour that are manifested in romances and conduct texts. The manuscript in question here is of course a well-known repository of both kinds of texts, and Critten argues that its overarching concern is with a bourgeois ethos, while examining the different approaches evident in the various texts.

In 'Regendering the *Festial* in British Library MSS Harley 2247 and Royal 18.B.XXV' (*Comitatus* 46[2015] 117–40), Gabriel F. Hill shows how the popular sermon collection by John Mirk was revised and edited in two of its so-called 'Revision' manuscripts. Hill contends that, along with the parochial material edited out of the Revision so that it might appeal to a more elite readership, it is possible to discern that in the *sanctorale* sermons female saints are also revised in order to diminish their authority and power.

A.S.G. Edwards contributes 'Notes on Middle English Heraldic Manuscripts' (*N&Q* 62[2015] 217–18), supplementing and correcting the work of George Keiser for volume 10 of the *Manual of the Writings in Middle English*. Mayumi Taguchi, in 'A Hitherto Unidentified Middle English Translation of "Les Quatre Requêtes de Notre-Dame à Jésus"' (*N&Q* 62[2015] 364–7), is concerned with the English text found in Cambridge, University Library, MS Ff.vi.33, and its French source, a dialogue that forms part of the *Passion Isabeau*, a Passion narrative translated from Latin at the request of Isabeau de Bavière in 1398. And David Scott McNab writes on 'Three Discontinuous Fragments of *The Boke of Marchlasi* in a Private Collection' (*N&Q* 62[2015] 529–34).

Finally, the *Journal of the Early Book Society* (*JEBS* 18[2015]) contains several relevant articles. Ralph Hanna describes 'Making Miscellaneous Manuscripts in Fifteenth-Century England: The Case of Sloane 2275' (*JEBS* 18[2015] 1–28), a manuscript which he describes as a 'thorough mess'. It preserves Latin texts of Richard Rolle with the Middle English *Prick of Conscience*. Hanna attributes its 'messy' state to the fact that it was a communal production carried out by amateur bookmen. His article is a description of the compilational procedures they used, in particular their use of BNF lat. 15700 as an exemplar. Hanna also contributes a short article to the journal: 'The Sizes of Middle English Books, *c*.1390–1430' (*JEBS* 18[2015] 181–7). Nicole Clifton, in '*Kyng Alisaunder* and Oxford, Bodleian Library, MS Laud. Misc. 622' (*JEBS* 18[2015] 29–49), calls attention to the role of the material artefact in recovering the late medieval reception of and reaction to two Middle English romances, *Kyng Alisaunder* and *Titus and Vespasian*. Kathryn Walls, in 'Oxford, Bodleian Library, MS Laud Misc. 740 and New York, Public Library, MS Spencer 19: A Common History?' (*JEBS* 18[2015] 192–207), examines a pair of manuscripts that were likely produced by the same workshop and that, Walls hypothesizes, remained together until the seventeenth century. In 'New Findings in a Late-Medieval Catechetic Prose Sequence' (*JEBS* 18[2015] 228–40), Michael Madrinkian looks at the occurrence of a text known as the 'Exposition on the Creed' in two previously overlooked witnesses: Trinity College MS B.14.54 and London, Westminster School, MS 3.

Various articles connected with the scribe Adam Pynkhurst are considered in Chapter IV of this volume.

## 4. Early Middle English

This year saw the publication of an absorbing new monograph on affect and emotion in early Middle English texts, as well as important chapters and articles on *Ancrene Wisse*, homilies and devotional texts, and Laȝamon's *Brut*. The *South English Legendary*, *The Owl and the Nightingale*, and *Dame Sirith* also received attention in chapters and articles concerned with related topics.

A.S. Lazikani describes her book *Cultivating the Heart: Feeling and Emotion in Twelfth- and Thirteenth-Century Religious Texts* as 'a cartography of affective pain' in high medieval English literature (p. 1). She positions her work as a contribution to the history of emotions. She also develops her own vocabulary of affect, speaking in particular of 'affective sentience', the 'sensitivity, malleability even, that enables affective pain to be felt' (p. 13), and 'affective constellations', where physical and cognitive processes are closely involved and hard to distinguish (p. 18). Chapter 1 concerns the Lambeth and Trinity homilies. Here, Lazikani looks to Quintilian and Augustine to theorize the way medieval homilists engaged their listeners' emotions. The homilies themselves stimulate and manage forms of affective pain that were considered essential to penitential practice in this period, positioning the preacher and his imagined audience as part of an 'emotional community'. Chapter 2 reads a selection of saints' lives from the early version of the *South English Legendary* from Bodleian MS Laud Misc. 108. Lakizani shows that, while many saints in the *Legendary* suffer physical torment, the text often has more to say about the spiritual significance of their suffering than about the experience of pain itself. Chapter 3 argues that the *Ancrene Wisse* and the texts of the Wooing Group encouraged their anchoritic readers in practices of 'co-feeling', where multiple subjects inhabit the same affective space. The Virgin Mary models the practice of 'co-feeling' in her relationship to Christ by virtue of their bodily connection as mother and son. The fourth chapter argues for the affective sophistication of a wide range of thirteenth-century lyrics. Lazikani draws particular attention to the use of English to encourage responses in the context of multilingual texts. Throughout, Lazikani makes connections with twelfth- and thirteenth-century parish church wall paintings, whose own affective strategies are shown to complement and supplement those of the texts she discusses.

In 'Remembrance and Time in the Wooing Group' (in Cox et al., eds., pp. 79–93), Lazikani considers the different instances of the word *munegunge* ('remembrance') in the Wooing Group texts, and argues that anchoresses made use of mnemonic techniques to re-create the scene of the Passion in their devotion, and to foster an intimacy with Christ that was tangible and immediate. In particular, she shows how the practice of kissing the wound-places on the crucifix served to stimulate an 'intimate affective-somatic response'.

In 'Bathing in Blood: The Medicinal Cures of Anchoritic Devotion' (in Yoshikawa, ed., pp. 85–102), Liz Herbert McAvoy locates the *Ancrene Wisse* in a tradition of religious writing that employed metaphors of medical blood-letting to conceptualize the salvific effects of the Passion. McAvoy shows how the *Ancrene Wisse* links the practice of phlebotomy in the anchorhold to Christ's bleeding on the cross, and argues that the text's image of God as a mother who prepares a bath of her own blood for her child alludes to the practice of bathing new mothers as a cure for postpartum bleeding, described in *De curis mulierum*. In its treatment of these images, McAvoy argues, the *Ancrene Wisse* foreshadowed Julian of Norwich's image of Christ as both physician and nurturing mother.

Laȝamon's *Brut* was the subject of three book chapters. In '"Blisse wes on londe": The Feeling of Peace in Laȝamon's *Brut*' (in Downes, Lynch, and O'Loughlin, eds., *Emotions and War: Medieval to Romantic Literature*, pp. 42–59), Andrew Lynch contends that, while Geoffrey and Wace celebrate peace primarily as a consequence of military victory, Laȝamon attempts a description of peace per se, deploying 'a shifting cluster of motifs and effects in various combinations' to communicate what the feeling of peace is like (p. 43). For Laȝamon, Lynch argues, periods of peace point beyond temporal experience to the atemporal joys of heaven. Lynch returns to emotion in Laȝamon's *Brut* in '"What cheer?": Emotion and Action in the Arthurian World' (in Brandsma, Larrington, and Saunders, eds., *Emotions in Medieval Arthurian Literature: Body, Mind, Voice*, pp. 47–63; also discussed in Section 11 below). At the height of his powers, Laȝamon's Arthur harnesses his own emotions and those of his followers successfully for political and military ends, but his dream of Guinevere and Mordred's treachery produces powerful feelings of sorrow that cannot be transformed into just or effective action. In 'Mingling with the English in Laȝamon's *Brut*' (in Watson and Somerset, eds., *Truth and Tales: Cultural Mobility and Medieval Media*, pp. 96–114), Fiona Somerset considers the complex relationship between land, people, and language in the *Brut*. She argues that, in Laȝamon, 'Cultural and linguistic identity and place overlap and coalesce rather than remaining distinctive' (p. 101), in a context where no one people can hold the land securely, and where kings are often required to reimagine the divine sanctions and popular allegiances that guarantee their control of the land. Somerset shows how Laȝamon identifies parallels for this complex situation in the natural world through his frequent use of human–animal similes: often in the *Brut*, 'people and animals go to ground or burst forth on land (or in water) where they variously do or do not belong' (p. 108).

Stephen Pelle, George Younge, and M.J. Toswell throw new light on early Middle English sermons and pastoralia. Pelle identifies sources for two passages in the early Middle English dialogue *Vices and Virtues*, and a close analogue for a third, in 'The Date and Intellectual Milieu of the Early Middle English *Vices and Virtues*' (*Neophil* 99[2015] 151–66): the dialogue borrows from Anselm's *De humanis moribus* (which the author probably knew in its later, more widely disseminated, version, *De similitudinibus*), and from Hugh of St Victor's recasting of Jerome's Letter 66 in his *De sacramentis Christiane fidei*, and includes a phrase that appears in a modified form in John of Salisbury's *Policraticus*. The author's use of these sources helps make the case that this text was written in the second half of the twelfth century, and also argues for his familiarity with texts emerging from the schools of Paris, where he may have been educated himself. In 'The New Heathens: Anti-Jewish Hostility in Early English Literature' (in Conti, Da Rold, and Shaw, eds., *Writing Europe, 500–1450: Texts and Contexts*, pp. 123–45), Younge shows that while pre-Conquest texts maintained a conceptual distinction between Jews who followed God's law and heathens who did not, Jews are repeatedly described as heathens in post-Conquest texts. Of the four early Middle English 'Lambeth homilies' that derive material from Ælfric, for example, one replaces Ælfric's neutral references to Jews with references to heathens in contexts where the Jews are hostile to Christ's teaching, while another systematically revises out Ælfric's account of the difference between Jews and heathens. Reading the Peterborough Chronicle entry for 1137, which describes both the 'anarchy' of Steven's reign and the reported murder by Jews of William of Norwich, Younge contends that the chronicler draws connections between the actions of the barons and of the Jews, eliding the latter group with the Vikings as archetypal enemies of the Christian community. Toswell offers a new reading of a homily on Psalm 126:6 that appears in both the Lambeth and Trinity collections, in 'The Exegesis of Tears in Lambeth Homily 17' (in Watson and Somerset, eds., pp. 79–95). Much recent scholarship on these collections has asked whether they provide evidence of an unbroken tradition of vernacular preaching that continued after the Conquest. Toswell questions whether this debate throws much light on Lambeth 17. She proposes instead to read the sermon alongside contemporary bilingual psalter commentaries, as evidence of a late twelfth-century project to translate Latin pastoralia into English.

The final chapter of Rebecca Pinner's *The Cult of St Edmund in Medieval East Anglia* addresses 'Texts beyond Bury: Legendary Collections', and includes a discussion of the life of St Edmund from the *South English Legendary*. Pinner argues that this text presents Edmund as an exemplary model for a lay audience to emulate, emphasizing 'his representative piety, rather than his actual historical role as ruler' (p. 228).

In 'The Meaning of Middle English *Gent and Smal*' (*ChauR* 49[2015] 371–5), Krista A. Murchison considers the word-pair *gent and smal*, which forms part of Alisoun's *descriptio* in the *Miller's Tale*, and argues that it describes a body that is well-built and attractive, rather than 'slender' as the glosses of many modern editions have it. *The Owl and the Nightingale*, which contains the earliest record of this word-pair, provides important evidence to support this claim. *The Owl and the Nightingale* also makes a brief appearance in Paul S. Langeslag's *Seasons in the Literatures of the Medieval North*. Although the poem is not itself a debate between the different seasons, Langeslag argues that it opposes summer and winter implicitly through the seasonal associations of the owl and the nightingale themselves.

Finally, Jamie McKinstry offers a brief discussion of *Dame Sirith* in the conclusion to *Middle English Romance and the Craft of Memory* (considered in detail in Section 11 below). McKinstry argues that the references to seasonal rituals in this text are in tension with the timeless and static quality of the narrative.

## 5. Secular Verse

Joanna Bellis has made a significant contribution to the field of secular verse studies this year with the publication of an excellent edition of John Page's *The Siege of Rouen*. The poem is an eyewitness account of Henry V's siege of Normandy's capital, between 1418 and 1419. If we take the poet at his word, which Bellis does, he was present at the siege, and his narrative offers an intriguing blend of patriotism and compassion, verse chronicle and historical romance. Bellis makes a persuasive case for the critically neglected poem as 'rich and sophisticated' (p. xiv) and sketches what she perceives to be the ideological fault-lines between patriotism and horror, literariness and historicity, which lie at the poem's heart. The previous edition, by Herbert Huscher [1927], emended the base manuscript, London, British Library, MS Egerton (E), on the grounds of metre, to produce a more metrically regular text. Bellis, in well-justified contrast, emends E only on the basis of mechanical error, and what is clearly corruption, therefore producing a less smooth and regular, but more faithful, version of the poem. Her introduction, which includes summaries of authorship, date, and audience, metre and verse form, language, genre, literary background, and reception, is clear and thorough. The poem itself is cleanly presented, with no facing glosses or notes, but the commentary, glossary, and index of names and places at the back make for easy navigation. Also included as an appendix is the prose paraphrase of the first half of the poem in the *Brut*, which helps to set *The Siege of Rouen* in its historical and literary context.

Bellis's essay '"I was enforced to become an eyed witnes": Documenting War in Medieval and Early Modern Literature' (in Downes et al., eds., pp. 133–51) uses a number of verse narratives to explore the role of eyewitness accounts in the medieval and early modern periods, and the emotions they elicit in a reader. Together with John Page's poem she examines the *Life of the Black Prince* [1385], a chivalric biography of Edward, Prince of Wales. In both poems she identifies a tension between 'historical truth and literary prestige' (p. 139), between admiration for their rulers and compassion for those who suffered during their campaigns. She labels this tension 'the emotional paradox of eyewitnessing' (p. 150), noting that recording battles conferred prestige but also brought acute pressure. Her astute readings justify the claims she makes in her edition of the *Siege of Rouen*—that this neglected genre of eyewitness accounts is far more complex and worthy of attention than has previously been realized. Andrew Lynch's '"Blisse wes on londe": The Feeling of Peace in Laȝamon's *Brut*' (pp. 42–59), in the same collection, is reviewed above (Section 4).

Victoria Flood casts the fourteenth-century alliterative poem *Wynnere and Wastoure* into a new, political context in her article '*Wynnere and Wastoure* and the Influence of Political Prophecy' (*ChauR* 49[2015] 227–48). The article explores the relationship between the poem and a long-lived culture of political prophecy, particularly relevant during the reign of Edward III. In it, Flood challenges the traditional assumption that the poem presents war as a waste of resources. She argues instead that, by considering *Wynnere and Wastoure* in tandem with prophetic material from the twelfth century onwards, a triumphal structure underlying the poem can be revealed. The political vision of the poem, her reading suggests, balances investment with expenditure with regard to warfare, and therefore both 'articulates and resolves' complaint about the cost of war (p. 447). This convincing reading also sheds new light on the apparently pessimistic, prophetic material in the prologue to the poem. Rather than understanding this material as a foreshadowing, Flood instead suggests that the poem, written during a period when King Edward still promised great things, moves deliberately from disorder (in the prologue) to royal orderliness.

Charles d'Orléans English lyrics have received attention this year from Gabriel Haley. 'A Story about Song: Narrative Ethics Versus Lyric Isolation in Charles d'Orléans's English Lyrics' (*EssaysMedSt* 31[2015] 11–23) focuses on the English mixed-form sequence in British Library, MS Harley 682, a sequence which consists of ballades and roundels alongside sections of narrative verse. It was written while Charles was imprisoned, between 1415 and 1440, but is less concerned with the circumstances of imprisonment and more, Haley argues, with poetic ambition. In this new reading, which borrows heavily from poetic theory, particular attention is paid to the language of religious solitude, which, Haley suggests, can only be understood as an attempt to 'create lyric for lyric's sake' (p. 20). He believes that in this sequence d'Orléans grapples with 'the potential for the lyric to withdraw from all social obligations', and that this withdrawal is deliberately figured in terms of religious solitude, as justification for such withdrawal (p. 12). Most usefully, perhaps, Haley's reading helps to explain the final section of the sequence, which critics have tended to consider as a 'lesser' section. According to Haley's argument, the poet attempts to depart from a traditional, poetic model of epistolary love but fails to find another convincing option—religious solitude is experimented with as an alternative, but does not entirely succeed. He must therefore return, but only 'half heartedly', to the traditional form with which he began the sequence (p. 18).

Ardis Butterfield also considers the form and theory of lyric in her article 'Why Medieval Lyric?' (*ELH* 82[2015] 319–43). This ambitious, wide-ranging analysis of medieval lyrics begins with two specific material examples of lyrics on the medieval page: a mixed-language epistolary expression of love from a man to a woman, written on the back of a fifteenth-century legal roll, and a lyric embedded in a page from a medieval sermon manuscript. Butterfield helpfully provides images of these pages and draws comparisons between the 'handwritten culture' of lyrics in medieval manuscripts and the unexpected, fragmented jottings of Emily Dickinson. More broadly she challenges critical assumptions that lyric is not a term which can properly be applied to medieval verse, and discusses the problems of its categorization. She also examines the problems of analysing lyrics through close reading, and the role of music.

Jake Walsh Morrisey continues to transcribe and analyse previously unnoticed excerpts of medical verse with 'Additions to the Index of Middle English Verse: Unpublished Verse "Longinus" and "Job" Charms in British Library, MS Sloane 2187' (*N&Q* 62[2015] 22–5). In this article he focuses on two charms in a fifteenth-century miscellany. The Longinus charm, copied in the remaining space after an extract of Trevisa's translation of *De proprietatibus rerum* (by Bartholomaeus Anglicus), is not obviously related to any of the recorded verse examples of Longinus charms. The Job charm is more typical, with Job sitting on a dunghill as its central motif. Both have irregular metre, and Walsh Morrisey shows how they can both be productively considered alongside other ritual counting charms.

Charles Wuest takes the short Middle English riddle 'I have a ȝong suster' as his focus in 'Sisters are Sisters: Identity in an Anonymous Middle English Poem' (*PLL* 51[2015] 373–87). This early fifteenth century riddle poem is frequently anthologized but, as Wuest notes, has rarely been the subject of serious analysis. By reading the language closely, and exploring the various ambiguities of terms and words used, Wuest is the first to suggest that 'suster' may refer to a female sibling rather than a sweetheart. Such an interpretation, he suggests, gives readers 'a more pronounced sense of female agency and a more subtle understanding of eros' (p. 374). Read in this way, the riddle becomes more a debate than a one-sided expression of love, with two female characters offering contrasting views on the same idea. This reading is an appealing one, as it suggests a more complex outcome for the riddle. Rather than ending the debate, he suggests, the final lines of the riddle resist closure and actually reinforce the inconclusive, contradictory nature of desire itself.

This year saw the publication of *Poems from BL MS Harley 913, 'The Kildare Manuscript'*, edited by Thorlac Turville-Petre for the Early English Text Society. The Kildare Manuscript is a small miscellany containing Latin prose and verse, and English and French poems. The manuscript also provides the only extant glimpse of English lyric verse circulating in Ireland in the early fourteenth century. As well as providing a detailed description of the manuscript and an analysis of language and historical context, the edition includes a very useful summary of the religious and political tensions from which much of the manuscript's contexts grow, specifically the role and context of Anglo-Irish Franciscans in Ireland. Moreover, this section highlights the practical value of many of the English poems in the manuscript, which were part of the day-to-day preaching mission of the friars. In the edition proper, each poem is given a concise but insightful introduction. The notes are exhaustive, and frequently offer translations of difficult phrases.

## 6. Religious Verse

Annie Sutherland's study of Middle English psalm translations, *English Psalms in the Middle Ages, 1300–1450*, is a wide-ranging examination of both prose and verse translations. Sutherland begins with a summary of the liturgical prominence of the psalms, and the relationship between monastic and secular Uses, pointing out that, within both traditions, 'one's daily prayer life would have been heavily inflected by the language and sentiments of the psalms'. Although the public liturgical use would have been entirely in Latin, the large number of vernacular psalm translations in the fourteenth and fifteenth centuries points towards, suggests Sutherland, the supplementation and even replacement of the Latin texts in private contexts. The processes and nature of such translations (ranging from the literal to free paraphrase) are discussed in their wider cultural context, particularly in terms of ongoing debates about the vernacular employment of biblical material. The first chapter focuses on the manuscript dissemination of the vernacular psalms, both in the translations of the complete Psalter and the many abbreviated and paraphrased versions which indicate that 'there was a hunger for a brief, digestible version of the Psalter among religious and lay readers'. Sutherland then considers the English psalms in terms of translation theory, before moving on in chapters 3 and 4 to an examination of the practice of psalm translation in medieval England. Chapter 3 examines the detail and practices of the five complete surviving Middle English translations of the Psalter: the *Metrical* version, Rolle's translation and commentary, the *Prose Psalter*, and the two Wycliffite translations. By the late fourteenth and early fifteenth centuries, these complete psalters were supplemented by an increasing number of paraphrased and abbreviated versions of the psalms, and these form the subject matter of chapter 4, with a detailed comparison of translations in English-language primers, followed by an analysis of the wide range of verse approaches from the simplicity of rhymed verse intended to be easily memorable (in the Auchinleck manuscript and the complete versions of the Penitential Psalms), to the aureate embellishment of Lydgate's poetry, and finally an examination of the English psalm commentaries. Chapters 5 and 6 are concerned with the reading of these English psalms in the context of biblical exegesis which takes account of historical context as well as affective interpretation, leading to an active and prayerful engagement with the texts. Sutherland suggests that the translations of and commentaries on the psalms suggested a dual attitude to reading, that the Psalter should be viewed as 'an inviolate mystery', demanding a literalized reading and translation, but also 'a book ripe for interpretive adornment ... engendering multiple readings'. Sutherland finally turns to the bilingual manuscript context where English psalms are presented alongside the texts of the Latin Psalter, in order to further understand the way in which the English psalms were read and used, and their relationship with the Latin texts. Examining the presentation of the two languages on the pages of the codex, Sutherland moves away from suggestions of hierarchies and competing demands to consider the ways in which the Latin and English texts operate 'in cooperation'. At its simplest level, the Latin incipits provide a form of referencing, but there is also evidence that reading these manuscripts involves a repeated movement back and forth between the Latin and English, with the variation in forms of presentation having clear implications for reading practices. As Sutherland concludes, 'interactions with the Vulgate stimulated some of the most remarkable English literary experiments of the late Middle Ages'.

*Cultivating the Heart: Feeling and Emotion in Twelfth- and Thirteenth-Century Religious Texts*, A.S. Lazikani's study of affectivity, is broad-ranging in scope, although its main focus is on the affective strategies of English texts of the twelfth and thirteenth centuries. It examines sermons (the Lambeth and Trinity Homilies), saints' lives (the Early South English Legendaries), the *Ancrene Wisse*, and the Wooing Group, and lyric poetry, examining how the affective language employed might influence religious practice through the focused engagement of emotions such as sorrow, compassion, and love. The focus is, however, largely on the way these coalesce into affective pain, and Lazikani demonstrates, through a range of textual and visual sources, the processes of 'shaping, apprehending and attempting to express affective pain for audiences and readers'. The introduction summarizes the current state of scholarship in terms of textual affectivity and the specific texts under discussion; it clarifies terminologies and processes, providing a useful trilingual table of affective vocabulary (Latin, Middle English, and Anglo-Norman); and finally it summarizes some of the ways in which church wall paintings operate in conjunction with, and sometimes mirror, the affective processes of the written texts under discussion. This section reviews the chapter on lyric poetry; other chapters are discussed in Section 4 above. Chapter 4, 'Call Me Bitter: Feeling and Sensing in Passion Lyrics' (pp. 93–120), considers a number of thirteenth-century lyrics in terms of their multilingual contexts and origins in order to develop a picture of poems which build a sophisticated degree of affectivity through their formal strategies, their engagement with the senses, and the figuring of the human voice. This chapter moves swiftly through close readings of a large number of lyrics, treating each only briefly, but alongside other lyrics which operate in a similar manner or which are associated with one another textually. Particularly important is the emphasis this study places on the 'multilingual hinterland' that informs these lyrics. Through a focus on some macaronic poems, and lyrics in multilingual manuscripts, Lazikani explores the affective subtleties of the movements between Latin, French, and English. Another form of multi-layered complexity in Passion lyrics is uncovered through an examination of the way in which different affective states and points of focus are simultaneously held by the reader. This leads into a revisiting of the two-way relationship of compassion in dialogic poems, and concludes with a survey of some poems which isolate particular elements of the Passion narrative to be employed as affective 'triggers'.

Thorlac Turville-Petre has produced new editions of seventeen Middle English poems for the Early English Text Society in *Poems from BL MS Harley 913 'The Kildare Manuscript'* (also discussed in Section 5 above). As well as secular lyrics in English, and a number of Latin and French texts, this fourteenth-century Irish miscellany manuscript also contains several religious poems, and Turville-Petre suggests that one of the functions of the manuscript is as 'a sermon notebook'. These religious poems include a group of five metrical verse 'sermons' (with poetic qualities Turville-Petre describes as 'unsophisticated', commenting on 'the dreary recitation of basic tenets of faith'): on the Seven Sins, the vanity of life, the fifteen signs heralding doomsday, the Ten Commandments, and Christ's sufferings as a result of man's sin. There are also religious lyrics of probable English rather than Irish origin: one on Christ's sufferings on the cross (embedded in a Latin devotional text), a secular lullaby (closely related to two religious lullabies addressed to the Christ-child in Grimestone's preaching book) which focuses relentlessly on the future miseries of life, the brief verse 'Five Evil Things', and an expanded version of the well-known 'Earth' poems based on the Ash Wednesday liturgy, with alternating stanzas in English and Latin.

A chapter by Ellen Rentz, 'Reading the *Prick of Conscience* in the Parish' (in her *Imagining the Parish in Late Medieval England*, pp. 122–48), explores the ways in which this text combines a focus on individual salvation with repeated references to communal worship, and demonstrates how this is played out in practice in the commissioning of a stained-glass representation of the poem in All Saints' Church, York, which employs both visual image and textual quotation. Rentz argues that the poem emphasizes the 'purgatorial reciprocity' of the living and the dead within the specific parish, through the enactment of prayer, almsgiving, and participation in Mass by both priest and congregation, and that this communal enterprise is related to the idea of a spiritual community in heaven (as delineated in Book VII of the poem). The representation of aspects of the poem in word and image in the stained-glass window expands the content of the poem to encompass its readers in, suggests Rentz, images of individual and collective responses to the warnings of the text and the horrors of the end times. These apocalyptic images are localized to represent images of the city of York, which serve to bring the impact of the Last Judgement into the everyday lives of parishioners, at the same time as the frame images offer a model for response in acts of collective prayer. The stained-glass adaptation of the text operates in conjunction with other visual images and religious practices to reinforce relationships between priest and lay worshippers in effecting salvation through a movement 'from fear to worship'.

Takami Matsuda, in his chapter 'Purgatory and Spiritual Healing in John Audelay's Poems' (in Yoshikawa, ed., pp. 123–37), considers the way in which Audelay's writings explore various aspects of the relationship between physical and spiritual health. Physical sickness is employed as metaphor, and as representative of a bodily reality, not least in terms of Audelay's frequently referenced blindness, but as Matsuda indicates, the organization of the material always points towards Purgatory as a necessary stage towards spiritual wholeness. His intention is to represent spiritual healing as 'a single process that begins in this world and is completed after death in Purgatory'. Physical suffering, then, can be seen as part of the purgatorial process that, with God's grace (and as the salutations demonstrate, through the Virgin Mary as the 'soul's physician'), leads to healing. The penitential aspect of worldly suffering (and of physical illness that cannot always be cured) as a purgatorial process leads ultimately to the assurance of spiritual recovery and 'cure'.

Natalie Jones also considers Middle English religious lyric in her article, '"Of al the knottes that I se / I prese the knot in Trinite": Trinitarian Iconography in the Middle English Lyric, *An Aungell fro Heuen gan Lyth*' (*Viator* 46[2015] 193–218). Jones presents a reading of this fifteenth-century carol focusing on the motif of the Trinitarian knot which is explicitly present in the poem's burden, but also functions throughout the five stanzas as a meditative device building into a summary of the five mysteries of faith. This article explores the development of this motif of the 'endless knot' as representative of 'the indivisibility of the triune God' in a range of textual and visual sources, originating in Patristic exegesis where various Old Testament texts employ threefold motifs which were glossed as Trinitarian symbols. Early Christian iconography employs various motifs of interlacing lines or geometrical shapes to represent the Trinity, with a circular image being the form most commonly adopted from Augustine onwards, in both textual and diagrammatic representations. Jones demonstrates that the structure of the poem, following that of the Apostles' Creed, and with the burden linked to each stanza through rhyme, mirrors the underlying theological framework: the Christological focus of man's redemption in each stanza is completed through the full power of God in Trinity as represented in the burden, and as such distinguishes this poem from the many Passion-focused lyrics of the fifteenth century.

The various Middle English lyric translations and adaptations of the *Homo Vide* (a Latin carol depicting Christ's appeal from the cross) are the subject of Nicole D. Smith's article, 'Middle English Lyrics, *Homo Vide*, and *A Christian Mannes Bileeve*' (*N&Q* 62[2015] 17–22). Smith explores the textual relationship between the two lyrics, 'Leerne þou vnkynde man to be kynde' and 'Vnkind man take heed of me' in terms of their context within a prose commentary on the Apostles' Creed, *A Christian Mannes Bileeve*. She adds to the current cataloguing of these poems by drawing attention to the other manuscript witnesses of this commentary containing the lyrics, and provides a new transcription of the text of the first of these two lyrics from Washington DC, Library of Congress, Rare Books and Special Collections MS 4, fos. 64$^r$–78$^r$, s. XV$^{in}$. Finally, Smith suggests that the distinctive manuscript context of the poem in *A Christian Mannes Bileeve* indicates an aristocratic female readership, where the other Middle English translations of the *Homo Vide* sit alongside sermons and other homiletic material, but the manuscripts under discussion here contain other catechetical works aimed directly at an aristocratic lay audience, without the intervention of a preacher, and this appears to be confirmed by evidence of female ownership of three of the four exemplars.

John Capgrave's verse *Life of St Katharine* is discussed alongside the *Revelation* of Julian of Norwich, in an article by Cristina Maria Cervone, 'Julian of Norwich and John Capgrave: Foul Black Dede Hame / Hame of Blyndnes' (*JEGP* 114[2015] 88–96). Cervone analyses the use of the relatively uncommon noun 'hame' in the works of the two writers, considering the similarities of context in terms of the idea of spiritual blindness, despite the differences of meaning (and the difficulties of interpretation due to the obscurity of the word and the problematic manuscript evidence in the case of Julian).

In '*The Sege of Melayne* and *The Siege of Jerusalem*: National Identity, Beleaguered Christendom, and Holy War During the Papal Schism' (*ChR* 49[2015] 402–26), Marco Nievergelt examines these two Middle English poems in the context of their composition at the time of the papal schism of 1378–1415. Nievergelt suggests that the psychological consequences of the schism in terms of 'generalized anxiety' and 'a shifting, threatened sense

of identity' were played out in these texts in terms of their narrative
engagement with ideas of the religious 'Other' (Jews and Saracens) being
successfully defeated by Christians, thus reinforcing the rhetoric of a stable
and unified Christian identity. However, the ambivalent representation of
both Jews and Romans in *Jerusalem*, and the self-inflicted violence of
martyrdom in *Melayne*, complicate the understanding of its contemporary
significance (the papal schism and the Hundred Years War), whereby the
religious Other is seen to be an 'inverted image' of the western Christian self.

## 7. Secular Prose

Several articles addressing secular literary prose appeared in 2015. Kari Anne
Rand extends her earlier work [1993] in 'The Authorship of the *Equatorie of
the Planetis* Revisited' (*SN* 87[2015] 15–35). She argues that the text in
Cambridge Peterhouse MS 75.I is an autograph of John Walsingham, a monk
of St Albans. The *Equatorie of the Planetis* is likely partly original and partly a
translation of a now lost Latin text. Rand traces Walsingham's life, which
included travels to Tynemouth and Flanders. Walsingham's hand may also be
found in Oxford Laud Misc. 657 and Cambridge, Pembroke College MS 82. In
'Sir John Mandeville's God(s)' (*ELH* 82[2015] 431–60) Theresa Tinkle
examines the ways in which God is represented in the *c*.1400 Defective
version of Mandeville's *Travels*. She argues that 'Mandeville's narrative
foregrounds the late medieval deity's discursive multiplicity, encompassing as
it does Crusade rhetoric, meditations on the life and Passion of Jesus,
scholastic philosophy about natural religion, the wonders of the east, and
assorted examples of Christian and non-Christian affective piety' (p. 454). In
'Failure before Print (The Case of Stephen Scrope)' (*Viator* 46[2015] 343–72),
Sonja Drimmer examines three manuscripts of Stephen Scrope's *Epistle of
Othea* to determine why Scrope failed to create relationships with his potential
patrons. Through a close reading of Scrope's prologues and of legal
documents related to Scrope, Drimmer demonstrates that the author's desires,
expressed in the prologues, were not well reflected by the ways in which the
manuscript objects themselves presented the text, and these manuscripts had a
great influence on the way their readers reacted to the work and its author.

William Caxton's books are at the heart of Merridee L. Bailey's exploration
of how political and social fears manifested themselves in literature aimed at
the mercantile classes and the children of merchants in 'Anxieties with Political
and Social Order in Fifteenth-Century England' (in Broomhall, ed., *Authority,
Gender, and Emotions in Late Medieval and Early Modern England*, pp. 84–
105). Peter Ramey, in 'The Poetics of Caxton's "Publique": The Construction
of Audience in the Prologues of William Caxton' (*ES* 96[2015] 731–46),
demonstrates how Caxton creates an 'aesthetics of access' (p. 735) in his
prologues and epilogues that actively courts a public readership from a broad
range of classes and dialects. Ramey uses the prologue to Caxton's *Le Morte
Darthur* to demonstrate how Caxton constructed his public audience.

Middle English mirrors for princes are explored by Matthew Giancarlo in
'Mirror, Mirror: Princely Hermeneutics, Practical Constitutionalism, and the

Genres of the English *Fürstenspiegel* (*Exemplaria* 27[2015] 35–54). Focusing in particular on the mirrors written by Hoccleve and Trevisa, he concentrates on their use during times of political instability as didactic, self-authorizing texts upholding sovereignty. *Fürstenspiegel* were composed of 'sedimented' or long-standing ideas about kingly authority and 'accreted' elements added to suit changing ideas about the role of a prince: 'the late medieval English mirror was uniquely important in its time not simply as practical *Fachliteratur* but for its critical reflection of images of rule and licit authority, and for the means it provided to think it through' (p. 50). Giancarlo makes a final feint towards placing the *Fürstenspiegel* at the root of modern notions of personal sovereignty. Caoimhe Whelan examines portions of James Yonge's Hiberno-English translation of the *Secreta secretorum* in 'The Notary's Tale' (in Booker and Peters, eds., *Tales of Medieval Dublin*, pp. 119–34). Whelan is particularly interested in Yonge's self-portrayal and his attempts to flatter the translation's patron, James Butler, fourth earl of Ormond. She draws particular attention to the political and personal factors at work in Yonge's interpolations.

Secular prose encompasses traditional literary prose texts, but scholars are increasingly exploring the literary merit of texts created for professional or practical uses; a number of studies of the latter type were published in 2015. In *Unwritten Verities: The Making of England's Vernacular Culture, 1463–1549*, Sebastian Sobecki explores the foundations and growth of the use of English and Anglo-French in common law and statute law. Treating texts related to the practice of law as literary texts, he argues that 'the oral education and practice of the common law paradoxically inscribed a normative consensus in the profession that came with its unwritten set of hermeneutics, an interpretive toolkit for the application of the law' (p. 8). This memorized and orally transmitted idea of law allowed flexibility as the oral legal culture shifted to a written culture in the early modern period. He divides his argument into two sections, 'Foundations' and 'Transformations'. 'Foundations' establishes the elements of late medieval law that would lead to the early modern 'Transformations': the growth of a printed textual body of law in English and the idea of consensual rule. His first chapter explores the oral underpinnings of the training of lawyers at the Inns of Court in the fifteenth century. He then considers the relationship of insular French to English in legal spheres. The two languages worked together as a single vernacular 'Franglais' (p. 45). For example, Osbern Bokenham uses law French alongside English in his *Mappa Angliae*, 'placing the two codes in a horizontal relationship with one another' (p. 55). Sobecki then focuses on Lancastrian political language, particularly the writings of John Fortescue, arguing that political language stemmed from the 'principle of consensual rule and institutionalized counsel' (p. 87). Chapter 4 explores the persistence of a largely unwritten common law in the face of the religious and political upheavals of the mid-sixteenth century. Sobecki then turns to John Rastell, arguing that Rastell's prefaces to his law books promote a type of law accessible to a broad audience and promoting a sense of 'Englishness'; '[Rastell's] law publications advocate a coherent ideology of political participation in a vernacular commonwealth' (p. 15). The final chapter further explores the practice and implications of the idea of the commonwealth

promoted by the vernacular legal writings of Fortescue, Rastell, and
Christopher St German. Sobecki's afterword contemplates the fate of the
common law in Tudor England and the pressures on its unwritten nature.
'Over the second half of the sixteenth century the crown eventually decided not
to codify or reform English law. Instead, a number of internal appointments at
the Inns of Court coupled with increased control of the law printing industry
provided checks on the independence of the profession and its hermeneutics of
unwritten verities' (p. 188). In treating legal works as literature, *Unwritten
Verities* provides a fresh foray into the study of late medieval and early
modern legal culture and its texts and encourages further similar
investigations.

Several of the chapters in *Language in Medieval Britain: Networks and
Exchanges*, edited by Mary Carruthers, address English prose in works and on
objects that are not traditionally considered literary. The collection of essays
as a whole focuses on the multilingual nature of language use in late medieval
Britain and Ireland. In '"Vestiges of Conversations"? The Medieval Building
Agreement and Architectural Language' (pp. 7–32), Alexandrina Buchanan
explores the language and uses of later medieval architectural contracts,
concluding that these contracts reflect contributions made by both builder and
patron. Christopher Woolgar, in 'The Language of Food and Cooking'
(pp. 33–47), concludes that language in the recipe books of upper-class
kitchens was often restricted to Anglo-French, but a large English vocabulary
existed among the lower classes for commonly used foods, such as cereals and
sauces. Paul Brand explores the use of language in the law courts *c.*1300 in
'The Languages of the Courtroom in England' (pp. 48–58), discovering heavy
use of Latin, some use of 'law French', and occasional use of English. He also
posits a difficult-to-trace language of gesture. In 'Text and Image: The
Language of Seals in Medieval England and Wales' (pp. 59–73), Elizabeth A.
New argues that seals, some with legends in English, have their own language
consisting of text and image; these elements work together in precise ways to
impart meaning within a particular cultural milieu. This language was legible
to individuals who would not normally be considered literate. In 'Language
and Register in English Medieval Surgery' (pp. 74–89), Peter Murray Jones
examines medical remedy books, particularly those of John Gaddesden, John
Mirfield, and John Arderne. Jones demonstrates that both Latin medical
writing and its English translations employ different registers—practical and
formulaic—to forge a relationship between the academic physician and the
more practical surgeon. In 'Rhetorical and Random Language Mixing in a
Fifteenth-Century Medical Manuscript (BL Harley MS 2390)' (pp. 90–103),
Linda Ehrsam Voigts concludes that English translations of Latin medical
books were more likely to be on the practical matters of treatment rather than
on the theoretical underpinnings of medical practice. In particular, she focuses
on the use of Latin words and phrases in two texts in BL Harley 2390, which
she concludes were used by a travelling physician who was bilingual in English
and Latin and who used Latin to underscore his skill to largely monolingual
audiences. Jessica Brantley focuses on multilingual Books of Hours from
England in 'Language Mixing in English Books of Hours' (pp. 104–16). The
Book of Hours composed and illuminated by John Lacy of Newcastle

(Oxford, St John's College MS 94) includes prayers in English. These prayers were an integral part of the manuscript, and reflect a conversation between Latin and vernacular cultures. Finally, Nicholas Orme, in 'Schools and Languages in Medieval England' (pp. 152–67), explores the use of vernaculars, including English, in translations of Latin school books and as a means of teaching Latin grammar.

Two articles in *Approaches to Middle English: Variation, Contact, and Change*, edited by Juan Camilo Conde-Silvestre and Javier Calle-Martín, deal with Middle English secular prose. In 'On Medieval Wills and the Rise of Written Monolingual English' (pp. 35–54), Laura Wright uses wills dating from the late fourteenth to the late fifteenth century to analyse the relative use of Latin, Anglo-Norman French, English, and mixed language during this century. After a brief discussion of the writers of wills and the constituent parts of wills, Wright demonstrates that the shift from Latin and French to English included a long period marked by code-switching and mixed-language documents prior to a final switch to monolingual English. Laura Esteban-Segura reports on the use of part-of-speech tagging software to analyse Middle English texts in 'Two Middle English Texts in the Light of the *Málaga POS Tagger of Middle English*' (pp. 149–59). The Middle English translation of Lanfranc of Milan's *Anatomia* and an anonymous Middle English text in a *Book of Astronomy* (London, Wellcome MS 411) are tagged, and Esteban-Segura analyses the errors and proposes solutions to them, promoting the software as a useful tool for analysis of Middle English.

Non-traditional secular prose texts, particularly practical treatises and reference works, were also well represented in journal articles. Matthew Boyd Goldie explores late medieval conceptions of geography in 'An Early English Rutter: The Sea and Spatial Hermeneutics in the Fourteenth and Fifteenth Centuries' (*Speculum* 90[2015] 701–27). This fifteenth-century navigational treatise, both in its text and the accompanying images, demonstrates a 'manner of experiencing space [that] is *horizontal* in that its somatic and visual experience is edged by the horizon and within a band that is parallel to the earth and sea' (pp. 726–7). In 'Mantic Alphabets in Late Medieval England, Early Modern Europe, and Modern America: The Reception and Afterlife of a Medieval Form of Dream Divination' (*Anglia* 132[2015] 641–75), László Sándor Chardonnens explores the transmission of alphabetic texts used for dream divination. He concludes that mantic alphabets died out in the seventeenth century. They were revived in North America in the nineteenth century as a system for selecting lucky numbers, and such alphabets persist to this day. The North American alphabets, however, are not textually related to the late medieval ones. Chardonnens also provides an edition of the fifteenth-century mantic alphabet in Oxford, Balliol College, MS 329, fo. 79ᵛ. Emily Steiner takes up the issue of genre in compendia, focusing in particular on those of Ranulph Higden and John Trevisa, in 'Compendious Genres: Higden, Trevisa, and the Medieval Encyclopedia' (*Exemplaria* 27[2015] 73–92). She argues that the genre of compendia helped shape other related genres. The accretive nature of compendia allowed Higden and Trevisa to define and move between genres of long texts, such as the encyclopedia and history, and shorter texts, such as the lyric.

Letters, contracts, and other personal correspondence also received attention. Bruce Watson offers an edition and image of the 1477 wedding invitation
sent to William FitzWilliam of Sprotborough, Yorkshire, in 'An Invitation to
the Wedding of Richard, Duke of York' (*Ricardian* 25[2015] 55–9). In 'Ends
and Beginnings in London Merchant Epistolary Rhetoric, *c*.1460–1520' (in
Donavin and Stodola, eds., *Public Declamations: Essays on Medieval Rhetoric,
Education, and Letters in Honor of Martin Camargo*, pp. 125–45), Malcolm
Richardson examines merchant education and analyses letters and guild
documents. He traces the rise of narrative in guild documents and the decline
of formulaic hypotaxis in the letters of merchants as their authors increasingly
used English and adopted forms that were more suitable to mercantile
requirements and relationships.

Unavailable for review was Jessica Berenbeim's Art of Documentation:
Documents and Visual Culture in Medieval England (PIMS).

## 8. Religious Prose

Annie Sutherland's monograph *English Psalms in the Middle Ages 1300–1450*
(also discussed in Section 6 above) provides a study of the vernacular psalm
tradition in late medieval England. Examining the psalms in the context of
translation theory and practice, Sutherland considers them as relating and
responding to the formal Latin liturgy. Of particular interest here are chapters
3 and 4, in which she offers a comparative textual analysis of Middle English
psalters, including Richard Rolle's *English Psalter*, the Wycliffite Psalms, the
Midland *Prose Psalter*, Walter Hilton's commentary on Psalms 90 and 91, and
Eleanor Hull's commentary on the Penitential Psalms. Sutherland argues
persuasively for 'a nexus of connections' between the versions of the Psalter
rather than patterns of direct influence. This extensive study offers valuable
insight into the processes, texts, and material products of the devotional
culture of the late Middle Ages.

Amy Appleford's *Learning to Die in London, 1380–1540* is discussed in
Section 1 above.

This year continuity, cross-faith, and English writing in a European context
emerge as something of a trend in the essays listed here. Sabrina Corbellini,
Margriet Hoogvliet, and Bart Ramakers, eds., *Discovering the Riches of the
Word: Religious Reading in Late Medieval and Early Modern Europe*, is a
collection of essays that explores a variety of approaches to biblical,
catechetical, and devotional texts. The material crosses the usual faith and
national boundaries to explore religious writing from the thirteenth to the
seventeenth century. Corbellini's introductory essay stresses continuity of
texts, and of earlier reading practices and strategies in the later period. Two of
the essays pertain to Middle English religious vernacular prose. Matti Peikola,
in 'Manuscript Paratexts in the Making: British Library MS Harley 6333 as a
Liturgical Compilation' (pp. 44–67), explores the paratextual material that
accompanies the Gospel Harmony *Oon of Foure* and the Later Versions (LV)
of the Wycliffite Bible in British Library MS Harley 6333. Ian Johnson's essay,
'From Nicholas Love's *Mirror* to John Heigham's *Life*: Paratextual

Displacements and Displaced Readers' (pp. 194–216), outlines a series of adaptations of the Middle English Love's *Mirror* which enabled its continuity among minority groups of readers in the seventeenth century. In a deftly written piece, he examines the *Mirror* against the 1606 Douai edition of Love's work and the 1622 revision of the *Mirror* by John Heigham, both printed by C. Boscard.

Also on the pseudo-Bonaventuran tradition, an essay by Alan F. Westphall, 'On Not Melting into Tears: Managing Meditative Reading in Michigan State University Library, MS 1 and Cambridge, Magdalen College, MS Pepys 2125' (*MÆ* 84[2015] 231–57), explores the Passion narrative found in two of the *Mirror* manuscripts, both of which are influenced by material from other sources. Westphall emphasizes the 'regulating and legitimizing' influence of these two versions of the Passion, which enabled readers to transpose experiences of spiritual aridity into human unworthiness, thereby leading to remorse and contrition. The European context and the *Meditationes Vitae Christi* also play a part in Mayumi Taguchi's article, 'A Hitherto Unidentified Middle English Translation of "Les Quatre Requêtes de Notre Dame à Jésus"' (*N&Q* 62[2015] 364–7). Taguchi introduces 'Of iiij requestes of Oure Lady made to hyr sone Ihesu', a short Middle English translation of a French Passion narrative found in Cambridge, University Library, MS Ff.vi.33 (fos. 33$^r$–37$^r$) and Cambridge, Magdalene College, Pepys Library, MS 2125 (fos. 144$^r$–145$^r$). An edition of the Middle English is presented in an appendix. As with the previous item, indexers of the *IMEP* volumes should take particular note of Jennifer Brown's discovery of the misattribution of four short Middle English Catherine of Siena excerpts which come, not from the *Dialogue* as is commonly understood, but from William Flete's *Documento Spirituale* and Raymond of Capua's *Legenda Major*. In 'The Many Misattributions of Catherine of Siena: Beyond *The Orchard* in England' (*JMRC* 41[2015] 67–84), Brown points to potential further study in the anthologizing of Catherine's writings and the connection with the Austin friars, of which Flete (who lived in Siena from 1357) was a member. Appended to the article is a useful list of the Catherine manuscripts in England.

The challenge of reconciling Julian of Norwich's compassionate view of human sin with the more condemnatory approach of the Church is the topic of Julian Sirko's article, 'Making "Penance Profitable": Julian of Norwich and the Sacrament of Penance' (*JMRC* 41[2015] 163–86). Sirko contends that Julian reappropriates the language of the sacrament of penance to form and create her own penitential practice, thereby transcending the Church's orthodox view of sin. Justin M. Byron-Davies identifies reformist tendencies in Julian of Norwich's *Revelations*. In his article, '"Holy Church shall be shaked": Reformist Tendencies in Julian of Norwich's *Revelations of Love*' (*Magistra* 21[2015] 68–89), he argues that each of the revelations 'exhort[s] and reprimand[s]'. Byron-Davies argues that Julian's focus is so positive, particularly in relation to soteriology and gender, that it implies criticism of the medieval Church's stance on these issues. He goes on to demonstrate her interest in the community of believers, which 'frames' the theme of 'repristination' at the heart of her work.

Fumiko Yoshikawa, in 'Julian of Norwich and the Medieval Rhetorical Arts of Preaching' (*Magistra* 21[2015] 90–109), addresses the challenge that Julian's desire to teach and preach poses to the Church, in which these activities are regarded as predominantly male. Using the *Forma praedicandi* by Robert Basevorn as her model, she suggests that one can identify rhetorical preaching devices of the new type of preaching (*sermo modernus*) in Julian's writing, but acknowledges the difficulty in establishing the source or intent of these devices. It is possible that Julian 'picked up' these strategies rather than deliberately studied the art of preaching.

Writing as a tool for memory informs Kisha G. Tracy's article, 'Julian of Norwich and the Sin of Forgetfulness' (*JMRC* 41[2015] 148–62). She argues that forgetfulness is blamed for sin because it separates the sinner from God, but it is also the mode to redemption because it provides Julian with the motivation to write. In turn, writing allows Julian to ruminate on her experience in order to deepen her understanding, and to seek repentance and forgiveness. Tracy argues persuasively that memory and its corollary, forgetfulness, are important elements in Julian's writing, including her consideration of forgetfulness as essential for those who wish to achieve spiritual perfection because it enables the sinner to forget worldly things and direct his or her sole attention to God. Cristina Maria Cervone, 'Julian of Norwich and John Capgrave: Foule Black Dede Hame / Hame of Blyndnes' (*JEGP* 114[2015] 88–96) draws attention to the unusual occurrence of the word 'hame' as referring to human skin or membrance in the writings of both Julian of Norwich and John Capgrave. In Julian of Norwich, the term refers to the 'skin' of humanity that hides Christ's divinity. In John Capgrave's *Life of St. Katherine* it is a reference to a membrane that shields Katherine from view of the priest as she is baptized. Cervone's work suggests that a side-by-side, comparative study of these two East Anglian writers might be a productive enterprise for future scholars. Paul Allen Miller briefly addresses Julian of Norwich's writing in 'Enjoyment Beyond the Pleasure Principle: Antigone, Julian of Norwich and the Use of Pleasure' (*The Comparatist* 39[Oct. 2015] 47–63).

Miller invokes Foucault, as does Kimberly Hope Belcher in '"My Body Free to God": Pilgrimage as a Technology of Self in the Book of Margery Kempe' (*Spiritus* 15[2015] 155–71). Belcher holds that Margery's spiritual identity is a combination of Christian identities (e.g. virgin, mystic, apostle), which are embodied in that of the pilgrim. Being a pilgrim allows Margery freedom from the traditional paths to female sanctity such as monastic enclosure or marriage, but at the same time offers other 'disciplinary practices' or 'technologies of the self', such as renunciation of the comforts of the world. Furthermore, through her writing about pilgrimage, Margery can shape her experiences into an 'accepted model' of feminine holiness, a saint in progress. Laura Varnam, 'The Crucifix, the Pietà, and the Female Mystic: Devotional Objects and Performative Identity in *The Book of Margery Kempe*' (*JMRC* 41[2015] 208–37), argues for the interplay of devotional objects and the devotional text as evidenced in the *Book of Margery Kempe*. For example, Margery's desire that the crucifix embrace her was taught her by devotional literature. Varnam holds that objects of devotion, such as the crucifix or Pietà, offered lay people the opportunity to enact and create moments and spaces of holiness outside the official Church, and therefore offered the opportunity for 'performative self-fashioning'.

Sebastian Sobecki published one of the ground-breaking pieces of research of 2015 in '"The writyng of this tretys": Margery Kempe's Son and the Authorship of Her Book' (*SAC* 37[2015] 257–83). His discovery of two documents builds the case for the historical reality of Kempe and her narrative, providing fresh insight into the process of composition of the *Book of Margery Kempe*. A letter written in 1431 in Danzig (modern-day Gdańsk) reveals the name of Margery's once wayward son and the purpose of his journey to Lynn, while a second document corroborates the identity of Robert Spryngolde as the cleric who had strong ties with Margery's family, and therefore as the probable clerical scribe behind her book. According to the letter, now held in the National Archives in Gdańsk, John (Margery's son) went to England to recover a debt. The second document (CP40/677, Norwich, 1430), previously unnoticed, links Spryngolde to Margery's elder brother (Robert Brunham) as the executor of the latter's will, and therefore having strong ties to Margery and her family. Sobecki calculates that John Kempe would have arrived at his mother's in late July or early August; he died there in September 1431, which corresponds with the second scribe's (Spryngolde's) claim to have begun writing the book in 1436, four years or more after the first attempt at her story was begun. Sobecki goes on to argue that the historical reality of Margery's story is the impetus for the 'anonymizing tendency' of the *Book*, which he claims removes it from the shadow of the 'Brunham dynasty'. In his deliberations on the compositional process of the *Book*, he recognizes its collaborative nature. Margery tells her story to a local audience, coloured with 'localized and historicized' detail. Spryngolde, on the other hand, employs a distancing technique, including the use of terms like 'creatur' and the anonymizing 'N', indicating his desire to create a story of universal experience with the same 'geographical mobility' as the protagonist. This is a compelling piece of research, persuasively delivered.

Barbara Zimbalist also stresses the universal appeal of *The Book of Margery Kempe* in her article 'Christ, Creature, and Reader: Verbal Devotion in *The Book of Margery Kempe*' (*JMRC* 41[2015] 1–23). She offers a detailed study of the 'literary representation' of conversations between Margery and Christ. Margery moves through quotation of Christ's speech, to imitation, to participation (by paraphrasing), instruction, and prayer, thereby providing a model of engagement with the Divine that moves beyond the affective corporeal response traditionally associated with the female devotee. Margery, by recording the dialogues between Christ and herself, offers future readers a 'textual exemplar' on how to imitate her encounters with the Divine.

Gabriel Hill, 'Pedagogy, Devotion and Marginalia: Using the *Pore Caitif* in Fifteenth-Century England' (*JMRC* 41[2015] 187–207), examines the marginalia in the manuscripts of the *Pore Caitif*, arguing that the catechetical material was of greater interest to medieval readers than any of the so-called Wycliffite and/or mystical material that often attracts the attention of modern scholars. His examination of six of the most heavily annotated manuscripts suggest that readers were more interested in the tracts on the Ten Commandments and the notes on instruction of children.

Joshua Easterling, '"Love will not be idle": Penance, Fantasy and Desire in Richard Rolle's *The Form of Living*' (*Exemplaria* 27[2015] 205–21), explores the tension in Rolle's distrust of bodily penitential practices. The anchorite's or contemplative's tendency towards askesis for the sake of spiritual redemption when faced with the incompleteness of one's self in the face of the Divine other, is fraught. Recognizing similarities to psychoanalytic approaches to the self, Easterling reads Rolle as cautious about ascetic practices because they maintain a focus on the body and spirit, keeping them in a circular, closed economy of exchange. Rolle's *Meditation on the Passion* is the subject of a detailed study by Daniel McCann in 'Medicine of Words, Purgative Reading in Richard Rolle's *Meditation on the Passion A*' (*MedJ* 5[2015] 53–83). McCann carefully illustrates how Rolle's use of medicinal terms goes beyond the figurative; it is also 'a statement of purpose'. He offers some contextual background on reading and its effect on affectivity before providing a close reading in which he demonstrates the 'adept use' that Rolle makes of poetic structures to induce an affective experience in his reader that will purge sin and heal the spirit. Kinga Lis, 'Richard Rolle's Psalter Rendition: The Work of a Language Purist?' (*StAPos* 50[2015] 45–70) challenges the linguistic purism that has been claimed for Rolle's psalter, arguing that the claim is anachronistic given the multilingual environment of medieval England. Lis tests nouns of the first fifty psalms in both Rolle's Psalter and the other Middle English prose psalters (Wycliffite and Middle English Glossed Prose Psalter). Through her comparative analysis, she concludes that the Rolle psalter used more Old Norse and Romance words than the other psalters, a fact that one might expect from a text produced in the north of England. Again, Daniel McCann looks at the use of interjectory words, grammars, and other texts in 'Words of Fire and Fruit: The Psychology of Prayer Words in the *Cloud of Unknowing*' (*MÆ* 84[2015] 213–30). He argues that in medieval psychology the interjection is perceived as an expression of the affective and irrational. Drawing on the writings of Augustine, Hugh of St Victor, Bacon, and others, he examines specifically the nouns *sinne*, *God*, and *fiir* in the *Cloud*. Although they are simple and monosyllabic, these words both evoke and express at once, thereby contradicting the commonly held notion that language has no place in contemplative experience.

Beth Alison Barr, in '"Sche hungryd ryth sor aftyr Goddys word": Female Piety and the Legacy of the Pastoral Programme in the Late Medieval English Sermons of Bodleian Library MS Greaves 54' (*JRH* 39[2015] 31–50), writes about a collection of sermons that covers both the *temporale* and *sanctorale*, including twelve sermons from the *Festial*. Citing gender-specific language in the opening addresses, biblical stories of women as exemplars, and other details, Barr argues that there is a deliberate shift in the pastoral programme of the late Middle Ages to include women as individuals who, like men, must take personal responsibility for their own salvation. Gabriel Hill argues for a contrary movement at work in two British Library manuscripts of the revised version of John Mirk's *Festial*. In 'Regendering the *Festial* in British Library MSS Harley 2247 and Royal 18.B.XXV' (*Comitatus* 46[2015] 117–40), he notes that many of the elements Barr identifies were 'edited or simply removed' in the so-called Revision. He highlights the increased passivity and dependence on male authority in the representation of female saints in the Revised *Sanctorale* sermons and argues that revision creates a more 'intellectualized, almost academic' version of the *Festial* probably intended for the hierarchical clergy rather than the less educated clergy or lay parishioners of the original sermon series.

Returning to the question of English writing in the larger European context, Sergey Ivanov and Svetlana Kleyner, in 'The English Versions of the Friday Legend: Three and Twelve' (*MÆ* 84[2015] 189–212), explore a number of short texts that deal with the veneration of Friday. Focusing exclusively on the list of Fridays tradition, the authors list and briefly describe extant manuscripts before arguing that the discrepancies in the English tradition, dismissed up to now as scribal error, are best understood against some of the European counterparts of the Friday tradition.

## 9. Piers Plowman

As in 2014, *Piers Plowman* scholarship is characterized by a wide range of approaches. David Aers's *Beyond Reformation? An Essay on William Langland's Piers Plowman and the End of Constantinian Christianity* is an extended close reading, a form which, according to Aers, presents dangers for articulating larger narratives of the poem and the historical events it describes. What Aers's book does very well is illustrate the poem's participation in an ongoing process of reformation as a kind of ideology, and to introduce its material to new readers, bridging the gap between its religious content and formal characteristics. Of special interest to students and teachers will be Aers's focus on the C-text and the translation of quotations from the poem.

*Taxonomies of Knowledge: Information and Order in Medieval Manuscripts*, edited by Emily Steiner and Lynne Ransom, includes Katharine Breen's 'Reading Step by Step: Pictorial Allegory and Pastoral Care in *Piers Plowman*' (pp. 90–135), which explores the 'taxonomy of the journey' (p. 92) as exemplified by the itinerary to Truth across the three versions of *Piers Plowman*. Contextualizing the poem with various pictorial depictions of allegories, some of which are printed in colour, Breen argues that '*Piers Plowman* is built upon picture maps that orient Christian pilgrims ever more securely in their journeys toward Truth' (p. 93). Stephen Yeager's 'The New Plow and the Old: Law, Orality, and the Figure of Piers the Plowman in B 19' (in Somerset and Watson, eds., pp. 60–78) suggests that Piers Plowman is a figure associated not only with ploughing but also with administration and law, which he tracks from the meaning of the ME *plouȝ*, a unit of land measurement. The implications for this argument are wide-ranging, and Yeager traces Piers as a figure recalling the history and value of justice from its Anglo-Saxon origins in England.

*The Yearbook of Langland Studies* predictably includes several relevant articles. In '*Panis Angelorum*: Rollean *Canor* and *Piers Plowman*' (*YLS* 29[2015] 3–23), Tekla Bude examines the ways in which the poem imagines sounds and how that depiction of sounds seems indebted to Richard Rolle's thought and writing. Examining not only Gluttony's misspent singing but also the nature of angelic singing in B.XVIII and XIX, Bude's article traces a relationship between Rolle's and *Pier*'s use of *canor*. R. James Goldstein's '*Ve Vobis Qui Ridetis* (Lk 6.25): Laughter in *Piers Plowman*' (*YLS* 29[2015] 25–60) describes Langland's frequent use of 'laugh' and words associated with laughter, which increases in the C-text, to show how *Piers* employs the term, especially beyond a simple reading of laughter as emblematic of the unruly body. Goldstein's article seems best when it moves on to the laughter centred on Will, and the connection between laughter and 'fiction-making' (p. 42). Paul Megna explores 'the theologies of love and dread' across the three versions of *Piers Plowman* in 'Dread, Love, and the Bodies of *Piers Plowman* A.10, B.9, and C.10' (*YLS* 29[2015] 61–88). Concentrating on Wit from the A-text to the C-text, Megna fleshes out how *Piers* imagines the relationships between love and dread. In 'Counting Sheep in the C Text of *Piers Plowman*' (*YLS* 29[2015] 89–116), Rosemary O'Neill contextualizes Langland's treatment of stewardship and agricultural management within a context of material from the period outlining an '*ethos of stewardship*' (p. 89). O'Neill uses this material to further explore the parable of the unjust steward, highlighting the anxieties of the poem regarding accounting and the care of estates, neighbours, and sheep in a fallen world. Finally, Sarah Wood's 'Confession and Compilation: The Seven Deadly Sins in Huntington Library, MS HM 114' (*YLS* 29[2015] 117–49) concentrates on the structure of the confession of the Seven Deadly Sins. Using evidence from the manuscript, Wood convincingly reconstructs the materials and motives of the fifteenth-century redactor, showing how this version reflects a fifteenth-century response to the poem.

Sarah Wood continued her examination of MS Hm 114 in 'Nonauthorial *Piers*: C-Text Interpolations in the Second Vision of *Piers Plowman* in Huntington Library, MS Hm 114' (*JEGP* 114:iv[2015] 482–503). She argues that the manuscript should be viewed an a non-authorial interpolation, with scribal readings inserted which prove nevertheless that the interpolator was an excellent reader of the poem.

Ian Cornelius's 'Passus Secundus De Dobest: On the Genesis of a Rubric in the Archetype of *Piers Plowman* B' (*RES* 84:i[2015] 1–15) examines the existence of rubrics. Cornelius sees the rubrication scheme of the B-archetype as shedding light on the poem as a whole.

Rebecca Davis, in 'Childish Things: Charity and the Liberal Arts' (*Postmed* 6[2015] 457–66), fleshes out the figure of Charity in *Piers Plowman*, giving shape to Charity's identity as 'a kind of shape-shifter' (p. 458). What proves valuable for this exposition of Charity is Davis's grappling with a divide between critical and creative modes of knowing, and its value in current debates about and over the liberal arts.

Conrad van Dijk's 'Nede hath no law": The State of Exception in Gower and Langland' (*Accessus* 2:ii[2015] 1–44) fleshes out the tensions surrounding necessity and law and the state of exception, as articulated by Giorgio Agamben. While not focused entirely on *Piers Plowman*, van Dijk illustrates how Langland's poem articulates need as a force that destabilizes both law and nature.

Ralph Hanna's 'The "Absent" Pardon-Tearing of *Piers Plowman* C' (*RES* 66[2015] 449–64) gives a new interpretation of the truncated episode of the tearing of the pardon, which is more complete in the A- and B-texts. What Hanna's article does very well is to show how modern reading habits— encountering the poem in parallel versions—conditions the reader to see a problem with this excision, when the lack of the scene actually presents a poem which demonstrates a careful handling of the changed conditions of the world outside the C-text.

Jocelyn Hargrave's 'Editorial Networks in Practice: Early-Modern Style Guides and the Editing of *Piers Plowman*' (*OResEng* 2[2015] 7–22) presents Thomas Dunham Whitaker's *Visio Willi de Petro Plouhman*, a nineteenth-century edition of *Piers Plowman*. She catalogues the various typographical and editorial features of the edition.

In 'Towards a Material Allegory: Allegory and Urban Space in Hoccleve, Langland, and Gower' (*Exemplaria* 27:i–ii[2015] 93–109), Ethan Knapp argues that 'the development of an urban poetics provides a conditioning historical context for a prominent set of late medieval English allegories' (p. 95). As well as looking at Gower, Knapp examines the connection between Langland's allegory and Hoccleve's own technique in *La Male Regle*.

Mark Miller's 'Sin and Structure in *Piers Plowman*: On the Medieval Split Subject' (*MLQ* 76[2015] 201–24) describes, in a cluster of articles centred on the 'inevitable', the inevitable split of the Christian subject in his or her nature regarding sin. Miller's argument that 'like Lacan, Langland views the subject's embeddedness in and division by social and political structures as a function of a fundamental ontological split that conditions human being' (p. 202) is compelling, and his connections between Langland's depiction of that split subject and the so-called 'death drive' will inevitably open new avenues for interpretation of the poem.

Andrew Pfrenger's 'Now Kynde me avenge": Emotion and the Love of Vengeance in *Piers Plowman*' (*ChauR* 50[2015] 55–87) offers a reading of Conscience's final call for vengeance that, Pfrenger argues, 'should be informed by a careful reading of Langland's discourse on the subject of justice in all its forms throughout the poem' (p. 57).

Lawrence Warner, in 'Impossible *Piers*' (*RES* 66[2015] 223–39), responds to the arguments of Robert Adams and Thorlac Turville-Petre (see *YWES* 95[2016] 266) about the copy of *Piers Plowman* in Aberystwyth, National Library of Wales, 733B, a conflation of A- and C-texts, and its similarities to the beta family of the B-text.

John Burrow, in '"Quod" and "Seide" in *Piers Plowman*' (*N&Q* 62[2015] 521–4), catalogues the number of uses and functions of *quod* and *seide*, asserting, for example, that *quod* is always used with direct speech and the quoted speech from what Burrow calls the 'first narrative level', which is introduced in the world of the dreams. Tristan Majo, in 'Pissede or Passede: *Piers Plowman* C VI.67' (*N&Q* 62[2015] 524–5), argues that the reading *pissede* is an allusion to several verses in the Old Testament.

Scholars of *Piers Plowman* will find Ellen K. Rentz's *Imagining the Parish in Late Medieval England* invaluable for its connections between literary depictions of ecclesiastical practice and sermon books and other liturgical texts of the period. Natanela Elias, *The Gnostic Paradigm: Forms of Knowing in English Literature of the Late Middle Ages*, is discussed in Section 1 above.

## 10. *Sir Gawain and the Green Knight, Pearl, Patience, Cleanness*

The most extensive single treatment of the Cotton Nero A.x poems this year is Cecilia Hatt's *God and the Gawain-Poet: Theology and Genre in Pearl, Cleanness, Patience and Sir Gawain and the Green Knight*. Hatt comprehensively discusses these poems, offering perceptive readings of all four, and significant new insights into these well-trodden works through a detailed engagement with the theological and literary contexts surrounding poem and poet. Hatt argues for a consistent theological vision that binds the four poems, moving away from previous arguments regarding the poet's possible connections and sympathies with the court and the wealthy. One of the most important prevailing themes of Hatt's discussion of the Cotton Nero poems is her notion of the poet's treatment of materiality, arguing for an Aristotelian celebration of art and nature. Natanela Elias, *The Gnostic Paradigm: Forms of Knowing in English Literature of the Late Middle Ages* which explores *Pearl, Patience*, and *Cleanness*, is discussed in Section 1 above.

Another important contribution to scholarship on the poems of Cotton Nero A.x is *Glossator* 9[2015], which is entirely devoted to commentary on *Pearl*. The volume includes an essay for each fitt of *Pearl*, offering a step-by-step close reading from beginning to end. The volume begins with Karl Steel's '"Innoghe": A Preface on Inexhaustibility' (*Glossator* 9[2015] i–vii), in which he discusses the commercial economies associated with the Jeweler, which 'break open to make way for unending generosity' (p. i). In this he offers a discussion of the two ways of not being satisfied in the poem, one insufficient, the other beyond sufficiency. As Steel notes, '*Pearl* tells us that God's infinite grace can never be used up, emptied, or satisfied, while also reminding us that, at least for now, we had better learn to be satisfied with our side of the river' (p. i). William M. Storm, in 'The Arbor and the Pearl: Encapsulating Meaning in "Spot"' (*Glossator* 9[2015] 1–19), offers a discussion of space and place in *Pearl*. He notes in particular the problems of interpretation in the poem, highlighting its ambiguity and multivalence of meaning. Kevin Marti's '*Pearl*, Fitt II' (*Glossator* 9[2015] 20–44) offers an insightful close reading as well as detailed engagement with the poem's sources and analogues. Marti discusses the Edenic setting of fitt II, demonstrating the increasing layers of artificiality and abstraction in the poem's three landscapes, the Arbor, Eden, and the heavenly city. Marti suggests further that recurring key words across the three settings stress parallels between the three landscapes, which in turn represent the three stages of the resurrection. Piotr Spyra's '*Pearl*, Fitt III ("More and More")' (*Glossator* 9[2015] 45–60) argues that the third fitt is organized around the recurring phrase 'more and more'. As Spyra demonstrates, Fitt III shifts its focus from a physical location to a 'sense of longing for something external to the narrator' (p. 45). In treating this sense of longing, Spyra discusses the dynamics of movement in the poem, which creates what he sees as a 'nightmarish' quality of the vision in stanzas 11–15. By forcing the

Dreamer to stop, he argues, the Maiden teases him with the illusion of satisfying his desire; yet her cold and immobile gaze also reinforces the incommensurable division between the movement of his earthly desire and the spiritual realm.

Daniel C. Remein, in '"Pyȝt": Ornament, Place, and Site—A Commentary on the Fourth Fitt of *Pearl*' (*Glossator* 9[2015] 61–90) conducts an in-depth linguistic analysis of the word *pyȝt* and its various semantic uses throughout the poem. The essay provides a useful continuity with the previous essay, building on Spyra's discussion of 'more and more' to further discuss the dynamics of desire, here from a more psychoanalytical perspective. Noelle Phillips, in 'Meeting One's Maker: The Jeweler in Fitt V of *Pearl*' (*Glossator* 9[2015] 91–108), discusses the changing nature of the repeated word *jeweler* and other related words. As Phillips argues, the shifting boundaries of signification show us that the Dreamer and the Maiden cannot be defined in only one plane of existence. Phillips also demonstrates the problems of interpretation, suggesting that 'the reader is never allowed to settle into one mode of reading, but is rather compelled to hold alternative hermeneutic models in mind simultaneously' (p. 91). Next, James C. Staples's '"Mercy schal hyr craftez kyþe": Learning to Perform Re-deeming Readings of Materiality in *Pearl*' (*Glossator* 9[2015] 109–31) discusses the concatenation on the word *demen* ('to judge') in Fitt VI. The reader is encouraged to read and 'deem' the poem, while simultaneously learning to re-read and re-deem the world. As Staples argues, the poem demonstrates that acts of judgement (whether aesthetic or the Last Judgement), are not necessarily wrathful, but might also be spaces for mercy and beauty. Paul Megna's 'Fitt 7: Blysse/ (Envy)' (*Glossator* 9[2015] 132–53) argues that the Dreamer evinces an acceptance of his loss and that the Maiden tries to render him desirous, even envious, of her existence in a celestial world, implying that people on earth should endure their envy of the bliss of heaven. Thus, they can comprehend, but not transcend, the gap between the world and the afterlife. While Megna makes the argument that 'In *Pearl*, envy can be ethical' (p. 135), however, one might wonder if this is a misuse of terms, since desirousness regarding the divine and the sin of envy would have been perceived as very distinct and different motivations.

In his second contribution to this volume, '*Pearl*, Fitt VIII' (*Glossator* 9[2015] 154–78), Kevin Marti continues his discussion of the correspondence between the stages of the vision and the stages of the ascent of the soul and the resurrection of the body in Christian Platonism. Marti here argues that Fitt VIII is a transitional structure, which is necessary to understand the nesting arrangement of the three main landscapes in *Pearl*. He discusses some small-scale images in this fitt that mirror larger structures in the poem, and sheds light on them through Platonist traditions. Walter Wadiak's '"Ther is no date": The Middle English *Pearl* and Its Work' (*Glossator* 9[2015] 179–97) explores questions of history and time in Fitt IX of *Pearl*, discussing the link-word *date* in this section. Focusing on the parable of the vineyard, he argues that the parable explores the measurement of time and the question of what time might be worth, materially and spiritually. Yet Wadiak also demonstrates the way in which *date* in the poem may also refer to the social concerns of the poet's own time. Ultimately, he argues that the poem shows the importance of history, even while offering a vision of its apocalyptic end. In 'Fitt X—More' (*Glossator* 9[2015] 198–216), Travis Neel continues a discussion of the parable of the vineyard in Fitt X. Neel discusses the Dreamer's perception of the parable as representing an unjust system of payment, arguing that 'the Dreamer may, in fact, be giving voice to a commonly held interpretation of the text—one that recognized the importance of worldly works within the economy of spiritual reward' (pp. 198–9). Neel compellingly supports this conclusion with reference to other Middle English texts as well as other exegetical and homiletic materials.

Monika Otter's 'Enough (Section XI)' (*Glossator* 9[2015] 217–25) discusses the link word *enough*, demonstrating its semantic complexity in the poem and its use as a juncture between desire and excess. In this position, she argues, the concept of *enough* navigates the relationship between the finite, earthly world and the transcendent limitlessness of heaven. In 'Fitt XII' (*Glossator* 9[2015] 226–50), Kay Miller offers an extremely detailed, line-by-line discussion of the twelfth fitt, in which she suggests that *Pearl* 'constructs an argument that aims to reconcile, and ultimately subjugate, reason to revelation, though without ever making any guarantees concerning individual salvation' (p. 227). A.W. Strouse, in '*Pearl*, Fytt XIII' (*Glossator* 9[2015] 251–63), departs from the other essays in conducting a comparative study of Fitt XIII with the poems of Emily Dickinson and their treatment of the 'pearl' motif. The study feels somewhat detached from the other essays, and it is not entirely clear how it positively contributes to the volume as a whole. Jane Beal's 'The Jerusalem Lamb of *Pearl*' (*Glossator* 9[2015] 264–85) treats Fitt XIV in relation to the poem's literary and cultural contexts, discussing the Maiden's response to the Dreamer's question about the lamb (ll. 771–2). Beal notes the Maiden's treatment of the practice of *lectio divina* and the four layers of Scripture, which he uses to inform the Dreamer, and prepare him for 'a future vision of the New Jerusalem. In 'Fitt 15—Lesse' (*Glossator* 9[2015] 286–307), Tekla Bude discusses Fitt XV's exploration of heaven and the grace of God through quantitative reasoning. In discussing the use of the word *lesse*, the essay builds on previous discussions of sufficiency in this volume of the journal, showing the poem's contrasting notion of plenitude. Ultimately, Bude demonstrates the tendency in *Pearl* to 'critique and then sublimate the tensions between a categorized, rational, and numbered world with an affective realm beyond—or prior to—the world of enumeration' (p. 307). Karen Bollermann's 'Out, Out, Damned Spot: *Mote* in *Pearl* and the Poems of the *Pearl* Manuscript' (*Glossator* 9[2015] 308–25) discusses the use of the word *mote(les)* in Fitt XVI, with reference to its usage in Fitts I, XIII, XIV, and XV, as well as the three other poems in the *Pearl* manuscript, all of which contribute to the word's lexical and semantic complexity.

Karen Elizabeth Gross's 'Seeing John: A Commentary on the Link Word of *Pearl* Fitt XVII' (*Glossator* 9[2015] 326–54) offers a close reading of Fitt XVII's treatment of the Heavenly Jerusalem, arguing against previous scholarly perceptions that its description is flat and unimaginative in comparison to other parts of the poem. Gross discusses the fitt's two repeated proper nouns, John and Jerusalem, with some compelling references to contemporary visual and material art. Rather than seeing the poet's deference to scriptural text as a simple authorizing strategy, Gross offers a rich interpretation of the exegetical traditions surrounding John as ways of reading *Pearl*. Bruno M. Shah, OP and Beth Sutherland, in 'Theoretical Lunacy: Moon, Text, and Vision in Fitt XVIII' (*Glossator* 9[2015] 355–79) discuss the link word *moon* in Fitt XVIII. As Shah and Sutherland suggest, 'Using the moon as a point and medium of vantage (in XVIII), the poet examines the interplay of light and matter as a means of displaying how poetry might unveil the indescribable realities of heaven' (p. 356).

Anne Baden-Daintree, '*Delyt* and Desire: Ways of Seeing in *Pearl*' (*Glossator* 9[2015] 380–99) discusses the importance of *delyt* in Fitt XIX and the word's semantic complexity, focusing particularly on the Dreamer's shifts of attention between various visual and sensory delights. As Baden-Daintree argues, these attention shifts distract the Dreamer, leading him to 'the (ultimately destructive) "delyt" and longing for his daughter's presence' (p. 383). This movement, Baden-Daintree demonstrates, leads the Dreamer to an exile from heavenly bliss to 'a perpetual situation of unfulfilled desire' (p. 399). The volume closes with David Coley's 'Fitt XX—"Paye"' (*Glossator* 9[2015] 400–22), which continues Baden-Daintree's focus on 'delight', discussing the final fitt's movement away from Fitt XIX, which dealt with divine delight, to a sensuous, human delight. As Coley notes, this notion of earthly delight brings with it notions of corruption, 'those stubbornly terrestrial traits that the Dreamer cannot expunge from his always corporeal, always desiring self' (p. 400). In discussing the mourning and grief that surround the poem's conclusion, Coley offers a compelling comparison with Shakespeare's Hamlet, describing the Dreamer's psychological state in Fitt XX as 'a madness arising from the struggle to experience the spiritual world through always-flawed human faculties' (pp. 401–2). Through this discussion of desire at the end of *Pearl*, Coley offers a thoughtful close to the volume with illuminating consideration of a wider contemporary literary milieu.

A number of other essays contribute to scholarship on the Cotton Nero poems. Arthur Bahr's 'The Manifold Singularity of Pearl' (*ELH* 82[2015] 729–58) draws connections between the beauty of the pearl in the poem and the aesthetic value of the poem itself. In this way, he endeavours to 'reassess the literary value of *Pearl* from the perspective of a new, historically and materially grounded formalism' (p. 729). Bahr's concept of 'manifold singularity' theorizes the notion of the poem's single attestation in Cotton Nero A.x, and explores the 'wide-ranging (manifold) forms of interpretive potential it would not otherwise have' (p. 729). This leads Bahr into some questions of authority in a single-manuscript text such as *Pearl*, which preserves no variant readings; though, as he acknowledges, this is in no way a situation unique to *Pearl*. What results is a kind of pluralist editorial theory, which sees the form of a singly-attested text as expanding and multiplying its interpretative potential.

Sarah McNamer, in 'The Literariness of Literature and the History of Emotion' (*PMLA* 130[2015] 1433–42), offers a compelling analysis of *Pearl* from the perspective of the history of emotion. McNamer argues that *Pearl* 'relies on the polyvalence and sensuous power of poetic language for its affective effects', and in this way 'scripts a therapeutic narrative of affective experience' (pp. 1433–4). McNamer offers an interdisciplinary analysis of *Pearl*, asking what the poem can tell us about the history of emotion and vice versa. McNamer also uses the opportunity to offer a broader discussion of the relationship between the history of emotion and the 'literariness of literature' (p. 1436), that is, how *Pearl*, as a literary text, can function as an instrument for the engagement with and refinement of feeling.

In 'Pendragons at the Chopping Block: Elements of *Sir Gawain and the Green Knight* in the BBC's *Merlin*' (*Arth* 25[2015] 101–12), Erin Chandler argues that the BBC television programme *Merlin* shows influence from *Gawain and the Green Knight*, comparing the trial of Arthur's court through Gawain in the poem to the trial of Uther's Camelot through Arthur in the television series. While the subject of this essay may be of some interest to scholars of modern medievalisms, it does not present a convincing case, beyond vague thematic parallels, that the creators of the BBC programme were consciously drawing from the fourteenth-century poem.

In contrast to the largely theoretical treatments of the Cotton Nero A.x poems, Edmund Miller offers a historical perspective on *Gawain and the Green Knight* in 'The Date and Occasion of *Sir Gawain and the Green Knight*' (*ANQ* 28[2015] 59–62). Miller discusses the internal resonances of the poem with late fourteenth-century social and political surroundings, speculating about the possible date and historical circumstances of *Gawain*'s composition. Somewhat disappointingly, this discussion does not present any historical evidence beyond such speculative association, and the short article does not offer much beyond what has already been said in past scholarship on the poem.

Eric Weiskott's 'Alliterative Metre and the Textual Criticism of the Gawain Group' (*YLS* 29[2015] 151–75) offers at once a broad-sweeping yet intricately detailed methodological argument about metre and the editing of Middle English verse, using ten examples from the Cotton Nero poems as case studies. Weiskott's essay ultimately concludes that 'metre can be utilized as one dimension of editorial assessment in conjunction with other considerations' (p. 152), yet also cautions the editor not to rely too heavily on emendation *metri causa*. As he notes, 'Editors and metrists must both resist the temptation to equate the answer to a textual question with the answer to a metrical one' (p. 164). Weiskott's important essay thus brings a fresh perspective to this year's treatment of the Cotton Nero poems, with wide-ranging applicability to late medieval textual scholarship.

## 11. Romance: Metrical, Alliterative, Prose

### (a) General

Editions of the Middle English romances *The King of Tars* and *Richard Coeur de Lyon* are discussed in Section 3 above. There are various studies related to romance manuscripts and their circulation in Nicholas Perkins, ed., *Medieval Romance and Material Culture*. In his introductory chapter, 'The Materiality of Medieval Romance and *The Erle of Toulous*' (pp. 1–22), Perkins focuses on *The Erle of Toulous*. He notes the close interrelation of 'thing' and romance on several levels here, since one of the surviving manuscripts of the romance was made as a gift, and the narrative itself not only deals with important 'things' like magic rings, but also treats people as 'things' at key moments. Rosalind Field's chapter, 'Courtly Culture and Emotional Intelligence in the *Romance of Horn*' (pp. 23–40), shows one of the key ways in which *Horn* expands its French sources, through the inclusion of lengthy descriptions of the material culture of courtly life. She argues that doing so adds depth to the portrayal of characters by allowing them to exhibit 'differing human responses to courtly splendour and activity' (p. 29). Robert Rouse's chapter, 'Emplaced Reading, or Towards a Spatial Hermeneutic for Medieval Romance' (pp. 41–57), is concerned with 'how the *material context* of a place might affect the reading of a text' (p. 41). In particular, he examines how *The Siege of Jerusalem* and *Titus and Vespasian*, both narratives of the conquest of a walled capital city, might be read within the city walls of medieval London, suggesting that they speak of a desire to rid the English capital of 'cultural and religious diversity' since 'the city must be wiped clean and made anew' (p. 56). Space in Siobhain Bly Calkin's essay, 'Devotional Objects, Saracen Spaces and Miracles in Two Matter of France Romances' (pp. 59–74), is centred on devotional objects in *The Sege of Melayne* and *Sir Ferumbras*. When these objects are captured and mistreated by Saracens in the *Sege*, reactions to the objects become the means of contesting space and territory too, with the result that the Saracens are miraculously turned into stone-like objects themselves. Relics in *Sir Ferumbras* provide repeated opportunities for 'cultural performances' and thus create the characters who handle them. Megan Leitch focuses on game as political metaphor and signifier in 'Ritual, Revenge and the Politics of Chess in Medieval Romance' (pp. 129–46), drawing on examples from a range of (late) romances. She notes how often chess does not so much substitute for violence as 'contribute to, or cause, violence and political turmoil' (p. 134). Ad Putter, 'Adventures in the Bob-and-Wheel Tradition: Narratives and Manuscripts' (pp. 147–63), seeks to remedy the paucity of scholarship on the metrical forms of romance, and in doing so reminds us that to understand these we need to look beyond romance to other narratives that shared the same forms. Raluca L. Radulescu, 'Reading *King Robert of Sicily*'s Text(s) and Manuscript Context(s)' (pp. 165–82), looks at the ways in which the varied contents of the manuscripts in which this romance is found affect how it is read. Aisling Byrne, 'The Circulation of Romances from England in Late-Medieval Ireland' (pp. 183–98), examines the translation and transmission of romances in Ireland, suggesting, first, that the prominent role that religious orders played in this process meant that romances would often be translated between vernaculars via Latin, rather than directly, and secondly that unusual texts may well survive in Ireland, currently unexplored, which could throw important light on wider medieval textual trends. Morgan Dickson, 'The Image of the Knightly Harper: Symbolism and Resonance' (pp. 199–214), examines the iconography of 'harper-heroes' (p. 205), chiefly in French texts but with reference to *Havelok the Dane* and the *Romance of Horn*. Anna Caughey's '"Ladyes war at thare avowing": The Female Gaze in Late-Medieval Scottish Romance' is discussed in Section 14 below.

For Jamie McKinstry in *Middle English Romance and the Craft of Memory*, 'romances are enjoyable because they reward the human aptitude for remembering past experiences and interpreting the present with reference to the past' (p. 2). After introductory chapters on memory and orality, and on classical and medieval theories of memory, the book proceeds to examine various ways in which memory and memory craft are structurally and thematically important to romance, especially in the shared endeavour of remembering undertaken by audience and characters alike. McKinstry draws attention to the ways in which, in line with medieval *ars memoria*, place is used in romance as an aid to memory, with the return to a specific location being an enactment of the process of remembering. In contrast, he points out that the forest, such a key location in many romances, 'had a role in medieval memory theory to conceptualize a mass of disordered material' (p. 76), which gives it an added significance as a place of testing and forming the identity and memory of characters that enter such places. Later chapters explore the importance of memory within romances, and what happens when characters forget things or otherwise offend against good memory by offering untrue accounts of what has taken place. In each chapter, the theoretical material is worked out in some detail with reference to one or two romances, and the overall range of coverage is impressive, with at least twenty-seven Middle English romances considered, as well as extensive commentary on works by Chaucer and Malory. The book concludes that 'Memory ... serves an essential, practical function in *episodic* narratives: the faculty allows a character to reaffirm and develop their identity whilst simultaneously maintaining the unity of a particular tale' (p. 217). Alongside this function, and the way in which 'romances reveal much about the processes, mechanisms, and abilities of memory itself' (p. 217), McKinstry offers the possibility that memory might 'unite' (he is careful not to say 'define') 'this disparate and often disputed genre' (p. 217). While this may be a step too far, the individual readings prove the first two points persuasively, and open up memory as a useful tool for reading romance.

There are various general studies in separate articles. Larissa Tracy, in 'Wounded Bodies: Kingship, National Identity and Illegitimate Torture in the English Arthurian Tradition' (*ArthL* 32[2015] 1–29), examines the depiction of torture as judicial procedure in the stanzaic *Morte Arthur* alongside the alliterative *Morte Arthure* and Malory's *Morte Darthur*, concluding that these romances were concerned with the nature of good kingship and government, and repudiated torture as inconsistent with this. Other general studies include Andrew Lynch's 'Good Knights and Holy Men: Reading the Virtues of Soldier-Saints in Medieval Literary Genres' (in von Contzen and Bernau, eds., *Sanctity as Literature in Late Medieval Britain*, pp. 38–59), which compares the ways in which hagiography and romance present knightly virtue. Lynch argues that the two genres, despite many similarities, ultimately differ in their conclusions on this matter. Romance, he says, depicts the knight as a political figure whose prowess is enmeshed with secular concerns. In hagiography, on the other hand, the martyrdom and spiritual service of the knight take precedence over military achievement. Andrew M. Richmond, in '"The broken schippus he ther fonde": Shipwrecks and the Human Costs of Investment Capital in Middle English Romance' (*Neophil* 99[2015] 315–33), examines the problems ingrained in romance characters reaping material rewards from shipwrecks. He argues that although these episodes are usually presented as being fortuitous, they also contain an undercurrent of unease that acknowledges both the human suffering behind such events and anxieties over the celebration of selfish material gain. In Frank Brandsma, Carolyne Larrington, and Corinne Saunders, eds., *Emotions in Medieval Arthurian Literature: Body, Mind, Voice*, which contains numerous studies on romance, Corinne Saunders, 'Mind, Body and Affect in Medieval English Arthurian Romance' (pp. 31–46), examines emotional affect in several well-known Arthurian texts. She presents a number of psychological episodes from *Ywain and Gawain*, *Sir Launfal*, *Sir Gawain and the Green Knight*, and *Le Morte Darthur* in which strongly felt emotion manifests itself in physical ways, and through these examples demonstrates the inextricable link that exists between mind and body in Arthurian romance texts.

Elsewhere, A.S.G. Edwards surveys 'Middle English Verse Romances: Manuscripts and Authorship' (*Poetica* 83[2015] 79–91). Other manuscript studies by Nicole Clifton (on *Kyng Alisaunder*) and Rory Critten (on Oxford, Bodleian Library MS Ashmole 61) are discussed in Section 3 above.

*(b) Metrical Romances*

There are various studies of individual romances. *Havelok the Dane* is examined by Ken Eckert in a rather laboured analysis: 'The Redemptive Hero and "Inconsistencies" in *Havelok the Dane*' (*PQ* 94[2015] 225–44) discusses the various characters in the poem. Jessica J. Lockhart, 'He Will Rock You: The Sports Wonders of *Havelok the Dane*' (*ChauR* 50[2015] 251–83), explores it in terms of 'discourses of sport' (p. 256), emphasizing the wider implications of his activities as wrestler and stone-thrower.

Wanchen Tai, in '"Al we wilniþ to ben old. wy is eld ihatid": Aging and Ageism in *Le Bone Florence of Rome*' (*SP* 112[2015] 656–79), employs medieval medicine to provide a context for assessing the romance's main figures, the youthful Florent and the aged Garcy.

Jamie Friedman makes use of the idea of racial borders in 'Making Whiteness Matter: *The King of Tars*' (*Postmed* 6[2015] 52–63). He argues here that the ideas of whiteness and racial distinction in *The King of Tars* are complicated by the fantasies of whiteness that are presented therein, and that these create a flexible bond between logic and desire in the representation of race within the romance. Borders are also the subject of Dominique Battles' 'The Middle English *Sir Degrevant* and the Architecture of the Border' (*ES* 96[2015] 853–72). She presents the castle residence of *Sir Degrevant* as being a particular form of architecture known as a 'tower house': a small-scale defensive structure that was built at sites on the Anglo-Scottish border in the late fourteenth and early fifteenth centuries. The article posits that this identification helps us to articulate the central conflict within the poem as being that of border politics.

Two articles make the case that particular romances offer critiques of key late medieval values. Sarah Lindsay, in 'The Courteous Monster: Chivalry, Violence, and Social Control in *The Carl of Carlisle*' (*JEGP* 114[2015] 401–18), argues that *Sir Gawain and the Carl of Carlisle* critiques chivalry, splitting noble action from noble birth and questioning the need for prowess shown through violence as an essential component of chivalry. In her reading, the romance ultimately casts doubt on whether chivalry can fully control violence as it purports to do (especially since, supposedly in order to demonstrate a chivalric obedience to his host, Gawain fights him and attempts to sleep with his wife).

Leah Haught's focus in 'In Pursuit of "Trewth": Ambiguity and Meaning in *Amis and Amiloun*' (*JEGP* 114[2015] 240–60) is on the varying values of *trewth* present in *Amis and Amiloun*, as she argues that 'the poem's reiteration of *trewth* simultaneously intensifies the word's many possible meanings and strips it of any manifest connotation' (p. 241). She suggests that the title figures and their relationships are not meant to be exemplary, but instead interrogate masculinist ideas of 'chivalric illustriousness' (p. 244). In particular, this is seen in the doubts cast on the wisdom of the oath made between Amis and Amiloun, and the ultimately self-serving and cruel actions that each takes in order to keep it.

Marco Nievergelt, in 'The Place of Emotion: Space, Silence and Interiority in the Stanzaic *Morte Arthur*' (*ArthL* 32[2015] 31–57), notes the difficulty that scholarship has had in evaluating the nature of the stanzaic *Morte Arthur*, since 'it lacks both the elaborate courtliness of a French romance and the "pulp" of an English one' (p. 33). He goes on to argue that the poem is able to achieve pathos through its careful attention to space in the narrative, especially in its use of beds and bedchambers (for example to feminize Lancelot) and to give a climactic sense of walls closing in on the main characters.

Although not specifically about romance, Aisling Byrne's *Otherworlds: Fantasy and History in Medieval Literature* is littered with references to Middle English romances. Perhaps unsurprisingly, the largest number relates to *Sir Orfeo*, the 'otherworld' of which Byrne argues persuasively is shaped by biblical texts rather more than by 'Celticity'. She also notes that, in a mode that scarcely tolerates the death of a hero, *Sir Orfeo* is remarkable not only for its emphasis on human limitation, but also its willingness to extend this to an examination of what it is to die. Both lines of argument are also applied to *The Buik of King Alexander the Conqueror*, one of several less studied romances that Byrne illuminates (others include *Of Arthour and Merlin* and *The Turke and Sir Gawain*). Other perceptive insights include the extent to which in *Sir Gawain and the Green Knight* not only the Green Chapel and its environs but also Castle Hautdesert are described in subtly otherworldly terms, and the fact that the absence of descriptive detail about the otherworld in *Sir Thopas* is one of the things that marks that parody as 'wrong' and thus funny.

Patricia A. DeMarco's study of 'Cultural Trauma and Christian Identity in the Late Medieval Heroic Epic, *The Siege of Jerusalem*' (*L&M* 33[2015] 279–301) is discussed in Section 2 above.


*(c) Alliterative Romance*
Much of Edward Donald Kennedy's 'The Prose *Brut*, Hardyng's *Chronicle* and the Alliterative *Morte Arthure*: The End of the Story' (in Whitman, ed.,

*Romance and History: Imagining Time from the Medieval to the Early Modern Period*, pp. 105–19) is, as its title suggests, concerned with chronicle rather than romance, and the third of his titular texts is, he argues, 'primarily derived from chronicles' (p. 105). He goes on to suggest that it presents Arthur's fall as a punishment for various 'misdeeds' (p. 114), and draws attention to parallels between his killing of Mordred's children and the actions of Herod (in Matthew's Gospel) and Pharaoh (in Exodus). Mordred here is, argues Kennedy, given his most complex medieval characterization; taken together, these two aspects mean that the romance 'raises the question of the extent to which traditional narratives permit complexity in characterizations if they are to be popular' (p. 117). Several articles focus specifically on the Alliterative *Morte Arthure*. Gillian Adler's '"ȝit þat traytour alls tite teris lete he fall": Arthur, Mordred, and Tragedy in the Alliterative *Morte Arthure*' (*Arth* 25:iii[2015] 3–21) presents the idea that the portrayal of Arthur's death in the *Morte* is not as heroic as it appears elsewhere, and particularly in Laȝamon's *Brut*. Instead, Adler argues, the *Morte* presents the demise of both Arthur and his court as a consequence of the king's hyper-masculinity and his approach to war and violence. Steven P.W. Bruso, in 'The Sword and the Scepter: Mordred, Arthur, and the Dual Roles of Kingship in the Alliterative *Morte Arthure*' (*Arth* 25:ii[2015] 44–66), also suggests that Arthur struggles with the role of kingship in the events leading up to his death, but focuses more on Mordred and the way in which the *Morte* presents him as a king with legitimate responsibilities rather than just as a traitor. Bruso argues that the text, contrary to pursuing the Mordred-as-traitor theme that is emphasized more strongly elsewhere, presents Mordred as a king who is perhaps better able to balance the dual governor-warrior roles ascribed to kingship than Arthur, who elevates his role as knight at the expense of his governance. Anne Baden-Daintree's 'Kingship and the Intimacy of Grief in the Alliterative *Morte Arthure*' (in Brandsma, Larrington, and Saunders, eds., pp. 87–104) examines the portrayal of Arthur's grief in the *Morte*. Arthur, it suggests, is permitted a public display of emotion following Gawain's death that would normally be conducted in a more private or intimate setting, and this transference of intimacy to the public sphere acts as a precursor for the open acts of vengeance that occur thereafter.

Elliott Kendall, in 'The Evolution of Cooperation in *The Avowyng of Arthur*' (in Perkins, ed., pp. 111–28), writes that *The Avowyng of Arthur* demonstrates an interest in economic exchange and theory (in particular game theory), and the potential of reciprocity to engender both material and symbolic forms of capital. Renée Ward, in 'The Politics of Translation: Sanitizing Violence in *William of Palerne*' (*SP* 112[2015] 469–89), compares the English *William of Palerne* with its French source, *Guillaume de Palerne*, and examines the ways in which the English author has sanitized martial passages in the French text, opting to eliminate or heavily abbreviate these. Ward suggests that the English author undertook these editorial decisions for the benefit of the text's patron, Humphrey de Bohun.

*(d) Prose Romance and Malory*

Megan Leitch's *Romancing Treason: The Literature of the Wars of the Roses* argues that the literature of the period *c*.1437–*c*.1497 is marked by 'its intense and admonitory concerns with the breakdown of social and political faith expressed in the idea of treason' (p. 2), especially treason as 'the antithesis of chivalry' (p. 3). Her analysis includes the prose *Siege of Thebes* and *Siege of Troy*. Contrasting these works and Malory, on the one hand, with earlier romance and the siege poems of Lydgate on the other, Leitch finds the later romances more questioning of providence, and more focused on the certainties provided by legal procedures and actions. This, she argues, reflects an uncertain political climate: 'If the divine cannot be relied upon, as the political and social upheavals of mid-fifteenth-century England seemed to indicate, then matters must be taken into human hands' (p. 81). An examination of the English prose and verse versions of *Melusine* highlights the foregrounding of treason in both (in contrast to their French source), a process which Leitch (in chapter 4) demonstrates in Malory's *Morte Darthur* as well. She points out that it is the necessary counterpoint to Malory's core interest in 'fellowship': treason 'often provides the language through which Malory defines community' (p. 98). This leads to more in-depth discussions of Balyn and especially Mordred, 'the incarnation of treason' (p. 118), illuminated particularly through comparison with other contemporary portrayals of him, in Scottish chronicles and the *Chronicle* of John Hardyng. A powerful close to the chapter puts Malory back into the context of other prose romances, and again argues that in his text the possibilities of romance are being challenged and extended. The final chapter turns to Caxton's prose romances, seeking to reclaim them from dismissal as mere Burgundian imports by showing their close thematic kinship to Malory's *Morte Darthur* (and other mid-century romances), not least in their preoccupation with questions of treason and Caxton's translation choices which intensify this focus. The postscript looks beyond 1500 and suggests that the romances of the sixteenth century were less preoccupied with treason, reverting to the providential framework of Lydgate's works.

Helen Cooper's 'Arthur in Transition: Malory's *Morte Darthur*' (in Whitman, ed., pp. 120–33) focuses on Malory, and she contrasts the dominant and far-reaching influence of his *Morte Darthur* on the medievalism of subsequent centuries (even inspiring 'T-shirts and excaliburgers', p. 120) with the small number of people who encountered it in manuscript. Her aim is to put the text back into the 1460s, and thus not merely a nostalgic and backward-looking culmination of the past, but a ground-breaking work, 'in tune with the contemporary fashion for prose' and 'the first Arthurian prose romance to be printed in any language' (p. 122). She argues that by reducing or excising the overt moral comment of his sources Malory produced a text that was more interested in realpolitik than abstract principle, and thus more adaptable by future readers and imitators.

Ralph Norris, in 'Another Source for Malory's "Tale of Sir Gareth"' (*ArthL* 32[2015] 59–73), carefully examines the changes made to the presentation of Lancelot in the *Tale of Sir Gareth* and concludes that Malory blended his presumed source with elements drawn deliberately from Chrétien's *Le*

*Chevalier de la Charette* and its prose redaction. Malory is also the focus of Lisa Robeson's essay "'Warre and Worshyppe": Depictions of Battle in Malory's *Le Morte Darthur*' (*ArthL* 32[2015] 75–103). She identifies four phases of battle descriptions through the text—Uther's wars, Arthur's early wars, the wars of the Round Table, and Arthur's final wars—and suggests that each has a distinct role to play in revealing 'conceptual layers of chivalry' (p. 76). Significantly, Robeson sees this as a matter not just for the knights but for the king, with Malory making Arthur's early wars a form of apprenticeship for rule, since '[a] chivalric king must be a great general' (p. 102). Richard Sévère, in 'Malory's "Chivalric Cliques": Public and Private *Felyshyp* in the Arthurian Community' (*ArthL* 32[2015] 105–22), reads Malory in the light of Cicero's *De amicitia*, focusing particularly on the friendship of Trystram and Lancelot, the public and private relationships forged by Dinadan, and the close ties between Lancelot and Gareth. He notes that private friendships in Malory have the power to undermine the wider social cohesion of the court, but that between Trystram and Lancelot is seen as an ideal, balanced between public and private demands. Lastly, David Eugene Clark, in 'Scribal Modifications to Concluding Formulae in the Winchester Manuscript' (*ArthL* 32[2015] 123–53), argues that scribes, rather than Malory himself, are responsible for the placing of five *explicits* in the manuscript, making 'relationships between stories and books in the first quarter of the narrative less clear' (p. 154), an important caution for how we interpret those stories and books.

David Eugene Clark explores the spiritual and chivalric rewards that can be attributed to the attendance of Mass in the *Morte Darthur* in 'Constructing Spiritual Hierarchy through Mass Attendance in the *Morte Darthur*' (*Arth* 25:i[2015] 128–53). He argues that Malory uses Mass as a means of secularizing faith within his text, and that he does so by offering concrete rewards to the participants who demonstrate the most diligence towards their faith. Siobhán Mary Wyatt, in '"Gyff me goodly langage, and than my care is paste": Reproach and Recognition in Malory's *Tale of Sir Gareth*' (*Arth* 25:ii[2015] 129–42), examines the portrayal of outspoken women in Malory's *Tale of Sir Gareth*. She focuses particularly on those who chide or remonstrate with the knights they encounter, and argues that Malory presents such women and their speeches as ultimately being beneficial to the careers of the knights within the tale. In Adam Bryant Marshall's 'Sir Lancelot at the Chapel Perelus: Malory's Adaptation of the *Perlesvaus*' (*Arth* 25:iii[2015] 33–48), the author compares Malory's portrayal of Lancelot's adventure at the Chapel Perelus with the same scene in its source text, the anonymous *Perlesvaus*. Marshall posits that Malory attempts to imbue his version of the episode with more terror than his predecessor in order to inflate the reader's opinion of Lancelot's courage. Richard Sévère, in 'Galahad, Percival, and Bors: Grail Knights and the Quest for Spiritual Friendship' (*Arth* 25:iii[2015] 49–65), offers a reading of Malory's Grail Quest that is based on the concept of spiritual friendship outlined in the work of that name by St Aelred. He argues that the authors of a number of Malory's source texts are likely to have been familiar with this work, and that it has informed Malory's own depiction of the Grail Quest and the spiritual friendships of the knights who partake in it.

Amanda D. Taylor, in 'The Body of Law: Embodied Justice in Sir Thomas Malory's *Morte Darthur*' (*Arth* 25:iii[2015] 66–97), argues that in the *Morte Darthur* Malory undermines divine, sovereign, and common law practices, and proposes instead an embodied law that relies primarily on three principles: the body as proof, the body as witness, and the body in debate. Through this line of discussion she highlights several complications with considering judicial practices in Malory's works.

Several studies on Malory and Arthurian romance occur in Brandsma, Larrington, and Saunders, eds., *Emotions in Medieval Arthurian Literature*. Andrew Lynch's chapter, '"What cheer?": Emotion and Action in the Arthurian World' (pp. 47–63), examines the transitional link between emotion and action in Laȝamon's *Brut*, Thomas Chestre's *Sir Launfal*, and Malory's *Morte Darthur*. Lynch argues that Arthurian emotion often acts as a precursor to forward action, but that the results are not always positive, and the needs embodied in the emotions are not always satisfied. Raluca L. Radulescu's chapter, 'Tears and Lies: Emotions and the Ideals of Malory's Arthurian World' (pp. 105–21) explores the displays of extreme emotion in the *Morte Darthur* that appear to be intended to effect external change, with particular attention to the scene in which Lancelot returns Guinevere to Arthur. She places this scene within a political context in order to examine the ways in which audiences might have reacted to a scene that was both emotionally and politically charged. Helen Cooper's afterword to the volume, 'Malory's Enigmatic Smiles' (pp. 181–8), explores the enigmatic displays of emotion that occur within Malory's text, ones that are either not easily read or not explicitly explained within the narrative. She notes in particular the elusive nature of smiles and laughter in the *Morte* compared to more extreme displays such as grief or weeping, and argues that these more subtle signs of emotion require detailed study in order to be better understood.

Several articles have focused on issues relating to Malory reception. Ruth Lexton, in 'Reading the Adulterous/Treasonous Queen in Early Modern England: Malory's Guinevere and Anne Boleyn' (*Exemplaria* 27[2015] 222–41), argues that the story of Guinevere's betrayal within the *Morte Darthur* provided a literary precedent for the execution of Anne Boleyn, who was accused of both treason and adultery. She posits that similar romance motifs provided an ideological basis with which the contemporaries of Boleyn could make sense of the events surrounding her death. Alec Gilmore, in 'Steinbeck's Translation of Malory's *Morte d'Arthur*: Success or Failure—An End or a New Beginning?' (*Steinbeck Review* 12[2015] 74–86), focuses on John Steinbeck's role as an interpreter of Malory. He argues that Steinbeck's interest in Malory informed his writing: in particular his early enthusiasm regarding the idea of the American dream, and his disillusionment following an abandoned attempt to retell Malory's stories in his own words. Kathy Cawsey, in 'The Once and Future Childslayer: Guy Gavriel Kay's Inversion of Malory's *Morte Darthur*' (*Arth* 25:ii[2015] 67–83), proposes that Guy Gavriel Kay's fantasy trilogy *The Fionavar Tapestry* holds Arthur to account for killing the children on Mayday in the *Morte Darthur*. She argues that Arthur's return is presented as a curse rather than a reward within this work, and that the child-killing episode has implications for Arthur's downfall that are not made explicit in the *Morte*. Joseph Brennan, in '"You could shame the great Arthur himself": A Queer Reading of Lancelot from BBC's *Merlin* with Respect to the Character in Malory, White, and Bradley' (*Arth* 25:ii[2015] 20–43), examines Lancelot's sexuality in the BBC's *Merlin* in the context of his forebears in Malory, T.H. White, and Marion Zimmer Bradley, and argues that his portrayal in each represents a paradox between idealization and secrecy that is comparable to secret sexuality and its capacity for both desire and anxiety.

*(e) Reception*

Nancy Mason Bradbury's 'The Victorian Afterlife of *The Thornton Romances*' (in Perkins, ed., pp. 253–74) examines the nineteenth-century publishing history of *Sir Perceval of Galles*, *Sir Isumbras*, *Sir Eglamour of Artois*, and *Sir Degrevant*.

There are two articles on the reception of *Sir Orfeo*. Kelley M. Wickham-Crowley, '"Mind to mind": Tolkien's Faërian Drama and the Middle English *Sir Orfeo*' (*TStud* 12[2015] 1–29), links the poem to Tolkien's writings about fairy stories and to his translation of *Sir Orfeo*. A.W. Strouse, in '*Sir Orfeo* as a Critical/Liberal/Art' (*Postmed* 6[2015] 478–84), evaluates the poem using a contemporary theoretical framework.

## 12. Gower

In 2015 *South Atlantic Review* released a special issue devoted to John Gower. Guest-edited by Kara L. McShane with the assistance of R. F. Yeager, the issue features a collection of essays originating in the Third International Congress of the John Gower Society held in Rochester, New York, in July 2014, and shows the diversity of current approaches to Gower's poetry and its afterlife. In the opening essay, 'Final *-e* in Gower's English Poetry, in Comparison with Chaucer's' (*SoAR* 79:iii–iv[2015] 6–19), Gyöngyi Werthmüller offers a comparative analysis of the phonological and metrical practice of Chaucer and Gower to demonstrate the remarkable degree of consistency in Gower's use of word-final *-e* in the *Confessio Amantis*. Werthmüller suggests that this consistency may be attributable in no small part to the impact of Gower's French on his English output. The regularity of Gowerian final *-e* is also the subject of another essay by the same author published this year, 'Final *-e* in Gower's and Chaucer's Monosyllabic Premodifying Adjectives: A Grammatical/Metrical Analysis' (in Conde-Silvestre and Calle-Martín, eds., pp. 179–97).

The next two essays in *South Atlantic Review*'s special issue consider Gower's posthumous reception by early copyists. In 'More Light on Ricardus Franciscus: Looking Again at Morgan M. 126' (*SoAR* 79:iii–iv[2015] 20–35), Martha W. Driver examines Pierpont Morgan Library, New York, MS M.126, a mid-fifteenth-century manuscript of the *Confessio Amantis* copied by the scribe Ricardus Franciscus. Driver's close analysis of Ricardus's scribal habits and emendations uncovers possible traces of his French origin and shows him to be an accurate copyist with equal competence in English and French. Whereas Morgan M. 126 is a complete copy of the *Confessio*, the manuscript discussed by Joseph Stadolnik in 'Excerpting Gower: Exemplary Reading in New Haven, Takamiya MS 32' (*SoAR* 79:iii–iv[2015] 36–50) is a miscellaneous compilation preserving only a handful of tales selected from the *Confessio*. As Stadolnik shows, these selections are stripped of the Latin glosses that appear in conventional *Confessio* manuscripts, and rearranged in such a way as to 'resist the thoroughgoing appropriation of the "lusty" matter of the *Confessio* for exemplary purposes' (p. 44). They thus attest to the various possibilities of reading open to the poem's earliest readers.

In Jeffery G. Stoyanoff, 'Beginnings and Endings: Narrative Framing in *Confessio Amantis*' (*SoAR* 79:iii–iv[2015] 51–64), the focus shifts away from scribal reception to the poem itself. Stoyanoff draws attention to how Gower gives a circular movement to the frame narrative by delaying until the end of the poem the disclosure of Amans as the aged poet. Stoyanoff argues that this circular frame triggers an interpretative process whereby readers engage in a retrospective contemplation of what they have read in light of the poem's final revelation. Concentrating on a tale that appears in Book VII of certain manuscripts of the *Confessio*, Emily Houlik-Ritchey's 'Fellows in the Wilderness: Neighborly Ethics in "The Tale of the Jew and the Pagan"' (*SoAR* 79:iii–iv[2015] 65–75) uncovers multiple layers of meaning in this tale by putting it in dialogue with current ethical theories. Houlik-Ritchey maintains that while the tale, on the surface, seems to deny Christianity's ethical indebtedness to Judaism by proposing an alternative ancestry in paganism, its 'dynamic landscape and multitudinous language obliquely recover the ethical-historical reality of a neighborly relation between Christianity and Judaism' (p. 66).

The three essays that follow are bound by their shared interest in the therapeutic function of Gowerian narrative. In 'Social Healing in Gower's *Visio Angliae*' (*SoAR* 79:iii–iv[2015] 76–88), Kara L. McShane explores the motif of the rudderless ship that figures centrally in the latter part of the *Visio Angliae*, a poetic account of the social and psychic fragmentation brought about by the Rising of 1381. McShane shows how this nautical image, common from vernacular romance, serves as a healing metaphor that enables the poet to articulate his traumatic experience in a way comprehensible both to himself and to his audience. In '"So schalt thou double hele finde": Narrative Medicine in the "Tale of Constantine and Sylvester"' (*SoAR* 79:iii–iv[2015] 89–104), Pamela M. Yee applies the concept of narrative medicine to her analysis of the last tale of Book II of the *Confessio*, proposing to read it as a series of medical encounters in which not only Constantine's capacity for charity but also the diagnostic skills of the doctor figures come under scrutiny. Yee's analysis is intended to show the tale's significance for the overall scheme of the *Confessio*, for, in her view, it can be seen as a miniature representation of the narrative healing that Genius seeks to enact with his patient-penitent Amans. William Rogers, 'Old Words Made New: Medea's Magic and Gower's Textual Healing' (*SoAR* 79:iii–iv[2015] 105–17), examines the scene describing Medea's attempt to rejuvenate Eson through magic in Book V of the

*Confessio*, and shows how closely this scene reflects language and imagery in a treatise on rejuvenation preserved in a late medieval medical manuscript: Cambridge, Trinity College MS R.14.52. Rogers suggests that Medea's magic not only highlights the blurring of the boundary between medical and literary texts in Gower's narrative, but also illuminates his strategy of breathing life into old stories for the moral edification of the present reader.

In '"The science of himself is trewe": Alchemy in John Gower's *Confessio Amantis*' (*SoAR* 79:iii–iv[2015] 118–31), Clare Fletcher examines the positive discussion of alchemy included in Book IV of the *Confessio*, which she sees as an integral part of Gower's project of ethical reform. Fletcher illuminates the ways in which the passage addresses the key themes underlying the argument of the poem—the postlapsarian deterioration of the world and the decline of language—and argues that 'the alchemical purgation of vice and retention of virtue' (p. 129) offer Gower the formula for transmuting the self and, by extension, the world at large. While Fletcher's essay focuses on the intermingling of science and ethics in Gower's alchemical exposition, Candace Barrington examines the intersection of legal and literary discourse in 'Common-Law and Penitential Intentionality in Gower's "Tale of Paris and Helen"' (*SoAR* 79:iii–iv[2015] 132–43). Noting that England's two dominant legal systems, the ecclesiastical and the common-law, had opposing attitudes towards intentionality, Barrington argues that, within the confessional framework surrounding the 'Tale of Paris and Helen', Gower dramatizes this conflict by having the confessor Genius prioritize intention over deed and having Amans adopt the opposite position associated with the common-law courts. As Barrington adroitly demonstrates, however, the tale gradually dismantles this dichotomy and begins to align itself exclusively with the common-law position as it limits its focus to a single, tangible offence—Paris's sacrilege—in preference to all the other deeds, both intended and committed, that better explain the outbreak of the Trojan War. Barrington concludes that in thus exposing the inadequacy of the common-law approach to justice, the tale points towards the need 'to incorporate intention into legal concepts and procedures' (p. 141).

Barrington's essay is followed by two articles on Lydgate's indebtedness to Gower, one by Stephen R. Reimer and the other by Robert R. Edwards, which are both discussed in Section 13 below. Continuing the theme of Gower's legacy, Jonathan Baldo concludes the special issue by turning to an early modern adaptation of Gower's tale of Apollonius. In 'Recovering Medieval Memory in Shakespeare's *Pericles*' (*SoAR* 79:iii–iv[2015] 171–89), Baldo shows how memory serves unequivocally to promote unity, virtue, and reconciliation in the play, in a way reminiscent of the idea repeatedly expressed in the *Confessio* that recollection of the past is the only way to ensure the recovery of psychological and political wholeness. Baldo argues that the play's emphasis on the moral function of memory, coupled with the role assigned to Gower as a chorus to the play, underlines its significance as 'a public, ceremonial restoration to life of the recently broken and buried culture of memory' (p. 183).

Sebastian Sobecki's '*Ecce patet tensus*: The Trentham Manuscript, *In Praise of Peace*, and John Gower's Autograph Hand' (*Speculum* 90[2015] 925–59) is a

penetrating discussion of the production and early provenance of the
Trentham manuscript by synthesizing codicological, palaeographical, and
literary-critical analyses. One of the most innovative aspects of Sobecki's study
is his revisionary reading of *In Praise of Peace*, the English poem included in
the manuscript, which has traditionally been interpreted as a Lancastrian
panegyric for the newly crowned Henry IV. Instead, Sobecki reads it against
the background of deteriorating Anglo-French relations during the first
months of Henry IV's reign, proposing to read it as an exhortation to the king
to affirm peace with France. In Sobecki's view, the physical arrangement of
texts in the manuscript is intended to convey the same message of Anglo-
French reconciliation, but Henry's confirmation of the truce with France in
May 1400 made it no longer necessary to present it to the king, with the result
that it remained in Gower's possession for the rest of his life. Sobecki's
discussion of Gower's continued ownership of the manuscript is based on a
close examination of codicological and palaeographical evidence, which also
leads to another important discovery: that one of the two scribes responsible
for copying the manuscript may be none other than Gower himself.

While Stoyanoff's essay, discussed above, argues that the circular frame of
the *Confessio* is designed to prompt retrospective reconsideration of the
poem's meaning, Lewis Beer makes an opposite claim in 'The Tactful Genius:
Abiding the End in the *Confessio Amantis*' (*SP* 112[2015] 234–63), contending
that the exemplary narratives in the main body of the poem are designed to
foreshadow its conclusion. Focusing on a sequence of tales from Book V, Beer
analyses the subtle narrative techniques employed by Genius to tactfully warn
Amans of the transience of earthly love and to urge him to renounce his
misdirected devotion. In thus highlighting the anticipatory aspect of Genius's
exempla and the inevitability of the poem's ending, Beer challenges a
pronounced tendency in recent Gower scholarship to emphasize the
*Confessio*'s incoherence as a main source of its interest.

In 'Figuring the Dangers of the "Greet Forneys": Chaucer and Gower's
Timely (Mis)Reporting of the Peasant Voice' (*Comitatus* 46[2015] 75–97),
Camille Marshall examines Gower's allegorical vision of the 1381 Rising in the
*Vox Clamantis* in an attempt to contextualize the Miller's portrait in the
*General Prologue* to the *Canterbury Tales*. Camille's analysis of the *Visio* is
chiefly concerned with the great emphasis that Gower places on the danger of
the peasants' voice and his use of the image of a fire-breathing beast to
describe its destructiveness—an image which provides a link with the Miller's
furnace-like mouth. Ethan Knapp also turns to the *Visio* in the last part of his
essay, 'Towards a Material Allegory: Allegory and Urban Space in Hoccleve,
Langland, and Gower' (*Exemplaria* 27[2015] 93–109), which examines the
shaping role that these poets assign to urban space in the structures of their
allegories. Knapp demonstrates the extent to which Gower's description of the
rebellion is filled with anxiety over the mutual penetration and contamination
of the city under attack and the surrounding wilderness. Knapp argues that
this anxiety explains why London is so energetically repressed in the *Visio* and
why Gower preferred the figuration of an allegorical New Troy.

Included in the same issue of *Exemplaria*, Ardis Butterfield's 'Afterwords:
Forms of Death' (*Exemplaria* 27[2015] 167–82) is a comparative study of

Gower's *Cinkante Balades* and Guillaume de Machaut's *Voir Dit*, which sheds light on the creative ways in which Gower engages with the closed system of French lyrical language to pursue fresh formal experimentation. One factor that facilitates this creative process is Gower's complete mastery of poetic truisms in French, but, as Butterfield shows, the *Cinkante Balades* also witnesses to Gower's acute sense of linguistic difference and his ability to employ 'linguistic alongside formal transposition/translation/metamorphosis to further his poetic ambitions' (p. 180).

Gower's awareness of linguistic difference is the issue also addressed by Richard Ingham and Michael Ingham in '"Pardonetz moi qe jeo de ceo forsvoie": Gower's Anglo-Norman Identity' (*Neophil* 99[2015] 667–84). Their investigation into the phonological and syntactic features of Gower's French verse reveals that, throughout his French writing career, Gower overwhelmingly retained insular usage at the linguistic-systemic levels even as his verse forms and metrical practice were orientated towards Continental style. On the basis of these findings, the authors suggest that Gower's unchanged predilection for insular usage may have been the result of a deliberate choice in his later years, made to position himself 'at a remove from the amatory poets across the water' (p. 682) and to assert his identity as 'a self-conscious moralist' (p. 683). William Sayers's 'Gower's "So nyh the weder thei wol love" (*Confessio Amantis*, 5, 7048)' (*ANQ* 28[2015] 135–9) offers a linguistic analysis of an often misinterpreted line from Book V of the *Confessio*. To clarify its meaning, Sayers focuses on the verb *loven*, the Middle English equivalent of the modern *luff*, and traces its semantic and morphological development from the Old Norse lexeme *úfr*.

In '"For it acordeth noght to kinde": Remediating Gower's *Confessio Amantis* in Machinima' (*Accessus* 2:i[2015] 1–61), medievalist and filmmaker Sarah L. Higley discusses her machinima adaptation of selections from the *Confessio*, which she characterizes as a creative response to the underlying philosophy of Gower's poetry: that writings of antiquity contain examples for the future. The essay begins by addressing technical and theoretical issues related to the reproduction of medieval tales in a 3-D virtual world, and proceeds to offer a close analysis of Gower's originals and Higley's adaptations, with particular emphasis placed on how her film both expresses and complicates Gower's views on love and nature. Conrad van Dijk's '"Nede hath no law": The State of Exception in Gower and Langland' (*Accessus* 2:ii[2015] 1–44) explores the two poets' understanding of the maxim *necessity has no law* and considers its resonance with postmodern reflections on the state of exception. As van Dijk shows, although Langland and Gower both relate necessity to nature, Gower, unlike Langland, is less interested in economic deprivation than in the needs generated by human sexuality. Through its association with the natural impulse to love, need in the *Confessio* becomes the rule and 'enshrined in natural law' (p. 29), thereby leaving no room for the exception and making it part of the all-encompassing law.

Another contribution by van Dijk, 'Vengeance and the Legal Person: John Gower's *Tale of Orestes*' (in Boboc, ed., *Theorizing Legal Personhood in Late Medieval England*, pp. 119–41), focuses on the concluding lines of the 'Tale of Orestes', in which Egiona's suicide is justified as retributive punishment in such a way as to deny her legal personhood. Drawing on a wide array of legal, theological, and narrative sources, van Dijk reveals that Gower's treatment of Egiona is based on multiple understandings of vengeance, including an Old Testament sense of retribution and contemporary notions about guilt by association, but van Dijk also emphasizes that the tale's ending is conditioned by the narrative needs of the genre of exemplum, which heavily relies on narrative closure and poetic justice for the production of meaning. Having thus demonstrated that 'both vengeance and legal personhood are shaped by narrative' (p. 120), van Dijk takes his argument a step further to suggest that such narrative constraints are 'hardly only a literary reality' (p. 138), but a helpful guide to understanding the legal self in late medieval society.

Gower also figures in two other essays in the same volume. In 'John Gower's Poetry and the "Lawyerly Habit of Mind"' (pp. 71–93), R.F. Yeager offers a fresh reading of the *Cronica Tripertita* as a poem bearing the marks of the 'lawyerly mind' of its author, capable of seeing more than one side to every situation and crafting a 'best case' for any side in a value-neutral manner. What emerges from Yeager's reading is a multifaceted text, not reducible to a straightforward piece of Lancastrian propaganda, which is 'carefully balanced to effect an admonitory purpose of the highest social import' (p. 88), while at the same time withholding little in its praise for the new king. Although adopting a different methodology to Yeager's, Candace Barrington's aim in 'The Spectral Advocate in John Gower's Trentham Manuscript' (pp. 94–118) is likewise to explicate the legal habits of mind that shaped Gower's poetry. To that end, Barrington looks at the trilingual poems in the Trentham manuscript to examine how they incorporate the lexical, procedural, and illocutionary gestures drawn from legal discourse as learned and practised in law-courts in late medieval England. Barrington argues that these gestures create legal arguments that demonstrate Henry IV's worthiness to rule without, nevertheless, condoning the extra-legal machinations that placed him on the throne.

Georgiana Donavin's '"Rex Celi Deus": John Gower's Heavenly Missive' (in Donavin and Stodola, eds., pp. 103–23) illuminates the composite nature of 'Rex Celi Deus'—one of the Latin laudatory poems copied into the Trentham manuscript—as an innovative conjunction of epistolary and musical conventions. Donavin discovers in the opening eight lines of the poem an allusion to 'Celi Deus Sanctissime', a popular hymn about creation. Combining this discovery with a close analysis of the epistolary rhetoric deployed in the poem and drawing attention to the ways in which the poem gestures to the coronation ceremony, Donavin convincingly argues that its 'blended dictaminal and musical rhetoric' is intended to 'celebrate God's sanctioning of the new king, include the people in this blessed event, and directly address Henry' (p. 119).

Amanda J. Gerber's *Medieval Ovid: Frame Narrative and Political Allegory* has a chapter on Gower and Lydgate, entitled 'Overlapping Mythologies: The Political Afterlives of Frame Narratives in Gower's *Confessio Amantis* and Lydgate's *Fall of Princes*' (pp. 102–33). In the section focusing on the *Confessio*, Gerber elucidates the compositional methodologies deployed by Gower to create a multivocal work endowed with the authority of the 'commun vois'. Among the methodologies that Gower derives from the works of Geoffrey of Vinsauf and medieval Ovidian commentators, Gerber places particular emphasis on the rhetorical device of *collocatio*, which enables Gower to interweave divergent voices, perspectives, and types of lore into a cohesive poetic text by means of hidden comparisons. In the chapter devoted to the *Confessio* in her book *The Gnostic Paradigm*, 'Gower's Bower of Bliss: A Successful Passing into Hermetic Gnosis' (pp. 119–46), Natanela Elias seeks to uncover Gnostic themes in Gower's poem, proposing to read Amans's quest for love as the process of gradual reawakening of his soul via the regaining of dormant knowledge. To support this claim, Elias examines key passages from the *Confessio* which show the importance of memory and self-reflection as the means to achieving salvific knowledge. Elias states in conclusion that the poet's final monologue in the poem represents an 'introspection' that eventually leads to 'a spiritual salvation' and 'poetic closure' (p. 146)

Finally, Jonathan Hsy's 'Disability' (in Hillman and Maude, eds., *The Cambridge Companion to the Body in Literature*, pp. 24–40) contains a brief discussion of how blindness offers new opportunities for poetic self-fashioning in Gower's later Latin lyrics.

## 13. Hoccleve and Lydgate

Although no monographs appeared in 2015 dedicated to either Thomas Hoccleve or John Lydgate, both authors figured individually and jointly in numerous articles and book chapters. Most refreshingly, much of this scholarship situates Hoccleve and Lydgate in relation to other key medieval authors or new thematic contexts, rather than considering each author in isolation.

### (a) Hoccleve

Simon Horobin suggests that Hoccleve may have been responsible for overseeing the production of both the Hengwrt and Ellesmere manuscripts of *The Canterbury Tales* (*ChauR* 50[2015] 228–50). Horobin notes that Hengwrt contains a number of 'textual additions that were made by one or more supplementary hands' (p. 229). He argues that palaeographical similarities and the nature of the scribal interventions in question indicate that the hands previously identified by A.I. Doyle and M.B. Parkes in Hengwrt as Hands D, E, and F are the work of a single scribe (p. 235). In the second part of his article, Horobin surveys the most distinctive elements of Hoccleve's hand in order to support his argument that 'Comparison of the text added by each of these Hands D-F with known instances of Hoccleve's hand suggests that all of these additions can be accommodated within the range of forms attested to in documents known to have been written by Hoccleve' (p. 236). Horobin reads Hoccleve's interventions in Hengwrt as evidence that suggests that Hoccleve 'was the supervisor responsible for overseeing, correcting, and completing the work of Pinkhurst. In short, Hoccleve was Chaucer's first editor' (p. 239). Horobin further argues that, both because of his professional position and as a writer who took pains to present himself as Chaucer's disciple, Hoccleve would have been a natural candidate to fill the role of Chaucer's literary executor. In the conclusion to his article, Horobin considers the implications of Hoccleve's potential supervisory role in the production of Hengwrt and Ellesmere for contemporary understandings of the late medieval London book trade. (Horobin's article is also discussed in Chapter IV in this volume.)

Hoccleve's role in textual production is also at the centre of a substantial article authored by Lawrence Warner, 'Scribes, Misattributed: Hoccleve and Pinkhurst' (*SAC* 37[2015] 55–100) in which he challenges the identification of Adam Pinkhurst as the scribe of Hengwrt and Ellesmere. Hoccleve is most present in the first half of Warner's article, which focuses on revisiting the identification by L.R. Mooney of London, British Library, Royal MS 17 D.XVIII as a Hoccleve holograph of the *Regiment of Princes*. Warner notes that the manuscript 'lacks the features one would expect to find' in a holograph—namely, 'textual proximity to the original version and unique signs of tinkering or even substantial changes' (p. 63), and that the language is 'unHocclevean' (p. 63). He concludes that 'difficulties attend the attribution of Royal 17 D.XVIII to Hoccleve from every side, while none attends the received conclusion that it is not a holograph' (p. 72). In the remainder of the article, Warner turns his attention to the case of Adam Pinkhurst, who, he argues, is *not* to be identified as the man responsible for the writing of Hengwrt and Ellesmere.

Jenni Nuttall's essay on Hoccleve for the *Oxford Handbooks Online* uses his biography and authorial personae in order to reassess the *balades* he composed in the first two years of Henry V's reign, as well as the *Remonstrance to Oldcastle* [1415]. As Nuttall points out, Hoccleve scholars benefit from what appears to be 'a mutually confirming relationship between what we know of Hoccleve's biography, what he records about himself and his life in his verse, and the genre and purpose of the works' (p. 2), a relationship that may encourage scholars to accept Hoccleve's poetic identity and agenda as straightforwardly intelligible and unproblematic (p. 3). Nuttall advocates a rereading of Hoccleve's works that takes account of ecclesiastical as well as political discourse in order to bring to light what she views as his 'clerical, moral voice speaking to royal authority on behalf of orthodoxy and the church' (p. 8).

Rory Critten takes up the relationship between Hoccleve's work and that of Christine de Pizan in 'Imagining the Author in Late Medieval England and France: The Transmission and Reception of Christine de Pizan's *Epistre au dieu d'Amours* and Thomas Hoccleve's *Letter of Cupid*' (*SP* 112[2015] 680–97; also discussed in Section 2 above). Critten argues that, because Christine had more control over the circulation and copying of her text than did Hoccleve, she therefore had more control over her literary reputation than did the English author. As Critten points out, 'While the artistic and political successes of Christine's text have already been pointed to, consideration of the extant manuscripts of the *Letter* reveals that any claims the English author made to poetic authority in this text most likely fell on deaf ears' (p. 684). This discrepancy is the focal point of Critten's article, which investigates the spotty reception of Hoccleve's poem, which he contrasts with the carefully controlled transmission of Christine's text in the medieval and early modern periods. Matthew Giancarlo considers Hoccleve's contribution to the 'mirror for princes' genre on the English *Fürstenspiegel* in 'Mirror, Mirror: Princely Hermeneutics, Practical Constitutionalism, and the Genres of the English *Fürstenspiegel*' (*Exemplaria* 27[2015] 35–54; also discussed in Sections 2 and 7 above). Giancarlo characterizes these 'mirror-texts' (as he terms them) as preeminently 'protean and accretive' in nature (p. 35). Mirror-texts 'are usually offered as instructions to the prince for his self-formation and for the sake of the commonweal or common good, but they are also addressed to the prince as the *source* of common good and sovereign authority' (p. 37; emphasis original), and it is this paradox that serves as the focal point for Giancarlo's argument. Drawing on the work of Fredric Jameson and Giorgio Agamben, Giancarlo proposes that English mirrors for princes might show us how a combination of genre theory and historical reading could revise our own conceptions of ourselves as sovereign individuals. While his article is concerned in general with late medieval English examples of the mirror for princes genre, Giancarlo notes in the case of Hoccleve's *Regiment of Princes* that 'his framing of a *De regimine* to his prince in the context of his own sociopolitical subordination, and in the broader context of a period of severe political instability, generates a significant reversal of key figures in the traditional pedagogical arrangement found in manuals of advice' (p. 41).

Hoccleve also features in Ethan Knapp's *Exemplaria* article on late medieval allegory (also reviewed in Section 12 above), which uses Walter Benjamin's discussion of the *flâneur* as a lens through which to reconsider texts such as Hoccleve's *La Male Regle*, Langland's *Piers Plowman*, and the opening *Visio* of John Gower's *Vox Clamantis* ('Towards a Material Allegory: Allegory and Urban Space in Hoccleve, Langland, and Gower', *Exemplaria* 27[2015] 93–109). Knapp explores the problem of the 'temporality' of interpreting allegory, 'the fact that an equal devotion to both tenor and vehicle can be maintained only in the moment before meaning is chosen' (p. 94), focusing in particular on the use of urban space in the three texts he discusses. He argues that, 'while Hoccleve and Langland share a very similar ambivalence about the crowd and urban space, Gower expresses mostly distaste and extreme anxiety' (p. 95). Knapp acknowledges that Hoccleve and Langland may seem like an unlikely pair for comparative analysis, but suggests that they share an interest in linking allegory to the depiction of urban space. Knapp shows how *La Male Regle* narrates what is in fact 'a mappable progression through London and Westminster' in four stages, each of which is marked by 'a new beginning in the form of an emphatic transition from allegory to literal representation' (p. 97).

Finally, Hoccleve plays a key role in Danila Sokolov's article on 'Renaissance Petrarchism and Medieval Begging in Robert Sidney's Sonnets' (*SEL* 55[2015] 21–43). Sokolov contends that the 'languages of sickness and penury' (p. 22) that permeate Sidney's and Shakespeare's sonnets owe much to style of medieval begging poems such as Hoccleve's *La Male Regle*, which Sokolov reads as 'the most illuminating instance of this form of discourse' (p. 27). While warning that Sidney's sonnets 'do not fall under the rubric of conscious medievalism' (p. 30), Sokolov proposes nevertheless that we might read early modern echoes of medieval begging poems as a form of discursive memory, a concept that might permit the consideration of chronologically distinct artefacts side by side.

*(b) Lydgate*

Anke Bernau published a chapter on 'Lydgate's Saintly Poetics' (in von Contzen and Bernau, eds., pp. 151–71). Bernau's essay contributes to a recent wave of publications on Lydgate's religious writings, and shows how Lydgate 'articulates a "saintly poetics"' (p. 151) in the verse life of *Saint Alban and Saint Amphibalus*. Bernau's discussion focuses on three aspects of Lydgate's *vita*: 'its engagement with the discourse of laureation, its treatment of "colours", and its temporal manoeuvres' (p. 152). Although Lydgate's laureate ambitions have been most frequently noted in his secular writings, Bernau shows how they also pervade the life of writings such as *Saint Alban and Saint Amphibalus*, in which the laurels of saints enable Lydgate 'to become the poet he claims not to be' and free him 'from having to follow in any poetic predecessor's "steppis aureat"' (p. 155). In this text, saints replace the Muses as the source of the rhetorical 'colours' that will 'enlumyne' Lydgate's verse. Bernau further argues that the poem emphasizes rupture rather than continuity between pagan Roman and Christian temporalities and customs in a way that enables Lydgate to use 'the stability that hagiography permits in order to valorize the "newness" of his articulation of sanctity, a sanctity that is also the sign of a poetic "new order"' (p. 165).

A second essay in the same volume by Eva von Contzen, 'Narrating Vernacular Sanctity: The *Scottish Legendary* as a Challenge to the "Literary Turn" in Fifteenth-Century Hagiography' (pp. 172–90), contends that Lydgate was acutely aware of 'the *formal* potential of hagiographic writing', a potential that led to the 'central loss or decline of hagiographic writing as a *narrative* genre in the fifteenth century' (p. 173; emphasis original). While scholars have tended to emphasize the exemplarity of hagiography at the expense of its narrativity, von Contzen argues, 'sanctity can be understood as the superordinate idea created by and transmitted through the dynamic processes of hagiographic narration' (p. 173). Von Contzen notes that Lydgate's hagiographical corpus stresses poetic form over narration in its depictions of sanctity. His approach contrasts sharply with that of the *Scottish Legendary*, which von Contzen proceeds to compare with Lydgate's legends (focusing particularly on their differing treatments of the life of St Margaret).

In a chapter of her *Anglo-Saxon Saints' Lives as History Writing in Late Medieval England*, Cynthia Turner Camp explores the presentation copy of Lydgate's *Lives of SS Edmund and Fremund* in London, British Library MS Harley 2278, focusing on what she describes as the manuscript's unusual lack of concern regarding historiographical matters in comparison with that evidenced by other contemporaneous saints' lives. Camp views *Edmund and Fremund* as 'less invested in meshing with chronicle history than its late medieval counterparts' (p. 176); instead, the poem makes use of what Camp identifies as the interplay between two spatio-temporal constructions: the monastic chronotype (a historiographical structure that focuses 'on a religious institution's origins, development, and traditions', p. 20), and the iconic chronotype (which privileges a saint's 'despatialized *virtus* and supratemporal exemplary potential over the supposed historical time and place of her *passio*', p. 20). She argues that from the interplay between these two concepts, which she identifies as occurring between the manuscript's text and its programme of illustration, 'emerges the figure of the shrinekeeper, the devout individual privileged to speak intimately with the saint and to intervene between saint and devotee' (pp. 178–9).

Like Camp, Timothy R. Jordan concentrates on the theme of shrine-keeping in the version of Lydgate's *Lives of SS Edmund and Fremund* contained in 'St. Edmund's Shrinekeepers: Monastic Self-Depiction in Harley 2278' (*ABR* 66[2015] 30–55). Jordan explores how the various models of kingship depicted in Lydgate's *Lives* might have benefited the poet's fellow monks at Bury St Edmunds, arguing that 'Lydgate uses the Edmund legend to assert concerns with royal privilege infringing on monastic authority' (p. 30). Jordan notes that shrine-keeping is a source of tremendous power for various characters in Lydgate's text, and suggests that the presentation of Harley 2278 to the king may have been viewed by Lydgate and his fellow-monks as an opportunity to represent themselves and their interests to the king. Jordan situates his discussion of Harley 2278 within the tense political climate of the mid-fifteenth century, when monastic houses struggled to maintain their autonomy in the face of Lancastrian pressure. Henry's visit to the abbey at Bury St Edmunds thus represented both an honour and an opportunity for its community to secure its favoured position with the king.

Seth Lerer's '"The Tongue": Chaucer, Lydgate, Charles d'Orléans, and the Making of a Late Medieval Lyric' (*ChauR* 49[2015] 474–98), on a poem in Cambridge University Library MS Ff.1.6 (the Findern manuscript), investigates how this composite text, made up of material from Chaucer's *Troilus and Criseyde*, Lydgate's *Fall of Princes* and one original stanza, engages with the broader concerns of the manuscript in which it appears, as well as the literary sensibility of Charles d'Orléans. The poem seemed to have moved in and out of existence in the eyes of contemporary scholars. Lerer's purpose is to 'restore a literary integrity to this assembly of stanzas', which he views as offering 'critical insight into notions of voice and poetic authority in late medieval manuscript culture' (p. 476). He investigates the changes made to the Chaucerian and Lydgatean material in 'The Tongue', and argues that it engages with 'the ideals of well-behaved speech' (p. 497) that characterize so much of the manuscript's contents.

In 'Lydgate's *Danse Macabre* and the Trauma of the Hundred Years War' (*L&M* 33[2015] 326–47), R.D. Perry argues that the poem's 'most distinctive literary features—its repetitive nature and its obsessive narration of death—become legible in modern terms as the narrative characteristics of trauma' (p. 326). Perry traces the influence of three separate genres—estates satire, tragedy, and the 'mirror for princes' genre—in Lydgate's poem, which he argues collectively enable Lydgate 'to present an overview of the trauma caused by warfare as a critique of the nobility' (p. 328). Reading the *Danse*

*Macabre* in light of the work of trauma theorists, Perry suggests that we can see some of the symptoms that have been associated with trauma for the past century at work in Lydgate's poem. Just as narratives of trauma 'have at their origin a lacuna that the subject repeatedly struggles to fill with content', the *Danse Macabre* 'contains exactly such a foundational lacuna' (p. 332), which Perry links to Lydgate's experience of the Hundred Years War. By merging estates satire with the 'mirror for princes' genre, Perry argues, Lydgate's *Danse Macabre* produces 'a particular kind of tragedy, one that allows Lydgate to show the traumatic effects of the king's failings on the entire body politic' (pp. 342–3).

Continuing this year's trend of focusing on Lydgate's shorter poems, Sebastian Sobecki's article 'Lydgate's Kneeling Retraction: The *Testament* as a Literary Palinode' (*ChauR* 49[2015] 265–93) argues that the poem constitutes 'a literary palinode rather than a genuine rejection of Lydgate's secular and laureate career' (p. 268). Whereas the *Testament* is often characterized 'as a genuine attempt by Lydgate either to remove himself from the poem in a textual exercise of piety or to retract his secular writings at the end of his extraordinarily productive literary career' (p. 267), Sobecki reads its depiction of Lydgate's misspent youth as precisely what facilitates the poem's spiritual conclusion. Indeed, Sobecki suggests that the 'fruitful tension between the often conflicting demands of the secular and the religious' not only lie at the heart of the *Testament*'s literary project, but might offer 'a unique yet apt conceptual framework for future explorations of the entire body of Lydgate's work' (p. 269). Sobecki's account focuses on the way the poem imagines its narrator as kneeling before Christ, a 'quintessentially affective and submissive gesture' (p. 275) that is reinforced by the poem's visual and thematic meditation on Jesus's name but also 'unsettled' by Lydgate's aureate style and classical allusions (p. 278). Sobecki characterizes this dynamic as a duality that seems to suggest that Lydgate's more courtly literary undertakings are not necessarily at odds with his religious writings. Pointing to the many illuminations in Lydgate manuscripts in which Lydgate is depicted as kneeling before both sovereigns and saints, Sobecki further suggests that Lydgate's fifteenth-century readers had no difficulty imagining him as a poet who moved within both secular and sacred circles, a concept that he argues might usefully shape future considerations of his work. In 'A Previously Unrecorded Manuscript Version of Lydgate's Testament' (*N&Q* 62[2015] 27–8), Mary Wellesley identifies a very late copy of one of Lydgate's most popular shorter poems in Liverpool Cathedral Library MS Radcliffe 16.

Lydgate features in two articles that appeared in a special issue of the *South Atlantic Review* on John Gower (discussed in Section 12). The first, by Stephen R. Reimer, 'A New Arion: Lydgate on Saints, Kings, and "Good Acord"' (*SoAR* 79:iii–iv[2015] 144–55), proposes a new reading of Lydgate's works as more closely aligned with the interests of Gower, rather than as most markedly Chaucerian. Reimer focuses on the poets' shared interest in a well-ordered society, and notes that Lydgate 'uses many of the same keywords and concepts that Gower uses' in his treatment of the subject (p. 144). After a brief overview of Lydgate's political themes, Reimer concentrates on how Lydgate's *Lives of SS Edmund and Fremund* and *Lives of SS Alban and Amphibal* depict saints who are 'active in the world, exemplifying the virtues of kings and knights, and are rewarded with martyrdom, as if achieving kingly or knightly perfection, through service to the common good, was a direct path to sainthood' (p. 146). The second article concerning Lydgate in this special issue is by Robert R. Edwards, 'Lydgate and the Trace of Gower' (*SoAR* 79:iii–iv[2015] 156–70), which explores the ways in which Lydgate might be viewed as following in the 'trace' of Gower. Like Reimer, Edwards suggests that we look to Gower as well as Chaucer for the inspiration behind much of Lydgate's verse, suggesting that 'Gower is the poetic interlocutor who shows how a writer of ethical conviction engages the profound contradictions that abide in the public sphere and the duties of official sponsorship' (p. 156). Edwards recounts the numerous occasions on which Lydgate's works reveal both acknowledged and unacknowledged debts to his predecessor, arguing that, in contrast with Chaucer, 'Gower marks a path for Lydgate into the substantive matter of writing in the public sphere' (p. 166).

Alaya Swann includes some discussion of Lydgate's *Life of Our Lady* in her article on late medieval English representations of the doubting midwife Salome who dares to insist on confirming the Virgin Mary's miraculous intactness by touch: '"By expresse experiment": The Doubting Midwife Salome in Late Medieval England' (*BHM* 89[2015] 1–24). Considering in turn evidence from sermon collections, devotional texts, the cycle nativity plays, and Lydgate's poem, Swann points to the different versions of this apocryphal story as narratives that present 'late medieval midwives as working outside the overlay of male, privileged, and theoretical knowledge', but which also confine 'female experiential knowledge inside the limits of prescribed areas; touch must be both careful and devotional' (p. 3). Swann notes that Lydgate's version of this narrative includes additional details that midwives would have recognized as confirmation of the Virgin's miraculous condition. This article positions Lydgate's *Life of Our Lady* within broader medieval debates about the value of experiential knowledge in medical practice.

An image from a manuscript of Lydgate's *Troy Book* features on the inside front cover of the *PN Review*, where it appears as 'Pictures from a Library: 18: "All That Glisters Is Not Gold": John Lydgate's *Troy Book*' (*PNR* 41[2015] inside front cover). Stella Halkyard introduces the illumination of the Trojan Horse being admitted into the city, an image that appears in Manchester, John Rylands Library, Rylands MS English 1 (fo. 145$^v$). Halkyard notes the illuminator's decision to render the wooden horse in gold leaf, a decision that she suggests is intended to highlight the deceitfulness of the Greeks, who 'know that they can dupe the Trojans into not looking this gift-horse in the mouth because they will interpret the gold as a sign of its incorruptibility'.

## 14. Older Scots

Two editions were published by the Scottish Text Society in 2015. Alasdair A. MacDonald's *The Gude and Godlie Ballatis* presents a comprehensive discussion of the print history and the witnesses for the text as well as giving an overview of previous textual scholarship on the material. He also includes verse that was added to later editions of the *Ballatis*. Significant textual commentary allows the reader to compare variant print editions, and a glossary is provided. Alasdair A. MacDonald also discusses the *Gude and Godlie Ballatis* in 'Writing Which, and Whose, Identity? The Challenges of the *Gude and Godlie Ballatis*' (*M&H* 41[2015] 157–67), in which he explores the scant evidence for (and warns against accepting) the assumed authorship of the work by the Wedderburn brothers. Joanna Martin, *The Maitland Quarto*, presents the first critical edition of all of the texts in the Maitland Quarto (Cambridge, Magdalene College, Pepys MS 1408). In her introduction Martin provides an overview of key areas of Maitland scholarship, including the manuscript's cultural and textual context as well as useful background to the Maitland family. A substantial part of the edition comprises headnotes and commentaries for each poem. This is a very welcome addition to the Scottish Text Society catalogue.

A special issue of *Medievalia et Humanistica* edited by Eva von Contzen and Luuk Houwen takes as its focus writing and identity in medieval and early modern Scotland. In 'Books Beyond Borders: Fresh Findings on Boethius's Reception in Twelfth-Century Scotland' (*M&H* 41[2015] 7–43), Kylie Murray presents evidence for the circulation of Boethius's *De Consolatione Philosophiae* and the *Liber Divisione* during the reign of David I. She challenges the 'prevailing theory' (p. 8) that Scottish engagement with Boethius's work was mediated through the literature of the fifteenth century. Rhiannon Purdie analyses Wyntoun's rhetorical skill in 'Malcolm, Margaret, Macbeth, and the Miller: Rhetoric and the Re-Shaping of History in Wyntoun's *Original Chronicle*' (*M&H* 41[2015] 45–63). Taking as her focus Wyntoun's chapters narrating the reign of Macbeth and the births and union of Malcom III and St Margaret, Purdie demonstrates how Wyntoun created an 'interlaced structure of multiple narratives' (p. 55) in order to present a version of Scottish history that was designed to appeal to a broad fifteenth-century audience. Ideas of rhetorical strategy also play a part in Claire Harrill's discussion in '"Ego sum Margarita olim Scotorum Regina": St Margaret and the Idea of the Scottish Nation in Walter Bower's *Scotichronicon*' (*M&H* 41[2015] 65–79). Harrill proposes that Bower's Margaret becomes a metonym for Scottish sovereignty through her roles as queen, mother, and saint. An examination of the rhetorical uses of historical narrative is also the subject of Kate Ash's chapter, 'St Margaret and the Literary Politics of Scottish Sainthood' (in von Contzen and Bernau, eds., pp. 18–37), in which she argues that Bower's interest in Margaret's sanctity serves both a literary and a political agenda in the mid-fifteenth century. In reading key episodes from the *Scotichronicon*'s narrative of Margaret, Ash suggests that Bower's use of sanctity as literary ornament demonstrates an awareness of the mechanisms by which historical narratives function for a contemporary audience. Other chapters in *Sanctity as Literature* are reviewed in Sections 11 and 13. In 'The Use of Virgil's *Eclogues* and *Georgics* in the *Eneados* of Gavin Douglas' (*M&H* 41[2015] 101–18), Conor Leahy traces the influence of key works of Virgil in prologues 4, 5, and 6 of Douglas's translation of the *Aeneid*. He argues that at these moments Douglas's use of paraphrase and assimila-tion—rather than faithful translation—demonstrates his own compositional techniques and poetic engagement that enrich his interpretation of the *Aeneid*. Also concerned with the *Eneados*, in 'Gavin Douglas's Humanist Identity' (*M&H* 41[2015] 119–36), Nicola Royan revisits the assumed humanism of Douglas to address the extent to which his concerns with kinship, patronage, and his status as a churchman as markers of identity influenced his approach to translation and, in particular, his choice of writing in the vernacular. Elizabeth Hanna considers John Mair's sustained engagement with Caxton's material in '"A Mass of Incoherencies": John Mair, William Caxton, and the Creation of British History in Early Sixteenth-Century Scotland' (*M&H* 41[2015] 137–55). She argues that, rather than dismissing Caxton's narrative of Anglo-Scottish relations, Mair's 'unionist agenda' (p. 150) prompts him to rebuke the English historical narrative by attempting to create a British historiography that engages with texts from both sides of the border. In '"Let all ȝour verse be literall": Innovation and Identity in Scottish Alliterative Verse' (*M&H* 41[2015] 169–93), Jeremy Scott Ecke makes the case for distinguishing between 'literall' and alliterative verse through a close reading of John Stewart of Baldynneis's *Ane Schersing out of Trew Felicitie* and 'Ane Literall Sonnet'. Through close consideration of Stewart's metrics, Ecke proposes that it is more appropriate to see Older Scots poets' deviation from the rules of alliterative metre not as a waning of an alliterative tradition but rather as a new height in 'alliterative consciousness' (p. 188). Alison Steenson's 'Writing Sonnets as a Scoto-Britane: Scottish Sonnets, the Union of the Crowns, and Negotiations of Identity' (*M&H* 41[2015] 195–210) also takes metrics as its focus to examine the ways in which choices made about sonnet patterns highlight complex negotiations of English and Scottish identities at the point of the Union of the Crowns. While Steenson points to the tensions between Scottish and British identities in the metrical choices of William Alexander and Alexander Craig, Jamie Reid Baxter's 'James Melville and the "Releife of the longing soule": A Scottish Presbyterian Song of Songs?' (*M&H* 41[2015] 211–30) considers how Melville's work was strongly influenced by English and Continental Calvinism. In particular, Reid Baxter notes how Melville's 'Releife' incorporates the works of Dudley Fenner, Thomas Wilcox, and George Gifford. Other articles in this special issue are not directly concerned with literary matters.

Joanna Martin argues for the development of a distinctive Protestant poetics in 'Alexander Arbuthnot and the Lyric in Post-Reformation Scotland' (*SSL* 41[2015] 62–87). Discussing the six poems attributed to Arbuthnot in the Maitland Quarto, and paying particular attention to the devotional lexis of the works, Martin ascertains the influence of contemporary theological debates on the poems' composition that provide evidence for the Protestant sympathies of the Maitland network of readers and writers. Scottish Presbyterian poetics are also a concern of Sarah C.E. Ross's study of Elizabeth Melville in the first chapter of *Women, Poetry, and Politics in Seventeenth-Century Britain*. This book is reviewed in Chapter IX.

In 'The Source and Significance of a Marginal Inscription in the *Buik of Alexander*' (*N&Q* 62[2015] 57–8), Priscilla Bawcutt sheds light on a marginal inscription in the single extant copy of the Scottish *Buik of Alexander* [*c*.1580]. She attributes the source of 'The pains departs bot vertue remaines' to the

*Treatise of Morall Philosophie* compiled by William Baldwin in 1547 and later expanded by Thomas Paulfreyman. Bawcutt points to further instances of its use in early modern Scotland. The concept of honour is the subject of Andrew James Johnston and Margitta Rouse's chapter, 'Facing the Mirror: Ekphrasis, Vision, and Knowledge in Gavin Douglas's Palice of Honour' (in Johnston et al., eds., pp. 166–83). Arguing that ekphrasis is used as a complex argumentative structure by Douglas, Johnston and Rouse demonstrate how different views of honour are contrasted through the allegorical narrative of the *Palice* in which 'ekphrasis as a dynamic literary *topos*' simultaneously 'veils the horrors of honourable violence, as well as allowing them to break to the surface' (p. 183).

In '"Hamelie Language" and *Translatio Studii* in Henryson's *Aesopic Fables*' (in Nicholson, Marquis, and Szamosi, eds., *Contested Identities: Literary Negotiations in Time and Place*, pp. 137–55), Roger Nicholson reflects on Henryson's translations from Latin to Scots to argue that, while literary translation sought to appropriate the ideas and experiences of Latinate culture, instances of code-switching in the *Fables* point to the possibility that Henryson's 'hamelie language' might naturalize Latin phrasings and borrowings. The *Fabillis* are also the focus of Laura Wang's 'Robert Henryson and the Animal in the Mirror' (*RES* 66[2015] 20–39), in which she seeks to demonstrate how Henryson both engages with and critiques fifteenth-century political theory. In arguing for a reformist reading of the *Fabillis*, Wang posits that Henryson's challenging of natural law and his mixing of the darker elements of fable, Reynardian epic, and Augustinian theology allow for the creation of a literary space in which the 'realities of political life and the possibility of reform' can be more effectively realised (p. 39). J.A. Burrow also examines ideas of natural law and the natural world in 'Nature in *King Hart*' (*RES* 66[2015] 624–33). Burrow illuminates the ways in which Hart's behaviour and feelings might be understood to be subject to natural influences throughout his transition from youth to old age. Continuing with ideas of ageing, Amber Dunai's '"Ane doolie sessoun" and "Ane cairfull dyte": Cresseid and the Narrator in Henryson's *Testament of Cresseid*' (*ChauR* 50[2015] 420–41) argues for the centrality of the narrator in Henryson's poem and suggests that his unperceptive response to Cresseid's story should act as an educative prompt for his own development.

Two chapters in *Children and Youth in Premodern Scotland*, edited by Janay Nugent and Elizabeth Ewan, are concerned with Older Scots literature. In 'Sons and Daughters, "young wyfis" and "barnis": Lyric, Gender, and the Imagining of Youth in the Maitland Manuscripts' (pp. 187–201), Sarah M. Dunnigan analyses the 'imaginative filiation' (p. 190) of the Maitland anthologies and situates Scottish texts within the broader European literary tradition of advice for children. Tracing the different responses to sons and daughters in the Maitland collections, Dunnigan demonstrates how the texts of the Folio and Quarto manuscripts encompass anxieties about familial and domestic relationships, and how the Quarto establishes a literary space for 'daughterly non-conformity' (p. 200). Jamie Reid Baxter's 'Elizabeth Melville, Lady Culross: Two Letters to Her Son James' (pp. 205–19) prints two letters from Melville for the first time.

Danila Sokolov reads the passion of the Casket Sonnets attributed to Mary, Queen of Scots against the *Kingis Quair*'s ideal of chaste sovereign love and Elizabeth I's cultivated virginity in '"Nat being (to my displesure) your wife as she": The Politics and Poetics of Sovereign Marriage in the Casket Sonnets' (*MP* 112[2015] 458–78). Sokolov argues that, as articulations of royal subjectivity, the Casket Sonnets threaten to disrupt the alliance between monarch and subject in the pursuit of the monarch's personal desire. Surveying the large number of begging poems in the Dunbar corpus, John Burrow examines the myriad ways in which a poet might beg for monetary rewards through close reading of a number of Dunbar's petitionary poems in 'Dunbar's Art of Asking' (*EIC* 65[2015] 1–11).

In arguing for the pig as a perfect comic hero despite (or perhaps because of) its reputation as a disruptive figure, Caitlin Flynn reads the comic subversion of legal language and community cohesion as an imaginative reworking of peacekeeping in late medieval Scotland in 'Mobbing, (Dis)order and the Literary Pig in *The Tale of Colkelbie Sow, Pars Prima*' (*SSL* 41[2015] 47–61). Published in 2014, but not received in time for review in last year's *YWES*, Greg Walker's 'The Popular Voice in Sir David Lyndsay's *Satire of the Thrie Estaitis*' (*SSL* 40[2014] 39–54) traces the development of the reforming voice in Lyndsay's drama from that of a single rural smallholder to two actors representing the figures, Pauper and John the Commonweal. Rather than being a comical figure like his comparable English counterparts, Walker argues, Lyndsay's Pauper provides an authentic (and authenticating) voice of the poor, whereas John speaks *for* the poor without being one of them.

Steve Boardman and Susan Foran's edited collection, *Barbour's Bruce and its Cultural Contexts: Politics, Chivalry and Literature in Late Medieval Scotland*, sets out to 'investigate diverse aspects' of Barbour's poem, specifically 'its manuscript history, the literary, intellectual and historical context(s) in which it was produced ... as well as the reception and recycling of the work in later medieval Scotland' (p. 25). While the volume in its entirety will be of interest to those working on Barbour's text and Older Scots more generally, the following chapters are the more literary in focus. In 'The Manuscript and Print Contexts of Barbour's *Bruce*' (pp. 33–50), Emily Wingfield surveys extant copies of the poem, providing detailed descriptions of the two surviving manuscript witnesses and detailing the transition from manuscript to print. She concludes that John Ramsay was responsible for both surviving manuscript witnesses. Rhiannon Purdie revisits the question of genre at work in the construction of the *Bruce* in 'Medieval Romance and the Generic Frictions of Barbour's *Bruce*' (pp. 51–74), analysing the ways in which Barbour was influenced by Old French *romans antiques* for his construction of the *Bruce*. Ultimately, Purdie concludes, while Barbour cannot escape the historicity of his subject matter, he relied on romance to structure a narrative that would appeal to his audience. Authorial intention and textual composition are also a concern for Theo van Heijnsbergen in 'Scripting the National Past: A Textual Community of the Realm' (pp. 75–99), in which he presents a detailed reading of the *Bruce*'s prologue to illustrate how Barbour very deliberately relied on rhetorical practice to negotiate the tensions between romance and history, thereby signalling the creation of a 'usable' collective past for his readership. Three chapters centre on discussions of chivalry. Chris Given-Wilson's 'Chivalric Biography and Medieval Life Writing (pp. 101–17) returns to the question of genre by discussing whether Barbour's poem might fruitfully be understood as a chivalric biography promoting ideals of collective aristocratic honour. The language of chivalry forms the basis of Diana B. Tyson's examination of Barbour's lexical choices compared to three Old French contemporary biographies in 'The Vocabulary of Chivalric Description in Late Fourteenth-Century Biography' (pp. 119–36). In outlining the construction of ideas of community and kingdom in 'A Nation of Knights? Chivalry and the Community of the Realm in Barbour's *Bruce*' (pp. 137–48), Susan Foran reads Barbour's poem as a foundation narrative for later Scottish histories and chronicles. Foran argues for the politicization of chivalry in the *Bruce* that is connected to the writing of a collective and cultural memory of a nation's past. In focusing on the Fife lairds who acted as both patrons to and audiences for the writers of literary texts, Michael Brown surveys the social and literary environment in which the manuscript copies of the *Bruce* were produced, in 'Barbour's *Bruce* in the 1480s: Literature and Locality' (pp. 213–31). In doing so, he calls attention to localized areas of literary production within late medieval Scotland. Biörn Tjällén, Dauvit Broun, and Steve Boardman's contributions focus on historical and cultural contexts for the *Bruce*.

In '"Ladyes war at thare avowing": The Female Gaze in Late-Medieval Scottish Romance' (in Perkins, ed., pp. 91–109), Anna Caughey identifies scopophiliac elements in the *Buik of Alexander*, *Lancelot of the Laik*, and *Clariodus*. In contrast to the trend in Scots texts whereby sexual love is seen as a distractive element to knightly action, Caughey argues that these three romances legitimize female sexuality through instances of them looking at men's martial bodies, and that this serves to motivate knightly endeavours, particularly in the service of the nation.

The *International Companion to Scottish Poetry*, edited by Carla Sassi, contains three survey chapters of interest to Older Scots studies. R.D.S. Jack provides an overview of major authors and genres in 'Scots Poetry in the Fourteenth and Fifteenth Centuries' (pp. 15–22), while Sim Innes and Alessandra Petrina cover 'The Sixteenth and Seventeenth Centuries' (pp. 44–53), paying particular attention to manuscript anthologies and the Marian period. J. Derrick McClure's 'Scots Poetic Forms' (pp. 109–20) also contains a significant discussion of Older Scots poetry.

Five articles on Scots drama in a special edition of *Medieval English Theatre* (37[2015]) are reviewed in Section 15.

## 15. Drama

This year has produced a number of works examining the ways in which medieval drama interacts with and fashions the identities of performer, spectator, and performance space. Andrea Louise Young's *Vision and Audience in Medieval Drama: A Study of the Castle of Perseverance* argues that vision is the organizing principle behind the staging, structure, and narrative of *The Castle of Perseverance* and its actor–audience relationships. In so doing, it makes an important contribution to the recent wave of work considering medieval spectatorship and the relationship between individual and communal acts. The volume provides a detailed study of medieval theories of vision and cognition; the morality of optics; and anxieties concerning the unstable meanings of visual signifiers and modern productions of the play. It argues that the play holds the acts of watching and being watched in a dynamic relationship that challenges audiences to learn new ways of looking.

Civic identities are also at the heart of Nicole R. Rice and Margaret Aziza Pappano's monograph, *The Civic Cycles: Artisan Drama and Identity in Pre-Modern England*. This focuses on the guilds of York and Chester and the ways in which their artisanal identities formed, and were formed by, their production of biblical drama. Rice and Pappano read the plays as products of the guilds' desire to consolidate their membership and to sacralize their values through collaborative production—as well as statements of connection between craft fellowship and civic responsibility and the guilds' claim over urban space. A comparative analysis of plays from York and Chester assesses their importance in constructing guild identities and distinguishing guild members from 'other' groups, including servants, wage labourers, and women, and in placing the master craftsman at the centre of the city community. This involves a more nuanced approach to the social make-up of these guilds than has generally been the case in previous criticism (which has often tended to assume guild homogeneity), while drawing intriguing parallels between the bodily processes of dramatic performance and practising a craft.

Questions of social power, resistance, and gender also form the basis of Robert Sturges's work *The Circulation of Power in Medieval Biblical Drama: Theaters of Authority*. This book offers a 'queer' response to the view that drama was used to sustain and perpetuate conventional power paradigms. Through a series of well-curated comparative case studies, and covering dramatic texts as diverse as *Quem quaeritis* and the Wakefield Master's *Second Shepherds' Pageant*, Sturges argues instead for the subversive potential of medieval drama. Focusing on the way power is made and sustained in biblical drama's engagement with the body, gender politics, money, and the law, the book suggests that these plays teach resistance at least as readily as they teach morality. Making an important case for reading medieval drama and dramatic culture as a way to engage with and rethink modern power relations and struggles, the book is part of a growing tendency among scholars of medieval theatre to read and value the past in terms of its ability to shed new light on the present.

An ongoing critical concern with the transmission and reception of plays as both text and performance is furthered by Frederick Kiefer's *English Drama from Everyman to 1660: Performance and Print*. One of a number of recent publications designed to catalogue early English drama, this book provides an indispensable toolkit for theatre practitioners and scholars of medieval and early modern drama. In an alphabetically arranged series of entries, it details the textual and performative histories of English plays from the earliest printed plays to the Restoration. The central focus of the catalogue is post-medieval drama, but it includes *Everyman* and early Tudor interludes.

Anne Lancashire and David Parkinson's three-volume *Civic London to 1558* is another immensely practical resource to have been published this year. It is a huge achievement, both in terms of its chronological scope and the wide range of performance documents it records. Historical records occupy the first two volumes. Volume 1 covers 1286–7 to 1520–3, and volume 2, 1521–2 to 1558–9. The third volume offers translations—largely the work of Abigail Ann Young—of non-English entries, as well as endnotes and glossaries. Adding substantially to the published evidence of early drama in London, these volumes shed new light on the performance of multi-day biblical plays, the sponsorship of performances by craft and trade guilds (and later royalty and the aristocracy), mummings at court and in company halls, and street performance including royal entries and mayoral inaugurations. The records are supported by a detailed introduction (in volume 1) that delineates the sources used (corporation and livery company records) and outlines the civic context, while a series of appendices covers materials including biographical records for key figures including musicians, players, and instrument makers as well as a comprehensive list of mayors and sheriffs. With the recently published volumes on *Ecclesiastical London* (Mary Erler, ed. *REED*, BL; UTorP [2008]) and *Inns of Court* (Alan H. Nelson and John R. Elliott, Jr., eds. *REED*, Brewer [2010]), it provides a near-exhaustive account of dramatic activity in medieval and early Renaissance London.

Douglas Gray's *Simple Forms: Essays on Medieval English Popular Literature* provides a study of popular or folk literature in the medieval period. The final chapter, 'Songs and Drama', discusses popular elements in medieval drama. Gray proposes not only that extant plays and interludes contain popular elements, but also that mystery cycles, which present the whole of Christian history to a lay audience, 'may well be the most important surviving example of English popular literature'. Noting the clerical auspices of many medieval plays, the learned and elite aspects of medieval drama have long been the focus of critical study. This essay offers a valuable corrective, and shows, explicitly, the dynamic relationship between oral traditions and book learning as testified by the various genres of medieval drama.

The relationship between play text and performance text continues to be an ongoing concern, and a number of works this year have sought to nuance these debates by considering spiritual engagement through spectacle and spiritual engagement through text. Tamara Atkin's 'Reforming Sanctity: The Digby *Mary Magdalen* and Lewis Wager's *The Life and Repentaunce of Marie Magdalene*' (in Bernau and von Contzen, eds., pp. 191–208) is part of a volume considering the manifestation and development of sanctity through literature. This chapter takes as its focus the different approaches to sanctity in the pre- and post-Reformation dramatizations of the hagiography of Mary Magdalene. Considering the plays' methods of giving holiness dramatic meaning, Atkin suggests that, while spectacle is used in the Digby *Mary Magdalen* as a means of illustrating and informing Mary's sanctity, in Wager's 1553 play spectacle and its trappings are established as emblematic both of Mary's sin and of the abuses of Roman Catholic piety. In doing so, she claims that Wager attempts a 'conversion of the saint play as genre' which is only partly successful.

The ways in which attitudes to material spectacle altered in the years leading up to the Reformation are also addressed in Gerhardt Ernst's discussion of the Croxton *Play*, which parallels the material and spiritual processes of production employed by the play's Jews and clergy. Re-examining Croxton's host-testing narrative as bringing the consecrated bread into contact with a series of culinary production techniques, recipes, and kitchen tools, 'Food Production in the Croxton *Play of the Sacrament*' (*CompD* 49[2015] 313–33) situates the play within a culinary, feasting, and trading culture in which the host is a 'twice-made' thing. In doing so, the article provides a detailed consideration of the play in relation to medieval Christian misunderstandings of Jewish Passover rituals; narratives of doubt concerning the combined material and spiritual labours of 'making' the Eucharist; and the increased focus on the host's materiality in Reformation satire.

Relationships between physicality and spirituality are central components of Susan Nakley's 'On the Unruly Power of Pain in Middle English Drama' (*L&M* 33[2015] 302–25). Nakley develops a theory about a 'dramaturgy of pain' as a way of exploring the relationship between pain and power in medieval dramatizations, specifically in the York *Play of the Crucifixion*, and the Wakefield Master's *Second Shepherds' Pageant*. These plays, despite their very different auspices, are often paired in critical treatment of medieval drama, which can result in a flattening of their very different performative circumstances. The article nonetheless teases out productive similarities that challenge prevailing ideas about pain and its relationship to divine punishment.

Frank M. Napolitano's essay, '"Here may we se a merveyl one": Miracles and the Psalter in the N-Town *Marriage of Mary and Joseph*' (*EarT* 18[2015] 37–56), examines Mary's reading of the Psalter as supplanting the miracle of Joseph's flowering wand in the N-Town *Marriage* pageant. It situates the play in relation to the comic elements of the flowering wand; miracle stories in medieval sermons and Mary's use of text and its relation to late medieval women's piety—suggesting that the blending of visual images with verbal and logical teaching performed related devotional functions. In doing so, it provides a new reading of the dialogue between God's intervention in the world through signs and angelic messengers and humanity's interaction with God's word through reading and prayer.

Links between plays and other forms of medieval performance are developed further in Ann Hubert's essay, 'Preaching Rhetorical Invention: Poeta and Paul in the Digby *Conversion of St Paul*' (*EarT* 18[2015] 9–32). This offers a reinterpretation of the figure of Poeta in the Digby *Conversion of St Paul*, and suggests he functions as far more than a framing device, as has traditionally been accepted. Rather, demonstrating and exploring his indebtedness to medieval preaching practices, Hubert argues his main function is to legitimize Paul as a credible Christian convert. Situating *St Paul* within the context of medieval sermons and preaching theory, this essay contributes to a broader critical discussion about the interrelatedness of drama and other performative genres.

Three essays by Mariana Lopez seek to broaden discussions of the experience of medieval spectatorship through investigating the acoustic properties of performance. 'Objective Evaluation of a Simulation of the Acoustics of a Medieval Urban Space Used for Dramatic Performances' (*Applied Acoustics* 88[2015] 38–43) employs computer modelling to study the acoustics of York's medieval Stonegate, which was one of the performance sites for the York Mystery Plays. This paper provides a context for and explains the technology used for the computer model which is then used as the basis for the analysis in the second article in the same journal, 'Using Multiple Computer Models to Study the Acoustics of a Sixteenth-Century Performance Space' (*Applied Acoustics* 94[2015] 14–19). Recognizing the importance of the *York Mystery Plays*' acoustic features, this article uses technological modelling techniques to show how architectures of space may have impacted the sonic experience of these plays in their original performance contexts. This argument is developed further in 'An Acoustical Approach to the Study of the Wagons of the York Mystery Plays: Structure and Orientation' (*EarT* 18[2015] 11–36), where the same model is used to calculate the impact of the introduction of wagons to the acoustics of four possible versions of the space. While providing a useful insight into the variables in the relationship between acoustics and performances spaces, the article hints at the further work these considerations might prompt—particularly concerning how a player might adapt their vocal performance to accommodate the demands of spaces and wagons with different acoustic properties. These articles contribute to a growing specialist field focused on aspects of the acoustics of street performance spaces. The emphasis on historic performance conditions illustrates how multiple computer models can offer new insights into the performance of medieval drama, and points to possibilities for potentially productive collaborations between scholars of medieval theatre and digital researchers.

Spectatorship and text have likewise been concerns in the essays contributed to this year's edition of *Medieval English Theatre*. The essays in this volume and those forthcoming in volume 38[2016] form a composite Festschrift celebrating the work of Professor John J. McGavin, and focus on his diverse interests in the early drama of England and, especially, of Scotland. Sarah Carpenter's essay, 'The Places of Foolery: Robert Armin and Fooling in Edinburgh' (*METh* 37[2015] 11–26), takes McGavin's *Theatricality and Narrative in Medieval and Early Modern Scotland* as its critical cornerstone, and offers a reading Robert Armin's *Foole upon Foole* [1600]—specifically, its depiction of the Scottish 'natural fool' Jemy Camber. Taking Camber and his home city, Edinburgh, as her case studies, Carpenter argues that narratives about fooling naturally lend themselves to the psychogeographical project of mapping the city's places of play. The focus is clearly post-medieval, but the implications will have interest and relevance to scholars of medieval drama in England and Scotland. Last year's critical work on David Lyndsay's *Satire of the Thrie Estaits* is built upon in three new essays. Janet Hadley Williams's 'George Bannatyne's "Sertane Mirry Interludis", and Sir David Lyndsay's Play' (*METh* 37[2015] 27–40) takes the play's textual history as its focus, and in particular its survival in a mid-sixteenth-century manuscript compiled by the Edinburgh merchant George Bannatyne. Considering the differences between this witness and the play as printed in 1602, and the relationship between the text and the various other items in Bannatyne's manuscript, the essay offers new ways of approaching Lyndsay's play in the light of the recent material turn in English studies. Greg Walker's essay, 'The Linlithgow Interlude of 1540 and Lyndsay's *Satire of the Thrie Estaitis*' (*METh* 37[2015] 41–56), reassesses the relationship between an unknown 'Interlude' played before James V in Linlithgow in 1540 (for which we have only a description), and Lyndsay's play of 1552 and 1554. He concludes that it is possible to map parts of *Ane Satire* back onto the description of the 'Interlude', therefore making Lyndsay's authorship of the earlier play indisputable. The third essay is Peter Happé's 'Stage Directions in Lyndsay's *Ane Satire of the Thrie Estaits*' (*METh* 37[2015] 57–72). This offers a comparative review of the stage directions in the two surviving texts and a discussion about what they reveal concerning the composition, publication, and performance of the work and the different objectives these fulfilled. Happé also situates the play within contemporary tensions between James VI and the Kirk concerning the morality of performance, and suggests that the *Satire*'s use of and deviation from a variety of dramatic genres constitutes an attempt to find a different kind of drama of protest.

Bob Godfrey's contribution, 'The Digby *Mary Magdalen* in Performance: A Merry Peripeteia' (*METh* 37[2015] 105–18), draws on his own work as a director as well as a close study of the play's stage directions to make a convincing case for the performance of the *Mary Magdalen* as medieval theatre in the round. This adds to previous work suggesting a round for this play, with the audience in promenade. Through analysing the multiple journeys made between dramatic loci, Godfrey focuses on the ways in which these journeys might affect the audience's experience of the play: the audience's concept of geography and travel, and the character journeys undergone by the players as they accommodate shifts of stance, status, and situation. This article works well in dialogue with the wider scope of Young's monograph (see above), and suggests that we are entering an exciting period of *Mary Magdalen* studies.

This year's *Medieval English Theatre* also includes an article by Tanya Hagen and Sally-Beth MacLean. 'How to Track a Bear in Southwark: A Learning Module' (*METh* 37[2015] 90–104) gives a summary of the recently developed *Early Modern London Theatres* online platform, and illustrates how its unique, accessible interface can serve not only as a research tool by providing an overview of the historical and archival record, but also as a broader educational resource. Given the nature of the historical material, it is not surprising that the focus is post-medieval. However, the essay offers useful insights into early drama pedagogy that will have application for medieval drama instructors.

Three essays engage with the plays and form of the Towneley manuscript. Garrett Epp is currently editing the manuscript for a new edition, and is therefore in a unique position to reappraise its form and function. His essay, '"Thus am I rent on rode": Taking Apart the Towneley *Crucifixion*' (*METh* 37[2015] 119–33), takes the position that it is a composite work, and reads the *Crucifixion* pageant as symptomatic of the manuscript's wider make-up, as a play imperfectly pieced together from a diverse range of sources. Over the course of the essay, Epp works to pull the pageant apart in order to examine its constituent parts and thereby speculate how the play might have been performed. While it is impossible to know if the play was written or intended for performance, Epp's approach nonetheless points the way to a reading of performance that takes fuller account of the material conditions of textual survival. Alexandra F. Johnston's '*The Second Shepherds' Play*: A Play for the Christmas Season' (*METh* 37[2015] 134–48) builds on her earlier arguments for an Easter play as a sub-genre of English biblical drama by claiming that there was also a genre of Christmas plays performed during the twelve Christmas feast days. This marks a development in the current focus on the nature of the plays of the Towneley and N-Town manuscripts as compilations of 'stand-alone' plays. Johnston first examines records suggesting the performance of plays alongside other Christmas revels around England, before arguing that the Towneley *Second Shepherds' Play* contains a number of elements which would have made it particularly amenable to an educated audience, possibly in a noble or monastic household, who would have been used to dramatic forms supporting social and political satire alongside farce. Meg Twycross's '"They did not come out of an Abbey in Lancashire": Francis Douce and the Manuscript of the Towneley Plays' (*METh* 37[2015] 149–65) grows out of the material researched for her long-awaited collection of essays on Towneley. In it, she shows how the scholar and antiquary Francis Douce may be responsible for arming critics with evidence for the two opposing and dominant views of the manuscript's provenance. Critics have argued over whether the document is a hidden heirloom, recording the Towneley family's recusant beliefs, or a more recent incomer, given to the family in the seventeenth century by a visiting Yorkshire antiquarian. Twycross traces the legacies of both these critical viewpoints back to Douce. It's a tantalizing essay, but one that frustrates the reader with the promise that all will be revealed when 'the book' is finally published.

This resurgence of interest in medieval dramatic manuscript culture is echoed elsewhere. Elza Tiner is one of a number of scholars currently working on the sole extant copy of Thomas Chaundler's *Liber apologeticus*, Cambridge, Trinity College Library, MS R.14.5—a presentation from the author to Thomas Bekynton, bishop of Bath and Wells. Her 'Performance Spaces in Thomas Chaundler's *Liber apologeticus*' (*EarT* 18[2015] 33–50) suggests three possible sites of original performance from the manuscript's various material and palaeographical clues. It demonstrates that even dramatic manuscripts designed for private reading could simultaneously recall the moment of original performance and provide hints for future performance. In '"This citie of insufficience": Heraldic Text and the Representation of Authority in York's 1486 Entertainment for Henry VII' (*EarT* 18[2015] 51–78) Lloyd Edward Kermode compares the two extant texts that record the York welcome pageants for King Henry VII in 1486. Exploring the profitable tensions between versions of the entry as recorded in the York House Books and the four-year 'Herald's memoir' in British Library MS Cotton Julius B.XIII, Kermode suggests that closer engagement with their contexts—their original form and function—explains why they remain incomplete and at odds. Matteo A. Pangallo's '"I will keep and character that name": Dramatis Personae Lists in Early Modern Manuscript Plays' (*EarT* 18[2015] 87–118) focuses on such lists as occur in late medieval and early modern dramatic manuscripts. His argument that character lists prove that pre-playhouse plays were intended for performance rather than reader consumption is a little over-stated, but this essay nonetheless offers a valuable contribution to the recent materially focused studies of early drama.

This year has also seen the emergence of a number of studies into the workings of time and temporality in medieval drama. Collective anticipation of the future is discussed in Jill Stevenson's 'Poised at the Threatening Edge: Feeling the Future in Medieval Last Judgment Performances' (*TJ* 67[2015] 273–93). Stevenson explores what she calls a 'dramaturgy of threat' intended to foster anxiety, simulating the experience of the Apocalypse in ways that collapse social distinctions and foster a collective sense of the reality of the Last Judgement. Taking a comparative approach, and usefully situating medieval English Judgement plays in a wider Continental context, Stevenson's essay is concerned with the ways in which time is figured and functions in medieval drama. Here it is shown to shore up the authority of the Church, creating in the audience a community of faithful, united in its belief in the End of Days.

Three contributions by Daisy Black examine the ways in which models of time and gender are intertwined and troubled in medieval drama. Black's 'A Man Out of Time: Joseph, Time and Space in the Marian Plays of the N-Town Manuscript' (in Cox, McAvoy, and Magnani, eds., pp. 147–62) illustrates how the N-Town Marian plays allow audiences to watch the biblical past in ways that respond to and are revised by the medieval present. In 'The Time of the Tree: Returning to Eden after the Fall in the Cornish *Creation of the World*' (*MFF* 50 [2015] 61–89), Black brings attention to the little-discussed *Gwreans an Bys*, which is often overlooked on account of its incompleteness and its relatively late survival in a post-medieval manuscript. Black makes a virtue of the play's sense of historical in-betweenness, and suggests that temporalities acting within and upon the play are reflected in its depiction of the Garden as Eden, which is imagined in the play as a site where biblical and historical time meet and interact in unexpected ways. Her essay contributes to a growing body of work exploring the temporality of medieval drama. '"Nayles Large and Lang": Masculine Identity and the Anachronic Object in the York *Crucifixion* Play' (*MFF* 50[2015] 85–104) also interrogates questions of temporality, here focusing on how the nails in the York *Crucifixion* pageant function as temporal agents that have startling consequences for the way masculine identities are formed and reformed in the context of performance.

This year has also seen a growth in interest in the reception of medieval plays by modern-day audiences. Amanda Wrigley's 'The Spaces of Medieval Mystery Plays on British Television' (*ShakB* 33[2015] 569–93) provides a history of televised dramatizations of medieval mystery plays. Evaluating a range of plays from the 1947 BBC production of the *Coventry Nativity Play* to the 2006 *Manchester Passion*, Wrigley observes a movement from television productions' early use of the imagery of medieval art and artefacts to establish setting to a focus on specific geographical places and localized communities. She also identifies an ongoing trend in which televised mystery play performances blur the genres of drama and documentary, focusing on elements such as audience response, (televisual and medieval) performance crafts, and the performances' pedagogical roles. This essay is a useful addition both to current discussions concerning mystery play spectatorship and to considerations of the plays as agents of civic identity. The afterlives of medieval plays are also given attention in Margaret Rogerson's chapter, 'Medieval Religious Plays in England: Afterlives and New Lives through Performance' (in Aston, ed. *Medieval Afterlives in Contemporary Culture*, pp. 32–47). Focusing on recent reinterpretations and reinventions of the tradition of medieval mystery plays in civic centres in the north of England, Rogerson's essay is complemented in the volume by other contributions on the performativity of medieval culture and its enduring appeal to modern audiences. However, though designed to be accessible to a non-academic audience, the collection as a whole suffers as a consequence of incomplete or erratic referencing. The essay nonetheless offers a lively account of the ways in which modern performances of the York and Chester mystery plays can provide insights to their original auspices, and offers a refreshing look at exactly what is at stake when we replay the drama of the medieval past.

## Books Reviewed

Adams, J.S. *Syon Abbey: Its Herbal, Medical Books and Care of the Sick: Healthcare in a Mixed Mediaeval Monastery* [2015]. Free from < https:// syonabbeysociety.files.wordpress.com/2012/09/syon-abbey-healthcare-and-medical-books-8-jan-2016.pdf >.

Aers, David. *Beyond Reformation? An Essay on William Langland's Piers Plowman and the End of Constantinian Christianity*. UNDP. [2015] pp. xix + 256. $35 ISBN 9 7802 6802 0460.

Appleford, Amy. *Learning to Die in London, 1380–1450*. UPenn. [2015] pp. 336. £42.50 ISBN 9 7808 1224 6698.

Aston, Gail, ed. *Medieval Afterlives in Contemporary Culture*. Bloomsbury. [2015] pp. xviii + 353. £130 ISBN 9 7814 4112 9604.

Bale, Anthony, ed. and trans. *The Book of Margery Kempe*. WC. OUP. [2015] pp. ix + 275. £8.99 ISBN 9 7801 9968 6643.

Bellis, Joanna, ed. *John Page's The Siege of Rouen*, edited from London, British Library, MS Egerton 1995. MET 51. Winter. [2015] pp. lxxvii + 158. €49 ISBN 9 7838 2536 4267.

Bernau, Anke, and Eva von Contzen, eds. *Sanctity as Literature in Late Medieval Britain*. ManUP. [2015] pp. x + 288. £70 ISBN 9 7807 1908 9701.

Boardman, Steve, and Susan Foran, eds. *Barbour's Bruce and Its Cultural Contexts*. Brewer. [2015] pp. 256. £50 ISBN 9 7818 4384 3573.

Boboc, Andreea D., ed. *Theorizing Legal Personhood in Late Medieval England*. Brill. [2015] pp. 310. €115 ISBN 9 7890 0428 0410.

Booker, Sparky, and Cherie N. Peters, eds. *Tales of Medieval Dublin*. FCP. [2014] pp. xii + 203. pb €25 ISBN 9 7818 4682 4975.

Brandsma, Frank, Carolyne Larrington, and Corinne Saunders, eds. *Emotions in Medieval Arthurian Literature: Body, Mind, Voice.* Brewer. [2015] pp. viii + 213. £60 ISBN 9 7818 4384 4211.

Broomhall, Susan, ed. *Authority, Gender, and Emotions in Late Medieval and Early Modern England.* Palgrave. [2015] pp. xvi + 229. £60 ISBN 9 7811 3753 1155.

Byrne, Aisling. *Otherworlds: Fantasy and History in Medieval Literature.* OUP. [2015] pp. 224. £55 ISBN 9 7801 9874 6003.

Camp, Cynthia Turner. *Anglo-Saxon Saints' Lives as History Writing in Late Medieval England.* Brewer. [2015] pp. xii + 260. £60 ISBN 9 7818 4384 4020.

Carruthers, Mary, ed. *Language in Medieval Britain: Networks and Exchanges.* Shaun Tyas. [2015] pp. xiv + 258 + 49 colour plates. £50 ISBN 9 7819 0773 0429.

Chandler, John H., ed. *The King of Tars.* TEAMS. MIP. [2015] pp. vii + 102. $14.95 ISBN 9 7815 8044 2046.

Conde-Silvestre, Juan Camilo, and Javier Calle-Martín, eds. *Approaches to Middle English: Variation, Contact and Change.* Studies in English Medieval Language and Literature 47. Lang. [2015] pp. 259. £45 ISBN 9 7836 5398 0004.

Connolly, Margaret, and Raluca Radulescu, eds. *Insular Books: Vernacular Manuscript Miscellanies in Late Medieval Britain.* Proceedings of the British Academy 201. OUP. [2015] pp. xii + 330. £70 ISBN 9 7801 9726 5833.

Conti, Aiden, Orietta Da Rold, and Philip Shaw, eds. *Writing Europe, 500– 1450: Texts and Contexts.* Brewer. [2015] pp. xviii + 198. £30 ISBN 9 7818 4384 4150.

Corbellini, Sabrina, Margriet Hoogvliet, and Bart Ramakers. *Discovering the Riches of the Word: Religious Reading in Late Medieval and Early Modern Europe.* Brill. [2015] pp. 378. €140 ISBN 9 7890 0429 0389.

Cowen, Janet, ed. *On Famous Women: The Middle English Translation of Boccaccio's De Mulieribus Claris,* edited from London, British Library, MS Additional 10304. MET 52. Winter. [2015] pp. li + 131. €66 ISBN 9 7838 2536 4557.

Cox, Elizabeth, Liz Herbert McAvoy, and Roberta Magnani, eds. *Reconsidering Gender, Time and Memory in Medieval Culture.* Brewer. [2015] pp. xii + 203 £60 ISBN 9 7818 4384 4037.

Donavin, Georgiana, and Denise Stodola, eds. *Public Declamations: Essays on Medieval Rhetoric, Education, and Letters in Honour of Martin Camargo.* Brepols. [2015] pp. xxvii + 292. €80 ISBN 9 7825 0354 7770.

Downes, Stephanie, Andrew Lynch, and Katrina O'Loughlin, eds. *Emotions and War: Medieval to Romantic Literature.* PalMac. [2015] pp. x + 274. £63 ISBN 9 7811 3736 6344.

Elias, Natanela. *The Gnostic Paradigm: Forms of Knowing in English Literature of the Late Middle Ages.* PalMac. [2015] pp. 208. $90 ISBN 9 7811 3747 4766.

Fein, Susanna, ed. and trans, with David Raybin and Jan Ziolkowski. *The Complete Harley 2253 Manuscript,* vol. 1. TEAMS. MIP. [2015] pp. 508. $24.95 ISBN 9 7815 8044 2053.

Fein, Susanna, ed. and trans, with David Raybin and Jan Ziolkowski. *The Complete Harley 2253 Manuscript*, vol. 3. TEAMS. MIP. [2015] pp. 420. $24.95 ISBN 9 7815 8044 1995.

Gerber, Amanda J. *Medieval Ovid: Frame Narrative and Political Allegory*. PalMac. [2015] pp. xvi + 163. $70 ISBN 9 7811 3748 8398.

Gray, Douglas. *Simple Forms: Essays on Medieval English Popular Literature*. OUP [2015] pp. 278. £55 ISBN 9 7801 9870 6090.

Hatt, Cecilia A. *God and the Gawain-Poet: Theology and Genre in Pearl, Cleanness, Patience and Sir Gawain and the Green Knight*. B&B. [2015] pp. 260. £60 ISBN 9 7818 4384 4198.

Hillman, David, and Ulrika Maude, eds. *The Cambridge Companion to the Body in Literature*. CUP. [2015] pp. 294. hb $93 ISBN 9 7811 0704 8096, pb $28.99 ISBN 9 7811 0764 4397.

Johnston, Andrew James, Ethan Knapp, and Margitta Rouse, eds. *The Art of Vision: Ekphrasis in Medieval Literature and Culture*. OSUP. [2015] pp. 336. £60 ISBN 9 7808 1421 2943.

Johnston, Michael, and Michael van Dussen, eds. *The Medieval Manuscript Book: Cultural Approaches*. Cambridge Studies in Medieval Literature 94. CUP. [2015] pp. xii + 302. £67 ISBN 9 7811 0706 6199.

Kiefer, Frederick. *English Drama from Everyman to 1660: Performance and Print*. Arizona Center for Medieval and Renaissance Studies. [2015] pp. xxiv + 930. £89 ISBN 9 7808 6698 4942.

Lancashire, Anne, and David J. Parkinson, eds. *Records of Early English Drama: Civic London to 1558*. 3 vols. Brewer. [2015] pp. cciv + 1,591. £195 ISBN 9 7818 4384 3993.

Langeslag, Paul S. *Seasons in the Literatures of the Medieval North*. Brewer. [2015] pp. viii + 258. £60 ISBN 9 7818 4384 4259.

Larkin, Peter, ed. *Richard Coer de Lyon*. TEAMS. MIP. [2015] pp. 300. $24.95 ISBN 9 7815 8044 2015.

Lazikani, A.S. *Cultivating the Heart: Feeling and Emotion in Twelfth- and Thirteenth-Century Religious Texts*. UWalesP. [2015] pp. xvi + 155. £95 ISBN 9 7817 8316 2611.

Leitch, Megan. *Romancing Treason: The Literature of the Wars of the Roses*. OUP. [2015] pp. 240. £55 ISBN 9 7801 9872 4599.

Martin, Joanna, ed. *The Maitland Quarto: A New Edition of Cambridge, Magdalen College, Pepys Library MS 1408*. Scottish Text Society. B&B. [2015] pp. 540. £40 ISBN 9 7818 9797 6401.

MacDonald, Alasdair A., ed. *The Gude and Godlie Ballatis*. Scottish Text Society. B&B. [2015] pp. 425. £40 ISBN 9 7818 9797 6418.

McKinstry, Jamie. *Middle English Romance and the Craft of Memory*. Brewer. [2015] pp. xii + 277. £60 ISBN 9 7818 4384 4174.

Mills, Robert. *Seeing Sodomy in the Middle Ages*. UChicP. [2015] pp. 400. $55 ISBN 9 7802 2616 9125.

Minnis, Alistair. *From Eden to Eternity: Creations of Paradise in the Later Middle Ages*. UPennP. [2015] pp. 384. £39 ISBN 9 7808 1224 7237.

Nicholson, Roger, Claudia Marquis, and Getrud Szamosi, eds. *Contested Identities: Literary Negotiations in Time and Place*. CambridgeSP. [2015] pp. 310. £52.99 ISBN 9 7814 4387 8463.

Nugent, Janay, and Elizabeth Ewan, eds. *Childhood and Youth in Premodern Scotland*. Boydell. [2015] pp. 251. £60 ISBN 9 7817 8327 0439.

Patterson, Paul J., ed. *A Mirror to Devout People (Speculum Devotorum)*. EETS 346. [2016 for 2015] pp. liv + 252. £50 ISBN 9 7801 9874 4979.

Patterson, Serina, ed. *Games and Gaming in Medieval Literature*. Palgrave. [2015] pp. 241. £55 ISBN 9 7811 3731 1030.

Perkins, Nicholas, ed. *Medieval Romance and Material Culture*. Brewer. [2015] pp. xiv + 285. £60 ISBN 9 7818 4384 3900.

Pinner, Rebecca. *The Cult of St Edmund in Medieval East Anglia*. Boydell. [2015] pp. xi + 276. £60 ISBN 9 7817 8327 0354.

Rentz, Ellen K. *Imagining the Parish in Late Medieval England*. OSUP. [2015] pp. 224. $62.95 ISBN 9 7808 1421 2752.

Rice, Nicole R., and Margaret Aziza Pappano, *The Civic Cycles: Artisan Drama and Identity in Pre-Modern England*. UNDP. [2015] pp. 376. $42 ISBN 9 7802 6803 9004.

Romero-Barranco, Jesús, ed. *The Late Middle English Version of Constantinus Africanus' Venerabilis Anatomia in London, Wellcome Library, MS 290 (ff. 1r–41v)*. CambridgeSP. [2015] pp. 109. £41.99 ISBN 9 7814 4388 0404.

Ross, Sarah C. F. *Women, Poetry, & Politics in Seventeenth-Century Britain*. [2015] PP. 264. £55 ISBN 9 7801 9872 4209.

Sassi, Carla, ed. *The International Companion to Scottish Poetry*. ASLS. [2015] pp. 256. £14.95 ISBN 9 7819 0898 0151.

Simpson, James, and Sarah Peverley, eds. *John Hardyng, Chronicle*, edited from British Library MS Lansdowne 204, vol. 1. TEAMS. MIP. [2015] pp. 342. $29.95 ISBN 9 7815 8044 2138.

Sobecki, Sebastian. *Unwritten Verities: The Making of England's Vernacular Culture, 1463–1549*. UNDP. [2015] pp. x + 257. $38 ISBN 9 7802 6804 1458.

Somerset, Fiona, and Nicholas Watson, eds. *Truth & Tales: Cultural Mobility and Medieval Media*. OSUP. [2015] pp. 360. $69.90 ISBN 9 7808 1421 2714.

Steiner, Emily, and Lynn Ransom. *Taxonomies of Knowledge: Information and Order in Medieval Manuscripts*. UPennP. [2015] pp. x + 163. $45 ISBN 9 7808 1224 7596.

Sturges, Robert, *The Circulation of Power in Medieval Biblical Drama: Theaters of Authority*. PalMac. [2015] pp. xvi + 230. £55 ISBN 9 7802 3011 5781.

Sutherland, Annie. *English Psalms in the Middle Ages 1300–1450*. OUP. [2015] pp. xvi + 322. £60 ISBN 9 7801 9872 6364.

Treharne, Elaine. *Medieval Literature: A Very Short Introduction*. OUP. [2015] pp. 160. £7.99 ISBN 9 7801 9966 8496.

Truitt, E.R. *Medieval Robots: Mechanism, Magic, Nature, and Art*. UPennP. [2015] pp. 296. £36 ISBN 9 7808 1224 6971.

Turville-Petre, Thorlac, ed. *Poems from BL MS Harley 913: 'The Kildare Manuscript'*. EETS os 345. OUP. [2015] pp. lxiv + 320. £45 ISBN 9 7801 9873 9166.

von Contzen, Eva, and Anke Bernau, eds. *Sanctity as Literature in Late Medieval Britain*. ManUP. [2015] pp. 288. £70 ISBN 9 7807 1908 9701.

Whitman, Jon, ed. *Romance and History: Imagining Time from the Medieval to the Early Modern Period*. CUP. [2015] pp. 338. £60 ISBN 9 7811 0704 2780.

Windeatt, Barry, ed. and trans. *Julian of Norwich, Revelations of Divine Love*. WC. OUP. [2015] pp. lviii + 214. £8.99 ISBN 9 7801 9964 1185.

Yoshikawa, Naoë Kukita, ed. *Medicine, Religion and Gender in Medieval Culture*. Brewer. [2015] pp. xvi + 293. £60 ISBN 9 7818 4384 4013.

Young, Andrea Louise. *Vision and Audience in Medieval Drama: A Study of the Castle of Perseverance*. PalMac. [2015] pp. xvii + 228. £55 ISBN 9 7811 3744 6077.

# IV

# Chaucer

## BEN PARSONS AND NATALIE JONES

This chapter has five sections: 1. General; 2. *The Canterbury Tales*; 3. *Troilus and Criseyde*; 4. Other Works; 5. Reception and Reputation. Sections 1, 3, and 5 are by Ben Parsons; section 2 is by Natalie Jones with contributions by Ben Parsons; section 4 is by Natalie Jones.

## 1. General

Alexander Gabrovsky's *Chaucer the Alchemist: Physics, Mutability, and the Medieval Imagination* provides an important re-evaluation of the influence of medieval sciences on Chaucer. By approaching the subject in terms of change and transformation, and as an attempt to schematize the necessary flux of worldly being, Gabrovsky expands the range of Chaucerian texts in which scientific thinking can be detected. After an opening chapter on the physics of sublunary existence, he reads the *House of Fame* as a thought-experiment on the human understanding of space. He finds Chaucer considering the ways in which sensory interpretation can be subject to distortion, not only by visual illusion but by hearing, as 'language (a product of sound)' proves to be 'the ultimate agent of distortion' (p. 60). The second section turns to alchemy, with two interconnected chapters looking at the *Franklin's Tale* and *Troilus and Criseyde*. The first discusses the principle of 'opposicion' evoked in Aurelius's prayer to Apollo, a term that recalls the idea that 'features of the alchemist's laboratory . . . have their natural counterparts in the actions of the sun' and other astral bodies (p. 106); this in turn provides a key for reading the ethical system of the tale, from the harmonization of disparate elements that underpins Arveragus and Dorigen's marriage, to the ability of the black rocks to 'transmute' human conduct into noble, self-sacrificing 'fredom', somewhat like the philosopher's stone. *Troilus* also situates alchemy within a complex network of symbols, one which focuses on the 'stiel' body of its hero and its failure to undergo transmutation, at least until Troilus's final, posthumous sublimation. Finally, the *Parlement of Fowls* is seen in terms of the new philosophical technology of modal logic, which provides the 'formal structure' underlying the 'surface elements' of *demande d'amour* and parliamentary

*The Year's Work in English Studies, Volume 96 (2017)* © *The Author 2017. Published by Oxford University Press on behalf of the English Association. All rights reserved.*
*For Permissions, please email: journals.permissions@oup.com*
doi:10.1093/ywes/max003

debate, and accounts for the poem's greater interest in raising possibilities than positing solutions (p. 202). As should be clear from the breadth of its survey, the work as a whole serves to stretch the limits of Chaucer's scientific engagement, showing how fully themes of chemical mutability pervade his work.

John Marenbon's *Pagans and Philosophers: The Problem of Paganism from Augustine to Leibniz* has a chapter on fourteenth-century English poetry. Langland and Chaucer prove especially important in the long history of engagement with paganism, as their formulations not only take radically different paths but often overstep the bounds of earlier scholastic engagement. While Langland raises profound questions by ascribing varying and uncertain levels of authority to his personifications, Chaucer takes a more relativistic tack. His attempts to reconstruct a pagan world in the *Knight's Tale* and *Troilus and Criseyde* refuse to set this world within a Christian eschatology or cosmology, instead allowing it to function by its own rules. Hence *Troilus* folds back into a pagan frame in its final passages, referring the reader to 'this worlde that passeth soone' even as Troilus achieves transcendence. Both texts are united by making 'inappropriate or incomplete' reference to Boethius, especially in Theseus's politicized 'First Moevere' speech, as though to underscore the selective and limited viewpoints their characters and narratives occupy (p. 230). Eve Salisbury also considers Chaucer's work against the subject positions created by larger discourses in 'Carried Away by the Law: Chaucer and the Poetry of Abduction' (in Boboc, ed., *Theorizing Legal Personhood in Late Medieval England*, pp. 50–70). Salisbury examines the legal concept of *raptus*, one of the slipperiest terms in medieval jurisprudence. Her discussion departs from earlier treatments, concentrating on male victims of abduction in Chaucer's work, such as Ganymede in the *House of Fame* or Chauntecleer in the *Nun's Priest's Tale*. She finds that Chaucer is able to conceive what medieval legal discourse cannot, broaching the possibility that the male body might also be subject to forcible seizure, aggression, and violation.

A.V.C. Schmidt's *Passion and Precision: Collected Essays on English Poetry* reprints articles from its author's lengthy career, with particular focus on Chaucer. 'Structure, Language and Myth in Chaucer's "The Former Age"' (pp. 2–16) examines the ways in which Chaucer reconstructs images of the Golden Age to present technology and trade as triggers, rather than symptoms, of a fall from a primal order. 'Nimrod in "The Former Age"' (pp. 21–4) considers the echoes of exegetic tradition embedded in Chaucer's 'Nembrot', and the ways in which he serves to bridge biblical and classical cultures. 'Telling the Truth About Love' (pp. 25–89) sees Troilus's love as a means by which he experiences inadvertent, unconscious contact with a Christian divinity. 'The Pity of It' (pp. 90–6) defends this position against Gerald Morgan's reading, especially his claim that Troilus is guilty of misguided idolatry in his love. Finally, 'The Tragedy of Arcite: Chaucer's Knight's Tale' (pp. 97–105) compares the endings of *Troilus* and the *Knight's Tale*, showing how their tragedies still seek to recoup the values of love and chivalry. In addition to these previously published items, Schmidt also includes a new piece, 'Questioning the Chivalric: Chaucer and the *Gawain*-Poet' (pp. 106–21). This offers a careful examination of the extent to which Chaucer and his north-western contemporary offer a critique of the ideals of knighthood. Against Huizinga's view of a culture in terminal decline, Schmidt offers a vigorous denial that fourteenth-century poetry 'had lost faith of in the robust and lucid values of the formative period of chivalry', tracing the continued vitality of chivalry's core virtues in the *Franklin's Tale*, and revisiting the triumphant conclusions of the *Knight's Tale* and *Troilus* (p. 110).

Chaucer's two adaptations from Boccaccio also draw the focus of Katarzyna Stadnik in *Chaucer's Choices: Through the Looking-Glass of Medieval Imagery*. Here Stadnik examines Chaucer's visual metaphors through the prism of cognitive linguistics. The first half of the study describes this complex system and its utility for literary analysis, observing how the use of visual images in written texts, especially those intended for oral performance before a particular community of listeners, might provide a means of shaping, rather than merely reflecting, the conceptual order of that community. The final, longest, chapter pursues these concerns across Chaucer's two great classical romances, tracing out the ways in which moments of spectacle and sight become a site of 'interplay between the individual's idiosyncrasy and their sociocultural situatedness' (p. 108). Stadnik investigates the ways in which images serve as conveyers of collective memory, showing how Chaucer's appeals to vision are both rooted in and expand upon Boethian philosophy; she herself draws on the work of Mary Carruthers to show how the human body serves as a particularly rich repository of communicative images. Linguistic concerns of a more traditional bent are investigated in Gyöngyi Werthmüller, 'Final -e in Gower's and Chaucer's Monosyllabic Premodifying Adjectives' (in Conde-Silvestre and Calle-Martín, eds., *Approaches to Middle English: Variation, Contact and Change*, pp. 179–98). Werthmüller finds a relatively stable pattern of practice across the work of the two poets, assembling copious evidence to show that terminal -e can have grammatical rather than purely metrical functions.

Discourse theory animates Nancy Mason Bradbury's 'The Proverb as Embedded Microgenre in Chaucer and *The Dialogue of Solomon and Marcolf*' (*Exemplaria* 27[2015] 55–72). Bradbury draws on Bakhtin's late, incomplete work on genre, and especially his account of the processes that occur when one genre is absorbed into the boundaries of another. As she writes, the effect of such integration is to switch rapidly between voices and worldviews in ways that can prove unstable and dynamic. Chaucer's inclusion of proverbs in *Troilus and Criseyde*, *Melibee*, and the *Miller's* and *Cook's Tales* show the fluidity of these quotations, as proverbs do not merely serve as tidy statements of conventional wisdom, but can become points of tension between competing truths, perceptions, and even social realities. A more localized use of proverbs is considered in E.G. Stanley's 'Proverbe of Chaucer' (*N&Q* 62[2015] 358–60). Stanley weighs up the rationales by which NIMEV 3914 has been ruled out as a genuine Chaucerian composition, despite the attribution it carries in several manuscripts. He finds such judgements wanting, and makes a plea for privileging stylistic over mechanistic philological or metrical features when identifying the authorship of medieval texts.

Chaucer's debt to demotic forms is further investigated in Douglas Gray's *Simple Forms: Essays on Medieval English Popular Literature*. In Gray's erudite discussion of oral narratives, Chaucer comes to participate in a far-reaching nexus of connections, not only through his use of proverbs and traditional topoi, but also in his references to charms, giants, rituals, and theories on the disappearance of the fairies.

Chaucer features at several points in Elaine Treharne's *Medieval Literature*, part of OUP's popular Very Short Introductions series. Chaucer's work is not only evoked in its own right, as the *Canterbury Tales* receives extensive discussion, but it appears as a witness to the conditions and the climate of ideas in which medieval authors worked. Hence the *Canterbury Tales* and *Troilus and Criseyde* are used to exemplify the variability of manuscript culture, and the 'information exchange and communal recollection' that underpins oral performance; likewise, the *Book of the Duchess* shows how personal and public registers might interact with one another, while the *Legend of Good Women* demonstrates the importance of patronage (p. 33). Ultimately, the breadth and detail of these references makes the book at least as useful for students of Chaucer as for those more generally interested in the Middle Ages as a whole.

Comparable in intent, although with a narrower focus, is Bernard O'Donoghue's *Reading Chaucer's Poems: A Guided Selection*. For the benefit of the novice reader, O'Donoghue draws together a varied and comprehensive collection of highlights from Chaucer's canon, supported with detailed glosses, a running commentary, and biographical material. Most of the major works are represented in part, from the *Book of the Duchess* to the *Canterbury Tales*, along with many shorter poems. Chaucer features in a further anthology for general readers, providing the capstone of Laura Ashe's *Early Fiction in England: From Geoffrey of Monmouth to Chaucer*. Interpreting 'English' culture with a similar generosity, the selection moves through Geoffrey of Monmouth, Wace, Marie de France, Walter Map, and the *Ancrene Wisse* before reaching *Troilus and Criseyde*, offering an implicit challenge to the popular idea of Chaucer as absolute origin of the English literary tradition.

Readers at every level are likely to benefit from Mark Allen and Stephanie Amsel, *Annotated Chaucer Bibliography 1997–2010*. This brings together synopses of 4,632 separate items of research on Chaucer, along with other resources and responses. The contents are based on the annual overviews of scholarship published in *Studies in the Age of Chaucer*, although these entries are supplemented by over 600 new items that had previously escaped the compilers' attention. What is of particular interest here, however, is the organizational scheme imposed on this formidable array of work. As well as placing criticism under the expected headings, dividing sources according to the works they address, there are also thematic divisions ('Style, Rhetoric, Prosody and Versification', 'Gender, Sexuality and Identity'), descriptions of audiovisual media, and a section on pedagogical materials. A further novelty in its taxonomy is the inclusion of modern fictional portrayals and adaptations. Lastly, the latest instalment of this larger project, the Annotated Chaucer Bibliography (*SAC* 37[2015] 347–400), remains a resource of central importance in its own right. The entries for 2013 give succinct overviews of 172 articles and books, as well as listing 28 reviews.

## 2. The Canterbury Tales

Complementing work on Chaucer's treatment of the sciences, and in several ways serving as a counterpoint to it, is Patricia Clare Ingham's *The Medieval New: Ambivalence in an Age of Innovation*. Ingham is less concerned with scientific discourse per se, and more with the ways in which mechanical developments were encoded as 'newfangelnesse' by medieval culture, and what concerns were projected into this term. Hence the wondrous technologies of the *Squire's Tale* are treated as meditations on human creativity in general, one in which poetry and machinery are equally implicated. Ingham sees Chaucer using the marvellous artefacts of Cambuskan to explore questions surrounding novelty and innovation. She reads the *Canon's Yeoman's Tale* in a similar light, paying particular attention to its depiction of the 'elvish' science of alchemy. Her unpicking of this term reveals a point at which conflicting ideas converge, as Chaucer shows that alchemy might function as a transformative resource akin to poetry, although it might also be empty, illusory quackery.

Creativity of a different kind informs Jameson S. Workman's *Chaucer and the Death of the Political Animal*. He offers an idiosyncratic reading of the *Canterbury Tales*, explicitly positioned as an alternative to the dominant historicist current of medieval scholarship. Rather than seeking to situate Chaucer's texts in a limited cultural moment, Workman treats them as nodes in a more extensive network of ideas, setting up lines of literary and philosophical continuity that stretch well beyond the Middle Ages. A key concern is the way in which language and lived experience, both readerly and authorial, are co-ordinated through art. Workman's reading of the *Miller's Tale* puts Chaucer into dialogue with voices as diverse as Plotinus, Dali, Alain of Lille, Samuel Butler, and Radiohead to show how the fallen world of the tale is beyond the power of poetry or God to fix. In the subsequent chapters, the *Manciple's Tale* is treated as an examination of mythopoetics as a whole, as the silencing of the bird becomes an originary moment for poetry itself, while the *Nun's Priest's Tale* returns to an even earlier point, moving back through the history of language, through imitation and animal cries into silence.

In *Desire in the Canterbury Tales*, Elizabeth Scala adopts a theoretical approach and argues that the overall frame of the poem, as well as the narratives of individual tales, engage in a complex 'discourse of desire' (p. 3). Although Scala examines the ways in which desire shapes the stories told by a number of pilgrims, she also considers how this impulse leads to acts of misrecognition and misreading which, in turn, contribute to the rivalry between some of the pilgrim narrators in the frame narrative. In order to sustain this approach to the *Canterbury Tales*, the discussion repeatedly engages with psychoanalysis, most notably the theories of Lacan and his work on desire and the relationship between the Subject and the Other. Chapter 1 reads the *Knight's Tale* as an 'elegant meditation on erotic and worldly desire' (p. 44). By focusing on the relationship between Palamon and Arcite, it is argued that the desire of the two Theban knights, rather than their object of desire, Emelye, forms the driving force behind the tale's narrative as both knights express a violent drive against the threat of the Other; as Scala asserts, 'their interest in the feminine object is sustained largely through a fantasy of what the other wants, perhaps even envy of what the other might attain' (p. 52). In Chapter 2, Scala examines the relationship between the *Reeve's Tale* and the *Miller's Tale*, focusing particularly on the Reeve's angry response to the Miller's story. It is proposed that the Reeve is pivotal to the exploration of desire in the *Canterbury Tales*, as he and his tale demonstrate how the desire of the Subject can be linked to misreading and misrecognition: the Reeve's desire to tell his tale is motivated not only by his inability to see the comedy in the Miller's story, but by his belief that the tale is a personal insult targeting his previous occupation as a carpenter. The relationship between wives and clerks in the *Canterbury Tales*, seen most acutely through the interaction between the Wife of Bath and the Clerk, forms the subject of chapter 3. Scala notes that the tales told by the Wife and Clerk share similar concerns, as both interrogate the concept of female desire: in the *Wife of Bath's Tale* it is overtly asserted through the will of Guinevere and the words of the old woman, while the *Clerk's Tale* relays the story of patient Griselda who relinquishes her will entirely to Walter's desire. Although these narratives seemingly run in opposition to one another, the Wife and Clerk are motivated by a shared desire to inhabit the morals or attributes embodied in their tales' protagonists; according to Scala, the magical old woman and Griselda serve, respectively, as 'ideal self-images imagined and projected by the Wife and Clerk' (p. 127). The pairing of the Wife and Clerk is furthered by the links that can be drawn between the ends of their tales, as both speakers withdraw from a position of mastery in order to recognize and identify with the Other (p. 151): both the Wife's latent desire to submit to a worthy husband and the Clerk's wish to obtain absolute mastery have been exposed. The final chapter of Scala's study demonstrates that desire is also an important shaping force in the religious tales. Focusing initially on the *Physician's Tale*, the chapter considers Chaucer's handling of the story in relation to its sources and analogues and notes how earthly desire, in the form of Apius's lust for Virginia, is the driving force behind Virginia's death. In spite of their acknowledgement of earthly desire, the religious tales typically place desire in a devotional context and, in keeping with the tradition of female hagiography, redefine it as a longing for union with God. This is seen most acutely in the *Second Nun's Tale* where, in spite of consenting to an earthly marriage, Cecilia's actions are untouched by, and typically counteract, all earthly desire.

The structural principles which underpin the *Canterbury Tales*, particularly with regard to the links between pilgrim narrators and their respective tales, are also explored by Warren Ginsberg in *Tellers, Tales, and Translation in Chaucer's Canterbury Tales*. Using the theories of Walter Benjamin, Ginsberg argues that the material on which we base our understanding of any one of Chaucer's pilgrim narrators (i.e. a pilgrim's portrait in the *General Prologue*; the tale and, where relevant, the prologue assigned to a pilgrim; and finally, a pilgrim's appearance in any links or episodes in the poem's frame narrative), should be read as 'translations' of one another, as each component serves to express 'in a different mode a coordinating idea or set of concerns' (p. 3). In addition to this, Ginsberg argues that certain events, motifs, and ideas are 'translated', in the sense that they reappear in different guises, throughout the

*Canterbury Tales*. In the first two chapters, Ginsberg suggests that Chaucer may have found a model for 'Benjamin-like intralingual translations' (p. 17) in the works of his favourite classical and contemporary authors. Chapter 1 looks at acts of textual transformation in Ovid, Statius, and Dante, while Chapter 2 examines Boccaccio's *Teseida* and *Filostrato* in relation to the *Knight's Tale* and the portrait of the Knight in the *General Prologue*. In chapter 3, Ginsberg turns to focus more closely on aspects of the *Canterbury Tales* by examining the role of interruption in the poem, which is seen as an act of 'interdiction' or 'a "speaking between"' that makes use of speech to cut off speech' (p. 80). This is seen particularly in the character of the Franklin, whose interruption of the Squire can be read as a reflection of his wish to prove that his status and nobility match the young knight's. The next chapter examines the textual relationship between the *Wife of Bath's Prologue* and *Tale*. By reading these two works as 'translations' of one another, Ginsberg notes that the Wife transforms in her tale a number of strategies that she had previously deployed in her prologue. In chapter 5 Ginsberg suggests that the Clerk and the Merchant can be read as 'translations' of one another. Through an examination of the Clerk's construction of his tale in relation to Petrarch's version, as well as a consideration of his portrait in the *General Prologue*, he argues that Chaucer depicts the Clerk as a figure 'with one foot in the physical world and the other in a world beyond it' (p. 155). Ginsberg suggests that this presentation of the Clerk is mirrored in that of the Merchant, who is also in a state of flux due to the world of commerce and exchange that he and his goods occupy. In chapter 6 Ginsberg examines the ways in which sacramental imagery is translated in the *Pardoner's Prologue* and *Tale*. The Pardoner intentionally corrupts the conventions of eucharistic imagery in order to 'translate' those he gulls, as is demonstrated by his unsuccessful attempt at mock-Communion with the Host at the end of the tale. Ginsberg concludes his study with a consideration of the Miller and Fragment I. According to Ginsberg, the Miller instigates a sequence of translation and repetition throughout the first fragment, as his insistence that he tell the next tale after the Knight 'echoes the Host and translates him' (p. 204). The Miller can be regarded as a 'figure in whom class translates itself' (p. 205), as he not only overturns the social ordering set up by the Host but entirely reframes the story told by the Knight by retelling it in a manner which accords with his own social level.

A number of smaller-scale studies have considered issues of narrative technique, voice, and form in relation to particular tales. In her monograph, *Medieval Ovid: Frame Narrative and Political Allegory*, Amanda J. Gerber devotes her fourth chapter, 'Clerical Expansion and Narrative Diminution in Chaucer's *Canterbury Tales*', to a consideration of the narrative style of the *Monk's Tale*. Gerber observes that although the Monk adheres to a Boccaccian *de casibus* model in his handling of classical and contemporary material, the form of his tale can be most fully understood in relation to developments in the clerical commentary tradition and models of Ovidian paraphrase. Indeed, the Monk's style of narration, which focuses on truncating and reshaping his classical material, mirrors the techniques found in clerical commentaries, which sought to condense classical or religious Latin works in order to accommodate a wider, lay, audience. The influence of clerical commentaries on the *Monk's Tale* also extends to its subject matter, as Gerber argues that Chaucer's knowledge of Ovid would have derived from his contact with the truncated paraphrases of classical myth contained in these sorts of commentary texts.

Another form of pagan survival is discussed in Alistair Minnis's 'Fragmentations of Medieval Religion: Thomas More, Chaucer, and the Volcano Lover' (*SAC* 37[2015] 3–27). Minnis's essay concerns popular or 'vernacular' religion, the host of practices and beliefs that lurk beneath the formally sanctioned dogma of the church authorities. He pays particular attention to the devotion of wax models of diseased body-parts at the shrines of particular saints, especially the replica genitals that often served as cures for impotence or infertility. The cults of these phallic saints might register at the conclusion of the *Pardoner's Tale*, when Bailly abuses its teller by wishing his genitals were torn from him and 'shryned in a hogges toord', as a more substantial replacement for his bogus relics. The insult might connect with phallic worship in two distinct ways, according to how we judge the Pardoner's claims to virility: if sincere, his body parts are indeed a fit subject for transformation into a fertility relic; if false, the line voices derisive, ironic praise of something of little worth. Abuse and satire also stand at the centre of Camille Marshall, 'Figuring the Dangers of the "Greet Fornys": Chaucer and Gower's Timely (Mis)Reporting of the Peasant Voice' (*Comitatus* 46[2015] 74–97). Marshall picks up on the work of Lee Patterson and Paul Strohm, also seeing the Miller's rebellion as a literary re-enactment of the chaos of 1381. She calls particular attention to the description of Robyn's mouth as a furnace, a manoeuvre that echoes chronicle accounts of the destruction, and recalls the caricatures of peasant speech found in Gower's *Vox Clamantis* and other sources.

Issues of narrative voice inform David Lavinsky's study of the Pardoner in 'Turned to Fables: Efficacy, Form, and Literary Making in the *Pardoner's Tale*' (*ChauR* 50[2015] 442–64). Lavinsky notes that in the context of Wycliffite thought, which criticized the use of exempla and fables in preaching, the Pardoner would have been regarded as a false preacher because of his choice of tale. However, the Pardoner's decision to tell a moral tale, rather than a story of 'myrthe or japes' as the Host requests, actually serves to reaffirm his role as both storyteller and preacher, as it not only instils his voice with authority, but subtly points to the moral efficacy of his choice of text. Indeed, Lavinsky argues that the Pardoner's exemplum can be read as a defence of the effectiveness of fiction as a form of moral instruction, as it demonstrates 'the potential of finding moral truth in fiction' and links 'efficacy to narrative form and verbal art' (p. 444). A similar concern with the relationship between voice and authority is also evident in Hwanhee Park's essay on the Prioress, entitled ' "To ben holden digne of reverence": The Tale-Telling Tactics of Chaucer's Prioress' (*Comitatus* 46[2015] 99–116). By reflecting on the Prioress's role as both reader and tale-teller, Park asserts that the Prioress intentionally ventriloquizes the voice of the 'litel clergeon' in order to instil the tale with authority. The Prioress's presentation of herself as an innocent and unlearned child, as seen most emphatically in her prologue, not only allows her to 'share in the Clergeon's authority to speak in public' (p. 100), but also heightens the devotional efficacy of her tale. Indeed, by emulating the voice of the martyred boy, the Prioress blurs the boundaries between teller and tale, providing her audience with 'the impression of having actually seen the miracle' that her tale describes (p. 99).

Eleanor Johnson's essay, 'English Law and the Man of Law's "Prose" Tale' (*JEGP* 114[2015] 504–25) situates the Man of Law in the context of English judicial and political history in order to consider the significance of his unfulfilled claim that he will tell his tale in prose. Johnson argues that throughout his prologue and tale the Man of Law is consistently aligned with the old English legal tradition in order to 'exonerate him from any blame in the kinds of legal corruption that motivated the dizzying array of antilegal sentiment in the later Middle Ages' (p. 504). The Man of Law's desire to depict himself as a representative of the old legal tradition directly informs his assertion that he will tell his tale in prose, as by recalling the popular assumption that prose is the medium of truth and accuracy, the Man of Law implies that his tale is 'a true and historical work in which the English, Christian law is the implicit hero' (p. 522). The legal context of the *Man of Law's Tale* is also considered by Brendan O'Connell in his article, '"Struglynge wel and myghtily": Resisting Rape in the *Man of Law's Tale*' (*M&AElig;* 84[2015] 16–39). O'Connell argues that Chaucer depicts the tale's attempted rape scene, in which Custance struggles with her attacker until he falls into the sea and drowns, in accordance with legal and ethical arguments relating to self-defence law. By considering Chaucer's handling of the episode in relation to the story in Gower and Trevet, O'Connell observes that Chaucer amends the scene in order to engage more directly with its contemporary legal implications. Indeed, by cutting material in order to add pace to the scene, as well as by drawing greater attention to the struggle which takes place between Custance and her attacker, Chaucer underlines the fact that the killing should be regarded as 'an act of non-felonious homicide committed in self-defence' (p. 35).

A consideration of the treatment of violence informs Ben Parsons's discussion of the *Wife of Bath's Prologue*, 'Beaten for a Book: Domestic and Pedagogic Violence in *The Wife of Bath's Prologue*' (*SAC* 37[2015] 163–94). Focusing on Jankyn's beating of the Wife as described in the prologue, Parsons argues that these acts of violence can only be fully understood if read in a pedagogical, rather than an exclusively marital, context. Indeed, it is observed that Jankyn is aligned with the schoolroom throughout the prologue and thus his instruction of Alisoun, as well as his beating of her, should be interpreted in this light. Although the two roles that Jankyn occupies, that of husband and schoolmaster, 'license him equally to use physical discipline against his wife-cum-pupil' (p. 171), Jankyn is unable to distinguish between the appropriate uses of violence in the marital and pedagogical sphere. By examining a range of texts which comment on the uses of violence in both contexts, it is noted that the two discourses of violence diverge sharply: in a marital context beating is seen as a means to curtail female agency, while in the context of education, the beating of pupils is regarded as 'a necessary step in the formation of adult subjectivity' (p. 177) and should thus be administered with self-restraint. These points of distinction highlight why Jankyn's beating of the Wife ultimately leads to the transference of 'maistrie' that occurs at the end of the prologue. Indeed, Jankyn has faltered not only by his lack of restraint when delivering the final blow, but also by beating and instructing the Wife in accordance with the rules of the classroom: 'The end result of the violence Alisoun undergoes is not subservience but subjectivity, as its effects do not limit her activity, but carve out a space from which her linguistic agency can be displayed in its own right' (p. 177).

The *Wife of Bath's Tale* is the subject of Susan Nakley's article, ' "Rowned she a pistel": National Institutions and Identities According to Chaucer's Wife of Bath' (*JEGP* 114[2015] 61–77). Nakley contends that in the *Wife of Bath's Tale* Chaucer explores ideas about national sovereignty, institutions, and identity in order to present a new and accessible model of English nobility. In order to present an inclusive vision of nationhood, the tale locates ideas about sovereignty in such cultural institutions as the household and gossip. The old woman in the tale becomes the advocate for this new form of national sovereignty, as from her very first meeting with the rapist-knight she challenges the importance he assigns to his own aristocratic lineage by 'replacing it with her concept of the nation as a class-crossing political and cultural family' (p. 75). The most dramatic demonstration of this new form of English identity is presented in the old woman's speech on 'gentillesse'. By drawing on Dante's understanding of nobility as inner moral worth, the tale not only celebrates the accessibility of this form of English Christian nobility but suggests that a diversion from this model can actually threaten England's sovereign future by hindering the success of such institutions as marriage and the law.

The *Knight's Tale* has been discussed by several commentators. Nora Corrigan's essay, 'The Knight's Earnest Game in Chaucer's *Canterbury Tales*' (in Patterson, ed., *Games and Gaming in Medieval Literature*, pp. 147–68), argues that games, and the risks involved in game-playing, are a central motif in the *Knight's Tale*. Although the tournament in which Palamon and Arcite fight at the end of the tale is the most obvious example of a game, as it initially serves as a form of entertainment for Theseus and positions Palamon and Arcite in the role of 'players', Corrigan also observes that the tale places an emphasis on the rigging of games through the workings of the gods. Moreover, the Knight's *demande d'amour* can be read as a form of game, reflecting his own role as a player in the wider storytelling contest of the pilgrimage. The mode of consolation offered by the *Knight's Tale* is re-examined in the fifth chapter of Chad D. Schrock's monograph, *Consolation in Medieval Narrative: Augustinian Authority and Open Form*. Schrock argues that the presence of the Theban narrative in the *Knight's Tale* repeatedly undermines its attempt to adhere to a linear model of Boethian consolation and instead encourages us to read the tale's ending in Augustinian, rather than Boethian, terms. According to Schrock, the 'Theban narrative is the cyclical equivalent of Augustinian secular historiography' (p. 116), which charts human history in terms of repetitions and cycles. The death of Arcite, which Schrock finds difficult to explain in relation to Boethian consolation, should instead be read as the 'Augustinian revelatory climax of the *Knight's Tale*' (p. 122), as the graciousness embodied in Arcite's dying words constructs a new model for imitation that replaces the cycle of violence seen up to this point. Lastly, Juliana Chapman considers the structural significance of music in the *Knight's Tale* in her article, '*Melody* and *Noyse*: An Aesthetic of *Musica* in the *Knight's Tale* and the *Miller's Tale*' (*SP* 112[2015] 633–55). Chapman maintains that both the *Knight's Tale* and the *Miller's Tale* use music as a structuring device to shape their narratives. Rather than focusing purely on music in the form of song or melody, Chapman proposes that both tales deploy a 'literary aesthetic of *musica*', which she defines as the 'literary use of music to shape a text's structure and guide its interpretation, even in the absence of notated or sounded music' (p. 634). In order to highlight the similarities in structural development between the two tales, Chapman suggests that both narratives work through the same six points of musical development: an initial musical episode, a generalized song from a female character, an explicit song from a male character, a confrontational juxtaposition, a scene of discordant disarray, and, finally, a conclusion. By demonstrating how these six aspects play out in both tales, Chapman's argument seeks to reinforce the evident interaction between the *Knight's Tale* and the *Miller's Tale*.

The *Franklin's Tale* is considered in Darragh Green's article, 'Moral Obligations, Virtue Ethics, and Gentil Character in Chaucer's *Franklin's Tale*' (*ChauR* 50[2015] 88–107). By considering how morality is treated in the tale, Greene argues that the Franklin promotes the values of virtue ethics through his focus on 'gentillesse'. That the Franklin himself embodies this virtue makes him a particularly fitting teller of his tale, as 'his most distinctive characteristic, generosity or liberality, is... essential to the solution of the ethical problem presented in his story' (p. 96). In order to draw attention to the value of virtue ethics, the *Franklin's Tale* questions the rigidity of law-based morality which does not accommodate the complexities of real life. For instance, Arveragus's fierce insistence on keeping one's *trouthe*, understood in the sense of keeping one's word, is rendered problematic given the fact that the *trouthe* Dorigen has pledged to him comes into conflict with the *trouthe* she has also sworn to Aurelius (p. 101). By highlighting that it is *franchise* rather than *trouthe* that is being tested in the tale, the answer to the Franklin's final question, 'Who was the mooste fre, as thynketh yow?', serves to encompass Dorigen, Arveragus, and Aurelius simultaneously: each character has acted in accordance with generosity and, in so doing, has demonstrated the 'need for good example in order to reform character' (p. 105). The treatment of time and 'literary time management' in the *Franklin's Tale* is explored by Kara Gaston in her essay, 'The Poetics of Time Management from the *Metamorphoses* to *Il Filocolo* and the *Franklin's Tale*' (*SAC* 37[2015] 227–56). Focusing particularly on the consequences of Dorigen's rash promise, Gaston views her complaint as a way for her to '"buy time" and postpone the fulfillment of her oath' (p. 228). Chaucer's interest in time-management can be traced back to his sources: for instance, in Boccaccio's *Filocolo* the manipulation of time is evinced by the conjuring of a May garden in January, while Boccaccio's source, Book VII of Ovid's *Metamorphoses*, details the account of Medea's rejuvenation of the aged Aeson. Gaston notes that, in contrast to the Christian perspective on time in the *Filocolo*, Chaucer's *Franklin's Tale* focuses more acutely on temporality and the desire to control earthly time. This is evinced most clearly through the character of Dorigen who, through her speech, seeks to manage her own time. Indeed, the rhetorical strategies deployed in her complaint, such as listing, excess, and a disorganization of material, can be read as a deliberate move on Chaucer's part to demonstrate the difficulties of time management. Thus, in contrast to Boccaccio's *Filocolo*, in the *Franklin's Tale* 'efforts to define the shape of time are associated not with divine intervention, but with earthly claims of political and sexual power' (p. 243).

The economic world of the *Shipman's Tale* is explored in Robert Epstein's article, 'The Lack of Interest in the *Shipman's Tale*: Chaucer and the Social Theory of the Gift' (*MP* 113[2015] 27–48). Challenging the popular reading of the *Shipman's Tale* as a story of self-interest and individual profit, Epstein argues that social theories of gift-giving can assist our understanding of the tale and can account more fully for the actions and motivations of its characters. Epstein argues that its sequence of borrowings and repayments can instead be regarded in terms of 'mutual indebtedness, communal value, and shared pleasures' (p. 29). The merchant's loan to Daun John, which is to be paid back by no set date and without any interest, can be interpreted as a gift which marks and perpetuates the friendship between the two men. The actions of the merchant's wife can also be seen to engage with social theories of gift-giving, as the tale's final scene, in which the wife simultaneously conceals her infidelity and 'repays' her husband with sex, 'reflects not the conclusive equivalence of the market transaction but rather the perpetual 'dynamic of indebtedness...in gift exchange' (p. 47). David K. Coley's essay, 'Money and the Plow, or the *Shipman's Tale* of Tithing' (*ChauR* 49[2015] 449–73), also focuses on the economy of the *Shipman's Tale* as it draws a link between the 100 francs that the merchant loans to Daun John and the payment of tithes. As one-tenth of the 1,000-franc profit that the merchant expects to procure from his transaction, his loan of 100 francs accords with the 'one in ten' rule for the payment of church tithes. Coley argues that although the 100 francs is a loan, the fact that the money is never repaid, at least not in monetary terms, demonstrates how 'the merchant's profit is subject to the same tithes as other modes of economic production' (p. 471). Chaucer draws attention to the increasingly mercantile world of the later Middle Ages, and highlights the role merchants played in England's economy.

An interest in situating Chaucer's *Canterbury Tales* in its wider, historical context is evident in ' "Soper at oure alle cost": The Politics of Food Supply in the *Canterbury Tales*' (*ChauR* 50[2015] 1–29), by Jayne Elisabeth Archer, Richard Marggraf Turley, and Howard Thomas. This study reads the *Canterbury Tales* as a 'game of food' as it directly engages with 'the politics and poetics of food supply' (p. 3). In order to demonstrate this, the study focuses particularly on the Plowman, who is described in the *General Prologue* but is not assigned a tale, and the *Reeve's Tale*. It is argued that Chaucer intentionally constructs the Plowman as a conspicuously silent figure in order to draw attention to the politicization of the food supply that had taken place after the Peasants' Revolt in 1381. That Chaucer's Plowman would have been read in these terms is evidenced by the apocryphal *Complaynte of the Plowman* (composed *c*.1400 and most likely written by a Lollard sympathizer), which directly engages with the socio-political importance of food. Chaucer's interest in this subject is demonstrated further by the *Reeve's Tale* through its depiction of a deceitful miller, and also by the decision to locate the tale's action in Trumpington in Cambridgeshire. It is demonstrated that food-supply politics were particularly fraught in Cambridgeshire at the end of the fourteenth century as a result of tensions between Trumpington Mill and the Cambridge colleges.

A very brief engagement with the *Canterbury Tales* is found in Matthew Beaumont's study of the history of nightwalking, *Nightwalking: A Nocturnal History of London*. In his opening chapter on the medieval context of nightwalking, Beaumont credits Chaucer as the first author to engage with the theme in literature. He notes that it is likely that Chaucer's character of the Cook in the *Canterbury Tales* was based on a real person, namely Roger de Ware, who is described in a record of 1373 as a 'common nightwalker' (p. 30). Although Chaucer makes no explicit reference to this fact in his character-ization of the Cook, Beaumont suggests that there may be a subtle allusion to nightwalking in the *Cook's Tale* through its depiction of Perkyn Revelour's disruptive behaviour at night.

Michelle Karnes's essay, 'Wonder, Marvels, and Metaphors in the *Squire's Tale*' (*ELH* 82[2015] 461–90), examines how the *Squire's Tale* uses language and metaphor to convey the supernatural. It is noted that, in contrast to some other Middle English romances, the *Squire's Tale* seeks to clarify more fully the magical objects it presents by focusing on the 'relationship between marvels and their mental representation' (p. 463). In particular, Karnes asserts that the tale demonstrates the marvellous nature of magical objects by focusing on the characters' responses of wonder: it is argued that these objects 'excite mental activity, prompting the formation of creative images that reveal the object and bring it to life more effectively than sensory ones' (p. 46). In this way, marvels can be read as a form of literature, as Canacee's magical ring or mirror, and even the unfaithful tercel in the tale's second half, become 'texts' which excite the imagination and require work to be understood. An interest in imagination and mental images is also evident in Hans Jürgen Scheuer's essay on the *Merchant's Tale*, 'The Soul of Ekphrasis: Chaucer's *Merchant's Tale* and the Marriage of the Senses' (in Johnston, Knapp, and Rouse, eds., *The Art of Vision: Ekphrasis in Medieval Literature and Culture*, pp. 224–42). According to Scheuer, 'medieval ekphrasis is essentially an engagement with the union of language and the inner senses' (p. 226) and thus, he argues, it can be understood as a form of mental picturing. In order to demonstrate this, Scheuer focuses on the depiction of marriage in the *Merchant's Tale* and the distinction made between a character's internal and external perceptions. Although Chaucer purposefully omits to offer an ekphrastic description of such concrete images as the garden or of the marriage of May and January, ekphrasis is deployed to describe a character's internal perception or cognition, such as January's desire to find a bride.

In ' "The gardyn is enclosed al aboute": The Inversion of Exclusivity in the *Merchant's Tale*' (*SP* 112[2015] 490–503), John Zedolik examines images of enclosure in the tale and argues that these serve to highlight the irony of January's situation. By working his way through the tale's narrative, Zedolik notes that images of enclosure are evident not only in the central image of January's walled garden, but also on a figurative level in January's speech, as evinced through his repetition of such words as 'kepere', 'kepe', and 'knyt' (p. 493). In spite of his desire to 'enclose' his young wife, May, it is January who ultimately becomes the victim. Indeed, while January's literal blindness can be read as a form of enclosure, it also takes on a symbolic quality and comes to signify his misguided belief that he is in control of his wife and marriage. According to Zedolik, the tale's use of a number of images of enclosure draws attention to the comic shift in power that marks the end of the narrative.

A number of studies have considered specific readings in the *Canterbury Tales*. A.S.G. Edwards's note, 'The Wife of Bath's Sixth Man (*Canterbury Tale*, III 21)' (*ChauR* 49[2015] 376–7), draws attention to the Wife's discussion of the Samaritan woman at lines 15–22 of her prologue, particularly lines 21–2 where the wife asks: 'But that I axe, why that the fifte man / Was noon housbonde to the Samaritan?' Edwards notes that the Wife's question about the Samaritan woman's 'fifth' husband does not make sense and should read 'sixth'. Thomas J. Farrell's 'The Meanings of Middle English *Wight*' (*ChauR* 50[2015] 178–97) reconsiders E.T. Donaldson's emendation of word 'wight' to 'wright' in Alisoun's reference to the Creator in the *Wife of Bath's Prologue* 115–17. While the reading has been rejected by the Variorum edition, it is supported by the editors of the *Riverside Chaucer*. Farrell argues that the range of potential meanings in the Middle English 'wight' does not exclude its application to divinity, as the word is not as narrowly restricted in its meanings as Donaldson infers.

A similar focus on word choice and language is evident in Ben Parsons's '*Collie* and Chaucer's "Colle"' (*N&Q* 62[2015] 525–9). Parsons examines the complex etymology of *Collie*, the name attributed to a particular breed of dog, and demonstrates that the term does not derive from the medieval pet name 'Colle'. Finally, Shawn Normandin's 'From Error to Anacoluthon: The Moral of the *Clerk's Tale*' (*N&Q* 62[2015] 218–19), focuses on the Clerk's words at the end of his tale, specifically lines 1153–61, which offer an explanation to the reader about Griselda's behaviour and her role as a model for imitation. Normandin notes that while lines 1153–61 correspond to Petrarch's text, they fail to include the full explanation that Petrarch offers regarding the purpose of the story and thus 'end in a syntactical pothole' (p. 218).

The manuscript context of the *Canterbury Tales* has been largely overlooked this year. One small-scale study, Salim E. Al-Ibia's 'Chaucer's *The Canterbury Tales*: The Position of Fragment VII' (*SLL* 11[2015] 57–61), discusses the theory of the Bradshaw Shift and agrees that Fragment VII should be placed after Fragment II. In addition to surveying the evidence to support this rearrangement, most notably the frame narrative's references to time and place, Al-Ibia also suggests that this new sequence would encourage readers of the *Canterbury Tales* to draw greater links between the fabliaux of the Miller, Reeve, and Shipman.

Finally, questions of audience are explored in Alfred Thomas's monograph, *Reading Women in Late Medieval Europe: Anne of Bohemia and Chaucer's Female Audience*. Thomas devotes considerable space to the *Canterbury Tales* in order to consider how Anne of Bohemia may have influenced Chaucer's works through her role as a possible reader and patron. In order to explore this association, Thomas situates a number of the *Canterbury Tales* in a wider literary context, reading them alongside contemporary works in Latin, German, and Czech that Anne may have known. In chapter 2, 'Writing Jews, Writing Women: Chaucer's *The Prioress's Tale* and the Sacred Drama of Europe' (pp. 45–77), Thomas suggests that Chaucer may have originally composed the *Prioress's Tale* either for Anne or with her in mind, and that the story recounted may have been informed by accounts of the Prague pogrom in 1389. By reading the tale alongside other Continental works, such as *The Passion of the Jews of Prague* written in Latin and *The Ointment Seller*, a mid-fourteenth-century Czech-Latin play, Thomas demonstrates the widespread tendency across Europe to depict Jews not only as perpetrators rather than victims, but as 'inverted projections of Christian doubts and fears about their own belief' (p. 66). Similarly, in chapter 3 (pp. 79–110), Thomas argues that Chaucer may have written his Life of Saint Cecilia for Anne. Indeed, it is noted that the prologue to the *Second Nun's Tale* features a subtle compliment to Anne through the praise it directs towards St Anne, the Virgin's mother. Thomas considers the Czech *Life of Saint Catherine*, the Middle English poem *Pearl*, and the *Second Nun's Tale* alongside one another and notes their shared emphasis on the virginity, learning, and nobility of the female protagonists. In light of this, it is argued that these three texts may have been the product of a courtly milieu and thus signify a 'royal female tradition', as they were written 'specifically with the devotion of pious lay women in mind' (p. 100). In chapter 4 (pp. 111–37), Thomas considers the *Knight's Tale* and investigates the origins of the common suggestion that the tale's depiction of Hippolyta and her Amazonian maidens can be read as a representation of Anne and her female entourage. Thomas suggests that this association may be due to Chaucer's familiarity with the story of the 'Bohemian Maidens' found in *The Dalimil Chronicle*, a Czech work of the early fourteenth century. While it is unlikely that Chaucer would have had access to the *Chronicle*, the legend of the 'Bohemian Maidens' may have been disseminated in court through Anne's entourage. Noting that Chaucer's handling of the Amazonian women in the *Knight's Tale* is similar to that in *The Dalimil Chronicle*, Thomas argues that the 'struggle between the Amazons/Maidens and the men in both narratives can be understood as enacting the struggle for influence between the adaptors and their *auctores*' (p. 113). Both Chaucer and the Czech author use the struggle of their female protagonists as a means to convey their own desire to break free from their source material and highlight the literary authority of the vernacular. Finally, chapter 5 (pp. 139–65) examines the *Wife of Bath's Tale*. Thomas argues that although there is no evidence to suggest that the tale was written for Anne, Anne's role as intercessor between Richard II and his subjects at court may have inspired the tale's narrative. Thomas examines the models of womanhood found in the *Wife of Bath's Tale* in relation to the depictions of women found in the chivalric romances of late medieval Bohemia, as well as *Sir Gawain and the Green Knight*. Chaucer's construction of Guinevere may evoke Anne's role as consort and intercessor, as the tale presents a scene where male power is replaced by female benevolence. Yet, unlike many Bohemian chivalric romances, which tend not only to depict a degree of equality in the relationship between men and women but typically present female characters as positive figures, Chaucer's tale presents a more masculine point of view where a woman is positioned more firmly under a man's control.

## 3. Troilus and Criseyde

New work on Chaucer's Trojan romance is fairly evenly split between its classicism and its treatment of chivalric and religious ideologies. Squarely in the first camp is Elizaveta Strakhov's '"And kis the steppes where as thow seest pace": Reconstituting the Spectral Canon in Statius and Chaucer' (in Davis and Nall, eds., *Chaucer and Fame: Reputation and Reception*, pp. 57–74). Strakhov offers a close consideration of Chaucer's tributes to six authoritative poets at the conclusion of *Troilus*, investigating the implications for his larger interweaving of vernacular and classical influences. She finds Chaucer revitalizing his material, unlike his model Statius, with his enervating and explicit debt to Ovid.

Occupying similar territory is Alcuin Blamires' essay, '"I nolde sette at al that noys a grote": Repudiating Infamy in *Troilus and Criseyde* and *The House of Fame*' (in Davis and Nall, eds., pp. 75–96). Blamires investigates the moment in Book IV when Criseyde finds herself drawn to 'the sceptical view that notoriety is not worth worrying about' (p. 75). He reviews various doubts about the validity of reputation raised by classical and medieval authors, ranging from Boethius to Lydgate. What interests Blamires is the fact that these moments of defiance are submerged as quickly as they surface; ultimately they remain isolated flickers, and cannot prevail against the chivalric logic that permeates Chaucer's thinking.

A somewhat different take on the culture of chivalry is given by Jennifer Garrison, 'Chaucer's *Troilus and Criseyde* and the Danger of Masculine Interiority' (*ChauR* 49[2015] 320–43). As Garrison argues, *Troilus* is often used to resist the Burckhardtian view that individual subjectivity is a creation of modernity; however, while the poem might be precocious in its understanding of selfhood, it does not treat interiority with particular sympathy. Rather, she contends, it can be read as a warning against the increased cultivation of the self among Richard II and his circle, especially through their usage of stylized love discourse. Through Troilus's reckless and perilous commitment to his inner life, Chaucer seems to be echoing other contemporary critics of Richard, rounding on his interest in self-fashioning and self-display, and his consequent neglect of wider political concerns. Chaucer's treatment of love discourse also forms the subject of Christopher Stampone's 'Choreographing *Fin'amor*: Dance and the Game of Love in Geoffrey Chaucer's *Troilus and Criseyde*' (*ChauR* 50[2015] 393–419). Stampone looks closely at the figurative references to dancing in *Troilus*, finding that they present the exchanges between Criseyde, Pandarus, Troilus, and Diomede not merely as a game but as a form of rhythmic movement. These terms, which are without parallel in the *Filocolo*, provide an important series of cues for understanding the course of the doomed affair, characterizing the characters' deployment of structured rhetoric, and the ultimate failure of Pandarus to contain the events within the bounds of his choreography.

The other major strand of scholarship on *Troilus* considers its treatment of Christian themes. Megan Murton's 'Praying with Boethius in *Troilus and Criseyde*' (*ChauR* 49[2015] 294–319) argues that Troilus's grasp of Boethian concepts is more complete than is often alleged. Concentrating on Troilus's hymn in Book III and his speech on destiny in Book IV, Murton disputes the common view that Boethian material provides a muted, ironic commentary on the action of *Troilus*. On the contrary, Troilus is made to voice a nuanced, expansive reading of the *Consolatio*, as his own movement from reflection to prayer recalls Boethius's insistence that the proper end of philosophy is devotion. Similar meanings also inform Lawrence Besserman's 'Biblical *Figura* in Chaucer's *Troilus and Criseyde*, ll. 1380–6: "As don thise rokkes or thise milnestones"' (*ChauR* 49[2015] 344–51). Besserman detects a subtle irony in the imagery with which Pandarus chivvies his despairing, lovelorn friend. While Pandarus's appeal to oaks, rocks, and millstones serves his immediate rhetorical purpose since all will swiftly collapse despite their initial obstinacy, the unmistakable echoes of the Gospels, and of the death of Abimelech, inject a more sinister undertone into his words. Maintaining religious criticism of the poem, although with emphasis on language rather than symbolism, is Laura Clark's 'Stretching the *Sooth:* Use, Overuse, and the Consolation of *Sooth* in Chaucer's *Troilus and Criseyde*' (*Neophil* 99[2015] 493–504). Clark considers the occurrences of the word *sooth* in the speeches of Troilus, Criseyde and especially Pandarus, and discovers that the term is not as rigidly defined as is often assumed. Although Middle English certainly differentiated between 'truth' in its empirical and moral senses, and used *sooth* and *trouthe* to separate the two levels of meaning, Chaucer seems to bring both into play, allowing one to overshadow and even compromise the other. This is particularly observable in Troilus's soliloquy in Book IV, where Criseyde's failure to disclose the *sooth* of her intentions calls her *trouthe* into doubt.

## 4. Other Works

The *Book of the Duchess* has attracted some scholarly attention this year. Jamie C. Fumo's monograph, *Making Chaucer's Book of the Duchess: Textuality and Reception*, consolidates the many strands of interpretation that make up the poem's critical history by charting its reception and dissemination in detail. In the introduction, Fumo states that her study not only seeks to 'provide a panoramic view of critical trends in [*Book of the Duchess's*] interpretation as they develop over time', but reflects on the materiality of the poem by considering its place 'within contemporary understandings of Chaucerian authorship and the culture of book production in the later Middle Ages and early modern period' (p. 3). The first two chapters of the work concentrate on the scholarly reception of the *Book of the Duchess* from the late nineteenth century onwards. Chapter 3 considers the self-conscious textuality of the *Book of the Duchess* by drawing attention to the poem's repeated emphasis on reading, writing, and authorship. In the final two chapters, Fumo considers the reception and dissemination of the poem in the fifteenth century and into the early modern period.

The, *Book of Duchess* has also been the subject of a number of smaller studies. Sarah Stanbury asserts, in 'The Place of the Bedchamber in Chaucer's *Book of the Duchess*' (*SAC* 37[2015] 133–61), that the bedchamber is an important framing device which serves to localize the poem in an English context. By drawing on documentary evidence, principally wills, that testifies to the economic value of beds and bedding in the late fourteenth century, Stanbury suggests that the description of the narrator's bedchamber serves to locate the text by pointing to 'economic surplus and bourgeois and gentry power' (p. 150). Stanbury also asserts that the English setting of the poem is further reflected in the poem's ending through the use of wordplay, where the references to 'Rich Hill' and 'Long Castle' point specifically to English locations and buildings, as well as people.

The relationship between language, memory, and consolation in the *Book of the Duchess* forms the subject of Reid Hardaway's essay, 'A Fallen Language and the Consolation of Art in the *Book of the Duchess*' (*ChauR* 50[2015] 159–77). Although the inability of language to express true suffering is a recurring motif throughout the *Book of the Duchess*, Hardaway argues that Chaucer, by looking to Ovid and the *Metamorphoses*, develops an 'Ovidian aesthetics' (p. 160) to suggest that the language of art functions as an effective means to articulate inner grief: 'By referring to Ovid, Chaucer situates art as a mode of transformation, where destructive emotions undergo conversion, and language, precisely by its indirection, can facilitate a metamorphosis of grief and loss into creativity and invention' (p. 164).

In 'Speaking Images? Iconographic Criticism and Chaucerian Ekphrasis' (in Johnston et al., eds., pp. 55–76), John M. Bowers examines Chaucer's approach to ekphrasis, focusing predominantly on the *Book of the Duchess* and the *House of Fame*. Bowers argues that an awareness of the rise in Lollard iconophobia directly informs Chaucer's use of ekphrasis, as his works focus on 'conspicuously literary, non-Christian images' (p. 56) in order to avoid any suspicion of idolatry. This preference for classical rather than Christian imagery is evident in the *Book of the Duchess*, where the windows of the dreamer's bedchamber are decorated with the story of Troy, as well as in the temple of Venus described in the *House of Fame*. As a result, 'Looking at an artwork is always, for Chaucer, looking into the past' (p. 70).

Chaucer's *House of Fame* is discussed in a number of essays in Davis and Nall, eds., *Chaucer and Fame*. The first essay in the volume, William T. Rossiter's 'Chaucer Joins the *Schiera*: The *House of Fame*, Italy and the Determination of Posterity' (pp. 21–42), considers Chaucer's response to the Trecento's conception of the poet, focusing particularly on the influence of Dante and Petrarch and the models of poetic fame they represent. Rossiter argues that, although Chaucer's examination of the role and function of the poet is seen most acutely in the *House of Fame*, this poem forms a 'discursive continuum' with the *Clerk's Prologue* and the end of *Troilus*, as together these texts 'constitute an intertextual discourse on poetic *claritas* and *fama*' (p. 21). The essay concludes with a consideration of the language of praise directed at

Petrarch in the *Clerk's Prologue* and argues that Chaucer uses this to establish 'his own posthumous poetic fame' (p. 36). The fifth chapter in *Chaucer and Fame*, 'The Early Reception of Chaucer's *The House of Fame*' (pp. 87–102) by Julia Boffey and A.S.G. Edwards, charts the poem's reception and influence on later texts and writers. They observe that the *House of Fame* appears to have made only a limited impression on later writers. The reasons for this lack of full engagement may be due to the poem's rather limited circulation, its unfinished state, and also the lack of attribution of the poem to Chaucer in the surviving manuscripts. It was not until Pope's *The Temple of Fame* that this focus on literary fame was fully acknowledged, as Pope's work re-established the 'conjunction of poetic identity and Fame' (p. 102).

The *House of Fame* is also the topic of Rebecca Davis's essay, 'Fugitive Poetics in Chaucer's *House of Fame*' (*SAC* 37[2015] 101–32). Davis argues that the poem's exploration of the relationship between form and motion can be described as a 'fugitive poetics', that is, 'a way of making poetry in a world in which "every kyndely thyng that is" reveals itself in transit' (p. 102). It is asserted that the attention the poem directs towards 'kyndely enclynyng' (l. 734), or natural inclination, is significant, as this force 'is not only responsible for the upward movement of "tydynges" to Fame's house', but reveals something about Chaucer's art as it 'serves more broadly as the basis of an *ars poetica* of material agency' (p. 102). Following a consideration of Boethius's theory of natural inclination in the *Consolation of Philosophy* and its relation to the *House of Fame*, Davis argues that the depiction of the field of sand which opens Book II, as well as the chaotic interior of the House of Rumour at the end of the poem, are deployed by Chaucer in order to comment on poetic matter. Davis asserts that these settings serve as liminal spaces and sites of motion, as is evinced by the frequent deployment of water imagery in both sections. However, while the field of sand can be read as a 'site of grappling, where a landscape and the processes that shape it represent the matter of poetry itself' (p. 113), the whirling structure of the House of Rumour demonstrates that poetic form is continually fluid and in motion. As a consequence, the poem overturns the idea of poetry as fixed and instead encourages us 'to think of poetic form not as an end point but as a conduit through which dynamic matter takes shape' (p. 105).

An interest in Chaucer's approach to poetry is shared by T.S. Miller in 'Chaucer's Sources and Chaucer's Lies: *Anelida and Arcite* and the Poetics of Fabrication' (*JEGP* 114[2015] 373–400). This study examines the way in which Chaucer handles his sources in *Anelida and Arcite* and argues that in the poem Chaucer 'carves out a space for himself as a poetic "fabricator"' (p. 375), rather than as author or compiler. This is reinforced not only by Chaucer's slippery use of source material, but by the construction of the poem's narrative voice, which is repeatedly presented as false and untrustworthy. While this may be typical of a number of voices found in Chaucer's works, Miller argues that the unreliability of the narrative voice throughout the *Anelida* allows Chaucer to emphasize the 'deception inherent in his poetic process of slyly integrating sources with material of his own invention' (p. 377).

In her discussion of Chaucer's *Parliament of Fowls*, 'Knowing and Willing in Chaucer's *Parliament of Fowls*' (*ChauR* 50[2015] 368–92), Sarah Powrie examines the influence of late medieval voluntarism. It is argued that throughout the poem Chaucer questions the classical view, as espoused by Thomas Aquinas, that reason's judgement is the basis of all moral action. Powrie notes that by depicting his learned dreamer-narrator as repeatedly unable to demonstrate true virtue, as evinced, for instance, by his lack of courage when confronted with the words on the garden's gates, Chaucer 'challenges classical assumptions that moral action can be rationally directed and consistently realized' (p. 378). The formel's decision to defer choosing a mate can be understood as the poem's most forceful demonstration of voluntarism, as she acts in opposition to Nature and Reason by failing to choose the royal tercel. Although this decision may initially appear to be morally dubious, Powrie notes that it is entirely in keeping with the poem's 'anti-intellectual objectives' (p. 390) and thus serves to demonstrate not only the virtue of free will, but the moral limitations of reason: 'the formel's morally motivated inaction would show that the will's freedom empowers individuals to resist what is ostensibly rational' (p. 392).

Marjorie Harrington considers Chaucer's engagement with the dream-vision tradition in her article, '"That swevene hath Daniel unloke": Interpreting Dreams with Chaucer' (*ChauR* 50[2015] 315–67). Harrington argues that, in addition to Macrobian or Augustinian dream theories, the *Somniale Danielis* (a popular manual of dream interpretation that derived its authority from the belief that the Old Testament prophet, Daniel, was an interpreter of dreams), was also a source of influence on Chaucer. However, unlike other contemporary writers who engage with the *Somniale* tradition, in Chaucer's works we can detect an 'ambiguity and skepticism in his references to *Somniale*-type dreambooks' (p. 320). In order to demonstrate the wider reception of the *Somniale Danielis*, Harrington examines two dream texts copied by the Harley scribe: *The Bok of Swevening* in London, British Library MS Harley 2253, and a Latin text of the *Somniale Danielis* in London, British Library MS Royal 12.C.xii (an edited and translated version of this work is supplied at the end of the article). Harrington's examination of these works demonstrates that there is no evidence that the scribe 'thought of dream manuals as anything other than practical knowledge made available by divine revelation' (p. 330) and, as a consequence, such a stance is in contrast to Chaucer's more sceptical attitude. This demonstrates that, although Chaucer's use of the dream-vision genre has often been seen as original, 'his attitude towards "Daniel" dreambooks was equally revolutionary' (p. 330).

The possible intended audience for the *Legend of Good Women* is considered in chapter 6 of Alfred Thomas's monograph *Reading Women in Late Medieval Europe* (also reviewed in Section 2 above). In keeping with his wider discussion about the influence of Anne of Bohemia on Chaucer's literary career, Thomas argues that the *Legend* was written for Anne, either as an imagined or actual audience. Thomas asserts that in order to appeal to the queen's love of female saints' lives, Chaucer sought to integrate the model of female hagiography into his accounts of classical women; however, this was an 'impossible task' (p. 169), as it sought to unite two contradictory discourses about women. As Thomas notes, 'Instead of presenting his heroines as strong and defiant, Chaucer's *Legend of Good Women* has the opposite effect of depicting them as weak and passive who became martyrs for human, not divine, love' (p. 170). By comparing the *Legend*'s handling of female characterization to that in other works from the Continent, specifically *The Little Weaver* (a Czech prose work of the early fifteenth century) and *The Plowman from Bohemia* (a German prose work of *c*.1400 which is a loose analogue of the Czech text), Thomas concludes that Chaucer's inability to reconcile his depiction of women in the *Legend* 'may be less a feature of deliberate irony than an index of the larger crisis of male authority in medieval Christendom at the end of the fourteenth century' (p. 194).

Finally, Sarah Stanbury considers Chaucer's short poem 'The Former Age' in her essay, 'Multilingual Lists and Chaucer's "The Former Age"' (in Johnston et al., eds., pp. 36–54). Through an examination of the poem's vocabulary, particularly its use of French and English words, Stanbury argues that Chaucer exploits the registers of language in order to engage with questions of 'historical change and linguistic translation' (p. 38). Stanbury regards the poem's use of listing as meaningful, examining it in the light of the popular French–English word lists that circulated throughout the later Middle Ages, as well as in relation to business inventories. It is claimed that Chaucer's technique of listing, as well as the mixing of French and English vocabulary, serves as a comment on history, as it not only charts a movement from an English Golden Age to a French fallen world, but depicts the present as a place where French and English sit rather uneasily together (p. 54).

## 5. Reception and Reputation

Chaucer's first copyists have been subject to several fresh readings, beginning with two radically differing interpretations of the Ellesmere and Hengwrt manuscripts. In the first place, Simon Horobin, in 'Thomas Hoccleve: Chaucer's First Editor' (*ChauR* 50[2015] 228–50), reiterates the attribution of these manuscripts to Adam Pinkhurst, although he raises the suggestion that Pinkhurst might have been supervised by Thomas Hoccleve. Two particular details lead him to this conclusion: the apparent presence of Hoccleve's hand in Hengwrt, especially at points that seem to organize its redrafting and reworking, and similarities between the Ellesmere and the two earliest copies of Hoccleve's own *Regiment of Princes*. Hoccleve's movement in the same circles as Pinkhurst, and his obvious interest in Chaucer, might also signal his oversight of these important formalizations of Chaucer's work. On the other hand, Lawrence Warner offers a reappraisal of the work of Linne Mooney, Horobin, and Estelle Stubbs in 'Scribes, Misattributed: Hoccleve and Pinkhurst' (*SAC* 37[2015] 55–100). While Warner's conclusions on Hoccleve are discussed at length in Chapter III above, his work also has implications for the attribution of Ellesmere and Hengwrt. As Warner writes, the claim that Chaucer's 'Adam scriveyn' is in fact Adam Pinkhurst has rapidly attained the status of a critical truism: not only has it received sanction from a string of commentators and by the editors of *ODNB*, it has achieved the rare feat of attracting notice beyond the confines of specialist scholarship. Nevertheless, as Warner argues, despite the appeal of this conclusion, the case has not been proven beyond all doubt. By revisiting Mooney's findings, Warner finds that the case for Pinkhurst rests largely on the 'repertoire of decorative motifs' thought to characterize his hand, such as the 'double slash and dot' that occurs in some enlarged capitals (p. 88). Far from being idiosyncratic, such features seem to be commonplace among a range of London scribes; even more problematically, they are generally absent from the two Chaucer manuscripts.

Pinkhurst and his circle also feature in Martha Carlin's 'Thomas Spencer, Southwark Scrivener (d.1428): Owner of a Copy of Chaucer's *Troilus* in 1394?' (*ChauR* 49[2015] 387–401), albeit as readers rather than scribes. Carlin might have uncovered an extremely rare reference to ownership of a Chaucerian text within Chaucer's own lifetime. Her find concerns the scrivener Thomas Spencer, who was sued at the Common Bench in 1405 for an outstanding debt of 100 shillings; in his defence, Spencer claimed that he had, eleven years earlier, surrendered a *librum vocatum Troylous* in partial lieu of the money. Although this is the sole mention of the book in the proceedings, Spencer gains added interest from his close contact with the tailor, hosteller, and book-collector John Brynchele, and from the fact that Spencer's admissions oath to the scriveners' company occurs next to that of Adam Pinkhurst. The relevant records are appended in a full translation. Chaucer's readership in his own lifetime is also a central concern for Stephanie Downes in 'After Deschamps: Chaucer's French Fame' (in Davis and Nall, eds., pp. 128–42). Looking to Deschamps's famous homage to the 'grant translateur, noble Geffrey Chaucier' in the 1390s, Downes considers how Deschamps might have gained access to Chaucer's work, and the extent to which this lone reference marks wider knowledge of Chaucer in medieval France. Despite evidence of some cross-pollination between francophone and anglophone culture, the *balade* and its request for more writing remains an isolated but tantalizing hint, difficult to site in a wider context.

Moving from material to literary culture, John Burrow, in 'The *Tale of Beryn*: An Appreciation' (*ChauR* 49[2015] 499–511), offers some remarks on the early fifteenth-century *Tale of Beryn* and its *Prologue*, both of which were grafted into an early manuscript of the *Canterbury Tales* in an effort to 'complete' the pilgrimage narrative. Burrow examines the poet's fidelity to his model: for instance, he suggests that the irregularity of *Beryn*'s lines might be explained by its author having read one of the *Canterbury Tales* manuscripts that includes *Gamelyn*; he also notes that the text shows an intelligent engagement with the realities of mercantile commerce, although it makes little attempt to replicate Chaucer's phrasing or portraiture. Andrew Galloway takes a wider view of Chaucer in the same period in 'Fame's Penitent: Deconstructive Chaucer among the Lancastrians' (in Davis and Nall, eds., pp. 103–26). Galloway's starting point is Thomas Gascoigne and his description of Chaucer's deathbed repentance, one of many texts from the period to visualize Chaucer as a penitent in the face of death. Galloway suggests that this trope develops a number of important functions: the likes of Hoccleve and Scogan replay Chaucer's apologetic posture in order to legitimize English poetry itself, creating a poetic voice that is founded in 'secular penance... a concern for good governance and social ethics, based on a form of sombre self-reflection tailored to the secular world' (p. 113).

Heather Blurton and Hannah Johnson look to Lydgate and Hoccleve to draw out a further aspect of Chaucer's fifteenth-century reputation in 'Reading the *Prioress's Tale* in the Fifteenth Century: Lydgate, Hoccleve, and Marian Devotion' (*ChauR* 50[2015] 134–58). They begin by noting the frequent circulation of the *Prioress's Tale* as an independent text, especially in devotional anthologies, effectively stripping away any irony embedded in its narrative persona. This in turn seems to indicate Chaucer's wider acceptance as a specifically Marian poet and the tale itself as an unproblematic account of a Marian miracle. This dimension of his work further feeds into the work of his earliest followers, as Lydgate's *Legend of Dan Joos* and Hoccleve's *Monk and the Virgin's Sleeves* show them using his Marian poems as 'important literary platforms upon which to engage with Chaucer's poetics and reputation' (p. 139). Similar customization of Chaucerian material is addressed in Seth Lerer's ' "The Tongue": Chaucer, Lydgate, Charles d'Orléans, and the Making of a Late Medieval Lyric' (*ChauR* 49[2015] 474–98). Lerer's subject is a minor text in the Findern manuscript, a piece on loose speech botched together from the *Fall of Princes* and *Troilus and Criseyde*. Despite the tendency to treat this poem as purely derivative, Lerer argues that it interrogates rather than reiterates its sources. By prying them from their original contexts, and bringing them into dialogue with the other, feminine-focused content of the manuscript, the copyist creates a complex set of new meanings; he also invites us to rethink our own critical definitions of text or lyric.

Another fifteenth-century reader is considered in Amber Dunai's ' "Ane Doolie Sessoun" and "Ane Cairfull Dyte": Cresseid and the Narrator in Henryson's *Testament of Cresseid*' (*ChauR* 50[2015] 420–41). Dunai takes issue with readings that see Henryson's text as a moralizing 'corrective' to Chaucer's work; instead, she argues that the narrator of the *Testament* is increasingly compromised as the text progresses, to the extent that he becomes 'the negative exemplar to Cresseid's positive one', only capable of lamenting his own suffering rather than learning from it (p. 440). Later in the same century, Chaucer's role in the emergence of print culture is assessed by Satoko Tokunaga, 'Wynkyn de Worde's Lost Manuscript of the *Canterbury Tales*: With New Light on HRC MS 46' (*ChauR* 50[2015] 30–54). It has long been known that De Worde consulted multiple copies of the *Canterbury Tales* when preparing his 1498 edition. Tokunaga builds on the hypothesis of Stephen Partridge regarding the likely line of descent of De Worde's text, examining a number of the tales and their marginalia in order to establish the likely character of the manuscripts De Worde had at his disposal. It is clear that De Worde's imprint is a valuable witness to the transmission of the *Canterbury Tales*, as it allows many of the family resemblances and groupings of the early manuscripts to be excavated. An appendix discusses the differences between De Worde's source-manuscripts and those available to Caxton before him.

The transition between medieval and modern cultures continues to be a vital turning-point in attitudes towards Chaucer. In 'Revenant Chaucer: Early Modern Celebrity' (in David and Nall, eds., pp. 185–99), Thomas Prendergast calls on Fred Inglis's notion of celebrity as a type of presence founded in the absence of the original person. He finds this idea a suggestive template for understanding different cultural uses to which Chaucer could be put. While late medieval scribes and readers might try to reconstitute Chaucer in ways that are 'authentically Chaucerian', albeit at times privileging wholeness over authenticity, their counterparts in the sixteenth and seventeenth centuries turned Chaucer into a free-floating voice into which more or less any concerns could be projected. Likewise, Joanna Bellis maps out another important discontinuity in Chaucer's early reception in ' "Fresh anamalit termes": The Contradictory Celebrity of Chaucer's Aureation' (in Davis and Nall, eds., pp. 143–63). While celebration of Chaucer's influence remains consistent across the fifteenth and sixteenth centuries, the conceptual ground shifts beneath this general approbation. Although Hoccleve, Lydgate, Ashby, and others praised Chaucer for introducing complex rhetorical diction into English, writers of the subsequent period usually followed a different path: Spenser, Sherry, and their contemporaries tended instead to salute the 'purity' and directness of his language. The movement from one standard of evaluation to another pinpoints a wider ambivalence, one bound up with nationalism and the necessity (or not) of embroidering English by looking to Continental cultures. Further disruptions are traced in Jamie C. Fumo's wide-ranging essay, 'Ancient Chaucer: Temporalities of Fame' (in Davis and Nall, eds., pp. 201–20). Fumo looks at the ways in which Chaucer's fame and supposed 'antiquity' orbit one another during the early modern period. She traces out the ways in which Chaucer's followers either see him as famous because of his longevity, or deserving of the label 'antique' because of his renown. Thus he is encountered as a poet from the distant past, whose language is filled with 'obscurities', but he also has antiquity thrust upon him: this tendency taken to its greatest extreme by Francis Kynaston's partial Latin translation of *Troilus and Criseyde*. Ironically, *Troilus* and other works contain an anticipation of these problems, as Chaucer insists on the timely rather than timeless quality of his poetry.

In the same volume, Mike Rodman-Jones examines Chaucer's insertion into seventeenth-century Anglican culture in 'Chaucer the Puritan' (in Davis and Nall, eds., pp. 165–84). Despite Chaucer's remarkable versatility as an authority as he could be made to support astrology, alchemy, grammar, and apiculture among other discourses, he is most commonly made to sanction the 'anticlerical . . . agenda of English Protestantism' (p. 167). Yet as Rodman-Jones demonstrates, this did not necessarily mean that Chaucer was used in a simplistic way, as a source of dour, dry axioms; on the contrary, many of his appropriations are lively, even comic, such as Samuel Harsnett's playful allusions to the *Miller's Tale*. Puritanism, albeit of the transatlantic variety, also concerns Nancy Bradley Warren, ' "Flying from the Depravities of *Europe*, to the *American Strand*": Chaucer and the Chaucer Tradition in Early America' (*ELH* 82[2015] 589–613). This essay studies allusions in the work of Cotton Mather, Anne Bradstreet, and Nathaniel Ward, noting that Chaucer becomes an important tool for staking out differences and continuities between the new and old worlds. Mather accepts Foxe's view of Chaucer as 'quasi-saint', a judgement that allows him to treat even snippets of the *Wife of Bath's Tale* as testaments of moral wisdom. Bradstreet likewise draws her posture from the Chaucerian apocrypha when upbraiding old England, while

Ward refers to Bradstreet sporting 'Chaucers boots' in a backhanded compliment to her art. For all three, Chaucer provides an anchorage in a proto-Protestant current of English history.

Material traces of Chaucer's sixteenth-century readership are reviewed in two separate articles by Mimi Ensley and Hope Johnston. Ensley's essay, 'Reading Chaucer in the Tower: The Person behind the Pen in an Early-Modern Copy of Chaucer's *Works*' (*JEBS* 18[2015] 136–57), concerns one John Harington of Stepney and his engagement with Thynne's *Workes* during his imprisonment in 1549–50. As well as putting biographical flesh on the bones of an early modern reader, her analysis is able to reconstruct Harington's reading practices: alongside modifying spelling and punctuation, his annotations isolate phrases of 'sententious or proverbial' value, and set up cross-references with other texts from Harington's reading (p. 140). In particular, his attraction to passages of immediate relevance to his predicament bear witness to a quasi-Boethian dialogue between this prisoner and his consolatory book. Johnston covers similar territory, albeit with a wider scope, in 'Readers' Memorials in Early Editions of Chaucer' (*SB* 59:i[2015] 45–69). Johnston surveys the inscriptions that occur in the surviving copies of sixteenth-century editions of Chaucer. These notations betray a particular interest in commemorating and celebrating Chaucer: the Westminster epitaph appears in no fewer than eleven copies, and is often augmented with further memorial verses or sketches; similarly, hand-drawn portraits of Chaucer appear in fifteen further volumes.

Chaucer is less a source of inspiration and more a target of ridicule in Kathryn Jacobs and D'andra White, 'Ben Jonson on Shakespeare's Chaucer' (*ChauR* 50[2015] 198–215). As Jacobs and White observe, Jonson's classicizing impulses drove him to deride the use of medieval forms and language among his contemporaries, seeing archaism as a perilous counter-influence to the literature of antiquity. Shakespeare and Spenser drew particular disdain for their addiction to 'Chaucerisms... best expung'd', especially since the former showed a greater commitment to medieval than Latin sources, with Holinshed, Chaucer, and Gower furnishing him with most of his theatrical narratives. One core in these criticisms is the sense that Chaucerian ideas are 'old' or 'stale', providing Jacobs and White with a key for interpreting some of the more cryptic snipes in Jonson's plays and poetry.

The relationship between Chaucer and his post-Reformation followers is addressed from the other direction in James Simpson, 'Not Yet: Chaucer and Anagogy' (*SAC* 37[2015] 31–54). Simpson coins the phrase 'anagogical posture': this term describes the tendency of some texts to 'recognize their own inadequacy, their own wounded, lapsarian and provisional state in time', as they gesture towards a future they will never see fulfilled (p. 33). Recognizing this stance offers a means of redirecting medieval studies, opening its habitual synchronicity into a more diachronic mode. The early modern reception of Chaucer's work signals its particular suitability for this approach, as Protestant readers such as Bale and Birkbeck did see him in exactly these terms, as a figure whose vision could reach beyond his own temporal horizons towards their own. What is more, despite Chaucer's scepticism towards oracular prophecy, there are points at which his work might actively invite such a response: the *Pardoner's Tale* in particular looks forward to a church crumbling into fragments, casting detectible 'ripples' beyond the frontiers of the Middle Ages (p. 54).

The ideological significance of the Victorian Chaucer is explored in two further articles. Stephanie Downes continues her examination of Chaucer's French reputation in 'Chaucer in Nineteenth-Century France' (*ChauR* 49[2015] 352–70). She traces out the ways in which Chaucerian scholarship was bound up with nationalistic concerns throughout the nineteenth century, as French literary historians such as E.G. Sandras and Emile Legouis sought to annex Chaucer to francophone culture, claiming him as an honorary French author: although clearly drawn to Chaucer by his Englishness, they sought to redress or reverse this quality, emphasizing his debt to Machaut and to De Meun rather than his poetic innovation. On the other side of the Channel, H.L. Spencer discusses one of Chaucer's most important editors, and one of Sandras's most vehement critics, in 'F.J. Furnivall's Six of the Best: The *Six-Text Canterbury Tales* and the *Chaucer Society*' (*RES* 66[2015] 601–23). Spencer weighs up Furnivall's motives in establishing the Chaucer Society in 1868, a mere four years after the foundation of the Early English Text Society. She finds that the decision rested equally on patriotic and logistical considerations, and that interaction between the two societies was often driven by financial concerns, but also notes Furnivall's commitment to high-minded Christian Socialist principles. The greatest monument to these impulses was Furnivall's parallel-text edition of the six (ultimately eight) 'best' witnesses to the *Canterbury Tales*, a deliberate attempt to democratize the editorial process, albeit one that led to Skeat's more authoritative (and authoritarian) edition.

Lastly, Chaucer is propelled into 1970s America by David Hamilton's 'Chaucer's Moose' (*ChauR* 49[2015] 378–86). Looking at sections of Elizabeth Bishop's 'The Moose' from her collection *Geography III*, Hamilton finds a string of hitherto undetected echoes of the opening lines of the *Canterbury Tales*. These are chiefly recognizable in the repeated use of prepositions, and the overall emphasis on travel; they also allow Hamilton to pick out several points of ironic interplay between Bishop's poem and its medieval model, as the connected issues of sickness and secularity are threads common to both. Hamilton speculates that Bishop may have come to Chaucer via Ezra Pound, perhaps drawing inspiration from Pound's characterization of Chaucer as a poet of international scope, a designation that mirrored Bishop's own ambitions.

## Books Reviewed

Allen, Mark, and Stephanie Amsel. *Annotated Chaucer Bibliography 1997–2010*. ManUP. [2015] pp. xx + 806. £75 ISBN 9 7807 1909 6099.

Ashe, Laura. *Early Fiction in England: From Geoffrey of Monmouth to Chaucer*. Penguin. [2015] pp. 464. £12.99 ISBN 9 7801 4139 2875.

Beaumont, Matthew. *Nightwalking: A Nocturnal History of London*. Verso. [2015] pp. 496. £20 ISBN 9 7817 8168 7956.

Boboc, Andreea, ed. *Theorizing Legal Personhood in Late Medieval England.* Brill. [2015] pp. 310. €115 ISBN 9 7890 0428 0410.

Conde-Silvestre, Juan Camilo, and Javier Calle-Martín. *Approaches to Middle English: Variation, Contact and Change.* Lang. [2015] pp. 259. £45 ISBN 9 7836 5398 0004.

Davis, Isabel, and Catherine Nall, eds. *Chaucer and Fame: Reputation and Reception.* Brewer. [2015] pp. 264. £60 ISBN 9 7818 4384 4075.

Fumo, Jamie C. *Making Chaucer's Book of the Duchess: Textuality and Reception.* UWalesP. [2015] pp. 272. £70 ISBN 9 7817 8316 3472.

Gabrovsky, Alexander N. *Chaucer the Alchemist: Physics, Mutability, and the Medieval Imagination.* PalMac. [2015] pp. 291. £72 ISBN 9 7811 3754 1345.

Gerber, Amanda J. *Medieval Ovid: Frame Narrative and Political Allegory.* PalMac. [2015] pp. 163. £47 ISBN 9 7811 3748 8398.

Ginsberg, Warren. *Tellers, Tales, and Translation in Chaucer's Canterbury Tales.* OUP. [2015]. pp. 250. £60 ISBN 9 7801 9874 8786.

Gray, Douglas. *Simple Forms: Essays on Medieval English Popular Literature.* OUP. [2015] pp. 278. £55 ISBN 9 7801 9870 6090.

Ingham, Patricia Clare. *The Medieval New: Ambivalence in an Age of Innovation.* UPennP. [2015]. pp. 288. £42.50 ISBN 9 7808 1224 7060.

Johnston, Andrew James, Ethan Knapp, and Margitta Rouse, eds. *The Art of Vision: Ekphrasis in Medieval Literature and Culture.* OSUP. [2015] pp. 336. $72.95 ISBN 9 7808 1421 2943.

Marenbon, John. *Pagans and Philosophers: The Problem of Paganism from Augustine to Leibniz.* PrincetonUP. [2015] pp. 368. £24.95 ISBN 9 7806 9114 2555.

McKinstry, Jamie. *Middle English Romance and the Craft of Memory.* B&B. [2015] pp. 289. £60 ISBN 9 7818 4384 4174.

O'Donoghue, Bernard. *Reading Chaucer's Poems: A Guided Selection.* Faber. [2015] pp. 256. £14.99 ISBN 9 7805 7123 0655.

Patterson, Serina, ed. *Games and Gaming in Medieval Literature.* PalMac. [2015] pp. 241. £55 ISBN 9 7811 3731 1030.

Scala, Elizabeth. *Desire in the Canterbury Tales.* OSUP. [2015] pp. 248. $62.95 ISBN 9 7808 1421 2783.

Schmidt, A.V.C. *Passion and Precision: Collected Essays on English Poetry from Geoffrey Chaucer to Geoffrey Hill.* CambridgeSP. [2015] pp. 475. £57.99 ISBN 9 7814 4387 1853.

Schrock, Chad D. *Consolation in Medieval Narrative: Augustinian Authority and Open Form.* PalMac. [2015] pp. 240. £55 ISBN 9 7811 3745 3358.

Stadnik, Katarzyna. *Chaucer's Choices: Through the Looking-Glass of Medieval Imagery.* Lang. [2015] pp. 222. £37 ISBN 9 7836 3166 3837.

Thomas, Alfred. *Reading Women in Late Medieval Europe: Anne of Bohemia and Chaucer's Female Audience.* PalMac. [2015] pp. 251. £58 ISBN 9 7811 3754 4193.

Treharne, Elaine. *Medieval Literature: A Very Short Introduction.* OUP. [2015] pp. 160. £7.99 ISBN 9 7801 9966 8496.

Workman, Jameson S. *Chaucer and the Death of the Political Animal.* PalMac. [2015] pp. 274. £58 ISBN 9 7811 3745 6519.

# V

# The Early Sixteenth Century

## GAVIN SCHWARTZ-LEEPER AND EDWARD SMITH

This chapter has six sections: 1. General: Drama and Prose; 2. General: Verse; 3. More; 4. Skelton; 5. Surrey; 6. Wyatt. Section 1 is by Gavin Schwartz-Leeper and Edward Smith; sections 2, 4, 5, and 6 are by Edward Smith; section 3 is by Gavin Schwartz-Leeper.

## 1. General: Drama and Prose

The publications on earlier Tudor drama and prose in 2015 have a broad reach. The latest instalment in the *Records of Early English Drama* is the highly-anticipated three-volume *Civic London to 1558*, edited by Anne Lancashire and David J. Parkinson. It will be a very welcome resource for any researcher interested in late medieval and early modern performative texts or contexts linked to London. The greatest strength of the series is its exhaustive approach. This is particularly true of the London volumes, which offer access to a wealth of materials that, thanks to the detailed coverage of the period 1286–1558/9, enable scholars to trace performative developments in and around London.

*Civic London to 1558* is divided into three volumes. Volume 1 contains an introduction via prefatory essays on 'Historical Background', 'Drama, Music, and Ceremonial Customs', 'The Documents', and 'Editorial Procedures'. The introductory materials also include a selected bibliography. The first volume then provides the civic records relating to performance from 1286 to 1523, with volume 2 covering the remainder of the records to 1558/9 and the appendices. The appendices incorporate a variety of related materials, including unclear, fragmented, or erroneous records. The final volume provides translations and glossaries for the texts, along with an index and detailed endnotes. The glossaries will be welcomed by interdisciplinary scholars in particular; while the glosses are useful for the Anglo-Norman and Latin records, the glossaries extend to the English records as well. (For further discussion of this book see Chapter III, Section 15.)

Karina F. Attar and Lynn Shutters' essay collection *Teaching Medieval and Early Modern Cross-Cultural Encounters* divides essays into three sections

*The Year's Work in English Studies, Volume 96 (2017)* © *The Author 2017. Published by Oxford University Press on behalf of the English Association. All rights reserved.*
*For Permissions, please email: journals.permissions@oup.com*
doi:10.1093/ywes/max005

on 'synchronic', 'synchronic and diachronic', and 'diachronic' studies of cross-cultural encounters, geared towards fostering a sense of what we might variously term 'cultural literacy' or 'intercultural intelligence' in historical studies. The editors present the essays as examples of pedagogical experiments that intend to shift discussions of how (and why) we teach the past towards activities that help students to learn from the past as they learn about the past. This goal is explicitly tied to what the editors (and several authors) identify as a growing awareness amongst students that modern cultural and geopolitical tensions shape readings of the past, and that historical conflicts or tropes shape our modern tensions.

*Teaching Medieval and Early Modern Cross-Cultural Encounters* covers a broad range of materials and contexts, ranging from Chaucer and Shakespeare to Sicilian *opera dei pupi*, ancient and modern depictions of Central Asians, and Nina Simone (to name just a selection of the diverse texts offered up in this collection). The essays are based around case studies explicating classroom practices that provide a wealth of exciting suggestions and opportunities. The essays provide concrete, often step-by-step, explorations of and reflections on the teaching of cross-cultural texts, blending authors' research with their classroom practices and student input.

There are a few issues thrown up by this collection that might have benefited from further exploration, however, particularly when we consider the cross-cultural aims of the volume. The editors and several of the authors frame their students' concerns with the interaction of past and present as being rooted in the 'post-9/11 world'; for a text concerned with global history, it is strange that such a label would be applied without further examination of that lens, especially when so many of the contributors' work pushes away from Eurocentric (or Western) analyses and texts. It is perhaps related (if otherwise circumstantially significant, if it is significant at all) that, of the sixteen contributors, only one is based outside the United States, and that one is in Canada. Despite the implications of this limitation, this is a useful and perceptive text that will provide exceptional inspiration for teachers (and researchers too) concerned with a very wide range of medieval and early modern texts.

Extending the focus on essay collections, *New Ways of Looking at Old Texts, V: Papers of the Renaissance English Text Society, 2007–2010*, the latest issue of the Renaissance English Text Society's (RETS) series, was published in 2014, edited by Michael Denbo. While many of the contributions to this volume will be familiar to readers of this section, given that the essays have grown from conference papers and other events over the past nine years, it is worth raising because of the wide range of useful and interesting contributions from so many leading researchers. In addition, the focus of many of the essays on practical aspects of early modern textual study—textual editing, digital editing, and pedagogy in particular—make this essay collection a wonderful resource.

The volume has three sections: 'Early Modern Digital Editing', 'Textual Criticism', and 'Editing the Early Modern Text', along with additional materials on the passing of former editor W. Speed Hill and recent RETS activities. In Section I, readers interested in the early sixteenth century may wish to focus first on Raymond G. Siemens's essay on using visualization approaches to better understand early modern writing communities and the collaborative effect of manuscript circulation. Using the Devonshire Manuscript (BL Add. MS 17492) as a case study, Siemens shows how to apply new digital editing and visualization tools, not just to illuminate aspects of the Devonshire Manuscript, but also to test the utility of those digital tools in manuscript scholarship.

A very welcome early addition Section II comes from Carolyn Diskant Muir, who discusses the production and patronage of Antoine Vérard's 1493/4 edition of the *Horologie de Sapience*. This will be of interest to readers interested both in the wider contexts of incunabula production and in aspects of print editing. Susan F. Felch's examination of the ways in which Katherine Parr reshaped Sir Thomas More's Tower Meditations into a reformist tool will be discussed further below. Section III generally focuses on the later sixteenth and the seventeenth centuries, but Paul A. Marquis's essay on editing the often overlooked second edition of Tottel's *Songes and Sonettes* will doubtless be of interest to those working on pre-Elizabethan poetry and textual editing.

The substantial collection *The Intellectual Culture of the English Country House, 1500–1700*, edited by Matthew Dimmock, Andrew Hadfield, and Margaret Healy, is a multifaceted collaboration between archivists, conservationists, historians, and literary specialists. It will be of interest to a wide range of readers involved in multidisciplinary approaches to early modern heritage, architecture, literature, intellectual history, book history, landscape history, and information networks. While the volume is of broad interest, readers of this section may want to focus first on the chapters that pertain to the early sixteenth century: Alden Gregory's essay on William Warham and architectural patronage at Otford (chapter 2); Matthew Neely's work on recovering aspects of the now lost Rycote House through materials held at the Bodleian Library (chapter 3); Richard Simpson's essay on the library of Sir Thomas Smith (1513–77) and his work as a humanist legal scholar (chapter 6); and James Raven's wide-ranging exploration of the link between early modern country houses and the development of bibliomania (chapter 10). Collectively, these essays provide a model for multidisciplinary analyses of early sixteenth-century intellectual culture; they are valuable not just in their own right, but as new and energizing considerations of extra-urban cultural change.

*The Oxford Handbook of the Bible in Early Modern England, c. 1530–1700*, co-edited by Kevin Killeen, Helen Smith, and Rachel Willie, includes three chapters which are wholly concerned with the period before and around the Elizabethan settlement of 1558-9. Susan Wabuda's ' "A Day After Doomsday": Cranmer and the Bible Translations of the 1530s' (pp. 23–37) demonstrates how Thomas Cranmer's interventions in the later 1530s set the course for a cautious implementation of the Bible in English across parishes in the kingdom. The Matthew Bible of 1537 and the Great Bible of 1540 both bore the imprint of Cranmer; the second served as the definitive English translation (derived in major part from William Tyndale's earlier version) until the Bishops' Bible in Elizabeth I's reign. Wabuda concludes her chapter with a discussion of Cranmer's preface to the Great Bible, which championed a 'seemly restraint' (p. 36) in parishioners' reception of the vernacular Bible and averred against open contestation or disputation of Scripture.

Femke Molekamp's 'Genevan Legacies: The Making of the English Geneva Bible' (pp. 38–53) draws out the strong pattern of derivation between the English translation, first printed in 1560, and the anterior French Geneva Bible of 1559. In particular, the English adapters exploited marginalia in a similar fashion to their French counterparts 'to open up the sense of the scriptures and thereby promote God's glory' (p. 45). These intellectuals also gained mileage out of other kinds of paratextual content, such as the 'Arguments' lifted from the French version, which emphasize that Christ's mercy and man's faith are contingent on predestination and therefore distil a Calvinist theology for the edification of their readership. Molekamp's final subsections concentrate on the Puritan scholar Laurence Tomson's 1587 revision of the Geneva Bible and the Bible's broader reception in England and Scotland.

Russ Leo's contribution, 'Scripture and Tragedy in the Reformation' (pp. 498–517), highlights the still obscure but fascinating 'rise of sacred tragedy in the early sixteenth century, its debts to antique poetics, and its exceptional capacities to express the most complex theological problems in dynamic and engaging terms' (p.498). Leo looks in particular at the significance that tragedy as a dramatic medium held for second-generation Reformers such as Martin Bucer, Philip Melanchthon, and George Buchanan, the dramatist of Latin tragedies. However, his chapter also takes in the work of other Reformed theologians who dabbled in tragic drama (several little-known in this capacity) such as Théodore de Bèze, Heinrich Bullinger, Francesco Negri, and Bernardino Ochino. The final part of his argument is on Buchanan's *Jephtes* [1539 × 43], reading its treatment of Jephthah's reaction to his rash vow against the rendition of the same scene in the Catholic theologian John Christopherson's *Iephte*, cast in both Greek and Latin between 1543 and 1547.

David J. Harvey's monograph, *The Law Emprynted and Englysshed: The Printing Press as an Agent of Change in Law and Legal Culture 1475–1642*, considers how the development of the movable type printing press transformed English law and legal culture from 1475 to 1642, contending that, as the English common law relies on precedent, the increase in access to newly printed legal texts allowed increase in access and the standardization of legal practice and theory impossible in a pre-print culture. Harvey adopts a chronological approach, beginning with the establishment of the Stationers' Guild in 1403 through to the beginning of the English Civil War, and discusses the role of proclamations, the Stationers' Guild, the role(s) of the royal printers, and the regulatory efforts of Star Chamber. Harvey presents a strong argument that while the printing press did replicate aspects of scribal legal text production and did not displace the role of manuscript coteries (particularly in training or the dissemination of new texts), the press did not simply scale up what had been produced under a scribal culture. Rather, Harvey argues that a confluence of cultural, political, and economic forces worked together with the increased output of the press to enable a new legal culture in England. This does not constitute a 'revolution', but Harvey's argument proposes a more complicated middle ground: a kind of evolution inextricable from the broader cultural changes of the period.

The 'Post Script' of Megan G. Leitch's *Romancing Treason: The Literature of the Wars of the Roses* examines the presence of treason as a motif in the texts that bridge earlier Lancastrian literary culture in the fifteenth century and that of the Tudor age. These are, in the main, romances produced between *c.*1437 and *c.*1497. Leitch's final chapter concentrates on earlier Tudor writers' treatments of treason in Stephen Hawes's *Example of Virtue* [1503–4] and *Pastime of Pleasure* [1505–6], the translation *Robert the Devil* [1500, 1517] and Henry Watson's prose *Oliver of Castile* [composed *c.*1500, published 1518] and *Valentine and Orson* [composed 1500 × 10]. Leitch concludes that in Tudor romances produced after 1500, 'treason content diminishes, and inclination towards or tolerance of unhappy endings also decreases' (p. 177).

Kirk Quinsland's 'Antitheatricalism and the Interpretation of Tudor Allegorical Performance' (*SEL* 55[2015] 365–89) argues that the Edwardian Protectorate's 1547 decision to permit lay scriptural reading led to the proliferation of public lay disputation regarding scriptural matters. As a result, Quinsland argues that much mid-Tudor theatrical writing actually exhibits an anti-theatrical theoretical positioning. Drawing on Thomas Heywood's 1612 *Apology for Actors* and discussing recent early modern performance theory scholarship, Quinsland traces the development and effects of this anti-theatricalism in performance texts (especially *Respublica* and *Gorboduc*), scriptural interpretations, legal and legislative documents and treatises spanning the early modern period.

Barrett L. Beer's 'Richard III: The Image of the King in Small Mid-Tudor Chronicles: 1540–1560' (*N&Q* 62[2015] 42–5) concentrates on the proliferation of private and state-sponsored historical texts in the mid-Tudor period, which spoke to attempts to put history to work in new ways. Beer's significant work in this area is well known, and this new examination of smaller and less well-known texts is to be welcomed. Prestige texts from major figures such as Holinshed, Foxe, Vergil, and Hall may have had wide impact, but that does not mean that they were ubiquitous. Smaller, cheaper texts filled a burgeoning desire for history-writing, and the effect of these texts is still largely a source for speculation. Beer's article takes as a case study the figure of Richard III. He traces the development of two texts, *A Cronicle of Yeres* (first printed in 1539 by John Byddell) and *A Breuiat Cronicle* (first printed in 1552 by John Mychell). He examines their departures from their source material—primarily Fabyan's *Chronicle*—and finds that their comparatively moderate treatment of Richard III speaks to a public interest not in the dynastic battles of the past, but in more recent events surrounding the royal supremacy and the Reformation. That these texts were edited and republished repeatedly strongly indicates that while more wealthy and powerful readers may have happily consumed histories that defined England's political and religious heritage (or, perhaps more to the point, justified those imagined and contested heritages), many lower-class readers were engaging with more recent and pressing events.

## 2. General: Verse

A.E.B. Coldiron's *Printers Without Borders: Translation and Textuality in the Renaissance* argues for the centrality of printed translations in the literary culture of Renaissance England. *Printers Without Borders* contains three chapters (1, 3, and 6) pertinent to verse in the first half of the sixteenth century, each of which illuminates a different strategy of translation ('appropriative', 'radiant', and 'compressed' in turn). The remaining chapters are reviewed in Chapter VI of this volume.

Chapter 2, 'Caxton, Translation, and the Renaissance Reprint Culture' (pp. 35–106), looks at three of William Caxton's translations: the *Recyuell of the Hystoryes of Troye*; the *Dictes and Sayengis of the Philosophres* (translated from French and Spanish renditions of the Arabic text *Mukhtar al-Hikam*); and the *Copy of a Lettre*, a translation from Alain Chartier's fifteenth-century anti-court *Curial* made at the time of Richard III's accession to the throne in 1483. Of particular interest to those of a mid-Tudor persuasion, Coldiron's discussion of Caxton's *Curial* translation brings in as a comparator Francis Seager's Englishing of the text as *A Brefe declaration* at the time of the rebellion of the commonwealth in 1549. The subject here is the differing appropriation of Chartier's paratextual colophon poem at two different points of national crisis. Whereas Caxton's poem replicates the slippery and 'ambiguous discourse' (p. 99) at court that the main text decries, Seager's version 'subtly recast[s]' (p. 100) the work to colour the dispraise of anti-court corruption with Protestant overtones and an unambiguous plea for loyalty to Edward VI.

Chapter 3, ' "Bastard allone": Radiant Translation and the State of English Letters' (pp. 107–59), takes as its subject the Frenchman Peter Derendel's 1553 translation into English of the *Quadrins historiques de la Bible* (the English title is *True and Lyuely Historyke Putreatures of the Woll Bible*). The *Quadrins* was a figure book comprising choice Old Testament scenes with accompanying poems, and was also turned into Italian, Spanish, Dutch, and Latin (Coldiron's principal focus is on the French and English versions). All of this six-language enterprise came from the printing press of Jean de Tournes. Coldiron discusses the project as 'a radiant pattern of transmission, in which one work is translated and printed in multiple languages at roughly the same time, radiating outward from one culture into several others' (p. 108). Derendel's decision to English the French original is akin to a 'missionary aim' in so far as he was one of a team of translators who needed to imagine dually a unified world audience for the text and a geographically nuanced one peculiar to the language of transmission. This is a keen insight, and Coldiron pursues it in her analysis of Derendel's efforts to raise the 'bastard' profile of English through his use of paratextual tools and the *mise-en-page*, and to communicate with an English audience on and in their own terms (as in the preface).

Chapter 6, 'Macaronic Verse, Plurilingual Printing, and the Uses of Translation' (pp. 255–82) represents the final contribution to a trio of studies on what Coldiron dubs a 'compressed pattern of transmission' (p. 32). This process is found in polyglot texts which bring multiple languages into the terrain of a single text. Macaronic verse is paradigmatic of this form of translation. Eschewing Skelton, Coldiron looks at the efforts of Caxton (in his English–Latin *Paruus Catho*), John Bale (in his English–Latin 'Song' in *A comedy concernyne thre lawes* [*c*.1538]) and Reginald Scot (in his Scots–Latin *Discoverie of Witchcraft* [1584]). Whereas Caxton's exploitation of macaronics caters to 'harmonized plurilingualism and pluriculturalism' (p. 262), Bale's emphasis falls on the discordant clashing of Protestant English and 'Papist' Latin. Coldiron's consideration of Scot is incorporated into a broader subsection on satirical macaronics and ironic performances.

Ruth Ahnert edited a special issue of *Renaissance Studies* (29:iv[2015] 493–680) dedicated to 'Re-forming the Psalms in Tudor England'. Ahnert's introduction surveys the current critical landscape on the Tudor psalms. She also discusses the psalms as a site of historical-cultural, political, and doctrinal tension in the period.

Hannibal Hamlin's article, 'My Tongue Shall Speak: Doing the Psalms in Different Voices' (*RS* 29:iv[2015] 509–30), on 'voice' in the psalms, highlights the multitude of voices that clamour to be heard when appraising them, which makes a critical understanding of them far from a univocal enterprise. These voices include: the word of God, King David, the congregations who sang psalms, other speakers, listeners, and the voice of the scholar or poet whose voice is added to the throng in the act of paraphrase or translation. Hamlin also considers whether the psalms can be considered prosopopoeic, that is, representations of the Davidic voice rather than the actual voice of David himself (pp. 516–17). In a sustained section on the presence of the translator's voice, he touches on examples from Edwin Sandys, Richard Stanyhurst, Sir Thomas Wyatt, Richard Robinson, George Gascoigne, and Henry Howard, earl of Surrey (pp. 518–26).

Nicholas Temperley's article, '"All skillful praises sing": How Congregations Sang the Psalms in Early Modern England' (*RS* 29:iv[2015] 493–680), is an instructive addition to an area of research which remains little-studied. He demonstrates that congregational singing began among the Marian exiles in Geneva. When congregational singing returned to England with the exiles, and their Geneva service book was printed as the *Whole Book of Psalms* in 1562, a number of tunes did not catch on as a result of their poor fit with iambic metre. The emergence of 'common tunes' (p. 551) in the 1590s (i.e. those not attached to a particular text) proved more popular than the 'proper tunes' included in the *Whole Book*.

Micheline White's article, 'The Psalms, War, and Royal Iconography: Katherine Parr's *Psalms or Prayers* (1544) and Henry VIII as David' (*RS* 29:iv[2015] 554–75), deals primarily with a prose item, but is included in this subsection for ease of reference. Her argument makes a valuable contribution to existing literature on Henry VIII's (and others') exploitation of a Davidic image to negotiate and figure his political power. White examines Katherine Parr's book *Psalms or Prayers*, which Thomas Berthelet printed in conjunction with a Latin version of the same text in 1544. White contends that the *Psalms or Prayers* performs valuable propagandist work, fashioning Henry with 'a wartime monarchical identity' (p. 555) at a time when the Crown was campaigning in Scotland and preparing for war in France. Of especial significance is Parr's 'Prayer for the King', serving with its Latin sibling as the first Crown-sponsored, non-liturgical prayers to be printed for Henry in England.

James Simpson's article, 'The Psalms and Threat in Sixteenth-Century English Court Culture' (*RS* 29:iv[2015] 576–94), contextualizes the vogue for metrical psalm paraphrase among imprisoned courtiers between 1539 and 1553. Simpson's protagonist is Henry Howard, earl of Surrey, together with other courtiers whom he believes to have been evangelical or evangelical-leaning in doctrinal affiliation: Sir Thomas Wyatt, Sir George Blage, Sir Thomas Smith, and John Dudley the Younger. To varying degrees, the psalm paraphrases of all these poets draw a sharp hermeneutic distinction between the literal, simple truth of God's word and an 'irredeemably duplicitous civil world' (p. 582) where the psalmist is ranged against earthly enemies.

Continuing the psalmic theme, Rebecca M. Rush's article 'Authority and Attribution in the Sternhold and Hopkins Psalter' (*Ren&R* 38[2015] 57–81) is another valuable addition to the corpus of writings on Tudor psalms. The Sternhold–Hopkins Psalter was an enduring bestseller after its initial publication in 1549; Rush's focus is on the paratextual apparatus (title pages, prefaces, marginal annotations) with which different sellers framed their printings of it. She examines how those involved in the publication of the Sternhold–Hopkins psalms (including Sternhold himself) understood them as verse creations with a human authority separate or additional to the scriptural.

Christopher Shirley's article, 'The Devonshire Manuscript: Reading Gender in the Henrician Court' (*ELR* 45[2015] 23–59), focuses on the poems to which Margaret Douglas and Mary Shelton either appended marginal annotations (as readers) or transcribed in full (as copyists). Shirley argues that the women's interventions in the manuscript allowed them to perform 'a variety of gender identities' (p. 52). These include both resistance to the anti-feminist common-places of courtly verse and, going beyond previous criticism, what Shirley terms 'misogynistic femininity' (p. 35).

It is rare to encounter criticism that considers Thomas Phaer's translation of Virgil's *Aeneid* (Books I–VII were published in 1558 and Books I–IX after his death in 1562). Sheldon Brammall's opening chapter, 'The Search for a Lofty British Virgil: The Early Elizabethan *Aeneid*s of Thomas Phaer, Thomas Twyne and Richard Stanyhurst', part of his monograph *The English Aeneid: Translations of Virgil, 1555–1646*, is therefore a welcome contribution to the meagre crop of studies on Phaer. He defines those qualities that made Phaer's translation such a hit with its Tudor readership: 'First, [Phaer] conveyed a loftiness of language and versification; second, he stressed the importance of historical Roman nobility in the poem … most importantly, he read the *Aeneid* as a humanistic expression of the lofty potential of man' (p. 22). Brammall's discussion of Phaer's adoption of the fourteener to match Virgil's dactylic hexameter line for line is masterful. It is to be hoped that Brammall's much-needed contribution to Phaer studies heralds future work on both him and his immediate heirs.

### 3. More

Susan F. Felch, 'Reforming Sir Thomas More in the Court of Katherine Parr' (in Denbo, ed., pp. 181–192), examines the devotional, textual, and material consequences of Katherine Parr's use of Thomas More's Tower Meditations evidenced in two manuscripts (BL MS Harley 2342 and Folger MS X.d.532) and one printed prayerbook (STC 16051). More's position was a fraught one; revered by many for his humanism, literacy, and intellectual acumen, his intractability on the Oath of Supremacy raised serious concerns for mid-century readers of the Meditations (and other works). Felch demonstrates through close material and textual analysis how Katherine Parr, that 'gospeller' so admired by no less a reformist than John Foxe, managed to employ and adapt More's devotional writing to evidence a bridge between her 'Lutheran-inflected ... reformist commitments' (p. 183) with the Christocentric devotional practices of the earlier age.

Daniel Eppley's 'A New Perspective on Islam in Henrician England: The Polemics of Christopher St. German' (*SCJ* 46[2015] 587–606) provides an opportunity to think about the ways in which Henrician reformists and conservatives employed Islam to shape their respective positions on English religious conflict. Eppley explores the manner in which reformist Christopher St German's use of Islam (in particular in *A lytell treatyse agaynst Mahumet and his cursed secte* [1531]) contrasts with those of Tyndale and More.

Kristin Dieter, in 'Building Opposition at the Early Tudor Tower of London: Thomas More's Dialogue of Comfort' (*Ren&R* 38[2015] 27–55), examines the ways in which Thomas More's 1534 *A Dialogue of Comfort Against Tribulation* adopts and adapts the iconography and symbolism of the Tower of London. Dieter contextualizes More's refashioning in several of his other texts (notably *Richard III*) and his developing sense of monarchical representation.

Robert E. Stillman's 'Philip Sidney, Thomas More, and Table Talk: Texts/ Contexts' (*ELR* 45[2015] 323–50) is primarily focused on Sidney and Elizabethan diplomacy. But it provides a translation of previously untranslated sections of Philip Camerarius's popular 1591 *Operae horarum subcisivarum sive meditationes historicae*, which provides an insight into early modern interest in Thomas More across Europe in the late sixteenth century.

Timothy D. Crowley, in 'More's "Neck" in Robinson's Translation of *Utopia* (1551 and 1556)' (*N&Q* 62[2015] 39–42), considers the stylistic features of Ralph Robinson's English translation of Thomas More's *Utopia* [1551/6] and their connections with Robinson's social and political contexts.

Travis Curtwright's 'From Thomas More's Workshop: *De Tristitia Christi* and the *Catena aurea*' (*Logos* 18[2015] 100–26) explores More's use of Thomas Aquinas's *Catena aurea* and John Gerson's *Monotessaron* in his *De Tristitia Christi*.

## 4. Skelton

Following his 2014 biography of Skelton is John Scattergood's revised edition of *The Complete English Poems of John Skelton*. This is the most substantial publication on Skelton in 2015. Scattergood's stated aim for the revised edition is to ensure its continuing utility for twenty-first-century scholars. There is little change to the texts themselves or to their chronology. But the annotation has been revised, as has the 'Table of Dates' and the section on 'Further Reading'.

David Carlson published two articles on John Skelton in 2015. In 'John Skelton's Autograph Verse Annotations on the *Chronique* of the Minstrel of Reims for Prince Henry's Education' (*Neophil* 99[2015] 167–74) he examines Skelton's use of a manuscript text of the *La chronique d'un menestrel de Reims* [*c*.1260] to instruct Prince Henry in the 1490s. In 'Skelton, Garnesche, and Henry VIII: Revels and Erudition at Court' (*RES* 66[2015] 240–57), Carlson contends that Skelton lost his bout with Garnesche in terms of royal favour.

Published in 2014, but not reviewed in last year's edition of *YWES*, Elizabeth Evershed's chapter, 'John Skelton's Courts, Real and Imagined' (in Gasper and McKinnell, eds., *Ambition and Anxiety: Courts and Courtly Discourse, c.700–1600*, pp. 39–63), engages with the intersections between Skelton's experiences in the courts of Henry VII and VIII and his poetical figurations of court settings.

Another 2014 publication omitted from last year's *YWES*, Emily Stockard's article 'Who Was Jane Scrope?' (*RenP* 53[2014] 1–16), performs some sleuthing to uncover details of the historical individual behind Skelton's character of the same name in *Phyllyp Sparowe*. She discovers that Jane was the longest-lived of eight daughters, three of whom 'were married to men on the opposite sides of a political power struggle (Elizabeth on the Tudor side, and Margaret and Eleanor on the de la Pole side)' (p. 5).

## 5. Surrey

The single article on Surrey is Joel Grossman's '"I can ne close in short and conning vearse": A New Poem for the Canon of Henry Howard, Earl of Surrey?' (*N&Q* 62[2015] 536–41). Grossman argues for Surrey's possible authorship of 'I ne can close in short and conning vearse', a poem in the Arundel Harington Manuscript and the 'Uncertain Authors' section of Richard Tottel's *Songes and Sonettes* [first published in 1557].

## 6. Wyatt

Mike Pincombe's 'Dream and Mystery in Sir Thomas Wyatt's '"Tagus, Farewell"' (*SN* 87[2015] 36–47) argues that the poem is best read with Robert Fabyan's *Chronicle*, and the account it gives of England's mythical founder Brutus petitioning Diana to help him find 'Troynovant' ('New Troy'). William T. Rossiter considers 'What Wyatt Really Did to Aretino's *Setti Salmi*' (*RS* 29:iv[2015] 595–614). Published in 2014, Chad Engbers's chapter, 'Aesthetic Activity in Sir Thomas Wyatt's Penitential Psalms' appears in his co-edited volume on the subject of dialogism in verse (Scanlon and Engbers, eds., *Poetry and Dialogism: Hearing Over*, pp. 39–56). The principal thrust of Engbers's argument is to relate his translation to Mikhail Bakhtin's 'Author and Hero in Aesthetic Activity'.

Also from 2014 is Chris Stamatakis's 'Image to Text: A Possible Visual Source for Sir Thomas Wyatt's Verse Epistles' (*Embl* 21[2014] 77–95), which hypothesizes that Wyatt derived inspiration for his 'Myne owne John Poyntz', not just from the exiled Italian poet Luigi Alamanni's words when penning his Horatian verse satire, but also from a woodcut device with which the Sessa family of printer-publishers prefaced their printed edition of Alamanni's *Opere toscane*.

Neil Powell includes a section on Wyatt's 'They flee from me' and the two satires addressed to John Poyntz in his short article 'The Poet Alone: (1) Continual Change' (*PNR* 42[2015] 66–70).

**Books Reviewed**

Attar, Karina F., and Lynn Shutters, *Teaching Medieval and Early Modern Cross-Cultural Encounters*. PalMac. [2015] pp. xxiv + 253. €83.19 ISBN 9 7811 3748 1337.

Brammall, Sheldon. *The English Aeneid: Translations of Virgil, 1555–1646*. EdinUP. [2015] pp. xii + 212. £70 ISBN 9 7807 4869 9087.

Brownlee, Victoria, and Laura Gallagher, eds. *Biblical Women in Early Modern Literary Culture, 1550–1700*. ManUP. [2015] pp. 264. £70 ISBN 9 7807 1909 1551.

Coldiron, A.E.B. *Printers Without Borders: Translation and Textuality in the Renaissance*. CUP. [2015] pp. xv + 399. £65 ISBN 9 7811 0707 3173.

Denbo, Michael, ed. *New Ways of Looking at Old Texts, V: Papers of the Renaissance English Text Society, 2007–2010*. RETS. [2014] pp. xxii + 362. £48 ISBN 9 7808 6698 5079.

Dimmock, Matthew, Andrew Hadfield, and Margaret Healy, eds. *The Intellectual Culture of the English Country House, 1500–1700*. ManUP. [2015] pp. 304. £70 ISBN 9 7807 1909 0202.

Gasper, G.E.M., and J. McKinnell, eds. *Ambition and Anxiety: Courts and Courtly Discourse, c.700–1600*. Brepols. [2014] pp. vi + 270. €80 ISBN 9 7808 8844 8620.

Harvey, David J. *The Law Emprynted and Englysshed: The Printing Press as an Agent of Change in Law and Legal Culture 1475–1642*. Hart. [Bloomsbury]. [2015] pp. 326. A$74.99 ISBN 9 7815 0991 4159.

Killeen, Kevin, Helen Smith, and Rachel Willie, eds. *The Oxford Handbook of the Bible in Early Modern England, c.1530–1700*. OUP. [2015] pp. xx + 783. £110 ISBN 9 7801 9968 6971.

Lancashire, Anne, and David J. Parkinson, eds. *Records of Early English Drama: Civic London to 1558*. 3 vols. Brewer. [2015] pp. cciv + 1,591. £195 ISBN 9 7818 4384 3993.

Leitch, Megan G. *Romancing Treason: The Literature of the Wars of the Roses*. OUP. [2015] pp. ix + 218. £55 ISBN 9 7801 9872 4599.

Scanlon, Mara, and Chad Engbers, eds. *Poetry and Dialogism: Hearing Over*. PalMac. [2014] pp. x + 205. €83 19 ISBN 9 7811 3740 1274.

Scattergood, John, ed. *The Complete English Poems of John Skelton*, rev. edn. LiverUP. [2015] pp. ix + 5566. £85 ISBN 9 7818 4631 9655.

# VI

# The Sixteenth Century: Excluding Drama after 1550

## HARRIET ARCHER AND RICHARD WOOD

This chapter has three sections: 1. General; 2. Sidney; 3. Spenser. Section 1 is by Harriet Archer; sections 2 and 3 are by Richard Wood.

## 1. General

Last year, myth featured in this review as a dominant theme; in 2015 studies in magic and alchemy seem to be undergoing a resurgence. The first three texts discussed here engage with this cluster of topics, taking a variety of approaches from the descriptive to the metaphorical. Katherine Eggert's hugely learned and original *Disknowledge: Literature, Alchemy, and the End of Humanism in Renaissance England* speaks to a sixteenth-century climate of post-truth anxiety. Alchemy is used as a trope with which to think about Elizabethan literature as much as a subject or motif, and Eggert's monograph is structured across five provocatively titled chapters which play on the strategic cultural stance Eggert defines as 'being acquainted with something and being ignorant of it, both at the same time' (p. 3). In the course of these chapters, Eggert addresses the literary expression of discomfort with a series of 'intellectual domains': transubstantiation, Kabbalah, and 'the study of female reproductive anatomy', fields 'that sixteenth- and seventeenth-century England had particular need of disknowing' (p. 9). The literary texts used as case studies are predominantly by canonical authors with their own *Year's Work* chapters, but the monograph offers a rich new reading of the period as a whole which should prove highly productive for Tudorists at large. The first chapter, 'How to Sustain Humanism', acts as a second introduction to establish the building blocks of Eggert's argument in general terms, and addresses the undoing of humanist modes of study and thought as scepticism was reintroduced to the philosophical canon, while 'humanism's faith in instilling personal and national virtue by means of rhetorical and philological training proved inadequate to the . . . challenges of the day' (p. 16). Eggert argues for 'the close relation between humanism and alchemy as knowledge-making systems'

*The Year's Work in English Studies, Volume 96 (2017)* © *The Author 2017. Published by Oxford University Press on behalf of the English Association. All rights reserved.*
*For Permissions, please email: journals.permissions@oup.com*
doi:10.1093/ywes/max007

(p. 243), including the ways in which both are simultaneously doubted and perpetuated, a relationship which sets up the framework for the ensuing investigations. Chapter 2, 'How to Forget Transubstantiation', moves into the seventeenth-century metaphysics of John Donne, George Herbert, and Henry Vaughan, while in 'How to Skim Kabbalah' the focus returns to the sixteenth century and John Dee, 'whose hopes of purifying the physical universe through the manipulation of symbols attracted him to the alchemical use of Kabbalah' (p. 10). Deeply indebted to Jewish learning, sixteenth-century alchemy rewrote Kabbalah as 'a Christian domain and a Christian creation' (p. 112). In order to effect this appropriation, Eggert argues, Christian scholars 'adopt[ed] an attractive veneer' of learning, skim-reading like Marlowe's Faustus, 'without having to accommodate Jewishness' (p. 116). Dee himself 'concertedly constructed his deeply kabbalistic natural magic out of as little Jewish Kabbalah as possible' (p. 129), and demonstrates a skill in skimming not shared by The Tempest's Prospero, who, Eggert suggests, fails wholly to suppress his magic's Jewish origins. Eggert considers the similarly evasive interest in parthenogenesis showcased in Ben Jonson's Mercury Vindicated from the Alchemists at Court [1616] in chapter 4, 'How to Avoid Gynecology'. The human reproductive equivalent to alchemy, masculine parthenogenesis proved to be a bizarre shaping factor in early modern biological theory, committed to the outdated Aristotelian–Galenic model, and representative of 'the choice to be wrong rather than right' (p. 158). The chapter concludes with a discussion of alchemical reproduction in The Faerie Queene and Love's Labour's Lost, texts in which alchemical discourse provides a language of avoidance and obfuscation put to work by misogynist intellectual systems. Finally, 'How to Make Fiction' explores the place of alchemy in Elizabethan literary theory, specifically the writings of George Puttenham and Philip Sidney, for whom the metaphor 'puts poetry in the category of a mode of learning that owes no necessary allegiance to the truth' (p. 207). The chapter then goes on to unpack the workings of Sidney's alchemical metaphor in Hamlet, Jonson's Alchemist, and Margaret Cavendish's The Blazing World [1666]. It is impossible to do justice to Eggert's argument and impressive synthesis of material in summary; instead I would refer readers directly to this enjoyable and, in its way, iconoclastic book.

In his extensively illustrated article, 'The "Ingendred" Stone: The Ripley Scrolls and the Generative Science of Alchemy' (HLQ 78[2015] 87–125), Aaron Kitch describes Huntington MS HM 30313; the manuscript text is also reproduced as an appendix. The 10-foot scroll, an anonymous work bearing alchemical symbols, allegorical images, English verses, and Latin labels, is one of the twenty so-called Ripley scrolls, dated to the second half of the sixteenth century—Kitch adjusts the dates slightly here—and could have been produced in association with John Dee, perhaps commissioned in Lübeck during Dee's tour of Europe in the 1580s. Kitch is interested in the metaphors of marriage and procreation which, as Carl Jung also noted, pervade alchemical discourse, and argues that 'we should approach the Ripley scrolls in the broader context of the history of sexuality' (p. 115), as the text's discursive framework informs and is informed by contemporary debates around human generation too.

He shows how language and myth are combined, filtered, and re-presented visually in the elaborate coded colour-schemes of the scroll and its narrative sequences of images, drawing on the corroborative evidence of a diverse sweep of scientific treatises from the medieval period through to the seventeenth century. This rich bibliography of the work tells us much about the state of alchemical thought in the Elizabethan period, and will be of value to scholars working on many kinds of sixteenth-century textual artefacts, well beyond its object of focus.

Francis Young's edition/translation of Cambridge University Library MS Additional 3544 plunges us headlong into the practicalities as set down in *The Cambridge Book of Magic: A Tudor Necromancer's Manual*, to the extent that this reviewer felt slightly unnerved to find herself in the text's possession. Young notes that 'Additional 3544 is a text in transition', representing the shift between medieval and early modern magical practices as they began to draw in and synthesize disparate traditions. As 'a complete treatise on the art of necromancy' rather than a series of notes or records, the text is uniquely placed to provide a window onto the practice of ritual magic in a turbulent period in history. Additional 3544 has been dated to the 1560s, although the original Latin and English text of the section of the manuscript in question was probably composed between 1532 and 1558—Young argues for earlier rather than later in this range—and 'embodies the final phase of medieval "clerical magic" in England' (pp. xi–xii). The critical introduction also provides a contextual overview of the reception and circulation of this kind of text across the sixteenth century. The manuscript itself, Young notes, was obviously carefully prepared to mimic the appearance of a printed book, and innovative in this regard. The writer also uses different scripts for English and Latin, and, Young argues, 'his use of novel orthographic conventions [seems to have come] from reading printed texts' (pp. xiii–xiv). The writer's identity is unknown, although the text is attributed to a 'Paul Foreman' whose name appears on the third folio; Young asserts that, despite the nominal similarity, 'there is no chance that Simon Forman was the author' (p. xvii), although the two held shared interests. Young begins his sixteenth-century history of magic with the role played by accusations of necromancy and other conjurations in the Reformation, when '"superstitious" practices, including magic, were routinely attributed to opponents of religious change' (p. xix). While later forms of more 'progressive' early modern magic have been more intensively studied, Young argues that liturgical conjuration, of which Additional 3544 is representative, has drawn less scholarly interest, with the result that the majority of sixteenth-century magic manuscripts have not been edited or published. It is the manuscript's conservatism and unexceptional nature, therefore, which make it a valuable object of study. The manual itself begins with instructions on how to acquire and consecrate the bats' blood and parchment needed to write out charms, before listing options for diverse scenarios, from 'To have a horse', and 'To raise up herbs', to 'That women should dance in the house' and 'lift up their skirts high whilst dancing' (there are three separate procedures recorded for this last), and the summoning of various spirits. The edition provides the original and translated texts in parallel columns, with modern English orthography facing the transcribed English portions. It also reproduces images and hieroglyphics, as well as appending the original Latin table of contents, and some brief explanatory notes; a classificatory table in the introduction breaks the experiments down by category, and calculates the percentage of the manual dedicated to each type, such as erotic magic (31%), theft-detection (8%), and harmful magic (just one entry, listed obliquely under 'Of the revenge of Troy'). The edition usefully makes this resource available to a wider audience, although it is perhaps best reserved for daytime reading.

Transnational exchanges characterize a fair proportion of the works reviewed here, befitting the escalation of debate around contemporary geopolitical configurations during the year of their publication. Martin McLaughlin, Ingrid D. Rowland, and Elisabetta Tarantino's edited collection, *Authority, Innovation and Early Modern Epistemology: Essays in Honour of Hilary Gatti*, does not advertise its focus on cross-cultural influence, except latently via Gatti's specialism, but one chapter in Part I, 'Authority and Innovation in Renaissance Literature', and three in Part II, 'Bruno, Campanella and Other Challenges to Religious Authority', treat the English Renaissance in conversation with other cultures, and in particular, of course, with Giordano Bruno. Well, Stephen Orgel, in 'Measuring Verse, Measuring Value in English Renaissance Poetry', reminds us that, in fact, 'Latin was not a foreign language' (p. 98) to the early modern educated classes, but instead profoundly familiar, and shows quantitative and qualitative metres in dialogue in a musical setting of 'Constant Penelope' by William Byrd [1588]. Instead, it was accent and dialect which, for the likes of the West Country Walter Ralegh, or Midlands-born Robert Laneham and William Shakespeare, made English itself as spoken and written in London 'a language that was not their own'; as a result, 'in a language as diverse and as much in flux as early modern English, surely one of the chief attractions of quantitative metres would have been precisely the fact that they were *not* tied to the spoken language' (p. 98). The late sixteenth-century metrical debate was not nearly as eccentric as scholarship would have us believe, Orgel suggests. Extending from Wyatt and Surrey in the early Tudor period through to Browning in the nineteenth century (and doubtless beyond), attention to quantitative metrics was necessarily a central concern for a literary moment preoccupied with nation, empire, and 'canons of order' (p. 97). The chapter's detailed reading of 'Constant Penelope' alongside Byrd's score, though, uncovers a 'rather baggy system' (p. 101), but nevertheless one which enables the interplay of defined classical metres, in spite of early modern English's orthographical and lexicographical shiftiness.

In Part II, Eugenio Canone contextualizes Bruno's anti-authority stance within his sojourn in England between 1583 and 1585, in 'Giordano Bruno: Portrait of a Philosopher Opposed to the Authority Principle'. Bruno's opposition to the arbitrary authority of both church and state, and his vilification of the popular ignorance which allowed for such authority to persist against the logic of Bruno's philosophical learning, permeated his works, whether more openly as in his *De gli eroici furori* [1585], or more latently as in the *Candelaio*, in which he showed 'justice to triumph over the pseudo-intellectual bourgeoisie' (p. 111). He dedicated both the *Furori* and his *Spaccio de la bestia trionfante* [1584] to Sidney, demonstrative of his participation in late Elizabethan intellectual culture, but Canone suggests that his relationship with Englishness and the English as evinced by his writings was a contradictory one: 'on the one side there was an elite of considerable cultural sophistication, even though plagued by religious questions, on the other a mass of plebs, who were uncultured, xenophobic, hostile to all forms of knowledge and intolerant of foreigners' (p. 110). Bruno certainly emerges as a cultural force to whom scholars of late Tudor English literature would do well to pay more attention; work begun by Gatti and pursued in Elisabetta Tarantino's subsequent chapter, 'Bruno's *Candelaio*, Shakespeare and Ben Jonson: Building on Hilary Gatti's Work'. Tiziana Provvidera returns to the 1580s and to the archives in 'Bruno, Charlewood and Munday: Politics, Culture and Religion during Bruno's Time in England' to reconsider what, if any, political agenda brought Bruno to England. Provvidera draws out a more detailed picture of Bruno's courtly and literary contacts, including his involvement with Sidney, Robert Dudley, and the earl of Essex, as well as Shakespeare and Marlowe. Positioning Bruno's anti-Protestantism between his Catholic past and his eventual execution by the Roman Inquisition in 1600, Provvidera situates his years in England amid a hardening of attitudes against Catholicism on the part of the English Crown, in response to the clustering of Catholic threats during the period. 'Protestant orthodoxy and Catholic conformity' were nevertheless 'two concepts often close and overlapping' in the 1580s (p. 140). Provvidera traces the interactions of the printer John Charlewood and Anthony Munday from the 1570s, to set up their associations with the Catholic Howards and the earl of Oxford, and their later adoption of a conformist standpoint, from which, Provvidera suggests, Charlewood was well placed to print Bruno's work. Henry Howard, 'a humanist and a refined man of letters with a deep interest in philosophy and theology' (p. 145), could have met Bruno at Salisbury Court, the residence of the French ambassador, Michel de Castelnau, where Bruno stayed. Following the thwarted Throckmorton plot of 1584, Castelnau and Bruno's position in England became particularly precarious, prompting, Provvidera argues, Bruno's revision of his *Cena de le ceneri*, an expensive business to be undertaken by Charlewood, 'a printer of popular literature apparently with little typographical experience of Italian texts' (p. 138). Having offended Leicester on their meeting in Oxford in 1583, Bruno might well have turned to 'one of Leicester's greatest enemies, Henry Howard' (p. 147), then enlisted the help of Howard's acquaintance Charlewood to help patch up the relationship the following year, along with mollifying nods to Walsingham and Lord Burghley, and an amplification of praise for Elizabeth I, interpolated in the new edition of the *Cena*. Provvidera's detailed reconstruction of the intricacies of courtly diplomacy during Bruno's stay is convincing, and points to 'a kind of political and religious irenicism' (p. 149) Bruno hoped to promote under Elizabeth and Henri III. The chapter concludes, though, by suggesting that Bruno's ultimate model was Philip Sidney, a patron better equipped to appreciate his controversial philosophy.

Helen Hackett's edited volume, *Early Modern Exchanges: Dialogues Between Nations and Cultures, 1550–1750*, features three particularly relevant essays, having begun with Hackett's consideration of Elizabeth I's Continental credentials under the grim topical irony of her first subheading, 'England in Europe'. Alessandra Petrina's chapter underscores the centrality of translation to early modern English literary culture and identity. Petrina foregrounds the prominent expression of the role of writing, and by extension of transcription and translation, as a tool for remembrance in Elizabeth I's own prose and poetry. She rejects the appropriation of '*any* Elizabethan translation as part of a grand project of cultural development', reminding us instead of Roger Ascham's prescription of translation exercises which demonstrate 'how language-learning was often not the prerequisite but the purpose of translation' (p. 56). Petrina and others are stumped, however, by the motivation behind Elizabeth's programme of translation, which she calls 'erratic' and 'capricious', 'inexplicably' rapid (p. 57), and 'divergent from common practice' (p. 58). She seeks answers in a case study of a translation of Petrarch's *Triumphus Eternitatis*, found within a manuscript anthology of sixteenth-century lyric verse and attributed to Elizabeth. By contrast with the writing of James VI/I, who 'appears to have been obsessed with authorship, and with the control not only over the composition of his works, but even over their circulation' (p. 61), the attribution is problematic, but suggestive. An unusual choice in itself, the translation 'captures, in fact, what many sixteenth-century translators of Petrarch often miss: his semantic compression, the turmoil under the deceptively smooth surface'; 'it might be closer to Elizabeth's intellectual attitude, as revealed by her writings, than much Petrarchan posturing imposed upon her figure by the poets and courtiers surrounding [her]' (p. 65). Petrina concludes that Elizabeth's translations must not be 'dismissed as mere pastimes' or 'linguistic exercises', but may instead be 'read as the attempt to set down in permanent form her intuition of a philosophical truth' (pp. 68–9).

Rayne Allinson and Geoffrey Parker also address royal writings in 'A King and Two Queens: The Holograph Correspondence of Philip II with Mary I and Elizabeth I' (in Hackett, ed., pp. 95–118). They present four 'remarkable but hitherto neglected' letters between the trio—lucky to have survived the careful routine destruction of sensitive holograph correspondence between the monarchs—and discuss the ways in which these documents 'help us to trace the emotional and political undercurrents that influenced Anglo-Spanish relations during the 1550s' (p. 96). Two letters in French from Mary to Philip demonstrate her confident wielding of rhetorical tropes and the tact with which she addressed him regarding controversial personal matters; Allinson and Parker are able to date the second of these with unprecedented precision thanks to the recorded travel of court personnel to whom Mary alludes. The first of the subsequent letters in Spanish from Philip to Elizabeth followed Mary's death, and 'formed the opening salvo in his reluctant plan to make Elizabeth his third wife' (p. 105). Three months passed before Elizabeth returned her response, followed by only eleven days until Philip's marriage to Elizabeth de Valois was confirmed; his next letter to the queen by contrast 'was explicitly intended as a political weapon' (p. 105), although Elizabeth responded neutrally to his veiled threats. The analysis is accompanied by transcripts of all four letters, translations, and a facsimile of Mary's second letter to Philip, of July 1557. In particular, these vividly depict the corrections and emendations made in Mary's hand which provide a fascinating insight into her process of composition. The formal presentation of the originals precludes this detail in Philip's communications to his sister-in-law, although his condescending evasion so as 'not to weary Your Highness with a long letter' (p. 114) still leaves the reader bristling.

Subsequently, Andrew Hadfield argues, in 'The Impact of Sir Thomas Smith' (in Hackett, ed., pp. 165–82), that a renewed interest in the Renaissance as 'a global phenomenon' (p. 166) might help to bring Smith's achievements back into focus in a field previously dominated by Latin and Italy where Smith, an eminent Elizabethan and 'public intellectual', favoured Greek and France. Framing the critical neglect of Smith's transnational educational reform efforts in cartographical terms—'his intellectual co-ordinates do not map easily onto current concerns' (p. 166)—Hadfield introduces readers to some of Smith's outstanding achievements, such as his house (Hill Hall), his library, and his contribution to humanist education, to demonstrate his neglected centrality to the development of anglophone culture. Smith's commissioning of French-inspired ekphrastic paintings, tiles, and panels for his house in Essex, his cultivation of his library 'as an alternative university' (p. 170), and his efforts in English orthography and Greek pronunciation provide a backdrop to his proposed significance in Gabriel Harvey and Edmund Spenser's intellectual interests. Spenser 'would have had access to Smith's library and papers' (p. 174) at Saffron Walden during his composition of *The Shepheardes Calender* [1579], for example, while Smith's *De Republica Anglorum* ('written in the early 1560s but not published until 1583'), to which Spenser had access in manuscript, would shape political discourse and the place of Roman history in debates over republicanism and tyranny in the final decades of the sixteenth century. The essays surveyed above showcase the productive eclecticism of the volume, whose work continues to build on the momentum gathered by translation studies in recent years.

Where Barbara Fuchs and Emily Weissbourd's *Representing Imperial Rivalry in the Early Modern Mediterranean* focuses on later sixteenth-century English writing, in Part II, 'Imagining the Mediterranean in Early Modern England', it is primarily interested in drama; Fuchs and Weissbourd explicitly note in their introduction that 'The early modern theatre is a particularly important site for analysing . . . English engagements with the Mediterranean, as both English and foreign identities are staged for a mass audience' (p. 7). But Brian C. Lockley's chapter, 'Catholics and Cosmopolitans Writing the Nation: The Pope's Scholars and the 1579 Student Rebellion at the English Roman College' (pp. 233–54), runs counter to this trend and is worth including here. Lockley asks, 'what was the relationship between the traditional notion of the Christian commonwealth and English national identity' (p. 234) between 1550 and 1600, and focuses on Rome, 'a complex locus of attraction and repulsion' (p. 233) for educated English Protestants. He suggests that there was more in common than has been thought between the cosmopolitan perspectives of Catholic recusants and Jesuits such as Edmund Campion, and conformist figures, notably John Harington and Anthony Munday, or the 'universal citizen' (p. 235), John Dee. Without sharing confessional sympathies with Campion, Harington and Munday sought, Lockley argues, to promote a closer relationship with Continental Europe, and may have championed 'a secular version of the papal or episcopal overseer, responsible for correcting an errant or tyrannical sovereign' (p. 237). Harington employed an intercontinental discourse of counsel, for example, in the *New Discourse of a Stale Subject, Called the Metamorphosis of Ajax* [1596], writing a letter of advice in the persona of a Bath magistrate to the Emperor Trajan, by way of offering contemporary commentary on the dealings of the earl of Essex. Meanwhile, Lockley suggests that Munday's and Robert Persons's confessionally antithetical accounts of the 1579 student rebellion against Father Morys Clynnog's new jurisdiction over the English College at Rome 'reveal a common view of papal intervention' (p. 241). Just as the students were able to appeal for the intercession of a higher power over a lower-ranking 'magistrate', both Munday and Persons advocate for the usefulness of a similar arrangement in England. Broadening the debate to consider its implications for the construction of English nationhood in relation to the historical legitimacy or otherwise of Catholicism's dominance in Britain, Lockley concludes that 'the widely accepted scholarly account of the early modern ideological production of English nationhood, according to which two opposing conceptions of the nation existed—one Protestant and the other Catholic—is erroneous. Conceptions of nationhood crossed confessional lines' (p. 247). The real opposition, he contends, lay between 'Catholic and Protestant cosmopolitans who saw England as an integral part of Christendom, or secular Europe, or Continental affairs, and Catholic and Protestant adherents to the myth of English or British national purity' (p. 247). *Plus ça change.*

Felicity Jane Stout's monograph, *Exploring Russia in the Elizabethan Commonwealth: The Muscovy Company and Giles Fletcher the Elder (1546–1611)*, discusses the ways in which international exchange shaped the discourses and structures of power in relation to the idea of 'commonwealth' in late sixteenth-century England. Stout's blurb states that 'this book seeks to redress the imbalance in scholarship of the "discovery era" that has so often looked to the "New World" of the Americas at the expense of northern sites of exploration and exploitation'. Stout achieves this aim admirably, but this is only one of the book's productive contributions. Giles Fletcher the elder became Elizabeth I's ambassador to Russia in 1588. His work, *Of the Russe Common Wealth or Maner of Governement by the Russe Emperour* [1591], reported first hand on another alien nation for an Elizabethan audience. Stout shows that Russia was 'a useful tool for Elizabethans to think with' (p. 1) with respect to interests in territory and monarchy closer to home. She makes the argument that ideas around trade and commonwealth should be brought back into dialogue with one another, and that the early 'discovery' of Russia, before English explorers had close contact with the Americas, offers an instructive object lesson. The first chapter, 'An Adventuring Commonwealth: English Mercantile and Diplomatic Encounters with Russia, 1553–88', describes English dealings with Russia from 1553 up until Fletcher's embassy in the late 1580s. Marred by diplomatic insensitivity in the face of an unfamiliar culture, it took this long for Elizabeth's ambassadors to hone interactions which allowed the nations to navigate between their rulers' conflicting international priorities. Moreover, the formation of the Muscovy Company was dogged by scandal, as corruption and private trading were rife; misdemeanours and the corresponding opprobrium, Stout notes, speak productively to the ways in which Elizabethans sought to construct and interpret their own common-wealth at home and abroad. The second chapter delves into Fletcher's humanist education and academic career to set up the backdrop to his embassy, and the ways in which his background shaped the construction of the path-breaking diplomatic role. The third and fourth chapters focus on Fletcher's textual construction of Russia—more on the reality of early modern Russia would be welcome, although beyond the scope of this monograph—while the fifth and sixth explore the uses to which his experiences were put in later sixteenth-century imaginative literature, including his sonnets, and the intersecting literature of counsel, such as Fletcher's *Richard III*, which Stout considers in the context of the expanding *Mirror for Magistrates* corpus, more on which below. A wealth of information unfurls from Stout's ostensibly confined subject matter. Situated squarely within a particular literary-historical critical milieu, this is a very helpful, deep contextual study, of interest to any scholar of the literature, history, and politics of Elizabeth's reign.

Returning to the old New World, in 'Thomas Hacket's Publication of Books about America in the 1560s' (*PBSA* 109[2015] 111–29) Philip Tromans reconsiders the scholarly reception of its eponymous subject matter, and focuses on Hacket's translation of Jean Ribaut's *The Whole and True Discovery of Terra Florida* [1563]. Detailed bibliographical description reveals that the Lambeth Palace Library's copy of the text 'represents a special issue with the dedication added for a specific clientele' (p. 113), although its purpose remains uncertain. While, Tromans suggests, an obvious reading would see the preparation of a unique presentation copy as a ploy to extract investment from Hacket's dedicatee for a future expedition to Florida, 'such an assumption is highly problematic' (p. 114). Rather than a straightforwardly pro-colonial text, Tromans argues, Hacket's *Terra Florida* and its depiction of a marvellous alien land would have held appeal for a wider book-buying public than a limited focus on expansionism allows. Rereading the anomalous dedication, Tromans draws attention to the distinction between commercial and colonial assays by the English explorers and their Iberian counterparts to whom Hacket alludes; further, he notes that Ribaut's main text claims Florida unequivocally for the French. When text and paratext are taken together, and in comparison to Richard Hakluyt's *Diuers Voyages* [1582], which does what Hacket's text has been said to do, Hacket's *Terra Florida* emerges as a less easily categorized work than a product of projected empire-building teleologies. Tromans concludes that close bibliographical attention to texts' individual printing histories is necessary to complicate the conclusions of a field 'too reliant on modern editions' (p. 128), and too quick to draw ideological inferences in preference to acknowledging 'newsworthiness and entertainment value' (p. 129).

Andrew Hadfield's capacious and playful article, 'A Red Herring?' (*ELR* 45[2015] 231–54), begins on the trail of the bookseller John Wolfe's 'news' pamphlet of 1598, *A Most Strange and Wonderfull Herring*, in which Wolfe describes an unusual recent catch off the coast of Norway. The fish is said to bear the image of two armed men fighting on one side, and on the other, five engraved characters. Wolfe takes the herring to be a portent of God's ire and imminent punishment. As such the pamphlet is typical of the body of ephemeral literature reporting and interpreting miraculous phenomena of the period. Hadfield notes, however, that the text itself draws attention to the tendency of such publications to elicit cynical responses from readers. And a reference to Marlowe's *Tamburlaine* suggests that Wolfe's frame of reference had a literary component. Through a synthesis of this literary backdrop with a potted history of the late sixteenth-century North Sea fishing industry, Hadfield traces the local significance of Wolfe's publication to a specific industry crisis, the Yarmouth–Lowestoft dispute over ancient fishing rights, which saw Robert Cecil, William Burghley, and Robert Devereux pitted against John Fortesque and Thomas Sackville in a landmark quarrel over statutory regulation. Wolfe, moreover, was an object of Thomas Nashe's invective, siding with Gabriel Harvey in their infamous feud; 'it would be odd', Hadfield argues, 'if there were no relationship between' Nashe's *Lenten Stuffe* [1599], 'the most famous work on herrings in English', and Wolfe's pamphlet (p. 247). Such a relationship proves slippery, however, and the article concludes with a reassessment of *Lenten Stuffe*, a work that 'looks like an allegory' but whose 'ostensible subject is sincere' (p. 252); it is 'a literary red herring precisely because it concerns the stuff of the real world' (p. 254).

A.E.B. Coldiron's *Printers Without Borders: Translation and Textuality in the Renaissance*, too, seeks to write early modern English literature back into its international networks of production. Reviewed at greater length in Chapter V above, the volume's fourth and fifth chapters are of particular relevance for this section. In a second outing for the printer in these pages, the fourth discusses John Wolfe's trilingual edition of Castiglione's *Il Cortegiano*, printed by Wolfe as *The Courtier of Count Baldessar Castilio* [1588]. Compiled as it was from Castiglione's Italian, Chappuy's French, and Hoby's English versions, to say nothing of the numerous Latin editions also available, Coldiron notes that the demand for another *Courtier* 'and the value it added to the English literary system are . . . not immediately obvious' (p. 163). But, she argues, the project foregrounded Castiglione's passing remarks about the ideal courtier's metropolitan credentials at a time when English ambivalence about the interrelationship of foreign and national identity was unusually pressing. Produced in the year of the Armada, Wolfe's *mise-en-page* demanded that readers engage with multiple languages almost simultaneously, heightening alterity rather than the appropriative assimilation common to other printed translations. Mirroring Castiglione's dialogic mode, Coldiron suggests, Wolfe's presentation enforced a heuristic encounter with the translated text, unmediated by marginalia or the 'framing thresholds' of prefatory paratexts (p. 191) to encourage 'comparative, contrastive, competitive, immediate' reception of the texts side by side (p. 185). Also printed in 1588 was the subject of chapter 5, the octolingual broadside 'Ad Serenissimam Elizabetham Reginam', a single sheet which presented versions of an epigram by Théodore de Bèze in Latin, Hebrew, English, Greek, Dutch, Italian, French, and Spanish. All conveying the same essentials—that the Armada was motivated by Spanish ambition or greed—their formally varied treatments each 'subtly brings to bear its own literary history and its own story about the transfer of empire and culture' (p. 202), enacting topical debates in literary theory as well as international rivalries. Although readers' appreciation of the poems' differences of approach would vary with their linguistic understanding, 'even a strictly monoglot reader . . . would still have received the clear visual message that the whole world, from every corner and in all its languages, knew of and celebrated the recent English success' (p. 228). The precise circumstances of the broadside's production by printers George Bishop and Ralph Newbery are unknown; Coldiron speculates about occasional commissions, and suggests that the contemporaneous Continental habits of printing single sheets and using vellum 'provide further international resonance and context' (p. 232), as well as speaking to the text's aspiration to different kinds of authority. By way of conclusion to the pair of chapters, Coldiron posits these texts' polyglot presentation as a means of elevating the late sixteenth-century construction of English literary and national identity into a transnational discourse, although 'the translated forms subtly betray that English naval actions and literary aspirations are not absolutely harmonized' (p. 254). While it is beyond the scope of this section to comment in more detail, the reader is wholeheartedly referred to Smith's review, and of course to Coldiron's book itself: an innovative, engaging, and highly valuable addition to the field.

Evgeny Kazartsev's article, 'Language and Meter in Early English, Dutch, German, and Russian Iambic Verse' (*CLS* 52[2015] 682–703), uses later sixteenth-century English poetry as a touchstone for a comparative analysis of iambic verse in four languages. The article sets out to explore 'why the rhythmic structures of verse in these various countries differ despite its having the same meters' (p. 683), and whether the language itself is behind this variation. By broadening the scholarly focus beyond 'a single national verse system' (p. 683) and conducting a statistical investigation, Kazartsev reveals significant differences between the patterns of deviation from metre across the data set. The Dutch iamb, for example, is subject to much greater variation than the German, despite the very similar demands imposed by the languages' average word lengths (just 0.1 syllables apart). English and Russian iambic verse, by contrast, shows much more similarity in this regard, despite English's lower average number of syllables. As a result, Kazartsev turns away from linguistic correlations to consider the historical conditions of poetic production. This portion of the article suggests that English syllabo-tonic versification's origins in French poetry meant that 'rhythm gradually led to the development of meter' (p. 690), not the other way around; the structure of the line was predicated on syllables rather than feet. Its notable freedom might be put down to the observation that 'in English verse practice . . . outpaced theory' (p. 691), while Dutch theory evolved in step with practice, and German syllabo-tonicism 'did not evolve, but came about as a revolutionary change' (p. 692). Although ultimately directed primarily at scholars of Russian iambic verse, the article has useful implications for the study of early modern English poetry as well, concluding that 'not only verse meter but also its rhythm is determined not so much by linguistic but by historical factors' (p. 698).

Worth reviewing here, despite its Shakespearean conclusion, is another article which treats the aural properties of the period's literature: John Wesley's engaging and revelatory 'Rhetorical Delivery for Renaissance

English: Voice, Gesture, Emotion, and the Sixteenth-Century Vernacular Turn' (*RenQ* 68[2015] 1265–96). Wesley resituates the Elizabethan elevation of the English language from rustic rudeness to classical standards of eloquence among contemporary linguistic, rather than literary, developments. By returning our attention to the vocal delivery of texts, he argues, in line with a growing interest in the Renaissance voice in the field, we may uncover a neglected history of English's battle with Latin for moral and rhetorical supremacy. The first section of the article, 'Roman Oratory for English Mouths', addresses the overlap between English and Latin rhetorical training, in the hands of familiar masterminds of humanist education such as Roger Ascham and Richard Mulcaster, and emphasizes the significance of the soundscape of the early modern schoolroom; inflected, in the case of pupils' Latin delivery at the Merchant Taylors' School, by Mulcaster's Carlisle accent. For George Puttenham, the ultimate marker of linguistic sophistication was delivery, a bodily rather than textual quality, which fed into the period's desire to codify English spelling and thus inscribe correct pronunciation. Wesley then goes on to discuss the role of delivery in the embodiment of history and emotion. Rehearsing the relationship between rhetorical imitation and persuasion, he deftly reintegrates the part delivery played in this equation, and its implications for attitudes towards neologisms and foreign borrowing, using illustrations from Elizabethan drama, including Kyd's *Spanish Tragedy*, and *Hamlet*. The third section, 'Renaissance Speech Therapy', sheds light on the interrelation of rhetorical training and physical exercise, where we find Demosthenes declaiming as he strides uphill (in Mulcaster), and imitating a dog the better to develop his vocal range (according to Ascham). Wesley notes in the article's penultimate part that the physicality of rhetoric necessarily points to a latent cultural relativism, while the dependence of delivery on performance 'demands a lacuna in the written form' (p. 1282). Wesley reads this as an opportunity which 'allowed for a sense of eloquence coming unstuck from its static classical past and adhering instead to English voices' (p. 1283), before focusing specifically on articulation through humanist learning in Shakespeare's *Titus Andronicus* to finish.

The *Renaissance Studies* special issue on the psalms is also reviewed in Section 2 of this chapter and in Chapter V. This section is able to comment on two articles, those by Clare Costley King'oo and Deirdre Serjeantson. King'oo's contribution, 'William Hunnis and the Success of the *Seven Sobs*' (*RS* 29[2015] 615–31), revisits Hunnis's overlooked verse paraphrase of the Penitential Psalms, printed in 1583. While scholarship has noted the essential attributes of the publication, King'oo observes, it has neglected to ask more searching questions about the work. She sets out to redress this, as well as to locate her interpretation of the text within the growing interest in everyday domestic devotional practices. The analysis begins with some number-crunching, to assess the relative and absolute popularity of the *Seven Sobs* in a marketplace already packed with books of psalms and their derivatives. Among close analogues, Hunnis's work was a clear winner, while King'oo's consultation of manuscript annotation to extant copies demonstrates that the book was not only purchased in large numbers but also circulated extensively. Its success, by comparison to Sir Thomas Wyatt's paraphrase which was only published once in the period, and the relative critical attention paid to the two works, bears witness, King'oo suggests, to notable scholarly bias. Analysis of the text itself reveals its engagement with an involved Augustinian hermeneutic tradition, and the productive formal and conceptual amplification facilitated by the paraphrastic process. Hunnis is also shown to push 'the inescapability of God's ire to an extreme known in the period only to the most fervent of evangelicals' (p. 627). King'oo concludes that Hunnis's 'dilatory method' (p. 629) points to 'a considerable degree of elasticity in the Penitential Psalms' (p. 630), which allowed the reworking of medieval Catholic material to innovative Protestant ends, and reinforces the ongoing importance of scholarship which rejects historical and confessional boundaries.

Deirdre Serjeantson turns, in 'The Books of Psalms and the Early Modern Sonnet' (*RS* 29[2015] 632–49), to the supposed opposition between the two verse forms in the early modern period. They are in fact, Serjeantson argues, 'closely intertwined' (p. 633). While contemporary commentators such as Edward Dering and Matthew Parker foregrounded the moral antithesis of the modes, Serjeantson suggests that the evidence of sixteenth-century poets participating in both traditions speaks to 'a peaceful co-existence' and even 'interdependence' of psalm and sonnet (p. 634). This alerts readers of the sonnet to the form's openness to biblical inflections which might otherwise be misinterpreted. Serjeantson urges the dissolution of binary readings which set up the Reformations' plain style and the intricacy of other kinds of poetry in opposition, and notes that both psalms and sonnets were considered 'songs' in the period. She locates Petrarch at the root of important developments for both genres, and behind their interrelation in the works of George Gascoigne and Philip Sidney, as well as the proliferation of religious sonnet sequences just as the amorous sonnet sequence was falling from favour. It makes perfect sense, then, that King David 'was, in the most literal terms, adopted as a Petrarchan lover' (p. 642) and specifically as a sonneteer, by Gascoigne, George Peele, and others. Through the fluidity of these associations, earthly sonneteers began laying claim to divine inspiration or prophetic agency for their own poems; Serjeantson looks forward to the seventeenth century here, to collections such as George Herbert's *Temple* [1633]. Meanwhile, 'the sonnet's connotations of interiority and self-scrutiny' (p. 646) also recommend the form for comparable psalmodic functions in prayer, meditation, and introspection.

Sonnets are also the subject of Danila Sokolov's piece, ' "Nat being (to my displesure) your wife as she": The Politics and Poetics of Sovereign Marriage in the Casket Sonnets' (*MP* 112[2015] 458–78). Sokolov rereads the so-called Casket Sonnets, a collection of twelve poems in French, accompanied by Anglo-Scots translations, alongside the medieval *Kingis Quair*, to shed light on the function of sovereign marriage in the political vocabulary of the late sixteenth century. Attributed to Mary Stewart, the sonnets were printed as part of *Ane Detectioun of the Duinges of Marie Quene of Scottes* [1571], a pamphlet which contributed to the propaganda campaign against the Scottish queen, and which accused Mary of conspiring with her lover James Hepburn, earl of Bothwell, to murder her husband Henry Stewart, Lord Darnley, in 1567. While the attribution of the sonnets has been controversial, Sokolov sidesteps this question with the observation that 'The voice of a monarch is never entirely his or her own; rather, it is a product of negotiation between representational and interpretative forces' (p. 461)—although one might argue that this applies to all voices, not just royal ones. In Sokolov's reading, the sonnets reconfigure marriage as a sexually violent and reciprocally traumatic act, framing Mary as an unstable and disloyal wife figure, whose 'Failure to govern [her]self translates into inability and unworthiness to govern others' (p. 467). By contrast, *The Kingis Quair* had insisted on the monarch's (James I's) chastity, by holding the language of erotic marital union at a remove, and reconciling passion with reason and right rule. Sokolov suggests that the rhetoric of the Casket Sonnets, as informed by the treatment of corresponding themes in the earlier poem, pertains not only to Mary's adulterous past but also to Elizabeth's matrimonial future, a subject of widespread anxiety in the 1560s and 1570s. The Casket Sonnets provided Elizabeth, Sokolov contends, 'with a kind of mirror for magistrates that showed her the dangers of an ill-suited marriage' (p. 470), propounding a 'tradition of monarchical government through self-governance' (p. 478) whose Anglo-Scottish origins also bespoke a more suitable way forward for Elizabeth's Anglo-Scottish successor.

So, this year's publications turn out strongly for Elizabethan advice literature, also the topic of the following three articles. In 'Masks of Impersonality in Burghley's "Ten Precepts" and Ralegh's *Instructions to his Son*' (*RES* 66[2015] 481–500), Fred B. Tromly takes issue with Richard Helgerson's claim, in *The Elizabethan Prodigals* [1976], that early modern fathers sought to inculcate their sons with a universal series of admonitory precepts, and suggests that instead his chosen examples demonstrate a high degree of personalization. The 'proudly individualistic, self-dramatizing Ralegh' (p. 481) could hardly have simply passed on a stock of commonplaces, Tromly argues, while also questioning whether it is even possible to reproduce a precept impersonally, given the unique inflection of context, placement, and occasion. Rather, a veneer of impersonality offered the opportunity to retain appropriate paternal detachment, while addressing affective concerns (a balancing act not necessary to be pursued, Tromly observes Helgerson noting, by early modern mothers). While Polonius-like Burghley performs this role commendably, suppressing personal history and politics in his axiomatic 'Ten Precepts' [1587], Tromly sees Ralegh as too 'idiosyncratic' and 'self-involved' (p. 484) for his Jacobean *Instructions* to be of benefit, or even relevance, to his son, a figure who is largely absent from the work. Part II of the article summarizes the essentials of Burghley's text, and Part III attends to Ralegh's delivery, while Part IV considers the occasion and purpose of the *Instructions*. Concluding with a teleological nod forward to Wat Ralegh's death while serving as the captain of his father's ship, the *Destiny*, Tromly reads Wat's lack of adequate training in military and filial discipline as a cause of his fatal impulsiveness—perhaps an unkind stretch in an otherwise nuanced extension of Helgerson's work.

Heralding a period of intensification in the field of *Mirror* studies, Scott C. Lucas returns to the text's complicated and shadowy genesis in his article, 'Henry Lord Stafford, "The Two Rogers", and the Creation of *A Mirror for Magistrates*, 1554–1563' (*RES* 66[2015] 845–58). Lucas has paid greater attention than any other scholar to the realities of the *Mirror for Magistrates'* composition, a topic which is frequently downplayed in favour of attention to the fictive narrative of the work's composition which makes up its metatextual prose frame. Despite its reputation as a radically polyvocal, collaborative enterprise, concrete evidence has only been presented for three named contributors: William Baldwin, George Ferrers, and Thomas Chaloner. Lucas offers a convincing case for Henry Lord Stafford to be added to this list. Known for his involvement in the printing and licensing of the benighted early edition of the text, Stafford was not thought to have had a hand in the compilation itself, but Lucas argues that Stafford was uniquely placed to allow access to the parliamentary rolls on which portions of the text are based. Building up a painstaking reconstruction of Stafford's motivations, rooted in his family history and financial misfortunes under Edward VI, as well as the early development of an association with Ferrers in whose manor Stafford and his wife planned to live in 1547, Lucas traces Stafford's growing attraction to the *Mirror* project's original Marian incarnation. He argues that the tragedy of 'The Two Rogers', an anomalous and, perhaps, sub-standard addition to the compilation, which uses material from the rolls of parliament to which Stafford alone among the known *Mirror* contributors had access, 'takes part in the same intellectual endeavor to which Stafford devoted the bulk of his historical research and writings' in his final decade (p. 853): affirming the right of due process of law for English peers through historical evidence. While it is impossible to confirm, Lucas's supposition persuasively ties up some loose ends in the story of the *Mirror*'s production, and usefully extends understanding of this enigmatic but central Elizabethan text.

Where is the line between panegyric and idolatry? Ethan John Guagliardo begins 'The Political Atheology of George Puttenham and Fulke Greville' (*MP* 112[2015] 591–614) with this question, citing Gabriel Harvey's 'puckish' (p. 591) use of the language of the pagan cult as a means of highlighting the awkward slippage between civil worship and the problematic deification of Elizabeth I. Guagliardo disagrees that Tudor political theology incorporated the rhetoric of idolatry as part of the 'migration of the holy' from religious to secular authority, arguing instead that the practice revealed 'the divine right of kings as something no less invented than the divine right of popes' (p. 594). Guagliardo points to the ways in which their ironizing of this invention has also been seen to offer poets their own blueprint for the construction of authority, before considering the writing of Puttenham and Greville who, he argues, interrogated and transformed 'the idol fashioning of the panegyrists' (p. 596). Pitting what he regards as Puttenham's atheistic tendencies against Greville's piety, Guagliardo suggests that both writers are exercised by the 'poetic origin of sovereign authority' (p. 597). Distinct from proto-secularists, Puttenham and Greville are presented, rather, as reconceiving political theology as 'a human project' and 'a work of atheological artifice': 'political atheology is the inner truth of political theology' (p. 598). A comparison of Puttenham's *Partheniades* and Greville's *Treatise of Monarchy* shows Greville 'echoing Puttenham's analysis of the invented nature of political theology but recoiling from its consequences' (p. 610). Ultimately, Guagliardo deploys his analysis to oppose the vilification of secular liberalism by Carl Schmitt and

Victoria Kahn; instead of a recourse to political theology, he suggests, we would do better to follow Puttenham and Greville's recognition that this reinvestment of authority is also a fiction, distinct from 'the truly transcendent sovereignty of God' (p. 614).

Alison V. Scott begins *Literature and the Idea of Luxury in Early Modern England* by telling the story of luxury's rehabilitation narrative. The concept is said to have been 'de-moralised' in the eighteenth century in its progress towards the neutral sense in which it is used today. Noting that this account leaves out the recent work on seventeenth-century consumption, Scott suggests that there is more work to be done to unpick the transition from medieval licentiousness to early modern indulgence. To address this lacuna, Scott focuses on 'particular fractures and discontinuities in luxury's conceptual development' (p. 3), complicating the homogeneous portrayal of early modern attitudes to luxury propounded by existing cultural histories. Drawing distinctions between classical and biblical senses of the term, and more nuanced subsets of these definitions, Scott offers a series of rich and layered dissections of familiar textual moments (*Hamlet*'s Denmark as a 'couch for luxury', for example, or *Paradise Lost*'s Eden as 'luxurious by restraint'). The suppleness of the term and the equal and opposing resistance with which such instability is greeted by contemporary commentators frequently shades, in the introduction, into discussion of the nature of language itself, early modern lexicography, and the interpretative history of conceptual change, a welcome metaleptic leap, which deepens the monograph's thematic analysis. Justifying her predominant focus on literary sources, Scott states that 'literature provides the most complete account of a concept's historical meanings and their shifts over time' (p. 10). Scott surveys the sixteenth and seventeenth centuries, although the book 'does not unfold chronologically because it does not argue for progressive change' (p. 21), focusing instead on three distinct frameworks: the moral, the material, and the political-economic.

The first chapter, on Spenser, the fourth, on staging luxury in early modern drama, and the last, 'Particularizing Abundance: Un-economic Luxury in Roman Political Tragedy', unfortunately fall outside this section's remit. The second chapter, 'Cleopatra's Spoils: Proto-Liberal Dimensions of Early Modern Luxury', concludes with Shakespeare, but approaches early modern uses of Cleopatra's legend in broad terms. Scott shows literary treatments of Cleopatra negotiating the conflicting Christian and pre-Christian attitudes towards, and accounts of, luxury which her history forced together, to explore depictions by Samuel Daniel, Thomas North, and Mary Sidney, via Plutarch and Pliny the elder. The figure of Cleopatra functions as a 'nexus of meanings' (p. 66) for luxury, from the dual concepts of spoils and despoliation, to positive, oppositional, or un-English connotations, as for William Rankins in *The English Ape* [1588]. Chapter 3, 'Sin City: Satirizing Luxury in Early Modern London', focuses on luxury's resonances against the contemporary backdrop of urban transformations at the turn of the century. Rankins, again, proves good value; his *Mirror of Monsters* [1587] decries the emerging social and economic changes with which luxury was associated, manifested in the Platonic unreality of 'early modern London and its temptations to self-abandon' (p. 83). Luxury also connotes riot, misgovernment, and disease, particularly for satirists Nashe, Marston, and Hall, for whom literature itself becomes a target. The fifth chapter uses Ben Jonson's *Entertainment at Britain's Burse* as a case study, but also contains productive insights for this review's area of interest. 'Bad Markets: Remoralized Luxury in Mercantile Literature' suggests that the rise of mercantilism depended on 'detaching particular . . . modes of consumption from the intensely moralized idea of luxury' (p. 142), and focuses more closely on the national dimensions of the discourse, including the foreignness of luxury, and a frivolous consumer culture upholding the interests of foreign merchants. Scott's book as a whole presents a dizzying multiplicity of significances which spool out of some well-worn binaries around luxury, morality, and pleasure, in an enjoyable new take on early modern urban culture.

This year's *Notes and Queries* contained another clutch of pertinent essays. First up is Timothy D. Crowley's piece, 'More's "Neck" in Robinson's Translation of *Utopia* (1551 and 1556)' (*N&Q* 62[2015] 39–42), in which Crowley explores the amplification of passages by *Utopia*'s first translator, Ralph Robinson, to reflect on More's political position after he composed the work. Following More's death, Robinson's translation draws out 'a vividly prophetic quality' (p. 40) in the character Hythloday's prediction about the fate of the counsellor, whereby 'the wickedness and folly of others shall be imputed to him and laid in his neck'; More's original is not so prescient. Crowley notes that the purpose of the interpolation, though, is more likely 'designed to complement Robinson's 1551 dedicatory epistle to his former schoolmate and fellow-Protestant William Cecil' (p. 41), which also warns of pursuing obstinate conciliar admonition to the death, a dedication that was later removed for the 1556 edition following Mary I's accession and the decline of Cecil's 'political prominence' (p. 42). The proleptic allusion to More's execution may be recast, under Catholic Mary, not as a cautionary tale for a capricious monarch's advisers, but as an 'open and sympathetic implication of martyrdom' (p. 42).

Barrett L. Beer argues, in 'Richard III: The Image of the King in Small Mid-Tudor Chronicles, 1540–1560' (*N&Q* 62[2015] 42–5), that said chronicles 'do not promote the familiar image of Richard III found in Tudor literature' (p. 42). While the larger and best known (Fabyan, Grafton, Hall, Holinshed, and Co.) do promulgate the villainous figure made most canonical by Shakespeare, the smaller chronicles, circulated among a significant non-elite readership, offer severely limited comment on his reign: readers of these sources alone 'would have concluded that Richard was an insignificant and colourless king scarcely worthy of mention' (p. 44)—he appends the 1540 account by John Byddell as an example. Beer speculates that the small chronicles' mid-century non-elite readers were more interested in recent history than 'the distant past', perhaps because of contemporary political and religious turmoil, and therefore their compilers gave greater weight to early sixteenth-century events. The extensive publication of these works therefore, Beer concludes, 'call[s] into question the depth of Richard III's notorious reputation' (p. 45). I would be interested in the complementary role the oral transmission of history might play in this narrative, but it should certainly give us pause.

In advance of his forthcoming monograph on Churchyard [2017], Matthew Woodcock proffers a note on 'Thomas Churchyard and Music' (*N&Q* 62[2015] 48–51). Churchyard's modest understanding of musical composition, theory, and notation, and perhaps also his actual composition, based on a Venetian galliard ascribed to him in the manuscript collection known as the Mulliner Book (British Library, Additional MS 30513), led to his deployment of various musical tropes throughout his oeuvre, as well as his participation in a pamphlet war with Thomas Brice in the early 1560s over the morality of secular arts, including music and rhyming poetry. Woodcock also comments on the musical afterlife of some of Churchyard's verse, such as a passage from his complaint of Jane Shore, first printed in the 1563 edition of the *Mirror for Magistrates*, which was later excerpted and set to music, while the tune ascribed to his poem, 'A matter of fonde Cupid, and vaine Venus', became one of the most popular ballad melodies of the early seventeenth century.

Gavin Alexander hunts down Gascoigne's metrical models in 'The Sources of the Verse Examples in George Gascoigne's *Certayne Notes of Instruction*' (*N&Q* 62[2015] 52–3), and notes Chaucer, Turberville, Wyatt, and Surrey. Amy Blakeway identifies 'A New Source for Holinshed's 1577 *Hystorie of Scotland*' (*N&Q* 62[2015] 53–6), observing that Francis Thynne's citation of John Lesley's Latin *History of Scotland* [1578] in his revisions to the *Hystorie of Scotland* for the *Chronicles*' second edition [1587] has not yet led to the recognition of Lesley's significance to Holinshed's 1577 version. In particular, Holinshed used Lesley's account for the 1488–1561 portion of his history. Blakeway provides three choice examples, and concludes by suggesting that Holinshed's access to Lesley's text 'implies that his *History* enjoyed a wider circulation than we have hitherto realized', which 'raises the possibility that his potential reach as a propagandist on behalf of the imprisoned Mary, Queen of Scots, was more widespread during the early 1570s than the few extant manuscripts imply' (p. 56).

Keeping to the Scottish theme, 'The Source and Significance of a Marginal Inscription in the *Buik of Alexander* (*c*.1580)' (*N&Q* 62[2015] 56–8) responds to Emily Wingfield's earlier note in the journal, where a marginal inscription to the *Buik* could not be interpreted. Priscilla Bawcutt suggests here that the inscription in question 'represents a truncated and imperfect witness to the remarkable popularity of an ancient topos or commonplace' (p. 56), drawn from William Baldwin's *Treatise of Morall Philosophie* [1547], which also found favour with Nicholas Grimald and George Herbert. In 'Nicholas Breton, Richard Jones, and Two Printed Verse Miscellanies' (*N&Q* 62[2015] 79–82), Hugh Gazzard turns to *Brittons Bowre of Delights* [1591] and *The Arbour of Amorous Deuises* [1597] to explore the relationship between author and printer, and Breton's interest in the miscellany form. While Breton remonstrated in the preface to *The Pilgrimage to Paradise* [1592] that Jones had printed the *Bowre* without his consent, Gazzard notes that this kind of spurious claim was common practice, and concludes that this is 'another case where assumptions and inferences drawn from the old inferences about Elizabethan "hacks" and "pirates" will not help us to understand trends and events in poetry publication' (p. 82).

'William Elderton's Ladie Marques Identified' (*N&Q* 62[2015] 541–2), by Jenni Hyde, pins down the eponymous heroine of Elderton's 1569 ballad as Elizabeth Parr, marchioness of Northampton and a close confidante of Elizabeth I, who died in 1565. Meanwhile in 'John Hopkinson of Grub Street: An Elizabethan Orientalist' (*N&Q* 62[2015] 545–9), Mordechai Feingold fleshes out the identity of the Hopkinson known only from a single reference in James Whitelocke's 1609 recollection of his studies at Merchant Taylors' School in the 1580s. New information is to be gleaned from his wife Katherine Hopkinson's petition to allow his return to England, after he had been driven, through a belief in the nation's disregard for learning, to seek a living teaching Hebrew and Greek, among other languages, in Heidelberg. Katherine had marshalled signatories including Lancelot Andrewes, the neo-Latinist William Goldingham, and Presbyterian preacher Thomas Barbar, and between her petition and recommendations from notable contacts on the Continent, Hopkinson's fortunes began to revive. However, Feingold notes, he died before reaching the level of recognition and financial security his reputation promised, despite subsequent recognition by Walter Ralegh, Joseph Scaliger, and George Buck, and his 'small, but important contribution to the development of Arabic studies in England' (p. 549).

Leticia Álvarez-Recio, in 'Chapters Translated by Anthony Munday in *The History of Palmendos* (1589): A Long-Standing Error' (*N&Q* 62[2015] 549–51), corrects a misapprehension regarding the number of chapters in the first section of Munday's translation of the French–Spanish *Primaleón de Grecia* [1512]: it's thirty-one. Confusion had arisen since Munday's work numbers one chapter fewer than his source text; Álvarez-Recio explores the ways in which Munday's translation relates to the original, and exhorts us not to perpetuate the error.

Rosalind Barber presents 'Sir John Davies as Guilpin's Fuscus' (*N&Q* 62[2015] 553–4), revisiting an epigram by Everard Guilpin [1598] which complains about the prevalence of profane verse by a poet identified by a pseudonym. Originally thought to have referred to John Marston—unlikely, Barber suggests, given Guilpin and Marston's close friendship—Davies is a more plausible object given his recent ridicule at the Middle Temple's 1597/8 Candlemas festivities.

Lastly, in 'Timon, Sir Thomas North and the *Loup-Garou*' (*N&Q* 62[2015] 572–4), Gerard Sargent notes the puzzling association made between Timon and the *loup-garou*, or werewolf, in Thomas North's translation of Plutarch's 'Life of Alcibiades' [1579]. The term, not found in Plutarch's Greek, was interpolated by the French translator Jacques Amyot, and appears to be 'French shorthand to describe someone of melancholic disposition' (p. 573). Sargent argues that to have translated the term into English would have been to miss the point, but by leaving it in the original French, North profits from a general equation of the lycanthropic and melancholic, traced back to the book of Daniel.

While anomalous among the other sorts of texts reviewed here, the books that follow demonstrate a field pushing at its own boundaries—always a mission to be celebrated. In *Teaching Early Modern English Literature from the Archives*, a publication in the MLA Options for Teaching series, Heidi

Brayman Hackel and Ian Frederick Moulton collate twenty-four chapters across five thematic sections on the possibilities of, particularly, electronic archival research and research-led teaching. Brayman Hackel and Moulton admit that this can only be a 'snapshot' (p. 2) of the digital revolution in the teaching of early modern literature, but it is a snapshot of a pivotal moment in the history of the archive; the very meaning of the word *archive*, the editors note, is itself in flux, and has come to signify 'both a place and a function' (p. 5). The volume provides extensive practical advice for instructors, though, and frequent caveats regarding the false dichotomy of print and digital, or the fallacy of digital completeness, and problems of access, in addition to a 'state of the field' pedagogical survey. Sarah Werner's 'Bringing Undergraduates into the Archives' (pp. 15–21) describes the Folger Undergraduate Program's seminar in Books and Early Modern Culture (2007–13), in which undergraduates from multiple disciplines were taught to combine theoretical knowledge and practical skills to interpret material texts effectively. Heather Wolfe's 'Manuscripts and Paleography for Undergraduates' (pp. 22–31) is also largely descriptive, and in some places addresses the reader with step-by-step lesson plans in the imperative, and provides URLs for open-access manuscript resources. In a stimulating chapter on 'The Work of the Book in an Age of Digital Reproduction'(pp. 39–44), Evelyn Tribble engages with the theory of the database to underscore the complex layers of representation, and, sometimes, error, in play in the process of digitization. Arnold Sanders builds on Tribble's wry acknowledgement of the generational divide in metaliteracy in 'The Death of the Editor and Printer: Teaching Early Modern Publishing Practices to Internet-Raised Undergraduates' (pp. 45–53). Facilitating the sorts of work seen being done earlier in this entry, Patrick M. Erben's 'The Translingual Archive' (pp. 54–63) reframes *Early English Books Online* as a starting point from which to consider 'the translingual nature of early modern English literature' (p. 55), before providing a series of sample assignments for students of different degree levels. Two multi-authored chapters address specific digital archives, the *Emory Women Writers Resource Project* in 'Engendering the Early Modern Archive' (pp. 82–89) by Sheila T. Cavanagh, Gitanjali Shahani, and Irene Middleton—the punning title contains both gendered and generative concerns involved in the archive's compilation—and the eponymous collection in Patricia Fumerton, Simone Chess, Tassie Gniay, and Kris McAbee's 'The *English Broadside Ballad Archive*: From Theory to Practice' (pp. 90–100). These chapters also make projections for their resources' outputs, from presentations and publications to graduate training and employment. Rebecca Laroche returns, in 'Early Modern Women in the Archives' (pp. 125–32), to the ways in which digital collections enable access to less canonical texts, notably those by female authors, using Isabella Whitney's *A Sweet Nosgay* [1573] as a case study for the sort of directed and contextual work that could be done. Joshua Eckhardt also opens 'Teaching Verse Miscellanies' (pp. 145–51) with a rueful campus anecdote to highlight the necessity of digitization for universities without extensive early modern library holdings. He goes on to summarize a seminar syllabus designed to integrate the study of canonical and noncanonical verse in early modern manuscript and print miscellanies, featuring texts made available by digital means. Additionally, the volume contains a selection of chapters on archival approaches to Shakespeare and other dramatists, on music and maps, and on other specific digital and historical resources. Although clearly a collection which courts imminent obsolescence, on a topic which might more readily have suggested online rather than print publication, this collection's reification in hard copy reflects hearteningly (if somewhat ironically) on the discipline's willingness to take digital archival work seriously as an object of, as well as a tool for, analytical engagement.

Finally, Carole Levin and associate editor Christine Stewart-Nuñez's *Scholars and Poets Talk about Queens* combines critical commentary and imaginative literature to reflect on a series of female leaders, and their early modern reception, 'to demonstrate the ongoing relevance and immediacy of these powerful women' (Levin, introduction, p. 1). Sections on Hecuba, Cleopatra, Boudicca, Matilda, Queen Margaret, Catherine of Aragon, Mary Stewart, Elizabeth I, and Gráinne Ní Mháille (or Grace O'Malley) present between one and five pieces each which reinterpret these figures from complementary academic and creative perspectives. A final section, called 'Gifts and Poison, Whispers and Letters', offers a broader take on early modern queenship and its representation in history and fiction. Particularly pertinent to this *YWES* entry are Marguerite A. Tassi's chapter, 'Tears for Hecuba: Empathy and Maternal Bereavement in Golding's Translation of Ovid's *Metamorphoses*' (pp. 7–24); Katarzyna Lecky's 'How the Iceni Became British: Holinshed's Boudicca and the Rhetoric of Naturalization' (pp. 55–74); 'The Widow of Scots: Examining Mary Stewart in Her Widowhoods', by Alyson Alvarez (pp. 165–80); Paul Strauss's 'The Virgin Queen as Nurse of the Church: Manipulating an Image of Elizabeth I in Court Sermons' (pp. 185–202); and 'Notorious: Gráinne Ní Mháille, Graven Memory, and the Uses of Irish Legend' by Brandie R. Siegfried (pp. 233–50); as well as their accompanying creative reworkings. Tassi's chapter focuses on the affective force of Golding's translation, reading the educative capacity of the early modern mirror trope and *Mirror for Magistrates* tradition through modern scientific understanding of mirror neurons, 'which fire in response to vivid, sensuous, emotive language and descriptive, penetrating characterization' (p. 9) to model the subject's emotional state. Tassi argues that by using rhetorical techniques like *prosopopoeia* Golding's translation elicits reciprocity between speaker, character, and reader.

Lecky's illuminating and timely chapter begins with the printer Reyner Wolfe's vision for Holinshed's *Chronicles*, and 'takes its cue from Wolfe's own status as a naturalized Englishman to study the ideal of naturalized citizenship at the heart of British identity in the *Chronicles*' (p. 56). Lecky notes that the 1577 edition's woodcut of Boudicca directly corresponds to the accompanying text, unlike many of the text's illustrations. Unusually heterogeneous, the image reflects the way in which Holinshed's Boudicca 'consistently highlights the radically contingent nature of Britishness' (p. 56). Lecky goes on to argue that this notion of Britishness is gendered and elective, with citizenship 'often constituted as a decision to align oneself with the land's women' (p. 59), embodied by Boudicca's composite English, Irish, and female identity.

In her essay on Mary Stewart, Alvarez comments on the same royal scandal as Danila Sokolov's article, discussed above, this time attending to condemnation of Mary's behaviour as inappropriate, not for a queen but for a widow. Such women 'were often treated with mockery, hostility, or contempt' (p. 166) in the early modern period, perhaps because of their enhanced legal rights, property ownership, and legitimized single status. Mary was widowed twice, first in 1560 on the death of her first husband Francis II of France, and of course again in 1567 when Henry Stewart, Lord Darnley, died in suspicious circumstances. Having conformed to expected French courtly mourning practices after Francis's death, Mary's reaction to Darnley's was less conventional, appearing in public the following day, failing to pursue justice for her husband's supposed murder in a timely fashion, and rapidly marrying again. Understanding the interplay between convention and Mary's actual conduct during her two widowhoods is, Alvarez concludes, important to her wider political history.

Strauss turns to Elizabeth I, and her presentation in court sermons by the likes of Lancelot Andrewes, Edward Dering, Richard Curteys, and John Jewel. The biblical metaphor of the monarch as a nursing mother helped to justify female rule and to structure the nation's relationship with its queen; as well as reconfiguring her authority, though, it allowed for the suggestion that such authority inhered in subordination to the commons. Strauss explores the shifting loci of power in the patronage, preaching, and publication of sermons, which integrated praise and admonition of Elizabeth, and notes that she 'exercised little direct control over this representation of herself' (p. 197).

Gráinne Ní Mháille, by contrast, is said to have extensively stage-managed her image when meeting Elizabeth in 1593. Siegfried's chapter assesses eighteenth- and nineteenth-century accounts of this meeting to interrogate the historiographical assembly of the Sea Queen of Connaught's legend. Siegfried locates the significance of Gráinne's folkloric eighteenth-century depiction in the 1751 Irish Tax Rebellion and 1793 French Revolution, a contextual backdrop which may have invited specific readers 'into the knowing circle of advocates for revolution in Ireland' (p. 245). It is beyond the *Year's Work*'s compass to comment on the accompanying imaginative prose, poetry, and drama, but the dialogue the volume encourages between critical and creative practice is instructive in all sorts of ways. Many of the creative pieces, too, focus on how past lives, particularly women's histories, are constructed: in the words of Erika Stevens in 'Grand Unified Theory' (pp. 51–4), how 'history is written by hegemonies of strong force that are often unkind to the smart, charismatic women we might have known as savvy or wily strategic planners— in the absence of the word *whore*' (p. 50). This is a story our field can and must tell, now more than ever.

## 2. Sidney

There were two issues of the *Sidney Journal* in 2015. The first, a special issue on William Scott's *The Model of Poesy*, begins with Gavin Alexander's article, 'Sidney, Scott, and the Proportions of Poetics' (*SidJ* 33:i[2015] 7–28).

Alexander's edition of Scott's *The Model of Poesy* [2013] is the stimulus for this special issue, and Alexander offers a useful introduction to the concerns of Scott's theory of poetry, as well as drawing out the significance of this approach for the study of Sidney's theory and practice. Scott's use of the word *proportion* is the particular focus, especially with respect to Scott's theoretical concern with 'the proportioning of poetry's parts to its wholes, and the proportionate arrangement—both conceptual and discursive—of poetics itself'. Alexander places Scott's approach in the context of other examples of early modern poetic theory, including Puttenham, Gascoigne, and Hoskyns, before concluding with Scott's equation of proportion with *decorum*: the 'decorous, analogical relatings of word to character to action, or mind to body to speech, or genre to verse form to occasion, or writing to painting that Sidney practices are illuminated by Scott's theory' (p. 7). This method is vividly demonstrated in Alexander's example from Book III of the revised *Arcadia*, where Cecropia is 'playing theatrical tricks on Pamela, Philoclea, and Pyrocles/Zelmane'. Here, in the responses of Cecropia's victims, Sidney makes 'an exemplary depiction of characters whose finely tuned ethical make-ups and profound mutual love can take them beyond tragedy into something that "stir[s] admiracion"' (p. 26; Alexander quotes John Hoskyns, *Directions for Speech and Style* [written *c*.1599], in Louise Brown Osborn, *The Life, Letters, and Writings of John Hoskyns, 1566–1638* [1937], p. 150).

Sarah Howe's article, '"Our Speaking Picture": William Scott's *Model of Poesy* and the Visual Imagination' (*SidJ* 33:i[2015] 29–67), continues this edition's examination of Scott's theory with respect to Sidney's 'alignment of poetry and painting'. Scott's approach is to draw together resources from Italian art theory—such as Giovanni Paolo Lomazzo's *Trattato dell'arte* [1584]—and ancient authorities such as Pliny and Quintilian, combining them into a 'pictorial poetics' that is peculiarly resonant with English poetry of the 1590s (p. 29). For Scott—who betrays a deep fascination for optics and optical metaphors—metaphors and allegories are 'like the period's perspective glasses, or trick mirrors, whose surfaces are tilted or curved in such a way that they do not reflect back exactly the same image they receive, but an altered or amplified one' (p. 43).

Peter Auger, in his article 'A Model of Creation? Scott, Sidney and Du Bartas' (*SidJ* 33:i[2015] 69–90), examines Scott's translation from Guillaume de Saluste Du Bartas's *La Sepmaine*, which follows Scott's *Model of Poesy* in the surviving manuscript. The two works have a great deal in common, as Auger delineates: 'images of making (e.g. gestation, architecture and agriculture) that describe the creation of poems in the *Model* and the creation of the world in Du Bartas evoke the analogy between the poetic maker and divine Maker' (p. 69). These aspects also occur, famously, in Sidney's *Defence of Poesy*. Interestingly, Du Bartas (in *La Sepmaine*) finds that 'mortal creation is incommensurable with divine creation' (p. 88), in contrast to 'the *Model*'s more positive assessment of the role of human reason in poetic composition' (p. 69). Nonetheless, for Auger, Scott's translation 'provides a model for how English poets can proceed given that insight into their deficiencies'. Moreover, given that Sidney is known to have begun a translation (now lost) of Du

Bartas's poetry, Scott's manuscript 'provides an outline for reading Du Bartas within Sidneian poetics' (p. 88).

Christian Anton Gerard's article, 'Within the Zodiac of Wit: Philip Sidney, William Scott, and the Right Reader Turned Right Poet' (*SidJ* 33:i[2015] 91–107), reads Scott's *Model of Poesy* as a continuation of, and evidence of the success of, Sidney's project (in his *Defence of Poesy*) to create an imagined community of right readers and right poets. Gerard sees Scott 'working alongside Sidney and incorporating the *Defence*'s trans-historical reading practices into his *Model*, thus making use of the English writing available to him that was not available to Sidney' (p. 91). In a highly persuasive argument, worth quoting at some length, Gerard shows that 'neither Scott nor Sidney wishes to produce a style manual or prescriptive formula for creating a certain kind of poet/poem, much less a certain sound practice in producing the material product of writing itself. For a William Scott following Philip Sidney's work, poetry's chief agent is its counter-factuality, its fictional world made from the poet's idea. The mental activity poetry produces is not to be used for reinforcing gentle or courtly doctrine, but for virtuous action. For Sidney, the difference between the poetry that upholds courtly decorum and the poetry that leads to virtuous action is that the poet un-attuned to the uses of reading and the "right" reason for making poetry "miss[es] the right use of the material point of Poesy"' (p. 103; Gerard quotes Sir Philip Sidney, *An Apology for Poetry (or The Defence of Poesy)*, ed. Geoffrey Shepherd, revised, edited, and expanded by R.W. Maslen [2002], p. 113).

Stuart Farley, in his article 'William Scott and Early Modern Prose Poetry' (*SidJ* 33:i[2015] 109–23), sees Scott theorizing a genre, prose poetry, that can be 'both prose with a poetic content, such as the Sidneian romance, as well as prose which approximates the measures of verse in the form of prose rhythms'. Drawing on Aristotle and Cicero, Scott (and Sidney) maintains that 'some instances of prose might be deemed to be poetic on account of their mimetic or fictive content, with verse being seen in such cases as merely incidental to the task of mimesis'. Scott, however, departs from Sidney 'in attributing to poetic prose certain formal qualities which are comparable to verse. The poem-in-prose, according to Scott, ought to aspire to "*concinnity*" [symmetry or 'tuneableness'] so as to impose form on the otherwise loose, open-ended sentences typical of prose as such' (p. 123).

The special issue concludes with Russ McDonald's short note, 'Great Scott' (*SidJ* 33:i[2015] 125–8), which summarizes the place of Scott's *Model of Poesy* in the artistic culture of its times. McDonald highlights 'Scott's determination to situate poetry among the several humanistic arts' (p. 126), and welcomes Scott as 'a valuable addition to the critical fellowship because he is an acute reader of Shakespeare—one of the first on record' (p. 128).

The second of the two issues of the *Sidney Journal* in 2015 includes three articles of interest here. The first, Roger Kuin's 'Hieroglyphics of Nobility: The Banners in Sir Philip Sidney's Funeral Procession' (*SidJ* 33:ii[2015] 1–25), examines the heraldry, both military and noble, of Thomas Lant's engravings of Sidney's funeral procession. Kuin decodes the heraldic symbols of the Ensign, the Guidon, the Standard, the Pennon, the Achievements, the Pall, the Bannerols, the Hearse, and the Pinnace. This is a detailed, informative, and highly suggestive piece of scholarship, which catalogues the relations and the affinities of the deceased knight as well as 'those relations that the survivors [the earl of Leicester, for example] wished to have known or emphasized' (p. 18).

I include two examples as illustration: the Ensign's 'imagery consists wholly of stars, probably silver, on a presumably blue background—in heraldic blazoning, this would be termed *azure, a semy of estoiles argent*—with the motto "Per Tenebras." This last is not especially original: usual phrases were "per tenebras ad lucem" (through darkness to light) or "per tenebras lucem quæro" (through darkness I seek the light) . . . In the Netherlands, then, we may imagine his regiment's companies . . . of foot carrying the large silk starry ensign with a motto of determination and hope: through darkness we will win through to light' (p. 5); the Guidon 'shows a fish with two eyes in the top of its head, the "uranoscopus" or Stargazer, lying on top of the water and looking at a starry sky. Of the motto, three words are visible: whether there were more is uncertain. What can be read is PULCHRUM PROPTER SE. "Pulcher," in this case, certainly does not mean "beautiful:" we need here to see the other meaning of the word, i.e. "noble" or "honorable." As 'The honorable (or: honor) for its own sake," the motto fits perfectly with Sidney's known other mottoes, "Vix ea nostra voco" (I hardly call these ours, meaning the famous deeds of ancestors), and "sic nos non nobis" (So we labor, but not for ourselves)' (p. 6).

Timothy D. Crowley's article, 'Diplomacy, Money, and Sidney's *Four Foster Children of Desire*' (*SidJ* 33:ii[2015] 27–60), examines Sidney's chivalric spectacle *The Four Foster Children of Desire* in the context of the poet's diplomatic career and financial affairs, with particular focus on the implications for Sidney of the second marriage of Robert Dudley, earl of Leicester. Crowley interprets the entertainment that Sidney presented to Elizabeth I as 'a multivalent symbolic appeal for financial aid that also conveyed an impression of political solidarity with both the queen and Leicester in condoning a political alliance with Anjou (marriage or no marriage)'. Building on the work of Steven May, who highlights little-known financial data ('Sir Philip Sidney and Queen Elizabeth', in Peter Beal and A.S.G. Edwards, eds., *English Manuscript Studies, 1100–1700*, vol. 2 [1990], pp. 257–68), Crowley presents 'a Sidney whose concern with his own financial debts revolved around how they affected his current and future political service: as a courtier who consistently enjoyed a high degree of royal favor, as a successful and esteemed ambassador, and (with Leicester) as a prospective military commander and political leader in the Netherlands' (p. 30).

Guillaume Coatalen, in 'Two Unpublished French Sonnets to Lady Sidney and Additional Verse by Anne de Rueil, a Huguenot Refugee' (*SidJ* 33:ii[2015] 61–80), examines, among other verse, two previously unknown sonnets addressed to Lady Frances Sidney (Philip's spouse) in French, written around 1590 by Anne de Rueil, a Huguenot refugee (see *Calendar of State Papers Domestic* 46: fos. 215–19). The article consists largely of an annotated bilingual edition of the verse as a whole (three sonnets and a complaint in total), but Coatalen also offers an insightful discussion of the author's background, the literary and political significance of the poems, and their importance for our understanding of 'the circulation of late sixteenth century

French political verse in England and cross-frontier female Protestant networks' (p. 61). In the collection as a whole, as well as exhorting the French nobility to support Henri IV, Rueil seeks to link herself, Lady Frances, Queen Elizabeth I, and the female allegory of France in 'a call to arms by women to women empowered by their faith' (pp. 79–80).

Away from the *Sidney Journal*, John Gouws, in 'Early Readers of Greville, *The Life of the Renowned Sir Philip Sidney* (1652)' (*N&Q* 62[2015] 595–7), discusses the initial reception of the 1652 publication of Greville's *Life of the Renowned Sir Philip Sidney*, with particular reference to Marchmont Nedham's reading, which co-opts Greville to the republican cause. Gouws, who is preparing a new edition of Greville's *Dedication to Sir Philip Sidney*, bemoans 'the lack of reader traction suffered by the [*Life*]' and asks readers of *Notes and Queries* if they, 'by way of serendipity, have encountered information which has eluded [him] over many years of research' (p. 597).

Andrew Hadfield's note, '"To Penshurst" and Sir Philip Sidney' (*ANQ* 28[2015] 21–2), alerts scholars to the echoes of Sidney's ninth sonnet of *Astrophil and Stella* in the opening lines of Jonson's poem. Hadfield sees Jonson referring to Sidney's sonnet sequence in order to signal his understanding that 'the grand houses associated with Sidneys were literary creations by great poets' rather than the trappings of new-found wealth. Jonson's reference to 'high-swol'n Medway' (l. 31) is a clever criticism of Jacobean arrivistes like Sir Robert Carr. This note is also considered in Chapter VIII, in the section on Jonson.

Robert E. Stillman, in 'Philip Sidney, Thomas More, and Table Talk: Texts/ Contexts' (*ELR* 45[2015] 323–50), asks why Philip Camerarius—a Protestant humanist who was part of the network of Continental humanists, jurists, and statesmen introduced to Sidney by his mentor Hubert Languet—introduced his Latin record of Sidney's table talk with an 'erudite celebration of Sir Thomas More', the famous Catholic martyr. Sidney's table talk, a disquisition on the absence of wolves from England, has often been 'read plainly' as 'a religious and political assault' against Roman Catholics (p. 324). Providing a large extract from Camerarius's *Operae horarum subcisivarum* (first published 1591; otherwise unavailable to English Renaissance scholars) and the relevant portion of John Molle's English translation of the *Operae* [1621], Stillman places the text in the context of the 'zealously moderate, ecumenically inclusive beliefs' shared by Camerarius, Languet, and Sidney, and familiar to those who have followed Stillman's assiduous work on Sidney's piety (see Stillman, *Philip Sidney and the Poetics of Renaissance Cosmopolitanism* [2008]). Along with his usual astute analysis, Stillman provides an extensive history of the text and its various incarnations, including the French translation of 1603 that excised the celebration of More; this was a surprising omission for the translator, Simon Goulart, whose ecumenical credentials rivalled those of Camerarius.

In his article, 'Friendship and Frustration: Counter-Affect in the Letters of Philip Sidney and Hubert Languet' (*TSLL* 57[2015] 412–32), Bradley J. Irish, in the light of the 'affective turn' in Renaissance studies, attempts to 'reassess the affective (and by extension, autobiographical) stakes of the Sidney/ Languet letters, with hopes of providing a more inclusive account of the correspondence's emotional architecture than has been offered by previous scholarship' (p. 412). Irish argues that the letters 'recall not only the conventions of classical friendship literature, but also the emotional fireworks of a sonnet sequence, primed with bitter ambivalence, latent aggression, and frustrated erotics'. He discovers 'the affective nodes that seem to challenge, subvert, or disrupt the overt aims of Sidney and Languet's epistolary relationship', highlighting 'the indirect operation of two competing frustrations: Languet's eroticized desire for his protégé, and Sidney's reciprocal struggle to escape his mentor's suffocating attention' (p. 413).

Samuel Fallon, in 'Astrophil, Philisides, and the Coterie in Print' (*ELR* 45[2015] 175–204), 'follows Sidney's personae from their origins in Sidney's own writings into their complicated textual afterlives'. Initially, Philisides and Astrophil 'seemed to mediate between an in-group of privileged readers and a larger world of outsiders, hinting at a subtext of biographical secrets that they nonetheless withheld from all but the most familiar audiences'. Nevertheless, in Fallon's reading, once the works were transferred to print, these personae 'offered themselves as a way to recover the exclusivity that the texts seemed to have lost': 'their invocation and reanimation in a range of epigrams, elegies, prefatory epistles, and pastoral romances' appear to be 'attempts to imagine Sidney once again as a poet of the coterie'. Matthew Roydon's 'An Elegie, or friends passion, for his Astrophill. Written vpon the death of the right Honorable sir Philip Sidney knight, Lord gouernor of Flushing', found in the quarto of Spenser's *Colin Clouts Come Home Againe* [1595], is one example, within a volume that 'convened a pastoral cast' of its own personae: Spenser's Colin, the shepherds Thestylis and Lycon, and Mary Sidney's alter ego, Clorinda. For Fallon, 'the poets in the volume used [Sidney's] personae to recall the scene of restricted production in which his poetry had originated, producing in its place a fictional coterie that was centered on Sidney, constituted in print, and projected before the reading public' (pp. 178–9).

Micha Lazarus, in 'Sidney's Greek *Poetics*' (*SP* 112[2015] 504–36), argues that—contrary to the view that sixteenth-century English readers such as Sidney had negligible access to Aristotle's *Poetics*—a passage of Sidney's *Defence* was directly translated from the *Poetics*. In an extensive philological analysis Lazarus suggests that 'Sidney's source was the Greek itself', offering a new model for assessing English encounters with this foundational classical text (p. 504).

Beginning with the observation that 'the biblical Psalm 139 is sewn up in images of needlework' (pp. 650–1), Michele Osherow's article in the *Renaissance Studies* special issue on the psalms (the remaining articles from which are reviewed in Section 1 of this chapter and in Chapter V), 'Mary Sidney's Embroidered Psalms' (*RS* 29[2015] 650–70), 'examines ways in which the Sidney psalms demonstrate an intertextual play between pen and needle'. For Osherow, in translating the psalms into English, Mary Sidney 'adorns holy articles by hand': the translations are 'linguistic embroidery of the biblical poems' characterized by 'Attention to colours and to cunning, to ornamentation and to pattern' (p. 652).

R.H. Winnick's note, 'An Onomastic Anagram in Sidney's *Astrophel and Stella*' (*N&Q* 62[2015] 551–3), identifies an example of onomastic wordplay in the penultimate line of *Astrophel and Stella*'s first sonnet. Winnick observes that 'the eight letters needed to form Lady Rich's given name [Penelope] . . . are sequentially dilated across the line': 'Byting my trewand PENnE, beating my seLfe fOr sPitE' (pp. 551–2).

Richard Wood's essay, ' "She made her courtiers learned": Sir Philip Sidney, the *Arcadia* and Step-Dame Elizabeth' (in Bamford and Miller, eds., *Maternity and Romance Narratives in Early Modern England*, pp. 49–73), examines Sidney's use of the popular trope of the cruel stepmother in the *Arcadia*. Helen of Corinth, a figure introduced in the revised *Arcadia*, serves as an image of Queen Elizabeth as ideal surrogate mother to the nation. Through the skilful deployment of his own education, Sidney casts Elizabeth as the learned monarch—in the *Arcadia* and his 'Letter to Queen Elizabeth'—who makes 'her courtiers learned', thus arrogating to himself the role of court counsellor (*The Countess of Pembroke's Arcadia (The New Arcadia)*, ed. Victor Skretkowicz [1987], p. 253). This essay follows Wood's earlier contribution to a collection on Robert Devereux, earl of Essex (' "Cleverly playing the stoic": The Earl of Essex, Sir Philip Sidney and Surviving Elizabeth's Court', in Annaliese Connolly and Lisa Hopkins, eds., *Essex: The Cultural Impact of an Elizabethan Courtier* [2013], pp. 25–46), in which Wood argues that Essex, often regarded as Sidney's literary, chivalric, and political heir, may also have inherited a pragmatic approach to political counsel suggested by a particular reading of the *Arcadia*. If the revised *Arcadia* is read in line with the philosophy of Sidney's sister, the countess of Pembroke— influenced by Philippe Duplessis-Mornay, a close ally of both Sidney and the countess—rather than the Tacitean philosophy of Fulke Greville, the philosophical outlook that Essex and his circle inherited from Sidney takes on a new conciliatory tone. A further two essays from Bamford and Miller's collection are discussed in the following section on Spenser.

Anne-Valérie Dulac's essay, 'Hilliard and Sidney's "Rule of the Eye" ' (in Chiari, ed., *The Circulation of Knowledge in Early Modern English Literature*, pp. 59–69), considers the relationship between Sidney's written work and Nicholas Hilliard's painting, an association that might have included personal tuition for the former from the latter in the art of limning. Dulac draws on Hilliard's own treatise, *The Art of Limning*, and Sidney's revised *Arcadia* to suggest that Sidney not only coined the word 'miniature' with reference to a small-scale representation under the influence of Hilliard, but also inaugurated a new kind of 'gentle sensuality' in his prose romance that can be traced to the miniaturist's art (pp. 65, 69).

A major publication in Sidney studies in 2015 was the two-volume *Ashgate Research Companion to the Sidneys, 1500–1700*, edited by Margaret P. Hannay, Michael G. Brennan and Mary Ellen Lamb. Volume 1 is subtitled *Lives* and, besides the extremely useful chronology, Sidney family tree, and high-quality illustrations, contains five sections: Part I, 'Overview'; Part II, 'Biographies'; Part III, 'The Sidneys in Ireland and Wales'; Part IV, 'The Sidneys and the Continent'; and Part V, 'The Sidneys and the Arts'. Part I, by Michael G. Brennan, covers the family networks of the Sidneys, Dudleys, and Herberts (pp. 3–19), and, like the other sections in these densely packed and highly authoritative volumes, includes helpful lists of manuscript, primary, and secondary sources. Part II, 'Biographies' (pp. 21–176), has generously proportioned biographies of an almost exhaustive list of the major figures in the aforementioned networks: 'Sir Henry Sidney (1529–86)', by Valerie McGowan-Doyle; 'Mary Dudley Sidney (c.1531–86) and Her Siblings', by Carole Levin and Catherine Medici; 'Philip Sidney (1554–86)', by Alan Stewart; 'Mary Sidney Herbert (1561–1621), Countess of Pembroke', by Margaret P. Hannay; 'Those Essex Girls: The Lives and Letters of Lettice Knollys, Penelope Rich, Dorothy Perrott Percy, and Frances Walsingham', by Grace Ioppolo; 'The Life of Robert Sidney (1563–1626), First Earl of Leicester', by Robert Shephard; 'Barbara Gamage Sidney (c.1562–1621), Countess of Leicester, Elizabeth Sidney Manners (1585–1612), Countess of Rutland, and Lady Mary Sidney Wroth (1587–1651)', by Margaret P. Hannay; 'Robert Sidney (1595–1677), Second Earl of Leicester', by Germaine Warkentin; 'A Triptych of Dorothy Percy Sidney (1598–1659), Countess of Leicester, Lucy Percy Hay (1599–1660), Countess of Carlisle, and Dorothy Sidney Spencer (1617–84), Countess of Sunderland', by Nadine Akkerman; 'Algernon Sidney's Life and Works (1623–83)', by Jonathan Scott; and 'Henry Sidney (1641–1704), Earl of Romney, and Robert Spencer (1641–1702), Second Earl of Sunderland', by Michael G. Brennan. Part III, 'The Sidneys in Ireland and Wales' (pp. 177–200), contains 'The Sidneys in Ireland', by Thomas Herron, and 'The Sidneys and Wales', by Willy Maley and Philip Schwyzer. Part IV, 'The Sidneys and the Continent' (pp. 201–38), contains 'The Sidneys and the Continent: The Tudor Period', by Roger Kuin, and 'The Sidneys and the Continent: The Stuart Period', by Michael G. Brennan. Part V, 'The Sidneys and the Arts' (pp. 239–327), contains: 'The Sidneys and Public Entertainments', by Arthur F. Kinney; 'The Sidneys and Literary Patronage', by Lisa Celovsky; 'Penshurst Place and Leicester House', by Susie West; 'The Sidneys and the Visual Arts', by Elizabeth Goldring; and 'The Sidneys and Music', by Katherine R. Larson.

Volume 2 is subtitled *Literature* and contains eight sections: Part I, 'Overview'; Part II, 'The Sidneys and the Circulation of Their Works in Manuscript and Print'; Part III, 'Prose Romance'; Part IV, 'Prose'; Part V, 'Drama'; Part VI, 'Poetry'; Part VII, 'Psalms'; and Part VIII, 'Conclusion'. Part I (pp. 1–20), is entitled 'The Sidneys and Their Books', and is written by Joseph L. Black. Part II, 'The Sidneys and the Circulation of Their Works in Manuscript and Print' (pp. 21–85), contains: 'The Circulation of the Sidney Psalter', by Noel J. Kinnamon; 'The Circulation of Sir Philip Sidney's *Arcadia*', by H.R. Woudhuysen; 'The Circulation of Writings by Mary Sidney Herbert, Countess of Pembroke', by Garth Bond; and 'The Circulation of Writings by Lady Mary Wroth', by Ilona Bell. Part III, 'Prose Romance' (pp. 87–149), contains: 'Sir Philip Sidney's *Arcadias*', by Kenneth Borris; 'Continuations and Imitations of the *Arcadia*', by Clare R. Kinney; and 'Lady Mary Sidney Wroth: *The Countess of Montgomery's Urania*', by Helen Hackett. Part IV, 'Prose' (pp. 151–95), contains: 'Sir Philip Sidney: *The Defence of Poesy*', by Robert E. Stillman; 'Tudor Political Theory and Sidneian Prose', by Joel B. Davis; and 'Mary Sidney Herbert, Countess of Pembroke: *A Discourse of Life and Death*', by Elaine V. Beilin. Part V, 'Drama' (pp. 197–221), contains: 'Mary Sidney Herbert, Countess of Pembroke: *Antonius* (1592)', by Barry Weller, and 'Lady Mary Wroth:

*Love's Victory*, by Alison Findlay. Part VI, 'Poetry' (pp. 223–79), contains: 'Sir Philip Sidney: *Astrophil and Stella*', by Danila Sokolov; 'Robert Sidney's Poetry', by Mary B. Moore; 'Lady Mary Wroth's Poetry', by Paul Salzman; and 'The Poetry of William Herbert, Third Earl of Pembroke', by Mary Ellen Lamb. Part VII, 'Psalms' (pp. 281–329), contains: 'Sir Philip Sidney's Psalms', by Anne Lake Prescott; 'The Psalms of Mary Sidney Herbert, Countess of Pembroke', by Danielle Clarke; and 'The Influence of the Sidney Psalter', by Hannibal Hamlin. Part VIII, 'Conclusion' (pp. 331–40), is entitled 'Future Directions for Sidney Studies', and written by Mary Ellen Lamb. This last section, like the other sections in these volumes, offers a number of opportunities for future study, all based on a strong sense of the variety of illuminating work that has been produced in this rich area of scholarship to date.

## 3. Spenser

Tara E. Pedersen's monograph *Mermaids and the Production of Knowledge in Early Modern England* contains a chapter entitled 'Perfect Pictures: The Mermaid's Half-Theater and the Anti-Theatrical Debates in Book II of Spenser's *The Faerie Queene*' (pp. 81–99). Pedersen's book is largely devoted to theatrical examples, but notably finds that Spenser's *Faerie Queene* 'calls into question the distinction between written and performed modes of artistic representation as it asks its reader to consider the transformative impact these varied forms of art have on the individual and society' (p. 83). Turning away from a discussion of 'how the mermaid engages questions of identity and agency as they pertain to a specific character or individual', in this chapter Pedersen focuses her readers' attention 'on the text itself as mermaid' (p. 82). Book II of Spenser's *The Faerie Queene* is read in the context of the contemporary anti-theatrical debates. Aware of scholars' tendency to look in the works of Lodge and Sidney for responses to anti-theatrical texts, Pedersen's reading, in which Spenser is seen to present 'an unusual defense of hybrid, mermaid-like, genres of art and the breaking down of social distinctions', is an intriguing intervention in a well-established field of scholarship. As Pedersen observes, 'Although Guyon attacks, with "rigour pittiless," the "goodly workmanship" of Acrasia's Bower, the mermaids, whose "half theatre" Guyon encounters on his Odyssean journey to the Bower ... arguably remain untouched within the world of the poem' (p. 83; *FQ* II.xii.83, 30).

Cyrus Moore's 2014 monograph, *Love, War, and Classical Tradition in the Early Modern Transatlantic World: Alonso de Ercilla and Edmund Spenser*, compares the employment of classical motifs in two early modern texts: Alonso de Ercilla's Chilean epic, *La Araucana* [1569–89], and Spenser's *The Faerie Queene*. Moore focuses on what he calls the 'venerable imagery of confrontation between love and strife', and two key images in particular for which Homer is an important source: 'the abandoned woman, enacted by Nausikaa in the episode of Odysseus among the Phaeacians (*Od.* 8.460 ff.), and the night raid, conducted by Odysseus and Diomedes during the Trojan war (*Il.* 10.252 ff.)' (p. 30). These images figure differently in the different texts. In the *Araucana*, they are invoked literally at points 'where attention shifts from the traditionally masculine world of conflict and violence to the ostensibly feminine concerns of beauty and chastity'. In *The Faerie Queene*, they are more often invoked figuratively, 'where conflict is as often psychomachic as physical and the distinctions between opposing forces more likely blur into unsettling similarities between the virtues and their opposites' (p. 33). This sensitivity to the complexity of Spenser's method is a welcome feature of Moore's discussion, and Moore offers an insightful reading of Spenser as following, while also significantly expanding the scope of, the allegorical practices of those who preceded him. For Moore, *The Faerie Queene* 'draws on multiple models, ancient, medieval, and early modern, native and imported, the separate identities of which are maintained and even accentuated rather than being subsumed in a newly unified product' (p. 142). Ercilla's *Araucana* manifests a comparable hybridity, but, whereas Ercilla performs 'a *renovatio* of classical epic, Petrarchism, and courtly discourse, with the last applied to the first to effect a real-life lesson in gallantry and the courtly defense of female virtue', Spenser stages 'nothing less than the *transformatio* of these traditions through reformed religion' (p. 144).

The Manchester Spenser series published by Manchester University Press added two publications in 2015. The first, Christopher Burlinson and Andrew Zurcher's edition of Ralph Knevet's *A Supplement of the Faery Queene*, will be invaluable to scholars interested in Spenser's reception in the early seventeenth century; Knevet completed his three-book continuation in 1635. As the editors note, 'Knevet's conformity to the Spenserian model . . . runs both broad and deep' (p. 10). He retains the formal presentation of *The Faerie Queene*, he writes in Spenserian stanzas, prefaces each canto with an argument in the same style as Spenser, and composed a preface in the style of Spenser's *Letter to Raleigh*. Knevet's poem is, however, much less complex than Spenser's, its author 'preferring instead the simpler, linear narrative of a single knight whose serial adventures illustrate philosophical and historical aspects of the virtue relevant to the book'; Knevet adds prudence, fortitude, and liberality to Spenser's six virtues (pp. 11–12). Stylistically, Knevet deviates from what the editors term 'Spenser's visual forms of representation': the 'use of emblem, ekphrasis, pageant, and other highly visual techniques'. Knevet's representations are generally 'tightly controlled presentations' that 'allude to well-established properties, which in turn are immediately moralized and applied'. This is in clear contrast to the 'association in Spenser's poetry between visual imagination and a complex play of ambiguity' (p. 21).

The second publication from the Manchester Spenser series, Maik Goth's *Monsters and the Poetic Imagination in The Faerie Queene: 'Most Ugly Shapes, and Horrible Aspects'*, furthers Goth's reading of Spenser as Prometheus, already highlighted in his article, 'Spenser as Prometheus: The Monstrous and the Idea of Poetic Creation' (*Connotations* 18[2008/9] 183–206). Divided into four parts—Part I, ' "Complicated Monsters Head and Tail": A Primer in Spenser, Monsters, and Teratology' (pp. 7–38); Part II, 'Reading the Monster: Taxonomy' (pp. 39–196); Part III, 'Making Monsters: The Monstrous Imagination and the Poet's Autonomy in *The Faerie Queene*' (pp. 197–313);

and Part IV, 'Conclusions' (pp. 315–19)—this highly original monograph places *The Faerie Queene* in the context of the monstrous, including: historical assessments of the monstrous; literary perspectives on the monstrous (including, more specifically, a survey of Spenser criticism with respect to monsters); a whole part devoted to a taxonomy of monsters; and a further part on the monstrous and the poetic imagination (including Spenser as Prometheus). Goth more than achieves his explicitly stated aim to 'analyse monsters and monstrous beings as signs interacting with the early modern discourse on the poet creating a secondary nature through the use of his transformative imagination, and as ciphers that need to be interpreted by the reader' (p. 2).

Karen Bamford and Naomi J. Miller's essay collection, *Maternity and Romance Narratives in Early Modern England* (also discussed in Section 2 above), contains two essays that focus on Spenser. Susan C. Staub's 'While She Was Sleeping: Spenser's "Goodly Storie" of Chrysogone' (pp. 13–31), reads Book III, canto vi of *The Faerie Queene*, in which Chrysogone gives birth to twins through a miraculous, asexual process, beside the Garden of Adonis, which immediately follows the story of Chrysogone. The 'asexual impregnation would seem to evade some of the commonplace anxieties about the maternal body' (p. 22). Nonetheless, Spenser's garden offers 'a consoling space where the land as maternal body can be manipulated'; 'just as the land must be husbanded ... so too, the maternal body must be managed' (pp. 28, 29). Anne-Marie Strohman's essay, 'Deferred Motherhood in Spenser's *The Faerie Queene*' (pp. 33–48), finds Britomart to be a more acceptable image of power to Spenser when she is disguised as a knight than she would be as a figure of maternity. As such, Britomart's maternity is continually delayed: 'Only by deferring Britomart's destiny can Spenser avoid both the maternal body and the anxiety of maternal authority' (p. 46).

Gordon Teskey's essay, 'The Thinking of History in Spenserian Romance' (in Whitman, ed., *Romance and History: Imagining Time from the Medieval to the Early Modern Period*, pp. 214–27), addresses the need, as he sees it, for 'better terms than the philosophical ones, *subject* and *object*', when we speak of 'objective historical study' and 'the subjective deployment of principles inherent to narrative'. This is especially so when considering 'how a poet such as Edmund Spenser can develop in narrative romance an immanent thinking of history that is comparable to the thought-work—that conceptual grasping from within—which Hegel sees taking place in history' (pp. 214–15). Teskey suggests replacing *subject* with *poiesis*, and *object* with *the other*, 'Something other within the work of art—a living, narrative voice, a speaking face, a heterocosm or fictional world, a hidden meaning' (p. 216). Of the genres that 'converge' in *The Faerie Queene*—allegory, epic, and romance—Teskey sees romance as 'the least suitable for thinking about history' (p. 218). Nonetheless, 'employing the conventions and stock situations of romance narrative', Spenser compresses past events, bringing them together 'incongruously ... with respect to historical time, but also with respect to decorum—entangling them in poetic thinking'. For Spenser, 'the historical "ruins" or "collapses" into the present and is there all around the poet ... to be excavated and meddled with now' (p. 223).

Elisabeth Chaghafi's article, '"Astrophel" and Spenser's 1595 Quarto' (*EIRC* 41[2015] 149–77), reads Spenser's 'Astrophel' in its original published context in an attempt to overcome the misconceptions of many earlier scholars, whose readings have been affected by the poem's decontextualization; rather than read it as an 'oddly unsuccessful elegy', Chaghafi prefers to highlight the 'shared characters, shared setting and the shared concept of the "sheapheards nation"' of the various contents of the 1595 quarto often referred to as *Colin Clouts Come Home Againe* (p. 150). Spenser places Colin Clout, his own alter ego, 'at the centre of the chorus of shepherds mourning Astrophel [Philip Sidney's alter ego]', thus 'declaring himself to be heir to the role of chief poet' and showing 'an acute awareness' of the fictional process by which such a poet emerges (pp. 172–3). Here, Chaghafi builds on the work of Richard McCabe, who notably observed that 'Spenser is given to "auto-fabrication"' (p. 173; see McCabe, *Edmund Spenser: The Shorter Poems* [1999], p. xvii).

Benjamin Parris, in his article '"Watching to banish Care": Sleep and Insomnia in Book 1 of *The Faerie Queene*' (*MP* 113[2015] 151–77), challenges the claims of Deborah Shuger and Northrop Frye (Shuger, '"Gums of glutinous heat" and the Stream of Consciousness: The Theology of Milton's *Maske*', *Rep* 60[1997] 1–21; Frye, *Fables of Identity: Studies in Poetic Mythology* [1963]) that sleep 'vexes Redcrosse as well as the author's Reformed political theology in book 1' (p. 151). Parris argues that sleep is merely 'a temporary and minor threat to [Redcrosse's] spiritual fortitude', and that Spenser sees insomnia 'as a greater threat to his well-being and his spiritual virtue'. Paradoxically, 'to sleep means to relax one's conscious guard against the forces of darkness and sin, but not to sleep means to refuse a crucial form of physiological and spiritual recovery that temporarily lifts the burden of worldly cares' (pp. 152–3).

William Palmer, in 'The Problem of Ideology in the Elizabethan Conquest of Ireland: A Comparative Approach?' (*NewHibR* 19:iii[2015] 128–42), looks at the role that ideology plays in the causal explanations of historical events. More specifically, Palmer interrogates whether certain courses of action were in fact influenced by certain texts that may or may not have been read by the historical agents involved. Of particular interest here is Palmer's discussion of 'the ideological importance [or otherwise] of such works as Edmund Spenser's *A View of the Present State of Ireland* for the 'governance' of Ireland in the Elizabethan period (p. 129). Palmer engages with Ciaran Brady's book *The Chief Governors: The Rise and Fall of Reform Government in Tudor Ireland, 1536–1588* [1994], questioning Brady's understanding of the role of ideology. Brady considers ideology 'to be almost superfluous to the story [of the English in Ireland]', dismissing ideological works often cited by historians, such as Spenser's *View*, as conventional, ambiguous, and contradictory (p. 133). For Palmer, contrary to Brady's interpretation, 'Historical actors do not read texts necessarily for their coherence and consistency. Nor does a text have to be original to be influential. Historical actors read to extract useful ideas and justifications for behaviors they are either pursuing or contemplating' (p. 135). Just as 'those who opposed aspects of royal policy from 1640–2 or who took up arms against the crown after the outbreak of civil war ... did not have to agree about why it should be done', the English in Ireland found 'justifications for conquest, violence, and extralegal behavior that could be extracted and tailored to fit the ideological needs of a range of people' (p. 141). For Palmer, Spenser's *A View of the Present State of Ireland* should be read in this context.

Sarah Van der Laan, in 'Songs of Experience: Confessions, Penitence, and the Value of Error in Tasso and Spenser' (*PMLA* 130[2015] 252–68), finds Spenser engaging with his near-contemporary Torquato Tasso on the subject of penance in order to 'expose and critique the void left by the English Reformers' rejection of penance'. Building on the work of previous scholars— who have 'long debated the sacramental theology of book 1 of *The Faerie Queene*, whose house of Holiness offers a model for a moderate reformation of penance into an efficacious penitential practice that enables Redcrosse Knight to overcome and learn from his errors'—Van der Laan focuses, for the most part, on Book II, where 'the moderate sacramental landscape of book 1 is reformed so completely that neither Catholic penance nor Reformed penitence retains its efficacy' (p. 253). Spenser, 'patterning Guyon's career on Tasso's narrative [from *Gerusalemme liberata*]', 'uses his Catholic predecessor to critique the fears and paradoxes he sees as born of a strict Calvinist ethos' (p. 254). Spenser depicts Catholic sacramental penance as 'a removal of sin *effected* through acts of penance rather than an interior motion of grace outwardly *represented* by acts of penitence'. In Book I, the amends Redcrosse makes for his errors 'enable a final heroic achievement that is available to Guyon [in Book II] only as long as he makes no errors at all'. For Van der Laan, Spenser shows 'the barrenness of an epic poetics reformed along the lines of book 2, the dangers to literature of seeing all human work as infused with sin' (pp. 265–6).

Brent Dawson's article, 'Making Sense of the World: Allegory, Globalization, and *The Faerie Queene*' (*NLH* 46[2015] 165–86), starts with the premise that 'Representations of the world or of world-making processes, whether in popular culture or in the social sciences, actively reshape the world, but they always sit at some distance from the world as it is.' As such, in Dawson's view, literary criticism 'needs to take account of [the] tension between the world as idea and as thing'. With reference to two examples of the 'Spenserian allegory of the world as a harmonious chain', the allegory of Concord in Book IV and the Cave of Mammon canto, Dawson argues that 'Spenser's poem reflects on the violence and disruption inherent in trying to bring the world together into a single allegorical system'. Spenser, who has 'often been read as a poet deeply nostalgic for what he sees as a fading medieval worldview ... shows [particularly in the Cave of Mammon canto] how medieval allegory continues to inform modern paradigms of global commerce' (p. 166).

Andrew Hadfield, in his article 'The Death of the Knight with the Scales and the Question of Justice in *The Faerie Queene*'(*EIC* 65[2015] 12–29), notes the critical consensus that Spenser's Book of Justice, published in the second edition of *The Faerie Queene* [1596], is rather distressing for readers. The poem takes us into 'areas where it is hard to know *what* we should think of the awful things that Artegall is doing' (p. 12). Nonetheless, Hadfield encourages critics to look again at this passage, one of 'the darkest sections of [Spenser's] work',

not least because in the Book of Justice the poet's 'analysis of justice and law
... may appear upon investigation more astute than is habitually thought'
(p. 13). Taking particular issue with John Carey's view of Spenser as guilty of
'craven power-worship' (see Carey, *The Unexpected Professor: An Oxford Life
in Books* [2014], p. 107), Hadfield finds that, on the contrary, for Spenser, 'the
problem of contemporary justice seems to lie with executive authority, which is
unbalanced and actually contains elements of injustice' (p. 21): 'It is no wonder
that Artegall cannot cope with the tasks he has been set: he does not know how
to read the icons of justice adequately ... Knights will inevitably make terrible
errors when their queen cannot confront the reality of the stony age' (p. 27).

Andrew Wadoski, in 'Spenser, Harvey, and the Strange Poetics of *The
Shepheardes Calender*' (*CollL* 42[2015] 420–41), examines *The Shepheardes
Calender* with reference to Sidney's critique of Spenser's 'little book' of poems:
'framing of his stile to an old rustick language, I dare not alowe: since neither
Theocritus in Greeke, Virgill in Latine, nor Sanazar in Italian did affect it' (*An
Apologie for Poetry* [1595], p. 64). Wadoski characterizes Sidney's objection
thus: 'in affecting "an old rusticke style," the *Calender*'s poet practices an
overly inclusive mimetic mode that necessarily distances him from the
metaphysically pre-existent ideas and ideals of those Plotinian "Reason-
Principles" that are the basis for, and ultimate justification of, poetic imitation
itself' (p. 423). And it is notable that, in the poems' glosses, 'E.K.'s description
of the English vernacular's rhetorical force notably dispenses with the notion
that transcendent ideals animate and sustain a poem. Rather, poetry's
conceptual power depends on its juxtaposing the varied forms of imitation and
invention' (p. 424). On the basis of this distinction, and effecting a useful
reappraisal of the literary reputation of Gabriel Harvey—no longer the man
whom Thomas Nashe satirized as a 'Pedantius' (p. 424; see Nashe's *Have With
You to Saffron Walden* [1596])—Wadoski is able to make a persuasive case for
reading Spenser's poems 'as embodying the principles of experimental self-
regard displayed in the margins of Harvey's *Courtyer*' (Harvey's annotated
copy of Thomas Hoby's *Courtyer of Count Baldessar Castilio* [1561]); The
*Shepheardes Calender*'s 'playful projection of Spenser and Harvey into various
personae'—'Spenser as Immerito, the New Poet, and Colin Clout; and Harvey
as both the Socratic master and the pastoral fiction, Hobbinol'—corroborates
Wadoski's contention (p. 432).

Andrew Wadoski also contributed a note on Spenser to *Notes & Queries* in
2015: 'Which Edition of Homer Did Spenser Read?' (*N&Q* 62[2015] 74–7).
Wadoski points to evidence that suggests Spenser might have used 'the 1583
commentary and parallel column Greek–Latin edition of Homer compiled by
the French Huguenot poet, jurist, and scholar Jean de Sponde from Andreus
Divus' 1537 Latin translation' (p. 76).

James D. Mardock's note from the same edition of *Notes & Queries*,
'The "Table" of Belphoebe's Forehead, *Faerie Queene* II.iii.24' (*N&Q* 62[2015]
72–4), corrects two misconceptions about the passage in question. Contrary to
the standard interpretation, in which Belphoebe's forehead is considered a
surface for painting, Mardock finds that it is a surface for writing: 'a
distinction central to Spenser's treatment of art, nature, and poesis—since
Love is explicitly considered to "engraue" his triumphs, and "write" his

battles, not to paint them' (pp. 72–3). The second error is 'the assumption that Love has already inscribed this table, written his battles, and engraved his triumphs on Belphoebe's forehead'. Conventionally, 'these inscriptions are to be distinguished from the actions of the "blinded god", who can kindle lust in her eyes' "rash beholders" (23.5), but fails in his attempts to do so in her eyes themselves'. Mardock points out that, actually, 'nothing in the diction indicates that Spenser has switched from the bad Cupid who fails in stanza 23 to a more positive, more successful version in stanza 24' (p. 73).

Rick Bowers's note, 'Harington's *Metamorphosis of Ajax* and Spenser's *Faerie Queene*' (*N&Q* 62[2015] 77–9), considers Harington's 'lukewarm' praise of *The Faerie Queene*: 'thirdly they descanted of the new Faerie Queene & the old both, and the greatest fault they could find in it, was that the last verse disordered their mouthes, and was like a trick of xvii in a sinkapace' (*The Metamorphosis of Ajax*, ed. Elizabeth Story Donno [1962], p. 207). The 'trick of xvii in a sinkapace' alludes to 'Spenser's use of the extra-footed alexandrine line' (p. 77). Perhaps more significantly, Bowers highlights Harington's 'tone of cheerful un-seriousness that is somewhat ridiculous but constantly entertaining at a curiously informative level of intelligence'. And we are reminded that 'Harington wants to be "thought of and talked of"' like Spenser'; and that, in the *Metamorphosis of Ajax*, where 'Harington, the courtier who would be a poet, meets Spenser, the poet who would be a courtier', the point is 'not about specific authorial intentions but about placement and effect, as well as about parody and self-promotion—two things at which Sir John Harington excelled' (p. 79; Bowers cites *Letters and Epigrams of Sir John Harington*, ed. N.E. McClure [1930], p. 66).

Julia MacDonald's article, 'Keeping Time in Spenser and Shakespeare: The Temporality of Spenserian Stanza and Shakespearean Blank Verse' (*BJJ* 22[2015] 83–100), analyses 'the contribution of the metrical and stanzaic form to the sense of time characteristic of Spenser's *Faerie Queene* and Shakespeare's drama'. MacDonald argues that 'Spenserian stanza and Shakespearean blank verse are constitutive of the reader's experience of time in significantly different ways': they present 'a foundational experience of each poet's sense of time as these are being elaborated on the increasingly conscious levels of plot and metaphor'; the 'Spenserian temporal imaginary ... is slow and cyclic, with a trajectory toward eternity', and the 'Shakespearean temporal imaginary ... is urgent and temporally precarious' (p. 84).

Andrew Smyth's essay, 'Impersonating Authority: Animals and the Anglo-Irish Social Order in Maria Edgeworth's *Ennui* and Edmund Spenser's *Mother Hubberds Tale*' (in Kirkpatrick and Faragó, eds., *Animals in Irish Literature and Culture*, pp. 135–48), is primarily concerned with Edgeworth's nineteenth-century fiction, but does offer a useful insight into the reception of Spenser's *Mother Hubberds Tale*. As Smyth notes, 'Edgeworth's intertextual engagement with Spenser ... represents an active attempt to critique the Elizabethan foundations of Anglo-Irish dominance' (p. 136). Smyth finds Edgeworth 'looking back over the colonial past for two purposes: to ascertain the problematic origins of English control and management of Ireland up to and continuing in her time, and to lay out possible solutions for Anglo-Irish relations with the indigenous Irish that would remain consistent with

Enlightenment principles of politics and economics'. Edgeworth's engagement with Spenser 'led her to a profound reconceptualization of social justice in Ireland away from the Ascendancy model developed during the seventeenth and eighteenth centuries, one that is mediated through human–animal relations in the literature of her adopted Irish home' (p. 137).

This year's volume of *Spenser Studies* is entitled 'Spenser and "the Human"'. It is divided into six sections, five of which end with a short response to the articles contained therein. Section I is entitled 'A Dialogue on Method'. It contains two articles, the first of which is Ayesha Ramachandran's 'Humanism and Its Discontents' (*SSt* 30[2015] 3–18). Ramachandran 'argues for a reappraisal of "humanism" as a philosophical tradition and suggests how the history of "the human" in the early modern period already contains its postmodern and posthumanist unraveling'. In this reappraisal, Spenser plays, for Ramachandran, an 'emblematic role' as a poet who 'anticipates a theory of distributed cognition in which the human is but one among many actors, one of which is literary figuration itself'. The effects of Spenser's 'merging of allegory and history in the chronicles of *The Faerie Queene*' 'make us wonder ... about the place and position of the human, who both makes these worlds and succumbs to their power' (pp. 3, 14–15). The second article, Melissa E. Sanchez's 'Posthumanist Spenser?' (*SSt* 30[2015] 19–31), delineates the 'key insights of the various schools of posthumanist theory (animal studies, ecocriticism and environmental studies, cyborg theory, actor-network theory [ANT], speculative realism [SR], object-oriented ontology [OOO], vitalism, thing theory)', before noting Spenser's place in this field of study (p. 19). For Sanchez, Spenser's qualities—'his benighted colonial politics; magical and estranging worlds; intricate stanzas; and willfully archaic vocabularies, spellings, and generic codes'—'help us to rethink the received history of enlightenment and progress that shape our work'. Posthumanism, in this understanding of it, teaches us that 'what frightens us with its unfamiliarity or inassimilability to who "we" are exercises no less power over us than that which attracts and comforts us with the illusion of sameness' (p. 27).

Section II is entitled 'Human Limits'. It contains three articles and a response. The first article, William A. Oram's 'Human Limitation and Spenserian Laughter' (*SSt* 30[2015] 35–56), looks at the treatment of characters in *The Faerie Queene* who attempt to transcend their humanity, such as Timias and Belphoebe in Book III, or those who fall below it, such as Sans Loy in Book I and Malbecco in Book III. The characters are mocked in comic episodes that 'insist on the limits of human possibility', and the narrator seems to assume 'godlike control of the poem'. Nonetheless, Spenser mocks his own attempt to know divine truth through the figure of Faunus in the *Mutabilitie Cantos*, whose foolishness is presented as the natural human condition (pp. 35, 52). Tullia Giersberg's article, ' "The art of mightie words, that men can charme": Language, Reason, and Humanity in *The Faerie Queene*' (*SSt* 30[2015] 57–74), examines the meaning of what Calidore in Book VI describes as 'inhumanitie' (VI.i.26, 9). Spenser seems to suggest, as in the *Letter to Raleigh*, that to be human is, in part, to be '*a gentleman or noble person in vertuous and gentle discipline*' (*Letter to Raleigh*, in *The Faerie Queene*, ed. A.C. Hamilton, Hiroshi Yamashita, and Toshiyuki Suzuki, rev.

2nd edn. [2007], p. 714). However, figures such as Grylle, the Salvage Man, and Talus put this formula in doubt: 'If to be human is to be intelligent, eloquent, and well-mannered, it is also to be brutish and animal-like' (p. 71). Matthew Zarnowiecki, in his article 'Spenser's Angels: Salvation, Retractation, and Superhuman *Poiesis* in *Fowre Hymnes*' (*SSt* 30[2015] 75–103), notes that Spenser 'neither renounces nor excises the first two poems [of *Fowre Hymnes*], on earthly love and beauty, in favour of the second two, on heavenly love and beauty', and goes on to argue that 'retractation is essential to [*Fowre Hymnes*] because it is an action angels cannot perform, since their salvation was determined once and for all after an initial moment of choosing'. This suggests a paradoxical superiority of humans to angels: 'Humans are corporeal, they are further from God than angels, and they follow angels temporally, yet they also are superior to angels since they are the form in which God chooses to become a hybridized being' (p. 75). This paradox is also reflected in the material state of *Fowre Hymnes*, printed with the elegy *Daphnaïda*, which was originally printed five years before. When read together, the latter returns humanity from the 'heights of heavenly love and beauty to human love and the anguish of grief', and 'reminds us that to be human is also to be creaturely, even beastly' (p. 95). Spenser, unlike the Calvinist doctrine of salvation, provides no assurance of redemption in an afterlife. David Quint's 'Response' (*SSt* 30[2015] 105–9) sees the three articles in this section as highlighting this aspect of Spenser's poetic vision. In an elegant synthesis of the articles' arguments, Quint finds these scholars wrestling Spenser's advocacy of human choice throughout: 'they defend humanism, even if that means accepting that the same human beings who can reach rational consensus and prudential wisdom through language and argument are also dying animals ... Spenser cannot quite accept *that*, but he does show that there are still worse things: degeneracy into brute, bestial nature or into Talus, a man-made destroying angel' (p. 108).

Section III, entitled 'The Politics of Humanism and Humanity', begins with James Ross MacDonald's article 'The Redcrosse Knight and the Limits of Human Holiness' (*SSt* 30[2015] 113–31). MacDonald shows Spenser, in his portrait of the Redcrosse Knight, rejecting a traditional, 'Pelagian-inflected' conception of the saint as 'an autonomous miracle-worker, even as [he] affirms the value of human spiritual effort against doctrines of absolute depravity'. The same conception is useful in 'bolstering [Queen] Elizabeth's authority against the destabilizing political claims implicit in Calvinist understandings of human nature' (p. 113). For MacDonald, 'in Spenser's hands, the career of Redcrosse seems to reveal how the impulses which led him blundering through the battle with Error can become a form of sanctity capable of defeating the devil-dragon. Something human within the saint ... persists through the onset of grace and is brought to full development through its steady application' (p. 123). Katarzyna Lecky, in 'Irish Nonhumanness and English Inhumanity in *A Vewe of the present state of Ireland*' (*SSt* 30[2015] 133–50), shows how, despite its justification of England's right to subjugate the 'nonhuman' Irish, Spenser's *View of the Present State of Ireland* also 'rends apart inhumane fictions fueling English hostilities in Ireland to view the raw life buried under theories of population, and to expose how the ideologies of violent empire dehumanize colonizers and colonized alike' (p. 133). Lecky characterizes Spenser's 'affective aesthetic' as one in which 'the speaker ... eloquently shares the emotional jolt of encountering life that extends past its human limits to expose its "naked, shivering nature"' (p. 143; Lecky quotes Edmund Burke, *Reflections on the Revolution in France*, ed. L.G. Mitchell [1993], p. 77). John Walters, in 'Human, All Too Human: Spenser and the Dangers of Irish Civilization' (*SSt* 30[2015] 151–65), highlights the possibility left open in Spenser's *A View* that Ireland's natural environment will 'perpetually threaten to draw English settlers away from their own ideas of civility' (p. 151). By the end of *A View*, 'its speakers have not succeeded in advancing beyond their uncertain beginning'; it is 'the all-consuming nature of the task of imposing human control of the environment ... that marks the dialogue's failure as an agenda for a successful colonial project' (p. 163). Anthony Welch's article, 'Anthropology and Anthropophagy in *The Faerie Queene*' (*SSt* 30[2015] 167–92), places Book VI of *The Faerie Queene* in the context of the humanist project that 'reject[ed] old legends of national origin in favor of evolutionary models of history' (p. 167). Spenser's cannibals and shepherds represent two contrasting visions of early human society: savagery and a golden age, respectively. Reflecting neither the legendary nor the evolutionary model to the exclusion of the other, Spenser's text is 'divided between the golden dream of an elementary stage of human culture and the nightmare of an alimentary one' (p. 186). Joseph Loewenstein's 'Response: "They speake like ghosts": Spenser, the Human, and the Humane' (*SSt* 30[2015] 193–7) finds a common 'therapeutic' element in these essays, noting in Lecky's reading in particular a desire to shield Spenser from his work. Loewenstein wonders whether, 'for Spenser, though not for us, the inhumanity of the conqueror does not exceed the disdained inhumanity of the victim' (p. 197).

Section IV is entitled 'Theorizing Life' and begins with Russ Leo's article, 'The Species-Life of Worldlings' (*SSt* 30[2015] 201–27). Leo examines Spenser's representations of work and distinctions between kinds of labour—'taking Marx's comments on labor and species-being as points of departure'—in a world before classes and capitalist class structures (p. 201). Focusing on the Cave of Mammon in Book II of *The Faerie Queene*, imagined as a mine by Spenser, Leo shows that Spenser's representations of Mammon's hoard are 'detailed treatments of labor and risk' (p. 204). The labourers presented by Mammon provoke Guyon's reproof: 'With such vaine shewes thy worldlings vile abuse' (II.vii.39, 5). The worldlings here are 'those worldly creatures which are susceptible to [Mammon's] wiles, those thoughtless participants in a market economy who are compelled and distracted by "vaine shewes" of wealth and power'. But the labourers also 'rank among Mammon's "worldlings"' (p. 214). Through a detailed analysis of the meanings of 'worldling', Leo finds Guyon paradoxically employing the term 'to understand the fiends' activity, to disparage that activity as unreflective, and to locate their work in relation to the economy that their work subsidizes, from which they are themselves estranged—an economy in which Guyon participates and emerges temperate' (p. 220). Steven Swarbrick, in his article 'The Life Aquatic: Liquid Poetics and the Discourse of Friendship in *The Faerie Queene*' (*SSt* 30[2015] 229–53), introduces several recent theories addressing 'the fluid co-mixture of bodies from which the discourse of friendship can and does emerge', and argues that 'an *aqua*centric account of relation is necessary to think the subject of friendship' in *The Faerie Queene* (p. 229). With reference to the address to Raleigh—'whose pseudonym "Ocean" provides the material and semantic substrate of Spenser's liquefacient verse' (p. 234)—in Book III and passages from Book IV, Swarbrick defines a 'liquid poetics' that allows us to read words like 'relent' in 'the scene in which "the proud Nymph" "relent[s]" to the Thames's sexual advances' in a new light (p. 244; see *FQ* IV.xi.8). Swarbrick presents a version of friendship 'in which one individual relents to another not by sacrificing one's will but by sacrificing one's wish for autonomy'; it is 'an anonymous and involuntary state of being dissolved through non-mastery' (pp. 248–9). Andrew Wallace, in 'Spenser's Dead' (*SSt* 30[2015] 255–70), proposes that posthumanist scholarship echoes Stanley Cavell's notion that 'in philosophizing we wish to escape our humanity' ('Reflections on Wallace Stevens at Mount Holyoke', in Christopher Benfey and Karen Remmler, eds., *Artists, Intellectuals and World War II: The Pontigny Encounters at Mount Holyoke, 1942–44* [2006], p. 78). Wallace sees both Spenser (in *The Faerie Queene*) and posthumanist scholarship 'working through the instincts that both constitute the human and spawn the philosophical enterprise' (p. 255). Spenser 'ceaselessly views the human through the strange and distorting lenses of all those other beings and things and places, as though hoping to get at what [he] wants us to see about humanity by throwing humanity's absence into high relief' (p. 259). Wallace concludes that 'Spenser's allegories bring before the eyes and imaginations of readers . . . not so much an actual breakdown of the barriers between the human and what surrounds it but rather a quintessentially human urge to violate, denigrate, and deface its own nature and integrity. The poem's composite, monstrous bodies mark the dominant strain of Spenser's efforts to track this wish'; 'his meditations on dead bodies in the House of Pride and the House of Holiness usher us into the "furthest part" of his experiment' (pp. 267–8; see *FQ* I.v.36, 5). Stephen Guy-Bray's 'Response' (*SSt* 30[2015] 271–3) sees the essays as potentially inaugurating 'a new humanism, one in which man is not the measure of all things, but rather only one more thing measured', and suggests 'Spenser's great poems' may be 'especially well suited to this project' (p. 273).

Section V is entitled 'Animal Life'. It begins with Joseph Campana's article 'Spenser's Inhumanity' (*SSt* 30[2015] 277–99). Campana seeks to explain the 'dearth of conversation in Spenser studies' on the subject of creaturely life in the Renaissance. The answer lies in 'forms of captivating inhumanity central to both Spenser and the critical tradition': the 'instances of dehumanization' in Spenser that have 'made it difficult to see beasts as anything more than aspects of the bestialization of humans'; and the 'inhumanity of allegorical reading and writing has made other forms of life hard to see in that certain allegorical reading strategies strip away creaturely life (human *and* nonhuman) to bare significance while allegorical writing has always been a complex and we might say inhuman mechanism of *humanization* and *personation* whose ultimate aim is to trap all life and all matter into some species of agentive, so-called humanity' (p. 277). There is in Spenser nonetheless 'the intimation of a world bristling with vitality', the catalogue of sea creatures faced by Guyon on the way to the Bower of Bliss being a notable example (p. 294). Sean Henry's article, 'Getting Spenser's Goat: Calepine, Spenser's Goats, and the Problem of Meaning' (*SSt* 30[2015] 301–16), examines the scene from Book IV of *The Faerie Queene* in which Spenser describes Calepine fleeing 'like a wilde goat' (IV.iii.49, 3). This simile, overlooked by editors, leads Henry into an insightful discussion of the 'blurred lines between human and animal' evident in Spenser's animal imagery (p. 301). As one might expect, the lustfulness signified by this goat attaches to Calepine, perhaps offering 'some small rebalance' considering the greater price paid by Serena for the 'solace' she shared with him; a sexual double standard is partially mitigated (p. 314; see *FQ* VI.iii.20, 2–9). Bradley Tuggle, in ' "Man is not like an ape": Facing Life in *PROSOPOPOIA. | Or | Mother Hubberds Tale*' (*SSt* 30[2015] 317–35), considers the title page and poem proper of *Mother Hubberds Tale*. The title page of Spenser's *Complaints* 'appears at first glance to present a hierarchical *scala naturae*', but closer attention reveals something more disorderly (pp. 320–1). This is reflected in the poem itself, where the ethically charged concept of 'the face as a locus of acknowledgment' allows a blurring of lines drawn between life-forms. The Fox 'puts on the disguise of, and fashions himself to be, the counsellor of the *Magnifico* Ape'; and the Ape-as-*Magnifico* revels in defacing others—'ioy'd others to deface, | Thinking that their disgracing did him grace' (pp. 317, 325; *Mother Hubberds Tale*, ll. 707–8); and when the Fox is unmasked by Mercury, Tuggle asks, 'how, if at all, is the uncasing of the Fox ethically differentiated from the defacing that the Ape performs on others?' (p. 326). This, in Tuggle's reading, is 'where Spenser's poem meets the radicality of [Giorgio] Agamben's thinking about bare life'; 'the Fox has been made *homo sacer*, sacred man, creature beyond the bounds of human ethics' (p. 326–7; see Agamben, *Homo Sacer: Sovereign Power and Bare Life*, trans. Daniel Heller-Roazen [1998]). Bruce Boehrer's 'Response: Equal Rights for All Dirt' (*SSt* 30[2015] 337–40) highlights the attention in these essays to 'tropes of anthropomorphic substitution such as personifica-tion and prosopopoeia, allegory and animal metaphor', all lending 'imagina-tive presence to the non-human' (p. 338).

Section VI is entitled 'Aesthetics, Objects, Things, and Matter' and begins with Rachel Eisendrath's article, 'Going Outside: Human Subjectivity and the Aesthetic Object, *The Faerie Queene*, Book III' (*SSt* 30[2015] 343–68). Eisendrath considers the work of 'thing-oriented posthumanist thinkers', who go outside the subject/object divide by focusing on things. Highlighting these thinkers' neglect of 'the fully complex humanist art object', Eisendrath draws the reader back to *The Faerie Queene*. Employing Theodor W. Adorno's aesthetics, Eisendrath finds Spenser's poem challenging its own status as a thing, and 'ultimately ... "non-identical" with itself' (p. 343). Focusing on 'a series of three moments in the beginning, middle, and ending of Book III when Britomart goes outside', the article shows how 'this going outside pertains to a crucial dynamic of the aesthetic as such'; 'the dynamic aesthetic object ... provides a dynamic model of processes of self-reflective human subjectivity' (p. 349). Eisendrath concludes that, 'Like subjectivity itself, the art object does not come to rest within itself; rather it strives toward a completion of meaning at which it can never fully arrive'; 'like Redcrosse, who no sooner completes his quest then heads out again, so too aesthetic meaning no sooner clarifies itself then it must break through again to a renewed state of incompleteness, forestalling closure until the end of time—at which point, we're told, subjectivity won't be subjectivity anymore' [*sic*] (p. 361). Michael West, in 'Wonder, Artifacts, and the Human in *The Faerie Queene*' (*SSt* 30[2015] 369–91), argues that Spenser 'understands the human in part as that creature capable of responding to and learning about artifacts with wonder and curiosity' (p. 369). Two encounters—Artegall's viewing of the False Florimell in V.iii, and Britomart's viewing of the tapestries and the masque of Cupid in the House of Busirane in III.xi–xii—form the basis of West's case that Britomart and Artegall represent 'two extreme poles' of model readers of *The Faerie Queene*; their responses—'all wonder and no cognition' and 'no wonder and all cognition', respectively—'mutually define the scope of the human's potential responses to artifacts' (p. 386). Tiffany Jo Werth, in ' "Degendered": Spenser's "Yron Man" in a "Stonie" Age' (*SSt* 30[2015] 393–413), examines Spenser's use of prosopopoeia on a larger scale than is usually considered: in *Prosopopoeia or Mother Hubberds Tale* 8 and *Faerie Queene* V, Proem, 2, 'mankind . . . lives in an Iron Age, an age full of "wicked maladie," a "stonie one" '; 'Spenser ascribes an insensible thing, an "age," with ethical and moral—but *in-* and *non-*human—characteristics; here, men of "flesh and bone" risk being "degendered," "transformed into hardest stone" (V.Proem.2)' (p. 393). By this means, Spenser challenges the 'categorical exclusives of "human" or "mineral" '. In Talus in particular, Spenser presents the reader with 'a lively congruent and transactional—as opposed to static hierarchical—view of "the human" ' (p. 408). Julian Yates's 'Response: Wonder, Stone, and the Outside: Edmund Spenser's Infra-Human Aesthetic' (*SSt* 30[2015] 415–19), which concludes this edition of *Spenser Studies*, welcomes the challenge that these essays present to 'the botched, faulty product we name "human" ', noting the 'predatory exclusions made in order to posit' this term (p. 418).

Theresa M. DiPasquale's article in *Studies in Philology*, 'Anti-Court Satire, Religious Polemic, and the Many Faces of Antichrist: An Intertextual Reading of Donne's "Satyre 4" and Spenser's *Faerie Queene*' (*SIP* 112[2015] 264–302), is prompted by Joseph Wybarne's *The New Age of Old Names* [1609], which suggests that Donne's 'Satyre 4' and Spenser's *Faerie Queene* 'portray the Antichrist in terms that evoke Roman Catholic polemical writing', especially the work of the Counter-Reformation polemicist Fr. Nicholas Sander (p. 264). DiPasquale examines the intertextual correspondences between Donne's poem and certain episodes in Spenser's epic, and identifies 'a strong misreading of Spenser's House of Pride' (see Harold Bloom, *The Anxiety of Influence: A Theory of Poetry*, 2nd edn. [1997]); Donne's 'Satyre 4' 'critiques not so much *The Faerie Queene* itself but the black-and-white distinction between Roman Catholicism and English Protestant conformity that, in the 1590s and early 1600s, some readers interpreted as an essential component of Spenser's allegory'. Reading Spenser 'through the eyes of Donne's satirical persona', DiPasquale discovers 'the degree to which both poets—despite their contrasting perspectives on Elizabethan Christianity—use the satiric portrayal of

Elizabeth's court and the interrogation of what passes for religion there to test poetry's capacity for the moral and religious education of readers' (p. 266). Donne comments upon 'the ironic degree to which the extreme and grotesque discourse of anti-"papist" polemic—including Spenser's *Faerie Queene* as it was read by some Elizabethan and Jacobean Protestants—mirrors the extreme and grotesque discourse of anti-Tudor polemic' (p. 267).

## Books Reviewed

Bamford, Karen, and Naomi J. Miller, eds. *Maternity and Romance Narratives in Early Modern England.* Ashgate. [2015] pp. xiv + 219. £60 ISBN 9 7814 7246 2244.

Brayman Hackel, Heidi, and Ian Frederick Moulton, eds. *Teaching Early Modern English Literature from the Archives.* MLA. [2015] pp. ix + 274. £48.50 ISBN 9 7816 0329 1552.

Burlinson, Christopher, and Andrew Zurcher, eds. *A Supplement of the Faery Queene* by Ralph Knevet. ManUP. [2015] pp. viii + 349. £75 ISBN 9 7807 1908 2597.

Chiari, Sophie, ed. *The Circulation of Knowledge in Early Modern English Literature.* Ashgate. [2015] pp. xx + 259. £67.99 ISBN 9 7814 7244 9153.

Coldiron, A.E.B. *Printers Without Borders: Translation and Textuality in the Renaissance.* CUP. [2015] pp. xv + 339. £67 ISBN 9 7811 0707 3173.

Connolly, Annaliese, and Lisa Hopkins, eds. *Essex: The Cultural Impact of an Elizabethan Courtier.* ManUP. [2013] pp. xii + 324. £65 ISBN 9 7807 1908 4942.

Eggert, Katherine. *Disknowledge: Literature, Alchemy, and the End of Humanism in Renaissance England.* UPennP. [2015] pp. 351. £44 ISBN 9 7808 1224 7510.

Fuchs, Barbara, and Emily Weissbourd, eds. *Representing Imperial Rivalry in the Early Modern Mediterranean.* UTorP. [2015] pp. vi + 282. £40.99 ISBN 9 7814 4264 9026.

Goth, Maik. *Monsters and the Poetic Imagination in The Faerie Queene: 'Most Ugly Shapes, and Horrible Aspects'.* ManUP. [2015] pp. viii + 365. £75 ISBN 9 7807 1909 5719.

Hackett, Helen, ed. *Early Modern Exchanges: Dialogues Between Nations and Cultures, 1550–1750.* Ashgate. [2015] pp. xi + 261. £65 ISBN 9 7814 7242 5294.

Hannay, Margaret P., Michael G. Brennan, and Mary Ellen Lamb, eds. *The Ashgate Research Companion to the Sidneys, 1500–1700*, vol. 1. Ashgate. [2015] pp. xliv + 340. £90 ISBN 9 7814 0945 0382.

Hannay, Margaret P., Michael G. Brennan, and Mary Ellen Lamb, eds. *The Ashgate Research Companion to the Sidneys, 1500–1700*, vol. 2. Ashgate. [2015] pp. xliv + 351. £90 ISBN 9 7814 0945 0405.

Kirkpatrick, Kathryn, and Borbála Faragó, eds. *Animals in Irish Literature and Culture.* PalMac. [2015] pp. xviii + 270. £55 ISBN 9 7811 3743 4791.

Levin, Carole, and Christine Stewart-Nuñez. *Scholars and Poets Talk about Queens*. PalMac. [2015] pp. xxii + 299. £60 ISBN 9 7811 3753 4897.

McLaughlin, Martin, Ingrid D. Rowland, and Elisabetta Tarantino, eds. *Authority, Innovation and Early Modern Epistemology: Essays in Honour of Hilary Gatti*. Legenda. [2015] pp. xi + 253. £55 ISBN 9 7819 0797 5752.

Moore, Cyrus. *Love, War, and Classical Tradition in the Early Modern Transatlantic World: Alonso de Ercilla and Edmund Spenser*. ACMRS. [2014] pp. 236. £54.40 ISBN 9 7808 6698 4928.

Pedersen, Tara E. *Mermaids and the Production of Knowledge in Early Modern England*. Ashgate. [2015] pp. x + 155. £62.99 ISBN 9 7814 7244 0013.

Scott, Alison V. *Literature and the Idea of Luxury in Early Modern England*. Ashgate. [2015] pp. 237. £62.99 ISBN 9 7807 5466 4031.

Stout, Felicity Jane. *Exploring Russia in the Elizabethan Commonwealth: The Muscovy Company and Giles Fletcher the Elder (1546–1611)*. ManUP. [2015] pp. xiii + 251. £94.22 ISBN 9 7807 1909 7003.

Whitman, Jon, ed. *Romance and History: Imagining Time from the Medieval to the Early Modern Period*. CUP. [2015] pp. xiv + 317. £83.06 ISBN 9 7811 0704 2780.

Young, Francis, trans. *The Cambridge Book of Magic: A Tudor Necromancer's Manual*, attrib. Paul Foreman. Texts in Early Modern Magic. [2015] pp. xl + 138. £24.99 ISBN 9 7809 9264 0422.

# VII

# Shakespeare

BRETT GREATLEY-HIRSCH, PETER J. SMITH,
ELISABETTA TARANTINO, DOMENICO LOVASCIO,
SHIRLEY BELL, CHRISTIAN GRIFFITHS,
KATE WILKINSON, SHEILAGH ILONA O'BRIEN, AND
LOUISE POWELL

This chapter has three sections: 1. Editions and Textual Studies; 2. Shakespeare in the Theatre; 3. Criticism. Section 1 is by Brett Greatley-Hirsch; section 2 is by Peter J. Smith; section 3(a) is by Elisabetta Tarantino; section 3(b) is by Domenico Lovascio; section 3(c) is by Shirley Bell; section 3(d) is by Christian Griffiths; section 3(e) is by Kate Wilkinson; section 3(f) is by Sheilagh Ilona O'Brien; section 3(g) is by Louise Powell.

## 1. Editions and Textual Studies

Readers will, I hope, forgive the relative brevity and narrow scope of this section as a necessary consequence of accepting the *YWES* brief three-quarters into the year. To avoid piecemeal, superficial treatment of the full range of this year's offerings in Shakespearean textual studies, I limit my focus to a more manageable section of scholarship: studies in authorship attribution and the apocrypha. My discussion thus excludes a great deal of interesting and important work across a field whose vibrancy and rapid evolution is reflected by the range of topics brought together in Margaret Jane Kidnie and Sonia Massai's *Shakespeare and Textual Studies* (CUP). My capacity as interim caretaker of this section similarly does not allow me to give the third edition of *The Norton Shakespeare* (Norton) and three impressive monographs — Laura Estill's *Dramatic Extracts in Seventeenth-Century English Manuscripts* (UDelP), Judith Milhous and Robert D. Hume's *The Publication of Plays in London 1660–1800* (BL), and Zachary Lesser's *Hamlet after Q1* (UPennP) — the due consideration and thorough assessment they deserve. No doubt my successor will wish to address these and other studies here neglected in a suitably enlarged section next year.

*The Year's Work in English Studies, Volume 96 (2017)* © *The Author 2017. Published by Oxford University Press on behalf of the English Association. All rights reserved.*
*For Permissions, please email: journals.permissions@oup.com*
doi:10.1093/ywes/max008

Aside from the *Norton* collected works, four single-text critical editions of Shakespeare's plays appeared in 2015. The second edition of *The Two Noble Kinsmen* for the Arden Shakespeare Third Series ('Arden3') gave Lois Potter an opportunity to revise the text and correct a number of errors and inconsistencies, mostly minor, identified by reviewers of the 1997 first edition (see especially John Jowett's review in *ShS* 51[1998] 309–10). More substantive textual changes are outlined in a new 'Additions and Reconsiderations' section appended to the introduction, in which Potter also surveys the effect of critical interest in 'collaboration', both authorial and theatrical, on scholarship on the play's language, Chaucerian source, patterns of casting and doubling, and editorial and publishing history, including its translation into Spanish (pp. 147–64). 'The topics discussed remain much the same', Potter observes, 'but they are now more likely to be interpreted as sites of contention between Shakespeare and Fletcher' (p. 150). Potter also briefly extends the original performance history to cover major stage productions in Britain and North America between 1997 and 2014, as well as the 2004 *Complete Arkangel Shakespeare* audio-recording (pp. 164–69).

Since critics of the 1998 first edition of the Arden3 *Troilus and Cressida* were universal in their praise for David Bevington's treatment of the text, it is unsurprising that the second edition is largely a reprint. The text, introduction, and appendices remain substantively unchanged, with the exception of an appended 'Additions and Reconsiderations' section extending the earlier edition's coverage of *Troilus and Cressida* in performance to include stage productions from Australia, Britain, Canada, New Zealand, and the United States from 1998 to 2014, and updating discussion of the play's critical reception. The 'Selective bibliography' has also been revised to cover the period 1998–2014 (pp. 503–6).

The 'Additions and Reconsiderations' appendage has become something of a convention for revised Arden3 editions. Although they may make it easier for owners of previous editions to identify *some* of the new content, I cannot help thinking the material might be more usefully integrated into relevant sections of the existing introductions. There is nothing in the table of contents in these editions to demarcate the various subsections of the 'Additions and Reconsiderations', rendering this approach particularly unhelpful for students and other first-time readers who may rightly expect a section of the introduction dedicated to, say, the play's performance history to provide all the pertinent information about that topic. After wading through an already substantial introduction, is it not equally frustrating for a reader to find interpretations and conclusions revised — and potentially rejected? That said, some editors are more careful (generous?) than others to construct a dialogue between material old and new. For example, Bevington modifies his earlier conclusion in the introductory section on Shakespeare's sources in light of new scholarship and provides a footnote to indicate extended discussion of this topic in the 'Additions and Reconsiderations'. By contrast, Potter refers readers of her 'Additions and Reconsiderations' section backward, but neglects to direct readers of the introduction forward. Potter's elaborate reconsideration of the play's 'unusual casting pattern' and doubling (pp. 159–63), for example, is couched in terms of 'Developing a view that I suggested earlier (pp. 73–5)', but there is nothing in those early pages to indicate this later addition. In the preface to the first edition of *Troilus and Cressida*, which also remains largely unchanged (save to reflect the passing of the series in the interim from Routledge to Bloomsbury), Bevington argues against having to produce a single-text edition of the play (in line with the series' general policy at the time) and laments the 'burdensomely numerous' textual notes such an edition requires (pp. xvi–xviii). The publication of editions of Q1, Q2, and F1 *Hamlet* in 2006 suggests that the Arden Shakespeare Third Series was no longer averse to version-based editing, at least in certain conditions. If those conditions include the 'prestige' and market share of the play in question, then reserving version-based editions for the texts of *Hamlet* is perhaps defensible on commercial grounds alone. However, in light of Bevington's persuasive arguments for a two-text edition of *Troilus and Cressida* and his obvious enthusiasm for its undertaking, merely publishing a revised single-text edition represents a lost opportunity for the Arden3. It is too early to tell whether the Arden4 will take this leap.

The late Thomas L. Berger remarked that Kenneth Muir's frequently reprinted 1984 revised Arden2 edition of *Macbeth* 'remains the edition to be first consulted by serious students of *Macbeth*' (in Ann Thompson et al, *Which Shakespeare? A User's Guide to Editions* [1991], p. 104). If Peter Kirwan's sober assessment of Sandra Clark and Pamela Mason's Arden3 edition is any indication, the situation is unlikely to change: 'This *Macbeth* breaks no new ground in text, interpretation or presentation, concentrating instead on marshalling existing scholarship' (*ShS* 69[2016] 484). There is a frustrating tendency in this edition's introduction to refer readers elsewhere. For example, the introduction opens with an outline of its contents, announcing that 'Textual matters are dealt with in Appendix 1' (p. 1). The decision to relegate 'textual matters' to an appendix devalues textual scholarship as secondary to criticism, but is not in itself uncommon in Arden editions. However, in some cases the extent of the 'textual matters' and detail of analysis justifies its relocation, at least in part, elsewhere in the edition. This is certainly not the case here. Appendix 1 is split into two brief sections: Mason's discussion of the text 'from the perspective of the editor' (as opposed to?) and Clark's evaluation of recent debates about revision and authorship (pp. 301–21, 321–36). The purpose of Mason's section, a revision of a paper previously published in an essay collection on *Macbeth*, is to demonstrate the 'primary concern of the editors of this edition to re-examine, consistently challenge and rethink the editorial tradition and practice surrounding the editing of *Macbeth* in an attempt to look at the text afresh, with new eyes, to reassess its particular qualities and characteristics' (p. 302). This may have read as a more radical departure, were it not for the stated 'editorial policy' taking 'a respect for the Folio text' as its 'lynchpin', with a concomitant 'allegiance to what [the Folio text] offers in the absence of coherent and compelling reasons to make emendations' (p. 301). Previous editors are taken to task for 'tidying up' the Folio's lineation and punctuation, features that Mason argues in 'some cases' are 'a means by which Shakespeare communicates the pressures, tensions, and complexities which the characters are experiencing' (p. 305). For Mason, 'editorial practice' in this regard 'seems to have gained nothing and lost a great deal' (p. 308). This is not a persuasive argument, and a conservative editorial approach such as this risks obscuring the meaning of the text for a modern readership for the sake of orthographical fidelity. Mason admits as much: 'To standardize the punctuation in order to help a modern reader is both a sensible and uncontested policy' (p. 308). Sensible and uncontested, perhaps, but not consistently applied. Two examples will suffice. The description of how Duncan's 'virtues/Will plead like angels, trumpet-tongued, against/The deep damnation of his taking off' (1.7.18–20) introduces a comma after *trumpet-tongued* not present in the Folio text. The editors unconvincingly argue that the word 'may modify either *virtues* or *angels*', but the imagery and pattern of language that immediately follows indicate that the word should be read as modifying *angels* alone. Although they acknowledge 'the completion of Macbeth's thought is interrupted by the entrance of his wife' at 1.7.28, the editors retain the Folio's period and reject the conventional addition of a dash to typographically indicate this interruption. On the topic of Lady Macbeth's entrances, Mason makes much of the speech prefixes for her and Macduff's wife (pp. 311–12), arguing that the names 'Lady Macbeth' and 'Lady Macduff' are products of the editorial tradition and do 'not exist in Shakespeare's play' (p. 311). This is certainly true — the Folio gives 'Lady' and 'Wife' as speech prefixes for these respective characters, though stage directions also use 'Macbeth's wife', 'Macbeth's Lady' and 'Macduff's wife'. Mason zealously imposes LADY in speech prefixes and stage directions, even when this interferes unnecessarily with the Folio text. For example, the Folio's '*Enter Macbeth's wife alone with a letter*' is perfectly sensible; Mason's editorial insertion of '[LADY]' after '*Macbeth's wife*' is wholly unnecessary (1.5.0 s.d.). There are other instances where the treatment of the text is at odds with the reading given in the annotation. Noting that the word is 'often emended', Clark and Mason retain the Folio's *time* in the Porter's speech, 'Come in time' (2.3.5), on the basis that the 'phrase can simply mean that the farmer's entry is timely'. If, as the note continues, 'The farmer, equivocator and tailor turn out to be parallel figures', then surely emending *time* to *time-saver*, *time-pleaser*, or simply *farmer* is justified so the line conforms to the verbal pattern established by 'come in, equivocator' (2.3.11) and 'Come in, tailor' (2.3.14).

Clark adopts an equally conservative approach for her portion of Appendix 1, 'The Folio Text and its Integrity', attending to the play's authorship and provenance. Again, readers anticipating a fuller discussion are directed elsewhere: 'there is no intention here to discuss these [issues] in any detail' (p. 321). Instead, Clark briefly summarizes scholarly arguments about the degree of textual revision in the Folio text and the play's relationship to Middleton's *The Witch*, concluding 'The Folio text of *Macbeth* is probably not the original version that Shakespeare wrote in 1606; but the extent to which it differs may well be very slight, and confined to 3.5 and two passages in 4.1' (p. 336). On the songs, Clark observes that 'it is impossible not to feel their incongruity' (329), but the decision not to print them denies readers the opportunity to make this assessment themselves. Slavish adherence to the Folio text might explain the decision not to interpolate the songs into the text, but failure to provide them in an appendix effectively cripples the edition. Yet again, readers are directed elsewhere for material — for example, the stage direction '*Sing within.* "Come away, come away, *etc.*"' (3.5.35) is glossed thus: 'The opening words of this song, sung offstage, are from a song given in full in Middleton's *The Witch*, and constitute one of the main pieces of evidence adduced for Middleton's authorship of the scene. Brooke, 162–5, includes the whole of the song in his text'.

If the wholesale exclusion of the songs renders the text of the edition incomplete, notable omissions in the introduction have a similar effect. While the section on '*Macbeth* and time' (pp. 62–82) attends admirably to this 'all-pervasive theme' (p. 82), Clark's discussion of language in the play (pp. 38–62) may have profitably engaged with recent stylistic analysis, such as Jonathan Hope and Michael Witmore's work on the topic for *Macbeth: The State of Play* (Bloomsbury [2014], pp. 183–208) — a collection to which Clark contributed an essay on *Macbeth* in performance. Given the wealth of available material, Clark's discussion of *Macbeth*'s stage history in the edition is remarkably brief and narrowly focused on 'a selection of themes and topics that have proved significant in productions in England over a long period' (p. 97). 'England' is something of a misnomer, since the vast majority of productions surveyed are from London and Stratford-upon-Avon. Film and television adaptations are given uncomfortably short shrift, meriting only a handful of references. The result is an entirely English — or, more specifically, London and Stratford — *Macbeth*, a picture that denies readers insight into the richness and variety of responses the play has inspired across different cultures, theatrical traditions, languages, and political contexts. Also absent is any consideration of the various experiments adapting the play to other media — the *Voyager Macbeth* (1994), for example, was one of the earliest forays into producing multimedia digital editions of Shakespeare, incorporating an audio-recording of a complete RSC production, film clips, critical essays, a concordance, and a delightful 'karaoke' function (in which Macbeth's or Lady Macbeth's audio is muted), all linked to a hypertext version of the New Cambridge text. In keeping with the rest of the edition, readers expecting a more comprehensive treatment are directed elsewhere.

Given the theoretically endless possibilities afforded by the medium, digital editions are often perceived as somewhat 'incomplete' if they fail to offer more than their counterparts in print. Even when they do, however, reviewers of digital editions are quick to tally the functions and features that are absent. For example, Stephen Wittek's 2015 review of Joost Daalder's edition of *1 The Honest Whore* for Digital Renaissance Editions (*This Rough Magic* [2015] 7 paras) praises Daalder's meticulously edited text, the extensive critical apparatus, and the 'striking and original features' offered by the platform before lamenting the inability to download the text for offline reading, create bookmarks, or adjust the text appearance (beyond the in-built function of the Web browser). 'Ultimately', Wittek concludes, 'one may safely assume that functionality will only improve as this very exciting, very ambitious project moves forward'. More telling is Francis X. Connor's review essay, '*The Cambridge Edition of the Works of Ben Jonson Online* and the Utility of the Digital Edition' (*PBSA* 109[2015] 247–63), whose title signals Connor's focus on that digital edition's 'utility' and not 'the editorial work itself' (p. 254).

Connor's review is more explicitly concerned with what the digital edition 'does not do' and, like Wittek, his critiques are couched in terms of features *in potentia*, written 'with the full knowledge that any criticism will hopefully read as outdated at some point in the future' (p. 254). Both of these reviews exemplify a tendency, if not an imperative, towards maximalism in both the evaluation and creation of digital editions. These thoughts are drawn from a paper Aaron T. Pratt and I delivered at the 2016 MLA conference, titled 'Infinite Riches in a Little ROM'.

But the 'digital' in 'digital edition' need not come with the maximalism that so often attaches to it, and quantity of content or features is not, in itself, a useful measure of a digital edition's quality. Although digital editions 'allow for more space and are able to do things beyond the scope of print', as Eoin Price suggests, 'there are times when brevity might be best' (*YWES* 95[2016] 526). Jessica Slights' 2015 digital edition of *Othello* for Internet Shakespeare Editions (ISE), internetshakespeare.uvic.ca, assembles an impressive collection of critical, editorial, and supplementary material, without overwhelming the reader/user (hereafter simply 'reader'). In keeping with other ISE editions, Slights' *Othello* includes a modern-spelling text with full critical apparatus, semi-diplomatic transcriptions of the Q1 and F1 texts, and photo-facsimiles of Q1, F1, F2, F3, F4, Rowe, and Theobald. The supplementary materials, lightly edited and in modern spelling, provide further context and are well suited to classroom discussion. These include relevant extracts from Peele's *The Battle of Alcazar* and the anonymous *Selimus*, the play's source from Cinthio and an analogous tale from Fenton's translation of Bandello, passages from contemporary manuals on household governance and treatises on the passions, selections on Venice from Coryate's *Crudities*, and Elizabeth I's letters on the deportation of blackamoors. Unlike the Arden editions mentioned above, Slights' edition is both 'born digital' (i.e., it has no prior existence in print) and 'open access' (i.e., freely available to anyone with access to the Internet). Slights' general introduction offers a sensitive and engaging reading of the play, arguing '*Othello*'s emotional power derives in part from its disconcerting insistence on both the participation and the impotence of its audience' ('Introduction', para. 2). Analysis of this strategy provides a framework for Slights to address tried and tested aspects of the play: characterization, questions of gender and power, early modern geopolitics and the Mediterranean setting, religion, race and ethnicity, and the themes of deception, abuse of language, and failure of the senses to distinguish appearance from reality (paras. 3–25).

Although described as 'sketches in broad strokes', Slights' discussion of *Othello*'s critical reception is admirably thorough, beginning with Thomas Rymer's late seventeenth-century denouncement of the play's depiction of 'a man of color as a tragic hero' and its 'violations of a natural hierarchy that positions people of color firmly below white Europeans, and non-Christians below Christians' ('A Survey of Criticism', paras. 2–3). The canonical eighteenth- and nineteenth-century critics (Johnson, Schlegel, Coleridge) are considered, and usefully juxtaposed with others less familiar. In so doing, Slights recovers the important — and frequently unacknowledged — contributions of women:

In addition to prompting a reassessment of Iago, the nineteenth-century view of Shakespeare's characters as expressions of fundamental truths about human nature stimulated a growing interest in Desdemona. This attentiveness to the play's tragic heroine intersected with a notable increase in the number of women's voices contributing to public conversations in the realm of literary criticism, as female actors began lecturing and publishing on the roles they performed on stage, and as women slowly began to be admitted to the ranks of professional scholars of Shakespeare. (para. 7)

Chief amongst these early pioneers is Anna Jameson, 'notable as the author of the first substantial and systematic discussion of Shakespeare's female characters' in 1832, and Slights' is the only modern edition of *Othello* I am aware of that not only mentions Jameson's study of Desdemona, but also recognizes its critical significance (paras. 7–8). In the remainder of the 'Survey of Criticism', Slights summarizes other influential literary-critical approaches to *Othello*, including character criticism, formalism, genre criticism, psychoanalysis, feminism and gender studies, New Historicism, postcolonial criticism, and critical race studies. Noting a 'consensus ... building around the notion of *Othello* as a text of the early modern Mediterranean', Slights concludes her survey by gesturing towards recent attempts to provide 'alternative historical contexts for the play', including 'new work on connections between early modern London's black community and the city's playhouses' and 'on links between sixteenth-century dyeing practices and the properties of Desdemona's handkerchief' (para. 21).

As one might expect, just over half of Slights' performance history traces various theatrical traditions of playing Othello, from white actors in blackface to black actors performing the role, as well as more recent experiments in cross-racial and 'photo negative' casting. Aside from an apartheid-era South African *Othello* mentioned in passing, all of the stage productions surveyed are professional and either British or American ('A History of Performance', paras. 1–14). The second half of Slights' performance history offers a detailed analysis of English-language film and television adaptations of *Othello*, from Orson Welles' 1952 Hollywood film to a 'self-consciously post–9/11' 2008 Canadian television production presenting 'Othello as a North African Muslim whose ethnic identity determines his relationships in ways that exceed his control' (paras. 15–21). Many cultures have made Othello their countryman, and the play has enjoyed a long tradition of non-Anglophone performance on both stage and screen. Slights' otherwise commendable performance history is marred by an exclusive focus on English-language productions.

In the 'Textual Introduction', Slights describes her editorial approach as broadly 'pragmatic'. The F1 text is used as copy, and Slights treats Folio-only passages 'as deliberate additions to an earlier, less complete text from which Q1 was derived' (para. 3). However, the Folio is not slavishly adhered to, and Slights frequently adopts readings from Q1 and Q2 'primarily in order either to correct likely errors in F1 or to regularize the meter of verse lines' (para. 3). Her collation, which can be displayed in note form and/or in-line using colour to distinguish between textual variants, is extensive but not without notable absences such as Theobald's conjectured reading (adopted by Hanmer without proper credit) of *make* for *mock* in 'It is the green-eyed monster, which doth mock/The meat it feeds on' (3.3; TLN 1781–82). Slights also admits some 'consistent intrusions from Q1' are 'not detailed in the notes', namely 'the many oaths and asseverations that do not appear in F1 but which seem likely to have enlivened the play early in its theatrical life' (para. 3). Her treatment of the text is sound, and Slights provides ample commentary. Many of these notes demonstrate an awareness of performance possibilities: for example, the opening stage direction, 'Enter Roderigo and Iago' (TLN 2), follows F1, but the note draws attention to how this is reversed in Q1–2 and 'playing the entrances in this order could operate as an early sign of the dominance that Iago has over Roderigo throughout the play'. The edition also makes use of the ISE's rendering of 'uncertain' stage directions in grayed out text. For example, Slights adopts F1's placement of Cassio's entrance at TLN 233, a line after Q1–2's placement, and signals this uncertainty visually with the greyed out text accompanied by a detailed commentary note on the effect of these options on performance. Slights' adoption of Q2 readings is often not simply 'pragmatic', but sensible. For example, editors typically retain Q1's and F1's 'This present wars against the Ottomites' (TLN 582), such as Michael Neill does for the Oxford, follow Malone in emending *This* to *These*, as Norman Sanders does for the New Cambridge, or retain *This* but give *war* as correcting a 'common error' in the printing of both Q1 and F1, as E.A.J. Honigmann does for the Arden3. Slights adopts the Q2 reading, 'This present war against the Ottomites', producing the same text as Honigmann without the need for elaborate arguments about transmission errors. Even so, the edition incorporates some questionable readings. For example, Slights retains F1's '*tongued* consuls' (TLN 27), which editors frequently emend to *toged* or *toga'd* to preserve the contrast between soldier-in-arms and toga-wearing consul. As support, Slights cites Neill's remark that *tongued* enables a 'chain of association' with 'spinster' (TLN 26) and 'prattle' (TLN 28) — but, as Slights notes, Neill opts for *toga'd* in his edition, and the emendation fits both meaning and metre. There are also instances where emendations of punctuation affecting the meaning of the text are not adequately noted. Slights introduces a period in Iago's speech ending 'For daws to peck at. I am not what I am' (TLN 71), for example, noting only the Q1 variant *doves* for *daws*. The F1 text gives 'peck at;' and both Q1 and Q2 give 'peck at,' — Slights' period severs the rhetorical sequence and breaks the conditional sense of the lines: 'For *when* my outward action [...] [*then*] I am not what I am' (TLN 67–71). These issues notwithstanding, Slights' *Othello* is an impressive addition to the Internet Shakespeare Editions, and one that shows that digital editions can more than hold their own against any commercial print counterpart.

One monograph on the apocrypha appeared this year. In fact, Peter Kirwan's *Shakespeare and the Idea of Apocrypha: Negotiating the Boundaries of the Dramatic Canon* is the first monograph-length study of the apocryphal plays as critical, theatrical, and editorial phenomena and not merely as a series of authorship attribution problems to be solved. This is an ambitious and provocative book, combining different critical-theoretical approaches to understand the canonical status of Shakespeare's plays as subject to exigencies of print and performance, shifting critical-theoretical priorities, and changing cultural tastes. In so doing, Kirwan marshals a breadth of material not typically brought together, which ultimately succeeds in demonstrating that the Shakespeare apocrypha merits sustained intellectual engagement. In 'Canonising the Apocrypha' (pp. 15–71), Kirwan showcases his aptitude for book history, skillfully tracing the fortunes of the apocryphal plays in print from early appearances in quarto to their collected incorporation into the 1663 Third Folio. From there, the '43-play canon' of the Third and Fourth Folios became 'a casualty of a burgeoning culture of Bardolatry' in the eighteenth century, which, following Theobald's ignominious defeat at the hands of Pope, 'treated aesthetic quality as a form of objective proof and prioritised authorial reputation over textual origins' (p. 34). Along the way, Kirwan draws attention to the importance of editions typically glossed over by other publishing histories, such as Robert Walker's *Dramatick works of William Shakespear* (1734–35). As the first to desegregate the disputed plays from the canonical and 'place equal authority on all forty-three plays', Walker's edition is a pertinent example of the arbitrary construction of the apocrypha (p. 26). According to Kirwan, two strands of scholarship on the apocrypha emerged in the eighteenth century: one implicating the 'increased degradation of the disputed plays' in 'the process of canonising Shakespeare as the British national poet', the other seeking to 'rehouse the [apocryphal] plays in more suitable formats, reflecting a new set of assumptions concerning authenticity' (p. 48). Key moments in the second strand include George Steevens' 1778 revision of Samuel Johnson's edition and Edmond Malone's 1780 *Supplement* in the eighteenth century, followed in the nineteenth century by Charles Knight's inclusion of a 'doubtful plays' volume in his *Pictorial Edition* (1838–41), William Hazlitt's revision of Malone's *Supplement* in 1852, and Henry Tyrrell's *Doubtful Plays of Shakspere* (c.1853). For Kirwan, C. F. Tucker Brooke's 1908 *Shakespeare Apocrypha* represents both a culmination of these previous efforts and a radical departure from them. By replacing 'supplement' and 'doubtful' with 'apocrypha', Brooke's anthology delivered 'a decisive blow in the death of nineteenth-century disintegration', introducing 'a category between "Shakespeare" and "not-Shakespeare"' that created 'a freestanding, defined canonical space' for the plays (p. 69).

In the second chapter, 'The Apocrypha in Rep' (72–114), Kirwan identifies common themes and dramatic strategies across Shakespeare's plays, canonical and apocryphal, as performed contemporaneously in the repertory of the Chamberlain's–King's Men. The repertory studies approach is invoked to privilege the shared content and thematic concerns of the plays over any need to establish Shakespeare's precise involvement with them — 'writer, reviser, adaptor, actor, selector, advisor, commissioner, mentor; the possibilities are multiple and ultimately unprovable' (p. 75). These dramatic commonalities suggest that 'distinctions between "Shakespeare" and "not-Shakespeare"' on the early modern stage 'were blurred enough not to preclude the attachment (prior or subsequent to print) of Shakespeare's name' (p. 75). Acknowledging that any reconstruction can only ever be partial (because only a fraction of the plays is extant), Kirwan proceeds to read plays in the Chamberlain's–King's Men repertory in juxtaposition with one another, regardless of authorship. These illuminating readings reveal a repertoire of plays bound together by common dramatic strategies, shared themes and subject matter, dominant motifs, and generic innovations, including prodigal husbands and patient wives (pp. 75–89), absent rulers and sympathetic commoners (pp. 89–98), 'romance and nostalgia' (pp. 98–106), and 'ensemble comedy' (pp. 106–111). Kirwan's lively and sensitive readings make a convincing case for renewed critical and theatrical interest in non-canonical plays.

In the remaining chapters, Kirwan turns to more contentious matters of authorship attribution and editorial theory. The treatment of these topics is less nuanced than those discussed earlier in the book. Chapter Three, 'Defining "Shakespeare"' (pp. 115–63), is a pessimistic assessment of Shakespearean authorship attribution study. Kirwan makes some sensible observations about the need for attribution studies 'to be brought into positive conversation with literary, theatrical and theoretical approaches' (p. 118), and the concomitant requirement that literary scholars 'develop the necessary skill sets to be able to properly critique it' (p. 163), but even these well-meaning assertions reflect an unsophisticated understanding of a complex field. For example, Kirwan either misrepresents or misunderstands the distinction between categories of 'external' and 'internal' evidence when discussing the title-page attribution of *Locrine* and other early playbooks. 'The notion of "external" evidence', he writes, 'implies an independent, separate or impartial witness, an outside corroboration of authorial origin' (p. 129). While relevant to considerations of its validity, notions of independence, distance, and impartiality are irrelevant to the classification of evidence as either internal or external. In *Attributing Authorship: An Introduction* (CUP [2002]), an important work curiously omitted from Kirwan's discussion, Harold Love distinguishes between these as follows: 'Broadly, internal evidence is that from the work itself and external evidence that from the social world within which the work is created, promulgated and read; but there will always be overlap' (p. 51). Thus, a claim in a diary to the authorship of a work published anonymously constitutes external evidence, whether penned by the author or another agent, because it is *external to the text of the work itself*. As with other so-called 'para-texts', title-page attributions are also typically classified as external evidence — even if, as Kirwan argues, 'they are brought into being at the same moment as the printed text' and are 'part of a simultaneous reconstitution of "author" and "work"' (p. 129). Other generalizing statements reflect a casualness toward authorship attribution study and its various methodologies. Again on *Locrine*, Kirwan argues that 'authorship tests are less accurate in ascertaining local revision' (p. 132), but fails to specify the tests to which he refers. Since he is not a practitioner, part of the problem undoubtedly stems from Kirwan's reliance on biased sources and on certain critics he mistakenly treats as representative of mainstream authorship attribution study, when in fact they operate at its fringes. The work of the Ward E. Y. Elliott and Robert J. Valenza, frequently cited throughout the chapter, is a case in point. Serious technical questions about their methods remain unanswered (see e.g. Thomas Merriam, 'Untangling the Derivatives:

Points for Clarification in the Findings of the Claremont Shakespeare Clinic' *L&LC* 24[2009] 403–16), and the pair have adopted an uncritical approach to text selection and processing, admitting to constructing their corpus 'with whatever text we could get, not troubling over which version we had, or what vagaries might be presented by the original-spelling text' (Ward E. Y. Elliott and Robert J. Valenza, 'And Then There Were None: Winnowing the Shakespeare Claimants' *CHum* 30[1996] 208). Equally troubling is Kirwan's characterization of Brian Vickers' 'Shakespeare and Authorship Studies in the Twenty-First Century' (*SQ* 62[2011] 106–42) as 'a magisterial survey of recent debates and the issues of practitioners prioritising their own methodologies and studies dating quickly' (p. 116). This is high praise for a review essay so ruthlessly antagonistic and biased in its treatment that it provoked a sobering thirty-eight page corrective (see John Burrows, 'A Second Opinion on "Shakespeare and Authorship Studies in the Twenty-First Century"' *SQ* 63[2012] 355–92).

In the final chapter, 'Apocryphising the Canon' (pp. 164–206), Kirwan turns his attention to the practical and 'implicit "end"' of authorship studies', namely, 'the constitution and presentation of the Canon' (p. 163). The chapter comprises three case studies, each exemplifying a particular paradigm of canon formation: 'bibliographical authorship (The Complete Books Attributed to William Shakespeare)', exemplified by Jonathan Bate and Eric Rasmussen's 2007 RSC *Complete Works* edition; 'individual authorship (The Complete Works to Which William Shakespeare Contributed Some Part)', as 'provocatively disturbed' by the inclusion of Shakespearean material in the 2007 Oxford Middleton; and 'the performative canon (The Complete Modern Shakespeare Repertoire)', represented by the RSC's Complete Works Festival of 2006–7 (p. 169). The first case study is marred by a confusion of terminology and the unhelpful introduction of neologisms. For example, Kirwan claims that the 'only single volume *Complete Works* that is theoretically constructed on principles of material bibliography' is the 2007 RSC edition (p. 170). He continues:

> This edition, following the ethos of edition-based editing, prioritises the 1623 folio as a material book: it begins with a physical moment of textual *incarnation* rather than a hypothesised moment of textual *origin*. While the core objective of edition-based editing, the retention of the distinctive features of an early authoritative manifestation of the text, is not new in itself, the edition's innovation here is in applying it to an early anthology. (p. 170)

Since the emphasis here is on the Folio as a material object, Kirwan probably intends *descriptive bibliography* where he writes 'material bibliography', since *physical bibliography* (another term for *analytical bibliography*, but 'physical' is a closer match with 'material') would render the claim absurd. 'Edition-based editing' is a similarly problematic construction, by which Kirwan presumably means 'version-based editing'. Issues of nomenclature aside, the RSC *Complete Works* certainly privileges readings from the F1 texts (except in cases where these do not exist), but not its material construction and 'distinctive features'. It does not, for example, preserve the Folio's setting of text in two columns or even retain F1's use of serif typefaces. The logical consequence of an editorial policy that 'prioritises the 1623 folio as a material book' is not the RSC *Complete Works*, but a facsimile edition. Later, Kirwan proposes a line-up of plays that a 'notional Complete Works of Shakespeare based on rigid bibliographical principles' would include (p. 173), but does not specify what these bibliographical principles might be. At times, the use of unorthodox terms renders completely obscure the sense: 'While the edition-based model remains constant, multivolume series are more flexible to the kind of dynamic canonizing and book-based editing that the paradigm requires' (p. 174). By 'edition-based model', does Kirwan mean *version-based editions* or *collected-works editions*? 'Multivolume series' presumably refers to *single-text editions*, but I am unsure what is meant by 'book-based editing'. To conclude this case study, Kirwan suggests the 'advent of hypertext editions' and 'online databases such as Early English Books Online, Eighteenth Century Collections Online and Literature Online' promises 'to democratise the availability of texts and allow "canons" to be constructed by readers' (p. 181). However, Kirwan offers no examples of 'hypertext editions' here or elsewhere in the book, and it is unclear how the 'online databases' he cites can possibly 'democratise the availability of texts' when access to them is limited by commercial, institution-based subscription. By contrast, Kirwan's other case studies are free of terminological issues and offer astute observations of their subjects. 'The key to interpreting the Oxford Middleton's inclusion of *Macbeth* and other plays', Kirwan suggests, 'is partially concealed by the author-centred marketing and the attempts to elevate Middleton's cultural status'. For Kirwan, the 'true achievement of this Middleton canon is, in fact, the decentring of Middleton within his own volume, to a point where even the text of an auditor's response to a Middleton pageant can be included'. Thus, in one of my favourite pithy statements in the study, 'Middleton becomes a motif or meme in his own book, acting as a link rather than a tyrannical bordering presence' (pp. 184–85). Kirwan's discussion of the 2006–7 RSC Complete Works Festival is similarly insightful, demonstrating the importance of performance in authorizing attribution: 'Whenever an early modern play is newly attributed, it is paramount to consolidate the attributions in performance; for a play to be saved, the word must be made flesh' (p. 189). However, as Kirwan cogently argues, the enterprise is fraught with complications:

> At one level, the very ephemerality of stage performance means that no one performance can ever be a 'complete' rendition of a work. Cuts, errors, interpolations, adaptation and interpretation all turn the theatrical experience into a performative engagement with the text, defying and rejecting the possibility of completion. The problems [...] of reaching a complete textual Shakespeare are even more apparent on stage, where a choice has to be made between textual variants: there is no performative equivalent of the 'Textual Variants' appendix. (pp. 191–2)

After a brief Epilogue (pp. 207–14), Kirwan provides a useful Appendix (pp. 215–29) tabling the first attribution and current scholarly consensus about the authorial status for all the apocryphal plays. Aside from its fresh readings and wealth of materials, which persuasively establish these oft-neglected plays as worthy objects of study, the chief value of *Shakespeare and the Idea of Apocrypha* lies in its call for a scholarship that engages with multiple critical-theoretical methodologies — including those outside one's usual comfort zone.

In "'I tell you what mine authors says": A Brief History of Stylometrics' (*ELH* 82[2015] 815–44), Jeffrey Kahan's intention is to make the field of stylometry appear ridiculous. To make his case, Kahan employs the same strategies for which he critiques stylometrists: cherry-picking case studies, distorting evidence, misrepresenting scholarship, and dubious logic. After a series of vignettes featuring 'some of the key historical moments in the mating of statistical methodologies and Shakespeare' (p. 816), Kahan hopes his potted history of the field may 'serve as its epitaph' (p. 837), concluding 'scientific inquiry (or, more accurately, pseudo-scientific inquiry) concerning such questions [of Shakespearean authorship] just doesn't add up' (p. 838). Consider the following short, self-contained vignette: '1980, UNIVERSITY OF MUENSTER. Marvin Spevack publishes the last of his nine-volume Shakespeare concordance. He lists 19,083 unique words. More recent counts have radically revised that number to 28,829 unique words. Spevack was off by nearly 50%. It seems, therefore, safe to say that for much of the history of stylometrics, scholars could not even count words properly. Without a proper count, statistics are virtually impossible' (p. 829). Kahan fails to realise that the disparity between the figures he cites reflects an application of different criteria for countable features that appear in (potentially different) Shakespearean texts. Kahan's use of the word 'unique' here is ambiguous, because these are not counts of words *unique* to Shakespeare's vocabulary. Rather, they are counts of word 'types', a term used to distinguish a word as an abstract entity from the concrete, particular instances of that word (or 'tokens'). For example, the line 'A horse! A horse! My kingdom for a horse!' from *Richard III* contains five word types (*a, horse, my, kingdom, for*) or nine tokens (with three instances of the types *a* and *horse*). Beyond the distinction between 'type' and 'token', the criteria for what defines a countable word may also differ. For example, scholars may wish to produce separate counts for homograph forms, count words as lemmas, expand or retain contractions, separate or retain compound words, and differ in their approach to orthography and spelling. As the source of the words to be counted, the choice of text(s) is another determining factor. Spevack uses the text of the *Riverside Shakespeare*, an edition that notably 'preserves' a selection of early modern word-forms and, following the dominant editorial practice at the time, conflates texts that survive in different versions. The 'more recent counts' to which Kahan refers are those automatically generated by the Open Source Shakespeare, opensourceshakespeare.org, an online edition based on the so-called 'Moby Shakespeare', derived from William George Clark and William Aldis Wright's 1864 *Globe Shakespeare*. The Open Source Shakespeare's concordance function treats compound words and contractions as distinct types and also counts words appearing in stage directions. (The inclusion of stage directions is problematic, since many are editorial insertions and the authorial statuses of those present in the early texts on which the edition is based are themselves uncertain. It also produces amusing results, such as counts for the Roman numerals designating various monarchs as they enter and exit.) In sum, what Kahan identifies are tallies of 'words' counted according to different criteria as they appear in radically different editions of Shakespeare's works. They are not a case of an inability to reach 'a proper count'. The only misleading arithmetic here is Kahan's calculation of Spevack's total as 'off by nearly 50%'. As a percentage, 19,083 out of 28,829 (Kahan's 'radically revised' target total) is just over 66%, meaning it was short by just under 34%. As Kahan's 'nearly 50%' ironically demonstrates, defective counting does not make it 'virtually impossible' to generate statistics; what matters is whether the statistics are accurate, relevant, and meaningful. Kahan's central argument rests on an assumption that 'a mathematical or scientific approach to reading literature' is to reject 'the humanist tradition' (p. 818), but this ignores the history of the concordance — a history going back at least to the Middle Ages — and the interest in counting features of language in texts it reflects. Kahan also misrepresents his subjects. For example, an unrelated statement about the limitations of raw statistics by Hugh Craig and Arthur F. Kinney is re-applied to dismiss Caroline Spurgeon's 'goal as nothing but a dream' and somehow support the notion that 'looking for a non-Shakespearean voice in a Shakespeare collaboration becomes virtually impossible' (p. 826). Kahan can also be casual in his handling of quotation. For example, on MacDonald P. Jackson's *Studies in Attribution: Middleton and Shakespeare*, Kahan writes 'He [Jackson] approaches his work with a self-described "deployment of forensic skill"' (p. 827). Kahan's term 'self-described' here suggests that Jackson is arrogating 'forensic skill' to himself, when Jackson does nothing of the sort, as is clear from the context of Jackson's original sentence: 'For demonstration in matters of attribution, as opposed to the formulating of hypotheses, the making of assertions, or the deployment of forensic skill in an attempt to persuade, quantification is necessary . . .' (p. 5). Kahan's carelessness extends not only to the names of plays, such as when he admonishes Jackson's later work for not comparing *The Miseries of Enforced Marriage* with '*The* [sic] *Yorkshire Tragedy*' (p. 828), but also to the ambiguous neologism of what he terms the 'block approach' in authorship attribution (p. 833 and *passim*), which unhelpfully conflates text segmentation with the tests themselves. Kahan's caution that 'The reader should now be sufficiently wary of such pronouncements' (p. 835) could serve as a disclaimer for his own article.

I turn now to consider articles from 2015 offering more serious treatment of Shakespearean stylometry and authorship attribution. A special issue of *Studia Metrica et Poetica* on the scholarship of Ants Oras prompted two articles relevant to this section. In 'Ants Oras and the Analysis of Early Modern English Dramatic Verse' (*SMP* 2:ii[2015] 48–57), MacDonald P. Jackson traces the contribution of Oras' *Pause Patterns in Elizabethan and Jacobean Drama: An Experiment in Prosody* (UFlorP [1960]) and its legacy in providing a method for research on authorship and chronology. Jackson concludes that the 'meticulous analysis of versification, based on the accumulation of quantitative data', as pioneered by Oras, 'remains a key to the understanding of individual playwrights' styles' (p. 55). In 'Shakespeare's Pauses, Authorship, and Early Chronology' (*SMP* 2:ii[2015] 25–47), Douglas

Bruster offers a series of case studies demonstrating how Oras' pause-pattern analysis can 'better place works of early modern drama in chronological order' (p. 30) and 'enrich our conversations about attribution even when they do not resolve specific questions' (p. 33). In 'Vocabulary Links between Shakespeare's Plays as a Guide to Chronology: A Reworking of Eliot Slater's Tables' (*Shakespeare* 11[2015] 446–58), Jackson reexamines the analysis of rare words published in Eliot Slater's *The Problem of 'The Reign of King Edward III': A Statistical Approach* (CUP [1988]) and corrects errors in calculation. The recalculated figures broadly support the chronology proposed by the Oxford Shakespeare *Complete Works* (OUP [1986]). The findings are promising, but Jackson notes the need to 'redo Slater's work on plays now [but not then] considered collaborative' (p. 453) to improve accuracy. By extending earlier methodologies and reworking the data produced by previous scholars to generate new findings, all three of these articles also poignantly repudiate Kahan's reductive narrative about stylometry's 'lack of progress' (p. 837).

In broad terms, Jackson's authorship attribution method is to search Literature Online (LION) for word sequences and collocations found in the text to be attributed, looking for those that are comparatively rare. Where a phrase or collocation is found in numbers of texts above a certain threshold, it is excluded. What remain are rare phrases- and collocations-in-common between the suspect text and the works of potential authorial candidates as represented in LION, which are tallied. According to the method, the greater the number of such rare 'links', the more likely a candidate's authorship of the text becomes. In 'Imitation or Collaboration? Marlowe and the Early Shakespeare Canon' (*ShS* 68[2015] 32–47), Gary Taylor and John V. Nance adapt Jackson's method to distinguish 'actual Shakespeare from Shakespeare imitating someone else' (p. 36), namely Christopher Marlowe, in short passages from *Titus Andronicus* and *1 Henry VI*. To validate the method, Taylor and Nance submit corresponding passages from Marlowe's *The Massacre at Paris* and *The Jew of Malta* to the same procedure. The article presents a useful conceptual model, contrasting identity, which is *cellular* and *systemic*, with imitation, which is *selective*, 'because we cannot (and early moderns certainly could not) identify and replicate all the fine-grained cellular detail of the huge complex changing system of any individual linguistic entity', as well as *semiotic*, 'because it depends on pattern recognition: the writer must first recognize a pattern in another person's lexical or gestural language and then replicate that pattern' such that readers 'also recognize those selected features as the sign of a particular identity' (pp. 33–4). The results are promising, but the application of Jackson's method as reported warrants closer scrutiny. While they are careful to ensure that the sample sizes are the same (i.e., 173 words), I am not convinced that Taylor and Nance adequately address the problem of class size asymmetry — in other words, the disparity in total words between the canons representing each of the candidate authors. In theory, at least, an author with a larger corpus has more opportunities to use the words and phrases that happen to be found in the suspect text. Although Taylor and Nance cite links identified between a passage of *Titus Andronicus* and *The Two Gentlemen of Verona* to suggest 'genre cannot explain the strong connection' (p. 37), there is inadequate discussion of the potential effect of genre, which represents another aspect of class asymmetry: not all genres are equally represented (or represented at all) in the works of the candidate authors. In theory, at least, we might expect certain phrases and collocations to be found more often in works of a particular genre. We might also expect to find a degree of self-repetition across the text of a play, which makes Taylor and Nance's failure to exclude the play from which the passage under investigation· is excerpted from the corpus of potential matches a highly questionable decision. Should it surprise us that two matches for words and collocations in a 173-word segment of *The Jew of Malta* (II.iii.176–99) are found elsewhere in the play, and should this count towards the likelihood of Marlowe's authorship? Taylor and Nance do not list the plays (and later, poems) included in their searches of texts in the LION, Early English Books Online Text Creation Partnership (EEBO-TCP), and Oxford Scholarly Editions Online (OSEO) databases, which frustrates any attempt to scrutinize their corpus as a whole. We can, however, critique what is reported. For example, a more conservative bibliographer might object to Taylor and Nance treating *Selimus* as Robert Greene's (pp. 35, 37), since the attribution (first proposed by Alexander Dyce) has received little sustained scholarly attention and falls short of constituting a consensus. Finally, Taylor and Nance use Fisher's Exact Probability Test to claim various 'chances' and probabilities of their results being random (p. 46-47). However, this is a misapplication of the test, which does not calculate probabilities, but frequencies — that is, how *often* a set of results will occur by chance alone, given prior conditions. Taylor has previously been taken to task for misusing the test in this way (see *YWES* 94[2015] 345; *YWES* 95[2016] 404), and this time is no different.

In 'Did Shakespeare Write Double Falsehood? Identifying Individuals by Creating Psychological Signatures with Text Analysis' (*Psychological Science* 26[2015] 570–82), Ryan L. Boyd and James W. Pennebaker use 'language-derived psychological signatures' for Shakespeare, Fletcher, and Theobald to compare with *Double Falsehood*. Their results 'offer consistent evidence against the notion that *Double Falsehood* is Theobald's whole-cloth forgery', finding 'a strong presence of Shakespeare's signature in the early parts' of the play and Fletcher's contributions 'greatest in the final two acts' (p. 579). Like Elliott and Valenza, Boyd and Pennebaker are not literary scholars or textual critics which, aside from notable differences in terminology that one might expect when reading psychological research, might also explain the mercenary attitude to text selection. 'Texts from each author were acquired from various sources' (p. 572), which, with the exception of Theobald, are not identified — even in the 'Text Sample Acquisition' section of the 'Supplemental Material' available to download from the journal's publisher. Electronic transcriptions of Theobald's plays were created by crowdsourcing the task using Amazon's *Mechanical Turk* online platform. With the exception of *Double Falsehood* itself, Boyd and Pennebaker sought to include only 'plays that are generally believed to have been written in solo', and while each text was 'manually stripped of extraneous information that did not directly reflect the author's language', stage directions 'were left intact' (p. 572). It is unclear on what basis this consensus on authorial status was reached, because the corpus of 55 plays listed in Table A1 (p. 580) includes a number of collaborative plays (e.g. the

*Henry VI* plays, *Macbeth*, and *Measure for Measure*) and translations (e.g. *Electra* and *Orestes*). It is also unclear whether Theobald's operatic pantomimes, which form the greatest portion of his corpus, are suitable for comparison. Along with genre, there is a class size asymmetry, with Shakespeare represented by 33 plays, Fletcher by 9, and Theobald by 12. Failure to provide total word-counts or list the sources of the texts frustrates any attempt to calculate the disparity between authors with more precision. Beyond the careless construction of the corpus and casual text preparation, Boyd and Pennebaker's study employs methods that are not designed to account for historical language use. The 'content-word measures' they describe work by grouping words into 40 predetermined (modern) categories, including 'positive and negative emotions, family members, sensory perceptions, religion, and death', whereas the 'meaning-extraction method' generated '13 broad themes' of words — 'Emotionality', 'Royalty', 'War/Battle', 'Tragedy', 'Nature', 'Social', 'Femininity', 'Youth', 'Greatness', 'Romance', 'Slumber', 'Nobility', and 'Family' (p. 573 and 'Supplemental Material'). The potential for error in classifying early modern words according to modern psychological categories and present-day usage and meaning should be readily apparent to the reader. For example, Boyd and Pennebaker categorize *sweet* as a 'Femininity' word, *happy* as 'Youth' word, *honest* as a 'Nobility' word, and, most curiously, *swear*, *vow*, and *oath* as 'Romance' words ('Supplemental Material'). While such errors do not necessarily invalidate Boyd and Pennebaker's findings, they do make it difficult to take their study seriously.

Finally, in a brief article, '*A Lover's Complaint* and Early English Books Online' (*N&Q* 62[2015] 586–9), MacDonald P. Jackson responds to criticism that his study published in *Determining the Shakespeare Canon* (CUP [2014]) failed to consider evidence from the EEBO-TCP corpus and searched only the LION database for matches with rare spellings found in *A Lover's Complaint* and its candidate authors. After repeating his searches using the EEBO-TCP corpus, Jackson finds added support for his earlier results, concluding 'the rare spellings shared by *A Lover's Complaint* and Shakespeare's plays originated in Shakespeare's own autograph manuscript and survived whatever stages of textual transmission led to their appearance in print' (p. 589).

## 2. Shakespeare in the Theatre

Michael Dobson's 'Shakespeare and the Idea of National Theatres' (*ShS* 67[2015] 234–46) is characteristically urbane and humorous. It is also unashamedly autobiographical, as Dobson name-checks his school tutor, 'the best teacher of English and drama ever, Wendy Williams' (p. 235), notes how his grandfather played the Ghost in *Hamlet* (p. 245), and mischievously relishes the chance to infuriate Dominic Dromgoole, former artistic director of the Globe: 'The last time I described Shakespeare's Globe as the folksiest theatre in London I received an abusive email from its artistic director, so I am going to do so again just in the hopes of annoying him' (p. 242). The essay charts the emergence and superimposition of three characteristics of national theatres: the historical involvement of royalty, the tradition of the actor-manager (Garrick to Olivier – and Branagh?) and 'what I am going to call the notion of a folk theatre [according to which] drama should be an expression of traditional immemorial indigenous popular culture' (p. 241). The essay ranges across France, Germany, and eastern Europe but ends, fittingly, in Dobson's office in the Shakespeare Institute with its offcut of 'royal carpet, with a pattern depicting all the kings from the history plays' (p. 245) which featured in the newly opened Shakespeare Memorial Theatre. Never mind presentist, this essay is autobiographicist!

'Actors' Conversations at the Rose Theatres' (*CahiersE* 88[2015] 155–68) is also animated by a distinctly personal perspective. Near the opening of his account of the first decade of the Kingston Rose, Frank Whately admits that 'this article offers some personal reflections, based on my experience as a founding director of the Kingston Theatre Trust' (p. 156). This is an insider's account which explores the relationship between the architecture of the space and playing styles. It also implicitly decries the pseudo 'Ye Olde Englande' sentimentality of historical reconstructions: 'there was no intention of building a chocolate box souvenir replica in Kingston' (p. 164). (No names are mentioned but it's a good job Dromgoole probably doesn't subscribe to *CahiersE*.) The theatre is less an archaeological reconstruction than a laboratory, a place to examine and reflect upon 'particular practitioners' discoveries' (p. 156). This shift, Whately concludes, is a current trend: theatres such as the Kingston Rose and the Sam Wanamaker 'reflect the design of the first public theatres in England [and] have begun to reveal acting styles which are very different from those which have predominated in actor training for the past century and in most stage practice since the Restoration' (p. 166). Whately underlines the similarities in terms of size between Philip Henslowe's 1587 Rose and its Kingston namesake: 'the external diameter of the 1587 Rose was 72 feet and that of the Kingston Rose is 73 feet 7 inches; the inner "yard" of the 1587 Rose was 49 feet and of its Kingston offspring 49 feet 6 inches' (p. 163). Of course, we should add that the Kingston Rose accommodates probably less than half the audience of Henslowe's crowded auditorium but, nevertheless, the similarity of dimensions allows practitioners a feel of what the original may have been like. Whately suggests that actors such as Barrie Rutter have spoken of the space's aptness for intimacy as well as its capacity 'to take epic readily' (p. 166). Whately finds in this empiricism an endorsement of the academic work of Bruce Smith and Robert Weimann: 'the Rose works most effectively when the acting is "presentational"' (p. 157). The space lends itself, perhaps as did the original Rose, to 'an extrovert physical and vocal quality' (p. 159).

Robert Shaughnessy reports on a collaborative research project between the University of Kent's School of Psychology and the Globe. 'Connecting the Globe: Actors, Audience and Entrainment' (*ShS* 67[2015] 294–305) discusses the various dynamics of the Globe audience, especially those standing in the yard, and the manner in which theatre critics and acting companies relate (in quite distinct ways) to them. The phenomenon of 'entrainment' is the process of synchronizing 'initially independent rhythmic systems' (p. 295) which, in the case of the groundlings, leads to a homogenizing of their responses to the live action played out in front of them. Shaughnessy draws on show reports from stage management, theatre reviews, and actors' interviews which variously document audience reaction to and interaction with the Globe's Playing Shakespeare 2013 production of *Romeo and Juliet*. Shaughnessy argues that 'Shakespeare's Globe is a highly emotionally contagious space: the audience is visibly and audibly on display to itself, thus maximizing the opportunities for behavioural mirroring' (p. 304). This mass observation (as it were) is treated distinctly in critics' and actors' accounts. Indeed, Shaughnessy regards the critics' contempt for the groundlings, on the one hand, and the actors' sometimes gushing admiration for them, on the other, as 'fairly polarized thinking' (p. 299). But just as the groundlings keep the actors on their toes, so they (as a large, homogenized force) can also be threatening: 'loss of control is a persistent worry, and there is constant concern that Globe performance can all too easily get out of hand, and that the audience can take charge' (p. 303). Shaughnessy cites how the show reports of the matinee on 18 March 2013 noted many missed cues and late entrances. The screams of the largely female teenage audience obscured several cues. Shaughnessy likens this crowd to the cacophonous reactions of teenyboppers at a rock concert. To Bieber or not to Bieber? What an awful question.

'Entrainment' also rears its head in another essay on the Globe audience. Penelope Woods, in 'Skilful Spectatorship? Doing (or Being) Audience at Shakespeare's Globe Theatre' (*ShakS* 43[2015] 99–113), notes that audience participation in 'clapping and bobbing and the likelihood of that audience joining in vocally when invited' (p. 107) is greater in productions preceded by 'a larger number of musical pieces performed before the play opens'. The audience, she suggests, uniquely at the Globe, 'is essential for the realization of performance', and she claims audience presence is a vital part of 'a "system" of performance' (p. 100). As she puts it, 'A porous and contingent site of interaction between performer, building, weather, play, and audience is produced that alters and subverts norms of audience behavior and assumptions around their passivity and quiescence' (p. 101). Woods is acute on the self-consciousness of those standing in the yard berated by Flavius at the opening of *Julius Caesar*: 'Hence! Home, you idle creatures, get you home: / Is this a holiday?' (she uses the 1999 production directed by Mark Rylance). The groundlings are both the plebeians whom the character berates and the audience at whom the actor is railing: 'Flavius's metatheatrical joke capitalizes on a latent shared suspicion that watching plays is unproductive, passive, voyeuristic' (p. 99). However, her conclusion is less convincing: she argues that the audience's 'capacity to switch between states of self-consciousness, absorption, laughter, nervousness [and] dread' (p. 111) demonstrates 'an emotional skilfulness in this audience'. It seems to me that the play's capacity to take an audience with it in spite of forcing it to encounter all these varied emotional states is evidence, rather, of the playwright's skills, not those of the audience.

In 'The International Language of Physical Theatre at the 2012 Globe to Globe Festival' (*ShJE* 151[2015] 101–15), Stephen Purcell also stresses the importance of the audience's contribution to the completion of the theatrical event: 'theatre is not a one-way act of signification, but a conversation' (p. 114). He examines some half a dozen productions from the 2012 Globe

Festival which were particularly concerned with physical gesturing as a way of overcoming the fact that they were played in a variety of languages: 'Clowning ... might be described not so much as a *language* but as a particular communicative strategy: self-aware, dialogic and playful' (p. 113). Purcell challenges the notion that gesture transcends culture, though, at the same time, he acknowledges that it may communicate to a wider audience than a particular spoken language: 'It is in translating Shakespeare's text into physical metaphor, I would argue, that such [theatrical] work achieves its broadest intercultural reach' (p. 110). Intriguingly, he suggests that through physicalizing these plays they were transformed 'in a double sense: transformed to the cultures of the companies themselves, but also *re*-transformed for the occasion of the Globe to Globe Festival in particular' (p. 113). This is an original and engaging essay, and Purcell has a good eye for performance details.

We move from the Globe to the RSC and Peter Kirwan's 'The Roared-at Boys? Repertory Casting and Gender Politics in the RSC's 2014 Swan Season' (*Shakespeare* 11[2015] 247–61). Kirwan examines the gap between the stated intention of the RSC's Roaring Girls season and its effects. The season, he opines, was marketed 'on the strength and specificity of its interest in women' (p. 248). Moreover it was to be 'a statement of intent in respect to women's roles both on and offstage at the RSC in this new era' (p. 252)—the new era being the reign of Greg Doran as artistic director. However, Kirwan goes on to demonstrate how the programming served to marginalize feminist concerns and reinforce the secondary status of the female-directed productions. Most obviously, while these peripheral plays were taking place in the Swan, the main house next door was mounting productions of the patriarchal *Henry IV* plays as well as *The Two Gentlemen of Verona*—a play not renowned for its feminist credentials. Nor was this sexism ameliorated by the choice of plays at the Swan. Of *The Roaring Girl* (directed by Jo Davies) Kirwan asserts that 'However the play is read, the *term* "roaring girl" remains the preferred phrase of the judgemental, misogynistic order for framing and situating Moll within a society that cannot fully accept her' (p. 249). The production was set somewhere between a Victorian slum and a contemporary music gig—it featured some (just terrible) rapping and rock songs. For Kirwan, this blending of different periods further undermined any feminist reading: 'The time-travelling feminism of this production risked rendering the resonance of the roaring girl so diffuse as to be meaningless' (p. 258). The other plays in the season are also challenged in feminist terms. Of *The White Devil*, for instance, Kirwan makes the point that 'The transgressive changeability or duplicitousness implied in the play's title ... already encodes a means of containing the disruptive or inexplicable woman', while the later addition of *The Witch of Edmonton* to the season (directed by Doran himself) 'did nothing, of course, to detract from the negative connotations of "roaring"'' (p. 250). Given Kirwan's acute and intelligent critique of the season's sexual politics, his conclusion is surprisingly conciliatory: the season 'reopened important conversations about female agency and the company's own positioning of women' (p. 260).

Christopher Baker, in '"Let me the curtains draw": *Othello* in Performance' (in Evans, ed., *Othello: A Critical Reader*, pp. 51–81), provides a thorough stage history concluding with the unsurprising pronouncement that it will continue to be 'as impossible to disengage productions of *Othello* from an awareness of contemporary racial friction as it has been for audiences to separate *The Merchant of Venice* from a post-Holocaust context' (p. 81). Baker, from the outset, emphasizes the play's meta-dramatic quality: 'it is not only the audience that is both involved in the play and yet outside it as observers of the performance, but likewise the hero himself who often seems conscious of his own identity within the story and of himself as the object of others' gaze' (p. 52). Perhaps this is the reason for the star quality of the play's title role, with performers including Betterton, Garrick, Cibber, Kean, Salvini, Aldridge (who 'at 17 appeared as Othello at the Royalty Theatre in London', p. 63), Robeson, Olivier, and Hopkins. Several of these stand out for Baker, who notes some general trends in terms of the performance history of this play. During the Romantic period, for instance, 'the stage conception of Othello was shifting, the pendulum swinging more towards a freer expression of his uninhibited side, an alteration also emerging in literary criticism' (p. 59). In illustrating this point, Evans cites Hazlitt, who 'was less concerned with Othello's social persona than with his tragic psyche'. The stage equivalent of this shift of focus was the performance of Edmund Kean, who prompted Keats to remark how he was 'direful and slaughterous to the deepest degree' (p. 60). But it was the black actor, Robeson, who brought to the play 'an intentional awareness of the racial predicament of his own society' (p. 64). In the wake of this there is, according to modern sensibilities, anyway, something clumsy or miscalculated about both Olivier and Hopkins blacking up to take the role. Evans notes of the latter that 'This was the last (and may perhaps be the final) time a major actor played Othello in blackface on film' (p. 70). Perceptively, given *Othello*'s domestic setting, Baker notes how from its first performances it was not only a Globe but a Blackfriars play, which suggests 'an enclosed space for audiences eager for more nuanced styles' (p. 54). Throughout this essay there is much that is familiar, but Baker's fluency and inclusiveness make this an obvious port of call for those recapitulating the play's theatrical history.

*Othello* is also the focus of Clare McManus's ' "Sing it like Poor Barbary"': *Othello* and Early Modern Women's Performance' (*ShakB* 33[2015] 99–120), in which she suggests that the combination of singing and speaking during the willow song of IV.iii 'can illuminate the interaction between English and continental theater, staging an embedded moment of opposition between English boy actor and continental actress' (p. 99). This is a suggestive idea, and McManus is thorough on 'the continental context of the circulating trope of the lamenting abandoned woman' (p. 115), but her argument that the willow song requires 'a high-wire act of exceptional confidence' (p. 108) or (repetitively) a 'high-wire act of talent, skillfully and charismatically executed' (p. 110) is over-egging the pudding. Yes, the boy actor is required to mix singing and speaking at the same time as changing costume, but is the co-ordination of these activities really so very difficult? While McManus is right to point out the competitive edge of the English theatre's rejection of the song's 'Italianate contexts in favour of the English ballad' (p. 113), that is not enough to convince me that the willow song constitutes a significant challenge to the mixed-sex theatre of the Continent from single-sex English theatre practice.

Another study of a single play, this time *The Tempest*. In his evocative and deftly balanced 'Airy Spirits: Winds, Bodies, and Ecological Force in Early Modern England' (*ShIntY* 15[2015] 21–38), Steve Mentz insists that wind is the driving force not only of Shakespeare's play but of the early modern world, writing of 'the wind–human exchanges that drove early globalization' (p. 22). He goes on, 'Shakespeare's stormy play presents a diverse accumulation of ideas about air and wind' (p. 34). Mentz neatly balances the abstract spirituality of the play against its maritime substance, juxtaposing Prospero's and the Boatswain's opposed conceptions of the weather: 'The anti-materialist wizard wants only Providence, while the physical mariner feels only disorderly wind. These two symbolic understandings of the human relation with the environment, Prospero's magic and the Boatswain's craft, define the play's attitudes toward air as immaterial force and material presence' (p. 25). It is the presence of this force in the theatre that animates the play: the task of the playwright and audience is 'to find within the insubstantial element traces of meaning' (p. 34). In this way, theatre-going itself becomes an ecological activity or at least one concerned with decoding the varieties of human attitudes to the non-human world—a bold and provocative idea.

Still concerned with the natural world, at least as a point of departure, Adam Rzepka unpacks the variety of ways in which the spectator's imagination is tested and utilized in the early modern theatre. His ' "How easy is a bush supposed a bear?"': Differentiating Imaginative Production in *A Midsummer Night's Dream*' (*SQ* 66[2015] 308–28) is a consideration of 'the collaboration between playwright, performer, and audience' and underlines 'the diversity of imaginative production' (p. 310) that this triangulated relationship produces. Rzepka notes the 'markedly experimental' way in which the play grafts 'imaginative landscapes onto the physical space of the theater' (p. 318). Techniques include evocative linguistic description and the suggestive use of classical names to summon up ideas of pastoral vistas, for instance. Elsewhere the suggestion of 'the microsphere' in the naming of Mustardseed, Peaseblossom, Moth, and Cobweb announces 'the theater's capacity to work comfortably within the apparent paradoxes of representation it is uniquely capable of posing' (p. 324). Throughout, Rzepka is adamant that this process is sophisticatedly self-conscious and that the play is explicit about the vulnerabilities of semblance. The audience is, he concludes, 'confronted with the heterogeneity of the modes of imagination that theater can demand of us' (p. 327).

Andrew Bozio cites some of the same theoretical sources as Rzepka (such as Evelyn Tribble and John Sutton's work on cognitive ecology), and his essay is also concerned with the conceptualization of space. 'Embodied Thought and the Perception of Place in *King Lear*' (*SEL* 55[2015] 263–84) examines the 'relationship between embodied thought and the environment' (p. 264). Bozio cites Gloucester's blinded pronouncement that he sees the world 'feelingly' as demonstrating that epistemology relies upon corporeality; therefore, he goes on, *King Lear* 'suggests that the embodied mind and its immediate environment are mutually constitutive of one another' (p. 265). In theatrical terms the importance of this suggestion is that theatre demands (and is reliant upon) the 'spatialization of thought' (p. 265) both within the terms of the narrative but also in order to make sense of *King Lear* itself in the theatre. Typically, for a play perched on the edge of its own theatrical cliff-top, while it 'foregrounds the role of experience in defining location, it invokes this intimacy between place and personhood precisely in order to stage its dissolution' (p. 279).

Paul Prescott's 'Shakespeare and the Dream of Olympism' (in Prescott and Sullivan, eds., *Shakespeare on the Global Stage: Performance and Festivity in the Olympic Year*, pp. 1–37) considers the ubiquity of the playwright in the year of the London Olympic Games [2012]. The so-called Cultural Olympiad featured the World Shakespeare Festival, an umbrella term which included visiting non-English productions in Stratford and London (the Globe's own 'Globe to Globe' festival), the 'Shakespeare Unlocked' season on the BBC, projects in schools, artistic exhibitions, *The Hollow Crown*, and so on *ad nauseam*. Prescott ponders Robert Dover's Cotswold Olympicks which, during the year of the London Olympics celebrated its 400th anniversary. Played just outside Chipping Campden—a mere 12 miles from Stratford-upon-Avon—the games may have been attended by Shakespeare himself but, in any case, they offer a 'reassuringly rural' (p. 6) nostalgia and 'an easy congruence between Shakespeareanism and Olympism' (p. 7). Perhaps most conspicuously and bewilderingly 'Shakespeare was threaded throughout the [2012] Olympic opening ceremony (estimated global TV audience: 900 million)' (p. 4), the function of which was 'to transmit and transfer images of Britain and Britishness that might easily be read and approvingly consumed by the national and global audience' (p. 22). There 'was little or no question as to why', Prescott asserts, 'the global study of Shakespeare might be a good thing or not' (p. 11). But the overwhelming optimism of the Shakespearean Olympic dream is punctured when Prescott considers some of the less ennobling manifestations of the Bard circulating at the same time, such as the footage of a Royal Marine sergeant murdering an Afghan insurgent in September 2011 with the words, 'There you are, shuffle off this mortal coil, you cunt.' The incident, filmed on a head-cam worn by another in the patrol, 'offered a painful reminder that the nightmare of history was very far from over' (p. 21). (Coincidentally, at the very time of writing, the *Guardian* [7 December 2016] reported that the soldier concerned, Alexander Blackman, is likely to have his conviction set aside on the grounds that he was suffering mental stress.) Prescott is also sceptical towards a sequence in the opening ceremony which dramatized the meeting and romantic involvement of a young couple via the Internet. Sir Tim Berners-Lee was revealed as 'a benign Prospero' (p. 24) whose World Wide Web drew them together. Prescott notes that the girl was mixed-race and the boy black, and insists that this apparently happy pairing should be read against the 'see-sawing [British] government attitudes to multiculturalism and immigration, and the London riots of summer 2011' which followed the police shooting of Mark Duggan (who was mixed-race). Prescott sombrely observes, 'At the time of the riots, pre-Olympic preparations were well underway for a new, semi-militarized infrastructure of defence systems and anti-terrorist surveillance' (p. 26). This is an eloquent and thoughtful essay which considers Brand Shakespeare as both a successful and problematic manifestation of Brand UK. Brand Shakespeare features at the end of Robert Ormsby's meticulous study of *Coriolanus* on stage. *Coriolanus: Shakespeare in Performance* concludes that 'the playwright's brand—based on star power, a cut script, "respectfully" interventionist direction and spectacle ... has prevailed in the theatre, on screen and in journalistic response to *Coriolanus* productions for most of the postwar era' (p. 243). The first of the book's eleven chapters deals with its stage history from first performance—'there is not much we know about the tragedy in early modern England' (p. 1)—through to its early twentieth-century productions, but things really get going when Ormsby discusses Olivier's 1959 performance, directed by Peter Hall (Olivier had played the role for the first time in 1938). This is the production which featured Olivier's death-doomed leap head first, to be caught by the ankles. Unsurprisingly, perhaps, the 'critics' response, collectively revealed a journalistic community largely in tune with the star system' (p. 43)—this, in spite of the RSC's avowed intention to assemble an ensemble company. (Though Ormsby cites Tynan's eloquent analysis, he misses perhaps the best sentence in theatre reviewing of the period. Laurence Kitchin vividly described Olivier's protagonist cursing the plebeians: 'There was a bizarre impression of one man lynching a crowd.') Between 1951 and 1971 several productions of the play were clearly influenced by Brecht, though Ormsby notes that the British reception of Brecht 'frequently coded Brechtian theatre as an ideologically hostile and distinctly foreign threat to Shakespeare' (p. 48). For instance, of the 1965 London residence of the Berliner Ensemble, Ormsby suggests that the company diluted Brecht and displayed 'an apolitical theatrical aesthetic, providing only an imprecise socialist gloss on their work' (p. 62). Günter Grass's adaptation, *The Plebeians Rehearse the Uprising* (RSC, 1970) ultimately did little politically. The diminution of Brecht's influence was a hallmark of the RSC's 1972–3 production with Nicol Williamson (directed by Trevor Nunn with Buzz Goodbody) as well as the 1977 RSC production starring Alan Howard (directed by Terry Hands). By 1984 and the BBC Shakespeare version, starring Howard and directed by Elijah Moshinsky, the plebs, servants, and crowds had been largely removed so that the focus had become psychological rather than political. Not till Peter Hall's 1985 production for the National, starring Ian McKellen, which took place against the protracted and violent miners' strike, was the play's staging 'explicitly engaged with its political context' (p. 140). Hall had been outspoken against cuts in public funding for the arts under Thatcher, though Ormsby notes awkwardly that labour problems at the National Theatre itself had 'provoked Hall to vote Tory in 1979' (p. 141).

There follow accounts of three overseas productions—Gábor Székeley's 1985 Budapest production (starring György Cserhalmi), Steven Berkoff's 1988 New York production (with Christopher Walken), and Robert Lepage's adaptation, *Coriolan* (starring Jules Philip, international tour, 1992–4). While Székeley's production was characterized by a lack of a particular political target, its topicality of design hinted at 'a melancholic recognition that the futility of participating in a degraded public sphere has a profoundly corrosive effect on anyone who attempts to do so' (p. 158). The American production 'coincided with an anxiety about specifically national identity (American or British) disrupting an idealized Shakespeare' (p. 189). Lepage's adaptation (translated by Michel Garneau) 'demonstrates how globalization can spur the reinvention of the local' (p. 192). In all these productions the politics seem generalized or, indeed, vague. But even this is better than the deep conservatism of Dominic Dromgoole's Globe version of 2006, starring Jonathan Cake. Ormsby cites Peter Holland, who was infuriated, describing this as 'the most reactionary production of the play I [Holland] had ever seen' and finding the 'racial politics' of *Coriolanus*'s publicity photograph, in which Cake kicks Mo Sesay's black Aufidius in the face, 'positively embarrassing' (p. 219). The production's humour targeted the theatre's groundlings, who equated to the play's lower classes, so that political grievances from below seemed merely humorous. Holland again: 'the patricians, RP-speaking, rational and ... clearly benign, could not but be the sympathetic centre of the politics of this divided society, for all the world like an old-fashioned Tory party, the core of a benevolent establishment' (p. 219).

Ormsby's final chapter is an account of Ralph Fiennes's feature film released in 2011 (screenplay by John Logan). Perhaps this film's most successful and conspicuous features are the involvement of the viewer in the battle sequences and the ways in which the film reworks the Hollywood figure of the action hero. Throughout this book Ormsby's analysis is eagle-eyed, though there are some tricks missed. Fiennes's 2000 stage performance of the role (directed by Jonathan Kent) could have figured more, especially since it took place in a film studio (Gainsborough) and formed an interesting contrast in scale. While the politically quietest thrust of Ormsby's book downplays the play's politics, some mention of more explicitly politicized productions would have offered valuable counter-examples—David Thacker's French Revolution RSC production (with Toby Stephens, 1994); Michael Bogdanov's ESC Brechtian epic (starring Michael Pennington, 1990), or Tim Supple's superb production, almost overrun by plebeians, staged at Chichester Festival in 1992 and starring Kenneth Branagh. And what, if any, might be the effects on a production of this macho play of a female director—Jane Howell directed Corin Redgrave in the role at the Young Vic in 1989? (Every one of Ormsby's directors is male.) Still, this is a valuable book for those boning up on the play's various manifestations (though it must be added that the quality of the black and white pictures is pretty poor).

## 3. Criticism

### (a) General

Oxford University Press has replaced its Very Short Introduction to *Shakespeare* by Germaine Greer with one to *William Shakespeare* by Stanley Wells: the new volume actually takes on the serial number (60) of the previous one. The move makes sense both as a better fit with the series remit and in updating the content (Greer's essay was originally published in 1986). This is evident in the new version's attention to Shakespeare's collaborative work and the inclusion in the 'Further Reading' of 'books that can be recommended to anyone tempted to question who wrote Shakespeare' (p. 120). The volume is especially aimed at readers who may not have encountered Shakespeare since their schooldays (pp. xiii–xv, 111). In fact, these readers may find some surprising information compared to what they would have learnt at school: that the dedication to Mr W.H. is not by Shakespeare but by the sonnets' printer (p. 44) and that the collection may not have been about one young friend but several (p. 45), or the idea that late in his career Shakespeare may have been 'encouraged' by his company 'to work with a colleague who was more attuned to popular taste' (p. 107). Character names ('A mischievous puck … Robin Goodfellow', p. 73; *Cymbeline*'s Giacomo), the chronological table on pages 116–17, and mentions of several textual issues all, obviously, refer to work done for the Oxford Shakespeare. The book is divided into eight chapters: 'Shakespeare and Stratford-upon-Avon', 'Theatre in Shakespeare's Time', 'Shakespeare in London', 'Plays of the 1590s', 'Shakespeare and Comic Form', 'Return to Tragedy', 'Classical Plays', and 'Tragicomedy', plus an 'Epilogue' on Shakespeare's afterlife. Up-to-the-minute scholarship is tempered by a real feel for the details of Shakespeare's life and times, as when the section on 'Shakespeare's Reading' in chapter 1 is enlivened by the remark that Holinshed had resided not far from Stratford in later life and that Shakespeare may therefore have met him as a boy (p. 16). Chapters 4–8 discuss each work's plots and themes, always with an awareness of their performance dimension and often including cross-references to the earlier background chapters as well as concentrated insights, such as the mention of Viola and Sebastian's 'antiphon of reunion' in *Twelfth Night* V.i (p. 80). In his substantial analysis, Wells finds room to express his opinion on the desirability of modern editions (p. 48), the relevance of biographical data (p. 88), and the unattainability of 'total authenticity' in the staging of the plays (p. 111). His final message to the addressees of this not so very short introduction is: 'Whether directly or indirectly, no one can remain untouched by Shakespeare. He is in the water supply; he is here to stay' (p. 115).

Unsurprisingly, some of the information and views in Wells's Very Short Introduction are also found in Paul Edmondson and Stanley Wells's edited collection *The Shakespeare Circle*. In her 'Afterword' to this book (pp. 335–9), Margaret Drabble hails its 'indirect and circular approach' to Shakespearean biography as 'a great success' (p. 339). The volume's combination of new archival research (mostly, though not only, in the Stratford chapters) and state-of-the-question reporting on various Shakespeare-related figures does indeed prove illuminating and, thanks to a detailed index and chapter-by-chapter bibliography, the book can serve as a useful reference tool. It contains a wealth of intriguing information, starting from the cover, which portrays a signet ring that may have belonged to Shakespeare (p. viii). Each of the book's three sections comes with an additional short introduction by the editors. On the crucial issue of religious background, the information gathered in Part I, 'Family', does seem to justify the editors' conclusion that the church of the time 'was catholic and reformed and could accommodate a wide-range of spiritual and religious beliefs among those who were happy outwardly to conform. Overall Shakespeare and his family, like most other people of their time, seem to have done just that' (p. 9). Another important issue in this section concerns the family's financial circumstances. Michael Wood (chapter 1, 'His Mother Mary Shakespeare', pp. 13–25) follows the traditional view that Shakespeare's father withdrew from public life after an economic downturn, while in chapter 2, 'His Father John Shakespeare' (pp. 26–39), David Fallow argues that John Shakespeare's involvement with the wool industry brought him prosperity in the end. Fallow further suggests that the reason why Shakespeare moved to London in the first instance was to do with his father's business (p. 32). Given the paucity of information on Shakespeare's three brothers, all of whom died unmarried before the dramatist and none of whom reached the age of 50, chapter 3, 'His Siblings' (pp. 40–8), by Catherine Richardson, deals with 'sibling experiences that must have seemed normal to Shakespeare' (p. 42), before focusing on the youngest brother, Edmund, sixteen years William's junior and a fellow-actor. In chapter 4, 'His Sister's Family: The Harts' (pp. 49–56), Cathy Shrank focuses on Joan, who was five years younger than her famous brother and the only one of his siblings to survive him: in fact, Joan buried her husband and her last surviving sibling within a week of each other. Chapter 5, by Katherine Scheil, summarizes the available information on 'His Wife Anne Shakespeare and the Hathaways' (pp. 57–70), using new archaeological evidence to illustrate the lifestyle at New Place. On the vexed question of the 'second-best bed', Scheil points out that the phrase could have been added by others. (As an alternative explanation, on pp. 156–7 Stanley Wells mentions Thomas Combe's will, which bequeathed all bedsteads to his wife, except the best bedstead, which went to his son.) In chapter 6, 'His Daughter Susanna Hall' (pp. 71–85), Lachlan Mackinnon discusses the Shakespeare family's funeral monuments, suggesting that Susanna wrote all their epitaphs. She is characterized as having 'Roman Catholic sympathies' despite being married to the Puritan John Hall (p. 77). On page 81 Mackinnon mentions a visit by Queen Henrietta Maria to New Place in 1643, and how Susanna later sent the queen a book that heavily criticized Catherine de' Medici, not least as the driving force behind the St Bartholomew's Day Massacre. Some of the information provided here is wrong, namely the presumed printer's name, the person to whom the book was given in the first instance (since an inscription in the book itself declares that it was gifted by Susanna to Richard Grace), and even the fact that Henrietta Maria was Catherine de' Medici's granddaughter (p. 82; the title of the book on p. 84 is also slightly misspelled). On the other hand, Susanna's possession of this book ties in with the fact that, as Greg Wells points out in chapter 7 ('His Son-in-Law John Hall', pp. 86–100), her being fined for absence from Easter Communion in 1606 could just as well be evidence of Puritan as of Catholic leanings (p. 92). Wells's essay includes a discussion of how medical figures evolved in Shakespeare's plays, though not necessarily by consequence of his daughter marrying a physician in 1607. On Shakespeare's son there is notoriously little to say and, perhaps influenced by the example of Joyce's speculations in *Ulysses* on the link between Hamnet's death and *Hamlet* (pp. 106–7), Graham Holderness flirts elegantly with creative non-fiction (chapter 8, 'His Son Hamnet Shakespeare', pp. 101–9). While not wishing to adjudicate on this supposed connection, Holderness does report an intriguing mistake in Shakespeare's will, where the neighbour after whom Hamnet Shakespeare was named is called 'Hamlett' (pp. 101, 106). Germaine Greer's essay on 'His Daughter Judith and the Quineys' (chapter 9, pp. 110–21) provides details that effectively bring the fantasy world of Shakespeare's comedies closer to his family's life in Stratford: for instance, how, in line with his Puritanism, the elder Quiney's first act as a bailiff was to forbid workmen's attendance at alehouses except at Christmas (while his family's mercer business then branched out into that of vintners). Along these lines, one wonders whether Greer's account of Judith's marriage to the caddish or naive Thomas is not more or less consciously shaped on that of Helena and Bertram in *All's Well That Ends Well*. An example of how divergent views are given equal space within this book is the fact that, according to Greer, Shakespeare was forced to make Susanna his sole heir by the conditions of her marriage settlement, while in chapter 10, 'His Granddaughter Lady Elizabeth Barnard' (pp. 122–34), René Weis reiterates that the playwright's will was changed in order to safeguard the estate from 'feckless' Thomas Quiney (p. 128). According to Weis, Elizabeth's birth and her father's medical profession may be reflected in *Pericles*. Prior to her death in 1670, she was her grandfather's last surviving direct descendant, which justifies the 'impulse to search for genuine Shakespeare materials from New Place among the descendants of the Barnards', her second husband's family (p. 131). A mention of a prolonged stay at Shakespeare's home, New Place, by 'His "cousin" Thomas Greene' gives Tara Hamling the opportunity to include a detailed description of the house in chapter 11 (pp. 135–43). Part II, on 'Friends and Neighbours', opens with chapter 12 by Stanley Wells on 'A Close Family Connection: The Combes' (pp. 149–60), a Protestant landowning family and owners of the largest house in Stratford (New Place being the second largest). Chapter 13, by Carol Chillington Rutter, is on 'Schoolfriend, Publisher and Printer Richard Field' (pp. 161–73), who also moved to London and managed the printing house that issued *Venus and Adonis* and *The Rape of Lucrece* after being apprenticed to printer Thomas Vautrollier, while chapter 14, by David Kathman, is on 'Living with the Mountjoys' (pp. 174–85)—thus these two chapters focus on Shakespeare's Huguenot connections. David Riggs discusses 'Ben Jonson' (chapter 15, pp. 186–98), including aspects of literary influence, for example on *Twelfth Night*, while Andrew Hadfield shows how references by 'Richard Barnfield, John Weever, William Basse and other encomiasts' do prove that a specific person named William Shakespeare was indeed the author of certain plays and poems (chapter 16, pp. 199–212). In Susan Brock's essay on 'Last Things: Shakespeare's Neighbours and Beneficiaries' (chapter 17, pp. 213–29), we learn that twenty-one out of twenty-five people mentioned in Shakespeare's will belonged to the Stratford rather than the London milieu and that, with the notable exceptions of his godson and the latter's father, his legatees were 'almost all ... mavericks in some way' (p. 226). These are all information-rich chapters, where details and opinions overlap with or supplement those given elsewhere in the book: see for instance Stanley Wells's opinion that there must be 'at least a small fire' behind the 'puffs of smoke' that point to Southampton providing Shakespeare with financial help towards a big purchase (p. 151). Several chapters link the factual information they provide with aspects of Shakespeare's works (e.g. on pp. 176–7, mentions of head-tires in the plays and Marie Mountjoy's profession as tirewoman). It should be pointed out that the notion that Field's master, Vautrollier, had been in trouble for printing heretical books by Giordano Bruno (p. 165) is at odds with what is generally believed by Bruno scholars. On the other hand, it is interesting to see that Shakespeare is now finally being credited with a 'first-rate classical education' (p. 186; see also p. 164), though this goes rather against the drift of Hadfield's chapter (who, however, is mostly referring to authors who were writing at the turn of the century, who seem only to have known Shakespeare's poems, *Romeo and Juliet*, and *Richard III*). In Part III, 'Colleagues and Patrons', Andy Kesson's essay on 'His Fellow Dramatists and Early Collaborators' (chapter 18, pp. 235–47) in fact focuses on *Greene's Groatsworth of Wit* and how it may not be by Greene, adding a general discussion of the issue of 'authorship'. John H. Astington gives a thorough account of 'His Theatre Friends: The Burbages' from the biographical and financial point of view (chapter 19, pp. 248–60), while Bart van Es explores the difference between the 'pan-European and domestic appeal' of Kemp and Armin respectively (p. 263) and its 'transformative effect' on Shakespeare's writing (p. 262); however, van Es believes that 'the old "row with Kemp" narrative' should be discounted (p. 269), and points out those aspects that did not make Robert Armin a pleasant character (chapter 20, 'His Fellow Actors Will Kemp, Robert Armin and Other Members of the Lord Chamberlain's Men and the King's Men', pp. 261–74; in fact, not much is said about the 'other members'). Alan H. Nelson rounds up 'His Literary Patrons' (chapter 21, pp. 275–88), that is, the patrons of Shakespeare's acting companies and the dedicatees of his works, focusing in particular on the earl of Southampton and his personal relationship with the dramatist. Nelson does not believe that the dedication to the sonnets is by Shakespeare (p. 284) and does not comment on the view, recorded in Kesson's chapter, that Mr W.H. is to be identified with 'publishing associate William Holme' (p. 232); however, he does point out that it is unlikely that an earl would be addressed by that title. Duncan Salkeld's essay (chapter 22, pp. 289–96) is especially credited by Margaret Drabble with providing the reader with a new 'sense of illumination' in relation to Shakespeare's work (p. 338) through its expert account of 'His Collaborator George Wilkins', a tavern and brothel keeper who played an important part in the writing of *Pericles*. In chapter 23, 'His Collaborator Thomas Middleton' (pp. 297–304), Emma Smith reports on current efforts to identify the younger dramatist's involvement in Shakespeare's plays thanks to an increased awareness of the collaborative nature of much early modern theatre and of Middleton's linguistic markers. Besides *Timon of Athens*, attention has focused on *Macbeth*, *Measure for Measure*, and, most recently, *All's Well that Ends Well*. Lucy Munro considers how the career of 'His Collaborator John Fletcher' (chapter 24, pp. 305–14) intersected with Shakespeare's: first in echoing his plays, then in collaborating with him on at least three works that are so unlike the 'romances' that they challenge the whole category of the 'late play', and finally taking Shakespeare's place as the King's men's dramatist. Munro's incidental reminder of the mixed recusant Catholic and Protestant family connections of the Beaumont and Fletcher firm again illustrates an important by-product of this book, which is to remind us that the reality of human connections at the time caused most people, including Shakespeare, to live a chequered existence in terms of religious allegiances. In the book's final chapter (chapter 25, pp. 315–28), drawing on recent research by David Kathman, Paul Edmondson documents the financial acumen and civic engagement of 'His Editors John Heminges and Henry Condell', which made them 'full-time London equivalents of Shakespeare' (though they left behind more children and less money), showing how 'All of them helped to represent the rising and respectable face of the professional theatre' (p. 326). The 'Closing Remarks' by the two editors weave factual information from the book into a brief, elegant narrative and suggest possible avenues of further investigation. The book is complemented by a website (theshakespearecircle.com), where it is possible to listen to dramatized narratives by some of the figures discussed in this work, read by familiar names in Shakespeare studies and important Shakespearean actors.

By general consensus, one of the most successful as well as original approaches to a combined biographical and critical study of Shakespeare is that adopted by James Shapiro in his *1599* (*YWES* 86[2007] 381) and in his 2012 BBC documentary on Shakespeare and the early years of the reign of James I (see, for instance, Grace Tiffany's essay, reviewed below). The 'sequel' to *1599* follows much the same format, but with even more emphasis on the plays that characterize the chosen year: *1606* is subtitled *William Shakespeare and the Year of Lear*, while the American (Simon & Schuster) edition changes the order to *The Year of Lear: Shakespeare in 1606*. This is also, as announced in the 'Prologue' (p. 10), the year of *Macbeth* and *Antony and Cleopatra* (Shapiro explains in a three-page note at the end of the book how he navigated the perilous waters of Shakespeare chronology). The book juxtaposes the year's events, cultural artefacts of a directly occasional nature, and Shakespeare's plays in order to show the underlying connections. This was the year of James's unsuccessful struggle to impose the union of his kingdoms—and the year in which Shakespeare's plays start talking less in 'English' and more in 'British' terms. The country is still reeling under the effect of the Gunpowder Plot, and its law-enforcement powers feel even more dangerously under attack by its moral equivalent and ally: the dreaded 'equivocation'—a word and concept that takes centre-stage in *Macbeth*, but that Shakespeare had already memorably used in the Gravedigger's scene in *Hamlet*. Another buzz-word of the year is 'allegiance', as this year sees Catholics forced to declare their loyalty to the king. For their part, players are forced to expunge all 'profanity' from their plays, leading to many a 'Jove' cropping up in unlikely places. Shapiro's book repays his readers with several insights like those on the wider significance of *King Lear* of the brutal world depicted in Harsnett's *Declaration of Egregious Popish Impostures*; or how details from 'The King's Book' on the Gunpowder Plot reappear in *Macbeth*, or those from the king of Denmark's state visit—something in which Shakespeare's company would have been involved as Grooms of the Chamber—find their way into *Antony and Cleopatra*; or *Macbeth* borrowing from the other two plays' sources, i.e. Harsnett (see pp. 217–18) and Plutarch's *Life of Antony* (see p. 267). Several of the essays in *Shakespeare the Man: New Decipherings* [2014], edited by R.W. Desai, purport to follow in Shapiro's footsteps. Desai's introduction (pp. ix–xxix) provides a whistle-stop tour of biographical lore on Shakespeare from Ben Jonson down to the most recent biographical studies, while arguably the most important and certainly the most substantial chapter in the book takes the place of a Conclusion. Grace Tiffany's essay (chapter 1, 'Shakespeare's Playwrights', pp. 1–16) also opens with a discussion of recent efforts to find 'Shakespeare the Man' in his works. Her own attempt in this chapter focuses on three historical events that she believes influenced Shakespeare's depiction of 'the plays' player-playwrights', identified as Jacques in *As You Like It*, *2 Henry IV*'s Pistol, Jupiter in *Cymbeline*, Vincentio in *Measure for Measure*, Paulina in *The Winter's Tale*, and *The Tempest*'s Prospero, these events being the 'War of the Poets' (1599–1601), the 1606 Act to 'Restrain Abuses of Players', or anti-profanity laws, and the 1572 Articles, that declared aspects of the Catholic religion to be fantasies and thus made them, and the figures of Catholic priests and friars, available for representation in works of fiction. In chapter 2, 'The History of the Shakespeares and the Shakespeares in the Histories' (pp. 17–52), Joseph Candido reads the second tetralogy in the light of Shakespeare's material and financial dealings with his father at the time of the play's composition. In chapter 3 (pp. 53–66), R.S. White conducts a 'thought experiment' (p. 54) on the subject of '1592–1594: Shakespeare's "Other" Lost Years', and in particular on how Shakespeare may have spent part of those years writing sonnets (and 'A Lover's Complaint') with a view to inserting them into a prose romance along the lines of Sidney's *Arcadia*. This allows the poems to be viewed as potentially spoken by different characters. Next, Mythili Kaul builds on and expands findings by other critics, from J.M. Brown in the nineteenth century to more recent work by Stephen Greenblatt, to show that if, in the character of Falstaff, 'Greene was caricatured in part through the lens of Harvey, Harvey, in turn, is caricatured through the lens of Nashe' (chapter 4, 'Greene, Harvey, Nashe, and the "Making" of Falstaff', pp. 67–84: 77). She also reports other links that have been adduced between her quarrelsome trio and characters from *Love's Labour's Lost*. After a methodological preamble, Subhajit Sen Gupta's essay (chapter 5, ' "Look in the calendar": *Julius Caesar* and Shakespeare's Cultural-Political Moment', pp. 85–99) covers ground that will be familiar to readers of Shapiro's *1599*, as it discusses *Julius Caesar* against the background of the building of the Globe theatre, the abolition of Catholic holidays and images, Essex's Irish campaign, the 'Protestant naturalization of unnatural phenomena' (p. 94), and the calendar reform. Chapter 6 (' "But I have that within which passeth show": Shakespeare's Ambivalence toward His Profession', pp. 101–20) is a version of an essay by R.W. Desai originally published in *The Shakespeare Newsletter* in 2006/7 (on which see *YWES* 88[2009] 463–4, though perhaps Desai's argument should be credited with a little more complexity). In chapter 7, ' "Those lips that love's own hand did make": Anne Hathaway and Shakespeare's *Venus and Adonis*' (pp. 121–34), Shormishtha Panja argues that in his poem Shakespeare recalls his early sexual desire for an older woman who would have been the pursuer in the relationship. Panja's adducing of *Faerie Queene* III.i as an additional source may not be quite as original as indicated, but she does remind us of some interesting connections, including a reference to two different Venuses in Plato's *Symposium*. In the next chapter, drawing on Shapiro, René Weis, and Charles Nicholl among others, Lisa Hopkins discusses the churches that had an actual or possible bearing on Shakespeare's life and works, with particular regard to *Hamlet* (chapter 8, 'Shakespeare's Churches', pp. 135–46). In chapter 9, 'Shakespeare and the Rhythms of Devotion' (pp. 147–55), Stuart Sillars finds parallels between 'the sounds and rhythms of liturgical prose' (p. 149) and passages in *Henry V* and *Hamlet*. (On a related topic, see David Bagchi's chapter in the Meek and Sullivan collection reviewed below.) John O'Meara (chapter 10, 'Outbraving Luther: Shakespeare's Final Evolution through the Tragedies into the Last Plays', pp. 157–81) identifies in *Hamlet* the moment when the dramatist 'plunges into a Luther-like confrontation with the very worst of human nature' (p. 162), which here refers mostly to lust, and in fact O'Meara's discussion at this point literally merges into *Othello*. O'Meara then goes on to analyse 'the transition from *King Lear* to the last plays' and the accompanying 'shift in focus away from the experience of his tragic characters to the transfigured mind of Shakespeare himself' (as we read on p. 157, in a summary prefixed to the chapter). John W. Mahon's 'Shakespeare among the Jesuits' (chapter 11, pp. 183–97) surveys the links that have been adduced between Shakespeare and the Society of Jesus in terms of actual references in and possible influences on his works, and any evidence of a personal connection. In Mahon's view, Shakespeare, unwilling to be martyred for any religious faith, 'was probably a Church Papist' (p. 184). Mahon's position contrasts—but perhaps more nominally than in substance?—with the final chapter in this collection, 'Was Shakespeare a "Church Papist" or a Prayer Book Anglican?' (chapter 12, pp. 199–264), in which Charles R. Forker decides that 'the second of the two is the more likely', i.e. that Shakespeare 'was a practicing Anglican with a strong residual sympathy for the old faith'. In the rest of the chapter Forker summarizes the evidence for both sides of the argument and then examines 'themes and details' in Shakespeare's works that support what he points out 'can only be' his 'inference' (p. 203). This essay is more substantial in every respect than an average book chapter. Alongside David Scott Kastan's *A Will to Believe: Shakespeare and Religion*, reviewed in *YWES* 95[2016], it provides a precious tool to help the reader evaluate the evidence and different critical positions on what Brian Cummings in a British Academy lecture called 'the last great mystery of Shakespeare studies' (quoted here on p. 199).

   Julia Reinhard Lupton's elegant essay, 'Birth Places: Shakespeare's Beliefs / Believing in Shakespeare' (*SQ* 65[2014] 399–420), also deals with Shakespeare and religion, but from two different angles. As helpfully summarized by the author (p. 400), the article is divided into three sections: a discussion of current scholarship on this topic; an analysis of 'abounding secularism' in *Cymbeline*; and a reading of Henry James's short story *The Birthplace*, which illustrates the religious connotations that can attach to the cult of Shakespeare himself. In relation to Shakespeare's play, Reinhard Lupton points out the 'multiple religious possibilities' (p. 401) derived from the fact that Christ's birth occurred at the time of King Cymbeline, but the play never alludes to that event. She focuses her analysis on Act III, scene ii, where Innogen leaves the court with Pisanio and her husband's murderous jealousy is revealed to her, a scene that ends in the 'suspension of sacrifice' and the unfolding of 'classical *virtù*' (p. 409) but also literally with a benediction (p. 411).

David Scott Kastan's volume, though published at the same time as Desai's collection, was based on the first series of the biennial Oxford Wells Lectures, from 2008. There's no escaping Sir Stanley in this year's review: as we move away from biographical or religious concerns, we turn to the book derived from the 2012 series of Wells Lectures: Lorna Hutson's *Circumstantial Shakespeare*. Hutson discusses circumstances—'the "five W's (and one H)" of journalism' (p. 76)—not in the post-Enlightenment understanding of proof, but in the classical rhetorical sense in which Shakespeare would still have understood them, of 'the finding out of figures and arguments in order to speak and write movingly and convincingly' (p. 77). By recovering the old meaning of this term from classical forensic rhetoric, Hutson intends to refute two assumptions: that there is no 'common ground between continental neoclassical theory and English dramatic practice', specifically Shakespeare's (p. 4), and that 'Shakespeare's plots are uniformly pants' (p. 37, quoting a *Guardian* reader) and that it pays to concentrate on character instead, a view that has resurfaced in a very different form from Johnsonian criticism in recent discussions of Shakespeare's works as collaborative and performance-centred enterprises. Hutson's contention is that questions of whether or not English drama followed the classical unities 'pale into insignificance' next to a shared concern with a 'rhetorical and dialectical invention' (pp. 19–20) that used 'circumstances' to arouse 'emotion through mental image-making' (p. 79). On the first level, the application of 'circumstances' in early modern plays is the dramaturgical equivalent of a novelist's 'show, not tell', where indications of time, place, and motive are naturally woven into the dialogue, as opposed to those plays castigated by Sidney, where a character 'must ever begin with telling where he is, or else the tale will not be conceived' (p. 23). Secondly, Hutson shows how in Shakespeare 'times, places and the events that occur in them seem more natural and vividly real' than in the plays of his contemporaries because 'these times and places are already implicitly shaped' (p. 54) by characters' discussions and assumptions about them. Besides Sidney, several ancient, early modern, and contemporary critics are taken into account, with special reference to Quintilian (though quotations from Castelvetro confirm the need for a reliable full English translation of his treatise on Aristotle's *Poetics*—as well as for turning the spellchecker off when quoting in other languages). Chapter 1 focuses on *Romeo and Juliet* as a '*locus classicus*' for illustrating Shakespeare's use of 'circumstances' (p. 55), and chapter 2 is on 'the connection between the forensic conception of Opportunity in *Lucrece* and the way time and place are imagined in *Lear*' (p. 75). Chapter 3 is mostly on *The Two Gentlemen of Verona*: what looks like an editorial blunder on Lance's 'my master's ship' joke (p. 120) within a discussion of ships, sheep, and travel by water between Milan and Verona, is in fact the Folio's reading—supporting, perhaps, Stanley Wells's defence of modern editions in his Very Short Introduction. Finally, chapter 4, on *Macbeth*, adds a political dimension to the discussion, and adduces a Ciceronian source that throws important light on the ambiguous mention of the additional sleepers in Duncan's chamber in Act II, scene ii.

Several books in this section bear out Hutson's evaluation that there is currently a resurgence of character-centred criticism, though this does not seem to be limited to textual and performance concerns.

One study that positively advocates a character-based approach is Neema Parvini's *Shakespeare and Cognition: Thinking Fast and Slow through Character*. This is a slim volume from the Palgrave Pivot series, where each chapter comes with its own abstract and DOI number. As the subtitle indicates, it takes as its starting point research done by Daniel Kahneman and Amos Tversky in the field of experimental psychology and behavioural economics and published in Kahneman's 2011 bestseller, *Thinking Fast and Slow*. Chapter 1 describes the current state of play in character analysis; chapter 2 introduces the key concepts to be utilized in the wake of Kahneman's book, i.e. dual-process theory, heuristics, and cognitive biases (including the practice of 'priming'); chapter 3 applies these concepts to two notorious instances of persuasion in Shakespeare, namely the wooing of Lady Anne in *Richard III* and Benedick accepting Beatrice's indictment of Claudio in *Much Ado About Nothing*; while chapters 4 and 5 offer two case studies, of Iago's persuasion of Othello and Hamlet's indecision respectively. As a matter of fact, one wonders whether we do need the new terminology and formal psychological perspective: the technical terms described in chapter 2 could be (and sometimes are) substituted by more intuitive concepts such as the contrast between reason and instinct or intuition, jumping to conclusions, or psychological and verbal manipulation. However, this is a work of undoubted brilliance, which makes several illuminating points, such as the idea that Iago at first resolves to attack Othello on the point of race, and only resorts to sexual jealousy once he has seen Plan A fail, or the analysis of personal pronouns in Hamlet's soliloquies to trace the shift from rational process to instinctive reaction. But it is worth remembering, with Hutson, that ultimately literary characters are the result of textual strategies and devices. One could object, for instance, that the baffling quality of the instances of persuasion analysed by Parvini is due to Shakespeare's foreshortening, to great dramatic effect, of a normally longer process of erosion of reason on the part of affect. In any case, for readers interested in pursuing this kind of methodology, Parvini concludes by indicating several possible avenues for further research.

Even the most theory-shy reader should not be put off by Julián Jiménez Heffernan's extensive references to Nietzsche, Derrida, and a variety of contemporary thinkers in his study of extraordinary characters, *Shakespeare's Extremes: Wild Man, Monster, Beast*. It is true that the fifty-page introduction does not so much summarize and introduce the book's argument as allow the author to give his opinion on a wide range of matters and critical theories related to the animal/human divide, but this is done in an ebullient and often entertaining style. Most importantly, there are many illuminating insights to be gathered from the intertextual parallels adduced in this book. The first chapter is a discussion of 'impasse' in Marlowe's drama that draws on the *pars destruens* of Alain Badiou's thought and his interest in 'subjective forms that cannot be either individual or communitarian' (p. 59; Heffernan quotes Badiou, *Logics of Worlds* [2009], p. 9). The three Shakespearean chapters that follow focus on Edgar as Poor Tom in *King Lear*, Caliban in *The Tempest*, and Julius Caesar. The obvious absentee from this line-up of extreme human beings is Richard III, who, however, features repeatedly in the book, especially in an extended comparison of the eponymous play with *The Tempest* on pages 144–9. The overarching thesis, that the main characteristic of Shakespeare's 'monsters' is how they retain a general humanity, gives way to effervescent readings of each character and their respective plays (tellingly, there is no concluding chapter). Chapter 2 convincingly demonstrates the important role played by the extended episode of Cardenio in Cervantes' *Don Quixote* in shaping several aspects of *King Lear*, in particular its transfer of location to the heath and Edgar's assumption of the Poor Tom disguise. Chapter 3 includes a discussion of Henry James's 'impressive misreading' (p. 115) of *The Tempest* in his novel *The Awkward Age*. Chapter 4 makes a case for keeping Ovid, Lucan, and Montaigne (and also, why not, Nietzsche) in mind as part of the intertextual/thematic scenario in *Julius Caesar*, and demonstrates the usefulness of this through an avowedly character-centred discussion (p. 158) that elegantly interweaves the theme of 'misunderstanding' and the trope of the lion as they occur in the play. The book's very liveliness is probably to blame for two easily corrected faults: its rather *too* ebullient appraisal of other critics' arguments, and some unaccountable textual disasters (for instance, in the quotations on pp. 176 and 183).

Robert Ellrodt's *Montaigne and Shakespeare: The Emergence of Modern Self-Consciousness* was originally published in French in 2011 under the title *Montaigne et Shakespeare: L'Émergence de la conscience moderne*. As the author explains (p. vii), the English version could not maintain the ambiguity between the two meanings of the French *conscience*, (self-)consciousness and moral conscience; thus the latter concept appears more clearly delimited and confined to chapter 6. Also, an 'annexe' in the French version entitled 'Et Shakespeare créa la jeune fille' has been left out because it focused only on the playwright (p. vii). The author's reflection on the issue of *la conscience moderne* began back in 1952 (see also his 1975 *Shakespeare Survey* article, reviewed in *YWES* 56[1977] 147). Notwithstanding up-to-date critical references this book is very much 'old school': not many critics today would dare produce a one-chapter overview of 'The Progress of Subjectivity from Antiquity to Montaigne' (chapter 2) in order to claim that the 'New Forms of Self-Consciousness in Montaigne', based on 'Calling the Self into Question' and the 'Persistence and Coherence of the Self' (as indicated in the titles of chapter 1 and its subsections) are not found anywhere before or around Shakespeare except perhaps in John Donne. After surveying manifestations of subjectivity in the literature of the Middle Ages and the Renaissance in England, chapter 3 analyses the sonnets. Ellrodt points out that Shakespeare used the word 'self' 'more often than his contemporaries and apparently created many compounds' with it (p. 72). He does not believe that the sonnets were influenced by Montaigne, but does find in them an understanding of the self as personal identity that is not recorded in the *OED* prior to Hume and

Berkeley (p. 72). This chapter then traces the relationship between the medieval monologue and the soliloquies in the dramatic works, before addressing the question of specific parallels between the *Essays* and Shakespeare. According to Ellrodt, these begin and are particularly strong in *Hamlet*, may then 'be found in plays performed between 1601 and 1606, particularly in *Troilus and Cressida*, *Measure for Measure* and *King Lear*' (p. 92)—and then subside, to resurface only in *The Tempest* (a play that Ellrodt does not specifically discuss in this book). Chapter 4 explores the 'Complexity and Coherence of the Shakespearean Characters' by taking into consideration Hamlet, Macbeth and Lady Macbeth, and King Lear, and argues for the presence of 'a self endowed with some permanent features' (p. 94) against modern theories to the contrary. Chapter 5 reviews the apprehension of time in Montaigne and Shakespeare, comparing it with that of their predecessors and contemporaries, but also focusing especially on the sonnets, where, Ellrodt points out, the word 'when' occurs with relatively high frequency in the 'young man' poems, while the word 'fate' occurs only once in the entire collection, in line with Shakespeare's non-deterministic view. Finally, chapter 6 finds a fundamental adherence to 'humanistic and modern' values beneath both writers' occasionally sceptical and relativistic stance (p. 144), a balanced view which is summed up in Ellrodt's 'Epilogue' by the word 'wisdom'.

Montaigne also features briefly in Jamey E. Graham's wide-ranging 'Consciousness, Self-Spectatorship, and Will to Power: Shakespeare's Stoic Conscience' (*ELR* 44[2014] 241–74). The first half of the article focuses on questions of morality and the self in Cicero and Machiavelli as a means to analyse the synthesis operated by Nietzsche between these two authors' positions. Graham turns specifically to Shakespeare in the second half of his article, after he has described aspects of the epistemology of morals in post-Reformation England with reference to Richard Hooker and William Perkins, and after he has briefly discussed Montaigne as an author in whose works 'A moral psychology emerges negatively, the result of allowing reality to push back against others' maxims'. Graham argues, with reference to Henry V, Shakespeare's 'most Machiavellian' hero (p. 257), that the playwright achieves a similar effect through his scepticism and dramatic irony. In his conclusion, Graham turns to *Hamlet* where, in his view, 'the shortcomings of Cicero's moral safeguards assert themselves, as Hamlet is unfree to choose a role suited to his talents and no amount of conscience or consciousness can supply him with an epistemology of morals' (p. 274).

The notion of character briefly surfaces also in David Hawkes's *Shakespeare and Economic Theory*, which is part of a new series, Arden Shakespeare and Theory, together with the volumes by Carolyn Brown and Gabriel Egan reviewed below. Hawkes examines the transition from a subjective, character-based view of economics as the science of utility (or the management of a household in the best possible way, which includes taking human relationships into account) to modern economics (what the ancients called chrematistics), i.e. the science of exchange. This transition was just beginning to take place in Shakespeare's time, and Hawkes finds in the dramatist an ultimately conservative attitude, but also 'enough sympathy' towards would-be upwardly mobile characters such as Jack Cade, Iago, and Edmund 'that we are forced to take their complaints and aspirations seriously' (p. 10). This becomes yet another aspect of Shakespeare's relevance today, since we are now returning to a notion of economics as influenced by subjective elements. The book is divided into two parts. Part I, a general introduction to 'Economics in History and Criticism', in fact never quite loses Shakespeare from sight. For instance, it includes a discussion of Marx's repeated engagement with Timon's speech on money (pp. 38–40) and of how, 'Having been praised by Marx and Engels, the Bard was ripe for appropriation by the forces of international Socialism' (p. 46). Part II focuses on Shakespeare's works mostly by means of an examination of economics-related keywords, such as 'commons' and 'commodity', 'price' and 'dear' (chapter 6), or 'worth' and 'value' (chapter 7); the concepts of wage labour, servitude, and slavery (chapter 8); 'the "restricted" economic significance of the word "use"' (p. 152) and the term 'advantage' (chapter 9); the terms 'property', 'counterfeit', and 'coining', and Francis Bacon's 'Idols of the Market-Place' as a way of deploring 'the autonomous power of liturgical, economic and verbal signs simultaneously' (p. 171, in chapter 10). The latter are an aspect of the common problem of 'taking signs for things' which, though the quotation dates back to Augustine (p. 157), was specifically felt to be arising in Shakespeare's time. In relation to the terms 'commodity' and 'usury' Hawkes also addresses parallels with attitudes towards sex. Plays that recur frequently in the discussion include the histories, *Coriolanus*, *Measure for Measure*, *The Merchant of Venice*, *Pericles*, *Troilus and Cressida*, and, of course, *Timon of Athens*, while the 'Conclusion' applies the key concepts explored in the book to a discussion of *The Tempest*.

'Money and Power' is also the theme of the 2014 *Shakespeare-Jahrbuch*, which includes papers from the spring 2013 conference of the Deutsche Shakespeare-Gesellschaft (*ShJE* 150[2014]). The first three articles address the issue to which most of Hawkes's volume is devoted: the way in which Shakespeare's works reflect the rise of a new form of economy. These include essays by Christina von Braun (in German, with English summary appended), who links the shift from money to credit to a growing belief in symbolism on the one hand and 'the monetary value of "human flesh"' on the other', and refers to *The Merchant of Venice* and *Measure for Measure* as revealing an 'almost sacral authentication of money, originating from sacrifice' (*ShJE* 150[2014] 11–29: 29); Jean E. Howard on 'Shakespeare and the Consequences of Early Capitalism' (*ShJE* 150[2014] 30–45), showing through examples from the histories, *King Lear*, and *Pericles* how the author both mourns the past and anticipates the future; and Isabel Karremann (in German, with English summary), who discusses *The Comedy of Errors* and the character of Falstaff to argue against the New Historicist 'anxiety-and-alienation paradigm' (*ShJE* 150[2014] 46–64: 64). These are followed by discussions of the materiality of the theatrical experience, with Tiffany Stern's article on the additional merchandise available and the overall costs of attending the theatre in Shakespeare's time, '"Fill thy purse with money": Financing Performance in Shakespearean England' (*ShJE* 150[2014] 65–78; reviewed in *YWES* 95[2016]), and essays on the transition from patronage to the commercial theatre by John Blakely, on *Love's Labour's Lost* and *Twelfth Night* ('Feste, *Twelfth Night's*

"Material Fool"') (*ShJE* 150[2014] 79–93), and Katherine A. Gillen, '"What he speaks is all in debt"': Credit, Representation and Theatrical Critique in *Timon of Athens*' (*ShJE* 150[2014] 94–109; reviewed in YWES 95[2016]). Finally, there are three articles on representations of Shakespeare in the last hundred years: Christopher Balme on 'the beginnings of the global theatre trade', including a discussion of British troupes in India and Southeast Asia at the start of the twentieth century, '"His means are in supposition": Shakespeare and the Beginnings of the Global Theatre Trade' (*ShJE* 150[2014] 110–27); Nicole Anae on Daniel E. Bandmann's Shylock in late nineteenth-century Australia, '"The majestic Hebrew ideal": Herr Daniel E. Bandmann's Shylock on the Australian Stage, 1880 - 1883' (*ShJE* 150[2014] 128–45); and a fascinating paper by Mark Thornton Burnett, 'Capital, Commodities, Cinema: Shakespeare and the Eastern European "Gypsy" Aesthetic' (*ShJE* 150[2014] 146–60), on the new genre of '"gypsy" Shakespearean cinema' (p. 146), represented by *Romani Kris*, a Hungarian adaptation of *King Lear* [1997], directed by Bence Gyöngyössy, and *Hamlet* [2007], by Serbian director Aleksandar Rajkovic, where Shakespeare's plays are used to describe the situation of the Roma people in eastern Europe after the fall of the socialist regimes.

Within the 'economy' in the old sense of household management, the preparation and handling of food would of course have held a place of primary importance. The 2014 issue of *Shakespeare Studies* is devoted to this subject. Two articles of general import within this volume (not reviewed in the previous issue of *YWES*) were written by authors of full-length studies on the topic. Ken Albala (author of *Food in Early Modern Europe* [2003]) contributes an essay on 'Shakespeare's Culinary Metaphors: A Practical Approach' (*ShakS* 42[2014] 63–74), which provides relevant early modern recipes in order to highlight, for instance, how the technical term for the crust of pies was 'coffin', which has obvious connotations with the funeral-cum-wedding pies in *Hamlet*, as well as explaining the literal sense of the term as used in a notorious scene in *Titus Andronicus* V.ii (one wonders whether this might not even be a source image for the scene itself, alongside its obvious classical antecedents). Also interesting is the way that references to culinary 'brine' (mostly in the comedies and in *Romeo and Juliet*) generally point to forms of mourning that are a little 'off'—too prolonged or exaggerated. Joan Fitzpatrick is the author of *Food in Shakespeare* [2007]. Here she writes on 'Diet and Identity in Early Modern Dietaries and Shakespeare: The Inflections of Nationality, Gender, Social Rank, and Age' (*ShakS* 42[2014] 75–90), showing how the dietaries by Thomas Elyot, Andrew Boorde, and William Bullein linked issues of food intake, health, and humoral balance. Fitzpatrick explains that through these works 'it is possible to trace patterns of consumption in Shakespeare's plays and what they might indicate about early modern attitudes to foreigners and Catholics, women, the poor, the old, and the social elite' (p. 76). Her article touches especially upon the *Henry IV* plays and *Merry Wives* (including a discussion of the name Bardolph), *King Lear*, and *Macbeth*.

An entirely different form of materiality is addressed in the 2015 issue of *Shakespeare Studies* with Mario DiGangi's survey of 'Shakespeare's "Bawdy"' (*ShakS* 43[2015] 131–53). DiGangi stresses the negative rather than pleasurable connotations of the word in the majority of cases in Shakespeare, and focuses on 'an eroticism that violates corporeal boundaries and pushes beyond subjective desires' (p. 132). His analysis of Shakespearean examples, concentrated in the first eight pages of the essay, focuses on 'the sexual disgust experienced by Diomedes [in *Troilus and Cressida*], Hamlet, Othello, and Leontes' (p. 133) and concludes with a discussion of Mercutio's joke about 'the bawdy hand of the dial' in *Romeo and Juliet* II.iii.

Three volumes focus on emotions in Shakespeare and his age: one authored book, Steven Mullaney's *The Reformation of Emotions in the Age of Shakespeare*, and two edited collections, by Richard Meek and Erin Sullivan, *The Renaissance of Emotion: Understanding Affect in Shakespeare and His Contemporaries*, and by R.S. White, Mark Houlahan, and Katrina O'Loughlin, *Shakespeare and Emotions: Inheritances, Enactments, Legacies*. This confirms that the 'emotional turn' is truly underway—a development on which Meek and Sullivan provide useful bibliographical references (see p. 18 n. 3), as well as generally bringing us up to date on the state of the question in emotion studies in their introduction. Their volume is divided into three parts. The four chapters in the first part explore non-fictional works that have a bearing on the perception of the emotions in early modern England. In an important chapter (chapter 1, 'The Passions of Thomas Wright: Renaissance Emotion across Body and Soul', pp. 25–44), Erin Sullivan discusses what has now become a 'classic' on the topic of emotions in early modern England, Thomas Wright's *The Passions of the Mind in General* [1601], addressing its relationship to the Jesuit's works of religious polemics, and also the work's interest in more 'disembodied' emotions, 'the emotionality of the rational soul' (p. 40). Chapter 2, '"The Scripture moveth us in sundry places": Framing Biblical Emotions in the *Book of Common Prayer* and the *Homilies*' (pp. 45–64), by David Bagchi, examines the 'emotional discourse' in the texts of the officially imposed Protestant religion (p. 49; on this topic see also Stuart Sillars's essay and section III of Charles Forker's chapter, both in the Desai collection reviewed above). In chapter 3, '"This was a way to thrive": Christian and Jewish Eudaimonism in *The Merchant of Venice*' (pp. 65–85), Sara Coodin reads *The Merchant of Venice* in the light of Christian and Jewish eudaimonism, or ideas on 'how to flourish' or do well in life. Coodin focuses on the parable of Jacob and Laban's cattle told by Shylock in Act I, scene iii, to justify his financial activities. Although she has earlier dismissed 'spirit-and-letter' readings of Shylock's attitude, it is not clear that this very episode could not be read along those lines: was the 'spirit' of Laban's contract with Jacob not that the latter would get a certain number of beasts, presumably 'statistically' estimated on the basis of previous years? And by applying his ingenuity to the alteration of that statistical average, was Jacob not effectively cheating his uncle of a number of cattle? However, it probably remains true that Shakespeare is bringing up the issue rather than offering a solution in one sense or the other. Part I concludes with chapter 4, by Mary Ann Lund, on 'Robert Burton, Perfect Happiness and the *Visio Dei*' (pp. 86–105). Part II is on 'Shakespeare and the Language of Emotion', and opens with an essay by Nigel Wood on 'Spleen in Shakespeare's Comedies' (chapter 5, pp. 109–29). Wood discusses the tragicomic potential of the word 'spleen', and how

Shakespeare 'favoured it as comprising a remarkably broad spectrum of meaning' and being especially related to 'the ungovernable qualities of emotional excess' (p. 113). This is followed by Richard Meek's chapter 6, ' "Rue e'en for ruth" : *Richard II* and the Imitation of Sympathy' (pp. 130–52). Meek describes the use of the term *sympathise* and its 'precursor' *rue* in the depiction of Queen Isabel's feelings towards her dispossessed husband in Samuel Daniel's *Civil Wars*, and links it to Shakespeare's exploration of the term *rue* and similar emotion terms in *Richard II*. Meek shows how, in borrowing from Daniel in Act V, scene i, Shakespeare 'makes the emphasis upon the emotional impact of narration far more explicit' (p. 143), using the verb *sympathise* in a way that 'represents a key moment in the history of the term' (p. 144). The final section of the chapter explores the parallel question of a monarch's pity for his subjects as applied to Richard in Act I and to Bolingbroke in Act V of the play. In chapter 7, 'What's Happiness in *Hamlet*?' (pp. 153–74), Richard Chamberlain takes the unusual step of attempting to discuss *Hamlet* from the point of view of its critics' happiness or otherwise, engaging in particular (from the chapter's very title) with John Dover Wilson's 1935 study, *What Happens in Hamlet*, and its stipulation that we should ask ourselves 'in what mood are the principal characters' when a scene begins (3rd edn. [1951], p. 174). The first chapter in Part III, which is on 'The Politics and Performance of Emotion', is Andy Kesson's ' "They that tread in a maze" : Movement and Emotion in John Lyly' (chapter 8, pp. 177–99). We return to Shakespeare with chapter 9, '(S)wept from Power: Two Versions of Tyrannicide in *Richard III*' (pp. 200–20), by Ann Kaegi, who, like Mullaney (see below), takes as her starting point the way in which the Reformation transformed 'the relationship between the living and the dead' (p. 200). Kaegi's chapter focuses on the lamentations of the women in *Richard III*, on how they contravene laws and regulations of Shakespeare's time, and how they ultimately constitute an alternative, effective form of tyrannicide. In chapter 10, 'The Affective Scripts of Early Modern Execution and Murder' (pp. 221–40), Frederika Bain draws upon 'broadside and pamphlet execution narratives from the late sixteenth to the mid-seventeenth century, including accounts of the regicide of Charles I, and upon Thomas Preston's … *Cambyses, King of Persia* and Shakespeare's *Richard III*' (p. 222), and discusses in turn the principal figures in execution scenes: the King, the Executioner, the Condemned, and the Spectators. The final chapter, chapter 11, 'Discrepant Emotional Awareness in Shakespeare' (pp. 241–63), is by R.S. White and Ciara Rawnsley. It shows how Shakespeare played off 'different emotional registers and patterns, allowing them to change, and finally merging them in harmony' (p. 242). The chapter focuses on Act IV, scene ii, of *The Two Gentlemen of Verona* and the 'transformation of suffering into joy' in *Cymbeline* (p. 251), 'examples chosen because they are driven by emotions rather than simply untangling narrative complications' (p. 244). Peter Holbrook's 'Afterword' (pp. 264–72) concludes this volume by highlighting Shakespeare's singularity in making 'the emotional life of human beings the essence of art' (p. 264), further showing how this is inextricably linked to the issue of freedom and free will. Holbrook thus puts forward a parallel claim to that made by Robert Ellrodt for the playwright's interest in individual self-consciousness.

Steven Mullaney's volume echoes episodes and critical references that are developed (often more fully) in Meek and Sullivan's collection, sometimes showing an uncanny complementarity: while Sullivan admittedly does not address Thomas Wright's 'interest in rhetoric and persuasion' (p. 40), this is the main focus in Mullaney's discussion of *The Passions of the Mind*. Mullaney offers new terminology for familiar concepts: for instance, 'affective technologies', which could be (and are) glossed as 'forms of cultural performance' (p. 150). In chapter 1, Mullaney discusses instances of 'affective irony', the emotional equivalent of dramatic irony, in Thomas Kyd's *Spanish Tragedy* and Shakespeare's *Titus Andronicus* (drawing also on modern productions of the play and focusing on audience reaction to Marcus' drawn-out rhetorical speech on the mutilated Lavinia) and in *The Merchant of Venice* (does the latter become a revenge play when seen from a Jew's point of view? It does not, because its 'genre cues' work against this interpretation; p. 90). Chapter 2, after adducing some fascinating examples from anthropology and neurology, examines how the first history tetralogy responds to the trauma of the Reformation and its attempt to erase memory by severing the affective links of the population with previous generations. A basic tenet in this work is that the early modern English theatre is for us now a privileged tool for the recovery of emotions from a different era: Shakespearean examples given are Antonio's sadness in *The Merchant of Venice* (pp. 35–6), and the visit by the Groom of the Stables to Richard II (pp. 38–9). This parallels its importance for the creation of a new public sphere in its time. This aspect is discussed especially in the third and final chapter, 'What's Hamlet to Habermas?', which in fact says much less on *Hamlet* than at several other points in the book.

It is interesting how discussions of emotions in Shakespeare tend to focus on the histories in the first instance, and then the comedies (including the problem plays). Of the twenty-three chapters in the volume on *Shakespeare and Emotions* co-edited by R.S. White, Mark Houlahan, and Katrina O'Loughlin only two deal with the tragedies. Chapter 1, 'Reclaiming Heartlands: Shakespeare and the History of Emotions in Literature' (pp. 1–14), functions as an introduction. In it Bob White describes the 'affective turn' (p. 1) that has occurred not only in the study of literature and drama but also in a variety of other fields, and sets the present 'pluralistic' collection (p. 2) against a long-term background, from Plato to current 'New Emotionalism' (p. 9), characterized by the polarity between the rational condemnation and the 'poetic' exaltation of emotions. Part I, 'Emotional Inheritances', shows how Shakespeare's representation of emotions is indebted more to his literary sources than to humoral theories. In chapter 2, '"Of comfort and dispaire": Plato's Philosophy of Love and Shakespeare's Sonnets' (pp. 17–28), Danijela Kambaskovic argues that a link with Plato's philosophy of love brings the young man and dark lady sections of the sonnets 'to an equivalent philosophical footing' (p. 18). In chapter 3, '*Locus amoenus* or *locus violens*? Shakespearean Emotions Expressed through an Ovidian Model' (pp. 29–38), Brid Phillips shows how *Titus Andronicus* reshapes and even 'undercut[s]'

(p. 29) the conventions of the *locus amoenus* that had already been used by Ovid to signal impending moments of 'emotional excess' (p. 30). Chapters 4 and 5, by Ciara Rawnsley and Andrew Lynch, are discussed below, with the late plays and the problem plays respectively. The section on sources in this collection concludes with two essays that glance at the intersection of sexual and political issues in the history plays: chapter 6, 'French Feeling: Language, Sex and Identity in *Henry V*' (pp. 59–68), by Stephanie Downes; and Mary-Rose McLaren's 'Power, Vulnerability and Sexuality: Representations of Margaret of Anjou in a London Chronicle and Shakespeare's *3 Henry VI*' (chapter 7, pp. 69–79), which draws on a mid-fifteenth-century commonplace book contained in fair copy in British Library MS Egerton 1995.

Part II, 'Shakespearean Enactments', focuses on readings of the plays themselves, literally so in Peter Groves's peroration in favour of keeping to the metre when speaking Shakespeare's lines because this will normally yield superior emotional sense than when the lines are accented according to a more banal conversational emphasis (see chapter 8, '"My heart dances": Performing Emotion through Shakespeare's Rhythms', pp. 83–94). In the next chapter, '"The teares of ten thousand spectators": Shakespeare's Experiments with Emotion from Talbot to Richard II' (chapter 9, pp. 95–104), Ruth Lunney describes the audience's emotional response to the character of Talbot in *1 Henry VI* and the eponymous figures in *Richard III* and *Richard II* by comparison with the 'response called for across a body of roughly contemporary texts' (p. 96), consisting mostly of history plays by other authors and works by Christopher Marlowe. Chapter 10, by Martin Dawes, is on 'Emotional Education and Leadership in the *Henriad*' (pp. 108–15), while Anthony Guy Patricia, in chapter 11, '"Say how I loved you": Queering the Emotion of Male Same-Sex Love in *The Merchant of Venice*' (pp. 116–23), brings together 'queer theory and emotionality studies' in his analysis of the Antonio and Bassanio relationship, taking issue with Joseph Pequigney's distinction between their relationship and that of Antonio and Sebastian in *Twelfth Night*, and adding an original reading in unselfish terms of Antonio's famous melancholy in the first scene of *The Merchant of Venice*. Chapters 12 and 13, by Alison V. Scott and Ronald Bedford respectively, are both on *Troilus and Cressida*, and are discussed in the problem play section below. In chapter 14, 'Displacement: Maps and Emotions in *Othello*' (pp. 146–54), Christopher Wortham links cartography (definitely relevant to his other example, the medieval play *The Castle of Perseverance*) with the account of Othello's adventures in Act I, scene ii. However, it is unclear why Wortham here refers to Waldseemüller for elements that are normally traced back to the medieval Mandeville narrative. In the next essay, 'Lear in the Storm: Shakespeare's Emotional Exploration of Sovereign Mortality' (chapter 15, pp. 155–63), Jennifer Hamilton insists on Lear's experience of shame and sees his fury in the storm 'as a tragic culmination of the emotional experience of embodying the paradox of sovereignty itself, the King's Two Bodies' (p. 162). Heather Kerr's '"Sociable" Tears in *The Tempest*' (chapter 16, pp. 164–72) finds that Prospero's emotional interaction with Gonzalo in Act V, scene i, manifests a kind of sympathy normally only found from the eighteenth century onwards.

Part III, 'Emotional Legacies and Re-enactments', consists of papers on the reception of Shakespeare: Philippa Kelly on her experience as a dramaturge (and as a bereaved sister) in chapter 17, 'Only Connect: Dramaturgy and a Living Shakespeare,' (pp. 175–85); Susan Broomhall on the 2012 British Museum exhibition *Shakespeare: Staging the World* (chapter 18, 'Cabbages and Kings: Curating the Objects and Emotions of English Encounter with the World through Shakespeare', pp. 186–97); Andrew Lawrence-King on a seventeenth-century musical setting of 'To be or not to be' believed to provide clues on the early modalities for delivering the speech (chapter 19, ''Tis Master's Voice: A Seventeenth-Century Shakespeare Recording?', pp. 198–217); Simon Haines on forms of recognition in Shakespeare and nineteenth-century philosophy, with examples from *Othello*, *King Lear*, and *Antony and Cleopatra* (chapter 20, 'Recognition in Shakespeare and Hegel', pp. 218–30); Rosemary Gaby on *The Hollow Crown* (chapter 21, reviewed in the histories section below); and Elizabeth Schafer on an Australian production of the Falstaff-centred comedy (chapter 22, 'Whose Nostalgia? Geoffrey Rush and *The Merry Wives of Windsor*, Brisbane 1987', pp. 240–50). Chapter 23 (pp. 251–5) contains an 'Afterword' in which Mark Houlahan summarizes the answers given in this volume to the problem of how we can know about emotions in the early modern world, arranging them under three headings: 'Archive', or written testimonies (including both primary and secondary literature) and material objects; 'Enactment', i.e. performances and accounts of performances; and 'Embodiment', a category for which Houlahan, in my view, fails to give a satisfactory exposition, beyond mentioning how a number of chapters in the book 'evoke Descartes as a key early modern philosopher of the body' (p. 254).

The theme for the 2014 volume of *Shakespeare Survey* was 'Shakespeare's Collaborative Work'. Two articles of more general import that were not mentioned in the last issue of *YWES* (95[2016] 396–402) have some bearing on the topic of emotions. With explicit reference to a 'much-maligned' 1967 essay by John Barth, and adducing examples from the sonnets, *Romeo and Juliet*, *Hamlet* (including a comparison with Book VI of Milton's *Paradise Lost*), and *The Tempest*, Stephan Laqué, 'Shakespeare's Literature of Exhaustion' (*ShS* 67[2014] 235–41), suggests that the richness of Shakespeare's plays may in fact stem 'from a kind of tiring surfeit and from a powerful sense of exhaustion' (p. 235); while in 'Why Ganymede Faints and the Duke of York Weeps: Passion Plays in Shakespeare' (*ShS* 67[2014] 265–78) Sujata Iyengar discusses the significance of the red-marked (in most instances bloodstained) cloth in *3 Henry VI*, *A Midsummer Night's Dream*, *As You Like It*, *Othello*, and *Cymbeline*.

The 2015 issue of *Shakespeare Survey* is entitled 'Origins and Originality' and includes three articles of a general character, alongside work-specific essays, or essays that deal with special topics such as translation. The volume opens with a contribution from Margreta De Grazia on 'Shakespeare's Anecdotal Character' (*ShS* 68[2015] 1–14), which includes a close reading of Rowe's 1709 biographical essay on Shakespeare and a discussion of the famous issue of 'blotting' lines (or not), raised by Ben Jonson and traced by Rowe back to its original in Horace. By reference to this and other eighteenth-century pronouncements, De Grazia concludes that the discrepancy between the 'wayward' anecdotal figure and the 'upright' Shakespeare of the biographies is due to the fact that, at this point in time, the anecdotes conveyed an image of the perceived unruliness of the writing rather than of the man himself. In 'What Is a Source? or, How Shakespeare Read His Marlowe' (*ShS* 68[2015] 15–31), Laurie Maguire and Emma Smith raise important methodological questions on the very concept of (Shakespearean) sources, and on the different planes on which one can discuss Shakespeare's relationship with his rival. They argue, partly on the basis of parallels first adduced by J.B. Steane, that the presence of Marlowe's *Dido* is felt not only in the First Player's speech in *Hamlet* but also and especially in *The Tempest*. The article perhaps exaggerates the distance between Marlowe's 'washed up' Aeneas (p. 23) and Virgil's 'triumphant' hero (p. 22), but it does make several points that will need to be incorporated in future discussions of *The Tempest*. It then draws on hauntology and trauma studies to investigate a different (unconscious) model of textual recollection, and concludes with a series of parallels between *Dido* and other plays in the Shakespeare canon. Farah Karim-Cooper's 'Shakespearian Gesture: Narrative and Iconography' (*ShS* 68[2015] 118–30) suggests that 'the context of a gesture is paramount to an interpretation of its meaning in a text' (p. 121), and illustrates this with reference to two gestures in Shakespeare: an involuntary, individual one in *The Rape of Lucrece* lines 386–7, where the heroine is asleep with her cheek resting on her hand, and the gestures with which, as Karim-Cooper states, Hamlet deliberately conveys his 'madness' to Ophelia, knowing that she will report it (as she does in Act II, scene i). In the latter case, Karim-Cooper adduces examples where 'taking by the wrist' signals a rape, thus highlighting the dangerous and dark connotations that the iconographical context lends to this passage in *Hamlet*.

The theme of the 2015 issue of *Shakespeare Jahrbuch* is 'Shakespearean Festivities', in line with the joint celebration in 2014 of the 450th anniversary of Shakespeare's birth and the 150th anniversary of the Deutsche Shakespeare-Gesellschaft. Most of the articles are on aspects of the reception of Shakespeare, including, rather prophetically, one by Heinrich Detering on 'Bob Dylan's Shakespeare' (*ShJE* 151[2015] 149–66; in German with English summary). The exception is 'Ominous Feasts: Celebration in Shakespeare's Drama', by Ina Habermann (*ShJE* 151[2015] 116–30), which discusses the plays themselves. Citing examples from across the canon, but focusing especially on *Antony and Cleopatra*, *The Winter's Tale*, and *A Midsummer Night's Dream*, Habermann illustrates the 'technique of syncopation' (p. 121), whereby general celebrations are marred by some ominous occurrence. On the other hand, real moments of happiness happen offstage as nostalgia for happy times past or anticipation of future celebrations, thus creating potential 'asynchrony' (p. 130) between the collective and the individual.

A similar concern is at the basis of *Shakespeare and Democracy: The Self-Renewing Politics of a Global Playwright*, in which Gabriel Chanan sifts through over half the plays in the canon asking a simple and direct question— What is Shakespeare's attitude towards democracy?—meaning not so much a system of political representation as a just and egalitarian society and culture.

Chanan's main conclusions could be summarized as follows: that Shakespeare's dialectical method, his way of showing both sides of an argument, in itself 'aligns naturally with democracy' (p. 197); that there are nevertheless 'social blind-spots in the plays' (back cover), particularly in the treatment of Shylock and Caliban; and that reading the plays in the order of composition highlights a development in Shakespeare's attitude, moments when his 'trajectory' towards democracy 'goes into reverse' (p. 189). This happens at those points in time when he is closest to the power structures of his day, that is, when he is writing the second historical tetralogy and the court is beginning to take note of this successful dramatist, and in late plays such as *Henry VIII* and *The Tempest* (in fact, one thing that I would definitely edit out of this very readable book, which does offer a number of arresting insights, is the close of chapter 5, where Chanan fantasizes that it was Shakespeare himself who, in a fit of disgust, set fire to the Globe during a performance of his final history play). On the other hand, *The Winter's Tale* is presented in the conclusion as 'an important stepping stone towards democracy' (p. 208) thanks to the character of Paulina, who, like the servant who dies trying to prevent the blinding of Gloucester in *King Lear* ('Shakespeare's greatest hero', p. 183), exemplifies the lower classes' prerogative to mitigate the dangerous arbitrariness of power.

*Celebrating Shakespeare*, edited by Clara Calvo and Coppélia Kahn, CUP, 2015 was not received in time for review, and will be covered with material from 2016.

*(b) Problem Plays*

*Measure for Measure* attracted by far the largest share of scholarly attention among Shakespeare's problem plays in 2015, and a strikingly diversified range of critical takes. Adrian Streete, in 'Lucretius, Calvin, and Natural Law in *Measure for Measure*' (in Loewenstein and Witmore, eds., *Shakespeare and Early Modern Religion*, pp. 131–54), is the first scholar ever to shed light on the extent to which the play's engagement with Lucretian philosophy seeks to criticize 'the dominant Protestantism of early modern England' by dramatizing 'a Calvinistic world becoming Lucretian' (p. 133). The contrast is exemplified by the play's attitudes towards sexuality, in particular in relation to Angelo's handling of his own, and others', sexual drive. Despite the strictly Protestant, puritanical bent of Angelo's rule—under which sexual pleasure 'is to be rigorously policed' (p. 141)—Act II, scene iv, makes him 'emerge as a Lucretian sensualist in thrall to his sexual desires', thereby exposing 'the keen tension between a Christian and a materialist understanding of sex' (p. 147). Although both Protestant and Lucretian philosophy conceive of humans as at the mercy of irresistible urges, 'the former sees this as tragic, the latter as inherently comic, a fact that may in part account for the bittersweet generic makeup of this play' (p. 146). Ultimately, *Measure for Measure* seems cautiously to suggest that 'a Lucretian universe where sexual pleasure and mutuality are valued is largely preferable to one that tries to control or deny human sexuality' (p. 150), even though the play blatantly 'doesn't end with a Calvinistic world turned *completely* Lucretian' (p. 154).

The negation of sexuality, in the form of virginity, takes centre stage in Andrew Lynch's essay ' "... another comfort": Virginity and Emotion in *Measure for Measure*' (in White et al., eds., pp. 49–58). For Lynch, the character of the 'traditional virgin martyr' offers a useful framework within which Isabella's 'emotional attachments', 'her defiance of unjust power and outspoken pursuit of truth' can be seen as exhibiting a higher degree of coherence and appropriateness to her situation than if one thinks of her as 'an intensely religious young woman of the very early seventeenth century' (p. 50). In particular, the importance Isabella places on virginity should be understood in relation to 'an independent and personal passion for the divine' (p. 53) typical of characters in the hagiographical tradition. Yet the play is not a virgin martyr's legend, where the protagonist 'is always perceived to be on the martyr's narrative path to God' and is therefore allowed considerable 'freedom of action and expression'. Hence, though initially setting up Isabella 'like a heroine in the virgin martyr genre', the play ends up 'disappoint[ing] her with bitter ironies' by 'subordinat[ing] the heaven-bound values of the virgin saint's life to those of a secular comedy concerned with earthly justice and the control of sexual passion through marriage' (p. 56).

Two essays deal with the question of genre, though from different perspectives. Genevieve Lheureux, 'Authority and Displacement: *Measure for Measure* or the Empty Chair Policy' (in Labaune-Demeule, ed., *Authority and Displacement in the English-Speaking World*, vol. 1: *Exploring Europe/from Europe*, pp. 11–23), argues that the intervention of providence that is necessary for *Measure for Measure* to end happily, 'placed as it is at the end of a series of rather unlikely developments' (p. 19), should be seen as an attempt on Shakespeare's part to expose the artificiality of the conventions and mechanical formulas that regulate comedy, as exemplified in the use the Duke makes 'of all available stage ploys to turn a potential tragedy into a comedy' (p. 18), such as 'the series of forced marriages that conclude Act V, or ... the indiscriminate mercy that [he] bestows on his subjects' (p. 12), with no distinctions made 'between lighter offences ... and heavier crimes' (p. 21). Moreover, said questioning of 'the very workings of comedy' cannot but lead the audience 'to question ... the relationship between justice and lawfulness' (p. 12) in a world where, rather than 'an expected prize', marriage 'has been turned into a paradoxical form of retribution' (p. 21), and any 'consolation of an ordered, meaningful world in which retribution and reward operate to guarantee that justice eventually prevails' (p. 22) is ultimately denied.

The unhappiness of the married characters at the end of the play, according to Igor Shaitanov in 'A Struggle of Genres, or a Dialogue: A Post-Bakhtinian View of Shakespeare's *Measure for Measure*' (*Style* 49[2015] 477–93), betrays 'the uncertainty in what generic terms and in what system of values' the play should be understood (p. 487). In Shaitanov's view, *Measure for Measure* should be read as having 'a morality play as its background and a tragicomedy as the final step in its development'. The fact that 'Angelo is prevented from committing ... the crimes ... of murder and seduction—and is thus saved from punishment' ought to be construed on a deeper level as a return 'to his own long-neglected humanity' (p. 488), in an implicit Shakespearean nod to *Everyman*. Despite the morality-like background, the play is nonetheless 'morally ambiguous, in part because of its shifting system of values', as evidenced by the final scene when only Angelo is pardoned (p. 491)—even though he and Lucio can be said to be 'extremes that meet' (p. 490) in their distortion of 'the topographic plane of myth', as 'Holiness in Angelo and carnival in Lucio are overdone' (p. 491).

François Laroque, 'Magic, Manipulation and Misrule in *Doctor Faustus* and *Measure for Measure*' (in Chiari, ed., *The Circulation of Knowledge in Early Modern English Literature*, pp. 123–32), argues that in the play 'transmission and transgression are presented ... as activities that are simultaneously contrasted and paralleled' (p. 130). The Duke's plan to delegate 'his authority ... in order to ... suppress sexual anarchy in Vienna while he himself safely hides' can be read as 'a cunning ploy to put Angelo's virtue to the test'. However, the Duke's incessant use of stratagems and devious tricks makes him appear corrupt as well, and ultimately shows that 'far from being extirpated, vice perpetuates itself in new forms' (p. 131), with transgression taking place 'through a form of interregnum which plays the role of a safety valve as in the traditional interval of festive misrule' (p. 132).

Sharing Laroque's focus on the Duke's manoeuvring, L. Joseph Hebert Jr., ' "When vice makes mercy": Classical, Christian, and Modern Humanism in Shakespeare's *Measure for Measure*' (in Radasanu, Balot, and Burns, eds., *In Search of Humanity: Essays in Honor of Clifford Orwin*, pp. 209–24), reads the play as 'a response to Machiavelli's radical critique' of 'classical and Christian humanism' (p. 209), as is made evident by the Duke's course of action. Whereas his overall conduct is 'redolent of Machiavellian *virtù*', his hesitation to have Barnardine executed (which significantly jeopardizes his elaborate plan) in fact reveals that, though 'tempted to follow the new modes and orders of *The Prince*, he is not ... willing to embrace core theoretical and practical features' (p. 219) of Machiavellianism. The play seems ultimately to suggest that society should be built on 'love and virtue rather than on the Machiavellian foundation of fear and desire' and that, in keeping with the classical humanist tradition, 'it is virtue, and not vice, that "makes" the mercy necessary to govern imperfect human beings' (p. 221).

Painstakingly scrutinizing language, structure, grammar, metrics, vocabulary, and imagery, as well as analysing a passage from *The Rape of Lucrece* informed by the same logic and sharing the same tone, John McGee, in 'The Lost Couplet Conjecture in Shakespeare's *Measure for Measure*' (*ES* 96[2015] 264–76), challenges J.W. Lever's influential conjecture that the Duke's monologue about the punishment of crime concluding Act III is missing a couplet. The speech contrasts 'two types of men and their respective capacities as law-implementing sovereigns': first, the Duke describes the ideal judge; then, he 'turns to his polar opposite—a judge who is at least as evil as the people he condemns' (p. 270). Here, argues McGee, when Vincentio mentions a 'likeness made in crimes / Making practice on the times', he has in mind a criminal-like judge who imposes his own version of justice on society; and when he imagines this same magistrate trying to 'draw with idle spiders' strings / The most ponderous and substantial things', he is actually portraying this judge's attempt to cleanse society from crime as inherently futile, because 'when a lawless man tries to implement the law, there can be no true justice' (p. 273). In a wider perspective, the Duke's speech clearly 'articulates ideas that appear to have been widely prevalent at the time of the play's composition' (p. 274), by 'addressing the far-reaching legal ramifications inextricably bound up in the person of the sovereign' (p. 276).

The issue of justice is also at the core of the discussion of the play by Paul S. Fiddes in 'Law and Divine Mercy in Shakespeare's Religious Imagination: *Measure for Measure* and *The Merchant of Venice*' (in Bugliani Knox and Lonsdale, eds., *Poetry and the Religious Imagination: The Power of the Word*, pp. 109–28), who sees *Measure for Measure* as wondering how 'divine mercy and justice [can] be applied in an imperfect world', thus confronting 'issues that concerned jurists and theologians in Shakespeare's time' without, however, 'offer[ing] a theory or a doctrine' but simply opening an imaginative space in which the complex tensions between 'human and divine justice ... can be explored' (p. 119) and 'in which we can work at a human approximation to transcendent justice and mercy' (p. 125). What Shakespeare seems to imply is that the best way to live within these tensions is by exercising the virtue of moderation, which in *Measure for Measure* seems to combine 'the classical virtues of Aristotle's "reasonableness" ... and Seneca's clemency ... together with the Reformer's ideal of Christian "equity"' (p. 118).

The Extended Mind hypothesis, i.e. the notion that 'human cognitive processes can be constituted by coalitions of biological and non-biological resources, rather than being confined to neural circuitry' (p. 1), underlies Miranda Anderson's discussion of *Measure for Measure* in *The Renaissance Extended Mind*, a discussion primarily focused on the significance of mirror motifs in the play. As Anderson points out, with the spread of 'new and improved mirrors' in the early modern era, mirror motifs started to be employed more and more often in literature for 'the representation of cognition and subjectivity', especially in relation to 'concerns about first-person versus third-person access to our own or to others' subjective cognitive experiences' (p. 179). This is exemplified in *Measure for Measure* by the contrast between Angelo's image of 'himself as Law personified' and his realization, prompted by Isabella, that he in fact plays 'a less exalted part in the more complex embodied and distributed cognitive system that comprises our flawed human world' (p. 189). In this sense, mirror motifs are shown as exposing 'a two-way relationship between the creation of the original by the image and the image by the original', as the 'mirror of the law is shown by Angelo's hypocrisy as operating humbly through the upholder of it, as a form of extended subjectivity' (p. 185).

Applying George Lakoff and Mark Johnson's cognitive metaphor theory to the numerous, polysemic uses of 'slip' and its cognate words in the play, Paul Yachnin and Patrick Neilson, 'Slips of Wilderness: Verbal and Gestural Language in *Measure for Measure*' (in Yachnin, ed., *Shakespeare's World of Words*, pp. 187–209), conclude that Shakespeare's use of metaphors in *Measure for Measure* 'exemplifies Lakoff and Johnson's argument for the metaphoricity of language itself and for the essentially metaphorical character of our descriptions of the world' (p. 191). All the major characters in *Measure*

*for Measure* variously 'slip', that is, 'deviate from', either 'law, ideology, power
or society' (p. 200) under the influence of some internal or external force, and
'the degree to which the characters slip under pressure demonstrates that none
of them is of metal sufficiently pure to take an impression straightforwardly'
(pp. 199–200). Yet 'all deviate in ways that reveal their individual qualities,
leading them along an irregular course toward something like a revelation of
self', in an adaptation of 'the "fortunate fall" of Adam and Eve' (p. 200).

Convinced that Thomas Middleton's modifications to the characterization
and story arc of *Measure for Measure* in *More Dissemblers Besides Women*
'perhaps account for revisions that he made to Shakespeare's play' in the early
1620s. Regina Buccola, in ' "Some woman is the father": Shakespeare,
Middleton, and the Criss-Crossed Composition of *Measure for Measure* and
*More Dissemblers Besides Women*' (*MRDE* 28[2015] 86–109), compares the
plays in order to highlight the differences between the two playwrights'
'conception[s] of female characters [who have a more prominent role in
Middleton] and figures of secular and religious authority' (p. 88). Buccola's
comparative discussion illustrates that, even though 'marriage, chastity, or
whoredom' are presented 'as the only viable options for their female
characters' by both dramatists, this choice is performed by Middleton's
women 'with the guidance of a maternal Duchess, whereas Shakespeare
depicts women as guided to their respective destinies by a paternal friar/Duke'
(p. 92).

The evidence for Middleton's early 1620s revision of *Measure for Measure* is
regarded by Richard Wilson, in ' "As mice by lions": Political Theology and
*Measure for Measure*' (*Shakespeare* 11[2015] 157–77), as both crucial for
examining the problematical nature of the play and 'fatal to the myth of
Shakespeare as a mystic royalist' (p. 169). On the one hand, Shakespeare's
portrayal of such a hapless and disrespected ruler as Vincentio could 'only be
ventured during the headless interregnum at the outset of the new reign, when
James delayed his entry into his southern capital for a year after he deserted
his northern one' (p. 161), so that the fictional Vienna must have strongly
reminded its audience of the real Edinburgh, to the point of prompting a
rewriting of the play. On the other hand, however, when Middleton tackled the
play in the 1620s he turned comedy into tragicomedy and transformed 'a
drama of demonic substitution ... into an allegory of divine sovereignty,
idealizing the monarch as a *deus ex machina*'. Hence, 'the real problems of
*Measure for Measure* reflect the contradiction of Jacobean ideas about election
and divine right, and the regression of Tudor parliamentarianism into Stuart
personal rule' (p. 168), with Middleton responsible for the insertion in
Shakespeare's play of 'the authoritarian ideal that runs throughout his canon,
of the great dictator' (p. 174).

The topicality of *Measure for Measure* is also taken up by Jane Rickard in
*Writing the Monarch in Jacobean England: Jonson, Donne, Shakespeare and the
Works of King James*, where she discusses the play's engagement with
*Basilikon Doron*, especially in relation to 'the conjunction in James's work of
the biblical phrase that gives the play its title with the issue of slander, one of
the play's central thematic concerns'. In particular, by 'draw[ing] upon the
phrase's wider biblical context', the play seems 'to interrogate the kind of

position James maintains' (p. 225) regarding 'how a ruler's public image is produced and may be contested' (p. 222) rather than straightforwardly making the new king the object of eulogy or satire. In so doing, 'the play highlights the ironies of associating the logic of measure for measure with the issue of slander': since James in *Basilikon Doron* advocates 'the right to speak freely while imposing limits on the speech of their subjects', and states that 'rulers are uniquely vulnerable to slander', no punishment exists 'for a subject that is exactly equivalent to the crime of slandering a ruler' (p. 226); therefore the play ultimately seems to suggest that 'the preoccupation of rulers with "slanderous" comment, epitomized in *Basilikon Doron*, may in effect produce what it seeks to prevent' (p. 227), namely criticism of the ruler.

In the context of a wider-ranging study of *Shakespeare's Folktale Sources*, Charlotte Artese sees the play as embodying 'the difficulty of adapting folktales, specifically by adding other folk narrative motifs to them' (p. 143), namely, in this specific case, those of the 'resistant sister', the 'disguised ruler', the 'bed trick', and the 'compassionate executioner', all added by Shakespeare—and, at the level of the plot, by the Duke—to the underlying 'Measure for Measure' folk-tale narrative. The situation is complicated further by the fact that the folk tale upon which Shakespeare's play draws had already been adapted by other writers, whose earlier versions of the story are 'preserved like fossils' and 'retained as counternarratives within the play' (p. 144). In the concluding scene, the Duke, 'as playwright-cum-folktale adapter' (p. 158), iterates all those versions one by one in order to reject them as lies, so as to present himself 'as the sole possessor of the one and only version of Isabella and Angelo's story' (p. 159). Yet, apart from the amusement Shakespeare might have wished the audience would feel 'at the lengths he [was] going [to] to torture the old story into a comedy' through recourse to considerably far-fetched solutions—for example, 'The double absurdity of a condemned criminal refusing to be executed and a pirate doppelgänger punctually dying' (p. 157)—'the audience is apt to have deep reservations about the marriage and the marriage plot' (p. 163) that leads Isabella to marry the Duke, so that the play turns out to be 'a failure in terms of creating a satisfying comic ending' as well as adapting the tale 'into a reassuringly romantic comedy' (p. 148).

Artese's monograph also examines another problem play, *All's Well That Ends Well*, and her contribution therefore deals with one of the three broad themes around which critical approaches to the play revolved in 2015: sources, economics, and desire. The story of Giletta as recounted by Boccaccio, Shakespeare's most immediate source, is in fact a version of the folk tale, 'The Man Who Deserted His Wife'. Shakespeare, argues Artese, makes very few departures from Boccaccio, but when he does, it is to insert 'details from the folktale not found in the *Decameron*' (p. 131)—for example the episode of the cure of the king—apparently in order to bring his plot increasingly 'into line with the "Deserted Wife" tradition' as the play progresses. This movement towards folk-tale lore produces 'a tension between the way a theater audience usually knows the motives and plans of characters, through dialogue and especially soliloquy, and the way an audience already familiar with the plot of a play knows a character's plans and motives, through prior acquaintance with the tale' (p. 121). This tension is evidenced by the fact that, 'while the audience gains privileged access to Helen's interiority through her speeches and dialogue in the first half of the play ... they lose contact with her in the second half' (pp. 121–2); in other words, 'when the plot of the "Deserted Wife" takes over, Helena's soliloquies disappear and her dialogue is much reduced, as if her speeches are redundant' (p. 122). Hence, Shakespeare must have assumed in the audience a certain familiarity with the folk tale; otherwise, play-goers would hardly have been able fully to appreciate the play's resolution.

In a plea for a return to the analysis of Shakespeare's changes to his sources as a way to appreciate his 'limited originality' (p. 63), Catherine Belsey, 'The Elephants' Graveyard Revisited: Shakespeare at Work in *Antony and Cleopatra*, *Romeo and Juliet* and *All's Well That Ends Well*' (*ShS* 68[2015] 62–72), interprets the structural modifications introduced by Shakespeare to Giovanni Boccaccio's novella of Giletta of Narbonne as intended to echo the parable of the Prodigal Son, especially its early modern declension as a favourite subject for moral plays such as *The Interlude of Youth* and *Lusty Juventus*, with which Shakespeare was familiar, as shown by echoes in *The Rape of Lucrece*, the sonnets, and *1 Henry IV*. The ending of the play, however, seems to act as a sort of counterpoint to that parable, where 'the father is God and divine forgiveness demands unreserved contrition' (p. 72), insofar as human relationships in the play look much less absolute and inevitably conditioned by human fallibility.

A concern for Shakespeare's transformation of his sources is shared by Ariana Traill's 'Shakespeare and the Roman Comic *Meretrix*' (in Dutsch, James, and Konstan, eds., *Women in Roman Republican Drama*, pp. 213–31). Resorting to Louise George Clubb's notion of theatergram as 'a dramaturgic element that exists within a common repertoire and is subject to permutation, combination, and gradual evolution' (p. 214), Traill considers a number of 'Roman comedy-derived theatergrams relating to the *meretrix mala* and associated types (*ancilla*, *lena*)'. As a result of the strict public moral standards that limited the opportunities for prostitutes to appear on the early modern stage, contends Traill, theatergrams centring 'on a *meretrix* in Plautus or Terence [had to] transfer ... to Shakespearian figures whose signal virtue is chastity', and who 'exhibit ... ingenuity, performance skill, and verbal facility in Roman-derived contexts, sometimes in contradiction to more conservative feminine virtues that they show elsewhere' (p. 215). In *All's Well*, Diana takes on these traits, inasmuch as she is 'the adolescent daughter of an old woman ... who plays something of the *lena*', and she 'attracts the unwanted attentions of a braggart soldier, Parolles, and an unhappily married *adulescens*, Bertram, who have both been ... offering a Terentian choice between poverty and prostitution' (p. 223). Diana's 'dedication to virtue' (p. 224), however, is never in doubt, and her taking upon herself 'the theatergrams of a *meretrix*' as some sort of secondary role ultimately 'requires the self-conscious performance of distinct theatergrams in order to dupe an internal audience' (p. 223).

Challenging the tendency of previous criticism 'to overlook the crucial roles money and class occupy in the play' and 'to romanticize the relationship between Helena, the Widow Capilet, and Diana' (p. 188), Emily C. Gerstell, in '*All's* [Not] *Well*: Female Service and "Vendible" Virginity in Shakespeare's

Problem Play' (*JEMS* 4[2015] 187–211), seeks to reassess Helena's role in the play. In Gerstell's view, far from being 'a passive victim of patriarchy', Helena is actually 'a woman keenly aware of both her own financial situation and that of those surrounding her, fluent in the market value of virginity, and masterful at getting what she wants' (p. 189). In Helena's construction of her relationship to Bertram as one of service, where he occupies an elevated position above her (with an inversion of the gender roles normally associated with chivalric romance and love poetry), and in her financial exploitation of her relationship with the other women in the play, not only does she bely 'any dichotomy between the rules that govern men and those that govern women' (pp. 203–4); more importantly, she 'demonstrates a profoundly economic and instrumental view of personal relations'. In its depiction of marriage as 'a manifestation of the power people have over one another' (p. 204) and its obsession with virginity as 'simultaneously the most important thing a woman can possess but [that she] must also dispense [with]' (p. 205), the play disturbingly ends up portraying Helena, the Widow, and Diana as 'not only resist[ing] but also participat[ing] in, benefit[ing] from, and perpetuat[ing] patriarchal structures of marriage and the household' (p. 208).

In *Shakespeare and Psychoanalytic Theory* Carolyn E. Brown discusses the incestuous overtones of the Countess's and Helena's relationship to Bertram, seeing the two women 'as active negotiators of the oedipal complex' (p. 108), in contrast to 'the standard view of early modern women as always victims[,] and illustrating they can enact their own sexual fantasies, even forbidden ones' (p. 129). Although Helena and Bertram are not consanguineous, their relationship is akin to 'that of a sister and brother, which makes a sexual relationship taboo' (p. 111). For Brown, Helena's attraction probably results from 'her projection or transference of her feelings for her father' onto Bertram as a mere substitute figure, which would explain 'her dedication to a man with whom she shares no compatibility and who displays no redeeming character traits' (p. 117). In addition, the incestuous nature of Helena's attraction to Bertram is borne out by her possessiveness and obsessive behaviour, which are typical traits in the perpetrators of incest. Moreover, argues Brown, Helena regularly 'enlists the defence mechanism of splitting ... typically employed by people involved in incestuous bonds' (p. 126), which 'allows her to engage in unchaste, immoral acts while disavowing them at the same time' (p. 127). Finally, the Countess's 'gradually attenuated role can suggest she symbolically becomes submerged into Helena, as Shakespeare correlates Bertram's having sex with Helena with his consummating his repressed oedipal desires for his mother' (p. 125).

The issue of desire is also at the core of Meredith Evans's discussion of the play in ' "Captious and inteemable": Reading Comprehension in Shakespeare' (in Yachnin, ed., *Shakespeare's World of Words*, pp. 211–35). Starting from a new reading of 'the captious and inteemable sieve' (I.i.204) to which Helena compares her own desire (and whose meaning has divided editors of the play for decades), Evans—taking ' "captious" possibly to mean deceitful; "inteemable" to mean bottomless' (p. 213)—argues that the description of Helena's desire, as characterized by 'infinite capacity and law-defying retention, tells of a miraculous performance she must replicate: to enter a scene where her integrity is tested and proved' (p. 216). This is made difficult by the fact that 'Helena's relationship to her own desire is defined by the object of desire and the sovereign power that can as easily obstruct as facilitate it' (p. 226): as a matter of fact, 'For *All's Well* to end well, the play must see its heroine legitimately coupled with the guy she somewhat inexplicably desires, and she must receive the King's benediction' (p. 229), so that the 'legitimate' heterosexual couple can, in turn, amplify sovereign power.

The analysis of the play's engagement with emotions was also one of the most trodden avenues in criticism of *Troilus and Cressida* over 2015. Alison V. Scott, in 'Making a Virtue of Giddiness: Rethinking Troilus' (E)Motion' (in White et al., eds., *Shakespeare and Emotions: Inheritances, Enactments, Legacies*, pp. 124–36) reads Troilus as engaging in a sort of 'emotional monitoring of the self' (p. 124), especially in the scene in which he admits to his own giddiness in the anticipation of the long-awaited sexual encounter with Cressida. Such an admission is, argues Scott, 'if not entirely unprecedented, certainly distinct and unusual' (p. 126) in Shakespeare's oeuvre. In this scene, 'Troilus first registers strong emotions triggered by his desire for Cressida, then realizes the physiological impact of those emotions, before reappraising the situation' (pp. 124–5). The scene is not meant merely to convey the idea of a straightforward 'failure of masculine self-government in the face of intense effeminizing emotion' (p. 126) in compliance with widespread contemporary moral discourse on the disruptive consequences of overflowing passions; more importantly, it seeks to construe giddiness 'as a force beyond control and problematically associated with positive energy and joy'. Troilus's unusual reflection—in itself a compelling dramatization of the complex 'intersection between emotional experience and cognitive appraisal' (p. 129)—should therefore be read as part of a larger attempt on his part to find 'a form of self-knowledge and self-mastery driven rather than threatened by emotion' (p. 125).

The issues of desire and self-governance are also taken up by Ronald Bedford's essay ' "I shall split all / In pleasure of my spleen!"': *Troilus and Cressida* and the Expression of Emotion' (in White et al., eds., pp. 137–45). In partial contrast to Scott's claims, Bedford contends that *Troilus and Cressida* 'demonstrates the futility of passion without reason, the folly of impulse over argument, the anarchy wrought by the self in the absence of grace' (p. 143). In Bedford's view, human values lose their meaning in the world of the play as a result of the characters' emotional incontinence, so that the 'disordered, undisciplined self ... becomes the site of subjugation: to self-delusion, self-ignorance, folly, rage, shame and disappointment—and finally becomes, in the moral vacuum of Achilles' empty, crowing ego, the subject of horror' (p. 144).

From a different standpoint, Unhae Langis, in ' "Desire is Death" in Shakespeare's *Troilus and Cressida*' (*EMLS* 24[2015] 1–31; special issue), suggests that the 'play's focus on choosing the right course of action in an alliance of reason and desire warrants an Aristotelian examination' (p. 9). For Langis, the play highlights 'a corrosive variant of a compelling convergence of *eros* and *thanatos*' in a decadent world where the Trojans and the Greeks 'are afflicted by akratic [i.e. lacking rational self-control] and vicious rather than virtuous desire' (p. 3). While it is true that the titular characters embody 'the play's potential for virtuous love', such possibility has to 'succumb to the inexorable forces of debased desire' (p. 21) pervading the play. This is especially exemplified by Cressida's fate. Finding herself alone at the Greek camp 'swarming with sex-starved soldiers' (p. 23), she gives herself up to Diomedes because she realizes that 'being the mistress of one man is preferable to being sexual prey for many' (p. 24). Even though she is taking the only possible course of action that can enable her to maintain an acceptable degree of integrity given her circumstances, she has to confront feelings of guilt and self-condemnation, insofar as she 'has internalized the patriarchal rebuke of the inconstant woman' (p. 23). From this perspective, the play therefore looks less like 'a condemnation of female inconstancy than a broad commentary on mutability as a shared human condition' (p. 26).

Cressida's destiny at the Greek camp and what it may suggest about gender construction in the play is also central to Lilly J. Goren's essay, 'Woman's Value on Trial in *Troilus and Cressida*' (in Howe Kritzer and López-Rodríguez, eds., *Woman on Trial: Gender and the Accused Woman in Plays from Ancient Greece to the Contemporary Stage*, pp. 67–86). Goren boldly likens Cressida to 'the women who have been systematically raped in a number of war zones throughout the world', inasmuch as Cressida 'has found herself displaced from her home, in an environment of insecurity where she and her body are under distinct threat' (p. 84). In Goren's view, the play 'poses questions about the position, power, autonomy, and agency of women treated as objects of consumption' (p. 69), and it does so by 'suggesting that the opposition between women who are virtuous and women who are corrupt is imposed on women by men'. More specifically, the play foregrounds the fact that 'the value placed on women's beauty, in a system where men view women as possessions, is constantly threatened by its association with sexuality' (p. 70), all the more so since honour seems to depend on a circular reasoning revolving around women's fidelity as judged by men, with women deprived of any agency whatsoever in the process, even though it is them who are ultimately held accountable for maintaining their own reputation untainted.

The last three critical contributions on *Troilus and Cressida* in this survey concentrate on aspects more closely connected to language and rhetoric. David Schalkwyk, in 'Proper Names and Common Bodies: The Case of Cressida' (in Yachnin, ed., pp. 59–76), observes that *Troilus and Cressida*, like *Romeo and Juliet*, 'explores the burden of the proper name, but ... in a different mode', namely by reflecting on the complex interplay between the abstractness of proper names on the page—where there are no bodies, which enables names to accumulate 'a series of descriptive properties passed on and reinvented, from poet to poet'—and their physical embodiment in the theatre, where 'the body cannot be reduced or eradicated', for on stage 'the common body of the actor is always forced to bear the burden of a proper name that is ... improper to it' (p. 64). This, in turn, leads to a de-idealization of paradigmatic names such as 'Troilus' and 'Cressida', which actually 'encapsulate the ideological process whereby these names come to epitomize the concepts of "fidelity" and "faithlessness"' (p. 68). This way, the play ends up turning 'rule back into sample, reducing paradigm to "instance"' (p. 65), and especially poses the question not so much 'whether Cressida is false or not, but whether her name is inevitably the epitome of falsehood' (p. 71). In *Figures of a Changing World: Metaphor and the Emergence of Modern Culture*, Harry J. Berger Jr. proceeds to an examination of Ulysses' speech in Act I, scene iii. Far from representing the 'defense of medieval metonymies' it was once believed to embody, the speech in fact illustrates, for Berger, 'the process by which metonymies get metaphorized' (p. 114). Distancing itself from the 'familiar medieval correspondence between macrocosm and body politic', Ulysses' description of the sun makes it emerge not as 'the metonymic double of a human ruler' but as 'a metaphor, an ideological fiction, a hyperbole by which the apprehensive ruler exalts his theatrical display of power to the skies' (p. 120). It is a sort of propaganda for royal success that, however, simultaneously betrays 'the precariousness, the anxiety, that motivates the propaganda' (p. 121). Ulysses' speech therefore challenges the medieval 'metonymy of active correspondence between the parts of a single universe' (p. 122) by exposing the image of the solar system and the order it purports to represent as a sophisticated metaphorical construction of the complexities inherent in, and exclusive to, court politics.

Touching upon the realms of both gender and rhetoric, Lucy Munro, in 'Staging Taste' (in Smith, Watson, and Kenny, eds., *The Senses in Early Modern England, 1558–1660*, pp. 19–38), discusses the figurative uses of taste that are interspersed throughout *Troilus and Cressida* as part of a broader examination of the varied 'imaginative and dramaturgical power' the sense of taste and its associations 'with both physical excess and spiritual endeavour, with cultivated appreciation and violent dislike' (p. 36) had for early modern playwrights. Taste repeatedly serves in *Troilus and Cressida* as a metaphor for both good and bad political advice; moreover, the play repeatedly associates 'correct and decorous acts of tasting with male martial valour', as well as '"distasting" with effeminate behaviour or female characters' (p. 31). All in all, taste seems to emerge as 'overpowering and uncontrollable, the domain of fevered appetites and famished kisses' (p. 32).

*(c) Poetry*

The year 2015 saw the publication of a book-length work on Shakespeare's sonnets, *Discovering the Hidden Figure of a Child in Shakespeare's Sonnets as the Key to a New Interpretation: From Literary Analysis to Historical Detection*, by Penny McCarthy. In chapter 1, McCarthy provides contextual information before drawing on similarities between Shakespeare's sonnets and Philip Sidney's *Astrophel and Stella* and Mary Wroth's 'Pamphilla to Amphilanthus'. In chapter 2, she looks at Sonnets 33–5, and suggests that the speaker's reputation is tarnished by the arrival of an illegitimate son, who, she suspects, could be Shakespeare's child. This idea is explored further in chapter 3, where McCarthy examines the possibility that Shakespeare ' "lived a life of crime" in engaging in an illicit sexual affair with a woman not his wife, but virtuously gives up the "fruit" of that crime—a child' (p. 76). Chapter 4 is concerned with the allusions to a baby in Sonnets 18–125. McCarthy argues that Sonnet 18 is 'addressed to an older woman, whose presence in the collection has not previously been recognized' (p. 90). She goes on to analyse Sonnets 74, 55, and 81, deducing that the speaker may not only be saying that, when he dies, his life will continue in the lines of the poems, but may actually be alluding to a bloodline, in that his life will continue through his child. McCarthy then turns her attention to shadows in Sonnets 37 and 53, and suggests that the 'shadows refer to the shadowy unborn babe' (p. 107). McCarthy addresses the theme of beauty in chapter 5, and notes that the poems seem to portray beauty being transmitted to a bastard child. She examines Sonnet 126 in chapter 6, and argues that this sonnet is 'addressed to two lovely boys of different generations'—the young man and a baby (p. 139). McCarthy, then, calls the reader's attention to Sonnet 26, suggesting that this poem is addressed to the same 'lovely boys' as 126. Chapter 7 focuses on the collection's dedication, drawing attention to its shape on the page and hourglass outline. She observes that 'this insight strengthens the general suspicion that the dedication is some way upside-down, and should be read from the bottom up' (p. 159). After examining all possible candidates for the identity of Mr W.H., to whom the poem is dedicated, McCarthy argues that there is a possibility that the Mr is indeed Master W.H.—the baby alluded to throughout the sonnets. Chapter 8 is concerned with the young man, and in an attempt to establish his identity McCarthy studies his character in the poetry as well as his potential existence as a real person. She examines play-scripts and historical documents to try to decipher whether or not Shakespeare's young man is based on William Herbert, earl of Pembroke, son of Mary Sidney, and cousin of Lady Mary Wroth, as previous critics have argued. The persona of the dark lady is considered in chapter 9, where McCarthy, again, looks for clues in the poetry and external documentation to investigate the possibility that Mary Wroth was the dark lady. Chapter 10 examines the reading of a possible Master W.H. further—McCarthy explores the love triangle between Herbert, Wroth, and Shakespeare, and places the child within this dynamic. The character of the older woman is studied in more detail in chapter 11. McCarthy suggests that her character is likely to have been based on Mary Sidney, and in the final chapter, McCarthy sums up her argument by concluding that Shakespeare seems to have fallen in love with a whole family. She claims that this is the key to an enriched understanding of his sonnets, and argues that in all likelihood, the family he fell in love with was the Sidney family.

Rebecca Laroche's chapter, 'Roses in Winter: Recipe Ecologies and Shakespeare's Sonnets' (in Munroe, Geisweidt, and Bruckner, eds., *Ecological Approaches to Early Modern English Texts: A Field Guide to Reading and Teaching*, pp. 51–60), provides a fresh reading of the eleven sonnets in Shakespeare's collection that make reference to roses. Laroche focuses her attention on one early modern recipe book, in which almost 20 per cent of the recipes include roses in some form, and observes that in Shakespeare's sonnets the roses mentioned are not only the preserved flowers, but living roses, which often get destroyed by worms and harsh weather, and that even distilled roses do not last for ever and must be replaced. Most importantly, she argues that the distillation process is described differently in each sonnet, just as the distillation processes of making rose oil and rose water differ, so, in a sense, the sonnets are their own mini-recipes.

In his article 'Revising Obsession in Shakespeare's Sonnets 153 and 154' (*SIP* 112[2015] 114–38) David Harper examines the 1609 quarto edition of these two poems, proposing that 154 had been unintentionally included in the collection by the printers. After observing inadvertent repetition in manuscripts of Shakespeare's earlier work, he argues that Sonnet 154 was a draft of Sonnet 153 added to the quarto for convenience. He also makes reference to the theme of sexual obsession in Sonnets 152, 153, and 154, and notes that 154 does not have the same intensity as the other two and does not seem to fit as well into the whole sonnet sequence as, perhaps, one would expect it to.

'Pyrrhonist Uncertainty in Shakespeare's Sonnets', by Amanda Ogden Kellogg (*Shakespeare* 11[2015] 408–24), explores the effect of Pyrrhonism on Shakespeare's poetry. Pyrrhonism, of course, encourages the thinker to consider multiple explanations to avoid making a judgement on a particular issue, in an attempt to reach tranquillity. Ogden Kellogg argues that Shakespeare's sonnets are ambiguous enough to appeal to Pyrrhonist philosophy in that they are susceptible to multiple interpretations, going beyond the Petrarchan convention of creating certainty by using metaphors which lead the reader to specific conclusions. She states that, although Shakespeare uses Petrarchan metaphors, they are used in a way that deviates from convention in that their meanings are unclear and subject to a number of different interpretations, which, according to Pyrrhonists, makes the reading experience a highly pleasurable one.

In her article, 'The Outmodedness of Shakespeare's Sonnets' (*ELH* 82[2015] 759–87), Emily Vasiliauskas argues that part of Shakespeare's sonnet collection was written after the trend for sonnets of love and passion had passed. Despite this, she observes, he indulges in outmodedness—'the persistence in a style after the expiration of its social utility' (p. 760). Style was closely associated with class in the period, with the people of a higher social standing setting new trends, and being outmoded was a sign of being of a lower class. But, by not striving to appeal to the fashion of the time, Vasiliauskas notes that Shakespeare, unlike Jonson and Hoskins, 'tried something different, remaining faithful to a style and discovering new energy within it, by virtue of its outmodedness' (p. 765). She adds that, by not following popular trends, he even forces style itself to question his poetic decisions.

There has also been a lot of scholarly interest in *The Rape of Lucrece* this year. In his article 'Rape and Republicanism in Shakespeare's *Lucrece*' (*SEL* 55[2015] 1–20), John Kunat investigates the topic of consent, arguing that it is not just a political issue, but an issue associated with gender and sexuality. Kunat looks as Shakespeare's poem alongside Livy's rape narrative, which discusses the beginning of the republic and how different forms of consent were related to sexual and gender politics.

'Hiding the Peacock's Legs: Rhetoric, Cosmetics and Deception in Shakespeare's *Lucrece* and Trussell's *Hellen*' (*EJES* 19[2015] 148–62), by Anna Swärdh, assesses the concepts of rhetorical and cosmetic deception in these two rape poems. By looking specifically at references to 'colouring' and 'cloaking', she observes that the colouring and cloaking metaphors are used to conceal the rapists' true intentions before they pounce on their innocent victims, and are also used by the women in different ways—for Lucrece through vocalizing her emotional state, and for Helen through using cosmetics—as ways to hide but also reveal their plight.

Christy Desmet, in her article 'Revenge, Rhetoric, and Recognition in *The Rape of Lucrece*' (*MultSh* 12[2015] 27–40), demonstrates how the poem associates justice with revenge, but 'also complicates its sense of public justice, mostly through Lucrece's own evolving ethics' (p. 29). She explores the concept of 'the borrowed bed' as an association with theft, debt, and crime, and notes that 'Shakespeare's poem also offers us a brief glimpse of a possible politics of recognition, located primarily in Lucrece's exploration of her physical and moral condition after the rape' (p. 34).

In his article, 'Shakespeare's Lady 8' (*SQ* 66[2015] 47–88), Douglas Bruster investigates the printers' ornament that was used on the title pages on the first publication of *The Rape of Lucrece* and *Venus and Adonis*, and examines the meanings and associations generated by the imprint it produced. Bruster states that the ornament was linked to the French and Huguenot print culture, and that it was very popular with Shakespeare's early followers as it provided a representation of the diverse content included in his work. Bruster adds that this stamp established Shakespeare's works as an 'Elizabethan brand' as well as establishing him as an author.

The two works published solely on *Venus and Adonis* this year both concern Ovid's influence on Shakespeare. In her book chapter 'Out-Oviding Ovid in Shakespeare's *Venus and Adonis*' (in Chiari, ed., pp. 175–87), Laetitia Sansonetti investigates Shakespeare's borrowings from Ovid, particularly those of sexual misdemeanours. She comments on the techniques used by Shakespeare in *Venus and Adonis*, and argues that 'criss-cross verbal quotation, narrative allusion and authorial recombination seem to have allowed Shakespeare not only to emulate Ovid, but also to overtake him' (p. 175).

Sarah Carter concentrates on the themes of love and death in her article '"With kissing him I should have killed him first": Death in Ovid and Shakespeare's *Venus and Adonis*' (*EMLS* 24[2015] 1–13; special issue). She explores the ways in which death is portrayed in both poems, and how death is seen to be continually linked with passion, desire, and unrequited love. Although she traces the influence of Ovid on Shakespeare with respect to the deployment of mythical characters, Carter focuses predominantly on Shakespeare's poem in this article, suggesting that the poem's use of irony and antithesis emphasizes irony in the poem's representation of the different types of love.

*(d) Histories*

Despite the fact that Shakespeare's history plays, with the exception of *Richard III*, have not often been popular in theatre repertory, they have somehow made a significant impact in film and television adaptations. The reason for this, perhaps, is that the relatively dry and uneven nature of the dramatic material has prompted practitioners to take experimental approaches to form and narrative. Laurence Olivier's *Henry V* [1944], Orson Welles's *Chimes at Midnight* [1965], and the BBC/RSC production of *The Wars of the Roses* [1965] are among the most prominent examples of this trend. Analyses of Olivier's *Henry V* are nothing new; however, historian Richard Inverne, in 'Henry V in the Cinema: Laurence Olivier's Charismatic Version of History' (*Historian* 127[2015] 24–9), contributes something original to the discussion by offering a comparative reading of Olivier's film and Kenneth Branagh's later adaptation to clarify how 'public attitudes' to the play's titular monarch have been shaped through the twentieth century (p. 24). Such an undertaking inevitably invites comparison with the recent popular re-evaluations of Richard III's reign that have occurred since the recovery of his remains in 2012. Inverne argues that Olivier's 'jingoistic' approach of portraying Henry as a national hero prompted the removal of the more 'controversial' moments in Shakespeare's play, such as the ruthless execution of French prisoners. As a result, the monarch is portrayed as heroic, but barely 'human' (p. 28). In contrast, Branagh's 'post-Vietnam' reworking is recognized as establishing Henry as a more fallible and human figure, one who is never quite sure if his campaign is anything more than an expression of vanity and pride (p. 29). However, Inverne observes that Branagh's film also falls short of historical iconoclasm in its failure to restore some of the textual cuts that Olivier made, perhaps in fear that it might result in the controversial depiction of a figure who has, accurately or otherwise, been established as a national hero in Britain.

During 2015, John Wyver published two separate articles relating to the RSC's tradition of filming stage productions of Shakespeare. The first article, 'Between Theatre and Television: Inside the Hybrid Space of the Wars of the Roses' (*CritSTV* 10:iii[2015] 23–36), addresses the BBC–RSC production of *The Wars of the Roses*, a 1965 adaptation of the first tetralogy by John Barton and Peter Hall. The article outlines the somewhat radical staging process of the production, whereby the RSC theatre was modified to function as a 'multi-camera' television studio for eight weeks of performances. Wyver's key focus here is on how this production created a hybrid performance idiom that combined elements of television and theatre staging, as well as editing techniques characteristic of both television and cinema (p. 33). Confirming the hypothesis about the difficulty of staging Shakespeare's history plays for modern audiences, Wyver asserts that the adaptation process was considered a necessity by Hall, an experienced director who felt that the *Henry VI* plays could not meet the needs of modern audiences without serious modification (p. 24; Wyver additionally notes that the heavily cut Shakespearean text was augmented by 'cod-Elizabethan' language written by its adapters). However, Wyver also cites instances of successful productions of uncut versions of the plays, thus casting doubt on Hall's hypothesis (pp. 25, 34).

The second of Wyver's articles, 'Screening the RSC Stage: The 2014 Live from Stratford-upon-Avon Cinema Broadcasts' (*Shakespeare* 11[2015] 286–302), takes this discussion of 'hybrid' performances to its most modern extreme by addressing the recent trend of screening filmed stage productions in cinemas. Wyver notes that this form has proliferated in the last five years, most notably with the *NTLive* template, which the RSC has followed belatedly (p. 292), but he also notes that this trend has not yet attracted proper critical analysis. In light of Wyver's first article, it appears that an approach that accounts for the hybridity of cinema, theatre, and television media will provide a suitable methodological basis for analysing this recent phenomenon in Shakespearean performance. The process of filming stage performance in more modern times, when cameras are both more sophisticated and much smaller, is, of course, easier than in 1965, and Wyver acknowledges that this feeds into the hybridizing process that these productions explore (p. 296). The article notes that the RSC's 2014 season of filmed productions uses both parts of *Henry IV*, although the survey of ongoing practices of filming stage performances in previous years has not given any special attention to the history plays. Interest in stage productions of *Henry IV* is often generated by the casting of a great actor in the role of Falstaff, in this case Antony Sher, and the degree to which these productions are successful is acknowledged to be related to the manner in which they mimic the experience of live theatre rather than making any attempt to employ cinematic values (p. 298).

Further supporting the premise that Shakespeare's history plays often attract a degree of innovation in performance to offset the dry and unfamiliar material of the texts, Cristina Gutierrez-Dennehy, in ' "Our lives and all are Bolingbroke's": Alternating Double Casting in *Richard II*' (*ThTop* 25[2015] 127–37), reports on a production of *Richard II* that identifies the duality of King Richard and Henry Bolingbroke as a point of experimental focus. The play was staged by the Poor Shadows of Elysium company in Austin, Texas, in 2013, and its central point of innovation was to cast two lead actors to alternate between the roles of Richard and Henry on a nightly basis. Central to this experiment was the use of a specially written prologue, during which a coin was tossed to determine which actor would play which role (p. 127). As the insertion of this prologue demonstrates, the value of such an innovation appears to be limited if it is not made visible to the audience; indeed, the apparent level of risk that is produced through this technique gives the performance the quality of 'theatre sports'—a performance spectacle that exists independently of the Shakespearean text that is being performed. However, Gutierrez is at pains to argue that the 'double casting' strategy actually serves to emphasize the thematic material of the play, which it does by illustrating the cyclical nature of history (p. 130). This, of course, assumes that Kott's post-Brechtian hypothesis, that the history plays are intended to elucidate this cycle, is authoritative. More recent critical approaches to the histories have sought to engage with analyses of the dominant ideologies of their time, and Kott's approach therefore reflects a residual methodology (see Ton Hoenselaars, 'Shakespeare's English History Plays', in Margreta De Grazia and Stanley Wells, eds., *The New Cambridge Companion to Shakespeare* [2011], pp. 137–52: 149). Considered in this light, Gutierrez-Dennehy's justification of the 'double casting' technique by citing its relevance to the themes of the text remains, at best, a selective perspective.

Countless sources assert that the most frequent dramatic conflict to occur in Shakespeare is that which breaks out between brothers over inheritances—a quality equally present in the tragedies, comedies, and histories. Some sources have asserted that the recurrence of this conflict is typological, such as we find in Heather Anne Hirschfeld's article, 'Hamlet's "First Corse": Repetition, Trauma, and the Displacement of Redemptive Typology' (*SQ* 54[2003] 424–48), which argues that the specific citation of the 'primal eldest curse' (III.iii.41) in *Hamlet* situates the play as a coded treatment of Genesis 4:1–16. Maurice Hunt, in 'Brothers and "Gentles" in *The Life of Henry the Fifth*' (*CompD* 49[2015] 71–93), notes that *Henry V* is an exception to the rule of fraternal conflict in Shakespeare, and argues that the positive images of brotherhood in the play support an image of the ideal Christian king as one whose reign is secured through brotherly bonds. This is explored through the play's thematic alignment of ideal brotherhood with the notion of 'gentility' that exemplifies a Christian ideal in social terms. The article focuses on the foot-soldier Williams who addresses the disguised king prior to Agincourt. Hunt analyses the exchange between the two to identify the limits of Henry's gentility and magnanimity, revealing in the play a critique of the ideal of 'brotherhood' that has been fostered by the 'We few, we happy few' speech of IV.iii.60–7. In contrast, Williams is characterized as an exemplar of 'imaginative empathy' (p. 76) and is compared several times to Prospero in *The Tempest*, whose 'discovery' of empathy in Act V, scene i, replaces vengeance with forgiveness, and moreover places the magician of Shakespeare's late play as the true ideal of noble gentility (p. 84). Taken in the wider perspective, then, Hunt's reading of *Henry V* finds in the play the same critiques of power that are present in the historical tragedies *Richard II* and *Richard III*; however, Hunt also sees this critique as being penned by a Shakespeare who believed in the possibility of an ideal kingship that could be attained by the ruler's rigorous and expansive application of Christian principles.

Further pursuing the hypothesis that Shakespeare's history plays may be read as critical meditations on the nature of kingship, Eric Pudney's analysis of *Henry V* and *Richard III*, in 'Mendacity and Kingship in Shakespeare's *Henry V* and *Richard III*' (*EJES* 19[2015] 163–75), proposes that these two plays may be interpreted as demonstrating how historical judgements of 'virtuous' or 'evil' rulers are largely a matter of effective rhetoric. Pudney locates in these plays articulations of public discourse, both within the drama and in the engagements that occur between the king and the audience, as a theme of central importance. He identifies in both kings a preoccupation with a self-image crafted through rhetorical strategies, the chief difference being that Henry crafts an image of heroism while Richard fashions himself as a villain. Pudney argues that this process is subject to tension in the dramas, whereby Henry's heroic rhetoric conceals qualities, if not of outright villainy, then at least ones that we may not easily reconcile with the image of the ideal Christian monarch; in Richard's case, the power of individualism that villainy brings is shown to exhaust itself long before the villain meets his destiny at Bosworth Field.

Rhetorical studies of Shakespeare are usually a safe bet, primarily because the exploration of tropes in the plays is so fruitful that it safely pushes the question of the author's ideological alignment further and further into the background. In this sense, the thorny problem of Tudor ideology in both of these plays can be neatly avoided by observing that their rhetorical designs are so complex, and their critical functions so developed, that they almost attain the status of being politically neutral. Pudney takes a broadly egalitarian approach to this question by citing the contemporary writings of Jean Bodin on kingship; Bodin's comparative approach to anatomizing 'good' kings and 'bad' tyrants becomes a framework for comparing Henry and Richard, and therefore sees the two plays as largely expositional exercises in rhetoric, in which the distinction between 'good' and 'bad' is further blurred. Nonetheless, as in Hunt's analysis, we are reassured by the presence of a liberal 'Shakespeare', who is concerned with revealing the rhetorical 'tricks' by which a ruler may assert power, and thereby arming the masses with a means of resisting them.

In his article 'Shakespeare's Machiavellian Moment: Discovering Ethics and Forming a Leadership Narrative in *Henry V*' (*Public Integrity* 17[2015] 265–78), Jerry E. Herbel Jr. takes an interdisciplinary approach to reading Shakespeare's *Henry V*, drawing on management theory and training manuals as a means of assessing the model of leadership that Shakespeare constructs in King Henry. Conversely, Herbel also cites Shakespeare's play as an effective manual of leadership ethics, one that may profitably be used by modern executives. Such a reading need hardly come as a surprise; recent scholarship on *Henry V* has moved away from the traditional reading of the play as a 'historical' or 'patriotic' epic, and found in it a penetrating critique of political power. Pudney's article, for example, asserts that the depiction of King Henry, in its own way, shows as cunning a political mind as that found in *Richard III*. This is not a point that Herbel disputes, but he is also at pains to note that the political focus of the play is not primarily critical, but presents an ideal of ethical management that surpasses in its impact any expedient shows of manipulation or deception. He notes that Machiavelli himself was not a cynic, but a realist who had observed that 'Christian ethics sometimes has a debilitating effect on politics by making leaders too weak and hesitant to rule well' (p. 269). This is not a new insight, but it is one that clearly bears repeating in view of the frequency with which the term 'Machiavellian' is conflated with 'malevolent' in our culture.

Herbel's article is simple and clear, and it makes its case effectively through reference to the play and text; however, as is often the case with interdisciplinary analyses, there is a risk of oversimplifying the discourses of one or the other discipline being cited. In this case, Herbel approaches *Henry V* via the problem of seeking a definitive reading of the play's purpose and meaning. The active Shakespeare scholar can readily accept that *Henry V* may be read in the light of early modern 'manuals' of ideal leadership, but the claim that this reflects Shakespeare's authorial intention should be met with resistance and scepticism. Herbel's analysis is both valid and original, but his observations should be understood within the dialectical framework that has long been the standard in the discipline, where the presence of any one literary genre is just one of many influences that have shaped the play's text.

Paul Brown has contributed a short but substantive article to *Vides*, an online journal produced by the students of the Department for Continuing Education, University of Oxford: 'Stealing Soldiers' Hearts: Appropriating

*Henry V* and Marching *Shakespeare's Boys* off to the Great War' (*Vides* 3[2015] 33–43). The article examines the reception of Shakespeare's *Henry V* in the period prior to the First World War, where it is interpreted largely as a patriotic epic, and it considers how the trauma of the war prompted a drastic reconsideration of the play's themes, where it came to be performed as an 'anti-war satire'. This reconsideration is aligned with Brown's own conviction that the play is a 'subversive attack on imperialism, military rhetoric, and the dangers of charismatic leaders' (p. 34). Brown uses the pathos of the Great War generation to make his case: he cites instances where the play's most jingoistic speeches are used in recruitment drives to condemn imperialistic or militaristic readings of Shakespeare.

While this is perhaps the most radically extreme reading of *Henry V* to emerge in 2015, Brown's analysis should not be taken as negating the viability of the more moderate or conservative readings of the play, such as those are outlined elsewhere in this section of *YWES*. Nonetheless, it remains an important piece for its acknowledgement that anti-establishment feeling permeates the history plays: like the ruthlessly violent tragedies, the histories were the mainstay of the public theatres, which were the site in which the early modern 'crisis of confidence' in the feudal order found its fullest expression (Jonathan Dollimore, *Radical Tragedy* [1984], p. 3). While it might be hasty to conclude that any Shakespeare play has a clearly articulated or single political purpose, we should always remain receptive to the possibility that such anti-establishment sentiments may frequently be found throughout the histories.

It is no surprise that Shakespeare's *Richard III* became something of a hot topic in Shakespeare studies after the 2012 recovery of the historical monarch's remains in Leicester; however, in many cases, the recent rise in interest has primarily benefited those scholars already working in the field established by the play's historical framework. Dana Percec, whose article 'Shakespeare and War: *Richard III*—The Long Shadows of Early Modern English History' (*Brukenthalia* 5[2015] 687–94) appears in a journal concerning itself with 'war studies', offers an overview of the recent trend in historical interest, identifying a significant tension between the Richard apologists and the mainstream perceptions of Richard as a historical villain. Percec argues that accounts of the historical figure feature enough 'dark spots' to make it difficult to dismiss Shakespeare's villainous characterization as wholly Tudor propaganda (p. 689). The centrepiece of Percec's analysis is a focus on how the tensions surrounding Richard's character impact on historical understandings of the battle of Bosworth. Percec identifies Richard as belonging to the late age of medieval 'warrior kings', and argues that Shakespeare's depiction of the battle, including the dream/ghost scene (V.iii) that precedes it, centres on the recurrent image of the king facing the enemy alone (p. 692). Like Pudney, Percec draws the comparison with Shakespeare's *Henry V*, whose own entry into battle is similarly couched in the trappings of a solitary endeavour, and argues that Shakespeare's vision of medieval kingship involves the conviction that leading an army into battle is a personal undertaking, akin to single combat but enacted on a national scale, with the king as the bodily focus of the process. Citing Michael Jones, Percec concludes with a familiar reading of Shakespearean politics, where Richard's defeat is shown to be predicated on his adherence to a medieval code of combat, which ultimately cannot withstand the pragmatism of Henry Tudor's modern invasion force, with its mercenary ranks and questionable legitimacy (p. 693).

Persisting with the familiar reading of Shakespeare's *Richard III* as Tudor 'propaganda', Elizabeth Zauderer, in '"... Neither mother, wife, nor England's queen": Re-visioning Queen Margaret of Anjou in Richard Loncraine's Film *Richard III* (1995)' (*LFQ* 43[2015] 146–59), addresses the ahistorical appearance of Margaret of Anjou in Shakespeare's play, as well the modification of the character in that mainstay of Shakespeare film studies, Richard Loncraine's 1995 adaptation of the play. Zauderer proposes that the figure of Margaret may have been intended to promote the Tudor world-view through the invocation of a historical warrior queen, supported by the earlier portrayal of Margaret in the *Henry VI* plays, Margaret's career loosely matching that of Elizabeth I; yet, as Zauderer argues, this claim stumbles on the corresponding portrayal of Margaret as a malevolent, curse-dispensing witch, an analogue unlikely to be taken as flattering the reigning monarch. Accepting these contradictions as part of the fabric of Shakespearean drama, the author then examines the conflation of Margaret with the Duchess of York (played by Maggie Smith) in the 1995 film. No plausible purpose of combining these characters is fully articulated in the article in terms of the play's ideological status, beyond the supposition that the Duchess's occasional use of Margaret's lines identifies her as the guarantor of legitimate rule in the face of Richard's usurpation. Although this replicates the function of Margaret in the play in the face of the claims of Yorkist illegitimacy, it does not clarify the recurrence of Tudor ideology in the film adaptation. There are some factual errors that a close reading of the play or its adaptations should eliminate, such as the claim that the dynastic dispute between York and Lancaster was resolved by the marriage of Princess Elizabeth and Edward of Lancaster (p. 147). These errors suggest that the article is perhaps attempting too much for its own good, and that its orientation to the discipline of film studies means that its historical claims are not being properly evaluated at the review or editing stages. There are perhaps interesting ideas yet to be explored in this film, which is still only twenty years old; this article suggests as much, but its own analysis retreats into somewhat safe and predictable analyses of how film language articulates what we may already know about the characters.

Rosemary Gaby, in her essay '"The days we have seen": The History of Regret in *Henry IV Parts One* and *Two, The Hollow Crown* (2012)' (in White et al., eds., pp. 231–9), highlights another reason why the history plays, while perhaps not totally engaging for modern audiences, have nonetheless remained a mainstay of theatre repertory: namely, that their reflections on monarchy have emerged as an important touchstone in British culture during periods of national importance. Citing the occasion of the 2012 London Olympics as the backdrop to the prestige adaptation of the second tetralogy as *The Hollow Crown*, Gaby observes that the emphatically dark tone of the plays, as well as their adaptation, seem somewhat at odds with the triumphal tone of the national occasion. Gaby offers an engaging analysis of the series from the perspective of performance tradition, noting, for example, that the portrayal of Henry IV by Jeremy Irons atypically overshadows the performance of

Simon Russell Beale as Falstaff (p. 234). Likewise, the portrayal of Henry V by Tom Hiddleston counters the recent critical readings of the character as Machiavellian, instead placing him as the 'heroic centre' of the series. Gaby's essay, which appears in a volume that has arisen out of the benighted 'History of Emotions' project that has dominated Shakespeare studies in Australia for several years, is relatively short, and it is to some extent hijacked by the need to discuss *The Hollow Crown* in terms of a nominated 'emotion'. So while Gaby begins and ends the essay by recognizing that the dark tone of the series is at odds with the celebratory spirit of Britain's 'Cultural Olympiad', the reason for this is left as an open question, with the concept of 'regret' being posited as a possible explanation. More welcome would have been a recognition of the tensions embodied in the 'national spirit' of the English people, and an acknowledgement of how such a latent tension may shape the works of the national poet, as well as the politics of the present.

Few Shakespeare scholars could have benefited from the discovery of Richard III's remains more than Philip Schwyzer: prior to 2012, Schwyzer had been heavily invested in the material analysis of the century that separates the eras of Richard III and William Shakespeare, tracing not only the significant cultural overlap between the late medieval and early modern periods, but also the discourses of historiography through which the image of Richard that dominated in Shakespeare's time had taken shape. Materialist analyses of this nature typically question the 'periodization' of history, where different eras are arbitrarily identified, distinguished, and made homogeneous, and Schwyzer is at pains to distinguish those elements of Richard's era that were still manifestly present in England by the late sixteenth century. The discovery of Richard's remains not only rendered this research area of increased value to scholarly and general readerships; the discovery itself also meant that the research would develop in exciting and unexpected new directions.

The resulting book, *Shakespeare and the Remains of Richard III* [2013; paperback published in 2015], is typified by this split between its pre-2012 and post-2012 impulses. The focus of the former is closer to the materialist criticism of Shakespeare that begins with Raymond Williams's concern with the 'crisis of confidence' in monarchy that drove the events of the seventeenth century, and which culminated in the Civil War and Commonwealth (Dollimore, *Radical Tragedy*, p. 3; Williams, *Marxism and Literature* [1977]). The primary historiographical shift this criticism represented was a rejection of the Tillyardian 'world picture' that had seemed to circumscribe and homogenize the eras of early modern England, and the move towards identifying the 'dominant', 'residual', and 'emergent' forces in culture (Dollimore, introduction to *Radical Tragedy*, p. 10). Schwyzer applies this historiography to the century that precedes Shakespeare's lifetime, and moreover identifies that the shift in perceptions of the last Plantagenet king was a dominating influence in a century that saw massive changes in English culture and society. For example, a large section of this book offers an impressive overview of the literary and dramatic folk traditions through which the image of Richard, as he appears in Shakespeare, was crafted; yet, this is contrasted with another section that outlines the substantial contribution that Richard made to English infrastructure, a legacy that stands even in spite of judgements of his historical villainy. As the analysis makes clear, it is no simple matter to identify any 'dominant' view of Richard.

Although such material is sufficiently engaging in its own terms, the archaeological discovery of 2012 appears to have subtly shifted Schwyzer's focus, with the result that the project has developed a characteristically New Historicist bent. In this context, the process of investigation is driven by a preoccupation with material particularities, arcane objects, and rituals, the gradually changing significance of which becomes a key site for questioning how we construct historical meaning. An apt example of this is found in the chapter that begins with the episode in which Richard woos Lady Anne (I.ii). Schwyzer draws a great deal of historical intrigue out of the presence of Henry VI's corpse throughout the scene; this develops into a detailed discussion of the rituals by which the bodies of monarchs were conventionally laid to rest. One of the key attractions of this type of analysis is how it prompts closer readings of the plays themselves, uncovering overlooked details. For example, Schwyzer observes that *Richard III* is one of the few Shakespearean tragedies in which the burial rites for the tragic protagonist are not discussed; instead, Richmond refers only to the burial of those who died nobly in battle. We cannot fail to see the significance of this reading of the play in light of the long-standing misplacing of Richard's remains. In respects such as these, *Shakespeare and the Remains of Richard III* not only forms a valuable response to the questions raised by the discovery of Richard's resting place, but also emerges as the essential companion piece to one of Shakespeare's better-known plays.

One point of criticism that this book has raised for me is that, while the type of analysis that Schwyzer offers is clearly indebted to the 'radical' readings of Shakespeare that began in the mid-1980s, as well to other sources of critical methodology, these sometimes appear to be used without adequate recognition of their origins. For example, a later chapter entitled 'Walking in the City' (pp. 158–72) identifies the detailed London geography that the first three acts of the play encompass, which centralizes the 'everyday' experience of the city into its dramatic framework (p. 158). Schwyzer connects this quality to the 'quotidian' details that inevitably accompany, and consequently personalize, the progress of history, as well as the experience of civic life. Is it a coincidence that French theorist Michel De Certeau's most famous essay, translated into English as 'Walking in the City', is also concerned with these matters, and that the essay appears in his book *L'Invention du quotidian* [1980], translated as *The Practice of Everyday Life* [1984; trans. Steven Rendall]? There appears to be a clear debt to Certeau, whose work aligns with the methodological innovations that cultural materialism and New Historicism applied to Shakespeare, yet the theorist is not mentioned in the book, even in passing. It is perhaps the case that the outcomes of these critical innovations have become so widespread that they are assumed to be commonplaces not originating in the work of individual innovators. Nonetheless, one would hope that a work of such penetrating historiography would be equipped with the means of recognizing one of its own antecedents.

*(e) Tragedies*

Nicolas Tredell's book *Shakespeare: The Tragedies* is a volume in Palgrave's Reader's Guides to Essential Criticism series, and as such the book presents discussion of criticism of the texts, introducing key critical debates and discussing the texts themselves at one remove. Tredell acknowledges that the 'critical response to the tragedies is itself, in microcosm, a history of global culture', but the book selects 'what seems essential from the Anglo-American strand of that response' (p. 1). The introduction addresses different versions and editions of the plays, issues of (co)authorship, and genre. There are then twelve chapters covering responses to the plays from the period 1693–2013. The first three chapters are chronological in their approach. There is then a chapter on A.C. Bradley's *Shakespearean Tragedy* [1904], and thereafter the chapters on twentieth- and twenty-first-century criticism are organized thematically. There are chapters on psychoanalytical approaches; important criticism from the 1930s and 1940s (presented under the heading 'Image and Form'); New Historicism, cultural materialism, and poststructuralism; gender and sexuality; ethnicity and ecology; philosophy and ethics; and religion. Critics covered include Stephen Greenblatt, Jonathan Dollimore, L.C. Knights, Ania Loomba, Jacques Derrida, and Jacques Lacan. The book concludes by suggesting possible directions for future study of Shakespeare's tragedies.

*Shakespeare's Roman Plays* by Paul Innes discusses the more obviously 'Roman' plays (*Titus Andronicus*, *Julius Caesar*, *Antony and Cleopatra*, and *Coriolanus*) along with the less obvious *Cymbeline*. Innes states that the theme of the book is the relationship between Rome and Britain and that he includes *Cymbeline* because of this. The intention of the book is to draw 'attention to the meanings of Rome as they are starting to be incorporated into the nascent British state contemporary to Shakespeare, and thus the emerging British Empire' (p. 4). The book treats each play separately while acknowledging points of contact across some or all of them. Chapter 1 covers *Titus Andronicus*, focusing especially on the first act and the potential of the Renaissance stage. Innes addresses the initial success of the play and later critical vilification. The social and dramatic construction of tragedy is also addressed. In chapter 2, Innes develops ideas from chapter 1 about the tragic form through the play *Julius Caesar*. He looks closely at the meanings that are generated by the figure of Caesar and the aftermath of his death. Chapter 3 focuses on *Antony and Cleopatra* and addresses the play's critical reception (rather than the text itself). Innes looks at historical material, reading Cleopatra as a figure in imperialist discourse. He adopts a 'doubled perspective' by which to talk about both the representation of Roman history and contemporary presentations of Rome. Using Brecht's well-known discussion of the opening of *Coriolanus*, the next (and longest) chapter looks at the meanings generated by the figure of Coriolanus in relation to the mixed constitution of the Roman Republic. Innes concludes the book with a chapter on *Cymbeline*, bringing discussions from the other chapters together under the title 'Empire Studies'. He addresses *translatio imperii*, but is more interested in the figure of Cymbeline, who hardly appears in the play named after him, seeing him as a figure who is 'enacted upon' (p. 7).

In *Shakespeare's Storms* Gwilym Jones poses three key questions, asking what Shakespeare understood weather to be; how the storms in his plays affect current critical discourse and change the way we experience early modern theatre; and how the storms achieve this. Jones writes of Shakespeare's storms as being both actual and metaphorical, and he argues that Shakespeare can be seen to be developing the dramatic immediacy of storms and their symbolic possibilities (p. 9). Across the book, he uses the approaches of performance history and ecocriticism to show how the storms have thus far been misread or ignored by critics. Each chapter on individual plays is preceded with a chapter on the various features of storms (such as thunder and wind) and early modern understanding of these meteorological phenomena. Jones argues that the storm in *Julius Caesar* (Shakespeare's first staged storm) is a 'prime example of theatrical bravado' by Shakespeare, who was at this point using spectacular stage elements to present the Globe theatre as an exciting venue (p. 32). In the chapter on *King Lear*, he argues that weather is used to show the separation of the body from the environment and that 'the external storm allows for the creation of the internal' (pp. 23–4). Jones links the weather in the play, and how it is created by and for those involved in it, to the developing field of ecocriticism. In the chapter on *Macbeth*, he 'details the way in which early modern anxieties about the supernatural allow for, or prompt, a play with discrete weather systems' (p. 24). Overall, he argues that Shakespeare's storms represent the 'evolving understanding of meteorological phenomena in late 16th and early 17th century England' (p. 24).

In the article, 'A Matter of Life and Death: The Fourth Act in Shakespearean Tragedy' (*BJJ* 22[2015] 188–207), Lisa Hopkins argues that the fourth acts of Shakespeare's tragedies provide far more than just a simple link between Acts III and V. Hopkins takes us through the fourth acts of the major tragedies (*Hamlet*, *Othello*, *Antony and Cleopatra*, *Coriolanus*, and *King Lear*), arguing that each play's Act IV offers alternative paths for characters to take, other modes of behaviour, alternative identities for the play itself, none of which are acted upon or followed through. Hopkins concludes that 'as the fourth act stops and breathes before the climax of the fifth, it is nevertheless a road which is glimpsed and whose possibilities haunt and energize the events that follow' (p. 205).

Dympna Callaghan's *Hamlet: Language and Writing* is aimed specifically at undergraduate students starting courses in Shakespeare studies. It is a book that acts as an introduction to the play, guiding students in writing about it. It has four chapters, all with self-contained subsections. Information is given about Shakespeare's development as a writer and the context of the play, and problems that students might encounter are addressed. Chapter 1 addresses the three different texts of the play, comparing and contrasting passages, and exploring the implications of the different versions. Chapter 2 looks at Shakespeare's use of, and his interest in, language. Among other elements, Callaghan covers soliloquies, asides, and blank verse. In chapter 3, Callaghan addresses why *Hamlet* is so important to theatre history and the play's significance in Shakespeare's own time. Each chapter ends with exercises for students to practise writing about Shakespeare, and chapter 4 is given over entirely to 'writing an essay'. This chapter offers guidelines for, for example, structuring an essay and constructing a thesis statement.

Rather than focusing on the isolation of Hamlet, in 'Ophelia's Loneliness' (*ELH* 82[2015] 521–51) Amelia Worsley investigates what she views as Shakespeare's 'new' concept of loneliness in relation to the character of Ophelia. Worsley contends that because Ophelia remains silent throughout Hamlet's soliloquy in Act III, scene i, she is more truly isolated than Hamlet because the act of speaking in itself conjures an audience. Worsley states that 'because Ophelia withholds her thoughts, she is less readable and more isolated onstage than Hamlet is. And perhaps this is why Shakespeare needs a new word to describe Ophelia, but not Hamlet' (p. 525). Worsley offers a review of previous approaches of critics, editors, and directors to Ophelia's loneliness, and invokes critical debates about inwardness and interiority in *Hamlet* to inform her discussion, in part because Ophelia has previously been omitted from such debates.

In 'Feigned Soliloquy, Feigned Argument: Hamlet's "To Be or Not To Be" Speech as Sophistic *Dissoi Logoi*' (*BJJ* 22[2015] 101–18), Phillip Arrington begins with James E. Hirsh's idea that Hamlet's 'To be or not to be' soliloquy is not 'real' but rather feigned to show that Hamlet is aware that he is being overheard (Hirsh, *Shakespeare and the History of Soliloquies* [2003]). Arrington builds on Hirsh in arguing that Hamlet overhears his own speech and in so doing adopts the sophistic rhetoric of *dissoi logoi* within the single speech. Arrington looks first at why Hirsh believes Hamlet's soliloquy to be feigned, before going on to examine *dissoi logoi* as the strategy best suited to 'To be or not to be'. He concludes that 'Hamlet's is a doubling argument of redoubling doubt, meant to give pause to any who overhear its vibrant, restless movements' (p. 114) before finally asserting that 'His *show* of *dissoi logoi* dramatizes why none of us, if we think about it, can ever *know*' (p. 115).

In 'Re-proofing the "Zero Part of Speech" in *Hamlet*' (*CompD* 49 [2015] 289–312), John Freeman readdresses the issue of 'O' and 'Oh' in Shakespeare's text. Freeman looks at how the difference between the two expressions has essentially been elided by scholars, and suggests this risks 'erasing an important discourse marker from the play' (p. 290). Freeman argues that work of discourse analysts can help editors to select the most appropriate form: put simply, 'O' is a marker in everyday speech, where 'Oh' is more refined. Freeman argues that these markers indicate the social class of the speaker. Furthermore, Freeman considers that the struggle of early modern compositors in choosing between the two represents efforts to define national character and a literary tradition distinct from those of Greek or Latin.

In 'Hamlet and the Limits of Narrative' (*EIC* 65[2015] 368–82), Rebecca Yearling judges *Hamlet* as having two possible narrative interpretations: Hamlet's own and that of Horatio at the end of the play. Yearling contends that Horatio's narrative might suggest a less favourable interpretation of the character, arguing that Horatio's story 'Of carnal, bloody, and unnatural acts' is about the messiness of human life (V.ii). Yearling concludes that neither account is 'correct' and that narrative itself is never innocent but always involves the selection and manipulation of facts.

In the short essay ' "Remember me": Hamlet's Corrupted Host and the Medieval Eucharistic Miracle' (*ANQ* 28[2015] 15–20), Courtney Bailey Parker argues that understanding of the eucharistic moment in *Hamlet* is darker than has been previously thought especially when read in the light of medieval miracle accounts of the eucharistic moment. Parker uses the Ghost's 'fleshy description' (p. 16) of the transformation of his flesh as a result of the poison to show how the speech actually presents a corrupted Eucharist. Parker concludes that Hamlet's experience of the eucharistic moment does not cause him to turn to Christ for renewal (as it should), but to rely on his own actions as revenger.

In his short essay 'Prince Hamlet and the Problem of Succession' (*ANQ* 28[2015] 63–7), Ronald B. Jenkins addresses the Danish elective monarchy in the play, asking why the Electors chose not to elect Hamlet as king. Jenkins provides evidence from the text that suggests sound reasons for finding the Prince unfit to rule.

In ' "O Jephthah, judge of Israel": From Original to Accreted Meanings in Hamlet's Allusion' (*ShS* 68[2015] 48–61), Péter Dávidházi discusses allusions as links in cultural memory. The essay is focused on this short line from Hamlet to Polonius in Act II, scene ii, which is from a ballad based on the biblical Jephthah, but also refers to the story of Jephthah in the book of Judges. Therefore, Dávidházi argues, Shakespeare is making both direct and indirect allusions. Through the article Dávidházi explores both what Hamlet meant (the details of the stories to which he alludes) and what function this allusion serves in the play, arguing that both the ballad and the book of Judges are appropriate comparisons for *Hamlet*. Dávidházi argues that Hamlet's allusion to Jephthah provides an interpretative model for the play, highlighting the 'interpretative significance of the suggested correspondences ... between the two fathers and daughters and [revealing] the ensuing relevance of such terms as sacrifice, burnt offering, victim, obedience, virginity, providence and responsibility' (p. 50). Dávidházi also explores meanings that are created by 'later and unintended accretion of meaning', arguing that 'Hamlet's reference is a striking example of an *accretive* allusion, unintended, but with grave consequences for interpretation. For a moment the ensuing new perspective shows the possible future of Ophelia as repeating the fate of Jephthah's daughter, yet not only as the biblical example of *holocaustum* but also as the first victim of what was to be called *the* Holocaust' (p. 57).

In 'My Kingdom for a Ghost: Counterfactual Thinking and *Hamlet*' (*SQ* 66[2015] 29–46), Amir Khan offers a counterfactual approach to tragedy and a new methodology for reading tragedy. Khan poses the questions of when we know that Claudius is guilty and how this affects our response to Hamlet's delay. In so doing, Khan discusses and refutes W.W. Greg's argument that the Ghost's story of murder is a fabrication.

Paul Cefalu's Iago-centric book *Tragic Cognition in Shakespeare's Othello: Beyond the Neural Sublime* is published as part of Arden's 'Shakespeare Now!' series. Cefalu addresses how recent theories of cognition inform our understanding of Othello and Iago, and raises questions about the relationship between cognition and consciousness. He begins with a discussion of how we can imagine what it is like to be Iago, positing that 'recent debates in the philosophy of mind can help us provide a more fine-grained context in which to describe Iago's discontentment' (p. 4). In introducing these debates, he also introduces key points of and contributors to cognitive theory. Cefalu posits phenomenology and psychoanalysis as means by which to gain insight into characters' 'consciousness'. The central argument of the book is that Iago is a 'neuro-reactionary' character: 'his well-known egotism and solipsism stand as a fragile bulwark against an assailing cognitive unconscious; he is a character for whom the neural sublime is so constricting that he stages, through the route of masochism and the eventual toppling of Othello, his own death' (p. 6). Cefalu argues that Iago comes close to closing the 'explanatory gap' between cognition and consciousness, which is unachievable for real people.

In 'Anxious Householders: Theft and Anti-Usury Discourse in Shakespeare's Venetian Plays' (*SC* 30[2015] 285–300), Jordi Coral's purpose is to refine understanding of the extent to which Shakespeare's Venice is 'constituted by the "psychological phenomenon" of usury' through discussion of the usurer's fear of theft (p. 287). Coral uses both *Othello* and *The Merchant of Venice* to do this, with the greater focus of the argument being on *Othello*. Coral sets up the argument with a discussion of the various responses to early modern capitalism, including credit systems and moral confusion, and explores how Elizabethans tended to read greed as the cause of all new instabilities. In the discussion of *Othello*, Iago is cast as the usurer, which is achieved through Iago 'using' Desdemona, thus presenting her as a commodity, in order to destroy Othello.

In '*Othello* and the Unweaponed City' (*SQ* 66[2015] 137–66), Andrew Sisson argues for a reading of the play in terms of the opposition between disarmed Venice and armed Rome. Sisson states that there is in Shakespeare's play a distinct self-consciousness about the nature of the division of the military and the political in Venice and the consequences of that division. There are three strands to Sisson's argument: in the first, he addresses the dialectic of the citizen-soldier and the mercenary as an interpretative scheme which is powerfully used in *Othello*. He then goes on to discuss one of the main sources of the play, Gasparo Contarini's *The Commonwealth and Government of Venice* (translated in 1599 by Lewes Lewkenor). Through this discussion, the choice between armed or disarmed citizenry is related to different kinds of virtue (which Sisson identifies as Roman and Venetian). In the third part of the article, Sisson argues that the tragedy of the play arises from the incommensurability of each of these virtues with the demands and expectations of its opposite.

Timothy A. Turner also addresses the unarmed aspect of *Othello* in 'Othello on the Rack' (*JEMCS* 15:iii[2015] 102–36). Turner discusses torture in the play, arguing that Iago, the 'unweaponed' Venetian, subjects Othello to psychological torture. He argues that Othello 'examines the effectiveness' of different types of torture against the backdrop of 'an early modern culture of pervasive, public, and brutal forms of corporal punishment' (p. 103). While looking at the contemporary context of the play, Tuner also addresses its sources, and looks to a more recent context, the KUBARK Counterintelligence Interrogation Manual produced by the CIA in 1963. He concludes that the way Iago's 'psychological approach unveils the mind's susceptibility to coercive refashioning, and not merely the body's vulnerability to corporal action, turns out to be the most chilling, and perhaps the most modern, feature of the play' (p. 129).

In Adam Hall's note, 'Othello as *Morisco*' (*ANQ* 28[2015] 68–73), Moorishness is put forward as being not about race but about religion. Hall reads Othello as a *Morisco*, a term contemporary with the play that was used in the West to refer to converts from Islam to Christianity. He discusses origins of the term and its contexts, explores elements of Othello's character that might be read as Islamic, and frames distrust felt by other characters towards Othello in terms of real-life concerns that *Moriscos* might not have really converted.

In ' "Too Gentle": Jealousy and Class in *Othello*' (*JEMCS* 15:i[2015] 3–25), Rebecca Olson addresses the notion that Shakespeare's most jealous husbands are married to only children of high-class men. In relation to *Othello*, Olson argues that Desdemona's social class is an important factor in the creation of Othello's jealousy and that this taps into contemporary anxieties around class. Olson shows how Othello attempts to claim equal status to his wife but that this is not achieved before it is fatally undermined. In this, Olson highlights the emasculating element of a lower-class man rising by virtue of his wife's social position. Olson concludes that 'Like a valuable garment, Desdemona deserves or even requires careful attention. The problem, for Othello and other Shakespearean husbands, is that their wives can also inspire tormenting imagined narratives, that in extreme cases such as Othello's, lead them to destroy what they most feared to lose' (p. 20). Olson finishes by acknowledging the implications of this view of tragedy for Shakespeare's comedies and their heroines.

In ' "Then let no man but I / Do execution on my flesh and blood": Filicide and Family Bonds in *Titus Andronicus*' (*MRDE* 28[2015] 110–22), Emily Detmer-Goebel looks at filicide in *Titus Andronicus* in order to address how Shakespeare invokes Roman law sanctioning the right of fathers to kill their children. By so doing, Detmer-Goebel argues that the play critiques *vitae necisque potestas* and confirms sixteenth-century systems limiting a father's power over his children. Thus, Detmer-Goebel explores attitudes to and treatises on the rights of parents and children. Detmer-Goebel discusses Titus's views of honour in the light of his behaviour, and contrasts them with the behaviour of Tamora, who is seen as the least honourable character in the play but displays the same behaviour. Detmer-Goebel concludes that the play dramatizes the danger of a father's power. However, in pointing out that fathers did not wield such power in Shakespeare's England, she also suggests similarities between the power of a father and the power of a monarch.

In ' "Groaning shadows that are gone": The Ghosts of *Titus Andronicus*' (*ES* 96[2015] 403–23), Lindsey Scott discusses the recurring presence of mutilated body parts as ghosts in *Titus Andronicus*. Scott examines the outcomes of subverted graves, and how and to what end characters are haunted by spectral returns. She argues that such spectres 'persistently hover at the margins of the play's presentation of violence' (p. 405), and that such returns reflect contemporary theological anxieties. In so doing, she discusses how it is the male characters (and not Lavinia as is usually assumed) who are haunted by such ghosts. Scott does much to establish the presence of such ghosts—addressing, for example, how the language used pictures Rome as neither living nor dead—and invokes the figures of Titus's dead sons. She demonstrates how the play suggests opposing cultures mix and seep into one another, thereby suggesting an overlap with anxieties regarding ghosts and burials in Catholicism and Protestantism. She argues that it is the attempt to appease the ghosts of Titus's already dead sons in the execution of Alarbus that sets the tragedy of the play in motion. Scott concludes that 'What remains so striking about *Titus*'s ghosts is the ways in which they meticulously document, often through gruesome permutations and violent spectacle, early modern relations between the living and the dead' (p. 421).

In 'Killing Time in *Titus Andronicus*: Timing, Rhetoric, and the Art of Defense' (*JEMCS* 15:iv[2015] 52–80), Dori Coblentz uses readings of interruptive good timing in early modern English and Continental fencing manuals to discuss inaction. Coblentz discusses how *Titus Andronicus* associates rhetoric with swordplay, and argues that Shakespeare explores the relationship between timing in both swordplay and rhetoric most fully in this play. Coblentz explores the tactics of waiting found in fencing texts and theories of *kairos*, and argues that such theories informed the pacing of the play.

In 'Hybrids: Animal Law and the Actaeon Myth in *Titus Andronicus*' (*ShIntY* 15[2015] 65–79), Miranda Garno Nesler discusses how *Titus Andronicus* is preoccupied with the Actaeon myth and notions of humanness, and shows how through this the play engages with Elizabethan debates on the legal definition of human and animal. Nesler focuses her argument primarily on the character of Lavinia, who is aligned with the Actaeon myth while also demonstrating rhetorical power, and posits her as a 'human-animal hybrid'. Nesler argues that such a character (with attributes which are also found in Tamora and Aaron) challenges the traditional status of 'non-human animals and human Others' (p. 66).

In ' "'Twixt two extremes of passion, joy and grief": Shakespeare's *King Lear* and Last Plays' (*YR* 103:i[2015] 26–47), Arthur Kirsch suggests that Shakespeare was less interested in writing about the orthodoxies of his time than we think, and that he seems rather, to have been more interested in creating a theatrical experience. The bulk of Kirsch's article discusses the relationship between joy and grief. He reads *King Lear* as prologue to the last plays, and argues that it 'relentlessly juxtaposes the hope for the joy of renewal in the play with the inexorability of death and grief' (p. 28). This is illustrated with various examples and close attention to the text. For example, Kirsch shows how the sense of characters' suffering is intensified through the love that characters feel (that of Edgar for Gloucester, and that of Kent, Cordelia, and the Fool for Lear) throughout the play. This discussion of *Lear* is then related to the last plays (*Pericles*, *Cymbeline*, *The Winter's Tale*, and *The Tempest*).

In 'Things I Should Have Known: Tardiness in *King Lear*' (*LitI* 17[2015] 131–52), Francisco Unger takes Kent's statement, 'Sir, I am too old to learn', as his starting point, asking 'can the person for whom it is too late to learn anything of consequence be pardoned, again and again? Does lateness obviate guilt, or make it frivolous in the greater scheme of expired possibilities for true justice?' (p. 131). Unger argues that lateness is a cathartic device in the play, and he relates the issue of tardiness to that of endurance and survival.

In ' "Where am I now?": The Articulation of Space in Shakespeare's *King Lear* and Marlowe's *Dido, Queen of Carthage*' (*CahiersE* 88[2015] 81–93), Andrew Duxfield discusses the fluid Elizabethan stage and the vagueness of location which is created by such stages. Although primarily discussing *Dido*, Duxfield uses *King Lear* to illustrate the flexibility of the stage, focusing on the scene between Gloucester and Edgar at Dover. He suggests that the blind Gloucester's experience is analogous to that of the audience: the audience themselves only 'see' what Edgar describes.

Robert N. Watson, in his article 'Lord Capulet's Lost Compromise: A Tragic Emendation and the Binary Dynamics of *Romeo and Juliet*' (*RenD* 43[2015] 53–84), addresses the attribution of III.i.184–8 to Lord Montague in all but one modern edition, despite early folios and Q2 and 3 attributing the lines to Lord Capulet. Watson poses the question of why editors and directors are so quick to assume that Shakespeare and/or his printers got the attribution wrong. Could not Lord Capulet defend Romeo against Tybalt? From this starting point, Watson goes on to explore the binary themes of the play. He argues that Shakespeare creates such binaries in order to knock them down, and that 'these invitations to facile binary distinctions can provoke editors and readers—as they provoke many of the play's characters—to overlook a more complicated and potentially redemptive blending of the seemingly paradoxical juxtapositions' (p. 58).

In the article 'Live Boys—Dead Girls: Death and False Death in *Romeo and Juliet*' (*LitI* 17[2015] 18–34), John Kleiner discusses the Renaissance interest in displaying the dead in relation to another contemporary interest: the idea of fake death. The instance of false death in *Romeo and Juliet* (Juliet in the Capulet tomb) is discussed in relation to its chief sources: Arthur Brooke's poem *The Tragical History of Romeus and Juliet* [1562] and Samuel Daniel's *The Complaint of Rosalind*. Kleiner argues that Shakespeare merges the sources to create a more complex dead girl than is presented in either source text. He states that in this scene Shakespeare 'brings into relief a constitutive problem with tragic spectacle; on the stage, as in the tomb, passion and its object are incommensurate' (p. 19). He argues that Shakespeare's Juliet is a 'hybrid corpse', one that is 'both Brooke's girl and Daniel's. She is, as she appears to Romeo, two women at once' (p. 23). Kleiner suggests that this shows Shakespeare developing a new theory of tragedy which will be seen in his later tragedies (he looks briefly at *Antony and Cleopatra*, *Othello*, *Hamlet*, and *King Lear*), arguing that 'Romeo's refusal of Juliet's vitality models the way subsequent characters will reject life and love, the way they will insist on death' (p. 33).

In 'Shakespeare's Franciscans' (*NewC* 33[2015] 19–24), Kenneth Colston addresses how Shakespeare 'gave several pivotal roles to characters belonging to an order that had virtually disappeared from England several generations earlier' and argues that in presenting Franciscans on the stage Shakespeare took a huge political risk. Colston focuses on Friar Lawrence in *Romeo and Juliet*, arguing that the character is 'the guardian of reckless virtue' (p. 20). He concludes that through Shakespeare's staging of Franciscans we see his attitude to religion and the Catholic Church.

In 'The Image of Both Theaters: Empire and Revelation in Shakespeare's *Antony and Cleopatra*' (*SQ* 66[2015] 167–87), William Junker juxtaposes two models of theatre: that practised by Caesar, of triumphal imperialism, and that performed by Cleopatra when she commits suicide. Junker argues first that through *Antony and Cleopatra* Shakespeare 'tracks the emergence of Caesar Augustus's imperium from the practice of triumphal procession that imperium both extends and displaces' (p. 167), before moving on to address the alternative theatrical model which is embodied in Cleopatra.

In 'Water, Absorption, and Cleopatra's Barge' (*ShIntY* 15[2015] 147–66), Ellen MacKay begins by referencing the various ways in which fire has been used to describe the audience's experience of theatrical absorption, before arguing that 'it is easy to underestimate the extent to which absorbing theatricality took place within an aquatic register, but the repeated citation of Cleopatra's barge brings out the metonymic relation the culture draws between the inventory of a royal boat's splendor and the incitement to thought-arresting, self-submerging awe' (p. 150).

*(f) Late Plays*

*Shakespeare in London*, by Hannah Crawforth, Sarah Dustagheer, and Jennifer Young, sets out to show the influence that the city of London had on Shakespeare and his works. It does so not only through the places in the city Shakespeare would have frequented, including the various theatres with which he was associated, but through the response of dramatists and literary figures in London, and the cultural and social influences of the city's teeming multitudes, from the wealthiest to the poorest. The final chapter, 'Experimentation in Shakespeare's London: *The Tempest* (1610–11) and Lime Street' (pp. 195–219), explores how 'Shakespeare's play draws on differing types of scientific knowledge circulating around his city' (p. 196). The chapter differentiates between and interrelates with two streams of scientific knowledge: natural sciences, on the one hand, and Renaissance magic on the other.

As Crawforth, Dustagheer, and Young point out, 'Shakespeare's writing absorbs and transfigures the wide ranging printed texts circulating around early modern London. The play in its own way displayed "the wonders reported therein for his playhouse audiences to marvel at", just as they had marvelled at sights from foreign lands and the New World, from the bodies of dead Native Americans to exotic beasts and birds' (p. 205). The nature of Prospero's arts, and their origins in his books, from astrology to alchemy, are discussed in relation to the emerging scientific culture of experimentation. Prospero is both a skilled and dynamic magus and an early modern scientist.

Donald Carlson's article on power, magic, and early science in *The Tempest* mines some similar ground to Crawforth, Dustagheer, and Young, but does not use London's geography as a starting point for his discussion. ' "'Tis new to thee": Power, Magic, and Early Science in Shakespeare's *The Tempest*' (*BJJ*

22[2015] 1–22) argues that the play is 'an especially fertile source for mining the playwright's mature perspectives on the intellectual climate for which and in which he composed the play' (p. 1). In the first half of the article Carlson explores the play's examination of theatricality and its use of both classical and contemporary conceptions of science and magic, in relation to architecture and thaumaturgy in particular. The connection between the mechanics of effects on stage and the relationships between the Renaissance magus and the Renaissance scientist is explored in part through the play's role as a court masque. The second half of the essay examines biblical resonances, particularly those which examine power and acts of 'magic'. At first glance these seem two different pieces that could almost be examined separately, but Carlson capably connects the two, and ably elucidates the connections between theology, magic, and science in early modern Europe.

Gwilym Jones's *Shakespeare's Storms* also addresses theatricality and the use of effects on stage in Shakespeare's plays, and the last two chapters focus on *The Tempest* and *Pericles, Prince of Tyre*. Jones connects physical effects with literary and dramatic effect. Chapter 8 (pp. 108–24) focuses on *Pericles*, and examines the play's biblical allusions, while chapter 9 (pp. 125–50), on *The Tempest*, focuses strongly on the theatricality of the storm in Act I. This chapter focuses not only on the storm's theatricality, and how both the effects and language were influenced by the original playhouse, but on the way that the storm itself is not natural. As with Carlson, Jones argues that there was a deliberate invocation of magic in the use of stage effects in plays.

Duke Pesta's ' "Thou dost here usurp the name thou ow'st not"': *The Tempest* and Intercultural Exchange' (*Renascence* 67[2015] 127–46), is another article that examines the problematic and reductive postmodern and postcolonial readings of Caliban. Pesta critiques noted Shakespearean Stephen Greenblatt's works on *The Tempest*, and argues that they contain internal inconsistencies of argument and problematic uses of sources. For Pesta this reading of *The Tempest* is anachronistic and deeply problematic: 'In the same way that Greenblatt's assumptions minimize a typically Renaissance commitment to polyglossic humanistic learning, so too they make a typically postmodern elision between historical reality and imaginative fiction' (p. 136). The article argues that postcolonial readings and postcolonial critics are 'forcing their shaping fantasies on other cultures and their texts' (p. 137).

Pesta's argument is pointed and thorough, but not entirely comfortable for those used to a postmodern reading of *The Tempest*. The concerns it raises over the anachronistic nature of postcolonial readings of the play are considerable and cogent. In previous years, works pointing to geographical inconsistencies between the site of the play and New World readings have been reviewed. Pesta takes a different approach, arguing that the context of the play lacked many of the preconceptions of Enlightenment and postmodern thinking. As he concludes, 'radical binary distinctions between colonizer and colonized [are] unable to accommodate a more humane vision of cultural and linguistic exchange, one readily available to Renaissance thinkers and poets and very much on display in *The Tempest*' (p. 145). However, just as Greenblatt's work is uncomfortable in its defence of Caliban, the lack of acknowledgement by Pesta that the exchange envisioned and understood by

Renaissance writers was experienced as violent and often destructive conquest in South and North America during the early modern period is this piece's major failing.

Theories related to the cultural history of emotions continue to be a strong area in early modern history, and are also appearing with more regularity as a framework for discussing literature. In a three-part discussion, Anne Sophie Refskou discusses in depth Shakespeare's *The Tempest* and *Titus Andronicus*, and briefly references the final scene of *The Winter's Tale*. The first and third of these sections will be discussed here. In 'Compassionate Perception and Touching Experiences in Shakespearean Drama' (*CS* 27:i[2015] 60–8) Refskou first examines theories of compassion and the importance of interaction to provoke it in relation to both Miranda's response to the shipwreck in Act I and Ariel and Prospero's discussion of the afflictions of the shipwrecked in Act V. It is from the second example that the two main points from the play are made clear: Ariel tells his master that if he saw the stranded survivors of the wreck he would be moved, and when Prospero questions whether he would, Ariel replies that he would, 'were I human' (p. 62).

Refskou's work examines not only the play's internal conceptions of emotion, but also how contemporaries viewed not only the emotions on display in the play but also their effect on the audience. A striking point is made on these contrasts, when Refskou points out that, while Miranda's horrified reaction to the shipwreck 'is a sign of her virtue (if not necessarily her reason) . . . [Stephen] Gosson sees both virtue and reason as overthrown by the sights, sounds, tastes and touches of the theatre' (p. 68). The discussion of compassion as a virtue or vice is one of the strongest parts of this article. While the underlying arguments are not wholly new, the relating of Gosson and Philip Sidney to *The Tempest* is ably done, and insightfully argued. Having discussed *The Tempest*, Refskou goes on to discuss compassion and reason in *Titus Andronicus*, and then finally *The Winter's Tale*'s last scene.

Refskou notes how 'King Leontes's sensory perception of the newly "awakened" warm hand of Hermione is followed by the somewhat enigmatic statement: "If this be magic, let it be an art / Lawful as eating" [V.iii.10–11]' (p. 79). Refskou uses this moment to 'reiterate and illuminate a question central to the discussions of this article: Is the experience of (com)passion "magically" provoked by theatre "lawful"?' (p. 79). The role of sensory perception in the plays, and in critics of theatre, from early modern England suggests a tactile or perceptive quality to the provocation of emotion.

Jessica Murphy's *Virtuous Necessity: Conduct Literature and the Making of the Virtuous Woman in Early Modern England* has several interesting underpinning ideas, including the use of digital humanities software, and the examination of a variety of sources on the cultural and behavioural expectations for women in early modern England. Murphy raises interesting questions about how virtue may have given those women who conformed a form of power of their own. However, the example from the late plays that Murphy uses here is Paulina, a woman who is obviously not conforming to the majority of the conduct literature in early modern England. She is contrasted with Ophelia, a young girl who, Murphy argues, receives the best of advice to no avail. But while Ophelia's failure ends in tragedy, another woman,

Hermione, who also does not conform to typical feminine virtues of obedience and silence and who openly, if honourably, disobeys both her husband and her king, ends her story in triumph.

However Murphy's discussion of *The Winter's Tale* has a problematic approach to the accusations of witchcraft in relation to Paulina. This is partly the result of the use of Diane Purkiss's problematic concept of counter-magic or '*un*witching', and partly the result of how Murphy frames witchcraft in the text (p. 71). Despite these problems, there is a thoughtful if brief exploration in *Virtuous Necessity* of the role of women as protectors of the domestic sphere in conduct literature, and their obligation 'to use their virtue to reform husbands' (p. 74). While underpinned by interesting new avenues of research, and examining an interesting concept in female virtue, conduct books, and the portrayal of women on the early modern stage, this work unfortunately falls short through its focus on problematic concepts related to witchcraft.

Sarah Beckwith's 'Are There Any Women in Shakespeare's Plays? Fiction, Representation, and Reality in Feminist Criticism' (*NLH* 46[2015] 241–60) uses ordinary language philosophy to interrogate feminist critiques of the representation of women in Shakespeare. Beckwith begins with Stanley Cavell's work on *King Lear* in 1966, using his discussion of the importance of each character's language—their words—and its context. For Beckwith, Cavell's questioning of how critics could forget the words a character uses, why they used them and in what context, is still as pertinent in 2015 as it was in 1966. Beckwith is attempting to move beyond questions of representation and gender and into the assessment of language as it relates to gender, and how fiction plays a role 'in our lives as event, expression, and act, to let it read us, as much as we read it'. Therefore Beckwith wishes to renew an effort 'to describe and justly respond to the fiction in our lives'; 'we might also restore some of the ancient pleasures of the text for feminism' (p. 257)

Judith Wolfe, in 'Hermione's Sophism: Ordinariness and Theatricality in *The Winter's Tale*' (*P&L* 39:i[2015] A83–A105), likewise begins with Cavell's— and Rush Rhees's—reading of *The Winter's Tale*, through an examination of the language and character of Hermione. Wolfe lays out Cavell's arguments regarding Leontes, and moves beyond them to examine Hermione, and to show how the play 'complicates both Cavell's and Rhees's accounts of the possibility of discourse' (p. A86). Wolfe then engages in a long discussion of how Hermione's use of language as a rhetorical form of play-acting (a performance designed to persuade) has an unsettling implication of falseness for her husband, and that this ultimately affects Leontes' mental state. In this reading of the play, Hermione's sophistry, her contrived behaviour, leave Leontes questioning every aspect of his wife's faithfulness and honesty, not only in the present but in the past.

Uncertainty, instability of the relationship between language and meaning, and the impossibility of truly knowing another's intent is a complex series of ideas, but Wolfe ably navigates them. Though Wolfe's arguments are based on Cavell's and Rhees's work, she takes them beyond the idea that Hermione, like Cordelia in *King Lear*, is a passive and 'entirely innocent victim of "skeptical" mania' (p. A91). But for Wolfe, a character like Hermione also contributes through her 'refusal to acknowledge the wider implications of her actions, to use language as more than a game in which she knows all the right moves'; this 'is, in its way, a failure almost as great as Leontes's to acknowledge others in their freedom and inscrutability' (p. A91). Performance of honesty and dishonesty itself unfolds as an ongoing theme for Wolfe, from Hermione's sophistry to the mask assumed by Florizel in his courtship of Perdita. The restoration of Hermione only occurs, for Wolfe, after her husband has renounced 'the claim that he can authoritatively decipher Hermione's behaviour' (p. A101).

Patricia Wareh's 'Literary Mirrors of Aristocratic Performance: Readers and Audience of *The Faerie Queene* and *The Winter's Tale*' (*RenD* 43[2015] 85–114) likewise begins with a discussion of Leontes' 'terrible recognition of what his jealous imagination has cost him' and moves on to declare that 'it also initiates the play's movement into the world of fairy tale' (p. 85). Wareh shows that Hermione, Leontes, and Polixenes are engaged in a game of courtly self-representation that undermines Leontes' confidence in his wife's integrity. For Wareh the courtly characters of *The Winter's Tale* are engaged in 'sprezzatura' rather than the sophistry of Wolfe's article.

Wareh argues, like Wolfe, that there is a contrast between the false courtesies and theatricality of the court scenes and the use of the pastoral, artful landscapes of Act IV. For Wareh those scenes engage with 'the question of aristocratic self-presentation' (p. 104). Furthermore Wareh argues that *The Winter's Tale* 'provokes reflection on the costs of the courtier's hidden arts by depicting how a culture of sprezzatura may lead to tragedy' while also making use 'of metatheatrical moments, especially in Perdita's reported recognition, in order to enlist the audience in the collaborative pleasure of recognizing the play's artfulness' (p. 104).

That artfulness reaches its high point in the final scene. The relationship between drama on stage and fiction on the page is played out in the final scenes, with the revelations and the tying up of all the play's narratives in romantic happy endings—including what Wareh calls the bizarre marrying off of Paulina and Camillo in response to the return of Hermione. For Wareh these final moments provide 'the audience with the happy ending of a comedy that it recognizes as all part of the fun, and which the play encourages it to accept, in the moment, despite any misgivings it may have' (p. 111).

Jeremy Tambling's '*The Winter's Tale*: Three Recognitions' (*EIC* 65[2015] 30–52) presents familiar themes of charge and forgiveness within an interesting framework of psychological recognitions and thematic dualisms, or as Tambling calls them 'double situations inscribed throughout the text' (p. 30). The appearance and reappearance of figures in Leontes' life are intertwined with the melancholy and regret that transform his personality over time. Tambling's work examines time, the psychology of loss and restoration, and the contrast between things that are and things that seem to be in *The Winter's Tale*.

While not focused solely on *The Winter's Tale*, Victoria Sparey's work on puberty in early modern drama does use the Old Shepherd's speech from Act III, scene iii, as an entry point into views of adolescence and their consequences in early modern drama. In 'Performing Puberty: Fertile Complexions in Shakespeare's Plays' (*ShakB* 33[2015] 441–67), Sparey analyses the presentation and representation of youth and youthfulness. Much of Sparey's analysis of adolescence relates to Perdita, and to how her social class—both actual and assumed—affected the portrayal of her 'ripeness', and burgeoning adulthood. At the shepherds' celebrations Perdita's exceptional qualities lead to a 'provocative framing of Perdita's maturation when she both is and is not viewed in the context of being a low-born pubescent woman' (p. 461). Sparey goes on to discuss how the physical attributes of youth and femininity functioned within the context of early modern performance in which 'adolescent male actors' bodies' acted out adolescent, female roles (p. 463). The role of gendered bodies is a central pillar of Sparey's work, not only on how both male and female teenage bodies were viewed and understood in early modern England, but also on how they were portrayed on stage.

Theology and religious denomination, particularly Protestant and Catholic influences, are once again a matter of discussion in relation to *The Winter's Tale*. Lysbeth Em Benkert envisions Hermione as a Marian figure, the font of grace and redemption for her husband Leontes. 'Faith and Redemption in *The Winter's Tale*' (*ReAr* 19[2015] 31–50) centralizes faith with respect not only to spiritual relationships, but also to temporal relationships. Unlike earlier interpretations of the play which focused on its apparent Roman Catholic origins, Benkert argues that the play presents 'an interpretation of faith consistent with the central Protestant doctrine of justification by faith rather than by works' (p. 35). While her argument is cogently presented, and the parts of the play cited can be interpreted as influenced by Protestant theology, there are other decidedly Catholic moments and themes that are inadequately covered here. Given Shakespeare's background and the period in which he lived, most people could not have avoided being influenced by both Protestant and Roman Catholic doctrine, as well as classical literature.

Maurice Hunt's works continue to be some of the most cogent examinations of theology in literature, and in particular of the conception of religion in Shakespeare's late plays. In *The Divine Face in Four Writers: Shakespeare, Dostoyevsky, Hesse, and C.S. Lewis*, Hunt examines the idea of the divine face in both Judaeo-Christian literature and classical literature. Shakespeare's works, from histories to tragedies and comedies, are examined and there is a discussion of *The Tempest*. This is not Hunt's first foray into religion and Shakespeare. In 2011 he published an article called 'Syncretistic Religion in Shakespeare's Late Romances' (*SCRev* 28:ii[2011] 57–79), which shares some features with *The Divine Face*. However the article also tackles religious questions in relation to other plays, in particular *Cymbeline*, with Hunt noting that 'Shakespeare crafts a calculated religious syncretism in *Cymbeline* through repeated allusions to the impending Nativity of Christ, which occurred during the historical Cymbeline's reign' (p. 64).

Indeed Hunt spends considerable time on his article's discussion of syncretistic religion in Shakespeare's late plays, with *Cymbeline*, *Pericles, Prince of Tyre*, and *The Winter's Tale* all having apt moments of both classical and Christian significance, often allusive or symbolic, but always present. It is worth noting that Stephen Greenblatt is once again criticized here, with Hunt using a statement by Greenblatt as his starting point, and returning to it at the end with: 'When Stephen Greenblatt speculates that Shakespeare's plays show him "at once Catholic, Protestant, and deeply skeptical of both," he possibly did not have the late romances in mind' (p. 74).

For Hunt, the late plays show Christian values which transcend denominational religious differences, and, for Hunt, reflect the 'primitive Christianity that Edmund Spenser and many Protestants believed that the Church of England could recover' (p. 74).

Hunt also points to the influence of classical literature in the late plays, arguing that 'Stephen Greenblatt did not consider the third religion that Greek and Roman mythology embedded in English versions of Hellenistic romance' and that this 'third religion' offered a comforting unifying alternative to' Elizabethans and Jacobeans disoriented by the ebb and flow of sixteenth-century Protestantism and Roman Catholicism and revolted by the horrific executions of hundreds of their dissenting countrymen and women' (p. 74)

Paul Raffield's article 'Common Law, *Cymbeline*, and the Jacobean *Aeneid*' (*LawL* 27[2015] 313–42), begins with the striking argument that *Cymbeline* is 'a Jacobean *Aeneid*: an epic poem, for a new century and an uncharted epoch' (p. 314). The article aims to explore the 'marked contrast between the absolutist leanings of James I and the artificial reason of common law' while reading *Cymbeline* 'not only as a dramatic symbol of national identity, but also as a representation of the journey of intellectual and political self-discovery upon which the subject of law was tentatively embarked in Jacobean England' (p. 314). These are ambitious goals, and are explored through several metaphors. Firstly, they are explored through the connection or disconnection between internal and external in the play, and the connection and disconnection between the English and Scottish states; secondly, Raffield explores journeys, both real and literary.

Connecting legal and political events and literary themes is complicated, but Raffield succeeds in drawing thematic links between the rival temporal and judicial jurisdictions and national jurisdictions with King James VI and I's realms, and the 'theme of rival jurisdictions is one only of several narrative threads that bind the central plot of Posthumus and his reconciliation with Innogen' (p. 326). Raffield concludes with a series of thematic connections between various events and legal conceptions from early modern England and events in *Cymbeline*, and while some are tenuously drawn, overall the argument is well made. Raffield concludes that in *Cymbeline* 'Shakespeare presents a myth of nationhood the allusion of which to aspects of Jacobean rule is compelling', and that the 'play provides a distorted image of a dysfunctional society, at the centre of which was an acephalous body politic' (p. 336).

J.K. Barret's article on *Cymbeline*, 'The Crowd in Imogen's Bedroom' (*SQ* 66[2015] 440–62), discusses in depth the role of allusion in the play. In particular it examines the way in which stories given in the play narrate events we have previously seen in relation to Iachimo's presence in Imogen's bedroom in Act II. The problematic nature of narrative and rhetoric, and the theatricality of performing a narrative, have also appeared in relation to *The Winter's Tale*, above. Barret draws particular attention to Iachimo's use of classical stories and allusions in both his foray into Imogen's bedroom and his recounting to Posthumus. The classical allusions in Iachimo's scenes are then echoed at a wider level with the appearance of a classical apparition of Jupiter.

Dana Percec, like Barret, also focuses on the scenes relating to Imogen's bedchamber, but focuses less on the use of allusion and memory, and more on how the scene relates to early modern conceptions of privacy, and its role as an emerging phenomenon. Gendered space, and its illustration in several Shakespearean plays, is approached in an onion style: 'proceed from the most visible level to the subtler ones, from evidence of material life, to the more intricate notions of domesticity and intimacy for families and individuals' (p. 91). Percec's 'It's a Private Matter: Space and Gender Issues in Shakespeare's *Cymbeline*' (*RJES* 12[2015] 88–94) also compares two spaces within the play, Imogen's richly decorated bedroom, which alludes to classical mythology and stories, and the 'rude' and 'savage' cave in which Belarius and her brothers are living (p. 93). The material objects of Imogen's bedroom are lavish and described in detail, yet the room is a locus of repeated dishonest narratives, while for Percec the cave is both more natural and more honest. For Imogen, a happy ending comes from the stripping away of lies that are related to material objects and space.

The last item on *Cymbeline* comes from a collection on emotions in Shakespeare. One of the fastest-growing areas of study over the last decade has been the study of emotions in history and literature. This year saw several publications on Shakespeare in the field of emotions, and more will undoubtedly appear in the years to come. Anne Sophie Refskou's work on emotion and tactile interaction is reviewed above in relation to *The Tempest*. Ciara Rawnsley's 'Once upon a Time: Cymbeline, Fairy Tales, and "the Terrifying Truths of the Inner Life"' (in White et al., eds., pp. 39–48), focuses on its more fantastical aspects, pointing to earlier examinations of *Cymbeline* which tend to dismiss the story as frivolous because of its fantastic elements, rather than recognizing the emotional impact of fairy tales. Rawnsley concludes that 'Embellishing the improbable, fairy-tale elements of the play ... does not trivialize the action or distance us from the emotional reality' (p. 46). Rawnsley's work on *Cymbeline* suggests we not dismiss the play's fantastical elements as detrimental to the plot and character development, but instead recognize how those elements appeal to and elicit emotional responses.

Jose Roberto Basto O'Shea's 'With a "Co-adjutor": Collaboration between William Shakespeare and John Fletcher in *The Two Noble Kinsmen*' (*Revista Letras* 92[2015] 49–65) argues that the play's authorship was a collaboration between an older, experienced dramatist and his junior colleague, John Fletcher. O'Shea uses half a dozen procedures to determine 'authorship and co-authorship', including verse tests, parallel passages, vocabulary, diction preferences, stylometry, and socio-historical linguistic evidence. Though the argument here is not new, the systematic approach is thorough and O'Shea presents a compelling argument.

Suparna Roychoudhury, in 'Mental Tempests, Seas of Trouble: The Perturbations of Shakespeare's *Pericles*' (*ELH* 82[2015] 1013–39), examines the layers of stormy metaphors in *Pericles, Prince of Tyre*. Images of storms, tempests, troubled waters, blowing winds, thunder, and shipwrecks appear in reference not only to Pericles, but to the experiences of his daughter Marina—

whose name and birth at sea are yet further allusions to the play's oceanic themes. In particular Roychoudhury creates a framework for thinking about the play as a metaphor for the troubled mind, and the 'plurality of . . . semantic possibilities, and dramatizing the challenge of navigating them' (p. 1037). Each character encounters and endures different forms of tempest, one in a journey both at sea and in his own mind, and one who faces down a series of external tempests while onshore.

Gwilym Jones's *Shakespeare's Storms* likewise examines the storm-tossed seas and coasts of Pericles' story, but with a focus on how the two authors of the play present storms in very different ways. Jones argues that while Shakespeare's co-author George Wilkins sees storms as 'heavenly judgement', Shakespeare's storm of Act III, scene i, is a 'personal experience', presented with both an 'intimacy' and 'immediacy' lacking in Wilkins's storm of Act II, scene i (p. 109).

Michelle M. Dowd's *The Dynamics of Inheritance on the Shakespearean Stage* is a striking work, well written and argued. However, there is an aspect of it that remains troubling. The conceit that literature, specifically Shakespearean drama, had the effect on early modern society claimed by the book's blurb is somewhat problematic. Thankfully the actual work itself limits this and instead aims to analyse 'the dramaturgical and rhetorical strategies that early modern playwrights deployed to represent and reimagine changing inheritance practices'. Dowd wants to show that 'attending to *how* the drama engaged its historical moment—not just to the fact of its doing so—can yield rich interpretive benefits, expanding the range of our practice as literary historicists' (p. 29).

The loss of an heir or heirs, and the problems of there being only female heirs, recur in many of Shakespeare's works, as does travel. In *Pericles* the lack of an heir is the 'issue' at hand, both literally and figuratively (p. 163). Dowd points to the frequent 'failure of wealthy families to produce a male heir' and the subsequent 'significant questions about the material stability of many landed estates' (p. 167). Like other rulers in the late plays, including King Cymbeline and King Leontes, Pericles' rule is made unstable throughout the play by the lack of an heir. The movement inherent in the romantic narrative lends the play its oft-derided episodic and dislocated quality. Dowd highlights the role of grief and the lack of offspring in Pericles' story, as well as the way in which 'physical and symbolic seclusion' provides 'opportunities to resist wayward expansion in both narrative and patrilineal terms' (p. 173). Dowd suggests that Gower, particularly in his chorus in Act IV, 'participates in a pattern of chorographic marking that permeates the play, drawing attention to the ways in which individual places encapsulate ... dynastic interests', ultimately imposing 'narrative order on disparate dramatic events'; 'spatial movement ... is ... dictated by the desire to solidify and recuperate lineage' (pp. 183, 185). Inheritance and heritage are important themes not only in Pericles' journey to his child and wife, but also in his rediscovery of his own heritage.

There are few themes to be found across the late plays this year, but within the works on each play there are some common elements: from storms in *Pericles, Prince of Tyre*, to connections between magic and science in *The*

*Tempest*, to theatrical falsehoods and courtly behaviour in *The Winter's Tale*. The influence of classical literature continues to play a role in the study of the late plays, along with works that reference geography and the role of religion. Although this year only two of the works on the late plays reviewed here focused on the study of emotions, it seems likely this is a trend that will continue in future years.

*(g) Comedies*

While no full-length monographs focusing solely on Shakespeare's comedies were published in 2015, many volumes devoted chapters to them. One full edited collection covered *The Merry Wives of Windsor*, and several edited collections featured more than one chapter on Shakespeare's comedies. Many journal articles relevant to this section were also published. These different forms of criticism were spread across a variety of approaches and texts, so many of them cannot be grouped easily together into a theme. What the 2015 criticism on Shakespeare's comedies does indicate, however, is a large difference in critical interest in the plays which fall under this remit. *A Midsummer Night's Dream* and *The Merchant of Venice* seemed to receive the most attention, while *Twelfth Night* and *The Comedy of Errors* received notably less.

One of the few clearly definable themes surrounding work on Shakespeare's comedies in 2015 was ecocriticism, with three monographs and one edited collection devoting full chapters, or significant sections of them, to this approach. Randall Martin's *Shakespeare and Ecology*, for example, assigns a chapter apiece to *The Merry Wives of Windsor* and *As You Like It*. In his chapter on the former play, 'Localism, Deforestation, and Environmental Activism in *The Merry Wives of Windsor*' (pp. 32–53), Martin convincingly argues for the influence of the increased levels of deforestation which were occurring around the time of its composition. He highlights how the Windsor community's naming of 'Herne's Oak' reflected one way of protecting certain trees that were in danger of being felled, and then rereads such objects as the Pages' fireplace as evidence of the high consumption of wood. The chapter 'Land-Uses and Convertible Husbandry in *As You Like It*' (pp. 56–77) locates the play in relation to enclosure. Martin examines various characters' attitudes towards the forest, and asserts that the comedy is an example of 'bioregional drama' (p. 61). This second chapter integrates early modern environmental issues with a reading of the play in a most effective and convincing fashion.

Tom MacFaul's monograph *Shakespeare and the Natural World* offers extensive commentaries on a number of the comedies. The 'second world' section of chapter 1, 'Country Matters' (pp. 45–90), focuses exclusively upon the role of the countryside in these types of plays. MacFaul asserts that *As You Like It*'s Duke Senior vainly tries to escape the court in the countryside, and highlights how the rural environment impacts upon Valentine of *Two Gentlemen of Verona*'s identity. MacFaul's discussion of *A Midsummer Night's Dream* reveals that the human characters are far more connected to the forest than the fairies because of their awareness of the transience of the seasons. The countryside of *Love's Labour's Lost*, meanwhile, is suggested 'not [to be] a place of happy meditation but a compromise based on the men's attempt to break their oath as little as possible' (p. 58), while such a place is linked with daily life in the treatment of *The Merry Wives of Windsor*. In his exploration of the countryside in these comedies, then, MacFaul interrogates its transformative nature, and convincingly demonstrates that 'while the rural world is a place of translation, it is never simply so, because people bring the weight of their own histories and identities to it' (p. 89). Chapter 2, 'Man and Other Animals' (pp. 91–131), argues among discussions of other plays that *As You Like It*'s reference to deer, and the interactions between Launce and Crab of *Two Gentlemen of Verona*, both suggest that animals can function to illuminate aspects of human relationships. In 'Lawful as Eating? Food, Natural Magic and the Arts of Health' (pp. 132–78), chapter 3's examination of diet, three comedies feature among the discussions of plays. MacFaul asserts that *Love's Labour's Lost* reveals the need to feed the body as well as the mind. He then illustrates that many of the problems in *The Comedy of Errors* arise because Adriana and Antipholus of Ephesus do not eat together at the correct time, and argues that *As You Like It*'s starving Adam reveals the importance of food and mercy. MacFaul handles his analysis of multiple plays in an accomplished manner, and his readings are consistently insightful.

Whilst Gabriel Egan's monograph *Shakespeare and Ecocritical Theory* does not devote chapters to any specific play, many of its discussions resonate with other works of ecocriticism that are relevant to this section. Chapter 1, 'The Rise of Ecocriticism' (pp. 17–40), offers an outline of significant works on ecocriticism, with chapter 2, 'Shakespeare and the Meaning of "Life" in the Twenty-First Century' (pp. 41–94), discussing nature, nurture, and the extent to which an unborn child can be affected by events which happened to their mother. Chapter 3, 'Animals in Shakespearean Ecocriticism' (pp. 95–120), is the most relevant to the comedies, as its treatment of the early modern uncertainty over the distinction between humans and animals is present in other ecocritical works. Among other plays, this chapter examines Theseus's attitude towards his dogs in *A Midsummer Night's Dream*, and how the relationship between Crab and Launce in *Two Gentlemen of Verona* ultimately reveals how similar humans and animals can be. 'Crowds and Social Networks in Shakespeare' (pp. 121–54) is the fourth and final chapter of Egan's monograph, and it explores the behaviour of various crowds. This work successfully outlines current thinking on ecocriticism, and demonstrates the relevance of that theoretical approach to Shakespeare studies.

An ecocritical approach is also evident in Jennifer Munroe, Edward J. Geisweidt, and Lynne Bruckner's edited collection *Ecological Approaches to Early Modern English Texts: A Field Guide to Reading and Teaching*, in which two chapters offer literary analyses of two comedies. Robert N. Watson's contribution, 'Tell Inconvenient Truths, But Tell Them Slant' (pp. 17–28), suggests that as *A Midsummer Night's Dream* is very aware of the interconnectedness of humans and other beings, it is a text which can help readers to become more informed environmental thinkers. Keith M. Botelho's chapter, 'The Beasts of Belmont and Venice' (pp. 71–80), on *The Merchant of Venice*, meanwhile, is informed by animal theory; stressing how intertwined humans and animals were held to be during the early modern period, it argues for the need to look past reading animals as metaphors. Botelho asserts that the Christian characters link Shylock with animality on account of his religion and personality, while the merchant responds by suggesting that the Christians already exhibit animal characteristics.

The following two monographs draw attention to the way in which Shakespeare was influenced by particular types of sources. Charlotte Artese's excellent *Shakespeare's Folktale Sources* is an engaging examination of how the playwright adapted the folk tales that directly influenced seven of his plays. Three of the works that she covers—*The Taming of the Shrew*, *The Merry Wives of Windsor*, and *The Merchant of Venice*—are relevant to this section. In chapter 1, ' "Tell thou the tale": Shakespeare's Taming of the Folktale in *The Taming of the Shrew*' (pp. 29–50), this comedy is linked to two folk tales which engage separately with ideas of gender and class. Artese highlights how Shakespeare makes Petruchio less violent, and Katherine more performatively submissive, than the folk-tale husband and wife. She also discusses how Shakespeare fails to end Christopher Sly's tale, which allows the audience to choose their own positive or negative ending from those which circulate in folk tales, and means that the playwright does not have to articulate a position on class hierarchies. In chapter 3, ' "Have I encompassed you?": Translating the Folktale into Honesty and English in *The Merry Wives of Windsor*' (pp. 79–98), Artese then explores how the women of this play are represented more sympathetically than in the folk tale which influenced it, while the men are rendered more ridiculous. She also illustrates the ways in which the original folk tale was anglicized. In chapter 4, ' "You shall not know": Portia, Power, and the Folktale Sources of *The Merchant of Venice*' (pp. 99–118), this comedy is shown to draw upon a number of folk tales which the audience would know, so Artese suggests that their pleasure in watching the play would come from knowing that the lead casket is the correct one, and that Shylock will not be able to exact his pound of flesh. To prevent the audience from feeling too masterful, however, Shakespeare includes the mysterious discovery of three of Antonio's ships, but never has Portia explain how they came to survive. With a bibliography of folk-tale sources at the end of each chapter on the plays, Artese's monograph is an admirably thorough work of scholarship. It is written with such clarity that it should be a source of interest and enjoyment for scholars with any level of familiarity with the field of folk-tale studies.

Stuart Sillars's equally excellent monograph *Shakespeare and the Visual Imagination* meanwhile offers a rich and compelling treatment of the way in which visual allusions function in four of the comedies. Chapter 2, 'Allusion and Idea in *The Taming of the Shrew*' (pp. 34–54), focuses upon the Sly episode, and highlights how allusions to artistic representations of classical figures raise questions around theatrical identity. In chapter 4, '*Love's Labour's Lost* and Visual Composition' (pp. 95–132), Sillars asserts that Shakespeare had moved from simply alluding to artworks to transferring aspects of their structure into his drama. It outlines how the artistic grouping of three people against a landscape is echoed in Shakespeare's placing of three characters together, and the many verbal references to that number. Chapter 6, 'Visual Identities in *A Midsummer Night's Dream*' (pp. 163–89), argues that Shakespeare's visual allusions are concentrated into four moments between

Acts II and IV. Titania is linked parodically to the 'reclining Venus' tradition, and Bottom in relation to the part-human, part-animal figure of the babwyne; in this way, classical and folk tales are merged. 'Emblem, Tradition, and Invention' (pp. 190–233), chapter 7's discussion of *As You Like It*, is perhaps the most important in the monograph, as Sillars maintains that this play reveals a shift in Shakespeare's references to the visual. By focusing on Jacques and the 'sobbing deer' and 'seven ages of man' extracts, which are both shown to be more allusive to the literary than to the visual, the author argues that 'The leisured variation of the early plays, as they absorb visual forms into their structures, has been displaced by something of far greater integration of the theatric and the literary' (p. 231). The monograph is not only impressive for the controlled and compelling way in which its argument develops over the chapters on the comedies, but also for how it makes compositional aspects of artwork easily understandable for a reader with no prior knowledge of such matters.

The last noticeable theme of the work published in 2015 on Shakespeare's comedies is the way in which early modern readers may have read them. In *Shakespeare's Verbal Art*, William Bellamy analyses that dramatist's use of anagrams, and argues that such a technique can either reinforce or contradict the surface meaning of his works. The final chapter, '*Twelfth Night*' (pp. 494–522), highlights various anagrammatical instances within the play which Bellamy believes would be detected by early modern readers. Anagrams are suggested to reveal references to the date, authorship, and sources of this comedy, as well as to indicate Shakespeare's response to John Marston's anagrammatical attack upon him. Bellamy declares that Malvolio represents Marston, and by extension Marsyas, the satyr who challenged Apollo (or Shakespeare in this instance), and was subsequently flayed alive. These likenesses are suggested to reveal more than Shakespeare's attitude towards Marston, for Bellamy maintains that they show the play's 'generic integrity . . . A coherent inter-relationship between the cruel and the comedic' (p. 519). The monograph is notably well presented, with anagrammatic letters capitalized whenever relevant, and the anagram itself is shown to the right of a passage of text. Readers can follow the argument clearly, and reflect upon early modern reading practices regarding anagrams as they do so.

Laura Estill's monograph *Dramatic Extracts in Seventeenth-Century English Manuscripts: Watching, Reading, Changing Plays* will be of interest to anyone working on early modern reading practices. Estill examines how extracts from various plays were copied into notebooks by seventeenth-century readers, and argues that they reveal insights into how drama related to life outside of the theatre. Chapter 6, 'Proverbial Shakespeare: The Print and Manuscript Circulation of Extracts from *Love's Labour's Lost*' (pp. 201–16), is of interest to this section. It considers the circulation of the extract 'fat paunches have lean pates, and dainty bits / Make rich the ribs, but bankrupt quite the wits' (I.i.26–7). Estill charts the appearances of the extract in print and manuscript, and highlights differences in phrasing. Since the extract is not always attributed to Shakespeare, Estill concludes that 'for early modern readers (and writers), a quotation by Shakespeare was not always a quotation from

Shakespeare, nor was it always meant to bring up associations with a particular play' (p. 211).

The final three monographs which are of relevance to this section cover very different topics and plays. In *Shakespeare and Abraham*, Ken Jackson examines how the playwright engages with Abraham's near-sacrifice of Isaac as told in Genesis 22. With remarkable clarity and efficiency, Jackson neatly presents the readings which such figures as Kierkegaard and Derrida offer of this episode, before turning his attention to Shakespeare's plays. His examination of *The Merchant of Venice* is much less interested in Shylock's conversion than the trial which precedes it, and Jackson convincingly argues that readers should obey Portia's suggestions to process events more slowly. He asserts that when Shylock pauses after Portia tells him that he must cut off exactly a pound of Antonio's flesh, he is placed in the Abrahamic position. Shylock realizes that because he has sworn an oath, he must fulfil it and kill Antonio even if he does not want to. Although he does not ultimately carry out the oath, Jackson maintains that this decision does not arise because he has forgiven Antonio, but because 'It is no more Shylock's choice to be merciful than it is Shylock's choice to kill Antonio' (p. 108).

In *At Work in the Early Modern English Theater: Valuing Labor*, Matthew Kendrick devotes half of chapter 5, 'Labor and Theatrical Value on the Shakespearean Stage: *A Midsummer Night's Dream* and *The Tempest*' (pp. 129–64), to one of Shakespeare's comedies. Kendrick focuses mainly on the Mechanicals, asserting that these characters are informed by medieval theatre because they privilege their identities as labourers over their identities as players. Bottom offers the most overt example of this mindset, for he still views himself as a labourer even when he has been physically transformed. Kendrick detects conflict between the moneymaking side of the theatre and the craft it required in order to function. He argues that 'The play attempts to resolve these tensions by representing the artisanal dimension of the professional theater as a nostalgic touchstone or criterion of communal value capable of pushing against the reifying logic of the market' (p. 130). Kendrick's chapter stands as evidence of the value of a Marxist approach to this comedy.

Astrology is the focus of Peter D. Usher's *Shakespeare and Saturn: Accounting for Appearances*. One of the monograph's key and somewhat unconvincing arguments is that Shakespeare was actually the controversial astronomer Leonard Digges. Usher asserts that because Digges had to keep a low profile on account of some of his ideas, he expressed his astrological findings in play form instead. In chapter 3, '*Much Ado About Nothing*' (pp. 125–62), Usher posits that the characters of Hero, Beatrice, Benedick, and Claudio are used to show that Saturn has two invisible rings. In the fourth chapter, '*The Comedy of Errors*' (pp. 163–99), Usher suggests that the play reveals various sub-cycles of Saturn. Both chapters tend to spend a considerable amount of time recounting the plots of the plays, which could have instead been used to show more of an awareness of the critical background surrounding them.

Evelyn Gajowski and Phyllis Rackin's edited collection *The Merry Wives of Windsor: New Critical Essays* is the most comprehensive work of its kind

published on any of Shakespeare's comedies in 2015. It features fifteen
different essays relevant to this section, which are split into six themed parts.
This work makes a varied and valuable contribution to scholarship on this
play, while remaining accessible enough for undergraduate students. The
editors' introduction concisely outlines the changing critical opinions surrounding the comedy since its first performance, and points towards its
burgeoning interest to historicist and feminist scholars. Catherine Belsey's
chapter, 'Agonistic Scenes of Provincial Life' (pp. 27–37), analyses the speech
patterns within the play, and highlights the very similar and supportive ways in
which Mistresses Ford and Quickly use language. Cristina León Alfar's
contribution, ' "Let's consult together": Women's Agency and the Gossip
Network in The Merry Wives of Windsor' (pp. 38–50), draws upon Judith
Butler's ideas surrounding power and agency in order to argue that the wives
do not allow Falstaff to impose a narrative on their bodies. While Falstaff
equates their hospitality with promiscuity, Quickly and Ford mobilize a strong
female community in order to disprove that connection. Rachel Prusko's
chapter, ' "Who hath got the right Anne?": Gossip, Resistance, and Anne Page
in Shakespeare's Merry Wives' (pp. 51–60), asserts that Anne does not only
resist the considerable amount of gossip which circulates about her, but
actually turns it to her advantage. In ' "May we, with the Warrant of
Womanhood and the witness of a good conscience, pursue him with any
further revenge?": Feminist Citizen Revenge Comedy in The Merry Wives of
Windsor' (pp. 60–9), Susanne Gushee O'Malley questions the extent to which
the play repays a feminist reading, and concludes that its middle section is the
most profitable part for such an approach.

Jean E. Howard's piece, 'Sharp-Tongued Women and Small-Town Social
Relations in Porter's Two Angry Women of Abington and Shakespeare's The
Merry Wives of Windsor' (pp. 73–83), highlights the existence of the former
play, which was contemporaneous with Shakespeare's comedy, is also set in a
small town, and similarly features older, married female protagonists. Howard
draws attention to the differences in setting, gender relations, and location
between the two comedies, but suggests that one play (unspecified) was written
in reaction to the other. Kay Stanton's essay, 'Shakespeare's Quantum
Physics: Merry Wives as a Feminist "Parallel Universe" of Henry IV, Part 2'
(pp. 84–95), argues that the differences in the Falstaff of the Henry IV plays
and The Merry Wives of Windsor can be explained as evidence that these
works are 'parallel universes' which the character travels between. In her
convincing argument for the value of The Merry Wives of Windsor's
apparently 'bad Quarto', Helen Ostovich's chapter, 'Bucking Tradition in
The Merry Wives of Windsor, 1602: Not a Bad Quarto, Really' (pp. 96–106),
explains that this version of the play functions effectively as a fast-paced farce.
Jennifer Higginbottom's wide-ranging chapter, 'Teaching Children Their
Behaviours in The Merry Wives of Windsor' (pp. 109–20), considers child
actors and characters as well as the quarto and Folio editions in order to
demonstrate how Shakespeare 'constructs childhood as a site of instruction in
theatrical and social performance' (pp. 110–11). Barbara Traister's piece, 'A
French Physician in an English Community' (pp. 121–9), discusses how
Doctor Caius's name and nationality confirm his medical occupation, then

highlights how he is both accepted into, and punished by, the Windsor community.

Wendy Wall's chapter, 'Finding Desire in Windsor: Gender, Consumption, and Animality in *Merry Wives*' (pp. 132–43), examines the problems and questions that arise when the desires of the play's characters—especially the female ones—are analysed, and she outlines the many different types of desire that are in evidence. Jessica McCall's article, 'Hysterical Shakespeare: Celebrations of Merry Sexuality' (pp. 144–53), argues that *The Merry Wives of Windsor* has been overlooked because of its portrayal of two older, married women who are in control of their sexuality. McCall asserts that the comedy is of extreme importance because it 'offers a unique site for explorations of established heterosexual relationships where chastity is obviously distanced from virginity' (pp. 151–2). Carolyn E. Brown's chapter, ' "Preposterous" Actions and "Tainted" Desires in *The Merry Wives of Windsor*' (pp. 154–68), is likely to provoke a good deal of debate, for it suggests that Falstaff is the innocent victim of the wives' masochism. She supplements this contentious reading with the more convincing suggestion that Ford suffers from dissociative personality disorder, which emerges on account of his wish to suffer from having an adulterous wife.

Rebecca Ann Bach's contribution, 'Falstaff Becomes the (Hu)man at the Expense of *The Merry Wives of Windsor*' (pp. 171–83), meanwhile takes issue with the prominent critical belief that Falstaff represents man. She argues that the Elizabethan audience would have understood him to be connected with animals, and then explains how his position has since shifted to seem totally human. The final chapter of relevance to this section is Rebecca Laroche's ' "Cabbage and Roots" and the Difference of *Merry Wives*' (pp. 184–93), which offers the fascinating argument that the comedy's use of vegetables is not linked so much to domestic matters as to the scatological and sexual features of the characters' and audience's bodies.

Other edited collections feature a number of chapters that are of relevance to this section. Paul Yachnin's edited collection *Shakespeare's World of Words* features three chapters which explore *The Merchant of Venice*, *Love's Labour's Lost*, and *The Comedy of Errors* respectively. Michael Bristol and Sara Coodin's article, 'Well-Won Thrift' (pp. 33–57), analyses the word 'well' and words connected to wealth in the first of these comedies. The authors refer to aspects of Jewish theology in order to argue that Shylock sees himself as earning his living through work that is respectable but necessary, as Jacob did with Laban. Jessica, meanwhile, is linked to both Dinah and Rachel, but the authors maintain that neither comparison is wholly satisfactory. Lucy Munro's chapter, 'Antique/Antic: Neologism and the Play of Shakespeare's Words in *Love's Labour's Lost* and *2 Henry IV*' (pp. 77–101), examines the uses of 'antique' and 'antic' in *Love's Labour's Lost* alongside *2 Henry IV*. Munro's discussion of the comedy focuses upon how artificial Armado's language sounds because of its use of old and new words—a combination which would resonate with Elizabethan discussions over language. Jennifer Roberts-Smith's article, ' "Time is their master": Men and Metre in *The Comedy of Errors*' (pp. 237–62), focuses upon the metre of *The Comedy of Errors*, particularly how accentual metre works in the 'lock-out' scene, and how its iambic counterpart functions in the final scene. The argument that the two types of metre affect how the characters interpret time is sound, but readers who have some knowledge of metrical terms would receive the full benefit of the detailed scholarship that is evident in this article.

Two chapters in the edited collection *Mapping the World of Anglo-American Studies at the Turn of the Century*, edited by Aleksandra Nikčević-Batrićević and Marija Krivokapić, focus on *The Merchant of Venice*. Esmerelda Subashi's chapter, 'The Universal and Timeless World of Shakespeare's Work' (pp. 65–73), offers a well-intentioned but sadly somewhat simplistic treatment of the comedy in order to argue that 'Shakespeare is as modern as contemporary writers who believe in feminism, the right of a person to their sexual preferences and the equality of all people' (p. 72). Subashi discusses the role of women, anti-Semitism, and homosexuality within the plays, but could have demonstrated a greater awareness of the critical complexities surrounding these topics, as there are a number of generalized arguments which impact upon the effectiveness of the readings. In her chapter 'Modern Critical Approaches to Shakespeare: New Readings of *The Merchant of Venice* and *Measure for Measure* (pp. 75–84), meanwhile, Tatjana Dumitrašković asserts that the trial scene of *The Merchant of Venice* has been the subject of the most critical interest. Dumitrašković explains the ideas of such critics as John Palmer, Stephen Greenblatt, and Terry Eagleton effectively, but the chapter could have benefited from a greater discussion of her own views on the play.

David Loewenstein and Michael Witmore's edited collection, *Shakespeare and Early Modern Religion*, contains two chapters that make Shakespeare's comedies the main focus of their arguments. Alison Shell's essay, 'Delusion in *A Midsummer Night's Dream*' (pp. 81–95), presents the intriguing possibility that Demetrius is not in love with Helena at the end of the play, but with an 'eidolon' or 'imaginative phantom' (p. 86) of her, and links this idea to notions of idolatry. Matthew Dimmock's chapter, 'Shakespeare's Non-Christian Religion' (pp. 280–99), meanwhile, uses Marlowe's *The Jew of Malta* to demonstrate how Shakespeare places Judaism to the side in *The Merchant of Venice*. Dimmock convincingly asserts that 'Shakespeare's recreation of Judaism for the early modern stage is ... one that is always already past, defeated by the truth of Christ' (p. 291).

Donald Beecher, Travis DeCook, Andrew Wallace, and Grant Williams's edited collection, *Taking Exception to the Law: Materializing Injustice in Early Modern English Literature*, contains two chapters that discuss Shakespeare's comedies. The first of these pieces, written by Tim Stretton, is entitled 'Conditional Promises and Legal Instruments in *The Merchant of Venice*' (pp. 72–89). Stretton compellingly links the comedy to anxieties surrounding people's ability to keep verbal or paper bonds. While the play reveals the harshness of certain types of legal practices and penalties surrounding bonds, Stretton maintains that Shakespeare does not identify the most secure way of making a bond; rather, he implies the importance of exercising mercy when engaging with the law. The second of the chapters, by Barbara Kreps, is entitled 'Two-Sided Legal Narratives: Slander, Evidence, Proof, and Turnarounds in *Much Ado About Nothing*' (pp. 162–78). Kreps argues that practices in this comedy would have been recognizable to contemporary law.

She posits that characters have 'contrasting attitudes towards the issues, fundamental to the play, of reliable evidence and what constitutes proof' (p. 163); while Leonato refuses to believe something he has been told until he has evidence of it, Claudio is nowhere near as discerning. Such impulsiveness combines with the unreliability of language to lead him to believe and perpetuate the slander that is made against Hero. As the defamed Hero is unrecognizable to the broader community, 'death provides her and her family with a singularly apt metaphor for slander' (p. 173).

Merry E. Wiesner-Hank's edited collection *Mapping Gendered Routes and Spaces in the Early Modern World* contains a chapter by Tara Pedersen, 'Bodies by the Book: Remapping Reputation in the Account of Anne Greene and Shakespeare's *Much Ado About Nothing*' (pp. 117–30), which has some resonance with Kreps's article. Pedersen examines *Much Ado About Nothing* in relation to a contemporaneous account of Anne Greene, a servant who was hanged for miscarrying her master's child, but somehow survived the ordeal. The author argues that Shakespeare's comedy interrogates whether a person comes to be recognized by performing an action, or by being seen to perform that action. She focuses primarily on the female body and reputation, and convincingly argues that Hero has to 'die' because her body seems to confirm the slanderous accusation made against her.

Stefan Horlacher's edited collection, *Configuring Masculinity in Theory and Literary Practice*, contains Mark Bracher's 'From Antisocial to Prosocial Manhood: Shakespeare's Rescripting of Masculinity in *As You Like It*' (pp. 95–125), which is a fascinating combination of psychology and literary analysis. Bracher explains how certain 'scripts' of dominant masculinity are initially acted through by Oliver and Orlando, but are shown to be harmful. The play then advocates alternative, less harmful, 'scripts' of masculinity through Corin and Duke Senior, as well as Rosalind's advice to Orlando.

Some of the journal articles which are of relevance to this section focused upon multiple plays of interest, but the vast majority treated them separately. One member of the former group is Kay Stanton's lively article, 'Intersections of Politics, Culture, Class, and Gender in Shakespeare's *Titus Andronicus, The Taming of the Shrew*, and *The Merchant of Venice*' (*MultSh* 12[2005] 41–54). Stanton uses the 'rabbit and duck' illustration that was popularized by Ludwig Wittgenstein in order to conceptualize the ambiguous nature of Shakespeare's works. For *The Taming of the Shrew*, Stanton argues that Katharine's speech on the role of wives is written so that the audience can choose whichever interpretation they like. She also highlights some of the ambiguities surrounding Antonio, Shylock, and Portia in *The Merchant of Venice*.

In her article 'Shakespeare and Thomas Underdowne's *Theseus and Ariadne*' (*RES* 66[2015] 465–79), Sarah Annes Brown considers how the latter's 1566 text may have influenced *A Midsummer Night's Dream* and *The Merchant of Venice*, as well as *The Tempest*, a play which is not covered by this section. She suggests that a prefatory poem of Underdowne's influences the way in which Egeus and Theseus talk about Hermia in *A Midsummer Night's Dream*. Brown goes on to discuss how Underdowne's Phaedra and Ariadne influence Shakespeare's Helena and Hermia, arguing that, while the latter pair are not sisters, they are as close and as jealous as Underdowne's characters are. Brown also suggests that the way in which Underdowne's sisters attempt to situate Ariadne in relation to classical heroines informs Jessica and Lorenzo's exchange in *The Merchant of Venice*: 'Jessica deploys her reference to Thisbe in order to reject any implications that she is a Cressida' (p. 474).

Of those articles which focus only upon one of the plays relevant to this section, *A Midsummer Night's Dream* is the most popular text to analyse, but critical approaches vary. Louise Geddes, for example, argues in her excellent article, 'Playing No Part But Pyramus: Bottom, Celebrity and the Early Modern Clown' (*MRDE* 28[2015] 70–85), that the role of the clown is split between Puck and Bottom so as to control the celebrity figure whose presence and improvisational skills had the potential to disrupt the entire play. Geddes discusses how playwrights would have to balance the audience's wish to see the clown with their own dramatic vision. She then outlines instances where Bottom's comic potential is diluted or contained, and Puck is given a controlled area for improvisation. In this way, Geddes concludes, the role the performer inhabits is privileged over the performer themselves.

Adam Rzepka's fascinating article, ' "How easy is a bush supposed a bear?" ': Differentiating Imaginative Production in *A Midsummer Night's Dream*' (*SQ* 66[2015] 308–28), meanwhile, draws upon Aristotelian and early modern understandings of imagination. It argues that the audience are made to participate in, or acknowledge, a number of imaginative practices. Through Titania's and Oberon's continued references to landscapes, Rzepka asserts, the audience is made to imagine something very different from what is onstage, and the flower juice is then designed to trick those watching the play into thinking that the lovers see more than they really do. Rzepka also discusses how the Mechanicals and Puck cause the audience to become aware of the limits or persistence of the imaginative process.

Andrew Barnaby's article, ' "The botome of Goddes secretes": 1 Corinthians and *A Midsummer Night's Dream*' (*RenD* 43[2015] 1–26), highlights the allusion which this comedy makes to the biblical book in the title. Barnaby argues that 1 Corinthians' criticism of the rich for failing to feed the poor has links to Theseus's relationship with the Mechanicals. While Theseus expects the Mechanicals to perform because they admire him, they expect to be paid. Theseus's attitude echoes that espoused by the criticized rich, so Barnaby suggests that the play encourages audience members who share that mindset to alter their ways.

In 'The Humorous Unseemly: Value, Contradiction and Consistency in the Comic Politics of Shakespeare's A Midsummer Night's Dream' (Shakespeare 11[2015] 425–45), an article which draws extensively upon critical and classical ideas surrounding humour and laughter, Daniel Derrin, argues that these two features can be used to both contradict and support the status quo. Focusing on *A Midsummer Night's Dream*, he argues that 'Shakespeare associates much of the play's humour with the political and rational power to make distinctions' (p. 439). Whether it is the lovers' inability to realize that they are acting on emotion rather than intellect, or Theseus's contradictory denigration of lovers and poets, humour has the potential to highlight societal problems, and to suggest a way of solving them.

Theseus's oft-quoted description of the figure of the poet is used by Christopher Thurman to frame his exploration of Shakespeare's ideas regarding poets in his article 'Fine Frenzies: Theseus, Shakespeare, and the Politics of Their Poets' (*Shakespeare* 11[2015] 115–34). By focusing on a number of Shakespearean references to poet-figures and poetry across various plays, Thurman convincingly argues that Shakespeare understands the many accusations levelled against poetry, but sees it as a form with the potential to create social change. While Thurman quite rightly does not engage only with *A Midsummer Night's Dream*, his article is an effective demonstration of how the play can prompt a broader examination of Shakespeare's works or attitudes.

In 'The Complexity of Dance in Shakespeare's *A Midsummer Night's Dream*' (*EMLS* 18:i–ii[2015] 1–26), Claire Gwendoline Hansen combines complexity theory with admirable close reading. She argues that 'Shakespeare uses dance in *A Midsummer Night's Dream* to create and negotiate turbulent communications and to transform the social and environmental systems and their various parts' (p. 10).

Joe Luna's article, 'Money, *die Ware*, and Marx's Shakespeare' (*TPr* [2015] 427–47), demonstrates another approach to *A Midsummer Night's Dream*. It examines Marx's use of the quotation 'the course of true love never did run smooth' from the play in the third chapter of *Das Kapital*. Luna is most concerned with what this quotation implies about the relationship between money and commodities, but he also comments upon why the play was relevant to Marx. He asserts that 'the plot ... is so deeply dependent on illusion and exchange, so riven with the entire spectacle of agency and unawareness ... that it provides not just a fitting or apposite reference, but a deeply ironical articulation of a state of mis-recognition' (p. 440).

*The Merchant of Venice* was also a popular text for analysis in journal articles, with a number of approaches to the comedy evident. Zachary Hutchins and Amy Lofgreen argue, in their article 'More Greek than Jonson Thought? Euripides' *Medea* and *The Merchant of Venice*' (*Shakespeare* 11[2015] 388–407), that contrary to general critical opinion, Shakespeare had read Greek drama. They convincingly outline the influence of the former titular play upon the latter, pointing out similarities in language and suggesting that Antonio, Portia, and Shylock all have Medea-like qualities. Hutchins and Lofgreen also assert that the influence of *Medea* supports the scholarly notion that Antonio has feelings for Bassanio, and contradicts the critical idea that Portia's cross-dressing is a homoerotic act. Matthew Scott Stenton's article, 'Unlocking Meaning: The Act of Reading in Shakespeare's *The Merchant of Venice*' (*C&L* 64[2015] 377–99), meanwhile, focuses upon the reading practices of characters within this play. Stenton argues that Bassanio is successful in the casket scene because he reads the caskets rather than the riddles, while Portia resolves the dilemma of the bond by reading it so literally as to make it seem ridiculous—a technique she learned from Shylock.

Jordi Coral's fascinating article, 'Anxious Householders: Theft and Anti-Usury Discourse in Shakespeare's Venetian Plays' (*SC* 30[2015] 285–300), argues that Shylock fears being robbed because he is uncomfortable with his profession as a usurer. Coral examines his reference to the biblical story of Jacob and Laban, and explores Jessica's own act of theft, before suggesting that Shylock's anxiety is also evident in Iago's victims. Huey-ling Lee's article, 'The Social Meaning of Money in Dekker's *The Shoemaker's Holiday* and Shakespeare's *The Merchant of Venice*' (*CD* 49[2015] 335–66), maintains that money had a vital part to play in perpetuating early modern social relations. Lee argues that the Christian and Jewish characters initially constitute two social groups which are connected by money because they trade with one another. After Jessica's elopement, however, this connection becomes more strained, and Shylock comes to view Antonio as an object he can own. The comedy thus offers examples wherein money supports relations between social groups, but it also illustrates how money may endanger them too.

Two other comedies, *Love's Labour's Lost* and *Twelfth Night*, are the focus of two journal articles apiece. In ' "Concolinel": Moth's Lost Song Recovered?' (*SQ* 66[2015] 84–94), Ross W. Duffin suggests that the French song 'Qvand Colinet faisoir l'amour' could be the song connected to Moth in *Love's Labour's Lost*. Duffin's argument is supported by a range of material, including the lyrics of the French song, an English translation, and a suggested score. Dermot Cavanagh's article, 'William Drummond of Hawthornden as Reader of Renaissance Drama' (*RES* 66[2015] 676–97), examines the way in which Drummond responded to a number of early modern plays, including *Love's Labour's Lost*. Through a fascinating examination of Drummond's commonplace books and annotations of the play, Cavanagh demonstrates that Drummond was not only searching for extracts as he read the play, but was also 'engaging with [its] moral process and concerns' (p. 690).

The two articles on *Twelfth Night*, meanwhile, take different approaches. J.A. Smith's article, 'Telling Love: *Twelfth Night* in Samuel Richardson, Teresia Constantia Phillips, and William Blake' (*SP* 112[2015] 194–212), discusses how Viola's 'She never told her love' speech was employed in a number of eighteenth-century texts written by the authors referred to in the title. Smith argues that Viola's speech has an ambiguous attitude towards virginity and the expression of love, then considers how Richardson, Phillips, and Blake employ the quotation to varying effect. These texts, Smith maintains, suggest that the eighteenth-century attitude towards Shakespearean quotation was far more complex than critics generally assume. James P. Bednaz's note, 'Suspect Evidence for the Late Dating of *Twelfth Night*' (*N&Q* 62[2015] 563–7), argues that this comedy was written before 1601. Bednaz suggests that, contrary to critical opinion, Shakespeare was not alluding to Dekker's parody of Jonson through Feste's 'out of my element' comment, but rather that Dekker alluded to Shakespeare.

Some of the other comedies were also discussed in journal articles. Tristan Samuk's piece, 'Satire and the Aesthetic in *As You Like It*' (*RenD* 43[2015] 117–42), examines how Jacques and Rosalind function as the play's two main satirists, with the latter being more successful than the former because she eventually realizes that art can alter the world. Rosalind's belief in the aesthetic is not wholly shared by Jacques, however, nor is it fully supported by the end of the comedy. In her article ' "I will be master of what is mine own": Fortune Hunters and Shrews in Early Modern London' (*SCJ* 46[2015] 331–58), Eleanor Hubbard convincingly argues for the connection between *The Taming of the Shrew* and a 1590 London divorce suit. Hubbard draws parallels between Petruchio's 'taming' methods and those attributed to Christopher Percy in the suit. She proposes that the case could have been a source for *The Taming of the Shrew*, or that Petruchio may have inspired Christopher Percy's behaviour, or that Margery Percy's friends and relatives linked her husband's actions with that character when they described them.

Last but certainly not least, Sophie Tomlinson's 'The Actress and Baroque Aesthetic Effects in Renaissance Drama' (*ShakB* 33[2015] 67–82) explores *Two Gentlemen of Verona* alongside other canonical and non-canonical works. Tomlinson explains that the figure of the suffering Ariadne was an important focus for baroque work, and argues that *Two Gentlemen of Verona* can be classified as such on account of the cross-dressed Julia's speech which recalls how s/he once played that character. Through a focus on this speech, Tomlinson asserts that there is 'a baroque *affect* that conjures and imparts theatrical pleasure' (p. 71) for the audience, who know that the boy-actress is highly conscious of expressing emotions.

**Books Reviewed**

Anderson, Miranda. *The Renaissance Extended Mind*. Palgrave. [2015] pp. xix + 278. £60 ISBN 9 7811 3741 2843.

Artese, Charlotte. *Shakespeare's Folktale Sources*. UDelP. [2015] pp. ix + 243. $80 ISBN 9 7816 1149 5553.

Beecher, Donald, Travis DeCook, Andrew Wallace, and Grant Williams, eds. *Taking Exception to the Law: Materializing Injustice in Early Modern English Literature*. UTorP. [2015] pp. 288. $52.50 ISBN 9 7814 4264 2010.

Bellamy, William. *Shakespeare's Verbal Art*. CambridgeSP. [2015] pp. 530. £62.99 ISBN 9 7814 4388 3849.

Berger, Harry Jr. *Figures of a Changing World: Metaphor and the Emergence of Modern Culture*. FordhamUP. [2015] pp. xi + 160. $20 ISBN 9 7808 2325 7485.

Bevington, David, ed. *Troilus and Cressida*. . ArdenS. Bloomsbury. [2015] pp. xxiii + 515. £12.99 ISBN 9 7814 7258 4748.

Brown, Carolyn E. *Shakespeare and Psychoanalytic Theory*. Bloomsbury. [2015] pp. xii + 226. hb £75 ISBN 9 7814 7250 3244, pb £21.99 ISBN 9 7814 7250 3237.

Bugliani Knox, Francesca, and David Lonsdale, eds. *Poetry and the Religious Imagination: The Power of the Word*. Ashgate. [2015] pp. xii + 268. £60 ISBN 9 7814 7242 6246.

Callaghan, Dympna. *Hamlet: Language and Writing*. Bloomsbury. [2015] pp. 232. £40 ISBN 9 7814 7252 0289.

Cefalu, Paul. *Tragic Cognition in Shakespeare's Othello: Beyond the Neural Sublime*. Bloomsbury. [2015] pp. 136. pb £16.99 ISBN 9 7814 7252 3464.

Chanan, Gabriel. *Shakespeare and Democracy: The Self-Renewing Politics of a Global Playwright*. Troubador. [2015] pp. x + 218. pb £12.99 ISBN 9 7817 8462 4248.

Chiari, Sophie, ed. *The Circulation of Knowledge in Early Modern English Literature*. Ashgate. [2015] pp. xxii + 268. £65 ISBN 9 7814 7244 9153.

Clark, Sandra, and Pamela Mason, eds. *Macbeth*. ArdenS. Bloomsbury. [2015] pp. xix + 381. £8.99 ISBN 9 7819 0427 1413.

Crawforth, Hannah, Sarah Dustagheer, and Jennifer Young. *Shakespeare in London*. Bloomsbury. [2015] pp. xviii + 262. $25.99 ISBN 9 7814 0815 1808.

Desai, R.W., ed. *Shakespeare the Man: New Decipherings*. FDUP. [2014] pp. xxx + 278. hb $90 ISBN 9 7816 1147 6750, pb $44.99 ISBN 9 7816 1147 8693.

Dowd, Michelle M. *The Dynamics of Inheritance on the Shakespearean Stage*, CUP. [2015] pp. xiii + 290. $99.99 ISBN 9 7811 0709 9777.

Dutsch, Dorota, Sharon L. James, and David Konstan, eds. *Women in Roman Republican Drama*. UWiscP. [2015] pp. vii + 260. $55 ISBN 9 7802 9930 3144.

Edmondson, Paul, and Stanley Wells. *The Shakespeare Circle*. CUP. [2015] pp. x + 358. pb £18.99 ISBN 9 7811 0769 9090.

Egan, Gabriel. *Shakespeare and Ecocritical Theory*. Bloomsbury. [2015] pp. 208. £15.39 ISBN 9 7814 4119 9300.

Ellrodt, Robert. *Montaigne and Shakespeare: The Emergence of Modern Self-Consciousness*. ManUP. [2015] pp. x + 192. £70 ISBN 9 7807 1909 1087.

Estill, Laura. *Dramatic Extracts in Seventeenth-Century English Manuscripts*. UDelP. [2015] pp. xxviii + 256. $39.99 ISBN 9 7816 1149 5546.

Evans, Robert C., ed. *Othello: A Critical Reader*. Bloomsbury. [2015] pp. xviii + 273. £22.99 ISBN 9 7814 7252 0364.

Gajowski, Evelyn, and Phyllis Rackin, eds. *The Merry Wives of Windsor: New Critical Essays*. Routledge. [2015] pp. 266. £95 ISBN 9 7804 1584 5045.

Hawkes, David. *Shakespeare and Economic Theory*. ArdenS&Theory. [2015] pp. xiv + 223. pb £21.99 ISBN 9 7814 7257 6972.

Heffernan, Julián Jiménez. *Shakespeare's Extremes: Wild Man, Monster, Beast*. Palgrave. [2015] pp. xi + 234. £55 ISBN 9 7811 3752 3570.

Horlacher, Stefan, ed. *Configuring Masculinity in Theory and Literary Practice*. Brill. [2015] pp. 328. $102 ISBN 9 7890 0429 8996.

Howe Kritzer, Amelia, and Miriam López-Rodríguez, eds. *Woman on Trial: Gender and the Accused Woman in Plays from Ancient Greece to the Contemporary Stage*. Teneo. [2015] pp. vi + 325. $35 ISBN 9 7819 3484 4595.

Hunt, Maurice. *The Divine Face in Four Writers: Shakespeare, Dostoyevsky, Hesse, and C.S. Lewis*. Bloomsbury. [2015] pp. xii + 175. $89.99 ISBN 9 7815 0131 1048.

Hutson, Lorna. *Circumstantial Shakespeare*. OUP. [2015] pp. x + 190. £25 ISBN 9 7801 9965 7100.

Innes, Paul. *Shakespeare's Roman Plays*. Palgrave. [2015] pp. 260. £55 ISBN 9 7811 3702 5913.

Jackson, Ken. *Shakespeare and Abraham*. UNDP. [2015] pp. 184. $27 ISBN 9 7802 6803 2715.

Jones, Gwilym. *Shakespeare's Storms*. ManUP. [2014] pp. xi + 198. £75 ISBN 9 7807 1908 9381.

Kendrick, Matthew. *At Work in the Early Modern English Theater: Valuing Labor*. FDUP. [2015] pp. 206. £49.95 ISBN 9 7816 1147 8242.

Kirwan, Peter. *Shakespeare and the Idea of Apocrypha: Negotiating the Boundaries of the Dramatic Canon.* CUP. [2015] pp. xii + 258. £62 ISBN 9 7811 0709 6172.

Labaune-Demeule, Florence, ed. *Authority and Displacement in the English-Speaking World,* vol. 1: *Exploring Europe/from Europe.* CambridgeSP. [2015] pp. xiv + 142. £41.99 ISBN 9 7814 4388 0947.

Loewenstein, David, and Michael Witmore, eds. *Shakespeare and Early Modern Religion.* CUP. [2015] pp. xii + 318. £65 ISBN 9 7811 0702 6612.

Martin, Randall. *Shakespeare and Ecology.* OUP. [2015] pp. 224. £16.99 ISBN 9 7801 9956 7010.

McCarthy, Penny. *Discovering the Hidden Figure of a Child in Shakespeare's Sonnets as the Key to a New Interpretation: From Literary Analysis to Historical Detection.* Mellen. [2015] pp. viii + 330. £147.04 ISBN 9 7814 9550 3030.

MacFaul, Tom. *Shakespeare and the Natural World.* CUP. [2015] pp. 220. £64.99 ISBN 9 7811 0711 7938.

Meek, Richard, and Erin Sullivan, eds. *The Renaissance of Emotion: Understanding Affect in Shakespeare and His Contemporaries.* ManUP. [2015] pp. xi + 276. £70 ISBN 9 7807 1909 0783.

Mullaney, Steven. *The Reformation of Emotions in the Age of Shakespeare.* UChicP. [2015] pp. x + 231. $35 ISBN 9 7802 2654 7633.

Munroe, Jennifer, J. Geisweidt Edward,, and Lynne Bruckner, eds. *Ecological Approaches to Early Modern English Texts: A Field Guide to Reading and Teaching.* Ashgate. [2015] pp. xviii + 256. £102.42 ISBN 9 7814 7241 6728.

Murphy, Jessica C. *Virtuous Necessity: Conduct Literature and the Making of the Virtuous Woman in Early Modern England.* UMichP. [2015] pp. x + 179. $60 ISBN 9780 4721 1957 8.

Nikčević-Batrićević, Aleksandra, and Marija Krivokapić, eds., *Mapping the World of Anglo-American Studies at the Turn of the Century.* CambridgeSP. [2015] pp. 315. £52.99 ISBN 9 7814 4387 6599.

Ormsby, Robert. *Coriolanus: Shakespeare in Performance.* ManUP. [2014] pp. xii + 281. £75 ISBN 9 7807 1907 8675.

Parvini, Neema. *Shakespeare and Cognition: Thinking Fast and Slow through Character.* Palgrave. [2015] pp. ix + 75. £45 ISBN 9 7811 3754 3158.

Potter, Lois, ed. *The Two Noble Kinsmen.* . ArdenS. Bloomsbury. [2015] pp. xix + 451. £12.99 ISBN 9 7814 7257 7542.

Prescott, Paul, and Erin Sullivan, eds. *Shakespeare on the Global Stage: Performance and Festivity in the Olympic Year.* Bloomsbury. [2015] pp. xvi + 356. £21.99 ISBN 9 7814 7252 0326.

Radasanu, Andrea, Ryan Balot, and Timothy W. Burns, eds. *In Search of Humanity: Essays in Honor of Clifford Orwin.* Lexington. [2015] pp. xi + 546. $140 ISBN 9 7807 3918 4165.

Rickard, Jane. *Writing the Monarch in Jacobean England: Jonson, Donne, Shakespeare, and the Works of King James.* CUP. [2015] pp. x + 278. $64.99 ISBN 9 7811 0712 0662.

Schwyzer, Philip. *Shakespeare and the Remains of Richard III.* OUP. [2015] pp. xii + 272. pb £27.50 ISBN 9 7801 9872 8030.

Shapiro, James. *1606: William Shakespeare and the Year of Lear*. Faber. [2015] pp. xi + 423. hb £20 ISBN 9 7805 7123 5780, pb £9.99 ISBN 9 7805 7123 5797.

Sillars, Stuart. *Shakespeare and the Visual Imagination*. CUP. [2015] pp. 333. £67 ISBN 9 7811 0702 9958.

Slights, Jessica, ed. *Othello*. ISE. [2015]. internetshakespeare.uvic.ca. Open access. ISBN 9 7815 5058 4660.

Smith, Simon, Jacqueline Watson, and Amy Kenny, eds. *The Senses in Early Modern England, 1558–1660*. ManUP. [2015] pp. xii + 243. £70 ISBN 9 7807 1909 1582.

Tredell, Nicolas. *Shakespeare: The Tragedies*. Palgrave. [2014] pp. 216. £60 ISBN 9 7811 3740 4893.

Usher, Peter D. *Shakespeare and Saturn: Accounting for Appearances*. Lang. [2015] pp. 241. £54 ISBN 9 7814 5419 2695.

Wells, Stanley. *William Shakespeare: A Very Short Introduction*. OUP. [2015] pp. xv + 125. pb £7.99 ISBN 9 7801 9871 8628.

White, R.S., Mark Houlahan, and Katrina O'Loughlin, eds. *Shakespeare and Emotions: Inheritances, Enactments, Legacies*. PalMac. [2015] pp. xii + 270. £58 ISBN 9 7813 4969 0749.

Wiesner-Hanks, Merry E., ed. *Mapping Gendered Routes and Spaces in the Early Modern World*. Routledge. [2015] pp. 398. £63.71 ISBN 9 7814 7242 9605.

Yachnin, Paul, ed. *Shakespeare's World of Words*. Bloomsbury. [2015] pp. xii + 292. £84.99 ISBN 9 7814 7251 5292.

# VIII

# Renaissance Drama: Excluding Shakespeare

EOIN PRICE, ELIZABETH SHARRETT, HELEN F. SMITH,
PER SIVEFORS, AND CLARE WHITEHEAD

This chapter has three sections: 1. Editions and Textual Matters; 2. Theatre
History; 3. Criticism. Section 1 is by Eoin Price; section 2 is by Elizabeth
Sharrett; section 3(a) is by Helen F. Smith; section 3(b) is by Per Sivefors;
section 3(c) is by Clare Whitehead.

## 1. Editions and Textual Matters

This year may well turn out to be a notable one for non-Shakespearean
Renaissance textual editions, but the fruits of its labours will not be evident for
some time. While there were very few new editions of Renaissance plays
published in 2015, the year has witnessed the initiation and continuation of
some exciting projects. Oxford University Press announced two major new
research projects related to the editing of Renaissance drama. Martin Butler
and Matthew Steggle will be general editors of the complete works of John
Marston; Joseph Black, Andrew Hadfield, Jennifer Richards, and Cathy
Shrank will be general editors of the complete works of Thomas Nashe. The
latter project will mostly feature prose, but two play editions—*Dido, Queen of
Carthage* and *Summer's Last Will and Testament*—are also planned. The
Oxford complete works of John Ford are on the horizon and the Oxford
complete James Shirley is also drawing closer to completion, so the future of
Renaissance textual editing looks bright, but this perhaps also explains why
2015 was relatively quiet. The spectre of Shakespeare was also a factor: major
new editions by Norton and Oxford have occupied many of the major editors
of Renaissance drama. Accordingly, there are only two editions to review:
Michael Neill's Norton edition of *The Duchess of Malfi* and the Malone
Society's *Collections XVII*.

Norton and Neill have been busy issuing informative editions of Renaissance
plays—Neill's Norton *Spanish Tragedy* was released in 2013—and *The
Duchess of Malfi* is a handsome addition to their catalogue. The edition is

*The Year's Work in English Studies, Volume 96 (2017)* © *The Author 2017. Published by Oxford
University Press on behalf of the English Association. All rights reserved.*
*For Permissions, please email: journals.permissions@oup.com*
doi:10.1093/ywes/max009

designed with students in mind and will be a valuable resource for many university modules. As well as an expertly edited and annotated text, Neill provides useful textual sources and some important critical essays. This material, together with a useful selected bibliography and a chronology of Webster's life, equips lecturers and students with information that can enliven class discussion. The essays range widely, from studies of theology by D.C. Gunby to Pascale Aebischer's analysis of Websterian adaptation, via essays on dramaturgy, gender, and socio-politics. The contextual section includes source material, contemporary responses, and documents relating to widows, and remembrance.

The Malone Society's latest collection (XVII) comprises four separate editions relating to Renaissance drama. The first section, edited by Eleanor Lowe, Martin Wiggins, and Janette Dillon, contains the accounts and inventories of the Revels Office for the years 1541–6. The second section is an edition of Edward Herbert's *The Amazon*, edited by Cristina Malcolmson, Matteo Pangallo, and Eugene Hill. The third section is an edition of Rachel Fane's 'Entertainments and Poems', edited by Marion O'Connor. The final section, edited by J. Caitlin Finlayson, is an edition of two lord mayor's shows: John Squire's *The Tryumphs of Peace* [1620] and John Taylor's *The Triumphs of Fame and Honour* [1634]. This is a wide-ranging collection of great interest to scholars working across Renaissance theatre history. The documents relating to the Revels Office help to flesh out the under-studied period of late Henrician drama, while the other editions also make valuable contributions to the study of civic drama, household drama, and early modern women's writing. The Malone Society continues to do important work by reminding scholars and students of the vast and eclectic nature of Renaissance drama, and this collection attests to the benefits of taking a more holistic view of the field. Each of the documents, many of which are previously unpublished, is newly edited and comes complete with a useful introduction, detailing date, authorship, and other useful information. The collection is therefore of great benefit to the study of Renaissance drama and an important addition to the Malone Society catalogue.

Although there were few new critical editions published in 2015, several important articles contributed much to the study of Renaissance printed drama. One such article is Aaron T. Pratt's 'Stab-Stitching and the Status of Early English Playbooks as Literature' (*Library* 16[2015] 304–28), which constitutes an important intervention in the study of bibliography and playbook publication. Attending to more than 2,500 surviving books printed before 1641, Pratt overturns the assumption that the physical appearance of playbooks can be used to determine literary credentials. In fact, for shorter books (including playbooks) stab-stitching was the dominant method of printing and binding: Pratt calculates that 'more than four fifths of playbook-length quartos were prepared for customers by being stab-stitched' (p. 315). Poetry, philosophical treatises, and other books dignified with the title of 'literature' were stab-stitched too. So, Pratt concludes, the practice of stab-stitching, so common amongst playbooks, was not, in fact, a marker of literariness. If anything, the fact that playbooks were stab-stitched connects them to, rather than distances them from, other forms of printed literature.

This thorough study of playbook materiality should have a major impact on all future considerations of drama as literature in Renaissance England. In 'John Ford's Substantive Accidentals in *Perkin Warbeck*' (*Library* 16[2015] 446–57), Gilles Monsarrat examines the use of capitalization and italicization in the 1634 quarto of Ford's history play. In an ingenious reading, Monsarrat argues against the standard assumption that Ford believed that Warbeck was an impostor, claiming instead that the presence of numerous accidentals demonstrated to the reader his belief that Warbeck was in fact Prince Richard. Monsarrat argues that Ford frequently employed the technique of capitalizing names and key words throughout his writing career; in *Perkin Warbeck*, Ford persistently capitalizes words linked to Warbeck's royalty. If accepted, Monsarrat's claims have considerable ramifications for the criticism on the play. The essay suggests that Ford, unable unambiguously to express his belief that Warbeck was really the king (given the sensitive political climate), articulated his belief covertly. Monsarrat ends playfully: 'the play Ford probably wanted to write might have been called *The Tragedy of Richard Duke of York* or even *The Tragedy of King Richard the Fourth*' (p. 457).

Two articles, printed in 2014 but not reviewed in the last issue, deserve inclusion in this review. In ' "High Designe": Beaumont and Fletcher Illustrated' (*ELR* 44[2014] 275–327) and 'Dramatic Pilcrows' (*PBSA* 108[2014] 413–52), Claire M.L. Bourne offers fascinating new ways of examining the effects of Renaissance printing practice. In the former, Bourne argues that the illustrations on editions of Beaumont and Fletcher plays are 'indicative of a publishing strategy aimed at adapting into print a new kind of suspenseful, plot-driven drama' (p. 276) heavily associated with Beaumont and Fletcher plays like *Philaster*, *A King and No King*, and *The Maid's Tragedy*. While these plays were evidently theatrically successful, there was no guarantee that they would have the same success in printed form, so publishers aimed to create suspense by including ambiguous illustrations that 'were designed to operate in conjunction with the plays' (p. 278) while also resisting the early disclosure of the plays' surprising resolutions. The playbooks attempt to replicate the pleasure that might be derived from the orchestrated confusion of Beaumont and Fletcher plays. This insightful essay shows how well attuned publishers were to the kinds of innovation taking place in the playhouses. While the article's principal achievement is to illuminate practices of printing and reading, it is also an excellent example of what might be gained by thinking about theatricality alongside the materiality of the text.

Bourne shows similar skill in 'Dramatic Pilcrows', an essay that focuses on the surprising power and versatility of typographical features. Bourne proposes that pilcrows and other special characters 'afforded printers a typographical means by which to render dramatic form and its effects legible in print' (p. 413). So, just as the illustrations in Beaumont and Fletcher texts aim to re-create something of the experience of attending a Beaumont and Fletcher play, so pilcrows create effects analogous to theatrical performance. So, for example, the 1565 first edition of *Gorboduc* uses pilcrows to help make visible to readers 'the play's status as classically-inspired, five-act tragedy' (p. 448), while the second quarto of John Heywood's *The Play of Love* [1548?]

uses pilcrows, fleurons, and manicules to create 'a typographic program for distinguishing speech, character, and action' (p. 437). Bourne's careful and detailed readings demonstrate thorough bibliographical skills, but they also show great theatrical imagination. Although published in a bibliographical journal, 'Dramatic Pilcrows' makes arguments that will be of interest to theatre historians and literary scholars.

## 2. Theatre History

The field of Renaissance theatre history continues to be thrown open further with the aid of the digital humanities, and a number of recent studies have benefited from the resources generated by this movement, perhaps most notably Matthew Steggle's *Digital Humanities and the Lost Drama of Early Modern England: Ten Case Studies*. This exciting research, which Steggle describes as situated at the intersection of historicized theatre studies and the digital humanities, explores ten lost plays in the period 1580–1642, providing new information about the content of these pieces. Steggle argues that recovering the accurate interpretation of the titles in question allows a new and innovative understanding of their subject matter. His research relies heavily upon the computer database Early English Books Online Text Creation Partnership, and the University of Toronto's Records of Early English Drama project. But he explains that his study is also 'in dialogue with both . . . current major projects looking at lost plays' (p. 6)—the *Lost Plays Database*, the website set up by David McInnis and Roslyn L. Knutson, and Martin Wiggins's catalogue of *British Drama 1533–1642*. In addition to the information now available thanks to the advances made possible by these incredible resources, Steggle credits the rise in study of lost plays with the increased attention given to repertory studies, as well as a turn away from the playscript-centric focus of years past, towards a broader interest in Renaissance theatrical culture as a whole, mining three crucial pieces of primary evidence: Henslowe's *Diary*, the *Office-Book* of Sir Henry Herbert, Master of the Revels 1623–73, and the Stationers' Register. As Steggle explains, his study raises theoretical questions about the conceptualization of lost plays and how to investigate them. Identifying that current approaches tend to organize them by author, repertory, or genre, Steggle distinguishes his study by focusing on textual criticism and exegesis. Indeed, his ten case studies are a pathway into a massive area of research, as the number of lost plays has long been underestimated, and now stands at roughly 2,500, with only 744 identifiable as lost. For instance, of the 280 plays identified in Henslowe's diary, only around eighty survive. He asserts, however, that the techniques utilized to conduct his research are not limited to the study of lost plays, but also have implications for the study of extant texts.

Lawrence Manley and Sally-Beth MacLean offer compelling insight into the London commercial theatre of the late 1580s and early 1590s. Uniting traditional theatre history narratives with the work of more recent trends, which have adopted patron and company-centric approaches to interpreting early modern plays, they make valuable contributions to repertory studies and offer insights into lost plays, in their comprehensive work *Lord Strange's Men and Their Plays*. Though they state that one of the central motives of the book is to establish connections between Shakespeare and Strange's Men and their influence on the playwright—indeed, they suggest that this may have been the company, or one of the companies, for whom Shakespeare acted and wrote during his early career—they also aim to provide a full view of the wider theatrical landscape. In so doing, they establish that from Lord Strange's Men 'passed the key theatrical innovators' (p. 2) who would have a profound impact on future decades of Renaissance theatre. Specifically and crucially, they identify the company as the source from which two of the major troupes of the period stemmed in June 1594. It hosted many of the eventual partners of the Lord Chamberlain's Men (later the King's Men), as well as Edward Alleyn, who became a principal figure of the Admiral's Men, another tremendously successful company, which likewise eventually enjoyed royal patronage as Prince Henry's Men, starting in 1603. The work also explores the relationship between theatrical success and professional stability, proposing that Strange's Men, with their impressive and unprecedented six court performances in the winter season of 1591/2, may have been the first company to 'attempt long-term residence and extended daily repertory in London' (p. 3). With such assertions they propose an answer to the perennial question of theatre historians—when did theatre companies become stabilized in Elizabethan London? Further still, the book connects the company and its repertory to the political and theatrical interests of its patron, Ferdinando Stanley. Indeed, it reveals that Stanley and his wife Lady Alice Spencer were actually part of a long family tradition of theatrical patronage, forcing a revaluation of the impetus for aristocratic patronage as a technical convenience to negotiate the 1572 Act of the Punishement of Vacabondes. They identify that the company's repertory of blank verse drama possessed a decidedly literary and learned style that distinguished it from the styles of theatrical artisans, and that the plays themselves addressed contemporary international political affairs of concern to Stanley. Manley and MacLean's thorough and important study contributes to a greater understanding of the workings of the wider theatrical business by shedding new light on the relationship between this acting company, its plays, and its patron.

Eoin Price makes significant contributions to the areas of theatre, book, and intellectual history in his impressive study, *'Public' and 'Private' Playhouses in Renaissance England: The Politics of Publication*. This valuable and comprehensive work engages an extensive range of evidence, including anti-theatrical writing, Privy Council correspondence, royal proclamations, and title pages, as well as the role of dramatists, theatre impresarios, booksellers, and legislators, to reconsider the meaning of the critical but complicated terms 'public' and 'private' in relation to the business of the London playhouses at this time. Revising entrenched narratives surrounding these terms, Price's study reveals that, while it was not uncommon to refer to outdoor commercial drama as 'public' in the sixteenth century, there is no evidence that performance in indoor commercial playhouses was in turn referred to as 'private', though the word had referred to domestic performances and academic drama. Indeed, the book tracks the emergence of the word 'private' in this context, investigating how it eventually came to be used to refer to indoor commercial performance in the seventeenth century. It argues that the complex process by which the term entered the wider theatrical discourse was due to a variety of social, political, and theatrical forces influencing the culture of the English theatre. In the process of negotiating and reconsidering the 'ideological baggage' (p. 3) associated with these two terms, the work also makes valuable contributions to wider conversations about the early modern English print market and the variety of ways in which bookmakers participated in promoting the play-texts they produced, offering insights into this emerging trade. The comprehensive yet detailed study covers a chronological range broader than most, devoting attention to areas frequently neglected by Renaissance theatre historians. It begins with the early Elizabethan period, exploring the beginnings of the London commercial theatre, before moving to analysis of the indoor theatres of the 1570s and 1580s, and examining the meaning of 'private' as it related to the second wave of indoor boy companies. It also considers the Caroline theatre, which, as Price describes, is all too often forgotten 'as a barren, post-Shakespearean landscape' (p. 7), and investigates the increased use of the word 'private' as it appeared on the title pages of indoor theatre playbooks of the late 1620s. The study crucially extends beyond the commonly used terminal date of Renaissance drama, 1642, concluding with an analysis of the under-studied period between the closing of the theatres and the Restoration, identifying that performance of Renaissance plays continued at commercial playhouses during this time, albeit illegally. Price's careful and detailed study introduces nuanced ways of understanding these critical terms and their relationship to the development of early modern theatre. This book is also considered in Section 3(a) of this chapter.

This was a bumper year for Martin Wiggins's ten-volume *British Drama 1533–1642*, as we welcomed the fifth and sixth instalments of the catalogue. These volumes, covering the years 1603–8 and 1609–16, arguably span the richest period of the series, and it is perhaps fitting that they stand at the very centre. Volume 5 begins with the unattributed St John's College, Oxford, drama *Narcissus* (entry 1380). Though dated to January of the year, Wiggins identifies that the prologue curiously refers to the performers as 'the King's own lovely subjects', which they would not have been until the queen's death two months later. He proposes that, perhaps, 'the point is to underline the burlesque qualities of the play by suggesting that it is fifty years old' (p. 1), or alternatively, and more likely, that the text was transcribed sometime after the queen's death on 24 March. The 1605 *Four Plays in One* (entry 1484) immediately precedes *A Yorkshire Tragedy* (entry 1484a), attributed to Thomas Middleton. Wiggins explores multiple theories about the existence of the two pieces and their relationship to one another, suggesting that though *A Yorkshire Tragedy* was printed separately from *Four Plays in One*, the reason for its brevity is perhaps that it was presented within an anthology by four scriptwriters. Wiggins believes it noteworthy that the play seems to have been written around the same time that another King's Men play, Shakespeare's *King Lear* (entry 1486), seems to have been delayed—perhaps because of plague closure of the London theatres, or because 'it was simply an uncommonly tough nut for a writer to crack, both intellectually and emotionally' (p. 253). Either way, it possibly explains the brevity of Middleton's tragedy. The volume also includes the lost Whitefriars play, *Torrismount* (entry 1561) of 1607, the evidence for which survives in the articles of agreement between shareholders of the Children of the King's Revels, quoted in the Chancery suit of George Andrew v. Martin Slater of 1609. Volume 5 concludes with the King's Men settled at the Blackfriars with Shakespeare's *Coriolanus* (entry 1589).

Volume 6 opens with the hitherto completely unknown play of 1609, *Cadmus* (entry 1590), which survives in a manuscript that may have been owned by Sir Henry Lee or a member of his family. The final entry of the same year is the partially surviving *Challenger for Meliadus' Combat at Barriers* (entry 1600). Like *Cadmus*, it too was previously unknown. The unattributed tournament challenge was issued on 31 December in the Presence Chamber at Whitehall Palace to an audience that included King James I, Queen Anne, and, presumably, Prince Henry. The volume also sheds considerable light on the previously obscure chronology of the middle period of John Fletcher's canon, including the reassigning of the date of his and Francis Beaumont's *The Scornful Lady* (entry 1626) from its traditional designation of 1613 to *circa* 1610. Fletcher, Philip Massinger, and an unknown collaborator's *Beggars' Bush* (entry 1799) is also shifted to 1616 from the previously designated year of 1622. The final entry of the sixth volume is the 1616 Oxford academic comedy *Mercurius Rusticans* (The Student in the Country) (entry 1811), which may usefully be collocated with *Work for Jupiter* (entry 1791), another academic piece of either Cambridge or, most likely, Oxford. An account of the performance of *Mercurius Rusticans*, by either John or Henry Sellar, recalls that the actors 'were so often out', or as Wiggins believes, they frequently forgot their lines, likening the actual performers to the very 'country bumpkins' (p. 560) they were impersonating. As Wiggins has demonstrated remarkably throughout his catalogues thus far, the series has provided users with the ability to see the familiar in a new way, and to see the familiar chronologically collocated with the unfamiliar.

Roger Clegg and Lucie Skeaping combine careful archival research with practical application for performers today in their book, *Singing Simpkin and Other Bawdy Jigs: Musical Comedy on the Shakespearean Stage. Scripts, Music, and Context*, which sheds light on the evolving history of the popular theatrical jig from the late sixteenth century to the Restoration. Clegg and Skeaping identify how, from its beginnings in the late 1570s as a brief simple satirical ballad, sung and danced by a clown to a popular tune, the jig evolved into a short sung drama, featured as an afterpiece to the main play, which was made famous largely by the talent of the clowns and actors such as Richard Tarlton, William Kemp, John Singer, John Shanks, and William Rowley, among others. Indeed, they credit Tarlton as 'London's first jigging clown' (p. 15). The book includes an extensive section which tracks the evolution of the jig, suggesting that its development was in part influenced by fashions in dance and early drama from the Continent, as seen in two of the surviving scripts, *Singing Simpkin* and *The Jig of St Denys' Ghost*. They also identify that, perhaps unsurprisingly, tension existed between the overwhelming personalities of the jig-makers and the playwrights. Clegg and Skeaping then consider the life of the jig throughout the period, exploring its presence during the Interregnum, as well as its post-Restoration life. This section is followed by a survey of nine jigs, which are, as far as possible, reunited with their original tunes. Each jig is presented usefully with its own brief introduction, including a synopsis, information regarding its provenance, and analysis of source material. The text of the jig is then presented with the tune, sometimes multiple ones. A substantial section then follows, broken into three subsections—Text, Music, and Dance—in which the individual jigs are analysed in relation to what they reveal about their nature and form, and which includes practical staging information for those wishing to stage them today. This incredibly rich resource, thoroughly and extensively researched, makes a valuable contribution to theatre history by ensuring that these dramatic works receive due attention, and are not overshadowed by the plays but situated in relation to the other forms of entertainment from the period. Clegg and Skeaping are sure to caution, however, that this book is not to be viewed as a manual for how to re-create jigs, as there is simply not enough surviving evidence to ensure exact accuracy. With that said, they encourage potential practitioners and performers to adopt the same creativity and ephemerality that characterized these popular entertainments on the early modern stage.

The year also saw important investigation into early modern women's performance and participation in the theatrical culture of the London commercial stage, with the contributions to a special issue of *Shakespeare Bulletin*, introduced by Clare McManus and Lucy Munro in their essay, 'Renaissance Women's Performance and the Dramatic Canon: Theater History, Evidence, and Narratives' (*ShakB* 33[2015] 1–7). The vital research presented in this issue, and outlined in McManus and Munro's introduction, addresses long-held assumptions about the gendering of the theatre at this time. It seeks to widen understanding of women's contribution to the making of Renaissance theatrical culture, and the roles they played to shape the work that appeared on its stages. In doing so, the studies in this issue reveal that women were heavily influential in a variety of ways. Some of the articles from this special issue are also discussed from the perspective of literary criticism in Sections 3(a) and 3(c) of this chapter.

In the first article, 'The Ongoing Exploration of Women and Performance in Early Modern England: Evidences, Issues, and Questions' (*ShakB* 33[2015] 9–31), James Stokes asserts that though the records reveal numerous accounts of women's participation in performance in the wider culture, the ideologies of moralist reformers had a 'strangling impact' (p. 28) on female involvement on the Elizabethan, Jacobean, and Caroline stage, which has continued to obscure the picture of this period. He suggests that the appearance of female performance on the commercial stage after 1660 was not so much unforeseen as it was a logical conclusion to the suppression of the radical views of anti-theatricalists. Andy Kesson follows with an exploration of the centrality of female characters to the works of John Lyly, calling for a reconsideration of the playwright's reputation among scholars as a sycophant to Queen Elizabeth I, in his article, '"It is a pity you are not a woman": John Lyly and the Creation of Woman' (*ShakB* 33[2015] 33–47). Kesson argues that the frequency with which Lyly places powerful female characters on stage in significant roles was not an attempt to curry favour with the monarch, but an example of the dramatist's importance to the development of the representation of women on the stage, eschewed by his contemporaries, as well as the sexism of the literary canon. The next piece, by Pamela Allen Brown, considers Thomas Kyd's characterization of Bel-Imperia in *The Spanish Tragedy* as a strong, plot-advancing woman, as well as the casting of her in the play-within-the-play, *Solimon and Perseda*, in relation to Continental performance practices, which included the use of female actresses in dramatic roles, in her article 'Anatomy of an Actress: Bel-Imperia as Tragic Diva' (*ShakB* 33[2015] 49–65). Brown draws attention to the character's 'theatrical virtuosity' (p. 55), arguing that Kyd created this sensational character as an icon, or diva, of boldness and revenge. Next, Sophie Tomlinson explores what Rachel Poulsen identifies as 'the actress effect' of the Continental baroque theatre, and the paradoxical notion 'of the actress in a theater marked by the physical absence of women' (p. 79) in her article, 'The Actress and Baroque Aesthetic Effects in Renaissance Drama' (*ShakB* 33[2015] 67–82). Roberta Barker then considers how boy players of the Renaissance stage and the aristocratic female performers of court masques may have influenced and affected each other's techniques, in her article 'The "Play-Boy", the Female Performer, and the Art of Portraying a Lady' (*ShakB* 33[2015] 83–97). She concludes that for both sets of actors the performance of each was an art that had to be learned and practised. Following Clare McManus's Shakespeare-focused article, ' "Sing it like poor Barbary": *Othello* and Early Modern Women's Performance' (*ShakB* 33[2015] 99–120), Natasha Korda provides an afterword to the issue (*ShakB* 33[2015] 121–8) in which she suggests that the essays gathered there gesture towards a 'newly conceived canon' (p. 125), which draws upon both canonical and non-canonical plays that shape and reshape each other, as well as the canon's gendering.

## 3. Criticism

### (a) General

In 2015 a number of monographs and publications approached the study of Renaissance and early modern drama in fresh and exciting ways. To start, Monica Matei-Chesnoiu's *Geoparsing Early Modern English Drama* uses the geoparsing technique in computer science in order to provide spatial co-ordinates to the geographical references found throughout early modern play-texts. This multidisciplinary approach enables the scholar to offer a new perspective on how the environment is both represented and responded to within the drama. In the introduction to the book, Matei-Chesnoiu explains that 'between 1550 and 1630, geographic space in early modern Europe ... was subject to a considerable social, economic, and political reformulation' (p. 1), highlighting the specific value of her research into the drama of this period. One of the chief ambitions of the monograph is to explore 'the influence of early modern geographic theories and cartographic practices on the playwrights discussed and the way these authors disrupted theatrical space to suit their dramatic purposes in order to represent a specific situational triangulation' (p. 9). In her next chapter, the author looks at both ancient and Renaissance geographical commentaries with the purpose of demonstrating 'the rejuvenating strength that ancient texts inflected into the fabric of early modern geography, and their enabling capacity to become a channel of communication among scholars, a useful tool in education, and a mode of dialogical thinking' (p. 27). Matei-Chesnoiu's following chapter progresses on to Ovid's influence on early modern English literature within the context of literary geologies, before early modern drama begins to be discussed in chapter 4. The focus of this fourth chapter is on hydrography, in which the author stresses the importance of rivers 'to the identities and economies of ancient and early modern societies' (p. 81), and discusses plays such as the anonymous *Caesar's Revenge* and *The Tragedy of Nero*, as well as *The Tragedy of Julia Agrippina* by Thomas May. For May's play, Matei-Chesnoiu thinks about the symbolic nature of geography and explores how 'the Rhine reflects the corruption of power in the hands of imperial individuals, as opposed to the relative freedoms of the republican period' (p. 91). In chapter 5, the book moves on to what Matei-Chesnoiu calls 'cities of the sea' and concentrates particularly on Constantinople as a site of mobility and cosmopolitanism, discussing plays including *The Tragical Reign of Selimus, Emperour of the Turkes*, attributed to Robert Greene. In this chapter the author shows how 'ichnographic perspectives of Constantinople as a city of the sea are dramatized in a multi-temporal and multi-spatial frame' (p. 164). Her penultimate chapter concerns island routes and incorporates a picture of the *Cosmographiae Universalis* to illustrate how the island 'was commonly represented as either as a place of corruption and dislocation or as a social and political utopia' (p. 136). Later in the chapter, in her discussion of the *Jew of Malta*, Matei-Chesnoiu argues effectively that the Malta of the play 'highlights the malleability of the archipelago space, the ease with which this space could be rearranged in different ways, as well as its ambiguity and openness to relocation' (p. 147). The final chapter of the monograph addresses the conclusions of the research, noting how, 'By extending into the geographical referent, drama transcends the simply aesthetic function and shows how it can actually participate in and inflect the history and cultural selfhood of the places in question' (pp. 163–4). While this is a complicated subject, Matei-Chesnoiu's use of metaphor and clear explanations help to break it down for those unfamiliar with geoparsing. In *Geoparsing Early Modern English Drama* she makes an original and intelligent contribution to the field.

Also focusing on literary geologies is Gavin Hollis's *The Absence of America: The London Stage 1576–1642*, which tackles the question of why America, as a contemporary subject of plot or dialogue (or as theatrical setting), features so little in early modern play-texts and performances. Hollis begins by acknowledging that, while there *are* allusions to the Americas, these 'tend to be fleeting and draw more on generalized associations with the New World . . . than specific associations with the English mission' (p. 2). One of the principal endeavours of the monograph is to explore how the experiences of London theatre-goers allow us to perceive their image of America and the

Virginia colony; the author argues that this picture was 'often slanderous and condemnatory, and, as it were, anti-American' (p. 3). The four chapters of the book are divided into two major sections of literary analysis: the first is 'Adventurers and Cannibals', in which Hollis concentrates on the Virginia Company adventurer; his second section, 'Indians and Londoners', addresses characters such as Virginian Indians. Hollis lucidly explains to the reader the broad cultural responses to America and the New World, and guides them step by step to show how this influenced early modern theatre. He explores a number of plays, from Dekker and Middleton's *The Roaring Girl* and Massinger and Fletcher's *The Sea Voyage* to Massinger's *The City Madam* and the anonymous play *The Fatal Marriage*. In the afterword to the monograph, he makes further observations about how the 'Virginian' character developed over time, progressing into the drama of Aphra Behn. The images reproduced from early modern literature add a fascinating insight to these contemporary perceptions of America. In this meticulously researched book, Hollis makes a vital and enjoyable contribution to a neglected topic of academic scholarship.

In *Architectural Involutions: Writing, Staging, and Building Space, c.1435–1650* Mimi Yiu broadly explores ideas of space in early modern drama, from the physical to the psychic, providing fresh new insight into theatre and theatre history. Over the six chapters of this engrossing and enthusiastically written monograph Yiu uses a range of evidence on architectural writing and practice in order to demonstrate the cultural impact on interiority in early modern thought as well as on the stage. In chapter 1, she explores how the Italian architect Leon Battista Alberti 'redirects the Vitruvian dialogue with his concept of a façade . . . an aesthetic "face" that makes the building cohere and thus signify on the public stage' (p. 9). Yiu then moves on in her following chapter to discuss how architecture performed a dramatic change both to the inside and outside of spaces in early modern England (p. 10). Shakespeare's *Hamlet* is the focus of chapter 3, which examines how spatial interiority 'becomes complicit in staging the human psyche' (p. 12), and argues that 'Hamlet's prolix madness not only prevents listeners from mapping his interiority, but also distances him from his desired identity' (p. 108). Yiu's fourth chapter continues with *Hamlet* but also turns to Great Britain, 'the center of an aspiring empire', as a space which influenced drama in the early modern period (p. 13). Here, she poses the question of what 'constitutes an inscriptural space in early modern England'. Moving on to Jonson, in her next chapter she is concerned with the play *Epicœne* and its architect Morose, who, she argues, 'creates a paternal icon of resistance to London's evolving identity' as an urban hermit 'whose hatred of noise supplies a pretext of living in the most enclosed, artificial house' (p. 183). The final chapter discusses Dutch artist Samuel van Hoogstraten and his trunk-like perspective box, painted 'to resemble the inside of an ordinary house' (p. 14), with its views through doorways playfully capturing an interior greater than the surface of the box—highlighting the illusiveness of space. This is a project which, as Yiu remarks, raises 'serious questions about the writing of space and subjectivity' (p. 209), and she uses this box to draw together the conclusions of all her chapters. This fresh monograph offers striking new analysis of dramatic space in the early modern period, and contains a number of fascinating and helpful panels and diagrams for the reader which clarify and punctuate its argument. Robert Henke's *Poverty and Charity in Early Modern Theater and Performance* provides an effective analysis of poverty and charity in drama using a wealth of resources from cultural history, such as German and Latin begging catalogues and evidence of popular songs performed in Italian piazzas. In his first chapter, Henke focuses on 'the range and complexity of responses to the poor in Italy and England, as well as across Europe' (p. 6), and he uses chapter 2 to explain the culture that shaped Shakespeare's 'Poor Tom' and its background in German texts of the fourteenth century. In his next chapter, Henke uses the emergence of printed literature in the early fifteenth century to explore how ideas about poverty, hunger, and economic inequality were disseminated in the form of pamphlets and songs and thus shaped both performances and cultural responses. He begins chapter 4 by observing that 'No early modern playwright addressed the problem of poverty and hunger in such direct, sustained, and complex ways as did the Paduan Angelo Beolco, known as Ruzante' (p. 84). In this chapter, he explores exactly how these plays were staged 'between official policy and actual practice, between authoritarian discourse and lived attitude' (p. 84), and compares Ruzante's plays with those of Shakespeare—thus providing a context of representations of poverty and charity in drama throughout Europe. In his fifth chapter, Henke moves on to the performances of *commedia dell'arte* troupes, and argues that the presence of travelling mendicant orders in Italy led to the *commedia dell'arte* inheriting a culture 'in which poverty, begging, itinerancy, and a certain disposition to perform degradation were in the air' (p. 109). His final chapter addresses the plays of Shakespeare, with a particular focus on *2 Henry VI*. The conclusion is used to reflect back over the cultural constructions of poverty through the ages and highlight the ways in which they are still relevant to us today. This is an engaging and illuminating body of research on a fascinating topic.

Poverty is also explored in *At Work in the Early Modern English Theatre: Valuing Labor* by Matthew Kendrick, which examines changing socio-economic perspectives of labour and how these can be seen in the play-texts and performances of early modern drama. In particular, Kendrick observes that 'most economic criticism focuses in literary representations of the circulation of commodities and money' and therefore examines 'how plays represent and evaluate the laborers underpinning this new economy' (p. xi). In his first chapter, Kendrick argues and explains how the stage was 'especially sensitive to changes in the way labor was understood' (p. xiv) and that in direct and indirect ways it gave rise to 'an early manifestation of working-class identity and resistance' (p. 2). Moving on to his second chapter, he then looks at the plays of Chapman, Jonson, and Marston in order to discuss how the representations of labourers seem to 'defy classification' (p. 33), thus reflecting contemporary changes in economic conditions. In chapter 3 he focuses on Beaumont's *The Knight of the Burning Pestle* which, he argues, offers a representation of 'the imbrication of labor and acting, depicting the stage as a point of resistance against perceived abuses within London's guild system' (p. 73). The following chapter then examines Dekker's *The Shoemaker's*

*Holiday* and Rowley's *A Shoemaker, a Gentleman*, which considers representations of aristocratic responses to labourers on the stage. Noting that labour
was taken for granted by the aristocracy, Kendrick discusses the 'aristocratic
disdain' (p. 93) for labour in Dekker's work, and uses this material to help
explain 'why London's laboring population, from vagrants to apprentices and
freemen, was attracted to the theater' (p. 93). Kendrick's final chapter
discusses the plays of Shakespeare who, he argues, 'captures the theatre's
transitional and mixed economy' better than anyone else (p. 129). The book
successfully delivers a complex understanding of the subject of labour on the
early modern stage and fully explores its topic across a number of disciplines.

   *Painted Devils, Siren Tongues: The Semiotic Universe of Jacobean Tragedy*,
by Justyna Laura Galant, is an accomplished monograph providing a fresh
perspective on the various ways in which meaning is created in Jacobean
tragedy. Across its four chapters, Galant explores the canonical tragedies of
Webster and Middleton as well as other, less well known, texts. In her initial
chapter, Galant first turns her attention to Middleton's *Revenger's Tragedy*
and examines what she terms the 'permutations' of revenge, noting that the
most complex semiotic entity in the play is the Revenger, for he 'undergoes the
most changes while employing his primary *modus operandi* consisting
principally in catering for the semiotic tastes or needs of the play's villains'
(p. 21). Moving on to *The True Tragedy of Herod and Antipater* by Gervase
Markham and William Samson, Galant focuses again on a protagonist, whom
she contrasts with Middleton's Revenger. In particular, she notes that, for
Antipater, 'the aesthetic joy at refashioning the dominant order is found not in
its successful imitation but in its direct and thorough negation' (p. 35). These
two plays are then compared with the anonymous *Lust's Dominion or the
Lascivious Queen*. For this play, Galant looks again at the motivations of the
central protagonist, and also considers how 'blackness' is used to create
meaning. The second chapter, 'Playing with Sentiments', first explores the uses
of mimicry in Middleton and Rowley's *The Changeling* before moving on to
Middleton's *Women Beware Women* to look in detail at the language of love,
game, and bargain. Galant's analysis of *The Maid's Tragedy* focuses on the
language of grief and romance. In her third chapter, Galant writes on *Thierry
and Theodoret* by Francis Beaumont and John Fletcher, as well as *The Wonder
of Women* by John Marston. Here, she turns her attention to the double
semiosis of female nature and carnivalesque justice. Chapter 4 is on
topographies of possible worlds, and explores the semiosis of private worlds
in *The Duchess of Malfi*, in addition to other plays. *Painted Devils, Siren
Tongues* delivers an effective analysis of meaning-creation in Jacobean drama,
in addition to providing a critical framework for studying semiotics in play-
texts and performances.

   *Metropolitan Tragedy: Genre, Justice, and the City in Early Modern England*,
by Marissa Greenberg, is another title from this year that is concerned with
geography. In this case, Greenberg provides a detailed study of urban
geography in early modern drama as well as subjects such as law, justice, and
punishment, using a wealth of historical sources as well as sources from visual
culture. The book is the first to study early modern tragedy as an urban genre,
for Greenberg notes that 'Metropolitan tragedy—even when seemingly

"about" sixteenth- and seventeenth-century London—often speaks to urban experiences that exceed its own temporality' (p. 139). Her first chapter discusses topography, murder, and domestic tragedy in the anonymous *A Warning for Fair Women* and Robert Yarington's *Two Lamentable Tragedies*, and argues that these plays 'locate murder and execution in a recognizable cityscape, thereby constructing a fantasy of London as chartable, exposed to view, and hence resistant to crime' (p. 17). She then progresses on to argue, in her second chapter, that Shakespeare's *Titus Andronicus* 'reveals how revenge tragedy invites a scrutiny of the implications of London's rise to national and international prominence' (p. 18). Chapter 3 is on the metropolitan tragedies of later Stuart England, with a particular focus on how the plays of this period 'disclose rising concerns about England's *camera regis* as the locus of royal prerogative and popular resistance' (p. 18). The final chapter is on the tragic closet drama *Samson Agonistes* by Milton. Here, the author discusses how the Great Fire of London is presented as an aural experience in the literature of the time in order to examine how *Samson Agonistes* 'registers sound's effects on audiences' (p. 110). In this monograph, Greenberg accomplishes an enjoyable and thorough exploration of early modern play-texts, the City of London, and even modern performances of early drama.

*Writing the Monarch in Jacobean England: Jonson, Donne, Shakespeare and the Works of King James*, by Jane Rickard, is a monograph which suggests that 'royal cultural "influence" is a matter of interaction rather than imposition' and recognizes that there are 'important continuities between James's relationship with literary culture in England, and between his "literary" and "political" activities' (p. 8). The book is split into three sections. Rickard first focuses on James, Jonson, and the Jacobean court. In her first chapter, she addresses the role of the court poet in the works of Jonson and King James. On Jonson, she notes that through his work he suggests that poets 'have an authority comparable to that of kings', and she observes that Jonson's literary celebration of King James 'is at the same time a carefully calculated act of self-promotion' (p. 59). In her next chapter Rickard continues with Jonson and King James and analyses their discussions of state affairs, such as the outbreak of war in Europe in 1618, foreign policy, and the relationship with Spain, utilizing both play-texts and poetry. The second section of the book concentrates on the politics of religion in Jacobean England in the works of both King James and Donne. However, it is in the third section that the theatre becomes the central focus, even though drama is considered over the chapters of the previous two sections. The single chapter in this section focuses on King James and Shakespeare, and discusses how *Measure for Measure* is not only 'acutely aware of the complex issues of control, agency, perception, interpretation and trust' but also actively 'dramatises the implications of his king's determination to control the ways he is represented and perceived' (p. 210). Shakespeare's response to James's work is also discussed. Overall, this is a well-argued book which covers Jonson, Donne, Shakespeare, and the works of King James over a range of genres, from drama and court masques to polemic and poetry, providing a thorough understanding of 'writing the monarch' in this period of early modern history. It is a valuable and engaging contribution to the field.

Rickard's book is also reviewed from a Jonsonian perspective in Section 3(c) below.

Michelle M. Dowd's *The Dynamics of Inheritance on the Shakespearean Stage* provides a thorough explanation of patrilineal inheritance and its effect upon the social order in the early modern period, and uses play-text and performance evidence to discuss the role of drama in shaping the cultural understanding of inheritance. In addition to Shakespeare, Dowd also focuses on the works of Webster, Jonson, and others over the five chapters of her monograph. Dowd's initial chapter is concerned with titles and estates, and thus 'how patrilineal inheritance was understood as a spatial story' (p. 33); it goes on to use the drama in support of her claims, discussing plays such as Jonson's *Staple of News* and Thomas Middleton's *Michaelmas Term*. This chapter is also helpfully illustrated with maps and armorial bearings. The second chapter is on Webster's *Duchess of Malfi* and the problems encountered by women, in particular the issues posed by a widow remarrying. Yet while this is the case in drama, Dowd also clarifies that 'wives and mothers exerted far more influence over property and inheritance in early modern England than scholars had previously assumed' (p. 81). Chapter 3 is on travel, displacement, and the prodigal son, and discusses Shakespeare's *Henry IV* as well as the plays of Inglend, Jonson, Fletcher, and Heywood. For these plays, the author discusses how the prodigality of sons affects the 'proper propagation of lineage' (p. 133). The fourth chapter is on Shakespeare and George Wilkin's *Pericles* and the familial responses to the lack of a male heir. In her final chapter, Dowd investigates Jonson's *Volpone* and *Epicœne* and how the playwright explores 'the ways in which the growth of England's urban economy demanded new conceptual approaches to inheritance' (p. 210). One of the general findings of Dowd's research is that early modern drama uses cultural fantasies of wealth transfer rather than the social realities, and these fantasies 'find vibrant expression in the realm of fictional drama, where what is imaginable takes precedence over what is actual or even historically possible' (p. 11). Dowd explains that this was done in order to make sense of the social and economic changes that were taking place. This is an accomplished and enjoyable piece of research.

*'Public' and 'Private' Playhouses in Renaissance England: The Politics of Publication*, by Eoin Price, is a shorter monograph published as part of the Palgrave Pivot series. The central focus of the book is to understand the public and the private spaces of theatrical performance and to use this fresh interpretation of performance spaces to shed new light on early modern drama. Dividing his chapters up by specific periods and events in theatre history, in the first section Price covers what he describes as 'public', 'private', and 'common' stages over the period 1559–1600 and analyses the implications of these terms and how they could be applied to the theatre in that time-frame. The second chapter focuses again on the private, and attempts to dispel the idea that 'private' performances of drama were 'primarily used to circumvent censorship' (p. 7). The plays discussed in this chapter include George Chapman's lost play *The Old Joiner of Aldgate* and Dekker's *Blurt Master Constable*. On *The Old Joiner of Aldgate*, Price examines its controversy, 'because performances of it at the St Paul's playhouse ran concurrently with a

court case which it was also satirising', which led to concern that the play 'might be part of an attempt to influence the ruling' (p. 31). This context of the performance of the play is part of an interesting discussion by Price regarding the private and public natures of the play, and he explores the idea 'that "private" could be used to evade attempts at "public" censure' (p. 31). The third and final chapter of the monograph addresses the 'public' and 'private' with regard to the indoor theatres between 1625 and 1640. The author covers the previous research on identifying 'public' and 'private' theatres and offers a fresh perspective on these distinctions. This monograph provides a complex, nuanced, and comprehensive analysis of early modern playhouses and makes a valuable contribution to the field.

Moving on to articles, in 'Allegorical Action and Elizabethan Staging' (*SEL* 55[2015] 391–402) Alan Dessen examines the ways in which allegory continued to take a role in plays beyond 1590, despite Spivak's assertion that there was a sharp decline in allegorical drama on the popular stage at the time. Dessen focuses on what he terms 'allegory in action, wherein such figures somehow enter into the play's dominant verisimilar world' (p. 392), and discusses how the character Honesty in *A Knack to Know a Knave* allegorizes the action of the play itself. The author also focuses on a number of other plays, as well as considering the different ways in which allegory can function in drama. For example, in addition to what is apparent to us today as allegory in action, Dessen also looks at 'actions less visible to us but resonant for the original playgoers and therefore only recovered through recourse to theater history' (p. 393). In this section, he makes mention of Robert Greene's *Friar Bacon and Friar Bungay*, Thomas Lodge and Greene's *A Looking-Glass for London and England*, and Ben Jonson's *The Staple of News* in addition to others, and goes on to speculate on how staging can affect both the play's meaning and our interpretation. This is an intelligent and thought-provoking article.

Andy Kesson's insightful essay, ' "It is a pity you are not a woman": John Lyly and the Creation of Woman' (*ShakB* 33[2015] 33–47), discusses how Lyly's plays, which 'regularly call attention to the queen and the elite women in the audience', also marginalize female characters (p. 33). In this article, Kesson provides a fresh new perspective on female roles, arguing that 'feminist and queer scholarship has overlooked or underestimated Lyly's work because of his reputation as a conservative sycophant to an all-powerful queen' (p. 33). He first turns his attention to representations of the female body in Lyly's first play, *Campaspe*, and discusses how 'Alexander's love for Campaspe is repeatedly expressed in terms of his power over her' (p. 36). He also considers the meaning of Apelles's portraiture of Campaspe, since the audience comes to learn 'that the painter's portfolio is entirely composed of images of rape and sexual abuse' (p. 38). Kesson then moves on to *The Woman in the Moon*, a play that he argues 'explicitly subordinates men to women on both the heavenly and human planes' (p. 40), and focuses on how it 'represents a stage investigation of female subjectivity' (pp. 39–40). This is an enlightening article that argues persuasively that 'Lyly has much to offer the history of women onstage' and sees his displacement from those narratives as 'itself a sign of the sexist history of literary canonization' (p. 42).

In 'The Performance of Divine Providence on the Early Modern Stage: Tumbling Canvases and History Plays' (*Bulletin of the Comediantes* 67:ii[2015] 49–67) Christopher Oechler offers a fascinating investigation of the staging effects of plays such as Damián Salustio del Poyo's *La próspera Fortuna de Ruy López de Ávalos* in the context of how special effects interact with the action of the play, and the meaning they create. In particular, Oechler discusses tumbling canvases, a staging effect which 'features prominently in several extant plays' (p. 49) including Poyo's *comedia*, Tirso de Molina's *La prudencia en la mujer*, Diego Ximénez de Enciso's *La mayor hazaña de Carlos V*, and *La Baltasara*. In this intriguing article, Oechler argues that 'the painting, thus imbued with animate potential, represents unseen divine forces and establishes an elaborate connection between art, history, and divinity' (p. 50), as well as that the falling painting 'reinforces art's moralizing and didactic function' and 'embodies the relationship between divine providence and early modern historiography' (p. 50). In his conclusion, he notes the 'cultural significance' (p. 61) of the falling canvas, and its potential to 'reinforce religion and divinely motivated history' (p. 61).

James Stokes's article on 'The Ongoing Exploration of Women and Performance in Early Modern England: Evidences, Issues, and Questions' (*ShakB* 33[2015] 9–31) provides a valuable discussion of women performers in pre-Reformist English culture, and how 'their absence from troupes and the tendency to consign them to something called "traditional culture" has encouraged the view that women's performance was marginal' (p. 9). In this endeavour, Stokes asks a number of critical questions—whether we need to 'expand our definition of what we mean by "performance record"', as well as 'How many general conclusions can be drawn from occasional items of factual information that are by their nature fragmentary' (p. 10). The author then moves on to look at the kinds of evidence that exist in terms of theatrical performances, commenting that 'records of specific performances exist in great variety, and more of them continue to emerge', including involvement by women 'ranging from the craft and yeoman classes to the royals, the nobility, and the gentry' (p. 10), as well as the different types of document that might record women's participation in the production and performance of early modern drama. Overall, this is a valuable piece of research providing a fresh overview of women's theatrical involvement.

Also on women and female roles, Sophie Tomlinson's essay, 'The Actress and Baroque Aesthetic Effects in Renaissance Drama' (*ShakB* 33[2015] 67–82), observes that it is the baroque period (1580–*c*.1700) that women became visible in drama 'in Italy, Spain, France, and subsequently in England' (p. 68). In this regard, Tomlinson discerns that 'we must read the representation of theatrical women within a historicized context' and that such readings 'should include aesthetic curiosity and responsiveness' (p. 68). She thereby discusses the suffering woman in the baroque age, utilizing Shakespeare's *The Two Gentlemen of Verona*. She then moves on to Beaumont and Fletcher's *The Maid's Tragedy*, in order to examine women's sexual and domestic identities, making a vital point that the 'play's figuration of an actress effect allows us to see Evadne and Aspatia as more intimately connected than critics have registered' (p. 73). Next, she turns her attention to

Lording Barry's *The Family of Love*, questioning whether his play 'bear[s] out Purge's view of his wife as a "dissembling strumpet," an actress-whore' (p. 75), and investigates the idea of the actress-whore in the context of this play. She concludes that this drama 'participates in an aesthetic that may aptly be conceived as baroque in its deployment of the bizarre paradox of the actress in a theater marked by the physical absence of women' (p. 79). This is an engaging and insightful contribution to literary criticism.

Cross-playing appears again as the focus in Roberta Barker's 'The "Play Boy," the Female Performer, and the Art of Portraying a Lady' (*ShakB* 33[2015] 83–97), which considers the intriguing question of how the 'boy players of the early modern English public stage and the aristocratic female performers of the early modern English court masques have considered, and perhaps even affected, one another's arts' (p. 83). Barker begins with a discussion of distinct versions of femininity in Jonson's *Masque of Queens*, before moving on to *Love Restored*, which is examined through a close reading of the text. These plays are later compared alongside Webster's *The Duchess of Malfi*. Barker notes that the first appearance of elite women in each of these texts 'is silent' (p. 90). She also makes the interesting observation that 'the Duchess's death scene transgresses the gender and class conventions of masquing even as it affirms them' (p. 92), and considers how the character might have been performed by a boy actor. In her conclusion, she acknowledges the distinction between the 'achievements of the boy actress and the elite woman performer' but also points out that can also be viewed 'as part of a continuum' (p. 94).

In 'Sin, Sacredness, and Childbirth in Early Modern Drama' (*MRDE* 28[2015] 30–48), Paige Martin Reynolds argues persuasively that 'representations of childbirth rituals' reflect 'male anxieties about the female-managed birth process and engage emerging Protestant perceptions of female piety' (p. 31). Reynolds uses in-depth analyses of Middleton's *A Chaste Maid in Cheapside*, Shakespeare's *The Winter's Tale*, and Webster's *The Duchess of Malfi* in this endeavour. In particular, she notes that 'these works offer views of pregnancy and childbirth that suggest contamination' (p. 31), and provides valuable historical context in support of her interpretations. Yet in addition to this contamination suggested in various narratives of childbirth, Reynolds also observes that childbirth could possess connotations of salvation and the sacred in the early modern period. This ambiguity is also discussed in relation to the plays. Reynolds offers the important reflection that both 'Shakespeare and Webster seem to make claims about the pollution of pregnancy and childbirth only to undermine them in the end' (p. 45).

In '"Some woman is the father": Shakespeare, Middleton, and the Criss-Crossed Composition of *Measure for Measure* and *More Dissemblers Besides Women*' (*MRDE* 28[2015] 86–109), Regina Buccola considers the interesting parallels between these plays and how they provide a 'glimpse of the dialogic nature of the early modern London theatre', demonstrating the way in which Middleton was influenced by 'predecessor playwrights such as Shakespeare' as well as 'the reciprocal influence that Middleton may have had on him' in turn (p. 87). Buccola goes on to consider the 'history of the performance and revision of these two plays' and highlights the ways in which they offer a 'fascinating view of the distinctions between Middleton's conception of female characters and figures of secular and religious authority and Shakespeare's' (p. 88). This is a valuable study of the reception, influence, and impact of drama in the early modern period.

The final article of this year is Judy H. Park's 'The Tragicomic Moment: Republicanism in Beaumont and Fletcher's *Philaster*' (*CompD* 49[2015] 23–47), which discusses tragicomedy, and poses the question of whether we can 'identify a republican politics in a genre and among authors typically considered antithetical to republican concerns' (p. 24). Park first examines Guarini's dramatic theory, and considers 'what republicanism might have meant prior to 1642' in order to gauge 'the nature of *Philaster*'s engagement with early seventeenth-century republican thought' (p. 25). She provides a close textual analysis of the play and discusses its plot to conclude that 'its political resonance lies in its republican affirmation of the participation of the people in the maintenance of the public good' (p. 35), and thereby concludes that the play's tragicomic resolution 'depends on the ability of the people to challenge the excesses and abuses of the monarchy and aristocracy' (p. 35). In this enjoyable and intelligent article, Park demonstrates persuasively that *Philaster* 'offers an important lens through which to examine tragicomedy' (p. 28).

*(b) Marlowe*

It may be relevant to open this review of Marlowe studies with some statistics. As is well known in the academic world, Ashgate Publishing was sold to Informa in 2015, and its back catalogue was transferred to Routledge. This is a transaction with potentially far-reaching consequences: in 2014, the only monograph on Marlowe plus four chapters in edited collections were published by Ashgate (see my review in the previous issue of *YWES*), and in 2015, the two new monographs on Marlowe (Duxfield, Martin) by major academic publishers were also from Ashgate, as were the only full anthology and one collection with significant contributions on *Doctor Faustus*. One wonders what the near future in Marlowe studies will look like. Is there going to be a significant drop in quantity (and, in the longer term, quality)? Available statistics for 2016 so far, i.e. until November, suggest that there is at least some reason for concern.

That said, the number of books published makes 2015 a fairly strong year in Marlowe criticism. *Doctor Faustus* unsurprisingly remains high on the agenda, with contributions on its political and intertextual dimensions, while the other plays and the poems receive less extensive treatment. Judging from the last few years, however, Marlowe's non-dramatic works seem to be gaining momentum in the critical discussion, which is welcome news considering the scant attention they still tend to get. *Hero and Leander* figures in two journal articles and a critical overview, and the translations are also represented in at least one full-length journal article.

As for the monographs, from its title alone, Andrew Duxfield's *Christopher Marlowe and the Failure to Unify* might seem to imply a return to a New

Critical concern with poetic and dramatic structure. This is not the case: Duxfield's focus is on unity as a political and religious concept in the early modern period. The claim that Marlowe's plays make unity in this sense problematic suggests various well-trodden critical paths, as Duxfield notes. However, he emphasizes that his study considers 'not just the ways in which Marlowe's plays negate unity, but also the way in which they focus on the pursuit and illusion of unity in the process of negating it' (p. 9). In Duxfield's reading, 'unity' and its hollowness have broad reverberations on, variously, the levels of politics, knowledge, sexuality, and religion; the politics of form remain relatively under-explored despite a suggestive hint that drama 'offers competing voices without a mediating narrative guide' (p. 10).

Duxfield's first chapter, on *Dido*, is suggestive in focusing on the expectations of learned audiences raised on Virgil, but also the Galfridian tradition according to which the English people were descendants of Aeneas's great-grandson Brutus; it is 'the conflict between personal desire and social duty' (p. 13) for both Aeneas and Dido that is at the centre of attention, with emphasis on Marlowe's transference of this conflict onto a canvas of 'moral indeterminacy' (p. 28) and subversion of imperial unity. A broader application of Duxfield's thesis can be found in the chapter on the *Tamburlaine* plays, which suggests that the protagonist's attempts to impose unity on the world he takes on are in the end defeated by the irreducible plurality and complexity of both the macrocosm (the world) and the microcosm (his own body). Tamburlaine's 'unified self-image' is thus shattered by his own 'religious, physical, familial and emotional inconsistencies' (p. 62). A similar drive towards unity characterizes Faustus, whose tragedy, to Duxfield, lies in the failure to attain a unified, consistent body of knowledge. His chapter, however, also addresses formal and generic unity, ever a notorious issue in criticism on this play. *The Jew of Malta* and *The Massacre at Paris* receive collective treatment in Duxfield's next chapter, which claims similarities between these plays in terms of their manipulation of audience sympathies: both begin as seeming perpetuations of moral outrages by 'recognizable "others"' (p. 109), but effectively turn into demonstrations of outrages by the faction with which English audiences were more likely to associate themselves. Unity, then, is exposed as the result of agendas, of political interests. Finally, Duxfield takes on 'the most genuinely ambiguous of Marlowe's plays' (p. 117), *Edward II*, in a discussion that emphasizes the fault-lines between the hierarchical world-views informing the play. A discourse with neither an obvious moral epicentre nor a towering Marlovian hero, *Edward II* in Duxfield's reading becomes a profound exploration of moral, sexual, and ideological ambiguity in a world where, again, unified world-views are showcased as the work of conflicting and equally unsympathetic factions.

Generally, while Duxfield's central claim has clear affinities with those of much previous Marlowe criticism, his book presents a series of thoughtful and nuanced readings of the plays. In one sense, Duxfield's close textual anchoring throughout comes off as both a virtue and a vice; it makes for a focused set of analytical studies, although the wide political and social ramifications of his argument leave the reader rather wanting more (something which the relative brevity of his book also suggests). On the whole, though, *Christopher Marlowe and the Failure to Unify* remains a solid contribution to scholarship on Marlovian drama.

Mathew Martin's *Tragedy and Trauma in the Plays of Christopher Marlowe* applies psychoanalysis and trauma theory to understand the impact of Marlovian violence. Drawing on Freud, Lacan, and Žižek, Martin claims to go beyond a mere aesthetic understanding of tragedy to understand how trauma in Marlowe's plays reconfigures the *de casibus* tradition on which it draws. With one notable exception, Martin's study follows the well-established tradition of a monograph arranged according to the mostly accepted chronology of Marlowe's plays. The first part of the chapter on *Dido* is devoted to a comparative study with trauma in the *Aeneid*; while Virgil's epic offers a redemptive narrative in its version of the *translatio imperii*, Marlowe's play by contrast 'foregrounds the trauma at the core of this myth of origin' (p. 25). The twin focus on Dido and Aeneas, and their conflicting stories, forestalls the notion of imperial foundation, with both protagonists rewriting Virgilian epic as trauma narrative. The *Tamburlaine* plays receive extended treatment in separate chapters. The protagonist of the first part exploits his otherness to be traumatizer rather than traumatized, elevating traumatic mimesis above tragedy rather than failing to conform with tragic standards; the second part enacts a rejection of the 'Oedipal closure' of tragedy. *The Jew of Malta* is placed more squarely in the realm of psychopathology—though, again, of a manifestly traumatic kind: the 'tragic mimesis' of this play 'does not work through and purge but acts out and perpetuates the psychopathology it dramatizes' (p. 86). Barabas—an uncanny Other throughout the play—renders its audience's laughter uneasy by becoming a fetish, a barrier both hiding and showcasing the spectators' own fears. Pain, history, and the suffering body come together in Martin's subsequent reading of *Edward II* as a play that juxtaposes a Christological paradigm of suffering to the myth of Actaeon and Diana, and exposes history as a strenuous attempt at concealing or erasing the hurtful moment of Edward's death. *The Massacre at Paris*—surely Marlowe's most overtly 'traumatic' play and one of Martin's most persuasive chapters—unfolds across the twin poles of memory and forgetting, in a 'refusal to reduce trauma to order' (p. 132) that ostentatiously relegates massacre to silence and forces its audience 'to recognize its ambivalent relation to and even complicity' in the events (p. 143). Finally, and somewhat surprisingly, Martin gives pride of place to *Doctor Faustus* as 'Marlowe's most powerful trauma narrative' (pp. 145, 147). Trauma here does not spell exterior violence so much as divine silence: Faustus in Martin's reading is a purveyor of theatrical fantasies, a traumatized figure for whom God is nothing more than an absence, and the audience of the play are left with 'no detached position from which to observe Faustus's tragedy' (p. 163).

It would clearly be unfair to require a more historically informed understanding of interiority and psychology than the one Martin offers, but taken on its own terms, *Tragedy and Trauma in the Plays of Christopher Marlowe* sometimes comes across as theoretically thinner than might be expected. Indeed, for a study that promises to 'elucidate the violence and trauma of Marlowe's plays by approaching them through Lacanian psychoanalysis and trauma theory' (p. 6), Martin's book shows surprisingly little engagement with Lacan's own writings, especially in its second half (where Lacan all but disappears from view). The connection to 'tragedy' as a concept is also somewhat patchy, although for example the chapters on *Tamburlaine* have valuable discussions on how the plays represent subversions of tragedy rather than aesthetic failures. In short, as a series of often quite perceptive readings of Marlowe's plays, Martin's book convinces more than his reductive theoretical framework suggests.

One anthology on Marlowe, edited by Sara Munson Deats and Robert Logan and covering the full canon of his works, was also published this year. Their third volume on the topic, *Christopher Marlowe at 450* sets out to provide an overview of existing scholarship on each of Marlowe's works, and a set of general theoretical perspectives that map current perspectives and indicate possible future directions. The first half of the collection contains a series of chapters that deal with each of the plays and the poems and translations. Ruth Lunney's contribution on *Dido* is an unusually well-informed and thoughtful piece that makes a broad case for this still under-examined play. Tom Rutter's chapter on *Tamburlaine* is insightful in its discussion of earlier criticism by Una Ellis-Fermor, Paul Kocher, and Harry Levin, but could perhaps have benefited from more attention to the contemporary critical context. Stephen Lynch's piece on *The Jew of Malta* contains a helpful overview of central aspects—including the morality tradition, the representation of race, and Machiavellianism—but has less focus on previous criticism than most of the other chapters. Robert Logan's discussion of *Edward II* reviews scholarly material but also, and usefully, identifies a whole series of particular ambiguities in the play that need further discussion, including aspects of historicity, sexuality, and politics. Sara Munson Deats's chapter on *Doctor Faustus* reads as a straightforward and well-structured introduction to the play, and while it skips relatively lightly over certain aspects such as sources or the much-debated textual dilemma, it remains a useful survey of critical issues. Leah Marcus discusses *The Massacre at Paris* in terms of its problematic history of transmission and ambiguous charting of religious conflict, making a case for Marlowe's shortest play as a complex work that might have more to offer both critics and theatres. Patrick Cheney offers a characteristically insightful and well-researched piece on *Hero and Leander* and 'The Passionate Shepherd'; and M.L. Stapleton considers not only Marlowe's translations but also, and importantly, how they colour his dramatic work. The contributions differ in length and in the amount of attention they give to the critical contexts, and vary in their degree of usefulness as resources for scholarship (for the latter, Cheney's and Lunney's chapters are particular standouts).

The second part is headed by Richard Wilson's magisterial 'Sceptres of Marlowe', which traces the political and theoretical implications of Anglo-American criticism since the 1980s and suggests that the recent compartmentalization of Marlowe studies enacts the recessional order of the new millennium. Part libel, part hagiography, Wilson's chapter provocatively contends that the 'particularist Marlowe' of recent criticism echoes 'the scaled-down age of Obama' (p. 248) in its concerns. Other chapters in the section may be less eye-catching than Wilson's but are quite valuable as summaries of

resources and criticism. David Bevington's overview of Marlovian performance history is comprehensive while necessarily episodic in its approach,
charting a vast number of productions from the 1590s until present time.
Christopher Matusiak contextualizes Marlovian drama in terms of early
modern theatrical practice and offers a thought-provoking insight into the
world of play-going—in which audiences may have paid less attention to the
playwright than most Marlowe criticism would be ready to admit. David
McInnis's chapter—a first of its kind—maps the digital resources currently
available on Marlowe and so provides what is surely one of the most useful
chapters in terms of research. Constance Brown Kuriyama, finally, discusses
issues in Marlovian biography, a topic she has previously explored in her
books and in her chapter in Deats and Logan's volume *Placing the Plays of
Christopher Marlowe*. As a whole, then, while pulling in somewhat different
directions in terms of purpose, *Christopher Marlowe at 450* both remains a
scholarly resource and brings new insights to a number of critical areas.

Dido Queen of Carthage is represented both in the previously mentioned
books and in two standalone articles. Lucy Potter's 'Telling Tales: Negotiating
"Fame" in Virgil's *Aeneid*, Ovid's *Metamorphoses*, and Christopher Marlowe's
*Tragedy of Dido, Queen of Carthage*' (in Kerr and Walker, eds., *Fama and Her
Sisters: Gossip and Rumor in Early Modern Europe*, pp. 37–63) engages with
the well-trodden critical path of classical intertexts in Marlowe's play. While
clearly acknowledging previous work on Marlowe's Ovidian intertexts by, for
example, Patrick Cheney, Potter suggests that the relationship between the two
classical poets in *Dido* is more complex than critics have claimed: Marlowe, in
this reading, primarily strives to outdo Ovid in 'taking the mastery of *Fama* to
a new level in [a] new genre' (pp. 40–1). However, despite its attempts at
reorientation, Potter's essay in the end becomes representative of the critical
impasse over the Virgil/Ovid interrelation that scholars have begun to
acknowledge.

A more unconventional take on *Dido* is represented by Kathryn Rebecca
Van Winkle's ' "Then speak, Aeneas, with Achilles' tongue": *Ethopoeia* and
Elizabethan Boyhood in Marlowe's *Dido Queen of Carthage*' (*Theatre
Symposium* 23[2015] 42–51). As its title suggests, *ethopoeia* or 'impersonation'
was one step in the humanist education that schoolboys in Marlowe's time
received, and Van Winkle suggests that Marlowe's focus on Dido as much as
Aeneas may be influenced by *ethopoeia* practice. Marlowe's grammar-school
room, in this reading, 'promoted alternative gender construction through
its practices of theatricality, fantasy, and identification across gender lines'
(p. 44). *Ethopoeia* is moreover practised in the play itself, according to Van
Winkle, for example in the initial scenes with Aeneas describing the fall of
Troy (p. 44). Van Winkle's account does not entirely manage to fuse the wide
contexts—humanist education, early modern boyhood, and theatrical practice—of her discussion, but her article remains an original investigation into
the educational dimensions of Marlowe's most classically influenced play.

As Wilson provocatively contends, the *Tamburlaine* plays received little
attention in 2015. An article by Roslyn Knutson, 'Dramatic Verse and Early
Modern Playgoers in Marlowe's Time' (in Netzloff, Ryner, and Farabee, eds.,
*Early Modern Drama in Performance: Essays in Honor of Lois Potter*, pp. 11–

24) does have a bearing on their immediate theatrical context. It is commonly thought that the *Tamburlaine* plays so electrified their audiences that other playwrights started to copy Marlowe's 'mighty line', but Knutson challenges this idea in emphasizing the 'continuing affection for familiar rhetorical devices and verse forms' (p. 10). Accordingly, she calls for a methodology that also accommodates the taste for established forms and figures, and that rehabilitates dramatists like Robert Greene from being imitators under the Tamburlainian sway to being writers on their own terms. In other words, Knutson suggests, reconsidering the impact of Marlowe's 'high astounding terms' may also help us to understand how other drama around 1590 was appreciated by its audiences. While necessarily speculative to some extent, Knutson's article is valuable in challenging one of the most persistent critical commonplaces on the *Tamburlaine* plays.

The Jew of Malta is juxtaposed to one of George Chapman's more rarely discussed plays in Bradley Ryner's short essay, 'The Usurer's Theatrical Body: Refiguring Profit in *The Jew of Malta* and *The Blind Beggar of Alexandria*' (in Netzloff et al., eds., pp. 25–34). While scholars have previously noted Chapman's indebtedness to Marlowe's play, Ryner suggests that the link extends to the economic ideas at work in *The Jew of Malta*. Barabas, on the one hand, troubles the then conventional stage representation of the usurer by becoming more of a proto-capitalist than a hoarder of money, and it is in the representation of his body that this conflict is located. By contrast, in Chapman's protagonist, who takes on a whole series of different identities, the conflict is enacted on the body of the actor, who is able to play '*both* the miserly usurer and the extravagant consumer of luxury goods' (p. 28).

It may be sheer coincidence that two other critical articles on *The Jew of Malta* focus on its conclusion. Clayton MacKenzie's short note, 'Marlowe's *The Jew of Malta* and the Murderers Pot' (*N&Q* 62[2015] 542–5), connects the cauldron episode to the pre-Reformation representations of murderers' fate in hell as found in medieval doom murals. By contrast, Mark Hutchings, in 'Barabas's Fall' (*TN* 69[2015] 2–16), examines the staging of the scene. Examining the actual evidence of the 1633 quarto and juxtaposing it to what we know about theatrical practices and playhouse design, Hutchings discusses the practical problems of displacing Barabas from the upper stage to the boiling cauldron where he dies. Hutchings establishes that the scene requires Barabas to appear 'aboue', and since the main stage is occupied by other characters, the cauldron must be located in the discovery space at the rear. This is consonant with the assumptions of modern editors, but Hutchings considers the complicating factor of differing theatrical venues (the outdoor theatre, the Cockpit, and the staging at court). Excluding the possibility of having the actor literally fall into the cauldron, Hutchings suggests that Barabas may have been briefly doubled by another actor to maintain the illusion of having fallen from the upper stage. This is, Hutchings argues, in line with the practices of Strange's men and Admiral's men, who had *The Jew of Malta* on their repertoire. Hutchings's argument, by his own admission, expands on a critical consensus rather than presenting any radically new findings, but as an analysis finely attuned to theatrical practice it is sensible and thoughtfully argued.

As for articles on *Doctor Faustus*, Jane Hwang Degenhardt's 'The Reformation, Inter-Imperial World History, and Marlowe's *Doctor Faustus*' (*PMLA* 130[2015] 402–11) suggests a wide set of contexts—empire and trade—for the play. Indeed, the religious dimension is, in Degenhardt's reading, even subsumed to such aspects: 'global commerce and its relation to empire provide an expansive historical framework in which the play locates the Reformation and Faustus's journey towards damnation' (p. 403). Instead of inaugurating the modern era, the 'myriad imperial references' (p. 403) of the play suggest the idea of history as an overall cyclical movement that emphasizes continuities between imperial-classical past and present. But the continuity stretches across space as well: as her title suggests, Degenhardt's prime theoretical tool is Laura Doyle's concept of 'inter-imperiality', which becomes a method for understanding both the dynamics of global trade and the 'shifting alliances and hostilities that characterized the Reformation and the Counter-Reformation' (p. 405). To Degenhardt, much of the gist of *Doctor Faustus* lies in its implicit denial of the Reformation as an inaugurator of the modern era and affirmation of the common pursuit of power across territories and times. This very broad framework is handled with skill and clarity, although the actual reading of the play could in the best of worlds have been more developed (for one thing, Faustus does not actually end up pursuing the empire-building that the play prepares, and he never travels outside Europe, so what position on empire and trade does that imply?). Clearly intended as part of a book project, Degenhardt's essay has an attractive theoretical and historical sweep which the relative brevity of her essay cannot entirely do justice to.

Further studies on *Doctor Faustus*, by veteran scholars, can be found in Sophie Chiari's edited collection, *The Circulation of Knowledge in Early Modern English Literature*. François Laroque offers a contrastive reading of 'Magic, Manipulation and Misrule in *Doctor Faustus* and *Measure for Measure*' (pp. 123–32). The plays, while obviously indebted to the morality tradition, differ in how they treat it: to Laroque, *Doctor Faustus* inverts the morality scheme into a regression towards hell, while *Measure for Measure* transposes the same scheme into urban sex comedy. 'Transmission' and 'transgression' are the main conceptual tools by which Laroque approaches this divergence: Faustus fails to transmit all human knowledge through his transgressive scheme, and transgression and transmission 'are thus tightly interwoven' (p. 125). By contrast, the transgression in *Measure for Measure* is enacted on the level of sexual vice and is therefore transmitted and perpetuated endlessly. While Faustus's transgression is 'an essentially individual and solitary enterprise' (p. 131), transgression in *Measure for Measure* takes the shape of an interregnum 'which plays the role of a safety valve as in the traditional interval of festive misrule' (p. 132)—a perspective well known from Laroque's ground-breaking research into seasonal entertainment and festivity.

Roy Eriksen's 'Marlowe's Political Balancing Act: Religion and *Translatio Imperii* in *Doctor Faustus (B)*' (in Chiari, ed., pp. 107–22) actually explores a critical position similar to Degenhardt's in its insistence that Marlowe's play has been read primarily in terms of theology despite the fact that it 'engages to no little extent with contemporary political issues' (p. 108). However, Eriksen's stated emphasis is on the courtly scenes of the B-text. While frequently dismissed as farcical additions, these parts form in Eriksen's reading a key to the overall political concerns of the play. As Eriksen suggests, Faustus's attack on predestination in the first scene of the play anticipates the pope's emphasis on infallibility in the courtly scenes, and 'the power relations between Pope and Emperor' (p. 112) come under close scrutiny in the play, with the emperor Charles V echoing the Tudor monarch's power struggle with the pope on issues of sovereignty. In other words, the seemingly marginal, comical and historical scenes set at the papal court become, in Eriksen's wide-ranging analysis, an acerbic comment on Elizabethan politics which touches 'a raw nerve in a society under threat from enemies without and within' (p. 120). Another, shorter, book chapter by Eriksen, 'Marlowe's Actæon: Synchretism on the Elizabethan Stage' (in Wåghäll Nivre, ed., Allusions and Reflections: Greek and Roman Mythology on Renaissance Europe, pp. 137–47), similarly explores the imperial scenes of the B-text and argues that these scenes draw on syncretist readings of myth in classical and medieval literature. Rather than assume a straightforward reading of Ovid on Marlowe's behalf, the allusions to the Actæon myth in Eriksen's reading are located in a complex interrelation with the Ovide moralisé tradition and, in the extension, the combination of Scripture with classical myth in the Cambridge milieu where Marlowe was a student.

Readings of Edward II tended, unsurprisingly perhaps, to focus on either early modern political contexts of the play or twentieth-century responses to it. Of the first category, Mark Hutchings's short note, 'Marlowe's "Greekish Strumpet"' (N&Q 62[2015] 66–9), speculates that Marlowe's allusions to the Helen of Troy myth may also allude to the Turkish sack of Constantinople, and that Edward II thus implicitly parallels medieval England with the Ottoman empire. Another approach which emphasizes the domestic political sphere is represented by Courtney Naum Scuro's 'Placing and Playing the Past: History, Politics, and Spatial Ambiguity in Richard Mulcaster's The Queen's Majesty's Passage and Christopher Marlowe's Edward II' (JMMLA 48:ii[2015] 71–94). Scuro's argument is essentially that Mulcaster's text, unlike Marlowe's, 'aims to reassert the unified values of a shared myth of origin' (p. 75) and that Edward II, by contrast, closes off its audience 'from an affirming sense of time's hopeful potentiality or redeeming capacity' (p. 91). Methodologically, Scuro's essay treads familiar New Historicist ground: for example, the basic and quite interesting idea of juxtaposing Marlowe's play to a non-dramatic representation of monarchic ritual may have benefited from some more theoretical reflection. In addition, an excursus to Derrida's discussion of the 'archive' to elucidate Mulcaster reads somewhat too much like a digression in the central section of her essay. Edward II and Mulcaster's text—the latter describing an event that took place before Marlowe was even born—raise all sorts of relevant questions concerning the past, present, and future of Elizabeth's reign (with Mulcaster and Marlowe approaching it as it were from opposite ends), and while Scuro's essay does not fully tease out the implications of this chronological opposition, her essay is suggestive in finding a new intertextual point of reference for Marlowe's play.

The second category of readings, which deal with the twentieth-century afterlife of the play, is represented by James Wallace's 'Marlowe and McKellen on screen: The Prospect Theatre Company Production of *Edward II* 1969–70' (*ShakB* 33[2015] 595–608). Featuring the first gay male kiss (in fact, the first six ones) on English television and a young Ian McKellen in the title role, the Prospect *Edward II* is discussed by Wallace in terms of background and artistic achievement. While there have been previous discussions of this production, Wallace is more thorough with his background material, noting for example that there had been a televised but unrecorded British performance as early as 1947, which is interestingly documented in his article. He then goes on to examine the various aesthetic and technical challenges that beset the Prospect production, with some notes also on its reception. Wallace's subsequent analysis emphasizes the 'detailed intensity' (p. 602) of McKellen's performance but also the 'broader social resonance' (p. 604) of the staging. A landmark production that opened just a couple of months after the Stonewall riots, the Prospect *Edward II* becomes notable in Wallace's analysis for its flaunting of 'transgressive same-sex desire' (p. 605); indeed, it even featured a kiss between Edward and the sadistic Lightborn. The production, in other words, established a paradigm for virtually all future productions of the play, as Wallace duly notes (p. 606).

Another 'presentist' article, which juxtaposes *Edward II* to Bertolt Brecht and Lion Feuchtwanger's adaptation, is Kristina Mendicino's 'Writing Coincidence: Brecht and Marlowe's History Play' (*Monatshefte für Deutschsprachige Literatur und Kultur* 107[2015] 46–63). As suggested by its title, Mendicino's article focuses on the presence of reading and writing in Marlowe's play—more specifically, with the argument that it stages history as constituted by all sorts of written documentation. There is a further twist to this argument in the sense that it also involves Brecht's oscillation between writing as a secure medium and writing as opening up an indeterminate space between writing and acting. Marlowe's play, in Mendicino's reading, 'multiplies the papers involved in the history of Edward II and dramatizes their troubling effects upon chronology and causality, the localization of event and agency' (p. 51). Brecht insists even more on the textual nature of the events, to such an extent that it becomes a 'determining structure of dramatic action' (p. 51). Mendicino's article is clearly more concerned with Brecht than with Marlowe's play as such, but overall she manages to find a new angle on a topic—writing and its power—that has previously been explored in Marlowe criticism.

*The Massacre at Paris* found scant representation outside the monographs, but it is the focus of Robin Hizme's 'Conversing with Affect, Genre and Identity in Marlowe's *The Massacre at Paris*' (in Bennett, ed. *Conversational Exchanges in Early Modern England (1549–1640)*, pp. 42–69), which argues that the violence of Marlowe's play and the emotive impact it had contributed to a sense of community among its early audiences. Affective response, in Hizme's reading, is fundamental in order to understand the sense of identity— collective in a general sense, but also, and specifically, English—that emerges from the play. While the central notion of 'affect' appears under-theorized (one wonders, for example, how the rich critical discussion on early modern passions relates to Hizme's argument), the analysis as a whole is wide-ranging and particularly efficient in emphasizing the multidimensional audience responses to the play. To Hizme, it is precisely in its ironies and polyvalent exposure of the outsider that *The Massacre at Paris* forges the sense of an 'English' community among its audience members.

As for Marlowe's poetry, Efterpi Mitsi's 'George Chapman's "Ancient Greek Souls": Translating Ekphrasis in *Hero and Leander*' (*W&I* 31[2015] 343–9) focuses on Chapman's continuation of *Hero and Leander* rather than on Marlowe's part, but has relevance for Marlowe scholars since it suggests that Chapman's use of ekphrasis exaggerates and amplifies Marlowe's own (exaggerated) descriptions of physical artefacts. Unlike in Marlowe, moreover, Hero becomes the subject rather than the object of sexual desire—a weaver and artist in her own right—and Chapman's ambition of turning Marlovian epyllion into grand epic results in a heightened significance of existing ekphrastic moments, but also in the introduction of further Ovidian myths into the complex narrative web.

The conjunction between textuality and sexuality is the theme of Gordon Braden's 'Hero and Leander in Bed (and the Morning After)' (*ELR* 45[2015] 205–30). Taking as its starting-point the familiar quandary over whether or not we can consider *Hero and Leander* a finished work, Braden's discussion focuses on the editorial problems of lines 753–85 in Marlowe's text, which have been rearranged by textual scholars: Tucker Brooke's moving of lines 773–84 to follow directly on line 762 has been accepted by most editors as the right one. Braden sheds light on the bibliographical assumptions behind it and examines the grounds on which the apparent non-linearity of Marlowe's original narration may be defended or rejected. Keeping the poem as it is may create an abrupt transition, but Braden shows that it can be made sense of in both psychological and narrative terms—as a description of a 'single experience compounded (realistically) of the emotions of both [Hero and Leander]' (p. 220). As for the question of whether *Hero and Leander* is finished, Braden, while acknowledging that Musaeus and Marlowe end their poems at the same moment, also examines the different significance conferred by the Ovidian and Christian contexts in which Marlowe operates. In Braden's reading, the ending of *Hero and Leander* may not be quite as bleak as some other critics have suggested, although the sexual fulfilment of desire also throws the comic register of the poem into a generically and temperamentally different mode. While Braden's combination of close textual focus, extensive (though necessary) quotation, and broad thematic scope can make his argument difficult to follow, his essay provides an insightful and poised response to a textual problem that is unlikely to be resolved any time soon.

Sexuality and textuality are similarly the focus of Jenny C. Mann's 'Marlowe's Slack Muse: *All Ovids Elegies* and an English Poetics of Softness' (*MP* 113[2015] 49–65). Suggesting that Marlowe's translations 'present "softness" and its gendered corollary—effeminacy—as the ground of masculine poetic invention' (p. 50), Mann goes on to argue that the translator's subordinate position becomes a source of enrichment to Marlowe, as Ovid's *Amores* precisely 'depict effeminization and even impotence as a means of poetic production' (p. 51). Mann's analysis is contextualized from the point of view of humanist rhetoric and its split between, on the one hand, the soft and effeminate and the vigorous and masculine on the other. The main thrust of her discussion, however, is located in the context of effeminacy, which is further connected to notions of *otium* and the associations it had with softness. Mann's analysis is, moreover, attentive to the formal requirements of the elegy as a genre, and her remarks on this matter pave the way for an insightful discussion of Marlowe's transferral of classical metre into English couplets. To Mann, Marlowe's paradoxical assertion of (sexual) non-performance as a ground for (textual) performance becomes the basis for a fascinating discussion of *All Ovids Elegies*, with its emphasis on the 'flaccid' and 'soft' as an aesthetic cornerstone. Claiming that effeminacy is 'one more code of masculinity' (p. 64) rather than its negation, Mann's study basically confines itself to effeminacy as a rhetorical construct, and while it might have benefited from a broader perspective on early modern masculinity provided by historians such as Alexandra Shepard or Elizabeth Foyster, her astute close readings of Marlowe's translations open up a new perspective on this still ignored work.

Marlowe also gets a full chapter, mostly and appropriately covering his poetry and translations, by Charles Martindale, in volume 2 of *The Oxford History of Classical Reception*, edited by Patrick Cheney and Philip Hardie (pp. 579–98). Obviously, the purpose of the chapter is to offer a synthesis of existing research, but Martindale also challenges, for example, tendencies to read Marlowe's biography into his works; his particular emphasis lies on Marlowe's radicalism as an aesthetic innovator. In particular, Marlowe's translations receive attention for their 'immediately decisive' (p. 587) use of blank verse and closed couplets in rendering classical metre. To Martindale, the fact that so much of Marlowe's career was devoted to translating—in a wide sense—the classics, itself says something crucial about 'Marlowe's singularity' (p. 593). While a comprehensive treatment of Marlowe's classicism is still waiting to be written, Martindale's chapter, and some of the other critical assessments from 2015, demonstrate just how diverse the field of Marlowe studies has become. Although focusing on Marlowe's canonical drama is still a clearly legitimate critical venture, the full range of Marlowe's oeuvre is increasingly, and rewardingly, at the centre of much critical attention.

*(c) Jonson*

One of the most significant publications in the field this year was, perhaps ironically, an edition of a text not actually authored by Jonson himself. *Ben Jonson's Walk to Scotland: An Annotated Edition of the 'Foot Voyage'*, edited by James Loxley, Anna Groundwater, and Julie Sanders, is a previously unpublished account of Ben Jonson's celebrated walk from London to Edinburgh in the summer of 1618. Until the discovery of this account, preserved among the papers of the Aldersey family in Cheshire, our picture of Jonson's walk was based on a patchwork of information pieced together from fragmentary sources by scholars such as David Masson, Ian Donaldson and

James Knowles. This edition, then, represents 'a major addition not just to our knowledge of this episode but to our broader understanding of Jonson's life and the history of the period' (p. 3). The text of the account is eminently readable, presented with modernized spelling, alongside meticulous annotations of the places Jonson visited, the people he met, and the activities he undertook along the way. The editors have also provided a wealth of secondary material, and the volume is bookended with introductory notes that deal with the status of the manuscript, its provenance, and questions of authorship (although internal details and evidence in this regard are 'ambiguous, indeterminate, or fleeting', p. 36), and a series of contextual essays that consider Jonson's reputation and status as celebrity, the inspiration for the walk, its place amongst other famous journeys of the time, and the possible ways in which it might have figured in Jonson's future work. Wider issues, such as early modern travel and relations between England and Scotland, are also considered as contexts for the account, and although, as the editors themselves point out, 'there is no doubt much more to say' about the journey, this volume represents the first steps towards 'assimilat[ing] the foot voyage into our critical accounts of Jonson's life, writing and times' (p. 3).

In terms of Jonson's own writings, his most popular plays remained very much the focus of scholarship this year, receiving attention from both critical and pedagogical standpoints. One student-oriented publication was Richard Willmott's edition of *The Alchemist*, which marks Jonson's first appearance in the Oxford Student Texts series, aimed at 'presenting literary texts to students in both a scholarly and an accessible way' (p. ix). Willmott takes a previously edited text (in this case, Gordon Campbell's 1995 edition for Oxford World's Classics) and augments it with various scholarly and pedagogical apparatus, including tasks to encourage close work with language and themes, chronologies and illustrations to support contextual understanding, and essay questions to help students prepare for assessment.

*Volpone* also features as one of two non-Shakespeare plays included in Palgrave's Shakespeare Handbooks series this year, alongside Christopher Marlowe's *Doctor Faustus*. These handbooks set out to provide readings of the plays in performance, and Marshall Botvinick deals ably with this brief, bringing a practitioner's eye to the text and offering insightful readings of the play within the scene-by-scene commentary that characterizes the series' approach to texts. As Peter Kirwan notes in a quoted review, the commentary 'enables the reader to visualise and work through the practical demands of the play in performance' (p. i), but the handbook more broadly provides other valuable notes on the play's various histories, including its cultural contexts and sources, early performances alongside stage and screen histories, and finally critical assessments by scholars through the ages.

Two articles took Jonson's *Bartholomew Fair* as their focus this year, approaching the play from two different perspectives. Andrew Moran won a Discoveries Award from the *Ben Jonson Journal* in 2015 for his article, 'An Emetic upon St. Bartholomew's Day: Purging, Stripping, and Reclothing the Pauline Body in *Bartholomew Fair*' (*BJJ* 22[2015] 23–40), in which he argues that Jonson's grotesque presentation of the human body in the play and his parodic use of Pauline theology 'affirm the sanctification of human things, including the body, against the Calvinist anthropology of the Puritans' (p. 36). In Moran's argument, the playwright's purpose is deliberately paradoxical, in that it directs attention to 'the hideousness of carnality' (p. 36) while at the same time suggesting that the body may be transformed into something glorified and worthy of visual representation. Katherine Gillen's 'Female Chastity and Commoditized Selfhood in *Bartholomew Fair*' (*SEL* 55[2015] 309–26) focuses on the market itself, suggesting that the play's male characters are helpless to resist its manifold temptations and thus incapable of maintaining autonomous selfhood. In contrast with these men, Gillen argues, the female character Grace Wellborn acquires autonomy and self-possession precisely because of the market, or rather because of the 'self-conscious commoditization [of her own sexual agency] as a strategy for navigating a commercial market' (p. 311). Through his presentation of Grace, the author posits, Jonson creates a position with which he can align himself and 'articulate a performative authorial self that is shaped through commercial constraints rather than in opposition to them' (p. 321).

*Eastward Ho!* also benefitted from two distinct approaches this year. The first, Kelly Stage, '*Eastward Ho!* and the Strength of Weak Ties for Playwrights and Patrons' (*BJJ* 22[2015] 208–28), brings network theory into play by examining the plot and conclusion of the play—written by Jonson with George Chapman and John Marston—alongside the playwrights' resulting imprisonment. Using the concepts of 'strong' and 'weak' ties to describe social relationships, Stage outlines the letter-writing campaign the playwrights undertook in the hope of securing their release, and demonstrates how Jonson and his colleagues were forced to embrace 'weak' ties rather than 'strong' ones in writing to contacts outside their immediate circle with enough social capital to plead their case at court. This reading of their letters is set against a reading of *Eastward Ho!* in which Quicksilver's imprisonment resonates with that of the playwrights, but also provides a fantastical contrast, as his charisma and performance prowess at the end of the play are figured as a 'wishful reordering of power structures' that allows 'exceptional personal agency' (pp. 209–10) to overpower the social conventions and stratified social credit to which Jonson, Chapman, and Marston were subject.

A second approach came from Emily Ruth Isaacson in 'Indulgent Masters and Sleights of Hand Servants and Apprentices in City Comedy' (*BJJ* 22[2015] 62–82), in which she provides close readings of *Eastward Ho!* and *The Alchemist* as city comedies that explore the disruptive potential of the servant figure. Isaacson sets these plays up alongside conduct books and other instructional texts from the period in order to reconstruct early modern expectations for servants and draw out the contrasting representations of family and household across the two genres. Citing servant relationships with other members of the household, such as apprentices and masters, and the instability these relationships lent to the definition of the servant role during this period, Isaacson approaches Jonson's plays as spaces in which the rigid homes of contemporary conduct books, which placed 'moral certitude at the center' (p. 64), could be interrogated and challenged.

Michael Saenger's chapter, 'Interlinguicity and *The Alchemist*' (in Delabastita and Hoenselaars, eds., *Multilingualism in the Drama of Shakespeare and his*

*Contemporaries*, pp. 179–202), also offered a close reading of Jonson's *The Alchemist*, this time in tandem with a polemical English Counter-Reformation pamphlet by the Catholic priest and translator Gregory Martin, and, more briefly, some passages from Shakespeare's plays. In juxtaposing these texts, Saenger highlights different theories of translation from the period, distinguishing between translation on a horizontal axis (which 'defines some languages are better than others', p. 182) and translation on a vertical axis (which 'figures them to be equivalent, even interchangeable', p. 182). Using Martin's 1582 pamphlet as a model for this distinction, the chapter moves on to demonstrate how Jonson negotiates 'horizontal' and 'vertical' translation in an expanded definition of 'language' that includes not only linguistic systems but also 'quasi-linguistic systems, like quarrelling, money, religious fanaticism, venture capitalism, cony-catching . . . [and] theatrical performance' (p. 187). Translation, therefore, does not just apply to the transformation of words but also of social standing, of reputations, of relationships. According to Saenger, it is the varying levels of opacity and translucency displayed in these 'languages' that not only allow different characters 'to practice various kinds of alchemy at each other's expense' (p. 195) but also allow Jonson to demonstrate, through the capturing of 'layered dialects, specialized vocabularies, and social desires', that 'the predominant language of this world is sin, from which only lucid repentance can "translate" us' (p. 179).

Jonson's *The Staple of News* formed one of three case studies for Stephen Wittek in *The Media Players: Shakespeare, Middleton, Jonson, and the Idea of the News*, in which the author emphasizes the 'coevolution of material innovations and the equally innovative development of the concept of news itself' (p. 1). Moving beyond advances in print technology and the development of new trade routes as the sole explanations for the development of early modern news culture, Wittek claims that theatres, in fact, created a 'unique discursive space . . . [that] helped to foster the conceptual framework that made news possible' (p. 1). In Jonson's earlier plays, the news is regarded as 'an overgrown form of gossip', offering a 'gaudy, exotic style of rhetoric . . . in place of actual substance' (pp. 88–9), and in *The Staple of News* the playwright moves one step further, making a claim for drama and the theatre as superior modes and platforms for public commentary and conversation. However, in maintaining this position, Wittek argues, Jonson acknowledges the common ground shared by the two forms, 'an awareness that, for better or worse, drama and news were complicit in, and dependent on, an escalation in opportunities for participation in public life and the new ways of thinking that came along with it' (p. 88).

Two articles this year focused on Jonson's relationship with contemporary writers, albeit of very different types. Kathryn Jacobs looked at Jonson in dialogue with two other literary giants in 'Ben Jonson on Shakespeare's Chaucer' (*ChauR* 50[2015] 198–215), offering a new lens through which to read Jonson's objections to the medieval origins and source material for several Shakespearean plays. She places Shakespeare alongside Spenser in this article by outlining the displeasure that both authors incurred at Jonson's hands, and suggesting that Jonson's objections stemmed from the borrowing of Chaucerian diction rather than Chaucerian efforts 'to "english" the writings of important classical authors' (p. 203). Examining evidence from across a range of Jonson's works, including *Timber, or Discoveries, Every Man in His Humour, Volpone*, and *Cynthia's Revels*, Jacobs maps his criticisms onto their Shakespearean targets and tentatively identifies a previously unnoticed allusion to *Hamlet* and a possible source for the character of Polonius in Chaucer's Pandarus.

In *Writing the Monarch in Jacobean England: Jonson, Donne, Shakespeare and the Works of King James*, Jane Rickard also looks at Jonson in dialogue, this time as one of three Jacobean writers, alongside Donne and Shakespeare, particularly engaged with the acknowledgement, reception, and reworking of the king's own writings. Over the course of two early chapters in the book, dealing with court masques, entertainments, and poetry, Rickard charts the familiar narrative of Jonson's career at court—peaking in 1616 and steadily declining thereafter—and suggests that it was not only political and cultural uncertainty and division that contributed to Jonson's compromised position at court post-1616 but also 'the literary responses they provoked in the King that put pressure on the role of court poet...that Jonson had so carefully constructed for himself' (p. 97). In this view, the king's writing career plays a significant role in Jonson's rise and fall at the Jacobean court. In the early years of the reign, Jonson acknowledges James as a fellow-writer but keeps him at a distance, contrasting his authorial role with that of the court poet as narrator of the reign; however, Rickard argues, Jonson's representation of court poet as mediator between the court and the people is eventually undermined by the king as he makes himself and his family more and more present to his subjects through his own writing.

Two further articles set up Jonson's relationship with other contemporary figures. In 'The Wrong Kind of Wonder: Ben Jonson and Cornelis Drebbel' (*RES* 66[2015] 60–70), Jennifer Speake sketches Jonson's relationship with the Dutch inventor and polymath Cornelis Drebbel through an examination of his 1609 *Entertainment at Britain's Burse*. Her close reading of the work identifies some of the earliest evidence of the antagonism that typically characterized the relationship between these men, while also revealing the debt Jonson owed to Drebbel for the appropriation of his automaton at the climax of the *Entertainment*. Kaara L. Peterson looks at a more distant relationship with monarchy in her article, 'Elizabeth I's Virginity and the Body of Evidence: Jonson's Notorious Crux' (*RenQ* 68[2015] 840–71), which re-examines Jonson's infamous claim that Elizabeth 'had a membrane on her which made her uncapable of man'. Peterson looked to the field of early modern medicine to help tell a fuller story about Jonson's comment, using contemporary medical commentary and documentary records of Elizabeth's health, combined with court gossip and common wisdom, to clarify the historical record of the queen's health, and also to uncover how early modern culture thought about lifelong virginity and its apparently attendant diseases.

Jonson's masques, and his success as a masque writer, received notable attention this year, notably from Roger D. Sell, who won a Discoveries Award from the *Ben Jonson Journal* for his article 'Political and Hedonic Re-contextualizations: Prince Charles's Spanish Journey in Beaumont, Jonson, and Middleton' (*BJJ* 22[2015] 163–87). Sell's study centres around Jonson's

*Neptune's Triumph for the Return of Albion*, Middleton's *A Game at Chess*, and some poems by Sir John Beaumont, all of which touch on Prince Charles's journey to Spain in 1623. His exploration of Jonson's unperformed masque highlights not only the political context in which the masque was written but also the literary contexts and conventions that Jonson both adhered to and broke away from in order to emphasize the pleasures of literary form that might arise from his text.

Other articles approached Jonson's masques as a means of reading other contemporary literary works. In 'The Visual Music of the Masque and George Herbert's *Temple*' (*ELR* 45[2015] 377–99), Simon Jackson begins by exploring the resonances between the altars represented in Jonson's *Hymenaei* and Herbert's *The Temple*, and suggests that Jonson's altar (an object transformed from a three-dimensional stage prop to a two-dimensional textual description) can be read in a similar way to Herbert's poetry, albeit in reverse (i.e. by configuring our reading of the text in terms of physically entering a church building). Jackson's aim is to examine the concepts of proportion across the disciplines, looking at 'the ways in which the masque presented harmonic ideals in visual terms in its proportionally conceived perspectival sets and in its formal choreography, and hear[ing] the echoes of this visual music resounding within Herbert's playful devotional lyrics' (p. 382).

In a different vein, Roberta Barker considered the relationship between boy players of the early modern public stage and aristocratic female performers of the court masque in her article, 'The "Play-Boy", the Female Performer, and the Art of Portraying a Lady' (*ShakB* 33[2015] 83–97). Focusing specifically on Jonson's *The Masque of Queens* and *Love Restored*, Barker suggests that these masques differentiate between male and female performance and allow for the representation of feminine power, both on a textual level (in their exposure of the flaws of boy actors and their exaltation of the virtues of women performers), and on a performance level (in providing opportunities for women to adhere to or refuse the conventions of the form, as Frances and Catherine Howard did when they refused to be taken out to dance by their male dance partners after *Love Restored*). Moving on from elite performance to professional performance, Barker makes the case for reading 'shared codes of class and gender embodiment' (p. 84) across the two cultures and looks at the ways in which these codes and their enactment in Jonson's masques help us better imagine the ways in which boy actors in plays such as Webster's *The Duchess of Malfi* might have performed their roles.

Eric Dunnum's 'Dauphine Was Right: Masques, the Authenticity of (Un)Performed Identity, and the Two Prologues of *Epicene*' (*BJJ* 22[2015] 229–51) addressed the interpretative problem posed by the two prologues to *Epicœne*, which, unlike the double prologues in Jonson's other plays, contain contradictory messages aimed at the same audience. Outlining the respective optimism and pessimism of the first and second prologues on the subject of performance and theatricality, Dunnum suggests that Jonson's stance in the first prologue is a result of his recent successes as a masque writer at court, which had prompted him to import 'a very un-Jonsonian pro-theatricality... from court culture to the public stage' (pp. 230–1). However, he argues, Jonson's more typical position is embedded throughout the play itself, so when the second prologue was occasioned by a complaint from Lady Arabella Stuart, 'the play was uncannily poised to revert to a typical Jonsonian anti-theatricality' (p. 231). Furthermore, Dunnum points out, the tonal tensions between the two prologues are a mirror for other tensions in *Epicœne*, not only between characters but also between conceptual ideas of performativity and essentialism.

Several articles provided a welcome focus on Jonson's poetry this year. In 'Ben Jonson's Sacramental Poetics: Manners as Mystery in his Poetry and Drama' (*BJJ* 22[2015] 41–61), Marshelle Woodward looked at a number of lyric poems alongside the *Discoveries* and *Cynthia's Revels* in order to interrogate the tensions surrounding Jonson's treatment of mystery and metaphysics. Tracing these tensions back to Jonson's relationship with Catholicism, Woodward creates an argument of two halves: the first contending that Jonson's frequent silence 'on matters of doctrine and metaphysics should be interpreted not as a marker of scepticism, but rather as a positive theological statement... that lay people should study moral rather than dogmatic theology', and the second suggesting that we can read in *Cynthia's Revels* the playwright's attempts to 'divorce mystery from its relation to ineffable or esoteric knowledge and align it instead with the "mysteries of manners, arms, and arts" that infuse a divine principle into human action' (p. 43).

In 'Temporality, Desire, Poetics: *Underwoods*' (*BJJ* 22[2015] 252–65), Amanda Henrichs built on the work of previous scholars who have noticed Jonson's frequent employment of the aged lover trope in his poetry, arguing that Jonson is not simply modelling himself on the old lover-poets of the classical period but rather 'inextricably link[ing] form, content and sexuality in order to create a newly sexualized poetic existence' (p. 254). Her argument follows Jonson through the *Underwoods* volume as he seeks to reframe the idea of the ideal lover, showing firstly that old poets are the best poets because they are most like the classical poets, and secondly that old poets like Jonson himself are able to inhabit the role of the youthful lover eternally through poetic skill, which is in fact acquired through age and worldly experience.

In 'The Ecology of Eating in Jonson's "To Penshurst"' (in Munroe, Geisweidt, and Bruckner, eds., *Ecological Approaches to Early Modern English Texts: A Field Guide to Reading and Teaching*, pp. 109–20), Amy Tigner read against traditional interpretations of indulgent eating in Jonson's 'To Penshurst', suggesting that the copiousness of food in the poem should be taken not as an instance of Rabelaisian, pastoral, or utopic fantasy but rather as a reflection of 'food practices of production, of preparation, and consumption at early modern rural estates' (pp. 109–10). She places the poem within the context of garden manuals, agricultural treatises, herbals, and household receipt books, and shows that Jonson's depiction of abundance, while participating in 'a rhetoric of the ideal', corresponds with 'the material realities of agriculture' on an estate such as Penshurst (p. 110). Tigner's chapter highlights the centrality of food production to ecological issues in the early modern period, but it also goes beyond this, showing how the death of animals and plants required for the abundance in the world of Jonson's poem 'denotes the temporal nature of all creatures—including the humans who consume the nonhumans' (p. 119). We conclude with several shorter notes and bibliographical studies that took Jonson's poems and entertainments as their subjects this year. James Doelman, 'The Dean of Dunstable' (*BJJ* 22[2015] 129–41), made a study of the reference to the 'Dean of Dunstable' in *The Gypsies Metamorphosed*, demonstrating the centrality of this fictional figure in 'a complex web of connections in early seventeenth-century satire' (p. 130). Doelman suggests that we might understand the Dean of Dunstable 'first as a caricatured figure of rustic simplicity, and secondly as a reference to the court fool, David Drummond' (p. 130). However, through a previously unprinted satirical poem in Brotherton MS Lt q 44 (reproduced in an appendix to his study), he also reveals the collation of this figure with Richard Corbett, the dean of Christ Church Oxford, and ponders the existence of other missing connections between Dunstable and Corbett that might further illuminate Jonson's reference. In ' "To Penshurst" and Sir Philip Sidney' (*ANQ* 28[2015] 21–2), Andrew Hadfield also focused on connections, pointing out the echoes of the ninth sonnet of Sidney's *Astrophil and Stella*, in Jonson's 'To Penshurst', and tracing the descriptions of touchstone, marble, and gold in both poems to suggest Jonson's acknowledgement of the Sidneys as a culturally rich but influentially and financially poor dynasty. And finally, in 'Ben Jonson at Althorp: Stage Directions as Memoir' (*N&Q* 62[2015] 224–7), Ralph Berry detailed the various stage directions included in Jonson's entertainment for Queen Anna and Prince Henry at Althorp in 1603, suggesting that Jonson eschews the present tense for his stage directions, instead using the past tense to convey his status and authority not only as the writer but also as the spectator of the performance on this esteemed occasion.

## Books Reviewed

Bennett, Kristen Abbott, ed. *Conversational Exchanges in Early Modern England (1549–1640)*. CambridgeSP. [2015] pp. 290. £47.99 ISBN 9 7814 4387 4465.

Botvinick, Marshall, ed. *Volpone* by Jonson Ben. PalMac. [2015] pp. 144. £50 ISBN 9 7811 3737 9818.

Cheney, Patrick, and Philip Hardie, eds. *The Oxford History of Classical Reception, vol. 2: 1558–1660*. OUP. [2015] pp. 808. £127.27 ISBN 9 7801 9954 7555.

Chiari, Sophie, ed. *The Circulation of Knowledge in Early Modern English Literature*. Ashgate. [2015] pp. 288. £67.99 ISBN 9 7814 7244 9153.

Clegg, Roger, and Lucie Skeaping. *Singing Simpkin and Other Bawdy Jigs: Musical Comedy on the Shakespearean Stage. Scripts, Music and Context*. ExeUP. [2014] pp. ix + 339 £30 ISBN 9 7808 5989 8782.

Deats, Sara Munson, and Robert A. Logan, eds. *Christopher Marlowe at 450*. Ashgate. [2015] pp. 382. £75 ISBN 9 7814 7240 9430.

Delabastita, Dirk, and Ton Hoenselaars, eds. *Multilingualism in the Drama of Shakespeare and His Contemporaries*. Benjamins. [2015] pp. 215. £76 ISBN 9 7890 2724 2617.

Dowd, Michelle M. *The Dynamics of Inheritance on the Shakespearean Stage*. CUP. [2015] pp. xii + 289. £64.99 ISBN 9 7811 0709 9777.

Duxfield, Andrew. *Christopher Marlowe and the Failure to Unify*. Ashgate. [2015] pp. 172. £62.99 ISBN 9 7814 7243 9512.

Galant, Justyna Laura. *Painted Devils, Siren Tongues: The Semiotic Universe of Jacobean Tragedy*. Lang. [2015] pp. 208. £34 ISBN 9 7836 3162 6269.

Greenberg, Marissa. *Metropolitan Tragedy: Genre, Justice, and the City in Early Modern England*. UTorP. [2015] pp. xiii + 248. £37.99 ISBN 9 7814 4264 8807.

Henke, Robert. *Poverty and Charity in Early Modern Theater and Performance*. UIowaP. [2015] pp. xi + 198. £59.50 ISBN 9 7816 0938 3619.

Hollis, Gavin. *The Absence of America: The London Stage, 1576–1642*. OUP. [2015] pp. 288. £55 ISBN 9 7801 9873 4321.

Kendrick, Matthew. *At Work in the Early Modern English Theatre: Valuing Labor*. FDUP. [2015] pp. xix + 184. £49.95 ISBN 9 7816 1147 8242.

Kerr, Heather, and Claire Walker, eds. *Fama and Her Sisters: Gossip and Rumour in Early Modern Europe*. Brepols. [2015] pp. 246. £80.02 ISBN 9 7825 0354 1846.

Lowe, Eleanor, Martin Wiggins, Janette Dillon, ., eds. *Malone Society Collections XVII*. ManUP. [2015] pp. 104. £45 ISBN 9 7897 1909 9274.

Loxley, James, Anna Groundwater, and Julie Sanders, eds. *Ben Jonson's Walk to Scotland: An Annotated Edition of the 'Foot Voyage'*. CUP. [2014] pp. 256. £67 ISBN 9 7811 0700 3330.

Manley, Lawrence, and Sally-Beth MacLean. *Lord Strange's Men and Their Plays*. YaleUP. [2014] pp. ix + 475. £35 ISBN 9 7803 0019 1998.

Martin, Mathew R. *Tragedy and Trauma in the Plays of Christopher Marlowe*. Ashgate. [2015] pp. 202. £62.99 ISBN 9 7814 7243 1561.

Matei-Chesnoiu, Monica. *Geoparsing Early Modern English Drama*. Palgrave. [2015] pp. 264. £58 ISBN 9 7811 3747 9686.

Munroe, Jennifer, Edward J. Geisweidt, and Lynne Bruckner. *Ecological Approaches to Early Modern English Texts: A Field Guide to Reading and Teaching*. Ashgate. [2015] pp. 274. £20.99 ISBN 9 7814 7241 6735.

Neill, Michael, ed. *The Duchess of Malfi* by John Webster. Norton. [2015] pp. 448. £8.95 ISBN 9 7803 9392 3254.

Netzloff, Mark, Bradley D. Ryner, and Darlene Farabee, eds. *Early Modern Drama in Performance: Essays in Honor of Lois Potter*. UDelP. [2014] pp. 204. £44.95 ISBN 9 7816 1149 5126.

Price, Eoin. *'Public' and 'Private' Playhouses in Renaissance England: The Politics of Publication*. PalMac. [2015] pp. vii + 95. £49.99 ISBN 9 7811 3749 4917.

Rickard, Jane. *Writing the Monarch in Jacobean England: Jonson, Donne, Shakespeare and the Works of King James*. CUP. [2015] pp. vii + 272. £64.99 ISBN 9 7811 0712 0662.

Steggle, Matthew. *Digital Humanities and the Lost Drama of Early Modern England: Ten Case Studies*. Routledge. [2015] pp. i + 200. £60 ISBN 9 7814 0944 4145.

Wåghäll Nivre, Elisabeth, ed. *Allusions and Reflections: Greek and Roman Mythology in Renaissance Europe*. CambridgeSP. [2015] pp. 488. £57.99 ISBN 9 7814 4387 4540.

Wiggins, Martin, and Catherine Richardson. *British Drama 1533–1642: A Catalogue, vol. 5: 1603–1608*. OUP. [2015] pp. vii + 530. £100 ISBN 9 7801 9871 9236.

Wiggins, Martin, and Catherine Richardson. *British Drama 1533–1642: A Catalogue, vol. 6: 1609–1616*. OUP. [2015] pp. vii + 592. £100 ISBN 9 7801 9873 9111.

Willmott, Richard, ed. *The Alchemist* by Jonson Ben. OUP. [2015] pp. 320. £11.99 ISBN 9 7801 9835 5397.

Wittek, Stephen. *The Media Players: Shakespeare, Middleton, Jonson, and the Idea of News*. UMichP. [2015] pp. 157. £69.50 ISBN 9 7804 7207 2811.

Yiu, Mimi. *Architectural Involutions: Writing, Staging, and Building Space, c.1435–1650*. NorthwesternUP. [2015] pp. 320. £96.95 ISBN 9 7808 1012 9863.

# IX

# The Earlier Seventeenth Century

## ELIZABETH BRADBURN, JOHN R. BURTON, AND WILLIAM BAKER

This chapter has five sections: 1. Women's Writing; 2. General; 3. Bacon; 4. Browne; 5. Burton. Section 1 is by Elizabeth Bradburn and is not confined to the early seventeenth century but extends throughout the century; section 2 also extends throughout the century: the opening paragraph is by William Baker; the rest of the section is by John R. Burton; sections 3, 4, and 5 are by William Baker. In a few instances some of the coverage in this chapter may overlap with materials covered elsewhere in the volume.

## 1. Women's Writing

The year 2015 saw two edited collections each devoted to a female writer. *Seventeenth Century* published a special issue, 'Lucy Hutchinson', edited by David Norbrook. Norbrook's introductory essay, 'Lucy Hutchinson: Theology, Gender and Translation' (*SC* 30:ii[2015] 139–62) provides an overview of the current set of questions regarding Hutchinson and then analyses her theological treatises, arguing that she both parallels and goes beyond typical women's theological writing of the period. Her theological writings also potentially offer information about her biography, especially her authorial ambitions. The essays in the special issue range from historical essays to formalist literary criticism. In ' "Every county had more or lesse the civill warr within it selfe": The Realities of War in Lucy Hutchinson's Midland Shire' (*SC* 30:ii[2015] 191–206), Martyn Bennett considers Hutchinson herself as a historian. Her history of the Civil War in the *Memoirs of the Life of Colonel Hutchinson* is limited by being local to Nottingham but her 'qualitative approach' (p. 204) is still very valuable. Two essays focus on Hutchinson's relationship to the theologian John Owen. Mark Burden's 'Lucy Hutchinson and Puritan Education' (*SC* 30:ii[2015] 163–78) draws in part on the *Memoirs*, but especially on a translation of Owen's theological treatise. Hutchinson adjusted existing Calvinist ideas of education, with a particular interest in the connection between the practices of education and theological principles. Crawford Gribben explores the connection between Hutchinson and Owen

*The Year's Work in English Studies, Volume 96 (2017)* © *The Author 2017. Published by Oxford University Press on behalf of the English Association. All rights reserved.*
*For Permissions, please email: journals.permissions@oup.com*
doi:10.1093/ywes/max011

further in 'John Owen, Lucy Hutchinson and the Experience of Defeat' (*SC* 30:ii[2015] 179–90), which says that women writers had a special relationship with Owen, whose importance is under-recognized. Three other essays in the special issue place Hutchinson's work in diverse cultural contexts. In 'No "Publick Funerall"'? Lucy Hutchinson's Elegy, Epitaph, Monument' (*SC* 30:ii[2015] 207–28), Susan Wiseman contextualizes Hutchinson's work in the study of mourning, following the interaction between her literary elegies and other kinds of traces, including topographical ones, that form a network with them. Mihoko Suzuki's 'Animals and the Political in Lucy Hutchinson and Margaret Cavendish' (*SC* 30:ii[2015] 229–47) studies the depiction and discussion of animals in Hutchinson's and Margaret Cavendish's writings, drawing a fascinating contrast with Milton's *Comus*. Both women, says Suzuki, flatten out the accepted hierarchical distinction between animals and humans, and both do so in a political context, though with some important differences. The intersection between feminist theory and queer theory is the context for Penelope Anderson's study, 'Lucy Hutchinson's Sodom and the Backward Glance of Feminist Queer Temporality' (*SC* 30:ii[2015] 249–64). Hutchinson approaches Sodom differently from male writers of the period, connecting sodomy with other kinds of disobedience; her works offer a potential way to bridge the divide between feminist and queer theory. Finally, Elizabeth Scott-Baumann takes up the poetics of *Order and Disorder* in 'Lucy Hutchinson, Gender and Poetic Form' (*SC* 30:ii[2015] 265–84), arguing that the genderedness of Hutchinson's form may be found in how she deploys the heroic couplets to reflect her themes.

Hutchinson received critical attention outside this special issue as well. In ' "I remain, an airy phantasm": Lucy Hutchinson's Civil War Ghost Writing' (*ELH* 82:i[2015] 87–113), Erin Murphy covers a number of Hutchinson's works, especially the *Memoirs* and *Order and Disorder*. The essay shows how Hutchinson, prompted by the civil wars to interpret the events of her time, depicts identity as inconstant and fluid—though she sees this changeability as divinely willed. *Studies in Philology* published two articles on Hutchinson. The first, ' "My victorious triumphs are all Thine": Romance and Elect Community in Lucy Hutchinson's *Order and Disorder*' (*SP* 112:i[2015] 162–93), by Emily Griffiths Jones, compares *Order and Disorder* with Dryden's *Astrea Redux*. In Jones's reading, both are 'romances', Dryden's historical and Hutchinson's biblical. Dryden's romance claims teleology and romance for all English subjects, whereas Hutchinson's limits these to the elect. In its following issue the same journal included Patricia Patrick's ' "All that appears most casuall to us": Fortune, Compassion, and Reason in Lucy Hutchinson's Exploratory Providentialism' (*SP* 112:ii[2015] 327–52). This study of Hutchinson's use of the word 'fortune' in the *Memoirs* argues that the word is actually experimental, questioning. Connected with a larger intellectual culture, it allows her to try to understand why providence is the way it is.

The other collection of essays on a woman writer is *The Noble Flame of Katherine Philips: A Poetics of Culture, Politics, and Friendship*, edited by David L. Orvis and Ryan Singh Paul. The book incorporates a selection of 'foundational' essays in the field with new prefatory notes by their authors. These include: 'Katherine Philips and the Post-Courtly Coterie' (pp. 41–63), by Catharine Gray, which is about the context and complexity of Philips's politics, showing the how the Society of Friendship maintained the ideals of the Caroline Court; 'Inventing the English Sappho: Katherine Philips's Donnean Poetry' (pp. 153–86), by Paula Loscocco, which investigates how Philips appropriates Donne's poetics to express female homoeroticism; '"Friendship so curst": Amor Impossibilis, the Homoerotic Lament, and the Nature of Lesbian Desire' (pp. 243–65), by Valerie Traub, which studies Philips's transformation of the pastoral and its images of nature to suggest the possibility of female same-sex love; and 'The Body of the Friend and the Woman Writer: Katherine Philips's Absence from Alan Bray's The Friend' (pp. 267–89), by Lorna Hutson, which is about the difficulty of writing at all about female friendship for Philips, who had no ethical or political discourse available for this subject.

A notable new essay in the book is 'The Conjuncture of Word, Music, and Performance Practice in Philips's Era' (pp. 213–41), by Linda Phyllis Austern. Austern demonstrates how music and performance are key to understanding Philips's poetry. Philips uses metaphors drawn from music, but also understands the aesthetic experience of reading poetry as drawing on historically specific ideas about music. Philips's complex royalism is addressed in three of the essays. Christopher Orchard's 'The Failure of Royalist Heroic Virtue: Philips's "On the 3. of September, 1651"' (pp. 65–86) argues that Philips was not a blind royalist, but in this poem questions royalist policies and presents an alternative model of heroism. In 'Biblical Poetics, Royalist Politics, and Anti-Eschatological Prophecy in Philips's Poetry' (pp. 87–123), David L. Orvis analyses the prophetic biblical language of Philips's poems, showing how she draws on the Old Testament rather than the language favoured by millenarian poets. Amy Scott-Douglass, in 'Restoring Orinda's Face: Puritan Iconoclasm and Philips's Poems as Royalist Remonumentalization' (pp. 125–52), discuss the poems prefacing the 1667 edition. These construct Philips's poems themselves as symbolizing the Restoration and the monarchy. Rounding out the volume are Harriette Andreadis's 'Versions of Pastoral: Philips and Women's Queer Spaces' (pp. 291–309), which puts Philips's poems in the context of the 'subversive' use of pastoral by women poets, and an afterword by Elizabeth H. Hageman entitled 'The Most Deservedly Admired Mrs. Katherine Philips—Her Books' (pp. 311–24), which offers evidence that Philips's reputation and influence did not disappear as soon after her death as is often assumed. The Noble Flame of Katherine Philips is complemented by one other essay on that writer that appeared in 2015: 'Katherine Philips's Pompey (1663); or the Importance of Being a Translator' (in Newman and Tylus, eds., Early Modern Cultures of Translation, pp. 221–35), by Line Cottegnies. Cottegnies discusses Philips's translation of Pierre Corneille's La Mort de Pompée, a work only occasionally mentioned in individual essays in the above-discussed collection. The article carries out a close reading of the play in terms of seventeenth-century controversies about translation, concluding that Philips takes a nuanced compromise position.

Of the six essays published on Margaret Cavendish, half were about The Blazing World. Two of these specifically explore the theme of motion in that work. Anne M. Thell's '"As lightly as two thoughts": Motion, Materialism, and Cavendish's Blazing World' (*Configurations* 23:i[2015] 1–33) argues that the travelogue form is an appropriate way to express and explore Cavendish's natural philosophy, because the latter depends on motion. *The Blazing World* isn't just a natural philosophical treatise, however, but a document that questions and experiments. Daniel P. Richards also considers motion in relation to Cavendish's natural philosophy, but with emphasis on female subjectivity. In 'The (Re)Naturalization of Margaret Cavendish: Making Active the Relationship between Nature and Female Subjectivity in Blazing World' (in Chappell, Stanton, and Saxton, eds., *Spectacle, Sex, and Property in Eighteenth-Century Literature and Culture*, pp. 83–103), he studies motion and the 'dynamic' relationship between nature and female subjectivity; female subjectivity emerges from power over nature, but not scientific experimentation. Delilah Bermudez Brataas's 'Shakespeare's Presence and Cavendish's Absence in *The League of Extraordinary Gentlemen*' (*Shakespeare* 11:i[2015] 39–57) analyses Alan Moore's appropriation of *The Blazing World* in his graphic novel—to my knowledge, the first critical essay to do so. The argument is that the use of Shakespeare as a common 'icon' in graphic novels and science fiction brings together the fluid worlds, blurs the difference between the real and the fictional, and ultimately reduces Cavendish's presence.

Several more articles on Cavendish focused on gender. In 'Art, Authority, and Domesticity in Margaret Cavendish's *Poems and Fancies*' (*EMW* 10:i[2015] 27–47), Megan J. Fung analyses the domestic motifs in these lyrics. Fung argues that these motifs are thematically and structurally important and have been under-studied because Cavendish said she didn't like housework. Cavendish's poems draw an analogy between domestic work and artistic methods. Marianne Micros's ' "Thus did he make her breeding his only business and employment": Absent Mothers and Male Mentors in Margaret Cavendish's Romances' (in Bamford, Miller, and Kinney, eds., *Maternity and Romance Narratives in Early Modern England*, pp. 155–74) points out that, in the romances, the female main characters, who are orphans, find male educators and mentors. In this way, says Micros, Cavendish argues that parenting doesn't have to be gendered female. Finally, Abdulhamit Arvas's 'Ecoerotic Imaginations in Early Modernity and Cavendish's *The Convent of Pleasure*' (in Oppermann, ed., *New International Voices in Ecocriticism*, pp. 147–57) argues from an ecocritical perspective that Cavendish's play is about female homoeroticism. Cavendish questions the naturalness of procreative sex. Nature is 'othered' and is linked with queer desire and acts.

Ecocriticism also provided the context for a new essay on Amelia Lanyer, ' "Bare and desolate now": Cultural Ecology and the ' "Description of Cookham" ' (in Munroe, Geisweidt, and Bruckner, eds., *Ecological Approaches to Early Modern English Texts: A Field Guide to Reading and Teaching*, pp. 99–108), by Louise Noble. Noble approaches Lanyer's poem with the assumption that literature is a form of cultural ecology. Lanyer, she says, interweaves the female speaker's subjugation and the corruption of the landscape. This allows the poem to criticize two kinds of hierarchy at the same time; it has a 'poetics of ecological awareness' (p. 99). Two more essays focused on Lanyer's *Salve Deus Rex Judaeorum*. Erin A. McCarthy's 'Speculation and Multiple Dedications in *Salve Deus Rex Judaeorum*' (*SEL* 55:i[2015] 45–72) is about the publisher's motivation for including so many dedications to the volume This was an effort to attract readers, specifically educated female readers. *Salve Deus* represents a transitional moment between patronage and professional authorship. Victoria Brownlee's 'Literal and Spiritual Births: Mary as Mother in Seventeenth-Century Women's Writing' (*RenQ* 68:iv[2015] 1297–1326) reads *Salve Deus* alongside Dorothy Leigh's *The Mother's Blessing*. The poets are alike in that they focus on Mary's physical maternity, but both poems ultimately conclude that true maternity is spiritual, not physical. For Lanyer this spiritual maternity can be a model of female authorship. Rounding out the scholarship on seventeenth-century women writers was 'The Language of Suffering in Anne Killigrew's "On the Birthday of Queen Katherine" and *Penelope to Ulysses*' (*Interactions* 24:i–ii[2015] 91–8), by Laura Linker. Linker argues that Killigrew identified with Queen Catherine, wife of Charles II, and that the language of sorrow in these poems is meant to express the suffering of the queen. All in all, critics attended to a range of female authors in 2015, and, with important collections on two major figures, scholarship on seventeenth-century women writers continues to grow.

## 2. General

A useful reference work published in 2015 is Robert C Evans's *Perspectives on Renaissance Poetry*. Texts of poems are followed by discussion using different critical approaches, offering paragraph-length accounts of twenty critical methodologies and showing, through application of one or several of them to individual poems, the ways in which they enrich thirty Renaissance poems. Mainly aimed at undergraduates, there is much to be gained from Evans's sensible discussions. Following Evans's introduction, 'Sir Walter Ralegh (1552–1616): "What Is Our Life?"' (pp. 1–20), there are chapters on 'Sir Thomas Wyatt (1503–42): "They flee from me"; "My lute, awake!"' (pp. 21–39); 'Henry Howard, Earl of Surrey (1517–47): "Love, that doth reign and live within my thought"; "Th' Assyrians' king, in peace with foul desire"' pp. 31–40); 'Anne Vaughan Locke (1534–after 1590): "And then not daring with presuming eye"; "Have mercy, God, for thy great mercy's sake"' (pp. 41–50); 'Sir Philip Sidney (1554–86): *Astrophil and Stella* 5 ("It is most true"); *Astrophil and Stella* 71 ("Who will in fairest book")' (pp. 51–60); 'Edmund Spenser (1552–99): *Amoretti* 68 ("Most glorious Lord of life"); *Amoretti* 75 ("One day I wrote her name"); *The Faerie Queene*, I. i–ii' (pp. 61–70); 'Christopher Marlowe (1564–93): "The Passionate Shepherd to His Love"; "Hero and Leander" (excerpt)' (pp. 71–80); 'William Shakespeare (1564–1616): Sonnets 3 and 147; "Venus and Adonis" (excerpt)' (pp. 81–90); 'John Donne (1572–1631): "The Flea"; "Holy Sonnet 14"' (pp. 91– 8); 'Aemilia Lanyer (1569–1645): "Eve's Apology in Defense of Women" (excerpt); "The Description of Cookham" (excerpt)' (pp. 99–108); 'Ben Jonson (1572–1637): "On My First Son"; "To Penshurst"' (excerpt)' (pp. 109–18); 'Lady Mary Wroth (1587–1651/3): "Like to the Indians"; Martha Moulsworth (1577–1646): "The Memorandum of

Martha Moulsworth, Widow" (excerpt)' (pp. 119–28); 'George Herbert (1593–1633): "Redemption"; "The Collar"' (pp. 129–38); 'Robert Herrick (1591–1674): "Corinna's Going A-Maying"; "To the Virgins, to Make Much of Time"' (pp. 139–48); 'Katherine Philips (1632–64): "Upon the Double Murder of King Charles"; "Friendship's Mystery"' (pp. 149–58); 'Andrew Marvell (1621–78): "To His Coy Mistress"; "The Mower against Gardens"' (pp. 159–68); 'John Milton (1608–74): "Lycidas" (excerpt); *Paradise Lost*, Book 12 (excerpt)' (pp. 169–80). There is an afterword, 'Critical Pluralism: "A Contemplation on Bassets-down-Hill" by Anne Kemp', that adopts different critical perspectives (pp. 181–92) followed by an appendix by Christina M. Garner, 'The Kinds of Questions Different Critics Ask' (pp. 193–214). An alphabetically arranged double-columned bibliography (pp. 215–16) is followed by a useful listing of further reading (pp. 217–19), and a helpful 'Index of Theories and Applications' starting with 'archetypal criticism' (p. 219) and concluding with 'traditional historical criticism' (p. 220).

The year 2015 saw a number of significant publications and studies of seventeenth-century literary culture, several of which will no doubt prove to be influential in future work. It would be difficult to over-state the significance of the Bible in the culture of the period, and this year's *Oxford Handbook of the Bible in Early Modern England*, edited by Kevin Killeen, Helen Smith, and Rachel Judith Willie, offers readers the benefit of more than forty scholars' contributions on a wide range of biblical topics including seventeenth-century interpretation, Milton and the Bible, the Jacobean political use of the Bible, Herbert and scriptural poetics, and Donne's biblical scholarship. Winner of the Sixteenth Century Society's Roland H. Bainton Prize for Reference Works, the volume is divided into six sections; 'Translations', 'Scholarship', 'Spreading the Word', 'The Political Bible', 'The Bible and Literature', and 'Reception Histories'. The editors are to be commended for bringing their expertise to bear on a topic of enormous import to scholars of the period. While the Bible can be said to be a locus of divine law, Christopher Warren provided scholars with the first book-length literary history of international law in the period in his *Literature and the Law of Nations, 1580–1680*. Arguing that early modern literary genres shaped and informed debates about the law of nations, he offers insightful readings of Sidney's *New Arcadia*, Shakespeare's *The Winter's Tale*, Bacon's *Aphorismi de Jure Gentium*, Hobbes's *Thucydides*, Milton's *Paradise Lost* and *Samson Agonistes*, and Grotius' *Sophompaneas*, among others. When the notion of a law of nations gave rise to the complex and overlapping landscape of international law (a term given significant analysis by Warren) it retained much from its literary roots, and Warren's study reveals that the conventions, customs, and treaties upon which international law came to be framed and constituted were fundamentally what early modern genres addressed. Thus, Warren argues, literature was the 'locus of accessible jurisprudence...a form of political participation' (p. 233). Warren's monograph is the result of a highly informed analysis, with thirty-six pages of bibliographical references, and will no doubt prove to become an important watershed in studies of the history of international law.

Fear and fascination prompted early modern authors to respond to the emergence in the sixteenth century of a new expansionist military, economic, and political power in the European and Mediterranean region. 'The mightie Empire of the Turks', as described by Richard Knolles (d.1610), had become 'the greatest terror of the world', as cited in Anders Ingram's study of this year *Writing the Ottomans: Turkish History in Early Modern England*. Ingram unpacks writing by Knolles, Paul Rycaut (1629–1700), and George Sandys (1577–1644), and translations by Abraham Hartwell (1553–1606) to explore the ways in which English writing on Turkish history often served as source material for a wide array of literary genres. In addition, Ingram explores how such authors furthered the role of historical writing as a method of not only accounting for the origins of the Ottomans, but also contextualizing their advance in moral, religious, philosophical, and political terms. The study necessarily engages fruitfully with theories surrounding historical writing, and here Ingram draws from J. Pocock, Quentin Skinner, and Anthony Grafton, and develops a critical approach that largely avoids controversies surrounding the figure of the 'Turk' as an oriental Other by focusing upon the discourse of Turkish history and the language used by English authors to articulate that history. What follows is an evolution of an English early modern historical discourse, one that relied upon a Continental discourse regarding the Turks, a process of repurposing European writing for a new audience that addressed both the fear of a new un-Christian world power and also a fascination regarding a foreign culture that offered new trading opportunities.

The literary texture of scientific writing in the period is examined by Claire Preston in *The Poetics of Scientific Investigation in Seventeenth-Century England*. Her central concern, how science was to be written by both literary and scientific writers, is explored by appealing to a wide range of early modern authors. Montaigne, Bacon, Donne, Browne, Lovelace, Boyle, Sprat, Oldenburg, Evelyn, Cowley, and Dryden are all given attention as she explores how scientists, laymen, and quasi-scientists gave rise to a new mode of expression and new hybrid literary forms. Exploring how spatial deixis operates in early modern lyric—terms such as here/there, this/that as they relate to space—leads Heather Dubrow to embark on a fascinating reading of works by Shakespeare, Donne, Spenser, and Wroth in her monograph *Deixis in Early Modern English Lyric: Unsettling Spatial Anchors like 'Here', 'This', 'Come'*. Dubrow's interest is focused both upon how a word like 'this' relates to spatial proximity and how as a deictic it 'demands to be read as a participant in a prolonged series of linguistic, cognitive, and possibly even physical events' (p. 2). Her selection of texts, each from lyric verse and chosen since lyric deixis appears to have received less critical attention than its counterparts in drama and narrative, necessarily requires an excellent discussion of the complex challenges in defining lyric. For Dubrow, deixis assists poets and their readers in ordering space, and a 'strategic spatiality' is the subject of her chapter on Spenser's *Epithalamion*, an exploration which yields surprising political references. In addressing Shakespeare's sonnets, Dubrow notes that the deictic 'this' appears in thirty-one of the couplets in the sequence, an often reflexive term that draws attention to the materiality of the poems themselves. A chapter on Wroth's pastoral Song 1 draws attention to the ways in which deictics can involve tensions within the pastoral world itself, rather than a simple country/city dichotomy. Donne's use of deictic, argues Dubrow, reveals unease about salvation, and here there are fascinating implications for the discussion of proximity and distance in relation to devotional lyric. A closing chapter allows Dubrow to address some recent developments in formalist analysis pertinent both to discussions of current critical methodologies and to her close reading of spatial deictic, confirming the value of this small volume and the task it performs so well.

In addition to contributions by Heather Dubrow and Emma Rhatigan's chapter on Donne's biblical encounters in the *Oxford Handbook of the Bible* mentioned above, further publications attest to 2015 being a highly productive year for Donne studies. A renewed interest in his non-poetic work has led key scholars in the field to embark on a complete reassessment of his sermons. Funded by an AHRC grant and managed under the general editorship of Peter McCullough, *The Oxford Edition of the Sermons of John Donne* will eventually run to sixteen volumes, offering the first major edition of the sermons since Potter and Simpson's offering. The first edition of the new series came to print in 2013, an edition of Donne's Carolinian sermons edited by David Colclough, coming as volume 3 of the series; 2015 saw the publication of two volumes: volume 1, covering 1615–19 and edited by McCullough, and volume 5, concerning sermons from 1620–3 and edited by Katrin Ettenhuber. Each edition offers a valuable commentary, and the series as a whole will eventually be furnished with a *Textual Companion* (volume 16), which will offer full bibliographical descriptions and analyses of all primary texts used, particularly important in Donne studies. Each sermon is presented in a clear format with marginal line numbering, old spelling, critical footnotes, textual variants, and all marginalia of the original copy. The commentaries offer introductory contextual headnotes, summaries of Donne's source material, and suggestions for further reading in addition to a line-by-line annotation giving obsolete diction and a translation of non-English words and phrases. Each edition is also augmented with an index of biblical texts, a biographical index of persons referred to by Donne, and an index of Donne's works, in addition to a general index. The series will prove to be of immense value to future scholarship and research.

Achsah Guibbory's contributions to the field of Donne studies rank her as insightful and erudite among her peers, and her most important essays have been collected and supplemented with three new essays in *Returning to Donne*. The collection is divided into three sections ('Time and History', 'Love', and 'Religion') and each section is given a brief explanatory introduction. Guibbory remains historicist in her critical approach, and yet in contrast to the general trend in recent Donne studies to look more to his prose, Guibbory's approach is equally sure-footed in his poetry, and this collection provides insights that will be of interest to scholars on both sides of the critical divide. It is perhaps her profound interest in both his poetry and prose works that allows Guibbory to be particularly sensitive to strands of continuity in Donne's writings. Testament to her wide scholarship are the expansive indexed references to Donne's works in the volume. Greg Kneidel aims to draw attention to an area of Donne's canon often overlooked; the 'Satyres'. Often aligned with illegality and subversion, the satirical poems are placed by Kneidel within the context of England's emerging legal culture of the 1590s, in his monograph *John Donne and Early Modern Legal Culture: The End of Equity in the Satyres*. Going beyond the more obvious point that Donne was well acquainted with the legal controversies of his day, Kneidel argues that Donne considered his satires as contributing to the practice of law, in that they attempt to draw together justice and law, aspects frequently in conflict. Few issues are of greater import to Donne scholars than his devotional loyalties, and Kimberly Anne Coles's article 'The Matter of Belief in John Donne's Holy Sonnets' (*RenQ* 68:iii[2015] 899–931) explores the somatic construction of religious identity in his Holy Sonnets. Coles argues persuasively that Donne frames his religious temperament and his body in terms of being changeable, a further reflection on how body and spirit are mutually imbricated to a profound degree in Donne's thinking and work. Mingjun Lu traces the genesis of the Arctic Northwest Passage as a route to China by examining historical and metaphorical associations of Donne's image of the Anyan Strait in his 'Hymn to God My God, in My Sickness' [1623] in her article 'The Anyan Strait and the Far East: John Donne's Global Vision and Theological Cosmopolitanism' (*Criticism* 57:iii[2015] 431–50). Lu argues that Donne's central metaphor involves a kind of globalism, the uniting of the East and West in an act of what she terms 'theological cosmopolitanism', an effort to align biblical discourse within a global context. Lu's article comes as her monograph *The Chinese Impact Upon English Renaissance Literature: A Globalization and Liberal Cosmopolitan Approach to Donne and Milton* comes to print. In it, she examines how English writers responded to the cultural shock caused by the first substantial encounters between East and West, arguing how Milton and Donne developed a respect for difference in light of Chinese culture, eventually becoming aware of their own monotheistic and Eurocentric assumptions. Of particular interest to readers of this section is her chapter entitled 'Chinese Chronology and Donne's Apologetic Exegesis in *Essayes in Divinity*', in which Donne has to negotiate the threat presented by Chinese chronology to the biblical system of time. M. Thomas Hester is interested in Donne's use of elegy, as he explores in his article 'The "Bitter Cost" of John Donne's "The Bracelet"' (*BJJ* 22:i[2015] 119–28). Hester engages with Donne's interest in Ovidian poetic daring and religio-political commentary.

What can account for the success of Baconian science and philosophy? While works on Francis Bacon run the risk of either relying solely upon an interpretation of his historical context or on an application of the history of science to a particular work, Tom van Malssen consciously turns to a number of works to support his argument that Bacon's thought can be brought to light only when his works are looked at as part of a combined historical and philosophical examination. Malssen's *The Political Philosophy of Francis Bacon: On the Unity of Knowledge* explores Bacon as a mainly political philosopher. In addition to this monograph, Bacon is further explored as Todd Butler examines how disputes over the cognitive processes that structure textual production helped establish and limit Jacobean state authority, in 'The Cognitive Politics of Writing in Jacobean England: Bacon, Coke, and the Case of Edmund Peacham' (*HLQ* 78:i[2015] 21–39), an article on the tense conflict between Francis Bacon, Edward Coke, and James I in the wake of the arrest and death of Edmund Peacham. Butler finds that the disputes over Peacham's arrest and Coke's *Reports* led to a greater philosophical struggle over individual and collective thought. Christopher Mead examines the intersection of print, anatomy, and eucharistic language in Robert Burton's *The Anatomy of Melancholy* in his article ' "Content to be pressed": Robert Burton and the *Editio Princeps Hominis*' (*Rep* 129:i[2015] 1–24). Mead convincingly argues that Burton conceived of his published work in somatic and eucharistic ways, as his 'body' is distributed and consumed by readers. Mary Ann Lund adds to this year's work on Burton by exploring happiness, a commodity in short supply in Burton's *Anatomy*, in her chapter 'Robert Burton, Perfect Happiness and the Visio Dei' (in Meek and Sullivan, eds., *The Renaissance of Emotion: Understanding Affect in Shakespeare and His Contemporaries*, pp. 86–108).

### 3. Bacon

Other interesting work on Bacon appeared in 2015. Salwa Khoddam's 'Looking into the "Enchanted Glass": C.S. Lewis and Francis Bacon on Methods of Perception and the Purpose of the "New Science" ' (in Khoddam, Hall, and Fisher, eds., *C.S. Lewis and the Inklings: Reflections on Faith, Imagination, and Modern Technology*, pp. 180–204) writes on the impact of Bacon's treatment of the natural sciences, the scientific-technological revolution, and the relation to fallacy and technocracy perceived in Bacon's writings by C.S. Lewis in his *The Abolition of Man*, published in 1943. Jenny C. Mann, in her 'Pygmalion's Wax: "Fruitful Knowledge" in Bacon and Montaigne' (*JMEMS* 45[2015] 367–93), compares the treatment of Pygmalion in Bacon's *The Advancement of Learning* [1605] and Montaigne: 'though this is not their avowed project, the allusions to Pygmalion in Montaigne's "Apology" and Bacon's *Advancement* show us how the enterprises of philosophy and poesis are intertwined in the early modern period' (p. 387). 'The Extrinsic Bible: Francis Bacon's *New Atlantis*, Concepts of Scripture, and the Question of Secularity' (*R&L* 47[2015] 99–121) is the subject of Travis DeCook's essay in *Religion and Literature*. DeCook's main text is Bacon's *New Atlantis* [1627]. For DeCook, 'God and religion very much determine natural philosophy in *New Atlantis*. However, the Bible imagined in Bacon's utopian narrative can counterintuitively be seen to raise the possibility of secularity more powerfully than his natural philosophical writings, which preserve a more mediated sense of the division between God and creation' (p. 113). Julianne Werline also focuses upon the *New Atlantis* in her 'Francis Bacon and the Art of Misinterpretation' (*PMLA* 130[2015] 236–51). Werline calls attention to symbolism, paradox, the treatment of characters, and knowledge and its relationship to the reader, plus misinterpretation. Her abstract observes that 'Recent research has shown how Francis Bacon drew on Renaissance practices of reading and writing to propose a new method for understanding nature. Yet Bacon was well aware that such techniques were vulnerable to error, miscommunication, and failure. Instances of misinterpretation in his utopian fantasy *New Atlantis* reveal that his dream of a legible world accounts for the possibility of misreading. Bacon's characters and his audience are invited to interpret the text's symbols, but they are denied the basis for adequate interpretation. The paradoxes that arise from this strange position affirm the utility of Bacon's method and expose some of its limits' (p. 527). Robert P. Ellis, in his biographical monograph *Francis Bacon: The Double-Edged Life of the Philosopher and Statesman* pays much attention to his subject's *The Advancement of Learning* [1605]. Virginia Lee Strain, in 'The "Snared Subject" and the General Pardon Statute in Late Elizabethan Coterie Literature' (in Beecher, DeCook, Wallace, and Williams, eds., *Taking Exception to the Law: Materializing Injustice in Early Modern English Literature*, pp. 100–19), while focusing upon coterie literary relationships and the idea of pardon in late Elizabethan circles discusses essays by Bacon, including his 'Of Judicature' (pp. 104–5), and 'Reading of the Statute of Users' and 'Of Tribute; or Giving That Which Is Due' (pp. 110–13). Todd Butler's 'The Cognitive Politics of Writing in Jacobean England: Bacon, Coke, and the Case of Edmund Peacham' (*HLQ* 78:i[2015] 21–39) is discussed elsewhere in the present chapter.

## 4. Browne

Giuliano Miro, in his 'Blending Theology with Science: Thomas Browne's *Pseudodoxia Epidemica* and the Tradition of Vulgar Errors' (*Viator* 46[2015] 353–84), explores Sir Thomas Browne's *Pseudodoxia Epidemica* [1646], its treatment of science and relationship to theological discourse, and Browne's perception of the ideas of error and his probable use of Sir Francis Bacon. Hugh Aldersey-Williams's *In Search of Sir Thomas Browne: The Life and Afterlife of the Seventeenth Century's Most Inquiring Mind* or, under its British title more accurately representing its content, *The Adventures of Sir Thomas Browne in the 21st Century*, is not so much a biography of the extraordinary writer, physician, and philosopher who spent the last forty years of his life in Norwich as an account of his importance and relevance to us in the second decade of the current century. Aldersey-Williams draws attention to Browne's influence upon such diverse thinkers as Jorge Luis Borges, Samuel Taylor Coleridge, and Virginia Woolf, admirers of Browne's Latinate prose, and on W.G. Sebald, who in his East Anglian essay-novel *The Rings of Saturn* [1995] pays homage to Browne and his celebration of human activity, interest, and puzzlement. Aldersey-Williams sees affinities between Vladimir Nabokov and Browne, in the first sentence of *Speak, Memory* [1951]: 'The cradle rocks above the abyss, and common sense tells us that our existence is but a brief crack of light between two eternities of darkness.' Browne, the virtuoso of prose style, introduced hundreds of words into English, including, to name but six: electricity, hallucination, medical, ferocious, deductive, and suicide. Chapters are structured around such themes as 'Animals' (pp. 78–111), 'Science' (pp. 143–69), 'Tolerance' (pp. 170–99), and 'Faith' (pp. 200–27), celebrating Browne's thirst for all kinds of knowledge, from tree-planting to birds to human burial rites. The book concludes with a detailed further reading section (pp. 301–12) and there is an extensive, helpful double-columned index (pp. 319–30). Reid Barbour and Claire Preston's 'Discursive and Speculative Writing' (in Cheney and Hardie, eds., *The Oxford History of Classical Reception in English Literature*, vol. 2: *1558–1660*, pp. 461–83) reviewed elsewhere in this volume of *YWES*, contains a discussion of Browne's style.

A very important study not only of Browne is Claire Preston's *The Poetics of Scientific Investigation in Seventeenth-Century England*, also reviewed above. Its concerns are reflected in the chapter headings: 'Introduction: "A Distemper of Learning": The Languages of Science' (pp. 1–33); '*Orlando Curioso*: The Lapsarian Style of Thomas Browne' (pp. 34–67); 'Equivocal Boyle and the Enamelled Telescope' (pp. 68–89); '"A blessing in the wilderness": Fictions of Polity and the Place of Science' (pp. 90–157); 'Dining Out in the Republic of Letters: The Rhetoric of Scientific Correspondence' (pp. 158–95); and 'The Counsel of Herbs: Scientific Georgic' (pp. 196–240; followed by the bibliography (pp. 241–72) and index (pp. 273–93). In her study Preston proposes that 'the available generic traditions of the early-modern period (elegy, epic, panegyric, epyllion, satire, dialogue, among others) became, or began developing as, natural philosophy's framework of scientific exposition, discussion and practice'. Preston considers 'the ways in which new literary forms ... (the experimental report, the journal article) emerged to support this framework, and the ways in which existing but evolving literary forms (the letter, the essay) were reshaped to meet its needs'. For Preston Sir Thomas Browne was 'possibly the most elaborately "literary" of any seventeenth-century savant, to the linguistic tools of investigation and of natural history'. Browne, unlike for instance Boyle, is 'only available to inference and by direct examination of the lexical, rhetorical, and revisionary discussion he makes in his major works'. Consequently Browne's 'liberal neologizing in encyclopedic works like *The Garden of Cyrus* and *Pseudodoxia Epidemica* suggests an almost complete openness to semantic invention'. Her 'discussion opens with extended consideration of Browne's neological and onomastic habits in *The Garden of Cyrus* in order to assess his attitudes and those of some of his contemporaries, to his semantic tools and to linguistic propriety in the writing of science'. Preston adds that 'his serial reconfiguration of some of *Pseudodoxia*'s chapters over twenty-five years is itself both a literary process and a scientific one, and an examination of these revisions' demonstrates Browne's increasing 'confidence in linguistic tools to convey matters of fact: we see the rhetorical and the empirical becoming seamless over its four editions' (p. 30). A considerable strength of Preston's monograph lies in her superb ability to convey complex ideas in excellent English and to make them exciting. Her work is a pleasure to read: this can rarely be said of academic monographs. It is difficult to resist giving a few other examples. She writes that 'the symphonic quality of Browne's splendid English we readily recognize in overtly spiritual works like *Religio Medici* and *Urne-Buriall* where he often speculates on matters of faith and morals by couching them in similitude to the empirically investigated world as if they were experimental assays or thought-experiments' (pp. 34–5). Preston observes that 'Thomas Browne clearly hungered for adjectives. Of his 157 original (including unique) words in *Cyrus*, eighty-three are adjectives, sixty-one are nouns, eleven are adverbs and only two are verbs' (p. 45). Hers is a most erudite work, with useful footnote documentation, an extensive bibliography (pp. 241–72) and a double-columned index (pp. 273–93).

## 5. Burton

There are two interesting Robert Burton items to report. Stephanie Shirilan's *Robert Burton and the Transformative Powers of Melancholy* appeared as part of Ashgate's Literary and Scientific Cultures of Early Modernity monograph series, now published by Routledge. Shirilan writes that 'in the third edition' of 1628 of his *Anatomy of Melancholy* (first published in 1621) Burton introduced a 'tag . . . taken from Horace: "Omne tulit punctum, qui miscuit utile dulci"— he who mingles the practical and the pleasurable wins the prize, or, more literally, "gets the point". The caption instructs the reader who hopes to profit from the book to approach it *sympathetically*, that is, with a willingness to be transformed, especially by the pleasures of the experience.' Shirilan's 'study is an attempt to demonstrate and elaborate this therapeutic principle by situating it in its rhetorical, physiological, theological contexts' (p. 1). In her introduction (pp. 1–28) she 'aims first, however, to contend with the history of critical resistance both to sympathetic readings of the *Anatomy* and to the positively transformative powers of the imagination in Burton's book' (p. 1). There are chapters on 'Democritus Junior: Discerning Care' (pp. 29–62), 'Heroic Hypochondria and the Sympathetic Delusions of Melancholy' (pp. 63–100), 'Exhilarating the Spirits: Study as Cure for Scholarly Melancholy' (pp. 101–36), and ' "Exonerating" Melancholy' (pp. 137–76), and an 'Epilogue: Loving Burton, or Burton for Amateurs' ( pp. 177–84). Shirilan's thematic exploration includes depression and melancholy in literature and mind–body therapies, topics of contemporary relevance. Her book concludes with an extensive list of works cited (pp. 185–204) and a double-columned index (pp. 205–17).

The other interesting Burton item is a somewhat surprising one, found in Robert D Denham's *Northrop Frye and Others: Twelve Writers Who Helped Shape His Thinking*. The writers who influenced him Frye wrote very little on. Denham draws upon Frye's notebooks, diaries, unpublished papers, student essays, and correspondence to reveal the impact of Aristotle, Lewis Carroll, Frances Yates, and others on him. Robert Burton is amongst these, and Denham's sixth chapter is devoted to 'Frye and Robert Burton' (pp. 131–46), in which Denham explores such issues as 'What Is an Anatomy?', 'Varieties of the Anatomy', 'Frye on Burton's *Anatomy*', and 'The Final Cause of Anatomy'. Denham cites Frye as observing of Burton that 'the greatest book ever written at Oxford is the *Anatomy of Melancholy*' (*Complete Works*, xiii. 132). For Frye 'the word anatomy in Shakespeare's day and a little later meant a dissection for a synthetic overview'. According to Denham, the author of *The Anatomy of Criticism* [1957] said that 'One of my favorite books in English literature—there are times when it is actually my favorite—is *Burton's Anatomy of Melancholy*.' Frye notes that 'of course, there were four humors then, but for Burton there was only the one, melancholy. That was the source of all mental and physical diseases in the world. So he writes an enormous survey of human life. It ranks with Chaucer and Dickens, except the characters are books rather than people. It was both an analysis of the causes and cures and treatment of melancholy and a kind of synthetic overview of human nature before it gets melancholy.' Denham also draws attention to Frye's observations made after his 1957 book that he retained his 'special affection for the literary genre I have called the anatomy, especially for Burton's *Anatomy of Melancholy*, with its schematic arrangements that are hardly those of any systematic medical treatment of melancholy, and yet correspond to something in the mind that yields a perhaps even deeper kind of comprehension. Such books as Burton's have an extraordinary pulling power: I understand very well what Samuel Johnson meant by saying that Burton's was the only book that got him out of bed earlier than he wanted to.' Furthermore, 'Frye's interest in the anatomy as a form of prose goes back to his teenage years.' Denham observes that Frye, during the summer of 1932 following his third year at Victoria College, began to form in his notes ' "an embryonic anatomy theory" ' (p. 131). Consequently by the time Frye attended a course on satire in 1934–5, he knew Burton's *Anatomy of Melancholy* well. Denham adds that 'Frye's ideas on the *Anatomy* continued to gestate during his Oxford years' (p. 131).

**Books Reviewed**

Aldersey-Williams, Hugh. *The Adventures of Sir Thomas Browne in the 21st Century*. Granta. [2015] pp 352. £20 ISBN 9 7818 4708 9007. Published in the United States as *In Search of Sir Thomas Browne: The Life and Afterlife of the Seventeenth Century's Most Inquiring Mind*. Norton. [2015] pp. xx + 330. $26.95 ISBN 9 7803 9324 1648.

Bamford, Karen, Naomi J. Miller, and Clare R. Kinney, eds. *Maternity and Romance Narratives in Early Modern England*. Ashgate. [2015] pp. 219. $104.95 ISBN 9 7814 7246 2244.

Beecher, Donald, Travis DeCook, Andrew Wallace, and Grant Williams, eds. *Taking Exception to the Law: Materializing Injustice in Early Modern English Literature*. UTorP. [2015] pp. ix + 315. $70 ISBN 9 7814 4264 2010.

Chappell, Julie A., Kamille Stone Stanton, and Kirsten T. Saxton, eds. *Spectacle, Sex, and Property in Eighteenth-Century Literature and Culture*. AMS. [2015] pp. 255. $39.50 ISBN 9 7804 0467 0030.

Cheney, Patrick and Philip Hardie, eds. *The Oxford History of Classical Reception 2: 1558–1660*. OUP[2015] pp.650. $215 ISBN 9 7801 9954 7555.

Denham, Robert D. *Northrop Frye and Others: Twelve Writers Who Helped Shape His Thinking*. UOttawaP. [2015] pp. viii + 295. $24.23 ISBN 9 7807 7662 3078.

Dubrow, Heather. *Deixis in Early Modern English Lyric: Unsettling Spatial Anchors like 'Here', 'This', 'Come'*. PalMac. [2015] pp. 135. $67.50 ISBN 9 7811 3741 1303.

Ellis, Robert P. *Francis Bacon: The Double-Edged Life of the Philosopher and Statesman.* McFarland. [2015] pp. vii + 213. $40 ISBN 9 7807 8649 7270.

Ettenhuber, Katrin, ed. *The Oxford Edition of the Sermons of John Donne, vol. 5: Sermons Preached at Lincoln's Inn, 1620–23.* OUP. [2015] pp. 448. £125 ISBN 9 7801 9956 3258.

Evans, Robert C. *Perspectives on Renaissance Poetry.* Bloomsbury. [2015] pp. x + 220. $29.95 ISBN 9 7814 7250 8676.

Guibbory, Achsah. *Returning to Donne.* Ashgate/Routledge. [2015] pp. 278. £67.99 ISBN 9 7814 0946 8783.

Ingram, Anders. *Writing the Ottomans: Turkish History in Early Modern England.* PalMac. [2015] pp. 195. $90 ISBN 9 7811 3740 1526.

Khoddam, Salwa, Mark R. Hall, and Jason Fisher, eds. *C.S. Lewis and the Inklings: Reflections on Faith, Imagination, and Modern Technology.* CambridgeSP. [2015] pp. xiv + 313. £44.99 ISBN 9 7814 4387 6292.

Killeen, Kevin, Helen Smith, and Rachel Judith Willie, eds. *The Oxford Handbook of the Bible in Early Modern England.* OUP. [2015] pp. 806. £110 ISBN 9 7801 9968 6971.

Kneidel, Gregory. *John Donne and Early Modern Legal Culture: The End of Equity in the Satyres.* Duquesne. [2015] pp. x + 246. $70 ISBN 9 7808 2070 4814.

Lu, Mingjun. *The Chinese Impact upon English Renaissance Literature: A Globalization and Liberal Cosmopolitan Approach to Donne and Milton.* Routledge. [2015] pp. 248. £62.99 ISBN 9 7814 7246 1254.

Malssen, Tom van. *The Political Philosophy of Francis Bacon: On the Unity of Knowledge.* SUNYP. [2015] pp. 336. $95 ISBN 9 7814 3845 4177.

McCullough, Peter, ed. *The Oxford Edition of the Sermons of John Donne, vol. 1: Sermons Preached at the Jacobean Courts, 1615–19.* OUP. [2015] pp. 368. £125 ISBN 9 7801 9957 9365.

Meek, Richard and Erin Sullivan, eds. *The Renaissance of Emotions: Understanding Affect in Shakespeare and His Contemporaries.* [2015] pp. 288. ISBN 97807 1909 0783.

Munroe, Jennifer, Edward J. Geisweidt, and Lynne Bruckner, eds. *Ecological Approaches to Early Modern English Texts: A Field Guide to Reading and Teaching.* Ashgate. [2015] pp. 256. $40.95 ISBN 9 7814 7241 6728.

Newman, Karen, and Jane Tylus, eds. *Early Modern Cultures of Translation.* UPennP. [2015] pp. 368. $55 ISBN 9 7808 1224 7404.

Oppermann, Serpil, ed. *New International Voices in Ecocriticism.* Lexington. [2015] pp. 217. $45.99 ISBN 9 7814 9850 1491.

Orvis, Daniel L., and Ryan Singh Paul, eds. *The Noble Flame of Katherine Philips: A Poetics of Culture, Politics, and Friendship.* Duquesne. [2015] pp. 454. $60 ISBN 9 7808 2070 4746.

Preston, Claire. *The Poetics of Scientific Investigation in Seventeenth-Century England.* OUP. [2015] pp. 320 £60. ISBN 9 7801 9870 4805.

Shirilan, Stephanie. *Robert Burton and the Transformative Powers of Melancholy.* Ashgate. [2015] pp. xii + 218. $109.95 ISBN 9 7814 7241 7015.

Warren, Christopher N. *Literature and the Law of Nations, 1580–1680.* OUP. [2015] pp. 304. £55 ISBN 9 7801 9871 9342.

# X

# Milton and Poetry 1603–1660

## WILLIAM BAKER, JAMES DOELMAN, ANNE JAMES, AND MATTHEW MROZ

This chapter has four sections: 1. General; 2. Herbert; 3. Donne; 4. Milton. Section 1 is by William Baker; section 2 is by James Doelman; section 3 is by Anne James; section 4 is by Matthew Mroz.

## 1. General

This section will focus on work published in 2015 on Cowley, Crashaw, and Herrick. There are two Cowley items of interest. Joseph Wallace, in his 'True Poetry and False Religion in Abraham Cowley's *Davideis*' (*RES* 66[2015] 895–914), is concerned with Cowley's poem as biblical poetry, its treatment of truth and relationship to paganism and religion. Wallace observes that 'Abraham Cowley's four-book biblical epic is about David's triumphs over various idolatrous pagan opponents. Cowley presents this story as an example of the "truth" that stands distinct from the fables of pagan poets.' Wallace argues that 'the poem's explicit claim to chronicle such religious and artistic distinctions provides the key to its significance. Cowley's meta-argument about his own poetry mirrors the subject matter of the poem.' According to Wallace's account, 'David struggles to exalt his people over the surrounding pagans and infidels, just as Cowley struggles to convert poetry from paganism. Paganism is a source of conflict for the poet because for Cowley and his contemporaries paganism signified a religious mistake with linguistic and ontological implications. Cowley's notes to his poem, which extensively cite contemporary biblical scholarship and are often considered overly pedantic, are in fact evidence of the poet's desire to alert his readers to the linguistic and intellectual compromises necessary to write a sacred Christian epic poem. The poem and its notes create a dialogue that is meant to protect against false religion by urging its readers outside of the poem and into the larger world of ideas' (p. 895). Simon Jarvis's 'Hyper-Pindaric: The Greater Irregular Lyric from Cowley to Keston Sutherland' (in Carr and Robinson, eds., *Active Romanticism: The Radical Impulse in Nineteenth-Century and Contemporary Poetic Practice*, pp. 127–44) draws attention to Cowley's use of the Pindaric

*The Year's Work in English Studies*, Volume 96 (2017) © The Author 2017. Published by Oxford University Press on behalf of the English Association. All rights reserved.
For Permissions, please email: journals.permissions@oup.com
doi:10.1093/ywes/max010

ode as the foundation for a discussion of contemporary poems by John Wilkinson, his 'Harmolodies', J.H. Prynne's 'Of Sanguine Fire', and, especially, Keston Sutherland's 'Hot White Andy'. For Jarvis the three poems are examples of 'hyper-excitable Pindaric' (p. 127).

Richard Crashaw is also the subject of two scholarly essays. N.K. Sugimura, in '"Divine Annihilations": Richard Crashaw's Religious Politics and the Poetics of Ecstasy' (*MP* 12[2105] 615–42), is concerned with Crashaw's treatment of mystical experience, his relationship to Catholicism, and the political context of his Laudianism. The approach 'emphasizes how the cultural politics of the Laudian Church exerted a powerful influence on Crashaw's poetic practice'. For Sugimura, 'the depictions of ecstatic religious experience in [Crashaw's] poetry reflect a deep yet subtle political engagement with the religious politics of the 1630s and 1640s'; Sagimura 'proposes that Crashaw's poetics of ecstasy allow him to enter the fray of religious controversy while at the same time appearing to stand to the side of it'. According to Sugimura, Crashaw's 'sensuous imagery, luxurious verse, and strange eroticism . . . [are] inseparable from the larger cultural, political, and aesthetic agenda of worship, in which the public, not private, dimension of religious experience is championed. Nowhere is this more marked than in Crashaw's treatment of ecstatic experiences.' Furthermore, Crashaw 'transformed individual experiences of ecstasy into an imaginatively shared—and, hence, communal—religious experience'. His article is divided into two main sections. 'The first section examines how Crashaw's poetry distinguishes ecstasy from (sectarian) enthusiasm. By exploring the impact Laudian affective theology had on Crashaw's poetry, it argues that experiences of ecstasy are brought in line with institutional authority. In setting up radically individual experiences of ecstasy as implicit critiques of Puritan enthusiasm, Crashaw's poetic practice not only expresses the religious politics of Laudian theology but also actively participates in an English response to Counter-Reformation spirituality.' His second section 'expands on this idea' and discusses 'the religious and political commitments in Crashaw's later poems on St. Teresa' and their 'advocating a poetics of ecstasy within an institutional framework'. Consequently, 'Crashaw's poetry sheds new light on how his ecclesiastical adherence to Laudianism allowed for, and actually encouraged, his conversion to Roman Catholicism' (pp. 616–17). Similarly complex is Nandra Perry's 'Turning the Tables: Richard Crashaw Reads the Protestant Altar' (*SP* 112[2015] 303–26). Perry is concerned with the treatment of ceremonies, the relationship to Protestantism, debate, and altars with especial reference to Crashaw's 'Blessed be the Paps which Thou hast Sucked', which Perry contextualizes within a contemporary debate about the proper role of ceremony in Protestant worship. More specifically, it 'identifies the scandalous feeding celebrated in the epigram with a pamphlet war raging in the mid- to late 1630s over the naming and placement of the altar. Far from articulating a clear "Laudian" position, Crashaw's imaginative invocation of Luke 11:27–8 exposes and explodes the shared hermeneutic underlying both pro-altar and pro-table arguments. Crashaw's poetic interrogation of the depth/surface hermeneutic informing the altar debate historicizes the affiliation between "literary" and "sacramental" habits of reading' (p. 303)

*(a) Herrick*

There are two contributions on Robert Herrick to note, both published in essay collections. Natalie K. Eschenbaum's subject is 'Robert Herrick and the Five (or Six) Senses' (in Smith, Watson, and Kenny, eds., *The Senses in Early Modern England, 1558–1660*, pp. 113–29). Eschenbaum writes that 'Throughout *Hesperides*, Herrick sings of things that enliven the senses, and he describes sensation as a process of absorption or consumption. For instance... the body absorbs the ambergris-based perfume through the sense of smell.' She argues that 'Herrick's poetics reveal that all objects act like fluids when they are seen, tasted, touched, heard or smelled—or, rather, when they are textualized or poeticized as sensible things' (pp. 113–14). Her focus is on sensory imagery; however, 'Herrick does not have a single poem, or a defined series of poems, that catalogues all five senses.' Furthermore, 'Even though his' *Hesperides* 'collection does not include a traditional poetic sensorium, and even though "Of Love. A Sonet" seems to dismiss the senses, Herrick writes dozens of poems about seeing, hearing, smelling, tasting and touching things and people. In *Hesperides* to sensually engage with things or people is usually to infuse with them, to melt into them, to liquefy.' According to Eschenbaum, 'Herrick's poems about seeing his beloved Julia are probably the best examples of the effects of intrusive, liquid sensation' (p. 115). Other poems that attract Eschenbaum's attention are 'Upon Julia's Clothes' and 'Julia's Petticoat'. She notes that 'in both of these poems, sounds have metamorphic power. They can change solids to liquids and people to things. Herrick gives scents this same power.' Another poem is one concerning smelling Julia. In 'Upon Julia's Sweat' Herrick's narrator asks if we would like 'oyle of Blossomes' or a floral perfume, and informs us that we can 'Take it from my *Julia*'s sweat' (ll. 1–2). Her sweat, he says, 'smells like lilies and lavender and should be bottled' (p. 117). Eschenbaum's conclusion is worth citing as it reveals the depth of her analysis and the way in which she illuminates Herrick's *Hesperides*. For her, 'It is Bacon's sixth sense that finally helps to explain Herrick's liquefying depictions of the five traditional senses. In *Hesperides* the desire for sexual pleasure defines the experience of sensation. Seeing, hearing, smelling, tasting and touching are all akin to sex. All are driven by the desire of individuals to (or not to) infuse with the people and objects they encounter. It is pleasurable to drink in a vision of Julia's undulating petticoat or to imagine inhaling her sweet scents. Even though Herrick's narrator cannot actually infuse with Julia (as Lucretius laments), poetic language can capture the truly desired terminus of love, which is the liquefaction and infusion of two sensual bodies.' In conclusion she observes that 'Herrick reminds us that poetry physically touches us; we are supposed to *feel* something when we read it, hear it, touch it, sense it. And because his poems are themselves sensible objects, we might imagine that a little bit of Herrick infuses with us every time we open our senses to his verse' (pp. 126–7).

Elizabeth Hodgson, in her 'Katherine Philips at the Wedding' (in Orvis and Paul, eds., *The Noble Flame of Katherine Philips: A Poetics of Culture, Politics, and Friendship*, pp. 187–212), is not primarily concerned with Robert Herrick but with Katherine Philips (1631–64). Hodgson's focus is Philips's wedding poems. Her discourse includes discussion of Donne's and Herrick's poetry. Both serve as 'examples of the male-authored epithalamic poems to which Philips's poems respond. Two particularly striking examples, to which Philips's poems are almost direct replies, are John Donne's "Epithalamion made at Lincolnes Inne," and Robert Herrick's "Nuptiall Song." These two marriage poems contain different balances of celebration, satirical critique', and what are referred to as 'anti-bridal . . . death[s]'. However, in Donne's and Herrick's poems 'the negotiations between the nuptial couple and the authority of the speaker as host, pandar, critic, and priest are emphatically central'. In her poems Philips clearly draws upon 'the cultural coding of the forms she uses, and very specifically on the precursors by both Donne and Herrick' (p. 193). Following a detailed discussion of a Donne poem (pp. 193–6), Hodgson turns to Herrick's '"A Nuptiall Song, or Epithalamie, on Sir Clipseby Crew and His Lady" [that] celebrates the marriage of Crew and Jane Pulteney in 1625'. Hodgson explains that 'Herrick's poem repeats the traditional Spenserian (Catullan) narrative structure for epithalamia, beginning with the procession of the bride and ending with her bedding. Herrick's "Nuptiall Song" is far less satirical than Donne's, as Herrick embraces the powerful agency of the narrator to create an alliance with the groom' (p. 196). Hodgson writes that 'Though the language is often as strenuous as Donne's, then, its tendency is to construct intimacy with the culture of marriage and sex rather than distance from it. Herrick's poem also constructs its sense of agency through violence. The speaker emphasizes, celebrates, and imaginatively initiates the annihilating effects of sexual consummation' (p. 197). She continues to make fine perceptive distinctions based upon close textual reading. 'The tension in Herrick's epithalamium, then, is slightly different from that in Donne's. "Lincolnes Inne" sits ambiguously between social satire, the separateness of the speaker from the event, and a kind of antagonistic celebration of the bride's loss of power. In "A Nuptiall Song" the speaker adopts the sexually aggressive mode of the groom to compel the bride into compliance with social necessity in an enactment of the gendered dependence within the cultural event'. Hodgson concludes that 'Both poems do illustrate the powerful dynamics of the narrative epithalamium in its conventional forms, especially the literarily functional teleology of the bride's loss of agency. Philips negotiates with this particular energy in her own marriage poems' (pp. 197–8).

## 2. Herbert

Although no scholarly monograph appeared, the year 2015 was a very rich one in Herbert studies, marked by a wealth of articles and a new edition of his poetry. The Penguin *George Herbert: The Complete Poetry* offers the English poetry as edited, introduced, and annotated by John Drury, and the Latin poetry edited and translated by Victoria Moul. The previous Penguin [1991], edited by John Tobin, had included the prose *A Priest to the Temple* and Izaak Walton's *Life* (both omitted here), but only a very small selection of Latin verse (with prose translations). The greatest value of the new edition, then, is the appearance of the Latin poems with a scholarly, poetic translation for the first time in a collected poetry. F.E. Hutchinson's 1945 edition of *The Works* had included all the Latin verse, but without translation, while Helen Wilcox's richly annotated edition of 2007 was of the English poems only. Most scholars have judged the only complete translation of the Latin verse by M. McCloskey and P. Murphy [1965] to fall short in scholarly accuracy. The new Penguin's inclusion of this substantial dimension of Herbert's output reflects the renewed interest in the neo-Latin poetry of the period. Moul's translations are scholarly, but perhaps aim to be more accessible than those provided by Catherine Freis, Richard Freis, and Greg Miller in *Memoriae Matris sacrum* [2012], which she reviewed favourably (*Bryn Mawr Classical Review* [2013]). (Freis, Freis, and Miller's edition of the rest of Herbert's Latin poetry is being published by *The George Herbert Journal* in 2017.) Moul offers a separate introduction to the Latin poems, in which she makes a compelling argument for the significance and richness of this often neglected part of Herbert's canon, and a helpful appendix on the technical aspects of Latin poetry and metre. A general introduction by Drury offers an accessible biography of Herbert and a useful guide to the poetry; the notes at the back of the volume include an engaging paragraph-length introductory commentary for each poem: these are more personal and reflective than is usual in such a volume. There are fewer and briefer individual annotations than in the old Penguin, and those omitted by Drury seem to suggest a more learned readership is expected. The relative scantiness of the notes, and that they are, as with all Penguins, at the back of the volume renders them less useful than those found in Wilcox.

In 'Devotion in the Present Progressive: Clothing and Lyric Renewal in *The Temple*' (*RenP* [2014] 95–108) Lisa Ulevich suggests that the past decade in Herbert scholarship has been dominated by historicist studies of Herbert, with rich explorations of the ecclesiastical and theological context (p. 98). If so, 2015 seems to mark a shift in another direction: towards close readings of individual poems and the artful linkages between poems within *The Temple*. While most articles published this year are still well informed by historical awareness, there nevertheless is a renewed concern with prosody, diction, and metaphor. This is reflected in the double issue of the *George Herbert Journal* (*GHJ* 38:i–ii [2014/15]), which drew upon the 2014 Herbert Conference in Phoenix whose theme was 'choyce Observations drawn out of the whole text'. Ulevich's article is typical of this shift: the rich senses of the word 'habit' ('both dress and customary action', p. 105) are the starting points for a consideration of clothing metaphors in 'Mans Medley' and 'Mortification'. In these poems mundane repetition of dressing and undressing becomes the stuff of spiritual edification. Ulevich goes further, by suggesting a parallel between the potentially transformative quality of church vestments and the elements of poetic craft and ornament: 'outward forms offer an interface with the divine, not a distraction from it' (p. 105). This leads to a reading of 'Aaron', where the repeated process of 'dressing' is a meditative act of repentance, one mirrored by the repetitive rhyme words of the poem. Ulevich concludes that 'Herbert repeatedly affirms the value of clothing holy thoughts in beautiful language' (p. 107).

Of all the poems on clothing elements in *The Temple*, none has attracted as much scholarly attention as 'The Collar', which Nicholas D. Nace explores in a rich and probing essay, 'On Not Choking in Herbert's "The Collar"' (*SEL* 55[2014] 73–94). He argues that this notoriously chaotic poem achieves a sort of coherence through the unspoken 'presence' of keywords such as 'choke', 'obligation', and 'sow/sew' (a similar argument about the unused word 'host' in 'Love (III)' has been advanced by Michael Schmidt and others). Overall, Nace suggests that 'The Collar' denies or conceals the unity that might arise from such linked words and images. He also revisits Levitt and Johnston's nautical reading of the poem, adding words with nautical connotations to their list but arguing that their reading falls short in its lack of attention to grammar and structure. He points especially toward the parable of the sower (Matthew 13), which has a nautical setting (Jesus speaks from a boat). Other poems inform this reading of 'The Collar': he notes 'The Pearl. *Matth. 13*' likewise brings together this parable with nautical terms, and 'L'Envoy' makes explicit the idea of establishing silence through choking. Finally, Nace turns to Harvey, Nashe, Thomas Drant, and Donne ('To Sir Henry Goodyer') to suggest 'that satire has provided a relevant language of affect for Herbert's stifled, choked rebellion' (p. 9). Rodney Stenning Edgecombe's essay 'Herbert's *Collar*, Bacon, Queen Elizabeth, and Burton' (*ANQ* 28[2015] 140–4) is a much more limited focus on the 'rope of sands' trope as similarly used by Francis Bacon, Queen Elizabeth, and Samuel Butler. Through this he suggests that Herbert's rebellion in 'The Collar' is a Baconian rejection of the scholasticism or 'crypto-monasticism' (p. 141) in which he finds himself mired.

Herbert's *The Temple* has often been read in relation to the ceremony of Christian worship that it directly invokes; Simon Jackson, 'The Visual Music of the Masque and George Herbert's *Temple*' (*ELR* 45[2015] 377–99), offers a more unlikely reading in reference to the ceremony of the secular masque. He convincingly argues that the theory and practice behind the multi-sensory experience of the 'visual music' of the masque is reflected in such poems as 'The Altar', 'The Windows', 'Easter Wings', and 'The Starr'. The same ideals of proportion and balance are found across the arts of the time: in architecture, music, the stage settings of masques, and *The Temple*. The two-dimensional words of Herbert's poetic page evoke music, perspectival depth, and the physical rhetoric of dance. The concrete poems 'The Altar' and 'Easter Wings' attract particular attention as they most fully reflect the paradoxical 'moving visual music of dancing'. However, the article also uses the conventions of physical illusion created by masque machinery and stage settings to present a compelling new understanding of the perplexing reference to 'perspective' at the end of 'Sinne (II)': that 'painted devils' are a way of giving flat and misperceived sin a perspectival depth that can be grasped and understood. A second article by Jackson, 'Putting Things in Perspective: George Herbert's 'Sinne (II)' (*GHJ* 38[2014/15] 120–34), covers much of the same ground as the preceding article, but limits its focus to 'Sinne (II)'.

A similar concern with perspective informs Claire Falck's ' "Full-ey'd love": Failing to See God in Herbert's "The Glance"' (*GHJ* 38[2014/15] 107–19). It offers a deep reading of 'The Glance' in the context of other poems in 'The Church' in which the speaker desires to see, and to be seen by, God.

The limitations to such experiences are a manifestation of earthly human perception, not divine presence: the grace of God's 'full-ey'd love' is continuing if not always felt. A multi-dimensional approach to the perception of the divine–human relationship is present not only in the *ideas* of Herbert's lyric poetry, but is part of the formal structure of the volume. The need to 'collate' the differing, and at times seemingly contradictory, experiences represented in the poems is itself a reflection of how Herbert understood that Scripture must be read. Falck argues that 'The Glance' represents a high point in the broader project of *The Temple*, which is 'to achieve new insight by juxtaposing many valid, but incomplete, visions of God' (p. 108).

Adele Davidson's ' "A more singular mirror": Herbert, Acrostics, and the Biblical Psalms' (*GHJ* 38[2014/15] 15–30) considers how Herbert's anagram and acrostic poems draw 'observations' from the very fabric of language, letters. She also traces the period's familiarity with acrostics in the biblical text, and how its poets extended that technique in their psalm paraphrases in verse. Davidson shows how Herbert's deep familiarity with the biblical text (particularly as reflected in the two 'H. Scriptures' poems) informed his own poetic practice. Davidson goes beyond the more obvious examples in Herbert's poetry ('JESU', 'Anagram [of the Virgin Mary], and 'Coloss. 3:3') by observing how the indentation patterns in the original 1633 edition of *The Temple* create acrostics and anagrams hidden by later editorial choices. Thus, for example, she finds a wealth of such effects in 'Love (III)', including an anagrammatic acrostic of 'DAILY TABLE', a fitting book-end to 'The Altar', which began the collection. Davidson sees a serious playfulness at work in these rhetorical figures, as the poetic text 'functions as an anagram or image of the reader's best self or ultimate desire' (p. 22).

Regina L. Walton, 'The Identity of the Friend and the Role of Spiritual Direction in George Herbert's "Love Unknown" ' (*GHJ* 38[2014/15] 94–106), challenges earlier readings of the poem that have identified the 'Friend' of the poem with Christ, or have seen the speaker engaging in an internal spiritual dialogue. In contrast, Walton argues that the interlocutor represents a living human friend, whose role as spiritual adviser is consistent with models of friendship in the period, such as that found in 'On Friendship' by Herbert's friend, Francis Bacon. In the last section of the article Walton suggests that a spiritual tale, 'The Anchoret and the Angel', found in the papers of Nicholas Ferrar, may have served as a source for 'Love Unknown'. Both use a tale to illustrate the divine purpose in seemingly destructive acts. As Ferrar may have served as a spiritual friend who guided Herbert through bewildering experiences, *The Temple* was offered by Herbert to fulfil a similar role for its readers.

In 'George Herbert's Bravery' (*EIC* 65[2015] 383–400), Tom MacFaul argues that Herbert brought to his devotional poetry an aristocratic sense of honour and manly conduct, which becomes manifest in *The Temple* as a bravery of proud defiance. At times this bravery takes the form of internal struggle, in other cases it is turned heavenward, as the speaker struggles to deal 'with the problem of gratitude to God' (p. 394). Herbert suggests that God allows this 'licensed pride' (p. 386) as part of the ongoing struggle of redemption. The article draws on a wide range of poems to show effectively how this 'oppositional stance is everywhere in Herbert' (p. 396). MacFaul's apt attention to metre, sound, structure, and diction brings about a rich series of close readings.

Unlike some earlier critics, Jennifer Downer, ' "Disorder'd clocks": Time, Grace, and the Mechanics of the Soul in George Herbert's "Even-song" ' (*GHJ* 38[2014/15] 41–53), understands 'Even-song' as a poem less concerned with liturgical time than with the ever-present 'now' of God's grace. She places the poem firmly in the tradition of an Augustinian and Calvinist understanding of time, in which the 'disorder'd clocks' of human beings constitute a falling short of divine temporality. The poem's oft-discussed reference to the 'ebony box' is read 'not simply as a rest or refuge for the speaker but also as a manifestation of divine grace.' (p. 47). Another article from the same collection also points to an Augustinian sense of time as foundational for Herbert: Daniel H. Strait's ' "Sudden passing": Herbert's Poetics of the Moment' (*GHJ* 38[2014/15] 54–65) begins with Herbert's translation of Cornaro's *Treatise of Temperance and Sobriety*, which presents temperance as a steadying of the tumultuous mortal life, so often reflected in *The Temple*. He argues that Herbert's poetry differs, however, in seeking a temperance grounded in 'the body in reaction' (p. 60) to the transitory nature of his experience of God. He convincingly argues (like Downer) that Herbert in this way reflects an Augustinian sense of time. In 'The Temper (II)' Strait identifies the 'unexpected suddenness' of God that Herbert is unable to reconcile with his own temporal experience. The article also offers a thorough reading of a similar dynamic in 'The Glimpse', where the speaker laments the regularity that even other elements of the natural world may enjoy. In the similarly titled 'The Glance' the speaker recognizes that the sudden grace of God is still at work, amidst his (often very physical) turmoils. The place of such sorrows, afflictions, and pain in the devotional life of *The Temple* is very evident to readers, but in contrast, Michael Schoenfeldt, 'Herbert and Pleasure' (*GHJ* 38[2014/15] 145–57), traces what he calls 'the astonishingly crucial role that pleasure assumes in the act of devotion' (p. 146). Ranging widely across Herbert's poetry, he demonstrates the undeniable place of a temperate pleasure that is both spiritual and sensuous (and, at times, sensual). Fittingly, he ends his article with 'Love (III)', which he aptly celebrates as capturing the 'deeply social pleasure' (p. 155) of this climactic experience.

The work of Daniel Doerksen has greatly enriched our understanding of Herbert's Calvinism by offering a far more nuanced and complex version of that theology than the severe caricature often found in literary scholarship. It is in that spirit that Russell M. Hillier's essay, ' "Tyes of gratefulness": Learning to Say Thank You in George Herbert's Lyrics' (*English* 64[2015] 268–92), responds to the suggestions of Stanley Fish, A.D. Nuttall, and Barbara Leah Harman that the poet's Calvinism ultimately undermines both the general human role in responding to God and Herbert's particular poetic role. He argues that gratitude is the required response repeatedly enacted by the poems to an all-powerful and all-sufficient divine grace. Grace is always first, enjoying 'divine precedence', and the speaker of *The Temple* often resists the passive role to which he is called. While ranging widely across the whole of *The Temple*, fully aware of the significance of sequencing and echoes between poems, the article particularly focuses on a pair of somewhat unlikely examples, 'Gratefulnesse' and 'Self-condemnation', which ironically express the need 'for human gratefulness through the use of negative example' (p. 281). The former presents an importune speaker, who is rather the opposite of the unworthy guest in 'Love (III)' and only comes to a fittingly grateful response to God's gift at the end of the poem. In the latter, the speaker steps forth as one not needing grace (and hence gratefulness), as he ironically encourages all others to judge themselves without ever turning that instruction inward, and in a final ironic twist Hillier suggests that the reader is prone to fall into the same trap in judging the speaker. These are fine close readings, ably placed in the context of *The Temple* as a whole and the broader biblical and theological context.

Grace in Herbert's verse is also the subject of Kensei Nishikawa's 'The Doctrine of Prevenient Grace in George Herbert's *The Temple*' (*GHJ* 38[2014/ 15] 66–79), which begins with the roots of Herbert's knowledge of the doctrine in St Augustine and the Book of Common Prayer. He rather surprisingly suggests that it was only 'possible' that Herbert knew the Protestant reformers on the topic (p. 68). Largely avoiding the debate over whether Herbert's understanding was more Calvinist or Arminian, Nishikawa suggests that his concern was with the 'radically preceding nature of the divine grace that surpasses a believer's understanding, rather than in the capacity of the believer to cooperate in response' (p. 68). He then offers careful readings of three well-known poems ('Redemption', 'Easter', and 'Love (III)'), which explore the repeated pattern of the speaker being 'prevented' by the prior actions of Christ from his intended steps in the relationship.

Like Hillier and Nishikawa, Kate Narveson, 'The Problem of Peace in Herbert's "Assurance" Sequence' (*GHJ* 38[2014/15] 1–14), adopts a theo-logical focus as she lays out the workings of the Calvinist theology of assurance: rather than being a placid state of blissful spiritual security, assurance was a devotional 'habit' (in the strongest sense of that word) that allowed believers to ride out the 'buffetings' that afflicted all. She traces this approach, not only in the published systematic theology and sermons of Herbert's time, but in surviving manuscript works of laypeople who gathered promises from Scripture as outward testimony to buttress their often vacillating emotional experiences of grace. All this provides a foundation upon which to explain the relative absence of peace in Herbert's 'Assurance' and surrounding poems. Narveson finds the dramatic conflict in 'Assurance' itself poetically compelling, but concludes that 'Clasping of Hands' 'is doctrinally sound but experientially thin' (p. 11).

Paul Cefalu's article, 'Johannine Poetics in George Herbert's Devotional Lyrics' (*ELH* 82[2015] 1041–71), begins by tracing the particular role of this gospel in formulating a theology of the Trinity, the Eucharist, and of love (*agape*). Despite this influence on the period's theology, he argues, there has not been sustained attention given to its significance for the religious poetry of the period, including Herbert's. He suggests that Paul's influence has been more consistently noted because of its place in Lutheran and Calvinist theology. In contrast, Cefalu asserts that 'Herbert embraces a much more traditional, high Christological account of Johannine theology, one which, on balance, elevates Christ's divinity over his humanity' (p. 1046), and then offers a series of theologically probing readings to illustrate this. He suggests that the emphasis of 'The Bag' is upon the joy and glory of the incarnate and crucified Christ rather than his debasement and suffering. Likewise, the image of the wine-press in the 'The Bunch of Grapes' distances Christ from the suffering on the cross and highlights instead the Johannine image of him as the true vine (p. 1060), and even in 'The Agonie' Herbert's emphasis is upon the spilled blood of Christ as an expression of love. Finally, the article traces the complex allegory of 'Love Unknown' to its roots in John's Gospel and the book of Isaiah. Ultimately, it is not only in its subject matter and theology that Cefalu finds Herbert to be indebted to John, but in his consistent use of a stable rather than paradoxical (and more Pauline) irony.

In 'George Herbert and the Jews: Purloin'd Blessings and Self-Condemnations' (*GHJ* 38[2014/15] 31–40) Christopher Hodgkins revisits the issue of the place of the Jews in Herbert's theology and poetry. The matter only emerges occasionally in *The Temple*, most prominently in 'The Jews' and 'Self-condemnation'. He argues that Herbert saw himself theologically as writing both from within and without Judaism, and that 'Self-condemnation' explores the complex dynamic of self-righteousness, of which all might be guilty. While these two lyric poems are at the heart of the article, Hodgkins opens and closes his discussion by placing it in the broader context of anti-Semitic rhetoric in Herbert's time and ours, and the appropriate place of evangelism in such a context.

In the essay ' "Who 'laid him in a manger'"? Biblical Women in Herbert, Vaughan and Traherne' (*EIRC* 41[2015] 56–74), Jean E. Graham explores the relative absence, or silence, of biblical women in the poetry of Herbert and the two other most significant devotional poets of the century. Her main argument is that the women in these poems are generally given far less agency and voice than in the biblical sources. While the article more heavily focuses on Vaughan, Graham also notes that Herbert's Mary Magdalene is more active than Vaughan's in the poem that bears her name, as 'she actively participates in her own absolution from sin' (p. 64). Herbert, however, depicts the Virgin Mary as largely a vehicle of divine power rather than an active participant, in 'To All Saints and Angels' and 'Anagram'.

To conclude, three articles consider the place of Herbert in the English literary tradition. Debra Rienstra, 'Scant Verses: Henry Lok as a Forerunner of George Herbert' (*GHJ* 38[2014/15] 80–93), explores a number of Henry Lok's hundreds of sonnets as suggestive precedents for Herbert's poems. She stops short of asserting a certain direct influence, but her claim that 'no other devotional poet before Herbert produces nearly the body of experimental theory and practice in devotional verse as does Lok' (p. 90) is accurate and establishes strong grounds for the comparisons the article offers. In a small selection of Lok's poems she traces his use of parable-like situations, anxiety over the application of a secular poetic form to divine purpose, a sense of unworthiness before God, and Christ supplying the deficiencies of both art and faith. Rienstra traces these same emphases in Herbert's 'Redemption', 'The Holdfast', 'Love (III)', 'A True Hymne', and 'Jordan (II)'. Overall, the discussion also shows how far Herbert surpassed his predecessors in poetic art and theological subtlety. In contrast to Rienstra, Chauncey Wood, ' "Patterns of Thought and Feeling" in Herbert's Easter Poems' (*GHJ* 38[2014/15] 135–44), considers a number of Herbert's poems in relation to the surrounding secular literary culture: as a poet Herbert and his initial coterie audience were deeply aware of such fashionable genres as the love sonnet, paradox, and answer poem. The article demonstrates the close connections between secular works by Sidney, Donne, and Jonson and specific individual Herbert poems such as 'The Sinner', 'Coloss. 3:3.', 'Easter Wings', and 'Easter'. In the last-mentioned poem's desire for a divinely rendered alchemical transformation from human dust to gold, Wood identifies a response to the closing prayer of Donne's 'Good Friday, 1613. Riding Westward.' Finally, Don W. King, in his chapter 'George Herbert, *The Temple*' (in Werther, Werther, and Downing, eds., *C.S. Lewis's List: The Ten Books That Influenced Him Most*, pp. 67–92), considers him in relation to a much later tradition. While C.S. Lewis identified Herbert's *The Temple* as among his most important influences, this is not immediately evident in the works for which he is most famous: his literary criticism and fiction. However, King argues that the effect of Herbert is clear in Lewis's religious poetry, letters of pastoral advice, and *A Grief Observed* (prompted by the death of his wife). King especially emphasizes the direct statement that Lewis made about Herbert, that in his depictions of lived experience he captivated Lewis before his own conversion: as he himself said, Herbert is 'a good poet and one who helped bring me back to the Faith' (p. 70). Especially convincing is King's exploration of the Herbert-like tone and spirit of Lewis's poetry. The pain and (at times) despair of *A Grief Observed* have proven difficult for some critics to integrate with Lewis's apologetics and pastoral writing, but King argues that the fully articulated sorrow and complaint in it find a precedent in such Herbert poems as 'Discipline' and 'Grief'.

## 3. Donne

Oxford University Press this year continued its commitment to Donne studies with two volumes of the *Oxford Edition of John Donne's Sermons* (discussed in Chapter IX) and a volume of selected poetic and prose works, *John Donne*, edited by Janel M. Mueller, in its Twenty-First-Century Oxford Authors series. Mueller's edition reflects the series' editorial principle of printing texts as much as possible as their first readers would have encountered them. Since much of Donne's poetry found its first audiences in manuscript rather than print, Mueller uses both early print and manuscript witnesses as copy-text for the edition's selections: the poetry, with the exception of the *Anniversaries*, is printed from the Dowden and Westmorland manuscripts; Donne's marriage letters from the Burley manuscript; and the *Anniversaries* [1610] and *Devotions upon Emergent Occasions* [1624] from the first print editions. To meet the goal of providing accessible texts, copy-texts are 'very lightly modernized' (p. xxxiii), with contractions expanded but punctuation and spelling changed only when required to avoid misreading (transcriptions of the manuscripts are available on the Donne Variorum website for readers wishing to compare

Mueller's readings and to trace her emendations). Elisions and diacritics have also been added to assist with scansion.

Although the presentation is appealing, it's difficult to determine the intended audience for this edition. The inclusion of the *Devotions* and the marriage letters suggests the volume is intended to appeal to general readers and students, and the notes providing short introductions to each genre also seem intended for such audiences. However, the focus on preserving early manuscript readings, including the titles found in these manuscripts rather than the more familiar ones, may frustrate such readers. The extensive notes on each poem, which direct readers mostly to primary works, seem suited to scholarly readers who may require a critical edition.

Donne critics in 2015 continued to discuss some of Donne's more neglected works, from the *Satyres* to *Pseudo-Martyr* and to engage Donne in conversations with his contemporaries. A number of these engagements are discussed in Chapter IX.

Donne's prose works continue to enjoy a resurgence of interest. In two chapters of her book *Writing the Monarch in Jacobean England: Jonson, Donne, Shakespeare and the Works of King James*, Jane Rickard takes up the question of how Donne responded to James I's writings. Her discussions provide strong evidence of how he cautiously but persistently challenged the ways in which James represented his own authority in his printed works, particularly through his use of biblical analogies. Chapter 3, on his early prose works, illustrates how Donne complicated James's analogy between himself and God by showing that the gulf between God and king is greater than that between king and people. Noting that Donne did not explicitly respond to James's work in *Pseudo-Martyr*, Rickard nevertheless argues that Donne relished the possibility of dialogue that James had authorized by 'descending' into print. Chapter 4, focusing particularly on Donne's two Paul's Cross sermons of 1622, argues for his concern with resisting 'James's exploitation of scripture', and the pulpit, 'for political purposes' (p. 171). Rickard's discussion in these chapters does much to illuminate and nuance the nature of Donne's relationship with James and with authority more generally.

In Chapter 3 of her book *Reading Humility in Early Modern England*, 'Kissing the Wound: Humility and Humiliation in John Donne's *Sermons* and *Devotions upon Emergent Occasions*', Jennifer Clement argues that, like most of his contemporaries, Donne saw illness as a bodily affliction leading, through mortification of the will, to humility. Juxtaposing his 1624/5 sermon celebrating Paul's conversion with the *Devotions upon Emergent Occasions*, Clement argues that Donne saw his illness as proof of God's intervention in his life and his own constant need for humiliation to avoid relapsing into sin. Clement begins by citing a passage from the sermon as 'one of the more strikingly masochistic passages of his sermons' (p. 57), which is unfortunate because the chapter moves resolutely away from the notion that Donne's focus on suffering is masochistic.

In a brief note, 'The "Holy Delight" of Donne's *Devotions*' (*N&Q* 62[2015] 247–9), Adam Bryant Marshall interrogates the phrase 'holy delight', which appears in a letter Donne wrote to Robert Ker enquiring about the propriety of sending his *Devotions* to Prince Charles. Examining Donne's use of the same phrase elsewhere, Marshall discovers that three of the four incidences, all from the sermons, relate directly to preaching rather than to private devotion. Marshall concludes that Donne may have thought of the *Devotions* 'as a kind of sermon intended for a popular readership' (p. 248) despite its origins in individual meditation.

In her essay ' "An anxious untangling and perplexing of consciences": John Donne and Catholic Recusant Mendacity' (*EJES* 19:ii[2015] 176–88), Shanyn Altman counters critics who believe Donne compromised himself by contributing *Pseudo-Martyr* to the king's side of the Oath of Allegiance controversy in 1610. She argues that Donne presents 'mendacity... as a crucial survival tactic for Catholics' (p. 176), who can fulfil their desires for martyrdom better by living through persecution than by dying. By urging Catholics to take the oath for public benefit, Donne effectively refused to countenance unquestioned obedience to any human authority, king or pope, that attempts to impose on private conscience.

In what may at first seem a surprising juxtaposition, Alison Bumke, in 'More than Skin Deep: Dissecting Donne's Imagery of Humours' (*RES* 66[2015] 655–75), compares the use of humoral theory in two of Donne's verse letters to female patrons and in his sermons, concluding that in both cases Donne employs it 'to raise questions about moral responsibilities, culminating in a call for action: for patronage in verse letters, and for repentance in sermons' (p. 656). Donne is aware that in flattering the complexions, and by implication the moral rectitude, of Lucy Russell, countess of Bedford ('T'have written then' [*c*.1610]) and Lady Elizabeth Carey ('Here where by All' [1612]) he risks going too far, but he hopes to get away with it 'just long enough to elicit their financial and social support' (p. 656). In his second sermon on Ezekiel 34:19, preached at Whitehall, Donne's logic is similar to that in the Carey letter, but instead of reassuring his listeners, he warns them to maintain continuous care of their souls. The comparison of verse letters with sermons proves to be fruitful in examining the extent to which Donne was aware not only of what was appropriate for various audiences, but also of what would move a particular audience to think or act in a certain way.

In another productive pairing, Theresa DiPasquale, in 'Anti-Court Satire, Religious Polemic, and the Many Faces of Antichrist: An Intertextual Reading of Donne's "Satyre 4" and Spenser's *Faerie Queene*' (*SP* 112:ii[2015] 264–302), brings these texts together through Joseph Wybarne, whose *New Age of Old Names* [1609] suggested that both poems portrayed the Antichrist. However, DiPasquale cautions that Donne's portrait of the Antichrist as a garrulous courtier is 'ambiguous and equivocal' (p. 296). The Catholic Church may be the Antichrist, but so may the Elizabethan court. Unlike Redcrosse, Donne's speaker recognizes there is always a danger of becoming like one's enemies.

Katherine Eggert, in *Disknowledge: Literature, Alchemy, and the End of Humanism in Renaissance England*, coins the term 'disknowledge' to describe 'the conscious and deliberate setting aside of one compelling mode of understanding the world—one discipline, one theory—in favor of another' (p. 3). In chapter 2, 'How to Forget Transubstantiation' (pp. 55–109), she argues that Protestant rejection of transubstantiation destroyed the underpinnings of medieval theories about matter. Consequently, Donne, George Herbert, and Henry Vaughan resorted to alchemy 'as a poetic device' for discussing the possibility of material transformation. Citing a selection of Donne's *Songs and Sonets* she shows how Donne treats both alchemy and transubstantiation as nonsense without entirely relinquishing them as impossible dreams.

Susan Wiseman's essay, ' "Did we lie down, because 'twas night?" ': John Donne, George Chapman and the Senses of Night in the 1590s' (in Smith et al., eds., pp. 130–47), engages the question of how these two poets coped, in different ways, with the doubt engendered by more precise methods of timekeeping and new ways of mapping 'official' time onto sensory time. Reading Donne's 'Lecture upon the Shadow' and 'A Nocturnall Upon St. Lucie's Day' against Chapman's 'Hymnus in Noctem', Wiseman concludes that in these poems, we see interplays of light, dark, and shadows that mark Donne's scepticism about whether one can believe one's senses.

## 4. Milton

Milton studies continued to be a lively intellectual space in 2015. This year saw the publication of two significant monographs wholly focused on our great epic poet: *Milton on Film*, by Eric C. Brown, and Helen Lynch's *Milton and the Politics of Public Speech*. Also striking this year is the groundbreaking nature of many of the journal articles published. While traditional themes and age-old questions in the field still drive much debate, there are many new and exciting approaches to Milton's work to be found this year. From investigations of the motivating factors behind Milton's work using 'Actor-Network Theory', to discussions of Milton and calculus, to articles examining Milton through an Islamic perspective, Milton's writings still inspire fresh ideas and drive scholars to uncover new and rich meanings in and around these early modern texts.

The first monograph, Eric C. Brown's *Milton on Film*, responds to and extends conversations about literature and pop culture in general as well as specific lines of enquiry regarding Milton and pop culture recently enlivened by the work of Laura Knoppers and Gregory Semenza. In setting the scene for his arguments in the book's introduction, Brown notes the 'competing and seemingly incompatible' twin responses to the idea of Miltonic film: that film is the ideal medium for capturing the extravagant imaginative scale and richness of Milton's story and the world he creates, and, in contrast, that Milton's work is far too 'serious', 'weighty', stodgy, or obscure to be successfully transferred to film (pp. 2, 3). Other obstacles noted are Milton's well-known source material, the problems involved with filming poetry, the wide but anonymous influence of Miltonic ideas in Western culture, and, of course, the inescapability of Milton's fierce personality and opinions. Lastly, Brown situates his study in relation to broader ongoing conversations regarding adaptation theory and the nature of 'Milton's visual imagination', which is alternately concretely pictorial and maddeningly abstract and unrepresentable (p. 18). Chapter 1, 'Milton and the Staging of Spectacle', examines the presence and influence of *Paradise Lost* in the production of 'spectacular entertainments in the first two hundred years after the poem's publication'. Brown first takes up the issue of Milton's attitudes towards spectacle, noting the disapproval expressed by some Puritans. Though Milton sometimes expresses a lack of comfort with the spectacular mode, Brown's reading of the poem clearly demonstrates that Milton makes complex use of spectacle in achieving the poem's aims. Brown spends the rest of the chapter providing in-depth analysis of a number of Miltonic spectacles produced between the 1670s and the 1870s. Some productions took the form of traditional drama, like Dryden's failed opera based on *Paradise Lost*, Servandoni's 1758 pantomime, and a musical Broadway production in 1874. Others employed advanced mechanisms and special effects of their day in order to capture Milton's imaginative world, including 1740's 'Eidophusikon', a complex, mechanized, multi-modal performance experience, and 'Infernal Regions', an 1829 waxworks exhibit. These examples demonstrate, Brown suggests, how Milton's material drives the development of representation techniques and technologies.

Chapter 2, 'Pre-Cinematic Entertainment', continues exploring the development of entertainment technology in the pre-cinematic era and makes some important connections between these technologies and *Paradise Lost*. First discussed is the panorama, an installation art piece designed to create an immersive, 360-degree illusion. Alongside descriptions of the technology and early uses of it to depict natural settings, Brown notes moments in Milton's work where panoramic vistas are prominent, all leading up to analysis of two separate instances where, instead of natural landscapes, panoramas are constructed to represent scenes from *Paradise Lost*. Brown also gives accounts of several stages of pre-cinematic projection technologies, such as magic lanterns, phantasmagorias, and more advanced Victorian lantern shows. Once again, Milton's influence is keenly felt. Not only do these 'ghostly' entertainments often treat subjects connected to Milton and clearly touched by his influence—scenes of heaven and hell, and the like—but Brown points to a number of shows that place Milton at the centre. Through all of these developments, Brown makes it clear how Miltonic subject matter lends itself to, and perhaps even inspires, these technologies. But the failure of many of the more explicitly Miltonic shows 'tease[s] out the roots of the resistance to the popularization of Milton' (p. 140).

The third chapter turns from these pre-cinematic technologies to consider 'Early Cinema and the Cinematic Sublime'. Brown argues here that the features of early cinema, 'unfiltered realism and strange manipulation' and effects, give rise to 'an important reconceptualization of the sublime, an attempt to synthesize the natural and artificial' (p. 142). This aesthetic atmosphere, he contends, draws on 'John Milton's own sublimity ... to give [it] shape' (p. 145). It is hardly surprising, then, that capturing *Paradise Lost* or Miltonic themes on film becomes something of a 'holy grail' for early cinema, desired, but largely unattainable, despite a number of attempts that Brown catalogues.

Chapter 4, 'The Ambivalence of the Miltonic Film', signals a substantial shift in the role and prominence of Milton in film of the mid- to late twentieth century. While a few serious attempts to continue the work of early cinema to capture a full-length *Paradise Lost* can be found, Brown notes that, by and large, Milton's existence in feature films is found in allusion to and appropriation of 'Milton as a preeminent poet of the establishment' (p. 194).

Brown leads the reader through a number of examples of films containing Miltonic references: *Animal House*, where Milton's stodginess is abused even as themes regarding temptation and the draw of misbehaving are developed; HBO's *Cheaters*, where *Paradise Lost* is used to draw parallels between the situation in a Chicago high school and Milton's hell; and others. Additionally, Brown examines numerous other more minor references to Milton's Satan, his Eden, to the title of *Paradise Lost*, to his less well known works, even the 'egregious presence of a Milton book' in a scene (p. 198). In all of these examples Milton is present, but his influence is often shallow and ephemeral. Adding to the 'ambivalence' of Milton in twentieth-century film, Brown provides convincing evidence that even in the most literary of films, Milton is often invoked only to be dismissed as obscure or unnecessary. Finally, Brown closes the chapter with an account of the most prominent attempt to make a feature-length film of Milton's famous epic: John Collier's *Paradise Lost*.

In Chapters 5 and 6, Brown moves from exploring somewhat fleeting Miltonic references to tracing the genres of contemporary film in which Milton's influence is most strongly felt: 'angelic warfare and diabolical horror' (p. 243). 'Winged Warriors and the War in Heaven' treats the rash of recent films depicting angelic combat in ways clearly influenced by Milton. Key markers of Miltonic influence include the representation of angels in militaristic ways and a response to Milton's choice not to allow angels to inflict lasting harm on each other. These films, Brown asserts, are aligned with 'the Milton of the Romantics', containing 'underdog heroes, an all-powerful but absent deity who has left the fight to others, moral codes that favor individual sacrifice, incessant drive, and unabated hope' (pp. 280–1). In addition, they return us once again to the realm of Miltonic spectacle. Chapter 6, ' "All hell broke loose": The Horror Film', covers spectacle of a different sort. Unlike films of other genres that reject Milton or demonstrate ambivalence about him even as he is invoked, horror films, in Brown's view, embrace Milton, even to the point of 'expressing an exclusivity or possessive-ness over him' (p. 284). Milton's Satan, of course, is a key source of influence for many horror films. But his Pandaemonium is another key place of inspiration for films desiring hellish landscapes. So common are Miltonic themes and references in horror films, it leads Brown to name the genre as the greatest hope for Milton's pop culture success.

After reading *Milton on Film*, I was greatly impressed by the depth of Milton's influence on film and other popular forms of entertainment, particularly given the lack of a Shakespeare-like Milton film industry. Brown's encyclopedic knowledge of Miltonic film references and knack for identifying Miltonic resonances allow him to make a compelling case for Milton's insistent presence in films that are indebted to him while attempting to mask or deny that debt. And his detailed scholarship regarding pre-cinematic entertainment technologies combined with insightful readings of Milton's poetry help establish a vocabulary for Milton's most cinematic themes and features and a performance history that provides crucial context for Milton's appearance on film.

In *Milton and the Politics of Public Speech*, Helen Lynch analyses attitudes towards public speech during the 1640s and 1650s, a time when political speech was plentiful but also contested, viewed both as the right of all citizens and as the driving factor in the tumult of the period. Lynch's aims in the book are threefold: (1) to give an account of the political culture of the time and the role public speech plays in it, drawing on Hannah Arendt's analysis of classical Greek political ideas; (2) to investigate 'seventeenth-century debates over the nature and condition of language' and to contextualize Milton's work in those conversations (p. 7); and (3) to use these contemporary concerns about speech to open up new readings of Milton's poetry, particularly Samson Agonistes. She argues that 'Milton is responding to contemporary preoccupation with the powers and dangers of public speech', particularly in relation to 'the debased, 'privatized', court world of the Restoration' (p. 8).

Lynch's first chapter, 'Milton and the Idea of Public Speech', outlines the concept of public speech as a means of public improvement, a concept endorsed by Milton. However, despite common acceptance of this notion, it was by no means universally or equally applied to all speech in this politically fractured time. As Lynch notes, 'for many... it becomes necessary to distinguish between the arguments voiced by one's own side and those in support of the opposing cause as different kinds of speech act altogether—with the latter frequently defined as non-speech. What becomes important to Milton and to so many others is defining the right kind of speech and speaker. The meat of the chapter is devoted to analyzing these distinctions and cataloguing the imagery applied to those who fall short of the ideal: "women, children, slaves, domestic animals"' (p. 45). Lynch gives particular attention to the ways in which these images are weighed down with gendered or religious markers. The chapter closes with an account of how the Arendtian model of public speech Lynch identifies in the seventeenth century relates to the later and more commonly known Habermasian model. Chapter 2, '"Two twins cleaving together": Rhetoric and "Knowing good by evil"', engages with the ambivalence towards rhetoric evident in much writing of the period, Milton's included. Does the study of rhetoric make one virtuous (p. 87)? Does its use mark a speech as suspect or deceptive, or is its value determined by the qualities of the rhetor and the cause to which it is applied (p. 90)? Which is more concerning, a lack of rhetoric in speech, or its misuse (p. 92)? Questions such as these are common in discussions of oratory, and Milton's poetry demonstrates that he, too, is concerned about them. In this chapter, Lynch traces the period's responses to the problem of rhetoric and language more broadly, including Milton's. Though Milton shares many of the concerns about rhetoric voiced by others, Lynch points to his poetry, particularly Jesus in Paradise Regained, for evidence that Milton, despite his concerns, was unwilling to dispense with so potent a tool as rhetoric, and instead put it to use in service of truth.

In her third chapter, '"Enchanting tongues persuasive": Rhetoric and Gender', Lynch unwraps the layers of gendered language and imagery associated with rhetoric and persuasion. Though oratory is commonly seen as a masculine pursuit and described in the masculine language of combat— constructions Milton himself uses at times—within Milton's work we also find references to reason as feminine, as well as many references to traditionally feminine activities like 'embroidery, application of cosmetics and flower gardening' in relation to rhetoric and speech (p. 120). Lynch presents in this chapter readings of Milton and others from the period that deepen our understanding of the ambiguous gendering of poets and poetry, and the ornaments of rhetoric more generally. Chapters 4 and 5 build on the conceptual foundation of the previous chapters through readings of the nature and power of public speech in *Samson Agonistes*. In 'Samson the Orator and the Redemption of Public Speech', Lynch presents Milton's closet drama as a reclamation of the Greek political notion of speech as action. Arendt argues that, within the Greek *polis*, 'it was through the active and public life, through deliberation and presentation of the self in public spaces, that humanity was realised' (p. 160). In contrast, modernity has lost this sense of public speech and action 'in the shift from speech to thought, action to contemplation, rhetoric to philosophy', moving 'from a focus on immortality... to a preoccupation with eternity' (p. 160). *Samson Agonistes*, Lynch argues, provides a model for how active public life can be reclaimed through the 'repoliticisation of both the hero and to some extent his "tribe"... through public interaction and debate' (p. 162). The story Milton tells about Samson, Lynch contends, demonstrates that he was equally interested in 'the eternal' and in immortality (p. 164).

Lynch's final chapter, '*Samson Agonistes* and the Temptations of Romance', turns from Samson's redemption to unpack the conditions of his original fall, and in the process ties together many of the book's earlier lines of enquiry. Just as Samson's victory comes from a repoliticization, a re-entry into the public sphere, his fall comes from his 'capitulation to the domestic realm' through the 'oratorical vice of unreserved or unsuitable speech' driven by Dalila's misuse of language (p. 200). Lynch also draws parallels between Samson's story and chivalric romance: it contains a woman who transgresses gender norms by engaging in political action and a man who engages in 'recreance from public duty' leading to 'emasculation' and causing him to become 'slavish, effeminate, infantilised'—all the markers of a non-citizen from chapter 1 (p. 206). Lynch pursues this argument by examining aspects of romance in Milton's representation of Dalila, as well as its reflection of Shakespeare's *Antony and Cleopatra* and *A Midsummer Night's Dream*. She also contends that 'Milton uses the tropes of Romance to represent the temptations of idolatrous sensuality and linguistic bombast' (p. 228) in his representation of the conflict between Samson and Harapha. Lynch closes her arguments with reflections on what the experience of Samson, with all of the gendered implications of his fall, means for Milton's view of the role of the poet and poetry, and on Milton's views on immortality. *Milton and the Politics of Public Speech* is a fascinating study of rhetoric and language that is not to be missed. Lynch's skilful application of Arendt's theories illuminates aspects of the public sphere that have been largely lost to modern readers but which were doubtless at work in the seventeenth-century context, as Lynch demonstrates. In addition, she uses her theorizations of gendered aspects of both rhetoric and language powerfully to draw out new dimensions of Milton's Samson, his fall, and his redemption.

*Milton Studies* 56[2015], edited by Laura L. Knoppers, features ten essays broken into four broad themes: 'Rhetoric, Recognition, Relationships';

'Intertextual Relations'; 'Milton and Philosophy'; and 'Milton and History'. The essays it contains once again meet or exceed the high bar of quality and creativity set by this yearly standard. The first section opens with none other than Stanley Fish. His essay, 'Milton and Interpretation' (*MiltonS* 56[2015] 3–16), points to a particular moment from Satan's conversation with Eve in *Paradise Lost* IX as laying the groundwork for the Fall: Satan's response of 'Indeed?' when Eve first protests that the fruit of the forbidden tree is off limits. With this one word, 'Satan invents interpretation', the process of creating meaning through reasoning, a process, Fish contends, that opens the door to the Fall (p. 3). In making this argument, Fish revisits work by Thomas Sloane that finds Milton to be lacking in '*controversia*' and operating in a non-rhetorical manner in relation to understanding and disseminating truth. He argues that Eve, by allowing God's command to be a matter of enquiry, subject to debate and the arts of rhetoric, cedes the ground of faith that would allow her to remain unfallen, in contrast to Jesus in *Paradise Regained*. Next, in her essay, 'Direct Address in *Paradise Lost*' (*MiltonS* 56[2015] 17–43), Calista McRae seeks to draw attention to a under-studied aspect of Milton's rhetorical strategy in *Paradise Lost*, his characters' use of direct address or vocatives. She argues that careful reading of how vocatives are employed by various characters opens up new avenues of interpretation by demonstrating how that character views and values his or her audience. Her study examines the use of direct address by Satan, the Father and Son, and Adam and Eve, showing the impact of the Fall on the human pair's 'intimacy and emotional connection' and bringing to light a surprising contrast between a dull and predictable Satan and an attentive and 'affectionate' Father (pp. 39, 40). The opening section is rounded out by Joseph Mansky's 'Does Relation Stand? Textual and Social Relations in *Paradise Regain'd*' (*MiltonS* 56[2015] 45–72), in which he reflects on Jesus's title in *Paradise Regained*, 'Son of God'. He raises the broader question of how Jesus's relationships (with the Father, with Satan, with Mary) are created and what they signify. Drawing on Milton's use of Scripture in the divorce tracts, 'in which comparing biblical verses can create or destroy marital, filial, and spiritual relations', Mansky argues that Jesus uses similar techniques to 'insert himself into his Father's hierarchy as the Son of God' (pp. 47, 48). Furthermore, he explores tensions between Jesus's relationship with God and his relationship with Mary (making an interesting connection between Mary's house and Restoration conventicles), as well as contrasting Jesus's model of relationship with the model theorized by Satan.

The second section of the volume, 'Intertextual Relations', begins with an essay by Maggie Kilgour: 'Odd Couplings: Hercules and Oedipus in *Paradise Regained* and *Samson Agonistes*' (*MiltonS* 56[2015] 75–113). In this study, Kilgour engages with one of the more enduring questions about Milton's 1671 volume: how do we understand the relationship between the stories of Jesus's passive resistance to Satan and Samson's violent response to the Philistines? Kilgour's approach is to examine an odd, extended simile at the end of *Paradise Regained* that evokes both Hercules and Oedipus, heroes many critics find alluded to throughout the second work of the volume, *Samson Agonistes*. Kilgour argues that Milton places this simile here in order to establish a connection between the seemingly different halves of the volume, specifically that 'both poems are concerned with the problem of heroic action; they depict protagonists who themselves are trying to figure out what it means to be a hero' and they consider 'how good can destroy evil without becoming it' (p. 101). Following Kilgour is 'Death and the "Paradise Within" in *Paradise Lost* and Margaret Atwood's *Oryx and Crake*' (*MiltonS* 56[2015] 115–50) by Lara Dodds. In this essay, Dodds deepens our understanding of Milton's impact on popular culture by tracing the impact of *Paradise Lost* on Margaret Atwood's *Oryx and Crake*. Noting Knoppers' and Semenza's idea that Milton's 'sublimity . . . accounts for Milton's influence on fantasy and science fiction', Dodds finds a second connection between Milton and the genre: reflections on 'the ethical dilemmas of creation' and on the Fall (p. 115). It is this aspect of Milton's work that Dodds finds to be most present in Atwood's novel. She argues that Atwood's depiction of impending 'environmental catastrophe' is driven by 'an extensive engagement with the Fall myth, which is also a story of origins and of catastrophe' (p. 116). 'Milton and Philosophy', the third section of *Milton Studies* 56, begins with Joshua Scodel's 'Edenic Freedoms' (*MiltonS* 56[2015] 153–200), which provides an extensive explication of the four categories of freedom he finds represented in *Paradise Lost*: the freedom to move, choices allowed by God, choices based on reason, and the 'choice to obey or disobey God' (p. 153). After defining and demonstrating each kind of freedom through examples from Edenic life, including an extensive engagement with the conversation between Adam and Raphael, Scodel examines the 'deeply paradoxical' relationship between the last freedom and the other three (p. 153). He concludes that 'in attempting a plausible, comprehensible depiction of how sinless Adam falls, Milton undermines his theodicy, which hinges on the justice of God's punishment of humankind for its free choice' (p. 189). Scodel is followed by Tzachi Zamir's 'Death, Life, and Agency in *Paradise Lost*' (*MiltonS* 56[2015] 201–30). In this essay, Zamir undertakes a deep examination of Milton's ideas about death and how they are built into the world and action of *Paradise Lost*. The heart of the essay is an attempt to come to terms with Milton's belief in 'living deadness' (p. 202), that is, categories of death (three of them) apart from our normal sense of bodily death, all involving one's spiritual status. To unpack this concept, Zamir considers definitions of life, discusses 'the experience of space', reflects on the work God gives to Adam and Eve (tending living things), and examines Book II's scene in *Pandaemonium* as presenting competing portraits of what living death looks like.

The final section of the volume is 'Milton and History'. Leading off, Erin Webster's ' "Presented with a universal blanc": The Physics of Vision in Milton's Invocation to Light' (*MiltonS* 56[2015] 233–71) extends the conversation surrounding Milton's discussion of blindness at the start of *Paradise Lost* III by connecting the usual 'Neoplatonic contexts and sources' for the figurative connection 'between bodily sight and spiritual insight' (p. 234) with early modern scientific understandings of how sight operated. Webster presents accounts of Kepler's and Descartes's theories of sight, arguing that Milton 'adopts not only Kepler's theory of the retinal image but also the analogy . . . between the eye and a camera obscura' (p. 235). Doing so, she contends, allows Milton to 'explore the theological and epistemological implications of having light at "one entrance quite shut out"' (p. 235). Next, in 'Paradise Regained and the Restoration Church of England: Pieties in Dialogue' (MiltonS 56[2015] 273–99), Edmund Christie White situates Milton's brief epic as part of a larger Restoration culture of piety. Drawing parallels between the most popular Anglican piety manuals of the period and aspects of Milton's poem that provide a 'poetical exposition of piety through dialogue' (p. 275), White argues that Milton makes use of this context in order to remake it. The poem pushes back on 'conformist' versions of 'holy living' as it 'redefines piety as a radical choice to live exclusively under one's own—and God's—restraints' (pp. 274, 275). Concluding the section and the collection is 'Milton and the Romance of History' (MiltonS 56[2015] 301–29), by Luke Taylor. This fascinating essay attempts to contrast the usual approach to history within Milton studies—the effort to properly contextualize Milton's work—by attempting to recapture Milton's understanding of history. Taylor's contention is that Milton views history as Romance: 'history is not an epic with an overarching telos but a romance concatenation of errors' (p. 302). Though Milton is seen rejecting the materials of Romance in his work, Taylor argues that Milton 'uses romance to perform—or even prophesy—the inner structure of history' (p. 303).

As I've mentioned, 2015 was a strong year for scholarly articles focusing on Milton. English Studies devoted an entire issue (96:i[2015]) to 'Reading Milton through Islam'. Milton Quarterly served up another fine quartet of issues full of scholarship related to Milton, and eight other journals reviewed here also featured Milton-themed work. All told, nearly thirty significant articles exploring Milton's work are covered in this review, divided for convenience into six topical groups: reception of Milton, seventeenth-century science and politics, religion and theology, Milton's influences, Milton's creative process, and Milton and Islam. The 'reception of Milton' group includes five essays, beginning with Leah S. Marcus's 'Ecocriticism and Vitalism in Paradise Lost' (MiltonQ 49:iii[2015] 96–111). While not a traditional literary-reception essay, Marcus's piece is included here because of her commitment to exploring the enduring importance of Milton within contemporary discussions of environmental issues. Her aim in this essay is to forge a necessary connection between recent sometimes anachronistic conversations about Milton and ecology and studies of Milton's vitalist materialism that are steeped in the context of seventeenth-century scientific controversies but rarely consider 'the implications of Milton's vitalism for modern environmentalism' (p. 100). Doing so, Marcus suggests, allows us to understand crucial differences between Milton's vitalism and today's ecological imperatives while still recognizing what Milton's views have to offer us today. Next, in '"Formed on ye Gr. Language": Benjamin Stillingfleet Reads Paradise Lost, 1745–46' (MiltonQ 49:iv[2015] 217–42), Hugh Adlington examines the reception of Milton's poem in the eighteenth century by bringing to light manuscripts for edited editions of Paradise Lost that never made it to print, but which give insight into the 'scholarly priorities, tastes, and habits of mind' of Milton's readers of this period (p. 217). Adlington's discussion of Stillingfleet's manuscript edition demonstrates the shadow cast by Bentley's edition, with its much maligned alterations of Milton's text, and draws attention to the importance of Greek scholarship to Stillingfleet and his contemporaries. Adlington is followed by another *Milton Quarterly* essay from the same issue, Paul Davis's 'Addison's Forgotten Poetic Response to *Paradise Lost*: "Milton's Stile Imitated, in a Translation of a Story out of the Third Aeneid" (1704): an Edited Text with Annotation and Commentary' (*MiltonQ* 49:iv[2015] 243–74). Davis's essay continues the issue's engagement with Milton in the eighteenth century in its treatment of a short poem by Addison in Milton's style. The poem in whole and accompanying notes and commentary are printed in order to 'retrieve "Milton's Stile Imitated" from critical obscurity' (p. 243) and to give insight into Milton's reception in the period and into the mind and context of one of Milton's 'first great critic[s]' (p. 243). Davis traces how Addison's poem draws attention to resonances between Milton and Virgil and how it perhaps betrays Addison's ambivalence about some of Milton's more controversial edges. ' "Dark with excessive light": Milton's *Paradise Lost* and the Nineteenth-Century Astronomical Imagination' (*NCC* 37:ii[2015] 107–26), by Gillian Daw, seeks to understand the resonance of Milton's work for nineteenth-century astronomers, who quoted and referenced him with great frequency in their texts. In responding to this phenomenon, Daw cites the 'natural allegiance with Milton' experienced by many at the time, and she contends that Milton's interest in and knowledge of astronomy plays a key role in this. Daw explores the period's 'pervasive fascination with Milton' (p. 108), parallels between the 'momentous progress in astronomy' experienced in both periods (p. 116), and the ways in which Milton's poetry gave astronomers words 'to help them express the wonder, awe, and fear they felt when beholding the bodies and spaces of the universe' (p. 122). Lastly, Nicholas McDowell, in 'Towards a Poetics of Civil War' (*EIC* 65:iv[2015] 341–67), draws together the poetry of several ages and cultures that have experienced civil war, from Lucan's epic, to the poetry of Milton and his contemporaries, and on to 'Northern Ireland during the "Troubles" ' in order to make an argument about 'civil war poetry' as 'a distinctive literary phenomenon in English, with its own characteristic and recurrent figures of speech, images, and themes' (pp. 343, 344).

Six essays explore Milton and seventeenth-century science and politics. First is 'John Milton's Beehive, from Polemic to Epic' (*SP* 112:iv[2015] 798–816), by Nicole A. Jacobs. In this essay, Jacobs reinterprets a brief image from Milton's *Eikonoklastes* in a way that opens up an entirely new context for his critique of Charles I and the royalist cause. Instead of reading a description of Charles as the 'Aegyptian Apis' as a reference to Egyptian mythology, Jacobs makes the case that Milton is instead making a connection between Charles and the Egyptian bee (p. 798). Jacob asserts that this reading solidifies Milton's argument that the royalists are 'a well-organized and potentially threatening group' (p. 799). But she also argues that this allusion 'places *Eikonoklastes* within the symbolically central and contextually rich culture of seventeenth-century entomology as it aligns with shifts in governmental authority' (p. 800). Next, Erin Webster's 'Milton's Pandaemonium and the Infinitesimal Calculus' (*ELR* 45:iii[2015] 425–58) highlights an important and perhaps under-recognized aspect of seventeenth-century life, the need to come to terms with the shifting scale of the world (both the infinitely large and the infinitely small) caused by developments in science and mathematics. She does this by bringing together two disciplines that are rarely paired: advanced mathematics and poetry, specifically Newton's and Leibniz's infinitesimal calculus and Milton's similes describing *Pandaemonium* in *Paradise Lost*. Webster contends that these two creations make use of the same technique, 'perspectival manipulation', 'to bring the incomprehensible concept of the infinite within the limits of human understanding' (p. 428). Following Webster is Christopher Crosbie's 'Publicizing the Science of God: Milton's Raphael and the Boundaries of Knowledge' (*Renascence* 67:iv[2015] 239–60). Crosbie's essay is an intriguing revisitation of the conversations between Raphael and Adam about the nature of the newly created world. While many discussions of this scene are concerned with the particular cosmology to which Milton subscribes, Crosbie endeavours to study what the format of the conversation can tell us about Milton's scientific attitudes. Focusing on the tension between Raphael's caution to Adam about enquiring further than he ought and his nevertheless provocative answers to Adam's questions, Crosbie argues that, on the one hand, Raphael presents us with an object lesson regarding the evil that comes of curtailing intellectual freedom (following *Areopagitica*) and that, on the other hand, the conversation between the two is reminiscent of 'the English coffee-houses where public debates over science...became an issue of increasing concern for moralists wary of unbounded discourse' (p. 241). Milton thus 'negotiat(es) between license and licensing' in his creation of a public sphere (p. 256). Giuseppina Iacono Lobo comes next, with 'John Milton, Oliver Cromwell, and the Cause of Conscience' (*SP* 112:iv[2015] 774–97). Her essay reopens arguments regarding the level of support Cromwell enjoyed from Milton and whether that support endured through Cromwell's protectorate. In contrast to many who find a break in the relationship because of Cromwell's act of dismissing the Rump Parliament, citing a passage in Milton's Second Defence, Lobo analyses an earlier work, Milton's 1652 sonnet to Cromwell, and its context. She argues that Milton found common cause with Cromwell against the Rump because of threats to freedom of conscience, and that Cromwell held fast to this cause so dear to Milton throughout his protectorate. The last two essays in this section are both found in *Milton Quarterly*'s third issue. Tobias Gregory, in 'Did Milton Have an Erastian Phase?' (*MiltonQ* 49:iii[2015] 159–66), responds to the claim by Michael Komorowski that Milton should be considered an Erastian, at least for a time in the 1640s. Arguing that Milton 'was never an Erastian', Gregory points to evidence within the poem, to the poem's relationship with the Erastian conflict among the Westminster Assembly and Parliament in the 1640s, and to evidence in Milton's other works. Finally, in 'Politics and Political Culture During the English Revolution: A Review Essay' (*MiltonQ* 49:iii[2015] 175–80), David L. Smith charts the contributions of three recent monographs by Bernard Capp, Julia Merritt, and Jason Peacey to an understanding of the English Revolution that is evolving away from 'Whiggish or Marxist' accounts. He finds a common theme within the works of 'the changing nature of political culture' and argues that they 'force us to reconsider the wide range of different forms that political action and expression could take' (p. 175).

Our third grouping of essays treats Milton and religion and theology, a perennial topic in Milton studies. Christopher Kendrick's 'Typological Impulses in *Samson Agonistes*' (*UTQ* 84:ii[2015] 1–30) takes up questions regarding typological interpretations of Milton's Samson. Kendrick maps out a set of four different positions on Samson's typology that have been presented by scholars: the common typological view of Samson's self-sacrifice as a prefigurement of Christ; an anti-typological view which holds Samson as a glaring contrast to Christ; a 'regenerationist' view that casts Samson as experiencing a kind of redemption; and a fourth position which has Samson 'interpreting the new law, rewriting Christ in Samson's profile' (p. 15). Kendrick works to build on the last position, arguing that Milton's Samson should be seen 'not as a Christianization of classical form, but rather as a radical return to it' (p. 2). He does so by examining 'two episodes of possible inspiration' in Samson's story and how we as readers respond to them (p. 16). In 'John Milton, Paradox, and the Atonement: Heresy, Orthodoxy, and the Son's Whole-Life Obedience' (*SP* 112:iv[2015] 817–36), David V. Urban joins with William Kolbrener, Michael Lieb, and Russell Hillier in seeking nuance in discussions of Milton's religious views. Though Milton's views are undeniably heretical in significant places, Urban seeks to demonstrate that 'Milton largely follows an orthodox Reformed understanding of Christ's atonement in his emphasis upon the salvific work of the whole of Jesus's earthy life' (p. 820). He pursues this enquiry through considerations of 'Upon the Circumcision', *Paradise Lost*, and *Paradise Regained*, arguing that Milton's representation of Christ's 'whole-life obedience' is a strikingly orthodox position paradoxically driven by Milton's 'Arian Christology' (p. 836). Next, Vladimir Brljak, in 'The Satanic "Or": Milton and Protestant Anti-Allegorism' (*RES* 66[2015] 403–22), provides a new reading of a seemingly small moment in *Paradise Regained* when Satan questions whether Jesus's kingdom is 'real or allegoric' (IV. 390). In contrast to other readings that ignore this moment or use it to demonstrate Milton's favourable view of allegory, Brljak connects the scene to a vein of Protestantism that rejects allegorical readings as 'the work of Satan' (p. 405), arguing that the scene signals Milton's own distaste for allegory and represents a turning point in the Protestant tradition. Following next is '"With such joy surcharg'd": The Predicament of Satiety in Patristic Theology and *Paradise Lost*' (*MiltonQ* 49:i[2015] 1–22), by Kristen Poole. This essay brings a controversy from early Christian theology, that of whether or not a soul can be sated or glutted on God's presence, into conversation with *Paradise Lost*. After outlining the ideas of Origen and other participants in the patristic debate and tracing the likelihood of Milton's familiarity with them, Poole makes the case that Milton dwells on this issue of satiety, on the 'difference between being filled and being overfilled' in many aspects of *Paradise Lost* (p. 12) and suggests that the poem is marked by Milton's frustration with this unresolved question. Jason A. Kerr's essay, 'Milton and the Anonymous Authority of *De Doctrina Christiana*' (*MiltonQ* 49:i[2015] 23–43) revisits questions of authorship with regard to *De Doctrina*, with a new twist. The authorship controversy, Kerr contends, obscures more subtle questions regarding how authorial presence and authority are practised within the work. He argues that, driven by generic concerns, the work 'anonymiz[es]' its author's 'personal authority by submerging it in the authority of Scripture' (p. 24). Further, he explores the ways in which these modes of authorship appear in *Paradise Lost*, albeit altered by the Restoration's changing spiritual context. The last essay in this grouping, Vladimir Brljak's 'Early Comments on Milton's Anti-Trinitarianism' (*MiltonQ* 49:i[2015] 44–50), investigates two reactions to Milton's work that have surfaced recently, to shed light on when Milton's heretical beliefs first began to attract the notice of readers. He discusses comments by Abraham Hill and John Dennis, argues for dates for each (1698 and 1704), and notes that the emergence of these sorts of comments about Milton's heretical beliefs at this time, 'a full generation after the first edition of *Paradise Lost*', can be attributed to renewed interest in theological questions regarding the Trinity during the period (p. 46).

The three scholars represented in the next section take on the work of tracing Milton's influences. Zoe Hawkins, in 'Spenser, Circe, and the Civil War: The Contexts of Milton's "Captain or Colonel" ' (*RES* 66[2015] 876–94), provides a surprising reading of Milton's sonnet 'Captain or Colonel' as an imitation of Spenser's Bower of Blisse scene in the *Faerie Queene*. Hawkins makes the case that, despite some significant differences in outward subject, Milton's 'diction and his moral purpose in writing the poem are Spenserian', and she suggests that 'the sonnet contains allusions both to the *Faerie Queene* and to the *Shepheardes Calender*' (p. 877). In pursing her reading of the poem, Hawkins gives an account of the context and purpose of Milton's poem, explores his engagement with Spenser, and describes the wider influence of Spenser on the literary tradition Milton operated in. Next is 'Milton's Spenser: Eden and the Work of Poetry' (*SEL* 55:i[2015] 175–96), by Andrew Wadoski. This study also takes on the task of tracing the influence of Spenser on Milton—a literary debt that many acknowledge but find difficult to pin down, as Wadoski explains. Wadoski's contention is that it is in Milton's Eden that the connection is to be found. While direct comparisons between the gardens in Spenser and Milton point more to difference than similarity, Wadoski argues that Spenser 'model[s] a poetics in which virtue is discovered not in our encounters with transcendent forms but rather in our movements through the mutable world' (p. 176). In this way, it is the ethos of action, the idea of 'redemptive work' which pervades Spenser's romance and is also the feature that is most reflected in Milton's Eden (p. 192). Lastly comes Ivana Bičak's 'Transmutations of Satan and Caesar: The Grotesque Mode in Milton's *Paradise Lost* and Lucan's *Pharsalia*' (*MiltonQ* 49:ii[2015] 112–25), which adds to a line of criticism that finds resemblance between Milton's Satan and Lucan's Caesar by examining the ways in which each author makes use of the grotesque in the construction of his character. Drawing on Michael Steig's theorization of the grotesque as 'the managing of the uncanny by the comic' (p. 113), Bičak demonstrates how the grotesque mode allows each author to show the actions of his character as 'simultaneously horrific and ludicrous: horrific enough to shake up readers ... but also ludicrous enough to convince them that the alternative world that is being offered by these villains could never stand on its own two feet' (p. 122).

The next three articles, grouped together as discussing Milton's creative process, all examine different aspects of the nuts and bolts of Milton's creative practice and how we should evaluate him as an artist. Jeffery P. Beck's 'Young Genius or Old Master? John Milton and the Two Life Cycles of Artistic Creativity' (*ILStud* 17:i[2015] 39–58) draws on David W. Galenson's work identifying two distinct models of creative accomplishment—young, revolutionary conceptual creators and older, more incremental experimental creators—in examining the oddly bifurcated creative career of Milton. Beck's analysis of Milton identifies him as a rare conceptual creator who continued to innovate into his later years, aided by the detour of his poetic career into politics during the 1640s and 1650s. Next, 'Milton and the Early Modern Social Network: The Case of the *Epitaphium Damonis*' (*MiltonQ* 49:ii[2015] 79–95), by Blaine Greteman, re-examines and overturns two commonly circulated memes regarding Milton: that he is an isolated, independent figure, and that the best way to understand him is by deeply examining those closest to him. In contrast, Greteman argues that Milton is a 'social poet', one whose writings are driven by and depend on a vast web of sometimes distant correspondents. Drawing on actor-network theory to help map Milton's wider social network, Greteman uses this context to draw out new readings of Milton's grief-poem for Charles Diodati, the *Epitaphium Damonis*. Last, but certainly not least, Barbara K. Lewalski's essay, 'Milton on Authorship: Personae and Poet-Characters' (*MiltonQ* 49:iii[2015] 167–74), catalogues and examines examples within Milton's poetry which contain an authorial persona or character as a speaker rather than Milton's own voice. In contrast to the common view that there is little distinction between Milton the poet and Milton the man, Lewalski argues that many of Milton's poems, including his great epic, contain characters that bring to life fragments of Milton's poetic self and provide opportunities for him to reflect upon 'what it is to be a poet and the many things poetry might be' (p. 173).

Our last grouping of articles for 2015 is an exciting one examining Milton and Islam. Leading the group is Nabil Matar's '*Paradise Lost* as an Islamic Epic: Muhammad 'Anānī's translation (2002/2010)' (*ES* 96:i[2015] 6–20). In this essay, Matar investigates the transformation that Milton's epic poem undergoes as it is translated into Arabic by Muhamad 'Anānī. The challenges facing such a translation are considerable, and Matar notes some of the more difficult decisions 'Anānī had to make as Western/pagan names and specific Miltonic coinages are rendered into a language that operates quite differently on the level of diction. However, the most significant challenges facing 'Anānī are theological, and Matar argues that 'Anānī consistently reworks the theology of *Paradise Lost* in order to make it more relevant to 'Anānī's Islamic readers. The result, Matar suggests, is a text that is as much 'Anānī's as it is Milton's (p. 7). Next is François-Xavier Gleyzon's essay, 'Holistic Typology. "Uniting the dissevered pieces": Quranic Retention and Protension in Milton's *Areopagitica* and Nativity Ode' (*ES* 96:i[2015] 21–43), which follows Derrida in suggesting that Milton studies 'recall and understand Islam' in relation to Milton's thought and work (p. 31). Noting the uncertain status of Islam in relation to Judaeo-Christian typological studies that are so much a part of discussing Milton's work, Gleyzon makes the case, with reference to *Areopagitica*, for Milton's openness to Islamic knowledge, and he argues that Milton's Nativity Ode displays 'a surprising symmetry' with the story of Jesus in the Qur'an (p. 38). Following Gleyzon is David Currell's 'Meditations on Mediation: John Milton and the Muslim Jesus' (*ES* 96:i[2015] 44–64). Currell's essay takes on a dual task: investigating the ways an Islamic context promotes new understandings of Milton's work and tracing the real, if sometimes thin, connecting threads between Milton and the Islamic (Ottoman) world of his time. Beginning with the latter aim, Currell examines the role of trade and the pursuit of classical knowledge as the motivating factors that 'mediate' the connection between Britain and the Middle East. Currell then points to the ways in which Islamic theology speaks to the theological controversies of Milton's day, particularly anti-Trinitarianism. Having established this foundation, Currell moves to consider the Jesus Milton presents in *Paradise Regained* in relation to the Islamic Jesus represented in the Qur'an, highlighting the similarities between the two representations of Jesus and arguing that both similarly participate in 'probing the tension established by the very structure of monotheistic narrative' (p. 57). Following this is a contribution by Feisal G. Mohamed, 'Milton's Enmity towards Islam and the *Intellectus Agens*' (*ES* 96:i[2015] 65–81). Mohamed's essay examines Milton's complex and conflicted relationship with the Ottoman world and Islamic thought. His two-pronged argument first considers Milton's 'direct mentions of Islam' (p. 67) or the Islamic world in his prose, identifying within them a shift from 'casual hostility' (p. 68) to an understanding of the size and power of the Islamic world. Mohamed then turns to examine the influence of Islamic thinkers within Milton's ideas regarding the *intellectus agens*. Rounding out the section are two works by Islam Issa. In 'Milton's *Areopagitica* in the Arab World Today' (*ES* 96:i[2015] 82–101), Issa investigates resonances between the political and religious discourse of Milton's England and the Islamic world today, particular with regard to censorship. Not only does Milton's biblically inspired work exhibit similarities with controversial religious art; Issa also contends that 'there are numerous similarities between a number of Milton's main arguments in *Areopagitica* and various aspects of Islamic belief and tradition' (p. 84). Issa's second article, 'Transforming Milton's *Paradise Lost* into Arabic' (*SEL* 55:i[2015] 197–214), seeks to open a new line of enquiry into the relationship between Milton and Islam by examining 'what Milton means to Sunni Muslims reading his works in Arabic in the Arab-speaking world today' (p. 197). Focusing on Mohamad Enani's translation of *Paradise Lost*, Issa discusses the challenges and choices involved in rendering the poem in Arabic, including Enani's use of qur'anic *ta'bir*, and how these choices 'significantly shape and color the Arab-Muslim reader's understanding of the poem', even to the point of reworking 'the basic characterization' of a figure like Satan in a way that is more 'domesticated' (p. 209).

The works reviewed above tell us a lot about the state of Milton studies in 2015. Questions about Milton's literary debts, his religious convictions, and his political views are all represented in this year's scholarship, and rightly so. But I can't help but be excited about all the fresh ideas scholars are connecting to

Milton's work. New knowledge about the seventeenth century is being brought to the surface that gives us new insights into what Milton's work means. Critics are reaching further afield than the usual literary and religious backgrounds to allow us to find richer contexts for interpreting Milton's poetry. And most exciting of all is the opportunity to see how his work resonates in new and different ways when it is translated into new cultural contexts. Good things lie ahead for Milton studies.

## Books Reviewed

Brown Eric C. *Milton on Film*. Duquesne. [2015] pp. xii + 419. $70 ISBN 9 7808 2070 4760.

Carr, Julie, and Jeffrey C. Robinson, eds. *Active Romanticism: The Radical Impulse in Nineteenth-Century and Contemporary Poetic Practice*. UAlaP. [2015] pp. vi + 276. $39.95 ISBN 9 7808 1735 7849.

Clement, Jennifer. *Reading Humility in Early Modern England*. Ashgate. [2015] pp. xi + 153. $112 ISBN 9 7814 7245 3778.

Drury, John, ed., and Moul Victoria, ed. and trans. George Herbert: The Complete Poetry. Penguin. [2015] pp. lvii + 578. £12.99 ISBN 9 7801 4139 2042.

Eggert, Katherine. *Disknowledge: Literature, Alchemy, and the End of Humanism in Renaissance England*. UPennP. [2015] pp. 351. $55 ISBN 9 7808 1224 7510.

Lynch, Helen. *Milton and the Politics of Public Speech*. Ashgate. [2015] pp. xvii + 283. $97.60 ISBN 9 7814 7241 5202.

Mueller, Janel M, ed. *John Donne*. OUP. [2015] pp. xxxv + 606. £95 ISBN 9 7801 9959 6560.

Orvis, David L., and Ryan Singh Paul, eds. *The Noble Flame of Katherine Philips: A Poetics of Culture, Politics, and Friendship*. Duquesne. [2015] pp. ix + 350. $60 ISBN 9 7808 2070 4746.

Rickard, Jane. *Writing the Monarch in Jacobean England: Jonson, Donne, Shakespeare and the Works of King James*. CUP. [2015] pp. x + 272. $99.99 ISBN 9 7811 0712 0662.

Smith, Simon, Jackie Watson, and Amy Kenny, eds. *The Senses in Early Modern England, 1558–1660*. ManUP. [2015] pp. xii + 243. £70 ISBN 9 7807 1909 1582.

Werther, David, Susan Werther, and David C. Downing, eds. *C.S. Lewis's List: The Ten Books That Influenced Him Most*. Bloomsbury. [2015] pp. xiii + 231 $21.99 ISBN 9 7816 2892 4152.

# XI

# The Later Seventeenth Century

JENNIFER L. AIREY, JAMES OGDEN,
ELIZABETH BRADBURN, AND WILLIAM BAKER

This chapter has five sections:1. Restoration Drama Excluding Dryden; 2 Dryden; 3 Marvell; 4 Other Poetry; 5. Prose. Section 1 is by Jennifer L. Airey; section 2 is by James Ogden; section 3 is by Elizabeth Bradburn; sections 4 and 5 are by William Baker.

## 1. Restoration Drama Excluding Dryden

For the second year in a row, criticism of Restoration drama was relatively scarce. Critics did, however, publish new perspectives on popular authors such as Behn, Rochester, and Congreve, provide new insights into Restoration staging practices, and present new interpretations of dramatic adaptations in the later seventeenth century.

Laura Estill offers a fascinating look at a little-known seventeenth-century practice in *Dramatic Extracts in Seventeenth-Century English Manuscripts: Watching, Reading, Changing Plays*. Throughout the seventeenth century, many fans of the theatre hand-copied favourite passages into 'miscellanies, composite volumes, commonplace books, and diaries' (p. 19). Estill has meticulously examined several hundred of these volumes, and argues quite convincingly that they provide new insight into 'our understanding of early modern reading habits, textuality, and theatre', and work as a 'corrective to author-centric and Shakespeare-centric scholarship' (p. 21). While much of the volume focuses on early modern works outside the scope of this section, chapter 4 examines compilations of extracts written after the restoration of Charles II. According to Estill, the extracts of this period reflect a continued interest in early-century plays, even as they begin to incorporate newer, contemporaneously authored works. In some cases, extracts reflect the owner's political concerns; in others, they serve as a form of 'proto-literary criticism' (p. 179), or simply as manifestations of the owner's personal taste. In chapter 5, Estill also examines extracts compiled by Archbishop William Sancroft, who 'copied thousands of extracts from a range of texts' both prior to the Restoration and after (p. 190). Sancroft's manuscripts, Estill argues, 'show us

*The Year's Work in English Studies, Volume 96 (2017)* © *The Author 2017. Published by Oxford University Press on behalf of the English Association. All rights reserved.*
*For Permissions, please email: journals.permissions@oup.com*
doi:10.1093/ywes/max012

how early readers understood play-texts' (p. 220). Despite his high-class standing, he was also a fan of the theatre, and 'one who engaged with dramatic texts like many other early modern readers, treating plays as works to be adapted for personal use' (p. 220). Estill's book is a remarkable achievement, and it will undoubtedly be of interest to all scholars of the early modern playhouse.

The afterlife of early modern plays in the later seventeenth century was also the focus of Huw Griffiths's 'Adapting Same-Sex Friendship: Fletcher and Shakespeare's *The Two Noble Kinsmen*, and Davenant's *The Rivals*' (*Shakespeare* 11:i[2015] 20–9). According to Griffiths, Davenant's changes to Shakespeare and Fletcher's script downplay homosocial friendships in favour of homosocial rivalries. The concept of *amicitia*, so important to *The Two Noble Kinsmen* and its source text by Boccaccio, is redirected into 'the *telos* of marriage' (p. 21). In making these changes, Davenant prioritizes Fletcher's contributions to the play over Shakespeare's, ultimately privileging 'a typically Fletcherian scepticism around the idealizing discourses of male friendship' (p. 21). He also excises the spectre of homoeroticism from the text, emphasizing instead heterosexual union. Griffiths's final point is particularly illuminating; by tracing Davenant's changes to the play, he argues, and by acknowledging Davenant's preference for Fletcher over Shakespeare, modern critics can gain greater insight into the 'rivalrous collaboration' of the two early modern playwrights (p. 27). Lines written by Fletcher often exist in tension with those of Shakespeare, conflicts that are exposed by Davenant's later authorial choices.

The works of Aphra Behn are a perennially popular topic of criticism, and were the subject of two essays published this year. In ' "*Jack Presbyter* in his proper habit": Subverting Whig Rhetoric in Aphra Behn's *The Roundheads*' (*WW* 22:i[2015] 34–55), Rachel Adcock sheds new light on Aphra Behn's *The Roundheads* [1682] by discussing it in the context of Exclusion Crisis-era pope-burning pageants. Adcock argues that, as a Tory play, *The Roundheads* foregrounds the 'seditious intent' of the pageants and mocks Elkanah Settle, the author of several such processions (p. 38). By invoking the memory of the English Civil Wars, Behn also seeks to link Whiggism with republicanism and 'Presbyterianism with popery' (p. 44). At the same time, however, she cannot resist the urge to criticize cavalier and Tory attitudes towards women and female sexuality. As Adcock points out, 'the downfall of the parliamentary buffoonish upstarts is celebrated, but there are some uncomfortable moments when cavalier behaviour merges with Whig nastiness' (p. 50). Whig noncon-formists might offer the greatest threat to the nation as a whole, but women must be equally wary of their Tory counterparts.

If *The Roundheads* evinces some discomfort with Tory ideology, at least in relation to gender, Behn's earlier plays are much more openly critical of monarchy. Taking as her central focus two of Behn's early works, *The Young King* [c.1660] and *The Forc'd Marriage* [1670], Anita Pacheco argues in ' "Where lies this power Divine?": The Representation of Kingship in Aphra Behn's Early Tragicomedies' (*JECS* 38:iii[2015] 317–34), that Behn's tragicomedies are deeply sceptical in their treatment of royalist political philosophy. Although Behn was undoubtedly a royalist, Pacheco argues, she believed that the concept of divine right freed the monarch from any responsibility to behave virtuously. Her 'disenchantment with divine right' thus led her to propose a new model of kingship 'based on intellectual freedom from Christian doctrine' (p. 332), and founded 'on obedience to a rational faculty liberated from the guilt and terrors instilled by Christian dogma' (p. 320–1). Pacheco offers a useful corrective to the critical tendency to accept Behn's royalism at face value. Even as she defended the Stuart kings, her political views may have been 'out of step with the absolutist tendency of Stuart royalism' (p. 332).

This year, two contributions to Matthew Augustine and Steven Zwicker's edited collection, *Lord Rochester in the Restoration World*, focused on John Wilmot, earl of Rochester's contributions to the Restoration playhouse. In 'Rochester, the Theatre, and Restoration Theatricality' (pp. 121–40), David Francis Taylor points out that while Rochester's theatrical output was not substantial, he was deeply immersed in and influential on the Restoration theatrical world. In his prologues and epilogues, Taylor argues, Rochester both satirizes the theatre and attempts to 'limit and shape the audience to which it speaks' (p. 136). He also foregrounds the nature of theatrical spectacle 'as hypnotically and corruptingly sensual' (p 139), a viewpoint he also explores in *Lucina's Rape*, his one full-length play. According to Taylor, Rochester stages the ways in which politicians and monarchs use spectacle as smoke-screen; he 'posits spectacle as a dangerous mode of fantasy... which blinds us to the wrongdoing that is always occurring elsewhere—offstage' (p. 145).

*Lucina's Rape* is also the subject of Melissa E. Sanchez's 'Sex and Sovereignty in Rochester's Writing' (pp. 184–206), a second relevant contribution to *Lord Rochester in the Restoration World*. According to Sanchez, Rochester emphasizes the violence of Valentinian's act of rape. Lucina is not merely a political symbol, but 'an actual political subject whose body has been violated' (p. 195). That Rochester treats her as an 'actual subject whose rights are violated rather than as the property of her husband' suggests his willingness to 'expand the definition of the political subject to include women' (p. 197). Sexual and political liberty are linked, and both 'are a matter of life and death' for individual subjects (p. 213). While I am loath to abandon wholesale the reading of Lucina as political symbol (indeed, I have myself written about her propagandistic value), Sanchez does offer a useful counterpoint to such readings, and encourages a more feminocentric view of Lucina's place within the text.

The plays of Congreve, too, remained a subject of discussion this year. In '"Drink up all the water in the sea": Contracting Relationships in Congreve's *Love for Love* and *The Way of the World*' (*ELH* 82:i[2015] 183–210), Lauren Caldwell argues that in both of Congreve's plays, contractual obligations take centre stage as the characters attempt to negotiate between individual desires and the demands of the law. According to Caldwell, 'comic marriage, no matter how apparently fantastical, is a self-consciously legal activity' (p. 187), and Congreve's characters must learn to live within the law while chafing at its boundaries. Caldwell points out that Congreve's engagement with the law is unique to plays of the period, and thus his works may offer new insight into Restoration comedic engagement with the concept of marriage. Perhaps, she suggests, 'we stand to gain more by approaching these Restoration and eighteenth-century plays as inquiries into the limits of obligation' (p. 206). It is an intriguing argument and a useful challenge to future critics writing on Congreve's comedy.

Theatrical representations of the New Exchange are the subject of Tim Keenan's 'Shopping and Flirting: Staging the New Exchange in Seventeenth- and Eighteenth-Century Comedies' (*RECTR* 30:i–ii[2015] 31–53). While the popularity of the New Exchange waned over the course of the eighteenth century, it was a popular gathering place throughout the seventeenth, and it is featured prominently in six plays authored between 1636 and 1719. Critics have long debated the extent to which Restoration audiences would have expected to see familiar locations represented realistically. Taking as his central focus Etherege's *She Would If She Could* [1668] and Wycherley's *The Country Wife* [1675], however, Keenan argues that the 'thrill of recognition' was 'very much the point' of theatrical scenes set in well-known locations (p. 34). As Keenan points out, 'entrances and exits' in both plays, 'together with spatial markers in the dialogue can be mapped...consistently onto a seventeenth-century plan of the Exchange' (p. 51). Such staging choices, combined with new 'perspective wings and backshutters' (p. 50), would have created for audiences a passable reproduction of the Exchange. By overlaying theatrical stage directions onto a map of the New Exchange, Keenan clarifies and deepens our understanding of the scenic capabilities of the Restoration theatre.

Although little work was published on Restoration actors and actresses this year, Riki Miyoshi's 'An Unpublished Document Relating to the Restoration Actor Michael Mohun' (*N&Q* 62[2015] 265–6) offers new insight into the final years of actor Michael Mohun. Although Mohun had enjoyed great professional success in his younger years, by the late 1670s the King's Company was on the brink of ruin, and Mohun himself increasingly under suspicion as a Catholic living in London during the unsettled years of the Popish Plot and Exclusion Crisis. Miyoshi has here unearthed a previously unpublished document dated 19 May 1678, in which Mohun 'was assessed for poll tax in Whitehall...and was consequently charged 5 shillings in total' (p. 266). Given the financial difficulties in which Mohun found himself, such an amount would have been considerable, adding fiscal insult to the injury of growing anti-Catholicism in England.

## 2. Dryden

As usual the online *Annual Bibliography of English Language and Literature* and *Modern Language Association International Bibliography* proved indispensable. But have they replaced scholars by scanners?—many items listed under Dryden had little or nothing to do with him. Where the bibliographies saved effort, my assistants and I wasted it. In 'Some Current Publications' (*Restoration* 39[2015] 205–25) Ben Neudorf, assisted by Anne Breyer, was more straightforwardly helpful. Another difficulty was that some journals have become less accessible: libraries that have not subscribed to them blame reduced funding, but I suspect changed priorities.

Several articles were mainly biographical. In 'Sir Robert Howard, Thomas Hobbes, and the Fall of Clarendon' (*SCent* 30[2015 ] 75–93), Christopher Marsh examines Howard's poem 'The Duell of the Stags', and finds that it throws light on his quarrel with Dryden over politics; Howard derived from Hobbes a more critical view of the Stuart monarchy than his brother-in-law did. In 'The Scrutiny of Poet Squab' (*MHRA: Working Papers in the Humanities* [2015] 10–20), Sean Whitfield outlines research on the roles of Dryden and coffee-house culture in developing bourgeois taste and criticism, and the consequent 'scrutiny' of the Poet Laureate's work and character by aristocratic contemporaries, notably Rochester and Buckingham. It should be pointed out that Rochester's portrayal of Dryden as 'Poet Squab' is especially outrageous, as the more likely of the two to 'cry cunt' in the hope of being thought 'a tearing blade' was Rochester himself; Whitfield notes that he has 'taken the liberty of censuring' the offensive word, but in fact he has not censored it. In 'Trading Places: Lord Rochester, the Laureate and the Making of Literary Reputations' (in Augustine and Zwicker, eds., pp. 58–78) Matthew C. Augustine suggests that the working relationship between the two men was closer than has been thought, and that it reflects the shift from script to print as a means of publication.

Two articles related directly to Dryden and his publishers. In 'Henry Herringman, Jacob Tonson, and John Dryden: The Creation of the English Literary Publisher' (*N&Q* 62[2015] 274–7), Stephen Bernard finds new significance in Dryden's changing from the conservative Herringman to the enterprising Tonson. Bernard supports the familiar ideas that Tonson was 'the first modern publisher' and that 'he created the English literary canon'. The former idea is true enough, in the sense that he discovered talents and sustained reputations, particularly among Whiggish authors. The latter is debatable, as few of his authors have remained required reading for students, or even scholars: George Stepney, for example, who according to Johnson 'professed himself a poet', is rarely mentioned in *YWES*. In 'Dryden's *Virgil* (1697): Gatherings and Politics' (*PBSA* 109[2015] 131–9), John Barnard discerns the political divide between Tory poet and Whig publisher, not only in their correspondence but also in the very gatherings or signatures of *The Works of Virgil*. Dryden easily subverted Tonson's plan of dedicating the whole collection to William IV, and dedicated the pastorals and georgics to two Tory noblemen. There is bibliographical evidence that Tonson tried unsuccessfully to stop him dedicating the *Aeneis* to Lord Chesterfield.

As a poet, Dryden appeared this year mostly in the company of precursors and contemporaries. In 'Edmund Waller's "Easy" Style and the Heroic Couplet' (*SEL* 55[2015] 93–123), Thomas Kaminski guides us over agreeable ground. He is mainly concerned with the sources and qualities of Waller's couplet verse, but adds that where Waller had been 'easy' Dryden was forceful, so he invented what we call the heroic couplet. Kaminski urges us to cultivate the proper manner of reading all verse in this tradition, and might have quoted Pope, 'the sound must seem an echo to the sense'. In ' "My victorious triumphs are all thine": Romance and Elect Community in Lucy Hutchinson's *Order and Disorder*' (*SP* 112[2015] 162–93), Emily Griffiths Jones includes a detailed consideration of *Astraea Redux* under the subheading 'Patriotic Romance and

Erotic Universalism' (pp. 166–70). She finds that 'a universalizing spirit of love, which proceeds from Charles II as the messianic prince of peace, inspires Dryden's ardent patriotism in *Astraea Redux*—and Hutchinson's burning contempt in *Order and Disorder*'. In ' "What passion cannot musick raise and quell!" ': The Pindaric Ode and the Musical Sublime in the History of the Emotions' (in Champion and Lynch, eds., *Understanding Emotions in Early Europe*, pp. 101–25), Miranda Stanyon analyses 'A Song for St Cecilia's Day' in the context of Pindaric odes about music and early theorizing about the sublime. I found her discussion of whether sublimity implied the excess or absence of passion interesting but problematic. In quoting an essay by William Jackson of Exeter [1783] she remarks on his 'somewhat opaquely situated' abstract terms: here I thought the new theoretical pot was calling the eighteenth-century kettle black. But if interest was sometimes quelled, it had previously been raised, and Stanyon's conclusion that the song 'shows the deep and generative roots of ambivalence towards the passions in discourses surrounding both music and the sublime' is plain and persuasive.

As a dramatist Dryden was still more elusive. In 'Literary Form and the Representation of Slavery in *Don Sebastian*' (*SECC* 44[2015] 101–20), Adam R. Beach remarks that critics have tended to reduce this play to either a quasi-allegorical reaction to the revolution of 1688, or a more straightforward account of conflict between Christianity and Islam. Beach brings out Dryden's interest in responses to slavery and its violations of body and spirit: the heroic resistance of Sebastian and Almeyda in the main plot, and the passive obedience of Antonio in the subplot. He believes Dryden sympathized most with Antonio, perhaps comparing his own 'drudgery' as a dramatist with Antonio's efforts at entertainment: while Sebastian and Almeyda suffer extraordinary misfortune, Antonio enjoys a fantastic escape. This is a lucid and illuminating essay. In 'A Shakespeare Allusion in *Love Triumphant*' (*N&Q* 62[2015] 270–1), Jason R. Denman draws attention to the phrase 'foot it featly', the memorable advice to dancers in Shakespeare's *The Tempest*, its Dryden–Davenant adaptation, and *Love Triumphant*. In Dryden's final tragicomedy, and in what Denman rightly calls 'the low plot', the phrase acquires irony at the celebration of a marriage more vicious than virtuous. I have not yet seen Rodney Stenning Edgecombe's 'An Allusion to *All for Love* in "Ode to a Nightingale" ' (*KSR* 29:i[2015] 11–12.

The life and the work came together forcibly in James Horowitz's 'Partisan Bodies: John Dryden, Jacobite Camp, and the Queering of 1688' (*Restoration* 39[2015] 17–60). Horowitz believes the Great and Glorious Revolution led to deplorable developments: the two-party and two-gender systems. Dryden—though not necessarily bisexual himself—in his late work explored the varieties of sexual experience, and implied that 'compulsory heterosexuality is as limiting for human desire as the labels Whig and Tory for a Jacobite'. His critique of 'political liberalism and the heteronormative values that have often been its ideological bedfellow', Horowitz suggests, should have a special interest for Anglo-American readers today. This essay is both lively and informative: for those unfamiliar with its ideas there are some twenty pages of notes and references.

Dryden's reputation and influence aroused more comment than usual. In 'The Typological Ego-Trip from "Dryden" to Prufrock' (in his *Swift and Others*, pp. 11–47) Claude Rawson argues that in the autobiographical elements of Dryden's dedications and prefaces Swift saw attempts at self-promotion which he thought were the beginnings of an objectionable trend towards Romantic egoism. This explanation of Swift's hostility to Dryden seems better than the well-known one, that 'cousin Swift' took umbrage when Dryden told him he would 'never be a poet', though to me the hostility still seems excessive. In 'Monarchy, Meritocracy, and Tragic Realism in the Work of Mary Leapor' (*TSWL* 34 [2015] 65–87), Anne Chandler regards Leapor's recurring pictures of Apollo and David as influenced by Dryden's typological approach to myth and his analyses of 'the kingly soul' in tragedy. She probably knew the mythic episodes in *Fables*, the political apologetics of *Absalom and Achitophel*, and the psychological studies of monarchs in *All for Love* and *Don Sebastian*. Dryden's influence on Leapor was less obvious than Pope's but more profound. In 'Choice Reading: Anthologies, Reading Practices and the Canon, 1680–1900' (*YES* 45[2015] 35–55), Barbara M. Benedict includes *The Covent-Garden Drollery* (Tonson, 1672), for which 'Dryden apparently wrote some fourteen poems', and the early volumes of *Miscellany Poems* (Tonson, 1684–94), of which he was in some sense editor. Such anthologies introduced a wider readership to his satires, songs, and translations. In 'Scott's Editing: History, Polyphony, Authority' (*MP* 112 [2015] 661–90), Robert Mayer remarks that in Scott's *Works of John Dryden* both the editor—authority on the author—and the author himself are sometimes reduced to silence by the voices of innumerable commentators quoted in the introductory 'Life' and the footnotes. We are given less an appraisal of Dryden than a history of his age. Mayer believes Scott has created 'a remarkable polyphony', though *The Edinburgh Review* complained that he had brought in 'loads of contemporary trash'.

## 3. Marvell

All of the scholarship on Marvell in 2015 was on the poetry, with one exception: Matthew C. Augustine's '"A mastery in fooling": Marvell, the Mock-Book, and the Surprising Life of "Mr. Bayes"' (*SP* 112[2015] 353–78). This essay details several 'points of imaginative contact' (p. 356; the phrase is intended to complicate and extend the notion of 'influence') between *The Rehearsal Transpros'd* and the satires of Swift and Pope. Augustine argues for a stronger connection between Marvell and eighteenth-century satire than has previously been noted. Marvell's poetic satires are the subject of a piece by Edward Holberton called 'Representing the Sea in Andrew Marvell's "Advice to a Painter" Satires' (*RES* 66 [2015] 71–86), which historicizes these poems in relation to England's complex maritime interests. The poems deploy the image of the sea to reveal the tensions and problems within the maritime community.

'Upon Appleton House' dominated studies of the poetry, with two journal articles and a book chapter on this work. In 'Andrew Marvell and the Epistemology of Carelessness' (*ELH* 82[2015] 553–88), David Carroll Simon takes up the topic of Marvell and science, beginning with a careful and critical survey of recent work in this area. Focusing first on the theme of civil war and then on that of optics, Simon argues that Marvell seems to 'do' science through what he calls 'effortless complexity' (p. 557). Marvell's apparent indifference or carelessness is not a constructed artifice, but rather a genuine openness, a form of 'experimentalism as affect' (p. 577). This fascinating essay should be of interest to students of literature and science beyond Marvell studies. Jeffrey Theis considers the same poem from an ecocritical perspective in 'Marvell's "Upon Appleton House" and Tree-Felling: A Political Woodpecker' (in Munroe, Geisweidt, and Bruckner, eds., *Ecological Approaches to Early Modern English Texts: A Field Guide to Reading and Teaching*, pp. 193–204). Theis suggests that teachers interested in historicizing ecocriticism should teach the poem with a focus on the 'Hewel' stanzas in order to help students understand the early modern relationship between nature and politics and to perceive trauma in both realms.

Ryan's Netzley's *Lyric Apocalypse: Milton, Marvell, and the Nature of Events* includes a chapter on 'Upon Appleton House'. The book analyses 'the present of apocalyptic transformation' (p. 3) in lyric poetry; in the case of 'Upon Appleton House', Netzley argues, Marvel deals not with projected past or future scenarios, but with revolution occurring in the present. Its literalized metaphors are important, and present events in the verse. In an earlier chapter, 'Apocalyptic Means: Allegiance, Force, and Events in Marvell's Cromwell Trilogy and Royalist Elegies', Netzley discusses Marvell's poems of praise, demonstrating that they praise not persons, but events and the force of apocalypse.

Several other poems received critical attention. In 'Marvell's Religious Dialogues: The *Ordo Salutis*, Home and Doubleness' (*ES* 96[2015] 139–56), A.D. Cousins considers the relationship among a group of poems not often studied together. He offers three contexts for this: the *ordo salutis*, the 'idea of home', and Marvell's 'doublenes'. The latter notion, which refers to Marvell's composition of verse that is both devotional and displays his own authorial powers, is one that Cousins began to develop in an essay on 'The Coronet' in 2014. Shannon Kelley's 'Amber, the Heliades, and the Poetics of Trauma in Marvell's "The Nymph Complaining"' (*SEL* 55[2015] 151–74) engages with trauma studies as well as offering a reading of the faun's amber tears in 'The Nymph Complaining'. Prefacing her analysis of the poem with a history of amber as a literary image, Kelley argues for the cultural significance of amber to trauma studies. Amber helps transform female grief to female agency, revealing how trauma can be both natural and creative. In 'Devouring Desire: Fear of the Abject in Marvell's *Daphnis and Chloe*' (*ANQ* 28:i[2015] 23–8), Laura Alexander reads Marvell's adaptation of Longus in the context of Kristevan psychoanalytic theory. She argues that Daphnis's flight is caused by abjection; he feels that desire is an all-consuming and deeply frightening force. Alexander also briefly comments on desire and language as Marvellian themes in other works.

As editor of the Longman Annotated English Poets edition of Marvell's poetry, Nigel Smith offers a retrospective reflection on the volume in 'Marvell Studies Ten Years After the Longman Annotated English Poets Edition of

Andrew Marvell's Poems' (*LitComp* 12:i[2015] 38–44). He describes the editing of the volume, its reception, and its influence, and surveys some archival finds since the book's publication. A recent find is discussed by Niall Allsopp in 'A Surreptitious State of Marvell's *Miscellaneous Poems* (1681)?' (*N&Q* 62[2015] 268–70). Allsopp analyses an anonymous title page, the one on the copy at the Senate House Library at the University of London. He argues that it represents a last-minute change made under political pressure, giving us a more detailed understanding of how seventeenth-century printers responded to such pressure. In sum, Marvell's poetry continues to receive study from a wide range of perspectives, perhaps fuelled by the Longman edition mentioned above.

## 4. Other Poetry

### (a) Rochester

This was an active year for studies of John Wilmot, second earl of Rochester, largely owing to Matthew C. Augustine and Steven N. Zwicker's edited collection of critical essays, *Lord Rochester in the Restoration World*. As Augustine and Zwicker observe in their introduction (pp. 1–16): 'to view Rochester as standing out, standing apart, so brilliantly from his age obscures how deeply he was embedded in Restoration sociabilities and especially in the sociability of writing' (p. 3). Moreover, 'His poems are echo chambers of voices, some distant—Latin poetry, cavalier song—some proximate—voices heard in fashionable resorts, but also, and of course, from below, in taverns and alleys, among bawds and whores, cutpurses and cheats. Rochester ventriloquized aristocratic peers and mere poseurs, and quite brilliantly and intimately he inhabited a range of female subjectivities: lovers and mistresses, women seduced and abandoned, as well as courtiers and aristocratic ladies and the king's own favourites and concubines. Dryden may well have caught the negligent masculinity of the king's bedchamber at the opening of *Absalom and Achitophel*, but it was Rochester who was capable of imagining himself into the pathos of female service' (pp. 6–7). Each contribution augments these and other areas of Rochester's achievement. Jonathan Sawday writes in detail on 'John Wilmot and the Writing of "Rochester"' (pp. 17–39). Paul Davis's subject is 'From Script to Print: Marketing Rochester' (pp. 40–57), and Matthew C. Augustine's contribution is 'Trading Places: Lord Rochester, the Laureate and the Making of Literary Reputation' (pp. 58–78), considered elsewhere in the present chapter. Steven N. Zwicker's subject is gossip in his 'Lord Rochester: A Life in Gossip' (pp. 79–98), and Nicholas von Maltzahn's concern is 'Rochester and the Satiric Underground' (pp. 99–120). David Francis Taylor's contribution, 'Rochester, the Theatre and Restoration Theatricality' (pp. 121–40), is considered elsewhere in this chapter. The role of scepticism engages Christopher Tilmouth in his 'Rochester and the Play of Values' (pp. 141–61). Tim Harris's subject is 'Sexual and Religious Libertinism in Restoration England' (pp. 162–83). Melissa E. Sanchez's discussion of drama in her 'Sex and Sovereignty in Rochester's Writing' (pp. 184–206) is treated elsewhere in the present chapter, although Ros Ballaster's 'Rochester, Behn and Enlightenment Liberty' (pp. 207–30), with its consideration of the treatment of the female libertine in Aphra Behn with its sources in Rochester, is not. The use of obscenity engages Tom Jones in his 'Unfit to Print: Rochester and the Politics of Obscenity' (pp. 231–49). Nicholas Fisher's topic is 'The Perspective of Rochester's Letters' (pp. 250–69). In the concluding essay in this challenging volume, Tom Lockwood writes on 'Rochester and Rhyme' (pp. 280–90). There is a useful double-columned index (pp. 291–3) but no overall bibliography or guide to further reading. Notation to individual contributions may be found at the conclusion of each chapter.

Leah Benedict's 'Generic Failures and Imperfect Enjoyments: Rochester and the Anatomy of Impotence' (*ECF* 28[2015] 59–84) primarily focuses upon Rochester's 'The Imperfect Enjoyment' and also *The Farce of Sodom, or the Quintessence of Debauchery*. Benedict's concern is the treatment of sexual problems, sexual passion, their relationship to social interaction, generic failures, and imperfect enjoyment in Rochester, compared to their treatment in Reinier de Graaf's (1641–73) *Tractatus Virorum Organis Generationi Inservientibus* [1668] and Walter Charleton's (1619–1707) *Natural History of the Passions* [1674]. Benedict observes in her abstract that 'in the late seventeenth century, literary descriptions of sexual failure attempted to synthesize the latest developments in anatomical science and material philosophy'. She explains that 'these branches of study pursued detailed accounts of passion and procreative capacity, including the many obstacles that stymied their perfect realization. Despite this interest in providing a comprehensive account of the body's inner workings, both fields obscure the relationship between passionate feelings and bodily performance in matters of sex, relying instead on stylish hints and obfuscation.' Her intention is to demonstrate 'how the silence around physical desire found in such thinkers as Regnier de Graaf and Walter Charleton found a voice in John Wilmot, Earl of Rochester's poem "The Imperfect Enjoyment" and in the under-appreciated Rochesterian drama *Sodom and Gomorah*. These literary revisions of scientific inquiry use coital mishaps to explore the ways in which anatomical and philosophical models of sexual congress create and impinge upon Sociality' (p. 59). Paul Davis, in his 'George Harbin and the Malet Family Manuscript of Rochester' (*PQ* 94[2015] 95–120), deals with manuscript study and the provenance of Rochester manuscripts, with especial attention to Sir John Malet (1623–86). Specifically, Davis focuses on the *Works of John Wilmot, Earl of Rochester*, edited by Harold Love [1999]. Topics covered include the significance of the Hartwell and Harbin documents, the life of English clergyman George Harbin (1665–1744), and the association between the English poet John Wilmot and politician Sir John Malet. Also presented in two appendices are the titles of the Rochester poems, 'Wiltshire, Longleat House, Library of the Marquess of Bath, Thynne Papers, Vol. XXVII' (pp. 110–12) that highlights the Rochester manuscripts and, in the second appendix, a family tree of 'The Harbin Family and the Malet Family' (p. 113). In the first part of his essay, Davis draws upon 'new archival evidence to plot the various stages of the "Harbin" manuscript's journey until its arrival in the hands of George Harbin. This provenance then forms the basis of an examination, in the second half of the essay, of the "private" purposes the manuscript served, in the decades after Rochester's death, for its original owners—members of his wife's extended family, the Malets of Somerset' (p. 96). Harbin's sister Anne married a Malet, a descendant of Rochester's wife; especially important regarding the poet's manuscripts is Alexander Malet (1704–75).

Peter DeGabriele, in his 'Clothes Make the Ape: The Satirical Animal in Rochester's Poetry' (*EMLS* 18:i–ii[2015]), writes on Rochester's satire, his treatment of monkeys, and his relationship to theriophilic discourse. DeGabriele pays especial attention to Rochester's verse satires 'A Satyr against Reason and Mankind', 'Tunbridge Wells', and 'A Letter from Artemisa in the Town to Chloe in the Country'. In his abstract, DeGabriele writes that his 'paper argues that by attending to the role of the ape, or monkey, in Rochester's satirical practice we can reevaluate both the role of the animal in Rochester's work, and the conceptual limits of early modern theriophilic discourse. Previous criticism, focusing on "A Satyr Against Reason and Mankind", has located Rochester within a stable and defined tradition of theriophily. Recent work in animal studies, however, has necessitated a revised look at the conceptual limits of theriophily, and this also provides an opportunity to look again at Rochester's most famous poem. I argue that Rochester pushes the limits of theriophily by producing an account of man that is not anthropocentric. In Laurie Shannon's terms [a reference to Shannon's *The Accommodated Animal* (*YWES* 94[2015] p. 413)] man is, for Rochester, an "unaccommodated animal" who has no proper place in nature. While Shannon focuses on man's tragic insufficiency', DeGabriele demonstrates that 'Rochester's satire shows man as always overgrown and monstrous, even in his nakedness. Rochester uses the imitative ape in his poems "Artemisia to Chloe" and "Tunbridge Wells" as a figure of the satirist. Because the ape naturally imitates man merely by mirroring him, man gets caught in the ape's reflective trap and is unable to establish the normative outside of the happy beast common to theriophily. Man is thus decentred in the world by his inability to distance himself from what Rochester calls "the ape's mock face".'

In Jim Owen's 'Lucretius and the Radical Imagination: John Wilmot and *The Nature of Things*' (*CEA* 77[2015] 344–9) attention is drawn to the treatment of Epicureanism and natural law in 'A Satyr against Reason and Mankind' with the sources in Lucretius' *De Rerum Natura* (*The Nature of Things*). According to Owen, 'Celebrating the philosophy of Epicurus, *The Nature of Things* depicts a universe composed of matter and void infinitely creating and recreating itself and presents the cosmos as the result of collisions and combinations of atoms with no help from an intelligent Designer. The lessons, Epicurus suggested, are that death is final, our actions can neither please nor displease any possible higher powers, and the key to living a good life is to seek pleasure and avoid pain.' Furthermore 'no poet of the age found Lucretius more fascinating than did John Wilmot, Earl of Rochester. Rochester took Lucretius's epicurean notion that one should live for pleasure a tad too far, however, dying of complications of venereal disease and drink at the age of thirty-three. He translated two passages from Lucretius and worked

Lucretius's ideas into his most famous work, "A Satyr against Reason and Mankind." Although Rochester never published his snippets of Lucretius, he shared them with others in his circle and thus influenced future generations of English writers, and his ironic allusion to *The Nature of Things* in his most famous satire shows that he expected some of his readers to be familiar with Lucretius's work.' (pp. 344–5). The implications of a February 1680 letter the Deist Charles Blount (1654–93) wrote to the famous libertine (and probable Deist) John Wilmot, earl of Rochester, to discuss the immortality of the soul (p. 266) concern Joanne Paul in her 'Disseminating the Renaissance in Seventeenth-Century English: Pomponazzi, Blount and the Three Impostors' (*N&Q* 62[2015] 266–8). The letter illuminates the role of Deism, the treatment of immortality, perceptions of the soul, and relationships to deception with sources in Pietro Pomponazzi (1462–1525) and *his De Immortalitate Animae* [1516].

*(b) Traherne*

There is only one Traherne item that has come to attention to report for 2015. Elizabeth S. Dodd, in ' "Perfect innocency by creation" in the Writings of Thomas Traherne' (*L&T* 29[2015] 216–36), draws upon 'Thomas Wilson's definition of "perfect innocency by creation" ', in Wilson's 'Innocence' (in J. Bagwell and A. Simson, eds., *A Complete Christian Dictionary*, 7th edn. [1661 [1612]], p. 336), to read ' the theme of innocence in the poetry and prose of Thomas Traherne through the doctrine of creation'. Such an approach allows Dodd to reveal 'the rich complexity of Traherne's innocence and uncovers its theological core. It provides the basis upon which to disinvest Traherne's works of disenchanted post-Enlightenment associations which have surrounded his concept of natural innocence.' According to Dodd's reading, 'in Traherne's works, "perfect innocency by creation" is not an absolute spiritual perfection or a bare natural innocence. Innocency by creation is a creaturely attribute characterized by the fragility and finitude of material existence. Innocency by creation means that one is created innocent by God, it is a relational status infused by grace and set in motion by love.' For Dodd, Traherne 'provides a good case study to illustrate both the misconceptions encouraged by superficial expositions of pre-modern innocence and the benefits of excavating and re-interpreting earlier traditions'. Consequently her article 'investigates Traherne's presentation of original innocence through Wilson's contemporary definition'. Such an 'approach demonstrates that, contrary to Henderson's account of pre-modern innocence', in his 'Innocence' entry found in J.F. Childress and J. Macquarrie, eds., *A New Dictionary of Christian Ethics* (SCM [1986]), pp. 302b–3033a, 'Traherne's original and Edenic innocence is not an absolute spiritual perfection but a complex and creaturely quality that is best understood in the context of relationship to God.' Dodd argues that her 'assessment uncovers the theological core of Traherne's idea of innocence. It thereby provides the basis upon which to disinvest Traherne's innocence of anachronistic associations with Enlightenment glorifications of nature, which are tied to the common reading of Traherne as a form of nature mystic.' However, Dodd 'does not deny the value Traherne places upon nature, but argues that Traherne's concept of original innocence might be better understood through the doctrine of creation than through 18th-century primitivism' (pp. 216–17).

Traherne's (1637–74) older contemporaries Henry Vaughan (1622–95) and his brother Thomas (1622–66) have recently received scant attention in these pages. Contributions of interest have recently appeared: two of these are from the hand of Jonathan Nauman. In 'Classicism and Conversion: The Role of the Poems and Letters of St. Paulinus of Nola in Henry Vaughan's *Silex Scintillans*' (*Scintilla* 18[2015] 13–26), Nauman argues that 'the figure of Paulinus came to hold a special position in Henry Vaughan's devotional regime, one that was central and even pivotal to his stance as a sacred poet' (p. 14). Nauman explores Vaughan's use of Paolino di Nola (355–*c*.431) in Vaughan's *Silex Scintillans* [1650]. In an earlier article, Nauman writes on 'With Patriarchs and Prophets: Herbert in Vaughan's Mount of Olives' (*GHJ* 37 [2013] 178–92), and isolates sources in George Herbert's 'Avarice' from *The Temple* [1633] in Vaughan's *Silex Scintillans* and *The Mount of Olives* [1652]. Mention should be made of Krzysztof Fordoński's 'The Subversive Power of Father Matthias: The Poetry of Maciej Kazimierz Sarbiewski as Vehicle for Political Propaganda in England of the 17th Century' (in Fabiszak, Urbaniak-Rybicka, and Wolski, eds., *Crossroads in Literature and Culture*, pp. 387–97). Although the subject is Polish literature and the poet Maciej Kazimierz Sarbiewski (1595–1640), neo-Latin poetry and its English reception are illuminated in Fordoński's essay. According to its abstract, on the European continent 'Maciej Kazimierz Sarbiewski seemed a pious Jesuit father, a benign neo-Latin poet, equal [to] if not better than Horace. When almost immediately after his death his poetry crossed the English Channel, [it] gained an unexpected subversive power. It gained a new territory not so much for what it was but thanks to a new purpose for which it could be used.' According to Fordoński, in an England 'controlled by the forces of the Parliament, acquaintance with the works of Sarbiewski became a telling sign for the Royalists. At the same time, regardless of his religious adherence, Sarbiewski gained popularity as a Neo-Stoic writer.' As a consequence 'several Royalist poets started to write and publish translations from Sarbiewski which departed from the originals in such ways which allowed the poets to express their true sentiments and bypass Parliamentary censorship'. Moreover, Fordoński observes that 'others would quote excerpts from his poems in their original works'. Fordoński's essay 'traces the way Sarbiewski's poems were used—translated, adapted, quoted, emulated etc.—by such Metaphysical poets as Richard Lovelace, Henry Vaughan, Abraham Cowley and Sir John Denham, to mention but a few' (p. 387).

More specific analysis of Vaughan is found in Daniel Juan Gill's 'The Resurrection of the Body and the Life of the Flesh in Henry Vaughan's Religious Verse' (*ELH* 82[2015] 59–86). Focusing on the treatment of the resurrection of the human body and its relationship to corporeality, and examining the notion of apocalyptic vision, Gill wishes 'to assess the impact of one very specific version of resurrection belief on how poetic language represents biological and corporeal life in relation to social life'. His focus is 'on Henry Vaughan and his collection of formally experimental religious verse entitled *Silex Scintillans* ("the flashing flint" in Welsh) which he published in two volumes, the first in 1650 and the second in 1655' (p. 59). Paying especial attention to poems such as 'Burial' (pp. 65–6), 'Repentance' (pp. 68–9), 'Distraction' (pp. 72–3), and 'In the Book' (pp. 80–1), amongst others, Gill concludes that 'Throughout Vaughan's poems, the material underpinnings of language are made visible and are imagined to have the power to persist as sounds and marks on the page even after the historical language community in which the poems are meaningful has passed away. As Vaughan puts it in "Vanity of Spirit," the material traces of language are destined to live on as "hieroglyphics quite dismembered, / And broken letters, scarce remembered" (23–4).' Moreover, according to Gill, 'by inviting readers to look upon his poems as though they were themselves already half-denatured, half-way to being hieroglyphs, Vaughan detaches readers from the particular language community in which words have the power to classify and catalog and carve the world (including human beings) into a particular historical shape. By doing so, the poems invite readers to contemplate the material stuff of the world and of persons that transcends any particular historical and linguistic world' (p. 82). This challenging essay concludes with twenty-seven informative notes (pp. 82–6).

Two contributions that appeared in 2013 are also of interest. The first mentions Vaughan and the second John Cleveland (1613–58). According to Ian C. Parker's 'Marvell's "Loyall Scot" and the "Humor" of Cleveland's Vein' (*N&Q* 60[2013] 530–5), Marvell's 'The Loyall Scot' is 'one of his most intriguing and under-appreciated poems'. Its final versions are made up of a number of distinct strata, composed at different times from 1667 onward; 'the poem in its most comprehensive composite form is a powerful plea for political unity and religious toleration and a devastating satire of prelatical abuses. From its first version (likely written in 1669–70) onward, the poem took the form of a continuation and parody of and reply to John Cleveland's Civil War satire, "The Rebell Scot" (composed, likely in early 1644, as a response to the Scottish army's entry into England in support of the Parliamentary side)' (p. 530).

Jeffrey S. Shoulson, in his *Fictions of Conversions: Jews, Christians, and Cultures of Change in Early Modern England* [2013], considers the treatment of the religious conversion of Jews and its relationship to church politics and cultural change during the English Reformation. His fourth chapter, 'Alchemies of Conversion: Shakespeare, Jonson, Vaughan, and the Science of Jewish Transmutation' (pp. 112–51), explains that 'in producing the elixir, the philosopher's stone, through an esoteric process of transmutation, the alchemist was also producing an agent of further changes and, perhaps most important, effecting his own transformation, his own conversion. In light of alchemy's inherently transformative and potentially destabilizing qualities, then', he is 'particularly concerned . . . with how alchemy was understood as a "Jewish" science in the period and served to figure the disruptive effects of conversion.' Shoulson uses 'alchemy's fictions of conversion as a means to read the relationship between Shakespeare's *The Merchant of Venice* and Ben Jonson's *The Alchemist*', and he concludes the chapter with 'an analysis of the alchemical imagery in Henry Vaughan's poetry in relation to mid-seventeenth-century millenarian expectations for Jewish conversion' (pp. 13–14).

## 5. Prose

### (a) Hobbes

This was a good year for writings about Thomas Hobbes. The *Journal of the History of Ideas* devoted a special section to Hobbes's *Leviathan* (*JHI* 76[2015] 237–314). This consists of a symposium stimulated by the publication of the three-volume Clarendon edition of Hobbes's *Leviathan*, edited by Noel Malcolm [2012]. Kinch Hoekstra, in 'The Clarendon Edition of Hobbes's *Leviathan*: *Leviathan* and Its Intellectual Context' (*JHI* 76[2015] 237–57), writes that 'Scholars generations hence will still talk about Noel Malcolm's edition of *Leviathan* as one of this century's outstanding editorial accomplishments. A great work is here available in a great edition' (p. 237). Hoekstra writes that 'Malcolm's work in this edition is simultaneously substantive, sweeping, and astoundingly detailed. He handles the biggest issues of the *Leviathan* with confidence; and yet he notes when there is a missing iota subscript in the Greek. We have here an edition that allows us to view the awesome monster whole, and at the same time to consider each capillary. The new *Leviathan* is a work breathtaking in range, insight, and judiciousness. Who knew that judiciousness could be breathtaking?' (p. 257). Sarah Mortimer and David Scott, in '*Leviathan* and the Wars of the Three Kingdoms' (*JHI* 76[2015] 259–70), write that 'The problems of the Stuart multiple monarchy provide an important context for Hobbes's *Leviathan*. His fellow Royalists were divided over whether to use Scottish or Irish assistance in regaining Charles's throne'; consequently, according to the abstract, 'Hobbes's work can be read as a qualified endorsement of his patrons' Scottish invasion strategy, to which a caustic assault on clerical power was then added. But *Leviathan* was more than a factional position paper; it was a Utopian masterpiece designed to secure lasting peace. *Leviathan* proposed to end the structural differences between the three kingdoms and to curb the power of an over-mighty British aristocracy.' Furthermore they conclude that 'Insofar as Hobbes's mid-century writings, and *Leviathan* in particular, can be said to have addressed the political and religious problems peculiar to the Stuart multiple monarchy, his project failed no less surely than did that of the Scottish Covenanters' (p. 270). Mónica Brito Vieira, in her '*Leviathan* contra *Leviathan*' (*JHI* 76[2015] 271–88), 'offers a comparative discussion of the two versions of Hobbes's masterpiece—the 1651 English *Leviathan* and the 1668 Latin *Leviathan*, with a view to examining the significance of some of the main continuities and differences between the two works'. She is referring to 'a parallel edition of the English and Latin versions of *Leviathan*, which makes it possible to trace any variations among the texts'. According to Vieira, 'there would be no better pretext for engaging in a comparison between the 1651 and 1668 versions of the book'. Her analysis is focused on 'the most meaningful changes, and on what these changes and the continuities discernible in them can tell us about the nature and purpose of Hobbes's project' (p. 271). She concludes that 'Hobbes's primary cause of concern was the tentacular reach of the system of oppression woven around falsehoods, dressed up as necessary truths, that these different groups—the aristocracy, the clergy, and the intellectual elite—had created, sometimes separately, sometimes in collusion with one another, to further their power and positions. This characterization of Hobbes's project works especially well with regard to the aspects of his philosophical system that Hobbes, sometimes bravely, chose not only to iterate, but also to reinforce and enlarge when revisiting *Leviathan* in Latin' (p. 288).

Jon Parkin, in his 'Hobbes and the Reception of *Leviathan*' (*JHI* 76[2015] 289–300), writes that 'Although there has been much discussion of the reception of Hobbes's work, Hobbes's response to his own reception has rarely received much consideration. This article looks at Hobbes's engagements with his critics. Far from being rearguard actions by a philosopher under siege, or disingenuous attempts to curry favour with those in power, they can be read as moments when Hobbes in fact sought to convert what he saw as the "truth of speculation into the utility of practice."' (p.289). Parkin adds that 'We are accustomed to thinking of Hobbes's encounters with his critics as rear-guard actions by a philosopher under siege, and often as slightly disingenuous attempts to curry favour with those in power. But this may be to misunderstand what Hobbes was up to when he turned and fought his opponents. It may be better to think of Hobbes's encounters with his critics rather as moments when Hobbes was in fact attempting to convert the truths of speculation into the utility of practice' (p. 300). Noel Malcolm, the editor of the Clarendon edition of *Leviathan*, responds to the other contributors in this symposium in 'On the Clarendon Edition of Hobbes's *Leviathan*: A Response' (*JHI* 76[2015] 301–14). He 'focuses in particular on points raised by Kinch Hoekstra, concerning such matters as Hobbes's theory about the nullity of grants of essential sovereign powers, the intended readership of the text, the nature of Hobbes's political re-positioning in the "Review, and Conclusion" at the end of the book, and the iconography of the famous engraved title page'. According to Malcolm, 'The edition is meant to provide the starting-point for future interpretative work, not an authoritatively final interpretation (were such a thing ever possible). And a natural consequence of this is that the editorial introduction is not expected to engage closely with' what is current 'in the modern interpretative secondary literature—which is just as well, since a text in itself, if correctly edited, may last for many decades, whereas any discussion tied to current interpretations will seem badly dated within one or two' (pp. 301–2).

To turn to other writing on Hobbes that appeared during 2015, although Hobbes is not the primary concern of Inger Sigrun Brodey in her 'Making Sense of Sensibility' (*Persuasions* 37[2015] 62–80), in her discussion of Jane Austen's treatment of sensibility, selfishness, and altruism in *Sense and Sensibility* [1811] she does draw attention to Hobbesian ideas. Brodey discusses the cult of sensibility that developed during the second half of the eighteenth century 'as a concept . . . to help resolve deeply troubling observations about humanity. It expresses a hope for goodness and virtue despite (ample) evidence of worldly corruption.' Brodey notes that 'in the background of this optimism hovers the specter of Thomas Hobbes', who argued that, 'without . . . a supreme power to hold us accountable, we cannot escape perpetual mistrust, competing desires, fear, isolation, and civil war'. Brodey adds that 'what Hobbes found dangerously delusional, sensibility embraced— at least on the surface' (p. 63), and she reads *Sense and Sensibility* with such ideas in the background.

A comparison between ideas on the treatment of democracy found in the contemporary French philosopher Jacques Rancière (1940– ) and their source in Thomas Hobbes is found in Patrick Craig's 'Jacques Rancière, Thomas Hobbes, and a Politics of the Part That Has No Part' (*Th&Text* 18:i[2015]). Craig observes that 'Jacques Rancière's political theory is well-known for its emphasis on equality, a non-representative form of democracy, and dissensus.' Craig argues that 'Rancière's conception of the demos is prefigured in, of all places, the political theory of Thomas Hobbes.' Craig's contention is that 'contrary to Rancière's treatment of him as a proponent of parapolitics, Hobbes can be seen to provide a radical theory of democracy, one that places his politics much closer to that of Rancière than the orthodox reading of Hobbes would suggest'. Craig argues that 'a subtractive conceptualization of democracy and the *demos* exists' in Hobbes. 'Against the orthodox reading of Hobbes as a staunch supporter of absolute, even authoritarian, sovereign power, of unchecked monarchical authority', Craig suggests 'a reading of Hobbes as presenting a subtractive conception of democracy, the *demos*, and equality, one that places him in close proximity to Rancière's work. Rather than read Hobbes as a theorist of, in Rancière's terms, the "police," I instead read Hobbes as a theorist of "the power of the people".' Craig reconsiders, 'first, the place of democracy in Hobbes's thought, and second, the place of Hobbes in the politics of Rancière'.

Paul Downes's monograph *Hobbes, Sovereignty, and Early American Literature* examines rereading's of *Leviathan* in early American literature with especial attention to the treatment of sovereignty, its relationship to perceptions of divinity, the body politic, and slavery. In his introduction, 'Hobbes and the Golden Calf' (pp. 1–18), Downes writes that 'anyone interested in rereading American literary and political history with an eye to understanding and critiquing the world that liberal (now "neoliberal") political philosophy has shaped (and misshaped) will find conceptual ammunition in the version of sovereignty and commonwealth that Hobbes unfolds in his *Leviathan*' (p. 1). Downes also argues that 'Hobbesian ideas have always been present, even in the myriad forms of their desperate disavowal, in the art and politics of the Anglo-American eighteenth and nineteenth centuries.' He adds that 'the texts addressed in this book are scanned for traces of Hobbesian sovereignty or for figurations of the antagonistic encounter between Hobbesian and liberal conceptions of political community' (p. 4). There are chapters on 'Sovereignty's New Clothes' (pp. 19–44); 'Rereading *Leviathan*: The "State of Nature" and the "Artificial Soul"' (pp. 45–68); 'Hobbes in America' (pp. 69–85); '"Heaven's Sugar Cake": Puritan Sovereignty' (pp. 86–112); 'Tyranny's Corpse: Jonathan Mayhew's Revolutionary Sermon on *Romans*' (pp. 113–41); '"Imperium in

Imperio": Founding Sovereignty' (pp. 142–67); 'Tar and Feathers: Hawthorne's Revolution' (pp. 168–90); and 'Hobbes, Slavery, and Sovereign Resistance' (pp. 191–206). The ninth chapter is on 'Nat Turner and the African American Revolution' (pp. 207–30). There are extensive notes (pp. 231–72), an alphabetically arranged enumerative listing of works cited (pp. 273–86), and a detailed double-columned index (pp. 287–97).

Rachelle Gold and Jim Pearce, in their 'Ferox or Fortis: Montaigne, Hobbes, and the Perils of Paradiastole' (P&R 48[2015] 186–210) compare and contrast Montaigne and Hobbes in their use of rhetoric. They explain that 'paradiastole as a trope becomes an emblem of the ability to reach contradictory conclusions regarding any particular event or action' (p. 189). For Gold and Pearce, 'beyond their skepticism, Montaigne and Hobbes share a concern for how phenomena can be interpreted and represented through language. Despite Hobbes's desire for a method that would ensure constant and determinate linguistic acts that would render rhetoric supererogatory, Leviathan demonstrates his unremarkable affinities with mainline Renaissance humanists alongside his uneasy affinities with the Sophists' (p. 186). Gold and Pearce maintain that from a rhetorical perspective they 'see in Leviathan a vibrant and creative set of textual innovations every bit as impressive as those found in the Essais' of Montaigne 'and equally mediated by the rich and capacious legacy of classical antiquity. Despite his ideologically motivated polemics against linguistic abuses, Hobbes retained the eloquence of the Renaissance humanist. Despite his quest for apodictic truths, Hobbes remained fully committed to the strategic and sometimes duplicitous use of the verbal arts in constructing the ideal commonwealth' (p. 204).

Qadri Ismail, in 'On Literature' (Phoenix: Sri Lanka Journal of English in the Commonwealth 12[2015] 131–9), finds traces of ideas found in Hobbes's Leviathan in Shelley's A Defence of Poetry [1821] and T.B. Macaulay's Minute on Indian Education [1835].

Jess Keiser, in ' "Very like a whale": Metaphor and Materialism in Hobbes and Swift' (MP 113[2015] 198–223), compares Hobbes and Swift, in his A Tale of a Tub [1704], in terms of their use of metaphor, treatment of human nature, relationship to materialism, and political philosophy. Keiser writes that 'Hobbes's first readers saw in the pages of Leviathan the efforts of a philosopher and a satirist. These readers recognized Hobbes's serious contributions to thought and were suitably alarmed by his materialist renderings of political philosophy, psychology, and theology. Nevertheless, these same readers also noted how quickly Hobbes's otherwise sincere philosophy shaded into ridicule and scorn.' Furthermore, according to Keiser, 'they saw how earnest defenses of sovereign authority gave way to vicious attacks on the orators and politicians who might subvert that authority, how discourses on the passions turned into expositions of madness and illusion, and how demonstrations of logic and reason became an opportunity to single out the nonsensical language of Scholastic philosophers and false prophets'. Basically 'these early readers captured the playfully caustic Leviathan that often eludes even the widest and sturdiest of modern nets'. Keiser's intention is to 'reclaim this older reading of Leviathan by stressing the close connection between Hobbes's materialist philosophy and his satire'. Keiser pays especial attention to 'that one wit who certainly did borrow his "weapons" from Hobbes...Jonathan Swift' (pp. 198–9). Keiser concludes that 'Hobbes's materialism does not give rise to a literalist flattening of reality; rather, it necessitates an analogical account of reality, one that can manage a subtle play of similarity and difference' (p. 223).

Wendy Anne Lee, in her 'The Scandal of Insensibility; or, the Bartleby Problem' (*PMLA* 130[2015] 1405–19), draws upon Melville's short stories and Adam Smith's *The Theory of Moral Sentiments* [1759] and Hobbes's writing in order to compare and contrast their treatment of sensibility, emotions, immobility, and resistance. She discusses 'the physical conundrum of impassivity in Hobbes's theory of resistance and trace[s] its resonances in contemporary affect theory' (p. 1407). In her abstract, Lee observes that 'reviving Thomas Hobbes's definition of the passions as interior motions that originate action, this essay considers the case of insensibility: an absence of feeling that results in immobility. Embodying this lack of feeling is the figure of the insensible, whose signature nonresponsiveness provokes the most vehement emotions in others.' She explains that 'through readings of Hobbes's theories of resistance and contempt, Adam Smith's condemnation of impassivity, and Herman Melville's tale of an "unmoving" scrivener', she will 'examine how insensibility challenges the model of emotions as causes, as accounts of how a moved body moves. Insensibility confuses distinctions between bad feeling and no feeling, agents and patients, living and dead. Finally', she argues 'for narrative's surprising dependence on the nonnarrative presence of the insensible, a subject that reaches back through the history of philosophy to Aristotle's unmoved mover, the first cause of the universe that makes all motion possible by not being subject to motion itself' (p. 1552).

The seventh chapter of Christopher Pye's monograph *The Storm at Sea: Political Aesthetics in the Time of Shakespeare* is titled 'Hobbes and the Hydrophobes: The Fate of the Aesthetic in the Time of the State' (pp. 158–80). Although Pye's book is primarily concerned with Shakespeare and Marlowe, he has illuminating points to make concerning the role of aesthetics and its relationship to politics in Hobbes. Pye sees a 'transformation of political aesthetics from its generative and creationist form...[in] a play like *The Tempest* to the thorough instrumentalization of art implied by Hobbes's automaton of state and his contractual fiction. Hobbes is the right place to look for an understanding of what informs such an aesthetic transformation' (p. 159). Detailed notes follow the text (pp. 181–228), and are followed by an enumerative, alphabetically arranged bibliography (pp. 229–48) and a thorough double-columned index (pp. 249–56).

Mark Reinhardt's 'Vision's Unseen: On Sovereignty, Race, and the Optical Unconscious' (*Th&Event* 18:iv[2015]). Reinhart's concern is the treatment of sovereignty, the visual, and race in the work of Hobbes, Walter Benjamin (1892–1940), and the installation art of Kara Elizabeth Walker (1969– ). Accompanied by seventeen pictorial illustrations, 'this article investigates what Walter Benjamin called "the optical unconscious." Focusing on photography but taking up representations and visual practices ranging from the frontispiece of Hobbes's *Leviathan* to audience interactions with Kara Walker's 2014 public installation, "A Subtlety," the article examines both the unconscious impulses and desires that guide visual perception and cases in which visual details are not noted consciously but may nevertheless register affectively. The examples make novel sense of Benjamin's enigmatic term while revealing how the visual construction of race and sovereignty are intertwined in ways involving not only what affect theorists call "side perceptions" but also the unconscious dynamics charted by Freud' (abstract).

Michael Squire, in '*Corpus Imperii*: Verbal and Visual Figurations of the Roman "Body Politic"' (*W&I* 31[2015] 305–30), examines *Leviathan* with attention to anatomical metaphor, the treatment of the body politic, the significance of its frontispiece, image–text relations, classical literature, and particularly ancient Roman sculpture. His article 'examines the political metaphor of the body in ancient Roman words and images' and its application to Hobbes's work. Squire observes in his abstract that 'to understand how the figure of the body was rendered into political metaphor in Late Republican/ Early Imperial Rome, no less than how that political metaphor was turned back into iconic figurative form', in for instance Hobbes, 'requires working across visual and verbal categories. No less importantly, it means tackling larger questions about how words and images construct ideas about the body in at once related and different ways' (p. 305).

Peter Stone, in 'Hobbes' Problem' (*Good Society* 24:i[2015] 1–14), assesses the treatment of social order and the relationship to agency in *Leviathan* and the theories of Philip Pettit (1945– ) amongst others. Stone writes that his paper 'considers the contribution positive political theory has made to the resolution of "Hobbes' Problem"—the problem of describing the nature of artificial persons, such as states. This problem plays a central role in both empirical and normative work in political science. Several areas of positive political theory, most notably social choice theory, have shed light on Hobbes' Problem, and the results have been generally negative. That is to say, they have suggested that the conditions necessary to generate an artificial collective agent out of the individual agents comprising it may be impossible to satisfy, at least if this is done in a nontrivial way. While efforts to establish the possibility of a collective agent continue—notably in recent work by [amongst others, Pettit]... the primary accomplishment of positive political theory has been to raise the question of whether Hobbes' Problem can be solved at all' (abstract). Furthermore, Stone writes that 'the quest to describe the nature of a collective agent—an "Artificiall man," to use Hobbes' term—has motivated a significant part of the field of positive political theory'. However, a 'positive political theory has not yet produced a definitive answer to Hobbes' Problem' (p. 11).

Finally in this review of work on Hobbes published in 2015, mention should be made of Ionut Untea's '*Leviathan*, the Bad Emperor and the Challenges of a Global Liberal Society' (in Raibaud, Symington, Untea, and Waterman, eds., *Cultures in Movement*, pp. 359–84). Untea uses Hobbes's relationship to liberalism to explore 'religious and philosophical questions. Using early modern perspectives on agency and voluntarism', Untea contributes to 'the ongoing philosophical debates related to the so-called incompatibility between Confucianism and democracy and argues that future philosophical and economic worldviews may benefit from a theoretical reevaluation of the role of agency and voluntarism in establishing social cohesion' (p. 6).

*(b) Bunyan*

Four items to report on Bunyan: the 2015 *Bunyan Studies* was not available for this assessment.

Interestingly, with the exception of the first item, by David Diamond, the other three are essentially reception or influence studies. David M. Diamond, in 'Sinners and "Standers By": Reading the Characters of Calvinism in *The Pilgrim's Progress*' (*ECS* 49:i[2015] 1–15), is concerned with the relationship between characterization and Calvinism. His essay 'considers the ways in which the need to determine the spiritual states of other professed believers bears on the representational status of Bunyan's literary characters' (p. 3). Diamond writes that 'Accounting for the points of continuity between *The Pilgrim's Progress* and eighteenth-century novels like [Henry Fielding's] *Tom Jones* means rethinking the literary afterlife of Calvinist theology. In the early novel, Calvinism lives on as an epistemology of character if not as a comprehensive system of meaning. It furnishes such disparate writers as Bunyan and Fielding with a framework through which to articulate the problem of knowing other people within and beyond ecclesiastical contexts.' Moreover, 'whether in the hands of a strict Calvinist like Bunyan or an Anglican Arminian like Fielding, novelistic character emerges as a substrate for experimenting with the resources and limitations of that framework. Figures like Talkative and Thwackum reveal a tension inherent to a Calvinist paradigm based on penetrative scrutiny of outward markers: the "real Character at the Bottom" of our self-presentations is both profoundly stable and potentially inscrutable.' According to Diamond, 'the Calvinist inheritance of the novel consists not in narrative technologies of interiority but in a model of literary character in which surfaces rather than interiors are the source of complexity' (p. 13).

The late Kirsty Milne, in her *At Vanity Fair: From Bunyan to Thackeray*, is concerned with the afterlife of Bunyan's novel and its section on 'Vanity Fair' that Thackeray used to name his 1847–8 novel. She is also concerned with Ben Jonson and his *Bartholomew Fair* [1614]. The focus of her attention is literary tradition, the treatment of vanity, and hedonism, and her approach is cultural-historical and social-economic. Her monograph is divided into an introduction and five main chapters. 'Introduction: The Boy at the Royal Exchange' (pp. 1–17); '"Copying from life": The Literal and the Literary in Bunyan's *Vanity Fair*' (pp. 18–38); 'Reforming *Bartholomew Fair*: Bunyan, Jonson and the Transmission of a Trope' (pp. 39–60); '"More moderate now than formerly": Re-writing *Vanity Fair*, 1684–1700' (pp. 61–81); '"Gay ideas of Vanity-Fair": Transforming Bunyan in the Eighteenth Century' (pp. 82–101); and '"Manager of the performance": Thackeray's *Vanity Fair*' (pp. 102–27); plus 'Conclusion: The Fair in Vogue' (pp. 128–38), and an 'Afterword' by Sharon Achinstein (pp. 139–42). These are followed by two appendices: the first to chapter 3 (p. 143) and the second to chapter 4 (pp. 144–6), followed by extensive notes (pp. 147–98), an alphabetically arranged enumerative bibliography (pp. 198–225), and a helpful double-columned index (pp. 226–8). Milne observes that, 'Although Vanity Fair is only one episode in the eventful narrative of *The Pilgrim's Progress*, taking up barely a dozen pages out of 267 in the first edition of 1678, it has had a potent and versatile afterlife' (p. 1). She writes in her introduction that 'Generations of readers have used Vanity Fair as a way of thinking about money and morality, commodification and conformity. New associations accumulated with William Makepeace Thackeray's choice of the name for his best-known novel [1847–8]; further layers of meaning accrued out of Condé Nast's decision to keep *Vanity Fair* as the title of the magazine that he bought and relaunched in 1914.' According to Milne's account, 'in this rich and complex process of transmission, the origins of the phrase have been obscured—and with them the paradox that a seventeenth-century puritan should have produced a familiar motif of modern consumerism'. For Milne, her 'study recovers the origins of this cultural trope, and shows how closely tied are the cultural legacies of puritanism within modern consumer society. Indeed, as shall be shown, Vanity Fair is an important image for modernity, one that may not reconcile the social and religious discipline of a hale puritanism with the insouciant freedoms of a market-driven economy, but one that is a flashpoint for these competing, and even complementary, energies' (pp. 2–3).

Greta Olson's 'Confessing Self, Confessing Nation: Life Narratives in the 2012 Presidential Election' (in Banita and Pöhlmann, eds., *Electoral Cultures: American Democracy and Choice*, pp. 341–66), seems somewhat irrelevant in the light of the 2016 presidential election. Olson's concern is narrative technique, confessional literature, life writing, the treatment of the self, national identity and redemption, and their relationship to the campaign leading up to the 2012 presidential election. Her texts for comparative discourse are Barack Obama's *Dreams from My Father: A Story of Race and Inheritance* [1995] and *The Audacity of Hope* [2006], Mitt Romney's *No Apology: The Case for American Greatness* [2010] and *Turnabout: Crisis, Leadership, and the Olympic Games* [2004] and Bunyan's *Grace Abounding to the Chief of Sinners* [1666].

David Reagles, 'The Atheist Bunyan: *The Pilgrim's Progress* and Organized Freethought in Victorian Britain' (*MdLSBC* 6:ii[2015]), is a reception study focusing on the Victorian and Edwardian period and its response to Bunyan's *The Pilgrim's Progress*. Reagles 'explores how freethinkers received John Bunyan and read his works in Victorian Britain. An analysis of freethinking periodicals, letters to editors, lectures, essays, and autobiography reveals a vexed relationship that was anything but monolithic.' Reagles's 'systematic analysis of how members of the freethought movement read and received Bunyan reveals two distinct reading strategies: one of resolute rejection, the other, of compromising appropriation'. The first section of his article examines 'those freethinkers who rejected Bunyan as a viable literary resource. It shows how their characterization of Bunyan was guided by a belief in the necessary connection between atheism and societal reform. The second section then describes the changing reception of Bunyan and attempts to explain why the shift occurred.' He instances two cases: 'In one case, there is Robert Cooper, who wrote off Bunyan as "holy trash." However, as with readers like Robert Blatchford [1851–1943], freethought contributed in meaningful ways to the project of seeking to reconcile the "divided self" of Victorian England into a complex whole during the Edwardian years. Bunyan had been placed within the familiar tendentious binary of faith versus reason, and for many freethinkers, there he remained. But that is not the whole story. Others who actively promoted secular ideals in British society accepted Bunyan as "the great teacher of us all".'

*(c) Aubrey*
The year 2015 witnessed the publication of two major works on John Aubrey (1626–97), the antiquary best known for the portraits of his contemporaries found in his *Brief Lives* 'first' published in a truncated version in 1813. Kate Bennett has produced the magnificent two-volume *John Aubrey: Brief Lives with an Apparatus for the Lives of Our English Mathematical Writer*, and Ruth Scurr, in her *John Aubrey, My Own Life* has—to use the words of Noel Malcolm in his lengthy review, 'Passions for the Past: The Aubrey Story' (*NYRB* 63[8 Dec. 2016] 36–8)—solved 'the problem of how to present Aubrey's life in a way that is both simple and radical. Scurr has trawled through Aubrey's writings, printed and manuscript, extracting anything that seems both significant and datable.' Furthermore, 'she has arranged these passages—some sentence-long, others consisting of lengthy paragraphs—in chronological order, starting with remarks about his birth in Wiltshire in 1626'. At times Scurr 'has converted the text into a first-person narrative format, but otherwise she has changed the wording as little as possible, just adding a minimum of explanatory or linking passages (which are presented also as Aubrey's own words)'. As Malcolm judiciously observes, 'the result is, as it were, the diary that Aubrey never actually wrote. The final entry is from 1697, the year of his death, in which he writes, "I have rescued what I could of the past from the teeth of time" ' (p. 37). In other words, Scurr has produced something that has rarely been done before. As Stuart Kelly observes in 'Enter John Aubrey', his review of Scurr (*TLS* [25 Feb. 2015]), 'as an experiment in the art of biography, it illuminates both its subject, himself a biographer, and the unquestioned presumptions behind biography itself'. Aubrey was an ' antiquarian, astrologer, scientist, toponymist, playwright, folklorist, educational theorist, hint-keeper, snapper-up of unconsidered trifles, assiduous collector' and 'as much as the form Scurr has chosen puts the subject, for once, centre stage, owing to the biographer's gracious retiring, it also cedes her absolute control over him. The centoic, diaristic method does, as Scurr hopes in her introduction, make him live again: it does so by reshaping and remoulding, by cutting and pasting.' In short 'Scurr emphasizes the fuzziness and partial nature of all biography, which reflects the ambiguity and unfinishedness of all life. Our actual lives are singular to ourselves; our afterlives are necessarily plural.' Scurr's book opens with a 'Dramatis Personae' (pp. ix–xxi) beginning with the 'King's, Queens and Lord Protectors in Aubrey's Lifetime' (p. ix), moving to 'Aubrey's Relations'

(p. x), 'Aubrey's Women' (p. xi), and then 'Aubrey's Contemporaries, Many of Them Friends, Some Also Patrons' (pp. xi–xxi). There is a list of illustrations (pp. xxiii–xxiv). The text of her biography is followed by an account of 'Aubrey's Afterlife' (pp. 425–32). Acknowledgements (p. 433) are followed by endnotes (pp. 435–73), an extensive, partially annotated, bibliography divided into manuscript sources (pp. 475–7) and alphabetically arranged enumerative printed sources (pp. 477–87), and a triple-columned, smaller typeface, detailed index (pp. 489–518).

To turn to Kate Bennett's two-volume edition *John Aubrey: Brief Lives with An Apparatus for the Lives of our English Mathematical Writer*. It is the first scholarly edition of *Brief Lives* since 1898 and is the first complete transcription of Aubrey's work. Its annotations are erudite and founded on an enormous mass of freshly uncovered manuscript evidence. In addition to a detailed, extensive introduction, there are twenty-five facsimile pages, and more than 160 images that reproduce for the first time Aubrey's horoscopes, pedigrees, coats of arms, and topographical sketches. Bennett's text pays respect to the unfinished, excessively revised manuscript, a work in progress, while presenting it as an edited text. Bennett's 'is one of the most astonishing feats of scholarly editing in recent decades'. Hers is an 'extensive, painstakingly exact... annotated edition of the original manuscripts'. According to Noel Malcolm, 'illuminatingly Bennett...characterizes the manuscripts as a "paper museum"—not just a text, but a set of objects including letters from third parties, drawings of buildings, tombs, and heraldic crests, specimens of handwriting, and astrological "genitures" (horoscopes cast for the precise time of a person's birth)'. Bennett's is a 'huge, huge and expensive, but altogether stupendous edition of *Brief Lives*' (*NYRB* [8 Dec. 2016] 37–8). Interestingly Aubrey excluded some lives from his *Brief Lives*, including, for instance, Thomas Hobbes. It is appropriate, however, to conclude this all too brief account of Bennett's monumental edition by quoting the words of Ruth Scurr in her review, 'Faithful Innovator' (*TLS* [16 Mar. 2016]): 'Kate Bennett's purpose is to remain faithful to Aubrey's own arrangement of his innovative collection. It is fitting that such scholarly devotion, extending over two decades, should have given rise to an edition that is an innovation in its own right. Nothing like it has appeared before, and it will last, if not forever, for a very long time. As Aubrey would have been the first to admit, the same cannot be said of the vast majority of other printed books.'

*(d) Pepys*

There are five items to report from 2015 in the world of Pepys studies. Two are articles and three books: one a monograph, a sumptuously illustrated, important collection of essays and a description of his library, now at Magdalene College, Cambridge. To start with the articles, Peter J. Tyldesley's 'Samuel Pepys and Edward Tyldesley' (*N&Q* 62[2015] 258–9) sheds light upon a reference in Pepys's diary that has hitherto eluded identification. Tyldesley writes that 'on 22 June 1662, shortly after the arrival in England of Catherine of Braganza, Samuel Pepys writes of a curious birth at Hampton Court Palace: "This day I am told of a Portugall lady at Hampton Court, that hath dropped a child already, since the Queenes coming. But the King would not have them searched whose it is; and so it is not commonly known yet."' From a 'prominent Lancashire family, noted for uncompromising adherence to the Catholic faith and staunch loyalty to the Stuart cause', Edward Tyldesley's (1632–85) 'greatest honour... came when he was asked to join the embassy sent to Portugal in 1661 to arrange the marriage of Charles II to Catherine of Braganza'. Tyldesley was married, to an Anne Fleetwood. Consequently, 'it was... regarded as particularly scandalous when it became clear that it was an affair he had conducted with one of Catherine's attendants which had led to the birth' of the child, a daughter, Lisbona. Further, 'Tyldesley was acquainted with Pepys, meeting him in London and writing to him in 1667 regarding the possibility of shipbuilding at the Pile of Foudray' (pp. 258–9).

Deborah C Payne's 'Theatrical Spectatorship in Pepys's *Diary*' (*RES* 66[2015] 87–105) is concerned with the treatment of the theatre-goer as spectator, as connoisseur, the relationship to interiority, pleasure, and sociability. In her abstract Payne writes that her article 'reads the diary diachronically and critically, looking closely at attendance patterns and shifting contexts to qualify the standard portrait of Pepys the avid, albeit remorseful, spectator'. According to Payne, 'professional aspirations, pecuniary ambitions, and declining health all affected [Pepys's] willingness to attend the theatre. Moreover, the performance of theatrical spectatorship allowed Pepys to select, adjust, and even at times reject the pleasures of the playhouse in order to create successive, idealized versions of himself.' In addition, 'whereas in the early 1660s, the diminution of playgoing made it possible for Pepys to become a "man of business", frequent attendance later in the decade promoted gentility and sociability, while friendships with actors in the King's Company reinforced the connoisseurship to which the diarist increasingly aspired' (p. 87). Payne concludes that, as Pepys's diary reveals, 'for Pepys, always ambitious and invariably restless, identity was fluid, fashioned by an ongoing process of selection and adjustment. To become a man of business, he put aside the playhouse; to become a gentleman and a connoisseur, he embraced its pleasures and came to understand its workings. To create the idealized self of the 1670s, Pepys would embark upon actions of another sort, well beyond the environs of the theatre with which his name even today is so intertwined' (p. 105).

Kate Loveman's excellent *Samuel Pepys and His Books: Reading, Newsgathering, and Sociability 1660–1703* centres on an obsessive collector of books, indeed a seventeenth-century bibliomaniac, Samuel Pepys. An arresting front dust-jacket image of Pepys is based on a portrait by John Hayls. Following her list of illustrations (p. xi), of which there are thirteen in black and white, there is a listing of abbreviations (pp. xiii–xiv). This gives a clear guide to Loveman's sources, including Latham and Matthews's eleven-volume edition of Pepys's diaries published between 1971 and 1983, Latham's seven-volume *Catalogue of the Pepys's Library at Magdalene College Cambridge* [1978–94], and the library itself at Magdalene College, Cambridge. A brief listing of conventions (p. xv) reveals that, in addition to the Julian calendar operating, which this 'ran ten days behind the Gregorian calendar which was widely used on the Continent ... in England, the new year officially began on 25 March (though this did not prevent people celebrating on 1 January' (p. xv). In her introduction, she writes that her 'interest' is not in 'the intimate accounts of [Pepys's] sexual activities and extramarital affairs' but 'in a different kind of passion, one which lasted throughout Pepys's life and, indeed shaped that life: his love of reading. In the wake of the Great Fire, it was the fate of his books rather than the fate of his cheese [during the Great Fire he buried his very expensive Parmesan cheese in order to keep it from the flames] that "mightily troubled" him, and "great joy" ensued when all of his book collection was safely returned to his study'. Furthermore, 'his love of books was such that even when he feared that reading was damaging his eyesight he struggled to stop ... he wrote of my "eyes, which would be reading"'. Consequently his 'voracious appetite for books, combined with his enthusiasm for record-keeping, makes his papers an extraordinarily rich resource for investigating reading, news-gathering, and collecting in the second half of the seventeenth century' (p. 1). Curiously Pepys rarely annotated the books he owned, probably because he was obsessive about their condition, and his library 'is first and foremost evidence of his collecting' (p. 16). Loveman's first chapter, ' "Multitude of Books": Patterns of Reading in Pepys's Diary' (pp. 20–49), 'presents an overview of Pepys's reading during the 1660s, examining his preferences in terms of topic as well as where, when, and with whom he commonly encountered books'. Loveman discusses 'reading behaviour in the Pepys household and the clues it provides about reading skills and attitudes to books among Restoration Londoners' (p. 17). Her second chapter, 'Books, Education, and Self-Advancement' (pp. 50–79), 'examines books as a means to education and self-improvement'. The chapter 'discusses Pepys's reading of ancient moral philosophers such as Epictetus and Cicero, before moving on to conduct writing by Francis Bacon and others, and then to instruction manuals on maths and mathematical instruments' (p. 17). Chapter 3, 'Pepys and News Networks in Restoration London' (pp. 80–107), and chapter 4, 'Reading History in the Restoration' (pp. 108–34), 'are united by an interest in news, gossip, and accounts of the recent past'. Chapter 3 'examines[s] the transmission of news in Restoration London through the media of print, manuscript, and conversation', whereas the fourth chapter discusses 'the challenges of history reading in the Restoration. Reading histories was one of Pepys's favourite pursuits and he read widely in this field: parliamentary histories, ecclesiastical histories, letter collections, and biographies feature heavily in his records' (pp. 17–18). The fifth chapter, ' "Books of Pleasure": Plays, Romances, and Novels' (pp. 135–64), as its title suggests, 'investigates the reading of imaginative literature among Pepys's kin and friends, focusing on plays, romances, and novels' (p. 18). Chapter 6, 'Buying Books in Restoration London' (pp. 165–94), and chapter 7, 'Books, Books, Manuscripts, Gifts: Scholarly and International Networks' (pp. 195–216), 'focus on the methods for obtaining books and manuscripts'. The sixth chapter 'describes Pepys's dealings with book trade professionals from the 1660s to the 1690s, using evidence from inventories, catalogues, trial records, and other book-buyers to build up a wider picture of developments in the trade'. The seventh chapter 'identifies the assumptions underlying the exchange of texts among Pepys and his associates, and uncovers the scholarly, governmental, and mercantile networks used to transmit ideas and augment collections' (p. 18). The penultimate chapter, '"Notes from Discourses touching Religion"': Religious and Scientific Enquiry' (pp. 217–44), places Pepys's 'religious and scientific reading in a political context' (p. 18). During his last years, following 'decades of book collecting, Samuel Pepys composed a paper describing the rationale behind a "Private Library" such as his'. He didn't collect for exhibition, or to build up a learned, specialized collection but for his own entertainment 'as a solitary unconfined enquirer into books' (p. 245). The final chapter, 'Libraries and Closets: The Uses of a Book Collection' (pp. 245–74), utilizes this paper now at the British Library in order to trace 'the development of Pepys's library and the changing nature of the various collections within his household' (p. 18). In her 'Afterword' (pp. 275–80), Loveman 'draw[s] out certain patterns in the ways Pepys's reading developed across the decades, along with the implications of [her] study for understanding the behaviour of other seventeenth-century readers and authors' (p. 275). An appendix, 'Notes from Discourses touching Religion' (pp. 281–6), transcribes and annotates Pepys's document, now at the Bodleian Library. The document 'provides evidence of the divisions Pepys instituted between his private and public beliefs, and between his private and public papers' (p. 18). The enumerative, alphabetically arranged select bibliography (pp. 287–97) is divided into 'Manuscripts', arranged alphabetically by location (pp. 287–8), a listing of 'Printed Editions of Pepys's Writings' (pp. 288–9), 'Printed and Online Primary Sources' (pp. 289–92), and 'Secondary Sources' (pp. 292–7). In a smaller font than the rest of the text and also used in footnote documentation, the index (pp. 299–308) is comprehensive. Loveman's *Samuel Pepys and His Books* is a very learned, well-written monograph that not only provides insight into Samuel Pepys's reading, his library and his circle during the second half of the seventeenth century but provides an illustration of how to approach and treat libraries, reading, and their relation to society.

M.E.J. Hughes, in *The Pepys Library and the Historic Collections of Magdalene College Cambridge* contains coloured illustrations and maps. Pepys's library of around 3,000 items was willed by Pepys to Magdalene College, which he attended in the 1650s. His library arrived at the college in 1724, and is housed in a new building. It includes medieval manuscripts; early printed books by, amongst others, William Caxton and Wynkyn de Worde; and a naval collection that reflects Pepys's role as Secretary to the Admiralty. There are works by Pepys's contemporaries and members of the Royal Society, including Newton's *Principia Mathematica*; and an unrivalled array of ephemera—letters, playbills, and invitations. The other collections at Magdalene evolve from benefactions across a nearly 500-year period, and include medieval manuscripts, incunabula, prints and papers, as well as the ancient records of the college. As Arnold Hunt observes in his 'Eye on Posterity' (*TLS* [16 Mar. 2016]), Hughes's short book 'provides an excellent companion to Loveman'. Hunt writes: 'generously illustrated, it reveals the extraordinary diversity of Pepys's collection and showcases some of its highlights, including the Elizabethan treatise on shipbuilding known to Pepys as "Fragments of Ancient Shipwrightry" (originally a loan from one of his colleagues in the Navy Office, which Pepys conveniently "forgot" to return to its owner) and the famous collection of sixteenth- and seventeenth-century black-letter ballads. The most remarkable item featured here is not a book at all, but Athanasius Kircher's "arca musarithmica", a machine for musical composition, which clearly appealed to the slightly geeky side of Pepys's character.'

Samuel Pepys: Plague, Fire, Revolution, edited by Margarette Lincoln, with an introduction by Claire Tomalin, was published to coincide with an exhibition that was on view to the public from 20 November 2015 to 28 March 2016 at the National Maritime Museum at Greenwich, and that brought 'fresh insights into Pepys's world'. 'It underlines Pepys's career as a naval administrator and his connection with Greenwich at key moments of his life.' Furthermore, 'it presents key objects from the material culture of seventeenth-century London and features many objects that Pepys himself owned or would have encountered' (p. 7). In addition to Claire Tomalin's introduction, entitled 'Samuel Pepys, Renaissance Man' (pp. 11–17), there are five parts with contributions by different hands. In the first, 'Turbulent Times' (pp. 18–59) there are essays by Mark Knight, 'Pepys's England: Revolutions and Transformations' (pp. 20–9); M.E.J. Hughes, 'Samuel Pepys: A Scholar and a Gentleman' (pp. 31–7); and Mark Jenner, 'Pepys and the Worlds of Medicine' (pp. 38–9), followed by 'Objects in Focus' (pp. 40–59) containing colour illustrations—the volume is replete with illustrations on almost every page—and commentary on the twenty-five objects, ranging from 'Gorget, forceps and scoops for performing a lithotomy' (p. 41) to 'Miniatures of Edward Montagu 1st Earl of Sandwich and Jemima Montague (née Crew),1st Countess of Sandwich' (p. 59). The second part, 'The Restoration' (pp. 60–139), has essays by Tim Harris, 'The Dissolute Court and Retribution' (pp. 62–71); Laura Gowing, 'Women in the World of Pepys' (pp. 73–9); Warren Cherniak, 'Pepys and the Restoration Theatre' (pp. 80–9); Catherine MacLeod, 'Stuart Portraiture' (pp. 90–1); and 'Charles II's Restoration and Marriage: Objects in Focus' (pp. 92–139). The third part, 'Pepys and the Navy' (pp. 140–93), has essays by James Davey ' "…and so to the office": Pepys at Work' (pp. 142–51); Margarette Lincoln, ' Pepys, Tangier and Islam' (pp. 152–9); Pieter van der Merwe, 'Pepys in Greenwich' (pp. 160–1); and 'Pepys and the Navy: Objects in Focus' (pp. 162–93). The fourth part, 'Scientific Enquiry' (pp. 194–227), has two essays: Robert Illiffe, 'Pepys and the New Science' (pp. 196–203), and Richard Dunn, 'A New Visible World' (pp. 204–5). These are followed by 'Scientific Enquiry: Objects in Focus' (pp. 206–27). Appropriately, the final part is on 'Revolution and Pepy's Retirement' (pp. 228–77) with essays by Clare Jackson on 'Pepys and Religion' (pp. 230–9); Kate Loveman, 'Pepy's Retirement' (pp. 240–7), followed by her 'Religious Tension-Objects in Focus' (pp. 248–53) and 'Religious Change and Pepy's Legacy' (pp. 254–69) and M.E.J.Hughes 'The Diary and its Later Life' (pp. 270–3). A map of the London frequented by Pepys (pp. 274–5) is followed by triple-columned notes to each of the authored sections (pp. 276–7), alphabetically arranged 'Sources and Further Reading' (pp. 278–9), picture credits (p. 280), and a list of contributors (p. 281). This sumptuous book, with over 260 colour illustrations in quarto format, concludes with a three-column (p. 282) and then a four-column detailed index (pp. 282–7).

*(e) Evelyn*

A slightly older diarist than Pepys is John Evelyn, the subject of Sean Silver's 'John Evelyn and Numismata: Material History and Autobiography' (*W&I* 31[2015] 331–42). Silver explores genre conventions, autobiography, the treatment of the past, medals, coins, and authority and their relationship to materiality and the Civil War as a backdrop. Silver, in his abstract, comments that 'material histories have tended to obscure, rather than illuminate, the materials upon which they depend; because we are seldom ultimately interested in things themselves, histories of the material sort tend to turn to objects only as stepping stones to analyses of cultural contexts'. His essay, however, 'is an experiment in a more symmetrical material history, seeking to take seriously the claims of a single historical object as it intersected with the life and autobiography of the historian who introduced it into discourse'. This 'object is one of the two surviving examples of the Kineton Medal, a coin minted in haste in 1643 to commemorate a high point of the English Civil War'. Silver is concerned with 'John Evelyn (1620–1706), minor statesman, antiquary, and diarist, whose *Numismata* (1697) assembled a national history entirely out of fragments like this one'. As Silver points out, 'Evelyn's life and the trajectory of the medal were fated to cross in a number of ways; among others, the medal was introduced into history in the same gesture with which Evelyn established himself as a historian. Bringing subject and object into alignment has lessons to teach about the ways the fortunes of an object might wax and wane, even while life-writing collects and shapes its materials.' Silver's essay, 'by way of a coda . . . traces the career of this coin, which was believed to have been lost to fire, from its birth to its current home in Birmingham' in the English Midlands (p. 331).

**Books Reviewed**

Augustine, Matthew C., and Steven N. Zwicker, eds. *Lord Rochester in the Restoration World*. CUP. [2015] pp. x + 293. $102 ISBN 9 7811 0706 4393.

Banita, Georgiana, and Sascha Pöhlmann, eds., *Electoral Cultures: American Democracy and Choice*. Publications of the Bavarian American Academy, Award Monographs 16. Winter. [2015] pp. 416. €45 ISBN 9 7838 2536 4571.

Bennett, Kate, ed. *Brief Lives, with An Apparatus for the Lives of Our English Mathematical Writers* by Aubrey John. 2 vols. OUP. [2015] pp. 1,968. £250 ($399) ISBN 9 7801 9968 9538.

Champion, Michael, and Andrew Lynch, eds. *Understanding Emotions in Early Europe*. Brepols. [2015] pp. xxxiv + 357. €90 ISBN 9 7825 0355 2644.

Downes, Paul. *Hobbes, Sovereignty, and Early American Literature*. CUP. [2015] pp. xiii + 297. $103 ISBN 9 7811 0708 5299.

Estill, Laura. *Dramatic Extracts in Seventeenth-Century English Manuscripts: Watching, Reading, Changing Plays*. UDelP. [2015] pp. 270. $80 ISBN 9 7816 1149 5546.

Fabiszak, Jacek, Ewa Urbaniak-Rybicka, and Bartosz Wolski, eds. *Crossroads in Literature and Culture*. Springer. [2013] pp. xvi + 530. $147.92 ISBN 9 7836 4221 9931.

Hughes, M.E.J. *The Pepys Library and the Historic Collections of Magdalene College Cambridge*. Scala. [2015] pp. 88. £14.95 ISBN 9 7818 5759 9534.

Lincoln, Margarette, ed. *Samuel Pepys: Plague, Fire, Revolution*. T&H. [2015] pp. 289. $50 (£29.25) ISBN 9 7805 0051 8144.

Loveman, Kate. *Samuel Pepys and His Books: Reading, Newsgathering, and Sociability, 1660–1703*. OUP. [2015] pp. xviii + 318. $99 ISBN 9 7801 9873 2686.

Milne, Kirsty. *At Vanity Fair: From Bunyan to Thackeray*. CUP. [2015] pp. ix + 229. $103 ISBN 9 7811 0710 5850.

Munroe, Jennifer, Edward J. Geisweidt, and Lynne Bruckner, eds. *Ecological Approaches to Early Modern English Texts: A Field Guide to Reading and Teaching*. Ashgate. [2015] pp. 256. $40.95 ISBN 9 7814 724 1 6728.

Netzley, Ryan. *Lyric Apocalypse: Milton, Marvell, and the Nature of Events*. FordUP. [2015] pp. 269. $45 ISBN 9 7808 2326 3479.

Pye, Christopher. *The Storm at Sea: Political Aesthetics in the Time of Shakespeare*. FordUP. [2015] pp. xii + 257. $105 ISBN 9 7808 2326 5046.

Raibaud, Martine, Micéala Symington, Ionut Untea, and David Waterman, eds. *Cultures in Movement*. CambridgeSP. [2015] pp. x + 395. £57.99 ISBN 9 7814 4387 1891.

Rawson, Claude. *Swift and Others*. CUP. [2015] pp. xiii + 301. $ 30.99 ISBN 9 7811 0761 0125.

Scurr, Ruth. *My Own Life* by Aubrey John. C&W and NYRB. [2015] pp. xxvi + 520. £25 ISBN 9 7807 0117 9076, $35 ISBN 9 7816 8137 0422.

Shoulson, Jeffrey, S. *Fictions of Conversions: Jews, Christians, and Cultures of Change in Early Modern England*. UPennP. [2013] pp. xii + 263. $65 ISBN 9 7808 1224 4823.

# XII

# The Eighteenth Century

## JILL DYE, JAMES A. SMITH, BYSSHE INIGO COFFEY, AND JAMES HARRIMAN-SMITH

This chapter has four sections: 1. General and Prose; 2. The Novel; 3. Poetry; 4. Drama. Section 1 is by Jill Dye; section 2 is by James A. Smith; section 3 is by Bysshe Inigo Coffey; section 4 is by James Harriman-Smith.

## 1. General and Prose

This has been a strong year for broad works centred on the eighteenth century, some reviewed elsewhere in this volume. Jacob Sider Jost's monograph *Prose Immortality, 1711–1819* is of interest to scholars of the eighteenth century and beyond, and will be covered in next year's YWES. The year also saw the publication of the three-volume *Encyclopedia of British Literature 1660–1789*, edited by Gary Day and Jack Lynch. The scope of the encyclopedia seems perhaps surprisingly narrow, with an alphabetical list of entries running only to five pages (vol. 1, pp. vii–xi), yet the work extends to three volumes (A–Ei, Em–Q, R–Z), attesting to the depth of the entries. It will undoubtedly prove most useful to students in its introduction to familiar eighteenth-century concepts such as masculinity (pp. 767–78), as well as specific individuals and genres as conceived in the period. For scholars, the inclusion of so many entries for writers of the period makes the work a useful starting point in investigating less well known names.

*Home and Nation in British Literature from the English to the French Revolutions*, edited by A.D. Cousins and Geoffrey Payne, covers the contested definition of both terms, 'home' and 'nation', and how they interacted with each other across a wide time span. The work is structured in three parts, of which this section is interested in Part II, 'Restoration, Glorious Revolution and Hanoverian Succession' (pp. 79–184). Comprising seven essays, it opens with two essays located in the seventeenth century: ' "Home to our People": Nation and Kingship in Late Seventeenth-Century Political Verse', by Abigail Williams (pp. 81–97), and William Walker's ' "Yet Israel still serves": Home and Nation in Milton's *Samson Agonistes*' (pp. 98–111), before moving firmly into the eighteenth century with ' "A thing remote": Defoe and the Home in

*The Year's Work in English Studies, Volume 96 (2017)* © *The Author 2017. Published by Oxford University Press on behalf of the English Association. All rights reserved.*
*For Permissions, please email: journals.permissions@oup.com*
doi:10.1093/ywes/max013

the Metropolis and New World', by Geoffrey Payne (pp. 111–26). This chapter assesses Defoe's attitudes towards Britain, a nation whose identity he was integral in shaping. It uncovers a 'complex attitude towards nationhood' (p. 112) by representing various functions of 'home space' through his texts, namely *A Journal of the Plague Year* [1722] and *The Life and Surprising Adventures of Robinson Crusoe* [1719], where instability of the material world challenges the viability of nationhood and national homeland. 'Pope's Homes: London, Windsor Forest, and Twickenham', by Pat Rogers (pp. 127–40), explores rootlessness in the work of Pope, despite his firmly England-based life. Rogers argues that Twickenham 'embodied a half-resolved contradiction between Pope's forest childhood and his engagement in the world of London', covering familiar dichotomies such as public/private and court/country. What London meant to Samuel Johnson is the topic for Evan Gottlieb's 'Samuel Johnson and London' (pp. 141–53), in which Gottlieb tracks the development of Johnson's attitudes towards London over time, from his personal home, to a literary and political centre, then onwards towards a global city. Catherine Ingrassia makes the first of two appearances in the review for 2015 with her chapter 11 in this volume, 'Contesting "Home" in Eighteenth-Century Women's Verse' (pp. 154–68), charting how female poets in the long eighteenth century capture the complex conception of home, as a place fraught with binaries such as labour/rest, public/private, local/global. Closing with chapter 12, 'Home, Homeland and the Gothic' by David Punter (pp. 169–83), the volume moves on to deal with revolutionary France, which will be of particular interest to readers of the chapter on the Romantic period (Chapter XIII).

Standing alone this year as the sole work on sport is *British Sporting Literature and Culture in the Long Eighteenth Century*, edited by Sharon Harrow. This is a collection of interdisciplinary essays charting 'the variety of literary and cultural representations of sporting events, and the evolution of sport from rural pastimes to organized, regular events of national and international importance' (p. 1). The introduction, written by the editor, places this change in its cultural context, going some way to explaining why the long eighteenth century was so ripe a time for sporting development. She cites the loosening of Puritan strictures as well as wider social developments including literacy, income, and transportation. The whole work is divided into three: 'Contexts', 'Sports', and 'People'. This review will focus primarily on the 'Contexts' section. It begins with Emma Griffin's ' "Wholesome recreations and cheering influences": Popular Recreation and Social Elites in Eighteenth-Century Britain' (pp. 19–34). Griffin assesses the intellectual context of criticism by elites on the sports and pastimes of the poor. She notes not hostility, but indifference, for much of the eighteenth century. 'Olympianism and Pastoralism in British Sporting Literature' is the topic for Jean Williams (pp. 35–54), who traces the legacy of the ancient Olympic Games 'as a topic, metaphor and sporting theme' (p. 35). This essay concludes that the emphasis of earlier studies on newspaper sources has 'been deployed to raise active leisure and physical culture about the level of mere sport into the domain of the spiritual and aesthetic' (p. 49). Further, the growth of Olympic revivals in the period had a lasting influence, with elements endowed with 'the necessary cultural validation to become a symbol of personal fulfilment and, subsequently, national character' (p. 50). Finally, Patricia Crown explores 'Sporting with Clothes: John Collet's Prints in the 1770s' (pp. 55–82). Her essay highlights the range of sources encompassed in this volume, which goes far beyond the field of literary studies. The second part, on 'Sports', looks at tennis, in Alexis Tadié's 'The Uses and Transformations of Early Modern Tennis' (pp. 83–104), archery, in Linda V. Troost's 'Archery in the Long Eighteenth Century' (pp. 105–24), and equestrianism, in Donal W. Nichol's 'Jockeying for Position: Horse Culture in Poetry, Prose and the New Foundling Hospital for Wit' (pp. 125–52). Part III, 'People', comprises two essays, Sharon Harrow's 'Boxing for England: Daniel Mendoza and the Theater of Sport' (pp. 153–78) and Jack D'Amico's 'Rehearsing Leander: Byron and Swimming in the Long Eighteenth Century' (pp. 179–93).

Gender, and women's writing particularly, has proven the basis for the overwhelming majority of general works on the eighteenth century this year. The *Cambridge Companion to Women's Writing in Britain 1660–1789*, edited by Catherine Ingrassia, is divided into two, the latter part focusing on genres, modes, and forms following the first section on 'Women in Print Culture' generally, which is most pertinent to this section and on which this review will therefore focus. Mark Towsey opens the work with 'Women as Readers and Writers' (pp. 21–36), a study of the role of women readers as 'an important force in the literary marketplace' of the eighteenth century (p. 21). He goes on to cover their access to books, and the reading experience more generally, and concludes with a turn towards the woman writer, not in the authorial sense but in the link between letter-writing and collective reading.

Betty A. Schellenberg's 'The Professional Female Writer' (pp. 37–54) takes the natural next step following Towsey's chapter by pursuing the woman as not only a writer, but also a professional. She charts the development of the professionalism of authorship as an eighteenth-century product before elaborating on the careers of five representative women: Aphra Behn, Eliza Haywood, Elizabeth Carter, Charlotte Lennox, and Anna Letitia Barbauld. The essay concludes with a brief look at the changing status of women writers at the turn of the century, when hierarchical structures within the literary field were to question women's right to produce high, public forms of poetry and political writing, a fight which, it is suggested, would have been unfamiliar to the previous generation.

Chapter 3, Sarah Prescott's 'Place and Publication' (pp. 55–69), charts the development of women's writing against the backdrop of the changing relationships in English counties and in Britain's constituent parts. She assesses the effect of geographical location on women and the reception of their writing, specifically in provincial locations, or where there are strong national affiliations, detailing the 'localized support networks' required for text dissemination, such as epistolary networks and the 'hub' of an aristocratic household (p. 56). After England and Wales, Scotland shows evidence of greater access to materials to those of lower social station, with a strong print capital in Edinburgh. The chapter ends, therefore, with a call to view archipelago authors not as token inclusions, but as examples of women writers from vastly different backgrounds, despite their similar class context.

Paula R. Backscheider's 'Women and Popular Culture' (pp. 70–85) ventures beyond the scope of the eighteenth century to link popular culture with the female author. The emphasis, therefore, is largely on drama and novels. The chapter sits well next to Kathryn R. King's 'Genre Crossings' (pp. 86–100), which warns against limiting women's writing to discussion solely of the novel, suggesting that poetry, drama, and memoirs ought also to take centre stage based on quantity of output. King charts the study of genre since the 1980s, before focusing on those writers who work across genres. She concludes that women read and wrote widely, far beyond the constrictions of 'gender-appropriate formal genres of fiction and drama', thus challenging once more the 'generic gridlines' previously imposed (p. 98).

The focus on women's writing continues in Teresa Barnard, ed., *British Women and the Intellectual World in the Long Eighteenth Century*. The volume begins with a useful chronology of women's writing from the period. Teresa Barnard and Ruth Watts's introduction sets up the volume to counteract the proliferation of scholarship concerning nineteenth-century women scholars without consideration of their forebears, with the aim of provoking further work on women's 'lives and achievements' (p. 11) in the long eighteenth century. Nine essays form the collection, broken into three trios (engagement with science, religious discourses, and politics/philosophy); four essays fall into the 1700–80 period and are outlined below.

In ' "To bring this useful invention into Fashion in England": Mary Wortley Montagu as Medical Expert' (pp. 15–32), Daniel Grey notes that, while Montagu is most famous for introducing smallpox inoculation to Britain, scholarly focus on her written output has centred on her as a diarist and fiction writer. He explores Montagu as a precarious 'female medical expert', and looks at her 'personal experience of smallpox' (p. 6) and her growing understanding of it. This analysis gives new insights into the role of women in eighteenth-century medicine as well as in the history of smallpox, the chapter concluding that her written interventions speeded up the process of bringing inoculation out of Turkey to wider Europe.

Also on the theme of women and science is Teresa Barnard's 'The Lure of the Volcano in the Female Literary Imagination' (pp. 33–52), which looks at women not as practitioners in science, but as witnesses, who saw literature as an easier field to enter than other fields of knowledge. Barnard looks at the poets Anna Seward and Eleanor Anne Porden Franklin and their use of volcanos, finding how their self-education (Franklin through travel, Seward through books), particularly in the field of geology, is evident in their poetic works.

Travel also becomes a recurring theme in Laura Mayer, ' "A longing to enjoy my liberty": The Patronage, Writing, and Picturesque Tours of Elizabeth Percy, 1st Duchess of Northumberland' (pp. 129–41), which charts the rise of Percy from her scandalous love-match to her 'social supremacy' (p. 10) in style, travel, and politics.

Writers such as Helen Maria Williams, Mary Anne Schimmelpenninck, Joanna Baillie, and Anna Barbauld form the subject of Natasha Duquette's 'Veiled Exegesis: Dissenting Women's Aesthetic Approach to Theological Hermeneutics and Social Action' (pp. 107–26) as exemplars of dissenting women introducing theological ideas through their individual and reciprocal contributions to print culture of the eighteenth century. Duquette unveils their hermeneutic claims through aesthetic and poetical works, seen as more acceptable modes for their gender. She finishes with a look at the impact of these collaborative writings on social change not just in Britain but in France and the United States.

Writing on women this year is not limited to the monograph or edited collection. Amy Culley's 'Women's Life-Writing in the Long 18th Century: A Critical Survey' (*LitComp* 12[2015] 1–11) gathers works in the field from the last twenty-five years. It celebrates the move from the binary autobiography/biography distinction into the more general category of 'life-writing'. It argues that only with the removal of binaries such as the male/female divide can the 'dynamic canon' of life-writing fully include female, slave, and working-class writers (p. 1). In a conclusion highlighting future avenues for research, Culley proposes that the inclusion of fragments and collaborative efforts, also as examples of 'life-writing', will further develop the field, for the study of women in particular, 'to create more inclusive and ambitious histories of this intriguing form' (p. 9).

*Heteronormativity in Eighteenth-Century Literature and Culture*, edited by Ana de Freitas Boe and Abby Coykendall, aims to gather into one volume the various developments which led towards the introduction of the 1753 Marriage Act, and to compare those developments with Enlightenment views of sex, gender, and sexuality. It characterizes the eighteenth century as the moment when sex/desire became heteronormative, setting up 'traditional' and non-traditional' marriages as a foil for straight and same-sex divisions that came in under the 2013 Marriage Act. As is clear from the ambitious aim, the chapters in the book are wide-ranging, from Chris M. Roulston's 'Marriage, Sexuality and the Meaning of the Wedding Night' (pp. 59–76) to Kirsten T. Saxton, Ajuan Maria Mance, and Rebekah Edwards, 'Teaching Eighteenth-Century Literature in a Transgendered Classroom' (pp. 167–88), exploring how transgender studies impact on the way eighteenth-century studies is taught, with a focus on modern inclusivity. Other chapters also of interest but not due full attention for this section are Theresa Braunschneider, 'Monstrous Gallantry: Protective Masculinity in the 1790s' (pp. 95–110) and George E. Haggerty, 'The Failure of Heteronormativity in the Gothic Novel' (pp. 131–50).

The division of public and private spheres forms the basis for many essays in this volume. In 'Conjugal Capitalism: The Domestication of Public Space' (pp. 41–58), Sally O'Driscoll posits that heteronormativity causes a new concept of public/private to emerge, in addition to new forms of femininity. She suggests that the move of eroticism from public to private spaces diminishes queer relationships, making middle-class heteronormative couples the omnipresent social norm, and thus invisible. The politics of privacy also forms the basis for Declan William Kavanagh's 'John Wilkes's "Closet": Hetero Privacy and the Annotation of Desire in *An Essay on Women*' (pp. 77–94). He assesses John Wilkes's *An Essay on Women*, re-characterizing it as not a war of words against Pope's *Essay on Man*, but as an attempt to separate sexuality (a private matter) from public politics.

In the same volume, the methodological issue of the heteronormative lens also dominates. Susan S. Lanser's 'Of Closed Doors and Open Hatches: Heteronormative Plots in Eighteenth-Century (Women's) Studies' (pp. 23–40) looks at the proper versus improper femininity of Hester Thrale's social circle and offers solutions to the problem identified: that women's studies previously have been conducted through a heteronormative lens. Such solutions to recognized methodological problems are posed in Abby Coykendall's 'Queer Counterhistory and the Specter of Effeminacy' (pp. 111–30), which covers queer/transgender masculinities through the reception of Thomas Grace and Horace Walpole. She notes that effeminacy troubles existing paradigms of gender and sexuality, concluding that a new type of counter-history is necessary to encompass gender embodiment and sexuality at once, along with whole host of other relationship types beyond sexuality alone.

With less in common with the rest of the volume, though of no less interest to readers of this section, is Ana de Freitas Boe's 'John Gabriel Steadman, Heteronormativity and White Men's Gender Trouble' (pp. 151–66), looking at the concept of masculinity in Suriname, and how racial difference and heteronormativity emerge in tandem.

Sociability is another theme which had a strong presence this year, especially when in relation to other popular themes, the Enlightenment or women. D.G. Tarbuck's 'Exercises in Women's Intellectual Sociability in the Eighteenth Century: The Fair Intellectual Club' (*HEI* 41[2015] 375–85) gives an overview of the earliest recorded female intellectual sociability (the Fair Intellectual Club), suggests motivations for its foundation, explores its reading, and assesses the type of philosophical understanding of sociability which inspired its participants. The Fair Intellectual Club provides a rare insight into the self-education of women, those in the society choosing to conduct this education publicly rather than individually in private. Reading, writing, and languages are unveiled as the most popular pursuits, though religion and virtue (inextricably linked to politics) made up the majority of the reading list. It is noted that Enlightenment sociability was not, therefore, linked to secularization, and that the club intended to be a reaction to the 'resentment of the fact that education and learning was designated for institutions' (p. 386).

Sociability and women form a strong part too of Amy Prendergast's *Literary Salons Across Britain and Ireland in the Long Eighteenth Century*, with women presiding over private mixed-gender gatherings of social elites at which topics such as literature, art, and philosophy were discussed. Given the nature of salons, much of the discussion focuses on sociability, using contemporary texts to shed light on such topics as conversation and the discussion of belles lettres. Salons existed at the same time as, yet are distinguished from, coffee-houses, taverns, and societies, set apart by the mix of gender; hence the volume's focus is on how a study of salons can shed light on women as participants in such discussions rather than passive observers. Prendergast begins by examining the literary salon in France, specifically the participation of foreign visitors, such as at the salons of Irish hostesses Anastasia Fitzmaurice, the countess of Kerry, and Bridget Plunkett, Marquise de Chastellux, before giving an account of changes in sociability during the French Revolution. She assesses the impact of French salons on their British counterparts, looking at Mary Monckton and Alison Rutherford Cockburn, before focusing on detailed case studies of the salons of Elizabeth Vesey and Lady Moira, their aims, influence, and participants, compiled from unpublished archival sources. The work also covers the role of the salon in the dissemination of literary materials in a provincial context, before ending by discussing the emergence of less elite reading groups and book clubs in an increasingly democratized society, and their relationship to salons as their forebears.

*Sociability in Enlightenment Thought* forms the subject of a special edition of *History of European Ideas* this year (*HEI* 41[2015] 571–698). In their introductory article, 'Between Morality and Anthropology—Sociability in Enlightenment Thought' (*HEI* 41[2015] 571–88), editors Eva Piirimäe and Alexander Schmidt outline the wide range of topics to which the concept of sociability contributes, before elaborating on the meaning of the term, its history, controversy, the impact of Rousseau, and its political implications. The rest of the issue works through Hugo Grotius, Thomas Abbt, and Michael Hissman before focusing again on Rousseau. One article focuses on the Scottish Enlightenment, Iain McDaniel's 'Unsocial Sociability in the Scottish Enlightenment: Ferguson and Kames on War, Sociability and the Foundations of Patriotism' (*HEI* 41[2015] 662–82), and aims to highlight the centrality of the controversies over human sociability in debates on the nature of international relations in the eighteenth century.

The Scottish Enlightenment is the subject for Leslie Ellen Brown, too, in *Artful Virtue: The Interplay of the Beautiful and the Good in the Scottish Enlightenment*. The monograph opens with the assertion that the Scots applied the Enlightenment landscape of moral philosophy to beauty, both in nature and the fine arts. The author thus proposes that this work, through a study of primary 'texts' (written and artistic) will reveal the transformation of the intellectual elite into a mainstream public, connecting the world of the academic author with a 'Scottish reading public who sought educational authority' (p. 3). The volume covers media far beyond the text, as is evidenced by the author's primary academic work in music, and by the myriad colour plates referred to throughout. These additions are not necessarily intended to give new insights into relevant texts. Instead Brown places them together in their artistic context, with the aim of shedding light on the particular period and place.

Again concerning the Scottish Enlightenment, R.J.W. Mills's article, 'Archibald Campbell's Necessity of Revelation (1739)—the Science of Human Nature's First Study of Religion' (*HEI* 41[2015] 728–46), identifies that Campbell's views on moral philosophy have eclipsed his views on revelation in current scholarship. Mills argues that Campbell's *Necessity of Revelation* marks the first time that the Scottish Enlightenment principle of 'the science of human nature' was applied to the study of religious belief. The article delves deeper into his methodology and the facts of Campbell's conclusion, moving on to reflect that there was very little interest in the work following its publication. We are encouraged to believe that its significance as 'the British Enlightenment's first application of the science of human nature to the study of religion' (p. 745), with its methodological uniqueness and rigour, deserve scholarly attention, despite the lack of interest of Campbell's contemporaries in the work. Luxury in the Scottish context is explored in Lisa Broussois's 'Francis Hutcheson on Luxury and Intemperance: The Mandeville Threat' (*HEI* 41[2015] 1093–1106). Broussois begins by emphasizing the strong link between luxury and development of trade in the eighteenth century. The paper first looks at how Hutcheson and Mandeville consider luxury as a moral good or as incompatible with old moral values. It then turns to explore Hutcheson's view on luxury as 'a moral, political and social issue' in its religious and Scottish context, in contrast to Mandeville's view, which Hutcheson describes as a threat. It concludes that Hutcheson is 'equally divided' between traditional Scottish values of temperance and the support of industrial development (p. 106).

Mandeville forms the basis of another article this year, Daniel Luban's 'Bernard Mandeville as Moralist and Materialist' (*HEI* 41[2015] 831–57). Luban notes that, through the lens of those who followed him, Mandeville is known as a 'figure from the prehistory of economic thought' (p. 831), yet this article aims to trace the eighteenth-century view of him through assessing reactions to his *Fable of the Bees* [1714]. 'Almost uniformly hostile' (p. 832), his harshest critics were defenders of the commercial society he proposed; instead, the threat was seen as tying luxury and prosperity to 'what they perceived as a corrosive and ultimately nihilistic moral philosophy', denying that humans could ever act virtuously (p. 832). An exploration of the relationship between virtue and vice forms the initial part of the essay, but it goes on to explore reality, pride, nature and culture, and hypocrisy as well as moral and literal economics. Luban concludes that Mandeville marks the transition between 'his Christian predecessors' and his 'social-scientific successors', successors who went on to develop ways of talking about human social life which were 'less ethically laden' (p. 857).

Two articles take Ireland as their subject: Sora Sato's 'Edmund Burke's Views of Irish History' (*HEI* 41[2015] 387–403) and Martyn J. Powell's 'The Army in Ireland and the Eighteenth-Century Press: Antimilitary Sentiment in an Atlantic Context' (*Éire* 50:iii–iv[2015] 138–72). Sato intends to form a comprehensive account of Irish history as viewed by Burke, around which debate in the eighteenth century is described as 'highly polemical, not a pure pursuit of historical truth' (p. 390). The essay outlines the debate on two controversial issues: the landing of Henry II and religious/civil liberties. Burke's early writing on Ireland, where historical figures carry his views and religious toleration is absent, serves to inform 'his concept of conquest and religious toleration, and his Enlightenment idea of society in general' (p. 401). Sato concludes that, although he acknowledges Irish improvement, Burke remains downbeat, preoccupied with the belief that 'there were still the remnants of unenlightened worlds in his native land' (p. 402). Powell's article tracks anti-military sentiments in the Irish press against a backdrop of the key role that the military played in society. He examines two newspapers run by printer Mathew Carey, first in Dublin, then in Philadelphia—the *Volunteer Journal* and the *Pennsylvania Evening Herald*. While this paper is more applicable to the Romantic period, its conclusions about the nationalism and patriotism of the printer being at odds with his religious identity are of note. Religion and print culture also form the basis for *The Textual Culture of English Protestant Dissent 1720–1800*. Tessa Whitehouse's work investigates the way in which a group of Protestant dissenters authored and edited texts to develop a 'reputation of candour, moderation and learning' (p. 1) with audiences in Britain and overseas. She particularly focuses on the printed discourse of Isaac Watts and Philip Doddridge, as well as their wider social circles, including figures such as John Jennings, Job Orton, and Samuel Palmer. The work provides a strong context for their printed output, in terms of textual culture and dissent (pp. 1–21), the make-up of the dissenting community and its social links (pp. 22–54), and the institutions within which the dissenters were educated (pp. 55–88). Doddridge's *A course of lectures* [1763] provides the focus for chapter 3, covering its publishing and editing in Britain and in Europe, as well as its 'intentions and effects' (p. 120). Chapters 4 and 5 cover Isaac Watts, first as educationalist, then as publisher, underlining his importance as pedagogue through means other than simply his hymn-writing. Whitehouse recasts Watts as 'a towering figure within dissent and leading participant in the international culture of enlightened evangelism' (p. 162) whose ideas, which during his lifetime circulated in prefaces, extracts, and tracts, were preserved in 'impressive physical editions that were posthumously published' (p. 163), about which chapter 6 concerns itself. The concluding chapter (pp. 197–217) briefly looks at the lives of these edited works in the period 1760–1800, arguing that these conservative cultural forms show the complex nature of the incoherent but growing body of dissent.

Still on the theme of nonconformist religion, Brett C. McInelly has produced a survey of literature surrounding the Methodist revival in 'Writing the Revival: The Intersections of Methodism and Literature in the Long 18th Century' (*LitComp* 12[2015] 12–21), which concerns not only the works written by key players in that revival, but also the reception of those works. It goes on to track works written about 'Methodism's relationship to wider literary and cultural developments' (p. 17), encompassing drama, the novel, and 'the Culture of Sensibility' (p. 18). It ends with a comment on the timeliness of works dealing with the 'literary reception of Methodism in the eighteenth century' (p. 19) to build on the existing foundation of scholarship by and about Methodist revival figures. In a similar vein, 'Recent Developments in 17th and 18th Century English Catholic Studies' by Karen Gevirtz (*LitComp* 12[2015] 47–58) charts the impact of new developments in the fields of New Historicism and gender studies on our understanding of English Catholicism from Henry VIII's break with Rome to the Catholic Relief Act in 1829. The section on eighteenth-century English Catholicism and Catholics (pp. 52–4) shows that this is an emerging field of study, which had previously been seen as the 'Sleeping Beauty' (p. 53) between the Glorious Revolution (1688) and Catholic Relief Act. It charts the impact of Colin Haydon's *Anti-Catholicism in Eighteenth-Century England* [1993] on English Catholic studies in the eighteenth century, concluding that literary studies is the pioneering field in which this study is taking place.

Further works on religion this year include 'Not Angles but Anglicans? Reformation and Post-Reformation Perspectives on the Anglo-Saxon Church. Part II: Seventeenth and Eighteenth Centuries', by Hugh Magennis (*ES* 96[2015] 363–78). A follow-up to his examination of Tudor writers, Magennis's article traces how Protestant authors appropriated (and Catholics dissociated themselves from) the Anglo-Saxon Church. He covers the authors James Ussher, Sharon Turner, and John Lingard, but, for the eighteenth century, only Elizabeth Elstob, despite identifying the early eighteenth century as 'a key period in the history of the [Anglo-Saxon] discipline' (p. 365).

In 'Towards a Post-Secular Eighteenth Century' (*LitComp* 12[2015] 565–74) Alison Conway and Corrinne Harol argue that 'eighteenth-century literary studies would benefit from an engagement with postsecular theory' (p. 565) because of its inextricable link to the Enlightenment. The essay defines post-secularism and explores its potential implications for eighteenth-century literary studies, breaking down the sharp divide between the 'fully secular' Enlightenment and the post-secular Romantic period (p. 569), as well as tracing accounts of things such as human emotion and agency which are already in existing studies but 'point towards post-secular developments' (p. 569). It concludes with the worry that 'eighteenth-century literary studies has lost its ability to advance secular critique, precisely because of its uncritical commitment to secularism' (p. 571).

A work that engages with both religion and science is Lucas Hardy's '"The practice of conveying and suffering the Small-pox": Inoculation as a means of Spiritual Conversion in Cotton Mather's Angel of Bethseda' (*SECC* 44[2015] 61–79). Hardy's essay serves to prove that Mather's view of inoculation was not solely medical, but that it also formed a 'new scientific means for inducing spiritual conversion' (p. 62), showing that the text is of interest to literary scholars as well as medical historians.

Science, this time without religion, is one of the themes explored in Morgan Vanek's 'The Uses of Travel: Science, Empire and Change in 18th-Century Travel Writing' (*LitComp* 12[2015] 555–64). A literature review of works on eighteenth-century travel and its records, and writing about travel writing, the article highlights contradictory views regarding the changeableness of the traveller through the experience of travel. Vanek focuses on 'studies of scientific travel in the service of empire' and the contrasting eighteenth-century novel. She concludes that understanding the 'journey within' and 'journey without' the traveller in novels, where the character develops internally while travel progresses, might inform interpretations of scientific travel texts (p. 563).

The developments in watch-making in the eighteenth century, which moved time-telling into the personal and private realm, are the subject of Marcus Tomalin's 'The Intriguing Complications of Pocket Watches in the Literature of the Long Eighteenth Century' (*RES* 66[2015] 300–21). His article explores how these developments impacted on the use of the pocket watch in literary depictions. He clusters this analysis into three dichotomies: public/private, truth/falsity, and male/female, but remarks that pocket watches can be utilized on both sides of each. He concludes that 'as distinct cultural objects [watches] never came to be associated with a stable set of connotations' (p. 321), in stark contrast to other time-telling devices such as sundials.

Networks, particularly for those involved in print culture, were another common theme this year. Pat Rogers's 'Family Kinship and the Evidence of Subscription Lists: Dorothy Stanley and *Arcadia Moderniz'd*' (*RES* 66[2015] 501–19) uses Dorothy Stanley's *Arcadia Moderniz'd* to explore the dangers of equating subscription lists with audience. Stanley's family (and their prominent business connections) are prevalent in the subscription lists, and the assessment goes on to highlight social, economic, and even political reasons for their inclusion. The assessment serves two purposes: to help Stanley 'to attain a more visible identity in light of a fuller sense of her social and familiar ties' and to show that the contents of a subscription list 'are always mediated by the arbitrary circumstances of a writer's life and milieu' (p. 519).

The epistolary world, and the letters and the networks which it comprises, form the subject of Lindsay O'Neill's *The Opened Letter: Networking in the Early Modern British World*. It begins with the permanent opening of the post office, charting the move forward from previous dependence on carriers or acquaintances, expanding personal postal networks in particular. The physical connections between letter writers are mapped in chapter 2, before O'Neill performs social network analysis on those connections (chapter 3). Chapter 4 then traces the evidence of communal connections within the content of the letters, before turning to more formal contractual and institutional networks of letter-writing, including social, religious, and intellectual societies. It ends with a look towards the challenge of the newspaper to letter networks as the main way of spreading news, concluding that letters retained their usefulness in maintaining personal bonds as well as being a means by which writers could question the truth of newspaper reporting. O'Neill reiterates the importance of letters in the eighteenth century as providing 'a way for the British elite to extend and monitor the fluid social networks on which their livelihoods depended' (p. 18) in the face of a changing social and geographical world.

Continuing with networks and the epistolary theme, the strained relationship between John Dunton and Daniel Defoe features in Rachael Scarborough King, '"Interloping with my Question-Project": Debating Genre in John Dunton's and Daniel Defoe's Epistolary Periodicals' (*SECC* 44[2015] 121–42), which looks at the impact of this relationship in 'developing concepts of authorship, publication, and authority' (p. 121), culminating in the epistolary periodical. The essay gathers together the fields of periodical and epistolary study to show the centrality of letters to periodicals, through a look at the epistolary community in Dunton's *The Athenian Mercury* and Defoe's *Review of the Affairs in France* and *The Storm*. It concludes that letters bridge the print/manuscript divide, 'offering a shortcut to authorship and readership for emerging constituencies' (p. 135).

The final work under review this year, *Passions, Sympathy and Print Culture*, edited by David Lemmings, Heather Kerr, and Robert Phiddian, maintains a focus on print culture, though from a new perspective. The introductory section, on the challenge of the passions in eighteenth-century studies, opens with a chapter by Heather Kerr, David Lemmings, and Robert Phiddian: 'Emotional Light on Eighteenth-Century Print Culture' (pp. 3–19), and argues that shifts in the experience and value of emotion are 'linked dialogically' with the cultural and social implications of the print revolution in the long eighteenth century which form the established narrative (p. 3). It outlines that the volume as a whole aims to cover not only expressions of feeling and self but also 'modes of community' (p. 4), with contributions from historians, psychologists, and philosophers. It concludes that public emotions, as part of public opinion, were different in the eighteenth century, and that it 'mattered crucially' (p. 18) that they were. W. Gerrod Parott's 'Psychological Perspectives on Emotion in Groups' (pp. 20–44) is a psychologist's account of emotions and their variability, to which the following essays respond.

Robert Phiddian's 'The Emotional Contents of Swift's *Saeva Indignatio*' (pp. 47–67) forms the first essay in the section 'Sympathy, Improvement and the Formation of Virtual Community'. Phiddian traces the negative emotions of satire in an assessment of the *saeva indignatio*, a 'remarkably harsh driving passion' (p. 49) that Swift included on his own epitaph, concluding that anger, contempt, and disgust were 'more naturally and socially valid' responses than they are today (p. 58). He tests this theory with a reading of Swift's 'A Beautiful Young Nymph Going to Bed'. This section continues with Jean McBain's '"Love, Marriages, Mistresses, and the Like": Daniel Defoe's Scandal Club and an Emotional Community in Print' (pp. 68–85), which acknowledges the usefulness of the corpus of the 'Scandal Club', Defoe's 1704–5 correspondence with readers of the *Review* [1704–13] to trace emotional preoccupations in the eighteenth century. She determines that authorial inauthenticity may lead to greater emotional authenticity, particularly in discussions about love.

Aleksondra Hultquist's 'Eliza Haywood's Progress through the Passions' (pp. 86–104) examines Eliza Haywood's *Reflections on the Various Effects of Love* [1726] and *Life's Progress through the Passions* [1748] as a 'discourse for the passions . . . in fictional narrative form' (p. 86). She posits Haywood as a good author for the study of the emotions, since they often are the starting point of her early fiction. She argues that Haywood contributes to the passion dialogue in the eighteenth century by emphasizing the 'private experience of passion' and the understanding of the self (p. 102). In 'That "Tremendous" Mr Dennis: The Sublime, Common Sense, and Criticism' (pp. 105–21), Kathrine Cuccuru continues the focus on individual authors, assessing John Dennis's account of the 'greatest sublime poetry' (p. 106) and, briefly, Pope's response to it. Laura J. Rosenthal concludes the section with 'Adam Smith and the Theatre in *Moral Sentiments*' (pp. 122–41).

Part III of the work concerns itself with the 'self', namely 'communicating feelings and identifying authentic humanity'. It opens with Emily Cock's ' "Off dropped the sympathetic snout": Shame, Sympathy, and Plastic Surgery at the Beginning of the Long Eighteenth Century' (pp. 145–64), followed by Amelia Dale's ' "Acting it as she reads": Affective Impressions in *Polly Honeycombe*' (pp. 165–82). Two chapters from this section warrant further review, given their contribution to the print culture theme already identified as prevalent this year. Eric Parisot's 'Framing Suicidal Emotions in the English Popular Press, 1750–80' (pp. 183–202) gives an account of the remarkably prevalent print accounts of suicide in the period. He reflects that the popular press 'attempted to limit' the impact of this 'disturbing record of a civilized society's inability to curtail a suicidal impulse' by 'discrediting the authenticity of suicidal emotions' (p. 197). The afterword for the volume is given to Conal Condren, whose 'Printed Passion: Sympathy, Satire, and the Translation of Homer (1675–1720)' (pp. 245–65) turns to the translation of Homer's work across Europe in the seventeenth and eighteenth centuries, 'other times and cultures' (p. 250), returning to the 'problematics of passion' (p. 261) in his conclusion. The volume also includes Glen Pettigrove's 'Passions, Perceptions, and Motives: Fault-Lines in Hutcheson's Account of Moral Sentiment' (pp. 203–22), reflecting again the Scottish Enlightenment theme this year, and Michael L. Frazer, 'Anatomist and Painter: Hume's Struggles as a Sentimental Stylist' (pp. 223–41).

In 2015 women's writing and work on gender in general were the most prevalent topics. Sociability, in particular pertaining to women or the Enlightenment, has also been a strong theme. The Scottish Enlightenment and its figures (Hutcheson particularly) have also received multiple treatments. Religion was ever present, this year often in tandem with epistolary networks and general print culture. Finally, works on travel and the history of science have shown that interdisciplinary work continues to flourish.

## 2. The Novel

Developing a trend noted in last year's review, Peter DeGabriele continues the transposition into eighteenth-century studies of one of the most important debates in political theory and philosophy of recent decades. *Sovereign Power and the Enlightenment: Eighteenth-Century Literature and the Problem of the Political* analyses Defoe's *Journal of the Plague Year* [1722], Richardson's *Clarissa* [1748], and Radcliffe's *The Italian* [1797]—along with the historical writing of Hume and Gibbon—with reference to the transition (if that's what it was) from the sovereignty of the divine right of monarchs to proto-liberal contractual government in the period. Like many political theorists and, increasingly, historians today, DeGabriele is interested in the subterranean survivals of the older system, identifying 'a heterodox tradition, sometimes inhabiting the very texts that support the civic republican or liberal narrative, that exhibits a continuing concern for, and anxiety about, sovereign power in the eighteenth century' (p. xvii). DeGabriele's discussions of the novels are thoughtful and dynamically integrated into current debates; his combination of literary analysis with a sophisticated grasp of eighteenth-century philosophy and political theory is particularly impressive.

Other kinds of 'heterodox tradition' are the concern of Lorri G. Nandrea's *Misfit Forms: Paths Not Taken by the British Novel*. Nandrea begins with the observation that, while scholars now have relatively sophisticated ways of tracing how the eighteenth-century English novel emerged from a 'messy and heterogeneous...primordial soup of other textual kinds' (p. 1), it is less commonly emphasized that eighteenth-century fiction can be pretty soup-like itself, and that the dominant forms it ended up engendering in the nineteenth century were in no way inevitable. Her introduction is an entertaining engagement with various thinkers who might help us in rethinking this kind of literary history: from Darwin to de Man and Deleuze. While anglophone eighteenth-century studies was always quite diffident about high Continental theory in its heyday, it is encouraging to find scholars making careful and original use of it now. Nandrea then turns to the famous decline in textual experimentation and exaggerated typography between its high-water mark in the mid-eighteenth-century novels of Sterne, and the more staid, self-effacing pages of nineteenth-century novels. Nandrea argues quite convincingly that this history can be mapped onto competing philosophical and physiological understandings of how feelings are produced and communicated. The book's subsequent chapters are mainly organized around pairings of eighteenth- and nineteenth-century novels, working to demonstrate a submerged survival in the second of some allegedly historically superseded quality in the first. Thus Sterne and Charlotte Brontë are examined with reference to the workings of sensibility; Defoe and Gaskell, from the point of view of what was assumed to constitute a 'plot'; and numerous examples from both periods to consider changing ideas of the 'wonder' that could be attributed to the material objects of everyday life. There is another version of this book imaginable, which would be weighted far more towards the many novels of the eighteenth century which, while having an audience at the time, fell out of view in subsequent periods. It is telling that, while the very specific elements of Defoe and Sterne identified by Nandrea might well represent 'paths not taken', their texts certainly did continue to have a reputation and an influence fairly consistently in the following centuries. But the book as it stands is an important one nonetheless.

Nandrea's preoccupation with afterlives and unexpected points of influence reads helpfully next to Daniel Cook and Nicholas Seager's edited collection, *The Afterlives of Eighteenth-Century Fiction*. As the editors note in their introduction, the terms of seminal works of adaptation theory published as recently as the 1990s and 2000s can already seem a little quaint 'in an age of fervent fan fiction, multimedia crossovers, mash-ups, remakes, and swedings' (p. 1). As Lisa Maruca's account of teaching 'Fielding, Print Culture, and the *Pamela* Media Event' (in this year's contribution to the Approaches to Teaching World Literature series, Wilson and Kraft, eds., *Approaches to Teaching the Novels of Henry Fielding*, pp. 100–9) implies, today's students are often willing to be surprised by how at home they feel among the often anarchically appropriative productions of eighteenth-century print culture. Cook's contribution to *The Afterlives of Eighteenth-Century Fiction* (Cook and Seager, eds., pp. 20–42) offers a helpful account of the trickiness of discussing 'appropriation' with reference to a historical time when literary property was considerably more ambiguous—and prone to flagrant trespass—than it would later become. This is followed by authoritative and lively accounts of the afterlives of particular tropes and genres by Michael McKeon (pp. 43–71) and Leah Orr (pp. 72–90), appropriations in popular culture such as musical theatre, anthology literature, and the puppet theatre by Michael Burden (pp. 192–211), M.-C. Newbould (pp. 133–52), and David A. Brewer (pp. 174–92), and newspapers and satirical cartoons by Nicholas Seager (pp. 111–32) and David Francis Taylor (pp. 212–32), as well as accounts of the afterlives of Defoe, Richardson, and Austen by Robert Mayer (pp. 232–52), Sarah Raff (pp. 91–110), Jillian Heydt-Stevenson (pp. 253–72), and Peter Sabor (pp. 273–89).

Continuing a generalized preoccupation with transmissions of this kind this year, Henry Power has written a superlative study of Henry Fielding's dealings with the Scriblerians, and of each of their dealings with Homer and the classics: *Epic into Novel: Henry Fielding, Scriblerian Satire, and the Consumption of Classical Literature.* Finding a curious clue in the ambivalent eighteenth-century reception of classical representations of eating, Power maps this onto the frequency with which too easy consumption provided a metaphor for the period's anxieties over making classical literature too palatable to modern audiences, in deference to a debased modern marketplace. While Swift, Pope, and Gay each negotiated differently the double bind that ancient epic be simultaneously the elevated counter-example to the consumerist shortcomings of the present *and* the privileged key to writing meaningfully about it, Power's Fielding has as his 'aim—and his great achievement…a series of fictions which reconcile epic spirit with consumable form' (p. 3). Providing valuable chapters on Fielding's three major novels, as well as original engagements with the Scriblerians on epic, this is a major monograph for the subject area.

Sterne studies, meanwhile, receives an eminent taking of stock in *Sterne, Tristram, Yorick: Tercentenary Essays on Laurence Sterne*, edited by Melvyn New, Peter de Voogd, and Judith Hawley. Collecting papers from 2013's tercentenary conference at Royal Holloway, University of London, the volume represents a highly international sector in rude health, with especially welcome contributions from younger scholars. Contributions reflecting reigning scholarly preoccupations such as material culture studies, by Stephanie DeGrooyer (pp. 201–18) and Amelia Dale (pp. 133–52), medical humanities, by Ashleigh Blackwood (pp. 101–20), and the construction of 'everyday life' in the period, by Brian Michael Norton (pp. 219–38), are joined by an outstanding keynote contribution by Thomas Keymer (pp. 3–24) situating Sterne as celebrity in a pan-eighteenth-century context.

Finally in books, of note for Defoe scholars is Judith Still's analysis of Jacques Derrida's late work, *Derrida and Other Animals: The Boundaries of the Human*, which provides the most 'useable' study yet for eighteenth-centuryists, of the philosopher's parting teachings on *Robinson Crusoe*. Situating Defoe alongside such Enlightenment thinkers as Hobbes, Buffon, Diderot, and Rousseau, Still offers a slightly more patiently historicized version of Derrida's path-breaking ideas about sovereignty and the bestial, as well as valuable pointers about how they can be applied in ethical literary criticism today.

In articles, Ros Ballaster, 'Satire and Embodiment: Allegorical Romance on Stage and Page in Mid-Eighteenth-Century Britain' (*ECF* 28[2015] 631–60), provides an invaluable account of the genealogical relations between those involved in the theatre in the run up to the 1737 Licensing Act, and the main contributors to the discourse of the early novel. Ballaster uses this to contend that 'the apparently inward turn of the novel in mid-eighteenth-century Britain is achieved not by repudiating but rather incorporating its allegorical and theatrical sources' (p. 657). Another excellent contribution is offered by Siv Gøril Brandtzæg. In 'Aversion to Imitation: The Rise of Literary Hierarchies in Eighteenth-Century Novel Reviews' (*FMLS* 51[2015] 171–85), Brandtzæg examines how reviewers in the second half of the century established norms of judgement around novels, but also established norms in reviewing itself: 'in charting how the novelists of the period used formulaic patterns, the reviewers themselves became repetitive, developing a very predictable reviewers' jargon and adopting idioms from each other' (p. 172). The eighteenth-century novel is examined panoramically, meanwhile, via Samuel Johnson's sometimes conflicting statements about the importance of particularized detail in writing, in Jenny Davidson's 'The "Minute Particular" in Life-Writing and the Novel' (*ECS* 38[2015] 263–81).

The debate over Defoe's canon continues in Ashley Marshall's 'Beyond Furbank and Owens: A New Consideration of the Evidence for the "Defoe" Canon' (*SB* 59[2015] 131–90). A series of publications by P.N. Furbank and W.R. Owens, beginning with *The Canonisation of Daniel Defoe* (YaleUP [1988]), have cut the number of texts attributed to the author virtually in half, relative to traditional accounts. While there have been any number of critiques of and objections to individual de-attributions, Marshall claims that it is time to move on from this form of response. Furbank and Owens divide the traditional Defoe canon into three categories: 'definite', 'probable', and 'de-attributed'; what Marshall sets out to show is that 'in quite a lot of particular cases a more nuanced and tentative judgment is as far as the evidence can carry us' (p. 132). Returning to Furbank and Owens's groundbreaking work with even more caution than they showed may present a yet more radical view of Defoe's texts and how they relate to each other. Indeed, Marshall finds, it may be one in which we have to get used to the fact that many of his most important works can no longer be taken for granted as being part of the canon at all.

Also on Defoe, Aparna Gollapudi has written an interesting article, 'Personhood, Property Rights, and the Child in John Locke's *Two Treatises of Government* and Daniel Defoe's Fiction' (*ECF* 28[2015] 25–58), dealing with the infrequent but suggestive appearances by children in Defoe's novels. Using Locke's *Two Treatises* instead of, say, his comments on education more commonly quoted in research on children in the period, Gollapudi argues that the figure of the child is more important to Defoe's representations of economic autonomy than has previously been thought.

On Richardson: while Richardson's relationship to tragedy has been the topic of several recent discussions, his use of comedy in *Clarissa* is Darryl P. Domingo's focus in 'Richardson's Unfamiliar Quotations: *Clarissa* and Early Eighteenth-Century Comedy' (*RES* 66[2015] 936–53), also discussed in Section 4 of this chapter. Domingo has helpfully spotted that alongside the better-known and often anthologized quotations from Shakespeare, Dryden, Otway, and others in *Clarissa*, Richardson also quotes Christopher Bullock's *A Woman is a Riddle* [1717] and Elizabeth Cooper's *The Rival Widows* [1735], and does so in contexts that belie his reputation for having puritanically disliked stage comedy in general. Richardson's quotations from comedy are also the topic of J.A. Smith's 'Telling Love: *Twelfth Night* in Samuel Richardson, Teresia Constantia Phillips, and William Blake' (*SP* 112[2015] 194–212), which situates Richardson's use of Shakespeare's play within other examples of authors quoting from it in the century. Two essays have considered the death of Clarissa in Richardson's novel: Stephanie Insley Hershinow, in 'Clarissa's Conjectural History: The Novel and the Novice' (*ECent* 56[2015] 297–319), argues that the heroine's death should be seen as the culmination of an uneasy kind of *Bildungsroman*; while Spencer Jackson, in '*Clarissa*'s Political Theology and the Alternative Modernity of God, Death, and Writing' (*ECent* 56[2015] 321–42), offers a highly original interpretation of the novel in light of recent work in political theology.

Sarah Fielding is the subject of a welcome dedicated article this year. In 'Circulating Stories and Moral Currency in *David Simple*' (*ECent* 56[2015] 1–19), Katherine Binhammer returns to arguments that the novel's pushing conventional Christian denouncement of riches into the realms of shared ownership represents a kind of 'proto-communism', arguing that the novel's many interpolated tales become a form of capital circulating around the text. While the old argument that sensibility was surreptitiously in temperamental sympathy with early capitalism has often come under strain in the face of specific examples (not least *David Simple* itself), Binhammer's argument provides a useful alterative model whereby we can see certain logics of capitalism in play, even in texts which seem to disavow them. Three other women novelists of the century are also given very welcome analyses this year: in Andrew Dicus's 'Everything Is Lost in Amoranda's Garden: Epistemology and Legitimacy in Mary Davys's *The Reform'd Coquet*' (*ECF* 28[2015] 263–85), Anna K. Segal's ' "Philosophy for the Ladies": Feminism, Pedagogy, and Natural Philosophy in Charlotte Lennox's *Lady's Museum*' (*ECF* 28[2015] 138–66), and David Oakleaf's ' "At the Margins of Utopia: Jamaica in Sarah Scott's *Millennium Hall*' (*ECF* 28[2015] 109–37).

Sterne's best-remembered Shakespeare citation provides a title for two essays this year: ' "Alas poor Yorick!": Sterne's Iconography of Mourning' by Helen Williams (*ECF* 28[2015] 313–44), and ' "Alas poor Yorick!": Elegiac Friendship in *Tristram Shandy*' by George E. Haggerty (*PMLA* 130[2015] 1450–6), both working to situate the famous scene of Yorick's death within older traditions and conventions. Williams continues her work of placing Sterne's visual, typographical, formal, and generic experiments in less explored contexts, seeing the representation of Yorick's death as continuing traditions of commemoration dating back to the early seventeenth century: not only at the level of content, but at the level of the minute visual qualities of the page. Haggerty, meanwhile, counter-intuitively pulls attention to the witness to Yorick's death, his friend Eugenius, the representation of whom Haggerty aligns with the important modern history of representations of friendship, running from Montaigne to Derrida. This famous moment's roots in *Hamlet*, meanwhile, are examined in a highly exploratory account of Sterne's relationship to the theatre in Emily Hodgson Anderson's 'Theatrical *Tristram*: Sterne and *Hamlet* Reconsidered' (*ECF* 28[2015] 661–80), covered fully in Section 4 of this chapter.

In editions, the year has seen O.M. Brack Jr., Leslie Chilton, and Walter H. Keithley's *The Miscellaneous Writings of Tobias Smollett*. This volume of ephemeral political, literary-critical, and medical writings provides important light and shade to Smollett as a novelist, and makes the medical writings conveniently available to scholars of medicine. The Cambridge edition of

Richardson's correspondence had two volumes added to it this year: *Correspondence Primarily on Sir Charles Grandison (1750–1754)*, edited by Betty A. Schellenberg, and *Correspondence with Sarah* [not, as long was thought, Sophia!] *Wescomb, Frances Grainger, and Laetitia Pilkington*, edited by John A. Dussinger. The ongoing development of this edition is of course a major event for the subject area.

### 3. Poetry

As scholars (in Britain at least) continued to adjust to the new REF cycle, there was a measurable impact on the number of monographs published on eighteenth-century poetry during 2015. The ambition and inventiveness of what there is, however, remain undiminished. One notable paperback reprint of a monograph from 2004 and two from 2010 appeared: G. Gabrielle Starr's influential and bristling *Lyric Generations: Poetry and the Novel in the Long Eighteenth Century*, Dustin Griffin's *Swift and Pope: Satirists in Dialogue*, and David Hopkins's *Conversing with Antiquity: English Poets and the Classics, from Shakespeare to Pope*. It is good to see these excellent texts reprinted and reasonably priced. Next year promises eighteenth-century fecundity, with British and American publishers preparing a wealth of exciting material. To give a taster, 2016 will see, among other things, Oxford University Press's mammoth tome *The Oxford Handbook of British Poetry, 1660–1800*, edited by Jack Lynch, and Laurie Langbauer's *The Juvenile Tradition: Young Writers and Prolepsis, 1750–1835*. As the discipline of medical humanities continues to spread, eighteenth-century verse is well represented in Bloomsbury's impishly titled *A Body of Work: An Anthology of Poetry and Medicine*, edited by Corinna Wagner and Andy Brown (eloquent champions of the discipline), but these will be covered next year. The year 2015 has been a good one by most measures. The restoration of marginalized voices has been a preponderant aim, as have articles focusing on the reach and play of genre. Whilst monographs have been scarce, then, fresh and exciting articles abound.

To begin with what was missing from the 2014 survey, that year saw the publication of two hefty tomes. The first was the third edition of Christine Gerrard's *A Companion to Eighteenth-Century Poetry*, which did not arrive in time for review. The second was the attendant volume from Wiley-Blackwell edited by Gerrard and David Fairer, *Eighteenth-Century Poetry: An Annotated Anthology*, which, again, did not arrive in time for review. These will be covered in next year's volume.

This year saw the publication of a work that takes on verse's various, knotty, and ultimately inventive arbitrations of religion. Timothy Whelan's *Other British Voices: Women, Poetry, and Religion, 1766–1784* centres on the lives and writings of Mary Steele, Mary Scott, Jane Attwater, and Elizabeth Coltman—four nonconformist, 'primarily Baptist' women at the heart of a thriving poetic circle in the West Country (p. 9). Whelan's monograph is a part of Palgrave's Nineteenth-Century Major Lives and Letters series, but the book offers fascinating insights into the poetic and religious culture of the eighteenth century too. Indeed, it is a text that strains and frets at periodization, despite its obvious list towards the nineteenth century; it is also a text that attempts to overhear sounds long silenced and restore them to anglophone scholarly communities.

Whelan makes full use of manuscript material, exploring the 'Steele Collection, Reeves Collection, Attwater Papers, and Saffery/Whitaker Papers (Angus Library), and Reeves Collection (Bodleian, uncatalogued)' (p. xi). *Other British Voices* attempts, as the title indicates, to re-create 'the lives and careers' of the poets above. One wonders how achievable this ambition is. There is also a more quotidian obstacle. Notably, 'these women employed literary pseudonyms within their private circle that shielded their proper identities from readers outside the circle (and, with graver consequences, to nearly all readers in succeeding centuries) while simultaneously providing them with literary identities that empowered their conscious determination to be writers' (p. xi). Whelan's monograph seeks to promote the achievements of these obscured and silenced poets. As he notes, 'the writings of these nonconformist women exemplify the variety of traditions present among women writers in the eighteenth and early nineteenth centuries' (p. 2). Whelan contends that these poets offer the possibility of hearing multiple female voices rather than one decidedly female voice. Imitative modes of expression, namely of masculine forms of discourse, are traced, but so too are distinctive modes of resistance.

Indeed, the admirable motif of hearing, or perhaps *overhearing*, is laced throughout the book. Importantly, 'Manuscript poetry and various forms of life writing central to the Steele circle have long been marginalized by historians of British nonconformity who have privileged church records and pastoral biographies' rather than 'other informal sources pertaining to the laity, especially women' (p. 11). As such, this book seeks to disrupt a history that has tended to be articulated by, and all about, men. But what is the relationship between voice as metaphor, voice in form, and the actuality of voice? There is a problem with this notional female voice and voice more generally. The study would have benefited from some conceptual, perhaps more broadly theoretical, and especially formal, clarification as to what we mean precisely when we speak of such things as a 'masculine discourse' and a female 'voice'. These are taken as read, but they are not. Those of us who do not subscribe to such formulations, or those who are waiting to do so, might want to know what is at stake. While the monograph seeks to displace a monolithic and contiguous account of a female voice, one wonders, in the end, what 'voice' means if indeed it means anything at all. The book suffers because of this.

Of course, that stubborn and tricky term, voice, has gained increasing traction in eighteenth-century and nineteenth-century studies recently. David Nowell Smith's *On Voice in Poetry: The Work of Animation*, another Palgrave book, opens up the term. While not specifically concerned with eighteenth-century verse, Nowell Smith's excellent, fresh and vibrant study for the Language, Discourse, Society Series for Palgrave tackles one of poetics' more problematic terms. Indeed, we should not think the answer to 'what do we mean by "voice" in poetry' all that simple: 'given the sheer diversity, and ambivalence, of poems' understandings, deployments, explorations of voice, their strategies of voicing, as well as the roles played by voice as trope, as prosodic resource, as ideology, so categorical a question could easily seem self defeating' (p. 1). Indeed, while it lies outside the immediate concerns of this section, the preponderance this year of the word 'voice' in books and articles suggests that eighteenth-century poetic scholarship might benefit from testing what is at stake when it uses this term. Again, voice is far from transparent or historically transcendent. It is muddy and involved; its hectic condition requires more caution.

Continuing the various themes of voices, listening, and recovery, a number of exciting journal articles on eighteenth-century poetry were published during 2015. *Tulsa Studies in Women's Literature*, under the guest editorship of Kerri Andrews, dedicated an issue to 'New Directions on Mary Leapor and Ann Yearsley' (*TWSL* 34[2015]). Andrews offers a synopsis of the current state of affairs, explaining that 'this special topics issue on the poetry of Mary Leapor (1722–46) and Ann Yearsley (1753–1806) adds to a steadily growing collection of work on previously forgotten, ignored, or neglected poets of eighteenth-century Britain' (p. 11). Many of the 'ignored' were from the labouring classes, or otherwise considered by posterity to sit outside the mainstream literary culture of the period' (p. 11). As such, since the 1970s and 1980s a process of decentring began, with 'Roger Lonsdale's field-changing anthologies in 1984 and 1989' leading the way (p. 11). Yet this decentring largely benefited labouring-class males and middle-class women. Andrews deftly summarizes the major contributions of figures such as John Barrell, Raymond Williams, E.P. Thompson, and Mary Poovey. The championing of middle-class women writers was also a gradual process, but 'strongly rooted in both these parallel recoveries of the neglected and noncanonical voices' is 'Donna Landry's ground-breaking study of labouring-class women's writing, *The Muses of Resistance: Labouring Class Women's Poetry in Britain, 1796* (1990)' (p. 11).

Indeed, the eight essays 'attempt, through various means, to refocus our attention on the cultural, material, and historical contexts of Leapor's and Yearsley's writing' (p. 13). The late Bill Overton's 'Mary Leapor's Verse and Genre' (*TWSL* 34[2015] 19–32) offers an enjoyable exploration of the 'issues of genre' and the scholarly inattention regarding her use of 'genre'. He explains that 'the essay attempts to outline how these gaps in scholarly knowledge might be filled by offering a quantitative analysis of Leapor's formal variety across her entire—if brief—literary career and a discussion of some of the genres with which she worked' (p. 19). The article contends that 'genre in eighteenth-century verse' is a topic that requires increased attention (p. 20). Indeed, for Overton, 'Given its importance for anyone writing or writing about poetry in the long eighteenth century, it is surprising that it has not attracted more notice' (p. 20). After reflecting on the preponderance of attitudes akin to Pope's neoclassicism, Overton then moves on to ably consider Leapor's negotiation of diverse poetic categories. Indeed, this focus on labouring women's mediation of genre is fascinating and novel.

William J. Christmas's 'Lyric Modes: The Soliloquy Poems of Mary Leapor and Ann Yearsley' (*TWSL* 34[2015] 33–50) begins with the forthright contention that within the poets' respective oeuvres there are 'interesting poems' still worthy of critical attention (p. 33). Indeed, despite their ' "collected works" treatment, their critical reputations nevertheless rest on a relatively small number of poems compared to their respective poetic *oeuvres*' (p. 33). Christmas intervenes, suggesting that 'even a cursory glance' at the contents page discloses each poet's generic inventiveness and range (p. 33). Examining the lyric potential of the soliloquy, he turns to Leapor's 'The Pocket-Book's Soliloquy'. Such poems indicate a familiarity with the 'invitational convention', but also the idea that Leapor's poem offers a sportive and almost parodic encounter with such conventions (p. 37). The article offers sympathetic and clever close readings expressed in a sparkling and pellucid style. It is an enjoyable addition to the collection and is a call to arms to read Leapor and Yearsley more broadly.

In 'Visiting the Country House: Generic Innovation in Mary Leapor's "Crumble-Hall"' (*TWSL* 34[2015] 51–64), Sharon Young, while endorsing biographical and socio-economic analyses of Leapor's poetry, attempts to move decidedly away from these types of explanation to focus instead on the poet's 'engagement with genre' and poetic practice more generally (p. 51). Leapor's most familiar poem, the delightful 'Crumble-Hall', takes readers on a tour of a country estate, and this is Young's principal focus. Indeed, 'as readers, we accompany the poem's speaker around the house, experiencing its delights and treasures much as eighteenth-century tourists accompanied the housekeeper of grand estates' (p. 51). However, far from being just another country house poem, Young contends, the poem participates in a wider repertoire of country house verse. Indeed, as she explains, 'Crumble-Hall' is often regarded as a late and atypical country house poem', but 'it may more accurately be seen as belonging to a much wider, yet for the most part critically unregarded, body of country house poetry of the mid-eighteenth century' (p. 61). According to Young, 'this poetry increasingly includes the house as an integral part of its discussion', but also indicates that we need to consider further the importance of generic contexts to the critical discussion of Mary Leapor's poetry and to labouring-class poetry more generally' (p. 61). The article constructs a compelling extension, and a couple of extra wings, perhaps, to the generic reach of the country house poem.

Continuing 2015's fascination with the protean identity afforded by personae and names, Anne Chandler's 'Monarchy, Meritocracy, and Tragic Realism in the Work of Mary Leapor' (*TWSL* 34[2015] 65–87) considers, among other things, the acuity of the alter ego's social consciousness. The article is ambitious and rewarding. It traces 'Leapor's recurring treatments of Apollo and David as influenced by Dryden's typological approach to myth and his analyses of the kingly soul in stage tragedy', but also 'observe[s] how motifs of divine kingship inform Leapor's own two tragedies' (p. 65). The article manages to 'redraw the lines of conflict and influence in Leapor's sadly truncated career and to reconsider her trajectory less through identity politics than through critical principles' (p. 81). As many of the scholarly productions this year have focused on unexamined, or suspiciously essentialist, formulations, this is a welcome (and sorely needed) lunge away from 'identity politics' towards 'critical principles'.

Brycchan Carey's 'The Poetics of Radical Abolitionism: Ann Yearsley's *Poem on the Inhumanity of the Slave Trade*' (*TWSL* 34[2015] 89–105) acknowledges the recent efforts of various scholars to establish Yearsley as an important poet of the eighteenth century, deserving 'comparison not only with other labouring-class poets but also with the most exalted writers of the age' (p. 89). Clearly this is an impossible, perhaps foolhardy, enterprise. Carey takes up the pairing of Yearsley with her quondam patron Hannah More. Yearsley and her work, Carey contends, have often been unfavourably contrasted with More to the extent that the former has suffered, with 'Yearsley's poetic vision' being 'subordinated to More's' (p. 89). The article sensitively and ably highlights the parallels and dialogue between Yearsley's thirty-page *Poem on the Inhumanity of the Slave Trade* [1788] and the complementary productions of such figures such as Thomas Chatterton, William Roscoe, William Cowper, John Bicknell, and Thomas Day. While, as Carey accepts, 'it is difficult to say whether or not Yearsley's radical abolitionism is merely an attempt to establish poetic difference between her and More', 'Bearing in mind the development of Yearsley's interests in the years to follow, particularly in *Earl Godwin* (1791) and *The Royal Captives* (1795), it seems more likely that she is developing a genuinely radical antislavery sensibility at this point' (p. 103). The article provides a fascinating and thorough beginning to what will no doubt prove to be a fruitful area for future scholars. Yet settling the question of whether Yearsley is first-rate is going to require a lot more work than this article.

Kerri Andrews, the editor of this capacious and energetic special edition, resumes the Yearsley–More contention, offering up an intriguing article on the subject of 'Ann Yearsley and the London Newspapers in 1787' (*TWSL* 34[2015] 107–24). Following their acrimonious and very public split, Yearsley went on to publish a second volume of verse, but also wrote four poems specifically for newspaper publication. Indeed, the essay is ideally placed, following as it does Carey's wonderful introduction to the Yearsley–More dissociation. As Andrews reminds the reader, 'In the summer of 1787, Ann Yearsley was preparing to publish her second volume of verse, *Poems, on Various Subjects*. It was to be her first new publication since the very public—and extremely bitter—breakdown of her patronage relationship with Hannah More' (p. 107). This fresh 'new volume' 'would include her defence against the charges of ingratitude and poor behaviour levelled at her, as well as a copy of the deed of trust over which Yearsley and More had quarrelled in 1785 with such unfortunate consequences'. Andrews then asks quite simply, 'why did Yearsley start publishing poetry in newspapers?' (p. 108). For Andrews, newspaper publication afforded Yearsley a wider audience and an opportunity to prove that she was a 'poet of national relevance' (p. 107). This essay beautifully complements the former and offers a fine reprise of the social and literary locale in which Yearsley wrote.

This fine special issue concludes with the familiar and welcome tones of David Fairer. He offers '"Flying atoms in the sightless air": Issues of Coherence and Scale in Leapor and Yearsley' (*TWSL* 34[2015] 141–62), which counsels that there is 'no embarrassment in focusing on the small, the insignificant, the awkward, and the specific in the poetry of Mary Leapor and Ann Yearsley' (p. 141). Rather, such atomic concerns might be seen as energetically displacing more conventional aesthetic concerns. In this brisk yet detailed contribution, Fairer encourages us to consider the small—the disjunctive and marginal. This is a welcome development in eighteenth-century poetics. Romantic and Victorian poetic criticism have been ambitiously enthused with an emphasis on process, marginalia, errata, and the stray. There is a scaling up that diminishes the small, and Fairer alerts us to this. He suggests that Leapor and Yearsley challenge 'the normally self-evident values of coherence and significance' (p. 141). Consequently, the small is 'creatively freed from mock-heroic, and their interest in the fragmented and dis-articulated (not the same as the inarticulate) raises questions about how meaning is made' (p. 141). This is a fascinating paper that will be a boon to those working outside the period too. Such references to the small, of course, encourage us to question why we call long poems long and short poems short, measuring poems in stretches of time, rather than in the demands of understanding. Why not big or small poems, wide or narrow, for instance? Fairer's analysis reveals that Leapor and Yearsley 'share this capacity to make incoherence articulate and small things significant', but in doing so they offer 'different approaches' (p. 158). Indeed, 'where Leapor's fundamentally comic vision challenges formality with her intriguing mixtures and informal perspectives, Yearsley confronts the centrifugal tendencies of the mind and the disturbing and potentially tragic implications of incoherence' (p. 158). This is a stimulating conclusion to this special edition of the journal.

Alexander Pope has made a brief, but exciting, showing this year. Two notable examples can be found in *Notes and Queries*. Stephen Bernard contributed 'Alexander Pope, Fame, Reputation and Advertising' (*N&Q* 62[2015] 277–9). Bernard explains that 'in the *Daily Currant* for Saturday 20 August 1715 (issue 4313), verso, there appeared an innocuous but momentous advertisement in the history of Popeiana' (p. 277). While Pope 'was already thought to be the leading light in poetry', despite the obstructions which resulted from his Catholicism, he 'was now a celebrity' (p. 277). This contained, if bursting, note probes Pope's attitudes towards advertising. Bernard suggests that advertisements 'had become more sophisticated as the poet's fame and reputation grew', but 'Obviously something larger in the book trade is taking place here over copyright and ownership of a poet's name, but Pope's celebrity is clearly exemplary of the battle, if not the war' (p. 279).

Another piece, Thomas McGeary's 'Opera-Loving Sons of Peers in *The Dunciad*' (*N&Q* 62[2015] 279–85), considers opera in *The Dunciad* [1728–43]. Here opera stands as a symbol of 'false taste in the arts pervading Britain, and more specifically as one of the preoccupations of the Grand Tourists returned from Italy' (p. 279). As McGeary highlights, 'The editor of the Twickenham Edition of *The Dunciad*, states, "Their sons (in Harcourt's case, grandson), were undistinguished, and, as Pope's line implies, patrons of the opera"' (p. 280). McGeary suggests that 'a variety of documentation allows us to confirm that these are likely the peers that Pope intended' and 'We learn that Pope must have chosen these five (grand)sons quite deliberately for their well-known passion for opera but that some had distinguished careers' (p. 280). Significantly, 'all five did go on Grand Tours, and it would have been known in polite circles (from letters home from sons and their tutors, and then as spread by gossip and sharing of letters) that they acquired or cultivated their opera-madness in Italy' (p. 280). This article provides a wealth of notable material on the Grand Tour and the reception of opera, and their place in *The Dunciad*.

Continuing this year's articles on Pope is Rebecca Roma Stoll's '"Ye soft illusions, dear deceits, arise!"': Apostrophe as Suture in "Eloise to Abelard"' (*ECent* 56[2015] 343–58), which turns to Pope's 'strange and starkly emotional poem' (p. 343). The article intelligently probes and questions the implications and play of genre. We witness a poem whose 'genre renders the poem technically incapable of responding to this desire, the very cries that emblematize Eloisa's isolation have intriguing formal consequences' as 'apostrophe provides Eloisa with a way of escaping her solitude by forcing the objects she calls to assume subject positions capable of calling back' (p. 343). At a time when sundry vibrant materialisms and object-oriented approaches are becoming increasingly and dully popular, Roma Stoll offers a fascinating examination of apostrophe's capacity to enfranchise objects into sounding while evading the lexical trappings of this intellectual fashion.

Although not particularly relevant to the concerns of poetry, if fascinating in relation to the visual and architectural, J. Vanessa Lyon considers Pope's grotto (*HLQ* 78[2015] 441–77), proposing an addition to the visual culture of Popeiana in the form of six previously unpublished period drawings. The images 'are examined in light of their proto-gothic qualities as well as the Catholic poet's pastoral retirement, artistic connections, and possible Jacobite leanings' (p. 441).

From the lush embellishments of opera to the call of objects, we now move on to the luxuries of panegyric in Noelle Dückmann Gallagher's article, 'The Embarrassments of Restoration Panegyric: Reconsidering an Unfashionable Genre' (*ECL* 39[2015] 33–54). Here, Dückmann Gallagher probes an often overlooked genre. Indeed, 'while the satiric works of this period have received sustained and extensive scholarly attention, its panegyrics have been left to fade quietly into the background, more a source of embarrassment to us than a legitimate subject for intellectual inquiry' (pp. 33–4). Again, the restoration of voices that has dominated this year's productions shifts to the recovery of an off-putting genre to contemporary sensibilities. She offers a compelling case for a reinvestigation of seventeenth-century and eighteenth-century panegyric, offering some 'observations on why—or rather, how— poems so prominent and ordinary in their own time have proven to be so discomfiting and so foreign in ours' (p. 50). This is a capacious and confident article with various readings of writers such as Behn, Swift, and Cibber.

James Thomson is represented in one article; Edward Holberton's 'James Thomson's *The Seasons* and the Empire of the Seas' (*HLQ* 78[2015] 41–60). Holberton explores 'a diplomatic controversy in the 1720s and 1730s over the freedom of the seas in the Caribbean' (p. 41). He contends that this debate offered Thomson 'innovative frameworks within which to examine Britain and its place in the world' (p. 41). The controversy had long-lasting implications for Thomson, influencing the reception of *Britannia*, but also revisions to *The Seasons* [1726–30]. This is a novel and intriguing article that offers a new approach to portions of this influential work.

Whatever we may now think of the transatlantic handshake, it is here given a historical treatment: Jared S. Richman's article, 'Anna Seward and the Many

(After) Lives of Major André: Trauma, Mourning, and Transatlantic Literary Legacy' (*ECS* 48[2015] 201–19), maps the publication history of Anna Seward's *Monody on Major André* [1781] and its reception history. Richman compellingly teases out and unravels 'Seward's personal connection to her poetic subject', evoking 'admiration and . . . sympathetic displays of emotion from others' (p. 215). Indeed, 'as Seward becomes the chief arbiter of André's memory, her poetic tribute becomes for Williams and her readers an exercise in transitive grieving' (p. 215). The article ably traces the tension between British Patriotism and American sympathy. Richman's examination of this tangled relationship parallels, in subtle ways, Kelly E. Battle's offering. In 'Anna Barbauld's Authorial Self-Fashioning: From "fair pedagogue" to "fatidical [*sic*] spinster"' (*ECS* 48[2015] 143–62), we see another instance of how another poet's intellectual development issues. In a year that has been dominated by reclamation of voices, Battle examines Barbauld's more strident process of self-fashioning.

## 4. Drama

Media and sociability were the keywords of research into eighteenth-century drama in 2015. This is due in no small part to the publication of a special double issue of *Eighteenth-Century Fiction*, edited by Daniel O'Quinn and Gillian Russell and entitled 'Georgian Theatre in an Information Age: Media, Performance, Sociability'. In their introduction to this volume (*ECF* 27[2015] 337–40), the editors describe the collection of fourteen articles as an attempt to 'orientate future research on the complex intermedial relations endemic to theatrical culture', in part to 'counteract the nascent tendency to separate sociability from its mediation and to isolate media archaeology from social relations' (p. 338). O'Quinn, Russell, and their contributors are not alone in this aim, and similar concerns run through much of the theatre research published in 2015. This review will thus begin with 'Georgian Theatre in an Information Age' before pursuing two of its key themes, media and sociability, through a number of other articles and books.

The special issue of *Eighteenth-Century Fiction* assembles writing from both theatre specialists and other scholars not previously known for their work in this area and covers the period from 1709 to 1812. It is divided into three thematic sections: 'Daily and Nightly Life', 'New Situations: The Historicity of the Repertoire', and 'Convergent Media: The Theatre–Novel Nexus'.

The first of these three overlapping sections tackles the integration of theatrical performance and the press. Stuart Sherman's article, ' "The general entertainment of my life": The *Tatler*, the *Spectator*, and the Quidnunc's Cure' (*ECF* 27[2015] 343–72), focuses on the figure of the news-hungry Quidnunc, born in the *Tatler* and then developed in this periodical, the *Spectator*, and on the stage. Sherman's work uses the Quidnunc to rethink press and stage relations, pointing out the significance of Richard Steele's 'core journalistic aperçu: that to print the theatre as news is to discover it as cornucopia' (p. 352). This culminates in a number of thought-provoking contrasts between the *Tatler* and the *Spectator*, summarized when Sherman claims that, in the

*Spectator*, 'the playhouse figures no longer as a teeming place of news, but as a psychological paradigm, a metaphor for the paper's mindset' (p. 363). For another, more heavily Habermasian approach to the Quidnunc also published this year, one may consult Uriel Heyd's 'News Craze: Public Sphere and the Eighteenth-Century Theatrical Depiction of Newspaper Culture' (*ECent* 56[2015] 59–84).

Sherman's article is followed by another standout piece, Leslie Ritchie's 'Pox on Both Your Houses: The Battle of the Romeos' (*ECF* 27[2015] 373–94). Ritchie begins with the observation that David Garrick's decision in 1750 to challenge the Romeo of his former protégé, Spranger Barry, entailed entering into 'an uncanny competition with his own textual and gestural interpretation of the play' (p. 379). The framing of this rivalry as a 'battle' is the result of the wide circulation of Garrick's prologues both on stage in the press, which may well have had significant ramifications far beyond the 1750–1 season: Ritchie points to both the potential for spouting clubs to re-enact the 'Battle' for decades afterwards and the extent to which Garrick's promotional techniques here would be further honed in the course of his career.

'New Situations: The Historicity of the Repertoire', this issue's second section, aims, in the words of the introduction, to demonstrate 'the political importance of engaging with the dynamic field of repetition itself' (p. 339). All six articles gathered here consider questions of repetition in their own particular ways. In 'The Scottish Play: Nationalism, Masculinity, and the Georgian Afterlife of *The Wonder: A Woman Keep a Secret*' (*ECF* 27[2015] 451–78), Misty G. Anderson demonstrates, through a series of well-wrought close readings, how Susannah Centlivre's work owes part of its slow-burning success to the way in which it 'uses parody to help audiences imagine British identity in broad imperial terms' (p. 451): a risky, Whiggish strategy when the play opened in 1714, the year of George I's coronation, but a popular angle by the middle of the century. 'Half-History, or The Function of *Cato* at the Present Time' by Daniel O'Quinn (*ECF* 27[2015] 479–508) offers a sophisticated analysis of three performances of Joseph Addison's *Cato* (at the Prince of Wales's residence in 1747, at Valley Forge in 1778, and at John Philip Kemble's Drury Lane in 1811), each of which allegorized George III at different points in his life through a process of 'forgetting' previous iterations, ultimately tending to the creation of a 'half-historical' *Cato*, an epithet which O'Quinn takes from Thomas Lawrence's own description of his famous 1812 portrait of Kemble as Cato. This section also contains a contribution from the issue's other editor, Gillian Russell, entitled 'Sara Sophia Banks's Private Theatricals: Ephemera, Sociability and the Archiving of Fashionable Life' (*ECF* 27[2015] 535–57). Russell's essay has a looser structure to it than O'Quinn's or Anderson's, and represents the kind of careful archival work on which the goal of writing about the theatre as an intermedial space relies. Russell's description of how, by organizing her collection of visiting cards according to Linnaean principles of classification, Banks 'defined the ruling elite . . . as an order analogous to that of the natural world' (p. 548) stands as a particularly good example of her fine attention to the material she is presenting.

The third and final section, entitled 'Convergent Media: The Theatre–Novel Nexus', contains four essays, and begins with Ros Ballaster's 'Satire and Embodiment: Allegorical Romance on Stage and Page in Mid-Eighteenth-Century Britain' (*ECF* 27[2015] 631–60), where she argues that 'with the introduction of stage censorship in the 1730s, allegorical prose romance mediates the transition from theatrical to novelistic modes of rendering plausible embodied character' (p. 631). Ballaster's work can profitably be read alongside Anne F. Widmayer's *Theatre and Novel* (reviewed below), with Ballaster sharing Widmayer's interest in framing and the effect of distance or intimacy it can create. Writing on Eliza Haywood's *The Adventures of Eovaai* [1736], Ballaster shows how the author found, through the framing conceit, 'the diegetic equivalent of the ambivalent play with the animated and embodied politics of theatrical satire' (p. 652), a kind of play Haywood had herself engaged in as an actress and one which Henry Fielding, prior to the Licensing Act, had explored extensively in *Pasquin* [1736]. Emily Hodgson Anderson's article, 'Theatrical *Tristram*: Sterne and *Hamlet* Reconsidered' (*ECF* 27[2015] 661–80), shows how Sterne's novel uses allusions to Shakespeare in order to 'highlight the theatre as a tool for memorialisation' (p. 661). Such an angle nicely connects Anderson's essays to the concerns of those earlier in this double issue, with a particular achievement of this piece being its ability to articulate the symbiotic relationship between Sterne's two personae of Tristram and Yorick, where 'it is through the character of Tristram that Yorick is remembered, and by playing one character Sterne enables the recurrent reanimation of the other' (p. 674).

Anderson's point owes a debt to Joseph Roach, whose work is constantly referenced throughout this collection of articles. Lisa A. Freeman's article, 'Mourning the "Dignity of the Siddonian Form"' (*ECF* 27[2015] 597–632), builds, for example, upon Roach's *Cities of the Dead* [1996] to present the ways in which Sarah Siddons—like many an ageing performer, albeit with more intensity—became 'an effigy to, and surrogate for, an earlier self' (p. 604). Roach himself provides a short 'Afterword' (*ECF* 27[2015] 731–4) to the collection, in which he praises its scope and provides some useful observations about the use of the word 'media': the term, he notes, is (like 'data') omnipresent in our society, while 'Neither a lonely medium nor a single datum dares intrude on media, which conveys the complex sense of a transmitting structure or vehicle of communication, including the enabling technology or protocols pertaining to that vehicle' (p. 732). Such a definition invites a rereading of the articles gathered here, even as it places them as the product of their own twenty-first-century standpoint, where, by reinserting the stage into its wider cultural context, their authors have undertaken an ironic reversal (as Roach notes in conclusion) of early theatre historians, who once 'cut the theatrical notices out of newspapers' (p. 734).

Overall, these fourteen articles represent a significant intervention in the field of eighteenth-century studies. The very best pieces here achieve their stated aim of using a simultaneous attentiveness to media, performance, and sociability to produce new insights. Yet this is risky stuff, and it is all too easy for such work to become burdened under an excess of context or theory. The interconnectedness of eighteenth-century theatre, so aptly demonstrated here, should not be over-emphasized; the best results in such scholarship are demonstrated through the use of restraint and discipline in their claims.

Such a level of focus is manifest in another edited journal issue published last year: the second of two special issues of *Restoration and Eighteenth-Century Theatre Research* on the subject of anti-theatre. The editor of both volumes, Logan Connors, shows a similar attentiveness to questions of media and sociability to O'Quinn and Russell, although he approaches them differently. Having noted how the first of these two volumes had focused on society's responses to the theatre, Connors's introduction, 'From Anti-Theater to Anti-Theatricality' (*RECTR* 29[2014] 5–8), then summarizes its companion as concentrating on 'anti-theatricality as a dramatic and critical construct used by playwrights, theatre critics, editors and other participants in the dramatic arts' (p. 5) in Europe. At its heart, this is what O'Quinn and Russell would call an intermedial process, which brings about, to quote Connors once more, 'the gradual collapse of powerful, autonomous arguments against the stage into an interesting theme in dramatic criticism and production' (p. 5). Three articles from this issue demonstrate such a phenomenon in English culture. Gillian Skinner's ' "Stage Plays... and a thousand other amusements now in use": Garrick's Response to Anti-Theatrical Discourse in the Mid Eighteenth Century' (*RECTR* 29[2014] 63–82) examines the actor-manager's ability, in such plays as *A Peep behind the Curtain* [1767], to write 'anti-theatrical' drama, using irony to weaken hostile attitudes to the theatre even as they are rehearsed. Skinner also helpfully locates such writing as part of a larger response against anti-theatrical attention to the variety of stage entertainments, namely that 'the fault lies not in theatrical representation, but in the choice of what to represent' (p. 64). A short piece by the writer of this review, entitled 'The Anti-Performance Prejudice of Shakespeare's Eighteenth-Century Editors' (*RECTR* 29[2014] 47–61), considers the anti-theatrical prejudices of Alexander Pope, Lewis Theobald, William Warburton, and Samuel Johnson, to the extent that each writer criticized the deleterious effects of performance on the preservation of Shakespeare's writing. Finally, 'Manipulating Reader-Actors: Eighteenth-Century Printed Harlequinades' (*RECTR* 29[2014] 83–104), an article by Anne F. Widmayer, offers an intriguing study of six of Newberry library's harlequinades, also known as turn-up or metamorphosis books, presenting them as an arena in which 'professionalism and naturalism... are devalued as unskilled reader-actors "play" their parts' (p. 84). In, for example, Robert Sayer's harlequinade of Garrick's *Harlequin's Invasion* [1770], not only is the harlequin 'rather static' (p. 86) but the format of the work allows for the production's concluding image of Shakespeare rising while Harlequin falls to be reversed. Widmayer continues with an analysis of Sayer's printing of *Harlequin Cherokee* [1772], which goes even further, replacing pantomimical tricks with 'metatheatrical scenes that remind the reader-actor of his or her dual role as spectator and actor' (p. 102).

In addition to a pair of articles, Widmayer's *Theatre and the Novel from Behn to Fielding* also appeared this year, published by OUP for the Voltaire Foundation. In this work, which could be placed in O'Quinn and Russell's category of 'Convergent Media: The Theatre–Novel Nexus', the author offers a lucid examination of the works of Aphra Behn, Delarivier Manley, William Congreve, and Henry Fielding, arguing that the 'great contribution Restoration and early eighteenth-century playwright novelists made to the developing novel was a highly satirical, fictional, self-awareness' (p. 231). Widmayer defines a number of dramatic techniques and shows how each of her subjects employed them to create self-conscious narratives: Behn's manipulation of space; Manley's focus on the performance of emotion, especially in 'discovery scenes'; Congreve's liaising scenes, with their satirical commentators; and Fielding's author-characters. Avoiding a focus on shared plot devices, Widmayer instead adopts a method which crosses 'performance and narrative critical practice' (p. 10). Perhaps the greatest virtue of this is that the book consistently demonstrates not simply the transfusion of theatrical technique into the early novel but rather the interchange between stage and page. Congreve, for example, acquires his plays' author-characters from French prose *nouvelles*, while Fielding brings such author-characters from his early plays into his later prose. In the final pages of this work, Widmayer also raises some fascinating ideas for future research, suggesting that Manley may have used her novels to explore dramatic effects unstageable in her contemporary theatre, such as sequential discovery scenes.

Widmayer, Ballaster, and the other contributors to *Eighteenth-Century Fiction* are not the only critics to have published on the 'Theatre–Novel Nexus' in 2015. Darryl P. Domingo's article, 'Richardson's Unfamiliar Quotations: *Clarissa* and Early Eighteenth-Century Comedy' (*RES* 66[2015] 936–53), after a slow start on Samuel Richardson's anti-theatricality, moves on to the much more interesting observation that, in *Clarissa*, 'the very texture of his characters' letters assimilates lesser-known lines from contemporary drama—including comedy' (p. 945). Domingo points out echoes of Christopher Bullock's *Woman is a Riddle* [1716, but revived in 1745] and, specifically in Anna Howe's letters, Elizabeth Cooper's *The Rival Widows* [1735]. He uses these echoes to warn critics that they 'can no more trust in the view of Richardson as "limited" in his reading than they can in truisms about a dramatic novelist' (p. 953). In 'Staging Sociability in *The Excursion*: Frances Brooke, David Garrick, and the King's Theatre Coterie' (*ECF* 27[2014] 257–84), Katherine G. Charles also examines theatre–novel relations, convincingly rereading Brooke's novel of 1777 as a 'bully pulpit for advancing her own vision of what the theatre should be and for criticizing what she sees as the bad practices of theatre managers, audience members, and governmental theatre policy' (p. 282), practices Brooke's own managerial experiences and her friendship with Mary Ann Yates made her all too aware of.

Beyond the relationship between published novels and the public theatre, considerable research has appeared this year on more fundamental questions about what happens when creative work is undertaken between media. Paul Goring's article, '*Gulliver's Travels* on the Mid-Eighteenth-Century Stage; or, What Is an Adaptation?' (*FMLS* 51[2015] 100–15), considers both Garrick's *Lilliput* [1756] and Charles Macklin's *True-born Irishman* [1761] as responses to Jonathan Swift's *Gulliver's Travels* in order to question current critical definitions of 'adaptation' by Julie Sanders, Linda Hutcheon, and others. A tendency to emphasize the importance of plot to adaptation has led works such as Garrick's to be considered adaptations when Macklin's is not; yet as Goring is right to suggest, 'Considering such non-narrative adaptation practices alongside more traditional story-based forms of adaptation can illuminate the breadth of an author's legacy as well as the variety of ways in which new authors relate to their literary forebears' (p. 114).

While Goring focuses on how playwrights adapted prose, Jayne Hildebrand considers what poetry gains from performance in this period. Her article, 'Cowper's Theatrical Blank Verse: Shakespeare, Garrick, and *The Task*' (*SEL* 55[2015] 579–602), looks beyond a superficial anti-theatricality to read Cowper's long poem as a work 'deeply preoccupied with the metaphorics of theatrical performance' (p. 579). Hildebrand's key points here are, first, that Cowper's desire to 'make verse speak the language of prose' correlates with Garrick's own innovative delivery of Shakespearean verse (p. 581); and, second, that a distinctly Garrickean understanding of the performer as one channelling the ideas of the author finds an echo in the centrality of an 'evacuated self' to Cowper's poetry (p. 582). Rather like Goring's meditation on adaptation, Hildebrand's work shows some of what may be achieved when one moves from a narrow definition of what is transferred between media.

Three other articles published in 2015 also consider stage–page relations, but in their case with respect to manuscripts. Hilary Havens, in her 'Omitting Lady Grace: *The Provok'd Husband* in Frances Burney's *Camilla* and *The Wanderer*' (*JECS* 38[2015] 413–24), follows Frances Burney's reworking of Colley Cibber's work [1728] in her drafts of *Camilla* [1796] and the published version of *The Wanderer* [1814]. Throughout the piece, Havens treats the play as a window onto both Burney's techniques for commenting on a contemporary vogue for private theatricals and her general editorial process. This is another piece that would not be out of place in O'Quinn and Russell's 'Theatre–Novel Nexus' subsection. The other two articles here, however, offer a different approach to handwritten sources. Robert W. Jones's 'Texts, Tools and Things: An Approach to Manuscripts of Richard Brinsley Sheridan's *The School for Scandal*' (*RES* 66[2015] 723–43) treats MS Harvard Thr 5.1 as a rich palimpsest of theatrical activity rather than a manifestation of Sheridan's sole intentions. This makes the document 'fundamentally a working life' (p. 739), gradually taking shape from 1770 onwards, and an important reminder that the 'amended and devolved' status of a text can be what makes it valuable to scholarship (p. 741). In an article entitled 'Possessing Parts and Owning Plays: Charles Macklin and the Prehistory of Dramatic Literary Property' (*ThS* 56[2015] 268–90), Jane Wessel refers to manuscript as part of an impressive discussion on how eighteenth-century limitations on literary property, such as the absence of performance copyright, affected actor-playwrights. Focusing on Charles Macklin, Wessel positions him as a prescient innovator, one who abandoned the traditional customs of part-possession in favour of a forceful assertion of his right to control performance. The latter approach entailed the use of Macklin's authorial rights to advance his career as an actor, as seen, for example, in his innovative decision to keep his *Love à la mode* [1759] as an unpublished manuscript, a technique later adopted by such actor-playwrights as Sheridan and George Colman.

Macklin is also the subject of an essay by Kristina Straub in 'Georgian Theatre in an Information Age', entitled 'The Newspaper "Trial" of Charles Macklin's *Macbeth* and the Theatre as Juridical Public Sphere' (*ECF* 27[2015] 395–418), which argues that the actor's frequent protests and claims for justice 'made him a figurehead for everything about the theatre as a space in which the lower classes, the not-English, actors, and women had voices that could challenge hegemonic systems of status, ethnicity and gender' (p. 403). Straub's analysis is exemplary of the intermingling of intermediality and sociability at which the special issue as a whole aims. A number of publications this year also seek to achieve this, with a particular emphasis—to repeat Straub—on the 'not-English' and 'women'.

A special issue of *Eighteenth-Century Life*, edited by David O'Shaughnessy and publishing proceedings from a 2012 conference on the London Irish of the long eighteenth century, contains two pieces on the role the theatre had to play in the constitution of this 'not-English' group. O'Shaughnessy's own contribution, 'Making a Play for Patronage: Dennis O'Bryen's *A Friend in Need Is a Friend Indeed* (1783)' (*ECLife* 39[2015] 183–211), assesses the neglected contribution of Irish playwrights to late eighteenth-century culture, with a detailed focus on Dennis O'Bryen (1755–1832). O'Bryen's only play emerges as the key means by which this man made his name: in the character of the Irish creditor Ragan, it simultaneously damned two of Charles James Fox's enemies, Lord Shelburne and the Jewish John King, and so helped bring its writer to the attention of Fox himself. Elsewhere in the volume, Helen Burke (also a contributor to O'Quinn and Russell's collection and producing here another intermedial piece) provides an article entitled 'The Irish Joke, Migrant Networks, and the London Irish in the 1680s' (*ECLife* 39[2015] 41–65), which examines mockery of the Irish on the stage and the page as a distorted record of the development of the London Irish community, and shows how the close reading of such gags unlocks a rich mine of material. Burke herself finishes her article with a glance at how 'the joke-book Irishman' (p. 61) evolves in the hands of the Derry-born George Farquhar in particular.

Farquhar is also to be found in James Evans's article, 'Adapting the Stratagem: Goldsmith's *She Stoops to Conquer*' (*ANQ* 28[2015] 34–8), which rereads Oliver Goldsmith's *She Stoops to Conquer* [1773] as an adaptation of *The Beaux' Stratagem* [1707]. Evans pays particular attention to Goldsmith's Kate as a role born from the hybridization of Farquhar's much more sharply distinguished characters, a process resulting in 'the creation of a new English heroine' (p. 37). Such an attention to what makes something English (as well as 'not-English') also runs through an article by Catherine Jaffe and Elisa Martín-Valdepeñas Yagüe's essay on 'Gender, Translation, and Eighteenth-Century Women Dramatists: Elizabeth Griffith's *The School for Rakes* (1769) and María Lorenza de los Ríos y Loyo's *El Eugenio* (1801)' (*ECent* 56[2015] 41–57). The authors show how both plays move away from Beaumarchais's *Eugénie* [1767] by developing the 'secondary female character, the go-between, and employ nationalistic discourse in order to introduce new possibilities for gender roles, modern roles for new times that they cast somewhat ironically as harking back to traditional national values' (p. 53).

One final area of not-Englishness present in this year's work concerns the Americas. A short piece by Matthew Duquès, 'John Dennis's Dramatis Personae' (*N&Q* 62[2015] 271–3), identifies a new source for Dennis's *Liberty Asserted* [1704], namely Louis Armand's *New Voyages to North America* [1703], which provided the names of two of the play's characters, Sakia and Okima. This decision reveals the plays 'multicultural roots' (p. 271), part of a larger pattern in theatrical writing of this period that sought to balance the unfamiliar and the probable. Such balancing constitutes the subject of Jace Weaver's overview of cultural interactions between Native Americans and Europe in a piece entitled 'Shakespeare among the "Salvages": The Bard in Red Atlantic Performance' (*TJ* 67[2015] 433–43), which includes passages on a number of Iroquois and Cherokee visits in the eighteenth century. Weaver emphasizes the role of Shakespeare in these visits, whose plays were performed by the British, he argues, as a kind of 'cultural imperialism' (p. 442).

All the above articles indicate the extent to which the theatre was, in Straub's assessment, a space where certain groups could challenge 'hegemonic systems of status'. Taken together, they also show how such challenges helped constitute these very systems, as Dennis puts down 'multicultural roots' and Goldsmith mines Farquhar for an English heroine. Such complex processes are at the heart of Helen E.M. Brooks's *Actresses, Gender, and the Eighteenth-Century Stage: Playing Women*, published by Palgrave Macmillan and presenting female performers from the late seventeenth to the early nineteenth century as 'the site of important cultural negotiations over radically shifting gender roles' (p. 6). She does this in the course of five remarkably lucid chapters: on the economic power of actresses ('Playing for Money'), on female rhetorical power ('Playing the Passions'), on travesty and breeches parts ('Playing Men'), on techniques of sincerity ('Playing Herself'), and on motherhood and performance ('Playing Mothers'). Dora Jordan and Sarah Siddons dominate the last two chapters and appear frequently elsewhere in this work, although Brooks also focuses on the careers of Peg Woffington, Susannah Cibber, and Anne Oldfield where appropriate, and even manages multiple references to second-tier and middling actresses. This book's range of dates and people is further supplemented by its careful attention to regional as well as London theatre, with Brooks arguing that it was when actresses were away from the capital that they had the greatest control over their business (p. 34). Overall, Brooks's comprehensive approach, along with her clear prose, makes this an excellent book for undergraduates as well as established scholars. While much of the material here may be familiar to the latter, Brooks is often able to cast things in a new light, not least by emphasizing the dynamics of performance over those of the text. She demonstrates how the performance of emotional women (such as Jane Shore) required a stereotype-defying level of self-control from actresses—a paradox male writers moved to contain, either by portraying actresses as deceptive sirens or by vaunting their own instruction of female performers. When discussing the performance of male roles by women, Brooks makes good use of the work of Thomas Laqueur to co-ordinate travesty with the one-sex gender model and breeches parts with the two-sex gender binary. The final chapters of the book, on the construction of actress's 'authenticity', reach their climax when connecting the work of

Jordan and Siddons to the interests of female writers of the eighteenth century, since both groups possessed a remarkable capacity for 'blurring the lines between sincerity and performance' (p. 116). The last section, on motherhood, is, unfortunately, the weakest part of the book, and, compared to the insights of earlier chapters adds little new, particularly given the recent publication of *Stage Mothers* (BuckUP [2014]), to which Brooks herself contributed a chapter (also, in part, on Jordan and Siddons).

Siddons's joy at inheriting Garrick's dressing room and, especially, its large mirror, constitutes a key example in a fascinating survey article by Terry F. Robinson, entitled ' "The glass of fashion and the mould of form": The Histrionic Mirror and Georgian-Era Performance' (*ECLife* 39[2015] 30–65). In this piece, Robinson charts 'the impact that mirrors had on . . . theatrical and social performance' (p. 32) in the long eighteenth century, a time when the theatre became not just a moral mirror but also a reflector of 'material and physical aspects of culture' (p. 31). Mirrors themselves appeared in theatre architecture, fostering 'a visual exchange that obscured the divide between auditorium and stage' (p. 38), and in acting manuals, frontispieces, poetry, and prints. Robinson shows how, in each medium, the mirror sharpens issues of theatrical authenticity, marking a 'split between imitation and morality, surface and depth' (p. 54). By the article's end, it is clear that the mirror has become something other than what the *Rover*'s Angellica calls an 'undeceiving glass' (p. 54).

While many publications examined in this chapter have pursued an interest in media and sociability in (roughly speaking) the Georgian era, *The Lively Arts of the London Stage, 1675–1725*, edited by Kathryn Lowerre and published by Ashgate, instead makes a deliberate choice to concentrate 'on an exciting period of theatrical and musical volatility at the turn of the century encompassing the span of a hypothetical audience member's actual theatre going' (p. 1). In the context of this year's other critical labours, Lowerre's introductory argument, which characterizes a period running from John Dryden to John Gay as one when all the arts were 'deeply interrelated' (p. 2), is significant. Such interrelation of artistic disciplines seems an important step towards the intermedial and sociable theatre articulated by O'Quinn and Russell. As for *The Lively Arts*, contributions to all three sections of the book provide ample evidence for artistic interrelation. Part I examines a competition between composers to set William Congreve's masque *The Judgement of Paris* [1701], with Olive Baldwin and Thelma Wilson focusing on the singers (pp. 11–26); Robert Rawson on one of the competitors, the composer Gottfried Finger (pp. 27–46); and Matt Robertson on the performance space and staging (pp. 47–62). All three essays are rich in detail, something that is also characteristic of the book as a whole. Later chapters, on eighteenth-century drama specifically, include a piece by Sean M. Parr entitled 'John Pepusch, Aesthetics, and the Sister Arts' (pp. 85–112), which presents Pepusch's *The Union of the Three Sister Arts*, an afterpiece composed for a St Cecilia's Day performance on 22 November 1723 at Lincoln's Inn Fields, as an innovative 'attempt to distinguish and unify the sister arts', making the cantata 'more than a pleasant light afterpiece—its aesthetic program elevates vocal music and promotes artistic unity' (p. 108). Elsewhere, a chapter by

Jennifer Thorp, 'From Scaramouche to Harlequin: Dances "in Grotesque Characters" on the London Stage' (pp. 113–28), offers another highly detailed study of stage phenomena, concluding on the observation that a tendency to equate grotesque with *commedia* dance reflects 'an era of constant transition and redefinition in theatrical dancing' (p. 126). Thorp's work is followed by a piece from Amanda Eubanks Winkler, 'Madness "Free from Vice": Musical Eroticism in the Pastoral World of *The Fickle Shepherdess*' (pp. 149–70), which, through careful musical and literary analysis, examines the 'stunt casting' (p. 169) of Anne Bracegirdle in a breeches role for a 1703 adaptation of Thomas Randolph's *Amyntas* [1632]. The adaptation added a musical mad scene for Bracegirdle which combined the titillation of a cross-dressed woman with the erotic potential of staged female insanity.

One final essay from this collection, by Melissa Bloom Bissonette, considers eighteenth-century drama. Under the title 'The Right to Write; or, Colley Cibber and *The Drury Lane Monster*' (pp. 243–58), Bissonette reveals how John Gay's *Three Hours After Marriage* 'offers a pointed commentary on farce, writers, and propriety which has been all but erased from history' (p. 244). This interpretation is all the more important as later critics have tended to read the piece as a satire on Cibber, when such assessments in fact 'originated as intentional devaluations of the play and the men involved on a social more than an aesthetic basis' (p. 244). Nicely summarizing contemporary responses to Cibber and popular entertainment as an example of how 'The battle for the high road was staged on "low" ground' (p. 258), Bissonette concludes with the observation that Gay's play may serve as an emblem of this period's 'new anxiety over generic instability, mob rule and the ascent of the low' (p. 258). Such work fulfils the aims of Lowerre's collection, while also looking forward to the concerns over media and sociability found in works from later in the 1700s by so much other research published in 2015.

Sociability and media together thus represent key themes for much work published this year, whether it be studies of anti-theatricality on page and stage, or the conditions and achievements of a performer's career. Four articles, however, fall outside such a summarization. The first of these, by Kate Novotny Owen, appears under the title 'Dramatic Entertainments of a Mixt Kind: The Form of Mixture in Early English Pantomime' (*ECS* 48[2015] 503–20). Having examined 2,650 individual pantomime performances, Owen identifies five forms of mixture: 'alternating, all serious, all grotesque, intermixed (grotesque and serious), and intermixed (grotesque and other)' (p. 506). Statistical analysis of these five categories gives some illuminating conclusions, notably that 'pantomime as a whole associates much more closely with *commedia dell'arte* than with the classical tradition' (p. 508). Yet this article also pays laudable attention to the problems of such statistical methods: Owens demonstrates how even an apparently homogeneous pantomime (all grotesque or all serious) may create a 'subtle homogeneity' as an afterpiece to a very different kind of work (p. 513). Indeed, such a mixture—illustrated here with reference not just to pantomime texts and performances but also parodies of pantomime—connects the genre to 'other places both within and beyond the theatre, where incompatible categories not only mingled but merged', such as the comic epilogues spoken by tragic actresses.

Owen's article is part of a special issue of *Eighteenth-Century Studies* on the topic of performance, edited by Kathleen Wilson. Wilson's introduction (*ECS* 48[2015] 375–90) presents three theses about performance and history, which share only some of O'Quinn and Russell's concerns: 'that understanding performance as a politically charged social practice draws attention to what people actually did'; 'that the embodiment at the heart of performance... underlines how bodies... can themselves disrupt or transform normative categories of "historical agency"'; and 'that performances of all kinds... reveal the existence of imaginaries that did not necessarily put the nation-state at their centre' (pp. 376–7). As well as Owen's piece, an article by John Robbins, 'Up in the Air: Balloonomania and Scientific Performance' (*ECS* 48[2015] 521–38), also focuses on eighteenth-century English culture, to argue that the activity (and showmanship) of ballooning provided eighteenth-century writers with 'a tool for actively shaping and modulating public perceptions about emerging technologies' (p. 522). Elizabeth Inchbald's popular farce, *The Mogul's Tale; or, the Descent of the Balloon* [1784], exemplifies this, intervening 'in contemporary public perspectives on ballooning... and providing a palliative against fears' over the threat of new aeronautical science (p. 522). Rather than using this insight to argue for the importance of the theatre to the sociable and intermedial dynamics of the eighteenth century (as would—perhaps—have been the case in 'Georgian Theatre in an Information Age'), Robbins instead ends his analysis (and the issue as a whole) by making a contiguous point about the extent and importance of collaboration between the humanities to the sciences in the eighteenth century, something modern scientists and humanists, he notes, would do well to continue today.

As well as the special issue of *Eighteenth-Century Studies*, two other publications diverge from O'Quinn and Russell's focus on media and sociability, and propose their own directions for future research. Daniel Cook and Nicholas Seager's edited collection, *The Afterlives of Eighteenth-Century Fiction*, reviewed fully in Section 2 above, contains David A. Brewer's 'Rethinking Fictionality in the Eighteenth-Century Puppet Theatre' (pp. 174–92). This essay turns to the high-end puppet productions of Henry Fielding's *The Author's Farce* and *The Covent Garden Tragedy* in order both to interrogate current theories of fictionality (notably the work of Catherine Gallagher and Nicholas Paige) and to reconstruct 'vernacular theories of fictionality' (p. 175). After providing a lively summary of the practices of eighteenth-century puppet theatre, he exposes the 'sheer dizziness' of a performance in which (for *The Author's Farce*) one might see 'a puppet recalling a live performer playing a puppet, who is playing the ghost of Sir Farcical Comick... who... recalls Cibber' (p. 183). Such a baroque situation ultimately 'blurs the line between persons and things in the realm of character' and questions 'the utility of insisting upon the difference between the material and the immaterial or the embodied and the disembodied' (p. 184). Current critical approaches, Brewer observes, are far less willing to accept such tangled simultaneity than eighteenth-century audiences seem to have been. To correct this, we are invited to treat the (admittedly esoteric) 'high-end puppet versions of Fielding's most metatheatrical plays' as 'the "normal exception": the seemingly oddball that nonetheless reveals a whole host of broader, often only half-articulated presumptions and desires' (p. 188).

Secondly, this reviewer's own article, '*Comédien*-Actor-*Paradoxe*: The Anglo-French Source of Diderot's *Paradoxe sur le comédien*' (*TJ* 67[2015] 83–96), examining the chain of translation and re-translation of acting treatises between France and England that resulted in Denis Diderot's *Paradoxe sur le comédien* (written throughout the 1770s, published 1830) is, with Robinson's article on mirrors, one of only a few pieces of research to reflect on the period's theoretical approaches to performance (for another, albeit exclusively on the French stage and so beyond my remit here, see Jeffrey M. Leichman's 'What They Talked About When they Talked About Acting: Clairon via Diderot and Talma' (*ECS* 48[2015] 417–36)). My article concludes with a warning that, even as we rightly emphasize how embedded the theatre is in its particular society, we should never lose sight of the very fluidity that allows such infiltration, remembering, as it were, 'the capacity for writing about performance in this period to cross political and aesthetic borders' (p. 96). In a year when drama's media and sociability have received great scrutiny, such a warning should remain in place for the work that builds upon the research of 2015.

**Books Reviewed**

Barnard, Teresa, ed. *British Women and the Intellectual World in the Long Eighteenth Century*. Ashgate. [2015] pp. xviii + 194. £62.99 ISBN 9 7814 7243 7457.

Brack, O.M., Jr., Leslie Chilton, and Walter H. Keithley, *The Miscellaneous Writings of Tobias Smollett*. Routledge. [2015] pp. 489. £110 ISBN 9 7818 4893 5037.

Brooks, Helen E.M. *Actresses, Gender, and the Eighteenth-Century Stage: Playing Women*. PalMac. [2015] pp. x + 201. £60 ISBN 9 7802 3029 8330.

Brown, Leslie Ellen. *Artful Virtue: The Interplay of the Beautiful and the Good in the Scottish Enlightenment*. Ashgate. [2015] pp. viii + 253. £73.99 ISBN 9 7814 7244 8484.

Cook, Daniel, and Nicholas Seager. *The Afterlives of Eighteenth-Century Fiction*. CUP. [2015] pp. ix + 304. £67 ISBN 9 7811 0705 4684.

Cousins, A.D., and Geoffrey Payne, eds. *Home and Nation in British Literature from the English to the French Revolutions*. CUP. [2015] pp. xi + 288. £64.99 ISBN 9 7811 0706 4409.

Day, Gary, and Jack Lynch, eds. *Encyclopedia of British Literature 1660–1789*. 3 vols. Wiley. [2015] pp. xxviii + 1,474. £385 ISBN 9 7814 4433 0205.

De Freitas Boe, Ana, and Abby Coykendall, eds. *Heteronormativity in Eighteenth-Century Literature and Culture*. Ashgate. [2015] pp. xi + 219. £62.99 ISBN 9 7814 7243 0175.

DeGabriele, Peter. *Sovereign Power and the Enlightenment: Eighteenth-Century Literature and the Problem of the Political*. BuckUP. [2015] pp. xxxiv + 181. £47.95 ISBN 9 7816 1148 6964.

Dussinger, John A., ed. *Correspondence with Sarah Wescomb, Frances Grainger, and Laetitia Pilkington* by Samuel Richardson. CUP. [2015] pp. lxix + 398. £82 ISBN 9 7811 3904 6015.

Griffin, Dustin. *Swift and Pope: Satirists in Dialogue.* CUP. [2014] pp. 260. pb £30.99 ISBN 9 7811 0742 2544.

Harrow, Sharon ed. *British Sporting Literature and Culture in the Long Eighteenth Century.* Ashgate. [2015] pp. xvi + 232. £62.99 ISBN 9 7814 7246 5085.

Hopkins, David. *Conversing with Antiquity: English Poets and the Classics, from Shakespeare to Pope.* OUP. [2014] pp. 352. pb £25 ISBN 9 7801 9870 6960.

Ingrassia, Catherine, ed. *The Cambridge Companion to Women's Writing in Britain 1660–1789.* CUP. [2015] pp. xx + 263. £19.99 ISBN 9 7811 0701 3162.

Lemmings, David, Heather Kerr, and Robert Phiddian, eds. *Passions, Sympathy and Print Culture.* PalMac. [2015] pp. xi + 290. $100 ISBN 9 7811 3745 5406.

Lowerre, Kathryn. *The Lively Arts of the London Stage, 1675–1725.* Ashgate. [2014] pp. 325. £65 ISBN 9 7814 0945 5332.

Nandrea, Lorri G. *Misfit Forms: Paths Not Taken by the British Novel.* FordUP. [2015] pp. x + 272. £45 ISBN 9 7808 2326 3431.

New, Melvyn, Peter de Voogd, and Judith Hawley, eds. *Sterne, Tristram, Yorick: Tercentenary Essays on Laurence Sterne.* UDelP. [2015] pp. xvi + 268. £65.94 ISBN 9 7816 1149 5706.

O'Neill, Lindsay. *The Opened Letter: Networking in the Early Modern British World.* UPennP. [2015] pp. 264. £31 ISBN 9 7808 1224 6483.

Power, Henry. *Epic into Novel: Henry Fielding, Scriblerian Satire, and the Consumption of Classical Literature.* OUP. [2015] pp. xiv + 232. £55 ISBN 9 7801 9872 3875.

Prendergast, Amy. *Literary Salons Across Britain and Ireland in the Long Eighteenth Century.* PalMac. [2015] pp. ix + 238. £55 ISBN 9 7811 3751 2727.

Schellenberg, Betty A., ed. *Correspondence Primarily on Sir Charles Grandison (1750–1754)* by Samuel Richardson. CUP. [2015] pp. xlvii + 288. £82. ISBN 9 7805 2183 2182.

Smith, David Nowell. *On Voice in Poetry: The Work of Animation.* PalMac. [2015] pp. 202. £58 ISBN 9 7811 3730 8221.

Starr, G. Gabrielle. *Lyric Generations: Poetry and the Novel in the Long Eighteenth Century.* JHUP. [2015] pp. 298. pb $29.95 ISBN 9 7814 2141 8223.

Still, Judith. *Derrida and Other Animals: The Boundaries of the Human.* EdinUP. [2015] pp. 416. £85 ISBN 9 7807 4868 0979.

Whelan, Timothy. *Other British Voices: Women, Poetry, and Religion, 1766–1840.* PalMac. [2015] pp. 265. £55 ISBN 9 7811 1373 43611.

Whitehouse, Tessa. *The Textual Culture of English Protestant Dissent 1720–1800.* OUP. [2015] pp. xii + 250. £55 ISBN 9 7801 9871 7843.

Widmayer, Anne F. *Theatre and the Novel from Behn to Fielding*. OUP. [2015] pp. xii + 264. £60 ISBN 9 7807 2941 1653.

Wilson, Jennifer Preston, and Elizabeth Kraft. *Approaches to Teaching the Novels of Henry Fielding*. MLA. [2015] pp. xii + 244. £22.50 ISBN 9 7816 0329 2245.

# XIII

# Literature 1780–1830: The Romantic Period

MAXINE BRANAGH-MISCAMPBELL, BARBARA LEONARDI,
PAUL WHICKMAN, MATTHEW WARD,
AND OMAR F. MIRANDA

This chapter has four sections: 1. General and Prose; 2. The Novel; 3. Poetry;
4. Drama. Section 1 is by Maxine Branagh-Miscampbell; section 2 is by
Barbara Leonardi; section 3 is by Matthew Ward and Paul Whickman; section
4 is by Omar F. Miranda.

## 1. General and Prose

Works focusing on political and philosophical writings of the Romantic period
published in 2015 include both author-specific studies and broader studies of
Romantic-era philosophy and its permeation in literary works. These works
will be dealt with in the first part of this section. It will then move on to discuss
recent work in the field of women's writing, focusing on three longer works,
and articles on Frances Burney, Mary Wollstonecraft, Felicia Hemans, Mary
Tighe, and specific male writers. Finally, this section will deal with works in
the field of material and print culture, which account for many of the general
and prose works published in 2015.

Kevin Gilmartin's book-length study of William Hazlitt, *William Hazlitt:
Political Essayist*, joins Stephen Burley's 2014 work, *Hazlitt the Dissenter:
Religion, Philosophy, and Politics, 1766–1816* (PalMac) in the field, proving
that, as Gilmartin argues in his introduction, 'William Hazlitt has enjoyed a
striking revival of interest among literary critics in recent decades' (p. 1).
Gilmartin's book seeks to offer a better understanding of Hazlitt's politics in
order to 'deepen our appreciation of the social and collective terms of his
literary achievement, and of the wider relations between early nineteenth-
century literary and aesthetic criticism and the British radical tradition' (p. 35).
The book is wide-ranging in its analysis of Hazlitt's political writings.
Gilmartin's combination of careful close reading of Hazlitt's 'distinctive
political voice' (p. 25), focusing on style and form, while also situating him in
relation to the wider press culture in the period, offers a fascinating and

*The Year's Work in English Studies, Volume 96 (2017)* © *The Author 2017. Published by Oxford
University Press on behalf of the English Association. All rights reserved.*
*For Permissions, please email: journals.permissions@oup.com*
doi:10.1093/ywes/max014

important insight into Hazlitt's contribution as a political writer within Romantic print culture.

Ulf Schulenberg's *Romanticism and Pragmatism: Richard Rorty and the Idea of a Poeticized Culture* asks, 'What role has Romanticism played for the development of pragmatism, and especially for the renaissance of pragmatism?' (p. 4). Schulenberg seeks to answer this question through a study of the philosopher Richard Rorty. However, the book's focus on the significance of pragmatism in the Romantic period in general is probably most valuable for readers of this section. The analysis of Rorty's writing in the first half of this work paves the way for a discussion of the relationship between pragmatism and Romanticism in the second half. The chapters in this second half focus on 'how Romantic writers prepared for the establishment of a poeticized culture' (p. 11) through a discussion of Thoreau, Emerson, and Whitman in chapters 4 and 5, and William James and John Dewey in chapters 6 and 7. This wide-ranging work offers a new perspective on the cross-over between pragmatism, humanism, anti-authoritarianism, and postmetaphysics.

Angela Esterhammer, Diane Piccitto, and Patrick Vincent's *Romanticism, Rousseau, Switzerland: New Prospects* is a collection of essays which seeks to position Rousseau in a Swiss context and offer new readings of his key philosophies in light of the recognition of the influence of Swiss philosophy, science, and the Swiss landscape on Rousseau's writings and the Romantic authors inspired by him. The work 'engages with numerous approaches in contemporary scholarship to undertake a re-evaluation of the significance of Rousseau and Switzerland for Romantic studies' (p. 16). The first essays in the collection focus on rereading some of Rousseau's major theories and their representation in Romantic-period works. These include his views on education in Enit K. Steiner's chapter, 'Romantic Education, Concealment, and Orchestrated Desire in Rousseau's *Émile* and Frances Brooke's *Julia Mandeville*' (pp. 21–37), and 'the formation of the Romantic conception of suicide' (p. 38) in Michelle Faubert's 'Romantic Suicide, Contagion, and Rousseau's *Julie*' (pp. 38–53). The next two essays offer different views of Rousseau's interest in 'organic and inorganic or mechanical life' (p. 13), with Rachel Corkle's essay 'Seeing Jean-Jacques' Nature: Rousseau's Call for a Botanist Reader' (pp. 54–67) arguing that Rousseau's *Lettres sur la botanique* and *Dialogues* offer 'a vision of the good botanist and of the good reader' (p. 63), while Wendy C. Nielsen's 'Rousseau's *Pygmalion* and Automata in the Romantic Period' (pp. 68–84) focuses on Rousseau's fascination with 'the artificial nature of society' (p. 69). The essays in the second half of the book focus more on the influence of the Swiss landscape on Rousseau and Romanticism more generally, with topics including literary tourism, in Nicola J. Watson's 'Rousseau on the Tourist Trail' (pp. 84–100), and alpine tourism more broadly in Simon Bainbridge's 'A 'Melancholy Occurrence' in the Alps: Switzerland, Mont Blanc, and an Early Critique of Mountaineering' (pp. 150–67). Other essays in the collection also focus on the influence of Switzerland and the Swiss landscape on a variety of Romantic writers, both in Britain and in Europe, including 'James Boswell and Rousseau in Môtiers: Re-inscribing Childhood and Its (Auto)biographical Prospects' (pp. 101–16) by Gordon Turnbull, Pamela Buck's 'Prints, Panoramas, and Picturesque

Travel in Dorothy Wordsworth's *Journal of a Tour on the* Continent' (pp. 117–31), and 'Visionary Republics: Virtual Representations of Switzerland and Wordsworth's Lake District' (pp. 132–49) by Patrick Vincent. These essays offer a diverse range of new perspectives on Rousseau's work and its impact on Romantic-period writing and thought, as well as the impact of the landscape of Switzerland both on his work and the work of a variety of Romantic writers.

Three articles published in *European Romantic Review* also focus on Romantic-period philosophy. Jonathan Kramnick's 'An Aesthetics and Ecology of Presence' (*ERR* 26[2015] 315–27) argues for 'an anti-representational model of perceptual experience' (p. 315) during the Romantic period by tracing connections between a variety of different writing forms by poets John Dyer and James Thomson, the letters and fiction of Laurence Sterne, Thomas Reid's *An Inquiry into the Human Mind on the Principles of Common Sense* [1764], and in the works of Hogarth and Lord Kames. In 'Hegel and the Prehistory of the Postracial' (*ERR* 26[2015] 289–99), Rei Terada examines Hegel's theory of race in light of what the author terms the 'post-racial', which he defines in two ways, as 'the rhetorical erasure of an actually existing racialized violence' and in a '*logical sense*, in that 'non-raciality' must carry assumptions about what 'race' is, and assume the responsibility for deciding what it looks like, in order to testify to its absence' (p. 290; emphasis in the original). Finally, in ' "Wandering beneath the Unthinkable": Organization and Probability in Romanticism and the Nineteenth Century' (*ERR* 26[2015] 301–14), Arkady Plotnitsky argues that Romanticism, and the nineteenth century, 'were characterized by their persistent attempts to find an effective *concept* of organization' (p. 301; emphasis in the original). Plotnitsky approaches this through an examination of ontological thinking in the works of Hölderlin and argues that 'the Romantics...introduced a new type of ontology' (p. 304).

Three studies of women writers, pertinent to 'General and Prose', were published in 2015. Two of these are also covered in Section 2 of this chapter. The first is Melissa Sodeman's *Sentimental Memorials: Women and the Novel in Literary History*. Sodeman aims to 'put the history of the novel and women's literary history in conversation with book history to better read the situation of later eighteenth-century women novelists' (p. 3). Though focusing specifically on novelists Sophia Lee, Ann Radcliffe, Charlotte Smith, and Mary Robinson, Sodeman's work takes a literary-historical approach and is therefore also of use to the reader interested in the history of women's writing, specifically the conditions under which women were writing and how they reflected upon these within their literary output. Each of the four chapters is devoted to one of the women writers named above and 'aim[s] to show how these novels meaningfully respond to changes in the cultural status of literature, authorship, and sentimentality at the end of the eighteenth century, changes that stranded sentimental genres and left their mostly female practitioners on the margins of literary history' (pp. 8–9). Of particular interest is Sodeman's argument that these women novelists were responding to developments in literary history in sentimental novels themselves, 'memorializing, quite self-consciously, the conditions of their writing' (p. 13). Chapter

1, which focuses on Sophia Lee, argues that her novel *The Recess; or, A Tale of Other Times* [1783–5] draws on the work of sentimental historiography by William Robertson and David Hume, whom Sodeman terms 'sentimental historians' (p. 21), and lost antiquarian texts, specifically Macpherson's Ossianic fragments. In so doing, Sodeman argues that Lee reveals how the 'shared methods' of these two approaches 'come to characterize the uses of the past in late eighteenth-century print culture' (p. 22). Chapter 2 deals with Ann Radcliffe's self-conscious reflections on reading practices of the late eighteenth century in her novels, especially *The Romance of the Forest* [1791]. Sodeman argues that these reflections reveal Radcliffe's anxiety about the ephemeral nature of her own literary output (p. 56), reflecting 'the situation of women novelists at this time' (p. 77). In chapter 3, Sodeman goes on to deal with Charlotte Smith's 'sense of literary exile, her precarious relation to the literary marketplace and estrangement from Britain's literary and intellectual circles' (p. 81). She argues that this literary exile, and Smith's interest in it, is 'inseparable from form' (p. 81). In the final chapter, focusing on Mary Robinson, Sodeman argues that Robinson 'seeks to guarantee the endurance of her literary fame' with her novels serving as 'literary memorials' (p. 114). The combination of these four studies achieves what Sodeman sets out to do: to illustrate the extent to which the sentimental fictions of four women writers are self-reflective of, and act as memorials to, the challenges and insecurities of female authorship at the end of the eighteenth century.

The second work on women writers, also covered in Section 2, is Charlotte Gordon's *Romantic Outlaws: The Extraordinary Lives of Mary Wollstonecraft & Mary Shelley*. This biographical work is the first to position these two women writers together in the same edition, as mother and daughter. In so doing, Gordon seeks to shed new light on both Wollstonecraft and Shelley by exploring the intersections of their lives. An extensive work, the forty chapters alternate between focusing on Mary Wollstonecraft and Mary Shelley, with the final chapter drawing the two together. This section will focus primarily on Mary Wollstonecraft, while Section 2 below deals with Mary Shelley. Despite being clearly written for the general reader, *Romantic Outlaws* does draw upon critical works, the writers' own works, and published collections of letters. However, the lack of careful footnotes or endnotes, and of a full bibliography, are frustrating for the academic reader. The originality of this work lies in its structure. The alternating narratives make the parallels between these two writers' lives, and the influence of Wollstonecraft's legacy on Shelley, thought-provoking. The chapters focusing specifically on Wollstonecraft tend to centre more on a dramatic retelling of her life rather than the works she produced. For example, in chapter 8, which deals with *On the Education of Daughters* [1786], there is little attention paid to the content and reception of the work itself, with Gordon instead emphasizing Wollstonecraft's feelings. This is, however, less of a problem in the short chapter (12) devoted to *Vindication of the Rights of Men* [1790], and chapter 14, on *Vindication of the Rights of Woman* [1792], which give more attention to the reception of these two works. Although nothing in Gordon's work will come as much of a surprise to Wollstonecraft scholars, it is nonetheless an entertaining read, and one which cleverly draws together two extensive biographies and intertwines them in an interesting way. The final work dealing with women's writing included here is *The Cambridge Companion to Women's Writing in the Romantic Period*, edited by Devoney Looser (also reviewed Section 4 below). This work includes a number of chapters of particular interest to readers interested in 'General and Prose', specifically Anne K. Mellor's chapter on 'Essays and Political Writing' (pp. 44–57), which focuses on Mary Wollstonecraft, Mary Hays, Hannah More, and Anna Letitia Barbauld, 'and the enduring contributions each made to political and cultural debates' (p. 44). Also of interest is Elizabeth A. Fay's chapter on 'Travel Writing' (pp. 73–87), which gives a broad overview of the variety of travel writing by women and argues that 'Travel writing provided the middle-class reader with an affordable, if imaginative rather than substantial, substitute for the elite experience of the Grand Tour' (p. 73). Crystal B. Lake's chapter on 'History Writing and Antiquarianism' focuses on the 'diversity of women writer's contributions to Romantic history' (pp. 99–100), first of all in the historical writing of Catharine Macaulay, but also in the novels, poetry, and periodical writings by women in the period. As well as these chapters concentrating on specific modes of writing, this edition includes chapters focusing on wider issues in Romantic women's writing, including the global literary marketplace (Deirdre Coleman's 'The Global Context', pp. 129–43), familial and literary networks (Julia A. Carlson's 'Social, Familial, and Literary Networks', pp. 144–57), the financial challenges these writers faced (Jacqueline M. Labbe's 'The Economics of Female Authorship', pp. 158–68), the role of age and ageing in the careers of women writers (Devoney Looser's 'Age and Aging', pp. 169–82), national identity (Fiona Price's 'National Identities and Regional Affiliations', pp. 183–97), and sexuality (Jillian Heydt-Stevenson's 'Sexualities', pp. 198–212). This collection of essays sheds light on both well-known and less well-known women writers in to order to create 'more nuanced literary histories in the generations to come' (p. xviii).

A number of articles were also published on women writers of the Romantic period in 2015. Harriet Kramer Linkin's 'Mary Tighe's Newly Discovered Letters and Journals to Caroline Hamilton' (*Romanticism* 21[2015] 207–27) looks at a collection of forty-one letters sent from Mary Blachford Tighe to her cousin and sister-in-law Caroline Tighe Hamilton between 1793 and 1808, which Linkin found in the Hamilton family papers at the National Library of Ireland. These letters 'provide intimately detailed and seemingly unreserved accounts of Tighe's feelings and activities' (p. 207), including journal entries. Linkin argues that these letters reveal a great deal about Tighe's biography and 'offer rare glimpses of her composition practices and psychological development as a poet and novelist'; more broadly, they uncover new insights into 'the permutations and power of female or "romantic" friendships' (p. 223). Cassandra Ulph's 'Frances Burney's Private Professionalism' (*JECS* 38[2015] 377–93) focuses on the role that the intellectual and artistic network of Burney's father's household played in the formation of her identity as a female author, which, Ulph argues, is a construct of 'a hybrid blend of domestic privacy with public professionalism' (p. 377). Through an examination of her correspondence and novels, Ulph argues that Burney creates a space which is 'compatible with both her own fiercely guarded privacy and her sense of professional and creative integrity', and in so doing 'maintains separate, and appropriately feminine, professional and social personas' (p. 392). Elizabeth Edwards's '"Lonely and voiceless your halls must remain": Romantic-Era National Song and Felicia Hemans's *Welsh Melodies* (1822)' (*JECS* 38[2015] 83–97) offers a close reading of Felicia Hemans's song collection, *A Selection of Welsh Melodies*, focusing on the paratextual elements of the collection, particularly the use of quotations in the songs' footnotes. By making her sources explicit, Edwards argues, Hemans is 'carefully resetting her sources in the new context of the national melody movement' and showing 'how both distant and recent myths and histories can be transformed via the cultural work of song' (p. 94). Finally, Laura Kirkley's '*Maria, ou Le Malheur d'être femme*: Translating Mary Wollstonecraft in Revolutionary France' (*JECS* 38[2015] 239–55) focuses on Basile-Joseph Ducos's translation of *Maria, or the Wrongs of Woman* [1798] as a case study in order to examine the translator's role in the reception of Wollstonecraft on the Continent. Kirkley argues that, 'although the strategy of the translator . . . evinces sympathy for many aspects of Wollstonecraft's Revolutionary feminism, his subtle but significant changes to the source text also elide some of its most controversial and pioneering elements' (p. 239). Through a careful analysis of differences between the source text and the translation, Kirkley argues that by 'drawing on a established lexicon of sentiment, [Ducos] undermines Wollstonecraft's attempts to rework the familiar seduction plot into a narrative of feminist resistance', which leads to French readers encountering 'a diluted version of Wollstonecraft's feminism' (p. 252).

Three other articles deal with the works of specific male writers. Like Sodeman's monograph discussed above, Alys Mostyn's article 'Leigh Hunt's "World of Books": Bibliomania and the Fancy' (*Romanticism* 21[2015] 238–49) also addresses questions of authorial professionalization. Mostyn argues, through an examination of the aesthetic category of 'the Fancy', that 'aspects of [Hunt's] work suggest that he too [alongside Byron] was troubled by the possibility of being little more than a fanciful pretender to the title of author' (pp. 238–9); in so doing, she aims 'to chart previously underexamined connections between the discourse of the Fancy and issues of professionalisation in the period' (p. 239). Katey Castellano's 'Cobbet's Commons: Monastic Economies in a History of the Protestant "Reformation"' (*ERR* 26[2015] 575–90) offers a reading of William Cobbett's *History of the Protestant Reformation in England and Ireland* [1829] which argues that it 'has little to do with championing the Catholic religion' (p. 575) and instead is 'countering the naturalization of private property through Malthusian discourse about the poor' (p. 586). She argues that Cobbett contrasts 'the medieval Catholic world to that of Protestant liberalism' (p. 576) by representing Catholic monasteries as places which '[check] over-consumption and facilitat[e] the distribution of community sources' (p. 586). Finally, Ewan James Jones's 'John "Walking" Stewart and the Ethics of Motion' (*Romanticism* 21[2015] 119–31) argues for a fuller consideration of John Stewart's work. In so doing, Jones makes two wider claims: 'that the span of "Walking" Stewart's career, and the temper of his interests, permit us to unsettle the standard account of the transition from the Enlightenment to the Romantic period; and secondly, that one of the principal ways in which Stewart effects this unsettling—through his idiosyncratic application of a philosophy of "matter and motion"—both anticipates and challenges recent criticism in so-called "vibrant" or "radical" materialism' (pp. 119–20).

A theme that pervades a number of the studies published in 2015 is that of material culture and its role in facilitating Romantic-period British culture's understanding of its recent past. Emma Peacocke's *Romanticism and the Museum* makes use of four case studies in order to argue that Romantic authors saw the museum space 'as integral to a society in the throes of reform and reaction' (p. 4). Each of the first three case studies focuses on representations of public museums in literary texts: Wordsworth's *The Prelude* [1850], Walter Scott's *Waverley* [1814], and Maria Edgeworth's *Harrington* [1817]. The final chapter focuses on the debate that occurred in the periodical press surrounding the British Museum's purchase of the Elgin Marbles in 1816. Chapter 1, focusing on *The Prelude*, states that 'explicit engagement with a museum is at the heart of Wordsworth's poetic opus' (p. 17), which centres on 'the displacement of *The Penitent Magdalene* from the Carmelite convent to the walls of the Louvre' (p. 18). By focusing on this, Peacocke argues, 'Wordsworth turned to the museum as a space that could comfortably accommodate opposing views of history in the making' (pp. 55–6). Chapter 2 argues for the important symbolic role of portraits in Walter Scott's *Waverley*, stating that 'They are a part of the apparatus of the novel for investigating the past' (p. 58), and that 'Ideas of the public gallery are essential to *Waverley*'s historiography, its contrast of the past and present' (p. 58). Peacocke's examination of Edgeworth's *Harrington* in chapter 3 argues that 'galleries and museums provide a tool to dissect the national imaginary' (p. 87) and that 'Both author and novel rejoice in images ensconced in one of the great British public museums, inspiring their viewers to re-imagine the national heritage' (p. 111). The final chapter moves away from fictional accounts and portrayals of museum spaces in order to examine debates surrounding 'proprietorship' (p. 112) and 'display strategy' (p. 113) in Byron's *The Curse of Minerva*, published in the *New Monthly Magazine* in 1815, and Horatio Smith's 'The Statue of Theseus, and the Sculpture Room of Phidias', printed in the *London Magazine* in 1821. These four chapters serve to illustrate the myriad ways in which Romantic authors conceptualized the museum space and how they 'saw their nation's and world's past, present, and future in the emergent public museum' (p. 15). Also focusing on antiquarianism and museums is Robert W. Rix's ' "In darkness they grope": Ancient Remains and Romanticism in Denmark' (*ERR* 26[2015] 435–51). Rix's article explores the establishment and early development of the Nordic Museum of Antiquities, later the National Museum. This is achieved through an examination of 'the desire for collecting ancient objects and for imaginatively transcending these same objects' (p. 436) in Adam Oehlenschläger's early poetry and the theological work of N.F.S. Grundtvig.

Neil Ramsey and Gillian Russell's edited collection *Tracing War in British Enlightenment and Romantic Culture*, meanwhile, brings together essays focusing on 'the pervasive effects of war in Enlightenment and Romantic-period culture' (p. 1) and takes an interdisciplinary approach in order to fulfil 'the need for a critical war studies that problematizes assumptions about the ontology of war by focusing on its multiple, divergent, and productive traces' (p. 8). The collection covers the period from 1750 to 1850, and so this review will focus on those essays which fall more clearly in the Romantic period, and more specifically those that centre on works which fall in the 'General and Prose' category. Three of the chapters focus on Romantic-period art in relation to the representation of war. R.S. White's chapter, 'Victims of War: Battlefield Casualties and Literary Sensibility' (pp. 61–76), looks at engravings produced by the London print-seller Edward Orme depicting scenes from the Battle of Waterloo. He argues that 'The images belong not only with the art generated by war but also with the politics of sensibility' (p. 62). In chapter 8, on 'Turner's Desert Storm' (pp. 151–70), Philip Shaw examines Turner's *The Army of the Medes* [1801], a lost painting which, he argues, 'responds to the culmination of the British campaign against the French in Egypt at the turn of the nineteenth century', despite focusing on 'the destruction of a military force in ancient Persia' (p. 151). Finally, Thomas H. Ford focuses on the atmosphere of war in the paintings of David Wilkie and Turner, and the writing of Carl von Clausewitz, in 'Narrative and Atmosphere: War by Other Media in Wilkie, Clausewitz and Turner' (pp. 171–87).

Other essays in the collection focus on the representation of war in the public space of Romantic-period Britain. In chapter 5, 'Romantic Militarisation: Sociability, Theatricality and Military Science in the Woolwich Rotunda, 1814–2013' (pp. 96–112), Gillian Russell argues that 'The Romantic period is a formative phase in the development of a modern militarised society based on the construction of credible fictions of knowledge about war' (p. 97). Russell 'trace[s] the phenomenon of Romantic militariza-tion, particularly the capacity of war to hide itself in plain sight' in relation to the Woolwich Rotunda (p. 98). Neil Ramsey's essay on 'Exhibiting Discipline: Military Science and the Naval and Military Library and Museum' (pp. 113–31) also argues that war became part of the public space in the Romantic period with the museum 'creating an almost religious historical aura around the nation's recent past' (p. 114). In chapter 7, 'Battling Bonaparte after Waterloo: Re-enactment, Representation and "The Napoleon Bust Business"' (pp. 132–50), Simon Bainbridge argues that 'the war with Bonaparte remained a profound presence in British society, fought not only through public re-stagings, representations, and re-enactments of Waterloo but also through the placement of cultural objects within the British domestic space' (p. 133). The final essay in the collection, Nick Mansfield's 'Destroyer and Bearer of Worlds: The Aesthetic Doubleness of War' (pp. 188–203), takes a slightly different approach and traces 'the connection between Romantic aesthetics through Romantic era thinking about war to modern constructions of war in aesthetic terms' (p. 188) through an examination of aesthetic discourse in Kant's *Critique of Judgement* and Clausewitz's *On War*. The essays in this edition work together to make a persuasive case for the pervasive impact of war on Romantic-period British culture.

Taking a material approach to Romantic-period print culture, Ina Ferris's *Book-Men, Book Clubs, and the Romantic Literary Sphere* takes a fresh look at the liminal figure of the 'bookman', a book collector or bibliophile, and his relationship to book clubs. Ferris defines these as 'in a literal sense *book* clubs in that they were organized around the book-object: formed to produce, sponsor, or obtain and circulate books' rather than 'reading societies' or 'reading communities', and the wider literary sphere (p. 3). Ferris's study is divided into two parts. The first looks at the 'friction between book culture and the literary sphere by focusing on the debate over the bookman's insertion of himself into the matrix of production' (p. 6), using case studies of urban book clubs: the Roxburghe Club and the Bannatyne Club. Part II focuses on rural book clubs in order to argue that these 'played a major role in the decentralization of literary culture and the fostering of regional consciousness' (p. 12). Ferris distinguishes her study from the field of the history of reading by focusing on the exchange and collection of books as physical objects. Her study of the bookman and book clubs makes a key distinction between book culture and literary culture, and offers an important new insight into our understanding of Romantic-period print culture.

The special issue of *Journal for Eighteenth-Century Studies* on 'Networks of Improvement' included a number of articles of interest. Timothy Whelan's 'Mary Steele, Mary Hays and the Convergence of Women's Literary Circles in the 1790s' (*JECS* 38[2015] 511–24) deals with the merging of two dissenting literary circles in the 1790s; that of Mary Steele of Broughton and Elizabeth Coltman of Leicester, and a London-based group revolving around William Godwin, Mary Hays, and Crabb Robinson. Whelan argues that the coming together of these two groups, as revealed in life-writings and poetry rather than through formal meetings, 'produced a diverse, cross-pollinated coterie of men and women' (p. 516). Jon Mee and Jennifer Wilkes's article, 'Transpennine Enlightenment: The Literary and Philosophical Societies and Knowledge Networks in the North, 1781–1830' (*JECS* 38[2015] 599–612), investigates literary and philosophical societies in Manchester and Newcastle and argues that these form part of a wider 'transpennine Enlightenment' which should not 'be understood only in terms of . . . "the science and technology interface"' (p. 599), and that these societies 'played a distinctive role in the Industrial Enlightenment' (p. 600). Turning to rural Scotland, Mark Towsey's article, '"Store their minds with much valuable knowledge": Agricultural Improvement at the Selkirk Subscription Library, 1799–1814' (*JECS* 38[2015] 569–84), examines 'the circulation of 'useful' books' in Selkirk in the Scottish Borders (p. 570). Through an examination of the Selkirk subscription library's records, Towsey argues that 'the library played a central role in the dissemination of new agricultural techniques in the town's immediate hinterland' (p. 570), and therefore in wider agricultural improvement, through 'the sociable life of reading and writing' (p. 582). Finally, Alexander Dick's '"A good deal of Trash": Reading Societies, Religious Controversy and Networks of Improvement in Eighteenth-Century Scotland' (*JECS* 38[2015] 585–98), argues for an approach to studying rural reading practices in the eighteenth century which takes into account both 'covenantal reading' (p. 588) and 'emulative reading' (p. 590) associated with the Enlightenment, stating that 'Improvement did not kill controversy . . . both the improvement agenda and the controversial tradition operated within a broad network of practices employed by readers' (p. 587).

Continuing on from works published in 2014, there has been a good deal of focus on women's writing in the Romantic period and a continuation of the desire to include less well-known women writers in the Romantic-period canon. There has also been a greater focus on material and print culture in the works published in 2015, which provides interesting new perspectives on Romantic-period culture with interpretations which move beyond the texts themselves.

## 2. The Novel

Literary criticism on the Romantic novel has been extremely prolific in 2015, with some single- and multi-author monographs of outstanding critical value. This section will begin by reviewing the monographs concerned with multiple Romantic novelists, it will then review the single-author monographs and edited volumes on Jane Austen, and will finally survey the articles and book chapters concerned with single authors, starting with the great bulk on Jane Austen, and then passing to Walter Scott, Ann Radcliffe, Frances Burney, Mary Shelley, Mary Wollstonecraft, William Godwin, Charlotte Smith, Sydney Owenson, and Elizabeth Hamilton in that order. Generally, there is a tendency to focus on the legacy of late eighteenth- and early nineteenth-century novels in the twenty-first century, particularly regarding their written and screen adaptations. Also important is the discussion of gender issues stimulated by these debates, exploring differences and similarities regarding equality of female and male rights in the past and today.

In *An Empire of Air and Water: Uncolonizable Space in the British Imagination, 1750–1850*, Siobhan Carroll explores the significance of places such as the poles, the ocean, the atmosphere, and the subterranean in literary texts during the eighteenth and nineteenth centuries. As areas resistant to 'cultivation and settlement' (p. 6), and thus to conversion into colonies because they could not be inhabited, such spaces came to assume different meanings when used as literary chronotopes. These range from representing sites of resistance to imperial dominion, as in the case of the poles, to spaces exhibiting the technical maritime skills of the British empire, as in the case of transoceanic navigation. Carroll names these areas 'atopias' because 'their intangibility, inhospitality, or inaccessibility' does not allow them to 'be converted into the locations of affective habitation known as "place"' (p. 6). Carroll contends that these atypical spaces contribute to constructing dialectically 'the inhabited places of home and community, providing a contrast to the familiarity, stability, and security implied by the idealized sites of dwelling' (p. 6). Carroll's book explores the formation of British identity not only in opposition to 'a continental colonial Other' but also 'in relation to supposedly empty spaces' (p. 11). In addition, Carroll argues that if Romantic authors such as Wordsworth, Goldsmith, and Clare turned to the local and rural landscape as a way to distance themselves from 'the globalized cityscapes of London and Manchester' (p. 13), the contemporary fascination for distant and abstract spaces served the same purpose. Carroll concludes by arguing that 'atopias offered authors opportunities to reflect on the role played by literature in British imperial expansion' (p. 187). Her fascinating book contributes to diverting the reader's habitual practice of visualizing the British empire as a power measured in terms of cultivated and tamed land to a power frustrated by inhospitable atopias that resist imperial conquest.

Drawing on eighteenth-century theories of music, the opera, and the ways in which some musical instruments galvanized the collective imagination, Pierre Dubois's *Music in the Georgian Novel* sheds new light on the significance of this art form on the creative process of the most important novelists of the eighteenth and early nineteenth centuries. Dubois's book 'investigate[s] the various representations of, and allusions to, music in the novels of the Georgian period' (p. 1), with the aim of clarifying its significance in the novelistic creative process. Of interest to this section are the third and fourth parts of his book, as these develop a noteworthy analysis of the influence of music on Ann Radcliffe's re-elaboration of the sublime, and on the writing of female authors such as Jane Austen, Anne Hughes, Jane West, Maria Edgeworth, Elizabeth Inchbald, Sydney Owenson, and Frances Burney. In their novels, Dubois argues, music plays an important role in defining 'female identity' (p. 8). Dubois's aim is to shed new light both on canonical and less well-known novels 'that could equally testify to the reality of the broadly shared conceptions of music in the period under study' (p. 7).

Another book of noteworthy interest to the development of the Romantic novel is the second volume of the Oxford History of the Novel in English series, entitled *English and British Fiction 1750–1820*, edited by Peter Garside and Karen O'Brien, particularly chapters 10–17 and 21. These are: 'Early Gothic Novels and the Belief in Fiction' (pp. 182–98) by Deidre Lynch, 'The Novel Wars of 1790–1804' (pp. 199–215) by Jon Mee, 'The National Tale' (pp. 216–33) by Claire Connolly, 'Gothic and Anti-Gothic, 1797–1820' (pp. 234–54) by Robert Miles, 'Evangelical Fiction' (pp. 255–72) by Anthony Mandal, 'Jane Austen's Domestic Realism' (pp. 273–95) by Vivien Jones, 'Historical Romance' (pp. 296–311) by Ina Ferris, and 'Walter Scott and the Historical Novel' (pp. 312–31) by Ian Duncan. Of interest also are the last two sections of Clara Tuite's chapter (ch. 21), 'Celebrity and Scandalous Fiction' (pp. 385–403), as they focus on the 1790s Jacobin, sentimental, and Gothic scandalous novels, and on the Regency period's silver-fork scandal and celebrity novels. The two editors, in their introduction to the volume, contend that, despite 'the large number of novels concerned with the themes of love, courtship, and marriage, this is not an inward or a nationally self-reflexive era for the novel, but one profoundly shaped by the economic and political transformations of the time, encompassing decades of continental and imperial warfare' (p. xviii). The aim of the volume is thus to 'offer a collective account of the novel within this process of transformation' (p. xviii). For the contexts related to the Romantic novel Part IV is also of interest, with three chapters shedding light on the historical events that influenced the novelistic writing process. These are Ruth Perry's 'All in the Family: Consanguinity, Marriage, and Property' (pp. 407–23), Thomas Keymer's 'Fictions of the Union' (pp. 424–41), and Deirdre Coleman's 'Imperial Commerce, Gender, Slavery' (pp. 442–58).

Also discussed in Section 1 of this chapter, Melissa Sodeman's *Sentimental Memorials: Women and the Novel in Literary History* explores the position of late eighteenth-century women novelists in the literary canon by juxtaposing the history of the novel, women's literary history, and book history, in order to challenge the general assumption that sentimental novels of this period are not suitable for inclusion in the 'august realms of literature' (p. 3). Sodeman contends that 'novels by Sophia Lee, Ann Radcliffe, Charlotte Smith, and Mary Robinson memorialize the literary-historical conditions of their writing' (p. 3). This was a moment when sentimental novels were at the peak of their popularity, though they commanded little respect as a literary genre. Nevertheless, these female novelists 'successfully navigated the professional marketplace', though they also 'struggled to position their works among more lasting literary monuments' (p. 3). Sodeman's book contributes to a re-evaluation of the late eighteenth-century sentimental novel written by women, and to the inclusion of this usually denigrated genre into the literary canon.

The second edition of Janet Todd's *The Cambridge Introduction to Jane Austen* is a lightly revised version of the first edition published in 2006, with the addition of a new chapter, 'Austenmania: Jane Austen's Global Life' (pp. 142–51), which contends that 'Like Shakespeare's, Jane Austen's characters are archetypes in the collective imagination' (p. 142). Yet, Todd explains, Austen's legacy has travelled beyond Shakespeare's, as her works have been rewritten as 'zombies, sea-monsters, and werewolves' (p. 142), with *Pride and Prejudice* as the most prolifically exploited both as written and screen adaptation, where its 'filmic versions . . . speak to previous adaptations as much as to the original novel' (p. 145).

Sheryl Craig's *Jane Austen and the State of the Nation* opens by arguing that the image of Austen on the forthcoming £10 note depicts the author in a 'calm', 'prosperous' and 'safe haven unaltered by time, war, and economic upheaval, exactly the way the Bank's Board of Directors would like the public to think of their financial institution—solid as the Bank of England' (pp. 1–2). However, Craig observes, Austen did not live in a financially comfortable situation and depended for most of her life on the generosity of her family's male members. Indeed, 'Georgian England and Jane Austen's life were much more economically and politically unstable than the reverse of the Bank of England's new £10 note indicates' (p. 2). Craig contends that the Regency period witnessed a series of economic disasters, hence 'how writers referred to the economy, how they depicted the rich and the poor, and the solutions they offered for their characters' economic problems were unavoidably politically charged' (p. 7). Craig observes that each of Austen's novels refers to England's financial situation at the time of writing. Through close analysis of the economic context of each novel, Craig thus contends that considering Austen's novels as a mere form of love-story escapism means missing 'the political message that would have been obvious to Austen's original readers' (p. 18). Her books focus not so much on 'considerations of the French Revolution, the Napoleonic Wars, or the British Empire' as on 'English politics in the House of Commons and national economic policies in England' (p. 19). Craig argues that Austen's 'concerns about the poor and the economic decline of her nation' are as 'relevant today as they were when they were written 200 years ago' (p. 19).

James Thompson's *Jane Austen and Modernization: Sociological Readings* draws on sociological studies such as Tönnies, Durkheim, Weber, Simmel, Parson, Goffman, and Bourdieu to apply 'a series of ideas from the first 60 or 70 years of professional sociological argument' (p. 2) to his reading of Austen's novels, engaging with both a deterministic, top-down 'explanation of institutions and practices' (p. 2) and a 'bottom-up view that focuses on the ways in which the individual subject negotiates his or her way among groups and institutions' (p. 2). Thompson contends that an interest in Austen's novels was reawoken at the same time as these sociological theories were elaborated, namely after the publication of her biography in 1870 by her nephew James Edward Austen-Leigh, and after the First World War, when a 'nostalgia for vanishing village life' (p. 4) boosted the reading of her novels again. Thompson claims that Austen's novels were revalued across this period because they provided a remedy for *anomie*, namely a model for 'shared rituals that would bind separate individuals into a coherent whole' (p. 5). According to Thompson, Austen's character construction has always been analysed 'in terms of psychological depth' (p. 7), but it is, rather, through the complexity of the relations established in the social milieu that Austen's novels achieve 'vividness and solidity' (p. 7). Thompson contends that 'Austen represents society as a web of obligations, with all its entanglements in legal, political, and religious discourse' (p. 72).

Margaret Doody's *Jane Austen's Names: Riddles, Persons, Places* is divided into three sections, 'England', 'Names', and 'Places', offering a fascinating analysis of Austen's subtle use of names in her works. Doody explains that Austen's names are never casual or arbitrary, as they convey an additional layer of meaning related to character construction and to the historical significance of places. Doody contends that the 'cultural forces that shape an English person include not only the social and financial status of the birth family, but also the place of birth' (p. 11). Finally, places in Austen's novels, 'are not permanent', as 'marriage, war, or financial fluctuations bring on change of location'. Such changes may indeed be either 'a stress or a tonic' to a character (p. 216). Doody concludes by arguing that 'Through the language of names and the language of place, Austen shows how each person is already shaped by the culture and history of the birthplace' (p. 389) and, with the sole exception of Emma, Austen's heroines are forced to move and change places, thus entering into contact with new and different cultures.

Kenneth R. Morefield's *Jane Austen's Emma: A Close Reading Companion*, volume 1, follows chapter by chapter the first volume of Austen's novel, providing a close reading through short synopsis with a descriptive title of the chapter's content. The main argument is that Austen's novel is more interested 'in what the events reveal about the central character than in the events themselves' (p. 79). The plot is formally linked to the development of Emma's character: a lady who, being born with the privileges of beauty, cleverness, and wealth, is used to 'having too much her own way' (p. 1) and, for this reason, needs to learn humility in order to become emotionally mature for marriage. Men in Austen's novels, on the other hand, need to be 'financially independent ("settled")' (p. 96) in order to be good husbands. Another important topic explored by the novel is that 'friendship and love are built on the same foundation' (p. 3), a lesson that Emma still has to learn. Austen's novel is also concerned with class mobility at a time characterized 'by increasing fluidity in the class system and resistance to class change' (p. 7). The first volume of this close reading of Austen's novel concludes by assuming that while Emma's 'disposition to think a little too well of herself' abates, her 'power of having rather too much her own way' does not, a flaw which may threaten her future happiness. Morefield's publication of volumes two and three of *Emma*'s close reading are thus eagerly anticipated, to see if and how the eponymous character will deal with her second character flaw.

Peter Sabor's edited collection of essays, *The Cambridge Companion to Emma*, is focused on the text and context of Austen's *Emma* with particular attention to the dedicatory and introductory sentences. The first four chapters are concerned with 'the circumstances of the novel's composition and publication, as well as with its literary, historical and economic context' (p. xii). Chapters 6 to 10 treat Austen's use of free indirect style, her portrayal of the heroine, the fictional setting of the novel, and the use of music and riddles. The last two chapters review a series of translations and adaptations of the novel up to the present day. Jan Fergus's 'Composition and Publication' (pp. 1–16) contends that *Emma* is Austen's most experimental novel, both in its composition and publication, as she moved from Thomas Egerton to John Murray II, 'the prestigious London publisher of Byron and the *Quarterly Review*' (p. 4). Walter Scott's 'thoughtful review' of *Emma*, published in the *Quarterly Review* of March 1816, Fergus explains, 'began the nineteenth-century canonisation of Austen as a novelist' (p. 13), even though Scott's positive review 'did not result in a sold-out edition' (p. 14) in Austen's time. Bharat Tandon's 'The Literary Context' (pp. 17–35) observes that Austen's literary allusions in *Emma* are not always self-evident. Yet one of the functions of intertextual reference is to give the reader a sense of the character's personality. Jonathan Sachs's 'The Historical Context' (pp. 36–51) points out that the visit to the poor by Emma and Harriet signals social inequalities in Austen's time as well as 'the connection between poverty and gender' (p. 38). Though Austen's novels have in general been judged by critics as being little concerned with the historical contexts of the French Revolution and the Napoleonic Wars, Sachs contends that, in *Emma*, 'Austen's relative silence might be read as a stronger, more subtle engagement with the pressing issues of her day' (pp. 43–4). Robert D. Hume's 'Money and Rank' (pp. 52–67) compares the value of the possessions of *Emma*'s characters with contemporary currency. Hume argues that 'Austen's families in *Emma* are not titled and do not seem terribly grand, but they are unquestionably part of an economic elite' (p. 57). The novel signals a world characterized 'by socio-economic change and issues of class and gender equity that were not so much unresolved as simply unrecognised' (p. 60). Edward Copeland's 'Contemporary Responses' (pp. 68–87) maintains that Austen's compilation of the 'Opinions of *Emma*', where she gathered comments of her friends, her family, and complete strangers about her novel, is 'an accurate snapshot of the issues that dominated discussions of *Emma* for the next fifty-five years, from 1815 to 1870' (p. 69). Copeland also reviews a series of 'fashionable novels' published between 1825 and 1840 directly influenced by Austen's *Emma*, and points out that by the 1850s *Emma* had come to be considered 'the touchstone of Austen's excellence' (p. 81). Linda Bree's 'Style, Structure, Language' (pp. 88–104) observes that Austen's letters to her niece Anna Austen Lefroy, herself a novelist, show some insights into her preferences regarding plot construction, thus shedding some light on *Emma*. John Wiltshire's 'The Heroine' (pp. 105–19) claims that through Emma's character Austen certainly wanted to confront her readers' expectations. This heroine is a complex character who unites snobbery with 'strength of character', 'intelligence', and 'vivacity' (p. 106), making it hard for the readers to despise her completely. Janine Barchas's 'Setting and Community' (pp. 120–34) observes that *Emma* is 'the most parochial of Jane Austen's novels' (p. 120), as the heroine never travels further than Highbury and Box Hill, thus 'emphasis[ing] physical confinement of all sorts' (p. 120). Her 'exactitude about place in *Emma* compels readers to...map her name-dropped locations and search for her interpretative purpose' (p. 125). Yet Barchas notices that such exactitude of place exposes the connections of its inhabitants 'to the country's larger economic and social grids, marking the towns' active participation in the Regency's trade economy and Britain's national identity' (p. 125). Ruth Perry's 'Music' (pp. 135–49) observes that music in *Emma* 'is used in a sophisticated manner to evoke class and gender status and as a pointer to moral character' (p. 135). Music is also an important element of 'entertainment and solace' (p. 139) in Highbury society. The novel itself displays a musical quality as 'many of its chapters are staged like operatic scenes' (p. 145), a fact that suggests some 'contribution of music to the architecture of this novel' (p. 147). Jillian Heydt-Stevenson's 'Games, Riddles and Charades' (pp. 150–65) points out that riddles in *Emma* are an important device to question characters' complacency and thus stimulate their deeper self-understanding. In addition, Heydt-Stevenson explains, in Austen's novel 'the riddle works at the literal and metaphorical levels, helping constitute the novel's larger meanings' (p. 151). Emma is not good at riddle-solving, but this does not seem to pose a problem for Austen as she sees this act as something to be done communally. Gillian Dow's 'Translations' (pp. 166–85) states that 'Austen's posthumous reception on the Continent was affected by her inability to fit the idea of what a novel should be doing as the nineteenth century progressed' (p. 169). Yet this 'did not prevent *Emma* from being translated' (p. 169). The first translation was published in Paris in 1816 as *La Nouvelle Emma*, three months after Murray's publication of its first edition. Its preface explains that a French audience would find Austen's novel 'problematic' primarily for its lack of action. In the twentieth century, *Emma* has met more success with foreign audiences, and has been translated into Spanish, Czech, Dutch, Italian, and Chinese. Deidre Shauna Lynch's 'Screen Version' (pp. 186–203), finally, focuses on *Emma*'s screen adaptations, contending that 'the Emmas of the past twenty years are...a group who nowadays...only intermittently appear to us in empire-line muslin gowns'

(p. 190), and sometimes she is 'no longer self-evidently white'. Though all 'this swerving from a familiar text can be disconcerting' (p. 191), it nevertheless proves the influential capacity of Austen's novel in the twenty-first century, two hundred years after its first publication.

Hanne Birk and Marion Gymnich's collection of essays, *Pride and Prejudice 2.0: Interpretations, Adaptations and Transformations of Jane Austen's Classic* centres on the legacy of Austen's novel *Pride and Prejudice* in the twenty-first century, and on its adaptation not only in book form but also in the plethora of new media that characterize the postmodern era. The famous 1995 BBC mini-series adaptation boosted a resurgence of interest in Austen's novel, and the iconic 'wet shirt scene' in Colin Firth's interpretation of Darcy helped to turn the focus on the female gaze. This scene, which does not exist in Austen's novel, has now entered into the twenty-first-century collective imagination, catalysing female erotic rewritings of Austen's novel centred on the fulfilment of Elizabeth Bennet's sexual desire. In her introduction, '200 Years of Reading Jane Austen's *Pride and Prejudice*; or Where the Literary Canon Meets Popular Culture' (p. 11–31), Marion Gymnich contends that this novel 'is a literary text that has aged remarkably well; at the beginning of the twenty-first century . . . [it] appear[s] to be as popular as ever'; this is proven by the fact that 'Beyond intertextual and intermedial references to Austen's novel in many movies, TV series and literary texts, there are several popular audiovisual adaptations, numerous sequels, rewritings and modernisations of *Pride and Prejudice*' (p. 11). The success of these adaptations lies in the 'intersection of the literary canon and popular culture' (p. 12). *Pride and Prejudice* has encountered enormous success in different cultures because its 'concerns . . . have been regarded as universal by many authors, readers and viewers' (p. 17). Marie-Josefine Joisten's 'The Serious Business of Mrs Bennet and the Consequences of a Mother's Fear' (pp. 33–50) contends that Austen's novel is primarily concerned with marriage and money, a fact that 'contradicts purely romantic readings of the text' (p. 33). Mrs Bennet's over-preoccupation with marrying her daughters reflects a 'general awareness of women's options in nineteenth-century England' (p. 35) who, as described in the subtitle of Deborah Logan's book, could only 'Marry, Stitch, Die or Do Worse' (p. 35). Nadežda Rumjanceva's '"And she beheld a striking resemblance to Mr. Darcy": Nineteenth-Century Illustrations of Jane Austen's *Pride and Prejudice*' (pp. 51–76) notices that the resurgence of Austen's popularity towards the end of the nineteenth century was due to the 'luxuriously illustrated editions of Austen's novels' (p. 51), which 'revived the humour and satire of *Pride and Prejudice*' (p. 63). Elena Baeva's ' "My name is Lizzie Bennet, and this is my [vlog]"—Adaptation and Metareference in *The Lizzie Bennet Diaries*' (pp. 151–65) reviews the reimagining of Austen's novel in a Web series of a hundred, three- to five-minute YouTube snap clips which focus on similarities and differences in female concerns between young women in the nineteenth and twenty-first centuries, as well as on 'the role of social media in today's life' (p. 152). The common denominator between the nineteenth-century novel and the modern media is 'prejudice': modern social media are biased because 'vlogs, like any type of opinion piece, are highly subjective' (p. 154). Stella Butter's 'Jane Austen Meets Bollywood: Forms and Functions of Transcultural Adaptations' (pp. 167–85) argues that Austen's heritage has gone beyond the British nation in a transnational movement that captures the 'cultural imaginary' of current Indian filmmakers, who are attracted by Austen's emphasis on the family, local communities, and 'the socio-economic dimension of marriage' (p. 167). Imke Lichterfeld's 'Mr Darcy's Shirt—An Icon of Popular Culture' (pp. 189–205) points out that the scene in the 1995 BBC version where Darcy's wet shirt clings to his body after he dives into the lake has turned this character into a pop cultural icon and prompted increased attention to Austen's novel. The statue of Darcy/Colin Firth in the wet shirt in Hyde Park, London, subsequently 'moved to Lyme Park in Cheshire, where the Pemberley scenes were filmed' (p. 191), celebrates 'the rejuvenation of Austen's popularity... fashioning a new, postmodern image' (p. 191). Today, *Pride and Prejudice* is perceived through the lens of the BBC adaptation, and this is revealed by a subsequent ITV mini-series *Lost in Austen* [2008], 'which is replete with intertextual and intermedial cross-references to Austen's novel and to previous audiovisual version(s)' (p. 199). Gislind Rohwer-Happe's 'The Mr. Darcy Complex—The Impact of a Literary Icon on Contemporary Chick Lit' (pp. 207–25) explains that the transformation of Darcy from a haughty and proud to a kind and gentle character has shaped a postmodern psychological complex which describes modern women's hope of true love and belief in the possibility that bad guys may actually hide a good side under the cover. This type of character has become recurrent in contemporary chick lit, 'with about 200 novels available at the moment that feature the name of Mr. Darcy in the title' (p. 209). The general plot of chick lit novels draws heavily on Austen's *Pride and Prejudice*, which can thus be considered as 'the grandmother of Chick Lit, while Helen Fielding's *Bridget Jones's Diary* can safely be called the mother of Chick Lit' (p. 209). Ulrike Zimmerman's 'Crime Comes to Pemberley—*Pride and Prejudice* Sequels in Contemporary Crime Fiction' (pp. 227–44) portrays a series of crime novels arising from the contact with Austen's novel and the 1995 BBC mini-series. These novels tend to 'deal with characters' lives after they were married off... or follow undeserving characters who would have been pushed unceremoniously off the scene in Austen' (p. 232). Crime sequels are 'part of the marketing strategies of the "Jane Austen" brand' and, most importantly, they 'cater to the readers' narrative greed' (p. 240), appealing to Austen's readers' desire to fill in the gaps in Austen's novel, with 'a noticeable urge to expose an underground world of Austen' (p. 241). Hanne Birk's 'Gothic Fiction Bites Back—The Gothification of Jane Austen at the Beginning of the 21st Century' (pp. 245–60) points out that Roland Barthes's assumption of 'The Death of the Author' is not borne out by the constant reappearance of Jane Austen as 'vampire protagonist' (p. 245) in Gothic versions of *Pride and Prejudice* produced in the twenty-first century. As these novels are 'highly successful' and 'widely read', they 'promise a considerable sociocultural "impact factor"' (p. 246). *Pride and Prejudice and Zombies* [2009], for example, 'has been turned into a video game, and a film adaptation is in progress and expected to be released in 2015' (p. 246). Yet Birk points out that in the latter Gothic adaptation, 'no matter how resourceful and professional... a woman possibly is' marriage is still depicted as the ultimate objective for her full realization

(p. 253), thereby suggesting that 'even for the best female zombie slayer a happy marriage is definitely preferable to enduring professionalism' (p. 255), an aspect that 'subverts any feminist reading of the text' (p. 257). Silke Meyer's '"Spank me Mr. Darcy": *Pride and Prejudice* in Contemporary Female (Hardcore) Erotica' (pp. 261–73) contends that the contrast between the prudery and repressed passion of the Regency period opens up fertile territory for 'female erotic rewriting of *Pride and Prejudice*' (p. 263). Uwe Küchler's 'Participatory Transfer/mations: Inviting *Pride and Prejudice* Adaptations into the Foreign Language Classroom' (pp. 275–90) argues that literary classics and their new media adaptations prove to be a 'stimulating choice of material' for the foreign language classroom because they enhance learners' creativity via a recognition of similarities and differences between source and target text. The recent TV adaptation *Lost in Austen*, for example, juxtaposes the nineteenth-century context of the novel's production with the twenty-first-century context of text adaptation, making useful 'intercultural juxtaposition(s)', with the female protagonist's time travel exposing the cultural clashes derived from the anachronisms and inconsistencies of the time-warp narrative expedient. Küchler contends that 'By creatively and intertextually transforming the original, the narrative material becomes accessible for a young generation: the digital natives' (p. 289). The original, however, is kept alive and its themes are brought into comparison with modern themes, thereby highlighting the relevance of the classic to the twenty-first century. Hanne Birk and Marion Gymnich's 'Elizabeth Bennet: A Heroine Past and/or Present?' (pp. 291–302) narrates their experience as university teachers of English literature and includes their students' perspective on what studying *Pride and Prejudice* means today. Denise Burkhard and Simone Fleischer's 'Have a Fan-tastic 200th Birthday, Lizzy!—Elizabeth Bennet in recent Fan Fiction' (pp. 311–22) points out that a 'fandom that is lively and thriving is an indicator of the topicality of a text' and, since the Internet is 'the most dynamic and interactive medium today', they have used online fan fiction to question 'whether Lizzy Bennet is a heroine of our times' (p. 311). Their aim was to see which features of Austen's heroine have been adopted and which ones have been reshaped. Fan fiction adaptations of *Pride and Prejudice* tend to emphasize the passion of the love affair between Elizabeth and Darcy (p. 315). Gender roles and sexuality are also revisited and changed in order to modernize the character of Elizabeth, who conforms to social rules only if these are in line with her own wishes. Birk and Gymnich's collection *Pride and Prejudice 2.0* is an outstanding contribution to Austen studies because it focuses on the interactive relationship between Austen's 200-year-old text and contemporary media of communication. It also highlights the fact that some gender issues are still present today, as shown in the still prevalent double standard of female and male sexuality. In addition, the book considers gender issues in intersectional relation with race and class, thus entering into conversation with current post-feminist and post-colonial academic debates.

The essays arising from the Jane Austen Society of North America's annual general meeting and gathered in *Persuasions* (37[2015]) explore the world of Austen's contemporaries, providing important information about 'practical' and 'village life, farming, beauty, fashion' and women's ageing in Georgian

England (p. 7). Some of the essays show a particularly considerate focus on the unstable financial condition of gentlewomen who, not allowed to work for their own support, depended on their husbands, fathers, or brothers for financial support. Miss Bates in *Emma* thoroughly illustrates the case of a middle-aged and unmarried woman of originally high condition later sunk into poverty after her father's death. Christine Alexander and Juliet McMaster's 'Children Writing in Jane Austen's Time' (*Persuasions* 37[2015] 13–29) explores the early writing of 'young authors and their creative and professional ambitions' (p. 13), focusing on both male and female writers such as Hannah More, Maria Edgeworth, Jane Austen, Anna Maria Porter, and Thomas Chatterton. They ponder how aware these authors may have been of their writing. For example, Porter wrote love stories with cross-dressing heroines at the tender age of 13, drawing on the sentimental tradition for the source of life experience she did not have; while Austen's early writing about love had a satirical tone that exposed the 'mercenary motives for marriage' (p. 20), a theme that she explored in her mature writing. Linda Slothouber's '"The holders of hay & the masters of meadows": Farmers in Jane Austen's World' (*Persuasions* 37[2015] 30–44) depicts the British agricultural system that informs the setting of Austen's novels. Farmers, who occupied the median position in the hierarchy, experienced increased economic stability during Austen's time, thus 'renegotiat[ing] their place in society and national affairs' (p. 30). Austen depicts the controversial figure of the gentleman farmer in *Persuasion* through the Hayters and in *Emma* through Robert Martin, highlighting how possession of money blurred the boundaries between the gentry and these new rich farmers. Sara Bowen's 'Village Life in Jane Austen's World: The View from the Parsonage' (*Persuasions* 37[2015] 45–64) gives an idea of 'the atmosphere of Jane Austen's village world' to the twenty-first-century reader by exploring the letters and diaries of parsons and parsons' wives (p. 45). Parsons not only dealt with spiritual issues but also attended to the medical, educational, legal, and social needs of the community. Inger Sigrun Brodey's 'Making Sense of Sensibility' (*Persuasions* 37[2015] 65–85) points out how the words of the title *Sense and Sensibility* are 'qualities that generate the same adjective: sensible' (p. 65), in that one can be both sensible 'as in having sense' and as in 'responding emotionally to something' (p. 65). Austen's book is meant to re-evaluate sensibility 'in its original philanthropic purposes and to teach her readers lessons about sympathy' (p. 66) by promoting the kind of sensibility embodied by Elinor's character: a sensibility that is 'social and not selfish, hidden rather than demanding' (p. 84). Rachel M. Brownstein's 'Character and Caricature: Jane Austen and James Gillray' (*Persuasions* 37[2015] 86–100) argues that Austen drew on her contemporary, caricaturist James Gillray, for the construction of some characters in order to expose their moral flaws as, for example, in the cases of Mr and Mrs John Dashwood in *Sense and Sensibility*. Brownstein contends that Austen's 'satire on selfishness and greed' is meant to expose the 'social structure and institutions that shape, alter, and inflect human nature—marriage and the family, primogeniture, assumptions about gender and rank' (p. 98). Jocelyn Harris's 'Jane Austen, the Prince of Wales, and John Thorpe' (*Persuasions* 37[2015] 101–14) argues that though Austen has always been considered more 'an ironist...than a satirist', her 'lacerating portrait of the Prince of Wales' through the character of John Thorpe 'speaks otherwise' (p. 101), showing that Austen 'based her patriotism on love of country, not loyalty to its rulers' (p. 112). Alden O'Brian's 'Achieving an "Air of Decided Fashion"': How Austen's Ladies Adapted the Latest from London' (*Persuasions* 37[2015] 115–28) relates what in Georgian society defined the ladies with an 'air of fashion' as distinguished from the Bennet sisters who, nevertheless, could manage 'to look fairly fashionable' (p. 115). O'Brian contends that the difference was in the way dresses were cut as well as in the time that provincial ladies would take to catch up with the latest London fashion magazines. Stephanie M. Eddleman's 'Past the Bloom: Aging and Beauty in the Novels of Jane Austen' (*Persuasions* 37[2015] 129–45) observes that women in Austen's time were considered old earlier than men, whose 'physical signs of aging...were declining strength and a loss of physical ability' (p. 141); indeed, 'Many eighteenth-century writers are not kind to characters no longer in the bloom of youth, treating them as mere caricatures or as people whose only purpose in life is to guide the young' (p. 130). Austen's culture 'privileges youth and beauty, especially for females, and her novels reflect this influence' (p. 131), though she also shows 'awareness of and resistance to this regrettable reality' (p. 132), as in the portrayal of Anne Elliot in *Persuasion*, through which Austen critiques society's restrictions 'of the joys of life only to the very young' (p. 134). Amanda Vickery's 'No Happy Ending? At Home with Miss Bates in Georgian England' (*Persuasions* 37[2015] 146–66) observes that, 'As the unmarried daughter of a widowed mother, dependent on familial favour, Austen had much more in common with poor Miss Bates than with blessed Miss Woodhouse' (p. 147). Austen lived in a familial nucleus composed of six women with her mother, sister, a friend, and two female servants forming a type of household known as 'the spinster cluster' which has not been thoroughly investigated by historians, as they are usually more devoted to exploring the history of the family. Fictional works do not depict such realities either, as they are generally perceived with 'a melancholy sense of blasted hopes and emotional failure' (p. 147). Nevertheless, widows and spinsters, though financially unstable, sometimes formed clusters rich in emotional comfort. Interestingly and in 'cruel contrast' (p. 149), men between the ages of 35 and 50 were viewed as at the height of their manhood. Gillian Dow's 'Reading at Godmersham: Edward's Library and Marianne's Books' (*Persuasions* 37[2015] 167–79) focuses on the libraries of two country houses, Godmersham Park in Kent and Chawton House, which belonged to Edward Austen, one of Jane Austen's brothers. These libraries collected books on various subjects such as travel, history, religion, conduct literature, architecture, painting, science, medicine, and dictionaries, reflecting the owner as aspirational and educated, a common feature that characterized many country houses of the period. The Austens' library differentiates itself by holding a significant collection of female-authored novels. In the 'Miscellany' section of *Persuasions*, Linda Zionkowski and Mimi Hart's ' "Aunt Jane began her day with music": Austen and the Female Amateur' (*Persuasions* 37[2015] 181–203) contends that defining Austen as a mere amateur of music does not do her justice as, for her entire life, she was committed to 'collecting, transcribing, and playing' (p. 182) music. Most importantly, though, music plays an important role in the development of Austen's characters as it 'can both express and conceal [their] feelings' (p. 200).

Elaine Bander's 'Jane Austen's World: Jane Austen's Words' (*Persuasions* 37[2015] 204–15) claims that the theme of the 2015 JASNA annual general meeting 'Living in Jane Austen's World' inspired a vibrant discussion on 'Austen's life and time' (p. 204). The focus on 'Austen's physical, social, and cultural world' (p. 204) is enlightening with respect to the metonymic value of the words that Austen used to create the worlds of her novels. Bander contends that even the best film adaptation in costume would not be able to mediate the true experience of the world of Austen's novels because it would be missing Austen's characteristic narrative voice. Aoife Byrne's ' "Very knowing gigs": Social Aspiration and the Gig Carriage in Jane Austen's Works' (*Persuasion* 37[2015] 216–26) illustrates that carriages were not just means to facilitate motion but also a way to show the owner's income and social status, 'revealing characterizations and modulations on class' (p. 216). In Austen's novels, the gig in particular reflects social mobility and 'its owner's status as *nouveau riche*' (p. 217). Lauren Wilwerding's 'Amatory Gifts in *Sense and Sensibility*' (*Persuasions* 37[2015] 227–37) draws on gift theory to explore the significance of gift exchange in the shift from 'economically motivated' to 'companionate' marriages, wondering whether in the latter case 'women still function as gifts' (p. 229). Patrick McGraw's ' "The world is not their's": The Plight of Jane Fairfax in *Emma*' (*Persuasions* 37[2015] 238–46) contends that the words pronounced by Emma when Jane Fairfax's secret engagement with Frank Churchill becomes public mark 'the unfairness of women's financial and legal inferiority in Regency society' (p. 239), in addition to showing Emma's growth as a character. According to McGraw, Austen condemns 'the social and legal conditions that restrict a poor woman's choices to marriage, spinsterhood, the governess trade, or, *in extremis*, prostitution' (p. 242), and her novel conveys 'the idea that the world's laws are un-Christian in their treatment of poor women' (p. 245). Anthony Domestico's 'Close Writing and Close Reading in *Emma*' (*Persuasions* 37[2015] 247–57) draws on D. A. Miller's *Jane Austen, or the Secret of Style*, which renames free indirect style as 'close writing'. Domestico contends that this is appropriate to a novel like *Emma* because, in addition to highlighting the fact that narrator and character collapse though remaining distinct, close writing also relates free indirect style to 'close reading', the careful analysis of the text. Domestico explains that, in *Emma*, 'characters attempt to read one another's thoughts as if they were texts' (p. 248) and on their own terms, a solipsism that, like the close reading developed by New Criticism, does not allow them to enter into a meaningful conversation with the other characters. Grace E. Miller's ' "This Peace": Naval Homecoming and Domestic Reintegration in *Persuasion*' (*Persuasions* 37[2015] 258–65) compares the novel's lack of attention to the emotional stability of naval officers returning home from war with the far greater consideration that the process of sailors' reintegration receives from the British navy in the twenty-first century. Miller's essay focuses on the 'multiple interactions between the naval and the domestic' (p. 258) in *Persuasion*, arguing that Austen transfers the responsibility of the homecoming process to the 'navy wife' (p. 259). The final essay by Isis Herrero López. 'Franco and Austen: Three 1945 Translations of *Northanger Abbey* and Their Gender Components' (*Persuasions* 37[2015] 266–77) explains why Austen's novels were not translated into Spanish until the twentieth century, when they entered the market because their restricted domestic environment was well suited to the type of subordinated woman endorsed by the Francoist regime. López compares three 1945 translations of *Northanger Abbey* based on a previous translation in 1925 by Isabel Oyarzábal, a feminist interested in women's emancipation. The differences between the three 1945 translations reveal different degrees of 'influence of Francoist ideology on the representation of women' (p. 267). Austen's ironic rejection of the idealized heroine disappears, while emphasis is given to 'the feminine roles of mother, virgin, and wife' (p. 269).

The essays of the Jane Austen Society of North America's annual general meeting collected in the volume of *Persuasions On-Line* (36[2015]) also explore Austen's world. The first part focuses on marriage law, economics, religion, Austen's material culture, disability, and Regency celebrities. The miscellanies look at further themes, providing details about Aristotle's influence on her novels, intertextualities with contemporary writer Sarah Harriet Burney (sister of Frances Burney), landscape description, and the presence of women in the navy. Martha Bailey's 'The Marriage Law of Jane Austen's World' (*Persuasions On-Line* 36[2015] 38 paras.) points out that if, on the one hand, in Austen's novels 'marriage for money alone is wrong', on the other, 'marriage without a fortune on at least one side is imprudent' (para. 2, ll. 5–6). Austen exposes the fact that the law of primogeniture, the purpose of which was to keep the family's estate intact, had serious consequences for unmarried women in particular, who were left at the mercy of their brothers and were not allowed to work for their subsistence. Marriage was thus necessary for women's survival, even though they would lose their legal personality because 'at common law, husband and wife are one person, and that person is the man' (para. 8, ll. 5–6). Bailey's essay also sheds light on how Austen's novels engage with the consequences of premarital sex, marrying relatives, clandestine and underage marriage, and divorce in Regency England. Katherine Toran's 'The Economics of Jane Austen's World' (*Persuasions On-Line* 36[2015] 22 paras.) helps the modern reader to translate the value of 'a nineteenth-century pound into a modern dollar' (para. 1, ll. 5–6). Ann Buermann Wass's '"I am the neatest worker of the party": Making and Mending the Family's Wardrobe' (*Persuasions On-Line* 36[2015] 25 paras.) explains that women in Austen's time were rarely idle, as they sewed and mended the garments of their family that showed signs of wear—an occupation that 'allow[ed] women to be productive while they chatted' (para. 1, ll. 20–2). Buermann Wass observes that, 'As most clothing could not, as Jane Austen noted, "be bought ready made" . . . the work of women's needles was indeed an important contribution to the household' (last para., ll. 7–9). Jill Ottoman's '"A woman never looks better than on horseback"' (*Persuasions On-Line* 36[2015] 30 paras.) explores the theme of women and horseriding in the Regency period. This activity, besides being excruciatingly expensive, put women's life at serious risk as they had to ride 'aside' for reasons of propriety: 'No woman who valued her reputation would ever attempt to ride astride' (para. 5, ll. 11–12). Ottoman maintains that a woman on horseback in Austen is always a 'telling device' that informs the reader of both the negative and positive traits of a character (last para., l. 12). Jeffrey A. Nigro and William A. Phillips's 'A Revolution in Masculine Style: How Beau Brummell Changed Jane Austen's World' (*Persuasions On-Line* 36[2015] 36 paras.) signals a change in male clothing style during Austen's time, arguing that George Brummell 'represents the zenith' (para. 6, l. 7) of the dandy style, a more sober and less exaggerated attire than the Macaroni style, 'an extreme form of appearance, exaggerated in costumes, cosmetics, and hairstyles' (para. 4, ll. 7–8), which Austen represents through the figure of Sir Walter Elliot in *Persuasion*. Nigro and Phillips point out that 'In place of outmoded displays of luxury and excess, Brummell emphasized the elegance and simplicity of the line and cut of clothes' (para. 17, ll. 1–2), thereby showing awareness of 'the dandy's desire to be noticed without drawing attention to himself' (para. 18, ll. 4–5). Sheryl Craig's 'Jane and the Master Spy' (*Persuasions On-Line* 36[2015] 28 paras.) contends that Austen draws on contemporary British spy William Wickham (1761–1840) to shape the duplicitous character of George Wickham in *Pride and Prejudice*. Robert Clark's 'Wilderness and Shrubbery in Austen's Works' (*Persuasions On-Line* 36[2015] 40 paras.) investigates the depiction of wilderness gardens in Austen's work. Clark points out that the wilderness's woodland walk would connote 'Christ's wandering in the wilderness to understand his relation to God', and Austen may have had this religious idea in mind 'when representing the Sotherton wilderness in *Mansfield Park*' (para. 13, ll. 4–8). Here the wilderness represents a space of sexual temptation that can be governed by 'moral rectitude' (para. 38, l. 4). Amanda Marie Kubic's 'Aristotelian Ethical Ideas in the Novels of Jane Austen' (*Persuasions On-Line* 36[2015] 31 paras.) maintains that, though there is no evidence that Austen read Aristotle, some of her works show awareness of this philosopher's ideas, which Austen may have known through her reading of seventeenth- and eighteenth-century didactic works. Christopher Toner's ' "With what intense desire she wants her home": Jane Austen on Home as *Telos*' (*Persuasions On-Line* 36[2015] 26 paras.) contends that in Austen's novels the themes of 'security, character', and the 'social comfort' deriving from 'participating in relationships based on mutual love and respect' are elements constitutive of 'a good home' (para. 1, ll. 12–16). The *telos* Austen describes concerns 'the finding of one's place in . . . marriage' (para. 1, l. 22), and characters achieve their happiness through 'economic' and 'relational security' (para. 8, ll. 13–14). Carmen María Fernández Rodríguez's 'Another Mistress of Deceit? Jane Austen's *Lady Susan* and Sarah Harriet Burney's *Geraldine Fauconberg*' (*Persuasions On-Line* 36[2015] 24 paras.) investigates the figure of the 'merry widow' in seventeenth- and eighteenth-century literature. Rodríguez argues that Austen draws on Burney's novel for the character of Lady Susan, and this is shown by the fact that even though the anti-heroines in both novels are not good models of benevolent motherhood, nevertheless they both have a capacity of penetration of which no male character is capable. Gillian Ballinger's 'Austen Writing Bristol: The City and Signification in *Northanger Abbey* and *Emma*' (*Persuasions On-Line* 36[2015] 23 paras.) contends that the depiction of Bristol and the nearby landscape in both novels exposes important traits of the characters that are connected to those places. Most importantly, Ballinger argues that not only does a 'novelist's topography [have] to be correct, but so does the portrayal of social behaviour within geographically-specific cultural groups' (para. 4, ll. 20–1). Austen's 'mimetic realism' is thus visible in her use of names belonging to the real world for her characters, as in *Emma*, where the connection of Mrs Elton to the Hawkins would enable Austen's contemporary readers to view her as an enslaving character, since the real Hawkins of Bristol were connected with the slave trade. Tsugumi Okabe's 'Jane Austen in Translation: On Sisterhood and Romance in Mochizuki Reiko's *Sense and Sensibility*' (*Persuasions On-Line* 36[2015] 39 paras.) points out that the translations of *Pride and Prejudice* in 1926 by Natsume Soseki, and of *Sense and Sensibility* in 1947, have contributed to the Westernization of Japan. The more recent popularity of Austen's novel, however, derives from modern film adaptations: Ang Lee's *Sense and Sensibility* and Douglas McGrath's *Emma*. This new revival has contributed to Japanese adaptations of Austen's novels in manga, Japanese comics that target a young female audience. Okabe observes that Mochizuki Reiko's graphic adaptation of *Sense and Sensibility* 'simultaneously borrows and deviates from Austen's novel to tell its own culturally relevant and original story' (para. 3, ll. 13–14). Haruko Takakuwa's '*Pride and Prejudice* as *Angels' Ladder*: Jane Austen's Novel Become Takarazuka Musical Theater' (*Persuasions On-Line* 36[2015] 16 paras.) investigates the adaptation of Austen's work into a Japanese musical. This adaptation, too, promotes an idealized modern woman, 'modest, upright, graceful and cheerful', namely 'fit' to be a potential urban wife and mother of the middle class (para. 5, ll. 15–16). Takarazuka's adaptation shows the early twentieth-century 'eagerness to embrace the Western world' (para. 6, l. 8). Penny Gay's 'A Hypothetical Map of Highbury' (*Persuasions On-Line* 36[2015] 7 paras.) sketches a conjectural map of *Emma*'s fictional world. Finally, Rowland McMaster's ' "I hate to hear of women on board": Women aboard War Ships' (*Persuasions On-Line* 36[2015] 32 paras.) provides a depiction of a wide range of women involved in the navy: from the ladies embodied by Mrs Croft in *Persuasion*, who experienced 'the pleasure and comfort on an admiral's man of war' (para. 9, ll. 14–15), to the wives of less socially prominent sailors, who worked in the lower deck, through prostitutes allowed to access the ship when anchored in a port, to women disguised as men who chose to serve in the navy.

The Eighteenth Century published a special issue in summer 2015 dedicated to 'Jane Austen and Her Contemporaries', edited by Devoney Looser (*ECent* 56[2015]). Notwithstanding the saturation of Austen studies, Looser argues that the relationship between Austen and her contemporaries needs a more in-depth analysis, and the issue aims at covering this gap. Cheryl A. Wilson's ' "Something like mine": Catherine Hutton, Jane Austen, and Feminist Recovery Work' (*ECent* 56[2015] 151–64) explores the relation between Hutton, a neglected woman writer, and Austen, arguing that a comparative study of the two female authors sheds new light on the rules of the literary marketplace in the 1810s. Both authors established the growth of the domestic novel and comment on the literature of their time in their works. Erin M. Goss's 'Homespun Gossip: Jane West, Jane Austen, and the Task of Literary

Criticism' (*ECent* 56[2015] 165–77) contends that the marriage plot of two sisters in Jane West's *A Gossip's Story* [1796] provided some elements for Austen's *Sense and Sensibility*. Goss suggests that in both Austen's and West's novels gossip functions as a social glue for the community and as a means of 'surveillance of that community' (p. 166). Toby R. Benis's 'The Neighborhoods of Northanger Abbey' (*ECent* 56[2015] 179–92) explores the significance of geographical spaces in Austen's novel in order to see the relation between the abbey, a local estate, and the nation, a 'geographical area whose inhabitants are unified by a shared cultural inheritance and religion' (p. 179). Benis is interested in exploring the neighbourhood as this is a layer situated between the state and the local estate. Bath is a town without neighbourhoods as people come and go for a relatively short period of time, while the estate of General Tilney is deeply connected to its surrounding environs which he governs in 'an authoritarian style' (p. 180). Danielle Spratt's 'Denaturalizing Lady Bountiful: Speaking the Silence of Poverty in Mary Brunton's *Discipline* and Jane Austen's *Emma*' (*ECent* 56[2015] 193–208) observes that the female protagonists of both novels end up assuming not only the 'normative domestic role as wife and mother' but also 'the more public role of Lady Bountiful' (p. 193), a lady of the upper class who, by showing a paternalistic philanthropy for her tenants, also maintains class differences. Spratt claims that both Austen and Brunton 'expose the mythological origins and the practical inadequacies of the Lady Bountiful model' (p. 194), as neither Ellen nor Emma is able 'to provide any true relief to the indigent who live in their communities' (p. 195). Olivera Jokic's 'The Odds and the Ends: What To Do with Some Letters of Catharine Macaulay' (*ECent* 56[2015] 209–25) investigates this female historian (1731–91), discussing how an eighteenth-century woman's professional reputation 'is tied up to the status of her letters and her correspondents' (p. 209). Jokic points out that Macaulay's letters have had an important influence on 'prominent figures in the history of feminism' (p. 210). Yet the politeness of her letters was also dictated by her gender as she never discussed personal matters with male correspondents. Laura E. Thomason's 'The Dilemma of Friendship in Austen's *Emma*' (*ECent* 56[2015] 227–41) observes that the titular character, even though 'handsome, clever, and rich' (p. 227), never experiences deep and true friendship, as characters 'are separated as much by social position as by difference in personality' (p. 228). Emma's 'circumstances and personality form a vicious cycle that prevents her from being a friend' (p. 233), and she can thus experience true friendship only in the companionate marriage with Mr Knightley. Misty Krueger's 'From Marginalia to Juvenilia: Jane Austen's Vindication of the Stuarts' (*ECent* 56[2015] 243–59) explores Austen's juvenile engagement with history-writing. In a parody of Oliver Goldsmith's *History of England* [1771], Austen recuperates and idealizes the historical figure of Mary Queen of Scots, 'engag[ing] with the traditions of martyrology and vindication' (p. 244). Krueger contends that before starting her *History* of the Stuarts, Austen drafted a 'defence' as shown in the marginal comments she wrote on the family's copies of Goldsmith's *History of England* and Knox's *Elegant Extracts*. 'Austen's marginalia', Krueger explains, 'act as prologue to the dramatization that is her *History of England*' (p. 250). Finally, Jodi L. Wyett's

'Female Quixotism Refashioned: *Northanger Abbey*, the Engaged Reader, and the Woman Writer' (*ECent* 56[2015] 261–76) maintains that in *Northanger Abbey* Austen revalued the figure of the supposedly uncritical, novel-reading, female Quixote. Austen uses this trope 'as a means of validating the intellectual labor of women readers and writers in *Northanger Abbey*' (p. 266). For Catherine Morland, her quixotism is the only way to 'understand her social world and the motives of those within it' (p. 268).

Various other articles have been published on Jane Austen's works, and some of them focus particularly on the re-adaptation of her novels in different media, and the success that such adaptations have brought Austen in the twenty-first century. Valerie Wainwright's 'On Being Tough-Minded: *Sense and Sensibility* and the Moral Psychology of "Helping"' (*P&L* 39:iA[2015] A195–A211) explores the Lockean notion of 'reasonable exertion', namely the 'rational assessment of one's circumstances and objectives' in explaining characters' behaviour in Austen's novel, arguing that not even so sensible a character as Elinor Dashwood is able to be 'invincibly rational' when pursuing her own interests (p. A195). According to Austen, Wainwright explains, even the most 'tough-minded of women' is vulnerable 'to the effects of the most potent of desires' (p. A197). Ashly Bennett's 'Shame and Sensibility: Jane Austen's Humiliated Heroines' (*SiR* 54[2015] 377–400) explores the shift in the perception of both the excess of sensibility and affected insensibility at the end of the eighteenth century. Not being able to command one's feelings was considered shameful. Nevertheless, Bennett points out that 'Across her novels, Austen fashions shame as a valuable mediator between sentimental absorption and what she terms, in *Northanger Abbey*, "affected indifference"' (p. 378). In her defence of the novel, Austen appears to place shame as a mediator between 'critical distance' and 'impassioned investment' for both the novelist and the novel reader (p. 380), as this feeling enables both the 'recognition and relishing of . . . one's own absorption' (p. 388). Enit Karafili Steiner's 'Between Cohesion and Reform in *Sense and Sensibility*' (*WW* 22[2015] 455–71) contends that in this novel Austen promotes a type of sociability derived from Addison's *Spectator* while recognizing, at the same time, the need to adjust this social behaviour to her post-revolutionary time. Austen's way, Steiner points out, is a forerunner of 'twentieth-century discussions of human interactions in the public sphere of civil society' (p. 455). Thomas W. Stanford III's ' "What do I not owe you!" ': An Examination of Gratitude in Jane Austen's *Pride and Prejudice*' (*LogosJ* 18[2015] 152–68) explores humility in Austen's novel 'as an antidote both to unjust pride and to the tendency to prejudice others' (p. 152), posing 'gratitude' as 'a sign and effect of authentic humility' (p. 153) and as 'the proper response to a gift' (p. 154). David Sigler's ' "It is unaccountable": Anxiety and the Cause of Desire in *Pride and Prejudice*' (in his *Sexual Enjoyment in British Romanticism: Gender and Psychoanalysis, 1753–1835*, pp. 57–91) argues that Austen's novels comment 'on sexual difference and its discursive, cultural, and economic implications, even as it trains readers to accept the inevitability and desirability of marriage' (p. 58). *Pride and Prejudice*, Sigler observes, is the most heteronormative among Austen's novels as Elizabeth Bennet can avoid choosing between 'marriage for sexual pleasure' and 'marriage for financial interest' because both options are embodied by the 'wealthy-but-sensual' Darcy (p. 58). Sigler contends that, according to Austen, the 'subject's anxiety stems from ... the restrictions on enjoyment that culture routinely imposes upon its membership' (p. 73). Deirdre Le Faye's 'The Archaeology of *Pride and Prejudice*' (in Baker ed., *Studies in Victorian and Modern Literature: A Tribute to John Sutherland*, pp. 263–73; this title is covered fully in Chapter XIV) explores changes between the creation of *First Impressions* in 1797 and its later version, *Pride and Prejudice*, in 1812, noticing that the closing stages of the plot reflect changes in the historical context of the text's production, thus bringing the action nearer to the world of readers in 1813. Brett Jenkins's 'I Love You to Meaninglessness: From Mortal Characters to Immortal Character Types in *P&P* Fanfiction' (*JPC* 48[2015] 371–85) contends that by taking the form of either prequel or sequel, or by exploring the narrative gaps of the canonical text, the fans of fanfiction become 'prosumers', namely 'both producers and consumers' of the canonical text by creating stories based on the source text. This activity allows fans to improve their 'social networking and community building' while also indulging their 'identification with characters from a particular novel, film, cartoon, game, or comic' (p. 372). However, the never-ending process of new character creation and plot extension empties the source characters of meaning, as 'The wholeness of the character is disrupted by supplementation and consequently a new whole and a new meaning is created' (p. 376). Ben Dew's 'Rewriting Popular Classics as Popular Fiction: Jane Austen, Zombies, Sex and Vampires' (in Berberich, ed., *The Bloomsbury Introduction to Popular Fiction*, pp. 282–95) observes that current novel adaptations of *Pride and Prejudice* tend to follow a pattern of 'four narrative strategies sometimes used in isolation, sometimes in combination' (p. 283). There can be an extension of the primary plot in the form of prequel or sequel, or a 'variation' which changes an element of the plotline and reimagines its consequences. A third type of novel adaptation is the change of focalization, providing the story from a different point of view. A fourth type is moving the action to a different cultural and historical context, as in Helen Fielding's *Bridget Jones's Diary* [1996], which describes the titular character's life in 1990s London. All types merge 'Austen's writing with a genre of popular fiction' (p. 285) such as zombies, vampires, or soft-core pornography. Glen Creeber's 'Romance Re-scripted: *Lost in Austen*'s Comparative Historical Analysis of Post-Feminist Culture' (*FeministMS* 15[2015] 562–75) contends that the aim of the television series adaptation of *Pride and Prejudice* is to make a modern audience reflect on the important 'social, cultural, and political changes that have taken place over the last two hundred years' (p. 563), particularly concerning women's freedom and emancipation. The time-travelling of *Lost in Austen*'s heroine is an excellent narrative strategy that allows the juxtaposition of women's condition between the nineteenth and twentieth centuries, hence treating a contemporary amnesia among young women in relation to the battle of feminist movements. *Lost in Austen*, Creeber claims, asks important questions about our 'increasingly hyper-sexualized culture, one that has cleverly re-objectified the female subject' (p. 564). Tammy Powley's 'Romance Fiction in Florida: The Crisscross of Jane Austen and Angela Hunt' (in Powley and Van Camp, eds., *Women of Florida Fiction: Essays on 12*

*Sunshine State Writers*, pp. 123–32), observes that Jane Austen's work has developed 'what is now a well-established formula for the perfect romance novel' (p. 123), and one twentieth-century author who draws extensively on Austen's formula is Florida writer Angela Hunt. Although academics tend to devalue contemporary commercial romance fiction, Powley argues that 'indulging fantasies and emotional values...attract readers to romance fiction'; this aspect makes it not 'that far removed from the classics and, therefore, worth exploring, at least in the sense of their relationship to one another' (p. 124). Douglas Murray's 'Donwell Abbey and Box Hill: Purity and Danger in Jane Austen's *Emma*' (*RES* 66[2015] 954–70) argues that though the often quoted passage of *Emma* describing the estate of Donwell Abbey is considered to be Austen's tacit 'contribution to the nation-defining discourse of the Napoleonic and post-Napoleonic era' (p. 954), this description is also a strategy Austen exploits to reveal the character of Emma. J.P.C. Brown's 'Screening Austen: The Case of *Emma*' (*Adaptation* 8[2015] 207–36) argues that some pages of Austen's novels are well suited to filmic adaption. One example of this, Brown contends, is the scene where 'Emma waits for Harriet to complete her purchase in Ford's' (p. 216), which 'invites filming and editing according to the principle of montage' with the juxtapositions of shots that show Emma's reaction to selected details and the perception of reality through her eyes. Jeanine M. Grenberg's 'Self-Deception and Self-Knowledge: Jane Austen's *Emma* as an example of Kant's Notion of Self-Deception' (*Con-Textos Kantianos* 2[2015] 162–76) addresses the Kantian notion of harmony, which a character can only achieve through the removal of self-deception as this is an obstacle to self-knowledge. Emma is an example of self-deception: 'because she is frightened to lose her happy situation at Hartfield, she constructs a belief that she never wants to marry' (p. 165). Lauren Miskin's '"True Indian muslin" and the Politics of Consumption in Jane Austen's *Northanger Abbey*' (*JEMCS* 15:ii[2015] 5–26) points out that the first flirtation between Henry Tilney and Catherine Morland brings about a conversation about muslin. Miskin intriguingly observes that Henry's 'fashionable taste' for Indian muslin shows a new masculine identity based on the consumption of the products derived from the expansion of the British empire, while 'his interest in "true Indian muslin" indicates...his political allegiance to larger structures of imperial and patriarchal oppression' (p. 6). Kate Nesbit's '"Taste in noises": Registering, Evaluating, and Creating Sound and Story in Jane Austen's *Persuasion*' (*SNNTS* 47[2015] 451–68) contends that the way Anne Elliot engages with her 'ingestion, evaluation', and 'creation of sound' signals a transition in her character from 'passive detachment' to 'critical engagement with the world around her' (p. 452). Gregory Tate's 'Austen's Literary Alembic: *Sanditon*, Medicine, and the Science of the Novel' (*NCL* 70[2015] 336–62) explores Austen's unfinished work, arguing that the period of illness during which she wrote it contributed to her ideas about the relationship between the novel and science. As voiced by the character of Sir Edward, *Sanditon* 'promotes a view of the novel as an objective and professional articulation of knowledge' (p. 338). Charlotte Brewer's '"That reliance on the ordinary": Jane Austen and the *Oxford English Dictionary*' (*RES* 66[2015] 744–65) compares Austen's quoted material in the non-surviving successive editions (c.1884–1928 *OED1* and 1972–86 Burchfield's Supplement) of the *OED* which have been preserved only in the *OED Online*. Brewer notes that Austen's novels 'have never been used, to any significant degree, to illustrate first use (or indeed any use) of morally or socially evaluative vocabulary, or, in general, vocabulary that is conceptual, aesthetic or "writerly"' (p. 746). Nevertheless, Brewer argues, Austen was quoted quite significantly in the first edition of the *OED*. Brewer concludes by arguing that, in its quotations, the *OED* might still mirror gender and other types of bias 'unconsciously reproduced' in the choice of its literary quotations. Finally, Barbara M. Benedict's 'Satire, Sentiment and Desacralization: The Relic and the Commodity in Jane Austen's Novels' (in Partenza, ed., *Dynamics of Desacralization: Disenchanted Literary Talents*, pp. 53–70) argues that Austen rarely describes objects or clothes, and when she does, her lingering on the character's obsession for materiality has the function of questioning her contemporary 'increasingly mercenary and crass' society and 'the degradation of spiritual values in a culture of superficiality, materialism and self-indulgence' (p. 53). Austen's focus on the objectification of women and marriage, Benedict concludes, 'portrays the transformation of what had been a sacred contract, marriage, into a mercenary calculation' (p. 63).

*Home and Nation in British Literature from English to French Revolutions*, edited by A.D. Cousins and Geoffrey Payne, contains three chapters of interest to scholars of the Romantic novel. The central argument of the book is an overview of the significance of home and the nation in the period between the Glorious Revolution and the French Revolution, 'a period when Britain fought an internecine war—with its devastating, traumatizing, effects on how Britons thought of the "nation" and "home"' (p. 1). The book aims to draw attention to the actuality of such themes, in an epoch of 'mass displacements and asylum-seeking', when 'a great many people are looking for "home" or struggling to establish the "nation"' (p. 1). The chapters on the novel focus on how writers discussed the notion of home and on 'how domestic economy mirrored that of the homeland', thereby questioning how 'the actuality of revolution—or fear of it—threaten[ed] the idea of home itself and ma[de] the domestic a microcosm of the debates over national concerns' (p. 11). David Punter's 'Home, Homeland, and the Gothic' (pp. 169–83), though focusing more on poetry, also explores the notion of home and the nation in the Gothic novel. The beginning of Ann Radcliffe's *The Italian* [1796] refers to the European world as the other, 'so long subjected to tyranny' (p. 176), which is doomed to increase in the aftermath of the French Revolution. The Gothic of the northern nations is viewed as 'organic growth' in opposition to the Gothic of southern Europe based on 'a set of impositions of a false order which condemn the inhabitants of those countries to repression and tyranny' (p. 177). However, Punter contends that such fear is a cover for another enemy, namely 'the radicals and supposed reductionists of the Revolution' who really threaten home and the nation. Matthew Lewis's *The Monk* [1794], on the other hand, 'positions England and the English as decisively superior to the benighted south' (p. 178). Gary Kelly's 'Jane Austen and the Modern Home' (pp. 219–33) explores the relation between home and the nation in Austen's oeuvre. Considering the notion of home in the Romantic period as 'the principal space for biological, cultural, and economic reproduction of the family' (p. 219), Kelly explores how Austen supported the notion of modern home in her novels, envisioned as a space of rational and social management, the improvement of which would provide material and physical comforts to its inhabitants. Dani Napton's 'Sir Walter Scott: Home, Nation, and the Denial of Revolution' (pp. 250–65) points out that in both *Waverley* and *Redgauntlet*, 'place, space, and landscape are fundamental to Scott's depiction of the...Hanoverian monarchy's consolidation of its political stature and stability', while 'rebellion is represented as delusional fanaticism' (p. 251). In Scott's novels, domestic harmony is only reserved to his 'counter-revolutionary characters' (p. 251).

Ten articles on Walter Scott were published this year. Maeve Adams's ' "The force of my narrative": Persuasion, Nation, and Paratext in Walter Scott's Early Waverley Novels' (*ELH* 82[2015] 937–67) focuses on the first three novels of the series and on how Scott built a rhetorical force to persuade his readers of their sense of 'national consensus and community' (p. 944). Christopher J. Scalia's 'Walter Scott's "everlasting said he's and said she's": Dialogue, Painting, and the Status of the Novel' (*ELH* 82[2015] 1159–77) contends that though Scott's use of speech in his works has been extensively explored, scholars have generally neglected the passages where Scott 'evaluates his approach to dialogues' (p. 1160). Padma Rangarajan's 'History's Rank Stew: Walter Scott, James Mill, and the Politics of Time' (*Romanticism* 21[2015] 59–71) views Walter Scott's *The Chronicles of the Canongate* 'as a single narrative' (p. 59) rather than separate stories. Rangarajan contends that these tales are united by the old Scottish neighbourhood, from which they 'geographically and historically radiat[e]' (p. 60). Tara Ghoshal Wallace's 'Historical *Redgauntlet*: Jacobite Delusions and Hanoverian Fantasies' (*Romanticism* 21[2015] 145–59) argues that Scott's construction of both narrative and characters are the result of historical forces, 'even when both are fictional' (p. 146). Wallace explains that 'Scott's fiction, though it depicts Redgauntlet's aims as delusional and as a misreading of diffuse malaise, nonetheless grounds them in a potent set of socio-political institutional instabilities under Hanoverian rule' (p. 153). Chad T. May's 'Sir Walter Scott's *The Monastery* and the Representation of Religious Belief' (*SSL* 41[2015] 191–208) observes that Scott's use of the supernatural makes this novel quite different from the rest. Nevertheless, May explains that here Scott exploits the supernatural dimension in order to express the impossibility of explaining 'certain elements of the human condition' (p. 191), particularly when they concern 'the psychological or emotional conflicts' that may overwhelm the individual before 'any type of religious conversion' (p. 205). Nancy Moore Goslee's 'Larder and Library: Revising Archives in *Castle Dangerous*' (*ScotLR* 7[2015] 63–73) maintains that if the episode of the Douglas larder in Scott's novel suggests 'the collapse of romance' and of 'chivalric ideals' (p. 65), and is a symbolic representation of *thanatos*, as the Scottish chief decides to destroy all provision rather than leave them in the hands of the English enemies; the tower library, on the other hands, 'points towards an *eros* that might re-energize some form of ongoing civilization, though only if we acknowledge and recall the threat of its opposite' (p. 66). Caroline McCracken-Flesher's 'Anxiety in the Archive: From the Antiquary to the Absent Author' (*ScotLR* 7[2015] 75–94) explains 'the anxiety that lies at the heart of any exercise in the archive' (p. 76) which describes the impossibility of grasping all its contents, as 'It is the nature of the archive to be incomplete and thereby excessive' (p. 89). Julie Watt's 'We Did Not Think That He Could Die: Letitia Elizabeth Landon and the Afterlife of Scott's Heroines' (*ScotLR* 7[2015] 119–34) contends that Scott's female characters are not well rounded, as the young heroines are usually idealizations while the older ones are caricatures. Yet when such characters are based on a real person they are more believable. Caroline McCracken-Flesher's 'Sir Walter Scott: Life-Writing as Anti-Romance' (*WC* 46[2015] 102–8) points out that 'Scott excelled in ordinariness' (p. 102) and that 'Scott's long career, from poetry through the novel and into prose constitute a life study in life-writing' (p. 107). The final article on Scott is Robert Mayer's 'Scott's Editing: History, Polyphony, Authority' (*MP* 112[2015] 661–90), which focuses on Scott's early editorial work of Border ballads and Dryden. Mayer argues that these early editions reveal important information 'about Scott as an author' (p. 662).

An issue of *Women's Writing* gathers a series of articles on Ann Radcliffe. JoEllen DeLucia's 'Radcliffe, George Robinson and Eighteenth-Century Print Culture: Beyond the Circulating Library' (*WW* 22[2015] 287–99) 'reconsiders the gendered and generic hierarchies that have shaped studies of the circulation and reception of Ann Radcliffe's work' (p. 287). Radcliffe's change of publisher and her experience of George Robinson's cultural milieu, in which he surrounded himself with radical authors and dealt with a wide range of publications, from translations to political works, positions Radcliffe in a wider cultural debate than the mere fashionable circulating libraries of London. Robert Miles's 'The Surprising Mrs Radcliffe: Udolpho's Artful Mysteries' (*WW* 22[2015] 300–16) contends that Radcliffe's practice of rationally explaining the supernatural is not an easy way to solve the plot but, rather, a device through which Radcliffe 'artfully managed to build meaning' (p. 300), as well as 'a means of keeping antithetical possibilities in solution' (p. 301). Andrew Smith's 'Radcliffe's Aesthetics; or, The Problem with Burke and Lewis' (*WW* 22[2015] 317–30) argues that Lewis's novel *The Monk* prompted Radcliffe to change her aesthetic of terror as she had elaborated it in *Udolpho*, and that in her subsequent novel, *The Italian*, she would 'conceal an all too self-conscious aesthetic of Terror' (p. 318), thereby renouncing its 'rhetorical construction' (p. 320). Jakub Lipski's 'The Masquerade in Ann Radcliffe's *The Mysteries of Udolpho* and *The Italian*' (*WW* 22[2015] 331–42) contends that the masquerade scenes in both novels project an ambiance of 'utopian fairyland' while simultaneously acting as 'a plot catalyst' (p. 331). Marianna D'Ezio's '"As like as peppermint water is to good French brandy": Ann Radcliffe and Hester Lynch Salusbury (Thrale) Piozzi' (*WW* 22[2015] 343–54) observes that though Radcliffe had never travelled to Italy, the southern landscape is where she set her novels. In order to be able to depict a believable geographical setting, Radcliffe drew heavily on Hester Piozzi's Grand Tour account, *Observations and Reflections Made in the Course of a Journey through France, Italy, and Germany* [1789]. D'Ezio claims that the two female writers mutually inspired each other's work, and that Radcliffe secretly admired Piozzi's nonconformist life experiences as a liberated woman. Another two articles and a book chapter on Ann Radcliffe explore the significance of materiality, death, and law in her novels. Yoon Sun Lee's 'Radcliffe's Materiality' (*RCPS* February[2015]) contends that 'Radcliffe's Gothic represents a certain materialist vision of the world', and that *The Mysteries of Udolpho* [1794] is 'a phenomenon of continuous material surfaces and folds, rather than...a reflection of consciousness or purposive ideological construction' (para. 3). Carol Margaret Davison's 'Trafficking in Death and (Un)dead Bodies: Necro-Politics and Poetics in the Works of Ann Radcliffe' (*IJGHS* 14[2015] 37–47) observes that *The Mysteries of Udolpho* mirrors the cultural changes concerning the relationship between the dead and the living in the late eighteenth century, a time which saw them 'negotiat[ing] a new social contract reflective of national values' (p. 37) that was 'decidedly Protestant in its make-up' (p. 40). Peter DeGabriele's chapter, 'The Witness and the Law: Ann Radcliffe's *The Italian*' (in his *Sovereign Power and the Enlightenment*, pp. 111–38), 'look[s] at the intellectual origins of the regime of the sovereignty of the laws in the work of Montesquieu and William Blackstone' while simultaneously exposing how Radcliffe's peculiar treatment of the Gothic 'manages to challenge the totalizing tendency of the law's knowledge' (p. 112), because 'the law cannot contain the form of knowledge represented by testimony' (p. 113). DeGabriele explains that by showing that 'the origin of the subject falls outside the cognizance of the law', Radcliffe's novel *The Italian* 'questions the law's supposed immortality and omniscience' (p. 135).

A series of eight articles and a book chapter focus on Frances Burney's major novels *Evelina* [1778], *Cecilia* [1782], *Camilla* [1796], and *The Wanderer* [1814]. Marcie Frank's 'Frances Burney's Theatricality' (*ELH* 82[2015] 615–35) explores the influence of the comedy of manners on the novel towards the end of the eighteenth century, focusing particularly on Frances Burney, 'who wrote plays alongside novels over the course of her career' (p. 616). Frank claims that Burney's modulation of distance between readers, narrator, and characters, such as the use of free indirect style, derives from 'the configuration of theater, shame, and narration in her oeuvre' (p. 616). F. Mark Vareschi's 'Motive, Intention, Anonymity, and *Evelina*' (*ELH* 82[2015] 1135–58) discusses the much-debated literary notion of author's intentionality in fiction by exploring anonymity in Burney's *Evelina*. Vareschi aims at 'reorient[ing] discussions of authorial anonymity from motive to intention', and he wants to 'recuperate intention...as a means of under-standing the context of...textual production' (p. 1136). Cassandra Ulph's 'Frances Burney's Private Professionalism' (*BJECS* 38[2015] 377–93) points out that Burney's literary circle of friends at her father's house in St Martin's Street, at Hester Thrale's literary salon in Streatham, and of the bluestockings at Montagu House, all contributed to condensing a mixture of 'domestic privacy' and 'artistic professionalism' of which Burney would make use in her more mature works. In *The Wanderer*, for example, Burney supports 'professional specialization' in a domestic environment where 'artistic virtu-osity can be practiced without commodification' (p. 388). Hilary Havens's

'Omitting Lady Grace: *The Provok'd Husband* in Frances Burney's *Camilla* and *The Wanderer*' (*BJECS* 38[2015] 413–24) considers Burney's use of Vanbrugh and Cibber's theatrical performance of *The Provok'd Husband* [1728] in *Camilla* and *The Wanderer* as a 'commentary on private theatrical traditions' (p. 415). Havens contends that the different use of such performances in the two novels shows Burney's changed view towards the figure of the 'virtuous heroine' (p. 415). Hilary Havens also published 'Revisions and Revelations in Frances Burney's *Cecilia* Manuscript' (*SEL* 55[2015] 537–58), where she contends that after the successful publication of her first novel *Evelina*, Burney wrote *The Witlings*, a play where she satirized the famous bluestocking Elizabeth Montagu. Burney's family, worried about the consequences this could imply, suggested that Burney write another novel instead. The *Witlings* play, Havens argues, is revived in *Cecilia*, a novel that shows a great deal of the sarcasm present in the play. However, the cuts she made to the 'incisive satire' in the manuscript draft of *Cecilia* held at the Berg Collection of the New York Public Library 'confirm...that *Cecilia* was subject to the same social and familial forces that stifled *The Witlings*' (p. 554). Meghan Jordan's 'Madness and Matrimony in Frances Burney's *Cecilia*' (*SEL* 55[2015] 559–78) notices that this work both 'subvert[s] and preserve[s] the ideological dominance of marital bliss' (p. 559). Burney, Jordan observes, revises the marriage plot by providing her heroine with 'individualization and social restoration' (p. 561), primarily because marriage fails to offer these things as, under its institution, women become invisible. The conclusion of the novel and the heroine's madness 'suggest that married women are just as "shackled" as single ones' (p. 567), and Cecilia's madness stands as a symbol of 'her cultural silencing...and of her rebellion in articulating her desire' (p. 575). Carmel Murphy's '"The stormy sea of politics": The French Revolution and Frances Burney's *The Wanderer*' (*WW* 22[2015] 485–504) contends that both Scott's *Waverley* and Burney's novel respond to the consequences of the French Revolution; however, they had a very different reception: to *Waverly*'s success, Murphy counterpoises the failure of Burney's novel, 'as a result of its cosmopolitan agenda and Burney's revival of revolutionary feminist concerns' (p. 488). In fact, Murphy explains, *The Wanderer* 'offered a nuanced exploration of the various social, economic and sexual injustices to which women of varying classes were subject' (p. 490), in addition to critiquing 'a dominant culture of militant nationalism and xenophobia' (p. 493). Yih-Dau Wu's '"I suppose it is not sentimental enough!": *Evelina* and the Power of Feeling' (*TkR* 45:ii[2015] 3–24) contends that feeling in *Evelina* is not intense enough to meet eighteenth-century standards for sentimental novels. While for Sterne and Mackenzie, 'to feel intensely means to feel spontaneously', for Burney 'the virtue of feeling lies in its ability to cement interpersonal connections' (p. 5). Heather King's 'Pictures of Women in Frances Burney's *Cecilia* and *Camilla*: How Cecilia Looks and what Camilla Sees' (in Peggy Thompson, ed., *Beyond Sense and Sensibility: Moral Formation and the Literary Imagination from Johnson to Wordsworth*, pp. 45–59) contends that the illustration in the frontispiece of the first edition of *Evelina* reminds readers that 'sentimental constructions of women's morally influential beauty and virtue are built implicitly on women's suffering' (p. 46).

King argues that in her following two novels, *Cecilia* and *Camilla*, Burney rejects this type of sensibility, which reduces 'the sight of suffering to an aesthetic object' (p. 48), by removing the pain of women's weeping from the reader's sight, and turning women's 'gaze inward on their own moral development' (p. 47).

Mary Shelley has also attracted a large number of publications, mainly focusing on her most famous novel *Frankenstein* [1818]. Shelley's less well-known novel, *The Last Man* [1826], has also drawn some attention, particularly for its concerns with the end of the world determined by geographical catastrophe and plague. Deanna P. Koretsky's '"Unhallowed arts": *Frankenstein* and the Poetics of Suicide' (*ERR* 26[2015] 241–60) argues that 'the Romantic period was one of repressed sensuality, ineluctable destiny, and irremediable malaise', all 'strong emotions' which 'were often understood to have suicide as their final result' (p. 241). Koretsky contends that suicide in *Frankenstein* functions as a trope through which Shelley critiques individualism and interprets 'Romanticism's interest in radical politics' (p. 241), as 'suicide may represent a political act' (p. 243). Stephen Bertman's 'The Role of the Golem in the Making of *Frankenstein*' (*KSR* 29[2015] 42–50) contends that there are some similarities between 'the Golem of Jewish folklore and the Creature that inhabits Shelley's novel' (p. 46). Bertman suggests that both are gigantic figures brought into existence by 'arcane knowledge' who then become dangerous to others. However, there is a reversal of roles because while the monster in Jewish folklore is 'an *opponent* of persecution' in Shelley's novel it becomes 'a Jew-like *object* of persecution because of its inherent otherness' (p. 46, emphasis original). Zoe Beenstock's 'Lyrical Sociability: The Social Contract and Mary Shelley's *Frankenstein*' (*P&L* 39:ii[2015] 406–21) observes that the predicament of the creature in *Frankenstein*, namely his condition as 'an inherently sociable being who cannot be socialized', invites us to think about 'one of the major questions of seventeenth- and eighteenth-century political theory: whether individualism is compatible with sociability' (pp. 406–7). The creature suffers rejection because he is 'formed of individual parts that share no common background' thus becoming a symbol of a 'corporate social body that fails to cohere' (p. 414). Erin Hawley's 'The Bride and Her Afterlife: Female Frankenstein Monsters on Page and Screen' (*LFQ* 43[2015] 218–31) maintains that Shelley's failure to give birth to a female counterpart for the creature has stimulated a series of literary and screen adaptations, making the female monster 'a cultural icon' (p. 218). Hawley questions '*why*' this female character has elicited 'such cultural fascination' and '*how*' she operates in cultural narratives about monstrous and posthuman presence' (p. 218, emphasis original). Christina Schneider's 'Monstrosity in the English Gothic Novel' (*Victorian* 3:i[2015] 1–11) argues that in *Frankenstein*, the 'moral degeneration of the creature, which occurs because he is rejected for his deformity, represents society's fear of the revenge of the outsider' (p. 4). He is also a symbol of the ' "civilization" of colonized people ... Once "civilized", these people cannot be returned to their savagery and therefore pose a threat to societal order with their "purposeful immorality" '. Lydia McDermott's 'Birthing Rhetorical Monsters: How Mary Shelley Infuses Mêtis with the Maternal in Her 1831 Introduction to *Frankenstein*' (*RhetR* 34[2015] 1–18) observes that Shelley uses a maternal rhetoric called mêtis, in vogue from classical times until the birth of professional obstetrics in the nineteenth century. According to folkloric beliefs, women had 'the power to deform their fetus' through their imagination. McDermott argues that though this popular belief diminished the credibility of women, in some ways it also gave them 'an important rhetorical power to "form"' (p. 2). McDermott claims that, in her 1831 introduction to *Frankenstein*, Shelley describes her creative process 'as distinct from the male Romantics' birth descriptions and as inscribed with the maternal imagination' (p. 10), thus reasserting her sole responsibility for the creation of the novel and establishing the correct contribution of her husband Percy to it. Donna Mitchell's ' "Being a mother is an attitude, not a biological relation": Mother as Monster in Mary Shelley's *Frankenstein*' (*JDS* special issue, 'Monstrous Shadows' [2015] 39–51) also deals with motherhood in Shelley's novel. Mitchell contends that *Frankenstein* challenges the traditional mother figure because Victor, the creator of the monster, takes on a matriarchal role which 'subverts the family's unity, and leads to social disorder as the mother ... is suddenly removed' (p. 39), while Victor fails to perform his parental role towards the creature. Melanie Friese's 'The Monster's Humanity: Racism and the Foreigner in *Frankenstein*' (*STDR* 12[2015] 91–100) observes that if on the one hand Shelley's creature 'represents all types of foreigners by being the most extreme foreign entity' (p. 95), on the other hand his articulate speech 'does not correspond with British stereotypes of foreigners' (p. 93). Jude Wright's 'Listening to the Monster: Eliding and Restoring the Creature's Voice in Adaptations of *Frankenstein*' (*JAFP* 8:iii[2015] 249–66) provides an overview of the monster's speech and/or silence in various adaptations of Shelley's novel. There are three further book chapters that engage with Shelley's *Frankenstein*. Charles E. Robinson's 'Percy Bysshe Shelley's Text(s) in Mary Wollstonecraft Shelley's *Frankenstein*' (in Weinberg and Webb, eds., *The Neglected Shelley*, pp. 117–36; fully reviewed in Section 3 of this chapter), explores the real contribution of Percy B. Shelley to his wife's novel, arguing that in addition to writing the preface to the 1818 edition as well as a review of the novel which was not published until 1832, a comparative analysis with Percy's literary works suggests that he may have 'contributed 4,000–5,000 of his own words to the novel' (p. 121). Sharon Ruston's 'Has Man "Paid too dear a price for his empire"? Monsters in Romantic-Era Literature' (in Calzoni and Perletti, eds., *Monstrous Anatomies: Literary and Scientific Imagination in Britain and Germany during the Long Nineteenth Century*, pp. 133–48; also covered in Chapter XIV) explores 'literary and medical theories of monstrosity in the 1790s and 1810s that reveal a change in the way monstrosity is viewed' (p. 133). Ruston explains that Edmund Burke's use of 'monstrous' in his *Reflections on the Revolution in France* [1790] likens the threatening populace to 'a healthy body politic, one that is animated by the vital principle of heredity' (p. 134), while Mary Shelley's *Frankenstein* shows that 'monsters are ... the responsibility of society', the result of 'Man's attempt to conquer nature' (p. 134). Finally, Jesse Weiner's 'Lucretius, Lucan, and Mary Shelley's *Frankenstein*' (in Rogers and Stevens, eds., *Classical Traditions in Science Fiction*, pp. 46–74) investigates the literary allusions to Lucretius's and Lucan's epic poems in Shelley's novel, arguing that such intertextualities prepare the ground for both ethical and scientific questions. Weiner claims that Victor Frankenstein's assemblage of body parts finds a correspondent in the atomism of Lucretius's *De Rerum Natura*, where he 'defines "monsters" as discordant assemblages of limbs' (p. 52), while a second model for Shelley's monster is to be found in 'the Erichtho's episode of Lucan's *Bellum Civile*' (p. 47), a 'necromantic episode' on which Shelley 'bases the life cycle of the corpse reanimated by Frankenstein' (p. 68). There are also two articles and a book chapter concerned with Shelley's less popular third novel, *The Last Man*. Melissa Bailes's 'The Psychologization of Geological Catastrophe in Mary Shelley's *The Last Man*' (*ELH* 82[2015] 671–99) argues that Shelley critiques contemporary scientific theories of geology and of cataclysmic destruction such as Cuvier's catastrophism, which 'established extinction as incontrovertible fact' (p. 672). To the various extinction theories, in *The Last Man* Shelley 'assert[s] the primacy of her chosen hypothesis, demonstrated in futurity: plague' (p. 682), thereby shifting the focus on to the individual rather than on a mass destruction comprehending all species. J. Jennifer Jones's 'The Art of Redundancy: Sublime Fiction and Mary Shelley's *The Last Man*' (*KSR* 29[2015] 25–41) contends that Shelley's novel critiques the limits of Burke's notion of the sublime, without, however, weakening the potential inherent in sublime fiction. Jones contends that the repetitiveness of the novel, for which it was 'most viciously attacked' (p. 27), represents its most important contribution, because through 'the concept of repetition, Shelley provides an analysis of Burke's theory of the sublime as well as an alternative to it' (p. 27). Of relevance to this section also are two chapters entitled 'Cruel and Unusual Romance: Beckford, Byron and the Abomination of Violence' (pp. 24–61) and 'Reasoning like a Turk: Indolence and Fatalism in *Sardanapalus* and *The Last Man*' (pp. 141–77) (both in Gerard Cohen-Vrignaud, ed., *Radical Orientalism: Rights, Reform, and Romanticism*), reviewed in greater depth in Section 3 of this chapter. Cohen-Vrignaud argues that 'Orientalism and the Gothic "monitor" the "abominations" of tyrants and enable readers to practice their moral sentiments' (p. 33), while 'licenses of Gothic villains depend on juridical inequality' (p. 38), as shown in the novels *Vathek* [1786] by William Beckford and *The Monk* [1796] by Matthew Gregory Lewis. On the other hand, Shelley's *The Last Man* 'locates in the East a refusal to live by the "happier" code of self-endurance and moderation' similarly to Byron's *Sardanapalus*. The plague in Shelley's novel originates in Turkey, thus playing on the orientalist stereotype according to which 'Muslim fatalists did not adequately protect themselves from infection' (p. 160). Shelley's Byronic hero Lord Raymond becomes 'a sensualist unworthy of the family unit that offers economic and sexual security' (p. 166). The plague thus acts as 'an insuperable force that dismantles human fallacies' (p. 170).

Three journal articles and one book chapter were devoted to the fictional work of Mary Wollstonecraft. Laura Kirkley's '*Maria, ou Le Malheur d'être femme*: Translating Mary Wollstonecraft in Revolutionary France' (*BJECS* 38[2015] 239–55), reviewed in Section 1, argues that *Maria, or the Wrongs of Woman* [1798] follows the same radical feminism of her *Vindication of the Rights of Woman* [1792] concerning both 'legal equality' and 'women's right to the experience and expression of sexual desire' (p. 239). A special issue of *Literature Compass* (*LitComp* 12[2015]), 'Romanticism and Suicide', also appeared in 2015, where in the introductory essay (pp. 641–51) the two editors, Michelle Faubert and Nicole Reynolds, argue that 'female suicide in the Romantic era emerges as a powerful trope through which a range of discourses—aesthetic, scientific, religious, philosophical, and political—converge to manage the culture's most unknowable, recalcitrant subjects and bodies, women and subalterns chief among these' (p. 641). Michelle Faubert's 'The Fictional Suicides of Mary Wollstonecraft' (*LitComp* 12[2015] 652–9) contends that while William Godwin's *Memoir* describes Wollstonecraft's suicide attempts as 'acts of passion', in her letters and her two novels Wollstonecraft defends the notion of suicide as a rational choice through which women can assert their agency. Heather Klemann's 'How to Think with Animals in Mary Wollstonecraft's *Original Stories* and *The Wrongs of Woman; or, Maria*' (*L&U* 39[2015] 1–22) points out that in these works Wollstonecraft exploits animal metaphors because they 'model the naturalness of maternal roles' (p. 2). Klemann maintains that 'In both these fictional works animal tropes at once reinforce and redefine gender roles ... and at the same time educate readers on the seemingly irresolvable contradictions of gender equality' (p. 4). Laura Kirkley's ' "Original Spirit": Literary Translations and Translational Literature in the Works of Mary Wollstonecraft' (in Goodman, ed., *Literature and the Development of Feminist Theory*, pp. 13–26) points out that Wollstonecraft's feminist agenda is also visible in her 'interventionist translation', entitled *Elements of Morality for the Use of Young Children* [1790], of Christian Gotthilf Salzmann's *Moralisches Elementarbuch* [1783], where Wollstonecraft 'translates, both literally and metaphorically, the figure of the mother-educator, who, in her final incarnation in *Maria, or the Wrongs of Woman* represents the most progressive stage in her revolutionary feminism' (p. 13), as here she promotes the 'rational mother who raises virtuous citizens' (p. 16). Kirkley contends that 'Wollstonecraft's goal was to form individuals who, far from conforming to the status quo, would exercise their reason to recognize and resist injustice or tyranny' (p. 20).

An article on William Godwin by Daniel DeWispelare entitled 'Fugitive Pieces: Language, Embodiment, and the Case of Caleb Williams' (*ECF* 28:ii[2015/16] 345–73) claims that 'fugitive advertising' provided 'a salient intertext for certain characterological and narrative strategies of the late eighteenth-century novel' (p. 345), and this is evident in Godwin's *Things as They are; or The Adventures of Caleb Williams* [1794]. DeWispelare contends that 'Anglophone communities used fugitive advertisements to invent and propagate ideas of human difference as they related to embodied social interaction' (p. 349), and that Godwin's novel uses 'a fugitive pursuit as a structural narrative element' (p. 352). Lisa Ottum's ' "Shallow" Estates and "Deep" Wild: The Landscapes of Charlotte Smith's Fiction' (*TSWL* 34[2015] 249–72) argues that in both her poetry and fiction Smith critiques 'idealised images of rural England'. To the prospect view of the gentry's gaze Smith counterposes her 'deep landscapes', in order to 'uncover the class and gender biases' (p. 252) of the former. In *Celestina* [1791] and *The Old Manor House*

[1793] 'landscape bears witness to the existence of a history far deeper than tradition, a history that contests the status quo' (p. 266). Jacqueline Labbe's 'Romantic Intertextuality: The Adaptive Weave' (*WC* 46[2015] 44–8) claims that the ' "adaptive weave" represents a network of allusive threads that, once plotted, enables an enhanced understanding of Romantic-period intertextuality' (p. 44). For example, Charlotte Smith transforms 'the standard male character of the novel of sensibility' into an 'inhabitant' of a conflictual 'modern world' (p. 44), as is visible in the character of Orlando in *The Old Manor House*, while 'Austen makes sustained use of most of Smith's novels in all of her own' (p. 46). Miranda Burgess's 'Sydney Owenson's Tropics' (*ERR* 26[2015] 281–8) notices that Owenson's novel *The Missionary: An Indian Tale* [1811] is in line with 'the emergent genre of writings on tropical medicine and tropical hygiene, which competed with the novel in attempting directly to *regulate* . . . the British-Indian world, seeking to shape the practices of colonists . . . and indigenous inhabitants alike' (pp. 282–3, emphasis original). Nicole Reynolds's 'Suicide, Romance, and Imperial Rebellion: Sati and the Lucretia Story in Sydney Owenson's *The Missionary: An Indian Tale*' (*LitComp* 12[2015] 675–82), an essay that is contained in the above-mentioned special issue 'Romanticism and Suicide', explores the politicization of the Hindu custom of widow-burning in Owenson's novel. Specifically, 'by reading the attempted sati of Owenson's female protagonist Luxima . . . as an iteration of the classical Lucretia story', Reynolds explores 'the novel's posited links between female chastity, inter-racial romance, and political community' (p. 675). Karen Steele's 'Irish Incognitos: Transnational Mobility in the National Tales of Maria Edgeworth and Sydney Owenson' (*Éire* 3&4[2015] 94–112) focuses on the 'The Irish Incognito', the penultimate chapter of Richard Lovell and Maria Edgeworth's *An Essay on Irish Bulls* [1802], on Edgeworth's *Ormond* [1817], and on Owenson's *O'Donnel* [1814], in order to explore the 'composite portrait of Irish men and women as cosmopolitan citizens of the world' (p. 95). Jeanne M. Britton's 'Fictional Footnotes, Romantic Orientalism, and the Remediated Novel: Elizabeth Hamilton's *Translation of the Letters of a Hindoo Rajah*' (*ERR* 26[2015] 773–87) points out that this heavily annotated epistolary novel performs a double function, as while the titular character learns the British culture in the main text, the British learn Hindu traditions in the notes. Britton explains that 'the pedagogical aim of Hamilton's notes indicates the very present concern of empire's intellectual and cultural ramifications' (p. 781). Finally, a chapter entitled 'The Stigma of Popularity' (in H. J. Jackson, *Those Who Write for Immortality: Romantic Reputations and the Dream of Lasting Fame*, pp. 63–106) is of interest to the present section on the Romantic novel as, in exploring the reasons behind the more durable legacy of some Romantic novelists than of poets, this chapter 'considers the careers and afterlives of Walter Scott, Jane Austen, and Mary Brunton in conjunction with their ideas about literary fame' (p. 63).

It is also worthwhile signalling Charlotte Gordon's double biography, *Romantic Outlaws: The Extraordinary Lives of Mary Wollstonecraft & Mary Shelley*. Shaped through alternating chapters on both mother and daughter, this section focuses on Mary Shelley while the chapters related to Mary Wollstonecraft are detailed above, in Section 1. This is 'the first full-length exploration of both women's lives', focusing on the influence of Wollstonecraft on her daughter Mary Shelley, and on the latter's 'obsession with her mother' (p. xvi). Gordon maintains that the parallels between the two women are numerous, as both 'mother and daughter attempted to free themselves from the stranglehold of polite society, and both struggled to balance their need for love and companionship with their need for independence' (p. xvii). Charlotte Gordon's biography of Mary Shelley is intense, provocative, and thought-provoking. It depicts an incredibly passionate circle of friends who mused in each other's company and who were deeply inspired by each other's intellect. It certainly shows the accomplishment of a young female writer who well deserved her mother's legacy.

## 3. Poetry

In this section, Matthew Ward covers work on Romantic poets from A to K; Paul Whickman covers poets from L to Z as well as general works on Romantic poetry.

There were a number of general works, either on Romantic poetry specifically or that predominantly featured Romantic poetry, produced in 2015. *Publishing, Editing, and Reception: Essays in Honor of Donald H. Reiman* is a case in point. Edited by Michael Edson, this is an excellent volume commemorating the career of Donald Reiman. The fact that of the twelve chapters in this Festschrift eight consider the work of Shelley, the Shelley circle, or the practice of editing Shelley in particular, reflects Reiman's most significant contribution to Romantic scholarship. Indeed, his influence is such that Michael Edson is right to say that his 'lifelong editorial efforts [have] transformed the field of Shelley studies' (p. xxiii).

*Publishing, Editing, and Reception* is primarily concerned with the multifaceted aspects of editing, particularly of Romantic poets. What is revealing is how these can influence a variety of critical approaches. To this end, the volume is arranged in four thematic units. The first two—'Romantic Publishing and Print Culture' and 'New Perspectives on the Shelley Circle' respectively—focus on Romantic-period 'context'; the final two—'Romantic Bards and Modern Editors' and 'Shelley's Afterlives'—instead consider modern reception and editorship (with Michael J. Neth's essay (pp. 215–44) an interesting exception). What is evident from this collection, however, is that an approach to Romantic writing or editing from the perspective of either temporal space cannot avoid the other entirely. A number of essays on approaches to modern editions of Romantic poetry for instance consider the vexed question of what the poets intended for their *original* readers and whether, in fact, such an 'intentionalist' approach is appropriate at all. Although one may invoke the 'intentional fallacy' in such considerations of intentionality in literary interpretation, this is arguably less suitable when reflecting on typographical presentation, punctuation, or even the idiosyncratic spellings of the author. Investigating an author's publication intentions is complex however, and involves greater examination than simply consulting manuscript drafts or first editions alone. This is the subject of both Hermione de Almeida's (pp. 3–24) and Alice Levine's (pp. 135–52) essays on the relationship between Byron and Murray. For Levine, Byron's published poetry should almost be viewed as a collaboration between poet and publisher, whereas de Almeida stresses Byron's own influence on Murray in championing poets such as Hogg. Similarly, David Greetham (pp. 153–70) explores what can be considered a 'primary' text in relation to the poetry of Shelley, arguing that it is more slippery than many modern editors appreciate, particularly since many poems exist only in a published form. Greetham also makes a convincing argument for Shelley's canonicity as being related to the editorial state of the various poetic editions available throughout history and also how editorial and critical practice are very much interrelated. Indeed, Michael O'Neill's (pp. 77–96) and Stuart Curran's (pp. 65–76) essays both demonstrate how consideration of manuscript drafts can enrich or reformulate readings of poetry. They both also remind us of how successful editors of poetry such as Reiman are also required to possess 'a good ear' as well as a firm grasp of editorial principles. O'Neill's essay, for instance, starts by relating Reiman's noting of the subtlety of rhyme in 'To Jane—The Recollection' that O'Neill was responsible for editing at the time. From this, O'Neill discusses the sophistication and subtlety of Shelley's rhyming, making superb and convincing readings, particularly of The Triumph of Life [1824].

B.C. Barker-Benfield and Michael J. Neth consider the role of the editor with regard to censorship (pp. 185–214, 215–44). Whereas the former considers this in relation to Lady Shelley's contradictory completionist and censorious attitudes to Percy Shelley's poetry after his death, the latter explores the oft-considered revisions to Laon and Cythna [1817], arguing, however, that many of these alterations were pre-emptive, and exist even in manuscript drafts to the poem. The posthumous legacy of Shelley was also explored in Nora Crook's essay, which relates, in a highly original way, Rudyard Kipling's comedic 'Steam Tactics' [1904] to Prometheus Unbound [1820].

Timothy Webb (pp. 245–62) and Charles E. Robinson (pp. 25–42) offer essays that can be seen as exemplifying the other key unifying theme of the volume: the questioning of concepts of single-author Romantic genius. Webb's essay for instance, 'Reading Aloud in the Shelley Circle', considers literary composition—as well as simple experience—to be far more collaborative than is usually thought. He notes too that the oral/aural nature of many of the Shelleys' literary experiences can in fact be observed in the surprisingly 'oral' nature of much of their written work. Robinson similarly considers the under-explored intertextual relationship between Byron and Hazlitt. This is, then, an excellent volume that is both wide-ranging and coherent, illustrating the importance and interrelation of editorial practices to readings of Romantic poetry. This is a fitting tribute to Reiman's career.

Tim Fulford's Romantic Poetry and Literary Coteries: The Dialect of the Tribe is another excellent 2015 publication that helps us to consider Romantic-period writing as not simply the original work of a 'sublime egotist' but as the result of 'literary production in groups' (p. 4). What follows is a convincing account of Romantic authorship as far more of a social experience than is popularly considered. Although his approach is ambitiously multifaceted, Fulford primarily focuses on three 'coteries', 'tribes', or 'sects' of writers: the

Southey/Coleridge (West Country) circle of the 1790s, the circles of labouring-class poets arranged around Clare and Bloomfield, and the so-called 'Cockney school' of poets associated with Leigh Hunt. As seems apparent, the relationship between the rural and the urban or the province and the capital, and the roles such groupings played in inculcating such consciousness, are an important part of the book. The formation of the 'Bristol coterie' of Southey, Coleridge, More, Yearsley, and Mary Robinson in the 1790s for instance, is considered in part to have resulted in a conscious removal from 'the culture of [the] conspicuous consumption and political repression' the poets saw in London (p. 23). The book's coteries become more complex than simple geographical groupings however. When discussing *Confessions of an English Opium Eater* [1821] for instance, and De Quincey's reading of the Solitary's account of an imagined city in Wordsworth's *The Excursion* [1814], Fulford interprets this as the view of 'an individual who speaks... from a rural community' and the scene as 'a rural vision of a heavenly city' (pp. 226–7). The fact that the Solitary's 'vision' is one that, despite his name, is formed from experience of community, and is then subsequently alluded to by De Quincey as a means to illustrate opium visions of London, shows literary 'coteries' working on a number of levels. Not only does De Quincey seemingly emphasize an aesthetic interconnection via intertextuality with Wordsworth, his allusion helps to connect the individual with the community, and the rural with the town. One of Fulford's central theses is that although 'the poetry led the group[s] to be defined by [their] critics' (p. 2), it nevertheless became an important part of the members' poetic self-identities. This manifested itself in a number of ways or, rather, was shaped by a number of factors that Fulford considers in depth. As well as considering the pressures of publication, such as poets banding together to help get their work into print, Fulford explores the individual writers' use of consistent tropes and allusions to the poetry of their peers. The example of De Quincey and Wordsworth is a case in point; other examples include the orientalist intertextuality between Coleridge and Southey as well as Mary Robinson's allusions to both poets in order to define herself as part of the Bristol school. The fact that this practice was also motivated by a need to maximize publication revenue helps to demonstrate how aesthetic considerations were not isolated from the realities of commerce.

Perhaps the most significant aspect of Fulford's book, however, is his work on authorial recovery. As well as more major figures like Coleridge, Fulford is particularly invested in the importance of more minor figures in these various coteries, Mary Robinson and Robert Bloomfield being the two most obvious examples. Whereas Robinson is considered as playing a significant role 'in shaping early Romanticism, as both the object and practitioner of allusions that signposted and cemented the literary partnerships she entered with the Bristol poets' (p. 25), Bloomfield 'had to *make* his locality an authentic site from which Englishness could be derived' (p. 133). Fulford's book, then, is both a fascinating and welcome addition to the study of Romantic poetry and not solely for his work in broadening the canon. Not only does his extensive primary research further emphasize the connections between poets, determining composition to be a communal experience, his attentiveness to the poetry allows us to see this manifesting aesthetically within the work itself.

Partly considered in Section 2 above, Gerard Cohen-Vrignaud's *Radical Orientalism: Rights, Reform and Romanticism* essentially explores the radical implications of orientalist discourse in Romantic-period literature. Cohen-Vrignaud's introductory example of the 1817 case of Thomas Wooler helps illustrate his central thesis. Wooler's comparison of the British people to Algerian slaves and the British government to the 'Great Mogul of the Indian Empire' shows how orientalizing practices became a way to challenge conceptions of British freedom (p. 1). Essentially, the assertion of superior British freedom compared to that encountered in other nations is readily challenged in the same way; the British state is either no different to these foreign powers or its illiberality is regarded as 'un-British' (p.1). As Cohen-Vrignaud puts it, orientalism 'offered pro-reform Britons a forceful way to articulate the rights they were due by society', thus deviating from Edward Said's claim 'that Orientalist art primarily voices imperial designs' (pp. 4–5). This thesis is interesting in its own right, but what is particularly original about the author's approach is his relation of the radical periodical press's invocation of a 'radical Orientalism' to the 'Oriental romances' and satires of Romantic poets such as Byron and Shelley (as well as Mary Shelley and William Beckford's novels, as discussed above). For Cohen-Vrignaud, this not only draws together such figures as Byron and Shelley as writers of a shared tradition, but also allows Byron in particular to be much more readily connected to 'plebeian radicals' than is often considered (p. 3). Indeed Byron, as the author of 'oriental' poems and plays that were both 'literary' and hugely popular, is the most prominently featured major author in the volume. A particular concern of Cohen-Vrignaud's throughout the book is thinking of how authors' use of orientalist tropes allows them to reflect on liberalism—and by extension humanism —in Britain. Chapter 1, for instance, considers Gothic orientalism and how its depiction of bodily violence highlighted the violation by the British state of the 'sanctification of the human body' which is 'at the core of liberalism' (p. 24). Conrad in Byron's *The Corsair* [1814], for instance, is considered as falling into a victimized and emasculated position towards the end of the poem that reflects Western 'liberal anxiety about male autonomy' (p. 60). Chapter 2 relates Shelley's *Hellas* and *The Revolt of Islam* most particularly to contemporary discussions concerning fears of the mob and how oriental-style despotism may lead to similarly 'oriental' 'popular violence' (p. 66). Cohen-Vrignaud reads *The Revolt of Islam* [1818], then, as a poem that eschews mob and popular violence for 'reform constitutionalism', arguing that it 'emphasizes the power of language, exemplifying liberalism's devotion to political change through discursive contestation' (p. 81). It is worth noting that Cohen-Vrignaud prefers *The Revolt of Islam* to the poem's original title *Laon and Cythna*, arguing that 'reform' more reflects the poem's 'constitutionalism' (p. 80). Although the poem's revisions have been widely discussed elsewhere, Cohen-Vrignaud himself does not consider these beyond the title. This is a shame, since some of the alterations might have benefited his argument or are, at least, worth considering. For instance, the tyrannical 'Christian Priest' in *Laon and Cythna* is more specifically an 'Iberian Priest' only in *The Revolt of Islam*. This alteration thus 'orientalizes' this figure in Cohen-Vrignaud's understanding, since he sees Gothic Catholicism as similarly 'oriental'. The final two chapters return to Byron (and Mary Shelley, as discussed in Section 2 above). The titular hero of *Sardanapalus* [1821] is read, on the one hand, as a strangely nuanced allegory of George IV. Sardanapalus's pavilions clearly allude to the 'orientalist' Brighton Pavilion of the British monarch, but Sardanapalus's redemption towards the end of the play suggests that such extravagance is not to be condemned outright. Rather, invoking a wasteful, slothful, and economically irrational oriental ruler who ultimately redeems himself is not simply to condemn a British monarch but to reflect on Western 'Economic Man' as a flawed model prompting present discontentment. The final chapter continues in this vein, but focuses instead on Byron's autonomy of the self, arrived at via his orientalism. As Cohen-Vrignaud puts it 'Byron's Orientalism promoted radical detachment from ideal systems of philosophy and poetry that would impose commitment to principle over the vagaries of desire' (p. 215). Cohen-Vrignaud's book, then, is an ambitious and well-researched work that provides a stimulating alternative to the standard Saidian approach to Romantic poetry's frequent orientalisms. Although guilty of imprecision with terms such as 'radical' and 'liberal'—they are certainly not interchangeable and are far more multifaceted than Cohen-Vrignaud implies—the exemplary research of a fairly niche trope among the radical press allows us to consider Byron and Shelley's poetry in a rather different climate.

Also considered in Section 2 above, H.J. Jackson's *Those Who Write for Immortality: Romantic Reputations and the Dream of Lasting Fame* contains chapters that deal with Wordsworth, Southey, Keats, Crabbe, Leigh Hunt, Blake, and Clare, among others, including Barry Cornwall and Robert Bloomfield, who stand as her counter-examples to canonical poets. The central and most important claim of the volume is that 'long-term survival has depended more on external circumstances and accidental advantages than on inherent literary worth' (p. 218), and Jackson's thorough and careful scholarship certainly backs this up. *Those Who Write for Immortality* wears its learning lightly, but it is nonetheless an important work not just for our period, but for all those interested in the vagaries of fame in literary history.

The twelve essays in Kostas Boyiopoulos and Mark Sandy's *Decadent Romanticism: 1780–1914* offer a range of approaches to the question of Romanticism and its relationship to 'Decadence'. Generally, the essays either consider the influence of Romanticism on the Decadence movement of the later nineteenth century or the Decadent tropes that are observable in earlier Romantic works. Anna Barton (pp. 15–26), for instance, reads the recovery of Blake in the later nineteenth century in relation to notions of literary 'perversity', that is seen by early Symbolist critics as evidence of Blakean Decadence (as limiting as this might be). Frederick Burwick (pp. 27–42), on the other hand, is more focused on the Romantic period itself in his discussion of depictions of incest on the Romantic stage, focusing on the dramas of Byron, Shelley, and Joanna Baillie. An important point that Burwick makes is that incest was far from taboo, and that 'No legal ban prohibited the stage representation' of it (p. 29). This is worth bearing in mind when we consider

Romantic-period censorship, such as of Shelley's *Laon and Cythna*, which is often seen to be concerned with matters of incest when evidence suggests the opposite. Bernard Beatty's essay (pp. 43–58) traces the influence of Byron and Wordsworth on later Decadence, noting that, although Byron's influence is more obvious, Wordsworth is 'usually regarded as the antithesis' of the movement (p. 43). Beatty traces the use by Decadent writers, such as Baudelaire, of Wordsworthian tropes through the lens of De Quincey, whereas Byron's relationship to Decadence produces 'the opposite problem' in that the 'path is all too well signposted' (p. 50). Essentially, Beatty convincingly concludes that when Byron and Wordsworth are either invoked or ignored by later writers, these writers are only really thinking of a mediated figure, a 'Byron' or a 'Wordsworth'. Boyiopoulos (pp. 59–74) and Sarah Wootton (pp. 75–88) offer different essays on Keats's influence on Decadent writers. Keats, superficially at least, appears the canonical Romantic poet who is most easily relatable to literary Decadence. Boyiopoulos reads the depictions of seeming intoxication or sensual euphoria in Keats's poetry as being important reference points for such depictions in the work of Arthur Symons and Ernest Dowson. Boyiopoulos's conclusion is that all three writers see writing and creativity itself as the 'ultimate intoxicant' (p. 74). Wootton's essay, on the other hand, starts from the position that, by 'the end of the nineteenth century, John Keats was no longer simply the author of "high" art, but the embodiment of art' (p. 75). To this end, Wootton explores the Keatsian books and images produced between 1888 and 1911, that served either as illustrations for editions of Keats's poetry or as visual attempts to capture a Keatsian aesthetic. This medium, it is worth noting, is often neglected by critics. Shelley's Decadent influence is the subject of essays by Michael O'Neill (pp. 103–18) and Lisa Vargo (pp. 119–30). O'Neill offers close comparisons between Shelley's poetry and that of the 'pseudo-Shelley' Algernon Swinburne (p. 103). At the same time, however, O'Neill stresses Swinburne's originality, who takes from allusions to 'Ode to the West Wind' [1820] and *The Triumph of Life* a modified Shelleyan poetics that is both creative and destructive. In a similar vein, Vargo argues that the poet Mathilde Blind's 'imaginative revisionism of the writings of Percy Bysshe Shelley' creates a 'distinctive contribution to British Decadent literature' (p. 119). Although this collection may well be of most use to scholars of the later rather than the earlier nineteenth century, there is nevertheless much rigorous Romantic scholarship that most importantly evidences the clear connections between the two movements and periods rather than simply relying on critical hearsay. To this end, this volume is a valuable contribution to studies of Romantic poetic legacies.

The legacy of Jonathan Wordsworth, who died in 2006, was evident in a 2015 volume. He was of course not only the great-great-great-nephew of William Wordsworth but a leading Wordsworthian and Romantic scholar in his own right. His most important books, *The Music of Humanity* [1969], which successfully recovered 'The Ruined Cottage', and his *The Borders of Vision* [1983], are two of the most influential works in the field of Wordsworth criticism. *The Invisible World* is a posthumous collection of ten of Jonathan Wordsworth's previously unpublished lectures, delivered at Wordsworth summer conferences and Wordsworth winter schools, both of which are held annually near Grasmere. Edited by Richard Haynes, the collection is an impressive array of raw, stimulating, and varied Romantic scholarship. It is regrettable that these lectures were not prepared for publication, since, although fluent, they are not quite at Jonathan Wordsworth's rigorous best, and the volume itself, designed primarily as an e-book, is lacking a little in typography. However, Haynes's editorship means that all essays are fully referenced and clearly presented; most importantly, the selection is both thought-provoking and wide-ranging. The essays are nevertheless unified by an overarching theme, the focus primarily being on different Romantic treatments of the imagination. The opening lecture on Wordsworth as a revolutionary poet, first delivered in 1989, argues for Wordsworth as maintaining his revolutionary fervour to a greater extent than is generally appreciated; essentially, that he was a 'passionate sympathiser with the ideal of revolution' (p. 17). Wordsworth is also 'revolutionary' in an aesthetic sense, in that he has the capacity to make the ordinary extraordinary. The third lecture, on Wordsworth's 'Sympathetic Imagination', similarly convincingly demonstrates Wordsworth's exceptional capacity to identify the poetical potential within an ordinary mind. Jonathan Wordsworth argues that, despite the young Wordsworth's limited contact with women, the success of his sympathetic female characters demonstrates a strong sympathetic imagination that aligns Wordsworth closely with the 'chamelion [sic] poet' figure of Keats, and does not see him simply as a poet of an 'egotistical sublime'. Keats is himself the focus of the following essay, on the 'Keatsian Imagination'. Jonathan Wordsworth describes Keats as 'yearn[ing]...for the power to paint...in the gleam of imagination...that consecrates, makes holy and also substantial' (p. 86). 'The Doors of Perception' is a broader lecture, considering the differing Romantic conceptions of imagination, taking in Blake, Wordsworth, Coleridge, and Keats, while two further lectures on Blake consider Blake's 'theory' of the imagination in depth, and the difficulty of *The First Book of Urizen* [1794]. As well as two further lectures on Wordsworth, another chapter considers Burns and Macpherson, exploring the success of Ossian and its influence on later Romanticism. Coleridge's own theory of the imagination is explored in depth through close attention to 'Frost at Midnight' [1817], taking into account the influence of Cowper's *The Task* [1785]. This collection reminds us of Jonathan Wordsworth's insightful scholarship, and will serve to inspire further generations of scholars, even if the lectures are not in themselves completed or polished pieces of work. It is a welcome addition to the body of Jonathan Wordsworth's criticism.

*Romanticism and Philosophy: Thinking with Literature* is a collection of sophisticated essays edited by Sophie Laniel-Musitelli and Thomas Constantinesco on Romantic-period engagements with philosophy. Considering Percy Shelley's position in *A Defence of Poetry* [1840] that poets and philosophers are virtually interchangeable, it almost goes without saying that poetry is prominent in the volume, and the work of Shelley and Wordsworth particularly so. It is worth emphasizing, as is indicated by the volume's subtitle, that these essays are not simply concerned with the poetry as a simple vehicle of the philosophical ideas of the authors; rather, they are 'bound by a common concern for literary writing as a form of thinking' (p. 2). Indeed, a number of the essays are interested in the 'afterlives' of Romantic writing; for instance, philosophical thinkers like Paul de Man and Stanley Cavell are considered as having approached their theoretical positions through their reading of Shelley and Wordsworth respectively. The essays are arranged in four sections. Part I, 'Romantic Confrontations', looks at both how Romanticism confronts previous philosophical certainties and how Romantic literature and philosophy are competitively engaged with each other. Mark Sandy's essay on the 'Ghostly Language' of Wordsworth's Salisbury Plain poems (pp. 60–74) explores how Wordsworth's poetry is both 'haunted and haunting' (p. 60). This works on a number of levels within the Salisbury Plain poems in particular; most simply, the traveller is haunted by 'the spectral presences' of the environment, while he himself becomes a 'haunter' of the plain, possessing a 'revenant-like impulse to return home' despite the impossibility of doing so (pp. 62–3). This parallels the textual situation, where the different versions of the poem, as well as Wordsworth's other poetry, are ghostly presences, informing and informed by each other. Similarly, Sandy discusses how the Spenserian stanza form suggests a haunting of, and by, the form of the older Romance of Spenser; the poem similarly echoes Milton. Most importantly, 'Salisbury Plain is haunted by shadowy historical and social realities, which reassert themselves in the main narrative as a series of presences' (p. 69). Arkady Plotnitsky's essay on Shelley's ontology (pp. 74–96) demonstrates how his poetry exceeds the investigation of Hume and Kant into the relationship between mind and matter, noting how Shelley's poetry does not commit to certainties. Indeed, because of this, poetry 'actively defines or redefines the field of possibilities, or of probabilities' (p. 91). Therefore, Shelley's poetry enables us to avoid the trap set by Alain Badiou that 'when you decide upon what exists you bind yourself to Being' (cited p. 74). Part II, on 'The Poetics of Thought', includes essays by Simon Jarvis (pp. 97–116), Pascale Guibert (pp. 117–30), and Yves Abrioux (pp. 131–46) on Shelley, Wordsworth, and Clare respectively. Jarvis's essay demonstrates, in a similar vein to Plotnitsky's, that Shelley's form and technique are central to how a poem such as The Triumph of Life 'thinks', and how verse itself leaves no original concept unchanged. In contrast to Plotnitsky and Jarvis, Guibert's essay shows, using Badiou, how the seeming separation of Wordsworth from a purely philosophical sphere means that 'truth' is something that can be objectively located for him. Abrioux's theoretically dense essay on Clare, offering close readings of three particularly 'minor' poems, considers Clare's 'minor' status as one that frees him 'from even the most implicit lip service to established philosophical or political hierarchies' (p. 131). Part III of the volume, on 'Romantic Selves', includes an essay by Laura Quinney (pp. 179–93) relating Blakean subjectivity to that proposed later by Kierkegaard, particularly in how both reject philosophical tradition that privileges 'objective' experience. At the same time, identity is really 'an intrusion of outwardness into the inner life' (p. 189); thus both Blake and Kierkegaard are seen to explore the difficulties in determining 'self' in relation to concepts of subjectivity. The volume ends with a 'Coda' by Edward T. Duffy (pp. 245–54) that, in focusing on Stanley Cavell's reading of Romantic poets and particularly his reading of Wordsworth, encapsulates the findings of the volume. Duffy sees Cavell not simply as having used Romantic poetry to 'carry' the weight of his philosophy for him, but also as expressing it and carrying it into being in the first place (p. 253). This complex volume is nevertheless a superb addition to Romantic scholarship. The essays demonstrate not only theoretical but philosophical rigour, and all attest to the sophisticated thoughts of the poets considered, as well as the philosophical potential within poetry itself.

This year also saw the publication of a number of scholarly versions of the works of more minor Romantic poets for the first time. Judith Thompson's *John Thelwall: Selected Poetry and Poetics*, for instance, is the first modern edition of Thelwall's poetry and poetic criticism. This seems remarkable when we consider the significance of Thelwall within the Romantic period, not only because he was a radical orator and writer of great political significance, but also because of his relationship and engagement with figures such as Wordsworth and Coleridge. Thompson herself has written on this relationship in her *John Thelwall in the Wordsworth Circle: The Silenced Partner* [2012], and this edition of poetry serves as a continuation of Thelwall's academic and poetical recovery. As the discoverer, in 2004, of Thelwall's 'Derby Manuscript', which has revolutionized our understanding of Thelwall's contribution to the literature and intellectual climate of the period, Thompson is well placed to be at the forefront of this process.

Part of the task awaiting those who wish to recover the works of less canonical writers is to assert their literary merit. Thompson certainly achieves this in her introductory chapter, noting that, despite Thelwall's strength lying primarily in an oral tradition—'voice was to him what vision was to other Romantics' (p. 3)—she nevertheless argues passionately not only for the breadth of forms with which Thelwall worked, but also for his originality and grasp of poetic style. For example, Thelwall is argued to have 'revolutionized...the sonnet' (p. 5) in much the same way that Coleridge had 'revolutionized' the ode. The relationship between the two men, beginning in the later 1790s, was not always cordial but is still seen as 'catalyz[ing] a new phase in the poetic careers of both men [that] changed the course of English literature' (p. 5). It seems churlish to dispute this claim, but it nevertheless feels an unnecessary one; the value of Thelwall's poetry could have perhaps been allowed to speak for itself more, with editorial comments limited to contextualizing the poems' biographical, political, social, and literary history. This is very minor criticism however, as otherwise the editorial decisions are to be highly commended. Indeed, Thompson's selections are well chosen, not only demonstrating Thelwall's versatility as a poet and poetical thinker, but also offering evidence of his extended work and experimentation in each form. To this end, the collection is arranged in eight sections, covering pastoral and peripatetic poems, comic ballads, sonnets, public and pindaric odes, conversational odes, love songs, epic, and autobiography. Each section is introduced with an appropriate extract from Thelwall's prose criticism or poetic theory, helping to establish his poetry as a manifestation of a poetic philosophy not too dissimilar, perhaps, to Wordsworth's. Thelwall is an amusing and skilful prose writer; his criticism of Alexander Pope, seen in his 'On Pastoral Poetry' (pp. 22–6), seems in part to tackle Pope on the grounds of Wordsworth's critique of Thomas Gray in the Preface to *Lyrical Ballads*. Thelwall is far less polite, however, dismissing Pope for his 'puerilities' and describing his poetic imagery as 'incongruous' (p. 23). His poetry, too, has the same direct wit, most obviously his satirical poetry. Thompson herself argues for his comic voice as his 'saving grace' (p. 51), which strangely seems to damn with faint praise; he is clearly an important poet in many other modes. In fact, what is most surprising about Thelwall's writing, considering what we know of his background and his reputation, is that so much of his best poetry, much of which was found in the Derby Manuscript, is erotic or amatory. His 'pastoral' poems clearly show the influence of Erasmus Darwin, as Thompson herself notes, but they frequently exceed even the eroticism of poems such as *The Botanic Garden* [1791]. Thompson's edition is an excellent introduction to Thelwall as poet. It is well presented and supported by superb original research, and the engaging and representative selection of poetry suggests a readership beyond a solely academic one. Despite this, it is nevertheless an important addition to Romantic studies and should be recommended reading to all scholars of the period. It is hoped that Thompson's work on Thelwall's biography will produce a similarly accomplished piece of scholarship.

In contrast to 2014, there were few single-author studies on female poets in 2015. A notable exception, however, was Sharon Smith's ' "I cannot harm thee now": The Ethics of Satire in Anna Barbauld's Mock-Heroic Poetry' (*ERR* 26[2015] 551–73). As Smith notes, Barbauld's satirical voice has been largely absent from poetry collections and critical studies of satire, despite Barbauld's command of the genre's traditions and cultural capital. Challenging the conventional view of satire as a masculine mode, and identifying the way Barbauld employs mock-heroic to question the ethics of readers and writers alike, Smith puts forward a convincing case for the inclusion of Barbauld's work amongst Romantic satire that will hopefully continue in future works. John Pierce, in 'The Suspension of Sensibility in Amelia Opie's Early Poetry' (*Romanticism* 21[2015] 238–49), considers, through study of an oft-neglected female writer of the period, the issue of sensibility within Romantic-period writing. Through close and careful reading of Amelia Opie's early volumes of poetry, Pierce demonstrates Opie's liminality in the history of sensibility. He argues that her poetry is 'rooted in the eighteenth century but also looking forward to the Romantic period' and 'registers a shift in its expression of traditional characteristics of sensibility while problematizing the nature of unconscious and self-conscious expressions of passion as identity emerges through temporal experience' (p. 229). Another less canonical female Romantic poet is the subject of Harriet Kramer Linkin's 'Mary Tighe's Newly Discovered Letters and Journals to Caroline Hamilton' (*Romanticism* 21[2015] 207–27), reviewed in Section 1 of this chapter. All three articles offer a generous recovery of female writers that particularly emphasizes their significance as well as their literary merit.

Tighe's literary merit is further evidenced by Linkin's publication of a substantial edition of her previously unpublished poetry, *Verses Transcribed for H.T.* on *Romantic Circles*. This makes a significant amount of manuscript and archival material available for the first time. *Verses Transcribed for H.T.* is a 266-page two-volume autograph manuscript of 121 original poems and seventy-two illustrations. Sixty-five of the poems have not appeared in any known print source, and, of those that have, seventeen are significantly different in the manuscript album version. The 'H.T.' of the volume's title is Henry Tighe, Mary's husband, who had urged her to prepare the collection for publication despite her reservations concerning the commercialization of her poetry. For Linkin then, this collection is important not only in unearthing previously unknown material, but also in revealing that Tighe was a determined figure when it came to the direction of her publishing career. This is detailed in depth in Linkin's introduction, which also offers an overview of Tighe's life and career more generally. Linkin's analysis of Tighe's poetry reveals Tighe to be a figure who self-consciously identifies herself as a poetess, despite her general disinclination for publication, as well as one aware of the paradoxes of representation. Of the benefits of an electronic edition, the most significant is the additional availability of the full-size page images of the original album manuscript. These are beautifully presented in a fine hand, and the images are of an exceedingly high quality. The fact that Tighe illustrated many of her poems suggests that, as with Blake, the relationship between text and image is not necessarily simply incidental. Making these images available allows the interpretation of the text and illustrations in unison to take place. Indeed, Linkin for instance explores the relationship between three of Tighe's poems—'The Faded Flowers', 'Sonnet VIII', and 'Address to My Harp'—and the accompanying 'tailpiece' illustrations: like the poems, they depict a paradoxically vibrant stasis. Tighe's poetry is very much in keeping with the poetic climate of the age: sonnets feature quite heavily in the first volume, and the relationship between art, artifice, and nature are important thematic concerns. This is a superb edition with excellent editorial work by Linkin. To publish without the illustrations would not do Tighe's artistry justice, and although a hard-copy facsimile edition would be a beautiful object, the electronic version is more practical. This edition plays an important role in re-evaluating Tighe's canonical position in literary history.

There were a number of valuable contributions to Blake studies this year, with several monographs, book chapters, and articles all offering new insights into this most bewitching and at times baffling of poets. Saree Makdisi, in *Reading William Blake*, draws attention to the bewitching and baffling, and the benefit of embracing both when teaching Blake. In the process Makdisi illustrates why he is one of the pre-eminent contemporary critics of Blake. Focused on Blake the author and printer of the illuminated books, this scholarly work goes much further than the introduction to the poet that such an edition is intended as. Makdisi's approach is imaginative and convincing, shedding important light on a range of topics pertinent to Blake studies. Each short chapter considers a particular area: image, text, desire, joy, power, time, making. *Songs of Innocence and of Experience* [1789–94] is used throughout to provide some consistency and grounding for the exploration. This has the added benefit of being the work that, for most students and critics, begins their fascination with Blake. Makdisi consistently focuses on the interplay between words and image, and combines discussion of the material nature of Blake's illuminated books and our interpretative strategies towards them. Reading Blake can so often be transformative, and yet the weight of scholarly apparatus that surrounds his work can sometimes minimize the intense experience of reading him. Thus, while keeping in view the need to elucidate much that is challenging in Blake's work, Makdisi rightly asserts that we run the risk of losing so much of what is exciting and potentially spellbinding in the lines of verse if we read Blake primarily through the filter of critical commentary. Informed, as he says, by his own teaching practices, Makdisi's work generously aims to offer a platform from which readers can think about Blake's works and find their own reading practices, rather than have Makdisi's imposed upon them. It is thus an open and liberating work of criticism very much in keeping with the beliefs of its subject.

The hugely dramatic nature of Blake's work encourages a sense of the theatrical. In both the popular and the scholarly imagination his verse has long been both appropriated to and examined through the performative. Recently we have had Susanne Sklar's *Blake's Jerusalem as Visionary Theatre* (OUP [2001]). Diane Piccitto seeks to add to our understanding of Blake's theatricality with *Blake's Drama, Theatre, Performance and Identity in the Illuminated Books*. She reflects on the relation between the poetic performer and his audience, or, as she puts it, on verse as 'dramatic performances of identity that create an active spectatorship' (p. 1). Piccitto focuses on the illuminated books because, as she explains, the combination of image and text illustrates the interplay between the verbal and visual that makes up the dramatic performance of Blake's forms and plays such a vital role in their reception. Piccitto's first chapter nicely situates Blake within his historical context, specifically the debates about popular theatre. This allows her to develop her argument as to why the illuminated books should be considered 'dramatic theatre' (p. 35) and the means by which the poet constructs 'Blakean spectatorship' (p. 52). Combining historicism, theory, and close readings, Piccitto offers another angle on Blake's relation to an important Romantic cultural context.

One chapter is dedicated to Blake in the late Marilyn Butler's *Mapping Mythologies: Countercurrents in Eighteenth-Century Poetry and Cultural History*. Butler selected the authors for her study because they shared a common interest in primitive religious beliefs or myths, while they also felt themselves to be patriotically speaking for the nation, and from an essentially country, rather than a city, perspective. Keen, as she puts it, to seek out 'the needs, beliefs and assumptions that governed' Blake and others and helped produce 'some of the most innovative, characteristic and influential British writings of the period 1730–1820' (p. 1), Butler's take on Blake is typically clear-sighted and illuminating. Butler identifies Blake not with a Romantic flight from the preceding decades, but as a figure whose own mythologizing stems in large part from the works of eighteenth-century British poets and thought. It was a pleasure to read an essay on Blake first written thirty years ago that still feels germane.

Two essays on Blake appeared in *British Romanticism in European Perspective*, edited by Steve Clark and Tristanne Connolly. Diane Piccitto, in 'Blake and the European (Pre)History of Melodrama: Beyond the Borders of Time and Stage' (pp. 193–209), considers the illuminated books as inspired by melodramatic techniques so as to place the Romantic Blake within a broader pan-European tradition. Theatrical melodrama is generally thought to have emerged in France in 1800 and in England in 1802. However, as well as exploring the interconnections in melodrama between England, France, and Germany, Piccitto identifies Blake's work as a way of detailing the earlier inception of the genre and its influence beyond the stage. Building further on the thesis of her book, *Blake's Drama, Theatre, Performance and Identity in the Illuminated Books* (reviewed above) Piccitto advances an important area in Blake studies. It will be interesting to see what other lines of enquiry are possible involving Blake and the theatre. Peter Otto meanwhile, in 'From the English to the French Revolution: The Body, the World, and Experience in Locke's *Essay*, Bentley's 'A Prospect of Vapourland', and Blake's *Songs*' (pp. 210–29), argues that Blake can be read as engaging with a pan-European phenomenon: that of a shift in political ideas from the sovereign head of state to the sovereignty of the people. By detailing Blake's interest in this transformation in the Romantic period, Otto also sheds light on debates that press upon our political experience today. John Harvey's *The Poetics of Sight*, reviewed in Chapter XIV, also contains a chapter on Blake (pp. 71–108), which will be fully reviewed in next year's *YWES*.

As well as his chapter in *British Romanticism in European Perspective*, Peter Otto also published 'Organizing the Passions: Minds, Bodies, Machines, and the Sexes in Blake and Swedenborg' (*ERR* 26[2015] 367–77). Perceptively comparing Emanuel Swedenborg's explanation for how bodies might be organized with Blake's revisionism, Otto methodically details Blake's radical development of Swedenborg's theories. The radical difference, Otto argues, not only exists in the contest between reason and the imagination, but also in Blake's and Swedenborg's contrasting perceptions of bodies and passions. In 'Blake's Body Without Organs: The Autogenesis of the System in the Lambeth Books' (*ERR* 26[2015] 357–66), Tilottama Rajan explores Urizen's body as a form for Blake's own body of writing and as a disfiguration of his idealistic ambitions. Rajan convincingly proposes that the Lambeth books serve as a 'primal scene... of the imaginary system that Blake elaborates in *Jerusalem*', because 'the grotesque body that dis-figures these books is an autoreferential figure for Blake's projection of his own corpus as a systematic body of work' (p. 358).

'Reluctant Ecology in Blake and Arendt: A Response to Robert Mitchell and Richard Sha' (*WC* 46[2015] 143–55), by Amanda Jo Goldstein, develops out of Mitchell's and Sha's investigations into, as Goldstein says, the 'risks and promises of Romantic(ist) enthusiasm for "the experience of experiment"' (p. 143). Goldstein examines the commitment to the Earth in Blake and Arendt—poets who are generally held to hold contempt for a materialist view of Nature, but who in Goldstein's reading are found to be curiously and intriguingly 'earth-bound' (p. 144), tethered to the natural world we inhabit. For all Blake's fascination with the extraterrestrial and supernatural at certain moments, Goldstein charts his terrestrial as well as cosmic poetic adventures.

Lucy Cogan's 'William Blake's *The Book of Los* and the Female Prophetic Tradition' (*Romanticism* 21[2015] 48–58) manages to find something new to say about Blake's visionary company. The critical positioning of Blake amidst a radical Dissenting community, too often uncritically assumed to be the domain of men, reaffirmed the sense of Blake's masculine poetic identity. But as Cogan points out, further evidence of the active and vital role women played in the Dissenting community allows us to rethink Blake's mythopoeia in relation to the significant female prophetic tradition at the time. This is thought-provoking and a pleasure to read.

Celebrity culture has been one of the most persistent trends in Byron studies since Tom Mole's *Byron's Romantic Celebrity* [2007]. Clara Tuite's *Lord Byron and Scandalous Celebrity* nonetheless manages to unearth thrilling new areas of investigation that should sustain this offshoot of Byromania and provide further readings of Byron's importance to culture. Taking a historical perspective Tuite engages thoughtfully with the phenomenon that was Byron, and the phenomenon of celebrity more widely during the Regency period. Examining Byron's persona in the literary, social, and political contexts of his time, Tuite suggests that the key to understanding his fascination lies in what Tuite calls 'scandalous celebrity' (p. xiv)—an ambivalent state of fame derived from a combination of notoriety and strutting a more traditional form of heroic distinction. This 'scandalous celebrity' rests on the 'charm of the celebrity figure and the affective ambivalence of the fan and reader' (p. xv), Tuite contends. It is how 'the famous and the notorious become newly intimate' and the 'rites and receptions that celebrate and denounce this intimacy' that form the focus of Tuite's important contribution to Byron studies (p. xv). Moreover, as with other works on celebrity culture in the Romantic period, Tuite makes a strong case for seeing the Regency period as a vital transitional moment for the emergence of our contemporary obsession with fame.

*The Byron Journal* continued its tradition of publishing some of the most engaging works on Byron by many of the field's most important voices. We live in a particularly rich time for Byron scholars, and many of them published in the *Journal* this year. In 'Byron at Home' (*ByronJ* 43[2015] 15–27) Bernard Beatty voyages across Byron's career to illustrate the poet's deft ability to make himself at home in both the world he inhabited and the world of poetry he found such refuge in. As Beatty notes, Byron is associated with particular geographical places, and is also famously a poetic figure of exile. Detailing Byron's various responses to the notion of home—whether literal or metaphorical—Beatty also once again proves perfectly at home with Byron's life and verse. Preceding Beatty's essay is 'Byron's Love Letters' (*ByronJ* 43[2015] 1–14) by Alan Rawes, which reads the love letters in light of key passages from the poetry in order to suggest that Byron's conventional approach to love letters is actually a way for him to steer through the expressive limitations of language while adapting its emotional force. Blurring the lines between writer and lover, Rawes suggests that Byron's seduction of the recipients of the love letters operates through the inadequacy of language. Byron's affection for canines is Michelle M. Taylor's focus in 'The Curious Case of "Epitaph to a Dog": Byron and *The Scourge*' (*ByronJ* 43[2015] 43–56). Reflecting on the two acknowledged versions of 'Epitaph to a Dog' as a means of considering textual history and reception, Taylor also details the satirical attacks on the verse at the time, and unearths Byron's place amidst a little-known magazine, *The Scourge*.

The journal's second issue of the year centred round the theme of 'Byron and the Bible'. Developing out of the conference held at Newstead Abbey in

May 2015, it produced a number of compelling essays on religious themes. 'Why Did Byron Have To Write *Cain* Before He Could Finish *The Vision of Judgement?*' (*ByronJ* 43[2015] 141–6), by the late Peter Cochran, employs manuscript evidence and intertextuality to show how these very divergent works are interrelated. Cochran proves the importance of the dramatic and foreboding *Cain* to the composition of the satirical *Vision*, and once again shows us why Cochran's voice will be missed. Bernard Beatty's ' "According to the old text": Byron and the Sacred Scriptures' (*ByronJ* 43[2015] 121–9) identifies a relationship between the Bible and Byron's oeuvre. Drawing attention to the interplay between history and storytelling in both the Bible and Byron, Beatty highlights the creative energy Byron derives from his use of Scripture and how his belief in the apparent meaninglessness of history, which might nonetheless hold meaning, is mirrored in sacred writing. In 'Byron and the Post-Secular: Quia Impossible' (*ByronJ* 43[2015] 91–108) Gavin Hopps skilfully proposes the sceptical Byron as a paradigm for a post-secular approach to our understanding of Romantic engagement with the other-worldly or mystical. For Hopps, Byron illustrates the Romantic combination of doubt and open-mindedness towards the possibility of religious transcendence. Catherine Redford, in ' "No love was left": The Failure of Christianity in Byron's "Darkness" ' (*ByronJ* 43[2015] 131–40) offered us an important religious context for one of Byron's most despairing works. She suggests that Byron's apocalyptic vision is evidence of his theological engagement since he can be seen responding to eighteenth-century Christian eschatology. Anna Camilleri's 'Sacrilegious Heroics: Biblical and Byronic Archetypes of the Vengeful Feminine' (*ByronJ* 43[2015] 109–20) uses sacramental matters as a means of delving into Byron's interest in female figures in the Bible. Pointing out that Byron likely drew on these women for inspiration, Camilleri focuses on the book of Judith in particular in order to offer a gendered reflection on Byron's interest in and portrayal of vengeance and violence.

Madeleine Callaghan also considers fearlessness and aggression in Byron, but from a markedly different perspective. In 'Forms of Conflict: Byron's Influence on Yeats' (*English* 64[2015] 81–98) Callaghan not only relays the vast shadow Byron casts over the Yeatsian imagination, but also provides a fascinating and convincing reading of the overlaps between their forms, voices, and themes. By highlighting the poetic kinship between the two poets, Callaghan gives us a thoughtful analysis of Byron as much as Yeats, and as such her reading does much to advance our appreciation of heroic forms and Romantic legacy.

Four articles on Byron appeared in *Studies in Romanticism* over the course of the year. Three concerned matters of race and depictions of the oriental 'other'. Yin Yuan's 'Invasion and Retreat: Gothic Representations of the Oriental Other in Byron's *The Giaour*' (*SiR* 54[2015] 3–31) reflects on Byron's formal strategies towards the orientalizing impulse witnessed in the Romantic period. Developing important lines of enquiry by Nigel Leask in *British Romantic Writers and the East* [1992] and considering in detail *The Giaour* [1813], Yuan suggests that Byron 'articulates *and* alleviates...[a] moral ambivalence through recourse to the gothic mode' (p. 4), utilizing the genre's aesthetic strategies so as to present the text's self-conscious perspective concerning its own orientalism. This permits Byron to both 'contemplate and indict the violent work of empire through its drama of psychic fragmentation' (p. 5). Fragmentation is also the subject of Mai-Lin Cheng's 'Lara's Stutter' (*SiR* 54[2015] 503–23). This details the various narrative and expressive breaks and falterings at play in this most self-reflexive and critically troubled poem in order to examine Byron's complicated engagement with oriental themes and appropriation of the Gothic genre. Detailing the interplay between hero and tale, Cheng discusses Byron's use of conventional literary tropes amidst an endeavour for an original and distinctive voice. 'Race, Writing, and *Don Juan*' (*SiR* 54[2015) 303–28), by Mark Canuel, meanwhile, looks to Byron's digressive and capacious epic in order to problematize the poet's response to the slave trade. Though Byron was on record as being an abolitionist and broad supporter of the work of William Wilberforce and others, Canuel detects a degree of ambivalence towards race issues in *Don Juan*, even as he acknowledges the poem's apparent voicing of support for the abolitionist movement. *Don Juan*, Canuel believes, relies on a 'subtle yet profound logic that insistently privileges the purity and beauty of white bodies' (p. 303). This is not a consequence of a racist ideology, but rather because the poem's 'intertwined configurations of political and aesthetic value are inseparable from a self-consciously constructed racial hierarchy' (p. 303)—a hierarchy Byron is both conscious of and seeking to satirize but which he is incapable of distancing himself from. Andrew McKendry's 'Will the Public Please Step Forward? Libel Law and Public Opinion in Byron's *The Vision of Judgement*' (*SiR* 54[2015] 525–49) diverges from most critical receptions of *Vision* [1822], which prioritize biographical matters—principally Southey's *A Vision of Judgement* [1821] that inspired Byron's work—or literary and political allusions and contexts, and concentrates instead on jurisprudence. As McKendry points out, *The Vision of Judgement* centres on a trial. McKendry builds a convincing case that Byron's captivating poem shows definite signs of a juridical issue created by changes to libel law, principally divergence between 'courtroom invocations of "the people" and the heterogeneous character of public opinion' (p. 528).

Lastly, 'Photographing Byron's Hand' (*ERR* 26[2015] 129–48), by Andrew Burkett, provides a fascinating account of William Henry Fox Talbot, protophotographer, who, at the inception of the photographic age in 1840, decided to photograph the final lines and signature of Byron's 'Ode to Napoleon Buonaparte' [1832]. Exploring publication history and posthumous reception, and offering a different perspective on Byronism, Burkett's cultural history and close literary analysis capture the role of Romantic poetry and identity in the development of the burgeoning art medium of photography in the middle of the nineteenth century.

There was much wonderful work on John Clare this year, adding to the rich reservoir of criticism that has developed in recent times. *New Essays on John Clare: Poetry, Culture, and Community*, edited by Simon Kövesi and Scott McEathron, fields a diverse range of approaches by ten distinguished scholars including practising poets as well as literary critics. In this varied collection we consistently find visions that are invaluable for our understanding of Clare's place within current debates on environmental ethics, aesthetics, literary history and periodization, and the nature of play and work. As the editors point out, it is now over twenty years since *John Clare in Context*, the first major critical essay collection focusing on Clare, appeared from Cambridge University Press. Since then there has been an enormous amount of material produced on Clare, while editorial practices continue to be debated and contested. Underpinning the collection is the belief that Clare has always been relevant to poets and readers alike, receiving 'quiet yet constant attention' (p. 6) since his death in 1864, not least because of the challenge he poses to periodization. Indeed, it is Clare's 'ongoing status as an uncategorizable literary and social misfit [that] might in the end serve him well' (p. 7). While Clare has remained relevant throughout the last 150 years, the appetite for his verse has never been greater, nor has Clare seemingly spoken with such weight to critical interests and contemporary matters. This new collection does an excellent job of detailing the breadth of Clare's relevance and his diversity, including the poet's engagement with poetic tradition, and the realization by his contemporaries of his deep environmental thinking. 'John Clare, William Cowper and the Eighteenth Century', by Adam Rounce (pp. 38–56), illustrates how Clare's engagement with Thomson and Cowper is foundational for his sense of his own poetic self and the construction of his verse. Fiona Stafford, in 'John Clare's Colours' (pp. 17–37), and Sarah M. Zimmerman, in 'John Clare's Conspiracy' (pp. 57–76), skilfully pursue the complexity of Clare's presentation of the natural world through his versification. Environmental approaches and interests are important refrains in this collection and in Clare studies more broadly. In his essay, 'John Clare's Natural History' (pp. 169–88), Robert Heyes reveals the social context out of which Clare's ecological voice emerges, so as to dispel some of the clichéd green myths that surround the poet. Clare was deeply informed by the natural history and the social and political writing of the time. In 'John Clare and the New Varieties of Enclosure: A Polemic' (pp. 79–96), John Burnside uses the nineteenth-century context in which Clare operated to engage powerfully and politically with our own ecological moment. Emma Mason, 'Ecology and Religion: Kinship in John Clare' (pp. 97–117), breaks new ground by unearthing the possible relation between Clare's green politics and his knowledge of divinity and ideas of faith. Scott McEathron, in 'The Lives of Frederick Martin and the First *Life of John Clare*' (pp. 118–45), meanwhile, reflects on the presentation and reception of Clare via the career of his first biographer—Frederick Martin. Simon Kövesi's 'John Clare's Deaths: Poverty, Education and Poetry' (pp. 146–66) also thinks about the reception and creation of Clare by others—this time how the 'jarring combination of poverty and poetry—of labour and literary culture—continued to inform his literary legacy and reputation' (p. 162) after his passing. Sam Ward's ' "This Radical Slang": John Clare, Admiral Lord Radstock and the Queen Caroline Affair' (pp. 189–208) does an excellent job of detailing Clare's complex relationships with patrons and promoters. Clare's relation to publishing is also the subject of the last essay in the collection, Richard Cronin's masterful 'John Clare and the *London Magazine*' (pp. 209–27), which relates the poet's prominence in both the London literary scene and the pages of the periodical, even as he remained distinct and distant from each.

The *John Clare Society Journal* continues to house excellent essays and offer an insight into the most pressing issues in Clare studies. On this occasion we were offered an essay on Clare's fen poems, followed by three articles on Clare's relationship to the American poet and nature-lover Henry David Thoreau. The works on Clare and Thoreau were all adapted from papers originally delivered at the 'John Clare in Space' conference in Oxford in May 2014. 'Syntax and World-View in John Clare's Fen Poems' (*JCSJ* 34[2015] 37–49), by Helen Pownall, attends to Clare's effusive verse describing the wild wetlands of his environment. Pownall focuses on Clare's syntax, which she admits is famously 'sinuous, his clauses long and meandering' (p. 37) in other works as well, but which, Pownall asserts, takes on a particularly meaningful significance in the fen poems that she finds to be mimetic of the topography of the landscape that also allows her to investigate Clare's world-view . Lance Newman, in 'John Clare, Henry David Thoreau, and Walking' (*JCSJ* 34[2015] 51–62), surveys how these two 'kindred spirits' shared a passion for getting out of doors. Walking, Newman argues, was not only a 'lifelong practice for both', but also 'shaped their thought and structured their art' in ways that led to them developing 'immersive ways of writing about walking that showed what kinds of vernacular experience were endangered by the privatisation of the commons' (p. 51). 'The Brighter Side of "Dark Ecology": John Clare and Henry David Thoreau' (*JCSJ* 34[2015] 63–73), by Markus Poetzsch, reflects on the various manifestations of ecological thought in Clare and recent environmental criticism, offering an ambivalent and thought-provoking picture of the poet and the subject's relation to the natural world. Poetzsch brings Thoreau and Clare together by detailing their shared sense of wonder at the world around them and their active and often ecologically problematic engagement with it. Jeremy Mynott, in 'Wonder: Some Reflections on John Clare and Henry David Thoreau' (*JCSJ* 34[2015] 75–86), also marvels at each poet's sense of wonder in order to get at their writing and reflect on our contemporary condition. Mynott details how Clare and Thoreau both evoke their fascination with the natural world through their use of the term 'wonder', and this is particularly evident in their respective close attention to local detail, fine and acute description, and deep understanding of the land and the creatures that inhabit it. These are matters which should also inform our appreciation of our environment today, as Mynott makes clear.

Clare's relation to others was also the subject of R.K.R. Thornton's 'Joseph Skipsey and John Clare: Two Labouring-Class Poets' (*JCSJ* 34[2015] 23–32). Deftly weaving intriguing parallels between these two labouring-class writers—their similar backgrounds and situations, their drive and will to achieve, their love of learning, whether in books or the wisdom found in nature—Thornton offers us both a detailed biographical account and thorough knowledge of the social and publishing scene at the time. In 'Clare on the Wane' (*English* 64[2015] 296–311) Andrew Hodgson focuses on Clare's style and form to offer perceptive insights into the poet's distinctive voice. Informed by other critical voices as well as the poet's own, Hodgson argues that Clare found a source of inspiration in the diminishment of his creative possibilities. Clare's poems, Hodgson asserts, 'rise to the peculiar challenge of writing successfully about imaginative failure' (p. 298).

As well as the piece on Clare's 'dark ecology' that appeared in the *John Clare Society Journal*, *Romanticism* also published work on Clare and ecology. '"Homeless at Home": John Clare's Uncommon Ecology' (*Romanticism* 21[2015] 171–81), by Shalon Noble, offers another perspective on Clare and ecocriticism—perhaps *the* topic currently doing the rounds in Clare studies if samples from this year are anything to go by. The subject of Clare and nature is nothing new of course: it has had a central place in the majority of studies on the poet since the start, just as Clare and his verse are said to be rooted in the landscape. As Noble points out, however, too frequently we make easy assumptions about what it means for us (or Clare) to have a relationship with nature, to be 'rooted' in it. More recent work on ecology has sought to question the assumptions surrounding nature's balance and stability, and it is this deconstructive approach to which Noble worthily contributes by offering us a new understanding of the poet as creative precisely because of the instability of the natural world and his place within it. There is, Noble argues, 'a singularly ecological creativity' in Clare's work, 'one that presents an experience of ecology as a restless and dynamic community' (p. 173).

Turning to Coleridge: Wayne Deakin produced some significant work on Coleridge in *Hegel and the English Romantic Tradition*. Deakin's canonical focus offers the reader a chance to re-examine English Romanticism by returning to the importance of Hegel, particularly his theory of recognition. Hegel's work continues to matter, Deakin believes, not only because of its philosophical value, but also for its assistance in understanding key moments of Romantic poetry. As with his other chapters, Deakin wisely avoids arguing for a direct influence of Hegel's writing on Coleridgean thought. Instead he proposes that key ideas in Hegel are also addressed and explored in Coleridge's verse. His chapter on Coleridge therefore seeks to 'examine the vacillation between receptivity and autonomy' (p. 35) in the poet's writing. For Deakin, Coleridge's attempt and failure to formulate a theory of knowledge based on the intuitive status of the imagination in chapter 13 of *Biographia Literaria* provides a springboard from which we can analyse Coleridge's poetry as productively centred around a tension between 'absolute idealism and an empirical-realism, or between imaginative autonomy and receptivity to the external world' (p. 35). Deakin argues that this tension is also evident in that play between *symbol* and *allegory* in Coleridgean thought and verse. Deakin's analysis of Coleridge's thinking and writing is suggestive, and makes an implicit case for seeing Coleridge as a more systematic operator than we sometimes allow for nowadays.

The journal *Romanticism* offered us two equally convincing essays on Coleridge. Timothy Whelan, 'Coleridge, Jonathan Edwards, and the 'edifice of Fatalism' (*Romanticism* 21[2015] 280–300), unearths a neglected yet apparently important figure for our appreciation of the life, work, and thought of Samuel Taylor Coleridge: one Jonathan Edwards—America's 'most influential and, at times, controversial theologian and philosopher' (p. 280) during the eighteenth century. Though Coleridge alludes to Edwards rarely, Whelan is persuasive in his contention that the poet's engagement with the theologian is significant, and touches on topics uppermost in Coleridge's religious thoughts from his earliest writings. In 'Coleridge, Employment and the Sorcery of

Wealth' (*Romanticism* 21[2015] 132–44), meanwhile, Barry Hough considered issues of wages and poverty, reflecting on Coleridge's engagement with the employment market of the eighteenth and early nineteenth centuries. The *Lay Sermons* explicitly advocates the need to moderate the socially and economically disruptive effects of laissez-faire liberalism, Hough suggests. Coleridge's ambition was to propose reform of the liberal marketplace that was more inclusive and worked for all members of society. Coleridge reminds us all that 'social justice requires a sophisticated inter-relationship between public and private initiative' (p. 142), and that a moral perspective should shape economic policy beyond the need for growth.

Ewan Jones's 'Split Lines in Shakespeare and Coleridge' (*EIC* 65[2015] 421–46) imaginatively assesses the broken line, that 'shifting, subterranean form' (p. 444) of verse, in part so as to reveal the interplay between dramatic performance and lyric, unsettling along the way critical narratives that 'pass as standard' (p. 444). Noting Coleridge's 'classical temper' (p. 422) in verse as in other respects, Jones charts the practical and imaginative relevance of the hemistich in Shakespeare and the Romantic poet, opening up another view of Shakespeare's influence on Romantic forms. This is a deeply rewarding read.

'Infinite Closure in "Kubla Khan" and the "Cave of Yordas"' (*WC* 46[2015] 48–52), by Peter Larkin, explores scenes of containment in Coleridge's verse. These spaces, Larkin points out, are ambivalent compressions, yet are also sites or situations that extend to an 'infinite degree' (p. 48) which, on a poetic level are 'encountered as immeasurably enwrapping', pulsing with mystery, 'put under pressure', and whereby an 'infinite space imitates a finite one and vice versa' (p. 48). Greg Ellermann's 'Late Coleridge and the Life of Idealism' (*SiR* 54[2015] 33–55) thinks again about what the concept of idealism offered the Romantics, and us as Romantic critics. Giving the 'romantic absolute another look' (p. 34) as he puts it, Ellermann wisely turns to Coleridge's late works so as to connect realism with Romantic idealism, and asks what an appreciation of this relation provides for our perspective on Coleridge and Romanticism more generally. In 'Coleridge, Politics, and the *Theory of Life*' (*SEL* 55[2015] 647–67) Jacob Risinger also approaches Coleridge's later work in order to explore the interplay between Romantic science, poetry, and politics. Emphasizing a 'convergence of political and natural philosophic considerations' (p. 648), we are offered two interconnected and intriguing lines of argument by Risinger. He contends that Coleridge's most important thinking on the political implications of organic life emerged not in the 1790s, as is more commonly supposed, but over two decades later. More expansively, Risinger makes a convincing case for seeing Coleridge's engagement with natural philosophy as a means of grappling with Britain's political constitutional existence. Coleridge's engagement with science is also the subject of Kevis Goodman's 'Reading Motion: Coleridge's "Free Spirit" and Its Medical Background' (*ERR* 26[2015] 349–56). Perceptively capturing the scientific spirit of the age, Goodman argues that Coleridge inherits eighteenth-century medical ideas concerning the relation between bodies and external forces and applies them to the poet's attention to and interest in the effect of poetic form upon the reader. Finally, 'Romantic Flashbacks: Coleridge, De Quincey, and Duration' (*ERR* 26[2015]

659–77), by Amanda Paxton, also engages with Romantic science in its exploration of temporality, agency, and ideas of memory. For Paxton, the writings of Coleridge and De Quincey, in importantly divergent ways, show signs of a later cognitive theory of memory: Henri Bergson's durational memory.

Gregory Leadbetter offered us two excellent essays involving Coleridge that were unavailable for review in last year's *YWES* (95[2016]). 'The Comic Imagination in Lamb and Coleridge' (*ChLB* 159[2014] 11–19) nicely draws out Coleridge's playfulness and mirth—both in life and in his lines of verse. Leadbetter is interested in the Janus-faced nature of the humorous—its capacity to create bonds with others and to be a means of distancing ourselves superiorly from others—but he also draws important distinctions between the comic and the intellectual freedom Coleridge (and Charles Lamb) held as sacrosanct. In 'Poetry, Politics and Portents: Coleridge and the Waters of Plynlimon' (*ColB* 43[2014] 29–36), meanwhile, Leadbetter charts the course of Coleridge's mind in the 1790s as he toured Wales and dreamt of Pantisocracy. Leadbetter proposes the walking tour as a medium for Coleridge's 'self-dramatization and, more obliquely, the drama of self-disclosure, where past behaviour and future hopes are held in tension' (p. 29) that leads to a present at once thrilling and troubled. It is the combination of a '*feeling for* the destiny he desired, with one eye on the darkness of his own psychological history' (p. 29), Leadbetter contends, that informs Coleridge's record of the tour.

Critical studies of Sara Coleridge continue to grow, with many expert voices leading important reassessments of her place in art and culture beyond her role in the posthumous life of her father. One such critic is Jeffrey W. Barbeau, whose *Sara Coleridge: Her Life and Thought* (reviewed in *YWES* 95[2016]) provided a thorough assessment of the intellectual as well as personal life of Sara Coleridge. This year we are lucky to have a nicely pitched essay in the *Wordsworth Circle*. Barbeau's 'Sara Coleridge on Love and Romance' (*WC* 46[2015] 36–44) shows how Sara may have 'inherited her father's genius and fashioned herself as heir to his thought' (p. 37), and also a Coleridgean idea of love. That concept of love is one tied to the unity of being, and a desire for complete unity with another. Barbeau shows that Sara not only loved deeply during her life but thought deeply about the subject and its philosophical as well as daily importance. '(Re-)Mapping the "Native Vale": Sara Coleridge's *Phantasmion*' (*Romanticism* 21[2015] 265–79), by Joanna E. Taylor, is a sensitive and erudite historicist approach that convincingly argues for the Fairyland of *Phantasmion* to be much more than a repetition of Wordsworthian Lake District tropes. Rather than simply being inspired by literary influences, Taylor suggests, Fairyland is a 'reconstruction of Sara's topographical childhood memories' (p. 265). Using a rough sketch that Sara drew some time between 1834 (when the idea of a fairy-tale *Phantasmion* was conceived) and 1837, when the poem was published, Taylor locates important differences between Fairyland and a Wordsworthian imaginative landscape and thus offers a new perspective on the individuality of Sara.

It was pleasing to find a chapter on Erasmus Darwin in *British Romanticism in European Perspective*. Tristanne Connolly's essay, '"Mistaken for natives of the soil": Translation and Erasmus Darwin's *Love of Plants*' (in Clark and

Connolly, eds., pp. 133–54), starts by acknowledging that the notion of translation is integral to Darwin's work—its cross-fertilization and interest in the exchange of ideas, themes, and languages. Connolly's deft handling of the material, and her use of Deleuzian theory and French sources, reminds us that the idea of translation is for Darwin a way of describing and enacting the transmission and transmutation that occur between various discourses, whether animal, vegetable, mineral, or linguistic.

Leigh Hunt was represented by only one article this year, reviewed in Section 1 above, Alys Mostyn's 'Leigh Hunt's "World of Books": Bibliomania and the Fancy' (*Romanticism* 21[2015] 238–49).

Like Saree Makdisi's *Reading William Blake* (reviewed above), Susan J. Wolfson's *Reading John Keats* is part of the new Reading Writers and Their Work series from Cambridge University Press. Just as with Makdisi's book, Wolfson's deep affection for and knowledge of the poet presents us with a work that is at once an introduction to Keats's life and writing and packed with perceptive insights. Through ten rapid chapters, Wolfson moves us from Keats's earliest literary inspirations and aspirations right up to the richness of his final works. And like her subject's distinctive idiom, Wolfson's writing is consistently a pleasure to peruse. She notices many fruitful connections between Keats's writing and his reading, while her playful style encourages readers to be lithe in their appreciation of Keats's whimsy and wordplay. The many archival images presented in the book are a nice touch, and lead Wolfson to engage most fully with Keats's poetic thinking. Though in some ways an abridged version of the compendia available in Wolfson's *Cambridge Companion to Keats* [2001], it is nonetheless helpful to find here suggested further reading, and a concise contextual timeline for Keats's life as well as a series of snippets from Keats's writing that serve as a brief summation of his extraordinary thoughts. For such a slim book, *Reading John Keats* is full of his expansive imagination and a valuable read, especially for those relatively new to Keats.

Brittany Pladek, in ' "In sickness not ignoble": Soul-Making and the Pains of Identity in the *Hyperion* Poems' (*SiR* 54[2015] 401–27), opens with a discussion of the medical issues surrounding Keats's final year, neatly suggesting that what has for a long time sounded like 'bad medicine' (the misdiagnosis of Keats's consumption) may well have been 'good bedside manner' (p. 402) from doctors keen to alleviate the concern of their patient, at a time when British medical ethics was just beginning to be codified. Such medical debates surrounding deception, pursuit of knowledge, and the alleviation of suffering are also in play in Keats's corpus, and Pladek suggests that, just as doctors in the Romantic period were arguing over whether or not they should reveal information that could do harm to their patients, so Keats examines 'whether poetry could provide relief for readers even while acknowledging...that "Sorrow is Wisdom" ' (p. 403). Nicholas Roe also advances our knowledge of Keats and medicine in 'Mr Keats' (*EIC* 65[2015] 274–88). This brilliant essay unearths new historical detail about Keats's medical life and its possible influence on his poetry. As Roe definitively shows, the alternative paths of poetry and medicine are not fully resolved by Keats the physician-poet; instead Keats's 'awareness of the one continued to define his consciousness of the other' (p. 274). Roe focuses on his discovery of a newly recovered first-hand account of Keats at work at Guy's Hospital to provide us with a fascinating version of the vibrant life of the poet. The essay also makes important connections between Keats's poetic works and his medical training more generally. During his training Keats took a trip to the seaside town of Margate, where he dedicated himself more fully to his poetry. It also commenced a period of engaging and thoughtful letter-writing. John Barnard delves into both the poems and the letters related to this important period of transition for Keats, in 'Keats's "Forebodings": Margate, Spring 1817, and After' (*Romanticism* 21[2015] 1–13). By reassessing Keats's writing from this time, Barnard identifies 'violent swings of emotion and artistic anxieties' that, while perhaps disguised by the 'performative nature of his letters' (p. 1), were much more severe than we have hitherto acknowledged. Barnard's essay tellingly speaks to the self-fashioning of the poet and the emotional life of a young and ambitious but also deeply apprehensive Keats.

Published in 2014, but not reviewed in last year's *YWES*, was Franca Dellarossa's *Talking Revolution: Edward Rushton's Rebellious Poetics, 1782– 1814*. This work coincides with the publication of Paul Baines's edition of Edward Rushton's works, *The Collected Writings of Edward Rushton* (reviewed in *YWES* 95[2016]), also published by Liverpool University Press. Dellarossa's monograph is the first full-length study of this important, yet hitherto non-canonical, Liverpool-based abolitionist poet. What is refreshing about Dellarossa's approach is that it actively avoids being a fairly limiting biographical reading, or what Dellarossa calls a narrowly ideological one. Instead, she focuses on the 'conjunction of the aesthetic and the ideological' in Rushton's work since 'his poetic language, and form itself, are knowingly determined by his politics' (p. 4). As Paul Baines's edition of Rushton's work reveals, Rushton is a writer of merit who is thoroughly deserving of literary recovery and, interestingly, was more prolific in poetry than in prose. The fact that Rushton is known *more* for his admittedly fascinating biography than his genuine literary talent is, in a sense, what Dellarossa seeks to overcome. This approach too is enlightening when contrasted with the literary criticism of so-called labouring-class poets of the period more generally, which often in fact ends up perpetuating the dichotomies of 'highbrow' and 'lowbrow' poetics that such studies superficially seek to undermine. Although Dellarossa's monograph is a single-author study, she is nevertheless at pains to consider Rushton's position within various networks of radical, abolitionist poets— both global and local—as well as within a poetic milieu more generally. To this end, the volume is structured in two sections, 'Local Radicalism' and 'Global Radicalism'. Although this implies a disjunction between these two sides of Rushton's poetics they are, in fact, very much connected, as Dellarossa reminds us. For instance, the opening chapter focusing on the late eighteenth-/ early nineteenth-century abolitionist movement and the situation within Rushton's home town of Liverpool is very interested in both the local and the global. Liverpool was, after all, at the heart of the global slave trade for much of the eighteenth century. Dellarossa reads Rushton's 'To a Redbreast in November, Written near one of the Docks of Liverpool', for instance, the opening poem of his 1806 collection, as very much a Romantic one that also performs the 'politics [that] epitomizes Edward Rushton's closeness to and distance from the world' (p. 42). The volume's second section explores Rushton's interest in global affairs, most particularly the slave trade in America and the Americas—the subject of Rushton's most famous *West Indian Eclogues* [1787]—as well as the Haitian Revolution. Regarding the latter, Dellarossa reads Rushton's ballad poem on the revolution's leader Toussaint L'Ouverture partly in the light of other poetic treatments of the figure, such as those by Southey and, most particularly, Wordsworth. For Dellarossa, Wordsworth's and Rushton's poems on L'Ouverture 'exemplify fundamentally distant ideological attitudes to the historical event and the historical character as such, which also influence the terms of their transmutation into poetic discourse' (p. 174). Dellarossa's monograph, then, is an important contribution to Romantic scholarship and an excellent work of literary recovery. We are offered not only a full-length study of a previously neglected poet that considers his work on his own terms, but also a reconsideration of the wider literary and historical context more broadly. A fine addition to the libraries of scholars of the period and of abolitionist writing more specifically.

It was a particularly rich year for publications on the life and work of Shelley. Jacqueline Mulhallen's short biography of Shelley for instance, *Percy Bysshe Shelley: Poet and Revolutionary*, is part of Pluto Press's Revolutionary Lives series. As the title and the series of which it is a part indicate, this biography focuses primarily on Shelley as a 'revolutionary' figure, contextualizing him amidst the political and social upheaval of his age. Such a reading of Shelley, as Mulhallen puts it herself, suggests a continuation of the work of P.M.S. Dawson (*The Unacknowledged Legislator* [1980]), Paul Foot (*Red Shelley* [1981]), and Michael Scrivener (*Radical Shelley* [1982]) from the 1980s (p. xiii). The brevity of the work, its informal style, and its limited end-noting, however, demonstrate that this is a book intended more for a wider, popular readership than for an academic one. In fact, for more 'academic' assessments of Shelley's life and literature more generally, scholars should still stick to the aforementioned works. Despite this, Mulhallen's informal, engaging style and her book's popular form often belie the extensive research or, at least, synthesis of research that underpins it. For example, a very brief discussion of the campaign of Shelley's friend Colonel Sergison in the Sussex election of May 1807 demonstrates a grasp of the minutiae of Horsham's local political history, despite this largely serving as a minor footnote in Shelley's adolescence (pp. 15–16). Mulhallen's earlier *The Theatre of Shelley* [2010] has already demonstrated her excellent grasp of Shelley's drama; this latest work is further evidence of her familiarity with the poet's work and, crucially, a number of more recent developments in Shelley studies. Although she does not discuss it in depth, Mulhallen does refer to *A Poetical Essay on the Existing State of Things* [1811], discovered fairly recently, as well as Shelley's relationship with disparate groups such as the Quakers and Spenceans (pp. 66–7). These brief accounts serve to demonstrate an awareness of critical debate as well as indicating potential areas of further research. Nevertheless, it is occasionally frustrating that Mulhallen does not develop each topic further, even if this is explained away by the space limitations of the volume. In fact, a reader's desire to know more pays Mulhallen's writing a great deal of credit. Mulhallen's knowledge of Shelley's poetry and prose is extensive, but her *reading* of the poems is cursory at points. Often the poetry is seen as an extension of Shelley's 'revolutionary' musings in other arenas or simple reflections of the social and political context rather than well-crafted pieces of art in their own right. Indeed, a more attentive reading of Shelley's poetry would have revealed the political implications of his poems' language, allowing a reader to see them as more than just a simple medium of delivery. The fact that Shelley decided to address political issues so often in verse is an important question; it is worth remembering that the *matter* under discussion is not so easily divorced from the *manner* of its expression. Mulhallen does seem to partly acknowledge this when she notes that 'Revolutionary artists can be innovators in art' (p. 86), but this still implies that politics and art are separate spheres. Nevertheless, this is an enjoyable, intellectual, and, crucially, accessible book. If it is polemical at points and not as nuanced with regard to Shelley's radicalism as other studies, it still serves as both a welcome introduction and a notable addition to an understanding of Shelley's political life.

Alan M. Weinberg and Timothy Webb produced a follow-up to *The Unfamiliar Shelley*, a 2009 edited collection of Shelley essays. This new collection, *The Neglected Shelley*, contains fourteen essays that attempt to reverse the common practice among academics who, in Weinberg and Webb's view, 'tend to focus on a narrow range of poems, thus excluding the larger and extraordinarily diverse corpus' of Shelley's works (p. 3). Weinberg and Webb suggest that Shelley's gifts as a great lyrical poet are partly to blame for why many of his longer poems—with the exception of *The Triumph of Life*—are neglected by critics. As well as exploring some of these longer poems in depth, a number of the essays consider Shelley's prose pieces or, in the case of Timothy Morton's essay on *Queen Mab* [1813], the overlooked paratextual elements of the poetry (pp. 77–94). Webb's opening essay is one that appreciates Shelley's letters as more than simple supplements to the poetry, but as interesting and frequently quite remarkable works of literary art in their own right. Not only do we discover a playful Shelley engaging in multiple epistolary personae, but also a number of poetic reveries that are, perhaps, reminiscent of the more widely appreciated letters of Keats. Diego Saglia (pp. 35–50) similarly reappraises Shelley's early Gothic fiction that is commonly regarded as adolescent, clichéd—if not outright derivative—and unrestrained. Saglia reads works such as *Zastrozzi* [1810] and *St Irvyne* [1811] as inaugurating Shelley's fixation on the physical human body that is often the subject of much of his later, more canonical, poetry. David Duff (pp. 51–76) similarly focuses on Shelley's Gothic juvenilia, most particularly his first two collections of poetry published in 1810: *Victor and Cazire* and *Posthumous Fragments of Margaret Nicholson*. Neither of these has received much critical attention, partly because, as Duff notes, these collections suffer from 'persistent plagiarism' (p. 56). Duff traces these borrowings, as well as reiterating the young Shelley's inheritance from the Gothic, arguing that the collections 'represent a vital stage in Shelley's literary development' (p. 75).

Weinberg and Stephen C. Behrendt offer essays on Shelley's unfinished or fragmentary works (pp. 157–76, 95–116), while Charles E. Robinson (pp. 117–36) argues that the c.4,000 words and corrections Shelley made to *Frankenstein* can be seen as fragmentary texts in their own right, and read alongside his poetry. Jack Donovan's essay on *Rosalind and Helen* (pp. 137–56), a poem surprisingly neglected considering it appeared at the height of Shelley's career in 1819, is read largely biographically and in relation to the incomplete 'Mazenghi', composed relatively contemporaneously. Richard Cronin (pp. 199–214), Timothy Webb (pp. 215–38), and Michael O'Neill (pp. 239–60) analyse *The Sensitive Plant*, the 'Hymn to Mercury', and *Hellas* respectively. Although all three poems are often covered in Shelley criticism, they are too often not given the focus or extended treatment they have been here. O'Neill's attentive reading of *Hellas*, for instance, reveals a poem of ambivalence more complex than is commonly thought, that 'tests the reader's mind and affects the reader's heart through its self-examining idealism' (p. 260). Maria Schoina's essay on Shelley's Cyclops translation similarly refigures our reading of the text to see Shelley's reworkings as engaging in a 'satyric' tradition, where our laughter is levelled at Odysseus. Finally, Nora Crook's essay on Shelley's attitude towards the Jews (pp. 261–80) is a further example of an area that is very much neglected in Shelley studies. Although much has been written on Byron and others in this regard, very little has been written on Shelley. Crook explores both Shelley's interest in the Old Testament/Hebrew Bible and his conception of wandering Judaism. This collection is a superb addition to Shelley studies. What is particularly successful is the additional space given to each chapter. Not only are we offered scholarly consideration of relatively less canonical aspects of Shelley's oeuvre, but it is given at length. This encourages the reader to see the particular works as far from minor, and therefore significant in their own right. That the contributors are some of the academy's leading Shelleyans also helps to situate this work as of central importance to the field.

Shelley's online presence was also boosted in 2015. *Romantic Circles* published two 'volumes' of Shelley essays as part of their excellent Praxis series. The first of these, *The Politics of Shelley: History, Theory, Form* edited by Matthew Borushko, is partly a follow-up to 2001's *Reading Shelley's Interventionist Poetry, 1819–1820* (http://www.rc.umd.edu/praxis/interventionist/). Like the earlier volume, this present work is interested in the relationship of Shelley's poetry to the political situation of his age while also emphasizing his autonomous poetics. A particular concern is in establishing that there is not in fact an impasse between the poetry's political interventionism and the aesthetic moment of art. This volume essentially, then, is one that reads Shelley's formal aesthetics as very much informing his political positions—or non-positions—and vice versa. Indeed, Joshua Lambier's essay, 'Shelley's Aesthetic Dimension: The Politics of Resistance and Reform', sees Shelley's aesthetic departures from the contemporary situation as allowing for the presentation of alternative ways of viewing the world. He makes use of Jacques Rancière's notion of 'dissensus' to describe Shelley's approach, where notions of 'common sense' are disrupted through an alternative aesthetics. Borushko's own essay, 'Aesthetics of Nonviolence: Shelley, Adorno,

Rancière', similarly engages with Rancière, as well as Theodor Adorno, in his consideration of Shelleyan 'non-violence'. Focusing particularly on Shelley's responses to the Peterloo massacre of 1819 and his poem 'The Mask of Anarchy' of the same year, Borushko sees Shelley as using it not simply as a vehicle for non-violent politics, but as an example of aestheticized non-violence. Again, there is a clear reading of the political and the poetic as informing each other. The fact that Shelley's sonnet 'England in 1819' is revolutionary in both form and content is not simply taken as read, however; Borushko reads the sonnet as one that disrupts conventional notions of causality and agency—in both form and argument—and thus avoids slipping into advocating for revolutionary violence. Rancière is again invoked in Jared McGeough's essay, 'Masks of An-Archy: Shelley, Rancière, and the Anarchist Turn'. McGeough moves away from considering 'The Mask of Anarchy' solely in terms of the mid-twentieth-century Marxist tradition and instead reads it in light of emerging anarchist theories. Although noting that some critics have read Shelley as an anarchist poet, McGeough does not quite commit to this. Instead, he is more interested in considering how recent theoretical developments allow for a consideration of an aesthetics of anarchism and how this can be read in Shelley's poem. Further than this, McGeough extends his reading to consider an anarchist aesthetic in the Romantic period more broadly, exploring the tensions highlighted by Rancière's concept of the 'aesthetic regime'. Mischa Willett's essay, 'Shelley's Spasmodic Afterlife', reads the vexed afterlives of Shelley in the later nineteenth century from a very original perspective; that is, his idolization by the school of poets referred to as the Spasmodics. As well as arguing for Shelley's immense political legacy, challenging Victorian notions of Shelley as 'apolitical' or, famously, his description as an 'ineffectual angel' by Matthew Arnold, Willetts argues that the Spasmodics were more Shelleyan than, as is often thought, Keatsian. This is precisely *because* of their politics. Lastly, Michael Demson offers a contribution to the consideration of post-Peterloo government repression in his essay on radical satire at this time, 'Remembering John Cahuac: Post-Peterloo Repression and the Fate of Radical-Romantic Satire'. Demson uses the example of the fate of the radical publisher John Cahuac to demonstrate how there was a general distaste for satire following a repressive government climate. Alongside this, Demson reads Shelley's relationship to satire as shifting and complex. The volume is an engaging and original consideration of Shelley's form in relation to his radical politics and is a fine contribution to the growing Romantic Praxis series.

The second Praxis volume of 2015 was *P.B. Shelley and the Delimitation of the Gothic*, edited by David Brookshire. Taking as its starting point the increased interest more recently in the relationship between the Gothic and the Romantic, the volume explores the role played by the Gothic in the literature of Percy Bysshe Shelley which, it is argued, has often been neglected. Shelley's engagement with the Gothic is often dismissed as a mere juvenile interest by critics; his short Gothic novels, for instance, were produced when he was a teenager. Indeed, the fact that these feature in Weinberg's and Webb's *The Neglected Shelley*, reviewed above, is quite telling. This volume instead seeks to trace the role played by the Gothic in Shelley's writing throughout his career, particularly in the way that Shelley 'delimits' it by unleashing its symbolic potential, trapped as the Gothic often is between reactionary and revolutionary impulses. Jerrold Hogle's essay, 'The "Gothic Complex" in Shelley: From *Zastrozzi* to *The Triumph of Life*', is perhaps the most exemplary of the volume's aims to indicate the Gothic influence on Shelley's works throughout his career, tracing the continuation of Gothic tropes from the early novels such as *Zastrozzi* to the final unfinished poem *The Triumph of Life*. Hogle sees the best work that Shelley produced in the final years of his life as essentially inspired by the Gothic's main traits, that is, the possibilities of symbolism, undecidability, and the contradictory aspects of Gothic's mixed modality. It is this 'Gothic complex', as Hogle calls it, that enables Shelley to critique contemporary society and to force his audiences to become aware of the choices they must make between the reactionary and the progressive paths towards humanity's improvement. Tilottama Rajan's essay, 'The Gothic Matrix: Shelley Between the Symbolic and Romantic', similarly notes the continuities between *Zastrozzi* and *The Triumph of Life*, although she refers to a 'Gothic Matrix' rather than Hogle's 'Gothic Complex'. Rajan is particularly interested in the opposition established by Hegel between the 'romantic' and the 'symbolic'; the Gothic is seen as a type of disfiguration of the Romantic but each mode is indispensable to the other in Shelley's poetry. Brookshire's own essay, 'Shelley's *Zastrozzi, A Romance*: Anti-Jacobin Paranoiac Fantasy and the Semblance of Subversion', also considers Shelley's *Zastrozzi*. Whereas Brookshire shows how scholars are often apologetic for Shelley's so-called 'Gothic phase', Brookshire is instead interested in attesting to the literary merit of Shelley's works from this period. In particular, Brookshire argues for the significant historical moment in which novels such as *Zastrozzi* were produced as well as the antagonisms that they illustrate. Reading largely through a Lacanian lens, Brookshire sees the novel as both a complex satire of (slightly) earlier 'anti-Jacobin' texts and a critique of ideological positions. Christopher Bundock, in 'Between Saints and Monsters: Elegy, Materialization, and Gothic Historiography in Percy Shelley's *Adonais* and *The Wandering Jew*', is similarly interested in the historical moment of Shelley's writing but in a rather different way. Offering a reading of *Adonaïs* [1821] and *The Wandering Jew* [1810, published 1877], Bundock's essay considers the historicizing impulse of the Gothic in Shelley's writing, that seeks to remind us of the attempted elision of the material or 'matter' of history. For instance, the uncanny relation between Catholicism and Judaism in Shelley's work is, for Bundock, a reminder that the increasing secularization via Protestantism of Shelley's age is essentially an eliding of these past religions. Robert Miles's closing essay, '*The Cenci*: Gothic Shelley', focuses on another of Shelley's later works, *The Cenci* [1819], exploring Shelley's engagement with the Gothic and Romantic. These are modes that, as we have seen, are not necessarily interchangeable. With attentive close reading, Miles demonstrates how Shelley's deployment of stock Gothic tropes—clichés even—in both the play and its preface illustrates a sophisticated self-consciousness. To this end, Miles concludes that Shelley's thought is dialectical. A theoretically dense and complex volume, *P.B. Shelley and the Delimitation of the Gothic* is a valuable contribution both to Shelley and to Gothic studies. The richness of the theoretical approaches is aided by the fact that the contributions are very much engaged with and even reference each other. To this end, the volume functions as a coherent and consistent whole rather than an assemblage of disparate essays.

Sophisticated readings and reinterpretations of Shelley's poetry also appeared in a number of articles in 2015. Anne C. McCarthy's article, 'The Aesthetics of Contingency in the Shelleyan "Universe of Things", or "Mont Blanc" without Mont Blanc' (*SiR* 54[2015] 355–76), for instance, is a fascinating rereading of one of Shelley's most complex poems. Whereas more traditional readings often focus on the poem's attempt to locate power or Mont Blanc, McCarthy's is one that sees the poem as undermining simple distinctions between subject and object in the face of sublime experience. McCarthy makes particular use of the philosopher Quentin Meillassoux's notion of 'the great outdoors' that unsettles conceptions of the relationship between 'thinking' and 'being' (p. 359). In this way, McCarthy's article can be read in relation to Arkady Plotnitsky's chapter in *Romanticism and Philosophy: Thinking with Literature* as discussed above. Madeleine Callaghan's article, 'Shelley and the Ambivalence of Idealism' (*KSJ* 64[2015] 92–104), is a superb consideration of Shelleyan ambivalence in such poems as *The Triumph of Life* and *Alastor*. Callaghan's reading is one that sees Shelley as a poet—or, rather, the Poet-figure within the poems themselves—refusing to commit to either outright 'idealism' or 'scepticism'. It is this very refusal to commit to either that is in fact not just at the heart of Shelley's poetic vision or quest, but the very mission itself: 'To commit to either choice would be to sacrifice an element of the poet, who requires both mortal and immortal facets to create "how beautiful an order . . . from the dust and blood of this fierce chaos!"' (p. 104). This ambivalence, Callaghan shows, is not simply something thematic but also aesthetic, demonstrating that factors like Shelley's verse form—such as terza rima in *The Triumph of Life*—similarly emphasize the poetry's 'fast-moving and ever-shifting interpretive possibilities' (p. 101).

Rosa Mucignat and Aileen Forbes both offered essays that at least partly considered Shelley's relationship with continental Europe and European writers in 'Characters in Time: Staël, Shelley, Leopardi, and the Construction of Italianness in Romantic Historicism' (*CL* 67[2015] 375–93) and 'Return of the Cenci: Theaters of Trauma in Shelley and Artaud' (*CL* 67[2015] 394–414) respectively. Mucignat's essay considers Shelley's role, alongside such writers as Germaine de Staël and Giacomo Leopardi, in establishing 'Romantic representations of Italians [that] were imbued with, and helped shape, a new type of historical consciousness that characterizes nineteenth-century thought and concepts of national identity' (p. 375). In Shelley's time, of course, there was no unified Italian state. Through close reading of 'Lines Written Among the Euganean Hills', Mucignat illustrates a tension in Shelley's mind between modern Italy and Italians, and the greatness of the (Romanticized) Italian past. Forbes's essay considers the representation of trauma in Shelley's play *The Cenci* in relation to the version produced by the French playwright and 'theatre of cruelty' theorist Antonin Artaud. Although Shelley and Artaud are often seen as rather different figures, Forbes notes how both treatments of the Cenci myth similarly react to historical trauma: 'because both Shelley and

Artaud wrote in the aftermath of historical cataclysm—the Napoleonic Wars and the Great War, respectively—their theaters reflect the traumatic tenor of their own historic moment' (p. 395). Forbes then offers an overview of contemporary trauma theory, applying this to her reading of Shelley's drama. Forbes notes how it reflects trauma's splitting of self through the character of Beatrice as well as dramatizing the difficulties of representing such trauma. In particular, Forbes focuses on Beatrice's inability to articulate her rape despite the representative burden falling on her shoulders, as well as the non-representation of it on stage.

Further to *Decadent Romanticism* discussed above, the posthumous nineteenth-century legacy of Shelley was also the subject of Michael Rossington's 'William Michael Rossetti and the Organization of Percy Bysshe Shelley in the Later Nineteenth Century' (*ERR* 26[2015] 387–93). Rossington considers Shelley's quasi-rehabilitation in the later nineteenth-century editing of his works but makes the case that William Michael Rossetti should be considered as having played a more major role than is often thought. Indeed, Rossington even goes as far as to argue that 'Rossetti has a right to be regarded, alongside Mary Shelley, as the most heroic nineteenth-century editor of Shelley's unfinished play *Charles the First* and the poem "The Boat on the Serchio"' (p. 389). Rossetti's argument at the time that unfinished works such as *The Triumph of Life* be placed among 'fragments' may not be popular among more modern editors but, as Rossington convincingly argues, Rossetti's 'life-long scholarly dedication to Shelley has nevertheless been of lasting value' (p. 391). Others also considered the issue of Shelley's 'fragment' works. Cian Duffy's 'Percy Shelley's "Unfinished Drama" and the Problem of the Jane Williams Poems' (*ERR* 26[2015] 615–32) returns to the key debates concerning the various Shelley fragments often called the 'Jane Williams poems'. An issue that has vexed critics is whether the 'Jane' of the poems relates to the historical Jane Williams. Through the example of Nancy Moore Goslee and William Ulmer in their reading of Shelley's *Epipsychidion* [1821], and through consultation of manuscript and draft evidence, Duffy argues that the 'Jane' in the fragments is very much a 'mediated' figure. We should not read these fragments as solely accurately reflecting biographical information, but neither would it be appropriate to ignore this entirely. As Duffy puts it, we should be cautious in using these poems 'to construct biographical hypotheses which are then reinscribed upon the very poems from which they originated' (p. 627).

Very little was published on Robert Southey in 2015; Stuart Andrews's 'Before the Laureateship: Robert Southey as Historian' (*Romanticism* 21[2015] 72–79) and 'Southey, Coleridge and Islam' (*WC* 46[2015] 109–15), by the same author, being the only two articles. In the first of these, Andrews revisits Southey's claim to Walter Savage Landor in 1810 that he would be remembered more as a historian than a poet, arguing 'he may have meant it' (p. 72). Of course, Southey did indeed write a number of successful prose histories, but Andrews investigates how the figure of 'Southey the historian' is very much evident even in the earlier poetry. His revisions to *Joan of Arc* (removing the supernatural aspects) show Southey's desire to capture historical veracity. Similarly, his correspondence demonstrates his desire to capture authentic historical events rather than imagined ones in his poetry, and even 'imagined' tales see Southey working to chase down appropriate sources. Andrews's second article considers Southey's intriguing relationship to, and interest in, Islam. Islam is of course not only the subject of a number of his poems, such as *Thalaba the Destroyer*, but also a recurrent theme in his correspondence with Coleridge. Andrews considers how Islam comes to be considered as a type of Unitarian Christianity for Southey, and notes that Southey's admiration or respect for the religion in its purest form is not necessarily extended to the faith practised by the Ottoman empire of his day, which Southey viewed as a corruption akin to 'the Christianity of the Vatican' (p. 113). Andrews also traces how both Coleridge and Southey move from Arabic Islam to a consideration of the Islam of the Iberian peninsula.

This year saw the publication of two very substantial reference works on the life and literature of William Wordsworth. To simply call them 'reference works', however, is to do them a disservice, since both show evidence of exemplary and often very original scholarship. *William Wordsworth in Context*, edited by Andrew Bennett, has thirty-five brief chapters divided between four sections that offer summaries of the multiple 'contexts' within which Wordsworth was living and working. The opening section provides us with context of the 'Life and Works' of Wordsworth. Stephen Gill interestingly offers autobiographical context to the writing of Wordsworth's autobiographical works (pp. 3–9). Susan Levin's chapter (pp. 10–18) details the life/practices of the Wordsworth circle, encompassing close family and friends as well as figures such as Thomas De Quincey. Judith Page (pp. 19–26) takes as her subject the role played by Dorothy Wordsworth, not only in the life of her brother, but also in his works and the cultivation of his poetic persona. Sally Bushell's following essay (pp. 27–37) reminds us that Wordsworth was an extensive redrafter. Using the example of the alterations made from 'Descriptions of a Beggar' to turn it into 'Old Man Travelling', Bushell argues 'how intertwined the relationship is between composition and revision for Wordsworth' (p. 35). Tim Milnes (pp. 38–44) reminds us of Wordsworth's standing as a prose writer, and how Wordsworth's poetic greatness 'means his contribution to Romantic prose is easily overlooked' (p. 38).

The book's second section considers both Wordsworth's critical reception and his subsequent influence on later writers. David Higgins (pp. 47–53) offers an account of Wordsworth's generally negative early reviews (1793–1806), but is at pains to point out that the common belief in the younger Wordsworth as a figure not beloved of contemporary reviewers is inaccurate. Peter Simonsen (pp. 54–60) is right to note that some of the most influential and significant criticism Wordsworth encountered in his lifetime is to be found in the mid-career period, 1807–18. Richard Cronin (pp. 61–8) covers the longest period, 1819–50, which sees the public perception of Wordsworth change significantly, so that by the time of his death he was 'recognized as the great English poet of the age' (p. 61).

The first three chapters of the book's third section offer superb detail concerning the literary traditions from which Wordsworth emerged and took influence from. These include the ballad tradition, as discussed by Daniel

Cook (pp. 101–10), the pastoral-georgic tradition, as discussed by David Fairer (pp. 111–18), and eighteenth-century poetry more generally, as considered by Kevis Goodman (pp. 91–100). These help us to see Wordsworth not simply as reacting against or moving away from these earlier forms but in deep and complex negotiation with them. The section then turns to consider the various literary forms popular in Wordsworth's age as well as historically; Wordsworth took inspiration from and even emulated these in his own writing. Ann Wierda Rowland reminds us of Wordsworth's seemingly contradictory attitude to 'popular' forms of poetry such as antiquarianism (pp. 119–26). Wordsworth's similarly vexed relationship with the sonnet—and the recent 'sonnet revival' of the late eighteenth century—is discussed by Daniel Robinson (pp. 136–44). The third section also includes chapters on 'Elegy' and 'Epitaphs', by Paul Fry (pp. 127–35) and Samantha Matthews (pp. 152–60) respectively, as well as 'Autobiography' by Joshua Wilner (pp. 145–51). This chapter's focus on *The Prelude* may well help explain the absence of a standalone chapter on the epic. James Chandler's chapter on 'Sensibility, Sympathy and Sentiment' (pp. 161–70) again discusses Wordsworth's work in relation to both popular literary forms of his age as well as earlier.

'Cultural and Historical Contexts' forms the final section. The very significant contexts of the French Revolution, the Napoleonic Wars, and Wordsworth's European travels are discussed by John Bugg (pp. 173–81), Michael Ferber (pp. 190–8), and Simon Bainbridge (pp. 199–206). As well as detailing the context, all three of these chapters closely relate this to the poetry. This is also the case with the chapters considering specifically 'English' context(s), such as 'London' by Christopher Stokes (pp. 215–23), 'Poverty and Crime' by Toby Benis (pp. 182–9), 'Education' by Frances Ferguson (pp. 232–40), and 'Family and Friendship' by Anne D. Wallace (pp. 224–31), as well as the chapters on walking, animals, and nature and the environment by Robin Jarvis (pp. 291–9), Scott Hess (pp. 207–14), and Kurt Fosso (pp. 241–9). Sophie Thomas sees Wordsworth's 'visual' poetics in the light of contemporary advances in visual technology such as the Eidophusikon and the Daguerreotype (pp. 300–7). The visual is of course at stake in Philip Shaw's and Noel Jackson's chapters on the 'Sublime' (pp. 283–90) and the 'Senses' (pp. 267–74) respectively. The context of Wordsworth's philosophical and religious beliefs is discussed by Stuart Allen (pp. 250–8) and Jonathan Roberts (pp. 259–66), while Alexander Regier's chapter on Wordsworth's language (pp. 275–82) addresses the 'language as really used by men' in relation to eighteenth-century linguistics. Despite the brevity of the chapters, they all nevertheless offer a detailed introduction to each topic. Bennett's enforcing of the tight chapter length, as well as the overall coherence of the volume, are to be commended. Wordsworth is successfully refigured not simply as an isolated 'poet of genius', but as a man deeply influenced by the tumultuous—and creative—period in which he was living.

Of the two major Wordsworth 'reference' works published in 2015, *The Oxford Handbook of William Wordsworth* is, despite its title, the one that is most clearly more than a simple guidebook for undergraduate students. This mammoth volume, approaching 1,000 pages and comprising fifty chapters including prefatory material, is produced by some of the leading scholars of

Wordsworth and Romanticism more widely. It is an astonishingly ambitious achievement. Far from simply offering a reference volume to key and well-known 'facts' of Wordsworth's life, the editors, Richard Gravil and Daniel Robinson, have established the work to be a forward-looking piece of scholarship, with the essays seeking 'to present where Wordsworth studies are and to open windows onto where they are going' (p. 11). This is most certainly the case; as well as reminding us of some of the major issues in Wordsworth criticism historically, useful reference points in their own right, these are also refigured and reconsidered in light of contemporary and potential future scholarship. It is impossible to consider all the essays here, but they generally follow this 'double pattern'. For instance, James Castell's superb essay on 'Wordsworth and "The Life of Things"' (pp. 733–48) partly revisits crucial debates concerning 'thingness' in Wordsworth, particularly the different readings of 'Lines Written a Few Miles Above Tintern Abbey' by Jonathan Bate and Marjorie Levinson amongst others. Whereas Bate's 'ecocritical reading' sees 'things' as an inclusive term, Levinson sees it instead as 'a symptom of exclusion' (p. 740). For Castell, citing Christopher Ricks's emphasis on the importance of 'doubleness' in Wordsworth's poetry, there is a potential 'co-presence of the two positions'; however, Castell's attentive close reading demonstrates how it ultimately has to remain ambiguous (pp. 741–2). This, as William Empson reminds us, is 'among the very roots of poetry' (*Seven Types of Ambiguity* [1930] Penguin edn. p. 3). In this sense, Castell's essay is both a concise summary of existing scholarship and also an insight into current and future developments.

It is the volume's own 'doubleness' that suggests it would be particularly suited to postgraduate students and those beginning a research career. The essays are nevertheless important works of criticism in their own right and likely to be cited by scholars at all career stages. Nicholas Roe's opening essay (pp. 35–50) on Wordsworth's early life, for instance, serves as a useful reference for students and scholars at all levels, offering both well-known and less well-known biographical accounts alongside close attention to the early poetry. A rather different essay by Michael O'Neill (pp. 237–53) is nevertheless similarly widely applicable. His essay on the Immortality Ode, as well as a useful summary of the poem's critical history, includes his own original interpretation of the poem that is a genuine contribution to scholarship. O'Neill's reading is one that helps us to consider the poem as one of slippery signification; a poem 'alive to the shifting meanings of words' (p. 239). O'Neill even goes so far as to read the poem in the light of Keatsian 'negative capability' (p. 239). His reading emphasizes, for instance, the paradox of memory and vision Wordsworth offers us; memory both reminds us of what is lost and is also 'something that doth live' (p. 250).

As well as reminding us of the immense variety and richness of both past and current Wordsworth criticism—for example, the strength of ecocritical, New Formalist, and New Historicist approaches—the handbook also helps to demonstrate that there remain some pivotal concerns that are not wholly satisfied within the field of Wordsworth studies. While analysis of Wordsworth's revisions has produced some superb scholarship over the years, this has nevertheless not solved the vexed issue of 'authoritative' versions of poems. This problem is at the heart of much of the discussion throughout the handbook; Gravil and Robinson's prefatory chapter, for instance, opens with an account of Charles Dickens's purchase of the 1850 *Prelude*, reminding us that the Victorian Wordsworth is different to the one we read today (pp. 1–13). Indeed, the final essay, 'Editing Wordsworth in the Twentieth Century' by Bruce Graver (pp. 816–32), while praising the excellent Cornell volumes, nevertheless partly concedes that 'the question of where we should draw the line between editorial principles and authoritative revisions' remains (p. 832). In this sense, this concern brings us full circle. The *Oxford Handbook of William Wordsworth* then, despite its prohibitive cost and unwieldy size, is a tremendous work. This is not solely for the quantity but for the quality of its academic chapters. These are exceptionally engaging and readable, and it is clear that this will be a superb acquisition for research and university libraries.

There was a similar scholarly richness to be found in the articles published on Wordsworth in 2015. Wordsworth's writing on infancy is the subject of Alexander Freer's article 'Wordsworth and the Infancy of Affection' (*SiR* 54[2015] 77–99). Focusing on 'Ode: Intimations of Immortality', Freer aims to not privilege either 'infancy' or 'adulthood' over the other but instead to read the poem as part of Wordsworth's 'productive ambivalence between the two states' (p. 79). Freer reads the 'I' of the poem productively, noting that in acknowledging one's origins one is also acknowledging their disappearance and loss. The 'I', then, 'marks the speaker as having fallen away from "celestial light"' (p. 81). Wordsworth's poetic education—the 'falling away' of his own celestial light perhaps—was the subject of two further articles. Pamela Woof's 'Wordsworth Learns to Write Elegy' (*WC* 46[2015] 70–9) both considers the influences that inspired Wordsworth's youthful elegiac writing and traces his honing of elegy into maturity. Major sources include classical writers such as Catullus and Virgil, but also Milton and Helen Maria Williams. Whereas Wordsworth's earlier elegy laid on the classical techniques a little thick—Woof refers to 'too much ... alliteration and repetition' and 'over-clear literary allusion' (p. 74)—his later elegy is the product of a poet who is 'irrepressibly himself' (p. 79). This is an excellent article, with very convincing close reading. Michael O'Neill's 'Poetic Education: Wordsworth, Yeats, Coleridge and Shelley' (*WC* 46[2015] 79–86) similarly discusses poetic development and influence, although it focuses more on the question of 'education', which is understood in various ways. For O'Neill, poetic education for Wordsworth is seemingly contradictory; it is 'at once anti- and post-Lockean' (p. 82). 'Nature' and some elements of human society are teachers for the nascent poet, yet the figure of the uneducated child is closer to the divine as seen in poems such as the Immortality Ode. O'Neill traces the connection to later writers such as Yeats, but also contemporaries such as Coleridge and Shelley. Coleridge's 'Frost at Midnight' is seen to demonstrate education as reciprocal; it is 'giving at the same time as asking' (p. 85). For O'Neill, this is reflected by the very verse form itself. Shelley's notion of education, O'Neill briefly asserts, is similar; although it is one based on error, the poet nevertheless unleashes an energy that both 'overwhelms and is controlled by him' (p. 86). This article benefits from O'Neill's trademark attentive close reading.

Wordsworth's poetic development is also central to Oliver Clarkson's 'Wordsworth's Lyric Moments' (*EIC* 65[2015] 125–43). This focuses on a number of Wordsworth's short lyric pieces produced in 1802 that were dismissed by some contemporary reviewers when they were published in 1807 as puerile or worse. Clarkson sensitively reads these 'lyric moments' as emerging at a time of Wordsworth's 'poetic in-betweenness' (p. 127), where the poet is wrestling with significant questions of poetic expression, such as the slipperiness of language. Clarkson superbly demonstrates these lyrics to be self-conscious works of art, where the poet considers resisting the fixities of naming, or is aware that 'a "moment" within the lyric becomes the "moment" *of* the lyric' (p. 129). In this elegantly written article, Clarkson helps in recovering these seemingly minor pieces as demonstrating a significant stage in Wordsworth's poetic career.

Three essays read Wordsworth through the lens of contemporary medical or scientific language. Arden Hegele's 'Romantic Autopsy and Wordsworth's Two-Part Prelude' (*ERR* 26[2015] 341–8) contextualizes the poem in the years surrounding the French Revolution in a fascinating and original way. He focuses in particular on the significance of the development of autopical dissection during this period. Exploring Wordsworth's use of dissection tropes in his poetry, Hegele considers it as a way of articulating poetic self-analysis that owes much to the use of similar metaphors in William Godwin's understanding of radical politics. As well as offering a thorough overview of Romantic and post-revolutionary period advances in medicine, Hegele notes how Wordsworth's attitude towards dissection altered in a manner analogous to his political ideals, evidenced through close reading of the poetry. Amy Mallory-Kani, in her ' "Contagious airs": Wordsworth's Poetics and Politics of Immunity' (*ERR* 26[2015] 699–717), similarly explores the use of medical discourse in Wordsworth's poetry as well as his politics. Mallory-Kani opens with Wordsworth's rhetoric of 1818 when he was campaigning for the Tories, which made use of the language of 'contagion' in describing the influence of French radicalism, noting that this was fairly typical of the time. Where, for Mallory-Kani, Wordsworth differs from this standard discourse, however, is in his 'biopolitical poetics' of immunity (p. 700). This discourse of pathology, then, is read through the lens of later 'biopolitics' as espoused by theorists such as Michel Foucault. The relationship of Wordsworth's poetics to the discourse relating the body to the state is one that seems to indicate Wordsworth as a poet whose metrics Mallory-Kani sees as inoculating the 'powerful feelings' within the poetry against spilling over into contagious Jacobinical actions. Mallory-Kani's short discussion of Wordsworthian imagination as something that is 'embodied' more than is often thought (p. 707) draws a connection to Lisa Ann Robertson's ' "Swallowed up in impression": Humphry Davy's Materialist Theory of Embodied Transcendence and William Wordsworth's "Tintern Abbey" ' (*ERR* 26[2015] 591–614). Noting how the chemist and inventor Humphry Davy had been inspired by Wordsworth's 'Tintern Abbey', Robertson offers an overview of Davy's unpublished theories of embodied cognition in which imaginative or transcendent experiences are simply seen as examples of intense emotion that is very material or corporeal. Therefore, Davy's more empirical concept of embodied transcendence is one that offers a different way of reading Romantic imagination. Robertson applies this to 'Tintern Abbey' and offers an original reading that argues that traditional interpretations of the poem as transcendental neglect its many physiological references.

Three further articles similarly considered Wordsworth's poetry and poetics in the light of contemporary discourse and events. Joshua Stanley's 'Wordsworth and "the most unhappy man of men"': Sentimentalism and Representation' (*ERR* 26[2015]185–204) reconsiders the traditional view of the relationship between Romanticism and earlier sentimentalism. Instead of considering Wordsworth's Romanticism as a 'turn away' from sentimentalism, it is read within the context of it (p. 185). Stanley's focus is on Wordsworth's sonnet 'TOUSSAINT! The most unhappy man of men' that first appeared in *Poems, in Two Volumes* and was later substantially revised by 1827. In a sophisticated reading, Stanley convincingly demonstrates the poem to be one in which Wordsworth, although 'draw[ing] on the techniques of sentimentalism to represent the radical force of Toussaint', is careful to keep his readers aware that it is a simple *representation* of sentiment (p. 202). To merely sentimentalize is to co-opt the experience and not to enact the necessary change. Essentially, 'only those who have suffered ... can make a just world out of an unjust one' (p. 203). Betsy Winakur Tontiplaphol's article, ' "Where Pastime only had been sought": Wordsworth at the Ballet' (*ERR* 26[2015] 205–24), offers an analysis of a rarely considered aspect of Romantic-period life: the ballet. Although Byron's contemptuous reference to ballet in *Don Juan* and the evident general disdain for it more widely establishes it as being somehow too frivolous and too French for the period, Tontiplaphol explores the oblique and largely positive allusions to the art in Wordsworth's poetry. In particular, Tontiplaphol is at pains to emphasize the significance of more general popular theatrical dancing in the period, despite its often being neglected by critics. Paying close attention to a number of Wordsworth's poems, Tontiplaphol not only illustrates the contextual importance of dancing and dance venues in the poetry, but also how the imagery of feet, and the rhythm and metre (or metrical 'feet') of Wordsworth's lines themselves, owe as much to balletic dance as they do to Wordsworthian walking. Richard Matlak's 'Wordsworth and the "Great Terror" of 1803–05' (*WC* 46[2015] 21–6) considers the poems Wordsworth wrote during the fear of French invasion in 1803–5. Matlak opens with an historical overview of the French and British military preparations for the invasion that ultimately never came. At the height of this anxiety in the latter half of 1803, Coleridge and William and Dorothy Wordsworth holidayed in Scotland. Although some have viewed this as a way to 'dodge the draft' into the military, Wordsworth did sign up for the 'Grasmere Volunteers' on his return (p. 23). Matlak, then, sees the Scottish tour as partly inspiring Wordsworth's decision to enlist; the Wordsworths did indeed meet with Walter Scott in Edinburgh, who was 'an enthusiastic poet-soldier' (p. 23). The sonnets of October 1803 seem to bear this out, adopting a seemingly 'populist sentiment' (p. 24). Matlak also contextualizes Wordsworth's other poetry of this period with his experience in the military and the fear of the invasion in an original and engaging way.

Eliza Borkowska's ' "But I am too particular for the limits of my paper' ':
Religion in Wordsworth's Poetry, Prose and Talk' (*Romanticism* 21[2015]
14–24) revisits an oft-explored aspect of Wordsworth's writing. This is not
without reason since, as Borkowska herself evidences, 'Statistically speaking,
religion is the second most important source of inspiration' in his poetry
(p. 14). Borkowska notes how the broad topic of 'religion' is less obvious in
Wordsworth's prose than his poetry. Whereas he is fastidious in describing, for
instance, the topography and weather in his depiction of the Alps in his prose
works, he essentially glosses his reflections on 'the Creator', arguing 'I am too
particular for the limits of my paper' (cited p. 15). This seeming 'taciturnity', as
Borkowska puts it, regarding religion in Wordsworth's prose as compared to
his poetry is seemingly at odds with Wordsworth's claim in the Preface to
*Lyrical Ballads* that there is little difference between the two. Explanations of
'religious' poems in Wordsworth's prose, Borkowska reveals, are similarly
cursory.

There were two 2015 articles that continued the glut of 2014 bicentenary
essays on *The Excursion*. Anthony Harding, in his '*The Excursion*: Life, Lives
and Writing' (*WC* 46[2015] 87–92), reads the poem as one of life-writing that
simply 'tells the stories of many lives' (p. 87). The dialogic nature of the poem,
Harding argues, is one that helps to engage readers with a significant 'cultural
moment' (p. 92) that is more than simply poetic reverie. Not only do
the various tales engage readers' sympathies, they also reflect anxieties about
the loss of an oral tradition of memorializing that, in Wordsworth's day, was
increasingly replaced by a commercialized print culture. The poem that
eventually formed Book I of *The Excursion* is the subject of Matthew
Rowney's 'Broken Arbour: "The Ruined Cottage" and Deforestation'
(*ERR* 26[2015] 719–41). Rowney reads the 'broken arbour' where Margaret
sits towards the end of 'The Ruined Cottage' in the context of the
deforestation of England between the seventeenth and nineteenth centuries.
Rowney's reading focuses partly on absence and loss. In particular, the 'vacant
and huge space' that surrounds the traveller in the poem 'illustrates a profound
historical and ecological transformation' (p. 721); what has been lost has been
lost forever. In this light, further readings of 'The Solitary Reaper' and *Goody
Blake and Harry Gill* help to demonstrate how Wordsworth's poetry of
deforestation—and the significance of trees—is connected to his writing about
memory, in that memory is an awareness of what has passed rather than any
sense of preservation. As Rowney puts it, 'the broken arbour illustrates the
broken bond between the human and the natural, reflected in Margaret's
anguished attempt to remember and reshape the past' (p. 734).

Memory was also considered in Michael Wiley's exploration of a central
Wordsworthian concept in his 'Wordsworth's Spots of Time in Space and
Time' (*WC* 46[2015] 52–8). As the title suggests, however, Wiley is interested in
locating potential influences on Wordsworth's famous concept, arguing that
he engages with 'the space-oriented writings and conversations of figures such
as Isaac Newton, David Hartley, the Common Sense philosopher Thomas
Reid, and Tom Wedgwood' as well as Gottfried Leibniz (p. 53). Although
Wordsworth is consistent with these philosophers in thinking of the 'physical
placedness of spots' (p. 53), the phrase 'spots of time' is exceedingly rare, and is

only used by the American educator Emma Willard in 1822 (who would not have read of the concept at this time). Wiley explores, through attentive research, echoes of Wordsworth's idea in the work of different poets, noting that none quite share Wordsworth's conceptual blending of space and time. Heidi Thomson's 'Wordsworth's "Song for the Wandering Jew" as a Poem for Coleridge' (*Romanticism* 21[2015] 37–47) considers a slightly under-appreciated poem of Wordsworth's that was first included in the 1800 *Lyrical Ballads* volume. Thomson's argument is that the poem's 'resistance to classification', and the fact that it a song *for* 'the Wandering Jew' as opposed to 'of', suggests it is a 'deflected address to Coleridge' (p. 37). Thomson notes that Wordsworth and Coleridge had already begun to differ in their poetic vision in the later 1790s (for example Coleridge's 'teleological aesthetic' versus 'Wordsworth's "lyrical and narrative inclination"', p. 39). The 'Song for the Wandering Jew', then, is seen as an ironically Coleridgean poem that 'reminds us of the experimental, new nature of [Wordsworth's] poetic work while at the same time issuing a declaration of independence from Coleridge's tutelage' (pp. 46–7). The subject of poetic intertextuality and influence is also investigated in Richard Gravil's '"The Reign of Nature"; or, Mr Bryant's Wordsworth' (*WC* 46[2015] 58–68). Gravil considers the early reception and influence of Wordsworth in the United States as well as his championing, alongside other Romantic poets, by William Cullen Bryant. As Gravil reminds us, Bryant was himself seen as the one great American poet of this time, and is a rather neglected figure in contemporary scholarship. Bearing this in mind, Gravil offers some close readings of Bryant's poetry, emphasizing its Wordsworthian influences, including such poems as the Immortality Ode and the Lucy poems. Interestingly, Gravil notes how the Solitary's ambivalence towards Native Americans in *The Excursion* in fact may have partly inspired Bryant's own (in 'The Prairies', Bryant's most 'Wordsworthian poem', p. 60). The fact that Bryant had some political influence, however, meant that although he 'wrote no more than a dozen genuinely remarkable poems . . . he exercised a legislative influence of which Wordsworth and Shelley could only dream' (p. 66).

The influence of continental Europe on Wordsworth was the subject of two articles. Eugene Stelzig's 'Vaudracour and William; or, a Tale of Two Different Recluses' (*WC* 46[2015] 120–4) offers a fascinating reading of the Vaudracour figure that appears in the 1805 *Prelude* (IX. 556–935), but is excluded from 1850. The lines were, however, published as *Vaudracour and Julia* in Wordsworth's *River Duddon* volume in 1820. Stelzig reads Vaudracour not simply as a disguised Wordsworth lamenting his lost love Annette, but as 'Wordsworth's version of a road not taken . . . his dark fictional double' who is a 'very different recluse' to the poet (p. 123). Stelzig's reading then is one that emphasizes both the romantic and the political analogies of Vaudracour's doomed relationship with Julia. 'Wordsworth and the Relief of Central Switzerland', by Julia Tejblum (*WC* 46[2015] 116–20), investigates Wordsworth's curious reference to a cartographic landscape model of Lake Lucerne and the neighbouring cantons that he encountered in Switzerland in 1790, and potentially again in 1820. Tejblum notes how Wordsworth uses the metaphor of the model—or 'relief'—in a number of versions of his *Guide to the*

*Lakes*, first appearing with a different title in 1810. What Wordsworth attempts to achieve with this allusion, Tejblum argues convincingly, is to capture what the poet sees as the relief's ability to be 'at once an aid to the future traveller and a retrospective tool, with which the reader can recast Wordsworth's experience' (p. 119).

In this light, it is a pleasing coincidence that *Romantic Circles* published an electronic edition of Wordsworth's *Guide to the Lakes*, edited by Nicholas Mason, Shannon Stimpson, and Paul Westover. Wordsworth's *Guide* was revised continually by the poet himself over twenty-five years, with five editions appearing in Wordsworth's lifetime alone. Although the second to fifth editions of the work are fairly easy to get hold of, the first edition is exceptionally rare and most of the available scholarly edited versions of the *Guide* are in extremely expensive volumes. This online version, that is of course open access, not only provides the text of the original 1810 edition, which was originally entitled *Selected Views in Cumberland, Westmorland and Lancashire*, but also the Reverend Joseph Wilkinson's accompanying engravings. This is very useful, as these high-quality images allow for easy consultation as well as reproduction. In addition, an annotated version of the 1835 edition is provided, along with page images of suggested 'Itineraries' provided by the then editors, published alongside the original. A heavily detailed PDF chart of parallel comparisons of all five editions is also provided, illustrating the extent of Wordsworth's revisionary practice as well as the diligent research undertaken by the editors. The thorough scholarly introduction provides an extensive overview of print history and the origins of Wordsworth's decision to write the *Guide* as well as a consideration of Wordsworth's potential influences regarding the writing of the Lake District. However, the editors stress Wordsworth's originality, arguing that he set out to write something that was far removed from a standard guidebook, and treated the Lake District as made up of something more than just 'scenes' to be observed from various viewing platforms. This treatment was very much informed by his poetic view of the landscape. As a final touch, there is also an interactive map where areas that Wordsworth discusses in the guides can be highlighted. This is an excellent resource for both general interest and Wordsworth scholars more specifically.

Finally, there were also two short *Notes & Queries* publications on Wordsworth. Stephanie Dumke's 'Wordsworth's Portraits of the Royal Children: A New Letter of 1850' (*N&Q* 62[2015] 415–17) details a previously unpublished letter from Wordsworth to Sir Charles Beaumont discovered in Coburg, Bavaria. Dumke notes that the status of the addressee means the paper used is expensive and the letter is very well presented. She then transcribes the letter in full, highlighting that it is written in 'a shaky hand' (p. 415); unsurprising considering Wordsworth's age (the letter was composed only two months prior to his death). The letter, as Dumke reminds us, also offers insights into Wordsworth's attitude to the Laureateship. Thomas Owens's '*Nature*'s Motto: Wordsworth and the Macmillans' (*N&Q* 62[2015] 430–5) is a fascinating consideration of Wordsworth's influence on the scientific journal *Nature*. Not only does Owens highlight that the magazine's motto was taken from Wordsworth's sonnet 'A VOLANT Tribe of Bards on earth are found', revised in 1827, but he also shows how it remained misquoted for so long. Owens correctly points out that, although the errors seem minor or superficial, they actually substantially change the meaning of Wordsworth's lines. In addition, Owens speculates, with persuasive evidence, that Wordsworth's lines may even have provided the inspiration for *Nature*'s title; after all, the early editors had a deep passion for Wordsworth's poetry. Amusingly, Owens notes that, had the editors chosen another Wordsworth quotation and taken the publication title in a different direction, it might not on occasion have been mistaken for a magazine for naturists. This article is an excellent, thorough, and entertaining piece of scholarship.

## 4. Drama

The scholarship from 2015 on the drama of the Romantic period sheds new light not only on the plays themselves but also on the many performances of them during these decades. While the attention to the latter concerns performances that took place at both major and less well-known theatres within and outside London, the emphasis on the stage speaks to a concerted critical effort from this year to foreground contextual readings of era plays.

This trend begins to become evident, for instance, in Frederick Burwick and Manushag N. Powell's transatlantic study, *British Pirates in Print and Performance*, which focuses on the period's fascination with the figure of the pirate in literary and theatre culture alike. Drawing on several works of the period and connecting them significantly to a time of maritime trade, exploration, and conflict, the authors trace a consequential history of piratical representation, which they contend offers a 'dramatic and performative affair' that is 'steeped in rebellion and chaos' (p. 14).

One of the major contributions of the book is the attention that Burwick and Powell give to the performative tendencies of the pirate, who is either 'striding the deck' or 'strutting the stage' (p. 1). After giving helpful background on an array of pirate representations and performances from the period, Burwick and Powell make clear that their book's purpose is to 'track the very interesting movement between pirate on stage and pirate in print' and how 'performance is continually, regardless of medium, the key to a pirate's successful mobility' (p. 11). The first three chapters of their book examine how piracy was realized as a performance on stage. Works by Lord Byron, Walter Scott, and James Fenimore Cooper are given significant attention. The final chapters of this impressive monograph then focus on matters of gender, including 'fraught pirate masculinity' and the possibilities of the 'she-pirate' in period works (p. 14). The book concludes with a brilliant chapter on the origins of several pirate clichés, including 'the "Pirate Code," pirate fashion (from peg legs to parrots), the Jolly Roger or skull-and-crossbones flag, pirate music and musical pirates, [and] walking the plank' (p. 14).

The next work reviewed also emphasizes the importance of stage history: a special volume of *DQR Studies in Literature* entitled 'The Romantic Stage: Holding the Mirror Up to Nature and Culture'. This excellent collection of essays re-examines the significance of the Romantic theatre from a myriad of perspectives. According to the introduction by its editors, Lilla Maria Crisafulli and Fabio Liberto (*DQR* 55[2015] 1–22), their volume aims to take into account the fact that these dramatic works 'were rich and innovative phenomena and that they made an essential contribution to the aesthetic and ideological complexity of British culture in the Romantic period' (p. 1). Crisafulli and Liberto contend that the essays in their collection contravene a long-standing critical bias that has maintained that the Romantics and the stage did not mix well. The essays 'seek to capture the richness and diversity of British Romantic theatre and drama and situate [them] at the centre of the multiple, and often radical, literary and social transformations that Romanticism brought about' (p. 20). Divided into four sections, the essays helpfully incorporate 'interdisciplinary, international and inter-generic perspectives' (p. 20).

The first section, 'Contextualizing Romantic Theatre and Drama', begins with Jeffrey Cox's essay, 'Editing Romantic Drama: Problems of Value, Volume, and Venue' (*DQR* 55[2015] 23–40), in which Cox argues that we are lacking 'a concerted effort to edit nineteenth-century drama so as to give us a complete picture of the dramatic and theatrical world during the Romantic era' (p. 25). He makes this claim as a recommendation to future editors of period dramas to include details about the evening at the theatre, especially since such evenings often included multiple performances. By the end of his essay, Cox proposes that more attention should even be paid to performing Romantic dramas themselves: 'Performance—whether in the theatre, the public reading, the classroom, or the closet stages of our own heads—provides particular historical embodiments of texts, the moments when these texts stop being marks on a page and become living works. An edition, which is finally marks on a page, may never be able to replicate the double life of performance works' (p. 40). Nicoletta Caputo's essay, 'Theatrical Periodicals and the Ethics of Theatre in the Romantic Age' (*DQR* 55[2015] 43–56), follows Cox's with an examination of the influence of periodicals on the theatre, including the 'strategies that such magazines adopted to arouse interest in the theatrical event and its protagonists, to influence public opinion, and to create an ideal audience and an "ideal theatre" ' (p. 43). In 'Romantic Drama and the Popular Theatre' (*DQR* 55[2015] 57–70), Michael Gamer considers the relationships between the Romantic stage and early nineteenth-century culture. For him, the theatres of the age provided cross-cultural spaces through which one can examine broader cultural and social issues: 'Here people and productions, both high and low, meet, contest, jostle, applaud, and constitute an evening of entertainment. Here issues of canon and class are raised face to face—between differing audience members, between rival actors, between competing cultural forms, between mainpiece and afterpiece. Romantic theatre audiences may have been segregated physically and economically—by ticket price as well by location in the theatre—but these divisions hardly stopped class interaction and frequently served as a cause for it' (p. 58).

The next section in the *DQR* volume, 'Drama across the Arts', begins with Carlotta Farese's 'The Strange Case of Herr von K: Further Reflections on the Reception of Kotzebue's Theatre in Britain' (*DQR* 55[2015] 71–84), and accomplishes precisely what its title suggests by offering an impressive analysis of August Friedrich Ferdinand von Kotzebue's influence on both Romantic drama and theatre. Next, Fabio Liberto's essay, 'Shakespeare's Visual Memorability during Romanticism' (*DQR* 55[2015] 87–110), stresses the importance of visual culture, especially painting, on drama and theatre of the era, particularly with regard to 'reconstructing the acting practices and dramatic conventions of the nineteenth-century stage' (p. 89). According to Liberto, 'paintings provide a different level of documentation and interpretation, offering a more immediate—and visually concrete—grasp of what was taking place in the London theatre'—especially in relation to the staging of Shakespeare's plays and heroes (p. 89). In 'Poses and Pauses: The Theatrical Portrait in English Romanticism' (*DQR* 55[2015] 111–34), Claudia Corti analyses the cultural fascination with celebrities by investigating the many circulating portraits of famous actors such as David Garrick, Sarah Siddons, and John Philip Kemble: 'the stars of the English theatre, who fascinated audiences and critics in the late eighteenth and early nineteenth centuries' (p. 111). In ' "A language in itself music": Salvatore Vaganò's Ballet en Action in Shelley's *Prometheus Unbound*' (*DQR* 55[2015] 135–59), Lilla Maria Crisafulli then turns to Percy Shelley's interests in multiple modes of performance, including choral drama, pantomime dance, and ballet. She does so by examining the influence of the Italian Romantic dancer and choreographer Salvatore Viganò on Shelley's *Prometheus*, which Shelley wrote in Italy, where he was able to experience 'new means of expression, new "languages", beyond the bounds of verbal discourse, capable to conjugate universality and subjectivism, personal emotions and human ties' (p. 137).

The next section, 'Staging the Gothic (Fear on Stage)', begins with Diego Saglia's 'Staging Gothic Flesh: Material and Spectral Bodies in Romantic-Period Theatre' (*DQR* 55[2015] 163–84). Saglia shows how Gothic drama in the period operated as a complex nexus of 'generic and performative codes caught between the competing claims of conservatism and subversion, masculinity and femininity, the comic, the tragic and the melodramatic, the natural and the supernatural'; he argues that Gothic drama's 'distinctively hybrid nature is fully visible and active in the figurations of the body', and it also includes 'oscillations between the cumbersome presence of the human physique and an evacuation of the physical into the immaterial, the evanescent and the spectral' (p. 164). In 'Matthew G. Lewis's Theatre: Fear on Stage' (*DQR* 55[2015] 185–97), Giovanna Silvani brings the discussion of Gothic drama specifically to Lewis's dramas, especially *Castle Spectre* [1797], a work in which Lewis 'succeeded in raising the popularity of Gothic drama to the level of that of the Gothic novel' (p. 185). She primarily argues that *Castle Spectre* 'provides an excellent example of a highly dynamic literary genre, often disharmonious in its various components, and teeming with inter- and intra-textual echoes and references'; for her, 'gothic drama ... becomes visible as a bridge linking past and future, tradition and innovation, a drama in progress, which inevitably seems to shun all classifications and clear-cut definitions' (p. 197). In the next essay, 'Vampire in Kilts' (*DQR* 55[2015] 199–214), Frederick Burwick traces the period's fascination with the figure of the vampire both on stage and on the page. Burwick specifically addresses how this figure transformed during the Romantic era into the aristocratic precursor to what many have considered the pinnacle of vampire literature, Bram Stoker's *Dracula* [1897]. In the final essay of the section, 'Dramatic Discourse and the Romantic Stage in Joanna Baillie's Theatre' (*DQR* 55[2015] 227–43), Franca Dellarossa takes on the task of examining Joanna Baillie's significant contribution to the Romantic stage. In analysing Baillie's plays, Dellarosa specifically takes 'into consideration the various ways in which dramatic discourse and the theatrical codes which define its Gothic characteristics interact, sometimes questioning the Gothic sign in the very act of reinforcing it' (p. 227).

The final section, 'Texts, Theories and Contexts', begins with Rosy Colombo's 'Closet Drama on the Stage of Revolution: Language on Trial in Wordsworth's *The Borderers*' (*DQR* 55[2015] 245–54). Through a careful analysis of Wordsworth's play, Colombo argues that the Romantics indeed focused on the performative aspects of their dramas by investing heavily in the 'theatrical performativity of their poetic language' (p. 245). In '*Sardanapalus*, or, Romantic Drama between History and Archaeology' (*DQR* 55[2015] 255–78), Carla Pomarè then transitions to discussing the convergence of historical knowledge and a 'new discipline touching upon the historical field, archaeology'; she shows quite lucidly how Byron's play offers a portal into this emergent field of study (p. 256). The last essay of the volume, 'The Sensory and the Ideal: S.T. Coleridge's Aesthetics in Romantic Theatrical Discourse' (*DQR* 55[2015] 279–92) by Valeria Pellis, offers a thorough and helpful exploration of the many critical readings of Coleridge's work as dramatist as well as his views on his contemporary stage culture.

This fruitful attention to Romantic stage history continues just as impressively with an issue of *Studies in Romanticism*, 'An Illegitimate History: Essays in Romantic Theater History in Memory of Jane Moody'. The collection is edited by Kevin Gilmartin, who authors a touching introductory tribute to Moody (*SiR* 54[2015] 151–8), whose dedicated career singlehandedly brought Romantic literary and cultural history into dialogue with theatre history. As Gilmartin states, the essays in the volume 'engage some aspect of Jane Moody's own interest in late Georgian illegitimate theater—its performance practices, its material forms and geographical distribution, its generic transgressions and innovations, its emotional range, and its relation to the licensed stage' (p. 157).

Jeffrey Cox's article, '"Illegitimate" Pantomime in the "Legitimate" Theater: Context as Text' (*SiR* 54[2015] 159–86), begins the series of essays, focusing on how 'action, sets and music displace language' in nineteenth-century drama (p. 160). For this reason, Cox argues, it is paramount to consider context (including 'paratexts, intertexts, and historical contexts') as much as the actual Romantic dramatic text itself, a line of argument consistent with Cox's previously cited essay (p. 168). In 'That "Fine Word" Illegitimate: Children in Late Georgian Theater' (*SiR* 54[2015] 187–209), Julia Carlson then argues that Romantic theatre became a conducive space not only for entertaining audiences but also for 'a child's mental flourishing'—what she calls the 'juvenile aspects of theater's aesthetic education [which was] central to the success of theater in facilitating mental transformation, not chronological stages of development' (p. 189). Next, Daniel O'Quinn addresses the 'heightened affective bonds between audience, player, and theatrical technology' in Romantic theatre in his essay, 'Anticipating Histories: Emotional Life at Covent Garden Theatre, February 1811' (*SiR* 54[2015] 211–39). Tracing the connections between legitimate and illegitimate theatres, O'Quinn draws on the specific case study of Covent Garden to show how emerging forms such as melodrama and spectacle offered a 'new form of affective engagement' at this specific moment in theatre history—one that targeted 'the bodily, visceral lives of the audience' (p. 212). In ' "Announcing each day the performances": Playbills, Ephemerality, and Romantic Period Media/Theater History' (*SiR* 54[2015] 241–68), Gillian Russell then turns to the significance of the playbill in relation to Romantic theatre as well as print culture: for her the playbill offers an 'ephemeral zone in which print textuality and theatricality are profoundly imbricated' (p. 242). Diego Saglia concludes the powerful series with his essay, ' "The frighted stage": The Sensational Proliferation of Ghost Melodrama in the 1820s' (*SiR* 54[2015] 269–93). As Saglia states, he sets out in his article to 'reappraise how in the 1820s . . . melodramatists and managers drew on earlier Gothic drama and melodrama to reinvent them with new stage technology that enabled their plays to capture audiences and, by the same token, represent (or indeed "ghost") topical questions and anxieties through the performance of the spectral' (p. 271). In the final pages of the special *Studies in Romanticism* volume, Greg Kucich (Moody's husband) provides a concluding response to the articles along with another tribute to Moody's life and prolific scholarship, noting how Moody captured the way that Romantic theatre was able to cross borders in so many ways—a feature that all of the contributors to this volume have successfully underscored.

The contexts of Romantic dramas receive further attention from Susan Valladares, whose brilliant monograph, *Staging the Peninsular War: English Theatres 1807–1815*, focuses on the intricacies of British wartime theatre. As she considers the relations between the Napoleonic Wars and theatrical responses to them in Britain, Valladares concentrates primarily on how Napoleon's invasion of Portugal, which led to Britain's involvement in the ensuing Peninsular Wars (the Iberian peninsula of Spain and Portugal), affected much of the era's theatre culture—both in London's licensed and its unlicensed theatres, as well as outside the metropolis in provincial theatres.

Valladares opens her first chapter, '*Pizarro*, "Political Proteus" ', with an analysis of Richard Brinsley Sheridan's *Pizarro* [1799] and how its interpretation varied from performance to performance. As she cleverly shows, Sheridan's play took on a new set of meanings during the Peninsular Wars, as the Spanish conquistador became a stand-in for French aggression, South American natives suddenly represented the British populace, and Spain was surprisingly transformed into an object of sympathy because of Napoleon's invasion of it (one need not forget the centuries-long adversarial relationship between both countries). In her next chapter, 'Performing Shakespeare', Valladares continues, showing how performances of dramatic texts offered an array of adaptations and interpretations. She focuses, for instance, on the staging of sympathies between Britain and Spain through the portrayal of Spaniards in Coleridge's *Remorse* [1797]. She turns her attention next to performances of Shakespeare's plays, arguing cogently that these dramas served as enactments of British nationalism during these specific years. Her third chapter, 'Spectacular Stages', shifts the direction of her analysis to the unlicensed theatres of London, where pantomime, burlesque, burletta, and melodrama received a new kind of status. According to her, these dramatic forms were indisputably in dialogue with the happenings in the Iberian peninsula. Her final chapter, 'Playing to the Provinces', then brings the reader to a specific case study outside London altogether: Bristol's Theatre Royal and Regency Theatre. Valladares demonstrates how Bristol's theatrical community became entangled in matters of the Peninsular Wars by virtue of the city's status as a consequential port of commercial and military traffic.

Valladares complements her fine pages of research with a series of indexed performances that occurred at the Bristol Theatre Royal, Covent Garden, and Drury Lane from 1807 to 1815, and this wealth of material is certainly a boon for drama scholars of the period. Through a book that introduces a new kind of methodology, given her performative objects of analysis, she does an admirable job of considering the valences of theatrical performance within an era in which considerable censoring practices took place. Valladares succeeds in showing how several dramas of the era were transformed time and time again through each of their individual enactments. She also makes the compelling case that the theatre of wartime Britain turned into a medium for celebrating military campaigns as well as shaping public sentiment—one that channelled the social and political influences of the day in new ways.

With an impressive essay in *Studies in English Literature*, 'Linguistic Instability in R.B. Sheridan's *Pizarro*' (*SEL* 55[2015] 603–20), Michael Wiley picks up Valladares's interest in the Anglo-Hispanic connections of the era as well as on what he calls the most popular play of the 1790s, Sheridan's *Pizarro*. As Wiley argues, '*Pizarro* engages extensively with the political and literary contexts and debates of the late 1790s and helps set the critical, political, and literary stage for the following decades. By engaging and even shifting such contexts, *Pizarro* details an antifoundational—and antityrannical—hermeneutics of linguistic and representational instability and change' (p. 604).

The next monograph reviewed also picks up on some of the themes of Valladares's work, offering exclusive attention to a form of theatre in mining towns, mill towns, and port cities dedicated to the labouring classes in both London and its provinces. Frederick Burwick's extraordinary *British Drama of the Industrial Revolution* provides a new account of the post-revolutionary effect on the world of the theatre, particularly as it represented the plight of exploited labourers, including weavers, miners, charcoal burners, steel mill workers, and field workers. Like Valladares, Burwick argues that the meanings of individual plays varied with each performance and audience. In making his argument, Burwick draws significant attention to political and cultural contexts that affected these local milieus, showing, for instance, how a melodramatic villain and victim on stage suddenly represent the factory owner and his underpaid, overworked employees.

Burwick argues that the performances he scrutinizes, including the emergence of a kind of industrial melodrama, offer a bridge between the failures of the French Revolution and the dawning of the Chartist movement.

He shows how these performances offered the labouring classes an opportunity for bonding through common purpose. Extending his compelling
argument across nine chapters of careful analysis, Burwick offers helpful
background on several labouring-class playwrights as well as a meditation on
the influence of various local organizations such as the Freemasons. He then
shifts his attention to the influence of specific industries, as well as leaders of
protest movements such as Captain Rock and King Ludd, on the era's dramas
and performances, taking his reader even to specific cases that called for
reform through the performances themselves. Burwick also considers the
theatrical representations of counterfeit coiners, poachers, and smugglers. All
in all, Burwick succeeds in shedding ample light on neglected subject matter,
and one can hope that his attention to the labouring classes and provincial
theatres—along with Valladares's—will begin to set a new direction for
scholarship of our period.

The final essays reviewed here provide important biographical analysis
pertaining to the dramas of women writers as well as Percy Shelley and Lord
Byron. Marcie Frank has contributed a wonderful essay in *English Literary
History* entitled 'Frances Burney's Theatricality' (*ELH* 82[2015] 615–35).
Frank argues that 'Burney's development of narrative techniques for
modulating distance, including free indirect discourse, grows out of the
configuration of theater, shame, and narration in her oeuvre. The narrative
innovations on view in her work are significant to the history of the novel not
simply because she precedes Austen, but also because they reorient our
attention to theatrical, indeed melodramatic, aspects especially prevalent in
some Romantic novels for whose extraordinarily labile features we still lack
a proper account' (pp. 616–17). In an essay on 'Drama' (in Looser, ed.,
pp. 32–44), Catherine Burroughs contributes an impressive analysis of this
subject matter by drawing on plays by women writers from the late sixteenth
century and culminating with an intensive focus on famous playwrights such
as Joanna Baillie, Elizabeth Inchbald, Frances Burney, and Frances Anne
Kemble. Burroughs sets out to 'paint a clear picture of the contributions made
to drama and theatre by British Romantic women writers so that what came
before and after them can be rendered with more nuance' (p. 32). In 'Percy
Shelley's "Unfinished Drama" and the Problem of the Jane Williams Poems'
(*ERR* 26[2015] 615–32), also discussed in Section 3 above, Cian Duffy maps
the relationship between the 'Jane' included in Shelley's late poetry and the
actual historical figure Jane Williams, whom Shelley had befriended during the
final months of his life. In presenting a thorough archival investigation of
manuscripts and poetic texts, Duffy also offers an extensive reading of
Shelley's 'Unfinished Drama', which treats the subject of unrequited love and
finds its inspiration, according to Duffy, in the fraught relationship between
Shelley and Williams. Duffy also contributed another fascinating essay, 'Percy
Shelley's Other Lyrical Drama and the Inception of *Hellas*' (*SEL* 55[2015]
817–40), in which he draws links between Shelley's plans for his Greek
revolutionary drama, *Hellas*, and his lifelong fascination with the book of Job
in the Old Testament. In 'Byron, Original Sin, Shadows of Death and the
Dramas of 1821' (*ByronJ* 43[2015] 29–42), Harold Ray Stevens brings all the
plays that Byron wrote in the same one year—*Marino Faliero* [1821], *The Two*

*Foscari* [1821], *Sardanapalus* [1821], *Cain* [1821], *Heaven and Earth* [1821], and *Werner* [1821]—into a single discussion: namely through how Byron treats the subject of original sin and its consequences. Stevens even sees a parallel between Byron's inclusion of this biblical subject matter, which also underscores the subject of death and dying, and what ultimately transpires through Byron's own death in Greece a few years later.

On a final note, a recent collaborative project between the New York University Department of English and the Red Bull Theater of New York City is worth mentioning. Spearheaded by this reviewer, this initiative has brought together scholars of Romantic drama and theatre experts through a common dramatic text of interest. Since 2012, the team has staged dramatic readings of Romantic plays with Red Bull, a theatre company dedicated to reviving neglected classics. Our productions have included Byron's *Sardanapalus* [November 2012], Shelley's *Prometheus Unbound* [November 2013], and Baillie's *De Montfort* [November 2014]. The joint project has aspired to be win-win for both communities: while theatre experts—including trained actors and directors—profit from literary scholars who serve as resident dramaturgs during rehearsals, literary critics benefit from experiencing these texts as performances in a number of ways (from rehearsals up to the final product). According to this reviewer, this approach indeed sheds new light on research, as Cox has persuasively written. All the while, the NYC community has benefited from encountering these texts—probably for the first time—on stage rather than through the page. Future productions of Romantic dramas with Red Bull will include Frances Burney's *The Woman Hater* and Byron's *Manfred*.

Based on all of the recent critical attention given to the contexts of Romantic drama, including analysing performances that took place during the period itself as well as scholarly efforts to reanimate Romantic dramas today, the direction of our scholarship is pushing well beyond the close readings of these dramatic texts. Such a propensity is sure to open new pathways and possibilities for what undoubtedly was the most popular of Romantic genres, and perhaps such an effort can help to redress the considerable imbalance between the era's criticism on plays and that devoted to both poetry and the novel.

**Books Reviewed**

Baker, William, ed. *Studies in Victorian and Modern Literature: A Tribute to John Sutherland*. FDUP. [2015] pp. xvi + 350. $90 ISBN 9 7816 1147 6927.

Bennett, Andrew, ed. *William Wordsworth in Context*. CUP. [2015] pp. xxviii + 331. £70 ISBN 9 7811 0702 8418.

Berberich, Christine, ed. *The Bloomsbury Introduction to Popular Fiction*. Bloomsbury. [2015] pp. 344. £25.99 ISBN 9 7814 4113 4318.

Birk, Hanne, and Marion Gymnich, eds. *Pride and Prejudice 2.0: Interpretations, Adaptations and Transformations of Jane Austen's Classic*. V&R. [2015] pp. 327. €50 ISBN 9 7838 4710 4520.

Borushko, Matthew, ed. *The Politics of Shelley: History, Theory, Form* . Praxis. RC. [2015]. https://www.rc.umd.edu/praxis/shelley_politics.

Boyiopoulos, Kostas, and Mark Sandy, eds. *Decadent Romanticism: 1780– 1914*. Ashgate. [2015] pp. xiii + 208. £60 ISBN 9 7814 7242 2422.

Brookshire, David, ed. *P.B. Shelley and the Delimitation of the Gothic* . Praxis. RC. [2015]. https://www.rc.umd.edu/praxis/gothic_shelley.

Burwick, Frederick. *British Drama of the Industrial Revolution*. CUP. [2015] pp. x + 322. £52.20 ISBN 9 7811 0711 1653.

Burwick, Frederick, and Manushag N. Powell. *British Pirates in Print and Performance*. PalMac. [2015] pp. x + 231. £55 ISBN 9 7811 3733 9928.

Butler, Marilyn. *Mapping Mythologies: Countercurrents in Eighteenth-Century Poetry and Cultural History*. CUP. [2015] pp. xxv + 214. £25 ISBN 9 7811 0711 6382.

Calzoni, Raul, and Greta Perletti, eds. *Monstrous Anatomies: Literary and Scientific Imagination in Britain and Germany during the Long Nineteenth Century*. V&R. [2015] pp. 316. £40. ISBN 9 7838 4710 4698.

Carroll, Siobhan. *An Empire of Air and Water: Uncolonizable Space in the British Imagination, 1750–1850*. UPennP. [2015] pp. 290. £39 ISBN 9 7808 1224 6780.

Clark, Steve, and Tristanne Connolly, eds. *British Romanticism in European Perspective*. PalMac. [2015] pp. xi + 286. £65 ISBN 9 7811 3746 1957.

Cohen-Vrignaud, Gerard. *Radical Orientalism: Rights, Reform, and Romanticism*. CUP. [2015] pp. ix + 261. £67 ISBN 9 7811 0711 0328.

Cousins, A.D., and Geoffrey Payne, eds. *Home and Nation in British Literature from the English to the French Revolutions*. CUP. [2015] pp. xi + 288. £64.99 ISBN 9 7811 0706 4409.

Craig, Sheryl. *Jane Austen and the State of the Nation*. PalMac [2015] pp. xi + 183. £55. ISBN 9 7811 3754 4544 (hbk).

Deakin, Wayne. *Hegel and the English Romantic Tradition*. PalMac. [2015] pp. ix + 198. £60 ISBN 9 7811 3748 2174.

Dellarossa, Franca. *Talking Revolution: Edward Rushton's Rebellious Poetics, 1782–1814*. LiverUP. [2014] pp. xxiii + 238. £75 ISBN 9 7817 8138 1441.

Doody, Margaret. *Jane Austen's Names: Riddles, Persons, Places*. UChicP. [2015] pp. xii + 438. £24.50 ISBN 9 7802 2615 7832.

Dubois, Pierre. *Music in the Georgian Novel*. CUP. [2015] pp. xi + 364. £74.99 ISBN 9 7811 0710 8509.

Edson, Michael, ed. *Publishing, Editing, and Reception: Essays in Honor of Donald H. Reiman*. UDelP. [2015] pp. xxxiv + 283. $90 ISBN 9 7816 1149 5782.

Esterhammer, Angela, Diane Piccitto, and Patrick Vincent, eds. *Romanticism, Rousseau, Switzerland: New Prospects*. PalMac. [2015] pp. xii + 229. £55 ISBN 9 7811 3747 5855.

Ferris, Ina, *Book-Men, Book Clubs, and the Romantic Literary Sphere*. PalMac. [2015] pp. x + 192. £55 ISBN 9 7811 3736 7594.

Fulford, Tim. *Romantic Poetry and Literary Coteries: The Dialect of the Tribe*. PalMac. [2015] pp. x + 264. £55 ISBN 9 7811 3753 3968.

Garside, Peter, and Karen O'Brien, eds. *English and British Fiction 1750–1820.* Oxford History of the Novel in English 2. OUP. [2015] pp. xix + 668. £95 ISBN 9 7801 9957 4803.

Gilmartin, Kevin, *William Hazlitt: Political Essayist.* OUP. [2015] pp. 368. £55 ISBN 9 7801 9870 9312.

Goodman, Robin Truth, ed., *Literature and the Development of Feminist Theory.* CUP. [2015] pp. 297. £80 ISBN 9 7811 0712 6084.

Gordon, Charlotte. *Romantic Outlaws: The Extraordinary Lives of Mary Wollstonecraft & Mary Shelley.* Hutchinson. [2015] pp. xviii + 649. £25 ISBN 9 7800 9195 8947.

Gravil, Richard, and Daniel Robinson, eds. *The Oxford Handbook of William Wordsworth.* OUP. [2015] pp. xxv + 868. £110 ISBN 9 7801 9966 2128.

Jackson, H.J. *Those Who Write for Immortality: Romantic Reputations and the Dream of Lasting Fame.* YaleUP. [2015] pp. 312. $35 ISBN 9 7803 0017 4793.

Kövesi, Simon, and Scott McEathron, eds. *New Essays on John Clare: Poetry, Culture, and Community.* CUP. [2015] pp. xii + 244. £57.99 ISBN 9 7811 0703 1111.

Laniel-Musitelli, Sophie, and Thomas Constantinesco, eds. *Romanticism and Philosophy: Thinking with Literature.* Routledge. [2015] pp. ix + 264. £95 ISBN 9 7811 3880 5507.

Linkin, Harriet Kramer, ed. *Verses Transcribed for H.T.* Romantic Circles. [2015]. https://www.rc.umd.edu/editions/tighe_verses.

Looser, Devoney, ed. *The Cambridge Companion to Women's Writing in the Romantic Period.* CUP. [2015] pp. 272. £57 ISBN 9 7811 3906 1315.

Makdisi, Saree. *Reading William Blake.* CUP. [2015] pp. xii + 137. £30 ISBN 9 7805 2176 3035.

Mason, Nicholas, Shannon Stimpson, and Paul Westover, eds. *Guide to the Lakes.* RC [2015]. https://www.rc.umd.edu/editions/guide_lakes.

Morefield, Kenneth R. *Jane Austen's Emma: A Close Reading Companion,* vol. 1. CambridgeSP. [2015] pp. ix + 103. £42 ISBN 9 7814 4387 4403.

Mulhallen, Jacqueline. *Percy Bysshe Shelley: Poet and Revolutionary.* Pluto. [2015] pp. xiv + 170. £11.50 ISBN 9 7807 4533 4615.

Partenza, Paola, ed. *Dynamics of Desacralization: Disenchanted Literary Talents.* V&R. [2015] pp. 179. £24 ISBN 9 7838 4710 3868.

Peacocke, Emma, *Romanticism and the Museum.* PalMac. [2015] pp. ix + 195. £58. ISBN 9 7811 3747 1437.

Piccitto, Diane. *Blake's Drama, Theatre, Performance and Identity in the Illuminated Books.* PalMac. [2014] pp. vii + 241. £55 ISBN 9 7811 3737 8002.

Powley, Tammy, and April Van Camp, eds. *Women of Florida Fiction: Essays on 12 Sunshine State Writers.* McFarland. [2015] pp. 236. $40. ISBN 9 7807 8647 8941.

Ramsey, Neil, and Russell Gillian,, eds. *Tracing War in British Enlightenment and Romantic Culture.* PalMac. [2015] pp. xiv + 239. £55 ISBN 9 7811 3747 4308.

Rogers, Brett M., and Benjamin Eldon Stevens, eds. *Classical Traditions in Science Fiction.* OUP. [2015] pp. 398. £64 ISBN 9 7801 9998 8419.

Sabor, Peter, ed. *The Cambridge Companion to Emma*. CUP. [2015] pp. xx + 219. £17.99 ISBN 9 7811 0744 2993.

Schulenberg, Ulf. *Romanticism and Pragmatism: Richard Rorty and the Idea of a Poeticized Culture*. PalMac. [2015] pp. vii + 251. £58 ISBN 9 7811 3747 4186.

Sigler, David. *Sexual Enjoyment in British Romanticism: Gender and Psychoanalysis, 1753–1835*. McG-QUP. [2015] pp. 288. $34.95 ISBN 9 7807 7354 5106.

Sodeman, Melissa. *Sentimental Memorials: Women and the Novel in Literary History*. StanfordUP. [2015] pp. 186. £37 ISBN 9 7808 0479 1328.

Thompson, James. *Jane Austen and Modernization: Sociological Readings*. PalMac. [2015] pp. x + 211. £55 ISBN 9 7811 3749 6010.

Thompson, Judith, ed. *John Thelwall: Selected Poetry and Poetics*. PalMac. [2015] pp. xiv + 324. £68 ISBN 9 7811 3734 4823.

Thompson, Peggy, ed. *Beyond Sense and Sensibility: Moral Formation and the Literary Imagination from Johnson to Wordsworth*. BuckUP. [2015] pp. xv + 214. $85. ISBN 9 7816 1148 6407.

Todd, Janet, ed. *The Cambridge Introduction to Jane Austen*, 2nd Edn. CUP. [2015] pp. 190. £35.99. ISBN 9 7811 0710 0251 (hbk); pp. 208. £ 12.99 ISBN 9 7811 0749 4701 (pbk).

Tuite, Clara. *Lord Byron and Scandalous Celebrity*. CUP. [2015] pp. xxv + 312. £67 ISBN 9 7811 0708 2595.

Valladares, Susan. *Staging the Peninsular Wars: English Theatres 1807–1815*. Routledge. [2015] pp. x + 472. £84 ISBN 9 7814 7241 8630.

Weinberg, Alan M., and Timothy Webb, eds. *The Neglected Shelley*. Ashgate. [2015] pp. xiv + 347. £75 ISBN 9 7814 7246 5641.

Wolfson, Susan J. *Reading John Keats*. CUP. [2015] pp. xviii + 179. £30.99 ISBN 9 7805 2151 3418.

Wordsworth, Jonathan. *The Invisible World: Lectures from the Wordsworth Summer Conference and Wordsworth Winter School*, ed. Haynes Richard. CreateSpace. [2015] pp. xxxiv + 280. £14.99 ISBN 9 7815 0329 0259.

# XIV

# The Victorian Period

KRISTEN POND, DANIEL SMITH, WILLIAM BAKER,
ARIANA REILLY, CHRISTIAN DICKINSON, CLARE
STAINTHORP, MICHAEL J. SULLIVAN, AND LUCY BARNES

This chapter is divided into four sections: 1. General and Prose; 2. The Novel; 3. Poetry; 4. Drama. Section 1 is by Kristen Pond, with assistance from Daniel Smith and William Baker; section 2 is by Ariana Reilly, with Christian Dickinson and William Baker; section 3 is by Clare Stainthorp and Michael J. Sullivan; section 4 is by Lucy Barnes.

## 1. General and Prose

In this section, William Baker reviews work covering George Borrow, Samuel Butler, Thomas Carlyle, Richard Jefferies, and other publications as noted. All general studies and works on other individual authors are reviewed by Kristen Pond, with assistance from Daniel Smith.

This year included several publications that honour prominent scholars in our field, and I begin with those. *Studies in Victorian and Modern Literature: A Tribute to John Sutherland*, edited by William Baker, is a Festschrift in honour of John Sutherland. The volume includes twenty-six essays that cover a remarkable range of topics modelled after Sutherland's intellectual interests and attempt to capture his intellectual spirit. Baker's introduction traces the trajectory of Sutherland's career, highlighting key works and their effect on Victorian studies. Baker also contributed chapter 24, 'John Sutherland: A Life', which offers an account of the major events in Sutherland's life and ends with Baker's memories of Sutherland. The following chapter titles, their content, and their style are meant to reflect and honour John Sutherland's provocative questions, compelling prose, and important contributions to the field. Reading the essays in this volume will make one want to run to the archives to explore further the fresh names and works held out to tantalize our intellectual curiosity, and to pull our well-worn favourite Victorian texts from the shelf to examine them again. In short, these essays provide just the sort of provocative readings one experiences when reading Sutherland's own work.

*The Year's Work in English Studies, Volume 96 (2017)* © *The Author 2017. Published by Oxford University Press on behalf of the English Association. All rights reserved.*
*For Permissions, please email: journals.permissions@oup.com*
doi:10.1093/ywes/max015

Section I, 'The Publishing Dimension', includes essays that explore dimensions of the Victorian publishing industry, one of Sutherland's primary interests. Chapter 1, 'Reconsidering the Unknown Public: A Puzzle of Literary Gains', by Simon Frost, discusses the changing publishing climate in the Victorian period famously coined by Collins as the 'Unknown Public'. Chapter 2, 'The Blackwood Female Literary Network, 1880–1910', by David Finkelstein, examines the publishing practices of the William Blackwood and Sons and their focus on attracting a network of female writers. In chapter 3, 'Trace Collaboration and the Problem of Evidence: Anna Jameson and Ottilie von Goethe', Linda K. Hughes, in the style of Sutherland's boldness and inquisitiveness, writes about Jameson's collaborations with Ottilie. Chapter 4, 'Margaret Oliphant and the Changing House of Blackwood', by Joanne Shattock, examines the publishing relationship between Oliphant and Blackwood. Chapter 5, 'Wheels of Desire: The Popular Adaptations of A.E.W. Mason's Thrillers from the 1900s to the 1930s', by Alexis Weedon, takes up the issues of adaptation in the publishing industry through a discussion of Mason's stories and their adaptations to film.

Section II, 'Victorians Major and Minor', exemplifies the kind of influence left on literary scholars by Sutherland's work, his methodologies, his questions, and his conclusions. Chapter 6, 'Moral Puzzles in Adam Bede', by Rosemary Ashton, engages with Sutherland's World's Classics volumes on puzzles. Ashton takes up the puzzling issue of how George Eliot handles Hetty's pregnancy. Chapter 7, 'Structure, Tone, and Temper in Charles Lever's Lord Kilgobbin', by Tony Bareham, represents scholarship on 'minor Victorians' in a discussion of Lever's novel focused on Anglo-Irish relationships. Chapter 8, 'Sister Acts: The Prevalence of Literary Families in the Victorian Period', by Troy J. Bassett, builds on Sutherland's claim, in an essay entitled 'The Victorian Novelists: Who Were They?', that most novelists were related to at least one other novelist. Using the database 'At the Circulating Library: A Database of Victorian Fiction, 1837–1901', Bassett examines this claim further. Chapter 9, 'Why Did William Butler Yeats Leave William Allingham Out?', by Simon Gatrell, takes up Sutherland's interest in the unwritten and excluded by tracing the story of why Yeats excluded Allingham from his literary ancestry. Chapter 10, 'Again the Zelig Effect: Israel Zangwill and the Modern Short Story', by Graham Law, takes up another 'minor' figure, though one that Law argues had a 'seminal role in modernizing the publishing format and the literary form of the short story' (p. 130). Chapter 11, 'Beyond Pickwick: Seymour's Sketches and Regency Print Culture', by Brian Maidment, discusses Robert Seymour, the only illustrator of The Pickwick Papers not given a separate entry in John Sutherland's Longman's Companion to Victorian Fiction. Chapter 12, 'Another "Spoiling Hand" at Work on Middlemarch?', by K.M. Newton, builds from Sutherland's essay entitled 'R.H. Hutton's Spoiling Hand', in which he discusses Hutton's criticisms that persuaded Eliot to alter the ending of Middlemarch. Newton takes up another critical letter from a lawyer that influenced Eliot's writing of the will-burning scene. Chapter 13, 'Rethinking the Endings of Great Expectations', by Robert L. Patten, aims to extend Sutherland's work on author–publisher relations by discussing the writing process and serialized form of *Great Expectations*. Chapter 14, "'Erect his statue and worship it'": A Victorian Shakespeare Souvenir', by Fred Schwarzbach, begins with the lessons Schwarzbach learned from Sutherland about 'thinking outside the box of literary studies' (p. 181) and offers one way of doing so through his discussion of the tourist souvenir bust. Chapter 15, 'The Satirist Satirized: Thackeray's Snobs and William North's Anti-Punch', by Patrick Scott, examines a little-known novella by William North, *Anti-Punch*, for what it reveals about the popular magazine *Punch* from the perspective of an outsider.

Section III, 'Non-Victorians and Puzzles', models the kind of work Sutherland did as a journalist. Sutherland 'retired' in 2004, but went on to publish an astonishing number of articles on diverse subjects in papers such as the *New York Times Book Review*, the *Los Angeles Times*, the London *Times*, the *Guardian*, and the *Daily Telegraph*. This section also plays off Sutherland's interest in puzzles and the big questions he raised that often sparked central debates in the field. Chapter 16, 'The Elephant in the Classroom', by Michael Caines, discusses Sutherland's work *Jumbo: The Unauthorized Biography of a Victorian Sensation*, and the case of the elephant Topsy and her public execution, which is still viewable on YouTube. This essay is also about the importance of offering unpopular critical opinions, which Sutherland did often with grace. Chapter 17, '*The Inheritors*: Conrad and Ford's Incursion into Wellsland', by Mario Curreli, explores the influence of H.G. Wells's science fiction work on Conrad and Ford's *The Inheritors*, which does not contain any immediately evident elements of science fiction. Chapter 18, 'Two Quiet Years: The University Press in Oxford in 1770 and 1845', by Simon Eliot, looks at 'years before the storms' (p. 231) to show that scholarly study can gain from examination of quiet years rather than always looking to revolutionary years. Chapter 19, '"Where are our moral foundations?"': Emily Dickinson and Henry James', by Philip Horne, models Sutherland's attention to 'negligible details' (p. 243) by tracing the connection between Dickinson and James. Chapter 20, 'The Archaeology of *Pride and Prejudice*', by Deirdre Le Faye, attempts to track the settings and dates of *Pride and Prejudice*, which, unlike Austen's other novels, does not offer explicit dating. Chapter 21, '*The Fallen Idol*: From Story to Screen', by David Lodge, is a reprint of an article originally published in the *Guardian Review* in 2006. Lodge details his discovery of an anomaly in the work of Graham Greene, a discovery made while studying the changes made by the author when the story was adapted for film. Chapter 22, 'My Collaboration with John Sutherland', by Cedric Watts, wittily writes about his experience working with Sutherland on one of the Oxford World's Classics puzzle books about Shakespeare. Chapter 23, 'Angelica's Susan: A Challenge From Real Life?', by René Weis, continues to tease vexed questions about details of Shakespeare's characters, which Sutherland addresses in his essay 'How Ancient is Lear? How Youthful is Juliet?' Here, Weis puzzles over names and the connection between Shakespeare's life and his plays.

*The Encyclopedia of Victorian Literature*, edited by Dino Franco Felluga with Pamela K. Gilbert and Linda K. Hughes (reviewed here by William Baker), is a broad-ranging encyclopedia, that assembles approximately 340 peer-reviewed contributions by nearly 300 critics, representing a mixture of eminent hands and new scholars writing on pertinent authors, topics, and genres within their respective scopes of expertise. Covering the period 1832–1901, essays vary significantly in length, ranging from about 1,000 to 7,000 words. In four volumes, the essayists reveal new directions, treating both cognitive and digital approaches to studies of Victorian literature. Coverage is universal and includes some neglected subjects, such as the English-language poetry of India. Inevitably, in such a wide-reaching reference work, there are omissions; notably, the novelist Richard Jefferies (1848–87) and the dramatist Sir Arthur Wing Pinero (1855–1934) do not have their own entries. Cross-references to related essays are followed in each case by the authors' suggestions for further reading; a few of these appear to need updating, however. A minor caveat aside, the quality of the contributions is uniformly interesting and thorough. The comprehensive nature of the set distinguishes it from similar earlier attempts at encyclopedic coverage of the Victorian era. Sturdily bound, well indexed by author and theme (pp. 1803–86), and illustrated with pertinent black-and-white figures, the computer-generated, double-column text is easy on the eye. An electronic version is also available on the *Wiley-Blackwell Encyclopedia of Literature* platform.

One of the finest publications this year has become even more meaningful as one of the last contributions we have from the late Linda Peterson. *The Cambridge Introduction to Victorian Women Writers*, edited by Peterson, begins with the growing sense that Victorian contemporaries, such as George Henry Lewes, John Stuart Mill, Anne Katherine Elwood, Julia Kavanagh, and other critics, recognized 'a distinctive women's literary tradition' (p. 1). In the introduction, Peterson argues that the nineteenth-century approach to women writers influenced the feminist approach to women's literature in the later twentieth century. The introduction thus provides a brief survey of scholarship on women writers from the Victorian period, the twentieth century, and more recent work. This volume joins this scholarship through its recuperative work, although Peterson thoughtfully meditates on the sometimes harmful connection between 'recuperation' and disease. The volume also aims to highlight the innovations that women writers brought to a wide range of genres. The chapters, written by key scholars in the field, cover an impressive range of writers and genres. Part I, 'Victorian Women Writers' Careers', covers more generally the situation of women writers and their careers, while Part II, 'Victorian Women Writers' Achievements: Genres and Modes', looks at specific women writers in key Victorian genres.

Chapter 1, 'Making a Debut' (pp. 15–28), by Alexis Easley, focuses on the obstacles women faced and their solutions to forming a career in the male-dominated literary marketplace. Easley's focus on the importance of networks sets the tone for an important approach to studying women writers in the following chapters. Chapter 2, 'Becoming a Professional Writer' (pp. 29–42), by Joanne Shattock, continues the focus on successful strategies these women adopted by focusing on the careers of Eliza Meteyard, Elizabeth Gaskell, and Margaret Oliphant. Shattock also emphasizes the importance of networks to these three writers as well as their use of the periodical press. Chapter 3, 'Working with Publishers' (pp. 43–58), by Linda Peterson, examines one specific facet of the literary career, the relationship that Victorian writers formed with publishers. Peterson surveys a number of women writers and their approach to this relationship. Chapter 4, 'Assuming the Role of Editor' (pp. 59–72), by Beth Palmer, looks at women as editors themselves. As Palmer argues, 'thinking about female editorship requires a relatively fluid understanding of professionalism in which the commercial and the social are interwoven' (p. 60). Chapter 5, 'Achieving Fame and Canonicity' (pp. 73–88), by Alison Chapman, concludes Part I with a compelling consideration of the issue of canon-formation generally alongside Victorian canon-formation more specifically. Women critics, reviewers, and biographers were central to shaping a female literary tradition and establishing canonicity for female writers.

Part II continues this contextual approach to women's writing in the period and considers all of the major genres, indicated by the title of each chapter. The essays comprising this part include chapter 6, 'Poetry' (pp. 89–104), by Linda K. Hughes; chapter 7, 'Silver-Fork, Industrial, and Gothic Fiction' (pp. 105–18), by Ella Dzelzainis; chapter 8, 'The Realist Novel' (pp. 119–32), by Deirdre D'Albertis; chapter 9, 'Sensation and New Woman Fiction' (pp. 133–43), by Lyn Pykett; chapter 10, 'Drama and Theater' (pp. 144–58), by Katherine Newey; chapter 11, 'Life-Writing' (pp. 159–74), by Carol Hanbery Mackay; chapter 12, 'Travel Writing' (pp. 175–89), by Tamara S. Wagner; chapter 13, 'Colonial and Imperial Writing' (pp. 189–205), by Mary Ellis Gibson and Jason R. Rudy; chapter 14, 'History Writing' (pp. 206–20), by Deborah A. Logan; chapter 15, 'Periodical Writing' (pp. 221–35), by Margaret Beetham; chapter 16, 'Reviewing' (pp. 236–50), by Joanne Wilkes; and chapter 17, 'Children's Writing' (pp. 251–64), by Claudia Nelson. The breadth of genres covered reveals the important presence of the woman writer and her career in this period.

Two other books are notable for their scope and their wide-ranging view of the Victorian period. *Reading and the Victorians*, edited by Matthew Bradley and Juliet John, traces two intellectual currents that follow 'micro' and 'macro' methodologies. The first current, exemplified in Philip Davis's 1997 *Real Voices on Reading*, focuses on actual reading experiences (the 'micro' perspective of the individual). The other current is a macro-level 'history of reading' approach of the sort in Richard Altick's *The English Common Reader* [1957]. More recent work by Robert Darnton and Nicholas Dames exemplifies the 'macro' approach that examines the reading experience by tracing material evidence. Despite the differences between these two approaches, Bradley and John emphasize the similarities in the way both find value in 'reading the Victorians, and reading the Victorians reading' (p. 9).

This book includes three parts. Part I, 'The Public Aspects of Private Reading', begins with Simon Eliot's 'Reading by Artificial Light in the Victorian Age' (pp. 15–30). Eliot focuses on the costs (financial and health) of reading by candlelight and how this influences the Victorian's experience of reading. In chapter 2, 'New Innovations in Audience Control: The *Select Library* and Sensation' (pp. 31–46), Stephen Colclough takes on Mudie's Select Library. Colclough draws attention to a neglected component of the library, *Mudie's Library Circular*, which he uses to question our understanding of Mudie's relationship to reading audiences and material through the library's attitude to stocking sensation fiction. Finally, with chapter 3,

'Reading Langham Place Periodicals at Number 19' (pp. 47–64), Beth Palmer explores the relationship between the editors of the feminist periodicals produced by the Langham Place group and their readership. Part II, 'The Reading Relationship', reconsiders the very notion of 'reading' itself. Philip Davis, in chapter 4, 'Deep Readings in the Manuscripts: Dickens and the Manuscript of *David Copperfield*' (pp. 65–78), examines Dickens's role as reader of his own work as he edits *David Copperfield*. In chapter 5, 'Telling All: Reading Women's Diaries in the 1890s' (pp. 79–88), Catherine Delafield examines texts that were written under the assumption that they would not be read, women's diaries in the 1890s, and the influence the textual practice of publishing diaries had on biography and autobiography. Sheila Cordner's chapter 6, 'Reading Across the Lines and Off the Page: Dickens's Model of Multiple Literacies in *Our Mutual Friend*' (pp. 89–98), compares 'observational' or non-textual literacy alongside more traditional conceptions of reading as both modes are represented in Dickens's novel.

Part III, 'Reading the Victorians Today', explores contemporary methodologies that take part in recent technological innovations used to study the reading Victorians. Two essays focus on marginalia. In chapter 7, 'Victorian Readers and Their Library Records Today' (pp. 99–110), K.E. Attard discusses how libraries catalogue reader annotations or marks in books and how electronic transcriptions of catalogues open this process to researchers. Rosalind Crone's chapter 8, 'Query: Victorian Reading' (pp. 111–26), looks to digitization efforts in the Reading Experience Database to see how quantitative data can be used with social network analysis to draw conclusions about how Victorians read. Matthew Bradley's chapter 9, 'Gladstone's Unfinished Synchrony: Reading Afterlives and the Gladstone Database' (pp. 127–42), illustrates the insights gained through digitization by tracing William Ewart Gladstone's marginal comments on the concept of the afterlife and the conclusions we can come to about his reading habits. In chapter 10, 'The Sharing of Stories, in Company with Mr Charles Dickens' (pp. 143–58), Clare Ellis looks at a Merseyside social outreach project called Get Into Reading, and the experience of reading *Great Expectations* as a group.

Norman Vance and Jennifer Wallace's *The Oxford History of Classical Reception in English Literature*, volume 4: *1790–1880*, is the fourth of a five-volume series that examines how English writers have responded to and refashioned literary texts of the classical world. The series covers from the Middle Ages to the present day, and volume 4 focuses on the years 1790–1880. The introduction offers a general sense of how the classics were viewed and used during this period. One of the most important components to the interdisciplinary nature of classical reception in this period was the variety of sources from which people could gain their knowledge of ancient Greece and Rome, which included art, music, and theatre, in addition to the classical texts themselves.

The volume is divided into two parts, Part I, 'Contexts and Genres', is discussed here. Chapter 1, 'Classical Authors 1790–1880' (pp. 29–56), by Norman Vance, discusses the classical authors who figure most prominently in this period, including Homer, Sappho, Theocritus, Anacreon, Plato, Aristotle, Sophocles, Euripides, and Horace. Chapter 2, 'Classical Translation' (pp. 57–78), by John Talbot, discusses the shifts in translation practices over the time period. Chapter 3, 'Education and Reading' (pp. 79–102), by Christopher Stray, discusses the reform and practices of education and learning that informed nineteenth-century literary practices. Chapter 4, 'Political Writing and Class' (pp. 103–30), by Edmund Richardson, looks at the class implications in the use of the classics. Chapter 5, 'Barbarism and Civilization: Political Writing, History, and Empire' (pp. 131–58), by Phiroze Vasunia, explores how notions of 'civilization' were being worked out in Britain with reference to classical writers. Chapter 6, 'American Literature and Classical Consciousness' (pp. 159–84), by Paul Giles, turns to the reception of the classics in America. Chapter 7, 'Myth and Religion' (pp. 185–202), by Norman Vance, discusses the fraught relationship between Christian culture and the classics. Chapter 8, 'Art, Aesthetics, and Archaeological Poetics' (pp. 203–42), by Jonah Siegel, examines the changing relationship between literature and the arts, especially the nature of archaeology and museum culture. Chapter 9, '"Greek under the trees": Classical Reception and Gender' (pp. 243–78), by Jennifer Wallace, explores the curriculum debates surrounding what woman should study in higher education. Chapter 10, 'The Novel' (pp. 279–98), by Norman Vance, discusses how the novel interacted with classical literature. Chapter 11, 'Shakespearean Sophocles: (Re)-discovering and Performing Greek Tragedy in the Nineteenth Century' (pp. 299–324), by Fiona Macintosh, traces the connections between ancient drama and nineteenth-century drama.

Part II comprises essays on single authors. Its contents are: chapter 12, 'William Wordsworth', by James Castell; chapter 13, 'Coleridge', by J.C.C. Mays; chapter 14, 'Walter Savage Landor and the Classics', by Adam Roberts; chapter 15, 'The Unexpected Latinist: Byron and the Roman Muse', by Timothy Webb; chapter 16, 'The Younger Romantics: Shelley and Keats', by Jennifer Wallace; chapter 17, 'Elizabeth Barrett Browning', by Isobel Hurst; chapter 18, 'Matthew Arnold', by Nicholas Shrimpton; chapter 19, 'Arthur Hugh Clough', by Isobel Hurst; chapter 20, 'Robert Browning', by Yopie Prins; chapter 21, 'Tennyson', by A.A. Markley; chapter 22, 'William Morris', by Stephen Harrison; chapter 23, 'George Eliot', by Shanyn Fiske; chapter 24, 'Thomas Hardy', by Ralph Pite; chapter 25, 'Swinburne', by Charlotte Ribeyrol; and chapter 26, 'Towards the *Fin de Siècle*: Walter Pater and John Addington Symonds', by Stefano Evangelista. These are reviewed in the appropriate sections.

These valuable books are representative of the quality of scholarship found in our field. Yet several publications this year suggest needs still to be met by Victorian scholarship. Caroline Levine's important monograph, *Forms: Whole, Rhythm, Hierarchy, Network*, falls into this classification. In this book, Levine seeks to close the gap between formalist and historical analysis. She expands the usual definition of form to include sociopolitical patterns and experiences. Levine works from an understanding of the heterogeneity of the term 'form' that cuts across many disciplines, but does operate with one common definition: form 'always indicates an arrangement of elements—an ordering, patterning, or shaping' (p. 3). To capture both the specificity and generality of forms, Levine borrows the concept of 'affordance' from design theory, as describing the uses or actions found in certain materials or designs. In her introduction, 'The Affordances of Form', Levine assures us that this capacious definition of form does not mean that everything counts as a form thereby rendering the term meaningless. For example, fissures and interstices, vagueness and indeterminacy, boundary-crossing and dissolution are areas and experiences that are essentially *formless*. The introduction posits different ways this theory of form might change the way critical schools approach literary analysis. For example, how new formalism and genre theory could be enriched by attending to the portability and endurance of forms over time. Four particular forms are the focus of each chapter in the book: whole, rhythm, hierarchy, and network.

Chapter 1, 'Whole', finds Levine arguing that scholars have focused on only one kind of affordance in relation to wholes, that 'totalities exclude and imprison' (p. 27). She looks at medieval church spaces, narrative closure, and the separate spheres ideology in Victorian culture. In chapter 2, 'Rhythm', she notes that the rhythm of social experience is multiple and heterogeneous, and these different temporal organizing principles often clash. Levine demonstrates why rhythm is a key form in both aesthetic and social realms. She examines 'institutional time', or the way institutions are themselves 'composed of overlapping repetitions and durations' that organize historicist scholarship (p. 52). Chapter 3, 'Hierarchy', argues that not all hierarchies work in the same direction, and when they collide 'they are capable of generating more disorder than order' (p. 85). Instead of always working to dismantle hierarchies, we can challenge their power by looking instead to where they intersect. She first looks at Sophocles' play *Antigone*, then more generally at how the gender binary functions as hierarchy, and finally she turns to the bureaucratic hierarchy. Her analysis in this chapter has implications for Victorian literary scholars in the ways that we conceive of power relations in this period. In chapter 4, 'Networks', Levine looks at the value gained from attention to the multiplicity of networks. This chapter also begins to bring together all four of the forms, so that in the first part of the chapter Levine looks at encounters between unified wholes and networked connections to see how they might work together. She then turns to how multiple networks work together by examining Trish Loughran's study of American print culture, *The Republic of Print*, and Charles Dickens's *Bleak House*. In her final chapter, '*The Wire*', Levine looks at David Simon's television series *The Wire* [2002–8]. The forms Levine has discussed, wholes, rhythms, hierarchies, and networks, here come together to create 'the system' that is portrayed in the show.

Two articles also address research methodologies. Elaine Freedgood's article 'We Are Not Yet Queer (in Victorian Studies): Response' (*VS* 57[2015] 445–8), introduces three graduate articles—Derek Bedenbaugh's 'Novel Violations: *The Hermaphrodite* and the Failure of Form'; Thomas J. Joudrey's 'Penetrating Boundaries: An Ethics of Anti-Perfectionism in Victorian Pornography'; and Natalie Prizel's 'The Non-Taxonomical Mayhew'. Freedgood argues that the unfinished nineteenth-century novel genre informs the ways we as readers approach gender performativity, alerting us to a fundamental inability to identify our reflexive sexual nomenclature as well as providing an exit strategy from this recurring feedback loop. She writes that 'we find our bodies and ourselves' through 'the unfinished novel maimed by a body that it cannot narrate' (p. 447), and concludes with an invitation to a fuller analysis to achieve an adequate queerness in nineteenth-century literary scholarship. Peter K. Andersson's article, 'How Civilized Were the Victorians?' (*JVC* 20[2015] 439–52), calls for what Andersson argues is a long-overdue reassessment of the ideas of civility and repression in the Victorian period. Reliance on published texts as source materials and a preference for looking at larger social and political structures contributed to stereotyped ideas about the period. Indeed, as Andersson contends, there needs to be more rigorous questioning of these received notions: 'The effortlessness with which scholars allow the literary version of Victorian culture to define our image of the period leads to a situation in which received notions such as the civilizing thesis are insufficiently questioned' (p. 442). Andersson provides a myriad of examples where misconstructions take place, such as surrounding the police force or prostitution, and examples where the 'backstage' of the Victorian period has been more accurately portrayed, such as through studies of photography. Perhaps less a critique than a love story that reminds Victorian scholars of the allure of archival research, *Love Among the Archives* by Helena Michie and Robyn Warhol concerns the process of discovery within the archives of an obscure Victorian personage: Sir George Scharf, the founding director of the National Portrait Gallery. Michie and Warhol call this book a 'love story', one that traces many forms of desire, both their own and Scharf's. The love in question is a love of other people, of work or vocation, of food, and of discovery. Although it is clear that Michie and Warhol pursued this work because they loved George Scharf the man, Scharf was also 'a way into and out of the larger stories that literary critics and historians tend to tell about Victorian life, especially those having to do with sexuality, class and profession' (p. xi). In captivating prose, Michie and Warhol tell the story of Scharf's life, intertwined with their own story of discovery, their 'archival fantasies' (p. 6). The book is divided between the story of Scharf's life and the story of Michie and Warhol's reconstruction of Scharf's life. They organize the chapters according to master-plots from nineteenth-century fiction.

The introduction, 'Adventures in Archives', explains the book's methodology and serves as an overview of the archival material and of Scharf's life. Chapter 2, 'Reading for Romance: The Marriage Plot', traces the process of sifting through material in search of mentions of love, and of the authors' findings concerning Jack Pattisson, who was an object of desire in Scharf's life. Chapter 3, 'Reading for Differentiation: The Family Romance', compares Scharf's life with the Bildungsroman. This chapter fills in details about Scharf's relationship with his parents and the family business. Chapter 4, 'Reading for Success: The Professional Plot', follows Scharf's working life in two country houses. Overall, Michie and Warhol's book introduces a Victorian figure lost amid the archives. Moreover, it presents new ways of thinking about archives and our relationship to them.

Moving to studies of teaching methodology in the field, readers will find Linda Hughes and Sarah Robbins's *Teaching Transatlanticism: Resources for Teaching Nineteenth-Century Anglo-American Print Culture* especially useful.

Hughes and Robbins begin their book with an introductory chapter, 'Tracing Currents and Joining Conversations', tracking the impulses that have kept British and American literature in separate curriculums. This volume comes out of the desire to address the need for further thinking about how to teach from a transatlantic perspective. Part I, 'Curricular Histories and Key Trends', functions as an introduction to transatlanticism. Chapter 2, 'On Not Knowing Any Better' (pp. 21–30), by Susan M. Griffin, traces her journey from graduate student to scholar and teacher of transatlanticism. Chapter 3, 'Transatlantic Networks in the Nineteenth Century' (pp. 31–9), by Susan David Bernstein, discusses the importance of genre, intertextuality, spatiality, and temporality in thinking about the pedagogical organization of transatlantic teaching. In chapter 4, 'Rewriting the Atlantic: Symbiosis, 1997–2014' (pp. 40–54), Christopher Gair, the founding editor of the seminal journal *Symbiosis: A Journal of Anglo-American Literary Relations*, discusses the aims of the journal, the conditions that led to its inception, and the historical narratives it attempts to rewrite.

Part II, 'Organizing Curriculum through Transatlantic Lenses', focuses on designs for entire courses structured around transatlanticism. Chapter 5, 'Anthologizing and Teaching Transatlantic Literature' (pp. 55–69), by Chris Koenig-Woodyard, discusses the difficulty of teaching a transatlantic course within the limitations of nationally based literature anthologies. His efforts to do so eventually led to the creation of *Transatlantic Romanticism* [2006]. Chapter 6, '"Flat Burglary"? A Course on Race, Appropriation, and Transatlantic Print Culture' (pp. 70–81), by Daniel Hack, discusses his transformation of a graduate course on print culture to the undergraduate classroom. Chapter 7, 'Dramatising the Black Atlantic: Live Action Projects in Classrooms' (pp. 82–94), by Alan Rice, shares a pedagogy that combines historiography with classroom performance.

Part III, 'Teaching Transatlantic Figures', shifts its focus from semester-long courses to single units that might be nestled within another course structure. Chapter 8, 'The Canadian Transatlantic: Susanna Moodie and Pauline Johnson' (pp. 95–106), by Kate Flint, offers suggestions for a unit on *Roughing It in the Bush* that includes comparative discussions of Canada, the United States, and Scotland. Chapter 9, 'Frederick Douglass, Maria Weston Chapman, and Harriet Martineau: Atlantic Abolitionist Networks and Transatlanticism's Binaries' (pp. 107–23), by Marjorie Stone, focuses on how teaching these three figures together emphasizes the commitment to blurring boundaries which is at the heart of transatlantic studies. Chapter 10, '"How did you get here? And where are you going?": Transatlantic Literary History, Exile and Textual Traces in Herman Melville's *Israel Potter*' (pp. 124–36), by Andrew Taylor, shows how to incorporate a single text into a course and yet reread it through a transatlantic lens. Chapter 11, 'Americans, Abroad: Reading *Portrait of A Lady* in a Transatlantic Context' (pp. 137–50), by Sandra Zagarell, similarly offers a rereading of one text within a transatlantic context.

Part IV, 'Teaching Genres in Transatlantic Context', focuses on specific genres. Chapter 12, 'Making Anglo-American Oratory Resonate' (pp. 151–63), by Tom F. Wright, discusses the genre of oratory. In chapter

13, 'Genre and Nationality in Nineteenth-Century British and American Poetry' (pp. 164–80), Meredith McGill and six students, Scott Challener, Isaac Cowell, Bakary Diaby, Lauren Kimball, Michael Monescalchi, and Melissa Parrish, discuss the experience of studying poetry in terms of circulation rather than authorial or national origins. Chapter 14, 'Teaching Transatlantic Sensations' (pp. 181–94), by John Cyril Barton, Kirstin Huston, Jennifer Phegley, and Jarrod Roark, discusses the experience of students and professors in a graduate seminar that studied American and British sensation fiction as part of a larger print culture. Chapter 15, 'Prophecy, Poetry and Democracy: Teaching through the International Lens of the *Fortnightly Review*' (pp. 195–210), by Linda Freedman, focuses on the *Fortnightly Review* as the basis for a transatlantic study.

Part V, 'Envisioning Digital Transatlanticism', examines the possibilities opened by digital humanities. Chapter 16, 'Transatlantic Mediations: Teaching Victorian Poetry in the New Print Media' (pp. 211–24), by Alison Chapman, shares how a course designed around Victorian poetry in digitized periodicals turned into a transatlantic seminar. Chapter 17, 'Digital Transatlanticism: An Experience of and Reflections on Undergraduate Research in the Humanities' (pp. 225–34), by Erik Simpson, discusses the digital project Simpson organized around work that students pulled together from one particular decade. Chapter 18, 'Twenty-First-Century Digital Publics and Nineteenth-Century Transatlantic Public Spheres' (pp. 235–44), by Tyler Branson, discusses the intersection between online projects and scholarship on the public sphere. In an Afterword, four students from Hughes and Robbins's 2010 class, Larisa Asaeli, Rachel Johnston, Molly Leverenz, and Marie Martinez, discuss how their experience with transatlantic pedagogy shaped their teaching and research.

One article also suggests teaching strategies. Joanne Nystrom Janssen's 'Teaching Students to Imagine Nineteenth-Century British Readers' (*CEA* 77[2015] 306–12) discusses two strategies she uses in her classroom to help her students replicate a nineteenth-century reading experience: reading aloud and creating a commonplace book. Janssen first discusses her overall course structure, arranged around the topics of reading, writing, and publishing. Janssen provides a wealth of details, from the length of time assignments and presentations take to the settings that are most conducive for encouraging student participation. This is a useful article for thinking through and implementing effective teaching strategies for a nineteenth-century literature course.

Victorian studies focused on imperialism or colonialism showcased the kind of new and nuanced work produced this year by Victorian scholars. Lauren Goodlad's *The Victorian Geopolitical Aesthetic: Realism, Sovereignty, and Transnational Experience* is mainly about the realist novel, but its overall argument and introductory chapter present a new understanding of liberalism and imperialism. She argues against critics, such as Amanda Anderson, who have described the Victorians as geopolitically naive. Rather, Goodlad recognizes the Victorian period as an important precursor to our own globalizing moment. The Victorian transnational experience included 'multifarious world perspectives, democratic projects, heterogeneous publics, and transnational encounters' (p. 22). Perhaps one of her most provocative claims, then, is that cosmopolitanism was at work already in the Victorian period and that we can study it not only as an ethos or process but as a form (p. 27). She argues that realist fiction was responsive and adaptive in the face of globalization, that it was more than a national literature: it was shaped by a 'transnational experience'. She attempts to rescue realism from the critics who saw it as either complicit with or ignoring the implications of imperialism.

Although Goodlad's textual discussions all centre on the novel, and Goodlad's readings of the novels are themselves impressive, the book engages with literary criticism, political theory, and historical context. She is also interested in the conflict between liberal ideals and an imperial ethic. The book engages with numerous critical conversations including Marxist analysis, surface reading, postcolonialism, and cosmopolitanism, to name a few. Goodlad's first chapter, 'Toward a Victorian Geopolitical Aesthetic', introduces the book by surveying recent approaches to cosmopolitanism and Atlantic studies. Her hopes for what the book might do for Victorian studies include the following: the joining of ethics and geopolitics; historical materialism that accounts for synchronic and diachronic history; attention to the normative tendencies in poststructuralism and the Enlightenment; and renewed attention to literary form (p. 21). Chapter 2, 'Imperial Sovereignty: The Limits of Liberalism and the Case of Mysore', examines the struggle to find language that would adequately describe the transnational experience of imperialism. Each of the chapters focuses on a specific realist novel.

Chapters 3 to 8 are entitled 'Trollopian "Foreign Policy": Rootedness and Cosmopolitanism in the Mid-Victorian Global Imaginary', '"India is a bore": Imperial Governmentality in *The Eustace Diamonds*', '"Dark, like me": Archeology and *Erfahrung* in *Armadale* and *The Moonstone*', 'The Adulterous Geopolitical Aesthetic: *Romola* contra *Madame Bovary*', 'Where Liberals Fear to Tread: E.M. Forster's Queer Internationalism', and 'The *Mad Men* in the Attic: Seriality and Identity in the Narrative of Capitalist Globalization'. Her coda, entitled 'The Way We Historicize Now', concludes the book with connections to recent debates about 'surface reading', 'distant reading', and the hermeneutics of suspicion.

*The Racial Hand in the Victorian Imagination* by Aviva Briefel—an interesting companion to Peter Capuano's *Changing Hands*, reviewed in Section 2 below—argues 'that racialized hands were vital to literary portrayals of colonial relationships in the latter part of the nineteenth century' (p. 2). In her introduction, Briefel traces the importance of hands to the Victorian period, from everything including proof of human exceptionalism to palmistry and other hand-reading techniques. The detached hand became a trusted signifier of identity, a fact that Briefel traces through several disciplines, including authorial identity, otherworldly identities in séances, and criminal detection. But the one area to which this widespread use and confidence in the hand as an identifier marker did not apply, as Briefel argues, was race. Despite attempts by various different disciplines, doubts persisted about the ability of the hand to serve as a racial signifier.

Chapter 1, 'The Case of the Blank Hand', discusses the fingerprinting discipline and its efforts to determine how fingers might be used to signify race.

Briefel illuminates the primary tension produced by looking to the hand for personal identity as well as racial identity, which defied the imperial logic that argued that these two things were mutually exclusive. She uses stories by Doyle and Kipling for support and context. Chapter 2, 'Potters and Prosthetics', turns to the Victorian concern over industrialization and the loss of British workers' hands, a loss that is lamented metaphorically through the Indian artisans' hands. Briefel turns to Flora Annie Steel's novel *The Potter's Thumb* [1894] as an example. Chapter 3, 'The Mummy's Hand', examines how hands become a Gothic duality—part person, part thing—that 'disrupts the evolutionary narratives emphasizing the progress and sophistication of British manual products' (p. 24). These hands also represent the damage a modern nation inflicts on the past, and narratives by Bram Stoker and H. Rider Haggard attempt to revive the past.

The last two chapters turn more explicitly to violence directed at racially marked hands. Chapter 4, 'A Hand for a Hand', centres on the amputation of Eastern women's hands for sexually deviant acts and the way such images were used to justify imperial intervention. Briefel examines a range of narratives by Kipling, Victoria Cross, Doyle, and the journalist William Le Queux that foreground the responses of horror and desire to these mutilations. Chapter 5, 'Crimes of the Hand', looks at responses to the amputation of Congolese subjects under Belgian King Leopold II. The narratives Briefel examines here include stories by Arthur Machen, Doyle, and R. Austin Freeman. In the coda, Briefel clarifies that 'amputation is a definitional process, one with a number of possible outcomes, rather than a finite act. It is a means of transforming hands, sites of corporeal agency, into human tools working in the service of a larger imperial body' (p. 154). The hands in Briefel's book thus offer a way to understand imperial sites of encoding on the other's body as well as sites of resistance performed by the racialized other.

Zoë Laidlaw and Alan Lester's edited collection, *Indigenous Communities and Settler Colonialism: Land Holding, Loss and Survival in an Interconnected World*, centres on the inception of settler colonialism from the perspective of displaced or dispossessed communities who nevertheless remained to 'cultivate space in specific localities around globe' (p. 3). The focus is thus on the literal ground occupied by indigenous people. The volume and its essays aim to encompass both the 'global scale of Indigenous dispossession and resilience' as well as the 'local particularities of these processes in individual Indigenous communities' (p. 5). Laidlaw and Lester argue that these indigenous sites are central to understanding several components of settler colonialism, including racial categorization and its relationship to land-holding, hybrid identity's challenge to settler sovereignty, and the methodological need to transcend distinctions between 'imperial, political, local, Indigenous, family and biographical histories' (p. 7).

The chapters are as follows: chapter 1, 'Indigenous Sites and Mobilities: Connected Struggles in the Long Nineteenth Century' (pp. 1–23), by Alan Lester and Zoë Laidlaw; chapter 2, 'Re-imagining Settler Sovereignty: The Call to Law at the Coranderrk Aboriginal Reserve, Victoria 1881 (and Beyond)' (pp. 24–44), by Julie Evans and Giordano Nanni; chapter 3, 'Indigenous Land Loss, Justice and Race: Anne Bon and the Contradictions of

Settler Humanitarianism' (pp. 45–61), by Joanna Cruickshank and Patricia
Grimshaw; chapter 4, '"On my ground": Indigenous Farmers at New Norcia,
1860s–1900' (pp. 62–85), by Tiffany Shellam; chapter 5, 'The Possession
and Dispossession of the Kat River Settlement' (pp. 86–101), by Robert
Ross; chapter 6, 'Discourses of Land Use, Land Access, and Land Rights
at Farmerfield and Loeriesfontein in Nineteenth Century South Africa'
(pp. 102–37), by Fiona Vernal; chapter 7, 'Living on the River's Edge at the
Taieri Native Reserve' (pp. 138–57), by Angela Wanhalla; chapter 8,
'Designing Dispossession: The Select Committee on the Hudson's Bay
Company, Fur-Trade Governance, Indigenous Peoples, and Settler
Possibility' (pp. 158–72), by Adele Perry; chapter 9, '"They would not give
up one inch of it": The Rise and Demise of St. Peter's Reserve, Manitoba'
(pp. 173–93), by Sarah Carter; chapter 10, 'Site of Dispossession, Site of
Persistence: The Haudenosaunee (Six Nations) at the Grand River Territory in
the Nineteenth and Twentieth Centuries' (pp. 194–213), by Cecilia Morgan;
chapter 11, 'Potawatomi Allotment in Kansas' (pp. 214–32), by Kelli
Mosteller; and chapter 12, 'Law, Identity and Dispossession: The Half-Caste
Act of 1886 and Contemporary Legal Definitions of Indigeneity in Australia'
(pp. 233–44), by Mark McMillan and Cosima McRae.

Three other articles on imperialism and empire include Robert Stilling's
'Warramou's Curse: Epic, Decadence, and the Colonial West Indies' (*VLC*
43[2015] 445–63). This essay explores the way writers from the colonies
challenged Britain's 'triumphal progressivism' through, surprisingly, the epic
form that often utilizes a historical progressivist narrative. Stilling examines
Horatio Nelson Huggin's epic *Hiroona*, composed in the last two decades of
the nineteenth century but set in the Anglo-Carib wars of the 1790s. John
Wallen's 'Burton's Personas: Imperialist Dissimulation or Parody/Hybridity?'
(*The Victorian* 3:i[2015] 1–24), is a meditation on Richard Burton's many
disguises, particularly as a Muslim. Wallen argues that these disguises served
Burton's personal desires rather than a larger agenda: 'The kind of subtle
identification with Easterners and, specifically, Muslims that Burton possessed
seems to suggest a nature that viewed a deeper understanding of himself and
the world around him as the primary goal of life' (p. 10). Dorice Williams
Elliott's essay, 'Transported to Botany Bay: Imagining Australia in
Nineteenth-Century Convict Broadsides' (*VLC* 43[2015] 235–59), discusses
the significance of broadsides in nineteenth-century England, focusing chiefly
on broadsides depicting criminal deportation to colonized Australia. Elliott
examines the role that broadsides played in popular culture, emphasizing how
even 'illiterate' individuals read them. She also considers visual properties
common to the genre. The balladic power invested in these convict broadsides
reinforced, more than anything, an attitude towards criminality, reform, and
ethics; very little attention was given to Australia itself. Elliott uses this elision
as a springboard for a look at how the distant continent was conflated with
other colonies.

India and China saw the most publications this year in studies of empire.
*The Australasian Journal of Victorian Studies* featured a special issue on China.
This special issue was formed from a panel at the annual meeting of the
Australasian Victorian Studies Association at the University of Hong Kong in

July 2014. Julia Kuehn's essay, 'The Victorians and China: Travels with Ships, Ideologies and Literature' (*AVSJ* 20:i[2015] 1–4), introduces the special issue by meditating on the difficulty of finding accurate representations of China in Victorian writings, due in part to the China's large size and its long history, but also due to the economic and imperial self-interest that guided many Victorian interactions with the country. Kuehn mentions the recent studies, few in number, that aim to more fully explore the relationship between China and Britain. This issue joins those studies. Stephan Davies's essay, 'Terminal Dilemma: Hong Kong's Waterfront, 1841–1891' (*AuVSJ* 20:i[2015] 5–23), tries to compare the transportation systems of the sea to railway transportation as one explanation for the differences between China and Britain's colonies. Davies focuses on the harbour and the lack of port planning and development. Ailise Bulfin focuses on trade practices, specifically coolie trade, in 'Guy Boothby and the "Yellow Peril": Representations of Chinese Immigrants in British Imperial Spaces in the Late Nineteenth Century' (*AVSJ* 20:i[2015] 24–40). Bulfin examines the travel writing, novels, and short fiction of Australian-born Guy Boothby. In 'Kipling in China: Empire of Noise' (*AVSJ* 20:i[2015] 41–9), Douglas Kerr emphasizes the vastness of China and its disorienting experience through his discussion of Rudyard Kipling's 1889 travel to China. In 'From Fire-Wheel Boats to Cities on the Sea: Changing Perceptions of the Steamships in the Late Qing, 1830s–1900s' (*AVSJ* 20:i[2015] 50–63), Jenny Huangfu Day also looks at the importance of the sea to the relationship between China and Britain. Steamships were important sites of contact between the British and the Chinese.

Three other essays also explored Victorian–Chinese relations. 'Civilized Depravity: Evangelical Representations of Early Nineteenth-Century China and the Redefinition of "True Civilization"' (*VLC* 43[2015] 409–29), by Benjamin Fischer, examines British evangelism abroad and how China, the most advanced of the Asiatic nations, presented a semantic problem: missionaries could not use their religion as a civilizing tool. He addresses existing scholarship and textual analysis on the interactions between Catholicism and the Chinese, shedding light on the gaps. Fischer discusses the light/dark paradigm that so coloured nineteenth-century evangelism, and he explains how missionaries had to modify their language so that the paradigm applied not to cultural progress but to the state of a nation's soul in relation to Christ.

Jennifer Hargrave, in 'Romantic Pretexts: Victorian Literary Appropriations in Anglo-Sino Discourse' (*NCC* 37:i[2015] 21–41), principally discusses the essays of Thomas De Quincey, which address the relations between the British empire and the Chinese. After a brief summary of the deteriorating affiliation shared by the two nations, Hargrave launches into a study of De Quincey's 1840 essay 'The Opium and China Question' and his 1857 *China* essays. She locates his agenda, which rests in a very specific moral superiority grounded upon Greek ideals, and she parses his use (and misuse) of Romantic poetry—both of which speak to his attempts to convey an increasingly nationalistic attitude towards war and revolution against China.

Three monographs this year focus on India. *Indian Arrivals, 1870–1915: Networks of British Empire* by Elleke Boehmer examines imperial encounters, but with a key distinction from other works in this rich area of study in Victorian literature. Boehmer looks at scenes of Indian arrivals in England. Her study is also unique in that she looks at how interpersonal negotiations between Indians and the British were conducted in writing and how such writing influenced British cultural and literary life. Boehmer is therefore interested in 'how textual forms mold and model intercultural contacts and relationships' (p. 11). The texts considered in the book are treated as both actual records of travel and encounters and as imaginative structures, with Boehmer arguing that 'the presence of Indian travelers and migrants needs to be seen as much more central to Britain's understanding of itself' (p. 5).

The chapters cover roughly the four decades from 1870 to 1915. Chapter 1, 'Passages to England: Suez, the Indian Pathway', traces Indian arrivals through the Suez Canal to London, focusing on the process of travelling to Britain as itself an important phase in the Indian–British encounter on British soil. Chapter 2, 'The Spasm of the Familiar: Indians in Late Nineteenth-Century London', looks specifically at Indian encounters in the metropolis, a site where strangers of all kinds encountered one another on busy streets. Chapter 3, 'Lotus Artists: Self-Orientalism and Decadence', examines Indian-English poets so as to further illuminate how Indians were constructed by them and how they helped to formulate notions of India and Indians. The final two chapters, 'Edwardian Extremes and Extremists, 1901–13' and 'Indian Salients', focus on the twentieth century and on the increasing radicalization of Indian politics.

Using the perspective of several different genres, including travel writing, correspondence, fiction, and poetry, Máire ni Fhlathúin examines the colonial literary culture in early nineteenth-century British India in *British India and Victorian Literary Culture*. All of the writers she discusses were British and living and working in British India. She examines a wide range of genres and extends the parameters of her study beyond those of most studies of British India in order to listen to a range of colonizing voices and to achieve a broader perspective on events such as the Indian Mutiny as part of the colonial history rather than a determining event. Fhlathúin divides the book into two sections, 'Experiences of India' and 'Representations of India'. As the title indicates, the first section concerns the actual experience of writing and publishing in India. Chapter 1, 'The Literary Marketplace of British India, 1780–1844', discusses the development of the publishing industry in India. Chapter 2, 'Exile', focuses on the émigré community's portrayal of home. Chapter 3, 'Consumed and Being Consumed', explores the metaphors used to portray the British role in India. These chapters consider prose and poetry in the periodical press, travel writing, and memoirs.

The second part of the book focuses on representations of India itself. Chapter 4, 'European Nationalism and British India', sets the stage for the literary analyses to follow. Fhlathúin examines the emerging nationalism in India at the beginning of the nineteenth century. Chapter 5, 'Romantic Heroes and Colonial Bandits', examines the representation of a predatory Indian masculinity. Chapter 6, 'Imagining India through *Annals and Antiquities of Rajas'han*', looks at female Indian agency in the story of the Rajput princess Kishen Kower. Chapter 7, 'Transformations of India after the Indian Mutiny', explores the influence of the mutiny on representations of British identity. The afterword discusses how the division in the book between 'lived experience and discursive representation' is never clear in practice (p. 185). To illustrate this complexity, Fhlathúin ends the book with a discussion of sati. Fhlathúin's final conclusion from an analysis of several different texts that feature the suttee is that representations of India are simultaneously representations of the colonial self.

*Nineteenth-Century Colonialism and the Great Indian Revolt* by Amit Kumar Gupta looks at the shift in British policy in India, which had allowed a feudalist system to prevail but in the nineteenth century began to realize better ways to protect its long-term interests by incorporating India into its own capitalist economy. The background for this shift lies in how the bourgeoisie that emerged from the industrial revolution successfully shifted Britain from a mercantilist to a capitalist society. Two changes were needed, 'supersession of the feudal mode of production with the capitalist order' and 'the supplantation of the medieval outlook with a rationalized world view' (p. 10). Gupta covers various approaches to reforming India in these two directions. For example, both utilitarians and Evangelicals sought to reform India, though for different reasons. Education was at the core of both programmes of reform, however, and Gupta covers in detail the different commissions, laws, and regulations that were passed in an attempt to modernize India.

The first chapter, entitled 'For Bourgeoization', lays the groundwork for what emerges in the later chapters: the problems that arose from Britain's efforts for 'elevating and bourgeoizing' India for their own interests rather than for India's interests. Chapter 2, 'Against Feudalism', details how the primary roadblock to Britain's efforts to modernize India was the feudal system so deeply entrenched in the countryside of India. The most successful route to upending feudalism proved to be the settlement and assessment of land. Chapter 3, 'For Rent Theory', examines how the success of British interests in India depended in large part on maintaining a balance between the success of those working the land and the amount of taxes levied to support the British government's efforts in India. The tension that emerged from this system, however, was the total dependence of the government on the 'men on the ground', those superintending and supervisory officials who were assessing the land.

Chapter 4, 'Against Peasantry', further explores this tension. In an effort to answer to the strict demands made on them, these supervisors often enacted taxes that created unliveable conditions for those working the land. Chapter 5, 'For Confrontation', traces the irony of how such conditions led to peasant revolts at a time when the peasants in India had perhaps their greatest number of sympathizers in Britain. Chapter 6, 'Against Qualitative Change', looks at the less obvious issues spurring the conflict as well as at the attempts to recover from it. The chapter ends with a nod to the beginning. As Gupta ironically points out, the adopted solution signalled the return to a kind of feudal society in the countryside. In his postscript, he describes how this decision has continued to negatively influence India. See also Deborah Denenholz Morse and Virginia Butler's essay, 'New Scholarship on Victorian India' (*VLC*

43[2015] 203–7) for a helpful review of recent works in the last decade on Victorian India.

Travel writing is implicated in Britain's imperialist ventures, and there was one interesting study this year in this field. *Britain and the Narration of Travel in the Nineteenth Century: Texts, Images, Objects*, edited by Kate Hill, traces how modernity and colonialism effect travel and how it was represented through different mediums. The essays utilize certain tropes and concepts in an effort to rethink how travel formulates the self and the other. They build on other works orbiting around travel narratives, but they also add to those conversations by providing a wide-ranging focus on different places and different types of narrative. For example, Mary Louise Pratt's concept of the 'contact zone' positions both the self and other as equally in question and deploys the literary concept of the chronotope to understand how time and space are interrelated elements that reconfigure travel and thus the world in the minds of individuals

Chapter 1, 'Arctic and European In-Betweens: The Production of Tourist Spaces in Late Nineteenth-Century Northern Norway' (pp. 13–26), by Ulrike Spring, looks at tourist reports from the urban centre of Tromsø. Chapter 2, '"The formation of a surface": European Travel in Charles Dickens's *Little Dorrit*' (pp. 37–52), by Charlotte Mathieson, focuses on Dickens's representations of permeable boundaries and the collapse of distance between Europe and England. Chapter 3, 'Female Space, Feminine Grace: Ladies and the Mid-Victorian Railway' (pp. 53–72), by Kara Tennant, examines the way railway travel affected understandings of identity as both time and space were reformulated. Chapter 4, 'Victorians in the Alps: A Case Study of Zermatt's Hotel Guest Books and Registers' (pp. 75–90), by Katarzyna Michalkiewicz and Patrick Vincent, discusses Victorian self-fashioning evident through hotel guest books and registers. Chapter 5, '"Nerves of the Empire": Submarine Telegraph Technological Travel Narratives as Imperial Adventure' (pp. 91–108), by Susan Shelangoskie, looks at two submarine telegraph accounts, W.H. Russell's *The Atlantic Telegraph* [1865] and J.C. Parkinson's *The Ocean Telegraph to India* [1870], analysing the discourses of 'managed economic competition' and 'dominant views of the empire'. Chapter 6, 'Thrills and Quills: Masculinity and Location in Three South African Travel Narratives (1834–1900)' (pp. 109–28), by Mathilda Slabbert, looks at travel narratives to South Africa by three white men, which demonstrate not only the typical othering move of travel narratives, but also the shifting ideas of manliness in the Victorian period. Chapter 7, 'Tourism in the Age of Mechanical Reproduction: Aesthetics and Advertisement in Travel Posters and Luggage Labels' (pp. 129–49), by Lori Brister, examines the material culture of travellers, specifically travel posters and luggage labels for what they say about touristic value systems.

Chapter 8, 'The Travelling Other: A Maori Narrative of a Visit to Australia in 1874' (pp. 153–74), by Conal McCarthy, examines an unpublished account of a Māori tribal leader's experience in Australia as an indigenous example of the way travel disrupted divisions between 'home' and 'away.' Chapter 9, 'Souvenirs: Narrating Overseas Violence in the Late Nineteenth-Century' (pp. 175–90), by Kate Hill, focuses on souvenirs and the way they intersected with emotional meanings of 'home' and 'away'. Chapter 10, 'British Travels in

China during the Opium Wars (1839–60): Shifting Images and Perceptions' (pp. 191–208), by Louise Tythacott, argues that the negative perception of China emerged directly from travellers' representations of China during the Opium wars. Chapter 11, ' "The untrammeled fancy of the scenic artist": Imagining and Encountering Zanzibar in the Late Nineteenth and Early Twentieth Centuries' (pp. 209–24), by Sarah Longair, examines the tension between orientalist ideas and British rule in the empire by looking specifically at constructions of Zanzibar.

Kristine Kelly's essay, 'Aesthetic Desire and Imperialist Disappointment in Trollope's *The Bertrams* and the Murray *Handbook for Travellers in Syria and Palestine*' (*VLC* 43[2015] 621–39), examines publisher John Murray's *Handbook for Travellers in Syria and Palestine* by J.L. Porter and Trollope's novel *The Bertrams* for the way they similarly pair spiritual pilgrimage and sightseeing. Kelly's analysis adds to our understanding of British attitudes towards travel and cultural contact by suggesting a specific imperialist aesthetic of dismissal. Both Trollope's travellers and Murray's handbook engage in a 'deliberate disengagement' that may at first seem benign but which reveals 'a strategy of devaluing sites and people which cannot be controlled so as to maintain the hierarchical authority of the viewing eye by the very act of looking away' (p. 622). This act of looking away allowed British travellers to devalue the Christian monuments located in foreign spaces and reappropriate them for representation in the English home. See also John Plunkett's essay, 'Peepshows for All: Performing Words and the Traveling Showman' (*ZAA* 63:i[2015] 7–30).

Finally, a special issue of note. 'The Nineteenth-Century Pacific Rim', in *Victorian Literature and Culture*, draws attention to a neglected region in colonial studies. In Tamara Wagner's introduction, 'The Nineteenth-Century Pacific Rim: Victorian Transoceanic Studies Beyond the Postcolonial Matrix', she explains how this special issue adds to our understanding of the Victorian empire by broadening its scope in two ways: going beyond Victorian canonical literature and covering the Pacific Rim, a region of the Victorian empire often overlooked. The issue adds to the growing interest in two-way exchanges in the colonies as well as places that were primarily of commercial interest rather than occupation or conquest. The introduction helpfully surveys the work done in three related areas: nineteenth-century global formations, settler colonialism, and the transpacific or transoceanic within transatlantic studies. Terra Walston Joseph's ' "Saving British Natives": Family Emigration and the Logic of Settler Colonialism in Charles Dickens and Caroline Chisholm' (*VLC* 43[2015] 261–80) discusses the conflict between Dickens and Chisholm, especially the satire of settlement projects in *Bleak House*, as one example of the debates about emigration and settlement throughout the period. Melissa Walker's 'Self-Made Maids: British Emigration to the Pacific Rim and Self-Help Narratives' (*VLC* 43[2015] 281–302) exposes the conflicting representations of the published and unpublished letters in the Female Middle-Class Emigration Society. Lilja Mareike Sautter's essay, 'Femininity and Community at Home and Away: Shipboard Diaries by Single Women Emigrants to New Zealand' (*VLC* 43[2015] 305–16), also considers gender ideology in discourses about empire through an examination of shipboard diaries that reveal the ambiguous space of the ship and what happened there. Hugh Roberts, in 'Chance, Providence, and Imperial Ennui in Alfred Domett's *Ranolf and Amohia: A South-Sea Day-Dream*' (*VLC* 43[2015] 317–41), draws attention to interpretative practices, first by examining an unfamiliar text and then by considering the role of context in performing an analysis of it. Philip Steer's essay, 'Romances of Uneven Development: Spatiality, Trade, and Form in Robert Louis Stevenson's Pacific Novels' (*VLC* 43[2015] 343–56), also draws attention to interpretative practices through his analysis of Stevenson's two novels that looks at how spatiality and economics work together, which departs from usual approaches to themes about space and form. Precious McKenzie Stearns, in 'Civilizing Hawaii: Isabella Bird Bishop in the Sandwich Islands' (*VLC* 43[2015] 357–70), reassesses Bird's travel memoir by focusing on her search for 'the real Hawaiian'. Joohun Jade Park's 'Missing Link Found, 1880: The Rhetoric of Colonial Progress in Isabella Bird's *Unbeaten Tracks in Japan*' (*VLC* 43[2015] 371–88) explores an important but overlooked aspect of one of Isabella Bird's major works, *Unbeaten Tracks in Japan*. Bird does not address the colonial relationship between the Japanese and the Ainu, an absence that scholars have not examined. Park argues that Bird's erasure of Ainu–Japanese relations results from her use of a hierarchical model that equates progress with cultivation. Stephen Keck's 'Involuntary Sightseeing: Soldiers as Travel Writers and the Construction of Colonial Burma' (*VLC* 43[2015] 389–407) argues that more attention needs to be paid to British Burma as an imperial colony and the three Anglo-Burmese wars. In order to recover some of this forgotten history, Keck examines four British war narratives that record details about the Anglo-Burmese Wars as well as the writers' assessments of Burma and the Burmese. One of the interesting and larger implications of this piece is the image of soldiers as travel writers. Keck argues that 'the soldier's stare' is 'an organizing concept to explore the traveler's perspective which can be found in military war narratives' (p. 392). Anna Peak, in 'The Chinese Language in the *Saturday Review*: A Case Study in Sinophobia's Scholarly Roots' (*VLC* 43[2015] 431–44), suggests that sinophobia has its roots in the first scholars of sinology in the late nineteenth century. She reads the scholarly discussion of China as it was transformed for a popular audience in the periodical *Saturday Review*. The contributions of Benjamin Fischer and Dorice Williams Elliott to this special issue are discussed above.

*19* had a special issue on the Crimean War, 'Charting the Crimean War: Contexts, Nationhood, Afterlives' (*19* 20[2015]). The issue comes from a 2013 conference organized by the National Army Museum and the University of Leicester. Its task was to 'look beyond the fragmentary British mythologies of the Crimean War', and this issue continues that effort, as the editors describe in the opening essay. Several essays reconsider historical assessments of the war, including medical reporting and misrepresentation of French supply lines by the British newspapers. Two articles look at the significance of relics from the war. Other articles turn to the relationships influenced by the media, including between the Crown and the army, the soldier and his family, and media representations of the war itself. The essay titles are as follows: 'Reporting the Crimean War: Misinformation and Misinterpretation' by Mike

Hinton (*19* 20[2015] 39 paras.), 'Russian Medical Service During the Crimean War: New Perspectives' by Yulia Naumova (*19* 20[2015] 26 paras.), 'The French Army and British Army Crimean War Reforms' by Anthony Dawson (*19* 20[2015] 43 paras.), ' "All touched my hand:" Queenly Sentiment and Royal Prerogative' by Rachel Bates (*19* 20[2015] 32 paras.), 'The Afterlife of Thomas Campbell and "The Soldier's Dream" in the Crimean War' by Tai-Chun Ho (*19* 20[2015] 27 paras.), 'Who Blew the Balaklava Bugle? The Charge of the Light Brigade and the Afterlife of the Crimean War' by Lara Kriegel (*19* 20[2015] 31 paras.), 'The Life and Afterlives of Captain Hedley Vicars: Evangelical Biography and the Crimean War' by Trev Broughton (*19* 20[2015] 29 paras.), 'Sebastopol: On the Fall of a City' by Trudi Tate (*19* 20[2015] 36 paras.), and 'Off the Chart: The Crimean War in British Public Consciousness' by A.L. Berridge (*19* 20[2015] 52 paras.). Also on nine-teenth-century wars, *Victorian Periodicals Review* 48:iv[2015] included a special series on Waterloo, introduced by Christopher Keirstead and Marysa Demoor: 'Waterloo and Its Afterlife in the Nineteenth-Century Periodical and Newspaper Press' (*VPR* 48[2015] 447–50). An event of mythic stature from the outset, Waterloo's significance only grew in the intervening decades, and this introduction makes the case that Waterloo, and so many paradigmatic conflicts that would follow, will continue to resurface in new and shifting forms. 'No such conflict...ever really achieves anything akin to ideological or historical "closure"...The battle, in some sense, continued to be refought in the press over the course of the nineteenth-century' (p. 451).

There were not as many publications this year related to science as in previous years, but the works that do focus on the connections between science and literature are provocative in the way they challenge our construction of how the Victorians understood science and its influence on other areas of culture. In *Science in Wonderland*, Melanie Keene begins with the educational debate about what children should be exposed to, both in terms of reading material and experiences. More specifically, Keene begins with the one of the most famous illustrations of this debate, Dickens's *Hard Times* and the figure of Gradgrind. Keene raises this example to show how Dickens's emphasis on facts was really only one side of the scientific educational programme of the period. Indeed, the stereotype that facts displaced fancy was one that many Victorian contemporaries themselves touted, and it has continued to erroneously colour our understanding of how science and education worked.

Keene's introduction includes a short history of the professionalization and specialization of the sciences. She makes a case for why the Victorian period was 'a fairy tale age' in general, and then how that translated to science. Each of the following chapters traces one branch of science and its relationship to the fairy world. Chapter 1, 'Once Upon a Time', looks at the geological sciences of palaeontology and mineralogy. Keene is interested in the relationship between changing conceptions of time and the 'once-upon-a-time' motif of fairy tales. In chapter 2, 'Real Fairy Folk', she argues that entomology, the study of butterflies, drew analogies between science and the fairy world both in its objects of study—butterflies and fairies shared many similar traits—and in its practices as a participatory science where anyone could have a 'fabulous story' or adventure (p. 56). Keene moves next to the wonderland of microscopy in chapter 3, 'Familiar Fairylands', where 'everyday substances could be revealed as homes to magical creatures, miraculous forces, and dangerous monsters' (p. 83). Next, Keene moves from the everyday world and its hidden states to the seemingly miraculous way the world has changed. Chapter 4, 'Wonderlands of Evolution', addresses how questions of faith and religion provoked by evolutionary theories were often the kind of questions broached in fairy tales. Chapter 5, 'Through Magic Glasses', looks at optical technologies that reveal the world in magical ways. Keene turns to the theatre in chapter 6, 'Modern Marvels', to explore 'the written and performed technological marvels of Victorian Britain, to reveal how they were compared, contrasted, and conflated with the tropes and characters of fairyland' (p. 155).

One of the most interesting claims Keene makes in arguing for the significance of blended fact and fancy is the way in which fairy tales offered a mode of thinking that could challenge the 'confident edifice of scientific truth' (p. 189). These diverse modes of understanding new phenomena, the scientific and the fantastical, in the Victorian period also point to the twentieth-century acceptance that truth is stranger than fiction. The book comes with an exquisite set of illustrations showcasing the fusion of science and fantasy Keene argues was so prominent in the period.

There was also an article on fairies and science by Laura Forsberg, 'Nature's Invisibilia: The Victorian Microscope and the Miniature Fairy' (*VS* 57[2015] 667–90). Beginning with a look at Fitz-James O'Brien's 'The Diamond Lens', Laure Forsberg launches into a study of the relationship between scientific advances actuated by the microscope, and the folk belief in fairies. 'During the nineteenth century', she writes, 'both the microscope and the fairy fostered a sense of wonder at the natural world by positing the existence of a miniature world of enchantment' (p. 639). She makes connections between fairies and bacteria, drawing on the work of Sabine Baring-Gould. She compares a child's maturation and concomitant adoption of nostalgia to the growth of the British empire in respect to empirical science, which allowed its citizenry to reflect upon their prior dalliances with fairy narratives. Victorian fairies 'were figures of nostalgia tied to the folk beliefs of England's past, but they were also figures of disenchantment, marking the end of true superstition and the repackaging of these past beliefs as childhood fantasy' (p. 650). Her essay considers popular fiction, literary works, and scientific textbooks.

*Transformation of Electricity in Nineteenth-Century Literature and Science* by Stella Pratt-Smith investigates the nineteenth-century fascination with electricity. Pratt-Smith argues that 'how electricity was written about shaped not just public perceptions of the phenomenon, but also the development of scientific understandings about it and its potential applications' (p. 1). Her introduction provides an overview of the different ways that novels in the period represented electricity, chiefly through metaphor. Chapter 2, 'Electrical Analogies, Science and Poetry', lays the groundwork for later chapters by explaining what information about electricity existed through key scientific developments in the period. Pratt-Smith is primarily interested in the relationship between mathematics and poetry as 'a means by which nineteenth-century scientists perceived and sought to understand electricity' (p. 45). Chapter 3, 'Electrical Practitioners', examines the process of popularization that resulted from new publication forums. This chapter traces the emergence of science as a popular field, a phenomenon traceable through the public's fascination with electricity, and in the engagement with electricity in periodicals such as *Punch* and *Once a Week*. Chapter 4, 'Electrical Shorts', looks at the literary response to electricity in the short fiction published in periodicals. Chapter 5, 'Electrical Utopias: *Another World*', turns to longer fictional accounts with a case study of Benjamin Lumley's novel. Pratt-Smith also gives careful attention to reviews as a way to analyse contemporary responses to literary constructions of science. By examining scientific ideas alongside fictions about electricity, Pratt-Smith argues that we gain a more accurate picture of how electricity was understood in the period. Beyond that, we also see new ways in which knowledge was formed.

Two articles focus on animals and natural history. Will Abberley's 'Animal Cunning: Deceptive Nature and Truthful Science in Charles Kingsley's Natural Theology' (*VS* 58[2015] 34–56) traces Kingsley's efforts to locate the moral in nature, despite emerging models of nature as 'ruthless'. Both nature and the Bible embodied moral truths for Kingsley, present in his version of liberal Anglicanism and a nationalist ideology of 'honesty of moderation' (p. 35). The essay's larger interest is in the relationship between Victorian science and religion, looking specifically at the strategies Kingsley used to hold them together through his 'rhetoric of unitary truth' (p. 35).

In 'Representing Animal Minds in Early Animal Autobiography: Charlotte Tucker's *The Rambles of a Rat* and Nineteenth-Century Natural History' (*VLC* 43[2015] 725–44), Julie Smith discusses the links between natural history and animal autobiographies, a genre that emerged in the late eighteenth century. Many writers of animal autobiographies used current scientific understandings of animals to represent animal minds as accurately as possible. Smith uses Charlotte Tucker's *The Rambles of a Rat* [1857] to illustrate this connection. Tucker explicitly identifies her source as a natural history essay on rats. Smith's essay adds to the critical conversation about natural history in the Victorian period by focusing on the involvement of an amateur public.

Several works address science and Darwin, of course. For these, see below. Two other essays focus on specific individuals also important to the field of science. An essay by Andrea Charise, 'G.H. Lewes and the Impossible Classification of Organic Life' (*VLC* 57[2015] 377–86), looks at the issue of ageing in G.H. Lewes's study *The Physiology of Common Life* [1859–60]. Charise is interested in this issue for the way it often confounds attempts to establish categories as it blends animal life with stone, petrifaction, and minerality. Furthermore, Charise contends that Lewes's presentation of ageing informed Victorian imaginings of human ageing. She looks to William Wordsworth and George Eliot as literary examples. For example, the bodily wasting in *Silas Marner* can be understood as a process of individual and social repair that was 'indispensable to lasting social cohesion' (p. 383).

In 'Statistical Criticism and the Eminent Man in Francis Galton's *Hereditary Genius*' (*VLC* 43[2015] 821–39), Sherrin Berezowsky discusses how Galton's attempts to demonstrate that eminence was inherited produced a new way of reading biography. In his work *Hereditary Genius* [1869], Galton builds from his programme of eugenics to explore some of Darwin's ideas about heredity. To prove his hypothesis that heredity can determine greatness Galton turns to 'great men' immortalized in biography. In doing so, Berezowsky argues, Dalton engages in a new way of reading biography that moves away from 'individualistic and didactic' qualities towards statistical analysis. Berezowsky's argument also illuminates the tension between Dalton's emphasis on statistical 'fact' and imagined vision for Britain's future, his inherently fictional and moral writing in *Hereditary Genius*.

In a year where there was a dearth of publications on ecocriticism, Jesse Oak Taylor's essay, 'Where Is Victorian Ecocriticism?' (*VLC* 43[2015] 877–94), seems especially pertinent. In this review essay, Taylor provocatively begins with the statement: 'The most striking thing about reviewing the field of Victorian ecocriticism is that there is so little of it' (p. 877). Victorian scholarship has some specific things to add to current ecocriticism, namely an attention to the city, empire, institutions, and a body of work that already merges literature and science. Taylor also spends some time discussing the Anthropocene. After surveying books that cover mainly ecology and Romanticism but include some chapters on Victorian ecocriticism, Taylor turns to the most important works by Victorian scholars on ecocriticism. These include: *William Wordsworth and the Ecology of Authorship: The Roots of Environmentalism in Nineteenth-Century Culture* [2012] by Scott Hess, *Natural Disasters and Victorian Empire: Famines, Fevers, and the Literary Cultures of South Asia* [2013] by Upamanyu Pablo Mukherjee, and *Victorian Literature, Energy, and the Ecological Imagination* [2014] by Allen MacDuffie.

As I move to discuss religion as an area of Victorian scholarship distinct from science, Peter Harrison's book *The Territories of Science and Religion* chastises me. Harrison's ambitious new book argues that we need to rethink how scholarly discussions have brought science and religion together (or, rather, kept them apart), because the historical relationship between these two suggests a different narrative. Using the metaphor of cartography, Harrison constructs an intellectual history of these two terms that debunks the 'conflict myth' as a current way of understanding the relationship between science and religion. Victorianists will be interested in this book for the prominent role the nineteenth century plays in shaping current understandings of religion. Beginning in chapter 4, 'Science and the Origins of "Religion"', Harrison traces what he calls a shift from the internal to the external. Although *scientia* and *religio* began as internal virtues, natural philosophy turned them into external ones.

This emphasis on the external in science can be seen through the rise of empiricism, and in religion there was renewed emphasis on texts and rituals. Chapter 5, 'Utility and Progress', traces the process by which science became the source of authority and knowledge over religion. These two chapters form an important backdrop to how Harrison approaches the nineteenth century, which he discusses in chapter 6, 'Professing Science'. Here, Harrison argues that the professionalization of scientists transformed a plurality of sciences into a singular entity. He traces this transformation in three steps: 'first, a new identity—the scientist—is forged for its practitioners; second, it is claimed that the sciences share a distinctive method, one that excludes reference to religious and moral considerations; and, third, following on from this, the character of this new science is consolidated by drawing sharp boundaries and positing the existence of contrast cases' (pp. 159–60). Harrison's book offers much for literary critics to ponder: how has the dominant historical narrative about science and religion influenced our approach to interpreting the representation of science and religion in Victorian literature?

There are two other giants this year in the area of religious studies. *The Dissenters*: volume 3: *The Crisis of Conscience of Nonconformity* by Michael Watts looks at dissent in the nineteenth century. Past *Dissenters* volumes have become standard works in the field. This third and final volume (Watts sadly passed away in 2011 just after completing it) will be of great interest to scholars of the Victorian period. The first section focuses on the influence of Romantic theology, the second on social dimensions of nonconformity, and the last on political dimensions of dissent. Watts's book reads like a series of tales strung together to suggest a timeline of events, issues, and influences that he traces through the years of the Victorian period. One of the greatest achievements of this text is its ability to be read as conversational and magisterial at once.

In Part I, ' "The very foundations of the Christian faith": The Crisis of Dissent', Watts begins by looking at the infallibility of the Bible. He traces how dissenters adapted their understanding of Genesis to geological findings. This scientific view also undermined the Romantic view of God. It was this threat to the authority of the scriptures, something laypeople and ministers knew intimately, that was perceived as the more imminent danger. After this, Watts looks at scepticism directed at the idea of miracles as well as dissenters' approaches to hell. Part II, ' "The hub and fount of social life": The Liberalization of Dissent', shows the effect on the church of the aforementioned crisis. Each chapter then takes a certain population, such as the poor or the suburban middle classes, and analyses the reasons why 'the social basis of their congregation was narrowing' (p. 101), plus the strategies different denominations used to attract converts.

Part III, ' "What is morally wrong can never be politically right": The Conscience of Dissent', begins with the influence of George Dawson, a liberal dissenter, and his efforts to make religion relevant in political and social life. Dawson's approach is representative of the general Evangelical movement from an emphasis on saving souls to improving the 'moral and material well-being of their fellow men' (p. 232). Education was again the focus of this movement, and the following chapters detail the complex debates, involving both church and state, over education—who should be educated, and how? Watts traces how the education debates fed into more overtly political debates and the nonconformist campaign to disestablish the Church of England. This campaign, as well as uprisings in Bulgaria and Ireland, was supported by the nonconformist belief that 'oppressed peoples had a right to overthrow tyrannical rulers in order to secure their liberty' (p. 255). In this final section, Watts delicately traces the different alliances and partnerships formed at different times between nonconformists and the Liberal Party, trade unionists, and figures like Gladstone. Watts concludes his book by looking at the growing philanthropic emphasis of nonconformists at home and abroad.

The other study that makes an important contribution this year is Joshua King's *Imagined Spiritual Communities in Britain's Age of Print*. The title alludes to Benedict Anderson's seminal work, *Imagined Communities* [1983], from which King extends Anderson's argument about national consciousness as a constructed image arising out of print media, but he departs from Anderson's contention that this was primarily a secular movement. King's book goes to great lengths, and is quite successful, in showing that it was often explicitly imagined religious communities that led to a national consciousness. King's book has many wider implications, not least of which are rethinking our categories of 'secular' and 'religious' and redefining our understanding of the relationship between religion, literature, and the nation in the nineteenth century. The book is divided into two parts. Part I, 'Apologists for Print-Mediated Spiritual Communities', looks at middle-class authors, clergy, and educators aligned with the Anglican tradition. Chapter 1, 'Coleridge's *Aids to Reflection*: The Clerisy and a National Spiritual Republic of Letters', discusses how Samuel Coleridge's *Aids to Reflection* [1825] projects an imagined classroom community that establishes the moral and spiritual truths Coleridge would deploy again in his call for a more literal classroom four years later, in *On the Constitution of the Church and State* [1829]. Chapter 2, 'F.D. Maurice's Universal Society: National Spiritual Community in a Sectarian Print Culture', discusses the Anglican clergyman, journalist, educator, and reformer Frederick Denison Maurice and his vision for how newspapers help construct a sense of community that combats the depersonalization of industrialism and capitalism. Chapter 3, 'Arnold's Poetic National Church: Anarchy and the Charming Force of Poetry', examines the way Matthew Arnold defines the role and meaning of 'religion' in public discourse. In grouping these three writers together, King aims to better illustrate what unites their common interests beyond the 'broad church' label. All three writers were united by their attempt to offset sectarian and class tensions through reading's potential to establish 'an imagined national Christian community' (p. 13).

Part II, 'Virtual Congregations and Printed Poetic Cycles', examines different poetic cycles and their influence on fostering 'extra-institutional communities of Christian readers' (p. 14). In chapter 4, 'John Keble's *Christian Year*: Private Reading and Imagined National Religious Community', King argues that under Keble's work, private poetry reading became a way to imagine a national Christian community. Chapter 5, 'Tennyson's "New Christian Year"': *In Memoriam* and the Minimum of Faith', reads Tennyson's *In Memoriam* alongside the context of Keble's *The Christian Year*. Chapter 6, '*In Memoriam*'s Open Secret: The Public Forms of Private Faith', continues with a provocative reading of Tennyson's *In Memoriam* that draws on the portrayal of the poem's emphasis on internal faith. Chapter 7, 'Christina Rossetti's *Verses*: A Multi-Fashioned Community of Strangers', turns to another poetic cycle inspired by *The Christian Year*, Christina Rossetti's *Verses*. Rossetti works against national and imperial forms of community in both Keble's and Tennyson's work, King argues, and instead emphasizes participation in a community 'under Christ' that emphasizes acts of love and justice (p. 17).

In his conclusion, King discusses the end of print-mediated Christian Britain in the twentieth century. Ironically, it was the very impulse at the heart of many of the texts discussed in this book, to create an imagined national Christian community through print, that would become outdated in the effort of churches and missions to become more international in their focus and outreach.

Two other books that have a different primary focus than religion, but which nonetheless have important implications for our understanding of religion in the Victorian period, are Mary Riso's *The Narrative of the Good Death: The Evangelical Deathbed in Victorian England* and Simon Goldhill's *The Buried Life of Things: How Objects Made History in Nineteenth-Century Britain*. Riso lists six factors that shaped beliefs about death among Evangelical nonconformists: denominational magazine obituaries, theology, social background, denominational variations, Romanticism, and the last words and experiences of the dying. The denominations Riso considers are Wesleyan Methodists, the Primitive Methodists, the Baptists, and the Congregationalists. The book includes 1,200 obituaries divided among the four denominations and covering three periods (1830s, 1850s, 1870s). Such a large sampling across so many years makes the book distinctive because it allows Riso to observe trends in nonconformist belief. Riso finds that there was a corollary between expectations concerning death and the afterlife and the social shifts towards middle-class respectability and a broader Evangelicalism.

Each chapter focuses on a specific aspect of death and how it changed over time. Chapter 2, 'Obituaries as Literature: Form and Content', examines the literary conventions of obituaries. Chapter 3, 'Evangelical Nonconformist Theology and Deathbed Piety', explores the theology connected to death and the afterlife of nonconformists. Chapter 4, 'The Claims of Heaven and Earth: Social Background and Social Mobility', considers social class, particularly social mobility, as it influenced expectations about death and the afterlife. Chapter 5, 'The Old Dissent and the New Dissent: Denominational Variations', takes a step back to look at the overall picture of death as it compares across the four different denominations. Chapter 6, 'The Infinite and the Finite: The Romantic Spirit and Nonconformist Death', examines the Romantic influence on both literary conventions in obituaries and overall world-views. Chapter 7, 'Last Words: The Experience of Death', takes a specific look at the words of the dying and the viewpoints of observers of death. Chapter 8, 'The Good Death and a Good Life', provides a summary of the study's findings related to each of the six factors listed above.

Goldhill explores the connection between history and things, how things 'become a way of telling the story of history' in the nineteenth century (p. 2). Goldhill's study brings together two ways of reconstructing history, through material objects and through narrative. The book's title highlights the interest Goldhill has in 'how things are used to make what is invisible visible' (p. 6). The title also refers to the trajectory Goldhill traces for each of the objects from their height of contested meaning to their life of obscurity.

Human skulls are the objects of focus in chapter 1, 'A Writer's Things: Edward Bulwer Lytton and the Archaeological Gaze'. Goldhill discusses both the literal skulls dug up in Pompeii and their presence in Edward Bulwer Lytton's novel *The Last Days of Pompeii*. The treatment of the literal and figurative skulls shows the contested boundary between history and fiction. Chapter 2, 'When Things Matter: Religion and the Physical World', turns to religious objects. Goldhill contends that religious conflicts in the nineteenth century were often based on histories of the Church, and the objects in this chapter, a Roman mosaic, a stone altar, and a ritual robe, are 'intricate acts of rebellious artistic representation' that form the centre of some of the most contentious debates (p. 4). Chapter 3, 'Imperial Landscapes, the Biblical Gaze, and Techniques of the Photo Album: Capturing the Real in Jerusalem and the Holy Land', continues the focus on religious objects. The thousands of photographs of Jerusalem and the Holy Land taken in the nineteenth century represent the competing discourses of the 'real' among photography, science, and religion. Chapter 4, 'Building History: A Mandate Coda', moves beyond the nineteenth century to the discussion of rebuilding Jerusalem. This chapter sets up the discussion in chapter 5, 'Restoration', about how restoration and reconstruction were 'key expressions of how the past can be expressed' for the Victorians (p. 6).

Also concerned with death and mourning, Deborah Lutz's *Relics of Death in Victorian Literature and Culture* examines Victorian death culture and its relationship to the body. In doing so she engages with other prominent theories, such as Thing theory. To that end, the book is not just interested in death per se but in the body as thing. Lutz is also interested in the issue of representation and the 'changing relations between language, image, and object' (p. 9). By looking at the representation of different relics of death in Victorian literature, Lutz can trace the cultural forces that took part in the changing beliefs about death: 'In the following pages novels and poetry are read as a means to understand the relic culture they elucidate, just as relics are "read" to theorize their begetting of signs, tales, and lyricism' (p. 3). Some of the cultural forces that influence Victorian relic culture include the rise of agnosticism and atheism, 'mechanical mementos' in photography, and a commodity culture (p. 9). One other interesting thread in the book is the relationship between secular and religious death relics. While it looks back to the connection between Victorian death culture and Catholic relics, the end of the book looks forward to 'The dematerialization and disembodiment of death's mementos' by the end of the First World War (p. 5).

Chapter 1, 'Infinite Materiality: Keats, D.G. Rossetti, and the Romantics', begins in the Romantic era with the collecting of corpse parts in the poetry of John Keats and Dante Gabriel Rossetti. Chapter 2, 'The Miracle of Ordinary Things: Brontë and *Wuthering Heights*', looks at the influence of Evangelicalism on relic culture, particularly commonplace objects in Brontë's *Wuthering Heights*. Chapter 3, 'The Many Faces of Death Masks: Dickens and *Great Expectations*', examines representations of the body as corpse both before and after death. Chapter 4, 'The Elegy as Shrine: Tennyson and *In Memoriam*', is reviewed below. Chapter 5, 'Hair Jewelry as Congealed Time: Hardy and *Far From the Madding Crowd*', turns to the end of the century and Hardy's work. Here Lutz examines the most common secular relic in the Victorian period, hair snippets, and how the meanings associated with this relic shifted towards the end of the century.

This year saw the publication of a range of works on gender, queer studies, and the family. Several of these focus on the body. In *Female Criminality: Infanticide, Moral Panics and the Female Body*, Annie Cossins participates in scholarly examinations of the female body and the moral regulation of women, particularly in the area of maternal infanticide. Cossins is interested in the social implications that would lead mothers to sell their children to infamous 'baby farmers'. To that end, this book is also a sociological study of the working class and conditions of poverty especially in the years 1861–72. In her introduction, 'Dumb Brutes and Murderous Mothers', Cossins claims that her particular contribution to other studies that engage with infanticide is her focus on 'the sexed female body whose biology, paradoxically, determined both her passive self-sacrifice and her immoral acts of wickedness and aggression' (p. 3). Using moral regulation theory, she provides a theoretical basis to understand the role of the sexed female body in moral panic.

Cossins traverses criminal law, social history of class, moral regulation theory, and gender theory, to name some of what this book covers. Cossins frequently isolates one of these areas as the focus of a chapter. In chapter 2, 'The Moral Panic Concept: Its History, Social Utility and Ability to Interpret Past Events', Cossins traces the political history of moral panic as a concept, evaluating whether or not the Victorian-era discourse surrounding infanticide constitutes a moral panic. Chapter 3, 'Regulation of the Female Body: Was Infanticide a Moral Panic of the Nineteenth Century?', looks more closely at the role of the female body in moral panic. Cossins identifies a causal model for the increasing moral regulation of the female body during the nineteenth century. Chapter 4, 'The Moral Regulation of Infanticidal Mothers', builds on this historical data to examine the modern-day cases of infanticide through case studies of four women. Chapter 5, 'The Implications of the Body for Female Criminality', considers in brief how Cossins's theoretical approach could be extended to other types of female criminality beyond infanticide. In focusing on the role of the sexed body in moral panic and moral regulation, Cossins provides a stronger theoretical basis for understanding how moral panic develops.

The journal *Victorian Network* produced a special issue this year, 'The Body'. In the introduction, Pamela K. Gilbert announces 'the body' as 'one of the most durable areas of inquiry in contemporary scholarship on Victorian literature and culture' (p. 1). Gilbert goes on to survey two of the most prominent areas of study, Foucault's study of how the body is represented and Judith Butler's construction of the body as 'doing'. The six essays included follow in these two traditions. Four are concerned with the novel, and are covered in the relevant section below, but the final pair of essays moves to other forms of writing. James Whitehead argues, in 'Biopower: Bodies, Minds, and Biographical Subjection in Victorian Lives of the Poets' (*VicNet* 6:i[2015] 7–31), that biographical discourse often connected the individual body with the textual material of biography. The 'poetic genius' was an exemplary case for biography, then, as Whitehead goes on to show through the case of Percy

Bysshe Shelley. Whitehead connects this to a larger argument about how Victorian biography influenced Victorian perceptions of Romantic poetry. Laura Fox Gill's 'Melting Bodies: The Dissolution of Bodily Boundaries in Milton and Swinburne' (*VicNet* 6:i[2015] 72–92), traces Milton's influence on Swinburne. Gill attributes Swinburne's melting metaphors not to classic sources most scholars assume but to Milton's use of 'melting' bodies in his portrayal of angelic and prelapsarian sexuality. Gill argues that Swinburne treats this image of the devouring lover as a positive one.

Several publications focused on women writers of magazine or periodical essays. *Women, Work and the Victorian Periodical: Living by the Press* by Marianne Van Remoortel takes up the divide between the public and private self in women's lives, focusing particularly on women who wrote for the burgeoning magazine industry in the nineteenth century. Van Remoortel adds to previous scholarship on women in the press by focusing on other activities related to the periodical press. These activities include editing, fancy-work instruction, poetry, typesetting, and illustration. Van Remoortel uses a broad array of primary sources, including birth, marriage, and death records, census returns, wills, letters, publishers' records, and pension applications. Expanding the kind of sources used in periodical research allows Van Remoortel to trace the tensions between these women's private lives and public work. In addition to exploring these women's lives, Van Remoortel also explores new research methodologies in periodical studies for dealing with the anonymity of the Victorian press.

Research methods are the focus of chapter 1, 'Women, Work, and the Victorian Press', as Van Remoortel explores the difficulties of studying print culture in relation to biography and the possibilities opened by the digital humanities. The rest of the chapters each focus on a specific type of work related to the magazine industry. Chapter 2, 'Selling Domesticity: Eliza Warren Francis and the *Ladies' Treasury*', looks at the work of magazine editors, using Eliza Warren Francis as a case study. Van Remoortel highlights the tension between Francis's magazine persona as a middle-class wife and mother and her lived reality as a childless, widowed woman. Chapter 3, 'Threads of Life: Matilda Marian Pullan and Needlework Instruction', turns to a specific type of contribution to magazines, fancywork patterns. Like Francis, Matilda Marian Pullan creates a public persona that departs markedly from her private life. Pullan's earnings were used to support an illegitimate child, an unhappy second marriage, and emigration to the United States.

Chapter 4, 'Christina Rossetti and the Economics of Periodical Poetry', is reviewed in Section 3 below. Chapter 5, 'The Fine Art of Satire: Florence and Adelaide Claxton and the Magazines', turns to visual contributions by women, including the graphic artists Florence and Adelaide Claxton and Mary Ellen Edwards. Van Remoortel argues that the less glamorous periodical art provided a forum for satirizing society. Chapter 6, 'Back-Room Workers Stepping Forward: Emily Faithfull and the Compositors of the Victoria Press', looks at the work of female compositors in the unique Victoria Press, run by Emily Faithfull, who hired only women in this traditionally male trade. This chapter traces the many tensions that emerged between Faithfull and the women who worked for her. Van Remoortel opens up these women's lives to us as well as new ways for exploring the work associated with the periodical press.

Barbara Korte's essay, 'Between Fashion and Feminism: History in Mid-Victorian Women's Magazines' (*ES* 96[2015] 424–43), looks at three market-leading middle-class women's magazines, *Englishwoman's Domestic Magazine*, *Ladies' Treasury*, and *Queen*, in addition to the feminist *English Woman's Journal*. Korte examines how history was constructed by women in these magazines. These magazines show 'mid-Victorian women were taking part in their period's historical interests and practices' (p. 425). The questions Korte is particularly interested in studying through the non-fiction articles in the four magazines she has chosen are as follows: 'What areas of history do the magazines take up and identify as particularly interesting and significant for their female readers? How do they utilize these areas to negotiate the social position of women and models of femininity? How does their presentation of history relate to dominant strands of historiography? and To what extent do they articulate their own gendered ways of historical thinking?' (p. 425).

Another article, 'Rivaling Conan Doyle: L.T. Meade's Medical Mysteries, New Woman Criminals, and Literary Celebrity at the Victorian *Fin de Siècle*' (*ELT* 58:i[2015] 54–72), examines the career of L.T. Meade at what Janice Dawson argues was a crucial turning point, her decision to leave her position as editor of the *Atalanta* to write fiction for the *Strand*. Dawson focuses on Meade's 'professionalism and market savvy' as an example of how women writers managed their careers in the *fin-de-siècle* literary marketplace.

Finally, William A. Davis's essay, 'Mary Jeune, Late-Victorian Essayist: Fallen Women, New Women, and Poor Children' (*ELT* 58[2015] 181–208), sketches the life and works of Victorian essayist Mary Jeune (1845–1931). He argues for the need for increased scholarship on her output, which totalled over fifty pieces on themes such as the state of poverty, women's issues and the New Woman question, politics, children, and culture at large. Although she wrote authoritatively, bolstering her periodical work with research and statistics, she has all but disappeared from the critical eye, and is often omitted from anthologies of women's prose. Having given ample context for her value, Davis proposes that future studies of Mary Jeune answer salient questions concerning style, intertextuality, personality, and comparative considerations of her views with those of Victorian academics and publishers.

There was an interesting cluster of work on women and the railway this year. *Women and the Railway 1850–1915* by Anna Despotopoulou finds that the railway is 'an ambiguously gendered space that highlights the artificiality of the private/public divide, giving prominence to woman's impulse to traverse boundaries, not only physically but also mentally and emotionally' (p. 2). Despotopoulou's introduction includes a helpful literature review of studies on the railway in Britain and studies on nineteenth-century women's movements in public spaces. She offers a careful summary of extant studies of the railway, including those that look specifically at women and the railway. She emphasizes how her book will focus on texts by and about women and texts that are fiction and non-fiction, whereas other studies either do not focus on gender at all, use a primarily historical rather than literary lens, or do not examine British women travellers. This fine study, tracing both the 'liberating and self-inventing' potential of the railway for women and the 'isolation or uprootedness' that it came to signify in the early twentieth century (p. 185), primarily focuses on fiction, and so is discussed at more length in Section 2 of this chapter. There were two articles on railways. 'Rape on the Railway: Women, Safety, and Moral Panic in Victorian Newspapers' (*JVC* 20[2015] 341–56) by Robin J. Barrow. The potential for sexual violence enabled by the intimate setting of the railway carriage was a fact of Victorian life that is often overlooked today (p. 341). This essay examines the connection between the rhetoric of sexualized women in newspapers and women's increasing presence in public spaces, particularly the railway. Barrow looks at two moral panics about railway travel in 1864 and 1875 as case studies. In 'The Railway Guide's Experiments in Cartography: Narrative, Information, Advertising' (*VS* 57[2015] 251–83), Tina Young Choi uses railway guides to trace 'train travel's cultural transformations', or the temporal and spatial shifts in the English imagination. The heterogeneous material gathered within a railway guide also provides a rich site for investigating the representational experiments in these guides. Choi argues these guides 'transformed and expanded the meaning of cartographic legibility and literacy for a popular audience over the course of the century' (p. 253). The essay includes several wonderful illustrations from the guides.

Some publications looked at gender's importance in concerns of empire and nationality. Susan Kingsley Kent's *Queen Victoria: Gender and Empire* is organized around the issues of gender and empire. Part of The World in a Life series from Oxford University Press, this volume is a short, accessible, and insightful look at Queen Victoria's life. A brief introduction explains the prominence of these themes in Victoria's life, from her own personal experiences to the political debates surrounding the women's movement as well as Britain's increasingly global reach. The book is organized around the notion of the split between public and private domains. The chapters are as follows: chapter 1, 'Childhood, 1819–1837: Transition to a New Social and Political Order'; chapter 2, 'Queen, Wife, Mother: Separate Sphere Ideology and the Paradox of Female Monarchy, 1840–61'; chapter 3, 'Co-Rulers, 1842–1861: Changing Ideologies of Gender and Race'; chapter 4, 'The Widowed Queen, 1861–1872'; chapter 5, 'Re-emergence, 1873–1887: New Imperialism and New Challenges to Separate Spheres'; chapter 6, 'The Height of Victoria's Reign, 1887–1901: Gender, Jubilees, and Colonial Wars'; and chapter 7, 'The Legacy of the Late Queen'. Kingsley Kent's book will be a useful teaching tool that opens up for students key historical debates of the Victorian period.

In *Jewish Feeling: Difference and Affect in Nineteenth-Century Jewish Women's Writing*, Richa Dwor argues that Anglo-Jewish women writers used the concept of midrash, the rabbinic interpretative form, to engage with affect. Dwor takes two Jewish writers, Grace Aguilar and Amy Levy, and reads their fiction and essays alongside the writing of George Eliot. Through this examination, she develops a distinctly Jewish form of affect. The book occupies itself with affect studies and theology in new and interesting ways, demonstrated by the intriguing readings of George Eliot within this framework. Dwor's introduction, 'Affect and Jewish Feeling', discusses the intersections between affect studies and theology, defines midrash, and situates it in relation to affect. Chapter 1, ' "The still undercurrent of deep feeling": History and Nation for Grace Aguilar', focuses on the work of Grace Aguilar through which she represents her model of reading with feeling and the midrashic concept of metonymy. Chapter 2, ' "Finer and finer discrimination": George Eliot's Feeling for the Jews', compares the theory of organicism prevalent in Eliot's work with the Jewish feeling used in Aguilar's. Chapter 3, ' "A fragment of the eternal truth": Futurity and Race for Amy Levy', turns to Amy Levy, and here Dwor is primarily interested in highlighting her differences from Aguilar and how she engages with Eliot. Dwor's work with these authors reveals a new category of affect in the nineteenth century, one that leads readers to an 'engagement with what they read rather than provid[ing] a solution to its ambiguities', where feeling becomes a way of knowing (p. 179).

Several works focused on masculinity and queer studies. *Visions of Queer Martyrdom from John Henry Newman to Derek Jarman*, by Dominic Janes, examines the role Christianity played in the history of homosexuality in Britain. Janes's term 'queer' refers to the 'creative blurrings between religious idealism and performances of non-normative gender and sexuality' (p. 5). Those outside the Church, such as Lytton Strachey, could use the construction of priesthood as a community of same-sex relationships to embody their own desire. The state of male Christian suffering that Janes traces throughout the book is contextualized with the ideologies of martyrdom and suffering as important theological concepts. The association with martyrdom is important because, as Janes argues, martyrdom was a 'culturally contestable state' and thus ideologies of martyrdom and sexual identity could play out in relation to one another (p. 10). For his source material Janes focuses primarily on the visual and material culture of religious display. His introduction, 'The Bitter Tears of John Henry Newman', includes a helpful review of scholarship on the topic of queer studies, including the troubled reception of studies that posit a relationship between Christianity and same-sex desire. Chapter 2, 'William Bennett and the Art of Ritualism', examines how the body of Christ provided the exemplary martyr for imagining pure forms of homoerotic expression. Janes uses a case study of William Bennett and his emphasis on the visual aspects of liturgy. Chapter 3, 'Father Ignatius's "Wonderful... Monastery Life"', focuses on the way communities of men acted as queer alternatives to the heterosexual family with a mixture of ascetic discipline and homoerotic pleasure. His case study in this chapter focuses on the community led by Joseph Leycester Lyne. Chapter 4, 'Frederick Rolfe's Scrapbook', explores material and visual bricolage in the form of Frederick Rolfe's scrapbook. Rolfe's private expression of queer identity reveals the limitations of queer self-expression within an ecclesiastical context. Chapter 5, 'Saint Oscar', re-examines Oscar Wilde's example of martyrdom within the context of the Victorian 'constitutive role of religion in the construction of queerness' (p. 136). Chapter 6, 'The Private Lives of David and Jonathan', turns to the Victorian focus on youth and the idealization of boyhood. The biblical relationship of David and Jonathan was used as a spiritual ideal which might offer an appropriate channel for otherwise deviant behaviour. In part, this chapter also attempts to explain why issues of sexuality in the Catholic Church so often coalesce around the figure of the boy or young man. Chapter 7, 'Derek Jarman and the Legacy of Queer Martyrdom', examines the twentieth-century queer filmmaker Derek Jarman, whose death as a result of AIDS made him a figure of martyrdom. Jarman's life and death encapsulate the very dynamic Janes has discussed throughout the book, in which 'secular and Christian viewpoints engage creatively with each other' (p. 185).

Duc Dau and Shale Preston's edited collection, *Queer Victorian Families: Curious Relations in Literature*, brings the family into queer studies. As the editors note, this volume 'is intended as a corrective against limited and traditionalist definitions of family' (p. 2). The essays in this volume join conversations about queer and same-sex relationships by focusing specifically on queer family formations. The essays are interdisciplinary and engage with fields as wide-ranging as childhood studies, nationalist studies, and animal studies. The editors intend these intersections among different fields to 'open up new avenues for understanding neglected types of affections and relationships, and thereby make for thought-provoking explorations of non-normativity within family relations' (p. 4). The essays offer a counter to theorists who align the family with middle-class heteronormativity.

Part I, 'Queervolutions', examine texts that interrogate contemporary understandings of the 'Victorian family' by turning to alternative perspectives present in literary texts. Chapter 1, 'The "Queer-Looking Party" Challenge to Family in *Alice*' (pp. 19–35), by Laura White, examines queer configurations of family structure in Lewis Carroll's *Alice* books. Chapter 2, 'Esther Summerson's Estate: The Queer, Quasi-Monarchical Line of Beauty, Family, and Inheritance in *Bleak House*' (pp. 36–56), by Shale Preston, reads Esther Summerson in Dickens's *Bleak House* as a character who challenges patriarchal imperatives as the head of a 'quasi-monarchical' queer family (p. 10). Chapter 3, 'Michael Field's Dramatically Queer Family Dynamics', by Tracy Olverson (pp. 57–76), explores the queer family relations in Michael Field's Roman dramas. Chapter 4, 'William Sharp's Neo-Paganism: Queer Identity and the National Family' (pp. 77–96), by Michael Shaw traces neo-paganism in the writing of William Sharp/Fiona Macleod as it challenges paternalistic hierarchies.

Part II, 'Queer Actually', explores queering structures within the more conventional family unit. Chapter 5, 'A "Strange Family Story": Count Fosco, His Animal Children, and the "Safe" Patriarch in Wilkie Collins's *The Woman in White*' (pp. 99–115), by Monica Flegel, examines the relationship between Count Fosco and his animal 'children' in Wilkie Collins's *The Woman in White*. Chapter 6, by Clare Walker Gore, explores the construction of alternative family structures through the inclusion of disabled characters in the work of Dinah Mulock Craik and Charlotte M. Yonge. Chapter 7, 'Two Girls in Love: Romantic Friendship and the Queer Family in Elizabeth Anna Hart's *The Runaway*' (pp. 134–54), by Ellen Brinks, reads the relationships between the adolescent girl protagonists in Elizabeth Anna Hart's *The Runaway* as a queer family space.

Part III, 'Queer Connections', explores networks of queer families across and beyond literature. Chapter 8, 'Reading on the Contrary: Cousin Marriage, *Mansfield Park*, and *Wuthering Heights*' (pp. 157–75), by Talia Schaffer, examines endogamous marriage in Emily Brontë's *Wuthering Heights* and Jane Austen's *Mansfield Park*. Chapter 9, 'The Queer, Statistical Kinship of Tennyson and Melville' (pp. 176–94), by Alec Magnet, explores the connections between the representation of same-sex attachments as family relationships in Alfred Tennyson's *In Memoriam* and Herman Melville's *Moby-Dick*. Chapter 10, 'The Victorian Family in Queer Time: Secrets, Sisters, and Lovers in *The Woman in White* and *Fingersmith*' (pp. 195–210), by Lauren N. Hoffer and Sarah E. Kersh, also looks at the connections between two texts, *The Woman in White* and Sarah Waters's Neo-Victorian novel *Fingersmith*. Both of these novels unsettle conceptions of the Victorian family through their representation of sisterhood.

Some other studies of the family take up more conventional themes of family and morality, but offer some interesting insights. *Pets and Domesticity in Victorian Literature and Culture: Animality, Queer Relations, and the Victorian Family* by Monica Flegel begins with a provocative opening example from Clara Balfour's 1861 novel *Drift*. Flegel sets up her main line of enquiry: how pets both constitute and disrupt domestic ideology. While unconventional families, as in *Drift*, are usually shown to be unsustainable, they also serve as uncanny doublings of traditional families to expose the desires that the bourgeois family structure represses. Flegel begins by looking at how pets help foster normative romantic relationships in chapter 1, 'Love Me, Love My Dog: The Role of the Pet in Rituals of Courtship and Romance'. The pet becomes a safe object to help characters develop their capacity for love. Flegel examines the pet as 'temporary placeholder for future partner' in Anne Brontë's *Agnes Grey* and *The Tenant of Wildfell Hall* and George Eliot's *Adam Bede* and *Middlemarch*. Chapter 2, 'Becoming Crazy Cat Lady: Women and Their Pets in the Domestic Circle', focuses on definitions of proper womanhood surrounding reproduction and the problem spinsters and their pets introduced into this ideology. Novels by Bulwer-Lytton and Clara Balfour as well as newspapers demonstrate that focusing on the spinster's affection for her pets helped to make her a more sympathetic figure. On the other hand, novels by Collins, Braddon, and Betsey Rayner Parkes represent the spinster's love of pets as a welcome separation from restrictive familial norms. Chapter 3, 'Pets and Patriarchy: Bachelors, Villains, and Their Animal Companions', examines a figure in even more direct opposition to domestic ideology, the villainous male and his pet. Through her exploration of Marryat's *The Dog Fiend; or, Snarley-yow*, Dickens's *Barnaby Rudge*, Eliot's *Adam Bede*, and Collins's *The Woman in White*, Flegel illuminates the divided identity of males as both savage and dependent on love, much like their animal counterparts. This chapter reveals that domesticity can be a repressive ideology for men as well as women.

If the previous chapters discussed the way pets illuminated the complicated status of men and women in the home, the final chapter turns to the same issue with children. 'Household Pets, Waifs, and Strays: Children and Animals Inside and Outside the Victorian Home' reveals the tension between two discourses surrounding children. In her conclusion, 'Animals and Their Families', Flegel turns to literary representations of animal families in texts such as Frances Power Cobbe's *Confessions of a Lost Dog* [1867] and Lucy D. Thornton's *The Story of a Poodle* [1890]. These animal families expose family as a concept that 'is both made and born' (p. 15). Flegel's examination of family pets helps develop a sense of the Victorian family as 'more capacious and more diverse' than previously understood (p. 8). While her book certainly helps us understand the place of animals in Victorian literature and culture, it also provides a rich and varied look at the Victorian family and adds much to our understanding of one of the most important institutions in the nineteenth century.

Thomas Joudrey's essay, 'Penetrating Boundaries: An Ethics of Anti-Perfectionism in Victorian Pornography' (*VS* 57[2015] 423–32), positions pornography as a challenge to the dominant public discourse, but he does not follow recent constructions of pornography in what he calls the 'perfectionist-porn thesis'. Instead, Joudrey argues that pornography is anti-perfectionist. Constructed this way, pornography resists two normative constructions of gender: the 'restrained gentleman and the modest virgin' (p. 424). Victorian pornography thus offers one way to examine Victorian attitudes towards bodily decay, suffering, and mortality.

Dara Rossman Regaignon argues, in 'Anxious Uptakes: Nineteenth-Century Advice Literature as a Rhetorical Genre' (*CE* 78[2015] 139–61), that advice literature cannot be read as a direct guide to social practices but rather 'should be read first and foremost as participating in a specific (generic) tradition' (p. 140). Though the essay focuses on one particular genre, the advice manual, Regiagnon's aims are much larger. She presents new methods for rhetorical genre studies to engage with historically distant texts and new ways for literary critics to attend to the way discursive formations shape experience. Her case study is Victorian medically authored child-rearing advice literature.

In an essay on the Victorian poster-child for morality and manners, Samuel Smiles, Vladimir Trendafilov's essay, 'The Origins of Self-Help: Samuel Smiles and the Formative Influences on an Ex-Seminal Work' (*The Victorian* 3:i[2015] 1–16), argues for the importance of Samuel Smiles and offers a corrective to the critical neglect he has faced since the close of the Victorian period. Trendafilov discusses the origins of the word and notion 'self-help' as one way to better understand Smiles and his work. See also Cara Murray's essay, 'Self-Help and the Helpless Subject: Samuel Smiles and Biography's Objects' (*NCL* 69[2015] 481–508), and Timothy L. Caren's essay, 'Idolatrous Reading: Subversive Fantasy and Domestic Ideology' (*NCL* 70[2015] 238–66).

Focusing specifically on conceptions of children in the Victorian family, Sally Shuttleworth's essay, 'Childhood, Severed Heads, and the Uncanny: Freudian Precursors' (*VS* 58:i[2015] 84–110), examines Freud's construction of the uncanny within the context of nineteenth-century psychology and anthropology. The essay sheds new light on Freud's theory of the uncanny as well as the Victorian's conceptions of childhood by comparing Freud's accounts with the work of psychologist James Sully and feminist Frances Power Cobbe. Nina Augustynowicz, in 'White Rosebud for Girlhood:

Victorian Floriography' (in Bemben, Borysławski, Jajszczok, and Gajda, eds., *Cryptohistories*, pp. 77–88), explores the sexual symbolism associated with flowers in the Victorian period. The essay includes a discussion of the range of connections made between 'the language of flowers' and sexuality, including sexual organs, innocence, and promiscuity, as well as the various ways Victorians engaged with flowers, such as botany and decorative books. Augustynowicz argues that flowers were most often associated with women, and thus the meanings of flowers were confined by the social roles of women.

Kimberly Wahl's essay, 'Picturing the Material/Manifesting the Visual: Aesthetic Dress in Late-Nineteenth-Century British Culture' (in Nicklas and Pollen, eds., *Dress History: New Directions in Theory and Practice*, pp. 97–112), is interested in the gaps that exist between 'the visual representation and literary framing' of clothes, as well as how clothes were acquired, adapted, and worn. Wahl examines two case studies of Aesthetic dress, a house dress/tea gown in the Royal Ontario Museum in Toronto, Canada, and a tea gown in the Royal Pavilion and Museums in the United Kingdom. In discussing these artefacts, Wahl highlights Aesthetic dress as a 'complex social practice' that is part of a 'contested visual culture' (p. 100).

For those interested in the late nineteenth-century and decadence, *The Decadent Short Story: An Annotated Anthology* (reviewed here by William Baker), edited by Kostas Boyiopoulos, Yoonjoung Choi, and Mathew Brinton Tildesley, consists of a collection of short stories published during the 1890s in 'the late Victorian Little Magazines' (pp. 297–8) and 'other sources' (pp. 299–391). Simon J. James's foreword (pp. xi–xii) is followed by a detailed introduction (pp. 1–24), and an introduction and endnotes for each specific story. There are three appendices: 'Parodies' (pp. 392–400); 'Background Sources' (pp. 400–20); and 'Further Reading: A Timeline' (pp. 420–6) beginning in 1840 and concluding in 1905. The notes (pp. 427–58) are helpful, and this useful anthology has a enumerative alphabetical select bibliography (pp. 459–61) followed by a double-columned index (pp. 460–6).

As Nancy Armstrong showed us long ago in *Desire and Domestic Fiction*, the family and domestic realm had important implications for the political realm. So from studies focused on the family we turn now to politics. In *Victorian Political Culture: Habits of Heart and Mind*, Angus Hawkins outlines several important principles that governed Victorian political culture, including the importance of history, the vision of politics as a moral activity, and the importance of community—rather than individual—interests. His introduction traces how these principles influenced the political climate in the nineteenth century. These principles also underlie the discussion in each of the following chapters. His analysis of political culture resists perceptions of Britain as a liberal modern state in the Victorian period.

Chapter 1, 'The Sovereignty of Parliament', examines constitutional language that evoked 'statute, landed status, and historical precedence as the embodiment of political values' (p. 21). Chapter 2, 'A Constitutional Turning Point: 1828–1836', explores the crisis of parliamentary agency from 1828 to 1836 and the reform of parliament that was essentially 'restorative' in its language and intent. Chapter 3, '"Parliamentary Government" and Its Critics: 1832–1867', examines the nature of parties between 1832 and 1867 influenced by the reliance on 'parliamentary government'. Chapter 4, 'Constituency Politics: 1832–1867', argues that the major political movements of the period were influenced by the changing ideology of 'constitutionalism' after the 1832 Reform Acts. Chapter 5, 'The Dynamics of Voting: 1832–1867', discusses the differences among England, Wales, Scotland, and Ireland between 1832 and 1867 in voting practices. Chapter 6, 'The Moral Climate of Reform: 1848–1867', traces the renewed importance of the morality of political activity following the Continental revolutions of 1848. The manners and customs of society came to be seen as integral to political stability and progress. Chapter 7, ' "Shooting Niagara": The 1867 Reform Acts', discusses the emphasis on morality for the 1867 Reform Acts, which considered 'respectability' the dominant qualification in discussions of voting rights for working-class men. The final two chapters, 'The Demise of "Parliamentary Government": 1868–1884' and 'Party, Society and the State: 1886–1905', trace the transition to 'party government' after 1867 as localism gave way to centralized government. 'Victorian politics was about the management of change' Hawkins writes in his epilogue; his book argues that large changes to the political culture did not actually take place until the 1880s and 1890s, rather than in the 1830s and 1840s. The emergence of liberal modernity in the nineteenth century, he contends, must be understood in relation to the conservative ideologies of the past, morality, and community that were so formative of Victorian political culture.

Thomas Dixon's *Weeping Britannia: Portrait of a Nation in Tears* is a magisterial march through six centuries of crying. This history of tears covers the Victorian period prominently in its middle section, as the book transitions from earlier centuries to the modern day. Dixon describes the book's aim as one that will 'anatomize, reconstitute, even reanimate, and feel once more, the experiences of tearful individuals, and those who witnessed them' (p. 9). He uses first-person accounts as well as literature, philosophy, science, and journalism to explore beliefs about tears. The book is organized around the tears of individuals (some of the most prominent being Oliver Cromwell, Queen Victoria, and Winston Churchill) as a way of examining large-scale social and cultural changes. This excellent book will be of interest to Victorian scholars for chapters 10–14 covering this period in sections entitled 'Pathos' and 'Restraint'. The chapters of note are entitled 'Strange Blessing on the Nation', 'Little Nell Without Laughing', 'Damp Justice', 'Old Ladies and Other Animals', and 'The "If" Upper Lip'. Dixon focuses on the duality of sentiment and restraint that he detects in Victorian discourse. He discusses Queen Victoria, Darwin's influence on theories of tears, educational theories, children's literature, imperial and military men, and the experience of reading Victorian fiction.

In 'Defending "the Principle of Representation": Andrew Bisset, The English Civil War, and *The History of the Struggle for Parliamentary Government in England*' (*JVC* 20[2015] 531–48), Michael J. Turner sets Andrew Bisset's *History of the Struggle for Parliamentary Government in England* [1877] in the wake of the professionalization of history as a discipline in the Victorian period. Bisset's work exemplifies the interplay between past and present and the view that history should be serviceable. Turner analyses how Bisset presents history in order to endorse the 'principle of representation' in contemporary debates about parliamentary government. Two articles discuss politics in relation to the Aesthetic movement. Matthew Potolsky's essay, 'Eros and Revolution: Rossetti and Swinburne on Continental Politics' (VS 57[2015] 585–610), joins other scholarship that attempts to change the long-standing view that the Aesthetic movement was disengaged from politics. Potolsky examines Dante Gabriel Rossetti and Algernon Charles Swinburne's comments on the political changes of the mid-nineteenth century effected by Continental events such as the 1848 revolutions, the Risorgimento in Italy, and the Franco-Prussian War. He argues that they identify 'an erotic motivation woven into the texture of politics as well as a political force underlying sexual desire' (p. 586). In 'Decadent Conservatism: Politics and Aesthetics in The Senate' (JVC 20[2015] 186–211), Alex Murray begins by reminding us how at odds Decadent writers and conservatives appear to be. He then provocatively argues that in the mid-1890s the 'lines of demarcation between conservatism and Decadence are much less clear' (p. 186). The common ground for Murray seems to be an aesthetic individualism that is actually at the heart of the British Conservative tradition. This symbiosis can best be seen in monthly journal The Senate, a largely forgotten journal that Murray works to recuperate in this essay.

Two other articles touch on war, revolution, and government. '"God'll send the bill to you": The Costs of War and the God Who Counts in W.T. Stead's Pro-Boer Peace Campaign' (JVC 20[2015] 168–85), by Ingrid Hanson, analyses the rhetoric in W.T. Stead's anti-Boer War pamphlet Methods of Barbarism [1901]. Hanson argues that Stead constructs a 'narrative of peace' as a response to 'the God who keeps accounts' (p. 168). The essay thus explores Stead's politicized version of faith, as he uses tactics from war reporting and warmongering to frame his appeal to war guilt and individual responsibility.

Lanya Lamouria argues, in 'Financial Revolution: Representing British Financial Crisis after the French Revolution of 1848' (VLC 43[2015] 489–510), that the French Revolution of 1848 gave new meaning to the financial crisis of the 1840s, essentially aligning the financial crisis with revolution as 'equivalent forms of social disruption' (p. 489). This mid-century moment was a 'formative moment in Victorian thinking about the financial system and its revolutionary potential' (p. 493). Lamouria uses two case studies to make this point: the press coverage of the bankruptcy of the duke of Buckingham and Chandos, and William North's novel The City of the Jugglers; or Free-Trade in Souls. A Romance of the 'Golden' Age [1850]. On such topics, see also Regenia Gagnier's article 'The Global Circulation of Victorian Actants and Ideas in the Niche of Nature, Culture, and Technology: Liberalism and Liberalization' (JELL 61[2015] 19–39).

There were a surprising number of studies this year on what I am broadly calling 'the city'. Nicholas Daly's The Demographic Imagination and the Nineteenth-Century City: Paris, London, New York describes a phenomenon he calls a demographic revolution—'suddenly there were a lot more people' (p. 1). Rather than envision a massive transition from country to city that prefigures an empty countryside, Daly argues there were more people everywhere. He argues that while urban concentration is only one part of an overall population explosion, it makes the overall demographic revolution more visible. He is interested in how the actual realities of demographic change registered in imaginative forms. Some of the variables he includes in 'demographic change' are population growth, longer lifespans (longevity), smaller families, and immigration. He labels five different responses to this population explosion as 'apocalyptic, criminal, supernatural, visual, and proto-ecological' (pp. 5–6). The genres he examines as case studies include volcanic disaster narratives, crime dramas, urban ghost stories, and urban genre painting. Chapter 1, 'Under the Volcano', examines disaster narratives and the way they project fear of the masses onto the natural world. Edward Bulwer Lytton's novel *The Last Days of Pompeii* [1834] serves as Daly's primary example. Lytton's novel establishes the conventions of the disaster narrative in which the city is destroyed by a natural disaster. Chapter 2, 'The Streets of Wherever', examines narratives that construct the city as a locus of crime. The popular figure of the stage detective emerges from these stories, which depict an underworld of thieves and a hero who restores order.

The next chapter, 'The Ghost Comes to Town', tackles the ghost story, which utilizes the Gothic conventions of the eighteenth century. Ghost story cities allow for nightmarish settings which serve as sites for hauntings of pedestrians and buildings alike. Here, Daly turns from fiction and drama to paintings and the way that artists such as William Powell Frith, George Clausen, and Jules Bastien-Lepage attempted to represent crowded urban areas and the masses. Chapter 4, 'The Frenzy of the Legible in the Age of Crowds', also examines the form of visual representation in advertising and mass journalism. Chapter 5, 'Fur and Feathers: Animas and the City in an Anthropocene Era', looks at the clash between the city and the natural world, as well as the Victorians' growing ecological awareness. As Daly explains, these chapters are not connected by any kind of trajectory mapping out the demographic imagination across the century, but are rather loosely connected case studies, each of which takes on some aspect of the demographic imagination. In his epilogue, Daly points to some of the ways *fin-de-siècle* works of fiction, such as those written by Bram Stoker and H.G. Wells, partake in this demographic imagination.

In her book *Anonymous Connections: The Body and Narratives of the Social in Victorian Britain*, Tina Young Choi is also interested in the implications of shifting urban demographics. Choi examines Victorians' changing conceptions of social belonging within the context of cultural and medical history. She considers the response of journalists, novelists, medical writers, and social reformers to urbanization and expansion, which produces new modes of transportation, epidemics, and new forms of contact with strangers. The social space in which actual bodies interact raises ethical, epistemological, and representational questions. Choi is interested in the interpersonal rather than institutional, and the central question her book asks is 'What happens when we foreground corporeal rather than affective social relations?' (p. 1).

Chapter 1, 'At Risk: Statistical Participation and the Victorian City', explores the social as 'a sphere of involuntary inclusion' (p. 10) in Gaskell's *Mary Barton*. Chapter 2, 'Miasmatic Texts: The Body's Excesses and Effects', explores unwanted physical contact with anonymous others in sanitary accounts. Chapter 3, 'Contagious Narratives: Distant Causality and the Emergence of Multiplot', argues that medical accounts of contagion produced new forms of narrative, such as the multiplot. Chapter 4, 'Radical Solutions, Conservative Systems: Narratives of Circulation and Closure', examines the recuperative potential of engineered structures, such as the sewer system in Mayhew's *London Labour and the London Poor* or the 'logic of reuse' in Dickens's *Our Mutual Friend* (p. 10). Chapter 5, 'Recollections of the Body: Anatomical Science and Fictions of Wholeness', turns to the implications of the Anatomy Act and the representation of the body as exchangeable and circulable. Chapter 6, 'Visions Global and Microbial: Germ Theory and Empire', explores narrative conventions for representing the germ in popular journalism, science, and fiction. Choi shows how these representations often intersect with narratives of and concerns about colonialism.

In *By Accident or Design: Writing the Victorian Metropolis*, Paul Fyfe traces one way of understanding the emergence of the modern metropolis, the lack of design in urban areas. The metropolis thus becomes an important arena for understanding Victorian notions of change, chance, and causation. Fyfe argues that his study of the Victorian metropolis 'offers a different vocabulary for the century's shifts towards probabilistic or relativistic paradigms by grounding them in the material contexts of the Victorian metropolis' (p. 3). To do so, Fyfe looks at representations of metropolitan life in texts and images from 1830–70, decades that mark important changes to metropolitan infrastructure. Each chapter offers a specific case study. Chapter 1, 'Accidents in the News', traces the increasing discourse of the 'accidental' especially prevalent in nineteenth-century newspapers. Chapter 2, 'Dickens and the Traffic of Accidents', examines one particular kind of accident associated with horse-drawn omnibuses as represented in Charles Dickens's *Sketches by Boz*. Chapter 3, 'Industrial Accidents and Novel Insurances', turns to industrial accidents as represented by Elizabeth Gaskell in *Mary Barton*. Chapter 4, 'Street Literature and the Remediation of Accident', discusses the chaotic feel of street literature as a commentary about Victorian anxieties about change reflected in mass media print culture. Chapter 5, 'Chaos and Connections on the Victorian Railway', discusses railway accidents in the work of Dickens and Trollope. In a brief Afterword, Fyfe discusses evolutionary discourse and Thomas Hardy's poem 'Hap'. The aim of his book is to 'establish the mid-century metropolis as an important domain of probability thinking and to demonstrate alternate, even accidental literary histories for the most conspicuous forms of its representation, from the newspaper to the realist novel' (p. 4).

Heather Shore examines how the language of police, writers, victims, witnesses, and criminals shaped visions of the underworld in London in *London's Criminal Underworlds, c.1720–c.1930: A Social and Cultural History*. The book begins in the early eighteenth century with the development of the idea of a criminal underworld and ends in the interwar period of the twentieth century where external factors heavily influenced the representation of crime and criminals. The four themes Shore is most concerned with are print culture, public crime, criminal networks, and territory. After an introduction, chapters

2, 3, and 4 focus on the eighteenth century and Romantic periods and the relationship between law enforcement and networks of criminals, and the narratives about the underworld that emerged. The chapter titles are ' "Now we have the informing dogs!": Crime Networks and Informing Cultures in the 1720s and 1730s'; ' "A Noted Virago": Moll Harvey and Her "Dangerous Crew", 1727–1738'; and ' "The pickpockets and hustlers had yesterday what is called a *grand day*": Changing Street Theft, c.1800–1850'. Chapter 5, ' "There goes Bill Sheen, the murderer": Crime, Kinship and Community in East London, 1827–1852', moves into the Victorian period with its examination of the life of William Sheen and his family. The theme of territory is prominent in this chapter as Shore focuses on the Wentworth Street area and narratives of family and local community. Chapter 6, ' "A new species of swindling": Coiners, Fraudsters, Swindlers and the "Long-Firm", c.1760–1913', discusses the emergence of more 'modern' ideas about crime in the Victorian period and the role of print culture. Chapter 7, ' "A London plague that must be swept away": Hooligans and Street Fighting Gangs, c.1882–1912', turns to the Victorian and Edwardian press and reports of street fighting gangs. The book ends with an exploration of these themes in the twentieth century in chapter 8, ' "The terror of the people": Organised Crime in Interwar London'.

An essay by Julian Wolfreys, ' "Otherwise in London" or, the "Essence of Things": Modernity and Estrangement in the Nineteenth-Century Cityscape' (*Victo* 5:i[2015] 17–35), examines the place of the city, specifically London, in the writing of the period. Wolfreys focuses on the way the cityscape often exists just beyond the limits of representation. The writers examined here, including Thomas De Quincey, William Wordsworth, Sarah Green, Pierce Egan, and Robert Southey, work to establish new ways of writing about urban landscape.

Because charity work was most often concentrated in the cities, Sarah Flew's essay, 'Unveiling the Anonymous Philanthropist: Charity in the Nineteenth Century' (*JVC* 20[2015] 20–33), adds an interesting perspective on the city. Rather than focus on the 'public and self-serving' aspect of charity, Flew highlights the prevalence of anonymous giving. Through an examination of the pseudonyms often used with these donations, Flew argues we can surmise the giver's relationship to the charity organization and the motivations behind the gift. As a case study, Flew compares anonymous giving to Anglican voluntary associations in London with those gifts made to welfare associations.

Geoffrey Cantor's 'Emotional Reactions to the Great Exhibition of 1851' (*JVC* 20[2015] 230–45) is an interesting essay that traces the various, and varied, responses to the Great Exhibition in order to demonstrate how it became an 'occasion for an outpouring of emotion, both private and public' (p. 232). Cantor also explores the language used to describe emotions, including the word 'wonder', and the problematic relationship between words and feelings.

Related to institutions that might be found in the city, Jane Hamlett's book *At Home in the Institution: Material Life in Asylums, Lodging Houses and Schools in Victorian and Edwardian England*, explores the ways that 'domestic objects, practices and relationships were transported into the institutional environment' (p. 2). She selects different institutions, asylums, lodging houses, and schools, each having different aims, organization, and social groups. With this range, Hamlett is able to show how hard Victorians worked to transport domesticity into such different contexts. Her exploration covers both how authorities constructed these spaces and how the inmates responded to them. During the Victorian period, each of these institutions underwent significant reforms, and Hamlett is interested in tracing intersecting discourses of domesticity with medicine, education, and morality. For example, drawing rooms and dining rooms were installed in female boarding houses, and asylums tried to instil the middle-class value of privacy as much as possible. But many of these attempts failed, as Hamlett explains: 'this book is particularly interested in what happened to inmates' feelings about home when they entered the institution and whether it was possible to transfer a sense of emotional attachment to these places' (p. 8).

Chapter 1, 'Public Asylums', looks at four different public asylums. Chapter 2, 'Asylums for the Middle and Upper Classes', compares two registered hospitals with a licensed house managed by a family of doctors. Chapter 3, 'Schools for Boys', looks at five different schools for boys, whereas chapter 4, 'Schools for Girls', in turn looks at schools for girls. Next, chapter 5, 'Common Lodging Houses' and chapter 6, 'Model Lodging Houses', turn their attention towards lodging houses. These final two chapters depend on slightly different sources, and by turns look at police records and the national census for evidence and support. The other chapters depend largely on autobiographies, memoirs, letters, diaries, and other personal documents. Hamlett's book attempts to bring together the spatial and material as controlling forces that worked together within institutions. But an important component of her argument is how the spatial and material at work in these institutions could also create opportunities for the inmates. Using examples such as the 'self-fashioning' practice of carving initials on desks or the act of adding buttons to asylum dress, this book shows the ways that the meaning of space and material objects are created by those who use them just as much as by those who control them.

Looking at the institution of the workhouse, Amber Cobb Vazquez's essay ' "The little world of poverty": Dread and Death in the Victorian Workhouse' (in Teodorescu, ed., *Death: Representations in Literature: Forms and Theories*, pp. 157–74) argues that death defines the space of the workhouse and the administration of the New Poor Law. Vazquez looks at memoirs, novels, poetry, and essays and shows how each of them represents paupers' 'fears of being mistreated as inmates and dying in the confines of the workhouse' (p. 159). The essay includes Charles Dickens's *Oliver Twist* [1838] alongside less well-known works, such as Thomas Doubleday's *A Political Pilgrim's Progress* [1839] and W.J. Linton's 'Bob Thin, Poorhouse Fugitive' [1845]. Ultimately Vazquez argues that death 'is a powerful symbol and force that these varied texts use to evoke sympathy, to humanize the inmates of the poorhouse, and to critique the treatment of the poor' (p. 160).

Another institution that connects the city with surrounding towns, the postal service, is the topic of Andrew A. Kuhn's essay, 'The Postal Imagination of Lady Gregory, Thomas Clarke, and Rabindranath Tagore:

Writing the Irish Post' (*ELT* 58[2015] 220–40). This article examines the relationship between literature and the postal service in the late nineteenth and early twentieth centuries. Kuhn argues that like other literary institutions such as publishers and printers, the postal service was 'a vital link in all of the stages between author and reader' (p. 221). Kuhn examines postal representations in Irish texts, including Lady Gregory's *Hyacinth Halvey: A Comedy* [1906], Thomas Clarke's *Glimpses of an Irish Felon's Prison Life* [1912–13; 1922], and Rabindranath Tagore's *The Post Office* [1913] and short story 'The Postmaster' [1918]. Kuhn focuses on the postal service in Ireland because it highlights where this 'grand communication network seemed to fray at the edges' (p. 220). In addition to its focus on the Royal Mail, then, this article also intersects with conversations about Irish politics.

'Nineteenth-Century London as Monstrous Body' by Laura Di Michele (in Calzoni and Perletti, eds., *Monstrous Anatomies: Literary and Scientific Imagination in Britain and Germany during the Long Nineteenth Century*, pp. 193–215), appears in a book collection about the abnormal body and its representations in literary and scientific texts. Di Michele discusses the way the city of London itself was constructed as a frightening place of slums, drunkards, beggars, and prostitutes. The essay discusses elements that contributed to this view, such as pollution and plagues, and provides interesting primary source quotations. One last article related to the city by virtue of its opposite, 'Villages and Village Life Observed, Remembered, and Imagined' (*Victo* 5[2015] 201–18), by Barry Sloan, uses a selection of novels, stories, and essays written between 1812 and 1912 to examine the village as a 'point of reference reflecting a variety of social and cultural concerns and changes' (p. 202). The essay examines Maria Edgeworth's *The Absentee*, Mary Mitford's *Our Village*, Richard Jefferies's 'My Old Village', George Moore's 'Home Sickness', and George Sturt's *Change in the Village*. By looking at this expanse of time, Sloan can analyse changes to how the village was represented as it evolved in relation to the city. Sloan is particularly interested in the 'complex emotional, psychological, and ideological questions prompted by relationship between individuals and the villages they have observed, remembered or imagined' (p. 217).

Print culture continues to be important to Victorian studies, as Barbara Leckie's review essay, 'On Print Culture: Mediation, Practice, Politics, Knowledge' (*VLC* 43[2015] 895–907) discusses. Leckie takes stock of what has happened to studies of print culture since Laurel Brake's 2001 essay 'On Print Culture: The State We're In'. Leckie reviews books that have engaged with the term, though she qualifies that she is not presenting a comprehensive survey of the field. She instead chooses works that help articulate some aspects of the term 'print culture' that help us to think of both the term's capaciousness and its boundaries. The books in her review include: Dallas Liddle's *The Dynamics of Genre: Journalism and the Practice of Literature in Mid-Victorian Britain* and Matthew Rubery's *The Novelty of Newspapers: Victorian Fiction after the Invention of the News*, both published in 2009, James Mussell's *The Nineteenth-Century Press in the Digital Age* [2012], Sukeshi Kamra's *The Indian Periodical Press and the Production of Nationalist Rhetoric* [2011], Ian Haywood's *The Revolution in Popular Literature: Print, Politics,*

*People, 1790–1840* [2004], Alberto Gabriele's *Reading Popular Culture in Victorian Print* [2009], Ann L. Ardis and Patrick C. Collier's edited collection, *Transatlantic Print Culture 1880–1940: Emerging Media, Emerging Modernisms* [2008], Elizabeth Miller's *Slow Print: Literary Radicalism and Late Victorian Print Culture* [2013], Paul Keen's *Revolutions in Romantic Literature: An Anthology of Print Culture, 1780–1832* [2004], Andrew King and Jon Plunkett's *Victorian Print Media: A Reader* [2005], Colette Colligan and Margaret Linley's edited collection, *Media, Technology, and Literature in the Nineteenth Century: Image, Sound, Touch* [2011], Beth Palmer and Arlene Buckland's edited collection, *A Return to the Common Reader: Print Culture and the Novel, 1850–1900* [2011], *How to Do Things with Books in Victorian Britain* [2012] by Leah Price, and Linda Hughes's 2014 essay, 'SIDEWAYS! Navigating the Material(ity) of Print Culture'.

While there was a wealth of articles on print culture and periodicals, only one monograph stands out this year, but it is exemplary of what a focus on print culture can produce. Mary L. Shannon's *Dickens, Reynolds, and Mayhew on Wellington Street: The Print Culture of a Victorian Street* begins with a photograph, which does indeed 'tantalize' us, as Shannon describes, for its unfulfilled glimpse of a side street off of the Strand. The image is of Wellington Street, and Wellington Street quickly becomes the captivating subject of Shannon's book as she details all of the important connections this street had to prominent authors and publishers. The kind of revelations produced by this focus on one street allow Shannon to make claims like 'this book reveals, for the first time, that Dickens, Reynolds, and Mayhew all had offices on the same London street' (p. 3). A small detail like this leads to important observations about literary networks and print culture from the period 1843–53. Further information about this geographical location also promotes a fuller understanding, Shannon argues, of these writers' works. Her book joins larger discussions about 'what kind of community, if any, is created by print culture' (p. 4).

The book reads like a 'life in the day of' Wellington Street, with each section organized around times of the day. Chapter 1, 'Morning', discusses the layout of the street and the community of editors as they arrive at work, a community used by Dickens when he addresses an imagined network of readers in 'The Preliminary Word'. Chapter 2, 'Afternoon', reconstructs the 'radical tradition' of Wellington Street and how this influenced the work of Reynolds. Chapter 3, 'Evening', examines the interactions between theatrical and print communities. Shannon argues that an awareness of theatre audiences influenced how Mayhew, Reynolds, and Dickens conceived of readers. Chapter 4, 'Night', traces the Wellington Street network out of its physical proximity to the network established in colonial Melbourne. Shannon analyses Marcus Clarke's 'A Night at the Immigrant's Home' to show the links between a night in Wellington Street and a night in Melbourne. The conclusion turns to Dickens's *Bleak House*, and Shannon illustrates how a close knowledge of one street can enhance a close reading of a novel. Shannon sets out to destroy the myth that city life is experienced by individuals in isolation, and her story of this one street helps to dispel that myth while providing a deeper understanding of Victorian print culture and literary networks.

Another monograph on print culture is really a biography, but Peter Blake's subject, George Augustus Sala, is an important figure in the world of Victorian journalism. *George Augustus Sala and the Nineteenth-Century Periodical Press: The Personal Style of a Public Writer* surveys the attention given to Sala, including two monographs published in 1942 and 1997, an edition of his letters to Yates, and the increased critical consideration alongside the body of work on nineteenth-century journalism. But Sala's status is still one 'we are more likely to stumble across while looking for something else' (p. 10). In this book, Blake is particularly interested in showing how influential Sala was on the New Journalism of the 1880s and 1890s. He aims to achieve this goal with a comprehensive look at Sala's work, including all of the various genres that make up Sala's oeuvre, fiction, essays, and visual innovations.

Chapter 1, 'A Visual Apprenticeship', covers Sala's childhood and early life, during which he was introduced into the illustrative world. His work with the visual medium, Blake argues, was a vital influence on his later writings. Chapters 2 and 3, 'Tale of Two Cities: Parts 1 and 2', cover Sala's work with Dickens on *Household Words*. Chapter 4, 'Interlude—A Russian Digression', follows Sala to Russia, where he first became interested in fiction writing. Chapter 5, 'Novelist and Man of Letters', assesses Sala's transition from journalist to novelist. Chapter 6, ' "There really is a world outside Fleet Street": Completing the Journalistic Education: Sala as Special Correspondent', traces Sala's career as a foreign correspondent for the *Daily Telegraph*. In chapter 7, ' "The flogging to be efficacious must be severe": Sala and Flagellation Pornography', Blake examines Sala's coverage of pornography (he published two books on this topic) as well as his work in the flagellant correspondence column phenomenon. Finally, in his conclusion, Blake reflects on Sala's influence on turn-of-the-century journalism. The breadth and depth of Blake's look at Sala's life and writing do much to position Sala as an important figure in Victorian literature.

One article demonstrates the importance of the print culture for inciting social action. In ' "[T]o bind together in mutual helpfulness": Genre and/as Social Action in the Victorian Antivivisection Press' (*JMPS* 6:ii[2015] 134–60), Susan Hamilton provides background on the state of anti-vivisection thought in the late nineteenth century before examining the formal similarities and differences of two anti-vivisection periodicals—*The Zoophilist* and the *Home Chronicler*. After the 1876 passing of the Cruelty to Animals Act, these publications and their public appeal entered a period of mass popularity. Hamilton addresses such questions as what advocacy they inspired in their readers, and how their presentation and generic format affected their audience and enabled it to attain a state of awareness and activity.

An essay by John Sutherland relates to one of print culture's import- ant institutions, the library. 'Literature and the Library in the Nineteenth Century' (in Crawford, ed., *The Meaning of the Library: A Cultural History*, pp. 124–50), appears in a collection that examines the human tendency to collect, contain, and sort books. Each essay focuses on the tensions that arise in the library's usefulness, structure, and practices. Sutherland explores two book phenomena in the Victorian period that were at odds with one another. On the one hand, books abounded and access was easier than ever. Here,

Sutherland traces legislation and technological improvements to show this proliferation of materials and literacy. In contrast to this access, libraries often functioned to control reading; Mudie's Select Library is the most famous example. The *Victorian Periodicals Review* continues to be instrumental in furthering the study of print culture. The articles reviewed here include a range of topics from state-of-the-field assessments to the periodical essay's engagement with politics, from analysis of the style of whole periodicals to individual texts. Articles about serialized novels are covered in the relevant section on the novel below.

Laurel Brake has an article in each issue this year. In 'London Letter: Researching the Historical Press, Now and Here' (*VPR* 48[2015] 245–53), part of the special issue discussed below, she looks at the 'inertness' of text in the digital age. Brake takes an inventory of the state of print, which 'is nudged towards the graveyard of the archaic'. She addresses particular problems to continued and future scholarship, such as failures to digitize particular periodicals and difficulties of access. Her argument is aimed against such limitations. In 'Looking Back' (*VPR* 48[2015] 312–22), from the special issue 'A Return to Theory' discussed below, Brake provides a retrospective of *VPR*, which began in 1989, looking at its progress through the years. Some of the most important advances include the popularization of new critical lenses and the extension of scholarship to authors' journalism and secondary works. And in 'Nineteenth-Century Newspaper Press Directories: The National Gallery of the British Press' (*VPR* 48[2015] 569–90), Brake focuses on the nineteenth-century move to gather 'information ... to measure, record, circulate, and take stock, as well as to facilitate oversight, improvement, and surveillance', which manifested most clearly in press directories such as *Index to the Times, Railway Timetables,* and *Index of Periodicals.* Laurel Brake looks at these texts, providing a thorough examination of their market, audience, evolution, and relationship to the press.

Hugh Craig and Alexis Antonia, in 'Six Authors and the *Saturday Review*: A Quantitative Approach to Style' (*VPR* 48[2015] 67–86), look at the innovative style of the *Saturday Review* by focusing on six frequent contributors: Walter Bagehot, Robert Cecil, G.H. Lewes, Eliza Lynn Linton, Anne Mozley, and Leslie Stephen. The authors' intent is to locate the position of the *Saturday Review* within the greater nineteenth-century periodical discourse. Dallas Liddle's 'Genre: "Distant Reading" and the Goals of Periodicals Research' (*VPR* 48[2015] 348–402) calls for scholarly awareness of 'forms and patterns of genre' (p. 384). He examines forms such as the 'leading article', but he also acknowledges the difficulties posed to generic analysis: for example, the issue of identifying genres, and, more importantly the inherent value in pursuing these questions.

Tom Gretton, in 'Richard Caton Woodville 1856–1927 at the *Illustrated London News*' (*VPR* 48[2015] 87–120), writes about artist Richard Caton Woodville's collaborations with the *Illustrated London News*. Gretton devotes special attention to Woodville's 'representations of encounters between Europeans and indigenous peoples in Oriental settings'. This essay focuses chiefly on the empowering active relationship and subsequent symbiotic authority resulting from the partnership of artist and media. Also by Tom Gretton, 'Waterloo in Richard Caton Woodville's "Battles of the British Army" Series for the *Illustrated London News*, 1893–99' (*VPR* 48[2015] 531–66), addresses Woodville's artistic representations of Waterloo. He looks at the artist's lack of traditional Britishness as a springboard for understanding these pieces of art and, ultimately, for understanding Britishness and the historiography of Waterloo.

Ann M. Hale's 'W.T. Stead and Participatory Reader Networks' (*VPR* 48[2015] 15–41), is this year's winner of the VanArsdel prize. The essay looks at the career of W.T. Stead and illuminates the ways in which he interacted with and encouraged his own readership, developed alter egos, and contributed to the growth of New Journalism. Annemarie McAllister, 'Onward: How a Regional Temperance Magazine for Children Survived and Flourished in the Victorian Marketplace' (*VPR* 48[2015] 42–66), looks at the child temperance periodical *Onward*. McAllister provides cultural background, identifying juvenile societies like the Band of Hope (later Hope UK) and the impressive readership of temperance publications. The author draws distinctions between *Onward* and some of its rival papers such as the *Band of Hope Review*, ultimately focusing on *Onward*'s family-friendliness and efforts to coincide with national and regional identity. Tom O'Malley, in 'Mitchell's *Newspaper Press Directory* and the Late Victorian and Early Twentieth-Century Press' (*VPR* 48[2015] 591–606), focuses on the *Newspaper Press Directory*. In this article, he qualifies its value for serious scholarship: 'the *Directory* represented dimensions of the industry over time, including its history, statistics, categories of publication, relationship to empire, and conception of a national press'.

Jeremy Parrott, in 'The Skeleton Out of the Closet: Authorship Identification in Dickens's *All the Year Round*' (*VPR* 48[2015] 557–68), tracks the work of the author to trace the authorship of *The Skeleton in the Closet*. He finds and works with a series of pencilled annotations, and suggests it may have been Dickens himself. By the end of the article, Parrott proposes a two-year endeavour: to 'produce a Lohrli-style index of contributors to *All the Year Round* that would replace Oppenlander's guide'. Margaret D. Stetz, in 'Internationalizing Authorship: Beyond *New Grub Street* to the *Bookman* in 1891' (*VPR* 48[2015] 1–14), looks both at *New Grub Street* and the *Bookman*, exploring their contrasting views on the future of literature. Stetz uses their diametrically opposed perspectives as a way of surveying the state of the Victorian literary climate. She links Gissing's pessimism to 'the incestuous nature of literary London'. The *Bookman*'s positivity, on the other hand, derived from an attitude of possibility. It 'was already oriented toward a newer and wide world' even in its early stages. Stetz brings up themes of imperialism and commercialism.

Mark Turner, in 'Sell's Dictionary of the World's Press: Chronicler and Promoter of the Media Industry' (*VPR* 48[2015] 607–24), addresses 'the ways the press directories help to reveal the shape and workings of the media industry in the late nineteenth century'. Turner's focus is Henry Sell's *Dictionary of the World's Press*. Turner outlines the history of Sell's enterprise (he founded a very successful advertising agency), and looks also at Sell's

*Directory of Telegraphic Addresses* and *Telegraphic Code*. Sell's publications 'bring attention to the ongoing movement of vast communication networks and systems ever outwards into the markets of the world'. Rosemary VanArsdel, in 'The Vann Victorian Collection' (*VPR* 48[2015] 138–41), covers Professor J. Don Vann, 'one of the first American scholars to become interested in first editions of Victorian fiction'. VanArsdel looks at the Vanns and their dedication to acquiring these texts. Vann was the official bibliographer for the Research Society of Victorian Periodicals. He had a passion for first-edition Dickens novels and periodicals. Much of his collection is at University of North Texas.

*VPR* 48:ii[2015] was a special issue, 'Digital Pedagogies', focused on the 'digital turn'. Clare Horrocks and Kim Edwards Keates's introductory essay, 'Digital Pedagogies: Building Learning Communities for Studying Victorian Periodicals' (*VPR* 48[2015] 157–60), highlights the practical effects this digital turn has on the ways that scholars and researchers approach Victorian periodicals. Anne DeWitt, in 'Advances in the Visualization of Data: The Network of Genre in the Victorian Periodical Press' (*VPR* 48[2015] 161–82), makes a case for how network analysis can assist in rediscovering 'genre as a social construction'. She provides graphs made using Gelphi to chart associations between works of a particular type, such as theological and religious novels. Her research leads her to conclude that *Robert Elsmere* spawned its own genre, and she calls for increased attention to network analysis of novels and of articles.

Jennifer Phegley, in 'Rethinking Student Research and Writing in the Digital Age: The *Punch* Historical Archive, 1841–1992 and the NINES Classroom Exhibit Scene' (*VPR* 48[2015] 183–96), presents strategies for formulating paper topics using digital resources. Praising the NINES platform, Jennifer Phegley addresses how she has her students incorporate primary, secondary, and visual sources, all of which can be found on NINES. This article presents NINES as an exemplary module for teaching students and reinforcing for faculty the collaborative nature of periodical scholarship. Caley Ehnes and Kylee-Anne Hingston, in 'Collaborative Knowledge and Merging Media: Teaching Victorian Periodical Print Using Digital Tools' (*VPR* 48[2015] 197–215), provide an overview of advances in the digital humanities, and then use their first-hand experience as teachers to discuss how implementing digital tools in Victorian classes can help students relate more intimately to the 'public and collaborative nature of Victorian periodical publishing firsthand'.

Kristin Mahoney and Kaitlyn Abrams, in 'Periodical Pedagogy in the Undergraduate Classroom' (*VPR* 48[2015] 216–31), discuss how faculty and their undergraduate students can use digital resources to animate their academic lives, even in spite of archival limitations. An example of student writing is presented to demonstrate the value of periodical pedagogy using archival research through *Bookman*. In anticipation of the online *Punch* archive, Seth Cayley and Clare Horrocks, in 'The Punch Historical Archive, 1841–1992: A Sustainable Brand for the Digital Age' (*VPR* 48[2015] 238–43), give a brief review of *Punch*'s cultural impact and enduring relevance for study.

The article emphasizes the archive's sleek user interface and helpful tools as well as stressing its value for contemporary digital scholarship. Bob Nicholson, in 'Tweeting the Victorians' (*VPR* 48[2015] 254–60), writes about social media and its involvement in academic discourse. He is especially concerned with Twitter's power. Nicholson, like many of his fellow essayists, is worried about access to digital archives. Basically, nobody can tweet about a critical article. He suggests that scholarship would be a much richer enterprise if data-mining were acceptable in a widespread fashion. Paul Fyfe, in 'Technologies of Serendipity' (*VPR* 48[2015] 261–6), responds to Patrick Leary's seminal essay 'Googling the Victorians'. Fyfe addresses the role of serendipity in the field of digital humanities. He cites random generation technology and increased enjoyment of discovery through Victorian periodical technology. Leary publishes a new article in this special issue. In 'Response: Search and Serendipity' (*VPR* 48[2015] 267–73), he responds to this issue's contributors. His greatest call is to deduce patterns within the surfeit of information that scholars are now presented with. As always, he concludes, it is the search that matters more than the answer.

*VPR* 48:iii[2015] was a special issue entitled 'A Return to Theory'. The issue begins with an article by Linda Hughes, 'Remembering Linda Peterson' (*VPR* 48[2015] 300–6), which memorializes Linda Peterson, who died on 25 June 2015. Hughes discusses Peterson's specific contribution to the field and her legacy. Margaret Beetham, in 'Time: Periodicals and the Time of the Now' (*VPR* 48[2015] 323–42), takes on the question of theory's utility. She wonders how twenty-first-century notions of time have changed scholarship's approach to periodicals. Her article encompasses advances in capitalism as well as key periodicals, *The Queen*, the *Lady's Newspaper*, and *Mothers' Magazine*. James Mussell, in 'Repetition: or, "In our last"' (*VPR* 48[2015] 343–58), addresses 'the relationship between seriality and materiality, particularly the way repetitive serial forms create particular ontological conditions, both in the present as periodicals are being published and in the past once publication has ceased'. Mussell uses *Household Words* as an example. He broaches questions of a reader's agency in relationship to formal and generic fixity. Finally, he praises how digital archives 'demonstrate how much more there is to know about print and print culture'. Nathan Hensley, in 'Andrew Lang and the Distributed Agencies of Literary Production' (*VPR* 48[2015] 359–82), looks at Andrew Lang's notion of literary networks, applies them to the sociological works of Latour and Pierre Bourdieu, and then concludes with an examination of Lang's fairy stories. The central idea is that of the relationship between continuity and modification. Dallas Liddle's 'Genre: "Distant Reading" and the Goals of Periodicals Research' (*VPR* 48[2015] 403–27) calls for scholarly awareness of 'forms and patterns of genre'. He examines forms such as the 'leading article', but he also acknowledges the difficulties posed to generic analysis: for example, the issue of identifying genres, and more importantly the inherent value in pursuing these questions.

*VPR* 48:iv[2015] included a special series on Waterloo, introduced by Christopher Keirstead and Marysa Demoor in 'Introduction: Waterloo and Its Afterlife in the Nineteenth-Century Periodical and Newspaper Press' (*VPR* 48[2015] 447–50). An event of mythic stature from the outset, Waterloo's significance only grew in the intervening decades, and this introduction makes the case that Waterloo, and so many paradigmatic conflicts that would follow, will continue to resurface in new and shifting forms. 'No such conflict ... ever really achieves anything akin to ideological or historical "closure" ... The battle, in some sense, continued to be refought in the press over the course of the nineteenth-century.' Marysa Demoor, in 'Waterloo as a Small "Realm of Memory"': British Writers, Tourism, and the Periodical Press' (*VPR* 48[2015] 453–68), looks at the efforts of such writers as William Makepeace Thackeray, Lord Byron, and William Wordsworth, who each visited the battlefield of Waterloo and then wrote about it. Their writings helped to bolster national pride and identity. Furthermore, she writes about the press's complicity in promoting these works, and the implications of this complex relationship to Waterloo. Ann Collins, in 'Courts Martial and Libel: A Waterloo Officer's Military Career and the Contemporary Press' (*VPR* 48[2015] 487–510), focuses on the protracted series of court martials issued against Captain John Tucker, as well as a libel case raised against Tucker by his former commander. The article emphasizes the role of the *Military Register* for its public involvement in these affairs.

Works in the area of art this year tended to focus on the Pre-Raphaelites or visual studies. In *Disillusioned: Victorian Photography and the Discerning Subject*, Jordan Bear writes that a study of photography is more than just 'one more chapter' in the study of Victorian representational and epistemological debates, forming instead a foundation for such enquiries into the production of knowledge. Bear provocatively contends that photography's objectivity was not a given in Victorian culture. In the introduction, 'The History of Photography and the Problem of Knowledge', Bear traces political liberalization and its connection to a consumer culture. Increased emphasis on policies such as laissez-faire economics resulted in increased pressure on individual discernment. The primary metaphor for this agency was visual, and visual discernment became the 'key for mediating the individual's agency and his place in the community' (p. 4). In tracing this social and cultural history, Bear shows that photography emerged amidst questions of representation. Photography grew less objective, emerging rather as another contested object for political agency and commercialized freedom of choice.

After the first chapter, 'See for Yourself: Visual Discernment and Photography's Appearance', Bear turns to two case studies. Chapter 2, 'Shadowy Organization: Combination Photography, Illusion, and Conspiracy', examines one of the most controversial images of the composite or combination photography method, Oscar Gustave Rejlander's *Two Ways of Life* [1857]. The subject matter of this photograph is industrial society, and Bear argues that the 'seams' were 'implicated in an urgent debate about how the bond between the individual worker and a collective industrial society was to be organized' (p. 6). Chapter 3, 'Same Time Tomorrow: Serial Photographs and the Structure of Industrial Vision', considers photography's mass production, the serial mode of production, and the 'emergence of an attendant mode of visual discernment' (p. 6). These serial images suggested how reality could no longer be found in one image, as Bear demonstrates through the work of Henry Peach Robinson. Bear next turns to issues of collaboration.

Chapter 4, 'Hand in Hand: Gender and Collaboration in Victorian Photography', examines the work of renowned photographer Julia Margaret Cameron and her photographs done in collaboration with Rejlander. Chapter 5, 'Signature Styles: Francis Frith and the Rise of Corporate Photographic Authorship', takes on the question of attribution. Chapter 6, 'Indistinct Relics: Discerning the Origins of Photography', continues to explore the previous chapter's questions about attribution as Bear engages with the efforts of the Photographic Society of London in the 1860s to decide who was responsible for inventing photography itself. The final chapter, 'The Limits of Looking: The Tiny, Distant, and Rapid Subjects of Photography', traces the conceptual changes that emerged once the new technologies of photography separated the photograph from vision, what Bear refers to as the 'denigrating of human vision' (p. 8). One of Bear's most interesting claims is that a study of photography helps foreground the inconsistencies and irregularities of knowledge production and the relationship between representation and reality that influenced so many areas of Victorian culture, including that of literature.

One article looks at another visual technology, the kaleidoscope. 'Kaleidoscopism: The Circulation of a Mid-Century Metaphor and Motif' (*JVC* 20[2015] 509–30), by Nicole Garrod Bush, examines the importance of the kaleidoscope to Victorian visuality and ideas about abstraction. Bush builds from Helen Groth's work on the 'kaleidoscopic metaphors' used in Romantic poetry to show how the kaleidoscope continued to be important in the Victorian period.

Julia Straub's essay, 'Nineteenth-Century Literature and Photography' (in Rippl, ed., *Handbook of Intermediality: Literature-Image-Sound-Music*, pp. 156–72) appears in a collection that is the first volume of the new De Gruyter series, Handbooks of English and American Studies: Text and Theory. Part II of this volume, 'Music, Sound and Performance', focuses on musico-literary relationships, theatrical intermediality, literature–dance encounters, and video games. In her essay Straub discusses how photography changed notions of seeing and representing. Importantly for realist practices in literature, photography influenced discourses about the real. Straub also examines how writers such as George Eliot, Nathaniel Hawthorne, Thomas Hardy, and Henry James engaged directly with photography in their works.

In 'Pre-Raphaelitism, Science, and the Arts in *The Germ*' (*VLC* 43[2015] 689–703), John Holmes asks: 'What should the place of science be in artistic renderings?' This question was debated in the Pre-Raphaelite periodical *The Germ* in several essays. Holmes reads these essays together to show how embedded a 'mid-Victorian ideal of science' was to the way Pre-Raphaelites theorized their artistic projects (p. 690). Together these essays also represent the early stages of what would emerge later as the polemical debate between Hunt and Rossetti over competing visions of Pre-Raphaelitism. Holmes also argues that the presence of this debate in *The Germ* marks the periodical's importance, despite its short-lived career, as forwarding an important theory of art modelled on science.

Shalini Gall's essay, 'A Pilgrimage to Bond Street: William Holman Hunt in the Middle East' (*JPRS* 24[2015] 63–77), examines Hunt's anthropological method of painting in his works that came from his Middle Eastern travels.

Hunt's paintings were seen as truthful representations of Jewish people, but did not conform to expectations for images of Christ. Hunt's work engaged with anthropological debates about 'the nature of human difference and its relationship to the concept of race' (p. 66). Through this examination of Hunt's paintings we see the intersections of art, religion, and science in discourses of orientalism and imperialism.

Replete with 180 colour and 120 black and white illustrations, the quarto-size volume *Samuel Palmer: Shadows on the Wall* by William Vaughan, emeritus professor of the history of art at Birkbeck College (reviewed here by William Baker), illuminates the life and work and times of Samuel Palmer (1805–81). Vaughan's work is a development from his long-standing concern with 'the connections between Samuel Palmer's extraordinary early landscapes and the transcendental aspects of the European-wide Romantic movement of his day'. Vaughan's study, in addition to examining in greater detail than has previously been undertaken 'aspects of Palmer's early life that have up to now remained obscure', also looks 'at Palmer's later career, suggesting that it played a more central role in the Victorian idealistic artistic movement than has previously been conceded' (p. ix). Following a detailed introduction (pp. 1–11), Vaughan's double-column printed text is divided into five sections: 'Beginnings, 1805–1822' (pp. 15–50); 'Discovering the Primitive, 1822–1826' (pp. 53–130); 'Shoreham, 1826–1835' (pp. 132–222); '"Real Life": The London Career, 1835–1861' (pp. 223–312); and 'Retreat and Recovery, 1861–1881' (pp. 314–78). Following the text is a listing of abbreviations (p. 379), triple-columned notes arranged by chapter (pp. 380–94), a selected bibliography (pp. 395–7), and a detailed triple-column index (pp. 398–411). Vaughan's final chapter, 'Reputations: Modernity and the Palmeresque' (pp. 365–78), examines the responses by Dante Gabriel Rossetti and other Victorians to Palmer's work, the 'initial response' following his death (p. 365), 'Yeats and the Symbolists' (pp. 366–7), 'Palmer and the Modernists' (pp. 367–70), and 'From Neo-Romanticism to Environmentalism' (pp. 371–6). This excellent book comes with a front and back jacket illustration of detail from Samuel Palmer's watercolour *Classical River Scene* (*c*.1878–81), now at the British Museum.

Neo-Victorian studies received some attention this year in the form of an intriguing monograph and a special issue. *Neo-Victorian Freakery: The Cultural Afterlife of the Victorian Freak Show* by Helen Davies begins with a reflection on the issues of representation inherent in the neo-Victorian act of reinterpreting the past. Davies turns to the Victorian freak show to ask questions of neo-Victorian representation. Each chapter looks at a specific performer to compare the nineteenth-century and neo-Victorian representations. Davies's study adds to neo-Victorian conversations around gender, sexuality, race, and class by adding the issue of disability, or more generally of bodily difference. She looks at the concern over appropriation as well as the possibility for identification as a move towards social justification. Her book is thoughtful and nuanced, navigating the ethical concerns in the act of remembering and representing a group whose perspective has been lost to history.

Chapter 1, 'Mixing (Re)Memory and Desire: Constructing Sarah Baartman', engages with the career of Sarah Baartman. Davies argues that '"re-membering" bodies marked as abnormal, freakish, or "other" raises crucial ethical questions about the author who reanimates such bodies, and the position of the reader who is encouraged to share in the process of textual/ corporeal reconstruction' (p. 6). Chapter 2, 'Separation Anxieties: Sex, Death, and Chang and Eng Bunker', examines the conjoined twins Chang and Eng and the speculation surrounding their sex lives. Davies examines several Mark Twain texts featuring twins, as well as neo-Victorian novels by Darin Strauss and Mark Slouka that adopt first-person narrative perspectives of the twins. Chapter 3, 'Excessively Feminine? Anna Swan, Gendering Giantesses, and the Genre of the "True Life Story" Pamphlet', considers two issues, one social and one generic, that converge in Anna Swan's life, how 'big' women trouble feminine ideals, and how the genre of the 'true life story' pamphlet resembles neo-Victorian writing. This chapter in particular illuminates the tension of freak shows between a site of agency and resistance for the performers and a space that commodifies their bodies. Chapter 4, 'Innocence, Experience, and Childhood Dramas: Charles Stratton and Lavinia Warren', examines how constructions of childhood are used by Victorians to structure discourses of dwarfism. In chapter 5, 'The Strange Case of Joseph and Jack: Joseph Merrick and Spectacles of Deviance', Davies reads Victorian fears and fantasies about 'monsters' like Joseph Merrick and Jack the Ripper alongside the spectacle of disfigured prostitutes. Representations of Merrick follow gendered discourse of 'moral monstrosity' (p. 21). In her afterword, 'The Neo-Victorian Enfreakment of P.T. Barnum', Davies examines three different representations of P.T. Barnum in the neo-Victorian works *Among the Wonderful*, *The Autobiography of Mrs. Tom Thumb*, and *Nights at the Circus*. This conclusion provides Davies with the opportunity to reflect on some of the main issues threaded throughout her text, which Davies describes as 'negotiating the politics of exhibition, of how cultural afterlives might be re-membered in an ethical fashion, and the metatextual lessons that the "enfreakment" of all Victorians, regardless of their bodies, can teach us as the "audience" for the neo-Victorian freak show' (p. 22).

The journal *Victoriographies* has an important assessment of neo-Victorian studies in its special issue 'Neo-Victorian Masculinities', edited by Ann Heilmann and Mark Llewellyn. Their introductory essay, 'To a Lesser Extent? Neo-Victorian Masculinities' (*Victo* 5:ii[2015] ??), begins by calling for a 'broader encapsulation of gender and its re-visioning that includes maleness and masculinity in neo-Victorian portrayals' (p. 99) and draws attention to the lack of attention to Victorian men and masculinity. The essays in this special issue aim to fill this hole by exploring 'the implications of using a portrayal of nineteenth century masculinity aimed at its own "imagined audience" to explore a contemporary sense of the masculine' (p. 101).

'The Late-Victorian "New Man" and the Neo-Victorian "Neo-Man"' (*Victo* 5:ii[2015] 105–21), by Margaret Stetz, traces the construction of the Victorian 'New Man' in neo-Victorian works. These depictions, Stetz argues, attempt to transform current readers' conceptions of gender. Neo-Victorianism has 'offered male and female authors alike a mask through which to speak about millennial masculinity and to express dissatisfaction with it' (p. 113). Stetz compares these neo-Victorian depictions to the way women writers in the late Victorian period represented the New Man.

In 'The Neo-Victorian Doctor and Resurrected Gothic Masculinities' (*Victo* 5:ii[2015] 122–42), Marie-Luise Kohlke examines the Victorian anxiety about professional men reflected in the trope of the Gothicized medical man. The films use conventional portrayals of masculinity contrasted with the film's emphasis of the physical rather than intellectual qualities of men.

Susanne Gruss traces a similar tension in her essay, 'Wilde Crimes: The Art of Murder and Decadent (Homo)Sexuality in Gyles Brandreth's Oscar Wilde Series' (*Victo* 5:ii[2015] 165–82). These mysteries downplay Wilde's sexual transgression but celebrate his flamboyant persona. As Heilmann's introduction reminds us, the neo-Victorian man is faced with 'competing archetypes' (p. 103) that the Victorian critic must remain attuned to. The special issue also includes Nadine Boehm-Schnitker's essay 'Adapting Victorian Masculinities: Oliver Parker's *Dorian Gray* (2009) and Guy Ritchie's *Sherlock Holmes* (2009)' (*Victo* 5:ii[2015] 143–64).

Digital humanities (DH) is vital to the growth of Victorian studies, and many of the publications this year focus on how it improves research methods and deepens our understanding of the period's literature and culture. Some of the articles discuss current DH projects, serving to both inform a wider audience of these resources and provide examples of how DH can work with more traditional forms of scholarly research.

'There is no fate but what we make', writes Dino Franco Felluga. This witty and informative essay, 'The Eventuality of the Digital' (*19* 21[2015] 15 paras.), heralds a new digital tool for nineteenth-century scholarship: COVE, the Central Online Victorian Educator, the spiritual successor of BRANCH—Britain, Representation, and Nineteenth-Century History, 1775–1925. Felluga addresses the cultural climate's spirit of possibility and sets ambitions for the COVE project, which he depicts as relying not on 'crowdsourcing' per se, but on 'insourcing'. He stresses the importance of annotative features in digital projects and lists the tools COVE would incorporate: gaming software, timeline-builders, iOS apps, and an exhibit-maker interface. He calls for funding, without which the COVE initiative will not be possible.

'Mapping "Wordsworthshire": A GIS Study of Literary Tourism in Victorian Lakeland' (*JVC* 20[2015] 287–307), by Christopher Donaldson, Ian N. Gregory, and Patricia Murrieta-Flores, is an essay that discusses the literary tourism of the Lake District in the nineteenth century. Unlike today, when tourists focus on Dove Cottage, in the Victorian period tourists made an attempt to visit a broader range of locations important to Wordsworth, including Rydal Mount, the gardens, his grave in St Oswald's churchyard, and places up and down the coastline. The authors use Geographic Information Systems to more accurately model the relationship between each of these locations.

Bob Nicholson's 'The Victorian Meme Machine: Remixing the Nineteenth-Century Archive' (*19* 21[2015] ?? paras.), begins with a problem: how do we gain a comprehensive understanding of the role of jokes in the Victorian period? Nicholson argues, 'If we want to understand the importance of humour within Victorian Britain, and to unpack the social, cultural, and political work that it performed, then we need to find a way to recover some of these long-forgotten jokes and open them up to scholarly analysis' (pp. 1–2). One way to recover them he suggests is by looking for them in the archives of nineteenth-century print culture, including newspapers, magazines, and periodicals. In order to make digital archives a viable option for searching for jokes, Nicholson argues we must have new ways for organizing digital collections. This article describes his project to do just that with the British Library's digital collections.

In 'Lost Visions: An Interview with Julia Thomas' (*19* 21[2015] ?? paras.), Luisa Calé, with Michael Goodman, Julia Thomas, Ana Parejo Vadillo, and Alexis Wolf, adapt a Twitter interview between Luisa Calé/Ana Parejo Vadillo and members of the Birkbeck Centre for Nineteenth-Century Studies' Lost Visions team in charge of *The Illustration Archive*. The Lost Visions team cites *The Database of Mid-Victorian Illustration*, the *William Blake Archive* (for its keywording system), and the *Rossetti Archive* as influences on their project. They also cite Zooniverse's crowdsourcing ethos. When asked about the philology of their endeavour within the digital humanities, they address the separation of image from text but admit that 'tagging is, after all, a textual act'. Through staging workshops, the team learned the value of testing their platform on blind audiences prior to going live. They broach the reality of crowdsourcing in the twenty-first century, and how crowdsourcing dovetails with image classification. *The Illustration Archives*, they hope, 'replicates leafing through a book for illustrations', but this hope must be tempered—a digital landscape 'emphasize[s] the materiality of the book, but they erase the specificity of the digital'. Nevertheless, an online archive allows for increased freedom of comparison between images and their historicity. One just needs to know how to mediate the pros and cons of separation from context. Luisa Calé asks whether *The Illustration Archives* achieves a 'poetics of illustration', to which the Lost Visions team agrees, stating that they hope that 'the relation between word and image that defines illustration is remediated in a new dynamics between the picture and the other texts that surround it: tags, descriptions, captions, iconographic, and bibliographic metadata'.

In 'Citizen Science: Sally Shuttleworth and Her Team Interviewed by Carolyn Burdett' (*19* 21[2015] ?? paras.), Carolyn Burdett, the editor of *19: Interdisciplinary Studies in the Long Nineteenth Century*, interviews Sally Shuttleworth, Professor of English Literature at St Anne's, University of Oxford, and her colleagues Gowan Dawson, Geoff Belknap, and Alison Moulds. They discuss their work with Zooniverse, the 'Web portal of the Citizen Science Alliance', which has a user base of 1.3 million; specifically, their focus is on science-specific periodicals from the nineteenth century. Gowan Dawson defines Citizen Scientists: 'volunteer workers in science who are producing real, genuine, elite, top-quality science and this, in part, is because of ... very large data sets. The Zooniverse motto is "The universe is too big to explore without you"'. Throughout the course of the interview, they discuss the parallels between the periodical-based 'information revolution' of the nineteenth century with the Internet-based one of the present. Burdett enquires as to the motivating force prompting ordinary laypeople to participate, the answer being that people like knowing that they're contributing to the future of science. Other topics broached in the interview include the intergenerational aspect of crowdsourcing projects; the salutary nature of public engagement; the Internet's 'imagined community' as life-giver for Citizen Science initiatives; transnational reactions to the phrase itself; and the hope that Zooniverse might one day 'transform the ways in which science is understood in its relationship to childhood and scholarly education'. They also touch upon how failure may be used as a positive parameter in understanding the future direction of various Citizen Science undertakings. Audio for the entire interview may be accessed on Soundcloud via a link in the article.

Virtual Victorians: Networks, Connections, Technologies by V. Alfano and A. Stauffer covers the intersection between reality, imagination, vision, mediation, and virtual technologies. This collection balances theoretical discussion and practical application. Each chapter selects one area related to virtual technologies and one specific writer or text as an example. Section I, 'Navigating Networks', explores current research methods in an age of online and digitized sources. The authors of each of these chapters will often share their own personal experiences with digital media use and creation. In chapter 1, 'How We Search Now: New and Old Ways of Digging Up Wolfe's "Sir John Moore"' (pp. 11–28), Catherine Robson discusses the hybrid nature of research that depends both on digital searches and close reading of non-digitized material, and how skills in both are required of researchers in the nineteenth century. Chapter 2, 'Viral Textuality in Nineteenth-Century Newspaper Exchanges' (pp. 29–56), by Ryan Cordell, tackles the idea of networks by tracing the circulation of texts, including reprints. Chapter 3, 'Networking Feminist Literary History: Recovering Eliza Meteyard's Web' (pp. 57–82), by Susan Brown, considers issues of feminist approaches to research by comparing the research tools of Google and the Orlando project. In chapter 4, 'Frances Trollope in a Victorian Network of Women's Biographies' (pp. 83–106), Alison Booth discusses her project Collective Biographies of Women (CBW), using Frances Trollope as a case study. Michael E. Sinatra begins chapter 5, 'Representing Leigh Hunt's Autobiography' (pp. 107–20), with a discussion of Hunt's textual revisions to Autobiography. Next, Sinatra highlights the planned Leigh Hunt Archive, explaining the benefit of digital editions, calling for them to 'visibly include both process and product', to be open to multiple contributors and community revisions (p. 114). Chapter 6, 'Visualizing the Cultural Field of Victorian Poetry' (pp. 121–43), by Natalie M. Houston, moves beyond the digital reproduction of one text to encompass the digital reproduction of a whole field.

The second part of this edition turns to Victorian virtuality. In chapter 7, 'Virtual Victorian Poetry' (pp. 145–66), Alison Chapman examines the technology of the serial form by analysing poetry in periodicals. This form of print has virtual resonances because of the hypertemporality of periodicals and their cyclical nature. The next few chapters take up Victorian pictorial technology. Peter Otto's chapter 8, 'Artificial Environments, Virtual Realities, and the Cultivation of Propensity in the London Colosseum' (pp. 167–88), looks at the nineteenth-century Panorama. Chapter 9, 'The Imperial Avatar in the Imagined Landscape: The Virtual Dynamics of the Prince of Wales's Tour of India in 1875–76' (pp. 189–214), by Ruth Brimacombe, focuses on the virtual effects of wood engravings in the periodical press. Chapter 10, 'Steampunk Technologies of Gender: Deryn Sharp's Nonbinary Gender Identity in Scott Westerfeld's *Leviathan* Series' (pp. 215–30), by Lisa Hager, turns to steampunk fiction as a virtual world where binaries are complicated. The final chapter of this volume, 'Strange Fascination: Kipling, Benjamin, and Early Cinema' (pp. 231–50), takes us to the end of the century and the phenomena of cinema, as Christopher Keep argues that the alterity of the virtual is what makes it so powerful. He approaches this claim through an exploration of how early cinema framed experience. Angela Courtney and Michael Courtney, in their essay 'Second Time Around, or, the Long Life of the Victorian Women Writers Project: Sustainability through Outreach' (in Baunstein and Golomb, eds., *Digital Humanities in the Library: Challenges and Opportunities for Subject Specialists*, pp. 263–75), trace the development of the Victorian Women Writers Project through its inception, respite, and revival. They look specifically at the roles of subject librarians in this as a model for other collaborations between subject librarians and digital humanities projects. The authors claim an important goal for their essay, to 'depict DH projects in a large and complex ecosystem that depends on much more than technical capacity' (p. 264). This is a informative article for anyone interested specifically in the Victorian Women Writers Project or in understanding digital humanities or forging their own digital humanities project.

Turning to individual prose writers, two interesting articles on Matthew Arnold discuss his influence on other writers. 'Listening to the Silence: Huxley, Arnold, and Wells' Scientific Humanity' (*Victo* 5[2015] 72–93), by Jan Vanvelk, explores the important debate between Matthew Arnold and Thomas Henry Huxley, a debate that informs many of our current understandings of the 'clash' between literature and science in the Victorian period. Recent scholars have drawn attention to the agreements between Arnold and Huxley, and Vanvelk continues that line of discussion. Vanvelk focuses on the convergence in the theories around the 'duty of the state educational system to establish a democratic citizenry through acculturation' (p. 73). Vanvelk then nuances the similarities and differences between them through a discussion of H.G. Wells, who relies more on Arnold than Huxley. In 'The Stephen Inheritance: Virginia Woolf and the Burden of the Arnoldian Critic' (*CQ* 44[2015] 119–45), Eleanor McNees traces Matthew Arnold's influence on Woolf, especially in her essays. While Woolf's contemporaries criticized Arnold, Woolf was influenced by her father's and uncle's public arguments in his favour. McNees compares Woolf's treatment of Arnold to T.S. Eliot's critical stance, one that both argues with and 'embeds' past critical voices in her work.

Turning to 2015 publications on George Borrow, he continues to receive attention from a group of devoted scholars. Two illustrated issues of the *George Borrow Bulletin* appeared during the year. Ann M. Ridler, in 'A Brief Visit to Istanbul, by the Editor' (*GBB* 10[2015] 3–4), describes a recent visit 'to follow just a little on Borrow's trial in 1844' (p. 3): this is accompanied by colour and black and white photographs (p. 21). The lead article in the spring 2015 number (second series) is also by Ann M. Ridler. Her 'Romantic Borrow and the Mind's Eye' (*GBB* 10[2015] 5–23) is 'primarily concerned with [Borrow's] use of language, with what the word "romantic" meant to him, the different senses in which he used it, and indeed what it might mean to present-day readers of Borrow' (*GBB* 10[2015] 6). A regular feature of the journal is its 'Notes and Queries' section, and in this issue there are nine of these. '(1) Richard Hayward's Love of *Lavengro*' by Paul Clements (*GBB* 10[2015] 23–6) is concerned with 'the Irish travel writer, Richard Hayward, [who] was hugely influenced in his writing by Borrow's *Lavengro* which he read as a young man in the early twentieth century', and draws upon Clements's biography *Romancing Ireland, Richard Hayward 1892–1964* [2014] (p. 23). '(2) "What say you, Sir Watkin?"' by Martin Murphy (*GBB* 10[2015] 27–9) focuses upon 'the name of Sir Watkin Williams Wynn [that] makes several appearance in the pages of Borrow's *Wild Wales* [1862]' (p. 27). '(3) Borrow and *The Sleeping Bard*' by Mark Mawtus (*GBB* 10[2015] 29–34) sheds light upon Ellis Wynne (1670/7–1734), a Welsh poet who took Holy Orders and translated various works into Welsh. Borrow introduced and translated into English his *The Sleeping Bard; or Visions of the World, Death and Hell* [1830]. Michael Skillman's '(4) Real People in *Wild Wales*' (*GBB* 10[2015] 35–41) is the first of three contributions from Skillman, a very active member of the George Borrow Society. In this note Skillman attempts to identify some of the people mentioned in Borrow's *Wild Wales*. His search is extended in his '(5) More Real People in *Wild Wales*: Borrow's Welsh-Speaking Guide' (*GBB* 10[2015] 41–4). Skillman's '(6) And Finally—the Church of England Cat—Out of the Bag?' (*GBB* 10[2015] 44–5) is a note on Borrow, a cat that was dirty, and its ill treatment. '(7). What's in a Name?' by Simon Keeton (*GBB* 10[2015] 45–52) interestingly explores the effect that the word 'Gypsy' had on Borrow and its origins and connotations in Borrow's time. '(8) Night Stirrings in Putney' by John Hentges (*GBB* 10[2015] 52–3 ) is a brief recall of childhood reading. '(9) Heroic Borrow?' by Ann M. Ridler (*GBB* 10[2015] 53–5) discusses 'Borrow's heroic rescue of men from an overturned boat off the shore at Yarmouth in September 1853' (p. 53). The remainder of this issue of the *George Borrow Bulletin* consists of reader's observations (*GBB* 10[2015] 55–8), book reviews, and accounts of recent publications and ephemera of interest to members of the George Borrow Society (*GBB* 10[2015] 58–76).

No less interesting is the autumn number (*GBB* 11[2015]), which opens with accounts of recent events including the April 2015 visit to Portugal by members of the George Borrow Society and future events (*GBB* 11[2015] 2–6). These are followed by Simon Keeton's detailed and extensively documented 'Borrow and the Bible in *Lavengro*' (*GBB* 11[2015] 7–16). There are seven 'Notes and Queries': '(1) *Wild Wales* and Wild Claims?' by Timothy Peters (*GBB* 11[2015] 16–20); '(2) William Mackay and His Acquaintance with George Borrow' by Ann M. Ridler (*GBB* 11[2015] 20–4); ' (3) A Note in Defence of Michael Scot' by Richard Hitchcock (*GBB* 11[2015] 24–5); '(4) George Borrow Out Loud', by Steve Gough (*GBB* 11[2015] 25–7); '(5) 'Our A5 Adventure' by Kate Skillman (*GBB* 11[2015] 27–30)—an account accompanied by colour photographs of exploring 'some more of the Wales that Borrow had described in ch. 23 of *Wild Wales*' (p. 27); '(6) Wrestling Jacob: Borrow and the Methodists' by Ann M. Ridler' (*GBB* 11[2015] 30–6); and '(7) Jeremiah Grant, Highwayman, and Sergeant Bagg', a query from Mark Mawtus (*GBB* 11[2015] 36–7). The remainder of the issue concerns publications, details of Lavengro Press publications (*GBB* 11[2015] 37–43), and Ann M. Ridler's review of Ivan A.W. Bunn's *George Borrow, Oulton and Beyond* (Green Man Publishing [2015]) (*GBB* 11[2015] 43–5). This is followed by a survey of 'Borrow On-Line' and other items of interest including 'Borrow First Editions for Sale' (*GBB* 11[2015] 45–9). Ann M. Ridler contributes 'Borrow Dreaming (1)' (*GBB* 11[2015] 49–50): she 'cannot think of another nineteenth-century writer who refers to dreams and dreaming quite so often as Borrow' (p. 49). There is an account accompanied with black and white plus colour illustrations of the 'Visit of the George Borrow Society to Lisbon and Évora 13–18 April 2015' by Mike Skillman (*GBB* 11[2015] 51–7). This is followed by Simon Hopkins's fascinating 'The Jews of Borrow's Portugal' (*GBB* 11[2015] 57–66). Ann M. Ridler's comments on one of her favourite passages from Borrow's *The Bible in Spain* in her 'A Magic Lantern Show in Fairyland, Ending Chapter 6 of *The Bible in Spain*' (*GBB* 11[2015] 66–70) are followed by the most detailed, well-documented 'A Rubik's Cube on the Road, or From Lisbon to Madrid by way of Évora, Badajoz and Wonderland' by Peter Missler (*GBB* 11[2015] 70–99). Missler demonstrates that 'there are convincing reasons to doubt the validity and veracity of previous reconstructions of the chronology' of George Borrow's journey from Lisbon to Madrid (p. 84).

The Lavengro Press (founded 2014), which produces materials relating to George Borrow, published three impressive works in 2015. The late Angus Fraser and Ann M. Ridler's *George Borrow and Dereham*, accompanied by black and white illustrations, provides a corrective to the perpetuation of 'some long-standing myths about Borrow and Dereham' found in the work of Borrow's first biographer, William Ireland Knapp, in his *Life, Writings & Correspondence of George Borrow* (John Murray [1899]). Ridler's introduction (pp. ix–xvi) is followed by her note on the late Sir Angus Fraser's (1928–2001) 'long planned…revision of his article of 1972 on "George Borrow's Birthplace and 'Gypsy' Ancestry"': Fraser died before being able to complete this (p. 1). His original finding appeared in 1972 in the *Journal of the Gypsy Lore Society* (3rd series, 51: 60–81) (p. 3). The text of his revised version with Ridler's small additions and slight revisions form the remainder of the text (pp. 3–26), followed by notes, including Ridler's additions (pp. 26–9), a reproduction of the 20 June 1906 auction particulars of the sale of Borrow's birthplace (p. 50), followed by a chronological 'George Borrow and Dereham: Select Bibliography' (pp. 31–2). There are six appendices, starting with 'The Reverend Thomas Howes Meets James Philo, by Ron Fiske' (pp. 33–6), the latter (1745–1829) was 'the Clerk of St. Nicholas Church, East Dereham'. Howes (1770–1848) was rector of Fritton church and met Philo during a 'jaunt' into north Norfolk in August 1816 (p. 35). The second appendix by Ridler focuses on 'G.A. Carthew and Borrow's "Inaccuracies"' (pp. 37–40): Carthew (1807–82) was a local historian, although 'there is no evidence that' he and Borrow ever met (p. 37). Ridler also contributes the third appendix, 'The Rev. Benjamin Armstrong and a Link with Borrow's Family' (pp. 41–3).

Armstrong wrote a Norfolk diary that was published in 1963, edited by his great-grandson H.B.J. Armstrong (Hodder & Stoughton), which in the printed version omitted Borrow material. The fourth appendix, by Clive Wilkins-Jones, sheds light on 'Goddard Johnson (1777–1860), Antiquary and Romani Scholar' (pp. 43–8). The fifth appendix consists of 'Samuel Henry Baldrey's Reminiscences of Borrow', by Ridler, with assistance from Ivan Bunn (pp. 48–50). Baldrey was the 'stepson of Burrow's solicitor' (p. 48). The final appendix concerns 'The Gypsy's Parson and Borrow Enthusiast Visits Dereham', a note by Ridler (p. 51). This is a reflection on George Hall's *The Gypsy's Parson, His Experiences and Adventures* [1916].

The second Lavengro Press publication is Angus Fraser's edition of *George Borrow's Tour of Galloway and the Borders 1866*. Ann M. Ridler explains in her foreword that 'this transcription of Borrow's tour of Galloway and the Borders was first produced for private circulation, in an edition of 30 copies to members of the George Borrow Society... in July 2000'. She adds that 'it was to be Fraser's last major study of Borrow's travel notebooks before his sudden death in May, 2001'. It is 'reproduced in its original form except for the addition of further illustrations, some further notes, and additional appendices on Borrow's admiration for Burns and on Borrow in Belfast' (p. x). Fraser's introduction (pp. 1–5) explains the background to Borrow's notebook of his tour, its relation to his other work, and its significance, including the reasons for Borrow's 'distaste for Walter Scott' (p. 5). Replete with black and white illustrations, an alphabetically arranged partly annotated bibliography, divided into works on 'The 1866 Diary', 'Galloway and Border Gypsies', and 'George Borrow and Scotland' (pp. 6–7), is followed by a 'Chronology and Itinerary' (pp. 8–9) and a map (p. 10). Fraser's transcription of 'Borrow's Notebook of his Scottish Tour of 17 July–11 August 1866' (pp. 11–41) is accompanied by footnote amplification. There are eight appendices: the first is 'Correspondence', containing 'the last extant letter from Mary Borrow to her husband. She died two and a half years later at the age of seventy-three. None of Borrow's letters from the Borders is known to have survived' (pp. 42–3). The second appendix relates to 'Borrow's Visit to Kirk Yetholm' (pp. 43–57), connected 'to the final chapter of his *Romana Lavo-Lil: Word Book of the Romany; or, English Gypsy Language* (London: John Murray, 1874)' (p. 43). Appendix 3, 'Galloway and Border Gypsies' (pp. 57–63), is a detailed account of the history of Gypsies in the area. Appendix 4, 'Materials Relating to the 1858 Scottish Tour' (pp. 64–5), is a record of materials relating to Borrow's 1858 expedition to Scotland and its linguistic background (p. 64). The fifth appendix is a partially annotated listing of 'Some Books on Borrow's Shelves (in Chronological Order of Publication)' (p. 65), followed by appendix 6, 'Borrow's Translations from Gaelic' (pp. 66–9), divided into those published (p. 66) and those unpublished (pp. 66–9) arranged by their locations at the Bodleian Library, Oxford, the British Library, the Fraser Collection at the National Library of Scotland, and the John Murray Archive at the same location, the Beineke Library, Yale, the Berg Collection, the New York Public Library, the Harry Ransom Humanities Research Center, Austin, Texas, the Library of the Hispanic Society of America, New York, Rutgers University Library, New Brunswick, New Jersey and the University of Kentucky Library,

Lexington, Kentucky (pp. 66–9). The seventh appendix, 'Borrow's Admiration for Robert Burns' (pp. 69–70), notes Borrow's 'great admiration for the poetry of Robert Burns' (p. 69). The final appendix, edited by Ridler and accompanied by many illustrations, as is the rest of the text, details what we know of Borrow's 1859 Belfast visit. 'Borrow in Belfast' (pp. 71–7) contains useful and at times extensive footnote documentation (see for instance pp. 72–3).

The last Lavengro Press Occasional Papers series to come to our attention published in 2015 is *George Borrow's Moorish Vocabulary (Tangiers 1839)*, edited with an introduction and notes by Simon Hopkins. Accompanied by colour photographic illustrations, Hopkins's richly annotated edition (pp. 41–103) is a transcription of Borrow's hitherto unpublished notebook that passed into the hands of his first biographer, W.I. Knapp, and 'together with much other Borrovian material from the Knapp collection, was subsequently acquired by the Hispanic Society of America in New York, in whose library, as MS Borrow Collection/Knapp 5, it has lain unread ever since' (p. 21). A listing of 'Facsimiles and Illustrations' (p. x), is followed by an alphabetically arranged enumerative bibliography (pp. xi–xiv) and a 'Map of Borrow's Morocco' (p. xv). Hopkins's introduction (pp. 1–39) is divided into ten sections: 'George Borrow (1803–81)' (pp. 1–2); 'Borrow's Approach to Language Study' (pp. 2–8); 'Borrow's Arabic Studies' (pp. 9–15); 'The Genesis of Borrow's *Moorish Vocabulary*' (pp. 15–18); 'The Study of Moroccan Arabic' (pp. 18–21); 'The Manuscript of the *Moorish Vocabulary*' (pp. 21–2); 'Borrow's Method of Transcription' (pp. 22–5); 'The Arabic Language of the *Moorish Vocabulary*' (pp. 25–6); 'Phonology' (pp. 26–31); 'Morphology' (pp. 31–4); 'The Source of the Material in the *Moorish Vocabulary*' (pp. 35–8); and 'The Edition of the Text' (pp. 38–9). Hopkins observes that 'it is not known from whom Borrow gathered his material, nor how many informants contributed to his *Moorish Vocabulary*'. However, its origins are likely to have been 'Jewish' as 'indicated by the presence of (a) Hebrew words and also by (b) specifically Jewish meanings' (p. 35). Hopkins concludes his introduction by writing that 'several of the words of the *Moorish Vocabulary* were subsequently to appear in some of Borrow's published works, in particular *The Zincali* and *The Bible in Spain*' (p. 39), and he points these occurrences out in his most detailed scholarly notes to his edition. The concluding note to this Lavengro Press Occasional Paper, 'About the Author' (p. 104), reveals that Hopkins, the editor of this splendid edition, is a Professor of Arabic at the Hebrew University of Jerusalem.

The neglected anti-Darwinian, pro-Lamarckian, anti-professionalism Samuel Butler (1835–1902) is the subject of David Gillott's *Samuel Butler against the Professionals: Rethinking Lamarckism 1860–1900*. An extensive introduction (pp. 1–19) outlines the parameters of Gillott's study. In his first chapter, 'The Origins of Butler's Lamarckism' (pp. 23–48), he 'traces the origins of Butler's Lamarckism via two routes: his early scepticism regarding the efficacy of infant baptism, and his use and specious misuse of analogy' (p. 17). The second chapter, 'The Attack on Darwin and Professional Science' (pp. 49–80), 'begins with an analysis of Butler's first response to' Charles Darwin's *The Origin of Species*, and shows how he, *inter alia*, draws a distinction between the professional and the layman that would become common in his later works. This chapter concludes 'with an account of Butler's ad hominem attack on Darwin in his later evolutionary works, which demonstrates that, for Butler, the author and the text were part of the same whole' (p. 18). The third chapter, 'The Evolution of Butler's Epistemology' (pp. 81–110), 'examines Butler's evolving epistemology through the lens of his theological writings' (p. 18). In the fourth chapter, 'Anti-Academicism and Lamarckian Aesthetics' (pp. 111–41), Gillott traces 'the connections between Butler's aesthetics, his epistemology, and his ethics' and shows 'that his theories of artistic appreciation and evaluation derive from the ideas set out in evolutionary works and thereby constitute a Lamarckian aesthetics' (p. 18). The fifth chapter, 'Towards a Posthumous Life' (pp. 142–71), considers 'three projects with which Butler was involved in the decade before his death: the *Life and Letters* of his grandfather (1896), his re-engagement with classical Greek literature, and *Shakespeare's Sonnets Reconsidered* (1899)' (p. 19). In his 'Conclusion' (pp. 173–9) Gillott observes that, 'for Butler, the shade of one's posthumous reputation was his alternative to an eternity of heavenly bliss or infernal damnation, and his careful construction of both respectable biological and literary genealogies was calculated to guarantee him the former, as well as to distinguish him from those mercenary professionals who sought only immediate recognition' (p. 173). Gillott concludes that in spite of Butler's 'shameless acts of self-fashioning... his outing of professional cant [that] serves to sensitize our modern-day spin-detectors' and 'the dangerous plausibility of some of the more egregious professional rhetoric, his legacy has not been entirely lost' (p. 178). Each chapter of this challenging monograph is followed by detailed documentation.

Carlyle studies saw an important publication with volume 43 of *The Collected Letters of Thomas and Jane Welsh Carlyle*, edited by Ian Campbell, Aileen Christianson, and David R. Sorensen. This volume contains the letters Carlyle wrote to Jane in the last year of her life. The period covered is October 1865 to June 1866. It should also be noted that the *Carlyle Letters Online* migrated to a new platform this year, hosted by the University of South Carolina's Center for Digital Humanities. *Carlyle Studies Annual* continues to publish interesting work, and the latest number to be published (*CStA* 31[2015/16]) is no exception. It opens with the 'Editors' Note' by Brent E. Kinser and David R. Sorenson (*CStA* 31[2015/16] 1–6), followed by a substantial contribution to scholarship by Kenneth J. Fielding and David R. Sorensen, ' "The supreme comfort of your presence": The Letters of John Forster to Thomas Carlyle, Part 1' (*CStA* 31[2015/16] 7–84). These are transcriptions with extensive annotation of letters now at the Armstrong Browning Library in Waco, Texas. The first part covers letters from 7 February 1849 to 17 August 1872. Bernard Richards, 'William Fox Talbot and Thomas Carlyle: Connections' (*CStA* 31[2015/16] 85–108), discusses Carlyle's recollections of his visits to Paris, and explores the connections between Carlyle and William Henry Talbot, whose own 1843 visit to Paris 'heralded a new age of photographic iconography' (p. 85). Peter L. Caracciolo's 'Microcosm, Macrocosm: Barbara Hardy, Wyndham Lewis, Mrs. Gaskell, and Nineteenth-Century Narrative' (*CStA* 31[2015/16] 109–22) is a tribute to the late scholar Barbara Hardy (1924–2016). Caracciolo movingly discusses Hardy's influence on his own writings. Owen Dudley Edwards, in his 'Carlyle, Burke, and Biography: Biographer Worship and the Biographical in History' (*CStA* 31[2015/16] [123–43), uses Richard Bourke's *Empire and Revolution: The Political Life of Edmund Burke* (Princeton [2015]) and the 'profusion of new writings on Burke' to investigate 'his relation to Thomas Carlyle' (p. 123). In the course of doing so, Edwards pays homage to the work of a friend and colleague, the late Conor Cruise O'Brien (1917–2008).

Travis Mullen and Rachel Mann, in their 'Jane Welsh Carlyle's Social Network and the Lexical Construction of "Home"' (*CStA* 31[2015/16] 145–58), utilize 'Latent Dirichlet Allocation (LDA) topics modeling' from the digital humanities in order to 'solidify the conceptual understanding of Welsh Carlyle's corpus of letters on a larger scale'. The aim of such an approach was 'to see what particular invocations of the concept of home meant on a broader scale within Welsh Carlyle's letters'. The results 'show that Jane Welsh Carlyle used the letter as a way to enter the public sphere and conceived of home as a kind of figurative hub created by and embodied in the act of writing and sending a letter' (p. 147). Sorenson's ' "The best club of all": Thomas Carlyle at the Athenæum, 1853–1872' (*CStA* 31[2015/16] 159–82) acknowledges previous scholarship in providing 'the record of [Carlyle's] participation in . . . the affairs for over thirty years' of the Athenæum. It suggests that Carlyle 'never quite lost the sense that he belonged to "the best club of all"' (p. 180). Helen O'Neill's 'The London Library and the Intelligentsia of Victorian London' (*CStA* 31[2015/16] 183–215) is accompanied by fifteen tables. These range from presenting in tabular format 'London Library members in *ONDB* [*Oxford Dictionary of National Biography*] by date of joining' (p. 193), the 'Frequency of occupation keywords from *ONDB* descriptors' (pp. 194–5), 'Novelists and poets in the dataset' (p. 197), and so on. In her listing of works cited (pp. 212–15), O'Neill refers to previous work on the early years of the London Library but doesn't actually cite most of the scholarship she lists. There is an implicit claim for newness in her article. Such a claim holds up in the context of computational analysis by using computers to count stuff: there is, however, nothing new in counting, just a different way of presenting material on the page. It comes, then, as something of a relief to turn to a new section of *Carlyle Studies Annual* called 'VLLC'. In this, Louisa Yates, Gary Butler, and Brent E. Kinser, 'The Reunification of the Gladstone Archives' (*CStA* 31[2015/16] 219–21), provide an introduction to 'a recently re-discovered notebook in the hand of W.E. Gladstone that will serve as the conceptual blueprint for the reunification of the Gladstone archives in London and in Hawarden, Wales' (pp. 219–20). It is followed by Brent E. Kinser's transcription of 'Gladstone's Notebook' (*CStA* 31[2015/16] 223–50). The 'Miscellanies' section of *Carlyle Studies Annual* includes Brent E. Kinser's 'A Burning Question Answered: The Manuscript of TC to William Graham, 22 April 1835' (*CStA* 31[2015/16] 253–9), which contains 'Carlyle's previous unpublished letter, now transcribed by Kinser from the previously missing manuscript, to his friend William Graham, 22 April 1835, in which he describes the burning of the *French Revolution*, unearthed by Melvin Schuetz at Armstrong Browning Library' (p. 3). The 'discovery in the Gilchrist family archive at the University of Pennsylvania of a hitherto unpublished letter from Captain Thomas Williams Nesham to Carlyle cited in a famous footnote in *The French Revolution*' forms the basis for Sorenson's '"A Trustworthy Gentleman": Carlyle and Admiral Nesham' (*CStA* 31[2015/16] 259–62).

David Southern's 'The Last Will and Testament of Stauros Dilberoglue' (*CStA* 31[2015/16] 262–70) introduces and transcribes the final will of a major figure among the Carlyle circle, the very wealthy and well-connected Stauros Dilberoglue, who 'came to England in 1835' and died in 1878 aged 60. 'He came into the Carlyles' circle through his association with the Jewsbury family, originally of Manchester, where he had worked as a cotton broker before moving to London' (p. 263). Brent E. Kinser's 'A Rather Dodgy Scheme: William Allingham's Pension, 1865' (*CStA* 31[2015] 271–7) describes the background to the poet William Allingham's (1824–89) efforts to get in 1865 an increase in the state pension he had earned in the customs service, and prints his letters to Tennyson, Robert Browning, and Thomas Carlyle, written in an effort to elicit their advocacy and support for his case. David Southern provides an account of 'Carlyleana at Auction' (*CStA* 31[2015/16] 278–90) and a note 'Nero Comes to Agrippina' (*CStA* 31[2015/16] 290–1) in which Southern introduces a newly discovered letter from Carlyle to the 'diarist and frequent correspondent of the Carlyles', Charlotte Williams Wayne (1807–69) (p. 290). The late and much-missed Kenneth J. Fielding's '"His humanity and cordiality as a tutor": Remembering C.S. Lewis' (*CStA* 31[2015/16] 291–7) is a 'memoir of his Oxford tutor C.S. Lewis'. It was written 'on 11 December 1989, at the request of a friend' (p. 291), and is very honest and moving.

'Portraying Presence: Thomas Carlyle, Portraiture, and Biography' (*VLC* 43[2015] 465–88), by Julian North, reads Carlyle's biographical techniques through his interest in portraiture. Just as others have argued that Carlyle's use of history in his biography is significant, North links visual and literary strategies for portraiture. This link is important, North argues, for understanding Carlyle not just as a historian but as someone connected to his contemporary culture. In a note by June Skye Szirotny, 'Thomas Carlyle—Misogynistic or Maligned?' (*N&Q* 62[2015] 418), Szirotny retraces how a misogynistic comment became attributed by scholars to Carlyle, when evidence shows it began as hearsay.

This year saw the publication of the fourth volume of the letters of prominent nineteenth-century British politician Richard Cobden. Edited by Anthony Howe and Simon Morgan, *The Letters of Richard Cobden*, volume 4: *1860–1865* spans a five-year period. The scope of this new volume includes Cobden's negotiation of the Anglo-French Commercial Treaty of 1860 as well as his advocacy for the enfranchisement of the working classes. This volume completes the first critical edition of Cobden's letters and, like the previous volumes, includes an introduction, headnotes to letters, and endnotes. The volume prints 359 of the more than 2,000 letters Cobden wrote during this period. The selection focuses on previously unprinted letters and those letters dealing with important themes in Cobden's personal life, key political events during these years, and those letters that provide insights into the personalities of major figures.

In *Louisa Stuart Costello: A Nineteenth-Century Writing Life*, Clare Broome
Saunders makes the case that Louisa Stuart Costello should be notable on two
accounts: her life spanned nearly the entire century and her work spanned
nearly every genre, including poetry, novels, travel writing, history, biography,
and art. Although she was acclaimed by her contemporaries, like so many
other women writers she 'fell out of fashion' in the twentieth century (p. 3).
Broome Saunders traces the fall and gradual recovery of Costello's reputation,
initially through the growing scholarly field of travel writing. The book is
organized into eight chapters, beginning with a biography and then seven
chapters that each take up a different genre of Costello's writing. The chapters
are as follows: chapter 1, 'Louisa Stuart Costello's Life'; chapter 2, 'Louisa
Stuart Costello's Translations and Medievalism'; chapter 3, 'Louisa Stuart
Costello and Arthurian Legend'; chapter 4, 'Louisa Stuart Costello and
Nineteenth-Century Journalism'; chapter 5, 'Louisa Stuart Costello and
Poetry'; chapter 6, 'Louisa Stuart Costello and Travel Writing'; chapter 7,
'Louisa Stuart Costello, History, and Historical Biography'; and chapter 8,
'Louisa Stuart Costello and Novels'. The book concludes with a transcription
of her obituary written by W.H. Hills.

Darwin garnered a lot of attention this year. Marco Solinas's book, *From
Aristotle's Teleology to Darwin's Genealogy: The Stamp of Inutility*, performs
two tasks at once: it compares the conceptions of living things in the
philosophies of Aristotle and Darwin, and it traces a lineage from Aristotle's
ideas to Darwin's that acts as a history of the life sciences. Solinas organizes
this rather large undertaking through the focus on inutility, or uselessness, as it
appears in concepts such as fixity, essentialism, and teleology from Aristotle
and the way that Darwin overturns each of these. Part I, 'The Aristotelian
Teleological Tradition', focuses on Aristotle, and Part II, 'The Evolutionary
Revolution', focuses on Darwin. Chapter 1, 'The Original Framework', begins
with the theoretical framework for the life sciences as constructed by Aristotle.
Chapter 2, 'For and Against Aristotle', investigates how Aristotle's framework
was revised in the late medieval and modern periods, particularly through
Galileo, but how some elements were retained in the life sciences. Chapter 3,
'Indirect Supremacy', focuses on the seventeenth and eighteenth centuries.
Solinas argues that even though there was widespread disavowal of many of
the Aristotelian principles, the 'theoretical nucleus' remained Aristotelian
(p. 8). His aim in Part I is to show how Aristotle's model survived. Until, that
is, the nineteenth century. Part II opens with the main turning point away
from an Aristotelian framework. Chapter 4, 'Crisis and Hegemony', traces the
'supremacy of fixism to the crisis which befell it' and focuses mainly on
Lamarck (p. 9). Chapter 5, 'Darwin's Breakthrough', turns to Darwin and
how he overturns the teleological system and final causes central to natural
theology. Chapter 6, 'Dry Branches', reveals that Aristotelian theory had not
completely disappeared from Darwinian theory. Yet Solinas reads this
presence as 'theoretical archaisms', evidence of 'the process of gradual
abandonment' (p. 11). Part II thus traces the evolutionary revolution as 'a
process of gradual overturning of the theoretical framework conceived by
Aristotle' (p. 11).

*Autobiologies: Charles Darwin and the Natural History of the Self*, by Alexis Harley, is a provocative take on autobiography in the Victorian period. She looks at the autobiographical writing of Charles Darwin, Herbert Spencer, Harriet Martineau, Oscar Wilde, Edmund Gosse, and Alfred, Lord Tennyson in the context of evolutionary ideas. Harley makes two claims: these writers construct their life stories to illustrate the working of evolutionary theories; at the same time specifics from the writers' lives are often in tension with these evolutionary theories, especially genotype and phenotype. Despite these writers' efforts to show continuity between their ideas about evolution and their self-representations, Harley reveals how they often clash. Her approach gives rise to such intriguing questions as: 'How was Herbert Spencer, who coined the phrase "survival of the fittest", to write a life in which he had neither married nor had children?' (p. xii). The first section focuses on Darwin and includes three chapters: chapter 1, 'Darwin's Family'; chapter 2, 'Naturalist Self-Fashioning and Seeing in Darwin's *Beagle* Diary'; and chapter 3, 'Animal Darwin and the Sympathy Instinct'. Part II then turns to other autobiographical writers with chapter 4, 'Theories of Self-Transformation'; chapter 5, ' "A Natural History of Myself": Herbert Spencer's Individuation'; and chapter 6, 'Harriet Martineau's Autothanatography and the Comtean Self'. The final section, 'Autobiologies', shows 'how readers of evolutionary ideas understood the self as inescapably defined by processes of biological change' (p. xii), and turns to chapter 7, '*De Profundis*, Degeneration and Wilde's Spencerian Individualism'; chapter 8, 'Father and Son: Darwinism and the Struggle of Two Temperaments', about Edmund Gosse; and chapter 9, '*In Memoriam* and the Consolations of Development'.

Harley includes a lucid and informing discussion of evolutionary thought in this period. Harley's is the first book to consider the influence of life-writing on the rise of evolutionism. Life-writing structured ways of experiencing that in turn influenced and gave rise to evolutionary theories. We see this most easily in the way Darwin's *Beagle* diaries enabled his theory to take the form it did, as Harley discusses. In her conclusion, Harley turns to the supplanting of evolutionary theory with genetic theory in the early twentieth century. But the more important change for the purposes of Harley's book was not shifts in evolutionary theory, but shifts away from autobiography as early twentieth-century writers turned away from 'referential discourses and away from the idea of the objective authority of the author' (p. 192). The argument of this book is about the intertextuality of texts and lives, about the 'co-constitution, relational becoming, ramification, elaboration, and transformation between texts, ideas and lives' (p. 193).

Dominika Oramus, in *Charles Darwin's Looking Glass: The Theory of Evolution and the Life of Its Author in Contemporary British Fiction and Non-Fiction*, as its title suggests is concerned with 'Darwinian fictions; Darwinian non-fictions; the theory of evolution as reflected in both of them; and Darwin's life as reflected in both of them'. In other words, 'why and how does today's culture gaze upon the myth of Darwin, his theory, and his life in order to find its own reflection? What image does it find there?—what kind of narcissistic pleasure does it get?—are our times the era of Charles Darwin?—If so, then why?' (p. 14). In addition to discussion of, for instance, 'References to the

Theory of Evolution in the Novels of John Fowles, A.S. Byatt, and Hilary Mantel' (pp. 67–79), other chapters encompass subjects such as 'Echoes of the Mid-19th-Century Spiritual Crisis in Selected Contemporary Texts Referencing Charles Darwin' (pp. 81–94), and 'Darwin's Problem with Human Ancestry as Reflected in Recent Fiction' (pp. 95–107).

Two articles consider Darwin in relation to naturalism. Peter Dear's essay, 'Romanticism and Victorian Scientific Naturalism' (*ERR* 26[2015] 329–40), examines Darwin's relationship to Romantic visions of nature as they are in tension with the more mechanistic view in the Victorian period. To do so, Dear focuses on two aspects of Darwin's work, the classification of organic beings and geological and evolutionary time. Dear argues that nature according to Darwin appears 'machine-like' because of his commitment to the uniformity of nature, and yet it is also infused with human characteristics. Dear thus posits that there is no ontological gap between mind and nature, and that we can therefore see Victorian scientific naturalism as aligned with Romantic sensibilities.

In an interesting piece by Stefan Dolgert, 'Listening in Order Not to Hear? Darwin, Politics, and Sacrifice' (*T&E* 18:i[2015]), Dolgert evaluates the turn in Darwin studies, particularly by feminist philosophers, that frame Darwin as a 'boundary-crossing figure'. Focusing specifically on Elizabeth Grosz's claims that sexual selection based on sexual difference, as described by Darwin, can form the basis for difference more generally. Dolgert raises the concern that such a presentation of Darwin risks anthropocentrism. He also finds some of the tensions in Darwin irreconcilable with feminist and posthumanist politics.

Also published this year on Darwin is volume 22 of the definitive edition of letters written by and to Charles Darwin, edited by Frederick Burkhardt and James Secord. *The Correspondence of Charles Darwin* publishes the letters chronologically, focusing on the year 1874. It includes over 650 letters written and received by Darwin in this single year, with explanatory notes and an introduction that focuses on the events of Darwin's life in 1874.

The recent development of ecological interest in literature has resulted in attention being paid to the life and work of Richard Jefferies (1848–87). A welcome contribution is John Plotz's 'Speculative Naturalism and the Problem of Scale: Richard Jefferies's *After London*, after Darwin' (*MLQ* 76[2015] 31–56), which discusses Jefferies *After London* [1885] in the context of 'naturalism' and observes that is 'an early and critically neglected work of British speculative fiction, [and] is a bellwether of the widely distributed naturalist impulses among novelists responding to the era of scientific naturalism marked by the appearance of Charles Darwin's *Origin of Species* (1859) and *Descent of Man* (1871)' (p. 31). Two issues of the *Richard Jefferies Society Journal* appeared in 2015. The summer issue includes the text of his short story 'A Little Stream' (*RJSJ* 28[Summer 2015] 3–4); a pencil sketch by Jefferies and John Price, 'Richard Jefferies' Broomrape Sketch' (*RJSJ* 28[Summer 2015] 4–7); Phyllis Hargrave's publication of 'Two Letters to Samuel Looker' (who single-handedly did much to revive and recover Jefferies's work in the pre- and post-1939–45 period) (*RJSJ* 28[Summer 2015] 8–10); Janice Langley's ' "Jefferies' Land" and Kipling's *Puck of Pook's Hill* Stories (Part 2)' (*RJSJ* 28[Summer 2015] 11–25)—the initial part appearing in the previous issue. Another comparative essay is found in Roger Ebbaston's 'The Marabar Echo: Forster and Jefferies' (*RJSJ* 28[Summer 2015] 26–9) and W.E. Henley writing on Jefferies followed by an 'Afterword about Henley' (*RJSJ* 28[Summer 2015] 30–5). The summer issue concludes with Rosamond Richardson's 'Richard Jefferies and the Metaphysics of Wild Flowers' (*RJSJ* 28[Summer 2015] 36–40). The winter 2015 issue opens with the text of a Jefferies short story, 'The Monkbourne Mystery' (*RJSJ* 29[Winter 2015] 2–12), and Jefferies's 'The Grave of the Last Abbot' (*RJSJ* 29[Winter 2015] 12–14), followed by George Miller's 'The Gothic Jefferies' (*RJSJ* 29[Winter 2015] 14–15). Peter Robins comments on 'William Strang: The Jefferies Portrait' (*RJSJ* 29[Winter 2015] 16–25). George Miller describes 'The Story of *The Scarlet Shawl*' (*RJSJ* 29[Winter 2015] 26–32). This is followed by Andrew Rossabi's 'Richard Jefferies, the Sensation Novel, and George Gissing's *New Grub Street*' (*RJSJ* 29[Winter 2015] 33–44).

An article on Henry Mayhew, 'The Non-Taxonomical Mayhew' (*VS* 57[2015] 433–44), by Natalie Prizel, offers a reading of Mayhew that emphasizes the non-taxonomical aspect of his work *London Labour and the London Poor*, focusing on its collaborative nature. Prizel focuses on the interaction between Mayhew and his subjects as portraits, where acts of performance and self-fashioning are key to understanding the ethics of representation in his work. Prizel is particularly interested in Mayhew's encounters with disabled or aberrant bodies, and she situates those encounters in what she calls a Victorian visual ethics, 'an ideal of relational looking' (p. 434). See also *Dickens, Reynolds, and Mayhew on Wellington Street: The Print Culture of a Victorian Street* by Mary Shannon, reviewed above.

Routledge Guidebooks has a new edition this year concerning Mill's *On Liberty*, edited by Jonathan Riley. *The Routledge Guidebook to Mill's On Liberty* is an updated version of the 1985 edition, and it includes a new section, 'Mill's Doctrine in Outline'. In this section, Riley attempts to convey Mill's utilitarian doctrine as he has come to better understand it since the first edition. Also added to this edition are substantial revisions, including assessments of recent criticism and clarifications based on Riley's own continued study. Riley also points out a few more specific changes to Part IV, where he frames Mill's form of argument in relation to twelve, rather than the original eleven, questions and adds to his discussion on each question. In this section also he alters his definition of harm to now refer to 'any type of perceptible damage excluding mere dislike or disgust' (p. xxi). Part I, 'General Introduction', provides contexts on Mill's life as well as critical reception, both contemporary and recent, of *On Liberty*. Part II, 'The Argument of *On Liberty*', provides a close analysis of individual chapters, while Part III, 'Mill's Doctrine in Outline', provides a broader analysis of his doctrine of liberty. Part IV, 'General Issues', takes a thematic approach to the work and focuses on liberal utilitarianism (chapter 8); liberty, individuality, and custom (chapter 9); and the doctrine of liberty in practice (chapter 10).

Volume 16 of *The Collected Works of F.A. Hayek* is devoted to Hayek's work on Mill. The entire project is edited by Bruce Caldwell, and this volume, *Hayek on Mill: The Mill-Taylor Friendship and Related Writings*, is edited by Sandra J. Peart. The editor's introduction highlights the primary issues and life events that Hayek followed in Mill's life and that came to light through the Mill–Taylor correspondence. Part I republishes Hayek's book *John Stuart Mill and Harriet Taylor: Their Friendship and Subsequent Marriage*, which first appeared in 1951. Part II, 'Related Writings', includes work by Hayek related to the research and publication concerning this volume; many of the essays are previously unpublished. These include his essay 'John Stuart Mill at the Age of Twenty-Five', published in 1942; 'J.S. Mill's Correspondence', published in the *Times Literary Supplement* in 1943; and 'The Dispersal of the Books and Papers of John Stuart Mill', which is a previously unpublished essay dated July 1944 that provides the starting point for his introduction to *The Earlier Letters of John Stuart Mill, 1812–1848*; also included is the actual introduction to the 1962 volume. Further essays include 'J.S. Mill, Mrs. Taylor, and Socialism', a manuscript discovered in Hayek's son's study; 'Portraits of J.S. Mill', published as a letter to the editor in the *Times Literary Supplement* in 1949; 'Preface to *The Life of John Stuart Mill*', which was published as the preface to Michael St John Packe's *The Life of John Stuart Mill* in 1954; 'Review of Mill and His Early Critics', published in 1957 as a review of J.C. Rees, *Mill and His Early Critics* [1956]; 'Review of John Mill's Boyhood Visit to France', a review published in 1961 of Anna Jean Mill's *John Mill's Boyhood Visit to France: Being a Journal and Notebook Written by John Stuart Mill in France, 1820–21* [1960]; an introduction to an edition of Mill's *Considerations on Representative Government*, which was published in 1962; and 'additional correspondence', which the editors describe as providing 'additional evidence of the enormity of the task before Hayek as he set out to collect the materials eventually published in 1951' (p. 384).

Turning to Morris, in 'William Morris, Extraction Capitalism, and the Aesthetics of Surface' (*VS* 57[2015] 395–404), Elizabeth Carolyn Miller argues that Morris's political writings exhibits eco-socialist views of capitalism. Morris was therefore an 'early adopter of the position that capitalism is fundamentally incompatible with Earth's ecological balance' (p. 395). This is a surprising position for a nineteenth-century critic given the pervasive ideology of classical political economy. 'Nordic Myths in **William Morris'** Works: Contextualization and Recontextualization' by Alessandro Zironi (in Fernandes, Serra, and Fonseca, eds., *The Power of Form: Recycling Myths*, pp. 29–56), argues that more attention needs to be paid to Morris's Nordic interests as they influenced his artistic and revolutionary ideas. Zironi traces the presence of Nordic myths in Morris's writings and lectures.

Another interesting essay on Morris was ' "The many shadows of Amiens": Morris's Early Essays' by Florence Boos. For the full review of her book, *History and Poetics in the Early Writings of William Morris, 1855–1870*, see Section 3 below. In this chapter focused on Morris's early essays, Boos examines how the essays develop Morris's view of a 'democratic art'. She outlines four ideals or principles that appear in his collections of essays such as *Hopes and Fears for Art* [1882] and *Signs of Change* [1888]. Those principles include: the importance of pleasure in labour; the need for simplicity (not privation) in a well-lived life; the role of craft and architecture as repositories of memory and history; and the conviction that humans must live in respectful harmony with the transcendent beauty of nature. Boos also discusses Morris's mentor, Ruskin, as an early precedent for many of Morris's ideas. Boos quotes liberally from an array of Morris's essays from throughout his career, thus providing a comprehensive picture of Morris's aesthetics and his work as an essayist.

There were two important studies on Newman this year. *John Henry Newman: A Portrait in Letters*, edited by Roderick Strange, begins with an assertion: 'More is known about Newman than about most Victorian writers and thinkers, yet people may still wonder who he really was.' This question is best answered by his correspondence: 'through his letters he helped shape his age and he also, vividly and unforgettably, revealed himself' (p. 2). Roderick Strange's introduction discusses the importance of letters to Newman, an explanation of why these particular letters were chosen from the thirty-two volumes. He also touches on some of the key ideas and moments in Newman's life highlighted by the particular letters chosen, such as some of the motives behind his path from Anglicanism to the Catholic Church, and the more practical (as opposed to theological) activities Newman engaged in, particularly once he joined the Catholic Church. Finally, this introduction offers a brief survey of some of Newman's most important friends and family. The collected letters that follow are organized chronologically, and each section is preceded by a short but helpful introduction.

*Receptions of Newman*, edited by Frederick D. Aquino and Benjamin J. King, is a collection of essays that looks not at 'what Newman thought' during various stages of his life, but at 'how others have interpreted his thought' during those various stages (p. 1). Parts I–III focus on the reception of *An Essay on the Development of Christian Doctrine*, *An Essay in Aid of a Grammar of Assent*, and *The Idea of a University*. Part IV provides a broader look at Newman's reception within specific regions and traditions, and Part V examines interpretations of some of Newman's theological thought. Chapter 1, 'The Protestant Reception of the *Essay on Development*, 1845–1925' (pp. 9–29), by Benjamin J. King, discusses Newman's influence on the development of doctrine, which was not an accepted Anglican practice at the start of the century but would be by its end. Chapter 2, 'The Catholic Reception of the *Essay on Development*' (pp. 30–51), by Kenneth Parker and C. Michael Shea, traces the more sympathetic Roman Catholic response to Newman's *Essay on Development*. Chapter 3, 'Philosophical Receptions of the *Grammar of Assent*, 1960–2012' (pp. 53–72), by Frederick D. Aquino, discusses *An Essay in Aid of a Grammar of Assent*, attesting to its relevance to contemporary philosophy. Chapter 4, 'Catholic Theological Receptions of the *Grammar of Assent*' (pp. 73–93), by Mark J. McInroy, traces Roman Catholic responses to *Grammar*. Chapter 5, 'Newman's Circle of Knowledge and Curriculum Wholeness in *The Idea of a University*' (pp. 95–113), by John Sullivan, moves to the reception of *The Idea of a University*, focusing on how the circle of knowledge and curriculum wholeness helped shape today's universities. Chapter 6, 'Historical (Mis)understandings of *The Idea of a University*' (pp. 114–35), by Colin Barr, takes a more historical approach to the *Idea*, tracing the various uses and understandings of the text, with special attention to the conflicted understandings that emerged from Newman's time in Ireland. Chapter 7, 'Newman's Tractarian Receptions' (pp. 137–55), by

Peter Nockles, traces the Tractarian responses to Newman's leadership of the
Oxford Movement. Chapter 8, 'The Reception of Newman in France at the
Time of the "Modernist Crisis"' (pp. 156–76), by Keith Beaumont, looks at
Newman's influence in France, with an emphasis on Newman's French
translator, Henri Bremond. Chapter 9, 'Orthodox Theological Receptions of
Newman' (pp. 177–95), by Daniel Lattier, transitions from the previous
chapters' emphasis on Tractarian thinkers to four prominent Orthodox
thinkers' interpretation to Newman. By looking at Georges Florovsky, George
Dragas, Andrew Louth, and Jaroslav Pelikan, Daniel Lattier argues that a
consideration of the Eastern Orthodox reception of Newman provides a fuller
picture of his thought. The last two chapters look at specific theological issues.
In chapter 10, 'Receptions of Newman on Revelation' (pp. 197–213), William
Abraham writes about Newman's vision of divine revelation. He argues that it
is, 'inescapably epistemic in nature' and should be treated as such. Chapter 11,
'Receptions of Newman the Saint' (pp. 214–32), by Cyril O'Regan, examines
Newman's sainthood and the contesting responses, using Newman's own
discussions of sanctity to shed light on how we can respond to his sainthood.
On Newman, see also Dominic Janes, *Visions of Queer Martyrdom from John
Henry Newman to Derek Jarman*, discussed above.

   Two articles on Pater focus on representations of his personality and
subjecthood. 'Reparative Pater: Retreat, Ecstasy, and Reparation in the
Writings of Walter Pater' (*ELH* 83[2015] 969–86), by Rachel O'Connell,
explores Pater's retreat from the public notoriety that came with his
association with homosexuality after *The Renaissance* and the homosexual
scandal at Oxford. This article aims to read that 'retreat' as neither a resistance
nor a defeat. As O'Connell argues, we need new ways of speaking about
marginalized subjects that 'neither turn that experience into a triumphant
narrative of political resistance nor read it as a defeatist narrative of political
oppression' (p. 971). O'Connell explores the 'fantasies, desires, and impulses'
behind the kind of subjecthood that Pater constructs. O'Connell describes this
subjecthood as 'neither abject nor obviously heroic' but with a 'stubborn core
of vitality' (p. 971). One way to understand this subject position is through
Pater's reconstitution of the notion of 'retreat', from withdrawal and defeat to
refuge, peace, and personal space. O'Connell offers this reading of Pater as a
model for understanding other subjects in queer history.

   In 'Walter Pater: Personality and Persons' (*Victo* 5:iii[2015] 234–50),
Stephen Cheeke tackles the vexed definition of 'personality' as it appears in
Pater's work, as something both essential to the self and yet a 'prison-house of
the self' (p. 236). While many critics, tracing back to T.S. Eliot, find Pater's use
of personality limiting, Cheeke argues for the term's capacious meaning as a
general framework for all of Pater's thinking: 'the primacy of the person is
asserted over and over again, which would seem therefore to offer an implicit
theory of the interpersonal as a kind of structuring principle: ethical, aesthetic
and religious' (p. 238). Cheeke then relates this to Pater's own personality and
how his uneventful life appears in stark contrast to his provocative work.

   This year saw the publication of the fifth and final volume of *The Collected
Letters of A.W.N. Pugin (1812–1852)*, designer, writer, and the leading
architect of the Gothic Revival. This volume, edited by Margaret Belcher,

contains letters dating from 1851 until his death in 1852. They include his work with and in the Great Exhibition as well as important conversations about his interest in faith and form. The volume also includes letters that appeared too late to for publication in the correct chronological volume. Belcher's excellent scholarship in the introduction and notes supplements these letters and showcases Pugin's significance.

Ruskin received considerable attention this year, including the *Cambridge Companion to John Ruskin*. The collection of essays in this volume serve as an introduction to Ruskin and attempt to capture the many vicissitudes of his life and work within the confines of a Cambridge *Companion*. Francis O'Gorman has organized a fine collection of scholars, and the essays cover a variety of topics important to Ruskin's life and work. In his introduction, O'Gorman provocatively states 'readers can have too much faith in him. And part—but not all—of that problem is that faith can outrun knowledge, or at least that faith can be in a complicated relationship with knowledge' (p. 2). This edition attempts to impart knowledge in just that spirit—to present the fullness of John Ruskin in all his complications so readers leave just a little more knowledgeable, and perhaps not the less faithful, about Ruskin. For a full description, see the review by Rachel Dickinson, 'The Cambridge Companion to John Ruskin' (CStA 31[2015] 311-323).

One of the more intriguing elements of Ruskin was his relationship to the visual arts. *Carrying Off the Palaces: John Ruskin's Lost Daguerreotypes*, by Ken Jacobson and Jenny Jacobson, is a tour de force of curiosities. The displays, with illustrations, showcase John Ruskin's collection of daguerreotypes and discuss the source of the photographs, many of which, the Jacobsons argue, were depicted by Ruskin himself. The Jacobsons use Ruskin's letters, diaries, and published writings to affirm his passion for photography, although the collection of images themselves is perhaps the most compelling evidence. One's fascination for this book extends, however, beyond the startling discoveries about Ruskin. The book itself is based on a startling discovery at an auction in Penrith in 2006: a box containing 188 daguerreotypes owned by Ruskin that had been assumed lost after the sale of his Lake District home, Brantwood. This book tells the story of this exciting discovery, the process of preserving and analysing the images, and the implications for our understanding of Ruskin.

'Ruskin's Copies' (*CI* 42[2015] 61–96), by Jeremy Melius, tackles the large question of how 'art and history came to be conjoined', a question for our scholarship today but also one that John Ruskin grappled with (p. 62). With attention to the 'confluence of didacticism and desire' in Ruskin's copies of Old Masters, Melius argues that we can better understand the Victorian period's investment in the historicity of art. Melius focuses his discussion on Ruskin's copy of Zipporah, rendered by Botticelli in his fresco of *The Trials and Calling of Moses* on the Sistine Chapel's south wall. Christiana Payne, in 'John Constable, John Ruskin, and the Pre-Raphaelites' (*BrAJ* 16:i[2015] 78–87), joins the recent reassessment of Ruskin's relationship to the Pre-Raphaelites that questions just how enthusiastically he supported their work. As Payne discusses, Pre-Raphaelite art does not really follow Ruskin's principles as laid out in his praise of Turner. Payne then turns to puzzle over other main sources of Pre-Raphaelite art and considers John Constable's influence. In the opening pages of his book *John Ruskin*, Andrew Ballantyne reminds us that Ruskin is 'one of the key figures for understanding nineteenth-century British culture' for two reasons: he was 'read so reverently and so widely', and his writing performed 'the role of the nation's conscience' (p. 11). The book begins by recounting Ruskin's unusual and complicated childhood. In chapter 1, 'A Start in Life', Ballantyne pays careful attention to those aspects of Ruskin's education and early travels that influenced his writings and paintings. Subsequent chapters discuss the major works of Ruskin's oeuvre, as well as the people who were most important to his critical writings. In chapter 2, 'Turner and the Picturesque', Ballantyne discusses the influence of modern painters on Ruskin, especially Turner. Chapter 3, 'The Pre-Raphaelites', focuses on the Pre-Raphaelites and their relationship to Ruskin. Ballantyne continues weaving details from Ruskin's life throughout each chapter; we learn in this chapter, for example, about Ruskin's marriage to Effie, its annulment, and her marriage to the Pre-Raphaelite John Everett Millais. Chapter 4, '*The Seven Lamps of Architecture*', discusses Ruskin's great work. Ballantyne carefully draws out Ruskin's aesthetic and moral values as they emerge from his critiques of architecture. Ballantyne also shows how unique Ruskin's work on architecture was in its use of empirical observations to draw moral conclusions. Ballantyne continues his focus on buildings and the Gothic in chapter 5, 'Lapping Waves, Living Stones', where he discusses Ruskin's *Deucalion: Collected Studies of the Lapse of Waves and the Life of Stones*, a collection of geological papers. Chapter 6, 'Reform', looks more closely at Ruskin's life after the dissolution of his marriage, charting the decades from the 1850s to the 1880s. Ballantyne is particularly interested in Ruskin's relationships with various women in this period, as well as his evolving political and artistic ideas. Chapter 7, 'Influence', serves as a review and summary of the key moments in Ruskin's life and works, as well as a brief discussion of how Ruskin remains relevant to contemporary ethical concerns and ideas.

Two articles are concerned with Ruskin and political theory. 'Atmospheres of Liberty: Ruskin in the Clouds' (*ELH* 82[2015] 141–82), by Daniel Williams, argues that Ruskin's 'cloud studies', present especially in *Modern Painters* but also appearing throughout his career, are an important aspect of Ruskin's 'inquiry into the character of human liberty' (p. 141). By attending to his arguments about cloud liberty, we can better understand the seemingly incompatible statements he made later about liberty. In the essay ' "Discipline and Interference": Ruskin's Political Economy, Natural Law, and the Moral Disorder of Victorian England' (*JVC* 20[2015] 50–64), Graham A. MacDonald explores Ruskin's turn towards political economy as the subject of his writings in the 1850s. His economic philosophy, as expressed, for instance, in *Unto This Last*, was unpopular with most of his reading audience, including his father. MacDonald outlines where Ruskin's ideas come from, and whether they were indeed so against the grain of dominant economic thought of the time. MacDonald examines the influence of Isaac Taylor's *Natural History of Enthusiasm* [1829], John Keble's edition of the *Laws of*

*Ecclesiastical Polity* by Elizabethan theologian Richard Hooker, and Ruskin's growing relationship with F.D. Maurice and Benjamin Jowett. One article looked at Ruskin and the environment. In 'The Earth-Veil: Ruskin and Environment' (*JPRS* 24[2015] 5–24), Sara Atwood asks what it means to call Ruskin a 'proto-environmentalist' in the context of his own time. Atwood argues that 'we must understand his ideas in the context of his worldview and of the intellectual and cultural forces that shaped it, drawing out his meaning rather than imposing our own' (p. 8). What we learn from the way Ruskin's ideas about the environment were so different from our own might be more valuable than aligning his environmentalism with modern notions of the term.

Marilynn Olson's essay, 'John Ruskin and the Mutual Influences of Children's Literature and the Avant-Garde' (in Duker and Kümmerling-Meibauer, eds., *Children's Literature and the Avant-Garde*, pp. 17–44) traces Ruskin's influence on children's literature, including his theories on the grotesque and the synthesis of image and text so important to picture books. As Olson discusses, Ruskin was an enthusiastic supporter of books for children and believed in their value. The connection between Ruskin and children's literature helps explain the use of the grotesque in books for children in this period. Olson argues that 'the importance he placed on the materials being offered to children is tied to his role as a social critic' (p. 41). In focusing on children's literature, then, this essay provides an interesting perspective on Ruskin.

The Ruskin journal *Eighth Lamp—Ruskin Studies Today* (10[2015]) features an article by Hiroship Emoto, 'A Treatise on The Seven Lamps of Architecture: The Seven Latin Lamps and Architectural Creation' (10[2015] 38-58) and this issue also discusses. Caroline Ings-Chambers, *Louisa Waterford and John Ruskin: 'For You Have Not Falsely Praised'* (reviewed here by William Baker), which centres around 'the life story of Louisa, Marchioness of Waterford' (1818–91) and her relationship with John Ruskin, who became her tutor. His correspondence with her 'comprises . . . a collection of sixty-three letters, all written by Ruskin, which span the dates 1853 to 1875'. These today are found 'in The John Ruskin Collection at the Huntington Library, San Marino, California' (pp. ix–x). In her introduction (pp. 1–7) Ings-Chambers observes that 'the purpose of this book is to transgress the boundaries and re-work the processes of time that for too long have held Louisa Waterford, the artist in obscurity and to emphasize the continuing value of her art today' (p. 6). There are chapters on 'Early Life and Artistic Development of the Artist' (pp. 1–23), 'The Occupations of Marriage' (pp. 24–36), 'A Nineteenth-Century Correspondence Course' dealing with the correspondence with Ruskin (pp. 37–73), 'The Letters' (pp. 74–104), 'The Revival of Monumental Art and Fresco Painting in Great Britain and Ireland' (pp. 105–41), 'The Murals at Ford' (Ford Castle, Northumberland where she moved following her husband's death in 1859) (pp. 142–91), and 'The "Companionship of Art" and the Later Years' (pp. 192–235). Each chapter closes with at times extensive notation: for instance the final chapter has 180 accompanying notes (pp. 228–35). The text contains black and white illustrative figures exemplifying Louisa Waterford's work.

There was a great deal of interest in Oscar Wilde this year. *Oscar Wilde's Chatterton: Literary History, Romanticism, and the Art of Forgery* is a fascinating exploration of Wilde. Joseph Bristow and Rebecca Mitchell examine Wilde's extensive notes on Chatterton, a forger who inspired countless nineteenth-century writers. They argue that his 'Chatterton' note-book is central to his development as a writer. The scholarship of this edition is astounding, not only covering the entire span of Wilde's career but also including archival research using previously undiscovered sources and a textual edition of the notebook with a separate editorial introduction. Chapter 1, 'Thomas Chatterton: Writing the Life, Editing the Poetry', focuses on Chatterton himself; his biographical information, including his tragic suicide at the age of 17; and the reception of his work. Chapter 2, 'The Chatterton Legend: Tributes, Adaptations, Memorials', traces the development of the myth of Chatterton and how it influenced Victorian constructions of the Romantic period. Chapter 3, 'Wilde's Discovery of Chatterton: The "Father of the Romantic Movement"', explores the reasons for Wilde's fascination with Chatterton and connects it to Wilde's fascination with Romantic poets. Chapter 4, 'Wilde's "Chatterton" Notebook: The Art of Forgery and the Charge of Plagiarism', examines the composition and structure of Wilde's notebook and traces ideas from the notebook in his later writing. Chapter 5, 'Wilde, Forgery, and Crime: Pen, Pencil and Poison, "The Decay of Lying," and the Short Fiction', examines the influence of Chatterton on some of Wilde's most important ideas in his later essays and fiction. Chapter 6, 'Forging Literary History: "The Portrait of Mr. W.H."', examines Wilde's engagement with forgery in his story 'The Portrait of Mr. W.H.' and his later interest in 'forged identity' such as we see in *The Picture of Dorian Gray*. The conclusion, 'Wilde's Writings and Chatterton's Reputation: The *Fin de Siècle* and Beyond', continues the exploration of the theme of forgery in Wilde's work, looking especially at *The Importance of Being Earnest*. The second half of the conclusion evaluates Chatterton's presence in the study of English literature and culture after Wilde's death. This book will surely inspire new ways of understanding and engaging with Oscar Wilde.

*The Evolution of Wilde's Wit* by Jure Gantar is a detailed exploration of Wilde's wit as exemplified in his epigrams. Gantar's introduction includes a historical exploration of the word 'wit' as well as a review of recent scholarship about wit. Related more specifically to Wilde himself, the introduction catalogues contemporary reactions to Wilde's wit. Gantar explains the scope of the book, which is limited to studying wit in thirty-five of Wilde's epigrams in seven chapters, which are grouped thematically. Chapter 1, 'Damp Squibs', focuses on failed epigrams; chapter 2, 'Comma in the Afternoon', examines the evolution of one group of epigrams; chapter 3, 'The Apparatus for Turning out "Oscarisms"', is a structural analysis of the epigrams. The next three chapters take a thematic approach. Chapter 4, 'Truth on a Tightrope', focuses on the relationship between wit and truth in the epigrams. Chapter 5, 'Laws and Exceptions', looks at epigrams that fail to achieve a balance between thought and expression, and Chapter 6, 'Expressing One's Self', examines the articulation of the Self in the epigrams. Chapter 7, 'Summaries of All Existence', provides a review of some of the epigrams in 'Phrases and

Philosophies'. The conclusion situates Wilde's wit in the larger context of his social environment.

In *Oscar Wilde's Elegant Republic: Transformation, Dislocation and Fantasy in Fin-de-Siècle Paris*, David Charles Rose sets out to 'understand Wilde's place in Paris, and that of Paris in Wilde' (p. xiii). It is simultaneously interested in studying Oscar Wilde the writer and Paris the city. The chapters are as follows: chapter 1, 'Paris Sighted'; chapter 2, 'Paris Mutuels'; chapter 3, 'Anglomania, Francophilia and Anglophobia'; chapter 4, 'Amis & Faux Amis in a Culture of Easy Duplicity'; chapter 5, 'Converse'; chapter 6, 'The Theatre of Paris'; chapter 7, 'Café au Fait'; chapter 8, 'Pervading Paris'; chapter 9, 'Walking with an Air'; chapter 10, 'Masquerade'; chapter 11, 'The Artist as Crisis'; chapter 12, 'Paris and the Good American'; chapter 13, 'A Question of Gender'; chapter 14, 'Phases of the Moon'; and chapter 15, 'Paris as Wilderness'. Rose's book is more than a biography of a single person or a sociological study of a place. It adds to our understanding of both Wilde the person and Wilde the writer. Accompanied by fourteen black and white illustrations, Giles Whitely's *Oscar Wilde and the Simulacrum The Truth of Masks* 'contends that Wilde's writing can only be approached through an understanding of the role masques play in the discourses of both philosophy and aesthetics as Wilde understands them, and the way in which this theory of masques problematizes the pretensions of philosophy to speak (of) the truth' (p. 4). Whitely's is a highly sophisticated study requiring knowledge of a whole range of Wilde's work including his journalism, letters, notebooks, and prose. Whitely also draws upon the complex writings of Gilles Deleuze, Jacques Derrida, Immanuel Kant, Pierre Klossowski, Friedrich Nietzsche, and Plato, amongst other philosophical thinkers. Extensive notation is found at the foot of the page.

A chapter that also explores the importance of place for Wilde, ' "Most people die in exile": **Oscar Wilde's** Final Personality, or the Queerness of the Non-Place' by Elizabeth Richmond-Garza (in Hartmann and Zapf, eds., *Censorship and Exile*, pp. 243–54) examines Wilde's presentation of a 'mobile, multiple and always potentially queer exilic self' (p. 244). Throughout Wilde's writings there is a strong connection between place and identity, as Richmond-Garza argues, 'For Wilde the decorum of location is crucial' (p. 243). An interesting essay by Joseph Portanova, 'Epistle from Prison: **Oscar Wilde's** *De Profundis*' (in Regan, ed., *Great Books Written in Prison: Essays on Classic Works from Plato to Martin Luther King, Jr.*, pp. 107–22), includes Wilde alongside Socrates, Thomas Paine, Gandhi, Hitler, and Martin Luther King Jr. Yet Portanova boldly begins his essay with the claim 'The circumstances surrounding Oscar Wilde's imprisonment and the writing of *De Profundis* are perhaps the most singular of any in this volume' (p. 107). And perhaps he is right. At any rate, there is something provocative about thinking about Wilde's work in the context of similar works completed in similar conditions but by writers from other nations and other times. The essay provides the background leading up to Wilde's imprisonment and then focuses on the writing of *De Profundis* itself and analyses some of the most important themes.

Rochelle Rives essay, 'Facing Wilde; or, Emotion's Image' (*PMLA* 130[2015] 1363–80), appearing in a special topic issue of *PMLA* on emotion,

uses recent debates about affect and the emotions to examine caricatures of
Wilde's face. After the trials of 1895, Wilde's face was linked to a
pathologically expressive personality type, and Rives is interested in exploring
this purely physiological notion of personality. ' "Cleverly Drawn": Oscar
Wilde, Charles Ricketts, and the Art of the *Woman's World* (*JVC* 20[2015]
375–400), by Petra Clark, explores the visual aesthetics of a late nineteenth-
century women's magazine, *Woman's World*, famously edited by Oscar Wilde.
Clark traces three important areas of exploration with this magazine: the
relationship between designer Charles Ricketts and the editor Oscar Wilde,
Wilde's aesthetic vision for the magazine, and how Ricketts's illustrations
cultivated a readership and modes of reading.

In 'Oscar Wilde's Multitudes: Against Limiting His Photographic
Iconography' (*ELT* 58[2015] 147–63), Laurence Dumortier offers a corrective
to the 'overprivileging of the 1882 Sarony session in Wilde's iconography' and
the effect this had on our understanding of Wilde as a cultural figure.
Dumortier joins other Wilde critics such as Linda Dowling, Alan Sinfield, and
Joseph Bristow in their attempts to 'nuance queer conceptions of Wilde'
(p. 148). Dumortier argues that this nuance has yet to be added to Wilde's
visual iconography, and this essay fills in that gap. Finally, in his provocative
essay, 'Wildean Interpretation and Formalist Reading' (*VS* 58:i[2015] 9–33),
Jonathan Loesberg suggests formalist critics have something to learn from
Wilde. Formalist's attention to paradox (Loesberg calls it 'an interpretive
indulgence' in paradox), he suggests, is a form of queering literary criticism,
and formalists need to embrace it as such. To do so would enable formalism to
foster a spirit of discovery, to 'shock us into an awareness of an artwork's
mystery' (p. 30).

## 2. The Novel

In this section Christian Dickinson reviews work covering Charles Dickens,
and William Baker reviews work covering Wilkie Collins, George Eliot, and
Anthony Trollope. All general studies of the novel and works on other
individual authors are reviewed by Ariana Reilly.

Two exceptional books on the Victorian novel were published this year,
both interrogating the primacy of the *Bildungsroman* in studies of the
Victorian novel: Rebecca Rainof's *The Victorian Novel of Adulthood: Plot and
Purgatory in Fictions and Maturity* and Elisha Cohn's *Still Life: Suspended
Development in the Victorian Novel*. In the first of these, Rainof convincingly
argues that our critical 'love affair' with the *Bildungsroman* has obscured from
sight the importance of another plot entirely, that of adulthood (p. 4). Fictions
of adulthood, Rainof contends, are not plotless; rather, they are characterized
by introspection, introversion, and 'epochs' of slow, thoughtful development
that gradually guide the protagonist to self-discovery or some other meaningful change (p. 11). Indeed, these slow plots of midlife are, as Rainof deftly
demonstrates, constitutive of many of the formal features we already associate
with the form of the nineteenth-century novel: 'its fascination with interiority,
its wealth of accumulative detail, and its ability to render these details into a

progressive, if at times uneventful, whole' (p. 5). In many ways, what Rainof proves in her monograph is that the formal features of the novel of adulthood are central to the ways in which we already think about the novel, but that we have been awkwardly insisting on the primacy of youth and narratives of eventful development even when our analysis does not support such a classification. By drawing our attention to this critical oversight, Rainof enables a far more coherent discussion of plot in Victorian fiction.

In addition to providing a skilful formal reassessment of the novel, Rainof also situates her study historically within debates surrounding Purgatory and the possibility of continued maturation and spiritual development in the afterlife. As Rainof notes, critics have long been aware of the Victorian interest in gradualism and incremental reform. However, for the most part, such discussions have been focused on evolution. What has received less attention is the gradualism present in Victorian theological debates at the time of, and following, the Oxford Movement. By asking us to consider the relationship between secular novels and theological tracts, Rainof contributes to the growing body of scholarship responding to post-secular theory. Those interested in developments in this area will certainly want to read her book with care.

The first chapter, ' "Strange Introversions": Newman, Mature Conversion, and the Poetics of Purgatory', lays the theological groundwork for the rest of the project, diving into Victorian discussions of Purgatory before focusing on Newman's essay on Aristotle's *Poetics* and *The Dream of Gerontius*. In these essays, Newman struggles with how to represent a 'state of change', a challenge that would continue to inspire novelists throughout the century (p. 18). Each of the remaining chapters examines a different figure who requires the slow plot of midlife—the miser, the widow, the bachelor, and the spinster. Chapter 2 examines two novels by George Eliot, *Silas Marner* and *Daniel Deronda*. Rainof connects Silas and Gwendolyn, both of whom undergo slow and uneventful interior transformations. Chapter 3 offers an important reading of *Little Dorrit*'s Arthur Clennam in terms of shadow folklore as well as an analysis of several of Henry James's bachelors. Rainof demonstrates how both novelists rely on counterfactual narratives in order to plot the uneventful lives of their bachelor protagonists. A final chapter, on Woolf's *The Years*, suggests that the figure of the spinster was crucial to modernist narrative experimentation, and a coda on myths of descent closes this excellent contribution to the field.

Where Rainof revises our understanding about the Victorian novel by questioning the primacy of the *Bildungsroman* and suggesting an equally important novel of slowly developing adulthood, Elisha Cohn maintains the central significance of the *Bildungsroman* in *Still Life*, but argues that we have overlooked the deep ambivalence towards development that often lies at the heart of these novels. Novels of development, Cohn contends, are filled with moments of suspended development where protagonists dream away their lives, enter trance states, sleep, or even read. These moments, which Cohn defines as 'lyrical', 'relieve the pressures of self-formation', and invite 'shifts of mood, tone, and voice [that] slow time, privilege feeling over action, and find plenitude in sensation' (p. 3). In order to make this argument, Cohn draws together affect theory as well as recent work on Victorian psychophysiology, finding much to applaud and critique in each. Affect theory's appreciation of non-purposive moods is useful for Cohn's description of suspended development, but she remains wary throughout of any suggestion that affect might open the door to alternative models of subject formation or agency. Cohn is similarly divided in her approach to historicist studies of Victorian science. While drawing on the work of these scholars as well as their primary sources, Cohn asserts that each writer in her study 'neither ratifies nor critiques the evidence of the sciences but instead conveys ambivalence about contemporary frameworks of attention, which privilege mental work, through formal strategies of mood, tone, and voice' (p. 17). Cohn tries to walk a fine line, here, one so fine we may ask whether it exists at all. If there is one shortcoming in Cohn's study, this is it. In her effort to be precise and to avoid the kind of critical heroics she associates with historicism, she sometimes allows her argument to become rather diffuse, adding a not always welcome performative quality to her argument about non-purposive action.

The first chapter, on Charlotte Brontë, argues that *Villette* 'juxtaposes a poetics of daydream . . . against discourses of self-culture', including, most significantly, phrenology (p. 26). Yet if the novel at times resists the forward movement of the *Bildungsroman*, it does not, in Cohn's account, ultimately overturn it. A second chapter, on Eliot's *The Mill on the Floss* and *Daniel Deronda*, zeros in on failures of omniscience as moments of valuable unknowing. Chapter 3 reads Meredith's *The Ordeal of Richard Feverel* followed by Meredith's long poem *Modern Love* to show how, in novel and poem alike, 'satire highlights the futility of excessive attentiveness, but scenes of reverie offer a more deeply dissociative means of dissenting from that ideal' (p. 28). A final chapter, on Thomas Hardy's *Tess of the D'Urbervilles* and *Jude the Obscure*, charts Hardy's growing dissatisfaction with the novel form (and increasing attraction to lyric) for exploring 'self-estranging aesthetic possibilities' (p. 28). Altogether, Cohn's first book is a valuable contribution to Victorian novel studies.

Felicia Bonaparte's *The Poetics of Poesis: The Making of Nineteenth-Century English Fiction* is another notable revision of critical approaches to the Victorian novel—the widespread assumption that realism was the most important generic mode for the period. Bonaparte argues that referring to the style of the nineteenth-century novel as 'realism' is a misunderstanding of a century deeply affected by German Romanticism as disseminated most successfully by Friedrich Schlegel and Thomas Carlyle. Nineteenth-century novelists, Bonaparte contends, wrote what Edward Bulwer Lytton called the 'novel of the double plot' (p. 7) in which the 'real' embodies the 'ideal'. In her well-researched and clearly articulated discussion, Bonaparte endeavours to revise our understanding of some of the symbols widely used in the nineteenth-century novel to gesture towards this double plot, and explains how such symbolic language addressed pressing concerns of the age. In the first three chapters, she shows how novels engaged the century's crises in religion, empiricism, and reason. She explains, for example, that novels of inheritance and disinheritance like *Great Expectations* signify that the 'legacy of heaven' has been lost in the 'crisis of faith', while the 'maze of rails' in *A Pair of Blue*

*Eyes*, the Wandering Jew in *Nina Balatka*, and the disorienting fogs in Dickens's fiction point to the century's loss of a grounding telos that gives order to the universe (pp. 34, 41, 42). Symbolic naming is another major concern of the study. Many novels, Bonaparte observes, include characters such as Sir Thomas Ashby in *Agnes Grey*, named after the doubting apostle Thomas who, like a good empiricist, needed to feel Christ's wounds to believe the apparition was real. Chapters 5 and 6, entitled 'The Need to Reconceive the World' and 'The Quest for a New Religion', show how the many characters bearing variants of the name Paul (e.g. Paul Dombey in *Dombey and Son*, Paula Power in *A Laodicean*, and Paul Emanuel and Paulina Mary Home in *Villette*) made nineteenth-century readers think of a saint who would, like St Paul, 'build the church that [would] house that [new] religion' (p. 102).

In chapters 7 to 9, Bonaparte argues that during the Victorian era imagination took faith's place as an 'epistemological tool' capable of apprehending truth (p. 127), and through art as *poesis* (a 'making'), rather than *mimesis*, novelists could constitute truth as what Naumann in *Middlemarch* refers to as 'the idealistic in the real' (p. 201). Here Bonaparte clarifies the misunderstanding which has resulted in viewing the nineteenth-century novel as a type of realism. Since in the Romantic understanding of art the ideal is embodied in the real, the novel presents a meticulous portrayal of the empirical surface of life, but that portrayal has been erroneously 'read "realistically" by those who begin with the assumption that this is all there is in the work' (p. 228). To express the inexpressible was the actual purpose of the concrete language of symbols created by the novel, Bonaparte claims, and the difficulty of this project is shown in many novels through a thematic interest in words per se. Bonaparte concludes by showing that towards the end of the century readers and novelists alike began to doubt that fiction could convey transcendent truth, a shift indicated by the prevalence of 'double endings' which suggest an irreconcilable division between truth and its realistic representation (p. 273).

Love was in the air in 2015—or at least in books on the Victorian novel. No fewer than four monographs appeared specifically on marriage. One of these looked at an actual marriage—the Disraelis'. Daisy Hay fashions her dual biography, *Mr. and Mrs. Disraeli: A Strange Romance*, from many sources, including letters, poems, novels, and over 10,000 papers collected by Mary Ann Disraeli over the course of her life such as 'reports of adultery hearings, frauds perpetrated by servants, women living into extreme old age, and family feuds' (p. 243). Mary Ann's papers are a decidedly rich trove but one hard to interpret. Hay reads them for insight not only into what interested this unusual woman, but also into what may have resonated with her own life. Drawing on methods learned from recent biographers of more obscure personages, Hay walks us through the more familiar details of the Disraelis' lives while, at the same time, 'watching for alternative narratives, listening to things not said' and weaving in the stories and experiences of those unremembered individuals on the periphery of the Disraelis' story (p. xii). Of particular interest to literary scholars is the way that Hay attends to the creativity of the Disraelis. Not only did Disraeli write fiction and his wife write stories; they also, according to Hay, incorporated style and subject matter from popular genres of the day into their self-presentations. Storytelling, in Hay's account, becomes, for the Disraelis, a way to understand the self, to project goals for the future, and to meet them. It is, in sum, a way of life. She finds that Mary Ann was, like Benjamin Disraeli, intent on self-fashioning with no strong attachment to reality. Both create for themselves flamboyant identities, patterning their letters to one another on those of epistolary novels like *Evelina* and *Cecilia*, and though their relationship was believed to be an alliance of convenience, 'it mattered to them both that they should be, and appear to be, swept up in a grand romance' (p. 81). Hay concludes with a discussion of *Endymion*, the novel Benjamin completed after Mary Ann's death, a fictional narrative based on his life which he wrote in response to the thousands of letters his wife saved from his friends, political associates, and relatives. In it the heroine states, 'I did not marry for love...though love came, and I brought happiness to one who made me happy' (p. 261). Unable to separate conclusively fact from fiction in the lives of this unlikely couple, Hay is content to end the biography with a fiction that probably has much truth in it.

Kirby Jane Hallum, in *Aestheticism and the Marriage Market in Victorian Popular Fiction: The Art of Female Beauty*, explores how Pre-Raphaelite notions of beauty and beauty's aesthetic value influenced the way novelists represented the marriage market in five works of popular Victorian fiction. Hallum bases her discussion on popular texts written by woman for women because they 'concurrently affirmed the woman reader's everyday emotions whilst offering her imagined escape from everyday domestic life' (p. 19). Chapter 1 examines Rhoda Broughton's *Cometh up as a Flower*, where Nell's self-representation in Pre-Raphaelite terms attests to her understanding of her aesthetic value to both Dick, a middle-class romantic hero, and Sir Hugh, an unattractive aristocrat more eligible as a match to whom she 'sells' herself in the socially acceptable prostitution of marriage. In chapter 2, Hallum sets aestheticism alongside Darwinism to understand how the selection of desirable attributes and pedigree directs the courtship of Willoughby and Clara in George Meredith's *The Egoist*. Hallum focuses on 'binaries between the natural and the artificial' in the depiction of Vere's and Lady Dolly's beauty in Ouida's *The Moths*, a novel where the 'boundary between people and objects blurs' (pp. 93, 97). In the next chapter, Hallum's discussion of Gaston Beauvais's characterization as an aesthete and sexual deviant in Marie Corelli's *Wormwood* shows the transition into decadence in late Victorian literature. Hallum's final chapter explores George du Maurier's satirical version of aestheticism in *Trilby*, and her conclusion looks towards aestheticism's continuation in modernism.

Melissa M. Adams-Campbell demonstrates the little-appreciated diversity of the eighteenth- and nineteenth-century novel's representations of courtship and marriage in *New World Courtships: Transatlantic Alternatives to Companionate Marriage*. In the introduction, Adams-Campbell gives a brief overview of the history of the conjugal or nuclear family and a summary of important feminist analyses of marriage in literature. She then discusses Lydia Maria Child's *Hobomok* as a clear example of a 'comparative marriage plot'. The novel's depiction of interracial marriage and family in the New England colony, Adams-Campbell argues, offers a critique of Puritan marriage laws of the seventeenth century as well as social and literary marriage conventions of the nineteenth century. In chapter 1, 'Why Marriage Mattered Then', Adams-Campbell surveys Enlightenment discussions of marriage rites and stadial theory to illuminate an eighteenth-century comparative marriage novel, *The Female American*. Chapter 2, 'Comparing Rights, Comparing Stories', considers shifts within the range of women's romantic choices when different cultural groups mingled in Canada during the eighteenth century as reflected in the eighteenth-century Canadian novel, *The History of Emily Montague*. Chapter 3, 'Making Room for Coquettes and Fallen Women', looks at the way *Secret History; or, The Horrors of St. Domingo* rejects both marriage and death as appropriate narrative ends, instead concluding with a homosocial community of women. Chapter 4, 'A Postcolonial Heroine "Writes Back"', finds in *The Woman of Colour* a postcolonial critique of British marriage conventions. In chapter 5, 'Bungling Bundling', Adams-Campbell discusses *The Life and Adventures of Obadiah Benjamin Franklin Bloomfield, M.D.*, a picaresque comparative marriage novel in which the titular hero experiments with a broad array of courtship practices. In the Epilogue, 'Why Marriage Matters Now', Adams-Campbell notes that the contemporary debate over same-sex marriage represents a relatively recent phenomenon of the state legislating the right to couple when for centuries more casual arrangements were accepted. She then calls for greater willingness within twenty-first-century society to explore the value of alternative family forms.

In *The Bigamy Plot: Sensation and Convention in the Victorian Novel*, Maia McAleavey looks at another type of unconventional marriage arrangement: bigamous ones. McAleavey argues that narratives involving bigamy or even the possibility of bigamy significantly challenged the conventional marriage plot of the nineteenth-century novel. Although novels are her primary focus, selecting plot as an organizing principle rather than genre, author, or critical reception gives McAleavey the opportunity to expand her purview beyond the novel to ballads, plays, and legal cases. Having assembled a list of over 270 Victorian novels which treat bigamy directly or tangentially, McAleavey notes that bigamy is gender-blind, may be deliberate as in *Lady Audley's Secret* or accidental because of a spouse's long absence or false death as in *Pendennis*, may involve a faked marriage as in *Romola* or an unofficial divorce as in *The Mayor of Casterbridge*, and may even be avoided at the last minute as in *Jane Eyre*. In the introduction she looks at historical factors which may have contributed to the rise of the bigamy plot and briefly explains that, since the stories of bigamist, first spouse, and second spouse 'proceed along two diverging [plot] lines' in a state of 'simultaneous "bothness"', the bigamy plot complicated *Bildung* or subject making, a presumed goal of the marriage-plot novel (p. 16). Part I includes chapters tracing the history of bigamy as a literary trope and argues that when marriage is sequential, but the first and second spouses have lived/live in the same house, a form of bigamy is at play in the narrative background. In Part II McAleavey looks first at *David Copperfield* and the question of how consecutive spouses of one person will work through the state of bigamy to come in heaven, and next at *Middlemarch* where Casaubon, after his death, inserts himself into Dorothea's second marriage through his will. Part III first examines *Pendennis* to show how the return of a spouse from the colonies challenges the Victorian assumption of firm separation between England and its imperial holdings, and next *Lady Audley's Secret* to explore the 'discontinuity of the colonial bigamous subject' (p. 117). The book concludes with a discussion of how the bigamy plots in *Aurora Floyd* and *Jude the Obscure* challenge two givens of the conventional courtship plot: personal choice and the marriage ending, thereby offering novelists a way to critique courtship as a dominant convention in both social and literary practice.

The marriage plot's close, less fortunate, cousin received attention in Maria Peker's book, *Gendered Time*, which revisits the fallen woman novel, maintaining that our monolithic approach to this crucial figure in nine-teenth-century literature and culture has obscured the diverse array of identities and life trajectories subsumed under this heading. In particular, criticism has failed to account for what Peker, drawing on Victorian terminology, labels 'the woman with a past'—an older woman whose illicit sexual history has not prevented her from achieving a certain level of security, happiness, and even respectability in society. These women do not, as Peker points out, uniformly meet with unhappy ends, and even when they ultimately do pay for their former transgressions, it is only after society has capitulated in some way to their alternative story line. Most important for Peker's thesis is the way that these women disrupt binary distinctions between male and female time. Peker follows Kristeva and, more recently, Patricia Murphy in identifying a gendered dynamic in Western representations of time, whereby men experience time linearly—and thus progressively—whereas women experience time cyclically and thus as a kind of stasis. Women with a past, however, 'usurp the male privilege of linear time and...construct their own life history after the masculine model both in mid- and late-Victorian novels' (p. 16). Time thus becomes one of the primary battlegrounds in Peker's reading for renegotiating gender in nineteenth-century literature and culture.

Peker's monograph is divided into two parts. The first provides the conceptual framework for thinking about time and gender in the Victorian novel. After discussing critical models for thinking about feminine and masculine temporalities in narrative, Peker turns to a discussion of Darwin and Freud in these terms. The second half of the book delves into readings of particular novels of the period by Thackeray, Braddon, Trollope, and Hardy, including *Vanity Fair*, *Lady Audley's Secret*, *Aurora Floyd*, *Barchester Towers*, *The Belton Estate*, *Phineas Finn*, and *The Mayor of Casterbridge*. A conclusion briefly treats Wilde's *Lady Windermere's Fan*. Peker is well aware that in describing the 'woman with a past' she is in some ways offering a character construct potentially as monolithic as the figure of the fallen woman. However, Peker's argument that we need 'literary types' to discuss and think through our literature, even though we know such types to be over-simplifications of the true diversity of literary creation, makes sense. The figure of the 'woman with a past' deserves more consideration and will hopefully be a continued topic for discussion in future.

Gretchen Braun also treats the fallen woman in her article, '"Untarnished Purity": Ethics, Agency, and the Victorian Fallen Woman' (*WS* 44[2015] 342–67). Braun calls our attention to the radical rewriting of the narrative of the fallen woman in Emily Jolly's novel *Witch-hampton Hall: Five Scenes in the Life of its Last Lady*. By drawing heavily on Gothic convention and locating 'gender-neutral moral virtue in an individual's commitment to act with responsibility and integrity toward those he or she loves' (p. 365), Jolly, in Braun's account, redefines purity such that she manages to award her fallen heroine with an ending typically reserved for the unfallen in *Bildungsromane* of the century.

In 'Victorian Women Novelists, Gossip, and Creativity' (*GSN* 59[2015] 9–15), Brenda McKay reflects on the importance of gossip to writers such as Gaskell, Eliot, and Charlotte Brontë. Perhaps most interesting is her suggestion that the importance of gossip lies in its bitter aftertaste. The guilt of having indulged in ungenerous gossip, McKay proposes, may encourage the gossips to re-evaluate their position and engage in a degree of self-reflection unlikely without this unpleasant incentive.

Two essays appeared dealing with the question of Charlotte Yonge's attitude towards gender and domesticity, a problem that has long puzzled those interested in bringing her work into the canon. Susan Walton's article, 'Suitable Work for Women? Florence Claxton's Illustrations for *The Clever Woman of the Family* by Charlotte Yonge' (*NCGS* 11:ii[2015] 26 paras.), part of a special issue of *Nineteenth-Century Gender Studies* on illustration and gender, adds to this debate by drawing our attention to drawings. Though rarely mentioned in the scholarship, *The Clever Woman of the Family* was first serialized with illustrations of a young independent woman whose life, it would seem, was very much at odds with the conservative message of the novel. Walton argues, however, that things are not what they at first appear, and that both text and pictures reveal a far more nuanced attitude towards female independence, one only complicated by the juxtaposition of the two media. Livia Arndal Woods also questions over-simplified accounts of Yonge's conservatism in her article, '"What are they to do with their lives?": Anglican Sisterhoods and Useful Angels in Three Novels by Charlotte Mary Yonge' (*NCC* 37[2015] 147–63). Woods argues that Yonge's interest in Anglican sisterhoods, which appear prominently in *The Clever Woman of the Family*, *The Heir of Redclyffe*, and *The Pillar of the House*, is evidence of her commitment to imagining 'alternatives to traditional familial roles and structures' even as she supported conventional practices by recreating them in modified form outside the home (p. 149).

Patrick Maume wandered even farther from the canonical camp in his discussion of nineteenth-century gender and genre. Maume's 'Containing Granuaile: Grace O'Malley in Two Nineteenth-Century Novels' (*NewHR* 19[2015] 98–114) attends to novelistic representations of a sixteenth-century female pirate and chieftain, Grace O'Malley. O'Malley's history, Maume argues, simply did not fit within the available narratives of nineteenth-century femininity. Thus, O'Malley never seems quite captured by these texts which seek to rewrite her history in terms of personal frustration, lost love, and an unfulfilled domesticity.

A considerable body of work was dedicated to the body as well. Derek Bendenbaugh's excellent essay, 'Novel Violations: *The Hermaphrodite* and the Failure of Form' (*VS* 57[2015] 413–22), focuses on a recently rediscovered, unfinished novel from the 1840s by American author Julia Ward Howe, which injects a hermaphroditic English aristocrat into the Victorian marriage plot. Drawing on Elizabeth Grosz's work, Bedenbaugh demonstrates how the unclassifiable body both confounds the conventions of the nineteenth-century novel, revealing them to be hopelessly dependent on stable gender categories and, at the same time, sets in motion 'plotlines that seek to categorize and erase the narrative problems raised by hermaphroditism' (p. 414). Bendenbaugh's was one of many essays on gender and sexuality. 'British Aestheticism, Sexology, and Erotica: Negotiating Sexual Discourses in *Telany*' (*VR* 41[2015] 163–79), by Frederick D. King, examines the way that Leonard Smithers's privately published erotic novel *Telany* drew on 'Decadent interpretations of British Aestheticism to question the taxonomical methods of sexology, the obscenity labels imposed on works that evoke erotic pleasure, and the consequences of the legal and moral alienation of same-sex desire' (p. 163). In the process, King argues, *Telany* also upsets divisions between 'sexology and smut' (p. 177), as well as those between British Aestheticism and erotica.

*Victorian Network* published a special issue on the body in 2015 with an introduction by Pamela K. Gilbert (*VicNet* 6[2015] 1–6). Gilbert provides a useful overview of work on the body as it relates to Victorian studies from Foucault through queer studies. Of the six essays, four treat Victorian novels. Molly Livingstone's essay, '"This little action": The Feminine Manner of Touching in Elizabeth Gaskell's *Wives and Daughters*' (*VicNet* 6[2015] 55–71), draws on Judith Butler's concept of performative gender in order to suggest that Victorian women telegraphed their femininity and potential for maternal and spousal care through carefully deployed touch between women. However, such touch had to be carefully regulated. In *Wives and Daughters*, Livingstone sees Gaskell using appropriate and inappropriate scenes of touch to flesh out the nature of her female characters. Livia Arndal Woods also reads the female body in 'Now You See It: Concealing and Revealing Pregnancy in *Wuthering Heights* and *The Clever Woman in the Family*' (*VicNet* 6[2015] 32–54), where she argues that describing the pregnant body amounts to a kind of punishment in the Victorian novel, almost always indicating that a woman has done something wrong. Turning from the female to the male body, Leslie Allin's 'Leaky Bodies: Masculinity, Narrative, and Imperial Decay in Richard Marsh's *The Beetle*' (*VicNet* 6[2015] 113–35) departs from previous work charging Richard Marsh's *The Beetle* with shoring up British imperial masculinity, arguing instead that by presenting the male body as porous and fragile, *The Beetle* actually 'critiques justifications of patriarchal governance and imperial legitimacy: which ultimately become leaky, grotesque, and thus profoundly unstable' (p. 114). The role of the body in imagining the nation is also the subject of Sanghee Lee's essay, 'The Farming Body in Thomas Hardy's *Far from the Madding Crowd*' (*VicNet* 6[2015] 93–111). According to Lee's interesting essay, the military and agricultural body were juxtaposed in Victorian literature and culture, often in ways that addressed anxieties about a changing national identity at home and abroad. In Hardy's novel, Lee sees the agricultural body as a privileged site for thinking through the moral, economic, and bodily improvement of an England suffering from a degenerate and outdated masculine identity based on violence and conquest.

Those interested in the interconnections between nineteenth-century spiritualism and gender will want to read Mohammed Hamdan's ' "Give me the table—all the rest, all the other effects, come afterwards": Sound and Sexual Communication in the Spiritualism Fiction of Marryat and Phelps' (*NCC* 37[2015] 341–58). Hamdan's essay finds female sexual agency in the sounds of spiritualist practice. Wood-rapping and other noises provide a space both within the home and in the other world for female voices at the same time that such sounds marginalize the voices of men, such that in the novels of Marryat and Phelps, male characters 'become bothered in the next world where hierarchical structures and gender roles are challenged and put on a basis of equality' (p. 342).

The New Woman made her appearance in a number of 2015 essays and played the starring role in a monograph on the spinster. Carrie Wadman's interdisciplinary *The Victorian Spinster and Emerging Female Identities: A Critical Study of the Fin-de-Siècle Literature and Culture* reads novels alongside travel narratives, newspapers, medical journals, and psychological texts in order to show how the figure of the spinster was essential to the discourse surrounding four emerging female identities at the end of the century: the New Woman, the female academic, the female invert, and the female explorer. Gissing's *The Odd Women* provides the primary text for analysis in chapter 1, in which Wadman argues that the New Woman was, herself, a reinvention or update of the spinster figure from earlier in the period—a spinster whose spinsterhood was chosen rather than forced upon her. In chapter 2, 'The Academic Uterus', Wadman turns to scientific and popular press articles in order to demonstrate how the figure of the spinster was used as a bogy to frighten young women pursuing higher education. Chapter 3 'charts the process by which inversion was consolidated through the spinster identity marker' (p. 160). As Wadman explains, sexologists needed a model to help them define the features of a woman with same-sex desire and found the already familiar mannish spinster ready to hand. The final chapter in the book, ' "A traveller in skirts": The Spinster Explorer', considers how the already established, masculine, asexual figure of the spinster enabled some women to become explorers despite the hyper-masculinity with which Rider Haggard and other adventure writers had defined that identity.

Whitney Standlee's *'Powers to Observe': Irish Women Novelists in Britain, 1890–1916* 'focuses on Irish women writers who were living and working in Britain during the period 1890 to 1916'. It is limited to the consideration of novels 'for the simple reason that the novel was by far the most popular format for literature at the turn of the twentieth century' (p. 7). Novelists and novels discussed range from Emily Lawless (1845–1913; pp. 25–63), L.T. Meade (Elizabeth Thomasina Meade Toulmin Smith, 1844–1914; pp. 65–99), George Egerton, and Katherine Cecil Thurston, née Madden (1875–1911; pp. 101–51), M.E. Francis (Mary Sweetman Blundell, 1859–1930; pp. 153–91), and Katharine Tynan (1859–1931; pp. 193–241). In her concluding sentence Standlee observes that these writers 'foresaw that Ireland's rebirth, in whatever form it was to take, would be a painful and protracted process' (p. 252).

Jad Adams provides a useful biography of an under-studied late-century New Woman novelist and travel writer, in 'Ménie Muriel Dowie: The "Modern" Woman of Choices' (*ELT* 58[2015] 313–40). Adams introduces Dowie's account of her foreign adventures, *A Girl in the Karpathians* [1892], as a text of interest to scholars working on the New Woman and Dowie's novel, *Gallia* [1895], as a critical text in debates surrounding eugenics at the end of the century. Adams, however, wasn't the only one to recognize Dowie's importance. Beth Rodgers asks how Dowie managed to succeed with *A Girl in the Karpathians* given its explicit treatment of themes and practices associated with the New Woman writing, in her article 'Ménie Muriel Dowie's *A Girl in the Karpathians* (1892): Girlhood and the Spirit of Adventure' (*VLC* 43[2015] 841–56). While conceding that the novel shares with other New Woman writing certain controversial themes, images, and motifs, Rodgers suggests that because Dowie's work 'coincided with and contributed to a burgeoning period in the history of girls' culture and girlhood' the text was in many ways less threatening than it otherwise might have been, much like L.T. Meade's "Wild Irish Girl" in her books of the 1880s and 90s' (pp. 845, 853).

Simon Joyce's *Modernism and Naturalism in British and Irish Fiction 1880–1930* (reviewed here by William Baker) is also of interest to scholars of late nineteenth-century fiction and the New Woman novel. He 'argues that the history of literary modernism is inextricably connected with that of naturalism'. He 'traces a complex response among aesthetes to the work of Émile Zola at the turn of the century, in the process recovering naturalism's assumed compatibility with impressionism as a central cause of their ambivalence' (p. i). An extensive introduction, 'A Modernisation on All Fours' (pp 1–28), clarifies Joyce's conceptual usage and is followed by his first chapter, 'How Zola Crossed (and Didn't Cross) the English Channel' (pp. 28–52), a second chapter on 'Portraits and Artists: Impressionism and Naturalism' (pp. 53–83), and third one on 'A Naturalism for Ireland' (pp. 84–118). The fourth chapter is concerned with 'Photo-Sensitivity: Naturalism, Aestheticism, and the New Women Novel' (pp. 119–50). In his fifth chapter Joyce writes on 'The Voice of Witlessness: Virginia Woolf and the Poor' (pp. 151–79), and there is an 'Afterword: Nietzsche contra Naturalism (contra Nietzscheans)' (pp. 180–9). Of particular interest to students of the late Victorian/Edwardian novel is Joyce's discussion, largely in his third and fourth chapters, of the work of George Moore (1852–1933), Sarah Grand, Frances Bellenden Clarke McFall (1854–1913), and George Egerton, Mary Chevelita Dunne Bright (1859–1945).

Emily Coit's excellent essay 'Mary Augusta Ward's "Perfect Economist" and the Logic of Anti-Suffragism' (*ELH* 82[2015] 1213–38) explores Ward's economic anti-suffragism within a novel rarely discussed in this context, *Marcella*. Coit reveals the novel's participation within a larger dialogue about gender and economics that included thinkers such as Beatrice Webb, John Ruskin, and Alfred Marshall. Jessica Grays takes a look at one way in which New Women managed to contribute to the economy in 'Typewriter Girls in Turn-of-the-Century Fiction: Feminism, Labor and Modernity' (*ELT* 58[2015] 486–502), which considers whether the new employment opportunities afforded women by the advent of the typewriter really offered the kinds of freedom often supposed. Using George Gissing's *The Odd Women*, Grant Allen's *The Type-writer Girl*, and Pratt Rayner's *The Questing Beast* as source texts, Grays concludes that typists did not radically rewrite femininity and suffered from the same objectification that troubled other women of the era. Particularly interesting is Grays's discussion of escapism in this context. Typists in these novels, Grays notes, often escape in their imaginations from the work that supposedly liberates them. '[S]uch moments', Grays argues, 'are a way to explore the notion of fantasizing as a mode of creativity' that contrasts to the mundane language production of the typewriter girl—a mode that could potentially be connected to a more fulfilling, creative form of labour to counter anxieties about feminism and modern forms of labour' (pp. 486–7). The New Woman's engagement with a different technological innovation, photography, is the subject of David Wanczyk's 'Framing Gertrude: Photographic Narration and the Subjectivity of the Artist-Observer in Levy's *The Romance of the Shop*' (*VLC* 43[2015] 131–48). Wanczyk suggestively argues that the figure of the photographic-observer was doubly useful to Levy. On the one hand it allowed her to explore the complicated position of the New Woman in late Victorian England—both active and passive, a part of the commercial world at the same time that she was kept at a distance. On the other hand, it also allowed her to reflect on the photographic realism of her style, which exhibits a complicated negotiation of passive reproduction and active organization much like that performed by the character Gertrude in relation to the other medium.

In monographs, however, men fared better than women, with three books appearing on masculinity and the nineteenth-century novel—one on the New Man. In *The New Man, Masculinity and Marriage in the Victorian Novel*, Tara MacDonald traces the Victorian novel's exploratory engagement with the emerging New Man before he was derided as effeminate by the press and celebrated as progressive by New Women writers towards the end of the century. Integrating the New Man into the marriage plot and the female *Bildungsroman* presented challenges that required reimagining traditional notions of both gender roles and marital models. In the mid-nineteenth century, novelists experimented with constructions of masculinity that blended the self-discipline of the gentleman with feminine attributes. Chapter 1 looks at the various incarnations of the moral gentleman in Dickens's *David Copperfield* and *Great Expectations* while condemning 'aggressive masculinity and unequal marriages' (p. 11). His heroes are 'home-bred and sensitive', as noted by Margaret Oliphant, and also 'adopt a female-inspired model' of sexual continence (p. 26). David's and Pip's observations of Tom Traddles and Herbert Pocket 'offer striking examples of a Victorian male's meditations on marriage, homosociality, and "proper" male sexuality' (p. 29), while their interactions with other men underscore undesirable attributes such as class bias and violent tendencies (James Steerforth), physical, racial, and sexual deviance (Uriah Heep), and working-class background (Joe the blacksmith). In chapter 2 MacDonald argues that Anne Brontë, in *The Tenant of Wildfell Hall*, and George Eliot, in *Adam Bede*, offer narratives of 'male healing' in the flawed characters of Gilbert Markham and Adam Bede, and that the marriages of Helen Huntingdon and Dinah Morris to these men are 'models of the future' even though the voices of these women are silenced and their careers abandoned at the end (pp. 21, 57). In chapter 3, MacDonald moves to *fin-de-siècle* rewritings of the marriage plot in Ella Hepworth Dixon's *The Story of a Modern Woman* and Sarah Grand's *The Beth Book*, and in chapter 4 finds in George Gissing's *The Odd Women* and Grant Allen's *The Type-writer Girl* versions of New Men unable to maintain their progressive ideals of New Womanhood. Chapter 5 explores colonial masculinity, finding that *The Story of an African Farm* and *Trooper Peter Halket* likewise depict failed incarnations of the New Man. The conclusion looks at Victoria Cross's *Anna Lombard* and Olive Schreiner's *From Man to Man*, where the New Man's 'ethics of sacrifice' threaten to 'impede artistic or personal pleasure' (p. 23).

In *The Measure of Manliness: Disability and Masculinity in the Mid-Victorian Novel*, Karen Bourrier reminds us that, before the New Man discussed in MacDonald's book, nineteenth-century novels were replete with men weakened by disability, deformity, or illness such as Rochester, Mordecai, and Philip Wakem. The novels, like contemporary medical literature, often implied that from such suffering a degree of sympathy and interiority otherwise alien to the male psyche could develop. It is for this reason, Bourrier maintains, that the man of weakness and, therefore, feeling was often paired with a strong, muscular, silent male such as Adam Bede, Daniel Deronda, and Tom Tulliver: the weaker man was able to offer insight into the stronger man's story. In *The Measure of Manliness*, Bourrier explores this dyad, arguing that 'in order to represent [the] new muscular yet silent hero Victorian novelists drew on what had become a naturalized connection between the weak, nervous body and the body that speaks' (p. 9). Connecting recent disability studies with established work on the culture of Victorian invalidism, Bourrier examines how little distinction Victorians drew between illness and disability and how 'cultural notions of masculine weakness inflected norms of healthy, red-blooded manliness' (p. 15). In chapter 1, she reads Charles Kingsley's *Westward Ho!* and *Two Years Ago* alongside Charlotte Yonge's *The Heir of Redclyffe* to highlight the 'dependence of Kingsley's strong heroes on weak or disabled companions' and to show how for both novelists 'spectacles of masculine suffering are central . . . in developing the hero's sense of Christian duty' (p. 21). In chapter 2, Bourrier turns to issues of class in Dinah Mulock Craik's *John Halifax, Gentleman*, arguing that with her invalid-narrator 'Craik presents writing as a type of worthwhile labor by virtue of its painfulness' (p. 21). Chapter 3 focuses on the schoolboy novel, finding that Thomas Hughes and George Eliot coupled their normative English schoolboy character with an 'odd and often disabled companion who bears the emotional and narrative burden of the novel' (p. 22). Chapter 4 focuses on the late nineteenth century when the invalid's role as observer 'has become painful and ineffective as he is no longer called into friendship and action with the strong man' (p. 23). In the concluding chapter, Bourrier looks beyond the nineteenth century, finding that the strong man/weak man trope continued to appear in schoolboy novels 'even as the pairing was increasingly pathologized and coded as queer', as in the novels of E.M. Forster and Somerset Maugham (p. 24).

Phillip Mallett's edited essay collection, *The Victorian Novel and Masculinity*, begins with Sara Lodge's 'Masculinity, Power and Play in the Work of the Brontës', in which she shows that the Angria writings consistently question, parody, and revise masculinity in ways that shed important light on the treatment of men in the Brontës' mature novels. In 'Working-Class Masculinity and the Victorian Novel', Chris Louttit examines portrayals of broken men in novels by Gaskell, Gissing, and Morrison who lose their power of control over the body, the home, and/or the work place. Natalie McKnight, in 'Dickens and Masculinity: The Necessity of the Nurturing Male', traces Dickens's changing attitudes towards the masculine standard he, early on, helped to establish, arguing that men in his novels are progressively androgynous, that the masculine ideal begins to be dismantled in *Dombey and Son*, that the conventional romantic plot is reversed in *Bleak House*, that the male ideal is subjected to lambast in *Hard Times*, and that 'the hero as failure' figures prominently in *A Tale of Two Cities*, *Great Expectations*, and *Our Mutual Friend* (p. 60). In 'Tomboys and Girly Boys in Eliot's Early Fiction', Shelley Trower finds in *The Mill on the Floss* that physical trembling signals what society reads as effeminacy in Tom and Philip. Richard Nemesvari, in 'Manful Sensations: Affect, Domesticity and Class Status Anxiety in *East Lynne* and *Aurora Floyd*', aims to give men in sensation novels their day in court, finding that male heads of household in a genre characterized by 'affective extremes' are placed in an untenable position when 'Domesticity, either imminent or actual... generates manful sensations of conflicting passion and restraint' (p. 89). Jane Thomas, in 'Growing Up To Be a Man: Thomas Hardy and Masculinity', turns to Judith Butler to explain the challenges facing men in Hardy's novels who, like Hardy himself, seem to experience a 'fragmented sensibility' as competing discourses of masculinity threaten to '"undo"...personhood, thereby undermining [their] capacity to persevere in a liveable life' (p. 122). Phillip Mallett, in 'Masculinity, Imperialism and the Novel', considers the less complicated ideals of masculinity enjoyed in the closely related genres of adventure novels and imperial novels, with special attention to Rider Haggard's *King Solomon's Mines*, Kipling's *The Light That Failed*, and Flora Steel's *On the Face of the Waters*. Emma Sutton, in 'Aestheticism, Resistance and the Realist Novel', turns to a diametrically opposite construction of manhood as, through close readings of Pater's *Marius*, she finds a clear critique of the realist novel and 'normative middle-class masculinity', i.e. the 'muscular Christian or the imperial hero' (p. 176). Linda Shires, in 'Conrad's Theatre of Masculinity', returns to Butler's notion of gender as performance in her discussion of the 'erotics of epistemology about masculinity' in Conrad's writings, arguing that 'what is distinctly Conradian is the total scepticism about the truth of identity, including gender identity' at the same time that his characters struggle to know themselves by being known (pp. 190, 195).

Masculinity was not forgotten in the journals either. In her article, 'Blue-Blooded or White-Collared? The Gradual Democratization of the Concept of Gentlemanliness in Selected Examples of Victorian Fiction' (*BAS* 21[2015] 61–9), Marlena Marciniak analyses the figure of the gentleman in four Victorian novels, *Nicholas Nickleby*, *John Halifax, Gentleman*, *The Woman in*

*White*, and *Evan Harrington*, in order to chart how the meaning of the term 'gentleman' evolved over the nineteenth century to reflect a series of moral traits rather than to denote a particular hereditary status. Such a shift is, as Marciniak points out, crucial to the rising middle class in their struggle for increased political and social influence. Nadine Boehm-Schnitker considers recent reworkings of Victorian masculinity in her timely article, 'Adapting Victorian Masculinities: Oliver Parker's *Dorian Gray* (2009) and Guy Ritchie's *Sherlock Holmes* (2009)' (*Victo* 5[2015] 143–64). Boehm-Schnitker considers both latent and explicit homoeroticism in each film as well as the way in which Victorian homosocial desire is packaged for consumption by twenty-first-century audiences eager to be titillated by the film industry's staged excavation of buried sexual histories.

Two monographs also appeared on adaptations of Victorian novels. The first, Valérie Hazette's *Wuthering Heights on Film and Television: A Journey Across Time and Cultures*, is covered below with the scholarship on Emily Brontë. In the second, *The Art of Adapting Victorian Literature, 1848–1920: Dramatizing Jane Eyre, David Copperfield, and The Woman in White*, Karen Laird treats early stage and film adaptations, aiming to quash the widespread belief that Victorian adapters were 'pirates and plunderers' cranking out uninspired imitations of high literary art for an undiscriminating market (p. 1). She argues that, although adapters were deeply motivated by commercial interests and novelists were often critical of stage versions of their works, adaptations and the novels upon which they were based actually promoted the success of one another. Laird's central claim is that dramatic adaptation in the Victorian era laid the foundation for narrative cinema. Beginning with adaptations of *Jane Eyre* in 'Upstairs, Downstairs: *Jane Eyre*'s Transatlantic Theatrical Debut', Laird points out that early stage versions in both England and America were attracted to class difference in the novel and focused as much on the servants as on Jane's inner struggle. Turning to film adaptations in 'Adapting Melodramatically: *Jane Eyre* of the Silent Screen', Laird further stresses her claim that 'adaptations often incorporate salient cultural concerns of their own historical moment' (p. 45). In the case of silent films of *Jane Eyre*, the working woman claimed a central focus and became the target audience in a culture where women were joining the workforce to replace men sent off to war. Laird also explains that silent films showed the tragedy in Bertha Mason's story, setting her history alongside Jane's as that of the luckless wife in an arranged marriage forced to make way for the successful New Woman. Chapter 3, 'Adapting the Seduction Plot: *David Copperfield* on the Victorian Stage', finds that all five of the Victorian dramatists of Dickens's novel foreground the plight of the fallen woman, 'correct[ing] Dickens' tendency to silence his female characters' (pp. 77–8). After looking at screen adaptations of *David Copperfield* in chapter 4, Laird turns to *The Woman in White* in chapters 5 and 6, explaining how J.M. Ware radically revised the novel's plot with his 'counterintuitive decision to unveil the sensation novel's central mysteries up front', a reflection of his understanding of his audience's prior experience as readers of the novel (p. 154). In her concluding remarks, Laird calls for greater appreciation of the artistry of talented writers for the Victorian stage and the early modern screen who 'boldly broke apart the dramatic structure [of novels] in their adaptation process and rebuilt it anew' in ways that spoke directly to the issues confronting their audiences (p. 205). Popular in its day, the sensation novel continues to grab scholarly attention. Janice M. Allan challenges our generic understanding of sensation fiction in 'Sensationalism Made Real: The Role of Realism in the Production of Sensational Affect' (*VLC* 43[2015] 97–112). Despite the sensation novel's status as a hybrid form, criticism has persisted, Allan notes, in defining sensation in opposition to realism. Allan challenges this critical commonplace, arguing that 'the sensational and the realistic are inextricably entwined in the production of sensational affect' (p. 99). Anne-Julia Zwierlein gives her attention to the complicated treatment of attention in sensation fiction, a genre often accused of distracting its readers from more respectable literature, in 'The Subject Escapes Me: Spellbinding Lectures and (In-)Attentive Audiences in Late-Victorian Serialized Sensation Fiction' (*ZAA* 63[2015] 69–88). In particular, Zwierlein discusses lecture scenes in *Armadale*, as well as serialized sensation fiction from penny weeklies. These scenes portray academic attention as troublingly indistinct from trance states more commonly associated with uneducated reading practices. Ultimately, these scenes question whether suggestibility is the exclusive purview of the uneducated and lower classes. Eileen Cleere discusses Ellen Wood's *East Lynne* along with a less well-known work in 'Chaste Polygamy: Mormon Marriage and the Fantasy of Sexual Privacy in *East Lynne* and *Verner's Pride*' (*VS* 57[2015] 199–224), where she argues that, though Wood was unsettled by the polygamy practised by Mormons in Salt Lake City, she nevertheless drew upon the conversation on monogamy sparked by Mormonism in order to imagine alternative models for female sexuality and domesticity. Cleere's thoughtful essay reminds us that the narrative of marital happiness in Victorian fiction and culture was far more contested than traditional accounts of the marriage plot and fallen woman novel typically allow. Sarah Fitzpatrick takes a fairly traditional approach to the sensation novel in 'Separate Spheres: A Closer Look at Ideological Gender Roles in Victorian England through the Sensation Novel' (*The Victorian* 3:ii[2015] 1–9), where she draws on Mary Poovey's 1988 *Uneven Developments* in order to argue that sensation novels like Wood's *East Lynne* and Collins's *The Woman in White* both support and trouble traditional gender roles, exposing the uneven and fissured nature of Victorian gender ideology. *East Lynne*'s many dramatic progeny are the subject of Mary A. Armstrong's 'Next Week!! Desire, Domestic Melodrama, and the Extravagant Proliferations of *East Lynne*' (*VLC* 43[2015] 745–64). Moving between the novel, the many stage versions, and a few film adaptations, Armstrong focuses our attention on the 'the beautiful domestic "thing"' as both the product and object of narrative desire.

Of course, Mary Elizabeth Braddon's fiction came in for considerable attention in this area. Elisabetta Marino's 'Challenging the Commodification of Victorian Femininity: The Sensation Novel' (in Rogobete, Sell, and Munton, eds., *The Silent Life of Things: Reading and Representing Commodified Objecthood*, pp. 165–81) examines the way that sensation fiction fought back against the commodification and objectification of women by dramatically exposing the villainous and, perhaps more importantly, autonomous core beneath the carefully cultivated exterior of the Victorian lady. In particular, Marino teases out the complicated negotiation between a woman and the objects that metonymically classify her as belonging to their ranks in *Lady Audley's Secret*, where the eponymous protagonist works to 'transform the sacred domestic hearth into a stage' and to employ 'the very objects she was assimilated to in order to reinvent her identity' (p. 166). Jennifer McCollum, in 'Robert Audley's Secret' (*The Victorian* 3:iii[2015] 1–18), asserts that Braddon's most famous novel was an important precursor to Jean-Martin Charcot's theories of male hysteria, significant for the way in which it managed not only to create a more gender-fluid hysterical body, but also to present that body as heroic rather than tragic or comical. *Lady Audley's Secret* 'is unusually saturated with precise travel times', notes Beth Seltzer in 'Fictions of Order in the Timetable: Railway Guides, Comic Spoofs, and *Lady Audley's Secret*' (*VR* 41[2015] 47–65). Reading the novel alongside actual timetables as well as comedic exaggerations of the tables in various media, Seltzer argues that *Lady Audley's Secret*, like such spoofs, calls attention to the fiction of order created by the railway timetable while questioning the epistemological grounds of the sensation novel itself. Timothy L. Carens offers new insight into the familiar narrative of middle-class domestic ideology and the subversive dangers of sensation fiction in 'Idolatrous Reading: Subversive Fantasy and Domestic Ideology' (*NCL* 70[2015] 238–66). Paying special attention to Mary Elizabeth Braddon's *The Doctor's Wife*, Carens demonstrates that idolatry was yet another figure for thinking about the relationship between female readers and sensation fiction, one that Braddon self-consciously employed to explore ways in which women might acquire power and escape the domestic order. Turning from novels to short fiction, Sylvia A. Pamboukian's essay, 'The "Wretched Italian Quack": Braddon's Critique of Medicine in "Good Lady Ducayne"' (*VLC* 43[2015] 559–75), claims that Braddon's 1896 story interrogates 'modern medical practice and the power dynamics of modern patienthood' (p. 560). The truly terrifying element in the tale, according to Pamboukian, is not vampires, but rather a technological 'nightmare of violated boundaries, human vulnerability, and encroaching medicalization' (p. 571). Those interested in Braddon's acting career will want to read Janine Hatter's 'Closing the Curtain: M.E. Braddon's Last Performance as Mary Seyton' (*N&Q* 62[2015] 426–9), which provides details concerning that event.

The sensation novel's closest generic family member, the Gothic novel, garnered perhaps even more attention than its younger relative. Stephan Karschay's monograph, *Degeneration, Normativity and the Gothic at the Fin de Siècle*, examines how notions of deviance and normalcy developed in nineteenth-century (pseudo)-science and the novel. His extensive analysis of Victorian theorists of degeneration includes Darwin and Huxley, whose ideas of evolution were 'partly transformed into a social theory of criminal and sexual behavior' (p. 41); Cesare Lombroso, who viewed 'criminality as an inborn quality' (p. 45); Henry Maudsley, who argued that hereditary psychological disturbances caused an underdeveloped moral sense; Richard von Krafft-Ebing, who understood deviant sexuality as symptomatic of a 'medical condition' (p. 63); and Max Nordau, who asserted that 'late-nineteenth-century trends in the fine arts, particularly in the literary sphere, were...the degenerate outcrops of sexually perverted minds' (pp. 71–2). Gothic literature, Karschay demonstrates, was part of the discourse on degeneration, and within it and scientific writings he finds the 'tripartite mechanism of "detection-Othering-normalisation"' to be dominant discursive strategies. He devotes a chapter to each of these strategies, and within each chapter focuses on two Gothic novels. In 'Detecting the Degenerate', Karschay reads *The Strange Case of Dr Jekyll and Mr Hyde* and *The Great God Pan*, detailing how both narratives 'engage their normative protagonists in a detective hunt for a degenerate monster' (p. 123). In 'Othering the Degenerate', Karschay's reading of *Dracula* and *The Beetle* finds that, while repudiating the deviants, both novels disregard the kinship between monster and victim, with the result that the distinction between degenerate and normal is compromised. 'Normalizing the Degenerate' identifies important concerns shared by *The Picture of Dorian Gray*, *The Sorrows of Satan*, and scientific degeneration discourse, such as the nature–nurture debate and the likely presence of deviance within the norm. In brief closing remarks, Karschay connects the *fin de siècle*'s discourse on degeneration with twentieth-century ideologies promoting eugenics, Nazism, and fascism.

Marie-Luise Kohlke's 'The Neo-Victorian Doctor and Resurrected Gothic Masculinity' (*Victo* 5[2015] 122–42) examines the recurring trope of the Gothic doctor in neo-Victorian fiction as a figure for post-Enlightenment masculinity in crisis and considers how these characters show us our complicated relationship to our Victorian past. Drawing on Georges Bataille's concept of *informe* and the formless, in her essay 'The Thing: Unidentified Monstrous Objects in Victorian Fiction' (in Calzoni and Perletti, eds., pp. 217–33), Maria Teresa Chialant attempts a geneaology of 'the thing' in Victorian fiction, paying especial attention to Edward Bulwer Lytton's ghost story, *The Haunted and the Haunters*, and H.G. Wells's *The Island of Doctor Moreau*. Intentionally gestural, the essay does not offer a coherent theory so much as some preliminary thoughts on a suggestive area for further consideration. The monstrous body is the subject of Jane M. Kubiesa's 'In Sickness and in Health: Physical Fascination and its Marriage to the Gothic Body at the *Fin de Siècle*' (*The Victorian* 3:i[2015] 1–8). Reading popular Gothic novels such as *Strange Case of Dr. Jekyll and Mr. Hyde*, *The Island of Doctor Moreau*, and *Dracula* alongside Arthur Munby's real-life obsession with masculine femininity, Kubiesa traces a shift from interest earlier in the century with ideal bodies to a more sinister fascination with abnormality towards its close. In 'Carrying on Like a Madman: Insanity and Responsibility in *Strange Case of Dr. Jekyll and Mr. Hyde*' (*NCL* 70[2015] 363–97), Melissa J. Ganz positions Stevenson's novel within current debates surrounding the nature of insanity and the attempts of James Cowles Prichard and Henry Maudsley to expand the definition of insanity to include those who cannot control their actions regardless of whether or not they know those actions to be wrong. Stevenson, Ganz argued, feared that such a broad definition would lead to a dangerous confusion of moral and philosophical distinctions.

*Dracula*, of course, received a fair bit of attention. Mario Ortiz-Robles's "Liminanimal" (*EJES* 19[2015] 10–23) offers an at times jargony account of the relation between animality and monstrosity in late Victorian Gothic fiction. Situating *Dracula*, *Strange Case of Dr. Jekyll and Mr. Hyde*, and *The Beetle* in the context of 'Darwinian evolution and its dynamics of random mutation and sexual selection' (p. 11), Ortiz-Robles claims that the monster of late Victorian Gothic fiction 'makes visible the animality of the human', which in turn suggests possible challenges to biopower (pp. 21–2). In 'Monstrosity in the English Gothic Novel' (*The Victorian* 3:i[2015] 1–11) Christina Schneider also treats monsters and monstrosity in *Dracula* and *Strange Case of Dr. Jekyll and Mr. Hyde*, as well as *Frankenstein*. Readers interested in the cultural history and spaces of London will enjoy Maria Peker's ' "The hours of the day and night are ours equally" ': Dracula and the Lightening Technologies of Victorian London' (in Bach and Degenring, eds., *Dark Nights, Bright Lights: Light, Darkness and Illumination in Literature*, pp. 35–55). Peker aims to decouple the traditionally aligned binaries of good/evil and light/dark by reading *Dracula* in terms of the evolving technology of street lighting in Victorian London. Against readings of the Victorian Gothic that stress the strict antagonism of opposing forces, Peker interestingly observes in her history of the Victorian nightscape 'a complex interplay of primitive natural darkness, archaic means of lighting, and their . . . successors, gas and electricity' (p. 38). In 'The Vampire's Night Light: Artificial Light, Hypnagogia, and Quality of Sleep in *Dracula*' (*CS* 27[2015] 50–66), Karen Beth Strovas likewise reads *Dracula* in the context of new lighting technologies, but adds to her analysis a consideration of how those technologies impacted both the theory and practice of sleep, a central, dynamic aspect of the plot and characterization in Stoker's novel. Strovas observes that the vampire, much like innovations in lighting, exercises a tremendous influence over the nature and quality of sleep, and that that influence has gendered implications. Scott Rogers's essay, ' "In God's name, what does it all mean?" ': Epistemological Crisis in *Dracula*' (*The Victorian* 3:iii[2015] 1–29), approaches the question concerning the fragmentary structure of *Dracula*—that it is a 'compilation of documents' (p. 11)—with an eye to a 'late Victorian epistemological crisis' concerning the nature of 'facts and facticity' (p. 4). The narrative, according to Rogers, expresses and reflects the period's confrontation with a 'proliferation of information' (p. 26) insofar as it offers the perspectives of a variety of characters in an array of different mediums. Aiming to redress a gap in the scholarship concerning *Dracula*'s reliance upon Slovaks and Gypsies, in 'The Slovaks and Gypsies of Bram Stoker's *Dracula*: Vampires in Human Flesh' (*ELT* 58[2015] 523–35), Stoyan Tchaprazov argues that Stoker's representation of them trades on such 'Victorian anxieties as Slavo-phobia' and 'Gypso-phobia' (p. 524). Ultimately, Tchaprazov sees Stoker's use of Slovaks and Gypsies as a part of the novel's 'imperialist ambitions' (p. 524) and an anticipation or precursor of the 'future fascist persecution' of European ethnic minorities (p. 532). Macy Todd, in 'What Bram Stoker's *Dracula* Reveals about Violence' (*ELT* 58[2015] 361–84), cannily observes that while many readings of *Dracula* perceive the sexuality latent in the novel's violence, few readers have truly explored what the novel has to tell readers about violence itself. Proposing the notion of 'violence-that-disappears' as the operative concept at play in the novel—evoking, among other things, the vampire's disappearing bite marks—Todd's essay raises important questions about the relation between violence and writing. Three books on transportation and mobility signal a burgeoning area of interest for Victorian novel studies. A fourth specifically on Gaskell's fiction, *Place and Progress in the Works of Elizabeth Gaskell* edited by Lesa Scholl, Emily Morris, and Sarina Gruver Moore, is covered with specific authors below. The essays in *Transport in British Fiction: Technologies of Movement, 1840–1940*, edited by Adrienne E. Gavin and Andrew F. Humphries, discuss the representation in fiction of transport in a century of major changes in transportation technology, investigating how new forms of transport, including train, tram, horse cab, bicycle, ship, air, and space, 'changed actual and literary perspectives' (p. 2). Elizabeth Bleicher, in 'The Democratization and Erasure of Travel in William Makepeace Thackeray's *Barry Lyndon*', argues that the eponymous 'peripatetic gentleman scoundrel' became an 'unwitting symbol of the worst social problems increased travel' could cause, i.e. 'class transgression, and the social and legal crimes that anonymity fosters', and that Thackeray's erasure of any references to the details of Lyndon's transportation adds to the reader's sense that time and space in the mid-nineteenth century have become fearfully compressed (pp. 29–30). Charlotte Mathieson, in ' "A perambulating mass of woolen goods": Travelling Bodies in the Nineteenth-Century Railway Journey', explains how the railway as depicted in *Dombey and Son* remade landscapes such as Stagg's garden in its own image. Jen Cadwallader, in 'Death by Train: Spectral Technology and Dickens' *Mugby Junction*', looks at how *Mugby Junction* showed the locomotive as 'a haunting, alien, uncontrollable force' sacrificing victims for its inscrutable ends (p. 58). Tamara S. Wagner, in 'Children on Board: Transoceanic Crossings in Victorian Literature', examines how pro and con literary treatments of emigration depict children on steamships. The complex but waning role of the horse for transport is the subject of 'The Living Transport Machine: George Eliot's *Middlemarch*' by Margaret Linley, while *Black Beauty*'s empathetic depiction of cab horses concerns Adrienne E. Gavin in ' "I saw a great deal of trouble amongst the horses in London" '. In 'The "Freedom Machine": The New Woman and the Bicycle', Lena Wånggren focuses on how the bicycle became a symbol of the New Woman, and Lorna Shelley in ' "Buses should... inspire writers": Omnibuses in *Fin-de-Siècle* Short Stories and Journalism' investigates the connection between omnibus transport and 'issues of urbanity, mobility, class, and gender' (p. 136). Courtney Salvey, in 'Transport, Technology, and Trust: The "Sustaining Illusion" in Joseph Conrad's *Heart of Darkness* and *Nostromo*', discusses Conrad's portrayal of rail and shipping technologies as a means of 'concealing the heart of darkness' (p. 152). How the early science fiction of Wells, Kipling, and others embraced technology's transformation of time and space is the subject of ' "Into the interstices of time": Speed and Perception in the Scientific Romance' by Paul March-Russell. Though the remaining essays address transportation issues in the early twentieth century, Benjamin Bateman's reading of Woolf alongside *Howards End*, in 'Train(ing) Modernism: Virginia Woolf, E.M. Forster, and the Moving Locations of Queerness', may be of interest to those wishing to consider rail travel in the long nineteenth century.

Charlotte Mathieson's *Mobility in the Victorian Novel: Placing the Nation* adds to nineteenth-century mobility studies by scholars such as Jonathan Grossman, Ruth Livesey, and Josephine McDonagh a particular focus on the 'corporeality of mobility' (p. 2). Beginning with a review of changes in transportation at mid-century and an overview of mobility theory, Mathieson discusses how changes in the transportation culture altered the concept of nation in the novel. The first half of the book 'places' the nation from within the body, first looking at how walking in *The Old Curiosity Shop*, *Jane Eyre*, and *Adam Bede* opens issues of class and gender, and second considering how in *Mary Barton*, *Dombey and Son*, and *Lady Audley's Secret* railway travel raises questions about physical safety while offering opportunity. The second half of the book focuses on the global experience of travel with attention to *Villette*, *Little Dorrit*, *Dombey and Son*, *David Copperfield*, *Cranford*, and *The Moonstone*.

Anna Despotopoulou's substantive contribution to mobility studies, *Women and the Railway, 1850–1915*, analyses Victorian and early modernist fictional and non-fictional depictions of the railway experience of women. She is especially interested in exploring the tension between the freedom afforded by train travel and the limits it imposed on women, limits which they challenged through 'strategies of masquerade and deception' before finding on the railway 'new opportunities for agency in terms of escape, emancipation, [and] sexual mobility' (p. 181). Beginning with an overview of studies of mobility in general and the railway in particular, as well as social space theories, Despotopoulou adds to the conversation a study of 'texts by and about women that exclusively deal with the railway as a gendered space within a British, European, and Imperial context' (p. 9). Since her study samples a broad range of texts including novels, short stories, news items, and graphic art, Despotopoulou devotes only a few pages to each of the Victorian novels she takes up, including James's *Portrait of a Lady*, Oliphant's *Salem Chapel*, Trollope's *He Knew He Was Right*, Braddon's *Lady Audley's Secret* and *Wyllard's Weird*, Collins' *No Name* and *Armadale*, Gaskell's *North and South*, Gissing's *The Odd Women*, and Hardy's *Jude the Obscure*. Chapter 1 treats the ways in which sensation fiction exploited the dangers of train travel to show women's vulnerability. Nevertheless, the anonymity afforded by the railway could be turned to a woman's advantage, as in the case of Lady Audley. Despotopoulou notes that, while Robert's pursuit of Lady Audley by train is narrated with ample detail from timetables and station locations, Lady Audley's flight is not described, leaving it up to Robert and the reader to guess how she 'eludes, via the railway, [their] surveillance techniques', and thereby adding another layer of mystification to her true nature (p. 50). Chapter 2 explores the association between fast trains and 'fast' women, flirtatious and promiscuous behaviour being made possible by the anonymity of travellers. In chapter 3, 'Breaching National Borders', Despotopoulou looks at questions of identity that arose for female tourists. Isabel Archer gains an 'expansion of consciousness as she experiences the permeability of boundaries between self and world', while for other women travel abroad initiates contact with imperial colonists whose status as disenfranchised subjects parallels their own (p. 19). The loss of community through spatial dislocation is the focus of chapter 4, in which Despotopoulou reads *North and South* and *Jude the Obscure*. Margaret Hale, travelling to Milton by rail, finds an 'impersonal geography of uniformity and automation' that threatens to 'sever permanent relations' to home and to fragment personal identity (p. 152). Sue Bridehead, like Margaret, resists the depersonalization of passengers, and her 'infamous volatility [which] matches the instability and fleetingness of location that the twists and turns of the railway plot precariously hinge upon' ironically saves her from becoming 'inert freight' like Little Father Time (p. 155).

Several notable articles on travelling to the empire appeared. In 'Guy Boothby and the "Yellow Peril": Representations of Chinese Immigrants in the British Imperial Spaces in the Late-Nineteenth Century' (*AVSJ* 20[2015] 24–40), Ailise Bulfin turns to late nineteenth-century Anglo-Australian novelist Guy Boothby in order to 'uncover how...superficially disinterested representations of the far-flung Chinese may have contributed to the developing myth of the yellow peril' (p. 27). Bulfin takes a close look at Boothby's Nikola novels, as well as his travelogue *On the Wallaby* [1894], in order to demonstrate the centrality of the Chinese in the British imperial imaginary. Terra Walston Joseph's 'Bulward-Lytton's *The Coming Race* and an Anglo-Saxon Global "Greater Britain"' (*NCC* 37[2015] 233–48) revisits Bulwer-Lytton's satirical novel, often read as a straightforward critique of American democracy and women's rights, arguing that 'its criticism of "philosophical reformers" [was] less than total' (p. 233). Bulwer-Lytton, Joseph asserts, explored 'the problem of Anglo-Saxon globality; that is, the problem of maintaining affective and political alliances over vast distances of empire as the settler colonies moved toward greater autonomy', offering a vision of governance based on establishing a shared enemy and promoting soft forms of privately disseminated power (p. 234). Published in 2014, but not received in time for review in last year's *YWES*, Jude Wright's ' "I had peopled else this isle with Dudleys": *The Tempest* in *Uncle Silas*' (*VIJ* 42[2014] 98–117) considers the many references to Shakespeare's comedy in LeFanu's novel. *The Tempest* haunts the Gothic novel, deepening the novel's engagement with colonialism and, ultimately, according to Wright, contributing to its critique of the imperial project and the violence it inflicts upon both colonizers and the colonized. ' "Curiously near akin": The Queer Imperial Gothic Heroes of Bertram Mitford and Victoria Cross' (*NCGS* 11[2015] 21 paras.), by Emily R. Lyons, also considers the intersections between empire and gender. Lyons looks at two little-read novels, Bertram Mitford's 1896 *The Sign of the Spider* and Victoria Cross's 1903 *Six Chapters of a Man's Life*, both of which, she argues, are notable for the ways in which they present queer masculinity as the modern ideal. Andrew Glazzard calls our attention to what to many will be an unfamiliar novel in 'Conan Doyle's *The Tragedy of the 'Korosko'*: The Clash of Civilizations and the Necessity of Empire' (*ELT* 53[2015] 164–80). A novel about a hostage crisis involving Islamist militants, *The Tragedy of the 'Korosko'* eerily evokes our own contemporary political climate. Glazzard teases out how the novel both supports British imperialism and questions its basic assumptions, ultimately concluding that texts like Conan Doyle's developed the narrative framework through which the West would understand twentieth- and twenty-first-century conflict in the region. Douglas Kerr takes an unexpected approach to Conrad's fiction in 'Conrad and the Comic Turn' (*VLC* 43[2015] 149–68), writing about the influence of the music hall in developing Joseph Conrad's comic aesthetic. Music halls were a popular destination for sailors on shore, and Conrad was no exception. Kerr examines the use of specific forms of comic speech Conrad may have learned from the music hall, such as *double entendre* in *The Nigger of the 'Narcissus'*, 'An Outpost of Progress', and *Heart of Darkness*.

Three articles dealt specifically with Rider Haggard's adventure novels. In 'Rider Haggard: A Triptych of Ambiguities on British Imperialism' (*Victo* 5[2015] 51–71), Gustavo Generani treats three Haggard novels, *King Solomon's Mines*, *Allan Quatermain*, and *She*, as making up a 'unity of tensions', sharing an ideology that they collectively work to support and destabilize (p. 54). By maintaining a distance from both the colonizer and the colonized, these three texts, Generani argues, expose the constructed nature of both categories in a manner self-destructive to British imperial interests. Julia Reid takes a different approach to Haggard's novels in her essay, '"She-who-must-be-obeyed": Anthropology and Matriarchy in H. Rider Haggard's *She*' (*JVC* 20[2015] 357–74). Reid places Haggard's novel in dialogue with writings on matriarchy by late Victorian anthropological theorists such as J.J. Bachofen and J.F. McLennan. In the accounts of a matriarchal past in both anthropology and the novel, Reid traces a deep ambivalence towards Victorian patriarchy. On a more personal note, Richard Pearson reads Haggard's novel *Montezuma's Daughter* in terms of the author's own traumatic experiences leading up to and during its composition. Pearson's psychoanalytical essay, 'Personal and National Trauma in H. Rider Haggard's *Montezuma's Daughter*' (*ELT* 58[2015] 30–53), uncovers a complicated story of repression, guilt, and grief in Haggard's dark novel.

In 'The Child's Resistance to Adulthood in Robert Louis Stevenson's *Treasure Island*: Refusing to Parrot' (*ELT* 58[2015] 3–29), Alexandra Valint argues, quite against the grain, that Dr Livesey is 'cruel, greedy, emotionless, and quick to punish those deemed inferior', taking Livesey's assumption of narratorial responsibility for a series of chapters as a singular mark of his disciplinary tendencies (p. 3). Valint's approach to the Livesey character, however novel, does leave us wondering why, if Livesey is indeed to be regarded as somehow villainous, most readers have, since the novel's initial publication, regarded him as a paragon of moral virtue. Philip Steer draws our attention to two of Stevenson's less well-received works, *The Wrecker* and *The Ebb-Tide*, in 'Romances of Uneven Development: Spatiality, Trade, and Form in Robert Louis Stevenson's Pacific Novels' (*VLC* 43[2015] 343–56). The very disjointedness of these novels that has long put off readers, Steer argues, is actually part of an intentional formal experiment to better capture the political and geographical reality of his subject matter. 'In these romances of uneven development', Steer writes, 'Stevenson finds a formal and thematic means to explore and critique the inherent instability of borderless flows of trade and capital across the region' (p. 544). Steer's essay is yet another fine contribution to the burgeoning field of literary criticism on the Pacific.

Two other articles dealt specifically with spatial aspects of the empire. Sally Bushell's interdisciplinary article, 'Mapping Victorian Adventure Fiction:

Silences, Doublings, and the Ur-Map in *Treasure Island* and *King Solomon's Mines*' (*VS* 57[2015] 611–37), draws on the terminology of critical cartography in order to demonstrate that 'fictional maps are not mere appendages' to the texts in which they appear, but 'rather form a vital, integrated part of their meaning' (p. 612). In particular, Bushell uses the concepts of 'accuracy', 'cartographic silence', and 'authenticity' in order to argue that maps not only aided in the imperial project, but also questioned the moral soundness of that enterprise. The organization of imperial space is also the subject of Jean Fernandez's '"A quaint house in the oldest quarter": Gendered Spaces of Empire in Flora Annie Steel's *On the Face of the Waters*' (*NCGS* 11:i[2015] 31 paras.). Identifying the spatial politics of empire as inherently patriarchal, Fernandez argues that women in the novel, no matter what their race, struggle to expose the narratives of conquest and expansion as a delusion while attempting to imagine spatial alternatives.

Spaces at home were mapped as well. Arina Cirstea considers space in the work of two Victorian writers in 'Women's Urban Modernity: Brontë, Gaskell and Woolf' (pp. 17–31), the first chapter of her monograph, *Mapping British Women Writers' Imaginaries: Space, Self and Spirituality*. The book's overarching thesis is that Fredric Jameson's 'theory of dysfunctional spatial change' in *Postmodernism*, his influential narrative of urban modernity, does not take into account the opposing urban experience found in women's writing. Cirstea describes Jameson's theory of 'hyperspace' as the notion that spatial changes in the postmodern urban West have been so overwhelming that they exceed the ability of humans, physically and cognitively, to grasp the map and locate themselves within it, with the result that they experience 'malaise and disorientation' (p. 17). Though this model excludes alternative perceptions based on gender and spirituality as well as the experience of earlier periods of urban expansion, it is accepted as a universally applicable narrative. Looking briefly at *Villette* and *North and South*, Cirstea finds a much more optimistic evaluation of urban space in Lucy Snow's and Margaret Hale's encounters with the metropolis than that predicted by Jameson's theory. Though Lucy Snow is disoriented upon her arrival in London, the setting generates within her a feeling of liberation and new possibilities. Similarly, Margaret in *North and South* moves from initial feelings of alienation and fear in Milton Northern to a more hopeful view of the city as the potential site of new identity and greater agency. Cirstea concludes her treatment of these novels by emphasizing that Jameson's hyperspace excludes the experiences of Victorian women in the city as represented by women writers.

Two essays considered the cleanliness (or uncleanliness) of urban spaces. Margaret S. Kennedy calls our attention to the way that Charles Kingsley uses miasmatic discourse, in her article 'Eco-Conscious Synaesthesia: Dirt in Kingsley's *Yeast* and *Alton Locke*' (*VicNet* 6[2015] 59–85). According to Kennedy, by making his characters feel the air they breathe and viscerally imagine the dirt invisibly contained within it, Kingsley sought to create an eco-consciousness in his readership that could be mobilized against environmentally hazardous industrial practices. Dirt is also the subject of Erika Kvistad's 'Bad Property: Unclean Houses in Victorian City Writing' (*VicNet* 6[2015] 86–108). Here, however, 'uncleanness is the point where ... scientifically driven social activism and superstitious horror meet' (p. 90). Originally a way for dealing with the horrors of urban poverty and justifying demolition in the writing of urban exploration writers, the dirt became a way for fiction writers such as Margaret Oliphant, W.T. Stead, and R.L. Stevenson to locate horror within the bourgeois interior.

Victorian industry received considerable notice. In *Changing Hands: Industry, Evolution, and the Reconfiguration of the Victorian Body*, Peter Capuano applies body studies theory to big data's finding that 'hands appear in nineteenth-century novels eight times more frequently than in all genres of eighteenth-century texts' and argues that the spike reflects Victorians' unwillingness to accede to the simultaneous assaults by industrial mechanization and evolutionary theory on their belief in the exceptionalism of the human hand (p. 12). While resisting the common critical practice of viewing this body part as a metaphorical or metonymical figure of speech, Capuano emphasizes his study's focus on 'embodied handedness' and his commitment to resurrecting dead metaphors like 'hand-to-hand combat' in *Vanity Fair*'s drawing rooms and 'having one's hand' in events in *Great Expectations* and *Daniel Deronda* (pp. 3, 4). His first chapter focuses on *Frankenstein*'s situation at the historical moment when a shift in cultural emphasis from eyes to hands occurred, and how the novel reflects 'anxieties about God's place in a world transforming from handicraft to industrial manufacture' (p. 4). Chapter 2 examines Charles Bell's 1833 Bridgewater Treatise on *The Hand*, a text which influenced the way subsequent industrial narratives and factory fiction approached mechanical approximations of God's perfect creation. Chapter 3 examines how 'contemporary etiquette literature, household training guides, and biomedical discourse on female "nature"' inform the role of the Victorian novel's 'most infamous manipulator, Becky Sharp' (p. 6). Chapters 5 and 6 argue that awareness of evolutionary theory is behind both the obsession with hands in *Great Expectations* and the hand's connection to Jewish identity in *Daniel Deronda*. The last chapters compare the incidence of hand references in eighteenth-century epistolary novels to their incidence in nineteenth-century suspense narratives, with the surprising conclusion that novels based on the pen show less interest in hands than Victorian novels which find clues to identity in penmanship.

In *The Industrial Novels: Charlotte Brontë's Shirley, Charles Dickens' Hard Times and Elizabeth Gaskell's North and South*, Mehmet Akif Balkaya offers undergraduates in history and literature classes a sound examination of the negative effects of the Industrial Revolution as depicted in three novels selected because they were to some degree written in response to a particular historical event, they take place in the England's northern manufacturing centre, and they call for social reform. In the introduction, Balkaya gives a useful overview of the technological innovations that transformed the Victorian era into a machine age where the working class was exploited in urban centres of production, and at the beginning of each subsequent chapter he gives a brief summary of the life of the author and the plot of his or her book. Chapter 1, 'The Luddite Riots as Reflected in Charlotte Brontë's *Shirley*', focuses on the Luddite riots, the Napoleonic Wars, and the Queen's Orders of Council of 1807. Balkaya draws examples from the novel to demonstrate that women of the period were considered to be on a par with workers, both groups being 'incompetent and unemployed' (p. 25). The next chapter, 'Charles Dickens' *Hard Times*: Utilitarianism as the Idea behind the Revolution', provides detailed examinations of Gradgrind and Bounderby to show how they are satirical portraits of the misguided principles of Utilitarianism and the injurious *modus operandi* of manufacturers, respectively. Chapter 3, 'Elizabeth Gaskell's *North and South* with Reference to Preston Lockout', gives particular attention to Gaskell's balanced depiction of division between the oppressed working class and the ruling class. Margaret, a mediator between the classes, demonstrates the possibility of dialogue to bridge the rift caused by miscommunication and prejudice between factions.

A different kind of work is the subject of Joshua Gooch's *The Victorian Novel, Service Work, and the Nineteenth-Century Economy*. Using works by Eliot, Dickens, Trollope, and Collins, Gooch examines the ways novels of the 1860s and 1870s depicted and influenced the appearance of the service economy, arguing that central to the emergence of service work as distinct from productive labour, i.e. labor that creates a material good, was a new subjectivity on the part of the worker. Adapting the work of Foucault, Marx, and Judith Butler, Gooch shows how novels participated in shaping work discipline in the minds of both characters and readers and in producing the new social relations upon which the service sector depended. In the first chapter Gooch traces the changes in how unproductive labour was understood by political economists such as Adam Smith, John Stuart Mill, and Karl Marx. In chapter 2, he looks in detail at how *Silas Marner* 'offers narration as a new form of socially productive work' in that it 'constructs new connections between author and reader' (p. 58). Chapter 3 focuses on *Our Mutual Friend*, arguing that its host of service workers, from river scavengers and pawnbrokers to teachers and lawyers, demonstrates both servility within the limits of scripted performative work and improvisation that challenges those limits. In chapter 4, Gooch suggests how Collins's character-narrators in *The Moonstone* show new features of the relationship between service work and narrative work. In chapter 5 he reads violence in *The Way We Live Now* as the particular form of coercion employed by the text to discipline the service work of language-production among its characters. Gooch ends the book with a conclusion entitled 'How I Stopped Worrying and Learned to Love my Work-Discipline', in which he argues that *Dracula* imagines one way 'work can become a joyful duty rather than a punishing necessity' when 'compensation [is] built into the fabric of [the worker's] subjectivity' (p. 183).

Those interested in literature and economics will also want to read Albert D. Pionke's though-provoking essay 'William North's *The City of the Jugglers* and the "Conventional Necessity" of Mid-Nineteenth-Century Fiction' (*SNNTS* 47[2015] 158–75). North's little-read novel, Pionke explains, centres around its financial plot, unlike so many other Victorian fictions, whose financial dramas form the backdrop to some other, more central, concern. In so doing, however, North doesn't simply depart from convention; he offers an entirely new perspective on these generic constraints. Pionke writes, 'By making financial speculation its sign rather than its signifier, *City* internalizes at the level of form the notion of unfettered free trade that it repudiates. That is, its critique of the market comes to look like the market: monstrously inclusive, with none of the aesthetic protections normally afforded to either the text or the reader by the generic convention' (p. 159). Abigail Boucher has contributed to the growing volume of work on the silver fork novel with another article related to nineteenth-century economics. In 'The Business Model of the Aristocracy: Class, Consumerism, and Commodification in the Silver Fork Novels' (*NCC* 38:iii[2015] 171–81), she demonstrates 'how the silver fork genre used economic language to investigate, clarify, and problematize the relationship between the middle classes and the aristocracy' (p. 173). The silver fork novel turns out to be a particularly useful genre for examining the commodification of identity and middle-class social aspiration because of the unusual degree to which these concerns are foregrounded in the novels.

The material conditions of publishing were another popular topic in the literature in 2015. In *Serialization and the Novel in Mid-Victorian Magazines*, Catherine Delafield looks at the original serial format of five Victorian novels (Gaskell's *Cranford* serialized in *Household Words*, Trollope's *Framley Parsonage* in *Cornhill Magazine*, Craik's *Mistress and Maid* in *Good Words*, and Collins's *The Moonstone* and *Poor Miss Finch* in *All the Year Round* and *Cassell's Magazine*, respectively) to better understand them as texts shaped in interesting ways by the serial market. In chapter 1, Delafield reviews the background of serialization in the nineteenth century and explains the factors such as the adverse critical climate, the serialized novel's juxtaposition with other texts, and the intriguing collaborative role of illustration that affected narratives embedded in periodicals. Chapter 2 considers authorship of the serial novel as collaboration between author, editor, and publisher as well as the way authors might acquire personae or roles as characters and how prior authorship could be leveraged for sales. In chapter 3 Delafield focuses on the role of editor and/or publisher as controlling the 'intertextual patterning' of the serialized novel in order to 'sell fiction and to promote the repeat purchase of the periodical' (p. 47). Chapter four looks at the periodicals which serialized the five novels under consideration, providing an overview of their 'layout, discourse and rationale for existence' (p. 73). For example, the publishing house of Cassell, Petter, and Galpin 'was several removes from its original foundation as a temperance organization', a fact which influenced the reception of *Poor Miss Finch*, while *Cassell's Illustrated Family Paper*, as suggested by the prominent inclusion of the word 'family' in its title, was a 'conservative, general interest, illustrated family miscellany intended for Sunday reading at home' (pp. 86–7). Chapter 5 examines the way each of the novels chosen for study attempted to design narrative strategies that would play to the periodical's commercial aspirations, and offers new interpretations of both forms of the novels. In chapter 6 Delafield explores the afterlife of the serials as fixed texts, drawing comparisons between the serialized version and the later book and finally summarizing a four-part model by which serialized novels can be studied by others: 'looking at the periodical frame, the function of authorship, the overall rhythm of production, and the intertextual patterns within and between numbers of the periodical' (p. 183). Delafield's thoroughly researched and clearly organized study concludes that the serial is not an 'imperfect original' but rather is a 'creative collaboration between author, editor, and periodical' (p. 184). 'Modulating Narrative Voice: Mary Russell Mitford's Sketches of Rural Character' (*WW* 22[2015] 505–24), by Kevin A. Morrison, examines Mitford's character sketches in their original context, the *Lady's Magazine*. Reading the sketches alongside the surrounding copy encourages a different interpretation of Mitford's text than that of later readers who came to it in book form. Drawing on the methodologies of book history, Morrison makes a compelling case that Mitford's distinctive narrative voice exists in the interrelation of text and context rather than in Mitford's formal choices alone. In 'Public Gains and Literary Goods: A Coeval Tale of Joseph Conrad, Rudyard Kipling and Francis Marion Crawford' (in Macdonald and Singer, eds., *Transitions in Middlebrow Writing, 1880–1930*, pp. 37–56), Simon Frost denies that large-scale publishers with commercial interests promoted low-brow literature while more aesthetically minded publishers preferred to support 'great' literature. In order to show what drove the nineteenth-century fiction market he sets aside current distinctions of literary merit and looks for what 'literary good' was purchased by book consumers, a good 'utterly below the critical radar'. Frost then identifies the literary good offered by three novelists who enjoyed both popular and critical acclaim around the turn of the century. Two—Conrad and Kipling—bridged the transition from the popular market to a new literary market while one—Marion Crawford—did not. Frost identifies the literary good Conrad, Kipling, and Crawford offered as the engrossing example of men who showed courage and honour in the dangerous domain of the Other.

In her interesting article, 'Investigating Charles Reade, the *Pall Mall Gazette* and the "Newspaper Novel"' (*JVC* 19[2015] 183–97), Beth Palmer argues for Reade's 'unrecognized but important place in [the] story of the relationship between the novel and the news' (p. 184). Unlike so many other writers of the period, Reade, according to Palmer, embraced the crossover between newspaper and novel, seeing the novelist as working under the same professional obligation to expose and report abuses of power to the public. 'The novelist and the journalist were not', Palmer writes, ' "sibling rival[s]" in Reade's eyes, but partners in enterprises of social reformism and public entertainment' (p. 185).

Three articles appeared on the work of George Gissing, mostly regarding his interaction with the publishing industry, but also concerned with biography and genre. Margaret D. Stetz sets out to balance *New Grub Street*'s pessimistic, masculine, and claustrophobic account of literary London by contrasting it with a periodical first published the same year as Gissing's novel in her essay, 'Internationalizing Authorship: Beyond *New Grub Street* to the *Bookman* in 1891' (*VPR* 48[2015] 1–14). Both Gissing and the *Bookman*'s founder, W. Robertson Nicoll, Stetz claims, realized that 'writing had become an industry inseparable from the concerns and demands of those who distributed, circulated, and consumed literature', and yet they reacted very differently (p. 11). Where Gissing saw reason for dejection, Nicoll saw an opportunity for new, more cosmopolitan literary networks. Ying Ying provides a helpful survey of largely untranslated Chinese criticism on Gissing's work from the 1920s, when Gissing's work was first noticed in China, until the late 1980s,

in her article, 'The Reception of George Gissing in China' (*ELT* 58[2015]
209–19). Amanda Kotch's suggestive essay, 'George Gissing and the Fictional
Work of Biography' (*SEL* 55[2015] 879–97), uses late Victorian attitudes
towards literary biography in order to theorize literary realism—in particular
as practised by Gissing. With readings of *The Unclassed*, *New Grub Street*, and
*Charles Dickens: A Critical Study*, Kotch argues that Gissing capitalized on
the slippage between biographical and fictional modes as part of his aesthetic
practice.

   A couple of important essays appeared on nineteenth-century criticism and
reading practices. In 'David Masson, Belles Lettres, and a Victorian Theory of
the Novel' (*VLC* 43[2015] 1–21), Jack M. Downs argues that the implicit
theory of the novel within Victorian era literary criticism can best be described
as a 'belles-lettres-influenced literary criticism' (p. 3). Distinct yet related to the
eighteenth-century discourse of belles-lettres from which it developed,
Victorian novel theory, according to Downs, was less systematic yet deeply
concerned with three principles borrowed from the earlier movement:
propriety, taste, and sublimity. Downs's well-researched essay is particularly
useful for restoring Victorian writers to a history of literary criticism in a
manner that emphasizes continuity and development while recognizing key
differences in the eighteenth- and nineteenth-century stances towards theory.
Cassandra Falke provides an important intervention in the conversation
surrounding the role of sympathy in nineteenth-century reading practices. Her
essay, 'On the Morality of Immoral Fiction: Reading Newgate Novels,
1830–1848' (*NCC* 38[2015] 183–93), demonstrates that crime fiction destabi-
lized the eighteenth-century account of sympathetic reading as a moral
practice. Instead, sympathy came to be seen as a dangerously automatic
reaction that might encourage illicit behaviour when evoked by immoral
characters. Newgate fiction, in Falke's account, thus becomes an important
chapter in the development of distanced reading practices, which came to be
seen as a powerful antidote to a sympathetic reading experience increasingly
coded as popular.

   Several contributions were made at the intersection of Victorian literature
and science. Will Abberley's *English Fiction and the Evolution of Language,
1850–1914* explores the interconnectedness of fiction and science in understanding the development of language, gathering evidence from a wide array
of minor as well as canonical authors. The introduction, 'Language under a
Microscope', explains that Victorians' self-consciously scientific attitude
towards the study of language infiltrated fictional accounts of linguistic
change. The writing of Herbert Spencer and Charles Darwin inspired
speculations on language's evolutionary future, while the work of Friedrich
Max Müller spawned fictions looking back to the oral foundation of language
in prehistory. At the same time, Abberley argues, fiction was a laboratory of
the imagination which tested and in turn influenced scientific discourse.
Chapter 1 examines how 'utopian and prophetic fiction both responded to and
framed the discourse of language progressivism' (p. 22). For example, H.G.
Wells's early scientific romances imagine speech forms (e.g. telepathy) 'which
seem to accomplish progressive goals' (p. 23). Although this apparent progress
resulted in 'breakdowns in sympathy and understanding' among characters

(p. 23), Wells ignored his own linguistic prognosis in order to defend the ideal of a world state based on a rationally devised lingua franca, and in *The War in the Air* showed 'linguistic nationalism as a driving force behind war and imperialism' (p. 53). Chapter 2 examines how archaeology's discovery of humans' prehistoric record fuelled interest in writing about the primitive linguistic past. Narrative 'visions of primitive language grew in tandem with forms of romance fiction' such as H.R. Haggard's depiction of 'Africans as frozen in the childhood of thought' (pp. 56, 60). In chapter 3, 'Organic Orality and the Historical Romance', Abberley argues that the historical romances of Charles Kingsley and R.M. Ballantyne sought 'ways of reconnecting with [the] organic verbal past', while the Viking fiction of James Frederick Hodgetts and Paul du Chaillu strove to use etymology to 'trigger racial impulses, reuniting speakers with their natural heritage' (pp. 92, 101). On the other hand, Victorian invasion fiction by George Chesney and Saki warned of the 'contamination of English' by Continental forces (p. 106). Looking further back in time, William Morris found evidence of linguistic commonality to support his vision of international socialism, but Thomas Hardy's novels 'lament the disappearance of regional dialects' (p. 121). In chapter 4, 'Instinctive Signs: Nature and Culture in Dialogue', Abberley notes that the *fin de siècle* 'explored speech as a pluralist dialogue between instinct and convention' (p. 128), as in Butler's *The Way of All Flesh* and Hardy's novels, where facial expression, gesture, and vocality communicate more honestly than conventional speech, prompting sympathetic understanding even between different species. In the conclusion, 'Widening the Lens', Abberley offers several topics deserving of further study, such as 'the relationship between instinct and convention in meaning' (p. 171).

Naturalism hasn't received much attention in Victorian studies of late, but John Plotz's fascinating essay 'Speculative Naturalism and the Problem of Scale: Richard Jefferies's *After London*, after Darwin' (*MLQ* 76[2015] 31–56) makes us wish it had. Plotz convincingly argues that naturalism, often treated as an unimportant offshoot of realism, actually encompassed a large body of work written in the wake of Darwin's *Origin of Species* and *Descent of Man*. Of particular interest is Plotz's claim that naturalism's impersonal approach to description brings into relief the often unrecognized affinity between realism and modernism, both of which prioritize 'felt individual experience as the evidentiary matrix on which their accounts of the world are based' (p. 33). Examining Jefferies's speculative fiction, *After London*, as his test case, Plotz contends that what makes naturalism distinct in literary history—and worth renewed consideration—is its experimental oscillations in scale. Shuttling between microscopic description and macroscopic abstraction while eschewing the personal and experiential, naturalism, in Plotz's estimation, suggests that 'many of the underlying assumptions of eighteenth- and nineteenth-century social realism were less obliterated in high modernist literature than we have long assumed' (p. 53).

Three final essays in this area consider the connections between literature and the mind—both human and animal. Using an obscure novel by Charlotte Tucker as her test case, Julie A. Smith demonstrates the close connection between the depiction of the animal mind in popular animal autobiographies of the period and the prevailing science of the day in her article, 'Representing Animal Minds in Early Animal Autobiography: Charlotte Tucker's *The Rambles of a Rat* and Nineteenth-Century Natural History' (*VLC* 43[2015] 725–44). In turning their animal protagonists into narrative heroes, however, writers like Tucker had to go beyond natural history, demonstrating in the process that the mysterious mental worlds of animals might be more complicated than the naturalists they based their stories on were willing to allow. In 'Faith and Hysteria: The Diagnosis of George Macdonald's *Adela Cathcart*' (*BAS* 21[2015] 101–7), István Szabadi argues that Macdonald's depiction of female hysteria and the medical community was ahead of its time. Hysteria in the novel, according to Szabadi, is presented as 'a sickness of the soul . . . more so, a sickness of faith, which is caused by social-gender problems' rather than by the inherent weakness of the softer sex (p. 101). Linda McDaniel provides a relatively straightforward psychiatric evaluation of Roy Richmond in 'The Manic-Depressive Father in George Meredith's *Harry Richmond*' (*VLC* 43[2015] 589–605). The article provides background on the history of the disorder and its classification in the nineteenth century as well as some biographical explanation for Meredith's personal interest in how the disease, when afflicting the patriarch, affects the family as well.

Religion was not to be outdone by science, however. Rebecca Rainof's *The Victorian Novel of Adulthood: Plot and Purgatory in Fictions and Maturity*, reviewed above, was a particularly notable contribution in this area, but so too is Richard Hughes Gibson's monograph, *Forgiveness in Victorian Literature: Grammar, Narrative, and Community*, which argues that forgiveness was a pervasive problem in Victorian discourse. Gibson argues that far from viewing forgiveness as a simple ethical principle, the Victorians questioned the origin of the impulse to forgive, how it works—if indeed it does work—and its implications for human psychology and community. To address these questions Gibson explores selected novels by major authors with regard to three topics. In chapter 1, drawing on the work of philosopher Robert Roberts and Shakespearean critic Sarah Beckwith, Gibson urges the importance of a *grammar* of forgiveness, i.e. a set of loose rules of usage to define this term within the context of related ethical concepts such as repentance and reconciliation. Secondly, in keeping with Charles Griswold's systematic discussion of forgiveness, Gibson stresses that forgiveness has a *narrative* dimension in that it first requires a retelling of the offending events, secondly has a 'timeful character', meaning that it is not bound by the moment but must endure in order to be genuine, and finally alters, not the events themselves, but the way the *story* of events is told (p. 16). Last, Gibson, like Beckwith, emphasizes that forgiveness is a part of community-building. Chapter 2 looks at the 'extravagance and excess of Dickensian forgiveness' in that it explodes rational boundaries of justice (p. 40). Tracing four redemption plots in *Dombey and Son*, Gibson finds different types of forgiveness stimulated not only by Christ's teachings but, when that ideal cannot be realized, by the secular ethics of duty. In Trollope's *The Vicar of Bullhampton* and Eliot's *Adam Bede*, Gibson finds that the focus on forgiveness broadens to embrace the community at large. Trollope 'raises the difficulty of communicating about forgiveness outside the context of the Christian faith' (p. 94), as will Hardy after him, but shows that community provides alternative models of forgiveness. George Eliot, like other freethinkers who questioned Christianity, remained committed to the value of forgiveness while disagreeing with the Bible on rationale. In particular, she shows that forgiveness cannot—and should not—cancel the deeds of the past; on the contrary, suffering the consequences of past offences is a necessary part of 'psychological and communal healing' (p. 103). Gibson closes the book with a pairing of Hardy and Wilde. Characters in *Jude the Obscure*, excepting Arabella, yearn for traditional Christian forgiveness, but are disappointed when well-intentioned acts of forgiveness injure the recipient. Though Wilde's *De Profundis* is a prison letter rather than a novel, Gibson includes an examination of this text because he sees it as a life narrative which reflects an understanding of forgiveness similar to Griswold's. Though he grounds his discussion of forgiveness in Christ's teaching, Wilde does not accept his society's assumptions about what constitutes sexual sin; rather, he reinterprets his personal history in the light of Christ's radical example of forgiving Mary Magdalene in that she 'loved much' (p. 153).

Katherine J. Anderson treats seven now obscure martyrological novels from the 1850s and 1860s in her suggestive essay, 'The Sensory Citizen-Witness: Liturgies of Torture in Mid-Victorian Martyrological Novels' (*VR* 41[2015] 143–61). Through vivid scenes of torture, Anderson argues, these texts 'provided readers with an experience that went bone-deep, infusing religious belief with urgent relevancy for the embodied citizens of the British nation and raising and shaping popular religious consciousness through their art rather than through sermons or treatises' (p. 158). The novel's ability to create intense sensory experiences made it a valuable tool in the religious recalibration of mid-century Britain. Finally, Anne DeWitt, in 'Advances in the Visualization of Data: The Network of Genre in the Victorian Periodical Press' (*VPR* 48[2015] 161–82), draws on the work of Franco Moretti and Ed Finn, employing network analysis in order to recover reader reactions to the neglected genre of the theological novel. The article includes exciting visual representations of the connections nineteenth-century readers drew between individual novels as reported in the periodical press. DeWitt does an exceptional job of explaining her methodology, and ends with a thoughtful discussion of how to introduce modelling and data analysis to the classroom, making her essay a valuable resource for anyone interested in exploring the digital humanities.

Turning to individual authors, it was an excellent year for biographical work on the Brontës, with the appearance of three books dedicated to their lives: a biography of Charlotte Brontë by Claire Harman, a creative study of the entire family by Deborah Lutz, and a book on the Brontës' Irishness by Edward Chitham. Harman's *Charlotte Brontë, A Life*, also published as *Charlotte Brontë: A Fiery Heart*, is added to her already impressive shelf of biographies, which includes books on Fanny Burney, Robert Louis Stevenson, and Jane Austen. Like most biographers of Charlotte Brontë, Harmon draws heavily on Gaskell's *Life*, following Gaskell in seeing Brontë as 'essentially a poet of suffering', but also insisting that Brontë was a spirited, often rebellious woman, untrammelled by Victorian notions of propriety (p. 227).

Significantly, Harman opens by recounting an 1843 incident Brontë confided in a letter to her sister and later revisited in *Villette*, an anguished walk through the streets of Brussels that landed her in a Catholic confession booth where she, presumably, lightened her heart by confiding her unrequited love for Professor Héger. This moment becomes a touchstone for Harman's biography, which offers as its major contribution an analysis of Brontë's writing as a form of confession, an outlet for a strong and emotional nature given to bouts of rage, depression, and passion. Harman interweaves Brontë's biography with her fictions to provide evidence of her view. This confessional technique, Harman contends, was in part responsible for the groundbreaking psychological penetration Brontë was able to achieve through first-person narration. The culminating example of her confessional style came, of course, in *Villette*, which Harman calls 'a landmark in the depiction of states of mind and self-perception, a thoroughly, peculiarly and disturbingly Modernist novel' (p. 314).

In *The Brontë Cabinet: Three Lives in Nine Objects*, Deborah Lutz follows up on her *Relics of Death in Victorian Literature and Culture* with a fascinating transformation of traditional biography from a linear account of life events into an evocation of the shared life of Charlotte, Anne, and Emily Brontë from the objects they touched. Beginning in the preface with a mental recreation of Catherine Earnshaw's bed cabinet in which she kept her library and on which she scratched her name, Lutz sets the tone of intimate encounter with ghosts of the past through the artefacts they left behind, suggesting that the oak case is an emblem of a 'portal' that can carry us 'to another sphere' (p. xx). In meticulously describing and imaginatively speculating about nine types of belongings important to the Brontës, Lutz endeavours to take advantage of material culture's uncanny powers of teleportation in order to illuminate the lives and writings of this literary family. In chapter 1, 'Tiny Books', Lutz focuses on the minute books 'published' by the Brontë children, about a hundred of which survive, written in microscopic minuscule in imitation of real book type. While reflecting on the scarcity of paper and the consequent repurposing of paper and books, Lutz inserts information about the mementos the Brontës kept between pages of books in the family library. In chapter 2, Lutz tours the numerous domestic jobs that kept the Brontë sisters busy, from peeling fruit and vegetables to the many forms of needlework Victorian girls and women did for livelihood or recreation. The title of the chapter—'Pillopatate'—comes from wordplay Emily formed in her 'diary papers' for 'peel a potato' as spoken in the Yorkshire accent of servant Tabby. Lutz explains that the Brontë girls kept writing paper handy while doing chores and offers examples of the experimental stream of consciousness style Emily developed as she 'exchanged her quill pen for a peeling knife', recording details of her kitchen work alongside glimpses of the fantasy narrative she is co-authoring with Anne. The chapter continues with examples of other work paraphernalia owned by the Brontë women and their fictional characters, items often hand-made and given as gifts by one friend to another—embroidery samplers, needlework boxes, needle cases, etc., all important in the shared consciousness of Victorian women. In the remaining seven chapters—'Out Walking', 'Keeper, Grasper, and Other Family

Animals', 'Fugitive Letters', 'The Alchemy of Desks', 'Death Made Material', 'Memory Albums', and 'Migrant Relics'—Lutz lovingly handles 'the belongings of authors [she] greatly admires' (p. xxiv). Illustrations and copious notes further enrich the discussion. Careful not to give her imagination too much play and grounding speculation in research, she knits together biography, close reading, history, and sociology in a seamless web within which the Brontës and their world come to life. *The Brontë Cabinet* is enthusiastically recommended to scholars and lay readers alike.

Expanding on his 1986 publication, *The Brontës' Irish Background*, Edward Chitham sets out, in *Western Winds: The Brontës' Irish Heritage*, to reinforce the importance of the Brontës' Irishness in their lives and in their writing. Noting that Charlotte and her father, Patrick, more than the other family members, sought to obscure their Irish background, Chitham suggests that we think of them as troubled by a double vision similar to that experienced by contemporary immigrants from the Asian subcontinent. Chitham devotes considerable attention to the problem of sources and gives a detailed rationale for his cautious use of William Wright's *The Brontës in Ireland* in spite of its errors and romantic embroidery. Wright, he observes, left the only record of Hugh Prunty, Patrick's father, and grew up close to Patrick's birthplace in Ireland. Always providing meticulous reasons for drawing his conclusions from scanty or vague sources, Chitham affixes Hugh Prunty's turn to Protestantism to the time of his employment as a servant to James Hernshaw and explains Patrick's ascent from blacksmith's assistant to weaver's apprentice to schoolmaster as arising from his bookishness as well as his father's unfulfilled wish to be 'a great scholar' himself (p. 83). Particularly interesting are Chitham's investigation of the considerable linguistic evidence he finds in the children's juvenilia of their Irish heritage and his excavation of Emily's recollections of stories told by her grandfather, Hugh Prunty, from within the text of *Wuthering Heights*.

*Brontë Studies* also published several essays dealing with the Brontës' lives and especially early years. Sarah Fermi's essay, 'A Question of Colour' (*BS* 40[2015] 334–42), examines the evangelical mission of the those who established the Clergy Daughter's School as well as the West Indian connections of some of the students who attended it. Fermi considers how the Brontë sisters' time at Cowan Bridge would have shaped their perception of race and imperialism. Turning to literary representation, Fermi argues that Quashia Quamina, a black character in the Brontës' juvenilia, was later developed in Emily and Charlotte's mature writing, most notably as Heathcliff. Olivia Malfait and Marysa Demoor consider the later literary dynamic between the sisters in 'Sibling Collaboration and Literary After-Life: The Case of the Brontës' (*BS* 40[2015] 187–200). Malfait and Demoor read Charlotte's editorial framing of and additions to Emily's work as an attempt to downplay the unfeminine quality in her younger sister's oeuvre, in part by presenting the material as co-authored. Stephen Whitehead provides an overview of existing theories on the origin of the Brontë pseudonyms, as well as his own conjectures on the subject, in 'The Bell Pseudonyms: A Brontë Connection?' (*BS* 40[2015] 59–64). Bob Duckett provides an improved catalogue of the Heaton family's library to which the Brontës had access and considers the possible role the collection played in their education and writing in 'The Library at Ponden Hall' (*BS* 40[2015] 104–49). In 'The Brontës, the Corset and the Condition of England' (*BS* 40[2015] 320–7), Birgitta Berglund revisits the letters and novels of the Brontë sisters in light of the controversies leading up to the dress reform movement. Though the Brontë sisters predate most of the public conversation Berglund considers, she, nevertheless, demonstrates how issues of surrounding dress, and especially the corset, informed their lives and fiction. Emma Butcher also considers early influences on the Brontë siblings in her article for *Victorian Periodical Review*, 'Napoleonic Periodicals and the Childhood Imagination: The Influence of War Commentary on Charlotte and Branwell Brontë's Glass Town and Angria' (*VPR* 48[2015] 469–86). Butcher treats Charlotte and Branwell's juvenilia as a fascinating early example of fan fiction written in response to the representation of Wellington and Napoleon in the periodical press. The presence of these two personalities in the children's fiction sheds light on Waterloo's afterlife in the public imaginary as well as the domineering heroes of Charlotte's mature fiction.

Gender was, as always, a popular topic for scholarship on *Jane Eyre*. Sarah Wootton, in 'Female Beauty and Portraits of Self-Effacement in Charlotte Brontë's *Jane Eyre*' (in O'Neill, Sandy, and Wootton, eds., *The Persistence of Beauty: Victorians to Moderns*, pp. 15–30), argues that *Jane Eyre* was a revolutionary novel for introducing a 'plain' heroine, but was also a novel 'rooted in . . . a mid-Victorian imprint of beauty' (p. 15). In close readings of selected passages from the novel as well as modern illustrations, Wootton finds that *Jane Eyre* inscribes a complex of conflicting attitudes towards beauty in which 'socially sanctioned beauty is invariably found wanting and proves to be more limiting . . . than Jane's professed plainness' (pp. 24–5). She concludes with evidence from the text and from Paula Rego's penetrating lithographic illustrations that Jane's actual appearance and the specific nature of her inner beauty are 'endlessly deferred', leaving open-ended the novel's insight into what constitutes her true beauty (p. 30). In 'What Jane Eyre Taught: The "Autobiographer" in *Jane Eyre* and Women's Education' (*BAS* 21[2015] 39–47), Violeta Craina attempts to make sense of the apparent disconnect between the education and marriage plots in the novel by rereading the narrative through the formal lens of autobiography. Rebecca Fraser, in her article 'The "Woman Question" and Charlotte Brontë' (*BS* 40[2015] 314–19), works through another disjunction, that between Charlotte Brontë's seemingly feminist message in *Jane Eyre* and her opposition to women's suffrage, by taking a closer look at the complicated history of the nineteenth-century woman question.

Other scholarship on the novel covered folklore, public health, birds, and translation. Reuben Sass's 'Swan Maidens and Spirits: The Archetype of the Fairy in *Jane Eyre*' (*VJ* 127[2015] 18–30) revisits Jane's association with the fairy world. Allusions to British folklore, scattered as they are throughout the entire text, Sass argues, offer a constant in a text whose protagonist changes drastically over the course of the narrative. Published in 2014, but not received in time for review in last year's *YWES*, Fran Thielman's excellent essay, '*Jane Eyre* and Public Health: A Closer Look at the Lowood

School Epidemic' (*VIJ* 42[2015] 179–98), urges us to attend to a group of victims often overshadowed by the consumptive Helen Burns: the mostly unnamed girls who die of the typhus epidemic at Lowood. Thielman argues that 'Brontë portrays the girls at Lowood as victims of institutional neglect' and suggests that the 'account of the actions of the wealthy people of Lowton to help the school provides a possible vision of a Board of Health' (p. 179). Kathleen Anderson and Heather R. Lawrence examine *Jane Eyre*'s abundant avian imagery in ' "No net ensnares me": Bird Imagery and the Dynamics of Dominance and Submission in Charlotte Brontë's *Jane Eyre*' (*BS* 40[2015] 240–51) in order to claim that Brontë's use of birds is far more complicated than previous critics have realized and evolves along with Jane's own personal and romantic development in the novel. Jane travels to Russia in Anna A. Syskina and Vitaly S. Kiselev's 'The Problem of Rendering Psychological Content in V. Vladimirov's Translation of *Jane Eyre* (1893)' (*BS* 40[2015] 181–6). Syskina and Kiselev compare Vladimirov's version to previous Russian translations as well as to the original novel, finding it more faithful, yet still more muted in its portrayal of Jane and Rochester's emotional excesses.

Several essays on *Shirley* also appeared. Comparing Brontë's fictional representations of mill owners to the idealized professional manufacturers described and lauded in the writings of Thomas Carlyle, Samuel Smiles, and John Ruskin, Erin Nyborg argues, in 'Captains of Industry and the Subversion of the Professional Ideal in Charlotte Brontë's *The Professor* and *Shirley*' (*BS* 40[2015] 306–13), that the novelist's mill owners problematize a code of commercial morality and professionalism fast becoming codified in the era. In particular, Brontë exposes these captains of industry as compromised by pride, paternalism, and a dependence on political and economic rather than moral investments. Religion, not economics, is the subject of Sara L. Pearson's essay, ' "God save it! God also reform it!": The Condition of England's Church in Charlotte Brontë's *Shirley*' (*BS* 40[2015] 290–6). According to Pearson, the question of social and economic reform in England was, for Brontë, inseparable from the need for spiritual reform in England's churches. Specifically, Brontë's novel counsels a middle road between High Church ritual and Low Church radicalism. Patsy Stoneman takes a different tack entirely in her essay '*Shirley* as Elegy' (*BS* 40[2015] 22–33). Taking seriously Brontë's reported assertion that the title character was intended to represent 'what Emily Brontë would have been, had she been placed in health and prosperity', Stoneman contends that *Shirley* is an elegiac novel, but in more ways than Brontë's strange comment might suggest (p. 24). If the title character seems like a strained tribute, Brontë succeeds better in her 'evocations of the natural world' which 'stand as her elegy, her memorial to Emily's love of mother earth, and as her own best claim to be a poet' (p. 32). *Shirley* also receives considerable attention in Marianne Thormählen's essay, 'The Brontë Novels as Historical Fiction' (*BS* 40[2015] 276–82). Thormählen asks why it is that all of the novels written by the Brontë sisters were set in the past, concluding that though always interested in the present, these backward-looking novels suggest that the sisters' 'deepest concern is never just the condition of England, but the condition of humanity' (p. 281).

Scholarship in 2015 on *Villette* included Beth Tressler's 'Illegible Minds: Charlotte Brontë's Early Writings and the Psychology of Moral Management in *Jane Eyre* and *Villette*' (*SNNTS* 47[2015] 1–19), which faults recent criticism on Victorian psychology for 'sustain[ing] the traditional Victorian binaries that put self-control in conflict with imaginative states' (p. 1). According to Tressler, Brontë's fiction works out a 'complex dialectic of self-control and ecstatic self-loss' and associates mental disease and insanity with a problematic insistence on the legibility of necessarily illegible psychic states (p. 1). Maria Ioannou examines the marriage subplots in '"I am the picture of Aunt Ginevra": Marriage Plotting, Sub-Plotting and the Spectacle of Beauty in *Villette*'s Economy of Female Worth' (*BS* 40[2015] 215–28). Analysing the plots of each of the female characters alongside one another, Ioannou concludes that in the social order described by *Villette* only unusual-looking women are allowed to rebel within their plots. Molly Ryder focuses on Lucy's imaginative reconstruction of space in her essay 'Dwelling in the Heart-Shrine: Lucy Snowe's Creative Architectural Metaphors in Charlotte Brontë's *Villette*' (*BS* 40[2015] 328–33). Challenging accounts of the novel that focus on the ways in which Lucy is confined and surveilled, Ryder turns our attention to what she terms 'architectural internalization, whereby an interior aspect of the mind or body is described metaphorically in architectural terms, allow[ing] authors to provide spatial extension to the intangible, housing thoughts and emptions within a material organ' (p. 328). Lucy, Ryder argues, utilizes this literary technique to build the kind of safe and nurturing interiors denied to her in the physical world. Finally, considering the range of Charlotte's fiction, Steven Earnshaw's essay, 'Charlotte Brontë's Fictional Epistles' (*BS* 40[2015] 201–14), posits that throughout the course of her career Brontë began to see in the 'ontology of letters... a potential bridge between souls' linking physical and spiritual being' (p. 201). Looking at Brontë's own letters, as well as those that feature in each of her major works, Earnshaw makes a convincing case for the metaphysical function of the epistle in Brontë's oeuvre.

An entire monograph appeared on film adaptations of Emily Brontë's novel, *Wuthering Heights*. Valérie Hazette's *Wuthering Heights on Film and Television: A Journey Across Time and Cultures* endeavours to provide a comprehensive examination of visual adaptations of *Wuthering Heights* across cultures as an 'ideologically charged journey during which archetypal structures and figures are dynamically translated and surreptitiously transmitted' (p. 59). Her project thus attends to the particularly rich mythical substrate of the novel that attracts and withstands translation across genres and to the cultural contexts governing filmmakers' aims and audience reception of the various adaptations. Part I briefly contextualizes the novel within Brontë's biography, identifies the novel's broader intertextual dimensions, and explains Hazette's methodology. For the chapters discussing the novel's reflection of myth and legend (Psyche, Beauty and the Beast, and Tristan and Iseult) and the Gothic as described in Georges Bataille's influential 1957 *Literature and Evil*, Hazette provides a chart. Part II endeavours to recover an understanding of the first feature film of *Wuthering Heights* based on Eliot Stannard's adaptation of the novel and directed by A.V. Bramble in 1920. In the absence of film footage, Hazette bases her discussion of the film on a ten-page programme, a frame enlargement, and two stills, all of which are reproduced in the text. She finds the cast list, textual 'foreword', and pictures in the advertising materials to be invaluable clues about, among other things, the film's degree of fidelity to the novel, its use of Brontë's gender as a sales gimmick, and its strong commitment to melodrama. To further suggest what the lost film was like, Hazette reproduces newspaper reviews from the 1920s and examines the films Bramble and Stannard made immediately before *Wuthering Heights*. Part III focuses on cross-heritage transformations, reading the Mexican adaptation, *Abismos de passion* [1953] directed by Luis Buñuel, alongside William Wyler's North American *Wuthering Heights* [1939]. The former represents a 'literary process of adaptation' where the novel is transformed into a surrealist staging of a fatal love attraction, while the latter is a Hollywood classic where the influential producer (Goldwyn) and the personalities of the main actors, especially Olivier, take a major role in shaping the novel (p. 2). After treating adaptations of British serialized drama for television, Hazette moves on to the British feature film's era of period drama inaugurated by the 1970 film by Tilly and Fuest and perfected over several decades to 'reflect the socio-historical truths depicted by Emily Brontë', notably making room for the second generation of lovers without stretching the film into a series (p. 3). Finally, Hazette looks at anti-period pieces, where she finds that bold changes such as switching Cathy's and Heathcliff's gender (*Sparkhouse* [2002]) or relocating the film in distant cultures (*Hurlevent* [1985]; *Onimaru* [1988]; and *Wuthering Heights* [2011]) test whether the novel's mythical subtext can survive translocation from the heath. Though Hazette presents important terms in bold out of concern for pedagogical clarity, the pervasiveness of these terms, often jargonistic, can be overwhelming. This, coupled with the decision to break up chapters into very short segments, impedes the flow and cohesiveness of this thorough and often insightful discussion.

Luis Rocha Antunes also published an article on an adaptation of *Wuthering Heights*. 'Adapting with the Senses: *Wuthering Heights* as a Perceptual Experience' (*The Victorian* 3:i[2015] 1–12) focuses on Andrea Arnold's 2011 adaptation of the novel. Antunes recognizes Arnold's film as participating in a recent cinematographic trend of representing 'the haptic and phenomenal appeal of human bodies and the landscape' in order to 'provide a new configuration of the materiality of the story world' (p. 2).

Several articles appeared just on the novel as well. According to Thomas J. Joudrey's ' "Well, we *must* be for ourselves in the long run": Selfishness and Sociality in *Wuthering Heights*' (*NCL* 70[2015] 165–93), Emily Brontë's only novel negotiates between selfish desires that tend towards a destructive and irresponsibly bounded solipsism and sociable ones that foster the community at the cost of interpersonal vulnerability and even shame. Most of the characters in the novel, Jourdrey argues, are object lessons in the dangers of selfishness, and yet Brontë, in Joudrey's reading, is unwilling to promote Victorian self-renunciation. Instead, a certain degree of self-preservation and distance is offered as a precondition for openness and successful sociality as epitomized by the relationship between Hareton and Cathy. Isabella Cooper's 'The Sinister Menagerie: Animality and Antipathy in *Wuthering Heights*'

(*BS* 40[2015] 252–62) makes two related claims: first that Brontë elides the human and animal, and second, that this elision, by refusing to acknowledge the concept of exclusionary humanity on which sympathetic feeling is based, renders Brontë's an 'antipathetic' novel that actively thwarts its reader's desire for identification. Graeme Tytler published two essays on Emily Brontë's novel this year. The first, 'Facets of Time Consciousness in *Wuthering Heights*' (*BS* 40[2015] 11–21), attends to the meticulous references to time in the novel as an important indicator of character as well as evidence of a metaphysical preoccupation on the part of the author. The second, 'House and Home in *Wuthering Heights*', investigates the novel's persistent homesickness as well as the manner in which houses and homes reflect back on those who live and pass through them. Moving from novel to biography, Christopher Cooper's essay, 'Was Emily Brontë an Amateur Geometer?' (*BS* 40[2015] 1–10), takes us to the Brontë parsonage library in order to examine a manuscript containing Brontë's geometric sketches and identify the manual from which she took her instructions. Christopher Heywood provides evidence for his belief that the original of a portrait of Emily Brontë declared lost by William Robertson Nicholl has resurfaced in 'Found: The "Lost" Portrait of Emily Brontë' (*BS* 40[2015] 85–103).

Very little scholarship appeared in 2015 on Anne Brontë. Carmen Pérez Ríu's essay, ' "Don't forget this is how I earn my living": Internal Focalization, Subjectivity and the Victorian Woman Artist in the Adaptation of Anne Brontë's *The Tenant of Wildfell Hall* (BBC Miniseries, 1996)' (*BS* 40[2015] 44–58), is a notable exception. Ríu thoughtfully connects contemporary adaptation to the way in which the novel focalizes the narrative through its own process of audiovisual translation in the form of Helen's paintings and diary. Nora Gilbert's fascinating essay, 'A Servitude of One's Own' (*NCL* 69[2015] 455–80), reads the letters and novels of Charlotte and Anne Brontë alongside the letters and writings of other nineteenth-century women who found themselves in this solitary and increasingly mythologized role. Writing, one of the few recreational activities available to the socially marginalized governess, Gilbert argues, became 'a key component of the governessorial mystique' (p. 457). According to Gilbert, these scribbling women were important figures both in literary and political history, and 'the governessing profession may be seen as an important stepping stone on the pathway to the "New Woman" movement and beyond, blurring as it does the lines between work and domesticity, between isolation and privacy, between subjugation and liberation' (p. 480).

Lewis Carroll received extended treatment in Robert Douglas-Fairhurst's *The Story of Alice: Lewis Carroll and the Secret History of Wonderland*. Douglas-Fairhurst explains that he wrote *The Story of Alice* to better understand the powerful 'emotional scramble of amusement, fear, bewilderment and sheer unexamined joy' he experienced when reading Lewis Carroll's Alice books as a child. His quest led him to investigate the elusive lives of both Charles Dodgson and Alice Liddell and the many reworkings of Alice's adventures in art, plays, film, fashion, pornography, and video games. Playing with numbers and type size in the spirit of Carroll's whimsical wit, Douglas-Fairhurst organizes his discussion into sections covering 'Before Alice', 'Alice', and 'After Alice'. In the first section, he combs through Dodgson's childhood scribblings and early poems, objects buried under the nursery floor, his mother's home-schooling records, home-made magazines, and letters to conclude that the boy evidenced the adult's later 'ambivalence about "the principle of submission to discipline"'—whether in adherence to the literary form of a limerick or the rules of playtime games (p. 36). The section on 'Alice' examines how 'making' rather than 'taking' photographs of Alice Liddell and others shows Dodgson's fascination with manipulating lighting, costume, props, and subject to tell an alternative story, for which he often drew inspiration from poetry, such as Tennyson's 'Beggar Maid' and 'The Daydream' (p. 92). But here and elsewhere Douglas-Fairhurst stops short of giving firm readings of Dodgson's artful photographs and his poetry, reminding us of how what is 'admirably clear on one level' is belied by what is 'oddly obscure on another' (p. 113); in other words, by what lurks down the rabbit hole. The discussion of how Dodgson's boating expeditions with the Liddell sisters evolved into Alice's unexpected descent into Wonderland is an especially good example of the book's attention to detail, both in its description of the outings and in its overview of the Western literary heritage of journeys underground. The section 'After Alice' samples the plethora of Alice remakes, beginning with 'Ernest', a boy who loses his ball down a well leading to Toad-land. Many spin-offs reflect the growing Victorian interest in fairies and the Romantic view of childhood as its own world. Some imitators simply exploited an easy target for parody, and others, like *Punch*, followed the 'satirical undercurrents in Carroll's writing' as in 'Alice in Blunderland', a term which quickly evolved to mean any dystopian world where 'ordinary events could be turned upside down to expose the ridiculous underside they usually tried to conceal' (pp. 226–7). This section also endeavours to show that, after Alice Liddell's mother tore up Dodgson's letters to her daughter and ended the friendship, Dodgson repeatedly attempted to rediscover Alice—whether the real girl or the fictional character or both—in other children, and that the immortalized fictional girl lived on in his life and work. The book concludes with the thought that Alice's questioning attitude never fails to restore its readers' childlike affirmation of mystery and bafflement, ensuring that Wonderland will live on within the cultural imagination.

Rasheed Tazudeen makes an unexpected and productive connection between the work of Lewis Carroll and Darwin in 'Immanent Metaphor, Branching Form(s), and the Unmaking of the Human in *Alice* and *The Origin of Species*' (*VLC* 43[2015] 533–58). In the case of the Alice books, 'events are detached from a sense of progressive necessity and time becomes endlessly reversible'. Further, at the same time that language and reality become confused, 'the anthropocentric logic of representation, as what upholds the form of the (human) subject and the ordering of events into narrative, becomes ungrounded' (p. 524). The result is a version of the world much closer to that presented by Darwin than Carroll's own hesitancy about evolutionary theory might suggest. Both authors, Tazudeen points out, destabilize human primacy and teleological progress, presenting instead a world of chance and unintentional change.

Turning to Wilkie Collins, the spring 2015 issue of the *Wilkie Collins Society Newsletter* is accompanied by Andrew Lycett's informative 'Collins the Campaigner', which originally appeared in *The Author* (126:i[2015] 20–1). The issue includes 'Unwritten Books' (*WCJ* 12[Summer 2015] 3–4) focusing on Collins's second series of *The Fallen Leaves* (the first series appeared in 1879); 'The *Moonstone Legacy* Trilogy' (*WCJ* 12[Spring 2015] 4–5) ('written mainly for younger readers', p. 5); and 'Wilkie at Work' (*WCJ* 12[Spring 2015] 7). This describes 'a newly discovered letter [that] has cast some light on Wilkie's working timetable when he was writing *No Name*'. It is written to the novelist and dramatist John Palgrave Simpson (1807–87), dated Monday, 14 July 1862. In the letter 'Wilkie sets out his writing timetable—he works every day except Sunday until 3pm. After that he is free' (p. 7). The full text with explanatory notes will be available with other newly discovered letters in the forthcoming 'The Collected Letters of Wilkie Collins: Addenda and Corrigenda (10)' to be assessed subsequently in this chapter.

The summer 2015 issue of the *Wilkie Collins Society Newsletter* includes 'New Collins Works in *All the Year Round*' (*WCJ* 12[Summer 2015] 1–3) and lists eight items that can be attributed to Collins (see www.djo.org.uk) and 'around 90 new Charles Collins pieces' (p. 3). Other items of interest include notes on a scarce edition of *Mr. Wray's Cash Box* published in Columbia, South Carolina in 1864 (*WCJ* 12[Summer 2015] 3), a digitized version of Collins's play *Black and White*, information on downloading *The Proceedings of the Seventh Anniversary Festival of the General Theatrical Fund*, a charitable institution of which Collins and Dickens were trustees (p. 4), and data on Frederick Walker (1840–75), 'an influential painter in oils and water-colours; he was also a friend of both Wilkie and Charles Collins' (p. 5). Lars-Erick Nygren has produced a bibliography of *Wilkie Collins in Sweden* [2010] which 'consists of 77 illustrated pages spanning Wilkie's works from 1845 to the present day' (p. 7), There is a note too on Collins's associations with the Garrick Club (*WCJ* 12[Summer 2015] 9–10) and Lewis Carroll's reading of Wilkie Collins's work (p. 10). Also of interest is 'Wilkie and Beethoven', which, after presenting the evidence, observes that he 'preferred Mozart' (*WCJ* 12[Summer 2015] 11).

Other notes include additional information on the publication of 'Collins's first identified short story, "Volpurno"' (*WCJ* 12[Winter 2015] 6), initially uncovered by Daniel Hack in his '*Volpurno*—Or the Student: A Forgotten Tale of Madness by Wilkie Collins' (*TLS* [2 January 2009] 14–15). Mention should be made too of 'French Bibliography' (*WCJ* 12[Winter 2015] 7), 'Wilkie Collins and Graphic Novels (Comic Books)' (*WCJ* 12[Winter 2015] 7–8), new printings of *The Haunted Hotel* and 'My Lady's Money' (*WCJ* 12[Winter 2015] 8–9), 'Wilkie's Tailor' (*WCJ* 12[Winter 2015] 9–10), concerning 'the Archives of Henry Poole & Co, the Savile Row tailor [that] are being opened to the public' (p. 9), 'Wilkie's School Bill' (*WCJ* 12[Winter 2015] 10–11), 'New Letters', of which 'almost 20 new letters have been identified in the last twelve months' (p. 1), and an article by Andrew Lycett, 'Where There's a Will' on *No Name* in *Slightly Foxed* (*WCJ* 12[Winter 2015] 58–62). Information on the availability of the *Wilkie Collins Society Newsletter* is found at www.wilkie-collins.info.

Accompanying the 2015 issues are three separate pamphlets including, besides Lycett's reprinted study, Paul Lewis's 'What Wilkie Earned from *All The Year Round*' dated 'August 2015' (pp. 1–8), which opens with the observation that 'scholars have largely overlooked the fact that Wilkie Collins was paid a one-eighth share of the profits of *All the Year Round* for two years from August 1860 to July 1862. Dickens paid Collins directly out of his own three-quarters share. It amounted in total to just over. £588.50' (p. 2): unfortunately Lewis doesn't provide modern equivalents. Andrew Gasson's '*The Woman in White*: Editions and Changes' (pp. 1–8) presents 'Errata and Chronological Changes in the Text' in tabular form (pp. 4–5). A Wilkie Collins Society pamphlet published in October 2013 and not previously reviewed is Graham Law's edition of 'Wilkie's Two Late "American Stories": Finds or Fakes?' (pp. 1–52). His detailed, clearly written introduction (pp. 1–18) concludes that 'the balance of evidence suggests that Wilkie Collins probably had no hand in the composition not only of "The Only Girl at Overview" but also of "One August Night in '61"'. Law judiciously adds that 'nevertheless, with the latter case so close to call, it seems right to provide the members of the Society not only with the main evidence in the case, but also the texts of the two stories themselves, so that they may play the part of the jury and make up their own minds' (p. 13). There then follows in tabulated format a 'Timeline: Wilkie Collins's Two "American Stories"' (pp. 14–16). A second table contains also in tabulated format the 'Two Story Sequences in US Sunday Papers in 1889' (pp. 16–17). This is followed by the illustrated texts in double-column format of 'The Only Girl at Overlook. Written for *The Dispatch* by Franklin File from a Plot by Wilkie Collins', *The Pittsburgh Dispatch*, Sunday 9 June 1889 (pp. 19–35), and, from the same newspaper of Sunday, 6 October 1889, the text of ' "One August Night in '61" Wilkie Collins' Last Story Plot. Written from his Original Sketch for *The Dispatch*' (pp. 36–51).

The *Wilkie Collins Journal* no longer appears in print form but is available online at http://wilkiecollinssociety.org/journal. Access to the latest issue, 13[2016] is only available to members of the Wilkie Collins Society, though earlier issues are now available. The 2013 issue, not previously covered in *YWES* and now accessible, opens with Jonathan Buckmaster's ' "Oh Doctor, Doctor, Doctor, don't expect too much of me! I'm only a woman, after all!"': The (Dis) Embodiment of Lydia Gwilt in Collins's *Miss Gwilt*' (*WCJ* 12[2013]). Buckmaster's illustrated account centres 'on the actress that Collins chose to play his title character, Ada Cavendish. Cavendish brought a variety of extra-textual associations to her embodiment of Lydia that affect our reading of the play and colour our re-reading of the novel as well. Through an examination of the reviews and advertisements for her performances, I will argue for her centrality to any critical appraisal we make of the play, as to some extent she even sidelines its official "author", Collins himself'. Helena Ifill's '**Wilkie Collins's Monomaniacs in** *Basil***,** *No Name* **and** *Man and Wife*' *(WCJ* 12[2013] ?? paras.) opens with an explanation of 'the term mono-mania…[that] became popular in Britain from the 1830s onwards as a means of describing a form of "partial insanity" in which a person was apparently insane in only one way'. Ifill applies it with refinements of meaning to three of Collins's novels. She concludes that 'for Collins, monomania was a means of explaining the kind of behaviour which fans of sensation fiction loved, but which its critics dismissed as unrealistic' and was 'a way of exploring the individual's relationship to society'. In three instances of monomania that Ilfill examines, Mannion in *Basil*, Magdalen in *No Name*, and Hester in *Man and Wife*, it is possible to 'identify a sense of injustice and helplessness which leads the characters to act in ways which are not dictated by their conscious selves'. Laurie Lydia's '*The New Magdalen* **and the Rhetoric of Prostitution: Restoring Mercy Merrick's Agency**' (*WCJ* 12[2013] ?? paras.) focuses upon one Collins novel, *The New Magdalen* **[1873], which has not received the critical attention it deserves. For the novel, as Lydia notes, 'is** not a simple redemption tale; Mercy's story transgresses the imagined boundaries of space and identity to reinvent the heroine as dynamic and capable, rather than as a maligned Angel of the House. This re-envisioning subverts the condescension and control that often motivated Victorian rhetoric about prostitution and presents a revelation: Disorderly women were capable of "ordering" themselves after all.'

Helen Williams, in her 'Redefining Bodies and Boundaries in Wilkie Collins's *Armadale* and *The Law and the Lady*' (*WCJ* 12[2013] ?? paras.) shows that 'Both texts . . . use poisons and cosmetics—problematic and indefinable substances in themselves—to highlight the essentially fluid and fluctuating states of bodies, but more importantly, to pose challenges to the medical and legal frameworks which sought to dispel such indeterminacy as a means to cementing their own knowledge and authority'. Jacqueline Banerjee's interesting and clearly written 'Authenticism and Post-Authenticism: Wilkie Collins's *Armadale* and Michael Cox's *The Meaning of Night: A Confession*' (*WCJ* 12[2013] ?? paras.), discusses Michael Cox's 2006 thriller and the ways in which it 'revisits the preoccupations' of *The Woman in White* [1860], *Armadale* [1866], and *The Moonstone* [1868]. Banerjee concludes 'like many of the other recent novels that tap into our fascination with all things Victorian, Michael Cox never brings his narrative up into the present. Yet he still participates in our continuing reassessment of the Victorian era, in this case by making us intensely aware of the sea-change in our cultural climate. *The Meaning of Night* also brings home to us, in this indirect way . . . one particular Victorian novelist's compelling moral and spiritual vision.' Hilary Newman's 'John Kitto's *The Lost Senses: Deafness and Blindness* and Wilkie Collins's *Hide and Seek* and *Poor Miss Finch*' (*WCJ* 12[2013] ?? paras.) demonstrates that 'Wilkie Collins wrote positively about deafness and blindness—the first in *Hide and Seek* and the second in *Poor Miss Finch*—in accordance with his views expressed in the dedication to the latter novel. He based these accounts on Dr Kitto's book *The Lost Senses: Deafness and Blindness*.' Moreover, 'while using fairytale or romance plot elements in both these novels, Collins's depiction of the disabilities of deafness and blindness were solidly based on fact. The novels reveal some degree of didacticism, as well as providing entertainment.' The keynote address to the Victorian Popular Fiction Association Conference, held at the School of Advanced Study, University of London, on 9 November 2013, William Baker's 'Wilkie Collins: Scholarship and Criticism Past, Present and Future [with a Bibliography]' assessing past, and present critical and scholarly work on Collins also appears in this issue (*WCJ* 12[2013] ?? paras.).

Other critical work on Wilkie Collins includes Alessandra Violi's 'Dead pro tem.: Suspended Animation and the Monstrosity of Death-Counterfeits' (in Calzoni and Perletti, eds., pp. 169–91), which compares and contrasts Collins's *Jezebel's Daughter* [1880] with H.G. Wells's *The Sleeper Awakes* [1910] in terms of their treatment of suspended animation. Flora DeGiovanni's 'Displaying the Anomalous Body: **Wilkie Collins**'s Freak Show', also in Calzoni and Perletti's collection, is concerned with the treatment of deformity in *Hide and Seek* (pp. 149–67). Laurence Talairach-Vielmas's 'Modern Phantasmagorias and Visual Culture in Wilkie Collins's *Basil*' (in Botting and Spooner, eds., *Monstrous Media/Spectral Subjects: Imaging Gothic from the Nineteenth Century to the Present*, pp. 56–70) reads Collins's early novel as a deliberate modernization of the Gothic and in the context of the monstrous and the spectral. **Peter Ackroyd's** *Wilkie Collins: A Brief Life* is a revised updated version of his Collins biography first published in 2012 (*YWES* 93[2014] 747). Sarah Fitzpatrick's 'Separate Spheres: A Closer Look at Ideological Gender Roles in Victorian England through the Sensation Novel' (*The Victorian* 3:ii[2015] 1–9) is concerned with the treatment of sex roles, the relationship to ideology and domesticity in *The Woman in White* compared to Ellen Wood's *East Lynne*, published a year after Collins's novel. In *Sensation and Professionalism in the Victorian Novel*, Mariaconcetta Costantini, in her exploration of 'the professional dilemmas articulated by...practitioners of the sensation genre' (p. 16), devotes considerable attention to various novels by Wilkie Collins, including *Armadale* [1864–6] (pp. 88–94, 98–105), *Basil* (pp. 105–10), *The Moonstone* (pp. 275–80), and *Poor Miss Finch* (pp. 306–11). Costantini writes that 'in anticipation of twentieth-century theories on diversity, *Armadale* offered to Victorian readers a provocative example of professional amelioration which question the legitimacy of social and racial assumptions' (p. 99).

Monica Flegel's 'A "Strange Family Story": Count Fosco, His Animal Children, and the "Safe" Patriarch in **Wilkie Collins**'s *The Woman in White*' (in Dau and Preston, eds., pp. 99–115) is concerned with its narrator's treatment of Count Fosco, especially in his relationship to family, animals, and domesticity, using the perspective of the application of queer theory. In the same collection, Lauren N Hoffer and Sarah E Kersh write on 'The Victorian Family in Queer Time: Secrets, Sisters, and Lovers in *The Woman in White* and *Fingersmith*' (pp. 195–210). They observe that, although Fosco is a members of an Italian secret society, 'it is the secret illegitimate sisterhood at the core of' the novel that 'drives the plot and unravels its enigmas' (p. 198). Further, Collins's *The Woman in White* 'is a novel replete with secrets' (p. 201) and Sarah Water's *Fingersmith* [2002] gained much from it. Meghan Self's 'Opium and Obsession: Alternative Causalities of Somnambulism' (*The Victorian* 3:i[2015] 1–9) primarily concerns the treatment of sleepwalking, its relationship to agency, and legal cases in *The Moonstone* compared to Edgar Allen Poe's short story 'Berenice' [1835]. Anne-Marie Dunbar's 'Making the Case: Detection and Confession in *Lady Audley's Secret* and *The Women in White*' (*VR* 40[2015] 97–116) examines the treatment of detection in M.E. Braddon's novel [1862] and Collins's novel, published two years earlier. Janice M. Allan, 'Sensationalism Made Real: The Role of Realism in the Production of Sensational Affect' (*VLC* 43[2015] 97–112), argues that focusing on Walter Hartright's encounter with Anne Catherick on the road to London 'illumin-ate[s] the extent to which the sensational and the realistic are inextricably entwined in the production of sensational affect, even as the former interrogates the epistemological and ideological foundations of the realistic impulse on which it depends' (p. 99). Jessica Durgan, in 'Wilkie Collins' Blue Period: Color, Aesthetics, and Race in *Poor Miss Finch*' (*VLC* 43[2015] 765–83), argues that in *Poor Miss Finch* Collins 'draws on his significant knowledge of the visual arts to reconsider the nature of color and its relationship to race and empire through the creation of a hero who is uniquely placed to question ideas of identity, belonging, and otherness through his color change' (p. 765).

Catherine Delafield's *Serialization and the Novel in Mid-Victorian Magazines* includes material on the serialization of Collins's *The Moonstone* (see for instance pp. 170–5), *Poor Miss Finch*, and Collins's relationship with *All The Year Round* (see pp. 135–47 and 151–9). Joshua Gooch's *The Victorian Novel, Service Work, and the Nineteenth-Century Economy* discusses '*The Moonstone*: Service Work as Narrative Work' (pp. 109–38): Gooch writes that the novel 'makes explicit the interrelation of service work and narrative work through its use of character-narrators' (p. 109). There are two articles dealing with different facets of Collins's *The Moonstone* in *Dickens Studies Annual*. Elisha Cohn's 'Suspending Detection: Collins, Dickens and the Will to Know' (*DSA* 46[2015] 253–76) 'argues that *The Moonstone* and [Dickens's] *The Mystery of Edwin Drood* suspend the detective fiction's efforts to know the mind as a comment on the physiology, aesthetics, and politics of the will to know'. Cohn explores 'how both novels complicate empiricism by exploring alternate epistemologies associated with opium and mesmerism' (p. 253). Christiane Gannon, in 'Hinduism, Spiritual Community, and Narrative Form in *The Moonstone*' (*DSA* 46[2015] 297–320), 'argues that Collins's fragmen-tation of narrative form in *The Moonstone* allows him to critique Victorian Christianity and reveal spiritual community as something that cannot coexist with modes of Western individuality'. Gannon makes large claims for Collins and his novel. She writes: 'Collins uses the ruptured unity of narrative form in *The Moonstone* to portray England in a state of chronic spiritual division, a consequence of Christian imperialism and of a national literature that nurtured an idea of salvation achieved through the cultivation of internalized subjectivity.' For Gannon, Collins's novel 'suggests that the price of annexing free nations'—an idea insufficiently explained by Gannon—'is the loss of England's own spiritual community, and the final scene of Hindu worship that concludes the novel suggests that the future of collective spirituality lies beyond Western nations' (p. 297).

Two studies included material on Collins and drama, and are reviewed elsewhere in this chapter: Richard Pearson's *Victorian Writers and the Stage*, which has two chapters concerned with Collins and Dickens, and Karen Laird's *The Art of Adapting Victorian Literature*, which contains two chapters on adaptations of *The Woman in White*. Lastly, in this survey of academic criticism on Collins published in 2015, mention should be made of Paul Fyfe's detailed discussion, in his *By Accident of Design: Writing the Victorian*

*Metropolis* (pp. 134–5,142–6), of the rhetoric of Collins's article 'The Unknown Public' in *Household Words* (21 August 1858, p. 217).

As always, Dickens received substantial attention in 2015. In *Dickens, Religion and Society*, author Robert Butterworth creates a simple but important argument: that Charles Dickens was a profoundly religious author. Contrary to what contemporary religious figures believed, Butterworth states that 'Dickens's religion is absolutely central to his work' (p. 2).

Butterworth follows this argument through what is practically the entirety of his oeuvre, beginning with early works like *Oliver Twist* and following the argument through to works published near the end of his life, such as *Tale of Two Cities*. However, before reaching his analysis of the novels, Butterworth sets the stage by placing Dickens within the context of the Christian social attitudes of the early Victorian era. Essentially, Butterworth argues that Dickens stands as a corrective to the religious opinion of his day, which viewed the poor or working classes as idle, selfish, extravagant, and brutish (p. 26). Often, religiously minded people would argue that poverty was in fact a judgement of God based on these moral failings. Analysing many of Dickens's novels, Butterworth demonstrates how the author provides Christian correctives to the divisive values and biases of his time. In *Oliver Twist*, for instance, he argues that Dickens provides, through the character of Fagin, a mirror to anti-Jewish sentiment. In *Barnaby Rudge*, Dickens takes the religiously motivated riots of a previous era to illustrate that a true Christianity seeks universal brotherhood. In *Bleak House*, Dickens plays on the social direction of the period of Chartism, and argues that a change in law is necessary for a truly Christian society to function.

Dickens is examined as a corrective influence to the beliefs of his age once again in *Dickens and the Imagined Child*, a collection of essays on the topic of children in Dickens's fiction edited by Peter Merchant and Catherine Waters. This collection gives the Dickensian of view of children as one that is incredibly distinct from the views of his era. The collection itself is divided into three sections and contains twelve chapters, including an introduction by Merchant and Waters (pp. 1–12). In order, the chapters themselves are entitled 'Dickens and the Knowing Child' (pp. 13–26), by Rosemarie Bodenheimer; 'Who Stole the Child? Missing Babies and Blank Identities in Early Dickens' (pp. 27–42), by Galia Benziman; ' "No magic dwelling-place in magic story": Time, Memory and the Enchanted Children of Dombey and Son' (pp. 43–56), by Carolyn W. de la L. Oulton; ' "In a state of bondage": The Children of *Bleak House*' (pp. 57–76), by Jennifer Gribble; 'The Adult Narrator's Memory of Childhood in David's, Esther's and Pip's Autobiographies' (pp. 77–92), by Maria Teresa Chialant; 'A Medway Childhood: The Dickensian "Arrière-pays" ' (pp. 93–110), by Jane Avner; ' "Ten thousand million delights": Charles Dickens and the Childhood Wonder of the Pantomime Clown' (pp. 111–30), by Jonathan Buckmaster; ' "A kind of odour of Salem House": *David Copperfield* and Thomas Anstey Guthrie' (pp. 131–50), by Peter Merchant; 'Savage Stories: Charles Dickens, "The Noble Savage" and the Childhood Imagination' (pp. 151–66), by Laura Peters; 'Child Readers in Dickens's Novels' (pp. 167–82), by Wu Di; and 'Playful "Assumption": Dickens's Early Performative Creativity and its Influence on His Sons' Family Newspaper, the

*Gad's Hill Gazette*' (pp. 183–206), by Christine Alexander. Of particular note are chapters 2 and 3. In the second chapter, Bodenheimer argues that the abnormality that is present in many of Dickens's childhood characters comes from the fact that they all seem to hide a secret store of knowledge. This reality violates the Romantic sensibility which sees children as innocent and uncorrupted. Dickens's children 'have to behave as if they were children, when, in secret, they know they are not' (p. 16). The next set of chapters in the first part of the text deal with early and late Dickens works. For example, in chapter 3 Benziman looks at *Oliver Twist* and *Pickwick* to argue that Dickens is adept at having his childhood characters be a 'blank slate' on which the shifting culture around them can write definitions. The 'fairy-tale' endings only add to this proof. The next two chapters deal with *Dombey and Son* and *Bleak House*, the first arguing that Dickens uses fairy tale and myth-making to set up his idea of the child while the second deals with the concept of childhood as related to the idea of original sin. The second part of the text deals exclusively with the theme of childhood and memory. Not surprisingly, two of these chapters deal with *David Copperfield* and the adult's reconceptualization of the child. The final part of the text takes a look at the many child readers in Dickens's novels, and the imaginative engagement his childhood characters always have with literature and story-telling. With this in mind, the final chapter asks, quite rightly, why we do not see this same imaginative engagement between Dickens and his own children.

Interestingly, discussions about Dickens's conceptions of childhood are closely linked to the treatment of death in his fiction. As the high priest of the cult of domestic sentimentality, Dickens understood the impact poignant death scenes had on his readers In *Dickens and the Business of Death*, Claire Wood deals with this aspect of Dickens's fiction, specifically, with the commercial side of the death trade. As she puts it in the introduction, 'Charles Dickens's career offers an ideal framework through which to explore death commodification' (p. 3). Wood takes us into this topic through some of Dickens's darkest novels. First, however, she sets the groundwork by giving the Victorian social and historical context to deathly commodification, starting with the death of the duke of Wellington, whose 'state solemnities...on 18 November 1852 marked the apogee of the Victorian funeral' (p. 13). This 'Public' funeral contrasts with 'Private' and 'Professional' affairs, such as the death of Little Nell and Clara Copperfield on the one hand and the deathly business of Mrs Gamp on the other. The second chapter, which discusses *The Old Curiosity Shop*, begins with John Ruskin's observation that Nell seemed to be killed for the market, as unsympathetically as a butcher slaughters a lamb. Using this as a foundation, the chapter goes on to discuss Dickensian manipulation of his audiences, in which there is, 'an almost mechanical link between sentimental stimulus and financial extraction' (p. 61); that is, influencing audience emotions for profit. The third chapter focuses on the commodification of death in *Bleak House* through the mechanism of inheritance law, which is of course a primary focus of the novel. As the author states, 'This "dead property" assumes numerous forms', and those characters who lack property soon die (p. 106). The final chapter deals with a text that seems to be hand-made for Wood's subject, as *Our Mutual Friend* begins with a man searching the Thames for a corpse, which he will later convert to financial gain. In this text, 'mortality frequently occurs in uncomfortable proximity to the commercial world' (p. 131).

In thinking of Dickens and commercialization, we must consider Dickens's penchant for commercializing and promoting his own image as an author of English national celebrity. With this in mind, it is safe to say that Dickens's 'lionization' was no more pronounced than when he made his first visit to the New World. However, in *Dickens and Massachusetts: The Lasting Legacy of the Commonwealth Visits*, editors Diana Archibald and Joel Brattin argue against the typical account of Dickens's view of America as a sub-par and 'bastardized' version of Britain. They take this even further, noting that while some scholars give a much more nuanced reading of Dickens's relationship with America, they do not examine the importance of Massachusetts. Essentially, Archibald argues that the Massachusetts visits were 'more significant than heretofore recognized, and that the people places, and institutions of Massachusetts left a lasting impact on Dickens' (p. 2). The collection opens with an introduction by Archibald and Brattin, 'Dickens and Massachusetts: A Tale of Power and Transformation; Exhibition Narrative with Illustrations' (pp. 13–95), which is a transcription of the original 'master text' of the exhibition held at Lowell National Historical Park from 30 March to 20 October in the bicentenary year. This introduction takes up the entirety of Part I. Part II is divided into seven chapters, each an essay examining one aspect of Dickens's relation with America, and Lowell Massachusetts in particular. In order, these chapters are 'The Lowell Mill Girls and the Making of *A Christmas Carol*' (pp. 99–112), by Natalie McKnight and Chelsea Bray; 'Visions of Lowell, Light and Dark, in *Our Mutual Friend*' (pp. 113–22), by André DeCuir; 'Dickens's Visit to the Perkins School and "Doctor Marigold"' (pp. 123–33), by Diana C. Archibald; 'Dickens, Longfellow, and the Village Blacksmith' (pp. 134–46), by Lillian Nayder; 'Slavery in Dickens's Manuscript of *American Notes for General Circulation*', by Joel J. Brattin (p. 147–62); 'Dickens's Visits to Springfield, Massachusetts, in 1842 and 1868' (p. 163–78), by Kit Polga; and 'Dickens, Martineau and Massachusetts: The Republic They Came to See' (p. 179–96), by Iain Crawford. Of particular interest in this collection are chapters 1, 2, 5, and 7. In the first chapter, McKnight and Bray examine Dickens's visit to the factories in Lowell. They argue that though such visits were common in the period (Martineau made similar visits herself), no critic has explored the impact these visits had on Dickens's fiction, particularly *A Christmas Carol*, which came out the year following his first American visit. In the second chapter, DeCuir argues that the impact of Dickens's visit to the Lowell Mill and the memory of the Lowell factory girls resonates all the way to Dickens's last complete novel: *Our Mutual Friend*. In his depiction of Lizzie, DeCuir argues that Dickens borrows from his memories of the Lowell Mill, using them to 'create [a]...utopian view of what mill life could be' (p. 116). Another extremely significant chapter from this text is chapter 5, in which Joel Brattin examines Dickens's views of slavery in *American Notes*. He makes no pretence of the fact that Dickens found slavery to be the most appalling reality about America. Brattin's argument then, is that Dickens viewed Massachusetts, and Boston in particular, as a corrective model for this peculiar institution, as many Boston ministers and journalists were prominent abolitionists. Finally, Iain Crawford examines the textual response to America from both Dickens and Harriet Martineau. Martineau, another literary 'lion' and contributor to *Household Words* until she and Dickens had a terrible falling-out, gives a much more optimistic account of the New World in *Society in America* than does Dickens in his *American Notes*.

From Dickens's response to America, we move to America's response to Dickens. In her work *Charles Dickens's Great Expectations: A Cultural Life, 1860–2012*, Mary Hammond states in her introduction: 'I have built here upon [the] notion of the novel as a cultural text that is still being written' (p. 3). Hammond focuses explicitly on the publication culture surrounding the novel. Her first chapter situates its production around the concurrent events in Dickens's life that seem to most inspire it, particularly his affair with Ellen Ternan and the subsequent falling-out with family and friends. The second chapter deals with the novel, and Dickens's fame as a whole, in light of his posthumous, *transatlantic* reputation. In Britain, despite late-career criticism, Dickens became a national treasure. American response, however, appears to have been more complex, as dime store novels, *Uncle Tom's Cabin*, and Mark Twain (i.e. the growth of an American literary canon) relegated the memory of Dickens to his early-novel glories. Hammond's third chapter deals with adaptations of the novel in the twentieth century. For nearly two decades, there were none, a function of *Great Expectations* simply not being among American's favourite works by Dickens. There did exist some early radio productions, but these did not match the post-war film adaptations, which are the focus of chapter 4. Of course, nearly all post-war adaptations are (and were) held up against David Lean's 1946 masterpiece. In the final chapter, Hammond argues that Dickens's cultural cachet in the twentieth century as the author of literary 'classics' enabled his work to undergo global 'translation' and 'remediation', not just as a text, but as a cultural artefact.

As with *Dickens and Massachusetts*, the Dickens bicentenary becomes a central focus once again in *Unsettling Dickens: Process, Progress and Change*. This collection, edited by Christine Huguet and Paul Vita, is compiled from the 2012 bicentenary 'travelling' conference and focuses on place, space, and anxieties about identity in Dickens's work. The collection divides into three sections: 'Dickensian Processes: Displacing Narrative Paradigms' (pp. 31–98); 'Progress in Dickens, Signifying Across Space' (pp. 99–192); and 'Changing the Dickensian: Texts in Becoming' (pp. 193–257). The sections divide into ten chapters. In order, these chapters are: 'Charles Dickens, Mental Time-Travelling and Autobiographical Memory' (pp. 33–54), by Simon J. James; 'Trial and Terror in Satis House: Great Expectations of Institutional Masculinity' (pp. 55–77), by Gilbert Pham-Thanh; 'Fluid Mechanics in *David Copperfield*' (pp. 78–98), by Jacqueline Fromonot; 'Ecstasy of Impatience: Some Notes on Travel in *Sketches by Boz*' (pp. 101–9), by Michael Hollington; ' "Drawn to the Loadstone Rock": Travelling Towards Imprisonment and Death in *A Tale of Two Cities*' (pp. 110–30), by Isabelle Hervouet-Farrar; ' "The weakest pilgrim going": Pilgrimage in Charles Dickens's *Great Expectations*' (pp. 131–56), by Ray Crosby; ' "Tramps": Dickens's Modern Rhapsody' (pp. 157–94), by Francesca Orestano; 'Dickens and Shakespeare' (pp. 195–209), by Michael Slater; 'Crossing Thresholds: The Aesthetics of an Urban Experience from *Oliver Twist* to *The Wire*' (pp. 210–34), by Clémence Follea; and 'From London to Sydney to Bougainville: Postcolonial Dickensian Gentleman' (pp. 235–57), by Louisa Hadley. Of particular note are chapters 1, 2, 4, 5, 6, 8, and 9. The book's first section, 'Process', focuses on processes in terms of both authorial composition and character development. James's essay examines the creation of the novel through the process of memory: his text, *David Copperfield*, is of course particularly apt. Pham-Thanh charts Pip's maturation process in *Great Expectations* as a function of the Victorian pressure to perform a very specific brand of masculinity. The second section, 'Progress', opens with an essay by Hollington that examines *Sketches by Boz* and other of Dickens's early works in connection with the anxieties associated with modern modes of travel. In her essay, Hervouet-Farrar examines *A Tale of Two Cities*, using the recurrent image of the Loadstone (from *Arabian Nights*, a book Dickens adored), to argue that each of the major characters is 'drawn' towards a death in some way—though possibly not theirs. Crosby focuses his chapter on the concept of pilgrimage in *Great Expectations*, noting its importance though the idea is mentioned only twice in the actual novel. The third section, 'Change', opens with the two essays that are arguably the collection's most fascinating: Slater's comparison of Dickens and Shakespeare, and Follea's analysis of the 'Dickensian' elements found in 'The Wire'. Slater explores how Dickens may have first encountered Shakespeare, and surveys the Bard's most notable moments of reference in his novels. Finally, Follea asks 'what makes *The Wire* "Dickensian"?'

Continuing with Dickens and the theme of change is one final edited collection from the year, *Charles Dickens as an Agent of Change*. Edited by Joachim Frenk and Lena Steveker, this collection divides into four parts, each examining an aspect of change inspired by Dickens personally, politically, and culturally: 'Dickens and Social Change' (pp. 3–60), 'Dickens and Changes of Power' (pp. 61–98), 'Dickens and Literary Change' (pp. 99–158), and 'Dickens and Changes in Popular Culture and in the Theater' (pp. 159–234). The essays themselves feature some of the top scholars in the Dickensian world, such as Jerome Meckier, David Paroissien, and Michael Hollington. In order, the essays are: 'Repetition and Reversal: Patterns for Social Change in *Pickwick Papers*' (pp. 3–18), by Jerome Meckier; 'Three Revolutions: Alternate Routes to Social Change in *Bleak House*' (pp. 19–32), by Joel J. Brattin; 'Dickens, Society, and Art: Change in Dickens's View of Effecting Social Reform' (pp. 33–46), by Robert Heaman; 'The World Changing Dickens, Dickens Changing the World' (pp. 47–60), by Bert Hornback; 'Parrots, Birds of Prey, and Snorting Cattle: Dickens's Whig Agenda' (pp. 61–74), by David Paroissien; ' "The tremendous potency of the small": Dickens, the Individual, and Social Change in a Post-America, Post-Catastrophist Age' (pp. 75–84), by Nancy Aycock Metz; 'Money, Power, and Appearance in *Dombey and Son*' (pp. 85–98), by Michael Hollington; 'The Passing of the *Pickwick* Moment' (pp. 99–110), by Malcolm Andrews; '*The Chimes* and the Rhythm of Life' (pp. 111–28), by Matthias Bauer; 'Radical Dickens: Dickens and the Tradition of Romantic Radicalism' (pp. 129–44), by Norbert

Lennartz; 'Modern Characters in the Late Novels of Charles Dickens' (pp. 145–58), by Herbert Foltinek; 'The Cultural Politics of Dickens's *Hard Times*' (pp. 159–72), by Doris Feldmann; 'Conjuring Dickens: Magic, Intellectual Property, and *The Old Curiosity Shop*' (pp. 173–90), by Christopher Pittard; 'Dickens on the Victorian Stage: Two East End Adaptations of *Bleak House*' (pp. 191–204), by Chris Louttit; 'The Frozen Deep: Gad's Hill, Summer 1857' (pp. 205–18), by Robert Tracy; and 'How to Read Dickens in English: A Last Retrospect' (pp. 219–20), by Edgar Rosenberg. The first section begins with Meckier's essay, which contrasts Dickens's views of personal change with Orwell's desire for a change in society as a whole. Meckier argues that, while Orwell criticized Dickens for offering no clear answers for the problems of society, Dickens affirms that social change is meaningless unless personal change happens first. The second section deals with Dickens's politics, or what seem to be the political foundations for his push towards social change. Paroissien examines Dickens's 'whiggery' through his literary friendship with Douglas Jerrold. Metz's essay explores Dickens's frustrated ambition to bring about social change, mirrored in the character of Martin Chuzzlewit, as the 'New World' immediately crushes his hopes for a better life. The third section examines Dickens's unique contribution to the literary turns of the period. Andrews's piece deals with Dickens's greatest contribution to the era— comedy. He argues that Dickens did not want to convert his audience to comedy alone, but to *Dickensian* comedy. The final section deals with the Dickensian influence on the popular culture of his time. The two most enjoyable pieces from this section are Pittard's, which explores Dickens's fascination with (and practice of) parlour magic, and Robert Tracy's essay, which examines the bizarre relationship between Dickens and Hans Christian Andersen.

In looking at the Dickens-focused chapters from the scholarly monographs this past year, one of the most recurrent analytical contexts is the view of Dickens as an author of 'The City'. In these texts, the importance of the Victorian metropolis of London to Dickens's authorial career and narratology takes central position. We begin with *Dickens, Reynolds and Mayhew on Wellington Street* by Mary Shannon, also covered in Section 1 above. In her first chapter, 'Morning: The Smallness of the World' (pp. 21–68), after giving a brief history of Wellington Street, including the various names for it and purposes that it served, Shannon introduces the reader to the editors and writers who had home offices on the street itself, giving particular attention to the literary rivalries that sprang up among such personalities as Dickens, Thackeray, Forster, and Lewes. Shannon then gives a geographical description of the street at this time, drawing an analytical connection between the 'composition' of the street and the 'composition' of its most famous product: Dickens's *Household Words*. The geographical layout of the great city is once again an important analytical framework in Paul Fyfe's *By Accident or Design: Writing the Victorian Metropolis*. In his second chapter, 'Dickens and the Traffic of Accidents' (pp. 67–99), after introducing readers to the comprehensive 'knowledge' test London cabbies must pass, foregrounding the urban sprawl that made Victorian London into the metropolis known today, Fyfe argues that Dickens's *Sketches by Boz* participates in discussions about both urbanization and commercial transport. In the first instance, Fyfe cites how Dickens's keen eye divides London taxonomically—each person in his 'sketches' described in nuanced detail as a member of the class, station, subculture, and personality group to which they belong. In the second instance, Dickens provides a sketch that marks the transition in commercial London transport from 'Hackney Cab' to 'Omnibus Cad'.

Though not necessarily central to London, the dual themes of accident and travel appear once again in *Transport in British Fiction: Technologies of Movement, 1840–1940*, edited by Adrienne E. Gavin and Andrew F. Humphries. In the third chapter of this collection, 'Death by Train: Spectral Technology and Dickens's *Mugby Junction*', Jen Cadwallader argues that in the 'Mugby Junction' collection of stories, Dickens and his fellow authors created a vision of technology that was 'spectral'—alien, other, and haunting rather than 'a tool for human betterment' (p. 58). Primarily, the characters killed in train accidents help the creation of this image most powerfully. Images of death associated with train travel played into the anxieties of the age regarding the new technology. Dickens in particular was the perfect author to write about these anxieties in light of the Staplehurst disaster, from which he never fully recovered.

The city of London and its peculiarities features once again in *London Fog: The Biography* by Christine L. Corton. Corton begins her second chapter, 'Dickensian Gloom' (pp. 37–76), by arguing that, for many Londoners, Dickens essentially *created* the London fog as envisioned in the popular consciousness. Beginning with *The Old Curiosity Shop*, Corton explores how the London fog becomes almost a central character, affecting the text in a profound way. Fog exemplifies (and perhaps brings about) Quilp's demise, it obscures and makes the already dangerous and mysterious city more dangerous and mysterious in *Martin Chuzzlewit*, serves as a metaphor for the obfuscation found throughout *Bleak House*, and colludes with the city to ensure its own destruction in *Our Mutual Friend*.

The reason Dickens was able to capture an ideal, romanticized vision of the city of London so well for his readers is because he knew it so intimately. This expertise came to him as the result of his night walks through the London streets, some of which would take several hours. This most Dickensian of Dickens's personal traits is examined in detail in two chapters from *Nightwalking: A Nocturnal History of London from Chaucer to Dickens* by Matthew Beaumont. In his twelfth chapter, Beaumont examines Dickens's compulsive habit of walking the streets of London throughout the night as a cure for his recurrent insomnia. Beaumont analyses this most unique of Dickens's habits by connecting it with similar scenes of nightwalking in the author's novels and surrounding life events. The scene Beaumont connects most specifically to Dickens's walks is that in *Great Expectations* in which Pip walks all night 'to tire himself out' after being warned not to return home. Beaumont, however, argues that Dickens's restlessness was linked to his father's recent death and his dissolving marriage with his wife Catherine, both events that occurred around the publication of *Great Expectations*.

In the thirteenth chapter of his text, Beaumont makes fascinating connections between Dickens's nightwalking and ideas from the era and his novels.

Beaumont mentions that walking attained a high degree of importance in the industrial era as workers walked 'briskly' from one task to another. A more disturbing connection exists between nightwalking and Dickens's *The Old Curiosity Shop*, in which a man walking the streets one night encounters Little Nell, who asks for directions. For Victorians, this scene suggests the nineteenth-century reality of child prostitutes, though Dickens is quick to reassure the reader of Nell's innocence.

Nightwalking again becomes a prominent feature of a text that examines one of the most prolific contributors to Dickens's *Household Words* in *George Augustus Sala and the Nineteenth-Century Periodical Press: The Personal Style of a Public Writer* by Peter Blake. In his second chapter, 'Tales of Two Cities: Part I—London' (pp. 65–102), he examines the journalistic relationship between Dickens and Sala. Underscoring Sala's love for the Dickensian style, Blake goes examines how Sala imitates that style throughout his many contributions to the periodical, even mentioning specific phrases that appear in both Dickens's and Sala's writing. The chapter then focuses on Sala's depiction of scenes on London streets at night during a walk he took after he had accidentally locked himself out of his home. Like Dickens, Sala places *himself* among the poorest of the London slums, petitioning the reader for redress of these wrongs.

A final connection can be made to the city (though not London) through the habit of nightwalking in Stephen Miller's *Walking New York: Reflections of American Writers from Walt Whitman to Teju Cole*. In his second chapter, 'Britons Visiting New York: Fanny Trollope, Anthony Trollope, Charles Dickens' (pp. 10–22), Miller examines the touring and walking habits of British writers in the great American city: Frances Trollope, Anthony Trollope, and Charles Dickens. Most of the chapter focuses on Dickens's visit, from which he wrote *American Notes*. During his visit, though hounded by journalists, Dickens still found time for one of his favourite habits: nightwalking. The chapter goes on to recount what one of these night walks might entail, and the social issues that it brings to his mind: Irish immigration, treatment of African Americans, the New York meat market, the American press, madrigal shows, and penitentiaries.

A second common theme in many of the works from this past year is industrialization and labour. We begin with *The Industrial Novels: Charlotte Brontë's Shirley, Charles Dickens' Hard Times and Elizabeth Gaskell's North and South* by Mehmet Akif Balkaya. In the second chapter, 'Charles Dickens's *Hard Times*: Utilitarianism as the Idea behind the Revolution' (pp. 43–66), Balkaya reads *Hard Times* in light of the Utilitarian philosophy of Jeremy Bentham, prevalent at the time. Balkaya surveys the characters in the text, showing how they originate from, or run contrary to, Bentham's ideology. In a fascinating reading, Louisa's marriage to Bounderby can be seen as driven by self-interest, as she marries not from feelings of love, but because the marriage would be 'the greatest good for the greatest number', i.e. the male authority figures in her life. Labour and capitalist ideals are also a feature of *The Victorian Novel, Service Work, and the Nineteenth-Century Economy* by Joshua Gooch, reviewed above in more detail. Gooch's third chapter, '*Our Mutual Friend:* Service Work as Subject-Work' (pp. 81–108), focuses on service work in *Our Mutual Friend*. The primary distinction made here is between the 'material' work of the professional gentleman and the 'immaterial' work of unproductive labour. As Gooch points out, 'Unproductive labour . . . underpins the novel's use of dust and finance as resonant motifs for waste and fraud' (p. 81). Gooch explores the motif of unproductive labour through the three primary 'villains' of the novel: Wegg, Headstone, and Riderhood. Gooch illustrates how each of these characters 'undertakes his plot as a result of personal experiences of subjugation in service, and so illustrates the potential for break-down in work discipline' (p. 99). Through depicting their service work, Dickens is again creating characters who seek to move beyond the class system that so rigidly circumscribes them.

A tangential concern to that of labour and industry is that of commercialization. The Victorian commercial culture is certainly one of the oddest in history, as Deborah Lutz makes clear in *Relics of Death in Victorian Literature and Culture*. In her third chapter, 'The Many Faces of Death Masks: Dickens and *Great Expectations*' (pp. 74–101), Lutz examines *Great Expectations* through the Victorian (and Dickensian) fascination with death-masks. After an examination of the fascination death-masks held for Victorians, Lutz argues that Dickens used the 'still body' in much of his writing to 'speak . . . about endings and their materiality' (p. 78). In *Great Expectations*, 'Death presses in from all sides' (p. 81): Magwitch envies the dead, Pip first understands himself as distinct from his dead siblings, Miss Havisham becomes an effigy when jilted, and Wemmick's face hardens as he approaches his offices. In all, Pip matures through his communion with the dead things around him.

Commercialization is also a primary focus of Peter Gurney's *Wanting and Having: Popular Politics and Liberal Consumerism in England*. In his sixth chapter, ' "Please Sir, I want some more": Dickens on Working-Class Scarcity and Middle-Class Excess' (pp. 183–219), Gurney examines Dickens's changing views regarding the means of poor relief. In his early work, *Oliver Twist* in particular, Dickens promoted 'paternalistic' charity motivated by 'non-sectarian, New Testament-inspired Christianity' (pp. 184–5). By *The Chimes*, however, Dickens has seemingly dismissed a paternalistic solution for the desire for a free trade market. Another shift in view appeared in *Dombey and Son*, in which Dickens explores 'the moral contradictions of the gospel of free trade' (p. 220). Ultimately, though Dickens himself gained tremendously from free trade, he became upon his death 'a man of the people' (p. 211).

Conceptions of gender form another group of the Dickens-centric chapters from this past year. We begin this group with *The Victorian Novel and Masculinity*, edited by Phillip Mallett. In the third chapter, 'Dickens and Masculinity: The Necessity of the Nurturing Male' (pp. 51–66), Natalie McKnight argues that, as Dickens aged, he began to write against the stereotyped depictions of gender that his period (and his early novels) helped to create. After a brief review of what Victorian depictions of gender roles might entail, helped by Sarah Ellis's conduct book *The Women of England*, McKnight surveys almost the entirety of Dickens's fictional oeuvre, pointing out how the male characters both adhere to and depart from typical norms of gendered behaviour. The two most extreme examples of this are Nicholas

Nickleby and Pip, who possess stereotypical masculine and feminine qualities respectively. In the fifth chapter of Heike Hartung's *Ageing, Gender and Illness in Anglophone Literature*, 'Figures of Childhood, Figures of Old Age: Charles Dickens's *Great Expectations*' (pp. 142–53), *Great Expectations* appears as a text that conflates childhood and adulthood in a number of interesting ways. Hartung reminds us that, even though Dickens is most commonly associated with childhood, his children find themselves in the most deplorable of situations, creating a portrait of childhood that is conflicted and 'aged'. She argues that Pip's maturation can be tracked through his various interactions with Miss Havisham. These interactions connect to Pip's development, which 'distinguishes between a static concept of childhood and youth ... and ... adulthood ... [marked by] an awareness of change and responsible agency' (p. 147).

Another text that deals with conceptions of the body is *Changing Hands: Industry, Evolution and the Reconfiguration of the Victorian Body* by Peter J. Capuano. In his fifth chapter, 'The Evolutionary Moment in Dickens's *Great Expectations*' (pp. 127–51), Capuano argues that while most descriptions of hands in Dickens serve as outward extensions of character, in *Great Expectations* they function as visible signs of the novel's identity politics. This connection appears in the description of Molly's powerful hands, whose animalism connects to an interest in Darwinian evolution and stereotyped descriptions of the Irish during this period. These hands are compared (in Pip's mind) to Estella's. This comparison, Gurney argues, emerges through Estella's delight in Pip's childhood beating of Herbert and her later marriage to the abusive Drummle; her condescending 'wave' a product of Miss Havisham's upbringing. In his seventh chapter, 'Handwriting and the Hermeneutics of Detection in Dickens's *Bleak House* (pp. 185–213), Capuano argues that Victorian texts expressed a fascination with hands because it was the part of the body most threatened. This 'threat' appears in the fact that the novel had moved from epistolary to chapter, thus making handwriting a less unique form of literary expression. Capuano focuses on *Bleak House*, whose plot revolves around the deciphering of an individual's penmanship. He goes on to tease out the distinctions between the individual and mechanic prevalent in the handwriting of the era, such as Hawdon's penmanship being recognizably individual, despite all clerks having to write in a prescribed 'Chancery-hand'.

A further set of publications from this year can be grouped by using the term 'historical analyses'. The first of these is *Greek and Roman Classics in the British Struggle for Social Reform*, edited by Henry Stead and Edith Hall. In chapter 6, 'Making It Really New: Dickens versus the Classics' (pp. 99–115), Edith Hall examines Dickens's reluctance to reference classical sources as many of his contemporaries did. In his novels, he parodies the classical referents that many of his fellow writers used to promote character or thematic ideals. Dickens's avoidance of the classics makes sense, she suggests, given that most classical heroines are much bolder than many of Dickens's own female characters, the learning of Latin by characters who have social aspirations seems to convey a dislikeable pretentiousness in his works, and filling his novels with classical references could have been seen as elitism.

A second text that falls into this category is *The Fiction of History*, edited by Alexander Lyon Macfie. In the fifth chapter of this collection, 'Dickens the Historian, Carlyle the Novelist, and Dickens, Carlyle and the French Revolution' (pp. 72–82), David Paroissien sets up an analytical comparison between Dickens's *Tale of Two Cities* and Carlyle's *The French Revolution*. After arguing that both authors wrote in order to break into English 'insularity' on the topic of the revolution, Paroissien begins by stating how much material each author worked with. Paroissien then examines how both authors approached history—Carlyle through his essays on the subject and Dickens through *Barnaby Rudge* and *A Tale of Two Cities*. Finally, Paroissien moves back and forth between novel and history, demonstrating how the one borrowed from the other.

Another pair of texts deals with the Victorian novel and religious belief in the era. The first of these is Richard Hughes Gibson's *Forgiveness in Victorian Literature: Grammar, Narrative and Community*. In his analysis of Dickens's uses of forgiveness, in chapter 2, 'Dickens and Forgiveness in 1846: Liberality and Liability' (pp. 39–78), Gibson argues that this virtue in Dickens's writings wavers constantly between two oppositional characteristics—liberality (the unconditional, extravagant expression of forgiveness) and liability (forgiveness dependent on moral self-correction and adherence to one's 'duty'). In *Life of Our Lord*, Dickens retells portions of the Gospels that highlight both these extremes. At the same time, however, Dickens relates stories from the Gospels in which forgiveness seems to be a 'reward of duty done'. Dickens's other works represented follow this same pattern. For example, liberality and liability are both seen in the plan of the reform house for fallen women. This text can be followed immediately by *Perplext in Faith: Essays on Victorian Beliefs and Doubts*, edited by Alisa Clapp-Itnyre and Julie Melnyk. In her essay for the second chapter in the third part, 'Dickens's *The Life of Our Lord* and the Problem of Jesus' (pp. 268–303), Jessica Hughes examines Dickens's *The Life of Our Lord* in light of popular Victorian religious and theological sentiment. After questioning why Dickens chooses to write on the life of Christ for his children rather than creating a fictional story that exemplifies Christian values, Hughes points to the shift in Victorian theology from a focus on Atonement to Incarnation. This focus on Jesus as God-Man, Hughes argues, created trouble for Dickens, as he had to write a *Bildungsroman* about a man who does not change, and has no flaws to overcome.

Another group of texts can be placed under the heading 'Stage and Screen'. The first of these is *Victorian Writers and the Stage* by Richard Pearson. Pearson's first chapter, 'Farce, Family and the Minor Theatres: Dickens as a Legitimate Playwright' (pp. 23–56), deals with the amateur plays written by Dickens. He begins by noting that, interestingly, though Dickens was undoubtedly the writer of the city, his plays 'are not directly concerned with the city' (p. 23), setting a marked distinction between them and his urban sketches. Pearson then goes through Dickens's career on the stage, teasing out the difficulties associated with being a nineteenth-century novelist who also writes plays and acts. Pearson traces Dickens's career through the minor theatre as a writer of farces. When he met with failure, Pearson suggests he expressed his frustrations through Crummles in *Nicholas Nickleby*. Chapter 4 of Pearson's text, 'Dramatic Collaboration: Dickens's and Collins's Melodramas' (pp. 124–45), deals with what is undoubtedly the best-known and most successful of all Dickens's theatrical enterprises: his collaboration with Wilkie Collins on *The Frozen Deep*. Because of the 'symbiotic' nature of this collaboration, Pearson suggests, the plays written by Dickens and Collins '[challenge] the notion that the play is always the adaptation of an original fiction' (p. 125). In speaking of the play's symbiotic creation, Pearson argues that one may trace Dickens's and Collins's own professional and personal relationship through their two major stage collaborations: *The Frozen Deep* and *No Thoroughfare*. Ironically, this last play marked both the beginning of Collins's popular career and Dickens's final complete publication.

*Remakes and Remaking: Concepts—Media—Practices*, edited by Rüdiger Heinze and Lucia Krämer, contains one chapter on adapting Dickens. 'The Remake as Re-adaptation of an English Classic: Charles Dickens's *Oliver Twist* on Film' (pp. 115–30), by Till Kinzel, explores several film adaptations of *Oliver Twist* and examines how they impact the concept of the 'remake' as a whole. Adaptations of the novel have been very popular since the time of its initial serialization. This is particularly true for the 'Death of Nancy' vignette, with which Dickens always ended his farewell readings. In fact, theatrical productions of this scene appeared before the serialization of the novel was even completed (p. 117). Kinzel does a brilliant job at dispelling the false correlation between quality and 'originality' before addressing both Bleasdale's and David Lean's films. Early on-screen adaptations are also examined in Deborah Cartmell's *Adaptations in the Sound Era: 1927–37*. In her third chapter, 'Sound Dickens' (pp. 55–76), Cartmell examines the early sound adaptations of Dickens's works, paying particular attention to the relationship between the written and spoken word. Cartmell begins by noting the 'cinematic' quality of Dickens's language, as many have done before her. She pays particular attention to the advertisements produced during the early sound film releases, noting how text and image suggest the films' fidelity to the Dickens original. The films themselves continue this play between text and image, such as 1935's *Tale of Two Cities*, which uses 'intertitles'—text appearing on screen—as a way of communicating theme.

Finally, there were a number of chapters on Dickens from a primarily theoretical perspective, beginning with *The Bigamy Plot: Sensation and Convention in the Victorian Novel* by Maia McAleavey, also discussed elsewhere in this chapter. McAleavey begins her third chapter, '*David Copperfield*'s Angelic Bigamy' (pp. 71–93), by addressing a particular instance of the bigamy plot: the dead first bride who returns miraculously to life. McAleavey argues that both *David Copperfield* and *Middlemarch* participate in this 'resurrection bigamy'. In *Copperfield*, resurrection bigamy occurs when David reunites with Dora in the afterlife. After examining typical Victorian readings of a verse in Matthew, the chapter looks at Victorian texts that seem to suggest that heaven provides a spiritual alternative to earthly marriage. The chapter then looks at Dickens's novel in light of David's early question to Peggotty about the possibility of someone marrying twice.

Next in this set is *Victorian Literature and the Physics of the Imponderable* by Sarah Alexander. Alexander's first chapter, 'Dickensian Physics: *Bleak House*,

*Our Mutual Friend* and the Luminiferous Ether', opens with discussion of the now famous feud between Dickens and George Henry Lewes over the scientific validity of Krook's spontaneous combustion in *Bleak House*. After remarking on a habitual critique of Dickens (lack of 'realism'), Alexander argues that the juxtaposition of Dickens's 'romanticism' with the 'realist' scientific empiricism prevalent during the age is not quite accurate, as very popular branches of Victorian scientific thought focused on the speculative and 'imponderables'. Alexander goes on to argue that Dickens's 'non-empirical science' both stimulates the imagination and provides an explanation for 'the invisible economic relationships that structure human societies' (p. 22). This is followed by *Mimesis, Desire, and the Novel: René Girard and Literary Criticism*, edited by Pierpaolo Antonello and Heather Webb. In the tenth chapter from this collection, David Quint applies Girard's novel theory to a reading of Dickens's *Little Dorrit*, arguing that Miss Wade enacts Girard's view of the novel as politically revolutionary and anti-authoritarian. The primary outworking of her revolutionary lifestyle occurs in her emotional resentment of 'Pet', the daughter of the upper-middle-class Meagles, who has all the advantages of the new aristocracy. Miss Wade's envious resentment is then contrasted with Esther Summerson, who, though also born into a condition of extreme marginality, does not grow bitter, but rather uses her birth to 'strive to be of use'.

We then come to *Reading and the Victorians*, edited by Matthew Bradley and Juliet John. In the fourth chapter of this collection, 'Deep Reading in the Manuscripts: Dickens and the Manuscript of *David Copperfield*' (pp. 65–78), Paul Davis argues that the most effective method for discovering Victorian reading practices is to look at an author's manuscript revisions and corrections. According to Davis, these revisions demonstrate 'imagined reception' (what an author believes the reader desires to see), the act of an author turning himself or herself into an 'expert reader', and the attention to 'minute specifics at a "micro" level ... which ... is crucial to the reader's sense of cumulatively registered meaning' (p. 65). One such moment is David's early 'flash-forward' to Little Em'ly's dark future when he sees her playing on the edge of a jetty. In the sixth chapter of this collection, 'Reading Across the Lines and Off the Page: Dickens's Model of Multiple Literacies in *Our Mutual Friend*' (pp. 89–98), Sheila Cordner argues that *Our Mutual Friend* engages with debates in the Victorian period regarding knowledge based on personal observation versus received authority. Cordner first contextualizes her argument by looking at giants of the era such as Ruskin, Charles Kingsley, and Huxley. She then analyses the character of Boffin, arguing that the illiterate may possess a power of seeing the world in way that those who can read do not. If Boffin represents the divide between the literate and illiterate, then Lizzie offers a possibility of their synthesis.

We next come to *The Poetics of Sight. Cultural Interactions: Studies in the Relationship between the Arts* by John Harvey. In chapter 4, '*Bleak House* to *Lighthouse*: The Optics of the Novel' (pp. 159–212), Harvey examines the importance of sight in extended narratives. He begins with a survey of some of the novel's early masters such as Defoe and Sterne, finally coming to Jane Austen. He argues that, while critics of Austen say she sees too little, the truth is that the visual imagery of the nineteenth-century novel is far too 'exorbitant'. Austen's economy of visual imagery matches her style beautifully. Most of the rest of the chapter deals with Dickens's *Bleak House*, a book in which 'failed sight', both metaphorically and literally, is a continual theme.

Looking at individual articles on the subject of Dickens from this past year, two primary themes stand out. The first is that of 'adaptation' or 'translation' (from one medium or language to another), and the second is that of 'language and linguistics'. In the first set, we begin with Laura Korobkin's 'Avoiding Aunt Tomasina' (*ELH* 81[2015] 115–40). This article takes a look at a short but fascinating episode in the life of Dickens. In April 1857 he was approached by Mary Webb, a black American 'freewoman' who had become a very well-known figure through her public readings of *Uncle Tom's Cabin*. Her request was to use Dickens's theatre to stage one of her readings. Dickens refused, and Korobkin argues that the refusal was given, not only for the stated reasons of cost and time, but because Dickens perhaps harboured the anxiety about race shared by many Englishman of his era. Korobkin also suggests that his refusal might relate to a private jealousy of Harriet Beecher Stowe, whose *Uncle Tom's Cabin* was even more popular in Britain than the United States, out-selling Dickens's own *Bleak House*.

Another article that examines a fascinating project in digital adaptation is 'Being John Rokesmith' (*19* 21[2015] 1–4) by Peter Orford. In this article, Orford takes on the persona of the protagonist in *Our Mutual Friend*. Through the voice of Rokesmith, Orford describes his character and comments on his transposition to the Internet. This piece is part of a larger project in which fictional characters from *Our Mutual Friend* are given Twitter accounts and handles, and send out daily tweets in their own unique voice. Throughout the piece, Orford analyses the essential differences between novel and Twitter and how character is represented in each. Film and television adaptations are a perennial favourite for Dickens scholars. Beside the chapter mentioned above, Rachel Carroll's 'Black Britain and the Classic Adaptation: Integrated Casting in Television Adaptations of *Oliver Twist* and *Little Dorrit*' (*Adaptation* 8[2015] 16–30) examines two recent adaptations of the above titles which include an African American actress in traditionally 'white' roles: Nancy and Tattycoram. Carroll argues that such integrated casting might more accurately represent the England of the period, in which thousands of people of African origin lived as a consequence of the transatlantic slave trade. She also connects these adaptations [2007 and 2008 respectively] to Ayanna Thompson's argument for 'colour-blind casting' in Shakespeare. The final article that can be classified under 'adaptation' is one that examines the theme in a pedagogical form, taking the performative aspects of Dickens's novels and placing them in the classroom. In 'Reading Communities in the Dickens Classroom' (*Pedagogy* 15[2015] 331–51), Susan Cook and Elizabeth Henley argue that the popular reading tours Dickens did of his own works exist beyond his life and find a new home in the contemporary community of elementary and secondary school classrooms. Cook tested this hypothesis by conducting a course in which students performed oral readings of Dickens's texts and responded to the insights these readings produced. Cook states that the primary conclusion drawn from this study is that the students respond quite differently when given face-to-face interaction than when asked to complete a project through digital means.

The most prevalent theme in this past year's articles can be classified as 'language and linguistics'. For example, in 'Belligerent Instruments: The Documentary Violence of *Bleak House*' (*SNNTS* 47[2015] 20–42), Suzanne Daly examines the destructive forces of the Jarndyce and Jarndyce suit on the Chancery wards. Building on J. Hillis Miller's argument that *Bleak House* is a 'document about documents', Daly analyses how the legal papers by which the suit is consumed cause great, though indirect, harm, through language and their own 'written-ness'. Daly also looks to the work of Slavoj Žižek, whose distinctions between 'objective' and 'subjective' violence form the basis of much of her argument. In 'Charles Dickens's *David Copperfield*: New Critical Reconsiderations' (*ELLS* 5[2015] 31–5), Ali Alhaj gives a 'bird's eye' view of the important contextual and thematic elements in *David Copperfield*. Alhaj touches on such subjects as Dickens's unique ability to create character, Dickens's own family and literary career (including the autobiographical nature of the novel), the Victorian notion of sentimentality, and, most importantly, the value the novel places on marriage and domesticity. Specialized vocabulary and 'Dickensian' language come to the fore in Leona Toker's 'Hypallage and the Lateralization of Metaphors in a Dickens Text' (*Style* 49[2015] 113–25). In this article, the author explores Dickens's *Tale of Two Cities* through the author's much-used imagistic vocabulary. As she states, 'One of the reasons for the famously "Inimitable" quality of Dickens's style is its oscillation between the literal and figurative uses of vocabulary' (p. 113). The device the article focuses on is 'hypallage', or the imagistic exchange between noun and adjective. Toker argues that the use of this device is a type of shorthand, creating a semantic tension between 'the abstract and the concrete' (p. 116). In 'Information in the Novel and the Novel as Information System: Charles Dickens's *Little Dorrit* and Margaret Drabble's *Radiant Way* Trilogy' (*Information & Culture* 50[2015] 339–71), Carol Colatrella argues that novels are not only made of language, but participate in a continual exchange of information. This exchange operates in particular when novels advocate social change, or illuminate society's social inequalities, using information to identify those institutions that are creating the inequality. Colatrella then looks at two novels (Dickens's *Little Dorrit* and Drabble's *Radiant Way* trilogy) which critique social inequalities by inserting historical and social information into their fictional plots and settings. Both novels demonstrate how information travels in society, and both prove that an excess of information does not equate to a solution for social ills. Finally, one of the most fascinating approaches to linguistic studies this year is in 'Mind-Modelling with Corpus Stylistics in *David Copperfield*' (*L&L* 24[2015] 129–47). In this article, Peter Stockwell and Michaela Mahlberg announce their goal as a characterization analysis of Dickens's *Copperfield* using 'corpus methods', or programs developed that analyse linguistics. Based on the argument that language use does not distinguish between real and fictional people, the authors create the idea of 'mind-modelling', or the ability we have as people to understand others as separate and distinct from ourselves. The authors then examine the character of Mr Dick (a representation of Dickens) using the corpus programs, citing statistically Mr Dick's language use in various contexts and as response to other characters.

Another common theme in articles from this past year was imperialism and colonialism. This theme is reflected first in 'Economic Imperialism and Financial Citizenship' (*JVC* 20[2015] 87–100). In this article, Jasper Schelstraete and Jennifer Scott analyse Dickens's *Martin Chuzzlewit* and Galt's *Lawrie Todd* in relation to the changing view of British economic protectionism as a response to global finance. During the 1820s, Britain was ready to re-engage in global finance as a means to build empire. The argument made is that, in both novels, America becomes the crux or linking point between global finance and the literary marketplace. This connection is seen in *Lawrie Todd* through its focus on land speculation. In *Chuzzlewit*, this connection is demonstrated through emigration and American settlement. In 'Saving British Natives' (*VLC* 43[2015] 261–80), Terra Walston Joseph argues that Caroline Chisolm (a Victorian philanthropist) and Charles Dickens each created narratives that worked to demystify the 'otherness' of the British colony of Australia. Joseph supports this argument by looking at the emigration of the Micawbers and Emily Peggotty in *David Copperfield*, and Chisolm's 'A Bundle of Emigrants' Letters'. In the latter, Chisolm demonstrates how 'family emigration' could support starving British households through the colonies' abundance. In *Copperfield*, Dickens 'imitates this use of emigration as a means of narrative closure' (p. 265). In both texts, Australia transforms into a second 'home' for Britons. Articles exploring this theme not only discussed how Dickens represented British colonies, but how the British colonies represented Dickens. In 'The Colonial Children Cry: Jo the Crossing-Sweep Goes to the Colonies' (*JVC* 20[2015] 308–25), Jane Lydon argues that the character of Jo from *Bleak House* was such a powerful symbol for neglected charity that variations existed as far afield as the English colonies of Australia and New Zealand. After discussing Dickens's own dramatic performance of his works, Lydon examines presentations of Jo in sketch art and photography. Lydon then looks at transmissions of Jo's story from England to the colonies. These included dramatized versions of *Bleak House* performed in imitation of Dickens, and artwork that came to the colonies through families and professionals. Unfortunately, any critical conversation regarding colonialism or imperialism in the Victorian era must include a discussion of the slave trade. In 'The Ghost of Slavery in *Our Mutual Friend*' (*VLC* 43[2015] 511–32), Alexandra Neel examines the subtle connections to the issue of slavery that underpin the text. After surveying recent scholarship that deals with these connections in works such as *American Notes*, *Bleak House*, and *Great Expectations*, Neel argues that these texts differ from *Our Mutual Friend* in that, rather than offering an autobiographical tale mobilizing tropes from slave narrative and the rhetoric of abolitionist reform, the character of Harmon/Rokesmith 'delivers fractured and fragmented monologues on his ghostlike identity' because he is 'a character devoid of personhood and civic attachment' (p. 512).

The next set of articles can be put under the heading 'Place and Space'. In her article 'Dickensian Blocks: East London's Contemporary Housing Landscape' (*Soundings* 60[2015] 95–106), Stephanie Polsky discusses the current state of Dickens's house, Gad's Hill Place. The house itself was in a severe state of disrepair, and local residents sought to apply to the council in an attempt to remedy the situation. The council was later rejected as residents opted to request repairs from Tower Hamlets Community Housing, a non-profit organization. In looking at the repair issues concerning the house, Polsky makes a comparison between the housing crisis in modern-day London and that of the Victorian era, noting several similarities. Thematically, 'place' moves from building houses to building narratives. In 'Mr. Pickwick and the Mighty Ponds of Hampstead' (*NCC* 37[2015] 91–106), Keith Crook writes against the critique that Dickens 'saved' his first serial novel through the inclusion of Samuel Weller. Rather, Crook argues, Dickens's plans for *Pickwick* were much more precisely laid out than critics suppose. One primary piece of evidence for this careful planning is the serious view Pickwick takes of popular science, particularly his interest in the nearby Hampstead Ponds, which Dickens chose as a geographical site many of his readers would know. It is here that Pickwick fishes for 'tittlebats', the focus of his scientific enquiries. Finally, place moves from local to global considerations in Jonathan Grossman's 'Living the Global Transport Network in *Great Expectations*' (*VS* 57[2015] 225–50). In this article, Grossman argues that Pip's 'biographical retrospective' is coloured by the existence of a growing transport network. The first section addresses Pip's unawareness of the geographical world that surrounds his boyhood (the isolation of the marshes and the bleakness of Satis House). In the second section, Pip becomes aware of global transport through the return of Magwitch from Australia. In the third section, we see how stagecoach transport works to make Pip a member of the greater London community. In the crowds of the fourth section, the opposite goal is reached.

Another set of articles from this past year set Dickens against another author or literary tradition. N. N. Starygina, M. A. Pershina, I. N. Mikheeva, O. S. Berezina and I. K. Klyukha in their 'Dickens's Christmas Story as an Intexteteme in Leskov's Yule Short Story' (REurSt 7[2015] 193 -200), conduct a textual comparison between the Christmas short stories of Dickens and those of Russian writer Leskov. They argue that the translation of Dickens's stories into Russian precipitated the growth of and interest in Russian 'Yule' stories that demonstrate similar thematic elements. Shared themes include the importance of 'home' or 'family', personal redemption from cruelty to childlike innocence, and the relationship between God and man. A common comparison made by 'transatlantic' literary scholars is that between Charles Dickens and the 'American' Dickens, Mark Twain. In 'The Spectre on the Stair: Intertextual Chains in *Great Expectations* and *The Adventures of Huckleberry Finn*' (*LitI* 17[2015] 71–94), Irene Morra argues that though Twain seemingly evinces a disdain for European 'book culture', he incorporates his version of these sensibilities into many of his novels. Morra states that such inclusion favours Dickens in particular, and that strong narrative and thematic parallels exist between *Great Expectations* and *The Adventures of Huckleberry Finn*. After some discussion regarding Twain's knowledge of

Dickens's work, Morra addresses her argument through the shared themes of social injustice (prison/slavery), *Bildungsroman* and agency, and the moral consciousness of children. Finally, one scholar compares Dickens to one of the masters of English literature in an attempt to determine Dickens's place in the canon. In 'Dickens and Chaucer' (*English* 64[2015] 42–64), Jeremy Tambling examines the possible link between these two giants. Interestingly, the beginning of Tambling's analysis involves comparisons between locations mentioned in Dickens's novels and scenes from Chaucer's own writing. The comparisons then end with Dickens's propensity to tell 'tales within tales'—or to break off the action of his novels to include local folklore. Of course, the strongest comparison made between the two authors is their depiction of character. Like those of Dickens, Tambling reminds us, 'Chaucer's characters all exist in the superlative' (p. 46).

A pair of articles from this past year can be placed under the heading 'Disease and Disability Studies'. In 'Conflicting Models of Care for People with Mental Disabilities in Charles Dickens's Fiction and Journalism' (*JLCDS* 9[2015] 89–105), Gillian Ray-Burruel examines Dickens's depiction of characters with either a mental or a physical disability (of which there are several). Looking at characters such as Smike, Mr Dick, and Barnaby Rudge, Ray-Burruel argues that, 'In contrast to the Malthusian principles of his own era, Dickens's fiction reflects eighteenth-century moral values such as community kinship and benevolence toward the less fortunate' (p. 93). Ray-Burruel's biggest criticism of Dickens is that his 'disabled' characters never marry—that they are 'not worthy' of becoming a part of their own intimate domestic community. A second article in this category is Ralph Smith's 'Narratives of Public Health in Dickens's Journalism' (*L&M* 33[2015] 157–83). Smith, after giving historical context to the sanitation reform of the Victorian era (and Dickens's connection to it), argues that Dickens's non-fiction 'undermine[s] the sanitarian version of public health' (p. 159). Smith's methodology compares Dickens's 'fever narratives' to the sanitarian argument. This comparison involves three different types of story—the visitor's tale, the history, and the fanciful story. In the visitor's tale, a fictional other observes and comments on the insanitary conditions caused by industrialization. The history relates past to current conditions, and the fable uses fancy to allegorize and parody fact.

Another pair of articles falls in the category 'Victorian Beliefs and Cultural Life'. First in this pair is 'Pigmies and Brobdignagians: Arts Writing, Dickensian Character, and the Vanishing Victorian Life-Size' (*VS* 57[2015] 667–90), by Dehn Gilmore. In this article, Gilmore argues that Dickens's 'larger-than-life' depictions of characters were, for the Victorians 'true to life', and reflect anxieties 'about the life-size as a mode of depiction or a standard for visual representation' (p. 668). As evidence for this argument Gilmore looks at the proliferation of Victorian 'life-size' figures, from Madame Tussaud's to the Great Exhibition. Gilmore then compares Ruskin to Whistler, two famous artists of the era who had vastly different ideas about the possibility of 'life-size'. After considering Victorian developments in sculpture, perspective, and photography, Gilmore ends with a discussion of public viewing of art. Secondly, in 'Reading Victorian Rags: Recycling,

Redemption and Dickens's Ragged Children' (*JVC* 20[2015] 34–49), Deborah Wynne compares the Victorian preoccupation with rags as material objects to Dickens's representation of 'ragged' children. Wynne argues that the two are comparable, in that Dickens saw these ragged children as the Victorians saw rags: capable of purification and social usefulness. Wynne begins her analysis with an examination of the 'rag-and-bone' shops that would encourage the poor to donate and recycle cloth. Wynne then examines the phenomenon of 'ragged children' and the growth of private charity and sentimentality. Finally, she examines Dickens's support for 'ragged schools'.

The last set of individual articles can be placed under the heading 'Manuscript Studies'. The first of these is 'The Skeleton Out of the Closet' (*VPR* 48[2015] 557–68), by Jeremy Parrott. In this article, Parrott examines a new find in Dickensian manuscript studies. In September 2014, Parrott tracked down a twenty-volume set of *All the Year Round* after a long and exhaustive search. In the margins of the pieces were pencilled in names of contributors, many of which were previously unknown. The most interesting discoveries are Dickens's collaborations with other authors, and pieces which were originally attributed to Dickens that were not actually written by him. Pieces originally attributed to Dickens and Collins were written by Collins's 'underrated' brother Charles (p. 565). Finally, in 'Tracking Pirates through the Digital Archive: The Case of Dickens' (*YES* 45[2015] 178–95), Mary Hammond examines the 'pleasures and pitfalls' of a digital archives project. The databases used for the search focus on the periodical press of the nineteenth century, the British Library's Nineteenth-Century Newspapers and the Library of Congress's Chronicling America. Hammond argues that the most profound 'pitfall' of this project is the tendency to view the habitual appearance or disappearance of a specific text as a marker of literary or cultural change. A 'pleasure', then, is the discovery of the many pirated versions of Dickens's novels that appeared throughout the era.

We now move on to the journals that specialize in Dickens, beginning with *Dickens Quarterly*. The March issue of this journal from 2015 featured themes of textual materiality that take the form of plagiarized publications, illustrations, and unusual correspondence. In 'Plagiarizing Pickwick: Imitations of Immortality' (*DQu* 32[2015] 5–20), Adam Abraham argues that the plagiarized imitations of *Pickwick Papers* popular during Dickens's time can be viewed as lights shining on Dickens's text. Abraham begins his analysis by examining *The Penny Pickwick*. Abraham argues of the imitations, 'Each prosthesis marks an intervention, a coming-to-terms with that which Dickens had wrought' (p. 8). The imitations fall into two categories—those that explore the past and future of Pickwick, and those that create alternative versions of the Pickwickians themselves. Finally, Abraham explores how these imitations explore issues of race and sexuality in their own time. In 'Illustrating Pip and the Terrible Stranger' (*DQu* 32[2015] 21–43), Jolene Zigarovich explores an important question: why did *Great Expectations* appear in print without accompanying illustrations? Fascinatingly, other than *Hard Times*, it was the only one of Dickens's novels to do so (p. 21). Zigarovich argues that one of the reasons for this, other than the speed at which this novel was serialized, is that the later novels of Dickens were far more complex, and thus did not need the accompanying illustrations that might mitigate their level of 'realism'. Zigarovich then goes on to trace the various artists that attempted an illustration of the novel, beginning with the American publication in *HarperCollins*. Finally, in ' "The Other Woman", Eliza Davis and Charles Dickens' (*DQu* 32[2015] 44–70), Murray Baumgarten argues that Dickens's correspondence with Davis, an English Jew, works to mitigate the anti-Semitic sentiments that Dickens held as a product of his age. For instance, Baumgarten states that Davis's friendship with Dickens led to his creation of Riah, the 'good Jew' in *Our Mutual Friend*. Riah, Baumgarten argues, exists as a type of atonement for Dickens's characterization of Fagin years earlier. Baumgarten states that, despite this maturation of racial awareness, 'stereotypes have a way of living on', citing Alec Guinness's portrayal of the character in David Lean's film as evidence.

The June issue of *Dickens Quarterly* can be divided into two categories: 'English Religious Sectarianism' and 'Italy'. The first begins with 'Dickens and Godparenting' (*DQu* 32[2015] 101–15) by William F. Long and Paul Schlicke. Dickens himself was godfather to several children, and the article explores the pattern of this relationship in Dickens's life as his growing popularity encouraged the growth of an ever-increasing circle of friends. Taking a fascinating direction, the article discusses Dickens's tumultuous relationship with Anglicanism and the Anglican Church, as christening was almost always a High Anglican practice. On the other side is 'Dantean Echoes in the *Old Curiosity Shop*' (*DQu* 32[2015] 116–28), by Adina Ciugureanu. In this article, Ciugureanu asks one simple question: 'Was Dickens familiar with the works of Dante?' Ciugureanu believes he was, and cites such historical evidence as the 1814 English translation of *The Divine Comedy* by Henry Francis Cary and Dickens's visit to 'the Stone of Dante' in *Pictures from Italy*. However, the strongest connection Ciugureanu draws between the two authors is in the similarities between the character of Dante's Beatrice and Little Nell from *The Old Curiosity Shop*. To Ciugureanu, the two characters can be compared in terms of their 'divine nature' (and Dickens's propensity to infantilize women), and Quilp is compared to Dante's Satan as grotesque and devouring. Coming back to the theme of religious sectarianism is 'Sources for the Characterization for Miss Miggs in *Barnaby Rudge*' (*DQu* 32[2015] 129–38) by Rodney Stenning Edgecombe. In this article, Edgecombe suggests types that Dickens may have used as a model for his Miss Miggs, whose characterization offers the 'definitive' rendering of the 'uncharitable Evangelical shrew' (p. 129). This characterization seems defined primarily by its 'thinness', which '*externalizes* the evidence of prayer' (p. 129). This character type, whose sparseness is linked to sexual frustration, gradually becomes physically abusive. Edgecombe connects this characterization to Elizabeth I, whose virgin status (he argues) manifested itself in aggressive behaviour. The final connection made to Miggs is Shakespeare's *Midsummer Night's Dream*—Elizabeth becomes Diana. We end this issue with another look at Italy, in 'Some Things About Italy: Dickensian Objects, Interiors and Pleasures' (*DQu* 32[2015] 139–52), by Mary A. Armstrong. In this article, Armstrong argues that Dickens's author-centric *Pictures from Italy* reveals the internal life of its creator through its engagement with things. Armstrong contextualizes her argument with some discussion of travelogue writing and previous critical approaches to thing theory. The 'things' analysed are at first unimpressive: a lottery ticket and a meal. As the objects observed by Dickens become more varied and unique, Armstrong posits that their accumulation 'triggers' a connection between the overall cumulative effect of the objects themselves and the text by which they are represented.

The September issue of *Dickens Quarterly* can also be divided into two categories: 'Fiction' and 'Fetish'. That is, articles that explore the boundaries between real and fictional accounts, or accounts that might be 'extra-fictional' (as in 'extratextual') and articles that explore the Victorian fetishization of the body and/or material culture. In 'Bumple Against Sludberry; or, Dickens Has an Early Encounter with Reform Politics' (*DQu* 32[2015] 181–98), William F. Long and Paul Schlicke compare a 'sketch by Boz', written early in Dickens's career about an actual court battle, to a fictional case that was created by Dickens years later in *David Copperfield*. This later case plays out in the novel while David is in his early career as a court reporter under Mr Spenlow. Though the two cases have been compared before, this article argues that while those involved in the actual case 'were respectable members of the community', those in the latter case 'were representatives of a self-perpetuating clique' (p. 195). In 'A Tale of Two Dwarfs' (*DQu* 32[2015] 199–210), Goldie Morgentaler takes an interesting look at two Dickensian characters that do not receive much critical attention at all—*The Old Curiosity Shop*'s Quilp and *David Copperfield*'s Miss Mowcher. Morgentaler's essential argument is that the negative connotations that are typically associated with these characters seem to originate from 'a perverse and malevolent sexuality' (p. 199). In attempting to discover the root of this connection, Morgentaler examines such disparate pieces of evidence as beliefs about physical deformity popular during the era, Dickens's own sexual proclivities and his interactions with women, his depiction of children, and Victorian beliefs regarding fairies and fairy tales. Ultimately, Morgentaler humanizes the dwarfs of the Victorian era, rescuing them from the 'Otherness' that comes from placing them within the fantasy of fairy tale or 'fancy' of the novel.

Continuing with the theme of fetishizing the Victorian body is Neil Forsyth's 'Hands in Dickens' (*DQu* 32[2015] 211–20). In this article, the author looks at two major Dickensian texts in which hands are focused on and 'fetishized'. Beginning with the focus on Molly's hands in *Great Expectations*, Forsyth explains how this points to a larger theme in the novel as a whole. He claims that this focus on hands, when combined with recent discoveries in neuroscience, helps us as readers understand the action of characters by recreating the sensory feelings of those actions in our own nervous system. Forsyth compares these moments in *Great Expectations* to Heep's rubbing his own hands in *David Copperfield* to produce the same effect. Switching back to the theme of extratextuality, we have Jerome Meckier's short article, 'Estella, Dead or Alive?' (*DQu* 32[2015] 221–8). This article asks a single, fascinating question: by the time Pip begins to publish the autobiographical account of his rise and fall, is the woman he has loved all his life living or dead? The inspiration for this fascinating conceit comes from the fact that Dickens published *Great Expectations* in *All the Year Round* using the device of the fictional author. He did not write 'Great Expectations by Charles Dickens' but published the story in its serial form as an autobiographical account of a rise in fortune told by one 'Mr. Phillip Pirrip'. Essentially, the argument goes like this: If Pip and those in his story are taken to be actual people, then by the time the story is published Estella must be dead. She must be dead because, in the story, Pip reveals Estella's parentage—something he promised Jaggers he would never divulge to her. The question of whether or not Pip is keeping this secret from a wife or a friend is irrelevant, as she would have heard about the revelation either way. This issue of the *Quarterly* ends with an article on commodification, the fetishization of commercial goods. In ' "The age of veneer": Charles Dickens and the Antinomies of Victorian Consumer Culture' (*DQu* 32[2015] 229–46), Peter Gurney argues that Dickens's critique of consumer culture points out a systematic 'disease' within the England of his time, one which places the 'consumption of material goods at the centre of personal as well as social and economic life' (p. 231). Gurney proves his argument by dividing the article into two—in the first section, he examines Dickens's tendency to turn objects into people and people into things. In the second, he explores Dickens's 'unsatisfactory resolution' of the contradictions extant in *Our Mutual Friend*.

The December issue of *Dickens Quarterly*, the final issue for this year, can be summed up in two words: 'digging' and 'discovery'. In two of the articles, scholars 'dig' through texts and manuscripts in an attempt to discover authorial authenticity to disputed writings. In the other two articles, actual digging and discovering take place. For their December article in *Dickens Quarterly*, William F. Long and Paul Schlicke examine a short allegorical sketch written in 1839 entitled 'The Man Who Couldn't Get Out. A Short Sketch—Not by "Boz" ' (*DQu* 32[2015] 277–82). The purpose of their examination is to delineate all the 'Dickensian' moments in the sketch itself after giving a brief summary of it and explaining the allegorical references. The sketch deals with the chiming of a clock in a large estate that the patriarch of the family cannot bear to listen to. The purpose of this sketch is to illuminate, through the use of allegory, the 6 May 'Bedchamber Affair'. The authors conclude that the sketch is indeed not by Dickens, but argue that the author believed that the absurdity of the actual events described stands up squarely against anything the greatest comic writer of the age could have produced. In 'Pickwick Plumbs the Hampstead Ponds' (*DQu* 32[2015] 283–92), Nancy Aycock Metz argues that chapter 1 of *Pickwick Papers*, in particular the discussion of Pickwick's scientific research interests, is a satire on the 'transactions' of the Royal Society of London. Metz's evidence for this connection appears in the satire of Joh Hill, a botanist refused entrance into the Royal Society. Dickens's satire relies on controversies closer to his own time. This satire was based on the British Association, which operated annual meetings that received constant condemnation from the press. Dickens's 'Mudfog' papers were his personal attacks on this body, soon recognized as such. In 'The Subterranean Topography of *Oliver Twist*' (*DQu* 32[2015] 293–312), Ruth Richardson argues that Dickens's representation of London is not 'Romantic' (or confused), but 'both accurate and truthful' (p. 302). The evidence for this argument comes from the parallels Richardson discovers between the novel and actual people and places existing in London. The location of the workhouse in which Oliver was born is in Hendon, a rural branch of the London workhouse in the central parish of Covent Garden. The identification of this location serves as linchpin for several others. Also of interest is the Covent Garden policy that banned second helpings of workhouse food. For his contribution to the December edition of *Dickens Quarterly*, 'Dickens and the Codebreakers: The Annotated Set of *All the Year Round*' (*DQu* 32[2015] 313–37), Leon Litvack discusses this fascinating manuscript discovery (an annotated edition of Dickens's *All the Year Round*). The marginalia in this edition give the names of several contributors to the journal whose offerings were printed anonymously. The marginalia include such names as Wilkie Collins, Lewis Carroll, and Elizabeth Gaskell. After a review of the edition by noted Dickensian scholars Michael Slater, John Drew, and Paul Lewis, Litvack himself confirmed that the marginalia is authentic and indeed in Dickens's own hand. Litvack acknowledges the early work done by Jeremy Parrott, whose article is included above. Litvack gives credit to Parrott's breakthrough discovery and even includes a short dialogue from an interview Parrott gave on BBC Radio 4's *Front Row* programme on July 14th.

The second speciality journal from this year that will be examined is *The Dickens Studies Annual*. In 'Whitewashing the Blacking Factory' (*DSA* 46[2015] 1–22), Robert L. Patten makes the claim that the 'autobiographical fragment' found in *David Copperfield* should not be considered strictly as such. Patten explores the truthfulness of the episode by comparing it to a simultaneous publication—*Dombey and Son*. He then charts the history of the writing of the fragment, as well as the events the fragment refers to. The purpose of this deception, Patten argues, is twofold: first, it is Dickens's own exploration of how he became a success; secondly, it is Dickens's attempt to present himself to his public as a competent author. In 'Dickens's Performances of Astonishment and Nicholas Nickleby' (*DSA* 46[2015] 23–50), Mark M. Hennelly argues that, given the strong ties between Dickens's novels and his interest in the theatre (he cites the oft-noted 'theatricality' of Dickens's fiction), it is surprising that more careful critical attention has not been given to the 'carefully scripted . . . scenes' of astonishment that proliferate in his novels. Hennelly argues that these scenes in Dickens's works find their origins in the English pantomime tradition, and appear most obviously in *Nicholas Nickleby*. In this novel, astonishment resides in the person of Crummles, who uses the word most effectively when first meeting Nicholas. Next, Alison Rutledge's 'Travelling Narrator, Travelling Characters' (*DSA* 46[2015] 51–70) examines Dickens's career as a novelist in the light of his travel writings; most particularly his *Pictures from Italy* and *American Notes*. Rutledge states that *Pictures from Italy* forms a dividing line of sorts in Dickens's career as a novelist, written during a year-long vacation in that country as a break from novel-writing after sales of *Martin Chuzzlewit* were not nearly what he hoped they would be. Ultimately, she hopes to show how 'the formal experiments found in *Pictures from Italy* evolve into the narrator–character relationship and character system of *Little Dorrit*' (p. 53).

As the name of the piece suggests, in 'Changes in Visual Interpretations of *A Christmas Carol*' (*DSA* 46[2015] 71–122), Philip Allingham traces the changes in the illustrated pages of nineteenth- and early twentieth-century editions of *A Christmas Carol*. Key to this analysis is 'Realization', which is defined as 'the faithful recreation of a text ("letterpress") in a stage adaptation or in an illustration' (p. 73). Allingham argues that in the original serialization, Dickens's desire would have been to enforce the primacy of the text, thus letting the illustrations have a much more active role in helping to shape the story in later editions. Brian Sabey's 'Ethical Metafiction in Dickens's Christmas Hauntings' (*DSA* 46[2015] 123–46) argues that Dickens concerned himself not only with the ethical choices of his characters (or their modelling of moral choice in society), but with the ethical choices of his readers. In analysing the 'metafictional' component of this view of ethics in Dickens's works, Sabey considers the introduction of the Spirit of Christmas Past (in which the narrator addresses the reader directly) before moving on to *A House to Let* in which the ethical metafiction 'explores how fiction can sometimes become an alternative to or an escape from ethical responsibility'.

In 'This Curious Association of Objects' (*DSA* 46[2015] 147–66), Jennifer Janechek focuses her analysis on a very specific sub-set of Dickensian characters: those who rely on transport by chair. The essay focuses primarily on Miss Havisham from *Great Expectations*, Mrs Skewton in *Dombey and Son*, and the ridiculous Grandfather Smallweed in *Bleak House*. Janechek argues, through the lens of 'thing theory', that characters in chairs alter the subject–object relationship, prejudicing the viewer, who gradually sees the chair-bound character as the thing itself, replacing subject with object. Mrs Skewton is treated as a dehumanized 'it' and Grandfather Smallweed uses and abuses his handicap for the sake of convenience (p. 159).

In 'Detective or Defective Vision: A Matter of Breathing or Dying in *Bleak House*' (*DSA* 46[2015] 185–208), Emily Kobayashi uses the figure of Krook as a symbol for the institutional blindness in the courts of Chancery. After his combustion, Krook leaves behind a line of red tape. Kobayashi conflates these two figures, stating that both illiteracy and red tape lead to a 'defective vision' that is blind to the ills of society. Kobayashi sets this vision of the 'Red Tapers' in opposition to the curative 'detective vision' demonstrated by characters such as Mr Bucket and Esther, who derive their empathy from the ability to 'read' texts, themselves, and others.

Michelle L. Wilson's 'Esther Summerson's Narrative Relations' (*DSA* 46[2015] 209–30) argues that Esther Summerson's self-penned narrative in *Bleak House* helps to do two things. Firstly, it provides an identity for the nameless, bastard orphan. Secondly, it functions as a counter-narrative to that which is dominated by Chancery, creating a set of personal relationships that operate 'outside the law' (p. 210). This is done in the novel by revealing that 'the law deals in fictions' (p. 211), creating a discrepancy between law and life. Wilson also argues that Esther keeps the public and private worlds, in constant danger of collapsing into one another, separate. Sarah Gates, in 'Pious Fraud and Secret Chamber: *Our Mutual Friend* and the Intertextual Marriage Plot' (*DSA* 46[2015] 231–52), argues in support of the Harmon marriage plot found in *Our Mutual Friend*, which has been ridiculed since the novel's first publication (p. 231). She does this by examining 'intertextual cues', recognizable to Victorian readers, though perhaps invisible to modern readers who may misinterpret such cues as an over-used brand of Dickensian sentimentality. Gates begins by looking at Dickens's inspiration for the 'pious fraud' of the novel: Knowles's *The Hunchback*. She then goes on to analyse how this appears in the John and Bella plot.

In 'Suspending Detection: Collins, Dickens and the Will to Know' (*DSA* 46[2015] 253–76), Elisha Cohn looks at two contemporaneous detective works: *Edwin Drood* and *The Moonstone*. After pointing out that both novels touch the subject of 'unconscious cerebration', Cohn states her argument: when a detective novel suspends consciousness in one of the characters, it also suspends its 'epistemic claims on behalf of English scientific and national culture' (p. 245). Secondly, states of altered consciousness are related to how reading itself is approached in both novels. Ultimately, Cohn is arguing against the idea that detective fiction reads as a symbolic meta-commentary on the Victorian age itself. In 'Beyond the Pale: *Edwin Drood* and the "Sanctity of Human Life"' (*DSA* 46[2015] 277–96), Gerard Cohen-Vrignaud argues that the conjectures about the various ways a murder might be accomplished that proliferate the novel function as more than just 'subtle clues'. Rather, they form the basis for Dickens's critique of Victorian progressivism; in particular, the idea that the modern state is responsible for the biological existence of the lives that occupy it. Cohen-Vrignaud pursues this argument through a study of characters such as Honeythunder and Sapsea, and ideas such as the Gothic and 'Orientalisms' that find their way into the novel itself.

Jonathan Farina's 'Mad Libs and Stupid Criticism' (*DSA* 46[2015] 325–38) argues that many of the characters in Dickens's novels participate in a linguistic creation similar to that which takes place in the modern game 'Mad Libs'. Characters cannot complete sentences, and those who do so on the characters' behalf often 'seem to be glaringly stupid' (p. 326). Farina goes on to demonstrate the range of ways 'Mad-Libbing' operates in Dickensian fiction, finally listing three ways in which this particular linguistic joke represents stupidity: Victorian psychology's associational disorder, concomitant narratives as a product of realism, and the critical view of Dickens's own intelligence. In 'Let Them Be: Dickens's Stupid Politics' (*DSA* 46[2015] 339–56), Daniel Wright engages in a comparative analysis of *Hard Times* and the contemporaneous *North and South*. In doing so, Wright looks for the moments of 'political fantasy', or the political beliefs in the novels that stem from dream-fulfilment rather than political reality. In *Hard Times*, the stupidity of political fantasy reveals itself in the obstinate 'hardness' of Gradgrind's utilitarianism while Sissy's imprecise fantasy forms the basis for her sympathy. In *North and South*, political fantasy is manifested in the tension between the busy bustle of Milton and the contemplative life of the country.

In 'Stupidity and Stupefaction' (*DSA* 46[2015] 357–76), Carolyn Williams analyses the most famous model of 'stupidity' in the entire Dickensian oeuvre: the childlike Barnaby Rudge. Williams first writes against the typical oppositional categories that criticism places *Barnaby Rudge* into ('melodrama' or 'historical novel'). Rather, she contends, the novel is a mixture of both. Williams also hopes to demonstrate that the 'novel's bifurcated structure'

(p. 358) makes complete sense when we consider the mixture of country/ Gothic setting that the novel introduces the reader to. She then ends with analysing the three representations of muteness in the characters of Barnaby, Grip, and John Willet. We close with an examination of the last Dickens speciality journal, *The Dickensian*. The spring issue of this year's *Dickensian* focuses on issues of both materiality and metaphysics. In 'Dickens at Furnvill's Inn: New Evidence of a Sub-Letting Agreement' (*Dickensian* 111:i[2015] 5–10), Leon Litvack examines a piece of Dickensian archival material discovered in 1935, belonging to a period in the author's life about which little is known. This period ranges from 1834 to 1838; at the beginning of these years Dickens was in his early twenties, single, and on the cusp of national celebrity. In the next two years, he would become engaged to Catherine Hogarth and his first series of published sketches (*Sketches by Boz*) would become so successful that he would soon be approached by Chapman and Hall with an offer to produce a second published work in twenty serial instalments. This lease shows us a fascinating period in Dickens's life—the slow yet sudden transition from clerk reporter to national celebrity.

From the materiality of archival scholarship to the unreality of supernatural symbolism, we move to an analysis of the raven, Grip, from *Barnaby Rudge* in ' "What mockery is this?": Dickens's Talking Bird' (*Dickensian* 111:i[2015] 11–22) by Francesca Mackenney. Mackenney's analysis begins with a review of this strange bird's typical associations—as a symbol of evil or ill omen. However, Mackenney then argues that Grip might actually have stronger associations with humour, albeit a very Dickensian brand of humour known as 'misplaced gravity'. Mackenney underscores Dickens's odd propensity at times for nearly uncontrollable laughter during a sermon or funeral service, and suggests Grip is written as mocking Victorian seriousness. This claim is supported by descriptions of the bird throughout the novel that parody Victorian gentility and manner.

In the next article, ' "A sort of spoiled child of the public": Dickens's Reception in Scotland in 1858' (*Dickensian* 111:i[2015] 26–33), Paul Schlicke examines the tumultuous year in Dickens's life in which he separated from his wife, Catherine. During the autumn of this year Dickens embarked on a reading tour of Scotland which met with immense success. However, the crowds that cheered him each night gave a much harsher greeting in response to the latest gossip of each day. On 7 June of this year, *The Times* published Dickens's infamous 'Personal' statement, revealing the truth regarding his domestic troubles to his reading public for the first time. The Scottish press responded viciously, criticizing Dickens for speaking publicly about such a personal, sacred matter. Unfortunately, this only added to the vitriol Dickens already received in the Scottish press for his pamphlet *Sunday Under Three Heads*, which criticized a recent reform that sought to curtail non-religious activities participated in by the lower classes on Sundays. Interestingly, the very next article, by Michael Slater, 'Munificence Declined: New Letters about the Guild of Literature and Art' (*Dickensian* 111:i[2015] 34–41), deals with the same troubled period in Dickens's life. At a certain point in this year, Dickens was contacted by Patrick Allan-Fraser, a Scottish landowner who expressed a desire to help fund an organization for the benefit of writers and artists throughout England. The organization itself was the brainchild of Dickens, Bulwer Lytton, John Forster, and others who believed in its cause. Unfortunately, the long-drawn-out legal processes required for acceptance of the generous financial gift (Hawkesbury Hall, an estate owned by Allan-Fraser), along with the conditions on which this acceptance was based, forced Dickens to ultimately decline the 'munificent offer'.

Finally, in 'Death(s) and *Great Expectations*' (*Dickensian* 111:i[2015] 42–51), Jerome Meckier examines the symbolic qualities of the many deaths that proliferate in this novel. He begins by pointing out the fact that deaths in the novel outnumber those in *Bleak House* and even *Hamlet*. *Great Expectations* is of course a far cry from the comic escapades of the Pickwickians, but how can Dickens get away with leaving so many bodies on the narrative stage without his motto of constant alteration between tragic and comic scenes being seriously called into question? Meckier provides an excellent answer: 'Dickens's masterpiece employs death ironically as the common denominator for human tragicomedy; it is the last not-so-great experience to expect from life, thus one of the many ironies in the title' (p. 42). Meckier then deals with each death in turn, analysing each one's 'tragicomic' aspects.

The summer issue of this year's *Dickensian* can perhaps be given the title 'At Home and Abroad', as the articles focus on the domestic life of the author and his characters, and on Dickens's reception outside his native England. In 'Tapley in the Trenches: Dickens and the Great War' (*Dickensian* 111:ii[2015] 109–22) Jerry White examines the Dickens mania that swept England during the First World War. This mania found its fullest representation in the Dickensian 'type' of the jovial, lower-class cockney; figures such as *Pickwick*'s Samuel Weller and *Martin Chuzzlewit*'s Mark Tapley. Tapley's irrepressible optimism served as a model for the British soldier (mostly provincial men like Tapley himself, rather than the upper-crust Londoners that they are portrayed as in films), to retain positivity in the face of the most horrific circumstances. Continuing with the Pickwickian theme, William F. Long's 'John Hill Powell and the Trial in *Pickwick Papers*' (*Dickensian* 111:ii[2015] 123–7) examines the first instance of Dickens's use of topicality. In comparing Pickwick and Bardell's 'breach of promise' case to a trial that actually took place one month before (*Norton v. Melbourne*), several similarities can be seen. However, Long argues that Dickens's involvement in a separate trial, not previously discussed, served as the true basis for the fictional trial's inclusion in the fifth number of *Pickwick*.

If Pickwick experienced trouble in his domestic affairs, they are as nothing when compared to those of his author. Yet, in 'A Dickens Photographer Identified: Adolphe Naudin' (*Dickensian* 111:ii[2015] 128–39), Leon Litvack examines a photograph taken in front of Gad's Hill Place in the last years of the author's life that suggests 'home' is still very much a place of peace and comfort for Dickens. In the article itself, Litvack examines each figure in turn from left to right, and suggests that their poses bespeak the relationship they may have had with Dickens. For example, Litvack notes that Mamie Dickens sits with her arm around Mrs Bessie Dickens in a gesture of affection, inclusion, and protection. This pose could speak to the fact that Bessie (the wife of Dickens's son Charley), most likely felt anxious around Dickens, as he and her publisher father had quarrelled over the 'Personal' statement Dickens gave to the *Times* regarding the collapse of his marriage.

Two issues of *George Eliot–George Henry Lewes Studies* appeared in 2015. The first opens with Molly Youngkin's ' "Narrative readings of the images she sees": Principles of Nineteenth-Century Painting in George Eliot's Fiction' (*GEGHLS* 67:i[2015] 1–29). Youngkin 'examines how George Eliot negotiated the nineteenth-century debate regarding connections and divergences between literature and the visual arts' (p. 1). Kathleen McCormack's 'Sundays at the Priory: Olga Novikoff and the Russian Presence' (*GEGHLS* 67:i[2015] 30–42) concentrates on a regular Russian visitor to the Sunday salons held at the Priory, the home of George Eliot and George Henry Lewes, and reveals 'that guests at Eliot's Priory often failed to absorb her own opinions, including those embodied in *Daniel Deronda*' (p. 40). Miyuki Amano's 'Recent George Eliot–George Henry Lewes Studies in Japan' (*GEGHLS* 67:i[2015] 43–55) provides an account of recent critical work on George Eliot and G.H. Lewes in Japan and includes an alphabetically arranged enumerative listing of works cited (pp. 52–5). Another useful guide to recent work is provided by Linda Reinert in her 'Articles on George Eliot in 2013: A Selective Survey and an Adaptation of *Middlemarch*' (*GEGHLS* 67:i[2015] 56–64). The theatrical adaptation was by Geoffrey Beevers, in three parts, performed from October through February 2013 at the Orange Theatre in Richmond, Surrey (p. 59). The remainder of the issue contains book reviews plus Martin Bidney's eighteen sonnets and his poem 'Early Morning Middle March' (*GEGHLS* 67:i[2015] 81–91). The second issue of *George Eliot–George Henry Lewes Studies* contains important primary material. It is mainly devoted to Michelle Eisenberg's transcription and edition with detailed annotation of two hitherto unpublished writings 'George Henry Lewes's 1869 Diary and Journal' (*GEGHLS* 67:ii[2015] 93–226). The first 'is a dated daily diary from the year 1869; the second piece comprises sections from his Journal, Volume XII, June 1866–May 1870, relating to that year'. As Eisenberg explains, 'the transcriptions and annotations, which locate or explain references, are followed by an alphabetically arranged listing of "Works Cited" as well as two appendices'. The first consists of an arranged and partly annotated listing of 'Books Read by George Henry Lewes in 1869' (pp. 181–8) and the second provides an alphabetically arranged guide to 'Friends, Acquaintances, and Visitors' (pp. 189–93) found in the holographs (p. 93). Eisenberg writes in her extensive introduction that 'Lewes's Chronicles show his vast readings, his varied activities, his community service, his great love for Eliot, and his tender care for his son.' Furthermore and 'most significantly, Lewes's diary and journal of 1869 gives readers insight into a year in which intellectual creativity and deepest feeling collide, and reveal not just a man of great intellect and talent but also just a man' (p. 113). Extensive 'Editorial Notes' (pp. 113–16) are followed by the transcription of 'The 1869 Diary and Journal' (pp. 116–80), the two appendices (pp. 181–93) and detailed notes (pp. 193–223), and an alphabetical listing of 'Works Consulted' (pp. 223–6). Eisenberg's important work is followed by the librettist Claudia Stevens's account of her 'A New Opera: *Middlemarch in Spring*' (*GEGHLS* 67:ii[2015] 227–33). This 'new chamber opera... based on George Eliot's *Middlemarch*, by composer Allen Shearer on a libretto by Claudia Stevens, received a high-profile, critically claimed premiere in San Francisco in March 2015. The librettist describes the opera's genesis from initial conception of a single scene, that of Dorothy and Celia dividing the jewelry, into a two-hour opera in six scenes and two acts' (p. 227).

The *George Eliot Review* for 2015 opens with Jen Davis's '*Silas Marner*: George Eliot's most Coleridgean Work? (Prize Essay)' (*GER* 46[2015] 8–14). Davis observes that 'the effect produced by... a high incidence of correlative language suggests a greater affinity between Coleridge and Eliot than has previously been established. Exploration of such compelling language similarities can open up a dialogic relationship between the texts of these two great writers' (p. 13). In her last years the late Barbara Hardy (1924–2016) was working on a book on Elizabeth Gaskell. In 'Elizabeth Gaskell in *Middlemarch*: Timothy Cooper, the Judgement of Solomon, and the Woman at the Window' (*GER* 46[2015] 16–20), she observes that Eliot gave Timothy Cooper, a farm labourer whose voice is heard in chapter 56 of *Middlemarch*, 'a Christian name taken from the Bible and a surname from an English craft, but it was also the name of a character in Gaskell's novella *Cousin Phillis* (1865)'. She explores the implications of this and other parallels between the two writers, especially between what she regards as 'Gaskell's best novel', *North and South*, and *Middlemarch*, which 'would have been a different novel without Gaskell, in particular without *North and South*, the novel which in spite of its difference in narrative scale, has a political and social scope which make it Gaskell's *Middlemarch*' (p. 20). Marianne Burton, in her 'How Much Did Dorothea and Celia Know? Sexual Ignorance and Knowledge Among Unmarried Girls in *Middlemarch*' (*GER* 46[2015] 21–8), draws upon contemporary articles in *The Lancet* and the *British Medical Journal* as well as other Victorian writing to 'suggest [that] sexual ignorance among unmarried girls in the nineteenth-century novel may not be as straightforward as readers sometimes imagine'. She concludes that 'it was Dorothea's lack of self-knowledge, not a simple lack of empirical knowledge about sexual mechanics, that caused her tragedy' (pp. 21, 26). Kate Osborne's 'Mr. Brooke's Thinking Organ' (*GER* 46[2015] 29–37) is concerned with the implications of a scene in chapter 30 of *Middlemarch* that 'has largely escaped critical attention' and 'describes how the creative process can slip out of other writers control' focusing upon Dorothea's request to 'her uncle, Mr. Brooke, to reply in her stead ' "to let Will [Ladislaw] know that Casaubon had been ill and that his health would not allow the reception of any visitors" ' (p. 29). John Rignall's '*Middlemarch* and the Franco-Prussian War' (*GER* 46[2015] 38–45) thinks 'it's important to underlined how momentous and profoundly disturbing, even traumatic... news of war was for both Lewes and George Eliot', who at was at work on *Middlemarch* when war was declared between France and Russia (p. 38). The issue Rignall addresses is 'what relationship might there be between the painfully absorbing historical context in which she began to work on what was to become a central part of *Middlemarch* and the finished novel?' (p. 39). Rignall's perceptive conclusion is that 'perhaps... George Eliot's most important response to the War was the act of writing *Middlemarch* itself, which involved creating a heroine who represented the opposite pole of human potential to that displayed on the battlefields and in the besieged cities of France. George Eliot beheld the tumult and was not still, but resolutely active with her pen; and if melancholy was never overcome, it was contained, and her vision of life, however much it had been disturbed, was ultimately reaffirmed' (p. 44).

Another George Eliot novel engages Rodney Stenning Edgecombe in his somewhat convoluted 'Felix Holt: The Radical and the Gusset of Cryptic Futurity' (GER 46[2015] 46–54). When not engaged in intertextual references, Edgecombe focuses upon the implications of a sentence in Eliot's novel 'located long before the conclusion' that provides a 'glimpse into the future' and is 'cryptic and irresolute'. In chapter 14 the narrator informs readers that 'There is a portrait of Mr. Philip Debarry still to be seen at Treby Manor, and a very fine bust of him at Rome, where he died fifteen years later, a convert to Catholicism.' For Edgecombe, Eliot here 'inlaid the narrative with a subtle, proto-Jamesian codetta'. The sentence is 'so unobtrusive as almost to pass us by, the sentence vibrates with implications for the character at hand and also for the novel as a whole' (pp. 46–7). It is something of a relief to turn to the next contribution, that by Rosemary J. Burges Woods on 'A Life Reclaimed: George Evans (1766–1857) of Norbury, Winster, Derby and Belper' (GER 46[2015] 55–9). She writes that 'George Evans, the elder brother of Robert Evans, George Eliot's father, has generally been disparaged as a drunkard who died young, but the following account of further research into his life aims to set the record straight' (p. 55). The life of George Evans 'was unremarkable, apart from his longevity, his (apparent) robust health and work routine well into his eighties and his somewhat unconventional domestic "setup"' (p. 57). A.G. van den Broek's report on the 'Annual George Eliot Conference: Middlemarch, Institute of English Studies, 22 November 2014' (GER 46[2015] 60–3) is useful and detailed and is followed by six reviews of recent books and a review of an audio reading of Silas Marner (GER 46[2015] 65–81). John Rignall contributes a brief 'Note: Alcharisi and the Redundant Definite Article' (GER 46[2015] 82). There is the text of Beryl Gray's address at the 'Wreath-Laying in Poets' Corner, Westminster Abbey 17 July 2014' (GER 46[2015] 83–4) that focused on Middlemarch. The final two items are John Burton's 'Chairman's Annual Report for 2014' (GER 46[2015] 85–8) and Eri Kobayashi's 'Japanese Branch Report' (GER 46[2015] 89–90), which once again provides a timely reminder of the considerable interest in George Eliot in Japan.

One monograph and a number of additional articles on George Eliot appeared in 2015. June Skye Szirotny's George Eliot's Feminism: 'The Right to Rebellion' demonstrates its author's thorough reading in and knowledge of George Eliot's life and work. For Szirotny, George Eliot's 'story is a battle between conservative and reformative influences'. She was 'driven by a passion for truth, relentlessly and methodically testing her arguments, she courageously moves toward a more radical, more feminist, perspective, forcefully, in the end, endorsing rebellion against the double standard restricting fulfillment and the doing of good—rebellion distinctly contrasting with the emphasis on submission in the early works' (p. 39). Carefully developing her case, and documenting it in detailed notes found at the end of her study (pp. 206–58), Szirotny provides an extensive enumerative 'Works Cited' (pp. 259–76). This engaged, thoughtful, well-written study is the fruit of a lifetime's engagement and passion for its subject. Ruth Abbott's thorough, well-researched, and clearly written 'George Eliot, Meter and the Matter of Ideas: The Yale Poetry Notebook' (*ELH* 82[2015] 1179–1211) is reviewed in Section 3 below. Leila Aouadi, in her 'Transgression in *Daniel Deronda*' (*The Victorian* 3:ii[2015] 1–29), 'defines transgression in literature, focuses on its manifestations in the novel, and links it to the depiction of Gwendolen's emotional and sexual dysfunction'. She argues, 'transgression is a method by which Eliot advances women's writings, and is manifested in the novel's conception and the new terrains Eliot is probing' (p. 1).

Jayne Elisabeth Archer, Richard Marggraf Turley, and Howard Thomas's triple-authored ' "Moving accidents by flood and field": The Arable and Tidal Worlds of George Eliot's *The Mill on the Floss*' (*ELH* 82[2015] 701–28) observes that '*The Mill on the Floss* is often regarded as a pastoral work. In fact, arable landscape informs the language, themes and events of George Eliot's novel.' Their essay 'recover[s] the original agri-environmental world described by Eliot and shows how the lives of the Tullivers and the fate of Dorlcote Mill are driven by the complex interaction of arable and tidal forces. Eliot's meticulous research into these arable and tidal worlds is reconstructed and it is argued that in this work the novelist reflects on the impact of free market economics on food production and distribution, on agricultural livings and rural communities and on river and land management across Britain' (p. 701). Rosemary Ashton, in her 'Moral Puzzles in *Adam Bede*' (in Baker, ed., pp. 83–92), is influenced by Sutherland's investigations of literary puzzles. For Ashton, in *Adam Bede* 'what is problematic is not so much the unmarried sex and unfortunate pregnancy—shameful and life-changing though these would be for a teenage girl of Hetty's time and class—but rather the fact that Hetty has, or *appears* to have, murdered her child. The criminal trial is for child murder, not unmarried motherhood' (pp. 84–5). This leads to the questions 'Does Hetty kill her baby? She is found guilty, but at the trial enters no plea' (p. 89), and 'why does George Eliot not present us with the full trial?' Ashton concludes that the strengths of George Eliot's novel 'lie in the author's unusual expressions of boldness and sympathy toward the tangled questions of sexuality and guilt' (pp. 90–1). Josie Billington, in her 'Gaskell's "Rooted" Prose Realism' (in Scholl, Morris, and Moore, eds., pp. 159–71) makes challenging comparisons between Eliot's prose realism and Elizabeth Gaskell (see for instance pp. 159–62). Karen Ann Bourrier, in the third chapter, 'Tom Tulliver's Schooldays' (pp. 76–102), of her *The Measure of Manliness: Disability and Masculinity in the Mid-Victorian Novel*, has interesting things to say about Tom Tulliver and Philip Wakem in *The Mill on the Floss*. Lauren Cameron, in 'Spencerian Evolutionary Psychology in *Daniel Deronda*' (*VLC* 43[2015] 63–81), is concerned with the 'central element of Eliot's final completed novel: the depth, development, and realism of its psychological portraiture. What made the psychology of Gwendolen Harleth especially, but the eponymous Daniel Deronda as well, resonate with discerning readers from that time to this?...it is the same cause that frustrates many readers: Eliot's engagement with the most famous and scientifically integrated psychological theory of her time—Herbert Spencer's' (p. 63).

Alicia Carroll adopts an ecocritical approach in her interesting ' "This is a sacred grove": Homosocial Ecologies in *Adam Bede*' (*GreenL* 19:ii[2015] 185–97). For Carroll 'Management of the woods is a labor of love negotiated between men in George Eliot's *Adam Bede* (1859). However, as a resilient and vital entity through which men enact the volatile pains and pleasures of homosocial desire, contest and reconciliation, the woods are vulnerable to becoming the primary vehicle through which Eliot naturalizes a sustainable, masculinist capitalism' (p. 185). She discusses the complexities of the discourses of forestry and improvement in the novel. The second chapter, 'Omniscience: Unknowing in George Eliot' (pp. 65–110), of Elisha Cohn's *Still Life: Suspended Development in the Victorian Novel* posits arresting challenges to our views of her novels, and especially *Daniel Deronda* in its author's treatment of narrative form; sleep; trance; stillness; self-consciousness; and knowledge production. 'Examining George Eliot's work in relation to theories of unconscious psychology in the work of G.H. Lewes and W.B. Carpenter', Cohn's second chapter 'argues that the logic of a developmental unconscious in these physiological accounts is not transposed into the literary domain. Rather, her famously omniscient narration breaks down, first in *The Mill on the Floss* (1860), and again in *Daniel Deronda* (1876)' (p. 26). Richa Dwor, in the second chapter of her *Jewish Feeling: Difference and Affect in Nineteenth-Century Jewish Women's Writing* (pp. 85–114), 'looks to George Eliot to introduce the contemporary theory of Organism as an epistemological model cognate to Jewish feeling. Eliot is drawn on here both to revisit the representations of the Jews in the context of Jewish feeling, and also as an important sounding board against which to read [Grace] Aguilar and [Amy] Levy' (p. 34). Richard Hughes Gibson, in his *Forgiveness in Victorian Literature: Grammar, Narrative and Community*, devotes considerable attention to *Adam Bede* (pp. 103–18) as 'the novel presents a number of scenes in which characters wrestle with forgiveness's meaning and practice (p. 103). This year saw four other short contributions on George Eliot from the prolific Rodney Stenning Edgecombe. Intertextual in nature, three of these are published in *Notes and Queries*: 'Allusions to Gray in *Silas Marner*' (*N&Q* 62[2015] 429–30), drawing attention to echoes of Gray's 'Elegy Written in a Country Churchyard' and his 'Ode on a Distant Prospect of Eton College' in the novel; 'An Allusion to Horace in George Eliot's "Brother Jacob"' (*N&Q* 62[2015] 429), on Eliot's use of Horace's 'Epistles' in her short tale; and 'A Heine Lyric and "The Lifted Veil"' (*N&Q* 62[2015] 423–5), drawing attention to the use of Heinrich Heine's 'Ich grolle nicht' in her novella. In 'Enriching Allusions in George Eliot's "The Lifted Veil"' (*ANQ* 28:i[2015] 51–3) Edgecombe also draws attention to allusions in Eliot's novella to, in this instance, prophecy, clairvoyance, and Thomas More. Edgecombe's insights would benefit from reference to the additional documentation from the actual texts/editions Eliot used. Kirsten Hall's ' "It is all one": Hetty Sorrel and the Myth of Cupid and Psyche' (*Renascence* 67[2015] 279–94) focuses on the character of Hetty Sorrel, selfishness, spiritual growth, Cupid, the figure of Psyche, and ancient Greek myth. Her essay 'examines the ways in which the

Cupid and Psyche myth brings the reader to a richer understanding of Hetty Sorrel's development throughout *Adam Bede*' (p. 279). Marcus K. Jones, in his 'Forming Reality through Perception and Imagination in *Middlemarch*' (*The Victorian* 3:i[2015] 1–13), is concerned with William Blake's 'The Clod and the Pebble'. Jones argues that 'it is plausible to draw connections between Eliot's philosophy of interpretation embedded within *Middlemarch* and Blake's theory of knowledge expounded throughout his poetry. This connection aids the reader in better understanding how Eliot's work addressed the Victorian anxiety of defining the general and particular aspects of the human condition by offering multiple perspectives of reality through her novel's characters, and illustrating the shaping of reality that each perspective creates' (p. 11). Sara Lyons's *Algernon Swinburne and Walter Pater: Victorian Aestheticism, Doubt, and Secularisation* raises questions such as 'by what acts of differentiation did Victorian aestheticism ever seek independence from religion?' and 'to what extent did its key representatives and detractors understand it not simply as a symptom but as an agent of secularization?' She 'explores these questions through a close study of the works of Algernon Charles Swinburne and Walter Pater' (p. 2). Her fourth chapter, ' "Inheriting its strange web of belief and unbelief": George Eliot's *Romola*, Pater's *Marius the Epicurean* and the Aura of Agnosticism' (pp. 215–51), 'reads Pater's *Marius the Epicurean* (1881) alongside George Eliot's Romola (1862–1863)' (p. 39) and includes an extensive discussion (pp. 230–44) of *Romola*, 'Pater's favourite among Eliot's novels' (p. 231).

The centre of attention in Kathleen McCormack's 'Yachting with Grandcourt: Gwendolen's Mutiny in *Daniel Deronda*' (*VLC* 43[2015] 83–95) is yachting and its association with British imperialism. McCormack notes that 'almost at the end of Book VI of Daniel Deronda, that is, with at least three-quarters of the novel over, Gwendolen Harleth's dreadful husband, Henleigh Mallinger Grandcourt, suddenly reveals a new side of himself. Whereas heretofore he has mentioned or engaged in recreations that include hunting, shooting (including tigers), and gambling, all as means of passing the time rather than achieving exhilaration or amusement, he now reveals himself as a yachtsman. After catching Gwendolen in their town house in Grosvenor Square in yet another of her contrived tête à têtes with Daniel, he declares he has already begun preparations for a Mediterranean cruise for himself and his wife, alone together' (p. 83). McCormack analyses the consequences of his decision and their reverberations. Brenda McKay includes discussion of George Eliot in her 'Victorian Women Novelists, Gossip and Creativity' (*GSN* 59[2015] 9–15), which concentrates on women novelists, letters, gossip, and creativity. Maia McAleavey, in her *The Bigamy Plot: Sensation and Conversion in the Victorian Novel*, reviewed fully above, discusses 'Dorothea's simultaneous remarriage' (pp. 94–112) in her fourth chapter. It tracks her 'two sequential marriages from their simultaneous origin in the honeymoon she shares with both Casaubon and Will Ladislaw to the continued presence of Casaubon's will after his death. Eliot's afterlife only appears through the earthly medium of will-making and nightmarish visions of haunting, but she uses the figure of the bigamy plot's conventional dead-yet-not-spouse to challenge the finality of the two classic fictional endings: marriage and death'

(p. 18). Jacek Mydla, in his 'Narrative Over-Reaching? Anachrony and Focalization in George Eliot's "The Lifted Veil"' (*BAS* 21[2015] 49–54), **is concerned with metafiction**, focalization, anachrony, and storytelling in the novella. K.M. Newton's 'Another "Spoiling Hand" at Work in *Middlemarch*' (*in Baker, ed.*, pp. 153–60) discusses the ramifications of Eliot's 'insertion of the paragraphs about the burning of' Featherstone's last will and testament, in his meeting with Mary in chapter 52 of the novel (p. 159). Kei Nijibayashi, in 'Dorothea Brooke's Political Economy: Romanticism and the Influence of John Ruskin on George Eliot's *Middlemarch*' (*JLC* 62[2015] 19–31), is concerned with the character of Dorothea Brooke, Romanticism, political economy, and the intertextual parallels with John Ruskin's *Unto This Last* and *Munera Pulveris* in *Middlemarch*. Nijibayashi, in the abstract to his article, writes: 'John Ruskin's influence on George Eliot, especially on her ideas about political economy, has attracted relatively little critical attention.' To redress this, his article 'offers a reading of *Middlemarch* which seeks to demonstrate that the thoughts of the novel's heroine, Dorothea Brooke, echo various ideas Ruskin put forward in his socio-political writings, including *Unto This Last* and *Munera Pulveris*' (p. 19). Caterina Tadlock's 'Boredom and Marriage in George Eliot's *Middlemarch*' (*Expl* 73[2015] 82–5) argues that 'it is not marriage itself nor the act of waiting for marriage that leads to boredom but the confinement that comes as a result of conforming to the feminine sphere. Dorothea's marriage to Ladislaw is a happy one because it allows her to break free of the confinements of the feminine sphere and thereby break free of boredom.' Of course the assumption is that Dorothea and Ladislaw's marriage is a 'happy' (p. 82) one!

There are two contributions of note to record in 2015 from Andrew Thompson. In 'George Eliot, Early and Late' (*NCP* 42[2015] 315–22), a review essay, he 'assesses two recently published studies that examine the public image of George Eliot early and late in her career: Fionnuala Dillane's *Before George Eliot: Marian Evans and the Periodical Press*' (*see YWES 94[2015] 756–7)* 'and Kathleen McCormack's *George Eliot in Society: Travels Abroad and Sundays at the Priory*' (*see YWES 94[2015] 757)*. Thompson's 'George Eliot On and Off the Beaten Track: "Recollections of Germany and Italy"', *in an interesting collection edited by Lisa* Colletta, *The Legacy of the Grand Tour: New Essays on Travel, Literature, and Culture* (pp. 71–91), draws upon Eliot's letters and journals written while visiting Germany and Italy to illuminate their author and her female characters. Finally, in a complex theoretical essay, Maria Su Wang's 'Realism's Operative Paradox: Character Autonomy vs Authorial Construction in *Middlemarch*' (*Narrative* 23[2015] 291–311) engages in dialogue with two articles by Peter J. Rabinowitz: '"The absence of her voice from that concord": The Value of the Implied Author' (*Style* 45 [2011] 99–108); and 'Truth in Fiction: A Reexamination of Audiences' (*CritI* 4 [1977] 121–41). For Wang, her 'reconsideration of *Middlemarch* in relation to Rabinowitz points to the significance of authorial construction, something that has been underplayed in novel theory and vigorously contested in some branches of narrative theory. While [her] argument here does not mean to intervene directly in those debates, [her] essay's attention to how Eliot inscribes uncertainty, even at the level of the sentence, highlights the role of authors as constructors. For *Middlemarch*, the concept of authorial agency usefully evokes the multiple layers of authorial construction, from plotting to characterization to focalization, and how they interact to produce the lifelikeness usually associated with realism' (pp. 306–7).

Two books of essays on Elizabeth Gaskell appeared this year, marking the 150th anniversary of her death. *Evil and Its Variations in the Works of Elizabeth Gaskell: Sesquicentennial Essays*, edited by Matsuoka Mitsuharu, includes essays written by thirty-two scholars from sixteen countries, and covers Gaskell's treatment of evil in her novels, novellas, short stories, and letters. Beginning with *Mary Barton*, Veronica Hoyt looks at Gaskell's use of tea-drinking to insinuate a critique of English imperialism, Fang Li considers Gaskell's depiction of the class divide in industrial England, and Francesco Marroni argues that John Barton's moral decline shows the human tendency to internalize social evil. Thomas Recchio shows that Gaskell, by invoking Wordsworth's pastoral poetry, depicts the 'truly evil' in *The Moorland Cottage*. Three contributors discuss how the community in *Cranford* manages to disarm potential evils: Yuji Miyamaru looks at the town's 'relativizing of values' while Emily Morris and Mark Weeks consider the serious work of humour in the novel in weakening evil (p. 86). Three contributors question the presence of evil in *Ruth*. Andrej Diniejko considers 'Gaskell's ambivalent attitude to the fallen woman question', Akiko Kawasaki explains Gaskell's refusal to follow moral stereotypes surrounding illness and sexual transgression, and E. Holly Pike sees that neither disease nor immorality is necessarily contagious when communities better understand the underlying causes (p. 122). Christine Huguet opens the discussion of *North and South* with the idea of *felix culpa*, that evil in the novel ends in good. Mary Haynes Kuhlman argues that Gaskell's Unitarian principles are behind the ultimate failure of evil in the novel, while Mitsuharu Matsuoka sees the novel's indictment of status quo mentality as an evil force. In the section on *The Life of Charlotte Brontë*, Tatsuhiro Ohno reports on his analysis of keywords having Christian significance, Matsuto Sowa finds Brontë to be a martyr to the cause of literature, and Manami Tamura reflects on the kinds of ill will the biography generated. Shu-Chuan Yan contributed the sole essay on *My Lady Ludlow*, using the novella to examine working-class literacy and class relations. Next, Akiko Kimura, Pirjo Koivuvaara, and Fumie Tamai discuss *Sylvia's Lovers*, finding evil in deception, alcohol, and political coercion, respectively. Anna Koustinoudi's essay on *A Dark Night's Work* applies psychoanalytic theory to illuminate the mystery of evil. For *Cousin Phillis*, Lizhen Chen discusses first-person narration as a strategy to 'detain information' and Paul's handling of secrets as part of his emergence into adulthood; Yoko Hatano explores Gaskell's ambivalence towards Holdsworth and Roman Catholicism, and Aya Yatsugi finds evidence of the negative influence of fairy tales (p. 358). In the three essays on *Wives and Daughters* Megumi Arai, Mitsuko Suzuki, and Tamara Wagner consider the menace of social ambitions, the education of women to allure, and 'domestic narratives of the everyday', respectively (p. 438). Short stories are the focus of Anne Enderwitz, Felicity James, Rebecca Styler, and Elmira Vasileva, who discuss sin and redemption, supernatural evil, misguided parenting, and quasi-Gothic narrative strategies, respectively. The collection closes with Miva Ota's exploration of the give and take between personal taste and religious duty in Gaskell's letters.

*Place and Progress in the Works of Elizabeth Gaskell*, edited by Lesa Scholl, Emily Morris, and Sarina Gruver Moore, gathers mobility studies sharing four thematic concerns. Opening the section entitled 'Home Geographies', Rob Burroughs, in 'Gaskell on the Waterfront: Leisure, Labor, and Maritime Space in the Mid-Nineteenth Century', and Nóra Séllei, in 'The Humanizing Transformations of the Space of the Home in Gaskell's Cranford', find a degree of liberation for women in waterfront excursions and uncanny textual intrusions. Divya Athmanathan, in '"You might pioneer a little at home": Hybrid Spaces, Identities, and Homes in Elizabeth Gaskell's *North and South*', discusses the flipped private/public spheres of Margaret and Thornton, while Emily K. Cody, in 'Grave Matters: Gothic Places and Kinetic Spaces in Elizabeth Gaskell's *Mary Barton*', considers the Gothic trope of entrapment within a realist framework. The second section, 'Mobility and Boundaries', begins with 'Unimagined Community and Disease in *Ruth*', in which Katherine Inglis traces Ruth's confused mental map of both space and human relationships. In 'Temporally out of Sync: Migration as Fiction and Philanthropy in Gaskell's Life and Work', Fariha Shaikh argues that Gaskell's stance on emigration changes from support in *Mary Barton* to the emigrant's regret in 'My French Master' and *Lois the Witch*. Lesa Scholl's 'Moving Between *North and South*: Cultural Signs and the Progress of Modernity in Elizabeth Gaskell's Novel' shows that an 'intrepid traveler' like Margaret Hale can adapt to the challenges posed by rail travel (p. 98). Mary Mullen closes the section with a critique of adherence to an 'imagined future' in *North and South*. The third section, 'Literary and Imagined Spaces', takes a look at Gaskell's letters about topics such as the railroad and the postal service. Anna Koustinoudi and Charalampos Passalis, in 'Gaskell the Ethnographer: The Case of "Modern Greek Song"', and Julia M. Chavez in 'Reading "An Every-Day Story" through Bifocals: Seriality and the Limits of Realism in Elizabeth Gaskell's *Wives and Daughters*', discuss Gaskell's extra-national interests. The 'busy, immersed, "natural" syntax' of Gaskell's style versus those of George Eliot and Charlotte Brontë is the focus of Josie Billington's 'Gaskell's "Rooted" Prose Realism', also noted above. Frances Twinn opens the fourth section, 'Cultural Performance and Visual Spaces', with an appreciation of Gaskell's scientific expertise in 'Applied Meteorology: Scientific Accuracy and Imaginative Writing in Elizabeth Gaskell's "Cousin Phillis" and *Wives and Daughters*'. Sophia Andres, in the next essay, 'Women's Voices in the Pre-Raphaelite Space of Elizabeth Gaskell's Novels', argues that Gaskell embedded 'narrative reconfigurations of Pre-Raphaelite paintings' in her novels to depict the subjectivity of women omitted from the beautiful but simplistic Pre-Raphaelite paintings (p. 94). In the final contribution in the volume, '"Look back at me": The Material Re-performance of the Victorian in *North and South* (2004)', Amy Montz locates the strong contemporary appeal of Victorian adaptations in the *mise-en-scène*'s 'proliferation of the material items' which enable a twenty-first-century audience to enter the Victorian world they expect to see (p. 210).

A handful of articles appeared on Gaskell as well. Carla Fusco covers familiar ground in her essay 'Ruth: An Unusual Prostitute: Elizabeth Gaskell's Speculative Gaze vs. Victorian Masculine Vision of Woman' (BAS 21[2015] 55–60), arguing that Gaskell's fallen woman novel troubled both the accepted figure of the Victorian prostitute and the phallocentric binary of Madonna and harlot that such a figure reinforced. A closing discussion of Ruth's passive agency in terms of Hannah Arendt's models of action is suggestive, but only roughly outlined. A more fully conceptualized model of agency in the novel is provided by Deborah M. Fratz in her essay ' "A feminine morbidness of conscience": Disability, Gender, and the Economy of Agency in Elizabeth Gaskell's Ruth' (VJ 127[2015] 4–17), which builds on Amanda Anderson's account of female agency in fallen woman novels in order to argue that the generic and social limitations placed on self-determination for the fallen woman are complicated in Gaskell's Ruth by the presence of male debility. Mr Benson's disability is, in some way, even more of an obstacle to agency than is Ruth's sexual fallenness. The feminization of the disabled Mr Benson, however, undermines the sexually progressive project Gaskell attempts with her title character. Those working on nineteenth-century science may be interested by Christie Harner's 'Physiognomic Discourse and the Trials of Cross-Class Sympathy in Mary Barton' (VLC 43[2015] 705–24), which attends to Gaskell's use of physiological descriptions evocative of characterological science. Gaskell turned to such discourse, Harner argues, originally to 'ease class biases ... and make visible similarities between the classes' (p. 708). The strategy is, however, ultimately unsuccessful, and Harner, like so many other critics of the novel, divides the work in half, claiming that when characterological science fails Gaskell seeks 'a kinship of subjectivity' rather than physiology (p. 709).

One of the finest publications on Hardy this year was Alicia Christoff's article 'Alone with Tess' (Novel 48[2015] 18–44), which received honourable mention for the Donald Gray Prize for best essay in Victorian studies. Christoff deftly explores the 'bidirectional exchange of ideas between the Victorian novel and post-Freudian psychoanalysis' (p. 19). Winnicott becomes a lens for viewing Hardy, but Hardy also exposes the force of narrative in Winnicott's relational theory. Ultimately, Christoff argues that novels do not, as we often imagine, keep us company in any straightforward sense; rather, they enable us 'to feel simultaneously alone and in the presence of someone else' (p. 19). Another excellent essay on Hardy, 'Obscure Forms: The Letter, the Law, and the Line in Hardy's Social Geometry' (Novel 48[2015] 1–17), appeared in the same issue. Allowing for a more nuanced and hopeful understanding of the law, Anna Kornbluh departs from recent scholars who have interpreted Jude's epigraph from Paul, 'The letter killeth', in terms of Agamben's revision of Foucauldian biopolitics in order to argue that Jude has a deeply geometric political imaginary, one in which the forms of writing and space exceed signification. Jude is not, as a biopolitical reading might suggest, a vitalist text, opposed to law of any kind. Quite the contrary, in Kornbluh's reading the novel embraces the possibilities of form while rejecting its particular application in the ways that destroy the lives of its main characters.

Everyone remembers the undelivered letters in Hardy. Kate McLoughlin, however, asks us to think about those that were never written at all in her article 'Missing Letters: Reading the Interstices in Archival Correspondence from the Napoleonic Wars and in Thomas Hardy's *The Trumpet-Major*' (*TPr* 29[2015] 1225–44). Reading the novel alongside an epistolary cache from the Napoleonic Wars, McLoughlin theorizes about the epistemological conditions of delay, desire, and hope. McLoughlin was not the only critic to write on Hardy's letters this year. Karin Koehler's ' "Essentially separated in spite of all uniting factors": Thomas Hardy and the Community of Letter Writers' (*VR* 41[2015] 125–42) examines the letters in three of Hardy's novels, *The Trumpet-Major, Under the Greenwood Tree,* and *Jude the Obscure,* in relation to contemporary postal reforms. On the one hand, Koehler argues, Hardy recognized the opportunities for inclusivity and community-building offered by an affordable and increasingly efficient national postal system. On the other hand, however, Koehler sees Hardy as deeply suspicious of the optimistic rhetoric in which postal reform was often couched. Hardy's characters attempt time and again to connect with others through their letters, but not always with success. Indeed, as Koehler writes, they often 'use the post to bridge otherwise insurmountable social barriers, only to make the painful discovery that their letters cannot bring them closer to the communities to which they aspire' (p. 127).

Jacqueline Dillion and Phillip Mallett explore the connection between the widespread folk tradition of the evil eye and its Dorset variant, 'overlooking', in *The Return of the Native.* Their essay, ' "The Evil Eye": Looking and Overlooking in *The Return of the Native*' (*THJ* 31[2015] 89–107), draws on the novel to identify 'something more powerful than envy' in the Dorset version, a 'fear that if events were to play out according to our secret wishes, hidden even from ourselves, the outcome might literally be fatal' (p. 104). Hardy's short fiction is the subject of Oindrila Ghosh's 'Breaking Victorian Taboos: "Unwelcome Motherhood" and the Case of Thomas Hardy's Short Stories' (*The Victorian* 3:iii[2015] 1–21). The plight of the unwed mother spills over from Hardy's long fiction into shorter works, where the human experience of these women is contrasted with the inhumane response they receive at the hands of their communities. In 'Killing the Pig' (*The Victorian* 3:iii[2015] 1–18), Jeremy Strong dissects the famously gruesome scene in *Jude the Obscure,* offering up tidbits on the humane treatment of animals, the likability of Arabella, and realism in the process. Moving from the animal to the animal-like, Nathalie Virgintino argues, in her article 'Survival and the Tragic Ending of Thomas Hardy's *The Woodlanders*' (*The Victorian* 3:i[2015] 1–18), that the fate of the characters in Hardy's fiction, like the fate of animals, is primarily a matter of how well they understand and react to their surroundings.

In 'A Weakness for Arguing with Anybody: G.K. Chesterton and Thomas Hardy' (*THJ* 31[2015] 108–29), Colin Cavendish-Jones examines the influence of Thomas Hardy on G.K. Chesterton, who famously accused the other writer of being 'a sort of village atheist brooding and blaspheming over the village idiot' (p. 112). Marion Dell also takes up the connection between Hardy and a later writer in 'Moments of Vision: Thomas Hardy and Virginia Woolf' (*THJ* 31[2015] 13–24). Hardy, Dell argues, provided an 'inter-generational link' between Woolf's present and that of her parents and a 'generic link' between realism and modernism, providing her with a literary technique—the moment of vision—for representing the simultaneous instability and arresting significance of memory (p. 13).

Julie Camarda reminds us that, before Morris was a socialist, he was deeply involved in liberal radicalism in 'Liberal Possibilities in a Communist Utopia: Minority Voices and Historical Consciousness in Morris's *News from Nowhere*' (*NCC* 37[2015] 301–20). Reading Morris's letters and two pieces in the *Commonweal* alongside the novel, Camarda uncovers the works' intellectual debt to John Stuart Mill, particularly in its representation of dissenting voices within the utopian community.

William Makepeace Thackeray received somewhat more attention than in recent years, beginning with Ellen Redling's *Allegorical Thackeray: Secularised Allegory in Thackeray's Major Novels*, which argues that since Thackeray's own time, critics have misunderstood the author's outlook on humanity and the formal context governing his major novels. Overemphasis on Thackeray's satirical style without an understanding of his novels' conformity to earlier 'Allegories of Mankind and God' such as *Piers Plowman*, *The Faerie Queene*, and *Pilgrim's Progress* tends to promote the false view, Redling maintains, that Thackeray was a 'dreary misanthrope' with little commitment to morality and religion (p. 1). She endeavours to show that, in fact, his mature novels are deeply indebted to those 'Allegories of Mankind and God' and that, although they do not show heaven as the destination, these novels nonetheless depict the journey of Everyman (p. 1). Redling explains that Thackeray's avoidance of first-person narration and psychological introspection is a strategy of depersonalization aimed at ensuring that the reader can identify with the novel's Everyman figure and follow his lead to do some personal soul-searching. After providing an overview of the history of allegory, Redling looks at techniques of satire and parody in *Catherine*, *Barry Lyndon*, *The Book of Snobs*, and *The English Humourists*, and then at the evidence for reading *Vanity Fair*, *Pendennis*, and *The Newcomes* as secularized allegories. The flawed Everyman figures in these novels—Dobbin, Pen, Colonel Newcome, Clive, and Ethel—are 'able to transform [their] misguided views and [obtain] some insight and contingent happiness' in their life journeys towards an unsentimental 'secularized redemption' (pp. 146, 173). That their progress is due, not so much to their own efforts, but to the help of others is part of what Redling sees as the Christian 'communitarian' view that all humans are fallible, a view which opposes the trend towards individual *Bildung* in the novels of so many of Thackeray's contemporaries (p. 6). The final chapters look at some of the novels of self-reliance of those contemporaries, *David Copperfield*, *Jane Eyre*, and *The Eustace Diamonds*, to demonstrate how Thackeray declined to follow the literary trends of his day.

In a unique article entitled ' "Becky Said"—"Cried Amelia": A Metaphonological Analysis of Speech in *Vanity Fair*' (*BAS* 21[2015] 165–72), Elisa Bolchi examines the representation of direct speech in Thackeray's novel without a hero. Attending to the manner in which Becky's speech makes its way onto the page, Bolchi argues, 'better allows the reader to figure Rebecca out not only as the female version of the typical

Victorian self-made man, but also as a plotter who, in order to climb the social ladder, manipulates those around her by altering their balance and control' (p. 172). Equally original is Nancy Marck Cantwell's approach to Thackeray's novel in 'Waist not, Want Not: The Corseted Body and Empire in *Vanity Fair*' (*NCGS* 11:ii[2015] 21 paras.). Cantwell reads the illustrations in *Vanity Fair* alongside the text, paying close attention to fashion, in order to identify a counter-narrative deeply attuned to national and imperial politics. The representations of corseted and uncorseted bodies becomes, in Cantwell's reading, a symbolic, yet profoundly physical, indicator of the performance and dissemination of national identity through processes of control and expansion. Ryan Francis Murray returns us to *Vanity Fair*'s much-discussed puppet show frame in 'The Puppet Narrator of *Vanity Fair*' (*Victo* 5[2015] 36–53). Murray argues, somewhat perversely, that the narrative inconsistencies in the novel are not accidental, but instead evidence of a masterful puppet show in which the narrator is himself an embodied fictional character, or puppet, whose lapses are evidence only of his careful manipulation by the author.

This year witnessed the celebration of Trollope's birth on 24 April 1815, and was marked by a flurry of publications, including the Folio Society's two-volume publication of Steven Amarnick's edition of Trollope's *The Duke's Children* (*The Last Chronicle of Omnium: The Rediscovery of The Duke's Children*) with an introduction by Joanna Trollope, and commentary by Robert F. Wiseman, Susan Lowell Humphreys, and Michael G. Williamson. Amarnick's introduction recounts the history of the book and its restoration, and discusses the significance of the restored passages. Wiseman provides an extensive listing of Trollope's major cuts and their importance. Lowell comments on the manuscript itself and what it reveals about Trollope's working methodology. Williamson supplies contextual notation on issues, institutions, fashions, customs, and etiquette, the position of women, parliament, the political process, sporting and allied activities, and gentlemen's club's. There is too in the second volume a detailed index of characters; this is cross-referenced with the remainder of Trollope's work. This edition spawned a host of review articles celebrating its achievement, and provided the opportunity for bicentenary reassessments of Trollope.

As John Sutherland notes in his 'A Father's Dilemma: Anthony Trollope's "Wonderful Late Phase"—and the Familial, Political, Physical and Financial Difficulties That Lay Behind It' (*TLS* 5847 [24 April 2015] 3–4), *The Duke's Children* includes the approximately 65,000 words 'Trollope shaved' from the earlier published version of the same name. This was its author's thirty-ninth novel and published in 1880: 'the pruning of *The Duke's Children* was an act of repackaging, not re-creation, and took a couple of months, in 1878'. Furthermore, 'what one has in the hitherto published version is a précis' and 'a comparison between the two differently "complete" versions of the *Duke's Children* therefore offers unique insight into Trollope's authorial efficiencies'. Sutherland observes 'the Folio Society have acquired Amarnick's ur-*Duke's Children* to prepare a limited edition de luxe, finely printed, handsomely bound, cased and endpapered and distributed *hors de commerce*. It is a beautiful thing' (pp. 3–4). For Charles McGrath in his 'Trollope Uncut', 'the new version will most likely not change anyone's view of *The Duke's*

*Children*, and yet all those tiny excisions do add up. The restored version is a fuller, richer book' (*New York Times Book Review* [9 October 2015] 29). Melanie Kirkpatrick's *Wall Street Journal* assessment is headed 'A Bigger, Better Trollope' and opens 'a restored version of Anthony Trollope's *The Duke's Children* more deeply explores characters and emotions, and has a surprising new ending' (*Wall Street Journal* [25 February 2015]). These reviews indicate the high praise heaped on Amarnick's labours.

Late 2014 and 2015 witnessed the publication, in the Oxford World's Classics series, of six carefully edited and annotated editions of Trollope's novels, and the appearance of Nicholas Shrimpton's edition of *An Autobiography and Other Writings*: a second edition of this is due to be published as an Oxford World's Classic in 2016. In addition to a detailed introduction (pp. xii–xx), followed by a 'Note on the Text' (pp. xxi–xxv), and a selected bibliography (pp. xxvi–xxvii), the text of *An Autobiography* (pp. 1–30) is followed by four critical essays by Trollope: 'Trollope on Jane Austen' (pp. 231–2), 'On English Prose Fiction as a Rational Amusement' (pp. 233–58), 'From Thackeray' (pp. 259–62), and 'From A Walk in a Wood' (pp. 266–73). An appendix is devoted to 'Passages Omitted from *An Autobiography*' (pp. 274–80) and is followed by detailed, helpful explanatory notes (pp. 281–300). A feature of the Oxford World's Classics editions of Trollope is their useful introductions and explanatory notation. John Bowen's edition of *Barchester Towers*, the late Simon Dentith's edition of *Doctor Thorne*, Katherine Mullan and Francis O'Gorman's edition of *Framley Parsonage*, Helen Small's edition of *The Last Chronicle of Barsetshire*, Dinah Birch's edition of *The Small House at Allington* and Nicholas Shrimpton's edition of *The Warden* follow a feature of the Oxford World's Classics Trollopes, a formulaic context pattern. A 'Biographical Preface' authored by Katherine Mullan and Francis O'Gorman (pp. vii–x) is followed by an introduction, usually of thirty pages or so in length, followed by a one- or two-page selected bibliography, then a just over three-page 'Chronology of Anthony Trollope' and 'Trollope's Map of Barsetshire'. The text of the novel follows. In the instance of *The Warden*, Shrimpton also reprints (pp. 173–231) the text of 'the novella "The Two Heroines of Plumpington", written as a Christmas story to appear in the magazine *Good Cheer* in December 1882' (p. xxvi). These are followed by appendices. For instance Helen Small's edition of *The Last Chronicle of Barset* has two. The first appendix is 'Trollope's Introduction to the Chronicles of Barsetshire (1878)' (p. 729) and the second, also by Nicholas Shrimpton, 'Trollope's Barsetshire Novels and the Church' (pp. 730–40). These remarkably valuable and inexpensive editions conclude with one of their considerable strengths, explanatory notes (in Small's edition pp. 741–71).

The hundredth issue of *Trollopiana*, the journal of the Trollope Society [Winter 2014/15] includes Michael Helm's 'A History of the Trollope Society' an account of the Society since its 1988 foundation (*Troll* 100[Winter 2014/15] 2–6). Nigel Starck's 'What They Said about Trollope at the Time: Part One 1847–1858' (*Troll* 100[Winter 2014/15] 7–10) is the first in a three-part assessment of Trollope's contemporaries' critical responses to his novels. Pamela Marshall Barrell's 'Cuts or Uncuts—What They Say Now. A Résumé of Recent Press Activity' (*Troll* 100[Winter 2014/15] 11) is an account of the critical reception of Amarnick's edition of *The Duke's Children*. Peter Blacklock's 'The First Celebrity: An Australian Odyssey' (*Troll* 100[Winter 2014/15] 14–17) reviews Nigel Starck's *The First Celebrity: Anthony Trollope's Australasian Odyssey* [2014], an account, accompanied by photographs, of Trollope's two Australasian visits during the 1870s. This is followed by the text of the 27th Annual Trollope Society Lecture, given by Steven Armarnick on the rediscovery of the complete 'Lost Chronicle of Omnium, The Duke's Children' (pp. 20–9), and an account of the new edition published by the Folio Society by the editor of *Trollopiana* (p. 29), Pamela Marshall Barrell. Three issues of *Trollopiana* appear annually and are available free to members of the Trollope Society (see its website https://trollopesociety.org/trollopiana). The summer 2015 issue includes the continuation of Nigel Starck's 'What They Said about Trollope at the Time' (*Troll* 101[Summer 2015]) in which he explores the contemporary reviews that Trollope received between 1858 and 1874, and 'Dispossession' (*Troll* 101[Summer 2015]) in which Simon Grennan discusses the thinking behind his new graphic novel, *Dispossession. A Novel of Few Words*, based on Trollope's *John Caldigate*. The autumn issue includes Michael Sheridan's exploration, in his 'The Beverley Election of 1868' (*Troll* 102[Autumn 2015]), of the circumstances surrounding Anthony Trollope's bid to become MP for Beverley. Starck, in 'What They Said about Trollope at the Time' (*Troll* 102[Autumn 2015]) concludes his exploration of contemporary reviews received by Trollope, reaching 1876–82. Peter Blacklock's 'Writing the Frontier' (*Troll* 102[Autumn 2015]) reviews the first extensive book-length study of the subject, John McCourt's *Writing the Frontier: Anthony Trollope between Britain and Ireland*. McCourt thoroughly considers Trollope's relationship with his adopted second home, Ireland and his career in Ireland as an official of the Post Office, and places in context Trollope's Irish novels and stories. Frederick Vaughan's 'Anthony Trollope: The Nose Has It' (*Troll* 102[Autumn 2015]) is an examination of Trollope's description of the noses of men and women in his novels. (Pagination unavailable: information from https://trollopesociety.org/trollopiana/numbers101–110/trollopiana.)

Rachel Cooke, in her 'The Best Graphic books of 2015' (*Observer* [7 December 2015]) recommends '*Dispossession* (Cape) by Simon Grennan... This beautiful-looking book, commissioned as part of the bicentenary of the birth of Anthony Trollope... is based on *John Caldigate*' [1877]. Cooke writes that Grennan's book is 'full of feeling for the' Victorian period. 'His drawing rooms and parlours, richly coloured yet deeply shadowed, speak to a society in which outward displays of moral rectitude—Hestor's parents are so protective of her reputation, they imprison her at home the better that she does not return to her "adulterer" husband—go hand in hand with repression and hypocrisy. Richly satisfying, *Dispossession* will make a charming, slightly surprising Christmas present for—doesn't every family have one?—the Trollope fan in your life, whether he or she likes comics, or not.' The other 2015 book on Trollope to be drawn to our attention is Simon Grennan and Laurence Grove's edited collection, *Transforming Anthony Trollope: Dispossession, Victorianism and Nineteenth-Century Word and Image*, consisting of cross-disciplinary essays providing a companion to Grennan's graphic novel. Grennan and Grove, in their introduction (pp. 7–12), observe that their 'companion volume to' Grennan's graphic novel 'is divided into three parts, each addressing different aspects of the adaptation process and surrounding context'. The first part '"*Dispossession*": Simon Grennan's Graphic Adaptation of Trollope's *John Caldigate*', directly analyses the techniques used by Grennan, both in comparison with other literary adaptations and conventions and on their own terms, via the interviewed words of Grennan himself. The second part, 'Nineteenth-Century Visualizations', moves from Grennan to Trollope. 'These analyses consider the visual nature of Trollope's work, the visualization of Trollope's work (using illustrations) and the visual context of Trollope's work, including the culture of Victorian comics.' The third part 'Using the Victorians: Appropriation, Adaptation and Historiography', bridges the first two parts. 'This section', the editors note, 'contextualizes the twenty-first-century adaptation of *John Caldigate* by comparison with other renditions of Victorian culture: from England, France and the USA, and into TV, novels and graphic novels' (p. 10).

There are three contributions to the first part: Jan Baetens, 'Adapting and Displaying Multiple Temporalities: What Became of Trollope's *John Caldigate* and Maupassant's *Boule de suif* in Simon Grennan's *Dispossession* and Dino Battaglia's *Contes et nouvelles de guerre*?' (pp. 15–32); 'John Miers in Conversation with Simon Grennan, Conducted by Email, July and August 2014: *Dispossession*: Time, Motion and Depictive Regimes' (pp. 33–53); and Hugo Frey's 'The Tactic for Illusion in Simon Grennan's *Dispossession*' (pp. 55–68). The second part has four contributions, beginning with Frederik Van Dam's 'Allegorical Landscapes: The Psychology of Seeing in Anthony Trollope's Later Novels' (pp. 71–87)—Van Dam has astute comments on Trollope's late style such as 'Trollope's later novels manipulate perspective through the use of internal focalisation' (p. 81). David Skilton's 'Complex Meanings in Illustrated Literature, 1860–1880' (pp. 89–106) includes helpful illustrations. Roger Sabin's object is to 'survey the discourses that emerge around early comics' (p. 107) in his 'Comics Versus Books: The New Criticism at the "Fin de Siècle"' (pp. 107–29), and Barbara Postema's subject is 'The Visual Culture of Comics in the Last Half of the Nineteenth Century: Comics Without Words' (pp. 131–47). The final part also has four contributions: Marie-Luise Kohlke considers '"Abominable pictures": Neo-Victorianism and the Tyranny of the Sexual Taboo' (pp. 151–74); Ian Hague's 'Drawing "The Apprenticeship of a Man of Letters": Adapting *Remembrance of Things Past* for "Bande dessinée"' (pp. 175–97) is a consideration of 'the visualisation of Victorian-age culture through the graphic novel and the specific example of Proust' (p. 12); Aarnould Rommens, 'Allegories of Graphiation: Alberto Breccia's Counter-Censorial Versions of E.A. Poe's *Valdemar*' (pp. 199–216), again does not concern Trollope but does underscore 'how cultural updates inevitably carry and convey changing political context' (p. 12). In the final essay of Grennan and Grove's collection, Peter Wilkins, in his 'An Incomplete Project: Graphic Adaptations of *Moby-Dick* and the Ethics of Response' (pp. 217–33), 'emphasizes the richness of ambiguity as compared to description of narrative, and the advantage of providing a visual equivalent, rather than an imitation of prose' (p. 12). *Transforming Anthony Trollope:*

*Dispossession, Victorianism and Nineteenth-Century Word and Image* concludes
with an extensive, helpful, double-columned index (pp. 235–45). It is followed
by a 'Gallery with Colour Figures' (pp. 249–63) containing seventeen
illustrative colour examples from Grennan's *Dispossession* and other works
discussed in this challenging, well-produced collection of essays.

The bicentennial witnessed a plethora of articles and essays in collections
devoted to Trollope. Robert D. Aguirre's '"Affairs of state": Mobilities,
Communication, and Race in Trollope's *The West Indies and the Spanish
Main*' (*NCC* 37[2015] 1–20) utilizes Trollope's *The West Indies and the Spanish
Main* [1860], a transatlantic travel narrative that reconceived an already well-
worn genre. Aguirre writes that 'Late in 1858, the British novelist Anthony
Trollope boarded the SS *Atrato*, owned and operated by the Royal Mail Steam
Packet Company, and took passage to the West Indies. Over the next several
months, traveling by ship, train, horseback, mule, and foot, Trollope made his
way through Britain's Caribbean colonies, Cuba, and the independent Central
American republics' (p. 1). Trollope's impressions are recorded in his travel
narrative. 'As a traveler along, and a colonial administrator of, this larger
network of mobilities, Trollope was well placed to understand its reach and
power, its limitations and exclusions. Far more than a catalogue of racial
oppositions, his travel narrative captures the tensions of a rapidly modernizing
world' (pp. 16–17). Drawing upon *The Small House at Allington* [1864] and
*The Way We Live Now* [1875] amongst other Trollope works, Kaelin B.C.
Alexander's 'Turning Mourning: Trollope's Ambivalent Widows' (*VLC*
43[2015] 607–20) 'proceeds from the claim that the widow is not necessarily
a figure for mourning, but rather for a radical form of ambivalence'.
Furthermore, 'The ambivalence of Trollope's widow characters offers an
important vantage point from which to reframe discussions about the place of
ideology, agency, and desire in the larger scope of Trollope's oeuvre' (p. 608).

Ayelet Ben-Yishai's 'Walking the Boundaries in Victorian Fiction: Realism
as Communal Epistemology' (*NCC* 37[2015] 197–214) 'examines the concept
of realism as communal epistemology in Victorian fiction. Topics discussed
include the relationship between epistemology and artifice and the contribution of the realist novel's success in creating a sense of commonality to its
prominence in the 19th century. Also discussed is the relationship between
correspondence and commonality based on the satirical novel *The Way We
Live Now*...published in 1875' (p. 197). **Oliver Bock, in 'Anthony Trollope's**
Novels and Their Reception on the Nineteenth-Century German Market'
(*Angermion* 8[2015] 109–25), gives an account of Trollope's reception in
Germany between 1848 and 1883. Carla Fusco, in her 'How Flexible Is the
Moral Code of a Businessman? **Anthony Trollope** and *The Way We Live Now*'
(in Çelikel and Taniyan, eds., *English Studies: New Perspectives*, pp. 61–6),
considers, in a short space amongst other topics, satire, the treatment of the
character of Augustus Melmotte as a self-made man, ethics, capitalism,
hypocrisy, facial expressions, and anti-Semitism in Trollope's novel. Paul
Fyfe's *By Accident of Design: Writing the Victorian Metropolis* contains a
detailed discussion (pp. 184–90) of *The Prime Minister* [1876] in the context of
the exploration of accidents and 'questions about railway design and
development' (p. 184). *The Way We Live Now* also engages Joshua Gooch,

who devotes a chapter to it in his *The Victorian Novel, Service Work, and the Nineteenth-Century Economy* (pp. 136–62).

For Richard Hughes Gibson in his *Forgiveness in Victorian Literature: Grammar, Narrative, and Community*, Trollope's *The Vicar of Bullhampton* [1870] 'is notable for a study of forgiveness not only because it explores the concept within the novel with particular richness but also . . . because it raises the issue in terms of the readers response' (p. 85; and see also pp. 86–99). Adam Gopnik, in 'Trollope Trending' (*New Yorker* [4 May 2015] 26–32), discusses Trollope's career and examines the reasons 'why he's still the novelist of the way we live now' (p. 28). Trollope's work discussed includes *The Last Chronicle of Barset, The Three Clerks,* and *Phineas Finn.* Attention is drawn to Trollope's depiction in his novels of modernization and how this leads to political reform, and the appearance of gossip. For Gopnik, Trollope's 'subject is always politics and his material is always gossip. Politics (the competition for status and power) and gossip (the shared information about who has it) remain the mostly benign stuff of human existence' (p. 32). Kristine Kelly, in 'Aesthetic Desire and Imperialist Disappointment in **Trollope's** *The Bertrams* and the *Murray Handbook for Travellers in Syria and Palestine*' (*VLC* 43[2015] 621–39), discusses the treatment of travel and pilgrimage to the Holy Land in both texts: Kelly, 'in [her] reading of these two traveling texts', has 'attempted to show a moment in the formation of a global aesthetic practice for British travelers in the Middle East'. However, 'the concomitance of desire for sublimity, that is, an experience of power in the world and in one's self, and of the disappointment of achieving this desire, because of the geographical and social context of the sites seen, leads to an aesthetic practice in which (paradoxically) aesthetic response is diverted' (p. 636). 'The Good Man and the Good Citizen: Political Philosophy in **Trollope's** Palliser Novels' concerns Peter Meilander (*FMLS* 51[2015] 394–416).

Ellen Moody, a most astute critic of Trollope, in her 'Epistolarity and Masculinity in Andrew Davies' **Trollope** Adaptations' (in Leggott, Taddeo, and de Groot, eds., *Upstairs and Downstairs: British Costume Drama Television from The Forsyte Saga to Downton Abbey*, pp. 79–94) discusses Davies's Trollope television adaptations of *He Knew He Was Right* and *The Way We Live Now*. Moody's focus is Davies's treatment of masculinity and his epistolary technique. George O'Brien includes discussion of Trollope's *Castle Richmond* [1860], set in Cork and London with its theme of inheritance and escape, in his *The Irish Novel, 1800–1910*. Melissa Raines, in 'Romantic Timing and Realist Implications in Hardy and **Trollope**' (*EIC* 65[2015] 53–74), **pays especial attention to romantic characters in Trollope's** *Rachel Ray* **[1863] and** *Phineas Redux* **[1873] and Hardy's** *Tess of the d'Urbervilles* **[1891] to make some fine distinctions. She considers stylistic concerns such as Trollope's use of 'the pluperfect tense' (p. 54) in her presentation of Rachel in** *Rachel Ray* **and astutely writes that** 'Hardy's texts are weighed down by the author's conviction that there is only one outcome—namely, that what "should" happen never does.' For Raines, 'Trollope's "shoulds" are always debatable because life is a process, a series of adaptations of the perceptions that are had in a particular moment. By recognizing the minute shades and inherent changeability within those perceptions in the present, characters in Trollope can validate their eventual chosen future stories in retrospect in an attempt to continue this sense of process, seeing more clearly the new nature of a missed "should" or "if" in terms of the reality of their own now' (p. 70). She concludes that 'Those who flounder romantically in Trollope's novels are often presented not as victims of fate, like Tess, but of themselves' (p. 73).

Supritha Rajan, in *A Tale of Two Capitalisms: Sacred Economics in Nineteenth-Century Britain* chapter 6, 'Household Gods Revisited in George Eliot and Anthony Trollope' (pp. 185–216), discusses the interconnections between Victorian political economy, anthropology, and literary discourse in order to show the ways in which they underpin capitalism. Sophie Ratcliffe's 'The Episodic **Trollope** and *An Editor's Tales*' (*VS* 5[2015] 57–83) concentrates on Trollope's collection of short stories *An Editor's Tales* [1869–70], and *The Way We Live Now* [1875], in order to 'argue that the idea of the editor, and the act of editing, provided **Trollope** with a productive metaphor for thinking about the idea of the self in time' (p. 57). Amy J. Robinson, in 'The Victorian Provincial Novel' (*LitComp* 12[2015] 548–54), examines the ramifications of the concept of the 'Victorian provincial novel' and by drawing upon instances from Trollope's and Gaskell's fiction demonstrates that it intertextually relates to discussions of 'regionalism, nationalism, cosmopolitanism, and empire' (p. 548). David Skilton and Simon Grennan write again on Grennan's comic adaptation of Trollope's John Caldigate in their 'Drawing Style, Genre and the Novel' (in Tabachnick and Saltzman, eds., *Drawn from the Classics: Essays on Graphic Adaptations of Literary Works*, pp. 147–60). Matthew Titolo's 'Sincerity and Reflexive Satire in **Anthony Trollope's** *The Struggles of Brown, Jones and Robinson*' (*VLC* 43[2015] 23–39) explores Trollope's 1861 satire on trade and advertising. Finally, in this account of 2015 publications on Trollope, mention should be made of Wayne W. Westbrook's 'Picking Trollope's Pocket, Again: James's use of *Barchester Towers* in *The Europeans*' (*N&Q* 62[2015] 419–24). Emphasis is placed upon Trollope's influence upon James's work and his use of Trollope's novel as source material. Westbrook discusses the roles of siblings in the novels, characters such as the Signora Vesey Neroni and Eugenia, and also James's personal writings reflecting on *The Europeans*.

Caroline Hovanec returns H.G. Wells to the genealogy of literary modernism, in 'Rereading H.G. Wells's *The Time Machine*: Empiricism, Aestheticism, Modernism' (*ELT* 58[2015] 459–85), arguing that he has been unfairly sidelined from the discussion of modernism's forebears, largely because critics have not recognized his peculiar, scientific form of aestheticism. According to Hovanec, Wells incorporates scientific observation in his novels but 'strips away its epistemological authority, leaving in its place a kernel of sensation that provides no evidence by aesthetic experience' (p. 459). Focusing on such aesthetic investments in novels like *The Time Machine*, Hovanec argues, links Wells to the modernist writers that followed him at the same time as it exposes modernism's scientific past. The relationship between science and aesthetics is also the topic of Jan Vanvelk's 'Listening to the Silence: Huxley, Arnold, and Wells' Scientific Humanity' (*Victo* 5[2015] 72–93). Drawing primarily from Wells' non-fiction prose, but from his novels as well, Vanvelk argues for Wells as a clarifying figure in the debate between Arnold and

Huxley over literature and science in education. Particularly notable for Wells scholars as well as those interested in the history of the novel is Christiane Gannon's 'H.G. Wells and the Aestheticized Individual: Critiquing the Bildungsroman in *The Bulpington of Blup*' (*MP* 112[2015] 503–21). Gannon convincingly argues that Wells resisted both the institutional *Bildungsroman* of the Victorian period and the aestheticized one of the modernist era. In *The Bulpington of Blup*, Cannon sees an ironic rendering of the ideal self that works towards a vision of art as integral to the democratic imaginary. For Wells, Cannon writes, 'the aesthetic state was an external, communal achievement, an ideal society that might be constructed in reality if reading and writing were regarded as active and shared—rather than contemplative and individual—pursuits' (p. 506). The relationship between Wells's politics and art is also the subject of Zoe Beenstock's 'Empiricist Political Theory and the Modern Novel: The Social Contract and H.G. Wells' (*MLQ* 76[2015] 57–77), which situates two of Wells's novels, *The Invisible Man* [1897] and *Love and Mr. Lewisham* [1899], within the novel's shared history with Enlightenment political theory. By attending exclusively to Wells as a figure of either late Victorianism or early modernism, critics have, according to Beenstock, overlooked the importance of social contract theory within Wells's work. The fear of microbes is the topic of Jens Lohfert Jørgenson's essay, 'Bacillophobia: Man and Microbes in *Dracula*, *The War of the Worlds*, and *The Nigger of the 'Narcissus'*' (*CS* 27[2015] 36–49). All three of these 1897 novels, Jørgenson claims, negotiate the anxiety that surrounds microbes, a scientific discovery that participated in the Weberian disenchantment of the world, while it worked, at the same time, to re-enchant it in fuelling a fear that science might not be able to halt infection.

A particularly strong contribution to Wilde studies came from Jonathan Loesberg. Those interested in histories of criticism as well as the more recent formalist turn will, in particular, benefit from reading Loesberg's 'Wildean Interpretation and Formalist Reading' (*VS* 58[2015] 9–33). In this suggestive essay, Loesberg draws our attention, through an analysis of Wilde's *The Portrait of Mr. W.H.* as well as the work of mid-century formalists, to the perversity of formalist reading with its insistence on privileging the paradoxical in language over the definitional non-contradiction of reality. Using Wilde's criticism as a model, Loesberg argues that formalist criticism needs to acknowledge the perversity or 'queerness' at its methodological and epistemological core. 'The difference between Wilde and the mid-century formalists', Loesberg writes, 'is that Wilde advocated for a criticism that would comment on the literariness of literature, doing for literature what literature did for us: as literature shocked us into an awareness of our lives through its artifice, criticism could shock us into an awareness of an artwork's mystery through its particular perspective on the work' (p. 30). 'Acting Out Gender: Performativity and Becoming Lord Henry Wotton in Oscar Wilde's *The Picture of Dorian Gray*' (*BAS* 21[2015] 77–82), by Burak Irmak, describes Wotton as a gender performer desperately trying to get off the predominant script of masculinity. He does so, in Irmak's account, by first arousing his own desires in Dorian and then living out these desires through the younger man. Acting and artifice is also the subject of Rebecka Klette's '*Fin de la réalité*:

Artificial Milieus and Hyperreality in Huysmans' *A Rebours* and Wilde's *The Picture of Dorian Gray*' (*The Victorian* 3:iii[2015] 1–14), where she draws on Jean Baudrillard's theory of hyperreality in order to argue that aesthetes in the nineteenth century reconfigured urban and natural space in an attempt to escape into an environment that privileged their own set of interests and preoccupations. Contributing to the growing body of recent scholarly work on the complicated interconnections of the religious and the secular, Ilona Urquhart's 'Devils, Souls, and the Spectre of Matthew Arnold in Oscar Wilde's *The Picture of Dorian Gray*' (*AVSJ* 20[2015] 14–27) reads Wilde's novel as a response to Matthew Arnold's assertion in 'The Function of Criticism at the Present Time' that religion is 'morality touched with emotion' and, thus, that art could be the moral force of the modern world (p. 14). Wilde's novel, Urquhart claims, does not simply reject the necessity for conventional moral norms; rather it 'utilizes the Faust myth . . . to propose the idea that art, and especially literature, is in some way "diabolical" and therefore unfit as a replacement for religion and guide to moral conduct' (pp. 14–15).

## 3. Poetry

In this section Clare Stainthorp reviews publications on the Rossettis, the Brownings, Morris, Swinburne, women poets, and poetry from 1870 to 1900. Michael J. Sullivan reviews publications on Arnold, Clough, Hopkins, Tennyson, Patmore, working-class poets, and poetry from 1830 to 1870.

Among the general works published this year was *Victorian Poetry and Modern Life: The Unpoetical Age*, by Natasha Moore. Her study ranges across mid-century poetry in order to consider how poets sought to establish the validity of everyday contemporary subjects as poetic. In her introduction Moore identifies the intersecting origins of 'the Victorian long poem of modern life' (p. 12); subsequent chapters chart a series of resemblances between poems that, while differing significantly on the surface, are part of this common movement. Chapter 1 situates Moore's research in the context of recent developments in the academic study of the quotidian as specifically modern. She goes on to focus upon Clough's *The Bothie* and *Amours de Voyage*, Patmore's *The Angel in the House*, and Barrett Browning's *Aurora Leigh*, considering these diverse poems in terms of their experimental engagement with everydayness, drawing out shared tensions between surface descriptions of routine and buried, more profound, meaning. Chapter 2 explores the formal choices made by these three poets, beginning with Tennyson in order to then consider specific developments in the long narrative poem during the mid-nineteenth century. Chapter 3 considers why it is that the most common focus of these poems is courtship or marriage plots. Moore suggests that the resultant 'series of concentric and sometimes overlapping personal, social and political circles' (p. 124) makes this an important narrative device through which to represent modern life; marriage becomes a vehicle to explore the potential for fulfilment, both personally and poetically. In chapter 4 Moore returns to the question of form, considering the generic hybridity of these poems. She is concerned with interrogating the term 'verse-novel', situating these poems in relation to the epic, identifying how metre demonstrates correspondence between form and content, reflecting upon their encyclopedic impulses, and showing the underlying tension between fragmentariness and unity. Moore concludes her book with a meditation on the centripetal 'ends' of these four poems—both their conclusions and their purpose—and provides a brief postscript on the failure of this form to persist by describing how Meredith's centrifugal ending to *Modern Love* diverges from the path laid out by Clough, Patmore, and Barrett Browning.

As will become evident over the course of this section, a significant theme in Victorian poetry studies in 2015 was the reception and reinterpretation of literary sources, with scholars keen to trace the significant influence of classical, medieval, and Romantic works upon a variety of poets. Norman Vance and Jennifer Wallace's impressive edited collection *The Oxford History of Classical Reception in English Literature*, volume 4: *1790–1880* marks an important contribution in this regard, as it covers the work of a broad range of writers. Its preliminary thematic section is reviewed in Section 1 above, and details of the chapters on individual poets appear below. Jalal Uddin Khan's chapter, 'Medievalism in Victorian Poetry and Prose' in his *Perspectives: Romantic, Victorian, and Modern Literature* (pp. 313–51) touches upon a wide range of canonical poetic works in order to provide an overview of medieval tropes and themes during the nineteenth century.

Annmarie Drury's pioneering book *Translation as Transformation in Victorian Poetry* provides an intervention into how we think about poetry alongside the 'incorporative impulse' of Victorian imperialism (p. 5), aiming to 'clarify our picture of Victorian translators ... and to reveal their pervasive legacy across the twentieth century' (p. 4). She begins by outlining the practice and study of translation, viewing it as 'a literary rather than linguistic phenomenon' (p. 9). The first chapter analyses texts from periodical contexts, and then reflects on six 'persistent habits of thought' in Victorian translation (p. 33): comparative evaluation, problems of metre, translations as ambassadors, translation as collecting, experiment and controversy, and the multivalence of the informant. Chapter 2 is concerned with '*Idylls of the King*, the *Mabinogion*, and Tennyson's faithless melancholy', showing how Tennyson drew on Charlotte Guest's translation of Welsh legends for the Geraint-Enid idylls while problematically 'draining ... Welshness from his source' (p. 81). Drury argues that 'his predicament as a faithless adapter of Guest's translation is represented through the struggle of Geraint, his literary foil' (p. 58). Chapter 3, 'In Poetry and Translation, Browning's Case for Innovation', considers how Browning's 'incorporative aesthetic' within his poetry-writing and translations generates a 'creative dialectic' between the two modes, and how 'hybridity in language operated as an essential creative tool' (p. 102). Drury finds an affinity between his translation of the *Agamemnon* and 'Caliban Upon Setebos', discussing the latter as pseudo-translation, which allows Browning to play with the 'expressive possibilities' of language (p. 119); she also draws out linguistic tensions in 'An Epistle Containing the Strange Medical Experience of Karshish, the Arab Physician' and 'Muléykeh', demonstrating the link he makes 'between Arab identity and poetic innovation' (p. 132). Chapter 4, 'The

*Rubáiyát* and Its Compass', focuses on the hybridity of the *Rubáiyát* and challenges common assumptions about FitzGerald's orientalism, considering more closely manoeuvres made when translating Khayyám's quatrains. It places the poem in dialogue with Swinburne's *Atalanta in Calydon* and Michael Field's *Underneath the Bough* in order to discuss 'a late-Victorian poetics of impersonation' (p. 168), as well as the parodies that proliferated, especially in America. Chapter 5 grapples with the largely unacknowledged pervasiveness of 'a "Victorian" sound' (as per the schemas drawn out over the course of Drury's book) in the translation of ' "exotic" languages' during the twentieth century (p. 193), focusing on William Hichen's translations of Swahili literature from the 1930s. Drury concludes by arguing that the creativity of Victorian translation practices is 'crucial to the story of world literature in formation' (p. 226).

A significant quantity of research that appeared in 2015 was concerned with poetry by women, with scholars seeking to recuperate less well-known voices and position these poets within their creative and social networks. Linda Hughes draws out key issues in Victorian women's poetry by focusing on Hemans, Barrett Browning, and Rossetti in her 'Poetry' (in Peterson, ed., *The Cambridge Companion to Victorian Women's Writing*, pp. 89–104; which is reviewed in Section 1 above). Fabienne Moine's book, *Women Poets in the Victorian Era: Cultural Practices and Nature Poetry*, is particularly impressive for its commitment to discussing a wide variety of works by less well-known poets alongside those more securely within the canon. Across five thematic chapters Moine considers 'Victorian women's poems about the natural world as sites of resistance to the forces of economic, social and cultural domination' (p. 2). She emphasizes how their use of nature as subject and metaphor differs from that of the Romantics, suggesting that these women 'generally had a much more concrete and empirical approach to nature'; they observed rather than contemplated (p. 6). The first chapter, 'A Woman's Place Is in the Garden', sets up the terms of engagement between the feminine and the natural during the nineteenth century. By considering women's 'alleged affinity' with the flower garden and its inhabitants (p. 46) and how they have been understood as feminine spaces Moine draws out tensions between empowerment and belittlement in a wide range of poems. In chapter 2 the focus turns to poems both as and about flowers. Delving into both the codified language of flowers and their wider symbolic resonances, Moine demonstrates the complex ways in which Victorian women poets negotiated a wealth of social, religious, and romantic issues. The focus of chapter 3, 'Digging for Identity', is the garden as an often hybrid space devoted to privacy and femininity; poetic gardens are shown to provide 'forms of cultural resistance' and symbolize both 'restriction and permissiveness' (pp. 105, 102) during this period in which amateur gardening became increasingly popular. Chapter 4 turns from plants to the question of animal identity, Moine finding that due to their 'physical and cultural proximity' it is birds and domestic pets that hold women's attention (p. 157). She shows that it is 'in avian poetry that women poets make the most radical use of gender identification' (p. 163), drawing on a large corpus of such writings; poems about dogs and cats speak more clearly to women's position in the social and economic sphere. Evolutionary themes come to dominate the final chapter, which focuses on women's 'rewriting, interpretation and appropriation' of scientific discourses about natural mechanisms (p. 217). Moine shows how women poets explicitly used contemporary scientific ideas to develop and support their own vision of the natural world, often 'using poetical tools that highlighted experimentation and observation' (p. 218) while seeking to imbue this perspective with morality and hope. Moine convincingly demonstrates the variety and complexity of women's poetry on natural themes in the nineteenth century, highlighting throughout the importance of attending to a breadth of (often neglected) voices in order to build up a fuller and more multifaceted understanding of their concerns.

Patricia Murphy offers another approach to women's nature poetry in 'Ecofeminist Whispers: The Interrogation of "Feminine Nature" in Mathilde Blind's Short Poetry' (*NCGS* 11:i[2015] 30 paras.). The article considers Blind's response to 'the problematic coupling of nature and woman' (p. 5) through close readings of 'Entangled', 'On a Forsaken Lark's Nest', 'The Sower', and 'A Parable'. She identifies how Blind makes a forceful case for the damage this gender alignment causes, admonishing those who make assumptions about either essential femininity or humanity's domination of nature. Lisa Vargo's chapter on Blind (in Boyiopoulos and Sandy, eds., *Decadent Romanticism, 1780–1914*, pp. 119–30; also reviewed in Chapter XIII of this volume), argues persuasively that her frequent allusions to 'Ode to the West Wind' and 'To a Skylark' are a jumping-off point from which to consider how she takes 'Shelley's vision of a union between the human and natural realms' and translates it via Darwinism into 'something more tentative and subject to doubt' (p. 119). Linda K. Hughes's contribution to the same volume is '"Phantoms of Delight": Amy Levy and Romantic Men' (pp. 161–76), in which Levy's lyrics 'The Old Poet', 'On the Wye in May', and (more obliquely) 'Sinfonia Eroica' are shown to be inspired by, to allude to, and to repurpose key themes within Wordsworth's poetry.

In *Networking the Nation: British and American Women's Poetry and Italy, 1840–1870* Alison Chapman focuses on connecting and repositioning the writings of Barrett Browning, Isa Blagden, Sophie May Eckley, Theodosia Garrow Trollope, Elizabeth Clementine Kinney, and Eliza Ogilvy, who were all expatriates based in Florence during the Risorgimento. Through reading these women's poetry, journalism, and other prose alongside the specific spaces they inhabited, Chapman argues that they 'predicated their writing identities on a political poetics that was circulated by a complex European and transatlantic print and manuscript culture' (p. xxvii). Throughout this carefully argued book Chapman's central concern is with women poets' personal, social, and political agency. The first section establishes the specifics of the salon culture that was built up by this network of poets, with chapter 1 arguing that Florence became a locus for such individuals because it 'offered social and professional connections as well as poetic inspiration' (p. 6). The subsequent chapters focus in turn on Villa Brichieri, where Blagden created a specifically female community, Villino Trollope, where the 'new Corinne' fostered gatherings of Italian and expatriate political and intellectual figures, and Casa Guidi, which Barrett Browning pitched as being in opposition to

Florentine salon culture but nonetheless functioned in an equivalent way. Section II focuses on the role of the poetess in this expatriate context. Chapman draws out how conceptions of the 'English poetess' were developed by periodical and annual poetry, and then subverted by *Aurora Leigh*, demonstrating how Barrett Browning and other women manipulated the expectations surrounding female authorship to shape their public identities. The following chapters respectively consider how Trollope took the idea of 'politicized poetess to its rhetorical extreme' (p. 124), the religious and political tensions underlying Blagden's multifaceted professional identity, and the way in which Ogilvy negotiated the terms of expatriatism and exile in relation to her Scottish literary identity. The third section considers the intertwining of spiritualism and politics during this period, dwelling on the personal and political resonances of the Risorgimento and revolution more broadly. Chapter 9 considers spiritualism (automatic writing and apparitions of hands in particular) through Barrett Browning's life and letters of the period, and into *Aurora Leigh*'s imagery. The following chapter is concerned with Barrett Browning's 'intense spiritual and textual affair' (p. 213) with American poet and medium Eckley, while in 'Vulgar Needs: EBB's Transatlantic Print Networks' Chapman discusses the thirteen political poems Barrett Browning published in the New York *Independent* in 1860–1. The final chapter, 'Performative Poetics', focuses on the lack of resolution in Barrett Browning's posthumous *Last Poems*, and Chapman concludes by arguing that she was pursuing in these a new poetics that broadly shunned metaphor.

Other networks are the focus of Kate Thomas's chapter, 'Lesbian Postmortem at the Fin de Siècle' (in Medd, ed., *The Cambridge Companion to Lesbian Literature*, pp. 122–35). She provocatively suggests that 'There was something about a dead lesbian that had, at the fin de siècle, oddly invigorating effects' (p. 122). Describing the connections between queer women writers that include Levy, Field, A. Mary F. Robinson, and Vernon Lee, Thomas finds that in their poetic writings death becomes not a sexless escape but 'an enigmatic region...beyond the bounds of law and the constrictions of life' (p. 124) through which passionate desire persisted. Sarah Parker's chapter, 'The Muse Writes Back: Lyric Poetry and Female Poetic Identity' (in Dowd and Rulyova, eds., *Genre Trajectories: Identifying, Mapping, Projecting*, pp. 89–108), also discusses the work of Robinson and Field, alongside that of Edith Nesbit, Constance Naden, and Olive Custance. Parker demonstrates how their works complicate and overturn the historical muse–poet relationship, transforming the lyric genre by subverting the identities of 'I' and 'you'.

Two pieces focus on women poets who straddle the Romantic and Victorian periods. One chapter of Clare Broome Saunders's *Louisa Stuart Costello: A Nineteenth-Century Writing Life* focuses on poetry (pp. 105–35; reviewed more fully in Section 1 above). Costello's publishing life spanned many genres and decades; while the majority of her poetry volumes were published before 1830, Broome Saunders provides commentary on, extracts from, and reviews of her well-received 1856 *The Lay of the Stork*, which turns medieval themes to political, anti-war ends. Aaron S. Kaiserman notes, in '"Wandering through bowers beloved": The Wandering Jew and the Woman Poet in Caroline Norton's *The Undying One*' (*NCGS* 11:i[2015] 27 paras.), how Norton exists at the intersection between the Romantic and Victorian eras. Her neglected long narrative poem from 1830 is here discussed as providing insights into this transitional period, blending 'sublime landscapes and the Gothic with Victorian domestic values and sentimentalism' (para. 1). The poem's characterization and narrative are shown to illuminate contemporary perspectives on Judaism, as well as Norton's figuration of herself as a woman poet.

Two articles take Augusta Webster's engagement with Robert Browning as their subject. Patricia Rigg's 'Augusta Webster, Dramatic Forms, and the Religious Aesthetic of Robert Browning's *The Ring and the Book*' (*VP* 53[2015] 1–14) explores how 'Webster's Preacher and Jeanne d'Arc might serve to illuminate the nuances of Browning's ongoing development as a dramatic poet' (p. 2). Rigg focuses on the interconnected terms 'monodrama' and 'dramatic monologue' in relation to these two poets, arguing that both are interested in creating performative spaces in their works. In 'Skepticism and the Dramatic Monologue: Webster against Browning' (*VP* 53[2015] 401–21) Joshua Taft focuses upon how, as a result of the reliability of her speakers, Webster's dramatic monologues are not typical of the genre and amount to a direct challenge to Browning's poems. He persuasively argues, through readings of 'Pilate', 'A Soul in Prison', and 'A Preacher', that Webster overturns Browning's scepticism, obscurity, and sympathy for religious faith; in her works 'Poetic clarity and epistemological accuracy . . . lead to the same place—a humble but convinced agnosticism' (p. 403).

Wolfgang Funk focuses on the resonances of non-Euclidean geometry in 'The Mathematics of Evolution: Dreaming about Four Dimensions with Edwin A. Abbott and May Kendall' (*CS* 27:ii[2015] 67–80). Beginning by introducing the development of theorizing about higher dimensions, Funk goes on to show how these ideas became entangled with evolutionary thinking in Abbott's *Flatland* and Kendall's 'A Pure Hypothesis'. Regarding the latter, he argues that Kendall is responding to scientific discourses regarding how 'thinking and existence in four dimensions really presupposes evolutionary progress' both physically and socially (p. 72).

Among the most exciting avenues in present-day English studies are the continued and accelerating advances in textual criticism: of manuscripts, drafts, unpublished fragments, and their revisionary potential for scholarship and stylistic criticism. In 'George Eliot, Meter, and the Matter of Ideas: The Yale Poetry Notebook' (*ELH* 82[2015] 1179–1211), Ruth Abbott presents an intricate and meticulously researched article on Eliot's 'unpublished manuscript collection of verse and critical prose' (p. 1186). This substantial piece of scholarship demonstrates how Eliot's research into metre in her commonplace books was bound up with a process of 'recopying, reorganizing, and indexing' (p. 1186), which 'transposes' her 'metrical research' for her published poetic volume, *The Spanish Gypsy*, 'into several new forms' (p. 1186). The weight and rigour of this research reinforce the value of substantial essays and articles as critical ends in themselves.

Scholarship relating to Matthew Arnold took different approaches to reading his work in context. Joshua King's *Imagined Spiritual Communities in Britain's Age of Print* includes one chapter on Arnold (reviewed above), which focuses on his dealings with religious and poetic discourse. In 'Arnold's

"Angelic" Shelley and an Image in *The Origin of Species*' (*N&Q* 62[2015] 435–6), Rodney Stenning Edgecombe probes potential allusions behind Arnold's famous description of Shelley: the 'beautiful and ineffectual angel, beating in the void his luminous wings in vain' (p. 435). Eschewing a possible inspiration in 1 Corinthians 9:26 ('so fight I, not as one that beateth the air'), Edgecombe asserts the likelihood that Arnold's phrase was prompted by Darwin's *The Origin of Species* [1859], in which he concluded that 'to discuss whether they ought to be called species or varieties, before any definition of these terms has been generally accepted, is vainly to beat the air' (p. 436). Nicholas Shrimpton, writing in *The Oxford History of Classical Reception*, has explored the wide range of classical origins for Arnold's writing (Vance and Wallace, eds., pp. 471–94). Shrimpton's article assesses Arnold's 'important works on classical topics in both verse and prose', his allusions to 'Greek and Latin texts in his poetry', and the 'classical models' which formed the basis of numerous poems (p. 471). 'Hellenism', as Arnold expressed it, became a 'key value' for *Culture and Anarchy* (p. 471), and classical works became both a 'corrective model' and an 'imaginative stimulus for modern literature' (p. 492). Isobel Hurst, in the same volume as Shrimpton, explores Clough's debt to classical literature, drawing on the poet's extensive classical education at Rugby School and Oxford (pp. 495–508). Clough's long poems are discussed at length in Moore's *Victorian Poetry and Modern Life*, as reviewed above.

Arnold's angelic description of Shelley clearly resonated with nineteenth-century readers, and still appeals today. By contrast, Coventry Patmore's *Angel in the House* now seems to signal the gulf between Patmore's culture and that of his present readers. Natasha Moore's article, 'The Realism of *The Angel in the House*: Coventry Patmore's Poem Reconsidered' (*VLC* 43[2015] 41–61), argues that the poem should be reread on its own terms, precisely for its incongruence with the twenty-first century. As Moore states, 'Through the lens of twenty-first-century Victorian literary studies, the upwardly-mobile *Aurora Leigh* seems to capitalize on every possible congruence between the nineteenth century and our own period, while *The Angel* manages only to hit one dissonant chord after another' (p. 58).

The dissonance or consonance of historical cultures with the present day is only one influence on the modern critical canon. In 'The Factory Exile: Ellen Johnston's *Autobiography, Poems and Songs*' (*VP* 53[2015] 77–99), Monica Smith Hart continues the work of highlighting the voices of Victorian working-class poets. Hart opens by noting how, over the last thirty years, 'scholars dedicated to reclaiming the historical and literary legacy of working-class writers have reintroduced Johnston and a handful of her literary peers into Romantic and Victorian studies' (p. 77). Johnston's reputation has now been revived through anthologies and biographical writings; however, as Hart indicates, she has been the subject of only one monograph. While the revival of her work has focused on 'our understanding of nineteenth-century working-class life and writing' (p. 78), Hart focuses on Johnston's 'poetic persona', and on close analysis of her poems. A further article, by R.K.R. Thornton, examines 'Joseph Skipsey and John Clare: Two Labouring-Class Poets' (*JCSJ* 34[2015] 23–32; also reviewed in Chapter XIII).

Decadent poetry garnered a significant amount of attention in 2015. In *Literature and the Politics of Post-Victorian Decadence* Kristin Mahoney is concerned with the critical function of decadence, taking as her subject writers and artists of the early twentieth century and considering their works in the context of their *fin-de-siècle* precursors. While not, therefore, focused on nineteenth-century poetry per se, this interesting book does offer some new perspectives on the reception and legacies of diverse works from the Yellow Nineties. Taking a similar approach, James Campbell's *Oscar Wilde, Wilfred Owen, and Male Desire: Begotten, Not Made* traces the development of Wilde's ideas on queer male desire into the twentieth century. While Wilde's poetry is not Campbell's chief concern, over the course of the book he offers readings of 'Charmides', 'The Sphinx', and 'The Ballad of Reading Gaol' among other poems in order to build an understanding of Wilde as a theorist of same-sex love. In 'Sex, Lies, and Poetry: *The Ballad of Reading Gaol*' (*CQ* 44[2015] 299–320) Peter Robinson is concerned with the interplay between subjectivity and truth in elements of Wilde's last poem. By considering the *Ballad* as a performative piece of writing Robinson teases apart lies that are not lies and exaggerated half-truths, describing its multivalence and concluding that it 'must have truth-values beyond its local inaccuracies of fact and emphasis' (p. 320). Joseph Bristow and Rebecca N. Mitchell's impressive *Oscar Wilde's Chatterton: Literary History, Romanticism, and the Art of Forgery* is not principally concerned with poetry. However, short sections on 'Wilde and the "Great Romantic Movement": From Keats to Rossetti' (pp. 129–49) and 'Watts, Rossetti, and Chatterton: "The New Romantic School"' (pp. 149–59) enlarge upon how Wilde positioned himself in relation to his poetic predecessors. Bristow and Mitchell argue that his identification with the Pre-Raphaelites 'had a political edge' (p. 132), highlight the importance of Keats to Wilde's preparation of *Poems*, and include as an annotated appendix Wilde's notes on D.G. Rossetti's *Ballads and Sonnets* (pp. 411–15). In 'Devils, Souls, and the Spectre of Matthew Arnold in Oscar Wilde's The Picture of Dorian Gray' (AVSJ 20:ii[2015] 14–27), Ilona Urquhart 'proposes that Wilde's only novel, *The Picture of Dorian Gray*, is responding to Arnold's claim that "most of what now passes with us for religion and philosophy will be replaced by poetry"' (p. 14).

Kostas Boyiopoulos's monograph *The Decadent Image: The Poetry of Wilde, Symons, and Dowson* focuses on 'lyrics preoccupied with art, artificiality, intense subjective states and self-analysis' published in the final decades of the nineteenth century. He argues that these reveal a crisis of language: 'as it can never escape its syntactic condition, it projects the poet's heightened sense of... unsatisfied yearnings' (p. 3). Beginning by teasing out important distinctions between the detachment of Aestheticism and the immersion inherent in Decadence, Boyiopoulos goes on to trace 'the development of the erotic encounter between the self and artifice' (p. 4) over three sections, beginning with Wilde, proceeding through Symons, and ending with Dowson. Chapter 2 focuses on the way Wilde's 1881 *Poems* was 'reincarnated' as a work of Decadence upon its reissue by the Bodley Head in 1892. By viewing this volume as a preface to British Decadence, Boyiopoulos constructs an argument whereby the 'dialectic between life and art, mind and pleasure, in

continuous irresolution' (p. 33) underpins the polarization between material
and ideal selfhood across the *fin de siècle*. Chapter 3 conducts parallel close
readings of Wilde's long poem 'Charmides' and the collection *The Sphinx*,
deftly drawing out the theme of futility, in regard to positioning actual
sensuality within poetic space, through analysis of the multiple 'barren
collisions and clashes' (p. 43) that characterize these poems' erotic participation with art objects and jewels. In the next section Boyiopoulos turns to
the city-poetics of Symons's volumes *Silhouettes* [1892] and *London Nights*
[1895/7]. In chapter 4 he demonstrates the self-reflexivity of Symons's poems in
relation to the concepts of fragmentation, strangeness, *flâneur*-ship, and
the subjectivity of the gaze. Chapter 5 is entitled 'Bianca's Body: Nerves and
the *Flâneurie* of Flesh', and engagingly considers encounters with the female
body and/as text and city in these two volumes. The final two chapters focus
on Dowson's *Verses* [1896] and *Decorations in Verse and Prose* [1897],
Boyiopoulos highlighting the 'elusive and paradoxical' relationship between
the self (or sensuality) and artifice in these works (p. 132). Chapter 6 provides
an analysis of states of liminality in relation to death in Dowson's poems,
including a consideration of how this is connected to the imagery of Catholic
ritual. In the final chapter the multifarious nature of Dowson's 'desiring of
desire' comes to the fore as Boyiopoulos demonstrates the 'tactics of non-
encounter' in these poems (p. 152), closing with an extended discussion of the
dead girl as a key aesthetic trope. Over the course of the monograph a clear
argument is constructed whereby the 'poetics of morbid dissatisfaction *in* and
*with* artifice' (p. 23) evident in these poets' work forms an important mid-point
between the discourses of Romanticism and modernism.

In addition, Boyiopoulos contributed the chapter ' "Enchanted Wine":
Symons, Dowson, and Keats's Intoxications' to Boyiopoulos and Sandy, eds.,
*Decadent Romanticism* (pp. 59–74). Boyiopoulos finds layers of connection
between these poets' works, whereby 'writing and creativity themselves are the
ultimate intoxicant' (p. 74). He finds continuity, as well as departures, within
the sensuousness of Keats's and Symons's poetry, and Dowson's Keatsian
preoccupation with melancholy as a drug.

Articles on Michael Field covered a variety of topics and approaches. Olivia
Malfait highlights how the process of co-authorship influenced Field's critical
reception in ' "Against the world": Michael Field, Female Marriage and the
Aura of Amateurism' (*ES* 96[2015] 157–72). Malfait demonstrates how the act
of collaboration was deemed by many a sign of amateurism, and suggests that
recent scholars' attempts to tease apart the contributions of each half of the
pair undermines Field's artistic and intellectual approach. Kristin Mahoney
also focuses on the specifics of collaboration. In her short article 'Michael
Field and Queer Community at the *Fin de Siècle*' (*VR* 41:i[2015] 35–40) she
identifies 'Bradley and Cooper's interest in models of alliance that destabilize
the boundary between self and other' (p. 37) as a queer sensibility. Mahoney
broadens the scope of this observation out from their shared writing practices
to consider their links to artistic communities such as the Century Guild, their
engagement with non-human animals, and the importance of intimate
friendship networks.

Rob Gallagher and Ana Parejo Vadillo describe and reflect upon their digital edition of Field's poem 'Antonello da Messina's *Saint Sebastian*' in 'Animating *Sight and Song*: A Meditation on Identity, Fair Use, and Collaboration' (*19* 21[2015] 31 paras.). Through their collaborative response to, and remediation of, this poem via layered images, hypertext annotations, and GIFs they demonstrate Field's relevance to contemporary concerns such as 'technological mediation, the role of archives in cultural production, the nature of collaborative and collective authorship, the function of avatars and aliases in identity work, and the changing relationship between art, life, and life writing' (para. 31). In ' "This hot-house of decadent chronicle": Michael Field, Nietzsche and the Dance of Modern Poetic Drama' (*Women* 26[2015] 195–220) Parejo Vadillo reads Field's later Roman dramas—*The World at Auction*, *The Race of Leaves*, and *Julia Domna*—as poetically experimental texts that prefigure modernism. She argues that these poetic dramas were badly received because they were too avant-garde, and that by positioning these works in relation to decadence, Nietzsche's philological criticism, and early twentieth-century ballet Field's radicalism and relevance become apparent.

Additional work on poets of the later Victorian period includes Mihail Evans's interest in 'figures who challenge our assumptions about the boundary between the realms of the living and the dead' (p. 857) in 'Housman's Spectral Shropshire' (*VLC* 43[2015] 857–73). Fixing upon the Derridean concepts of spectrality and hauntology, Evans demonstrates important parallels with Housman's poetic approach to engaging with the realm of the dead; he argues not for a model of influence or theoretical application but for observing the mutuality of their concerns. Francis O'Gorman uses Walter Pater's 'sense of exactness' (p. 79) to guide his reading of 'Lionel Johnson and Charing Cross' (*JPRS* 24[2015] 78–96). Reproducing in full 'By the Statue of King Charles the First at Charing Cross Station' (composed 1889, published 1892), O'Gorman proceeds to draw out the composition history of Johnson's poem, identifying several specific contexts that embed it in a time and place and arguing that this was a provocative poem about contemporary politics and the new.

Important work also appeared on Thomas Hardy, led by Indy Clark's *Thomas Hardy's Pastoral: An Unkindly May*. This monograph focuses principally upon his poetic works, arguing that Hardy's adaptation of the pastoral tradition enacts both a crisis of social mobility and a crisis of form. Chapter 1 demonstrates how Hardy's Arcadian landscapes are not simple idylls, but evoke the knowable rural geography and society of Wessex. His poems therefore delineate dialectical spaces that reveal a complex relationship between labour and class. In chapter 2 Clark focuses on the importance of Hardy as observer and draws out the influence of the Romantics and Darwin upon his perception of pastoral and representations of landscape, nature, and work. Hardy's attitudes to the rural working class underpin chapter 3, which is concerned with his characterization of labourers; while none of his novels has a member of this class as a protagonist, Clark observes that his poetic use of first-person narrative techniques gives such individuals a voice. The eloquence of these speakers, he argues, is both empowering to the labouring classes and confounds the expectations of Hardy's largely middle-class, metropolitan readership. Clark goes on to deftly interrogate the use of the term 'peasant' in Hardy's poetry and prose, and his use of the name 'Hodge' to denote a stereotypical agricultural labourer, demonstrating that these signify neither ridicule nor idealization and bringing these to bear upon Hardy's own social mobility. In his final chapter Clark goes on to explore more explicitly the pastoral of modernity, considering how Hardy's later poems negotiate with early twentieth-century contexts.

The focus of Linda M. Shires's innovative article 'Matter, Consciousness, and the Human in *Wessex Poems*' (*SEL* 55[2015] 899–924) is the function of the thirty-one rarely reproduced and often ignored illustrations that accompany Hardy's *Wessex Poems and Other Verses*. She considers 'all potential ways of producing meaning between image and text' via W.J.T. Mitchell's conception of 'image X text relationships' (p. 900), offering several illuminating close readings of these two facets of Hardy's 1898 volume. Ralph Pite's chapter on Thomas Hardy for Vance and Wallace, eds., *The Oxford History of Classical Reception* (pp. 601–18) engages with the georgic strain of Hardy's early poetry, while focusing more broadly upon the influence of classical literature upon his novels.

Much of the research described above and below touches upon the ramifications of periodical publication. However, 2015 saw fewer pieces taking periodical poetry as their explicit focus. Two such articles did appear in *Victorian Periodicals Review* however. The first was Caley Ehnes and Kylee-Anne Hingston's pedagogical 'Collaborative Knowledge and Merging Media: Teaching Victorian Periodical Print Using Digital Tools' (*VPR* 48[2015] 197–215). The section by Ehnes, 'Teaching Victorian Poetry in Context' (pp. 199–203), reflects on teaching practices that encourage students to conceptualize poetry as part of periodical culture while critically evaluating the curated nature of digital databases. She also recounts her experience of developing a wiki project, *Victorian Poetry, Poetics, and Contexts*, whereby students produced work that grew out of their engagement with *Victorian Poetry Network*. Barbara Barrow's article is ' "The Waterloo of democracy against despotism": Chartist Internationalism and Poetic Repetition in the *Labourer*, 1847–48' (*VPR* 48[2015] 511–30). She uses the contents of this short-lived periodical to construct an argument regarding 'unity in miscellany' within this publication context. Barrow convincingly identifies how, through the poetic techniques of repetition and refrain, writers co-opted and revised the legacy of the battle of Waterloo for the workers' cause 'as a powerful symbol of international cooperation and armed resistance' (pp. 512, 513).

Marjorie Stone's important article 'The "Advent" of *Aurora Leigh*: Critical Myths and Periodical Debates' (*Branch* [2015] 83 paras.) contextualizes the publication of Barrett Browning's poem in 1856 and effectively overturns received opinions about the overwhelmingly negative critical response to it. By drawing on a breadth of periodical sources—British and American quarterlies, monthlies, literary magazines, and newspapers—Stone supplements the regularly cited condemnatory reviews printed in some influential British periodicals, demonstrating that early readers responded in a variety of ways to the form, themes, and narrative of *Aurora Leigh*, and that many were impressed by its power and originality. Barbara Barrow is interested in Barrett

Browning's political woman-centred poetics in 'Gender, Language, and the Politics of Disembodiment in *Aurora Leigh*' (*VP* 53[2015] 243–62). She asserts that the poem is built upon a fundamental conflict between the social body, the communal body of readers, and the poet's embodied sensibility, and identifies a subtext in *Aurora Leigh* whereby 'images of abstracted, vanishing, and intangible bodies' (p. 243) function as an intervention into gendered conceptions of embodiment. As discussed above, much of Chapman's book *Networking the Nation* is concerned with Barrett Browning and her Florentine circle.

In 'Material Spirits and Immaterial Forms: The Immaterial Materiality of Elizabeth Barrett Browning's Abolitionist Poetry' (*VP* 53[2015] 353–74) Rebecca D. Soares proposes that recent material culture approaches should be counterbalanced by the idea that 'even the physical object of the book is infused with immaterial significance' (p. 354). Soares contends that Barrett Browning's interest in spiritualism points to her desire to transcend material boundaries, her political poetry seeking to develop a transnational perspective that uses the liminality of poetic form to bridge the material/immaterial binary. Olivia Loksing Moy traces echoes of *The Mysteries of Udolpho* in poems by Wordsworth, Keats, and Barrett Browning in 'Radcliffe's Poetic Legacy: Female Confinement in the "Gothic Sonnet"' (*WW* 22[2015] 376–94). She discusses 1790s novelistic tropes in Barrett Browning's metasonnet 'The Soul's Expression', showing how 'the discourse of entrapment and liberation is re-imagined through the theme of Gothic motherhood' (p. 388).

Besides her chapter on Clough, Isobel Hurst contributes a chapter on Barrett Browning to Vance and Wallace, eds., *The Oxford History of Classical Reception* (pp. 449–70). She identifies how Barrett Browning's classical education enabled her to try out 'a variety of strategies for placing herself within a literary tradition dominated by men' (p. 452). For example she challenged epic tradition directly in early works such as *The Battle of Marathon*, but later distanced herself from imitation by writing 'poems of everyday life in which ancient images and characters are often to be found' (p. 467). In the same volume Yopie Prins's chapter, 'Translating Tragedy: Robert Browning's Greek Decade' (pp. 509–38), focuses not on his 'poetic negotiations' of classical texts but his publication of three ' "transcripts" of Greek tragedy within elaborate frames of his own poetic design' during the 1870s (p. 509). She argues that these translations are 'highly performative' (p. 534) and a direct contribution to nineteenth-century debates surrounding the practice of translation and the contemporary relevance and reception of Hellenism. Chapter 3 of Annmarie Drury's book *Translation as Transformation*, reviewed in full above, is concerned with similar themes in Browning's works. Alan Barr draws Barrett Browning and Browning's masterpieces into dialogue in 'The Making of the Poet, the Making of a Poem: *Aurora Leigh* and *The Ring and the Book*' (*VJCL* 127[2015] 46–59). He draws out their complementarity with regard to the themes of artistic creation and poetic self-fashioning, and argues that 'the subject of the first anticipates the subject of the latter' (p. 57).

Volume 22 of the Wedgestone Press's fully annotated edition of *The Brownings' Correspondence* was published in 2015, edited by Philip Kelley,

Scott Lewis, Edward Hagan, Joseph Phelan, and Rhian Williams. It covers November 1855 to June 1856 (Letters 3678–3809). The couple were living in Paris during this period, which saw Browning's *Men and Women* published in the UK and America, alongside Barrett Browning's 'A Curse for a Nation'. The appendices include useful biographical sketches of principal correspondents, a list of supporting documents, and a large number of contemporary reviews of the Brownings' works. Marcus Waithe's chapter, ' "Another sort of writing"? Invalidism and Poetic Labour in the Letters of Elizabeth Barrett Browning' (in Ellis, ed., *Letter Writing Among Poets: From William Wordsworth to Elizabeth Bishop*, pp. 126–40), focuses on the Brownings' courtship correspondence. He argues that 'Barrett's letters eluded secondary status, and became a testing ground for unconventional work ethics and excluded modes of production' (pp. 128–9), as she asserts agency and authorship in ways that transcend her ill health.

Richard Cronin and Dorothy McMillan state that their 'principal aim' in editing the impressive 21st-Century Oxford Authors annotated edition of Robert Browning's poetry is 'to represent Browning as a poet' (p. xxviii). In order to facilitate tracing the development of his writings across his life, the selections are ordered chronologically by publication in book form, and are printed as they were first published. The editors' decision not to include extracts of longer poems—which either appear in their entirety or not at all—means that *The Ring and the Book* is not represented within their selection, although *The Inn Album* is present 'to introduce a 21st-century audience to a little-read and shockingly modern work' (p. xli). The comprehensive selections from the rest of his corpus are interspersed with three pieces of correspondence, Browning's essay on Shelley, and several illustrations (principally reproducing manuscript or title pages). In the introduction a balance is struck between biographical and critical details, and the 200 pages of notes include a brief but illuminating headnote for each poem.

In 'Sordello and the Poetics of Reception' (*EIC* 65[2015] 144–62) Clara Dawson provides a new perspective on Browning's supposed obscurity by addressing how he 'openly portrays the self-conscious making of a poetic persona whose identity is formed very explicitly through a relation to his perceived audiences' (p. 146). Dawson argues that the underlying tension between words and deeds in the poem is ultimately unresolved, highlighting Browning's appeals to the reader to attend to the creation of a multivalent narrative with a multiplicity of auditors. In ' "Let the rank tongue blossom": Browning's Stuttering' (*VP* 53[2015] 103–32) Ewan Jones draws out how a range of critics have come to apply the terms 'stammering' and 'stuttering' to Browning's corpus, and their presence in his poems themselves. Jones's focus is upon 'stuttering both as literal theme and as a variety of novel technical effects' (p. 105) in *Sordello*, and he compellingly shows how the hesitations and emphases of phonemic reproduction both underlie and propel metre, narrative, and characterization over the course of this long poem.

Several articles seek to read Browning alongside significant intertexts. Stefan Hawlin argues for the importance of Keats to Browning's poetic development in 'Reading Browning Intertextually: "A Toccata of Galuppi's" and "Ode on a Grecian Urn"' (*VP* 53[2015] 263–79). Hawlin builds upon the formal and thematic parallels by suggesting that Browning was not echoing but renegotiating the religious–aesthetic binary at work in Keats's poem through his presentation of speakers, choice of location, and overarching poignant message. Margaret A. Loose finds a 'range of intertextual Lucrezias' (p. 133) in 'Blended Selves and the Spectacle of Subjection in Browning's "Andrea del Sarto"' (*VP* 53[2015] 133–49). She argues that in this poem Browning is concerned with the policing and disempowerment of women, and through a series of close readings shows how he blurs the characters' separate selves and gender identities in this poem to illuminate the far-reaching consequences of this type of social control upon both men and women. Emily Walker Heady argues, in 'Robert Browning, Theologian: The Incarnational Politics of "Fra Lippo Lippi"' (*Renascence* 67[2015] 147–61), that Browning's poetry and Lippo's art both indicate that they 'see clearly the disruptive political and aesthetic implications of religion' (p. 151). By discussing 'the intersections between aesthetics and ethics, poetic praxis and politics' (p. 147) Heady suggests that Browning critiques contemporary religious practices that too often divide spiritual life from what is conceived as the real world. Finally, Jennifer McDonell explores Henry James's conception of two Brownings—the private genius and the public personality, which demonstrate the mobility of the writing self—in her consideration of these two men's intertwined responses to discourses surrounding celebrity and the public, in her article 'Henry James, Literary Fame, and the Problem of Robert Browning' (*CS* 27:iii[2015] 43–62).

Major editorial advances have continued to transform the landscape of Hopkins criticism and scholarship. For the third consecutive year, a new volume of Hopkins's collected works was released by Oxford University Press. Edited by Lesley Higgins, volume 3 focuses on Hopkins's diaries, journals, and notebooks, and is reviewed in Chapter XIX. 'Passion and Playfulness in the Letters of Gerard Manley Hopkins' (in Ellis, ed., pp. 141–54), by Michael D. Hurley, treats the recently published correspondence from the same series as 'a vital resource' for understanding Hopkins's 'achievement as a poet' (p. 153). Hurley animates the literary criticism contained within these letters in relation to the style of the correspondence itself, revealing aspects of Hopkins's poetic thought that have rarely been noticed. 'Hopkins's Dividing Errors', by Jane Wright, is an eloquent and nuanced exploration of Hopkins's notion of vice, and its relationship with the perfections and errors inherent in artistic endeavour (*LI* 17[2015] 183–97). Hopkins famously described 'inscape' as 'the vice of distinctiveness', and Wright's article teases out the various theological and artistic implications of this statement through close readings of Hopkins's poetry and his own reading of Duns Scotus.

Hopkins's relationship to artistic 'beauty' acted as a starting point for two essays, by Angela Leighton and Michael O'Neill. Leighton's chapter, 'Something in the Works: Frost, Bishop and the Idea of Beauty' (in O'Neill, Sandy, and Wootton, eds., *The Persistence of Beauty: Victorians to Moderns*, pp. 103–16), hears in Elizabeth Bishop's poem 'Sandpiper' the echoes of Hopkins's line, 'beauty, beauty, beauty', from 'The Leaden Echo and the Golden Echo'. She thus reconnects nineteenth-century notions of beauty to poets such as Bishop, whose relationship with the word has been characterized as more distant, wary, or oblique. O'Neill's chapter in the same volume, 'The

Difficulty of Beauty: Hopkins, Yeats, Hart Crane, Spender' (pp. 117–33), finds new insights even in poems as well-studied as 'The Windhover' and 'To what serves Mortal Beauty?', as his usual flair for close reading allows the effects of the poetry to enter his critical prose. Kate Hext's 'Decadence and the Fate of the Romantic Sublime' (in Boyiopoulos and Sandy, eds., pp. 145–60) considers how aesthetes and decadents were 'self-conscious', 'selective', and 'unsystematic' inheritors of Romantic poets'. Her chapter focuses on the 'nostalgia' of Hopkins and Pater for the 'unrecapturable past of Romanticism' (p. 160).

'Stem and Skein: Order and Evolution in Hopkins', by Daniel Williams (*VP* 53[2015] 423–54), pursues the poet's notions of order through 'instress' and beats. The article also argues for Hopkins's intellectual absorption of 'counter-Darwinian materials' (p. 445) as a central part of his 'energetic vision of order' (p. 445). Norman White's 'The Journals of Gerard Manley Hopkins' (*HQ* 42[2015] 23–48) investigates the poet's journals with a keen eye to their contemporary context, depictions of nature, and limited perspectives on 'people outside the cloister' (p. 48). Justin Tackett (*HQ* 42[2015] 1–22) examines Hopkins's initial reception, and the influence of 'global events'—from war to commercialization—on the publishing practices of Oxford University Press in the early twentieth century. In 'Translating Hopkins' (*HQ* 42[2015] 85–101), Dmitri Manin speaks from his own experiences as a translator of Hopkins and argues for the merits of poetic, rather than literal, translation. Michael Meeuwis considers how Herbert Spencer's 'The Philosophy of Language' enables an understanding of Hopkins's concern with 'public influence' in his poetry, in 'Herbert Spencer, Gerard Hopkins, and the Force of Poetic Expression' (*MP* 113[2015] 246–66).

New historical and biographical parameters for Hopkins's poetry were explored in several further articles. In 'Robert Frost's Encounters with Robert Bridges' (*HQ* 42[2015] 49–63), Patrick Samway S.J. speculates that Frost had read Hopkins, drawing on new and 'solid evidence' (p. 51). That word, 'solid', masks what might otherwise be termed an informed guess. Samway maintains that during Frost's 1914 dinner with Bridges, 'Bridges most likely mentioned the poetry of Hopkins' (p. 56), and 'Frost most likely mentioned his inchoate views on the relationship of sound and sense' (p. 54). Similarly, of Harriet Monroe's 1913 *Poetry*, he writes that 'It can be assumed that Frost read this important manifesto, since he knew both Flint and Pound' (p. 58). The essay's confidence in its assumptions, however, cannot sustain the strength of its scholarly conclusions. In 'Grace Notes: The Provenance of a Fragment of Hopkins's "The Loss of Eurydice"' (*N&Q* 62[2015] 438–40), Melinda Creech investigates the journey of a manuscript fragment at the University of Texas at Austin. Her article suggests that the fragment of 'The Loss of Eurydice' may have been sent to Hopkins's sister, Grace, in sympathy for the loss of her *fiancé*. The narrative, if verified, would join the wider literary phenomenon of epistolary poems and manuscripts, relevant to nineteenth-century poets from Wordsworth to Tennyson.

The most prominent contribution to the study of Morris's poetry this year was Florence S. Boos's *History and Poetics in the Early Writings of William Morris, 1855–1870* (also reviewed in Section 1 above). This book traces the stages of his literary development across genres through a close engagement with manuscripts, periodical publications, and unpublished works. Chapter 1, ' "If I can": Morris's Early Writings' (pp. 1–17), introduces key features of his work, particularly regarding his engagement with history. Chapter 3 is concerned with reassessing 'Morris's Earliest Poems: Preparation for *The Defence of Guenevere*' (pp. 69–96); Boos demonstrates how reading his juvenilia and earliest drafts provides insights into Morris's precocious intellectual independence and traces the development of themes such as his secularism and medievalism. Chapter 6 turns to 'The Sources of *The Defence of Guenevere*' and his strategies for engaging with these (pp. 159–94). In the following chapter, 'Gender Polarities in *The Defence*' (pp. 195–230), Boos considers in depth how in this poem Morris created an ethical framework through which to explore the polarized nature of social and sexual roles for women and show how rhetorical resistance might offer liberation from these, · thus anticipating the progressive plurality and complexity of female characters in his later works. Boos's article 'Unprintable Lyrics: The Unpublished Poems of William Morris' (*VP* 53[2015] 193–225) provides an important reassessment of the later personal lyrics that were written during his estrangement from Jane Morris; while some went on to appear in print, many remained unpublished at Morris's death. Boos traces the composition and publication histories of these poems, which range across a wide variety of forms. The well-illustrated article reproduces many of these lyrics, and provides readings that demonstrate how Morris often effaced and displaced their introspective tendencies upon their inclusion in later volumes.

Katja Lindskog argues, in ' "Well-known things": Experience, Distance, and Perspective in William Morris's "The Defence of Guenevere" ' (*VP* 53[2015] 455–74), that well-documented tensions underlying Morris's artistic and social goals can be resolved through a model of ideal readerly participation, which amounts to 'a collective and collaborative engagement with the past' (p. 456). Through Lindskog's innovative approach to the *Defence* we are encouraged to understand the poem as enabling an experience of, rather than being a story about, the past. In 'William Morris, Extraction Capitalism, and the Aesthetics of Surface' (*VS* 57[2015] 395–404), Elizabeth Carolyn Miller uses the prologue to *The Earthly Paradise* to support her argument that 'an emphasis on cleanliness runs through Morris's environmental critique' (p. 399), but otherwise focuses on his prose works as exemplifying his eco-socialism.

Stephen Harrison contributes a chapter on Morris to Vance and Wallace, eds., *The Oxford History of Classical Reception* (pp. 559–78). Spanning a range of Morris's original poems and translations, Harrison identifies how Morris's works 'represent a very individual (and unclassical) approach to the Graeco-Roman heritage which met the favour of the mid-Victorian period' (p. 559), creating hybrid texts that merge classical sources with medieval and Renaissance elements. Jack Mitchell offers a reassessment of Morris's translation practices in 'William Morris' Synthetic *Aeneids*: Virgil as Physical Object' (*T&L* 24[2015] 1–22). He argues that in *The Aeneids of Virgil* [1875] Morris layered 'heroic, classical, Dark Ages, medieval, and Renaissance material' to signal the chronological layering and textual history of the source, and aspired to convey a sense of artistic unity through its publication in the form of an illuminated manuscript (an argument supported by several helpful images). Also concerned with Morris's medievalism is Yoshiko Seki's monograph, *The Rhetoric of Retelling Old Romances*, which is reviewed in full below.

In *To Build a Shadowy Isle of Bliss: William Morris's Radicalism and the Embodiment of Dreams*, edited by Michelle Weinroth and Paul Leduc Browne, two chapters are concerned with Morris's poetry. 'Telling Time: Song's Rhythms in Morris's Late Work', by Elizabeth Helsinger (pp. 106–23), considers lyric strategies in *Chants for Socialists*. Helsinger provides a series of close readings that amount to a reconsideration of Morris's late poetry; she argues that his actively political poetry that draws on historic forms is crucially underpinned by rhythm, which is used to 'forge a social body and sustain it in the complex time it must inhabit' (p. 107). She concludes by considering prosody in the lyrics that are embedded within his late romances. In 'The Pre-Raphaelite Tongue: The Politics of Antiquarian Poetics' (pp. 124–48) David Latham makes a case for the importance of Morris's desire to transform archetypes and overturn paradigms through his works. Focusing on *The Defence* and *The Earthly Paradise* alongside Morris's prose, Latham argues that 'he is developing the prose poem as a new genre of art' (p. 139).

This year saw a large quantity of publications on the Rossettis and Pre-Raphaelite poetry. Laura Kilbride nonetheless contends that scholarship of the last decade on literary Pre-Raphaelitism has not kept pace with that on the movement's visual arts. In her useful article 'The Pre-Raphaelite School: Recent Approaches' (*LitComp* 12[2015] 615–26) Kilbride questions what we are to understand by the label Pre-Raphaelite when seeking to define a school of poetry, and provides an overview of recent debates regarding this appellation under the headings ambidexterity, brotherhood, and style.

Marianne Van Remoortel's chapter, 'Christina Rossetti and the Economics of Periodical Poetry' (in her *Women, Work and the Victorian Periodical*, pp. 71–91), illuminates Rossetti's publication strategy. Van Remoortel demonstrates the 'profound preoccupation with the materiality and economics of writing' (p. 71) that can be found when reading the poems that appeared in *Macmillan's* alongside contemporary correspondence; these 'pot-boilers', as Rossetti called them, imply an underlying tension between monetary and artistic value in her oeuvre. The reprinting, setting to music, and parodying of 'A Birthday' is shown to be indicative of the transactions inherent in the circulation of texts within periodical contexts. Joshua King's *Imagined Spiritual Communities in Britain's Age of Print* (also reviewed in Section 1 above) closes with the chapter 'Christina Rossetti's *Verses*: A Multi-Fashioned Community of Strangers' (pp. 232–88). King argues that in her final volume of poetry Rossetti constructed an imagined transnational community founded on spiritual citizenship and the communion of saints. He demonstrates how the poetic cycle's language, form, and structure encourage readers of various denominations 'to imagine their membership in a community that hopes for an eternal society in which all will fully achieve their unique selfhood in unity with God and others' (p. 233). David A. Kent introduces 'Four Unpublished Letters by Christina Rossetti' (*JPRS* 24:i[2015] 44–66), the transcriptions and photos of which are reproduced in his article. Located in the Clara Thomas

Archives and Special Collections at York University Toronto, these letters to Lady Welby date from the summer of 1881 and concern a seeming attempt to commission Rossetti to write a poem about a significant spiritual event experienced by Welby.

'Goblin Market' continues to be approached from a variety of perspectives. Robbie McLaughlan reads the poem alongside Susan Sontag's 'The Artist as Exemplary Sufferer' and the Bakhtinian grotesque and carnivalesque, setting out the 'perverse logic' (p. 252) of the formula laid out in the article's title: 'The Rossettian Formula: No Love without Suffering' (*Victo* 5[2015] 251–68). He places Rossetti's poem within the nineteenth-century sphere of consumerism, and deftly draws out the importance of (Christian and artistic) suffering in her conceptualization of desire and love. Anna E. MacDonald argues, in 'Edible Women and Milk Markets: The Linguistic and Lactational Exchanges of "Goblin Market"' (*NCGS* 11:iii[2015] 17 paras.), that 'Rossetti employs the female, *liquid* expression vested in lactation imagery to signify the female *linguistic* expression of an emerging women's poetry' (para. 1). Relating imagery in 'Goblin Market' to Victorian anxieties about breastfeeding that surfaced in the late 1850s and early 1860s, MacDonald seeks to reconcile literal and symbolic readings of Rossetti's often discussed food imagery. In 'Rehearsing Social Justice: Temporal Ghettos and the Poetic Way Out in "Goblin Market" and "The Song of the Shirt"' (*VP* 53[2015] 151–69) Jennifer MaClure approaches the theme of disenfranchisement by placing Rossetti's poem in dialogue with Thomas Hood's (and also discusses the latter alongside Barrett Browning's 'The Cry of the Children'). She convincingly argues that these poems centre upon individuals 'marginalized through their experience of time' and that 'Goblin Market' offers 'a poetic solution' to those marginalized by 'temporal injustice' (p. 152), offering a new perspective upon the oppression of repetitive time for women and workers.

Elsewhere connections are drawn between Rossetti and other significant poetic figures. In 'Voices at the Convent Threshold: An Exchange between Christina Rossetti and Gerard Hopkins' (*JPRS* 24:i[2015] 67–75) Gerald Roberts identifies how Hopkins's early fragmentary poem 'Beyond the Cloister' began life as 'an answer to Miss Rossetti's Convent Threshold' (p. 67) and draws out ways in which the two poets were motivated by shared concerns. Simon Humphries identifies and interrogates echoes of Tennyson throughout her poetic career, in 'Christina Rossetti's Tennysonianism' (*CQ* 44[2015] 43–61). He seeks to demonstrate that Rossetti was acutely aware of these borrowings; she sought to elide them in several instances, but on other occasions embraced them as opening up intertextual responses that demonstrate her 'formidable poetic intelligence' (p. 61). Humphries adeptly interrogates how Rossetti has been associated with poetesses by nineteenth-century and recent critics alike, and suggests that in aligning herself with Tennyson Rossetti was attempting to remove herself from an explicitly gendered mode of literary production. Rebecca N. Mitchell demonstrates how the varied work of Robert Herrick (1591–1674) was appropriated and adapted, in 'Robert Herrick, Victorian Poet: Christina Rossetti, George Meredith, and the Victorian Recovery of Hesperides' (*MP* 113[2015] 88–115). Mitchell highlights how allusions to Herrick underscore the multiplicity and ambivalence that characterize much of Rossetti's work, identifying links between his 'Cherrie-Ripe' and 'Goblin Market' and formal echoes in *Sing-Song*. She goes on to show how Meredith's early poems use Herrick as a model through which to 'question social and sexual norms' (p. 105), and that elements of Herrick's distinctive verse surface in works of the 1890s. In 'Christina Rossetti and *Sir Gawayne and the Green Knight*' (*SEL* 55[2015] 861–78) Laura Forsberg argues that the Early English Text Society's 1864 edition of *Gawayne* was a key source for Rossetti's long 1865 poem 'The Prince's Progress'. Through a discussion of the former poem's Victorian reception, and attending to the form and content of both, Forberg demonstrates ways in which Rossetti critiques and 'reconceptualizes the medievalist quest epic as a narrative of spiritual discernment and a warning against moral thoughtlessness for the Victorian age' (p. 862).

In 'Sacramental Memorializing: Upon the Death of Dante Gabriel Rossetti' (*NCC* 37[2015] 215–31) Karen Dieleman discusses the form and function of Christina Rossetti's poem 'Birchington Churchyard', alongside the other memorials her family created for her brother: his tombstone and stained-glass window. Dieleman argues that locational memory played an important role in 'confirm[ing] spiritual hope as her principal posture toward Gabriel's life and death' (p. 220). In ' "Love that releases no beloved from loving": Christina and Dante Rossetti's Reaction to the Courtly Love Convention of Dante Alighieri and the Idealization of the Female Muse' (*JPRS* 24:2[2015] 47–62) Azelina Flint suggests that both poets 'align themselves with a shared tradition of troubadour poetry through investing themselves with the authority to reinterpret Dante' (p. 48), although this manifests in distinct ways. Flint's discussion focuses on D.G. Rossetti's paintings and Christina Rossetti's sonnet sequence 'Monna Innominata'.

Brian Donnelly highlights the need to make connections across disciplinary boundaries in *Reading Dante Gabriel Rossetti: The Painter as Poet*, arguing that in his corpus the discourses of sexuality and representation are fundamentally intertextual. Donnelly begins this well-illustrated book with a reading of *Helen of Troy* as a double portrait representing both the celebrated and the marginalized parts of Helen's mythology, and suggests that this 'visible deconstruction of woman' is fundamental to Rossetti's prose and poetry. Chapter 1, 'Inscribing Mary', centres upon reading the two sonnets 'Mary's Girlhood (For a Picture)' alongside *The Girlhood of the Virgin Mary* and *Ecce Ancilla Domini!*, and then considering these in connection with the structurally similar 'Found' and *Found*. Donnelly argues that the latter amounts to a secular reconfiguration of the former, and draws out the importance of Rossetti's undermining of traditional expectations surrounding the Virgin Mary, and Victorian womanhood, here and elsewhere. In chapter 2, 'The Poetics of Ownership', Donnelly demonstrates how Rossetti responded to medieval sources through a deliberately modern Victorian lens. Beginning by drawing out the theme of artistic and representational limitation in the story 'St Agnes of Intercession', he goes on to trace this concern through several poems, later turning to Rossetti's re-evaluations of love and life after death. The following chapter, 'Fleshy Designs', dwells upon the acts of looking and speaking, and the dynamic of absence and presence in Rossetti's poetry and paintings of the 1860s. These are read as commentary upon women's developing public existence, and are considered in dialogue with his sister's engagement with these themes in 'Goblin Market'. In the final chapter, ' "Found" in the City', Donnelly reads 'Found' and 'Jenny', both poems with a contemporary setting, against novelists' deployment of urban spaces in *The Mayor of Casterbridge*, *A Pair of Blue Eyes*, *David Copperfield*, and *Oliver Twist*. This opens up into an analysis of ownership and impotence, betrayal and revelation, in relation to ambiguities in gender relations in Rossetti's works. Donnelly's afterword draws our attention to poem and painting *Astarte Syriaca*, and concludes that Rossetti's intertexts 'realize for the spectator the inherent doubling created when images and texts are brought together, of the possibilities they embrace, the limitlessness they attempt to encompass' (p. 162).

The final chapter of Dometa Wiegand Brothers's monograph *The Romantic Imagination and Astronomy: On All Sides Infinity* is entitled 'Rossetti: Reconciliation and Recursivity' (pp. 142–76). Brothers argues that, despite D.G. Rossetti's aversion to science, the influence of Keats and others led to 'the inculcation of the operating metaphors left from the previous Romantic scientific exploration ... demystification, and destruction of the beauty of nature' (p. 142). By suggesting 'that science is *not* inherently different to art' (p. 150) she finds points of identification between astronomical models and perspectives and conceits used in Rossetti's paintings and sonnets, specifically 'Soul's Sphere' and 'Willowwood'. Deborah Lutz also situates Rossetti alongside Keats, in the chapter 'Infinite Materiality' in her *Relics of Death in Victorian Literature and Culture* (pp. 14–51). She does so in order to consider the locating of memories in secular relics in association with the idea of the beautiful death, showing how Rossetti 'sacralized' literary figures in his 'epigraph poems that embody death, hold or inscribe remains' (p. 45). Lutz discusses the narrative surrounding the interment and retrieval of his poems from Siddal's grave as linked to Rossetti's figuring and reimagining of death as materialized and aestheticized in poems and paintings. In 'Eros and Revolution: Rossetti and Swinburne on Continental Politics' (*VS* 57[2015] 585–610) Matthew Potolsky identifies and explores how these two poets responded to the 1848 revolutions, focusing on D.G. Rossetti's 'After the French Liberation of Italy, 1859' and 'After the German Subjugation of France'. He argues that, in related but distinct ways, they use 'innovative aestheticist language' (p. 586) to express their anger at what they conceived to be the conservative betrayal of revolutionary ideals; thus 'sexuality is fundamentally political and, more presciently, politics is shot through with erotic energies' (p. 588).

The idea of empathy via the communication of an 'inner standing-point' preoccupies D.M.R. Bentley in 'Dante Gabriel Rossetti's "For an Annunciation, Early German": *Einfühlung*, Inspiration, and Significance' (*JPRS* 24:ii[2015] 35–47). He discusses how in this manuscript poem Rossetti presents us with 'not only the perspectives and emotions of an imagined other, but also an alternative way of perceiving and responding to the world' (p. 36). Bentley also describes his impressive attempts to identify the specific painting of the Annunciation that inspired this poem, Rossetti's earliest sonnet for a picture.

In 'Pre-Raphaelitism, Science, and the Arts in *The Germ*' (*VLC* 43[2015] 689–703) John Holmes demonstrates how *The Germ* provided a forum for the ongoing debate surrounding the relation of science to art; while his focus is primarily on essays and reviews in the short-lived periodical, Holmes also draws out how many of the poems published therein engage in different ways with scientific themes. Holmes then convincingly argues that 'poetry itself becomes a mode of scientific enquiry' (p. 16) in 'Poetry on Pre-Raphaelite Principles: Science, Nature, and Knowledge in William Michael Rossetti's "Fancies at Leisure" and "Mrs. Holmes Grey"' (*VP* 53[2015] 15–39). Focusing upon tropes including 'observation, investigation, experiment, the "adherence to fact," and the "search after truth"' (p. 16), Holmes suggests that in the late 1840s W.M. Rossetti undertook deliberate poetic experiments that engaged with contemporary scientific discourses; these aspired to shared values 'at once to enhance knowledge and to advance the "moral purposes of the Arts"' (p. 37). In 'Speaking with the Dead: The Séance Diary of William Michael Rossetti, 1865–68' (*JPRS* 24:i[2015] 35–43) Andrew Stauffer introduces W.M. Rossetti's diary of séances held with his brother, during which they communicated eight times with Siddal's spirit, and makes intriguing connections between these records and Siddal's presence in D.G. Rossetti's 1880 *Poems*. Michael Rossington's short article, 'William Michael Rossetti and the Organization of Percy Bysshe Shelley in the Later Nineteenth Century' (*ERR* 26[2015] 387–93), illuminates W.M. Rossetti's approach to editing poetry, through which he sought to respect texts' resistance to organization.

Charlotte Ribeyrol argues that Swinburne's poetry shows how he 'both revered and yet distorted' ancient Greek culture 'in accordance with his more personal "fleshy" conception of antiquity' in her chapter for Vance and Wallace, eds., *The Oxford History of Classical Reception* (pp. 619–42). She describes the development of his classicism across his corpus, and suggests that towards the end of his career Swinburne had turned towards the creation of new, more personal myths. Ribeyrol published two further articles, in which she identifies key features of Swinburne's foot-fetishism. In 'Poetic Podophilia: Gautier, Baudelaire, Swinburne, and Classical Foot-Fetishism' (*JVC* 20[2015] 212–29) she focuses upon specifically French influences, beginning by observing that podophilia is 'a critically neglected form of sexual deviance that late nineteenth-century medical writings frequently discussed' (p. 215). Ribeyrol demonstrates how it is the foot in motion that elicits desire in Swinburne's poetry, displacing traditional paradigms of statuesque beauty and metre with 'more subversive and erotically charged forms of versification' (p. 228). While in '"The Feet of Love": Pagan Podophilia from A.C. Swinburne to Isadora Duncan' (*Miranda* 11[2015] 36 paras.) Ribeyrol identifies further important 'liberating prospects offered by such erotic displacements', drawing comparisons between rhythmical treading in Swinburne's poems and 'hellenophile dancer Isadora Duncan who was also an enthusiastic reader of Swinburne's poetry' (para. 6).

In 'Swinburne Reads Keats: Prostitution, Pornography and the Decadence of Aesthetic Critique' (*CogAH* 2[2015] 1–20) Joshua David Gonsalves argues that reading Swinburne's Decadence as looking back to and building upon themes inherent in Keats's Romanticism renegotiates the terms of nineteenth-century masculinity and aestheticism. He interrogates the *appearance* of a gender-transgressing poetics' in Swinburne's *Poems and Ballads* (p. 9, my emphasis), and focuses on both the prostitute and the act of flagellation as 'contradictory "site[s]" of subjectification' (p. 2). Michael O'Neill also considers Swinburne in the light of Romanticism. His chapter ' "Stars caught in my branches": Swinburne and Shelley' (in Boyiopoulos and Sandy, eds., pp. 103–18), identifies how Swinburne's poetry 'invites us to reanimate our understanding of Decadence' via the 'intense reworking' of Shelley's poems (p. 103). This is done through convincing paired readings of generically similar poems: 'To a Seamew' and 'To a Skylark', *Atalanta in Calydon* and *Prometheus Unbound*, *Ave atque Vale* and *Adonaïs*, and 'Thalassius' and *Epipsychidion*. In addition, Francis O'Gorman reads Swinburne alongside Tennyson in an article that is reviewed below (*ES* 96[2015] 277–92) and Potolsky's article, 'Eros and Revolution: Rossetti and Swinburne on Continental Politics' (*VS* 57[2015] 585–610), reviewed above, is concerned with Swinburne's reaction to the 1848 revolutions in 'Les Noyades', 'Arthur's Flogging', and his unfinished novel *Lesbia Brandon*. Laura Fox Gill's 'Melting Bodies: The Dissolution of Bodily Boundaries in Milton and Swinburne' (*VicNet* 6:i[2015] 72–92) is also reviewed above in Section 1. Sara Lyons' study, *Algernon Swinburne and Walter Pater: Victorian Aestheticism, Doubt and Secularisation*, was not received in time for review in this section and will be covered with 2016 works.

In Tennyson studies, two articles by Jane Wright drew on a prodigious frame of reference to reassert the lyrical and cultural significance of bees in the poet's work. 'Tennyson's Bees' (*TRB* 10[2015] 321–39) identifies an etymological connection between the word 'mellifluous', which has so often been used to describe Tennyson's musical style, and the Latin terms for 'honey' and 'to flow'. Wright's commanding style and impressive knowledge—spanning from antiquity to nineteenth-century politics—work to retune our sense of the relations between Tennyson's verse and its literary traditions. The article traces Tennyson's references to humming or murmuring across his works, from 'A Dirge' to 'Lancelot and Elaine'. Another such poem is *The Princess*, where bees are apprehended partly as a sound effect, mimicking or competing with narrative. In 'The Princess and the Bee', Wright shows how this motif also shines new light on the narrative's uneasy social and gender politics (*CQ* 44[2015] 251–73). Wright's proof for these powerful conclusions and observations lies in the meticulous layering of examples, the unmistakable characteristics of scholarly rigour and prolonged thought.

Tennyson's poetry often relies not only on its mellifluousness, but also on its many noises and bizarre effects of sound. In 'Tennyson's Strange Noises: "Dwelling amid these yellowing bowers / to himself he talks" ' (*TRB* 10[2015] 357–71), Phoebe Braithwaite organizes her readings around ideas of onomatopoeia. Pauses between sound patterns form Owen Boynton's subject, in 'Tennyson and the Weight of a Pause' (*VP* 53[2015] 229–42). Rhetorical sources of Tennyson's patterns of sound are further explored in Erik Gray's insightful article, 'Polyptoton in *In Memoriam*: Evolution, Speculation, Elegy'

(*SEL* 55[2015] 841–60). Critics from Christopher Ricks to Seamus Perry have noted the enfolding and renewing impulses of lines such as 'Tears, idle **tears**'. Gray focuses exclusively on polyptoton: 'the repetition of a single root word either in different grammatical cases or as different parts of speech' (p. 842). He finds, in this prevalent rhetorical device, genuine sources of *In Memoriam*'s swerves of thought and crises of faith: 'The year is **dying** in the night; | Ring out, wild bells, and let him **die** . . . . The year is **going**, let him **go**. (p. 851). As Gray writes, polyptoton demonstrates 'at the most fundamental linguistic level the possibilities of perpetual variation', playing 'an essential role in the adaptive work of mourning that elegy undertakes' (p. 856). Opening with another example of polyptoton, Kiera Allison, in 'The Repression of the Return: Tennyson's *In Memoriam* and the Art of the Unheard Echo' (*VP* 53[2015] 41–56), considers the relationship of repetitions to prosody and psychology.

The role of rhetoric in Victorian poetry is also the subject of Yoshiko Seki's monograph, *The Rhetoric of Retelling Old Romances: Medievalist Poetry by Alfred Tennyson and William Morris*. This monograph examines two 'oppositional concepts', 'Medievalism and Victorianism' (p. 3), in order to assess Tennyson's and Morris's Arthurian works. Such *-isms* are increasingly unfashionable, characterized as reductive or ill-defined; yet the book's introduction historicizes these terms, drawing on John Ruskin's categories of '*Classicalism, Mediævalism*, and *Modernism*' (p. 3). Following a preliminary survey of the 'cultural climate' (p. 14) of Victorian Britain, Seki proceeds with a reading of *Idylls of the King*, dwelling on their original order of publication. In the second chapter, Seki considers Tennyson's early Arthurian plans, before focusing on the work's major female voices: Enid, Vivien, Elaine, and Guinevere. Turning to William Morris, Seki attempts a broad characterization of the poet's development, 'from his early Arthurian poems to *The Earthly Paradise*' (p. 15). In the fifth and sixth chapters, Seki examines 'the period when Morris published *The Defence of Guinevere and Other Poems*', and their relations to Tennyson and Browning (p. 15). Finally, the monograph's two closing chapters consider *The Earthly Paradise*, drawing on Walter Pater. By the monograph's end, the 'rhetoric', or vocabulary, mentioned throughout turns out to signal what Seki claims to be entirely different approaches to the medieval. Seki's conclusion asserts that 'The opposing rhetorics' that these poets 'achieved represent two divided attitudes toward art in the Victorian age: either to regard art as inseparable from the concerns of society', in the case of Tennyson, or, as with Morris, 'to demand the autonomy of art' (p. 176). The formulation is neat, and no doubt contains some truth, though it necessarily flattens the texture of the poetry, and, indeed, this book's appealing chapters on Tennyson's medieval inheritance.

The poet's Latin and Greek inheritance was explored in the fourth volume of *The Oxford History of Classical Reception* (Vance and Wallace, eds., pp. 539–57). It is well known that Tennyson's father—a clergyman and, as A.A. Markley states, 'a devoted classical scholar'—had among his library 'eighteenth-century editions of the classics that he used in educating his sons' (p. 539). Not only did these works include 'the poetry of Anacreon, Callimachus, Catullus, Horace, and Theocritus'; they encompassed 'the tragedies of Aeschylus, Sophocles, and Euripides; and the works of Juvenal, Lucretius, Martial, Ovid, Pliny, Plutarch, Tacitus, and Thucydides' (p. 539). At least three of these books contain inscriptions by the Tennyson children, apparently 'composed in Greek and Latin' (p. 540). Having surveyed Tennyson's classical reading, Markley proceeds to examine the influence of Latin and Greek literature on Tennyson's metres and verse forms. Illuminating Tennyson's biblical and Romantic influences, Sibylle Erle reports on 'Lord Tennyson's Copy of Blake's *Illustrations of the Book of Job* (1826)' (*Blake* 49:ii[2015] 9 paras.). As discussed above, chapter 2 of Drury's *Translation as Transformation* brings *Idylls of the King* into dialogue with Guest's translations of Welsh legends in the *Mabinogion*, considering how translation might be understood as domestication.

Tennyson's own reception and his influence on Victorian material culture were discussed in several books and articles. Joshua King's *Imagined Spiritual Communities in Britain's Age of Print* contains two chapters on *In Memoriam*, reviewed above in Section 1. For Deborah Lutz, writing in *Relics of Death* (pp. 102–27), copies of *In Memoriam* were treated as relics by their readers. Lutz's wide-ranging monograph embraces the recent burgeoning of 'thing theory', drawing parallels between elegy and the power of relics to prompt memories of the deceased. Her chapter on 'The Elegy as Shrine: Tennyson and *In Memoriam*' places the poem in its cultural contexts, likening the poem to shrines and memorials. That simile is asked to perform much work, since the comparison is the critic's, and the powerful emotive and formal forces of *In Memoriam* attempt far more than material shrines. Where this impressively detailed book most excels, however, is in the biographical accounts and anecdotes that connect literature's reception to the many forms of grief in nineteenth-century culture.

The Poet Laureate's reputation at the end of the nineteenth century was the focus of Elizabeth Carolyn Miller's article, 'Twilight of the Idylls: Wilde, Tennyson, and *Fin-de-Siècle* Anti-Idealism' (*VLC* 43[2015] 113–30). Miller views Oscar Wilde, 'along with writers like Henrik Ibsen, Friedrich Nietzsche, and George Bernard Shaw, as part of a late-nineteenth-century reaction against moral and aesthetic idealism' (p. 114). Her article argues that *Idylls of the King* had been received as an idealizing text, in the sense of a moralizing work of art. In his 1891 work *The Quintessence of Ibsenism*, which Wilde knew and liked, Shaw launched an 'attack on idealist literature', including the poems of Tennyson (p. 114).

Tennyson has famously been attacked on many counts, not least of all his intelligence. For Auden, Tennyson was 'undoubtedly the stupidest' of English poets. In 'Stupid Like Tennyson' (*Raritan* 35:i[2015] 97–113), David Russell distinguishes between the state of being 'stupid' and that of being 'stupefied'. Poetry, after all, entertains states of wonder, astonishment, or stupefaction: 'a condition of utter receptivity in which difference is perceived', as Gertrude Stein has it, before objection or qualification sets in. Of course, Russell suggests, to be permanently or 'absolutely stupefied is to be stupid' (p. 99); and yet Tennyson, he states, is 'often stupefied in just this philosophical' and productive sense (p. 100). Clearly not all of Tennyson's artistic and personal choices were perceived as wise, moralizing, or characteristic of wonder. In

'Tennyson's *Come into the Garden, Maud*: The Goddess at Sunrise' (*Expl* 73[2015] 86–91), Tim L. Sadenwasser performs a critical commentary on the poem's narrative, finding sexual undercurrents submerged beneath the poem's images. Beatrice Sanford Russell's 'How to Exist Where You Are: A Lesson in Lotos-Eating' (*VP* 53[2015] 375–99) focuses on the psychological and political undercurrents of Tennyson's verse. Her aim is to reconsider the young Tennyson's aesthetics, in order to reassess Alan Sinfield's charge against his late 'capitalism and imperialism' (p. 375).

In 'Longfellow, Tennyson, and Transatlantic Celebrity' (*CS* 27:iii[2015] 6–23), John Morton explores how Tennyson's 'celebrity' allegedly sowed the seeds of the decline in his reputation in the twentieth century. The article draws parallels with the 'ultimate American literary celebrity of the period' (p. 6), Henry Wadsworth Longfellow, whom Tennyson met on the Isle of Wight in 1868, and who allegedly hunted down the Poet Laureate. Similarly, James Tozer's article 'Tennyson's Popularity' (*TRB* 10[2015] 372–86) is an elegant and probing account of Tennyson's early success and public recognition. In 'Swinburne and Tennyson's Peerage' (*ES* 96[2015] 277–92), Francis O'Gorman assembles an impressive array of contemporary newspaper reports on Tennyson's barony, arguing how three of Swinburne's sonnets referred directly to the Poet Laureate. First printed in the *Pall Mall Gazette* in 1883, the three sonnets 'Vos Deos Laudamus' represent, according to O'Gorman, Swinburne's republican opposition to Tennyson's acceptance of a peerage: a move from the unacknowledged legislator, in Shelley's terms, to the all-too-acknowledged one (p. 282). A further article on Tennyson's reception is reviewed alongside criticism on Christina Rossetti: an eloquent piece by Simon Humphries, entitled 'Christina Rossetti's Tennysonianism' (*CQ* 44[2015] 43–61), reviewed above.

Tennyson's intellectual connections extended far beyond the established Victorian literati. Three articles this year dealt with his encounters with evolutionary and geological thinkers, and their relationship to philology. In 'Tennyson and the Geologists, Part 1: the Early Years and Charles Peach' (*TRB* 10[2015] 340–56), Lyall Anderson and James Taylor seek to 'explore the connection' between Charles Peach, Tennyson, and the geologist Adam Sedgwick (p. 340). By Tennyson's 1848 visit to Cornwall, 'he was undoubtedly interested in the science', though his 'early involvement in geology', the article claims, 'was much weaker, and slower to develop, than is sometimes argued' (p. 340). Scientific discourses and evolutionary thought were key concerns for Matthew Margini's 'The Beast with the Broken Lance: Humanism and Posthumanism in Tennyson's *Idylls of the King*' (*VP* 53[2015] 171–92). The article's opening risks misreading Tennyson's 'The Epic' to illustrate the poet's concern with an 'anthropocentric cosmology' (p. 171); yet evolutionary and scientific knowledge is genuinely interwoven with Tennyson's poems, and, as Margini's essay proceeds to examine, *Idylls of the King*. The link between evolution, geology, and figures of speech in the wider nineteenth century is also central to Sarah Weaver's 'Victorian Philology and the Metaphors of Language' (*LitComp* 12[2015] 333–43). Weaver's article 'contextualizes philology within the milieu of Victorian intellectual pursuits and investigates its relation to metaphor' (p. 333). Among its several strands of argument, it dwells on Emerson's statement that 'Language is fossil poetry', comprising 'images, or tropes, which now, in their secondary use, have long ceased to remind us of their poetic origin' (p. 339). The article continues a growing trend of examining poetic developments alongside the origins of modern literary criticism.

## 4. Drama

Jeffrey Richards begins *The Golden Age of Pantomime: Slapstick, Spectacle and Subversion in Victorian England* by noting the frequent repetition of the critical lament, ' "the pantomime is not what it was" ' (p. 2). This authoritative account of the development of the pantomime form throughout the nineteenth century demonstrates that one of the great strengths of the genre was its capacity to evolve and absorb new influences. Richards begins by establishing the importance of transformation, pointing to the impact of the Theatre Regulation Act of 1843 that officially sanctioned spoken language on the stages of the minor theatres, allowing lengthier pantomimes that could employ puns, rhyming couplets, and satirical comments on current events. Richards also details technological, artistic, and social transformations, and describes the shift from literary and historical subjects to fairy stories. Despite this apparently apolitical subject matter, Richards argues that a celebration of British imperialism was part of the texture of many of these plays. Chapter 1 introduces the four figures who were the key figures in the development of the form, according to Richards: the playwright James Robinson Planché, the scene painter William Roxby Beverley, the playwright Edward Leman Blanchard, and the impresario Sir Augustus Harris. The rest of the book traces the influence of these men: Planché developed the fairy extravaganza; Beverley expanded the visual range of pantomime and, simultaneously, the importance of scene painting as an art form in its own right; Blanchard established the Drury Lane pantomime as an important event in London life; and Augustus Harris oversaw the increasing influence of music hall on the genre, as stars such as Dan Leno and Marie Lloyd began to perform in pantomimes. The first half of the book is taken up with discussion of different pantomime forms, including the classical and fairy extravaganzas, as well as Beverley's scenic creations, but the second half contains a detailed and extended look at every Christmas pantomime staged at Drury Lane until 1901, using reviews and other contemporary accounts to provide a rich history of the evolutions of this supremely popular theatrical form.

*Staging the Other in Nineteenth-Century British Drama*, edited by Tiziana Morosetti, is a collection of essays that explores the exotic and its representation on the nineteenth-century stage. The first two essays focus on the exoticized Jewish body. ' "By a Nose" or "By a Hair": Bearding the Jew on the Georgian Stage' by Toni Wein compares Charles Macklin's clean-shaven Shylock with Edmund Kean's famous and hairy incarnation of the character to suggest that the beard reduced the exoticized body of the Jew to a type composed of fragments. Michael Bradshaw's essay, 'The Jew on Stage and on the Page: Intertextual Exotic' explores Henry Hart Milman's *Fazio* and Thomas Wade's *The Jew of Arragon; or, The Hebrew Queen* to argue that both plays engage with Shakespeare and Marlowe's famously rapacious Jewish characters, Shylock and Barabas, to negotiate the opposing impulses to include and to expel the Jewish 'other', whose exotic body is marked by the hidden but known fact of circumcision. In 'Edwin Forrest: The Exotic American Body on the Nineteenth-Century English Stage', Arthur W. Bloom suggests that the American actor Edwin Forrest's performance of Spartacus in Robert Montgomery Bird's *The Gladiator* in 1836 exuded a physicality that was seen as barbarically, yet authentically, American. Forrest cultivated a 'fabricated otherness' (p. 61) that seemed to represent American freedom while simultaneously recording its disappearance. Tiziana Morosetti's essay, 'Constructing the Zulus: The "African" Body and Its Narratives' discusses a different kind of spectacular physicality in her examination of the ethnological exhibition of the 'Zulu Kaffirs' on the English stage in 1854 and the 'Friendly Zulus' in 1880. She argues that earlier theatrical representations of Zulus developed a politically inflected portrayal that was contextualized and historicized by these later exhibitions, but despite this, the Zulus were still seen as representative of the whole of Africa.

In ' "An interest must be strong now-a-days to raise much enthusiasm in an audience, but it may be, at the same time, of an unpleasant nature": Māori, New Zealand and Empire on Stage, 1862–1864', Marianne Schultz describes the conflict between representations of 'civilized' culture and 'savage' authenticity in the performances of both European and Māori performers on the mid-nineteenth-century stage. Peter Yeandle, like Richards, examines pantomime's engagement with imperialist ideologies in 'Performing the Other on the Popular London Stage: Exotic People and Places in Victorian Pantomime'. Yeandle focuses on the Indian Rebellion of 1857 and its impact on *Jack and the Beanstalk* in the form of topical references, particularly with regard to the villainous Giant. In 'Impressment, Exoticism and Enslavement: Revisiting the Theatre of War through Thomas Hardy's *The Trumpet-Major* (1880)', Sara Malton examines the influence of the Harlequin and the Italian *commedia dell'arte* on the depiction of impressment in Thomas Hardy's *The Trumpet-Major*.

Zara Barlas, in 'Transcultural Operatics: India on the British Stage in *The Nautch Girl; or, The Rajah of Chutneypore*', argues that the transculturality of operetta allowed its stigmatized Indian female characters to represent aspects of British society, while their exoticization simultaneously provided sufficient distance for the production to avoid controversy as a result. Serena Guarracino also explores a musical form in 'Singing the Exotic Body across the Atlantic: From *The Mikado* to the *Swing Mikado* and Beyond'. She contrasts productions of Gilbert and Sullivan's opera performed by a predominately white cast with a 1939 all-black staging in Chicago to argue that the representation of Japanese bodies by white performers paradoxically created an opportunity for non-white performing bodies to claim normativity. Finally, Sophia Duncan explores a neo-Victorian retelling of the life of Ira Aldridge, in 'A Progressive *Othello*: Modern Blackness in Chakrabarti's *Red Velvet* (2012)'. Duncan argues that Chakrabarti associates Aldridge's exoticized blackness with modernity and progressivism, allowing modern audiences to be comfortable with Aldridge's exoticization, which was historically more complex. Another work that engages with both neo-Victorian fictionalizations and the 'other' is Helen Davies's book, *Neo-Victorian Freakery: The Cultural Afterlife of the Victorian Freakshow*. Davies is primarily concerned with the potential for neo-Victorian representations of the freakshow to be both an ethical recuperation and a problematic restaging of the performance of freakishness; she is also interested in freakish as an embodiment of neo-Victorianism itself, but it is her discussions of the Victorian performers involved that are most relevant for those of us interested in the nineteenth-century stage. The chapters are organized around each performer: Sarah Baartman, 'The Hottentot Venus'; Chang and Eng Bunker, the original 'Siamese Twins'; Anna Swan, the 'giantess'; Charles Sherwood Stratton, 'General Tom Thumb', and Lavinia Warren, his wife; and Joseph Carey Merrick, the 'Elephant Man'. Of particular interest is chapter 1, which discusses various representations of Sarah Baartman in nineteenth-century ballads and plays, and explores ways in which 'the signifiers of race, gender and sexuality which shape her persona are a mode of performance' (p. 19), and also chapter 3, which devotes some attention to Albert Smith's 1846 American play *Hop O' My Thumb*, performed by Stratton in Britain.

A number of books and articles written this year examine Oscar Wilde and his reputation, whether influenced by his own self-fashioning or the judgement of others. In *Oscar Wilde's Chatterton: Literary History, Romanticism, and the Art of Forgery*, also reviewed elsewhere in this chapter, Joseph Bristow and Rebecca N. Mitchell take issue with the claim that Wilde's 'Chatterton' notebook, a substantial book of notes and clippings the author kept during the mid-1880s that detailed his fascination with the controversial eighteenth-century poet Thomas Chatterton, was evidence of his plagiarism. Instead, they argue that Wilde used his notebooks as a 'testing ground for ideas and phrasing' (p. 213) and 'a repository of information' (p. 171). They disagree with critics such as Paul K. Saint Amour, Josephine M. Guy, and Geoff Dibb that the notebook constitutes writerly theft, arguing instead that it shows us 'the ways in which he was reshaping his career' and 'inspired many of the remarkable shifts that took place during the mid and late 1880s in Wilde's evolving emergence as a major *fin-de-siècle* author' (p. 21). Of particular interest in relation to Wilde's drama is the concluding chapter, which uses the portrait of Dorian Gray to discuss forgery, lying, and finally false identities in *The Importance of Being Earnest*.

Elizabeth Carolyn Miller's essay, 'Twilight of the Idylls: Wilde, Tennyson, and *Fin-de Siècle* Anti-Idealism' (*VLC* 43[2015] 113–30), also deals with Wilde's literary self-fashioning, drawing out the echoes of Alfred Lord Tennyson's *Idylls of the King* in Wilde's play *An Ideal Husband* to argue that Wilde offers 'a caricatured version of Tennyson's idealism against which his play can define a new modern sensibility' (p. 116). Miller suggests that Wilde's 'modern sensibility' is compromised by an attachment to several of the ideals he apparently disavows, but positions him as an anti-idealist alongside Henrik Ibsen, George Bernard Shaw, and Friedrich Nietzsche.

Julia D. Atkinson examines Wilde's reputation in the years immediately following his imprisonment by considering the extent to which it impacted on touring productions of his plays. In ' "An author not just now familiar to ears polite": *The Importance of Being Earnest* and *Lady Windermere's Fan* on Tour, 1895–1900' (*TW* 47[2015] 21–37) she concludes that his plays were increasingly popular during this time, identifying two particularly successful touring companies led by Nina Cressy and Elsie Lanham, which unsettle the prevailing assumption that George Alexander's production of *Earnest* at the Coronet Theatre in Notting Hill in 1901 was the first sign of Wilde's theatrical recuperation. Timothy Peltason's 'Oscar in Earnest' (*Raritan* 35:i[2015] 114–44) argues that *The Importance of Being Earnest* was central to the 'last, tragic chapter' (p. 116) of Wilde's life, and demonstrates the play's links to his own earlier works and to precursors such as John Ruskin and Charles Dickens, while suggesting its influence on writers such as Eliot and Yeats. Finally, Bulbul Gupta's 'Oscar Wilde—The Individualist' (*TW* 47[2015) 118–23) suggests that the eponymous Vera from *The Nihilists* embodies her creator's 'vision of individualism' (p. 122).

Theatrical adaptation is a topic that has gained a significant amount of attention this year. Karen E. Laird's book, *The Art of Adapting Victorian Literature, 1848–1920: Dramatizing Jane Eyre, David Copperfield, and The Woman in White*, links Victorian drama with the early days of cinema by arguing that nineteenth-century playwrights 'established a language, theory, and practice of adaptation that was foundational to the development of narrative cinema' (p. 2). She organizes her project around three novels by Charlotte Brontë, Dickens, and Wilkie Collins, and devotes two chapters to each, one of which focuses on the nineteenth-century stage adaptations and the other on the later films. There is a further tripartite subdivision within the argument, as Laird argues that the operation of the themes of gender, class, and nation within these novels was altered to create new meanings in the adaptations.

Laird maintains that mid-nineteenth-century stage adaptations of *Jane Eyre* were interested in the socio-economic aspect of Jane's position in Rochester's house, and amplified the roles of the servants to give more weight to the class dynamics at play. The films of the early twentieth century, however, were directed at a female audience and paid more attention to gender, which aligned with critical interest in Brontë at the time. The theatrical adaptations of *David Copperfield* also developed the roles of the female characters, moving away from the *Künstlerroman* plot of the novel to focus on Emily and Martha, the fallen women, while the films, which were made around the time of Dickens's bicentenary and formed part of the growing Dickens industry, reclaimed Copperfield—widely viewed as a proto-Dickens—as the central character.

In her chapter on *The Woman in White* and its stage adaptations, Laird challenges the claim made by Janice Norwood that Collins's own adaptation of his novel was original because it eschewed the conventions of sensation drama in favour of a focus on character. Laird suggests that Collins borrowed this approach from J.R. Ware, who had adapted the novel himself some years previously. Finally, Laird argues in her final chapter that the Victorian novel was kept alive by cinema because it was rewritten, and that consequently in the cinematic adaptations of Collins's novel, the silent film form was altered to recreate the thrills of sensation fiction. A special issue of *Nineteenth Century Theatre and Film* (43[2015]) also focused on adaptation. Jackie Bratton's essay 'William Thomas Moncrieff' (*NCTFilm* 43[2015] 9–21) sets out to recuperate the playwright and prolific adapter from the attacks he received from Dickens, and for which he is now probably best remembered. Bratton argues that Moncrieff's 'eclectic, wide-ranging, syncretic' approach to adaptation (p. 19) requires re-examination, and suggests that Moncrieff's use of song to build the drama anticipated the techniques of musical theatre by some hundred years. In 'Adaptation, Originality and Law: Dion Boucicault and Charles Reade' (*NCTFilm* 43[2015] 22–38), Sarah Meer argues that the court cases contested by Dion Boucicault and his sometime collaborator, Charles Reade, not only affected the practice of adaptation but made the law courts, and not only the theatre, an important venue in which 'the ethics of adaptation' were 'examined and established' (p. 35).

Tracy Cattell makes the case for the recognition of stage managers' prompt books as a record of the continuing adaptation of plays in performance, in her article, 'Transmitting the Thinking: The Nineteenth-Century Stage Manager and the Adaptation of Text for Performance' (*NCTFilm* 43[2015] 39–49). Cattell follows Bratton's appreciation for Moncrieff's adaptability by noting that this was also an essential quality of the successful stage manager. In my own article, Lucy Barnes, 'A Crowded Stage: The Legitimate Borrowings of Henry Milner's *Mazeppa*' (*NCTFilm* 43[2015] 50–65), I argue that the equestrian adaptation of Byron's poem *Mazeppa* also reworked several Shakespeare plays, and in so doing negotiated the fraught divide between legitimate and illegitimate theatre to shed light on broader cultural shifts in the early nineteenth-century theatre. Kate Mattacks, in her essay '(Per)forming the Adaptive: Watts Phillips's *The Woman in Mauve* (1864/65) and the Sensation Genre as Commodity' (*NCTFilm* 43[2015] 66–79), argues that Phillips's play 'renegotiates the sensational tropes of authentic repetition as a self-referential theatricalized commodity' (p. 71), exposing the commodification of the sensation genre, in an example of adaptation that was self-aware and challenged the conditions within which it operated. Finally, Caroline Radcliffe examines two of Collins's dramas, his adaptation of his novel *The Moonstone*, and *The Red Vial*, which he later rewrote as a novel, *Jezebel's Daughter*. 'Behind Closed Doors: The Theatrical Uncanny and the Panoptical Viewer in the Dramas of Wilkie Collins' (*NCTFilm* 43[2015] 80–98) proposes that Collins skilfully makes the offstage space into the 'site of the uncanny' (p. 83).

Several other articles and book chapters have investigated a broad variety of nineteenth-century stage adaptations. Mary A. Armstrong in 'Next Week!! Desire, Domestic Melodrama, and the Extravagant Proliferations of *East Lynne*' (*VLC* 43[2015] 745–64) explores dramatizations of Ellen Wood's frequently-adapted novel to argue that, while the novel uses desire for the domestic object to express other forms of transgressive yearning, the dramas and film adaptations of *East Lynne* transformed the play itself into a 'consumable domestic spectacle' (p. 747), making its portrayal of private domesticity both an object of purchase and, consequently, an articulation of loss.

Meredith Conti's chapter, 'Ungentlemanly Habits: The Dramaturgy of Drug Addiction in Fin-de-Siècle Theatrical Adaptations of the Sherlock Holmes Stories and The [sic] Strange Case of Dr Jekyll and Mr Hyde' (in Penner and Sparks, eds., Victorian Medicine and Popular Culture, pp. 109–24), argues that William Hooker Gillette's play Sherlock Holmes and Thomas R. Sullivan's Dr Jekyll and Mr Hyde are the first major representations of drug addiction on the popular stage, and that they embody two different Victorian theories of addiction. In 'Alternative Family and Textual Citizenship in Frances Hodgson Burnett's Little Lord Fauntleroy: A Drama in Three Acts' (ChildLAQ 40[2015] 339–54), Deanna Stover examines Burnett's own adaptation of her novel, suggesting that, while the novel valorizes reading as a means of fostering relationships, both familial and social, the play focuses on the spoken word as a source of power and democratic representation.

Finally, the Journal of Adaptation in Film and Performance included two articles this year that discussed nineteenth-century stage adaptation. In '"His knife and hands bloody": Sweeney Todd's Journey from Page to Stage—Melodrama, Adaptation and the Original 1847 Manuscript' (JAFP 8[2015] 233–47), Sarah A. Winter compares George Dibdin Pitt's 1847 manuscript for his play The String of Pearls; or, The Fiend of Fleet Street, an adaptation of the serialized story The String of Pearls. A Romance, with the 1883 published version of the same play. Winter argues that the earlier version contains similarities to various crimes that were reported in the press at the time, while the published play replaces these with stagecraft such as the use of the vampire trap to dispatch Todd's victims, which is more recognizable to those familiar with later iterations of the Demon Barber. Jude Wright's essay 'Listening to the Monster: Eliding and Restoring the Creature's Voice in Adaptations of Frankenstein' (JAFP 8[2015] 249–66) explores three adaptations of Mary Shelley's novel, only one of which is from the nineteenth century. Richard Brinsley Peake's 1823 play Presumption; or, The Fate of Frankenstein is highlighted because it deprives the Creature of speech, an adaptation that Wright ascribes to the legislation that forbade dialogue on the stages of the minor theatres before the 1843 Theatre Regulation Act. Wright then traces the recuperation of the Creature's voice in later adaptations.

Two further books deal at least partly with the practice of adaptation. Victorian Classical Burlesques: A Critical Anthology by Laura Monrós-Gaspar presents four important classical burlesques, with an introduction and notes: Antigone Travestie [1845] by Edward L. Blanchard, Medea; or, The Best of Mothers with a Brute of a Husband [1856] by Robert Brough, Alcestis; The Original Strong-Minded Woman [1850], and Electra in a New Electric Light [1859] by Francis Talfourd. The careful annotations reflect the alterations made to the manuscripts that were sent to the Lord Chamberlain, and explore the satirical allusions and contemporary events that are referenced. The introduction presents the history of the burlesque form and the growing enthusiasm for the classics during the nineteenth century while arguing that social changes created 'a new negotiation of gender relations that was mirrored in Victorian classical burlesque' (p. 1). The notes on the different plays provide a wealth of information about the classical myths the burlesques are based on, as well as information about production choices and performance practices. Richard Pearson's book *Victorian Writers and the Stage*, also covered elsewhere in this chapter, explores those dramas, or writing about drama, produced by authors better known for their work in other genres. This includes Dickens's early plays and the melodramas he wrote with Collins; William Makepeace Thackeray's reviews and his fictional theatrical characters; Collins's theatrical adaptations of his own novels; and Tennyson's and Robert Browning's plays. Pearson argues that much nineteenth-century drama, and these plays in particular, failed to achieve the popular longevity and critical consideration afforded to novels and poetry because of 'the difficulty of forming a coherent authorial identity' (p.3) as a nineteenth-century playwright. However, the literary fame of writers such as Dickens and Collins made their dramas attractive to theatre managers who wanted to draw audiences. In chapter 1, Pearson explores Dickens's relationship with the Tottenham-street Theatre and St James's Theatre to explore the construction of 'Dickens' the author and the identity of the playwright-author in the nineteenth-century theatre. Browning's difficult relationship with Macready, and the battle between the roles of author and the performer, is discussed in chapter 2. Chapter 3 examines Dickens's and Thackeray's engagement with the theatrical in their writing, including Dickens's integration of theatrical elements into his fiction and Thackeray's critique of the industry, while chapter 4 discusses Dickens and Collins's theatrical collaborations, including *The Frozen Deep* and *No Thoroughfare*. Chapter 5 explores Collins's many theatrical adaptations of his own novels and his difficulty in negotiating his audiences' expectations, while chapter 6 examines Tennyson's dramas, arguing that a metanarrative about their potential to rescue the nineteenth-century theatre from itself led to the reification of a hierarchy that condemned the drama of the period and influenced subsequent critical opinion.

Race is at issue in Laura Korobkin's 'Avoiding "Aunt Tomasina"': Charles Dickens Responds to Harriet Beecher Stowe's Black American Reader, Mary Webb' (*ELH* 82[2015] 115–40), which explores Dickens's response to a request from Mary Webb, the reader and actress who was closely associated with Harriet Beecher Stowe. Korobkin examines Dickens's letter recounting their unfulfilled meeting, arguing that it not only revealed Dickens's racist attitude towards a successful black reader—a role (that of reader) he was himself soon to take on—and also the effect of his rivalry with Stowe.

Barry Anthony's book, *Murder, Mayhem and Music Hall: The Dark Side of Victorian London* presents us with a panoramic view of the boisterous and sometimes criminal life that abounded in the streets, pubs, and performance venues of the Strand, using individual accounts to give focus to his broader descriptions of the texture of everyday life. Discussions of the variety of entertainments available in this part of London, and how they changed over time with the arrival of new theatres and overlooked varieties of performance, form a backdrop to the narratives of individuals who inhabited the area, whether for work or pleasure. Particularly striking is chapter 4, which describes Renton Nicholson and his success in bringing mock-trials to the public houses of the area. Chapter 6 discusses Thomas Boulton and Frederick

Park, famously arrested for wearing women's clothes, as an introduction to the consideration of musical burlesques and cross-gender impersonation on stage, while chapter 8 discusses music-hall performance, the 'skirt dance', and Lottie Collins's success. The examination of performance, however, is often secondary to the human dramas with which the book is concerned. Also of interest to those studying music hall is 'Conrad and the Comic Turn' by Douglas Kerr (*VLC* 43[2015] 149–68), which examines various music-hall techniques that appear in Conrad's fiction, establishing his appreciation of the form before exploring the chorus in *The Nigger of the 'Narcissus'*, cross-talk in 'An Outpost of Progress', and repartee, double entendre, and comic collusion in 'Heart of Darkness'.

Just touching on this period is Frederick Burwick's *British Drama of the Industrial Revolution*, which explores provincial drama between the 1780s and 1890s, but since its material belongs mostly outside the period covered by this review, it is discussed in Chapter XIII above. Burwick has also co-written *British Pirates in Print and Performance* with Manushag N. Powell, which explores the pirate as a figure at the centre of a negotiation between literary text, theatrical performance and popular reception. It likewise is concerned mostly with drama before 1830, and the review can be found in Chapter XIII.

Anna Farkas's essay, ' "Highly superior 'variety turns' ": The Orthodox Roots of Suffrage Theatre' in the special issue *Victorian Oral Cultures* (*VOC* 63[2015] 101–17), explores the influence of private theatricals and the socially conservative variety theatre of the 1890s upon the politically and—it has been argued—theatrically radical suffragette drama of the early twentieth century. Farkas argues that the prevalence of female performers and writers, the unorthodox performance spaces, and the common forms of monologue, duologue, and one-act plays in suffrage theatre all have their roots in the workings of a drama whose aims were very different. Kate Newey's chapter, 'Drama and Theater', in *The Cambridge Companion to Victorian Women's Writing*, edited by Linda H. Peterson, is reviewed by Kristen Pond in Section 1 above.

Nineteenth-century stagecraft has received some attention this year. *Bandits! or The Collapsing Bridge: An Early Film and a Late-Victorian Stage* by Bryony Dixon and David Mayer, examines the earliest known surviving motion picture filmed in a London theatre. *The Bandits* was performed in 1902 at the London Hippodrome and the film records a spectacular scene in which an avalanche is sparked by a gunshot fired by a bandit queen, sweeping away a bridge that is being traversed by a group of horses and riders, causing choreographed chaos. The film is significant as much for what it tells us about late nineteenth-century performance practices as for the record of this particular production: Bryony Dixon recounts its discovery in the BFI archives and the gradual process of identifying its contents, while David Mayer explores the theatre history that lies behind the film, describing the water tanks that were first used at Sadler's Wells in 1804, the use of horses in performance, and the rise and fall in popularity of such sketches at the London Hippodrome at the turn of the century. Russell Burdekin's essay, 'Pepper's Ghost at the Opera' (*TN* 69[2015] 152–64), describes the stage technology involving mirrors and lighting that enabled ghosts and other illusions to be projected on the nineteenth-century stage, arguing that the device was more commonly used—particularly by touring companies—than has previously been supposed. Finally, Michael Gilmour has written a survey of criticism on melodrama in his essay 'Victorian Melodrama' (*LitComp* 12[2015] 344–57), which also argues briefly that further work on the connection between melodrama and neuroscience might shed new light on drama and the production of affect.

## Books Reviewed

Abberley, Will. *English Fiction and the Evolution of Language, 1850–1914.* CUP. [2015] pp. vii + 234. £65 ISBN 9 7811 0710 1166.

Ackroyd, Peter. *Wilkie Collins: A Brief Life.* Vintage. [2015] pp. viii + 252. £12.99 ISBN 9 7803 8553 7391.

Adams-Campbell, Melissa M. *New World Courtships: Transatlantic Alternatives to Companionate Marriage.* Dartmouth. [2015] pp. xii + 204. hb $85 ISBN 9 7816 1168 8313, pb $45 ISBN 9 7816 1168 8320.

Alexander, Sarah. *Victorian Literature and the Physics of the Imponderable.* P&C. [2015] pp. ix + 204. $45 ISBN 9 7818 4893 5662.

Alfano, Veronica, and Andrew Stauffer, eds. *Virtual Victorians: Networks, Connections, Technologies.* PalMac. [2015] pp. ix + 281. £55 ISBN 9 7811 3739 3296.

Amarnick, Steven, ed., introd. Trollope Joanna, commentary Wiseman Robert F., Susan Lowell Humphreys, and Michael G. Williamson. The Duke's Children [The Last Chronicle of Omnium: The Rediscovery of The Duke's Children] by Trollope Anthony. 2 vols. Folio. [2015] pp. 724 + 150. £195 ISBN unavailable.

Anthony, Barry. *Murder, Mayhem and Music Hall: The Dark Side of Victorian London.* Tauris. [2015] pp. xi + 244. £20 ISBN 9 7817 8076 6348.

Antonello, Pierpaolo, and Heather Webb. *Mimesis, Desire, and the Novel: René Girard and Literary Criticism.* MSUP. [2015] pp. liii + 303. $29.95 ISBN 9 7816 1186 1655.

Aquino, Frederick D., and Benjamin J. King. *Receptions of Newman.* OUP. [2015] pp. 264. $110 ISBN 9 7801 9968 7589.

Archibald, Diana C., and Joel J Brattin. *Dickens and Massachusetts: The Lasting Legacy of the Commonwealth Visits.* UMassP. [2015] pp. xii + 212. $90 ISBN 9 7816 2534 1365.

Bach, Susanne, and Folkert Degenring, eds. *Dark Nights, Bright Lights: Light, Darkness and Illumination in Literature.* MGruyter. [2015] pp. vii + 234. £75 ISBN 9 7831 1041 5292.

Baker, William, ed. *Studies in Victorian and Modern Literature: A Tribute to John Sutherland.* FDUP. [2015] pp. xvi + 350. $90 ISBN 9 7816 1147 6927.

Balkaya, Mehmet Akif. *The Industrial Novels: Charlotte Brontë's Shirley, Charles Dickens' Hard Times and Elizabeth Gaskell's North and South.* CambridgeSP. [2015] pp. x + 96. £42 ISBN 9 7814 4388 2187.

Ballantyne, Andrew. *John Ruskin*. UChicP. [2015] pp. 252. $16.95 ISBN 9 7817 8023 4298.

Baunstein, Laura and Liorah Golomb, eds. *Digital Humanities in the Library: Challenges and Opportunities for Subject Specialists*. Chicago: ACRL. [2015]. pp. 291. $68.00. ISBN 9 7808 3898 7674.

Bear, Jordan. *Disillusioned: Victorian Photography and the Discerning Subject*. PSUP. [2015] pp. 216. $74.95 ISBN 9 7802 7106 5014.

Beaumont, Matthew. *Nightwalking: A Nocturnal History of London, Chaucer to Dickens*. Verso. [2015] pp. 496. $29.95 ISBN 9 7817 8168 7956.

Belcher, Margaret, ed. *The Collected Letters of A.W.N. Pugin, vol. 5: 1851–1852*. OUP. [2015] pp. 800. $250 ISBN 9 7801 9871 3913.

Birch, Dinah, ed. *The Small House at Allington*, by Trollope Anthony. OUP. [2015] pp. xlii + 582. £9.99 ISBN 9 7801 9966 2777.

Blake, Peter. *George Augustus Sala and the Nineteenth-Century Periodical Press: The Personal Style of a Public Writer*. Routledge. [2015] pp. 296. $119.95 ISBN 9 7814 7241 6070.

Boehmer, Elleke. *Indian Arrivals, 1870–1915: Networks of British Empire*. OUP. [2015] pp. 288. $50 ISBN 9 7801 9874 4184.

Bonaparte, Felicia. *The Poetics of Poesis: The Making of Nineteenth-Century English Fiction*. UVirginiaP. [2015] pp. xi + 322. £54 ISBN 9 7808 1393 7328.

Boos, Florence Saunders. *History and Poetics in the Early Writings of William Morris, 1855–1870*. OhioUP. [2015] pp. xi + 373. $91.95 ISBN 9 7808 1421 2899.

Botting, Fred, and Catherine Spooner, eds. *Monstrous Media/Spectral Subjects: Imaging Gothic from the Nineteenth Century to the Present*. ManUP. [2015] pp. xii + 175. £70 ISBN 9 7807 1908 9770.

Bourrier, Karen Ann. *The Measure of Manliness: Disability and Masculinity in the Mid-Victorian Novel*. UMichP. [2015] pp. 184. $65 ISBN 9 7804 7207 2484.

Bowen, John, ed. *Barchester Towers* by Trollope Anthony. OUP. [2014] pp. xlii + 486. £9.99 ISBN 9 7801 9966 5860.

Boyiopoulos, Kostas. *The Decadent Image: The Poetry of Wilde, Symons, and Dowson*. EdinUP. [2015] pp. xii + 219. £63 ISBN 9 7807 4869 0923.

Boyiopoulas, Kostas, Yoonjoung Choi, and Mathew Brinton Tildesley, eds. *The Decadent Short Story: An Annotated Anthology*. EdinUP. [2015] pp. xiv + 466. $40 ISBN 9 7807 4869 2149.

Boyiopoulos, Kostas, and Mark Sandy, eds. *Decadent Romanticism, 1780–1914*. Ashgate. [2015] pp. 226. £60 ISBN 9 7814 7242 2422.

Bradley, Matthew, and Juliet John, eds. *Reading and the Victorians*. Routledge. [2015] pp. 194. $109.95 ISBN 9 7814 0944 0802.

Briefel, Aviva. *The Racial Hand in the Victorian Imagination*. CUP. [2015] pp. 236. $99.99 ISBN 9 7811 0711 6580.

Bristow, Joseph, and Rebecca N. Mitchell. *Oscar Wilde's Chatterton: Literary History, Romanticism, and the Art of Forgery*. YaleUP. [2015] pp. xii + 470. £25 ISBN 9 7803 0020 8306.

Broome Saunders, Clare. *Louisa Stuart Costello: A Nineteenth-Century Writing Life*. PalMac. [2015] pp. xi + 254. hb £55 ISBN 9 7811 3734 0115, pb £55 ISBN 9 7813 4967 4084.

Brothers, Dometa Wiegand. *The Romantic Imagination and Astronomy: On All Sides Infinity*. PalMac. [2015] pp. x + 203. £55 ISBN 9 7811 3747 4339.

Burkhardt, Frederick, and James Secord, eds. *The Correspondence of Charles Darwin, vol. 22: 1874*. CUP. [2015] pp. 904. $152 ISBN 9 7811 0070 88726.

Butterworth, Robert. *Dickens, Religion and Society*. PalMac. [2016] pp. 237. $90 ISBN 9 7811 3755 8701.

Calzoni, Raul, and Greta Perletti, eds. *Monstrous Anatomies: Literary and Scientific Imagination in Britain and Germany during the Long Nineteenth Century*. V&R. [2015] pp. 316. £40 ISBN 9 7838 4710 4698.

Campbell, Ian, Aileen Christianson, David R. Sorensen, ., eds. *The Collected Letters of Thomas and Jane Welsh Carlyle, vol. 43: October 1865–June 1866*. DukeUP. [2015] pp. xxxvii + 304 pp. $70 ISBN?

Campbell, James. *Oscar Wilde, Wilfred Owen, and Male Desire: Begotten, Not Made*. PalMac. [2015] pp. x + 241. £45.99 ISBN 9 7811 3755 0637.

Capuano, Peter J. *Changing Hands: Industry, Evolution, and the Reconfiguration of the Victorian Body*. UMichP. [2015] pp. xv + 323. hb $80 ISBN 9 7804 7207 2842, pb $40 ISBN 9 7804 7205 2844.

Cartmell, Deborah. *Adaptations in the Sound Era, 1927-37*. Bloomsbury. [2015] pp. 176 $90.00 ISBN 9 7816 2356 0423.

Cohn, Elisha. *Still Life: Suspended Development in the Victorian Novel*.OUP. [2015]. pp. 272. $65 ISBN 9 7801 9049 3479.

Çelikel, Mehmet Ali, and Baysar Taniyan, eds. *English Studies: New Perspectives*. CambridgeSP. [2015] pp. x + 363 pp. $90.99 ISBN 9 7814 4387 7275.

Chapman, Alison. *Networking the Nation: British and American Women's Poetry and Italy, 1840–1870*. OUP. [2015] pp. xl + 303. £60 ISBN 9 7801 9872 3578.

Chitham, Edward. *Western Winds: The Brontës' Irish Heritage*. History Press Ireland. [2015] pp. 224. pb £15 ISBN 9 7818 4588 8336.

Choi, Tina Young. *Anonymous Connections: The Body and Narratives of the Social in Victorian Britain*. UMichP. [2015] pp. 192. $65 ISBN 9 7804 7211 9721.

Cirstea, Arina. *Mapping British Women Writers' Imaginaries: Space, Self and Spirituality*. PalMac. [2015] pp. ?? £58 ISBN 9 7811 3753 0905.

Clapp-Itnyre, Alisa, and Julie Melnyk, eds. *Perplext in Faith: Essays on Victorian Beliefs and Doubts*. CambridgeSP. [2015] pp. 340. £52.99 ISBN 9 7814 4386 8143.

Clark, Indy. *Thomas Hardy's Pastoral: An Unkindly May*. PalMac. [2015] pp. ix + 217. £55 ISBN 9 7811 3750 5019.

Cohn, Elisha. *Still Life: Suspended Development in the Victorian Novel*. OUP. [2015]. pp. 272. $65 ISBN 9 7801 9049 3479.

Colletta, Lisa, ed. *The Legacy of the Grand Tour: New Essays on Travel, Literature, and Culture*. FDUP. [2015] pp. xx + 206. $75 ISBN 9 7816 1147 7979.

Corton, Christine L. *London Fog: The Biography*. HarvardUP. [2015] pp. 408. £22.95 ISBN 9 7806 7408 8351.

Cossins, Annie. *Female Criminality: Infanticide, Moral Panics and the Female Body*. PalMac. [2015] pp. 302. $105 ISBN 9 7811 3729 9413.

Costantini, Mariaconcetta. *Sensation and Professionalism in the Victorian Novel.* Lang. [2015] pp. 366. $105.95 ISBN 9 7830 3431 5883.

Crawford, Alice, ed. *The Meaning of the Library: A Cultural History.* Princeton UP. [2015]. pp. 336. £27.95 ISBN 9 7806 9116 6391.

Cronin, Richard, and Dorothy McMillan, eds. *Robert Browning.* 21st-Century Oxford Authors. OUP. [2015] pp. xliii + 861. £95 ISBN 9 7801 9959 9424.

Daly, Nicholas. *The Demographic Imagination and the Nineteenth-Century City: Paris, London, New York.* CUP. [2015] pp. 288. $98 ISBN 9 7813 1615 5295.

Dau, Duc, and Shale Preston, eds. *Queer Victorian Families: Curious Relations in Literature.* Routledge. [2015] pp. xi + 219. £95 ISBN 9 7811 3879 2456.

Davies, Helen. *Neo-Victorian Freakery: The Cultural Afterlife of the Victorian Freak Show.* PalMac. [2015] pp. 239. £58 ISBN 9 7811 3740 2554.

Delafield, Catherine. *Serialization and the Novel in Mid-Victorian Magazines.* Ashgate/Routledge. [2015] pp. viii + 212. $95 ISBN 9 7814 7245 0906.

Dentith, Simon, *Doctor Thorne* by Anthony Trollope. OUP. [2014] pp. xl + 504. £9.99 ISBN 9 7801 9966 2784.

Despotopoulou, Anna. *Women and the Railway, 1850–1915.* EdinUP. [2015] pp. x + 202. £70 ISBN 9 7807 4867 6941.

Dixon, Bryony, and David Mayer. *Bandits! or The Collapsing Bridge: An Early Film and a Late-Victorian Stage.* STR. [2015] pp. 84. £24 ISBN 9 7808 5430 0808.

Dixon, Thomas. *Weeping Britannia: Portrait of a Nation in Tears.* OUP. [2015] pp. 400. $45 ISBN 9 7801 9967 6057.

Donnelly, Brian. *Reading Dante Gabriel Rossetti: The Painter as Poet.* Ashgate. [2015] pp. viii + 178. £62.99 ISBN 9 7814 7244 6688.

Douglas-Fairhurst, Robert. *The Story of Alice: Lewis Carroll and the Secret History of Wonderland.* HarvardUP. [2015] pp. viii + 488. hb £24 ISBN 9 7806 7496 7793, pb £15 ISBN 9 7806 7497 0762.

Dowd, Garin, and Natalia Rulyova. *Genre Trajectories: Identifying, Mapping, Projecting.* PalMac. [2015] pp. xi + 255. £60 ISBN 9 7811 3750 5477.

Drury, Annmarie. *Translation as Transformation in Victorian Poetry.* CUP. [2015] pp. vii + 293. £67 ISBN 9 7811 0707 9243.

Duker, Elina and Bettina Kümmerling-Meibauer, eds., *Children's Literature and the Avant-Garde.* John Benjamins Publishing Company. [2015]. pp. 307. $149 ISBN 9 7890 2720 1591.

Dwor, Richa. *Jewish Feeling: Difference and Affect in Nineteenth-Century Jewish Women's Writing.* Bloomsbury. [2015] pp. 208. $72.99 ISBN 9 7814 7258 9804.

Ellis, Jonathan, ed. *Letter Writing Among Poets: From William Wordsworth to Elizabeth Bishop.* EdinUP. [2015] pp. xii + 252. hb £70 ISBN 9 7807 4868 1327, pb £19.99 ISBN 9 7814 7441 4128.

Felluga Dino Franco, with Gilbert Pamela K., and Linda K. Hughes, eds. *The Encyclopedia of Victorian Literature.* Wiley. [2015] vol. 1, pp. xxxii + 486; vol. 2, pp. vi + 487–966; vol. 3, pp. vi + 967–1,398; vol. 4, pp. vi + 1,399–1,888. $795 ISBN 9 7811 1840 5383.

Fernandes, Ana Raquel, José Pedro Serra, and Rui Carlos Fonseca, eds. *The Power of Form: Recycling Myths.* Cambridge Scholars Publishing. [2015]. pp. 250. £47.99. ISBN 9 7814 4387 1945.

Fhlathúin, Máire ni. *British India and Victorian Literary Culture.* EdinUP. [2015] pp. 272. $110 ISBN 9 7807 4864 0683.

Flegel, Monica. *Pets and Domesticity in Victorian Literature and Culture: Animality, Queer Relations, and the Victorian Family.* Routledge. [2015] pp. 204. $145 ISBN 9 7811 3883 2831.

Fraser, Angus, ed. *George Borrow's Tour of Galloway and the Borders 1866.* Lavengro Press. [2015]. pp. [xii] + 80. £10 ISBN 9 7809 9284 6343.

Fraser, Angus and Ann M. Ridler. *George Borrow and Dereham.* Lavengro Press. [2015]. pp. 56. £10.00. ISBN 9 7809 9284 6336.

Frenk, Joachim, and Lena Steveker. *Charles Dickens as an Agent of Change.* AMS. [2015] pp. xx + 242. $84.50 ISBN 9 7804 0464 4826.

Fyfe, Paul. *By Accident or Design: Writing the Victorian Metropolis.* OUP. [2015] pp. 256. $90 ISBN 9 7801 9873 2334.

Gantar, Jure. *The Evolution of Wilde's Wit.* PalMac. [2015] pp. ix + 199. $95 ISBN 9 7811 3748 8480.

Gavin, Adrian E., and Andrew F. Humphries, eds. *Transport in British Fiction: Technologies of Movement, 1840–1940.* PalMac. [2015] pp. xii + 273. £58 ISBN 9 7811 3749 9035.

Gibson, Richard Hughes. *Forgiveness in Victorian Literature: Grammar, Narrative, and Community.* Bloomsbury. [2015] pp. xiv + 170. $90 ISBN 9 7817 8093 7113.

Gillott, David. *Samuel Butler against the Professionals: Rethinking Lamarckism 1860–1900.* Legenda. [2015] pp. x + 198. £55 ISBN 9 7819 0996 2254.

Goldhill, Simon. *The Buried Life of Things: How Objects Made History in Nineteenth-Century Britain.* CUP. [2015] pp. 268. $55 ISBN 9 7811 0708 7484.

Gooch, Joshua. *The Victorian Novel, Service Work, and the Nineteenth-Century Economy.* PalMac. [2015] pp. vii + 233. $90 ISBN 9 7811 3752 5505.

Goodlad, Lauren M.E. *The Victorian Geopolitical Aesthetic: Realism, Sovereignty, and Transnational Experience.* OUP. [2015] pp. 320. $95 ISBN 9 7801 9872 8276.

Grennan, Simon. *Dispossession: A Novel of Few Words. After John Caldigate by Anthony Trollope.* Cape. [2015] pp. 104. $25.50 ISBN 9 7814 7352 0998.

Grennan, Simon, and Laurence Grove, eds. *Transforming Anthony Trollope: Dispossession, Victorianism and Nineteenth-Century Word and Image.* LeuvenUP. [2015] pp. 264. €55 ISBN 9 7894 6270 0413.

Gupta, Amit Kumar. *Nineteenth-Century Colonialism and the Great Indian Revolt.* Routledge. [2015] pp. 208. $160 ISBN 9 7811 3893 5440.

Gurney, Peter. *Wanting and Having: Popular Politics and Liberal Consumerism in England, 1830–1870.* ManUP. [2015] pp. 320. £75 ISBN 9 7807 1909 1452.

Hallum, Kirby-Jane. *Aestheticism and the Marriage Market in Victorian Popular Fiction: The Art of Female Beauty.* P&C. [2015] pp. ix + 217. £75 ISBN 9 7818 4893 4818.

Hamlett, Jane. *At Home in the Institution: Material Life in Asylums, Lodging Houses and Schools in Victorian and Edwardian England.* PalMac. [2015] pp. 225. £60 ISBN 9 7811 3732 2388.

Hammond, Mary. *Charles Dickens's Great Expectations: A Cultural Life, 1860–2012.* Ashgate. [2015] pp. 312. $103.70 ISBN 9 7814 0942 5878.

Harley, Alexis. *Autobiologies: Charles Darwin and the Natural History of the Self.* BuckUP. [2015] pp. 234. $85.14 ISBN 9 7816 1148 6001.

Harman, Claire. *Charlotte Brontë: A Life.* Viking. [2015] pp. 464. £25 ISBN 9 7806 7092 2260.

Harris, Peter. *The Territories of Science and Religion.* UChicP. [2015]. pp. 320. $30 ISBN 9 7802 2618 4487.

Hartmann, Johanna and Hubert Zapf, eds. *Censorship and Exile.* Göttingen: Vandenhoeck & Ruprecht. [2015]. pp. 285. €45.00. ISBN 9 7838 4700 4264.

Hartung, Heike. *Ageing, Gender and Illness in Anglophone Literature: Narrating Age in the Bildungsroman.* Routledge. [2015] pp. xii + 245. $125.80 ISBN 9 7811 3885 8503.

Harvey, John. *The Poetics of Sight. Cultural Interactions: Studies in the Relationship between the Arts,* ed. J.B. Bullen. Lang. [2015] pp. 309. $64.95 ISBN 9 7830 3539 9240.

Hawkins, Angus. *Victorian Political Culture: Habits of Heart and Mind.* OUP. [2015] pp. 400. $110 ISBN 9 7801 9872 8481.

Hay, Daisy. *Mr. and Mrs. Disraeli: A Strange Romance.* C&W. [2015] pp. xii + 308. £20 ISBN 9 7807 0118 9129.

Hazette, Valérie. *Wuthering Heights on Film and Television: A Journey Across Time and Cultures.* Intellect. [2015] pp. xiv + 359. £30 ISBN 9 7817 8320 4922.

Heinze, Rudiger, and Lucia Kramer, eds. *Remakes and Remaking: Concepts—Media—Practices.* ColUP. [2015] pp. 184. $35 ISBN 9 7838 3762 8944.

Higgins, Lesley, ed. *The Collected Works of Gerard Manley Hopkins, vol. 3: Diaries, Journals and Notebooks.* OUP. [2015] pp. 1+726. $150 ISBN 9 7801 9953 4005.

Hill, Kate. *Britain and the Narration of Travel in the Nineteenth Century: Texts, Images, Objects.* Routledge. [2015] pp. 246. $149.95 ISBN 9 7814 7245 8353.

Hopkins, Simon, ed. *George Borrow's Moorish Vocabulary (Tangiers 1839).* Lavengro Press. [2015]. pp. [xvi] + 104. £15 ISBN 9 7809 9284 6350.

Howe, Anthony, and Simon Morgan, eds. *The Letters of Richard Cobden, vol. 4: 1860–1865.* OUP. [2015] pp. 552. $225 ISBN 9 7801 9921 1982.

Hughes, Linda, and Sarah Robbins, eds. *Teaching Transatlanticism: Resources for Teaching Nineteenth-Century Anglo-American Print Culture.* EdinUP. [2015] pp. 312. $160 ISBN 9 7807 4869 4457.

Huguet, Christine, and Paul Vita, eds. *Unsettling Dickens: Process, Progress and Change.* Sagittaire. [2015] pp. 260. $23 ISBN 9 7829 1720 2326.

Ings-Chambers, Caroline. *Louisa Waterford and John Ruskin: 'For you have not Falsely Praised'.* Legenda. [2015] pp. xii + 252. £55 ISBN 9 7819 0966 2476.

Jacobson, Ken, and Jenny Jacobson. *Carrying Off the Palaces: John Ruskin's Lost Daguerreotypes.* Quaritch. [2015] pp. xxvi + 406. £85 ISBN 9 7809 5630 1277.

Janes, Dominic. *Visions of Queer Martyrdom, from John Henry Newman to Derek Jarman.* UChicP. [2015] pp. 240. $50 ISBN 9 7802 2625 0618.

Joyce, Simon. *Modernism and Naturalism in British and Irish Fiction 1880–1930.* CUP. [2015] viii + 216. $90 ISBN 9 7811 0708 3882.

Karschay, Stephan. *Degeneration, Normativity and the Gothic at the Fin de Siècle.* PalMac. [2015] pp. ix + 29. hb $110 ISBN 9 7811 1374 5032 6, pb $105 ISBN 9 7813 4949 6990.

Keene, Melanie. *Science in Wonderland.* OUP. [2015] pp. 256. $29.95 ISBN 9 7801 9966 2654.

Kelley, Philip, Scott Lewis, Edward Hagan, Joseph Phelan, and Rhian Williams, eds. *The Brownings' Correspondence,* vol. 22. Wedgestone. [2015] pp. xiii + 432. $110 ISBN 9 7809 1145 9395.

Khan, Jalal Uddin. *Perspectives: Romantic, Victorian, and Modern Literature.* CambridgeSP. [2015] pp. xix + 478. £57.99 ISBN 9 7814 4387 2089.

King, Joshua. *Imagined Spiritual Communities in Britain's Age of Print.* OSUP. [2015] pp. xi + 338. $86.95 ISBN 9 7808 1421 2936.

Kingsley Kent, Susan. *Queen Victoria: Gender and Empire.* OUP. [2015] pp. 232. $16.95 ISBN 9 7801 9025 0003.

Laidlaw, Zoë, and Alan Lester. *Indigenous Communities and Settler Colonialism: Land Holding, Loss and Survival in an Interconnected World.* PalMac. [2015] pp. 270. £63 ISBN 9 7811 3745 2351.

Laird, Karen E. *The Art of Adapting Victorian Literature, 1848–1920: Dramatizing Jane Eyre, David Copperfield, and The Woman in White.* Ashgate. [2015] pp. xi + 230. £47 ISBN 9 7814 7242 4396.

Leggott, James, Julie Anne Taddeo, and Jerome de Groot, eds. *Upstairs and Downstairs: British Costume Drama Television from The Forsyte Saga to Downton Abbey.* R&L. [2014] pp. xxx + 298. $70 ISBN 9 7814 4224 4825.

Levine, Caroline. *Forms: Whole, Rhythm, Hierarchy, Network.* PrincetonUP. [2015] pp. 192. $29.95 ISBN 9 7814 0085 2604.

Lutz, Deborah. *The Brontë Cabinet: Three Lives in Nine Objects.* Norton. [2015] pp. xx + 310. £18 ISBN 9 7803 9335 2702.

Lutz, Deborah. *Relics of Death in Victorian Literature and Culture.* CUP. [2015] pp. xii + 244. £62 ISBN 9 7811 0707 7447.

Lyons, Sara. *Algernon Swinburne and Walter Pater: Victorian Aestheticism, Doubt, and Secularisation.* Legenda. [2015] pp. x + 292. $99 ISBN 9 7819 0966 2483.

Macdonald, Kate, and Christof Singer, eds. *Transitions in Middlebrow Writing, 1880–1930.* PalMac. [2015] pp. 272. hb £58 ISBN 9 7811 3748 6769, pb £56 ISBN 9 7813 4950 3889.

MacDonald, Tara. *The New Man, Masculinity and Marriage in the Victorian Novel.* P&C. [2015] pp. x + 218. £100 ISBN 9 7818 4893 4917.

Macfie, Alexander Lyon, ed. *The Fiction of History.* Routledge. [2015] pp. x + 221. $125.80 ISBN 9 7804 1572 3015.

Mahoney, Kristin. *Literature and the Politics of Post-Victorian Decadence.* CUP. [2015] pp. xii + 252. £67 ISBN 9 7811 0710 9742.

Mallet, Phillip, ed. *The Victorian Novel and Masculinity*. PalMac. [2015] pp. xv + 217. hb $95 ISBN 9 7802 3027 2323, pb $90 ISBN 9 7813 4932 3135.

Mathieson, Charlotte. *Mobility in the Victorian Novel: Placing the Nation*. PalMac. [2015] pp. viii + 217. $99 ISBN 9 7811 1375 4546 6.

McAleavey, Maia. *The Bigamy Plot: Sensation and Conversion in the Victorian Novel*. CUP. [2015] pp. x + 250. $95 ISBN 9 7811 0710 3160.

McCourt, John. *Writing the Frontier: Anthony Trollope between Britain and Ireland*. OUP. [2015] pp. 304. $99 ISBN 9 7801 9872 9600.

Medd, Jodie. *The Cambridge Companion to Lesbian Literature*. CUP. [2015] pp. xxxii + 258. hb £54.99 ISBN 9 7811 0705 4004, pb £18.99 ISBN 9 7811 0766 3435.

Merchant, Peter, and Catherine Waters, eds. *Dickens and the Imagined Child*. Ashgate. [2015] pp. xv + 226. $107 ISBN 9 7814 7242 3818.

Michie, Helena, and Robyn Warhol. *Love Among the Archives: Writing the Lives of George Scharf, Victorian Bachelor*. EdinUP. [2015] pp. 256. $34.95 ISBN 9 7814 7440 6642.

Miller, Stephen. *Walking New York: Reflections of American Writers from Walt Whitman to Teju Cole*. FordUP. [2015] pp. 272. $80 ISBN 9 7808 2326 3158.

Mitsuharu, Matsuoka, ed. *Evil and Its Variations in the Works of Elizabeth Gaskell: Sesquicentennial Essays*. Osaka Kyoiku UP. [2015] pp. ??. £30 ISBN 9 7842 7121 0399.

Moine, Fabienne. *Women Poets in the Victorian Era: Cultural Practices and Nature Poetry*. Ashgate. [2015] pp. vii + 305. £70 ISBN 9 7814 7246 4774.

Monrós-Gaspar, Laura. *Victorian Classical Burlesques: A Critical Anthology*. Bloomsbury. [2015] pp. x + 298. £85 ISBN 9 7814 7253 7850.

Moore, Natasha. *Victorian Poetry and Modern Life: The Unpoetical Age*. PalMac. [2015] pp. vi + 239. £58 ISBN 9 7811 3753 7799.

Morosetti, Tiziana, ed. *Staging the Other in Nineteenth-Century British Drama*. Lang. [2015] pp. viii + 272. £60 ISBN 9 7830 3539 6164.

Mullan, Katherine, and Francis O'Gorman, eds. *Framley Parsonage* by Trollope Anthony. OUP. [2014] pp. xxxix + 488. £9.99 ISBN 9 7801 9966 3156.

Nicklas, Charlotte and Annabella Pollen, eds. *Dress History: New Directions in Theory and Practice*. Bloomsbury. [2015]. pp. 240. $114 ISBN 9 7808 5785 5411.

O'Brien, George. *The Irish Novel, 1800–1910*. CorkUP. [2015] pp. 296. €39 ISBN 9 7817 8205 1251.

O'Gorman, Francis, ed. *The Cambridge Companion to John Ruskin*. CUP. [2015] pp. xxiv + 289. £54.99 ISBN 9 7811 0705 4899.

O'Neill, Michael, Mark Sandy, and Sarah Wootton, eds. *The Persistence of Beauty: Victorians to Moderns*. P&C. [2015] pp. xi + 195. £84.99 ISBN 9 7818 4893 5112.

Oramus, Dominika. *Charles Darwin's Looking Glass: The Theory of Evolution and the Life of Its Author in Contemporary British Fiction and Non-Fiction*. Lang. [2015] pp. 152. $46. 95 ISBN 9 7836 3165 8703.

Pearson, Richard. *Victorian Writers and the Stage: The Plays of Dickens, Browning, Collins and Tennyson*. PalMac. [2015] pp. xii + 250. $90 ISBN 9 7811 3750 4678.

Peart, Sandra J., ed. *Hayek on Mill: The Mill–Taylor Friendship and Related Writings*. UChicP. [2015] pp. 440. $65 ISBN 9 7802 2610 6397.

Peker, Maria. *Gendered Time: Woman with a Past in the Victorian Novel*. Wissenschaftlicher. [2015] pp. 222. €2600 ISBN 9 7838 6821 6325.

Penner, Louise, and Tabitha Sparks, eds. *Victorian Medicine and Popular Culture*. P&C. [2015] pp. xiii + 182. $45 ISBN 9 7818 4893 5693.

Peterson, Linda H., ed. *The Cambridge Companion to Victorian Women's Writing*. CUP. [2015] pp. 319. $29.99 ISBN 9 7811 0765 9612.

Pratt-Smith, Stella. *Transformation of Electricity in Nineteenth-Century Literature and Science*. Routledge. [2015] pp. 216. $149.95 ISBN 9 7814 7241 9408.

Rainof, Rebecca Elise. *The Victorian Novel of Adulthood: Plot and Purgatory in Fictions of Maturity*. OhioUP. [2015] pp. xii + 252. $59.95 ISBN 9 7808 2142 1789.

Rajan, Supritha. *A Tale of Two Capitalisms: Sacred Economics in Nineteenth-Century Britain*. UMichP. [2015] pp. viii + 354. $90 ISBN 9 7804 7207 2552.

Redling, Ellen. *Allegorical Thackeray: Secularised Allegory in Thackeray's Major Novels*. LIT. [2015] pp. 307. £30 ISBN 9 7836 4390 6731.

Regan, J. Ward, ed. *Great Books Written in Prison: Essays on Classic Works from Plato to Martin Luther King, Jr.* McFarland and Company. [2015]. pp. 268. $45. ISBN 9 7807 8647 8033.

Richards, Jeffrey. *The Golden Age of Pantomime: Slapstick, Spectacle and Subversion in Victorian England*. Tauris. [2015] pp. xiii + 438. £25 ISBN 9 7817 8076 2937.

Riley, Jonathan. *The Routledge Guidebook to Mill's On Liberty*. Routledge. [2015] pp. 354. $130 ISBN 9 7804 1566 5391.

Rippl, Gabriele, ed. *Handbook of Intermediality: Literature-Image-Sound-Music*. De Gruyter. [2015]. pp. 691. £149.99. ISBN 9 7831 1031 1075.

Riso, Mary. *The Narrative of the Good Death: The Evangelical Deathbed in Victorian England*. Routledge. [2015] pp. 292. $109.95 ISBN 9 7814 7244 6961.

Rogobete, Daniela, Jonathon P.A. Sell, and Alan Munton, eds. *The Silent Life of Things: Reading and Representing Commodified Objecthood*. CambridgeSP. [2015] pp. vi + 211. £48 ISBN 9 7814 4388 3689.

Rose, David Charles. *Oscar Wilde's Elegant Republic: Transformation, Dislocation and Fantasy in Fin-de-Siècle Paris*. CambridgeSP. [2015] pp. 610. $125.95 ISBN 9 7814 4388 3603.

Scholl, Lesa, Emily Morris, and Sarina Gruver Moore, eds. *Place and Progress in the Works of Elizabeth Gaskell*. Ashgate. [2015] pp. xii + 231. $107 ISBN 9 7814 7242 9636.

Seki, Yoshiko. *The Rhetoric of Retelling Old Romances: Medievalist Poetry by Alfred Tennyson and William Morris*. Eihosha. [2015] pp. x + 195. £22 ISBN 9 7842 6974 0310.

Shannon, Mary L. *Dickens, Reynolds, and Mayhew on Wellington Street: The Print Culture of a Victorian Street.* Routledge. [2015] pp. 278. $119.95 ISBN 9 7814 7244 2048.

Shore, Heather. *London's Criminal Underworlds, c.1720–c.1930: A Social and Cultural History.* PalMac. [2015] pp. 286. $95 ISBN 9 7802 3030 4048.

Shrimpton, Nicholas, ed. *An Autobiography and Other Writings* by Trollope Anthony. OUP. [2014] pp. xxviii + 300. £ 14.99 ISBN 9 7801 9967 5289.

Shrimpton, Nicholas, ed. *The Warden* by Trollope Anthony. OUP. [2014] pp. xliv + 292. £6.99 ISBN 9 7801 9966 5440.

Small, Helen, ed. *The Last Chronicle of Barsetshire* by Trollope Anthony. OUP. [2014] pp. 816. £10.99 ISBN 9 7801 9967 5999.

Solinas, Marco. *From Aristotle's Teleology to Darwin's Genealogy: The Stamp of Inutility.* PalMac. [2015] pp. 182. £60 ISBN 9 7811 3744 5766.

Standlee, Whitney. *'Powers to Observe': Irish Women Novelists in Britain, 1890–1916.* Lang. [2015] pp. x + 286. £40 ISBN 9 7830 3431 8372.

Starck, Nigel. *The First Celebrity: An Australasian Odyssey.* Trollope Society. [2014]. pp. 192. £25 ISBN 9 7809 5735 7013.

Stead, Henry and Edith Hall, eds. *Greek and Roman Classics in the British Struggle for Social Reform.* Bloomsbury. [2015] pp. 384 $133.93 ISBN 9 7814 7258 4267.

Strange, Roderick, ed. *John Henry Newman: A Portrait in Letters.* OUP. [2015] pp. 608. $49.50 ISBN 9 7801 9960 4142.

Szirotny, June Skye. *George Eliot's Feminism: 'The Right to Rebellion'.* PalMac. [2015] pp. xii + 288. £60 ISBN 9 7811 3740 6149.

Tabachnick, Stephen E., and Esther Bendit Saltzman, eds. *Drawn from the Classics: Essays on Graphic Adaptations of Literary Works.* McFarland. [2015] pp. viii + 283. $35 ISBN 9 7807 8647 8798.

Teodorescu, Adriana, ed., *Death: Representations in Literature: Forms and Theories.* Cambridge Scholars Publishing. [2015]. pp. 450. £57.99. ISBN 9 7814 4387 1587.

Van Remoortel, Marianne. *Women, Work and the Victorian Periodical: Living by the Press.* PalMac. [2015] pp. ix + 189. £55 ISBN 9 7811 3743 5989.

Vance, Norman, and Jennifer Wallace, eds. *The Oxford History of Classical Reception in English Literature, vol. 4: 1790–1880.* OUP. [2015] pp. xiv + 746. £140 ISBN 9 7801 9959 4603.

Vaughan, William. *Samuel Palmer: Shadows on the Wall.* YaleUP. [2015] pp. xii + 412. $85 ISBN 9 7803 0020 9853.

Wadman, Carrie. *The Victorian Spinster and Emerging Female Identities: A Critical Study of the Fin-de-Siècle Literature and Culture.* Mellen. [2015] pp. 360. £173 ISBN 9 7814 9550 2972.

Watts, Michael R. *The Dissenters, vol. 3: The Crisis of Conscience of Nonconformity.* OUP. [2015] pp. 600. $125 ISBN 9 7801 9822 9698.

Weinroth, Michelle, and Paul Leduc Browne, eds. *To Build a Shadowy Isle of Bliss: William Morris's Radicalism and the Embodiment of Dreams.* McG-QUP. [2015] pp. xiv + 372. $39.95 ISBN 9 7807 7354 4611.

Welby, Lizzy. *Rudyard Kipling's Fiction: Mapping Psychic Spaces.* EdinUP. [2015] pp. vii + 246. £70 ISBN 9 7807 4869 8554.

Whitely, Giles. *Oscar Wilde and the Simulacrum The Truth of Masks.* Legenda. [2015] pp. xvi + 356. $99 ISBN 9 7819 0966 2506.
Wood, Claire. *Dickens and the Business of Death.* CUP. [2015] pp. x + 225. $95 ISBN 9 7811 0709 8633.

# XV

# Modern Literature

MATTHEW LEVAY, ANDREW RADFORD, SOPHIE VLACOS,
ANDREW KEESE, MARIA-DANIELLA DICK, CLARA JONES,
HANNAH TWEED, REBECCA D'MONTÉ,
GRAHAM SAUNDERS, NEIL MILES, MATTHEW CREASY,
MATTHEW SPERLING, AND ADAM HANNA

This chapter has eight sections: 1. General; 2. Pre-1945 Fiction; 3. British Fiction, 1945–2000; 4. Pre-1950 Drama; 5. Post-1950 Drama; 6. Poetry; 7. British Poetry Post-1950; 8. Modern Irish Poetry. Section 1 is by Matthew Levay; section 2(a) is by Andrew Radford; section 2(b) is by Sophie Vlacos; Section 2(c) is by Maria-Daniella Dick; section 2(d) is by Andrew Keese; section 2(e) is by Clara Jones; section 3 is by Hannah Tweed; section 4 is by Rebecca D'Monte; section 5 is by Graham Saunders; 6(a) is by Neil Miles; section 6(b) is by Matthew Creasy; section 7 is by Matthew Sperling; section 8 is by Adam Hanna

## 1. General

In assessing the direction of modernist studies in 2015, one notes two related phenomena: firstly, the expansion of modernism as a historical period, as a formal designation that registers various levels of commitment to experimental aesthetics and as a broad artistic response to the experience of modernity continues unabated. Secondly, critics remain steadfast in their efforts to map the intellectual, social, political, and national cultures that fostered modernism as a formal and conceptual category. Many of the books published in 2015 exemplify both of these trends, understanding modernism as a pluralistic array of artistic practices dominant in the first half of the twentieth century (though by no means limited to that chronology) while also attending to the specific contexts and environments that made such practices possible. Thus, modernist studies is still firmly committed to a combination of formalism and literary history, and to research that views the aesthetic productions of the era within and across diverse cultural milieus. Such commitment is increasingly urgent, acknowledging as it does the fact that the expansionism of modernist studies

*The Year's Work in English Studies, Volume 96 (2017)* © *The Author 2017. Published by Oxford University Press on behalf of the English Association. All rights reserved.*
*For Permissions, please email: journals.permissions@oup.com*
doi:10.1093/ywes/max016

raises pressing questions about just how elastic the concept of modernism can or should be. As 'modernism' continues to bear more weight as a critical descriptor, we need scholarship that explains more concretely what the term signifies, not to stem the flow of formerly neglected authors and texts into the canon, but rather to theorize how those authors and texts participate in specific versions of modernism, and to what ends. Several of 2015's most significant books in modernist studies do precisely that, pressuring the limits of modernism in order to understand how the concept operated differently (or similarly) in non-Anglo-American contexts, popular genres, and art forms beyond the literary. The result is a body of work that demonstrates the sizeable influence of place and time on modernist aesthetics while also showing how flagrantly modernism crossed those borders, effectively reintegrating modernist cultural productions into the various contexts that fostered them but also noting the latter's essential permeability.

As this brief overview might indicate, modernist studies has become increasingly ambitious in its scope, and, as a result, potentially intimidating to students. With terminology up for debate and geographical and temporal borders continually being crossed, the field can appear alternately groundbreaking and disorienting. One of 2015's most welcome developments, then, was the release of several edited collections, each devoted to either a broad survey of modernism across time and space or a more intensive overview of one of the period's central elements, aimed specifically at student readers and library reference collections. Perhaps the most ambitious of these volumes is Stephen Ross and Allana C. Lindgren's *The Modernist World*, which, as its title suggests, situates modernism within an expansive, global frame. Divided into eight parts, with each covering a specific region—East and Southeast Asia, South Asia, sub-Saharan Africa, Australia and Oceania, Europe, Latin America, the Middle East and the Arab world, and Canada and the United States—the book boasts more than sixty chapters devoted to key aspects of modernist cultural production, from literature, visual art, and cinema to architecture, dance, and music. Such comprehensiveness not only affirms the diversity of modernist artistic practice, but also allows for comparative readings of modernism as a global occurrence, locating it within local and national communities while also illustrating the possibilities for international exchange. Throughout, *The Modernist World* presents a consistently multiform notion of modernism as both transnational and interdisciplinary, rooted and wandering. As Ross and Lindgren explain, the book 'is perhaps best understood as an experiment in n-dimensional scholarly cartography', which 'does not merely map Modernism around the world, but seeks to determine how the global orientation of new modernist studies is understood across arts disciplines and geopolitical regions' (p. 3). Bolstered by a strong, international list of contributors, each of whom takes a meticulous approach to his or her subject, Ross and Lindgren's volume proposes a modernism that is both defined by the locations of its production and able to traverse those boundaries with relative ease. What unfolds is a modernism that means different things within different national and artistic traditions, but that ultimately signifies a wealth of cultural activity that deserves an overview of this magnitude; as the editors assert, a collection of this size and scope is necessary precisely because 'disputes about terms like modern, Modernism, and modernity will remain unresolvable in large part because they are so context-dependent' (p. 2). *The Modernist World* provides one of the most expansive versions of that context one could imagine, and in so doing gives the field a practical, searching account of itself that should inspire equally probing and attentive work.

Whereas *The Modernist World* surveys its subject as a fundamentally global enterprise, other edited collections approach modernism in more focused yet equally thoughtful ways. Indeed, one of the most informative and enjoyable books of the year is the *Cambridge Companion to Modernist Culture*, edited by Celia Marshik, whose lively sense of the period makes for a welcome addition to Cambridge's longstanding Companions to Culture series. In her introduction, Marshik acknowledges that modernism's expansion has created substantial challenges. As she argues, 'While the interdisciplinary turn in Modernist studies has produced volumes of exciting scholarship, it presents a high barrier to students and scholars, who are now expected not only to familiarize themselves with texts like *Ulysses* and *The Great Gatsby* and with movements such as Futurism, Symbolism, and the Harlem Renaissance but also to understand the significance of the Charleston, the gramophone, little magazines, "talkies", the bias cut, and numerous other cultural phenomena' (p. 2). Marshik is right to point out that modernism's interdisciplinarity can vex novice and experienced scholars alike, as modernist expansionism demands that one go beyond traditional frames of reference to understand the period in a more holistic, comprehensive fashion. In part, this means understanding modernism not solely in terms of literature, but also in terms of an exceptionally rich and varied cultural scene, and so Marshik's book provides needed guidance by introducing readers to the contexts, both material and intellectual, in which modernism came to exist. Its chapters are eclectic yet add up to an absorbing narrative of the early twentieth century's defining concepts, artistic practices, and amusements: we have Suzanne Hobson on 'Religion and Spirituality', Ulrika Maude on 'Science, Technology, and the Body', Allison Pease on 'Sexuality', Ellen Ross on 'Militarism, Pacifism, and Internationalism', Elizabeth Outka on 'Consumer Culture', Ilya Parkins on 'Fashion', Susan McCabe on 'Modernist Film and Cinema Culture', Carrie J. Preston on 'Dance', Jessica Burstein on 'Visual Art', Judith Walkowitz on 'Urban Pleasures', Allen Guttmann on 'Sport', Helen Carr on 'Travel', Len Platt on 'Popular Theater', and George Bornstein on 'Publishing'. Each contribution is impressive in its own right; taken as a whole, they detail a cultural moment of profound transformation and contradiction for individuals and collectives alike. Many pivot on the idea that modernism brings a renewed emphasis on subjectivity to both aesthetic and everyday experience, and that early twentieth-century culture reflected and enabled that emphasis in myriad ways; Parkins, for instance, argues that 'fashion dramatized the underside of modern life, the alternative narratives that structure everyday, lived experiences of modernity, highlighting the gap between ideals and representations' (p. 97), while Burstein claims that 'the subjectivity of objectivity is what modernism shows us again and again' (p. 156). Other essays, meanwhile, focus on the transnational exchange of ideas and cultural forms, or on the period's unique blending of high, low, and middlebrow culture; some, like Preston and Platt's terrific contributions on dance and popular theatre respectively, do both, situating the idea of modernism in relation to avant-garde and mass cultural forms and demonstrating its circulation in multiple national contexts. In all of its essays, the *Cambridge Companion to Modernist Culture* adopts a rigorous historical focus, framing the early twentieth century as a period of astonishing ingenuity and flux.

Gregory Castle's *A History of the Modernist Novel* complements the previous two collections while also distinguishing itself as a vital resource for those interested in the permutations of modernist fiction. By examining significant themes in the modernist novel in England, America, France, Germany, Russia, Ireland, South Africa, and India, this volume offers a refreshing account of late nineteenth- and early twentieth-century fiction that shirks modernists' own aesthetic pronouncements in favour of a more historically grounded approach to the novel's prolonged evolution during the period. Castle's introduction emphasizes one of the central paradoxes at the heart of the modernist novel—namely, the fact that it is 'always in an experimental mode' at the same time as it is 'always engaged with realism'— and several chapters take up one or both of those poles to demonstrate how some of the most repeated critical narratives about modernist fiction are, if not wholly untrue, at least less uniformly true than has been supposed (p. 3). David Bradshaw's excellent study of the Edwardian novel, for example, casts deserved suspicion on Virginia Woolf's infamous dismissal of H.G. Wells, Arnold Bennett, and John Galsworthy in 'Mr Bennett and Mrs Brown' and 'Character in Fiction', memorably asserting that Woolf's 'emphasis on severance and exceptionality, on there being a categorical distinction between the modernists and those who flourished just before them, occludes crucial debts and continuities. Modernism did not burst forth in full bloom "about the year 1910" but grew organically yet aberrantly from its Edwardian mulch' (p. 139). Other contributions revise the history of the modernist novel by placing it within a longer history of popular forms, audiences, and institutional contexts, showing how modernism's publication and reception histories can shed needed light on the vaunted experimentalism of its narratives. Sean Latham's 'Serial Modernism' makes an especially convincing case for the magazine—particularly its physical shape and serial temporality—as a galvanizing force for modernism's experimental aesthetics, while David Earle's essay proposes increased attention to what he terms 'The Modernist Genre Novel', in which 'Modernist authors examine their own relationships to reading, audience, and modernity while using the tropes and generic conventions of popular fiction, sometimes as métier and sometimes as a means of satire' (pp. 345–6). In both cases, the modernist novel ceases to appear as a monolithic, uniformly experimental formation, but as a much more complex negotiation between generic and other formal categories that alternately conflict and overlap.

In addition to its focus on the circumstances of a work's publication and the various genres to which it might be attached, Castle's collection follows Ross and Lindgen's in proposing an expansive, global framework for tracking the literary history of the modernist novel. Here Jessica Berman's essay on 'Modernist Cosmopolitanism' and Laura Winkiel's 'The Modernist Novel in the World-System' make welcome contributions to the interpretation of modernist fiction as a transnational enterprise. For Berman, the term 'cosmopolitanism' does not necessarily denote the kind of privileged border crossing available only to the economic elite for which it is sometimes derided, and she proposes instead the idea of 'cosmopolitan communities', or 'new models of cosmopolitanism that are intimately bound to community affiliation', providing ways of being in the world that are both local and global, public and private (p. 430). For modernist novelists, the cosmopolitan becomes a vehicle for re-evaluating local concerns through global frameworks, and of decentring the nation from its central position as the defining feature of cultural life. Winkiel makes a similar intervention by applying world-systems theory, particularly as articulated in Immanuel Wallerstein's work, to modernist and postcolonial fiction, arguing that such novels represent everyday experience in a diverse swath of locations and thereby allow readers to see how such experience is mediated through local and global sociopolitical forces. Here and elsewhere, the idea of the modernist novel appears increasingly dynamic, characterized by authors' willingness to pressure traditional formal, national, and material boundaries on a scale we are only beginning to grasp, and by our own abilities as critics to take in the broad range of aesthetic manoeuvres that the form of the novel affords. What *A History of the Modernist Novel* contributes to this discussion, then, is a uniquely expansive vision of its subject that never fails to confront some of the most widely accepted yet ultimately tenuous narratives of modernist aesthetics. Castle and his contributors are admirably attuned to the modernist novel's most fundamental and most idiosyncratic attributes, and do an exceptional job of showing where and why the two intersect.

Alongside the surge of edited collections in modernist studies, monograph series devoted to the period have continued to emerge. Complementing well-regarded series from university presses at Oxford, Columbia, Penn State, Johns Hopkins, and Edinburgh, as well as the 'Modernism and' series at Palgrave, Bloomsbury inaugurated a new series of monographs on modernism and modernist studies, designed to familiarize readers with the field's current debates. The debut volume in the New Modernisms series is the excellent *Modernism: Evolution of an Idea*, co-written by series editors Sean Latham and Gayle Rogers. An engaging introduction to the fraught history of modernism as a critical and aesthetic category, the book makes a substantive case for the lability of its subject, beginning with its provocative yet undeniable charge that 'there is no such thing as Modernism', in that there exists 'no singular definition capable of bringing order to the diverse multitude of creators, manifestoes, practices, and politics that have been variously constellated around this enigmatic term' (p. 1). Indeed, Latham and Rogers assert, this period, which 'insists on a kind of ahistorical, even paradoxical presentism, an art for a boundless now', is notoriously resistant to categorization not only because of the immense formal variations between works associated with it, but also due to the myriad investments and predispositions by which critics have defined it (pp. 1–2). Consequently, their focus is not on modernism per se, but rather the critical history of the concept itself, and the debates over form, politics, and interdisciplinarity that have led scholars to their current positions in accounting for modernism within a larger cultural field. Their volume expertly traces the history of this vexed concept, moving from early twentieth-century disputes over the autonomy of literary form to more contemporary conversations in which changing attitudes towards the concept of modernism mirror the transformation of the university and its practices; in the process, it gives students and scholars alike a handy guide for making their own way through the thicket of past and present critical approaches. This is disciplinary historiography at its most lucid, and the narrative it weaves introduces readers to or reminds them of an impressive number of arguments without ever feeling rushed, over-stuffed, or, most importantly, tangential. And while it may seem like faint praise to commend a book for its back matter, Latham and Rogers append an extensive critical bibliography of significant works in modernist studies, which should prove invaluable to students and early researchers looking for direction in navigating such a diverse field. The detail of this apparatus speaks to the utility of *Modernism* as a whole, a book that should become a staple in modernist classrooms and dissertation reading lists for the foreseeable future.

Equally impressive for its breadth and depth is Daniel Albright's *Putting Modernism Together: Literature, Music, and Painting, 1872–1927*. Throughout his career, Albright, who passed away in 2015, produced innovative accounts of modernism across the arts, advocating with verve and clarity for interdisciplinary approaches that situate modernism's best-known literary contributions alongside other experimental achievements in the visual arts and, especially, music. *Putting Modernism Together* serves as a fitting tribute to that legacy. It begins with a wide-ranging account of modernism's definitions, yet unlike other, comparable, introductions, Albright's moves deftly from Nietzsche and Pound to Shakespeare and Genesis, landing on the assertion that modernism is best defined as 'a testing of the limits of aesthetic construction', and thereby understood as a perennial challenge to prevailing standards of value (p. 5). The connections between canonical modernist works and texts from much earlier periods are persuasive and never strained, offering a genealogy of 'Modernism' that seeks to portray its subject as a distinctive part of a longer literary history. Other chapters highlight this extraordinary range, as the majority of the book is devoted to a series of penetrating chapters on those movements and collectives that comprised the modernist period. Whether discussing standards like Impressionism and Cubism or less known but equally significant concepts like Corporealism (defined as a rejection of abstraction, particularly evident in the work of D.H. Lawrence) and Totalizing Art (that is, the encyclopedic aspirations of Eliot, Joyce, Pound, and composer Alban Berg), Albright's arguments are rich and suggestive, provoking new constellations of modernist creation and influence. He is also, one should add, a delight to read: what modernist would want to argue with the proposal that, 'after the nineteenth century had established a remarkably safe, intimate centre where the artist and the audience could dwell, the Modernist age reaches out to the freakish circumferences of art' (p. 5)? In these and other moments, Albright's immersion in his subject is absolutely clear, his delight in modernism's creative and interpretative possibilities immediately transferred to his readers.

Whereas Albright showcases modernism's range of innovations across the arts, Barry McCrae, in his short, elegant book *Languages of the Night: Minor Languages and the Literary Imagination in Twentieth-Century Ireland and Europe*, carefully argues for the centrality of multilingualism to modernist fiction and poetry. Persuasively demonstrating how several modernists' overwhelming impression that language itself needed revitalization coincided with the gradual disappearance of minor European languages and dialects from daily speech, McCrae contends that 'as they became rarer, or threatened to become so, these languages and dialects went on to have second, post-vernacular lives as literary mediums or sites of projection for writers for whom they were not a native language' (p. xiii). In so doing, he reframes the dominant narrative of modernism as an urban phenomenon by showing how authors like Joyce, Proust, Seán Ó Ríordáin, and Pier Paolo Pasolini drew upon these primarily rural languages and dialects in their search for more vigorous modes of expression. He is also commendably attuned to the distinctions between fiction and poetry in their use of these 'languages of the night' (a phrase borrowed from Ó Ríordáin's description of Irish as a language spoken largely by the elderly, outside everyday, public discourse). Modernist fiction, McCrae argues, often employs such minor languages in subtle ways, sometimes as an idea to be considered rather than an actual, viable language to be used, as in the ghostly, at times elegiac presence of Irish in Joyce's fiction, for instance. But modernist poets employ the expressions of fading vernacular speech in order to infuse their verse with 'a purer alternative to what they saw as their own compromised or degraded major mother tongues' (p. xiv). McCrae makes a sustained case for both points in all of his chapters, most notably in his illuminating section on Ó Ríordáin, who wrote all of his poetry in Irish despite the fact that it was not his native language. Identifying Ó Ríordáin's Irish-language poetry as part of a 'minor literary tradition of lyric poetry in the waning peasant languages of Europe, far removed from the cosmopolitan experiments of Paris, London, and Vienna', McCrae notes that such a tradition was not 'a last remnant of a premodern world that was bound to fade', but instead 'another, later strain of European Modernism' that has yet to be fully recognized (p. 120). Inverting the typical association of rural and premodern spaces, McCrae makes a valuable contribution by directing the growing critical awareness of regional modernisms toward the long-established interest in polyglot modernism, effectively bridging the divide between a modernism traditionally viewed as a metropolitan phenomenon and the creative possibilities present in rural communities.

While, for McCrae, modernism's aesthetic and cultural aims become more legible through authors' investment in the minor languages that once characterized rural, peasant life, according to Susan Stanford Friedman, such aims are legible everywhere. Friedman's newest book, *Planetary Modernisms: Provocations on Modernity Across Time*, advances a bold set of claims in its effort to debunk the common perception of modernity as originating in sixteenth-century Western cultures, replacing that narrative with a global history of modernity characterized by ruptures occurring across the world, over vast spans of time. Arguing that modernist studies today is necessarily animated by the concerns of the present—most notably the geopolitical and economic forces of globalization, coupled with the spread of communication networks enabled by ascendant digital technologies—Friedman nonetheless takes contemporary criticism to task for failing to recognize its most persistent and potentially insidious assumptions. As critics of modernity, she suggests, we are invariably informed by our current condition of global interconnectedness, and yet, however pluralistic our conception of modernism might be, it is nonetheless based on a disingenuous notion of modernity as a singular, fundamentally Eurocentric occurrence: 'in Modernist studies, Eurocentrism is the dominant centrism to confront because the West's narrative of itself is the story of its own invention of modernity' (p. 54). Confronting this imbalance head-on, her book proposes 'a fundamental rethinking of modernity that posits it as a geohistorical condition that is multiple, contradictory, interconnected, polycentric, and recurrent for millennia and across the globe' (p. 4). By this formulation, modernism is not the response to a singular, Western modernity, but rather a set of responses to a recurring condition of rupture with the dominant forms and ideologies of a particular era. To illustrate the point, Friedman details the modernity of a number of historical moments and the texts produced within their borders, many of which have existed well beyond the markers typically used to cordon modernism off from other periods; thus, her study has much to say about Joyce and Woolf, but also about Theresa Hak Kung Cha, Arundhati Roy, the Tang and Song dynasties, and the Mongol empire. These choices are deliberately provocative—Friedman notes at several points that readers may well quarrel with her examples—but they are also well considered given the scope of Friedman's thesis. Indeed, as its subtitle suggests, *Planetary Modernisms* derives much of its force from its bold attempt to unsettle the foundations of modernist studies, an attempt grounded in the idea that modernism, as a concept, is far older, more global, and ultimately more prevalent than even the most vocal of expansionist critics have assumed.

Another 2015 book that has made an immediate contribution to the field is Paul K. Saint-Amour's magisterial *Tense Future: Modernism, Total War, Encyclopedic Form*, a profound and impressively researched account of modernism's engagement with the traumatic repercussions of mass warfare. Beautifully written and astutely argued, *Tense Future* examines the period between the First and Second World Wars as a time when citizens not only ruminated upon the war that had just concluded, but were also conditioned by that conflict to view the future with anxiety, and so existed in a state of total war, in which disaster was perpetually poised to strike. Saint-Amour draws together a diverse array of literary texts, notably Woolf's *Mrs Dalloway* and *The Years*, Joyce's *Ulysses*, and Ford's *Parade's End* tetralogy, as well as less canonical pieces like Cicely Hamilton's *Theodore Savage* [1922] and the memoirs of conscientious objector L.E.O. Charlton, and then places them alongside government reports and other documentary materials on the employment of air warfare. The book thus constructs a voluminous archive to sustain its position that the interwar period was one of intense anticipation and pervasive dread. In so doing, it challenges trauma theory's model of anxiety as a gesture of self-protection, claiming instead that the constant state of awareness demanded by modern military technologies led to a 'pre-traumatic stress syndrome' among an expectant civilian populace (pp. 7–8). Saint-Amour's intensive close readings, buttressed by thick historicization, are all extremely persuasive, and his account of encyclopedic form is especially convincing in this regard, highlighting as it does some of the book's most fundamental arguments. He advocates that works traditionally deemed modernist epics, such as *Ulysses*, *Parade's End*, and Robert Musil's *The Man Without Qualities*, should be relabelled as encyclopedic fictions, which 'attempt to furnish an alternative world-picture to modern warfare's portrait of the social totality' (p. 183). In overwhelming detail, these novels attempt to preserve a comprehensive representation of societies that now live under the threat of annihilation. Yet in their distinctly fragmented styles they all attempt to avoid falling victim to the traditional dictates of epic form, which tend to present social relations as mediated by war and militarism. Modernist encyclopedism, then, becomes a way of rebuking the totalizing logics of epic by presenting grand social narratives through remarkably limited perspectives (a novel that takes place over a single day, for example, or multi-volume novels in which each volume in some way undermines or contradicts perspectives shared in the previous one), making literature a profound site for thinking otherwise about a future that appears radically under siege. Perhaps the most admirable element of *Tense Future* is the unflinching urgency that Saint-Amour brings to the study of war while resolutely refusing to surrender to the banalities of expression that war can easily engender; 'To speak of "the shadow of war"', he remarks at the outset of his chapter on Ford, 'is to walk in the valley of cliché' (p. 263). Saint-Amour, by contrast, consistently approaches his subject with empathy and assiduousness, and crafts an eerie but insistent account of literary form as it responded to situations deemed at once inconceivable and all too likely to occur.

Other monographs also explored the depth of modernism's historical imagination, among them Seamus O'Malley's careful study *Making History New: Modernism and Historical Narrative*, which explains how the work of modernists like Joseph Conrad, Ford Madox Ford, and Rebecca West tests the limits of narrative in order to pursue new modes of representing historical experience. Reclaiming the historical novel from previous and subsequent literary periods—particularly its association with the nineteenth century and the historiographical metafictions of late twentieth-century postmodernism—O'Malley makes a sophisticated case for the modernist investment in historical narrative. Examining his chosen texts as instances of 'Modernist historiography', he maintains that critics should not simply interpret these works as containing historical reference, but instead perceive them as examples of narrative history, as modernists attempt to write history through narrative techniques that communicate both the factuality of past events and the indeterminacy of narrative in representing them fully. Beginning with an introduction that seamlessly connects modernist fiction and poetry, historiography, and narratology, and ends with a considered assessment of Paul Ricoeur's work on history, narrative, and the problem of forgetting, the book continues through a series of chapters focusing on deeply historical readings of canonical modernist novels: Conrad's *Nostromo*, Ford's *The Good Soldier* and *Parade's End*, and West's *The Return of the Soldier* and *Black Lamb and Grey Falcon*. In each, O'Malley presents history as something that these three authors felt compelled to preserve through narrative at the same time that they thought such preservation potentially impossible given the available means at hand. Ford, for instance, evinces a 'radical scepticism regarding memory and impressions, and also regarding our ability to record or narrate events', which is what makes his *Parade's End* tetralogy so intriguing, focused as it is on a protagonist whose memory is severely damaged during his time at the Western Front (p. 129). Likewise, West's *Return of the Soldier* reveals 'a suspicion of the self-confidence of orthodox historiography, which believes that it renders history by naming its objects', and instead attempts to 'surround the historical events in other forms of textuality' (p. 117). Throughout, O'Malley proposes subtle variations in each modernist's approach to historical narrative while also tracing key connections between the three. As a result, his tight focus on a small selection of novels makes for an extremely persuasive, conceptually rigorous argument, and helps the reader understand historiography not just in relation to modernism, but as an unexpectedly yet incontrovertibly modernist practice.

Whereas O'Malley's discussion of historical representation occurs primarily in a British context, Nicole M. Rizzuto establishes deep connections among Europe, the Caribbean, and Africa in her *Insurgent Testimonies: Witnessing Colonial Trauma in Modern and Anglophone Literature*. Like O'Malley's, her book also takes up the problem of historical memory in twentieth-century literature, but does so by scrutinizing the traumatic legacy of insurgency in modernist, colonial, and postcolonial writing. Focused largely on novels by West, Joseph Conrad, H.G. de Lisser, V.S. Reid, and Ngũgĩ wa Thiong'o, Rizzuto presents a wide constellation of voices that facilitates a much more nuanced exchange between modernist and postcolonial literature, a decision that, in turn, makes modernism appear far more responsive to imperial history, and postcolonial writing far less 'indebted' to modernism, than has traditionally been the case. Rather than reading modernism and traumatic events as instances of rupture—an early twentieth-century poem that shouts its departures from Victorian verse, or a Great War that shatters the placidity of a peaceful European continent—*Insurgent Testimonies* interprets both within the parameters of a long-standing imperial project. The authors Rizzuto examines 'reimagine revolutions, insurgencies, counterinsurgencies, treason, and war as tears in the fabric of the nation and empire, but the formal practices that constitute testimony relate that each of these events is enmeshed within historical processes that predate them and is the product of contemporaneous forces that extend beyond the particular region, nation, or continent in which they are shown to occur' (p. 8). The book is divided into two halves, the first exploring how the form of modernist writing was affected by authors' attempts to bear witness to state violence and colonial unrest, while the second surveys anglophone literature that takes similar positions, under conditions and pressures specific to its location. Rizzuto's interpretations of these texts are consistently impressive, emerging from a combination of postcolonial theory and exceptional close reading, and should lend even

more momentum to critics searching for new transnational approaches to
continue altering the dynamics of modernist studies.

Some 2015 books, meanwhile, fit uneasily into the trends of current
modernist scholarship, yet this is precisely what makes them such welcome
additions to the field. Nico Israel opens his engaging book *Spirals: The
Whirled Image in Twentieth-Century Literature and Art* with an admission that
his focus on a century's worth of art and writing 'runs counter to the current
penchant for a narrower, more archival brand of historicism predominant in
Modernist studies in literature ... or to the still-prevalent tendency in early-
twenty-first-century art history to concentrate monographically on individual
artists or on chronologically circumscribed movements' (p. 4). *Spirals*, by
contrast, offers an energetic theorization of the spiral as an image combining
aesthetics and politics, recurrence and endlessness, in a dialectic of forms that
allowed artists and writers unique opportunities to think through the historical
moment in which they found themselves. Generously illustrated and beautifully designed, it is a thoughtful blend of art history, aesthetic theory, and
literary criticism that generates a surprising amount of reflection on what
might initially seem either a dauntingly broad or oddly narrow topic. In its
chapters, one finds dazzling assessments of individual artists and authors like
W.B. Yeats, Vladimir Tatlin, Marcel Duchamp, James Joyce, Robert
Smithson, and Samuel Beckett, as well as insightful reflections on wider
avant-garde movements (most notably Futurism, Vorticism, and
Constructivism). Each seamlessly shifts between the textual and the visual,
and the result is not only an admirably interdisciplinary study of one of the
twentieth century's most enduring images, but also, much like Albright's book,
a fine indication of what critics can achieve through a concentrated
examination of modernism across the arts. Take, for example, the chapter
on Smithson and Beckett, which pairs the latter's *L'Innommable* with the
former's *Spiral Jetty*. As Israel demonstrates, it is not enough to see Beckett as
an influence on Smithson; instead, he proposes that we understand both works
as 'expos[ing] the presumptions and limits of the project of philosophical
modernity', and as 'reveal[ing] the multiple temporalities of the geopolitical,
problematizing (by spiralizing) the relation of the "local" to the "global"'
(p. 167). Other chapters serve a similar function, situating authors and artists
in relation to one another through a dialectical rather than comparative
approach, and in the process begin to form spiralling chains of association and
fluctuating yet consistently pointed arguments that blend politics, aesthetics,
and ethics in expert and often surprising ways. The book's claims thus begin to
mirror their subject, resulting in a monograph whose form knowingly alludes
to the winding history of the spiral in order to craft an appropriately twisting
narrative of twentieth-century art and thought.

In arguing for the centrality of a particular image across time and space,
*Spirals* is concerned with the permutations of a modern concept as it
repeatedly inflects the twentieth century's artistic and political imaginations.
In contrast, Kevin Ohi's *Dead Letters Sent: Queer Literary Transmission*
analyses the aporias that arise in the queer transmission of knowledge, as
information is addressed to but often fails to reach its intended recipients
(students, readers, subjects of desire, and so on), and thereby short-circuits the

processes of influence and inheritance. Proposing a model of transmission that encompasses, first, the passing of knowledge and desires specific to queer culture from one generation to the next, and second, the essential queerness of cultural knowledge more generally, Ohi offers the metaphor of the dead letter, or the object that marks the failure of transmission that occurs through forgetting, loss, or misinterpretation. How, he asks, can one transmit literary knowledge? And how does blocked or otherwise unsuccessful transmission figure as the thematization of queer desire and literary knowledge? Put differently: what does the thwarted transmission of queer eroticism tell us about the inability of the literary object to be passed from one to another as a bearer of cultural knowledge? Though not entirely concerned with modern literature (Ohi's early chapters centre on Plato, Shakespeare, Algernon Charles Swinburne, and Walter Pater) the second half of the book turns more firmly towards late Victorian and modernist figures, including Oscar Wilde, Henry James, and William Faulkner, in order to address these questions. The chapters on James, in particular, are fascinating for their evocative close readings of that author's late fiction, focused on scenes of failed pedagogy and the seeming inability to receive knowledge and therefore arrive at a greater sense of oneself or of others; 'It is a striking aspect of Henry James's fiction', Ohi wryly notes, 'that no one ever learns anything—or, more precisely, no one is represented learning' (p. 143). Here the lines between action and representation grow fuzzy, and transmission is thwarted both for the characters of James's fiction and for its readers. Other chapters, too, solidify their claims through smart, graceful close readings, making Ohi's that paradoxical monograph that teaches its audience a great deal, even when its subject is those texts that make teaching and learning appear as a necessarily frustrating, perhaps even doomed, endeavour.

If so many of the books on modernism and modern literature published in 2015 adopt expansive critical agendas, positioning the period within much wider aesthetic, cultural, and political histories, then it seems fitting to end this survey of the year's work by broadening our perspective even further—that is, by considering modernism's relationship to the discipline of English studies as a whole. For this purpose, we have Rónán McDonald's edited volume, *The Values of Literary Studies: Critical Institutions, Scholarly Agendas*, which powerfully endorses the fundamental value of literary criticism at a historical moment in which the discipline is under exceptional scrutiny. The goal of the collection, McDonald argues, is to demonstrate how 'we find the values *of* literary studies, at least in part, by identifying and articulating the values *in* literary studies' (p. 3). In other words, while this collection aims to promote literary studies as a valuable enterprise, it does so not through a tautological restatement of a belief in criticism's utility, but through a detailed interrogation of the discipline's competing conceptions of value and how it deploys them in the act of criticism. An important endeavour in itself, what is so remarkable about McDonald's collection is the fact that several of the book's contributors turn to modernism in their efforts to identify the various forms of value that circulate in both literary and critical texts. In some ways this is unsurprising, as *The Values of Literary Studies* is populated with several notable modernist critics—among them Charles Altieri, Derek Attridge,

Simon During, McDonald, Julian Murphet, Jean-Michel Rabaté, and Dirk Van Hulle. At the same time, it is significant that modernism is put to so many related uses throughout the book, as a way of articulating the values of critical practice without merely pronouncing literary study a valid intellectual pursuit. Anthony J. Cascardi's contribution follows the connections made and missed between modernism and literary criticism, and claims that 'assessing the value of Modernism' is largely 'a matter of understanding how literature has come to self-awareness through a critical engagement with its own underpinnings in forms of representation and of *their* associations with value that did not sufficiently account for the open-endedness of the human project' (p. 17). Thus, modernism can reveal to us 'the fact that as a form of critique, literature is not *about* anything wholly external to it', and that 'indeed, the very notion of "aboutness" undermines the force of its assertions' (p. 26). Julian Murphet makes a related point when he suggests that 'Literature does nothing, changes nothing, makes nothing happen, and the very best that can be asked of any act of literary criticism is that it might work to *shelter the nothing* that is at permanent risk of vanishing from the text, of being flattened out into sanctioned semantics that flatter social ideologies' (p. 118). In both essays, modernism allows us to think through questions of aesthetic autonomy, critical interpretation, and social utility that revolve around the literary object, and to see literature not just in relation to the world outside it, but also, and more importantly, in relation to itself, as a cultural production worthy of self-directed scrutiny. These and other contributions demonstrate modernism's continued relevance for literary studies, and make persuasive cases for perceiving the values that inform modernist criticism as those inherent within the discipline as a whole. It is a testament to modernism's enduring value in the twenty-first century, and to its potential to continue shaping, challenging, and provoking literary study even further in the future.

## 2. Pre-1945 Fiction

### (a) British Fiction 1900–1930

A striking range of monographs, symposia, and scholarly articles in 2015 featured British women writers whose fiction does not, for one reason or another, fit smoothly into the 'authorized version' of the high modernist canon. Researchers have been assiduous in reinstating long-smothered aesthetic dialogues and thematic links between devalued figures such as Mary Butts, Evelyn Underhill, Sylvia Townsend Warner, and Rose Macaulay and more well-established authors like Dorothy Richardson, May Sinclair, and Katherine Mansfield.

One positive facet of Mansfield scholarship in 2015 has been the increasing attention to her status as both canny participant in and sardonic observer of various transnational literary factions, cadres, and constellations. The special issue of 'Virginia Woolf and Katherine Mansfield' (*VWM* 86[2015] 1–25), co-edited by Kathryn Simpson and Melinda Harvey, and Janka Kascakova and Gerri Kimber's edited collection, *Katherine Mansfield and Continental Europe:*

*Connections and Influences* merit particular mention. The latter foregrounds how Mansfield's fiction links concerns about colonialism in anglophone modernist aesthetics to developments in European literary and visual culture. Contributors variously explore Mansfield's physical and generic border-crossing; her figurations of voluntary and enforced exile; her imaginative terrain of cheerless hotels, guest-houses, and liminal spaces. Overall, the volume depicts the nomadic Mansfield as a mordantly shrewd chronicler of the tangled politics of patronage, salon, and coterie culture, the modish instruments of design, publication, and circulation of ideas that affected the social visibility of writers in this historical epoch. Patricia Moran's essay 'The "Dream of roots and the mirage of the journey": Writing as Homeland in Katherine Mansfield' (pp. 202–21) is especially effective in showing Mansfield's authorial identity as defined by spirited resistance to rigid conceptions of national and class affiliation.

Anna Plumridge's fine edition of Mansfield's *Urewera Notebook* brings into sharp relief the writer's intense 'attitudes to New Zealand, not in adulthood when memory is tempered by time or in fiction where memory is reworked through the act of writing, but as a nineteen-year-old living in the colony' (pp. 1–2). Mansfield continues to be construed through the critical prism of the 'affective turn', prioritizing those webs of collaboration and dissemination that span linguistic, cross-channel, and global expanses. This topic also receives treatment in Julie Taylor's edited collection, *Modernism and Affect*. Taylor conceptualizes the modernist 'mood' as an affective phenomenon that challenges 'humanist understandings of selfhood and psychology' (p. 5). What makes this collection so useful for scholars who privilege Mansfield's subtle rendering of heightened consciousness—as well as 'mood disorders' such as depression and anxiety—is Taylor's cogent discussion of 'a competing and overlapping cluster of terms surrounding affect' (p. 6).

Adrienne E. Gavin and Andrew F. Humphries's *Transport in British Fiction: Technologies of Movement, 1840–1940* will resonate powerfully with re-searchers who view Mansfield's work as a vivid portrait of a modernist age enraptured by 'newness' (technology) and 'nowness' (dizzying speed). Like Robert Burden's *Travel, Modernism and Modernity*, this edited collection addresses the transport and communication technologies that reconfigured the pace and patterns of diurnal existence during and after the First World War. Andrew F. Humphries's chapter (pp. 199–219) prioritizes 'Trains as Settings of Disturbance and Dislocation' in the short stories 'The Little Governess' [1915] and 'An Indiscreet Journey' [1915]. Humphries demonstrates that, in addition to rendering railway encounters as acute 'sites of conflict', Mansfield's formally innovative narrative art also frames women as intrepid 'passenger-explorers who defy male and/or military conventions of travel', so connecting 'female dissent to transport experience' (pp. 200–1). This volume also examines the cultural politics of place and depictions of transport technologies in E.M. Forster's *Howards End* (pp. 185–98), Joseph Conrad's *Heart of Darkness*, and *Nostromo* (pp. 151–66), as well as less well-known interwar texts such as J.B. Priestley's *The Good Companions* (pp. 235–49).

Dan Shen's 'Dual Textual Dynamics and Dual Readerly Dynamics' (*Style* 49:iv[2015] 411–38) throws into sharper relief the narrative fabric of

Mansfield's short stories. Karen Shaup's 'Consuming Beauty: Aesthetic Experience in Katherine Mansfield's "The Garden Party"' (*PLL* 51:iii[2015] 221–43) focuses on the articulation of social mobility, class affiliation, and economic inequality in one of Mansfield's most complex short stories. Kate McLoughlin's 'The Modernist Party as Pedagogy' (*JML* 38:iii[2015] 86–98) ponders how social gatherings are represented in a range of modernist texts, including Mansfield's 'The Garden Party'. Simon During's 'Katherine Mansfield's World' (*JNZL* 33[2015] 33–66) considers Mansfield through the prism of world literature and idealist philosophy. Also of interest here are Todd W. Martin's review essay 'Katherine Mansfield Among the Moderns' (*SoAR* 80:i–ii[2015] 178–90); Sebnem Kaya's 'Katherine Mansfield's "The Canary" as a Pointer to Deep Ecology' (*Expl* 73:ii[2015] 97–100); and Jane Nardin's 'Katherine Mansfield and Elizabeth von Arnim's *Vera*' (*N&Q* 62[2015] 450–1), which measures 'The Garden Party' against Von Arnim's blackly comic 1921 novel.

Mansfield aficionados should also consult Shannon McMahon's 'Freespinsters and Bondspinsters: Negotiating Identity Categories in *The Freewoman*' (*JModPerS* 6:i[2015] 60–79), which treats the 'spinster' as an identity category circulated, debated, and ultimately debunked in *The Freewoman*. Readers of McMahon's lucid and percipient account will be mindful of influential criticism such as Emma Liggins's *Odd Women?* [2014] and especially Suzette A. Henke's *Herspace: Women, Writing, and Solitude* [2003], which code the spinster as an 'implicitly deviant and dangerous figure', threatening to the gatekeepers of bourgeois hegemony. McMahon contends that *The Freewoman*'s myriad 'conversational threads about spinsterhood' permit researchers to rethink how an overlooked 'identity category' resonated within 'Edwardian feminist discourse' (pp. 60–1).

Kate Kennedy's '"A Tribute to My Brother": Women's Literature and Its Post-War Ghosts' (*JW&CS* 8:i[2015] 7–23) situates Rose Macaulay's *Non-Combatants and Others* [1915] and Katherine Mansfield's short stories in relation to imperfect recall, mourning, and the fictional evocations of the First World War canvassed by Anna Branach-Kallas and Nelly Strehlau's edited collection, *Re-Imagining the First World War* as well as Claire Buck in *Conceiving Strangeness in British First World War Writings*. Macaulay and Mansfield emerge from Kennedy's shrewd assessment as writers preoccupied with what the critic Nicholas Andrew Miller calls 'a memorial medium'. Macaulay and Mansfield variously participate in a fraught cultural conversation about how post-war communities salvage their traumatic past so as to confront the profound mysteries of human affect.

Courtney Andree's essay 'Non-Combatants and Other Peace Activists: "Everyday" Disability in a Time of War' (*DSQ* 34:iii[2014] 23 paras) focuses on *Non-Combatants and Others* in relation to recent trends in 'disability studies', a field of academic enquiry that, according to Andree, explores how fractured subjectivities are managed, categorized, and processed. Kabi Hartman's 'Male Pacifists in British Women's World War I Novels: Toward an "Enlightened Civilisation"' (*ELT* 58:iv[2015] 536–50) considers portrayals of conscientious objectors to the Great War in fiction by female authors who exploit links between metaphysical awareness and Christ-like authority. The 'conchie' character in many of these short stories and novels is the epitome of stoical self-abnegation and numinous wisdom. Hartman is particularly interested in how these self-sacrificing pacifists are frequently coded as queer dissidents. Indeed, Rose Macaulay's fiction published during and after the Great War offers a vivid case study in what Hartman theorizes as 'crosswriting': the experiences of 'closeted lesbians' are woven into 'narratives about gay men' (pp. 536–7). Hartman concludes that Macaulay seeks to counteract debilitating feelings of cultural invisibility after the war by devising fictions that affirm quiet endurance as opposed to the battlefield bravado lauded by the popular press. Hartman demonstrates that Macaulay's texts imagine a post-war nation in which conventional gender roles are radically reimagined, giving voice to those stifled and stymied on the home front. These insights typify a notable strand of academic research in 2015: the reappraisal of neglected female authors becomes key to extending ideas of modernist cultural production in the domains of peace activism, war propaganda, mainstream reportage, and pro-suffrage literary narrative.

Beci Carver's 'What Women Want: The Modernist Kimono' (*Mo/Mo* 22:ii[2015] 303–14) analyses the appropriation of the paraphernalia of Japanese culture in early twentieth-century Anglo-American literary culture. Carver's argument illuminates how the aspiring female consumer's affinity for the glamorously exotic connotations of the 'Japanese kimono' is rendered in Ford Madox Ford's narratives.

Jane Potter's essay, ' "Khaki and Kisses": Reading the Romance Novel in the Great War' (in Towheed and King, eds., *Reading and the First World War*, pp. 29–44), not only scrutinizes the reading habits and preferences of combatants and civilians; Potter also foregrounds less well-known texts such as Joseph Hocking's *All for a Scrap of Paper* [1915], Mrs Humphry Ward's *Missing* [1915], and Boyd Cable's *Action Front* [1916].

Anna Andes's 'The Evolution of Cicely Hamilton's Edwardian Marriage Discourse: Embracing Conversion Dramaturgy' (*ELT* 58:iv[2015] 503–22) scrutinizes Hamilton's play *Marriage as a Trade*, which appeared at the height of the suffrage movement, as well as her thematic emphases in her searching novel of pre-war suffrage *William—An Englishman* [1919].

Anthony Patterson's 'Maverick Vices: Sexual Felicity and the Edwardian Sex Novel' (in Patterson and Choi, eds., *We Speak a Different Tongue: Maverick Voices and Modernity 1890–1939*, pp. 35–50) explores Edwardian novels of sexual manners such as Elinor Glyn's *Three Weeks* [1907], H.G. Wells's *Ann Veronica* [1909], Hubert Wales's *The Spinster* [1912], and Victoria Cross's *Life's Shop Window* [1907]. Patterson illustrates that these novels variously generate polemical momentum by aestheticizing—even sacralizing—sexuality in a way that the New Woman fiction of the previous fifteen years could not (pp. 40–1). Ultimately, however, many of these popular narratives can be seen as disappointingly complicit in 'a reactionary appropriation of science which re-inscribes as much as it transgresses the gender values of earlier Victorian fiction' (p. 46).

Mimi Winick's 'Modernist Feminist Witchcraft: Margaret Murray's Fantastic Scholarship and Sylvia Townsend Warner's Realist Fantasy' (*Mo/Mo* 22:iii[2015] 565–92) raises lively questions not only about Townsend

Warner's generically diverse oeuvre but also on how her writing confronts and revises contemporary definitions of feminism. Winick demonstrates that both *Lolly Willowes* and Margaret Murray's *The Witch-Cult in Western Europe* are centrally concerned with what the critic Lucy Delap has labelled 'avant-garde feminism'. What makes Winick 's critical approach so striking is her notion that feminist aesthetic innovation should not be seen as synonymous only with the technical radicalism of, say, Mary Butts and Virginia Woolf; but also with popular and middlebrow fiction as well as scholarly texts. Winick's article will prove helpful to scholars who view Townsend Warner's narrative art in terms of how she, and we, classify interwar reading communities as a zone of bitter disagreement between so-called highbrow, middlebrow, and mainstream tastes.

Mary Pollock's 'Animal Companions in Sylvia Townsend Warner's More-than-Marxist World' (*Mosaic* 48:i[2015] 65–81) and Meyrav Koren-Kuik's 'From *Lolly Willowes* to Kingdoms of Elfin: The Poetics of Socio-Political Commentary in Sylvia Townsend Warner's Fantasy Narratives' (in Croft, ed., *Baptism of Fire: The Birth of the Modern British Fantastic in World War I*, pp. 245–62) each bring a welcome focus to Townsend Warner's generic experiments, especially the manner in which her interwar narratives question gender and sexuality, race and empire, and a range of religious affiliations, both orthodox and recondite.

Aficionados of Townsend Warner's fictional explorations of queer or liminal femininities will find much to ponder in Kristen Renzi's 'Dough Girls and Biscuit Boys: The Queer Potential of the Countercommunal Grotesque Body within Modernist Literature' (*Mo/Mo* 22:i[2015] 57–80). Renzi illustrates that the 'grotesque' announces a lexical and formal sense of disturbed estrangement from standard judgements and perceptions. However, Renzi is more preoccupied with the somatic location of 'grotesquerie'—the outsider 'difference' that 'spectacularly appears' on the physical form (p. 57). For Renzi, this somatic grotesque needs to be foregrounded by textual scholars in both disability studies and queer theory. This argument prompts us to rethink the correspondences and conflicts between 'queerness' and 'freakishness', especially bodily 'hybridity, along with excess and absence' (pp. 57–8).

In 2015 scholars continued to investigate Ford Madox Ford's fiction in relation to the politics of class, cultural geographies, gendered subjectivity, and canon formation. David Quint's 'Uneasy Riders: Some Literary Modernists and the Aristocracy' (*Neoh* 42:i[2015] 17–42) focuses on *The Good Soldier* in relation to the narrative treatment of patrician mores and manners. Youngjo Kim's 'A Troubling Sign of Englishness: The Country House Novels of Henry James, Ford Madox Ford and E.M. Forster' (BAF1900 22:ii[2015] 93–114) is alert to the genre conventions and contested ideologies of Englishness in Ford's *The Good Soldier* and Forster's *Howards End*.

Randi Saloman's review article 'Making Modernism Fit' (*JML* 38:iv[2015] 192–6) furnishes an astute discussion of Rob Hawkes's recent research into Ford Madox Ford as novelist and memoirist, as well as other 'misfit' early twentieth-century authors who remain—to some literary historians at least—partly or completely estranged from 'high' modernist circles, such as Arnold

Bennett, G.K. Chesterton, H.G. Wells, the Powys brothers, and John Galsworthy.

Elizabeth Steedley's 'Fordian Confiteor: Catholicism and Social Disengagement in *The Good Soldier*' (*TCL* 61:ii[2015] 173–208) focuses on figurations of Catholicism in *The Good Soldier*. Steedley contends that Ford's protagonists often turn to religious pieties and 'unauthorized' confessional modes as a means of protecting themselves from the demoralizing effects of a tightening technocracy (p. 173). Steedley makes a compelling case for reading John Dowell's impressionistic narrative as a parable about the psychic risks of civic and political disaffiliation. The essay also examines Ford's historical references to the English Reformation and the covert links between the characters' remarks and activities and the 'antimodernist' position of the Catholic Church during the early years of the twentieth century (pp. 173–4). This fine article should be measured against C.J.T. Talar and Lawrence F. Barmann's edited collection, *Roman Catholic Modernists Confront the Great War*, which carefully traces the thought of several Roman Catholic modernists (and one especially virulent anti-modernist) as they decoded the intellectual challenges posed by an era of seismic upheaval.

Rod Rosenquist's 'A Transatlantic "Field of Stars": Redrawing the Borders of English Literature in the Late Nineteenth Century' (*CS* 27:iii[2015] 105–23) weighs the function of charts and map-making in promoting a strong sense of national and regional belonging in Ford's fictional and autobiographical texts.

Trevor Dodman's *Shell Shock, Memory, and the Novel in the Wake of World War I* and Paul K. Saint-Amour's *Tense Future: Modernism, Total War, Encyclopedic Form* demonstrate that Ford's oeuvre—especially the hugely ambitious *Parade's End*—is central to any discussion about the encounter between aesthetic modernism and geopolitical strife. Drawing inspiration from Vincent Sherry's *The Great War and the Language of Modernism* [2003], these projects permit us to see how the restless innovation synonymous with 'high' modernist modes, tropes, and concepts was sustained or modified during and after the Great War itself. Max Saunders's 'Impressions of War: Ford Madox Ford, Reading and *Parade's End*' (in Towheed and King, eds., pp. 63–77), and Rebekah Lockyer's 'Ford Madox Ford's Musical Legacy: *Parade's End* and Wagner' (*FMLS* 50:iv[2014] 426–52) are also relevant in this respect.

Nancy Martin's ' "And all because it is war!": First World War Diaries, Authenticity and Combatant Identity' (*TPr* 29[2015] 1245–63) considers the complexities of the image of the soldier as expressed through combatant diaries. Martin argues that the diary, as 'a private, self-reflexive form', allows a reassessment of what Michael Roper views as a misconstrued facet of Great War scholarship: 'the behaviour and emotional dispositions of individual men' as they witness the casual brutalities of industrialized combat (pp. 1245–6). This work belongs to a strand in recent modernist scholarship that canvasses the literary and cultural resonance of correspondence, trench journals and hospital magazines, war ephemera, and paintings by official war artists. Martin is especially acute on how the Great War diary stages and interrogates the diarist's newly militarized, masculine identity using a wide array of figurative devices, such as references to classical lore.

Andrzej Gąsiorek and Nathan Waddell's edited collection, *Wyndham Lewis: A Critical Guide* is compelling reading for anyone interested in the full range of Lewis's published corpus. Postgraduate researchers will find this an elegantly structured and affordable guide that puts a welcome emphasis on Lewis's swingeing cultural criticism (pp. 64–81), elaborate satirical strategies (pp. 82–96), and pre-war narratives (pp. 5–19). As Louise Kane explains, during this pre-war period Lewis was devising what would become *Tarr* [1918] and *Mrs Duke's Millions* [1908–9] as well as a dazzling number of short stories and controversial periodical publications. Faith Binckes is eloquent about the experience of 'Reading *Tarr*' (pp. 35–48), while Nathan Waddell tackles the hugely complex problem of 'Lewis and Politics' (pp. 128–42) with the same stylistic verve and attention to telling detail that characterizes his contribution to *Wyndham Lewis and the Cultures of Modernity* [2012].

Jamie Wood's ' "On or about December 1910": F.T. Marinetti's Onslaught on London and Recursive Structures in Modernism' (*ModCult* 10:ii[2015] 135–58) addresses Wyndham Lewis's formally and politically radical early narratives and how they influenced the thought of F.T. Marinetti. Literary and textual historians fascinated by Marinetti and other major figures of the European avant-garde will find subtle material in Arthur Sabatini's 'Vorticism Revitalized' (*JML* 38:iv[2015] 178–83).

David Dwan's 'The Problem of Romanticism in Wyndham Lewis' (*EIC* 65:ii[2015]163–86) measures Lewis's most acclaimed novel *Tarr* and his journalism against Carl Schmitt's *Political Romanticism* [1919]. Dwan explains that Schmitt perceived Lewis as a 'related soul' given their shared distaste for the political structures of a liberal representative democracy as well as the Romantic literary-cultural lexicon that seemed to buttress it (pp. 163–4). Dwan focuses well on Lewis's conceptual engagement with Romanticism as a poorly designed framework for promoting the politics of subjective freedom. For Lewis, and for those who inspired his stinging critique of 'Romantic decadence' (Nietzsche and Hulme), 'Romanticism' was an umbrella term for all types of whimsical self-regard and jejune 'nature-sentiment' (pp. 164–5). Lewis's reframing of Romantic lyrical subjectivity as solipsistic self-indulgence and psychotic extremity colours Lewis's text 'Franciscan Adventures' [1927]. Lewis's fiction also features in Toshiaki Onishi's 'The Psychic Prison of Manliness: A Reflexive Gaze into the Male Subjectivity in *Decline and Fall*' (*SELit* 56[2015] 57–73), which assesses codes of masculinity in Waugh's novel and Aldous Huxley's *Antic Hay*.

Caroline Maclean's *The Vogue for Russia* reflects the recent scholarly emphasis on cross-cultural debates, transactions, and collaborations, exploiting Virginia Woolf's much-quoted 1919 observation that 'the most inconclusive remarks upon modern English fiction can hardly avoid some mention of the Russian influence'. Maclean's sustained meditation on this 'influence' will appeal to aficionados of Mary Butts's published oeuvre. Butts's fiction and numerous book reviews furnish a trenchant commentary on the reception, adaptation, and diffusion of Russian political concepts and literary idioms in this era. Indeed, her journals offer a nuanced portrait of an interwar culture profoundly affected by Soviet cinema and ballet, the moral and ethical quandaries dramatized by Chekhov, and the social and spiritual credos of

Tolstoy and Dostoevsky, as well as translations by Constance Garnett. Maclean's third chapter, 'Voices of Stones: Mary Butts and Petr Ouspensky's Fourth Dimension' (pp. 103–35), prompts us to revisit Butts's posthumously published memoir *The Crystal Cabinet*, a text which links in complex ways the portrayal of megalithic survivals and moments of multiplied consciousness. Maclean also invites readers to gauge Butts's oeuvre as the epitome of 'obscure modernism'. Like Ian Patterson, Maclean is intrigued by how Butts has been wilfully misconstrued or unfairly dismissed. Yet there is also a sense of Butts purposely adopting—and relishing—an encrypted writerly register so as to mock or derail institutionalized habits of critical scrutiny.

In 2015 Joseph Conrad continued to exert a binding fascination for scholars keen to explore the sophisticated scepticism at the heart of the fiction. Vincent Sherry's *Modernism and the Reinvention of Decadence* furnishes an incisive account of *The Secret Agent* [1907] in terms of its evocation of 'exhausted civility', which 'represents both a civilization at its end and a stylization of this extremity' (p. 120). Sherry measures the 'specifically textual politics' of Conrad's novel against another narrative that scrutinizes the malign workings of metropolitan anarchism, G.K. Chesterton's *The Man Who Was Thursday* (pp. 123–7). Chesterton experts should also consult Michael Shallcross's '"This odd game called war": The Ethics of Game Playing in the War Writing of H.G. Wells, G.K. Chesterton, and Wyndham Lewis' (*Wellsian* 38[2015] 41–56) and Julia Stapleton's 'The Battle of Plutocracy: G.K. Chesterton, Wells, Masterman and the Future of Democracy' (*Wellsian* 38[2015] 57–69).

Linda Dryden's *Joseph Conrad and H.G. Wells* chronicles the literary friendship between Conrad and Wells from their early correspondence through to the disagreements that triggered their estrangement, including their published reactions to the Great War. Dryden is probing about the literary collaboration between Conrad and Ford Madox Ford—a 'concerted attempt to transform the form and content of the novel' with Wells 'failing, or resolutely refusing to comprehend their purpose' (p. 158).

Anne Enderwitz's *Modernist Melancholia* provides detailed analysis of Conrad and Ford Madox Ford in terms of their shared interest in an evolutionary and archaeological framework of thought that powerfully influenced modernist conceptions of temporality and subjectivity. Enderwitz's fourth chapter, 'From Melancholia to Wish-Fulfillment: *The Inheritors* and *Romance*' (pp. 146–86), is perspicacious about the decade of creative collaboration between Conrad and Ford. Enderwitz also includes a brief discussion of the long short story *The Nature of a Crime* [1909], whose depiction of 'a materialistic and amoral society' prompts close comparison with *The Inheritors* (pp. 147–9).

Marta Puxan-Oliva's 'Racial Stereotypes as Narrative Forms: Staging the English Gentleman in Joseph Conrad's *Lord Jim*' (*JNT* 45:iii[2015] 333–69) addresses the novel's intricate treatment of national identity in relation to the malign workings of the British empire. Jessica Martell and Zackary Vernon's '"Of great gabasidy": Joseph Conrad's *Lord Jim* and F. Scott Fitzgerald's *The Great Gatsby*' (*JML* 38:iii[2015] 56–70) suggests that Fitzgerald likely gleaned the title for *The Great Gatsby* from an enigmatic passage in Joseph Conrad's *Lord Jim*, in which the eponymous character is said to be 'of great gabasidy'—

a polyglot's pronunciation of formidable intellectual skill. But the parallels between Conrad's and Fitzgerald's novels, according to Martell and Vernon, go well beyond the title, most notably in the way that Fitzgerald fashions Gatsby in the image of Jim.

Soonbae Kim's 'Exiled Space and Political Agonism in *Lord Jim*' (BAF1900 22:ii[2015] 71–91) ponders cross-cultural relations in this novel, while Jeffrey Meyers examines 'Allusions and Meaning in Conrad's *The Shadow-Line*' (*Style* 49:ii[2015] 149–52). Brian Richardson's 'Representing Social Minds: "We" and "They" Narratives, Natural and Unnatural' (*Narrative* 23:ii[2015] 200–12) assesses *The Nigger of the 'Narcissus'* in terms of its complexities of narrative voice. Robert Higney's ' "Law, good faith, order, security": Joseph Conrad's Institutions' (*Novel* 48:i[2015] 85–102) throws into bolder relief the machinery of imperialist institutions in *Nostromo* [1904].

Andrew Francis's *Culture and Commerce in Conrad's Asian Fiction* is the first book-length critical analysis of commercial concerns and tropes in Conrad's oeuvre. Francis is sure-footed when gauging the associations between cultural power and entrepreneurial aspiration in those fictions which map colonial Southeast Asia. Francis shows how Conrad's portrayal of Arab, Chinese, Malay, and European commerce divulges a fault-line in developed European imperialism. Francis's close discussion of both literary and non-literary sources will be of particular interest to postcolonial scholars who focus on how modernist fiction depicts and debunks the interplay between entrepreneurial capitalism, colonialism, and globalization.

This topic is extended by Regina Martin's 'Absentee Capitalism and the Politics of Conrad's Imperial Novels' (*PMLA* 130:iii[2015] 584–98), which posits that *Lord Jim*, *Nostromo*, and *Victory* scrutinize and subvert an emerging system of imperialism orchestrated around the modern, investor-owned corporation (pp. 584–5). This system, referred to here as 'absentee capitalism', was replacing the nineteenth-century British system of relatively modest, family-based firms. Martin proposes that these novels idealize the family-owned firm as having an 'affective' resonance and humane structure that sharply contrasts with the 'squandered value' synonymous with absentee capitalism's invisible and fluid framework of social contacts (pp. 584–5). According to Martin's account, the relatively marginalized novel *Victory* takes on renewed import for its canny insight into the relation among imperialism, romance conventions, and aesthetic modernism.

Rachel Hollander's 'Thinking Otherwise: Ethics and Politics in Joseph Conrad's *Under Western Eyes*' (*JML* 38:iii[2015] 1–19) indicates that Conrad is frequently coded as a politically cagey or evasive figure. This discerning and detailed analysis of his late novel, *Under Western Eyes*, as an illustration of the association between ethics and politics, rightly complicates this assessment. Hollander describes *Under Western Eyes* as a text whose keynote is ambivalent cynicism. It stages, she argues, a conflict between Russia's 'non-viable' political extremes (autocracy and revolution) and a 'Levinasian ethics of alterity' (pp. 1–2).

Taylor Eggan's 'Revolutionary Temporality and Modernist Politics of Form: Reading Ngũgĩ wa Thiong'o Reading Joseph Conrad' (*JML* 38:iii[2015] 38–55) queries the critical consensus regarding 'the politics of intertextuality' between Ngũgĩ wa Thiong'o's *A Grain of Wheat* and the novel it rewrites, Conrad's *Under Western Eyes* (p. 38). Eggan does not add to the already substantial body of academic scholarship that interprets the political concerns of 'betrayal and disenchantment'. Rather, this essay concentrates on a subtle 'politics of form' by parsing Conrad's account of the 'temporality of revolution': a 'contradictory flux that ejects the subject from a stable experience of time' (pp. 38–9). This essay is part of a special edition of the *Journal of Modern Literature* on 'Joseph Conrad Re-seen and Re-appropriated'.

Charlie Wesley's 'Inscriptions of Resistance in Joseph Conrad's *Heart of Darkness*' (*JML* 38:iii[2015] 20–37) finds an anxiety in this much-discussed text concerning 'the possibility of native resistance to colonial tyranny' (pp. 20–1). Wesley argues that recent pundits have overlooked these 'inscriptions of resistance' in Conrad's novella.

In 'The Revolutionary Pole in Late Victorian and Early Edwardian Dynamite Fiction' (*Conradian* 40:ii[2015] 98–108), David Mulry assesses the representation of anarchist insurgency in Conrad's more political fictions. Mark D. Larabee's 'Conrad and the Great War at Sea' (*Conradian* 40:ii[2015] 55–77) examines the depiction of naval warfare in *The Shadow-Line* [1917]. Aaron Jaffe's 'Total Unconscious: Jameson, Conrad, and James' (*HJRev* 36[2015] 257–66) scrutinizes and compares Fredric Jameson's reading of Henry James with his ideas about Joseph Conrad's literary career. Jameson construes James as the last in a long line of nineteenth-century mimetic realist authors, while Conrad emerges as the first modernist who tests the realist rubric in surprising ways.

Other notable contributions to Conrad scholarship in 2015 include Kai Mikkonen's *Narrative Paths: African Travel in Modern Fiction and Nonfiction* which gauges the African forest as imaginative locality in a range of Conrad's literary works. Colin Bower's 'Against Moral Seriousness as a Literary Value: Casement, Conrad, and Leavis' (*CQ* 44:i[2015] 62–8) focuses on Leavis's famous—or notorious—assessment of Conrad and the moral and ethical implications of the short story 'The Secret Sharer'. Then there is also Tina Skouen's 'Ciceronian Oratory and the Idea of Civilization in *Heart of Darkness*' (*Conradian* 40:ii[2015] 1–6); Jeremy Lakoff's ' "A variable and yet perfectly precise mechanism": Temporal Prosthesis in *The Secret Agent*' (*Conradian* 40:ii[2015] 23–35); Nic Panagopoulos's 'Civic Virtue in *Under Western Eyes*' (*Conradian* 40:ii[2015] 36–53); J.H. Stape's 'Additional Supplementary Notes and Corrigenda to *The Collected Letters of Joseph Conrad*' (*Conradian* 40:ii[2015] 130–8); and Douglas Kerr's 'Conrad and the Comic Turn' (*VLC* 43:i[2015] 149–68). Gillian Bright's ' "Paper, ink, and the blood-stained inanity": The Aesthetics of Terrorist Violence in Joseph Conrad's *The Secret Agent*, Paul Theroux's *The Family Arsenal*, and Doris Lessing's *The Good Terrorist*' (*Critique* 56:ii[2015] 190–206) adds to a substantial body of recent academic work on the troubled (and troubling) representations of psychic and physical cruelty in Conrad's fiction.

While Kipling's 'Wireless' [1902] has frequently been interpreted as the epitome of a defunct realist narration, Heather Fielding's 'Kipling's Wireless Impressionism: Telecommunication and Narration in Early Modernism'

(*MFS* 61:i[2015] 24–46) makes a persuasive case for viewing the text as an intriguing early experiment in Impressionism. Fielding proposes that midway through the narrative, the 'narrator's point of view suddenly becomes distorted and private' and the story clarifies this shift through 'the figure of the wireless telegraph, which Kipling uses to imagine a dizzying excess of technological chatter', so making 'communication impossible' (pp. 24–5). Claire Buck's *Conceiving Strangeness in British First World War Writing* devotes an incisive chapter to 'E.M. Forster and the War's Colonial Aspect' (pp. 81–116). Buck draws attention to how Forster disentangles 'the connections among nationalism, Englishness, masculinity, and colonialism'. She also ponders the ways in which Forster situates non-normative textual and sexual identities at the very core of his nuanced 'anti-colonial politics' (pp. 95–6). Buck also sheds much-needed light on the war writing of Enid Bagnold, whose *Diary without Dates* [1918] 'explores the relationship between front line and home front' (p. 133).

Dustin Friedman's 'E.M. Forster, the Clapham Sect, and the Secular Public Sphere' (*JML* 39:i[2015] 19–37) indicates that critics have characterized Forster as an eloquent exponent of what Jürgen Habermas terms the 'secular public sphere'. Friedman's article, like many published on Forster in 2015, gauges Forster's legacy in English literature and cultural history (pp. 19–20). Friedman is interested in Forster's less often canvassed narrative texts and tactics; but he also appraises the international values Forster endorsed almost half a century after his death (p. 20). Friedman concludes that we can scrutinize *A Passage to India* [1924], for example, in terms of how its spiritual themes mould and express a politically relevant alternative to a 'rationalized religiosity and Bloomsbury's secular insularity' (p. 20). This is because Forster's depiction of the Hindu religious festival of Gokul Ashtami adumbrates a different model of social togetherness that cannot be dissected using the narrow terms of a strictly secular or forensic discourse.

Adam Kirsch's chapter on Forster in his collection *Rocket and Lightship: Essays on Literature and Ideas* (pp. 233–52) weighs 'the difficulty of connecting' everyday 'conventional personalities' with 'transgressive sexual desires' (p. 233) in the fiction. Kirsch encourages us to rethink the presence and legacy of Forster in recent British literature and film. Jo Ann Cruz's 'Attending to Reading E.M. Forster: *Howards End* and Ruth Wilcox's Unattended Death' (*MFS* 61:iii[2015] 404–22) assesses the semantic and cultural resonances surrounding Forster's searching treatment of the dying and death in relation to Mrs Wilcox from *Howards End*. Cruz's subtle argument underscores the value of revisiting the nature and role of silences, evasions, and ambiguities in the imaginative fabric of this novel.

Stephen Ross's 'Thinking Modernist Ethics with Animals in *A Passage to India*' (*TCL* 61:iii[2015] 305–29) contends that the most significant happening in Forster's *A Passage to India* is not the much-debated episode at the Marabar Caves, but the car accident preceding the trek to these caves. Ross considers the textual nuances of the accident, particularly the figure of 'the hyena' upon which the accident is blamed (pp. 305–6), furnishing a lively account of the novel's 'indeterminate ethics of alterity' that foreshadows the thinking of Emmanuel Levinas and Jacques Derrida. Forster scholars will find much of interest here, especially Ross's alertness to 'the cultural histories of the hyena in West and South Asia, as well as in England' (pp. 306–7). Ross concludes that Forster deploys the trope of the hyena to imply the radical indeterminacy surrounding issues of racial and sexual identity in *A Passage to India*.

Nisha Manocha's 'Leonard Woolf and the Book in the Jungle' (*JCL* 50:i[2015] 75–86) analyses the representation of 'the book' in Leonard Woolf's *The Village in the Jungle* [1913]. Manocha construes the 'act of writing in the colonial context' as an 'event'—inspiring wonder or hostility in the illiterate indigenous population, or bittersweet memories of the colonial mandarin's more comfortable life at 'home' (pp. 75–6). This is not by any means a narrative strategy found only in Leonard Woolf's fiction. However, what makes Woolf's descriptions of the act of writing unusual is his vivid sense of the book in 'colonial Sri Lanka' as a kind of 'fetish' (pp. 75–6).

Michael Bell's 'Towards a Definition of the "Long Modernist Novel"' (*ModCult* 10:iii[2015] 282–98) gauges a number of long fictions from the modernist period to see how far their length serves specifically modernist concerns, especially the dynamics of temporality and history. Kate McLoughlin's 'Moments of Insight in Long Novels by Henry James and Dorothy Richardson' (*ModCult* 10:iii[2015] 299–315) argues that James and Richardson composed long novels in response to what they construed as a crisis in 'transferable experience', a crisis traced by Walter Benjamin to the Great War (pp. 299–300).

Eveline Kilian's 'Alternative Temporalities: Queer Time in Marcel Proust's *A la recherche du temps perdu* and Dorothy Richardson's *Pilgrimage*' (*ModCult* 10:iii[2015] 336–56) employs the concept of 'queer time' to examine the functions of the alternative temporalities created in Proust's multivolume opus and Richardson's *Pilgrimage*. Kilian argues that despite similarities between the two texts in the relevance they ascribe to those privileged 'moments' in which 'linear time' is seemingly transcended, there are also marked differences which are at least partly related to the complexities of gendered subjectivity (pp. 337–8). In *Pilgrimage*, Kilian concludes, the female protagonist's 'moments of being' generate a 'life-sustaining queer energy' that imbues the narrative fabric and helps her combat the myriad pressures of a heteronormative and technocratic culture.

Jeremy Tambling's 'Judaism and Heterogeneity in the Modernist Long Novel' (*ModCult* 10:iii[2015] 357–79) prioritizes the representation of Judaism in non-Jewish writers of the nineteenth century (for example George Eliot) and in modernist long novels, such as those by Dorothy Richardson and Proust (p. 358). Tambling finds a striking connection between the length of the long novel, 'as a meaningful category in itself' and the concern of these novels with Judaism and anti-Semitism 'as something which cannot be easily assimilated into the narratives which the writers mentioned are interested in' (pp. 357–8).

Ria Banerjee's 'Nihilistic Femininity in the Early Twentieth Century: Allison Pease's *Modernism, Feminism, and the Culture of Boredom*' (*JML* 38:iii[2015] 119–23) investigates Allison Pease's recent research, especially how boredom, banality, and stoical endurance are markers for a feminist critique of women's enforced social exclusion in novels by May Sinclair and Dorothy

Richardson, even as a literary device that proclaims a feminine independence of mind. Mhairi Pooler's ' "The strange happiness of being abroad": Dorothy Richardson's *Oberland* (*Journeys* 16:i[2015] 75–97) appraises Richardson's 1927 text in relation to women's travel writing tropes from the interwar period. Ellen Turner's 'E.M. Hull's *Camping in the Sahara*: Desert Romance Meets Desert Reality' (*StTW* 19:ii[2015] 127–46) focuses on the publication of *Camping in the Sahara*, seven years after E.M. Hull's bestselling debut novel, *The Sheik* [1919]. Turner argues that Hull's travelogue throws into sharper relief her surprisingly detailed understanding of the North African Saharan localities in which her most popular fiction was set.

Suzanne Hobson's ' "Looking all lost towards a Cook's guide for beauty": The Art of Literature and the Lessons of the Guidebook in Modernist Writing' (*StTW* 19[2015] 30–47) explores the signal impact of the guidebook, especially the Baedeker series, on modernist literary culture. Hobson treats the guidebook as a multifaceted aesthetic object in its own right. E.M. Forster emerges from this discerning essay as an author unusually concerned with the guidebook as a textual device by which to rethink the cultural politics of space and place, contested ideologies of Englishness, and the utility of aesthetic categories such as the picturesque and the sublime.

Sam Wiseman's 'Cosmopolitanism and Environmental Ethics in Mary Butts's Dorset' (*TCL* 61:iii[2015] 373–91) provides fresh topographical trajectories into the oeuvre of a conceptually bold female author who was obsessed with the *genius loci* or 'spirit of place', especially in her critically lauded *Armed with Madness* [1928]. Wiseman demonstrates that the Dorset-born Mary Butts addresses a modernist tension between an intensely lyrical feeling of attachment to agrarian England and the compelling allure of urban modernity. Wiseman's monograph, *The Reimagining of Place in English Modernism* builds on the scholarly virtues of this essay by appraising 'land-consciousness' in the fiction of Mary Butts and John Cowper Powys. Wiseman is certainly mindful of Ezra Pound's brash sloganeering ('Art is a matter of capitals', 'Provincialism the Enemy') as he delineates a rival strand of aesthetic modernism receptive to pastoral edge-lands and sparsely populated border zones. *The Reimagining of Place* affirms Powys and Butts as trenchant yet radically ambivalent commentators on the socio-economic and technological innovations of the era. This is a particularly welcome intervention that challenges received opinion by offering dynamic close readings of literary figures who feature only briefly in standard accounts of the high modernist project. The energetically eccentric, place-oriented strand of interwar modernism that emerges from Wiseman's book will resonate with cultural geographers such as David Matless, whose work documents the archaeologically rich Celtic corners of the island nation. Perhaps the key strength of Wiseman's thesis is his nimble approach to the stratified sense of 'place' in Butts's non-historical novels and short stories. So we are presented with a Mary Butts who maps and communes with the pre-Christian shrines of her natal homeland even as she acknowledges that avant-garde aesthetics can be partly construed—to quote Malcolm Bradbury—as 'an art of cities'. Wiseman also presents a Mary Butts with strident views on class struggle, radical feminism, and democratic politics, who struggles to find her social and cultural 'place' among literary forebears, peers, and vanguard networking clusters—resulting in embittered polemics such as her unpublished article on 'Bloomsbury'.

Wiseman's project should be measured against Jeffrey Mathes McCarthy's *Green Modernism: Nature and the English Novel, 1900 to 1930*, from the Palgrave series Literatures, Cultures, and the Environment, which skilfully fuses cultural history and contemporary theory to explore the textual representations of natural terrain in fiction by Conrad, Ford, and Butts. McCarthy is fascinated by how modernist fiction confronts and re-visions traditions and tropes synonymous with pastoral and the georgic. Kimberly Anne Coles, Ralph Bauer, Zita Nunes, and Carla L. Peterson's edited collection, *The Cultural Politics of Blood, 1500–1900* and Scott Freer's *Modernist Mythopoeia: The Twilight of the Gods* will also be useful resources for scholars of Mary Butts's fiction.

Elizabeth Brunton's 'May Sinclair's Modernism, and the Death of the Baby' (in Patterson and Choi, eds., pp. 52–67) discusses the critical commonplace of Sinclair seeming more of a generous 'maiden aunt' to the high modernist movement rather than one of its most visionary, prolific, and radically experimental voices (p. 52). Virginia Woolf reflected in 1929 that women 'remain even at this moment *almost unclassified*'. Sinclair's writing remains peculiarly difficult to classify, and Brunton responds to this challenge by showing a confident grasp of a notable array of Sinclair's fiction as well as the gendered politics of modernist form more generally. Her core contention is that the trope of the 'death of the baby' signals upheaval in 'the social, medical, and cultural landscape of the times' (p. 55). Brunton also notes that this trope leads into a complex discussion about Sinclair's resolve 'to kill the ghosts of the past but by pursuing this line so doggedly, she is frequently guilty of invoking the very morality inherent in the thinking she despises' (p. 67).

Elizabeth A. Mosimann's 'Postwar New Feminisms: May Sinclair and Colette' (in Rabaté, ed., *1922: Literature, Culture, Politics*, pp. 196–208) should be read alongside Diana Collecott's ' "The Women of 1914": Women's Networks in Literary London during World War One' (in Baumann, ed., *Ezra Pound and London: New Perspectives*, pp. 53–64).

Emma Heaney's 'The New Woman: Sexology, Literary Modernism, and the Trans Feminine Remainder' (*Genre* 48:i[2015] 1–33) analyses Aldous Huxley's first published narrative, *The Farcical History of Richard Greenow* [1920]. Heaney scrutinizes Huxley's fictional treatment of transsexuality in relation to the modernist novel. Huxley's text is shaped by misgivings about 'authorship and sexual identity' that were shared by other interwar modernist male writers. His protagonist considers himself a spiritual hermaphrodite because his body is inhabited by two personalities: a male intellectual and an increasingly powerful and popular female novelist and war propagandist named Pearl Bellairs. Heaney contends that this female figure affords a way for protagonist and author to defend themselves against 'same-sex eroticism' (pp. 1–2).

Helen Green's 'Mystical Mavericks: The Influence of Gustav Fechner and Henri Bergson on Algernon Blackwood's *The Centaur*' (in Patterson and Choi, eds., pp. 136–53) treats Blackwood's 1911 novella as a thorough exploration of mystical affect and its precise relation to a strand of aesthetic modernism that promotes dissident or heretical forms of spirituality. This should be read alongside James Thompson's 'Selfhood and Bodily Transformation in Algernon Blackwood's "The Wendigo"' (*Expl* 73:iv[2015] 283–5). Richard J. Bleiler's *The Strange Case of 'The Angels of Mons': Arthur Machen's World War I Story, the Insistent Believers, and His Refutations* considers the textual and cultural significance of Machen's fiction concerned with the psychic and civic impact of the Great War.

Kristin Mahoney's *Literature and the Politics of Post-Victorian Decadence* contains a perceptive chapter on Vernon Lee and her vexed relationship to practitioners of aesthetic modernism. Mahoney posits that the early twentieth century was an era in which *fin-de-siècle* tropes and narrative tactics exerted a compelling hold on the modernist cultural imagination and emergent vanguard experimentalists. Mahoney construes Lee as a writer for whom numerous modernist aesthetic, social, and political innovations were both profoundly unsettling and disillusioning. In Mahoney's incisive account, Lee emerges as one dependent on decadent strategies to reshape urgent debates about social activism and feminist protest, the emergence of the Labour Party, and shifting gender roles. Elke D'hoker and Stephanie Eggermont's '*Fin-de-Siècle* Women Writers and the Modern Short Story' (*ELT* 58:iii[2015] 291–312) explores the contribution of Vernon Lee to histories and theories of the modernist short story.

The scholarly interest in the stylistic and generic features of middlebrow literature that has burgeoned since Nicola Humble's *The Feminine Middlebrow Novel* [2001] was reflected in 2015 by the publication of Kristin Ewins's '"Revolutionizing a mode of life": Leftist Middlebrow Fiction by Women in the 1930s' (*ELH* 82:i[2015] 251–79) and Kate Macdonald and Christoph Singer's edited collection, *Transitions in Middlebrow Writing*. The latter assesses the links evident between the simultaneous emergence of British modernism and middlebrow literary culture from 1880 to the 1930s. Contributors scrutinize the mutual influences of modernist and middlebrow authors, critics, publishers, and monthly magazines grapple with a tricky problem: how to define 'the middlebrow' given that it is not a discrete or fixed cultural category, but instead restlessly repackages tropes of high modernist literary aesthetics and popular narrative modes alike. Emma Miller's chapter on H.G. Wells (pp. 121–40) focuses on *The Sea Lady* [1902], while Simon Frost (pp. 37–56) canvasses Kipling, Conrad, and F. Marion Crawford. Alison Hurlburt furnishes a striking account of the 'anti-modernism' of John Galsworthy's *The White Monkey* (pp. 103–20).

Paul March-Russell's cogent *Modernism and Science Fiction* asks whether the future-oriented narratives of science fiction, evolving alongside aesthetic modernism during the closing years of the nineteenth century, can be accurately labelled as 'modernist'. This is a limpid, witty, and engaging account that traces how modernist authors such as Conrad and Ford reacted imaginatively to the ground-breaking discoveries of Darwin, Edison, and Einstein, and how these major novelists exploited a vivid repertoire of figurations and thematic emphases that we would describe nowadays as 'science fiction'. March-Russell makes an effective case for Conrad's sly subversion of psychical research as well as social Darwinism in *The Secret*

*Agent* as well as his earlier text *The Inheritors* [1907], his first collaboration with Ford Madox Ford and 'their only foray into Wellsian scientific romance' (p. 35). Conrad aficionados will appreciate March-Russell's positioning of *The Inheritors* as a thought-provoking 'meta-commentary upon nineteenth-century sf' (p. 37). March-Russell also draws attention to other scientific romances from the early years of the twentieth century, such as Allen Upward's *The Discovery of the Dead* [1910], William Hope Hodgson's *The House on the Borderland* [1908], and *The Night Land* [1912].

Grevel Lindop's *Charles Williams: The Third Inkling* claims to be the first complete biography of a formidably prolific writer who was a core member of a group of Oxford writers that included C.S. Lewis and J.R.R. Tolkien. Lindop's patiently plotted enterprise will prove helpful for philosophers of religion and, especially, literary scholars who analyse the early novels, such as *War in Heaven* [1930] and *Many Dimensions* [1930]. Lindop is interested in how these texts reflect and refract the grave moral and political concerns of interwar culture, especially the category of evil, and how it emerges in and infects close-knit communities or nation-states. The Williams who emerges from this exceptionally detailed biography—a tireless yet deeply troubled metaphysical voyager—also foresees the temper of our own time, characterized by what Gilles Châtelet termed 'the complete triumph of the individual' in which current notions of the 'soul' and 'selfhood' require radical reformulation. Lindop is astute about the imaginative fabric of Williams's occult thrillers; how they disclose a subtle theological mind that is surprisingly and keenly responsive to a range of recondite lore.

Edited by Erik Tonning, Matthew Feldman, and David Addyman, *Modernism, Christianity and Apocalypse* argues convincingly that the function of Christianity is essential to any nuanced chronicle of aesthetic modernism. Contributors assess how religious tropes resonate in the published narratives of male authors such as G.K. Chesterton, Ezra Pound, and T.S. Eliot. But the volume is comparatively reticent about what Kristin Bluemel calls those 'vital figures' that 'disappear in discussions of modernism'—spiritually attuned novelists such as Naomi Mitchison, Evelyn Underhill, Mary Butts, Hope Mirrlees, and Winifred Holtby, and the Rebecca West that emerges from Laura Cowan's *Rebecca West's Subversive Use of Hybrid Genres*. Tonning's volume should be scrutinized alongside Leigh Wilson's *Modernism and Magic: Experiments with Spiritualism, Theosophy, and the Occult* and Lynne Hinojosa's *Puritanism and Modernist Novels: From Moral Character to the Ethical Self*. With admirable attention to textual nuance, Hinojosa interrogates conventional accounts of the modernist novel as a defiantly secular product by demonstrating that the British novel tradition is formed by Puritan hermeneutics and Bible-reading habits.

West's deployment of genre is also pertinent to Timothy Wientzen's article 'An Epic of Atmosphere: Rebecca West, *Black Lamb*, and Reflex' (*JML* 38:iv[2015] pp 57–73). By framing West's capacious travelogue in the context of modernist anti-fascist writing and contemporary preoccupations with conditioned and Pavlovian behaviours, Wientzen establishes a surprising line of filiation between Virginia Woolf's *Three Guineas* and West's extended reflections on travelling in the Balkans. The relation is surprising because West in many ways disdained the politics of Bloomsbury. Yet, like Woolf and the anti-fascist philosopher Hannah Arendt, West was intellectually intrigued by the perceived link between fascistic societies and modes of physiological conditioning. Woolf's *Three Guineas* began life as an ambitious epic on the role of social environment or 'atmosphere', one that she ultimately abandoned. West's *Black Lamb* is the epic on social conditioning that Woolf never wrote, and a defining work for in what Wientzen terms the 'modernist politics of reflex'.

Finally, Patrick Parrinder's 'John Buchan and the Spy Thriller' (in Berberich, ed., *The Bloomsbury Introduction to Popular Fiction*, pp. 200–12) sheds light on Buchan's complex engagement with a mainstream fictional mode as a vehicle for caustic socio-economic critique.

*(b) Fiction 1930–1945*
This year saw a significant number of publications devoted to materialist modes of reading, confirming the productive relationship currently enjoyed by late modernist and interwar studies with recent post-dualist theories of materiality and agency. Questions relating to embodiment, affective landscape, material objects, intertext, and the intermedial effects of networks (be they broadcasting networks or artistic transnational networks) were prevalent themes. Continued emphasis upon archival research in the period either provided further testament to this materialist trend or signalled a converse historicist impetus. Either way, the expansion of publicly accessible archives in recent years was an oft-cited catalyst for many projects.

This was certainly the case with the year's work in Beckett studies. From the Bloomsbury Historicizing Modernism series came Iain Bailey's *Samuel Beckett and the Bible*, a study of biblical intertextuality across Beckett's oeuvre. The Bible, following Bailey's approach, is neither a parent text nor a body of ahistorical teachings. Indeed, Bailey argues that within our increasingly secular literary culture, Beckett's biblical allusions are all too often taken for granted, overlooked in the criticism or hastily elided with timeless philosophical themes. Yet this kind of timeless abstraction is incongruous to contemporary Beckett studies in general, where the disclosure of new and previously private documents has encouraged a turn towards material history and the archive in recent years. Accordingly, Bailey's study seeks to redress this incongruity with an analysis of Beckett and the Bible as historically situated intertexts. The Bible is thus more than a stable storehouse of tropes and idioms for Beckett; it is, Bailey suggests, a 'canon or corpus' (p. 7) riven by internal inconsistencies and repetitions, which Beckett then tracks and traces in the recurrences of his own writings, and still very much a living, responsive component of his predominantly Christian cultural context. The question Bailey seeks to pursue therefore is 'how something in Beckett comes to count as "biblical"' (p. 9). Clearly this entails far more than a simple decoding or allegorizing of latent textual content. One of Bailey's central contentions is that the Bible was not a mere source text amongst many for Beckett; its living fealty (personal, national, or pedagogical) was something he sought to explore rather than contain through stable allusion, with the result that 'there are not a fixed, finite number of biblical presences in the Beckett oeuvre, waiting to be found' (p. 11).

Another fallacy he seeks to unpick is the largely biographical assumption that Beckett's Bible was forged, and so to a large extent fixed, in Beckett's imagination early on in childhood. Of particular interest in this context is the discussion in chapter 5 of Beckett's bilingualism and contrasting attitudes to French and English biblical allusion. These divergent modes of interpolation underscore the material and textual (as opposed to fixed or purely intellectual) bases behind Beckett's biblical appropriations.

Critiquing naively historicist or biographical interpretations of Beckett's Bible, Bailey deploys a broadly genetic and intertextual approach to the Beckett archive (he elaborates upon the methods and merits of genetic intertextuality in chapter 3). As a pervasive and productive cultural force at the time of writing, the Bible's influence suffuses many inexplicit elements of Beckett, he claims. By bringing those energies to light with archival methods, Bailey also helps to illuminate those tacit cultural influences explored by Beckett at the time of writing.

Another study to issue from new archival access is Natka Bianchini's *Samuel Beckett's Theatre in the America*, which focuses upon Beckett's theatrical productions and his working relationship with the American director Alan Schneider. The study comes as part of a new series devoted to Beckett's interdisciplinary legacy for subsequent artists, writers, and thinkers and is intended to 'reconnect Beckett with his own cultural and historical situation'. Bianchini's project is explicitly motivated by new archival access and aims at recovering Beckett studies from what the series editor terms its 'ahistorical phase'.

Two notable works of philosophical criticism in Beckett studies were S. E Gontarski's *Creative Involution: Bergson, Beckett, Deleuze* and David Kleinberg-Levin's *Beckett's Words: The Promise of Happiness in a Time of Mourning*. The latter sets out to enrich our understanding of Beckett's philosophical relation to language from the perspectives of Walter Benjamin and Theodor Adorno. Significantly, *Beckett's Words* is the third volume in a trilogy of works by Kleinberg-Levin dedicated to what Gerald Bruns refers to as 'an exclic philosophy of hope'. The promise of hope in the title of this study is a paradoxical potential evinced, so Kleinberg-Levin claims, by the experience of mourning and catastrophe. Following the dialectical models of Benjamin and Adorno, Kleinberg-Levin argues that Beckett presents disaster as the condition for the possibility of hope; and it is hope for the future, rather than any indwelling property, which constitutes the essence of happiness in the precarious desublimated universe of Beckett and the Frankfurt school. The fact that Kleinberg-Levin chooses to focus predominantly on Beckett's middle and later works, *How It Is* [1964], *The Trilogy* [1953], and *Texts for Nothing* [1967], is also significant, since Beckett for Kleinberg-Levin was clearly much closer to his modernist forebears than late modernist ascriptions generally admit. Indeed, the high modernist trope of redemption through artistic freedom or, in this case, poetic freedom is the guiding axiom for this work and receives explicit treatment in the context of Benjamin's secular messianism.

With respect to these redemptive strains, one of work's signal achievements is Kleinberg-Levin's attention to philosophical energies less frequently discussed in Beckett studies. Whilst more orthodox references, such as Schopenhauerian or Nietzschean nihilism, or the absurdist affirmations of existentialism or the aporetics of poststructuralism, tend to consolidate a pessimistically monadic Beckettian world view, Kleinberg-Levin philosophical references point to something quite different. Accordingly, in *How It Is*, Kleinberg-Levin elicits a 'theological dimension' to the work's pervasive gloom, 'illuminated', he claims, 'by the remembrance of the promise of social reconciliation, a redemption of our humanity borne by language' (p. 196). It is the social dimension to Kleinberg-Levin's eschatological reading which makes his claims for language distinctive.

Gontarski also invokes creative sociality or being-with-others in Beckett, albeit to markedly different ends. The 'involution' of the title derives from Deleuze and Guattari, for whom the term articulates, among other things, a mode of deterritorialized or post-dualist becoming characterized by multiplicity and the dissolution of boundaries. Neither evolutionary nor devolutionary, lacking both telos and determinate ground, 'creative involution' also describes the shape of Beckettian imagination according to Gontarski. Beckett's withdrawal from figure and ground, his commitment to summoning thoughts beyond rationalist representation, involves the dissolution of unified identity and the proliferation of ambiguously related minds or mental states which, whilst clearly not determinate beings, are evidently something other than nothing. As a becoming-other-than-identity, 'creative involution' also invokes the all-important mediatory figure of Henri Bergson, whose *Creative Evolution* [1907] proposed an alternative to Darwinist evolution based upon the principle of a creative spark or *élan vital*, an imperceptible *something* that distinguishes human propagation from the merely animal and material. Gontarski's genealogy of involution and creativity pivots upon the perception of a shared approach to non-Cartesian ontology between the three figures, and one to which a critique of rationalist empiricism, rationalist representation, and rationalist conceptions of nothingness and zero are central. Gontarski reads canonical texts like *Murphy*, *Watt*, and *The Unnameable* alongside less explored theatrical works such as 'Ohio Impromptu' [1981] and 'That Time' [1974].

The intellectual affinities of Beckett and Deleuze were also the subject of S.E. Wilmer and AudrorèŽukauskaite's edited collection, *Deleuze and Beckett*, which includes a previously published article by Gontarski on the subject (pp. 36–59), as well as an essay on '*Ideas* in Beckett and Deleuze' by Anthony Uhlmann (pp. 23–35). Other contributions include an essay on Beckett, Deleuze, and schizophrenia by Benjamin Keatinge (pp. 81–96); Isabelle Ost on Beckett, Deleuze, and Lacan (pp. 97–110); and David Addyman on Beckett, Deleuze, and Bergson (pp. 137–51).

Edited by Dirk Van Hulle, the *New Cambridge Companion to Samuel Beckett* is split into three sections, 'Canon', Poetics', and 'Topics', containing fifteen essays by an impressive roll-call of Beckett scholars that include Anthony Uhlmann's 'Beckett's Intertexts' (pp. 103–13); Jean-Michel Rabaté's 'Love and Lobsters: Beckett's Meta-Ethics' (pp. 158–69), S.E Gontarski's 'Samuel Beckett and the "Idea" of Theatre: Performance through

Artaud and Deleuze' (pp. 136–43); Peter Boxall's 'Still Stirrings: Beckett's Prose from "Texts for Nothing" to "Stirrings Still"' (pp. 33–47); and Ulrika Maude's 'Beckett, Body and Mind' (pp. 170–84).

Finally, with regard to Beckett studies, Andrew Gaedtke's 'Prey to Communications: Samuel Beckett and the Simulation of Psychosis' (*ModCult* 10:ii[2015] 227–49) explores the author's evolving treatment of psychosis, from a thematic feature of the early narratives to a formal and phenomenological principle of his later radio plays. Gaedtke argues that Beckett's theatrical successes following *The Unnameable* and the creative impasse commonly ascribed to its completion have tended to mask the critical importance of his radio work for his development overall. Radio offered Beckett the opportunity to explore and in some ways to directly instantiate the kind of psychological and ontological ambiguities previously only described in narrative form. Since its inception radio technology has prompted speculative anxieties regarding the transmission of personal mental frequencies, brain-waves, and inner thoughts. As such, it provided Beckett with an ideal medium to interrogate conditions of personal identity and the kinds of narrative dissolution associated with psychotic breakdown. Through readings of the radio plays *Embers* [1959] and *Rough for Radio, I* [1973], Gaedtke demon-strates that mental illness was far more than a casual or prurient interest for Beckett, and that the questions Beckett interrogates through the formal and technical constraints of radio were also being asked by clinicians and psychologists of the era. With plays such as *Embers*, Beckett trades on the restrictions of radio, not least the lack of visual cues and the centrality of disembodied voices, to enact the ontological confusions of schizophrenic hallucination. Gaedtke asserts the ethical importance of these experiential renderings and their historical significance for Beckett studies.

The social and aesthetic potential of radio is also at the heart of Melissa Dinsman's *Modernism at the Microphone: Radio, Propaganda, and Literary Aesthetics During World War II*, which focuses specifically upon the various 'turns to radio' enacted by modernist and late modernist writers, including Ezra Pound, Archibald MacLeish, T.S Eliot, Thomas Mann, E.M. Forster, Louis MacNeice, Dorothy Sayers, George Orwell, and Mulk Raj Anand during the Second World War. Dinsman combines socio-intellectual history, citing radio's import for the Frankfurt school of critical theory for instance, with the individual histories of these literary turns, which were often the result of restricted literary opportunities during the war. The introductory chapter provides an informative overview of radio in relation to key modernist figures and to modernist aesthetics more generally. It conveys both contemporary reservations regarding radio as a form of mass communication and some of the ways in which it helped to inspire modernist innovation. This discussion, concerning largely the 1920s and 1930s, establishes key questions which are then pursued in specific contexts. Not least of these is whether radio can move and educate its listeners by means other than passive or propagandistic instruction. And this question is central to the chapter on George Orwell, since it preoccupied him, and goes some way to explaining the ambivalence of his wartime relation to the BBC, and the apparent contradiction of Orwell's attacks on propaganda in *Homage to Catalonia* [1938] and *Nineteen Eighty-*

*Four* [1949]. In Dinsman's summation, whilst Orwell was critical of propaganda, it was the uses rather than the medium to which he ultimately objected. This chapter also provides an important rejoinder to the assumed insularity of late modernism; Orwell's work with the BBC in Burma was arranged on imperialist and propagandistic grounds, but his work there was international in outlook. Contrary to Orwell's own darker visions of mass media and thought control, the radio proved a medium for cultural enlargement and exchange. In Dinsman's words: 'Orwell's Indian Section work proves a material instance of the extreme inter-connectedness of modernist networks made possible by media' in war-torn Europe. Like American radio in the hands of Louis MacNeice, Orwell's radio was an instrument 'of transnational networks in an era of extreme Nationalism' (p. 99).

The growth in critical middlebrow studies continued in 2015 with Ann Rea's edited collection, *Middlebrow Wodehouse: P.G. Wodehouse's Work in Context*, which includes an excellent introduction (pp. 16–33). As a paradigm for reading, the middlebrow category affords serious consideration of class-bound values and judgements and, for Rea, an important frame through which to reconsider Wodehouse's literary style and preoccupations. Wodehouse was sidelined as a populist or trite entertainer by critics of the twentieth century; this volume redresses the dearth of serious critical attention previously paid to him and to middlebrow culture more generally. One of the main ways in which it seeks to do this is by contesting the common perception of Wodehouse as an entertainer blithely out of kilter with his historical situation. In his day, Wodehouse was criticized for failing to take the Great War seriously, for what the critic Robert McCrum latterly referred to as his 'aworldly' quality. High-minded literary types dismissed this lack of historical sensibility accordingly. But by the close of the Second World War, matters had deteriorated significantly for Wodehouse: following civilian capture by the Germans in France, he emerged to make a series of rambling and in no way partisan broadcasts on the Nazi radio network. Branded a traitor in Britain, his books were withdrawn from libraries and his name was tarnished with political disrepute. Although he was never fully exonerated, the general perception of his unworldliness and lack of historical sensibility has served him well in this respect; like one of his own characters, Wodehouse the bumbling aristocrat wound up in a situation graver than he was capable of countenancing. But this view fails to add up if, as this volume suggests, unworldliness was only a ruse. Although Caleb Richardson's contribution addresses this woeful period in Wodehouse's life (pp. 87–105), the main objective of the collection is to contest his reputation for unworldliness and historical insensitivity. Accordingly, Ann-Marie Einhaus examines Wodehouse's self-conscious positioning in the literary marketplace (pp. 16–33) and Ann Rea explores his literary representation of that marketplace (pp. 35–50). *Middlebrow Wodehouse* also contains many thoughtful essays relating to the historical particularity of thematic content such as food, pigs, class, and the musical innovations of Wodehouse's libretti.

Samantha Walton's *Guilty but Insane: Mind and Law in Golden Age Detective Fiction* also deals the populist middlebrow. Her study provides an intriguing analysis of detective fiction writers' conceptions of guilt, responsibility, and psychology between the 1920s and 1940s. The study combines social, medical, and juridical history with a series of literary case studies of work largely produced by women, such as Gladys Mitchell, Marjorie Allingham, and Christianna Brand, during the 1930s. Dismissed by 'hard-boiled' writers like Raymond Chandler, these Queens of Crime were in fact rather more ambivalent and discomfiting in their social portrayals than their reputation suggests. Biological determinism, inherited deviance, and eugenics were hot topics in the interwar period, as was the diagnostic potential of psychology and psychoanalysis. Walton demonstrates how Golden Age writers capitalized on these questions narratologically whilst challenging readers to reassess their moral assumptions. Chapter 1 explores diagnosed insanity as a plot device for murder mysteries. Enlarging upon the genre's contribution to the spread of psychological and psychoanalytic methods within the popular imagination, Walton also demonstrates how crime writers used these new categories of judgement to destabilize conventional ideas of fairness and justice. Subsequent chapters examine texts which probe the M'Naghten Rule, the principle that defendants are assumed to be sane and responsible for their actions unless medically proven otherwise. Walton explores engagements with philosophical questions in these texts regarding free will and conceptions of breakdown and neurosis in the wake of the Great War. Gladys Mitchell's *The Saltmarsh Murderers* [1932] and *St Peter's Finger* [1938] are singled out for their up-to-date psychoanalytic handling of sanity and criminal culpability and for drawing attention to the shortfalls of contemporary legal definitions of insanity. One of the Golden Age's most prolific authors, Mitchell's *When Last I Died* [1941] also receives special attention in the context of inherent or inherited criminality. Other works covered include Agatha Christie's *The ABC Murders* [1936], Christianna Brand's *Heads You Lose* [1941] and *Police at the Funeral* [1931], and *Traitors Purse* [1941] by Margery Allingham. The latter text is discussed in the context of a culminating discussion about irrationality in crime fiction. Walton demonstrates how modernist and psychoanalytic energies inspired authors such as Allingham to subvert the crime genre's rationalist conventions.

In keeping with materialist trends in modernism and intermodernism, the *Journal of Modern Literature* devoted an issue to 'Space and Place' which includes two articles on buildings in Jean Rhys: Emma Zimmerman's ' "Always the same stairs, always the same room": The Uncanny Architecture of Jean Rhys's *Good Morning, Midnight*' (*JML* 38:iv[2015] 74–92) identifies Sasha Jansen's Parisian hotel in *Good Morning, Midnight* [1939] as more than a mere backdrop to her wandering existence. The hotel functions not only as a symbol for modern transience and urban detachment, but as a central structuring device for Rhys's tale. Just as Freud's essay, *The Uncanny* performs a certain undecidability or uncanniness in the relaying of its argument, so Rhys's narrative structure in *Good Morning, Midnight* refuses any clear and determinate psycho-spatial logic. Sasha's narrowly circumscribed wandering to and from the hotel evoke the experiences of a deracinated modern urban condition; the hotel's ambivalent status as both sanctuary from the streets and public meeting ground epitomizes the erosion of public and private boundaries in the modern era. Moreover, the familiar impersonality of

Sasha's hotel room functions as a synecdoche and spur for voluntary and involuntary remembrances and the continued return of her repressed past. Katherine C. Henderson's 'Claims of Heritage: Restoring the English Country House in *Wide Sargasso Sea*' (*JML* 38:iv[2015] 93–109) identifies the great house of Thornfield Hall in *Wide Sargasso Sea* as wholly constitutive for Rhys's message. Critical opinion of this novel, which was begun in the 1940s but not published until 1966, has been divided: for many of Rhys's British contemporaries in the 1960s its meaning was dependent on a reading of Brontë's 'parent text', *Jane Eyre*; for subsequent postcolonial critics, it works as an autonomous Caribbean novel. Contesting this critical division, Henderson argues for a re-evaluation of the novel's position in the British and postcolonial canon. Central here is Henderson's account of British preservationist impulses in the mid-century, when the English country house was pushed to the forefront of national culture and identity, courtesy of the National Trust. The exploitative and turbulent relations upon which these great houses were built was consciously nullified, their sturdy foundations repackaged as emblems of British endurance, domestic stability, and timeless grandeur. For Henderson, this conscious reinscription of the past, with its convenient erasure of colonial history, is a direct target for Rhys. Hence the insufficiency conventional interpretations of the novel: through Thornfield Hall, *Wide Sargasso Sea* dramatizes 'the multiplicity and conflict *within* the space of "essential Englishness"' (p. 96). Rhys's country house asserts the impossibility of purging either English heritage or modern postcolonial consciousness from the past oppressions of empire.

*Wide Sargasso Sea* was also the subject of Ambreen Hai's '"There is always the other side, always": Black Servants' Laughter, Knowledge, and Power in Jean Rhys's *Wide Sargasso Sea*' (*Mo/Mo* 22:iii[2015] 493–521), which discusses recent postcolonial debates concerning the critical agency of Christophine, Rhys's previously overlooked servant character.

This year marked the seventieth anniversary of the first publication of Evelyn Waugh's *Brideshead Revisited* on 28 May 1945 and D. Marcel DeCoste's *The Vocation of Evelyn Waugh: Faith and Art in the Post-War Fiction* begins with a discussion of aestheticism in that novel as a response to declining faith. DeCoste presents Waugh's cautionary message here and in the less favoured later fictions, such as *Love Among the Ruins* [1953], *The Ordeal of Gilbert Pinfold* [1957], and *Unconditional Surrender* [1961], as both an artistic endeavour and an enactment of his Catholic vocation. Articles on Waugh's life and oeuvre elsewhere include Alex Murray's 'Decadence Revisited: Evelyn Waugh and the Afterlife of the 1890s' (*Mo/Mo* 23:ii[2015] 593–607), which addresses incidental elements of Waugh's aesthetic decadence and disdain for periodization; Muireann Leech's '"Do Not Analyse the Self": A Little Learning as Evelyn Waugh's Catholic Anti-Autobiography' (*PSt* 37:ii[2015] 112–27) examines Waugh's impersonal or anti-subjective approach to auto-biography writing; Sławomir Koziol's 'Between a Butterfly and a Cathedral: The Question of Art in *Brideshead Revisited*' (*Misc* 52[2105] 69–87) explores Waugh's aesthetic attitudes and the influence of Roger Fry in *Brideshead Revisited*; Robert G. Walker's 'The Rough-Hewn Patterns of Evelyn Waugh's

*Sword of Honour*' (*SR* 123:iv[2015] 674–84) addresses Waugh's late trilogy of novels.

*C.S Lewis's List: the Ten Books that Influenced Him Most*, edited by David Werther and Susan Werther, contains ten essays on ten books identified by Lewis as the most influential for his vocational and philosophical outlook on life. As David C. Downing points out in the foreword (pp. xi–xiii), Lewis was a voracious reader, and this was not the only list of influential books he was invited to compile. This particular list of 'dead white males' is handled by a roster of esteemed philosophers and literary critics, most with expertise in aspects of Christian or spiritual exegesis. Whether or not Lewis's list would 'make an excellent starting point for a Great Books curriculum' (p. xii) is open to debate, but as a starting point for this particular dead white male the collection is a rich resource. Of course, for Lewis scholars, the chapters on less predictable entries will be of greatest interest. George MacDonald was Lewis's self-professed 'master', and David L. Neuhouser provides a masterful opening chapter on the influence of his *Fantastes*, with appendices detailing concrete examples of his influence and a chronology for Lewis's reading of his works (pp. 9–30). Perhaps less anticipated in Lewis's list is his poetic preference for George Herbert's *The Temple* over the great epics of Dante or Milton. Don W. King uses archival material to demonstrate the poet's role in reviving his faith, in part thanks to Herbert's evocations of a very personal relation, lived out in his day-to-day existence (pp. 67–92). Another potentially surprising entry is Charles Taliaferro's account of the little-known *Theism and Humanism* by Arthur James Balfour, the first earl of Balfour and British prime minister between 1902 and 1905 (pp. 201–17). Lewis's work lacks decisive allusions to Balfour, and so Taliaferro combines correspondence records with an in-depth analysis of Balfour's theistic philosophy, which, based upon his self-professed import for Lewis, can endow our appreciation of his philosophical reasoning.

The faith referenced in Michael Tomko's *Beyond the Willing Suspension of Disbelief: Poetic Faith from Coleridge to Tolkien* has less to do with theism and more to do with artistic redemption and the possibility for modes of imaginative enlargement in an age of critical scepticism. The discussion is pitched rather more towards Coleridge, Romanticism, and Shakespeare than it is towards Tolkien or the twentieth century. Nevertheless, chapter 1 presents *The Hobbit* [1937] as an allegory for imaginative adventure and the transgression of bourgeois norms (pp. 19–64). A final chapter presents a distinction between poetic 'enchantment', which is collaborative and product-ive, and poetic 'magic', understood as a mode of domination, analogous to ideology or propaganda (pp. 109–44). Tomko frames this distinction through an exchange between the wizard characters Saruman and Gandalf in *The Lord of the Rings* [1954–5].

A vocational quality also permeates Ronald Zigler's treatment of socio-ideological prophecy in *The Educational Prophecies of Aldous Huxley; The Visionary Legacy of 'Brave New World', 'Ape and Essence' and 'Island'*. Drawing upon Huxley's manifold non-fiction publications, Zigler reads Huxley's one utopian and two dystopian novels in light of his progressive and countercultural lifestyle practices and beliefs, which included yoga, drug-taking, and pacifism. More specifically, Zigler reads these works in light of what he fulsomely conceptualizes as the portrayal of distinctive 'neurocultural ecosystems' (p. 19). As the term suggests, these ecosystems involve more than ideology alone; or rather, they invoke worlds wherein the cultural, institutional, and technological components of ideology are supplemented by neurochemical elements. Ideology is thus reconceived as an all-encompassing 'neurocultural' landscape. The novels under consideration present three such distinctive landscapes: the soma-suffused *Brave New World* [1931], the irradiated *Ape and Essence* [1948], and the utopian hallucinogenic *Island* [1962]. They are cautionary tales from the mid-century with identifiable elements in our own twenty-first-century environment. Huxley's percipience in these novels merits serious attention, Zigler argues, despite the critical contempt commonly reserved for later works like *Island*. The aim of the study is both 'descriptive' and 'prescriptive' (p. xi), however, and Zigler identifies the works' contemporary foreshadowings in order to promote Huxley as both writer and social pedagogue.

In *A Guide to the Graham Greene Archives*, John Wise and Mike Hill continue collating an authoritative index of Greene's writings. The first volume, published in 2012, listed and contextualized his published output. In this volume, they provide an invaluable guide to the nearly sixty worldwide repositories of archival material relating to Greene. The majority of the archives detailed are not widely known; they incorporate a fascinating array of documents including dream diaries, notebooks, business transactions, working manuscripts, and Greene's prolific correspondence with family, friends, and an array of public and literary figures including Edith Sitwell, Tom Stoppard, Kim Philby, and Ronald Harwood.

*(c) James Joyce*

Among the highlights of 2015 in Joyce studies are two methodologically distinct but equally significant monographs. Luke Gibbons's *Joyce's Ghosts: Ireland, Modernism and Memory* provides a working through of historical legacy that represents a fitting return of the repressed: as the centenary year of the Easter Rising approached, Gibbons's title calls up the spectral form in all its manifestations. The central argument is that ghosts in Joyce do not have a primarily personal dimension but represent a failure to internalize memory of events that have not yet attained the aspect of history. It encapsulates all the ghosts of modernity, its unseen forces political and economic, and, in this case particularly, colonial, suggesting that social history is inseparable from personal trauma and that the failure to process that trauma results in its breaking through as hauntings; these are spectres not of the Gothic but the Freudian tradition. In this way, ghosts escape psychological explanation and personal subjectivity, attaining a public dimension; interiority in Joyce therefore becomes expressive of permeable bounds, even within the mind itself. This liminal blurring of inner and outer trauma becomes a condition of modernity both personal and political, as colonialism itself prevents self-formation: thus Joycean ghosts cannot be explained away by recourse to models of the self understood as contained by proper limits. Instead, they are indicative of that subjection, the permeability at the limits of which is itself a formation of a haunting that is collective and, moreover, modernist in character. In this, the urban city and the subject interact as ghosts, and trouble the distinction between self and environment, private memory and communal experience: the past enters the present as a revenant of a history not yet constituted, creating an alter-metropolis wherein the dead occupy the space of the living, and a coexistent temporality in which the living are shadowed by a colonial history that divides the present from itself. These phantom forms of modernity are also literary, an aesthetic radicalism called up by Ireland's own haunted past, occupied doubly by two languages. Gibbons argues that Joyce creates formal techniques to represent and respond to that state and to mark it in a language containing its own phantom, an absence called into presence indicative of the irruption of that haunting in Joyce, such that in his writing 'Ireland achieves articulation as ... *form*' (p. xiv). *Joyce's Ghosts* also contributes to the recent emergence of 'vernacular modernism', and is important theoretically lending its own dimension to the term whereby the vernacular indicates unstable barriers between inside and outside, linguistically, culturally, and politically. In its concentration on absence and language, Gibbons's work has links to the first chapter of Barry McCrea's *Joyce in Languages of the Night*, which discusses the loss of Irish as vernacular (pp. 20–46), contending that 'After "Eveline," Irish makes its appearance in Joyce's work mostly as an idea rather than as a language' (p. 21). Reading 'The Dead', McCrea suggests that Irish represents a lost language embodying a dream of connection to the other that is fated to be unrealized.

In *Joyce's Creative Process and the Construction of Characters in Ulysses: Becoming the Blooms*, Luca Crispi has produced a magisterial genetic reading of the text that aims also to contextualize genetic criticism beyond Joyce studies and to relate it to critical approaches with which it intersects. Crispi focuses on the construction of the characters of Leopold and Molly Bloom, in seven chapters and a textual apparatus containing four appendices—an overview and glossary of kinds of *Ulysses* manuscripts and documents; a census of extant *Ulysses* manuscripts by episode; a chronological list of extant *Ulysses* manuscripts and typescripts; and a chronological list of *Ulysses* in proof—alongside an explanatory introduction setting out the rationale for the project. *Joyce's Creative Process* serves the dual purpose of reconstructing the compositional history of *Ulysses* through a genetic study of its *avant-texte* that reveals Joyce's creation of the Blooms, both individually and as a couple. Across all the extant notes and manuscripts for the novel, including those acquired by the National Library of Ireland since 2000, Crispi examines the construction of Leopold and Molly as characters and how that construction creates and, in the critical analysis, illuminates, the narratological structure of the text. Mapping the individual and intertwined histories of the Blooms enables the history of the text to be reconstructed and an exposition of a genetic *Ulysses* presented to the new reader, evidencing at the same time how the work of the reader and that of the writer are united in the process of character creation. This survey of genetic material is replete with insights: for example, Crispi notes that we now know that many fundamental facts of the novel were only established late in its construction, which alters our understanding of the function of characters in the text. Among other findings, he contends that the function of Milly is to serve as a subsidiary character by which we may better understand the Blooms; that the early introduction of the adultery plot is interdependent with the love story of the Blooms that Joyce was writing in 1918, thereby connecting beginning to end; and that Molly's recollections of her early life in Gibraltar are intended to remain essentially private, as evidenced by the fact that when Joyce constructs them he does not revise earlier sections in order to allow Bloom to reference these memories. Crispi thereby destabilizes critical readings on the stability of the Blooms, and 'focuses on the more general fluidity of their composition … until the juncture when *Ulysses* was published as a book' (p. 12). By exploring the creation of Molly and Bloom, their courtship and early life together, the years of Rudy's death and Bloom's unemployment, and their situation in Eccles Street, and by coupling this with an examination of other characters both incidental and significant (Blazes Boylan among them), Crispi demonstrates how memory and events are interwoven throughout *Ulysses* for strategic purposes of narrative formation.

Michael Patrick Gillespie's *James Joyce and the Exilic Imagination* employs exile studies to elucidate his reading of Joyce's attitude to Ireland, offering nuanced understandings of states of exile, from the physical to the ontological, through the concept of the exilic experience. It overlaps Nels Pearson's *Irish Cosmopolitanism: Location and Dislocation in James Joyce, Elizabeth Bowen, and Samuel Beckett*, in which two chapters, '*Ulysses*, the Sea, and the Paradox of Irish Internationalism' (pp. 19–41) and ' "Forget! Remember!": Joyce's Voices and the Haunted Cosmos' (pp. 42–62) are dedicated to theorizing how the national and international are mutually influential. Combining cosmopolitan and postcolonial theory with transnational and exile studies, *Irish Cosmopolitanism* aims to complicate simplistic readings of exile to examine Joyce's contribution to international modernism and his ties to an Ireland in the process of decolonization from a position of artistic exile; Pearson advances what he calls the 'Irish-Cosmopolitan paradox' (p. 5) whereby, in postcolonial states, the national does not constitute a pre-existing environment but a colonial appropriation of nation that fundamentally destabilizes a position of racination from which to be exiled. The search for an international identity would thus become the search for an always deferred national identity; through a reading of Joyce, he shows that the exiled subject nuances a exilic position poised on metaphorical and literal borders.

Written from the ecocritical perspective, Alison Lacivita's *The Ecology of Finnegans Wake* also adopts a genetic critical methodology to read *Finnegans Wake* through its sources, notebooks, and proofs as a development of the ecological thematic. Nor does the text offer its own retreat: it is alert to the 'Politics of Nature' (a chapter title) and to the means by which conceptions of the natural are politically encoded. Concentrating particularly on the technology of nature and the urban landscape as it relates to ecological environments, Lacivita develops concerns addressed in Robert Brazeau and Derek Gladwin's landmark collection, *Eco-Joyce* [2014], contributing to both Irish studies and modernist studies as well, which, as the author notes in the introduction, requires further engagement with ecocriticism.

*Modernists at Odds: Reconsidering Joyce and Lawrence*, edited by Matthew J. Kochis and Heather L. Lusty, proposes a reorientation of the pairing of Joyce and Lawrence, two writers conventionally considered antinomic. Essays outline sympathies in their work, thematics, and lives; contributors including Zack Bowen, Enda Duffy, and Margot Norris canvass comparisons across the oeuvres of both writers, under rubrics of religion, myth, social constructs, and cultural pastimes.

Kimberly J. Devlin and Christine Smedley's edited collection, *Joyce's Allmaziful Plurabilities: Polyvocal Explorations of Finnegans Wake*, proposes seventeen new and methodologically diverse readings of the *Wake*, concentrated through a particular attention to Joycean wordplay and the form of Wakean words. The editors focus on the multiple layering of (and between) words to expose a polyvocality of the text, wherein each word speaks in many different voices; they insist on this multiplicity as a principle of the text that cannot be rendered univocal in the interests of accessibility, since to do so is to 'level' the text and deny the formal 'prodigal experimentalism' of the *Wake*, which they describe as a prodigious and excessive text, in the sense of a 'lavish' and abundant effort whose richness is repaid by a concomitant readerly effort (pp. 2–3). Individual contributors mine the depths of this treasure, exploring the texture of the *Wake* in its multiple dimensions. John Terrill ventures a biblical exposition of the text, while Jim LeBlanc adopts an existentialist approach to sin. Tim Conley unites form and theory by gauging the 'atmosphere' of the *Wake*, as both an ecology and a formal mode; Margot Norris also takes an ecocritical approach to the aqueous females of the book, while Kimberly J. Devlin 'saves' on waste by following homophonic equivalences between salvation and salvage. Mia L. McIver's study focuses on corporeal bodies, and Colleen Jaurretche combines word and image to view the readerly response to the text; Christine Smedley also focuses on vision, in an essay that brings the Famine into its purview. Jeffrey Drouin, too, argues a visual approach to the space of the text, wherein he suggests its voices are made visible. Sean Latham plays with the meaning of game theory, Enda Duffy charts the conflicts of Irish history in II.3, and Sheldon Brivic focuses on the family, as does Richard Brown, who uses the Porters to examine mimesis in the novel. Patrick A. McCarthy's genetic reading compares excerpts from the published text with their *transition* counterparts. Carol Loeb Shloss is concerned with female desire, and David Spurr reads the kiss as a means of accessing the language of the *Wake*, while Vicki Mahaffey examines the import of fire and water as creative forces in the text. The proliferation of approaches is well suited to the organizing principle of the text, evoking the luxuriousness that is contained in the unit of the word as in the work.

A further approach to voice is that of Phillip Mahoney, whose 'Bloom's Neume: The Object Voice in the "Sirens" Episode in Joyce's *Ulysses*' (in Sacido-Romero and Mieszkowski, eds., *Sound Effects: The Object Voice in Fiction*, pp. 131–55) is a Lacanian spin on Joyce's voices, arguing that the experience of epiphany and artistic calling is underscored by the voice, and specifically by the concept of 'hearing voices'. Mahoney focuses on 'Sirens' to expound further phonological theory as it relates to the text, including that of

Mladen Dolar on the 'object voice' and Garrett Stewart, to develop insight into Joyce's 'posterior monologue'.

Materialist approaches, particularly in textual editing and genetic criticism, continue to be strongly represented in 2015, as do historicist methodologies. *James Joyce, The Little Review 'Ulysses'*, edited by Mark Gaipa, Sean Latham, and Robert Scholes, replicates the print publication of *Ulysses* as it was released in the *Little Review* in 1918–20 and provides an important contextual history of its censorship. The serialization of the novel constitutes the text; it is accompanied by colour plates and tables of contents to place each issue in context, as well as a textual apparatus comprising a general introduction; composition history of *Ulysses*; the magazine context for the *Little Review 'Ulysses'*; and a section of essays, letters, and comments on *Ulysses* in the *Little Review* between 1918 and 1921 that situates the novel in serial form within the wider dynamic of modernist textual production and reception.

Combining art and science, Jeffrey S. Drouin's *James Joyce, Science, and Modernist Print Culture: 'The Einstein of English Fiction'* examines how Joyce's work exemplifies aspects of the Einsteinian theory of relativity, an empirical approach to modernist print culture that focuses not only on the publication of *Ulysses* and *Finnegans Wake* in the little magazines, and the engagement of aesthetic modernism with scientific discovery through those reviews, but also the wider social milieu of material print culture as it constructed arguments on science that the author traces back to the compositional history of the text. In doing so, Drouin forwards the claim that both novels assume their structure from the humanities' relation to scientific debate in the period.

Edited by Anne Fogarty and Fran O'Rourke, *Voices on Joyce* has its genesis in the ReJoyce *Ulysses* celebrations at University College Dublin during 2004. Lee Miller's photographs of Dublin from 1946, accompanied by an essay from Terence Killeen, are a notable inclusion. Subjects range from the socio-historical context of 1904 Ireland as investigated in essays by Michael Laffan and Joseph Brady, to Bloom's Jewishness and Judaism in Dublin, by Cormac Ó Gráda; from Anne Fogarty's interrogation of Joyce and Parnell to Adrian Hardiman's legal account of *Ulysses*; and from Donal McCartney's treatment of Joyce's UCD and its relationship to the city, to discussions of music and sport by Harry White and Conal Hooper respectively. Articles on Joycean writing abound, examples of which include Terence Dolan on etymology and Richard Kearney on the epiphany, and comparative studies of influence from Aristotle, the classics, and Vico by Fran O'Rourke, Fritz Senn, and Daragh O'Connell. James Pribek, Joseph Long, and Frank McGuinness's treatments continue this thematic, with essays on the influence of Newman; of Dante and Homer on Joyce and Beckett; and on Ibsen. There are further contributions from Declan Kiberd ('*Ulysses* and Us'), and from Christopher Murray on the specifically Irish 'problem play' of *Exiles*, while Gerardine Meaney's consideration of Joyce's contemporary status concludes the volume.

Arguing that Joyce had anarchist tendencies, chapter 3 of Jeff Shantz's *Specters of Anarchy: Literature and the Anarchist Imagination* examines *Ulysses* in the light of nineteenth-century discussions of anarchy and the co-implication of anarchy with gender and sexuality in his writing (pp. 77–102).

Shantz claims Joyce's relationship to nationalism and imperialism evinces a suspicion of the state, and traces what he perceives to be anarchist leanings based on the list given to Herbert Gorman of writers he was reading, Bakunin and Kropotkin among them, imagining *Ulysses* as espousing the latter's ideal of society as interdependent mutual aid and a Bakunian antipathy towards religion and nationalism. Gerry Smyth's *The Judas Kiss: Treason and Betrayal in Six Modern Irish Novels* makes a different invention into the political sphere. Chapter 3 examines a Joycean preoccupation with traitorous betrayal, originating in the historico-political with Parnell and extending throughout his life and early writings to the psychosexual dimensions of adultery in *Ulysses* (pp. 69–91).

In 'Bloom's Job: The Role of the Advertisement Canvasser in Joyce's Dublin' (*Mo/Mo* 22:iv[2015] 651–66), Matthew Hayward aims to historicize the debate on Joyce and advertising in the twenty-first century. He produces a materialist reading that advances claims regarding the role of advertising in *Ulysses* by placing Bloom within what he argues is the historical particularity of Dublin advertising culture during 1904. John McGuigan's 'To Go and Sin Once More: Confession and Joyce's "Nausicaa" Episode' (*ModCult* 10:ii[2015] 201–26) discusses the linguistic presence of contemporary Catholic form in 'Nausicaa', focusing on the discourse of the confessional as a means of mediating sexuality in the consciousness of Gerty and, by extension, that of Ireland.

Edited by Martha Carpentier, *Joycean Legacies* is a collection of wide-ranging essays surveying Joycean influences in contemporary writing, with chapters focused on Kate O'Brien; Brendan Behan; J.G. Farrell; Patrick McCabe; George Orwell; J.R.R. Tolkien; Anthony Burgess; Frank McCourt; Raymond Carver; Derek Walcott; Sadeq Hedayat; and post-1984 British fiction. The volume aims not only to read Joyce in contemporary writing, but to propose new readings of the contemporary through the lens of Joyce; its foreword by Derek Attridge is important in its own right, excavating Joyce's legacies in Irish writing. Also within the contemporary strand is Catherine Lanone's 'Clarity of Insight and Commonplaces: Alice Munro, James Joyce and Alex Colville' (in Guignery, ed., *The Inside of a Shell: Alice Munro's 'Dance of the Happy Shades'*, pp. 169–86), which claims that Munro employs cliché in order to effect a process of defamiliarization through the use of textual fragments such as the newspaper story. Lanone suggests that Munro's reworking of the short story format and the epiphany issue from the influence of Joyce, and particularly from 'A Painful Case'.

Chapter 3 of *Modernism and Homer: The Odysseys of H.D., James Joyce, Osip Mandelstam, and Ezra Pound*, by Leah Culligan Flack, argues that Joyce employs a classical schema in response to a censorious audience, subverting mythological and heroic discourse to eschew sentimental nationalism (pp. 95–123). Tracing the censorship history of *Ulysses*, she offers 'Cyclops' as an example of confrontation aimed at the censors through its insistence on the word 'bloody' and ventures that, at the time of writing *Ulysses*, the *Odyssey* did not represent a solid classical precursor for Joyce, but an unstable text that impelled the stylistic experimentation of *Ulysses*. The enduring preoccupation with Joyce and the classics signalled here is also evident in David Weir's accessible *Ulysses Explained: How Homer, Dante, and Shakespeare Inform Joyce's Modernist Vision* and Theodore Ziolkowski's *Classicism of the Twenties: Art, Music & Literature*, which offers a synoptic account of classically inflected modernism drawing on references to Joyce throughout, from the 'classical temper' of *A Portrait of the Artist as a Young Man* to the Homeric order of *Ulysses*.

Geert Lernout's slim and elegant *Cain: But Are You Able? The Bible, Byron and Joyce* charts Joyce's fascination with the biblical tale of Cain and its refraction through Byron, for whose play, *Cain*, Joyce wished to develop the libretto. Lernout places Joyce's interest in the context of an ongoing struggle with Christianity and the Bible, and argues that both writers were influenced by biblical interpretation of the Cain story; furthermore, he claims that it is Byron's interpretation of the story that shadows *Finnegans Wake*. Peter Cochran's *Byron's European Impact* contains chapter on Joyce that provides a general, conversational account from a non-specialist of Byronic instances in Joyce's writing and a comparative discussion of *Don Juan* and *Ulysses* (pp. 436–64).

Catherine E. Paul's edited collection, *Writing Modern Ireland*, contains two comparative essays which are of a musical note: Wim Van Mierlo's '"I have met you too late": James Joyce, W.B. Yeats and the Making of *Chamber Music*' (pp. 43–66) concentrates on an unpublished early notebook by Joyce in order to argue for its centrality to our understanding of his early writing. Van Mierlo situates this notebook within the conditions and period of its production and suggests more broadly that it can help revise the commonly held view of Joyce and Yeats as oppositional figures. Using evidence from the notebook, Van Mierlo illuminates the relationship between Joyce and Yeats and resituates *Chamber Music*. Wayne K. Chapman's '"Notes chirruping answer": Language as Music in James Joyce and Virginia Woolf' (pp. 229–36) also ventures a comparative analysis, proposing that Woolf's reading of *Ulysses* in *The Little Review* influenced her writing of *Monday or Tuesday*, the musical prose of which he traces to 'Sirens'. The Yeatsian note continues with Tudor Balinisteanu's *Religion and Aesthetic Experience in Joyce and Yeats*, which compares the poetics of Joyce and Yeats through the lens of Georges Sorel's social myth, in which aesthetic experience represents a form of religious experience. Balinisteanu explores their use of myth to offer a potential resistance against capitalist forces of modernity. Like Shantz, Balinisteanu draws parallels between Joyce's art and the anarchist politics embodied in Sorel's theory to argue that an interpretation of the former through the latter evinces the possibility of art to provoke social change. Elsewhere, Philip Keel Geheber's 'A Return to Revivalist Myth in *Finnegans Wake*' (in Fernandes and Serra, eds., *The Power of Form: Recycling Myths*, pp. 170–83) outlines how *Finnegans Wake* inscribes Irish myth, claiming that Revivalist models anticipate modernist mythic treatment. As such, Geheber argues, the *Wake* can be viewed simultaneously as a work of high modernism and the endpoint of the Irish Literary Revival.

Gabrielle McIntire's 'Uncanny *Semblables* and Serendipitous Publications: T.S. Eliot's the *Criterion*, and *The Waste Land* and James Joyce's *Ulysses*' (in Rabaté, ed., *1922: Literature, Culture, Politics*, pp. 15–28) examines the

*Criterion* as a fulcrum for epic publications of 1922 and the uncanny twinning of the Eliotic and Joycean texts as radical departures in literary form, offering challenges to social mores. Elsewhere, Donald Phillip Verene's contribution Matthew Feldman and Karim Mamdani's edited collection, *Beckett/ Philosophy*, 'On Vico, Joyce and Beckett' (pp. 51–74) ventures a triangulation, elucidating the presence of Vico in the *Wake* via Beckett's 'Dante... Bruno. Vico.. Joyce'. Russell McDonald's 'Pedestrian Perils on the Road to Irish Identity in Joyce and Bowen' (*ISR* 23:iv[2015] 385–406) argues that both writers share an interest in walking, denuded of Romantic and English nationalist connotations, as a means to articulate what he suggests is a shared materialist construction of Irishness.

There was a notable minor trend this year, namely an emphasis on Judaism in Joyce, from Ó Gráda's essay in *Voices on Joyce* (discussed above) to Jeremy Tambling's 'Judaism and Heterogeneity in the Modernist Long Novel' (*ModCult* 10:ii[2015] 357–79), also discussed above, which suggests that there is a parallel relation within the modernist long novel, including *Ulysses*, between narratological length and an interest in Judaism and anti-Semitism. Stephen Watt's *'Something Dreadful and Grand': American Literature and the Irish-Jewish Unconscious*, establishes a reading of diasporic Irish Jewish identity in America through a discussion of Joyce's 'Irish Jews', ranging across the Joycean canon to posit that Joyce adopts alternative approaches by both equating Irishness with Judaism and separating them into an antagonism to reflect contemporary historical positions on race and nationality. Watt offers that in fact 'the most famous Irish Jew of the modern era may well have been Joyce himself' (p. 17), on the basis of his concern for Jewish culture in his life and works.

A concern with affect can also be discerned across recent work on Joyce. Maria-Daniella Dick's 'Bloom-Space of Theory: The Pleasure and the Bliss of Gerty MacDowell' (in Taylor, ed., *Modernism and Affect*, pp. 167–84) argues for an affective reading of 'Nausicaa' through the work of Roland Barthes. Paul K. Saint-Amour's *Tense Future: Modernism, Total War, Encyclopedic Form* also contains a chapter on 'The Shield of Ulysses' (pp. 222–62) that engages with the affective imagination of interwar writing in a colonial and global context. Considering *Ulysses* as a total representation of Dublin intended to archive the city against war, Saint-Amour draws on the metaphor of Achilles' shield in the *Iliad*, arguing for *Ulysses* as a modern analogy. *Ulysses*, he contends, encapsulates the 'political logic of epic—the logic whereby war offers the primary occasion for an organic, coherentist portrait of a social totality' (p. 225). Furthermore, Saint-Amour argues, it 'both attempts and renounces' the model of 'social totality at war' and the portrait of 'total war as *the* occasion for perceiving and theorizing social totality' (p. 225). Against this synoptic portrait, he suggests, *Ulysses* ventures the encyclopedic form, which emphasizes the partial over the total.

Dedicated to 'Irish Modernism', the Winter 2015 issue of the *Journal of Modern Literature* contains several articles on Joyce. Echoing Gibbons's work, an interest in the vernacular and in modernism's conceptual geographies is salient. The Joycean readings herein intervene into contexts of modernity, its philosophy and history of ideas as well as its material history. David P.

Rando's 'Storytelling and Alienated Labor: Joyce, Benjamin, and the Narrative Wording Class' (*JML* 38:ii[2015] 29–44) posits that *Ulysses* offers a model for regarding narrative as alienated labour through the figure of the Arranger, postulating a challenge to Benjamin's reading of the novel under capitalism. In ' "Khaki Hamlets don't hesitate": A Semiological Reading of References to the Boer War and Concentration Camps in Joyce's *Ulysses*' (*JML* 38:ii[2015] 45–58), Leona Toker advances a semiological reading of concentration camp history that argues for a futurity of reference in *Ulysses*. Erik H. Schneider's ' "Welcomers": James Joyce and Frederic W.H. Myers' (*JML* 38:ii[2015] 59–70) sheds welcome light on the little-read essay, 'The Portrait of the Artist' [1904], arguing that it founds spiritual and occultist thematics in Joyce, influenced by his reading of Myers and ultimately leading to his reconceptualizing of the concept of epiphany. In Roy Benjamin's 'Looking for the Bilder: The Subversion of Ocularcentrism in *Finnegans Wake*' (*JML* 38:ii[2015] 71–85) the metaphor of the eye in the *Wake* is examined as it allows for the subversion of the Western 'world-picture' as theorized by Heidegger.

In his introduction to an important issue of *James Joyce Quarterly* on 'Legal Joyce' Jonathan Goldman situates this topic within the context and long history of a comparative interest in Joyce and the law (*JJQ* 50:iv[2013] 943–9), arguing that a study of the linguistic basis of the law befits current empirical approaches to Joyce and modernist studies and creates the opportunity to evidence how 'literature inflects, rather than reflects, how a culture thinks—that narrative works have mutually influential relationships with their historical contexts' (p. 947). Conceiving law as both discipline and discourse, Goldman avers that 'In Joyce, the law is a language that creates its own reality' (p. 947). Robert Spoo's 'Judging Woolsey Judging Obscenity: Elitism, Aestheticism, and the Reasonable Libido in the *Ulysses* Custom Case' (*JJQ* 50:iv[2013] 1027–49) investigates Judge Woolsey's 1933 verdict, arguing that his decision has been mischaracterized in critical discourse and should be re-evaluated as a sophisticated and creative judicial response. The essay is one of three on Woolsey: Kevin Birmingham's 'The Prestige of the Law: Revisiting Obscenity Law and Judge Woolsey's *Ulysses* Decision' (*JJQ* 50:iv[2013] 991–1009) examines the man himself and views the case through the lens of 'prestige' both literary and personal, while John Gleeson, himself a sitting judge, argues that the 1920 and 1933 cases have an enduring use today in providing a perspective on the legal and judicial world in 'The *Ulysses* Cases and What They Reveal about Lawyers and the Law' (*JJQ* 50:iv[2013] 1001–25). Gleeson avers that judicial decision tends to ratify public opinion rather than lead it. Among the other essays in the volume: Andrew Gibson's ' "Nobody Owns": *Ulysses*, Tenancy, and Property Law' (*JJQ* 50:iv [2013] 951–62) studies the politics of property law in a British-Irish context through *Ulysses*; Celia Marshik's 'Dublin, Inc.: Municipal Corporation Reform in "Ivy Day in the Committee Room" ' (*JJQ* 50:iv[2013] 963–76) utilizes references to the Dublin Corporation to claim that Joyce wishes to emphasize the issue of local government in a colonized state, balancing the city against the nation; and Robert Brazeau's '*Pro Bono Publico*: Urban Space in "Cyclops" '

(*JJQ* 50:iv[2013] 977–90) looks at the laws of alcohol consumption in Ireland as a means of redistributing public space. A special issue of the *Dublin James Joyce Journal* on *Finnegans Wake*, edited by Luca Crispi and Anne Fogarty, contains a host of illuminating articles. Chrissie Van Mierlo's ' "Greedo!": Joyce, John MacHale, and the First Vatican Council from "Grace" to *Finnegans Wake*' (*DJJJ* 8[2015] 1–14) considers Joyce's inscription of the Great Council of 1869–70 into 'Grace' and his return to it in the *Wake*, suggesting that his interest in the council's decree regarding papal infallibility resounds throughout the *Wake*'s treatment of Catholicism. In 'Time and Space: The Opposition of Professor Jones in *Finnegans Wake* I.6' (*DJJJ* 8[2015] 15–34), Robert Baines revisits the Professor Jones lecture in I.6, examining the interconnections of its personages to argue that they demonstrate Joyce's use of the lecture to forward a thinking of opposition. Terence Killeen's 'From Notes to Text: The Role of the Notebooks in the Composition of *Finnegans Wake*' (*DJJJ* 8[2015] 35–46) reconsiders Danis Rose's claim that the *Wake* constitutes an assemblage from the notebooks, in light of more recently available material. Daniel Ferrer's 'From Tristan to Finnegan: A Re-telling' (*DJJJ* 8[2015] 47–62) considers the *Wake*'s beginnings via manuscript holdings at the National Library, examining the role of *Tristan and Isolde* in these initial pages. Dirk Van Hulle uses the ALP episode to investigate the newspapers at Buffalo in 'Textual Enactment: The Cognitive "riverrun" and the "Fluid Text" of Joyce's "Anna Livia Plurabelle" ' (*DJJJ* 8[2015] 63–94) in order to chart the earliest reception of the fragments of 'Work in Progress', arguing that these constitute a 'feedback loop' that re-enters the public reception into the ongoing imagination of the text, such that the process can be considered the textual performance of a cognitive theory of embodied mind. Finally, this issue contains the proclamation by Finn Fordham, Robbert-Jan Henkes, and Erik Bindervoet, 'Announcing: An Emended *Finnegans Wake* with Full Explanatory Apparatuses: A Sample of Pages 3–9' (*DJJJ* 8[2015] 95–113), an article heralding the publication of a critical edition of *Finnegans Wake* with Oxford University Press, in two volumes with an emended text and apparatus. The article states the principles of the edition and a sample of that apparatus, for the first six pages of the text.

*Hypermedia Joyce Studies* is dedicated to Joycean poetry in 2015, offering a challenge to its ostensibly marginal status in Joyce studies. Fritz Senn's 'Logodaedalian Bypaths: Evading the Obvious' (*HMJ* 14:i[2015]) proposes a poetic reading of verbal performance and linguistic excess in *Ulysses*. In ' "*Bella Poetria!*" (*U* 16.346): Rereading the Poetic in Joyce's Prose and the Prosaic in His Poetry' (*HMJ* 14:i[2015]), Onno Kosters considers poetic effect in Joycean prose, offering a reading of 'Flood' from *Pomes Penyeach* to illuminate the wider argument on prose poetics. In an important contribution, a 'Wordlist' to accompany that volume is published for the first time here. In ' "Cultic Twalettes": Joyce, Jonson and the Performance of Katharsis' (*HMJ* 14:i[2015]), David Pascoe claims that Joyce's satirical mode in 'The Holy Office' was centrally indebted to Ben Jonson, reading there a poetics of purgation, influenced by Aristotle and Jonson, that is at once physical and cultural. Tim Conley's ' "Easier than the dreamy creamy stuff": On Joyce's

Limericks' (*HMJ* 14:i[2015]) seeks to reinstate the importance of the limerick as a form both particular and general, arguing that in Joyce it serves to inscribe personal and social history. Two articles are concerned with poetic influence in America. Katherine Ebury's '"Serve, Serve' it sang, and it sang all that day": James Joyce and John Berryman' (*HMJ* 14:i[2015]) considers how Berryman's poetry utilized a Joycean prose influence, while David Vichnar's 'From Poetriarchy to Proteiformity: Joyce, Jolas, Stein . . . McCaffery' (*HMJ* 14:i[2015]) traces a relationship between the American writer Steve McCaffery and Joyce by way of the latter's absorption into Language poetry. Bridget O'Rourke's 'RoaraTORio: A Senescent Circus on *Finnegans Wake*' (*HMJ* 14:i[2015]) offers a glimpse of the possibility of the digital journal: she supplies an audio composition inspired by John Cage on the moving theme of the writer's father and his dementia, to which 'realm' *Finnegans Wake* provides a 'means of access'.

Within a wide-ranging volume of the *Joyce Studies Annual*, Garry Leonard's 'Soul Survivor: Stephen Dedalus as the Priest of the Eternal Imagination' (*JoyceSA* [2015] 3–27) reads the discourse of the soul in *Portrait*, moving from a religious understanding thereof to artistic rebirth. We then move from the numinous to the corporeal, with Ethan King's ' "All that the hand says when you touch": Intercorporeal Ethics in Joyce's *Ulysses*' (*JoyceSA* [2015] 55–72), a haptic perspective on Bloom and the radical politics of touch in *Ulysses* as a means for understanding alterity. In 'From "Dear Dirty Dublin" to "Hibernian Metropolis": A Vision of the City through the Tramways of *Ulysses*' (*JoyceSA* [2015] 28–54), Julie McCormick Weng presents a materialist argument, predicated upon tram technology, for the modernity of Dublin as a resistance to stereotypical views of Ireland. Frank Callanan contributes to the study of Joyce's relation to Parnell in 'The Parnellism of James Joyce: "Ivy Day in the Committee Room" ' (*JoyceSA* [2015] 73–97), advocating for the enduring influence of his shade in Joyce, while Richard Gerber considers the influence of James Clarence Mangan in 'Joyce's "Araby" and the Mystery of Mangan's Sister' (*JoyceSA* [2015] 186–94). There are four contributions on the *Wake*: Margaret McBride's 'St. Martin and HCE in Joyce's "Loonacied . . . Madwake" ' (*JoyceSA* [2015] 98–127) focuses on the legend of St Martin of Tours in the *Wake*, positing that the linguistic composition and dream logic of the text offers a portrait of madness, while John Gordon argues that is contained as a 'letter in a bottle' in 'Noble Rot' (*JoyceSA* [2015] 178–85). Boriana Alexandrova's 'Wakeful Translations: An Initiation into the Russian Translations of *Finnegans Wake*' (*JoyceSA* [2015] 128–67) examines the representative diverse strategies of two Russian translations of Henri Volokhonsky's *Weik Finneganov* and Konstantin Belyaev's transliteration of 'Anna Livia Plurabelle', while Colleen Jaurretche proposes that the voice of ALP constitutes a dramatic form, revealed through her ' "Leafy Speafing": Drama and *Finnegans Wake*' (*JoyceSA* [2015] 171–7).

Elsewhere in the *James Joyce Quarterly*, Colin Gillis's 'James Joyce and the Masturbating Boy' (*JJQ* 50:iii[2013] 611–34) views *A Portrait of the Artist as a Young Man* through Havelock Ellis's sexology, linking Stephen Dedalus's autonomy to masturbation; Janina Levin's 'Empathy, Cuckoldry, and the Helper's Vicarious Imagination in *Ulysses*' (*JJQ* 50:iv[2013] 653–4) interrogates Bloom's position as a cuckold—with echoes of Crispi's work, she argues that Bloom's cuckoldry serves a primarily narrative function, developing themes of empathy and altruism in the text; in 'How to Listen to "Sirens"': Narrative Distraction at the Ormond Hotel' (*JJQ* 50:iv[2013] 655–74), Andrew Warren argues that 'Sirens' represents a rendering of Books XXI and XXII of the *Odyssey*, a textual resonance from which the musicality of the scene distracts. John Lurz's 'Literal Darkness: *Finnegans Wake* and the Limits of Print' (*JJQ* 50:iv[2013] 675–92) focuses on the oppositions print evokes in the *Wake* between space and time, phonicity and aurality, a concern similar to those of Devlin and Smedley's volume. Other contributions on the subject of the corpus and corporeal include Stephen Abblitt's fictive hybrid essay, touching on the touch, the body, and the relationship between reading and mourning staged through a Derridean encounter with a first edition of *Ulysses* (*JJQ* 50:iv[2013] 693–708); and Tim Conley's 'The Stephen Dedalus Diet' (*JJQ* 50:iv [2013] 725–40) offers an original treatment of eating in *Ulysses*, examining how it has traditionally been treated as indicative of allegorical readings and suggesting that study of Stephen might refute and destabilize both reductive allegory and mimetic realism in the novel. Michael Patrick Gillespie takes up one of the themes of his book (discussed above) in 'Re-Viewing Richard: A Look at the Impact of Nostalgia and Rancor on Characterization in *Exiles*' (*JJQ* 50:iv[2013] 709–24). Two final essays focus on archival work: Neil R. Davison's '"Not a propagandist for the better treatment of minorities": The Richard Ellmann–Louis Hyman Correspondence' (*JJQ* 50:iv[2013] 741–66) reads the exchange between Ellmann and Hyman to extrapolate a reading of Jewish intellectual sensibility in the mid-twentieth century, exemplified by the positions they took and tracing those positions within their interpretation of Judaism in the novel; as such, it lends to the body of scholarship produced on *Ulysses* and Judaism in 2015. Lise Jaillant produces research from the Random House archives at the Columbia Rare Book and Manuscript Library in 'Blurring the Boundaries: *Fourteen Great Detective Stories* and Joyce's *A Portrait of the Artist as a Young Man* in the Modern Library Series' (*JJQ* 50:iv[2013] 767–96) to examine these simultaneous publications in March 1928 in the Modern Library as a means of subverting binary oppositions between high modernism and popular fiction.

Margaret McBride's 'Vicking with the Censors: Joyce's Bold Use of the Suppressed in an Unsuppressed *Finnegans Wake*' (*JJQ* 51:i[2013] 21–45) argues that veiled sexual references in the *Wake* allow it to evade legal censorship; continuing the legal theme, Jonathan Goldman's '*Ulysses* and the Fiction of Trademark' (*JJQ* 51:i[2013] 47–62) examines trademark registration, arguing that Joyce shares the same structural concerns with recognition and distinction, in which authorial stance and trademark law are linked. Logan Wiedenfeld's 'The Other Ancient Quarrel: *Ulysses* and Classical Rhetoric' (*JJQ* 51:i[2013] 63–79) sites 'Aeolus' within classical treatises on rhetoric and, alongside 'Scylla and Charybdis', within the debate on rhetoric between philosophers and sophists. Susan E. Lorsch also focuses on classical themes, reading 'Freddy, Gabriel, Gretta, Nietzsche, and Joyce's "The Dead"' (*JJQ* 51:i[2013] 129–46) through *The Birth of Tragedy* as occupying a dynamic between Apollonian Gabriel and Dionysian Freddy, synthesized into final tragedy by re-examining the implication of Gretta's pregnancy the end of 'The Dead'. Luca Crispi's 'Molly, Mr. Stanhope, and Hester: A Genetic Reading of a Love Triangle in *Ulysses*' (*JJQ* 51:i[2013] 97–117) retraces the presentation of Molly's friend Hester Stanhope and complements his own monograph by demonstrating how the Stanhopes intervene in the creative process of Joyce's mapping out of minor characters in *Ulysses*. Taking an interdisciplinary approach, Jesse Meyers's 'Found: Frank Budgen's Three Views of *Finnegans Wake*' (*JJQ* 51:i[2013] 81–95) draws attention to three oil paintings by Budgen representing his perspective on the *Wake*. These have never been presented collectively to Joyceans and two of them are now unavailable to the public. Li Weiping and Cheng Huijuan round out the volume with 'A Portrait of the Artist as a Literary Giant: Thirty Years of Joyce Scholarship in China' (*JJQ* 51:i[2013] 119–28), citing how studies of Joyce in China have followed political patternings of the country, as well as modelling trends in ideology and aesthetics.

   *Genetic Joyce Studies* contains articles from Viviana Braslasu on '*Imirce, ou la Fille de la Nature*' (*GJS* 15[2015] 1–12), which examines the 'pious Aeneas' fragment of the *Wake* and Buffalo notebook VI.B.9 in light of Joyce's reading of *Imirce ou la fille de la nature* [1765] by Henri-Joseph Dulaurens. Daniel Ferrer's 'VI.B.17: A Reconstruction and Some Sources' (*GJS* 15[2015] 1–68) is a Herculean effort that conceptually puts back together this physically dilapidated resource, identifying sources that allow for the sequence of the notebook to be reconstructed. Ronan Crowley isolates an anomaly in the received account of the rejection of 'Work in Progress' by the *Dial* in 'Dial M for Marianne: The *Dial*'s Refusals of "Work in Progress"' (*GJS* 15[2015] 1–16), while, with Steven Bond, he has a second contribution on cartomancy in *Ulysses*: 'SD was on the Cards: P.R.S. Foli's *Fortune-Telling by Cards* [1904] in "Penelope"' (*GJS* 15[2015] 1–16). From ghost stories to fortune-telling, the review of Joyce studies 2015 here concludes.

### (d) D.H. Lawrence

The recent resurgence of D.H. Lawrence studies continued in 2015. David Ellis's *Love and Sex in D.H. Lawrence* surveys Lawrence's biographical views on love and sex and how he worked them into his creative works. For Ellis, one of the authors of the three-volume Cambridge biography on Lawrence, love and sex 'are not the most comfortable topics for academics to discuss' (p. xiv). What Ellis offers is not necessarily 'new knowledge': he puts 'into order what we already know' (p. xii). Chapter 1 discusses the beginnings of Lawrence's thought on love and sex, including his childhood relationship with Jessie Chambers, their eventual love affair, and her fictionalized appearances in *The White Peacock* and *Sons and Lovers*. Arthur Schopenhauer's essay 'Metaphysics of Love' 'made a deep and powerful impression on' Lawrence (p. 3), particularly the idea that all love is rooted in the so-called 'instinct of sex' (p. 3). Chapter 2 moves on to Lawrence's affair with Frieda Weekley and their subsequent marriage. Ellis discusses how Lawrence's thoughts were complicated and enriched by his readings of Sigmund Freud and relates this to the ideas presented in *The Rainbow* and *Women in Love*. Chapter 3 discusses the influence of Walt Whitman, Lawrence's book of poetry, *Birds, Beasts and Flowers*, and his novels, *The Lost Girl*, *Aaron's Rod*, and *Mr Noon*. Much of this chapter concerns Lawrence's evolving feelings about sexual relations with men and adulterous sexual encounters.

In chapter 4, Ellis writes about Lawrence's experiences in the New World, his novels *Kangaroo* and *The Plumed Serpent*, and his novellas *St Mawr* and *The Woman Who Rode Away*. Ellis addresses Kate Millett's charge that Lawrence was a misogynist, characterizing the misogyny of the work he wrote in America and Mexico as 'a more complicated business than Millett imagined' (p. 126). Chapter 5 concerns the evolution of *Lady Chatterley's Lover* in its various drafts and Lawrence's explicit and frank accounts of sex between Oliver Mellors and Connie Chatterley. A final chapter outlines Lawrence's reaction to the criticism of *Lady Chatterley's Lover*: Ellis takes issue with the logical consistency of *A Propos of 'Lady Chatterley's Lover'*. 'Here', observes Ellis, 'at the end of his life and career, he is as confused and contradictory as he ever was' on love and sex (p. 179), and he bemoans the lack of scholarship in this area.

In her introduction to *The American Lawrence*, Lee M. Jenkins observes that Lawrence has not been given enough credit for his contribution to American literature. Her book concerns the three-year period from 1922 to 1925, during which Lawrence lived and wrote from New Mexico and Mexico. Jenkins states that her 'book is an attempt to flesh out the American, or Americano, Lawrence' (p. 12). Instead of dismissing Lawrence's place in American literature as irrelevant because of his status as a British citizen, she examines Lawrence's impact on how American literature is understood and his contribution to both American modernist poetry and fiction. For a period in his life, Jenkins sees Lawrence as fitting into American literature, helping link the contributions of the great nineteenth-century American artists to their modernists.

*The American Lawrence* is not a long work, with only three chapters, not including the introduction or conclusion. Chapter 1 deals with Lawrence's attempt at American literary criticism: *Studies in Classic American Literature*, which Jenkins calls 'creative criticism, of course, and with a vengeance' (p. 27). Lawrence, she notes, tells Americans that the future of their literature is to look beyond their ' "perfected" European past' to their own 'continental and pre-Columbian spirit of place' (p. 46). Chapter 2 looks at Lawrence's book of poetry, *Birds, Beasts and Flowers*, and explores the relationship between him and American poets. This includes the influence of Walt Whitman and, in turn, Lawrence's influence on William Carlos Williams and H.D. Chapter 3 tackles Lawrence's American fiction: *St Mawr*, 'The Princess', and *The Woman Who Rode Away*. *St Mawr*, Jenkins asserts, 'is surely a precursor for Cormac McCarthy's *Border Trilogy*, in which the horse is again the avatar of chthonic powers' (p. 91). Lawrence's fiction, she concludes, illustrates 'the slippage between American romance and American reality, and between genre and gender, and genre and ethnicity' (p. 101). His writings offer a dose of reality about American place and people that complicates rather than simplifies. For Jenkins, 'Lawrence was a working writer and a ranchero, a pro tem Americano who not only "brings 'Englishness' itself into question" but who also queries our definitions of American identity and of American literature' (p. 109). Time will tell whether Jenkins's argument about Lawrence's place in American literature is accepted, but she certainly succeeds in showing his impacts in the United States.

Lawrence wrote eight finished plays and left two unfinished. In *The Theatre of D.H. Lawrence*, James Moran seeks to understand his development as a dramatist. Moran writes that 'Lawrence remained deeply concerned with performed drama throughout his career, proved himself a skilled if somewhat undeveloped playwright', and that 'the theatrical element of his work is key to understanding Lawrence's development and his over achievement as a writer' (p. xiii). An introduction explains shifts in Lawrence's reputation as a playwright, including the admiration of George Bernard Shaw, who watched Lawrence's *The Widowing of Mrs Holroyd* in 1926. Chapter 1 provides a biographical assessment of theatrical influences on Lawrence, including a travelling theatre that regularly visited Eastwood and his participation in readings from Shakespeare at the Chambers farm. Moran sets out the circumstances behind the early plays, including *A Collier's Friday Night*, *The Widowing of Mrs Holroyd*, and *The Merry-Go-Round*. Chapter 2 describes the writing of *The Fight for Barbara*, *Touch and Go*, and *David*, and attempts to put them on stage.

Chapter 3 relates instances of dramatic performance in Lawrence's novels, providing further biographical details of plays he saw and their appearance in his fiction. Moran also identifies Christmas acting games in the Lawrence household as an important tradition that left a lasting impression, reflected in *The White Peacock* and *The Rainbow*. This is even reflected in Lawrence's first, pseudonymous, short story, 'A Prelude', printed in the *Nottingham Guardian* in December 1907. Chapter 4 examines Lawrence's theatrical development over his career. For Moran, *Lady Chatterley's Lover* 'exemplifies the way in which his prose fiction incorporated the dramatic ideas that a successful playwright might have explored in his scripts, and reveals the influence of various experimental theatrical ideas' (p. 136). Chapter 5 is an interview with director Peter Gill, and the final three chapters are written by playwright Stephen Lowe, screenwriter William Ivory, and Iranian scholar Soudabeh Ananisarab. Concluding, Moran observes that 'the young Lawrence showed an impressive ability to craft plays; the mature writer channeled that theatrical sensibility into his novel writing; and throughout his career Lawrence showed an engagement with dramatic experiment' (p. 192). This book greatly expands how Lawrence is understood and should encourage further scholarship into Lawrence's plays and the impact that theatre had on him as a writer.

Matthew Kochis and Heather Lusty's edited collection *Modernists at Odds: Reconsidering Lawrence and Joyce* is one of the more exciting works to come out in 2015. Despite the bitter rivalry between Lawrence and Joyce and differences between the scholars who work on them, Lusty notes 'striking similarities' between their 'lives and careers'. Both men 'wrote across genres, including essays, plays, poems, short stories, and novels, and incorporated music and singing into their writing' (p. 2). The marriage of Lawrence and Joyce studies at this level has been long overdue. A posthumously reprinted essay from 1985, Zack Bowen's '*Lady Chatterley's Lover* and *Ulysses*', compares the treatment of sex in both novels and their differing outcomes. Leopold Boom from *Ulysses*, Bowen suggests, 'is not unlike Clifford, when he assumes initially that he will triumph over the men who merely plant seeds in Connie's womb and that the mental bond of friendship will overpower the passionate bond of sex. Clifford is wrong; sex wins. But the case of Bloom is more ambiguous' (p. 15). Covering similar territory, Margot Norris's 'Love, Bodies, and Nature in *Lady Chatterley's Lover* and *Ulysses*' focuses on Connie Chatterley and Molly Bloom, whereas Earl G. Ingersoll's 'The "Odd Couple" Constructing the "New Man": Bloom and Mellors in *Ulysses* and *Lady Chatterley's Lover*' considers new ideas of masculinity in these leading male characters.

Eight further essays provide a varied treatment of Lawrence and Joyce with some overlapping. Gerald Doherty's 'The End of Sacrifice: Joyce's "The Dead" and Lawrence's "The Man Who Died"' compares each author's treatment of sacrifice. Doherty focuses on neither religion nor sexuality, but 'sacrifice—a direct offspring of both' (p. 61). Martin Brick's 'The Isis Effect: How Joyce and Lawrence Revitalize Christianity through Foreignization' looks at *Finnegans Wake* and 'The Man Who Died'. Louise Kane's ' "In Europe They Usually Mention Us Together": Joyce, Lawrence, and the Little Magazines' examines how similarly in style and philosophy each of these authors presents himself in the literary periodicals that they depended upon. Eleni Loukopoulou's 'Lawrence and Joyce in T.S. Eliot's *Criterion* Miscellany Series' looks at how this single literary publication helped both authors. Hidenaga Arai turns to French psychology in 'An Encounter with the Real: A Lacanian Motif in Joyce's "The Dead" and Lawrence's "The Shadow in the Rose Garden" ', which deals, in part, with disillusionment in both stories. In 'Masochism and Marriage in *The Rainbow* and *Ulysses*', Johannes Hendrikus Burgers and Jennifer Mitchell turn to Lawrence's and Joyce's biographies in addition to the content of these novels to explain the dynamic of marriage outside traditional norms. Enda Duffy's 'That Long Kiss: Comparing Joyce and Lawrence' considers each author's treatment of the kiss and how their public received them. The final essay, ' "Result of the Rockinghorse Races": The Ironic Culture of Racing in Joyce's *Ulysses* and Lawrence's "The Rocking-Horse Winner" ', by Carl F. Miller, considers the treatment of horseracing in each work, comparing it to the general interest in the sport. While subjective differences between Lawrence and Joyce scholars do occasionally appear in places, this collection is a genial success that feels like it is only the starting point of joint Lawrence and Joyce studies.

David Game's *D.H. Lawrence's Australia: Anxiety at the Edge of Empire* provides a thorough examination into Australia's impact on Lawrence and his writings. 'Lawrence's engagement with Australia', Game writes, 'is informed and mediated by a plethora of images he derived from literature, anthropology, his personal interactions with Australians and his responses to a range of discourses that underpinned Britain's sense of itself as the centre of a vast global empire, including those associated with migration, gender, race relations and colonialism' (p. 3). The book covers the period during which Frieda and Lawrence lived in Australia and offers chapters that examine obvious Australian works, *The Boy in the Bush* and *Kangaroo*. But Australia, as chapter 4 details, also enters Lawrence's imagination in *The White Peacock*, *The Lost Girl*, *Aaron's Rod*, *Mr. Noon*, and even the play *The Daughter-in-Law*. Later chapters cover the impact of Australians in *St Mawr* and the unexpurgated edition of Lawrence's poetry, *Pansies*. Chapter 8, 'The Race for the Bush: The Australian Aboriginal Presence and the British Race Regeneration in *Kangaroo* and *The Boy in the Bush*', is particularly remarkable for its postcolonial approach. Game writes that 'In a powerful, if somewhat oblique way, *Kangaroo* challenges contemporary assumptions about British colonial hegemony, well before [Edward] Said's postcolonial theorising. Aboriginal "darkness" is an unsettling ingredient in Lawrence's critique of Australianness in *Kangaroo*' (p. 175).

Despite a publication date of 2014, the second issue of volume 39 of the US-based *D.H. Lawrence Review* only appeared during 2015. In his introduction to this special edition on *Sons and Lovers* (*DHLR* 39:ii[2014] 1–10), Richard Kaye (co-editor with Keith Cushman) notes that seven of the articles it contains started off as presentations at a conference at the City University of New York during September 2013 to mark the centenary of Lawrence's *Bildungsroman*. The highlight is Andrew Harrison's '"I tell you it has got form—*form*": Plot, Structure and Meaning in *Sons and Lovers*' (*DHLR* 39:ii[2014] 11–24), which provides an overview of the novel's evolution through its various drafts, including the influence of Lawrence's first lover, Jessie Chambers, and Edward Garnett, a literary agent who acted as the Lawrence's editor. Among the useful details that Harrison includes is an observation about the novel's form by Virginia Woolf, who states that it 'is perpetually in process of cohesion and dissolution' (p. 20). In ' "The final aim is the flower": Wild and Domestic Nature in *Sons and Lovers*' (*DHLR* 39:ii[2014] 25–45), Seamus O'Malley uses Lawrence's *A Study of Thomas Hardy* to explain what he terms as 'floral mythology' in the novel (p. 26). Keith Cushman's 'Feeling "Oceanic": Civilization and Discontented Paul' (*DHLR* 39:ii[2014] 46–58) states that 'Lawrence embraces the idea that Freud refers to as a "sensation of 'eternity', a feeling as of something limitless, unbounded—as it were, 'oceanic'"' (p. 47). Howard J. Booth also channels Freud in his examination of the relationship between Paul Morrel and Baxter Dawes in ' "They had met in a naked extremity of hate, and it was a bond": The Later Chapters of *Sons and Lovers*, Psychoanalysis, and Male–Male Intimacy' (*DHLR* 39:ii[2014] 59–76). Jane Eldridge Miller explores contemporary influences and the influence of Lawrence's reading on the novel in ' "The penumbra of its own time and place and circumstance": Modern Women, the Edwardian Novel, and *Sons and Lovers*' (*DHLR* 39:ii[2014] 77–96). Robert L. Caserio's 'Beyond Oedipal Psychology in *Sons and Lovers*: Lawrence's "Foreword" to Being and History' (*DHLR* 39:ii[2014] 97–115), uses Lawrence's foreword as a basis to understand Paul Morel. Finally, Maria DiBattista, who gave a keynote address at the 2013 conference celebrating the hundredth anniversary of *Sons and Lovers*, contributes 'Dereliction' (*DHLR* 39:ii[2014] 116–27). She focuses especially on the last chapter of the novel, 'Derelict', and Paul Morel's future.

The next volume of *D.H. Lawrence Review* is also a special edition, with the theme 'Lawrence and the Arts'. In their introduction, 'D.H. Lawrence and the Arts: A Sketch of the Critical Heritage' (*DHLR* 40:i[2015] 1–20), editors Paul Poplawski and Stefania Michelucci affirm not only Lawrence's skill as a writer, but also 'a performance-oriented dramatist with the ability to compose his own music, as for his last play, *David* a skilled draughtsman in drawing and painting from his early years; and, in his later years, the creator of a number of striking original paintings on canvas worthy of their own exhibition in London in 1929' (p. 1). They also note that Lawrence made frequent reference 'to music and the visual arts, to dance, sculpture, architecture, and to film, music hall, and other aspects of popular culture' in his fiction (p. 1). Seven essays by women follow, a deliberate choice intended 'to call attention to certain recurring concerns of women critics, and to celebrate ways of writing that integrate lived experience with academic knowledge' (p. 2). The highlight is Margaret Storch's 'Abstraction and the "Heat of Life": Lawrence and Contemporary Art' (*DHLR* 40:i[2015] 21–36), which focuses on Lawrence's paintings, his view of the term 'abstract', and his reaction to the art of other modernist painters. In 'Reading Lawrence through Film: The Horse Dealer's Western' (*DHLR* 40:i[2015] 37–58), Jason Mark Ward looks at a short film adaptation of Lawrence's 'The Horse Dealer's Daughter'. 'Accepting adaptations as part of the critical discourse surrounding a literary text', Ward writes, 'enables the reader to respond constructively and mindfully when liberties are taken with literary works and established readings' (p. 47). Nora Foster Stovel's 'Minerva *Victrix*: *The Daughter-in-Law*, A Power Play' (*DHLR* 40:i[2015] 59–72) champions the quality and originality of this play. In 'From the Pits to the Kitchens: The Dynamics of Food and Eating in *The Fight for Barbara* and *The Daughter-in-Law*' (*DHLR* 40:i[2015] 73–89), Zeynep Z. Atayurt-Fenge looks at the importance of kitchen scenes in both of these plays by Lawrence, including the influence of his first visit to Italy on these representations. Fiona Richards's 'The Goat-God in England: A Musical Context for Lawrence's Fascination with Pan' (*DHLR* 40:i[2015] 90–106), examines the work of three English composers who, like Lawrence, were inspired by Pan. In 'From Rope-Dancer to Wrestler: The Figure of the Artist as Performer in *Women in Love*' (*DHLR* 40:i[2015] 107–27), Susan Reid looks in the influence of modernist music on Lawrence.

In her introduction to the British *Journal of D.H. Lawrence Studies* (*JDHLS* 4:i[2015] 3–4), Susan Reid states that 'Lawrence's concerns with a civilization gone wrong and the urgent need for "a new heaven and a new earth" are scrutinized from a number of fresh perspectives' (p. 3). Of particular interest is Crispian Neill's 'D.H. Lawrence and Dogs: Canines and the Critique of Civilisation' (*JDHLS* 4:i[2015] 95–118), which pays special attention to the intimacy that dogs have with humans. Neill examines Lawrence's 'Reflections on the Death of a Porcupine', 'Rex', and 'St Mawr', concluding that 'Dogs, transformed through their mutual co-habitation with human beings, remain recognisably animal, suggests Lawrence, but are irrevocably contaminated by domestication; they are as removed from their wild antecedents, and consequently as compromised and constrained, as their civilized human companions' (p. 114). Howard J. Booth's '"At last to newness": D.H.

Lawrence's *The Rainbow* and the Dream of a Better World' (*JDHLS* 4:i[2015] 19–44) grew out of a Lawrence birthday lecture. In '*All of Us*: D.H. Lawrence's First World War Poems for the People' (*JDHLS* 4:i[2015] 45–66), Kate McLoughlin examines a group of poems Lawrence wrote in 1916 that were not published in their entirety until the Cambridge University Press edition of his poems in 2013. In 'Getting It Off His Chest: Some Implications of D.H. Lawrence's Affair with Alice Dax' (*JDHLS* 4:i[2015] 67–94), Barbara Kearns re-examines Lawrence's relationship with Dax and looks at her impact on his writings. Gemma Moss's 'A "Beginning Rather Than an End": Popular Culture and Modernity in D.H. Lawrence's *St Mawr*' (*JDHLS* 4:i[2015] 119–39) uses the lens of Frankfurt school critical theory to examine parts of 'St Mawr'. 'Rather than offering any definite solution', Moss writes, Lawrence suggests 'that the trajectory of modernity is not inevitable and that individual resistance is possible' (p. 136).

Entitled 'D.H. Lawrence, His Contemporaries and the First World War', the 2015 issue of *Études lawrenciennes* addresses the impact the Great War had on Lawrence and his contemporaries. This extended edition features sixteen articles. A highlight is Luke Ferretter's ' "A prison for the infinite": D.H. Lawrence and Bertrand Russell on the War' (*EL* 46[2015] 38 paras.), which looks at the dialogue between Lawrence and Russell. 'Lawrence sees the philosopher's ideas as part of the shell', Ferretter writes, 'part of the democratic, Christian form of life that has caused the war and that cannot therefore constitute a way to end it or to live better after it' (para. 37). Michael Bell's 'Freud and Lawrence: Thoughts on War and Instinct' (*EL* 46[2015] 26 paras.), helps provide context and deeper understanding of Freud and Lawrence's views, which occasionally overlap. According to Bell: 'Lawrence's opposition to Freud was partly based on a common reductive understanding of him' (para. 2), but this article helps to clear that up. Other articles in this themed collection include Jean-Paul Rosaye's 'A Not-So-Distant Mirror: The Modern Predicament in the Early Twentieth Century' (*EL* 46[2015] 24 paras.), Sarah Bouttier's 'War and Continuity in D.H. Lawrence's Works' (*EL* 46[2015] 29 paras.), Cornelius Crowley's 'War and Words: Broken Writing and Modest Inflections of Brutality' (*EL* 46[2015] 20 paras.), Elise Brault-Dreux's 'Limbs at War: Amputation, Mutilation and Paralysis—Wilfred Owen, Blaise Cendrars and D.H. Lawrence' (*EL* 46[2015] 35 paras.), Juliette Feyel's 'Self and Suffering: Virginia Woolf, D.H. Lawrence and the War' (*EL* 46[2015] 26 paras.), Keith Cushman's ' "I wish that story at the bottom of the sea": The Making and Re-Making of "England, My England" ' (*EL* 46[2015] 45 paras.), Gaku Iwai's 'Wartime Ideology in "The Thimble": A Comparative Study of Popular Wartime Romance and the Anti-Romance of D.H. Lawrence' (*EL* 46[2015] 26 paras.), Shirley Bricout's 'War through the Prism of Time in the Post-War Novels of Woolf and Lawrence' (*EL* 46[2015] 37 paras.), Marina Ragachewskaya's 'War Trauma and Madness in the Fiction of D.H. Lawrence and Virginia Woolf' (*EL* 46[2015] 42 paras.), Stefania Michelucci's 'D.H. Lawrence's (Un)happy Islands' (*EL* 46[2015] 22 paras.), Brigitte Macadré-Nguyên's ' "The colour of tears": Fernand Léger's and D.H. Lawrence's Experiences of the Great War' (*EL* 46[2015] 33 paras.), Jane Costin's 'A Sense of Touch: Henry Moore and D.H. Lawrence' (*EL* 46[2015]

33 paras.), Kumiko Hoshi's 'D.H. Lawrence and Hannah Höch: Representing Einstein and the Post-World War I World' (*EL* 46[2015] 18 paras.), and Jonathan Long's 'D.H. Lawrence and Book Publication during the Great War: A Study in Stagnation' (*EL* 46[2015] 26 paras.).

*(e) Virginia Woolf*
Amongst rich pickings for Virginia Woolf scholars in 2015, Marion Dell's well-researched and comprehensive monograph *Virginia Woolf's Influential Forebears* draws attention to the legacies of Julia Margaret Cameron, Anny Thackeray Ritchie, and Julia Prinsep Stephen in Woolf's writing and the ambivalent way in which she negotiated these. There is a valuable work of recovery driving this project, which does an admirable job of drawing attention to the late Victorian influences on Woolf's work. Chapter 1 offers a useful biographical introduction to the three 'influential forebears' of Dell's title and reminds us of Woolf's significant Anglo-Indian links on her mother's side. These are important in terms of thinking about Woolf and empire, as there has tended to be greater familiarity with her paternal relations and their anti-imperialist activities. Chapter 2 focuses on Woolf's second novel, *Night and Day*, and makes a strong case for the ambivalence that characterizes Woolf's engagement with the past, introducing the importance of Ritchie as a model in this novel. Chapters 3, 4, and 5 take Ritchie, Cameron, and Stephen respectively as their focus and explore Woolf's complicated engagement with them. Dell argues that this combines deliberate obscuration and covert celebration and makes convincing claims for the proto-modernist qualities of Ritchie and Cameron, suggesting Woolf builds on these in various ways. The chapter on Ritchie is at its best when Dell is making the case for Woolf's indebtedness as an essayist and stylist to Ritchie's 'Spinsters and Toilers'. Dell makes a solid case for these women as models of female professionalism, and the chapter on Stephen successfully detaches Woolf's mother from the romanticized image cultivated by Lesley Stephen. I wonder if Woolf's failure to acknowledge or celebrate her mother's philanthropic pursuits and her pamphlets on domestic service might be on account of her scepticism about the power politics she judged to be involved in these activities? This point gets a little obscured and Dell glosses over the fact of Julia Stephen's anti-suffragism and what this might have meant for her daughter. A final chapter on *The Years* draws attention to Woolf's continued preoccupation with questions of heredity, and Dell's conclusion explores Woolf's ambivalence and failure to acknowledge the influence of these women in the context of various theories of influence.

Monica Latham's *A Poetics of Postmodernism and Neomodernism: Rewriting Mrs Dalloway* charts a range of contemporary responses to Woolf's 1925 novel, including texts by Christopher Isherwood, Ian McEwan, Rachel Cusk, and Ali Smith, across its five chapters. In her introduction, Latham draws a distinction between Woolf's neo-modernist and postmodernist heirs: 'the two rewriting trends have divergent concerns and impulses: both borrow from modernist aesthetics, but while postmodernism confronts, provokes and talks back to modernism, neomodernism prolongs and surpasses modernist innovations' (p. 8). In chapter 1, Latham makes a preliminary study of Woolf's novel itself, adopting a genetic approach to show how key 'Dallowayisms' (a term Latham coins here to designate a range of aesthetic and thematic features, including moments of being, fragmentation and free indirect discourse) emerge in pre-texts to the novel, including 'Mrs Dalloway on Bond Street', and in drafts of the text itself. Chapter 2 focuses on Michael Cunningham's *The Hours* and Robin Lippincott's *Mr Dalloway*, paying particular attention to how these rewritings draw out and foreground the 'gender and political implications of Woolf's novel' (p. 94). Latham writes against criticism of these novels as parasitical pastiches, suggesting they instead represent layered engagements with the hypotext, citing their figuring of Woolf's own biography and reception as instances of this. By contrast, Chapter 3 is dedicated to parodies that, rather than paying homage, 'challenge [and] exaggerate the hypotext' (p. 99). Chapter 4 focuses on Woolf's 'neomodernist heirs', considering the way circadian novels by Isherwood, McEwan, and Hynes engage with Woolf's legacies. Chapter 5 explores a different set of neo-modernist rewritings of *Mrs Dalloway* by Rachel Cusk, Jon McGreggor, and Ali Smith, drawing attention to their revival of 'Woolf's Dalloway-esque formal innovation' (p. 167), particularly through their engagement with the everyday. There is lively close reading throughout this chapter, but Latham could perhaps have said more about Ali Smith's engagement with class in her novel, especially her figuring of the beggar, Else, who might represent a more critical reworking of Woolf's presentation of the beggar woman by Regent's Park tube station.

Edited by Jeanne Dubino, Gill Lowe, Vara Neverow, and Kathryn Simpson, *Virginia Woolf: Twenty-First Century Approaches* aims to show the 'protean possibilities for reading Woolf's writing using a wide range of critical and theoretical frameworks' (p. 11) across eleven rich and varied essays. The collection's editors offer a lucid overview of the project in their introduction, supplying not only useful glosses for the substantive chapters but also a detailed account of recent work in Woolf studies. The decision to cluster essays 'into five interconnected sections' is a smart one and this collection contains some pieces of strong original research.

Section I, on 'Self and Identity', includes chapters on Woolf's 1897 diary by Gill Lowe and on Woolf's commemorative house museum by Nuala Hancock, which complement each other nicely. Lowe reads Virginia Stephen's diary in the light of recent autobiography theory and developments in neuroscience in order to cast light on her engagements with the first person, offering a particularly stimulating reading of her alter-ego 'Miss Jan'. Hancock's chapter gives an overview of Woolf's literary tourism as a writer, touching on her well-known reports of visits to Carlyle's House and Haworth Parsonage, as well as an experiential account of visiting Woolf's house museum at Monk's House in Rodmell. The most interesting part of this chapter is the final section, which details the history of the National Trust's acquisition of and subsequent dealings with Monk's House.

Section II, 'Language and Translation', contains stimulating essays by Diane F. Gillespie and Claire Davison. In her engrossing piece on the Hogarth

Press's publication of actress and agony aunt Violet Tree's etiquette book, *Can I Help You?* Gillespie gives an overview of the book itself, pointing out 'several verbal nods to Bloomsbury and Virginia Woolf' (p. 61). She then offers an astute and subtle cross-reading of this book on manners with Woolf's *Three Guineas*, published a year later: 'I think it appealed to Woolf for several reasons. She saw parallels to her own experiences in society and to ways she had reflected social life in her fiction. She also valued candid glimpses of women's lives, and Tree's was a fascinating one' (p. 65). Taking Richard Dalloway's ambiguous use of the word 'outlandish' in his marginal additions to his wife's letter in *The Voyage Out* as a point of departure, Claire Davison explores 'Woolf's experiments in thinking "outlandishly" across borders, languages, and translations' (p. 73).

In Section III, 'Culture and Commodification', Ann Martin argues that 'The car's association with apparently oppositional impulses—modern and traditional; democratic and hierarchical; private and public—signals its cultural mobility' (p. 94), making it a particularly suggestive motif in Woolf's work. Martin does a fine job of tracing its significance, especially in terms of Woolf's thinking about the individual and community, through a range of her work from *Mrs Dalloway* to *The Years* to *Between the Acts*. Martin sets out the historical and biographical contexts of Woolf's engagement with the motor-car, her status as an enthusiastic car owner, and her awareness of the debates around motoring, class, and rural preservation. Kathryn Simpson's chapter on Woolf and Jewishness follows, and focuses on her ambiguous portrayal of Jewish characters in 'Lappin and Lapinova' and *The Years*. Simpson describes how 'Woolf's antisemitism can be seen as a vehicle to articulate wider cultural anxieties and criticism than those related to only to race and ethnicity' (p. 112), demonstrating how Woolf's anxieties about commercial success seem to be played out via anti-Semitic tropes in these stories.

Section IV, 'Human, Animal, and Non-Human', opens with Jeanne Dubino's chapter, which borrows the scientific term of co-evolution in a reading of *Flush* that focuses on that dog's 'cross-species encounters' (p. 132) and the way Woolf depicts the relationship between dogs and humans. Derek Ryan's chapter on ecology and ethology in *The Waves* follows, focusing on the ten italicized interludes in the novel and arguing that these passages are crucial in showing the relationship between Woolf's political and ecological interests. The final section, 'Genders, Sexualities and Multiplicities', includes three chapters offering fresh takes on well-established themes in Woolf studies. Eileen Barrett's subtle chapter on indecency in *Jacob's Room* reads Woolf's third novel in the context of her relationships with queer Bloomsbury figures including Lytton Strachey and E.M. Forster, suggesting that these men informed both her rendering of the novel's eponymous protagonist and her take on the First World War. In the engaging chapter that follows, Vara Neverow explores the relationship between Henry Fielding's *The Female Husband* [1746] and Woolf's *Orlando*. The final chapter of the volume, by Kristin Czarnecki, offers another original way into *Orlando*, this time through the work of contemporary Native American writer Louise Erdrich.

*The Cambridge Companion to To the Lighthouse*, edited by Allison Pease, makes a valuable contribution to the study of what is often thought Woolf's most successful novel. Its thirteen chapters showcase a range of critical approaches, from the formalist to the historicist to the genetic. The greatest strength of this collection is that it exceeds one's expectations of a companion, with many chapters driven by original research, offering fresh new takes on this most familiar of Woolf's novels. Pease's useful introduction is followed by Anne Fernald's chapter, which reads the novel in the context of Woolf's life and diaries and valuably sets up many of the biographical parallels that subsequent contributors probe, while also drawing attention to the intriguing 'asymmetrics between art and life' (p. 6). Next Michael Levenson considers questions of narrative perspective in the novel, returning to Erich Auerbach's foundational reading of the novel, productively querying some of its assumptions through a wonderful reading of omniscience. Jane Goldman's chapter continues to pursue these stylistic questions by focusing on Woolf's use of language and form. There is much that's compelling about this chapter, including Goldman's reading of Woolf's use of parenthesis as a form of literary 'mosaicking' (p. 30) and the sources she proposes for the 'two blocks joined by a corridor' (p. 33) structure of the novel. The chapter that follows on time in the novel by Paul Sheehan offers subtle readings of the different temporalities of each of its three sections, and is followed by a highly original reading of embodied cognition by Melba Cuddy-Keane. Proceeding from the 'premise that the body thinks' (p. 58), Cuddy-Keane explores the implications of gestures made by Cam Ramsay and Lily Briscoe. Emily Dalgarno's chapter on philosophical approaches to the novel offers a useful account of key readings of Woolf and philosophy, including work by Auerbach, Mark Hussey, Gillian Beer, and, most recently, Anne Banfield, while addressing the daunting question: 'what access to philosophy does *To the Lighthouse* provide that is unavailable in other forms of writing?' (p. 69).

With chapter 7 the collection shifts in focus to consider questions of social and historical context through three chapters on gender, race, and class. Gabrielle McIntire's piece on gender and feminism in the novel offers a useful gloss on existing readings that centre on these questions and draws out the relationship between the traditional gender roles the novel presents and its radical poetics. McIntire, unlike the majority of contributors to the collection, makes an effort to draw links between her chapter and others—a particularly welcome feature of this piece. Urmila Seshagari's chapter on the 'Art of Race' reads Woolf's engagement with racial difference in the context of Roger Fry's writing on non-Western artistic traditions and suggests the subversive political and artistic possibilities of Lily Briscoe's ' "Oriental" vision' (p. 104). Kathryn Simpson's chapter on social class grapples brilliantly with the 'slippery' (p. 118) nature of Woolf's class politics, offering convincing readings of the oft-neglected character Charles Tansley, and of Mrs McNab. Ana Parejo Vadillo's chapter on 'Generational Difference in *To the Lighthouse*' reads Woolf's depiction of Mrs Ramsay in the context of models of femininity crafted by two Victorian writers, John Ruskin and Coventry Patmore. Particularly interesting are the social connections Parejo Vadillo reveals between Woolf's mother and grandmother and the Patmores. The highlight of this piece is the case the writer makes for Woolf's effacement of the *fin de siècle* in *To the Lighthouse*, her refusal to acknowledge the late Victorian generation that separated her from her parents and the Ramsays. Chapters follow on the visual arts in the novel by Suzanne Bellamy, who detects 'transmodernist resonances' (p. 143) in Woolf's depiction of Lily Briscoe, and on genetic approaches to this novel by Hans Walter Gabler. The collection finishes with Jean Mills's account of the novel's critical heritage, which gives an overview of contemporary responses to the novel, its reception by feminist scholars in the 1970s and 1980s (particularly interesting are Mrs Ramsay's changing critical fortunes), and how digital approaches to literary study have transformed our reading of this text.

Michael Whitworth's guide to key critical material relating to *Mrs Dalloway* for Palgrave will make an extremely absorbing read for undergraduate students of Woolf and scholars alike. It takes in an impressive and often unexpected range of criticism, including reviews, articles, chapters, and books, and it is particularly strong on contemporary and early reviews of Woolf's novel, as well as criticism from the 1950s and 1960s, a period often perceived as a nadir in Woolf criticism. This book usefully challenges some of the assumptions about the history of Woolf criticism. Whitworth is a scrupulous close reader and is judicious in his criticism; he offers an exemplary critical model here, and I would heartily recommend this book to students.

Chapter 1, on 'Early Responses' to the novel, gives an overview of contemporary reviews and points out interesting ways in which they anticipate later Woolf criticism. Whitworth gives a valuable gloss on Leavis and the Scrutineers and their opinions of Woolf, and nods to the first Ph.D. thesis written on Woolf (p. 17). Chapter 2, on 'Recovering Woolf: Criticism in the Era of Second Wave Feminism', is a thoughtful account of Woolf's changing fortunes and those of *Mrs Dalloway*, and is especially interesting on the critical impact of comparisons with James Joyce's *Ulysses*. Chapter 3, on Woolf and philosophy, includes measured discussions of Roger Poole's well-known and controversial book, *The Unknown Virginia Woolf*, Mark Hussey's *Virginia Woolf and the Singing of the Real World* and other less well-known work. Whitworth is good on the question of Bergson's influence on Woolf and the problems that emerge when attempting to read her as a philosopher. Chapter 4, on structuralist and poststructuralist readings of *Mrs Dalloway*, will be useful to students, not only for its thorough account of theoretical readings of the novel, but also for its readable and clear glosses on the principles of these reading strategies and their origins and development. The same can be said for the chapter that follows, on Woolf and psychoanalysis, which is careful in its delineation of Freudian and post-Freudian incarnations of these approaches. Chapters on 'Sexuality and the Body', 'Historicist Approaches', and '*Mrs Dalloway* and *The Hours*' follow, and all feel scrupulously researched.

Daniel T. O'Hara's beautifully written *Virginia Woolf and the Modern Sublime: The Invisible Tribunal* shows the degree to which Woolf's modernist experimentation involves revision of canonical Romantic notions of the sublime. This book takes in a range of texts, including *Jacob's Room*, *A Room of One's Own*, and *On Being Ill*, and reads productively across genres. In chapter 1, O'Hara offers a fine close reading of Woolf's short story 'Moments of Being: Slater's Pins Have No Points', and introduces a number of the concepts central to chapters to come, such as the sublime and uncanny. In his chapter on *Jacob's Room*, O'Hara homes in on the 'distinctive voice' we encounter in this novel and considers what happens when this voice juxtaposes 'virtually textbook' (p. 14) versions of the Romantic sublime with the quotidian, often banal domestic concerns of the novel's characters, facilitating observations about the role of the sublime in the novel's social criticism. Chapter 3 offers a creative review of the new Cambridge edition of *Mrs Dalloway*, while Chapter 4 returns to Erich Auerbach's reading of representation in *To the Lighthouse*, before offering a close reading of the dinner-party episode of the novel in the context of Longinus's concept of sublime judgement. In chapter 5, O'Hara concentrates on Woolf's often overlooked essay, *On Not Being Ill*, and gives a suggestive reading of its concluding 'tableau' (p. 63) and the politics of Woolf's revisionism here, while in chapter 6 O'Hara turns to *The Waves* and the 'paradoxical intention' (p. 72) that, he argues, haunts this novel—its desire to continue tradition and dispense with it. The closing chapter of this book focuses on the idea of female genius in *A Room of One's Own*, while its 'Coda' is devoted to a cross-reading of *Between the Acts* and poems by Walt Whitman and Percy Shelley, in order to further gloss O'Hara's conception of 'revisionism'.

Steve Ellis's *British Writers and the Approach of World War II* will be of interest to Woolf scholars for its final chapter on *Between the Acts*, 'Virginia Woolf and the Theatre of War' (pp. 188–233), which contributes to our understanding of Woolf's complicated engagement with her fraught historical moment in the late 1930s. Ellis's project in this thoughtful book is to offer an appraisal of the varied ways in which a range of writers, including T.S. Eliot, H.G. Wells, J.B. Priestley, and both Leonard and Virginia Woolf, interrogated and gave expression to 'the 1939 state', a phrase Ellis borrows from E.M. Forster. Here Ellis offers a 'literary "year study" of what might be called the "long 1939"' (p. 7), sampling texts from September 1938 to May 1940. The result is a richly contextualized study that brings Woolf into conversation with writers familiar and unfamiliar. Ellis succeeds in his aim of reasserting the claims of an older generation of writers (Eliot, Wells, and Woolf) on the political and literary landscape of the late 1930s so frequently identified with the 'Auden generation' (p. 9).

The chapter on Woolf's final novel is valuable for its revisiting of a number of familiar debates. Ellis is particularly circumspect in his treatment of Woolf's reading of Freud and the way in which the anxiety this wrought in her was, in turn, written into her novel. A significant part of the chapter is given over to a discussion of the relationship between Woolf and her fictional pageant-maker, Miss La Trobe. Many critics have argued that writer may be identified with creation here, and that *Between the Acts* represents a celebration of the communal possibilities of the play replacing the individual appeal of the printed book. Ellis argues staunchly against such readings, drawing to light how La Trobe is identified with authoritarian voices that dominated the wireless at the time Woolf drafted the novel. He also shows how Woolf continued to prize the political possibilities private reading offered the individual in her late writing, *Three Guineas*, 'The Leaning Tower', and the unfinished work tentatively titled 'Reading at Random'.

*Personal Effects: Essays on Memoir, Teaching, and Culture in the Work of Louise DeSalvo*, edited by Nancy Caronia and Edvige Giunta, includes many stimulating chapters, and two in particular that will concern Woolf scholars. In 'Furthering the Voyage: Reconsidering DeSalvo in Contemporary Woolf Studies' (pp. 140–52), Benjamin B. Hagen returns to DeSalvo's work on the draft material of *The Voyage Out* that led to her publication of her edition of *Melymbrosia* [1982] and her *Virginia Woolf's First Voyage: A Novel in the Making* [1980]. Hagen describes the 'archival labour' (p. 141) undertaken by DeSalvo and the criticism her decision to publish a clean edition of *Melymbrosia* elicited from other Woolf scholars. This chapter concludes with a moving tribute to DeSalvo through a reading of sadness and style in Woolf. Mark Hussey's 'The Context of Louise DeSalvo's *Impact*: Incest in Virginia Woolf's Biography' (pp. 155–68) offers a valuable account of the scholarly and political contexts out of which emerged DeSalvo's controversial *Virginia Woolf: The Impact of Childhood Sexual Abuse on Her Life and Writing* [1989]. This chapter begins with a succinct overview of Woolf's relationship to life-writing before moving on to set DeSalvo's book in the context of 'the revolutionary work in incest and trauma studies that emerged in the late 1970s' (p. 160).

Like Marion Dell's monograph discussed above, Eleanor McNees's 'The Stephen Inheritance: Virginia Woolf and the Burden of the Arnoldian Critic' (*CQ* 44:ii[2015] 119–45) contributes to the thriving sub-field of Woolf studies concerned with her Victorian inheritance. It foregrounds Woolf's 'preoccupation with the role of the Arnoldian critic and the burden this role entails' (p. 133) in essays including 'Hours in the Library' [1916], 'How it Strikes a Contemporary' [1923], and 'Phases of Fiction', many of which feature titles borrowed from her Victorian forebears. The article opens with a detailed account of the critical rivalry between Matthew Arnold and both Fitzjames and Leslie Stephen, which played out across the pages of the *Saturday Review*, *Cornhill Magazine*, and *Pall Mall Gazette*. The tenor and content of these debates, which took in questions of philistinism, middle-class complacency, chauvinism, and education, had a profound influence on Woolf's voice and approach in her non-fiction. Woolf recognizes her debt to Arnold as well as her inheritance from Stephen by adopting 'both Leslie Stephen's prosaic voice and Matthew Arnold's poetic one in her own essays' (p. 134). Yet McNees also draws attention to how tribute is tempered by challenge in these essays, in which Woolf responds to and complicates these Victorians' 'critical tenets'. This is convincingly managed in a close reading of Woolf's engagement with the figure of the 'disinterested critic' in 'How It Strikes a Contemporary' (p. 140).

In ' "What a weathercock of sensibility I am!": Sensory Self-Observation in the Diaries of Virginia Woolf and "A Human Experiment in Nerve Division" by Henry Head and W.H.R. Rivers' (*TPr* 29:vi[2015] 1117–42), Susie Christensen builds on recent scholarship on the relationship between neurology and modernism, exploring the 'intellectual connections' between Woolf and her one-time doctor Henry Head. Christensen compares both writers' attempts at 'sensory self observation' (p. 1122), Woolf in her accounts of illness in her diaries and Head in his 'A Human Experiment in Nerve Division', for which he had two nerves severed in his left arm in order to experience the return of sensation to that limb. Before turning to a close reading of these texts, Christensen gives a valuable account of the place of 'Attention and Sensation' in modernism and modernity, its centrality to modernist approaches such as literary Impressionism, and the significance of these ideas to modernist tracts such as Eliot's 'Tradition and the Individual Talent'. Here she gestures to the affinities between 'modernist neurologist' (p. 1122) Head and modernist writers, including Woolf. In the following two sections, Christensen borrows and imaginatively rehabilitates Woolf's 'self-mocking' use of the phrase 'weathercock of sensibility' to describe her aptness to be 'led quickly from one feeling to another' (p. 1129), suggesting this metaphor can usefully 'explain the way in which she depicted herself observing herself and her sensations when she was ill' (p. 1130).

Anna Jones Abramson's 'Beyond Modernist Shock: Virginia Woolf's Absorbing Atmosphere' (*JML* 38:iv[2015] 39–56) aims to reconfigure the critical conversation surrounding 'modernist shock' (p. 55), drawing on developments in affect theory and casting light on the significance of absorption to Woolf's 'historical, psychological, and formal concerns' (p. 40) in *Mrs Dalloway*. Abrahamson suggests a familiar narrative of modernity (with its roots in Simmel's and Benjamin's theories) that privileges shock and its relationship to technological developments, urbanization, and war trauma. Literary critics have supported the primacy of shock to this modern moment, locating examples of rupture, discontinuity, and fragmentation in modernist literature. By contrast, Abramson convincingly reads episodes frequently associated with shock in the novel, such as the car backfiring and the news of Septimus's death, and foregrounds Woolf's understanding of absorption as an integral response to the trauma of modernity: 'Free indirect discourse is a narrative strategy driven by the logic of absorption: the narrator absorbs and is absorbed by the voices of the novel's extensive cast of characters' (p. 47).

Paul Tolliver Brown's 'The Spatial Topography of Virginia Woolf's *Mrs Dalloway*: Capturing Britain's Transition to a Relative Society' (*JML* 38:iv[2015] 20–38) reads Woolf's novel in dialogue with Einstein's theory of relativity, focusing on the way it potentially informs her understanding of the relationship between space and time in this text. Brown opens with an account of existing scholarship concerning Woolf and science, particularly developments in physics in the first half of the twentieth century. He goes on to show how Woolf 'entangles time and topography' in the novel in order to draw attention to 'Britain's transition into a postwar era that is distinctly relative' (p. 22). This argument is supported through a number of close readings, most strikingly of the specific and discrepant responses of two observers of the famous skywriting episode—Mr Bentley in Greenwich and the unnamed man outside St Paul's.

Caroline Marie's 'Virginia Woolf's Cinegraphic Poetics in *The Years*' (*CLS* 52:iii[2015] 510–35) is a lively article that seeks to reassert the aesthetic qualities of Woolf's novel, which she suggests have been neglected in favour of its social commentary and documentary qualities. This is achieved via an engagement with the novel's 'cinegraphic' qualities, focusing on Woolf's treatment of time and space and her reliance on techniques of cutting and shifts in focalization. Marie also weighs in to familiar arguments about the relationship between modernism and realism in the novel: 'My hypothesis is that the fundamental tension between modernism and realism central to that novel is better understood when articulated to the way other artistic fields handled it at the time, 1920s and 1930s cinema in particular' (p. 511). Although Marie is keen to retain a 'poetical' 'outlook' (p. 520) on the novel, this article supplies interesting details of films Woolf was familiar with, including René Clair's *Entr'acte* [1926], and her reactions to the Charlie Chaplin craze.

The *Woolf Studies Annual* for 2015 includes three stimulating articles that show the range of research being undertaken across the field. In 'About Face: The *Three Guineas* Photographs in Cultural Contexts' (*WStA* 21[2015] 1–49), Rebecca Wisor continues her invaluable research on Woolf's pacifist polemic by focusing on the four photographs to feature in that work, which were only reinstated in Michèle Barrett's 1993 Penguin edition in the UK, and later in Jane Marcus's edition in the US. Wisor argues that the cultural and political contexts of these photographs, of Stanley Baldwin, Robert Baden-Powell, Cosmo Gordon Lang, Gordon Hewart, and the Household Cavalry's state trumpeters, have been overlooked. What follows is a rigorously contextualized reading of each figure and photograph that will surely enhance our understanding of this text. Kristin Czarnecki's 'Melted Flesh and Tangled Threads: War Trauma and Modes of Healing in Virginia Woolf's *Mrs Dalloway* and Leslie Marmon Silko's *Ceremony*' (*WStA* 21[2015] 50–77) offers another engaging relational reading that brings *Mrs Dalloway* into fruitful dialogue with Native American writer Leslie Marmon Silko's *Ceremony*. Both novels deal with war trauma, and Czarnecki draws attention to the ways in which both allot responsibility for this mental strain to patriarchal culture and in doing so finds points of overlap between Woolf's philosophy and that of Native Americans. Bethany Layne's 'The "Supreme Portrait Artist" and the "Mistress of the Phrase": Contesting Oppositional Portrayals of Woolf and Bell, Life and Art, in Susan Sellers's *Vanessa and Virginia*' (*WStA* 21[2015] 78–106) focuses on Susan Sellers's recent work of biofiction. As well as offering a valuable overview of the protocols of this genre, Layne shows the various ways in which Sellers refigures the relationship between these artist sisters and in so doing queries myths that have grown up around both women and their relationship.

As usual, *Virginia Woolf Miscellany* offered a range of stimulating work on the author. This edition began with a series of moving tributes to the late Jane Marcus and Shari Benstock, both pioneering scholars of modernist women's writing who will be greatly missed. The rest of the journal, guest-edited by Erica Delsandro, is themed around '1930s Woolf' and includes short but rigorous pieces of research on a range of work from this era, including *Flush*, *Three Guineas*, *The Years*, and 'America, Which I have Never Seen'. Peter Stansky's 'Virginia Woolf and Edward Upward' (*VWM* 87[2015] 17–18) casts interesting light upon 'two significant connections' (p. 17) between these

writers: the Hogarth Press's publication of Upward's *Journey to the Border*
and 'The Falling Tower', his reply to 'The Leaning Tower'. Alice Keane's
essay on language, economy, and fascism, ' "Miserably devaluated currency":
Language, Economy, and Fascism in Christopher Isherwood's *The Berlin
Stories* and Virginia Woolf's *The Years*' (*VWM* 87[2015] 18–21) draws
productive attention to 'economic motifs' in both texts (p. 19). Matthew
Beeber's Virginia Woolf, Victoria Ocampo, and the National/Transnational
Dialectic in *Three Guineas*' (*VWM* 87[2015] 21–3) is also worthy of mention.

Alexandra Harris delivered a paper called *Woolf in Winter* as the sixteenth
annual Virginia Woolf Lecture, which has since been published by the Virginia
Woolf Society of Great Britain. In this lively piece, Harris explores Woolf's
reactions to the winter months in her life and writing, taking in diverse works
including *Night and Day* and, of course, *Orlando*, which includes Woolf's most
enraptured winter scene: the carnival on the frozen Thames.

### 3. British Fiction, 1945–2000

Following on from Bloomsbury's Contemporary Decades series, 2015 saw the
publication of further texts attempting a systematic survey of contemporary
literature. David James's *The Cambridge Companion to British Fiction since
1945* is a comprehensive and accessible survey volume, covering a wide range
of primary material and critical developments. In his preface, James
summarizes the collection as exploring 'the myriad cultural movements and
literary genres that have affected the development of postwar British fiction,
showing how writers have given voice to matters of racial, regional, and sexual
identity' (p. iii). The text opens with a chronology of key historical events and
publications, ranging from the publication of George Orwell's *Animal Farm*
and the bombing of Hiroshima in 1945, to Ishiguro's *The Buried Giant* and the
Scottish National Party's landslide victory in the 2015 UK general election.
This prefatory material provides useful contextual material, particularly for
younger scholars to whom the mid-twentieth century is not 'contemporary'.
As James observes, 'the ever-expanding end-dates for "post-1945" as a
periodizing rubric make comprehensive accounts of so many decades of
cultural transformation seem increasingly unviable' (p. 1).

The focus on political change in the chronology is also mirrored in the
structure of the collection as a whole, with Part I of the text focused on
'Reformation of National Identity'. Dominic Head's 'Mapping Rural and
Regional Identities' discusses the shift in attitudes towards novels set in
regional or provincial environments. Head suggests that with the radical
changes to rural life after 1945 (and increasingly urban populations) 'rural
fiction became more concerned with *ideas* about the countryside ... rather
than with the verisimilitudinous depiction of a settled rural existence' (p. 25).
Such a shift, focused as it is on nostalgia for the past, combined with 'anxiety
about the future' (p. 25), encourages the reading of texts such as Kazuo
Ishiguro's *The Remains of the Day* or Graham Swift's *Waterland* as novels
written as part of a rural tradition, even as they also engage with

postmodernism and 'familiar questions of ethnicity, identity, community, and exclusivity' (p. 25).

Addressing national boundaries, Kirsti Bohata's 'Welsh Fiction' engages with a wide range of novelists, including Emyr Humphreys, Gwyn Thomas, Menna Gallie, Ron Berry, Alun Richards, Paul Ferris, Robert Watson, Charlotte Williams, Trezza Azzopardi, and Erica Wooff. Bohata's brief history of post-War Welsh literature situates Welsh political devolution in 1997 as a 'watershed' moment for 'novels exploring the intersections of national, gender, sexual, linguistic, and class identities' (p. 40) and highlights a focus on trauma fiction and disability writing in the late 1990s. Disability, Bohata suggests, is no longer used to comment on 'class relations and the exploitations of workers', but for more symbolic representations of national identity (p. 41). This rather divided summary of recent Welsh literature is mirrored in David Goldie's 'Scottish Fiction'. This field has been critically praised in recent years for its 'formal and linguistic inventiveness, its diversity, and the sense it gives of an increasingly self-confident culture edging closer to a distinctive expression of national self-determination', but Goldie observes that it was 'much less ambitious, less focused, and less self-assured' in the mid- to late twentieth century (p. 46). He also highlights the 'new wave' of Scottish fiction writing led by Alasdair Gray and James Kelman, a literary experimentation that reflected the 'more self-confident Scottish political and cultural nationalism that has emerged since the failed devolution referendum of 1979 and which culminated in the referendum on Scottish independence in 2014' (p. 49). Such a summary also encompasses the importance of Gray, Iain Banks, Irvine Welsh, and James Robertson in writing in Scots and the vernacular, and their use of postmodern, multi-layered narratives.

The final chapter in this section, by Aarthi Vadde, discusses narratives of migration and immigration in British fiction. Providing historical context to the *Windrush* generation, Vadde discusses Lamming's *The Emigrants* [1954] and Selvon's *The Lonely Londoners* [1956] as emblematic of a generation who combined 'West Indian and minority British identity' (p. 63). Salman Rushdie, Hanif Kureishi, and Kazuo Ishiguro are presented as the second generation of black British writing, sharing what Vadde refers to as a 'migrant theory of identity', imagining identity collectivities as 'more deeply indebted to performance practices than to any innate differences among races and nationalities' (p. 70). Finally, Vadde introduces Zadie Smith's work as spanning both the global and the local, and suggests that 'global network novels', which actively analyse and critique interconnectivity, are 'at the vanguard of British fiction' (p. 74).

The second part of *The Cambridge Companion to British Fiction since* 1945 focuses on the politics of culture, subjectivity, and the environment. With thematic chapters on feminist fiction (Emma Parker), queer writing (Sarah Brophy and Kasim Husain), ecocriticism and nature writing (Daniel Weston), and the posthuman (Peter Boxall), this section provides a useful survey of a range of key critical trends in modern and contemporary literature and culture. The final section focuses on form and genre and opens with Julia Jordan's analysis of 'fiction after modernism' (p. 145), and the avant-garde writing of the 1960s and 1970s. Joseph Brooker's 'Reanimating Historical

Fiction' engages with a genre that he presents as a frequent 'locus of critical theory' (p. 165), as it engages with the ideas of historical truth in work by Jeanette Winterson, Salman Rushdie, and Angela Carter. Brooker also introduces Kazuo Ishiguro's and Pat Barker's fiction as 'revisionist' (p. 169), before citing Hilary Mantel's work to show how historical fiction can 'bring us to think about the ways in which we know the past, especially the ways that narrative shapes our conception of history' (p. 175). Michael Lemahieu's chapter on 'The Novel of Ideas' presents a hybrid genre, engaging with classic debates: 'faith versus reason, religion versus science, logic versus emotion' (p. 182). Continuing the focus on globally interconnected politics, Matthew Hart's chapter, 'Globalism and Historical Romance', introduces Salman Rushdie and David Mitchell as authors whose work should be considered as historical romances. Nicky Marsh, meanwhile, presents the financial novel as a specific form of literary thriller, one which 'offers a generic paradigm through which the peculiar spatial and temporal logics of finance can be understood' (p. 192). Marsh's chapter offers a lively analysis of a range of financial fictions, from Muriel Spark to J.G. Ballard, Ian McEwan to Martin Amis. She presents the significance of these novels as not merely concerned with the rise of financial markets after 1945, but also engaged with the 'difficult, fraying social relations of those that exist beyond ... this still-growing political and cultural power' (p. 204). Finally, Weishin Gui, writing on transnational forms in British fiction, offers a defence and analysis of genre and criticism in contemporary writing, querying how 'the play of a certain genre with other genres and elements, both within and without the text, enable[s] a kind of reading and interpretation that constitutes a formative movement' (p. 226). Overall, this collection presents a varied critique of literary trends since 1945.

In addition to Marsh's analysis, J.G. Ballard was also the subject of one of Glyphi's Critical Studies in Science Fiction, with David Ian Paddy's *The Empires of J.G. Ballard: An Imagined Geography*. Opening with a discussion of the difficulty of placing Ballard amongst a field of representative contemporaries in twentieth- and twenty-first-century writing, Paddy identifies Ballard as an author as comfortable with international politics and global economics as with science fiction or transgressive writing. *The Empires of J.G. Ballard* presents Ballard's work as 'a sustained examination of the evolution of imperialism ... and of the cultural, social, economic and psychological dynamics of international imperial networks' in contemporary society (pp. 6–7). Along with specific close readings of Ballard's 'reverse colonisation narratives' (p. 9) and subversion of the 'imperial legacy of science fiction' (p. 10), Paddy also tracks the global nature of Ballard's writing. For example, Paddy and Patty Jula's map of the geographical locations of Ballard's fiction (p. 26) makes for instructive illustration of the breadth of Ballard's oeuvre, before proceeding to more detailed assessment of geography and global politics in key Ballard texts across the late twentieth century.

Continuing the focus on single authors, Glyphi also published *Maggie Gee: Critical Essays*, edited by Sarah Dillon and Caroline Edwards, the second publication in their Contemporary Writers: Critical Essays series. One of the distinctive features of this series is the involvement of the named contemporary author in each publication. As such, in addition to ten chapters on Gee's novels, the collection also includes a foreword by Gee, and concludes with an amended version of her 1996 William Matthews lecture, 'How May I Speak in My Own Voice? Language and the Forbidden', where Gee presents fiction as the space where 'the unsayable can be said' (p. 13), particularly on topics which are elided in public conversation. Monika Szuba opens the collection with her analysis of transgressive aesthetics and politics in *The Burning Book* [1983]. Szuba presents this text as an experimentally realist novel, using inventive typography to represent a disintegrating political world and looming nuclear apocalypse (p. 44). Alexander Beaumont's 'Reproductive Politics and the Public Sphere: Natalism, Natality, and Apocalypse' critiques the dooms-day theme in Gee, from *The Burning Book* to *The Flood*. Of particular interest to Beaumont is Lauren Berlant and Hannah Arendt's theorizing of natality, where hope and potential futurity are explicitly linked to the infant, who 'possesses the capacity of beginning as something anew, that is, of acting' (p. 75). In the third chapter of this collection, Sarah Falcus analyses familial roles in *Where Are the Snows* [1991], using escapism to 'reflect upon contemporary discourses of aging', particularly with regard to women (p. 17). Finally, Sarah Dillon's 'Literary Equivocation: Reproductive Futurism and *The Ice People*' draws on the work of Lee Edelman to position Gee's work on 'reproductive futurism' (p. 102) within a wider range of contemporary dystopian novels concerned with familial relationships. The collection presents a coherent and engaging analysis of her fiction as a whole, including a breadth of work on *The Flood* [2004], and discussion of Gee's most recent publication, *Virginia Woolf in Manhattan* [2014].

Other single-author monographs and collections published in 2015 include Peter Childs's *Julian Barnes*, part of Manchester University Press's Contemporary British Novelists series. Childs provides a clear and concise introduction to Barnes and his work. Of particular interest to Barnes scholars will be the inclusion of previously unpublished archival material from the Harry Ransom Research Centre. Childs balances his discussion of key texts, including *Metroland* [1980], *Flaubert's Parrot* [1984], *A History of the World in 10½ Chapters* [1989], and *England, England* [1998], with extracts from Barnes's letters and manuscript drafts.

Focusing on a twentieth-century author with a more explicitly political element to his work, Paula Martín Salván's *The Language of Ethics and Community in Graham Greene's Fiction* presents a systematic analysis of the linguistics of Greene's fiction. Martín Salván's monograph is structured around her seven chosen keywords (or key pairings): peace, bargain, despair, pity and compassion, commitment, and *caritas*. She proposes a reading of Greene that focuses on the ethical implications of his over-use of those key terms, as a 'lexico-conceptual articulation ... shaped as ethical conflict dramatized in narrative form' (p. 1). Drawing on a wide range of his work, Martín Salván successfully showcases Greene's persistent use of these keywords, combining close reading, critical theory, and quantitative assess-ment of the key terms and the ethics of Greene's select word choice in a manner that is useful to both English literature and language scholars alike.

Kate Macdonald's *Novelists Against Social Change: Conservative Popular Fiction*, 1920–1960 centres on popular mid-twentieth-century novelists who are now significantly less well known than Greene. Macdonald focuses on the fiction of John Buchan, Dornford Yates, and Angela Thirkell, investigating their public reception and the key themes and concerns of their novels. In Macdonald's words, these novels 'preserve the views, and fears, of the authors, like asparagus in aspic' (p. 3). Macdonald proposes that this focus on popular reception can also be used to cross-examine contemporary assumptions about early and mid-twentieth-century readers. She summarizes the work of Yates as 'tense and highly strung thrillers' featuring 'dramatic set-piece social dramas to illustrate the dangers of failing to obey social rules' (p. 5), and Thirkell's fiction as 'reassuring and regressive, extolling the comfort and desirability of Victorian ideals ... untouched by the twentieth century' (p. 7). Yet while there is an undeniable regressive trend to both authors' work, Macdonald successfully argues for their innovation, too—in consistently using fiction to attempt to preserve 'the old order against the onslaught of the new' (p. 7) over several decades, with a wide readership. For example, in her chapter on Yates and Thirkell in the post-war period, Macdonald presents the strategic exhaustion of many of Thirkell's female characters: where 'managing women' were previously portrayed as physically and emotionally worn out by the war (p. 196). Meanwhile, the nineteenth century is presented as a nostalgic ideal by both authors—and used to criticize the 'slipping social standards' of the 1940s and 1950s (p. 200). Such narratives were already dated by the interwar period; yet Macdonald argues that these popular conservative narratives are nevertheless critically relevant, in that they suggest that 'fiction read for pleasure has a political dimension, and that the political elements function as a natural circumscriber of taste' (p. 223).

Addressing very different texts, Lykke Guanio-Uluru also focuses on literary ethics, in *Ethics and Form in Fantasy Literature: Tolkien, Rowling and Meyer*. Guanio-Uluru's key texts, *The Lord of the Rings*, the *Harry Potter* series, and the *Twilight* franchise, are presented as popular catalysts in 'the development and commercialization of fantasy as a genre' (p. 1). Of particular interest is her analysis of the quest narratives and Judaeo-Christian belief systems and ethics in *Lord of the Rings* and *Harry Potter*, and the contrasts between their ethical 'visions' (p. 2) and Meyer's work.

Also focusing on genre and fiction, Alan McCluskey's *Materiality and the Modern Cosmopolitan Novel* explicitly engages with questions of class, alongside geopolitics, race, and gender. In three parts that examine Caryl Phillips, J.M. Coetzee, and Philip Roth in turn, McCluskey focuses on cosmopolitanism with regard to home and subjectivity, material ethics, and tragedy and silence. The volume interrogates the term 'cosmopolitan' and queries the degree to which supposedly cosmopolitan texts can engage with 'issues of socio-political relevance' (p. 1). Tracing common themes of empathy and sympathy in the work of all three novelists, McCluskey suggests that the problematic empathy engendered by characters such as Eva Stern, the Holocaust survivor in *The Nature of Blood*, prompts readers to acknowledge linguistic limitations in expressing trauma and contemporary experience. Thus empathy becomes 'intertwined with a haunting sense of self-reflectivity, with the reader being made aware of the fact that they are ultimately responsible for its production' (p. 15). Self-reflectivity also plays a more formal role in

McCluskey's chosen texts. For example, the intratextual narratives of *The Nature of Blood*, spanning a range of time periods and geographical locations, also query concepts of truth and historical narrative.

*End of Empire and the English Novel since* 1945, edited by Rachael Gilmour and Bill Schwarz, continues this concern with issues of citizenship, particularly as it pertains to minority identity categories in twentieth-century British literature. Analysing authors from George Orwell to Alan Hollinghurst, William Golding to Ian McEwan, the volume encompasses a wide range of genres in its discussion of imperial disintegration and racial diversity in modern and contemporary English fiction. In the introduction, Schwarz states that the collection aims not to challenge postcolonialism, but to 'extend its remit to those works which at first glance do not first fall within' the category (p. 17). In reflecting on English culture of the mid- to late twentieth century, the authors trace metropolitan responses to decolonization, and 'parochial' attitudes to popular English literature (p. 18). Thus, Patrick Parrinder analyses the significance of Anglo-American relations in reactions to mid-twentieth-century English fiction in the opening chapter of the collection; Cora Kaplan introduces Josephine Tey as an example of 'conservative modernity and the female crime novel' (p. 53); John Masters's family sagas are presented as popular liberal-colonial reading material. Rachael Gilmore is also a contributor to this collection, here working on William Golding, and the illusions of empire in his work. Building on her earlier monograph *Writing Romance: Post-War Women's Fiction* 1945–2005 [2014], Deborah Philips writes on empire and romance fiction, specifically the publications of the Mills & Boon imprint, while William Boyd's novels are analysed as 'comedies of imperial decline' (p. 134) by Michael L. Ross. Huw Marsh concentrates on the metaphors of imperialism in Penelope Lively's Moon Tiger [*1987*] and Salman Rushdie's *Midnight's Children* [*1981*], alongside wider discussions of historical metafiction. James Proctor's comparison of the regional fiction of Pat Barker and David Peace, and the ghosts of empire, pairs well with David Alderson's 'Saturday's Enlightenment' in addressing the controversies of twenty-first-century novels and British foreign policy. Susan Hobson critiques the role of the British empire in travel fiction from D.H. Lawrence to Tim Parks, and Sarah Brophy discusses queer theory, history, and 'postcolonial intimacies' (p. 184) in Alan Hollinghurst's writing. The collection closes with an afterword from Elleke Boehmer, presenting a new globalization of empire for contemporary British fiction.

Finally, select chapters of *The History of British Literature on Film*, 1896–2015, edited by Greg M. Colón Semenza and Bob Hasenfratz, are of potential use to scholars working on post-1945 literature and culture. This work presents a wide-ranging survey of adaptations of classic British novels across the long twentieth century, with analysis engaging equally with literary and film studies theory. Overall, the depth and range of publications on British fiction from 1945 to 2000 produced in 2015 indicated a lively and politically charged interest in twentieth-century cultural productions and their continued relevance in the twenty-first century.

## 4. Pre-1950 Drama

There has been a fine crop of recent theatre history books focusing on pre-1950 drama. This has ranged from single-subject works on D.H. Lawrence, Noël Coward, and Donald Wolfit to several works on Irish drama, especially George Bernard Shaw, the Abbey Theatre, and political theatre. Rebecca D'Monté's survey of *British Theatre and Performance* 1900–1950 sees the two world wars as crucial transitional moments in the development of the theatre, and Andrew Maunder also gives a fresh perspective on the Great War of 1914–18.

Crime has always been a major topic of English literature, but studies have tended to focus on novels and short stories. *The English Crime Play in the Twentieth Century* by Beatrix Hesse instead looks at drama and makes a distinction between the dead body on a page of 'dead, written' language, and that in the theatre, where it exists amongst 'living bodies' (p. 1). There are three main areas to the book. The first section provides socio-historical contexts by which to read crime drama, and gives a useful survey of previous criticism of the subject. The second part presents a poetics of crime drama by looking at staging, structure, and genre, while the third focuses on stage adaptations of Agatha Christie's work, and of others such as Joe Orton and Tom Stoppard.

Bloomsbury Methuen Drama's Critical Companions series continues to produce excellent additions to theatre studies, such as James Moran's *The Theatre of D.H. Lawrence*. This is the first major work on the subject in over forty years and, one hopes, will do much to resurrect Lawrence's flagging reputation (the introduction shows the ways in which his critical fortunes have risen and fallen). The plays that make up the 'Eastwood Trilogy'—*The Daughter-in-Law* [1912], *The Widowing of Mrs Holroyd* [1914], and *A Collier's Friday Night* [1934]—are examined, alongside less well-known drama such as *The Fight for Barbara* [1933] and *The Married Man* [1940]. Moran presses for Lawrence's theatrical experimentation, naming Brecht, Beckett, Artaud, and Joyce as influences on his work. Viewing Lawrence not just as a realist but as a modernist does much to expand his position in twentieth-century drama. As with other books in the Critical Companions series, there are three further contributions in addition to Moran's central thesis, providing studies by a playwright, Stephen Lowe (pp. 157–66), a screenwriter, William Ivory (pp. 167–80), and Soudabeh Ananisarab on the subject of interculturality (pp. 181–90). Moran himself gives the director's perspective in conversation with Peter Gill (pp. 143–56), and there is a foreword by Sir Richard Eyre (pp. viii–x). Altogether, this is an important work that adds much to Laurentian studies.

Noël Coward is another writer whose academic standing is being reappraised. Whilst initially dismissive of film as a medium, Coward was approached during the Second World War to write for the cinema. In *Noël Coward Screenplays*, Barry Day continues his exhaustive editing of Coward's work with the screenplays for *In Which We Serve* [1942], *Brief Encounter* [1945], and *The Astonished Heart* [1950]. The latter two are the most relevant, appearing as they did as part of Coward's cycle of ten stage plays, *Tonight at 8.30* [1936]. Filmed plays tended to stick to their stage origins, as happened with *The Astonished Heart*. This centres on a psychiatrist who becomes obsessed with one of his wife's friends, but its melodramatic theatricality did not translate well to the cinema. In contrast, *Brief Encounter* was opened up for the screen to become a separate entity. The director David Lean wanted to excise the subplot of the working-class Myrtle Bagot and Albert Godby, but Coward insisted that their putative romance remain, so as to provide comic relief from the tragedy of the main plot. The film was not an immediate success but has since been seen as a classic of the British cinema. Day's editing skills are as sharp as ever, though one hopes for a more academic view of the adaptation process. He provides introductions to each of the screenplays and gives useful information on *Tonight at 8.30*, the development of the narrative and characters, as well as insights into the production process. Included are also some stills of the films and original posters.

Another towering figure of the time was the actor-manager Donald Wolfit. Laurence Raw's *Theatre of the People: Donald Wolfit's Shakespearean Productions* 1937–1953 does much to go beyond the myths that have grown up around this actor. Raw's book looks at a similar period and subject to those depicted in Ronald Harwood's play *The Dresser* [1980], based on the famous actor. In this, 'Sir' is ageing, eccentric, and vulnerable, crippled by his ego as he struggles with touring Shakespeare to provincial theatres during the Second World War. Raw shows the tenacity with which Wolfit pursued his dream of bringing the works of Shakespeare to large swaths of the country under almost impossible conditions. The introductory chapter is rather too subjective for my liking, but this is a minor quibble. The book is good at providing background information about touring away from the major cities and the problems encountered in putting on theatre during the war. More than this, though, Raw has done extensive archival research amongst Wolfit's personal papers and builds a compelling picture of a man who was both part of the 'old guard' of actor managers and looked forward to the community theatre of the future.

D'Monté's monograph, *British Theatre and Performance* 1900–1950 re-evaluates this period and questions the view that theatre in the first part of the twentieth century lacks interest when measured against that in the post-war period. The introduction sets out the seismic political, social, and theatrical changes taking place at this time. The chapter divisions relate to the way in which 'Britain was either anticipating war, involved in war or recovering from war' (p. 6). Thus, there are sections on the Edwardian theatre, First World War theatre, interwar theatre, and Second World War theatre and after. A secondary aspect of this is that the periods of theatre history rarely covered—1939–45 and the immediate post-war period—are explored in finer detail. Further thematic chapters by Claire Cochrane (pp. 199–211), Penny Farfan (pp. 213–22), and Steve Nicholson (pp. 223–39) cover the role of the director, gender and sexuality, and Hitler and censorship respectively.

Theatre and war is a growing area of interest and *British Theatre and the Great War, 1914–1919: New Perspectives* develops our understanding of drama in this period. The editor, Andrew Maunder, has amassed a noteworthy collection of contributors. The book is divided into four parts, some of which shift slightly into other areas: 'Mobilization and Propaganda' (Steve

Nicholson on representations of war, Anselm Heinrich on Shakespeare, Maunder on melodrama); 'Women and War' (Sos Eltis on depictions of women's work, Katharine Cockin on the Pioneer Players, Veronica Kelly on Edith Cavell); 'Popular Theatre' (Viv Gardner on musical comedy, Simon Featherstone on music hall, Emma Hanna on cinema); and 'Alternative Spaces' (Claire Cochrane on Birmingham theatres, Ailsa Grant Ferguson on performances for Anzacs, Margaret Leask on touring concert parties, Victor Emeljanou on POW camps). Thus a wide range of theatrical material is covered, allowing this fruitful period to be further explored. Maunder's book gives a sense of the richness and range of theatre during the First World War and is much to be commended.

Anthony Roche takes a chronological approach in *The Irish Dramatic Revival 1899–1939* to show the development of a national identity through theatre. Starting with the late nineteenth century, he looks at the foundations of this movement with the work of Dion Boucicault, Oscar Wilde, and George Bernard Shaw (who later gets a chapter of his own), as well as attesting to the influence of Ibsen. Roche then explores the role taken by W.B. Yeats, J.M. Synge, Lady Gregory, and Sean O'Casey. Further chapters are on performance in modern Irish theatre, by Paige Reynolds (pp. 161–71), Synge and cultural debates, by P.J. Mathews (pp. 172–81), and the supernatural on the Irish stage, by Conor McPherson (pp. 182–93). It is pleasing to see Gregory being given her due, not just as a co-founder of the Abbey Theatre but as a significant dramatist in her own right, with Roche stressing her comedic skills and use of realistic language. The most interesting parts of the book are about the playwrights' experimentation and global influence. For example, Synge and Yeats had a major influence on Beckett; Yeats's *At the Hawk's Well* [perf. 1916; pub. 1917] and *Purgatory* [1938] were particularly important to *Waiting for Godot* [1953] and *Endgame* [1957].

Roche convincingly argues for George Bernard Shaw to be included as part of the Irish Revival movement. This is taken up in David Clare's *Bernard Shaw's Irish Outlook*. In this, Clare shows how Shaw's early life in Ireland had a major impact upon his drama, even though only three plays were set there: *John Bull's Other Island* [1904], *O'Flaherty, VC* [1917], and *Tragedy of an Elderly Gentleman* [1923]. Shaw makes use of Irish-born, Irish diasporic, surrogate Irish, and stage English characters to both celebrate and mock his fellow countrymen and critique Anglo-Irish relations. This could be to blistering effect in a play like the censored *O Flaherty, VC*, or more comically as, for example, in *Pygmalion* [1913]. Clare insightfully notes that Henry Higgins's name reveals his Irish nationality and his occupation deliberately chosen to puncture the 'linguistic pride of their English overlords' (p. 22).

Brad Kent's *George Bernard Shaw in Context* is an excellent companion to the two previously mentioned books. Amply illustrated, it explores Shaw's relationship with both his native country and his adopted one, as well as looking at the role that the Abbey Theatre took in his life. Kent's edited volume, though, is much wider in scope, covering 'People and Places', 'Theatre', 'Writing and the Arts', 'Politics', 'Culture and Society', and 'Reception and Afterlife'. This could easily have been an unwieldy project, given its huge range of topics (forty-two essays in total). However, Kent has marshalled an impressive range of contributions and edited them with a fine touch. One of the strengths of the book is that it is not hagiographical, but rather provides a critical study of the man and his work and ideas. It also points to other areas still to be explored, such as Shaw's relationship with modernism. It is difficult to privilege one contribution over another, but certainly the second section, on theatre, provides the most pertinent commentary, particularly the essays by J. Ellen Gainor on Fabian drama (pp. 76–84), Kerry Powell on farcical comedy (pp. 85–93) and Jean Chothia on the new drama (pp. 109–16). Nevertheless, the whole book is highly recommended and an essential guide to George Bernard Shaw.

Elsewhere, contributions to Donald E. Morse's edited collection, *Irish Theatre in Transition: From the Late Nineteenth to the Early Twenty-First Century* include Christopher Murray's famous view of the Abbey Theatre as holding 'a mirror up to nation', showing how it developed from a small arts theatre to the Abbey Theatre and finally to what is now simply known as 'the Irish theatre' (pp. 13–31). While there is plenty on contemporary Irish dramatists, such as Brian Friel, Conor McPherson, Frank McGuinness, and Stella Feehily, this collection is much weaker on earlier writers, though there is useful material on Synge, Yeats, and O'Casey. Pleasingly, José Lanters (pp. 54–67) also comments on the less well-known Mary Manning, who wrote *Youth's the Season* [1931].

Finally, Fearghal McGarry's *The Abbey Rebels of 1916: A Lost Revolution* provides an unusual perspective on the Abbey Theatre by viewing its position in relation to the Easter Rising of 1916. The relationship between Irish theatre and political revolution has been carefully researched using original archival material and the book throws up some fascinating information. For example, Máire Nic Shiubhlaigh was one of the founding members of the Abbey Theatre, taking the leading role in W.B. Yeats's *Cathleen Ni Houlihan* on its opening night in 1904. A fervent nationalist, she took an active part in the Easter Rising. Other actors included Maude Gonne, Arthur Shields, and Seán Connolly, who became the first rebel to die. An interesting connection is forged between the performativity of theatre on stage and the performativity of war outside the theatre, as well as the possible culpability of dramatists in inciting political action. As Yeats asked provocatively (and proudly) of *Cathleen Ni Houlihan* 'Did that play of mine send out / Certain men the English shot?'

## 5. Post-1950 Drama

One monograph and one essay collection this year make major contributions to work on black British dramatists. Edited by Mary F. Brewer, Lynette Goddard, and Deidre Osborne, *Modern and Contemporary Black British Drama* is divided into three sections: 'Post-War Migration', 'Second Generation', and 'Neo-Millennial'. Together, these encompass work from the 1950s to the present, with introductory essays that contextualize the work of each section. The book mainly comprises individual case studies, including: Brian Crow's 'Identity Politics in the Plays of Mustapha Matura' (pp. 32–46);

Mary F. Brewer's 'Staging Social Change: Three Plays by Barry Reckford' (pp. 47–61); Suzanne Scafe's 'Home/lessness, Exile and Triangular Identities in the Drama of Caryl Philips' (pp. 62–78); Nicola Abram's 'Looking Back: Winsome Pinnock's Politics of Representation' (pp. 95–111); Lynette Goddard's '(Black) Masculinity, Race and Nation in Roy Williams' Sports Plays' (pp. 112–27); 'Michael Pearce's 'Kwame Kwei-Armah's African American Inspired Triptych' (pp. 128–46); Deidre Osborne's 'Resisting the Standard and Displaying Her Colours: debbie tucker green at British Drama's Vanguard' (pp. 161–77); Ekua Ekumah's 'Bola Agbjae: Voicing a New Africa on the British Stage' (pp. 178–93); and Victor Ukaegbu's 'Witnessing to, in and from the Centre: Oladipo Agboluaje's Theatre of Dialogic Centrism' (pp. 194–209). Lynette Goddard approaches the same subject in *Contemporary Black British Playwrights: Margins to Mainstream* by focusing on a more recent group of largely London-based black British playwrights who rose to prominence around 2000. These include Roy Williams, Kwame Kwei-Armah, debbie tucker green, and Bola Agbaje. The book's main approach can be found in its title as it charts the rise of these playwrights through twenty-two plays that take us from marginal spaces to their occupation of the stages of major London theatres such as the Royal Court and National Theatre. Goddard also points towards external events such as the murder of Stephen Lawrence in 1993, an act which she sees as reverberating across the arts and cultural policy in helping to promoting greater diversity. At the same time, Goddard discusses some of the inherent dangers that accompany this higher profile through the effects of the work being exposed mainly within a culture whose patronage is aimed mainly at white middle-class audiences. She explores how this might change the reception of work as it is produced, together with future commissions and the dangers of the work stereotyping black masculinity and youth gang culture.

James Reynolds and Andy Smith's edited collection, *Howard Barker's Theatre: Wrestling with Catastrophe* includes contributions from scholars and practitioners of Howard Barker's theatre. In a three-part structure the book examines accounts of the working practices of The Wrestling School, a company originally formed to produce Barker's work; there is then a section of scholarly essays on Barker's work. These include Andy Smith's 'To Experience a Thing is Beautiful: The Photographic Practice of Howard Barker' (pp. 95–112), which looks at Barker's own photography of Wrestling School productions, taken under the alias of Eduardo Houth; James Hudson's 'Vintage Barker: New Writing in Old Bottles' (pp. 113–30), which considers Barker's current status in contemporary British playwriting culture, and the widening gap between the increasingly experimental course his drama has taken and the conservative turn Hudson identifies in much contemporary new writing; Peter A. Groves's 'Howard Barker and the Return of Religion' (pp. 131–48), a somewhat perplexing offering that attempts to make a case for Barker's work following some of the precepts of the Christian mystic Meister Eckhart; and James Reynold's 'Going Underground' (pp. 149–68), which looks at the use of subterranean spaces in Barker's theatrical imagination. The third section, 'Other Barkers', examines non-Wrestling School productions. This includes an interview with the actress Fiona Shaw, where she discusses her 2012 performance as Galactia in the National Theatre's 2012 production of *Scenes from an Execution* [1984] at the National Theatre (pp. 175–88); there are also accounts by American directors of Barker's work (pp. 189–98) as well as productions in Scotland (pp. 215–24) and Wales (pp. 225–40).

Elaine Aston and Mark O'Thomas's *Royal Court: International* is the first major study to look the Royal Court's longstanding commitment to international drama, an area that has been relatively neglected by scholars. The introduction argues that the development of an internationalist policy was always at the very heart of the theatre's mission since its inception in 1956, while other chapters look at the development of the work itself through methods of international exchange such as writing and acting workshops. Chapter 3, 'Conversations', is given over to seven interviews with writers, directors, and translators. One of these involves the playwright Mark Ravenhill, who discuss aspects of the Royal Court's international work. Chapter 4 looks at the reception of some of this work in the UK, while the final chapter looks at the legacy of the Royal Court's work abroad.

Maggie Inchley's *Voice and New Writing, 1997–2007: Articulating the Demos* provides a fascinating riposte to an age where mission statements deploy terms such as 'empowerment', 'diversity', and 'plurality' as buzzwords for any self-respecting theatre that promotes new writing. Another ubiquitous phrase is 'new voices', and Inchley's book explores the implications of this phrase, both literally and culturally. In her provocative analysis, 'voice' is stripped back to its original praxis and value in drama training. In an extensive and wide-ranging analysis that takes in the work of, among others, debbie tucker green, Dennis Kelly, and Tania Gupta, she also demonstrates how crucibles of new writing culture such as the Royal Court, the Traverse, and the National Theatre respond to new or marginalized voices. Inchley's book asks some difficult questions and provides some troubling answers about the limits, in a supposedly liberal theatre culture, on how far these new voices are permitted to speak, and how these voices are covertly policed and controlled by theatre institutions.

Carl Lavery and Clare Finburgh's edited collection, *Rethinking the Theatre of the Absurd: Ecology, the Environment and the Greening of the Modern Stage* is a major reconsideration of the school of theatre that lent its name to Martin Esslin's highly influential *The Theatre of the Absurd* in 1960. Here they resituate and reassess the term through a consideration of the ecological and environmental implications set up by this group of dramatists. In the editors' introduction the plays are reread as a reflection of mankind's negative impact on the environment (p. 40). Some essays return to the British and Irish playwrights that Esslin originally included in his study: Joe Kelleher's 'Recycling Beckett' (pp. 127–46) looks at the ways in which his work has been appropriated, or 'recycled', in photography and art installations, where Beckett's human protagonists are erased, allowing a contemplation of the denuded landscapes of the stage plays, particularly *Happy Days* [1961]. Mark Taylor Batty and Carl Lavery's jointly authored 'The Secluded Voice: The Impossible Call Home in Early Pinter' (pp. 219–40) considers the use of the hearth as a place of belonging in Esslin's reading of Harold Pinter's *The Room* [1957], *The Birthday Party* [1958], *The Caretaker* [1960], and *The Homecoming*

[1965]. For Batty and Lavery these sanctuaries become instead 'shifting, unsettling sites of displacement' (p. 50). Yet the authors go on to argue that these states are not negative; rather, they offer a resistance against a taming domesticity. In 'Caryl Churchill's "Dark Ecology"' (pp. 59–76), Elaine Aston looks at work ranging from *The Ants* [1962] to *The Skriker* [1994] and *Far Away* [2000], demonstrating Churchill's formal credentials as an absurdist, but also exploring how these plays dramatize risk to the non-human world (p. 62). This becomes the fate of figures in these plays who are ejected from the domestic space to take up 'modes of dwelling that while unsettling and disrupted, avoid the stasis of reactionary discourses' (p. 50). Climate change also concerns Una Chauduri in 'Anthropo-Scenes: Theater and Climate Change' (*JCDE* 3:i[2015] 12–27), which discusses Churchill's *Far Away* alongside Wallace Shawn's work. His term 'the drama of bad ideas' (p. 21) is applied to the final scene in Churchill's play, and nature is shown to be at war with itself. Chauduri links this dystopian scenario to recent reports on climate change and the repercussions for animal and plant life attempting to colonize new areas in a bid to escape rising temperatures.

Several articles in the same volume take a global view of history and politics. In ' "Provincializing" Post-Wall Europe: Transcultural Critique of Eurocentric Historicism in *Pentecost*, *Europe* and *The Break of Day*' (*JCDE* 3:i[2015] 28–46), Janine Hauthal takes three works by David Edgar, David Greig, and Timberlake Wertenbaker, respectively, to represent transnational narratives in the 1990s. She charts a shift between an old Europe and one being reshaped by the collapse of communism, and argues that the three plays articulate the consequences of these changes that are reflected in a crisis of national identity. The communist regime in China is the subject of Christiane Schlote's 'A Historiography of Protest and Politics of Commemoration in Lucy Kirkwood's *Chimerica*' (*JCDE* 3:i[2015] 56–76). This article forms part of a larger ongoing research project that focuses on the role of the war photographer in contemporary plays. Schlote looks at the figure of the iconic 'tankman' photograph from the 1989 Tiananmen Square protests and its representation in Lucy Kirkwood's play.

David Ian Rabey's *The Theatre and Films of Jez Butterworth* is the first study devoted to a playwright whose work first appeared on the main stage at the Royal Court in 1995 with *Mojo*. The book contextualizes Butterworth's work and his influences, offering an assessment of his place within contemporary British drama. Butterworth's uniqueness, Rabey argues, arises principally from the way his work forms a series of distinctly English vignettes, with an emphasis on rural communities. Examining Butterworth's best-known play, *Jerusalem* [2009], Rabey locates a recovery of tragic form through its appropriation of neo-Shakespearean motifs and English pagan mythology that principally involves the sacrifice of its larger-than-life protagonist Johnny 'Rooster' Byron. Rabey also traces this pattern back through earlier work, including *The Night Heron* [2002] and *Parlour Song* [2009]. There is close attention here to the distinctive settings in Butterworth's work too, including the urban settings of *Mojo*; suburbia in *Parlour Song* and the film *Birthday Girl* [2002]; and the rural in *The Night Heron* and *Jerusalem*. Rabey's analysis is complemented by chapters from other contributors. These include James D.

Balestrieri's discussion of the Broadway production of *Jerusalem* (pp. 165–72), Mary Karen Dahl's analysis of *The River* [2012] (pp. 173–84), and Elisabeth Angel Perez's consideration of ghosts and the spectral in Butterworth's work (pp. 185–93).

Cristina Delgado-Garcia's *Rethinking Character in Contemporary British Theatre: Aesthetics, Politics, Subjectivity* makes a distinctive intervention in the way character in drama can be understood, arguing that this configuration permits the extension of notions of subjectivity. In her analysis of Sarah Kane's *Crave* [1998] and *4.48 Psychosis* [1999], Tim Crouch's *ENGLAND* [2007], and Ed Thomas's *Stone City Blue* [2004], Delgado-Garcia builds on Elinor Fuchs and Hans Thies-Lehmann's ideas on character and introduces readers to some significant, but overlooked, voices from France and Spain, Robert Abirached and Juan Antonio Hormigon. In her case studies, Delgado-Garcia presents new insights into the understanding of character. Addressing Sarah Kane, for example, she challenges the received idea that abstraction of character is a feature of her work in a most productive way, also addressing similar preoccupations about her late work being concerned with inner mindscapes and Cartesian divisions between mind and body. Kane's *4.48 Psychosis* is also the subject of Matthew Robert's 'Vanishing Acts: Sarah Kane's Texts for Performance and Postdramatic Theatre' (*MD* 58:i[2015] 94–110), which looks at the connection between the idea of the play as text and its inscription through performance. In a reading based on Hans-Thies-Lehmann's notion of postdramatic theatre, Roberts argues that demarcation between the two forms is misguided: we need to 'examine the assumptions that determine, or at least inform, how performance is theoretically elucidated' (p. 97).

Tom Stoppard's work is the subject of several articles this year. Christopher Innes's 'Utopian Histories: Transforming Past Ideals in Stoppard's Plays' (*JCDE* 3:i[2015] 47–55) considers his trilogy, *The Coast of Utopia* [2002], and *Rock and Roll* [2006] and explores how these plays chart the history of revolutionary socialist ideas to form an ideal of social existence, through to its practice in communist regimes in Czechoslovakia and its reception and interpretation by British Marxists. Innes concludes that in both plays Stoppard comes down on the side of the arts in painting, music, and poetry as containing 'ideals, which trump politics' (p. 55). R. Darren Gobert's 'The Field of Modern Drama, or *Arcadia*' (*MD* 58:iii[2015] 285–301) uses archival sources to examine three productions, in 1992, 1995, and 2009 of *Arcadia*, in order to test its reception, both from the perspective of changing critical reactions and the shifting interpretations the play has received within the academic community. Gobert rightly uses his article to champion textual criticism based on the various versions of the play as they have been altered by Stoppard.

Samuel Beckett's theatre work continues to be explored in several highly detailed articles. Paul Lawley's 'Krapp at the Hawk's Well: Beckett, Yeats and Joyce' (*MD* 58:iii[2015] 370–90) is a comparative close reading based on thematic and biographical similarities between the work of Joyce and Yeats. Here, *Krapp's Last Tape* [1958] is held up for comparison with Yeats's Noh-inspired *At the Hawk's Well* [1917], a play that Beckett much admired. Pim

Verhulst's '"There are differences": Variants and Errors in the Texts of Beckett's Radio Plays' (*JBeckS* 24:i[2015] 57–74) highlights in great detail published textual variants in English of all of Beckett's wireless dramas. Elaine Wood's 'Cript Sexuality in *Happy Days*' (*JBeckS* 24:ii[2015] 210–22) is a more discursive piece that discusses the body of Winnie, the hapless female protagonist of *Happy Days* [1961]. Wood concentrates on Winnie's snatches of song throughout the play, arguing that it might be read to disperse pleasure throughout [her] body' (p. 211). Wood argues that this access to pleasure is important within a drama that seems to focus itself on discomfort and imprisonment of the body. Wood also sees Winnie's body as disabled, and yet able to experience pleasure and desire, by employing Robert McRurer and Michael Berube's 'crip theory' in her analysis. The same issue also contains an interview with the director Natalie Abrahami (*JBeckS* 24:ii[2015] 247–58), who discusses her 2005 production of *Play* [1963] and *Not I* [1972] at the Battersea Arts Centre in London and her production of *Happy Days* with Juliet Stephenson at London's Young Vic in 2014. In a wide-ranging conversation, Abrahami discusses her methods of preparation for rehearsals and approach to the text, which she likens to a score (p. 248) and a map (p. 250). Abrahami also talks about interpreting *Happy Days* as a play that has resonance in terms of how it can be interpreted as a commentary about climate change (p. 256).

Simon Stephens's work continues to attract attention. Seda Ilter's 'Rethinking Play Texts in the Age of Medialization: Simon Stephens's *Pornography*' (*MD* 58:ii[2015] 238–62) considers how Stephens's play utilizes new technologies in what she describes as 'mediatized dramaturgy' based on an understanding of 'how a play is affected by the media and the culture it generates rather than ... what theatrical dramaturgies are deployed and how they incorporate technology into performance' (p. 240). In terms of Stephens's *Pornography* [2007], Ilter considers how these technologies impinge on the consciousness of characters set against the background of a surveillance culture at the time of the 7/7 bombings in London. The article also discusses recent productions of the play in the UK and Germany.

The treatment and interpretation of history has also been the subject of several articles. Ian Brown and Sim Innes's 'Parody, Satire and Intertextuality in the Songs of *The Cheviot, the Stag and the Black Black Oil*' (*STP* 35:ii[2015] 204–20) considers the use of music in John McGrath's landmark play. The authors show this to be a subversive exercise in taking popular and sentimental ballads, such as 'These Are My Mountains', and giving them a different, politicized, meaning through their incorporation within the play. The article also considers how McGrath manipulated historical sources for the purposes of a play that focuses around the Highland Clearances and the discovery of offshore oil, by pointing out that they took place in different geographical locations (p. 215). Amelia Howe Kritzer's 'Women and Historical Agency in Contemporary British Plays' (*JCDE* 3:i[2015] 127–41) considers the 2010 series of plays at the Tricycle Theatre in London, *Women, Power and Politics*, and the ways in which the dramatists in this project used the history play to explore resistance to society's exclusion on the basis of gender. Vicky Angelaki's 'From History to "Ourstories" in Martin Crimp's Metanarratives' (*JCDE*

3:i[2015] 142–55) considers the dramatist's work with respect to his use of classical texts in plays such as *Cruel and Tender* [2004] (an adaptation of Sophocles' *Trachiniae*). For Angelaki, this produces what she sees as the coexistence of the past and the present. In the same volume, Mark Ravenhill discusses the use of history in his work in an interview, 'Locating History on the Contemporary Stage' (*JCDE* 3:i[2015] 156–73).

Markus Wessendorf's 'David Greig's *The American Pilot* and Earlier Dramatizations of Political Hostage Takers' (*JCDE* 3:i[2015] 93–109) considers the lure of hostage-taking as a dramatic scenario in dramas that focus on terrorism. Wessendorf considers Greig's play in the light of a tradition stretching back to Brendan Behan's *The Hostage* [1958] and Christopher Hampton's *Savages* [1974]. But his main focus is *The American Pilot* [2005] and how Greig relates the pilot's rescue (in an unnamed country that closely resembles Afghanistan), to one of America's foundational myths: the rescue of Pocahontas by John Smith. In the same volume, Janina Wirzoch's 'Time and Temporalities in Contemporary British War Plays—Roy Williams' *Days of Significance* and Owen Sheer's *The Two Worlds of Charlie F*' (*JCDE* 3:i[2015] 110–26) explores two plays that have addressed conflicts in Afghanistan and Iraq, where personal narratives and history are shown to intersect.

Aleks Sierz provides a useful round-up and critique of new drama in his annual review of 'New Writing in the UK in 2014' (*CTR* 25:i[2015] 135–49), noting the preponderance of plays such as Tim Price's *The Internet is Serious Business* [2014], Alecky Blythe's *Little Revolution* [2014], and Duncan Macmillan and Chris Rapley's 2071 [2014], which he perceptively terms 'soft socialism', in which 'the radical gesture is more important than any radical content' (p. 136). He also expresses concerns over the Royal Court's artistic policy under Vicky Featherstone, which has seen its new writing disrupted by stage adaptations such as *Let the Right One In* [2014] and *The Mistress Contract* [2014]. Sierz complements this review in a later edition of the same journal with 'New Writing in the UK 2015: A Mid-Year Overview' (*CTR* 25:iv[2015] 590–9), where he is similarly pessimistic, despite adding his praise, like many others, to Alistair McDowall's *Pomona* [2014] and Alice Birch's *Little Light* [2015] and *We Want You To Watch* [2015].

## 6. Poetry

### (a) 1900–1950

Increasing scholarly attention to the work of Edward Thomas continued in 2015 with Jean Moorcroft Wilson's new biography of the poet, *From Adlestrop to Arras*. Following Wilson's biographies of Siegfried Sassoon, Isaac Rosenberg, and Charles Hamilton Sorley, this book begins by arguing for Thomas's modern sensibility, one 'in tune with our twenty-first century outlook' (pp. 1–2), and proceeds on the basis that his work still deserves wider recognition and greater understanding. Among the reasons offered for the relative neglect of his work is a lack of consensus regarding how best to place him, since categories such as 'Georgian', 'pastoral', or 'war poet' serve to obfuscate as much as to clarify. Similarly, as Wilson aptly notes, myths surrounding Thomas's personal life and the circumstances of his death inevitably threaten to obscure his worth as a writer. Indeed, Wilson argues that it is distortions around Thomas's character which most urgently give rise to the need for a new biography; in particular, the construction of the terminally fragile tortured genius, sensitive to a fault and 'almost permanently depressed' (p. 6). She rightly points out that a fuller understanding of Thomas's complex character is integral to any true appreciation of his work. That said, there are times when the book (perhaps inevitably) seems to underline the very myths it purports to challenge, and certainly the poet's proneness to depression is a recurrent presence. As is made clear, however, such traits should be understood in the context of the material and circumstantial difficulties Thomas was obliged to face.

One of the facets of Thomas's character which comes through strongly, especially in the earlier sections of the book, is his capacity for forming friendships, including with Gordon Bottomley (who affectionately called him 'Edward the Confessor', p. 113), Walter de la Mare, and Eleanor Farjeon, among others. The account of Thomas's best-known friendship, with Robert Frost, is prefaced by a warning against giving the relationship more than due prominence: Wilson suggests that Thomas's shift to poetry was already under way and would have occurred without Frost's intervention. Yet the affinity between the two is never in doubt. The transition from writing prose to poetry is sensitively covered, giving a strong sense of the developing marriage of sensibility and remarkable poetic ability which ultimately emerged. Wilson astutely observes that it is Thomas's 'naturalist's eye and poet's ear which distinguish him most sharply, his interest in the smaller details' (p. 228). More generally, she is adept at focusing attention on those features of Thomas's work which mark him out as a distinct and influential voice within the modern canon. Certainly there is much here to incline the reader towards visiting Thomas's work anew; surely one of the principal aims of any such book.

Further work on Thomas is found in David Farrier's 'Reading Edward Thomas in the Anthropocene' (*GLetters* 18:ii[2014] 132–42), which was unavailable at the time of writing last year. Noting that he was 'well versed in paying attention to the ground beneath him', this article offers Thomas as an early eco-poet, arguing that the 'uncanny landscapes of Thomas's poetry and prose can be read as anterior echoes of the darker inflections of contemporary ecological thinking' (pp. 134–5). Thus, to the extent that Thomas's work (in exhibiting traits and effects which might previously have been described as pastoral) manifests an 'acute sense of ecological history', it is situated against one of the more recent and still burgeoning areas of modern critical enquiry (p. 135).

Moving on to modernist studies, Henry Mead's *T.E. Hulme and the Ideological Politics of Early Modernism* is a further addition to the Historicizing Modernism series. Ultimately aiming at an expanded definition and understanding of modernism (and thus aligning itself with much recent work), the author sets out by asking which of modernism's ideological components 'might be salvageable as part of a liberal democratic tradition'

(p. 1). The study aims at refining received notions of the modernist canon as typically affiliated with right-wing politics, instead emphasizing an earlier stage of 'modernist anarchism', and exploring the project's affinities with radical individualism. Far from being proto-fascist, Hulme is positioned in conjunction with such figures as *New Age* editor Alfred Richard Orage as exemplifying 'a distinctive modernist synthesis of left-and right-wing ideology' (p. 4). Indeed, Mead proposes that Hulme's relationship with Orage requires a study of its own as a notable element of the modernist project, reflecting larger patterns of collaboration between the radical left and right across Europe. Divided into five chapters, the book first covers Hulme's 1906–7 notebooks and his 1908 'Lecture on Modern Poetry', showing his disillusion with philosophical systems and early, complicated engagement with the 'ancient problem of universals' (p. 26). This is turn is linked to the development both of Hulme's aesthetic and his political ideas. Chapter 2 analyses Hulme's relation to the radical socialist journal *New Age*, and in particular the perhaps unlikely convergence between the latter's conservative tendency and Orage's vitalist politics. The starting point of chapter 3 is Hulme's famous lecture of 1912, 'Romanticism and Classicism', taking up again the conservative traits in Hulme's work in relation to his interest in the French neo-royalist group Action française. Chapter 4 addresses Hulme's interest in the visual arts from 1911 onwards, pointing to how this interest stemmed 'from the same preoccupations as his philosophical and literary writings' (p. 140). Hulme is seen to have adopted an (arguably) unlikely pragmatic stance, favouring an art which 'reflected a desire for absolutes while keeping in view the troublingly messy sensory realm that was its spur' (p. 141). Mead's final chapter maps the continued evolution of Hulme's thought against the backdrop of the First World War, the experience of which served to make tangible ideas previously approached only in the abstract. Following on from Oliver Tearle's valuable study of 2013, this is a thorough and well-argued account which represents an undoubtedly useful further step on the ongoing reappraisal of Hulme's contribution to the modernist project.

Mark Jacobs's 'Contemporary Misogyny: Laura Riding, William Empson and the Critics: A Survey of Mis-History' (*English* 64:ccxlvi[2015] 222–40) takes as its topic the complicity of Empson himself, and subsequent critics and reviewers (singling out John Haffenden's biography of Empson as especially indicative) in the overlooking of Laura Riding's co-authorship (with Robert Graves) of *A Survey of Modernist Poetry* [1927]. This, the author argues, has had the effect of misdirecting understanding of the book, and consequently the critical assumptions which have since followed from it. The article points to the fact that Empson's acknowledgement of *Modernist Poetry*'s examination of Shakespeare's Sonnet 129 in *Seven Types of Ambiguity* [1930] (which in turn was significant in the development of New Criticism) omits Laura Riding as the first-named author. It is essentially argued that such an omission is less peripheral in its effects than might be assumed, having caused scholars to look to Robert Graves alone in furtherance of their understanding of the themes and critical methodology of both books.

Thomas Hardy's influence on the war poets (in particular Sassoon and Owen) is the subject of Oindrila Ghosh's ' "Quaint and curious war is": Hardy

and the Poets of the First World War' (*THJ* 31[2015] 130–9). While
acknowledging Hardy's reliance on second-hand experience of war, Ghosh
persuasively argues for a 'complex and ambivalent response to the Great War'
on Hardy's part (p. 139). Attention is drawn to the alternations in Hardy's war
poetry between optimism, dark humour, and irony, which are presented as
anticipating the treatment in, for example, Owen's 'Strange Meeting', of the
inexorable inhumanity latent in war. The author shows how the publication of
*Satires of Circumstance* [1914] and *Moments of Vision* [1917] supplied the war
poets with a model for expressing their own sense of moral disillusionment.

Robert Magella's 'Rupert Brooke and Isaac Rosenberg: Myth, Modernity,
and the Destabilization of "Georgian War Poetry" ' (*WarL&A* 27[2015] 55–86)
takes as its starting point the marginalization of non-modernist literatures of
the period, in particular Georgian war poetry as distinct from pre-war
Georgian poetry. The essay focuses its attention on two poets: Rupert Brooke
and Isaac Rosenberg, taking them in turn. While Brooke's death is posited as
'the first literary milestone of the First World War' (p. 59), arguing that its
manner and timing have been unfairly factored into the appraisal of his work,
Rosenberg's poetry, the author contends, represented a clear break with the
formal conservatism of the Georgians.

Also of relevance here is Sarah Montin's ' "Not flowers for poet's tearful
foolings": First World War Poetry, Flowers and the Pastoral Failure'
(*WarL&A* 27[2015] 1–14). Starting from Paul Fussell's classic, *The Great
War and Modern Memory* [1975], Montin suggests that the experience of the
First World War, in generating a need for escape and re-enchantment, could
be said to have encouraged a revival of the pastoral tradition in English
poetry. While the war poets' use of the pastoral permitted a symbolic, textual
escape, Montin argues, the contradictions inherent in 'holding war and
pastoral in the same frame' (p. 2) did not in the end permit any sustainable
sense of refuge or consolation. Rather, it is argued that the war pastoral
'generally demonstrates an incapacity for symbolic and formal closure' (p. 10).

George M. Johnson's *Mourning and Mysticism in First World Literature and
Beyond* contains two chapters of relevance to this section: entitled 'E.W.H.
Myers: Loss and the Obsessive Study of Survival' (pp. 28–59), chapter 1
follows a strongly biographical, slightly speculative thread, the main thrust of
which is that Myers responded to the traumatic emotional events of his youth
(in particular the death of the love of his life, Annie Marshall) by embarking
on an 'obsessional quest to prove that human personality survived bodily
death' (p. 39). The ensuing psychical research, the author argues, played an
important role for the Edwardians and emerging modernists, particularly in
the context of finding a means of coping with the mass trauma of war loss.
Chapter 6 is entitled 'Purgatorial Passions: "The Ghost" (aka Wilfred Owen)
in Owen's Poetry' (pp. 187–200), and assesses the implications of Owen's
sexual orientation and the 'homoerotic sensibility' of poems such as 'Strange
Meeting'. Johnson identifies here a 'ghostly other' (p. 189), which he argues
serves as a covert expression by Owen of a homosexual self which could not be
expressed openly. Also discussed is the significant role played by Owen's
mother, with reference to object relations theory. Johnson argues that poetry
itself was for Owen a 'transitional object', a means by which he might 'express

those passions and other unacceptable feelings that could not be acted upon' (p. 192). Overall, while the originality of this approach seems clear, the imaginative scene-setting at the beginning of these and other chapters is among those aspects of the book that demand some degree of indulgence from the reader keen to get to the essence of what is being argued.

New work on Owen also appeared in Christina Laubenthal's 'Wilfred Owen's Onomatopoeic Critique of War' (*Expl* 73:iii[2015] 163–7), which sets itself at the audiolinguistic dimensions of Owen's work. Citing Derek Attridge's claim that poetry has 'the capacity to heal the breach between signified and signifier' Laubenthal ably and aptly focuses attention on the ways in which Owen's poetry persistently uses onomatopoeia in order to bring his audience closer to an 'experiential understanding' of war from the soldier's perspective, intensifying reader involvement through the elimination of the narrator (p. 163).

Amongst the essays in A.G.G. Gibson's edited collection, *Robert Graves and the Classical Tradition*, John Burnside's interesting discussion of Graves's love poems (pp. 221–32) focuses on the poet's explorations of the relationship between love and selfhood. Citing Graves's retelling of the Narcissus myth, the essay argues that his earlier poetry is preoccupied with the potential loss of self through 'needy attachment'; that is, by 'the threat to selfhood occasioned by sexual and/or romantic love in its debased forms' (p. 222). Meanwhile, Tom Palaima's essay, 'Robert Graves at Troy, Marathon, and the End of Sandy Road' (pp. 233–54) also takes Graves's poetry as its subject, but follows a different line. Among the points considered is the question of why only a few of the poems have clear classical themes, given the poet's extensive work in the classics elsewhere (though this may of course be the reason). The author nonetheless notes how Graves the war poet keeps his own feelings at a remove, in contrast to, say, Sassoon and Owen. Suggesting some distaste on Graves's part at the vicarious experience which certain war poems might be seen to supply, Palaima's somewhat discursive account offers the former's response as marked, rather, by an ironically couched rhetorical distancing. These essays, together with others in this volume, represent a worthwhile contribution to an important and familiar, yet still unsettled, aspect of Graves's contribution to twentieth-century literature.

New work on A.E. Housman appeared in the form of Jasmine Jagger's 'Tongue-Tied and Contorting: The Comic Body in A.E. Housman' (*LitI* 17:iii[2015] 311–26). Noting the prevalent focus on the 'emotional darkness' surrounding the poet's work, Jagger seeks instead to draw attention to a more complex sensibility than is allowed for amidst more familiar constructions of Housman the terminal melancholic. Broadly centred upon the function of humour within Housman's work, this essay includes a number of close readings from the selection of hitherto neglected light verses published in the poet's brother's memoir. Written for close family and friends, these reveal an unfamiliar side to Housman's character, featuring as a principal trope the exploitation of the body for comic effect. This, in turn, is linked to Housman's statement on the physicality of poetic language. Jagger aptly touches upon Bergson's *Laughter* [1900] and the argument that poetry is 'not the thing said but a *way* of saying it'. Overall this is a welcome consideration of a clearly under-remarked aspect of Housman and his work.

New work on W.H. Auden appeared in Jacek Partyka's 'The Double Man: W.H. Auden's Transatlantic Transformation' (*TextM* 5:v[2015] 129–47), which revisits the relatively familiar territory of the implications of Auden's infamous departure for the United States in 1939. Invoking works including 'The Sea and the Mirror' and the 'An Elegy for W.B. Yeats', Partyka argues that the poet's 'American adventure' was less the ideological volte-face it has often been cast as than a further stage in the poet's ongoing personal and poetic evolution. In essentially arguing (correctly) that Auden's earlier work had contexts other than the international political situation of the time, it is not, however, entirely apparent where the newness of insight lies.

Collected under the editorship of Bonnie Costello and Rachel Galvin, *Auden at Work* aims to attend more closely to Auden's writing and artistic practices, and in particular the restless revision of his work at every stage of his career. The collection begins with a consideration by Hannah Sullivan of Auden's compositional habits (pp. 5–23). Looking to dispel the notion that Auden's aversion to the typewriter was mere technophobia, Sullivan seeks instead to present it as a more complex aesthetic decision, linked to his interest in 'certain kinds of involuted syntax, to retroactive, revisionary temporal structures, and to a mastery of traditional forms' (p. 16). Rachel Galvin's contribution (pp. 24–48) focuses on Auden's 1939 journal, which came to light only in 2013, having been acquired by the British Library from a private owner. As Galvin notes, foremost among the anxieties expressed in the journal is that over 'making art in a time of war' (p. 34), and the consequent search to define the role of the civilian writer in wartime conditions. Evan Kindley attends to Auden's preface to *Oxford Poetry* 1926 and *The Orators* as expressive of his preoccupation with the English educational system (pp. 216–30), while Michael Wood's 'Shakespeare's Auden' (pp. 179–90) takes as its point of departure the 'small car-crash' of quotations from Shakespeare in 'The Sea and the Mirror'. Jonathan Foltz's essay 'Vehicles of the Ordinary: W.H. Auden and Cinematic Address' (pp. 49–68), offers a useful discussion of Auden's documentary film work and its relationship to his poetry, while Claire Seiler revisits Auden's final long poem, *The Age of Anxiety*, in view of 'shadow text' *The Hidden Damage* (p. 252). The latter, published in 1947, is a travel book by Auden's friend, James Stern, covering his and Auden's service in the Morale Division of the United States Strategic Bombing Survey, which Auden had initially agreed to co-author. The poem is read in light of Auden's thinking, in a professional capacity, about bombing and its affective effects, such as can be inferred from Stern's account. Lastly, Tony Sharpe's '"No permission to be idle": W.H. Auden's Work Ethics' (pp. 275–93), invokes—among others—Yeats, Trollope, and Nijinsky as models for the poet's authorial pragmatism and purportedly 'workmanlike' approach to his craft. Overall, this worthwhile collection does much to illuminate the character of Auden's working practices and their implications for, and impact on, his work.

Unfortunately, *Thomas Hardy, Poet: New Perspectives*, edited by Adrian Grafe and Laurence Estanove, was not available at the time of writing.

*(b) T.S. Eliot*

The most significant event of 2015 for anyone interested in T.S. Eliot was the publication of his *Complete Poems* in two volumes edited by Christopher Ricks and Jim McCue. Unevenly distributed across two volumes, the first of these includes those poems Eliot chose to collect and publish in his lifetime, followed by uncollected material from drafts, manuscripts, and *Valerie Her Book*—a commonplace book Eliot prepared for his second wife, containing handwritten versions of his published poems and some previously unpublished poems. Volume 2 contains the *Practical Cats*, further uncollected verse derived largely from Eliot's correspondence, and coterie poems written for friends and acquaintance at Faber and Gwyer. This volume also includes a 'Textual History' providing an extensive and detailed collation of published texts and manuscripts relating to the poems across both volumes. It's clear from this that the establishment of the texts of Eliot's poems is an impressive feat of scholarship in its own right, but these volumes are also characterized by copious scholarly notes. In some respect these annotations are unusual: keen to preserve a neutral stance, the editors avoid imposing critical opinion by sticking to factual, rather than interpretative, statements and by supplying quotation from Eliot's own writings for context and comparison. The sheer extent of these quotations is what distinguishes these volumes from standard editorial practice, but it is also what makes them a joy to read. Moving back and forth between the poems and the notes is a journey through some of Eliot's most salient critical statements, as well as reflections upon his own practice. Public reaction to these volumes in the press has tended to focus upon previously unpublished erotic verses Eliot wrote to Valerie, but the editorial and scholarly achievement represented in this edition will have a longer-lasting impact upon our understanding and appreciation of Eliot's craft as a poet.

This was a bumper year for Eliot studies. In addition to the poems, two further volumes of his prose were published as part of the ongoing project under the general editorial supervision of Ronald Schuchard. The third volume, *Literature, Politics, Belief, 1927–1929*, edited by Frances Dickey and Jennifer Formichelli, and the fourth volume, *English Lion, 1930–1933*, edited by Jason Harding, chart Eliot's continuing public engagement into the 1930s as editor of the *Criterion* and the increasing prominence he assumed as an Anglo-Catholic. This public role saw him defending the right-wing French philosopher and activist Charles Maurras, espousing the poetry of Dante, and pronouncing upon the policies and doctrines of the Church through pamphlets such as *Thoughts After Lambert* [1931]. Elsewhere he explores the relationship between poetry and belief through critical tussles with I.A. Richards and John Middleton Murry, as well as his engagement with the humanism of Irving Babbitt. Of particular interest are Eliot's unsigned contributions to the *Times Literary Supplement* and his contributions to the *Criterion*, since many of these have not previously been collected. Eliot's close scrutiny of detective fiction in these articles, from contemporary potboilers to the origins of the genre in work by Wilkie Collins, Edgar Allan Poe, and others, has also attracted particular attention. Likewise, in documenting Eliot's radio broadcasts for the BBC during this period, the editors return to the typescripts submitted to the *Listener*, restoring passages excised by the magazine's editor.

Volume 4 documents Eliot's lecture tours in the United States during 1933, previously published as *The Use of Poetry and the Use of Criticism* and incorporated into Schuchard's *Varieties of Metaphysical Poetry* [1996]. The editors also attempt to reconstruct some of Eliot's other American lectures from this period on the basis of newspaper reports and other accounts from those present. Such composite texts enjoy a dubious, secondary authority, but they do provide insights into Eliot's views on the poetry of Edward Lear (amongst other topics) to which we would otherwise lack access of any kind. As with the first two volumes in this series, Schuchard's team are assiduous in their annotations and bibliographical scholarship.

A third welcome contribution to textual scholarship on Eliot's work is the latest volume in the ongoing edition of *The Letters of T.S. Eliot*. Under the editorship of John Haffenden, Volume 5 covers the years 1930 and 1931. A preface details the contribution made by Valerie Eliot (who died in 2012) to this edition, describing her extensive efforts to track down letters and notes written by the poet. The end result is a volume of over 800 pages that covers only two years of his life. The impulse towards bibliographical completeness is understandable in relation to a writer of Eliot's stature and influence, but this book contains both Eliot's correspondence with the archbishop of Canterbury and the poet's tax returns. There *are* letters of literary, biographical, and bibliographical interest here in relation to Eliot's life and work, but its real value lies in the abundance of its accompanying notes and biographical sketches. Even seemingly trivial material helps form this volume's fascinating gateway into the world of publishing and letters during the 1930s. It constitutes an important act of recovery extending beyond Eliot's career to a host of his contemporaries, from publishers to poets, to scholars and figures from the religious establishment.

One problem for Eliot's biographers has been his repeated insistence that poetry is 'impersonal', that the poet's own emotions and experience are not the end point of a literary work, but a point of departure—the material with which he or she works. Robert Crawford's *Young Eliot: From St Louis to The Wasteland* negotiates this cautiously, generally resisting the temptation to read Eliot's poems biographically, but also making repeated and insistent biographical connections. Crawford is similarly cautious about other poten-tially contentious aspects of the poet's life, exercising both tact and a sensible refusal to gloss over matters in relation to Eliot's sexuality and his wife's adultery. Crawford's insistence on referring intimately to Eliot as 'Tom' throughout is cloying, but the strength of this biography lies in the sheer depth of detail with which it probes Eliot's most seemingly casual reading encounters to find material of potential relevance. *Young Eliot* stops at the publication of *The Waste Land*, but another volume is anticipated. Flawed in some places, this is now by far and away the best of currently available biographies of Eliot.

Turning to academic criticism of Eliot's work, 'The Beauties of T.S. Eliot', Seamus Perry's contribution to Michael O'Neill, Mark Sandy and Sarah Wootton's volume, *The Persistence of Beauty* (pp. 59–70), examines with great insight not only those occasions when Eliot uses the term 'beauty' in his critical writings, but also his general aversion to the concept as tainted by its association with the Impressionist criticism of Arthur Symons and Walter Pater. Eliot's reconciliation with this word, Perry argues convincingly, comes through the location of the beautiful and the poetic within a sense of some fuller dramatic situation.

Gabrielle McIntire's collection of essays, *The Cambridge Companion to The Waste Land* is unusual, but not exceptional within the Cambridge Companions series since it focuses upon one seminal text rather than a broader topic, period, or oeuvre. There is no doubt that a poem like *The Waste Land* can bear the weight of scrutiny, but the collection feels a little stretched in places, and its claim to present 'the most current lenses of critical thinking' (p. 4) does not always seem justified.

Jean-Michel Rabaté's contribution on the First World War (pp. ??) ranges widely and deploys an unusual form, close to bullet points in places, in order to outline parallels between Eliot's personal experiences and broader events in Europe. Rabaté draws upon Eliot's reading in Dostoevsky in order to identify a 'double unreality' (p. 18) in *The Waste Land*, juxtaposing the domestic unreality of Eliot's marriage to Vivien—her infidelity with Bertrand Russell and the demands of her mental illness—with the effects of war on the Continent. Spencer Morrison's essay on the geography of *The Waste Land* (pp. ??) explores the tension between Eliot's sense of a present crisis in London and the cycles of imperial history. Morrison draws upon theories of urban experience in the work of Michel de Certeau and Henri Lefebvre. He examines the concept of the 'ruin' in particular, mapping tensions between public and personal histories within the phrase '*my* ruins' (p. 30; emphasis added) in the final section of the poem. A ruin, Morrison suggests, may paradoxically be the site for rebuilding as well as a place of devastation. In this way, the poem moves between social collapse and the assertion of 'governance' (p. 35).

Drawing upon her experience as Eliot's biographer, Lyndall Gordon attempts to read *The Waste Land* as 'rooted' in 'personal issues and preoccupations' (p. 39), although she struggles to reconcile the obscenity, misogyny, racism, and levity of Eliot's contemporary 'Bolo' verses with her sense of his serious purposes in *The Waste Land*. Barry Spurr reads *The Waste Land* in terms of its religious implications, warning against dividing Eliot's career too strongly around the watershed of his public conversion to Anglo-Catholicism in the 1920s after the completion of *The Waste Land*. Spurr finds the notion of a quest or journey more attractive, propounding a sense of Eliot's 'protracted struggle to attain meaning' (p. 55) in *The Waste Land* as representative of concerns similar to his later, explicitly Christian, poetry. He acknowledges Eliot's interest in Buddhist and Hindu religion, but connects Eliot to Anglican theology.

David Chinitz and Julia Daniel revisit Chinitz's previous work on Eliot and 'popular culture' to explore the productive 'engagement' (p. 71) with various popular forms in *The Waste Land*, from jazz and cars to contemporary perfumes. Jewel Spears Brooker offers a summary of the composition of *The Waste Land* through the manuscripts, describing Ezra Pound's role in editing them and the interventions of Eliot's first wife, Vivien.

Michael Levenson's essay on 'voice' in *The Waste Land* offers the most protracted and detailed engagement with the form and technical achievement of the poem. Levenson explores phasal shifts within the voicing of each section of the poem, identifying 'a tonal rhythm that repeatedly passes from gnomic generality to ardent utterance' (p. 89). His reading turns upon the tensions in Eliot's poem between forms of impersonal speech (such as allusion) and situated utterance. Michael Coyle reads Eliot's allusive practice in *The Waste Land* in terms of 'pastiche', and argues that the poem played a role in subsequent debate between Fredric Jameson and Linda Hutcheon about the nature and value of 'pastiche' in relation to 'parody'. Coyle sees Eliot's use of pastiche as part of his relationship with previous literary history. By this means, *The Waste Land* measures both continuity and separation from its precursors.

As part of the collection's attempt to engage with recent approaches to Eliot, it concludes with four essays that read *The Waste Land* through 'critical and theoretical approaches'. Rachel Potter explores the place of gender and obscenity in *The Waste Land*, arguing that Eliot 'tethers female physicality to the obscene' (p. 135), drawing upon details that Eliot (or Pound) excised from manuscript drafts of the poem. Although Potter is concerned that Eliot conflates different female characters within *The Waste Land*, she concludes the essay by affirming a sense of shared physicality between the women in the poem as a site of potential resistance to official forms of censorship. Richard Badenhausen proposes an analysis of Eliot's poem in terms of contemporary trauma theory, drawing in particular upon work by Sara Cole on the links between modernism and trauma. The figure of Tiresias lies at the heart of this essay, as Badenhausen explores the degree to which he witnesses or suffers traumatizing experiences within the poem. He reads 'Death by Water' as a failed elegy, and suggests that *The Waste Land* is sanguine about the possibility of recovering from the traumatic after-effects of the First World War. Eve Sorum reads the poem in terms of 'Psychology, Psychoanalysis and New Subjectivities'. Citing Eliot's reading of F.H. Bradley on the nature of experience and his own experiences of psychoanalytic treatment at the hands of Roger Vittoz, Sorum explores polyphony in *The Waste Land* and the failure of various attempts at empathy by characters within the poem.

Finally, McIntire supplies an essay on 'ecocritique' in *The Waste Land*. The premise—that Eliot expresses his sense of broader collapse through devastated landscapes and oppressive cityscapes—is promising. McIntire notes the 'compromised environmental exteriors and a complex range of similarly polluted interior states' within the poem (p. 178). This sounds a bit like what Ruskin called the 'pathetic fallacy', and the essay's attempt to present Eliot as an eco-poet sounds inconclusive at some points ('I begin to wonder', p. 190). The whole volume is capped by Anthony Cuda's descriptive summary of critical responses to *The Waste Land* since its publication. Although it contains little critical comment, this survey is probably a more useful and direct guide for students than some of the essays in the collection.

Scott Freer's monograph, *Modernist Mythopoeia* includes a chapter on Eliot's attitude towards myth in *The Waste Land* (pp. 45–77). This occupies an important position within Freer's larger argument that 'modernist mythopoeia is a continuation of a metaphorical theology that rejected logo-centrism and regarded spiritual truth as poetic or metaphoric by nature' (p. 8), since Eliot's avowal of Anglo-Catholicism in the 1920s would seem to complicate or contradict this. Indeed, Freer argues, Eliot saw myth as 'a defunct moral base' (p. 51) even while he was drawn to classical sources, because he was 'aware that deep layers of human impulses were played out in the classics' (p. 50). The 'underlying purpose' of *The Waste Land*, Freer claims, was 'to induce the reader to make a choice between the non-redemptive aesthetic way of myth or the redeeming agency of Christian faith' (p. 45).

Paved with good intentions, *Reading 'The Waste Land' from the Bottom Up* by Allyson Booth is not quite a work of annotation, but nevertheless aims to provide information for first-time students and readers of *The Waste Land* that will ease the difficulties they may experience in negotiating its different languages and points of cultural reference. After two general sections on the First World War and Eliot's use of comparative anthropological work by Jessie Weston and James Frazer, the body of Booth's book is structured around explicating the allusive cues provided by Eliot in his notes to *The Waste Land* in short sections of three or four pages. At its best, *Reading 'The Waste Land' from the Bottom Up* takes Eliot's sources seriously, probing the textual and dramatic contexts that inform Eliot's allusive practice. Elsewhere, it is over-familiar in its choice of language and simile; and it is tantalizing— there's an argument here about the play of similarity and difference running through *The Waste Land* that never quite coalesces.

Amongst the essays in Alex Davis and Lee Jenkins's extensive edited collection, *A History of Modernist Poetry*, Miranda Hickman provides a brusque survey of 'early' Eliot, alongside H.D. and Ezra Pound (pp. 186–203), focused upon the poems in *Prufrock and Other Observations*. Davis and Jenkins's own contribution summarizes Pound and Eliot in the 1920s and 1930s (pp. 303–23). These useful introductory essays tend to cover familiar ground, but provide a good starting point for students of modernism.

Derived in part from a conference of the T.S. Eliot Society held in Paris in 2011, *T.S. Eliot, France and the Mind of Europe*, edited by Jayme Stayer, aims to re-examine Eliot's engagement with French poetry and philosophical thought and the implications of his understanding of Europe. Charlotte Webb's essay on Eliot and 'hyper-consciousness' (pp. ??) seeks to show how the poet's work 'seems to anticipate' (p. 40) the findings of the psychologists Louis Sass and Iain McGilchrist. Webb rereads early poems, including 'The Love Song of J. Alfred Prufrock', 'Hysteria', and 'Rhapsody on a Windy Night', and emphasizes the degree to which speakers are shown to be 'absorbed in the winding labyrinths of their own thought' (p. 43). Jean-Michel Rabaté (pp. ??) ranges across the work of Mallarmé, Edouard Dujardin, Charles-Louis Philippe, André Gide and Proust, amongst others, in order to provide 'a French context for Eliot's sense of a homology between his personal death and the collective death entailed by the idea of tradition' (p. 3). Elizabeth Däumer (pp. ??) traces the influence upon Eliot of Jean Epstein's 'physiological theory of literature' in terms of a 'neuropathic aristocracy' (p. 115). Whilst their understandings of 'sensibility' do not quite mesh, Däumer establishes connections between Epstein's work and Eliot's 'conflicted, fascinated, revolted' (p. 123) treatment of the relationship between modern technology and feeling in his poetry.

Many of these contributions focus upon the year that Eliot spent in Paris in 1910 after graduating from Harvard. Nancy Hargrove revisits her monograph *T.S. Eliot's Parisian Year* [2009] (pp. ??), offering a general survey of the 'Parisian influences' upon 'The Lovesong of J. Alfred Prufrock' from contemporary fashions to *The Martyrdom of Saint Sebastian* by Gabriele D'Annunzio, which was performed at the Théâtre du Châtelet in May 1911. Jayme Stayer (pp. ??) reconstructs Eliot's initial 'culture shock' upon his arrival in Paris and before he had acquired any fluency in French. This experience, Stayer argues, reverberates through a series of audiences that are imagined as uncomprehending in Eliot's early poetry. Jennifer Kilgore-Caradec (pp. ??) suggests that Eliot's awareness of Charles Péguy dates from his Parisian sojourn, through his contact with Henri-Alain Fournier. She then charts allusions to Péguy and connections to his work through Eliot's subsequent career as a critic and poet. Benjamin Lockerd's contribution on 'Eliot's Critique of Evolutionary History' (pp. ??) updates an article on the same topic from 2012, arguing that Eliot aligned himself with Catholic historiography of Christopher Dawson and Hilaire Belloc, against the 'pseudo-scientific historiography and the progressivism' of Herbert Spencer and H.G. Wells. Whilst Lockerd's argument mostly concerns Eliot's writings from the 1930s, he traces this position back to Eliot's Parisian encounter with Bergson and the French philosopher's critique of Spencer.

In her contribution, Jewel Spears Brooker (pp. ??) re-examines Eliot's 'temporary conversion to Bergsonism' during his visit to Paris in 1909 (p. 24). This essay covers very similar ground here to Brooker's article, 'Eliot and Bergson: "Rhapsody on a Windy Night" and the Intractability of Dualism' (*PAns* 13:i[2015] 1–17), which provides a cogent summary of Eliot's engagement with the French philosopher, from attendance at lectures by Bergson to his influence upon Eliot's early poem 'Rhapsody on a Windy Night' and the philosophical papers Eliot wrote upon his return to Harvard. Condensing Bergson's philosophy into his claim to have reconciled binary pairings such as body and mind by subsuming the quantitative into the qualitative, Brooker reads this into the problematic self-splitting dialogue form of 'Rhapsody'. He may have rejected Bergson's philosophy, but Eliot's 'longing to transcend dualism', Brooker concludes, remained 'a significant factor' in his 'creative and spiritual life' (p. 16).

Returning to *The Mind of Europe*, other contributors place Eliot's work in broader, although not exclusively European, contexts. Thus Joyce Wexler (pp. ??) charts Eliot's fascination with nineteenth-century French Symbolism as it transformed into an aesthetic she sees as holding stronger affinities with the expressionism of Kurt Pinthus and Gottfried Benn, amongst others. William Blissett (pp. ??) traces the elemental presence of wind and air across Eliot's poetic oeuvre, drawing connections and comparisons with the work of Gaston Bachelard at the close of his contribution. Although Michael Webster claims 'to restore Eliot to a Cummings-context (and vice versa)' (p. 76), his contribution (pp. ??) largely charts echoes of Eliot's form and technique in the poetry of e.e. cummings, taking in the mutual suspicions tempered by the occasional entente between the two poets on the way. Tomislav Brlek's contribution, 'Eliot and Theory' (pp. ??), does not so much justify reading Eliot's work through the lens of subsequent literary theory as urge Eliot's own qualifications as a theoretical thinker in his criticism. In his defence of Eliot, Brlek highlights misapprehensions of his work by Christopher Norris, Edward Said, and others.

Fabio Vericat (pp. ??) explores the impact of Eliot's experience as a radio broadcaster upon his poetry, arguing that it helped him 'to pinpoint legitimate poetic sounds by understanding writing as inherently performative as speech' (p. 171). Comparing Eliot's scripts with recordings of his broadcasts, Vericat suggests that his work on the radio provided Eliot with a more practical understanding of the 'auditory imagination'. Margery Palmer McCulloch (pp. ??) compares and contrasts Eliot's work with that of Edwin Muir, finding a point of contact in their mutual investment in European literature. Eliot recruited Muir to the *Criterion* for his writings on German literature and later wrote a preface to a posthumous edition of his *Selected Poems* [1965]. Despite this, McCulloch laments, Muir has yet to find recognition for his contribution to modern writing.

A.V.C. Schmidt devotes considerable space to Eliot in *Passion and Precision: Collected Essays on English Poetry from Geoffrey Chaucer to Geoffrey Hill*, which draws together previously published articles from the Oxford don's lengthy career as a scholar. Five essays on various aspects of Eliot's work, from his concern with linguistic precision to the influence of his conversion to Christianity upon his poetry and criticism, are republished here from journals such as *Essays in Criticism*, alongside five short notes on aspects of Eliot previously published in *Notes and Queries* (pp. 267–78). Elsewhere, in *T.S. Eliot and Spirituality*, Richard Brock offers a reading of *Four Quartets* that is 'an attempt to bring Eliot's poem down from its elevated place on the bookshelves of scholars and literary critics' (p. 3). This is a strongly personal account, anchored in Brock's own experience of 'spirituality' as well the themes and content of Eliot's poetry.

Within scholarly journals during 2015, 'Interpretation and Reality: Anthropological Hauntings in *The Waste Land*' (*Mo/Mo* 22:i[2015] 237–54) by Sheela Banerjee reads the figure of Tiresias in the light of Eliot's graduate writings on 'primitive religion', arguing that Eliot combines 'the traditional qualities of a literary ghost' with 'modern anthropological anxieties over questions of knowledge, truth, and interpretation' (p. 238). As a graduate, Eliot used the work of Lucien Lévy-Bruhl to probe the degree to which it was possible to access states of mind associated with other cultures and beliefs. Banerjee sees the ambivalence Eliot expressed in his philosophical enquiries as condensed into the attenuated experiences of Tiresias as they become fractured and split across various voices in Eliot's poem.

Anita Patterson's 'T.S. Eliot and Transpacific Modernism' (*AmLH* 27:iv[2015] 665–82) explores Eliot's 'concern with transpacific crossculturality' (p. 666). Centred upon his early, unpublished poem 'Mandarins', Patterson's essay traces Eliot's interest in neo-Confucian Buddhism, through the writings of Emerson and others and through personal contact in Boston with the art historian Kakuzo Okakura and the scholar of comparative religion Masaharu Anesaki. Patterson then outlines the place of Buddhist philosophies of indifference and detachment within later work, including *Coriolan, Murder in the Cathedral*, and *Four Quartets*. Connecting Eliot's interest in these questions to his formative intellectual experiences in Boston, 'a world city' and 'cosmopolitan centre' (pp. 678–9), Patterson posits 'transpacific dialogue' as a source of Eliot's power as a 'great and representative poet' (p. 679).

Margaret Greaves, 'The Spanish Copla in T.S. Eliot's "Landscapes"' (*JML* 37:iv[2014] 130–42), begins with Eliot's observation to a Spanish correspondent that 'Virginia' was indebted to the 'copla', a Spanish poetic form associated with expressions of love for a local landscape. Laying out other uses of this form by his contemporaries, Greaves reads all five of Eliot's 'Landscapes' as 'a cohesive sequence' characterized by 'the tensions between human desire and religious devotion' (p. 131). In this way, the landscape poems anticipate allusion to the Spanish mystics in *Four Quartets*.

Brian Cheadle's '*Four Quartets*: Structure and Surprise' (*CQ* 44:iii[2015] 233–50) takes the lapse of seventy years since the completions of *Four Quartets* as the occasion to review the poem's reception and explore Eliot's turn of thought. Weighing up objections from Orwell, Leavis, and Hill, Cheadle probes the language and form of *Four Quartets* for moments of pleasure.

A. Banerjee's 'T.S. Eliot and the *Criterion*' (*SR* 123:ii[2015] 231–40) uses the ongoing edition of Eliot's correspondence to retell the poet's experiences in setting up the *Criterion*. Largely biographical, this essay also covers Eliot's beginnings at Faber & Dwyer and the transition to the *New Criterion*. Banerjee traces the poet's distinguished career in publishing to his 'fortuitous' entry into journalism in 1916 (p. 240). Finally, no annual survey of scholarship on Eliot's work would be complete without the inclusion of a short work by G. Douglas Atkins, who has published at least one such volume with Palgrave every year since 2012. *Strategy and Purpose in T.S. Eliot's Major Poems* contains chapters on *The Waste Land, Ash Wednesday*, and *Four Quartets*.

## 7. British Poetry Post-1950

Heavily publicized and widely reviewed, Jonathan Bate's *Ted Hughes: The Unauthorised Life* provoked strong disagreements during 2015. Many of these centred on Bate's discussion of Hughes's sex life and, relatedly, his ' "sadistic" tendencies' (p. 438)—a word attributed to Sylvia Plath, which Bate quotes at second hand from the transcripts of a 1987 libel trial in which Hughes was the defendant. More fruitfully from a scholarly perspective, critical debate also focused on Bate's reading of Hughes's oeuvre. Such discussion drew attention to the wide range of credible disagreement that is possible about the true strengths of Hughes's poetry. At moments in Bate's biography, it seems as though all of Hughes's work is leading up to *Birthday Letters* [1998], the final, posthumously published book in which he speaks with 'unprecedented candour' (p. 11) about his marriage to Plath and her death, taken by Bate to be the most important event in his life. Yet for many scholars and readers of Hughes, the more important works are the early poems collected in *The Hawk in the Rain* [1957] and *Lupercal* [1960], in which Hughes invents his lyric voice with extraordinary gusto and clarity; or *Crow: From the Life and Songs of the Crow* [1970], in which the accomplishments of that voice are broken into a more jagged-edged rhetoric, as the urgency of the theme required. Others find volumes such as *Moortown* [1979] and *River* [1983] compelling, in which we find perhaps Hughes's most supple and alert nature writing, or *Tales from Ovid* [1997], his late masterpiece of creative translation. That each of these positions has been argued persuasively lends some conviction to Bate's treatment of Hughes as a figure with the stature of Wordsworth or Eliot (p. 555)—or indeed Shakespeare. Among all the discussion of *The Unauthorized Life*, it has not been emphasized enough how much new ground the book breaks in its archival research: the highlight here is Bate's extended discussion of the unpublished long poem 'Trial', dating from the 1980s (pp. 442–8).

*Ted Hughes's South Yorkshire: Made in Mexborough* by Steve Ely focuses on a very early period of Hughes's life (1938 to 1951) and reorients the focus on Hughes's early move away from Mytholmroyd, the Yorkshire town where he spent the first eight years of his life, and towards Mexborough, the Yorkshire town where he spent the next thirteen years. This may seem a rather slight difference, since the towns are only forty miles apart, but Ely's elegant study argues that it makes quite a lot of difference: Mexborough, in the coal and steel belt of the West Riding, becomes the site for Hughes's developing ecological awareness and literary consciousness, as well as the location for the grammar school which furthered him on the path towards Cambridge and the bright lights of the literary world. Ely is, as Hughes was, 'a Yorkshire poet from a coalfield background' (p. 7), and his highly rewarding and lucidly written book evinces a deep appreciation of Hughes's particular qualities and of how they were fostered by history and culture of the area.

Adding to the book-length studies by Bate and Ely in 2015 were two admirable articles on Hughes by Yvonne Reddick. The first, ' "Throttle College"? Ted Hughes's Cambridge Poetry' (*CQ* 44:iii[2015] 213–32), continues the recent scrutiny given to Hughes's own self-mythologizing about his undergraduate experience, and concludes that 'Hughes's time at Cambridge was certainly not a fallow period' (p. 231) in the process of his artistic and intellectual formation. The second, 'Icthyologue: Freshwater Biology in the Poetry of Ted Hughes' (*Isle* 22:ii[2015] 264–83), reframes the question of Hughes and nature by considering it in the light of his reading of scientific work in ecology, his interactions with his son Nicholas, a freshwater biologist, and his occasional deployment of scientific data and other technical content in his poetry.

Hughes is one of the subjects of William Wooten's *The Alvarez Generation: Thom Gunn, Geoffrey Hill, Ted Hughes, Sylvia Plath and Peter Porter*, which is stylishly described on its dustwrapper as 'the biography of a taste in poetry and its consequences'. Wooten's starting point is the Penguin anthology *The New Poetry* [1962], edited by A. Alvarez, which brought together the poets mentioned in Wooten's title along with four American confessional poets (Berryman, Lowell, Plath, Sexton), seemingly as a way of propagandizing on behalf of a poetry that would go 'beyond the gentility principle', in Alvarez's words, represented by the poets of the so-called Movement. The task is to reconstruct the intellectual biography of a cluster of associated ideas central to Alvarez's critical ambitions, which Sean O'Brien summarized in 1998 as 'nature-violence-the-Holocaust-psychic-crisis', while noting that some features of this 'emotional style' seem 'barely comprehensible' from today's perspective (p. x). Wooten does an excellent job of reconstruction, supported by careful research in the Penguin Books archive at Bristol University and other archives. His title may initially seem excessive: the fact of having been anthologized by A. Alvarez in 1962 has relatively little importance in the context of the lives and extensive oeuvres of the five poets treated. Yet Wooten persuasively shows that the anthology's 'timeliness and lack of timelessness give it a literary-historical importance a less period-bound anthology would not possess' (p. xiii). He shows how 'Alvarez's taste ... was to become a significant factor in the writing, publishing and reading of poetry throughout the 1960s and into the early 1970s' (p. xvi). He also convincingly argues for the afterlife of Alvarez's idea of psychic and stylistic 'extremity' in Hill's later work of the 1990s and early part of this century (pp. 193–8).

Geoffrey Hill is also the subject of four essays in *European Voices in the Poetry of W.B. Yeats and Geoffrey Hill*, edited by Ineke Bockting, Jennifer Kilgore-Caradec, and Elizabeth Muller. Hill appears here alongside Yeats but also Ezra Pound, T.S. Eliot, Charles Péguy, Cesare Pavese, and sculptor Ernst Barlach. Perhaps the most valuable item for Hill scholars is the concluding interview between Hill and Kenneth Haynes, the editor of his collected poetry and criticism and the scholar who worked most closely with him in the last two decades of his life. Among many highlights here are the details about the composition of *The Mystery of the Charity of Charles Péguy*, much influenced by C.H. Sisson, and the image of Seamus Heaney 'dancing like my Uncle Len, from the knees down ... a peasant way of dancing' (pp. 165–6). Two further articles on Hill appeared in 2015. 'Geoffrey Hill's Complex Affinities with American Agrarian Poetry' by Steven Matthews (*CQ* 44:iv[2015] 321–40) traces the shape of Hill's engagement with precursors, among whom Allen Tate looms largest, from Hill's earliest years as a poet to the publication of his revised *Broken Hierarchies: Poems* 1952–2012. Matthews argues persuasively that agrarian poetry needs to be seen as a shaping influence on Hill's relation to poetic modernism and to social and political matters. Alex Pestell's 'Vision, Commerce and Society in Geoffrey Hill's Early Poetry' (*TPr* 29:v[2015] 905–25) approaches the thorny question of the 'visionary' tendency in Hill and its political implications with considerable sophistication, arguing, with the help of Gillian Rose's notion of the 'speculative proposition', that rather than embodying either a reactionary belief in poetry's transcendence or a purely negative view of the possibilities of vision, 'Hill's prosody and mythical themes encode a particular attitude towards the temporality of visionary thought' (p. 907).

British experimental poetry was the focus of some distinguished scholarly work in 2015. The subject of Alex Latter's impressive and valuable first scholarly book, *Late Modernism and the English Intelligencer: On the Poetics of Community*, is one of the founding documents of the post-war poetic avant-garde, *The English Intelligencer*, a publication that ran from early 1966 to mid-

1968. 'Magazine' is not quite the word for it, because *The English Intelligencer* was a series of home-duplicated circulars; some participants called it a 'poetry worksheet'. J.H. Prynne, who printed the sheets himself on the mimeograph machine in his Cambridge college, loomed large in the line-up of contributors, alongside poets including Peter Riley, Andrew Crozier, John Hall, John James, and Barry MacSweeney. The worksheets were sent gratis to a mailing list of interested parties that never exceeded sixty people. The poets on the mailing list, who were mainly English, were all interested in developing a mode of writing which could learn from and outmatch the advances they saw happening in the 'New American Poetry', and the pages of *The English Intelligencer* were a site for ardent exchanges about poetry's relation to the history and scope of knowledge. But it was a fractious and uneven community from the start, and Latter's excellent treatment of the 'breakdown' of late modernism, richly supported by original archival scholarship, shows how quickly the moment of late 1960s cultural optimism was dissipated.

In Prynne's view, the breakdown of the *Intelligencer* project signified 'a fault in the world seam', and after the 1960s his poetry would never again place the same trust in the possibilities of human community and communication. Instead, Prynne's ambition was 'to establish relations not personally with the reader, but with the world and its layers of shifted but recognizable usage'. Matthew Hall's first monograph, *On Violence in the Work of J.H. Prynne*, begins with this quotation (p. 1), and immediately moves into an extended chapter on Prynne's elegy for Paul Celan, 'Es Lebe der König', published in *Brass* [1971], the book which marked a decisive break with Prynne's 1960s style. That chapter considers the poem's movement from grief to consolation in a pastoral mode criss-crossed by images of bodily harm and social violence, attempting, in Hall's words, 'to render through language the horror facing Holocaust victims, rather than to represent and comment upon this horror' (p. 18). That subtle distinction is characteristic of Hall's sensitive and inventive mode of reading Prynne's exceptionally challenging poetry. *On Violence in the Work of J.H. Prynne* is perhaps the most valuable single book yet written on Prynne's work, and the one which makes best headway with the accelerating strangeness of late works such as *Acrylic Tips* [2002] and *Refuse Collection* [2004] (pp. 127–202).

Several articles explored the work of less heralded writers of experimental poetry. Veronica Forrest-Thomson was the subject of Calum Gardner's '"Residence at C___": Veronica Forrest-Thomson and Lisa Robertson Writing Cambridge' (*CWW* 10:i[2015] 67–84), which rescued the term 'Cambridge poetry' from the air of uselessness that has hung about it in recent years, by reading Forrest-Thomson's work 'with, and in, Cambridge, through its constructed spaces, both intellectual and architectural', arguing that her challenging poetry is fruitfully understood as being, 'in a new and innovative sense, site-specific' (pp. 67–8). The online *Journal of British and Irish Innovative Poetry*, meanwhile, ran articles entitled 'Following John Wilkinson' by Joe Luna (*JBIIP* 7:ii[2015] 1–19) and '"A new geography of delight": Communist Poetics and Politics in Sean Bonney's *The Commons*' by Jon Clay (*JBIIP* 7:i[2015] 1–26), both of which were sensitively alert to the contradictions involved in conceiving a poetics of radical political ambitions within unpropitious existing conditions.

Some of the most intellectually invigorating writing on recent British poetry in 2015 was found in two books with a general span and introductory purpose: the *Cambridge Introduction to British Poetry* 1945–2010 by Eric Falci and *Contemporary British Poetry* by David Wheatley (published in Palgrave's valuable Readers' Guides to Essential Criticism series). The books have several things in common. Both put postcolonial issues near the front of their consideration, Wheatley in a chapter on 'Postcolonialism' which begins by discussing Ireland as 'The Colony Within' (p. 56) and also includes discussions of the devolutionary poetics of Scottish and Welsh writers, and Falci in a fascinating chapter on 'Decolonizing Poetry' (pp. 42–67) which sets post-war writing in the context of the dizzying speed of British decolonization. Both treat a rewardingly wide range of poets to extended attention, covering a broad spectrum of aesthetic and political positions in the busy world of recent poetry; between them, they take seriously not just academic favourites like Hill, Heaney, Larkin, and Prynne, but also Roy Fisher, Caroline Bergvall, Edward Kamau Brathwaite, Alice Oswald, and Carol Rumens. And both are committed to a practice of deft close reading, even while this practice is informed by a familiarity with theoretical and philosophical perspectives which have sometimes worked against it in the history of criticism. 'The advent of gender studies or postcolonialism', Wheatley writes, 'no more renders the art of close reading poems redundant than a Schoenberg string quartet replaces our favourite folk songs' (p. 8). Falci's book covers more ground, beginning in 1945, than Wheatley's does—*Contemporary British Poetry* mainly restricts itself to work produced since the 1990s. But both books point the road ahead to a genuinely pluralist and even-handed way of writing about poetry of the recent past and present moment, while doing justice to its literary qualities and maintaining academic rigour, which is much to be welcomed.

## 8. Modern Irish Poetry

As in the previous year, articles and book chapters prompted by the death of Seamus Heaney made up a very large proportion of all the critical work on modern Irish poetry that was published in 2015. Many of these pieces appeared in special editions of two journals: the *Hungarian Journal of English and American Studies* and the *Irish Review*. The autumn edition of the former journal begins with a reminiscence by Helen Vendler, 'Remembering Seamus Heaney' (*HJEAS* 21[2015] 273–6), that details the poet's personal qualities and reflects on the lightly worn mastery of some of his lines. Taking a suitably grief-stricken example, Vendler points to the extraordinary compression Heaney achieved in his description of a mother who 'coughed out angry tearless sighs' in his early poem 'Mid-Term Break'. This is followed by Bernard O'Donoghue's short reflection, 'Remembering Seamus Heaney II' (*HJEAS* 21[2015] 277–80), in which he notes the distance between Heaney's origins and his adult life. O'Donoghue writes of Heaney that he learned to play a 'subtle, wary and socially accomplished game' (p. 278). Edward

Larrissy's 'Crossing Common Ground: W.B. Yeats and Seamus Heaney' (*HJEAS* 21[2015] 281–300) not only points out where the younger poet emulated the elder, but 'seeks to identify those seams of literary and cultural history that both poets were mining' (p. 283). This search leads Larrissy to challenge and at times invert the terms with which both poets are commonly associated. So, the earthy matter-of-factness of Yeats's *The Celtic Twilight* [1893] is brought to the fore, as are Heaney's poems of the mystical and the marvellous. Rosie Lavan's 'Screening Belfast: "Heaney in Limboland" and the Language of Belonging' (*HJEAS* 21[2015] 301–16) considers the poet's relationship with Belfast through the lens of a 1970 documentary. Lavan suggests the urban sites that formed the poet have been given less attention than the rural ones and associates the 'we' Heaney speaks of in the documentary with the poet's sense of civic communality. She goes on to provide a new reading of 'Whatever You Say Say Nothing', resituating it as a Belfast poem. Stephen Regan's 'Seamus Heaney and the Making of *Sweeney Astray*' (*HJEAS* 21[2015] 317–40) makes use of Heaney's notebooks to illuminate the status of his poem as a political and personal allegory. Highlighting the profound differences in style between Heaney's two attempts at the poem, Regan concludes that Heaney's translation of the medieval Irish text was a pivotal point in his work: 'after some cautious preliminary flittings, then, Sweeney would take flight and determine the direction of Heaney's poetry towards a new aerial authority and vision' (p. 338). Michael Parker's closing tribute, ' "Now, and ever / After": Familial and Literary Legacies in Seamus Heaney's *Human Chain*' (*HJEAS* 21[2015] 341–60) identifies the discernible shadow of mortality that falls across Heaney's work from the early 1990s onwards. It goes on to provide close, sonically attentive, readings of several poems from Heaney's last collection of lyric poetry, *Human Chain* [2010], showing how the poems are imbued with a sense of the transitoriness of life and the fragility of the body.

The Heaney tribute in the *Irish Review* has its origins in a commemorative conference that was held at Queen's University Belfast in April 2014. It begins with Neil Corcoran's 'The Melt of the Real Thing' (*IR* 49–50[2015] 5–18), which first focuses on the cross-grained materiality of the worlds Heaney's poems conjure, then identifies the note of mourning for the transience of the material that is such a consistent element of his work. Corcoran notes that 'the term "homesickness" seems consistently appropriate to it, and in several ramifying senses. For all his Aristotelian relish of the actual, the real melts too' (p. 7). Angela Leighton's 'Heaney and the Music' (*IR* 49–50[2015] 19–32) explores how the musicality of his poetry, and the use of musical imagery in it, are both ways in which Heaney invites his readers 'to listen beyond what is told ... to something other than what we think we understand', and thereby to approach an inaccessible mystery (p. 30). Michael Longley's 'Room to Rhyme: Some Memories of Seamus Heaney' (*IR* 49–50[2015] 33–7) provides a series of short vignettes that are both clear-eyed and affecting. He pictures the two poets in their twenties, flopping on top of Slemish to smoke; he shows them dedicating poems to each other as 'something of a business transaction'; and he reproduces the affectionate postcard he sent Heaney two weeks before his death (p. 34). Jahan Ramazani's 'Seamus Heaney's Globe' (*IR* 49–50[2015] 38–

53) beguilingly laces together Heaney's imagery of the globe with the 'global' elements of his poetry, providing illuminating readings of a handful of poems including 'Electric Light' and 'Alphabets'. Throughout, Ramazani makes clear that, despite its ubiquity in corporate buzzspeak, the 'global' can be a fecund point of departure for literary scholarship. Rosie Lavan's 'Explorations: Seamus Heaney's Education' (*IR* 49–50[2015] 54–70) examines how Heaney's experiences as both an educator and a student informed his literary output and his work as a broadcaster. This piece focuses on a series of 1974 radio programmes, called 'Explorations', which he wrote and presented for the BBC Northern Ireland Schools Service. In this piece, Lavan does valuable work in situating these broadcasts in a wider landscape than the troubled Belfast in which they were recorded, bringing to light the social, political, and educational worlds out of which they arose.

Peter McDonald's 'Heaney's Implications' (*IR* 49–50[2015] 71–89) gives a masterful reading of 'The Harvest Bow', convincingly questioning the meliorative readings that its most famous line, 'The end of art is peace', has garnered. Connal Parr's 'Definitively Other: Seamus Heaney and Ulster Protestantism' (*IR* 49–50[2015] 90–101), in spite of the oppositional implications of its title, centres on the sympathies as much as the antipathies that are part of Heaney's many engagements in poetry and prose with Ulster's Protestants. Parr discusses Heaney's demurrals from Thomas Kinsella's unflattering depictions of Protestants in *Butcher's Dozen* [1972], Heaney's description of a massacre of Protestant workers in his Nobel speech, and his statement during the Belfast 'flags protests' in the last year of his life that there is 'never going to be a united Ireland' (p. 97). Nick Laird's short piece, 'Making Strange' (*IR* 49–50[2015] 102–5), argues that Heaney's writing 'allowed something like a space to grow where second thoughts were not only possible but imperative' and was 'a kind of secret weightless place where one could consider issues outside the old received notions and arguments with which we were imprinted' (p. 104). Catriona Clutterbuck's ' "Pilot and stray in one": Sustaining Nothingness in the Travel Poems of Early Heaney' (*IR* 49–50[2015] 106–21) considers both the political and personal elements of Heaney's work, focusing on how it is haunted by ideas of death and absence. John Wilson Foster's 'Fraught Pleasures: Engaging Seamus Heaney' (*IR* 49–50[2015] 122–36) benefits from the half-century its author has spent reading and thinking about Heaney's work. In it, Foster writes with affection and authority of the dilemmas and sources out of which Heaney's poetry grew. Sinéad Morrissey's ' "And fostered me and sent me out": Muldoon Reading Heaney' (*IR* 49–50[2015] 137–40) takes Muldoon's reading of Heaney's poems at a tribute event as its starting point. Morrissey goes on to note how Muldoon's powerful live readings of Heaney's work often draw attention to the poets' shared background on Ulster farms. Alan Gillis's valuable piece, 'Heaney's Legacy' (*IR* 49–50[2015] 141–6), looks ahead to how Heaney's posthumous reputation might develop, pointing out that the vivid, sensory immediacy of his work has a countercultural value in an 'age of disembodied corporate utilitarian anonymity', and that his revivification of the pastoral form has worth in a time of ecological crisis (p. 145). It also anticipates a time when Heaney's work will be read in contexts beyond those of the Troubles with which they have so long been associated. Rui Carvalho Homem's 'On Authorship and Intermediality in Seamus Heaney: "I can connect / Some bits and pieces" ' (*IR* 49–50[2015] 151–64) pays particular attention to the pictorial and ekphrastic elements in Heaney's work. Homem skilfully weaves an argument that Heaney's writing, in spite of its coming from an era in which notions of subjectivity have come under suspicion, constitutes an 'evolving but sustained vindication of selfhood and the human' (p. 162). Patricia Craig's ' "Station Island": A Kind of Valediction' (*IR* 49–50[2015] 165–72) combines recollections of the mid-century Ulster Catholic upbringing that she and Heaney shared with an analysis of his long mid-1980s poem *Station Island*, arguing that it is a compound of literary, religious, and personal influences. Nicholas Allen's 'Seamus Heaney and Water' (*IR* 49–50[2015] 173–82) takes its subject from a different element from the terrestrial one with which the poet is so often associated. Allen demonstrates the lifelong centrality of water to Heaney's poetry, examining the pump in his farmyard home, the eel fishery in nearby Lough Neagh and other watery sites near and far. Throughout, he engagingly discusses how arterial rivers and lakes and their connections to the ocean form a continuum both in Heaney's imagination and in his work. Anne Devlin's 'Seamus Heaney and the Mantle of Aeschylus: The Aftermath of the War' (*IR* 49–50[2015] 183–93) examines how Heaney drew on the work of his Greek precursor, in particular in his paradoxically bloody peacetime poem, 'Mycenae Lookout'. Devlin argues that the poem is profoundly influenced by theatre, noting the origins of the poem in a piece of drama. Hugh Haughton's 'Seamus Heaney: First and Last Things' (*IR* 49–50[2015] 194–207) takes its theme from Heaney's statement 'my last things will be first things slipping from me'. It authoritatively shows how preoccupations, ideas, and images from Heaney's earliest life and work are present in his final volume. Finally, Leontia Flynn's 'Radically Necessary: Heaney's Defence of Poetry' (*IR* 49–50[2015] 208–18) charts her own relationship with the elder poet's work. Flynn comes around to the idea that, in an increasingly digitized and professionalized world, Heaney's belief in the self-appeasing sphere of the poem can buttress his readers' attempts to resist an increasingly commodified system of values.

Eugene McNulty and Ciarán Mac Murchaidh's edited collection, *Hearing Heaney: The Sixth Seamus Heaney Lectures*, was not initially designed as a tribute volume though circumstances turned it into one. It has its origins in the 2011 round of a biennial series of lectures named in Heaney's honour that take place at St Patrick's College, Dublin City University. Heaney's associations with the college, and with education more widely, are delineated by Pauric Travers in a short opening piece, 'The Seamus Heaney Lecture Series' (pp. 29–32). The volume that follows contains pieces by poets and literary scholars that sit alongside ones by historians, an educationalist, a legal scholar, and a journalist. In Vona Groarke's essay, 'Between the Lines: The Writer's Heaney' (pp. 33–48), she reflects on Heaney the poet, exploring the idea of the line: Heaney's train lines, borderlines, lines of connection, and, of course, lines of verse. In the next essay, 'Reluctant Amoralist: Seamus Heaney's Physical World' (pp. 49–61), the poet Harry Clifton begins by reflecting on his early reading of Heaney's work, writing that what stayed with him above all was

Heaney's ability to summon the tangible world in all its vividness and specificity. Two pieces by poets are followed by two that link Heaney to his troubled historical context. Olivia O'Leary writes, in 'Seamus Heaney: Part of What We Are' (pp. 62–74), of how *North* [1975], with its linguistic subtlety and doubled perspectives, was a corrective to the unthinking sloganeering that made up the political discourse in which her job as a journalist immersed her. Pauric Travers also writes of Heaney's role as a public voice during the Troubles in 'Crossing Borders: Heaney and the "Ulster Thing"' (pp. 75–92). Carla King takes a historian's perspective in 'Of Bogs, Bodies and Sagas...' (pp. 93–110), analysing Heaney's poems alongside the histories of the archaeological finds that inspired him. Eugene McNulty writes of Heaney the dramatist in 'Words into Action: Re-hearing Antigone's Claim in *The Burial at Thebes*' (pp. 111–23), discussing how Heaney meditated over visions of justice in his 2004 version of the Greek play. His piece is followed by a wide-ranging essay by Michael Cronin, 'Ireland's Fractal Futures: Seamus Heaney and the Cultures of Possibility' (pp. 124–35), which sees Heaney's work through the lens of what he terms 'micro-cosmopolitanism'. From a legal perspective, Yxta Maya Murray provides a fascinating account of teaching Heaney's 'Punishment' in the United States in 'Punishment and the Costs of Knowledge' (pp. 136–54). The last piece in the collection is entitled 'Learning from Heaney: The Poet and Arts-Based Educational Research' (pp. 155–66). In it, writing from her perspective as an educationalist, Regina Murphy reflects on the preceding chapters while exploring the implications for researchers in education of the profound but enabling uncertainties that face readers of Heaney's poetry.

Ashley Bland Crowder's 'Seamus Heaney's Revisions for *Death of a Naturalist*' (*NewHibR* 19[2015] 94–112) looks at Heaney's first published volume in the context of his association with the famed Belfast 'Group' of the early 1960s. In this well-informed work, Crowder advances the hypothesis that Heaney's revisions to these 1960s poems were influenced by the group's close-reading practices. Helen Vendler's *The Ocean, the Bird and the Scholar: Essays on Poets & Poetry* contains two pieces about Heaney, one of the poets most closely associated with her. The chapter, 'Seamus Heaney's "Sweeney Redivivus": Its Plot and Its Poems' (pp. 332–55) is a detailed look at Heaney's revisitation in *Station Island* [1984] of the ground he covered in *Sweeney Astray* [1983]. Taking a typically close and affectionate look at Heaney's work, Vendler examines the forms as well as the themes of the sequence to bring to light how it relates to Heaney's self-image after his relocation from Northern Ireland to the Republic. She claims it 'gave Heaney a model for hardness, purpose, and venture, for the courage of alienation, even of outlawry' (p. 355). Another chapter, 'Seamus Heaney and the *Oresteia*: "Mycenae Lookout": and the Usefulness of Tradition' (pp. 130–43), engagingly associates the sanguinary imagery of Heaney's poem 'Mycenae Lookout' with the mid-1990s IRA ceasefire. Vendler argues that the violence of feeling that Heaney suppressed during the Troubles was given greater scope for expression by the end of the hostilities: 'if Heaney's voice was born to joy, the undeclared war in the North forced him—once the cease-fire gave him permission to unleash his long-suppressed anger and disgust—to take up the "pneumatic drill" of "Mycenae Lookout" ' (p. 143).

John Dennison's *Seamus Heaney and the Adequacy of Poetry* is a nuanced exploration of Heaney's critical prose that contends that a 'transcendentalist humanism' and 'latter-day Arnoldianism' lie at the base of the poet's world view (p. 11). In this book Dennison pays close attention to the tonal and structural echoes of Christianity that ring in Heaney's work, while identifying at its heart a substitutive Arnoldian 'expansive trust in the arts' (p. 8). The author expands on this theme in six substantive, chronologically ordered chapters, carefully marking the poet's subtle shifts in emphasis across the decades. Though, at times, the tone of the book perhaps passes from the unsparing to the fussy, this is nevertheless a highly valuable study. A particular strength lies in the way it goes beyond Heaney's better-known works, mining ore from vast numbers of occasional pieces, pamphlets, introductions, interviews, and documents from the archive. The book that results from this painstaking approach is a subtle and unflinching exploration of Heaney's evolving thought.

Though other poets from Northern Ireland received attention in 2015, the number of critical works on them was dwarfed by those on Heaney. Brendan Corcoran's ' "Antarctica" and Derek Mahon's "Topography of the Void" ' (*NCentR* 15:iii[2015] 17–48) examines the many wastelands that form the landscapes of Derek Mahon's mid-1980s poetry, arguing that his preoccupation with physical limits at this time is matched by poems which question artistic ones. The more meliorative elements of Mahon's poetry are explored by Ahmed Badrideen in 'The Counter-Apocalyptic Moment in Derek Mahon's Poetry' (*NewHibR* 19[2015] 93–108), which argues that a consistent, if intermittent, 'counter-apocalyptic' sentiment that is in evidence across Mahon's career shows how the poet 'recognises the inescapability and, more positively, the potentiality and richness of the present' (p. 94). Though this reading risks underplaying the desire for oblivion that imbues so much of Mahon's poetry, it nevertheless represents an attempt to read Mahon's work against the grain of much recent criticism.

Two 2015 monographs look at the work of a range of poets from Northern Ireland. Adam Hanna's *Northern Irish Poetry and Domestic Space* examines why houses, in some ways the most private of spaces, have taken up such visibly public positions in the work of Seamus Heaney, Michael Longley, Derek Mahon, and Medbh McGuckian. In his book, Hanna argues that the work of poets from Northern Ireland demonstrates that the imaginative draw of the house lies in its status both as a site of contestation and as a place that can offer an insulated refuge from political conflict. In this way, the house parallels lyric poetry itself: both are forms that compel by seeming to offer a personal space for private expression, but that also have the potential to provide a position from which to engage with the world. Julia Obert's *Postcolonial Overtures: The Politics of Sound in Contemporary Northern Irish Poetry* is a perceptive and innovative look at the work of Ciaran Carson, Paul Muldoon, Derek Mahon, and others. Its introduction moves illuminatingly between the sounds of the present-day city of Belfast, the echoes of the past that shaped the city, and the music of the poetry it inspired. The chapters are attuned to theories of acoustic ecology and are informed by recent work in both sound theory and literary criticism. In one especially engaging chapter, Obert reads the lyrics and rhythms of the music of Paul Muldoon's former band, Rackett, with the ear and eye of a literary critic. In the light of Bob Dylan's recent Nobel Prize, Obert's focus on the points where popular music and poetry fuse with each other looks prescient. The final section focuses on a handful of younger poets, Gearóid Mac Lochlainn, Leontia Flynn, and Alan Gillis, connecting their sensitivity to the city's soundscapes to the increasing interest in sound as a subject for academic study. As well informed as it is original, this book maps out new directions in the study of Irish poetry.

This year saw the publication of several other books with an Ulster focus. These included *Close Readings: Essays on Irish Poetry*, a posthumous collection of Michael Allen's essays edited by his former colleague Fran Brearton. This collection is divided into two parts: the first consists of eight previously published essays; the second is an extended essay, unpublished during the author's lifetime, on development in the poetry of Michael Longley. Brearton's foreword usefully sets out Allen's preoccupations as a critic, stating that reading poetry was for him both a matter of being carried away by it and attending closely to it. The essays, on Patrick Kavanagh, Medbh McGuckian, Seamus Heaney, Michael Longley, Derek Mahon, and Paul Muldoon constitute a major new contribution to the study of Irish poetry. In particular, the essay on Kavanagh and provincialism is as insightful about the poetry as it is about the history of the term 'provincial' and its many implications. The volume ends with a personal reflection by Edna Longley that gives an account of the workings of the famous 'Group' of Belfast that diverges intriguingly from the literary history of the period that was propounded in Heather Clark's monograph a decade ago. The poets of this famous generation, as well as their predecessors and successors, are the subject of the second chapter of Guy Woodward's *Culture, Northern Ireland, and the Second World War*. This examines how the war is present in the work of well-known poets and their less famous contemporaries. It is particularly concerned with the older generation, of which Robert Greacen (1920–2008) and Roy McFadden (1921–99) were part, 'who lived through the war as young adults and were unable to keep it at a distance from their work' (p. 82). Co-edited by Woodward with Dorothea Depner, *Irish Culture and Wartime Europe, 1938–48* looks at Irish literature and culture during the same period. This includes Simon Workman's ' "Poised on the edge of absence": Kavanagh and MacNeice in the Shadow of War' (pp. 23–40), a considered look at how the war (or, to Irish officialdom, 'the Emergency'), shaped the work of both poets.

Maureen E. Ruprecht Fadem's *The Literature of Northern Ireland: Spectral Borderlands* contains a chapter that focuses on poetry, 'Outlining Silence in the Poetry of Medbh McGuckian' (pp. 99–135). In it, the author consistently links politics and poetics, writing in a theoretically informed way of how McGuckian's work illustrates the condition of spectrality. To Fadem, McGuckian's poems are the 'dream language of the collective, political unconscious' (p. 135). This book, with its focus on borders, has a timeliness that has become more apparent with the hardening of borders that is expected to accompany Northern Ireland's exit from the transnational European structures it shares with the Republic. Kenneth Keating's 'Medbh McGuckian's Source Texts and the Challenge to Authorial Identity in "The Good Wife Taught her Daughter"' (*ISR* 23[2015] 310–30) seeks to chart a middle ground between the opposing critical approaches to McGuckian's work. In it, Keating highlights the limitations associated with both hunting her sources and reading her work independently of the clues that her source-texts provide. Keating argues that the resistance of the poems to coherent explanation via either mode of analysis demonstrates the challenge her work offers to 'the critical desire for singular meaning' (p 327). From the same generation as McGuckian, Paul Muldoon is the subject of Wit Pietrzak's '(Self-)In-Mourning: Paul Muldoon's Early Elegies' (*HJEAS* 21[2015] 361–76). This appreciative article includes readings of the poems 'The Soap-Pig' and 'Incantata', and argues that Muldoon's elegies achieve 'a triumph of empathy and self-quest(ion)ing' (p. 374).

Looking to older poets from Northern Ireland, 2015 saw the publication of W.J. McCormack's deeply informed biography *Northman: John Hewitt, (1907–87): An Irish Writer, His World, and His Times*. It begins with an account of the belated publication of Hewitt's first volume of poetry when he was over 40, and brings to light the mid-century literary and artistic networks that supported Hewitt, and that he supported in turn. Having charted this critical moment, McCormack goes back to Hewitt's early life and works forwards from there, making use of many sources, not least among them Hewitt's wife's journal. There are rewarding chapter-length diversions that allow for detailed exploration of one of the poet's works or notebooks, making this volume one for scholars rather than general readers. One of the pleasures of this book is the richly evocative way in which McCormack brings Hewitt's mid-century world, with its ration books and typewriters, to life. Another is the way that the author's reflections on Hewitt expand outwards into meditations on Ireland, Ulster, and the past, so that what starts as the exploration of a single author's work becomes a panoptic survey of a place and a time.

Tom Walker's *Louis MacNeice and the Irish Poetry of his Time* is a beautifully written study that places MacNeice in his Irish context. In the past, analyses of MacNeice's place in Ireland have situated him as an inheritor (of Yeats) or a progenitor (of the Northern poets who came to prominence in the 1960s). Innovatively, Walker gives a portrait of MacNeice alongside the Irish poets of his time, one that shows him as both contemporary and collaborator. His first chapter shows how MacNeice's early poetry was influenced by Yeats's and, more unusually, brings to light Yeats's engagement with the younger poet. The central chapters consider MacNeice's relationships with, among others, Austin Clarke, Patrick Kavanagh, Thomas Kinsella, and W.R. Rodgers, the last of whom planned with MacNeice an unpublished collaborative work, 'The Character of Ireland'. Intriguingly, Walker reappraises MacNeice's relationship with F.R. Higgins, looking beyond the antagonism of their famous broadcast encounter. A final chapter revisits the question of MacNeice's engagement with Yeats in his late poetry, paying special attention to the younger poet's refrains and repetitions as points of contact between the two. This highly original reassessment of MacNeice is a great boon to scholars of his work, as well as to readers with an interest in Irish poetry in the twentieth century more generally. There is also a chapter on MacNeice in C.D. Blanton's *Epic Negation: The Dialectical Poetics of Late Modernism*, that reads MacNeice's *Autumn Journal* [1939] alongside Auden's poems of 1938–9 (pp. 233–83). Through a series of deft and illuminating close readings, Blanton argues that MacNeice's long poem 'confesses the conclusion that MacNeice himself sought to resist throughout the thirties: the force of events is sufficient to conscript even poetry under another's voice' (p. 283).

Examining the work of poets from both Northern Ireland and the Republic, Lucy Collins's *Contemporary Irish Women Poets: Memory and Estrangement* covers a broad array of writers. The introduction sets out the major preoccupations of the study: Irish women poets' negotiations with memory; how recording an event in writing can be as much a licence to forget and move on as a means of remembering; how recording a memory in words can change the memory itself; and how the personal memories recorded in poems can, at times, be dramatically at odds with accepted communal narratives. These are fascinating points of departure, and Collins does them full justice in chapters that focus on Eavan Boland, Eiléan Ní Chuilleanáin, Medbh McGuckian, Catherine Walsh, and Vona Groarke. The conclusion, 'Memories of the Future', provides articulate and thoughtful close readings of works by poets including Sinéad Morrissey, Leontia Flynn, and Sara Berkeley. Between this monograph and her 2012 critical anthology *Poetry by Women in Ireland*, Collins has done a great service for the study of women's poetry in Ireland.

Modern Irish poetry is central to several of the sixteen chapters in Kathryn Kirkpatrick and Borbála Faragó's edited collection, *Animals in Irish Literature and Culture*. Many of these chapters connect poets' representations of animals to their sensitivity to other, ignored, kinds of exploitation. Amanda Sperry's 'Dennis O'Driscoll's Beef with the Celtic Tiger' (pp. 42–54) argues that the poet's work 'presents a continuum wherein the exploitation of animals is connected to the exploitation of human workers' (p. 42); Katarzyna Poloczek's ' "Their disembodied voices cry": Marine Animals and Their Songs of Absence in the Poetry of Sinéad Morrissey, Caitríona O'Reilly, and Mary O'Donoghue' (pp. 75–91) links Irish women's reclamation of their voices as poets to 'their attentive listening to the hushed or ignored voices of animals' (p. 75); Luz Mar González-Arias's ' "A pedigree bitch, like myself": (Non)Human Illness and Death in Dorothy Molloy's Poetry' (pp. 119–34) examines the poet's depictions of the deaths of pets, pointing out that the shared corporeality of animals and humans means that writing about the former can be a way of writing about the latter; Liam Young's ' "Do you dance, Minnaloushe?": Yeats's Animal Questions' (pp. 149–64) contains observations on a handful of Yeats's poems, mainly from later in his career, arguing that his poems 'acknowledge that we become who we are, materially and imaginatively, through and with other animals' (p. 150); Donna Potts's ' "Room for Creatures": Francis Harvey's Bestiary' (pp. 165–81) argues that the poet's works remind their readers that 'wilderness is not as far removed as it might seem' from human life (p. 171); Christine Cusick's ' "A capacity for sustained flight": Contemporary Irish Poetry and the Ecology of Avian Encounter' (pp. 182–98) takes examples from the work of poets including

Francis Harvey and Michael Longley to argue that the depiction of encounters between humans and birds can be a means of 'reimagining and revaluing the inadequacies of human perception and knowledge of animal life' (p. 183); Borbála Faragó's 'Transnational—Transanimal: Reading the Insect in Migrant Irish Poetry' (pp. 231–43) focuses on the entomological elements of the poetry of Eva Bourke. Finally, Tom Herron's 'Strange Becomings: Paul Muldoon's *Maggot*' (pp. 244–58) argues that both the destructive and the regenerative activities of that unglamorous creature, the maggot, inform the volume that shares its name. Another edited collection, Catherine E. Paul's *Writing Modern Ireland*, was not received in time for review, and will be covered with material from 2016.

Iain Twiddy's second monograph, *Cancer Poetry*, convincingly shows the centrality of the disease to the imagination of Paul Muldoon and Michael Longley, among others, arguing persuasively that it has helped to shape the content and even the form of their poems. In the second chapter, Twiddy arrestingly links the complex rhyme-scheme of Muldoon's 'Yarrow' to the patterns of replication involved in metastasis; he also analyses Michael Longley's responses in poetry to the cancer, linked to his war wounds, that killed the poet's father. In this section, Twiddy explores how Longley's elegy 'Wounds' links his father's condition to the 'metastasis' of violence: from Ulster, to the killing fields of the Somme, to a new generation of Ulstermen. Chapter 6 brings the focus back to Paul Muldoon, this time offering illuminating readings of several poems, including 'Incantata', to demonstrate how 'the structural principles of the disease—replication, invasion and metastasis—elicited mimetic correlatives' (p. 144). Chapter 7 contains a section that revisits Muldoon's 'Incantata', this time from the perspective of imaginative redress, and one on Muldoon's collection *Maggot* that unteases some of its poems' dense admixtures of religious, mythological, and medical imagery. This chapter concludes that in Muldoon's poetry, as in that of others who write of cancer, 'what remains inextinguishable is the attempt to make sense' (p. 188).

Despite its title, David Wheatley's wide-ranging *Contemporary British Poetry* is required reading for those with an interest in contemporary Irish poetry. Indeed, Wheatley makes the case for how difficult it is to separate the two categories. The book is divided into thematic chapters, each broken down into pithy, readable, author-based sections. Chapter 2 sets out some of the debates that the conflicted national status of Northern Irish poets has engendered. Chapter 3, on postcolonialism, argues that 'the poetry written in the shadow of the Northern Irish Troubles has lent itself eloquently to the post-colonial debate' (p. 56). In surveying this field, Wheatley points out the critical oddities that are produced by consistent misreadings of the writings of Edna Longley by her peers, and questions the 'sanitised Heaney' that overly meliorative readings of his works have created (p. 57). Chapter 4, on gender, sexuality, and class, sets out the critical arguments surrounding the works of Vona Groarke and Medbh McGuckian. Chapter 5, 'Experiment and Language', draws attention to less discussed poets like Trevor Joyce, Catherine Walsh, and Maurice Scully. Chapter 6, 'New Environments', contains sections that address the works of Michael Longley and Ciaran

Carson. Throughout, Wheatley's writing is incisive and vivid, and shows a refreshing lack of obeisance to dogmas and precepts of all kinds.

David Lynch's monograph, *Confronting Shadows: An Introduction to the Poetry of Thomas Kinsella*, contains the author's insights into various poems from across his career. It is, according to Lynch, not aimed at academics but, rather, was written in the hope that it 'will provide a helpful introduction to other general readers eager to enter the work, but who are searching for a little guidance' (p. 5). The book is written in a style suited to this intended readership, though general readers who are looking for guidance with individual poems may be stumped by both the author's self-confessed tendency to 'jump from one poem to another that was published decades later' (p. 10), by chapter titles that do not orient the reader in specific decades or volumes, and by the lack of an index. Heather H. Yeung's *Spatial Engagement with Poetry* contains a chapter on the poetry of Thomas Kinsella, 'Economies of Poetic Production: The Poetry of Thomas Kinsella' (pp. 79–109). This piece notes the economic arguments that Kinsella incorporates into his poetics, showing how his critique of 'verbal excess' maps on to Enlightenment-era ideas of political philosophy.

As in previous years, 2015 saw many publications that either took the poetry of W.B. Yeats as their sole focus or examined it in comparison with the work of others. Barry Sheils's *W.B. Yeats and World Literature: The Subject of Poetry* opens with a short account of how the poet was denied an allowance by a shipowning uncle who was displeased with his political views. The monograph that follows makes clear how the poet and his work, like the vessels owned by his mother's family, crossed the seas back and forth from Ireland; it also brings to light the centrality of capital and politics to these ventures. At the heart of this book are two linked tensions: between the modern and the pre-modern, and between the global and the national. The book contains particularly illuminating new readings of 'Easter 1916' and 'An Irish Airman Foresees His Death', examining the former in terms of a sacrificial 'economy of ... transmission and exchange' (p. 146) and the latter in a way that is mindful of 'the real technology of flight' (p. 29). Of course, reading as 'world literature' the work of a poet who embraced Indian and Japanese models, but who also worried that English and American influences were 'denationalising' Ireland, is far from a straightforward task. However, Sheils does deft, convincing work in identifying the syntheses and contradictions that form Yeats's writing.

This year also saw a number of journal articles on Yeats. Grigory Kruzhkov's 'Once More on a "Discarded Poem": Yeats, Auden, and Brodsky' (*NewHibR* 19[2015] 130–41) points out the elements of Auden's 'September 1, 1939' that were inspired by Yeats, locating parallels between its title, diction, and imagery and various works by the Irish poet including 'Nineteen Hundred and Nineteen', 'The Second Coming', and 'Vacillation'. Kevin Riel's ' "I do not love": Rethinking W.B. Yeats's "Elegies" of Major Robert Gregory' (*JML* 38:ii[2015] 1–15) attempts to reframe Yeats's ambiguous elegies as condemnations of a 'sociopathic mercenary ... fighting to further the colonial power of an empire that fiercely maintains control over his "country" ' (pp. 11–12). This article perhaps suffers from a mischaracterization of the subtleties that conditioned Yeats's attitude to the First World War. Jules Brody's refreshingly readable and intelligent 'Reading Yeats: "The Fascination of What's Difficult"' (*P&L* 39[2015] 487–94) makes a convincing case for reimagining a poem that is often read solely in its biographical context as a meditation on the act of writing poetry. Nels Pearson's densely written '"Postponement and Prophecy": Northrop Frye and the "Great Code" of Yeats's "Byzantium"' (*UTQ* 84[2015] 19–33) examines the parallels between Yeats's poem and 'the process of signalling and postponing revelation that drives Biblical language' (p. 21). Denis Corish provides an admiring reading of several of Yeats's better-known poems in ' "The Artifice of Eternity": Reading Yeats' (*SR* 123[2015] 102–17), an article that centres on themes of permanence and transience in the poet's work.

Alex Davis and Lee M. Jenkins's edited collection *A History of Modernist Poetry* complicates the idea of modernist poetry as an Anglo-American enterprise. The editors memorably frame their challenge to this concept in nautical terms in their introduction: 'Anglophone modernist poetry, like the *Titanic*, was launched and fitted out in 1911–12, the product, as was the White Star Liner, of American, British and Irish interests' (p. 1). A chapter by Gregory Castle, 'Yeats, Modernism, and the Irish Revival' (pp. 204–26), demonstrates how central this Irish poet is to the exercise in reappraisal that is at the heart of the book. In this chapter, Castle explores the continuities between Yeats's earlier works that are associated with the Irish Revival and his modernist masterpieces of the 1920s and 1930s. In doing so, his chapter calls for a reassessment of ideas of the Irish Revival as a retrograde or backward-looking enterprise: 'I want to suggest that Yeats's modernism is rooted in and continuous with Revival, in part because Revival taught the poet that faith in transcendence, in an *otherworld* of eternal Beauty, could only be grounded in the historical world he occupied' (p. 205).

The essays that Margaret Mills Harper published on *A Vision* in 2014 have now been joined by her and Catherine E. Paul's 1937 edition of Yeats's late esoteric work. This begins with an introductory essay that sets out in detail how the first version of this mysterious treatise (dated 1925 but actually published in early 1926) turned, through many revisions and additions, into the second one over a decade later. Letters, diary entries, and drafts are all pressed into service in this massive work of investigation. A valuable feature of the volume is its retrieval of critical judgements on this puzzling book by Yeats's contemporaries. Perhaps Yeats himself hit on the book's true value in a letter (quoted by the editors) in which he writes that he longs to finish the 1926 version so that he 'may write the poetry it seems to have made possible' (p. xxviii). Just as *A Vision* made new poetry possible for Yeats, this new edition of it will enable new scholarship on his work.

**Books Reviewed**

Albright, Daniel. *Putting Modernism Together: Literature, Music, and Painting, 1872–1927*. JHUP. [2015] pp. x + 328. pb £22 ISBN 9 7814 2141 6441.

Aston, Elaine, and Mark O'Thomas. *Royal Court: International*. PalMac. [2015] pp. 248. pb £18.99 ISBN 9 7811 3746 1827.

Atkins, G. Douglas. *Strategy and Purpose in T.S. Eliot's Major Poems: Language, Hermeneutics and Ancient Truth in 'New Verse'*. PalMac. [2015] pp. x + 71. £45 ISBN 9 7811 3759 0572.

Bailey, Iain. *Samuel Beckett and the Bible*. Bloomsbury. [2015] pp. 208. £85 ISBN 9 7817 8093 6888.

Balinisteanu, Tudor. *Religion and Aesthetic Experience in Joyce and Yeats*. PalMac. [2015] pp. 225. £55 ISBN 9 7811 3743 4760.

Bate, Jonathan. *Ted Hughes: The Unauthorised Life*. Collins. [2015] pp. 662. £30 ISBN 9 7800 0811 8228.

Baumann, Walter, ed. *Ezra Pound and London: New Perspectives*. AMS. [2015] pp. xi + 213. £95.50 ISBN 9 7804 0465 5334.

Berberich, Christine, ed. *The Bloomsbury Introduction to Popular Fiction*. Bloomsbury. [2015] pp. xv + 326. £65 ISBN 9 7814 4113 4318.

Bianchini, Natka. *Samuel Beckett's Theatre in the America: The Legacy of Alan Schneider as Beckett's American Director*. PalMac. [2015] pp. 204. £58 ISBN 9 7811 3743 9857.

Blanton, C.D. *Epic Negation: The Dialectical Poetics of Late Modernism*. OUP. [2015] pp. ix + 367. £44.49 ISBN 9 7801 9984 4715.

Bleiler, Richard J. *The Strange Case of 'The Angels of Mons': Arthur Machen's World War I Story, the Insistent Believers, and His Refutations*. McFarland. [2015] pp. viii + 236. £36.95 ISBN 9 7807 8649 8673.

Bockting, Ineke, Jennifer Kilgore-Caradec, and Elizabeth Muller, eds. *European Voices in the Poetry of W.B. Yeats and Geoffrey Hill*. Lang. [2015] pp. 172. £51.58 ISBN 9 7830 3431 6897.

Booth, Allyson. *Reading 'The Waste Land' from the Bottom Up*. PalMac. [2015] pp. xx + 273. £55 ISBN 9 7811 3748 8381.

Branach-Kallas, Anna, and Nelly Strehlau, eds. *Re-imagining the First World War: New Perspectives in Anglophone Literature and Culture*. CambridgeSP. [2015] pp. xviii + 393. £57.99 ISBN 9 7814 4387 7480.

Brearton, Fran, ed. *Michael Allen: Close Readings: Essays on Irish Poetry*. IAP. [2015] pp. xviii + 318. pb £24.99 ISBN 9 7807 1653 3047.

Brewer, Mary F, Lynette Goddard, and Deidre Osborne, eds. *Modern and Contemporary Black British Drama*. PalMac. [2015] pp. 240. pb £19.99 ISBN 9 7802 3030 3195.

Brock, Richard. *Four Quartets: T.S. Eliot and Spirituality*. Patrician. [2015] pp 119. £7.95 ISBN 9 7809 9323 8802.

Buck, Claire. *Conceiving Strangeness in British First World War Writings*. PalMac. [2015] pp. x + 249. £55 ISBN 9 7811 3747 1642.

Burden, Robert. *Travel, Modernism and Modernity*. Ashgate. [2015] pp. vii + 269. £67.99 ISBN 9 7814 7245 2863.

Caronia, Nancy, and Edvige Giunta, eds. *Personal Effects: Essays on Memoir, Teaching, and Culture in the Work of Louise DeSalvo*. FordUP. [2014] pp. 288. $45 ISBN 9 7808 2326 2274.

Carpentier, Martha C., ed. *Joycean Legacies*. PalMac. [2015] pp. 290. £55 ISBN 9 7811 3750 3619.

Castle, Gregory, ed. *A History of the Modernist Novel.* CUP. [2015] pp. xvi + 532. £75 ISBN 9 7811 0703 4952.

Childs, Peter. *Julian Barnes.* OUP. [2015] pp. 174. £22.75 ISBN 9 7807 1909 7607.

Clare, David. *Bernard Shaw's Irish Outlook.* PalMac. [2015] pp. x + 207. £60 ISBN 9 7811 3754 3554.

Cochran, Peter. *Byron's European Impact.* CambridgeSP. [2015] pp. 550. £62.99 ISBN 9 7814 4387 5417.

Coles, Kimberly Anne, Ralph Bauer, Zita Nunes, and Carla L. Peterson, eds. *The Cultural Politics of Blood, 1500–1900.* PalMac. [2015] pp. xvi + 274. £60 ISBN 9 7811 3733 8204.

Collins, Lucy. *Contemporary Irish Women Poets: Memory and Estrangement.* LiverUP. [2015] pp. xiii + 248. £75 ISBN 9 7817 8138 1878.

Colón Semenza, Greg M., and Bob Hasenfratz. *The History of British Literature on Film, 1895–2015.* Bloomsbury. [2015] pp. 488. £82.60 ISBN 9 7816 2356 0430.

Costello, Bonnie, and Rachel Galvin, eds. *Auden at Work.* PalMac. [2015] pp. xi + 309. £66.99 ISBN 9 7811 3745 2924.

Cowan, Laura. *Rebecca West's Subversive Use of Hybrid Genres: 1911–41.* Bloomsbury. [2015] pp. x + 195. £28.99 ISBN 9 7814 4114 4171.

Crawford, Robert. *Young Eliot: From St Louis to The Waste Land.* Cape. [2015] pp. 493. £25 ISBN 9 7800 9955 4950.

Crispi, Luca. *Joyce's Creative Process and the Construction of Characters in Ulysses: Becoming the Blooms.* OUP. [2015] pp. 368. £60 ISBN 9 7801 9871 8857.

Croft, Janet Brennan, ed. *Baptism of Fire: The Birth of the Modern British Fantastic in World War I.* Mythopoeic. [2015] pp. 332. £12.73 ISBN 9 7818 8772 6030.

Davis, Alex, and Lee M. Jenkins, eds. *A History of Modernist Poetry.* CUP. [2015] pp. xxxvii + 532. £65 ISBN 9 7811 0703 8677.

Day, Barry, ed. *Noël Coward Screenplays.* Methuen. [2015] pp. 512. pb £21.99 ISBN 9 7814 7256 8090.

DeCoste, D. Marcel. *The Vocation of Evelyn Waugh; Faith and Art in the Post-War Fiction.* Ashgate. [2015] pp. 196. £62.99 ISBN 9 7814 0947 0847.

Delgado-Garcia, Cristina. *Rethinking Character in Contemporary British Theatre: Aesthetics, Politics, Subjectivity.* Gruyter. [2015] pp. viii + 228. £74.99 ISBN 9 7831 1040 3909.

Dell, Marion, *Virginia Woolf's Influential Forebears.* PalMac. [2015] pp. 222. £58 ISBN 9 7811 3749 7277.

Dennison, John. *Seamus Heaney and the Adequacy of Poetry.* OUP. [2015] pp. xii + 244. £55 ISBN 9 7801 9873 9197.

Depner, Dorothea, and Guy Woodward, eds. *Irish Culture and Wartime Europe, 1938–48.* FCP. [2015] pp. 205. €55 ISBN 9 7818 4682 5620.

Devlin, Kimberley J., and Christine Smedley, eds. *Joyce's Allmaziful Plurabilities: Polyvocal Explorations of Finnegans Wake.* UFlorP. [2015] pp. 336. £73.50 ISBN 9 7808 1306 1542.

Dickey, Frances, and Jennifer Formichelli, eds. *The Complete Prose of T.S. Eliot: The Critical Edition. Literature, Politics, Belief, 1927–1929*. JHUP. [2015] pp. 786. Price not available. ISBN 9 7814 2141 8902.

Dillon, Sarah, and Caroline Edwards, eds. *Maggie Gee: Critical Essays*. Glyphi. [2015] pp. 312. £16.99 ISBN 9 7817 8024 0336.

Dinsman, Melissa. *Modernism at the Microphone: Radio, Propaganda, and Literary Aesthetics During World War II*. Bloomsbury. [2015] pp. xiv + 247. £79.99 ISBN 9 7814 7259 5072.

D'Monté, Rebecca. *British Theatre and Performance 1900–1950*. Methuen. [2015] pp. 352. pb £21.99 ISBN 9 7814 0816 5652.

Dodman, Trevor. *Shell Shock, Memory, and the Novel in the Wake of World War I*. CUP. [2015] pp. ix + 244. £58.70 ISBN 9 7811 0711 4203.

Drouin, Jeffrey S. *James Joyce, Science, and Modernist Print Culture: 'The Einstein of English Fiction'*. Routledge. [2015] pp. 160. £85 ISBN 9 7804 1589 5521.

Dryden, Linda. *Joseph Conrad and H.G. Wells: The Fin-de-Siècle Literary Scene*. PalMac. [2015] pp. x + 216. £55 ISBN 9 7811 3750 0113.

Dubino, Jeanne, Gill Lowe, Vara Neverow, and Kathryn Simpson, eds. *Virginia Woolf: Twenty-First Century Approaches*. EdinUP. [2015] pp. 250. £19.99 ISBN 9 7814 7441 4135.

Ellis, David. *Love and Sex in D.H. Lawrence*. ClemsonUP. [2015] pp. xi + 202. £75 ISBN 9 7819 4295 4026.

Ellis, Steve, *British Writers and the Approach of World War II*. CUP. [2015] pp. 260. £60 ISBN 9 7811 0705 4585.

Ely, Steve. *Ted Hughes's South Yorkshire: Made in Mexborough*. PalMac. [2015] pp. 231. £55 ISBN 9 7811 3749 9349.

Enderwitz, Anne. *Modernist Melancholia: Freud, Conrad and Ford*. PalMac. [2015] pp. viii + 229. £55 ISBN 9 7811 3744 4318.

Fadem, Maureen E. Ruprecht. *The Literature of Northern Ireland: Spectral Borderlands*. PalMac. [2015] pp. x + 218. $95 ISBN 9 7811 3747 4742.

Falci, Eric, ed. *The Cambridge Introduction to British Poetry 1945–2010*. CUP. [2015] pp. 279. pb £17.99 ISBN 9 7811 0754 2570.

Feldman, Matthew, and Karin Mandoni, eds. *Beckett/Philosophy: A Collection*. Ibidem. [2015] pp. 344. £40 ISBN 9 7838 3826 7012.

Fernandes, Ana Raquel, and José Pedro Serra, eds. *The Power of Form: Recycling Myths*. CambridgeSP. [2015] pp. 250. £47.99 ISBN 9 7814 4387 1945.

Flack, Leah Culligan. *Modernism and Homer: The Odysseys of H.D., James Joyce, Osip Mandelstam, and Ezra Pound*. CUP. [2015] pp. 248. £67 ISBN 9 7811 0710 8035.

Fogarty, Anne, and Fran O'Rourke, eds. *Voices on Joyce*. UCDubP. [2015] pp. 320. £61.50 ISBN 9 7819 0635 9799.

Francis, Andrew. *Culture and Commerce in Conrad's Asian Fiction*. CUP. [2015] pp. xvii + 228. £64.99 ISBN 9 7811 0709 3980.

Freer, Scott. *Modernist Mythopoeia: The Twilight of the Gods*. PalMac. [2015] pp. 246. £55 ISBN 9 7811 3703 5509.

Friedman, Susan Stanford. *Planetary Modernisms: Provocations on Modernity Across Time*. ColUP. [2015] pp. xii + 451. £37 ISBN 9 7802 3117 0901.

Gaipa, Mark, Sean Latham, and Robert Scholes, eds. *James Joyce, The Little Review 'Ulysses'*. YaleUP. [2015] pp. 448. £17.99 ISBN 9 7803 0018 1777.

Game, David. *D.H. Lawrence's Australia: Anxiety at the Edge of Empire*. Ashgate. [2015] pp. xxi + 325. $138 ISBN 9 7814 7241 5059.

Gąsiorek, Andrzej, and Nathan Waddell, eds. *Wyndham Lewis: A Critical Guide*. EdinUP. [2015] pp. 288. £24.99 ISBN 9 7807 4868 5684.

Gavin, Adrienne E, and Andrew Humphries, eds. *Transport in British Fiction: Technologies of Movement, 1840–1940*. Palgrave. [2015] pp. xii + 273. £60. ISBN 9 7811 3749 9035.

Gibbons, Luke. *Joyce's Ghosts: Ireland, Modernism and Memory*. UChicP. [2015] pp. 286. £34 ISBN 9 7802 2623 6179.

Gibson, A.G.G. *Robert Graves and the Classical Tradition*. OUP. [2015] pp. viii + 370. £75 ISBN 9 7801 9873 8053.

Gillespie, Michael Patrick. *James Joyce and the Exilic Imagination*. UFlorP. [2015] pp. 192. £73.50 ISBN 9 7808 1306 0651.

Gilmour, Rachael, and Bill Schwarz, eds. *End of Empire and the English Novel Since 1945*. OUP. [2015] pp. 256. £27.46 ISBN 9 7807 1909 7454.

Goddard, Lynette. *Contemporary Black British Playwrights: Margins to Mainstream*. PalMac. [2015] pp. xii + 255. £50 ISBN 9 7892 3023 7483.

Gontarski, S.E. *Creative Involution: Bergson, Beckett, Deleuze*. EdinUP. [2015] pp. 208. £70 ISBN 9 7814 7440 8356.

Guanio-Uluru, Lykke. *Ethics and Form in Fantasy Literature: Tolkien, Rowling, and Meyer*. PalMac. [2015] pp. 261. £43.99 ISBN 9 7811 3746 9687.

Guignery, Vanessa, ed. *The Inside of a Shell: Alice Munro's Dance of the Happy Shades*. CambridgeSP. [2015] pp. 305. £52.99 ISBN 9 7814 4387 5967.

Haffenden, John, and Valerie Eliot, eds. *The Letters of T.S. Eliot - Volume 5: 1930–1931*. Faber. [2014] pp. lxi + 862. £40. ISBN 9 7805 7131 6328.

Hall, Matthew. *On Violence in the Work of J.H. Prynne*. CambridgeSP. [2015] pp. 226. £47.99 ISBN 9 7814 4388 0145.

Hanna, Adam. *Northern Irish Poetry and Domestic Space*. PalMac. [2015] pp. xxiv + 188. £55 ISBN 9 7811 3749 3705.

Harding, Jason, ed. *The Complete Prose of T.S. Eliot: The Critical Edition. English Lion, 1930–1933*. JHUP. [2015] pp. xlvii + 873. Price not available. ISBN 9 7814 2141 8919.

Harper, Margaret Mills, and Catherine E. Paul, eds. *A Vision: The Revised 1937 Edition. The Collected Works of W.B. Yeats*, vol. 14. Scribner. [2015] pp. li + 503. $60 ISBN 9 7806 8480 7348.

Harris, Alexandra. *Woolf in Winter: 2015 Virginia Woolf Birthday Lecture*. VWSGB. [2015] pp. 24. £4 ISBN 9 7809 5557 1787.

Hesse, Beatrix. *The English Crime Play in the Twentieth Century*. PalMac. [2015] pp. 298. £55 ISBN 9 7811 3746 3036.

Hinojosa, Lynne. *Puritanism and Modernist Novels: From Moral Character to the Ethical Self*. OSUP. [2015] pp. x + 218. £55 ISBN 9 7808 1421 2738.

Inchley, Maggie. *Voice and New Writing, 1997–2007: Articulating the Demos*. PalMac. [2015] pp. vii + 204. £55 ISBN 9 7811 3743 2322.

Israel, Nico. *Spirals: The Whirled Image in Twentieth-Century Literature and Art*. ColUP. [2015] pp. xiv + 299. £37 ISBN 9 7802 3115 3027.

James, David, ed. *The Cambridge Companion to British Fiction since 1945.* CUP. [2015] pp. 275. £45.95 ISBN 9 7811 0704 0236.

Jenkins, Lee M. *The American Lawrence.* UPFlorida. [2015] pp. ix + 159. $74.95 ISBN 9 7808 1306 0507.

Johnson, George M. *Mourning and Mysticism in First World Literature and Beyond.* PalMac. [2015] pp. xiv + 256. £55 ISBN 9 8711 3733 2028.

Kascakova, Janka, and Gerri Kimber, eds. *Katherine Mansfield and Continental Europe: Connections and Influences.* PalMac. [2015] pp. xii + 269. £55 ISBN 9 7811 3742 9964.

Kent, Brad, ed. *George Bernard Shaw in Context.* CUP. [2015] pp. 418. £74.99 ISBN 9 7811 0704 7457.

Kirkpatrick, Kathryn, and Borbála Faragó, eds. *Animals in Irish Literature and Culture.* PalMac. [2015] pp. xviii + 270. £58 ISBN 9 7811 3743 4791.

Kirsch, Adam. *Rocket and Lightship: Essays on Literature and Ideas.* Norton. [2015] pp. xi + 305. £17.99 ISBN 9 7803 9324 3468.

Kleinberg-Levin, David. *Beckett's Words: The Promise of Happiness in a Time of Mourning.* Bloomsbury. [2015] pp. 328. £90 ISBN 9 7814 7421 6852.

Kochis, Matthew J., and Heather L. Lusty, eds. *Modernists at Odds: Reconsidering Joyce and Lawrence.* UFlorP. [2015] pp. 256. £73.50 ISBN 9 7808 1306 0477.

Lacivita, Alison. *The Ecology of Finnegans Wake.* UFlorP. [2015] pp. 288. £73.50 ISBN 9 7808 1306 0620.

Latham, Monica. *A Poetics of Postmodernism and Neomodernism: Rewriting Mrs Dalloway.* PalMac. [2015] pp. 282. £55 ISBN 9 7811 3749 0797.

Latham, Sean, and Gayle Rogers. *Modernism: Evolution of an Idea.* Bloomsbury. [2015] pp. vi + 266. pb £21.99 ISBN 9 7814 7252 3778.

Latter, Alex. *Late Modernism and The English Intelligencer: On the Poetics of Community.* Bloomsbury. [2015] pp. 276. £84.99 ISBN 9 7814 7257 5821.

Lavery, Carl, and Clare Finburgh, eds. *Rethinking the Theatre of the Absurd: Ecology, the Environment and the Greening of the Modern Stage.* Bloomsbury. [2015] pp. 312. £60 ISBN 9 7814 7250 6672.

Lernout, Geert. *Cain: But Are You Able? The Bible, Byron and Joyce.* Bulzoni. [2015] pp. 150. €12 ISBN 9 7888 6897 0178.

Lindop, Grevel. *Charles Williams: The Third Inkling.* OUP. [2015] pp. 544. £25 ISBN 9 7801 9928 4153.

Lynch, David. *Confronting Shadows: An Introduction to the Poetry of Thomas Kinsella.* New Island. [2015] pp. 306. £20.99 ISBN 9 7818 4840 2874.

Macdonald, Kate. *Novelists Against Social Change: Conservative Popular Fiction 1920–1960.* PalMac. [2015] pp. 271. £58 ISBN 9 7811 3745 7714.

Macdonald, Kate, and Christoph Singer, eds. *Transitions in Middlebrow Writing.* PalMac. [2015] pp. 284. £58 ISBN 9 7811 3748 6769.

Maclean, Caroline. *The Vogue for Russia: Modernism and the Unseen in Britain 1900–1930.* EdinUP. [2015] pp. 240. £70 ISBN 9 7807 4864 7293.

Mahoney, Kristin. *Literature and the Politics of Post-Victorian Decadence.* CUP. [2015] pp. xi + 259. £70 ISBN 9 7811 0710 9742.

March-Russell, Paul. *Modernism and Science Fiction.* PalMac. [2015] pp. xii + 193. £19.99 ISBN 9 7802 3027 3481.

Marshik, Celia, ed. *The Cambridge Companion to Modernist Culture*. CUP. [2015] pp. xxii + 257. pb £18.99 ISBN 9 7811 0762 7390.

Martín Salván, Paula. *The Language of Ethics and Community in Graham Greene's Fiction*. PalMac. [2015] pp. 171. £43.99 ISBN 9 7811 3754 0102.

Maunder, Andrew, ed. *British Theatre and the Great War, 1914—1919: New Perspectives*. PalMac. [2015] pp. xvi + 333. £55 ISBN 9 7811 3740 1991.

McCarthy, Jeffrey Mathes. *Green Modernism: Nature and the English Novel, 1900 to 1930*. PalMac. [2015] pp. 276. £70 ISBN 9 7811 3754 9358.

McCluskey, Alan. *Materiality and the Modern Cosmopolitan Novel*. PalMac. [2015] pp. 213. £45.99 ISBN 9 7811 3750 3374.

McCormack, W.J. *Northman: John Hewitt, (1907–87): An Irish Writer, His World, and His Times*. OUP. [2015] pp. xx + 294. £45 ISBN 9 7801 9873 9821.

McCrae, Barry. *Languages of the Night: Minor Languages and the Literary Imagination in Twentieth-Century Ireland and Europe*. YaleUP. [2015] pp. xviii + 177. £25 ISBN 9 7803 0018 5157.

McDonald, Rónán, ed. *The Values of Literary Studies: Critical Institutions, Scholarly Agendas*. CUP. [2015] pp. xi + 265. pb £18.99 ISBN 9 7811 0757 5684.

McGarry, Fearghal. *The Abbey Rebels of 1916: A Lost Revolution*. G&M. [2015] pp. 376. £26.99 ISBN 9 7807 1716 8811.

McIntire, Gabrielle, ed. *The Cambridge Companion to The Waste Land*. CUP. [2015] pp. xxii + 224. pb £19.99. ISBN 9 7811 0767 2574.

McNulty, Eugene, and Ciarán Mac Murchaidh, eds. *Hearing Heaney: The Sixth Seamus Heaney Lectures*. FCP. [2015] pp. 176. €45 ISBN 9 7818 4682 5279.

Mead, Henry. *T.E. Hulme and the Ideological Politics of Early Modernism*. Bloomsbury. [2015] pp. 288. £80 ISBN 9 7814 7258 2027.

Mikkonen, Kai. *Narrative Paths: African Travel in Modern Fiction and Nonfiction*. OSUP. [2015] pp. x + 324. $76.95 ISBN 9 7808 1421 2745.

Moran, James. *The Theatre of D.H. Lawrence*. Methuen. [2015] pp. xv + 244. pb £21.99 ISBN 9 7814 7257 0376.

Morse, Donald E., ed. *Irish Theatre in Transition: From the Late Nineteenth to the Early Twenty-First Century*. PalMac. [2015] pp. xvii + 265. £58 ISBN 9 7811 3745 0685.

Obert, Julia. *Postcolonial Overtures: The Politics of Sound in Contemporary Northern Irish Poetry*. SyracuseUP. [2015] pp. x + 236. $34.95 ISBN 9 7808 1563 4003.

O'Hara, Daniel T. *Virginia Woolf and the Modern Sublime: The Invisible Tribunal*. PalMac. [2015] pp. 134. £45 ISBN 9 7811 3759 0596.

Ohi, Kevin. *Dead Letters Sent: Queer Literary Transmission*. UMinnP. [2015] pp. 326. pb £22.38 ISBN 9 7808 1669 4785.

O'Malley, Seamus. *Making History New: Modernism and Historical Narrative*. OUP. [2015] pp. xxii + 271. £32.99 ISBN 9 7801 9936 4237.

O'Neill, Michael, Mark Sandy, and Sarah Wootton, eds. *The Persistence of Beauty: Victorians to Moderns*. P&C. [2015] pp. xi + 195. £70 ISBN 9 7818 4893 5112.

Paddy, David Ian. *The Empires of J.G. Ballard: An Imagined Geography.* Glyphi. [2015] pp. 370. £18.99 ISBN 9 7817 8024 0183.

Patterson, Anthony, and Yoonjoung Choi, eds. *We Speak a Different Tongue: Maverick Voices and Modernity 1890–1939.* CambridgeSP. [2015] pp. xix + 271. £47.99 ISBN 9 7814 4387 7022.

Paul, Catherine E., ed. *Writing Modern Ireland.* LiverUP. [2015] pp. 279. £75 ISBN 9 7809 8908 2693.

Pearson, Nels. *Irish Cosmopolitanism: Location and Dislocation in James Joyce, Elizabeth Bowen, and Samuel Beckett.* UFlorP. [2015] pp. 192. £73.50 ISBN 9 7808 1306 0521.

Pease, Alison, ed. *The Cambridge Companion to To the Lighthouse.* CUP. [2015] pp. 208. £17.99 ISBN 9 7811 0768 2313.

Plumridge, Anna, ed. *The Urewera Notebook by Katherine Mansfield.* EdinUP. [2015] pp. ix + 118. £60 ISBN 9 7814 7440 0152.

Rabaté, Jean-Michel, ed. *1922: Literature, Culture, Politics.* CUP. [2015] pp. xvi + 279. £67 ISBN 9 7811 0704 0540.

Rabey, David Ian. *The Theatre and Films of Jez Butterworth.* Methuen. [2015] pp. 225. pb £19.99 ISBN 9 7814 0818 360.

Raw, Laurence. *Theatre of the People: Donald Wolfit's Shakespearean Productions 1937—1953.* R&L. [2015] pp. 240. £52.95 ISBN 9 7814 4225 7344.

Rea, Ann, ed. *Middlebrow Wodehouse: P.G. Wodehouse's Work in Context.* Routledge. [2015] pp. 312. £95 ISBN 9 7814 7245 4485.

Reynolds, James, and Andy W.H. Smith, eds. *Howard Barker's Theatre: Wrestling with Catastrophe.* Bloomsbury. [2015] pp. 267. pb £18. 99 ISBN 9 7814 0818 4318.

Ricks, Christopher, and Jim McCue, eds. *The Poems of T.S. Eliot, vol. 1: Collected and Uncollected Poems.* Faber. [2015] pp. 1,311. £40 ISBN 9 7805 7128 3905.

Ricks, Christopher, and Jim McCue, eds. *The Poems of T.S. Eliot, vol. 2: Practical Cats and Further Verse.* Faber. [2015] pp. 667. £40 ISBN 9 7805 7123 8712.

Rizzuto, Nicole M. *Insurgent Testimonies: Witnessing Colonial Trauma in Modern and Anglophone Literature.* FordUP. [2015] pp. x + 272. pb £24.99 ISBN 9 7808 2326 7828.

Roche, Anthony. *The Irish Dramatic Revival 1899–1939.* Methuen. [2015] pp. 272. pb £21.99 ISBN 9 7814 0817 5286.

Ross, Stephen, and Allana C. Lindgren, eds. *The Modernist World.* Routledge. [2015] pp. xxxiii + 615. £137 ISBN 9 7804 1584 5038.

Sacido-Romero, Jorge, and Sylvia Mieszkowski, eds. *Sound Effects: The Object Voice in Fiction.* Brill. [2015] pp. 340. €91 ISBN 9 7890 0430 4383.

Saint-Amour, Paul K. *Tense Future: Modernism, Total War, Encyclopedic Form.* OUP. [2015] pp. xiii + 347. £64 ISBN 9 7801 9020 0947.

Schmidt, A.V.C. *Passion and Precision: Collected Essays on English Poetry from Geoffrey Chaucer to Geoffrey Hill.* CambridgeSP. [2015] pp. xv + 460. £25 ISBN 9 7814 4387 1853.

Shantz, Jeff. *Specters of Anarchy: Literature and the Anarchist Imagination.* Algora. [2015] pp. 296. $22.95 ISBN 9 7816 2894 1418.

Sheils, Barry. *W.B. Yeats and World Literature: The Subject of Poetry*. Ashgate. [2015] pp. x + 200. £60 ISBN 9 7814 7242 5539.

Sherry, Vincent. *Modernism and the Reinvention of Decadence*. CUP. [2015] pp. xi + 333. £70 ISBN 9 7801 9874 4887.

Smyth, Gerry. *The Judas Kiss: Treason and Betrayal in Six Modern Irish Novels*. ManUP. [2015] pp. 240. £70 ISBN 9 7807 1908 8537.

Stayer, Jayme, ed. *T.S. Eliot, France and the Mind of Europe*. CambridgeSP. [2015] pp. xxi + 259. £47.99 ISBN 9 7814 4387 7381.

Talar, C.J.T., and Lawrence F. Barmann, eds. *Roman Catholic Modernists Confront the Great War*. PalMac. [2015] pp. vii + 165. £45 ISBN 9 7811 3754 6845.

Taylor, Julie, ed. *Modernism and Affect*. EdinUP. [2015] pp. ix + 230. £70 ISBN 9 7807 4869 3252.

Tomko, Michael. *Beyond the Willing Suspension of Disbelief: Poetic Faith from Coleridge to Tolkien*. Bloomsbury. [2015] pp. 192. £65 ISBN 9 7817 8093 7304.

Tonning, Erik, Matthew Feldman, and David Addyman, eds. *Modernism, Christianity and Apocalypse*. Brill. [2015] pp. xvi + 391. £100 ISBN 9 7890 0427 8264.

Towheed, Shafquat, and Edmund G.C. King, eds. *Reading and the First World War: Readers, Texts, Archives*. PalMac. [2015] pp. xi + 266. £70 ISBN 9 7811 3730 2700.

Twiddy, Iain. *Cancer Poetry*. PalMac. [2015] pp. ix + 232. £55 ISBN 9 7811 3736 2001.

Van Hulle, Dirk, ed. *The New Cambridge Companion to Samuel Beckett*. CUP. [2015] pp. 266. pb. £19.99 ISBN 9 7811 0742 7815.

Vendler, Helen. *The Ocean, the Bird and the Scholar: Essays on Poets & Poetry*. HarvardUP. [2015] pp. viii + 444. £25.95 ISBN 9 7806 7473 6566.

Walker, Tom. *Louis MacNeice and the Irish Poetry of His Time*. OUP. [2015] pp. v + 216. £55 ISBN 9 7801 9874 5150.

Walton, Samantha. *Guilty But Insane: Mind and Law in Golden Age Detective Fiction*. OUP. [2015] pp. xiv + 304. £20 ISBN 9 7801 9872 3325.

Watt, Stephen. *'Something Dreadful and Grand': American Literature and the Irish-Jewish Unconscious*. OUP. [2015] pp. 272. £47.99 ISBN 9 7801 9022 7951.

Weir, David. *Ulysses Explained: How Homer, Dante, and Shakespeare Inform Joyce's Modernist Vision*. PalMac. [2015] pp. 254. $90 ISBN 9 7811 3748 8404.

Werther, David, and Susan Werther, eds. *C.S Lewis's List: The Ten Books that Influenced Him Most*. Bloomsbury. [2015] pp. 248. £64 ISBN 9 7816 2892 4145.

Wheatley, David. *Contemporary British Poetry*. PalMac. [2015] pp. vii + 203. pb £18.99 ISBN 9 7802 3036 2536.

Whitworth, Michael. *Virginia Woolf—Mrs Dalloway*. Readers' Guides to Essential Criticism. PalMac. [2015] pp. 192. £13.99 ISBN 9 7802 3050 6428.

Wilmer, S.E., and Audronė Žukauskaite, eds. *Deleuze and Beckett*. PalMac. [2015] pp. xii + 253. $90 ISBN 9 7811 3748 1139.

Wilson, Jean Moorcroft. *Edward Thomas: From Adlestrop to Arras*. Bloomsbury. [2015] pp. xii + 480. £25 ISBN 9 7814 0818 7135.

Wilson, Leigh. *Modernism and Magic: Experiments with Spiritualism, Theosophy and the Occult*. EdinUP. [2015] pp. 224. £24.99 ISBN 9 7807 4862 7707.

Wise, John, and Mike Hill, eds. *The Works of Graham Greene, vol. 2: A Guide to the Graham Greene Archives*. Bloomsbury. [2015] pp. 336. £94.99 ISBN 9 7814 7252 8193.

Wiseman, Sam. *The Reimagining of Place in English Modernism*. LiverUP. [2015] pp. 220. £75 ISBN 9 7809 9089 5886.

Woodward, Guy. *Culture, Northern Ireland, and the Second World War*. OUP. [2015] pp. xiv + 266. £50 ISBN 9 7802 3036 2536.

Wooten, William. *The Alvarez Generation: Thom Gunn, Geoffrey Hill, Ted Hughes, Sylvia Plath and Peter Porter*. LiverUP. [2015] pp. 228. £25 ISBN 9 7817 8138 1632.

Yeung, Heather H. *Spatial Engagement with Poetry*. PalMac. [2015] pp. xiv + 209. €74.99 ISBN 9 7811 3748 8367.

Zigler, Ronald. *The Educational Prophecies of Aldous Huxley; The Visionary Legacy of 'Brave New World', 'Ape' and 'Essence and Island'*. Routledge. [2015] pp. 208. £100 ISBN 9 7811 3883 2497.

Ziolkowski, Theodore. *Classicism of the Twenties: Art, Music & Literature*. UChicP. [2015] pp. 224. $40 ISBN 9 7802 2618 3985.

# XVI

# American Literature to 1900

## HELENA GOODWYN, THERESA SAXON, AND REBECCA WHITE

This chapter has two sections: 1 General; 2 American Literature to 1900. Section 1 is by Theresa Saxon; section 2 is by Helena Goodwyn and Rebecca White.

### 1. General

*American Literary History*, in 2015, produced a number of essays relating to the study of the nineteenth century. Joe Shapiro, in 'The Providence of Class: Catharine Maria Sedgwick, Political Economy, and Sentimental Fiction in the 1830s' (*AmLH* 27:ii[2015] 199–225), posits a specific definition of class in his examination of 'sentimental' fictions, *The Poor Rich Man* and *Live and Let Live*. Such fictions, Shapiro argues, locate class-based economic inequality as intrinsically underpinned by Christian values. Focusing on Pauline Hopkins's 1900 novel, *Contending Forces: A Romance Illustrative of Negro Life North and South*, Daniel Hack argues for a consideration of the ways in which African writers have 'contended' with voices of Victorian literary gravitas in their writing, in 'Contending with Tennyson: Pauline Hopkins and the Victorian Presence in African American Literature' (*AmLH* 27:iii[2015] 484–511). In 'James Fenimore Cooper and the NSA: Security, Property, Liberalism' (*AmLH* 27:iv[2015] 677–701) Russ Castronovo locates *The Pioneers* as a significant challenge to concepts of state surveillance, in an assessment of the role of the NSA in contemporary America.

The first volume in *Nineteenth-Century Literature* for 2015 consists of a special edition dedicated to George Lippard's *The Quaker City*. The introductory essay in this edition, Christopher Looby's 'Lippard in Part(s): Seriality and Secrecy in *The Quaker City*' (*NCL* 70:i[2015] 1–35), examines the serialization of the novel between 1844 and 1845 as a product of Lippard's journalistic training which, while preparing him for writing longer-form fiction, also provided a platform from which the writer could negotiate the value of secrecy—intrinsic both to the novel and to the process of writing—as demonstrated by the subsequent publication of the 'Key'. David S. Reynolds

*The Year's Work in English Studies, Volume 96 (2017)* © *The Author 2017. Published by Oxford University Press on behalf of the English Association. All rights reserved.*
*For Permissions, please email: journals.permissions@oup.com*
doi:10.1093/ywes/max020

examines the more recognizable aspect of *The Quaker City*, as a city mystery, in 'Deformance, Performativity, Posthumanism: The Subversive Style and Radical Politics of George Lippard's *The Quaker City*' (*NCL* 70:i[2015] 36–64), suggesting that Lippard's novel constitutes a satire of literary and social conventions of detection through an overview of the novel's transgressions of detection's generic format. In ' "Picture it all, Darley": Race Politics and the Media History of George Lippard's *The Quaker City*' (*NCL* 70:i[2015] 65–101), Sari Altschuler explores the intertwined contexts of media and race and a growing awareness of antislavery agitation, recognizing Lippard's experience as playwright and journalist on his most famous novel. D. Berton Emerson's essay, 'George Lippard's *The Quaker City*: Disjointed Text, Dismembered Bodies, Regenerated Democracy' (*NCL* 70:i[2015] 102–31), argues it should be remembered as a novel with a sequel, revealing the writer's own literary turn from seduction plot to anti-democracy narrative transgressions. The concluding essay, 'In Search of Monk Hall: A Publishing History of George Lippard's *The Quaker City*' (*NCL* 70:i[2015] 132–49), Michael Winship explores the available archive to examine the chronology of serialization and the relationship between writer and publisher.

In issue ii of this volume, we find 'Whitman's Atlantic Noise' by Christopher Hanlon (*NCL* 70:ii[2015] 194–220), which considers 'A Word Out of the Sea', from the 1860 edition of *Leaves of Grass*, for its aural qualities, linking the poem to a wider antebellum interest in the sound patterns of telegraphy, examining the poem alongside songsheets, poems, fiction, and technical commentary. Also in this issue is Adam Ochonicky's ' "A Better Civilization" through Tourism: Cultural Appropriation in *The Marble Faun*' (*NCL* 70:ii[2015] 221–37), which argues that Nathaniel Hawthorne's 1860 novel locates the United States as a part of a heritage of 'great' nations through its locus of tourism, particularly through an association of art objects, literature, and cultural sites with constructions of sophisticated national identity/ies. Issue 70:iii provides us with Karen L. Kilcup's essay, 'Feeling American in the Poetic Republic' (*NCL* 70:iii[2015] 299–355), which argues for a reconceptualization of frameworks to resist the oversimplification of nineteenth-century American poetry. Reviews written between 1820 and 1840, Kilcup contends, reveal a more effective calibration of, in her terms, a 'poetic republic' that accounts for tastes and identities, both individual and national, taking issue with Benedict Anderson's assertion of newspapers and novels over the national body politic. Poetry, she argues, represented here by William Cullen Bryant and Lydia Sigourney, was the frame through which American culture of this period was most receptive to unspoken fears about nation-building in this period. Issue 70:iv also yields material for scholars of nineteenth-century American literature. Seth McKelvey, in ' "But One Kind" of Life: Thoreau's Subjective Theory of Value in *Walden*' (*NCL* 70:iv[2016] 448–72), through the framework of Austrian economist Carl Menger, relocates Henry David Thoreau within a lineage of free-market thinkers, revising understandings of the writer as hostile to market exchange. Also exploring the theme of the market, Henry B. Wonham's 'Realism and the Stock Market: The Rise of *Silas Lapham*' (*NCL* 70:iv[2016] 473–95) examines W.D. Howells's 1885 novel through a reassessment of its titular lead's investment career, which complicates narratives of realism as traditionalist supporters of honest industry over speculation.

English Literary History also featured a small selection of essays relevant to American letters of the nineteenth century. In 'The Tragic Immigrant: Duality, Hybridity and the Discovery of Blackness in Mark Twain and James Weldon Johnson' (ELH 82:i[2015] 211–49), Richard Hardack contests analyses of race in Pudd'nhead Wilson and The Autobiography of an Ex-Colored Man, arguing that while, in the former, European culture, as an externalizing pole to explore double consciousness, consolidated difference, in the latter it fosters hybridity, though such attitudes are not easily transferred to American contexts. Henry B. Wonham has an essay in this issue entitled, 'The Art of Arbitrage: Reimagining Mark' (ELH 82:iv[2015] 1239–66), which argues that Mark Twain's imaginative engagement with capital, particularly investment returns, was an integral aspect of his life and fiction.

The Journal of American Studies offered readings of nineteenth-century literary culture in 2015, specifically issue ii, a special collection edited by Fionnghuala Sweeney and Karen Salt, entitled 'Acts of Emancipation in the Art, Culture and Politics of the Black Diaspora'. Fionnghuala Sweeney's introductory essay, ' "It will come at last": Acts of Emancipation in the Art, Culture and Politics of the Black Diaspora' (JAS 49:ii[2015] 225–39), explores new scholarship in the field of emancipation, 150 years after the declaration proclamation. The stand-out essay in this special collection is Celeste-Marie Bernier's 'A Visual Call to Arms against the "Caracature of my own face": From Fugitive Slave to Fugitive Image in Frederick Douglass's Theory of Portraiture' (JAS 49:ii[2015] 323–57), which argues that Douglass's work with visual signification validated an alternative form of iconography that debunked an aesthetics of 'sameness' for the appearance of African Americans.

## 2. American Literature to 1900

John A. Casey's New Men: Reconstructing the Image of the Veteran in Late-Nineteenth-Century American Literature and Culture addresses the often overlooked need to remember the living as well as the dead, exploring the Civil War as a transition point in experiencing and expressing conflict. As Casey maintains, 'no longer the marker of a temporary status, 'veteran' came to connote a new identity that was associated with a new state of consciousness. This shift in the understanding of what it meant to be a veteran was a different type of reconstruction that would influence how later generations of US authors wrote about war.' Offering revisionary textual readings and new perspectives on the simultaneous tension and sympathy between Northern and Southern former soldiers, Casey's book presents 'an alternative to examining the era's cultural production exclusively through the lens of race and reconciliation or sectionalist politics'. Comparing and contrasting a wide array of fiction and non-fiction instead enables fresh insight into Civil War writing, countering the myth that it was a conflict left 'unwritten'. Chapter 1 upturns the sentimental image, propagated by postbellum civilians, of the disabled warrior in need of care, and demonstrates the ways in which veterans resisted this stereotype, retrieving comparatively obscure writers (such as John William De Forest and Sidney Lanier) at the same time. Chapter 2 examines the notion, held by both Northern and Southern veterans, that civilian employment would function as a restorative to 'normal' life; work often became another site of conflict instead. Chapter 3 follows on from veterans' practical disillusionment with the post-war world to show how their memories imprisoned them in further pain and displacement, as men became caught between recollections of an idealized youth and the reawakened trauma of the battlefield. Chapter 4 outlines the ways in which veterans (from 1890 to 1900) increasingly demarcated themselves as a separate social group, exploring the consequences of this emerging 'veteran identity' (especially the tension between former soldiers and the succeeding generation of white, middle-class males, and the influence of this on conceptions of masculinity in the 1890s—an issue which has received little attention in gender studies). Veteran identity assumes specific characteristics when attached to racial identity, as demonstrated in chapter 5, which considers the reintegration process faced by African American Union soldiers. Casey's engagingly written, highly readable study is fascinatingly illustrated (including photographs of soldiers and battle sites), and places other art forms (such as painting) alongside literary works. Almost forgotten texts and authors (such as Albion Tourgée's *Figs and Thistles*) are unburied, and celebrated stories (notably *The Red Badge of Courage*) are read in a new light (linking Crane's tale with his journalism, for example, and interpreting it as 'the contradictory product of a transitional age', re-creating 'the experience of Civil War combat only to undercut it'). Wider issues are also reconsidered. While the lack of black Civil War writing is often attributed to deteriorating race relations in the 'Jim Crow' era, for instance, Casey uncovers the 'equally important factor' of the growing tension within the black community surrounding the subject of military service during the conflict. Although scholars have 'not typically viewed the Civil War as a defining moment in America's cultural understanding of what it meant to be a veteran', Casey's timely research will 'encourage not only a new approach to academic inquiry on the Civil War and the culture it spawned, but also the growth of a new "veteran studies" movement', placating Walt Whitman's fear that 'the real war will never get in the books'.

Networking the Nation: British and American Women's Poetry and Italy, 1840–1870, by Alison Chapman, opens with an extensive and useful timeline that begins with Germaine de Staël's *Corinne; or Italy* published in 1807, and ends with the death of Isabella (Isa) Blagden and the publication of Elizabeth Clementine Kinney's *Bianca Cappello*. Chapman writes of the poets studied here—Elizabeth Barrett Browning, Isa Blagden, Elizabeth Kinney, Eliza Ogilvy, and Theodosia Garrow Trollope—that they saw their literary identity as transnational. *Networking the Nation* tells us there is much to be gleaned from the published and unpublished writings of these women poets about the nature of female authority, agency, and political endeavour in the nineteenth century. Chapman demonstrates the importance of salon culture to the networking of these expatriate poets who created spaces that were at once private and public, socially safe but politically liberal. In chapter 2 Chapman describes Blagden's salon at Villa Brichieri, Bellosguardo, as a space coded as feminine and spiritualist, showing how Blagden's cohabitation with others and her creation of a fluid private–public environment made for a productive literary sphere. Villino Trollope is the subject of the next chapter, and the artistic works of Theodosia Garrow Trollope, whose translations from Italian to English are convincingly presented by Chapman as works of mediation and powerful political energy. We next encounter Casa Guidi: memorialized in Elizabeth Barrett Browning's (EBB) 1851 collection *Casa Guidi Windows*. Parts I and II of *Casa Guidi Windows*, this chapter establishes, are shot through with the negotiation between domestic ideology and political rhetoric. Considering *Aurora Leigh* as the ultimate text of the expatriate woman poet, chapter five solidifies the arguments presented by Chapman throughout *Networking the Nation* that compellingly show how poetry produced by the networks of American and British middle-class women living in Florence during the Risorgimento established a distinctly transnational, and significantly female voice of political engagement. In the later chapters entitled 'Spirit Hands: Writing, Spiritualism, and Political Agency' and 'Spirit Sisters: EBB, Sophia May Eckley, and *Poems before Congress*', Chapman explores the networks of association between a Risorgimento politics and spiritualism. Chapman explains why poetry, particularly women's poetry, was the appropriate vessel for an exploration of the productive ties between spiritualism and an expatriate expression of Italian patriotism. In the final chapter, entitled 'Performative Poetics', Chapman looks at EBB's *Last Poems* published posthumously in 1862 and argues that Barrett Browning was attempting to achieve a new performativity in her final poems that married politics and emotions without resorting to overblown sentimentality.

*Transnational Na(rra)tion: Home and Homeland in Nineteenth-Century American Literature* by John Dolis opens with a bold, perhaps even aggressively so, statement of what this book is *not*. It is not, writes Dolis, morally righteous, not an attempt to change society, not a means of correcting or fixing a problem with the field of literary studies, and not an easy read. It *is*, our author tells us, a piece of performance criticism beginning with a chapter addressing Benjamin Franklin's biography and letters. Dolis then turns to Washington Irving and argues (contrary to what we're told in the prefatory note *won't* be happening) that as a corrective to 'critics' who have 'domesticated' Irving, Dolis finds contained in Irving's work a 'larger context of romantic irony' in which the bachelor figures as a repressed other 'embedded' in the family unit and the national identity. In a chapter on Louisa May Alcott's *Little Women*, Dolis asks us to 'Notice' things repeatedly in the closing pages of the chapter. It is difficult to know, in a book so self-consciously performative, whether or not this insistent 'Notice' is an affective mode or the result of the fragmentary structure of *Transnational Na(rra)tion*.

In her unusual, refreshing, and compellingly written study, *Embroidering the Scarlet A: Unwed Mothers and Illegitimate Children in American Fiction and Film*, Janet Mason Ellerby offers an 'uncommon perspective to literary analysis', practising Elaine Showalter's concept of autobiographical criticism as a means of exploring the often stigmatized concept of female sexual 'transgression' in American culture. Taking Nathaniel Hawthorne's *The*

*Scarlet Letter* as a pivotal trope, and placing close analyses of his novel alongside an examination of its cultural afterlives, the contemporary relevance of Hester's story is embodied by Ellerby's own personal response to the text; her study of the unwed mother plot is shaped by her 'own embroidered experiences with unwed pregnancy, enduring shame, and irrevocable regret'. However, in 'tracing the numerous literary representations of Hester … and by interrogating the letter's cultural and social ramifications', Ellerby 're-embroiders' it 'with imagination and creativity rather than shame and humiliation'. The condemnation of female sexuality in twenty-first-century America is shown to have deep historical and cultural roots, stemming from the influence of classical literature and the eighteenth-century notion of the 'fallen woman', the subject of Ellerby's first chapter ('The Unwed Mothers of the Early American Novel'). Taking Franklin's *Polly Baker* as a point of departure, she examines the first three novels published in independent America (William Hill Brown's *The Power of Sympathy*, Hannah Webster Foster's *The Coquette*, and Susann Rowson's *Charlotte Temple*), exposing the seduction narrative as moral lesson ('fallen women' are punished, often by death, in order to promote female virtue). Although the book's subsequent chapters focus on post-1900 writers (such as William Faulkner, Alice Walker, and Theodore Dreiser) and film, Ellerby often examines them in relation to pre-1900 ideological values (maintaining that Dreiser's Jennie Gerhardt reiterates Coventry Patmore's 'Angel in the House', for instance), while Hawthorne's *Scarlet Letter* is returned to throughout. Aligned with her desire to give voice to the disenfranchised, Ellerby retrieves more obscure writers (such as Sandra Cisneros and Dorothy Allison), as well as less well-known texts by canonical authors. Her colourful study presents a broad, yet richly detailed, canvas, her historical sweep considering a range of issues and genres on both the page and the screen. Crucially, Ellerby's conclusion incorporates real-life female accounts regarding the discrimination and shame which still confront women who transgress social expectations in twenty-first-century America, testifying to the timeliness and significance of her study. As Ellerby hopes, her book will encourage 'new, fresh, and empowering narratives' regarding unwed motherhood, illegitimacy, and adoption, finally countering Alexander Pope's contention that 'every woman is, at heart, a rake'.

Shelley Fisher Fishkin has produced an impressive study of over 150 National Register historic sites in *Writing America: Literary Landmarks from Walden Pond to Wounded Knee (A Reader's Companion)*. Fishkin begins from the understanding that if place is important to literature, as it undoubtedly is, then to return to significant places will help us to gain further meaning from those texts. Chapter 1 looks at Walt Whitman's birthplace, built by his father, before examining Whitman's house in New Jersey, the Fulton Ferry Historic District in Brooklyn, New York, the Seaport Museum, and Langston Hughes House, both also in New York. Next we visit Walden Pond state reservation, where Henry David Thoreau built his cabin in 1845. Fishkin efficiently reminds us of Thoreau's importance to American literature, demonstrating that his connection to that place has become a philosophy that continues to inspire readers today. The related sites in this case are Thoreau–Alcott House, Sleepy Hollow Cemetery, Orchard House, Ralph Waldo Emerson House,

Margaret Fuller House, Yosemite National Park, and Bryce Canyon National Park. The Rotch–Jones–Duff House, the only whaling mansion in New England that is open to the public, is pictured at the opening of chapter 3, in which Frederick Douglass and Herman Melville are examined together through the lens of their experiences in New Bedford, Massachusetts. Chapter 4 is dedicated to 'The House That *Uncle Tom's Cabin* Bought', and explores Harriet Beecher Stowe's anticipation of Virginia Woolf's *A Room of One's Own* in Stowe's confirmed opinion that to write she must have her own space away from the domestic obligations of the home. Over the course of the next nine chapters we encounter Mark Twain's boyhood home, Wounded Knee national historic landmark at the Pine Ridge Indian Reservation in South Dakota where the 1890 massacre occurred, and a host of other locations. Writers such as Anzia Yezierska, Sinclair Lewis, Maxine Hong Kingston, and Gloria Anzaldúa make up this scholarly tribute to sites of great historical import. Each chapter delineates its chosen place, supported by illustrations, and brings in the works of numerous writers by providing generous quotations that further illuminate our understanding of the American literary canon.

In *Black Print Unbound: The Christian Recorder, African American Literature, and Periodical Culture*, Eric Gardner addresses the layers of critical neglect and myth-making that have covered American, and especially African American, history. In this, he sheds new—and often challenging and uncomfortable—light on iconic figures (such as Abraham Lincoln) and events (such as the Civil War) through a privileging of black perspectives. Compellingly and colourfully written, Gardner's study retrieves the often overlooked African American paper, the *Christian Recorder*, and places it at the centre of 'any sense of American and African American history, culture, and literature'. The ability of the periodical to literally and metaphorically present black thought unbound is emulated by Gardner, as his study likewise gives voice to the forgotten, and unearths the obscure. Upturning conventional narratives, he maintains that 'Lincoln was not the nation. The myth we have made of that man has often taken away from our consideration of the other men and women—including Black men and women . . . who worked for social and political change during that period. This book is part of a scholarly tradition that values *their* experiences.' Gardner's welcome and timely recovery project, rich in fascinating detail and exhaustive archival work, confronts the critical disregard of black newspapers (a trend exacerbated by the dismissal of church print and periodicals more generally), and offers the fullest study to date of the *Christian Recorder*, spanning both its practical workings and its ideological, political, and aesthetic development. At the same time, Gardner also joins recent scholarship which reconceptualizes African American literature, and argues against rigidly constructed canons, terms, and boundaries (appreciating the diversity of black writing beyond slave narratives, for example). While well-known writers, such as Frederick Douglass and Frances Ellen Watkins Harper, are referenced, Gardner's key motivation is to recover non-canonical writers (Edmonia Highgate, George Vashon, and Julia Collins, for example), and thereby present new perspectives on wider discourses (such as American Transcendentalism). Chapter 1 outlines prior work on black print, acknowledging critics such as Jacqueline Bacon, William

Andrews, and Lois Brown. Chapter 2 provides a detailed account of the *Christian Recorder*'s origins, its activity during the Civil War, and the significant influence of the under-studied black editor, Elisha Weaver. Chapter 3 explores the paper's production, physical spaces, and distribution, in dialogue with denominational, regional, and racial politics. Chapter 4 analyses its distribution more closely, focusing on the period between 1861 and 1867. The ways in which the paper recorded acts of reading and writing are considered in chapter 5, while chapter 6 uncovers its frequently forgotten printed correspondence, emphasizing the periodical's development as 'a multifaceted nexus of genres and concerns that challenge contemporary conceptions of both American epistolarity and Black press traditions'. Chapter 7 then considers the *Recorder*'s poetry (especially in elegiac form), and the final section provides a close reading of Julia Collins's *The Curse of Caste*. Incorporating fascinating illustrations, from portraits to photographs of people and places, Gardner's study allows intriguing glimpses into lost lives, asserting the need to 'rethink our conclusions about African American and broader American literature and print culture', considering approaches to '"book history" that open possibilities for under-represented texts [and] authors'. Intending to be 'both a catalyst for and an example of the continuing recovery of nineteenth-century African American print in all its diversity', Gardner's work embodies the *Recorder*'s observation that 'such a narration be worth reading'.

   *Transatlantic Romanticism: British and American Art and Literature, 1790–1860*, edited by Andrew Hemingway and Alan Wallach, is a beautifully illustrated book that recognizes the 'need of fresh work that addresses the relations between artistic focus and the larger history of ideas', and highlights the rich possibilities offered by an interdisciplinary study of visual art and literature. Although Romanticism tends to be characterized by a narrow, national focus, Hemingway and Wallach offer a new direction, interrogating instead the international exchanges which promoted the development of the movement in England and the United States, and noting that 'there is a value in considering American Romanticism from a transatlantic perspective in that the American viewpoint gave a particular character to the Romantic sense of loss'. Building upon the work of critics such as Michael Löwy and Robert Sayre, they argue that the frequently discarded notion of 'Weltanschauung' (a 'comprehensive world view') needs to be reconsidered. In following this line of enquiry, dynamic and refreshing perspectives are explored in the book's thirteen chapters, which are organized helpfully into thematic categories ('The City', 'History', 'Landscape', and 'Race'). In 'Urban Convalescence in Lamb, Poe, and Baudelaire', Matthew Beaumont explores the way in which urban experience was given literary form, where the 'neurasthenia of the convalescent becomes the signature of a modern consciousness characterised by its distance from quotidian concerns' and reacts against capitalist utilitarianism. William Vaughan, in 'Peace and Ambition in the London Art World', and Dell Upton, in 'The Urban Ecology of Art in Antebellum New York', both explore the ways in which the metropolis influenced the arts, while Nicholas Grindle, in 'Sublime and Fall: Benjamin West and the Politics of the Sublime in Early Nineteenth-Century Marylebone', considers its effects upon an individual artist. Although Romantic sensibilities rejected commercialism, Romantic art was a monetary phenomenon, as shown by Leo Costello in 'Turner, Cole, and Transatlantic Ideas of Decline', which outlines the corrupting effects of exhibitions. 'Thomas Cole and Transatlantic Romanticism', by Alan Wallach, explores the artist's calculating negotiation of the New York and London art world. As Löwy and Sayre argue, Romanticism was, in many ways, a reaction against capitalist society, infused with the loss of a stable former time, and aligned with the Burkean notion that traditional social and political institutions ought to be upheld. Religion therefore became a key means of resisting the dominance of capitalism, and religious belief and experience coloured Romantic attitudes, as explored in Wayne Franklin's 'James Fenimore Cooper and American Artists in Europe', in which writers and painters were forced to confront Catholicism. Capitalist modernity is also related to racial questions, especially in the United States during the nineteenth century, as demonstrated by Sayre's essay, 'The Romantic Indian Commodified: Text and Image in George Catlin's *Letters and Notes* (1841)'; racialized modes of representation became part of Romanticism, valorizing national differences over Enlightenment universalism, while Sayre also provides a fresh perspective on Catlin's writing, appreciating it as travel literature set specifically within Indian territory. The role of Romanticism in ideological justifications for North American slavery is likewise considered. In her especially readable and compelling contribution, Janet Koenig explores 'Romantic Racialism and the Antislavery Novels of Stowe, Hildreth, and Melville', placing the comparatively obscure Hildreth alongside his more celebrated counterparts, and reading his work *The Slave* as a possible source for *Uncle Tom's Cabin*. While Hildreth's writing is seen as more radical than Stowe's, such radicalism is then taken to a new height by Melville's democratic Romanticism in *Benito Cereno*. Incorporating a wealth of illustrations (including colour reproductions), many of the essays (such as William Truettner's 'Picturing the Murder of Jane McCrea: A Critical Moment in Transatlantic Romanticism') are highly readable, enriched with fascinating and engaging factual and analytical detail. Presenting unusual insights into familiar writers and artists, and retrieving the less well-known, this collection above all presents 'a unifying outlook that links many of its most substantive works of art and literature with larger perspectives on religion and their organisation of social and political life, a particular Weltanschauung that is distinct from other possible belief systems in the period'.

Cody Marrs's *Nineteenth-Century American Literature and the Long Civil War* counters the critical tradition of separating the antebellum and postbellum eras, offering, like John A. Casey's *New Men* (reviewed above), a refreshing approach to this iconic conflict. As Marrs contends, the Civil War often functions 'as a constitutive absence in American literary history', perceived largely as 'a transition that matters only to the extent that it demarcates what precedes and follows it'; as such, the conflict holds a 'paradoxical status' as 'both the structural pivot and the empty centre of the nineteenth century'. Marrs argues instead for 'a different realisation', presenting the war 'not as a discrete instance of overturning but as a rupture with a stunning array of . . . afterlives'. Regarding the Civil War as an 'ongoing imaginative conflict across much of the nineteenth century' therefore generates revisionary readings of familiar figures, focusing upon Walt Whitman, Frederick Douglass, Herman Melville, and Emily Dickinson. Although they are usually perceived as antebellum writers, Marrs's line of enquiry reveals that their work is legible as part of a 'transbellum literature that stretches ... across and beyond the war itself', as they returned to the conflict as a subject after its conclusion, and recast its historicity. Chapter 1 roots Walt Whitman's *Leaves of Grass* in turmoil rather than tranquillity, following the author's own assertion that the war was 'the centre, circumference, umbilicus, of my whole career'. He notes that Whitman's writing life 'bridges the very epochal boundaries and periodic subsets that have long structured American literary studies; it is not so much antebellum or postbellum as it is interperiodic' (defined by Marrs as 'transbellum'). Reading Douglass as a 'transbellum' writer offers similarly revisionary perspectives in chapter 2, as he traces abolitionism back to earlier struggles for religious liberty and promotes an 'extraordinarily long view of freedom that enables emancipation to be retimed and reframed'. Chapter 3 considers Melville as a poet (a sometimes overlooked element of his oeuvre), exploring the presentation of the Civil War in his poems as a 'cyclical event that assumes a variety of forms', as historical patterns re-emerge in the conflict. Marrs's study concludes with Dickinson, observing that, 'for much of the twentieth century, the bellum context of Dickinson's verse was construed as a matter of coincidence', as the external clashes of the battlefield seemingly held no interest for the most inward-looking of poets. By contrast, Marrs recontextualizes her work within the rhetoric and ideologies of the war, and demonstrates the ways in which the conflict is presented as a 'vast destruction that is unmoored from chronology' in her writing. An Afterword then considers other, often less canonical, authors, offering new directions for their study and contending that the current reassessment of the rigidity of geographical borders in US literature ought to be broadened to include the fluidity of temporal borders; in doing so, Marrs considers, and yet counters, Whitman's refrain that 'the war, the war is over'.

Carla J. Mulford's *Benjamin Franklin and the Ends of Empire* is both a literary biography and an analysis of the evolution of the Founding Father's imperial theories. In contrast to much scholarly work on Franklin, Mulford is sensitive to the 'literariness of [his] expression', examining a rich array of material authored by him (including private and published letters, pamphlets, newspaper articles, notes, and speeches), and appreciating his intellectual life within the contexts of early modern liberalism and political theory. In tracing the intricate and deep roots of Franklin's thought, conventional images of him as a 'chameleon-like' figure are exploded, shifting standard interpretations which perceive his turn against the British empire as a sudden move and recognizing instead the gradual development of his disillusionment with imperial rule. Her study provides valuable new insight at both the micro and macro levels, presenting rich detail about Franklin specifically, yet placing it within a detailed outline of eighteenth-century political thought and the workings of the British empire. Consequently, as 'an intellectual history of British colonial relations articulated by and through Benjamin Franklin, it is the first of its kind'. Drawing on, yet developing, older scholarship (most especially Alan Houston's *Benjamin Franklin and the Politics of Improvement* [2008] and Douglas Anderson's *The Radical Enlightenments of Benjamin Franklin* [2000]), Mulford's book is organized both roughly chronologically and thematically. The introduction presents an overview of the intellectual roots of Franklin's early modern liberalism, then chapters 1 and 2 trace his family history, particularly in England. Most notably, Mulford demonstrates the ways in which his knowledge of British culture and imperialism influenced his writings about free trade and peoples. Chapters 3, 4, and 5 follow Franklin from young adulthood to middle age, as his developing socio-economic opinions gradually supported his belief in the advantages of a commonwealth, and his view that freedom was a natural right that ought to be available to all British Americans was formed. Franklin's disillusionment with British colonial administration, far from marking a rapid change, therefore stemmed from such beliefs, as examined in chapters 6 and 7. Chapter 8 recounts the revolution against Britain, emphasizing Franklin's stance on sovereignty and human justice, while chapter 9 outlines his last years, as the ageing Founding Father widened his concerns to encompass the subjection of peoples throughout the world. Mulford's study is meticulously researched and intricately detailed, albeit a little densely written and repetitive at times. Nevertheless, through stressing Franklin's relative modernity and enabling his voice to emerge (through extensive quotations from his writings and speeches), Mulford's biography embodies his desire 'to be acquainted with the truth'.

Kevin Pelletier's *Apocalyptic Sentimentalism: Love and Fear in U.S. Antebellum Literature* presents a simple yet surprising thesis: that terror played a significant role in the sentimentalism of nineteenth-century antislavery writings. Fear, in particular fear of God's vengeance, was a tool used by writers like Stowe when love and sympathy were deemed not quite effective enough at pressing a point. Pelletier aligns his study in opposition to the work of Ann Douglas, whose 1977 work *The Feminization of American Culture* has, according to Pelletier, skewed critical understandings of the sentimental tradition. Part I explores apocalyptic sentimentalism's beginnings in David Walker's *An Appeal to the Coloured Citizens of the World* [1829] and Nat Turner's *The Confessions of Nat Turner: The Leader of the Late Insurrection in Southampton, Virginia* [1831]. Maria W. Stewart, who has become known as the first African-American woman to speak to men and women, white and black, in a public setting, is the subject of chapter 2, along with Catherine Beecher and Lydia Maria Child. In his discussion of them Pelletier builds an illuminating picture of influences for later sentimental writers. Each abolitionist and women's rights activist, in their representation of the American home and domesticity as spaces of racial conflict, are demonstrated to have laid the groundwork for Harriet Beecher Stowe's *Uncle Tom's Cabin* which is the subject of the next chapter. Chapter 4 considers Stowe's 1856 novel *Dred* and black violence as abolitionist stratagem; Nat Turner's influence is reiterated and excavated. In Part III contemporary responses to John Brown's raid on Harpers Ferry are considered as sentimental in form. Pelletier argues that the preceding analysis leads to Brown as the 'irrepressible fantasy of nineteenth-century abolitionist sentimentality', and as the ultimate example of antislavery activity read in an apocalyptic-sentimental way. Turning, to some general conjectures relating to our present moment in the Coda, Pelletier discerns a fascination with terror in modern America. A sense of impending apocalypse, he suggests, continues to animate and inspire sentimental discourse.

*Performatively Speaking: Speech and Action in Antebellum American Literature* by Debra J. Rosenthal is as canonical in focus as they come. Looking at the work of mid-nineteenth-century American writers Fanny Fern, Nathaniel Hawthorne, Herman Melville, and Harriet Beecher Stowe, Rosenthal presents a work of literary criticism that is engaged in a consideration of words that do what they say: that perform the very action they describe. The slim volume opens with a description of Timothy Shay Arthur's *Ten Nights in a Bar-room and What I Saw There* and the scene in which the character Joe promises his daughter Mary that he will give up alcohol. The words of the promise, Rosenthal explains, are performative. The British philosopher of language John Langshaw Austin (or J.L. Austin) is the guiding theoretical voice for this study. The lecture series, that became *How To Do Things with Words*, published posthumously in 1962, and his other works on speech acts inform *Performatively Speaking*. However, Rosenthal carves the space for her critical intervention out of Austin's theory in relation to literary performance. Whilst Austin argued that in the poem, or the soliloquy, the fact that the situation and speech acts aren't 'real' renders them "'hollow or void'", Rosenthal's study begins from the premise that the authors included in her book were 'practitioners of performativity before such a theory was codified'. Potential problems with this aside, the following discussion of Fanny Fern's 1854 novel *Ruth Hall* reads the production of the signature in the novel, using Derrida's 'Declarations of Independence'. In the chapter addressing *The Scarlet Letter* Rosenthal attempts to show that the letter in question—the *A*— embodies both punitive language and performative dissent. She then turns to think about Stowe's *Uncle Tom's Cabin* and a moment of violent potential between Cassy and Sambo. Finally, using Judith Butler and J.L. Austin, Rosenthal comes to *Moby-Dick* to examine linguistic injury. *Performatively Speaking* is in one sense ambitious, but in another it is cursory, and therefore somewhat insubstantial.

Shawn Salvant's *Blood Work: Imagining Race in American Literature, 1890–1940* draws on anthropological and sociological research, maintaining that race is 'largely an effect of language', a metaphorical conception. In this, 'blood' performs a key function in the construction of racialism in late nineteenth- and early twentieth-century American literature, forming perhaps 'the most significant device by which American racialism has made sense of its ... historically contingent racial projects'. Although 'blood' emblematizes race across nations and cultures, Salvant argues that it becomes 'a particular substance' in the United States, coloured by slavery and race riots, the revolution and the Civil War. As such, the literary readings in *Blood Work* are motivated by the premise that 'the concept of blood, as the core image of American racial rhetoric, signifies a uniquely American racial formation characterised by particularly American cultural, legal, rhetorical, and literary constructions of the relationships between race, identity, and society'. An introductory chapter outlines the early roots of 'blood' in the birth of the nation, as American history and culture became underwritten by an interplay between literal and metaphorical blood, often tied to anti-black and anti-immigrant violence. In chapter 1, Salvant explores the ways in which blood works differently in scientific racial discourse and American race law, focusing on Mark Twain's *Pudd'nhead Wilson*. In chapter 2, the religious symbolism of blood is associated with racial identity and sacrifice in Frances Ellen Watkins Harper's *Iola Leroy*, together with her (often overlooked) poetry. In this, Harper is seen in relation to other African American writers (such as W.E.B. Du Bois), as well as differentiated from them, as her 'rebuttal against scientific determinism originates from sources unlike any of these others'. Subsequent chapters explore twentieth-century works (Pauline Hopkins's *Of One Blood* and William Faulkner's *Light in August*). While drawing on earlier scholarship, such as Betsy Erkkila's *Mixed Blood and Other Crosses*, Salvant offers refreshing insights and revisionary readings. Countering other critical assessments of Twain and Harper, for example, he demonstrates the ways in which they reinstate 'an alternative relationship between blood and racial identity that allows race to become reconstituted and practiced in non-biological terms'. Meticulously researched and encompassing an array of scholarly fields and approaches (from metaphor theory to legal, theological, and anthropological discourses), the span of Salvant's study embodies its central thesis—that there is no single meaning behind 'blood'. Above all, *Blood Work* illustrates 'how blood filters and frames our perceptions of race', shifting the standard focus of racial blood 'away from race and more toward the cultural and discursive meanings of blood'.

Vanessa Meikle Schulman's *Work Sights: the Visual Culture of Industry in Nineteenth-Century America*, published in the University of Massachusetts Press Science/Technology/Culture series, seeks to question why so many images of industry flooded the 'visual realm' between the years 1857 and 1887. Schulman investigates the tension between positive and negative responses to technical and industrial change that shaped the three decades focused on here. In chapter 1, 'Between Materialist and Magic: Representing the Railroad and the Telegraph', we see how visual artists represented a map of the nation by way of the railroad and the telegraph, creating a sense of national identity in an otherwise expansive and divided country. Chapter 2 examines John Ferguson Weir's *The Gun Foundry* and *Forging the Shaft*, two paintings that, according to Schulman, have been held up as examples of visual works that celebrate advancing technological developments in the Northern States. Schulman argues for a more complex view of Weir's artistic creations, and she identifies a number of tensions or ambivalences in the artworks, for example between labour and leisure, in an approach similar to chapter 1's examination of how these visual images depict technology as magical. In the case of Weir, the author argues, this enchantment is due to the alchemical properties of painting, that add a layer of sublimity to the representation of metalwork in these canvases. Chapters 3 and 4 illustrate how technological systems, in the decades following the Civil War, were figured increasingly as national in character. Chapter 5 argues that a certain type of image appears in conjunction with managerial capitalism that attempts to give the viewer the feeling of control over the production of commodities. In this chapter we are taken authoritatively through the ways in which proto-Progressive Era politics were supported by representations of managerial control published in *Harper's Weekly*, *Scientific American*, and *Scribner's Monthly*. Concluding *Work Sights*, Schulman articulates the modest yet meaningful importance of this contribution to nineteenth-century American studies: that while the Civil War may have been the dominant force moulding national identity at this time, representations of the changing scale of industry between 1857 and 1887 played a part in shaping how the population understood the relationship between work and technological progress as a constituent part of the national character.

Daneen Wardrop's *Civil War Nurse Narratives 1863–1870* begins with a discussion of Louisa May Alcott's *Hospital Sketches* and the ways in which Alcott established her style through multiple revisions of the sketches. Wardrop argues that Alcott's attention to her readership, who showered an amount of praise on the pieces that baffled the author, can be seen in the way she developed the sketches from letters, to articles, to a book. By increasing the variety of methods employed for creating rapport between her narrative voice and the reader in each new format Alcott created a distinctive, energetic voice that captivated her audience with its blend of fiction and nonfiction, levity and seriousness. In doing so she produced the perfect vehicle for her underlying abolitionist message. Of the twelve Union women nurses who published single-author studies of the war period, six others are included in Wardrop's study: Georgeanna Woolsey's *Three Weeks at Gettysburg*, Julia Dunlap's *Notes of Hospital Life*, Elvira Powers's *Hospital Pencillings*, Anna Morris Holstein's *Three Years in Field Hospitals of the Army of the Potomac*, Sophronia Bucklin's *In Hospital and Camp*, and Julia Wheelock's *The Boys in White*. In her introduction to *Civil War Nurse Narratives* the author explains that her study does not include the narratives of Confederate nurses. Commenting on the 'healing' decade—the 1870s—during which time the American populace 'recovered', Wardrop argues that those nurse narratives published from 1880 onwards were more conciliatory, accepting, nostalgic even. Thus, this book focuses on the 1860s, and those texts composed and published *during* the conflict and in its immediate aftermath. Elvira J. Powers is the focus of chapter 4, 'Travel, Dissent, and Cultural Ties'. In her book *Hospital Pencillings* [1866], Powers aligned herself forcefully, we are told, with the rhetoric of the women's rights movement and battled patriarchal, institutional codes of behaviour in her time as a civil war nurse. Chapter 7 looks at Julia S. Wheelock's *The Boys in White*, describing Wheelock's transformation from schoolteacher to writer, urging the public to give donations to the newly formed army hospitals and war effort, the novel performing as representative of the main discursive threads of *Civil War Nurse Narratives 1863–1870*. Wheelock's 1870 text, the 'last nurse narrative written for a decade', is convincingly articulated by Wardrop as resistant to the possibilities of sentimental closure. Concluding her study, the author maintains the measured tone established early on in this well-evidenced and illuminating study of a neglected area of Civil War history. Wardrop makes a quiet yet persuasive claim for Civil War nurse narratives as engagements with concerns that would become the politics of the New

Woman, and in doing so connects this 'small arena' of self-expression to larger concerns facing the republic.

Cindy Weinstein's *Time, Tense, and American Literature: When is Now?* establishes a 'rather surprising tradition' of American writing, tracing the ways in which time is focused on by authors ranging from Charles Brockden Brown to Edward P. Jones. Weinstein takes Edgar Allan Poe's *Pym*—a novel infused with temporal references—as a central point of departure, maintaining that time, in each of the texts included, 'discloses a fascinating literary sensibility that is inextricably linked to a historical context without which that sensibility would not ... be so able to express itself'. Building upon prior studies of temporality (such as Wai Chee Dimock's *Through Other Continents: American Literature Across Deep Time*), she posits that key moments of cultural upheaval (the Civil War and race riots, for instance) find expression in literary uncertainty about time, defined as 'tempo(e)rality'. Consequently, *When Is Now?* is 'as much about how to read time as it is about time'. Engagingly written, Weinstein's book presents astute and invigorating analyses at both the macro and micro levels, examining temporal patterns in relation to historical contexts and offering close readings of individual texts (informed by Barthes's structural analysis of tenses and Genette's theories of analepsis and prolepsis). The first three chapters focus on pre-1900 texts (Brockden Brown's *Edgar Huntly*, Poe's *Pym*, and Elizabeth Stuart Phelps's *The Gates Ajar*), before moving on to later writers and works (Theodore Dreiser's *An American Tragedy* and Jones's *The Known World*). While the specificity of each novel is recognized (highlighting Phelps's preoccupation with Civil War mortality, Dreiser's modernism, and Jones's concern with race and slavery, for example), intertextual connections are also drawn, as each 'registers some shock to consciousness that is imagined as an irreparable break in the American Gestalt, dislodging its past from its present, making its future insecure'. Such a critical focus therefore presents 'a new trajectory for American literature', while enabling fresh interpretations of well-studied texts and embedded ideas (for example, although Brown and Poe are often linked thematically—through their interest in issues ranging from Gothicism to racial difference—Weinstein connects them at the level of diction instead, interrogating their shared language of time). Chapter 1 offers a close analysis of the rhythm of Brown's prose, caught between paralysis and action, and notes how it recalls the debates about the ratification of the Constitution (which was contemporaneous to the novel's story [1787]). Chapter 2 examines temporal fluidity and confusion in Poe, set within the context of his racism. Phelps's use of tense is considered in chapter 3, as the temporal disorderliness of *The Gates Ajar* reflects the rupturing trauma of the Civil War, prior to an examination of Dreiser and Jones in chapters 4 and 5. Although Weinstein's study is organized chronologically, from Brockden Brown to Jones, its interconnected analyses, moving backwards and forwards between texts, embody her recognition of the complexity, and confusion, of time.

*Kate Chopin in Context: New Approaches*, edited by Heather Ostman and Kate O'Donoghue, and published by Palgrave Macmillan, is the latest in the American Literature Readings in the 21st Century series, edited by Linda Wagner-Martin. The collection is divided into two parts: Part I, containing six chapters, is devoted to 'New Contextual Approaches', and Part II, also consisting of six chapters, is focused on 'New Pedagogical Approaches'. In a work dedicated to 'New' approaches there are some strange critical omissions. There is one reference to the 2008 *Cambridge Companion to Kate Chopin* and only one reference to the even more recent Critical Insights collection devoted to *The Awakening* and published in 2014. Both of these feature in Bernard Koloski's opening chapter, 'Chopin's Enlightened Men', which begins from the somewhat risky premise that hitherto Chopin scholarship has been 'woman-centric'. In his discussion of Chopin's 'worthy' men Koloski moves through a number of the short stories, including 'A No-Account Creole', 'Charlie', 'Athénaïse', and the novel *At Fault*. Analysing Offdean, Mr Laborde, Gouvernail, and Hosmer as characters with redeemable qualities is all very well, but these men exist in a universe concerned with female experience, female agency, female suffering. Rafael Walker's 'Kate Chopin and the Dilemma of Individualism' is, again, not critically engaged with that which has gone before, nor is it 'new' in its discussion of swimming, sexual desire, and suicide. There are substantial discussions of individualism in Janet Beer and Helena Goodwyn's 'Kate Chopin's *The Awakening*: Authenticity and the Artist', Erik Margraf's 'Kate Chopin's *The Awakening* as a Naturalistic Novel', and John Glendening's 'Evolution, Narcissism, and Maladaptation in Kate Chopin's *The Awakening*', to name but a few chapters that deal with *The Awakening* alone. Diana Epelbaum's 'Pioneering Kate Chopin's Feminism: Elizabeth Stoddard's *The Morgesons* as Patchwork Precursor to *The Awakening*' is one of the collection's more successful moments. Epelbaum models the work of a comparative approach to *The Awakening*, providing an example of a fruitful 'compare and contrast' essay for students. Kate O'Donoghue's description of the relationship between digital humanities, pedagogy, and student engagement is interesting, as is Mohanalakshmi Rajakumar and Geetha Rajeswar's discussion of Qatari students' responses to 'The Story of an Hour', but to argue that their engagement with the story demonstrates 'the relevance of her [Chopin's] work for contemporary readers' is, at best, a prosaic observation. Emily Toth's contribution is three or so pages long and in some ways reflective of the overarching problem with this collection. There is not much here that adds anything of substance to serious Chopin scholarship.

*A Kiss from Thermopylae: Emily Dickinson and Law* by James R. Guthrie is divided into seven chapters and begins by explaining that Dickinson's life was imbued with the legal profession and its language. Emily Dickinson's father, Edward Dickinson, and her brother, William Austin Dickinson (known as Austin), were both lawyers in the family practice. Chapter 2 considers how Dickinson dealt with the idea of equity in her poetry and focuses in particular on the poem 'Alone and in a Circumstance'. As in chapter 2, in chapter 3 Shakespeare's *The Merchant of Venice* provides appropriate legal and literary context for Dickinson's works. A later chapter, entitled 'Felonies, Trials, and Transcendental Prisons: Crime and Punishment', analyses metaphors of crime, trial, and punishment in Dickinson's poetry and makes links to Guthrie's previous work, *Emily Dickinson's Vision: Illness and Identity in Her Poetry*, published by the University Press of Florida in 1998. In the final chapter, from which this book takes its name, Guthrie considers the last few decades of Dickinson's life in the aftermath of Lincoln's and Garfield's assassinations. Beginning with a brief discussion of 'the rule of law', and then turning to a consideration of Dickinson's oft-used image of the battle of Thermopylae as a 'metatrope', Guthrie ends his study by declaring that 'law and love' were often synonymous for Dickinson as they both represent a powerful and binding form of commitment.

*Jack London: A Writer's Fight for a Better America* by Cecelia Tichi calls for more emphasis on London as a public intellectual alongside all the other monikers he has achieved, including travel writer, novelist, social essayist, and journalist. Tichi makes some bold claims for London as a figure who 'laid the foundation for a refashioned, better world'. Written in a style that suggests that this is what has come to be known as a 'crossover' book, *Jack London* presents the reader with a number of vignettes from London's life that go some way to construct what, at times, feels very much like a biography, and it is difficult to know if this is the intended effect. There are a number of attractive illustrations contained within this volume, including London's own photography, as well as wide-ranging reference to his prolific writings. Nonetheless, it is difficult to find a clear sense of what *A Writer's Fight for a Better America*'s leading line of argument is. If, as the title suggests, this is a study of London as social crusader, then this idea is of course not new but one that has been examined by a number of critics, including Carolyn Johnston, Joan D. Hedrick, Rebecca Stefoff, and Jeanne Campbell Reesman. Enjoyable but lacking critical focus, this is a knowledgeable work that suffers from an absence of a central organizing principle.

Brian Yothers's *Sacred Uncertainty: Religious Difference and the Shape of Melville's Career*, published by Northwestern University Press, proposes that throughout his literary life Herman Melville was engaged in a consideration of faith, doubt, knowledge, and hope. His negotiation of the relationships between these with characteristic humour does *not*, Yothers insists, negate the seriousness of the endeavour. This diligent work begins with a consideration of William Rounseville Alger's *The Solitudes of Nature and Man; or, The Loneliness of Human Life* and Melville's marginalia. Yothers argues that Melville's markings in *The Solitudes of Nature and Man* are indicative of his preoccupation with solitude and sociability. Elsewhere in the chapter Yothers highlights the still (relatively) new work that digital methodologies allow, and the work of Steven Olsen-Smith with *Melville's Marginalia Online*. In the next chapter, concerned with the five-year period between *Typee* and *Moby-Dick* (1846–51), the author examines Melville's interest in religious difference. Noting that *Typee* and *Omoo* are not prominent in the critical attention paid to Melville, Yothers says that they were, however, the most read by Melville's contemporaries. By tracing 'missionary encounters' in these two texts one can discern a triangular pattern, argues Yothers, which pits hollow missionary hypocrites against sympathetic yet othered indigenous peoples, and thirdly us, plus Melville and his narrators. This chapter considers the human to contain a fundamental duality—'the sharkish and the divine'—which Yothers sees everywhere in Melville's oeuvre, even after the 'landlessness' of the early works. Chapter 3 discusses Melville's engagement with the range of religions operating in his contemporary America in the 1850s and the debates that informed them. Chapter 4 charts the move to poetry made by Melville in response to the Civil War and contends that *Battle-Pieces* marks the 'major turning point' in Melville's career. Chapter 5 considers *Clarel, A Poem and Pilgrimage in the Holy Land* Melville's 18,000-line epic, and concludes that Melville was, with qualification, a Unitarian. Lastly, *Billy Budd* and Melville's late poetry are considered together in chapter 6. Yothers makes much of the idea that we should not separate Melville's poetry and prose works altogether, but instead read them as part of a continuous, if not linear, development. Melville's late poetry has been, according to Yothers, 'egregiously ignored' by other critics. In this, the final discussion of doubt presented in *Sacred Uncertainty*, Yothers revels in a sense of Melville's works as 'unfinished ... thought', endlessly incomplete, resistant to any attempt at a final reading.

Hsuan L. Hsu has contributed to the relatively new transnational turn in literary studies with his second critical book *Sitting in Darkness: Mark Twain's Asia and Comparative Racialization*. His first, *Geography and the Production of Space in Nineteenth-Century American Literature*, was published by Cambridge University Press in 2010. That book was grounded in the theoretics of space and the 1980s works of Henri Lefebvre, Edward Soja, and others. In *Sitting in Darkness* Hsu takes on an area of Twain's writings that has been under-studied: his engagement with Asia and Asian Americans. Hsu employs frameworks of legal scholarship, comparative ethnic studies, and transnational studies to consider the comparisons that Twain made between racial groups, critiquing comparative racialization while also making a case for the usefulness of comparative studies. Hsu lays out the terms of his argument methodically and persuasively in the introduction, emphasizing the importance of connecting our understanding of imperialism, Chinese Exclusion, Jim Crow, the rise of corporations, and the development of the US West. Chapter 1 begins this work with Twain's play *Ah Sin*, written collaboratively with Bret Harte. Hsu demonstrates how the 1854 case *People v. Hall*, which prohibited Chinese Americans and Chinese immigrants from testifying against white citizens, generated the very debates that *Ah Sin* took part in. Chapter 2 considers the legal and cultural connections between vagrancy and racialization in *Huckleberry Finn* and *The Adventures of Tom Sawyer*, skilfully weaving a wealth of intertexts through the discussion, such as 'Three Vagabonds of Trinidad' by Bret Harte and other texts by Twain. In chapter 3 *The Comedy of Those Extraordinary Twins* and *The Tragedy of Pudd'nhead Wilson* are the texts through which Hsu examines Twain's engagement with the 'legal fiction of corporate personhood'. Chapter 4 brings in the writings of Yung Wing, the first Chinese person to graduate from a US university, and Wong Chin Foo, activist and journalist. Both writers were interested in the movement for Chinese and Chinese American modernization. *A Connecticut Yankee*, Hsu convincingly argues, is informed by Twain's understanding of China's 'Self-Strengthening' movement in the latter half of the nineteenth century. Chapter 5 looks at Twain's allegorical non-fiction as a movement away from creating individual characters to looking at populations. Twain's critique of how racist and imperialist regimes count and discount the dead is the final topic of this thorough and compelling work of criticism. Concluding his study Hsu makes a case for Twain as precursor to twentieth- and twenty-first-century writers who reveal institutional racisms in their works.

## Books Reviewed

Casey, John A. *New Men: Reconstructing the Image of the Veteran in Late-Nineteenth-Century American Literature and Culture*. FordUP. [2015] pp. 248. $55 ISBN 9 7808 2326 5398.

Chapman, Alison. *Networking the Nation: British and American Women's Poetry and Italy, 1840–1870*. OUP. [2015] pp. xxii + 303. £60 ISBN 9 7801 9872 3578.

Dolis, John. *Transnational Na(rra)tion: Home and Homeland in Nineteenth-Century American Literature*. FDUP. [2015] pp. xii + 199. £49.95 ISBN 9 7816 1147 8150.

Ellerby, Janet Mason. *Embroidering the Scarlet A: Unwed Mothers and Illegitimate Children in American Fiction and Film*. UMichP. [2015] pp. 290. $34 ISBN 9 7804 7205 2639.

Fishkin, Shelley Fisher. *Writing America: Literary Landmarks from Walden Pond to Wounded Knee (A Reader's Companion)*. RutgersUP. [2015] pp. xi + 381. $34.95 ISBN 9 7808 1357 5971.

Gardner, Eric. *Black Print Unbound: The Christian Recorder, African American Literature, and Periodical Culture*. OUP. [2015] pp. 352. £19.99 ISBN 9 7801 9023 7097.

Guthrie, James R. *A Kiss from Thermopylae: Emily Dickinson and Law*. UMassP. [2015] pp. ix + 256. $25.95 ISBN 9 7816 2534 1136.

Hemingway, Andrew, and Alan Wallach, eds. *Transatlantic Romanticism: British and American Art and Literature, 1790–1860*. UMassP. [2015] pp. 336. $29.95 ISBN 9 7816 2534 1143.

Hsu, Hsuan L. *Sitting in Darkness: Mark Twain's Asia and Comparative Racialization*. NYUP. [2015] pp. xii + 244. $89 ISBN 9 7814 7988 0416.

Marrs, Cody. *Nineteenth-Century American Literature and the Long Civil War*. CUP. [2015] pp. 206. £67 ISBN 9 7811 0710 9834.

Mulford, Carla J. *Benjamin Franklin and the Ends of Empire*. OUP. [2015] pp. 448. £41.99 ISBN 9 7801 9938 4198.

Ostman, Heather, and Kate O'Donoghue. *Kate Chopin in Context: New Approaches*. PalMac. [2015] pp. vii + 216. £43.99 ISBN 9 7811 3755 1795.

Pelletier, Kevin. *Apocalyptic Sentimentalism: Love and Fear in U.S. Antebellum Literature*. UGeoP. [2015] pp. xii + 256. $49.95 ISBN 9 7808 2033 9481.

Rosenthal, Debra J. *Performatively Speaking: Speech and Action in Antebellum American Literature*. UPVirginia. [2015] pp. ix + 136. $59.50 ISBN 9 7808 1393 6963.

Salvant, Shawn. *Blood Work: Imagining Race in American Literature, 1890–1940*. LSUP. [2015] pp. 240. $45 ISBN 9 7808 0715 7848.

Schulman, Vanessa Meikle. *Work Sights: The Visual Culture of Industry in Nineteenth-Century America*. UMassP. [2015] pp. xi + 287. $29.95 ISBN 9 7816 2534 1952.

Tichi, Cecelia. *Jack London: A Writer's Fight for a Better America*. UNCP. [2015] pp. 281. $34.95 ISBN 9 7814 6962 2668.

Wardrop, Daneen. *Civil War Nurse Narratives, 1863–1870*. UIowaP. [2015] pp. ix + 267. $55 ISBN 9 7816 0938 3671.

Weinstein, Cindy. *Time, Tense, and American Literature: When Is Now?* CUP. [2015] pp. xi + 181. £72 ISBN 9 7811 0709 9876.

Yothers, Brian. *Sacred Uncertainty: Religious Difference and the Shape of Melville's Career*. NorthwesternUP. [2015] pp. xii + 244. $99.95 ISBN 9 7808 1013 0715.

# XVII

# American Literature: The Twentieth Century

JAMES GIFFORD, MARGARET KONKOL,
JAMES M. CLAWSON, MARY FOLTZ,
SOPHIE MARUÉJOULS-KOCH, ORION USSNER KIDDER,
JOLENE ARMSTRONG, AND LINDSAY PARKER

This chapter has eight sections: 1. Poetry; 2. Fiction 1900–1945; 3. Fiction since 1945; 4. Drama; 5. Comics; 6. African American Writing; 7. Native Writing; 8. Latino/a, Asian American, and General Ethnic Writing. Section 1 is by James Gifford and Margaret Konkol; section 2 is by James M. Clawson; section 3 is by Mary Foltz; section 4 is by Sophie Maruéjouls-Koch; section 5 is by Orion Ussner Kidder, section 6 is by Jolene Armstrong; section 7 is by James Gifford; section 8 is by Lindsay Parker.

## 1. Poetry

Several major edited collections on American poetry have come to completion through Cambridge University Press in 2015, including *The Cambridge History of American Poetry*, edited by Alfred Bendixen and Stephen Burt, *A History of Modernist Poetry*, edited by Alex Davis and Lee Jenkins, *The Cambridge Companion to American Poets*, edited by Mark Richardson, and *The Cambridge Companion to Modern American Poetry*, edited by Walter Kalaidjian. All four are excellent, but to have them as a set side by side and published in a single year is remarkable. All four also overlap extensively with recent work, and many of their contributors have been productive beyond the norm in recent years, so they call to recent developments in American poetry and to the most recent textual, archival, and biographical studies. The four are also deeply overlapping while entirely distinct in orientation and approach. Richardson opens *The Cambridge Companion to American Poets* by setting patriotic American exceptionalism in contrast to the equally American tradition of the jeremiad. This focus gives his volume a strong tendency towards the twentieth century, and as with his opening focus on the jeremiad

*The Year's Work in English Studies, Volume 96 (2017)* © *The Author 2017. Published by Oxford University Press on behalf of the English Association. All rights reserved. For Permissions, please email: journals.permissions@oup.com*
doi:10.1093/ywes/max018

through Frederick Douglass, a nineteenth century focused on the familiar figures of the fireside poets, Poe, Emerson, Whitman, Melville, and Dickinson all in respective chapters. This is both what makes the volume perfect for use in a survey course that must 'cover all the bases' in sequence but also distinct from Bendixen and Burt's *The Cambridge History of American Poetry*. Bendixen and Burt's introduction stresses the historical inclusivity of their project, setting aside the canonical excisions of time in order to find new contexts and companion pieces for the familiar figures and works. In their phrasing, too many survey projects have touched vaguely on the Puritan poets to 'give a nod to Poe and the Transcendentalists and a dismissive shake of the head for the old Fireside Poets and a declaration that the two poets from this century who mattered—Walt Whitman and Emily Dickinson—achieved greatness by writing poetry in a way that poetry had not been written before' (p. 2). They astutely point to how this privileges the twentieth century and the modernist privileging of the new, which in effect has reshaped our critical vision to understand the past through the lens of modernism just as much as it leads us to understand the present twenty-first century through the same. By stressing the historical, they offer a distinct narrative that not only recuperates lost voices, such as opening the volume with indigenous oral traditions (a move as much a political as it is a scholarly corrective), but also redraws the way we have framed modern works, which they consider up to the year 2000 on the convenient marking of a shift in American culture in 2001. They have organized the book's opening with Betty Booth Donohue's 'Remembering Muskrat: Native Poetics and the American Indian Oral Tradition' to point, per the introduction (p. 9) forward into the twenty-first century to the rise of performance of embodied poetics through American Sign Language and poetry composed through computational methods. Both of these future directions read well back into the twentieth century but give a jumping off point for further work and also connect the volume to current scholarship, such as Rebecca Sanchez's *Deafening Modernism*, which is reviewed below. The history as a whole closes with Burt's own quasi-polemical call to Hart Crane's *The Bridge*. By contrast, Kalaidjian's *Cambridge Companion to Modern American Poetry* stresses the globalized community that shaped the local conditions in America, while Davis and Jenkins make this globalized frame the major part of their project in *A History of Modernist Poetry*, which opens with international anglophone poetics and the new modernist studies. These last two volumes also open with detailed chronologies. Taken together, the 104 chapters and four introductions, two chronologies, and four guides to further reading (a chapter-by-chapter selected bibliography for *The Cambridge History of American Poetry*) in these volumes together form the signal critical resource on American poetry published in 2015.

Richardson's *Cambridge Companion to American Poets* opens the twentieth century with his own chapter on Robert Frost that follows on his editing last year of *Robert Frost in Context* (CUP [2014]; reviewed in *YWES* 95[2016]), in which he included a number of the same contributors as this volume, such as the major scholars John Xiros Cooper and Steven Gould Axelrod, here authoring the chapters 'T.S. Eliot and American Poetry' and 'The Three

Voices of Robert Lowell' respectively. Although there are no chapters dedicated to Robert Duncan or H.D., both appear in Alan Golding's excellent summary chapter on 'The Black Mountain School', and H.D. is discussed in both Alec Marsh's 'Ezra Pound' and Celeste Goodridge's 'Marianne Moore'. Daniel Katz's dedicated chapter, 'Jack Spicer', follows in the path of much recent work, much of it Katz's own or prompted by his work, including his 'Jack Spicer's *After Lorca*: Translation as Decomposition' (*TPr* 18[2004] 83–103; reviewed in *YWES* 85[2006]) and the final chapter of *American Modernism's Expatriate Scene: Labour of Translation* (EdinUP [2007]; reviewed in *YWES* 89[2010]). Other chapters are dedicated specifically to Allen Ginsberg, Gwendolyn Brooks, Adrienne Rich, Elizabeth Bishop, Langston Hughes, Hart Crane, Marianne Moore, William Carlos Williams, Wallace Stevens, and Gertrude Stein, with other chapters on groups, the Harlem Renaissance, confessional poetry (focused on Anne Sexton and Sylvia Plath), the New York school, and the Black Mountain school. David Kirby closes the book with a consideration of the contemporary scene. He opens with a lament on the universal accessibility of production such that just as our various technologies now allow anyone the studio musician experience to record and make music regardless of talent or training, so too is poetry more easily produced and distributed than ever before, resulting in the unrecognizability of most current writers even to critics as capacious and as Catholic in taste as Kirby. From here he moves to the 'War of the Anthologies' (pp. 426–7) dividing the academic and confessional poets from the Black Mountain school and San Francisco Renaissance. The key argument of this closing point is in favour of what Kirby calls 'three-dimensional' poetry, by which he means poetry in a lyrical tradition with a speaker and/or interlocutor, poetry of its moment but aware of broader spans of time, poetry holding both tragedy and comedy, poetry that may be performed just as well as read, and poetry with an explicit or implicit form of narrative. It is no surprise that Language poetry receives a quietly caustic rejoinder here in the form of a quip on its potential for engaging with Marxist interests. However, as a gesture to navigating the breadth of contemporary poetry, Kirby's stance is clearly both sincere and polemical, meaning it argues its position while obviously inviting disagreement and dispute.

Bendixen and Burt's *The Cambridge History of American Poetry* has fifty chapters, twenty-nine of which focus on the twentieth century, which is divided in two sections for 'Forms of Modernism, 1900–1950' and 'Beyond Modernism: American Poetry 1950–2000'. Siobhan Phillips's chapter, 'Robert Frost and Tradition', sits very well next to John Xiros Cooper's polemical call for the inclusion of Frost in the new modernist studies in Jason Harding's *Robert Frost in Context* (CUP [2014]; reviewed in *YWES* 95[2016])—where Cooper's polemical and casual tone calls for a major reconsideration, Phillips has in a more historical context set out a series of finer points that support this polemic inexorably while reading across Frost's career and closing with his influence on poets most active after 1950. Charles Altieri's excellent chapter on T.S. Eliot connects beautifully through its consideration of the importance of the French Symbolists to McGuiness's *Poetry & Radical Politics in Fin de Siècle France* (OUP [2015]; reviewed below).

Cristanne Miller's 'Finding "Only Words" Mysterious' challenges the national distinctions that plague studies of British versus English writers, firmly setting Mina Loy and H.D. as American poets despite attempts to shift their affiliations, as happens with Eliot and Pound. Mark Scroggins, whose *Intricate Thicket* (UAlaP [2015]) is reviewed below, contributes 'The Objectivists and the Left', in which his opening on the conflict between leftist politics oriented towards socialist realism in both poetry and prose versus reactionary modernist experimentation provides the rationale for the emergence of Objectivist poetry. Scroggins firmly reads the Objectivists as second-generation modernists with a distinct political affiliation and hence social aim and subject matter: what he later examples through reading Louis Zukofsky's '*A*' as 'something of a Marxist *Cantos*' (p. 737), leading in to his approach to Lorine Niedecker and George Oppen. Bob Perelman writes the dedicated chapter on William Carlos Williams, Robin G. Schulz on Marianne Moore, George S. Lensing on Wallace Stevens, and David Chioni Moore on Langston Hughes. There is no dedicated chapter on Ezra Pound, though he is discussed throughout and in Matthew Hofer's 'Ezra Pound, William Carlos Williams, and the East Coast Projectivists'. Other thematic chapters in the modernism section include Ernest Suarez's 'Writing the South', Richard Flynn on feeling in Elizabeth Bishop and Randall Jarrell, David Wojahn on Robert Lowell's influence on the confessional school, Lesley Wheeler on formalism, and an excellent summative historicizing chapter, 'The Twentieth Century Begins', by John Timberman Newcomb, whose recent *How Did Poetry Survive?* has been widely lauded (UIllP [2013]; reviewed in *YWES* 94[2015]). The fourth section of the volume from 1950 to 2000 is more oriented to movements and groups than individual figures. It opens with Stephen Fredman's 'San Francisco and the Beats' and Brian M. Reed's 'The New York School'. Fredman's great strength here is opening the social networks and community that bound the Beats and San Francisco Renaissance together, and likewise Reed emphasizes what ties the New York school poets together despite their stylistic and topical variety. Rigoberto González's 'Latino Poetry and Poetics' takes on the dauntingly capacious field across the twentieth century as a whole, dividing his attention by ethnicity with sections on Chicano, Puerto Rican, and Cuban American poetries under a grudgingly pan-Latino identity that is oriented to activism as much as poetics. Juliana Spahr's 'Multilingualism in Contemporary American Poetry' attends to the daunting combination of World Englishes and migration as well as the appropriation of terms by bilingual writers from a mother tongue. This is particularly detailed for indigenous North American languages far beyond the twentieth century here (and including Hawaiian), but also Spanish, Greek, German, Korean, and so forth, which she closes through the ethical call to speak of our complicity in the violence of language yet relations among difference.

Kalaidjian's *Cambridge Companion to Modern American Poetry* focuses on movements or groups without chapters on representative figures, although Pound and Eliot appear across the volume more than any other two poets. Rachel Blau DuPlessis's 'Objectivist Poetry and Poetics' sits informatively beside Scroggins's chapter reviewed above and recalls her *The Objectivist Nexus* co-edited with Peter Quartermain (UAlaP [1999]; reviewed in *YWES*

80[2001]). In contrast to Scroggins, though not in conflict, DuPlessis presents the Objectivists as 'a late modernist set of leftists and realists', yet 'objectivist work is not Popular Front poetry' (p. 91), which emphasizes the materialism of the Objectivists over their deeply related political commitments. This leads her to privilege their deployment of Pound's poetical influence into a distinct political programme. Burt, who co-edited and wrote the final chapter for the *Cambridge History of American Poetry*, contributes the 'Mid-Century Modernism' chapter here, in which he presents Jarrell, Lowell, Elizabeth Bishop, James Merrill, and Richard Wilbur as a highly successful generation without the same unifying focus as their predecessors and with a liberal trouble over ideological certainties caused by the genocides of the Second World War. Burt productively turns to Diederik Oosdijk's *Among the Nightmare Fighters* (USCP [2010]; reviewed in *YWES* 91[2012]) and Alan Filreis's influential *Counter-Revolution of the Word* (UNCP [2008]; reviewed in *YWES* 89[2010]). Kaplan Harris's 'Black Mountain Poetry' follows on his co-edited *The Selected Letters of Robert Creeley* with Rod Smith and Peter Baker (UCalP [2014]; reviewed in *YWES* 95[2016]). He presents a central critical problem at the outset between those who consider the Black Mountain school through Black Mountain College and hence with Charles Olson as the central and unifying figure, versus those to look to Robert Creeley's *Black Mountain Review*, with its more heterogeneous and international set of contributors, in particular the emergent Beats. Cary Nelson's 'The Legacy of New York' is deceptively focused more on the city than a movement or group, shifting from Mina Loy and Pound to Moore and indigenous writers. He also emphatically returns attention, unexpectedly, to the major recuperative collection *Changing is Not Vanishing*, edited by Robert Dale Parker (UPennP [2011]; reviewed in *YWES* 92[2013]), which enlivens the Native American Renaissance that gained ground in the 1960s, but not without long and deep roots in the previous century and earlier. By using the city as a locus, Nelson stresses the diversity, internationalism, and deep connections across forms of difference that characterize this segment of American poetry and poetics. Anne Day Dewey's 'The Modern American Long Poem' also needs special notice for its work sewing together Eliot, Pound, H.D., Hart Crane, and Williams to John Berryman, Langston Hughes, Creeley, Duncan, and Ginsberg, with a suggested brief consideration of Marilyn Hacker. Janet McAdams also extends Nelson's provocations in 'Land, Place, and Nation: Toward an Indigenous American Poetics'. She deftly sets out the reclaiming of indigeneity following on the Native American Renaissance as a neoliberal critical conceptualization privileging the heroic individual in a Cold War climate and cultural context to instead consider how rootedness in place and community differ in the nationalist and localist paradigms. The chapter is both excellent scholarship and an accessible introduction to the field and its critical debates for students—for student readers, the chapter would work admirably in conjunction with Sean Kicummah Teuton's 'Cities of Refuge: Indigenous Cosmopolitan Writers and the International Imaginary' (*AmLH* 25:i[2013] 33–53; reviewed in *YWES* 94[2015]).

Davis and Jenkins's *A History of Modernist Poetry* is more focused than any of the four collections on modernism as a movement and concept, which is reflected in the relatively few single or joint point-focused chapters and their thematic continuities. Some of the finest scholars at work on literary modernism today are included in the volume and contribute to the themes on which they are most experienced. Vincent Sherry contributes 'Decadence and Poetic Modernism', which connects closely with his *Modernism and the Reinvention of Decadence* (CUP [2014]; reviewed in *YWES* 95[2016]). Adam Piette wrote 'War Modernism, 1918–1945' following on his *Imagination at War: British Fiction and Poetry 1939–1945* (Macmillan [1995]; reviewed in *YWES* 76[1998]) and more recent *Edinburgh Companion to Twentieth-Century British and American War Literature* (EdinUP [2012]; *YWES* 93[2014]). Scroggins appears again with 'Objectivist Poets', and Helen Carr remains close to her excellent *The Verse Revolutionaries* (Cape [2009]) with 'Edwardians, Georgians, Imagist, Vorticist, and "Amygist" Poetry'. Miranda Hickman contributes 'Early Eliot, H.D., and Pound', again so near to her expertise established in *The Geometry of Modernism* (UTexP [2005]; reviewed in *YWES* 87[2008]) and her edition of *One Must Not Go Altogether with the Tide: The Letters of Ezra Pound and Stanley Nott* (McG-QUP [2011]; reviewed in *YWES* 92[2013]). Hickman's chapter is followed later in the volume by Jason Harding's 'Later Eliot and Pound', lamentably without H.D. but remarkable in its direct comparison of the later cantos, notably 'Rock-Drill', with *Four Quartets*. Harding's work follows just after his edited collections *T.S. Eliot in Context* (CUP [2011]; reviewed in *YWES* 92[2013]) and, with Giovanni Cianci, *T.S. Eliot and the Concept of Tradition* (CUP [2007]; reviewed in *YWES* 88[2009]). Charles Bernstein's chapter on Gertrude Stein is wide-ranging as well, looking forward to Language poetry and dwelling on Stein in relation to Freud. The collection closes with Anthony Mellors on 'Modernism After Modernism' as a coda, and again it connects intimately to his work in *Late Modernist Poetics: From Pound to Prynne* (ManUP [2005]; reviewed in *YWES* 86[2007]). In it he takes on Objectivist, Projectivist, San Francisco Renaissance, and New York school poets, to close with the anti-lyrical innovations that neo-modernists are content to set beside subjective reflections critics would be uncomfortable containing within the postmodern. It may seem to stress the obvious, but the great advantage of Davis and Jenkins's *A History of Modernist Poetry* is not merely that they have excellent contributors doing very fine work but that they have consistently assembled the leading voices for each topic covered on modernism. The focus of each chapter privileges the summative rather than making new innovative additions to scholarship, but both occur, which makes this book as much a help for scholars as for students. However, for the pedagogical context, it would be difficult to imagine a book taking up this project in any comparable way for at least a generation.

A late arrival from 2014, Jesse Cohn's *Underground Passages: Anarchist Resistance Culture 1848–2011* offers both critical engagement with American poetry, particularly working-class poetry, and a theoretical modelling of an anarchist literary theory built from his influential *Anarchism and the Crisis of Representation: Hermeneutics, Aesthetics, Politics* (SusquehannaUP [2006]). Cohn's aim is to outline how anarchist politics are expressed aesthetically in a 'culture of resistance', which marks his distinction from McGuinness's project of this year that instead attends to the reactionary potential inside seemingly radical artistic innovations. Cohn is careful from the very start to clarify how a culture of resistance does not romanticize away the hegemonic forces in culture and to which literary critics will most naturally attend through critical cultural theory as enmeshed in problems of inoculation and neoliberal bourgeois individualism. Cohn's richly historicized and theorized analyses are presented in a lucid and nearly narrative form in the body of the text with scholarly, critical, and theoretical discussions in the footnotes to each page. This makes the book work as two conversations: one for the reader and one for the scholar. This is particularly effective in the opening conceit of a tunnel, literally an underground passage for the title, from prison to freedom. The two locations are later transformed into a mall and theatre respectively. This permits Cohn to give the general reader a pathway into fraught disputes, such as his own with David Weir's *Anarchy & Culture* (UMassP [1997]) on anarchist aesthetics that falls closer to McGuinness's work insofar as art displaces praxis, while with Cohn art is a part of praxis among active practitioners. A central question, then, is whether anarchism is taken as a prefigurative politics. If so, in what ways is anarchist art likewise prefigurative and based in not only the conditions of social change but the personal transformations that prefigure such change? This is, effectively, the underground passage, and, most emphatically for Cohn (in a memorable image of the introduction), both the art and praxis emphasize the liminal passage itself over its ends. They are defined by the passage itself and not its undefined utopian aim or problematic origins. Cohn's work is set firmly in the paradigm grown from post-anarchist theory, and this brings particularly provocative readings of Robert Duncan, Diane di Prima, Kenneth Rexroth, the Black Mountain poets, and the San Francisco Renaissance that demand responses from current criticism. For instance, Duncan and di Prima in relation to Surrealism also connect to Kenneth Patchen, and both Ezra Pound and Denise Levertov figure, as well as the New York school poets, and all of their British counterparts. However, Cohn is broadly international, with working-class and activist poets from diverse traditions woven into this wide-reaching network, and recent work on modernist periodicals (see the review of Matthew Chambers's *Modernism, Periodicals, and Cultural Poetics* below) would do very well to attend to Cohn's extensive critical history here of anarchist little magazines. His project would readily and very productively sit next to works like Adam McKibble's recently reissued *The Space and Place of Modernism* (Routledge [2013]; reviewed in *YWES* 94[2015]) and Eric B. White's *Transatlantic Avant-Gardes: Little Magazines and Localist Modernism* (EdinUP [2013]; reviewed in *YWES* 94[2015]).

Jean-Michel Rabaté's *1922: Literature, Culture, Politics* follows in a lengthy and daunting path of works to take up the *annus mirabilis* of modernism, most obviously Michael North's *Reading 1922: A Return to the Scene of the Modern* (OUP [1999]; reviewed in *YWES* 80[2001]) and Michael Levenson's *A Genealogy of Modernism: A Study of English Literary Doctrine 1908–1922* (CUP [1986]; reviewed in *YWES* 66[1988]), as well as Rabaté's own monograph *1913: The Cradle of Modernism* (Blackwell [2007]; reviewed in *YWES* 88[2009]). This is a well-trod approach with long shadows, and Rabaté draws together contributors who are entirely convincing as they take on the challenge. The short and highly readable 'Editor's Introduction' makes clear the work's combination of a new contribution to scholarship with accessibility and utility to the classroom with its concomitant need for background information, elucidation, and clarity. Rabaté uses the plot of a light 1922 novel, Beverly Nichols's *Self*, to open the context of conflict and international progressive and reactionary forces, all to more deftly lead the reader into Evelyn Waugh, futurism, Georg Lukács, Carl Schmitt, and Ludwig Wittgenstein, then inevitably to Pound, Eliot, Woolf, Joyce, Proust, and the high modernists in general. The titular allusion for Rabaté's introduction is to E.E. Cummings's *The Enormous Room*, which binds to the postwar context while also opening the European focus of the volume, pointing as it does not only to Americans in Paris or Europe generally in 1922 but also the return to New York in the close of the novel and the 'immensity' of America as contrast to the 'enormity' of the war, or, per Rabaté, the greatness in contrast to the out-of-rule violation of the norm. The seventeen chapters fall into three loosely distinguished sections: the first on the high modernists, the second focused on art and movements, and the third on anthropological and sociological new epistemologies for postwar modernity. Of these, Gabrielle McIntire's 'Uncanny *Semblances* and Serendipitous Publications' focuses on Eliot and Genevieve Abravanel's 'Anglophones in Paris' on Gertrude Stein and Ernest Hemingway. McIntire opens with what Levenson has called the 'institution-alization' of modernism (*Genealogy*, CUP [1986], p. 213), the founding of *The Criterion*, as a quasi-pedagogical training of modernist taste for difficulty and its pan-European forms. This then leads her to compare Eliot's *The Waste Land* with Joyce's *Ulysses*, particularly the importance of Eliot's reading of Joyce during the composition of the poem. Abravanel moves widely among the American expatriate scene in Paris to set Stein's queer and feminine coteries as distinct from the networks around Joyce. Much as with Niall Munro's work on Hart Crane reviewed below, the impulse here is to show the overlapping nature of queerness and modernism. The contrast to Joyce repeats in Sherwood Anderson's defence of Stein that also recasts her work as 'a study in American masculinity' (p. 93) and nationalism, and again in most detail in the well-known shift from mentorship to conflict between Stein and Hemingway. Abravanel is particularly helpful here for her clarity outlining the responses by Hemingway to Stein and Anderson. Pound appears across the volume, most strikingly in Elizabeth A. Mosimann's 'Postwar New Feminisms', as does Eliot in Angeliki Spiropoulou's '"In or about 1922": Virginia Woolf, Katherine Mansfield, and Modern Fiction', as a way to emphasize Bloomsbury over Joyce's and others' influences on experimental form and innovation. Like Rabaté's most recent edited collection, *A Handbook of Modernism Studies* (Blackwell [2013]; reviewed in *YWES* 94[2015]), *1922* will benefit scholars, teachers, and students together.

Another capacious project, Andrzej Gąsiorek's *A History of Modernist Literature*, surveys modernism with a focus from 1900 to 1940, but opening more than a decade earlier with the New Woman well within the paradigm of Victorian literature and with an internationalized English focus. That is, Gąsiorek insists from the opening pages on the framework of English modernism in England as the purview of this literary history while at the same time recognizing the internationalized nature of that localized perspective with an array of American talents both on site and of deep influence, from Henry James to Eliot and Pound to less frequent commentary on H.D. and Mina Loy, as well as other internationals from Joseph Conrad and Wyndham Lewis to Joyce and Samuel Beckett. In fact, no author is referred to more frequently than Eliot and Pound across the book, followed by Lewis, each of whom eclipses any English author in the study. The writing is consistently lucid and clearly set for an anticipated audience of undergraduate and postgraduate student readers while still providing a text of record for researchers. As a history, Gąsiorek's book frequently engages with the entanglements of political and aesthetic commitments for the various figures in each chronological section of the project, while through the extensive footnotes pointing the reader to current scholarly debates or conflicted interpretations. He is also generous in pointing to other kindred works, including Chris Baldick's exceptional *The Modern Movement: 1910–1940* in *The Oxford English Literary History* (OUP [2005]; reviewed in *YWES* 86[2007]) and Christopher MacGowan's forthcoming *Blackwell History of American Literature 1900–1950*. Full bibliographical materials and annotations fall at the end of each chapter for easy excerpting of materials, which further marks the pedagogical intentions of the project. The scope of *A History of Modernist Literature* is also no surprise, following on the diversity of Gąsiorek's previous monographs *Postwar British Fiction: Realism and After* ([1995]; reviewed in *YWES* 76[1998]) and *J.G. Ballard* (ManUP [2005]; reviewed in *YWES* 86[2007]), as well as his many diverse co-edited projects from Lewis and Ford Madox Ford to various forms of modernism, including the recent *Wyndham Lewis and the Cultures of Modernity* (Ashgate [2011]; reviewed in *YWES* 92[2013]), edited with Alice Reeve-Tucker and Nathan Waddell. The book is a commendable and exhaustive addition to scholarship, and the reviewer has already made it suggested reading for the modernism module.

It is rare for a reviewer to be able to hold together three volumes that trace an illustrious career through to a resounding climax. Albert Gelpi delivers this in his *American Poetry after Modernism: The Power of the Word*, which follows on his well-known *The Tenth Muse: The Psyche of the American Poet* (HarvardUP [1975]; reviewed in *YWES* 57[1978]) about American poetry from the Puritans into the nineteenth century, and his *A Coherent Splendor: The American Poetic Renaissance 1910–1950* (CUP [1987]; reviewed in *YWES* 68[1990]), which relates American modernist poetry to its Romantic predecessors. Gelpi describes this complete trilogy in terms that relate to his teaching the survey of American poetry at Harvard and Stanford, and the teacher's well-polished movement from clarity to brilliant observation is clear here. This is a book that has been many, many years in the making. It is original for researchers, but may find its truest home among other instructors teaching such surveys who are seeking a way to communicate to students a coherent narrative across the broad sweep of the nation's poetic history as a reflection of its intellectual growth. Since the first two volumes, Gelpi has been most active in, again, widely lauded editorial projects, including, with Robert Bertholf, *The Letters of Robert Duncan and Denise Levertov* (StanfordUP

[2004]; reviewed in *YWES* 86[2007]) and the companion edited collection *Robert Duncan and Denise Levertov: The Poetry of Politics, the Politics of Poetry* (StanfordUP [2006]; reviewed in *YWES* 87[2008]) among others. The long gestation makes *American Poetry after Modernism* densely suggestive. By tracing questions of form and language from the Confessional poets through to the Language poets, Gelpi narrates a long, red thread of concerns from Romanticism's privileging of the individual's aesthetic experience in conflict with Enlightenment rationality to modernism's struggle with the rupture of meaning and form (understood here as an intensification of Romanticism), leading to the making of new notions of form as a creative struggle against indeterminacy. From this point, the present study takes up postmodern American poetry as, first and foremost, in dialogue with modernism but also with neo-Romanticism, and hence only having a full rupture with the appearance of the materialism of the Language poets. In this respect, the postmodern is, for Gelpi, the shift forward from the Beats, Black Mountain school, and San Francisco Renaissance to L=A=N=G=U=A=G=E, in which Romanticism is excised by eliminating the lyrical 'I'. His acknowledged exclusion of poetic traditions after the Second World War that attend to identity politics is, however, also partially the answer he suggests in his 'Coda', which also supplies the book's subtitle. That is, the struggles of Romanticism in its various forms appear to continue, perhaps amidst the conditions of late capitalism or late modernism, yet still a defining trait of American poetry. This is not a monograph to be missed. It is a remarkable gift forward from Gelpi's rich and long teaching career to the classrooms of his readers.

Greg Barnhisel offers a project covering the same period as Gelpi's. *Cold War Modernists: Art, Literature, and American Culture Diplomacy* concentrates on American modernism after the Second World War as understood through the critical lens of government, business, and institutional interests. Barnhisel is overt in signalling his development of arguments set out recently by Allan Filreis in *Counter-Revolution of the Word* (UNCP [2009]; reviewed in *YWES* 87[2008]) and Robert Genter in *Late Modernism* (UPennP [2001]; reviewed in *YWES* 91[2012]) in relation to the conservatism of Cold War cultural attitudes towards modernism. This is a modernism after its heyday, a modernism grown tired, a modernism now retooled for fostering American Cold War interests through discourses of 'freedom' running in parallel to the avant-garde. Tellingly, he opens the book with twinned references to Daniel Bell's *The Cultural Contradictions of Capitalism* (Basic Books [1976]) and Philip Larkin's famous derogation of Ezra Pound, Pablo Picasso, and Charlie Parker. The degeneracy of this modernism is then set against a cultural programme with deep roots in the Central Intelligence Agency, American diplomacy, capitalist investment, and elite American cultural institutions. Barhisel's extensive archival work shines in this excavation of cultural diplomacy and ties closely to his previous projects on New Directions publishing and James Laughlin in *James Laughlin, New Directions, and the Remaking of Ezra Pound* (UMassP [2005]). For example, in the introduction he quickly points to William J. Casey moving from the Office of Strategic Services to the board of directors for Laughlin's Intercultural Publications and back to the CIA during Ronald Reagan's presidential term, as well as Norman Holmes Pearson's term in the same Office of Strategic Services in relation to his work on H.D. and Pound and his co-founding of American studies at Yale University. While these are already recognized but representative examples, Barnhisel's excavation of the details and extent of this cultural programme for promoting scholarship and artistic work as an avenue for Cold War cultural diplomacy is exceptional. The crux of his analysis is explicit near the opening of the book, but unfolds in detail: that a programme of cultural diplomacy would foster and disseminate a narrative that the various radical avant-gardes of modernism 'had come into being and found fertile ground in America because of the West's valorization of freedom and individualism' (p. 10), and that this narrative would receive indirect support from government. This casts modernism in the American century as an expression of bourgeois liberalism with deep ties to the private sector, cultural institutions, and institutions of higher education, particularly the Ivy League. The conception leads to 'freedom' understood principally in a liberal rather than a republican form, meaning freedom of personal expression rather than free participation in one's community, and hence individualism set in conflict against facelessness or infiltration by the crowd. Barnhisel is impressive here in defining and periodizing modernism (in a form particularly helpful for the classroom) while setting it amidst cultural propaganda and popular content of the period, such as American films that set the rugged individual of liberalism against the creeping communitarian blob, alien invaders, or Manchurian candidate, while at the same time showing the parallels to Soviet models of realism. The first two thematic sections, the introduction and first chapter, are followed by medium-specific chapters on the visual arts, the book (meaning book publishing as well as the industry, content, and scholarly studies), two chapters on periodicals (*Encounter* and *Perspectives*), and broadcasting. The archival work in the two chapters on periodicals is impressive, the latter of which builds from Barnhisel's previous work on Laughlin and New Directions. The chapter on broadcasting largely focuses on Voice of America as straddling modernism and the middlebrow, and sits in the comfortable company of recent work on broadcasting and modernism, such as Todd Avery's *Radio Modernism* (Ashgate [2006]; reviewed in *YWES* 87[2008]), Debra Rae Cohen, Michael Coyle, and Jane Lewty's edited collection, *Broadcasting Modernism* (UFlorP [2009]), and Matthew Feldman, Henry Mead, and Erik Tonning's *Broadcasting in the Modernist Era* (Bloomsbury [2014]; reviewed in *YWES* 94[2015]). The conclusion ends the project with the incoming Kennedy administration in 1961 and the expansion of exchange programmes, such as international students in the USA that fostered person-to-person interactions as part of the cultural propaganda system, and the move from print culture to mass media through, implicitly for Barnhisel, colourized television. This closing also opens the project out to a meta-level discussion of the conflicts between conservative and Marxist critical readings of modernism and late modernism, moving across Fredric Jameson, Irving Kristol, Theodor Adorno, and Jürgen Habermas. Barnhisel's project of bringing modernism to the 1950s is exemplary, building from the continued vitality of the topic. It particularly benefits from being read beside Eric Bennett's *Workshops of Empire: Stegner,*

*Engle, and American Creative Writing During the Cold War*, reviewed in Section 3 below.

Zhaoming Qian's edition of Ezra Pound's *Cathay* seamlessly combines the commercial edition of New Directions with Ernest Fenollosa's notes, which are vital to understanding Pound's work, and also includes a new foreword by Mary de Rachewiltz. Qian's work on the notes is more than half the book itself, and as de Rachewiltz writes, he is the perfect editor for the project based on his previous work on Pound's knowledge of written Chinese at different points in time from his *Ezra Pound's Chinese Friends: Stories in Letters* (OUP [2008]; reviewed in *YWES* 89[2010]), as well as his earlier *Orientalism and Modernism: The Legacy of China in Pound and Williams* (DukeUP [1995]). Both Qian and de Rachewiltz focus on Pound's enormous influence on modern poetry, particularly Western conceptualizations of China and translation in general, with particular attention to Pound's famous use of Fenollosa. Here, the natural companion volume is Haun Saussy, Jonathan Stalling, and Lucas Klein's exquisitely edited *The Chinese Character as a Medium for Poetry* (FordUP [2008]; reviewed in *YWES* 89[2010]) and Steven G. Yao's article 'Toward a Prehistory of Asian American Verse: Pound, *Cathay*, and the Poetics of Chineseness' (*Rep* 99[2007] 130–58; reviewed in *YWES* 88[2009]). Qian stresses the in-betweenness of *Cathay* as a translation and as original poetry, the former open to critique (yet widely influential) and the latter supported by Pound's inclusion of *Seafarer* as well as his deliberate alterations of meaning to suit his own anti-war values at the time amidst his Vorticist and Imagist period, the same moment as his anarchist politics before his later turn, which was articulated very well in Mark Antliff and Scott Klein's collection *Vorticism: New Perspectives* (OUP [2014]; reviewed in *YWES* 94[2015]). Qian's deep scholarship and the affordability of the New Directions paperback make this the ideal teaching text for *Cathay* in English and comparative literature courses as well as translation studies. Ira B. Nadel's very brief *Cathay: Ezra Pound's Orient* in the Penguin Specials series is an ideal historical and biographical companion piece to this edition of *Cathay*, offering a distillation of his approach to Pound in his earlier *Ezra Pound: A Literary Life* (Palgrave [2004]) with extensive updates based on David Weir's *American Orient: Imagining the East from the Colonial Era through the Twentieth Century* (UMassP [2011]).

Pound is also discussed at several points in Jeffrey Herlihy-Mera and Vamsi Koneru's *Paris in American Literatures: On Distance as a Literary Resource*, most especially Carl Miller's chapter on Sherwood Anderson 'Forget Paris' and Jonathan Austad's 'From Dada to Nada' on Hemingway, both of which consider Pound's role as editor, and in passing in Chase Dimock's 'The Nightinghols of Paris' on Robert McAlmon. A more extensive city focus on Pound comes in the conference proceedings *Ezra Pound and London: New Perspectives* edited by Walter Baumann and William Pratt. The papers are expanded from conference form to full chapters but retain their more conversational tone, which makes the volume highly accessible while clearly intended for a specialized audience. De Rachewiltz opens this volume as well, with 'Kinship and Friendship' in the same vein as her foreword to the centennial edition of *Cathay*. Ira B. Nadel's 'Picasso and Pound' and Stephen

Romer's '"Building Ornamentation!"': E.P.'s Architectural Walkabouts in London' are standout chapters, though Romer's is much more focused on London. Nadel approaches Pound and Picasso comparatively, on the basis of Philip Larkin's complaint about both—this is the same reference as the one that opens Barnhisel's *Cold War Modernists* (reviewed above). However, the real focus here is recuperating their respective networks and the political context around the Second World War. This enters much-disputed terrain, and Nadel's stance is clear when he argues, via Peter Nicholls's *Ezra Pound: Politics, Economics and Writing* (Macmillan [1984]; reviewed in *YWES* 66[1988]), that fascism for Pound was 'something visionary and cultural rather than a fixed political program' (pp. 147–8), while Picasso 'accepted' (p. 147) the Nazi occupation of France and Gertrude Stein 'outrageously suggested Hitler be awarded the Nobel Prize' (p. 149). This will surely provoke reactions, contradicting as it does work like Patricia Leighton's *Re-ordering the Universe: Picasso and Anarchism, 1897–1914* (PrincetonUP [1989]), yet Nadel's point that Pound's fascistic works need further critical discussion and nuanced contextualization is sound. There are also natural comparisons here to much recent work, particularly Mark Antliff and Scott W. Klein's *Vorticism: New Perspectives* (OUP [2013]; reviewed in *YWES* 94[2015]) and Matthew Feldman's *Ezra Pound's Fascist Propaganda, 1935–45* (Palgrave [2013]; reviewed in *YWES* 94[2015]). Romer's chapter offers a careful poetic sense of Pound's *Cantos* in nuanced relation to London architecture, including helpful illustrations that lead the reader through the walking tour-cum-hermeneutical exegesis. William Pratt and Gavin Selerie both contribute chapters focused on London in the *Cantos*, and other collections of chapters include 'Pound and Other Writers', 'Pound and the Classics', and 'Pound and the Fine Arts', which sets Romer and Nadel with Jo Brantley Berryman and Evelyn Haller, and 'Pound and Politics'. In the final section, Roxana Preda turns to Pound and Henri Gaudier-Brzeska, which benefits from being read beside Mark Antliff's chapter, 'Politicizing the New Sculpture', in his *Vorticism*, mentioned above. Stephen Wilson closes the political discussion through Pound's advocacy of the American entry to the First World War. That the recent work on Pound and anarchism does not enter the discussion in the volume may provoke questions, but the conference from which the papers derive was in 2011.

Alec Marsh opens *John Kasper and Ezra Pound: Saving the Republic* with a bold gesture to the Ku Klux Klan in a quintessential example of what Ted Bishop terms the 'archival jolt' (*Riding with Rilke*, Viking [2005], p. 36). Marsh is direct in confronting Pound's problematic politics and contact with 'a thing, fairly reeking of the heart of American darkness' (p. x) in his preface, before beginning the book with a focus on the poetics of American extremism. By questioning Pound as a Southern writer against the Civil Rights Movement, Marsh broadens the more widespread discussion of his anti-Semitism and exhaustively contextualizes his work during the 'St Elizabeths period' in relation to wider progressive and reactionary movements such as the National Association for the Advancement of Colored People and the Ku Klux Klan respectively. The book's erudition and exceptionally detailed index are to be commended, and the argument that literary studies of McCarthyism must include consideration of Pound seems impossible to overlook. This sets

Marsh's work beside important recent work. Readers already familiar with Alan Filreis's *Counter-Revolution of the Word: The Conservative Attack on Modern Poetry, 1945–1960* (UNCP [2008]; reviewed in *YWES* 89[2010]), Robert Genter's *Late Modernism: Art, Culture, and Politics in Cold War America* (UPennP [2010]; reviewed in *YWES* 91[2012]), and Barnhisel's *Cold War Modernists* (reviewed above) will find this volume a very helpful companion and expansion on those discussions. Marsh's book not only builds on Pound scholarship but cements the value and rapid development of Bloomsbury's Historicizing Modernism series edited by Matthew Feldman and Erik Tonning.

Pound and Eliot both appear repeatedly in Patrick McGuinness's very fine *Poetry & Radical Politics in Fin de Siècle France: From Anarchism to Action Française*. McGuinness's insistence on the continuities from the closing decade of the nineteenth century to the opening of the twentieth challenges many approaches to modernism, but he is very convincing. Setting Pound (and several others) as obfuscating some of the anarchist legacies in poetic form, he regards Pound and Eliot together as poets of reactionary politics with experimental or progressive aesthetics, which he identifies as a reactionary modernism fraught around form—the point is to instead explore those instances in which literary form and political praxis cohabit, and in which anarchism is not reduced to a purely symbolic set of actions. This confrontation permeates the book and is set at the opening between three equidistant and conflicted possibilities: Bakunin's creative destruction, Marx's economism, and Baudelaire and Verlaine and Swinburne's inward quietist Symbolism. He deftly sets aside overtly political poetry or agitprop poetics that may leave the reader without inclination to change the witnessed pathos, while at the same time opening questions of radical form attached to reactionary ambitions. While the book's concerns are with nineteenth-century French poetry and poetics, the deep influence and extensive literature on Symbolist influences on the high modernists and American experimental poetry make McGuinness's arguments here widely important. The approach to anarchism is primarily historical and concerned with the culture of radical politics more than with the nuances of its theorizations, but with the potential for significant reconsiderations of Eliot, Pound, Stevens, Crane, Williams, and so forth. It is tempting to think of Andrew Cornell's *Unruly Equality: U.S. Anarchism in the Twentieth Century* (UCalP [2016]) as a potential continuation of this argument, but it was not received for review. Dean Irvine and Smaro Kamboureli's *Editing as Cultural Practice in Canada* is likewise incidentally connected to American literary modernism, with an extended section of Irene Gammel and Benjamin Lefebvre's chapter, 'Editing in Canada: The Case of L.M. Montgomery', dedicated to Margaret Anderson, Jane Heap, and Pound. The focus for Gammel and Lefebvre is to contrast the editorial history and strong editorial interventions in Montgomery's *Anne of Green Gables* to the editorial praxis of *The Little Review* and more broadly its ties to Hemingway's work and posthumous publication.

*Modernism, Periodicals, and Cultural Poetics* shows Matthew Chambers's efforts to extend discussion of modernist periodical studies. The new ground struck with the founding of the *Journal of Modern Periodical Studies* and the completion of the *Oxford Critical and Cultural History of Modernist Magazines* series (OUP [2009, 2012, 2013]; reviewed in *YWES* 90[2011], 93[2014], *and* 94[2015]) has both supported and reflected increasing work in periodical studies in relation to modernism. Chambers's project focuses on British periodicals from the 1920s to the 1940s, including those published in France, through the prism of two contrasting figures: T.S. Eliot and I.A. Richards. This leads him to four chapters, each of which is set around the conflicted nature of allegiances such as those to Eliot or Richards, as well as politics. The first chapter, 'The Standards of Criticism', focuses on the question of the critic through Eliot and Richards across the 1920s. The second chapter, 'The English in English Surrealism', is concerned with the divisions in English Surrealism, such as those that emerged between Charles Madge and David Gascoyne, as well as against Surrealism in its English and French forms. The closely related third chapter, 'Popular Poetry and Mass-Observation', is more openly politicized, and here comparison with Thomas Davis's *The Extinct Scene: Late Modernism and Everyday Life* (ColUP [2016]) is much merited. Where Davis pursues a theoretically focused investigation of Humphrey Jennings's politics, Chambers takes up the rift between English Surrealism and Mass-Observation in relation to Richards's sense of the task of the critic and theories of poetic value. By recuperating a history of Richards's influence on Madge and Jennings, Chambers provides unexpected expansion of avenues into Mass-Observation and its connections to a number of politicized periodicals. When read after Davis's excellent theoretical project (as this reader did), Chambers's historical recuperation is a helpful extension. The fourth chapter, 'The Politics of Reception', sets the Auden-generation poets in contrast to the later generation, oriented here, in Chambers's articulation, around James Meary Tambimuttu, whom he sees as working in Eliot's shadow; these would become the Scottish Renaissance poets and the Welsh poets, the most famous of whom is Dylan Thomas. but also Lynette Roberts, Alun Lewis, R.S. Thomas, Keidrych Rhys, and Vernon Watkins. This is again focused through the influence of the strong poets Eliot and Richards, but as an under-studied set of groups. Chambers has done work here that future scholarship is charged with building upon. Despite focusing on periodicals produced in the United Kingdom, Chambers also spends more time working through Pound and Eliot than any two other poets, and all of his networks are thick with interactions with the publications of American figures too often overlooked.

Mark Scroggins, who has been so very well represented in edited collections this year, has also published *Intricate Thicket: Reading Late Modernist Poetries*, which collects his incidental writings of the past fifteen years. He opens with a plain statement that his scholarship and critical reading have increasingly shifted away from postmodernism and towards the less divisive concept of late modernism. In this, his work coincides with the rise of the new modernist studies in the late 1990s, with its own privileging of a capacious modernism, and extension of the period and its concerns through late modernism. The theoretical terrain of this break is likewise overt, with Scroggins's continuing admiration for David Harvey and Fredric Jameson yet dissatisfaction with the notion of postmodernism as the aesthetic and cultural manifestation of the conditions of late-stage capitalism. In the first section of the book, 'Longer Views', the chapters on Olson, Duncan, and Creeley; Louis Zukofsky; and Guy Davenport all reflect this critical shift to lateness and a continuity with modernism. The second section, 'Shorter Takes', is composed of brief pieces on poets ranging from Oppen to John Taggert to Ian Hamilton Finlay. He closes the collection with two chapters on poetics that reflect on his own praxis as a biographer and poet. Although these works have been previously published, they are updated here. Writing as he does with wit and clarity, Scroggins's scholarship is very current. His opening chapter on Duncan draws on the collected works, and his chapters on Zukofsky and Anne Carson engage with the latest critical works, in Carson's case returning attention to her *Eros of the Bittersweet* (PrincetonUP [1986]) as a way of approaching her subsequent poetry. Scroggins's work here on Zukofsky is, of course, excellent, but his detailed thoughts on Peter Gizzi and Theodore Enslin are also very engaged.

Ann Keniston's *Ghostly Figures: Memory and Belatedness in Postwar American Poetry* takes a very different approach to late modernist poetics through the trope of belatedness and mortality. Her work on Sylvia Plath's Holocaust poems is familiar from Keniston's 'The Holocaust Again' in Anita Helle's important edited collection, *The Unravelling Archive: Essays on Sylvia Plath* (UMichP [2007]; reviewed in *YWES* 89[2010]). A key contention in the project is that postwar American poetry is not only belated historically by virtue of its postwar creation, but that this manifests itself thematically in an indistinct or obstructed remembrance of the past and formally through distortions, fractured syntax, or other structural fragmentations (literal versus figurative belatedness in Keniston's discussion). The fifth chapter, on Susan Howe's *The Midnight* (ND [2003]), offers a reconceptualization of the figurative form of belatedness that looks back across the rest of the book, shifting how she attends to comparisons. Her particular attention is given to the spatialization of time through objects infused with metonymical potency. In this, the elimination of the lyrical subject akin to Language poetry (yet distinct from it as a movement for Keniston) presses a materialist approach to the displaced objects such that the displaced original concept replaced by its metonym is a new formal enactment of the more literal displacements of text on page (such as negative leading in the type production) in Howe's previous works. This is a remarkable innovation in reading Howe that contrasts sharply with, for example, Stephen Collis's emphasis in *Through Words of Others: Susan Howe and Anarcho-Scholasticism* (ELS [2006]; reviewed in *YWES* 88[2009]) when reading in *The Midnight* on the 'immediate and personal' from Howe's archive (p. 72).

*Listening for the Heartbeat of Being: The Arts of Robert Bringhurst* is a special addition to 2016, edited by Brent Wood and Mark Dickinson. Its subtitle stresses the challenge and boon of any work on Bringhurst: the plural nature of his talents in poetry, typography, and translation. The contributors are also unusual for an academic volume, combining outstanding scholars with primarily creative artists, including Margaret Atwood, Crispin Elsted, Erica Wagner, Dennis Lee, and Clare Goulet, as well as Indigenous storytellers Ishmael Hope and Káawan Sangáa, and the publishers Scott

McIntyre and Peter Rutledge Koch. This scope gives the volume traditional scholarly work on Bringhurst as well as highly readable chapters that show a practitioner's attentive care for Bringhurst's craft. The artists' chapters, unsurprisingly, tend towards narrative. Elsted's 'Grace in Two-and-a-Half Dimensions: Robert Bringhurst, Typographer' is perhaps the most sensitive to the relations among poetics, translation, and typography (all three being Elsted's own areas of expertise), and it also tellingly takes up its subject as the familiar 'Robert' whose *The Blue Roofs of Japan: A Score for Interpenetrating Voices* [1986] was published by Elsted's own Barbarian Press. The work is a remarkable letterpress publication with contrasting voices, one of which is in blind (impressed in the paper but without ink). In this collection, Katherine McLeod's chapter, 'Water Music', studies *The Blue Roofs of Japan* in detail. Wood and Dickinson's introduction stresses Bringhurst as an important yet oddly under-studied literary artist whose 'mission is the drive to access modes of consciousness not shaped by the industrial world but evolving from cultures outside it, beyond it, and prior to it' (p. 5). This specific focus drives the political, aesthetic, and ethnographic approaches to his work as well as the craft of its material production. The chapters are organized in roughly two parts with no explicit division, the first being approaches to Bringhurst's poetry, which inevitably engages deeply with his work in typography, book design, and publishing, closing with McIntyre's chapter, 'Bringhurst in West Coast Book Design and Publishing'. The second half of the collection takes up his work as a translator and his engagement with Indigenous peoples of the West Coast, although again, like typography and book design, this work is inextricable from his poetry. Wagner and Atwood here both emphasize his American background, coming to the Canadian coast and encountering Haida storytelling and culture. Sangáa and Hope's very brief chapters stand out here as endorsements of his care when engaging with Indigenous cultures, and Nicholas Bradley's 'At Land's End' gives a scholarly entrance to ways of reading Bringhurst's Haida trilogy with emphasis on *A Story as Sharp as a Knife: The Classical Haida Mythtellers and Their World* (Douglas & McIntyre [1999]).

A second title from McGill-Queen's University Press expands on recent work on Wallace Stevens. David Jarraway's *Wallace Stevens among Others: Diva-Dames, Deleuze, and American Culture* seeks to use Stevens to look outward to other figures, the titular 'Others', both for an anxious legacy of influence but also for affinities and kinships. Jarraway is explicit that *Wallace Stevens among Others* is the kind of project made possible by his previous two studies, *Wallace Stevens and the Question of Belief: Metaphysician in the Dark* (Louisiana State University Press [1993]; reviewed in *YWES* 75[1997]) and *Going the Distance: Dissident Subjectivity in Modernist American Literature* (LSUP [2003]). Both earlier books attended more specifically to Stevens and conceptually set the ground, the latter taking Stevens *passim* in relation to dedicated chapters on Stein, Williams, Langston Hughes, O'Hara, and Elizabeth Bishop. The project here begins with the problem of subjectivity from *Going the Distance*: a challenge to the individual lyric subject so long praised in relation to pragmatism and exceptionalism, but more recently connected to wider critiques in American literature. Here this is updated through Deleuze. This updating opens the volume with a Deleuzian reading of Stevens and a Stevens-shaped approach to Deleuze. With the conceptual paradigm set, Jarraway continues to chapters on queer theory through Cormac McCarthy, Michael Cunningham, and Mark Doty; contemporary fiction via John Updike, Joyce Carol Oates, and Philip Roth; masculinities and George Cukor's films; the New York school poets, particularly John Ashbery, O'Hara, and James Schuyler; and finally a closing through Stevens's readings in Freud in relation to subjectivity, although with a diversion to Elizabeth Bishop (in many respects a follow-up to *Going the Distance*) in the conclusion. This approach, to take a single author as a point of conceptual contact among several others from which to extract the 'red thread' of the mystery narrative (here the problem of subjectivity), works well, even though few readers are likely to be intimately familiar with the breadth of authors. The obvious appeal is to Stevens scholars reading more widely while reconsidering Stevens's works as well. How the book works through queer theory and masculinities to aim for a general revision is particularly productive, which is still much needed for work on Stevens and is a lively concern in American literature. Jarraway makes good use of David Halperin's foundational *Saint Foucault* (OUP [1995]) to assert queerness, and Eric Keenghan's *Queering Cold War Poetry* (OSUP [2009]) suggestively appears via a footnote, which could do much for contextualizing current definitional care. The struggle of the book will be for readers coming to it after recent work on Stevens and the everyday or seeking an explicit articulation of how these 'Stevensian' readings of 'others' revise the direction of scholarship on their works (perhaps Roth in particular). Recent books on Stevens such as Edward Ragg's *Wallace Stevens and the Aesthetics of Abstraction* (CUP [2010]; reviewed in *YWES* 92[2013]), Siobhan Phillips's *The Poetics of the Everyday* (ColUP [2010]; reviewed in *YWES* 91[2012]), Alan Filreis's extension of his earlier work in *Counter-Revolution of the Word* (UNCP [2008]; reviewed in *YWES* 89[2010]), and Liesl Olson's *Modernism and the Ordinary* (OUP [2009]; reviewed in *YWES* 90[2011]), do not appear here, even though this project would be important to them and would extend their discussions. Likewise, scholarship on urban space and painterly traditions in the New York school poets is caught in the same timeline, without response to recent work by Mark Silverberg or Ellen Levy as exemplars, such as their respective *The New York School Poets and the Neo-Avant-Garde* (Ashgate [2010]; reviewed in *YWES* 91[2012]) and *Criminal Ingenuity: Moore, Cornell, Ashbery, and the Struggle between the Arts* (OUP [2011]; reviewed in *YWES* 92[2013]). This may be an unfair critique of what is most likely a limitation of production timelines rather than scholarship. At the opening, Jarraway signals his preparatory work for this project over the past dozen or more years, and the late arrival near the final stages of the book (p. 11) of Mark C. Taylor's *Rewiring the Real* (ColUP [2013]), titled throughout as 'Rewriting' - both point to a project written before these other closely related recent projects appeared in print. However, most readers will come to the project with these past five years of Stevens scholarship mentally ready to hand, so it will be an inevitable query. Readers may have questions about how Jarraway's very fine work suggests interventions in more recent materials, which would make for very welcome rejoinders. As a project of primary critical study, this is strong work.

Niall Munro's *Hart Crane's Queer Modernist Aesthetics* takes momentum from the recent burst of activity on Crane, in part leading to and continuing from the founding of the Hart Crane Society at the American Literature Association conference in 2014. The critical queer theory here, in juxtaposition to Jarraway, is quite current with developments forward from Lee Edelman's *No Future: Queer Theory and the Death Drive* (DukeUP [2004]), Christopher Nealon's *Foundlings* (DukeUP [2001]), and Judith Halberstam's *The Queer Art of Failure* (DukeUP [2011]), as well as the most recent work on Crane and, contextually, the new modernist studies in general. Munro's careful work on Crane's manuscripts enriches his critical readings throughout the volume, as does his care in dealing with the transatlantic networks and little magazines that contextualize American works of this period. This puts his project methodologically on track with the growing Bloomsbury Historicizing Modernism series and the archival consciousness of the new modernist studies, which Munro marks out by detailing his debt to Eric B. White's *Transatlantic Avant-Gardes: Little Magazines and Localist Modernism* (EdinUP [2013]; reviewed in *YWES* 94[2015]). Munro is also meticulous in pointing to his work's growth from recent scholarship, particularly the concurrent publication in 2011 of Lawrence Kramer's *Hart Crane's 'The Bridge': An Annotated Edition* (FordUP [2011]) and John T. Irwin's expansive *Hart Crane's Poetry: 'Apollinaire lived in Paris, I live in Cleveland, Ohio'* (JHUP [2011]; reviewed in *YWES* 93[2014]), which he points out early in the study (p. 12). A key combination made by Munro is the non-incidental pairing of modernism and queerness, which he stresses as co-relational. The destabilizing modernist traits readily seen in Crane are, to Munro's reading, also key queer traits to his work, and vice versa. This gives vitality to the genetic approach to manuscript states, concerns with subjectivity, and engineered space. The project works towards a final chapter focused on Crane's *The Bridge* as a modernist queer technology, but earlier analyses across Crane's work are also groundbreaking, including extended analyses of 'Voyages', 'The Broken Tower', and *White Buildings*. The opening chapter shows Crane's growth from the Decadence of Oscar Wilde and Walter Pater, growing into a reading of *White Buildings* in the second chapter as in the ekphrastic tradition. The closing provocation, 'Towards a Queer Community', is timely for the new modernist studies, gently taking to task the disjointed approach taken by Cassandra Laity in 2010 in the 'Queer Modernisms' special section of *Modernism/Modernity* (*Mo/Mo* 17:iii[2010]) and by Heather Love the prior year (*PMLA* 124:iii[2009]). Rather than critiquing the work done, Munro points to its fragmented nature to argue that this forces 'queer' as an umbrella term rather than a theoretical paradigm with remarkably adept kinship to 'modernism'. Munro's book will be necessary reading for future work on Crane, but also makes a significant contribution more generally to modernist studies and particularly its close relations with queer theory.

C.D. Blanton brings a theoretically grounded reading to high modernist and late modernist texts in *Epic Negation: The Dialectical Poetics of Late Modernism*, the intimations of which are, in retrospect, clearly present in his

'London' chapter in Jason Harding's edited collection *T.S. Eliot in Context* (CUP [2011]; reviewed in *YWES* 92[2013]) and 'Invisible Times: Modernism as Ruptural Unity' in Stephen Ross's outstanding *Modernism and Theory: A Critical Debate* (Routledge [2009]; reviewed in *YWES* 90[2011]) that combined Louis Althusser and periodization with a study of Pound and Eliot much akin to the more developed work here. The book is in two parts, the first of which is largely concerned with Eliot's and Pound's high modernist works, and the second moving forward to late modernism with W.H. Auden and Louis MacNeice, and finally closing with H.D. The chapter on 'Eliotic Marxism: Culture as Praxis' (pp. 146–57) will call attention. The close work on Eliot's editorship of *The Criterion* and Joseph Needham's description of the impossibility of a secular Marxism is impressive, moving to read the symptomatic nature of the attempt more than the failures intrinsic to it. By focusing on Eliot's radical reading notes in *The Criterion*, Blanton reveals an Eliot sympathetic to socialism, though ultimately reactionary and deeply ironical in that sympathy (it is always contingent in the quotations Blanton presents), and his close reading of Trotsky. The chapter on MacNeice is also polemical and will conflict with scholars like Helen Goethals who are working on MacNeice and liberalism. The closing chapter on H.D. focuses on her relationship with and writings about Freud as a means of approaching her *Trilogy*. This reads H.D. as inextricably belated in her mature works and also as the culmination of the work to make epic poetry properly dialectical among the Auden generation of poets in and around the Spanish Civil War (seemingly more broadly conceived through the passing references to poets immediately following them, such as George Barker, who were of a quite distinct political orientation). Blanton's book is a tribute to the robust work coming from the Modernist Literature & Culture series edited by Kevin J.H. Dettmar and Mark Wollaeger for Oxford University Press. *Epic Negations* is also an exciting companion volume to Thomas Davis's *The Extinct Scene* (ColUP [2016]), each drawing on kindred methods to approach poetry and prose, respectively.

Two volumes in 2015 discuss poetry in relation to science. Peter Middleton's *Physics Envy: American Poetry and Science in the Cold War and After* opens with Robert Oppenheimer's famous dismissal of poetry as juvenile in order to set the position of poets during the Cold War against the cultural capital enjoyed by scientists, physicists especially. The book is in three sections with seven short chapters, as well as an introduction and coda, broadly devised as 'Poetry and Science', 'Midcentury', and 'Scientific Americans'. This structure allows Middleton to overlap his interests through Muriel Rukeyser, Charles Olson, Duncan, Rae Armantrout, Jackson Mac Low, Oppen, and Amiri Baraka. The degree of detail given here to each poet's engagements or arguments with science in general and physics in particular is remarkable and continuously convincing. Chapter 5, 'Stories, Geometries, and Angels', makes it difficult to envision work on Rukeyser that would not take into account her interests in physics, and likewise for Olson's investment in Alfred North Whitehead and his syntax. Duncan is distinct with his occult, mystical, and theological concepts, beside which he puts Olson's composition by field via Whitehead. Duncan returns again in the next chapter as a transition to Mac

Low and interests in *Scientific American* as a source of allusions and borrowed language or terminology. The coda turns to genetics to suggest a different field of study that eclipsed physics in the mid-1970s to call out for poetic responses and to challenge poetry. Middleton's work here is excellent. It is surprising that the scientist-poets of American literature do not figure, such as Bern Porter, who would seem to work particularly well both thematically and formally for Middleton's methodology. Mark Noble's *American Poetic Materialism from Whitman to Stevens* opens with Lucretius observing dust motes in a sunbeam, from which Noble moves to atomic particles as the materialist thesis of the book in relation to contemporary epistemologies of cultural liberalism and Enlightenment rationality as the crux of modernity via Stephen Greenblatt and Michel Serres. He provocatively compares William James and Theodor Adorno early in the volume through early American poetry, moving forward to Whitman and Emerson as the book proceeds, and closing with two chapters that take up George Santayana's naturalist poetics and his importance as a mentor to Wallace Steven. Noble offers a theoretical coda to the volume concentrated on Gilles Deleuze and Félix Guattari.

A very welcome addition to 2015 is Jonathan F.S. Post's monograph on Anthony Hecht that follows on his edition, *The Selected Letters of Anthony Hecht* (JHUP [2012]; reviewed in *YWES* 94[2015]). Post's book, *A Thickness of Particulars: The Poetry of Anthony Hecht*, opens with reflections on his personal relationship with the poet, as student and correspondent, even house-sitting. This level of personal detail and exceptionally attentive reading carries across each of the book's nine chapters, moving across major works of Hecht's career. The preface precedes the table of contents, as if to separate its personal commentary and observations of Hecht as an important individual for the author, even a friend, from its critical attention to his work. Post's primary work in early modern English literature shines at several moments, marking out not only an ideal critic for Hecht but an ideal reader. Post moves as readily between Hecht's interactions with Elizabeth Bishop and W.H. Auden or the influence of T.S. Eliot as he does between John Donne, Shakespeare, and even John Dowland in Hecht's 'Clair de Lune' (p. 81). Post's critical work editing *The Oxford Handbook of Shakespeare's Poetry* (OUP [2013]; reviewed in *YWES* 94[2015]) and especially *Green Thoughts, Green Shades: Essays by Contemporary Poets on the Early Modern Lyric* (UCalP [2002]; reviewed in *YWES* 83[2004]) very clearly establishes the background necessary for the careful readings of Hecht's poetic works that he unfolds across the book.

Michael Golston's *Poetic Machinations: Allegory, Surrealism, and Postmodern Poetic Form* asserts Surrealism as an allegorical art form, and, more centrally for his study, allegory as a defining element of a stream of American poetry running from Lorine Niedecker and Louis Zukofsky to Susan Howe, with suggestive gestures to Christian Bök. The materialism implicit in the chosen subject matter, poets, and critical methodologies is overt, hence the conceptual 'red thread' leading the reader along this mystery of unravelling from Objectivism to L=A=N=G=U=A=G=E, which remains a constant throughout the project. Golston's style is by turns casual, even chatty, and complex—this will challenge some readers, but it is also a way of reflecting on his subject matter. The opening dismissal of the reactionary notion of allegory, which Golston associates with the American high modernists, will surely find answers excited and disputational. It is an openly polemical gesture, and to contend that the likes of Pound and Williams are utterly without allegory will stir response. The crux, though, is allegorical *form*. Golston's project recalls Stephen Voyce's *Poetic Community: Avant-Garde Activism and Cold War Culture* (UTorP [2013]; reviewed in *YWES* 94[2015]), but will contrast sharply with projects such as Stephen Collis's *Through Words of Others: Susan Howe and Anarcho-Scholasticism* (ELS [2006]; reviewed in *YWES* 88[2009]) or Dani Spinosa's 'Freely Revised and Edited: Anarchist Authorship in Jackson Mac Low's *The Stein Poems*' (*ESC* 41:ii–iii[2015] 91–107) and 'Cagean Silence and the Comunis of Communication' (*Canadian Review of American Studies* 46:i[2016] 22–41).

The Gdańsk Transatlantic Studies in British and North American Culture series has added *Image in Modern(ist) Verse*, edited by Janusz Semrau and Marek Wilczyński. The six chapters predominantly relate to Imagism in a wide sense of the term. Andrzej Kopcewicz has the most substantial contribution, on the image and objective correlative (translated from the original Polish publication), in which he moves capaciously across poets ranging from Eliot, H.D., and Pound, as would be expected, to Dylan Thomas, William Carlos Williams, W.B. Yeats, Edgar Allen Poe, and T.E. Hulme. Pound and Eliot take by far the largest share of Kopcewicz's attention, with profitable returns to modernist spatial form and the new critics. Paulina Ambrozy builds out from Helen Carr's *The Verse Revolutionaries* (Cape [2009]) and relies on Andrew Thacker's *The Imagist Poets* (Northcote House [2011]; reviewed in *YWES* 92[2013]) to argue for the broad reach of Imagism as a movement, through to Louis Zukofsky. Jørgen Veisland likewise stresses Imagism's influence forward, opening with Robert Duncan's *The H.D. Book* in the recent scholarly edition by Michael Boughn and Victor Coleman (UCalP [2011]; reviewed in *YWES* 92[2013]) but reaching conceptually through the image as a concentration of modernist concerns that is unified yet brief and impermanent, which he then uses to link to other proto-modernist and late modernist figures. Joseph Kuhn's chapter connects back to Kopcewicz's interests in the new criticism through John Crowe Ransom to argue for the importance of Imagism's influence on his thought and creative work. Paweł Stachura takes a comparative approach to the 'singing poet' Vachel Lindsay and Eliot through Deleuze and Guattari's *Kafka: Toward a Minor Literature*. His argument stresses the value of conceiving of Lindsay as a minor poet, not as a limiting but rather as an expansive category. He avoids linking this to revolutionary literatures and instead focuses on minor literatures, not as reterritorializing a culture but rather as deterritorializing by virtue of intensity of expression. Finally, Miłosz Wojtyna also takes up Imagism's afterlife through Pound's imagist influence on Basil Bunting and Simon Armitage.

The edited collection *Traditions sur mesure: Exploration des poétiques expérimentales américaines, de H.D. à Michael Heller / Tailor Made Traditions: The Poetics of U.S. Experimental Verse from H.D. to Michael Heller* appears both in book format and doubling as a special issue of *Anglophonia: French Journal of English Studies*. It also extends the discussion of Imagism, for which Pound and Vorticism are continual references again. Clément Oudart's introduction sets a Pound–H.D.–Williams tradition in concert with an Imagist-Objectivist trajectory. Part of the impulse for the work is the addition of H.D. to the *agrégation* examination in France, and it seems this provokes an introductory or summative approach in several contributions. The result is a collection ideal for classroom use, particularly so given the OpenEdition access online to the periodical format, which allows free downloads of each chapter. The first five chapters focus strongly on H.D., including contributions by Antoine Cazé, Jane Augustine, Claire Conilleau, Natalia Carbajosa, and Matte Robinson, whose edition of the *Hirslanden Notebooks* with Demetres Tryphonopoulos was also released this year (reviewed below). The remaining eight chapters move from William Carlos Williams to Robert Creeley, Objectivism, Language poetry, and finally, from Michael Heller: a memoir on his interactions with George Oppen leading him to a meditation on Walter Benjamin and other Frankfurt school writers and, second, a closing interview he gave with Fiona McMahon. A second French publication, in English, relates to H.D. for the same reason of new examinations in France. Hélène Aji, Agnès Derail-Imbert Cazé, and Clément Oudart's edited collection *H.D.'s Trilogy and Beyond* contains excellent focused chapters by Aji, Augustine, Annette Debo, Susan McCabe, Fiona McMahon, and others, closing with four comparative chapters that open H.D.'s work to modernist studies more generally. Cristanne Miller offers a feminist reading of H.D. in relation to Walt Whitman; Cyrena Pondrom looks to H.D. in comparison with Eliot; Matte Robinson writes on a topic near to his *The Astral H.D.: Occult and Religious Sources and Contexts for H.D.'s Poetry and Prose* (Bloomsbury [2016]), which will be reviewed next year; and David Ten Eyck undertakes an impressive comparative study of H.D.'s *Trilogy* and Pound's *Pisan Cantos*.

ELS Editions has produced another critical edition of H.D.'s work to build on its beautifully designed yet affordable works over the past decade. *Hirslanden Notebooks: An Annotated Scholarly Edition* is edited by Matte Robinson and Demetres Tryphonopoulos, who previously collaborated to complete the final editorial work on Nephie J. Christodoulides' edition of *Magic Mirror, Compassionate Friendship, Thorn Thicket: A Tribute to Erich Heydt* (ELS [2001]; reviewed in *YWES* 92[2013]). This edition is dedicated to Christodoulides and was inspired by her work towards an edition of it before her untimely death, although she had not begun the transcription process, so this is entirely the editors' project. Robinson contributes the introduction to the edition and Tryphonopoulos 'A Note on the Edition and Text', both of which are essential for contextualizing H.D.'s very late writings. The notebooks themselves are from H.D.'s time in the Hirslanden clinic in Zürich at the end of her life, much of which would be difficult for readers to access without the extensive annotations from the editors. The annotations are particularly successful in linking the notebooks to H.D.'s previous writings and complex allusions, and in some instances notes towards future works not realized. The critical apparatus is impressive as well, with the appendices (including facsimiles of manuscripts and letters) and critical notes equal in length to the body of the text. Caroline Zilboorg's edition of H.D.'s *Bid Me to Live* (UFlorP [2011]) was also reissued in paperback format, making it more easily adoptable for the classroom. The new edition contains an extended introduction that contextualizes the autobiographical contents of the novel and the circumstances under which it was written, as well as the editorial process between H.D. and Norman Holmes Pearson for its original publication through New Directions (with Pearson being closest to New York while H.D. was in Switzerland). The text is richly annotated with endnotes, has photographs of the major locations and people involved, and contains a character key to explain the *roman-à-clef*. Likewise, Annette Debo's edition of *Within the Walls and What Do I Love?* (UFlorP [2015]) has been published in a paperback release in 2016 but was not received for review. The signal chapter of Rebecca Walsh's *The Geopoetics of Modernism* is also on H.D. and the overlapping geographical spaces of her *Trilogy*, combining Egypt and London. She shows much care with H.D.'s access to Bryher's copy of Ellen Churchill Semple's *Geography of the Mediterranean Region: Its Relation to Ancient History* (Constable [1931]), a geographer whose work crosses the book. This is a striking reading of H.D.'s *Trilogy*, most especially 'The Walls Do Not Fall' and its attendant fixation on the bombed landscape of wartime London leading on to increasing overlaps with historical and mythological Egypt. It seems difficult to resist the reading Walsh offers based on the indirect yet very strong evidence that H.D. had read Semple's work. The introduction takes up the possibilities of reading American poetics through theories of geography of the late nineteenth and early twentieth centuries that attend less to national boundaries than to relations between geography and economics or culture. This leads her to the first chapter, which establishes a method and set of concerns for the rest of the book, 'Academic and Popular Geography', for which the popularizations of geography matter as much as the original works. The more focused literary readings begin in the second chapter, 'The "Terraqueous" Globe', on Walt Whitman and Alexander von Humboldt, followed by 'African Diasporic Re-placing' on Helene Johnson and Langston Hughes and their alignment with anthropological challenges to the environmental determinism of essentialist geographical theories of their time. The book closes with a fourth chapter, on Gertrude Stein's *Geographical History of America*, and its strongest chapter, 'H.D.'s *Trilogy* as Transnational Palimpsest'.

Leah Culligan Flack also contributes work that should appeal to H.D. scholars widely, *Modernism and Homer: The Odysseys of H.D., James Joyce, Osip Mandelstam, and Ezra Pound*; it will also appeal to readers of *Antiquity Now*, reviewed below in Section 3. The book is second in the new Classics After Antiquity series edited by Alistair Blanshard, Shane Butler, and Emily Greenwood for Cambridge University Press, the premise of which is to work through classical reception studies in a way that contributes to the second field and provokes re-evaluation of how modern histories respond to the Greek and Roman worlds. This is a strong start to the series. Flack divides her project between two sections, 'High Modernism and Homer' and 'Late Modernism and Homer'. The first covers familiar terrain leading from Pound to Mandelstam to Joyce, which seems an inevitable progression. The opening with Pound's epic ambitions is refreshing in that she moves from his early works towards the *Cantos*, with excellent detailed work on the ur-Cantos. The second section, however, sets Pound's Pisan Cantos and *A Draft of XXX*

*Cantos* beside H.D.'s shorter poetry and *Helen in Egypt*. The work here on Pound's correspondence with W.H.D. Rouse is excellent, at several points responding to the recent scholarship. The turn to the new modernist studies and to Greek modernism in the conclusion is also highly provocative, and although she focuses attention on the reception studies context for classics in Greek modernism through C.P. Cavafy, George Seferis, and Nikos Kazantzakis, the provocation to set these plural modernisms together is implicit and strong.

Also in relation to Eliot, Noriko Takeda has published a third slim volume in the project begun in her *A Flowering Word: The Modernist Expression in Stéphane Mallarmé, T.S. Eliot, and Yosano Akiko* (Lang [2000]) and continued in *The Modernist Human: The Configuration of Humanness in Stéphane Mallarmé's Hérodiade, T.S. Eliot's Cats, and Modernist Lyrical Poetry* (Lang [2008]; reviewed in *YWES* 89[2010]). Building from this, *Translating as Oneself: The Re-creative Modernism in Stéphane Mallarmé's Late Sonnets, T.S. Eliot's Poems, and the Prose Poetry since Charles-Pierre Baudelaire* considers translation in its figurative and literal meanings as an interpretative process, and hence Takeda's focus here is on works not taken up in her previous books, most importantly Eliot's 1920 *Poems* originally published in 1919 as *Ara Vus Prec*, from which 'Gerontion' captures her attention the most.

The collection *Spatial Perspectives: Essays on Literature and Architecture*, edited by Terri Mullholland and Nicole Sierra, takes up designed and urban spaces with particular interests in New York City, Ted Berrigan, James Baldwin, and Don DeLillo. Julian Ferrara's chapter also analyses the comic artist Seth through architectural and urban space, and Greg Thomas relates Scottish concrete poetry to architectural form. Yasmine Shamma's ' "Room in the room that you room in?": Ted Berrigan's Structures' takes on the New York school poet Berrigan through reading approaches based on Frank O'Hara, emphasizing indecision through spatial form. By drawing out Berrigan's self-description of *The Sonnets* as growing from thoughts about architectural space, she focuses on contrasts between interior urban domestic space and capacious cityscapes outside, which suggests that the formal traits of lists and directionless wandering in poetry reflect the urban experience of confined interiors and large exploration-ready exteriors. The effect is to conflate poetry itself, New York City, and the lyrical subject's selfhood.

Rebecca Sanchez's *Deafening Modernism: Embodied Language and Visual Poetics in American Literature* brings together the discussions of disability studies and new modernist studies, both as part of a long-emerging trend that has already had further work published in 2016, such as Maren Linett's *Bodies of Modernism: Physical Disability in Transatlantic Modernist Literature* (UMichP [2016]), but also as a pressing reinvestigation of the bridging concerns of modernist studies and new modernist studies. This brief book, which is 150 pages prior to its notes, is in four chapters with an introduction and epilogue, each chapter near to the thirty-page mark. Each takes up a traditional modernist concept: impersonality, primitivism, difficulty, and the image, the last of which is broadened into the visual beyond only Imagism as a literary movement. For obvious reasons, Pound and Eliot play a major role in these thematic concerns, although with rich discussions of Hart Crane, H.D.,

Sherwood Anderson, and Gertrude Stein. Much of Sanchez's work is to reinvigorate modernist concepts by bringing them into conversation with the embodied poetics of American Sign Language through problems such as simultaneity of expression, visual communication, and so forth. The natural question at several points, such as with simultaneity (p. 96) and visual poetics (p. 122), is how the juxtaposition of materials such as the text and image in modernist works or the fact of print as a visual medium necessitates a more specific trait for ASL, which would privilege the embodied over the visual as its distinction. The matter of embodiment is particularly effective here for her critique of impersonality, although as she points out, a strictly Eliotic impersonality has been vigorously disrupted by Aaron Jaffe in *Modernism and the Culture of Celebrity* (CUP [2005]; reviewed in *YWES* 86[2007]), Jonathan Goldman in *Modernism is the Literature of Celebrity* (UTexP [2011]), and Melissa Bradshaw in *Amy Lowell: Diva Poet* (Ashgate [2011]; reviewed in *YWES* 92[2013]). Sanchez's work here is deeply entangled with contemporary currents in new modernist studies, and while this at times becomes repetitive in its presentation, it is also helpful to see a critical intervention invested in the varied projects variously afoot in studies of modernism.

Justin Quinn richly asserts the international series of networks informing American poetry during the Cold War, particularly writing reaching American poets from behind the Iron Curtain that reconfigures how we approach world literature as so-called 'literature that moves', per David Damrosch. In *Between Two Fires: Transnationalism and Cold War Poetry*, Quinn reconsiders foundational figures like Robert Lowell, Derek Walcott, Lawrence Ferlinghetti, Allen Ginsberg, and Seamus Heaney. While the internationalism and leftist orientation of many of these authors is well established, Quinn's insistence on their work's impact on Czech writers in particular and the echoing back of their work presses a new interpretation sensitive to the ideological context of those behind the Iron Curtain, such as Miroslav Holub. This challenges any distinction between the aesthetic and the political. Quinn adopts a highly sectionalized approach to the book, with subsections in each chapter—the slim collection is in four chapters with an introduction and conclusion as well, but with a further thirty subsections, very often one every few pages. At first, this is disruptive, but given the complexities of translation and Quinn's extensive footnotes to each page (often with lengthy original passages in Czech), this also means that preparatory materials to a subsequent argument are very clearly set off as such. A repeated gesture in the book is to make clear the author's stance at the close of chapters as well, lest an overly committed dedication to either side of the Cold War (and its very many others) seem implicit.

In *The Ecology of Modernism: American Environments and Avant-Garde Poetics* Joshua Schuster offers a welcome perspective on modernist environmental aesthetics. Some of the expected figures, such as William Carlos Williams, make appearances, but the five chapters that make up the study describe how Marianne Moore, Gertrude Stein, and less well-known blues poets and musicians engaged with new ideas about the environment yet stopped short of developing an activist ethos. Acknowledging the gap between interest in changing environmental conditions and actual activist positions,

*The Ecology of Modernism* as a useful counter to ecocriticism focused on ethical exemplariness. Yet the study spans from the 1920s to the early 1960s in order to include also John Cage and Rachel Carson, as it draws together writers who share an abiding interest in the non-human and explore this through formally heterogeneous experiments with representation. In comparison to Robin Schulze's explicitly historical, rather than ecocritical, *The Degenerate Muse: American Nature, Modernist Poetry, and the Problem of Cultural Hygiene* (OUP [2013]; reviewed in *YWES* 94[2015]), which examines the reactionary forces that propelled Back to Nature movements into the cultural foreground in the 1920s and focuses on Marianne Moore, Harriet Monroe, and Ezra Pound, *The Ecology of Modernism* embraces an ecocritical framework and more varied archive, linking discussion to theory like that of Timothy Morton and to environmentalist concerns like monocropping. The first chapter, 'On the Morals of Marianne Moore's Animal Monologues', follows the critical consensus that Moore eschewed allegory in favour of highlighting animal opacity, and used style to foreground animal expressivity. In the second chapter Schuster takes a broad view with Stein, charting a development in her work inclusive of *Tender Buttons*, *The Making of Americans*, and *Everybody's Geography*. What the study calls Stein's ambient poetics is the result of her growing interest in the relationship between a person's habits, perspectives, language, and natural environment. The third chapter posits blues as a vehicle well positioned to document American racial environmental experience, especially in the rural South. Among others, Schuster addresses the work of Langston Hughes and Sterling Brown. The fourth chapter regards noise as an ecological aesthetic in Cage. In sympathy with Jesse Oak Taylor's *The Sky of Our Manufacture* (UPVirginia [2016]), the final chapter addresses Rachel Carson's Cold War ethos-infused but nonetheless continuingly relevant warning about the danger of pervasive toxic pollution.

## 2. Fiction 1900–1945

With *Literary Careers in the Modern Era*, Guy Davidson and Nicola Evans unsurprisingly offer a wide study of the idea of literary careers. What is surprising is the depth they bring to a study that is otherwise so well suited to broad scope. Ranging from authors like G.K. Chesterton to those whose works were born digital, this collection explores the changing idea of what it means and has meant to be a writer. Davidson and Evans open their introduction by discussing Edward Said's first book, *Beginnings: Intention and Method* (ColUP [1975]), probing the connection between the writer as a person and the writer as a role. As they explain, the collection does not provide a comprehensive and final analysis so much as it builds upon previous 'piecemeal' analyses (p. 4). In this way, they suggest, an author's career 'may productively be thought of as a category of analysis in its own right' (p. 5). With attention, this category puts the 'plot' of an author's life back into play with the works he or she writes (p. 6). Of the essays in the collection, many stand out as impressive studies of literary careers, but only one extensively relates to modernist American fiction. Jeff Solomon's 'Broadly Queer and Specifically Gay: The Celebrity and Career of Gertrude Stein' presents a fascinating distinction between otherness at large and homosexuality at a point. As Solomon describes her, 'In her personal life, Stein was specifically gay... [and this] specific homosexuality interacted in complex ways with her broad queerness' (p. 78). In considering Stein's *Autobiography of Alice B. Toklas*, Solomon shows, too, the impact Stein felt from the overwhelming success of that work on her literary career. From the resulting anxiety of celebrity (p. 79), Solomon traces three 'case studies' of Stein's life: right after publication of *Three Lives* [1909–10], after the armory show (1912), and as an 'opium queen' image of decadence (1910s–1930s). In this, Solomon's chapter is an impressive example of the collection's scope and focus.

Edinburgh University Press's *The Modernist Party*, edited by Kate McLoughlin, presents a collection of views, gathered together as for a party of parties, understanding modernist literature by its lively social lives. The volume offers a convincing perspective. Introducing the collection, McLoughlin situates theories of social gatherings historically, touching on 'the Roman *convivium*, the Victorian dinner-party' before arriving at parties of the modernist period: 'from tea-parties to cocktail-parties, from lunch- and dinner-parties to extended house-parties, from breakfast-parties to parties held in venues such as nightclubs, restaurants and artists' studios, from at-homes to dinner-dances to soirées' (p. 2). While later chapters bear out McLoughlin's claim that the party offers new opportunities in the modernist period to study 'a forum for testing the relationship of the individual to other people, exploring the nature of the self and critiquing the state' (p. 2), she nevertheless offers consideration for some of these herself: in examples of literal and actual parties with Joseph Conrad, Ford Madox Ford, and others at a children's birthday party (p. 3); in literary depictions of parties in the writing of F. Scott Fitzgerald, Arthur Ransome, and Virginia Woolf, among others (pp. 3–4); and in glimpses of parties that are at times something of both, as in Alice B. Toklas's cookbook (p. 4). While some of the volume's twelve chapters offer consideration for modernist American fiction, most focus on European works or works of poetry. For instance, although Alex Goody's chapter glances on Gertrude's Stein's fiction and reflects on her personal life, it focuses mostly on her plays *What Happened: A Play in Five Acts* and *A Play Called Not and Now*. As such, the chapter is only partially relevant to this section's interest in American modernist fiction, but it nevertheless provides some useful context. Most significantly, Margo Natalie Crawford's chapter, 'The Interracial Party of Modernist Primitivism and the Black "After-Party"', avoids studying the rent-party—what might seem a tempting approach to black literature of the period. Instead, she visualizes modernist primitivism by drawing forth the image of a mixed-race party with white hosts and black guests (pp. 164–5). Reading Nella Larsen, Langston Hughes, and Jean Toomer, among others, Crawford finds modernist authors relating the performance of racialized primitivism varyingly as degrading, as potentially rehabilitative, and as beautiful (pp. 166–9). Ultimately, she shows the African American response to modernist primitivism to offer more than just a response, 'a cultural moment that was "somewhere" and "nowhere"' (p. 175).

This was a good year for readers of Hemingway. James M. Hutchisson's study *Ernest Hemingway: A New Life* is biographical, but it is tempting to call it something more than just a biography. In reading the life of '*the* American writer' (p. 1), Hutchisson also offers significant insights into the works that align with the author's life, reaching his stated goal of avoiding the paths of previous Hemingway biographies, arriving at something contradictory and, internally, anything but simplified (pp. 1–2). The resulting volume is equally useful for scholars of Hemingway's writing or readers interested in his life. The introduction promises 'several specific angles of entry into understanding Hemingway' (p. 3): his relationships with women, with place, and with medicine. Of these angles, those of relationships with women and with place are the strongest: chapters chart his wanderings in love life and across continents in titles including 'Italy and Agnes von Kurowsky', 'Pauline, Key West, and *A Farewell to Arms*', and 'Jane Mason and Africa', among others. Starting in Hemingway's childhood, Hutchisson develops the importance of the author's religious upbringing (p. 5) and marks his fascination with nature, drawing connections to *A Farewell to Arms* and *The Sun Also Rises* (p. 15). Hutchisson makes useful connections like these throughout, whether in relating Hemingway's childhood reading to later writing (pp. 19–20); in showing his writing style as influenced by his time as a journalist in Kansas City (p. 22); or in linking Hemingway's time with the Red Cross to specific moments in *A Farewell to Arms*, 'A Natural History of the Dead', 'A Way You'll Never Be', 'Soldier's Home', 'Now I Lay Me', and others (pp. 23–8). But Hemingway's relationships with other authors and with women might be the strongest connections throughout the work. For instance, Hutchisson helpfully relates the waning of Hemingway's marriage to his first wife to the beginning of a new relationship and the finishing of *The Sun Also Rises* (p. 83). Fifteen plates of images show further aspects of the life of the author and those around him, but even without these photographs Hutchisson's wide-ranging study already brings a new life to Hemingway and his writing.

Along with Hutchisson's biography, James Gifford's editions of the 1923 and 1924 versions of one of Hemingway's most significant works, *In Our Time*, add to the year's catalogue of works on the novelist. With each version, Gifford provides a nine-page introduction granting adept readings of the sketches themselves and the work as a whole. Gifford calls Hemingway 'a pedagogical writer' (1924 edn., p. v) for teaching the reader how to read the stories closely, and the examples he provides show the reasonableness of this understanding. The introductions further offer details to accompany and explain the autobiographical elements in the text, and they provide much-needed contextualization, placing the vignettes in a specific place in history and in culture (1924 edn., pp. v–viii). Outside the introductions, the texts are displayed cleanly and are well laid out. The 1923 edition includes 'In Our Time', three pages, and 'They All Made Peace—What Is Peace?', two pages, as first published in *The Little Review*, along with two pages of original endnotes and a two-page bibliography of further suggested reading. The 1924 edition, by contrast, reprints the twenty pages of *in our time* as first published by Three Mountains Press, along with two and a half pages of endnotes and a two-page bibliography. In making available two earlier editions of such a canonical work of modern American fiction,

Gifford has himself prepared a pedagogical text of this pedagogical writer that is well suited to both scholar and classroom.

Finally, editor Kevin J. Hayes's collection *A History of Virginia Literature* differs from the other works this year for a focus on the literature of one state. In it, Hayes makes the case for Virginia's prominence in the context of American letters, touching on its early pre-eminence, its sometime omission from curricula, and its resurgence in the canon (pp. 1–3). Despite all this, he explains, the collection presents 'the first major collaborative literary history of Virginia ever attempted' (p. 5). The resulting volume is useful for any reader of American literature, and the fourth section, on 'Modern Virginia', is especially relevant to modernist fiction. For instance, the first chapter in the section rehabilitates the work of Ellen Glasgow to whom, as Susan Goodman writes, 'Literary history has not been... kind' (p. 297). As Goodman explains, part of Glasgow's lack of recognition comes from the difficulty placing her works: when readers favoured romanticized images of the South, Glasgow offered realism (p. 298) and addressed fear of 'the race question' (p. 301). While Goodman's single-author focus allows for depth in studying the work of one Virginian, Tom Barden's chapter on the Virginia Writers' Project shines light on the community of writers formed by Franklin Delano Roosevelt's Federal Writers' Project, a subset of the president's Depression-era Works Progress Administration (p. 309). Barden ultimately shows that scholarship so far has merely scratched the surface of the full vein of works contributed as part of the Virginia Writers' Project. While Goodman's and Barden's contributions read works of particular authors, John David Miles's chapter on 'Science Fiction and Fantasy' reads by genre. From chronicling the 'new founde' land's fantastic dimensions and properties in sixteenth-century depictions, Miles moves swiftly into nineteenth-century and modern speculative fiction of the state, touching down on names like William Jenkins, Nelson Bond, and James Branch Cabel. In these authors of the early twentieth century, Miles largely finds continuation of the work in speculative fiction earlier honed by writers like Edgar Allen Poe (p. 327), and he notes themes related to Virginians' identity (p. 328). Finally, Adam N. Jabbur's contribution, on 'Virginians at a Distance: Willa Cather and Tom Wolfe', further expands the consideration of Virginia writers to include treatment of topics predominantly outside the state. Most relevant to modern fiction, Jabbur's treatment of Cather is highly biographical—an approach that makes sense given the limits of the novelist's formative experience in Virginia. In fact, as Jabbur points out, Cather seemed to reject the state, finding 'little in Virginia to inspire the emotive nostalgia that characterizes her best fiction' (p. 349). Returning full circle in this section on modern fiction in Virginia, he reports, too, on Cather's declining an invitation Ellen Glasgow extended to her, thereby underscoring Cather's appellation as a 'Virginian at a distance'.

## 3. Fiction since 1945

In general, literary criticism published in 2015 that focuses on works of the post-1945 period shows a consistent focus upon and development of theoretical analyses of literary representations of globalization and late capitalism, environmental crises, biopolitics and thanatopolitics, and violence in the society of the spectacle. The opening portion of this section of the review situates recent monographs within these broader topics in literary criticism before addressing works that examine aesthetic shifts in the 1990s that, for multiple scholars, mark divergences from postmodernism. Whether they focus on the rise of digitization, developments of global capitalism after the end of the Cold War, or the philosophical and aesthetic legacy of postmodernism to which literary writers respond, monographs discussed in the second portion of the review contribute to critical debates about periodization by tracing both formal and contextual changes in literary production around and beyond the millennial turn. Following this section, the review addresses criticism that returns to discussions of literary appropriations and revisions of canonical texts in post-1945 texts with particular attention to aesthetic reworkings of classical texts, American literary classics, and Romantic poetics. Building from this discussion, the review also explores monographs that examine how contemporary authors address and challenge myths of the frontier in recent literary works. This portion of the review will conclude with a discussion of one published collection that focuses upon feminist works of the post-1945 period as well as an overview of critical texts focused on single authors such as Barbara Kingsolver, Sara Paretsky, William Gaddis, Edward Abbey, Don DeLillo, David Foster Wallace, Richard Ford, and Lee Smith.

In terms of wide-reaching theoretical implications for the understanding of contemporary aesthetic production, Christian Moraru's *Reading for the Planet: Toward a Geomethodology* is the most important book published in 2015. The book is an intervention into the 'global turn' and the conceptualization of 'globalization', 'globalism', or the 'global age' within humanistic disciplines. To this end, Moraru seeks to outline the limitations of the commonplaces of recent studies in this area and to propose an alternative to them through his elucidation of planetarism, the planetary imaginary, and geomethodology. His critique of the scholarship of the global turn revolves around its totalizing impulses; he writes, 'The global world is...a well-rounded, integrated, definitive—and in that existentially and politically hopeless—closed system and happily confirmed teleology enforced from a political and economic if not geometrical center or centers and by a plethora of feedback loops, symmetries, parallels, and exchange procedures effectuated and conveyed across a relational web progressively overlapping with the world itself. The world worlds itself into globe, goes global, once the infinite, the unlimited, the multitudinous, the boundless, and the boundlessly different...have been quantified and repurposed materially and conceptually as domains of one, the homogenous, the circular, the repetitive, and the selfsame' (p. 29). Building from work by Masao Miyoshi, Gayatri Chakravorty Spivak, Hardt and Negri, and Paul Gilroy, to name just a few of the theorists that Moraru claims as influence, he traces in aesthetic and philosophical works a 'planetary counterdiscourse' that is 'sensitive to formations, workings, and implications of world relationality that escape or are disadvantaged by the co-opting fury of corporations, markets, and empires, by the serial, the formulaic, the routine, the "universal," the easily or apparently classifiable and profitable' (p. 51). In terms of periodization, Moraru views the end of the Cold War and the fall of the Berlin Wall as the opening through which a planetary imaginary appears. Across literary and philosophical texts he traces a 'planetary epistemology' defined by its 'emblematic mind-set, *Weltanschauung*, or world picture sponsored by the insight that fewer and fewer separate or presumably discrete places, groups, and undertakings are sitting out the transnational and transcultural protocols that link up, intertwine, and inflect things, people, and cultural iconologies on a steadily widening scale' and 'a sensitivity to the planetary articulations and problematics, which supply increasingly central, formal metaphors and foci to artists and critics alike' (p. 74). Because Moraru's aim is to provide a schematic overview as well as a rich conceptual framework for the planetary imagination, his work is a kind of manifesto for ways of reading and analysing post-1989 fiction and theory and therefore does not offer many detailed readings of specific works from this period. However, the allusions to various fictional texts as well as the detailed engagement with a few key novels, like Joseph O'Neill's *Netherland*, will be incredibly generative for scholars. For example, he suggests that 'authors like O'Neill, DeLillo, Kunzru, Hamid, Pynchon, and Richard Powers . . . push us to envisage a world *demotikón* . . . [and] prompt us to follow the dialectical ontology of the macro and micro all the way to its end, where the planet's face turns—and turns us as well—to the faces of those around us and to the problematic of care "in" or, better still, across "territory," to a responsibility idea and practice notionally and nationally reterritorialized, extended conceptually and physically to other spaces and people' (p. 176). This leads Moraru to an engagement with the ethics of such fictional works as well as the ethical work of criticism attuned to the planetary imagination. For him, works by the aforementioned authors and others engage in an '*ethic beyond the ethnic*: an ethic that neither erases nor dismisses ethnic background and all backgrounds, grounds, and *Gründe*, but, to the contrary, one that acknowledges and honors them by working with, through, and over their contested geography, their territoriality and ethno-culturally demarcated spaces, turfs, and discourses' (p. 180). Inspired by Levinas, Moraru ultimately concludes his book with a call for criticism to reformulate conceptions of the global turn with attention to 'planetary stewardship', which reflects and continues the ethic of work by authors like O'Neill, DeLillo, and Pynchon. This monograph inevitably will inspire much future critical conversation because of its compelling take on literary and philosophical work of the late twentieth and early twenty-first century, its detailed proposal for a geomethodology beyond the limitations of previous work associated with the global turn, and its nuanced and beautiful elucidation of the import as well as ethics of planetarism.

Although not directly focused on the environment, Moraru's work also will contribute provocatively to environmental literary criticism, as will two other major monographs published in 2015. Adam Trexler's *Anthropocene Fictions: The Novel in a Time of Climate Change* asks how 'climate change make[s] new demands on the novel, forcing formal and narrative innovation' (p. 10). Although works from the 1970s and 1980s certainly addressed a wide variety of environmental crises, including global warming, Trexler argues that the

1990s mark the beginning of an explosion in literary treatment of climate. He suggests, 'Al Gore's 1999 presidential campaign ensured that climate change was a central issue in American politics at the same time that a new wave of novels came into print... [that address] the historical tension between the existence of catastrophic global warming and the failed obligation to act. Under these conditions, fiction offered a medium to explain, predict, implore, and lament' (p. 9). Providing a schematic overview of the major characteristics of novels focused upon climate change, Trexler offers four different ways to group novels of the late twentieth century that reflect recent understandings of a new period in Earth's history named the Anthropocene. The term denotes the way that human activity has become the major force that impacts climate and the environment. He argues 'that dozens of works successfully reconfigure the historical relationship between fiction and truth-telling', especially scientific truth claims, 'alter assumptions of how humans relate to place; reimagine social and political organization; or rearticulate the global, mechanized, consumer economies of the twenty-first century' (p. 16). Each chapter of the monograph targets one of these topics—truth, place, politics, and economics—in aesthetic production by documenting a larger trend with reference to numerous novels and offering detailed analysis of a few key texts. For example, the third chapter of the book, which focuses upon representations of politics and climate change, outlines three different trends in numerous works: an investigation of 'a central conflict between states to explore the geopolitical dimensions of climate change', a presentation of 'structural conflict between radical environmentalist groups and a capitalist establishment bent on ignoring climate change', and the exploration of 'a composite political entity with sufficient agency to redress climate change' (pp. 121–2). The full chapter fleshes out these broad strokes with examination of novels by Bruce Sterling, T.C. Boyle, Arthur Herzog, Clive Cussler, Kim Stanley Robinson, Michael Glass, and Paul McAuley, to name a few of the authors addressed. Ultimately, Trexler argues that 'the most politically engaged novels are not those that threaten the public with annihilation, but rather those that show the alliances between readers and institutions that might lead to a climate of abrupt action' (p. 169). Each chapter of Trexler's work offers multiple nuanced insights both into the broad field of anthropocene fiction and into specific exemplary texts; thus, this monograph will be essential reading for environmental literary critics. Still, as Trexler suggests that 'all contemporary fiction could be said to reflect a condemned "greenhouse culture" ', he offers a rich variety of ways in which we might approach aesthetic works in which climate change is not the primary focus and yet inevitably shapes the cultural, political, and environmental contexts in which contemporary authors write (p. 27). With this larger claim, Trexler's work assuredly will be important for conversations about shifts in narrative form and content at the end of the twentieth century and into the twenty-first.

A second work of environmental literary criticism, Jeffrey Bilbro's *Loving God's Wildness: The Christian Roots of Ecological Ethics in American Literature*, intervenes in environmental literary criticism that eschews the import of Christianity for key writers associated with nineteenth- and twentieth-century American environmentalism. Although Bilbro acknowledges damaging usages of Christian ideology that justify 'turning nature into profitable resources' (p. 4), he seeks to trace a tension in Puritan thinking between viewing wilderness as the 'Devil's Territories' and, alternatively, as 'God's temple' that influences later writers like Thoreau, Muir, Willa Cather, and Wendell Berry. Rather than abandon Puritan religious thinking, Bilbro shows how all four of these authors turn to previous generations' exploration of what Muir calls 'God's wilderness' to explore how American Christianity's Puritan roots make room for an ethics of care for the world beyond the exploitation of it for economic gain (p. 8). He writes, 'despite the Puritans' ambivalence over how the physical and spiritual worlds were connected, their faith that these spheres are indeed related led some to articulate a theological framework in which humans should love and participate in God's wild order. And from this belief, haltingly expressed by John Winthrop, Cotton Mather, and Jonathan Edwards, emerged an American literary tradition that imagines more complex, sustainable ways for humans to live with the rest of creation' (p. 8). Attention to the ecological imagination in Puritan works and how nineteenth- and twentieth-century authors have engaged such texts should be integral to environmental literary criticism in Bilbro's account, because authors themselves view Christianity as providing a counterpoint to destructive engagement with the natural world (pp. 15–16). In this way, Bilbro follows important environmental literary critics like Lawrence Buell, Bill McKibben, and John Gaata, who recognize 'that American Christianity has a deeply conflicted track record with regard to the environment' while also affirming that prominent authors, like those listed above, continue to think theologically about human impact upon and responsibility for the world (p. 16). To understand the American ecological imagination, for Bilbro, requires a deep engagement with theological underpinnings that inspire ways of seeing 'creation' and exploring human interactions with it that honour the 'sacred' world. The chapter that focuses on Wendell Berry's works examines a variety of essays and novels with particular attention to *Jayber Crow* and *The Memory of Old Jack*. Overall, Bilbro addresses Berry's 'understanding of the troubled history of Europeans' settlement in America, the Christian tradition, the economy or order of the Kingdom of God, the human place within this economy, the faithful, particular, imaginative work required to care for this place' (p. 141). Because of the focus on the religious ecological imagination and the beautiful interpretations of literary works, *Loving God's Wildness* will appeal to scholars invested in environmental literary criticism and history, the legacy of Puritan theology into the twentieth century, and the Christian vision of authors like Cather and Berry as counterpoint to the damage of industrialization, militarism, and agribusiness.

Beyond these two major works of environmental literary criticism, editors Scott Slovic, James E. Bishop, and Kyhl Lyndgaard's *Currents of the Universal Being: Explorations in the Literature of Energy* is a useful anthology that offers a variety of short literary works—poetry, fiction, and literary non-fiction—that reflect upon energy crises. With the aim of 'assembl[ing] a suggestive compendium of texts to stimulate discussions about energy consumption, to reflect upon and explore energy but not to reduce opinions into simple polemics about lifestyle choices' (p. 7), the editors provide useful primary material for the undergraduate classroom as well as effective short introductory essays to major trends in aesthetic works that focus broadly on energy. For example, introductory essays to specific sections of the anthology address how authors attend to fossil fuels and the atomic age, alternative sources of energy such as solar and wind power, and the environmental costs of energy production. The anthology ends with three sample syllabi designed by the editors that supply educators with ideas for constructing interdisciplinary courses with energy as the primary theme. In addition to this collection, Jon Gordon's *Unsustainable Oil: Facts, Counterfacts and Fictions* also addresses energy with a particular focus on aesthetic works that address petroleum extraction with an emphasis on literary engagement with Alberta's bituminous sands. Like Ross Barrett and Daniel Worden's edited collection *Oil Culture* (UMinnP [2014]; reviewed in *YWES* 95[2016]), both of these works suggest an increased critical engagement with aesthetic grappling with energy production and its environmental impact as well as literary contributions to imagining environmental justice.

In addition to this focus on human impact on the environment, one late arrival continues a critical trend that addresses literary renderings of and resistance to biopolitics and thanatopolitics. Christopher Breu's *Insistence of the Material: Literature in the Age of Biopolitics* is a pivotal and provocative monograph that traces a literary 'countertradition' within postmodern literature for which he proposes the name 'late-capitalist literature of materiality' (p. 4). He argues that this literature emerges during the post-Second World War period, in which 'the built environment, modes of representation, the figuration of the body, and the experience of everyday life are profoundly intertwined with late-capitalist production, consumption, and signification practices that both remake the material world and produce an ever-growing fantasy of transcendence' (p. 26). In contrast to a critical focus on 'metafictional forms' as the defining feature of postmodern aesthetic production, Breu suggests that authors like Burroughs, Pynchon, J.G. Ballard, Silko, and Dodie Bellamy 'use language experimentally to engage the increasingly obscured yet ever proliferating material underpinnings of everyday life ... [and] our globalizing world' (pp. 26–7). As a contribution to the material turn in literary studies, Breu's work addresses the 'insistence' on the material within aesthetic works that counter 'fantasies of dematerialization and complete socialization' (pp. 26–7). For example, with astute analytical power, Breu shows how William S. Burroughs's *Naked Lunch*, inspired by his inhabitance of the interzone of Tangiers, offers 'a fictional landscape that is built around biopolitical production, including sex work, the trade in narcotics, the biomedical economy, and the traffic in life and death that would only become a more dominant part of the world system ... in our own moment' (p. 37). For Breu, the prevalence of the abject as well as mutilated bodies in this work showcases the damages of 'biopolitical and thanatopolitical commerce' that 'violently exploit[s] and reform[s] bodies' (p. 55). Ultimately, he argues that it is through bodies made expendable that the text proposes a 'locus of political resistance in the biopolitical and deregulated world presciently imagined by Burroughs' (p. 55). Drawing on theorists such as Michael Hardt and Antonio Negri, Giorgio Agamben, and Jacques Lacan and providing brilliant readings of Thomas Pynchon's *V*, J.G. Ballard's *Crash*, Dodie Bellamy's *The Letters of Mina Harker*, and Leslie Marmon Silko's *Almanac of the Dead*, Breu's monograph is essential reading as it calls for a re-evaluation of the material in major works of the postmodern period and persuasively argues that such attention to the material is necessary for charting diverse responses to the biopolitical and thanatopolitical forces. Concluding with a manifesto of sorts for scholarship of the material turn, Breu's monograph finally serves as a call for literary criticism and theory that 'refuse[s] to validate our fantasies of transcending the material' (p. 190).

Also focusing on the insistence of the material in post-1945 literature, Raymond Malewitz's *The Practice of Misuse: Rugged Consumerism in Contemporary American Culture* builds from 'thing theory' and work by critics like Bill Brown, Bruno Latour, and Jane Bennett to address the status of human–object relations in contemporary culture, visual art, plays, and novels. With a particular emphasis on the oppositional and creative misuse of consumer goods, Malewitz outlines the emergence of what he calls 'rugged consumers'—'who creatively misuse, reuse, and repurpose the objects within their social environments to suit their idiosyncratic needs and desires' (p. 6). Although rugged consumers' 'misuse' of objects may 'temporarily suspend the various networks of power that dictate the proper use of a given artefact and to allow those networks of power to be understood as contingent strategies that must be perpetually renewed and reinforced' (pp. 6–7), Malewitz is clear that they 'simultaneously embody and critique [consumer] culture' (p. 8). Additionally, he views rugged consumerism as 'a left- and right-libertarian response to economic and political developments within the United States' that is 'skeptical of both traditional political institutions and . . . globalized corporate capitalism' (p. 8). Drawing upon 'American myths of primal nature', and 'rugged individualism', rugged consumers 'become mediating figures between mythic models of productive self-sufficiency conceived during the country's older frontier history and the modern interdependent realities that characterize the country's transition to a neoliberal globalized economy' (p. 8). Addressing countercultural theatre of the late 1960s, Pynchon's *Gravity's Rainbow*, Palahniuk's *Fight Club*, Don DeLillo's *Underworld*, and Cormac McCarthy's novels, Malewitz traces how 'early forms of rugged consumerism are presented as Utopian alternatives to the institutions and modes available to consumers under late capitalism' in Sam Shepard's plays and Pynchon's novel, and how works published in the following two decades reveal a shift in understandings of rugged consumerism as 'instances of creative repurposing [that] reinforce the structural conditions [of late capitalism] that they purport to combat' (p. 40). Like Breu's work, Malewitz's monograph is a stunning rendering of literary engagement with and resistance to capitalist ideologies of value as well as a provocative account of the shifting aesthetic accounts of the practice of misuse across the late twentieth century. In addition, Malewitz powerfully concludes his monograph with an exploration of how 'the literary imagination offers partial solutions to the cognitive, industrial, and ecological endgames of late capitalism by not simply reflecting the current repurposing culture but also by asking us to reimagine the creative relationships between humans and all objects that populate our world' (p. 189). Thus, Malewitz charts a few ways in which scholarship of 'vibrant matter' in literary works of the post-1945 period as well as the 'various economic and geopolitical crises of the twenty-first century might now create a desire to reimagine or to remythologize human–object relationships in ways that serve progressive rather than negative ends' (pp. 189–90).

With an emphasis on the relationships between humans in the age of biopolitics, Arne De Boever's *Narrative Care: Biopolitics and the Novel*, another late arrival, focuses upon how contemporary anglophone novelists acknowledge 'complicit[y] with biopower' while simultaneously experimenting with literary works as sites for exploring 'care for the self and others' (p. 13). Addressing one US author—Paul Auster—in his monograph, De Boever uncovers 'Auster's concern [in *The Book of Illusions*] with life-writing and the power-relation of novelists to characters, a concern that takes on biopolitical significance when it is considered in light of the history of the Holocaust that lies occluded in the book' (p. 12). More Foucauldian than Breu's text, De Boever's monograph also engages with theoretical work by Agamben, Derrida, and Judith Butler in his close readings of the textual incorporation and troubling of biopolitics as well as imaginative renderings of care for others.

Although not situated directly within theoretical discussions on biopolitics, a few monographs published in 2015 connect with this critical emphasis by addressing representations of violence with a specific focus on contemporary aesthetic engagement with the society of the spectacle and literary renderings of the Shoah. *Disappear Here: Violence after Generation X*, by Naomi Mandel, examines representations of violence produced by artists born between 1960 and 1980 as well as artists who reflect upon the specific world view of Generation X. Mandel draws from a number of studies of Generation X to explore 'violence's forms and functions in the world that Xers grew up in. In this world, the line between fiction and fact is permeable, fungible; the relationship of violence to action is characterized by complicity, giving pause to ethics; "reality" is produced for television and marketed for consumption, and fiction—in the sense of fashioning and fabricating, as well as illusion and delusion—assumes an important role in the creation, construction, and preservation of "real violence"' (pp. 211–12). Arguing that aesthetic works produced by Generation X writers and those interested in the political, cultural, and technological developments of their youth reveal a 'unique attitude toward violence', Mandel analyses work by Bret Easton Ellis, Jay McInerney, Douglas Coupland, Colson Whitehead, Jess Walter, Claire Messud, Ken Kalfus, Jonathan Safran Foer, Don DeLillo, and Chuck Palahniuk. Offering compelling interpretations of Ellis's work, for example, Mandel shows how his novels 'trace the disappearance of the sign of the real and document a subtraction of reality from representation in the quarter century between 1985... and 2010' (p. 212). Countering criticism that has treated Ellis's work as 'trashy' and 'substanceless', Mandel highlights the 'philosophical seriousness' of his work to elucidate how his fiction captures the problem of violence for Generation X as the lines between 'reality' and representation are blurred (p. 83). She writes, 'Rather than separating "violence" or fact from fiction, I trace how Ellis's novels subtract epistemic certainty from violence and tease apart violence and the reality attributed to it. [His novels] blur distinctions between reality and fiction, object and agent, violence and "violence," underlining the mobile or unstable nature of the ground from which such judgments may be made' (pp. 82–3). Turning to works produced in the twenty-first century, Mandel shows how Generation X's earlier insights into violence continue to shape more recent fiction. Her study of 9/11 novels challenges claims that such fiction marks a 'return to the real'; as Xers have come of age, their take on the tragedy that occurred on 9/11 'attests repeatedly to the inextricability of the real from mass media' (p. 213). More than focus on the spectacle of violence, novels by authors like Messud and Walter, '[open] up an approach to violence that refuses the affective ethos of trauma, the singularity of U.S. exceptionalism, and the presumption of fidelity that, in the informal patriotic fervor and official bellicose rhetoric, assumed such murderous manifestations in the months and years following the attacks' (p. 115). In this way, Mandel powerfully shows how attention to the fiction of Xers and those who write about or are influenced by them reveals a complex ethical navigation of violence in contrast to an assumed detachment from philosophical engagement with representations of it.

Like Mandel's monograph, Emily Miller Budick's *The Subject of Holocaust Fiction* also investigates representations of violence, albeit with a different focus to *Disappear Here* in that Budick examines how specific literary renderings of the Shoah 'call into question the motivations and actions not only of the characters in the text and of its author, but ultimately and more importantly, for reasons both ethical and epistemological, also of the reader' (pp. 10–11). Thus, she builds from scholarly works that address literary accounts of trauma to address 'the fantasies, wishes, and fears [that texts entertain] in relation to the events [they] narrate so as to be able to examine what in us as readers and Holocaust scholars represents both legitimate and illegitimate investments in the subject' (p. 14). Budick is particularly interested in how texts like Cynthia Ozick's *The Shawl* trouble readers' desire for detailed renderings of others' suffering and violation. For example, she argues that Ozick's novel 'forc[es] readers to interrogate their own subjectivities when they hear or read . . . stories [about the Holocaust] . . . [and] suggests that in order to be good listeners and good historians we might need to separate out our own needs in relation to the events of the past from the responsibility we have to hear other people's stories of pain' (p. 70). Budick positions Ozick's *The Shawl* in conversation with Art Spiegelman's *Maus: A Survivor's Tale* and Aryeh Lev Stollman's *The Far Euphrates* in order to examine how all three works challenge readers to address their own subject positions and desire for narration of the Holocaust. Budick also addresses mourning and melancholy in a number of works, including novels by Philip Roth, Nicole Krauss, Jonathan Safran Foer, and Michael Chabon. In particular, she is interested in multiple novels' critical engagement with 'incomplete mourning' in which 'both characters in the texts and the texts themselves become involved in forms of conjuring and idol worship, escapist fantasies, and the production of golems and messiahs' even as they also explore 'healthier, more productive' ways to mourn (p. 124). In the concluding section of the monograph, Budick examines novels written by non-Jewish authors and the ways in which 'the Holocaust can become fused with and thereby become a cover for other subjects and interests' (p. 17). *The Subject of Holocaust Fiction* is a deeply moving and beautifully written contemplation of how Jewish authors grapple with their own and readers' desire for representations of the Holocaust, the difficulty of mourning, and how the Holocaust is presented by non-Jewish writers, including W.G. Sebald, William Styron, and J.M. Coetzee.

Like Budick's work, Laurie Vickroy's *Reading Trauma Narratives: The Contemporary Novel and the Psychology of Oppression* addresses representations of trauma and how such representations gesture towards strategies for readers to respond to suffering. '[B]y employing theories of trauma, narrative, and cognition to analyse the ways in which . . . texts engage readers cognitively and ethically in a reading process that immerses them in, while providing perspective on, the flawed thinking and behavior of the traumatized, and by exploring how the psychology of fear drives individuals and society' Vickroy highlights how specific writers 'want readers to understand their own role in systems of power and how they have internalized systems' ideologies' (pp. xii–xiii). Her chapters address novels by Margaret Atwood, Toni Morrison, William Faulkner, Jeanette Winterson, and Chuck Palahniuk. Although she discusses various forms of trauma, Vickroy argues that works by these authors 'condemn a rampant, dehumanizing materialism that has driven and haunted our culture from its beginnings' (p. 184). Her work with Palahniuk's *Fight Club* and *Invisible Monsters* especially is useful on this point, as she explores how 'the framework of trauma helps readers conceptualize characters' behaviors as symptomatic: their repetitions, dissociations, defenses, and acting out are the emotional consequences of destructive social and sexual designations and human objectification' (p. 155).

In addition to Budick's work, Leah Garrett's *Young Lions: How Jewish Authors Reinvented the American War Novel* will be of interest to scholars focused on representations of the Holocaust. With attention to best-selling war novels by Jewish authors from 1948 to 1961, Garrett argues that, 'since authors of the war novels were composing their work for mainstream readers, their "use" of the Holocaust highlighted their liberal notions about pluralism and equality. . . . In their rendering, the Jewish soldier is a fighter against, rather than a victim of, the Germans and because of this he serves as an emblem of the American war against totalitarianism. . . . He thus becomes a symbol of all victims of hate, a wakeup call to American readers that in the postwar era they must treat all members of society equally' (p. 13). Analysing novels by Norman Mailer, Ira Wolfert, Irwin Shaw, Herman Wouk, Leon Uris, and Joseph Heller as well as many other authors, Garrett provides a strong overview of 'a genre of war writing that made the topic of Jewishness, in its many and varied forms, a central lens through which the war was filtered' (p. 20). While she addresses early representations of the Holocaust, she also explores how the 'Jewish soldier was an ideal symbol for shifting concerns of postwar America' as authors engaged with anti-communism, McCarthyism, and the social conservatism of the 1950s (p. 21). Ultimately arguing that best-selling novels by the aforementioned authors shaped larger national narratives about war, Garrett's work, while clearly focused on the figure of the Jewish soldier, importantly addresses the major themes of best-selling war novels and thus contributes to scholarly discussion of 'middlebrow' novels and renderings of combat in popular fiction in the decade following the conclusion of the Second World War. Beyond this attention to the Second World War, one recent collection of essays edited by Brenda M. Boyle offers new readings of Vietnam War literature. Essays in *The Vietnam War: Topics in Contemporary North American Literature* revisit well-known texts like Michael Herr's *Dispatches*, Tim O'Brien's *The Things They Carried* and *In the Lake of the Woods*, Larry Heinemann's *Paco's Story*, and Bobbie Ann Mason's *In Country*, but also address under-studied works by Vietnamese Americans as well as works that reflect upon the experience of Vietnamese people during the war. In terms of focus, essayists examine renderings of trauma and mourning, literary engagement with masculinity 'to critique Vietnam war narratives', and the influence of 9/11 on Vietnam narratives written after the attacks (p. 20). The strength of the collection is in authors' attention to novels about the North Vietnamese and Vietnamese refugees' experience, with analysis of works by Dương Thu Hương, Bảo Ninh, and lê thị diễm thúy, evaluation of how the Vietnam War is refigured in the wake of 9/11 in aesthetic works, and close readings of canonical texts with nuanced engagement with new directions in trauma theory, such as Marianne Hirsch's work on postmemory.

Although the works of Moraru, Trexler, and Mandel have been situated here as contributions to criticism of the global turn, environmental literary criticism, or representations of violence in the society of the spectacle, they also point towards increasing critical attention to and nuanced theoretical development of frameworks to address fiction of the 1990s and the twenty-first century. Even as authors like Breu importantly call for scholarly reimagination of postmodern texts for their insight into biopolitics across the mid-twentieth century, a number of scholarly monographs trace formal shifts in aesthetic production that reflect literary wrangling with the rise and instantiation of digitization and the legacy of postmodernism. Despite the thematic differences between the following monographs, each of their authors, like Moraru, Trexler and Mandel, understands the 1990s to instantiate significant changes in aesthetic works. For example, Alexander Starre's provocative *Metamedia: American Book Fictions and Literary Print Culture* addresses how a number of authors have engaged with the status of printed literary books as new mediums for the dissemination of aesthetic works emerged. Showing that the 'technological ensemble of carrier media for digital texts passed a crucial threshold in the late 1990s', Starre addresses how such media 'prompt[ed] an ever-growing number of American writers and readers to acknowledge the changing media environment and to respond to it' (p. 4). In his account, multiple texts from the late 1990s to the present exhibit a 'literary phenomenon' called 'metamediality' (p. 8). He writes, 'A literary work becomes a metamedium once it uses a specific devise to reflexively engage with the specific material medium to which it is affixed or in which it is displayed' (p. 8). Because of the rise of digitization, 'literary texts can no longer take a specific medium for granted', and thus authors like Dave Eggers, Mark Z. Danielewski, Jonathan Safran Foer, Chip Kidd, Salvador Plascencia, and Reif Larsen produce works that 'merge the medial properties of the printed book with their discursive content... [which] fosters the experience of metamediality' (p. 24). With the aim of revealing how authors participate in a 'literary dialectic of digitization' both in the discursive content and the embodied form of printed books, Starre is also keen to explore the various ways in which the aforementioned authors explore the value of print in a digital world. For example, he argues that 'metamedial forms of expression... qualify as elements of an evolving semantics within contemporary literature that attempts to rationalize the hypercomplex media environment constituted by the diverse channels through which texts circulate' (p. 64). Using Danielewski's *House of Leaves* as a case study, Starre builds from and counters readings of this influential novel posed by N. Katherine Hayles in order to argue that 'its truly unique quality lies in its finite bibliographic form' and 'its textual stability' (pp. 129, 133). Rather than viewing the novel as a 'rhizomatic assemblage', Starre proposes that 'the novel appears to embrace its position as ordering device within a hyper-complex communication system' (p. 133). For Starre, the fixity of the text's 'bibliographic codes' as well as the 'marginality of the few differences' in 'fonts', 'colors', and 'layout' within two published editions—despite erroneous claims that the novel appeared in four different editions—support this claim. He further explores 'five metamedial dimensions of printed literature' that appear in *House of Leaves* and other twenty-first-century fiction, including a commitment to exploring 'external design; typography and visual elements; paratextual framing; diegetic reflexivity; medial mise en abyme and metalepsis' (p. 134). Analysing the literary journal *Timothy McSweeney's Quarterly Concern*, Eggers's *A Heartbreaking Work of Staggering Genius* and *You Shall Know Our Velocity*, and Foer's *Tree of Codes*, among other novels, Starre's monograph will inspire much critical discussion, especially in relation to the status of the printed book in the early years of the twenty-first century and reflexive engagement with the medial properties of the contemporary printed book influenced by the complexities of technological innovations in digitization.

Like Starre, Laura Shackelford engages with systems theory, including pivotal work by Niklas Luhmann, to address 'American fictions published between 1991 and 2002, in the midst of the "digital revolution," to retrospectively unfold their literary contributions to understanding digital cultures' (p. 1). Still, Shackelford's *Tactics of the Human: Experimental Technics in American Fictions* maintains a broader scope than *Metamedia* as her monograph also draws on research in 'feminist science studies, gender studies, phenomenological philosophy, and critical geographies', including work by Sara Ahmed, Karen Barad, Doreen Masey, and Elizabeth Grosz (p. 17). Thus, her approach traces how literary texts of the period not only register how 'digital technics enter into, transform, and recapitulate print cultures and values' but also 'think through the material, technological, social, and cultural dimensions to technics... [as they] recursively reenter subjectivities, social systems and material spaces' (pp. 16–17). In this way, Shackelford's work allows readers to see the way in which contemporary authors grapple with how new digital technics 'enter into and rerealize social systems' (p. 21). Each chapter of the book addresses different authors' engagement with the impact of digital technics upon the 'scene of writing', 'gendered and racialized subject formation', 'materially realized social spaces such as transnational economic networks and the U.S. nation-state', and the 'micropractices of eating, food production, sex, reproduction, family, and the closely affiliated affective economies subtending the nation-state' (p. 21). Analysing work by John Barth, Shelley Jackson, Leslie Marmon Silko, Ruth L. Ozeki, and Jeffrey Eugenides, Shackelford takes readers through the different albeit interrelated scales through which 'the deadly and affirmative forces of technics . . . are incorporated into and play themselves out politically and socially in contemporary U.S. social systems' and the short stories and novels that address them (p. 21). Although Shackelford attends to the 'deadly force of technics', she does maintain an emphasis on the tactical relationship that authors explore between humans and technology. Utilizing Michel de Certeau's theorization of tactics, Shackelford shows how literary texts explore negotiations with digital technics 'by those who have only temporary and imperfect access to the resources they borrow and hope to lead astray' (p. 20). Because technics are 'socially embedded practices', 'there is room to maneuver' and 'to explore select technics as tactics of the human that reorient us toward the world' (p. 20). Shackelford concludes her book with a discussion of the 'bioinformatic circulatory systems of "late capitalism"' as well as a discussion of 'the modes of becoming American U.S. biopower encourages or overlooks' (p. 21). Because of this attention to biopower in the 'digital age', Shackelford's monograph nicely connects with Breu's work discussed above and picks up on the insistence on the material and the import of new materialism more broadly in understanding contemporary fiction, even as she focuses on the reciprocal relationship between digital technics and lived experience and works produced from the 1990s to the present. Despite some divergences in theoretical framing, their texts share not only close readings of Silko's *Almanac of the Dead*, but also an emphasis on how literary works are important sites through which to chart the movement of biopolitical and thanatopolitial forces and to envision creative tactics in responses to such forces.

Susanne Wegener's *Restless Subjects in Rigid Systems: Risk and Speculation in Millennial Fictions of the North American Pacific Rim*, a late arrival, continues this critical trend of focusing on artistic considerations of the digital age with a particular emphasis on aesthetic engagement with the 'hypercapitalist' North American Pacific Rim and 'the digitized semiotic immateriality that has become a hallmark of globalized capitalism' (p. 31). Analysing Kathryn Bigelow's *Strange Days*, Karen T. Yamashita's *Tropic of Orange*, and Larissa Lai's *Salt Fish Girl*, Wegener explores how all three works 'comment on the world-making strategies of factual discourses of globalization, economic liberalization, and risk management' and counter the neoliberal utopian rhetoric of free trade and economic growth that has speculated about the transnational economic future of the Pacific region (pp. 9–10). Wegener argues that the 'bleak dystopias' created by the aforementioned artists critique 'the pervasive economization of the state, the social, and the subject' as well as engaging with 'the re-configurations of race, class, and gender within a new political rationality formed by the alliance of neoliberalism and neoconservatism' (p. 10). Despite a thematic convergence with works discussed above, Wegener's monograph is unique in its focus on the relationship between speculative fiction and economic speculation appearing in discourses about the Pacific Rim as well as her attention to risk theory. Ultimately, Wegener's work calls for a rethinking of how particular speculative fictions 'historiciz[e] risk as a dispostif and a political rationality, delineat[e] the calculating operations of its underlying logic of speculation, and expos[e] the disembodied semiotics of electronic information transfer as its unprecedented medial condition' (p. 290). Beyond critique, the fictions she analyses utilize allegory and 'fantastic elements' as they participate in a 'self-reflexive mediation on the relation between sign and referent, representation and presence' as well as negotiating 'the social and political changes in North American societies that came with the growing currency of the ideal borderless world market' (pp. 31, 290).

One other late arrival deserves mention here quickly because, like Starre's and Shackelford's books, it also engages theoretical work by Luhmann and Hayles and addresses the changing status of the human across the full twentieth century. Mads Rosendahl Thomsen's *The New Human in Literature: Posthuman Visions of Changes in Body, Mind and Society after 1900* analyses works by Virginia Woolf, Carlos Williams, Orhan Pamuk, Don DeLillo, Michel Houellebecq, and others. His work on DeLillo's novels outlines how biotechnology and cyberspace operate in texts to explore a dual focus on the author's 'fascination with the idea of a transformation into a new way of being that could be furthered by technology' and his 'critical' evaluation of 'what that world might look like' (p. 194).

Two other monographs focus on fiction of the 1990s and the twenty-first century with an emphasis on the relationship between such works and authors associated with postmodernism. Allard den Dulk's *Existentialist Engagement in Wallace, Eggers, and Foer: A Philosophical Analysis of Contemporary American Literature* expands upon discussions of 'new sincerity' or 'post-postmodern' fiction by attending to the existentialist philosophical influences of Kierkegaard, Sartre, Wittgenstein, and Camus on his selected authors while exploring how they address 'the problems that characterize contemporary Western existence (hyperreflexivity and endless irony)' as well as how 'these problems can be overcome' through 'sincerity', human 'commitment' to each other 'within the finite, uncertain *reality* of existence', and 'community' (pp. 4, xii). Contrasting works by Wallace, Eggers, and Foer with Barth's metafiction and Ellis's 'postmodernist minimalism', den Dulk argues that the former writers critique both the 'endless reflexive-ironic strategy' of metafiction and 'the extreme irony' of writers like Ellis that centres on the 'impossibil[ity] [of] formulat[ing] any meaning or value, at all' (pp. 19–20). Because of den Dulk's careful attention to philosophical influences, nuanced readings of how Wallace, Eggers, and Foer build from such influences to address existential struggles in the late twentieth century and early twenty-first century, and careful renderings of consistent literary thematic emphases on sincerity and community, his monograph will appeal to scholars invested in providing a more substantial philosophical basis for literature of the so-called 'new sincerity', a term that den Dulk feels 'does not fully communicate [the] complexity' or import of novels by his featured authors (p. 9).

A late arrival, Adam Kelly's *American Fiction in Transition: Observer-Hero Narrative, the 1990s, and Postmodernism* also addresses late twentieth-century works' engagement with the legacy of postmodernism. With a focus on Roth's *The Human Stain*, Paul Auster's *Leviathan*, Jeffrey Eugenides' *The Virgin Suicides*, and E.L. Doctorow's *The Waterworks*, Kelly traces the development and import of the observer-hero genre for writers at the turn of the century. Building from Lawrence Buell and Kenneth Bruffee's foundational works on the genre, Kelly identifies the observer-hero narrative as containing 'a dramatized first-person narrator [who] retrospectively tells the story of an important figure in his or her life who has died. In these 1990s novels, the deceased figure seems to embody a certain kind of heroism, in that his or her life seems to offer a model of decision and temporal agency set against a postmodern backdrop that has placed these qualities out of bounds' (p. 2). Although Kelly shows a long history in American letters of the observer-hero narrative, his aim is to highlight how the four aforementioned authors utilize conventions of the genre in order to grapple with the legacy of postmodernism. For Kelly, 'these writers are... concerned to explore... the consequences of the theoretical de-centering of the subject, and to offer intimations of human agency that can challenge that worldview' (p. 32). Drawing on Derrida's and Jameson's work, Kelly ultimately showcases how the observer-hero narrative at the end of the twentieth century is a 'site of contemporary resistance to postmodern fragmentation and stasis, a place where the postmodern diagnosis we find most clearly in Jameson can be incorporated and staged as simply one possible mode of interpretation among others' (pp. 3–4). Like den Dulk, Kelly argues that novelists of the 1990s should be read with an eye towards how they 'relate to their postmodern inheritance in new and valuable ways' (p. 32).

A final work, Michael Keren's *Politics and Literature at the Turn of the Millennium*, contributes to critical evaluations of the political themes of import within novels of this period. Contributing to a movement in political science to take aesthetic works seriously, Keren sets out to 'illustrate the contribution of fiction to political understanding by questioning, updating, and altering accepted political theories; by deepening our comprehension of otherwise incomprehensible political phenomena; by uncovering the past as a way to help us cope with the present; and by extrapolating from the present political conditions where we may be heading and what alternative paths are available to us' (p. 20). Addressing novels by José Saramago, Gil Courtemanche, Anosh Irani, Cormac McCarthy, and others, Keren adeptly examines how literary works remain an important resource for political scientists, especially in contrast to the dominant approaches in the field of 'realism in the study of international relations and behaviouralism in the study of domestic politics' (p. 13). In reference to McCarthy's *The Road*, Keren traces how the text updates Camus's earlier engagement with 'absurdity and revolt' to address the twenty-first century (p. 66).

Although not focused exclusively on literary works from the 1990s, Michael L. Ross's *Designing Fictions: Literature Confronts Advertising* will have relevance for scholars of the millennial turn because it traces the development of literary attention to advertising and promotional culture across the full twentieth century and up to our current moment. Rather than highlighting a clear oppositional stance towards the promotion of consumer culture and the increasingly invasive nature of advertisements across the full twentieth century, Ross sets out to explore the tensions within contemporary fiction as American, British, and Canadian authors grapple with the relationship between art and the more utilitarian creative endeavours of advertising. By examining 'how a number of fictional texts have engaged with advertising as a social praxis and/or a means of professional livelihood', Ross shows 'how such narratives pit promotional business against "artistic" pursuits, often though not always, to the detriment of promotion' (p. 3). He further argues that novelistic 'critiques tend inevitably to be conditioned by their own participation in modern commodity culture... [and] manifest, again and again, a tension between an oppositional view of advertising as an enterprise and identification with those engaged in it' (p. 3). Opening with a thorough overview of theoretical analyses of advertising that draws on work by Baudrillard, Zygmunt Bauman, Roland Barthes, Marshall McLuhan, Judith Williamson, and Andrew Wernick, Ross moves on to structure chapters around different moments in the history of advertising and literary responses to them. The first chapter, for example, addresses early twentieth-century work by H.G. Wells and Henry James and a 'buoyant new wave of promotion', while the second chapter examines the years following the First World War and an intense surge of advertising that impacted the work of Christopher Morley and George Orwell. With the third chapter, Ross examines Frederick Wakeman's *The Hucksters* and Herman Wouk's *Aurora Dream* with an emphasis on the impact of commercial radio on literary renderings of the 'invasiveness' of advertising and the 'abuses of commercial promotion', including the 'hoggish arrogance of sponsors or the shallowness and vulgarity of some promotional techniques' (p. 102). While both novels do provide resistant readings to consumer culture and advertising, Ross argues that the texts only provide a naive 'alternative to the established system... [with] unlikely retreat[s] from money-grubbing, urbanized modernity into a modest existence within an unspoiled American "heartland"' (p. 103). Further, he shows that the 'energetic mass marketing of both Wouk's novel and Wakeman's harmonizes with the basically conservative nature of the fables they produced; the whole commercial logic of the bestseller works against a more searching and abrasive treatment of contentious issues' (p. 103). Ross's analysis of US author Joshua Ferris's *Then We Came to the End* brings readers into aesthetic reflections on 'the exponential growth of promotional culture's magnitude and diffusion' in the 1980s and beyond (p. 129). With nuance, Ross ultimately argues that 'because promotional work is central to the modern capitalist system, Ferris's treatment of the business is broadly representative, commenting on many elements that go to compose twenty-first-century American, or for that matter global, experience' even as 'the malignant offshoots of promotional work are made troublingly clear' (pp. 146–7). Ross's book also includes analysis of Atwood's *Edible Woman*, Blake Morrison's *South of the River*, the television show *Mad Men*, and brief concluding comments on Franzen's *The Corrections*. In sum, *Designing Fictions* offers a rich rendering of the conflicted representations of promotional culture within pertinent works of the twentieth century while showcasing the appearance of related and divergent concerns as such culture extended its reach.

Beyond a surge in critical attention to the 1990s and early twenty-first century, a number of recently published monographs analyse the variety of post-1945 fictional appropriations and revisions of canonical literary texts. *Antiquity Now: The Classical World in the Contemporary American Imagination* by Thomas E. Jenkins is a jubilant examination of how contemporary artists appropriate classical works to address 'ideological concerns', with a particular focus on 'gender studies; ethnic studies; and American politics, including eco-criticism' (p. 25). Analysing poetry, drama, and fiction, Jenkins showcases a variety of works that riff upon classical texts in order to explore specific concerns of the contemporary period. He writes, 'it's *precisely* in classical texts' ability to remain sites of cultural contestation that the works remain "classical"; it's *precisely* because marginalized (or empowered) groups appeal to classical texts that such texts' authority is thereby reinforced and reconstituted. It's not enough to say, however grandiloquently, that classics remain classics because they appeal to universal concerns; classics remain classics because they appeal to *specific* concerns' (p. 29). With the first full chapter of the book, Jenkins explores recent GLBTQ receptions of the ancient world, emphasizing creative revisions of Plato's *Symposium* in theatrical performances of *Hedwig and the Angry Inch* and *All About Love*, Euripides' *Bacchae* in *Dionysus in 69*, and Sophocles' *Philoctetes* in Mark Merlis's novel *An Arrow's Flight*, to name a few key texts. Although Jenkins unites his analyses of various texts with the claim that 'gay and lesbian appropriations of antiquity nearly always represent ancient homosexuality as a phenomenon analogous to modern homosexuality' (p. 34), his larger aim is to survey the 'metaphors employed when adapting classical myths to modern American contexts' (p. 61). For example, with Merlis's novel, he powerfully shows how the text explores 'both the possibilities of Greek metaphors for American life, but, also . . . the limits of metaphor in the age of AIDS' (p. 71). Beyond his attention to GLBTQ receptions of classical texts, Jenkins also addresses 'September 11th on the Western Stage' (pp. 129–57), 'race and the classics—and musical theater' (pp. 159–65), 'recent Greek tragedies by Chicano playwright and activist Louis Alfaro' (pp. 165–83), feminist 'versions of ancient heroic epic', namely Ursula K. Le Guin's *Lavinia* and Margaret Atwood's *The Penelopiad* (pp. 184–204), and 'classics and the environment' (pp. 205–11). In reference to Le Guin's and Atwood's work, Jenkins traces how these authors utilize the 'problematic construction of gender relations' in the classical text as 'impetus for a new, "corrective," version, one that redresses the ancient's poem's flawed depiction of female subjectivity' (p. 184). Because of its careful attention to classical texts as well as detailed and inspired readings of contemporary revisions, *Antiquity Now* provides an erudite and impassioned plea for attention to how the classics are reimagined brilliantly and provocatively to address key specific issues of our time. With delicious prose and its intersectional focus on the wide variety of revisions of classical texts in which contemporary artists address sexuality, gender, race, the environment, and labour, Jenkins succeeds in producing a monograph that will appeal broadly to scholars of post-1945 aesthetic works.

Betina Entzminger (a late arrival from 2013) also evaluates contemporary appropriations and revisions of texts, albeit canonical American novels and short stories, in her monograph *Contemporary Reconfigurations of American Literary Classics: The Origin and Evolution of American Stories*. Entzminger focuses mainly on works published from the 1990s to the early years of the twenty-first century and produces astute analyses of a broad array of contemporary 'reconfigurations' of work by Poe, Hawthorne, Melville, Alcott, Twain, Chopin, and Faulkner. Although her primary aim is not to distinguish work of the past two decades from postmodern intertextuality, Entzminger does position recent work within a shift from the self-reflexivity and parody of authors like Ishmael Reed to greater emphasis on cross-historical engagement with national identity. She writes of her project, 'As in historiographic metafictional novels, the themes and plots of the more recent reconfigurations...often reveal a sophisticated examination of the process and implications of narrative constructions, but in contrast these authors refrain from self-reflexive peek-a-boo games that interfere with the reader's immersion in the narratives.... These authors also produce new versions that—rather than abuse or denigrate—respectfully add to or engage in a civil dialogue with the classic literary ancestors' (p. 2). As a monograph that traces how contemporary authors engage with American literary history as well as the aims of such revisions, there is much in this text to admire, especially because of Entzminger's attention to contemporary women writers' revisionary efforts. For example, Entzminger provides analyses of Bharati Mukherjee's reconfiguration of Hawthorne's *The Scarlet Letter* in *The Holder of the World*, Sena Jeter Naslund's creative play with Melville's *Moby-Dick* in *Ahab's Wife*, Judith Rossner, Barbara Kingsolver, and Geraldine Brooks's reworkings of Alcott's *Little Women*, Nancy Rawles's engagement with Twain's *The Adventures of Huckleberry Finn* in *My Jim*, Anne Tyler's imaginative exploration of Chopin's *The Awakening* in *Ladder of Years*, and Toni Morrison's reconfiguration of Faulkner's *Absalom, Absalom!* in *Beloved*. She also addresses work by Richard Powers, John Updike, John Seelye, and David Bradley. As in Jenkins's work, the strength of this monograph lies in its careful exploration of the texts with which contemporary authors engage even as Entzminger's primary aim is to showcase how recent works 'acknowledge narrative as an ongoing process connected to identity and call attention to the power of narrative to shape individuality and to form community' (p. 18). Although Entzminger draws on recent studies of cognitive psychology and evolutionary literary criticism to support her work with contemporary narrative, this monograph will appeal to scholars not necessarily invested in the turn to cognitive science in literary study as it contributes to larger conversations about the legacy of postmodern intertextuality at the end of the twentieth century and into our current moment.

Another late arrival, Lauren Rule Maxwell's *Romantic Revisions in Novels from the Americas*, also examines intertextuality in twentieth-century fiction with a focus on engagement with Romantic poetics in five novels: Jamaica Kincaid's *Lucy*, Margaret Atwood's *The Handmaid's Tale*, Cormac McCarthy's *Blood Meridian*, F. Scott Fitzgerald's *The Great Gatsby*, and Wilson Harris's *Palace of the Peacock*. With a transnational focus, Maxwell shows how these novels' 'reformulation of Romantic poetics works to change our conceptions of the Americas through new understanding of how the legacies of British colonialism influence our own social and political realities... [and provide] critiques of American manifestations of British imperialism' (p. 13). The chapter that addresses McCarthy's work nicely traces the novel's engagement with Byron's celebratory take on America 'as a nation that has freed itself from the chains of (British) empire' (p. 70). Ultimately, Maxwell argues that 'the preoccupation with Americanness is what ties *Don Juan* to *Blood Meridian*, and that *Blood Meridian* responds to and critiques the figuration of America within *Don Juan*, the rest of Byron's poetry, and the generic Western by using Byron's own mode of romantic irony' (p. 73). Other chapters address contemporary revisions of and engagement with poetry by Wordsworth, Keats, Coleridge, and Blake.

Although not focused on literary revisions of specific canonical texts, James J. Donahue's *Failed Frontiersmen: White Men and Myth in the Post-Sixties American Historical Romance* does investigate how contemporary authors like E.L. Doctorow, John Barth, Thomas Pynchon, Ishmael Reed, Gerald Vizenor, and Cormac McCarthy engage with the tradition of historical romance and frontier mythology. With the aim of situating contemporary works within the longer history of historical romance developed by authors like James Fenimore Cooper and Nathaniel Hawthorne, Donahue argues that that post-1960s authors 'rewrite the mythology of the American frontier by injecting into it the progressive social and cultural values embodied by the protest movements of the 1960s' (p. 5). Critiquing the 'hegemonic masculinity' of the white frontiersman as well as the racism and sexism of frontier mythology, and revisiting how celebratory accounts of westward expansion are built at the expense of 'Native American sovereignty and African-American self-determination' (p. 5), Donahue argues that historical romances of the late twentieth century address how 'the positive progressive aspects of the frontier came as a result of the violence inflicted by warfare and attempted genocide' (p. 21). Analysing Doctorow's *Welcome to Hard Times*, Barth's *The Sot-Weed Factor*, Pynchon's *Mason & Dixon*, Reed's *Yellow Back Radio Broke-Down*, Vizenor's *The Heirs of Columbus*, and McCarthy's *Blood Meridian* and Border Trilogy, Donahue offers rich and compelling renderings of major works that reveal their continuation of the historical romance tradition as well as their critical stance on American myths of progress that eschew the violence of the nation.

Geoff Hamilton's late arrival, *The Life and Undeath of Autonomy in American Literature*, also examines how McCarthy's work in *Blood Meridian* 'uses its nineteenth-century setting in the southwestern borderlands—a moment and place permitting the most extreme expressions of self-law—in order to illustrate' the dangers of certain conceptualizations of human autonomy that 'threat[en]...the entire natural world' (pp. 14, 99). Still, Hamilton's focus is much wider than an emphasis on late twentieth-century visions of individualism associated with the frontier, as he takes a longer view of American literary production by examining shifting conceptions of autonomy across works produced from the late eighteenth century to the present. Opening with a discussion of the concept of autonomy in ancient Greece, Hamilton turns to Jefferson to explore how his conceptualization of autonomy exhibits an 'optimistic endorsement of reduced human governance' that 'prepares the way for the more extreme notions of personal autonomy articulated by the Transcendentalists' (p. 13). Analysing work by Charles Brockden Brown, turning to a discussion of nineteenth-century works by John Filson, Timothy Flint, James Fenimore Cooper, Emerson, Thoreau, and Whitman, and concluding with an examination of twentieth-century novels by Hemingway, Norman Mailer, Cormac McCarthy, and Don DeLillo, Hamilton argues for a more nuanced understanding of the evolution of the concept of autonomy across the long history of American letters. Although his work is contextualized here within critical discussions of frontier ideologies, this monograph provides a powerful map of a shifting accounts of autonomy that speak not just to contemporary aesthetic engagement with the dangers of American individualism but also to the various and divergent ways that autonomy has been understood and mobilized in literary works.

   Like Donahue, Carl Abbott examines the evolution of frontier mythology in his monograph *Imagined Frontiers: Contemporary American and Beyond*, with a broader focus on capacious usages of such mythology in literary, filmic, and televisual texts to address representations of 'the metropolitan frontier of suburban development, the classic continental frontier of American settlement, and yet unrealized frontiers beyond the bound of a single planet' (p. 5). This wide-reaching monograph powerfully illuminates how contemporary authors grapple with development, national progress, and growth by updating and drawing on understandings of the frontier as 'zones of settlement and displacement where, historically, one numerous people or nation has assumed political and military control and occupied "empty" or "underutilized" land' (p. 4). Addressing the 'suburban frontier' in the first section of the monograph, Abbott offers a particularly nuanced reading of novels focused on Sunbelt cities, including John Nichols's *The Milagro Beanfield War*, Leslie Marmon Silko's *Almanac of the Dead*, Rudolfo Anaya's *Albuquerque*, and T.C. Boyle's *The Tortilla Curtain*. Arguing that these novels 'describe, embody, and make visible the pathways through which capital accumulates in real estate [thereby]... offer[ing] insight into the social and political dynamics of the modern southwestern Sunbelt... [and] highlight[ing] the way in which Anglo-Americans continue to act as if western North America is *terra nullius*, land without prior ownership that is open for the taking' (p. 15). Utilizing and updating frontier mythology to address 'modern methods of dispossession', Abbott ultimately shows how key novels 'remind [readers] that contests over land and its uses remain central public issues in any region like the Southwest, where population is growing and settlement is still in process' (p. 32). Building from the first section of the monograph, Abbott turns to analysis of literary texts, such as Peter Matthiessen's *Florida Trilogy*, that address other areas of regional development while referencing 'tropes characteristic of western myth and fiction' (p. 95). The monograph concludes with a section on 'Planetary Pioneering' in contemporary science fiction, with a particularly effective engagement with the West in fiction by Kim Stanley Robinson. Because of its consistent emphasis on situating aesthetic works within discussion of urban planning and development, its breadth in documenting a trend in literary and visual arts that rework frontier mythology to address contemporary struggles within specific regions around land use, and its attention to science-fictional utilizations of the genre of the Western, *Imagined Frontiers* will appeal broadly to scholars of late twentieth-century fiction.

While not specifically focused upon re-evaluations of the frontier, Ann Brigham's *American Road Narratives: Reimagining Mobility in Literature and Film* also critically examines national conceptions of space and the visions of freedom and conflict that appear in fiction and film focused on the open road. She explores 'how the American... national imaginary has been profoundly shaped by the promise of mobility: the freedom to go anywhere and become anyone. The road trip [in fiction and film] epitomizes the linkage between the two: spatial mobility—the movement between places or across space—has often been understood as a way to achieve a range of other mobilities, from the social and economic to the psychological and sexual' (p. 3). Rather than confirming that the American road novel represents a quest for freedom, Brigham traces the tension within road narratives between mobility as a means of engaging with the heterogeneity of the nation—both in terms of geographical and social diversity—and as a threat to the cohesion of the nation as well as rooted communities, neighbourhoods, and families. Following Tim Cresswell's theorization of mobility, Brigham argues that movement in road narratives does not 'function as an exit from society/home/the familiar, but instead emerges as a dynamic process for engaging with social conflicts. This makes sense because road stories themselves are plotted around unsettling processes: the crossing of borders, the courting and conquering of distance, the reinvention of identity, and the access, negotiation, and disruption of space' (p. 8). Opening with analysis of early twentieth-century works by Thomas W. Wilby and Agnes A. Wilby as well as Sinclair Lewis, Brigham moves into post-1945 literary renderings of the road by addressing Kerouac's *On the Road*, John Howard Griffin's *Black Like Me*, John Steinbeck's *Travels with Charley: In Search of America*, and John A. Williams's *This Is My Country Too*. Invested in showing how these various road-trip narratives '[act] out the fantasy of a borderless world, which reincorporates and rescales white masculinity as a figure of expansion that obliterates or subsumes other scales and identities', Brigham further shows how authors like Williams critique privileged visions of white masculine mobility (p. 14). Addressing the road narrative in the age of identity politics in later chapters, Brigham examines works by Mona Simpson and Barbara Kingsolver to show how specific women writers intervene in the genre by using 'women's mobility... to bring domesticity out into the open' and to showcase the 'disenfranchisement' of 'women and others' at the 'scales of city, state, and federal jurisdiction' (pp. 14–15). Brigham further examines work by David Seals and Sherman Alexie to explore two Native American road narratives that chart 'landscape as a site of struggle' and 'challenge the history of erasure and containment that has defined Euro-American incorporation' (p. 15). Concluding with a discussion of the post-9/11 road film and narrative, Brigham gives readers a provocative overview of developments in the genre over the full twentieth century into the twenty-first, while providing a number of insightful renderings of works that challenge previous critical conceptualizations of the genre.

Although Brigham and other critics discussed above certainly draw on and contribute to feminist literary criticism and theory, editors Jaime Harker and

Cecilia Konchar Farr's collection, *This Book is an Action: Feminist Print Culture and Activist Aesthetics* is the most important work in this area of 2015 because of its focus on feminist literary works and publishing of the late 1960s to the 1970s. With the aim of countering limiting understandings of this period that emphasize the consciousness-raising novel, essays in the collection examine a wide variety of feminist literary production during this period in order to showcase authors' various forms of aesthetic experimentation as well as the intersectional qualities of second-wave feminist works. Rather than assuming that literary works of the period focus narrowly on white 'women's issues' or even 'white lady feminism' (p. 11), essayists seek to complicate this critical narrative by analysing diverse topics addressed by multiple authors. The editors write, 'when we read the literature of second-wave feminism only for its depiction of "women's issues," we artificially limit its narrative reach and miss its many other critical and cultural engagements—something this collection of essays aimed to avoid. Instead, these essays delve into the material conditions of publishing (both mainstream and alternative), frame issues within unexpected historical and cultural contexts, explore the intersection of social movements and capitalism, interrogate queer women's desires, and perform superb close readings of formally distinctive literary artifacts' (p. 17). The opening four essays in the collection examine feminist publishing, including Jennifer Gilley's analysis of the publishing history of two major works of the period (*Sisterhood is Powerful* and *This Bridge Called My Back*) and Agatha Beins's analysis of feminist newsletters and periodicals published in five different cities during the 1970s. Julie Enszer's discussion of Women in Distribution, a feminist book distribution company, and Yung-Hsing Wu's essay on close reading as a consciousness-raising practice also provide provocative archival research that emphasizes the 'lively revolutionary spirit that pervaded the material productions of the early Women's Liberation Movement' (p. 13). The remaining essays in the collection focus on specific works, such as Atwood's *Surfacing* and *The Edible Woman*, Anne Roiphe's *Up the Sandbox!*, Erica Jong's *Fear of Flying*, Bertha Harris's *Lover*, Alice Walker's *The Color Purple*, and Sara Paretsky's *Indemnity Only*. Laura Christine Godfrey's work on the epigraphs in Harris's *Lover* is particularly effective in her exploration of the 'uses of saints' narratives to provide alternative biological and familial connections in [Harris's] creation of a nonpatriarchal lineage of women who seek to escape the confines of traditional gender roles' (p. 188). Still, Phillip Gordon's '*The Color Purple* and the Wine-Dark Kiss of Death: How a Second-Wave Feminist Wrote the First American AIDS Narrative' is the most provocative essay in the collection. He argues, 'By considering the sexual economy, the emphasis on illness and sexual contact, the post-colonial interests (which is to say, considering Africa), and the time and place of its writing, I argue that *The Color Purple* should be read as the first AIDS narrative in American literature' (p. 206). In his account, such a reading challenges not only 'the current model of AIDS literature' but also the continued lack of attention to 'the current AIDS crisis among black women' (pp. 206–7). As a whole, the collection succeeds in re-evaluating key works associated with women's liberation and offering provocations for future study of this important period in feminist literary production and publishing.

To close this portion of the review, one more monograph deserves mention for its contribution to literary criticism of the post-1945 period with a focus on the programme era. Eric Bennett's *Workshops of Empire: Stegner, Engle, and American Creative Writing During the Cold War* builds from and critiques Mark McGurl's work with a particular focus on philosophical and political influences on major figures who 'laid the groundwork for a future nation of Master of Fine Arts programs' (p. 6). Analysing creative writing programmes through discussions of 'program founders, institutional structures, and intellectual and literary influences', Bennett produces a provocative account of how 'the New Humanism' of Irving Babbitt promoted by Norman Foerster shaped 'the postwar literary outlook' as well as creative writing programme directors like Paul Engle and Wallace Stegner, both of whom worked with Foerster (pp. 7–8). Additionally, Bennett pays close attention to how the Cold War shaped programme directors; for example, he argues that Paul Engle's successful fundraising for the Iowa Writers' Workshop in the 1950s revolved around promoting the idea that 'writers could serve in the soft diplomatic struggle against the Soviet Union' and that the creative writing programme was 'crucial to a liberal democratic capitalistic America' (p. 11). Because of its careful and nuanced attention to 'the genesis of the early workshops within the context of ideas prevailing in the United States in the 1940s and 1950s' as well as its critical engagement with McGurl's influential work, *Workshops of Empire* will be of import for scholars of creative writing programmes in the United States as well as how these programmes and the ideas that inspired their structure and focus continued to impact a number of writers who trained in Iowa and Stanford's programmes and who emerged with force onto the literary scene in the later years of the Cold War.

In addition to the provocative monographs discussed above, a number of works were published in 2015 that focus on single authors. *Barbara Kingsolver's World: Nature, Art, and the Twenty-First Century*, by Linda Wagner-Martin, provides detailed analysis of each of Kingsolver's novels as well as discussion of her non-fiction writing and poetry. With the aim of 'fus[ing] discussion of Kingsolver's use of different lines of scientifically based knowledge with readings of her fourteen books' (p. x), Wagner-Martin positions her book within environmental literary criticism that attends to the interconnection between social justice and environmental justice. Following Barbara Bennett's definition of ecofeminism, Wagner-Martin address how Kingsolver's oeuvre treats 'science and nature, politics, human and animal rights, spirituality, and feminism holistically rather than in isolation'; in this way, she argues that approaches to this author's work require attention to how 'social history [merges] with the biology of the natural world' (p. xi). Starting with analysis of the recent *Flight Behavior*, Wagner-Martin suggests that critical reviews of the lack of subtlety in Kingsolver's focus on the impact of climate change miss the larger stakes of her attention to how communities and individuals, in the face of scientific and experiential proof of it, respond with hostility 'in the face of obvious global change' (p. 14). In her account, the novel contrasts the narratives of marginalized communities as they navigate the disastrous flooding that impacts agriculture and witness the decimation of Monarch butterflies with the erudite and different 'vocabularies... [of] the scientific community' in order to address the contemporary moment in which many impacted by climate change, such as rural farmers, remain sceptical of it (p. 9). As the novel offers different narrative forms about climate change, from scientific rhetoric and research through the character of Ovid to religious rhetoric, which posits that 'saving the earth and its people, its animals, and its living organisms is a spiritual act' (p. 9), it suggests that environmentalists, scientists, and rural communities need to listen to seemingly opposed stories about human connectivity and impact on the world and create new narratives that might inspire greater care for the world upon which we depend. Although the novel serves as a primer of sorts for readers to engage with scientific research about climate change, it also calls for a shift in the narrative strategies of scientists to connect more emotionally, perhaps, with the lives of those most impacted by climate change and with a broader public. In sum, Wagner-Martin argues that this is a novel that asks what would be 'an appropriate language to discuss the fact that towns are sinking, cataclysmic storms are wiping out areas... and the warming of the earth increases the volume of water in the ocean, resulting in rising sea levels and "acidified oceans"' (p. 15). Bringing scientific narrative, agricultural family histories of hardship due to global climate change, and religious accounts of human responsibility for the world together in one novel, Kingsolver engages with the import of multiple narrative forms and strategies for encouraging wider public understanding of climate change as well as investment in individual, communal, and governmental action to address it. Having given readers this powerful close reading of *Flight Behavior*, Wagner-Martin goes back to Kingsolver's first published novel—*The Bean Trees*—to suggest that this concern with the interconnection of environmental and social history is at the heart of Kingsolver's literary endeavours, albeit with less force in the earlier novels. Tracing thematic elements that appear across texts, including working-class women's labour, motherhood and parenting, interracial working-class communities and tensions, and community responses to social injustice as well as environmental devastation, Wagner-Martin ultimately provides a comprehensive and compelling account of the import of Kingsolver's work. Because she situates her readings at the conclusions of chapters within recent critical debates, her monograph also provides nice coverage of up-to-date commentary on Kingsolver's connection to women's literary history and the political novel of the late twentieth and early twenty-first century.

   Like Wagner-Martin's work, editor John A. Murray's collection, *Abbey in America: A Philosopher's Legacy in a New Century*, explores the import of a single author—Edward Abbey—for our contemporary moment, with a particular emphasis on the prescience of his texts for contemporary discussions of climate change, fracking, and environmental pollution, or what Abbey identified broadly as 'planetary biocide' (p. 28). Opening with a series of essays by academic authors, the anthology brings Abbey into the twenty-first century to ask 'What fine adjectives would [Abbey] find for the drilling rigs on fracking pads spattered all the way from the Uinta Basin to the San Juan River?... What would he say when he climbed to the hidden springs... to find the water gone, poisoned and forced underground to fracture the rock to release the natural gas to earn a fat CEO $22 million a year? What would he say about the silent masses, the corrupted science, the solipsistic consumers and the sociopathic corporations?' (p. 27). Kathleen Dean Moore's essay, 'Equal Parts Anger and Love: A Posthumous Interview with Edward Abbey', answers these questions with an inspired piece in which she calls Abbey up from the grave to address contemporary environmental crises and splices together sentences from multiple non-fictional and fictional works to provide insight into how he might speak to readers and activists in the present. A second essay, by Michael Branch, 'One Man's Terrorist: Reclaiming Edward Abbey for the Post-9/11 Era', examines Abbey's radicalism and call for active dissent to environmental devastation in light of the increased usage of 'terrorism' to apply not only to 'harming people' but also to 'harming property' (p. 40). Calling for a more careful evaluation of the direct action of environmental activists, Branch ultimately suggests the development of 'a semantics that is sufficiently nuanced to distinguish between a person who murders runners at the Boston Marathon and another who occupies an old-growth redwood in an attempt to prevent its destruction' (pp. 40–1). Another highlight is John Alcock's essay, which addresses Abbey's problematic views on immigration into the United States from Latin America with an eye towards how his disdain for immigrants is echoed in contemporary xenophobic political rhetoric and policy. These three pieces would be useful for the undergraduate classroom, as they situate his works within our contemporary political moment. The remaining sections of the anthology provide essays by independent authors and a new generation of writers influenced by Abbey as well as reflective pieces by his friends and colleagues. Many of these essays offer wonderful anecdotes about Abbey. John A. Murray's 'The Age of Abbey' is particularly fine, as it recalls encounters with Abbey, has recollections of Abbey's thoughts about key writers such as Annie Dillard and Barry Lopez, and provides a lovely narrative about Murray's interactions with Hunter S. Thompson as well as his recollections of other key authors who made up the literary scene that influenced both Thompson and Abbey.

A number of other monographs also return to major literary figures of the twentieth century who have already received substantial critical attention to offer new insights. *Richard Ford and the Ends of Realism* by Ian McGuire provides a critique of literary criticism that assumes contemporary realism to be a degraded continuation of a pre-modernist project. Countering critics like Fredric Jameson and noting a lack of engagement with realism in criticism by authors like Mark McGurl, McGuire sets out to explore what he defines as Ford's 'pragmatic realism', which is indebted to 'the traditional realist claims to represent or grasp reality' but is also 'tempered by a pragmatic, antifoundationalist awareness that any reality that the realist grasps is only ever temporary and that any act of grasping is only ever partial' (p. xvii). Building from Ford's acknowledged 'enthusiasm for Emerson', McGuire positions Ford's work within the 1980s return to American pragmatism as evidenced by philosophical works by Richard Rorty and Hilary Putnam and interdisciplinary renewed critical investment in exploring pragmatist philosophy 'derived from Emerson, William James, and John Dewey' (pp. xvii–xviii).

With a focus on elucidating Ford's pragmatic realism beginning with the first two novels of the Frank Bascombe trilogy, McGuire powerfully showcases why Ford's work serves as a criticism of the minimalism of writers, like Carver and Hemingway, before him as well as postmodernist literary works. Drawing on Ford's essay, 'The Three Kings: Faulkner, Hemingway, Fitzgerald', McGuire illustrates that Ford's work in *The Sportswriter* contrasts with his deployment of minimalism in *Rock Springs* and reveals a writer working through the possibilities and drawbacks of Hemingwayesque silences. For McGuire, Ford understands minimalism as representing a 'certain attitude toward loss and thus by extension with a particular phase of his own . . . maturational processes' (p. 9). Although he 'reject[s] the methods and presuppositions of his own earlier work and of the work of the contemporary minimalist school more generally', Ford's usage of minimalist tendencies in *Rock Springs* while writing the more 'loquacious' *The Sportswriter* allowed him to explore the inadequacies of minimalism for moving through mourning to return to 'normal life' (pp. 9–10). McGuire writes, 'Whereas *The Sportswriter* . . . is devoted quite explicitly to the mourner's effort to return to normal life by reconnecting with a substitute love object, *Rock Springs*, in contrast, is given over almost completely to the more primitive and painful task of learning and relearning the fact that the mother is lost and will never return' (p. 10). Situating both texts within in the context of Ford's mother's death, McGuire provides close readings of passages that forward an argument about Ford's movement from minimalism's ability to point towards the difficulty of loss to the more pragmatic approach offered by a realism attuned to working through loss towards re-engagement with the world. As minimalism fails to offer a pragmatic approach to grappling with death and loss, so, too, Ford critiques postmodernist solipsism and relativism that threaten the novelist's and reader's ability to engage with morality and meaning. With analysis of *A Multitude of Sins*, McGuire argues that Ford counters a postmodernist position that 'meaning is primarily limiting or oppressive, an effect of power or coercion' by engaging with a realist pragmatism that 'suggests that meaning is (or can be) an effect of conversation and democratic consensus' (p. 66). Ultimately, McGuire posits that 'rather than being merely postmodernism's crudely representational, deterministic, or essentialist Other, Ford's work raises the possibility that contemporary realism may, to the extent that it aligns itself with pragmatism, offer a plausible and sophisticated correction to postmodernism's relativizing or dehumanizing tendencies' (p. 71). It is gestures like these, which reach out to position Ford's work within larger debates in literary criticism of the post-1945 period, that make McGuire's book more than a study of Ford's aesthetic production. While this work clearly will interest scholars of Ford's work, it will also be relevant for those invested in examining the longer history and shifting emphases of American realism and addressing contemporary explorations of philosophical influences, especially the renewed interest in pragmatism, on literary production.

William Gaddis, Don DeLillo, and David Foster Wallace also continued to be a focus in 2015. Joseph Tabbi's *Nobody Grew But the Business: On the Life and Work of William Gaddis* will delight, provoke, and dazzle scholars of this renowned author. With the aim of producing a literary life, Tabbi 'accounts for the way . . . [Gaddis's] life entered into his art' as he drew upon his 'own life and the lives, words, and recounted experiences of people he knew and family members he knew about going back to America's founding apostasy, migration, speculation, noise, and sheer recklessness' (pp. 12, 8). For all of its details of Gaddis's life, nuanced interpretations of literary texts with reference to such biographical details, and exploration of Gaddis's engagement with capitalism as well as 'alternatives to markets and corporate systems', Tabbi's work will assuredly provoke renewed critical interest in Gaddis, a writer that Tabbi deems to be 'the novelist of our time' (p. 11).

*Understanding Don DeLillo* by Henry Veggian provides a nice overview of the formal and thematic elements of DeLillo's fiction from the early novels through his twenty-first-century publications. Veggian divides the chapters of his monograph into periods of literary production focusing primarily on the novels, beginning with the period 1971–85, turning to 1985–97 and DeLillo's rise to great acclaim, and concluding with works published in the twenty-first century. Although he is attentive to consistencies across these periods, Veggian utilizes this periodization to showcase the major characteristics that groupings of novels share. For example, in his discussion of *Americana, End Zone*, and *Great Jones Street*, Veggian focuses on two aspects of these works, namely, DeLillo's engagement with 'specialized jargon' and 'variants of American English' as well as his 'heightened and increasingly refined sense of how to combine genres' (pp. 44–5). This chapter on the early novels as well as subsequent chapters succinctly capture critical debates and thus serve as a useful introduction to trends in literary criticism of DeLillo's work.

*Freedom and the Self: Essays on the Philosophy of David Foster Wallace*, edited by Steven M. Cahn and Maureen Eckert, offers six essays written by philosophers who primarily address Wallace's engagement with Richard Taylor's arguments about fatalism. William Hasker's 'David Foster Wallace and the Fallacies of Fatalism' opens the collection and provides a discussion of Taylor's argument, criticism of Taylor's work, and examination of Wallace's philosophy honours thesis as well as his criticisms of Taylor's argument that appear in it. Three other essays—Gila Sher's 'Wallace, Free Choice, and Fatalism', M. Oreste Fiocco's 'Fatalism and the Metaphysics of Contingency', and Maureen Eckert's 'Fatalism, Time Travel, and System J'—also examine Wallace's thesis and give readers a sense of the philosophical debates around fatalism, free choice, and contingency that shaped Wallace's later literary production. Because of this extensive focus on Wallace's early philosophical work, *Freedom and the Self* will be valuable for scholars interested in the philosophical debates the shaped Wallace as well as his interventions in them that evolve across his later literary production.

Finally, beyond Linda Wagner-Martin's work on Barbara Kingsolver, two other monographs of 2015 focused on women writers. *Sara Paretsky: Detective Fiction as Trauma Literature*, by Cynthia S. Hamilton, provides detailed analysis of Paretsky's fiction. Engaging with larger claims about the conservatism of crime fiction more broadly, Hamilton makes the case for re-examining the subversive potential of recent works in the genre like those by Paretsky by situating them within discussions of 'trauma literature and historiographical discourse' (p. 7). Rather than assume 'the restoration of the status quo through the detective's actions' as a defining feature of detective fiction (p. 12), Hamilton utilizes theoretical discussions of trauma forwarded by Dori Laub, Cathy Caruth, Dominick LaCapra, and, especially, Judith Herman to argue that detective fiction can usefully be read as a 'therapeutic narrative' in which the 'narrative structure ... recounts the process by which a healing narrative can be constructed from the confused, fragmented testimonies available' (pp. 18–19, 17). As readers identify with the figure of the detective, they may be empowered in Hamilton's account to explore the import of communal responses to the trauma of individuals while simultaneously exploring how such responses require a connection between the 'therapeutic and the political' (p. 21). While the detective is a listener-witness, she also is a figure that calls for a wider social response to the trauma addressed; turning to discussion of Paretsky's V.I. Warshawski, Hamilton posits that it is representations of the detective's experiences with trauma as well as her commitment to addressing the trauma of others with the aid of a 'surrogate family' structure that operates in texts to call both for 'consciousness-raising' around specific forms of violence and social change (p. 21). Having explored the fruitful positioning of detective fiction in connection to critical accounts of trauma literature, Hamilton discusses her second intervention in criticism of the genre by turning to Hayden White and LaCapra's discussion of historical narrative forms that might destabilize rather than secure dominant master-narratives. Highlighting how the traumatic events at the centre of detective fiction have the 'power to challenge conceptual frameworks', Hamilton argues that 'built into the very fabric of the detective novel is a mechanism that enables discussion of the constructed nature of historical narratives and that suggests the high stakes involved in securing definitive status for a particular narrative. The space opened up by this enabling structure has the power to deconstruct the definitive account presented at the end of the novel' (p. 33). Following her introduction, Hamilton fully focuses on Paretsky's work with an eye towards her engagement with second- and third-wave feminism, her investment in community responses to trauma and the empowerment of marginalized populations, her engagement with global capital, and finally her strategic 'expos[ure] [of] the interests served by ideological master narratives of history' as well as their 'marginalisation of particular groups' (p. 137). Because of her focus on the political power of Paretsky's 'disruption of patriarchal discourse and assertion of a feminist perspective', 'her privileging of community values over either competitive individualism or a corporate ethos', and 'her indictment of the failure of the institutions charged with protecting the public good' (p. 137), Hamilton's work will be of interest to feminist literary critics, scholars of detective fiction, and critics invested in post-1945 trauma literature and historiographical fiction.

   'I have been so many people': A Study of Lee Smith's Novels by Tanya Long Bennett provides short close readings of Smith's novels with the focus on how she explores the 'postmodern Southern subject' (p. 4). Beginning with her earliest published novels and proceeding through the later more acclaimed works, Bennett traces Smith's turn against the traditional ideological narratives of the South as her characters '[push] against the boundaries of their cultures' prescribed values' (p. 10). Further, she argues that as Smith's characters '[chafe] against prescribed Southern roles ... [Smith] posit[s] what a "liberated" self would mean' in the face of 'experience[s] not prescribed by the old categories' (p. 10). In tandem with her argument about Smith's challenge to the limitations of nostalgic narratives of the South, Bennett explores Smith's investigation of the 'problematic self-conscious postmodern experience of the world, the constant and somewhat tragic self-construction of the postmodern subject, and the resulting difficulty of achieving unselfconscious experience' (p. 7). Engaging with criticism of Michael Kreyling's *Inventing Southern Literature* (UPMissip [2012]) and Patricia Yaeger's *Dirt and Desire: Reconstructing Southern Women's Writing, 1930–1990* (UChicP [2009]), Bennett nicely situates her analyses of Smith's work within larger critical conversations that re-evaluate categorizations of Southern literature, and thus her monograph will be useful not only for scholars of Smith's work but also for those invested in studies of late twentieth-century Southern aesthetic production.

## 4. Drama

In *Anti-War Theatre after Brecht*, Lara Stevens analyses a selection of politically engaged, post-9/11 plays through the lens of Brecht's aesthetics and theory for the theatre. Drawing upon Marx's early writings, she convincingly demonstrates that the Brechtian concept of epic theatre has evolved into 'dialectical theatre', a form of theatre that uses contradiction as a means of unsettling the public's frames of reference. The relevancy of Brecht's theory for today's politically engaged playwrights and theatre-makers is upheld by recent developments in Brechtian studies. Jacques Rancière's re-examination of the relation between politics and art and David Barnett's notion of 'epistemological uncertainty' indeed provide the author with efficient critical tools, enabling her to show how Brecht's ideas have found their way to the post-political and digital age. The six anti-war plays examined in the book give the reader a small but representative sample of how engaged Western artists responded to the 'war on terror' that followed the 9/11 attacks. Tony Kuchner's *Homebody/Kabul* [2001] and *Only We Who Guard the Mystery Shall Be Unhappy* [2003–4], Théâtre du Soleil's *Le Dernier Caravansérail* [2005], Elfriede Jelinek's *Bambiland* [2004], and Caryl Churchill's *Iraq.doc* [2003] and *Seven Jewish Children: A Play for Gaza* [2009] are all given in-depth analyses. Not only are their dramatic and linguistic structures thoroughly examined, but the context in which they were created, distributed, and eventually received is also explored at length in an effort to place the plays in conversation with the cultural, political, and social issues of the post-9/11 period. This emphasis on the theatrical experience, on the play as an ongoing process meant to trigger discussions and debates among members of the public, corresponds to the Rancièrian model of an 'emancipated spectator' and constitutes one of the strongest points of the book. It is what enables the author to update Brechtian ideas and move from the pedagogical model that Rancière criticized to a post-Brechtian theatre that expands the potentialities of dialectical thinking to challenge the spectators' certainties, initiating a fruitful questioning of the status quo.

*Experiments in Democracy: Interracial and Cross-Cultural Exchange in American Theatre, 1912–1945* takes its title from a 1932 statement published in a Chicago African American newspaper. The expression refers to the interracial and collaborative dynamics that characterized the productions of the Pennsylvania's Hedgerow Theatre at a time when racial segregation was institutional in the United States. Editors Cheryl Black and Jonathan Shandell's anthology is an attempt at showing that the Hedgerow Theatre, far from being an isolated case, was but one example of the broader impulse towards a more egalitarian democracy that found in theatrical performance the means to express itself in the period preceding the Civil Rights Movement. Bringing together plays, musicals, dance performances, and radio series, the anthology explores an eclectic range of works, promoting a vision of diversity inspired by intellectuals such as Randolph Bourne and Horace Kallen, who criticized the homogenizing tendency of the melting-pot model. Heterogeneity therefore appears to be the main thread weaving the thirteen chronologically ordered chapters together, but heterogeneity in the sense of a 'symphonic cultural variety', which corresponds to the vision promoted by Bourne and Kallen's progressive democratic ideals. Among the catalysts for a more diverse and interracial theatre, the major roles played by community theatres, leftist theatres, and the Federal Theatre Project are worth noting. Their active participation in the elaboration of a discourse that criticized segregation and racial exclusion is examined by Eric Mayer-Garcia in chapter 3, Cheryl Black and Anne Fletcher in chapter 5, Margaret F. Savilonis in chapter 8, and Elizabeth A. Osborne in chapter 9. However imperfect and fraught with stereotypes these experiments might appear, they all, in their own specific ways, draw the contours of a new, more racially inclusive America. But Broadway also had its share of experiments, as Ju Yon Kim's comparative analysis of the 1912 and 1928 Broadway productions of *The Yellow Jacket* exemplifies in a very interesting first chapter which underlines the ambiguities and contradictions prevailing both in the public and in the authors' perceptions of Chinese people through a period of sixteen years. The introduction of jazz in Broadway musicals in the 1920s—at a time when the Broadway scene was largely controlled by Jewish producers—is examined by Stuart J. Hecht in chapter 2, which reveals how African and Jewish Americans combined their artistic sensibilities to counter the nativist sentiment that emerged after the First World War. Finally, the 1943 Broadway production of *Othello* is analysed by Lisa Jackson-Schebetta (chapter 11) through the lens of the Spanish Civil War in an illuminating attempt at defining and updating the concept of race as 'a nuanced and complex identity category, inclusive of colonial histories and bound up with language, ethnicity, nation, and religion as well as skin color' (p. 218). W. Douglas Powers, Elizabeth Coonrod Martinez, and Harry J. Elam Jr. focus on the marginalized voices of playwrights like Rollie Lynn Riggs (chapter 4), Josefina Niggli (chapter 6), and Theodore Browne (chapter 7), in contributions that explore the way each writer uses a particular strategy to break through stereotypes and give a vision of identity as multi-layered and essentially plural. Powers's description of the celebrated Broadway musical *Oklahoma!* as 'a white-washed patriotic revision' (p. 80) of Riggs's work *Green Grow the Lilacs* raises a further issue that is expounded by Jonathan Shandell in chapter 12, namely the paradoxical position of marginalized voices when they find their way to the centre. Shandell's examination of the evolution of the play *Anna Lucasta* from Harlem to Broadway and of the disastrous consequences of its success for the American Negro Theatre, which brought the play into being, points out the utopian dimension of such 'experiments in democracy'. This utopian aspect prevails in chapters 10 and 13, which show how the context of the Second World War prompted American people to reaffirm their diversity as a nation through the 1941 'Fun to be Free' anti-fascist venue and the 'Stage Door Canteen' wartime experiment. Cheryl Black's conclusion to the anthology therefore sounds rather pessimistic, but her insistence on theatre practitioners' continuing effort to promote tolerance and equality leaves the reader with the belief that art, as an ongoing process, may have the power, not only to reflect, but also to 'help create reality'.

In *Tennessee Williams and Italy*, Alessandro Clericuzio broaches a topic that has so far been little explored by scholars, namely Williams's critical reception outside the United States. In his well-documented book, he examines many aspects of the special relationship between Williams and Italy during the second half of the playwright's life. Approaching this special relationship from various angles, Clericuzio not only deals with the critical reception of Williams's works in Italy, but also tackles the issues of censorship and influence, examining the way Williams's fascination for Italy was perceived by Italian critics and appropriated by Italian artists. The book therefore offers a chronological overview of the evolution of the playwright's reputation in Italy interspersed with aesthetic forays into the role played by encounters with Italian artists like filmmaker Luchino Visconti or actress Anna Magnani in the development of Williams's theatrical language. With examples ranging from the Italian productions of the plays, the film adaptations, the novels, and the short stories, the book evinces a desire for exhaustiveness that does not always find its way easily into the chronological progression announced in the table of contents. What serves as a thread of connection throughout the book is the parallel evolution of Williams's critical reception in the United States and in Italy, and the way homophobic biases shaped the public's reception of Williams's work in both countries. Another interesting issue raised by the book is the patriotic rejection of the American playwright in post-fascist Italy in the years immediately following the Second World War. Clericuzio's book thus opens up new vistas for Williams studies. In his conclusion indeed, the author insists on what he calls 'the transcultural potential' (p. 15) of Williams's work, returning to a 1946 radio interview quoted at length in the second chapter in which Williams mentioned the idea of a 'world theatre' meant to 'fight fundamentalisms, suspicion, hatred and all that creates barriers between people in the world' (p. 12). The notion of a 'world theatre' might therefore replace Williams's well-known statements about 'plastic theatre'.

In *Steppenwolf Theatre Company of Chicago in Their Own Words*, John Mayer tells the success story of the Steppenwolf Theatre Company from its

1974 debuts in the suburbs of Chicago to its current position as one of the major ensemble theatres in the English-speaking world. With a foreword by Jeff Perry, one of the co-founders of the company, and in-depth interviews with the ensemble members, this captivating book traces the trial-and-error development and expansion of a community-based theatre company which started out as the adventurous enterprise of a few inspired high school students. The first chapter goes back to the early years when Jeff Perry, Gary Sinise, Terry Kinney, John Malkovich, Laurie Metcalf, and a few others developed their theatre in the basement space of an elementary school in the suburbs of Chicago. There, in the late 1970s, they sowed the seeds of what was to become the Steppenwolf style. The involvement of the company members in every aspect of production, their intense acting, their choice of challenging texts, and their unwavering belief in the value of collaborative work are some of the characteristics that contributed to their success, starting with their move to Chicago in 1980, which established them as a tightly knit ensemble whose performances surpassed the critics' expectations and delighted audiences. The second chapter traces the development of Malkovich's 'electrifying' production of Lanford Wilson's *Balm in Gilead* in September 1980. The critical acclaim the play received resulted in an extended sold-out run in Chicago and helped the Steppenwolf members gain national recognition, while positioning Chicago as the vanguard of American theatre. The business adjustments and upheavals in leadership the company had to deal with in the period following the immense success of *Balm in Gilead* proved its ability to adapt to its newly acquired status. Kinney and Sinise's productions of *Of Mice and Men* and *True West*, in 1981 and 1982 respectively, further reinforced Steppenwolf's position as a leading theatre company, a position that reached new heights with the move of *True West* to New York in October 1982 and its subsequent television showing on PBS's *American Playhouse* in 1983. The third chapter focuses on the production of *The Grapes of Wrath*, which premiered in Chicago in 1988 and then moved to the London National Theatre in 1989 to finally make it through Broadway in 1990 to great critical acclaim. The company's ability to manage a huge Broadway production while carrying out the project of opening its own theatre in Chicago evinces an exceptional ability to combine high artistic ambitions with an acute sense of business. The fourth chapter is a continuation of the company's maturing process. It spans the nineteen-year period separating *The Grapes of Wrath* from the 2007 premiere of *August: Osage County*, a play written, directed, and acted by Steppenwolf members, which was a first in the history of the company. The new millennium is marked by the members' attempts at diversifying the company in terms of race and gender and by their initiatives to support original scripts by up-and-coming playwrights. The adding of dynamic female artists like Amy Morton, Tina Landau and Anna D. Shapiro, or the opening of Steppenwolf to the world at large proved to be decisive steps for the future of the company. These new developments and the challenges they inevitably brought about show that the story of the Steppenwolf theatre company is far from being over, and that a future full of promise still lies ahead for its members.

The title of Cynthia Baron's book reveals an ambitious project that challenges a number of prevailing ideas about the history of acting in the

United States. In *Modern Acting: The Lost Chapter of American Film and Theatre*, the author unearths a diversity of acting strategies that emerged in the 1930s and 1940s as a response to the new challenges brought about by the transition to the sound era. Choosing to focus on these two decades, Baron fills in a blank in the history of the performing arts, engaging her readers in a reassessment exercise meant to give its rightful place to a period whose legacy has been obscured by the popularity of Lee Strasberg's Method. Exploring the work and ideas of acting teachers like Josephine Dillon, Sophie Rosenstein, and Stella Adler, Baron brings together a coherent set of principles she names 'Modern acting', after the title of Dillon's and Rosenstein's manuals. Concomitant with the development of Strasberg's Method, Modern acting aims at adapting performances both to the new forms of drama defined by the plays of Ibsen and Chekhov and to the development of new stagecraft. It is therefore mainly concerned with 'truth', or rather, with a 'truthful' rendering of the characters' emotions and feelings, an objective that highlights the intricacy of the threads weaving stage and screen performances together in a period marked by economic and institutional alliances between Broadway and Hollywood. Essentially defined as different from Strasberg's Method, Modern acting tenets as described in Baron's book create a sense of continuity between the Stanislavsky system from which Strasberg strove to emancipate himself and today's new developments in the performing arts industry. Baron's expansive approach provides a historical and economic context as well as an aesthetic background to a set of principles drawn from a plurality of people and places. Her book therefore touches on many fields of study. As an attempt at acknowledging the role and value of a significant number of women who contributed to shape American theatre within their limited status as acting coaches and teachers, the book will be of great interest to feminist studies scholars. But the part played by anti-communist political activism during the Cold War period in the success of Method acting advocates over the more dispersed and politically engaged proponents of Modern acting adds yet another dimension to it. Drawing on an impressive amount of material, Baron succeeds in gathering the scattered elements she needed to give the reader an illuminating glimpse into the way some narratives are told while others are lost. The result is a major, exceptional book: a convincing rewriting of the history of American acting.

Another major book is Lindsay B. Cummings's rethinking of the complex notion of empathy. In *Empathy as Dialogue in Theatre and Performance*, Cummings tackles the many paradoxes inherent to that notion, exploiting the works of philosophers, sociologists, and psychologists to finally come up with a rather challenging definition of empathy as a process, as a multi-directional exchange involving critical distance as well as affective engagement. Her dialectical approach allows her to reconcile Brecht's *Verfremdungseffekt* with the emotional appeal the idea of empathy inevitably entails. Through what appears to be a reassessment of Brecht's theories reminiscent of Lara Stevens's own re-examination of Brechtian concepts in *Anti-War Theatre after Brecht* (Palgrave [2016]), Cummings aptly highlights the relevancy of the Brechtian model for today's theatre. Choosing to explore the techniques of interruption, repetition, and rehearsal in a selection of plays and performances, she persuasively demonstrates the validity of her thesis. Her second chapter begins with the example of *Black Watch*, a 2006 testimonial-based play about the Iraq War written by Scottish playwright Gregory Burke. Analysing the function of interruptions in this play, Cummings suggests that interruptions take part in a dialogue whereby empathy is challenged rather than simply rejected. Her further exploration of the gaps created by interruptions in the 2008 collaborative musical *BETSY!* and the 2009 workshop performance *BOP: The North Star*, which were both performed in New York, reinforces the notion of empathy as a dialectical process through which history is understood as a series of gaps and contradictions that somehow have to find their way into the public's consciousness as parts of the narrative of the past. The third chapter of the book focuses on two 'repetitions' of Robert F. Kennedy's 1968 tour of Kentucky: the 2004 three-day re-enactment of Kennedy's visit entitled *RFK in EKY: The Robert F. Kennedy Performance Project* and Senator John Edwards's 2007 'Road to One America Tour', a political citation of Kennedy's tour. Pitting the collaborative, participative, and deeply affective dimension of *RFK in EKY* against the politically oriented visit of Edwards, Cummings further supports her conception of empathy as a democratic process bringing together the individual and the collective, the critical and the affective, the past and the future, into the dialectical, ever-shifting present moment of the performance. In the fourth chapter the technique of rehearsal is analysed through two plays by Naomi Wallace—*In the Heart of America* [1994] and *The Trestle at Pope Lick Creek* [2001]—to reveal how Wallace's use of rehearsal techniques within the fictional world of a play calls for a re-evaluation of the relationship between empathy and estrangement. Cummings's thorough exploration of the two plays serves to further define her concept of empathy as a collaborative, conscious process meant to challenge the boundaries between self and other. Finally, it is towards the political dimension of empathy that Cummings leads us, for her last chapter deals with performances about and by refugees and asylum seekers. Grounding her argument in contemporary issues about the way asylum seekers' stories are shaped and exploited by Western frames of thought, she demonstrates how a participative enterprise like *Journey of Asylum—Waiting*, produced in 2010 in Melbourne, Australia, makes use of dialogic empathy to create an 'active, collaborative space in which to engage others' (p. 188), allowing both the performers and the spectator to be together in 'the moment of interpersonal encounter, while at the same time making space for consideration, exploration, and analysis' (p. 193). Cummings's theoretically extensive study of the conflicting tensions of empathy therefore considerably expands the limits of its definition, making it a rich and challenging notion that will undoubtedly attract the attention of scholars in various fields of study.

## 5. Comics

M. Keith Booker's *Comics through Time: A History of Icons, Idols, and Ideas* is a massive, four-volume encyclopedia-style series that contains hundreds of individual entries on creators/influential individuals, comics (books, strips, 'graphic novels'), characters, genres, and publishers. The series focuses on American comics and major British works, with some attention to Japanese and Franco-Belgian comics. The volumes are divided by time period: the nineteenth century to 1960, 1960 to 1980, 1980 to 1995, and 1995 to the present. Booker's introduction makes it clear that this division is along conventional lines: the nineteenth century as the prehistory of American comic books and the 1930/1940s as the time of the 'Golden Age' of superheroes, the 1960s as the after-effects of the Comics Code and thus the split between mainstream and underground comics, the 1980s as the reintroduction of underground sensibilities into the mainstream, and then the present as the period after the total dissolution of the Code. This history is quite familiar in American comics scholarship as the superhero-centric model: not exclusive to them, but very much focused on them. It is perfectly serviceable for these purposes, but in this series it also literally makes the most room for comics that fit into the model (i.e. superheroes). Each volume includes an introduction that details the development of comics largely in terms of sociopolitical context, market position, and industry practice. There are few revelations in these introductions, but they do provide a broadly cultural-studies underpinning to each period. Each volume also includes a chronology of significant publications or events, for example Richard Outcault hired away from Pulitzer by William Randolph Hearst (in volume 1), or the first appearance of Spider-Man (in volume 2). The individual entries are arranged alphabetically but marked with an icon for four different topics: comics publishing (a dollar sign), genres and themes (a pencil), individuals (a conventionally male silhouette), and characters/titles (a lightning bolt). Both alphabetical and topic-specific tables of contents are provided. As to the individual entries, like the introductions, they are written for novice readers. The volume 1 genre/theme entry for 'Race', for example, takes the time to define racism, the Other, and stereotype—in very broad terms—before providing examples of creators of colour as well as racist imagery in comics of the era. Entries for titles, characters, and people are written in a loosely similar style: chronology, historical notes, dates, and issue numbers. Each entry contains an individual byline as well, thus personalizing it. Finally, sprinkled throughout the book are 'Sidebar' boxes that contain short notes on related topics, such as a box on William Hogarth in the 'Satire' entry or one on short-lived superhero characters of the 1940s in the 'Superhero' entry (both examples from volume 2). All in all, the series is a true encyclopedia. The format maximizes ease of access through alphabetization and indexical icons, and the text is uniformly written to inform rather than make specific critical arguments. Nevertheless, both the format and the content contain implications about American comics: that they were essentially invented in the 1930s, that the superhero is their most important figure, and that politics and economics were prime forces in their creation.

Randy Duncan, Matthew J. Smith, and Paul Levitz's *The Power of Comics: History, Form and Culture* is a revised edition of the 2009 book that contains two new chapters. It is a textbook, complete with chapter summaries and discussion questions, that mounts a familiar but well-constructed historical survey of comics in America, so it would be most suitable for an introductory course on comics *if* the instructor were interested exclusively in America and its influences. This approach strongly contrasts with Shane Densen, Christina Meyer, and Daniel Stein's *Transnational Perspectives on Graphic Narratives* (Bloomsbury [2014]; reviewed in *YWES* 95[2016]). The introduction performs a familiar but clearly laid out explanation of how comics are a medium, not a genre; offers the standard definition of that medium as sequential; and, finally, attempts to justify the scholarly study of comics, arguing in essence that it is a unique and powerful art form that is historically significant. Such a justification seems more fitting for a book published in 1995 than 2015 (or even 2009), but it is a solid introductory text in that it lays the groundwork for a novice while containing nothing objectionable to an informed comics scholar. The book contains ten chapters divided into three 'units', in addition to the introduction. Unit I, 'History', includes the first three chapters. Chapter 1, 'The History of Comics Books, Part I: Developing a Medium', gestures towards European comics but then launches into an 'eras' model of comics in America that is divided largely by genre. Chapter 2, 'The History of Comics Books, Part II: The Maturation of the Medium', focuses on underground and independent comics and the feedback loop of influence that they had on the American 'mainstream' (i.e. superheroes). Chapter 3, 'The History of Comics Books, Part III: The Diversification of the Medium', is new to this edition, and it examines more recent comics that have been created using new distribution networks and technologies. Unit II, 'Form', includes the fifth to eighth chapters. Chapter 4, 'Creating the Story', and Chapter 5, 'Experiencing the Story', look at imprinting (creator) and extracting (audience) the information in comics as a form. Chapter 6, 'Comic Book Genres: Classifying Comics', establishes a general theory of genre and then surveys several genres common to American comics. Chapters 7 and 8, respectively, examine what are arguably the most popular genres of comics in America: the superhero and the memoir. Chapter 8 is new to this edition. Unit III, 'Culture', looks at the culture(s) of comics and includes the ninth to twelfth chapters. Chapter 9, 'The Business of Comics', looks at the distribution chain and its influences, including the limited number of publishers and the retailers' reliance on the collector mentality. Chapter 10: 'The Comic Book Readers', focuses on 'fandom', what defines it, how it formed, and its potentially problematic relationship to the comic-book industry. Chapter 11, 'Exploring Meanings in Comic Book Texts', surveys methodological approaches to comics: qualitative (media studies, pedagogy), quantitative (content analysis, myth), and finally critical theory (focusing on feminism/gender theory). Finally, Chapter 12, 'Comics Culture Around the World', examines Japanese, Franco-Belgian, Canadian, Mexican, British, and (briefly) Indian comics, but does so only in terms of influences on or from America, including its discussion of cultural imperialism.

Cody Walker's *The Anatomy of Zur-en-Arrh: Understanding Grant Morrison's Batman* comes from the Sequart Organization, a publisher that deliberately sits between academic and popular scholarship. Its texts assume no knowledge of criticism or theory and generally contain a good deal of summary, but they are thesis-driven works. The scope of Walker's book is

Grant Morrison's specific presentation of the character, the goal of which, Morrison has in various places explicitly stated, was to incorporate all eras of Batman comics into one character, from the grim revenger to the camp icon. The implied argument of the book, then, is that Morrison's Batman breaks continuity by embracing it; he includes seemingly self-contradictory elements of the character in order to create one, seemingly complete, character. The body of the book bears out that implied thesis across nine chapters, not including the introduction, that focus on specific elements or story arcs within Morrison's tenure writing Batman: his comics before he took over the title in 2006 (e.g. *Arkham Asylum* and *Justice League*), 'Batman and Son', the foils of Dick Grayson as Batman, Damien Wayne, the Joker's battle with Dr Hurt, the reintroduction of Bruce Wayne, Batman Inc., Talia al Ghul, and finally the last chapter attempts to integrate into Morrison's narrative logic the continuity contradictions created by DC's relaunch in the 'New 52'. The book includes a chronology of Morrison's Batman and ends with a lengthy interview with Morrison, who had by then read Walker's analysis.

Barbara Brownie and Dannie Graydon's *The Superhero Costume: Identity and Disguise in Fact and Fiction* discusses the superhero costume in the context of comics/film, cosplay, political protest, and real-world vigilantes. They assert that its visual presence contains the core of the genre. The book mixes theories of performed identities (as split identities) and anthropological notions of masks (as liminal identities) to characterize the superhero costume. Specifically, they argue that it both creates and marks a hyper-masculine body and a divided identity. Although the book occasionally addresses the female superhero's costume, it is not the focus; superheroines are treated as exceptional. The book contains four sections, each of which has three chapters. Part I, 'Origins and Evolution', discusses Superman as the archetype for the superhero costume (chapter 1), the costume as separating and stabilizing split identities (chapter 2), and film's struggle between fidelity and realism. Part II, 'Identities and Ideals', addresses nationalist costumes (chapter 4), the superhero's street clothes as costumes (chapter 5), and animal-themed costumes as rationalizing beastly behaviour (chapter 6). Part III, 'Harsh Realities', analyses the superhero costume's resistance to being fashionable (chapter 7), the identities that attend to cosplay (chapter 8), and political motivations behind wearing costumes, including vigilantism. Finally, Part IV contains three case studies: *Watchmen* as deconstruction (chapter 10), Iron-Man as overdetermined costume (chapter 11), and the X-Men's costume as a uniform (chapter 12).

Liam Burke's *The Comic Book Film Adaptation: Exploring Modern Hollywood's Leading Genre* focuses on Hollywood adaptations of comic books, post-2000 (i.e. after the first *X-Men* film). Its goal is to understand how and why, in a fairly brief period of time, comic-book adaptations have come to dominate American film, as well as the kinds of films that have been produced within that trend. It does reference television adaptations (e.g. CW's *Arrow*), film adaptations that arrived there via other media (e.g. *Annie*), and comic-book-like films (e.g. *The Matrix*), but those are not the primary objects of study. It roots itself in adaptation theory, specifically a taxonomy that separates them into direct (retaining plots and visual design), loose (retaining character designs and premises but creating new plots), and self-reflexive (often commenting on the process of adaptation itself). While the book's scope may be limited, the tight focus allows it to come to thoroughly sound conclusions about a multi-billion-dollar trend in Hollywood that has, as yet, not been thoroughly studied in comics scholarship. Comics scholars, specifically those who work in cultural studies and communications, will find this book valuable. In addition to the introduction, which contains an extended survey of adaptation theory and other studies on adaptation to film, there are five chapters, a short conclusion, and an appendix. Chapter 1, 'The Golden Age of Comic Book Filmmaking', offers four causes for why comic-book adaptations presently dominate in Hollywood: the ability to reflect on post-9/11 trauma, advances in special effects, pre-existing fan bases, and finally a generation shift in the film industry. Chapter 2, 'The Comic Book Movie Genre', argues that the effect of this trend has been to create a genre, the comic-book film, which can be defined in terms of production, promotion, and reception. Chapter 3, 'Fans, Fidelity, and the Grammar of Value', posits that comic-book fans were already accustomed to being in dialogue with creators, and the Web offered them the same dialogue with film creators. Chapter 4, 'A Comic Aesthetic', follows the logic, illustrating how comic-book fans pushed for fidelity to comic-book aesthetics in comic-book films. Finally, 'How to Adapt Comics the Marvel Way' demonstrates that there is a direct influence between *How To Draw Comics the Marvel Way* (published in 1984) and the way that all comic-book films are constructed today, although most especially the superhero films. The conclusion very usefully reviews the main points of the book, and the appendix is a list of box-office earnings of comic-book movies between 2010 and 1978, in reverse chronological order.

Chris Gavaler's *On the Origin of Superheroes: From the Big Bang to Action Comics No. 1* is a prehistory of the genre figure called the 'superhero'. His introduction uses an extremely useful image to define the scope of the book: an hourglass. The top of the glass is the prehistory of superheroes, and the bottom is the superhero since *Action Comics #1* in 1938. The neck is Superman, the single character that defines the genre today even though he was prefigured for at least a century. In this model, Superman is not the origin of the genre but the transition between phases of development. Superman, and the superhero as we know it, is only possible because it was preceded by centuries (arguably millennia) of superhero characters. That is to say that he is retroactively perceived as the origin point specifically because he is not the origin point. This way of looking at the development of the superhero—and arguably any genre figure—is extremely valuable. It points us away from origins and towards these moments of transition. The book is written in a very casual style that includes much autobiographical detail, and it does not include in-text citations. Gavaler is an academic by training, though, so the text is alive with scholarly ideas, but the casual and personal qualities of the prose seem to free him to speak directly to his subject. It is a very lucid text. The book contains eight chapters in addition to his introduction, in which he describes his hourglass model and demonstrates the concept, as well as an epilogue. The chapters are chronological. Chapter 1, 'In the Beginning', covers world mythology with specific attention to Judaeo-Christianity. Chapter 2,

'Revolution', addresses characters from the French and American revolutions. Chapter 3, 'A Parliament of Monsters', examines Gothic and horror literature of the nineteenth century. Chapter 4, 'Indians and Cowboys', looks at Westerns, including the John Carter series. Chapter 5, 'Evolution', essentially looks at genetically determined superheroes and villains (Nazis, *Harry Potter*, biological experiments, noble heroes). Chapter 6, 'Thou Shalt Not Kill', discusses the moratorium on killing in the superhero genre with special attention to Batman. Chapter 7, 'The Superhero Guide to Love and Sex', addresses dual identity in terms of a costumed, sexualized self as separate from a nerdy, mundane self. Chapter 8, 'Best of Both Worlds', takes a close look at the years just before the emergence of Superman, specifically the conglomeration of genre influences that created him. Finally, the epilogue, 'Magneto's Giftshop', is in truth an elaborate, autobiographical introduction to the bibliography, which contains the only organized citations in the book.

Mel Gibson's *Remembered Reading: Memory, Comics, and Post-War Constructions of British Girlhood* is an interdisciplinary study of British girls who read comics and their adult memories of them, both comics marketed to girls specifically and those marketed to boys. Gibson's tone and delivery are entirely scholarly, but unusually in scholarship she foregrounds her personal experience as part of the study. The book also periodically reprints whole black-and-white pages from British girls comics, which significantly aids the reader given that these books have all but disappeared from circulation. The consistent focus of the book is on how these comics constructed femininity and how their readers responded to that construction. Ultimately, she argues that since femininity *has* to be taught in media like comics, it is essentially amorphous and unnatural. The book contains five chapters—each one broken down into many subsections—a conclusion, and two appendices as well as the introduction. The first three chapters establish the methodology and situate the study in history. Chapter 1, 'Picture This', describes Gibson's interdisciplinary approach. Chapter 2, 'The Rise and Fall of the British Girls' Comic', describes their history and how they were marginalized. Chapter 3, 'Mediating the Text', demonstrates how the larger cultural context understood those girls comics. The last two chapters focus on women's memories of reading these girls' comics. Chapter 4, 'The Readers' Tale', focuses on the pleasure of reading and girls' social experiences in relation to the comics, and locates them within Britain's class structure. Chapter 5, 'You Can't Read Them, They're For Boys!', focuses on girl readers who read comics that were marketed to boys, and thus were exposed to very different models of girlhood. Her conclusion is a detailed review of the specific arguments the book makes. The first appendix is a short explanation of some problematic aspects of interviews with children used in the book—not done by Gibson but by another researcher—and the second appendix is an alphabetized list of comics that fall into the scope of the book.

Casey Brienza's *Manga in America: Transnational Book Publishing and the Domestication of Japanese Comics* is a sociological case study of how manga was, in her terms, *domesticated* into American culture. She studies the industry that performed that labour of cultural importation—editors, translators, printers, etc.—and she posits this industry as the driving force behind that importation, rather than the formal power of the medium itself or the ostensibly unique Japaneseness of the content. She argues that in the process of bringing manga to America, usually fuelled by a sincere love of the material, it was Americanized. She stresses that the Japanese manga industry is arranged not primarily by genre, as American entertainment is, but by gender and age—young children, boys, girls, men, and women—although within those demarcations is a much wider available range of genres and styles than in Anglo-American comics; however, what is popular in America tends towards a relatively narrow bands of fantasy, science fiction, horror, and sexually explicit material, material that tends to be rendered in a distinctive big-eyes/small-mouth style. This expectation, she implies, effectively defines the features of what Americans think of as 'manga', and therefore creates space for American-made comics to qualify as manga if they display those features. This process of Americanizing manga so thoroughly that Japanese comics have been affected by it is the culmination of what she calls 'domestication'. In addition to the introduction, labelled 'chapter 1', the book contains six more chapters, including the conclusion, labelled 'chapter 7'. Chapter 2, 'Theorizing Domestication', explains the theoretical underpinnings of domestication, as she uses the term. Chapter 3, 'Book Trade', traces the history of manga publishing in America to the 1980s but argues that it became professionalized in 2005. Chapter 4, 'A License to Produce', describes the licensing difficulties of reproducing Japanese comics in America. Chapter 5, 'Working from Home', describes the manual work of preparing these Japanese texts for English readers (translators, letterers, editors, etc.) and the insecure labourers who perform it. Chapter 6, 'Off the Page', contrasts the move of prose books to digital with the attempt to do so with comics and how it contributes to manga's domestication. Finally, chapter 7, 'Making Manga American', concludes that American manga is decreasingly dependent on Japanese licensing as American creators make their own 'manga' and even influence how manga is made in Japan.

Rikke Platz Cortsen and Erin La Cour's *Comics and Power: Representing and Questioning Culture, Subjects and Communities* is a collection of essays that address how comics participate in power dynamics that are both fluid and defined in the relationships between texts/genres, audiences, and institutions. The book is mostly about European comics, except for Sacco's *Footnotes from Gaza* and DC Comics' *Red Son*, but it consistently speaks from a European, specifically Nordic, perspective. The book has three sections that work their way from the art form itself, to the individual, and finally to groups. Section I, 'Power and Institutionalization', contains chapters on comics in relation to other art forms and thus constructs an understanding of them as a specific form of artistic expression. Øystein Sjåstad's 'Comics: This Bitter Art' examines the relationship between comics and the (institutionally legitimized) art world. Andreas Gregersen's 'You Wouldn't Get It' studies the remarkably successful webcomic *Penny Arcade*, a media company. Fred Andersson's 'Nordic Contribution to the Understanding of Comics in Art' studies Elis Eriksson's *Pavan*, an avant-garde comic strip, and explains Continental/ Nordic comics theory in the process. Katja Konturri's 'Fantasy and Intertextuality' analyses Don Rosa's *Escape from Forbidden Valley* as a narrative powered by intertextual references to the 'lost world' fantasy genre. Section II, 'Power and the Subject', looks at documentary and auto/biographical comics in terms of how they construct subjects in relation to social norms. The editors, Cortsen and La Cour, argue that comics constitute a 'thirdspace' of liminality in 'The Unmasking Effect of Comics'. Kristina Arnerud Mejhammer's 'Politics, Everyday Life, and Humor' analyses Cecilia Torudd's *Ensamma mamman*, partly to make the point that comics are well suited to life-writing. Øyvind Vågnes's 'Comics Reenactment' uses *comic re-enactment* to understand Joe Sacco's *Footnotes in Gaza*. Martin Lund's '[A] matter of SAVED or LOST' examines a subset of Chick Tracts that defines the 'saved' versus the 'lost' (i.e. Evangelical Christians versus Catholics, Jews, and Muslims). Section III, 'Power and Society', examines comics that help define and/or contest national or cultural identities. Dennis Meyhoff Brink's 'Fearing Religious Satire' argues that critiquing religion—as seen in religious satire comics—is a formative element of European society. Ralf Kauranen's 'Transnationalism in the Finnish 1950s Debate on Comics' details Finnish fears of comics as foreign and threatening to children by placing them in the context of other countries' parallel fears. Margareta Wallin Wictorin's 'Comics in Postcolonial Senegal' describes how Senegalese comics have participated in that nation's internal debate about its postcolonial identity. Gunhild Borggreen's 'Drawing Disaster' situates the manga *Santetsu* as an activist document designed to remind the Japanese government of the need for continuing support for the region affected by the 2011 earthquake. Finally, Mervi Miettinen's 'All Men Are Not Created Equal' describes how changing Superman into an idealistic Marxist in DC Comics' *Red Son* is a self-critical gesture that demonstrates how superhero comics define identity and power.

John A. Lent's *Asian Comics* is the result of decades of work and research. Lent is a familiar figure to comics scholars because of his *International Journal of Comic Art*, and he has had a special interest in comics from Asia for some time. The book contains a lengthy introduction that sketches out the wider field of Asian comics: their great variety in both form and content, developments in their various national industries since the 1980s, the manner in which they are purchased and consumed, and, more briefly, the status of women creators. This introduction provides a sense of just how much variation there is in the region and hints at the stated goal of the book, which is to be comprehensive, to cover all recognizable forms of comics (books, magazines, strips, etc.) in all of Asia, with the exception of Japan, which Lent does not cover at all given how much scholarship already exists on the subject. In addition to traditional textual scholarship, Lent supports his research with lengthy interviews collected over the last twenty-plus years with, as he is wont to point out, very little research performed online. Finally, it is also worth mentioning that *Asian Comics* is laid out somewhat like an art book (heavier paper, wide margins, illustrations on almost every page, full-page illustrations for each section) and with a distinctive cover design (a solid background colour with floating panels) that marks it as part of Mississippi University Press's line. (For example, compare the volume to Barbara Postema's *Narrative Structure in Comics* (RITP [2013]; reviewed in *YWES* 94[2013]).) *Asian Comics* is divided into three sections—East Asia, Southeast Asia, and

South Asia—and further subdivided by country on the logic that their politics and/or languages are quite distinct. Lent's opening chapter, before the regional/ national chapters, is a survey of comic art in Asia before the current era. It broadly traces patterns of caricature, humour, parody, and wit as well as, very briefly, narrative/sequence. The rest of the chapters are specific to a nation (or area, in Hong Kong's case) and discuss the formats and styles their unique historical circumstances created: politics, economics, industry structures, and artistic influences. The East Asia section contains chapters on China, Hong Kong, Korea, and Taiwan. The Southeast Asia section has chapters on Cambodia, Indonesia, Malaysia, Myanmar, the Philippines, Singapore, Thailand, and Vietnam. Finally, the South Asia chapter covers Bangladesh, India, Nepal, and Sri Lanka. Each chapter is a separate discussion with its own citations, although many of the historical and political circumstances are interrelated of course. There is no conclusion to *Asian Studies*, as befits a comprehensive survey that emphasizes variety and is consistently reluctant to draw general conclusions about sixteen different national traditional.

Robert Moses Peaslee and Robert G. Weiner's essay collection, *The Joker: A Serious Study of the Clown Prince of Crime*, takes two specific ideas as its premise. First, the Joker is probably the most famous of all supervillains—the rise in popularity of Loki and Harley Quinn notwithstanding—and second, that the defining trait of the character is chaos, so declaring any one origin or meaning to him would be a categorical error. As such, he represents the existential uncertainty of contemporary culture, and/but the collection contains a great number of perspectives on the character with no obligation to be consistent. It is worth noting, as well, that the book's design reflects this sense of chaos just a little in its typography; author names in the table of contents contain random spacing and capitalization. It is a small gesture, but it does make the point, and the collection is consistent in its broadness, including essays on the character in four different categories, across three media, and in a variety of subject areas. The sections are essentially about tricksters, politics, digital and online incarnations, and applications of theory. The first section discusses the Joker in physical performance (Dan Hasoun), his visible depiction in comics (Roy T. Cook), parallels with Lady Gaga (Eric Garneau), and his non-lethal behaviour in children's cartoons (David Ray Carter). The second section, on politics, discusses the Joker as deployed by the American 'Tea Party' (Emmanuelle Wessels and Mark Martinez), his abusive relationship with Harley Quinn (Tosha Taylor), and the Joker as Marxist (Richard D. Heldenfels). The third section, on the Joker across media, addresses the Joker as Internet troll (Vyshali Manivanna), as twisted game-master in the video game *Arkham Asylum* (Kristin M.S. Bezio), and as viral marketing tool (Kim Owczarski). Finally, the theory section discusses the Joker as satirical figure (Johan Nilsson), as Nietzschean superman (Ryan Litsey), and as Žižekian symptom (Mark P. Williams), and finally, it discusses Morrison and McKean's *Arkham Asylum* as an underworld.

Julian Darius's *Classics on Infinite Earths: The Justice League and DC Crossover Canon* comes from the Sequart Organization, a publisher that straddles popular and academic criticism. This book leans more towards a fan text;

Darius specifically calls it a 'critical celebration' written to encourage people to 'fall in love' with the characters. It is the first in a series of Sequart books that will propose 'canons' within DC Comics as tools for critique. Darius justifies the narrowness of this proposed canon—just one publisher—by claiming that DC is the older of the two major American superhero publishers and that its characters are more iconic, but it is a somewhat contrived distinction. The book itself consists of two sections, one on the Justice League, DC's most prominent hero team, and one on DC's summer crossovers in which a mini-series depicts a major conflict within their shared universe and all or nearly all of DC's superhero comics include a single issue that relates to that conflict. The chapters are very short, under ten pages each, and focus on either specific, short-run series or 'runs' within an ongoing series (i.e. a specific creative team on ongoing series). Darius's criteria for inclusion are quality—which for him results in comics that are unusual or self-critical—and historical significance: i.e. usually what the fan community celebrates. Thus, the first section addresses *Kingdom Come*, *JLA: Earth 2*, *Identity Crisis*, Giffen and DeMatteis's *Justice League International*, O'Neil and Dillin's *Justice League of America*, and *Super Powers*. The second section addresses *Crisis on Infinite Earths*, *Infinite Crisis*, *DC One Million*, *Invasion*, *Armageddon 2001*, and *Underworld Unleashed*. The sequence of chapters is based on ranking within Darius's proposed canon. They largely consist of summaries with commentary, the argument being that they deserve the rank Darius gives them. Finally, the canon appears to end in the mid-2000s, for reasons not fully explained. Contrariwise, each section also ends with an 'Other Works' chapter that surveys those comics that Darius decided *not* to include in his canon. They are much longer—sixty-seven pages and seventy-eight pages, respectively—and far more critically interesting. They still contain a great deal of summary, but by virtue of being surveys they juxtapose DC's comics to each other, thus tracing creative influences, and they acknowledge the influence of the profit motive.

Rich Handley and Joseph F. Berenato's *The Sacred Scrolls: Comics on the Planet of the Apes* is an essay collection from the aforementioned Sequart Organization that looks specifically, as its title suggests, at comic-book adaptations of the film series *Planet of the Apes*. The book does not have a formal introduction, instead opting for two chapters in which the editors describe their personal relationships with *Planet of the Apes*, and a foreword that speaks in broad terms, from personal experience, about adapting it for BOOM! Studios (2011 to the present). The remaining sixteen chapters vary from around fifteen to thirty pages, and most of them directly address one particular publisher's adaptation: Marvel (Sam Agro, John Roche, Joe Bongiorno), Dark Horse (Lou Tambone), Mr. Comics (Edward Gross), BOOM! Studios (Joseph Dilworth Jr.), and IDW (Joseph F. Berenato). The remaining chapters discuss more specific elements of the comics, including sketching out a timeline of all of them (Zaki Hasan), publishing them with playable records (Dan Greenfield), exporting them to the UK (Jim Beard), time travel as narrative device (Dayton Ward), and unpublished *Apes* comics. In keeping with Sequart's house style, the chapters contain a good deal of summary and praise along with a running commentary on the comics themselves.

*The Future of Comics, the Future of Men: Matt Fraction's Casanova* is written by Geoff Klock, who made himself known to comics scholarship in his *How to Read Superhero Comics and Why* [2002], and it comes from the aforementioned Sequart Organization, the house style of which is casual and often somewhat fan-oriented. This book is no different. It is a short manuscript on the first three volumes of Matt Fraction, Gabriel Bá, and Fábio Moon's series, and Klock makes it explicit that he is a fan and would like more people to support the series (i.e. both read and pay for). He is also a scholar, though, so he explains his methodology quite directly. He argues that *Casanova* is constructed on the same principle as 'wall-of-sound' music recording in which many tracks are layered such that individual tracks are inaudible even though listeners feel their effects. The plot, for example, frequently leaves out major details but proceeds at speed such that audiences either do not notice or learn not to care. Therefore, Klock's approach is to isolate individual 'tracks' of *Casanova* for analysis, separating them so that they are individually appreciable as discrete elements of the wall of sound. The book contains two major sections, thesis-driven arguments of around fifty pages each, and one thirty-page section filled with observations unconnected by a single thesis. It is worth mentioning that while *Future of Comics, Future of Men* is slightly more academic than most of this year's Sequart books, Klock's writing is the most conscious of that separation. The first section contains three topics: formal self-consciousness; artistic influences on *Casanova* primarily, from music and film but also comics; and finally, speculation about the future of comics as a medium. In essence, it emphasizes and explains *Casanova*'s argument about what comics ought to be. The second section, 'The Future of Men', examines the series' commentary on masculinity, that it is a performance of 'freedom, sexuality, and violence', and finally that the series presents a counterpoint to that performance in the character Kaito Best. The last section contains gleefully random commentaries on elements of *Casanova* such as race, music, media references, dialogue, lettering effects, costuming, fun bits of art, use of titles, references that require research, possible mistakes, and a section in the 'Other Commentaries' chapter labelled 'Other Things'. This last section is very chaotic, and Klock is both honest about and comfortable with that fact.

Logan Ludwig's *Moving Panels: Translating Comics to Film* comes from the Sequart Organization, which situates itself between the overlapping worlds of popular and academic scholarship, and Ludwig's book leans heavily towards scholarship, the only exception to which is his willingness to make claims of quality or artistic success on the part of the adaptations, although his claims are by no means unwarranted. The book uses five major case studies, and one brief one in the first chapter, that collectively argue two related points: first, comics and film are unique media, not parallel although strongly analogous in some ways, and as such, second, good adaptations of comics have to translate their unique features into the analogous features of film. He makes this point, in part, by specifically employing a formalist methodology and paying specific attention to action/movement, sound/sound effect text, and time. The book contains seven chapters, and although they are not labelled as such, the first is clearly an introduction—including an explanation of methodology and a critical review—and the last is a conclusion. The body of the book, then, is a series of comparisons between comics and the films that adapted their material. Chapter 2, 'The Cinematic Comic', examines how *The Invincible Iron Man* employs a cinematic style to match the *Iron Man* film of 2008. Chapter 3, 'Sinful Motion', looks at the opposite effect: how the *Sin City* film goes out of its way to replicate the aesthetics of the comic-book page. Chapter 4, 'A Moving *Persepolis*', is specifically concerned with motion, something comics have to imply where film can depict it directly. It is also the only chapter in which the film is co-directed by the creator of the comic book *and* in which the adaptation is animation rather than live action. Chapter 5, 'Why Adapt *Watchmen*?', parallels the *Sin City* discussion, arguing that the film overwhelmingly replicates the appearance of the comic book rather than truly adapting it. Chapter 6, 'Scott Pilgrim vs. the Adaptation', argues the opposite, that Wright's film replicates the formal *effects* of O'Malley's comic book by using the unique features of film. Finally, the last chapter, 'To Be Continued', is a traditional conclusion that reviews the big ideas lurking behind the chapters of the book and restates Ludwig's ultimate point: that the two media are distinctly different and that adaptations should take that into account.

Bart Beaty's *Twelve Cent Archie* is quite consistent with the author's tendency towards contrarianism and his communications background. Rather than looking at what Beaty calls *auteurist* comics (single-author, often autobiographical), or the faux-popular (superhero comics), he focuses on the statistically popular Archie comics, which outsold *Fantastic Four* at the height of its popularity. In the same vein, he argues that Archie comics are culturally ubiquitous and seemingly without significance aside from being used as exemplars of comics as 'low' culture, and he points out that there has been almost no published research on them. Beaty chooses a narrow focus on what he identifies as the best years of Archie—1961 to 1969—when three specific creators worked for Archie. This period coincides with the years in which the cover price was US¢12, hence the title, which is also a play on David Hajdu's *Ten Cent Plague* (Macmillan [2008]). Beaty is aware that this focus betrays his attempt to argue by example against auteurism. The structure of the collection mimics Archie comics themselves: many short narratives that have little if any continuity or consequence such that they can be read at any time and in any order. *Twelve Cent Archie*, likewise, contains a hundred chapters, many of which close-read individual Archie shorts, a methodology that betrays the book's cordially anti-literary premise. The chapters are arranged loosely chronologically, but there are a few more conceptual patterns in their sequence. The first five form a collective introduction: scope and methodology, Archie's narrative formula, the typical length of Archie stories (typically six, anywhere from a half-page to twenty-two pages), the structure of the Archie titles, and finally Archie himself: a normative lead with very few stable character traits. There are sporadic chapters on the remaining cast members as well as other permanent fixtures of Archie comics, and several extrapolate broader ideas from specific stories: racism, gender, and so on. These 'idea' chapters tend to be a little longer, at two or three pages, than the others, which are often a single paragraph. The remaining chapters are typically close readings that point out a technique or a notable feature in a given Archie story. The collection then ends with three chapters that function as a collective conclusion, describing the closest stories that include all the elements Beaty identifies, applying Eco's 'The Myth of Superman' to Archie, and finally, the author describing his personal relationship with Archie comics.

Bill Schelly's *Harvey Kurtzman: The Man Who Created Mad and Revolutionized Humor in America* is not written as an academic book. Instead, it is a biography in a journalistic style. However, the consistent, if often implied, argument of the book is that despite his humility and enduring American attitudes towards comics, Kurtzman has been a major influence on the satire of the country. Although the claims are sometimes a little overblown, the book does make the case that *Mad Magazine*'s early years were a formative influence on the artists who would create the underground, which was a major element of the protest culture of the 1960s. At nearly 650 pages, it is exhaustive. The book is divided into three sections—'Cartoonist', 'Editor', and 'Icon'—but they are, in essence, pre-comics, comics (mostly *Mad*/EC), and post-comics. The first section, then, describes Kurtzman's upbringing, social context, and war experiences: the man before *Mad*, in essence. The second section details his time as an editor, first of EC's remarkably grounded war comics, then *Mad*'s self-conscious satirical work, and lastly his attempts to replicate *Mad*'s success outside EC. It contains a great number of insider stories about the comic-book marketplace and, thus, Kurtzman's opportunities for social commentary and satirical expression. Marxists, materialist historians, and cultural studies critics will find it particularly interesting. Finally, the third section essentially describes life after *Mad* and its continuing influence, both on his life and on his successors in the world of satirical comics. Given that it is not an academic book, it is worth noting that Schelly also includes complete citations in the form of endnotes as well as a chronology of Kurtzman's life and a robust index.

Christian W. Schneider's *Framing Fear: The Gothic Mode in Graphic Literature* is a lightly revised version of his dissertation, some chapters of which have been published as papers. It argues that the Gothic is multifaceted by nature, pushing the boundaries of 'taste', shifting rapidly between the horrific and the erotic, and the comic-book Gothic reflects these traits. Further, it uses Gothic criticism, comic-book formalism, and cognitive theory to examine how and why the Gothic is present in contemporary comics, specifically in terms of emotions, aesthetics, and narrativity/non-narrativity. The book has the default structure of a literature review in the introductory chapter and then two lengthy chapters of theory that lead into four chapters of case studies. The theory chapters address the Gothic and comics (defined as 'Gothic literature'), respectively. Schneider defines the Gothic in terms of horror, transgression, the uncanny, and poststructuralist and postmodernist representation, including intertextuality. He defines comics as visual literature, a hybrid medium, and in terms of cognition and space/time. Tying the two together, he makes the somewhat familiar argument that comics are inherently fragmentary, and their imagery is especially affective, thus they are particularly suited to representing the Gothic. The remaining four chapters perform close readings of Gothic comics/the Gothic in comics. Chapter 5, ' "Fear in their hearts": 1950s Horror Comics', describes EC's horror comics, specifically *Haunt of Fear*, *Tales from the Crypt*, and *Vault of Horror*, as well as their crime and SF comics, which have similarly horrific elements. Chapter 6, '"In the midst of death...": Neil Gaiman's *The Sandman*', discusses this work as a particularly obvious example of the Gothic in comics. Chapter 7, 'Behind the Spandex Wall: Gothic Superheroes', looks closely at Batman and *Watchmen*. Chapter 8, '"Looks like skulls": Alison Bechdel's *Fun Home*', defines Bechdel's graphic memoir as Goth by virtue of its dominant patriarch, violation of sexual taboo (i.e. homosexuality), and the spectre of death that hangs over the narrative. The conclusion returns to the case study of the introduction, Moore and Burrows's *Neonomicon*, a Gothic metacomic.

Gabriel N. Mendes's *Under the Strain of Color: Harlem's Lafargue Clinic and the Promise of an Antiracist Psychiatry* is not a work of comics scholarship. Rather, it is a history of the Lafargue Clinic, co-founded by Richard Wright and Fredric Wertham, the latter of whom is often seen within American comic-book fan communities as a hysterical killjoy and a scold rather than a humanitarian scientist who attempted to reveal the negative social effects of racism, sexism, and violence depicted in children's mass media. Mendes describes how liberal thinkers and policymakers in the era attempted to view mental health problems among African Americans not as a marker of inherent inferiority but rather as the result of systemic oppression. He places this shift in attitudes into the context of postwar liberalism as well as part of the attempt to integrate large numbers of black Americans into northern cities such as New York. The Lafargue Clinic, he argues, put that theory into action, offering mental health services to the poor black residents of Harlem in a conscious attempt to help them become mentally healthy enough to fight against their oppressive surroundings. Thus, the book is a history of one particular moment of the intersection of psychiatry and anti-racism, with only a small amount of attention paid to Wertham's mass media analyses. For comics scholars, it is an extremely useful way to understand the whole of Wertham's career rather than just the thin slice that is Wertham's *Seduction of the Innocent* (Rinehart [1955]), which makes it akin to Bart Beaty's *Fredric Wertham and the Critique of Mass Culture* (UPMissip [2005]). The book contains four chapters, the first two of which establish Wright and Wertham's respective biographies and intellectual influences, both scientific and political. The third chapter describes the Lafargue Clinic itself and argues that it was a radical attempt to place the psyche of African Americans into the context of racial oppression, thus promoting social justice through the mental health of the individual. Finally, the fourth chapter briefly describes Wertham's critique of comic books but only for the purposes of putting his larger anti-racist critiques in a context so that Mendes can then describe the clinic's collective contributions to the successful 1954 fight against racial segregation in American schools, a fight that Wertham was instrumental in but also cut out of, in the end. The book ends with a conclusion that places the clinic's anti-racist efforts in the context of present-day psychological notions of how race and racism function, and it relates how the clinic was eventually closed in 1958.

Gavin Parkinson's *Surrealism, Science Fiction, and Comics* is an essay collection that, as its title makes plain, looks at the intersection of surrealism,

SF, and comics, but specifically from an Anglo-European perspective rather than from the Anglo-American perspective that is conventional in English-language comics scholarship. Parkinson argues that surrealism was, in its day, critiqued as having more in common with popular media, including SF and comics, than with the abstract art that was ascendant at the time—a commonality that he celebrates rather than condemning. However, he also asserts that there has rarely been an academic exploration of that connection. Despite the cover image—Captain Marvel battling a collection of radio equipment—only four of the ten chapters examine connections between surrealism in comics, while the rest look at prose SF/F. The bulk of the comic-book-oriented chapters are about francophone comics, with one that covers anglophone comic strips. Barnaby Dicker's 'André Breton, Rodolphe Töpffer and the Automatic Message' argues that these comic-book creators used a method akin to surrealist automatism. Jonathan P. Eburne's 'Approximate Life' places the bédé *Les Tribulations de Monsieur Wzz...* in the context of Dadaist technophilia. Gilda Axelroud's 'René Magritte's "Vache" Paintings and "Les Pieds nickelés"' unearths the (at the time openly acknowledged) connections between Magritte's then dismissed series and contemporary bédé. Jeannette Baxter's 'The Comic Book Conditions of Chicago Surrealism' describes how that group of artists became interested in comic strips of the day, including Herriman, McCay, and Capp. The remaining chapters examine Jules Verne, SF's mid-century reception in France, Alan Burns, J.G. Ballard, and Salvador Dali. It is worth noting that none of these chapters address the *Captain Marvel* comic depicted on the cover of the book.

Noah Berlatsky's *Wonder Woman: Bondage and Feminism in the Marston/Peter Comics, 1941–1948* is the last of a small group of books on Wonder Woman and/or her creator, William Moulton Marston, including Jill Lepore's *The Secret History of Wonder Woman* (Knopf [2015]), which was not received for review, and Tim Hanley's *Wonder Woman Unbound: The Curious History of the World's Most Famous Heroine* (ChiR [2014]; reviewed in *YWES* 95[2016]). This trend is fuelled by the sexuality that clings to the character, as hinted in the titles that play up bondage and secrets. That said, both Berlatsky and Hanley are largely quite frank about the subject, neither titillating nor shameful, as discussed last year (*YWES* 95[2016]). Berlatsky looks at early Wonder Woman comics as written by Martson and in terms of theories he used to construct them. In addition to the introduction and conclusion, the book is thus divided into three chapters, each of which discusses a broad element of his theories: feminism, pacifism, and queerness. Berlatsky argues that these concepts also imply their obverse: bondage, violence, and heterosexuality. The chapters are not, he claims, arranged to be read in order but rather to continuously reference each other, as Martson/Peter's comics did. Chapter 1, 'The Pink Bondage Goo of Feminism', argues that Martson's theories of bondage underpinned his concept of feminism, and it looks closely at *Wonder Woman* #16, arguing that it uses fantasies of bondage and incest to empower women. Chapter 2, 'Castration in Paradise', is subdivided into four sections that examine, first, the concept of the male Just Warrior (i.e. the warrior who is just in his actions) and then three theories/permutations of the female Just Warrior. Chapter 3, 'Candy You Can Eat', looks at Marston's 'lesbophilia' and essentialist notions of femininity as feminist, in opposition to recent queer/feminist theories that would argue otherwise. Finally, at forty pages long, the conclusion is truly a chapter in itself. It looks at three versions of Wonder Woman that Berlatsky identifies as being of unusually high quality (as compared to other Wonder Woman work): comics by Azarello and Chiang as well as Simone and Dodson, and finally a single image by Nicole Eisenman. He concludes by lamenting how much Wonder Woman without Marston retains some of the surface details of the original comics but little if any of their complexity or radical politics.

## 6. African American Writing

In *Dancing on the Color Line: African American Tricksters in Nineteenth-Century American Literature*, Gretchen Martin endeavours to explore the influence of black-authored works on white-authored works, specifically looking for instances of black oral culture and the presence of a trickster figure as found in many seminal African American texts. While black characters created by white authors are generally either demeaning caricatures of the black minstrel type, or simply inconsequential bit players, Martin argues that by re-examining these characters and refiguring their minstrelsy as wisdom and trickery, the influence that black aesthetics and culture have had on key pieces of American literature by white authors can be illuminated. Martin claims that white-authored black characters are often overlooked and misinterpreted. At play in Martin's argument is a teasing out of the social, cultural, legal, and scientific categories of black and white identity during the years prior to, and following, the Civil War, through the post-Reconstruction era. Accordingly, she argues that racial essentialism has had an impact on American history, fictional as it is. To Martin, writers such as Kennedy, Stowe, Melville, Harris, and Twain have used African American aesthetics to demythologize racial definitions, and these constructions signal a shift in attitudes towards racial categorization. As part of her argument, Martin traces changes in labour laws as they pertained to race, as well as tracing race theory via nineteenth-century race ethnologists whose theories of racial superiority/inferiority were used to justify the master–slave relationship in the Southern states prior to the Civil War. Martin continues by arguing that it was precisely the paternalistic system and relationship between master and slave that unintendedly led to the slaves developing systems of defence: adopting a religion that preached love and asked its adherents to value each other, to take a critical view of their masters, and to reject ideologies of enslavement. Additionally, equally important was the legacy of folktales in slave communities. Rather than simply providing entertainment, these tales offered a means of solidarity within slave populations. The trickster figure itself offered a means of countering the master–slave relationship, of usurping the power structure in covert ways, and offered a means of resistance. Martin traces the evolution of the coded communication strategies in black folktales as being the result of the culture of slavery and its many structures, such as prohibiting the education of slaves, the physically demanding forced labour, restricted mobility, the panopticon of invasiveness in the living quarters of the slaves, and so on. From these realities, the figures of the trickster and the fugitive are born. At the heart of the trickster tradition lies the aesthetic of signifying, a way of speaking resistance, a way in which the slaves could voice that which is otherwise unspeakable due to the absolute control which masters exerted over the slaves. To Martin, signifying is a doubling of speech: a compliant surface which encodes a deeper layer of subversion. Also, bound up in the practice of signifying is W.E.B. Du Bois's theory of the double consciousness: signifying offers a way out of the double-consciousness bind of always seeing oneself through the eyes of others. Nevertheless, Martin's main purpose in this book is to examine white authors' use of black characters, one which seeks to challenge the notion that the figures are simply reinforcing racist stereotypes. Martin asserts that the adoption of black aesthetics offers the opportunity for subversive possibility. Martin's argument hinges on the observation that the appearance of minstrel or trickster figures in works by white authors is a perpetuation of the trickster figure as subversive as found in black folktales; that the figures possess the signifying features and double consciousness of their originals.

In the edited collection *Post-Soul Satire: Black Identity after Civil Rights*, which is released in trade paperback this year, Derek C. Maus and James J. Donahue seek to address the critical gap in literature on African American satire, as well as to address why there is so little satirical work being produced by black American writers. The editors believe that there is indeed a healthy production of satirical work, but that it has largely gone unnoticed, or has been displaced by studies that seek to profile more serious or weighty discussions of black aesthetics, relegating satire to the bottom of the rank. They argue that, in the past, seriousness was valued and indeed demanded in order to legitimize black works vis-à-vis white mainstream American works. Nevertheless, the editors note that circa 1989 there was a shift due to Trey Ellis's essay, 'The New Black Aesthetic', which liberated artists to pursue a broader scope of genres, including satire, and thus this anthology focuses its attention on works, including television, film, theatre, music, stand-up comedy, the visual arts, and the Internet, produced since 1989. Maus and Donahue explain that the unifying thread in their collection is its focus on the 'dual-vectored nature' of the subjects of study. On one level, 'post-soul satire' is aimed at the in-group, African Americans, and contains mild ridicule, commentary on trends and follies; on another level, post-soul satire levels a scathing critique of political institutions, social practices, and cultural discourses from outside the black community. Somewhat controversially, I think, Maus and Donahue suggest that the trend is towards the former, as many artists of what has been termed the New Black Aesthetic, as well as the community itself, are what they term 'cultural mulattoes', a term which points not only to the mixing of black and white peoples, but also to a population educated by a multi-racial mix of cultures; it is also a term that is widely viewed as denigrating. The editors see this trend as liberating for black artists, who are no longer bound to a responsibility or obligation of representation of blackness. The essays contained within this anthology establish a critical discourse for post-soul satire, of 'blaxploration', and offer discussions around three significant authors (Paul Beatty, Percival Everett, and Touré), works that the authors argue are departure points for other works. Finally, the essays reveal affinities between the literary satires and non-literary modes of satire in other media.

Carol Bunch Davis begins her critical assessment in *Prefiguring Postblackness: Cultural Memory, Drama, and the African American Freedom Struggle of the 1960s* with an analysis of the Rosa Parks incident, not refiguring it simply as a chronological marker for the Civil Rights Movement's beginning, but rather asserting that the figure of Parks serves a number of purposes: sympathetic protagonist and impetus for national reflection of racial injustice and subsequent movements towards racial equality. She symbolizes the means of resolution and the result of the refusal. Nevertheless, Bunch Davis concludes that the folk hero appropriation of Parks as a symbol of civil rights is a one-dimensional view of her life which omits the complexities and also her involvement in civil rights activism prior to the bus incident, and, furthermore, denies the ongoing troubles of racial relations in the United States, as both her life and her death have come to signify that racial inequality has also been laid to rest. Bunch Davis's book aims to address the limitations of representation of African American identity with the Civil Rights Movement, narratives of which seek to neatly contain the movement to Martin Luther King's non-violent protests, or what Bunch Davis refers to as tidy narratives, and instead seeks to give fuller attention to the era's messiness—the complexities of the movement. Bunch Davis's book revises the racial uplift ideologies and Black Arts' cultural nationalism by instead positing a 'postblack ethos', a phrase that marks 'a temporal distinction' between the 1960s and the late 1980s, the former acting as prescient representations that reject, embrace, satirize, magnify, and revise African American identity codes. Bunch Davis focuses her attention on a number of plays, offering close readings of not only the plays themselves but also the theatre reviews, thereby enabling a critical analysis of the era as represented by the era, noting in particular the confluence between print media reviews and politics and history, and the way in which these discussions both construct and draw upon cultural memory for context for the representations on stage. Bunch Davis's critical foundation for her study stems from Marianne DeKoven's postmodern theorizations and her contentions that 1960s counterculture and radical politics enabled the shift from modern to postmodern, and notes the contribution of the freedom struggle in aiding this shift, citing specifically the identity politics of the era, relying on a shift from the universal to particular subject politics, as being a key paradigm change that enabled civil rights gains. Two key elements that Bunch Davis locates in the plays she discusses are a critique of essentialism and a refusal to engage in cultural nostalgia or allegiance to the past. Instead, Bunch Davis argues that the plays in her study tend to flout the usual proving of moral and civic fitness, opting to envision black identity not how it appears vis-à-vis white identity but on its own terms, when it is not bound up in arguments geared towards achieving collective freedoms, pointing to the strategy of 'troubling blackness'. Bunch Davis's book focuses on plays by Beneatha Younger, Leroi Jones, Howard Sackler, Alice Childress, and Charles Gordone.

In their edited collection *The Blacker the Ink: Constructions of Black Identity in Comics and Sequential Art*, Frances Gateward and John Jennings initiate discussions around the concept of blackness as a type of medium and the way in which the medium has been used to certain effect. The title refers dually to the ink used in the creation of comics, as well as the title of Wallace Thruman's seminal text on colour and racial identity, *The Blacker the Berry*. The editors explain that their collection of essays was designed to address the representation of blackness, including black agency and identity in comics. The collection is conceived to address the black identity as expressed in the comics' medium. Acknowledging that comics are generally associated with white male superheroes, the collection aims to examine the black male figure and its various roles and manifestations. The editors begin by pointing out the relative dearth of black comic heroes in the conventional comic series, describing how, when in 2011 DC comics re-released their entire line of comics, entitled The New 52, only five of the fifty-two comics featured a black character in the titular role. The authors note how in every case of the black character in the series, there were problems with the various representations. The editors trace the evolution of black comic writers from the 1930s and 1940s to the present day. This edited collection showcases scholarly work on the little-known subgenre of black comics. The collection is large, featuring thirteen essays that forge critical scholarship into the topic of black comics. The book opens the pathway for critical discourse on this topic by covering a notable breadth of works in a scholarly manner.

In *Things That Fly in the Night: Female Vampires in Literature of the Circum-Caribbean and African Diaspora*, Giselle Liza Anatol provides an ambitious and thorough examination of the soucouyant in Caribbean and African diasporic literatures, in particular tracking ways in which the legend appears in contemporary works. Anatol's aim is to dig deeply into the legend and beliefs, the contemporary manifestations, in order to reveal the root of the figure. She notes that while many studies of the figure have critically examined the intersections between sexuality, gender, violence, and 'respectability' of the form, few have focused on how it appears in folk narrative and various literary genres. Anatol's goal with her critical book is to reveal and thereby loosen the constraints placed upon female bodies, as they are used in various literatures to disempower and demobilize women. Anatol points to the transgressive nature of the soucouyant as a monstrous entity; the female body as monstrous must contain her sexuality or at least confine it to private spaces. Anatol demonstrates that many contemporary works of fiction urge a refiguring of the female body, freeing it to be privately and publicly erotic, in effect bringing the female body out of obscurity and at the same time resisting the privatization of violence, abuse, and terror and restoring female sovereignty. Anatol juxtaposes the soucouyant with European versions of the vampire figure, who, generally, is understood as a symbol of rebellion against social order and convention. In North America, the vampire often symbolizes contagion, rampant or perverse sexuality, and even stoicism and divinity. Often the vampire has been read as a colonizing force in the Caribbean and other formerly colonized places. Anatol offers a thorough review of the way in which the vampire figure has been read as a critique of capitalism, but points out that, in each case, the gender dynamics of the figure have failed to be addressed. Anatol points to the act of the draining of blood that is a particularly ripe symbol of colonialism and enslavement, but also an expression of the fear of miscegenation between Europeans and colonized peoples. Alternatively, Anatol cites the presence of the soucouyant and other monstrous figures as a remnant of slavery and the way in which enslavement turned people into monstrous beasts. Anatol asserts that as the soucouyant stories become more and more distant from slavery, the fear associated with this figures remains, but the agency shifts so that the soucouyant is no longer objectified or subjugated but rather is the agent of her own monstrosity. Bolstering this manifestation are prevalent anxieties over female menses, and as Anatol asserts, the universality of this attitude reinforces the taboo nature of blood. Given the female nature of the soucouyant, Anatol develops a theory that situates the female body as the primary recipient of the violence that is generally used to police a society. Anatol is interested in pursuing the way in which the soucouyant stories have generated from colonial and postcolonial spaces, tracking the shifts that have occurred, and examining the way in which the vampire myths of the African diaspora offer a means by which the people grapple with their historical legacy, even as it continues to unfold.

Editors Houston A. Baker Jr. and K. Merinda Simmons have compiled a collection of essays in *The Trouble with Post-Blackness* that challenge the notion of post-blackness as expressed by Touré, on the one hand, but also offer a much broader discussion around the rhetorics of conceptual categories such as 'post-black', and, in the process, interrogate the discourses that occupy the spaces in which the concept of race is concerned. The editors identify a basic pitfall in discussions of black identity wherein the category of white hegemony is left untroubled, arguing that whiteness needs to also be viewed as constructed and contingent, rather than a cohesive whole that is rarely interrogated in the way that other marginalized identities are. As a starting point, Baker and Simmons interrogate the assumed neutral norm of whiteness against which black identities are constructed. In so doing, they assert a new premise that all identities are constructed and political. They argue that deconstructing the assumed norms is critical to understanding blackness. They suggest that post-blackness demands a move beyond double consciousness and the adoption instead of another type of doubling: a double standard. The editors ask, 'how might we talk about blackness and performance in complicated ways, troubling the notion of post-blackness for a number of different reasons and from a number of different perspectives?' (p. 15). The essays in this collection address this broad enquiry, including topics of blackness in aesthetics, blackness in time and technology, blackness in globalization, blackness in authorship, and blackness in institutions.

Earle V. Bryant's compilation of over one hundred of Richard Wright's journal articles, published during his time as a reporter at the *Daily Worker* and the *New Masses*, is an attempt to retrieve much of Wright's forgotten written work that is generally overlooked in favour of his fiction and autobiographical writing. It is well known that Wright held communist views, and his time at these two papers reveals how deeply involved in workers' struggles and anti-capitalist discourses Wright was. The compilation *Byline*

*Richard Wright: Articles from the Daily Worker and New Masses* broadens readers' understanding of Wright's later fictional writings, giving a deeper context for his beliefs. It also gives readers a deeper appreciation for Wright's overall knowledge of the tumultuous times that he not only wrote about but also lived and participated in. It reminds readers that Harlem is not only the setting for some of America's best literatures, but also a historical player in the United States, the site of civil unrest, racial injustice, poverty, and workers' protests, and that black Americans were major participants in that history. Accordingly, many of Wright's articles in the *Daily Worker* cover stories that were not covered by mainstream black or white journals, and thus this anthology gives a fuller impression of the era, featuring coverage of such issues as the rent strikes and deplorable housing conditions, as well as coverage of the African American soldiers who fought in the Spanish Civil War, and coverage of white-on-black assaults carried out in the neighbourhood. The compilation is an effort to bring Wright's newspaper work out of obscurity to provide a fuller understanding of this important American writer.

Using Du Bois's *The Souls of Black Folk* as a springboard for her study, Rebecka Rutledge Fisher offers readers a complex examination of African American identity as a psychosocial experience, as she develops what she calls a 'poetics of black being' in *Habitations of the Veil: Metaphor and the Poetics of Black Being in African American Literature*. The poetics is developed by drawing upon commonly observed metaphors in African American literature spanning the eighteenth century all the way through to the postmodern period. Rutledge Fisher develops her theory of black being by drawing upon Heidegger's theory of being-in-the-world, or Dasein. Following Heidegger's notions of care, Rutledge Fisher detects in the works she studies an extension of that central notion to include humanistic action in response to the racially driven horrors experienced by black Americans, from slavery to the civil rights era. Rutledge Fisher sees in Heidegger's Dasein the potential for confronting racist thought and practice, although this emphasis on race and confronting racism is generally lacking in American and European philosophical texts on being. In particular she cites Ellison and Wright as having provided important metaphors for being that address the issue of race and racism. Rutledge Fisher offers a thorough examination of the way in which blackness-as-being is constructed, even against philosophical theories that inadequately provide space for blackness when whiteness is privileged within philosophical schools of thought, but does not dismiss these philosophies entirely, as she finds ways, points of entry, that enable a wider discourse on being as a universal category, and specifically as a means by which to understand black American experience. For Rutledge Fisher, metaphor becomes the entry point through the gates which, in traditional Continental philosophy, bar blackness from entry. They appear in various works of literature in different forms, including what she refers to as the philosophy of plain language, as conceptual metaphors that engage directly in debate, as challenges to Freudian psycho-analysis; in common, Rutledge Fisher contends that they are ontological and onto-theological, orientational. For instance, she cites the frequency of the form 'to be', and the presence of linguistic and literary modes of personifi-cation, speaking one's place in the world, or displacement as resulting from oppression, marked by deviations in conventional language use and challenges to traditional categories of meaning. Finding that existing modes of expression lack the ability to express their lived experience, black American writers have had to make ordinary language into a conceptual discourse that establishes new meanings and calls to activism; Rutledge Fisher argues that this is primarily achieved through metaphorization.

In *Cultural Melancholy: Readings of Race, Impossible Mourning, and African American Ritual*, Jermain Singleton explores the pervasive manner in which the past claims the present through various cultural productions. He focuses on racialized identities as formations, and on the intersections of social difference, nation-making, and concealed social memory. He explores various narratives for the purpose of deconstructing the legacy of racial subjugation and inequality. Singleton's central theory rests in the idea that racialized subjects of multiple generations are bound across time through social loss, and that it is this binding that results in continued struggles with the nearly impalpable remains of slavery and subjugation, that it is the inability of later generations to be able to claim this loss, yet still being bound to it intergenerationally, that results in legacies of social and racial unrest. Singleton seeks to explore new territory by bringing together various fields such as critical race studies, psychoanalysis, and performance studies in a challenge to scholarship which insists on the separation of ethnic studies and psychoanalysis, as well as the separation of psychoanalysis and socioeconomic histories. Instead Singleton develops a theory of cultural melancholy that seeks to address the ideology and psychic claims that result from a history of slavery and racial subjugation on contemporary American racialized subjects. According to Singleton, these intersections of disciplines enable a way to articulate the intergenerational experience of melancholy and also enable a space for performance studies to offer a political and cultural transformation experience. As a starting point, Singleton draws upon Freud's notion of melancholy as loss retained and barred from conscious recognition, as the unhealthy response to loss, as a sort of internal darkness that infiltrates people—in the case of Singleton's subject matter, the lives of African Americans. Singleton cites an instability that can be located in the subject formation at the intersection of racialization and melancholia; however, Singleton challenges Freud's binary supposition of mourning and melancholia, offering instead a theory that sees the binary as more ambivalent, that racialized subjects experience something that sees loss as more dynamically experienced in which the self is disavowed and retained. This melancholia can be expressed through ritual or, according to Singleton, can be used to circumvent the past's claim on the present. Accordingly, Singleton sees theatre as a vehicle that through its reliance on ritual can harness the emotional intelligence and critical awareness needed for the mitigation of trauma and the ensuing melancholy. Singleton's historical, cultural materialist, and interdisciplinary approach draws upon James Baldwin, August Wilson, Alice Walker, and Tony Kushner to exemplify the proposed theory.

Claudia Rankine, Beth Loffreda, and Max King Cap's *The Racial Imaginary: Writers on Race in the Life of the Mind* originates from a number of premises: that we are bearers of unwanted and/or shunned memory, and that race is more readily spoken about in relation to scandal. The authors describe discourse about race in additional ways through sentimentality, or in discourse that harnesses the past tense, or in jaded, cynical language. This collection is premised on the notion that discussions about race are worth subsequent multiple attempts. The editors acknowledge and wish to highlight the literary and intellectual conventions that writers sometimes use and struggle to reinvent, and simultaneously to query the aesthetics that writers use to depict and carry racial identities and conversations about race. The editors identify a number of tropes that writers might use. For instance, they cite encounters with others; the treatment of race as something exotic, or hard to find; race as racism, and race as a binary of black and white. In particular, the books takes critical aim at racialized depictions by non-racialized others, challenging the notion that imagination is a free space. The writers use the term 'racial imaginary' to describe the way in which race resides in a creative act. The book offers a number of essays that take a critical look at the way in which race operates in the act of creativity, and by extension how creative depictions of race can induce anxieties about racism given the oftentimes ephemeral nature of racism, and, as the editors note, the way in which racism can undermine one's ability to determine whether something is racist. Included in this critical collection are both academic and artistic critical responses to the depiction of race.

In *The Repeating Body: Slavery's Visual Resonance in the Contemporary*, Kimberly Juanita Brown aims to trace the memory of slavery in black women's visual and literary works, paying particular attention to the way in which black artists reconcile the duality of representation and memory. Central to her discussion is Toni Morrison's novel *Beloved* for its vivid and plentiful descriptions of the way in which memory is inscribed in female flesh. Also central to her argument is the assertion of critical arguments which give prominence to the violence that has shaped black female identity as it is tied to and continues to be shaped by the experience of physical violence in the past of the black Atlantic. A key thematic structure of Brown's book is the notion of repetition as it can be found in the idea of an after-image, double exposure, hyperembodiment, or in the form of a riff. Overall, the book aims to expose multiple sites upon which slavery reoccurs and repeats upon the black female body in both literature and the visual arts. Kathy Lowinger's *Give Me Wings: How a Choir of Former Slaves Took on the World* is a historical recovery effort that details the life of Ella Sheppard (b. 1851), who after having been born a slave went on to become a teacher, musician, and an international celebrity. Relying heavily on Sheppard's letters and diaries, Lowinger reconstructs the remarkable life of a woman whose life straddled the slavery and post-slavery eras and who charted territory hitherto unheard of for a black woman at the time. The book is scholarly but accessible to a broad range of readers and features a variety of historical photographs and details that are little known.

Lindsay R. Swindall's *Paul Robeson: A Life of Activism and Art* is a homage to Robeson not simply as an artist, but as an artist and activist, and the book sets out to examine the events that shaped Robeson's career, the ideas that drove his actions, and the principles that shaped his activism. The book traces Robeson's development from the scholar athlete, very much in the light of Du

Bois's theory of the talented tenth, through his career as not simply an artist but as an artist who used his position, his popularity, and his skill to advance the rights and lives of black Americans. Swindall uses historical markers such as the Roaring 20s, the Depression, the Second World War, the Cold War, and the civil rights era as markers to highlight Robeson's continued and ever-evolving involvement in events of national and global importance. Downplaying his association with the Communist Party, which in Swindall's opinion was overplayed and never formalized, the author seeks to rehabilitate Robeson's reputation as being larger than simply his socialist and communist associations, asserting that, in privileging these, several key actions are overlooked. For instance, Swindall makes the case for Robeson's support of the Bill of Rights, and that, more precisely, his political leanings were socialist in that he supported workers' rights and a more equitable distribution of wealth. Additionally, Robeson's adoption of a distinctly 'African' identity and the ensuing identity politics that arose from this movement in general is equally important to understanding Robeson's work during his lifetime, in particular his anti-fascist work and his advocacy for anti-colonialism and civil rights. These associations more than any association with communists are responsible for his reputation as a radical, argues Swindall. Overall, the book aims to reposition his artistic work alongside the contributions he made in the realm of his activist work, and his embracing of African identity was key to elevating civil rights work beyond the post-slavery identity; he reconnected black Americans with their cultural heritage, thereby bolstering their sense of cultural right and dignity beyond that which Du Bois had been able to achieve.

The reprinting of Bill V. Mullen's *Popular Fronts: Chicago and African-American Cultural Politics, 1935–46* (UIllP [1999]) includes a new preface situating the book as a product of its time. The updated preface serves to acknowledge work that immediately followed the original publication, citing specifically a proliferation of work on African Americana and communist and radical left collaboration. Mullen notes that the period was ripe for these discussions because of the thawing of Cold War prohibitions. By noting these trends, Mullen situates his own scholarship within a shifting discourse on communist history and a revitalization of scholarship seeking to assess the implications of the former shift. Rather than circling around the centrality that communist or radical left politics played in the Chicago renaissance, Mullen argues that the shifting discourses of the 1990s enable a more thorough discussion of the role of communism itself. Mullen also addresses the idea that, despite the first black president having been elected, little has changed in black Chicago in terms of the managed segregation and restrictions experienced, alongside the neoliberal clawbacks of public and social services, schools, unions, and so on. Overall, Mullen offers an argument reiterating that, despite many changes since 1999, the book's central thesis and discussion concerning culture remain relevant.

Stéphane Robolin's *Grounds of Engagement: Apartheid-Era African American and South African Writing* begins by drawing an essential literary connection between Langston Hughes and South African writers, in particular Richard Rive, in the 1950s. The connection leads to a fertile exchange of literary and other ideas about identity and racial politics, as writers from before and during the civil rights era in the United States and writers living under apartheid in South Africa cultivated a relationship. The particular relationship establishes a comparative ground of place, culture, racialization, and racial struggle—as well as a resulting transnational solidarity—that comprises the focus of the book. Of particular interest to Robolin are the social and physical geographies of segregation, that space dictates racial experience. So, rather than treating space as the setting, Robolin views spaces as a necessarily dynamic and active constituent of the social, especially after centuries of white supremacy being played out in that space. Accordingly, Robolin also asserts that spatiality can also impact subjectivity, citing specifically the notion of the colour line as asserted by Du Bois, and the way in which colour politics and space reinforce each other by determining who may go where on the basis of shades of difference. Robolin locates a spatial literacy in highly segregated communities, a way of knowing where and how to move about space according to racial colour lines. Robolin argues that similar effects can be detected in both African American and South African racial geographies. Robolin asserts that through this comparison we can better understand black spatial expression and transnational relationships between racialized populations. Robolin discusses writers such as Richard Wright, Peter Abrahams, Keorapetse Kgositsile, Nikki Giovanni, Toni Morrison, Alice Walker, Michelle Cliff, Bessie Head, Audre Lourde, and Gwendolyn Brooks, to name a few.

In *Funk the Erotic: Transaesthetics and Black Sexual Cultures*, L.H. Stallings offers an unusual approach to cultural critique in that eros and eroticism are privileged as key elements in efforts at decolonization, in particular examining the way in which funk music harnesses eros and functions as a music of resistance. Further, the author is quick to point out that it is not just music that harnesses a spirit of funk; literature, such as that by Toni Morrison, employs similar techniques in a different medium. Funk is a philosophy, epistemology, and ontology. Additionally, Stallings highlights the multiple meanings that funk can inspire—sexual act, dismissal, stink—explaining that each is significant to the overall agency of the word to generate power. Moreover, Stallings postulates that the notion of funk applied as a philosophical category enables a way to think about sexuality, gender, and their agencies that is not anti-black. Stallings defines funk as an aesthetic mode which blurs the boundaries between nature, technology, and culture—the aesthetics do not originate in only one cultural or sensory form, but rather a multiplicity of forms and origins, human and non-human. Funk also displaces other divides such as life and death. Funk can also, in Stallings's estimation, be a creative force for myth and other originating narrative structures. Stallings also argues that funk has critical capacities as well, and provides effective means of critiquing capitalism and Western morality; in particular, Stallings views funk in terms of reproductive sex and transaesthetics of culture. It is a philosophy of art that focuses not on beauty but rather on what is 'funky'—its stance being inherently anti-Western in its aesthetic value. In other words, Stallings proposes funk as an aesthetic category that operates outside the liberal humanist tradition that has dominated aesthetic discourses, offering instead alternative orders of knowledge about the body and imagination as sensually experienced; thus, Stallings advocates rehabilitating the link to smell that funk can signify. Stallings asserts the notion of transaesthetics as the underlying principle at play in black art and funk: a reorganization of the senses; transaesthetics as a practice provides a new way to discuss representation, agency, and sexuality, which Stallings sees as representative of art as experience. Throughout the book, Stallings invokes relationships and antagonisms amongst sensory experience, sex and sexuality, sacredness and profanity, secularity and spirituality, the body, the senses and sensory experience. As a result the book is an invigorating contribution to a field of feminist and critical race studies.

James Donald begins *Some of These Days: Black Stars, Jazz, Aesthetics, and Modernist Culture* by tracing the introduction and establishment of jazz as a black cultural symbol in Europe through the early twentieth century, and as definitive of modernity. His narrative draws together Jean-Paul Sartre, Josephine Baker, a variety of 1920s-era jazz musicians who found themselves working in Paris and Berlin, and a host of other prominent musicians and artists, both black and European, who identify a defining spirit of the modern age in jazz and black musical arts from America. Additionally, Donald points to the proliferation of technology in this period as working in concert with black American culture: the radio, for instance, but also the new phenomenon of mass production and mass consumption of proliferating, repeating goods that need no longer be experienced in reality but rather reach the masses through radio, cinema, photography, and a spirit of virtuality in which humans become the subjects of their own experience. Even black American culture as it is experienced in Europe is a reduction, offering an experience through performers such as Baker and Robeson, but it is a conjuring rather than a transportation of the culture itself. In other words, black culture is performance. In summary, the book asserts that jazz was a vehicle through which modernism is communicated; jazz modernism contains a history of migrations, ideas, and influences between the United States and Europe and across racial divisions; jazz 'principles' are evident in other types of modernist artistic expression. The book aims to trace the intersections between transatlantic modernism and the black Atlantic.

In *Origins of the Dream: Hughes's Poetry and King's Rhetoric*, W. Jason Miller seeks to highlight the acknowledged but little-known or -studied influence that poets such as Langston Hughes had upon Martin Luther King's speeches; Miller refers to Hughes's influence as an inflection upon the words and ideas that King expresses, in particular, but not limited to his most widely known 'Dream' speech. Despite the relationship between King and Hughes, and King's acknowledgement of Hughes as an influence and inspiration, Miller detects a measurable distance between the two. In bringing the two together Miller aims to illuminate a fuller understanding of many of King's metaphors, and to elevate the integral relationship between poetry and politics at this time. Miller sees King's use of poetry and metaphor as a subversive act, but says that it also reveals King's poetic sensibilities as they are employed to inspire resistance. The poetic structure of King's own speeches, drawn and inspired by his own love of poetry, reveals the cultural pride that King possessed, and also his own poetic capabilities. Miller asserts that King was also a poet. Miller explores four critical facets that are brought to light in a comparative study of these two men's poetics: metaphors from Hughes are transformed by King into political principles; King's willingness to integrate a poet who was simultaneously renowned for his poems but reviled as a communist demonstrates a larger truth to power that through metaphors is larger, more important, than day-to-day politics; the creative exchange between the two was reciprocal; King selected Hughes's poetry with intentionality. The chapters trace King's engagement with Hughes's poetry, highlighting particular poems, such as 'Mother to Son', 'Brotherly Love', 'Dream Deferred', and 'Youth' to name but a few. The book offers close comparative readings of both King's and Hughes's work.

In *Playing in the White: Black Writers, White Subjects*, Stephanie Li strives to examine how racial representation works in novels, identifying where they undermine simplistic attempts at authenticity in depictions of both black and white characters by black authors, in particular focusing on works that are frequently neglected by critical studies. Li identifies a number of common themes, such as rape in marriage, false master narratives, collapsing of black and white speech, and the failure of white characters to live up to various expectations of whiteness. Underpinning her analysis are the assertions that novels cannot be 'non-racial', or 'beyond race', since the most divisive social category in America is race, and that even novels that do not explicitly explore racial conflict or identity need to be read as racial novels. Failure to do so results in a lack of recognition for the way in which dominant subjectivities that are unmarked by race are complicit in racial and gendered hierarchies. Li contends that texts portray a specific set of cultural dynamics rooted in their era of production and reveal conceptions of social relations held by the authors. Li theorizes that black-authored texts about whiteness offer insight into how blackness and whiteness are social constructions that are both limiting and liberating of imaginative potential for African American writers. Li's book offers both close readings of a variety of texts and discussions about their critical reception. Li's critical assessment of depictions of white characters by black authors demonstrates that whiteness is both confining and exploitative; that, like blackness, whiteness is unstable as a site of power, for instance. Whiteness as a social category has been ever-shifting since the end of slavery, according to Li, and tracing the shift via depictions of whiteness is enlightening for understanding social discourses on race in the United States. Li's book offers chapters on Zora Neale Hurston's *Seraph on the Suwanee*, Richard Wright's *The Outsider* and *Savage Holliday*, Ann Petry's *Country Place*, James Baldwin's *Giovanni's Room*, and William M. Kelley's *A Different Drummer*.

Steven C. Tracy asserts that *Hot Music, Ragmentation, and the Bluing of American Literature* takes a cue from the three major elements of African American music: ragtime, blues, and the concept of in the moment, newness of hot music—and the passion, the unbridled sexuality. The book focuses on the blues tradition, but recognizes the intertwining nature of music at the turn of the century, and also traces the way in which musical trends influence and become part of an intertextual conversation with other forms of expression. The title also captures the explicitly racial nature of the subject matter, pertaining as it does specifically to African American music. Tracy's book aims to chart the emergence and influence of the blues on literature and other media through the 1920s, and covers as much as possible in this 500-page book. Tracy notes specifically the way in which the blues affirms and privileges orality over textuality in both music and its influence over the written word. Overall, Tracy makes the case for social, cultural, aesthetic, and cross-racial contexts and influences between the blues tradition and literature during this decade. Tracy aims to identify the elements that can be traced to a blues tradition, whether they are conscious or unconscious uses of the blues as an aesthetic. Tracy is careful to qualify that the blues is not simply an emotional state, although it is that too, but rather that, when we refer to 'the blues', an entire cultural, historical, and racial creative expression is being transmitted, one that is specifically rooted in an experience and memory of slavery. The book is a comprehensive study of the mutual influence and expression of blues in music and literature throughout the 1920s.

Robert E. Crafton begins *The African American Experience in Crime Fiction: A Critical Study* by addressing the critical lack of inclusion in education wherein ethnic voices are still considered new, and the experiences that they write about remain wholly unfamiliar to the dominant white American population, despite forty years of integration in American schools. Crafton moves to detail the way in which black crime fiction as an intersection of pop culture and minority experience provides a medium and entry point for multi-ethnic studies for students, and so he details the emergence of murder mystery in African American literature from the early twentieth century to the present day. Crafton views each of the works studied as a historical artefact that expresses the prevailing anxieties and prejudices that African Americans have faced at various times—legal, medical, educational, literary, and cultural. Spanning 2001 to 2014, Crafton's study includes works by Stephen L. Carter, Walter Mosley, Rudolph Fisher, Chester Himes, Pauline Hopkins, Ishmael Reed, and John Edward Bruce, among others.

Leslie Larkin's *Race and the Literary Encounter: Black Literature from James Weldon Johnson to Percival Everett* addresses not only the representation of black people, but also the reception of that representation; Larkin's critical discussion encompasses reader-response and reader reception studies, as well as poststructural theory. Larkin uses works that have stirred controversy in order to understand how literary reception works as a site of racial formation in relation to reader agency. Larkin claims that contemporary black literature is capable of articulating strategies for reading race and imagining the reading subject—in other words that texts are agents that engage readers, and that the works should be analysed as performative subjects rather than static objects, and likewise that readers are agents, too, rather than passive receptors. Larkin notes that reading itself has always been a sign of outlaw freedom in that reading was prohibited amongst slave populations; therefore, the very act of reading and, by extension, writing is a performative and intentional act, and an act that writes out of the experience of race consciousness, that by virtue of its existence disrupts racial hierarchy and constructions of identity. Black writers challenge the notion that writing is race-neutral and that the reader is an abstracted subject. Larkin describes the

AMERICAN LITERATURE: THE TWENTIETH CENTURY 1143

texts discussed in the book as having been chosen because they offer reading as a predominant theme, address conflicts past and present in education and publishing, address the relationship between reading and freedom, position reading as an experience of racialization, and anticipate the experience of readers. Larkin aims to develop a theory and practice of critical reading from African American literature, introducing concepts such as speakerly reading, collaborative reading, and critical self-reflexivity, thereby challenging the longstanding notion that reading is private and solitary, and that the reader is unraced. Underpinning this theory is a desire to use the socializing force of literature for racial justice. Larkin offers a critical methodology that requires both the performativity of literature and the agency of readers to meet in the encounter of literature. This methodology is outlined as comprising three components: that the politics of reading and literacy is a prominent theme in black literary criticism; that the tradition possesses a wealth of aesthetic and performative strategies capable of intervening in scenes of reading that are also scenes of racialization; and that African American literature is in a unique position to offer a theory of reader ethics. To develop this theory and methodology, Larkin uses works by James Weldon Johnson, Zora Neale Hurston, Ralph Ellison, Sapphire and Percival Everett, Jamaica Kincaid, and Toni Morrison.

Bernard A. Drew describes his book *Black Stereotypes in Popular Series Fiction, 1851–1955: Jim Crow Era Authors and Their Characters* as an examination of popular, humorous American literature featuring continuing black characters written by white authors for periodicals and newspapers in the late Jim Crow era. Drew asserts that these stories were racist, featuring denigrating stereotypes of black Americans, created in ways that comforted white readers, who felt reassured by the stereotypes that reinforced views that blacks were inferior, bolstering what Drew refers to as Jim Crow etiquettes. Drew relates that characters were depicted as subhuman—stripped of masculinity or femininity, mocked, spoofed, and generally of a clownish nature. Drew explains that his purpose in performing this study was to examine the way in which early twentieth-century depictions of black Americans have impacted ongoing race relations and characterizations of blacks in popular culture. Drew studies 101 writers and artists, twenty-two closely. Drew cites the affordable proliferation of paper periodicals, and the way in which syndicated regional newspapers carried stories from further afield, and how pulp paper magazines were the vehicles through which the serial stories depicting scenes of local colour, black comedic characters, and the like were able to spread nationally, putting readers who might not otherwise have sought out fiction about black Americans in touch with the characterization. Drew sees the tradition of the black comedic figure as growing out of the Civil War era and emancipation as a way to dampen white fears of freed black people and neutralize white fear over their growing list of rights by denigrating the figure in other ways, such as through caricature and comedy. However, continued depiction of black people as poorly educated, superstitious, lazy, conniving, lustful, and untrustworthy worked to bolster white superiority and ensure that Jim Crow laws kept black Americans in low positions. Drew addresses the use and abuse of 'dialect' as both a tool for claiming language (by writers such as Hurston and Hughes) and a way to reinforce negative stereotypes of Southern blacks, and provides careful analysis through numerous examples. Drew's analysis draws links between the evolution of these serial publications and the evolving situation of segregation and race relations in the United States through the post-Civil War period and the Jim Crow era to the civil rights era. While Drew offers a thorough discussion, he concludes his study by asserting that these white writers who featured comedic and stereotypical black characters in serial publications did little to advance black literature; while these stories did not overtly incite violence, their passivity reinforced the worst stereotypes and bolstered white feelings of superiority.

Inspired by Richard Wright's poem 'The F.B. Eye Blues', William J. Maxwell's *F.B. Eyes: How J. Edgar Hoover's Ghostreaders Framed African American Literature* begins by examining the way in which the FBI's attempt at blackmailing Martin Luther King was actually a larger, more calculated attempt at undermining the Civil Rights Movement and black American writers in general, discrediting the movement through infiltration and blackmail. Moreover, Maxwell asserts that FBI harassment of black political leaders was linked to a deeper white fear of black writing. Maxwell's book examines public documents written by African American writers and FBI literary commentary to discern and critique the depth of contact between these two groups. In order to carry out this analysis, Maxwell examines multiple declassified FBI files on various authors and thus is able to establish the extent of the influence that Afro-modernist writing had in America, as well as the extent to which this writing was viewed as threatening to the state, or to the current state of white–black relations. The book is fascinating mediation on the relationship between literature's disruptive and revolutionary potential and government forces keen to contain agitation and disruption.

Carter Mathes's *Imagine the Sound: Experimental African American Literature after Civil Rights* explores the expression of radical thought in the post-civil rights era, looking at the literary creations and manipulations of sound by writers who seek to tap into African American cultural and political identity that is consciously post-civil rights. Mathes examines sonic effects and states, noting how they work to bridge the aural and literary, and the political dimensions that inform this literature. In privileging sound, Mathes seeks to illuminate the way in which categories such as rationality, progress, and liberty align with legislated civil rights-era equality as espoused by the state. Mathes sees sound as a useful entry point into what would be categorized as black postmodern literature, a category that Mathes feels is insufficient to encapsulate the breadth of activity. For Mathes, sound represents a useful point of entry for analysing experience of black consciousness; sound offers artists a valuable tool for disrupting state processes and racial formations of identity, fusing the sensory and the political and challenging white supremacy. Unlike words, Mathes argues, sound offers a means for black artists to challenge homogenizing logics that inform institutions through their very nature. Sound betrays the illusion of pluralism to reveal the true nature of a state as racialized, according to Mathes. While this use of sound can be traced to pre-Civil War enslavement, during which black slaves used aural expression for communication and resistance, identity formation and solidarity, post-civil rights-era uses of aurality reflect a desire to envision alternative configurations of subjectivity outside mainstream movements. Mathes offers discussion of Amiri Baraka, Henry Dumas, Arry Neal, James Baldwin, Toni Cade Bambara, and Gayl Jones as exemplary of the sonic culture born of the jazz era and the post-Civil Rights Movement. Moreover, Mathes establishes a connection between musical experimentation and literature and radical ideas of black consciousness and resistance.

Mary Helen Washington begins her book *The Other Blacklist: The African American Literary and Cultural Left of the 1950s* by positioning the discussion in the convergence of Cold War politics and racial integration in the 1950s, asserting that it was an era that was an anti-black period underwritten by fragile white tolerance and black invisibility, a time during which blacks policed blacks for 'acting black', lest they draw attention to themselves. Washington uses personal anecdotes to establish the way in which animosity to civil rights was an undercurrent in the US Cold War era, pushing many activists towards communism as the antithesis of white supremacy. Moreover, agencies like the FBI determined that anyone agitating for racial equality must also be a communist sympathizer, so that people like Richard Wright and even James Baldwin were considered dangerous communist agitators as civil rights work was seen as a sign of disloyalty. Washington's argument that the Cold War was a black–red war counters popular conceptions that the Cold War was white in the national imaginary: white America versus red Soviet Union. Washington asserts that nearly every black writer from the 1940s and 1950s was blacklisted because of real or imagined ties to communist or leftist organizations, yet the left wing tends to signify a white history and black absence. What is often overlooked is the fact that leftist organizations were amongst the most racially integrated groups at the time. Washington's book is a retrieval project wherein she seeks to highlight the often overlooked work of black activists in the union and labour organizations, the leftist poets and writers, thereby revealing important facts about the Communist Party's stance on race, and restoring black contributions to these counter-movements. After establishing a clear relationship between communist and labour organizations and black American participation, Washington turns her attention to the relationship between the black left and African American literature. In so doing, Washington seeks to rehabilitate the role of leftist politics in the formation of the black literary canon through the first half of the twentieth century, arguing that it is not sufficient to label the works from the period as merely realist, naturalist, or modernist without acknowledging the role of the left in that formation. Washington goes so far as to charge that there was an intentional attempt to distance Cold War writers from their leftist participation, a move which Washington believes dismisses the social consciousness of the literature. Washington's book proposes a counternarrative that reinserts the black left movement and participation in the literary history of the African American canon. Washington focuses on Lloyd L. Brown, Charles White, Alice Childress, Gwendolyn Brooks, Frank London Brown, and Julian Mayfield.

Judith Madera's *Black Atlas: Geography and Flow in Nineteenth-Century African American Literature* examines the way in which place is a space that is generated not simply by geography but also by participation, about how places are used and with whom they are shared. According to Madera, place is semiotic and material. Focusing initially on African American literature from 1849 to 1900, Madera works towards the Reconstruction period, citing the unsettling of history as it pushes against place. Madera makes an argument for the organization of geographical meaning as arranged by African American literature. Madera asserts that black writers had to overwrite white geographical boundaries, reterritorializing the space that white discourse sought to contain. Rather than simply mapping space, Madera suggests that mid-nineteenth-century African American writing maps subjectivity. Using concepts of deterritorialization, Madera demonstrates how the literature of black flow, as she explains, is the speech or movement of culture and capital through space. Madera points to the creative potential of deterritorialization, the decoding and recoding of dominant structures to better express and disrupt racist structures of confinement and reclaim them on their own terms. Madera locates narrative strategies in African American literature that use space as a location for dissension, not merely reactive, but productive, purposeful, a type of aesthetics. For Madera, place offers opportunities for creative strategies, and highlights space not simply as cartography, but as a productive receptacle of memory, experience. Madera emphasizes the difference between space as freedom and space as enclosure, and the way that narrative can challenge the geography of both place and space by offering counternarratives, reconfiguring it often against the dominant discourse that defined it in the first place. For Madera, nineteenth-century African American literature is geographical, centring as it does on debates about free soil, regionalist scales of production, Indian deterritorialization, internal diasporas, colour line spatialities, pan-American expansionism, and hemispheric circuitry; however, it is also working to defamiliarize the dominant delineations of these concepts by reconfiguring through difference in signification. Finally, Madera asserts that the black geographies that are produced in this literature offer possibility.

Nadia Ellis explains that her book *Territories of the Soul: Queered Belonging in the Black Diaspora* is about examining queer diasporic space because the space in which Caribbean and African American artists engage in black aesthetics is an intersection between queerness and diaspora, a horizon of possibility, a sense of insufficiency in existing modes of belonging being challenged, and the elusiveness of new forms. It is a longing for an outside— outside traditional geography, politics and genealogy, chronology, and spatiality. Ellis admits that the authors who occupy a queer diasporic space are not numerous; however, theorizing their particular aesthetics and contribution is enlightening in understanding the art of alternatives. Ellis's book is a theoretical exploration that at once uses and challenges traditional theories of both queerness and diaspora, working at the intersection in order to elucidate the longings of writers to belong elsewhere, what Ellis describes as both an affinity and a desire for separation. Ellis focuses on the writings of C.L.R. James, George Lamming, James Baldwin, Andrew Salkey, Nathaniel Mackey, and Burning Spear. Ellis explains that each chapter is intended to effect a consideration of eccentric, troubling, or failed attempts to create diasporic communities that aim for something better. Ellis links the notion of the territory of the soul—the interior space of the art, culture, and music of black subjects—with queered forms of identification, which for Ellis are found on the horizon of possibility, an elsewhere of imaginative possibility belonging to a diasporic elsewhere.

## 7. Native Writing

The signal work of 2015 is the publication of the *Final Report of the Truth and Reconciliation Commission of Canada* in six volumes. It is the product of a six-year investigation of the residential school system for Indigenous children as part of Canada's Aboriginal policy, which is acknowledged in the opening paragraph of the first volume as a policy of 'cultural genocide' (p. 1). Across more than a century, approximately a third of Indigenous children were incarcerated in the residential school system with limited parental access. They experienced profound damage to their cultural heritage, many were sexually and physically abused, and mortality rates were greatly increased. The fourth volume, *Missing Children and Unmarked Burials*, details the extent of recorded and unrecorded deaths—for a third of the confirmed deaths from school or government records, the student's name was not recorded, for a quarter the gender was not recorded, and without a policy for the return of the body to the home community, many of the school cemeteries were abandoned or built over. Notably, the Truth and Reconciliation Commission was mandated on the basis of the Indian Residential Schools Settlement Agreement in 2006, the largest class action settlement in the history of Canada. As a document of cultural damage and historical recuperation, and as a call for reconciliation, the materials will be important to anyone at work on Native literatures of North America or indigeneity in general, as well as those at work on Native American literature of nations bisected by the Canada–United States border. The complete six volumes are published by McGill-Queen's University Press, but are also in the public domain and distributed freely under a creative commons licence through the National Centre for Truth and Reconciliation out of the University of Manitoba (http://nctr.ca). Only the first volume as published by Lorimer was received for review, *Honouring the Truth, Reconciling for the Future*, but the electronic editions have also been reviewed. These include six further volumes in addition to those mentioned: *The History, Part 1, Origins to 1939*; *The History, Part 2, 1939 to 2000*; *The Inuit and Northern Experience*; *The Métis Experience*; *The Legacy*; and *Reconciliation*; as well as the shorter *What We Have Learned: Principles of Truth and Reconciliation*. While the reports are formal documents with particular emphasis on government policy and law, they extensively incorporate survivors' narratives, actions to preserve linguistic and cultural heritage in both Canada and the United States, educational policy reforms, and comparative analyses of similar programmes in relation to Indigenous populations around the world. The forced use of English and prohibition against Indigenous languages, the separation of children from family, and the severing of cultural traditions are detailed across each volume. Direct references to literary works are rare, but the historical materials and personal narratives are directly relevant to literary studies. Given the free public access and the absence of a comparable report for the Native American boarding schools through the Bureau of Indian Affairs, which share many traits with Canada's, the Truth and Reconciliation Commission Reports are ideal for classroom use, both as historical documents and as ancillary resources for literary works that depict the residential school system or its consequences. The companion volume, *A Knock on the Door: The Essential History of Residential Schools from the Truth and Reconciliation Commission of Canada, Edited and Abridged* (UManitobaP [2016]) suggests such uses and will be reviewed next year.

The critical edition of Mini Aodla Freeman's *Life among the Qallunaat* continues the University of Manitoba Press's First Voices, First Texts series, edited by Warren Cariou, the first of which was Anahareo's *Devil in Deerskins: My Life with Grey Owl*, edited by Sophie McCall (UManitobaP [2014]; reviewed in *YWES* 95[2016]). The text is edited by Keavy Martin, Julie Rak, and Norma Dunning, and opens with an interview with Freeman by Martin as well as a map of James Bay. The text explains life among non-Inuit westerners, the 'Qallunaat', in short fragments or chapters, some of several pages and others of only a paragraph, much like a memoir or diary entries except here with the added dimension of explaining cultural difference. This makes it less narrative-driven than Mitiarjuk Nappaaluk's *Sanaaq: An Inuit Novel* (UManitobaP [2014]; reviewed in *YWES* 95[2016]) but akin in references, their sense of orality, and storytelling, although the subjectivity expressed in the two works is very different, especially the memoir form that Freeman develops. The 'Afterword' by Rak, Martin, and Dunning provides both the publication and reception history of the book and a helpful explanation of the rationale for its reissue. The historical contextualization of the narrative for travel among the Qallunaat by Inuit of James Bay, such as for treatment of pulmonary tuberculosis (10 per cent of the eastern Arctic Inuit by 1957) and in the shadow of the residential school system, is particularly important. A closing comment that half the original publication's print run (more than 3,000 copies) was purchased and then kept in storage by the Department of Indian and Northern Affairs is far more suggestive than the editors argue (p. 274), seemingly intentionally so, and it clearly impacted the availability of the text to readers at the height of its publicity. For classroom use, reading the 'Afterword' would productively precede reading the text, and the documentary film *Nunaaluk: A Forgotten Story* is noted several times for its images of the author. This edition of *Life among the Qallunaat* also details the restoration of altered or cut sections of the text from the original typescript, which was done with Freeman's assistance.

Robert Alexander Innes and Kim Anderson's edited collection, *Indigenous Men and Masculinities: Legacies, Identities, Regeneration*, carries on the discussions seen last year in *Masculindians: Conversations about Indigenous Manhood*, edited by Sam McKegney (UManitobaP [2014]; reviewed in *YWES* 95[2016]). Where McKegney emphasized a conversational series of engagements, Innes and Anderson take a more formal approach with social-scientific content. They open the volume by carefully distinguishing masculinities as understood through an intersectional methodology from the various men's movements. The emphasis across the chapters is clearly on the intersection of Eurocentric, patriarchal norms imposed by settler colonialism on Indigenous cultural practices and the concomitant contradictions experienced within that population. Movingly, they open with gestures to reconciliation and the recognition of violence against women, or at least the opening of dialogue around missing and murdered Indigenous women, while at the same time pointing to the very high levels of violence and homicide experienced by Indigenous men in comparison to white women. Hence, the perpetuation of a mainstream cultural mythos of Indigenous men as victimizers rather than victims (even if Indigenous men are most frequently victims of Indigenous men in homicides), or as protectors rather than those who are in need of protection, reflects imposed colonial norms of masculinity that operate hegemonically. The first section of the book is composed of four chapters that emphasize theoretical approaches to understanding masculinity, and all four tacitly adopt a performative understanding of gender. The second section of four chapters covers representations of Indigenous masculinities in the arts. Lisa Tatonetti's '"Tales of Burning Love": Female Masculinity in Contemporary Native Literature' opens with Judith Halberstam and Judith Butler rethought through Craig Womack's work, eventually to approach Leslie Marmon Silko and particularly Louise Erdrich's *The Beet Queen* (HC [1986]). This leads her through the discussion of Erdrich to argue that female masculinities in Indigenous literatures disrupt the Western normativity imposed as part of the colonial legacy, which is further developed by the addition of affect theory and Two-Spirit histories. Niigaanwewidam James Sinclair's chapter, 'Oshiki Ishkode, New Fire', follows, and demonstrates a storytelling tradition rich in implications for the discussion of masculinities across the book (indirectly arguing for the vital productive possibilities of storytelling as a positive contribution to academic projects such as this, particularly its capacity to recuperate those relations and subjectivities elided by scholarly enterprise). The third section focuses on lived Indigenous masculinities, and the final, fourth, section of the book returns to the thematic of conversation seen in McKegney. The fourteenth chapter of the book is in this final section and brings together the novelists Richard Van Camp and Daniel Heath Justice, the prose writer Warren Cariou, and the poet Gregory Scofield in conversation with McKegney. Their discussions inform their works as well as the themes of the book as a whole. Each writer talks about coming to understand masculinity, most frequently in relation to matriarchal elders or parents, and the social demands of masculinity in different cultural environments. While they do not specifically address their own writing, the strong female figures discussed by Van Camp, Scofield, and Justice are connected with their creative works, in particular *The Lesser Blessed* (D&M [1996]), *I Knew Two Métis Women* (Polestar Press [1999]), and the series *The Way of Thorn and Thunder*, which is now available in a single volume (UNMP [2011]) respectively. Cariou presents a contrast with his father's influence and social role as well, which stands in relation to his memoir *Lake of the Prairies* (Doubleday [2002]).

A major critical intervention in 2015 comes in Marieke Neuhaus's *The Decolonizing Poetics of Indigenous Literatures*, which follows on her linked project, *'That's Raven Talk': Holophrastic Readings of Contemporary Indigenous Literatures* (URegP [2011]). The reading of poetics here centres on holophrasis in contemporary Indigenous literatures in conjunction with arguments about Indigenous languages perhaps most familiar to readers through Ngũgĩ wa Thiong'o's *Decolonising the Mind: The Politics of Language in African Literature* (HeinemannC [1986]) and Chinua Achebe's 'Politics and Politicians of Language in African Literature' collected in his *The Education of a British-Protected Child: Essays* (Knopf [2009] 96–106). Where their general argument is over the legacy of decolonization in the subsequent language of a national literature, Neuhaus seems to pointedly avoid discussing their work in order to assert the legacy of Indigenous languages in the poetics of contemporary writing and even Indigenous use of colonial languages. The holophrase is her most striking example. Most typically, a holophrase occurs when a single word stands in for a complete phrase or sentence, or a complex concept, but Neuhaus means the more nuanced challenge of a mother tongue or cultural context in which the complex grammar of a complete statement can be expressed in a single agglutinative expression, such as in her example from the opening page, 'the Plains Cree word ki-nohte-h-âcimo-stâ-tinâwâw, which translates as "I want to tell you folks a story"' (p. 1). Her contention, richly traced through several literary examples and assembled in an appendix of phrases in English reflecting holophrastic statements in Indigenous languages, is that this tradition manifests in the poetics and cultural foci of Indigenous literatures. Her reading of Richard Van Camp's *The Lesser Blessed* (D&M [1996]), for instance, moves through relational word bundles that emerge from a holophrastic oral tradition as a way of accessing the healing narrative at work as a return to Dogrib culture. The poetics of the relational word bundles in this case draws attention to the thematics of the novel and encourages a hermeneutical reading attentive to recurrence and the transformation of the images of trauma into images of recuperation. The first three chapters can stand on their own to outline a reading method, here set as a group to form a primer on holophrastic reading, and the second chapter, 'Holophrastic Reading: A Heuristic' (pp. 31–56), may be particularly useful as an excerpt. The index has a number of omissions—Pauline Wakeham and Eden Robinson appear a number of times but are not listed—but this is a relatively minor difficulty since it relates mainly to passing references to authors in the opening theoretical chapters and to critics whom one might not expect to be indexed at all (hence an incomplete set of references is not especially problematic). The close of each chapter includes suggestions for further reading, and while the book makes a clear critical argument, this shows its deep value for the classroom and teaching. Although it is not presented as such, the final two chapters also make a critical gesture towards cosmopolitan and nationalist paradigms in Indigenous studies, and the suggestions for further reading are the most detailed of the book, suggesting that the ethical and critical concerns here are at the heart of the project's purpose even though it most prominently features its methodology. Neuhaus seems to deliberately avoid gestures to arguments over language and national literature familiar through Ngũgĩ and

Achebe, but methodologically this is suggestive, and could bring her work into conversation with Glen Sean Coulthard's *Red Skin, White Masks* (UMinnP [2014]; reviewed in *YWES* 95[2016]) and Sean Kicummah Teuton's *Red Land, Red Power* (DukeUP [2008]).

Arnold Krupat edited *Companion to James Welch's The Heartsong of Charging Elk*, which will be essential to teachers and students responding to Welch's seminal work. Three of the eleven chapters have previously appeared in print, so there is much new material here as well as an introduction, three interviews, and an excerpt from Welch's *The Marseilles Grace*. The writing is highly accessible and introduces key concepts of indigeneity, Indigenous literary studies, and historical context for the work that will benefit teachers approaching the novel or the Native American Renaissance in general. Students can also access the materials in the book directly and with ease, even at an early undergraduate level. Arnold Krupat's 'Issues of Identity' is helpful and highly accessible, and Craig Womack's following 'The Fatal Blow Job' narrates his personal response while first reading *The Heartsong of Charging Elk*, both admiring and being disturbed by the work. The honesty of his discussion of homophobia in the novel is paired with the importance of its depiction of the Lakota adventurer. Womack makes several viscerally striking critical turns in the chapter while retaining a prose style and mode of discourse accessible to any reader, which is very effective in his unpacking of Romanticism and irony. A further chapter by Krupat follows Womack's, and closes the collection: 'History, Language, and Culture in James Welch's *The Heartsong of Charging Elk*'. The repetition of some historical materials indicates the intended excerptable nature of the chapters for the classroom. This will be a necessary resource, and it may be hoped a paperback edition will come available in the future.

Gabrielle L'Hirondelle Hill and Sophie McCall edit contributions of artists and writers in *The Land We Are: Artists and Writers Unsettle the Politics of Reconciliation* to assert independence from demands for reconciliation between Indigenous people and settler colonialism. The project was financially supported by the Truth and Reconciliation Commission of Canada (discussed above) and focuses its critique on the politics of recognition as a product of liberalism, a republican form of individualism that locates claims and reconciliation under the purview of the nation state. That is, formal policies of reconciliation are here understood as a strategy for containing and delegitimizing forms of activism that resist the settler colonial state, or alternatively see reconciliation as a process of recognition without redress, and accommodation only through Indigenous integration. The chapters are in four distinct sections: the first focuses on the city of Vancouver and neoliberalism, the second takes up the strategies of apology as political reconciliation, the third concentrates on aporias of colonial narratives, and the fourth is dedicated to decolonizing pedagogies, performances, and artistic practices. The book is richly illustrated in colour and frequently makes use of different colours of ink for the body of the text and the integration of visual cues into the textual materials themselves. Clifford E. Trafzer's *A Chemehuevi Song: The Resilience of a Southern Paiute Tribe* is a largely historical and anthropological study of the Chemehuevi of the Twenty-Nine a Palms tribe of southern

California with an extensive study of the role of song. The opening gesture is to Chemehuevi songs as a living tradition, strikingly the public sharing of several songs of mourning (Salt Songs) following the terrorist attacks of 11 September 2001. The discussion emphasizes both the sharing of the songs as way of perpetuating the living culture from one generation to the next and connecting to the contemporary world and American identity. The first five chapters, after the foreword and introduction, concentrate on a historical recuperation of the Chemeheuvi experience, primarily of the nineteenth century. The sixth chapter opens at the turn of the century and Twenty-Nine Palms Chemehuevi with the murder of (and limited information about) William Mike by Willie Boy. This prompted the Office of Indian Affairs to relocate the people to the Cabazon Reservation, which broke many cultural traditions, in particular hunting and their ties to space, further prompting them to seek wage labour and employment. The closing seventh chapter emphasizes the preservation and revitalization of Chemeheuvi culture and traditions through ethnogenesis, or the process of coming into an ethnic identity in the new social and material context, including socialization and upbringing in relation to other groups, such as the Cahuilla, which caused language deterioration. The relationship between revitalization and education is clearly outlined here, with self-determination, regaining material artefacts of the culture, and linguistically and culturally relevant education programming playing central roles.

The biography of Clyde Warrior adds an important history to the Red Power movement. Paul R. McKenzie-Jones recounts first discovering Warrior in his graduate studies in history, and *Clyde Warrior: Tradition, Community, and Red Power* shows this historical approach to biography thoroughly, as well as the inextricable overlapping of community and history in Warrior's life. The opening gesture of the biography is to place Warrior in the context of the Cold War and the Black Power movement, although McKenzie-Jones stresses that this was not a one-directional influence as the limited scholarly work might suggest. He also points to Warrior's willingness to draw on Cold War cultural movements from different Indigenous and decolonizing movements in order to focus the early thinking of Red Power. He is also overt in showing his reliance on and attempts to develop a more complete historical context for Warrior in relation to earlier works, such as Cobb's *Native Activism in Cold War America: The Struggle for Sovereignty* (UKanP [2008]) and Bradley G. Shreve's *Red Power Rising: The National Indian Youth Council and the Origins of Native Activism* (ND [2011]). The first chapter is a Ponca history that materially positions Warrior's life as a consequence of the history of his community while also contextualizing his personal struggles within a history of conflict between assimilationist and nationalist movements. McKenzie-Jones also shows much sensitivity to Warrior's struggles with alcoholism, in later chapters detailing the difficulties he experienced moving between his community and the outside world with conflicted interests and pressures: 'As comfortable as Warrior felt in these circles, he was going back and forth between two worlds' (p. 153), with congressional hearings, graduate studies, and ceremonies in White Eagle, leading to time in rehab that used unacceptably degrading methods. A diagnosis of cirrhosis of the liver led to his death seventeen months later, aged only 28. Despite Warrior's early death,

McKenzie-Jones compellingly closes the biography with a chapter on his legacy in activism, education reforms, and his community. The biography draws extensively on interviews with Warrior's family and fellow-activists in the National Indian Youth Council. Its aim, to provoke further work on Warrior and to cement his importance to the Red Power movements and the intellectual development of Indigenous studies, is clear.

Jon Reyhner's edited collection *Teaching Indigenous Students: Honoring Place, Community, and Culture* opens with Reyhner and Navin Kumar Singh's chapter 'Overcoming the Legacy of Assimilationist Schooling', which examines colonialist assumptions in education that measure outcomes through assimilationist achievements. The focus is various approaches to reverse declining graduation rates for Indigenous youth in the United States by indigenizing the curriculum and making it more relevant to and culturally accessible by Indigenous youth, as well as by recognizing the need for linguistically appropriate curricula. The second chapter, 'The Continuum of Literacy in Native American Classrooms', is by Sheilah E. Nicholas and Teresa L. McCarty. They take up connected challenges to literacy by recognizing the role of socialization in linguistic interactions and the differences in literacy testing outcomes based on such interactions. By seeing literacy as a social and cultural practice, resolving the culturally inappropriate approaches in curricula offers the opportunity to improve student achievement. Reyhner and Ward Cockrum follow up, in 'Promoting Indigenous Literacy', and subsequent chapters turn to mathematics, the sciences, social sciences, music, and physical education before the book closes with two chapters on sustainability and immersion, followed by a series of appendices with suggested reading on literacy, sample lesson plans, resources, and advice for the production of instructional resources.

*Voices of Fire: Reweaving the Literary Lei of Pele and Hi'iaka* is a late arrival from 2014 by Ku'ualoha Ho'omanawanui. She considers the Kanaka Maoli literary traditions of Pele and Hi'iaka in what is the first book-length study of Indigenous Hawaiian literature. Pele is the deity of lava and Hi'aka is her younger sister, and the epic narratives about them have been translated, as Ho'omanawanui shows, as part of colonial expropriation and violence after the ceremonies that told their stories were suppressed. The crux of Ho'omanawanui's approach is to contextualize, across the first two chapters respectively, Hawaiian history and the formal and stylistic devices of traditional narratives. The third to fifth chapters take up the Pele and Hi'iaka narratives from 1860 to 1928 on the basis of their serial publication, which is partial, and of the archival recovery of manuscripts that record Indigenous Kanaka Maoli tellings. This leads to a discussion of Hawaiian literary nationalism, theorized significantly through Daniel Heath Justice's Indigenous literary nationalism. By setting aside the major translations as settler colonial displacements, Ho'omanawanui stresses how expressions of Indigenous nationalism surface in the surviving print and manuscript Pele and Hi'aka narratives in ways that show agency and women's knowledge as part of the community. The final chapter then turns to Pele and Hi'aka as inspirations for contemporary literary production in which recovery and retelling are a vital weaving together of poetics and politics. As oral narrative traditions bridge into written as well as Indigenous English-language tellings, Ho'omanawanui underscores their operation as a vehicle for conceiving the Hawaiian nation in fact and affect through cultural knowledge and the maintenance of community. In contemporary conditions, she shows how new poetics and English-language works by Kanaka Maoli continue to draw inspiration from Pele and Hi'aka for the same purposes of nationalism and cultural community. The obvious value of the excellent work here is establishing a context in which further scholarship will develop; but more, Ho'omanawanui has persuasively demonstrated a method for recuperating voices of dissent from among a wider community of Indigenous knowledge systems and nationalisms.

## 8. Latino/a, Asian American, and General Ethnic Writing

Insufficient materials were received from 2015 for distinct topical divisions in this section. Steven S. Lee's *The Ethnic Avant-Garde: Minority Cultures and World Revolution* appears in Columbia University Press's Modernist Latitudes series, edited by Jessica Berman and Paul K. Saint-Amour. Lee sets out to recuperate the bonds among ethnic or racial minority writers in the United States with the Soviet avant-garde in alliance for a revolutionary end to discrimination and transformation of US society. The ties of Harlem Renaissance writers to Soviet support and communism are already thoroughly documented, but Lee extends this through deep archival work on Russian records and writers as well as careful attention to form and technique in creative works. While Lee opens the book by recognizing that Soviet artistic innovation and anti-racism are both well-trod areas of scholarly work, the two together are less so and offer a productive tension between the cultivation and maintenance of tradition typically found in minority cultural products and the radically new of the avant-garde. Claude McKay and Langston Hughes attract Lee's most extensive attention, particularly Hughes's attachment to Vladimir Mayakovsky, but the study is wide-ranging and moves among the arts without being confined to literary studies. Lee also deftly avoids a 'partisan' reading, moving from the repeatedly dream-like vision of Soviet revolutions in society and the arts experienced by minority writers in the United States to the disillusionment with Stalinism and the Cold War, or what he calls via Richard Wright the horror and glory of communism. As Lee explains, the origins of the project in a study of the forced removal of Koreans from the Russian Far East to Central Asia prompted his vision of the multinationalist nature of the Soviet avant-garde and its meaning to American writers. The closing discussion of Karen Tei Yamashita's *I Hotel* moves through the end of the Cold War and revelations of the deep ethnic divisions in the former Yugoslavia and Soviet Union (waking from the previous multinationalist 'dream') to Maoism in the 1960s and 1970s as offering a continuing framework for revolution to those disillusioned with Moscow, although juxtaposed to Maxine Hong Kingston's anti-communism.

The path cut by Josephine Nock-Hee Park in *Apparitions of Asia* (OUP [2008]; reviewed in *YWES* 89[2010]) is developed by Audrey Wu Clark in *The*

*Asian American Avant-Garde: Universalist Aspirations in Modernist Literature and Art*, which asserts the vitality of modernism for studying Asian American literature prior to the 1965 Immigration Act and in particular during the Exclusion Era. Clark retraces the problematic reification of Asia as a static orientalist vision among several authors who were, while drawn to modernism's cosmopolitanism, also racialized as 'other' in the United States. Since this collective grouping of Asian American writers from diverse linguistic and cultural backgrounds did not have the unifying identity that can be ascribed to other movements such as the Harlem Renaissance, Clark established continuity through their experience of otherness and resentment of exclusion. In this, the emergence of an Asian American identity in the interwar years is made possible despite pre-dating the universalist movement after 1965 that brought a unifying sense of identity founded on political agency and a developed pan-ethnicity of Americanness. By dealing with several authors' engagement with American exceptionalism and failures of the 'American Dream', Clark unifies four chapters: the first on Sui Sin Far and Chinese American literature, the second on haiku and Japanese exclusion, the third on Indian and Korean American authors Dhan Gopal Mukerji and Younghill Kang (both first-generation immigrants), and Filipino American writing through Carlos Bulosan. The internalization of the orientalism of high modernists such as Pound, Eliot, Stein, and others is compelling as a lineage running through writing of the interwar and war years, and Clark's work closes by suggesting how extensive the scholarship yet to be done remains for Asian American literature prior to 1965, tellingly with a specific gesture (p. 173) to social realism and the political affiliations explored by Lee in *The Ethnic Avant-Garde*.

In *Salvage Work: U.S. and Caribbean Literatures amid the Debris of Legal Personhood*, Angela Naimou presents a timely and relentlessly searching examination of legal personhood. The broad scope here is the movement from legal fictions of personhood constructed as a response to slavery and its dialectical conflict with citizenship, which moves towards economic pressures on personhood of the contemporary Western world and global capitalism. By taking legal personhood as the debris or legacy of slavery, and relating this legal narrative to literary representations of slavery in contemporary writing, Naimou richly traces colonial paradigms at work today that compose the framework of global capital. Hence, salvaging identity and personhood in Caribbean literature, most strikingly via Derek Walcott's poetry, becomes a decolonizing process fraught with the conflation of waste and the marginalized who are to be salvaged or saved. The fissures between the 'person' and the 'human' as categories in liberalism and democratic traditions develop in each chapter, and the fourth chapter in particular makes the careful work of distinguishing the 'human' as a category placed over the 'person' in a universal understanding of rights that still bears the legacies of labour, gender, and race as social categories shaping the subject and all altered by migration in relation to the nation state under which personhood, rights, and the human are defined. By setting biopolitics and liberal humanism in conversation, Naimou provokes deeply here, and offers a revision of Giorgio Agamben's *Homo Sacer: Sovereign Power and Bare Life* (StanfordUP [1998]). Each of the four chapters takes a close focus on one or two authors but ranges widely. The first chapter takes up Francisco Goldman's *The Ordinary Seaman* and the trope of salvage from the introduction. The second explores Edwidge Danticat and Rosario Ferré, while the third takes on sanctuary in relation to personhood through Gayl Jones. The fourth chapter concerns John Edgar Wideman's *Fanon* as an attempt to construct personhood in a mobile form that evades legal powers of definition through prosopopoeia. The epilogue confronts neoliberal globalization and its damage to 'wasted' lives and the elision of discourses of rights produced by statelessness. This is a remarkable book made all the more urgent by the times in which it will be read.

In *The Autobiography of Citizenship: Assimilation and Resistance in U.S. Education* Tova Cooper draws out the relations among citizenship and populations for which Americanization and curricular innovation were as much oppressive as progressive. Indigenous and African Americans take up the majority of her focus across the first three chapters that make up the bulk of the project, with a fourth and fifth chapter each dedicated to Jewish immigrants and Emma Goldman's Modern School. The first two chapters concentrate on assimilationist education in the programme of American Indian boarding schools, and in this respect the methodology here would benefit from being read in conjunction with the *Final Report of the Truth and Reconciliation Commission of Canada*, reviewed above. Cooper locates assimilationist curricula in relation to understandings of republican individualism that are detached from community, tribe, language, and culture. In the first chapter, this is focused through Charles Alexander Eastman's *From the Deep Woods to Civilization* as a conflicted work between assimilation and resistance, at once used in curricula of the Assimilation Era for purposes of indoctrinating consent while at the same time resisting forms of subjectivity divorced from Indigenous cultural identity. The second chapter continues to Frances Benjamin Johnston as a photographer and superintendent of the Indian boarding schools, in particular her photographs of the Hampton Institute that educated both Indigenous and African Americans, thereby connecting with Booker T. Washington and Samuel Chapman Armstrong and W.E.B. Du Bois. In this, Johnston's Social Darwinism and assimilationist ideology conflict with (or in a neoliberal sense compound) her other progressive views on education reform. Du Bois returns in greater detail in the third chapter's focus on cosmopolitanism and the conflict between cultural integration and education for citizenship for upward class mobility in conflict with cultural identity. The challenges of assimilation are again focal for the fourth chapter on east European Jewish immigrants, and Emma Goldman's Modern School closes the fifth chapter by showing more open forms of resistance to integrationist policies, although not exclusively in relation to immigrant populations here, instead focusing on working-class students. The final chapter emphasizes Goldman's interest in education policy and sexual liberation while minimizing (almost entirely excluding) her anarchism, which is here 'libertarian' and focused on the liberation of women from the nuclear family and patriarchal sexual mores through claiming control of reproduction.

Maria McGarrity's *Allusions in Omeros: Notes and Guide to Derek Walcott's Masterpiece* delivers on its titular promise. McGarrity opens with a detailed introduction outlining a summation of the importance of Walcott's *Omeros* and the function of allusion within it, with special attention to its influence on Caribbean writing and its approach to language. The introduction is divided into sections of a page or two each to address a specific element of *Omeros*, followed by chapters dedicated to each book of the poem. Each chapter contains an opening summary of the book of the poem, and there is a chapter-by-chapter annotation of allusions to the poem. The format of noting 'page number.line number' allows the reader to move between the Faber & Faber and Farrar, Strauss & Giroux editions of *Omeros*, and hence the book is the de facto scholarly apparatus for an annotated edition of the poem. Most annotations are brief, such as translations of terms from foreign languages, but some are longer than a full page. The book would be invaluable for students, teachers, and scholars alike when approaching Walcott's epic poem, and while an annotated edition is not available, this format is the 'next best' option, allowing the reader to set the two books side by side and move between them as needed, which is in many respects easier than the use of endnotes in a scholarly edition. The inclusion of a detailed index to the annotations is particularly helpful, allowing a backward reading of the poem from themes, references, and allusions as starting points to re-enter the original text at various points.

## Books Reviewed

Abbott, Carl. *Imagined Frontiers: Contemporary American and Beyond.* UOklaP. [2015] pp. 270. $19.95 ISBN 9 7808 0614 8366.

Aji, Hélène, Antoine Cazé, Agnès Derail-Imbert, and Clément Oudart. *H.D.'s Trilogy and Beyond.* PUPOuest. [2014] pp. 180. €12 ISBN 9 7828 4016 1936.

Anatol, Gizelle Liza. *Things That Fly in the Night: Female Vampires in Literature of the Circum-Caribbean and African Diaspora.* RutgersUP. [2015] pp. 312. $90 ISBN 9 7808 1356 5743.

Baker Houston A. Jr., and K. Merinda Simmons, eds. *The Trouble with Post-Blackness.* ColUP. [2015] pp. 288. $35 ISBN 9 7802 3116 9349.

Barnhisel, Greg. *Cold War Modernists: Art, Literature, and American Cultural Diplomacy.* ColUP. [2015] pp. 336. $40 ISBN 9 7802 3116 2302.

Baron, Cynthia. *Modern Acting: The Lost Chapter of American Film and Theatre.* Palgrave. [2015] pp. 300. £67 ISBN 9 7811 3740 6545.

Baumann, Walter, and William Pratt, eds. *Ezra Pound and London: New Perspectives.* AMS. [2015] pp. 213. $97.50 ISBN 9 7804 0465 5334.

Beaty, Bart. *Twelve Cent Archie.* RutgersUP. [2015] pp. 232. $26.95 ISBN 9 7808 1356 3848.

Bendixen, Alfred, and Stephen Burt, eds. *The Cambridge History of American Poetry.* CUP. [2015] pp. 1,326. £100 ISBN 9 7811 0700 3361.

Bennett, Eric. *Workshops of Empire: Stegner, Engle, and American Creative Writing During the Cold War.* UIowaP. [2015] pp. 232. $22.50 ISBN 9 7816 0938 3718.

Bennett, Tanya Long. 'I have been so many people': A Study of Lee Smith's Novels. UNGP. [2014] pp. 120. $29.95 9 7819 4077 1076.
Berlatsky, Noah. Wonder Woman: Bondage and Feminism in the Marston/ Peter Comics, 1941–1948. RutgersUP. [2015] pp. 264. $26.95 ISBN 9 7808 1356 4180.
Bilbro, Jeffrey. Loving God's Wildness: The Christian Roots of Ecological Fiction in American Literature. UAlaP. [2015] pp. 240. $54.95 ISBN 9 7808 1731 8974.
Black, Cheryl, and Jonathan Shandell, eds. Experiments in Democracy: Interracial and Cross-Cultural Exchange in American Theatre, 1912–1945. SIUP. [2015] pp. 320. $40 ISBN 9 7808 0933 4681.
Blanton, C.D. Epic Negation: The Dialectical Poetics of Late Modernism. OUP. [2015] pp. 384. $65 ISBN 9 7801 9984 4715.
Booker, M. Keith, ed. Comics through Time: A History of Icons, Idols, and Ideas, vols. 1–4. Greenwood. [2014]. pp. 1,921. $415 ISBN 9 7803 1339 7509.
Boyle, Brenda M., ed. The Vietnam War: Topics in Contemporary North American Literature. Bloomsbury. [2015] pp. 205. £21.99 ISBN 9 7814 7250 6269.
Breu, Christopher. Insistence of the Material: Literature in the Age of Biopolitics. UMinnP. [2014] pp. 264. $25 ISBN 9 7808 1668 9460.
Brienza, Casey. Manga in America: Transnational Book Publishing and the Domestication of Japanese Comics. Bloomsbury. [2015] pp. 245. $29.95 ISBN 9 7814 7259 5874.
Brigham, Ann. American Road Narratives: Reimagining Mobility in Literature and Film. UPVirginia. [2015] pp. 262. $29.50 ISBN 9 7808 1393 7502.
Brown, Kimberly Juanita. The Repeating Body: Slavery's Visual Resonance in the Contemporary. DukeUP. [2015] pp. 264. $89.95 ISBN 9 7808 2235 9098.
Brownie, Barbara, and Dannie Graydon. The Superhero Costume: Identity and Disguise in Fact and Fiction. Bloombsury. [2015] pp. 208. £19.99 ISBN 9 7814 7259 5935.
Bryant, Earle V., ed. Byline Richard Wright: Articles from the Daily Worker and New Masses. UPMissip. [2015] pp. 304. $60 ISBN 9 7808 2622 0202.
Budick, Emily Miller. The Subject of Holocaust Fiction. IndUP. [2015] pp. 250. $32 ISBN 9 7802 5301 6300.
Bunch Davis, Carol. Prefiguring Postblackness: Cultural Memory, Drama, and the African American Freedom Struggle of the 1960s. UPMissip. [2015] pp. 224. $65 ISBN 9 7814 9680 2989.
Burke, Liam. The Comic Book Film Adaptation: Exploring Modern Hollywood's Leading Genre. UPMissip. [2015] pp. 352. $60 ISBN 9 7816 2846 2036.
Cahn, Steven M., and Maureen Eckert, eds. Freedom and the Self: Essays on the Philosophy of David Foster Wallace. ColUP. [2015] pp. 179. $27 ISBN 9 7802 3116 1534.
Chambers, Matthew. Modernism, Periodicals, and Cultural Poetics. Palgrave. [2015] pp. 208. £55 ISBN 9 7811 3754 1352.
Clark, Audrey Wu. The Asian American Avant-Garde: Universalist Aspirations in Modernist Literature and Art. TempleUP. [2015] pp. 222. $84.50 ISBN 9 7814 3991 2263.

Clericuzio, Alessandro. *Tennessee Williams and Italy*. Palgrave. [2015] pp. 225. £66.99 ISBN 9 7833 1931 9261.

Cohn, Jesse. *Underground Passages: Anarchist Resistance Culture, 1848–2011*. AKP. [2014] pp. 421. £18 ISBN 9 7818 4935 2017.

Cooper, Tova. *The Autobiography of Citizenship: Assimilation and Resistance in U.S. Education*. RutgersUP. [2015] pp. 280. $90 ISBN 9 7808 1357 0150.

Cortsen, Rikke Platz, and Erin La Cour. *Comics and Power: Representing and Questioning Culture, Subjects and Communities*. CambridgeSP. [2015] pp. 385. £52.99 ISBN 9 7814 4387 0863.

Crafton, Robert E. *The African American Experience in Crime Fiction: A Critical Study*. McFarland. [2015] pp. 212. $29.95 ISBN 9 7807 8649 9380.

Cummings, Lindsay B. *Empathy as Dialogue in Theatre and Performance*. Palgrave. [2015] pp. 220. £63.99 ISBN 9 7811 3759 3252.

Darius, Julian. *Classics on Infinite Earths: The Justice League and DC Crossover Canon*. Sequart. [2015] pp. 428. US$19.99 ISBN 9 7819 4058 9107.

Davidson, Guy, and Nicola Evans, eds. *Literary Careers in the Modern Era*. Palgrave. [2015] pp. 214. £55 ISBN 9 7811 3747 8498.

Davis, Alex, and Lee M. Jenkins, eds. *A History of Modernist Poetry*. CUP. [2015] pp. 352. £65 ISBN 9 7811 0703 8677.

De Boever, Arne. *Narrative Care: Biopolitics and the Novel*. Bloomsbury. [2013] pp. 181. $100 ISBN 9 7814 4119 9992.

Den Dulk, Allard. *Existentialist Engagement in Wallace, Eggers, and Foer: A Philosophical Analysis of Contemporary American Literature*. Bloomsbury. [2015] pp. 301. $120 ISBN 9 7816 2892 3315.

Donahue, James J. *Failed Frontiersmen: White Men and Myth in Post-Sixties American Historical Romance*. UPVirginia. [2015]. pp. 222. $27.5 ISBN 9 7808 1393 6833.

Donald, James. *Some of These Days: Black Stars, Jazz, Aesthetics, and Modernist Culture*. OUP. [2015] pp. 280. $35 ISBN 9 7801 9935 4016.

Drew, Bernard A. *Black Stereotypes in Popular Series Fiction, 1851–1955: Jim Crow Era Authors and Their Characters*. McFarland. [2015] pp. 292. $55 ISBN 9 7807 8647 4103.

Duncan, Randy, Matthew J. Smith, and Paul Levitz. *The Power of Comics: History, Form, and Culture*. Bloomsbury. [2014] pp. 445. $29.95 ISBN 9 7814 7253 5702.

Ellis, Nadia. *Territories of the Soul: Queered Belonging in the Black Diaspora*. DukeUP. [2015] pp. 256. $84.95 ISBN 9 7808 2235 9159.

Entzminger, Betina. *Contemporary Reconfigurations of American Literary Classics: The Origin and Evolution of American Stories*. Routledge. [2013] pp. 242. £90 ISBN 9 7804 1553 9647.

Flack, Leah Culligan. *Modernism and Homer: The Odysseys of H.D., James Joyce, Osip Mandelstam, and Ezra Pound*. CUP. [2015] pp. 232. £67 ISBN 9 7811 0710 8035.

Freeman, Mini Aodla. *Life among the Qallunaat*. UManitobaP. [2015] pp. 264. $24.95 ISBN 9 7808 8755 7750.

Garrett, Leah. *Young Lions: How Jewish Authors Reinvented the War Novel*. NorthwesternUP. [2015] pp. 275. $34.95 ISBN 9 7808 1013 1750.

Gąsiorek, Andrzej. *A History of Modernist Literature*. Wiley. [2015] pp. 632. $99.95 ISBN 9 7814 0517 7160.

Gateward, Frances, and John Jennings, eds. *The Blacker the Ink: Constructions of Black Identity in Comics and Sequential Art*. RutgersUP. [2015] pp. 356. $90 ISBN 9 7808 1357 2345.

Gavaler, Chris. *On the Origin of Superheroes: From the Big Bang to Action Comics No. 1*. UIowaP. [2015] pp. 264. $18 ISBN 9 7816 0938 3817.

Gelpi, Albert. *American Poetry after Modernism: The Power of the Word*. CUP. [2015] pp. 308. £67 ISBN 9 7811 0702 5240.

Gibson, Mel. *Remembered Reading: Memory, Comics, and Post-War Constructions of British Girlhood*. LeuvenUP. [2015] pp. 272. $75 ISBN 9 7894 6270 0307.

Gifford, James. *In our time: The 1924 Text*. MVP. [2015] pp. ix + 27.

Gifford, James. *'In Our Time' and 'They All Made Peace—What Is Peace?': The 1923 Text*. MVP. [2015] pp. ix + 30.

Golston, Michael. *Poetic Machinations: Allegory, Surrealism, and Postmodern Poetic Form*. ColUP. [2015] pp. xvi + 247. $60 ISBN 9 7802 3116 4306.

Gordon, Jon. *Unsustainable Oil: Facts, Counterfacts and Fictions*. UAlbertaP. [2015] pp. 234. $45 ISBN 9 7817 7212 0363.

Hamilton, Cynthia S. *Sara Paretsky: Detective Fiction as Trauma Literature*. ManUP. [2015] pp. 190. £70 ISBN 9 7807 1909 6952.

Hamilton, Geoff. *The Life and Undeath of Autonomy in American Literature*. UPVirginia. [2014] pp. 152. $24.50 ISBN 9 7808 1393 5294.

Handley, Rich, and Joseph F. Berenato, eds. *The Sacred Scrolls: Comics on the Planet of the Apes*. Sequart. [2015] pp. 312. $16.99 ISBN 9 7819 4058 9114.

Harker, Jaime, and Cecilia Konchar Farr, eds. *This Book is an Action: Feminist Print Culture and Activist Aesthetics*. UIllP. [2015] pp. 250. $28 ISBN 9 7802 5208 1347.

Hayes, Kevin J., ed. *A History of Virginia Literature*. CUP. [2015] pp. xv + 420. £77 ISBN 9 7811 0705 7777.

Herlihy-Mera, Jeffrey, and Vamsi K. Koneru, eds. *Paris in American Literatures: On Distance as a Literary Resource*. FDUP. [2013] pp. 188. $39.99 ISBN 9 7816 1147 8105.

L'Hirondelle, Gabrielle, and Sophie McCall, eds. *The Land We Are: Artists and Writers Unsettle the Politics of Reconciliation*. Arbeiter. [2015] pp. 240. $24.95 ISBN 9 7818 9403 7631.

Ho'omanawanui, Ku'ualoha. *Voices of Fire: Reweaving the Literary Lei of Pele and Hi'iaka*. UMinnP. [2014] pp. 312. $75 ISBN 9 7808 1667 9218.

Hutchisson, James M. *Ernest Hemingway: A New Life*. PSUP. [2015] pp. 291. $38 ISBN 9 7802 7107 5341.

Innes, Robert Alexander, and Kim Anderson, eds. *Indigenous Men and Masculinities: Legacies, Identities, Regeneration*. UManitobaP. [2015] pp. 304. $27.95 ISBN 9 7808 8755 7903.

Irvine, Dean, and Smaro Kamboureli, eds. *Editing as Cultural Practice in Canada*. WLUP. [2015] pp. x + 294. $42.99 ISBN 9 7817 7112 1118.

Jarraway, David R. *Wallace Stevens among Others: Diva-Dames, Deleuze, and American Culture*. McG-QUP. [2015] pp. 332. $60 ISBN 9 7807 7354 6028.

Jenkins, Thomas E. *Antiquity Now: The Classical World in the Contemporary American Imagination*. CUP. [2015] pp. 253. $145.45 ISBN 9 7805 2119 6260.

Kalaidjian, Walter. *The Cambridge Companion to Modern American Poetry*. CUP. [2015] pp. 290. £52 ISBN 9 7811 0704 0366.

Kelly, Adam. *American Fiction in Transition: Observer-Hero Narrative, the 1990s, and Postmodernism*. Bloomsbury. [2013] pp. 147. $100 ISBN 9 7814 4111 2859.

Keniston, Ann. *Ghostly Figures: Memory and Belatedness in Postwar American Poetry*. UIowaP. [2015] pp. 228. $49.95 ISBN 9 7816 0938 3534.

Keren, Michael. *Politics and Literature at the Turn of the Millennium*. UCalgaryP. [2015] pp. 255. £24.95 ISBN 9 7815 5238 7993.

Klock, Geoff. *The Future of Comics, the Future of Men: Matt Fraction's Casanova*. Sequart. [2015] pp. 136. $12.99 ISBN 9 7819 4058 9084.

Krupat, Arnold. *Companion to James Welch's The Heartsong of Charging Elk*. UNebP. [2015] pp. xx + 279. $60 ISBN 9 7808 0325 4329.

Larkin, Leslie. *Race and the Literary Encounter: Black Literature from James Weldon Johnson to Percival Everett*. IUP. [2015] pp. 294. $80 ISBN 9 7802 5301 7581.

Lee, Steven S. *The Ethnic Avant-Garde: Minority Cultures and World Revolution*. ColUP. [2015] pp. 304. $60 ISBN 9 7802 3117 3520.

Lent, John A. *Asian Comics*. UPMissip. [2015] pp. 400. $60 ISBN 9 7816 2846 1589.

Li, Stephanie. *Playing in the White: Black Writers, White Subjects*. OUP. [2015] pp. 248. $65 ISBN 9 7801 9939 8881.

Lowinger, Kathy. *Give Me Wings: How a Choir of Former Slaves Took on the World*. Annick. [2015] pp. 148. $21.95 ISBN 9 7815 5451 7473.

Ludwig, Logan. *Moving Panels: Translating Comics to Film*. Sequart. [2015] pp. 144. $12.99 ISBN 9 7819 4058 9091.

Madera, Judith. *Black Atlas: Geography and Flow in Nineteenth-Century African American Literature*. DukeUP. [2015] pp. 312. $94.95 ISBN 9 7808 2235 7971.

Malewitz, Raymond. *The Practice of Misuse: Rugged Consumerism in Contemporary American Culture*. StanfordUP. [2014] pp. 227. $55 ISBN 9 7808 0479 1960.

Mandel, Naomi. *Disappear Here: Violence after Generation X*. OSUP. [2015] pp. 254. $54.95 ISBN 9 7808 1421 2868.

Marsh, Alec. *John Kasper and Ezra Pound: Saving the Republic*. Bloomsbury. [2015] pp. 272. £80 ISBN 9 7814 7250 8867.

Martin, Gretchen. *Dancing on the Color Line: African American Tricksters in Nineteenth-Century American Literature*. UPMissip. [2015] pp. 224. $65 ISBN 9 7814 9680 4150.

Mathes, Carter. *Imagine the Sound: Experimental African American Literature after Civil Rights*. UMinnP. [2015] pp. 264. $75 ISBN 9 7808 1669 3054.

Maus, Derek C., and James J. Donahue, eds. *Post-Soul Satire: Black Identity after Civil Rights*. UPMissip. [2015] pp. 342. pb $30 ISBN 9 7814 9680 4563.

Maxwell, Lauren Rule. *Romantic Revisions in Novels from the Americas*. PurdueUP. [2013] pp. 177. $45 ISBN 9 7815 5753 6419.

Maxwell, William J. *F.B. Eyes: How J. Edgar Hoover's Ghostreaders Framed African American Literature*. PrincetonUP. [2015] pp. 384. $29.95 ISBN 9 7806 9113 0200.

Mayer, John. *Steppenwolf Theatre Company of Chicago in Their Own Words*. Bloomsbury. [2015] pp. 249. £70 ISBN 9 7814 7423 9448.

McGarrity, Maria. *Allusions in Omeros: Notes and a Guide to Derek Walcott's Masterpiece*. UFlorP. [2015] pp. 240. $74.95 ISBN 9 7808 1306 1009.

McGuinness, Patrick. *Poetry and Radical Politics in Fin de Siècle France: From Anarchism to Action Française*. OUP. [2015] pp. x + 289. £55 ISBN 9 7801 9870 6106.

McGuire, Ian. *Richard Ford and the Ends of Realism*. UIowaP. [2015] pp. 128. $50 ISBN 9 7816 0938 3435.

McKenzie-Jones, Paul R. *Clyde Warrior: Tradition, Community, and Red Power*. UOklaP. [2015] pp. 256. $29.96 ISBN 9 7808 0614 7055.

McLoughlin, Kate, ed. *The Modernist Party*. EdinUP. [2015] pp. viii + 232. £70 ISBN 9 7814 7440 1418.

Mendes, Gabriel N. *Under the Strain of Color: Harlem's Lafargue Clinic and the Promise of an Antiracist Psychiatry*. CornUP. [2015] pp. xii + 196. $39.95 ISBN 9 7808 0145 3502.

Middleton, Peter. *Physics Envy: American Poetry and Science in the Cold War and After*. UChicP. [2015] pp. 272. $45 ISBN 9 7802 2629 0003.

Miller, W. Jason. *Origins of the Dream: Hughes's Poetry and King's Rhetoric*. UPFlorida. [2015] pp. 256. $34.95 ISBN 9 7808 1306 0446.

Moraru, Christian. *Reading for the Planet: Toward a Geomethodology*. UMichP. [2015] pp. 248. $39.95 ISBN 9 7804 7205 2790.

Mullen, Bill V. *Popular Fronts: Chicago and African-American Cultural Politics, 1935–46*. UIllP. [2015] pp. 272. $30 ISBN 9 7802 5208 1071.

Mullholland, Terri, and Nicole Sierra, eds. *Spatial Perspectives: Essays on Literature and Architecture*. Lang. [2015] pp. 258. £45 ISBN 9 7830 3431 7719.

Munro, Niall. *Hart Crane's Queer Modernist Aesthetic*. Palgrave. [2015] pp. 232. £58 ISBN 9 7811 3740 7757.

Murray, John A., ed. *Abbey in America: A Philosopher's Legacy in a New Century*. UNMP. [2015] pp. 218. $24.95 ISBN 9 7808 2635 5171.

Nadel, Ira B. *Cathay: Ezra Pound's Orient*. Penguin. [2015] pp. 1,024. £7.99 ISBN 9 7807 3439 9533.

Naimou, Angela. *Salvage Work: U.S. and Caribbean Literatures amid the Debris of Legal Personhood*. FordUP. [2015] pp. 320. $55 ISBN 9 7808 2326 4766.

Neuhaus, Mareike. *The Decolonizing Poetics of Indigenous Literatures*. URegP. [2015] pp. 295. $29.95 ISBN 9 7808 8977 3905.

Noble, Mark. *American Poetic Materialism from Whitman to Stevens*. CUP. [2015] pp. 238. £60 ISBN 9 7811 0708 4506.

Oudart, Clément, ed. *Traditions sur mesure: Exploration des poétiques expérimentales américaines de H.D. à Michael Heller / Tailor-Made Traditions: The Poetics of US Experimental Verse from H.D. to Michael Heller*. UMirail-ToulouseP. [2014] pp. 242. €22 ISBN 9 7828 1070 2930.

Parkinson, Gavin. *Surrealism, Science Fiction, and Comics.* LiverUP. [2015] pp. 288. £75 ISBN 9 7817 8138 1434.

Peaslee, Robert Moses, and Robert G. Weiner, *The Joker: A Serious Study of the Clown Prince of Crime.* UPMissip. [2015] pp. 288. $60 ISBN 9 7814 9680 7816.

Post, Jonathan F.S. *A Thickness of Particulars: The Poetry of Anthony Hecht.* OUP. [2015] pp. xviii + 294. £20 ISBN 9 7801 9966 0711.

Quinn, Justin. *Between Two Fires: Transnationalism and Cold War Poetry.* OUP. [2015] pp. 218. £55 ISBN 9 7801 9874 4436.

Rabaté, Jean-Michel. *1922: Literature, Culture, Politics.* CUP. [2015] pp. 286. £65 ISBN 9 7811 0704 0540.

Rankine, Claudia, Beth Loffreda, and Max King Cap, eds. *The Racial Imaginary: Writers on Race in the Life of the Mind.* Fence. [2015] pp. 256. $19.95 ISBN 9 7819 3420 0797.

Reyhner, Jon. *Teaching Indigenous Students: Honoring Place, Community, and Culture.* UOklaP. [2015] pp. 232 $24.95 ISBN 9 7808 0614 6997.

Richardson, Mark. *The Cambridge Companion to American Poets.* CUP. [2015] pp. 492. £49.99 ISBN 9 7811 0712 3823.

Robinson, Matte, and Demetres P. Tryphonopoulos, eds. *Hirslanden Notebooks: An Annotated Scholarly Edition.* ELS. [2015] pp. 158. $35 ISBN 9 7815 5058 3915.

Robolin, Stéphane. *Grounds of Engagement: Apartheid-Era African American and South African Writing.* UIllP. [2015] pp. 256. $45 ISBN 9 7802 5203 9478.

Ross, Michael L. *Designing Fictions: Literature Confronts Advertising.* McG-QUP. [2015] pp. 198. $24.95 ISBN 9 7807 7354 5366.

Rutledge Fisher, Rebecka. *Habitations of the Veil: Metaphor and the Poetics of Black Being in African American Literature.* SUNYP. [2014] pp. 442. $29.95 ISBN 9 7814 3844 9326.

Sanchez, Rebecca. *Deafening Modernism: Embodied Language and Visual Poetics in Twentieth-Century American Literature.* NYUP. [2015] pp. 240. $89 ISBN 9 7814 7982 8869.

Schelly, Bill. *Harvey Kurtzman: The Man Who Created Mad and Revolutionized Humor in America.* Fantagraphics. [2015] pp. 644. $34.99 ISBN 9 7816 0699 7611.

Schneider, Christian W. *Framing Fear: The Gothic Mode in Graphic Literature.* WVT. [2014] pp. 300. €35 ISBN 9 7838 6821 5113.

Schuster, Joshua. *The Ecology of Modernism: American Environments and Avant-Garde Poetics.* UAlaP. [2015] pp. 272. $39.95 ISBN 9 7808 1735 8297.

Scroggins, Mark. *Intricate Thicket: Reading Late Modernist Poetries.* UAlaP. [2015] pp. 304. $49.95 ISBN 9 7808 1735 8044.

Semrau, Janusz, and Marek Wilczyński, eds. *Image in Modern(ist) Verse.* Lang. [2015] pp. 170. £32 ISBN 9 7836 3165 6969.

Shackelford, Laura. *Tactics of the Human: Experimental Technics in American Fiction.* UMichP. [2014] pp. 265. $35 ISBN 9 7804 7205 2387.

Singleton, Jermaine. *Cultural Melancholy: Readings of Race, Impossible Mourning, and African American Ritual.* UIllP. [2015] pp. 168. $50 ISBN 9 7802 5203 9621.

Slovic, Scott, James E. Bishop, and Kyhl Lyndgaard, eds. *Current of the Universal Being: Explorations in the Literature of Energy*. TTUP. [2015] pp. 193. $39.95 ISBN 9 7808 9672 9285.

Stallings, L.H. *Funk the Erotic: Transaesthetics and Black Sexual Cultures*. UIllP. [2015] pp. 296. $95 ISBN 9 7802 5203 9591.

Starre, Alexander. *Metamedia: American Book Fictions and Literary Culture after Digitization*. UIowaP. [2015] pp. 310. $55 ISBN 9 7816 0938 3596.

Stevens, Lara. *Anti-War Theatre after Brecht*. Palgrave. [2015] pp. x + 224. £55 ISBN 9 7811 3753 8871.

Swindall, Lindsey R. *Paul Robeson: A Life of Activism and Art*. R&L. [2015] pp. 212. $19.95 ISBN 9 7814 4220 7943.

Tabbi, Joseph. *Nobody Grew But the Business: On the Life and Work of William Gaddis*. NorthwesternUP. [2015] pp. 255. $35 ISBN 9 7808 1013 1422.

Takeda, Noriko. *Translation as Oneself: The Re-creative Modernism in Stéphane Mallarmé's Late Sonnets, T.S. Eliot's Poems, and the Prose Poetry since Charles-Pierre Baudelaire*. Lang. [2014] pp. 119. £46 ISBN 9 7814 3312 4525.

Thomsen, Mads Rosendahl. *The New Human in Literature: Posthuman Visions of Changes in Body, Mind and Society after 1900*. Bloomsbury. [2013] pp. 258. $114 ISBN 9 7814 4118 3194.

Tracy, Steven C. *Hot Music, Ragmentation, and the Bluing of American Literature*. UAlaP. [2015] pp. 537. $64.95 ISBN 9 7808 1731 8659.

Traftzer, Clifford E. *A Chemehuevi Song: The Resilience of a Southern Paiute Tribe*. UWashP. [2015] pp. 328. $45 ISBN 9 7802 9599 4581.

Trexler, Adam. *Anthropocene Fictions: The Novel in a Time of Climate Change*. UPVirginia. [2015] pp. 260. $29.50 ISBN 9 7808 1393 6925.

Truth and Reconciliation Commission. *Final Report of the Truth and Reconciliation Commission of Canada, vol. 1: Summary: Honouring the Truth, Reconciling for the Future*. Lorimer. [2015] pp. 544. $22.95 ISBN 9 7814 5941 0671.

Truth and Reconciliation Commission. *Canada's Residential Schools: The History, Part 1, Origins to 1939: The Final Report of the Truth and Reconciliation Commission of Canada*, vol. 1. McG-QUP. [2015] pp. 978. $0 ISBN 9 7807 7359 8171.

Truth and Reconciliation Commission. *Canada's Residential Schools: The History, Part 2, 1939 to 2000: The Final Report of the Truth and Reconciliation Commission of Canada*, vol. 1. McG-QUP. [2015] pp. 978. $0 ISBN 9 7807 7359 8195.

Truth and Reconciliation Commission. *Canada's Residential Schools: The Inuit and Northern Experience: The Final Report of the Truth and Reconciliation Commission of Canada*, vol. 2. McG-QUP. [2015] pp. 276. $0 ISBN 9 7807 7359 8218.

Truth and Reconciliation Commission. *Canada's Residential Schools: The Métis Experience: The Final Report of the Truth and Reconciliation Commission of Canada*, vol. 3. McG-QUP. [2015] pp. 88. $0 ISBN 9 7807 7359 8232.

Truth and Reconciliation Commission. *Canada's Residential Schools: Missing Children and Unmarked Burials: The Final Report of the Truth and Reconciliation Commission of Canada*, vol. 4. McG-QUP. [2015] pp. 272. $0 ISBN 9 7807 7359 8256.

Truth and Reconciliation Commission. *Canada's Residential Schools: The Legacy: The Final Report of the Truth and Reconciliation Commission of Canada*, vol. 5. McG-QUP. [2015] pp. 392. $0 ISBN 9 7807 7359 8270.

Truth and Reconciliation Commission. *Canada's Residential Schools: Reconciliation: The Final Report of the Truth and Reconciliation Commission of Canada*, vol. 6. McG-QUP. [2015] pp. 296. $0 ISBN 9 7807 7359 8294.

Truth and Reconciliation Commission. *What We Have Learned: Principles of Truth and Reconciliation*. McG-QUP. [2015] pp. 193. $0 ISBN 9 7806 6002 0730.

Veggian, Henry. *Understanding Don DeLillo*. USCP. [2015] pp. 147. $39.95 ISBN 9 7816 1117 4441.

Vickroy, Laura. *Reading Trauma Narratives: The Contemporary Novel and the Psychology of Oppression*. UPVirginia. [2015] pp. 198. $24.5 ISBN 9 7808 1393 7380.

Wagner-Martin, Linda. *Barbara Kingsolver's World: Nature, Art, and the Twenty-First Century*. Bloomsbury. [2014] pp. 218. $29.95 ISBN 9 7816 2356 4469.

Walker, Cody. *The Anatomy of Zur-en-Arrh: Understanding Grant Morrison's Batman*. Sequart. [2014] pp. 272. $16.99 ISBN 9 7819 4058 9046.

Walsh, Rebecca. *The Geopoetics of Modernism*. UPFlorida. [2015] pp. 208. $74.95 ISBN 9 7808 1306 0514.

Washington, Mary Helen. *The Other Blacklist: The African American Literary and Cultural Left of the 1950s*. ColUP. [2015]. pp. 368. $26 ISBN 9 7802 3115 2716.

Wegener, Susanne. *Restless Subjects in Rigid Systems: Risk and Speculation in Millennial Fictions of the North American Pacific Rim*. Transcript. [2014] pp. 311. $50 ISBN 9 7838 3762 4168.

Wood, Brent, and Mark Dickinson. *Listening for the Heartbeat of Being: The Arts of Robert Bringhurst*. McG-QUP. [2015] pp. x + 265. $60 ISBN 9 7807 7354 6349.

Zhaoming, Qian, ed. *Cathay* by Ezra Pound. Centenniel Edition. ND. [2015] pp. 136. $15.95 ISBN 9 7808 1122 3522.

Zilboorg, Caroline, ed. *Bid Me to Live*. UFlorP. [2015] pp. lxxx + 146. $19.95 ISBN 9 7808 1306 1955.

# XVIII

# New Literatures

MARGARET DAYMOND, ROANNA GONSALVES,
WEISHIN GUI, MICHAEL GRIFFITHS, MADHU KRISHNAN,
CHRISTINE LORRE-JOHNSTON, DOUGAL MCNEILL,
IRA RAJA, GISELLE RAMPAUL, PAUL SHARRAD,
GERALDINE SKEETE, LYNDA GICHANDA SPENCER,
TINA STEINER, AND MARK WILLIAMS

This chapter has seven sections: 1. Africa; 2. Australia; 3. Canada; 4. The Caribbean; 5. South Asia; 6. New Zealand and Pacific; 7. Southeast Asia. Section 1 is by Margaret Daymond, Madhu Krishna, Lynda Gichanda Spencer, and Tina Steiner; section 2 is by Paul Sharrad and Michael Griffiths; section 3 is by Christine Lorre-Johnston and Mark Williams; section 4 is by Giselle Rampaul and Geraldine Skeete; section 5 is by Ira Raja and Roanna Gonsalves; section 6 is by Dougal McNeill; section 7 is by Weishin Gui.

## 1. Africa

### (a) Southern Africa
Apart from Antjie Krog's having had two studies of her work in English published in the past two years (essays reviewed in 2016 and monograph below), the big names in South African writing, past and present, are not the subject of single-focus studies in this year's production of books and journal articles. Attention remains on the struggle to live with cruel histories of colonialism and other forms of oppressive power, but the focus of study is now more comparative and is turning to new or less well-known writers as well as to thematic matters.

Embarking on her wide-ranging and original conception of 'comparative research [into women's writing], while combin[ing] historical and cross-cultural perspectives' (p. 3), Ksenia Robbe, in *Conversations of Motherhood: South African Women's Writing Across Traditions*, points to both the particular need for such inclusive work 'in the wake of the political transformation following the first democratic elections of 1994' and the problems still attendant on a

doi:10.1093/ywes/max022

cross-cultural reading of texts written in English and Afrikaans (p. 2). Robbe does not include South Africa's other languages in her study. She observes that she chose the representation of motherhood, its discourses and metaphors, in order to create a space in which texts by 'authors of very diverse backgrounds could be read *in dialogue*' and to find a way of considering how women in varied circumstances in the late apartheid and post-apartheid periods shape 'their positions as *writing* subjects' (p. 4; emphasis original). Robbe recognizes women in relation to 'motherhood' as 'both... subjects of patriarchal discourses and as agents in traditional and countertraditional practices' (p. 13) and therefore sees the field as 'a heterogeneous... [one] of conflicting perspectives and intersecting imaginaries' (p. 15). On the question of traditions, she acknowledges at the outset their 'inherently unstable and shifting contours... in South Africa' (p. 9), but is confident that this instability allows comparative initiatives while warding off unifying approaches. Because literary traditions have marginalized women, particularly black women, tradition is a concept which Robbe is concerned to 'translocate'—that is, to trace and shift its conventional socio-cultural boundaries (p. 5)—by, for example, challenging the idea of the nation and its historical configurations, and of any nation-building agenda. The eight texts she has chosen all touch on important historical events and processes in South Africa and contain representations of mother–daughter and/or mother–mother relationships. The linked texts are Elsa Joubert's *Die Swerfjare van Poppie Nongena* [1978] and Wilma Stockenström's *Die Kremetartekspedisie* [1981]; Sindiwe Magona's *Mother to Mother* [1998] and Marlene van Niekerk's *Agaat* [2004]; Zoë Wicomb's *You Can't Get Lost in Cape Town* [1987] and Pamphilia Hlapa's *A Daughter's Legacy* [2006]; and Ellen Kuzwayo's *Call Me Woman* [1985] and Antjie Krog's *A Change of Tongue* [2003]. Robbe keeps to the original titles for works first published in Afrikaans.

The conceptual framework that Robbe uses for her study comes from Mikhail Bakhtin, and there is a careful exposition of several of his key concepts so this study will be valuable to students of Bakhtin as well as to those interested in its thematic debate. Bakhtin's theorizations of speech as fundamentally dialogic and co-creative, of communication as context-shaped (the chronotope), and of texts as 'replies in a socio-cultural dialogue' (p. 17) are all taken up. The latter wording is a reminder of Bakhtin's allowing agency to all participants in a dialogue, even those who do not speak. Postcolonial critics such as Peter Hitchcock have, Robbe points out, developed this framework to emphasize the dialogic relations between text and critic as well as the dialogic moments within a text. In addition, Robbe suggests, Bakhtin's concept of 'outsideness' by which 'our real exterior can be seen and understood only by other people, because they are located outside us in space and because they are *others*' (Bakhtin, *Speech Genres and Other Late Essays*, p. 7; emphasis original) goes some way to de-centre the self–other opposition which has become so predictable in much postcolonial reading.

Robbe's reading of her selected novels ranges from passages of extremely close textual analysis to intense theoretical exposition. In her survey of textualized approaches to 'motherhood' she emphasizes that as a concept and as a practice it is 'deeply implicated in relations of power in societies that have experienced colonialism and its consequences including global capitalist exploitation' (p. 39). As her intent is translocational, she emphasizes the particular historical properties of motherhood, observing that her study will attend to its use in integrating women into industrial economies (p. 34), and its use in nationalist discourses (p. 35). She is also interested in how the clashing of traditions and modernities produces ambiguity in motherhood through contradictory demands and outcomes (p. 36). In view of South Africa's having socio-cultural traditions that 'can be seen as separated, rather than separate' (p. 46; emphasis original), Robbe gives a brief indication of the incipient dialogues between these traditions, such as that in the 1970s and 1980s when Afrikaans women writers such as Antjie Krog, Welma Odendaal, Jeanne Goosen, Lettie Viljoen, Emma Huismans, and Joan Hambidge first began to produce distinctly feminist, modernist, and anti-apartheid texts, and black women writers such as Miriam Tlali, Noni Jabavu, Bessie Head, Lauretta Ngcobo, and Ellen Kuzwayo first embarked on self-representation in their writing (p. 48). Another occurred in writing in English by white, black, and coloured women in the 1980s and 1990s when autobiographical forms were favoured in efforts to 'develop a consciousness of gender oppression and to articulate a feminist politics' (p. 50). In critical studies of that time too, there were several significant articles which found it valuable to use the trope of motherhood in order to embark on the issue of cross-cultural relations. In South Africa's intellectual history, maternal stereotypes have also offered comparable although differently originating possibilities (p. 52), a crucial idea for her study which Robbe takes from the pioneering 1995 work by Deborah Gaitskell and Elaine Unterhalter, 'Mothers of the Nation: a Comparative Analysis of Nation, Race and Motherhood in Afrikaner Nationalism and the African National Congress' (in NiraYuval-Davis, Floya Anthias, and Jo Campling, eds., *Woman–Nation–State*, pp. 58–78). For black and Afrikaner women writers, nationalist thought offered a base, whereas in the English tradition liberal political convictions and feminist principles were foundational for women. In the former instance the *volksmoeder* became a significant figure for Afrikaner culture from the Boer War onwards, while for black groupings around the African National Congress in the 1950s the 'mother of the nation' took on a comparable importance as consciousness of the potential wholeness of the nation, its unifying and homogenizing function, was developed. But there remained a crucial difference: the former figure was racially exclusive whereas the latter was not. In the 1990s a new, historically specific *volksmoeder* figure emerged as the 'rainbow nation' was celebrated. This was Krotoa-Eva, who stood for hybridity in 'yet another exercise in mythologisation' (p. 55, quoting Natasha Distiller and Meg Samuelson, ' "Denying the Coloured Mother": Gender and Race in South Africa', *L'Homme* 16:ii[2005] 28–46).

The texts Robbe has chosen for comparison are generically heterogeneous, and the paired texts are sometimes deliberately but creatively mismatched, so that they are read through their differences as much as through their similarities. In the first of her detailed comparisons, between Joubert's and Stockenström's novels, Robbe makes particular use of Bakhtin's concept of 'outsideness' in order to discuss the relations between white Afrikaner authors and black mothers in what are landmark texts for her purposes. In their use of black protagonist-narrators, they stand as examples from the apartheid years of white writers ventriloquizing black mothers' 'self-reflexive engagement with issues of gendered identity and cross-cultural relations' (p. 68). The protagonists' stories differ in many ways, but touch at a major point: both experience motherhood as a condition of 'constant questioning and loss' (p. 71), Poppie because she has to send her children to the care of her distant parents-in-law while she works to provide for them, and Stockenström's anonymous slave woman because her children are taken away and traded as commodities, as she has been herself.

Acknowledging the vigorous debates which accompanied the publication of these two novels, Robbe reads them in their chronotope (the decade of the Soweto uprising), as 'histories from below' which try to 'find ways of rendering the experiences of black women as extremely marginalized subjects in colonial systems of oppression' and thus as 'both aesthetic and ethical interventions' (p. 78). Both protagonists try to escape control over their physical mothering, one by sterilization and the other by abortion, but their efforts are ambiguous in that they could render the women even more exploitable commodities. Robbe points out that both women are endlessly relocated through others' exercise of power and that dispossession and dislocation are constants in their stories as mothers. The loss of control over time in their lives—of their histories, families, and cultures (p. 97)—is integral to this experience of loss in motherhood. Within the loss of time, however, there is a possibility of recovered agency when the regular rhythm of things is momentarily disrupted, a pattern is broken, and what Bakhtin calls an 'extrarhythmic' moment can be identified. Robbe reads one such moment at the end of Poppie's story when, tired and dispirited by yet another failure in her efforts to protect her children, she entrusts responsibility for their future to them (p. 109). In Stockenström's novel there is a similar moment when the protagonist accepts the gift of poison and takes her own life, thus turning to her own purposes what seemed to be yet another attempt to control her.

In her comparison of Marlene van Niekerk's *Agaat* with Sindiwe Magona's *Mother to Mother*, Robbe again pairs texts which seem not to offer immediate, easy alignment, but the processes of her approach are always interesting. At the core of her comparison are texts 'in which black and white mothers are shown interacting and imagining ("authoring") each other' (p. 116). Even if this 'dialogicity of cross-cultural encounters . . . is mostly only attempted, "hidden" or impaired' (p. 116), suggests Robbe, its staging is a sign of new possibilities being felt in the late 1990s and early 2000s. In both narratives, mother–son relations are recast and, in keeping with the Truth and Reconciliation Commission (TRC) being the chronotope of these fictions, the mother-narrators are moved to resist being reinscribed into the prevailing emphasis on victimhood in their accounts of suffering. Robbe uses Bakhtin's concept of co-authoring—an interplay of responsibility and complicity between characters and between characters and author in the creative process: 'a questioning, provoking, answering, agreeing, objecting activity' (p. 125)—to suggest how the power of the official discourse and resistance to it is at play. She also takes up the ambiguity of the maternal as a sanctioned speaking position (it can be circumscribing as well as enabling; excluding as well as inclusive) and suggests, again from Bakhtin, that the outcome of utterance needs to be an understanding of difference, leading to a mutual change and enrichment.

In writing of her child, each narrator tells her own life story in order to ask where and how it all began (p. 134). Mandisa in *Mother to Mother* needs to understand how and why her son became a murderer, and Milla in *Agaat* broods on her loss of the affection of both her birth child and her adopted child. Each narrator tries to bring her misunderstandings to an apotheosis which might result in some mutual communion but, says Robbe, their efforts remain at the level of longing imbued with the hope that to articulate failure may have a potential for the future (p. 149). This technique has raised the question for many critics of whether the child in each novel is able to speak/ can be heard. Robbe points out that each narrator becomes aware of sounding like her own authoritative, patriarchal mother (p. 161) but fails to achieve a reciprocity with her child. Such reciprocity remains, like the longed-for understanding, in the realm of the imagined future.

In her third comparison, Robbe deals with texts in which daughters' relationships with their mothers are 'laden with mutual blame, guilt and dissatisfaction...at least until the...protagonists...[make] choices with regard to their own motherhood' (p. 173). In these stories of 'inheritance and legacy' (p. 179), Robbe sees Zoë Wicomb's *You Can't Get Lost in Cape Town* and Pamphilia Hlapa's *A Daughter's Legacy* as postcolonial 'transformations' (p. 176)—choosing Bakhtin's term over 'rewriting'—of the *Bildungsroman* which, in Wicomb's case in particular, is represented as a conflict with male authority. The mother-figures function somewhat ambiguously as embodiments of the legacy of the past (p. 180) against which the daughters need to emerge, and *Bildung* thus becomes a genre of postcolonial modernity (p. 189). In Wicomb's story cycle, the mother is an ambiguous figure of authority in espousing English (rather than Afrikaans) as the language of progress and power, despite its being the colonizer's language; in Hlapa's novel the mother's ambiguous authority is as a teacher who advocates the skills of modernity while affirming patriarchal social norms. In this way, both women live in what Achille Mbembe calls 'interlocking visions of time' (quoted p. 197).

The *actions* of the mother figures in each text render them barriers to their daughter's independence; but the *idea* of maternity is, suggests Robbe, a converse stimulus and this is most clear when the choice of abortion arises in each story. Kedibone, the protagonist of Hlapa's novel, recalls her mother saying that if she really is pregnant then 'It was the end of me' (p. 207), thus giving her a choice between the unborn child and her identity-hopes for the future. Frieda, Wicomb's protagonist, does not tell her family about her decision to abort but again it is clear that her choice is between 'the assumed wholeness of becoming a fully fledged subject' (p. 209) or bearing a child. As the father is white, Robbe points out, Frieda's decision also carries the separatist logic of the apartheid chronotope deep into her personal life. In Wicomb's text the generational and filial divisions are, as in the novels discussed in the previous chapter, resolved at a symbolic level when her mother shows Frieda that a protea, which was a central apartheid-era symbol, can be reclaimed as a beautiful flower. In Hlapa's novel, on the other hand, Kedibone's decision to have a child and thereby to gain her psychological as well as practical independence carries a material as well as symbolic promise. In the last of her comparative readings, between Ellen Kuzwayo's *Call Me Woman* and Antjie Krog's *Change of Tongue*, Robbe concentrates on the ways in which each text represents intricate connections between personal and collective becoming (p. 232). Although reflecting different chronotopes, each text can be read as a female protagonist's dialogue with tradition as she seeks 'an enabling position [of speaking] in changing social circumstances' (p. 233). In Krog's case this entails a 'process of becoming different from [her]self' (p. 233), in which discursive, rather than just linguistic, change is essential so that the processes may carry over to the cultural traditions in which she remains firmly rooted even while seeking to transform them.

Robbe compares the 'dialogics of belonging' in these two texts (p. 238) by reading 'motherhood' and 'daughterhood' as they are shared in family and social relationships, and in writing. In both texts, she suggests, belonging is 'achieved in the complex process of departing from the initial (familial) spaces and coming back, [each protagonist] having developed their own, alternative stances' (p. 256). From here, Robbe considers the 'contradictions of "fighting, being mothers and writing"... [and how the texts] translate between these activities and the respective identity categories' (p. 257). For both writers 'notions of collaboration and communal being' (p. 264) are always important, although particular episodes indicate that they find it difficult to create such bonds 'across cultural and national borders' (p. 266). A quotation from an essay by Antjie Krog sums up the aspirational focus Robbe gives this chapter: 'One can only reach ... [one's] fullest self ... through and with others, which include ancestors and the universe' (p. 274).

The comic is not often the mode of fiction from South Africa, but Michiel Heyns is now widely appreciated for his wry, witty approach. His recent novel, which does not have a local setting, is discussed by J.U. Jacobs in '(Mis)appropriating Caravaggio in Michiel Heyns's *A Sportful Malice*' (*JLST* 31:iv[2015] 1–21). He argues that Caravaggio's double self-portrait in his painting *David with the Head of Goliath* as the novel's iconic intertext suggests comparable degrees of authorial self-reflection. The tortured note in Fred Khumalo's novel *Seven Steps to Heaven* [2007] is perhaps more characteristic of the prevailing mood in South Africa. It is discussed in 'Between the Kafkaesque and the Grotesque: The Monstrous Idea of South Africa in Fred Khumalo's Historiographic Metafiction' by Kgomotso Masemola (*JLST* 31:iii[2015] 16–29). He sets the idea of being South African represented in Nelson Mandela's *A Long Walk to Freedom* against the parodic possibilities in Khumalo's novel.

Two edited collections of essays from 2014 whose contributors come from across the humanities and social sciences—Peter Vale, Lawrence Hamilton, and Estelle H. Prinsloo's *Intellectual Traditions in South Africa* and Meghan Healy-Clancy and Jason Hickel's *Ekhaya: The Politics of Home in KwaZulu-Natal*—are of considerable interest in addressing issues and texts currently preoccupying literary scholars.

Each essay in *Intellectual Traditions in South Africa* focuses on one of the ideas or practices which played out in the regional events of the twentieth century; each indicates the origins of these traditions, and then examines their migration to South Africa and their 'local footprint' (p. 4). The topical point of the collection is, as Peter Vale states, that 'only by rethinking the ideas that made us can we reimagine our country' (p. 5). The volume is divided into three sections; the first covers the obvious, powerful, and most-discussed ideas that have played a role in the country's history: liberalism, Marxism, and Afrikaner intellectual history, the latter having been dominated by Calvinism and, more recently, nationalism (Pieter Duvenage, 'Afrikaner Intellectual History: An Interpretation', pp. 73–94). As the outside/inside origins of the ideas in question are contentious in South Africa, the second section covers what could be seen as local alternatives to the Western emphasis in the first: African nationalism, Pan-Africanism, Black Consciousness, Gandhi, and a somewhat oddly placed but 'truly incendiary' (p. 19) piece on feminism by Helen Moffett, 'Feminism and the South African Polity: A Failed Marriage' (pp. 218–41). The final section considers the intellectual impact of the great religions that meet in South Africa: Christianity, Hinduism, Judaism, and Islam. The introduction stresses that the collection is 'only a moment in our understanding' (p. 23) of those intellectual traditions which make us even as we make them; the editors hope it is only the beginning of a vital conversation about South Africanness.

Not unexpectedly, South African writers feature large in the making of the traditions discussed. In this respect, pride of place probably goes to Olive Schreiner who, with Anton Lembede, N.P. van Wyk Louw, and Rick Turner, is said to have contributed significantly to 'a genuine South African strain of intellectual thought' (p. 10). Her writing features in Andrew Nash's essay 'The Double Lives of South African Marxism' (pp. 51–72) because her criticism of monopoly capital (that of Cecil John Rhodes in particular) placed great emphasis on the human cost of policies in which people are regarded merely as tools for creating wealth (p. 56). She raised, suggests Nash, questions which South African Marxists later tended to overlook: 'but the question of what kind of human being would take the place of the class divisions of capitalism did not disappear just because it was not acknowledged' (p. 57). Another literary figure who features in Nash's essay is Dora Taylor. Her Trotskyist views were, in the 1930s–1950s, at odds with those of the Communist Party of South Africa in that, amongst other concerns, she took up the point raised by Schreiner of the 'interconnected destinies of black and white' (p. 63). In her discussion of writing by black South Africans, Taylor turned away from the orthodox focus on forces in the industrialized West as having shaped world history to argue that the 'African struggle against oppression and exploitation will most surely express itself in the growth of a new culture' (p. 65).

The important contribution of literary figures is also mentioned by Mabogo P. More in 'The Black Consciousness Movement' (pp. 173–96). Arguing that it must be seen as a philosophy as well as a politico-cultural movement, More links Black Consciousness to Africana existential philosophy, including *négritude*, and says that its animating questions are 'infused with ontological and teleological significance ... identity and liberation' (p. 180). Steve Biko's formulation of these questions was central to the movement; the writing of

Chabane Manganyi made explicit the philosophical links with Sartre and Fanon, and the work of poets such as Mafika Gwala, Mongane Wally Serote, Oswald Mtshali, Don Mattera, Sipho Sepamla, and Mbulelo Mzamane in the *SASO Newsletter*, *Staffrider* and *New Classic* took up its 'political and cultural dimension' (p. 183). In 'Christianity as an Intellectual Tradition in South Africa' (pp. 245–67) Anthony Egan argues that Christianity really only began to be a progressive intellectual discourse resistant to apartheid in the pivotal period of the 1960s and 1970s. He says that three books published in this period were crucial; they each 'looked backwards to the traumas of Sharpeville [the massacre] and Cottesloe [the Statement issued by South African members of the World Council of Churches rejecting racial discrimination], state repression and limited popular resistance ... and tried to find meaning amidst the muddle' (p. 250). These were *The Eye of the Needle* [1972] by Rick Turner; *Black Theology: The South African Voice* [1973], edited by Basil Moore (who smuggled it to London for publication because the authors had all been banned or put under house arrest in South Africa); and *Jesus Before Christianity* by Albert Nolan [1976]. Even before mentioning authors and titles, Egan points out that the first of these texts was by 'an atheist philosopher' (p. 250) who held to a brand of humanistic Marxism and was friendly with Steve Biko, and the other two by a group of young black ministers and seminarians, and a Dominican friar. The ironies of this seemingly unlikely mix, which Egan relishes, are explained by the authors' having known each other 'through the complex, intellectually incestuous circles that linked South Africa's 1960's internal opposition' (p. 250). On Turner's book, Egan comments that today, as 'a new apartheid of wealth' (p. 254) is being formed, some leaders are revisiting the 'participatory democratic socialism' (p. 253), which it advocated, but within the church it is 'sadly ... forgotten' (p. 254).

Uma Dhupelia-Mesthrie points out that Gandhi himself cautioned that he had not attempted to carve out 'a systematic ideology' (p. 197) and thus she calls her essay 'Gandhian Ways: The South African Experience and its Legacy' (pp. 197–217), but she nevertheless indicates that what he advocated made up a 'total package' in which 'the body and inner self-development were linked to political and social activism' (p. 197). Dhupelia-Mesthrie lays great emphasis on Gandhi's use of journalism to propagate his ideas, and his founding of the weekly newspaper *Indian Opinion* in order to counter the 'hostile, white-owned, colonial press, which reflected and shaped anti-Indian sentiments' (p. 199) in Durban. She also draws attention to Gandhi's eclectic reading as he defined the principles of Satyahgraha and communal living at the Phoenix settlement. Besides ancient Indian texts like the *Ramayana* were Tolstoy; the Bible (specifically the Sermon on the Mount); Thoreau; Mazzini; the lives of Socrates, Martin Luther, and the Prophet Muhammad; and Ruskin. The printing press which Gandhi established became central to the promotion of reading and buying books which had an ethical and moral influence. Dhupelia-Mesthrie quotes Isabel Hofmeyr's observation that 'Gandhi was an early open source man ... [who] envisaged a utopian zone in which texts circulated freely beyond the constraints of the market and the state' (p. 208; Dhupelia-Mesthrie's ellipsis).

In outlining the origin of the traditions that they discuss, several essays point to inner tensions or contradictions in these ideas in order to consider their impact on South African developments. In 'The Ambiguous Legacy of Liberalism: Less a Theory of Society, More a State of Mind?' (pp. 29–50), for example, Steven Friedman points to Western liberalism's being both the basis for the principles of liberty, equality, and justice on which the new democratic constitution is based and, in its economic, free-market form, the rationale for a pursuit of profit at the expense of (black) workers. The tendency of liberalism to regard Western civilization as the norm has, Friedman suggests, lived on after 1994 so that the world of the suburbs (as against the townships) and 'the Anglo-Saxon cultures...[are seen as] the sole arbiters of "civilised" values'; liberalism here 'often resembles a tribal cult more than a political philosophy' (p. 44). In his discussion of Marxism in South Africa (title given above), Nash points to the tension between 'the privileged place its theory gives to the industrialised West in the process of social change...and its claim to provide a vision of global emancipation in which the most oppressed and exploited have a leading role to play' (p. 60) and he suggests that not resolving this tension led to a 'failure to establish a philosophical basis for Marxist ideas in a South African context' (p. 69). The division in African nationalism to which Raymond Suttner points in 'African Nationalism' (pp. 121–45) is between its inclusivity and its Africanism (p. 121); everything hinges on how the question 'To whom does South Africa belong?' is answered. Another tension emerges when he deals with a recent phase in the thinking of the African National Congress; it is a 'change in the character of nationalism from the mass popular, self-empowering towards the supportive, leadership-driven version' (p. 141), which came as the ANC assumed the reins of government. The chapter 'Pan Africanism in South Africa: A Confluence of Local Origin and Diasporic Inspiration' by Mcebisi Ndletyana (pp. 146–72) also rests on a division. As the title indicates it is over the question of whether Pan-Africanism has local or international origins. Ndletyana's answer is 'both' as he points to the early importance of W.E.B. du Bois, Edward Blyden, and Marcus Garvey, on the one hand, and South Africans such as Tiyo Soga and John Langalibalele Dube on the other. Once the Pan-African Congress had been formed under the leadership of Robert Sobukwe in South Africa in 1959, it found a ready alliance with Senghor's *négritude* in West Africa. Ndletyana sees South African Pan-Africanism as predominantly assimilationist, and unlike those of some of the other authors, his own position does not remain bifurcated; when he quotes the novelist Ezekiel Mphahlele saying he feels himself to be 'the personification of a paradox, a paradox that is a meeting point between acceptance and rejection' (p. 169) his sense that he too enjoys a hybrid, multiply influenced African identity is evident.

The remaining chapters on religious traditions in South Africa also point to divisions and their resolutions which have affected the behaviour of adherents. These are Vashna Jagarnath's 'The Hindu Intellectual Tradition in South Africa: The Importation and Adaptation of Hindu Universalism' (pp. 268–90); Muhammed Haron's 'Islam, Intellectuals and the South African Question' (pp. 313–32); and Sally Gross's 'Jewish Responses: "Neither the Same nor Different"' (pp. 291–312). Lawrence Hamilton, in his concluding chapter,

'The Power of the Past: The Future of Intellectual History in South Africa (pp. 333–48), suggests that 'despite the best efforts of high apartheid' the traditions discussed have come from 'ideas and languages... [that] have mixed and re-mixed over and over again' (p. 333), and that 'the ferment of imported or indigenous ideas has been healthy and strong for some time' (p. 336).

The second volume of essays deals with the topic of home and how its meanings have been changed over three periods of rule in KwaZulu-Natal: colonial, apartheid, and post-apartheid regimes. As its title indicates, *Ekhaya: The Politics of Home in KwaZulu-Natal* is focused on Zulu people's experience of being 'at home' (*ekhaya*) in the region ('*i*khaya' means 'home'). The essays challenge misperceptions in African studies such as the tendency to see public, urban settings as 'sites of the making of modernity, and the homes as spaces where traditional roles are entrenched and re-enacted without innovation and change' (p. 2). Countering this view, the collection demonstrates that 'throughout the modern history of this region, the constitution of the domestic domain—be it the rural homestead, the Christian home, the township house or the urban shack—has been crucial to organising activities in the political realm' (p. 17). Jeff Guy's essay, 'Colonial Transformations and the Home' (pp. 23–47), sets the scene by looking at what was assumed to have been an age-old, spatio-symbolic and material pattern—formed around gender (specifically women's reproductive and labour capacities) and cattle—for the homestead (*umuzi*) and tracing what actually continued and what changed over the 'long nineteenth century' (p. 26) when the farming peoples of southern Africa were conquered. The crucial underlying shift was 'from a system creating people to one producing things' (p. 45) but, suggests Guy, despite such a fundamental change what has survived is the least material thing of all: 'the idea of the home' (p. 45).

The essay by Eva Jackson, 'Familial Authority, Political Authority and the Life of a Female Chief in Colonial Natal' (pp. 48–82), continues the challenge to standard assumptions about domestic life, this time by demonstrating that the patriarchy was much more 'porous' (p. 79) than was recognized. Jackson recounts the case of Vundlazi, a widow of Frank Fynn, who was ' "Queen of the Umtwalume" from 1838 and stepped down as chief before 1880, remaining politically influential up until her death in approximately 1890' (p. 48). She ruled by popular acclaim and despite the occasional interference of the colonial authorities. To indicate that Vundlazi's challenging example was not particularly rare, Jackson also cites the contemporaneous example of two other women in southern Natal (as it was then) who took over as chief after the death of their husbands, and who seem to have 'performed a new gender role, which included "symbolic celibacy" and sometimes self-identification as a man' (p. 75). In 1908 the colonial authorities decided to impose an administrative system of wards in Natal's Lower Thukela division. This meant attempting to map colonially demarcated territories onto the customary pattern of 'space, authority and the homestead political economy' (p. 83). Percy Ngonyama examines, in 'Bounding Chiefly Authority in Colonial Natal' (pp. 83–106), the problems which arose when an *umuzi* had to be re-sited and the accompanying difficulties in fulfilling their responsibilities that were experienced by chiefs as well as household heads, problems which were greatly exacerbated by shortages of land under chiefly control as more and more was given over to commercial farming. In the early twentieth century, many women who 'no longer wanted to be (or no longer could be) at home' (p. 107) found an alternative place to live and feel 'emotionally comfortable' (p. 108) in the church that had been founded in Natal by Isaiah Shembe. The significance of this alternative home is examined by Lauren V. Jarvis in 'Gender, Violence and Home in the Nazareth Baptist Church, 1906–1939' (pp. 107–30) with particular reference to women's actions in violently defending what they saw as a threat to the person and authority of J.G. Shembe, Isaiah Shembe's son and successor.

To answer his question of why the principles of national democratic revolution took hold in Natal's urban townships in the 1980s and 1990s but not as readily in the rural areas, Jason Hickel, in 'Engineering the Township Home: Domestic Transformation and Urban Revolutionary Consciousness' (pp. 131–61), looks to three versions of domestic living to which African people in Natal were subject. The first is the rural homestead through which colonial authorities practised indirect rule; the second is the urban 'slum' which developed as people flocked to towns in search of work and where a 'subaltern counterpublic' (p. 139) developed; the third is the peri-urban township to which these 'slum' dwellers were forcibly removed. Apartheid planners saw standardized rows of tiny, detached houses in the townships as a means of producing docile, nuclear families on a Western pattern, but the ironic result was, says Hickel, 'an incubator for political agitation' (p. 149), for 'a revolutionary movement that had a distinctly liberal, egalitarian and class-oriented character' (p. 155).

As state housing policy now enables young women to acquire a house of their own, increasing numbers choose to live apart from their families. Judith L. Singleton, in ' "House" and "Home": Changing Meanings and Practices in a Post-Apartheid Township' (pp. 162–89), looks at some of the changes that are happening in the township of Mphophomeni (near Pietermaritzburg), changes which she reads back to profound gender and generational shifts (p. 163) occurring across the country. In KwaZulu-Natal, for example, '91 per cent of all black households are female-headed' (p. 164) and women need the 'bargaining power and extra income' (p. 185) that access to a house can provide. With the changes in meaning that new living patterns entail, 'house' is used to refer only to a material and spatial entity, while 'home' is a socio-spatial concept. In Mphophomeni, however, these distinctions became aligned (in ways that cut across some of the advantages accruing to women) with labour and political matters when workers at the major employer in the area went on strike, the longest strike in the country's history; imported scab labour tended to live in houses provided by the factory while the strikers lived in their homes in the township. The relationship of young women to their home is also taken up by Emily Margaretten in 'Parting Homes in KwaZulu-Natal' (pp. 190–213), in which she looks at the attitudes of young people who leave their home to live on the streets of Durban, and at those of their families who have lost their children. On the one hand, the youth can create kinship structures in the temporary dwellings they find in the city, for kinship does not depend on biology. On the other, the familial loss is not always total, especially when newborn children are involved, for the youngsters on the streets often take their infants home, where the ancestors (the *amadlozi*) are believed to dwell, in order for the children, and possibly all the family members, to benefit from their benevolence. In these cases, while the traditional kinship structures which the youth may have felt to be oppressive may still be in abeyance, the authority of those kin attachments is not completely lost.

The last chapter in the book turns to a case on which, the editors say, hinged much of the discussion that initiated the book—an example of homestead building which has, somewhat confusingly, been both a national scandal and a source of pride to many, especially women, in KwaZulu-Natal: Jacob Zuma's exorbitantly expensive homestead developed at taxpayers' expense at Nkandla. Mark Hunter, in 'Beneath the "Zunami": Jacob Zuma and the Gendered Politics of Social Reproduction in South Africa' (pp. 241–6), argues that Zuma's controversial presidential gestures (such as the homestead, his behaviour at the rape trial, and his polygamous marriages) can be understood in their popularity as part of the way in which 'political processes . . . unfold in relation to seismic recent changes to the home perhaps best captured by the rapid decline in marriage rates' (p. 214). Against drastic threats to the meaning of the home, Zuma, at the time of his election, could be understood as embodying both older values and fresh hope: 'For the young, he brings hope of work, service delivery and a re-mooring of gender relations . . . for the old, he can also stand for a renewed sense of generational respect' (p. 239). As a coda to the collection, Mwelela Cele, in 'Eposini Elidala: A Modern Umuzi, in Words and Images' (pp. 247–59), presents an account of the Reverend Posselt J. Gumede and his family, residents of Inanda (outside Durban) whose home functioned in the early decades of the twentieth century as a 'prominent social landmark' (p. 248). It was meeting place for many of the region's important intellectual and political figures, as well being known as the Pastor's Place, the Doctor's Surgery, and the Post Office through the achievements and services of the Gumede family.

Anthea Garman, herself a journalist during the states of emergency of the 1980s and the dramatic shift to democratic rule in South Africa in the early 1990s and now a lecturer at Rhodes University, analyses Antjie Krog's emergence as a public intellectual writing in English and concentrates on her approaches to issues of race, conflict, and justice in South Africa. Every concept used in her book, *Antjie Krog and the Post-Apartheid Public Sphere: Speaking Poetry to Power*, is extremely carefully explained and the steps of the argument are set out with exemplary clarity. Although the study makes it clear that Krog is a special case, as any public figure would be, it would serve as an excellent general model for anyone undertaking such an enquiry.

By the early 1990s, Krog was a celebrated poet in Afrikaans, but with the publication of *Country of My Skull* [1999], which represented her experiences as a radio reporter of the Truth and Reconciliation Commission, she moved to writing more and more prose, and to the medium of English. This was a time, as Garman says in her preface, when the public sphere was taking on a new shape and public intellectuals were increasingly called on 'to help think the country into a new space' (p. xi). The then president, Thabo Mbeki, was foremost among these voices, and the Palestinian writer Edward Said was frequently invoked. Habermas is a framing influence on Garman's study, and Bourdieu and Said are the major, immediate theoretical resources for her work. Apart from her consideration of Krog's self-positioning in her poetry, Garman does not concentrate on literary criticism, unlike the 2014 collection of essays on Krog reviewed last year (Judith Lütge Coullie and Andries Visagie, eds., *Antjie Krog: An Ethics of Body and Otherness*), in which Garman herself had two essays. Rather, she concentrates on analysing the historical processes through which Krog has acquired sufficient cultural-political capital for her writing to be accepted locally and internationally as 'speaking truth to power'.

Garman places the decades when Krog's poetry first came to public notice as a period in which it was peculiarly difficult for a young white Afrikaner woman poet to gain respect on all sides. Since the 1980s the public sphere had both required 'spoken consultation...[that was] institutionalised in a variety of instruments, organisations, and policies' and shown evidence of 'silencing, self-silencing and...evasion' (p. 6). Since the 1990s in particular, many white people who were once active in the resistance to apartheid had felt marginalized (Garman cites Raymond Suttner), so that Krog's rise as an authoritative voice able to play a key role in society raises a number of questions which Garman investigates. She begins by looking at Krog's own account of her 'originary story' (p. 39) in *A Change of Tongue* [2003]. It starts with a poem, 'My Beautiful Land', which was published in Afrikaans in a school magazine when she was 17. Its nascent anti-apartheid sentiments caused a furore in her home town, which then spread nationally because of her youth and the eminence of her mother as a loyal Afrikaans writer. There was a more muted reaction in the press when the poem was republished without Krog's knowledge in London in *Sechaba*, the in-house magazine of the ANC in exile. After this brief appearance on the international political stage, Krog lived predominantly in the poetic realm, consolidating her remarkable talents as a stylistic and linguistic dissident in Afrikaner poetic circles. Garman argues that Krog's publishing three prize-wining volumes of poetry while still at university indicates her increasingly astute understanding of the literary field she occupies and, within this trajectory, the creation of the poetic subjectivity she needs.

Garman then shows that Krog's subjective-poetic and public political development were increasingly interwoven. At the time that she received significant 'consecration' (p. 56) from political figures in the ANC, both in South Africa and abroad, as well as from the comrades (the radical black youth) with whom she worked in Kroonstad (her home town), she was awarded the Herzog Prize, the most prestigious award for an Afrikaans poet. To trace the poet's subjective development, Garman studies Krog's celebrated volume *Lady Anne* [1989], in which the poet takes as her guide a minor aristocrat who lived at the Cape at the end of the eighteenth century, and whose voluminous letters, journals, and diaries record what she saw, thought, and felt while representing an imperial rule to which she herself, as a Scottish woman and an astute political observer, was not particularly partial. For Anne Barnard's complex subjectivity as a sympathetic stranger in a new land, the critic Dorothy Driver coined the term 'self-othering' in order to convey the consciousness that rendered 'the self engaged in dialogue with an "otherness" within' (quoted p. 78). This, Garman suggests, is what Krog found so useful in *Lady Anne* that she chose her as an 'interlocutor' (p. 80), and she supports her claim chiefly in a discussion of the poem 'Lady Anne at Genadendal' (pp. 89–94).

From Krog's poetry, Garman turns to the radio reporting and the lead-up to the publication of *Country of My Skull*, the volume which gained a huge response internationally as well as in South Africa. In a careful exploration of why the blend of autobiography and testimony-report should have gained the authority it did, Garman uses Gillian Whitlock's theorizing of testimony: a transaction which, when reported, has to rest on both a 'first person' (the narrator) and a 'second person' (the hearer) voice. And she uses Mark Sanders's recognition of Krog's writing as 'being host to their [the testifiers'] words' (quoted p. 125) rather than an expert, overwhelming presence. Garman also places great weight on Krog's having announced that she witnessed the testimonies not as an impartial observer but a conscience-stricken beneficiary of apartheid.

In the last part of the book, Garman considers Krog's developing role as a celebrity and the importance of such figures in the self-fashioning of those who respond to her. She has been granted this status at a time when suspicion of Western intellectual traditions is extremely strong in South Africa (Garman refers in her epilogue to the 'fees-must-fall' campaign as the time of her own writing), but, suggests Garman, there is still 'a desire for exemplary human beings who will speak in ways that are universalising and visionary and not merely particular' (p. 163). It is this that Krog, by taking the personal voice of her poetry, including 'the extremes of emotion such as shame, mourning, frustration, helplessness, irrational love' (p. 71), into the realm of what would once have been dispassionate reportage, has manage to achieve.

The first half of *Interviews with Neville Alexander: The Power of Languages against the Language of Power*, edited by Brigitta Busch, Lucijan Busch, and Karen Press, consists of biographical interviews with Neville Alexander recorded between 2006 and 2010 by Brigitta Busch and Lucijan Busch, and the second half consists of six essays by Alexander which have been selected to represent his views on developing an egalitarian multilingualism after the monolingual policies of colonial and apartheid South Africa. As this collection has been prepared for publication in South Africa by Karen Press (an earlier German version of the interviews was edited by Lucijan Busch), where Alexander is presumably widely known, no chronologically arranged information about his work in language policy is given—although the selected bibliography of his writings (pp. 178–80) is a useful guide—and the focus is chiefly on the dialectical interactions between his experiences of various languages, his studies, his political activism, his views on language policy, and his practice.

As Alexander is insistent that theoretical understanding and policy cannot be separated from historical context, it is useful to remember that the span of his own life was from pre- to post-apartheid: he was born in 1936 in Cradock in the Eastern Cape and died in Cape Town in 2012. He reveals in the interviews that the home in which he grew up was thoroughly bilingual (in English and Afrikaans), and that because he had many Xhosa childhood friends, he grew up speaking colloquial isiXhosa too. In itself his background indicates both the ease with which, free of political interference, people can accommodate to living with and between several often very distinct languages, as well as the contradiction between their choices and the notion of racial purity on which apartheid was built. His grandmother was English-speaking because she had been 'reared as a slave girl, a freed slave, in the London Missionary Society mission station in Bethelsdorp' (p. 15) outside Port Elizabeth. Her first language was Oromiffa (from Ethiopia), to which she reverted in extreme old age. Alexander's mother, a schoolteacher, married an Afrikaans-speaking carpenter and stonemason whose father was a Scot, 'totally illiterate and really white, white, white' (p. 16), who had married a woman of 'mixed descent, mostly Khoi I would say', and who was also Afrikaans-speaking. Alexander's early education gave him further contact with isiXhosa, and once he reached high school he began his acquaintance with German as many of the nuns who taught him were from Germany. Attending mass at school (although he was not a Catholic) gave Alexander a lasting fascination with Latin which in his mind was 'strongly linked to philosophy and theology and a sort of metaphysical vision' (p. 26). Thus by adolescence he had a vigorous knowledge of five languages.

At university, Alexander chose to continue his studies in German and history with English literature as a subsidiary subject. These courses gave him a 'much clearer sense of what being European means as opposed to being African or Afrikaner' (p. 43) and, although as a student in Cape Town he was involved in anti-apartheid activities (through the Unity Movement), it was not until he had returned from doctoral studies in Germany and had been arrested and sent to Robben Island for ten years because of his increasingly radical activism, that he gained a balancing insight into matters African. He describes his reintroduction to Xhosa, and to other African languages while in jail, as 'very much a musical experience' (p. 72) because of the prisoners' singing traditional songs and those of migrant workers longing for home. When formal studies were allowed, it was through his postgraduate historical coursework that Alexander gained access to the *Communist Manifesto*, which he then decided to translate into English so that other prisoner-students might read it, observing that 'It took me about two weeks' (p. 91). It is interesting to note that an equivalent translation project for certain postgraduate students is one of the steps that he advocates in an essay about the intellectualization of African languages (p. 282).

'[B]ecause of the whole colonial history of the country it never entered into anybody's mind that the African languages themselves could become powerful, could become languages of power' (p. 116). In the remaining three interviews, Alexander recounts how he came to understand for himself, and tried to persuade those in authority, that for a unified nation to be built, and the damage done by centuries of racial oppression to be counteracted, a language development policy which included, equally, all eleven official languages was needed for South Africa. He recounts how he began to work intensively in planning and policy-making as he sought a way of 'integrating language planning with economic planning... [and] with identity politics'

(p. 130), and describes the various bodies through which this was done. Persuading the politicians that the issue was important was not easy. As Alexander puts it, "language is a little bit like air. You only become aware of the importance of air when there is no air. Or when the air is dirty... It's only the strategic, visionary insight of a few people who realise that you can do a lot with language from the point of view of power. People like Mandela, they never saw that; even Mbeki, he never understood, he still doesn't understand' (p. 136).

In the early 1990s, leading up to the first democratic elections and the creation of the constitution, it was (ironically enough) Afrikaners who saw eye to eye with Alexander's team and who 'created the political space within which multilingualism could thrive in the new South Africa' (p. 138) because they were determined that their language should have equal status and function with English. Then the Pan South African Language Board (PanSALB) was created in order to formulate principles and policy on matters that included the improvement of the status of African languages. It had, says Alexander, the good fortune of discussing its deliberations with Ben Ngubane, then the Minister of Arts and Culture. As a Zulu he took matters of language and culture as seriously as did the Afrikaners, and so PanSALB had a propitious start. At first those on the board were there in their professional capacity and not to represent a particular language, but this changed as an increasingly centralized, bureaucratic spirit took over. Eventually PanSALB ceased to function as first envisaged, and other bodies, such as the Project of the Study of Alternative Education in South Africa (PRAESA), had to undertake a visionary role.

As he withdrew from the local quasi-governmental function, Alexander found it valuable to reach out to similar bodies in countries throughout Africa, a move which enabled him to promote the idea of the 'multilingual *habitus*' (p. 166) of ordinary people who would draw on all forms of expression (speech, writing, mime, gesture, drawing, etc.) in order to communicate, a practice which has been largely ignored by Western intellectuals. This was his own experience as a child, and thus he affirms that language is not 'a sort of abstract linguistic schema... [That view is] what kills our understanding of the capacity of language to transform things' (p. 166).

In the first of the essays (pp. 181–208) that have been selected for inclusion in this volume, Alexander discusses his understanding of 'nation' in relation to the struggle for national liberation in South Africa. Published in 1979, shortly after his release from Robben Island, Alexander's radical and optimistic political rhetoric is much in evidence: he argues that 'The working people have resolved in the field of action to create a new South Africa in which the barriers of caste can no longer rise up to tower above the nation and imprison its members in separate cells (whereby the capitalist gaolers of the country can the more easily control them)' (p. 203). In similar vein he conveys his confidence that working-class unity will ensure 'the legal enforcement of equality of all languages' (p. 200). In the last selected essay (pp. 305–23), published thirty years later, in 2010, he is still championing the cause of the African languages in a multilingualism project for South Africa, and is now considering the means of their intellectualization so that they might play their proper role in education and thence in economic life. In the pieces between these two essays he argues that it is only a fully multilingual policy which can bring about real national unity (pp. 209–38); explains why he prefers to replace the descriptors 'major' and 'minor' for African languages with 'high-status' and 'low-status' (as well as 'endangered') because these latter terms do not carry implications about the intrinsic qualities and capacities of the languages concerned (pp. 239–55); argues that in view of globalization and the 'counter-hegemonic currents' (p. 260) that it is producing, the use of African languages in tertiary education becomes ever more important—particularly in relation to the economy, democracy, and identity (pp. 256–91); that in formulating language policies, a rigid standardization must be avoided; and that in order to be non-prescriptive language should for certain purposes be treated as a process, and for others 'as a (temporarily) stable category' (p. 296). In relation to South Africa, Alexander says that he and his team have developed a 'strategic pedagogical objective...[which is] the establishment of a mother-tongue-based bilingual education system...[in which] English...[is] taken to be the constant element in the equation' (p. 265).

A recognition of the still hidden history of homosexuality is argued for in 'A Novel Archive of Intimacy: Sex and the Struggle in Gerald Kraak's *Ice in the Lungs*' by Andy Carolin (*JLST* 31:iii[2015] 49–66). The novel, published in 2006, is set during the 'escalating violence and political activism' (p. 51) of 1976, and subverts the currently idealized representation of the struggle against apartheid. Carolin argues that one matter suppressed by that idealizing is gay and lesbian culture, and that fiction can function as an important dialogue with that silencing.

Lewis R. Gordon's *What Fanon Said: A Philosophical Introduction to His Life and Thought*, published by Wits University Press, is an edition of a relatively brief but comprehensive study of Frantz Fanon for distribution in Africa only (an American edition also appeared from Fordham University Press in 2015). Gordon concentrates on Fanon's first book, *Black Skin, White Masks*, as one in which, he said, 'A new type of text was born' (p. 73) and which 'challenges the viability of any single science of the study of human beings' (p. 70). Gordon treats this—rather than Fanon's last book, *The Wretched of the Earth*, which he calls 'a masterpiece of political writing' (p. 112)—as the major philosophical work

Emerging from the distinction between ontogenic and phylogenic approaches, a third factor, the sociogenic approach—attending to the 'intersubjective world of culture, history, language, and economics' (p. 22)—is what Fanon was concerned to explore. Gordon in turn emphasizes sociogenic factors in his analysis of Fanon's insider's account of anti-black racism. He also addresses Fanon's response to the dominant, and still lingering, assumption that black writers produce experience while white thinkers produce theory (p. 5), and claims that Fanon is both the experiencing black and 'the voice about the text' (p. 25).

Fanon's exploration of the tools of living—'language, sex, labour (material and aesthetic), socializing (reciprocal recognition), consciousness, and the "soul"'—as they are framed by modern Western thought, led to the discovery that as he tried to live 'an adult human existence' of his choice as a black man he found himself called to live 'simply as a white', as whiteness sets the '"normal" mode of "humanness"' (p. 24), and so each part of his narrative becomes a record of failure. Gordon also points to Fanon's psychoanalytical view that 'theoretical articulations of the nègre's condition on the basis of Self-Other relations fail...[because they] presuppose the subtle symmetry of "otherness"' (p. 69). As blacks struggle to rise out of the 'zone of nonbeing, struggle to achieve Otherness...[they struggle] *for the ethical to emerge*, for ethics and morality...are relationships between human beings' (p. 69; emphasis original).

Gordon explains that Fanon's despair continued partly because of Sartre's essay 'Black Orpheus', in which he suggested that *négritude* was a negative moment of descent prior to, and necessary for, a black ascent to a universal revolutionary consciousness (p. 56); Fanon saw this as yet another reminder that his '*négritude* was only a minor term' (quoted p. 57) to be absorbed eventually into the light of whiteness.

Gordon sees Fanon's approach as profoundly ironic: 'He spoke and wrote as truthfully as possible in the hope that he was, in the end, wrong' (p. 7), but in discussing the first of his more political works, *A Dying Colonialism*, Gordon shows that Fanon found the promise of radical change in activism: 'the victory of dignity is already won in fighting for it' (p. 98). His discussion of Fanon's account of women and the veil during the FLN war against the French in Algeria endorses the claim made by the Algerian writer, Assia Djebar, and others that, across the spectrum of possibilities and loyalties for women, the choices they made in the changing conditions of war led directly into the subsequent feminist struggles for freedom in Algeria.

Gordon offers a robust rebuttal of a much-repeated perception that from the opening sentence onwards of *The Wretched of the Earth* ('decolonization is always a violent phenomenon') Fanon was advocating violence, declaring that 'Fanon is not arguing that violence is, in and of itself, revolutionary. He had no interest in valorizing violence, which he detested...Fanon was offering his usual difficult dose of reality' (p. 118). As both colonizers (settlers) and colonized see themselves in the right over issues such as land ownership, for example, the conflict between two rights and the overturning of one is likely to be a violent and even tragic process. Finally Gordon considers Fanon's having asked Sartre to write the foreword to his book—a interesting request in the light of the 'Black Orpheus' essay—and suggests that Sartre demonstrated a full understanding of Fanon's real point: the ultimate irrelevance of the colonizer. Gordon's own tribute is: 'Fanon dedicated his life to breaking free of the weighted expectations of consciousness without freedom' (p. 140).

In discussing Fanon's concern with what would be required for colonies to build successfully on their newly acquired independence, Gordon observes that 'Fanon is careful to raise the question of *how* a transition could be made from neo-colonialism to a genuine *post*colonialism instead of, as Achille Mbembe has observed, the emergence of a "postcolony", that is, a legally independent entity with all the sociological and material trappings of a colony' (p. 121; emphasis original). As this cross-reference reminds us, these two thinkers, Fanon and Mbembe, share an intellectual tradition, have many concerns in common, and have explored many similar conclusions; it is thus pleasing that with Lewis Gordon's book on Fanon, Wits University Press has decided to reissue, again for distribution only in Africa, Mbembe's *On the Postcolony*. The reissue has a foreword by Isabel Hofmeyr and a 'Preface to the African Edition' by Mbembe.

In explaining the need for republication, Hofmeyr points to Mbembe's text's status as one that is always on students' reading lists but is so regularly stolen from South African libraries and bookshops that it is never available. Currently Fanon and Steve Biko are the other two favourites. More seriously, Hofmeyr also points to the intellectual connections between these three thinkers: they do not approach their subject (the shaping of the political present by the 'residues and remainders of colonial violence') through state and civil society but through a central focus 'on psychic questions of the self: existential liberation, subjectivity, self-writing' (p. vi). As Mbembe was writing some forty years later than Fanon, his focus is on fully fledged 'postcolonial African authoritarianisms' and what he called in an interview 'the logic of mutual corruption and conviviality' (p. 46) in newly independent African states. Hofmeyr concludes her preface by pointing out the continuing relevance of Mbembe's essay to South Africa: 'As the . . . order becomes more neo-patrimonial, *On the Postcolony* emerges as an evermore important handbook to help us make sense of the cruel absurdities of contemporary . . . life—the libidinal President, the genuflection to gerontocratic patriarchs, new forms of populist authoritarianism . . . the omnipresence of "eating" as the key metaphor of dominant political culture . . . structures of insiders and outsiders . . . idioms of the useful citizen and the criminalised surplus' (p. xi).

In his preface, Mbembe describes the kind of writing he wanted to achieve, again providing echoes of Fanon. He begins with a tribute to the 'emotional sublimity' of Congolese music and his wish to write 'with the musicality of one's own flesh' (p. xiii) in acknowledgement that in Africa 'music has always been a celebration of the ineradicability of life, in a long life-denying history' (p. xiv). Again this is a reminder of the affinities and differences between Fanon and Mbembe, both deeply stirred by music, in their different times and places of writing. Gordon gives great insight into Fanon's sense that a blues idiom serves only to trap its listeners in the era of slavery from which it emerged, a view which he says is limited by 'the fallacy of causal permanence' (Gordon, p. 88) and which prevented Fanon from recognizing that blues, with its tragi-comic lyricism, is what Gordon calls 'the leitmotif of modern life' (p. 89). Mbembe also acknowledges the African novel as the other 'direct biographical element' (p. xiv) of his work—once again echoing Fanon's turning to fiction for insight into the (in)human condition he needed to explore. But again there is a slight difference: Mbembe found himself liberated by the experimental fiction of the francophone novelists Sony Labou Tansi and Yambo Ouologuem, and by Amos Tutuola's *The Palm Wine Drinkard*. Striking a very different note from Fanon's use of the theme of racialized entrapment in more realist fiction, he says that in them 'contingency, uncertainty and ephemerality appeared to offer a vast reservoir of freedom and free play' (p. xiv). But then he turns squarely into Fanon's territory when he writes that his work 'is an attempt to uncover what lies underneath the mask of the Father', and his indebtedness is clear as he says that in writing he felt required first to 'dwell in the chaos of the night in order precisely to break through into the dazzling light of the day' (p. xv).

Writing *from* the past is discussed by Ayub Sheik in 'B.D. Lalla's *The Black Coolie*: A Struggle for a Voice' (*CW* 27:i[2015] 50–60), in which he discusses Lalla's poems from the 1940s as 'romanticised reveries of the Indian diaspora to the Natal sugar belt'. Past writing is also the subject matter of 'Whiteness Visible: The Representation of Race in Daphne Rooke's *Mittee*' (*CW* 27:i[2015] 1–12) by Bridget Grogan, who argues that this novel, published in 1951, is 'potent in its critique of white society' but finally able to produce its 'coloured' narrator Selina, only in relation to 'the bounds of whiteness' (p. 1). Writing *about* the past is discussed by J.U. Jacobs in 'Performing the Precolonial: Zakes Mda's *The Sculptors of Mapungubwe*' (*CW* 27:i[2015] 13–25). He argues that, while Mda explores 'the Kung cultural heritage in southern Africa' and 'recreates the physical and human geography of the precolonial Kingdom of Mapungubwe' (p. 13), he does not undertake to suggest the present-day relevance of the events he depicts. Representing the colonial past is the subject matter of Cuthbeth Tagwirei's article, 'Dealing with a Troubled Rhodesian Past: Narrative Detachment and Intimacy in Peter Godwin's *Mukiwa* (1966)' (*JLST* 31:iii[2015] 1–15). He argues that the use of a child's consciousness enables Godwin to represent the past in all its imperfections and to show why whites are estranged from present realities.

An article by Sofia Kostelac, 'The Singularity of Damon Galgut's Small Circle of Beings' (*JLST* 31:iii[2015] 67–80), takes an unusual line on apartheid-era writing. In light of the neglect of Galgut's novella, published in 1988, Kostelac argues that not every production of that period has to be overtly or analogously political in order to be legitimate and significant. Two other somewhat unusual pieces on fiction are Estelle Trengrove's 'Lightning and Fiction: An Engineer Reads Phaswane Mpe's Brooding Clouds' (*CW* 21i[2015] 38–49) and 'In Search of a "Rock Star": Commemorating Kabelo Sello Duiker's Life and Work Ten Years On' (*CW* 21:i[2015] 26–37) by Danyela Demir, Olivier Moreillon, and Alan Muller. Trengrove's article comes out of her interest, as an electrical engineer, in 'myths, beliefs and misconceptions' (p. 38) about lightning, particularly the belief that witches can send lightning to kill a person. As she finds Mpe's posthumously published short story an important source in understanding the holding of such a belief, and as it shows that tradition can be 'creative and nurturing' or 'destructive' (p. 47), she suggests it would be mistaken simply to ridicule the belief in witches and lightning. The collectively written article by Demir et al. records conversations with Duiker's mother and brother about his life, family relationships, and writing habits. It also looks via intertextual references to his novels, *Thirteen Cents* [2000] and *The Quiet Violence of Dreams* [2001], at the influence his work has had on other, more recent, South African fiction.

Two important editions of letters were published this year: *Flame in the Snow: The Love Letters of André Brink and Ingrid Jonker*, edited by Francis Galloway, and *Everyday Matters: Selected Letters of Dora Taylor, Bessie Head and Lilian Ngoyi*, edited by M.J. Daymond.

The Brink–Jonker letters were written in Afrikaans in the years 1963–5, and have been published simultaneously in separate volumes in the original and in English. The translations were done by Leon de Kok (translating Brink's letters) and Karin Schimke (translating Ingrid Jonker's letters). Shortly after the correspondence ended, Jonker drowned herself. During her 'tempestuous life... [she had published] three volumes of poetry, a play and a handful of short stories' (pp. 10–11) and is still celebrated today; Brink, slightly younger than Jonker, was at the beginning of a long and illustrious career as a novelist and literary critic (the volume does not include a bibliography). The letters show that during their passionate affair they had a strong influence on each other's work. They are filled with literary interest, particularly in giving a subjective view of each writer's work in progress. As Willie Burger says in his introduction, the intimate revelations in the letters may yet startle some readers, but as the note on the text explains, three months before his death in 2015, André Brink himself offered the letters to Penguin Random House, having kept carbon copies of everything that he wrote to Jonker. This suggests that at the time he may have needed their words for his own work, and that he also saw the correspondence as having a future interest to the public.

Bessie Head was another writer who kept and filed copies of all of her voluminous correspondence, largely because she used her letters as notebooks for her fiction-writing and to try out her ideas on suitably sympathetic correspondents. This is also why, to date, three collections of her letters to particular people—Bessie Head and Randolphe Vigne in *A Gesture of Belonging: Letters from Bessie Head, 1965–1979* [1991]; Patrick and Wendy Cullinan in *Imaginative Trespasser: Letters Between Bessie Head and Patrick and Wendy Cullinan, 1963–1977* [2005]; and now the letters to Paddy Kitchen in *Everyday Matters*—have been relatively readily published. But so far, although Bessie Head is acknowledged as one of the greatest of Africa's literary letter-writers, neither a collected nor a selected letters has been published.

*Everyday Matters* assembles three sets of letters written to different correspondents by writers who did not know each other and were writing during slightly different periods in South Africa. The volume has a general introduction by the editor, M.J. Daymond, who has also written a substantial biographical introduction to each set of letters as well as an afterword on the experience of reading letters. The book is held together by the writers' profound opposition to apartheid and by the fact that the letters are domestically located, and show the extent to which the dictates of a racist regime affected the everyday lives of women who were simultaneously ordinary and extraordinary in their resolute anger. The earliest, Dora Taylor, was a writer and a political activist; her fiction was not published in her lifetime but two novels and a set of short stories were released during the 1990s. Her literary criticism and extensive political commentary were published in the 1930s–1950s, chiefly in the journal *Trek*. She was also a significant behind-the-scenes figure in the Non-European Unity Movement and so, when the regime cracked down on its opponents after the Sharpeville massacre in 1960, she was advised that the country was now too dangerous for her. The letters chosen for *Everyday Matters* record her anguish as she guides her daughter on the shutting down of her beloved home in Cape Town, a home which had been a centre of her active political and literary life. Dora Taylor, Scottish born, died in what she considered to be exile from South Africa.

Paddy Kitchen's correspondence with Bessie Head began in 1969 when she conducted an interview by post for a London journal with this remote, unknown writer whose remarkable first novel, *When Rain Clouds Gather*, had just been published. Kitchen was herself a novelist and the two women clearly hit it off from the beginning; the correspondence continued, with one longish break when Head was ill, for the rest of Bessie Head's life. It reached particular intensity while Head was writing *A Question of Power* so the letters, which range over gardening, children, fiction for children, cookery, jazz, favourite authors, politics and village people (Kitchen had a beloved house in the village of Barnwell as well as a home in London), may be particularly interesting to readers of Head's major, peculiarly demanding, novel.

Lilian Ngoyi was nationally known in the 1950s as a trade unionist, a leading member of the ANC, and a founding member of the Federation of South African Women, but once she was banned in the early 1960s she disappeared from public view. Although she is remembered as a powerful orator, almost nothing of her words has survived in print, and so these letters, written some ten years after her first banning, are a rare direct record of her voice. She was writing to Belinda Allan, who had begun by sending a small monthly grant to her on behalf of Amnesty International and had continued doing so in her personal capacity. The letters, which began as routine records of receipt, developed into a warm friendship and show that in the loneliness of virtual house arrest, Ngoyi found much-needed support and solace in the correspondence. It continued until a month before her death and, while Ngoyi knew that police surveillance required her to be careful, her letters contain strikingly expressed, moving details about her struggles with poverty and her delight when unexpected help arrived, her despair when the uprising known as Soweto '76 erupted, and her fury when the inquest into Steve Biko's death exonerated those who, she believed, should have been held responsible.

A special issue on teaching creative writing was published by *Current Writing* in October under the guest editorship of Kobus Moolman. It comes out of a colloquium on the teaching of creative writing held at Rhodes University in 2014 and includes contributions from other practitioners, including a young MA graduate, Sindiswa Busuku-Mathese, in 'It's Not Personal, It's Just Business: Market or Artistic Value when Credentialing Creative Writing Graduates at South African Universities?' (*CW* 27:ii[2015] 174–80). She has just published a poetry collection of her own; here she writes from a student's point of view. In his introduction (*CW* 27:ii[2015] 82–5) Moolman points out that, as a comparatively new discipline in the South African academy, creative writing is under-researched and under-theorized; there is no local journal devoted to the subject and this is the first journal special issue given to it. There are two essays on community writing projects: in 'Demystifying Writing and the Democratisation of the Story and Knowledge' (*CW* 27:ii[2015] 86–94), Angifi Dladla, himself a published poet, writes about the Femba Writing Project, which works with groups in a maximum-security prison and various townships in Gauteng. He describes how his own education destroyed the idea of reading or writing for pleasure and outlines the egalitarian techniques for interaction and participation that he now uses. Vonani Bila describes a poetry project in 'Building Socially Committed Writers through the Timbila Writing Model' (*CW* 27:ii[2015] 95–102), which is based in Polokwane, Limpopo. It works chiefly with indigenous African languages, and produces an annual, multilingual journal, *Timbila—a Journal of Onion Skin Poetry*.

Besides the journal, the project liaises with poets elsewhere and brings them into local festivals, and it works in schools 'to teach poetry that is grounded in people's awareness of reality' (p. 96). Several teachers reflect on their methodology: because he encourages his student to write without pausing for correction and then to read aloud the results to each other, Anton Krueger, in 'Whose Voice Is It Anyway? Implications of Free Writing' (*CW* 27:ii[2015] 103–10), enquires into the nature of the voice, both physical and textual; Meg Vandermerwe, in 'Grace Paley's Six Lies: A Practical Tool to Enable Creative Writing Students to Refine Their Imaginative Writing' (*CW* 27:ii[2015] 111–16), explains how she presents these 'lies' to students in order to encourage them in redrafting their work; in 'Minute Particulars and Global Flows: Place and Interconnectedness in a Creative Nonfiction Class' (*CW* 27:ii[2015] 117–23) Julia Martin describes how, without becoming too parochial, she uses an intense focus on place to develop ecological sensitivity in her students' writing; in 'Teaching the Practice of Writing Poetry in an Academic Environment' (*CW* 27:ii[2015] 124–31) Kobus Moolman writes about teaching students to recognize the inner logic of the poem they are writing, why the poem has to be, as Coleridge said, as it is, and not otherwise. Several contributors comment that they try to show their students that a poem may start out as what they want it to say, but if it is any good it soon takes over with a life of its own. Jean McNeil reports on the methods used at one of the long-established schools of creative writing, in 'The Rhetoric of the Prose Fiction Workshop—an Analysis of Teaching Methods at the University of East Anglia' (*CW* 27:ii[2015] 132–8). Robert Berold describes the approach used nearer to home, in 'What Do Writing Students Need? The Rhodes Masters in Creative Writing' (*CW* 27:ii[2015] 139–44). He argues for the emphasis on reading, 'how to read a text for its pace and music, and ultimately how to read one's own work' (p. 139); Paul Wessels continues the focus on the course at Rhodes University in 'To Practice What We Teach' (*CW* 27:ii[2015] 145–50); so does Denis Hirson in 'Ukutshona Kwelanga: The Drowning of the Sun: Introducing Translation into Creative Writing Courses' (*CW* 27:ii[2015] 154–8), and because he encourages his students to write without pausing for correction and then to read aloud the results to each other, he argues, via several illustrations, that the inclusion of translation in multilingual poems enables 'remarkably rich and strong' (p. 154) results. Stacy Hardy also argues for the value of the vernacular in poetry, in 'Multilingualism in Creative Writing' (*CW* 27:ii[2015] 159–64), and says that currently at Rhodes students are able to write their theses in several South African languages. Consuelo Roland writes 'Preliminary Thoughts on the Supervisor's Role in Getting Creative Writing MA Candidates across the Finish Line' (*CW* 27:ii[2015] 165–73), and Henning Pieterse explores the possibilities and practices of 'The PhD in Creative Writing and the Teaching Thereof at South African Universities' (*CW* 27:ii[2015] 181–9). Paul Munden considers the relationship between the 'international writing community' (p. 190) and higher education in Britain as it is reflected in *Beyond the Benchmark*, a report by the National Association of Writers in Education. He titles his article '(In and) Out with the Academy' (*CW* 27:ii[2015] 190–8) as a prelude to looking beyond the orthodoxies, the assumptions, the knowledge, and the discipline of creative writing, in order to support the claim that it 'produces creative, flexible, literate, resourceful people' (p. 195). One of South Africa's better-known performance poets, Lesego Rampolokeng, writes 'What Gets Me Teaching, and How' (*CW* 27:ii[2015] 199–206), in what the editor calls his 'idiosyncratic language and condensed poetic form' (p. 84). The other poet-contributor who uses a non-discursive mode is Noy Holland, in 'On Creative Ambivalence' (*CW* 27:ii[2015] 151–3), in order to ask the question how to 'stay hungry', to 'practice the code [of academe], without becoming clowns to ourselves, fraudulent' (p. 151).

Translating literature is also discussed by Rose Masubelele in 'Do Literary Translators Have a Style of Their Own? Lessons from C.S.Z. Ntuli's Translation of D.B.Z. Ntuli's Short Story *Uthingo Iwenkosazana* (The Rainbow)' (*JLST* 31:iv[2015] 42–55). She examines the translation in order to show that the target language, English, is not purely derivative of the original Zulu but has its own 'trademark' (p. 42) while preserving effects similar to those found in the source text.

The essays and interviews in *Gaze Regimes: Film and Feminisms in South Africa*, edited by Jyoti Mistry and Antje Schuhmann, come in part from a forum for African women filmmakers hosted by the Goethe Institute in Johannesburg in 2010, and have been supplemented with one or two other pieces. The volume brings together film practitioners, academic theorists, and festival organizers who explore 'the conditions of making films in post-colonial Africa with a gender-sensitive and feminist analysis', and it discusses 'individual and/or collective positioning when art meets politics and vice versa' (p. xii). The four main themes in the collection are historical and theoretical contextualization; the construction of gender; conditions of production; and curators and exhibition platforms in the value chain of meaning. There are interviews with nine women and one man currently active in the film world: Taghreed Elsanhouri, filmmaker from Sudan, and Christina von Braun, filmmaker and academic from Berlin (pp. 10–17); the Lebanese-born filmmaker, Jihan El-Tahri who now lives in France and works in Egypt (pp. 33–43); Djo Tunda Wa Munga from the Democratic Republic of Congo and Rumbi Katedza from Zimbabwe (pp. 44–54); Shannon Walsh, who is based in Hong Kong and made a film with Arya Lalloo in Johannesburg (pp. 133–47); the Mozambican filmmaker Isabel Noronha (pp. 148–60); the Indian-born and now South African-based scriptwriter and producer Anita Khanna, who has also directed documentaries and is a film festival director (pp. 168–73); and Tsitsi Dangarembga, the Zimbabwean novelist turned filmmaker (pp. 201–10). She drafted a brief manifesto for the forum which is included in her interview; it asks that women film practitioners in Africa get a

50 per cent share in resources and broadcasting content, and a 50 per cent representation on decision-making bodies. The essays begin with 'African Women in Cinema: An Overview' by Beti Ellerson (pp. 1–9), which covers developments from the beginning in the 1950s and 1960s. One of the interviewees, Christina von Braun, writes 'Staged Authenticity: Femininity in Photography and Film' (pp. 18–32) in which she considers the 'collective imaginary', that is, 'historically variable models or ideals thrown up by every epoch which contribute to the formation of the self-image and visage of society' (p. 19) as it is recognizable in retrospect in photography and film. In view of the difficulty of seeing the ' "staging" behind the "authentic" ' (p. 29) in gender, of seeing 'one's own existence . . . as culturally coded' (p. 30), her concluding suggestion is that their centuries-old memory of having been excluded from culture serves today to energize the cultural critique of women cinematographers (p. 30). Antje Schuhmann writes, in 'Shooting Violence and Trauma: Traversing Visual and Social Topographies in Zanele Muholi's Work' (pp. 55–80), an account of this acclaimed South African artist's representation of black lesbian and transgender people through the medium of photography as well as film, installations, and beadwork. The kind of question which Muholi faces in her work, says Schuhmann, is 'How to tell a counter-story without referencing the very normative politics of Otherness ones aims to counter? How to intervene in hegemonic white feminist imaginaries of the black Other as a poor, abused, black shemale without restating or denying it?' (p. 61). In the next essay, Antje Schuhmann co-authors, with Jyoti Mistry, '*Puk Nini*—a Filmic Instruction in Seduction: Exploring Class and Sexuality in Gender Relations' (pp. 81–96). Their article records a student discussion of the film *Puk Nini* [1995] made by Fanta Regina Nacro, who also made the full-length feature film *Night of Truth* [2004], from Burkina Faso. The objective of the discussion was to 'gauge how much gender relations might have changed since the making of [*Puk Nini* and] . . . to explore its reception in a different geosocial environment' (p. 81) such as South Africa. Two films about Saartjie Baartman by Zola Maseko are critiqued in Nobunye Levin's article 'I am Saartjie Baartman' (pp. 97–117). She suggests that this iconic woman is seen as a victim without any capacity for self-determination. Levin suggests that this depiction of Baartman served an immediately post-apartheid nation-building outlook and now wishes to counter it with her own research and film project which has the same title as her article. It is a 'short experimental film shot on digital video' (p. 103), which Levin describes in some detail. In 'Filmmaking at the Margins of a Community: On Co-producing *Elelwani*' (pp. 118–32), Jyoti Mistry writes about her experiences working on a film directed by Nshavheni Wa Luruli which was based on the first novel, *Elelwani* [1954], meaning 'promise', to be written in Tshivenda, by Dr Titus Maumela. He was a schoolteacher, who wrote it so that he would have a suitable text to teach to his Tshivenda-speaking pupils; the director read it as a school set work. The film tells the story of a young woman who is compelled to forgo the emancipated life opened to her by her university education and to marry the chief who has (unknown to her) been sponsoring that education. Allison Anders, Mira Nair, Lisa Cholodenko, Djamila Sahraoui, and Regina Nacro

are instanced by Anita Khanna, in 'Dark and Personal' (pp. 161–7), as examples of women filmmakers whose work, while very varied in form and content, has in common the struggle it took these women to get their films realized. It is a struggle which results in a particular quality of 'candour' (p. 166) in their films. Katarina Hedrén writes about one of these filmmakers, Djamila Sahraoui, in '*Barakat!* Means Enough' (pp. 174–81). Made in 2006 and set in Algeria during political revolution in the early 1990s, *Barakat!* presents two women dealing with choices such as 'when to veil and when to choose to be unveiled' (p. 174); in Hedrén's account of the film, these choices are precipitated and/or blocked by men's patriarchal behaviour.

The last of the articles is 'Post-Colonial Film Collaboration and Festival Politics' by Dorothee Wenner (pp. 188–200). She reflects on the difficulties facing filmmakers in Africa, particularly women, and on the collaborative success that women such as Tagreed Elsanhouri (Sudan) and Jihan El-Tahri (Egypt) have had, as well as the filmic energy current among young women in Kenya. Funding and technical collaboration with sources in Europe and the Americas tend to raise questions such as 'What is an African film?' and, unfortunately, films such as Mark Dornford-May's *U-Carmen eKayelitsha* [2005] have been accused of appropriating European culture. This, suggests Wenner, is to impose a colonial essentialism about Africa. Audience-building is still a crucial task, for while films from Egypt, Senegal, or South Africa are eagerly awaited at festivals, even masterpieces from Africa attract little interest on the commercial circuit in Europe.

## (b) West Africa

This year saw a diverse range of scholarship on West African literature in English. As has been the case in previous years, a substantial body of criticism focused on the work of Chinua Achebe, whose passing in 2013 remains a focus of West African literary scholarship. David Borman's 'Playful Ethnography: Chinua Achebe's *Things Fall Apart* and Nigerian Education' (*ArielE* 46:iii[2015] 91–112) returns to Achebe's foundational novel, reading it as an 'insider' account of Igbo culture and society which plays with the ethnographic tropes circulated in contemporary accounts of Nigerian village life. Drawing on the novel's intertextual relationship to small magazines and university publications from Nigeria in the 1950s, the essay convincingly situates Achebe's novel within a complex discursive landscape which reaches beyond the simple act of 'writing back' to Empire. *Things Fall Apart* is also the subject of Mahshid Tajilrou's 'Postcolonial Study of Chinua Achebe's *Things Fall Apart*: Foregrounding Marginal Elements' (in Çelikel and Taniyan, eds., *English Studies: New Perspectives*, pp. 194–206). Tajilrou uses Homi K. Bhabha's notion of postcolonial hybridity as a lens through which to analyse the cultural and linguistic 'third spaces' created within the novel. Best placed as an overview and introduction to Achebe and postcolonialism, the essay concludes that the author presents a balanced view of African society through a hybridization of the novel form and oral traditions. Three further essays published in 2015 focus on Achebe's first novel. Ernest Cole's 'Demystifying the Unfamiliar: Competing Discourses and the Pedagogy of Agency in *Things Fall Apart* and Poems from Sierra Leone' (*JALA* 9:i[2015] 10–31) takes a comparative perspective in order to consider the pedagogical uses and purposes of the novel as an encounter with the unknown. Mads Rosendahl Thomsen's 'African Mediations: Transcultural Writing in Achebe, Gourevitch, Eggers, and Okri' (in Helgesson and Vermeulen, eds., *Institutions of World Literature: Writing, Translation, Markets*, pp. 126–40), similarly takes a comparative perspective to *Things Fall Apart*, here setting it in dialogue with Ben Okri's *Starbook*, Dave Eggers's *What Is the What*, and Philip Gourevitch's *We Wish To Inform You That Tomorrow We Will Be Killed With Our Families*. Arguing that each work is inherently transcultural in its purview, Thomsen situates each as a study in violence and atrocity (p. 127). *Things Fall Apart* is thus read as a novel which 'create[s] a space where questions of both universality and uniqueness are made void by a series of more complex renderings of African culture and the process of colonization' (p. 128), in contrast to Okri's more allegorical, counter-supplemental rendering. Finally, Ignatius Chukwumah's 'Retheorising the Pharmakos: The Nso Concept in Narratives of the Igbo of Nigeria' (*TvL* 31:iv[2015] 23–41) reads *Things Fall Apart* alongside Buchi Emecheta's *The Joys of Motherhood* through the twinned concepts of the pharmakos, the figure whose suffering stands in excess of his or her sin, and *nso*, the Igbo code of order and taboo. Contributing to the localization of Western critical concepts through indigenous forms, the essay suggests that these two ideas, when placed together, open up 'the possibility of the pharmakos being suitably requited within the existing logic of persecution and suffering as an innocent, or not too guilty, figure' (p. 24), supported by close readings of Achebe's and Emecheta's works.

Two essays published in 2015 examine Achebe's work through the framework of literature and law as part of a special issue of the *Cambridge Journal of Postcolonial Literary Inquiry*. Neil ten Kortenaar's 'The Rule, the Law and the Rule of Law in Achebe's Novels of Colonization' (*CJPLI* 2:i[2015] 33–51) reads *Things Fall Apart* and *Arrow of God* as 'parables of political philosophy' (p. 33) which dramatize the threat of war, British intervention, and the imposition of a colonial rule of law. In ten Kortenaar's reading, these novels foreground the question of reciprocity as functioning in opposition to the law, drawing on the distinction between the gift economy of the former and role of the sovereign in allegedly disinterested forms of arbitration of the latter. While asserting that Achebe moves from a position which foregrounds reciprocity as a system which functions outside the law to one which is more state-based, following the creation of the Nigerian nation-state, the essay ultimately finds in both texts a deep ambivalence towards the role of the law with respect to violence. Taiwo Adetunji Osinubi, meanwhile, turns to *No Longer at Ease* to explore the institution of Osu slavery in 'Abolition, Law, and the Osu Marriage Novel' (*CJPLI* 2:i[2015] 53–71). Placing Achebe's literary text in dialogue with abolition discourse, the essay situates *No Longer at Ease* as a novel which narrativizes the impasse between international law, colonial law, and indigenous tradition.

Two further essays on Achebe's other works appeared this year. Danica Savonick's important essay, '"The Problem of Locomotion": Infrastructure and Automobility in Three Postcolonial Urban Nigerian Novels' (*MFS* 61:iv[2015] 669–89), examines the imagined potency of urban infrastructure as a materialization of colonial modernity through readings of Achebe's *No Longer at Ease*, Chika Unigwe's *On Black Sisters Street*, and Chris Abani's *GraceLand*. For Savonick, the disjuncture between the idea of modernity and the material realities of its infrastructure offers an avenue for constructing a bottom-up vision of Nigerian society. *No Longer at Ease*, for instance, exposes 'the fantasy that a good (English) education will lead to a government job, wealth, a foreign car, and prosperity' (p. 672), linking together the degeneration of nationalist promises and the myths of progress and modernization and ultimately functioning 'as a response to a history in which British colonial rule erected a Nigeria in its image, orchestrated through both material infrastructures and affective fantasies of the good life as forms of indirect rule' (p. 675). Chioma Opara's 'Decadent Space: Women, Language and Crime in Chinua Achebe's *A Man of the People*' (in Diala-Ogamba and Sykes, eds., *Literary Crossroads: An International Exploration of Women, Gender, and Otherhood*, pp. 111–21), examines the intersection of politics, corruption, and language through the lens of femininity and spatiality. Fernanda Alencar Pereira's 'Language Contact in Novels by Chinua Achebe and Pepetela' (in Gorovitz and Mozzillo, eds., *Language Contact: Mobility, Borders and Urbanization*, pp. 69–77) similarly focused on language, examines Achebe's oeuvre as a whole through its modification of English by Igbo as a form of contact zone. Further linguistic criticism of Achebe's work includes Njemanze Queen's 'A Structuralist Study of Chinua Achebe's *Anthills of the Savannah*' (*ALLS* 6:iii[2015] 93–100), which uses formalist analysis based on the work of Propp, Greimas, Barthes, Todorov, and Genette to explore the linguistic underpinnings of Achebe's critique of dictatorship, power, and corruption in the post-independence African nation. Daniel Oppong Adjei's 'An Analysis of the Language of Humour in Chinua Achebe's *A Man of the People*' (*ALLS* 6:iv[2015] 195–202) shifts focus to apply Veatch's theory of incongruity to the development of humour in the novel, while Joseph Eke's 'Postcoloniality, Idiomatic Allusion and Intercultural Communication in the Translation of *Things Fall Apart* and *Arrow of God* into German' (*JALA* 9:ii[2015] 112–39) explores the ways in which the translations of Achebe's novels function as examples of intercultural communication.

Along with Achebe, Wole Soyinka was a subject of significant critical enquiry in 2015. Ato Quayson's 'Wole Soyinka's *Death and the King's Horseman* in Comparative Frameworks' (*CJPLI* 2:ii[2015] 287–96) examines Soyinka's seminal text in a range of comparative contexts including Achebe's *Things Fall Apart* and *Arrow of God*, as part of a tradition of literary tragedy and through the topos of world literature. In a crucial resource for all teachers of the play, Quayson elucidates the pitfalls of teaching African literature in a European and American context, making practical suggestions for navigating the cultural negotiations so required. Ali Jimale Ahmed's 'Wole Soyinka: An African Balzac?' (*Ufahamu* 38:iii[2015] 217–29) takes a broader view of the author as public intellectual. Beginning from the polemical stance that

Soyinka shows a 'total lack of respect for the African toiling masses which he views as "cowed", "defenseless" and docile' (p. 217), the essay traces his engagement as a bourgeois intellectual mired in contradictions. Drawing connections with Balzac's position as a public intellectual in the nineteenth century, the essay concludes that it is precisely Soyinka's position that allows him to expose the 'rotten underbelly' of Nigerian society, even as he attempts to hide his own complicity as part of the elite in his works (p. 226). More salutatory towards the author is Saeed Talajooy's 'Intellectuals as Sacrificial Heroes: A Comparative Study of Bahram Beyzaie and Wole Soyinka' (*CLS* 52:ii[2015] 379–408), which foregrounds the ways that, across his work, Soyinka 'demythologize[s] the traditional and modern superstitions haunting [his] people, depict[s] the fallacy of the artificial constructs that distort [his] people's lives, and mythologize[s] the positive aspects of [his] cultures to redefine the narratives of nationhood produced to form collective identities for [his] people' (p. 380). Focusing on the figure of the dissenting intellectual as sacrificial victim, the essay draws together autobiographical analysis and close reading to position Soyinka as an organic intellectual in the Gramscian style.

A chapter in Gbemisola Adeoti's edited collection, *African Literature and the Future*, written by the editor and titled 'Requiem for Absolutism: Soyinka and the Re-visioning of Governance in Twenty-First-Century Africa' (pp. 33–48), focuses on Soyinka's career as a dramaturge. In this reading, Soyinka's dramaturgy is held as an ideal exemplar of engaged art, using the examples of *The Beatification of Area Boy* and *King Baabu* to explore the ways in which the author 'advocates for a relentless war of attrition, fought on all fronts, including through cultural productions and drama, against despots, tyrants, autocrats and other purveyors of undemocratic rule, wherever they are found on the continent' (p. 33). Positioning Soyinka's use of satire as part of 'an onslaught against absolutism' and 'the first step towards the recovery of popular will' (p. 33), the essay argues for the centrality of cultural forms in the re-envisioning of governance in the African context. *The Beatification of Area Boy* is also the subject of Niyi Akingbe's 'Contextualizing the Contours of Subjugation: Dramatizing Conflicted Image of the Military in Wole Soyinka's *The Beatification of Area Boy* and Esiaba Irobi's *Cemetery Road*' (*SATJ* 28:ii[2015] 129–42), which sets the play in dialogue with the work of Soyinka's countryman. For Akingbe, Soyinka's engagement is best seen in his depiction of the military as a key historical driver of Nigeria's failed democracy and his historicization of authoritarian rule.

Like Achebe, Soyinka's work attracted a range of studies focused on language. Moussa Pourya Asl's 'Power in Play: A Foucauldian Reading of A.O. Soyinka's *The Trials of Brother Jero*' (*ALLS* 6:vi[2015] 63–8) uses Foucault's conception of power and the subject to analyse Soyinka's play, focusing particularly on the use of language and dialogue as an enactment of power and agency. In 'Protest against Military Regime in Wole Soyinka's *King Baabu*' (*TPLS* 5:viii[2015] 1543–51), Mashhoor Abdu Al-Moghales and Abdulrahman Mokbel Mahyoub Hezam focus on the play of power, revolt, and protest to portray a revolutionary spirit in the play. As they argue, *King Baabu* 'emphasizes that continuous struggle and protest must be crowned with the victory of the oppressed over the oppressor' (p. 1550) and acts as a historical document of sorts of the immediate post-dictatorship era. Marzieh Shamsi, Sohila Faghfori, and Seyed Ali's 'Ritual/Carnival Performance in Wole Soyinka's *The Road*' (TPLS 5:ix[2015] 1935–9) situates *The Road* as a text inherently linked to Yoruba rituals of transition and passage, notably the Ogun festival. Viewing theatre as a collective and community-building experience, the essay explores the play's use of Yoruba metaphysics as a means of engendering self-awareness and actualization.

Ben Okri, too, attracted significant critical attention in 2015. Most significantly, *Callaloo* devoted a special issue to the writer and his work, featuring critical essays, tributes, personal reflections, and a broad selection of fiction, poetry, and reflection by the author himself (*Callaloo* 38:v[2015]). Notable amongst the contributions are Vanessa Guignery's introduction, 'Ben Okri: A Man of Many Arts' (*Callaloo* 38:v[2015] 997–1003), which situates the issue as an examination of 'Ben Okri's multiple metamorphoses as a storyteller who borrows from West African traditions but maintains his attachment to European models' (p. 997). Drawing on Okri's transcultural and transnational childhood, Guignery cites Okri's 'awareness of a multiplicity of worlds and ways of living and seeing' (p. 998) as central to his work, imbued both with 'the tradition of social realism inherited from European masters' and 'West African folktales steeped in the supernatural and the fantastic' (p. 998). The issue also contains a personal essay by Elleke Boehmer, 'Ben Okri: My Neighbour and Friend' (*Callaloo* 38:v[2015] 1007–11), which recalls a period spent living next to the author in London, and tributes from former collaborators, fellow poets, and friends including Baroness Helena Kennedy, Nii Ayikewi Parkes, Per Wästberg and Hanna Westerlund, Elly Strik, and Peter Krüger. A number of academic essays complete the issue. Kathie Birat's 'The Dialogue of the Big and the Small: The Poetry of Ben Okri' (*Callaloo* 38:v[2015] 1065–86) uncovers 'the dialogue he establishes between Africa and the world, between the poets, both ancient and modern, who have affected his work, and between the different forms or genres which make up his artistic universe' (p. 1066). Chris Ringrose's ' "Redreaming the World": The Poetry of Ben Okri' (*Callaloo* 38:v[2015] 1135–50) similarly considers the writer as poet, focusing on *An African Elegy* and *Wild*. For Ringrose, 'Okri's poetic project involves a high-risk strategy' (p. 1135) through its practices of rhetorical address and its engagement with and commitment to a vision of literature as high art. Meanwhile, Mariaconcetta Costantini's 'Transcending Historical Violence: Uses of Myth and Fable in Ben Okri's *Starbook*' (*Callaloo* 38:v[2015] 1118–34) turns its attention to the author's novelistic output. Arguing that violence serves as a central leitmotif to African literature, the essay situates *Starbook* as a study in the trauma of transatlantic slavery, which 'narrates the Black Atlantic diaspora from an ahistorical perspective that transcends culturally limited boundaries' (p. 1132). Eleni Coundouriotis's 'Things of Poverty and War: Ben Okri and Thing Theory' (*Callaloo* 38:v[2015] 1087–99) 'uses the representation of the camera in *The Famished Road* as a springboard to examine Okri's use of objects to mediate the realms of the spiritual and the real' (p. 1088). For Coundouriotis, the slippage between objects and things in Okri's work signifies a deep critique of late modernity that seeks to rehabilitate the possibilities of history. 'The Famished Road after Postmodernism: African

Modernism and the Politics of Subalternity', by Mark Mathuray (*Callaloo* 38:v[2015] 1100–17), similarly focuses on the Booker Prize-winning text, examining the ways in which the novel places postcolonialism and postmodernism in a sometimes conflictual dialogue which resists their conflation. Instead, Mathuray argues for a reading of *The Famished Road* as a text imbued with the aesthetic practices of modernism, which highlights postcolonialism's own modernist influences. José-Santiago Fernández-Vázquez, in 'Journeys of Artistic and Social Exploration: Katabatic Influences in Ben Okri's Fiction' (*Callaloo* 38:v[2015] 1151–69), turns to 'When the Lights Return' and *In Arcadia* to explore Okri's use of the Orphic myth and the katabasis to foreground an opposition to binary modes of thinking and highlight the role of the artist and cultural producer through a re-envisioning of the descent to the underworld.

Okri is also briefly mentioned in Timothy Clark's *Ecocriticism on the Edge: The Anthropocene as a Threshold Concept*, appearing in a chapter on scale framing that sets Okri's story 'What the Tapster Saw' in comparative dialogue with the work of Raymond Carver. Kathie Birat, in ' "Through a Bending Light": Ben Okri's Poetic Commitment' (*CE&S* 38:i[2015] 45–55), reads *Wild* in order to produce an understanding of artistic commitment indebted less to specific forms of activism and political engagement and more to a longer poetic practice rooted in Graeco-Roman tradition which functions 'in terms of the paradoxical relation between political engagement and aesthetic distance' (p. 45). Finally, Wendy B. Faris's 'Scenes of Enchantment: Visionary Style in Ben Okri's *Dangerous Love*' (*RAL* 46:i[2015] 127–41) concentrates on narrative style, identifying Okri's use of scenic lists (defined as a sequence of brief sentences which evoke a scene) as a means of 'creating [one of those] epiphanic moment[s] of defamiliarization suggesting the onset of visionary power' which ultimately define Okri's singular style (p. 127).

This year saw a number of essays on the writing of Chimamanda Ngozi Adichie. Several essays appeared on the topic of Adichie's latest novel, *Americanah*. Katherine Hallemeier's ' "To be from the country of people who gave": National Allegory and the United States of Adichie's *Americanah*' (*SitN* 47:ii[2015] 231–45) situates the novel within 'ongoing debates about the function and failures of the representation of "Africa" and "Africans" in Euro-America broadly and the United States specifically' (p. 232). For Hallemeier, '*Americanah* presents an alternative, utopic vision of global power in which the United States stands as a foil to the promising future of late Nigerian capitalism' (p. 232) through a depiction of economically empowered Nigerians and dispossessed Americans which 'envisions a global capitalist system in which race does not exhaustively and exhaustingly delimit the affective bonds that enable financial success' (p. 243). Caren Irr's 'Neomedievalism in Three Contemporary City Novels: Tobar, Adichie, Lee' (*CRCL* 42:iv[2015] 439–553) places *Americanah* in dialogue with Héctor Tobar's *The Tattooed Soldier* and Chang-rae Lee's *On Such a Full Sea* in order to explore the ways in which the unsettling of medieval tropes through neo-medieval urban forms complicates Benedict Anderson's notion of the 'homogenous, empty time' of the nation-state. In ' "The Strange Familiar": Structure, Infrastructure and Adichie's *Americanah*' (*MFS* 61:iv[2015]

587–605), Caroline Levine examines the relationship between structures and infrastructure, using the examples of electricity and racism in Adichie's novel. The essay argues that the novel's preoccupation with the *Bildung* and migration, as forms and plots, allow it to defamiliarize both concepts to productively enable their rethinking. A final essay on *Americanah* is Patrycja Austin's 'Searching for One's Self at the Crossroads of the Cosmopolitan World: Determining the Importance of Roots for Those who Travel through Diversities in Chimamanda Ngozi Adichie's *Americanah*' (*OJEP* 7:i[2015] 7–16).

Adichie's short fiction was also the subject of much critical attention. Susan VanZanten's ' "The Headstrong Historian": Writing with *Things Fall Apart*' (*RAL* 46:ii[2015] 85–103) imagines Adichie's short story as a revisioning of and conclusion to Achebe's seminal novel. The essay argues that ' "The Headstrong Historian" positions itself in ironic juxtaposition with the District Commissioner's reduction of Okonkwo's history to a paragraph' (p. 99), augmenting the story by abbreviating the text. Ultimately, the story is positioned as a text about history and history-making which engages with larger questions around narrative and power in its making. Heba M. Sharobeem's 'Space as Representation of Cultural Conflict and Gender Relations in Chimamanda Ngozi Adichie's *The Thing Around Your Neck*' (*RMR* 69:i[2015] 18–36) looks at the collection as a whole in order to consider the various spaces inhabited by women, dwelling on the intersection between space, place, race, gender, and power. Two essays in Robert C. Evan's edited collection, *Critical Insights: Contemporary Immigrant Short Fiction*, place Adichie's short stories in dialogue with short stories by South Asian women writers: Anupama Arora's 'Forbidden Desires: Interracial Relationships in Chimamanda Ngozi Adichie and Jhumpa Lahiri's Short Fiction' (pp. 52–67) and Maryse Jayasuriya's 'Irony and Epistolary Form in Chitra Banerjee Divakaruni's "Mrs. Dutta Writes a Letter" and Chimamanda Ngozi Adichie's "The Thing Around Your Neck" ' (pp. 195–207). Finally, in 'Christianity Brewed in an African Pot: Reading Chimamanda Ngozi Adichie's "The Shivering" ' (*AGON* 7[2015] 5–23), William F. Purcell considers the various forms of religious and cultural hybridity in Adichie's work.

Adichie's contemporary, Chris Abani, was also a major focus of scholarship in 2015. Dustin Crowley, in his *Africa's Narrative Geographies: Charting the Intersections of Geocriticism and Postcolonial Studies*, features an extended discussion of Abani's novelistic output in his chapter 'Half Slum, Half Paradise: Abani's Global Cities' (pp. 129–54). In this chapter, Crowley focuses on the ways in which 'world cities like Los Angeles and Lagos are seen as simultaneously situated within and a conduit for complex cultural, economic, and political relations across many scales' (p. 130) in novels such as *GraceLand*, *The Secret History of Las Vegas*, and *The Virgin of Flames*. For Crowley, Abani depicts cities in a manner which foregrounds their ability to enable flexible subjectivities and alternative forms of world-making. Despite the promise of the city, however, Crowley sees a pessimism at work in Abani's depiction of the cities of the global South, places dedicated to 'whitewashing poverty with conspicuous wealth and shallow opulence' (p. 142) whose appearance unmasks 'urbanization as a process itself made unequal through its transnational relations' (p. 146).

Abani's 2006 novella of sex trafficking, *Becoming Abigail*, is the subject of a number of important critical works. Susan L. Hall's 'The Uncanny Sacrifice: Sex Trafficking in Chis Abani's *Becoming Abigail*' (*Crit* 56:i[2015] 42–60) suggests that the novella 'offers a vital rethinking of both mainstream trafficking discourse and governmental policies with respect to the ways that they frame understandings of female sexuality and of migration issues' (p. 42). *Becoming Abigail*, the essay argues, resists mainstream discourse around trafficking through 'its exposure of both the damaging effects of constraining the trafficked person to the status of victim and the reinscription of colonial hierarchies' (p. 43). Pamela McCallum's 'Between Life and Death: Representing Trafficked Persons in Chris Abani's *Becoming Abigail* and Justin Chadwick's *Stolen*' (*Mosaic* 48:ii[2015] 29–44) sets the novella in a comparative framework. Drawing on Butler's conception of precarious lives, the essay foregrounds the experience of vulnerable children as agents who function without meaningful connections to the state and who strive nonetheless to make meaningful change and take action in their bleak worlds.

In 'Elvis Has Left the Country: Marronage in Chris Abani's *GraceLand*' (*CollL* 42:i[2015] 90–111), Erin M. Fehskens turns to Abani's second novel in a discussion of the self-displacement of protagonist Elvis from the city of Lagos and from the notion of masculinity. Drawing on linguistic analysis and spatial readings, the essay develops a reading of the text as a response to capitalism and the militarized state with clear links to the search for autonomy. Linking the movement of *GraceLand*'s protagonist to the act of marronage as acts of refusal and attempts to forge alternative communities, the novel highlights the tension between the effort at self-creation and the force of the state under global capitalism. Annalisa Oboe's ' "As there are hyena-men and panther-men . . . ": Chris Abani, Pieter Hugo, and the Shocking Life of Images' (*JPW* 51:i[2015] 95–107) addresses Abani's less well-known collaboration with Hugo in the 2009 volume *Nollywood*. The object of much furious criticism on its release, *Nollywood*, Oboe argues, creates a space which moves beyond established aesthetic and ethical paradigms through its unsettling visual and textual compositions.

Aminatta Forna's *The Memory of Love* was the subject of two essays in 2015. Dave Gunning's 'Dissociation, Spirit Possession, and the Languages of Trauma in Some Recent African-British Novels' (*RAS* 46:iv[2015] 119–32) places Forna's novel in a comparative framework with Zimbabwean Brian Chikwava's *Harare North* and Nigerian-British Helen Oyeyemi's *The Icarus Girl*. For Gunning, Forna's novel largely conforms to a traditional model of trauma and traumatic experience, in contrast to the non-realist forms seen in Oyeyemi's work. While noting the desire in *The Memory of Love* to create a space for local understandings and contextualized definitions of trauma, the essay nonetheless concludes that the novel ultimately serves 'to endorse a rather conservative Western model of trauma: the "local" explanation that insists on spirit worlds is in practice dismissed and the medicalized model instead prevails' (p 123). *The Icarus Girl*, by contrast, is read as a work that refuses the demand to adhere to a single, dominant discourse of trauma, maintaining a connection to and wariness towards both Western models derived from psychologies of dispossession and Indigenous models of spirit possession. Madhu Krishnan's 'Affect, Empathy and Engagement: Reading African Conflict in the Global Literary Marketplace' (*JCL* [online, 3 August 2015] 1–19) explores the ways in which unreliable narration and temporal dislocation function in *The Memory of Love* to displace the expertise of Western models for decoding African civil conflict. Foregrounding the role of fallibility in the novel as a form of strategic empathy-formation, the essay argues that *The Memory of Love* forces the reader to reckon with his or her own unreliability as interpreter and thereby enables a form of distancing that predicates affective responsibility.

Amongst studies of other writers in 2015, Walter P. Collins III's collection *Writing Contemporary Nigeria: How Sefi Atta Illuminates African Culture and Tradition* stands as a significant work which is the most in-depth engagement with the author to date. The book is organized in four sections: 'Sisterhood, Womanhood, and Rites of Passage'; 'The City'; 'Dark Aspects of Atta's Works'; and 'Atta's Literature in Application'. These interrelated sections foreground themes of gender and patriarchy; geography and politics with chapters on motherhood and marriage; alternative visions for society and alternative publics for women's participation; dictatorship and corruption; and education. The collection ends with an extended interview with Atta. The role of the female writer continues as a theme in Folasade Hunsu's 'Redefining Otherness: Writing Fictional (Auto)biography and Centring Female Subjectivity in Akachi Adimora-Ezeigbo's *Children of the Eagle* (*TvL* 52:i[2015] 168–78). The essay examines how the centrality of female subjectivity through the development of female narrative voices in the novels determines its ability to transform sexual otherness into a position of resilience, and includes pedagogical suggestions for bringing this material to the classroom. Ultimately, Hunsu concludes, the novel 'underlines the potency of the speaking subject and strengthens the view that the sub-genre of fictional autobiography enables the redefinition of otherness as a favourable concept capable of accentuating women's positions as critical members of their societies' (p. 177). Nnedi Okorafor is the subject of Joshua Yu Burnett's 'The Great Change and the Great Book: Nnedi Okorafor's Postcolonial, Post-Apocalyptic Africa and the Promise of Black Speculative Fiction' (*RAL* 46:iv[2015] 133–50). In this essay, Burnett examines *The Shadow Speaker* and *Who Fears Death* as postcolonial reimaginings of speculative fiction, using the figure of the trickster and the trickster trope to critique postcolonial dichotomies of good and bad, colonized and colonizer, and create a counter-hegemonic narrative landscape that gestures towards a different future. The essay argues that 'Okorafor's post-apocalyptic Africa, a land where juju is reality, reality is shifting, and the very basis of Western rationalism has been undermined, becomes a space where a true postcolonialism is at least possible' (p. 134) which stands in contrast to the neocolonial realities of the present.

In addition to the work already discussed, 2015 saw the publication of two important interviews with contemporary female Nigerian writers: Elisabeth Bekers, 'Writing Africa in Belgium: A Conversation with Chika Unigwe'

(*RAL* 46:iv[2015] 26–34), and Nicklas Hållén and Janet Remmington, ' "You want people to see you in all your nuanced variety": An Interview with Noo Saro-Wiwa' (*StTW* 19:iii[2015] 274–82).

Noo Saro-Wiwa's late father, Kenule, is the subject of Erin James's 'Immersed in the Storyworld: Oil, Nigeria, and You in Ken Saro-Wiwa's *Sozaboy*' (*JNT* 45:iii[2015] 419–46). In this essay, James focuses on protagonist Mene's 'rotten English' and use of orality to read *Sozaboy* as a counter-narrative to the story of the Ogoni people and oil, contributing to the field of environmental justice writing as much as discourse around oil in southern Nigeria. The essay argues that rotten English enables the narrative to foreground 'Ogoni disenfranchisement from the rhetoric and politics of oil' (p. 422) and to imagine alternatives through a focus on systems of oppression which remain opaque despite their prevalence. Rebecca Fasselt's 'Reassessing Thematic Crossings between South Africa and Nigeria: Postcolonial Leadership and Power in Mandla Langa's *The Lost Colours of the Chameleon* and Helon Habila's *Waiting for an Angel*' (*ArielE* 46:iii[2015] 23–53) also focuses on the relationship between literature, space, and politics in its reading of Habila's novel. For Fasselt, the novel's engagement with Nigeria's postcolonial military dictatorships evokes a sense of placelessness that exceeds its national boundaries. At the same time, Habila's novel is read as a reflection on leadership which unwrites both the utopian myths of cultural nationalism and the crude vision of power as operating through a dichotomy between ruler and ruled. Space is also a key theme in Madhu Krishnan's 'Postcoloniality, Spatiality and Cosmopolitanism in the *Open City*' (*TPr* 29:iv[2015] 675–96). In this essay Krishnan reads Teju Cole's *Open City* through the lens of spatial theory, drawing on the work of Henri Lefebvre and Doreen Massey to suggest that the cosmopolitan preoccupations of the novel deliberately engage with a performative aesthetic which unmasks the originary violence from which this cosmopolitanism arises. Arguing more broadly that postcolonial space functions as an extension of colonial space and its violent destruction, rather than a break from it, the essay positions Cole's novel as a text that self-consciously unmasks the solipsism at its core.

Two notable essays move back in time to consider earlier West African writers. Notably, Stephen Ney's 'Samuel Ajaui Crowther and the Age of Literature' (*RAL* 46:i[2015] 37–52) looks at the work of the nineteenth-century Yoruba scholar and bishop. Ney establishes Crowther's intentional role as the founder of a literary tradition through his own writing which, while not considered 'literary' in the elevated sense, significantly impacted the development of linguistic and religious writing, as well as his deliberate engagement with Indigenous literatures. Ney centres his argument through a reading of Femi Osofisan's *Ajayi Crowther: The Triumphs and Travails of a Legend* and, importantly, draws links which foreground an African literary tradition pre-dating the era of high colonialism. While not as foundational as Crowther, Ayi Kwei Armah, a significant figure in mid-twentieth-century West African writing, is at the centre of Minna Niemi's 'Revising Postcolonial Trauma: Multidirectional Identifications in Ayi Kwei Armah's *Fragments* and Nuruddin Farah's *Maps*' (*JPW* 51:iii[2015] 283–95). Expanding Rotherberg's notion that there is no singular, universal notion of trauma, the essay proposes the idea of insidious trauma as a means of understanding the complex subject positions depicted in Armah's novel. Applying a notion of multidirectionality to the text, Niemi foregrounds the novel's depiction of Ghana as a nation of corruption and exploitation which generates new and more insidious forms of inequity, felt as trauma by its populations.

Cultural studies make their mark on scholarship on West African writing in 2015. A key example is Terri Ochiagha's *Achebe and Friends: The Making of a Literary Elite*, a must-read monograph for all scholars of West African literature. The study centres on Government College, Umuahia, in the 1930s, 1940s, and 1950s, a period in which the college served as host to a number of students who would go on to become pioneers of anglophone African writing, including Achebe, Elechi Amadi, Chike Momah, Chukwuemeka Ike, Christopher Okigbo, Gabriel Okara, Ken Saro-Wiwa, and I.N.C. Aniebo. Ochiagha's key concern is to elucidate why it was that Government College became such a creatively vital place and the legacy of each writer's tenure there. Drawing on close readings, archival research, and personal testimonies, the study opens by setting the context in which the college was established and the subsequent development of a vibrant culture of magazines, reading, and extracurricular engagement by its students. The second half of the study focuses on close readings of later writing by Ike, Momah, and Okigbo to unpack the lasting influences of, and traces of a network instilled by, the college. Ochiagha has also published 'Decolonizing the Mind Onitsha-Stle: Reexamining Ogali A. Ogali's Cultural Nationalism in *The Juju Priest*' (*RAL* 46:i[2016] 90–106), exploring the ways in which *The Juju Priest* provides an outlet for understanding non-elite experiences with colonization and cultural nationalism. Reading the novel as an allegory for Ogali's own trajectory, the essay links to both Ogali's career as an Onitsha market pamphleteer and to his later influence by Achebe's *Things Fall Apart*. Two chapters in Frieda Ekotto and Kenneth W. Harrow's *Rethinking African Cultural Production* take a cultural studies approach to material, which will interest scholars of West African literature. Olabode Ibironke's chapter, 'African Writers Challenge Conventions of Postcolonial Literary History' (pp. 29–51), contains extended discussions of the work of Femi Osofisan, Chinua Achebe, Ayi Kwei Armah, and Wole Soyinka, focusing particularly on their reflections around the role of the African writer and question of audience. Examining less read essays which express a radical politics committed to '"moving the centre" of cultural production' (p. 37), the chapter explores the ways in which globalization and extroversion have complicated questions of commitment and engagement for the African writer. In the same volume, Tejumolan Olaniyan's 'African Cultural Studies: Of Travels, Accents, and Epistemologies' (pp. 94–108) contains a brief discussion on the work of Biodun Jeyifo, Wole Soyinka, and Chinweizu as part of a longer reflection on the continued asymmetries in the location and training of academics from Africa.

Poetry was another area of focus in scholarship this year. Henri Oripeloye's 'The Development of Exilic Poetry in Anglophone West Africa' (*TvL* 52:i[2015] 155–67) is an important study of the ways in which exilic poetry has emerged in West Africa as a deliberate process predicated on 'the sordid social, political and economic realities in the sub-region' (p. 155). Drawing on an impressive array of authors and individual works, the essay exposes the vast range of personal subjectivities and migrator responses which this body of work has encapsulated. Christopher Anyokwu's 'The Essentials of Niyi Osundare's Poetry' (*TransL* 8:i[2015] 3–11) explores the theme of rural dispossession at the heart of Osundare's poetry, reading his oeuvre as a testament to class struggle which aspires to a classless future. Amongst the key features that allow for this are Osundare's use of multivalent form, limpid diction, wordplay, the interconnections between nature and man, animism, collectivism, and a revolutionary ideal. Enajite Eseoghene Ojaruega's 'The Place of Urhobo Folklore in Tanure Ojaide's Poetry' (*TvL* 52:ii [2015] 138–58) examines the use of Urhobo folklore in the writer's poetry, drawing links between Ojaide's cultural background and education and his complex rendering of folkloric themes in his work. Isidore Diala turns to music in 'Okigbo's Drum Elegies' (*RAL* 46:iii[2015] 85–111) to consider Okigbo's creation of 'a music of words' (p. 85), which references contemporary Nigerian politics through the use of funeral drum music which gives rise to surrealism. The article ultimately sees in Okigbo's poetry 'the possibility of surrealistic African funeral drumming, by daring meaninglessness through transcending its formulaic restrictions, breaking new frontiers of meaning, though that musical meaning may well lie beyond the clarities of denotative language' (p. 106).

*(c) East Africa*

This year saw engaged debates on different strands of East African literary scholarship, in particular the discussion of the shifting contact zones between Swahili and English in the literature of the region became a central strand of discussion. Chief among the publications dealing with this issue is the well-timed, scholarly, and diverse collection of essays, 'Habari ya English? What About Kiswahili? East Africa as a Literary and Linguistic Contact Zone' in a special issue of *Matatu* (46[2015] 1–274), edited by Lutz Diegner and Frank Schulze-Engler. Diegner and Schulze-Engler have drawn together various East African writers and academics in robust conversations that offer often trenchant analysis of the fluid relations between Kiswahili and English. In their introduction, 'Habari ya Contact Zone? East African Literature revisited' (*Matatu* (46[2015] 1–22), the editors sketch developments in Tanzania and Kenya regarding literature written in English and in Swahili to arrive at the following questions: 'How do the different literatures and literary histories relate to each other? What are thematic, stylistic, generic and diegetic similarities and differences? Has literature in English and Swahili developed along regional trajectories or has it mainly been shaped by national imperatives? What is the role of regional or national contexts in transcultural and transnational literatures?' (pp. 4–5). The articles that follow take up these questions in various ways to explore how the linguistic contact zone between English and Swahili has shaped the artistic production of the region. While the academic fields of Swahili studies and New Literatures in English (or anglophone postcolonial literature) seem quite distant, the editors are quick to point out that the contributions to this special issue belie this separation and instead explore prevalent innovative linguistic and literary practices that speak of much more hybrid linguistic landscapes. A particular strength of the volume is the combination of reflections by creative writers, translators, and academics on the two languages—this crossing of disciplinary boundaries itself represents a productive and engaging contact zone.

Abdulrazak Gurnah's thoughtful autobiographical reflection in 'Learning to Read' (*Matatu* 46[2015] 23–32) beautifully demonstrates the multiple entanglements of Swahili and English (among other languages such as Arabic, Kutchi, and Somali) in Zanzibar, where he grew up. And while his experience of childhood encounters of the contact zone between Swahili and English had a profound influence on him, migrancy and becoming a reader and writer in Europe did too; he observes that 'in England I was able to read widely, and slowly English came to seem to me to be hospitable and roomy and spacious... . I believe that writers come to writing though reading and that it is out of the process of accumulation, of hearing and of creating, of echoes and repetitions, that they fashion a register which enables them to write, a register of their own' (p. 31). Gurnah ends his reflections by suggesting that while English is the language he learned to write in, the past is not lost and continues to influence his writing in profound if intangible ways. Sissy Helff's piece on two of Gurnah's novels, 'Measuring Silence: Dialogic Contact Zones in Abdulrazak Gurnah's *By the Sea* and *Desertion*' (*Matatu* 46[2015] 153–68), provides insightful examples of cultural encounter embedded within multilingual and culturally diverse contexts that illustrate the entangled history of the author and his subject matter. She concludes: 'All in all, it can be said that Gurnah's novels, by combining different life- and storylines, create dialogic contact zones in which the past comes alive in the present' (p. 166). Another creative response comes from the dynamic Kenyan writer Yvonne Adhiambo Owuor, who in her piece 'O-Swahili' (*Matatu* 46[2015] 141–52) picks up on Gurnah's point about the capaciousness of languages, yet also remarks that language may function as a marker to determine friend or foe in times of conflict and war. She homes in on the linguistic diversity in Kenya and suggests that Swahili and English are but two strands in the multilingual dynamic of the country, which thrives on code-switching, hybrid dialects, and creative appropriation of diverse language material. Her reflections end by cautiously celebrating the opportunities and challenges this poses for the creative writer, who has 'to accept and recognize the various voices in and of story' (p. 150). The third autobiographical piece, 'The Role of Translations in the Development of Swahili Language and Literature' (*Matatu* 46[2015] 255–66), is that of the translator Gabriel Ruhumbika, who attributes his attachment to and continued creative expression in Swahili to the national climate in Tanzania after the 1967 Arusha declaration, which saw to the active promotion of Swahili as part of its policies on socialism and self-reliance. Looking back on his long career as translator, he suggests that continued translation from and to Swahili is crucial to keep the contact zone alive, and he recommends an end to the 'preoccupation with Kiswahili "Sanifu" ("Standard" Kiswahili)' in favour of attending to 'the whole range of Kiswahili varieties' (p. 264).

The first cluster of academic papers takes up the issue of asymmetrical power relations in contact zones, which Mary Louise Pratt, in *Imperial Eyes: Travel Writing and Transculturation*, defines as 'social spaces where disparate cultures meet, clash and grapple with each other' (p. 9). Euphrase Kezilahabi's 'Dialogic Swahili Literature: Key to Harmonization in Diversity' (*Matatu* 46[2015] 33–48) homes in on the enduring hegemony of the languages of the erstwhile colonizers which, along with contemporary pressure to adopt English, calls for a conscious effort to promote Swahili since it 'can be singled out as the essential inter-ethnic and cross-border language for constructing postcolonial identities', particularly in Tanzania and Kenya (p. 45). With a view to African indigenous knowledge systems, Kezilahabi goes even further to suggest that Swahili should not be allowed to replace local ethnic languages since these constitute important interpretative matrices of knowledge production. He concludes his piece by exhorting writers not to forget the significant role they play in keeping the multiplicity of local worlds alive. Said A.M. Khamis, in 'Nguvu versus Power: Resilience of Swahili language as Shown in Literature and Translation' (*Matatu* 46[2015] 49–66), echoes Kezilahabi's sentiment that Swahili is a resilient border-crossing language, but, unlike Kezilahabi, Khamis does not feel that the language is embattled; on the contrary, he interprets the prevalent presence of Swahili-language material in the literature of anglophone East African writers as diverse as Abdulrazak Gurnah, Moyez G. Vassanji, and Ngũgĩ wa Thiong'o as a sign of its enduring mutual cross-fertilization with English that far exceeds attempts to introduce 'local colour' (p. 55). In the second part of the essay Khamis turns to issues of translation and, like Ruhumbika, suggests that more translation from Swahili is needed to showcase this rich literary archive to a wider international audience.

Mikhail D. Gromov, in 'Regional or Local: On "Literary Trajectories" in Recent Swahili Writing' (*Matatu* 46[2015] 60–79), moves from the international arena to take a detailed look at the way in which Swahili literature in Tanzania and Kenya has developed from the 1960s until today. He identifies three distinct phases: from the 1960s literature contributes mainly to nation-building and the respective national imperatives that go along with this; from the 1980s literary production enters a period of consolidation and maturation of the local specificity with a new openness to the experimentation with literary form; during the 1990s and 2000s he identifies a turn in Swahili literature to take on a regional character as new literary forms reach beyond national borders to a regional readership. He attributes this latest regional shift to a number of factors which he carefully delineates as follows: 'this development was driven by political changes on the East African scene, internal changes in language policy (in Kenya), as well as "intra-literary" factors (such as the emergence of the "new novel"' (p. 78). Clarissa Vierke's piece, 'Comparing the Incomparable: On the Poetic Use of Language in Swahili Hip-Hop and "Classical" Swahili Poetry' (*Matatu* 46[2015] 81–112), makes the convincing, if somewhat surprising, discovery that contemporary Swahili hip hop exhibits similar linguistic 'contact phenomena' to those utilized in 'pre-twentieth century' practices of Swahili poetry (p. 81). Her comparative lexical analysis across the poetic genres and historical epochs reveals that the commonalities of linguistic experimentation, code-switching, and hybridization are much greater than expected. She concludes that, while the linguistic practices are quite similar, the impetus behind these practices is different for the two genres: 'In the *utendi* and other pre-twentieth century genres, poetic speech is expected to be elevated above the conventional form found in ordinary conversations', whereas contemporary hip hop seeks to 'approximate everyday speech in an urban context' (p. 95). Various aspects of linguistic hybridization form the focus of the last cluster of papers in this collection.

Ute Reuster-Jahn, in 'Literary Code-Switching in Contemporary Popular Fiction in Tanzania' (*Matatu* 46[2015] 113–40), explores code-switching in the fiction of the Tanzanian writer Eric James Shigongo to suggest that 'English in contemporary Tanzania embracing neoliberalism is strongly associated with social achievement and success and is seen as a highly desirable commodity' (p. 113). While most popular fiction is written in Swahili, Shigongo's work stands out because of his frequent incorporation of English dialogue in the otherwise Swahili text. Reuster-Jahn attributes this practice to the increasing social prestige of English and its promise of upward social mobility (p. 114). She offers an illuminating reading of Shigongo's work and biography to explain the place he occupies in the contemporary publishing industry in Tanzania. She ends her paper by comparing Shigongo to the Kenyan writer David G. Maillu, whose code-switching is more radical, as explored in Kyallo Wadi Wamitila's 'Mapping Hybridity, Transgression, and Literary Experimentalism in Kenyan Literature: David G. Maillu' (*Matatu* 46[2015] 207–22). Wamitila explains that David Maillu's recent novels construct an unusual and idiosyncratic linguistic contact zone out of a 'peculiar' mix of English and Swahili, which, while superficially resembling Sheng or Engsh, turns out to be an artistic invention by the author. Maillu's hybrid language challenges readers who have to confront linguistic liminality, a sign of 'the cultural/urban dissonances that pervade the society in which the narratives are set' (p. 207). Wamitila concludes his careful analysis by suggesting that Maillu's linguistic choices challenge the exclusionary and exclusive claims of the monolingual (p. 20), but wonders whether the relatively poor reception from readers suggests that the highly experimental nature of the texts does not in itself also represent a form of exclusion.

Alina N. Rinkanya's contribution also discusses code-switching from a Kenyan perspective: 'Code-Switching in Kenyan Women's Literature After 2000' (*Matatu* 46[2015] 169–84). The enhanced status of Swahili in Kenya, Rinkanya points out, has contributed to 'one of the most persistent and vital contact zones between Swahili and English' (p. 169). Rinkanya's analysis lends support to Gromov's assertion discussed earlier that contemporary 'East African writers promote a sense of regional identity and common belonging as well as a common future' (p. 169). The women writers she discusses have mainly used the online publishing platforms provided by *Kwani?* and *Storymoja*, and they include Haakasa Renja, Christine Bukana, Mary Kariuki, Connie Mutua, Yvonne Adhiambo Owuor, Wambui wa Wanjiru, and Juliet Maruru. For readers wishing to get a sense of contemporary women writers in Kenya, this article provides a good starting point. In the conclusion, Rinkanya asserts that the various strategies of code-switching lead to an

'Africanization' of English 'by turning it into the language not only of Kenyan but also of regional East African literature' (p. 181). This strategy, she argues, may bode well for imagining a common future for the region.

As we have seen, many papers in this collection touch briefly on the urban hybrid languages of Engsh and Sheng—these are more fully explored in Lilian Kaviti's essay 'From Stigma to Status: Sheng and Engsh in Kenya's Linguistic and Literary Space' (*Matatu* 46[2015] 223–54). Kaviti explains that these hybrid codes are spoken in quite distinct social settings: 'while Engsh is mainly spoken by upwardly mobile middle-class youth in Western Nairobi, Sheng is spoken by a much larger proportion of urban youth and has evolved from a stigmatized "ghetto" code in eastern Nairobi into a prestigious code' (p. 223). Both of these codes however, provide a bridge between local and global expression as well as a sense of regional identity, and are increasingly likely to be incorporated into the literary medium. Aldin K. Mutembi's piece, 'HIV/AIDS in Kiswahili and English Literary Works' (*Matatu* 46[2015] 185–206), supports this claim to a new sense of regional identity as he shows how writers from Kenya and Tanzania utilizing both languages 'have not only contributed to furthering an open debate that is needed to make people aware of HIV/AIDS but have also helped to set Swahili and English writing in Kenya and Tanzania onto converging trajectories' with regard to their approach to represent HIV/AIDS in their work (p. 185). As the foregoing discussion shows, this special issue of *Matatu* offers a major intervention in reframing the literary landscape of East African creative production by breaking down the imaginary walls between the disciplines of Swahili studies and anglophone African literary studies.

Two other publications grapple with similar themes: Rémi Armand Tchokothe, in 'Globalectical Swahili literature' (*JACS* 27:i[2015] 30–9), takes issue with the idea that Swahili literature is seen as minor and limited to the East African region. In his discussion he turns to Ngũgĩ wa Thiong'o's concept of 'globalectics' in order to argue convincingly that the two Swahili novels he investigates indeed have a 'glocal' reach, in terms of both content and form. Tchokothe explains that 'Nguũgĩ insists on the need to regard literature as a space for reconsidering established discourses and as a material for global interconnectedness and intercultural communication' (p. 31). The biography and the works of the two Swahili writers upon which the analysis focuses, namely *Babu Alipofufuka* ('When Grandfather Came to Life Again' [2001]) by the Tanzanian author Said A. Mohamed and *Bina-Adamu!* ('God's Wretched Sons' [2002]) by the Kenyan writer Kyallo Wamitila, suggest that movement, cosmopolitan concerns, and a non-nationalist orientation shift the debate in interesting ways. Tchokothe argues that 'the way texts enable parts of the world to enter in a dialogue that is on the ground of the globalectic traits they exhibit' (p. 31) should be enough to ensure they be granted their place in world literature, particularly as both novels offer a sophisticated critique of the way in which global capitalism structures local environments. He concludes by appealing for more concerted translation efforts in order to bring this literature to the attention of global critics so that 'Swahili [can] enter into a dialogue with works in other languages through translation' (p. 38). Mikhail D. Gromov's 'Bilingual Literature of Tanzania as a Specific Inter-Literary

Community' (*JLT&EA* 6:i[2015] 1–15) argues that the two branches in Tanzanian literature, anglophone and Swahili, emerge out of two different literary traditions. On the one hand, anglophone literature was influenced by classical and modern European literature; on the other hand, Swahili literature was shaped by 'the traditions of classical ancient Swahili writing' (p. 2); however, the two branches cannot be read as distinct literatures. By drawing on the theories of inter-literary communities as espoused by comparative literature scholar Dionýz Ďurišin, Gromov demonstrates that Tanzanian literature may have simultaneously developed into two different languages, Swahili and English, but it is possible to trace common traits between the two. In other words, both branches emerge out of similar historical, cultural, and ideological contexts. By focusing on selected works by Tanzanian authors such as Peter Palangyo, Gabriel Ruhumbika, Ebrahim Hussein, and Hamza Sokko, he clearly illustrates how we can appreciate the 'differentiating', 'integrative', and 'complementary' functions of the two branches of Tanzanian literature. In addition, he shows how the growth of anglophone popular writing in Tanzania 'confirmed the tendency towards the generic and typological levelling with its Swahili branch' (p. 12) by adapting from Swahili popular genres such as detective fiction and didactic melodrama. He concludes by noting that his observations in relation to inter-literary communities in Tanzania can be extended to larger literary systems in the East African region.

In a detailed and thoughtful study on the multi-dimensional meanings of belonging and home in Malawian poetry, *From Home and Exile: A Negotiation of Ideas about Home in Malawian Poetry*, published in Cameroon, Joanna Woods brings conventional close reading into conversation with the findings of her anthropological fieldwork. The author's note and chapters 1 and 2 could have been combined into an introduction, as all the pieces are quite brief and variously explain certain aspects of approach and methodology. What is particularly engaging about this study is the meticulous theoretical framing of the discussion in chapter 3, where Woods clearly delineates scholarly debates about the concept of home, exile, self, and community. It's a wide-ranging discussion that provides an astute overview of the theoretical terrain and is applicable to various contexts and literatures. In the next chapter, Woods presents us with a useful sketch of Malawian history and the biographical background of the five well-known Malawian poets whose poetry forms the focus of the analysis: Felix Mnthali, Frank Chipasula, Jack Mapanje, Lupenga Mphande, and Steve Chimombo (the poems are included in full at the back of the book in a separate appendix (pp. 149–210), and this in itself represents a valuable resource). Chapter 5 presents the core analysis of the poetry during the repressive Banda years (1966–94) and the way in which each poet engages with features of Malawi as home: its natural world, its myths and oral tales, its political conditions, and the resilience of its people. Woods comes to the following conclusion regarding her analyses: 'I see that home can be arrived at by way of two core themes: "landscape" and "relationship"' (p. 137). Whether these themes are tackled as utopian or dystopian visions, in both cases the poems create and re-create ideas of home in dynamic ways. The book concludes by returning to situating the findings in the disciplines of anthropology and literary studies.

Malawian poetry is also the focus of Nick Mdika Tembo's article, 'Representations of "Economic Hit Men" in Selected Malawian Poetry' (*Marang* 26[2015] 173–90). In this article Tembo uses the phrase 'economic hit men' to refer to international aid agencies that use financial and political power to control and dictate how developing countries should run their economies. This paper attempts to address the following questions: 'What choices have been made by Less Developed Countries by opening their economy to the outside world and how have those choices affected the living standards of people? When is foreign aid genuine and when is it greedy and self-serving? What is literature's (especially poetry's) place and potential as a mode of representation of, and resistance to, neo-colonialism and international aid agencies in sub-Saharan Africa?' (p. 174). By focusing on Malawian poets David Rubadiri, Felix Mnthali, and Bright Molande, Tembo examines how they use their poetry to offer a critique of the exploitative nature of international aid agencies. He argues that, drawing on postcolonial resistance theories, these poems can be read as a radical resistance and protest against neocolonialism. Put differently, Tembo contends that the poems selected address how unjust neoliberal ideologies have contributed negatively to the social and political conditions in Africa.

Ezinwanyi E. Adam's article, 'Postcolonialism and Socio-Political Development in Africa: Learning through the Literary Eyes of Ngugi Wa Thiong'o' (*JLAS* 5:vii[2015] 521–30), offers a related critique of the negative impact of capitalism in post-independence Kenya. While Nick Tembo's article focuses on neocolonial aid agencies, Adam returns to Ngũgĩ's murder mystery, *Petals of Blood*, to examine how the renowned author represents the negative impact of postcolonialism on the sociopolitical development of post-independent Kenya. Using ethnicity as well as hybridity and comparative models of postcolonial theory, Adam explores how *Petals of Blood* focuses on issues of betrayal of love, exploitation, violence, oppression, and death to show how these themes have contributed to the corruption and disintegration of most African nations in the post-independence era. He argues that, in spite of the demise of colonialism, the black imperialists and capitalists who took over continued to enrich themselves by exploiting the nation's resources and the masses. In other words, Adam notes that in *Petals of Blood* for most Kenyans, and by extension other African nations, it is not yet uhuru (Swahili for 'freedom') because life after independence has not transformed the livelihoods of the majority of the masses; instead it has benefited a small class of the elite bourgeoisie.

On a different variant of how global capital shapes labour relations, Jen Dickinson's article 'Chronicling Kenyan Asian Diasporic Histories: "Newcomers", "Established" Migrants, and the Post-Colonial Practices of Time-Work' (*PSP* 22[2015] 736–49) offers a cogent account of how Asian migrants to Kenya narrate time and belonging. She argues that the temporal production of distinctions between those migrants perceived as 'newcomers' and those who are deemed to be 'established' affords the diasporic communities the chance to navigate the continuing ambiguities of citizenship. The paper shows how contemporary labour patterns, dominated by temporary labour migrants and entrepreneurs, are quite distinct from historical forms of kin-chain migration between the 1890s and the 1960s (p. 737). Key to documenting these new patterns is the move away from space and place as principal analytical frames to a temporal frame: the picture that emerges from interviews and discourse analysis of newspapers and online fora is a complex collage of chronologies in which 'newcomers' are judged negatively against the 'established' narrative histories of diaspora formation within colonial migratory circuits and even pre-colonial trading networks that seek to cement a 'singularized Kenyan Asian history' (p. 742). Dickinson concludes that 'newcomers', those temporary workers who use their time in Kenya to secure other contract work, are perceived as a threat to such carefully constructed narratives of Kenyan Asianness.

Lynda Gichanda Spencer's timely piece, 'Visible Wars and Invisible Women: Interrogating Women's Roles During Wartime in Goretti Kyomuhendo's *Waiting: A Novel of Uganda at War*' (*EinA* 42:ii[2015] 109–28), situates her discussion within an increasingly expanding revisionist project by African women writers to represent the lives of women during war and its aftermath. She convincingly argues that women's various kinds of participation in war make a neat separation between various 'home fronts' and the 'frontlines' impossible (p. 110). In this way, the paper provides answers to the following questions: How does the novel reflect on the lived experiences of the individual, the family unit, and the community during times of conflict? How does Kyomuhendo represent the experience of violence and the disintegration of the home? What new forms of agency emerge during conditions of repression? Kyomuhendo's novel follows the life of 13-year-old Alinda during the last months of the 1979 civil war in Uganda that saw the end of the Idi Amin era. The novel insists that there are no safe spaces, that women find themselves on shifting ground that requires them to fulfil multiple roles: of active combatants, of survivors and victims of trauma, of suppliers of food, medical care, and other forms of assistance, whether required amidst the battle or in moments of ceasefire. This expanded agency, Spencer argues, causes conflicts once peace has been restored, because women are expected to fit neatly back into their more restricted roles within post-war patriarchal society. In fact, this tension already exists during times of war, as Kyomuhendo portrays conventional motherly roles as well as 'exceptional and transgressive female figures' (p. 115). Spencer concludes her article by suggesting that Kyomuhendo strikes a careful balance in portraying war as providing women with the possibility of redefining their capabilities and identities without romanticizing the devastation and trauma that it simultaneously inflicts on their lives.

Taking up the issue of conflict in a related context is Danson S. Kahyana's 'Writing Dictatorship and Misrule in Uganda: Susan N. Kiguli's *The African Saga*' (*SD* 4:iii[2015] 502–15). In this article Kahyana explores the various poetic techniques that Susan Kiguli deploys in her collection of poems *The African Saga*, to critique various forms of dictatorship and misrule. Although most of her poems focus on the dictatorship in Uganda, she also makes reference to repressive regimes in Malawi and Nigeria. Kahyana argues that she not only focuses on repressive political structures that exist in the public domain, but also explores how traditional patriarchal structures continue to marginalize women. For Kahyana, Kiguli's writing is important, because it allows the reader to understand the destructiveness of tyrannical regimes in exposing social ills, while also attempting to reconstruct a disintegrated society. Staying with the thematics of regional armed conflicts, Nick Mdika Tembo's article 'Paranoia, "Chosen Trauma" and Forgiveness in Leah Chishugi's *A Long Way from Paradise*' (*EAR* 32:ii[2015] 70–87) identifies signs of paranoia in Chishugi's memoir detailing her experiences during the Rwandan genocide. Tembo argues that, while such paranoia obviously finds its origins in the traumatic past, it may inhibit opportunities for reconciliation. Tembo situates Chishugi's text within the kind of life-writing that attempts therapeutically to re-enact the traumatic past in order to evince certain truth claims. Cautioning the reader against the way in which autobiography and memoir express such truth claims, Tembo convincingly shows how contesting truths compete for the reader's attention. On the one hand, there is Chishugi's overwhelming sense of distrust of fellow-Africans that results in her migration to the UK (she flees via Uganda, Kenya, Tanzania, Zambia, Malawi, Mozambique, and South Africa). But even there, the trauma resurfaces and prevents Chishugi from achieving emotional well-being and from re-establishing trusting relationships. This constitutes what the article identifies as 'chosen trauma'—unhealed and unaddressed, it has the power to influence even future generations (p. 80). Tembo concludes the paper by issuing a critique of the kind of memorialization of the genocide in Rwanda which prevents true reconciliation by casting people into the rigid categories of victims and perpetrators. Chishugi's memoir, he points out, supports this critique towards the end, when she comes to the realization that her own healing depends on confronting her past trauma in order to arrive at a more inclusive conception of Rwandans, regardless of their ethnicity.

The emerging interest in the intersection between disability studies and literary analysis has also shaped the debate in East African literary studies this year: Ken Junior Lipenga's article 'Voicing Marginality: Disability in Leila Aboulela's *Lyrics Alley*' (*JACS* [2015] 1–11) focuses on the representation of the disabled body in Aboulela's *Lyrics Alley*. He argues that the novel allows us to understand the difficulties experienced by those who find themselves in this marginal space. Of importance in Lipenga's article is an attempt to illustrate that, although disability tends to be seen or regarded as marginal, Aboulela's novel has imagined spaces in which this marginality becomes an enabling condition in that it encourages alternative forms of subjectivity, especially in relation to masculinity in an African context. Lipenga observes that in her earlier novels Aboulela focuses on those who exist on the periphery of society; likewise in *Lyrics Alley* the spotlight is on how the disabled male protagonist finds alternative ways of asserting his masculinity. In other words, Lipenga argues that, in a society that places a great deal of emphasis on 'hegemonic standards of desirability and sexuality' (p. 6), the protagonist, through his disability, discovers that poetry offers alternative forms of expression and an articulation of a patriotism that in turn enables a sense of belonging and of self. The article is important to disability studies because of its focus on the experiences of disability in African literary representations.

## 2. Australia

### (a) General Studies

David Throsby, Jan Zwar, and Tom Longden have published the second in a series of research papers on the book industry in Australia. *Book Authors and Their Changing Circumstances: Survey Method and Results* surveys over a thousand authors to assess how they are adapting to technological changes affecting the industry worldwide. Small details such as exports of children's books holding up national sales in 2014 are of interest. Larger-scale findings (that professional writers do not in the main earn very much, or that novelists and poets are most likely to seek grants) are less surprising, though it is worth knowing that seemingly better conditions for writers today are not all they appear to be. Poetry pays the least ($4,000 a year), while creative writing brings in between $9,000 and $15,000 on average, educational books earning the most. The survey shows that 'three quarters of all authors write trade books, with genre fiction writers making up the largest single category within this group'. Women dominate overall, and children's writers are mostly female. Average annual production was 1.6 books per person, with education and genre writers most prolific and literary fiction authors least so. Every group of writers has published some electronic work in recent times, with poets the least likely to do so and genre fiction writers the most 'with it'. Piracy, mainly via the electronic media, had affected 30 per cent of respondents however. Writers are mostly beyond middle age, with genre fiction having a high youthful quotient, followed by children's fiction and poetry.

The Australian government has committed to a new Book Council, despite downgrading the Literature Board. In 'When They Come To Save Books, What Will They Save?' (*Overland* 218[2015] 10–16), Stuart Glover offers a genealogy of the relation between the cultural value of literature and the commercial intellectual property of authors and publishers in order to explain the shift to the latter and offer strategies to avoid capture of the former by interests that do not prioritize such cultural value.

Another publishing study, but of the history (and possible future) of Australia's little magazines comes from Phillip Edmonds. *Tilting at Windmills: The Literary Magazine in Australia, 1968–2012* offers 'a history informed by political economy' (p. 2) to overcome common fixations on personalities, coteries, and mythicized reputations. Following a brief history of older production (*Meanjin, Realist Writer, Overland, Quadrant, Southerly, Westerly, Poetry Australia*), he concentrates on the proliferation in the 1970s (lots of ephemeral poetry mags and student newspapers partly connected to the counterculture around the Vietnam War and spreading beyond the major cities). Edmonds sees a calmer sorting out in the following decade, changes to editors and society in the 1990s, and changes induced by the Internet since 2000. Little magazines are depicted as 'democratic moments' providing a wide range of outlets and gatekeepers (p. 5) for a small intellectual class otherwise lacking real social power (p. 6). The small scale of these 'unreliable commodities' is set against their importance as social weathervanes (feminism expressed in *Hecate* and, later, 'migrant writing' in *Outrider*). This is despite their operating, in the main, separately from newspapers and popular magazines. They are problematically located between private reading, elite thinking, and the public arena, and require good organization, links to a university, and government subsidies while often expressing an anti-establishment and anti-commodity capitalism ethos. Operating at the literary 'cutting edge' can either render a publication disposable or confer belated value on it for having included writers who subsequently became famous.

As a guide to who was writing in which journals, and to key influences (such as the innovative *Tabloid Story*, which piggy-backed on other journals and newspapers and re-established the short story in the national literary scene), *Tilting at Windmills* is the book to read. Chapters 7 and 8 are of particular interest for tracking shifts from a national to a global outlook, the impact of creative writing courses, and the acceptance of contemporary literary theory. Edmonds is thorough, though he devotes a lot of space to *Quadrant* when more on *Southerly* might have been expected. There's a solid case study of *HEAT*, and he usefully points to the wealth of production from his home town, Adelaide (including lots on *Wet Ink*), and from several sites in Queensland. He laments the government ranking of research and creative outputs that favours international and refereed publications, doesn't see much benefit from the growth of writers' centres or the academic turn to 'creative industries', and, while noting the importance of online magazines such as *Jacket* and *Mascara*, suspects that under the new electronic forms there is less reflection and less provocation of the status quo.

Supplementing Edmond's comprehensive overview, Jim Davidson's 'Harmony with Discord: The Christensens and the Palmers' (*Meanjin* 74:ii[2015] 82–91) shows the relations between Clem and Nina Christensen and Vance and Nettie Palmer, based on the latter pair's contributions to *Meanjin*. Less respectably, *Man* magazine was an Australian forerunner to *Playboy* and significant in publishing some literary writers. Chelsea Barnett in '*Man*'s Man: Representations of Australian Post-War Masculinity in *Man* Magazine' (*JAS* 39:ii[2015] 151–69) cites some of its (bad) verse and several cartoons to chart the maintenance of 'he-man' masculinity in the face of 1950s anxiety about a national ideal of suburban domesticity, on the one hand, and increasing numbers of women in the workforce on the other. It makes useful contrasts to its later American replacement.

In ' "Something that makes us ponder": A Virtual Book Club in Central Queensland, 1928–38' (*QR* 22:i[2015] 15–28) Patrick Buckridge identifies a 1930s reading group mediated through reader contributions to the *Capricornian* newspaper, and Ken Gelder and Rachael Weaver enlist examples from Rolf Boldrewood, Mary Fortune, and the magazine *Heads of the People* [1847–8] to work 'Towards a Genealogy of Minor Colonial Australian Character Types' (*Interventions* 17:ii[2015] 211–28). They consider how the 'generic colonial figure or type of "white man" can be 'fractured and dispersed' (pp. 212–13) by representations of minor types such as the dandy, the roustabout, the 'night auctioneer', the pieman, and 'the inspector of nuisances'.

The nineteenth century is the focus for the third issue of *Australian Literary Studies* in 2015, slanted towards 'circuitry': movements of texts, people, and ideas around the globe. Anne Maxwell, in ' "The Beast Within"': Degeneration in *Dr Jekyll and Mr Hyde* and Three Australian Short Stories' (*ALS* 30:iii[2015] 47–61), notes the popularity of the Gothic mode in early Australian writing, suggesting (after Andrew McCann and others) its function as an encrypted outlet for colonial anxieties, one being that progress could be undone by degeneration as the lower classes 'infected' the morals and physique of the population. Stevenson's concerns are anticipated five years earlier by Marcus Clarke in his story 'The Mystery of Major Molineux'. Maxwell canvases possible sources of inspiration and suggests the influence of both tales on other Australian writers (Campbell McKellar's 'The Premier's Secret' and Ernest Favenc's 'My Only Murder'). All texts show the degeneracy of the bourgeois male, but the Australians are less inclined to moralize about it. Maxwell discusses medical thinking about deviant behaviour that might have informed the stories.

Her essay is followed by Kylie Mirmohamadi's 'Strange in the Cold Blue Light: Sensation and Science in the *Australian Journal*' (*ALS* 30:iii[2015] 62–78). The Melbourne-based periodical was a conduit for the latest European ideas, which were incorporated into colonial writing and reflected back in a mix of sensation plot, modern technology, 'scientific' observation of nature, and new ideas such as those promulgated by Huxley and Darwin. Several short stories are adduced as examples, Mary Fortune being one writer. The bush is a site of lurking violence and boundaries are dangerously unstable.

Philip Butterss, 'The Tennysons in Literary Adelaide' (*ALS* 30:iii[2015] 110–120), considers the link between Tennyson and South Australia, as forged by the poet's son being governor there. Butterss tracks local responses to the poet (as in Catherine Helen Spence's use of his work in *Clara Morison*, library borrowing patterns and press commentary), notes his popularity for connecting parts of the empire and suggesting the continued relevance of spiritual beliefs. Hallam Tennyson was feted for consolidating Adelaide's sense of itself as the literary capital of Australia. Other essays from this issue are listed in Sections 2(d), 'Drama', and 2(e), 'Author Studies'.

Nicholas Birns, editor of *Antipodes*—North America's major Australian and New Zealand literature journal—was confirmed this year by *The Australian* newspaper as Australian literature's 'honest umpire'. His *Contemporary Australian Literature: A World Not Yet Dead* is unabashedly autobiographical in its framing and reads Australian literature in relation to the normalization of neoliberalism as a global political discourse. Birns's discovery of Australian literature came about as a means to escape the hold of Reagan-era values on US ideas about culture, and his book works as a rare balance of the anecdotal and the analytic. Birns moves deftly through his own experience with Patrick White and Les Murray to provide a kind of allegory for the place of Australian literature on the world stage. He shows the way the discourse of economic rationalism smuggled neoliberalism in through the back door of Australian public discourse. He answers the question: 'Was hyper-capitalism the price required in order to achieve racial justice?' by asserting that 'Neoliberalism may pay lip service to diversity, but it often deepens the social inequality that is racism's legacy' (p. 15). The title's 'contemporary' is a loose term, the text winding back to Christina Stead and smuggling in Eleanor

Catton's New Zealand novel. For Birns, if an author provides insight into the Antipodean embrace of—or, at times, resistance to—neoliberalism, then she or he is worthy of survey. The book moves in a space of several pages from the question of a book's length and its relative sales to close, appreciative reading of figures from Peter Carey to Alexis Wright. The honest umpire delivers a balanced, optimistic, but nonetheless critical evaluation of a country that has fascinated him for thirty years.

David Carter continues to promote interest in Australian literature overseas, here co-editing *Australian Studies: Proceedings of the 14th International Conference of Australian Studies in China* with Liang Zhongxian and Han Feng. Tony Moore and Mark Gibson chart the long history of coterie artists crossing into the commercial realm as a basis for contemporary arts policies ('Fringe to Famous: Bohemians, Entrepreneurs, Audiences and the Enabling State', pp. 20–34), Zhengfa Chen looks at 'Patrick White Studies in China' (pp. 73–8), and Xiang Lan ('Nature Writ Large', pp. 86–97) essays an 'eco-interpretation' of White's novels. White also supplies material for Xing Chunli in 'Becoming Indigenous: A Comparative Analysis of Patrick White's *A Fringe of Leaves* and Gail Jones *Sorry*' (pp. 123–31). Xing uses Deleuze's notion of 'becoming' to look at white settler desire to become Indigenous. A different concept of ecology frames Diao Keli's overview of the networks behind literary production, in which he relates contemporary writers' work to past constructions of identity by Australian nationalism ('Australian Literature: A Perspective on the Ecology of Literature', pp. 79–85). Zhang Rongsheng and Ding Wei read Michael Wilding's *Academia Nuts* and Elizabeth Jolley's *The Sugar Mother* against other fiction dealing with universities ('Interpretation of Academic Fiction in Britain, America and Australia', pp. 102–9), while Zhang Geping takes a biographical approach to the latter author ('Elizabeth Jolley's Life Experience's Influence on her Literary Creation', pp. 98–101). Indigeneity features again in ' "Their Own Voices"—On the Hybrid Construction of Aboriginality in *Carpentaria*' by Zhan Chunjuan (pp. 117–22), and Xu Xianjing picks up the ecological theme again in 'From Conquest to Collapse: Ecological Thoughts in the Depiction of Wheatbelt in *Cloudstreet* and *Dirt Music*' (pp. 132–45). There's also a paper on the film *Crocodile Dundee* and the Australian Dream by Wei Xutao (pp. 110–16).

Writing continues in Anhui University's *Oceanic Literary Studies*. Its 2015 issue contains essays on Bush realism, Alex Miller's *The Ancestor Game*, and Peter Carey's *The Fat Man in History*. Continuing the transnational turn, Ouyang Yu reflects on his own shuttling between Australia and China, his translations of Chinese poems and their reception in Australia, and the production of 'rubbish' or 'shit' poems (his and others') as marks of disaffection with both countries, in 'A Poetic Revolution in Keywords: On Contemporary Chinese Poetry 1' (*Antipodes* 29:i[2015] 193–215).

Fiona Polack calls for a renewal of the comparative work once regularly done between Australia and Canada in 'Juxtaposing Australian and Canadian Writing' (*JASAL* 15:iii[2015] 11 pages). Claiming that a non-hierarchical 'juxtaposition' can 'produce off-kilter reflections that undermine entrenched notions of national exceptionalism, and draw our attention to textual and cultural phenomena that might otherwise go unnoticed' (p. 1), she pairs Melissa Lukashenko's *Steam Pigs* with Eden Robinson's *Monkey Beach*, Kate Grenville's *The Secret River* with Michael Crummey's *River Thieves*, and Michelle de Kretser's *Questions of Travel* with Will Ferguson's *419*. Juxtaposing texts rather than undertaking fully fledged comparative reading fails to show much about how one text illuminates the other, but the readings are sound and the general proposition is well worth attention.

This idea of Australian literature as an international network is developed further in *JASAL* 15:iii[2015] under the subheading 'Borders, Skins, Mappings', introduced by Brigid Rooney and Brigitta Olubas. General discussions come from Suvendrini Perera ('Burning our Boats', the 2015 Dorothy Green Lecture, with an Afterword from Joseph Pugliese), Vilashini Cooppan ('The Corpus of the Continent: Embodiments of Australia in World Literature'), and a panel comprising Robert Dixon ('National Literatures, Scale and the Problem of the World'), Nicholas Birns ('Is Australian Literature Global Enough?'), Paul Giles ('Transnationalism and National Literatures: The Australian Case'), and Sneja Gunew ('Scenes of Reading: Australia–Canada–Australia').

Perera takes the image of the ship in flames and works from Ondaatje's *The Cat's Table* and Amitav Ghosh's distinction between purposeful exodus and disruptive dispersal to rigorously and roundly criticize Australia's refugee exclusion policies. The burning boats are reconfigured in the burning bodies of suicide protests, and the mirrored violent excess of state and dispersed person requires (after Debrix and Barder) an ethic of 'inventorying the scattered', not as an impossible attempt to recover and remedy, but as an opening to resist closing borders when confronted with horror.

As a way of emphasizing the local nuance, Vilashini Cooppan mounts a case for bringing affect into world literature studies, rehearsing her personal journey to and into Australia alongside commentary on White's *Voss*, Malouf's *Remembering Babylon*, and the transnational settings of Joan London's *Gilgamesh, a Novel*. Playing on the conceptual implications of occupying a 'continent', Cooppan shows how the sense of space, borders, and the deep time of geology it gives rise to interrupts notions of nation, region, and globe. Invoking Aboriginal concepts and an understanding of genre as network and process, she looks (following Manuel De Landa) to a sense of history as a dynamic of non-linear intersecting forces.

Robert Dixon uses Henri Lefebvre, Neil Brenner, Nirvana Tanoukhi, and other analysts of space and scale to question the value of accepting national or global frames for literary study. Usefully, he asks what scale a book favours (body, home, suburb, nation, region, etc.) and what scale/s we read in/from. He wonders whether Kim Scott's and Alexis Wright's locally situated novels have not bypassed the national scale to reach a world intertext and readership, and critiques the idea implicit in World Literature that there is a transcendent point from which a reader can view the field, insisting on historically and geographically interested analysis.

Nicholas Birns canvases many of the transnational flows in and around Australian literature, arguing that its vitality lies in its lack of a set canon, and noting different ideas of its features depending on the position of the viewer

(Herbert Jaffa in New York, or British literati championing the otherwise little-known expatriate Michael Thwaites).

Paul Giles sees transnationalism 'as a critical method, not as a description of inherent cultural forms' (p. 1) and notes how the drive to establish a national literature has been supplanted by a cultural studies paradigm in which literary texts are read as data evidencing some social phenomenon. This seems, for him, to be linked with the underfunding of Australian universities and a general anti-intellectual culture (that he tracks from Joseph Furphy's parodic satire to Les Murray's verse). World Literature's attention to 'processes of reciprocity' allows us to see beyond narrow national assessments (Murray's international reach; Alexis Wright's links with magic realism and Carlos Fuentes). Overlooking the contradiction of speaking from a Department of *English* Literature, Giles declares that 'the notion of an undergraduate degree in "Australian Literature" seems... as intellectually absurd as one in "Australian Philosophy"', and mounts a case for Henry Handel Richardson being read as part of modernism (read Virginia Woolf and E.M. Forster), though he also concedes that broad global formations 'should always be counterpointed by the thick descriptions of particular situations' (p. 5).

Sneja Gunew, after twenty years of teaching in Canada, takes a critical look at the monolingual norm in Australian literature and argues for 'intra-cosmopolitan multilingualism' (p. 1), noting Kim Scott's play with Noongar language under his English prose in *That Deadman Dance*, Christos Tsiolkas's mix of 'ocker' and migrant English in *Barracuda*, and Antigone Kefala's writing. She observes that 'race' (including 'whiteness studies') has become a productive frame in which to re-read Australian texts, and cites work from Canada alongside Maxine Beneba Clarke's stories. David Malouf's work also comes in for some comment, with a final exhortation to attend to 'moments of eloquence that do not communicate easily', particularly in connection to asylum seekers.

Wenche Ommundsen and Zhong Huang look at an early Chinese community newspaper ('Towards a Multilingual National Literature: The *Tung Wah Times* and the origins of Chinese Australian Writing') and their archival opening up of Australian literary history to include work in languages other than English is matched by Michael Jacklin's '*El contestador australiano* and the transnational flows of Australian writing in Spanish'. The issue also contains articles on individual writers, which are listed below.

Situating itself in a wider space of international comparative cultural studies, *Transcultural Writers and Novels in the Age of Global Mobility* by Arianna Dagnino includes interviews with Australian writers Inez Baranay and Brian Castro. There is also analysis of their work in the context of the multiple negotiations entailed in working across national and cultural boundaries. Castro gets his deserved share of critical attention, but the more peripatetic Baranay slips off the Aust. Lit. radar, so it is good to see her getting some notice in an appropriate context.

Transnational movements of culture have always been subject to some kind of control, and Nicole Moore follows up her book-length study of censorship in Australia with an edited collection *Censorship and the Limits of the Literary*, in which her chapter, 'Surrealism to Pulp: The Limits of the Literary and

Australian Customs' (pp. 105–18) takes up Felski, Attridge, Taussig, Blanchot, and Frow to rethink the uses as well as the anti-utilitarian nature of the literary; to consider the literary as performative event; and to ask, 'when is the literary? At which reading moment does it happen?' (p. 106). In this context, censorship becomes part of a dynamic shaping of what is/is not offensive, what is/is not literary value. With nods to Catholic Ireland and Apartheid South Africa, Moore looks at the Australian Censorship Board's 1944 treatment of *Les Chants du Maldoror* and of a New York pulp novel *Furnished Room* in 1936. The Minister for Customs declared the former a Satanic obscenity, but Board opinion differed: it was too literary to be censored, or not literary enough to be worth censoring (p. 112). The pulp novel was considered either so trite it was not worth worrying about or such bad writing that the public should be protected from it. By admitting or denying entry to texts, censorship acted alongside other modes of nation-making to define the literary field.

Censorship is also represented in the collection by Jeremy Fisher's 'Out of the Shadows: The Emergence of Overt Gay Narratives in Australia' (pp. 192–204). Fisher surveys the legal and publishing situation from the 1950s onwards, with Australia banning books by Gore Vidal, James Baldwin, and its own G.M. Glaskin. With legal and social changes in the 1970s, censorship was relaxed. Gay activist newsletter *Camp Ink* began including poetry, and 1972 saw more gay magazines appearing and a novel, *Wayward Warriors*, by Wal Watkins. Popular publishers such as Horwitz began issuing gay fiction; Frank Moorhouse included gay material in his stories. Longer work (Gary Dunne *If Blood Should Stain the Lino* and Simon Payne's *The Beat*) appeared in the 1980s and the mainstream Penguin published Sasha Soldatow's *Private—Do Not Open* in 1987. AIDS-related writing is mentioned, and the chapter closes noting work by Graeme Aitken and Christos Tsiolkas.

Tom Lynch sketches a comparative outline of how the pastoral ideal was put into social practice in settlement schemes in 'Ecopastoralism: Settler Colonial Pastoral Imagery in the US West and Australian Outback' (*ALS* 30: ii[2015] 144–57). Elimination of native peoples and plants by the introduction of sheep and cattle was motivated by images of wilderness being civilized, though settlement on the land meant the unsettling removal of an authentic ecology. As environmentalism takes hold, pastoralists shift from being heroes of settlement to villains of destruction. Lynch notes that sustainable 'New Ranching' in the US finds little echo in Australia because cattle do not as easily substitute for kangaroos as for bison. The article is fairly 'broad-brush' and more attentive to America than Australia.

The humanities have moved through critiquing boundaries of race and gender to questioning the human/animal divide and how it is represented and operates discursively. *JASAL* 15:ii[2015] is themed as 'On Species'. One of the guest editors, Ken Gelder, considers Foucault and Agamben's work on Linnaeus as a path into examining the animal fable in 'Colonial Modernity, Native Species and E.J. Brady's "The Friar Bird's Sermon: An Australian Fable"' (*JASAL* 15:ii[2015] 9 pages). He asks whether it is always about humans or sometimes about 'the conditions of animals themselves, as species' (p. 1). Gelder tracks Linnaeus's influence on Solander, Banks, and John Gould in their recording of Australian nature, noting Gould's comment that some birds thrived on European settlement, the friar bird becoming both a household companion and a major crop-eating pest. Brady's story has the friar bird defending Australia's birds against Adam Lindsay Gordon's disparaging descriptions, berating the curlew for depressing Australian poetry with its mournful cry and preaching a positive outlook on the nascent nation. If Foucault saw Linnaeus as stripping animals of language and history, Gould and Brady restore both to them, if only to implicate them in the colonial project.

In the same issue, Rachael Weaver writes on 'Ecologies of the Beachcomber in Colonial Australian Literature' (*JASAL* 15:ii[2015] 14 pages). She compares the work of Louis Becke with that of the naturalist E.J. Banfield, whose 1908 *The Confessions of a Beachcomber* she takes as marking a shift from the vagabond scrounger to the ecologically minded isolate. Becke's fiction uses specific reference to species to differentiate native populations from white intruders (who see islands as undifferentiated colourful backdrops), even though he displays a detailed knowledge of island fauna and flora himself. Ecological interest is, however, matched by interests in hunting and trade. A similar biographical and textual reading of Banfield's work on Dunk Island points up his more nature-centred outlook, though Banfield is also caught in contradiction—between preserving the island as a nature reserve and favouring economic development, between indigenizing himself and disparaging Aborigines.

Timothy Clark's *Ecocriticism on the Edge* reads the Anthropocene as a crucial concept for thinking about past and contemporary cultural artefacts. He includes Henry Lawson's story 'Telling Mrs Baker' as a case study for examining the relationship with the non-human in narratives whose nationalist ideology is typically thought of in anthropocentric terms.

'Australian Film in the Australian Literature Classroom' is the subject of Theodore F. Sheckels's article (*Antipodes* 29:i[2015] 105–15). He notes that many teachers outside Australia first encountered that country by way of films promoted by the national government in the late 1970s and through the 1980s. After a quick history of Australian feature films, Sheckels quickly considers *Australian Rules*, *Rabbit-Proof Fence*, *Beneath Clouds*, *Samson and Delilah*, and *The Sapphires* as illustrations of race relations and insertions of black voices into the national imaginary. He asks what 'the classics' (*Breaker Morant*, *Gallipoli*, etc.) say about the nation they represent, and suggests links to literary versions. There's not a lot to argue with, but not much that is surprising either.

*Narrative and Identity Construction in the Pacific Islands*, edited by Farzana Gounder, includes Dorothea Hoffman's 'Moving through Space and (Not?) Time: North Australian Dreamtime Narratives' (pp. 15–35), Clive Moore's 'Australian South Sea Islanders' Narratives of Belonging' (pp. 155–76), and Hannah Birk's ' "[P]ulling tomorrow's sky from [the] kete": Culture-Specific Narrative Representations of Re/membering in Contemporary Māori and First Australian Novels' (pp. 209–23). Moore's piece is of relevance to the study of Faith Bandler's writing, while Birk's focuses on Patricia Grace and on Bruce Pascoe's *Earth* [2001].

In another slightly tangential work, Valentyna Skybina offers 'A Cultural Portrait of Australia' by surveying 'Australian Diachronic Dictionaries' (in Karpova, Kartashkova, Egorov, and del Bianco, eds., *Life Beyond Dictionaries*, pp. 42–53). Marije van Hattum also looks at language change, examining the preservation of minority language in diaspora and its effects on Australian English in ' "Queensland for ever & Augus un ballybug go braugh": The Expression of Identity in Nineteenth-Century Irish Emigrant Letters' (pp. 105–22). This is a chapter in *Language and Identity: Discourse in the World*, edited by David Evans, which champions the cause of minority cultures across the world.

One of the first dictionaries in Australia was a list of words of the Eora people compiled by Lieutenant William Dawes. His diaries are the source of critical and philosophical enquiry for Ross Gibson, whose book *26 Views of the Starburst World* [2012] is examined by Catherine Noske in 'Seeing the Cosmos: Ross Gibson's "Simultaneous Living Map" ' (*JASAL* 15:iii[2015] 11 pages). Noske and Gibson both turn from rational categorization to thinking of language through 'views', or experiential fragments in the hope that we may learn to see anew. Gibson extends Barbara Bender's work on landscape, and his meditations on Dawes's Eora words are a self-aware critique of critical reading and writing that sits alongside Jane Rogers's *The Promised Lands* [1997], Kate Grenville's *The Lieutenant* [2008], and Bangarra Dance Theatre's *Patyegarang* [2014]. Noske also alludes to work by Katrina Schlunk and Stephen Muecke and relates Gibson's ideas to Vilashini Cooppan's view of world literature as shifting nexuses of localities. Noske turns to reading her own place, invoking Kim Mahood's *Craft for a Dry Lake* [2000], John Kinsella's writing, local history, Aboriginal lore, and Paul Burman's *The Snowing and Greening of Thomas Passmore* [2008].

Of tangential interest as a study in book history and the circulation of works under colonialism, Michael Organ salvages the work of an Australian artist illustrating a 1924 school-reader publication of *Alice in Wonderland* in 'Pre-Raphaelite Wonderland: Christian Yandell's Alice' (*Antipodes* 29:i[2015] 181–91). Also working in and around popular magazines and artwork, with attention to influential public intellectuals and writers, Louise D'Arcens examines the uses of medieval ideas and iconography in 'Australian Medievalism: Time and Paradox' (in Ashton, ed., *Medieval Afterlives in Contemporary Culture*, pp. 177–86).

Adam Aitken considers discourses of race and imperial governance in a 1985 publication by 'Chinese' Morrison, in 'Australians Going Native: Race, Hybridity and Cultural Anamorphism in G.E. Morrison's *An Australian in China*' (*JEASA* 6:i[2015] 12 pages). In 'Home Was Where the Hearth Is: Fire, Destruction and Displacement in Nineteenth-Century Settler Narratives' (*Antipodes* 29:i[2015] 29–42), Grace Moore uses some old illustrations of burnt-out homes to consider 'how old associations between fire and domesticity were challenged ... in the bush' (p. 30). Moore observes that bushfire served as a marker of distance from 'home' (identified with Britain and Dickensian Christmas cheer) and forced a new figuring of fire's place in Australian story.

While the comparison of Australian works of fiction to global postcolonial works is now commonplace, it is heartening to see the rigour with which this is extended to life-writing in Gillian Whitlock's latest work, *Postcolonial Life Narratives: Testimonial Transactions*. Whitlock's book is broad in historical and temporal scope, covering, for instance, Watkin Tench's journals (which are intriguingly compared to the writing of Olaudah Equiano, published in London at a similar time), as well as Bennelong's letter, and an authoritative revisiting of Sally Morgan's *My Place* and its reception in academic and non-academic circles. The book is detailed and wide-reaching, ranging in its methodology from consideration of the material circulation of life-narrative texts to the analysis of their production and reception.

Life narrative also features in *Southerly*'s issue on 'The Naked Writer' (75:ii[2015]). Kristina Olsson reflects sensitively on her 'family memoir' and how it nearly was not written in 'On Writing *Boy, Lost*' (*Southerly* 75:ii[2015] 55–70). Paul Genoni and Tanya Dalziell analyse a perhaps exceptional family memoir, 'Desperately Seeking Suzanne: Suzanne Chick's Adoptee-Narrative *Searching for Charmian*' (*LW* 12:iv[2015] 385–99). The autobiography's subject, adoptee Suzanne Chick, was unable to meet her birth mother because she had committed suicide. Chick plays with tensions between third- and first-person voice in a narrative without a reconciliation, its gaps partially filled by photographs. Susan Hosking delves into the correspondence between George Meredith, a prominent free settler in 1820s Tasmania, and his second wife, Mary Anne Meredith. Her family and estate management involves cultivating a garden, and his management of his wife is couched in metaphors of horticulture: 'Saying It With Flowers: A Marriage Made in Hobart' (in Blaber, ed., *Whaddya Know? Writings for Syd Harrex*, pp. 28–40).

Juliana de Nooy, in 'Postfeminist Worldmaking in Australian Memoirs of Life in France' (*JLLC* 62:i[2015] 55–61), makes the startling observation: 'While only one book-length memoir of an Australian in France was published in the 1990s, thirty-seven have appeared since 2000.' Nearly all of these are tales of 'self-reformation' by women for women, in which France figures as a magical site of sophistication and luxury. Consumerism and the individual feature in postfeminist narratives, though this vision is challenged by working-class and older women. Nonetheless the transformation myth holds for all work. De Nooy provides another overview of these memoirs—particularly those surreptitiously themed on language learning—in 'Encountering Language Difference in Australian Memoirs of Living in France' (*LW* 12:i[2015] 25–42). Focusing on Ellie Nielsen's *Buying a Piece of Paris*, she argues that it is a 'model [of] an alternative way of negotiating language difference for the reader', improving on other anglophone accounts of linguistic alienation (p. 39).

In a meditation on homeliness and nomadology, centred at first around *Reading the Country* by Paddy Roe, Stephen Muecke, and Krim Benterrak, Ken Gelder considers how the terms are intertwined, as are 'becoming indigenous' and 'becoming modern'. In 'Thirty Years On: Reading the Country and Indigenous Homelessness' (*AuHR* 58[2015] 17–27) he draws on intersections between cultural criticism and anthropology, alluding to work by

John Frow and Elizabeth Povinelli, to end with some criticism of Alison Ravenscroft's recent work.

While some components of *The Blackwords Essays* began in 2014, this year saw the completion of this set of resources hosted on AustLit and focused on Aboriginal literature, written by Anita Heiss. Nine essays are predominantly introductory and very comprehensive. As well as a general introduction to Aboriginal writing and related issues of identity, topics include the Aboriginal concept of country, the Stolen Generations, collective storytelling, children's literature, and Indigenous literacy. Another important resource comes from Anne Brewster, who begins *Giving this Country a Memory: Contemporary Aboriginal Voices of Australia* with the assertion that the 'expressive modern individual' of the Western author-position has been withheld from Indigenous writers (p. xi). Brewster's book is structured around single-author-focused chapters engaging with a range of Aboriginal writers including Kim Scott, Romaine Moreton, Jeanine Leane, Melissa Lucashenko, Marie Munkara, Alf Taylor, and Doris Pilkington Garimara. Each chapter provides a survey of the author's career and work followed by an edited selection from extensive interviews that Brewster conducted with her subjects. The book functions effectively both as an introduction to the field and as a work of scholarship in its own right. Brewster's point is not only to restore the privilege of speech to Aboriginal authors, but to show how the author position itself might change in light of such a methodology, giving rise to readings of ideas ranging from sovereignty to Aboriginal humour.

Work centred on Indigenous issues includes Rohan Wilson's examination of 'extinction narrative' (after Patrick Brantlinger) in a nineteenth-century colonist poem and two twentieth-century novels, 'Extinction Discourse in *Wanting* and *Doctor Wooreddy's Prescription for Enduring the Ending of the World*' (*Antipodes* 29:i[2015] 5–17). Wilson faults Beth Roberts's *Manganinnie*, Richard Flanagan's *Wanting*, Robert Drewe's *The Savage Crows*, and even Mudrooroo's book for 'reviving a discourse through commentary [rather than] confronting it as the monument to a crueller time' (p. 8). Neither Flanagan's indignation at colonialist power nor Mudrooroo's subversive reversal of perspective prevents melancholic presentations of inevitable death. The former corrects himself only by commenting on survival outside his novel's frame, and the latter by reworking his materials in *Masters of the Ghost Dreaming*. Robert Edric's *Elysium* and Brian Castro's *Drift* more effectively allow for racial adaptation and survival.

The centenary of the First World War continues to generate literary reflections. Anna Branach-Kallas and Nelly Strehlau have edited *Re-imagining the First World War: New Perspectives in Anglophone Literature and Culture*. This collection of conference papers from mostly Polish academics includes, under the section heading of '(De)Mythologization', Ryszard W. Wolny's 'The War Quandary: Some Notes on the Images of the Great War in Pre–1939 Australian Literature' (pp. 224–34), and 'The Anzac Legend and Australian National Identity One Hundred Years after the Great War' by Tomasz Gadzina (pp. 234–46)—mainly focused on film and television.

Diaspora writing takes an unusual turn in Amit Sarwal's *Labels and Locations: Gender, Family, Class and Caste—The Short Narratives of South*

*Asian Diaspora in Australia.* Most attention of late has gone to writers of East
and Southeast Asian heritage, so analysis of the often quite different dynamics
of South Asian migration (including the double migration of Indo-Fijians) is
welcome. Familiar names appear (Yasmine Gooneratne, Chitra Fernando,
Satendra Nandan, and Adib Khan), supplemented by newer generations
(Christopher Cyrill, Sunil Badami, Manik Datar, Suneeta Peres da Costa,
Sunil Govinnage) and less well-known voices (Sujhatha Fernandes, Rashmere
Bhatti, Shrishti Sharma). The subtitle indicates their thematic treatment, and
texts are somewhat overwhelmed by lengthy coverage of social theory. More
attention to the different kinds of text being examined might deepen the
commentary centred on 'location', and the publishing editor should have
prevented repetition of the same material in different chapters, but it's a useful
start on this expanding field.

Kylie Cardell and Kate Douglas have edited *Telling Tales: Autobiographies
of Childhood and Youth*, the book of a 2013 special issue of *Prose Studies*. It
includes Pamela Graham's 'Alice Pung's *Growing Up in Australia*: The
Cultural Work of Anthologized Asian-Australian Narratives of Childhood'
(pp. 67–83). Graham uses Graham Huggan's distinction between integrative
and interventionary anthologies and analysis of paratextual features to show
how Pung's collection tries to appeal to a wide readership and to lever
perceptions of national identity by presenting a range of differences and family
relationships under a universal 'coming-of-age' narrative and incorporating
stereotypic taxonomies ('Battlers', 'Mates') and humour.

*(b) Fiction*
Children's literature and its connection to postcolonial memory is the subject
of Troy Potter's 'Ghosts of Australia's Past: Postcolonial Haunting in
Australian Adolescent Novels' (*IRCL* 8:ii[2015] 185–200). He analyses Victor
Kelleher's *Baily's Bones* [1988] and Anthony Eaton's *A New Kind of Dreaming*
[2001] in the contexts of Reconciliation and of the Boat People crisis. Both
books use the mystery/detective genre to explore past disorder in the hope of
re-establishing social harmony. Their adolescent 'investigators' do not simply
mature into adults but remain at odds with most adults in their communities.
The books animate the landscape; hauntings lead to the exposing of past
killings. These figure a postcolonial anxiety/amnesia in need of correction, but
each book fails to achieve its ideological goals. In Kelleher, white suffering
displaces black deaths and the past is ritually buried. Eaton allows a 'female
racial other who is silenced [to be] rescued and spoken for by a white male'
(p. 196) and, though there are implied links, refugee and Aboriginal issues fail
to connect.

Another study of young adult fiction is 'The Perfect Place to Set a Novel
about the End of the World? Trends in Australian Post-Nuclear Fiction for
Young Adults' (*Bookbird* 53:ii[2015] 22–9) by Elizabeth Brathwaite. The
author posits a difference between Australian writing (interested in how
disaster allows discussion of national issues such as the treatment of refugees
and Aborigines) and overseas work (more focused on the causes of apocalypse

and how to prevent another). Brathwaite sketches Australia's official relation to nuclear activities and uses Anthony Eaton's *Nightpeople* and Claire Zorn's *The Sky So Heavy* as case studies.

'Love on the Land: Australian Rural Romance in Place' (*ES* 98:ii[2015] 204–24) by Kylie Mirmohamadi inspects a relatively new popular genre—a version of 'chick lit' set in the farmlands of Australia's interior. Sampling works set in the Mallee (dry sandy scrub) country of South and Western Australia, the author points not just to the generic blend of Western, female romance and colonial adventure romance, but to how these books sit in the Australian market (covers with 'big sky' landscapes and a woman at the centre, populist website support) and how they address local social concerns (the decline of rural communities, settler-colonial history, and ecology). Australian literary traditions of horse-riding and resourceful country women are invoked (Catherine Martin and Rosa Praed are forerunners). Revegetation of over-cleared land and romantic tales of homecoming suggest white settlers assuming the custodianship of country commonly accorded to Aborigines and making their home on Aboriginal land. Kerry McGinnis's *Mallee Sky* [2013] acknowledges some of this problematic: other books tend to gloss over it.

Graham Huggan, 'Australian Literature, Risk, and the Global Climate Challenge' (*LIT* 26:ii[2015] 85–105), investigates Australian climate-change novels to ask whether the social realist novel can function adequately in the Anthropocene—a question answered more or less in the affirmative. He surveys Kate Grenville's *The Idea of Perfection* and Tim Winton's *Breath* to argue that each novel's engagement with the ongoing effects of devastation is better parsed through Ulrich Beck's notion of 'risk society' than through evocations of apocalypse. For Huggan, social realism's engagement with everyday lived exposure to risk allows such texts to evoke the exigencies of climate change.

Isabel Carrera Suárez examines 'The Stranger *Flâneuse* and the Aesthetics of Pedestrianism' (*Interventions* 17:vi[2015] 853–65), thinking (aided by Sara Ahmed) about how post-diasporic women walk cities challenging older modernist ideas about the *flâneur*. Along with other works, the author considers Simone Lazaroo's *The Australian Fiancé* (with attention to the book's use of photography) and Tsu Ming Teo's *Behind the Moon* (highlighting how the city street is not neutral when it comes to race and sexuality). Diaspora also frames Lachlan Brown's sensitive and considered account of recent Australian short fictions, which explores the relative international success of writers like Ali Alizadeh and Nam Le as well as analysing their style to the level of the sentence: 'Worlds Apart: Nam Le's *The Boat* and Ali Alizadeh's *Transactions*' (*TransL* 7:ii[2015] 12 pages).

In 'Excruciating Moments: On Writing Cross-Cultural Agency in the Novel' (*NW* 12:iii[2015] 339–48), Annee Lawrence theorizes the writing of her novel, set in Indonesia and featuring Indonesian characters. Lawrence draws on Gadamer to suggest strategies for literary representations of alterity.

Simon Castles muses over the absence of novels about cricket in Australia, despite the sport's heavy cultural weight and the comparable influence of baseball on US literature (*KYD* 20[2015] 13 pages).

*(c) Poetry*

In 'Transported to Botany Bay: Imagining Australia in Nineteenth-Century Convict Broadsides' (*VLC* 43[2015] 235–59), Dorice Williams Elliot considers the popular verse of transportation that was published in English broadside newspapers from 1790 to 1860.

*Coolabah* contains a paper on 'two Australian writers whose work captures in verse a sense of connection to rugged and remote terrains' (p. 48): Lynda Hawryluk and Leni Shilton, 'Negotiating "Negative Capability": The Role of Place in Writing' (*Coolabah* 16[2015] 48–73). The two are the authors themselves, and their 'artist statements' draw from Keats (negative capability), Elizabeth Gilbert, Les Murray, Martin Harrison, and others. They posit 'being in the poem' as analogous to 'being in the landscape', and work with the notion of the glimpse, sourced from Mary Oliver—a suggestive compendium of ideas and poems rather than a rigorous argument.

A collaborative essay and poetry suite produced by John Kinsella and Charmaine Papertalk-Green, 'Eclogue Failure or Success: The Collaborative Activism of Poetry' (*Southerly* 75:ii[2015] 92–118), reflects on the environment and environmentalism. The pair, each with connections to Geraldton, Western Australia, and its surrounds—Kinsella's is settler, Papertalk-Green is Indigenous of Yamaji heritage—provides an absorbing reflection on mining, exploitation, and other crucial issues in the region.

Traditional owners of Stradbroke Island have resolved to end sand mining by 2019. It is appropriate then, that in 'Kath Walker (Oodgeroo Noonuccal), Judith Wright and Decolonised Transcultural Ecopoetics in Frank Heimans' *Shadow Sister*' (*SSEng* 41[2015] 61–74), Peter Minter begins an analysis of the relationship between Judith Wright and Oodgeroo Noonuccal with a meditation on Oodgeroo's poetic critique of sand mining in 'Minjerriba'. Minter focuses on a moment in Heimans's documentary about the pair when Walker offers a native flower to Wright and they disagree on its name as the basis for appraisal of the role of ecology in a cross-cultural poetics of sisterhood.

Poet Michael Farrell has published his doctoral study, *Writing Australian Unsettlement*. It follows Philip Mead (*Networked Language* [2008]), Marjorie Perloff, Martin Harrison, Eve Kosofsky Sedgwick, and others in examining historical texts 'networked' to poetry in a quest to rethink Australia's 'heritage of poetics' (p. 2). Starting with the first piece of writing by an Aboriginal (Bennelong's letter), and comparing it with Ned Kelly's 'Jerilderie letter' under the trope of hunting, Farrell moves on to consider less well-known texts (Jong Ah Sing's diary of his trial, Dorothea Mackellar's diaries, 'peripheral' work by Charles Harpur, Christopher Brennan, drawings, writing by drovers). Farrell unsettles the official settler narrative by suggesting that these texts constitute 'an experimental poetics, pre-empting the modern' (p. 4) and challenging histories of Australian literature that tell of maturation towards separation from the colonial parent. The dual meanings of Deleuze and Guattari's *agencement* (assemblage, agenting) lead Farrell to anthologies (the *Macquarie PEN* in particular) and the kind of relationship they imply between Indigenous and settler histories. He makes the point that these days few people know there is a canon of Australian literature, so he is not revising it, but rather seeking to 'enliven and enrich Australian poetics by creating more interest in the colonial era' (p. 11).

This he certainly manages to do, but as a poet Farrell gets caught up in imagery (and intertextual breadth) and blurs real possibility with textual probability: 'Kelly is hunting down a rhythm: one strong enough to transform settlement' (p. 21). We do find productive observations (Kelly's shift in style as he confronts the Stringybark Creek killings, his unusual use of 'creole', the fact that similar Aboriginal rebels were not made into icons). Our response to this book depends on how far we are prepared to indulge the poet's enthusiasms (it's useful and instructive to read a Chinese miner's diary of incarceration, but its interesting hybrid style can't be said to do much cultural work if it was unknown outside the archive until 2000). Nonetheless, Farrell's often *very* close readings and his range of critical reference are impressive; his chapter on boredom, Harpur, and Mary Fullerton is cogent, as is 'Writing to Order' for its specific focus on the Moore River Settlement. Farrell's overall project of 'Recovering the diversity and energy of the field of Australian poetry [via] a critical openness to form and a willingness to read texts beyond their immediate contexts' (p. 152) is a worthy one, and the book has the merits and shortcomings of trying to do a lot on the basis of poetic assemblage.

Stuart Cooke and Dan Disney also write 'On Australasian Poetics' in a Pacific-focused issue of *CapR* (3:xxvi[2015] 76–9), but their piece was not sighted in time for reviewing.

*(d) Drama*

Emma Cox's *Performing Noncitizenship: Asylum Seekers in Australian Theatre, Film and Activism* turns on the degree to which differentiation of citizen-subject from asylum seeker could potentially and unwittingly 'entrench... distinctions artists and activists might hope to breach' (p. 2). Cox's book provides a compelling account of the mode by which Australia's zealous border-protection regime constructs border and body, the refugee in camp and in the community. Cox's book applies the thought of Agamben, Butler, Ahmed, and Hage and, at its finer moments, innovates through application to the Australian experience. The study uses close analysis of texts as diverse as verbatim plays like Ros Horin's *Through the Wire* and documentaries like Steve Thomas's *Hope*.

*Australasian Drama Studies* 67[2015] focuses on music and theatre, including a general calculation of music's role based on a year's theatre-going in Kim Baston's 'Not Just "Evocative": The Function of Music in Theatre' (*ADS* 67[2015] 4–27), and a reflection by Bagryana Popov on her collaboration with Elissa Goodrich in scoring for plays, including a description of her own work for *Subclass 26A* [2005] and *Café Scheherazade* [2011]. Drawing on ideas about listening and relationality from Heidegger and Levinas, the gist of the essay is conveyed in the title: 'Music, Silence and the Single Note in the Creation of Meaning in Theatre' (*ADS* 67[2015] 28–48). In 'Music and Sound Design: A Round Table Discussion' (*ADS* 67[2015] 76–94) chaired by Kim Baston, musicians from several Australian cities stress the difference between 'composer' and 'sound designer', and discuss working in collaboration with visual artists and theatre workers. Baston also interviews Jethro Woodward (*ADS* 67[2015] 95–108) covering similar topics, and his work on *Antigone* and for film.

Daniel Schlusser, Darrin Verhagen, and James Paul, in 'Sound (Image, Text): Audiovisual Relationships in *M+M*' (*ADS* 67[2015] 109–30), discuss the collaborative production of *M+M*, a version of Bulgakov's novel *The Master and Margarita* informed by contemporary Russia and centring on 'love, sacrifice, and individual acts of artistic creation as a ritualistic defence of the polis' (p. 76). There's some interesting comment on how the rehearsal process messes with being faithful to the source text, and on differences between sound design evolving in rehearsal and being set beforehand. *M+M* and *Peer Gynt* both tried to extend the time an audience would be attentive through 'long form climax' and music could be used to both keep control of a situation and break it up. It's an intelligent discussion, but phrases like a 'horizontal dramaturgy of means, dependent on a reality-based rehearsal process' are not helpful.

Veronica Kelly digs once more into theatre history, this time making a study of the long-successful Tivoli theatre, in 'David N. Martin and the Post-War "Acts and Actors" of Australian Variety' (*ADS* 67[2015] 131–54). With the expansion of international travel after the Second World War, Tivoli could select overseas performers subject to affordability and their fit with ideas of Australian audience tastes. Existing biographies tend to provide an incomplete picture based on anecdotes, whereas company papers show definite patterns such as the shift from patriotic performances to exotic acts, or that from performer-centred management to hard-nosed business. Martin brought to Australia black musicians (Winifred Atwell, Shirley Bassey), Russian dancers, and the Folies-Bergère. Tivoli sought to combat the rise of television by putting on more musical comedies, and hired people it could get PR mileage from in extra radio and magazine pieces. In the process it trained managers who would go on to engage performers for television until Tivoli's variety acts had to end.

Less related to Australia, but nonetheless centred on her production of Bloomsday performances in Melbourne and her earlier work with the Australian Censorship Board, Frances Devlin-Glass reflects on good taste, bodily abjection, and performing *Ulysses* in 'Reading and Performing Abjection: Staging Joyce, a Professional Reflection' (*ADS* 67[2015] 155–75).

Another work of theatre history is 'Political Theatre and the State: Melbourne and Sydney, 1936–1953' (*HA* 12:iii[2015] 113–36) by Phillip Deary and Lisa Milner. They concentrate on the New Theatre, a left-wing mix of conventional and experimental work that originated in Sydney's Workers Arts Club (1931) and Melbourne's Workers' Theatre Group (1935) and became two theatre ensembles in 1939. Its activist socialist realism and mix of international and Australian material attracted government attention, and the article surveys the censoring of Clifford Odet's *Till the Day I Die* and raids during 1940s anti-communist controls. Leftist support for the war reduced government attacks, but the *Sydney Morning Herald* refused to review productions until 1960, and security services kept Melbourne's theatre under surveillance. Productions declined under 1950s Cold War conditions, though the folkloric *Reedy River* [1953] was a hit, and the New Theatre survives to uphold a radical tradition in Australia. Milner joins Cathy Brigden to extend the study to Britain in 'Radical Theatre Mobility: Unity Theatre, UK, and the New Theatre, Australia' (*NTQ* 31:iv[2015] 328–42). They give a detailed account of the economic and sociocultural conditions (such as association with unions and their fortunes and the relation to new media) that precipitated (and then increasingly limited) the mobility of these theatres.

Terence Crawford focuses on a 1982 Newcastle-born 'backyard' vaudeville-style group that he claims 'turned Australian cabaret on its head' in 'The Castanet Club: History, Provenance and Influence' (*ADS* 66[2015] 225–52). He records their rise through big-city arts festivals to performing in Edinburgh, the shift from big musical performances to smaller actor-centred ones, and the struggle to combine professional smoothness with original messy vitality.

In 'Australian Gothic Drama: Mapping a Nation's Trauma: Convicts to the Stolen Generation' (*ADS* 66[2015] 11–39), Stephen Carleton seeks out persistent cultural memories and foundational traumas via a survey of 140 years of theatre texts. Carleton extends work by Turcotte and Gelder, and looks to include more than 'Bush Gothic' works, using Jeffrey Cox's model of Gothic theatre. He considers Marcus Clarke as typifying the 'convict Gothic', ranges through Esson's *Shipwreck* and the effects of the First World War, mentions work by Max Afford, Alan Seymour, Anthony Coburn, and Patrick White, then jumps to Louis Nowra (adding *The Language of the Gods* to extant discussion) and Stephen Sewell (*Hate*). More contemporary work shows a continuation of the 'isolated heroine-villain and lost child motifs' (p. 28) and expresses white guilt in plays dealing with Stolen Generation experience. An appendix lists plays with Gothic content from 1992.

Rob Conkie, 'Holofernes, Peregrine and I: Australian Campus Shakespeare' (*ADS* 66[2015] 153–67), contributes this nation's experiences to Andre James Hartley's wide-reaching collection, *Shakespeare on the University Stage*. Sarah French, in 'Radical Adaptation: Hypertextuality, Feminism and Motherhood in *The Rabble's Frankenstein* (after Mary Shelley)' (*ADS* 66[2015] 81–108), expands on the practice of adapting overseas works, supporting Alison Croggon's rejection of claims that such work displaces Australian material from the national stage. French uses Genette to read the 2014 Melbourne production by an independent company known for its transformative adaptations. Substituting women for Shelley's original male roles, *The Rabble* highlights feminist issues implicit in the original while pointing to contemporary Australian concerns around technologies of childbirth and the value of motherhood.

Also dealing with adaptation, Sue Thomas, in 'Transforming *Jane Eyre*: Its Australian Stage Adaptations' (*ALS* 30:iii[2015] 134–48), applies her psycho-analytic approach to Jean Rhys's work to readings of how Helen Jerome and David Malouf represent the affect between Jane and Rochester (passion versus sympathy) in the former's 1936 stage version and the latter's contribution to the 2000 opera. (How each work uses doors and windows provides an interpretative key.) She also touches on the earliest trans-Tasman adaptation, Rose Evans's melodrama, *Quite Alone* [1872] and its hostile Melbourne reviews, and lists early film versions of the novel.

Angela Campbell takes up the mix of memory, desire, history, politics, and myth that is cultural heritage to examine three representations of the Eureka uprising on the goldfields of Ballarat in 1854. Performances of three site-specific 'Living Heritage, Ballarat' as part of the city's annual celebrations are examined, noting shifts from 2013's theatrical walking tour devised by students at the regional university to a well-funded 2015 re-enactment of the first Anzac Day parade involving local and state government and UNESCO. In *The Sovereign Wife*, Sisters Grimm (a 'DIY drag theatre troupe') blended the contemporary rave party and nineteenth-century melodrama with a multi-ethnic and cross-dressing cast to both show and deconstruct figures from the Eureka story not commonly included in official versions. This contrasts with the more sedate outdoor theme park of mining history at Sovereign Hill and its son-et-lumière 'Blood on the Southern Cross' version of Eureka.

Similar kinds of work supply the subject of Hannah Böttcher and Alexandra Ludewig's 'Performing Haunting Histories: A Psychogeographical Reading of Two Site-Specific Performance Projects on Rottnest Island' (*ADS* 66[2015] 179–201). Julia Jarel and Helen Hunt devised 'Open House' and 'After Dark' in 2013 at different locations on the island, disturbing its contemporary reputation as a holiday venue by performing aspects of its past as an internment site for convicts, Aborigines, and suspected First World War 'enemy aliens'. The authors invoke Said, De Certeau, and Paris's Situationists while describing how unfamiliar aspects of history are dramatized by actors voicing the lives of Rottnest's former inhabitants. Also in 2013 the people of Gladstone, Queensland, took part in drumming, bell-ringing, bike-riding, and tugboat 'dances' to perform the history of their town, adding more personal touches to its image as an industrial port. Danielle Carter describes the event in 'Community Engagement of Community Conversation? *Boomtown*, a Large-Scale Regional Outdoor Community Theatrical Event' (*ADS* 66[2015] 202–24), giving a brief history of community engagement in the arts and director Sean Mee's other theatrical ventures. The process of incorporating participants' ideas led to productive conversations about how the community might progress.

Culminating in readings of *Box the Pony* and *The Seven Stages of Grieving*, Karen Austin traverses the National Black Theatre's 1973 *Basically Black* and *Bran Nue Dae*, theorizing black humour by reference to Bergson and Freud in 'Talkin Blak: Humour in Indigenous Australian Theatre, 1970–2000' (*Philament* 20[2015] 129–64).

Denise Varney, in the 'species' issue of *JASAL* (15:ii[2015]), considers 'the relative slowness of theatre to engage with human and animal ecology' (p. 1). She cites Una Chaudhuri among others, and goes on to survey theatre that takes up the challenge of animal studies, concentrating on Justine Campbell's and Sarah Hamilton's 2013 work, *They Saw a Thylacine*, in ' "Beauty Tigress Queen": Staging the Thylacine in a Theatre of Species' (*JASAL* (15:ii[2015] 13 pages). Two monologues record the hunting down and the captivity of Tasmanian tigers in the context of Depression-era society; another voices a spectral thylacine, one that haunts Australia still with tales of sightings and guilt about extinctions of species. Varney suggests that listening to the monologues (in which the female hunter and zookeeper speak of 'becoming animal' in their different quests) on a bare cage-like stage allows the audience to forget the human-centred drama and centre on the species extinction story. She cites Theresa J. May's ecodramaturgy and calls for Australian applications of it.

*(e) Author Studies*

Randa Abdel-Fattah's popular novel about a girl in Australia who decides to wear the hijab is Colin Hains's subject in 'Challenging Stereotypes: Randa Abdel-Fattah's use of parody in *Does My Head Look Big in This?*' (*Bookbird* 53:ii[2015] 30–5). Using Chinua Achebe's and Judith Butler's work, Hains argues that the writer deploys stereotypes parodically to expose the ignorance of anti-Muslim Australians; she overdoes the lists of stereotypes, asserting the personal agency of her protagonist and making cross-ethnic comparisons to ensure that readers cannot simply take the book as reconfirming them.

Francis Adams, author of *The Australians* [1893], is examined for his transmission of ideas to and fro between colony and imperial centre by Meg Tasker in 'Francis Adams: Realism and Sensation in the 1880s' (*ALS* 30:iii[2015] 79–95). Adams's five Australian novels, mostly dismissed as 'pot boilers', contain critique of the social status quo. Tasker looks at Adams's first two novels, *Leicester: An Autobiography* [1885] and *Madeleine Brown's Murderer* [1887], one literary (published in England), the other popular (published in Melbourne), but both showing the author's interest in modern uses of realism and sensation and his debt to Zola and 'New Fiction'.

'Jessica Anderson's *Tirra Lirra by the River*' (*AuBR* 369[2015] 30–2) is revisited by Kerryn Goldsworthy. We get a brief biography (mentioning Anderson's work for radio, an often overlooked aspect of Australian literary history), comment on the mistaken marketing of her early novels, and details of key prizes and other writers with whom Anderson effected a turn in attention to women's fiction. The book itself—'one long act of remembering' and a quest to align the country of the mind with the actual place of residence—is also about many other things, including the frailty of old age, and employs intricate poetic structuring.

In '"A Landscape with Figures": Thea Astley's Aesthetic' (*AuS* 7:ii[2015] 13 pages) Susan Sheridan takes the novelist's description of *Girl with a Monkey* [1958] as defining her modernist attempt to have landscape suggest characters' emotions and their significance. Using a detailed realist regionalism rather an impressionistic figuring more akin to 1980s 'spatial consciousness', Astley undoes nationalist identity constructed on the land and employs a postcolonial critique of race relations, but differs from Judith Wright's sense of landscape and from current conceptions of the literary 'sacred'. Landscape does have a metaphysical aspect in which 'presence is transcendent' but meaning is carried not in things but in metaphor. It is apprehended as sensations, and later work situates these in historical as well as spiritual contexts. Sheridan notes Astley's links to painting and mentions her lonely male characters, who move through the landscape wanting to disappear into it. She points to the importance of weather and emphasizes Astley's contrast between the ugly, dry inland and beautiful, lush coast, seeing the 'drylands' of 'rainshadow' country as a metaphor for masculinist violence, barren materialism, and the waste of white mistreatment of Indigenous Australia.

Inez Baranay is an Australian writer who was born overseas and later travelled widely, writing about places such as Papua New Guinea and India. In 'Questions of Identity' (*JEASA* 6:i[2015] 11 pages), she describes her process of working through identity positions to self-identify as 'a writer in the English language', 'a writer of Australian citizenship', 'a writer of immigrant background', a writer of transnational culture', 'a writer of cosmopolitan temperament'.

Since the fixation on A.D. Hope and Judith Wright lost hold, apart from Les Murray, amongst Australian poets, Bruce Beaver has seemed to attract the most international attention. Tegan Jane Schetrumpf provides an interesting comparative reading in 'Diminished but Never Dismissed: The Confessional Poetry of Sylvia Plath and Bruce Beaver' (*Antipodes* 29:i[2015] 117–27). She reads against the 'bad press' and prurient interest that confessional poetry generates to compare the two writers, both post-Holocaust, both mentally disturbed, both read for biography rather than craft. The critic examines 'lyric address' and central symbols in both writers, finding Beaver to be more varied and wider in his addressees. Schetrumpf lists all the names referred to in *Letters to Live Poets* and relates them to a postmodern compilation of possible selves as antidote to bipolar fragmentation. Beaver also slides his addressees around in his handling of Vietnam and trauma so that 'we' readers find ourselves implicated. He can also register simultaneous psychotic fantasy and poetic appreciation of it, horrific mortality and calm reflection on it. The critic adds a perceptive comment: 'There is no rationalization to be done here. Beaver merely asks us to keep our sensitivity to sorrow' (p. 124). Schetrumpf tends towards Jungian analysis of symbols, noting Beaver's motifs of blindness and landscapes 'filled with dualities', ugliness, and waste counterpointing implied beauty (p. 126).

Robert Dixon develops his application of geographical ideas to the mapping of transnational literary circuits in 'Before the Nation: Rolf Boldrewood and the Problem of Scale in National Literatures' (*ALS* 30:iii[2015] 6–27). Cheap colonial edition series, and the cultural impetus provided by federation, allowed a proto-canon of Australian novels to appear—Clarke, Kingsley, and Boldrewood—but before this, Boldrewood's *Babes in the Bush* had appeared as the serialized *An Australian Squire* in a pre-national colonial context that utilized an international range of intertextual connections. Dixon asks, 'What are the consequences of approaching a pre-national literature from the scale of the nation, or a national literature from the scale of the world?' (p. 7). Boldrewood's novel is set during the expansion of squatter holdings from Tasmania and New South Wales into Victoria, when maps were partial and changing, and he relocates his story from his own lands in the Western District to a location west of where Canberra now is. This local movement is matched by a transnational textual movement of citation (British, Indian, French, and

American) that finds an echo in Cooper's American writing (including debate about incursions on Indigenous territory). Dixon wonders whether a nation-based dismissal of *An Australian Squire* as a colonial curiosity ought not to attend more carefully to such a mix of pre-national flux and transnational networking. He also questions where the point of observation is for the world literature scholar and how that might also distort views of local writing at a specific point in history.

Ailise Bulfin sets out the history of anti-Chinese sentiment in Australia and how it is insistently manifest in the work of Guy Boothby, in 'Guy Boothby and "The Yellow Peril": Representations of Chinese Immigrants in British Imperial Spaces' (*AJVS* 20:i[2015] 5–23). There's little new in this, but Bulfin follows Ross Forman's pointing to a more interactive sense of colonial relations than the centre–periphery model, and tracks Boothby's writing in relation to his travels through the empire, seeing his racist tropes as confessions about the 'coolie trade' on which empire was reliant.

In 'Andrew Bovell's *When the Rain Stops Falling*: Theatre in the Age of "Hyperobjects"' (*ADS* 66[2015] 40–62) Mohebat Ahmadi surveys phases in the development of ecocriticism and applies Timothy Morton's concepts of 'hyperobjects', 'mesh', dark gaps, and the agency of things to Bovell's 2008 collaborative apocalyptic work grounded in concern over climate change. A family drama on the surface, the play's deployment of hyperobjects (climate change; references to rain and floods) displaces humans from its centre, so that we see, for example, one character's paedophilia in terms of 'dark ecology' of melancholia, pain, and Earth's vengeance on the Anthropocene. Ahmadi points out the links between the play's settings (Uluru, the Coorong) and real ecological crises, and analyses the theatrical handling of space in relation to a discourse of restoring balance.

Peter Carey's *My Life as a Fake* is not the easiest novel to understand, even if you know the story of how two poets faked some modernist verse by a working-class unknown, Ern Malley, to embarrass Australia's avant-garde. Anthony J. Hassall, 'High Wire Act: Peter Carey's *My Life as a Fake*' (*JEASA* 6:i[2015] 10 pages), tracks the three unreliable narrating voices (female English editor, dissolute expatriate Australian poet Chubb, and the Frankenstein reanimation of character Bob McCorkle), but argues that Carey's cleverness in pointing up the fakeries inherent in all fiction leaves his characters hard to relate to, his story beyond credence, and some of the parodic prose strained. Hassall usefully links the book to Carey's other 'damaged' characters and to *Theft*, though some credit might be given Carey for his evocation of the Conradian/Maugham-esque steamy squalor of the back streets of tropical cities and (in another faking of old tropes) the collapse of reason in colonial folk abroad.

Carey the short-story writer is examined by Claire Corbett in 'Must Australia Always Be Imaginary? Cartography as Creation in Peter Carey's "Do you love me?"' (*Antipodes* 29:i[2015] 43–54). The importance of cartography as fixing a real Australia once deemed a fantasy in Europe is part of Carey's 'complex emulsion of genres' (p. 45) in his tale, where landmarks and people disappear from lack of love. The story is read against 'science fiction' conventions (blurred with speculative fiction) and the close reading looks to allegories in which the inadequate mapping/census shows up the holes in official narratives (their lack of affective pull, for example) and the echoing absence of Aborigines underlies the anxiety amongst settler characters. The particular significances of some buildings Carey mentions are explained.

In the same issue, Nathanael O'Reilly expounds on 'Mythology, History and Truth: Teaching Peter Carey's *The True History of the Kelly Gang*' (*Antipodes* 29:i[2015] 71–81). Students find the novel engaging and it introduces them to cultural traits such as anti-authoritarianism and egalitarianism while prompting consideration of the appeal of historical fiction. Outside Australian literature courses, time is required for cultural and historical contextualizing, the style is compared to the original Jerilderie Letter to show Carey's strategic polishing. The text is studied in three tranches accompanied by activities around themes of justice, Irish–English relations, the nature of the hero, and the outlaw. Contextual reading moves into close reading followed by some work on reception. O'Reilly lists discussion topics for each of the thirteen sections of the novel, and written assignments, including quick in-class reflections on one of the topics discussed. Some comparison with Delia Falconer's story 'The Republic of Love' is included, and supplementary teaching resources are listed.

*The Unusual Life of Tristan Smith* is not a commonly studied work, but James Dahlstrom, in 'The Unusual Life of Gough Whitlam: Peter Carey's *Tristan Smith*' (*JLLC* 62:i[2015] 32–47), relates the book to Richard White and Benedict Anderson, tracking how Eficans struggle to construct a national identity in opposition to the powerful Voorstand as an allegory of Australian–US relations and reading the ultimate defeat of Efican democratic process as reflecting the 1975 dismissal of Prime Minister Whitlam.

Antonio Cassella went on to write a thesis about representations of Italy in Australian literature, but before that he wrote a novel, *The Sensualist* [1991]. Giovanni Messina turns the tables on the author by examining his representations of Sicily in relation to Australia in ' "A comfortable distance": Weird Melancholy and Escapism in Casella's *The Sensualist*' (*JEASA* 6:i[2015] 14 pages). Messina uses Freud and Kristeva, plus readings of the Gothic, to suggest that the Australian characters suffer from a melancholy born of the inability to shed the colonial past, and that they need a comfortably distanced location such as Sicily onto which to project their dreams. The first part of the essay locates the dynamic in the author's struggle against both 1960s assimilation to Anglo-Australia and being ghettoized under later multiculturalism as a 'migrant writer'. Sicily as both barbarism and lost Eden has its own literary archive, inflected by emigrant desire (Venero Armanno's *The Volcano* is cited), but Cassella creates Anglo-Australian characters who compare the island to their outback. The essay swings between close attention to textual detail and broad theorizing.

Brian Castro's work is considered by Marjorie Ambrosio in the context of critical struggles between reading 'multicultural' work for ideological content/effect and reading it for aesthetic qualities. Castro uses a 'minor key' to slip through and between such boundaries in 'Une esthétique du non-positionnement? Du questionnement de l'idéologie dans les oeuvres de Brian Castro'

('An Aesthetic of Non-Positioning? Questioning Ideology in the Work of Brian Castro) (in Gonzalez and Agostini, eds., *Aesthetics and Ideology in Contemporary Literature and Drama*, pp. 149–60). Castro's shifting experiments with form and voices point to 'zones of contact and exchange' and 'masks' rather than quests to excavate some original/definitive identity—reflected in the shifting architecture of the hotel in *After China*. Castro's musical metaphor of writing in a minor key deflects Deleuze and Guattari's politicized 'minor literature'; defamiliarization and heterotopia are more pertinent concepts. In line with Althusser and Bakhtin, Castro works at a subtle ideology underpinning his assertion that 'every novel...must make an ethical gesture towards the end of suffering' (p. 158).

A different reading of Castro comes from Wang Guanglin, 'Translating Fragments: Disorientation in Brian Castro's *Shanghai Dancing*' (*Antipodes* 29:i[2015] 129–43). Wang links Castro's mobile network of auto/biographical, linguistic, and photographic fragments to Benjamin's ideas on translation and his Arcade Project. There is a brief diversion into trauma and the labyrinth. It is a rich essay, though the assertion that Castro is more high modernist than postmodernist seems undercut by the 'deconstructive' techniques set forth.

Agnes Balajthy, in ' "In the labyrinth of invisible pathways": Tropes of Aboriginal Australia in Bruce Chatwin's *The Songlines*' (*JEASA* 6:i[2015] 9 pages), attends to the tropes of map and labyrinth to show how the celebrated traveller reworked the colonial idea of unmappable desert at the country's heart, appropriating Aboriginal ideas while simultaneously suggesting the land's resistance to appropriation. The double act is reflected in the text's play between documentary and fiction, author and narrator, and informant Arkady's roles as enthusiast and analyst, attention to desert otherness and intertextual framing in Eurocentric ideas.

Literary networks are the frame for Tim Dolin's study, 'Marcus Clarke, the Two George Eliots, and the History of Two Newspapers' (*ALS* 30:iii[2015] 28–46). Clarke 'discovered' an 'unknown late work' by George Eliot in French, his translation of which he serialized in the Melbourne *Leader*. It turned out to be Eliot's own translation of her much earlier story 'The Lifted Veil', published anonymously in *Blackwood's Magazine*. Melbourne's *Argus*, with which Clarke had quarrelled, pilloried him for his error. Dolin meditates on the readings we give to texts, knowing or not knowing their actual historical context, and points to a culture of 'appropriation' of overseas texts and impersonation of other identities by colonial writers and newspapers. Eliot's story on the limits of realism is transformed by Clarke's longer romance version, and Dolin attributes much of the shape-shifting to rivalry between newspapers, the *Argus* and *Age* having propriety over Eliot and the *Leader*, until Clarke's intervention, relying on Wilkie Collins—realism versus romance mapped over local political differences.

Jessica Gildersleeve, ' "Ropes of stories": Jean Rhys, Vivienne Cleven and Melissa Lucashenko' (*QR* 22:i[2015] 75–84), develops Melissa Lucashenko's metaphor of 'ropes of stories' connecting Aboriginal writers and readers, and examines how Lucashenko and Vivien Cleven use Jean Rhys as an inspiration point—Cleven explicitly has a character identify with Rhys.

In *Transnational Literature*, Shadi Neimneh, 'Autofiction and Fictionalisation: J.M. Coetzee's Novels and *Boyhood*' (*TransL* 7:ii[2015] 12 pages), sets Coetzee's fictive autobiographies against his novels. David Attwell takes a similar approach in the much longer *J.M. Coetzee and the Life of Writing: Face to Face with Time*. Attwell insists that 'Coetzee's writing is a huge existential exercise, grounded in fictional autobiography' (p. 26). The book results from research in the Coetzee papers in the Harry Ransom Center at the University of Texas at Austin. Grounded in the *longue durée* of Coetzee's career, Attwell's book is not overly concerned with the writer's relocation to Adelaide in 2002. Nonetheless, for students of Australian literature eager to understand Coetzee in that context, it offers useful reflections. Attwell moves from considering the importance of Roland Barthes and T.S. Eliot in Coetzee's own attempted 'escape from personality' through writing (p. 33) towards a contextualization of the South African author's early suspension between the cultural meaning of Afrikaans—sign of both a linguistically mobile Karoo farm upbringing and of membership of an oppressive community—and English—sign of high culture, international lingua franca, and protest against parochialism. Attwell finds Coetzee shaping a suspicion of monolingualism and a 'recusant' attitude to Afrikaaner identity that cannot be resolved by English. What Coetzee calls (in a letter to Paul Auster) the 'Anglo weltanschauung' dominant in largely monolingual Australia leaves him slightly out of place (p. 35). Attwell focuses on *Slow Man* and *The Childhood of Jesus*, written in Australia, in the final chapter.

Eleanor Dark's *Sun Across the Sky* has been overshadowed by *The Timeless Land*, and it was 'pipped at the post' for the sesquicentennial literary prize by Herbert's *Capricornia*, notes Helen O'Reilly in 'The Poet in Her Past: Eleanor Dark and Christopher Brennan' (*Southerly* 75:ii[2015] 217–23), a consideration of the mark left by Christopher Brennan on that short work. This also appears in the 'Naked Writer' issue of *Southerly*.

Jack Davis's account of his brother Harold's war experience in *A Boy's Life* is discussed by Tim Rowse in 'Dangers and Revelations: World War II in Indigenous Autobiography' (*GriffithR* 48[2015] 137–48). Other reminiscences, by Ruth Hegarty, Claire Henty-Gebert, Roy McIvor, Willie Gordon, Hilda Jarman Muir, Ellie Gaffney, Connie Nungalla McDonald, Dick Roughsey, Alec Kruger, and Bill Cohen, are surveyed, one insight being the positive impact of military service on breaking racist structures.

Davis came to public life as an activist and public servant in the early 1970s, before recognition of Aboriginal rights. In 'Spinning *The Dreamers*: Jack Davis and the Drama of Assimilation' (*Westerly* 60:i[2016] 24–39), Tony Hughes D'Aeth offers thoughtful comment on the temporality and generic conditions of the play, which manoeuvres between social realism and a more mythic space of dreaming associated with the character Worru that Davis also played on stage in several performances.

Reviews of Australian literary studies tend, on the whole, to refer to such themes as nation, colonization, and the struggle between the bush and the suburbs. This focus is somewhat shifted by attention to the hard-SF writer Greg Egan. N. Katherine Hayles writes about Egan's experiment with settings and characters to offer accounts of differing modes of consciousness in 'Greg

Egan's *Quarantine* and *Teranesia*: Contributions to the Millennial Reassessment of Consciousness and the Cognitive Nonconscious' (*SFS* 42[2015] 56–77).

In ' "Addressing a great silence": Black Diggers and the Aboriginal Experience of War' (*NTQ* 31:iii[2015] 223–31), Liza Mare-Syron juxtaposes Wesley Enoch's *Black Diggers* and Tony Albert's Sydney monument to Aboriginal servicemen *Yininmadyemi Thou Didst Let Fall*. The extent of Aboriginal soldiers' contribution is well known through oral accounts, but difficult to reckon from archival records because a 1909 Act prevented non-European enlistment. Consequently, many Aboriginal servicemen passed as European in order to serve. This tension produces both limits on and new possibilities for artistic practices of counter-hegemonic remembering.

Ffion Murphy and Richard Nile, in 'Wounded Storyteller: Revisiting Albert Facey's Fortunate Life' (*Westerly* 60:ii[2015] 87–100), offer a reconsideration of the war survivor memoir *A Fortunate Life*, reflecting on the autobiographical truth of the text in the face of evidence that Facey's account of the Gallipoli landings does not fit with historical record.

Gabrielle Dixon-Ritchie shows that avant-garde poetry is alive and well in 2015, with a rich analysis of the work of Kate Fagan, in ' "Aesthetics in welcome crisis": Kate Fagan's *The Long Moment* as New-Lyricist, Post-Romantic, Transversal, Post-Language Poetry' (*Southerly* 75:i[2015] 153–71). Dixon-Ritchie may attribute an excess of poetic inheritances to Fagan, but the essay is anchored in an aesthetics of space and land that derives from a reading of Fagan's own academic work, in particular her thesis, a Deleuzian-Guattarian analysis of Lyn Heijinian.

Bernadette Brennan writes on Helen Garner's *The Children's Bach* in the 'Reading Australia' series (*AuBR* 371[2015] 49–51). She recalls criticism of Garner's earlier work for its attention to small-scale domestic concerns and diary-based story, but points to the importance of rooms and houses as places where women live out the liberties and constraints of marriage and childrearing—or of rejecting either. The later novel opens up the home, setting a contemporary family against Tennyson's Victorian one, and subjecting it to the vicissitudes of more bohemian lives. The role of music is discussed: 'Marriage, life and playing music are all complex tasks requiring dedication and hard work' (p. 50). Female desire is allowed, but consequences are also shown, and family somehow muddles through as a kind of song.

Geoffrey Lehmann, ('Jamie Grant: Form with Feeling', *Quadrant* 59:i–ii[2015] 108–9), positively reviews Jamie Grant's latest collection, *Glass on the Chimney and Other Poems*, to find instances of and reasons for Grant's tapping of Dylan Thomas and T.S. Eliot for his formal bases.

Syd Harrex was best known for his promotion of postcolonial literatures, but he also published books of poetry. These are reviewed by Molly Murn, ' "No Man is an island": Crossing Thresholds—Journeying with the Recent Poetry of Syd Harrex' (*Asiatic* 9:i[2015] 22–30), who examines how failing eyesight induced changes in writing and turned the poet to earlier times in Tasmania as well as his later house on Kangaroo Island. Murn worked with the poet to assemble his *Five Seasons* [2011], and she marks a shift from crafted modernist writing to bursts of inner thought, memories, and music, setting forth notebook jottings and poems against a biographical backdrop.

Samuel Finegan, in 'Adolescent Occultism and the Philosophy of Things in Three Novels' (*TransL* 7:ii[2015] 11 pages), draws attention to the phenomenology of Sonya Hartnett's under-appreciated novel *Butterfly* alongside similar considerations in work by US and British writers.

In *Southerly* Brigitta Olubas continues her work on Shirley Hazzard—who has since passed away—with an essay exploring the amateur circuits of scholarship and influence that radiated out from Hazzard and her husband Francis Steegmuller: ' "I think you're my wife": Translation, Marriage and the Literary Lives of Shirley Hazzard and Frances Steegmuller' (*Southerly* 75:ii[2015] 73–87).

In ' "The pretty and the political didn't seem to blend well": Anita Heiss's Chick Lit and the Destabilisation of a Genre' (*JASAL* 15:iii[2015] 11 pages), Imogen Mathew takes up Wenche Ommudsen's suggestion that chick lit offers the globally marginal a vehicle to provide different views to Western capitalist romance, arguing that altering one element of the formula (race) undoes the whole genre package. Mathew surveys critical work on chick lit, then reads *Not Meeting Mr Right* and *Manhattan Dreaming*, showing their strategic management of humour, their conservative reproduction of gender roles and sexuality, and how race throws the conventions of the genre (such as consumption) into an implicitly politicized critical light. The tension between being co-opted into the mainstream and resisting it is a central concern.

In 'Years of Agony and Joy: The Sadie and Xavier Herbert Collection' (*QR* 22:i[2015] 96–8), Simon Farley celebrates the Sadie and Xavier Herbert papers at the Fryer Library—offering a brief overview of the latter's career and of the collection.

The Jindyworobaks have gone out of fashion as misguided white folk usurping Aboriginal culture to indigenize settler society, but Jayne Regan adds nuance to their reputation in 'A Cosmopolitan Jindyworobak: Flexmore Hudson, Nationalism and World-Mindedness' (*JASAL* 15:iii[2015] 14 pages). Hudson wrote advocating world citizenship in *Jindyworobak Review* [1948]; his poetry shifted focus from love and nature to war and politics. Regan describes Hudson's non Anglocentric history of Australia in the educational comic book *Discovery*, and contextualizes his little magazine, *Poetry* [1941–7], showing its international reach. Hudson's ties to and disagreements with the Jindyworobaks are charted, particularly his opposition to a narrow focus on Aboriginal culture (which he thought had little to offer) and to nationalism's attraction to fascism. Hudson's use of rural nature as a source of inspiration permitted him to keep up his association with the group, but his own reading was international, and he inclined to Buddhism and ecological concerns.

Simon Ryan, '*Lasseter's Last Ride* and the Gothic Narrative of Failure' (*JAusS* 39:iii[2015] 381–95), details the claims on modernity of the final prospecting expedition of Lasseter, equipped with a plane and specialized truck. Technology failed and Lasseter lost his camels, his supposed gold-seam, and his life. Popular writer Ion Idriess rewrote the venture as a heroic narrative, surrounding its failures with Gothic devices (hostile land, primitive natives, cursed objects) as culpably perverse forces that left national aspirations to modernity intact.

The Lebanese diaspora and what prompts return is the subject of Luma Balaa's reading of Nada Awaar Jarrar, 'Exile, Return, and Nationalism in *A Goodland*' (*Antipodes* 29:i[2015] 91–104). Balaa argues that Jarrar mixes positive views of displacement with naturalistic attention to suffering. Said and others provide a framework of 'contrapuntal consciousness' for discussion of protagonist Layla's doubled diasporic life in Australia, which she solves by returning to Lebanon. There is a slight problem in Balaa's emphasizing the 'restorative' aspect of nostalgia in that, when Layla does go home, it is no longer the nurturing place of memory; but return assuages guilt, and Layla learns to live in present reality, with hopes for Lebanon's future, though she does romanticize the homeland. Balaa relates Jarrar to the Beirut Decentrists: women writers who stayed in Lebanon during the civil war but scattered across the country.

George Johnston's *Clean Straw for Nothing* [1969] and Charmian Clift's *Peel me a Lotus* [1959] record their sojourn in the Greek islands, distanced from the metropolitan centres usually focused on in studies of Australian expatriates. Tanya Dalziell and Paul Genoni push further to examine the expatriate story through photographs rather than writing in 'Australians in Aspic: Picturing Charmian Clift and George Johnston's Hydra Expatriation' (*JASAL* 15:iii[2016] 23 pages). American photographer for *Life* magazine James Burke stayed on Hydra, and his photo archive has now been digitized, allowing a new glimpse of Johnston's 'being Australian in the world' (p. 3). Burke's pictures record the heyday of the artistic community, but show some of the social changes that led eventually to the couple's return to Australia in 1964. Clift's descriptions of a colourful, primitive retreat are 'framed' by photos pointing to the touristic tropes and capitalist world system that would eventually impinge on the idyll. Photos of Johnston show complicity in construction of an image of the brooding artist, but also record the author's slide into depression. A shot of Martin reading a local paper underlines his parents' expatriate isolation in that they never learned more than basic Greek. Clift's written mistrust of young footloose wanderers is offset by pictures of the community swimming and dining, though these also bring out the separation between sojourners and Hydriots. The article (with recourse to Berger and Sontag) stresses that photos do not constitute a fully authoritative substitute for the writing, nor do they 'preserve meaning' (p. 23), but constitute another set of signs expressing the pleasures and limitations of expatriate experience.

Monique Rooney writes on 'Mute Eloquence: Elizabeth Jolley's *The Well* as Encrypted Melodrama' (*JASAL* 15:i[2015] 16 pages), arguing that the novel's use of song and speech provides a key to its dark secrets of allegorical melodrama. She finds a continuity from Rousseau's *mélodrame* of Pygmalion's transformations to Jolley's use of musico-theatrical elements to animate melodramatic interest in 'terrestrial death and sub-terrestrial life'. Jolley's use of cinematic devices and critics' identification of her play with voices take *The Well* beyond readings of cultural exile linked to Jolley's own migration into mythic echoes of fertility cults. Derrida on the crypt and Catherine Malabou on post-Enlightenment self-sculpting support a careful reading of extant criticism and textual musical references, to close with Katherine being 'turned to stone' (silenced) while Hester is given the voice to begin writing.

In the context of white responses to the *Bringing Them Home* report, Valerie-Anne Bellflamme discusses the avoidance of speaking for others' suffering in ' "Shakespeare was wrong": Counter-Discursive Intertextuality in Gail Jones's *Sorry*' (*JPW* 51:vi[2015] 661–71), and how it courts the danger of making Perdita's traumatized silence seem to express white suffering (victim surrogacy) rather than that of her childhood Aboriginal friend Mary, who goes to prison on her behalf. The article also considers how Jones's Shakespearean references show the limitations of official history and literature when applied to Australia, and how that incommensurate difference suggests the 'insufficiency of reconciliation' (p. 665). If reciting the Bard saves Perdita from muteness, her learning sign language indicates alternative modes of knowing/speaking, and the novel, while invoking Western culture, also alienates it to point to a need for ongoing painful negotiation of ethical handling of colonialist abuses and cross-racial relations.

Thomas Keneally celebrated fifty years of publishing novels in 2014, and a conference held at the University of Wollongong led to a special issue of *Australian Literary Studies* in which he surveys his career in 'Since 1964' (*ALS* 30:i[2015] 1–8) and Paul Sharrad, 'Back to Whitton Week: Tracking Tom Keneally's Career' (*ALS* 30:i[2015] 9–26), and Peter Pierce, 'The Making of Tom Keneally' (*ALS* 30:i[2015] 40–51), analyse its principal features. More specific focus is provided by Maureen Clark, 'Colonialism, Racial Violence and Loss: *The Chant of Jimmie Blacksmith* and *The Roving Party*' (*ALS* 30:i[2015] 27–39), Irene Lucchitti, 'From the Harp of Erin to Erin of the Harp with Thomas Keneally' (*ALS* 30:i[2015] 52–62), and John Scheckter, 'In Custody: Thomas Keneally and American Stories' (*ALS* 30:i[2015] 63–75). There is also an interview with the author.

Another Keneally interview, dating from 1984, mounts a defence of *The Chant of Jimmie Blacksmith* as attempting a decolonizing narrative in advance of later more sophisticated approaches to racial representation. Bruce Harding's 'An Interview with Thomas Keneally: *The Chant of Jimmie Blacksmith* and the politics of Australian Aboriginality' (*JPW* 51:iii[2015] 310–23) provides historical context to the book and an Afterword assessing it in the light of Bhabha and others. The revisionary approach to Keneally's landmark novel is echoed by Tony Birch (*AuBR* 372[2015] 50–2).

Kim Don'o was an early contributor to 'migrant writing' in Australia, and as Kun Jong Lee points out in ' "Quo Vadis, Terra Australis?": Don'o Kim's *The Chinaman*' (*JAusS* 39:iv[2015] 461–76) his work has been largely overlooked, possibly because critics did not want fully to accept the critique of racism presented. *The Chinaman*, more polyphonic and intertextual than previous work, is also strongly autobiographical and uses relationships on a Barrier Reef tourist ship (centred on the bigoted captain and a Japanese passenger) to question the direction of a nation bordering Asia. This close reading explains some intertextual and historical allusions.

A case is made for Peter King's place among the influential creators of Australian theatre in Jim Daly's first-person account of details of performing

King's play at La Mama in 2013, 'Grotesque and Gothic in Peter King's *John Gabriel Borkman*: A Reflection from the Inside' (*ADS* 66[2015] 109–30).

Henry George Lamond is a somewhat forgotten Queensland writer who nonetheless was widely published, reviewed, translated, and read (in England, the United States, and Australia) in the 1930s. In 'Nostalgia and Belonging: Henry George Lamond Writing the Whitsunday Islands' (*QR* 22:i[2015] 49–61) Celmara Pocock delves into a particular regional corner of his writing and his use of the perspectives of animals. It can only be hoped that Pocock's interest will salvage Lamond from the dustheap of literature.

Lucy Treep reconsiders Eve Langley's *The Pea-Pickers*, surveying intriguing details such as the transvestism enabling the story and the multicultural vicissitudes of East Gippsland, in '*The Pea-Pickers*: An Introduction' (*Westerly* 60:ii[2015] 106–13).

Anne Holden Rønning, 'Louisa Lawson and the Woman Question' (*Coolabah* 16[2015] 74–86), surveys the contents of *The Dawn*, mentions some novel marketing strategies, and summarizes public responses. It is a descriptive piece owing much to existing scholarship, and is perhaps most interesting for its comparisons to other papers of the time.

Simone Lazaroo is revisited by Rosalind Nicole McFarlane in 'A "Bay of Whispers": Seascape in Simone Lazaroo's *The Australian Fiancé*' (*Antipodes* 29:i[2015] 163–73). Connecting with recent scholarship (by Elizabeth DeLoughrey, Suvendrini Perera, and Elizabeth McMahon) about the ocean and 'boat people' as links and threats to Australia's island and regional being, McFarlane points to its underlying importance to the commonly discussed themes of racism and diaspora in Lazaroo's novel. The three central characters meet, live and die by the sea, which figures desire for intimacy, promise of escape, limits to movement, separation. See also the discussion of Carrera Suárez in Section 2(b) above.

Caroline Leakey, best known for her novel *The Broad Arrow* [1859], also wrote poetry, some collected in *Lyra Australis* [1854]. Katie Hansord, in 'Symbolism and the Antipodes: The Fallen Woman in Caroline Leakey's *Lyra Australis, or Attempts to Sing in a Strange Land*' (*ALS* 30: iii[2015] 121–33), tracks the title's trope through stories and poems, relating her Tasmanian work to transnational movements of thought, and comparing it with British Romantic writing (Caroline Norton's in particular).

Jack Lindsay was famously an 'expat', living in Britain from 1926. As an Australian writer or otherwise, his connections to the rise of the New Left in the1950s are charted by John T. Connor in 'Jack Lindsay, Socialist Humanism and the Communist Historical Novel' (*RES* 66[2015] 342–63).

*Southerly*'s 'Naked Writer,' issue includes Shaun Bell's consideration of the complexities of literary expatriation, '"But even memory is fiction": The [fictional] Life and (Self) Writing of Sumner Locke Elliot' (*Southerly* 75:ii[2015] 172–92).

Ruth Blair takes up the work of an under-examined author in 'Amanda Lohrey's *Vertigo*: An Australian Pastoral' (*ALS* 30: ii[2015] 117–31). As is appropriate to a writer usually read for her sociopolitical engagement, Blair takes up Empson's view of pastoral as being about social relations to consider Lohrey's fictional treatment of environmental issues. Historically and geographically, Australia has been post- or anti-pastoral, but has continued to work the urban–rural contrast, giving Arcadia (in Peter Kirkpatrick's words) a 'prophetic rather than a representational purpose' (p. 120). Lohrey depicts the 'sea change/tree change' move away from cities, noting the appeal of ownership of a *locus amoenus*, the dialogue with older residents (sheep farmers), the *et in Arcadia ego* threats of snakes and fires. The pastoral presents rather than resolves endemic contradictions in which the non-human world provides a sort of grace as a hint of future blessing in the real imperfect (and world-aware) present, even when that is manifest as vertigo—the obverse of epiphany. Blair argues that 'anti-pastoral' is in fact 'anti-Arcadia' and that there is no 'post-pastoral', as Lohrey's admitting into the story of the non-human world shows how pastoral is still being renegotiated.

Melissa Lucashenko is considered in Jessica Gildersleeve's article listed above in relation to Vivien Cleven.

David Malouf's well-known 'postcolonial' novel is given an ecocritical reading by Clare Archer-Lean and Gary Crew in 'Tracing Practice-Led Research to Locate a "Nature" in *Remembering Babylon*' (*JLLC* 62:iii[2015] 182–90). The trendy label would seem to indicate what any novelist does in researching material for a book; more interesting is the discussion of Malouf's citations and how they set up a relationship between humans and imagined nature, and how the text suggests moments beyond language as indicative (after Kate Rigby) of the 'non-equation' of the word and thus of human power over any 'natural' referent.

The same novel is analysed by Nicolette Bragg in 'Between Longing and Dwelling: The Hospitality of David Malouf's *Remembering Babylon*' (*CulSR* 21:ii[2015] 208–22). The reading uses Derrida and Lorenzo Veracini as a basis for showing the disruptions to home and hospitality at the heart of colonial settlement (who is host, who the guest?). The novel appears after the Mabo land-rights case and seems to allow a history of disturbance of boundaries while reinscribing that disturbance into a national narrative, though its engagement with the notion of hospitality suggests a deeper critique that acknowledges the host–guest relationship rests on an unequal split (one that Gemmy as both self *and* other shows up). There is no reconciliation or satisfactory mourning in the novel: the national home is shaken.

Suzie Gibson returns to the early Malouf and finds connections between the then Italy-based writer and the work of Italo Calvino in 'Malouf's Invisible City: The Intertwining of Place and Identity in *Johnno*' (*QR* 22:i[2015] 85–95). Stephen McInerney, in 'James McAuley: Strength in Weakness' (*Quadrant* 59:xii[2015] 94–6), compares two James McAuley poems in order to render possible observations about the political and ethical import of religious poetry.

Drusilla Modjeska's 'sometimes idiosyncratic feminism' is examined by Ulla Rahbek in 'Developing a Connective Feminine Discourse: Drusilla Modjeska on Women's Lives, Love and Art' (*Coolabah* 16[2015] 101–11), who applies the figure of the triptych and 'hinging tropes' of weaving, folding, and talking to a reading of *The Mountain, Stravinsky's Lunch, Secrets, Timepieces*, and *Poppy*—with brief mention of *Exiles at Home*—as a means of elucidating the writer's representation of women's experiences. Modjeska develops a female aesthetic out of friendships, conversations, love affairs, and female art practice, not so much as social critique as 'a form of positioning' (p. 102). She employs images of threads, stitching, braiding, weaving (and, later, photography) as signs of pulling together and composing memories in her slippery first-person-narrative locations.

The socialist realist writer John Morrison was a master of the short story and also a novelist, fêted by critics from A.A. Philips to Ivor Indyk to David Carter. 'Morrison's writing', writes Paul Galimond in the online *Sydney Review of Books*, 'is invariably witness to the relationship between the social and the economic' ('John Morrison: Writer of Proletarian Life' [August 2015] n.p.). Yet his work is entirely out of print. Galimond's interest encourages new editions of Morrison's work.

*JASAL* 15:i[2015] is a themed issue on voice, sound, and space. Anthony Uhlmann, 'Silence and Sound in the Sentences of Gerald Murnane's *A Million Windows*' (*JASAL* 15:i[2015] 9 pages), cites Murnane's comments on how he strives after sentences that have a 'sound shape that fits the contours of the thought', the mix being the voice of the writer (p. 1). Uhlmann argues that *A Million Windows* is 'a meditation on sound and silence', and as such gives the lie to critics who see his later work as less compelling. The novel links silence with secret and nervous disorder: 'One addresses, resolves, or stops the breakdown by finding the right sentences.' Looking for patterns in life, a process reflecting the emergence of meaning in fiction, the narrator/writer charts a series of dark-haired women, real, imagined, and written. Murnane's fourteen-year silence following *Emerald Blue* [1995] underlies this and other late work. Uhlmann suggests links between the 'chapter' numbers and Dante's writing, echoes of Hal Porter's work, and notes allusions to Henry James, Pascal, and Turgenev.

In 'Les Murray and the Purpose of Poetry' (*Quadrant* 59:vi[2015] 64–7), Clive James reflects on Murray's *Waiting for the Past*. It seems that because the political right has held on to perhaps Australia's greatest living poetic talent, James feels justified in dismissing those who write from the left. Their supposed lack of poetic achievement is blamed on Whitlam's democratization of education. James conscripts Murray's greatness more for advancing his own social agenda than for enhancing appreciation of the poet.

'Bill Neidjie's *Story About Feeling*: Notes on Its Themes and Philosophy' (*JASAL* 15:ii[2015] 11 pages), by Phillip Morrissey, is another piece in the 'species' issue of *JASAL*. The transcribed oral 'lectures' to a white readership and younger Aboriginals about Indigenous knowing stress embodied experience and speaker-listener/writer-reader engagement ('feeling') that are also connected to the land in general and with specific sites of power and ceremony. Use of Kriol removes distinctions between genders and between humans and nature. Morrissey concludes with a contrast between the modern subject of Joyce's Dedalus and the more positive conception from Neidjie and other Indigenous philosophers.

Eric Partridge, if he is known, is known as a lexicographer, born in New Zealand and educated in Queensland. In 'Worthwhile Rarities? The Fiction of Eric Partridge' (*S&P* 39:iii[2015] 182–90), John Arnold identifies three obscure, self-published novels by this 'chronicler of slang' (p. 182): *Why Not?*, *Glimpses*, and *Chronicle*, all published under pseudonyms.

Jessica White's '"I actually hear you think of me": Voices, Mediums and Deafness in the Writing of Rosa Praed' (*JASAL* 15:i[2015] 12 pages) considers Rosa Praed's interest in telepathy along with her relationship with deaf daughter Maud, who was subjected to a German training in speech rather than a French one in sign language. Ideas about deafness are connected with colonial discourses and Praed's fiction, which is alive with the (mostly threatening) sounds of the bush against which the human voice is comfort. Silent communication with the spirit world (her dead mother and then her dead companion) found 'voice' in automatic writing that also gave comfort. All this inclined Praed to have her daughter lip-read rather than assume her own 'voice' through signing. Maud's decline into madness drives troubled expressions in Praed's depictions of disability.

Ellen Smith's 'Different Workers: Political Commitment and Subaltern Labour in Katharine Susannah Prichard's *Brumby Innes*' (*JPW* 51:vi[2015] 648–60) puts the play into the context of leftist discourses about race, and argues that it shows the inability of socialism to address black exploitation. Smith's nuanced reading shows that while Prichard's fiction of the time, such as *Black Opal* [1921] and *Working Bullocks* [1926], gave voice to white male workers, and while later writings on Aboriginal labour offered the relatively standard Communist Party line, Aboriginal work for rations took labour relations beyond standard political analysis, so that 'Despite its radical presentation of Aboriginal exploitation and rage, the play, at times, falls back upon the language and the tropes of the nationalist left that it otherwise questions' (p. 658).

Nathan Hobby—writing a biography of Katharine Susannah Prichard's early life—reflects on Prichard's framing of her life through a 1926 fictionalized account of a crisis in her family around 1895 in her children's novel, in '"The memory of a storm": *The Wild Oats of Han* and the Childhood of Katharine Susannah Prichard, 1887 to 1895' (*Westerly* 60:ii[2015] 116–27). Hobby gives a detailed account of father Tom Prichard's professional and personal difficulties, speculating on little Katherine's experiences of them and how she deftly weaves them into her 1963 autobiography *Child of the Hurricane* and elsewhere in essays and other adult reflections.

Gig Ryan is fêted by Corey Wakeling in 'Anxiety and Antigone: An Introduction to Gig Ryan's *New and Selected Poems*' (*Westerly* 60:ii[2015] 35–47.

Kim Scott provides a meditation on history and language, working with stories from Noongar picture books and material connected to *That Deadman Dance* and *Kayang and Me*, in 'Not So Easy: Language for a Shared History' (*GriffithR* 47[2015] 200–14). Maggie Nolan considers the ethical and pragmatic consequences of cross-cultural appropriation in 'Shedding Clothes: Performing Cross-Cultural Exchange through Costume and Writing in Kim Scott's *That Deadman Dance*' (*Southerly* 75:ii[2015] 124–44).

Much recent criticism on Kenneth Slessor, including, for instance, work by Philip Mead and Peter Kirkpatrick, draws connections between the poet's journalistic career and his formation as a poet. Rod Grant will surely cause more ink to be spilled on the topic as he reconsiders the relationship in 'Kenneth Slessor and Bertha Blither: Two Sides of an Australian Writer

Between the Wars' (*SSEng* 41[2015] 92–110). This is especially so since Grant argues that the connection between Slessor's journalism and his poetry is 'dissonant rather than supportive' (p. 94). On a different tack, Slessor's first published poem (about a dying soldier after the Gallipoli landings) leads Julian Croft into an account of the poet's time as a war correspondent and its relationship to the composing of 'Beach Burial', in 'Kenneth Slessor's 'Other Front' (in Blaber, ed., pp. 43–52).

Christina Stead's less widely studied work is examined by William Lane in 'Narrative Origins in Christina Stead's "The Triskelion"' (*JLLC* 62:ii[2015] 100–6). The story was an early work and, according to Lane, deals with the nature of narrative, hidden drives, and narrative's capacity to create a world.

'Christina Stead's Poor Women of Sydney, Travelling into Our Times' (*JASAL* 15:iii[2015] 16 pages) has Carole Ferrier tracking 'the imaginary psychic territories' behind Stead's first novel, *Seven Poor Men of Sydney*, as indicated from her life at the time. Following Dorothy Green's reading of Catherine as the central figure, Ferrier considers three portraits of Catherine (possibly based on Esther Waite, sister of Stead's friend at teachers' college), depicting her struggle to be free but also to find an outlet for her passions. Ferrier connects these to the inner and outer worlds of Sydney's leftist intellectuals in the late 1920s, caught up with local struggles to survive but also reading and thinking about their place in world-historical movements. The novel's engagement with post-First World War surrealism, Marxism, and psychoanalysis and women's liberation 'travels with a strange or odd familiarity into the early twenty-first century, intersecting with recent preoccupations [with] trauma, femininities and masculinities [and] interactions of the global and the local' (p. 3).

Stead's encounter with a recording of Joyce reading from *Finnegans Wake* leads Helen Groth to examine modernism's engagement with modes of communication in 'Modernist Voices and the Desire for Communication in Christina Stead's *Seven Poor Men of Sydney*' (*JASAL* 15:i[2015] 14 pages). Stead's cosmopolitan outlook is countered by her Sydney settings and their giving voice to a modernism beyond its usual Anglo-American location. Her characters strive to communicate in a text infused with acoustic metaphors, and Stead's reading of *transition* and Joyce makes her conscious of language and dissonance. She deploys sensory impressions to suggest rather than describe characters, and produces broken sentences and conversations that go nowhere. The novel is not 'homely': written from a distance, it distances itself from its author and demands that we hear it across distances.

Stead is also considered in an issue of *Australian Literary Studies* focused on the pastoral. William Lane provides 'A Pastoral Reading of Christine Stead's *Cotter's England*' (*ALS* 30: ii[2015] 94–104), using Paul Alpers's work on Virgil's *Eclogues* and voice as a point of differentiation from criticism focused on realist engagement with politics and gender in Stead's novel. This work relies on the provincial background of characters and contrasts to metropolitan London; it also features conversations, songs, and an awareness of the power of voice, recalling the shepherds of pastoral, whose voice is their weapon of seduction and plaint. Tom evokes a rustic past and a yearning for continuous connections to it, disrupted by the recent war; Nellie more cynically uses her regional roots as a ploy to impress or cow others. Specifics also function within a generalized frame, as in pastoral.

Shaun Tan's popularity continues to grow in multiple circles. This year finds him used as a means to develop pedagogical skills—visual and otherwise—in 'Using Shaun Tan's Work to Foster Multiliteracies in 21st-Century Classrooms', by Ashley Dallacqua, Sara Kersten, and Mindi Rhoades (*TRT* 69:ii[2015] 207–17). Martin Blok Johansen offers an unusual approach to the work of this visual storyteller in ' "Darkness overcomes you": Saun Tan and Søren Kierkegaard' (*CLE* 46:i[2015] 38–52). The girl in *The Red Tree* undergoes a splitting and despair but undertakes the task of consolidating herself in a manner that accords with the Dane's existential philosophy. It is a careful reading of images and text, well situated within existing work on Tan.

Alf Taylor's poetry in *Singer Songwriter* [1992] and *Winds* [1994] provides Danica Čerče with an opportunity to argue that Aboriginal writing is more than just 'mere propaganda' or social-protest reportage. Based on interviews and thematic reading of texts, she gives a good description of the work, but even personal poems of 'sadness and despair' and anger from someone who declares 'The pencil is my weapon' (p. 27) call the overall thesis into question (*Coolabah* 16[2015] 25–33).

Revisions of Australian identity (ethnic, homosexual, female) are the focus of Catalina Ribas Segura's 'Identity and Friendship in Hsu-Ming Teo's *Behind the Moon*' (*Coolabah* 16[2015] 112–21). Using identity-construction theory from Manuel Castells, Raewyn Connell, and Maria Pallotta Chiarolli, Segura reads the quest for belonging in each of the three central characters. See also the discussion of Carrera Suárez in Section 2(b) above.

Catherine Seaton investigates 'Salvador Torrents and the Birth of Crónica Writing in Australia' (*JASAL* 15:iii[2015] 9 pages). Torrents, a Spanish cane-cutter in north Queensland, published internationally from 1915 to 1950, using the documentary-essay-story form popular in European and Latin American newspapers to voice the experiences of Australian labour and migration. Torrents went into exile owing to his anarchist beliefs. He mixed hard labour with wide reading, translation, and writing across a range of genres, publishing in Spanish in New York and Barcelona. As 'a community moralist' (p. 4), Torrents comments on Australia's egalitarian ethos, its addiction to alcohol, its insistence on speaking English, its mindless physical violence and racism, carrying through his Spanish emphasis on 'honor', and advocating gender equality. His work is an important basis for studying later writing by Hispanic immigrants.

P.L. Travers, despite her expatriation and Anglophilia, was a Queenslander by birth, and so it is appropriate that Sharyn Pearce, in 'The Business of Myth-Making: *Mary Poppins*, P.L. Travers and the Disney Effect' (*QR* 22:i[2015] 62–74), offers a more detailed account in *Queensland Review* of what has recently become common knowledge since the biopic *Saving Mr Banks*. Pearce adds the irony that Disney went against the wishes of Travers twice over in this recent project.

Andrew McCann, from the outset of his *Christos Tsiolkas and the Fiction of Critique: Politics, Obscenity, Celebrity*, foregrounds a distinction in Frankfurt school critical theory between lived experience and 'a more robust order of consciousness bound up with memory, temporality and futurity' (p. 1). The latter of these is disordered, he argues, by capitalist consumer life. For McCann, Tsiolkas presents an unusual example of a writer who is both embedded in this culture by virtue of his own celebrity and one who fosters a persona capable of challenging it. This is not a position, however, that remains fixed across Tsiolkas's oeuvre. That the politics of Tsiolkas's critique of capitalism is vested in a mode of obscenity deriving from Pasolini suggests that sexuality and the body can be a site of resistance, but the theoretical distinction McCann makes allows him to complicate this premise. As he notes, 'for both Pasolini and Tsiolkas, the possibility of remaining outside these circuits [of capitalist commodification] produced a visceral intensity that would also, ultimately, be the basis on which atomized subjects are assimilated into the hedonism of consumer society and global capitalism' (p. 133). A problem arises in that while libidinal investment in alternatives to the commodified self can act to resist consumer logics, it also threatens to sink the more temporally complex sense of self into the merely visceral response to experience's commodification. McCann suggests that the body disfigured as a mode of resistance 'can still appear to be an irruption into the space of culture' (p. 8). Hence McCann posits celebrity as a new mode of resistance to the commodification of authorship that emerges with *The Slap* (pp. 16–17). This is a difficult book but its difficulty is both true to the spirit of Tsiolkas and resists the circuits of recommodification that it claims Tsiolkas's work also refuses.

In 'Subaltern Cosmopolitanism: The Question of Hospitality in Christos Tsiolkas's *Dead Europe*' (*JASAL* 15:iii[2015] 10 pages), Jessica Brooks takes up the book's critique of multicultural cosmopolitanism and free-market capitalism to consider 'the global treatment of the migrant and asylum seeker' (p. 1). The hauntings are signs of violations of hospitality. Isaac, the cosmopolitan tourist-vampire is thrown to the extra-legal fringes of Europe where the contradictions of unconditional hospitality and border protection (after McCann, Derrida, and Nikos Papastergiadis) are exposed. Isaac's family history shows how Australia is not a safe haven from the viruses of money and racism, and his story looks to some new subaltern collectivity on which emancipation might be founded.

*Dead Europe* is also examined from the perspective of Caryl Phillips's *The European Tribe* by Janine Hauthal in 'Writing Back or Writing Off? Europe as "Tribe" and "Traumascape" in Caryl Phillips and Christos Tsiolkas' (*JPW* 51:ii[2015] 208–19), to show the greater degree of disturbance of genre, of narrative reliability, and (through using photography to establish 'traumascapes') of readers, by engaging them in the struggle to handle transcultural difference and determine the book's position on anti-Semitism. There is no sense of looking for a Europe of convivial multicultural cosmopolitanism, and Australia is no clean refuge from conflict and haunting. The article attends to Tsiokas's varying of narrative position and recourse to uncertain magic realism and hallucination.

'One of the most sonically intense Australian novels ever written' is how Joseph Cummins describes Christos Tsiolkas's *Loaded* in '"I turn up the volume and walk towards home": Mapping the Soundscapes of *Loaded*' (*JASAL* 15:i[2015] 11 pages). Ari's discovery of identity occurs partly through his selection of a variety of popular music and against the sounds of Melbourne city life. This reading floats on a raft of media theorists connecting sound, space, technology, and identity formation, making links between the *flâneur* and the Walkman, music and dance, and choreographed self-construction.

'Patrick White, Composer Manqué: The Centrality of Music in White's Artistic Aspiration' by John J. Carmody (*Antipodes* 29:i[2015] 153–61) keeps the great man in the critical limelight. Carmody tracks White's attention to music via textual and biographical material. The argument is clear, though perhaps unsurprising, given White's modernist aesthetic, and there are three previous works pointing up the connection by Bruce Nesbitt, Fiona Richards, and Rodney Stenning-Edgecombe.

Jackson Moore, 'Is Prowse's Rectum a Grave? Jouissance, Reparative Transnationalism and Patrick White's *The Twyborn Affair*' (*JASAL* 15:iii[2015] 10 pages), links Don Prowse to Australia's masculine nationalist literary tradition, and, rather than repeating suspicions of that, uses Eve Sedgewick and Leo Bersani to explore how a queer outlook might offer a new 'rhetoric of belonging'. The argument uses dense theoretical phrasing to compact a long line from text to world. It turns from Prowse's brutish physicality to Eddie's desiring view of him, reading through conventions of gay porn. Admitting the ('paranoid', p. 5) criticism that shows the misogyny and homophobia in the book, Moore points to homoerotic pleasure in Eddie's experience as a possible queering of standard interpretations and undoing the dominant literary historical myth and White's canonical/oppositional relationship to it. Moore then runs his argument through Vilashini Cooppan's work about affect, nation, and transnation. It needs time to tease out the links and test their validity, but it's an interesting take on both novel and literary tradition.

Focusing on *Memoirs of Many in One* [1986], Nourit Melcer-Padon, in 'Patrick White's Hungarian Connection' (*JASAL* 15:iii[2015] 16 pages), argues that a brief intertextual reference to Hungarian Imre Madách's poem 'The Tragedy of Man' serves White as a framework for his book's double narrative (Alex's story and the story of her editor, Patrick) in which the protagonist is both set up and questioned. With reference to Said's *On Late Style*, and to Flaubert's identification with Madame Bovary, plus some biographical detail on White and a quick survey of critical reception, the article suggests that the book's fragmented, disruptive structure is actually carefully crafted and points to a wholeness beyond its protagonist's grasp. Madách's debate between Lucifer and God informs White's 'medieval mystery play' about artistic creation and creative lack of control. Textual detail is mixed with some archetype analysis to produce a compelling reading.

White studies received an international reboot in 2010, with a conference at the University of London, papers from which have been edited by Ian Henderson and Anouk Lang as *Patrick White Beyond the Grave: New Critical Perspectives*. Henderson's introduction (pp. 1–13) looks to a shift from literary criticism to a livelier 'performance of literary reading' (p. 1). He surveys the main trends in White criticism from Simon During onwards, pointing to the continuing relevance of the writing to Australian society, and noting how

White's plays have kept his name alive, helped in more recent times by the discovery of manuscripts and the centenary of his birth.

In the first section ('Resurrected Papers'), Margaret Harris and Elizabeth Webby tell the story of the National Library's acquisition of White's papers in 'The Evidence of the Archive' (pp. 17– 34) and Angus Nicholls returns to 'Leichhardt and *Voss* Revisited' (pp. 35–63). Harris and Webby outline the contents of the NLA collection, from notebooks containing wartime diaries, notes on Australian language, and jottings towards many books ('the challenge is to see what scrap gets worked up', p. 23). There are letters, drafts of plays, manuscripts of later work, and 'big tranches of unpublished longer fiction', plus photographs, an index to his music collection, theatre programmes—all survivors of many fires and White's denials that he kept papers.

The result shows how little he relied on his income as a writer, how intricately he worked his life-fiction identity, and how early he experimented across genres. It gives insights into his process of composition and his historical research. The collection has since generated publication of the unfinished *The Hanging Garden*.

Angus Nicholls goes to the notebooks to determine exactly White's use of Leichhardt's writing and of material relating to his journeys, arguing for his closer reliance on his letters than his journals. Nicholls considers the construction of the explorer's negative image and his place as letter-writer in German Romantic travel writing.

Part II ('Many in One') begins with David Marr's 'White's London' (pp. 67–80). Escaping from becoming a sterile London intellectual, White nonetheless declared he felt himself to be a Londoner; he always subscribed to the *Observer*, even though it gave him his worst reviews; he hated boarding school, but it gave him access to London theatre and inspired his early writing. London inducted him into homosexual society and subjected him to the Blitz that figured in his later writing. After his long association with New York, his London base with Jonathan Cape produced his later fiction.

Mark McKenna ('Elective Affinities: Manning Clark, Patrick White, Sidney Nolan', pp. 81–100) tells of White's friendship with Clark, relating its vicissitudes to their mutual involvement with Nolan's paintings and the efforts of a small artistic elite to create a new vision of Australia. The focus is on Clark, how he was inspired by *The Tree of Man*, how 'Since 1961, Clark...clipped and filed every press report he read on White and Nolan and would continue to do so until his death' (p. 85). They both supported Whitlam's re-election and read each other's work while writing their own, but parted company in the wake of the Dismissal and Clark's acceptance of an award from Prime Minister Malcolm Fraser.

Georgina Loveridge ('Dismantled and Re-Constructed: *Flaws in the Glass* Re-visioned' pp. 101–15) argues that the fictive autobiography is 'both a sample of White's aesthetic and a commentary upon it...a reading guide to his fictions' that may not tell us '*the* truth but *about* truth' (p. 101). Loveridge claims that many have read the work as a guide to the author's personality despite White's record of unreliable self-presentation. Her demonstration (with mention of Paul de Man) of the book's attention to the impossibility of complete autobiographical veracity is well made. She charts critical uses of the text and gives a detailed reading of White's use of houses, overlaying Blake, Hayley, Banjo Paterson, and childhood to argue that disconnected fragments become their own symbol, multiplying rather than limiting referents to locate meaning in the nexus between elements rather than in the elements themselves.

Andrew McCann writes of 'Patrick White's Late Style' (pp. 117–28), sketching the critical mix of postcolonial analysis and interest in the sacred as a project aimed at discovering modes of belonging apart from 'secular instrumentalized society' and in tune with Indigenous connection to land that makes White into a vehicle for becoming 'properly postcolonial'. He argues that the later work in fact shows as travesty and ruin 'the very signifiers of its own theological orientation' (pp. 118–19). Aligning himself with Elizabeth McMahon and Adorno, McCann uses *Memoirs of Many in One* to point to a 'playful incongruity' in which 'the performativity of the sacred' is undone by 'the textual apparatus... now too burdened by its materiality to function in any other mode but that of parody' (p. 120). He reads the text as a confusion of and struggle between symbol and allegory, the saintly and the abject, indicating 'the ruin of art itself' (pp. 120–1). This is one of the strongest chapters in the collection.

Part III is labelled 'The Performance of Reading'. It comprises Ivor Indyk's 'Patrick White's Expressionism' (pp. 131–40), Aruna Wittman on 'The Doubling of Reality in Patrick White's *The Aunt's Story* and Paul Schreber's *Memories of my Nervous Illness*' (pp. 141–53), Gail Jones's 'Desperate, Marvellous Shuttling: White's Ambivalent Modernism' (pp. 155–62), and Brigid Rooney's '"Time and its fellow conspirator space": Patrick White's *A Fringe of Leaves*' (pp. 163–77). Indyk finds a 'meteoro-logical' dynamic flow of emotions around a static situation in *The Eye of the Storm* that immerses the reader, a rise and fall that leaves enough disturbance to spark another cycle. White's modernism is tinged with the baroque and with German expressionism, a Catholic emotionality vying with Protestant guilt and restraint, though 'the emotion itself is social rather than religious in origin' and may be quite small but attended to so closely that it is magnified, partly by being embedded within other emotions (pp. 134, 136–7). Indyk perceptively points to the long sequence of scenes wherein a rhythm of alternating 'extended awkwardness and momentary grace' is created (p. 139).

Aruna Wittman juxtaposes White's fictional account of madness with a non-fiction memoir to show the former's 'erasure of narrative presence, the mixing of narrative viewpoints and the doubling of narration in which two point of view co-exist' (p. 141). Love and home are themes underlying the transition from early to later styles marked by *The Aunt's Story*, with a possible connection to authorial fears of madness, madness being feminized in both texts and negotiated through cross-dressing (in actuality with Schreber, through fictive performance with White).

Adorno's attack on modernism as occult compensation for brute reality is employed by Gail Jones as a lens through which to read *The Aunt's Story*. She attends to the painterly 'imagistic exorbitance' and 'baroque embodiment' that accompany moments of 'mystification', an 'individualist quest for the past as future...typical...of high modernist disillusion' and both echoed and countered by 'assertive vulgar materialism'. The Jardin exotique is read against Benjamin, with the nautilus seen as an 'icon of both integrity and destruction', a 'natural fetish [that] prepares the way for the pastoral resolution of the novel' (pp. 156–9). White seeks to refuse commodity but retain materialism.

Rooney suggests that two attempts at writing *A Fringe of Leaves* inform the book's 'doubled temporalities' and recurring chronotopes. As with other chapters, this one looks at White's shape-shifting: 'All that is solid melts and all that melts solidifies' in a cycle of 'revelation and encryption' (p. 164). Rooney surveys divided responses to the novel, hearing echoes in the text's dualities, and asserting the book's unique working of 'the zone of the edge' as theme and form. Vehicles shuttle to and fro, create inside and outside spaces, echo the workings of earlier novels of sentiment; pregnancy vies with rupture, colonist with captive, prolepsis with analepsis, figured in White's use of the conditional mood (p. 170), all in a theatre of (post)colonial drama.

A final section, 'Queer White', has Ian Henderson improbably but entertainingly bringing White together with a British comedian and radio presenter ('Knockabout World: Patrick White, Kenneth Williams and the Queer World' pp. 181–92), while Anouk Lang closes with 'Queering Sarsaparilla: Patrick White's Deviant Modernism' (pp. 193–204). Henderson provides a personal account of coming to read White to assess Williams's negative response to *The Living and the Dead*. Williams and White are linked by performances in writing that negotiate a time of socially enforced closeting of homosexuality. Camp is a mode of expressing this and queerness emerges in *The Twyborn Affair* and afterwards. Henderson suggests these are indirectly informed by what Williams overtly mentions: the gay theatre language called Polari. He closes by echoing other chapters in stressing White's focus on the material and corporeal.

Lang seeks to reposition White within contemporary work on queer modernism, both to value the writer's work and to shift modernist studies a little. White requires none of the creative misreading that queers otherwise normative modernists because he directly figures queer lives. Moreover, his Australian location gives his work an unusual sense of transnational and postcolonial energies that supplement current work on queer modernists. Lang considers the 'queer' coded nature of *The Aunt's Story* and White's androgynous challenges to gendering, especially of masculinity, in 'an extended commentary on suburban normalcy' that makes his queerness integral to his modernism (p. 200).

Denise Varney and Sandra D'Urso, in 'Patrick White and Aesthetic Modernism in Mid-Century Australia' (*ADS* 66[2015] 63–80), track modernist tropes across *The Ham Funeral* and *Signal Driver* to assess White's post-war criticism of materialist Australia in terms of a paradox of critiquing nation via the modernism that helped shape it, noting the ambivalence in critical depiction of theatre modernism as both non-conformist and anti-bourgeois, on the one hand, and elitist and complex on the other. White offsets his attention to something transcendent with an accumulation of material objects, signalling something beyond and with language, beyond and within modernity. Following Veronica Kelly, Varney and D'Urso take up Julian Murphet's views on the uneven presence of the modern within the postmodern, the centrality of 'the nothing' in its aesthetics that opposes utility and consumerism. *Signal Driver* engages with the modernist 'nothing' (an empty bus) in its 'maudlin sentimentality and capacity for critique' (pp. 69, 74). White's links with Dobell in shaping *The Ham Funeral* are canvassed.

*Southerly* 75:ii[2015] is themed 'The Naked Writer'. It begins with an essay by Fiona McFarlane, 'On Reading *The Aunt's Story* by Patrick White' (*Southerly* 75:ii[2015] 17–31)—a thoughtful, finely wrought reflection on Patrick White's third novel as 'an argument against our lives as they are ordinarily lived' (p. 30) in complacency and comfort.

In 'White's Brown Woman' (*Meanjin* 74:iv[2015] 11–12), Denise Varney speculates on the racial identity of Miss Docker, a character in Patrick White's play of the early 1960s, *A Cheery Soul*.

William Willis was best known in Australia as a corrupt politician in the first decade of the twentieth century. He fled to Singapore and then London, writing popular accounts of everything from racing to white slavery. He helped to establish the 'Anglo-Eastern Publishing Co.', but John Arnold and James Doig, in 'William Nicholas Willis, Père, Fils and Family and the Anglo-Eastern Publishing Company' (*S&P* 39:iv[2015] 197–220), show that much work issued under the pseudonym 'Bree Narran' that might have been attributed to Willis (the company's most prolific author) was probably the work of Mercy Lehane Willis, his wife.

Tim Winton is interviewed by Madeleine Watts in 'Contending with a Blank Page: On Writing, Wealth and Being a West-Coaster' (*GriffithR* 47[2015] 105–15). Discussion ranges widely, with some commentary on *Eyrie*. Stephen Harris, 'Tim Winton's *Dirt Music*: Sounding Country/Re-Siting Place' (*JASAL* 15:i[2015] 15 pages), draws our attention to the circular drone of the didgeridoo in Winton's novel, a sound that 'earths' in its embodied production while dissolving the body/world boundary in a trance of song/breathing. This 'soundsculpture' suggests ways of connecting to the natural environment. 'Music, then, becomes at once earthly force and imaginative source' (p. 2). The novel distinguishes acoustic from electric music, in the process linking the former to 'dirt', the sound of the poor, and of the land. Other writers and sound artists (notably Ros Bandt) are brought in to show possibilities and limitations of white men connecting to 'country' in the same way as Aboriginals, some 'practical mysticism' of self-emptying and transformation—some 'resonance'—being required. Bill Neidjie and *Breath* are sources used to illuminate Fox's quest in *Dirt Music*. Lyn McCredden's article, 'Tim Winton's Poetics of Resurrection', reviewed in its online version last year, has now appeared as *L&T* 29:iii[2015] 323–34.

'Chris Womersley's *Bereft*: Ghosts that Dwell on the Margins of Traumatic Memory' by Dolores Herrero (*Anglia* 133:iii[2015] 511–27) applies trauma theory to a close reading of the novel about small-town murder, memory, and the effects of the First World War on returning soldiers. Womersley employs elements of the Gothic in a postcolonial context, reversing some of the usual binaries of strength/weakness and law/criminality. Herrero argues that reading via trauma theory allows an allegorical interpretation in which marginal figures 'come to the fore as Derridean ghosts in order to reclaim their rightful place and presence and demand justice' (p. 515), opening up the 'crypt' of traumatized mourning in the protagonist. The ambiguous figure of Sadie and the open ending of the book suggest literature's role of pushing the reader out into ongoing processes of memorializing and reconciling.

Alexis Wright receives detailed attention in Ben Holgate's 'Unsettling Narratives: Re-evaluating Magic Realism as Postcolonial Discourse through Alexis Wright's *Carpentaria* and *The Swan Book*' (*JPW* 51:vi[2015] 634–47). Holgate argues that Slemon's analysis of the disturbing clash of magic and real as a postcolonial literary strategy 'does not adequately allow for the complexity of problems that arise from a situation in which there is ongoing colonization in a supposedly postcolonial country' and insists that transnational capital is a necessary dimension in considering Indigenous magical realist texts composed and set in settler colonies (p. 643). He tends to slip too loosely from textual operations into contextual issues of fourth world politics and global economics, but usefully invokes Mudrooroo's idea of 'maban reality' in Aboriginal fiction to show a difference between Wright's subscribing to the ontological reality of Indigenous belief in spirit powers and writers who use magic realism simply as a literary device, although it is acknowledged that Wright follows such literary invention as well.

Arnaud Barras reads allegorically, in 'The Law of Storytelling: The Hermeneutics of Relationality in Alexis Wright's *The Swan Book*' (*JASAL* 15:iii[2015] 12 pages), to argue that the novel points Australian literature beyond national boundaries to transcultural and world-directed connections. He uses Jauss's ideas of fields within which texts and readings operate, plus notions of the relational self taken from Val Plumwood, Deborah Bird, and Doreen Massey, along with Alison Ravenscroft's reading of the novel to suggest the book's refusal of access to any fixed Aboriginal knowledge. Its deployment of polysemy, self-aware intertextuality (white and black swan stories from both hemispheres), and circulating stories ('musical, bodily, ecological and literary', p. 8) 'trigger[s] a horizon change' (p. 3) in both characters and readers, and boundaries between dreaming, thinking, telling, writing, reading, and listening are broken down.

Judith Wright is the central figure in a broader treatment, 'Refiguring the Silence of Euro-Australian Landscapes', by Nicholas Kankhainen (*JASAL* 15:i[2015] 12 pages). Early settlers commonly spoke of the silence of the land and began imposing European words and urban noises onto it. Wright's ecologically sensitive poetry (and perhaps her own experience of deafness) suggests that the silence of the landscape is a positive phenomenon that should be maintained. Heidegger, Derrida, Val Plumwood, and Wright's writings are adduced to explore the limits of language, especially in the encounter with the non-human.

## 3. Canada

### (a) Books

Several books have been published in 2015 that make important contributions to the critical discussion of Canadian literature and culture and their role in the defining of the nation. This is the case in particular with Margery Fee's *Literary Land Claims: The 'Indian Land Question' from Pontiac's War to Attawapiskat*, on the question of land and relations with Indigenous people; *Public Poetics: Critical Issues in Canadian Poetry and Poetics*, edited by Bart Vautour, Erin Wunker, Travis V. Mason, and Christl Verduyn, on the role of poetry in community; and *Magazines, Travel, and Middlebrow Culture: Canadian Periodicals in English and French, 1925–1960*, by Faye Hammill and Michelle Smith, on the impact of magazines on Canadian culture and lifestyle.

Fee's *Literary Land Claims* illustrates and reflects on an important development in the approach to land in Canada. The book's publication coincides with that in December 2015 of the final report of the Truth and Reconciliation Commission (TRC), which started its activity in 2008 and was part of the Indian Residential Schools Settlement Agreement (IRSSA, 2007). As the subtitle of Fee's book suggests, the corpus of works studied in its seven chapters spans the period starting with Pontiac's War (1763–5), a successful First Nations war against European invasion in the Great Lakes area led by Ottawa chief Pontiac. It stretches into the contemporary period and Chief Theresa Spence's appeal in 2011 to the Canadian Red Cross to address the housing conditions of Attawapiskat First Nation in northern Ontario. Fee's central concern is with contemporary land claims, euphemistically called the 'Indian land question' in the past, and the role literature, in its most inclusive sense, and literary studies can play in this debate. The selection of texts deliberately includes speakers and writers who cannot easily be categorized as Indigenous or Canadian, because these categories are themselves products of colonization. The texts and speeches studied thus destabilize the notion of state and literary canon, the two being closely linked in the process of the definition of national identity. However, the variety of experiences represented simultaneously emphasizes the fact that the notion of identity is connected to land rights. This is also true of the identity of the settlers, as evidenced in two now classic essays, Northrop Frye's 'Conclusion' to the *Literary History of Canada* [1965] and Margaret Atwood's *Survival* [1972]. But in this relation to the land, Fee points out the epistemological difference between the Romantic nationalism in which Nature is terrifying, and the Indigenous world-view which consists in identifying with it. To Fee, it is crucial to listen to Indigenous voices: by 'moving away from narrowly nationalist histories and perspectives to those that better articulate the multiple dilemmas of colonization' (p. 226), these voices have a role to play, together with literary studies, in the process of finding good ways to share the land. Fee starts by positioning herself as an 'uninvited guest' in Musqueam territory (p. 17)—this practice is a significant development among academics in parts of Canada that are treaty land—while also examining the long-lasting effect in discourse of the opposition between white civilization and primitive savagery. In the six subsequent chapters, her aim is to 'find the points of friction where [the texts] rub against both the dominant discourses of their times and those of their more recent reception' (p. 13). She studies John Richardson's novels, *Wacousta* [1832] and *The Canadian Brothers* [1840], as those of 'a disaffected, pessimistic, and even traumatised chronicler of a dark time in colonial history' (p. 13). She then examines the 'Constitutive Rhetoric in the Courtroom Addresses of Louis Riel (1844–1885)' of 1885 and considers how Riel's vision for the nation differed from that of Prime Minister John A. Macdonald. She studies 'Performance, Authenticity, Disidentification, and E. Pauline Johnson/Tekahionwake (1861–1913)', showing how Johnson tried to transform what was seen as her dual identity through her performances. Similarly, 'Imposture, Animism, Ecosystem, and Archibald Belaney/Grey Owl (1888–1938)' examines how Grey Owl 'transgressed the Nature/Culture divide' (p. 15). Last, reading Harry Robinson's (1900–90) oral story of origin, 'Coyote Makes a Deal with the King of England', Fee analyses the connections between the white man's double theft of literacy and of Indigenous land.

To pursue the theme of Indigenous writing, Tomson Highway, in an autobiographical essay entitled 'First Nations Writing: A Personal History' (in Däwes, Fitz, and Meyer, eds., *Twenty-First Century Perspectives on Indigenous Studies: Native North America in (Trans)Motion*, pp. 42–60), gives an evocative sense of the richness of Indigenous culture and languages. He retraces the fast development of an Indigenous literature in Canada in the past thirty years or so, largely as a reaction to the threat of 'Pierre Elliott Trudeau's infamous White Paper' of 1969, which 'proposed the elimination of the reserve system and the wholesale assimilation of Indian people into white society' (p. 53). As a result, Native youngsters now 'have a literature that validates their existence, that gives them dignity, that tells them that they, and their culture, their ideas, their languages, are important if not downright essential to the long-term survival of the planet' (p. 58).

Evelyn P. Mayer, in 'Indigenous Interstitial Spaces: Liminality in Thomas King's "Borders"' (in Achilles and Bergmann, eds., *Liminality and the Short Story: Boundary Crossings in American, Canadian, and British Writing*, pp. 263–73), studies the well-known and well-loved short story by Thomas King, 'Borders', focusing on the potential of Indigenous interstitial spaces and storytelling. Borders in King's oeuvre have already attracted a lot of attention, with a whole book devoted to the theme of border crossing in his work, and this article adds little to one previously published by the same author in 2011.

To go back to the question of the land: Claire Omhovère, in 'Landscapes in Transit: The Displacement of the Western Landscape Tradition in English Canada' (in Labaune-Demeule and Pesso-Miquel, eds., *Authority and Displacement in the English-Speaking World*, vol. 2: *Exploring American Shores*, pp. 93–115), expertly analyses the processes whereby space has been transformed into place and landscape in Canada, through readings of texts by John Richardson, Ruby Wiebe, Jane Urquhart, Joy Kogawa, Aritha van Herk, and others. Omhovère also confronts the representations of landscape in these works with a number of visual artworks, framing the discussion in the tradition of Western art, which she contrasts with Eastern landscape traditions, and observing by comparison what happened in various parts of the English-speaking world, so that the essay gives accrued depth of resonance to landscape in narrative.

Although *Nature in Translation: Japanese Tourism Encounters the Canadian Rockies*, by Shiho Satsuka, primarily belongs to the field of anthropology, it also presents fruitful intersections with literature, which makes it relevant to include here. The book analyses the role of tour guides in translating the relationship between man and nature for the Japanese tourists who started travelling en masse to Banff in the 1980s and 1990s. The main argument is that nature is always in translation, and that the translation of nature is a philosophical, but also a political and economic, question. The literary interest of the book hinges on the notions of translation and narrative it studies. The guides' translation work is linguistic—for instance, they translated a book about the first ascent of Mount Alberta by the Japanese Maki Yuko, as told by a local historian—as well as cultural. At first the guides translated the cultural narrative 'of discovery and exploration from the point of view of European explorers and settlers' (p. 14), before gradually elaborating on this script, adding context or explaining knowledge. Through their translations, they turned the natural landscape into an object of admiration—Canada's 'magnificent nature'—and they also shaped social interactions, particularly through translation words such as 'nature', subject', and 'freedom'. Their translations of sensibilities of nature had an impact on the lives of ordinary people in contemporary Japan, opening them up to sensibilities of modernity. And their own life stories, which consist in having left the Japanese corporate system and chosen to become guides in the Canadian Rockies, driven by the notion of freedom, have contributed to the construction of a global space. Satsuka's book about the process of transcultural perspectives on landscape will no doubt be of interest to those concerned with the different literary forms of perception and representation of landscape.

The shaping of one's views and the factors that contribute to that shaping is a leading thread in *Magazines, Travel, and Middlebrow Culture*, by Faye Hammill and Michelle Smith, a book at the crossroads of cultural studies, literary studies, Canadian studies, periodical studies, and other fields of research. Although its primary corpus is not literary, literary writing is part of the material it examines, by way of the fiction published in the magazines selected: *Mayfair, Chatelaine, Maclean's, La Revue Moderne*, the *Canadian Home Journal*, and *La Revue Populaire*. To the authors, these magazines 'illuminate the relationships amongst nationalism, consumerism, and print culture, three defining features of the last century'; as for literature, 'The fiction and poetry [these magazines] circulated tell us about shared ideals and value systems, while the disappearance of many of their authors from literary history hints at cultural hierarchies that came into play as the magazines went into decline' (p. 2). The term 'middlebrow' implies a set of aesthetic values: 'books or artworks which are conventional rather than experimental in form, and accessible rather than challenging to audiences, yet which are not formulaic or sensational' (p. 9). However, what is categorized as middlebrow varies over time, and there is ambivalence in the mediation the term implies, between high culture and mass culture. So the authors shift the perspective: 'What we find much more useful is to consider the middlebrow as a mode of circulation, reception, and consumption of cultural products, and also as a space where high and popular culture meet, and where art encounters consumerism' (p. 10). Further, the theme of travel and 'mobility locates Canadian magazines in the context of an increasingly global modern culture' (p. 20), inscribing Canada into a larger network of circulation. The four chapters of the book focus on aspects of magazines that contribute to various fields of enquiry: periodical history ('Marketplace'), print culture studies ('Pages'), discourses of modernism ('Fashion'), and social and cultural capital ('Consumers'). Through the chosen angle of study of magazines, the book paves the way for the study of an important, but until now insufficiently explored, aspect of Canadian culture.

Several books investigate various grounds of newness and creativity. *Pathways of Creativity in Contemporary Newfoundland and Labrador*, edited by María Jesús Hernáez Lerena, maps out the literature and arts of a region which has considerably developed culturally since the 1970s. As the editor points out, one of the aims of the book is 'to identify the juncture points—ideological as well as aesthetic—in which a range of contemporary writers and visual artists become both inheritors of past definitions of national and regional identity and individual creators of narratives, poems, plays, films and paintings which address the roots but also the fractures threatening their society' (pp. 2–3). The book deals with the identity of a region, and as 'many critics have argued, a region is not a location, it is an ideology produced by a set of rhetorical devices' (p. 5). The idea of region is complicated by 'the interaction between locality and globalism in a place that was historically regarded as marginal to Canada' (p. 8). It is further complicated by the association of Newfoundland, an island settled by British and Irish settlers, and Labrador, which is part of the Canadian mainland and where the Inuit population is a majority, into a single province. The book comprises chapters written by academics and artists from Newfoundland and Labrador, and it ends with a series of interviews with artists and writers conducted by the editor, which gives a vivid sense of the questions at stake in artistic (literary) creation. The book has a comprehensive ambition so the topics of the twelve chapters are varied, ranging through history, travelling, fiction, Aboriginal writing, poetry, theatre, film, storytelling, painting, and sculpture. The volume thus achieves its goal of providing an overall view of contemporary Newfoundland and Labrador culture.

In *The Canadian Fantastic in Focus: New Perspectives*, editor Allan Weiss pursues his work of mapping out the fantastic in Canadian literature and culture. The collection gathers the proceedings of the Academic Conference on Canadian Science Fiction and Fantasy, from 2005 to 2013. The conference first took place in 1995, and Weiss, who has been acting as its chair, edited two earlier volumes [1998, 2005]. In the introduction (pp. 1–13), he brings up the question of whether there is something distinctive about science fiction and fantasy created by Canadians, but remains cautious about generalizations. The literature has been written both in English and in French, and some regional differences can be traced. The themes of identity and alienation are present, but these are not particularly Canadian. In the early literature, political themes predominated: 'Much of the fantastic literature written during the late nineteenth and early twentieth centuries was part of a nationalist literary agenda' (p. 4), with utopias dominated by a superior 'Canadian race', and corresponding agrarian utopias in French Canada. The Cold War and potential nuclear disaster from the 1950s to the 1970s, and scientific and technological advances, have influenced the genre since. According to Weiss, the 'true flowering of Canadian science fiction and fantasy occurred in the 1980s' (p. 7), with fanzines, conventions, and anthologies appearing. The volume opens with a survey by Robert Runté of writing and scholarship in the field ('Why I Read Canadian Speculative Fiction: The Social Dimension of Reading', pp. 14–33), and a paper by Veronica Hollinger about writing as a scholar on science fiction ('The Body on the Slab', pp. 34–43). The fifteen papers of the volume are then organized into three parts, by genre: 'Canadian Science Fiction', 'Canadian Fantasy and Dark Fantasy', and 'Media Expressions'. Two essays are devoted to Nalo Hopkinson's work, 'New-Half-Way Tree and the Second World: Themes of Nation and Colonization in Nalo Hopkinson's *Midnight Robber*', by Brecken Hancock (pp. 95–105) and 'Navigating the Darkness: Blindness and Vampirism in Tanya Huff's *Blood Books*' by Derek Newman-Stille (pp. 186–98); one by Tammy Dasti focuses on Rikki Ducornet, 'The Word and the Flesh: Natural Law vs. Catholic Dogma in Rikki Ducornet's *The Stain*' (pp. 120–30). These are two of the established writers in the genre. The posthuman and vampirism are some of the themes examined.

*Cultural Mapping and the Digital Sphere: Place and Space*, edited by Ruth Panofsky, Kathleen Kellett, Susan Brown, and Mary-Jo Romaniuk, will draw the attention of researchers interested in digital humanities, as it largely deals with infrastructure (rather than research per se). It results from the second conference of the Canadian Writing Research Collaboratory (CWRC), held in October 2011 at Ryerson University. In the contemporary context of a digital environment, CWRC 'aims to create a new forum for literary research in and about Canada. [It] will make it easier for scholars to work together and share the raw materials of their research . . . with each other and the wider scholarly community. It will also offer an innovative, non-traditional online venue for publishing and connecting research results' (p. viii). The book is the product of 'a four-way collaboration among the University of Alberta Libraries, the University of Alberta Press, CWRC, and SSHRC [Social Science and Humanities Research Council]' (p. ix). The first part, 'Place and the Digital Frontier' (seven chapters), is particularly valuable in the way it deals with various aspects of digital humanities. Two chapters are devoted to maps. 'Mapping Tags and Tagging Maps' (pp. 3–24), by a group of five authors, evokes the challenge of 'devising even a basic generalized system of mapping' (p. 5). 'How to Play with Maps' (pp. 107–28), by Bethany Nowviskie, points at the possibilities that maps offer to not only represent reality but also experiment with the telling of lies. 'Modelling Collaboration in Digital Humanities Scholarship' (pp. 25–50) by Paul Hjartarson and a group of authors, reflects on the drafting of a charter to guide collaborative editorial work. The seven chapters of the second part of the book, 'Writers and Readers: Mapping Textual Space', look at the broader theme of the subjective construction of space in artistic or literary works across a range of works.

'Languages as Spaces, Translation as Play' (pp. 215–30), by Lori Saint-Martin, is a personal piece in which she reflects on place, writing, and translation. Critical essays on space analyse the work of Anne Hébert (Stéphanie Walsh Matthews), Marguerite Andersen (Kathleen Kellett), and Grace Irwin (Patricia Demers). Reingard M. Nischik, the editor of *The Palgrave Handbook of Comparative North American Literature* [2014], makes a claim for developing an innovative comparative approach to American and Canadian literature, one that in her eyes has too rarely been used but that 'results in a balanced view of the literatures and cultures involved and works against stereotypes, preconceived ideas, and traditionally hierarchical views' (p. 19). In the introductory first chapter, 'Comparative North American Studies and Its Contexts: An Introduction' (pp. 3–31), the editor first draws attention to the instability of such commonly used terms as 'America', 'Canada', and 'North America', and to the defining role of the concepts of hemispheres and borders. She then evokes the shifts from national to transnational to global frameworks of study, and reassesses the place of a comparative approach of literature in that context, locating comparative North American studies between 'nationally circumscribed fields of study on the one hand and hemispheric or global studies on the other hand' (p. 18). The handbook, meant as a guidebook to that new field, then unfolds in sixteen other chapters that map the ground thematically, with a cultural studies approach. All chapters but two (which compare respectively Canadian/Québécois literary studies and the North in English Canada and Quebec) systematically adopt a comparative perspective between Canada and the United States, dealing with a variety of topics: mapping, multiculturalism, race studies, Indigenous literatures, naturalization and citizenship, francophone borderlands, the Mexico–US and Canada–US borders, regionalism, urban fiction, modernism, postmodernism, literary celebrity, and global studies.

  *Public Poetics: Critical Issues in Canadian Poetry and Poetics*, edited by Bart Vautour, Erin Wunker, Travis V. Mason, and Christl Verduyn, is part of the TransCanada series edited by Smaro Kamboureli, and the outcome of a conference that was held in Sackville, New Brunswick, in 2012. Starting from theories of poetry and the lyric (Warner, Altieri, Frye), editors Erin Wunker and Travis V. Mason, in 'Introduction: Public Poetics' (pp. 1–24), 'posit that lyric speech has the potential not only to cite specific temporal and geographic events, but also to activate the urgency with which those events are uttered' (p. 3). The discussion is about poetry's potential in public, its ability to forge not only culture but also community. Importantly, the contributors 'reposition discourses about poetics in Canada so that they inhabit traditional literary-critical spaces as well as non-traditional and technological spaces' (p. 14). Editors Bart Vautour and Christl Verdun, in '*Nota Bene*; or, Notes Towards a Poetics of Work...' (pp. 333–40), conclude that poetry is valued as an alternative language economy (the dominant one being prose) that 'requires us to understand shifting modes of valuation in order for intelligibility to materialize' (p. 334).

  The fifteen chapters that analyse public poetics in Canada in its historicity, present manifestations, and future possibilities, deal first with 'The

Contemporary Field' (Section I) by looking at the poet as public figure, her private life, and the making of community (Sina Queyras), racial prejudice (El Jones), the body in pain (Tanis MacDonald), feminist poetics, the body, and body politic in an age dominated by technology and the marketplace (Heather Milne), and experimental poetry (John Stout). 'The Embedded Field' (Section II) focuses on public aspects in the work of several poets: Peter Sanger as public poet (Amanda Jennigan), Raymond Souster and Dennis Lee as Toronto poets (Will Smith), Dionne Brand's activism in a context of cuts to social programming (Geordie Miller), Sachiko Murakami and issues of urban alienation and unaffordable housing (Emily Ballantyne), and Gillian Jerome and Brad Cran as Vancouver poets (Kevin McNeilly). 'Expanding the Field' (Section III) is turned towards future possibilities: the role of the pamphlet in formal protest (Andrea Hasenbank), the radio broadcast (Katherine McLeod), the poetry reading (Erin Mouré and Karis Shearer), the human microphone (Michael Nardone), and public poetry from a global perspective (Diana Brydon). The valuable view that the contributors and editors of this book stand for may be encapsulated in the words of Derek Beaulieu, who is quoted in the conclusion: 'Art is a conversation, not a patent office' (p. 337).

In *Anthologizing Canadian Literature: Theoretical and Cultural Perspectives*, editor Robert Lecker pursues his work on the Canadian literary canon and anthology (see his *Canadian Canons* [1991], and *Keepers of the Code* [2013]). The guiding question of this collection of essays is the following: 'to what extent do [Canadian anthologies] transmit ideas about the nature and value of the nation whose literature they represent?' (p. 3). In the introduction Lecker points out that anthology editors are subject to criticism for upsetting the status quo, or making choices that are too conservative, or too subversive (pp. 1–34). The national subject is unstable, 'the idea of Canada is multiple and evolving', so 'the anthological construction of the nation today is in many ways about the deconstruction of national identity' (p. 5). Further, material restrictions, in particular the book budget, often mean that certain texts have to be left out (for instance the famous Canadian long poem, because of its length) and tend to distort the idea of nation; as a result, 'the presentation of national literary canons is always restricted and partial, and always a function of the corporate material resources available to the companies that produce them' (p. 10). Anthologies are ritualized objects that convey conflicted narratives of the nation, so that they also tell the story of their own attempt 'to capture a dream of nation' (p. 14). The thirteen chapters of the book, which Lecker had hoped would be more consistent, explore and reflect this conflicted story. Richard Cavell demonstrates that anthologies are a testimony to the fluid status of the nation ('Anthems and Anthologies', pp. 35–50). Margery Fee comments on the inclusion (or not) of 'Indian poems' by Pauline Johnson and Duncan Campbell Scott in anthologies ('Publications, Performances, and Politics: The "Indian Poems" of E. Pauline Johnson/Tekahionwake (1861–1913) and Duncan Campbell Scott (1862–1947)', pp. 51–78). D.M.R. Bentley studies the critiques raised by W.D. Lighthall's 1889 anthology ('The Poetry of the Canoe: William Dough Lighthall's *Songs of the Great Dominion*', pp. 79–106). Cheryl Cundel analyses the significance of exploration writing in a selection of anthologies ('Excerpts of Exploration Writing in Anthologies in

English Canadian Literature', pp. 107–26). Peggy Lynn Kelly demonstrates the gender imbalance in anthologies published between 1920 and 1950 ('Anthology and the Canonization Process: A Case Study of the English-Canadian Literary Field, 1920–1950', pp. 127–44). Bonnie Hughes analyses the selection of work by Susanna Moodie and John Richardson in anthologies published in the 'literary nationalist' phase of the 1950s and 1960s ('Nation Building, the Literary Tradition, and English-Canadian Anthologies: Presentations of John Richardson and Susanna Moodie in Anthologies of the 1950s and 1960s', pp. 145–66). Joel Deshaye examines how Robert Weaver's CBC Radio *Anthology* fell into line with the CBC's nationalist mandate ('Anthology on the Radio: Robert Weaver and CBC Radio's *Anthology*', pp. 167–82). Janet B. Friskney surveys the historical trends of literary anthology publishing over two centuries ('Canadian Literary Anthologies through the Lens of Publishing History: A Preliminary Exploration of Historical Trends to 1997', pp. 183–208). Gary Geddes recalls how existential rather than academic criteria presided over his selection of texts for the influential 1970 *15 Canadian Poets* anthology ('Confessions of an Unrepentant Anthologist', pp. 209–18). Karis Shearer demonstrates how the publication of Michael Ondaatje's *The Long Poem Anthology* [1979] partly undermined the subversive value associated with that form ('The Poet-Editor and the Small Press: Michael Ondaatje and *The Long Poem Anthology*', pp. 219–52). Lorraine York shows how the humour of quirkily themed anthologies nonetheless leads to a reaffirmation of national values ('Why So Serious? The Quirky Canadian Anthology', pp. 253–70). Frank Davey, in 'Reading Anthologies' (pp. 271–8), studies the impact of the course pack that replaced the anthology, removing the sense of community conveyed by the latter. Anne Compton's essay, 'The Poet and Her Libraries: Anthologies Read, Anthologies Made' (pp. 279–96), reflects on the impact of anthologies on 'your mind, your taste, and future reading' (p. 285).

Beverly Rasporich, in *Made-in-Canada Humour: Literary, Folk and Popular Culture*, undertakes 'a literary and cultural survey of humour, primarily in English Canada, from the 19th century until the close of the 20th' (p. xiii). Rasporich's study is broad, with a view to recording cultural history, so it includes literary humour, cartooning and comic strips, oral folk humour, and stage, radio, and television comedy. The term 'humour' is taken in an open sense, including irony, satire, parody, and burlesque. The author successively analyses the colonial literary humourists Thomas McCulloch and Thomas Haliburton and the cartoonist J.W. Bengough (chapter 1, 'Antique Humour: New Eden Dreamers and Sam Slick', pp. 1–36), Stephen Leacock (chapter 2, 'Canada's Remarkable Humourist Stephen Leacock: Bridging Uncle Sam and Mother England', pp. 37–76), Calgary humourist Bob Edwards, who was part of cowboy folk culture and the Canadian western frontier (chapter 3, 'Folk Humour in the Country and in the City: The Side Hill Gouger and Other Myths', pp. 77–110). She then moves on to postcolonial and postmodern writers: Montreal Jewish writers, Paul Hiebert, Robinson Davies, Basil Johnston, Jacques Ferron, Roch Carrier, Mordecai Richler, Robert Kroetsch, Leonard Cohen, Alice Munro, and Margaret Atwood (in chapter 4, '20th Century Literary Humour: Protest and Resistance', pp. 111–62), then to twentieth-century print humourists and cartoonists (chapter 5, '20th Century Print Humour and Cartoons: Amusing the People and Provoking the Politicians', pp. 163–208), humour based on ethnicity, race, and gender (chapter 6, 'Joking at the Margins: Ethnicity, Race and Gender', pp. 209–40), and humour in popular culture on stage, radio, and television (chapter 7, 'Popular Comedy on Stage and in the Media: Towards a Continental Humour', pp. 241–74). Canada's middling position, between the United States and Britain, has always been a source of humour, whether through joking about Americans or in the form of self-derision. Canada thus 'presents a unique humorous tradition that reflects its emergence from a colonial country to a postcolonial and postmodern nation' (p. 275). The comprehensive approach to the topic means that the various chapters have a survey quality to them, which is the author's intention: to provide a starting point for discussion on humour, 'the beginning of a conversation about a cultural topic that invites attention' (p. xx).

In the genre of drama, Krištof Jacek Kozak studies Sharon Pollock's play *Doc* [1984] in his *Contemporary Tragedy: The Tragic Subject in B.-M. Koltès, S. Pollock and D. Greig* (pp. 182–201). Kozak briefly refers to Friedrich Hebbel's notion of 'tragedy of common life' to argue that, in *Doc*, the tragic is passive and internalized, but then goes on to write what is a plain psychological analysis of the characters along a number of 'lines of conflict'.

Criticism of the literature of various diasporas often adopts a relevant transnational perspective. This is the case especially with studies of Caribbean literature, which may comprise the work of Canadian writers of Caribbean origin. Elena Machado Sáez, in *Market Aesthetics: The Purchase of the Past in Caribbean Diasporic Fiction*, examines 'the ways that the style and content of the historical fiction [of the Caribbean] articulate a conflict between the pedagogical ethical imperative and the market lens of the reader' (p. 1). In 'Kinship Routes: Contextualizing Diaspora via the Market in Andrea Levy and David Chariandy' (pp. 46–81), the author reads Chariandy's *Soucouyant* [2007], along with Levy's *Fruit of the Lemon* [1999], as novels that 'foreground how consumerism enables and delimits the narration of Caribbean diasporic subjectivity' (p. 80). She argues that the characters in *Soucouyant* are depicted against a Canadian nation defined by its market multiculturalism, while their Caribbean past is tied to global histories of economic and sexual exploitation. Consumer citizenship is seen as a mode of diasporic belonging, notably through the circulation of US commodities and culture. In 'Messy Intimacies: Postcolonial Romance in Ana Menéndez, Dionne Brand, and Monique Roffey' (pp. 120–53), Machado Sáez engages with historical novels that explore the postcolonial inheritance of anti-colonial discourse through romance, demonstrating how these novels aim to recuperate women as agents of history. She thus shows how, in Brand's *In Another Place, Not Here*, women try to come to terms with their past marginalization in the context of 1960s anti-colonial revolution.

Giselle Liza Anatol, in 'Reconstructing a Nation of Strangers: Soucouyants in the Work of Tessa McWatt, David Chariandy, and Helen Oyeyemi' (in her *The Things That Fly in the Night: Female Vampires in Literature of the Circum-Caribbean and African Diaspora*, pp. 189–220), examines 'the notion that the true vampiric figure in world history is not the foreigner... but the colonial or neocolonial nation that greedily sucks the lifeblood of foreign lands and foreign people via economic, political, sexual, cultural, and ecological exploitation' (p. 190). Through a fine analysis of the character of Adele and of the eponymous figure of the soucouyant in Chariandy's novel, she shows how members of the Caribbean community in Canada eventually 'turn on themselves and each other' (p. 205).

Jameela F. Dallis, in ' "Life refusing to end": The Transformative Gothic in Shani Mootoo's *Cereus Blooms at Night*' (in Anderson, Hagood, and Turner, eds., *Undead Souths: The Gothic and Beyond in Southern Literature and Culture*, pp. 224–35), analyses how Mootoo uses the Gothic mode, in its US Southern version, its gardens and exotic flora and fauna, to create a space of terrific sublimity and transformation.

Esther L. Jones's 'Organ Donation, Mythic Medicine, and Madness in Nalo Hopkinson's *Brown Girl in the Ring*' (in her *Medicine and Ethics in Black Women's Speculative Fiction*, pp. 91–112) deals with a familiar theme in Hopkinson's work by examining the ways in which her young adult fantasy novel 'challenges the hierarchical binaries of religion and science to blend Western and Afro-Caribbean practices. By dissolving these binaries, an alternative ethics can emerge that confers dignity on multiple modes of knowledge production' (p. 93).

Michael A. Bucknor, in 'Beyond *Windrush* and the Original Black Atlantic Routes: Austin Clarke, Race, and Canada's Influence on Anglophone Caribbean Literature' (in Brown and Rosenberg, eds., *Beyond Windrush: Rethinking Postwar Anglophone Caribbean Literature*, pp. 206–21), draws on archival documents to evoke the crucial role of Austin Clarke, 'the granddaddy of Caribbean/Canadian writing' (p. 217), through publishing, broadcasting, literary community, and political activism in the emergence of anglophone Caribbean literature. Bucknor thus convincingly advocates the pivotal place of Canada in the transnational circuits of exchange that make up what Paul Gilroy has called the Black Atlantic. See also the discussion of *Beyond Windrush* in Section 4(b) below.

Studies of Canadian writers of Asian origin are also conducted trans-nationally. Klara Szmańko proposes a fine reading of *Obasan* in 'Representation of Whiteness in Joy Kogawa's *Obasan*' (in her *Visions of Whiteness in Selected Works of Asian American Literature*, pp. 137–48), by approaching whiteness not only as a sign of racial difference and antagonism, but also from an aesthetic standpoint that conjures both negative and positive images.

The Yiddish diaspora is now mostly part of history. Rebecca Margolis, in 'Remembering Two of Montreal's Yiddish Women Poets: Esther Segal and Ida Maza' (in Horowitz, ed., *Women Writers of Yiddish Literature: Critical Essays*, pp. 248–69; originally published as a journal article), evokes the literary career of two Yiddish women poets 'during the brief period when modern Yiddish culture was a global mass phenomenon' (p. 250). With the decline of Yiddish culture, Maza is now remembered for her salon, which gave her a role as nurturer in the community, while Segal's leftist poetry has not lasted well beyond the historical moment. This article is a form of tribute to the role they played.

Michael Keren, in 'A Canadian Alternative to the Clash of Civilization: Yann Martel's *Life of Pi*' (in his *Politics and Literature at the Turn of the Millennium*, pp. 207–25), identifies insights on world politics in Martel's fictional tale. Keren first recalls the defining role of Canadian secretary of state Lester Pearson in the 1950s in durably shaping Canada's foreign policy, and then reads *Life of Pi* as a strong criticism of Samuel Huntington's 'clash of civilizations' theory: 'it provides a profound examination of the theory's philosophical foundations and proposes an alternative of coexistence between civilizations, consistent with Pearson's vision' (p. 210).

*Margaret Atwood: Crime Fiction Writer: The Reworking of a Popular Genre*, a study by Jackie Shead, 'considers how Atwood reimagines both the role of the detective-investigator and the nature of the crimes and secrets being uncovered, linking both these matters to issues of gender, class and colonialism' (p. 2). Atwood uses the crime fiction tradition—the whodunit, the clue puzzle, and the spy thriller—in a number of her novels; the works considered here include *Surfacing, Bodily Harm, Alias Grace, The Blind Assassin*, and a selection of short stories. In contrast with the tradition established by writers such as Sherlock Holmes or Agatha Christie, in which the interpretation of perceived phenomena leads to the solving of mysteries, Atwood's heroines 'struggle for understanding' and 'must dismantle their current mindsets in order to construct new ways of looking' (p. 26). 'While they come to recognize themselves as subjects of abuse, coercion or manipulation, [they] also discover they are far from innocent, owing to their interpellation by, and collusion with, damaging social forces' (p. 34). Atwood thus 'sees detection as an activity properly exercised upon oneself... because self-scrutiny unearths interpellation and leads characters to a greater under-standing of their involvement in social injustices' (p. 193). Shead's study focuses on and expertly analyses the elements of crime fiction. One wishes her argument also took a step back and showed how crime fiction interacts with other competing genres and discourses in Atwood's novels for the writer to make her points.

Daniel Cojocaru, in *Violence and Dystopia: Mimesis and Sacrifice in Contemporary Western Dystopian Narratives*, devotes a section to Margaret Atwood's *The Handmaid's Tale* and *Oryx and Crake*. Based on René Girard's ideas of scapegoating violence and sacrifice, Cojocaru convincingly demon-strates that 'both [of Atwood's] novels read together reveal the gradual exhaustion of the scapegoat mechanism, culminating in social entropy and the potential end of the human race in *Oryx*' (p. 252). Regrettably the book was not edited to lose its form as a Ph.D. thesis.

Zhange Ni, in 'Wonder Tale, Pagan Utopia, and Margaret Atwood's Radical Hope' (in her *The Pagan Writes Back: When World Religion Meets World Literature*, pp. 97–121), 'explores Atwood's project to write back the pagan' (p. 97) into her trilogy—*Oryx and Crake* [2003], *The Year of the Flood* [2009], and *Maddaddam* [2013]—as well as *The Handmaid's Tale* [1985], four works which Ni considers together as a tetralogy. The concept of pagan, which at times seems a bit forced onto Atwood's novels, is part of Ni's larger thesis and refers here to how 'Atwood's utopian/dystopian projects go postsecular or postreligious together with the "real" world that gives rise to them' (p. 99). Michael Keren, in 'Body and Mind in Margaret Atwood's *Oryx and Crake*' (in Keren, pp. 185–205), provides a luminous reading of Atwood's novel by first 'discuss[ing] briefly the conversation about science and technology in recent decades' and moving on to 'show how Atwood's fictional subordination of the mind to the body in the realms of genetic engineering and digital technology contributes to that conversation and enlightens us about the brave new world we live in' (p. 186). Keren concludes by making a strong point about the role of narrative in contemporary posthuman society.

Janine Rogers, in 'Beautiful Infestations: Margaret Atwood's *Cat's Eye*, Entomology, and the Superorganism' (in her *Unified Fields: Science and Literary Form*, pp. 112–40), also adopts a scientific perspective, through the scientific study of insects. She shows how 'Entomology provides Atwood with a set of shifting references for depicting human emotional and social life' (p. 115), in particular the notion of 'superorganism', 'an overarching view of organic systems' (p. 116) that can be applied to human or insect societies. Rogers beautifully demonstrates that 'As in its scientific context, the superorganism theory in *Cat's Eye* sheds some light on our understanding of larger social and discursive entities, including some intangible and powerful qualities, such as the potential for mass communication in a collective unconsciousness' (p. 139).

Laurie Vickroy, in 'Re-creating the Split Self in Margaret Atwood's *The Blind Assassin* and *Alias Grace*' (in her *Reading Trauma Narratives: The Contemporary Novel and the Psychology of Oppression*, pp. 33–65), starts with a fairly general argument about the 'intricate connections between power relations and personal trauma' in Atwood's two novels (p. 34). Using the work of psychoanalyst Judith Hermann and the dialectical nature of the experience of trauma, and focusing on the flawed thinking of Iris and Grace, Vickroy goes on to illuminate how Atwood's works complicate the idea of responsibility, shame, and guilt by putting them in specific historical contexts.

*Anne Carson: Ecstatic Lyre*, edited by Joshua Marie Wilkinson, is published in the Under Discussion series edited by Marilyn Hacker and Kazim Ali, which 'is concerned with contemporary American and English poets', so presumably Carson is considered an American poet here. (She was born in Toronto in 1950, studied at the University of Toronto and taught at McGill before teaching in the United States; in Canada she is claimed as a Canadian writer.) The editor's interest is in how Carson seems 'to obliterate genre itself, from inside out' (p. 1), by writing in 'every genre imaginable . . . lyric, epic, dramatic poetry; the fragment, epitaph, and elegy; her translations cover ancient comedy and tragic drama' (p. 3), while her essays offer equal variety in style. The book brings together forty-two short essays by poets, 'dissimilar writers who all recognize the influence and import of Carson's work on their own' (p. 4), most of whom are also academics, and American. The editor comments on how the approaches to Carson's work are varied and open, 'from critical and scholarly to personal and lyrical' (p. 5)—in fact, most essays adopt a combination of these approaches. They also reveal a deep appreciation of Carson's 'genre-bending and genre-obliterating books' (p. 5). The volume ends with a 2001 interview with Carson, following the inaugural performance of her opera *Decreation* in San Francisco.

*Northrop Frye and Others: Twelve Writers Who Helped Shape His Thinking* is the work of Robert D. Denham, who edited several volumes of the collected works of Frye, now in print at the University of Toronto Press in twenty-nine volumes (plus the index). To Denham, the availability of previously unpublished material means that 'the material is ripe for developing more complex and revisionary views of Frye' (p. 6). Frye was a prolific writer, and in his late notebooks especially, which Denham edited, he returns 'again and again to the archetypes of his mental landscape in an effort to get the architecture and the verbal formulation [of his ideas] right' (p. 12), discussing the thinkers that inspired him in the process. Denham thus investigates Frye's links with twelve thinkers who have been influential, judging by the notebooks—Aristotle, Longinus, Joachim de Floris, Giordano Bruno, Henry Reynolds, Robert Burton, Søren Kierkegaard, Lewis Carroll, Stéphane Mallarmé, Colin Still, Paul Tillich and Frances A. Yates. Frye is approached as both reader and thinker: there is a wealth of facts and details about his readings, and how they relate to his writing—for instance, how Lewis Carroll's Alice books are put to the test of Frye's account of the descent and ascent themes. This erudite study, by a scholar who has been working on Frye for fifty years, will be useful to those interested in the history of ideas and the cultural, intellectual, and literary contexts of Frye's theoretical writings.

Claude Le Fustec, in *Northrop Frye and American Fiction*, draws on Frye's religious and biblical theory (in *The Great Code*, *Words with Power*, and *The Double Vision*) to read American literary texts and investigate the interiorization of religion and the renewal of our bond with transcendence in secular, twentieth-century culture. The study is 'the result of twenty years' teaching American literature to a French public, [and] stems from an acute awareness of the "religious valence" of fiction in the United States' (p. 11). It is also the reflection of the author's personal view of literature and spirituality. Le Fustec adheres to Frye's view of not only 'the mere continuing relevance of the biblical text to our present age, but its ongoing influence on the Western psyche' (p. 12). She distinguishes between the terms 'religious', which is synonymous with Christian and theological, and 'spiritual', which refers to what goes beyond the limits of Christian theology, and in Frye's view, is 'the highest intensity of consciousness' (p. 16). Frye's concept of 'kerygma' is central to this study: the term refers to 'the intersection of a metaphorically "horizontal" dimension of consciousness, connecting us to our daily secular environment, with a "vertical", spiritual one, relating us to the whole of humankind's experience. In [Frye's] view, this intersection marks the point where a potential experience of revelation...may take place through language' (p. 20). In short, kerygma is 'a kind of linguistics of revelation' (p. 22) that conveys the transforming power of literature. Because American literature is so linked originally to religious dogma, Le Fustec sees it as the perfect ground to test Frye's theory of the Bible as the 'great code' of Western secular literature. The secular journey represented in the six novels chosen—Hawthorne's *The Scarlet Letter*, James's *The Europeans*, Fitzgerald's *The Great Gatsby*, Steinbeck's *The Grapes of Wrath*, Kerouac's *On the Road*, and

Morrison's *Beloved*—is psychological rather than religious, yet one that makes biblical cosmology relevant in a new way.

In *Apostate Englishman: Grey Owl the Writer and the Myths*, Albert Braz discusses the life and vision of Archie Belaney, aka Grey Owl, the Englishman 'gone native' in the early twentieth century. Apart from Grey Owl's own writings, the book largely draws on two biographies of 1973 and 1990. Braz also uses a viewpoint expressed by Anishinaabe leader Gary Potts, which is that 'what troubles white people the most about Archie Belaney's transformation into Grey Owl is precisely that he favoured Indigenous ways over European ones' (p. 172). Braz reformulates this idea into his central argument: that Grey Owl had committed cultural apostasy in the eyes of Europeans, and was criticized for this very reason. Going against this trend, Braz sees Grey Owl as 'a famous white...conservationist', 'the champion of the beaver' (pp. 165–6), and rehabilitates his Romantic vision of nature in Canada. What is striking is that the book refers only allusively to the history of colonization, while no broader analysis of the encounter between Europeans and Indigenous people (repeatedly referred to as the 'Indigenous populace') is undertaken. Grey Owl's story and persona are thus nostalgically restored some of the reputation they enjoyed before Archie Belaney was found out, in a way that is remarkably out of touch with contemporary questions.

Alice Munro's work has received substantial attention. Several book publications were initiated by French scholars after *Dance of the Happy Shades* was included in the 2015 and 2016 curriculum for students preparing for the *agrégation* (a yearly competitive national teaching exam). *Sunlight and Shadows, Past and Present: Alice Munro's Dance of the Happy Shades*, by Corinne Bigot and Catherine Lanone, identifies key themes and motifs that are explored through close readings of the stories and careful attention to narrative details. In *The Mind's Eye: Alice Munro's Dance of the Happy Shades*, Ailsa Cox reads several stories using the phenomenologist approach that she defined in her *Alice Munro* [2004], in particular through Bergson's analysis of time, while Christine Lorre-Johnston studies Munro's style by examining various archival drafts of 'Red Dress—1946' and 'Images'. *'With a Roar from Underground': Alice Munro's Dance of the Happy Shades*, edited by Corinne Bigot and Catherine Lanone, proposes a variety of thematic approaches to the stories, as found for instance in 'The Strumpet of Jubilee: Tragi-comedy, Burlesque and Charivari in "Postcard"', by Héliane Ventura (pp. 35–44), 'Munro and Gender Construction in *Dance of the Happy Shades*', by Linda Collinge-Germain (pp. 65–76), 'Fitting, Cutting and Matching: Dressing in Alice Munro's *Dance of the Happy Shades*', by Catherine Delesalle-Nancey (p. 77–96), and '"In Lovely Blue": Seeing Outside "The Shining Houses"', by Thomas Dutoit (pp. 145–64).

*The Inside of a Shell: Alice Munro's Dance of the Happy Shades*, edited by Vanessa Guignery, includes seventeen chapters, among which two are reprinted articles (by Robert Thacker and Magdalene Redekop). Several chapters are particularly innovative in their approach; for instance Jacob Hovind's 'The Epiphany Concept and Its Undoing in Alice Munro's Early Stories' (pp. 114–28), Catherine Lanone's 'Clarity of Insight and Commonplaces: Alice Munro, James Joyce and Alex Colville' (pp. 169–85),

Jean-Marc Victor's 'Happy Shades of "June Recital" in "Dance of the Happy Shades": Munro's Dance with Welty' (pp. 186–99), Matthieu Duplay's ' "The Other Country where she lives": Opera and its Doubles in Alice Munro's "Dance of the Happy Shades" ' (pp. 200–17), Claude Maisonnat's 'Grandmothers Beware: Deadly Feminine Desires in Alice Munro's "A Trip to the Coast" ' (pp. 244–57), and Pascale Tollance's 'Alice Munro's "The Peace of Utrecht" or How to Deal with Remains' (pp. 258–70). Other contributions provide enlightening syntheses on key aspects of Munro's work that go beyond this particular collection; so it is with Claire Omhovère's ' "For there is no easy way to get to Jubilee from anywhere on earth": Place in Alice Munro's *Dance of the Happy Shades*' (pp. 26–45) and Ulrika Skagert's 'The Rupture of the Ordinary as an "Awkward Little Space": Evental Moments in Alice Munro's "Dance of the Happy Shades" ' (pp. 271–82). Altogether, what this series of publications on Munro's first collection shows is how the stories already establish the themes that she would develop in her later work, and the richness of her style at this early stage, despite the fact that she later dismissed some of them as 'exercises'.

*Alice Munro: Reminiscence, Interpretation, Adaptation and Comparison*, edited by Miroslawa Buchholtz and Eugenia Sojka, is not yet available for reviewing.

Ailsa Cox, in ' "Almost like a ghost": Spectral Figures in Alice Munro's Short Fiction' (in Achilles and Bergmann, eds., *Liminality and the Short Story*, pp. 238–50), pursues her reading of Munro's fiction through the prism of Henri Bergson's theory of matter and memory to analyse liminal states of consciousness across a selection of stories that include 'The Peace of Utrecht', 'Dimensions', 'Chance', 'Amundsen', and 'In Sight of the Lake'.

Katherine Orr, in 'Liminality, Metamorphic Experience, and the Short-Story Form: Alice Munro's "Wenlock Edge" ' (in Achilles and Bergmann, eds., pp. 251–62), convincingly reads 'Wenlock Edge' as an incomplete, transgressive, and haunting rite of initiation, one in which Munro plays on 'borderlines of meaning' (Ricoeur), particularly through multiple interpretations associated with the body.

## (b) Journals

Multiculturalism has long had a central role in defining Canadian identity, as authors have anatomized the economic and existential anxieties of first-wave immigrants, the ambivalences of following generations, and the ongoing difficulties presented by both separateness and assimilation. Critics and scholars in Canada have also responded to a literature increasingly attuned to the discriminations within, and overlappings of, identity in a 'postnational' society, as well as to the multiple perspectives of colonial history (Charles Foran, 'The Canada Experiment: Is This the World's First "Postnational" Country?', *Guardian*, 4 January 2017). If the field falls into familiar categories—historical, settler, Indigenous, prairie, multicultural, feminist— these are continually revised and updated by new critical, cultural, and theoretical perspectives.

In 2015 the range not only of ethnicities represented but also of the kinds, combinations, and conditions of cultural identity has been notable. The varieties of attention directed at multicultural citizens, their communities, and their traditions have also been notable, sometimes migrating into surprising but fruitful territories for exploration. Rebecca Romdhani offers an ingenious political reading of Nalo Hopkinson's *Brown Girl in the Ring*, investigating the legacy of African and Caribbean migrants by way of the exotically apposite literary figure of the zombie, in 'Zombies Go to Toronto: Zombifying Shame in Nalo Hopkinson's *Brown Girl in the Ring*' (*RAL* 46:iv[2015] 72–89). Romdhani sees the zombie as a means of exploring the complex legacy of the African diaspora, observing both the abject mechanism of internalizing the shame associated with white racism and the affirmative one of reclaiming traditional religious beliefs so as to 'help prevent and heal emotional zombification' while 'reclaim[ing] ownership of the zombie in all its transformations' (p. 88). The Gothic element is also applied inventively by Esra Melikoğlu to Carol Shields's beautifully composed novel on death and domesticity in '*Unless: A Covert Postcolonial and Transnational Gothic Novel, or The Haunted House (of Fiction) Is Falling Apart*' (*SCL* 40:ii[2015] 211–25). In *Unless* the unexplained suicide of a Muslim woman shatters the assured surface of literate, liberal, middle-class life. Melikoğlu offers a persuasive way into Shields's novel, even if one feels uncertain that, however renovated, the gothic genre is the exact vehicle by which to enter the profound confrontations Shields provokes with the undefined terror that lies underneath Reta's efforts to restore order and familiarity to her house, its inhabitants, and by extension her country.

Moving on from ghoulish themes, Desi Valentine, in 'Contesting Clarke: Towards a De-Racialized African-Canadian Literature' (*ArielE* 45:iv[2014] 111–32), starts from her own personal experience of being African Canadian to 'interrogate George Elliott Clarke's conceptualizations of a Black Canadian literature and a racialized African-Canadian literary canon' (p. 111). Attesting to the complexity of contemporary multicultural experience, Valentine contests the notion that racial identity can underpin separate and self-contained cultures, arguing that 'a racialized African-Canadian literary canon excludes the multiple Canadian cultures in which our literatures are formed, and supports racial constructs that no longer fit the shapes of our multi-ethnic, diasporic, postcolonial skins' (p. 111). Pilar Cuder Dominguez, in 'In Search of a "Grammar for Black": Africa and Africans in Lawrence Hill's Works' (*RAL* 46:iv[2015] 90–106), encompasses both sides of the Atlantic in her reading of Hill's concern with the different meanings of Africa for black Canadians and the differences *within* black Canadianness.

Natalia Aponiuk, in '"... No longer quite Ukrainian but not quite Canadian either ...": The Ukrainian Immigrant in Canadian English-Language Literature' (*CES* 47:iv–v[2015] 49–65), evokes the familiar migrant narrative of displacement, maladjustment, and being in between, while observing optimistically a breakthrough by Ukrainian authors of fiction and theatre in Canada since national adoption of multiculturalism. Mumbi Tindyebwa's 'A Multicultural Stage' (*CTR* 163[2015] 25–9) calls for a Canadian theatre that truly and radically reflects the cultural diversity of contemporary society, while Karen E.H. Skinazi, in 'Kol Isha: 'Malka Zipora's *Lekhaim* as the Voice of the Hasidic Woman in Quebec' (*Shofar* 33:ii[2015] 1–26), defends the lives of Hasidic women against mainstream social claims that they suffer gender oppression. Emily Ballantyne, in 'Exile Beyond Return: Zionism and Diaspora in A.M. Klein's Journalism' (*SCL* 40:ii[2015] 164–88), considers the role played by Klein's non-fiction, especially his journalism, in negotiating the personal and political pulls exerted on him by his affinities both to Zionism and to Jewish spirituality.

In a sophisticated and sensitive response to a demanding writer, Dominic Williams and Milena Marinkova's 'Affective Trans-scapes: Affect, Translation, and Landscape in Erín Moure's *The Unmemntioable*' (*CWW* 9:i[2015] 73–92), undertake an important consideration of Moure's registration of multicultural subjectivity that looks at literary strategies such as disruption rather than the textual representations of cultural displacement. In Moure's work they find 'a significant meditation on translation: of self, place, and language. Mobilizing affect, Moure allows other ways of being a self to be explored, a self that exists between spaces and languages as much as within them' (p. 90).

Literary multiculturalism and its critical exponents are not universally celebrated in the critical writing surveyed here. The blindness of multicultural criticism's attention to religion is explored by Shoshannah Ganz in 'A Buddhist Blessing: Meditations and Mindfulness in Souvankham Thammavongsa's *Small Arguments*' (*BJCS* 28:i[2015] 105–20). Ganz finds a connection between her work and other Canadian literature, not in her migrant status, but in the Buddhism Thammavongsa shares with Phyllis Webb, for example. Ganz also argues that the cultural emphasis deflates the author's literary merits, pointing out that existing criticism of Thammavongsa's work pays too much attention to her 'refugee origins rather than the intricacies of her poetry' (p. 105). Rodolphe Solbiac, in 'Ramabai Espinet's *The Swinging Bridge* as a Refunctioning of Neil Bissoondath's *A Casual Brutality* and *the Worlds Within Her*' (*IJCS* 51[2015] 57–68), casts an affirmative eye on Espinet's rewriting of Bissoondath, finding less damaging outcomes for the unsettled subject in respect of both a traumatic past elsewhere and a transcultural present.

Literary study of race and religion requires critical distance from, as well as familiarity with, the contemporary contexts of cultural discussion, notably those shaped by multiculturalism and its discontents. Atef Laouyene, in 'Race, Gender, and the Exotic in Ann-Marie MacDonald's *Fall on Your Knees*' (*JCL* 50:ii[2015] 197–215), attends to 'the cultural politics of the exotic', tracing a persistent exoticism that has structured views of Muslims and, more generally, ethnic and gender minorities in North America since the early twentieth century (p. 197). This reading focuses on MacDonald's 1996 novel's critique of contemporary debates about multiculturalism 'by warning its readers against the superficial posturing of boutique multiculturalism' (p. 211). Lindy Ledohowski, in ' "White Settler Guilt": Contemporary Ukrainian Canadian Prairie Literature' (*CES* 47:iv–v[2015] 67–83), considers a difficulty for multiculturalism by critically examining the claim of Ukrainian Canadians from the 1960s to founding status as first prairie settlers and the uncomfortable relation in which this places them with respect to First Nation Canadians.

Scholarship on nineteenth- and early twentieth-century Canadian literature in 2015 tends to avoid the harsher binaries of postcolonial criticism, without exculpating settler culture or sanitizing its writing. Corinne Bigot, in 'Did They Go Native? Representations of First Encounters and Personal Interrelations with First Nations Canadians in the Writings of Susanna Moodie and Catharine Parr Traill' (*JCL* 49:i[2015] 99–111), applies a nuanced critical reading to her two 'British gentlewomen' in respect of their relations with Indigenous peoples (p. 99). Bigot observes that the structure of racial thought and feeling is modified in the writing of her authors over time, observing that in limited ways they actually 'went native' (p. 99). Alison Calder, in 'Hiding in Plain Sight: A New Narrative for Canadian Literary History' (*JCSR* 49:ii[2015] 87–105), revisits the well-tilled field of prairie literature. Arguing that, by concentrating on a body of canonical texts that depict a 'White space' (p. 5), previous criticism has overlooked the evidence of recognition of Indigenous presence, Calder turns to less well-known works that 'engage with and reenact' Indigenous 'removal' (p. 87). Calder's close reading is convincing, allowing her to conclude that Christine van der Mark's 1947 novel *In Due Season* 'denaturalizes the idea of progress, showing the seams in the historical narrative and suggesting that choice, not destiny, shaped the Canadian West' (p. 102). Indeed, she argues that 'Reopening the Prairie canon by rereading early texts has the potential to construct a new genealogy for contemporary prairie writing, one that stresses a connection with the past rather than a rupture from it' and that such 'continuities are particularly important to keep in mind as we strive to decolonize critical practices' (p. 102). In 'Imagining the Canadian Agrarian Landscape: Prairie Settler Life Writing as Colonial Discourse' (*ArielE* 46:iv[2015] 155–84) Shirley Ann McDonald looks back to the georgic as a mode of writing about farming life and uses pioneer memoirs to consider the place of myth—classical and colonizing—in entitling settlers to their appropriations of Indigenous land. The life writings she examines show the failure of these writers, whether their literary worlds are figured as 'gracious lifestyles or on frontier ranches', to 'imagine living in peaceful cohabitation with Indigenous peoples' (p. 180).

Other critics find new or particular approaches to the study of colonial writing. Angela Byrne, in a notable revaluation of a crucial colonial author, ' "My Little Readers": *Catharine Parr Traill's* Natural Histories for Children' (*JL&Sci* 8:i[2015] 86–101), argues against the view of her author's conservatism in respect of science as well as society. Byrne focuses on Traill's 'natural histories for children', where she finds 'a form of cross-genre nature writing that presents a holistic vision of Canadian ecology, interweaving as they do the scientific, settler, and Indigenous forms of knowledge to which Traill had access' (p. 86). Shelley Hulan's 'My Letter of Confession: Sara Jeannette Duncan's Late Imperial Rhetoric and Risk-Taking' (*UTQ* 84:i[2015] 1–18) employs a recently discovered cache of Duncan's letters to show the complexity of Duncan's registration of empire. Jessica Langston sets out to liberate the criticism of historical fiction by moving attention to the peripheries of the texts so as to destabilize relations between narrative and history.

Trawling through major figures Wiebe, Atwood, and Marlatt in 'Supplementing the Supplement: Looking at the Function of Afterwords and Acknowledgements in Some Canadian Historical Novels' (*ESC* 40:ii–iii[2014] 155–72), Langston considers the front- and endmatter of her texts in terms of incompleteness, representation, and the past.

Barbara Bruce, in 'Collecting, Gifting, and Hoarding: The Cabinet of Curiosities and Imperial Governance in John Richardson's *Wacousta*' (*IJCS* 52[2015] 61–81), brings to the study of historical literature the whole range of contemporary approaches—'postcolonial, historical, psychological, cultural-studies, and gender-studies'—focusing especially on the use of material culture in *Wacousta* 'as an index of imperialist and Aboriginal attitudes that shaped frontier encounters between European and Native peoples' (p. 62). Bruce connects the collecting of items from a 'dying' culture to the institution of the reservation, which also relegated Native people to the past, while observing, justly, that 'this newer form of collection as an attempt to contain and to control Indigenous peoples is also subject to Native resistance' (p. 79).

In articles on late twentieth-century and contemporary Canadian literature we also find critics seeking to avoid over-explanatory systems of thought or to rejuvenate familiar ones. David Callahan, in 'Canada's Humanitarian Reach and Maggie Helwig's *Where She Was Standing*' (*JCL* 49:i[2014] 113–26), examines Helwig's novel in terms of its questioning of Western, and particularly Canadian, sympathy for humanitarian causes. We also find adventurously synthetic interpretative contexts in which to read familiar writers. In Tina Northrup's 'Aesthetics of the Sublime and Don McKay's Poetics of Deep Time' (*CanL* 224[2015] 83–99) ethics and aesthetics are realigned as she reconsiders the poet's critique of Romanticism by way of his attention to the sublime. Geopoetry here is part of a project of forcing reconsideration of how we attend to nature without recourse to the tropes of sublime experience. Perhaps the most impressive piece of literary criticism here surveyed is Neil ten Kortenaar's essay, '"Touching them into words": Running with Michael Ondaatje among the Dead' (*UTQ* 84:iv[2015] 15–28), which manages to be both critically brave and moving. Reflecting on the place of the dead in Ondaatje's fiction, particularly the way writing allows communication between the living and the dead, ten Koortenaar develops an ingenious treatment of narrative presence and absence to encompass both the reader and the recently dead Sri Lankan Canadian critic Chelva Kanaganayakam, who did so much to extend knowledge of Tamil and South Asian writing and to uncover and encourage the South Asian dimension in Canadian literature.

The *University of Toronto Quarterly*'s critical summations of Canadian literature in 2013 offer an opportunity to respected critics to evaluate the state of the various genres through notable examples (*UTQ* 84:iii[2015]). The critics take this opportunity, briskly and authoritatively sorting the memorable from the minor, as when David Staines, surveying 'Established Fiction' (*UTQ* 84:iii[2015] 25–42), concludes that 2013 was not a 'startling' year, the most formidable presence being that of Alice Munro. The authors adroitly survey large fields with admirable precision. Still, although cramped for space, the essays might have benefited from more engagement with the climate of critical reception. Reinhold Kramer, in 'Emergent Fiction' (*UTQ* 84:iii[2015] 1–24), observes that 'To argue that the works that follow are the most notable prose works by emergent Canadian writers in 2013 is... not to claim that they give us the proper way to frame a particular issue or that they have (by virtue of their authorship) special implications for the Canadian polity', only to settle for a familiar generality: 'each of these works... gives us a compelling way to understand what it is to be alive and human' (p. 2). Brent Wood, writing on 'Poetry' (*UTQ* 84:iii[2015] 42–69), notes the inverse relation between the 'tiny' readership for Canadian poetry and 'the energy, quality, and range of the work being created by poets born or living in Canada'. Wood also observes that the rising popularity of slam poetry indicates an opportunity for 'cross-pollination between spoken and printed forms as a means to address the accelerated cultural and techno-biological evolution of our times' (p. 65). Certainly, the prospect of mutual cross-fertilization by such opposing ends of the spectrum of literary taste is enticing, although it is questionable whether it would produce more readers of contemporary poetry. Ann Wilson, reviewing 'Drama' (*UTQ* 84:iii[2015] 69–92), exposes the shallowness of a predictable kind of politics of the theatre when she critiques Michael Healey's successful play *Proud* for appealing 'to those who already share its political perspective' (p. 70). What, she asks, is the point of 'staging a well-reported aspect of Harper's style of governing' given that the 'relatively few Canadians [who] go to the theatre 'are likely not fans of Harper?' (p. 70).

Two special issues of journals in 2015 indicate the resilience of both culturalist interpretation and of a more specifically literary kind. *Commonwealth Essays and Studies* based at the Sorbonne Nouvelle, Paris-3, dedicates an issue to Alice Munro, edited by Corinne Bigot, while *Studies in Canadian Literature* explores multicultural literature and theatre in Canada, in an issue edited by Mariam Pirbhai.

Introducing the *CE&S* issue entitled 'Alice Munro: Writing for Dear Life' (*CE&S* 37:ii[2015] 1–104), Bigot cites Michel de Certeau in *The Practice of Everyday Life* and observes that 'Objects and places... "have hollow places in which a past sleeps"', while living spaces are haunted by the '"presences of diverse absences"' (p. 6). The essays in this issue explore the memories stored in objects, the reserve in literary language that accumulates enigmatic force for readers, and the felt absences worked into Munro's fiction, and they do so by way of continuous exactingly close attention to the particulars of literary language and narrative form. Several focus on Munro's 2012 collection, *Dear Life*, and there is a sense throughout the issue of memory operating *within* Munro's work, revealed by a connective tissue of echoes and reverberations, as it approaches a whole. W.H. New speaks tellingly of 'the allegory of inheritance that the reader learns to appreciate over time' (p. 14). New here is referring to a particular story in a brief but astute essay that opens the issue and that looks closely at the title of Munro's iconic story, 'The Peace of Utrecht', using the word 'allegory' to open up questions about choice, order, and history (*CE&S* 37:ii[2015] 11–14). Editor Bigot returns in an essay, 'Forsaken Objects, Haunted Houses, Female Bodies, and "the Squalor of Tragedy in Everyday Life": Reading *Dance of the Happy Shades* with Later Stories' (*CE&S* 37:ii[2015] 15–26), to the early stories and the collection in which 'The Peace of Utrecht' appeared, bringing them into relation with the later stories. Eleonora Rao, in ' "Home" and the Narrative of an Impossible *Nostos*' (*CE&S* 37:ii[2015] 27–34), focuses on the story 'Home' with its complex registrations of desire, memory, disappointment, and shame caught up in the narrator's return to her childhood house.

In the same issue Lucile Rouet-Bentley's ' "I meant the risk. The secrecy. The power": When Secrets Become Weapons' (*CE&S* 37:ii[2015] 35–44) reconsiders the usual association of secrets with embarrassment and conceal-ment in Munro's stories, finding in them, rather, a capacity for agency and power. Lynn Blin, in 'Sweet Dissonance in Alice Munro's "The Progress of Love," "Friend of My Youth," and "Free Radicals" ' (*CE&S* 37:ii[2015] 45–56), uncovers a musical structure of pleasing discord in the opening sections of Munro's stories. To read Munro properly tuned one must attend closely to the grammatical sleights cunningly worked into these openings. Isla Duncan, in ' "A cavity everywhere": The Postponement of Knowing in "Corrie" ' (*CE&S* 37:ii[2015] 57–68), also adopts a narratological approach, one that demon-strates how foreshadowing works for the reader alert to Munro's 'dextrous means': by intimating the importance of some detail the reader is vouchsafed a 'reward' when 'the pattern is observed' (p. 57). Miroslawa Buchholtz, in 'Alice Munro's Legacy: The Finale of *Dear Life*' (*CE&S* 37:ii[2015] 69–78), follows Bigot in linking the early and late work, focusing on 'Finale' as a key to interpreting Munro's fictional legacy from beginning to end of her oeuvre. Christine Berthin, in 'Of Wounds and Cracks and Pits: A Reading of *Dear Life*' (*CE&S* 37:ii[2015] 79–88), also settles on this late collection, considering it as a whole structure whose careful patterning and inward reverberations illuminate the parts. The issue concludes its rich critical engagement with a writer who both tempts and teases readerly desire to close the distance between literature and 'life' with an interview (conducted in 2004) with the author by Eleanor Wachtel (*CE&S* 37:ii[2015] 89–104).

Among the countries covered in 'New Literatures' Canada is the most comprehensively served by a range of journals providing qualitative academic attention to the national literature. Special issues of these journals are particularly important in continually directing attention not only to major authors like Munro, but also to neglected areas in the field or to finding new ways of looking at familiar ones. In 2015 Mariam Pirbhai edited a special issue of *Studies in Canadian Literature* (*SCL* 40:i[2015] 1–244); 'South Asian Canadian Literature: A Centennial Journey' is focused on cultural memory in the South Asian diasporic community, with particular attention paid to the 1914 incident in which 352 Indian would-be immigrants and citizens of the empire on the Komagata Maru were turned back by Canadian authorities.

In 'Discontinuous Journeys: South Asian Canadian Migrations' (*SCL* 40:i[2015] 5–26), an essay introducing the issue, Pirbhai reflects on the relation of the Komagata Maru incident to cultural memory, or rather memor*ies*, as each reading of such traumatic events is always partial, never closing the narrative, and is thus in dialogue with other possibilities. The turning back in memory and critical conscience becomes a multiply faceted point of entry not just into white racism 100 years ago but also into the unresolved condition of Asians in contemporary Canada. For Pirbhai, the afterlife of such events in consciousness—Indian and Canadian—is of deep interest, and their registrations in literature, theatre, and scholarship mean that they 'accrue significance' (p. 5). Indeed, the brief period since the collection appeared has made more urgent the multiple implications represented by the 1914 act of rejection of the imperial citizens aboard the Japanese ship for our own time in which race, migration, and refuge have become, again, fearful existential issues for countries as well as communities and individuals.

Nandi Bhatia's contribution to Pirbhai's issue, 'Revisiting the Theatre of the Komagata Maru Incident' (*SCL* 40:i[2015] 27–44), observes the variety of fiction, film, and theatre that has drawn on the event. By examining its shifting representations, Bhati endorses the national and cultural value of works that memorialize history, notably in this case a moment that involves a negative model for the present. Here the arts become an educative reminder of a truism (no less potent for being conventional) of Canadian self-understanding as a community 'whose future lies in the coexistence, recognition, and celebration of its diversity' (p. 42). Anne Murphy also follows the fitful line of memory of the event by way of theatre in 'Performing the Komagata Maru: Theatre and the Work of Memory' (*SCL* 40:i[2015] 45–73). Like Bhati, Murphy ends on an instructive note, urging the social value of theatre that calls on 'Punjabis *and* whites to discern the complexity of the seeming monolith of white exclusion' (p. 69). Thus Murphy points to the role of 'the enduring political interventions of these plays in making our particular present' (p. 69).

Alia Somani, in 'What Is Remembered and What Is Forgotten? South Asian Diasporic Histories and the Shifting National Imaginary' (*SCL* 40:i[2015] 74–92), considers the Komagata alongside a more recent act of extreme political violence with racial implications: the 1985 bombing of Air India Flight 182 with the loss of 329 people. Tanis MacDonald's 'Un/Authorized Exhibits: Elegiac Necropolitics in Renée Sarojini Saklikar's Children of Air India' (*SCL* 40:i[2015] 93–110) considers tragedy and memory in the light of elegy as a form that serves as a vehicle for mourning. In 'Official Apology, Creative Remembrances, and Management of the Air India Tragedy' (*SCL* 40:i[2015] 111–30) Chandrima Chakraborty anatomizes the terror attacks on Air Canada planes in terms of the government's response and eventual apology, and of the implications for Canadian multiculturalism. As she points out, 'even while pointing to an apparent crisis in multiculturalism, the text of the apology . . . does not put the state's official policy of multiculturalism into question' (p. 112).

In the same issue, Alan Filewod, in 'Family Business: Affect and Reconciliation in *A Brimful of Asha*' (*SCL* 40:i[2015] 131–45), adopts a somewhat disconcertingly personal stance towards his experience and interpretative response to the performance of a play as a means of prying open its cultural implications: 'the samosa that I ate at the start of the performance was an ambivalent token. It was a talismanic device that personalized the experience of the show to create an affective, somatic relationship with the text that would continue long after the performance was finished' (p. 131). James W. Johnson, in ' "Beggaring the Nation": Bodily Inscription and the Body Politic in Rohinton Mistry's *A Fine Balance*' (*SCL* 40:i[2015] 146–65), explores the connections between imagery of bodily decline and the decaying condition of the body politic in Indira Gandhi's India.

Nandi Bhatia, in 'Revisiting the Theatre of the Komagata Maru Incident' (*SCL* 40:i[2015] 27–44), considers Sharon Pollock's *The Komagata Maru Incident* [1976] and other plays 'as performative enactments that contribute to memorialization of the episode (p. 28), allowing for the limited memory of the event in both Canada and India. In 'Physiognomy of War: Ruins of Memory in Michael Ondaatje's *Anil's Ghost*' (*SCL* 40:i[2015] 166–83), a reading that gracefully draws on Walter Benjamin, Lichung Yang sees *Anil's Ghost* as one of those novels where the horrors or war are conveyed 'in an intricate or aesthetically conceived form' (p. 166). Arun Nedra Rodrigo, in 'A "Just Hearing": Reading Shyam Selvadurai's *The Hungry Ghosts* as Counter to State Practice' (*SCL* 40:i[2015] 184–204), argues that the novel 'gives the reader a sense of what it means to really hear a refugee voice', even if within that voice 'multiple layers of truth and meaning [are] not revealed or resolved' (p. 202). Aliyah Khan, in 'Indigeneity and the Indo-Caribbean in Cyril Dabydeen's *Dark Swirl*' (*SCL* 40:i[2015] 205–26), follows the great Wilson Harris in uncovering the buried Indigenous presence in Caribbean history, reminding us that 'the Guyanese Indigenous presence persists despite dislocation and erasure from land and literature' (p. 222). Turning to the present, Khan reminds us that Dabydeen's work demonstrates that migrant communities can themselves 'politically and physically displace marginalized Indigenous communities and that the national substitution of one historically oppressed minority group with another does nothing, without the alliance of those groups, to remedy the systemic injustices of the colonial legacy' (p. 222). The issue closes with Pirbhai's 'On "Moving Forward" Toward the Un/familiar: An Interview with Shani Mootoo' (*SCL* 40:i[2015] 227–41), where the Trinidadian Canadian writer reflects, among other things, on her family difficulties as a young writer dealing with sexual abuse and queer lifestyles.

Literary theory as well as close literary reading inform the essays in both these issues, even if the focus on the 'literary'—as a category that richly includes drama—rather than the cultural is stronger in *CE&S* than in *SCL*, in part, no doubt, because Munro so richly rewards such attention. The choice between the literary and the cultural as modes of critical analysis is not as sharp as that drawn by Albert Braz in 'The Good and the Read: Literary Value and Readership in Canadian Literature' (*CRCL* 41:ii[2014] 174–82). Reviewing two books which address contemporary critical practice—Colin Hill's *Modern Realism in English-Canadian Fiction* and Smaro Kamboureli and Robert Zakarias's edited book, *Shifting the Ground of Canadian Literary Studies* (both 2012)—Braz compares the aesthetic values of early twentieth-century fiction and Hill's criticism that grants agency to the author with the critical method of Kamboureli and Zakarias, which announces a 'shift toward a foregrounding of the situational and the material conditions that influence the production of Canadian literary texts' (p. 177). Braz's corrective is in favour of a criticism that has something 'to say about the workings of literary texts' (p. 181).

Also in this issue of *Canadian Review of Comparative Literature*, Jen-chieh Tsai uses rhetorical analysis to explore Yann Martel's *Life of Pi*. In 'On the

Migration of Pi: Toward a Rhetoric of Identification' (*CRCL* 42:i[2015] 94–106), Tsai turns this timely topic back against imperial assumptions around European concepts of travel, indicating a way of thinking about difference that draws on Kenneth Burke's 'rhetoric of identification'. Martel is an apt example of the Canadian author as a global citizen, born in Spain, and not confined as a writer by nationality. It might seem, then, inappropriate to approach his work, which deals in universal themes, by way of a national literature. Yet he is a Canadian literary intellectual actively committed to the progressive politics associated with Canada, and Canadian writing has long been able to combine a global view with local, regional, and national modes of attention. Criticism of Canada's canonical authors has benefited from their being placed on both sides of the national/international divide that in the past has hampered the reception and valuing of Canadian literature.

Mavis Gallant, certainly, speaks eloquently to an expansive view of national belonging, and Jacob von Baeyer considers both the registrations of nation and the cosmopolitanism in her work in 'The Displaced Cosmopolitan: Canadian Nationality and World Citizenship in the Fiction of Mavis Gallant' (*BJCS* 28:ii[2015] 187–203). Von Baeyer uses the 'slippery Canadian identity' he finds in Gallant's fiction as a way into the cosmopolitanism of her fiction. The theme is pursued indirectly by Jason Blake in 'A Canadian Icon in a "Cretinous Provincial Dump"—Glenn Gould and Thomas Bernhard's Novel *The Loser*' (*BJCS* 28:i[2015] 71–88). An Austrian novelist, Bernhard inserts the Canadian pianist into his novel, while scarcely noticing his Canadianness. This provides Blake with an unusually detached but effective point from which to view the debates about Canadianness and its responsibilities (or lack thereof) for the author or the critic.

Michael Ondaatje receives clever attention from Michael Barry, whose essay, 'Archaeology and Teleology in Ondaatje's *Anil's Ghost*' (*Crit* 56:ii[2015] 138–54), probes the structure and philosophical implications of arguably his finest novel. Barry counters the established focus on what he calls the 'aerial view' (p. 138) in approaching Ondaatje's work by setting it in dialectical relation to the figuring in his fiction of excavation, both literal and figurative. This allows Barry to draw out the novel's recognition of the difficulty as well as the desirability of maintaining cultural difference in light of the increasing commonality of our human 'fate' (p. 152).

Margaret Atwood receives her deserved share of interpretation in 2015, extending a richly varied background of study that ranges across the modes of her writing from speculative fiction to political critique. Alaina Kaus, in 'Liberalities of Feeling: Free Market Subjectivities in Margaret Atwood's *The Blind Assassin*' (*Crit* 56:iv[2015] 369–82), identifies two strains of investigation, loosely the postmodern and the political, in Atwood's 2000 novel that 'juxtaposes Depression-era politics against those at the end of the twentieth century' (p. 369). Drawing on *The Blind Assassin*'s interrogation of both selfhood and its representation of class and gender oppression, Kaus seeks a critical reconciliation by demonstrating that market liberalism is 'itself a theory of human subjectivity that discursively structures human experience in the novel' (p. 370). J. Paul Narkunas's 'Between Words, Numbers, and Things: Transgenics and Other Objects of Life in Margaret Atwood's *MaddAddams*'

(*Crit* 56:i[2015] 1–25) offers a substantive reading of the MaddAddam trilogy, arguing that in it Atwood mounts an attack on the instrumentalization of human life by way of an odd assortment of opponents: 'transgenics and critical theology and ecological discourses' (p. 3). Thus the trilogy responds to the threats posed by an unholy intersection of technology, synthetic biology, and capitalism in reducing humans to tools. Here the aesthetic serves a critical purpose: by 'acknowledging the human's perpetual creation' in her speculative fictions Atwood opposes a civilization progressively eroding the status of humans (p. 22).

Two examples of ethically turned criticism, one on MaddAddam, are found in *Studies in Canadian Literature*. Lucy Rowland follows a bioethical line of criticism in Atwood's work in 'Speculative Solutions: The Development of Environmental and Ecofeminist Discourse in Margaret Atwood's *MaddAddam*' (*SCL* 40:ii[2015] 46–68). Rowland argues that Atwood adds 'new potential solutions to ever-pervasive patriarchal and totalitarian world views', and closes with a list of the unexceptionable values the novel serves: 'inclusivity, equality, and democracy' (p. 67). Laura Moss, in ' "A science of uncertainty": Bioethics, Narrative Competence, and Turning to the "What If" of Fiction' (*SCL* 40:ii[2015] 5–24), investigates the value of pursuing literary studies by reference to the discipline of medicine, looking to the model of the doctor as interpreter who must proceed to a treatment in a condition of uncertainty. Moss's chosen novels—Kathleen Winter's *Annabel*, Emma Donoghue's *Room*, and Vincent Lam's *Bloodletting and Miraculous Cures*—allow her to connect, richly yet cautiously, the two fields around the notion of 'narrative competence'. This is an important essay for the study of literature and narrative within the field of the medical humanities that enriches each of the seemingly distant disciplines it joins—ethically, critically, and productively—by looking both ways.

Introducing a special Alice Munro issue of the *American Review of Canadian Studies* (*ARCS* 45:ii[2015] 144–7), Robert Thacker observes that the 2013 award of the Nobel Prize had 'jump-started' critical attention to her work (p. 147). In Thacker's own contribution to the issue, ' "Evocative and luminous phrases": Reading Alice Munro's *Hateship, Friendship, Courtship, Loveship, Marriage*' (*ARCS* 45:ii[2015] 187–95) (which first appeared in Mandarin in 2014), the commingled literary and humanist values which he celebrates in the introduction—she is 'ever gauging questions of human understanding, of human knowing, of human happiness'—open out into endless narrative equivocations (p. 147). Munro is, as Thacker's introduction puts it, 'ever there, shaping the point-of-view, creating its profound effects', but the reader is not conducted to easy affirmations (p. 147). Carol L. Beran places Munro in a national-canonical line-up in 'Beautiful Girlhood, a Double Life: Lucy Maud Montgomery, Margaret Laurence, and Alice Munro' (*ARCS* 45:ii[2015] 148–60), tracing the influence of Montgomery's young adult fiction on the later writers. Montgomery's concept of 'beautiful girlhood' is shown to inform the social questioning of both authors, 'particularly as the construct pertains to the female artist, available to the Canadian imaginary, that set of beliefs that help define the imagined community that is Canada' (p. 7). Children's literature here facilitates a more direct connection between the national and the international, serving both to establish a thematic of national identity and to throw up texts that speak fluently to all cultures, albeit with pleasingly local accents.

Dennis Duffy, in 'Alice Munro's Narrative Historicism: "Too Much Happiness"' (*ARCS* 45:ii[2015] 196–207), considers the titular story in terms of its curious focus on a nineteenth-century Russian writer, Sophia Kovalevsky, and Munro's impact on feminism, which he understands in non-theoretical terms. Lives such as Kovalevsky's he sees as part of a continuum of Munro's female figures 'from the quotidian realistic to the historical to the exemplary' (pp. 204–5). Duffy thus positions the story within the arc of Munro's fiction, observing that, by 'blending the actual with the symbolic and imaginative, Munro has swung her style of narrative far enough forward to have it whip back far into the past, into the conditions of the exemplary narrative' (p. 203). Nadine Fladd, in 'Alice Munro, Charles McGrath, and the Shaping of "The Turkey Season"' (*ARCS* 45:ii[2015] 174–86), considers the literary relationship between Munro and her *New Yorker* editor, Charles McGrath. Timothy McIntyre's '"This is not enough": Gesturing Beyond the Aesthetics of Failure in Alice Munro's "Material"' (*ARCS* 45:ii[2015] 161–73), applies pressure to the complex failures of narrative and language in Munro's story by focusing both on the limits of language it exposes and the affirmation of creative value it implies. McIntyre thus supports both an aesthetic reading of 'Material' and offers a deconstructive reading of a text that, he observes, indicates 'a mode of literature beyond the logocentric, or at least phallogocentric'. The critical exercise is supported by the analogies drawn between D.H. Lawrence's Mellors in *Lady Chatterley's Lover* and the narrator's husband.

Stephen Bernstein's '"LONGING TO SEE DOCUMENTS": Writing and Desire in Alice Munro's Longest Stories' (*Crit* 56:iv[2015] 355–68) focuses on the long stories, where he argues Munro was able to 'achieve the fullest rendering of desiring consciousness' (p. 355). Bernstein's tentative conclusion from his examination of Munro's 'lengthy explorations of characters who write' is that she was preparing for a shift towards exploration of the writing self, moving, that is, 'toward a different kind of exploration of someone who writes—herself' (p. 367). Marlene Goldman and Sarah Powell, in 'Alzheimer's, Ambiguity, and Irony: Alice Munro's "The Bear Came Over the Mountain" and Sarah Polley's *Away from Her*' (*CanL* 225[2015] 82–99), consider Munro's fictional treatment of Alzheimer's and Polley's film version in terms of the Lockean model of selfhood, which they both recognize and resist. Both text and film confront us with the confusion and ambiguity that arise from 'unwilled illness coupled with "tempestuous and turbulent passion"' (p. 97). The essay thus construes the way Munro and Polley see 'the affective and embodied nature of memory' as a means of deepening our perception of and response to identity and subjectivity (p. 83).

Munro is also considered by Chantel Lavoie in 'Good Enough, Bad Enough, Animal, Monster: Mothers in Alice Munro's *The Love of a Good Woman*' (*SCL* 40:ii[2015] 69–87) in terms of the mother figure, obliged to be monstrous because of the monstrous experience of childbirth. Lavoie observes that 'a legacy of unforgiveness is implicit in [Munro's] writing about memory and her memory about writing' (p. 84). Pilar Somacarrera returns to a critical avenue somewhat sidelined in contemporary culture and theory, religion of an orthodox kind, in '"The unavoidable collision of religion and life": Scots Presbyterianism in Alice Munro's Fiction' (*SCL* 40:ii[2015] 88–107). Somacarrera notes the ill effects of the 'repressive ideology' of Presbyterianism in Munro's fiction, but moves beyond this predictable and worn critique to observe also the author's gratitude for the drama and 'structuring pattern' that belief, however cramping of characters, allows to the novelist (p. 105).

An earlier hero of the novel in Canada, Ethel Wilson, is reconsidered not only for her complex negotiation of realism and modernism but also for the compassion of her modernism in Kait Pinder's 'Difficult Compassion, Compassionate Modernism: Ethel Wilson's *Swamp Angel* (*CanL* 225[2015] 101–18). Calling for attention to 'the intricacies of Wilson's theory of compassion', Pinder locates the author within the history of thinking about compassion and argues that it offers a means of re-evaluating Wilson's modernism 'at a moment when critics of modernism are also reevaluating the "still-pervasive notions of modernism's hostility to notions of feelings for others"' (p. 116).

A still earlier engagement with modernism and a rather different Canadian modernity are addressed by Will Smith in '"First and foremost a writer of fiction": Revisiting Two Toronto Novels: Hopkins Moorhouse's *Every Man for Himself* and Peter Donovan's *Late Spring*' (*BJCS* 28:ii[2015] 167–86). Smith's essay valuably contributes attention to an early modernism aligned with realism and the urban places these long-neglected early twentieth-century novelists register in their appropriate contexts in nuanced and complex terms. This article appears in an issue of the *British Journal of Canadian Studies*, which features 'New Voices in Canada' written by scholars in the United Kingdom or elsewhere in Europe. The editors, Christopher Kirkey and Tony McCulloch, chose to focus on younger scholars and collected a strong body of essays offering a fresh sense of critical enterprise. The articles are treated separately in this section, but Sarah Galletly's 'L.M. Montgomery and Canadian Mass-Market Magazines' (*BJCS* 28:ii[2015] 145–65) is a representative example. Galletly places Montgomery's career in a specifically Canadian context of the magazines *Chatelaine* and *Canadian Home Journal*, where Montgomery shaped her career and celebrity status through the publication of more than 300 short stories. Not focused on the fiction itself, the article does much more than simply register the contexts of reception. Instead, Galletly makes us aware of Montgomery as an author constructed by editors and advertising, but also one who navigated the magazine industry/culture of her day and the shaping of an image of herself as an author at the intersections of literature and marketplace, high and low culture, middlebrow and modern.

The major publication in Indigenous literary studies in Canada in 2015 is Margery Fee's *Literary Land Claims: The 'Indian Land Question' from Pontiac's War to Attiwapiskat*, considered elsewhere in this section. Critical articles, while less ambitious in scope, continued to contest white literary representations of Indigenous history and culture.

Renée Jackson-Harper, in 'Forests, Clearings, and the Spaces in Between: Reading Land Claims and the Actuality of Context in *Ana Historic*' (*SCL* 40:ii[2015] 128–43), suggests a point of potentially healing agreement between white and Indigenous stories and lifeways by following Daphne Marlatt's repudiation of 'white male narratives' in favour of an imagined ecological and 'ab-original' selfhood (p. 14). Kaitlin Debicki, in 'Returning to the Kaswéntah River: A Trans-Indigenous Reading of Land-Centred Citizenship in Thomas King's *Truth and Bright Water*' (*SCL 40:ii[2015] 109–27*), argues that ethnic difference within Canada can be maintained within a unity constructed around common assent to ecological principle and practice. Julia A. Boyd, in ' "Fugitive Visions": Cultural Pseudomemory and the Death of the Indigenous Child in the Indian Poems of Duncan Campbell Scott' (*SCL 40:ii[2015] 143–63*), addresses the appalling record of mortality among Indigenous children under bureaucratic regimens in the early twentieth century. Scott directly contributed to the educational system that savagely impacted on Indigenous children, who also figure in his poems and stories. Scott is thus a fascinating subject as an administrator and poet in whose life and work the two fields of activity are entangled. Representing the 'racial violence' resulting in the deaths of so many children, his writing is deeply significant for national cultural memory (p. 143) and opens up the figure of the author-administrator who played an ambiguous, sometimes deeply disturbing, role in colonial and early modern settler societies.

Michèle Lacombe, in 'More Than Where the Heart Is: Meeting Places in Wabanaki Poetry by Cheryl Savageau and Mihku Paul' (*JCSR* 49:ii[2015] 133–49), observes that 'there are not many literary studies of Indigenous meeting places in the borderlands of New England, Quebec, and the Maritimes'. Lacombe sets about addressing that lack by focusing on a small body of contemporary writers from the 'Wabanaki' confederation of First Nation and Native American peoples, whose work overrules the distinction between the nation states on either side of the 49th Parallel. Where the nation state, ignoring the habitation, history, and cultural being of First Nation peoples remains so problematic for the Indigenous writer, one welcomes such engagement with Indigenous studies as a transnational phenomenon complementing a contemporary emphasis in, for example, the Pacific.

Thomas King invests border-crossing in the late twentieth century with his caustic satirical humour in *Green Grass, Running Water*, a novel still deservedly attracting strong critical attention for its testing of the intersection between popular culture and the political, and especially the image-making that imprisons whole peoples for generations. Joel Deshaye, in 'Tom King's John Wayne: The Western in *Green Grass, Running Water*' (*CanL* 225[2015] 66–80), argues compellingly that King's vision of Wayne reframes other Canadian Westerns about Billy the Kid and Jesse James '*as a collective phantasy of the death of American celebrity*—or at least as an attempted subversion of American pop-cultural influence' (p. 66). At a time when the Canadian Western, with its long history, is resurgent, Deshaye looks to a popular culture that has become 'a threat bigger than history' (p. 62). Canadian fiction focused on American heroes like Wayne is certainly 'part of a general commentary on American-Canadian relations'; more importantly

King, by killing John Wayne in *Green Grass, Running Water*, is offering those most demeaned by American popular culture a kind of justice that is '*creative*, *fantastic*, not *real* retribution' (p. 78).

David Creelman, in 'Refashioning Mi'kmaw Narratives into Maritime Fictions: Theodore Goodridge Roberts, Frank Parker Day, and Alden Nowlan' (*JCSR* 49:ii[2015] 150–70), examines translated stories of Mi'kmaq people from the late nineteenth to the late twentieth centuries, asking what it means for a non-Indigenous author to write a text as if it is aboriginal. Desiree Hellegers, in 'From Poisson Road to Poison Road: Mapping the Toxic Trail of Windigo Capital in Linda Hogan's *Solar Storms*' (*SAIL* 27:ii[2015] 1–28), develops a decolonizing stance directed at 'Healing the effects of intergenerational trauma' (p. 3). While Hellegers is keen that history told from a colonial perspective must give way to Indigenous perspectives and world views, this is not to be effected merely by way of vague generalities about culture and belief structures. Instead, the essay traces the 'intergenerational life of capital' in Indigenous communities (p. 3). The Hudson Bay Company is given special attention here, from its fur-trading posts to modern consumerism. For Hellegers, there is hope in the 'fragile alliances' that are emerging in opposition to corporate power to exploit native land. Chickasaw writer Linda Hogan's *Solar Storms* shows Indigenous communities' opposition not by the 'embrace [of] Eurocentric models of liberation, but in a deepening exploration of and engagement with Indigenous stories, practices, and cultural traditions—of survival, struggle, and resistance' (p. 22).

David Gaertner, in ' "Something in between": *Monkey Beach* and the Haisla Return of the Return of the Repressed' (*CanL* 225[2015] 47–63), argues against the importation of Western knowledge such as psychoanalysis into Indigenous texts already 'populated with [their] own systems of knowledge and hermeneutics' (p. 47). The Indigenous author is shown employing psychoanalytic tropes that 'pre-date Freud and are built out of their own histories, cultures and experiences' (p. 61). Critical attention here is a means of casting back to forms of memory deeper than those preserved by and predicated on literature.

From a contrarian position, Albert Braz, in 'Minus Literature: The Curious Canonisation of Len Findlay's "Always Indigenize!" ' (*BJCS* 28:i[2015] 89–104), directs energetic criticism at Len Findlay's much cited and affirmed 2000 essay, 'Always Indigenize! The Radical Humanities in the Postcolonial Canadian University'. As Braz points out, Findlay does not much engage with either literature or Indigenous literature, so is an odd model to be adopted by the humanities or by Indigenous scholars. Braz critiques Findlay's article both for not practising what it advocates and for the general acceptance it has received. His complaint against the compliant reception of Findlay's piece asserts that to be 'critical' scholars need to resist the lure of all rallying cries. Moreover, to reform literary studies by concentrating its attention on the rejection of colonization is to overlook the broader frame of scholarly and critical activity. Braz might argue more persuasively for what he proposes in place of Findlay's cure for the humanities. And he might have looked more broadly at Indigenous studies. Braz observes, carpingly, Findlay's high praise of Māori scholar, Linda Tuhiwai Smith's *Decolonizing Methodologies*. Here he might have explored more generously both the trans-national purview of current Indigenous studies and the differences and similarities presented within such a field.

The political and cultural implications of literary texts are sometimes approached in less familiar ways, as when Vikki Visvas in 'The Sounds of the North: Political Efficacy and the "Listening Self" in Elizabeth Hay's *Late Nights on Air*' (*CanL* 225[2015] 29–45) observes a shift from the ecological association of sound with 'hazardous background noise' in the 1970s to its contemporary identification with cultural inclusiveness and 'political advocacy' (p. 43). Shannon Maguire's 'Parasite Poetics: Noise and Queer Hospitality in Erín Mouré's *O Cidadán*' appears in a special issue of *Canadian Literature* on 'Queer Frontiers' (*CanL* 224[2015] 47–63). Maguire argues that Moure uses 'noise as both poetic medium and tool in *O Cidadán*' (p. 47). The object is to confront, estrange, and disrupt the reader so as to signal new understandings of belonging as citizens and of 'queer hospitality'. Shirley McDonald, in 'Finding Common Ground: Purposeful Disarticulation in the Poetry of Erin Mouré' (*ESC* 41:ii[2015] 109–31), meditates on the 'hermeneutical poetics' of this elegantly deconstructive and notably resistant writer (p. 129). Informed by posthumanist philosophy and phenomenology, the essay explores the patterns of growth in the author's work. Through close reading, McDonald explores not only the poet's hints of sublimity and representations of actuality but also, critically, 'the politics of self-identity' and the limits of those borders that enforce the idea of national identity (p. 111).

In the 1970s British expatriate novelist Malcolm Lowry was inducted into the Canadian literary canon largely on the basis of his habitation of a beach near Vancouver. In fact, his sense of affiliation to place as an author was multiple, and Canada had as demonstrable a claim as Mexico or the Wirral peninsula. Contemporary Canadian multicultural writing prefers to accommodate rather than eliminate the variety of nationalities or ethnicities that might claim its authors. Lisa Grekul, in 'Guns and Tender Cotton: Feminized States in Rawi Hage's *De Niro's Game*' (*UTQ* 84:ii[2015] 48–69), approaches Lebanese Canadian Hage's depiction of Lebanon's unrest by way of its narrator's struggle towards manhood. Lebanese women, however, have no capacity in a patriarchal society to discover and express identity. Almas Khan's 'Poetic Justice: Slavery, Law, and the (Anti-)Elegiac Form in M. NourbeSe Philip's *Zong!*' (*CJPLI* 2:i[2015] 5–32) reads the poem as an unpacking of the legal language used to describe the murder of a ship's 'freight' of slaves. The writer employs the words included in the official narrative but also employs poetry as an 'elegiac counter-narrative' to show 'language's complicity with violence' (p. 6). This is a rewarding essay, attending closely to literary language and readerly involvement in a text that uses a specific literary form and a technique of stylistic antithesis both to oppose savage legality and to re-establish battered humanity.

Ian James MacRae, in ' "In all things, a slippage in the works": Reading Place, Gender, and Genre in Michael Helm's *In the Place of Last Things*' (*ESC* 41:ii[2015] 65–89), argues that Helm deploys multiple genres in his narrative to reinvent entrenched paradigms, as well as rooted notions of subjectivity, not just in respect of the literature of the North American West but also in respect of Western literature generally. So moving beyond masculine and regionalist modes of reading traditional prairie literature will allow the transformation of the genre (as in Robert Kroetsch's beautifully ambivalent renditions). Vanja Polić approaches similar issues of genre and region in 'The Reworkings of the Western from the Northern Side of the Medicine Line: Caple's *In Calamity's Wake*, Vanderhaeghe's *The Englishman's Boy* and Stenson's *Lightning*' (*BJCS* 28:ii[2015] 205–21). Observing the emergence of a renewed Western genre in Canadian writing, Polić demonstrates that this 'is visible through the replacement of certain tropes and schematic plots from the traditional Western with more complex postmodern narrative techniques such as historiographic metafiction; dialogism and polyglossia; and a greater prominence of ex-centric characters such as women, peoples of the First Nations, and atypical cowboys' (p. 206).

One notes a welcome encroachment on literary criticism of a contiguous discipline in Anna Mongibello's linguistically based ' "Translators of the old ways": The Reinvention of Canadian English in "Jacob" by Maria Campbell (Métis)' (*BJCS* 28:ii 247–63). Mongibello analyses the 'métisation' of Standard Canadian English in the story 'Jacob'. The active mixing of Cree, French, and Canadian English, she states, aims 'to claim the right to speak through [Campbell's] own culture with its influences, interruptions, and fragmentations each destabilising the grammars of standard Canadian English' (p. 259). This suggests a promising linguistic approach to comparative Indigenous literatures involving what we might call subversive code-switching that would also speak to Alexis Wright in Australia and Patricia Grace in New Zealand.

Liedeke Plate, in 'How To Do Things with Literature in the Digital Age: Anne Carson's *Nox*, Multimodality, and the Ethics of Bookishness' (*CWW* 9:i[2015] 93–111), treats Carson's curious tribute to her dead brother to the attention she claims it has not received. A kind of assemblage or scrapbook comprising literary and non-literary elements, *Nox*'s formal oddness is read by Plate as 'embody[ing] a theory of "moving words": carrying them across languages, transporting them to new contexts, making them convey meaning; but also, moving readers affectively, cognitively, and physically'. Elizabeth Reimer, in 'Desire, "Narrative Hunger," and Alterity: Framing Biography as Dialogic Encounter in Carol Shields's *Jane Austen* and Alice Munro's "Meneseteung" ' (*CWW* 9:ii[2015] 200–18), focuses a Bakhtinian lens on the biographer-narrators of Shields's *Jane Austen* and Munro's 'Meneseteung' to reflect on moments of recognition, 'those startling moments . . . when the biographer makes a tentative connection and then doubles back on her own constructions' (p. 216). Cautioning that 'the biographical enterprise itself is untidy and unpredictable' and 'should be launched in a spirit of interrogation and humility', Reimer also acknowledges enthusiastically its opportunities for dialogic connection and discovery. Kevin Shaw's 'Ekphrastic Drag: Temporal Transgressions in John Barton's *West of Darkness: Emily Carr: A Self-Portrait*' (*CanL* 224[2015] 65–81) takes the fashionable critical interest in ekphrasis in a particular direction, arguing that John Barton's 'poetic "self portrait" ' of Emily Carr functions as a queer form of Canadian (auto)biography' (p. 65). Here 'drag' is uncovered as a vehicle for nationalist discourse, particularly in 'the reiterative presence of iconic figures' (p. 67).

Dystopian futures, posthumanist theory and fantasy, and conscriptions of outré popular fashions—Libe García Zarranz adopts a Deleuzian approach to the nightmarish vision of contemporary dehumanization in 'Necropolitical Assemblages and Cross-Border Ethics in Hiromi Goto's *Darkest Light*' (*CanL* 224[2015] 17–31). Zarranz extends the concept of 'necropolitics' to include not only the state's power to determine life and death but also the way death is often capitalized as a productive source of capitalist intervention', and proceeds to interrogate the 'new forms of necropower' she identifies (p. 18). Aesthetic practice in this dark vision of contemporary reality indicates modes of resistance (even if one wonders how effectively dystopian novels or poems might mobilize fundamental change when contemporary politics have themselves appropriated the techniques of fantasy and exaggeration). Sonia Villegas-López, in 'Body Technologies: Posthuman Figurations in Larissa Lai's *Salt Fish Girl* and Jeanette Winterson's *The Stone Gods*' (*Crit* 56:i[2015] 26–41), considers two dystopian novels 'that ponder the relationship between body and self in the context of technological societies' (p. 26). At the intersection of feminism and science fiction, of genetics, robotics, and cyborgian politics, Villegas-López finds space to reflect on gender and 'interbreeding' in two novels, one by a British writer, the other by the Chinese Canadian, Larissa Lai. In her fictional Vancouver, Lai depicts a divided society threatened by ecological disaster and misused technology. Fortunately, 'Non-conventional sexual liaisons' offer a form of remedy by opposing heteronormativity and the economic system (p. 36).

## 4. The Caribbean

*(a) Journal Articles and Chapters in Edited Volumes*

Alison Donnell's revisionist essay, ' "The African Presence in Caribbean Literature" Revisited: Recovering the Politics of Imagined Co-Belonging 1930–2005' (*RAL* 46:iv[2015] 35–55), turns to recent writing by Nalo Hopkinson and Charlotte Williams to address and reconstruct the historical engagements with Africa by earlier Caribbean writers and thinkers. Arguing that 'West Indian literary and critical discourses that reached toward Africa in their attempts to redress colonial bias and bypass European perspectives were consistently troubled as well as valuable', Donnell observes that ultimately they allowed Caribbean critics and writers to articulate 'the distinctive and celebrated Caribbeanness of the Caribbean situation' (p. 36). Candace Ward, in ' "In the Free": The Work of Emancipation in the Anglo-Caribbean Historical Novel' (*JAmS* 49:ii[2015] 359–81), also looks back to the historical novel in her exploration of the tensions and pitfalls of the genre and to what it says about the Caribbean now. Her study focuses on E.L. Joseph's *Warner Arundell: The Adventures of a Creole* [1838], Paule Marshall's *The Chosen Place, the Timeless People* [1969], and Erna Brodber's *The Rainmaker's Mistake* [2007].

Victoria J. Collis-Buthelezi, in 'Caribbean Regionalism, South Africa, and Mapping New World Studies' (*SmAx* 19:i[2015] 37–54), reconsiders the attempts by Caribbean scholars to articulate the sense of place and the character of the Caribbean in the post-independence period of the 1970s. By examining the physical and literary 'detours' to the Cape and South Africa taken by many Caribbean migrants and seafarers, she argues that earlier definitions of 'what the Caribbean is—where it starts and stops—and what exactly it has to do with Africa' (p. 40) are limiting. The map of the Caribbean has to be expanded.

Gwen Bergner's essay, 'Zoning in on the American Tropics' (*AmLH* 27:iv[2015] 831–42), acts as a critical survey of recent publications that examine the American Tropics as an expanded space sharing a colonial history of colonialism and slavery, a zone of contact among Africans, Europeans, and Indigenous peoples. Concerned with ecocriticism and literary geography, the concept of an American Tropics shifts attention away from the relations between and demarcations among nations and ushers us into 'a region united by its history of plantation slavery, near genocide of native peoples, and tropical environment' (p. 831).

Examining another 'zone' of conflict as well as contact, Ifeona Fulani, in 'New Ethnicities: Literary Representations of West Indians in London, 1948–2001' (*CarQ* 61:iv[2015] 82–99), juxtaposes the inflammatory remarks by British historian David Starkey in the wake of the 2011 London riots with Jamaican poet Louise Bennett's 'Colonisation in Reverse' to examine race and the social relations between Caribbean immigrants and Britons in London. She focuses on the post-war wave of migration to the metropolis, on the Brixton and Tottenham uprisings of 1981 that signalled a change in black politics in London, and on second- and third-generation West Indians. The immigrant novel is also the subject of Alicia E. Ellis's article, 'The Imperfect Longing: Sam Selvon's *The Lonely Londoners* and the Dance of Doubt' (*ABD* 8:ii[2015] 178–89). Her essay brings into focus the various linguistic strategies and discourses immigrants use to articulate their particular situations, and 'the various, sometimes conflicting ways in which the idea of home can be invoked and maintained' (p. 178).

The revisionist approach continues in James Robertson's article, 'Rewriting *Dr No* in 1962: James Bond and the End of the British Empire in Jamaica' (*SmAx* 19:ii[2015] 56–76). Robertson examines Ian Fleming's 1958 novel alongside multiple drafts of the screenplay that began the James Bond franchise to show the ways in which Jamaican concerns about independence from British rule were overwritten by more glamourous issues such as the Cold War and technological developments. The film, however, was also responsible in many ways for the 'self-imagination' of Jamaica and the Caribbean at large (p. 60).

The influence of the British canon on Caribbean literature was also the focus of two essays in 2015. In ' "The Last Syllable of Modernity": Chaucer in the Caribbean' (*Postmed* 6:i[2015] 79–93), Michelle R. Warren examines Caribbean writers' engagement with their colonial literary legacy through 'Chaucerian allusions' in their work (p. 81). She argues that 'Chaucerian allusion can challenge the very concept of modernity that underwrites the racial politics of imperialism' (p. 81). The essay focuses on the use of Chaucer in critical essays on the racial politics of the Caribbean, in Jean Rhys's short story 'Again the Antilles', and in more recent writing about diaspora, race, and gender. Sarah Ficke turns her attention to the influence of later writing—specifically the adventure novels of the Victorian period—on Trinidadian Stephen Cobham's 1907 novel, *Rupert Gray* in 'Constructing a Post-Victorian Empire: *Rupert Gray, A Tale in Black and White*' (*SN* 47:iv[2015] 514–31).

Beginning with an anecdote about an enslaved seamstress's embroidered writing on her garments, Danielle C. Skeehan explores the ways in which the 'material text' of African and Caribbean writing disrupts traditional Western ideas about literacy, authorship, and texts and can be read in the context of colonization, in 'Caribbean Women, Creole Fashioning, and the Fabric of Black Atlantic Writing' (*ECent* 56:i[2015] 105–23).

Phanuel Antwi turns his attention to Jamaican dub poetry as a way of recording and reflecting the rhythms of a complex Caribbean history that includes translocation and the reverberations of ancestral homes, in 'Dub Poetry as a Black Atlantic Body-Archive' (*SmAx* 19:iii[2015] 65–83). The incompleteness of dub poetry is not only part of its function and theme; it is also a form of expression that embodies 'the erotics of the black body' (p. 66).

In 'Rereading the Diminutive: Caribbean Chaos Theory in Antonio Benítez-Rojo, Edouard Glissant, and Wilson Harris' (*SmAx* 19:i[2015] 20–36), Jeannine Murray-Román examines these three writers' encounters with the scientific discourse of chaos theory and the ways in which it has provided 'a model for recasting the region's place on the map and in contemporary geopolitical relations'. Caribbean cultures, she argues, might be understood according to a different framework, one that emphasizes repetition and 'revaloriz[es] smallness' (p. 21).

*Small Axe* (19:i[2015]) devotes a section to Stuart Hall. Essays include Kobena Mercer's 'Stuart Hall and the Visual Arts' (*SmAx* 19:i[2015] 76–87); Michelle Stephens's 'New Points of Recognition: Stuart Hall's Gift of Blackness' (*SmAx* 19:i[2015] 88–99); Maxime Cervulle and David Scott's 'What Is To Be Done (at the University)? Stuart Hall, Critique, and the Institution' (*SmAx* 19:i[2015] 100–8); and Liv Sovik's 'Stuart Hall and Writing Structured Like Music' (*SmAx* 19:i[2015] 109–17), which considers his influence on—and the difficulties he posed for—Brazilian readers of his intellectual work.

In 'A Postcolonial Appraisal of V.S. Naipaul's *A House for Mr Biswas*' (*IJALEL* 4:ii[2015] 104–11), Tahereh Siamardi and Riza Didari use Homi Bhabha's theorizing of the relationship between the colonizer and the colonized to examine the complexities of Naipaul's characters' cultural identities. Bahareh Shojaan takes this issue further by analysing the ambivalence experienced by the Indian immigrant characters living in 'the creole society' of colonial Trinidad, in 'A Postcolonial Survey of *A House for Mr Biswas* by V.S. Naipaul' (*ALLS* 6:iv[2015] 72–9). An interview with the writer was also conducted and published by Bharati Mukherjee and Robert Boyers: 'A Conversation with V.S. Naipaul' (*Salmagundi* 185/186[2015] 584–606).

Intertextuality is the focus of the Fawzia Mustafa's essay, 'Gurnah and Naipaul: Intersections of *Paradise* and *A Bend in the River*' (*TCL* 61:ii[2015] 232–63). Both novels centre on postcolonial Africa, focused especially through Conrad's *Heart of Darkness*. As Mustafa demonstrates, teasing out

NEW LITERATURES

generational differences and repetitions within literary postcolonialism, Naipaul's historical inaccuracy is countered by Gurnah's parodic writing.

In 'Geo- and Ecocritical Considerations of Derek Walcott's Multitasking, Omnipresent Sea' (*IJALEL* 4:vi[2015]196–203), Doris Hambuch picks up from the conclusion of Ben T. Jefferson's essay 'The Sea as Place in Derek Walcott's Poetry' [2013], in which he argues that 'Walcott's representations of the sea favour phenomenological understanding as they challenge notions of nation' (p. 196). Hambuch proceeds to examine the 'agency' of the sea by discussing its self-referential, historical, communicative, and spiritual functions in Walcott's work. Ishion Hutchinson's 'A Voice at the Edge of the Sea: An Interview with Derek Walcott' appeared in *Virginia Quarterly Review* (*VQR* 91:i[2015] 172–5). 'After six decades of making the language that has elevated his Antillean world into the permanence of poetry', as the introduction puts it (p. 172), the poet reflects on place, friends, and poetry. Hutchinson prompts humour, wry insight, and honesty from the poet who, as the brief introduction elegantly observes, possessed a 'genius for breaching the membrane between metaphor and metonymy' (p. 173).

A significant amount of critical attention was directed at Caribbean women writers in 2015. Jamaica Kincaid's travel writing is the subject of ' "The leeches are the least of the worries": Blankscapes and Another Other in Jamaica Kincaid's *Among Flowers* and Biyi Bandele's *The King's Rifle*' (*RAL* 46:i[2015] 19–36), in which Pallavi Rastogi explores the ways in which an Antiguan writer and a Nigerian writer, both influenced by colonization, depict other colonized places and people. Burma and Nepal, notably, are both depicted as 'Another Other'. Ricia Anne Chansky's 'Between Selves: An Intertextual Approach to Jamaica Kincaid's *Among Flowers*' (*Biography* 38:i[2015] 135–51) fills the gap in scholarship on this particular travel narrative, and argues for its importance to understanding 'Kincaid and her diasporic identity construction' (p. 135). Chansky examines this text apropos of *A Small Place* to make fuller observations about Caribbean diasporic subjectivities.

In ' "There is always the other side, always": Black Servants' Laughter, Knowledge, and Power in Jean Rhys's *Wide Sargasso Sea*' (*Mo/Mo* 22:iii[2015] 493–521) Ambreen Hai draws attention to the black servant Christophene in the novel to uncover the complexities of the condition of servitude that involves 'affective interpersonal relations, paradoxical intimacies, and dependencies' (p. 494). However, unlike previous critics, Hai chooses to 'relocat[e] her as one of a *constellation* of figures of black servitude' (p. 495) in her analysis of domestic servitude in modern narratives about the post-emancipation period.

Jean Rhys is again the subject in Emma Zimmerman's ' "Always the same stairs, always the same room": The Uncanny Architecture of Jean Rhys's *Good Morning, Midnight*' (*JML* 38:iv[2015] 74–92). Zimmerman examines the ways in which the Parisian hotel's thematic and formal functions intersect with Rhys's exploration of memory in the novel. Freud's 'The Uncanny' serves as a lens through which Zimmerman analyses the 'psychological symptoms of the deracinated modern urban condition' (p. 74).

Katherine C. Henderson also considers the significance of architecture in 'Claims of Heritage: Restoring the English Country House in *Wide Sargasso*

*Sea*' (*JML* 38:iv[2015] 93–109). Thornfield Hall, the English country house, allows for an examination of the ways in which race functions in a post-imperial context. Henderson uses the vehicle of the country house, 'an icon of national history' (p. 94), to interrogate ideas of nostalgia and preservation during this period.

In 'Ghostly Presences: James Potter Lockhart and Jane Maxwell Lockhart in Jean Rhys's Writing' (*TSLL* 57:iv[2015] 389–411), Sue Thomas re-creates the history and examines the influence of Rhys's forebears on her writing. Family history becomes a means of interrogating identity and colonial history in her texts. Patricia Moran compares the work of Norwegian writer Coral Sandel and Jean Rhys in relation to shame and affect in her essay, 'Shame, Subjectivity, and Self-Expression in Coral Sandel and Jean Rhys' (*Mo/Mo* 22:iv[2015] 713–34). She draws attention to their common themes of 'female development and female subjectivity' (p. 713), and shows how their creative and artistic expressions help to manage the crippling effects of shame.

Edward Kamau Brathwaite's 1974 contention that 'white creoles have forfeited their claim to the spiritual life of the Caribbean' led to a questioning as to whether Jean Rhys's *Wide Sargasso Sea* deserves to be included in the Caribbean canon. In 'Recrossing the Sargasso Sea: Trauma, Edward Kamau Brathwaite, and His Critics' (*ArielE* 46:iv[2015] 89–121), Jeremy Metz contradicts and complicates Brathwaite's argument through an examination of the complexity of the Caribbean trauma where the lines between victimhood and perpetration are blurred.

Opening up yet another 'zone of contact', one not limited by region, Jairus Omuteche discusses his pedagogical approach to Dionne Brand's *In Another Place, Not Here* and Erna Brodber's *Myal* in his article 'Case Study: Teaching Two Caribbean Texts in Kenyan Universities' (*REIL* 46:i–ii[2015] 211–38). Approaching these two black diasporic novels from 'an implied comparatist, multi-disciplinary, and translational mode' allows for 'inquiry into the wider black cultural and historical encounter with European imperialism and the resultant power dynamics' prevalent in the African diaspora (p. 211).

In 'Human Together: Into the Interior of Auto/OntoPoesis' (*Symploke* 23:i–ii[2015] 153–71), Mina Karavanta considers texts by Sylvia Wynter and Michelle Cliff to offer posthumanist readings of their work. She argues that these writers 'creolise the myth of the national community as a homogeneous fraternity that shares the same imaginary of a national community and project a history of the human from within the ground of an unevenly differentiated temporality lived by heterogeneous constituencies and communities' (pp. 156–7). Their texts therefore offer alternative 'decolonializing' ways of reading the Caribbean subject (p. 157).

*(b) Books*

*Beyond Windrush: Rethinking Postwar Anglophone Caribbean Literature*, edited by J. Dillon Brown and Leah Reade Rosenberg, gathers together sixteen essays by eminent scholars who take counter-discursive views of the defining period in Caribbean migration and writing which began with the 1948 sailing of the SS *Empire Windrush* to England. On board were the future canonical writers George Lamming, Samuel Selvon, and V.S. Naipaul; nevertheless, as the blurb confidently announces, this collection of essays presents a 'challenge to the primacy of the Windrush generation [of writers] as the sole founders of Caribbean literature'. *Beyond Windrush* both revisits and looks beyond the terms in which these foundational writers have been regarded (and canonized) to focus on aspects of the *Windrush* era previously overlooked or under-investigated. Writers like John Hearne, Roger Mais, Andrew Salkey, Ismith Khan, Austin Clarke, Elma Napier, Joyce Gladwell, and Marie Chauvet are revalued. Genres besides the novel, such as the short story, memoir, and journalistic writing, are reconsidered. Strenuous subjects such as non-heterosexuality and environmental urgencies are given prominence. And a generous range of geographical locations other than London, all pertinent to the period and its writing, are visited and explored: the anglophone and francophone Caribbean, Canada, and the United States.

*Beyond Windrush* is divided into four parts which speak to the specific modes of attention that govern this general revisioning: 'Negotiating National Belonging' (pp. 27–78), 'Genre and Gender' (pp. 79–128), 'The Politics of Literary Production and Reception' (pp. 129–78), and 'Alternate Geographies' (pp. 179–248). The aim is to do more than simply rehearse familiar themes and assumptions of Caribbean literary foundations. The collection interrogates the status of the *Windrush* era as 'the predominant origin myth of Anglophone Caribbean literature' (p. 18) with essays that busily unearth 'forgotten facets of genre, gender, sexuality, ethnicity, transnationalism, and the local in the era's writing' (p. 12).

Angelique V. Nixon's *Resisting Paradise: Tourism, Diaspora, and Sexuality in Caribbean Culture* is relevant here for the attention it directs to literary works and criticism that serve to illustrate the author's assertion that 'paradise is always on some level signifying colonial, sexualized, racialized, and gendered space/object/desire' (p. 3). Somewhat weightily, Nixon problematizes 'the complex and often overlooked relationship between sex and culture within the production of paradise and the Caribbean neo-colonial tourist industry [and offers] possibilities and sites of resistance through the vexed relationships among tourism, diaspora, and sexuality' (p. 25). Exploring 'the myriad ways' the creative writer, among the scholar, intellectual, activist, and artist, engages in 'negotiating and transforming ideas of tourism' (p. 25), *Resisting Paradise* references both canonical and popular literature. Nixon examines how writers such as Derek Walcott, Kamau Brathwaite, and Sylvia Wynter have confronted the master-narratives of Caribbean history. She observes Jamaica Kincaid's laying bare her 'resistance to tourism and neocolonialism' in *A Small Place* (p. 207), and follows scholar/theorist Patricia Saunders's analysis of the representation of the Caribbean in Terry McMillan's novel, *How Stella Got Her Groove Back*. In addition, Audre Lorde's *Zami: A New Spelling of Her Name* and Paule Marshall's *Praisesong for the Widow* are examined for their discussions of the politics of place, identity, migration, and travel. Nixon also considers in these terms V.S. Naipaul's *The Middle Passage*, Erna Brodber's *Myal*, and Michelle Cliff's *Abeng* and *No Telephone to Heaven*.

Alison Donnell, Maria McGarrity, and Evelyn O'Callaghan's edited collection of seventeen essays, *Caribbean Irish Connections: Interdisciplinary Perspectives* with a foreword by eminent historian Hilary McD. Beckles, like Nixon's book, is largely a cultural and historical study employing literary discourse to pursue its argument. The book is structured in three parts: 'Histories of Encounter and Exchange' (pp. 17–102), 'Cultural Performance and Exchange' (pp. 103–88), and 'Comparative Readings and Critical Encounters' (pp. 189–304). Poetic, prose, and dramatic forms are examined throughout *Caribbean Irish Connections*. In Part II, of especial note is McGarrity's chapter, 'Cataloguing Ireland: Exile and Indigeneity in Derek Walcott's *Omeros*' (pp. 140–56). In Part III, Jamaican poetry and the works of Derek Walcott, Dionne Brand, Jean Rhys, and Kamau Brathwaite are explored in relation to Irish canonical writers. Lee M. Jenkins's 'Water Songs: "The Lake Isle of Innisfree" and Jamaican Poetry' (pp. 189–202) brings into alignment literary traditions not often connected. Also of note are Leif Schenstead-Harris's 'The Haunted Ocean: Mourning Language with J.M. Synge and Derek Walcott' (pp. 203–20), 'Medbh McGuckian's *Shelmalier* and Dionne Brand's *Inventory*: Elegiac Ecopoetics' (pp. 236–57) by Elaine Savory; Richard McGuire's '"Two Tunes": Settler-Colonist Worlds in Elizabeth Bowen's *The Last September* and Jean Rhys's *Voyage in the Dark*' (pp. 258–71); and 'Mutual Obsessions: Walcott, Beckett and Brathwaite' (pp. 272–89) by Jean Antoine-Dunne. In answering Jamaican Erna Brodber's question, 'What did the Irish contribute to the Caribbean creole literary mix?' the editors declare that 'the essays in [the third] section amply demonstrate how Caribbean writers have connected with and been profoundly influenced by aspects of the writings of Joyce, Yeats, Heaney, Synge and Beckett, among others' (pp. 9–10).

In this perhaps unexpected, but certainly rich, comparison of peoples and literary traditions connected by histories of colonization and dispersion, the chapters find points of contact, exchange, and commonalities in the ways in which writers express histories of suffering, persistence, and discovery. By shifting away from the United States as the focus of both Irish and Caribbean migration—by looking sideways, in a sense—this book deepens the ways in which we think about diasporas and their complicated networks of connection and encounter.

Veronique Maisier's *Violence in Caribbean Literature: Stories of Stones and Blood* and Giselle Liza Anatol's *The Things That Fly in the Night: Female Vampires in Literature of the Circum-Caribbean and African Diaspora* both look at narratives of trauma and the supernatural embedded in Caribbean history as well as in storytelling and folk traditions. Maisier's readings of the historical, educational, sociopolitical, psychological, and gendered realities of the Caribbean are informed by works of anglophone writers Jean Rhys, Merle Hodge, and Michelle Cliff among those of their francophone counterparts. Anatol's main focus is on the soucouyant figure and, like Maisier, she analyses both francophone and anglophone writing, with the latter including work by science fiction and fantasy writer Nalo Hopkinson. Traditional materials such as vampire narratives have been turned to exciting literary use and cultural revision by writers from Caribbean and African backgrounds. Above all, these long-despised sub-cultural forms have become important and critically respected literary and cultural means for asserting power and agency in the face of debilitating histories. In addition to examining 'the range of Black female vampires in literature of the African diaspora', the work considers 'how people of the Caribbean and African diasporas have appropriated these stories to suit their artistic, social and political goals' (p. xi).

## 5. South Asia

*(a) Books*

Few single-author studies came out this year; edited volumes were also scarce, and not all were available for review, while the number of monographs went up. Salman Rushdie again emerged as a figure of concern in all but two books, while, thematically speaking, cosmopolitan connections and the question of Islamic identities, especially as articulated by writers from Pakistan, dominated critical attention.

Pheng Cheah's *What Is a World? On Postcolonial Literature as World Literature* makes a powerful intervention in current debates on world literature, arguing for the literary text to be seen as an ethico-political force in the world rather than just a commodity whose global trajectory is best understood in terms of existing networks of influence and exchange. Cheah argues for the need to see literature not only as a site for what he calls 'world making' but also as an agent that intervenes and participates in such processes. Part of the value of trying to understand world literature as a world-making activity, Cheah contends, lies in the way it clarifies the connections between literature and cosmopolitanism, paving the way for recognition of the salience of literature to the formulation of normative cosmopolitan principles for regulating the operations of institutional players on the global stage and for the study of the associations and networks that are proliferating across the globe (p. 3). Cheah's discussion of Amitav Ghosh's *The Hungry Tide* [2004] as a robust example of world literature that attempts to give visibility to the world of the subaltern inhabitants of the Sundarban islands forms the subject of chapter 7, in a book that also discusses a number of other works of narrative literature from the postcolonial South, including those by Michelle Cliff, Nuruddin Farah, Ninotchka Rosca, and Timothy Mo. The novel, it is argued, is predicated on the hope that global recognition of the threat facing the subalterns of the Sundarbans from the combined forces of an international interest in world heritage preservation, environmental and ecological movements, global capitalist interests, and economic development, will give the ordinary people of the Sundarbans a voice that in turn will enable them to renew their world.

*The Hungry Tide*, which combines the phenomenological concept of worlding with a neo-Marxist understanding of the Sundarbans' place within the Indian nation and of India as part of the global capitalist system, finally underscores for Cheah 'the superiority of literature as a modality of worlding over other forms of discursive knowledge' (p. 248). It is the novel's dissemination of stories about divine forces, he argues, that gives meaning to the subaltern's continuing struggle with the landscape and keeps the subaltern world together as a whole—processes that are fundamental to its reworlding. The educated, middle-class, Western subject who cannot visualize the Earth as a meaningful place governed by divine forces becomes, in this scheme of things, directly culpable for the plight of the subalterns, only to become radically transformed by the novel's end, and moved to responsible action through her contact with subaltern cultural practices and religious rituals (p. 248).

The concept of translation is central to Cheah's analysis of the novel, which he describes as a 'complex labyrinth of interwoven translations' (p. 276). Regardless of its literary complexity, however, he argues that the novel subscribes to a rather simplistic view of translation as the perfect transference of meaning between minds and cultures, rendering them completely transparent to each other. While the novel strives to read the blankness that lies at the heart of its narrative—the lost diary and the storm that leads to its loss—as something meaningfully destined by divine forces, Cheah contends that they are both completely devoid of meaning: there is no reason for the storm to take place. At the same time, though, the storm is the origin of meanings and interpretations; it was the loss in the storm of the diary that was to be the basis of the narrative that led to attempts to retrieve the diary's missing narrative. The storm, in other words, becomes the very condition of possibility for the novel to emerge. The divine presence celebrated by subaltern stories becomes in Cheah's analysis a blankness constituted by a radical Other that escapes appropriation by human reason or belief, making the meaningful stories that the divine presence gives rise to open to interpretation and even rebuttal (p. 274). The important point, as Cheah warns, is not that translation or mediation has the potential to distort meaning but that the possibility of distortion is structural to the creation of meaning because the unity that constitutes meaningfulness is finally impossible to explain. As the author puts it, 'because this unity comes from what is entirely other to reason, it is always unstable and cannot be guaranteed' (p. 275). On a more optimistic note, however, to the extent that this inappropriable blankness at the heart of the novel is what enables the telling of stories about the subaltern world, including Ghosh's novel, it also holds a promise for the future, albeit one without 'the secure guarantee of an ideal telos' (p. 277).

Cheah's concern with a theoretical and substantive explication of the role of literature as a moral and political force in the world is continued in Dillet and Puri's *The Political Space of Art*, which examines the work of five contemporary artists, spanning the period from the 1990s to the present: filmmakers the Dardenne Brothers, novelist Arundhati Roy, artist Ai WeiWei, and electronic recording artist Burial. The book comprises individual studies on their gesture and oeuvre to show how all five artists strive to create a space for politics within their work at the same time as they attempt to speak to the political context in which this work is produced. In the chapter 'Arundhati Roy's Language of Politics' (pp. 47–65), the authors focus on the screenplay of Roy's early film *In Which Annie Gives It Those Ones* [1989] as well as some of her recent essays on the political struggles of the Naxalites, the Kashmiris, and the *Narmada Bachao Andolan*, to trace a continuity of commitment and vision in which social marginalization is understood not just as a lack of access to resources but also as a lack of access to a certain kind of language. It is through her use of language—'the surface of the text and the texture of words'—the authors argue, that Roy creates in her work a space for the political (p. 52). Language, a fluid mix of English, Hindi, and Punjabi, emerges as one of the prominent characters in the film, serving to give voice to the 'confused, fractured, hybrid selves' of the young generation of urban, middle-class Indians. Roy's political essays also make imaginative use of language, forcing it to yield sudden insights at the same time as they also help expose the ways in which media use language to dehumanize and diminish the other. While the book attempts to initiate an important debate on the meaning and function of contemporary art, it perhaps ends up sounding too much in awe of its subject, preventing the kind of critical engagement that would do it full justice.

Arundhati Roy is also a subject of Kelly A. Marsh's monograph on the fictional stereotype of motherless daughters. In *The Submerged Plot and the Mother's Pleasure*, Marsh argues that in many novels in which women are central, the story of the mother's hardship and death is known but the story of her pleasure is elided. Through a close reading of novels from Austen's *Persuasion* to Roy's *The God of Small Things*, Marsh draws attention to narrative structures which may not give voice to the mother, but which reveal her story and emphasize that the daughter protagonist's progress depends on that story. Although culture demands disciplining of the eroticized mother, the daughters in these novels nevertheless seek knowledge of their mother's pleasure (p. 4). Under the plot of 'maternal absence and filial disidentification', Marsh contends, we can locate 'a submerged plot' of the daughter's search for the mother's story that surfaces at times and exerts continuous pressure on the surface plot. Although the mother's story is typically not narrated, the daughter discovers it in her own experience, which is narrated to the reader (p. 6). *The God of Small Things* [1997], alongside the British novelist Helen Dunmore's *Talking to the Dead* [1996], is the subject of discussion in chapter 5. Both novels narrate how the daughter's knowledge of the certain end of the mother's pleasure thwarts the daughter's own ability to seek and feel pleasure (p. 206). The ending of Roy's novel, which Marsh argues has not received the sustained critical attention that has been devoted to the rest of the text, raises a number of significant questions that have remained unaddressed by previous scholarship. Why the novel offers incestuous sex as the only means for the twins, Estha and Rahel, to reach out to each other, and why readers are left with this image without any indication of its aftermath, are questions that cannot be answered without reference to the submerged plot. Through a meticulous analysis of the parallels between the lives of mother and daughter, Ammu and Rahel, Marsh makes a case for reading the incestuous relationship between the twins as a repetition of the transgressive relationship between their mother and the low-caste Velutha, as one that finally allows the twins a means of accessing the mother's pleasure. Like Ammu and Velutha, Marsh argues, Rahel and Estha too are guilty of breaking the Love Laws 'that lay down who should be loved. And how much' (p. 242). But in thus enabling their transgression, the author also succeeds in rewriting the social and generic stereotypes that have hitherto demanded that the mother's pleasure remain unnarratable (p. 243).

Mrinalini Chakravorty's *In Stereotype: South Asia in the Global Literary Imaginary* undertakes an even closer, more self-conscious engagement with the use of literary stereotypes, to unearth, beneath the deceptive simplicity of the term itself, a complex and labile discourse about fear and desire, power and responsibility, politics and history. Chapter 1 considers the contradictory resonances of stereotypes about crowds and overpopulation, mainly in Rushdie's *Midnight's Children* [1981]. Drawing on the work of Michael Hart and Antonio Negri, the author strives to track the tension between conceptualizing the multitude as a form of collectivity potentially capable of challenging the autonomy and authority that liberal democracies invest in the individual, on the one hand, while being mindful of the singularities that go on to constitute the multitude, on the other—a tension that comes to represent the uncertain prospect of India's decolonial moment in the novel (p. 58). These contradictory views of the multitude are further complicated by glimpses of minor collectives that exist on the fringes of the primary stereotype, undermining its stability over time. Chapter 3 discusses the stereotype of slums in Aravind Adiga's *The White Tiger* [2008] alongside the film *Slumdog Millionaire* [2009] to show how the slum becomes at once a stereotype for the most abject subalternity and the enchanted space of community under globalization. Chapter 4 turns to the stereotype of violent death in the postcolony, as viewed in Ondaatje's *Anil's Ghost* [2000], to examine the ethical demands that are made on readers, who are invited to rethink their entanglements with the deaths of others, while chapter 5 looks at what happens when stereotypes about South Asia cross borders in an instance of diasporic fiction. Writing with reference to Monica Ali's *Brick Lane* [2003] Chakravorty examines the reinvention of stereotypes attached to Bangladesh and its migrants, such as feminization of the garment industry, the dereliction of estate housing for immigrants, and the spectre of unassimilable migrants in a way that appears to plunge into crisis the very idea of Britishness. The last chapter turns to Mohsin Hamid's *The Reluctant Fundamentalist* [2007] to think about how this novel invites the reader to pursue a psychic identification with stereotypes about South Asia's place in the world, only to disrupt them again and again.

A critical engagement with stereotypes also underwrites the concerns and preoccupations of a series of books focused on the question of Islamic identity published in the year under review. Anshuman Mondal's scrupulously researched *Islam and Controversy: The Politics of Free Speech After Rushdie* uses case studies of a number of Muslim-related freedom-of-speech controversies surrounding four texts—*The Satanic Verses* [1988], *The Jewel of Medina* [2008], the Danish cartoons of Muhammad [2005], and the film *Submission* by Theo van Gogh [2004]—to address two questions: Were these authors, artists, and filmmakers right to do what they did in the manner in which they did it? And were the Muslims who opposed them right to have read these texts as offensive? Mondal deploys a reading strategy that utilizes the critical protocols and insights of secular literary criticism while at the same time subjecting that criticism to the pressure of an opposing perspective, and in so doing also subjecting this *other* perspective to the same pressure as well (p. 98). The task, he explains, is not to judge Rushdie's responsibility to his 'evidence' in terms of the extent to which he departs from some supposedly unproblematic and uncontested historical truth about the life of the Prophet. Rather, the task is to establish how Rushdie reworks the material he draws upon and to what purpose (p. 104). Through an acutely clarifying discussion of a passage from the 'Return to Jahilia' section of the novel, Mondal shows Rushdie to be guilty of erroneously showing qur'anic revelation to be excessively and fundamentally legalistic, when in fact Islamic jurisprudence only began some two hundred years after the death of the Prophet. Rushdie's historical departures involve a series of essentializing gestures which suggest that the Islamic religion, at the time of its origin, inaugurated the kind of totalitarian Islamic state envisaged by contemporary radical Islamists and embodied in the Islamic republic of Iran (p. 110). Such sweeping gestures not only deny fourteen hundred years of Islamic history but also disavow Rushdie's claim that the novel was meant to attack 'the narrower definition of Islam' as opposed to Islam as a whole. In fact, as Mondal notes drily, it is difficult to imagine an Islam that would meet with Rushdie's approval (p. 111). In a penetrating critique, Mondal charges *The Satanic Verses* with approaching its Islamic material as an Other in a manner reminiscent of medieval Christian and nineteenth-century orientalist discourses. Rushdie's exploration of faith, in his view, finally appears to subscribe to precisely the kinds of conceptual binarisms that the writer has so volubly challenged elsewhere in the name of the 'hybrid', the postmodern, and the postcolonial (p. 140).

Madeline Clements's *Writing Islam from a South Asian Muslim Perspective* undertakes a close, chapter-wise study of selected works of four writers, Salman Rushdie, Mohsin Hamid, Nadeem Aslam, and Kamila Shamsie, to explore a range of Muslim experiences of ordinary cosmopolitan contact, co-operation, and strife in a post–9/11 world (p. 34). In a conclusion that echoes Anshuman Mondal's critique of Rushdie reprised above, Clements makes a case for reading Rushdie's post-9/11 as part of a wave of 'new atheist' fiction evidently not equipped to do justice to the non-secular perspective, viewing Islam rigidly, as it does, as an embodiment of the irrationality, immorality, and violence of religion in general (p. 48). To the extent that *The Enchantress of Florence* [2008] gives greater credit to non-spiritual forms of enchantment, it may be seen as an altogether more philosophical work than *Shalimar the Clown* [2005]. Ultimately, however, both novels seem unable to engage seriously with feelings of affiliation and affinity that are experienced from *within* the spaces of religious faith. Rushdie's failure to see beneath the well-worn stereotypes of an orthodox, fundamentalist Islam, Clements argues, finally distinguishes his work from novels by a younger generation of Pakistani Muslim writers who by contrast are more successful in contesting monolithic perceptions of 'Muslims' in a polarizing world (p. 58). Amongst the new writers, Mohsin Hamid's fiction attempts to complicate the idea of South Asian Muslim affiliation by avoiding a commitment to any of the identities available to him, while Shamsie's novels repeatedly question the widespread tendency to pass judgement on others with whom we share this world on the basis of a partial view and a limited understanding of things. Together Hamid and Shamsie offer a nice contrast to Nadeem Aslam, whose novels strive to illuminate precisely those areas of darkness in the lives of his Pakistani and Afghan Muslim protagonists which Hamid's novels tend to occlude and which Shamsie's fiction shies away from judging (p. 87). Although Aslam appears to invite readers to consider how greater access to the secular, expressive, and faith-inflected arts—particularly local ones—could have helped troubled Muslims get back in touch with their humanity, his fiction finally shows these efforts to have failed to achieve their aim. Thus the attempts of characters like Marcus and Dunia to refine Casa using Sufi practices and Buddhist artefacts are shown to fail to make any impression on the unmovable Islamic subject (p. 121).

The subject of Aroosa Kanwal's critical gaze in *Rethinking Identities in Contemporary Pakistani Fiction: Beyond 9/11* is not just the national and international religious and political dimensions of extremism but also Anglo-American foreign policy in the Muslim world, whose operations are similarly seen to recall forms of terrorism. Kanwal is particularly interested in the ways in which three second-generation writers, Kamila Shamsie, Nadeem Aslam, and Uzma Aslam Khan, negotiate the identity crises resulting from current antagonisms towards Muslims and Islam, paying special attention to the struggles of Pakistani migrants with hyphenated identities (p. 2). Aslam Khan's fiction, especially her novels *Trespassing* [2003] and *The Geometry of God* [2008], is concerned with the phenomenon of Muslim stereotyping and the rhetoric of 'war on terror'. Rather than viewing 9/11 as the primary marker of Muslim identity formation, Khan recontextualizes the post-9/11 framing of Pakistani identities in terms of the increasing visibility and involvement of self-proclaimed Islamic terrorist organizations in sectarian conflicts within the subcontinent and the Middle East as also to the Islamization of Pakistan under the regime of Zia ul Haq (p. 73). Much like those of Aslam Khan, the novels of Kamila Shamsie—*Salt and Saffron* [2000], *Kartography* [2002], and *Burnt Shadows* [2009]—link the post-9/11 phenomenon of Islamophobia back to the rise of religious extremism during Zia's regime, and to US interventions in the region since the late 1970s, thereby underscoring the political and historical causes that lay behind the global stereotyping of Muslims and the discourse of 'war on terror' (p. 113). By contrast, in the work on Nadeem Aslam—*Maps for Lost Lovers* [2004], *The Wasted Vigil* [2008], and *The Blind Man's Garden* [2013]—Kanwal detects a problematic conflation of Islam and Islamic extremism which not only contributes to Islamophobic narratives but also risks overlooking US imperialistic ventures in the subcontinent and the Middle East. Finally, she contends, Aslam's work demonstrates a limited understanding of the Qur'an and Islam that undermines the validity of his critique of Islamic radicalism.

Authorial ignorance is clearly an issue for Kanwal, who holds Aslam to account for a form of ignorance that enables the author to cross the line between a critique of radical Islamists and a critique of Islamic faith. Kanwal here appears to share ground with Anshuman Mondal, for whom the strategic guise of an unreliable narrator does not finally excuse Rushdie's many sins of commission and omission. The ignorant and unreliable narrator, however, presents less of a dilemma for Areti Dragas when writing with reference to Rushdie's earlier, greatly celebrated but less controversial novel, *Midnight's Children*. In *The Return of the Storyteller in Contemporary Fiction* Dragas takes as her point of departure Walter Benjamin's claim that the birth of print culture has led to the silencing of the voice of the storyteller, at the same time as it has precipitated the rise of the author. Dragas's study identifies how the storyteller has been appropriated by contemporary writers not simply as a trope or figure within the novel, but as a more rebellious entity, one that challenges the dominant conceptualization surrounding the novelistic author, and calls for its re-evaluation. As a figure that traditionally represents communal rather than individual truths, the storyteller emerges defiantly as one who is capable of wearing all narrative masks and assuming all authorial positions: narrator, novelist, author. This capacity to shape-shift into various figures, all of whom insist on telling stories (as opposed to truths), invests the storyteller with the ability to bypass the authority and responsibility for the text that are normally viewed as being synonymous with the author (p. 2). The first two chapters of the book lay the theoretical grounds for reconceptualizing the storyteller in contemporary fiction, while the following six chapters explore how the figure of the storyteller makes a reappearance in the work of contemporary writers, including Jim Crace, Mario Vargas Llosa, John Barth, A.S. Byatt, J.M. Coetzee, and Salman Rushdie, whose three novels, *Midnight's Children*, *The Satanic Verses*, and *Haroun and the Sea of Stories* [1990] are the subject of chapter 5, 'The Oral Storyteller' (pp. 141–90). Rushdie's texts, the author argues, blur the line between *telling* stories and *writing* novels. The storyteller is the figure that shapes and drives the narrative voice of these novels, a voice which not only highlights the 'telling of stories', but also employs storytelling and story as a means of contesting other discourses which present themselves as bearing 'truth(s)'. All three texts juxtapose the grand narratives of science, history, divine history (revelation), and religion against little narratives or stories.

The critical frames of Rushdie's fiction continue to pose new and intriguing challenges for his readers, as is evident from Stuti Khanna's *The Contemporary Novel and the City: Re-conceiving National and Narrative Form*, a comparative study of Rushdie and James Joyce. Khanna adopts a postcolonial approach to examine a series of important themes that figure in the work of the two writers, including the status of the nation, nationalism, diaspora, conflicts over class, race, and ethnicity, and, not least, the meaning of art and the role of the artist in turbulent times. The city in the work of both Joyce and Rushdie functions importantly, she argues, as a critique of nationalist and neo-nationalist standpoints that valorize certain versions of tradition, the past, and by extension the rural as constituting the essential spirit of the nation (p. 40). By offering instead the dissonant, chaotic and impure realities of the city as components for a more adequate narrative of the post/colonial nation, the fictions of Joyce and Rushdie posit alternative, more inclusive ways of conceiving the nation and the national. At the same time though, what these texts demonstrate is the city's recalcitrance against any such co-option, its refusal to submit to the excisions and exclusions that underwrite nationalist agendas. The city, she suggests is posited not as a symbol of but as a model for the nation (p. 41). The linguistic energy of Joyce's and Rushdie's texts, Khanna argues, derives from the interaction of the acts of reading and writing with the modes in which the city itself speaks—shop signs, advertisement jingles, street slang, polyglot construction. Contesting scholarly positions that praise Rushdie for the authenticity of his pan-Indian argot or that castigate him for the inauthenticity of his language, Khanna contends that the language of Rushdie's novels cannot be seen outside its relationship to the city of Bombay, as it enacts the heterogeneities and contradictions of a Third World postcolonial metropolis (p. 83). Rushdie, she argues, deploys a particular linguistic register almost invariably throughout the landscape of his novels, especially the later ones. A real-life Aurora Zogoiby, for instance, would speak in one register with her servants, in quite another with her family, and in yet another with her socialite crowd. But Rushdie's writing style nowhere seems to recognize this linguistic elasticity, a move that allows him to homogenize a deeply fractured postcolonial landscape (p. 97). Khanna's insightful analysis is at its best in the chapter 'Artist's City, City's Artist'. Writing with reference to artist figures from three novels, *Midnight's Children*, *The Ground Beneath her Feet*, and *The Moor's Last Sigh*, Khanna argues that the artist's negotiation with the 'teeming' city of Bombay invariably and insistently takes the form of a confrontation with the crowd, an encounter that reveals the artists, for all the idealism associated with their persona, to be marked by their inherited class anxieties, in which fear and guilt remain prominent.

Rushdie is also one of the subjects of Sam Knowles's *Travel Writing and the Transnational Author*, a cross-generic study that also focuses on the travelogues of Michael Ondaatje, Vikram Seth, and Amitav Ghosh in order to establish the important role that the authors' travelogues play within their later work. Chapter 1 reads the travel memoir of the Canadian Sri Lankan author Michael Ondaatje, *Running in the Family* [1982], in tandem with his later novel, *Anil's Ghost*, to contest the critique of Ondaatje's memoir for its 'failure' to engage with the history of Sri Lanka. Knowles argues that Ondaatje's work is based on ideas of the importance of travel to a sense of self, which complicates easy binaries such as 'Canada/Sri Lanka', and in doing so it presents itself as transnational literature. This is enacted not only through the dependence of this writing on ideas of travel and movement but also in its deployment of narrative forms and strategies such as fragmentation, slippage, ellipses, and silence, to suggest not a lack of ethical responsibility so much as a critique of the 'linear grid of national affiliations' (pp. 28–30). Chapter 2 reads Vikram Seth's *Heaven Lake: Travels through Sinkiang and Tibet* [1983] alongside his novel *An Equal Music* [1999] to trace the ways in which Seth's travelogue itself exposes the limitations of the concept of performance, and moves towards the conclusion that his travel writing gestures towards the innate instability of artistic and literary performance. Chapter 3 turns to Amitav Ghosh's *In an Antique Land* [1993] to foreground a particular set of India–Egypt–Arabian sea relationships, which lay the textual groundwork for a back-and-forth traffic across the Bay of Bengal in *The Glass Palace* [2000], while the last chapter examines two of Rushdie's relatively neglected works, *The Jaguar Smile: A Nicaraguan Journey* [1987] and *Fury* [2001], the second published novel after the end of his fatwa-induced years in hiding, to show once again how the generic and formal features of the novel rely on his early work of travel writing (p. 154).

Pavan Kumar Malreddy's *Orientalism, Terrorism, Indigenism: South Asian Readings in Postcolonialism*, a collection of previously published essays on postcolonialism from a South Asian perspective, includes at least one chapter of relevance to readers of this section. In 'Cosmopolitanism Within: The Case of R.K. Narayan's Fictional Malgudi' (pp. 89–105) Malreddy strives to show how the fictional space of Narayan's Malgudi foregrounds the local as an active site of cultivating cosmopolitan ethics and experience. While it is great to see how Narayan's work continues to excite and engage new scholarship, the author's delicately ironic vision does not seem particularly well served by the heavy overlay of critical theory. From Hannerz to Harvey, Malreddy wheels in all the big guns of postcolonial and cosmopolitan theory, completely overwhelming the fictional world of Narayan that he purportedly sets out to examine. However, on the occasions when we do get to glimpse his analysis of this world, as in his discussion of the short story 'A Willing Slave' from *Malgudi Days*, the insights are well worth it.

### (b) Chapters in Edited Volumes

Ulka Anjaria's edited volume *A History of the Indian Novel in English* is a well-conceived collection of twenty-five short, incisive, and insightful essays that together seek to retell a familiar story from a series of new and varying perspectives. While the Indian English novel has mainly been periodized in terms of its emergence, its realist phase, followed by its modernist one, Anjaria's volume is more interested in what happens to the novel between and within these ostensibly distinct eras. The first fifteen chapters focus variously on the Indian novel's nineteenth-century beginnings, the rise of the nationalist novel, of which the 'progressive' and 'Gandhian' novels of Ahmed Ali, Mulk Raj Anand, and Raja Rao constituted a sub-genre, the legacy of Partition, the foregrounding of gender issues in the novels of Anita Desai and Shashi Deshpande, the Emergency novels of Nayantara Sahgal in addition to those by Rushdie and Mistry, and finally the meta-historical novels of Amitav Ghosh, Githa Hariharan, and M.G. Vassanji. Another five chapters are given over to examining the different forms of novel writing that have emerged over the last decade, including pulp fiction, 'chick lit', fantasy fiction, the graphic novel, and 'filmi lit' (or novels written with a film adaptation already in mind). Questions of linguistic experimentation and aesthetic innovation form the focus of another two chapters, while the remaining three are given over to elaborating variously on the violence of neoliberalism, the complicity between human rights discourse and the violence it is meant to condemn, and finally the question of caste in relation to the contemporary. Together these essays draw attention to how traditions not only develop but also intersect and interact and gain richness and meaning from contemporaneous trends and transhistorical forms, rather than only as revisions of their own past. Contesting a solely historical approach that can potentially reduce authors to being mouthpieces of their age, Anjaria emphasizes the need for scholars to pay attention to questions of genre, form, and aesthetics. This line of enquiry, as evidenced by many of the essays in Anjaria's volume, has far-reaching consequences for how we understand the contemporary novel, which cannot, as Anjaria cautions in her excellent introduction, be seen as a mere continuation of or development on the Rushdie generation.

Abigail Ward's edited collection of essays *Postcolonial Trauma: Memory, Narrative, Resistance* explores new possibilities for understanding a diversity of traumatic experiences, both personal and collective, from around the globe. One essay in particular, Alberto Fernandez Carbajal's 'From Colonial to Postcolonial Trauma: Rushdie, Forster and the Problem of Indian Communalism in *Midnight's Children* and *The Moor's Last Sigh*' (pp. 112–26), should be of special interest to readers of this section. The three novels discussed by Carbajal, namely E.M. Forster's *A Passage to India* [1924] and the two Rushdie novels referenced in the chapter title, are all concerned with foregrounding the significance of personal connections in challenging the divisive boundaries of race, faith, and education in colonial and postcolonial India. Forster's text invests a heroic degree of faith in the friendship between Aziz and Fielding, deeply nurtured as it is by the novel's homosocial structures. The bond between the two men, however, is finally undone by the pressures brought to bear upon it by the claims of the community, and their friendship is deferred until the end of the colonial subjugation of India. In response, Rushdie adopts the secularist, if troubled, political position of Forster's Dr Aziz and transforms it into the explicitly Nehruvian nationalist sentiments embodied by Dr Aadam Aziz. In Rushdie's text, the failed politics of friendship is recalibrated in order to interrogate not colonialism but communalism, characterized as the growing tension between Hindus and Muslims. The pessimism that attaches to the failure to connect across differences of race and faith, in colonial and postcolonial India, in *A Passage to India* and *Midnight's Children* scarcely gives way to greater hope in Rushdie's later work, namely *The Moor's Last Sigh* [1995], a novel that self-consciously charts in greater detail the legacy of Aadam Aziz's secularism turned into communalism. Finally, Carbajal argues, the deferral of political harmony in Rushdie's novels speaks to a liberal impasse and individual trauma not dissimilar to the one delineated by Forster.

*(c) Journals*

This was a year of contention when debates and discussions about the urgent issues of our time found their voice in numerous scholarly journals. In English studies focused on Indian and Sri Lankan literatures in international journals the preoccupying issues were the uneasy relations between democracy and resistance, the failures of neoliberalism, the multiple negotiations of gender, the poetics of urban spaces, the role and relevancy of aesthetics, speculative fiction, and a renewed interest in literary cultures. As well, respectful and fond tributes were recorded in memory of two eminent scholars in the field who died in 2014, Stuart Hall and Chelva Kanaganayakam.

The rise of another wave of authoritarian regimes in the early years of this decade and the hyper-masculine nationalism that accompanied this rightward lurch in the global political landscape were deliberated on in the scholarly journals surveyed. In *Sanglap*, Vineet Mehta's 'Hydrocarbon Genre: The Oil Encounter in Abdel Munif's *Cities of Salt* and Amitav Ghosh's *The Circle of Reason*' (*Sanglap* 1:i[2015] 170–9) points to the curious dearth of what Amitav Ghosh has termed 'petrofiction', or literary production in relation to the oil trade. Mehta argues that Ghosh's novel (like Munif's) anatomizes the encounter effected by oil extraction of capital, the Indigenous, and the migrant (who remains especially outside). Thus the narrative's subversiveness is focused through the viewpoint of the outcast.

In *Interventions*, Amit Baishya draws our attention to the ways in which sovereign power manifests itself through multiple modalities in the critical and contested geopolitical area of India's north-eastern region. In 'The Act of Watching with One's Own Eyes: "Strange Recognitions" in *An Outline of the Republic*' (*Interventions* 17:iv[2015] 603–20), he provides a brief discussion of Arupa Patangia Kalita's Assamese novel *Felanee*, but the focus of his work is a nuanced discussion of Siddhartha Deb's novel *An Outline of a Republic*. Baishya suggests that 'strange' recognitions facilitate not only an ethical metamorphosis as the narrator empathizes with the demands of the dispossessed but also an intertwined political metamorphosis as the narratives 'stage possibilities of alternative forms of ethical identification and political solidarity with supposedly "abjected" others' (p. 18). In 'Speech of the Nation and Conversations at the Margins of the Nation-State' (*Interventions* 17:v[2015] 669–85), Papori Bohra moves the discussion about the north-east to a focus on representation and voice at the margins of the postcolonial nation state where political dialogue is built upon a foundation of inequality. She locates her argument in the space between the categories of the postcolonial and the transnational, that is, between the Spivakian linking of representation and speech which points to the impossibility of the subaltern speaking due to the irretrievable loss of subject position, and the process of dialogue and solidarity enabled by the transnational.

Roger McNamara directs attention to discussions of the Anglo-Indians, another peripheral community within the Indian postcolonial nation state. In 'The Uneven Aesthetics of I. Allan Sealy's *The Trotter-Nama*: Secularization, Nationalism, and the Marginalization of the Anglo-Indian Community' (*PocoT* 10:ii[2015] 1–21), McNamara eschews the convention of discussing literature about minority communities through the lens of nationalism, and chooses instead to focus on the process of secularization in the text, in which the marginalized status of the Anglo-Indian community is viewed not as a result of nationalism, but as a consequence of the community's own choices in the reformulation of its identity.

The contestations of nationalism, and ruminations upon democracy and resistance, are broadened in 2015 into sustained critiques of neoliberalism, *Textual Practice* devoting a special issue to this subject, entitled 'Neoliberalism and the Novel'. Here a trenchant critique is levelled at neoliberalism, notably in 'The Betrayals of Neoliberalism in Shyam Selvadurai's *Funny Boy*' (*TPr* 29:ii[2015] 215–33), where Emily Davis dissects the ways in which deeply ingrained understandings of individual and group identity are perpetuated as well as produced by economic policy.

*Postcolonial Text* carries an altogether different reading of Selvadurai's novel, where the contestations of heteronormative masculinity playing out in South Asian nation states in 2014–15 resonate in the concerns of literary scholarship. Kaustav Bakshi draws attention to the potential for disruption within the genre of the English school story, as he focuses on 'The Best School of All' in '*Funny Boy* and the Pleasure of Breaking Rules: Bending Genre and Gender in "The Best School of All"' (*PocoT* 10:iii–iv[2015] 1–18). Bakshi notes that Selvadurai transfigures the overtly masculinist discourse that has come to be accepted in the genre of the school story, and infuses his narrative with the concerns of not just ethnic marginalization but sexual minoritization as well. Selvadurai's own privileged class position is noted in this reading, but despite this, Bakshi notes, 'Borrowing an established English genre and collapsing its "boundaries and limits" to narrate the reality of a queer Sri Lankan Tamil boy definitely has in it the political charge of the queer "empire writing back"' (p. 15).

In *Journal of Postcolonial Writing*, Sandeep Bakshi also engages with representations of same-sex male desire in Selvadurai's work, as well as in the work of Leslie de Noronha. In 'Past Matters: Queer Contestations of Colonial Masculinity in Leslie de Noronha's *The Dew Drop Inn* and Shyam Selvadurai's *Cinnamon Gardens*' (*JPW* 51:v[2015] 543–55), and following on from Leela Gandhi's work 'Loving Well: Homosexuality and Utopian Thought in Post/Colonial India' (in Ruth Vanita, ed., *Queering India: Same-Sex Love and Eroticism in Indian Culture and Society* [2002], pp. 87–99), he returns to the scene of the colonial encounter to argue that Selvadurai's and Noronha's examinations of same-sex male desire in an interracial context refigure Kipling's and Forster's tropes of interracial desire. He notes, 'My reading of Selvadurai's and Noronha's novels does not salvage the queer agency of the colonized South Asian subject. Instead, it asks whether connecting colonial histories to current homophobic laws in postcolonial South Asia can help dismantle hegemonic notions of heteronormative masculinity' (p. 553).

These concerns about gender were taken up through rich textual readings in numerous journals. In the *Journal of Postcolonial Writing*, Youngsuk Chae's 'Postcolonial Ecofeminism in Arundhati Roy's *The God of Small Things*' (*JPW* 51:v[2015] 519–30) examines the critique of particular patriarchal, economically rationalized exploitations of the environment in Roy's novel with a nuanced postcolonial and ecofeminist engagement with the text. The *Journal of Women's History* carries an article by Srirupa Prasad, 'Sanitizing the Domestic: Hygiene and Gender in Late Colonial Bengal' (*JWH* 27:iii[2015] 132–53), which analyses the work of Bhudeb Mukhopadhyay, Radha Gobinda Kar, and Saratkumari Chaudhurani, three famous writers and educators who wrote about health, hygiene, and domesticity in the late nineteenth and early twentieth centuries. Prasad also considers critically the classed and gendered concepts of 'cleanliness' and 'care', upon which discourses on hygiene pivoted during that period, as they continue to do today.

In *Postcolonial Text*, Teresa Hubel's passionately argued article, 'Dutiful Daughters (or not) and the Sins of the Fathers in Iqbalunnisa Hussain's

*Purdah and Polygamy*' (*PocoT* 10:ii[2015] 1–19) locates Hussain's work within an illustrious literary tradition of critique of patriarchal imperialism in the pre-independence years where male, upper-caste, Hindu writers were privileged. This is a tradition of women's writing, particularly Indian women with a Muslim cultural heritage, such as the illustrious line that includes Rashid Jahan, Ismat Chughtai, Rokeya Sakhawat Hossain, and Sakinatul Fatima Wazir Hasan, that has not been legitimized as iconically nor examined as prolifically as the work of Mulk Raj Anand, Raja Rao, and R.K. Narayan. As Hubel justly observes, 'Since India's nationalist ideal of secularism seems to be on the run from these new forms of religious fundamentalism, it is an appropriate moment to be reminded about the history of women's resistance to fundamentalism and their opposition to forms of communalism that would confine them and their daughters, sisters, and mothers within categories best conducive to patriarchal control and would seek to use them as justifications for violence' (p. 14).

The city and the idea of urbanity were decidedly of concern to literary scholarship in 2015. *Interventions* devoted a special issue to the idea of the postcolonial city—the taking apart, refashioning, and perpetuation of colonialism in urban spaces across the world. In an intriguing essay in this special issue, 'Seeing Double: Is Old Delhi Modern?' (*Interventions* 17:vi[2015] 814–25), Karl Mendonca reflects on the creation of a short film to think through the conditions of modernity in the postcolonial urban space that is Old Delhi. In so doing he usefully mobilizes Jyoti Hosagrahar's idea of 'indigenous modernity', and Ravi Sundaram's 'pirate modernity', alongside the Barthesian collapsing of the distance between writing and reading of a text.

Alex Tickell's wide-ranging interview with Manju Kapur in the *Journal of Postcolonial Writing* (*JPW* 51:iii[2015] 340–50) provides a nuanced picture of Kapur's writerly life. Elleke Boehmer and Dominic Davies, in 'Literature, Planning and Infrastructure: Investigating the Southern City through Postcolonial Texts' (*JPW* 51:iv[2015] 395–409), place (among other texts) Manju Kapur's novel *Home* [2006] in conversation with Rana Dasgupta's non-fiction tome *Capital: A Portrait of Twenty-First-Century Delhi* [2014]. In doing so they compellingly argue that the mappings of urban spaces in literary texts do not merely represent urban space but can interrogate and reconstruct the fluid relationship between the organization of public space, urban planning, other forms of human intervention, and 'planned violence', and that they 'plot resilient conceptual pathways for the reader through, around and beyond the city's delimitations' (p. 396).

Shifting the focus to the urbanscape of the city of Bombay/Mumbai, Emma Bird, '*Beautiful Thing*: Literary Reportage and Bombay' (*JPW* 51:iv[2015] 380–94), productively juxtaposes the rendering of this city in the work of Sonia Faleiro's *Beautiful Thing* [2010] which, she suggests, draws from as it interrogates the popular view of the city as a site of hyper-real cosmopolitanism, against Suketu Mehta's *Maximum City* [2004] a gendered picture of this metropole.

*Postcolonial Text* also nods at the interrogation of aspects of urbanity through the work of Rajender Kaur, who examines the effects of Partition in

'Lamenting a Lost Cultural Imaginary: Lahore and Amritsar in Manju Kapur's *Difficult Daughters*' (*PocoT* 10:iii–iv[2015] 1–21).

Debjani Ganguly's introduction, as guest editor, to the special issue of *South Asia*, 'The Subaltern after Subaltern Studies: Genealogies and Transformation' (*SA* 38:i[2015] 1–9), serves as a lively and useful map not only of the special issue, but especially of the intellectual trajectory of the project of subaltern studies, of its founders, and of the fecund transformations it continues to enable across English studies as well as other scholarly fields, over thirty years after the publication of the first volume of *Subaltern Studies*. In the erudite and elegant essay, '"Ye Haath Mujhe De Dey, Thakur!"': The Dacoit, the Insurgent and the Long Arm of the Law' (*SA* 38:i[2015] 84–99) Mridula Nath Chakraborty applies her formidable expertise as a literary scholar to a sparkling discussion of three 'dacoit' characters from Bombay cinema, to suggest that the 'dacoit' as a particular representation of the subaltern cannot be confined 'within its institutional framework' (p. 86). She suggests that the 'dacoit' 'is interpellated by, and yet cannot be contained by, the strictures of "modern" law in a newly-independent post-colonial state. . . . Thus, Bombay cinema continues to rely on the subaltern as idea and concept in order to map the tension between a nationalist/statist history and a narrative of rebellion and resistance from below, particularly in caste terms' (p. 84). Chakraborty's examination of the cinematic figure of the dacoit may be usefully read alongside Charu Gupta's essay, 'Embodying Resistance: Representing Dalits in Colonial India' in the same issue (*SA* 38:i[2015] 100–18), where Gupta notes a sense of embodied resistance in the self-representation of Dalits in colonial Hindi literature. Also of interest here is Pietro Deandrea's 'The Spectralized Camp: Cultural Representations of British New Slaveries' (*Interventions* 17:iv[2015] 488–502), which mobilizes both postcolonial studies and Holocaust studies to reflect on the tropes of the ghost and the concentration camp present within the new forms of slavery associated with large-scale global migrations, a critical discussion which suggests useful resonances with Simon During's reflections on the 'precariat' in 'Choosing Precarity' (*SA* 38:i[2015] 19–38).

Gayatri Chakravorty Spivak pays eloquent tribute to the memory of Stuart Hall in 'From the Last Dancer' (*CulC* 89[2015] 129–35), as does Homi Bhabha in the long essay '"The beginning of their real enunciation": Stuart Hall and the Work of Culture' (*CritI* 42 [2015] 1–30).

With characteristic clarity, Bill Ashcroft turns his attention to the vexed relationship between postcolonial theory and aesthetics in his essay, 'Towards a Postcolonial Aesthetics' (*JPW* 51:iv[2015] 410–21). He suggests, right at the start, that a discrete 'postcolonial aesthetic' is an unlikely category, noting two very different definitions of aesthetics: one as cultural ideology with its attendant hegemonic, racialized, classed, and colonized exclusions, and the other as the much more fecund function of reception in which the aesthetic object calls forth a perception of values which give consideration to the nature and the context of the aesthetic encounter, rather than any inherent, absolute, or fixed value that is ideologically determined by the dominant group. Drawing attention to the materiality of language, Ashcroft suggests that the aesthetic is 'a feature of both the production and consumption of the text' (p.

415) and thus 'a form of engagement, of act and response, opening a space for continual transformation' (p. 417). It is this sense of there always being something more with every encounter with the text, its 'material resonance' (p. 420), that Ashcroft productively suggests as 'a path towards a postcolonial aesthetics' (p. 420).

In the same issue, Neetu Khanna's 'Poetics of Progressive Feeling: The Visceral Aesthetics of Mulk Raj Anand' (*JPW* 51:iv[2015] 449–61) examines Anand's best-known novel, *Untouchable* [1940], in conjunction with his less well-known short story 'Lament on a Death of a Master of Arts' [1938]. Khanna argues for the value of the term 'progressive' in relation to Anand's texts and his work with the All-India Progressive Writers' Association during the process of decolonization, asserting that it 'brings [in]to focus their dynamic aesthetic grapplings with revolutionary feeling and the revolution of feelings: "the critical spirit", defined against the forces of complicity that sustain the visceral logics of empire' (p. 459).

Neil ten Kortenaar pays respect to Chelva Kanaganayakam in an inventive essay on Michael Ondaatje, ' "Touching them into words": Running with Michael Ondaatje among the Dead' (*UTQ* 84:iv[2015] 15–28). *Postcolonial Text* devotes a special issue to the memory of the esteemed Tamil Canadian author, academic, and translator. Most notably, Vasugi Kailasam continues the conversation about the aesthetics of postcolonial writing in 'Notes on a Postcolonial Sri Lankan Tamil Diasporic Aesthetic: Reading Cheran Rudhramoorthy's Poetry' (*PocoT* 10:iii–iv[2015] 1–18). Following the formulation suggested by Kanaganayakam, Kailasam thinks through the ways in which the literary history of Sri Lankan Tamil literature created out of the civil conflict may be illuminated by literary form. Kailasam examines the work of Cheran Rudhramoorthy through this lens, arguing that Cheran's poetic work 'underscores an important dimension of postcolonial diasporic writing shaped by conflict, in which aesthetic form itself, when read as being migratory, opens rich possibilities. It illustrates that Sri Lankan Tamil diasporic writing, when read as a prototype of a literary aesthetic shaped by displacement, stands as both product and critique of a postcolonial, migratory world' (p. 14).

In their introduction to the speculative, fiction-focused issue of *Sanglap*, Sourit Bhattacharya and Arka Chattopadhyay home in on the conjectural aspects of speculation in fiction, an area of scholarship within English studies that is gaining currency (*Sanglap* 2:i[2015] 1–24). Writing within the speculative fiction sub-genre of future-war fiction, Dibyadyuti Roy's article 'Of Men, Machines and Apocalypses: Masculine Anxieties in Indian Speculative Fiction' (*Sanglap* 2:i[2015] 50–71) is an examination of the apocalyptic settings in Sami Ahmad Khan's speculative novel *Red Jihaad* [2012] and M.V. Ramana's speculative commentary *Bombing Bombay? Effects of Nuclear Weapons and a Case Study of a Hypothetical Explosion* [1999]. Roy argues that the terrain upon which these texts unfold, the catastrophic bombings of the urban centres of Mumbai and Lahore, 'provide a topos for enacting postcolonial masculine anxieties, which are subsequently countered through making male bodies contingent on the volatile performances of destructive military technology' (p. 51).

The illuminating discussions in the essays on print culture in South Asia in *Modern Asian Studies* in 2014 found new voices again in 2015, in *MAS* as well as in other journals. In 'Print, Religion, and Canon in Colonial India: The Publication of Ramalinga Adigal's *Tiruvarutpa*' (*MAS* 49:iii[2015] 650–77), Richard Weiss notes the importance that Ramalinga and his disciples accorded not just to the religious content but also to the materiality of the printed object, the medium in which the text is made accessible to the reader/audience and to how this focus on the material aspects of print perpetuated ideas of authority and legitimacy in relation to the religious canon in the Shaiva tradition. In *South Asia* Francesca Orsini's 'Booklets and Sants: Religious Publics and Literary History' (*SA* 38:iii[2015] 435–49) turns our attention to the Belvedere Press, Allahabad, and its publishing of sant orature (*bani*), particularly the *Santbani Pustakmala*. Orsini meticulously maps the trajectory of this project in relation to an early twentieth-century religious-devotional north Indian public. In *Cultural Sociology*, Roanna Gonsalves' ethnographic account of contemporary Indian literary cultures, 'The Survival of the Friendliest: Contemporary Indian Publishing in English at the Frankfurt Book Fair' (*CultSoc* 9:iii[2015] 425–46) mobilizes Bourdieu-based theoretical framework to examine some of the strategies used by the gatekeepers of contemporary Indian publishing in English at an international literary marketplace.

The customary annual nod to Salman Rushdie in the field of English studies finds an interesting form in the pages of *Marvels and Tales* by way of Meenakshi Bharat's essay 'Creative Fear in Salman Rushdie's *Haroun* and *Luka*: The "Safe House" of Children's Literature' (*M&T* 29:ii[2015] 304–23). Bharat tackles the ongoing concern with fear in Salman Rushdie's books written for children and dedicated to his own children, *Haroun and the Sea of Stories* [1990] and *Luka and the Fire of Life* [2010]. Locating the texts within the tradition of the fairytale and the cautionary narrative, Bharat shows 'how the particular choice of writing for children is both a means of examining these fears and the identification of a safe house for creativity' (p. 304).

There were cogent and lucid discussions presented in the pages of *IACLALS* (journal of the Indian Association for Commonwealth Language and Literature Studies). The gap in knowledge between disability theory and postcolonial theory is bridged persuasively by Someshwar Sati in 'Towards Abling Postcolonial Discourse: Revising the Field from a Disability Perspective' (*IACLALS* 1[2015] 153–64). Critiquing the glaring occlusions of and derogatory references to disability in speeches made by Indian nationalist leaders, and through an incisive reading of Megan Mylan's *Smile Pinki*, Sati powerfully concludes with a call to a political strategy in response to the current dominant homogenizing/fetishizing discourse around disability, 'to withstand the totalizing and therefore despotic tendencies of hegemonizing ideological structures. This can be only achieved through reemphasizing "difference" and "marginality" as the basis to our individuality' (p. 163).

Jaydeep Sarangi's 'Conversation with Jatin Bala: An Account of Refugee Dalit Life' (*IACLALS* 1[2015] 50–9) is an account of the Bengali author Jatin Bala's life in refugee camps and his encounters with the stratifications of society. In 'Invisible People/Citizens: Re-engaging with Hijras in India'

(*IACLALS* 1[2015] 124–36), an essay that tackles a subject of crucial import, Shaweta Nanda looks at 'how hijra discourses force us to revise our understanding of family, sexuality, identity, and citizenship that is marked not only by series of rejections, refusals, oppression and humiliation, but also by resistance, recreation and re-envisioning of the past and future' (p. 124).

In a nuanced reading of O.V. Vijayan's *The Legends of Khasak*, 'Civilization and Its Malcontents: Reading Novel Nomadic Spaces' (*IACLALS* 1[2015] 31–8), Sandhya Devesan Nambiar works with Rosi Braidotti's notions of the nomadic subject contingent upon Deleuze's conceptualization of nomadology. Nambiar examines nomadic consciousness as a way in which resistance may take place, in both the political as well as the literary sense, in the work of Vijayan. As she observes, 'Towards the end, the novel abandons the project of achieving a totalized unified meaning. Human agency fails Ravi, and the state of alterity that he is striving towards ultimately collapses into becoming the absolute other—the post-human, through death' before the closing image of 'man becoming nature' (p. 37).

## 6. New Zealand and Pacific

There were fewer works in New Zealand and Pacific studies in 2015 than in previous years, although critics have covered a wider range of modern and contemporary writers in their articles. The major canonical figures, in particular Janet Frame and Katherine Mansfield, continue to be the focus of much critical work, but a developing, and pleasing, diversity of Māori and Indigenous literary subjects counteract the dangers of monocultural cultivation techniques in the fields of literary studies. Two anniversaries—ten years since Janet Frame's death in 2014, and the ongoing commemorations of the First World War—structured critical reflections in special journal issues of the *Journal of New Zealand Literature* and the *Journal of Postcolonial Writing*.

'Janet Frame has just had her second most prolific decade in a career going back to the 1950s' (p. 67). So claims David Callahan in his 'Other Countries and the Terrain of Representation in *The Adaptable Man*' (*JNZL* 33[2015] 67–84). This must, he continues, 'be considered a healthy rate [of publication] for someone who has been dead ten years' (p. 67). A slew of publications this year marks the decade since Frame's death, and indicates also—in their focus on her work and its literary allusions over more well-worn biographical claims—the continuing vitality of Frame studies, not to say industry. Callahan's own contribution he describes as a 'partial illumination' (p. 81), tracing images of 'mobilization' (p. 68) in *The Adaptable Man*—other countries, postage stamps, aeroplanes—in order to follow some of the ways the text deploys these tropes to 'do duty as explorations of ways in which representation is always already indirect, asking us to reflect upon what this might mean without ever telling us what exactly to conclude' (p. 69). Callahan's illuminations are partial, he suggests, because the text's richly ambiguous complexity ought not to be reduced to a lock waiting for one correct interpretative key. Taking a similar approach, Manon-Lili Morand's 'Fiction and Freedom: Janet Frame's Commitment' (*CE&S* 38:i[2015] 21–31) treats the 'puzzling' (p. 21) qualities of Frame's work as central to her aesthetic achievement and not as dilemmas in need of resolution. Like Callahan, Morand stresses the importance of Frame's posthumous publications, finding *Towards Another Summer* [2007] 'a keystone to her whole corpus and its wide network of echoes' (p. 22). Frame's 'commitment', for Morand, is to writing as a form of freedom and imaginative movement in a 'poetics of expression' (p. 22). The discussion tends towards summary and description over analysis, but there are insights stacked in the essay for its careful readers. Combining critical commentary with notes on how Frame can be deployed in the literature classroom, Josie McQuail's '"How can Life be still?": Teaching Janet Frame's *A State of Siege* and Virginia Woolf's *To the Lighthouse*' (*Antipodes* 29:i[2015] 57–70) displays the multi-faceted political-literary achievements of Frame's novel, although her decision to position this comparison, following journalist Naomi Wolf, as one between 'the "victim feminism" of Frame' and 'the "power feminism" of Woolf' (p. 69) is unfortunate and limiting.

Janet Wilson introduces a special issue of the *Journal of Postcolonial Writing* on 'Janet Frame: Ten Years On' by noting the particular fascination Frame's posthumous publications have for critics currently, and by seeing in these publications the suggestion 'that some more comprehensive reassessment of Frame's oeuvre is desirable' (*JPW* 51:v[2015] 574–8). The essays she gathers together—two of which were first presented as papers to a colloquium on Frame 'ten years on' hosted by the New Zealand Studies Network at Birkbeck, University of London, in November 2013—all develop critical accounts of the posthumous fiction self-consciously turning away from earlier biographical models. Alice Braun's '*In the Memorial Room*: The Conditions of Being a Writer' (*JPW* 51:v[2015] 591–602) pursues two interconnected arguments. She reads *In the Memorial Room* [2013] as 'a blueprint for *Living in the Maniototo*' (p. 592), not just in its anticipation of the later novel's themes—*Living in the Maniototo* was published just five years after *In the Memorial's Room*'s composition—but also in the ways in which the earlier novel is 'metafictionally embedded' (p. 592) in the later. This textual argument is then used to make the case that '*In the Memorial Room* deconstructs the discourse built around what an artist should be' (p. 594), exulting in the 'disappearance' (p. 594) of the author from the world of the story alongside the aesthetic disappearance of the author from Frame's own texts. Nuanced and measured, Braun's argument shows the distance between current readings and the biographical approaches that were once dominant. Andreia Sarabando's '"The dreadful mass neighbourhood of objects" in the Fiction of Janet Frame' (*JPW* 51:v[2015] 603–14) concentrates on novels from Frame's astonishingly productive mid-career period, and reads them with Bill Brown's 'thing theory' in mind to trace the 'encounters with everyday objects' (p. 604) represented in these fictions. Sarabando pays attention to what she calls Frame's sense of 'the contingency of things' (p. 605) and how, in the novels, characters invest, or attempt to invest, objects with meaning, and her reading of the treatment of chairs, household objects, and sanitary napkins in Frame novels reveals 'an ontological vertigo in which everything can be connected, but in which no connection is inevitable' (p. 613), destabilizing and energizing Frame's art. Pursuing similar themes of disappearance and the aesthetic and personal attractions of invisibility, Marc Delrez, in his 'Embarrassment in the Posthumous Fiction of Janet Frame' (*JPW* 51:v[2015] 579–90), follows blushes, moments of shame, and personal discomfort in the posthumous fiction back into better-known earlier works, suggesting that the posthumous novels 'provide an extension of the corpus apt to modify the overall architecture of the oeuvre' (p. 579).

Other contributions for this year have been more uneven. Cindy Gabrielle asks her readers, in *The Unharnessed World: Janet Frame and Buddhist Thought*, to follow her 'in the meanders of a Buddhist exploration of Frame's oeuvre' (pp. 18–19). This is a maddeningly meandering text, and one studded with strange asides: because of 'the negative reputation of Buddhism in the rational West, gesturing towards the East is always a bold move' (p. x). Gabrielle's own gestures are energetic and imprecise, but point at enough biographical and textual information for the text to serve its own purpose well. Her opening suggestion that critics have passed over Frame's own intellectual interests, including in Buddhism, in favour of more familiarly citable academic sources such as Heidegger is well made. Continuing biographical approaches of earlier critical periods, Annette M. Krizanich's 'The Pen is Mightier than the Dominant Discourse' (*ILStud* 17:iii[2015] 396–425) treats Frame's *Faces in the Water* as an example of 'scriptotherapy', or writing as healing, documenting the experience of institutionalization in order to resist its effects.

The only real rival to Frame's popularity in contemporary criticism is Katherine Mansfield, and the critical industry around her work continues at its hectic pace. There have been two great waves of Katherine Mansfield textual scholarship. The first, John Middleton Murry's energetic, dubious, and financially lucrative clip through the archives, set the popular and critical view of Mansfield for the inter- and post-war periods. Then Vincent O'Sullivan and Margaret Scott's edition of the letters [1984–2008] crashed on the shore, washing Middleton Murry's detritus in its wake. A third tidal movement seems to be under way with the Edinburgh University Press collected works project, a related publication of which is Anna Plumridge's edition of *The Urewera Notebook*. Plumridge and Edinburgh have done scholars in New Zealand literary studies a great service with this fine new edition. Plumridge provides thorough general-contextual (pp. 1–22) and textual (pp. 23–42) introductions, and provides clear accounts of how her approach differs from previous editors Middleton Murry, Ian A. Gordon, and Margaret Scott. After all this, the *Notebook* itself (pp. 87–112) seems rather slight, but this new edition renders it usefully accessible to critics. Of particular interest for literary critics is Plumridge's dissection of the critical assumptions informing earlier editions: her own becomes something of a history of Mansfield's New Zealand reception. After years of condescension and neglect, Mansfield is now seen—as evidenced by the frequent scholarly publications on her work, the existence of the Mansfield *Yearbook* and Society, and the presence of her work in discussions of others writers—as a significant figure in global anglophone modernism. Critical work on Mansfield is thus discussed in Chapter XV of this volume of *YWES*. This section provides details on criticism with a specifically New Zealand application. Sarah Ailwood and Melinda Harvey's collection *Katherine Mansfield and Literary Influence* is particularly welcome for its emphasis on literary rather than biographical analysis, and a chapter from Janet Wilson is of special interest to students of New Zealand literature. In 'The "Burden" of the Feminine: Frank Sargeson's Encounter with Katherine Mansfield' (pp. 207–18) Wilson makes the case for Mansfield's influence on Sargeson by way of a close reading of the latter's 'A Man and his Wife' [1939]. The results are satisfyingly provocative. The liveliest contribution this year is Simon During's 'Mansfield's World' (*JNZL* 33[2015] 33–66), an argument, via contextualizing accounts of Mansfield and the Beauchamp family's social position in shifting British and New Zealand economics and politics, and of Murry and Mansfield's intellectual work, that 'her project was simultaneously creative and philosophical, and that flows between her imaginative writing and a criticism out of British idealism enabled her to make literary worlds' (p. 59). Mansfield's is 'world literature' for During in the ways in which her stories create or shape worlds: 'she writes self-contained stories that communicate a coherent experience by virtue of their concreteness' (p. 34). His division of her important stories into three sub-genres—'switch' stories, 'brutal' stories, and anti-nostalgic 'childhood reminiscences' (pp. 40–1)—is nicely re-energizing, as is his overall irreverence towards Mansfield, a writer, in this account, important because of, and not despite, her aesthetic-aristocratic anti-democratic project.

The most exciting work in Indigenous studies these last years has been transnational in focus, stressing inter-Indigenous connections and boundary-crossing imaginative voyages in Oceania's 'sea of islands' over the more familiar settler–indigene encounter. Jeffrey Carroll, Brandy Nālani, and Georganne Nordstrom continue this new work with their edited collection *Huihui: Navigating Art and Literature in the Pacific*, the 'first work to be devoted entirely to the aesthetics and rhetorics of Oceania' (p. 4). Three chapters in particular stand out. Selina Tusitala Marsh's 'Un/Civilized Girls, Unruly Poems: Jully Makini (Solomon Islands)' (pp. 46–62) offers a richly detailed, attentive, and appreciative reading of two poems by Makini, the first, and to date only, Solomon Islands woman to have published sole-authored poetry collections. Marsh subjects each line of 'Civilized Girl' [1981] and 'Roviana Girl' [1986] to careful attention, her close reading itself offering an implicit rebuke to wider critical neglect of this poet. Hers is not a purely critical exercise, however, and this neo-formalist approach elaborates the ways in which Makini's poems depart 'from the popular oppositional politics of the 1970s, which romanticized Indigenous traditions and vilified the colonizing West' (p. 49) in favour of a more politically and aesthetically complex Indigenous feminism, alive to both the patriarchal and colonial pressures shaping women's writing and experience. Taking issue with reductive critical approaches that have treated Apirana Taylor's 'Sad Joke on a Marae' [1979] as nothing more than a lament for a lost and irrecoverable culture, Alice Te Punga Somerville's chapter, 'Nau mai, hoki mai: Approaching the Ancestral House' (pp. 71–88), begins with an account of the 'productively ambiguous' (p. 75) treatment of dispossession and dislocation in Taylor's poem. Māori aesthetic forms, Te Punga Somerville suggests, 'are not mere signs of Māoriness, but are active participants in a complex intergenerational negotiation of homecoming and connection' (p. 71). In similar ways, therefore, poems representing ancestral houses 'do not merely describe homecoming but produce it' (p. 86). Writing becomes, in new ways, an ancestral house of its own. Finally, Steven Gin's 'Adventures in Chronicling: the Relational Web of Albert Wendt's *The Adventures of Vela*' (pp. 283–97) uses the metaphor of a 'relational web' (p. 295) to explore Wendt's genre-defying, form-shifting epic. Impatient with the classificatory divisions of Eurocentric aesthetic theory, *Huihui* illustrates its own claims by including poetry, fiction, and creative writing, from Albert Wendt, Michael Puleloa, and Steven Winduo among others, as well as these literary-critical chapters.

David O'Donnell's brisk survey 'Staging Modernity in the New Oceania: Modernism in Australian, New Zealand and Pacific Islands Theatre' (in Ross and Lindgren, eds., *The Modernist World*, pp. 282–92), pays particular attention to Māori and Pasifika playwrights, many of them prolific and celebrated authors still under-discussed by theatre scholars. O'Donnell's organizing conceit—that 'modernism' in the New Zealand and Pacific context was as often inspired by realist theatre forms as by anti-representational Western avant-gardes—makes for a useful fusion of survey and argument. 'Hinenuitepo begins as a dread goddess yet ends as a Great Mother' (p. 97): this is the central claim of Simon Perris's 'Witi Ihimaera and the Dread Goddess' (*JNZL* 33[2015] 85–109), and he establishes his case through careful reconstruction of Ihimaera's revisions of his early career novels. Taking Ihimaera's revisions as a 'rewriting project' (p. 86) involving its own aesthetic and political aims, Perris sees the novelist's 'long-term, on-again, off-again relationship' (p. 100) with the goddess as 'unique' in Māori literature. Tracing his revisions, then, tells us much, and not only about his own aesthetics. The shifting representations of the 'Great Mother' reveal the impact of shifts in scholarship, Māori politics, and feminist and postcolonial criticism as Ihimaera's narrators' descriptions of 'an archetypal...maternal, female deity present in Māori, Greco-Roman, and Near Eastern traditions' are rewritten by later passages which 'develop, revise, and even correct the image built up in earlier passages' (p. 88). There are two brief but fecund and suggestive readings of Patricia Grace and Keri Hulme in Ato Quayson's *Cambridge Companion to the Postcolonial Novel*. Clare Barker's chapter, 'Disability and the Postcolonial Novel' (pp. 99–115), notes the varied ways in which critics have treated the child Simon Gillayley in Keri Hulme's *The Bone People* in 'symbolic terms' (p. 109) as either Christ-like sacrificial figure, Maui-like trickster, or sacrifice. Without discounting this work, Barker encourages critics to note also how 'the novel has a lot to say about Simon's *experiences* as a disabled child' (p. 109); the novel, in classic realist terms, produces information about its social world. Demonstrating a similar openness to the ongoing creative and critical possibilities of the realist tradition, Anthony Carrigan's 'Nature, Ecocriticism, and the Postcolonial Novel' (pp. 81–98) shows the ways in which postcolonial novelists have been 'motivated by a refusal to treat the nonhuman world as passive "setting" or backdrop in literary texts' (p. 82). This ambition has involved, Carrigan suggests, 'not simply rejecting but also building on the legacies of social realism, which in its canonical form is by no means divorced from broader ecological and economics processes' (p. 83). His inventive treatment of Patricia Grace's *Potiki* and *Dogside Story* illustrates the point well. Both novels 'grapple' with the impact of the 'ambivalent industry' (p. 89) of tourism in Māori communities, a source of both economic advance and environmental degradation. Grace's achievement, in Carrigan's reading, is to do with her stories, and the skill with which she explores the complex and multifaceted political dimensions to community responses to development, and a result of her formal agility. 'Grace's innovative use of the novel', he suggests, 'functions as a correlative to the process of cultural adaptation she depicts with respect to tourism and environmental agency' (p. 90). The realist novel, a European form, is, in Grace's masterful hands, bent and adapted to Indigenous ends; her 'adaptive approach to...the novel form' (p. 90) thus contains within it suggestions for Indigenous political strategy.

Ihimaera, Hulme, and Grace are of course major figures in anglophone world literature, and these chapters as well as Perris's article are welcome additions to the critical body of work studying this fiction. It can sometimes feel, however, when reading critical articles, as if these three were the only important Māori writers active today. There has in fact been a decade of new voices producing important work for critics to contend with, and Justine Seran's 'Photography's Long Shadow: Ekphrasis and Maori Literature' (*JPW* 51:iv[2015] 436–48) is therefore particularly welcome. Seran explores the place of painting and photography in Paula Morris's *Rangatira* [2011] and Kelly Ana Morey's *Bloom* [2003], both as a way of thinking about the ambiguous presence of photographic representation in Indigenous people's imaginations—symbol as it so often is of colonial control as much as memory or family history—as well as the wider aesthetic challenges the verbal representation of visual representation poses to narrative. Morris's is a historical novel, and Morey's is set in contemporary Aotearoa/New Zealand, but both use ekphrasis as a device to affirm 'self-representation and the rejection of representations by non-Indigenous outsiders' (p. 437). Seran's is a satisfying account of two important contemporary novels.

The varied offerings around nineteenth-century and colonial literatures reinforce my sense from previous years that this remains the site of the most adventurous scholarship in New Zealand literary studies. J.E. Traue's 'Submerged Below the Codex Line: New Zealand's Neglected Nineteenth Century Serial Novels' (*JNZS* 20[2015] 2–9) reveals the surprising number of novels published only in serial form during the nineteenth century. 'A number of hitherto unrecognised novelists will need to be admitted to the literary pantheon' (p. 7), he concludes, and his article mixes bibliographical documentation with critical reflections on how considering these serially published works might shift our view of literary history. Pursuing a similarly intellectually sharp but methodologically 'blurry' interdisciplinary approach, Helen Bones's ' "A book is a book, all the world over": New Zealand and the Colonial Writing World 1890–1945' (*JICH* 43:v[2015] 861–81) usefully straddles book history and literary history in order to unsettle some dominant assumptions about the literature of the colonial and cultural nationalist period. Eileen Duggan, despite never leaving New Zealand, enjoyed a decades-long and very successful literary career. What might this tell us, Bones wonders, about some of the myths of cultural nationalism about the colonial period? Duggan's story is 'not so unusual' (p. 863), Bones suggests, but other successful literary careers 'have been obscured by the centrality of "the nation" to New Zealand literary criticism' (p. 863). Placing New Zealand authors' publishing practices, with prose works in particular, as part of a 'British world system' (p. 865), Bones's quantitative and historical work shows how much author-driven myth-making has passed into the historical-critical record unchallenged. Drawing on many years' reflecting and writing about W.E. Maning and *Old New Zealand*, Alex Calder's chatty and free-wheeling 'Accounting for Pakeha: Value and Cross-Cultural Exchange in *Old New Zealand*' (*JNZL* 33[2015] 1–32) makes the case for a 'fundamental instability' (p. 18) in Maning's humour. Neither an objective ethnological record nor simply a racist screed, *Old New Zealand*'s literary qualities, 'rather than closing down indigenous perspectives' (p. 15) manage to open them up. The book, Calder argues, 'presents a more perceptive view' (p. 15) of the early years of settlement than its own author may have intended.

The centenary years of the First World War continue their lumbering roll, publishing programmes, books, and features spilling from each one along the way. The results, for literary studies, have so far been disappointing. Rod Edmond and Janet Wilson's special issue of the *Journal of New Zealand Literature* on 'New Zealand and the First World War' (*JNZL* 32:ii[2015]) is concerned mainly with music, history, and memory studies, but does contain two notable pieces on literary themes. Murray Edmond's ' "Whatiwhati taku pene": Three First World War Poems from *The Penguin Book of New Zealand Verse*' (*JNZL* 32:ii[2015] 38–49) takes up the opportunity presented by Ian Wedde and Harvey McQueen's bi-cultural organization of their *Penguin Book of New Zealand Verse* [1985], one surprisingly under-utilized by scholars thus far, to unsettle the idea that there is a 'remarkable silence about an event that is often referred to as nation-forming' (p. 38) in New Zealand poetry. When Katherine Mansfield's sonnet on the death of her brother is read alongside Māori-language *waiata* by Paraire Henare Tomoana and Te Puea Herangi, a very different sense of the war's presence in the literatures of New Zealand emerges. Edmond's essay is written in a relaxed, discursive style but carries considerable scholarly force. Perhaps the literary history of the First World War will never be written: like Lytton Strachey's Victorian Age, 'we know too much about it'. This, at any rate, is the conceit Harry Ricketts toys with in 'Fear's Head Hid in Joke: Donald H. Lea and Alfred Clark, Two New Zealand First World War Poets' (*JNZL* 32:ii[2015] 50–71). Starting with an overview of the familiar and much-anthologized world of the 'war poets', Ricketts suggests that 'to see and read poets like' Lea and Clark 'we need somehow to go behind, to get backstage of, the now mythically powerful idea of the First World War as a theatre of pathetic curiosity and regard' (p. 54). Neither poet is as 'great' as Owen or Sassoon, but what of it? Poetry is not a competition. Both writers' curious lives and styles made them unsuitable for the canonizing work which would go on in New Zealand literature following the cultural nationalists, and their periodical publishing practices further facilitated this neglect. Rediscovering Lea and Clark as British migrants writing comfortably in a range of registers, including Scots and Cockney, adds nuance to our accounts of twentieth-century literature produced in New Zealand. One hopes Ricketts's discoveries are followed up by other researchers. His article adds to the critical sense that the literature of 'Maoriland' persisted much later in the twentieth century than has previously been acknowledged, and his subjects' use of Scots in their poetry in particular gives weight to recent work around non- or anti-modernist poetics being practised in the inter-war years. Ricketts, although he does not pursue these arguments himself, sets up further readings to come.

A rattle-bag of general and miscellaneous articles and books to round up the year's work. Picking up a sentence-long paragraph from *Man Alone*, Heidi Thomson's 'Poets Had Moved in this Country Once: John Mulgan and Romantic Poetry' (*JNZS* 21[2015] 13–18) finds affinities to the world views and work of William Cowper, John Clare, and Lord Byron in Mulgan's novel and his letters. Igor Maver's 'War and Race in C.K. Stead's *Talking About O'Dwyer*' (*JLLC* 62:iii[2015] 176–81) concludes that 'Stead maintains a tolerant stance towards the Maori in [his] novel and they are never exoticized' (p. 180). Maver's appreciative survey highlights many of the novel's successes, but is untuned to the controversies around Stead's work in the New Zealand context. This gives his work a refreshingly formalist focus but also, perhaps, drains it of some critical-contextual juices. Drawing on international poetics and avant-garde writers as well as local antecedents, Janet Newman's 'Listening Harder: Reticulating Poetic Tradition in Michele Leggott's "Blue Irises"' (*JNZL* 33[2015] 110–27) follows the sources of Leggott's poem in order to better appreciate its project of drawing 'the voices of female poets from different time periods together and to join her voice with theirs in a poetic of reconstruction' (p. 112). Leggott's *Blue Irises* [1994] divided critics on its first publication; the subsequent two decades have, Newman argues, established Leggott as a major poetic voice. Many of the allusions and quotations laced through 'Blue Irises' are unattributed or only partially accounted for, and so Newman's diligent pursuit of Leggott's various inspirations provides much helpful critical lighting for future readers.

Religious thought has long been important to New Zealand literature, from James K. Baxter's troubled relationship with his Roman Catholicism to Janet Frame's interest in Buddhist thought, and yet the secular mindset dominant in contemporary universities leaves critics ill suited for treating religious themes. Two very different articles on starkly different poets—one from early in the twentieth century and now not much read, one living and a recent Laureate—show what can be done when a critic brings theological sensitivity and open-minded attention to a writer's religious views. Peter Whiteford's 'Shall the Garden be a Paradise? Ursula Bethell's Encounter with Eden' (*L&T* 29:ii[2015] 138–52) demonstrates that the religious references in *From a Garden in the Antipodes* [1929], Bethell's first volume of poetry, are more pervasive than critics have realized. These references, for Whiteford, 'operate in a way that frequently calls to mind the traditional narrative of the Garden of Eden, and the loss of Paradise, alluding both to the biblical source of that narrative, and at times to its later expressions in English literature' (p. 139). His article traces these allusions, noting also how Bethell draws on 'traditional associations that link the activity of gardening to the narrative of the Garden of Eden' (p. 140), and offers along the way some informative remarks on Bethell's 'translation'

(p. 150) of traditional imagery from one hemisphere to another as well as on the 'sidelong glance that is the mark of Bethell's allusiveness' (p. 145).

In a very different register, but drawing on the same biblically informed appreciation of literary form, Joanna Osborne's 'Encountering the Song of Spring in Ralph Hotere and Cilla McQueen's *Song of Solomon*' (*BCT* 11:i[2015] 55–65) is itself a kind of ekphrasis, combining art-historical discussion of Hotere and McQueen's collaborative series *Song of Solomon*, a mixed-media work on fourteen sheets of paper involving McQueen's poem with Hotere's visual imagery, close reading of McQueen's original poem, and biblical commentary and sourcing. McQueen wrote her poem 'Warpath' as a response to the first Gulf War, composing it out of found phrases in commentary from *Time* and *Newsweek*. She then, in collaboration with Hotere, interspersed these fragments with lines from the biblical Song of Songs. Osborne provides a thorough account of the visual work and of the process of composition, and then details the ways in which the Song of Songs has been deployed by poet and painter. She makes a good case for the 'sonic and visual potential of language as art, or language in art' (p. 64).

Finally, two book-length single-author surveys will provide useful resources for scholars, particularly those based outside New Zealand, seeking information about sources and publications in drama. Modern professional New Zealand theatre began with Bruce Mason, John Smythe claims in his *The Plays of Bruce Mason: A Survey*, and his book provides synopses, production details, and critical commentary on all of Mason's plays, published and unpublished. His subject's neglect leads Smythe to the occasional jeremiad lamenting the theatre's neglect in New Zealand currently but, overall, this is a solid work of reference. Judith Dell Panny's *Let the Writer Stand: The Work of Vincent O'Sullivan* provides an overview of all parts of O'Sullivan's writing career, with brief chapters surveying his work as poet, anthologist, novelist, short-story writer, and Mansfield scholar. Panny also includes chapters by Paul Millar on O'Sullivan's novel *Believers to the Bright Coast* and Sebastian Black on O'Sullivan's plays, both reprinted from the 2007 Festschrift volume *Still Shines When You Think On It*. Peter Whiteford contributes a chapter, written especially for Panny's book, on O'Sullivan's biography of John Mulgan. *Let the Writer Stand* contains a full bibliography of O'Sullivan's publications to date (pp. 212–18), and each chapter is helpfully referenced with suggestions for further reading. Murray Edmond's memoir of his early literary encounters, 'Who Would a Would-Be Be?' (*JNZL* 33[2015] 128–49), is as much a primary source itself as a work in English studies, but its charm, generous readings, and loving detail make it the ideal essay with which to conclude this survey.

## 7. Southeast Asia

### (a) General

A special issue of the *Journal of English Studies and Comparative Literature* on 'Rewor(l)dings: Contestations and Reconfigurations in the Literatures and Cultures of the Asia Pacific Region' features key essays that focus on

Southeast Asian literature as a whole or through comparative analyses. Poet and academic Dennis Haskell blends both personal and scholarly perspectives in his account of the difficulties and the promises of spearheading the ongoing creation of an anthology of Southeast Asian writing, a project that was started in 1995 and has seen several editors and contributors come and go. In 'A Jumble of Words: Studying the Literatures of South-East Asia' (*JESCL* 15:i[2015] 3–16) Haskell's difficulties gathering parts of this anthology due to the multitude of different languages, cultures, and ethnicities in the region speak to the problems concerning Southeast Asia as a singular entity created during the Second World War and the Cold War. Yet Haskell also observes the common ties that bind the different countries in the region, together with Australia, where Haskell is based. Haskell also observes the difficulty of recruiting editors to write introductions for and find primary materials from particular national literatures such as that of Laos and Brunei, and the challenges of translating poetry and fiction from their original languages into English when no qualified translators are available. However, Haskell remains optimistic that the anthology will highlight certain common concerns among Southeast Asian writers, such as the vexed relationship between literature and sociopolitical authority and the difficulties of maintaining a sense of tradition and history in the face of a rapidly modernizing present.

Also essaying an overview of Southeast Asian literature is Vijay Devadas, whose 'When Postcolonialism Is Insufficient: Reconfiguring the Literatures of Southeast Asia' (*JESCL* 15:i[2015] 245–59) highlights the limited usefulness of using postcolonial theory to cognitively map or categorize Southeast Asian literature. Devadas begins by tracing the productive connections between postcolonial critique and Southeast Asian literary criticism from the 1980s to the present day, presenting an overview of several scholarly texts as well as creative works in different languages that are informed or inspired by postcolonial thinking. The limits of postcolonialism are then broached: it tends to homogenize diverse literatures and cultures and is institutionally too focused on anglophone writing. Devadas ends by proposing a politics of border crossing (the transgression of national, linguistic, and disciplinary borders) as a more suitable paradigm by which to study Southeast Asian literature today.

In a more lyrical and theoretical vein, Ashraf Jamal's 'A Soft Slab of Fresh Clay: Musings on a Broken Land and a Funny Piece of Water' (*JESCL* 15:i[2015] 17–29) uses Gaston Bachelard's and Gilles Deleuze's theoretical writings to conceptualize Southeast Asia as a maritime culture, 'an imaginary zone defined first and foremost by the littoral' (p. 17). Jamal turns to the work of modernist Joseph Conrad and a short story by Thai writer Rattawut Lapcharoensap to discuss how both authors convey the fragility and viscosity of Southeast Asia's maritime world in their fiction. Such a visceral representation of Southeast Asia is non-dialectical and requires a fluid or flowing logic for comprehension. Applying a different theoretical frame, Chitra Sankaran uses Gayatri Chakravorty Spivak's notion of worlding to perform a comparative analysis, in 'Reworlding Asian Female Locations through Literature: An Analysis of Three Novels by Asian Women Writers' (*JESCL* 15:i[2015] 260–9). Sankaran looks at novels by Lydia Kwa

(Singapore/Canada), Shirley Geok-lin Lim (Malaysia/Singapore/USA), and Kiran Desai (India/USA), arguing that they 'realign and reassign the relations among space, time, and memory to subvert colonial imaging(s) of Asia' (p. 263). The literary process of re-worlding Asia in these novels problematizes a singular version of Asia and instead produces multiple and competing feminist visions of Asia rather than a normative ideal of it.

Moving back in time, Judy Celine Ick discusses productions of Shakespeare's plays in Malaysia and the Philippines during these countries' respective colonial periods. In 'Unknown Accents, Unborn States: The Renegade Shakespeares of Colonial Southeast Asia' (*JESCL* 15:i[2015] 291–304) Ick acknowledges that Shakespeare was often part of an educational curriculum spreading British and American colonial ideology. However, Ick proposes what she calls 'renegade' Shakespeares that 'flagrantly defy the very colonial authority Shakespeare was meant to shore up' (p. 293). Ick traces the history of Shakespeare's translation into Malay and Tagalog and argues that these local translations helped Shakespeare's plays become popular outside the official colonial education system. This in turn made the plays ripe material for adaptation, particularly through the *bangsawan* or Malay opera, which dramatically reworked the original plays to suit local tastes.

In a different venue, Dennis Haskell also looks at writing from different regions in his essay ' "we . . . head back to English": Anglophone Lyric in Hong Kong, Singapore and the Philippines' (*Asiatic* 9:i[2015] 146–59). Examining the poetry of Agnes Lam (Hong Kong), Kirpal Singh (Singapore), and Isabela Banzon (the Philippines), Haskell argues that English, no longer seen as just a colonial legacy, has become part of the literary culture of these societies and is a suitable language for authentic creative expression. Furthermore, the English language allows these poets to write in a committed yet critical manner about their respective societies. Confronting the cultural politics of language and education, Ruanni Tupas's essay 'Inequalities of Multilingualism: Challenges to Mother Tongue-Based Multilingual Education' (*Lang&Edu* 29:ii[2015] 112–24) describes the problems faced in Southeast Asian countries regarding mother-tongue-based multilingual education. Although providing educational instruction in the mother tongue or first language of a particular ethnic group is an admirable ideal, this is often hampered in various Southeast Asian societies because of a process of nation formation that did not incorporate the mother-tongue language, a hierarchy of languages corresponding with divisive social inequalities, and authoritarian or draconian measures of cultural and hence linguistic assimilation. Tupas uses the example of the Philippines to describe 'the everyday enactments of inequalities of multilingualism' (p. 117) that occur elsewhere in the region.

*(b) The Philippines*
One important strand of criticism regarding literature from the Philippines concerns the history of American colonialism and the continuing hegemony of the United States over the country's society, culture, and politics after official independence in 1946. Epifanio San Juan Jr., in his book *Between Empire and*

*Insurgency: The Philippines in the New Millennium*, repeats an argument made in his earlier writings about the need for more pointed and materialist critiques of the history of American colonialism, its neo-colonial influence on the Philippines' national sovereignty, and the effects of the US-led 'war on terror' on Muslim minorities in the archipelago. Two of the chapters in this book are concerned with literature. In 'The Insurgent Imagination and the Case of Jose Garcia Villa' (pp. 66–110), San Juan Jr., in a rather convoluted fashion, reads Villa's poetry as evidence of 'an emergent Filipino-American culture on the margins of the canonical Eurocentric mainstream' (p. 91) against the grain of other critics who see him as a nationalist or cosmopolitan writer. 'Writers in Exile: Wrestling with the Minotaur' (pp. 111–29) is a more coherent piece that employs warfare as both trope and material history (the Spanish Civil War; the Second World War; the Cold War; the 'war on terror') to explicate the work of various Filipino and Filipino American writers such as Carlos Bulosan, Jessica Hagedorn, and Ninotchka Rosca. Denise Cruz and Erin Suzuki's chapter on 'America's Empire and the Asia-Pacific: Constructing Hawai'i and the Philippines' (in Parikh and Kim, eds., *The Cambridge Companion to Asian American Literature*, pp. 16–28) analyses the literatures of both island polities through the perspective of their fateful encounters with US colonialism and neocolonialism from the early twentieth century to the present. Chronologically, Cruz and Suzuki trace moments of political resistance, cultural nationalism, and transnational community formation in the works of Filipino and Filipino American writers. Examining Hawai'ian and Filipino literatures in this manner not only underscores historical and ongoing American imperial hegemony in the Asia Pacific region but also highlights the ways in which Filipino writers, both in the nation and in diaspora, challenge this hegemony.

On the question of national identity, Ruanni Tupas discusses the history and cultural politics behind the three different names given to the national language of the Philippines (Tagalog, Pilipino, and Filipino) in 'The Politics of "P" and "F": A Linguistic History of Nation Building in the Philippines' (*JMMD* 36:vi[2015] 587–97). Tupas argues that these different names arose as part of a nation-building effort (on the one hand) against American colonialism, and the hegemony of English (on the other hand) against other local languages. Tagalog first emerged as the national language in the 1930s because it was the language that dominated in the capital of metro Manila. After independence in 1946, however, the shift between Pilipino and Filipino was a sign of a struggle for national identity: the former 'helped puncture the symbolic and material dominance of English' while the latter 'affirmed the power of the national language to marginalize all other Philippine languages' (p. 588).

David Keoni Lawrimore's 'Imperial Ambivalence: Gender, Discourse, and Empire in Early Twentieth-Century Women's Travel Narratives of the Philippines' (*Interventions* 17:iv[2015] 585–602) examines the travel writing of two white American women, Emily Bronson Conger and Mary Helen Fee, who lived and worked in the Philippines. Lawrimore's essay shows how these women employed their roles within the US colonial regime 'as domesticators and as stewards of racial uplift' (p. 586) in order to empower themselves and push back against gender constraints in contemporary American society. However, even as they may have expanded the sphere of white women's lives, their role as agents of change is problematic as their empowerment is inscribed within a white-supremacist discourse of colonial racism and racial hierarchy. The history of American influence in the Philippines and the sustained migration of Filipinos to the United States form the backdrop of two other essays concerned with national institutions and transnational communities. Talitha Espiritu's study, 'The Marcos Romance and the Cultural Center of the Philippines: The Melodrama of a Therapeutic Cultural Policy' (*JNT* 45:i[2015] 141–62), employs genre theory (specifically that of melodrama) to analyse the discourse surrounding the Marcos presidency and Imelda Marcos's support for and establishment of the Cultural Center in 1969. Although this centre was meant to promote a populist national culture, it gradually became more of a tourist attraction over time. The Marcos regime 'shifted the Center's cultural priorities away from the social empowerment of the folk' (p. 159), members of which were employed as cultural providers to entertain a global audience and clientele. Catherine Ceniza Choy's chapter, 'The Awesome and Mundane Adventures of *Flor de Manila y San Francisco*' (in Chiu, ed., *Drawing New Color Lines: Transnational Asian American Graphic Narratives*, pp. 209–24), focuses on Jenifer K. Wofford's unconventional graphic narrative about Flor Villanueva, a nurse from the Philippines who emigrates to the United States but maintains active ties to her family in Manila and fellow diasporic Filipinos in San Francisco. Instead of a published volume, Wofford's graphic narrative takes the form of six kiosk posters publicly displayed on San Francisco streets. Wofford's innovative depiction of Flor's life challenges the invisibility of migrant health workers in American society and 'reminds the viewer that the Filipino nurse immigrant is not a perpetual newcomer, but rather has a history over time and space' (p. 211).

Another important topic that emerged this year is the problem of literary form. Several essays in the 'Rewor(l)ding' special issue of *JESCL* address this problem. Jose Dalisay Jr.'s short but polemical essay, 'Why We Don't Write More Novels But Should (The Challenge to the Filipino Fictionist)' (*JESCL* 15:i[2015] 50–5), contends that not enough novels have been written in the Philippines because local writers lack both grand imaginative vision and sweeping historical consciousness to work well in this form, whereas short stories and poetry seem better suited to the shorter attention span of Filipinos as a people. Dalisay Jr. challenges fiction writers to try writing novels in popular genres, and to write novels that both help Filipinos better understand themselves and make a global audience take literature from the Philippines seriously. In 'On the Poet's Craft or Sullen Art' (*JESCL* 15:i[2015] 121–39) literary critic and poet Gemino H. Abad makes a case for a more sensitive and meticulous approach to the connection between language, land, and culture when reading poetry from the Philippines. Abad suggests that for Filipino poets, 'our sense of country is essentially a *poetic sense*, for it is work of imagination in and through language *upon our own ground*' (p. 131). A sense of being Filipino and of a national and cultural identity is created and shared through the poetic imagination rather than through state policies and slogans.

A similar concern with close reading appears in Rajeev Patke's essay 'Formalisms Revisited: A Reading of Angela Manalang Gloria and Edith Tiempo' (*JESCL* 15:i[2015] 140–59). Patke advances an expanded but also ambivalent notion of form 'as hovering between interpretive recovery and interpretive (mis-)appropriation' (p. 141). His analysis of Gloria's and Tiempo's poetry reveals how the former hewed more closely to an American tradition of early twentieth-century women's poetry while the latter achieves a formal combination of intellectual wit and emotional tenderness celebrated by modernist critics such as Cleanth Brooks. One particularly famous modernist poem by T.S. Eliot is the subject of Bienvenido Lumbera's essay 'The Impulse Toward Modernity and *The Waste Land* in Tagalog Translation: Receptivity and Resistance in the Reworlding of a Modern Classic' (*JESCL* 15:i[2015] 160–8). Lumbera gives a brief overview regarding the history of the translation of Eliot's poem into Tagalog and its influence on three young poets at the University of the East in the 1960s: Virgilio S. Almario, Rogelio Mangahas, and Lamberto E. Antonio. Despite the important differences between the milieu of Eliot's poem and the Philippines in the 1960s, in the writings of these three poets 'the mood of dark despair may have been borrowed from Western poetry, but the sense of loss is authentic' (p. 165) as they struggled to negotiate a very difficult decade in the country's history.

Although Eileen R. Tabios's *Against Misanthropy: A Life in Poetry* is a collection of interviews with and occasional lectures or essays written by Tabios herself, it is covered in this section because the work included can be regarded as self-studies of her development as a poet, an intellectual, and a cultural activist. Two key refrains emerge from the various pieces in this collection: first, her insistence that choosing to write in the English language (a legacy of American colonialism) does not make her less of a Filipino poet because she incorporates what she calls 'Babaylan Poetics', which are 'based on indigenous Filipino practices' (p. 33) and connects people across socio-cultural and politico-historical divides; second, her development of a hybrid poetic form called the 'hay(na)ku', an adaptation of the haiku that draws on 'the Filipino exclamation "Hay naku" ' and is made up of tercets [comprising] one-, two-, and three-word lines' (p. 48). Poetry is also the subject of Maria Ancheta's 'In Stitches: Con/Refiguring the Language of Wit and Humour in Contemporary Filipino Poetry in English' (*Asiatic* 9:ii[2015] 74–88). Ancheta argues that the period from the 1970s to the present has seen the emergence of a crucial but often neglected strand of Filipino poetry employing humour in reflective and critical ways. She focuses on the poems of Paolo Manalo and Isabela Banzon; the former uses lively wordplay and language mixing to depict the underside of Filipino society while the latter represents the plight of Filipinos working overseas in a comic but poignant light. In the same journal issue, Dinah Roma's essay 'Of Histories, Erasures and the Beloved: Glimpses into Philippine Contemporary Poetry' (*Asiatic* 9:ii[2015] 60–73) discusses three poets whose emerging work exemplifies innovative directions in the development of poetry in the twenty-first-century Philippines. Charlie Veric Samuya's verse spotlights the versatile power of the first-person speaker in lyric poetry; Mesandel Virtusio Arguelles's poetry of erasure selectively effaces an existing Filipino play to produce a new text; Genevieve Asenjo vividly evokes her native island of Panay in poems originally written in Kinaray-a but translated into English.

Another cluster of critical studies takes up the problem of literary form and representations of things past. Ryan Canlas's 'But For the Apocalypse: Wilfrido Nolledo's Dark Mirror of Empire' (*KK* 24[2015] 157–78) reads Nolledo's novel *But For the Lovers* as showing how American colonialism in the Philippines is a natural result of American westward expansion on the continental United States and its Manifest Destiny. Canlas takes issue with scholars such as E. San Juan Jr. who criticize postmodern anglophone Filipino novels for being apolitical. Instead, he proposes that the failure of Nolledo's novel to substantively resolve issues of national sovereignty and colonial violence must be balanced by an understanding of how 'the novel constantly inscribes the horizon of genocide into its very structure and form' (p. 175). The depiction of past violence is also the subject of Shu-ching Chen's 'Affect and History in Ninotchka Rosca's *State of War*' (*EurAmerica* 45:i[2015] 1–38). Rosca's debut novel links three main characters from different families across various turbulent periods in history: Spanish and American colonialism; the Japanese military occupation during the Second World War; the authoritarian Marcos regime; and the People Power revolution that overthrew it. Chen reads the novel as departing from conventional ways of representing the past in other postcolonial historical novels. She argues that Rosca's 'writing of the affective history of the everyday disrupts the opposition between the public and the private' (p. 7) and shows us how affect can help characters strategize and survive in brutal circumstances.

Turning from state violence to migration, Gloria Gonzales's essay 'The Alien, the Citizen, and the Triumphant Capitalist' (*KK* 25[2015] 426–66) examines Charlson Ong's historical novel *Banyaga: The Song of War* in the context of the Chinese diaspora in Southeast Asia, transnational capital flows, and the marginalization of the ethnic Chinese in the Philippines. The term *banyaga* means 'alien' or 'foreigner', and is symptomatic of how Filipino Chinese are treated as strangers in their own home. Gonzales shows how Ong's novel, in depicting the interconnected lives of five young men through the frame of important historical events, 're-writes history to make the Chinese visible in various subjectivities', and traces their transformation 'from alien to citizen' (p. 429) rather than perpetual foreigners. A different kind of marginalization is of primary concern for Cristina Pantoja Hidalgo, whose book *To Remember, to Remember: Reflections on the Literary Memoirs of Filipino Women* argues that memoirs by women authors in the Philippines have been relatively neglected in critical scholarship. Reading the memoirs of seven women writers, Hidalgo proposes that, despite their differences, all are pioneering exponents of the literary memoir because earlier women authors described their self-writing simply as essays or non-fiction prose. These seven writers also share a commitment to 'rewriting the stories that have been told about women, deconstructing the old myths, and creating new narratives that embody their true goals' (p. 15), despite their differing backgrounds. Hidalgo's journal article 'Reading and Writing Creative Nonfiction' (*JESCL* 15[2015] 56–69) touches on similar themes to the book, but is more focused on the travel writing of two Filipina writers (Kerima Polotan and Sylvia Mayuga) and on Hidalgo's own experience as a practitioner of creative non-fiction. Hidalgo argues that travel writing is not only a descriptive rendition of another place and time but also an elaborate self-portrait of the writer, who is inevitably rootless.

Two essays explore the links between literature from the Philippines and the growing fields of literary ecocriticism and environmental studies. Rina Garcia Chua's 'Dismantling Disaster, Death, and Survival in Philippine Ecopoetry' (*KK* 25[2015] 26–45) introduces the concept of dismantling as a way of linking the inner life of people who survive natural disasters and the exterior and physical spaces affected by such disasters. In her discussion of the poetry of Merlie Alunan and Abercio V. Rotor, Chua explores 'the wisdom in the Filipino ecopoetry of disaster, death, and survival in order to bring about sustainable ideas and change in society' (p. 28). Chua argues that ecopoetry in the Philippines can be both a witness to the tragedies wrought by natural disasters and a call for sustainable action to prevent future disasters. Kelly Adams draws on Rob Nixon's concept of slow violence in her discussion of 'Postcolonial Environmentalism in Carlos Bulosan's *The Cry and the Dedication*' (*Isle* 22:iii[2015] 582–601). Adams argues that Bulosan's last novel is not primarily about the historical Huk rebellion; rather, Bulosan deploys this historical event to connect the political crises affecting the postcolonial Philippines and 'the less visible environmental damage that incrementally worsened with each colonial administration' (p. 585). The dislocation of the Filipino people in diaspora is therefore closely linked with the degradation and destruction of the country's natural environment.

### (c) Malaysia

In Malaysia, English has recently been re-emphasized in the national education system in response to the demands of the global economy, and academic proficiency in the language is now required for admission to local universities. In 'English Language Literacies of Undergraduate Students in Malaysia's Culturally and Linguistically Diverse Environment: Casualties of National Language Policies and Globalisation?' (*ERP* 42[2015] 329–62) Wahiza Wahi examines several difficulties faced by undergraduates at a Malaysian university with regard to English language acquisition. Wahiza observes that unsupportive secondary school teachers, a weak English foundation at the secondary education level, peer pressure against the use of English in conversation, a family environment where English is seldom spoken, and a general attitude that perceives English as a foreign language are challenges faced by Malaysian undergraduates. The inclusion of literature in English as a compulsory part of the Malaysian secondary school English-language syllabus has created a demand for teachers trained to teach such literature and also placed a strain on existing teachers to be retrained to perform such teaching often in an ESL (English as a Second Language) context. Florence G. Kayad, writing in the same issue on 'Teacher Education: English Language and Literature in a Culturally and Linguistically Diverse Environment' (*ERP* 42[2015] 286–328), examines the challenges faced by trainee teachers as well as primary school teachers, who are being retrained to teach literature in English at the secondary level. Kayad concludes with apt propositions to help improve teacher training in this area, such as strengthening the connections between teaching programmes at the university and teaching practices in secondary schools and fostering a greater awareness of a culturally and linguistically diverse milieu in Malaysia. Malaysia's multilingual milieu is also an important topic in Sze Seau Lee and Yew Lie Koo's essay, 'Examining Linguistic Proficiency in the Multilingual Glocal Workplace: A Malaysian Case Study' (*L&IC* 15:i[2015] 46–61). Through their fieldwork done in a Malaysian company with transnational business connections, Lee and Koo argue that an idealized version of Standard English might not be best suited for multilingual and globally connected workplaces in Malaysia. Instead, the 'diverse linguistic task requirements' of these venues require 'the use of repertoires of linguistic codes' (p. 58); employees at all levels must switch between different registers of English and also between English and other languages. The physical environments of Malaysian cities are also multilingual, as Syed Abdul Manan, Maya Khemlani David, Francisco Perlas Dumanig and Khan Naqeebullah explore in their essay 'Politics, Economics and Identity: Mapping the Linguistic Landscape of Kuala Lumpur, Malaysia' (*IJM* 12:i[2015] 31–50). In their study of signs and other public displays in the capital city of Kuala Lumpur the authors observe that, although Malay is officially the country's national language, the English language is used more frequently in urban signage compared to other languages. The authors conclude that English 'performs a moderating role, facilitating communication across' users of different languages (p. 44) and is also popular because of its informative role in commercials and advertisements.

Starting with colonial-era literature, Krishnavanie Shunmugam's 'The Creative Style of C.W. Harrison and J.L. Humphreys in Malay Pantun Translation' (*JMLang* 25:i[2015] 107–25) brings to light English translations of traditional Malay pantun poems by two British colonial officials, C.W. Harrison and J.L. Humphreys, whose translations are not widely known compared to those of Sir R.O. Winstedt. The author notes that the original Malay poem on which Harrison's translation is based cannot be found, so the discussion of that poem lays the ground for a more detailed analysis of Humphrey's translation of a linked pantun. Humphrey's translation, while creative, performs a degree of 'linguistic domestication' that 'smacks of Englishness throughout' and its form and structure 'echo the ease and naturalness of lines typical in an English poem of the early twentieth century' (p. 121).

Rare is the essay that looks at literatures from all four official languages in Malaysia, but Nor Faridah Abdul Manaf's 'Debunking the Myth of Submissive Women in Asia: Strong Women in Post-Independence Malaysian Literatures' (*JESCL* 15[2015] 305–19) is such a piece. Focusing mainly on novels and short fiction written in Malay, English, Chinese, and Tamil since national independence in 1957, the author stresses the portrayal of strong female characters as a way of challenging the stereotype of the submissive Asian woman propagated during the colonial era and also by male nationalist writers. The essay positions these representations of women within the sociopolitical context of gender relations in Malaysia, and concludes that there has overall been an increase in the number of positive female role models in literature for a younger generation of readers.

Turning from feminist writing to genre fiction, Mohd Nazri Latiff Azmi's 'East Meets West: The Reader Response Theory in Thriller Fictions' (*Procedia* 174[2015] 58–63) looks at the thrillers of Malaysian writer Ramlee Awang Murshid and American author Sidney Sheldon. The popular novels of these two writers are examined in terms of their formal characteristics, such as the use of flashbacks, detailed descriptions, and presentation of factual informa- tion. The author concludes with the perhaps obvious point that, because of their personal backgrounds, Ramlee is concerned about Islamic culture and religious beliefs while Sheldon focuses more on the role of women and creates stronger female characters. Fateha Aziz also undertakes comparative work in 'The Dark Side of Society in Two Malaysian Short Stories: A Grotesque Reading' (*Asiatic* 9:i[2015] 177–92), which looks at two pieces of short fiction by Lee Kok Liang and Lisa Ho King Li. Fateha argues that the grotesque aesthetic in both short stories has a critical function that goes beyond unsettling readers through feelings of fear and horror. The protagonists in both stories are trapped in twisted and perverse social situations, and 'their deaths ironically grant them freedom from the grotesque predicaments they are in and the seemingly bleak future in a society' that discriminates against them (p. 190).

A number of essays this year focused on the works of a single poet or author. Zainor Izat Zainal's essay 'Yang-May Ooi's *The Flame Tree* and the Politics of Environment in Malaysia' (*Pertanika* 23[2015] 159–71) is centred on a novel by a Malaysia-born author who now resides in Britain. The plot of *The Flame Tree* concerns an ambitious project to build a new university along a mountain range that will adversely affect the biodiversity of the area as well as the environmental integrity of two neighbouring towns. Zainal argues that the novel's tragic ending (the activists are unable to prevent the environmentally damaging construction) reveals a need to focus more on ideological rather than coercive forms of power and domination. Ecocriticism is combined with critical race analysis in Agnes S.K. Yeow's 'Place, Race and Environment in the Poetry of Muhammad Haji Salleh' (*TPr* 29:i[2015] 173–99). Going against the grain of criticism that views Muhammad as a poet exclusively concerned with Malay culture and identity, Yeow observes that his poetry advocates 'a stewardship of the land and transnational spaces which is based on the idea of a shared space of collective duty and responsibility' (p. 175). An ecocritical perspective problematizes and expands the politics of racial identity that are unmistakably evident in his poetry. Muhammad Haji Salleh is also discussed in contrast to another poet originally from Malaysia, Ee Tiang Hong, in Shirley Geok-lin Lim's 'English in Malaysia: Identity and the Market Place' (*Asiatic* 9:ii[2015] 1–25). Ee, who wrote in English, emigrated to Australia after anglophone literature was officially designated a sectional or secondary literature in Malaysia, whereas Muhammad advocated a Malay-language poetics and eschewed English. However, Lim points out that Muhammad has begun republishing his earlier anglophone poetry and has had his works translated into English, thus showing that the language still has currency in

Malaysia. Lim's writing is the subject of Chingyen Yang Mayer's essay 'Entangled Allegiances and Multiple Belongings in Shirley Geok-lin Lim's *Among the White Moon Faces: An Asian American Memoir of Homelands*' (*Asiatic* 9:i[2015] 94–109). As the title suggests, Mayer traces a bifurcated subjectivity in Lim's memoir (Asian American and Malaysian Singaporean), arguing that the constituent parts are distinct but not easily extricable from each other. Cherishing but not confined by her various attachments, Lim's narrative self 'simultaneously traverses multiple national, cultural and linguistic borders' (p. 107).

Multiple cultural identities are also important in the fiction of Indian Malaysian writer K.S. Maniam. In 'Cultural Identity in K.S. Maniam's "Ratnamuni"' (*JLC* 2:i[2015] 27–34) Ruzbeh Babaee, Kamelia Talebian Sedehi, and Rosli Talif argue that, unlike other writers of the Indian diaspora, Maniam creates fictional characters who gradually come to see Malaysia as their homeland rather than harbouring a nostalgic longing for an ancestral India. But Maniam also employs 'the resources of his diasporic experience to fashion alternative cultural and historical politics' (p. 32) to contest the marginalization of the minority Indian community in Malaysia. Daniel McKay performs a provocative trans-colonial reading of Magnus Pretorius, a Boer War veteran who appears in Tan Twan Eng's second novel. In 'Don't Hate the British: Old Boer Wisdom in Tan Twan Eng's *The Garden of Evening Mists*' (*Wasafiri* 30:iii[2015] 50–6), McKay suggests that Magnus's presence in the novel should be understood in the light of South Africa's historical connections with Southeast Asia and also Tan's own personal connections with the country. Magnus's sense of justice, which might be influenced by contemporary discussions regarding South Africa's Truth and Reconciliation Commission, is seen as a contrast to the main character Yun Ling's own desire for truth and reckoning.

*(d) Singapore*

As Singapore is a multilingual society with four official languages (English, Chinese, Malay, and Tamil), shifts in language usage and style as well as translations between different languages are important topics in scholarly criticism. Zhiming Bao's book *The Making of Vernacular Singapore English: System, Transfer, and Filter* discusses the grammatical structure of a local-national strand of English in Singapore in relation to two other languages in Singapore's multilingual milieu: Chinese and Malay. Singapore English, or Singlish, should be considered a type of New English rather than a pidgin or creole because its grammatical structure is constantly being informed and modified by other languages in its linguistic substratum. The individual chapters of Bao's book focus on particular grammatical features in Singapore English borrowed and adapted from Chinese and Malay. Although Singapore puts a lot of emphasis on primary and secondary education, the place of literature and the space for reading literary texts in schools is a troubled one, especially since literature is now an optional subject at the secondary level. Rozita Dass's essay 'English Literatures in Postcolonial Singapore' (*ERP*

42[2015] 134–65) does not discuss specific texts or authors, focusing instead on the way English literature is regarded in Singaporean society and taught within the educational system. Although the Singapore state's avowed desire to become a global city might suggest that literature has an important role to play in its cultural development, the achievement-oriented mindset of most students and parents means that literature is often not chosen in secondary schools because it is perceived as a harder humanities subject to score well in. Dass offers four propositions that might help make literature more popular among Singaporean students. In 'Towards a Transnational Model of Critical Values Education: The Case for Literature Education in Singapore' (*APJLE* 35:ii[2015] 226–40) Suzanne Choo focuses on values education as the primary objective for teaching and studying literature in Singapore. Choo is mindful that English literature was one vector for the transmission of colonial values when Singapore was a British colony. However, she argues that, today, reading contemporary literature in English closely and thoughtfully can aid in the development of ethical selves by 'equipping students in transnational negotiations, critical-ethical reasoning, and affective engagements with values' (p. 232). Making a case for literary studies in Singapore, Angelia Poon argues for a critical cosmopolitan perspective, a global outlook that is also ethically self-reflective and open to otherness 'Being in the World: Literary Practice and Pedagogy in Global Times' (*ArielE* 46:iii[2015] 257–73) discusses two novels by Mohamed Latif Mohamed and Mohsin Hamid as exemplary texts for a critical cosmopolitan pedagogy. Although both novels deal with different contexts and themes, they can be useful in 'developing ethical alternatives to neoliberal' world views and subject positions (p. 264) and helping students become more sensitive and understanding towards other cultures and peoples.

Chin Ee Loh, in 'Building a Reading Culture in a Singapore School: Identifying Spaces for Change through a Socio-Spatial Approach' (*ChE* 22:ii[2015] 209–21), argues that to develop a deeper appreciation for literature, a desire to read for pleasure and leisure should be inculcated in Singaporean students rather than limiting their encounter with literature to classroom teaching of set texts. Spaces such as school libraries can be made more conducive for students' leisure-reading activities. Sally Ann Jones also draws on her own fieldwork with primary school students for her essay 'Children Reading Series Books: Ways into Peer Culture and Reading Development' (*ChE* 22:iii[2015] 307–25). Jones examines the popularity of children's series books such as *Geronimo Stilton* and finds that they not only 'provide suitable conditions for the advance of [students'] reading skills and fluency' but also help students connect with their peer groups (p. 321). Children's books are also the subject of Tom Ue's essay "Holmes in Singapore: Sherlock Sam in Context' (*NW* 12:iii[2015] 355–62). Ue focuses on Sherlock Sam, a Singapore-based and -set series of books for young readers, and talks to Adam Jimenez and Felicia Low-Jimenez, the husband-and-wife creative team behind it. The creators came up with a character like Sherlock Sam because 'there aren't a lot of stories set in Singapore that Singaporean kids can see themselves in' (p. 360) and they believe that the stories' setting is more important than ascribing to Sherlock Sam a specific race or ethnicity.

In scholarship on Singaporean literature in English for the past year, the question of space and place emerges frequently. In ' "A delicate pellet of dust": Dissident Flash Fictions from Contemporary Singapore' (*JPW* 51:vi[2015] 723–36) Joanne Leow examines how the particular genre of flash fiction (extremely short stories) can both represent and interrogate the construction of social spaces in Singapore by drawing on Henri Lefebvre's theories on the production of space. On the one hand, the compact physical environment of Singapore lends itself to depiction in short fiction of extreme brevity. On the other hand, a writer such as Alfian Sa'at is able to use flash fiction's 'polyphonic structure' and 'multiple focalizations' to represent 'a diverse range of Malay perspectives that contest Singapore's highly regulated built environment and racially motivated spatial politics' (p. 726). Lefebvre's conceptualization of space and its production also serves as a framework in María Concepción Brito Vera's chapter 'A Spatial Reading of Fiona Cheong's *Shadow Theatre*: The Production of Subversive Female Spaces' (in Lázaro Lafuente and Porto Requejo, eds., *English and American Studies in Spain: New Developments and Trends*, pp. 69–75). Vera argues that Cheong's novel represents Singapore as a complex space not only physically but also socially and mentally by employing multiple narrators and points of view. Furthermore, the novel's emphasis on round shapes and horizontal lines in its visual descriptions runs counter to the Singapore state's modernizing project symbolized in the vertical lines of skyscrapers and other towering structures.

Another essay examining city spaces is Isabel Carrera Suárez's 'The Stranger *Flâneuse* and the Aesthetics of Pedestrianism' (*Interventions* 17:vi[2015] 853–65). Suárez juxtaposes four novels about different cities (Toronto, Sydney, Singapore, London) by women of colour who are either immigrants or descendants of immigrants. She argues that these 'texts create embodied (and at times exposed) pedestrians rather than detached modernist flâneurs' (p. 856). Suárez's discussion of Hsu-ming Teo's *Behind the Moon* is relevant to this section. Although Teo was born in Malaysia and lives in Australia, one of the main characters in her novel is Justin, the gay, Australian-born son of Chinese Singaporean immigrants. He asserts his identity and sexuality while negotiating the attractive but sometimes hostile neighbourhoods and streets of Sydney. Catalina Ribas Segura's essay focuses exclusively on Teo's novel. In 'Identity and Friendship in Hsu-ming Teo's *Behind the Moon*' (*Coolabah* 16[2015] 112–21) Segura shows how the three main characters' struggles over their ethnic identity reflect a change in Australia's official multicultural policy, one that moves away from an equation of Australianness with racial whiteness towards a more inclusive but also more inchoate sense of national identity and culture. Segura employs Manuel Castells's three-part formulation of identity in *The Information Age: Social Formations in the Age of Information* (vol. 2 [1997] pp. 8–10) as 'legitimizing', 'resistance', and 'project' to perform detailed analyses of the three protagonists' identity development.

There are also essays dealing with multiple cultural and national identities. In her meditative essay, 'Irresponsible Sex, Responsible Love, & Marriage Somewhere in Between: A Singapore Butterfly's Perspective' (*JESCL* 15[2015]

335–42), Suchen Christine Lim uses the metaphor of a butterfly to describe how, as a writer, she straddles two cultures just as a butterfly is symmetrically shaped. Also, she likens the writerly and poetic spirit's refusal to be defined by the pragmatic and rational imperatives of Singapore's national development to the divagations of a butterfly's flight path. Lim briefly discusses the representation of women's lives and their choices regarding love, sex, and marriage in two of her novels, and concludes that there is a lot more to be explored regarding these topics by future writers. Edwin Thumboo's poem 'Uncle Never Knew' is the subject of two essays in the same issue with very different interpretative lenses. In '"Uncle Never Knew": What Can Never Fully Be Known' (*JESCL* 15[2015] 353–67), Jonathan J. Webster situates Thumboo's poem within a set of intertextual relations with classical and modern Chinese literary texts by Tao Qian, Du Fu, Lu Xun, and Mao Zedong. Webster also uses the number eleven, which features prominently in the poem, to make connections with the *I Ching* or *Book of Changes* and other features of Chinese cosmology. What emerges is not so much an explication of the poem as a catalogue of its multiple allusions and references. Carlotta L. Abrams's treatment of the poem situates it within the history of Chinese migration in the region. In '"Uncle Never Knew": Exploring Edwin Thumboo's Poem— Cultural Adaptation, Immigration, and Family Ties in Southeast Asia' (*JESCL* 15[2015] 368–76) Abrams focuses on how the poem gives readers a detailed description of Uncle's background and personality. The poem and Uncle's significance as a transplanted figure who eventually integrates into Singapore are further explicated with reference to an interview with and essays written by Thumboo.

Turning from literature to theatre and performance, four essays discuss the significance of performance spaces in Singapore, the productions of plays by well-known dramatists. Adelina Ong's 'Creating Places of Radical Openness in Singapore' (*RDE* 20:iii[2015] 271–7) draws on her own experience as a theatre practitioner and organizer of dance and street art events. Ong proposes 'the dance battle as a metaphor that extends the critical analysis of discourse related to national identity' (p. 271) as well as a tripartite analytical framework derived from dance kineaesthetics: toprock, floorwork, and power moves. Dance battles become a space through which conflict and anger can be expressed and national identities negotiated in fluid and protean ways. The equation of English proficiency with a Singaporean national identity is challenged in Philip Smith's analysis of a play by Alfian Sa'at. In 'The Gaps Between Us: Multilingualism and Immigration in Alfian Sa'at's *Cook a Pot of Curry*' (*ATJ* 32:i[2015] 259–79) Smith explains how Alfian's play, which draws on an actual incident involving an immigrant family from China and their curry-cooking neighbours, advocates 'forms of nonstandard and badly translated English' that can possibly 'heal the fissures between Singaporean citizens and their immigrant neighbors' (p. 262). The play also suggests that an emphasis on English in both Singaporean theatre and society at large marginalizes non-English speakers and other hybrid forms of linguistic expression. The use of multiple languages on stage is an important topic in Levi Shen's essay in the same journal issue. In 'Decoding Kuo Pao Kun: A Close Reading of *No Parking on Odd Days* and *The Coffin Is Too Big for the*

*Hole*' (*ATJ* 32:i[2015] 280–94) Shen analyses four distinctive linguistic features in these two monologues written by Kuo: slang, jargon, code, and expression. Through this analysis, Shen observes that Kuo's language reveals 'the alienation between the state and the people' resulting in 'a submissive and conformist citizenry' (p. 201). However, Kuo's oblique and veiled language can also serve as a means to avoid censorship and as a social survival strategy.

## Books Reviewed

Achilles, Jochen, and Ina Bergmann, eds. *Liminality and the Short Story: Boundary Crossings in American, Canadian, and British Writing*. Routledge. [2015] pp. 282. £95 ISBN 9 7804 1573 8910.

Adeoti, Gbemisola, ed. *African Literature and the Future*. Codesria. [2015] pp. 112. £14 ISBN 9 7828 6978 6332.

Ailwood, Sarah, and Melinda Harvey, eds. *Katherine Mansfield and Literary Influence*. EdinUP. [2015] pp. 262 + viii. £75 ISBN 9 7807 4869 4419.

Anatol, Giselle Liza. *The Things That Fly in the Night: Female Vampires in Literature of the Circum-Caribbean and African Diaspora*. RutgersUP. [2015] pp. 312. $32.95 ISBN 9 7808 1356 5736.

Anderson, Eric Gary, Taylor Hagood, and Daniel Cross Turner, eds. *Undead Souths: The Gothic and Beyond in Southern Literature and Culture*. LSUP. [2015] pp. 320. $42.50 ISBN 9 7808 0716 1074.

Anjaria, Ulka, ed. *A History of the Indian Novel in English*. CUP. [2015] pp. 430. $120 ISBN 9 7811 0707 9960.

Ashton, Gail, ed. *Medieval Afterlives in Contemporary Culture*. Bloomsbury. [2015] pp. 368. $200 ISBN 9 7814 4112 9604.

Attwell, David. *J.M. Coetzee and the Life of Writing: Face to Face with Time*. Viking/OUP. [2015] pp. 272. £19.99 ISBN 9 7801 9874 6331.

Bao, Zhiming. *The Making of Vernacular Singapore English: System, Transfer, and Filter*. CUP. [2015] pp. xvi + 214. $113 ISBN 9 7811 0702 2089.

Bigot, Corinne, and Catherine Lanone. *Sunlight and Shadows, Past and Present: Alice Munro's Dance of the Happy Shades*. PUF. [2014] pp. 164. €21 ISBN 9 7821 3063 2931.

Bigot, Corinne, and Catherine Lanone, eds. *'With a Roar from Underground': Alice Munro's Dance of the Happy Shades*. Presses Universitaires de Paris Ouest. [2015] pp. 190. €12 ISBN 9 7828 4016 2353.

Birns, Nicholas. *Contemporary Australian Literature: A World Not Yet Dead*. SydneyUP. [2015] pp. 280. A$30 ISBN 9 7817 4332 4363.

Blaber, Ron, ed. *Whaddya Know? Writings for Syd Harrex*. Wakefield. [2015] pp. 183. A$24.95 ISBN 9 7817 4305 3409.

Branach-Kallas, Anna, and Nelly Strehlau, eds. *Re-imagining the First World War: New Perspectives in Anglophone Literature and Culture*. CambridgeSP. [2015] pp. 410. £57.99 ISBN 9 7814 4387 7480.

Braz, Albert. *Apostate Englishman: Grey Owl the Writer and the Myths*. UManitobaP. [2015] pp. 216. C$27.95 ISBN 9 7808 8755 7781.

Brewster, Anne, ed. *Giving This Country a Memory: Contemporary Aboriginal Voices of Australia.* Cambria. [2015] pp. 300 $114.99 ISBN 9 7816 0497 9114.

Brown, J. Dillon, and Leah Reade Rosenberg, eds., *Beyond Windrush: Rethinking Postwar Anglophone Caribbean Literature.* UMP. [2015] pp. 260. $60 ISBN 9 7816 2846 4757.

Buchholtz, Miroslawa, and Eugenia Sojka, eds. *Alice Munro: Reminiscence, Interpretation, Adaptation and Comparison.* Lang. [2015] pp. 225. £37 ISBN 9 7836 3165 4149.

Busch, Brigitta, Lucijan Busch, and Karen Press. *Interviews with Neville Alexander: The Power of Languages against the Language of Power.* UKwaZulu-NatalP. [2014] pp. x + 342. ZAR350 ISBN 9 7818 6914 2773.

Cardell, Kylie, and Kate Douglas, eds. *Telling Tales: Autobiographies of Childhood and Youth.* Routledge. [2015] pp. 144. £95 ISBN 9 7811 3877 4988.

Carroll, Jeffrey, Brandy Nālani McDougall, and Georganne Nordstrom, eds. *Huihui: Navigating Art and Literature in the Pacific.* UHawaiiP. [2015] pp. ix + 308. $29 ISBN 9 7808 2483 8959.

Carter, David, Liang Zhongxian, and Han Feng, eds. *Australian Studies: Proceedings of the 14th International Conference of Australian Studies in China.* Shanghai JiaotongUP. [2015] pp. 289. Y48 ISBN 9 7873 1313 7098.

Mehmet Ali Çelikel, and Baysar Taniyan, eds. *English Studies: New Perspectives.* CambridgeSP. [2015] pp. 375. £52.99 ISBN 9 7814 4387 7275.

Chakravorty, Mrinalini. *In Stereotype: South Asia in the Global Literary Imaginary.* ColUP. [2014] pp. 320. $60 ISBN 9 7802 3116 5969.

Chan, Kenneth. *Yonfan's Bugis Street.* HongKongUP. [2015] pp. xiii + 173. $25 ISBN 9 7898 8820 8753.

Cheah, Pheng. *What Is a World? On Postcolonial Literature as World Literature.* DukeUP. [2016] pp. 408. $28.95 ISBN 9 7808 2236 0926.

Chiu, Monica, ed. *Drawing New Color Lines: Transnational Asian American Graphic Narratives.* HongKongUP. [2015] pp. xv + 336. $69 ISBN 9 7898 8813 9385.

Clark, Timothy. *Ecocriticism on the Edge: The Anthropocene as a Threshold Concept.* Bloomsbury. [2015] pp. 232. $130 ISBN 9 7814 7250 6481.

Clements, Madeline. *Writing Islam from a South Asian Muslim Perspective: Rushdie, Hamid, Aslam, Shamsie.* Palgrave. [2016] pp. 196. £55 ISBN 9 7811 3755 4376.

Cojocaru, Daniel. *Violence and Dystopia: Mimesis and Sacrifice in Contemporary Western Dystopian Narratives.* CambridgeSP. [2015] pp. 335. £52.99 ISBN 9 7814 4387 6131.

Collins, Walter P. III. *Writing Contemporary Nigeria: How Sefi Atta Illuminates African Culture and Tradition.* Cambria. [2015] pp. 240. $104.99 ISBN 9 7816 0497 9091.

Cox, Ailsa, and Christine Lorre-Johnston. *The Mind's Eye: Alice Munro's Dance of the Happy Shades.* Fahrenheit. [2015] pp. 197. €19 ISBN 9 7910 9426 5000.

Cox, Emma. *Performing Noncitizenship: Asylum Seekers in Australian Theatre, Film and Activism.* Anthem. [2015] pp. 202 £60 ISBN 9 7817 8208 4005.

Crowley, Dustin. *Africa's Narrative Geographies: Charting the Intersections of Geocriticism and Postcolonial Studies*. Palgrave. [2015] pp. 192. £55 ISBN 9 7811 3751 8996.

Dagnino. Arianna. *Transcultural Writers and Novels in the Age of Global Mobility*. PurdueUP. [2015] pp. 250. $45 ISBN 9 7815 5753 7065.

Däwes, Birgit, Karsten Fitz, and Sabine N. Meyer, eds. *Twenty-First-Century Perspectives on Indigenous Studies: Native North America in (Trans)Motion*. Routledge. [2015] pp. 269. £90 ISBN 9 7811 3886 0292.

Daymond, M.J. *Everyday Matters: Selected Letters of Dora Taylor, Bessie Head and Lilian Ngoyi*. Jacana. [2015] pp. xxi + 360. R259 ISBN 9 7814 3140 9488.

Denham, Robert D. *Northrop Frye and Others: Twelve Writers Who Helped Shape His Thinking*. UOttawaP. [2015] pp. 295. C$29.95 ISBN 9 7807 7662 3078.

Diala-Ogamba, Blessing, and Elaine Sykes, eds. *Literary Crossroads: An International Exploration of Women, Gender, and Otherhood*. Lexington. [2015] pp. 196. $80 ISBN 9 7814 9850 2085.

Dillet, Benoit, and Tara Puri, eds. *The Political Space of Art: The Dardenne Brothers, Arundhati Roy, Ai WeiWei and Burial*. R&L. [2016] pp. 144. £34.95 ISBN 9 7817 8348 5680.

Donnell, Alison, Maria McGarrity, and Evelyn O'Callaghan, eds. *Caribbean Irish Connections: Interdisciplinary Perspectives*. UWIndiesP. [2015] pp. 341. $45 ISBN 9 7897 6640 5045.

Dragas, Areti. *The Return of the Storyteller in Contemporary Fiction*. Bloomsbury. [2014] pp. 312. £90 ISBN 9 7808 2643 9901.

Edmonds, Phillip. *Tilting at Windmills: The Literary Magazine in Australia, 1968–2012*. UAdelaideP. [2015] pp. 304. A$44 ISBN 9 7819 2526 1042.

Ekotto, Frieda, and Kenneth W. Harrow, eds. *Rethinking African Cultural Production*. IndUP. [2015] pp. 212. $30 ISBN 9 7802 5301 6034.

Evan, Robert C., ed. *Critical Insights: Contemporary Immigrant Short Fiction*. SalemP. [2015] pp. 300. $105 ISBN 9 7816 1925 8327.

Evans, David, ed. *Language and Identity: Discourse in the World*. Bloomsbury. [2015] pp. 256. $36.99 ISBN 9 7805 6756 6140.

Farrell, Michael. *Writing Australian Unsettlement: Modes of Poetic Invention 1796–1945*. PalMac. [2015] pp. 223. €79.99 ISBN 9 7811 3748 5717.

Fee, Margery. *Literary Land Claims: The 'Indian Land Question' from Pontiac's War to Attawapiskat*. WLUP. [2015] pp. x + 316. C$31.19 ISBN 9 7817 7112 1194.

Gabrielle, Cindy. *The Unharnessed World: Janet Frame and Buddhist Thought*. CambridgeSP. [2015] pp. xi + 274. £47.99 ISBN 9 7814 4387 2034.

Galloway, Francis, ed. *Flame in the Snow: The Love Letters of André Brink and Ingrid Jonker*. Umuzi. [2015] pp. 453. R298 ISBN 9 7814 1520 8786.

Garman, Anthea. *Antjie Krog and the Post-Apartheid Public Sphere: Speaking Poetry to Power*. UKwaZulu-NatalP. [2015] pp. xv + 204. R225 ISBN 9 7818 6914 2933.

Gonzalez, Madelena, and René Agostini, eds. *Aesthetics and Ideology in Contemporary Literature and Drama*. CambridgeSP. [2015] pp. 365. £52.99 ISBN 9 7814 4387 7633.

Gordon, Lewis R. *What Fanon Said: A Philosophical Introduction to His Life and Thought*. Wits. [2015] pp. xvii + 191. ZAR275 ISBN 9 7818 6814 8608.

Gorovitz, Sabine, and Isabella Mozzillo, eds. *Language Contact: Mobility, Borders and Urbanization*. CambridgeSP. [2015] pp. 170. £41.99 ISBN 9 7814 4387 0627.

Gounder, Farzana, ed. *Narrative and Identity Construction in the Pacific Islands*. Studies in Narrative 21. Benjamins. [2015] pp. xvi + 260 €99 ISBN 9 7890 2724 9340.

Guignery, Vanessa, ed. *The Inside of a Shell: Alice Munro's Dance of the Happy Shades*. CambridgeSP. [2015] pp. x + 296. £52.99 ISBN 9 7814 4387 5967.

Hammill, Faye, and Michelle Smith. *Magazines, Travel, and Middlebrow Culture: Canadian Periodicals in English and French, 1925–1960*. UAlbertaP. [2015] pp. xi + 212. C$49.95 ISBN 9 7817 7212 0837.

Hartley, Andre James, ed. *Shakespeare on the University Stage*. CUP. [2014] pp. 304. A$145 ISBN 9 7811 0704 8553.

Healy-Clancy, Meghan, and Jason Hickel, eds. *Ekhaya: The Politics of Home in KwaZulu-Natal*. UKwaZulu-NatalP. [2014] pp. ix + 278. R310 ISBN 9 7818 6914 2544.

Heiss, Anita. *The BlackWords Essays*, ed. Worby Gus and Kerry Kilner. [2015]. www.austlit.edu.au.

Helgesson, Stefan, and Pieter Vermeulen, eds. *Institutions of World Literature: Writing, Translation, Markets*. Routledge. [2015] pp. 234. £95 ISBN 9 7811 3883 2541.

Henderson, Ian, and Anouk Lang, eds. *Patrick White beyond the Grave: New Critical Perspectives*. Anthem. [2015] pp. vi + 211. £60 ISBN 9 7817 8308 3978.

Hidalgo, Cristina Pantoja. *To Remember, to Remember: Reflections on Literary Memoirs of Philippine Women*. UST. [2015] pp. xvii + 181. $22 ISBN 9 7897 1506 7737.

Hill, Colin. *Modern Realism in English-Canadian Fiction*. UTorP. [2012] pp. 340. $54 ISBN 9 7814 4266 4913.

Horowitz, Rosemary, ed. *Women Writers of Yiddish Literature: Critical Essays*. McFarland. [2015] pp. 320. $45 ISBN 9 7807 8646 8812.

Jones, Esther L. *Medicine and Ethics in Black Women's Speculative Fiction*. PalMac. [2015] pp. x + 190. €77.99 ISBN 9 7811 3752 0609.

Kamboureli, Smaro, and Robert Zakarias, eds. *Shifting the Ground of Canadian Literary Studies*. WLUP. [2012] pp. xviii + 350. C$42.95 ISBN 9 7815 5458 3652.

Kanwal, Aroosa. *Rethinking Identities in Contemporary Pakistani Fiction: Beyond 9/11*. Palgrave. [2015] pp. 223. $95 ISBN 9 7811 3747 8436.

Karpova, Olga M., Faina I. Kartashkova, Vladimir Egorov, and Paolo del Bianco, eds. *Life Beyond Dictionaries*. CambridgeSP. [2015] pp. 220. £47.99 ISBN 9 7814 4387 7947.

Keren, Michael. *Politics and Literature at the Turn of the Millennium*. UCalgaryP. [2015] pp. 272. C$34.95 ISBN 9 7815 5238 7993.

Khanna, Stuti. *The Contemporary Novel and the City: Re-conceiving National and Narrative Form*. Palgrave. [2013] pp. 229. $95 ISBN 9 7811 3733 6248.

Knowles, Sam. *Travel Writing and the Transnational Author*. Palgrave. [2014] pp. 244. $95 ISBN 9 7811 3733 2455.

Kozak, Krištof Jacek. *Contemporary Tragedy: The Tragic Subject in B.-M. Koltès, S. Pollock and D. Greig*. Champion. [2015] pp. 240. €50 ISBN 9 7827 4532 7062.

Labaune-Demeule, Florence, and Catherine Pesso-Miquel, eds. *Authority and Displacement in the English-Speaking World, vol. 2: Exploring American Shores*. CambridgeSP. [2015] pp. xiii + 185. £47.99 ISBN 9 7814 4388 0879.

Lázaro Lafuente, Alberto, and María Dolores Porto Requejo, eds. *English and American Studies in Spain: New Developments and Trends*. Universidad de Alcalá. [2015] pp. 275. ISBN 9 7884 1659 9110.

Le Fustec, Claude. *Northrop Frye and American Fiction*. UTorP. [2015] pp. ix + 248. C$41.25 ISBN 9 7814 4264 7695.

Lecker, Robert, ed. *Anthologizing Canadian Literature: Theoretical and Cultural Perspectives*. WLUP. [2015] pp. vii + 334. C$39.79 ISBN 9 7817 7112 1071.

Lerena, María Jesús Hernáez, ed. *Pathways of Creativity in Contemporary Newfoundland and Labrador*. CambridgeSP. [2015] pp. xiv + 341. £52.99 ISBN 9 7814 4387 7459.

Machado Sáez, Elena. *Market Aesthetics: The Purchase of the Past in Caribbean Diasporic Fiction*. UPVirginia. [2015] pp. x + 264. $29.50 ISBN 9 7808 1393 7052.

Maisier, Veronique. *Violence in Caribbean Literature: Stories of Stones and Blood*. Lexington. [2015] pp. 170. $111.33 ISBN 9 7807 3919 7134.

Malreddy, Pavan Kumar. *Orientalism, Terrorism, Indigenism: South Asian Readings in Postcolonialism*. Sage. [2015] pp. 170. $39.95 ISBN 9 7893 5150 1428.

Marsh, Kelly A. *The Submerged Plot and the Mother's Pleasure*. OSUP. [2016] pp. 296. $84.95 ISBN 9 7808 1421 2974.

Mbembe, Achille. *On the Postcolony*. Wits. [2015] pp. xvi + 274. $30.95 ISBN 9 7818 6814 6918.

McCann, Andrew. *Christos Tsiolkas and the Fiction of Critique: Politics, Obscenity, Celebrity*. Anthem. [2015] pp. 176 £60 ISBN 9 7817 8308 4036.

Mistry, Jyoti, and Antje Schuhmann, eds. *Gaze Regimes: Film and Feminisms in South Africa*. Wits. [2015] pp. xxxi + 229. ZAR320 ISBN 9 7818 6814 8561.

Mondal, Anshuman. *Islam and Controversy: The Politics of Free Speech after Rushdie*. Palgrave. [2014] pp. 248. $100 ISBN 9 7811 3746 6075.

Moore, Nicole, ed. *Censorship and the Limits of the Literary: A Global View*. Bloomsbury. [2015] pp. 272. £74 ISBN 9 7816 2892 0093.

Ni, Zhange. *The Pagan Writes Back: When World Religion Meets World Literature*. UPVirginia. [2015] pp. 248. $27.50 ISBN 9 7808 1393 7687.

Nischik, Reingard M., ed. *The Palgrave Handbook of Comparative North American Literature*. Palgrave. [2014] pp. x + 417. $54.99 ISBN 9 7813 4949 0066.

Nixon, Angelique V. *Resisting Paradise: Tourism, Diaspora, and Sexuality in Caribbean Culture*. UPMissip. [2015] pp. 229. ISBN 9 7816 2846 2180.

Ochiagha, Terri. *Achebe and Friends: The Making of a Literary Elite*. Currey. [2015] pp. 216. £45 ISBN 9 7817 8204 4659.

Osofisan, Femi. *Ajayi Crowther: The Triumphs and Travails of a Legend*. Bookcraft. [2015] pp. 114. N1000 ISBN 9 7897 8813 5920.

Panny, Judith Dell. *Let the Writer Stand: The Work of Vincent O'Sullivan*. Steele Roberts. [2015] pp. 225. NZ$29.99 ISBN 9 7819 2724 2803.

Panofsky, Ruth, Kathleen Kellett, Susan Brown, and Mary-Jo Romaniuk, eds. *Cultural Mapping and the Digital Sphere: Place and Space*. UAlbertaP. [2015] pp. 310. £28.99 ISBN 9 7817 7212 0493.

Parikh, Crystal, and Daniel Y. Kim, eds. *The Cambridge Companion to Asian American Literature*. CUP. [2015] pp. xxiv + 242. $28.99 ISBN 9 7813 1615 5011.

Plumridge, Anna, ed. *The Urewera Notebook by Katherine Mansfield*. EdinUP. [2015] pp. ix + 118. £30 ISBN 9 7814 7440 0152.

Quayson, Ato, ed. *The Cambridge Companion to the Postcolonial Novel*. CUP. [2015] pp. 332. £18.99 ISBN 9 7811 0758 8059.

Rasporich, Beverly J. *Made-in-Canada Humour: Literary, Folk and Popular Culture*. Benjamins. [2015] pp. xxi + 300. €99 ISBN 9 7890 2720 2307.

Robbe, Ksenia. *Conversations of Motherhood: South African Women's Writing Across Traditions*. UKwaZulu-NatalP. [2015] pp. x + 317. ZAR 325 ISBN 9 7818 6914 2889.

Rogers, Janine. *Unified Fields: Science and Literary Form*. McG-QUP. [2014] pp. 256. C$32.95 ISBN 9 7807 7354 4239.

Ross, Stephen, and Allana C. Lindgren, eds. *The Modernist World*. Routledge. [2015] pp. xxxiii + 614. £137 ISBN 9 7804 1584 5038.

San Juan, Epifanio Jr.. *Between Empire and Insurgency: The Philippines in the New Millennium*. UPhilP. [2015] pp. xxv + 318. $39 ISBN 9 7154 27626.

Sarwal, Amit. *Labels and Locations: Gender, Family, Class and Caste: The Short Narratives of South Asian Diaspora in Australia*. CambridgeSP. [2015] pp. xi + 164. £41.99 ISBN 9 7814 4387 1983.

Satsuka, Shiho. *Nature in Translation: Japanese Tourism Encounters the Canadian Rockies*. DukeUP. [2015] pp. xii + 263. $25.95 ISBN 9 7808 2235 8800.

Shead, Jackie. *Margaret Atwood, Crime Fiction Writer: The Reworking of a Popular Genre*. Routledge. [2015] pp. 232. £60 ISBN 9 7814 7245 0630.

Smythe, John. *The Plays of Bruce Mason: A Survey*. VictUP. [2015] pp. xiii + 266. NZ$40 ISBN 9 7817 7656 0554.

Szmańko, Klara. *Visions of Whiteness in Selected Works of Asian American Literature*. McFarland. [2015] pp. 216. €45 ISBN 9 7807 8649 7010.

Tabios, Eileen R. *Against Misanthropy: A Life in Poetry*. BlazeVOX Books. [2015] pp. 169. $16 ISBN 9 7816 0964 2075.

Throsby, David, Jan Zwar, and Tom Longden. *Book Authors and Their Changing Circumstances: Survey Method and Results*. Macquarie Economics Research Papers 2/2015. Macquarie University. [2015] pp. 59. ISSN 1833 5020; online ISSN 1834 2469.

Vale, Peter, Lawrence Hamilton, and Estelle H. Prinsloo, eds. *Intellectual Traditions in South Africa: Ideas, Individuals and Institutions*. UKwaZulu-NatalP. [2014] pp. xii + 364. R349 ISBN 9 7818 6914 2582.

Vanita, Ruth, ed. *Queering India: Same-Sex Love and Eroticism in Indian Culture and Society*. Routledge. [2002] pp. 264. £33.99 ISBN 9 7804 1592 9509.

Vautour, Bart, Erin Wunker, Travis V. Mason, and Christl Verduyn, eds. *Public Poetics: Critical Issues in Canadian Poetry and Poetics*. WLUP. [2015] pp. x + 375. C$31.99 ISBN 9 7817 7112 0470.

Vickroy, Laurie. *Reading Trauma Narratives: The Contemporary Novel and the Psychology of Oppression*. UPVirginia. [2015] pp. xv + 198. $24.50 ISBN 9 7808 1393 7380.

Ward, Abigail, ed. *Postcolonial Trauma: Memory, Narrative, Resistance*. Palgrave. [2015] pp. 235. $90 ISBN 9 7811 3752 6427.

Weiss, Allan, ed. *The Canadian Fantastic in Focus: New Perspectives*. McFarland. [2015] pp. 245. $35 ISBN 9 7807 8649 5924.

Whitlock, Gillian. *Postcolonial Life Narratives: Testimonial Transactions*. OUP. [2015] pp. 256. £37.50 ISBN 9 7801 9956 0622.

Wilkinson, Joshua Marie, ed. *Anne Carson: Ecstatic Lyre*. UMichP. [2015] pp. 240. $29.95 ISBN 9 7804 7205 2530.

Woods, Joanna. *From Home and Exile: A Negotiation of Ideas about Home in Malawian Poetry*. Langaa. [2015] pp. 236. £16 ISBN 9 7899 5679 2771.

# XIX

# Bibliography, Textual Criticism, and Reference Works

## WILLIAM BAKER

This chapter has five sections: 1. Periodicals; 2. Books; 3. Bibliography and Associated Books and Articles; 4. Histories and Companions; 5. Shakespeare, History of Libraries, and Collections. With some exceptions this review of the year's work published in 2015 in the areas of bibliography, textual criticism, and reference materials is alphabetically arranged. Within the alphabetical arrangement by author there are some exceptions where publications are grouped under their respective authors rather than under editors of, for instance, their correspondence. There is also included in this chapter work that has been missed in some of the other chapters in this volume. Readers should be aware that coverage is mainly limited to those items that have been received by the contributor, who would like to thank James E. May, James Fergusson, and Patrick Scott for their assistance.

## 1. Periodicals

The last *Studies in Bibliography* to be noticed in these pages (*YWES* 90[2012] 1030–3) was volume 58 (*SB* 58[2007–8]) published in September 2010. Volume 59 (*SB* 59[2015]) appeared in January 2016 with fourteen contributors, one of whom, Geoffrey Hargreaves, dying in 2012, did not live to see his most useful essay appear in print. Hargreaves, born in 1941, 'retired from Scottish University librarianship and was a former editor of *The Bibliotheck*' whose 'volumes of bibliography and book history and of the Brontë family and their contemporaries now constitute the Hargreaves Collection in Special Collections at St. Andrews University Library': 'Notes on Contributors' (*SB* 59[2015] 325). Accompanied by a black and white illustration of a binding 'of Wilkie Collins, *The Dead Secret* (London: Smith, Elder, 1865) at Emory University, Manuscript, Archives and Rare Book Library (p. 273), Hargreaves's 'Wilkie Collins in Smith, Elder Boards 1865–66' (*SB* 59[2015] 269–80) provides a descriptive account of Smith, Elder's 1860s publication of Wilkie Collins's novels. Hargreaves usefully draws upon the Smith, Elder

*The Year's Work in English Studies, Volume 96 (2017)* © *The Author 2017. Published by Oxford University Press on behalf of the English Association. All rights reserved.*
*For Permissions, please email: journals.permissions@oup.com*
doi:10.1093/ywes/max017

ledgers formerly at John Murray's and now at the National Library of Scotland, and copies of Smith Elder's Collins volumes today in various institutional and other collections, although his trawl, for instance in what may be held in private libraries, is far from exhaustive.

Studies in Bibliography volume 59 opens with G. Thomas Tanselle's 'Extracts from "The Living Room: A Memoir"' (SB 59[2015] 1–26). Tanselle writes 'in the weeks preceding and following my seventy-fifth birthday in January 2009, I wrote a memoir in the form of a tour guide to my living room, with descriptions of the objects it contains and the associations they have for me' (p. 1). This memoir will be published: what we have here are extracts from various memoir sections. To take instances from many in the description of objects and their associations, over the years Tanselle acquired innumerable bookshelves. A 'large group of shelves came in the early 1970s from Grace Hughes, the widow of Merritt Y. Hughes the famous University of Wisconsin Miltonist (whose intensely learned performances at oral examinations furnish my most distinct recollections of him)'. The bookshelves provide the opportunity also to reflect upon those he had whilst living in Madison, in New York, and so on. To take one other example: 'on top of the three-shelf bookcase in the foyer of four broad species. Two of them, a small bowl and a basket with a large handle, came from [Tanselle's] family house. The other two are eighteenth-century French candlesticks-or so I was told by Joe Tucker, who gave them to me. Joseph Eagon Tucker, a professor of French at the University of Wisconsin, was one of my first acquaintances after I moved to Wisconsin in September of 1960' (p. 8). There then follow recollections relating to Tucker, their association and Tucker's work. One further illustration from the memoir will convey a flavour of content, tone, and method. Memories of Tucker lead into memories of the great Fredson Bowers, who 'dominated the fields of bibliographical scholarship and textual criticism in the English-speaking world during the second half of the twentieth century'. It is somewhat surprising to learn that Tanselle was not a student or colleague of Bowers—their contact began in 1962 when Tanselle sent a submission for Studies in Bibliography, then edited by Bowers. Tanselle writes of their subsequent meetings, the copies of Bowers's writings he has on his shelves, and his collection 'of the writings of Fredson's wife, the novelist and short-story writer Nancy Hale' (pp. 10, 13).

Tanselle's article is followed by Dirk Van Hulle and Peter Shillingsburg's 'Orientations to Text, Revisited' (SB 59[2015] 27–44). The authors' 'initial purpose was to add a "genetic orientation" to the list of orientations presented in Shillingsburg's Scholarly Editing in the Computer Age, 3rd edn. (1996): documentary, sociological, authorial, bibliographic, aesthetic. However, in working through them to add a genetic one, we discovered ways to improve the original design. We offer here a re-orientation to orientations to text' (p. 27). They conclude that 'an awareness of orientations to text can ... Be useful, not only to the individual scholarly editor who tries to be consistent in his or her approach to reading and editing, but also to editors as a community of scholars with an openness to understanding and respecting other editors' approaches and priorities' (p. 44). Hope Johnston writes on 'Readers' Memorials in Early Editions of Chaucer' (SB 59[2015] 45–69). Her concern is to 'consider how individuals took printed books and re-crafted them in ways that reflect the high cultural status accorded to Chaucer. Intentional alterations made by book owners to their sixteenth-century editions of Chaucer include memorial inscriptions, title-page embellishments, and portraits inserted as frontispieces' (p. 45). Her contribution is accompanied by thirteen black and white figures exemplifying early, largely sixteenth-century editions of Chaucer. Michael Johnston's '*Sir Degrevant* in the "Findern Anthology" (Cambridge, University Library MS FF.1.6)' (*SB* 59[2015] 71–84), discusses 'the copy of the romance *Sir Degrevant*' (p. 73) in the 'Cambridge, University Library MS FF.1.6, known as the Findern Anthology'. Johnston writes that this 'has long been recognized as one of the most interesting and noteworthy surviving manuscripts of Middle English Literature' (p. 71). The extant manuscript demonstrates 'the wide range of gentry readers who handled this manuscript'. Additionally 'it shows ... the central place that Middle English romance played in their literary and cultural world' (p. 84). In another most detailed contribution, Joseph J. Gwara, 'Robert Copland and *The Judgement of Love*' (*SB* 59[2015] 85–113) considers the ramifications of Frank Stubbings's 1993 announcement of 'the sensational discovery of three sixteenth-century English printed fragments in the library of Emmanuel College, Cambridge ... . These fragments together formed a single complete folio' (p. 85). Gwara discusses 'a number of technical issues concerning the production' of the printed fragment and 'based on an analysis of its types and ornamental initial [assigns] the leaf to the Rose Garland press of Robert Copland (d.1547?)'. Additionally Gwara proposes 'a revised printing date of either 1531 or 1533'. Furthermore, he uses 'the French translation ... to reconstruct the English edition from which the Emmanuel College leaf derives'. Gwara concludes 'that the anonymous translator was almost certainly Copland himself. This deduction suggests that although Copland's known translations of French romances date from the time of his apprenticeship with [Wynkyn] de Worde (probably 1505–13) he continued to translate such works throughout his printing career' (p. 87). Gwara's article is accompanied by three black and white figures and two tables. His first appendix, 'Grotesque "I" in the Books of Robert Copland, William Copland, and William Hill, 1514–1550' (pp. 105–8) is accompanied by images. His second appendix discusses 'Editions of *The Judgement of Love* and *Le Iugement D'Amour*' (pp. 108–13) and concludes with a listing of 'Variant Readings' (pp. 112–13).

Gabriel Egan writes on 'Press Variants in Q2 *Hamlet*: An Accident on N(Outer)' (*SB* 59[2015] 115–29). Accompanied by six illustrative figures, three of which are in black and white (pp. 120–1), Egan's essay is a tour-de-force display of speculative analytical bibliographical ability. He provides two appendices. The first is a tabular form containing 'Type-Width (in Millimetres) of Thirty-Six Pages in the Seven Surviving Exemplars of Q 2 *Hamlet*' (pp. 126–7). The second is an account of 'Statistical Analysis' (pp. 128–9), introduced with the sentence 'Regarding the printer's measure used by compositors X and Y, we can say with some confidence that they were different and by how much' (p. 128). In his 'Conclusion' Egan gives precedence to 'the first round of changes, witnessed uniquely in the British Library exemplar, having authority arising from the compositor's likely consultation of copy when recovering from it' (p. 125). But so what? Egan's findings are mostly so tentatively expressed and hedged by reservations conveyed in word usage—'suggests' and 'if' for instance (pp. 125–6)—that apart from displaying his own skills at analytical bibliography, one wonders what is the actual point of his article. The same caveat could not be made regarding Ashley Marshall's 'Beyond Furbank and Owens: A New Consideration of the Evidence for the "Defoe" Canon' (*SB* 59[2015] 131–90). Her 'aim is to put forward an alternative representation of their results', that is, those of P.N. Furbank and W.R. Owens, 'in a format designed to communicate more clearly the realities of the "Defoe" canon—to sensitize us to the nature and solidity (or lack of the same) of the evidence we have'. She adds 'Furbank and Owens offer three possible verdicts: definite, probable, and de-attributed. I want to demonstrate that in quite a lot of particular cases a more nuanced and tentative judgment is as far as the evidence can carry us' (p. 132). Her contribution is divided into five sections: 'The Logic of the Furbank and Owens Canon' (pp. 132–4); 'Practical and Conceptual Issues' (pp. 134–9); 'The Evidentiary Basis of the Furbank and Owens Canon' (pp. 139–43); 'Some Facts, Statistics, and Observations' (pp. 143–6); and 'Some Problems and Suggestions' (pp. 146–52). These are followed by a lengthy appendix, 'A Tabular Representation of the Furbank and Owens Canon', in which there are columns for 'Title', 'Evidence', 'Date', 'Imprint', then below 'Author's Name', 'Early ed.', 'Reprint', 'Epithet', then below 'Time of Attribution', 'Lifetime', 'Later 18c', 'After 18c', and 'Other Evidence': this appendix has 133 footnotes (pp. 153–90).

Hao Tianhu's 'Lines Per Page, Engravings and Catchwords in Milton's 1720 *Poetical Works*' (*SB* 59[2015] 191–5) is a brief analytical bibliographical account of compositorial changes in Jacob Tonson II's 1720 publication of Milton's *Poetical Works*. Accompanied by a table instancing 'Pages with 21 lines in Milton's *Poetical Works* (1720)' (p. 193), Tianhu concludes that 'careful attention to a frequently overlooked physical feature of a book, the number of lines per page, provides insight into the way that workers three centuries ago dealt with some everyday challenges of their craft'. Additionally, 'In Tonson's 1720 edition of Milton's poetry this scrutiny shows how the compositors accommodated the presence of engraved ornaments, white also helps us understand how small inconsistencies, here with catchwords, arose in the course of their labors' (p. 195). Another fine illustration of analytical bibliography is displayed in James E May's 'Offset Evidence in Edward Young's *The Centaur Not Fabulous* (1755)' (*SB* 59[2015] 197–223). May clearly writes in his opening sentence, 'this paper examines offset (sometimes called "set off") principally on the sixteen leaves that were canceled or printed impartial gatherings for the first edition of Edward Young's prose satire and homily *The Centaur Not Fabulous* (1755), printed by Samuel Richardson' (p. 197). May's 'study can offer a tentative answer to the question whether a damp leaf was more prone to discharge (express) or to receive (absorb) offset' (p. 214). There are two appendices: the first lists 'Copies Examined' (pp. 216–18); the second tabulates 'Offset Evidence in Copies Examined' (pp. 218–23). William McCarthy's 'Uncollected Periodical Prose by Anna Letitia Barbauld' (*SB* 59[2015] 225–48) draws upon various methods of attributing authorship.

Following a detailed evidence review, McCarthy produces a descriptive listing of nineteen uncollected pieces, including summary of their individual content which he definitely assigns to Barbauld (pp. 234–42), followed by 'a list of twenty titles' that he believes 'more or less likely to be Barbauld's for reasons given in each case, but which' he attributes 'with less confidence than' the thirteen that he definitely attributes to her hand (pp. 243–48). Gary Simons, 'Thackeray's Articles in *The Morning Chronicle*' (ca.1838–48)' (*SB* 59[2015] 249–68), firstly 'overviews Thackeray's contribution to rearrangements with the *Morning Chronicle*', secondly 'summarizes and assesses prior attributions', and thirdly 'proposes additional attributions to flesh out an understanding of Thackeray's contributions to this periodical' (p. 250). Following the introduction to this clearly written article, he considers 'Thackeray and *The Morning Chronicle*' (pp. 250–2), 'Previous Attributions' (pp. 252–4), and 'Attribution Analyses' (pp. 254–63). His 'A Thackeray *Morning Chronicle* Bibliography' (pp. 263–4) provides an introduction to the table that 'lists Thackeray's attributed contributions to the *Morning Chronicle*'. Simons writes that 'without doubt the forty-eight listed entries still understate Thackeray's total contribution' and that 'the currently attributed *Morning Chronicle* writings may not be fully representative of his contributions'. However 'the articles that have been identified as Thackeray's do add substantially to our understanding of his ideas and his times. Most of Thackeray's anonymous art criticism was published in the *Morning Chronicle*, and these articles document his views' (p. 263). Simons's table of 'Thackeray's Contributions to the *Morning Chronicle*' (pp. 264–7) is chronologically arranged in three columns: by 'Date'; by the title of the 'Article'; and 'Attribution' source such as a reference in Thackeray's letters. This most valuable addition to our knowledge of Thackeray's output is concluded by an alphabetically arranged enumerative listing of works cited (pp. 267–8).

The penultimate contribution to the fifty-ninth volume of *Studies in Bibliography* is Richard Bucci's 'Mark Twain and Bret Harte: A Mysterious Early Piracy in Context' (*SB* 59[2015] 281–317), which focuses upon advertisements in order to reassess 'evidence of the early national esteem of California's two leading authors, and invite questions relating to the progress of their careers'. Furthermore, 'as these questions are pursued, particular revelations about Bret Harte and Mark Twain disclose connections to a larger literary landscape, and its commercial and artistic dimensions, during the transformative 1860s' (p. 287), especially in the context of piracy. In the final article, Michael Winship writes on 'Directories of American Bookstores to 1950: Addenda and Corrigenda' (*SB* 59[2015] 319–21). In this, five additional directories are added to his ' "The Tragedy of the Book Industry"? Bookstores and Book Distribution in the United States to 1950' (*SB* 58[2007–8] 145–84). So, to conclude this account of the latest *Studies in Bibliography* to be published: chronologically in coverage it ranges from early readers' reactions to Chaucer to late nineteenth-century American publishing activities, the memoirs of a late twentieth-century eminent bibliographer and textual scholar and the revisiting of early twenty-first-century scholarly editing utilizing the computer; approaches also encompass instances of analytical bibliography and authorial attribution. Hopefully, given the amount of time many of the contributors have had to wait to see their work appear in print, another *Studies in Bibliography* will appear and we won't have to wait another five years for the sixtieth volume to be published.

The *Book Collector*, although it is relatively expensive, continues to provide fascinating material for those interested in book history and collecting. The spring issue for 2013 opens with Nicolas Barker's discussion of 'Chromolithography' (*BC* 64:i[2015] 11–23) and a detailed highly favourable assessment of Michael Twyman's *A History of Chromolithography*. Charles Chadwyck-Healey's 'The Literature of the Liberation 1944–6' (*BC* 64:i[2015] 41–58) is accompanied by four compelling illustrative figures (pp. 43, 50, 55, 57). John Sellars writes on his 'Collecting Stoicism' (*BC* 64:i[2015] 59–71). he observes that 'The Stoic books that surround [him] are a mixture of modern academic studies that form a working library and a number of early printed editions of Stoic and Stoic-related authors. [His] book collecting grew out of [his] academic interest and it always felt like a natural and inevitable progression' (p. 59), and his is a fascinating account of an obsession. Mirjam M. Foot, in her 'A London Binding for the Earl or Countess of Warwick, c. 1575' ('English and Foreign Bookbindings 122') (*BC* 64:i[2015] 72–4) describes the binding and the history of the binding of Martin Luther's *A Commentarie … upon the Epistle of S. Paul to the Galatians* (London: T. Vautrollier, 1575) now at the University Library, Cambridge: there is also an illustration of the binding (p. 72). 'Jeff Towns in Conversation with Sheila Markham. The Markham Interviews (New Series) 12' (*BC* 64:i[2015] 76–82) is particularly interesting, as Towns is an obsessive Dylan Thomas collector and seller: he also collects Bruce Chatwin. In addition to other customers, some of whom he discusses, Towns was close to the dealer Eric Korn, and relates anecdotes concerning Korn, and their travels together. Ian Jackson's ' "How to Understand …": Cesi Kellinger, 1922–2104' (*BC* 64:i[2015] 83–7) recalls the life of the dealer who 'throughout the 1970s', 1980s, and into the 1990s, 'was a diligent dealer in books on arts and crafts, and especially women artists' (p. 85). John Saumarez Smith's 'Shoeless in the Library at Chequers' (*BC* 64:i[2015] 89–93) relates his time as librarian at the prime minister's country residence and his supplying it with books. There is too an encounter with a prime minister, Tony Blair who confessed when 'asked what constituted his holiday reading "You'd be surprised; I'm happiest with theology" ' (p. 92). James Fergusson, who will succeed Nicolas Barker as editor of *The Book Collector*, continues his account of literary author societies with 'The Trollope Society: Author Societies 25' (*BC* 64:i[2015] 95–7). There is an arresting opening sentence: 'Anthony Trollope was undone by his *Autobiography*', and Fergusson probably hits the nail on the head when he writes that 'Trollope's frank worldliness may be a key to his enduring popularity'. The Trollope Society was created in 1987 with the intent of 'making Trollope's enormous corpus available all at once for the first time'; it instantly gained 1,700 members. Fergusson observes that 'even after the fulfillment of its great project, at 900 the size of the Trollope Society's membership is astonishing for a UK author society (the US has its own, separate branch, founded in 1989)' and 'attracts the great and the good, the City and the law; its dinners have been huge affairs' (p. 96). In addition to describing 2015 events to mark 'the bicentenary of Trollope's birth', Fergusson draws attention to 'Trollopiana, the journal of the Trollope Society ... published three times a year' and to its recent contributions and contributors (pp. 95–7). Regular features include 'News and Comment' (BC 64:i[2015] 25–40), accounts of 'Sales' (BC 64:i[2015] 99–114), 'Catalogues' (BC 64:i[2015] 115–28), 'Exhibitions' (BC 64:i[2015] 129–32), 'From the Archive' (BC 64:i[2015] 133–4), followed by 'Obituaries' (BC 64:i[2015]135–46). In this instance there are three of these: Janet Ing Freeman writes on 'William H. Scheide' (1914–2014), the collector (BC 64:i[2015]135–8); James Fergusson writes on the collector and book seller 'John Chancellor' (1927–2014) (BC 64:i[2015] 139–43); and Nicolas Barker writes on the custodian of the Wing Collection at the Newberry Library Chicago, 'James M. Wells' (1917–2014) (BC 64:i[2015] 143–5). The regular 'Bibliographical Notes & Queries' contains Ian Jackson's 'An Unrecorded Attack on Thoreau' (BC 64:i[2015] 147–9). There is too a listing of 'Books Received' (BC 64:i[2015] 151–2) and 'Book Reviews' (BC 64:i[2015] 153–64).

The summer issue contains much of interest. In the opening contribution, 'Old Books and New Technologies' (BC 64:ii[2015] 179–90), Nicolas Barker considers David McKitterick's Old Books and New Technologies: The Representation, Conservation and Transformation of Books Since 1700 published by the Cambridge University Press [2013]. Nicolas Barker also writes on 'Robert S Pirie 1934–2015' (BC 64:ii[2015] 203–10), who 'collected books for over sixty years' (p. 203). This is followed by James Carley's description of 'Hannibal Gamon and Two Strays from the Library of King Henry VIII' (BC 64:ii[2015] 213–19). Hannibal Gamon (c.1582–1650/1) was a 'Church of England clergyman and rector of the north Cornish parish of St Mawgan'. He possessed an incunable, 'William of Ockham's Dialogi aduesus haereticos [Lyons: Iohannes Trechsel, not before 12 September 1494].' He also owned 'a rebacked volume still in its original sixteenth-century English binding containing Ockham's Opus nonaginta dierum et dialogi and Michael de Cesana's Litterae, the title page reading Summaria seu epitomata CXXIIII Capitulorum operis XC dierum M. Guilhelmi de Ocham diligenter collecta (Lyons: Iohannes Trechsel, 16 July 1495)' (pp. 214–15). Carley writes that 'Ockham was one of the most learned and influential of the English Franciscans of the fourteenth century'. Interestingly, 'in his political writings, of which the Dialogi was meant to be a complete summary, Ockham undertook a refutation of Pope John XXII's condemnation of the Franciscan views on evangelical poverty and he argued as well against the spiritual and temporal supremacy of the Pope, insisting on the independence of the monarch's authority'. Carley finds in them evidence of Gamon's ownership and their provenance in Henry VIII's library. Ockham's volume 'must therefore be added to the group of texts that were consulted and annotated in the crucial years leading up to the break with Rome and the establishment of the ecclesia Anglicana'. Carley closes his fascinating contribution by observing 'why the arguments Ockham put forth were not fully exploited by Henry's advisors in their official publications, however, remains a mystery' (pp. 217–18). Richard Foster, in his 'An Unpublished Grolier at Winchester College' (BC 64:ii[2015] 221–3), gives an account of 'a copy of the edition of Pontanus printed by Aldus in 1505; a hitherto unrecorded volume from the library of

Jean Grolier (1489–1565)' now at Winchester College (p. 221). Anthony Davis's '"But do you actually read them?": Contemporary Collectors LX' (*BC* 64:ii[2015] 225–38) is an account of a contemporary collector who writes 'about how [he] got started, what [he] collect[s], what makes it fun and why'. Davis has 'around 500 volumes chosen for their fine bindings. They are mostly British, and mostly after 1660 and before 1825' with some earlier French bindings too with 'the strengths of the collection ... in the Restoration period and the late eighteenth-century/Regency period, possibly the only time when the standard of British bookbinding was high enough to compete internationally' (pp. 225–6). Interestingly 'the most popular author in [his] collection is Richard Allestree, who wrote long books about how to be a good Christian in the late seventeenth century'. Further, 'the next most popular are half-forgotten poets like Cowper, Rogers and Campbell. So, do I read them? Almost never' (p. 228). So why then does Davis buy them, especially as he doesn't read them? He 'buy[s] books that speak to [him]—usually, they are books with a story' (p. 229). The books may, for instance, have interesting inscriptions. He also reflects upon the issue of why one should collect books, the future of book collecting, the future of his personal book collection, and dealing with wives who don't collect or necessarily appreciate books! Davis's article concludes with nine illustrative figures from his collection (pp. 236–8). Karen Limper-Herz describes 'A Binding Possibly by Alexander Cleeve, c.1688. English and Foreign Bookbindings 123' (*BC* 64:ii[2015] 240–2). Her account is prefaced by a figurative illustration of the binding of Thomas Coomber's *Short Discourses upon the Whole Common-Prayer* (London, 1688), now at the British Library (p. 240). Richard Ovenden, the librarian of the Bodleian, contributes 'The Weston Library: A First Report' (*BC* 64:ii[2015] 243–7). On 21 March 2015 the Weston Library, the Bodleian Library's new home for its special collections, formally marked its opening with an exhibition, 'Marks of Genius' (p. 243). Ovenden's is a report on the new library, its construction, and contents which has replaced Duke Humfrey's Library 'as the main reading room for special collections' (p. 244). This is followed by Sheila Markham's 'Bennett & Kerr: Edmund Bennett and Andrew Kerr, the Markham Interviews (New Series) 13' (*BC* 64:ii[2015] 248–55). Edward Bennett's father was a colleague of C.S. Lewis at Magdalen College, Oxford, and subsequently succeeded him in the chair of medieval and Renaissance English at Cambridge . Andrew Kerr's father, Lord John Kerr, 'worked in the book trade for fifty years or so', ran Sothebys Book Department from 1965, and subsequently became involved with Bloomsbury Book Auctions (p. 253). John Saumarez Smith's 'Stanley Olson's Non-Existent Literary Archives' (*BC* 64:ii[2015] 257–62) recalls a young American working on a doctorate on the Hogarth Press who was on the fringes of London book dealers and shop activities during the 1970s and 1980s. James Fergusson's 'The Sherlock Holmes Society of London: Author Societies 26' (*BC* 64:ii[2015] 263–5) is an account of a society founded in 1951 'to encourage the pursuit of knowledge of the public and private lives of Sherlock Holmes and Dr. Watson'. It has a membership of around 1,200 and there is a 'Victorian Cricket Match, against the P.G. Wodehouse Society' (p. 265). 'Richard Lancelyn Green (1953–2004), the greatest of Conan Doyle collectors' was of course a member, from the age of 12. 'He bequeathed to the city [of Portsmouth] his collection of Doyle books, letters, photographs and memorabilia: hip flask, police whistle and all' (p. 263). There then follows an account of 'Sales' (*BC* 64:ii[2015] 269–79), information on recent 'Catalogues' (*BC* 64:ii[2015] 281–90), and 'Exhibitions' (*BC* 64:ii[2015] 291–6). There are three obituaries in this issue. 'Oliver Neighbour' (1923–2015) is by Nicolas Bell (*BC* 64:ii[2015] 297–9). Neighbour 'devoted his working life to expanding and cataloguing the British Library's music collections, as well as making many important contributions to musical scholarship in a diverse range of fields' (p. 297). Nicolas Barker writes on 'Marni Hodgkin' (1917–2015) (*BC* 64:ii[2015] 299–301), the children's book editor who was born in New York and died in Cambridge. 'The musician, bibliographer, editor and printer' (p. 301) 'Robert Threlfall' (1918–2014) is the subject of an obituary by Stephen Roe (*BC* 64:ii[2015] 301–2). The summer issue of *The Book Collector* concludes with a listing of 'Books Received' (*BC* 64:ii[2015] 305–6) followed by books reviews written by Rupert Neelands, Nicolas Barker, Roger Gaskell, Thomas Woodcock, James Fergusson, Elizabeth James, Joel Silver, Gail King, A.S.G. Edwards, Stephen Colclough, and Bob Richardson (*BC* 64:ii[2015] 307–28).

The autumn *Book Collector* opens with Nicolas Barker's 'The Tenth Muse' (*BC* 64:iii[2015] 347–57)—his reflections on what he refers to as 'a monumental work' (p. 347), Roger E. Stoddard and David R. Whitesell's *A Bibliographical Description of Books and Pamphlets of American Verse Printed from 1610 through 1820* published in 2012 (*YWES* 94[2015] 1249). Nigel Stoughton's 'The First Foreign Phrasebook: Noel van Barlement's *Colloquia et dictionarolum* (1626?)' (*BC* 64:iii[2015] 373–86) discusses the 'first example of what is now the familiar everyday foreign-language reference book and guide for travelers'. Noel van Barlement's book 'remained continuously in print for nearly 200 years running to well over 100 editions' (p. 373). Stoughton's account concludes with illustrations from early editions of the work (pp. 384–6). B.J. McMullin, in his 'Joseph Crawhall, His Chap-book Chaplets and the Leadenhall Press' (*BC* 64:iii[2015] 387–400), writes that 'one of the more productive collaborations involving the London firm of printers and publishers Field & Tuer, the Leadenhall Press in the late nineteenth century was that between the firm and Joseph Crawhall, the Newcastle upon Tyne wood engraver, a collaboration that resulted in Crawhall's being the author or illustrator of a number of Leadenhall Press books, three of which are the subject of [his] article'. The three consist of 'miscellaneous collections predominantly of ballads, with some prose narratives and even one short play'. The 'identifiable' texts 'appear to range in date from early in the sixteenth century to early in the nineteenth'. McMullin describes them enumerative-bibliographically as well as descriptively. The article concludes with three illustrative figures: '*Olde Tayles | Newlye Relayted* (publication has been dated to *circa* 1883 but is now suggested to be not before mid-1890' (p. 398); the title page for *The Babes in the Wood* [1883]; and the 'colophon for *Olde ffrendes wyth new Faces* (1884)' (pp. 399–400). Mark Byford's 'A John Marbeck Presentation Copy: Collector's Piece X' (*BC* 64:iii[2015] 401–11) is an account of Byford's copy of Marbeck's 'A Booke of Notes and Common Places, with their expositions, collected and gathered out of the works of divers singular writers, and brought Alphabeticall into order printed by Thomas East, in London, in 1581' (p. 402). The volume is not in pristine condition; however, it has interesting inscriptions that 'yield up a few more of the secrets of its ownership, and therefore give it more layers of meaning as an object' (p. 401). It is a presentation copy from the author 'to his patron, Henry Hastings, the third earl of Huntington, often called the "Puritan earl"' with Marbeck's 'carefully crafted inscription "Your Honnors petitioner to the Lord of Hostes, John Marbecke"' (p. 402). Marbecke was born 'around 1505 and died about eighty years later; and was, for most of his life, a lay clerk and organist in St. George's Chapel, Windsor' (p. 401). Marbecke had a far from uneventful life. He was condemned to burn for heresy in the early 1540s and was reprieved at the last moment 'by a royal pardon, possibly instigated by Stephen Gardiner, the Bishop of Winchester, who was a great admirer of his singing' (p. 402), although as late as 1563 he was described as having been burnt at the stake in John Foxe's *Actes and Monuments*. In addition to examining the ramifications of Marbecke's dedication, Byford also discusses other inscriptions found in the volume: that of 'James Mayttes', probably a clergyman from 'the East Riding of Yorkshire in the parish of Thornegumbald in 1592', and 'Thomas Bilcliffe', a rector 'in the diocese of Lincolnshire, who died in 1638'. The volume then eventually ended up 'at the Colgate Rochester divinity school in New York State, from where it was subsequently deaccessioned' (p. 409). Byford's article is accompanied by four illustrations from Marbeck (pp. 403–10) and Foxe's *Actes and Monuments* [1570] (p. 411). Mirjam M. Foot's 'A Binding Probably Made at Charenton, c.1652: English and Foreign Bookbindings 124' (*BC* 64:iii[2015] 412–13), with illustrations a French binding. 'Anthony Surtees in Conversation with Sheila Markham Contemporary Collectors LXI' (*BC* 64:iii[2015] 414–20) concerns the retired solicitor and collector 'of fiction in English from 1600 to 1900' (p. 415). His memories include with affection Andrew Block, 'a delightful man and extremely knowledgeable about the English novel', and 'Sally Edgecombe of J. Clarke-Hall behind Fleet Street' (p. 416). He 'ended up with large number of odd volumes, which have always had a fascination for [him]. Currently [he has] about 300 odd volumes, and buys some 35 a year', and he manages 'to make up a title every other year' and in his house has approximately 40,000 books (p. 419). Charles Elliott, in his 'Deconstructing an Envelope' (*BC* 64:iii[2015] 421–7), observes that 'Book collecting need not always involve books. Just as we may prize the first edition for its proximity to the author, other objects can possess the same magical aura, in a perhaps even more intensely affecting way. This is about such an object, an old envelope.' The envelope in question 'is brown, tattered, about 10in x 7½'. There is a typed address on the envelope and that is 'Ezra Pound., Esq., | 5 Holland Place | Kensington, W'. On both sides of the envelope 'Mostly in pencil with a smattering of black ink splotches, are words that cannot fail to draw the attention of anyone with even a passing interest in literary history.' These words are 'Joyce | Am copies | Eliot' accompanied by 'some squiggles that resemble musical notes. On the other side of the envelope is a label in red pencil reading in block capitals the word 'Photographs' and 'a date ("apr.27"), and what seems to be titles in Provençal or some other language'. Elliott discusses these, including 'the photographs—photostats actually—[that] consist of thirty-six pages copied from medieval manuscripts' (pp. 421–2). Elliott concludes that 'taken together, the evidence of the envelope serves to remind us of Pound's ceaseless but rarely rewarded determination to "Make It New"—to break down the old patterns and encourage fresh ones. Still, what we can pick out here is bound to be partial, scarcely more than a snapshot of a moment in the dazzling range of Pound's activities in this period' that he attributes to the years 1916 to early 1918 (p. 425). This fascinating article is accompanied by two illustrative figures of 'Ezra Pound's envelope and contents' (p. 427). An article that should be mentioned is John Saumarez Smith's mischievously titled 'China, Diplomacy and Espionage: The Books of David and Evangeline Bruce' (*BC* 64:iii[2015] 429–33), an account of a former United States ambassador to the court of St James and his wife Evangeline plus their book-collecting activities which barely mentions China! James Fergusson's 'The R.S. Surtees Society: Author Societies 27' (*BC* 64:iii[2015] 435–7) describes 'The R.S. Surtees Society', founded in 1979, that aims 'to stimulate interest in the works of Robert Smith Surtees (1805–64) and keep them in print', that has a membership of 300 and annually publishes *The Surteesian* (p. 437). This is followed by an account of 'Sales' (*BC* 64:iii[2015] 441–59), recent 'Catalogues' (*BC* 64:iii[2015] 461–8), and 'Exhibitions' (*BC* 64:ii[2015] 469–77). Obituaries include Nicolas Barker on the type designer 'Hermann Zapf' (1918–2015) (*BC* 64:iii[2015] 479–80), who 'left his mark on the shape of letters in our time' (p. 479), and Nicolas Barker on the distinguished Jane Austen bibliographer and librarian at the Taylor Institution Oxford, 'David Gilson' (1935–2015) (*BC* 64:iii[2015] 480–1). There then follow 'Books Received' (*BC* 64:iii[2015] 483–4) and two 'Bibliographical Notes & Queries'. Note 584 is Patrick Scott's 'William McGill's Meditations and Prayers (Kilmarnock: John Wilson, 1789)' (*BC* 64:iii[2015] 485–7). Scott utilizes evidence from two incomplete copies, in Glasgow University Library and the Burns Monument Museum, Kilmarnock, Ayrshire, in order to identify the author, printer, and circumstances of publication for a pamphlet, given only partial data in cataloguing records. Scott adds a further title to the Wilson imprint bibliography. Richard Healey. in Note 585. 'A Ghost Edition of the Novels of Jane Austen' (*BC* 64:iii[2015] 487–8). supplements Gilson's labours. The autumn issue concludes with book reviews by Andrea Immel, Nicolas Barker, A.S.G. Edwards, and James Fergusson (*BC* 64:iii[2015] 489–95).

The last issue of *The Book Collector* for 2015, is the final one under the editorship of Nicolas Barker, the distinguished editor since 1965, whose introductory essay opens with his 'Texts in Transit' (*BC* 64:iv[2015] 511–18). Barker's essay is a reflection on Lotte Hellinga's *Manuscripts to Proof and Print in the Fifteenth Century*, assessed elsewhere in the present chapter. Barker's contribution is followed by his 'News & Comment' (*BC* 64:iv[2015] 521–31) on the book trade, interesting items and other matters including the appearance of '*Go Set a Watchman* the "Prequel" to [Harper Lee's] *To Kill a Mockingbird*' (p. 521). Murray C.T. Simpson describes 'Brodick Castle Library: Unfamiliar Libraries XXXIX' (*BC* 64:iv[2015] 533–50). In 1957 'the castle passed to the National Trust for Scotland'. 'The total number of printed books at Brodick is just over a thousand, which thus makes it a small collection, but individual titles and small groups of items reflect the general history of the castle and its owners, and mirror its other contents ... ensuring that it is of considerable interest.' There are books bound for William Beckford, a family connection, displaying 'his cross and cinquefoil motifs' (pp. 534–6). The Beckford association copies include *Contarini Fleming*, published in London in 1832, 'inscribed to Beckford by Benjamin Disraeli' (p. 540). Simpson includes as an appendix 'Books Owned by William Beckford, Now at Brodick Castle' (pp. 545–50): there are forty-eight listed with annotations or presentations described and whether or not in a Beckford binding. Simpson's account is accompanied by three illustrative figures. Elizabeth Grice contributes 'Norman Janes and Barbara Greg' (*BC* 64:iv[2015] 553–64). The present writer rented a room from one of Janes's daughters in Kentish Town—the flat must be worth a bomb today—during the mid-1960s as a young graduate student. Norman Janes (1892–1980), watercolourist and teacher, and his wife Barbara Greg (1900–83) 'were book illustrators and print-makers working in the golden age of wood-engraving between the wars' (p. 554). Janes survived some of the fiercest battles of the 1914–18 war; 'he recorded life in the trenches' and was 'commissioned ... to make drawings from artillery observations posts for intelligence purposes'. Janes 'never spoke of what he had seen and done in the First World War, but a haunting self-portrait and experimental woodcut from his student days at the Slade suggests a bleakness beyond words'. The woodcut self-portrait is exemplified in figure 1 (pp. 555–6). Grice's account draws upon hitherto unavailable archival material: as Grice observes 'it was a privilege to rediscover' (p. 564) Norman Janes and Barbara Greg. The article is accompanied by three figurative illustrations, and serves as a taster for Grice's *Norman Janes: Wood Engravings & the Man*, published by the Evergreen Press [2015]. Mark Valentine's 'Cope & Fenwick: A Reminiscence, and a Checklist' (*BC* 64:iv[2015] 565–78) concerns 'the liturgical publisher Cope & Fenwick, an Edwardian imprint' (p. 566), those concerned with it, the subsequent history, and 'Cope & Fenwick: A First Annotated Checklist of Publications' starting in 1908 and concluding in 1949 (pp. 572–8). Karen Limper-Herz describes 'A Binding Probably Made for Thomas Grenville by John Mackenzie, c.1820: English and Foreign Bookbindings 125' (*BC* 64:iv[2015] 580–2); this is accompanied by an illustration of binding of a work published in Italian in Venice between 1560 and 1565. 'John Mackenzie was born around 1788 and probably worked for Staggemeier & Welcher before setting up his own bindery around 1817. He later became Royal Binder to George IV and William IV and worked in London until c.1850' (p. 582). A.S.G. Edwards, in his 'A.I. Doyle: A Tribute at 90' (*BC* 64:iv[2015] 583–90), provides details of Doyle's career: 'his tutor [at Downing College Cambridge] was the redoubtable F.R. Leavis. After he graduated with a double First in 1945 he stayed on at Downing to undertake a PhD, teaching Middle English and Shakespeare with success and reviewing (including modern poetry) for Leavis's journal *Scrutiny*. In 1950 he left Cambridge for Durham, to become Assistant Librarian at the University Library' where he spent his career (p. 583). According to Edwards, 'a central achievement is undoubtedly his work on the production of Middle English manuscripts, a subject to which he has given form and authority'. The tribute concludes with a checklist recording Doyle's 'writings from his 70th birthday to the present' (pp. 585–6)—'The Publications of A.I. Doyle: 1995–2014' (pp. 586–90). Sheila Markham's 'Lars Forberg: Contemporary Collectors LXII' (*BC* 64:iv[2015] 592–8) concerns the Swedish book collector and dealer. John Saumarez Smith's 'Is This Mr Gulbenkian?' (*BC* 64:iv[2015] 599–602) relates his experience in 1982 advising the then headmaster of Winchester concerning 'the school's long-established bookshop' (p. 599) and his disposal of books belonging 'to a bibliophile Wykehamist called George Harwood' (p. 600), who owned William Beckford's 'fine copies of his illustrated books about Fonthill' and, amongst other interesting items, 'a full shelf of Walter Savage Landor'. Twenty years later Harwood's son asked Smith to assist him in 'culling his considerable collection' that included 'a copy of Marlowe's *Hero and Leander*, 1637, and some handsome eighteenth-century bindings'. He also possessed on his death *Poor Poems and Rotten Rhymes* 'A.P. Herbert's first published book' (pp. 601–2). James Fergusson, who takes up the editorship of *The Book Collector* in what is likely to be his final contribution in this series at least for a while, writes on 'The Thomas Hardy Society: Author Societies 28' (*BC* 64:iv[2015] 603–5). He begins with a Mark Twain anecdote before relating that 'it wasn't until 1968 … that a Thomas Hardy Festival Society was established' and draws attention to Michael Millgate's 'virtual "reconstruction" of the library' at Max Gate 'to be found at http://hardy.library.utoronto. ca/. It is a work of marvellous imaginative diligence.' 'Membership of the Thomas Hardy Society brings with it the annual, peer-reviewed *Thomas Hardy Journal* and two issues a year of *The Hardy Society Journal*' (pp. 603–5). This issue of *The Book Collector*, the last for 2015, concludes with notices of 'Sales' (*BC* 64:iv[2015] 609–18), 'Catalogues' (*BC* 64:iv[2015] 621–9), and 'Exhibitions' (*BC* 64:iv[2015] 631–7). Obituaries include Ann Payne and Christopher Wright on 'Michael Borrie' (1934–2015) of the British Museum and then British Library (*BC* 64:iv[2015] 639–43); Tony Cox on 'John Blatchly' (1932–2015), headmaster of Ipswich School (*BC* 64:iv[2015] 643–6); and, last but by no means least, James Fergusson on 'Toby English' (1956–2015), the bookseller and dealer (*BC* 64:iv[2015] 646–7). There are 'Book Reviews' by James Fergusson, Clive Hurst, Adri K. Offenberg, David Pearson, Jason Scott-Warren, and Edmund M.B. King (*BC* 64:iv[2015] 651–60), and finally a listing of 'Books Received' (*BC* 64:iv[2015] 649–50). If the present contributor had one journal to take to the legendary desert island it would be *The Book Collector*. In spite of the high cost of its postage overseas owing to its thickness and plethora of content, the journal rarely disappoints, with more than a few items of absorbing interest and enlightenment.

The March issue of *The Library* includes Niall Allsopp's '"Lett none our Lombard author rudely blame for's righteous paine": An Annotated Copy of Sir William Davenant's *Gondibert* (1651)' (*Library* 16:i[2015] 24–50). Allsopp examines an annotated copy of the 1651 quarto edition of Sir William Davenant's epic poem 'Gondibert', now at the National Library of Scotland. The annotations are negative in their response to the epic poem. Allsopp 'describes the problems of interpreting the annotations; their likely date, social context, and political stance; the secondary reading used alongside

"Gondibert"; and their literary-critical responses to the text. The annotations can be related to the satires on "Gondibert" written by the circle around Sir John Denham.' Allsopp argues that 'one of the annotators may indeed have been Denham himself. The annotators were employing traditional humanist collaborative reading practices in a manner designed to make nonsense of Davenant's poem, objecting to Davenant's departures from the humanist tradition' (p. 24). In their 'Book-Buying and the Grand Tour: the Italian Books at Belton House in Lincolnshire' (*Library* 16:i[2015] 51–79), Abigail Brundin and Dunstan Roberts 'examine the Italian books in the library at Belton House in Lincolnshire', purchased by the family on their continental journeys during the early modern period. Brundin and Roberts describe 'the growing prevalence of books at Belton House from its construction in the late seventeenth century' and they pay particular attention to 'the significance of two foreign tours: the first undertaken by Sir John Brownlow (1690–1754), later Viscount Tyrconnel, in the years 1710–11, and the second by John Cust (1779–1853), later Earl Brownlow, in the years 1801–2'. The 'article considers the ways in which books prepared tourists for going abroad, assisted them whilst they were in foreign countries, and helped them afterwards to recollect their travels' (p. 51). In a 'Bibliographical Note', Sebastian Sobecki's 'A New Manuscript of John Peyton's *A Relation of the State of Polonia* (1598–1619)' (*Library* 16:i[2015] 80–7) investigates the anonymous *A Relation of the State of Polonia and the Provinces United with that Crowne, Anno 1598* that 'has only been known to have survived in a single manuscript, British Library, MS Royal 18 B I'. Attributed to 'George Carew (c.1556–1612) or William Bruce (c.1560–after 1613)', 'having established that the text was composed by John Peyton (1579–1635), son of Sir John Peyton (1544–1630), Lieutenant of the Tower', Sobecki has 'been able to demonstrate that a lost complete copy of the text, named *A Relation of the Kingdome of Polonia and the Provinces United with that Crowne*, must have existed between 1751 and 1898. This copy surfaced in May 2013 and is now held by St Andrews University Library as MS 38902'. His article 'discusses the provenance, history, and date of the St Andrews manuscript, as well as its relationship with the British Library copy' (p. 80). Of interest to *YWES* readers in the June issue of *The Library* is John Barnard's 'Bibliographical Note' on 'The Inventory of William Norton (1527–93), Master of the Stationers' Company' (*Library* 16:ii[2015] 179–84) that 'offers a transcription of and commentary on the inventory of William Norton (1527–93), Master of the Stationers' Company. The document gives a detailed account of the contents, room by room, of a major London bookseller together with an incomplete account of his wealth at his death' (p. 179).

The September issue opens with Oliver Bock's 'C. Maier's Use of a Reagent in the Vercelli Book' (*Library* 16:iii[2015] 249–81). Bock writes that 'More than a millennium after its scribe put pen to parchment, the Vercelli Book continues to fascinate researchers and students of Old English and its palaeography.' Bock 'examines the mutilations the Vercelli Book suffered at the hands of C. Maier, a German scholar who prepared the manuscript's first modern transcript in 1834'. Bock adds that 'through reconstructing the possible working procedure of the transcriber and his motivations for reagent use [in order to enhance the legibility of medieval handwriting], [his] article ...

contributes to a better understanding of nineteenth-century philologists' attitudes towards the material integrity of manuscripts' (p. 249). James P. Carley's 'The Libraries of King Henry VIII: An Update of the Westminster Inventory of 1542' (*Library* 16:iii[2015] 282–303) 'provides an update to the author's *The Libraries of King Henry VIII* published in the Corpus of British Medieval Library Catalogues [2000]'. Carley adds that 'the most substantial list in that volume (H2) consisted of an inventory in two alphabetical sequences of 910 books contained in the Upper Library at Westminster Palace in 1542. Each book had a number corresponding to its place in the inventory entered in it'. In addition 'over the next five or six years further books were added, especially after Henry VIII's death, and these too were arranged alphabetically with matching numbers inserted in the books themselves'. Carley explains that 'since 2000 fifteen more Westminster books have been found in a variety of locations, some unexpected. An annotated list of these is provided' in his article (pp. 298–303) 'as well as an introduction explaining the significance of the discoveries and the means by which they found their way to their present locations' (p. 282). Aaron T. Pratt, in his 'Stab-Stitching and the Status of Early English Playbooks as Literature' (*Library* 16:iii[2015] 304–28), puts his 'obsession with small holes in the gutters of books' (p. 329) to good use. His 'article reevaluates the significance of buying and reading English play quartos in stab-stitched copies'. For Pratt a 'survey of more than 2,500 surviving books from the period before 1641 demonstrates that stab-stitching was the dominant choice for short quartos of all forms and genres—not only playbooks and "ephemeral" publications—forcing us to abandon orthodox narratives that use the physical appearance of playbooks as a way to gauge their literary credentials'. He adds that 'poetry by Sidney and Spenser was also sold stab-stitched, and so too were books ranging from humanist classics like More's *Utopia* to philosophical treatises written in Latin'. Consequently 'early-modern stab-stitching reminds us that the meaning of bibliographical features is almost always relative, contingent upon book-trade norms and consumer expectations. Playbooks may have been "cheap quartos", but this identity was one that served to connect rather than distance them from other literature' (p. 304). Pratt's fascinating contribution is accompanied by five figures that electronic access enhances. Similarly the three figures accompanying Nancy Peters Maude's 'Bibliographical Note', 'The Extended Collaboration of John Danter and Edward Allde' (*Library* 16:iii[2015] 329–42), enhance it through electronic access. Maude explains that 'In 1596, the earthy humour of *A New Discourse of a Stale Subject* scandalized Elizabethan society, but the book was a runaway bestseller, with four editions printed in one year. Its later editions sold simultaneously with another book, *Ulysses upon Ajax*, an equally scandalous text that harshly criticized the low tone of the *New Discourse*, and the book's high-born author John Harington.' Maude 'presents evidence that printers John Danter and Edward Allde joined forces to print both the later two editions of the *New Discourse* and the sole two editions of *Ulysses*, likely to increase commercial success'. Her 'evidence includes both historic research and fresh analysis of the founts, type, and ornamentation of the books, and' provides further evidence to show 'that Danter and Allde jointly printed *Romeo and Juliet (Q1)*' (p. 329). The December 2015 issue of *The Library* contains three articles of interest to *YWES* readers. These include Ralph Hanna and Thorlac Turville-Petre's 'Medieval Manuscript Fragments at the Staffordshire Record Office' (*Library* 16:iv[2015] 405–28), that 'draws attention to two largely untapped resources for manuscript study. Perhaps primarily, it exposes the potential riches still unexamined in local record offices.' They 'chronicle but a single example, the Staffordshire Record Office, where [they] uncovered more than sixty folios of medieval materials from bindings (presented in a brief catalogue [pp. 425–8]). But more broadly', Hanna and Turville-Petre 'argue the need for investigation of medieval materials now extant as fragments within bindings of all sorts' (p. 405). Gilles Monsarrat's 'John Ford's Substantive Accidentals in *Perkin Warbeck*' (*Library* 16:iv[2015] 446–57) examines 'The 1634 quarto' which 'contains an unusual number of words in capitals or italics'. According to Monsarrat, 'all the capitalized and many italicized words highlight Warbeck's claim' to be Prince Richard rather than an imposter. Several politically important words are italicized only with reference to Warbeck; '"*Vsurpers of our throne and right*" and "O Divinitie Of *royall birth*!" (IV.5.6 and 56–7) can be contrasted with Henry's "our owne royall birth-right" (I.1.9). The princes' skeletons had not yet been found and, like some others, Ford seems to have thought Richard had been spared. He conveyed this to the reader by using numerous but fairly unobtrusive accidentals' (p. 446). Supported by four illustrative figures, A.B. Kraebel's 'A Further Book Annotated by Stephan Batman, with New Material for his Biography' (*Library* 16:iv[2015] 458–66) examines 'BL MS Arundel 158, a copy of Richard Rolle's *English Psalter*, [that] contains a series of annotations in the hand of Stephan Batman, providing one further example to illustrate Batman's interest in Middle English biblical literature, and also identifying the precise date of Batman's birth' (p. 458). W.G. Day's 'Surreptitious Publication of the Spurious Volume IX of *Tristram Shandy*' (*Library* 16:iv[2015] 467–71) 'provides a brief survey of the problems that have been caused in translation and criticism, and to librarians and collectors, by the three editions of the anonymous spurious Volume IX of *Tristram Shandy*. All three were declared to be published by Durham and Caslon; this note identifies the printer and the actual publisher of the second edition' (p. 467).

The Papers of the Bibliographical Society of America appear regularly on a quarterly basis. Sandro Jung's 'Thomson, Macpherson, Ramsay, and the Making and Marketing of Illustrated Scottish Literary Editions in the 1790s' (*PBSA* 109:i[2015] 5–61) is accompanied by fifteen illustrative figures. Jung's focus is the 'relatively neglected' area of 'the study of Scottish book illustration' (p. 6). Jung writes that 'in this article, illustrated editions are understood as the products of a complex series of negotiations among various participants in the trades for engraved illustration, the printing and marketing of editions of literature, and the shaping of authorial and textual reputations through interpretive visualization' (p. 5). Specific titles discussed include 'James Thomson's *The Seasons*' (pp. 13–35), 'The Poems of Ossian' (pp. 35–46), and 'The Poems of Allan Ramsay' (pp. 46–61). The second half of the twentieth century and a far different literary landscape preoccupy Paul Ardoin in his '"The courage to be a writer": Theorizing Writerly Courage in Burroughs's *Blade Runner: A Movie*' (*PBSA* 109:i[2015] 63–81). Ardoin draws upon the first and second drafts of Burroughs's text 'held in the Florida State University archive' as the foundation for his consideration of *Blade Runner: A Movie* '*BR:AM* as a test case for Burroughs's own theory of writerly courage'. Ardoin 'positions Burroughs's project as akin to a strain of genetic criticism tied to acknowledging possible alternative texts alongside a published version'. Ardoin writes that 'revision, for Burroughs, is not only wise but also courageous and creatively necessary; and inflexible approach to composition is, in fiction or life, cowardly' (pp. 64–5). Accompanied by three black and white figurative illustrations, Ardoin's article demonstrates that 'we see in both the example of *BR:AM* itself, and in examples *from BR:AM*, Burroughs's theory of writerly courage practiced at all levels' (p. 80). A totally different area of bibliography preoccupies Todd Samuelson and Christopher L Morrow in their 'Empirical Bibliography: A Decade of Book History at Texas A&M' (*PBSA* 109:i[2015] 83–109). They draw upon Ronald B. McKerrow's strictures in his 'Notes on Bibliographical Evidence for Literary Students and Editors of English Works of the Sixteenth and Seventeenth Centuries' (*Transactions of the Bibliographical Society* 12[1911–13]). McKerrow wrote that 'a student or scholar should experience "all the processes through which the matter of the work before them has passed, from its first being written down by the pen of its author to its appearance in the finished volume"'. Furthermore, 'seeing the work "from the point of view of those who composed, corrected, printed, folded, and bound it" could yield invaluable perspectives about a book's authorship and the forces that continued to shape it through its material production—even more, perhaps, then other modes of academic inquiry' (p. 83, citing McKerrow, p. 220). Samuelson and Morrow provide an account of 'the formation and first decade of the Book History Workshop at Texas A&M University in the context of McKerrow 's initial prompt and early attempts to fulfill' his vision (p. 84). In spite of caveats, they conclude that 'over the past thirteen years, the Book History Workshop has taken great strides towards achieving a form of empirical bibliography in the spirit of R.B. McKerrow's initial call' (p. 108). Philip Tromans 'Thomas Hacket's Publication of Books about America in the 1650s' (*PBSA* 109:i[2015] 111–29) is accompanied by four illustrative black and white figures (pp. 116–19) from 'Jean Ribaut's 1563 *The Whole and True Discovery of Terra Florida* ..., one of the earlies extant books on the New World printed in English'. Published in London by Rowland Hall for Thomas Hacket in 1563, 'only two copies of *Terra Florida* are known, both in London'. The Lambeth Palace Library copy is more complete than the copy 'held in the British Library'. Both are the subject of Tromans's 'close bibliographical analysis' (pp. 111, 112, 114). Hacket's dedication to Sir Martin Bowes, a London alderman, present in the Lambeth Palace Library copy in the form of 'an additional bifolium dedication inserted between the first two leaves of the initial gathering' (p. 112), is also the subject of considerable discussion (pp. 115–20), as are Hacket's 'other publishing activities in the 1560s' (pp. 121–7). Tromans finds 'it too easy to read Hacket's publications as part of a grand, emerging, and overarching English colonial design, one that reached fruition in later centuries'. He adds that 'although *Terra Florida* was later reconceived by Hakluyt as a colonial manual for North American enterprises, we must recognize that Hackett's original publication was at least partly marketed at a general readership'. The dedication to Bowes complicates the issue as it 'was not meant for general consumption': 'the very real possibility that' the Lambeth Palace Library copy in which the dedication is found 'is unique or the last surviving representative of only a few copies may indicate Hackett was not that interested in colonialism, if indeed he was interested at all'. Tromans concludes his fascinating article by writing that 'the physical evidence of' the works he discusses 'not only ... problematize[s] readings of the marketing strategies behind their publication but also challenge[s] the considerable field of English travel and colonial writing to pay more attention to the particularities of original copies' (pp. 127–8). This issue of *The Papers of the Bibliographical Society of America* concludes with John Barnard's 'Bibliographical Note' on 'Dryden's *Virgil* (1697): Gatherings and Politics' (*PBSA* 109:i[2015] 131–9), consisting of an analytical bibliographical analysis and the political implications of 'John Dryden's translation of *The Works of Virgil*, the first example of a major literary work by a living English writer published by subscription' (p. 131). Barnard's analysis concludes with an appendix conveying 'the sequence of printing for John Dryden's *The Works of Virgil*' (p. 139).

The June 2015 *PBSA* opens with Michael Thompson's 'The 2014 Whitney Biennial: The Book as a Medium in Contemporary American Art' (*PBSA* 109:ii[2015] 147–92). In 2014 this biennial was made 'a literary event'. The curators at the Whitney Museum of American Art in New York 'selected artists known for being writers' or 'selected artists known for being poets as well as artists' and two publishers. There was a 'semiotic theme' (pp. 147–9). The article is accompanied by twelve black and white figurative illustrations, including Susan Howe's '*Or, at the silent haply* (from *Tom Tit Tot*) (one of twenty-two) 2013. Letterpress print' (p. 164), and 'David Foster Wallace, page from *The Pale King* materials, "Midwesternisms," notebook' (p. 182). There are two appendices: the first is an alphabetically arranged enumerative listing of 'Titles in Matthew Deleget Installation, *Zero-Sum* (2011–present)' (pp. 184–6). The second is similarly arranged and consists of 'Titles Included in *Semiotext(e)* [the publisher's] New Series, 2014' (pp. 187–8). Thompson's account concludes with six colour plates illustrating some of the items exhibited (pp. 189–92). Kathryn Gucer's 'Beyond the Fronde: Jacques Cailloué's Border-Crossing Books' (*PBSA* 109:ii[2015] 193–221) throws light upon Anglo-French publishing interconnections in the middle of the seventeenth century with especial reference to the years 1648 to 1653. Accompanied by six illustrative black and white figures, it investigates the ways in which 'the Rouen-based Protestant publisher' Cailloué 'explored a space created by the process of transporting books beyond their local origins, whether in England or in France' (pp. 193–4). A more recent period of book production and publishing activities is the concern of Patricia Pender's 'Constructing a Canonical Colonial Poet: Abram E. Cutter's *Bradstreetiana* and the 1867 *Works*' (*PBSA* 109:ii[2015] 223–46). The first edition of Anne Bradstreet's poem to be published in over a century was published by Abram E. Cutter in 1867 and edited by John Harvard Ellis. Pender writes that 'Cutter's motivations in the publishing the *Works* are harder to assess' than Ellis's 'editorial strategy' contained in his introduction 'or have been, until the recent recovery of two scrapbooks Cutter compiled about his production of the text'. For Pender 'the *Bradstreetiana* scrapbooks, preserved in the Boston Public Library Rare Books and Manuscript Collection, provide a fascinating insight into Cutter's efforts to present and promote Bradstreet to his contemporary nineteenth-century audience'. Her contribution 'introduces and analyzes the new source materials included in the *Bradstreetiana* volumes, with the aim of illuminating their potential significance for Bradstreet's publication history' (pp. 223–4). An appendix contains a 'List of the Contents of the *Bradstreetiana* Volumes, Boston Public Library' (pp. 244–6). Francis X. Connor's '*The Cambridge Edition of the Works of Ben Jonson Online* and the Utility of the Digital Editions' (*PBSA* 109:ii[2015] 247–63) is an extensive review essay of the 2014 Cambridge edition edited by David Bevington, Martin Butler, and Ian Donaldson. Following a judicious assessment of its strengths and weaknesses, Connor observes 'whether [it] remains a viable archive six decades after its creation or it drifts into obsolescence as a relic of the early internet, its general editors have earned similar gratitude and awe for stewarding Jonson into our modern knowledge economy' (p. 263)—his reference is to C.H. Herford, Percy Simpson, and Evelyn Simpson's *Ben Jonson* published in eleven volumes at the Clarendon Press, Oxford, between 1925 and 1952.

The September 2015 *PBSA*, in addition to 'Book Reviews' (*PBSA* 109:iii[2015] 421–8) contains Melissa Conway and Lisa Fagin Davis's 'Directory of Collections in the United States and Canada with Pre-1600 Manuscript Holdings' (*PBSA* 109:iii[2015] 273–420). Alphabetically arranged by state, although within individual states arrangement seems to be by city, 'with public collections listed first for each city, followed by private collections .... The Canadian Provinces are listed separately at the end of the directory.' Conway and Davis explain that 'The *Directory of Collections* is a continuation of the *Census of Medieval and Renaissance Manuscripts in the United States and Canada*, published in 1935 and 1937, and its 1962 supplement'. Moreover 'the present *Directory* details, when known, the current location of the collections listed in the original *Census* and *Supplement*. ... For each of the 499 North American repositories, this *Directory* provides updated contact data and general information on pre-1600 manuscript holdings'. In short they update Seymour de Ricci and W.J. Wilson's *Census of Medieval and Renaissance Manuscripts in the United States and Canada*, first published in 1935, and C.U. Faye and W.H. Bond's *Supplement*, published in 1962. However, Conway and Davis observe that 'detailed descriptions of individual manuscripts are outside the scope of this *Directory*, but detailed bibliographical references to published catalogues and internet addresses giving access to online cataloguing records are provided when available' (pp. 273–4).

The December issue contains some fascinating materials too. There are three main articles. The first is Craig Kallendorf's 'The Medium Is the Message: From Manuscript to the Hand Press to the Computer Age' (*PBSA* 109:iv[2015] 429–59), who reflects upon his forty years of 'indulging' his 'passion' in which he has 'encountered ... the full range of bibliographical experience' (p. 430) as an academic and a collector. His essay is illustrated with five black and white figures from copies of Virgil, 'the author [he is] most passionate about' (p. 429). The second article is Jeffrey Mala's 'The Early History of Stereotyping in the United States: Mathew Carey and the Quarto Bible Marketplace' (*PBSA* 109:iv[2015] 461–89). Accompanied by five black and white illustrative figures and drawing upon the accounts of Mathew Carey, whose 'business was the largest and most well-capitalized publishing firm in America' in 1813 (p. 464), now at the Lea and Febiger Collection at the Historical Society of Pennsylvania, Mala 'investigates the earliest days of stereotyping in the United States following its introduction as a new technological process from England in 1812' (p. 462). Brief mention should be made of the third contribution, Huub Van Der Linden's 'Printing Music in Italy Around 1700: Workshop Practices at the Silvani Firm in Bologna' (*PBSA* 109:iv[2015] 491–532). Probably of more concern to present readers are the Bibliographical Society of America's 'Minutes of the 2015 Annual Meeting' (*PBSA* 109:iv[2015] 533–54). The volume concludes with a double-columned index (*PBSA* 109:iv[2015] 563–71).

*Textual Cultures* 'In Honor of David Greetham' pays tribute to the magisterial book historian, pioneer in, and authority on, the digital humanities, textual theorist, and critic who retired during 2014 from CCNY. Tributes include 'Marking the Body, Marking the Text: David Greetham's "Archive Fever"', by Katherine D. Harris (*TC* 9:i[2014] 1–21), a fascinating account of Harris's graduate training with Greetham and of Harris's subsequent work represented by her *Forget Me Not: The Rise of the British Literary Annual, 1823–1835*, reviewed elsewhere in this chapter. 'Iconoclastic Textuality: The Ecclesiastical Proust Archive', by Jeffrey Drouin (*TC* 9:i[2014] 22–39), is a tribute to David Greetham's encouragement of 'the theoretical and methodological flexibility towards text that led [Drouin] down the path of digital humanities'. Greetham's 'introduction of archival and textual theories inspired the Ecclesiastical Proust Archive, an open-ended experimental project investigating the nature of digital textuality as it embodies the massive *A la recherche du temps perdu*' (p. 22). 'Down the Rabbit Hole with David Greetham', by Emily Lauer (*TC* 9:i[2014] 40–54), 'addresses the influence Greetham has had on [Lauer's] scholarship and pedagogy' in the area of analysing 'the illustration history of the book *Alice's Adventures in Wonderland*' (p. 40). 'Txtual [*sic*] Forensics', by Matthew Kirschenbaum (*TC* 9:i[2014] 55–64), 'explores David Greetham's notions of "textual forensics" in light of new forms of textual analytics practiced upon born-digital materials'. Kirschenbaum 'argues that computers and computational environments ask us to rethink basic evidentiary categories, i.e. "internal" vs. "external," as well as such concepts as normality, agency, and intentionality in relation to textual criticism'. Additionally, 'through a forensic examination of one specific piece of digital media we also learn something about David's own personal computing habits' (p. 55). 'Scholar', by Jerome McGann (*TC* 9:i[2014] 65), is a three-verse of three lines each poem by one great scholar to another entitled 'For David Greetham, Precepts from His Example' (p. 65). These tributes are followed by five articles. In '*A Few Figs from Thistles*: Edna St. Vincent Millay—"Constant only to the Muse" and Not to be Taken Lightly' (*TC* 9:i[2014] 66–96), Geffrey [*sic*] Davis 'reconsiders the complicated production and reception of Edna St. Vincent Millay's early poetry, especially that of *A Few Figs from Thistles* first published in 1920' (p. 66). In 'Ernest Hemingway: Teasing, Typewriting, Editing' (*TC* 9:i[2014] 95–111), E.J.F. Allen uses the publication of the first volume of Hemingway's *Collected Letters*, edited by Sandra Spanier and Robert W. Trogdon, 'as a case study' in order to offer an 'interpretive approach to matters of textuality, typographical expression, and mechanical accident that lie at the heart of Hemingway's early life writing' (p. 95). Antonio T. Bly, in his ' "By her unveil'd each horrid crime appears": Authorship, Text and Subtext in Phyllis Wheatley's Variant Poems' (*TC* 9:i[2014]112–41), illuminates Phyllis Wheatley's 1773 collection *Poems on Various Subjects, Religious and Moral*. Bly pays attention to something 'ironically missing' in the 'discourse' on 'the African-born poet ... [her] diacritical critical marks that underscores [*sic*] not only the power of words to mean, but also subversive readings' (p. 112). In 'Reading and Rendering: Notes on the Edited Shakespeare Page' (*TC* 9:i[2014] 142–9), using the eighteenth-century editor William Warburton's emendations and 'the speculative writing of Lawrence Lipking, and the editorial provocations of James Joyce, as well as Shakespeare himself', Paul J. Hecht 'argues for a greater variety of approaches to editing Shakespeare, including editors who may creatively and productively read, fashion or distort the text, not just clarify it' (p. 142). Mention should be made too of the final essay in this fascinating issue of *Textual Cultures*, which is available in print and online at www. textualcultures.org. Paolo Trovoto, in his 'Bédier's Contribution to the Accomplishment of Stemmatic Method: An Italian Perspective' (*TC* 9:i[2014] 160–76), draws attention to the work of the French scholar Joseph Bédier (1864–1938). Trovoto writes that 'through [Bédier's] statements, critical editions produced with a single copy text regained ... academic prestige' (p. 160). Trovoto's contribution is followed by three reviews of recent books of interest to readers of *Textual Cultures* (*TC* 9:i[2014] 177–85).

The eighteenth volume of *Book History*, edited by Greg Barnhisel, Beth le Roux and Jonathan Rose, contains twelve most interesting contributions. R.W. McCutcheon's 'Silent Reading in Antiquity and the Future History of the Book' (*BoH* 18[2015] 1–32), whilst focusing on readings of classical Roman and Greek texts, contains much that is pertinent and contemporary. McCutcheon writes that 'the new textual and literary culture that the digital revolution is inaugurating may find some useful *comparanda* in ancient scroll culture, particularly with regard to how to negotiate and interact with a less stable form of textuality'. Additionally, 'as we move further into this brave new digital world, I would recommend that we look back and give attention to the ancient scroll, particularly the sociology of this textual culture. After all, the past—the ancient past, in this case—may very well be prologue when it comes to the book' (p. 24). McCutcheon's contribution has 150 accompanying notes (pp. 24–32) following its text (pp. 1–24): lengthy notation is not uncommon in *Book History* and its editors might well find a way to truncate some of the unnecessary ones. Their value rests in the documentation of work that has been undertaken previously and in the citation of the sources upon which an article is based. Anthony McGrath writes on 'Using Religious Art as Pictorial Evidence for Medieval Book History' (*BoH* 18[2015] 33–47). There are only thirty-one notes (pp. 45–7) accompanying his text (pp. 33–47), and there are seven illustrative black and white figures. McGrath's interest is the 'pictures of saints ... A popular form of religious art from the thirteenth century onwards, and in many cases the Saints were portrayed holding books. These books are seen as attributes, as representing the Word of God, or indicating a particular vocational or calling.' His immediate concern is 'the detail that sometimes exists in these images of books [that] may provide information about the form and appearance of medieval bindings. This would be useful given the shortage of physical evidence that has survived': specifically McGrath focuses upon 'gold-tooling, whereby a designing gold leaf is applied to a leather cover, using a metal die' (pp. 33–4). English diarists rather than Italian medieval craftsmanship is the direction of the article that follows. Gillian Wright's 'Delight in Good Books: Family, Devotional Practice, and Textual Circulation in Sarah Savage's Diaries' (*BoH* 18[2015] 48–74) draws upon the diaries of 'Sarah Savage (1664–1752) ... one of the best attested English diarists of the late seventeenth and early eighteenth centuries'. Her 'diary is an important and intriguing resource for book historians and scholars of women's writing. Of special interest to the former are the many references in the diary to the production, circulation, and reception of written texts in both manuscript and print.' Wright traces 'the connections between textual production, family, and religion as witnessed by Savage's diaries' (p. 48). Elizabeth Della Zazzera's 'Translating Revolutionary Time: French Republican Almanacs in the United States' (*BoH* 18[2015] 75–102) demonstrates that the 'French republican almanacs printed in the United States highlight ... the ideological power almanacs could have, and were believed to have, outside of their practical use'. Della Zazzera adds, 'the practicality of almanacs, and their concomitant commonality, might be what makes almanacs potentially powerful, but by the 1790s that power had long been established and impractical or symbolic almanacs could call on that generic power to exert political influence' (p. 96).

Amanda Watson's 'Shared Reading at a Distance: The Commonplace Books of the Stockton Family, 1812–40' (*BoH* 18[2015] 103–33) draws upon 'the five surviving commonplace books of the Stockton family [which] include large shared clusters of favorite poems, which the compilers evidently read together, copied again and again, and handed on to later generations'. These 'reveal an under-examined function of commonplacing in antebellum America: that of maintaining family ties by extending the communal reading that typically took place at home—one person reading aloud as other family members listen while working at domestic tasks—across the dimensions of space and time' (p. 103). Watson provides an alphabetically arranged first appendix of 'Poems transcribed by three or more members of the Stockton family' beginning with Arthur Brooke's 'Ballad Stanza's (When pain and hatred hemmed me round)' and concluding with an 'Unknown' author's poem titled 'The offspring of Mercy'. The second appendix is 'a partial Stockton family tree, showing persons mentioned in this article' beginning with 'Richard Stockton (1730–81)' and concluding with 'Mary Rotch (1823–73)' (pp. 126–7). The article that follows chronologically moves into a more recent period. Devin Griffiths 'The Radical's Catalogue: Antonio Panizzi, Virginia Woolf, and the British Museum Library's *Catalogue of Printed Books*' (*BoH* 18[2015]

134–65) is accompanied by seven illustrative black and white figures. Griffiths is 'interested in how the archival practices of the British Museum's catalogue of printed books, particularly decisions about structure that were communicated through features of script, format, and institutional design, liberalized access to the printed word in far-reaching ways'. The opening section of the contribution explores 'the implications of the institutional design of Panizzi'—the Keeper of Printed Books (1837–56) and then chief librarian (1856–66)—the 'catalogue, its schemes of classification and its layout'. The second section 'takes Virginia Woolf's *A Room of One's Own* (1929) as an influential evaluation of 'Panizzi's and his associates' *Catalogues* operation in the world, both in terms of its physical format about the institutional structures that built up around it' (pp. 136–8). Library activities, albeit on a different scale, are the subject of Bernadette A. Lear's 'Libraries and Reading Culture at the Carlisle Indian Industrial School [Pennsylvania], 1879–1918' (*BoH* 18[2015] 166–96). Lear's contribution is accompanied by five black and white illustrative figures and three appendices: the 'Occurrence of Selected Themes in Books at Academic Library, Carlisle Indian Industrial School, 1918'; the 'Number of Library Books by Subject and Estimated Age, Academic Library at Carlisle Indian Industrial School, 1918'; and 'Self-Reported "Favorite Books" of Selected Carlisle Students, ca. 1912' (pp. 187–90). Lear judiciously observes that 'although study of such phenomena has just begun, this article offers compelling evidence that the history of library development and reading culture for American Indians is far more complex and interesting than scholars have previously realized' (p. 186). A different area of book history engages Sydney Bufkin. In her 'Resisting Naturalism: Purpose and Literary Value in the Reception of Frank Norris's *The Octopus*' (*BoH* 18[2015] 197–234), Bufkin observes 'naturalism is largely a category invented by twentieth-century literary scholars to explain nineteenth-century literary production'. Her 'essay argues that scholars of American literature need to re-think naturalism's outsized place in American literary history, and to pay more attention to the late nineteenth-century ways of reading that have been neglected in favor of naturalism'. Bufkin illustrates 'the kinds of reading that an excessive attention to naturalism can obscure' by examining 'the reception of Frank Norris's *The Octopus*, generally considered a classic work of naturalism by the only American author to label himself a naturalist. The reviews of *The Octopus* demonstrate that naturalism as a fully realized category played a relatively minor role in the book's reception' (p. 198). In her conclusion Bufkin writes, 'we might do well to ask what else our scholarly fixation on naturalism has kept us from seeing about American literary history' (p. 229).

Replete with 122 notes, L. Ashley Squires's 'All the News Worth Reading: The *Christian Science Monitor* and the Professionalization of Journalism' (*BoH* 18[2015] 235–72) draws upon materials at the archives of the Mary Baker Eddy Library in Boston. She 'demonstrates just how the Christian Science Publishing Society self-consciously and with a sense of spiritual purpose produced a paper that both embodied and helped shape the content and stylistic standards that would define respectable journalism—intellectualism, discretion, and an ethos of impartiality—in the subsequent decades' (p. 237). John B. Hench's 'The Publishers Who Lunch: The Social Networking of American Book Publishers' (*BoH* 18[2015] 273–301) has four more notes than Squires's contribution: Hench largely utilizes 'the Publishers' Lunch Club Collection' at Princeton University Library (p. 296). Hench writes that 'for a century or more American book publishers have demonstrated a high degree of sociability, with an even without the stimulation of alcohol' (p. 273). Drawing upon its archives, Hench examines the activities of a publishers' lunch club that was established 'in April 1915' probably by 'Joseph H. Sears of D. Appleton' and included representatives from most of the eminent publishing firms from the New York area. 'Throughout the period covered by the club's records (1915–59) … The group met almost always at the Yale Club across Vanderbilt Avenue from Grand Central Station, on the first Thursday of each month, except June, July, and August' (p. 278). In his concluding paragraph Hench notes that 'the club has always reflected the highest levels of major American publishing companies, and that is no less true over the last couple of generations that it was in the early days … . The Publishers' Lunch Club celebrated its centennial in April 2015.' Hench cites 'William Strachan, a past president', who in an October 2014 email to Hench observed: 'clearly the business is very different now from what it was' in the past 'and it changes daily with the advent of new technologies and new business models. Nonetheless, we gather our monthly to help each other keep abreast of the changes with speakers who addressed the issues and conversations that are the old-fashioned equivalents of "social media." It's still a community' (p. 295). A different universe is documented in Evelyn Ellerman's '"Who should you write for?": Competing Spheres of Print Culture Production in Colonial Papua and New Guinea' (*BoH* 18[2015] 302–31). The article examines the work of 'the primary institutional sponsors of print culture in Papua and New Guinea—the colonial administration, the University, and the Christian missions [and] the relations' between them in the second half of the twentieth century and especially 'during the final years of formal colonialism in Papua and New Guinea, from the mid-1960s to the mid-1970s' (pp. 302–3). Ellerman concludes her account by observing that in the post-independence period 'the personalities may have changed and the colonial ideologies faded as primary drivers of print culture production, but the institutions and programs established in the late colonial era content to shape the field of print culture production in [Papua New Guinea]. Writers, on the other hand, could now make their publishing choices in a less heated environment' (p. 326). Given the direction of some of the essays, it is by no means inappropriate that the 2015 *Book History* ends with interested reflections by Elizabeth Yale on archives and their history. Her 'The History of Archives: The State of the Discipline' (*BoH* 18[2015] 332–59), following a five-paragraph introduction, is divided into six sections followed by a conclusion. In the concluding paragraph of her introduction Yale writes that 'historians of archives, consider the social, political, and institutional frameworks that govern the production, storage, and accessibility of archival documents' (*BoH* 18[2015] 334). The six sections are: 'Archives in Critical Theory', consisting of a discussion of work by Jacques Derrida—his 'extended meditation on archives, *Archive Fever: A Freudian Impression* (1994)'—and Michel Foucault—his *The Archaeology of Knowledge and the Discourse on*

*Language* (1972)' (pp. 334–5); 'Archives and Global Institutions in the Early Modern World' (pp. 336–41); 'Archives, Nationalism, and Empire' (pp. 341–4); 'Archives and Justice in a Postcolonial World' (pp. 344–7); 'Reading Against the Grain: Archival Methodology and the History of Women and Gender' (pp. 348–50); and 'Personal Archives' (pp. 350–4). In her 'Conclusion' Yale writes that the examination of issues such as 'failures of access, secrecy, the accidental order to bring destruction of records, ambiguous borders between public and private, all are just as important as the positive actions that archives make possible. Indeed, such "negatives" are part and parcel of how archives function as political, cultural, and intellectual tools' (pp. 355–6). Such concerns are a most appropriate ending to a highly instructive and stimulating volume of *Book History*. The volume under review maintains the high standards of scholarship to be found up to now in *Book History*. It can only be hoped that subsequent volumes will continue this tradition and that its readers will be as assiduous as they have been till now.

The *Eighteenth-Century Intelligencer*, edited by James May in two issues during 2015, contains a number of articles related to publishing, editing, and bibliography. The March issue included 'Two Talks/Lectures on Scholarly Publishing Delivered at Emory' by Greg Clingham, director of Bucknell University Press (*ECIntell* 29:i[2015] 6–16). The two lectures, delivered on 18 September 2014 at Emory University, had separate topics. The first, 'The Serendipity of Scholarly Publishing', was focused particularly on this university press and its leadership up to the present, but also celebrates the role of university presses generally (several paragraphs with grateful and appreciative remarks regarding individuals at Bucknell University and other less generalized topics were omitted from the transcript). In his forward-looking second lecture, 'The Monograph, Open Access, and the Future of Scholarship in the Humanities', Clingham reflects on what is sometimes called the 'crisis' of university presses in more competitive times (cuts to budgets, reductions in copies sold), and offers strategies to allow them to continue contributing to scholarship with the widest distribution possible. In '"The Glory and the Nothing of a Name": Sources of Charles Churchill's Scottophobia', Corey Andrews examines the sources of Churchill's attacks on Scots in such poems as *The Apology Addressed the Critical Reviewers* (particularly attacking Tobias Smollett for an anonymous review in that journal's March 1761 issue), *Night: An Epistle to Robert Lloyd* (a parody attacking *Day* by the Scottish poet and physician John Armstrong, who assisted Smollett in founding *The Critical Review*), and *The Prophecy of Famine*,Churchill's broadest attack on the Scots (*ECIntell* 29:i[2015] 35–43). The hostility to the Scots, Andrews contends, goes beyond Churchill's desire to oppose the Scottish prime minster the earl of Bute, which was the focus of *The North Briton*, the periodical collaboration of Churchill and John Wilkes, and beyond the desire to feed on English prejudice against those migrating south out of Scotland. Churchill's animus is directly related to his being criticized and unappreciated by Scottish men of letters, who were 'conspiring against him in the literary field' (p. 41). Andrews's article begins with a discussion of William Hogarth's satirical print of Churchill, *The Bruiser* [1763], provoked by Churchill's angry defence of Wilkes, *Epistle to William Hogarth* (that print is reproduced on the March issue's cover). Anthony W. Lee's review essay, 'Editing, Editions, Essays, and Lives: Johnson, Boswell, and Other Usual / Unusual Suspects', examines two books with important contributions to textual studies: Jesse G. Swan, ed., *Editing Lives: Essays in Contemporary Textual and Biographical Studies in Honor of O.M. Brack, Jr* [2013] and Paul Tankard, with the assistance of Lisa Marr, eds., *Facts and Inventions: Selections from the Journalism of James Boswell* [2014] (*ECIntell* 29:i[2015] 43–50). And an important tool for Swift studies is reviewed by Ashley Marshall, *The Index* compiled by Hermann J. Real and Dirk F. Passmann [2014] to complement, as volume 5, the four-volume edition *The Correspondence of Jonathan Swift, D.D.*, edited by the late David Woolley (*ECIntell* 29:i[2015] 56–7).

The October 2015 issue contains a lengthy critique by the authoritative Robert D. Hume, 'A Quantitative and Comparative Approach to Restoration Comedy' (*ECIntell* 29:ii[2015] 6–18), offering corrections and valuable advice for the future of an important bibliographical project centred at the University of Seville. The occasion is the publication of the project's first volume, *Restoration Comedy, 1660–1670: A Catalogue*, edited by Manuel J. Gómez-Lara, María José Mora, Paula de Pando Mena, Rafael Portillo, Juan A. Prieto-Pablos, and Rafael Vélez Núñez [2014]. The review section includes Máire Kennedy's account of *Tommy Thumb's Pretty Song Book: The First Collection of English Nursery Rhymes*, a facsimile edition with a history and annotations by Andrea Immel and Brian Alderson [2013] (*ECIntell* 29:ii[2015] 35–6), and James E. May's of *The Irish Poet and the Natural World: An Anthology of Verse in English from the Tudors to the Romantics* [2014], edited by Andrew Carpenter and Lucy Collins (*ECIntell* 29:ii[2015] 40–3). The news section contains memorial tributes to three recently deceased editors and textual scholars active in the East-Central American Society for Eighteenth-Century Studies, the organization publishing *The East-Central Intelligencer*. The editor of Fielding, Martin C. Battestin, is remembered by the editor (James E. May), aided by an anonymous obituary (*ECIntell* 29:ii[2015] 44–6); the Swift scholar John Irwin Fischer is recollected by the editor Kit Kincade, Hermann J. Real, and Donald C. Mell (*ECIntell* 29:ii[2015] 46–50); and Alvaro Ribeiro, S.J., the editor of Charles Burney's correspondence, is memorialized by the editor, drawing in part on published tributes (*ECIntell* 29:ii[2015] 50–1).

*Script & Print* (*S&P* 39:i–iv[2015]), edited by Shef Rogers, continues to publish fascinating articles. Bryony Cosgrove's 'Editorial Practice and Epistolarity: Silent and Not So Silent' (*S&P* 39:i[2015] 5–20) argues that 'all epistolary editors, whether scholars, trained editors, or family members, add other layers of meaning to published letter collections through decisions concerning content, interpretation, presentation and market'. Furthermore, 'even as they work with the original author's voice, editors inevitably produce different versions of the correspondence: shadow letters'. For Cosgrove, 'these should not be read as primary sources but rather as another form of the originals, related but not quite the same, and with an appreciation of the intended market' (p. 20). She supports her contention by drawing upon case studies and in particular, amongst other editions, *The Letters of Rachel*

*Henning*, edited by David Adams [1952], her own editing in her *Portrait of a Friendship: The Letters of Barbara Blackman and Judith Wright 1950–2000* [2007], and *With Love and Fury: Selected Letters of Judith Wright*, edited by Wright's daughter Meredith McKinney and the historian Patricia Clark [2006]. The opening sentence of Patrick Spedding's 'Thomas Lucy and Helen Lasher Gardner, Opposite St. Clement's Church in the Strand, 1739–1805' (*S&P* 39:i[2015] 21–58) succinctly describes his contribution, which occupies most of the remaining pages of this first issue of *Script & Print* for 2015. It is accompanied by 173 footnotes, some of which are very detailed—see for instance note 33 on the exact location of Henry Gardner's shop (p. 28)—and six black and white illustrative figures. Spedding writes: 'the following essay was written with the intention of expanding the information available on Thomas Gardner, his wife Lucy and son Henry Lasher, a family of print-publishers who ran their business opposite St. Clement's Church in the Strand from 1739–1805'. Spedding also points out that hitherto Thomas 'has attracted only a modest amount of scholarly attention and probably his greatest claims to fame are as the publisher of Richard Rolt and Christopher Smart's *The Universal Visitor* (1756)'. Furthermore, he was 'the printer and publisher of most of Eliza Haywood's later, and most highly-regarded, works, included both *The Female Spectator* (1744–6) and *The History of Miss Betsy Thoughtless* (1751)' (p. 21). Spedding's explorations include three appendices: 'Inventory of Furniture at no. 200, the Strand, in 1775' (pp. 52–3); 'John Brett at no. 201, the Strand' (pp. 54–6); and 'no. 200, the Strand, after 1805' (pp. 56–8). This first issue contains the only review present in the four 2015 issues of *Script & Print*: Thomas A Darragh reviews Michael Tywman's *A History of Chromolithography: Printed Colour for All*, published by the British Library and the Oak Knoll Press in 2013 (*S&P* 39:i[2015] 59–61).

*Script & Print* 39:ii[2015] contains two articles. In the first, Patrick Spedding continues to explore the activities of the eighteenth-century printer Thomas Gardner. Spedding's 'Thomas Gardner's Ornament Stoke: A Checklist' (*S&P* 39:ii[2015] 69–111) is divided into a detailed introductory account (pp. 69–82) and an explanation of his bibliographical arrangement (pp. 82–4). The bibliography itself is partially annotated and 'is arranged alphabetically (by or for and title) within years' (p. 83). There are two parts: '(Part A): Items that Contain Only Gardner Ornaments' (pp. 84–93) and '(Part B): Items with Ornaments of Uncertain Evidential Value or that Contain No Gardner Ornaments' (pp. 94–7). These are followed by an illustrated 'Checklist of Garner Ornaments' (pp. 98–110). Spedding's erudite work concludes with an illustrated appendix: 'Henry Gardner's Publisher's Device' (p. 111). The second contribution is a splendid illustration of analytical bibliography, B.J. McMullin's pictorially illustrated '"A Nightmare," "Very Complicated": Towards a Bibliographical Description of Pierre Bizot's *Histoire métallique de la République de Hollande*, 1688, 1690' (*S&P* 39:ii[2015] 112–22). Although McMullin's subject is not a book in English, his application of analytical bibliographical technique and description provides an object lesson and exemplar from which much may be learnt and applied to books in English and other languages.

There are four contributions to *Script & Print* 39:iii[2015]. The first is Chris Vening's 'Henry Dashboard and Fisher's Ghost' (*S&P* 39:iii[2015] 133–62). Vening writes, 'in the year 1832 there appeared in an obscure and short-lived Sydney newspaper the first published account of the legend of Fisher's Ghost, a tale that still exerts a powerful grip on the imagination of Australians. It was presented in an anonymous thirty-stanza poem, "The Sprite of the Creek!"'. . . . Its authorship has been a puzzle.' Vening's research 'reveals a likely candidate: James Riley (ca. 1795–1860), Irish-born ex-convict, "bush tutor" and associate of the Hume family, early explorers and settlers of the southern districts of New South Wales' (p. 133). In addition to three illustrative figures, Vening's explorations are accompanied by a partially annotated appendix, 'Works Attributable to James Riley' (pp. 158–62). Jocelyn Hargrave begins her 'Joseph Moxon: A Re-fashioned Appraisal' (*S&P* 39:iii[2015] 163–81) by writing: 'Printer Joseph Moxon's legacy to print culture has suffered from myriad, often conflicted interpretations by book historians from the late nineteenth century to present day.' Hargrave's essay attempts to answer the question, 'who really was Joseph Moxon (1627–1691)?' By examining 'Moxon's professional interests and associations with the Stationers' Company and the Royal Society of London' and an 'analysis of specific editorial aspects of' Moxon's *Mechanick Exercises or, The Doctrine of Handy-Works. Applied to the Art of Printing*, initially published in 1683, she provides 'a clearer picture of Joseph Moxon as self-fashioning pragmatist'; then Hargrave 'redefine[s] his place within print culture—that is, as a pivotal contributor not only to the mechanical art of printing but also to the standardisation of editorial practice' (p. 163). Accompanied by two illustrative figures, there are three sections to Hargrave's account: 'Critical Perceptions of Joseph Moxon' (pp. 163–5); 'Moxon: Self-Fashioning Pragmatist' (pp. 165–75); and '*Mechanick Exercises*: Moxon's Editorial Legacy' (pp. 175–80). In her 'Conclusion' Hargrave writes that 'Moxon's published output was both politically and professionally necessitated' and 'his influence on the mechan-ical art of printing is undeniable and enduring; however, he should also be remembered for his vital contribution to the standardization of editorial practice' (p. 181). The third contribution to this issue of *Script & Print* focuses on a different century and a different kind of author. John Arnold, in his 'Worthwhile Rarities? The Fiction of Eric Partridge' (*S&P* 39:iii[2015] 182–90), observes that the New Zealand-born Eric Honeywood Partridge (1894–1979) 'is rightly known as a major lexicographer and *the* chronicler of slang'. However 'very few people know that Eric Partridge also wrote and published fiction' (p. 182). Arnold's essay, accompanied by two illustrative figures, examines that fiction and concludes that 'after *Why Not?* (pseudonymously published in 1931) / *The Scene is Changed* [a revised version] and *Chronicle* (1933) Partridge never again wrote or at least never published any fiction. Which, one has to say, was probably a good thing' (p. 190). The final contribution is yet another illustration of fine analytical bibliography from B.J. McMullin. In this instance his subject is 'An Eighteenmo in Thirty-Six' (*S&P* 39:iii[2015] 191–2). This is in effect an addendum to an earlier report in these pages (*S&P* 38:ii[2014] 110–14: *YWES* 95[2014] 1402) 'on the make-up of early-nineteenth-century children's "chapbooks" printed in the eighteenmo' (p. 191).

The final issue of *Script & Print* for 2015 contains three articles. In the first, John Arnold and James Doig look at 'William Nicholas Willis, Père, Fils and Family and the Anglo-Eastern Publishing Company' (*S&P* 39:iv[2015] 197–220). They write, 'William Nicholas Willis (1858–1922) is one of the more obscure Australian writers and publishers of the first half of the twentieth century ... . As well as being a writer, Willis was also a publisher. He established the Anglo-Eastern publishing company in London around 1914, mainly to publish his own books and pulp fiction novels.' Accompanied by four illustrative figures, the article 'briefly chronicle[s] Willis's life, survey[s] his books and then focus[es] on his publishing activities including those of his son, also William Nicholas Willis, who took over the Anglo-Eastern publishing company after his father's death' (p. 197). They conclude with an annotated 'Checklist of Books by W.N. Willis, "Bree Narran" [his pseudonym] and Titles Published by the Anglo-Eastern Publishing Company' (pp. 216–20). Rosi Crane, in her 'Creating Parker & Haswell's *A Textbook of Zoology* (1897)' (*S&P* 39:iv[2015] 221–40), replete with 116 footnotes, 'explores the creation of *A Textbook of Zoology*, principally through the eyes of one of its joint authors, Dunedin-based Thomas Jeffery Parker, FRS (1850–97)' (p. 221). Crane concludes that Parker and Haswell's textbook 'helped to provide a finite and stable view of comparative anatomy. More broadly the creation of this single textbook illuminates how textbooks synthesize knowledge but also place it in a straitjacket' (p. 240). The third and concluding contribution to the 2015 issues of *Script & Print* is appropriately another insightful one on analytical bibliography by B.J. McMullin. In this instance his subject is 'Gatherings and Signatures in Conflict' (*S&P* 39:iv[2015] 241–7). Importantly, McMullin indicates that 'signatures constitute a source of information about the production of the volumes in which they appear' (p. 221). His footnotes should not be ignored; for instance, McMullin's note 14 on 'the presence of two sequences of signatures in certain editions' of Henry James, and James bibliographers lack of providing 'details about the relative incidence of issues gathered in particular' or 'reporting the location of copies' (p. 245) is most useful.

Mention should be made of items of interest that may be overlooked as they are found in non-bibliographical, textual, or reference periodicals. Such an instance is Kathryn Sutherland's 'From Kitty to Catharine: James Edward Austen's hand in *Volume the Third*' (*RES* 66[2015] 124–43). Sutherland argues, 'from the evidence of handwriting in a range of his own teenage fictions, for a shorter time span than previously suggested for James Edward Austen's continuation to the second novella, usually referred to by its revised name "Catharine, or the Bower"'. She also raises 'the possibility that numerous revisions to Austen's original text, presumed to be hers, are also in her nephew's hand' (p. 124). Her discussion is based upon an examination of the manuscript copybook, 'one of three ... to survive containing samples of [Jane Austen's] teenage writings' (p. 124). And 'preserved in Winchester, Hampshire Record Office' (p. 128). *Clues: A Journal of Detection* contains an article of interest to students of bibliography and textuality. Jacqui Miller's 'The

Tremors of Forgery: The Palimpsest of Tom Ripley's Identity' (*Clues* 33:ii[2015] 56–66) is found in an issue entitled 'Re-Evaluating Patricia Highsmith'. Miller writes that 'forgery is a recurrent theme in Patricia Highsmith's work, both as a transgressive act and a metaphor for transformation'. By 'positioning the films' of the novels 'within their socio-historical context' she 'examine[s] the ways in which Tom Ripley is reconstructed or "forged" in the adaptations of Highsmith' (p. 56). William Baker and Shang Biwu's 'Fruitful Collaborations: Ethical Literary Criticism in Chinese Academe' (*TLS* [31 July 2015] 14–15, Commentary) explicates the ideas of the Chinese 'ethical critic' Zhenzhao Nie and surveys recent explorations in the field of 'ethical theory' and criticism (p. 15).

## 2. Books

Frances Burney has been well served by scholarly editions and editors. Peter Sabor, the general editor of *The Additional Journals and Letters of Frances Burney*, published by the Oxford University Press, writes in his preface that Stewart Cooke's volume 'is the first of two ... . Volume 1 of the present edition prints in their entirety Burney's journals and letters from the beginning of 1784 until her move to Court in July 1786, as well as any letters written before 1784 that were not published in the series of early journals.' These were published in five volumes by the Clarendon Press and McGill-Queen's University Press between 1988 and 2012. The second volume, edited by Sabor, 'will consist of all the letters, and journal and diary entries, written between 1791 and 1840', the year of Burney's death, 'that's were not included in the series of later journals' (p. v) published in twelve volumes by the Clarendon Press between 1972 and 1984. John Abbott writes in his introduction to this first volume that 'the journals and letters here amplify Burney's full induction into the cultural and social order of her world that *Evelina*', anonymously published in 1778, 'initially generated and detail exhaustively the terrain of the life she could have only dreamed about'. Furthermore, between 1784 and 1786 'Burney's life changed in ways she had never before experienced, in ways equalled only in the distant future in a harrowing surgical experience and a nearly fatal escape from France in the turmoil of war' (p. xv). This introduction is followed by a 'History of the Manuscripts and Earlier Editions' (pp. xxi–xxiv). Stewart Cooke, in his remarks on 'The Present Edition', observes that 'the goal of this edition of Burney's additional journals and letters is to print the surviving manuscripts in their entirety, while recovering, as far as possible the original texts' (p. xxv). 'Short Titles and Abbreviations' (pp. xxix–xxxiv), a 'Burney Genealogy' (pp. xxxv–xxxvi), and a very useful short 'Biographical Notes' on 'The Burney Family' (pp. xxxviii–xliii) are followed by the texts of the letters accompanied by extensive footnote documentation. The first letter is dated '6–8 January [1784]' (pp. 1–5) and the last, the 123rd letter '[11] July 1786' (pp. 443–4). There are four appendices: 'Letter from Francis Burney to Samuel Crisp, 15 January 1779'—this is a fragment (pp. 445–6); 'Letter from Francis Burney to Hester Lynch Thrale, 26 January 1783'—a previously misdated letter (pp. 447–9); 'Letter from Francis

Burney to Sarah Rose Burney, 12 September 1783' (pp. 451–2)—reasons for its inclusion are not given, presumably it illuminates the 1784 letters; and 'Fragments of Letters Between Mr. Crisp and F:B. in the Year 1782' (p. 453). In addition to the frontispiece, 'Hester Lynch Piozzi, Etching by Charles William Sherborn, after Robert Edge Pine, 1887', there are seven black and white illustrations included in this edition (see p. xi). Well bound, with a readable, computer-generated typeface and not too minuscule footnotes, an additional virtue of this first volume lies in its double-columned index (pp. 455–88) that includes 'all proper names in the text and appendices, and . . . selected names in the annotations' (p. 455).

The Oxford Edition of the Works of Robert Burns, vol. 1: Commonplace Books, Tour Journals, and Miscellaneous Prose is edited by Nigel Leask. Following 'Acknowledgements' (pp. v–vi) and 'Abbreviations' (pp. viii–x), the 'Note on the Text' opens with the observation that its 'editorial observations . . . are relatively straightforward, to the extent that in the majority of cases the principal copy-texts are manuscript books unpublished during [Robert Burns's: 'RB'] lifetime, and published subsequently only in a lightly edited format, when they had been edited at all'. Leask's volume 'adopts a chronological approach, but the circulation and transmission history of the manuscript texts presented here is often very different from that of published poetry and song'. As 'the rapid digitalization of RB's manuscripts will soon make all of the originals available on line . . . this is not a Quixotic attempt to "remediate" the manuscript page in print (in any case an impossible task), but rather to create an edition that opens up facets of the original manuscript text that might otherwise have remained concealed from the uninformed reader'. The volume 'offers diplomatic transcriptions that adhere as closely as possible to RB's original manuscript page, retaining his eccentric spellings, capitalization, punctuation, and use of ampersands, as well as marking revisions, elisions, and superscriptions'. In addition, 'this is the first edition to provide for annotation of RB's prose and associated items, now cross-referenced with his poetry and correspondence' (pp. xi–xii). These ambitious goals, are followed by three black and white 'Maps of Burns's Tours' (pp. xiii–xv) and a 'General Introduction' (pp. 1–5). In this Leask raises 'a problem of nomenclature' as 'drafts of poems and songs embedded in Commonplace Books and Tour Journals make up a substantial proportion of the volumes contents, the title "Prose Works" would be a misnomer'. For Leask 'the title Commonplace Books, Tour Journals, and Miscellaneous Prose offers a more accurate description of the variegated body of writings collected together here, for the first time'. Furthermore, the first volume is not a complete edition; there are exclusions. Leask's 'main criterion has been to collect material with a bearing on RB's literary career as a poet'. There are eleven chapters, and the strength of Leask's edition rests in the detailed introductions to each, which include 'a brief textual history of the materials contained in each' (pp. 1–2). This is followed by discussion of the materials' relation to the author's life and ideas, a description of the extant manuscript and details of its present location. Notation is found at the end of the texts (pp. 303–415) rather than in footnote format, and is followed by an enumerative alphabetically arranged bibliography divided into 'Primary' (pp. 416–19) and 'Secondary' (pp. 419–22) works and a double-columned 'General Index' (pp. 423–30), followed by a similarly arranged 'Index of Robert Burns's Poems and Songs' (pp. 431–2). The volume is well bound; however, the computer-generated typeface is by no means easy on the eye. The importance of this edition is rather modestly described at the conclusion of its 'General Introduction'. Leask writes that 'the material presented in *Commonplace Books, Tour Journals, and Miscellaneous Prose* has never before been properly transcribed and edited, or even published together in a single volume: and for much of the nineteenth and part of the twentieth centuries it was available only in abridged and bowdlerized form. To this extent the present edition marks a new epoch in Robert Burns studies' (p. 5).

The late Peter Cochran's (1944–2015) *Manfred: An Edition of Byron's Manuscripts and a Collection of Essays* is an important addition to Byron studies. Following 'Abbreviations' (pp. ix–x) Cochran's introduction, '*Manfred* and Drury Lane' (pp. 1–22), has material on 'The writing of *Manfred*' (p. 1) in which Cochran explains that there are two extant manuscripts of the work that he has examined: 'the rough draft is in the Pierpont Morgan Library in New York; and the printers fair copy is in the John Murray Archive (now at the National Library of Scotland)' (p. 1). Material on 'The Role of Douglas Kinnard: *Manfred* as an Intended Theatre Event' (pp. 1–7)—Cochran believes that *Manfred* displays its author's wish to have a drama produced in Drury Lane with the great Edmund Kean in its leading role—'The Incantation, and Byron's "Nightmare of my own delinquencies"' (pp. 10–16), and 'Contemporary Reactions' (pp. 19–22), is followed by detailed accounts of the Pierpont Morgan and National Library of Scotland copies (pp. 24–30). It is clearly stated that Cochran's text 'is based on the rough draft at the Pierpont Morgan Library . . . and principally on the fair copy and associated letter'—that is, Byron to his publisher John Murray, dated 15 February 1817 (the text is included in this edition as the first appendix (pp. 218–25)—'collated with the first edition and the editions of E.H. Coleridge (1898–1904) and J.J. McGann['s]' Clarendon edition published in 1986. Unlike McGann's edition, Cochran 'presents the play in a form as close as possible to the way in which it was written—with Byron's spelling, capitalization, and a plethora of dashes, which readers can interpret in various ways' (p. 24). The text (pp. 31–124), in common with the rest of this edition, is very well documented with accompanying explanatory notes at the foot of each page. Unlike McGann, who relegates an earlier version to his notes, Cochran includes both versions of the third and final act (pp. 85–124) . The text is followed by essays on '*Manfred* and Thomas Taylor' (pp. 125–35), in which parallels with Taylor's *Pausanias* [1794] are demonstrated (pp. 126–9)— an intertextual influence ignored by McGann. Other neglected parallels are indicated too in Cochran's '*Manfred* and Zoroastrianism' (pp. 136–43). '*Manfred* and Orthodox Christianity' (pp. 144–8) is followed by another area ignored by McGann, '*Manfred* and Shelley's *Alastor*' (pp. 149–55), '*Manfred* and *Frankenstein*' (pp. 156–63), '*Manfred* and the *Prometheus* of Aeschylus' (pp. 164–6), '*Manfred* and *Doctor Faustus*' (pp. 167–72), '*Manfred* and *Faust*' (pp. 173–80), '*Manfred* and Pellico's *Francesca Da Rimini*' (pp. 181–94), and an equally fascinating '*Manfred* and Shakespeare' (pp. 195–200). Parallels are also drawn with '*Manfred* and *Vathek*' (pp. 201–6) and '*Manfred* and

Wordsworth' (pp. 207–12). This is followed by what must be the first comprehensive 'Manfred: A Stage History' (pp. 213–17). There are three appendices. The first is 'Byron's First Letter to John Murray Announcing Manfred' (pp. 218–25), which 'has never been published complete' before this edition (p. 218). The second appendix concerns 'Two Proposed Productions of Manfred' (pp. 226–33). Cochran bravely writes, 'If left to my own devices, I wouldn't do a production of Manfred at all. As a poem by Byron it may be fascinating, but as a play it's rubbish' (p. 227). The third appendix, headed 'Man-Fred' (pp. 234–48), comments on and prints the text of a parody by 'Gilbert à Beckett (1811–56) ... A lawyer, journalist, and comic writer and lyricist [who] was on the staff of the first Punch' (p. 234). This parody is at times rather funny; for instance a character called Ann appears with the lines 'apples, here—apples, oh!—in vain I roar / No one will buy—it cuts me to the core' (p. 239). This edition concludes with a descriptive primary and secondary enumerative bibliography that includes a listing of contemporary reviews, and translations as well as 'Criticism' and a listing of theatrical productions (pp. 249–56) and a detailed index (pp. 257–63). Short of a major Byron discovery, Cochran's splendid edition is almost the final word on the subject and a worthy monument to a scholar who had an unparalleled knowledge of Byron. The Cambridge Scholars Publishing Edition is clearly reproduced, tightly bound, and reasonably priced.

James Gifford edits and introduces Lawrence Durrell's From the Elephant's Back: Collected Essays & Travel Writings. In his introduction (pp. xiii–xxxii) Gifford writes 'this collection has a straightforward ambition: to redirect the interpretive perspective that readers bring to Lawrence Durrell's literary works by returning their attention to the short prose'. Three areas of 'critical intervention' are necessary: 'reconsidering Durrell's political postures over time, reassessing his position in English literature as a Late Modernist, and addressing the role of the poignant suffering surrounding the Second World War in his travel writing' (p. xiii). In addition to a foreword (pp. vii–ix) from Peter Baldwin, a Durrell collector who runs the Delos Press that has published Durrell, the collection opens with 'From the Elephant's Back' (pp. 1–24) from a 1981 lecture that 'sets his childhood as a subject of empire in relief against the homelessness he felt when he was returned to the centre of empire: his Indian childhood and his adolescent migration to London' (p. xxiv). The essays and travel writings are divided into: five on 'Personal Positions' (pp. 27–58); eleven on 'Ideas about Literature' (pp. 63–180); eleven on 'Eternal Contemporaries' (pp. 183–283) on personalities including Ezra Pound (pp. 235–7), Dylan Thomas (pp. 239–46), the now largely forgotten Bernard Spencer (pp. 247–56), and T.S. Eliot (pp. 257–69); and ten on 'Spirit of Place: Travel Writing' (pp. 287–378). These essays are previously unpublished or out of print. At the conclusion of each is very helpful notation on individuals, places, and the content of the essays. Gifford's is 'a full critical edition with a scholarly apparatus, detailed annotations, and bibliography'. On the whole Gifford has 'left Durrell's idiosyncratic grammar untouched although spellings have been standardized'; furthermore, he has 'attempted to remain faithful to the original English typescripts, even though they are not as editorially polished as the subsequent French publication'. Gifford, 'for the final selection of material

[has] limited [himself] to works not otherwise accessible and particularly those that appeared in exceedingly rare publications or that exist only in typescript' (pp. xxix–xxx). The essays are followed by an alphabetically arranged list of works cited (pp. 379–90) and a detailed, double-columned index (pp. 391–406). Durrell knew figures who are now obscure, especially those who wandered in the shades of the disintegrating British empire: Gifford's selection is valuable for Durrell's essays and for bringing back into focus voices such as the fascist poet and editor Count Geoffrey Potocki de Montalk (1903–97), the editor James Meary Tambimuttu (1915–83), the American poet Michael Fraenkel (1897–1957), and, to name one other, Bernard Spencer (1909–63).

The first volume of Christopher Ricks and Jim McCue's annotated two-volume edition of *The Poems of T.S. Eliot* begins with *Collected Poems 1909–1962* 'as issued by' (p. xi) the poet just before he died (pp. 1–219), followed by the '"Uncollected Poems"' (pp. 221–319), and '*The Waste Land*: An Editorial Composite' (pp. 321–46). This 'is a 68-line reading text of the earliest available drafts of the various passages of the poem. By showing TSE's [T.S. Eliot's] earliest surviving thoughts as a contrast to the published poem, it aims to illustrate how radically it changed during composition' (p. 321). There then follows an extensive 'Commentary' (pp. 351–1227) on each of the poems. The first volume concludes with an annotated, alphabetically arranged bibliography (pp. 1229–49), in which for instance the reader learns that 'TSE's copy of' the first volume 'only, unopened (uncut)' of Spinoza's *Opera*, edited by J. van Vloten and J.P.N. Land, published in two volumes in 1895, is now at King's College, Cambridge (p. 1247). Somewhat confusingly the bibliography is immediately followed by '"Where Every Word is at Home"' (pp. 1250–2), consisting of citations from Eliot's prose and letters referring to words and their meanings and concluding with comments by 'Robert Burchfield (then editor of the *OED*)' relating to Valerie Eliot's confirmation 'that her husband possessed a copy of the *Shorter Oxford* but not of the *OED* itself'. Rick and McCue then comment on the '*OED* and the Present Edition' (p. 1252). There is then a commentary (pp. 1253–4) on the 'Index of Identifying Titles for Prose by T.S. Eliot' followed by an alphabetically arranged partially annotated 'Index of Identifying Titles' (pp. 1255–74) including 'jacket material'—see for instance Charles Williams's *The Greater Trumps* [1954] (p. 1261). The first volume concludes with two additional extensive indexes: 'Index to the Editorial Material' (pp. 1275–1300)—arranged in double columns—and 'Index to Titles and First Lines' (pp. 1301–11). The strength of this edition lies in its wealth of detail and commentary. There are some caveats. For instance, the 'Index to Editorial Material' under 'Eliot, George' refers to '*Daniel Deronda* 376' (p. 1282) and concerns the opening four lines of '*The Love Song of J. Alfred Prufrock*'—'Let us go then, you and I, |When the evening is spread out against the sky| Like a patient etherized upon a table; | Let us go, through certain half-deserted streets' (p. 5). In their commentary Ricks and McCue note 'George Eliot: "Let us go now ... We will get down at the end of the street", *Daniel Deronda* ch. XL, closely following "See the sky, how it is slowly fading"' (p. 376). There is such a plethora of detail in this edition that the present reviewer may have missèd it; however, he cannot find in the first volume evidence that T.S. Eliot read *Daniel Deronda*: such verbal parallels are interesting but speculative.

The second volume, as Ricks and McCue explain in their 'This Edition' found at the beginning of their first volume, 'contains the children's book *Old Possum's Book of Practical Cats* (pp. 5–35) and Eliot's only sustained translation, *Anabasis* (pp. 82–129), each followed by a commentary (pp. 37–77: 131–46), plus, within contextual notes, three categories of private verses: "*Other Verses*", *Noctes Binanianoe* and "Improper Rhymes" (pp. 147–290)' (vol. 1, p, xi). There then follows in the second volume an extensive 'Textual History' constituting most of the text (pp. 291–650): it 'provides information about the writing of the poems and their history in print' (p. 291). Two indexes complete this volume: a double-columned 'Index to the Editorial Material in Volume II' (pp. 651–5); and 'Index to Titles and First Lines' in both volumes (pp. 657–67). The first volume begins with 'This Edition' with the subheadings 'Arrangement of the Present Edition', '*The Waste Land*: A Composite', 'Titles', 'Text of the Poems', 'Spacing and Punctuation', and 'TSE on Treatments of his Poems', in which the editors draw, as they do throughout their two volumes, on published and hitherto unpublished Eliot correspondence (pp. xi–xvii). Extensive 'Acknowledgements' (pp. xix–xxii) are followed by a glossary (p. xxiii) and 'Abbreviations and Symbols' (pp. xxiv–xxv). The introductory arrangement of the second volume is different. It begins with Eliot's 'An Autobiographical Sketch' that he 'Sent to M.A. Frank-Duchesne, 5 November 1945': there is no explanatory note on who the recipient may be or why Eliot sent it! The 'Sketch' concludes: 'My chief function is to write verse, and verse plays and to publish the poetry of other writers: everything else I do is a *Nebenfach* [ancillary study]' (p. xi). This is followed by a 'Table of Dates' (pp. xiii–xv) that would have been more appropriate at the beginning of the first volume. The glossary (p. xvii) and explanatory listing of 'Abbreviations and Symbols' (pp. xviii–xix) also found in the first volume are repeated. This second volume contains black and white illustrations, for instance of the title page of *Old Possum's Book of Practical Cats* (p. 1). Extensive commentary follows each poetry collection, for instance '*Old Possum's Book of Practical Cats*: Commentary' is extensive. It is arranged by a commentary on '*Possum*' (pp. 37–8), the title (pp. 38–9), 'Composition' (pp. 39–43), 'Broadcasts' (pp. 43–4), 'Publication' (pp. 45–7), 'With and Without Illustrations' (pp. 47–50), 'TSE's Recording', including a short note on musical adaptations (p. 50), and then 'Apropos of *Practical Cats* by Valerie Eliot' (pp. 51–3): 'The following note from *Cats: The Book of the Musical* is taken from the version prepared for the (1982) American production. The version in the original British printing of 1981 was shorter and not illustrated by drawings.' His widow's account concludes with a fascinating 'P.S. Whenever he was unwell or could not sleep, TSE would recite the verses under his breath' (pp. 51–3). Such fascinating insights are followed by notes on each of the poems (pp. 53–77) and so on. As stated, a major portion of this second volume consists of 'Textual History' (pp. 291–650) to the material in both volumes. For instance the 'Textual History' of *Old Possum's Book of Practical Cats* (pp. 621–4) contains two general introductory paragraphs. The first discusses the 'many editions' that have appeared and the complex nature of the 'emendations', followed by a discussion of the various typescripts, notes arranged by year of publication on 'Published Texts and Post-Publication Emendations' and then 'A Word About the Musical Settings' (pp. 621–5). Then there follow textual notes on individual poems. In short there are infinite riches in these most reasonably priced two volumes. My major caveat is tactile: the paper is thin and irritating; the typesize rather small, no doubt to encompass the plethora of data packed into this edition. At times the editors assume too much: there ought, to take one instance from many, to be a note on Wolf Mankowitz (1924–98) the author, playwright, and scriptwriter, who at the time Eliot wrote to him in 1947 saying that 'I cannot give my consent to ... [his poems] in an annotated edition' (vol. 1, p. xv), graduated from Cambridge where he had been a student of F.R. Leavis at Downing College, and was editing, with Raymond Williams and Clifford Collins, *Politics and Letters*. However, it would be misleading to conclude on a negative note. Adam Kirsch observes in his lengthy assessment of Ricks and McCue's edition in the *TLS*, its 'real importance' is in their 'notes and commentaries, which are so comprehensive and authoritative that one can't imagine their being superseded' (*TLS* [11 March 2016] 4).

The third volume of *The Collected Works of Gerard Manley Hopkins: Diaries, Journals and Notebooks* is superbly edited by Lesley Higgins. Illustrated, an extensive 'Chronology' (pp. xv–l) is followed by Higgins's introduction (pp. 1–46) fully documented with footnotes on each page. She observes that 'this volume represents Hopkins the man of extremes, both emotionally and psychologically. There are mundane memoranda about neckties to purchase or letters to write, but also exacting revisions of poems.' Furthermore, 'there are entries of quiet rapture, his attention caught by the unexpected sight of a bluebell'. In addition 'paintings, sculptures, and works of literature are stringently assessed, his aesthetic principles freely exercised. There are also nightmares relived; undergraduate "sins" unsparingly recorded' and so on (p. 1). For Higgins, 'the Hopkins who emerges from the pages of the diaries is intellectually sophisticated and emotionally mercurial—all too capable of lacerating self-scrutiny and the resultant "despondency", but so vividly responsive when, in Wordsworth's phrase, he was "surprised by joy"' (p. 44). The diary entries extend from September 1863, 'just before his second term at Oxford' (p. 6), until February 1875, when he was studying theology as a Jesuit in Wales, and from February 1884 until July 1885, the period when he was living in Dublin as a professor of classics at University College and Fellow of the Royal University of Ireland. 'Editorial Notes' (pp. 47–55) encompass 'The Manuscripts' (p. 47), 'Principles of Transcription and Translation' (pp. 47–50), a note on 'Citing Other Works by Hopkins' (p. 50), and a listing of 'Poems and Poetry Fragments by Hopkins' (pp. 51–5). An alphabetically arranged, comprehensive 'Biographical Register' (pp. 56–94), beginning with 'Addis, William Edward (1844–1917)' (p. 56) concludes with 'Woollcombe, Edward Cooper (1816–80)' (p. 94). There is too a listing and explanation of 'Major "Feasts" in the Church of England and Roman Catholic Calendars' (pp. 95–102). This is followed by Hopkins's 'Diaries, Journals, and Notebooks' (pp. 105–631) accompanied by at times extensive footnoting. There are three appendices: 'Appendix A: Examples of Unedited Pages from

C.I and C.II'—Hopkins's diary at the Hopkins Collection, Campion Hall, Oxford (pp. 633–7); 'Appendix B: Architectural Terms Used by Hopkins' (pp. 638–51), arranged alphabetically beginning with 'Abacus' (p. 639) and concluding with 'Zig-zag' (p. 651); and 'Appendix C: The "Monita" or Community Rules for St Mary's Hall (Stonyhurst)' (pp. 652–3), the 'Jesuit Philosophate' where Hopkins spent 'a three year-course of study' beginning in September 1870 (p. xxvii). There is a detailed, alphabetically arranged, enumerative bibliography divided into 'Hopkins's Manuscripts' (p. 654) and 'Primary and Secondary Sources' (pp. 654–73), followed by an extensive alphabetically arranged index (pp. 675–722). A notable feature of this volume is its printing: Oxford University Press's printers have done a magnificent job with Hopkins's underlinings, erasures, and other idiosyncratic writing habits.

*Ben Jonson's Walk to Scotland: An Annotated Edition of the 'Foot Voyage'* has been edited by James Loxley, Anna Groundwater, and Julie Sanders. It is an edition of a previously unpublished third-person account of Ben Jonson's famed walk from London to Edinburgh during the summer of 1618. Jonson's account has not survived although it resulted in a meeting between Jonson and William Drummond of Hawthornden, 'recalled in the latter's notes of his guest's conversation and opinions'. However, 'unknown to scholars until recently ... a record of the journey did survive the centuries, preserved from fire and other threats among the papers of the Aldersey family of Aldersey Hall in Cheshire'. Now held in the 'Cheshire Archives and Local Studies' this '7,000-word account entitled "My Gossip Joh[n]son /his foot voyage / and myne into / Scotland' (pp. 1–2) is published in this annotated scholarly edition accompanied by five black and white illustrative figures. 'Acknowledgements' (pp. vii–viii), are followed by 'A Note on Names' (pp. ix–xi), which opens with an important statement of editorial method: 'this edition provides a modernised text of the "Foot Voyage," in the belief that the task of comprehending the difficult aspects of the account—which is for the most part a matter of understanding names and references or making sense of elliptical, abbreviated or compressed passages—should not be made any harder than necessary by the preservation of archaic habits of spelling and punctuation which differ from contemporary practice' (p. ix). A listing of a plethora of abbreviations (pp. xii–xvii) is followed by an extensive introduction, 'Jonson's "Foot Voyage" and the Aldersey Manuscript' (pp. 1–36), in which the editors 'focus on the manuscript witness, addressing the status of the surviving text, the provenance of the manuscript in which it is found, and—as far as is possible—the question of authorship, in order to provide a detailed context for [the] annotated edition of the "Foot Voyage" itself' (p. 3). The text (pp. 39–97) is accompanied by double-columned, extensive footnotes in a smaller, computer-generated typeface than the text. Personal names in the text and the footnotes are included in the double-columned comprehensive index (pp. 219–37). Three appendices follow the text: 'Brief Additional Passages' (p. 98); 'Canesco' (pp. 99–101), '"Canesco" Is PseudoItalian, of Sorts, for "Dogs" Language' (p. 99); 'Notes on Bothal and York' (pp. 103–5). Three 'Contextual Essays' essays then follow that 'invoke a more expansive notion of context, in an attempt to begin the process of assimilating the "Foot Voyage" into our critical accounts of Jonson's life, writing and times' (p. 3): 'The

Genres of a Walk' (pp. 109–33); 'Jonson's Foot Work' (pp. 134–70); 'Scenes of Hospitality' (pp. 171–98). The fascinating annotated edition concludes with an enumerative, alphabetically arranged listing of 'Printed Works Cited' (pp. 199–218), followed by the index.

Sir Thomas Malory's *Whole Book of King Arthur and of His Noble Knights of the Round Table* has been the recipient over the years of some most distinguished editions including those based upon the Winchester manuscript that came to light in1934 (for instance that edited by Eugène Vinaver published by Oxford in 1971) and William Caxton's edition of 1485. Joseph Glaser's *Condensed and Modernized* version is based, as he explains in his preface (pp. vii–xviii), on the 1485 text. Although Glaser notes that 'the textual situation, like so many other things about Malory, remains a muddle', he has 'chosen the Caxton text as the basis for [his] work because the Penguin Classics *Morte D'Arthur* edited by Janet Cowen [published 1962] is the version [he knows] best and because Caxton's chapter and book divisions best lend themselves to indexing the text' (p. xiv). Glaser's preface includes discussions of the question 'Who Was Malory?' 'Who Was King Arthur?' 'Malory's Sources', 'Tournaments and Chivalry', 'The Grail', 'Caxton and the Winchester Manuscript', and 'Sources for Further Study'. This latter section of the preface is arranged by date of publication and is enumerative. It is divided into 'Editions of the Full Text', 'Facsimile Editions', 'Discussions', 'Adaptations' (both alphabetically arranged), 'Films', and 'Arthurian Websites' (usefully annotated). The preface concludes with 'A Note on the Text and Graphics' that interestingly observes that 'the headpieces and ornaments throughout the text are taken, often in interesting form, from the work of Arthur Rackham (1867–1939), a prolific British artist whose illustrations remain as lively as ever' and that 'the typeface is Goudy Old Style' (pp. x–xviii). Textual annotations are sparse, although there is an extensive alphabetical index beginning with 'Abel' (p. 309) and concluding with 'Wisshard' (p. 348) arranged 'by book and chapter as in the Caxton text. . . .When a character has a significant part to play, the entry is descriptive' (p. 309).

This year witnessed the publication of two additions to the magisterial *Cambridge Edition of the Correspondence of Samuel Richardson*. Betty A. Schellenberg's edition of *Richardson's Correspondence Primarily on 'Sir Charles Grandison' (1750–1754)*, as she points out in her 'General Introduction' (pp. xxxv–xlvii), encompasses his 'correspondence with London-based authors and other members of the print trade; clergyman friends and other leading professional men; admirers and critics of Sir Charles Grandison; Irish book pirates and Continental translators; and collaborators in various publishing projects'. Consequently her 'volume supports a print-culture or sociological understanding of the author as an agent operating within a communications circuit or intercultural field that will at once shape and in turn be shaped by his own activity' (pp. xxxvi–xxxvii). Following Thomas Keymer and Peter Sabor's extensive 'General Editors' Preface' (pp. ix–xxii), 'Acknowledgements' to this volume (pp. xxiii–xxiv), a 'Chronology' (pp. xxv–xxxii), also found in the other volumes in the series, and 'Abbreviations' (pp. xxxiii–xxxiv), is Schellenberg's 'General Introduction'.

This is divided into sections on: 'An Author's Miscellaneous Correspondence in the Age of Print' (pp. xxxv–xxxvii); 'Samuel Richardson from 1750 to 1754' (pp. xxxvii–xxxix); 'Richardson and his Correspondents' (pp. xxxix–xlii); 'Sir Charles Grandison' (pp. xlii–xliii); and a very clear statement of 'Editorial Issues and Procedures for Volume 10' (pp. xliii–xlvii). The text of the letters (pp. 3–280) is fully annotated with extensive footnote documentation that is both textual and informational. This excellent volume concludes with a double-columned, alphabetically arranged 'Index of Richardson's Correspondence in' the volume (pp. 281–2) and a 'General Index' (pp. 283–8).

The introductory material to John A. Dussinger's volume in *The Cambridge Edition of the Correspondence of Samuel Richardson*, his *Correspondence with Sarah Wescomb, Frances Grainger and Laetitia Pilkington*, is organized upon similar lines. Facing the title page of both volumes are, in black and white, striking contemporary portraits of Samuel Richardson. Dussinger's 'General Introduction' (pp. xxxiv–lxix) is divided into three sections: 'Richardson's Correspondence with Sarah (née Wescomb) Scudamore' (pp. xxxi–lv), of which there are 152 letters, '52 are written by Richardson and 89 are written by Wescomb' (p. xxxv); 'Richardson's Correspondence with Frances Grainger' (pp. l–lxii), of which there are seventeen letters, 'a mere fragment of the original correspondence' (p. lxi); and 'Richardson's Correspondence with Laetitia Pilkington', of which there are twenty letters (pp. lxii–lxix). The text of the letters is once again accompanied by textual and informational footnotes (pp. 3–386). An appendix contains the triple-columned 'Richardson's List of Worthy Women in Letter to Frances Grainger, 8 September 1750' (pp. 387–92), with annotative details below the name of the lady, for instance 'A Miss S'. is 'Isabella Sutton (d. November 1768), unmarried daughter of Sir Robert Sutton' (p. 390). Curiously neither is referred to in the name-orientated index (pp. 393–8).

William E. Fredeman died in 1999. His great enduring edition of *The Correspondence of Dante Gabriel Rossetti* has now been completed by Roger C. Lewis and Jane Cowan with a tenth volume, containing the *Index, Undated Letters and Bibliography*. This final volume reveals the sheer wealth of material in the nine volumes and the extent of Fredeman's erudition. The volume begins with 'Abbreviations, Including Manuscript and Major Printed Sources of Letter Texts' (pp. ix–xxviii). The alphabetically arranged, double-columned 'Biographical and Analytical Index' (pp. 1–282) opens with an explanation, an example, and an 'Index [of] Abbreviations' (pp. 1–2). Lewis and Cowan write that 'this analytical and biographical index is designed to give researchers the widest possible contextual access to all names of persons, places, works of art, writings, organizations, and activities, both physical and intellectual, mentioned in Rossetti's letters and in the notes for the years 1835–82'. The compilers add that 'the Index is more than a simple listing of names: it also serves as a subject index, providing miniprécis descriptions of the information detailed in the entries'. Furthermore, 'since Dante Gabriel Rossetti is the lens through which all other entries are filtered, his own entry is divided into multiple subheadings to facilitate access'. It must be admitted that the arrangement of the index is far from self-evident, as its compilers admit when they write 'while some users may feel that this index is overly complex, the ultimate test will be in its usefulness to scholars, students, and readers who consult it'. The index is followed by the 'Full Version of a Letter Previously Published in Part'—Rossetti writes to Joanna Boyce in a letter dated '18 April 1857' (pp. 283–4)—and 'Undated, Unpublished Letters' (pp. 285–328). The volume concludes with a lengthy enumerative, alphabetically arranged bibliography (pp. 329–67). The computer-generated typeface of the index although small, is not unpleasant to the eye, and spatially well organized on the page; the volume is sturdily bound.

Thomas E. Schneider's edition in the ongoing edition of the *Selected Writings of James Fitzjames Stephen* (1829–94), the eminent judge, legal historian, author of *Liberty, Equality, Fraternity* [1873], and also a prolific journalist, includes thirty-six of his essays. Schneider observes in his introduction (pp. xvii–xxviii) that 'signs of intellectual disability prompted his retirement from the bench in 1891, at the age of sixty-two .... Stephen's preoccupation with problems of society, religion, and government is fully displayed in his journalistic writings from the previous four decades, a selection of which make up this volume' (p. xvii). The edition is accompanied by four black and white figures. An alphabetical listing of 'Abbreviations and Short Titles' (pp. x–xiii) is followed by a 'Note on Attributions' pointing out that 'most of the essays collected here were published anonymously, in accordance with mid-Victorian journalistic conventions' and that Schneider for identification purposes has drawn upon extant files of his subjects' journalistic contributions (p. xiv). In his 'Note on the Texts' (pp. xv–xvi) the editor observes that 'no effort has been made to impose uniformity of spelling or punctuation on' the texts 'with two exceptions', and these are the 'two essays [that] are excerpted for this volume, "Tom Brown" and "Ecce Homo"' (p. xv). Schneider observes in his introductory headnote to the first: 'given here are the opening and closing paragraphs of the review and two sections on English public schools and [Thomas] Arnold's views concerning them' (p. 16); of 'Ecce Homo' Stephen writes that it constitutes 'nearly the first attempt which has been made to write in English a life of Christ'. In Schneider's 'excerpt [Stephen] examines the "enthusiasm of humanity" that' the author of the works reviewed by Stephen, J.R. Seeley, 'has attributed to his subject' (p. 200). In neither instance does Schneider sufficiently explain why he chose to publish these two of his subject's periodical essays in as abridged form. His 'Note on the Texts' explains that the texts are based upon printed forms: there is little attempt to examine Stephen's manuscripts. Schneider's detailed introduction (pp. xvii–xxviii) discusses 'Stephen the Journalist' (pp. xix–xxii), the topic of 'Theology for Politicians' (pp. xxii–xxiv), 'Politics for Theologians' (pp. xxiv–xxvii), and Stephen's personal political commitment under the heading 'Sustain and Counteract' (pp. xxvii–xxviii). Footnote documentation to the texts is not extensive. Two of Stephen's 'Metaphysical Society papers' are included in Schneider's selection. A sole appendix includes the text of Richard Holt Hutton's 'The Metaphysical Society: A Reminiscence' from the *Nineteenth Century* in 1885 (pp. 295–310). The volume concludes with an alphabetically arranged, brief, enumerative 'Select Bibliography' (p. 311) and a double-columned, alphabetically arranged brief index (pp. 313–15). The paper used in this edition is irritating, it is well bound, and the computer-generated typeface of Stephen's text is slightly larger than that of Schneider's footnote documentation.

Anne E. Fernald's edition of Virginia Woolf's *Mrs Dalloway* is an excellent addition to *The Cambridge Edition of the Works of Virginia Woolf*. There are, in addition to the frontispiece, Vanessa Bell's 'dust jacket for the first British edition of *Mrs. Dalloway*' (p. iv), five other illustrations prior to the text of the novel. Jane Goldman's and Susan Sellers's 'General Editors' Preface' (pp. ix–xvii) discusses issues such as 'how should we edit the writings of Virginia Woolf?' (p. xiv) and 'Annotating Woolf' (pp. xv–xvii). Goldman and Sellers write that 'the Cambridge edition ... has invited editors of the novels normally to map out published and proof variants from the first British edition as copy text, with minimal interference on the page where possible, and with no silent emendation' (p. xiv). In 'Notes on the Edition' the general editors state that 'Virginia Woolf's sometimes idiosyncratic spelling and punctuation have been retained' (p. xviii). 'Acknowledgements' (pp. xx–xxi) are followed by a 'Chronology of Virginia Woolf's Life and Work' (pp. xxiii–xxvii), a listing of abbreviations divided by alphabetical arrangement into 'Archive Locations' (p. xxviii), 'Works by Virginia Woolf' (pp. xxviii–xxx), 'Texts of *Mrs. Dalloway* in Chronological Order' (pp. xxx–xxxi), and 'Shakespeare Works Cited in This Volume' (p. xxxi): 'as for Shakespeare, his importance to Woolf cannot be overstated. Woolf alludes to and quotes Shakespeare throughout'. Fernald adds that *Cymbeline* was the drama 'that converted Woolf herself to a love of Shakespeare' (p. lxi). There is a listing of reference works (pp. xxxi–xxxii), and also an alphabetically arranged enumeration of 'Archival Sources for Manuscript, Typescript and Proof Material Relating to *Mrs Dalloway*' (pp. xxxiii–xxxiv) and 'Editorial Symbols' (p. xxxv). Fernald's extensive introduction (pp. xxxix–xcvi) discusses 'Composition History' (pp. xli–lxxv), 'Publication History' (pp. lxxv–lxxx), accompanied by two black and white marked-up illustrations from the American proofs (pp. lxxvi–lxxvii)—Fernald writes that 'the British proofs have not survived' (p. lxxxv)—the novels' 'Early Critical Reception' (pp. lxxxi–lxxxiii), and 'Editing *Mrs Dalloway*' (pp. lxxxiv–xc). 'There are over 300 differences between the first British edition of *Mrs Dalloway* and the first American edition.' A third of these differences involve commas; there are other changes involving other kinds of punctuation such as semi-colons or exclamation points. Consequently the Hogarth Press's 'first British edition ... is more heavily and more strongly punctuated than the first American edition' published by Harcourt (p. lxxxix). Sixty-five notes (pp. xc–xcvi), some of which are most detailed (see for instance note 8 (pp. xci–xcii)) accompany the introduction. A tabulated 'Chronology of the Composition of *Mrs Dalloway*' (pp. xcvii–ciii) precedes the text (pp. 3–174). Each page of the text is accompanied by the number of lines on it and at its foot rather cumbersome indications of where 'Explanatory Notes', referred to as 'EN', 'TA'—Textual Apparatus—and 'TN'—Textual Notes—are located (see p. xxxv, and for instance the first page of the text of the novel, p. 3). The 'Explanatory Notes' that follow the text (pp. 175–311) are very useful and are followed by the 'Textual Apparatus' (pp. 312–31) distinguishing different textual states, and 'Textual Notes' (pp. 332–55) in which we learn for instance that 'the words *plunge* or *plunged* appear five times in the novel' (p. 332). An appendix (pp. 356–8) prints 'Virginia Woolf's Introduction to the Second American Edition of *Mrs Dalloway* (New York: Random House/Modern Library, 1928)' (p. 356). Anne E. Fernald's edition concludes with an alphabetically arranged, enumerative bibliography (pp. 359–76) followed by an alphabetical listing of 'Works by Virginia Woolf Not Listed in Abbreviations' (pp. 376–8). Sturdily bound with acceptable computer-generated typeface, Fernald's is *the* definitive edition of *Mrs Dalloway*.

Four additions to the Norton Critical Editions, very reasonably priced paperbacks primarily for the undergraduate market, published in 2015 should not be ignored: Willa Cather's *My Ántonia*, edited by Sharon O'Brien; Joseph Conrad's *The Secret Sharer and Other Stories*, edited by John G. Peters; James Weldon Johnson's *The Autobiography of an Ex-Colored Man*, edited by Jacqueline Goldsby; and John Webster's *The Duchess of Malfi*, edited by Michael Neill. O'Brien's edition of *My Ántonia* first 'published by Houghton Mifflin in September 1918' (p. xxv), in which 'Cather most fully transformed memory into art and created her most autobiographical novel' (p. vii), contains a detailed introduction (pp. vii–xxiii). This contains a 'Publishing History' (pp. xi–xv), and observations on its 'Reception' (pp. xvi–xxiii) that curiously ignore David Daiches's penetrating remarks on *My Ántonia* in his pioneering monograph *Willa Cather: A Critical Introduction*, published by Cornell University Press in 1951, although it is referenced in the enumerative 'Selected Bibliography' (p. 503) that concludes O'Brien's edition. Her 'Note on the Text' indicates that the first edition 'was printed unchanged until 1926, when a revised version was published. The major changes were to the introduction, which Cather shortened by more than a third.' This present edition 'incorporates the 1926 introduction into the 1918 text (the version that represents Cather's original conception of the work)' (p. xxv). The text, incorporating explanatory notes at the foot of the page (pp. 1–179), is followed by 'Contexts and Backgrounds' (pp. 183–328) that include 'Biographical and Autobiographical Writings' (pp. 183–217), extracts from letters pertinent to the novel (pp. 218–50), a section on 'Americanization and Immigration' (pp. 251–328)—not without its relevance to today—and then 'Criticism', organized by 'Contemporary Reviews' (pp. 331–52) and 'Modern Critical Views' (pp. 353–497), all accompanied by brief, sensible footnote annotation. This admirable edition concludes with 'Willa Cather: A Chronology' (pp. 499–502), an alphabetically arranged, enumerative 'Selected Bibliography' divided into books and articles on 'Willa Cather' (pp. 503–4), '*My Ántonia*' (pp. 504–5), and 'Backgrounds and Contexts' (pp. 505–6). The eminent Conrad scholar and critic John G. Peters's edition of *The Secret Sharer and Other Stories* contains his preface (pp. ix–xii) explaining his selective criteria, followed by 'Acknowledgments' (p. xiii), and an alphabetical listing of abbreviations (pp. xv–xvii). In his 'Note on the Texts' (pp. xix–xx) Peters writes: 'Throughout this edition, I have used the first English book edition as my copy text for the stories and the first American edition for my copy text for the "Author's Note" for *The Shadow Line*, *Typhoon* and *The Secret Sharer*' (p. xix); in other words the choice of copy texts is carefully calibrated in this volume. On occasions detailed, helpful explanatory annotations are found in notes at the foot of the texts (pp. 3–324): see for instance page 3. Peters provides a listing of 'Textual Emendations' (pp. 325–31). 'Backgrounds and Contexts' (pp. 333–437) opens with eight black and white illustrations depicting maps of voyages, and various perspectives on the kind of three-mast sailing vessel depicted by Conrad (pp. 335–42), followed by a useful, alphabetically arranged 'Glossary of Nautical Terms' (pp. 343–62), and pertinent extracts from Conrad's correspondence (pp. 363–79). 'Contemporary Reviews' (pp. 381–420) are followed by 'Contemporary Accounts' (pp. 421–37) of voyage disasters. This excellent edition concludes with 'Contemporary Criticism' (pp. 441–582). There is too a 'Joseph Conrad Chronology' (pp. 583–5) and an enumerative alphabetical 'Selected Bibliography' (pp. 587–99) on the Conrad texts included in Peters's edition.

The Norton Critical Edition of James Weldon Johnson's *The Autobiography of an Ex-Colored Man*, initially published in 1912 by the Boston firm of Sherman, French & Company, has been edited by Jacqueline Goldsby. James Weldon Johnson was born in 1871 in Jacksonville, Florida; he attended 'the all-black campus' of Atlantic University (p. xli). Goldsby writes in her detailed introduction (pp. ix–lvi) that 'perhaps the most devastating event that shaped Johnson's life and [*The Autobiography of an Ex-Colored Man*] *ECM*'s composition was his near-death at the hands of a lynch mob in Jacksonville' in 1901. This 'incident ... traumatized Johnson profoundly, fueled his later activism ... and inspired him to cast that incident as the turning point of an ex-colored man's life.' Furthermore, 'like so many African-Americans who migrated out of the South before World War I, Johnson left Jacksonville permanently after his near-lynching, relocating North in New York City' (p. xliii). Subsequently he obtained diplomatic postings with the 'U.S. State Department' (p. xxxiii) followed by academic positions. The annotated text (pp. 5–110) is followed by four appendices: the text of 'Revisions to Chapter X' (pp. 111–14); the text of the 'Original Conclusion' (pp. 115–19) followed by an 'Index of Sentence-Level Revisions to Chapter XI Draft Manuscript' (pp. 119–21); Carl Van Vechten's 'Introduction to Mr. Knopf's New Edition' of 1927 (pp. 121–4); and 'Introduction to the 1928 German Edition' (pp. 124–8), including 'a brief accompanying essay commissioned from the British composer Frederick Delius': Delius 'spent a few years near Jacksonville .... There, Delius first heard African-American folk music, which proved to be a significant influence in his later compositions' (pp. 124–5). 'Backgrounds and Sources' (pp. 131–337) includes material 'On the Life of James Weldon Johnson' (pp. 131–77); 'On the Cultural History and Milieu' of the work (pp. 179–219); and on 'Composition and Publication Correspondence' (pp. 221–52); 'Related Writings by James Weldon Johnson' (pp. 253–65); six black and white illustrations (pp. 266–71) including one of Johnson (p. 266); 'Contemporary Reviews' of the 1912, 1927 and 1948 editions (pp. 273–337); and four examples of subsequent criticism (pp. 341–428). This fascinating edition concludes with a tabulated 'James Weldon Johnson's Life and Times: A Chronology' (pp. 429–33), followed by an alphabetically arranged, enumerative 'Selected Bibliography' (pp. 435–9).

Michael Neill's Norton Critical Edition of John Webster's *The Duchess of Malfi* contains four black and white accompanying illustrations. Following an alphabetically arranged listing of abbreviations (pp. ix–x) there is an extensive introduction (pp. xiii–xliii) although its 'scope ... does not allow for a full performance history' (p. xiii). The annotated text (pp. 5–115), is followed by '*Malfi*: Collation' (pp. 117–24) that lacks an explanatory headnote, and curiously there seems to be no explanation of the text upon which Neill's edition is based. There is a note following the initial item listed in the 'Selected Bibliography' under the heading '*Quartos*'. Neill observes that the play 'was printed in four quarto editions in the hundred years after its first performance: Q1 (1623); Q2 (1640); Q3 (1678); Q4 (1708)'. He then comments without explanation 'of these only Q1 has any claim to independent textual authority' (p. 401). 'Contexts' (pp. 127–88) contains material on the play's 'Sources and Analogues' (pp. 127–67), 'Widows' (pp. 169–70), 'Remembering the Dead' (pp. 171–86), 'Contemporary Responses' (pp. 187–8). 'Criticism' (pp. 191–398) is divided by material—in most instances reprints from one critical essay only rather than several—on 'Sociopolitical Background' (pp. 191–9), 'Webster's Reputation, Seventeenth through Nineteenth Centuries' (pp. 201–17), 'The Play in its Own Time' (pp. 219–39), 'Theatrically Orientated Readings' (pp. 241–57); 'Dramaturgical Approaches' (pp. 259–312), 'Feminist Accounts' (pp. 313–34), 'Monuments and Ruins' (pp. 335–53), 'The Bonds of Service' (pp. 355–78), and 'Afterlife' (pp. 379–98). There is too the tabulated 'John Webster: A Chronology' (pp. 399–400), followed by an alphabetically arranged, largely enumerative 'Selected Bibliography' (pp. 401–5).

Amanda Gailey, in her *Proofs of Genius: Collected Editions from the American Revolution to the Digital Age*, 'examines how collected editions helped shape American literature, erecting monuments to individual people on the cultural landscape. [Her] study does not attempt to be comprehensive, but instead examines several important periods and cases in the development of the genre within the American national context' (p. 2). Her introduction (pp. 1–9) 'describes the book's working definition of "collected edition," discuss[es] how the concept of genius provided a motivation for many of the volumes, and offers a brief overview of how the collected edition has helped build a national literary identity' (p. 2). In her first chapter, 'American Collecting Itself: National Identity and Intellectual Property in the Early Republic' (pp. 10–32), she 'examines the early history of the collected edition in the United States'. Interestingly the 'early collected editions were more flexible than the ones we know today, sometimes including multiple authors or writings by still living the authors'. Developments in the book industry, such as for instance in bookbinding itself, led to 'collections based on authorial identity [that] became an uncontroversial way of organizing materials for sale, which contributed to the standardization of the form' (pp. 7–8). The second and third chapters, 'Dickinson's Remains' (pp. 33–54) and 'Whitman's Shrines' (pp. 55–82), 'focus on how the nineteenth-century collected edition influenced the publication history of two giants of the American poetry canon, Emily Dickinson and Walt Whitman'. In the case of Emily Dickinson, 'what has been lost in discussions of the first edition is how it was edited, published, and received as part of the long, feminized genre of literary or poetical remains, posthumous collections of work by authors who were typically but not always single, amateur women or girls' (p. 33). The initial collected Whitman, *The Complete Writings of Walt Whitman*, was published by his executors ten years after his 1892 death. However, during his lifetime his 'own efforts to control his literary legacy offer a case study in how the late nineteenth-century collected edition mirrored other death customs as a way of marking a dead poet's cultural prominence' (p. 55). The tenth and final volume of *The Complete Writings of Walt Whitman* contains 'a prefatory photograph ... depicting [Whitman's] tomb: there lie Whitman's remains in the granite monuments, next to the literary remains that lie in his textual one' (p. 82). The fourth chapter, 'Cold War Editing and the Rise of the American Literary Industry' (pp. 83–106), draws a fascinating parallel between literary editing and the formation of an ideological vision. The chapter 'studies the influential midcentury Greg–Bowers method for editing texts, and examines how the professional, scholarly editing of American authors arose in the context of the Cold War academy'. Gailey observes that 'government-funded editions from this period helped produce a vision of an American national literature and the American academy that was anchored in the Cold War political climate of the United States, exerting soft power as the United States attempted to concretize and spread its values'. Furthermore, 'these editions, the first to apply rigorous, academic methodologies and apparatuses to American literature, were both embraced as cultural accomplishments that uplifted American authors by purifying their texts and vilified as pedantic enemies of traditional literary scholarship' (pp. 8–9). In the 1980s there was a shift in editorial focus away from the Bowers line towards the views represented by Jerome McGann, who 'laid the groundwork for collected editions of American authors in the digital era' (p. 106). In the fifth and final chapter, 'The Death of the Author Has Been Greatly Exaggerated' (pp. 107–40), Gailey 'argue[s] that technological limitations have contributed to the singular status of author-centric collected editions in the digital age'. She 'conclude[s] by considering some potential alternative digital methodologies that might more robustly support the heterogeneous approaches of the modern academy-alongside ... this flexible, powerful, underexamined genre that has silently shaped American literature'— the collected edition (p. 9). There are notes (pp. 141–56) but no bibliography. Fourteen illustrative figures accompany this thought-provoking monograph that concludes with a double-columned index (pp. 157–62).

Amy E. Earhart's *Traces of the Old Uses of the New: The Emergence of Digital Literary Studies* 'analyzes the emergence of digital literary scholarship over the last 25 years'. Earhart, as she explains in her introduction, 'Digital Literary Studies in the United States' (pp. 1–10), 'uses the scholarship and products of the digital turn to define historical and emergent trends; [she] analyze[s] a range of materials including digital editions, digital archives, etexts, scholarly writing, digital artifacts (including tools and metadata), and interviews with key players in the field'. Further, she 'reveals that many of the theoretical elements of literary studies are retained in digital literary studies'. Earhart 'defines and analyzes four dominant areas of work in what [she calls] digital literary studies: the digital edition form, the digital archive form, cultural studies approaches, and literary data approaches' (p. 7). In her first chapter, 'The Rationale of Holism: Textual Studies, the Edition, and the Legacy of the Text Empire' (pp. 11–37), she traces 'the foundational form of digital literary production, the digital edition'. She 'argues that the centrality of the digital edition form that emerged from the combative field of textual studies transferred key ideas regarding texts and materiality to digital literary studies'. Amongst the 'key concepts examined in the chapter [are] a distrust of the digital environment, the holistic text and the desire for editorial control of the text'. Further, 'textual studies work has not neatly transferred into the digital nor has textual studies remained the dominant mode within digital literary studies, but the impact of textual studies on the field is undeniable' (pp. 7–8). The second chapter, 'The Era of the Archive: The New Historicist Movement and Digital Literary Studies' (pp. 38–61), 'tracks the archive fever that took over digital humanities in the 1990s, arguing that the digital archive was a contradictory form that sought to create an idealized archive'. Drawing upon work by Jerome McGann, Alan Liu, and others, Earhart examines 'how specific tenets of new historicism, such as the use of an anecdote within a complex social system, form the digital archive model'. Moreover, 'examination of theorists including Clifford Geertz, Jacques Derrida and Michel Foucault exposes the impact of new historicist thinking on digital literary studies' treatment of power structures, canon and apparatus' (p. 8). The third chapter, 'What's In and What's Out? Digital Canon Cautions' (pp. 62–89), 'charts the impact of cultural studies approaches on digital humanities' (p. 8). Chapter 4, 'Data and the Fragmented Text: Tools, Visualization, and Datamining, or Is Bigger Better?' (pp. 90–116), 'focuses on tool development, visualization, and data mining, three crucial subareas of the interpretive bent of digital studies'. Earhart's 'chapter argues that there is an unresolved and long-standing division between interpretive and representational uses of technology within digital literary studies, particularly in the development of tools' (p. 9). Her final chapter, 'Notes on the Future of Digital Literary Studies' (pp. 117–27), 'examines the current contours of debate in digital literary studies, with particular attention to formations of inside/outsider and resistance to the field by traditional literary scholars'. Chapter 5 'calls for a return to activist digital innovation that is divergent, not convergent' (p. 10). Notes (pp. 129–49), at times detailed, follow the text and stand in for an absent bibliography. There is a useful double-columned index (pp. 151–61) and black and white illustrative figures to this thought-provoking study that does attempt to clarify nomenclature and place 'Digital Literary Studies' (p. 11) within a historical context, although its author inevitably has her own agenda.

## 3. Bibliography and Associated Books and Articles

Philip W. Errington, a director at Sotheby's in London in the Department of Printed Books and Manuscripts, has produced *J.K. Rowling: A Bibliography 1997–2013*. In her short 'A Word from J.K. Rowling' dated 'November 2014' she writes: 'as someone who respects comprehensive research, I am in awe of the level of detail and amount of time Philip Errington has dedicated to this slavishly fine and somewhat mind-boggling bibliography'. She adds, 'I could never have anticipated that an idea that occurred to me on a train to Manchester could have spawned this amount of verbiage and prose in every language under the sun', for which she is 'humbled and deeply flattered'

(p. xvix). The 'Contents' pages (pp. vii–xv) reveal the cope of Errington's bibliography, beginning with 'A. Books and Pamphlets by J.K. Rowling'; Errington's 'A1', is *Harry Potter and the Philosopher's Stone* [1997]' and the final item is 'A17 *The Cuckoo's Calling* (2013)' (pp. vii–xii). There is a separate section 'AA. Proof Copies/Advance Reader's Copies of Books by J.K. Rowling' with five separate titles (p. xii). This is followed by 'B. Books and Pamphlets with Contributions by J.K. Rowling' beginning with 'B1 *Bloomsbury Autumn Highlights ... June to December 1997*' and concluding with 'B20 Joseph Galliona, *Dear Me: More Letters to My Sixteen-Years-Old-Self*' (pp. xii–xv). Section 'C' consists of 'Contributions to Newspapers and Periodicals by J.K. Rowling' and the final section, 'D', describes eight 'Items Created by J.K. Rowling Specifically for Sale at Auction' (p. xv). The book is well illustrated in colour and black and white. Errington observes in his introduction (pp. xxi–xxviii) 'This is a book about books. A descriptive bibliography looks at books as objects and describes them as such (often in painstaking detail). It can also tell some of the story behind the books themselves' (p. xxi). He also provides a 'flowchart' that may assist in answering the question '"have I got a *valuable* first edition?"' (p. xxiii). In his introduction Errington carefully explains each of the four sections he divides his Rowling bibliography into. Section A (pp. 1–455) includes title-page transcription, collation, page contents, paper description, running title, binding, dust-jacket detail—if one exists, the publication date, and how many copies were printed, the price, the content, and extensive notation that also includes reprint details. This plethora of data is continued throughout section B too (pp. 479–510). Section C, 'Contributions to Newspapers and Periodicals by J.K. Rowling' (pp. 507–10), gives the title, the newspaper or periodical where published, and on occasions brief detail. The final 'D. Items Created by J.K. Rowling Specifically for Sale at Auction' (pp. 511–14) has more information that in the previous section. There is a splendid illustrated dust-jacket but no index to Philip W. Errington's magnificent, well-bound and computer-generated printed *J.K. Rowling A Bibliography 1997–2013* that, like its subject's work, must surely become a collector's item too.

The sixth volume of Martin Wiggins, in association with Catherine Richardson, *British Drama 1533–1642: A Catalogue* covers the years 1609–1616. This is, to quote from the introduction to the first volume published in 2012, 'an enumerative, descriptive, and analytical catalogue of identifiable dramatic works, both extant and lost, written by English, Welsh, Irish and Scottish authors, in all languages, during the 110 years between 1 January 1533 and 31 December 1642' (p. ix; cf. *YWES* 93[2014] 247–8). This sixth volume, in common with the other five volumes so far published [2012–14], includes, in addition to a detailed abbreviations listing (pp. vi–x), a chronological double-columned list of entries (pp. xi–xiii), in this instance beginning in 1609 with '*Cadmus*' 'for performance at St. Oxford' (p. 2), and concluding in 1616 with '*Mercurius rusticans* [The Student in the Country]' that was 'probably performed at Corpus Christi College, Oxford, during the Christmas season' (p. 559). The main double-columned body of the volume, 'British Drama, 1609–1616' then follows (pp. 1–560). There are then triple-columned indexes of 'Persons' (pp. 561–81), 'Places' (pp. 583–5), and 'Plays' (pp. 587–92). In this monumental edition items are described in terms of title, text with location of the manuscript if extant, the genre, and explanation of the title, commentary on the date, details of the original production, plot description, scene designation, roles, the main speaking parts, brief description of other characters, the settings, sources, language, form—the metre, the rhyme and so on—the staging, music, props, costumes, the early stage history and then early textual history, editions if they exist, and references (see, for example, pp. 1–2; cf. *YWES* 94[2015] 1305). There is no doubt that these volumes contain a plethora of most useful information.

The eminent eighteenth-century scholar and critic Claude Rawson concludes a most enthusiastic lengthy assessment of Judith Milhous and Robert D. Hume's *The Publication of Plays in London 1660–1800: Playwrights, Publishers and the Market* by observing 'it is hard to imagine how the multifarious documentation of this stupendous volume will be surpassed anytime soon' (*TLS* [4 March 2016] 25). Milhous and Hume write in their preface (pp. xi–xiii) that their 'principal subject ... is published plays that were professionally performed in London' between 1660 and 1800. 'Of the 2,300 professionally performed plays, some 1530 were published—about 66%'. Replete with many black and white illustrations (see pp. xv–xxi) and accompanying tabulations (listed pp. xxii–xxiii), a short, alphabetically arranged listing of abbreviations (p. xxiv) is followed by a paragraph containing 'An Explanation of Pre-Decimal English Currency' and a paragraph explaining Milhous and Hume's 'Policy on Names and Titles' (pp. xxv–xxvi). A 'Prologue' on 'Play Publication Before 1660' (pp. 1–30) is followed by the first part of the study, dealing with 'The Publication of New Plays after 1600' (pp. 33–122), which has two chapters: 'The Age of the Quarto, 1660–1715' (pp. 33–76) and 'The Era of Octavo and Duodecimo 1715–1800' (pp. 77–122). The second part is headed 'Financial Contexts' (pp. 125–206). This also has two chapters: the first on 'Income Levels, the Value of Money, and the Price of Plays' (pp. 125–62); the second on 'Playwrights' Remuneration' (pp. 163–206). This concludes with a section answering the question 'Could an Author Make a Living from Plays?' (pp. 202–6). Milhous and Hume write, in the final sentence of their section, 'with a bit of luck, an eighteenth-century writer might make quite a lot of money from a particular play, but basically what one could *not* earn from playwriting was a living' (p. 206). The third part is on the subject of 'Catalogues, Reprints, Collections, and Illustrations' (pp. 209–359). This includes sections on: 'Catalogues and "Lives of the English Dramatick Poets" ' (pp. 209–14) answering the basic question 'How did booksellers and readers know what plays had been published?' (p. 209); 'Singleton Reprints' (pp. 214–25); 'Playwright Collections' (pp. 225–31), in which tabulations indicate which authors received the most reprints, for instance in the 'Early 18th Century' William Congreve, with thirteen collections, and Sir Richard Steele, with seventeen, were 'perennial favorite[s]' (p. 226); 'Collected Editions of Shakespeare from 1709' (pp. 231–45). Judiciously, Milhous and Hume write that their 'aim here is merely to report facts, problems, and puzzles, as we attempt to explain how the publication of Shakespeare fits in the larger context of publication of plays in our period' (p. 231). The fifth section, on

'Thomas Johnson and Early Collections' (pp. 245–9), begins with the activities of 'the noted pirate T. Johnson', who, between 1710 and 1712, at the Hague, 'published new editions of forty English plays' (p. 245). There is detail on 'Three Experimental Collections' (pp. 248–9), followed by 'Specialty Collections' (pp. 249–54) such as 'genre collections' (pp. 253–4). 'New Directions' focuses on 'John Bell's Three Editions of Shakespeare, 1773–1774, 1775–1776, and 1785–1788' (pp. 254–62) and is followed by material on 'General Drama Series: John Bell, His Predecessors and Competitors' (pp. 262–9). This fascinating fifth chapter concludes with 'Some Figures on Cost, Wholesale Price, and Print Runs' (pp. 269–72). The sixth chapter, 'Illustrations in Eighteenth-Century English Playbooks' (pp. 273–359), focuses on 'the seriously understudied subject of illustrations' (p. 272) and is accompanied by many black and white illustrative examples. As the authors observe, it was the publisher John Bell who 'had foreseen the potential value of widely distributable portraits of actors in character that photography would later make easy, and he had struggled with the complexities of getting excellent results, even if his auspices turned out to be not quite the right ones for generating and controlling the images' (p. 359). The brief 'Epilogue: Print and Theatre in the Long Eighteenth Century' (pp. 361–3) concludes that 'on average, playwrights got much higher copy fees than novelists for two very good reasons. Their published products got potent free publicity from performance, and a whole lot more people could afford to buy them' (p. 363). There are five appendices accompanied by tables and footnotes at their end rather than at the foot of the page as in the main text: 'Copyright Payments for Plays' (pp. 365–74); 'Plays Included in Major Multi-Author Collections Published in London from T. Johnson (1710) to John Bell (1773–1778 and 1791–1797)' (pp. 375–86); Bernard Lintott was an important publisher whose 'Copyright Transfer Agreements with Authors as Reported by [John] Nicholls' in his self-published eighth volume of Nicholls's nine-volume *Literary Anecdotes of the Eighteenth Century* (1812–15) constitutes the third appendix, followed by extensive footnote documentation (pp. 387–95). The fourth appendix, 'Author–Publisher Copyright Transfer Agreements in the Upcott Collection' (pp. 397–418) at the British Library is accompanied, following the listing of the transfer agreements, by 204 footnotes (pp. 397–418). The final appendix contains '*The Publication Order of* Bell's British Theatre, 1791–97' (pp. 419–23). A partially annotated bibliography is divided into 'Primary Sources (in Chronological Order)' (pp. 425–8) and an alphabetically arranged listing of 'Secondary Sources' (pp. 428–51). There are two double-columned indexes: the 'General Index' (pp. 453–75) and an 'Author-Title Index to Appendices III and IV' (pp. 477–83). To cite Claude Rawson again, among its other considerable strengths 'as well as being a hugely informative history of theatrical publication, its evolving relationship with theatrical practices, changing attitudes to plays and to authors, and publishing conditions, this volume is a magisterial account of the economics of publication and bookselling, as well as of the theatre' (*TLS* [4 March 2016] 25). The volume is a pleasure to handle and well designed, the computer-generated typeface setting is congenial, the plates and illustrative figures are reproduced clearly, and the volume is well bound. On a micro rather than macro level, Robert W.

Jones's 'Text, Tools and Things: An Approach to Manuscripts of Richard Brinsley Sheridan's *The School for Scandal*' (*RES* 66[2015] 723–43) investigates 'a manuscript' '*The School for Scandal*, Harvard Thr 5.1, Harvard Theatre College, Houghton Library, Harvard University', focusing 'on the ways in which the document discloses its own history'. Jones adds that 'the manuscript, which was created from two separate texts, reveals much about the nature of Georgian theatre and its practices' and 'the improvised and social nature of theatrical production' (p. 733). His article clearly demonstrates that the dramatist is 'only one element in a complex and multi-layered working environment' (p. 743).

A volume written by an eminent scholar and published in 2014 that was missed in our previous review is Lotte Hellinga's *Texts in Transit: Manuscript to Proof and Print in the Fifteenth Century*. She explains in her introduction (pp. 1–7) that 'in this book a selection of studies and essays are brought together, most of which were published in earlier forms in the course of the last forty years. Their common theme is following the transformation of texts during the time they spent in printing houses of the fifteenth century' (p. 1). The fifteen essays range from subjects such as 'Press and Text in the First Decades of Printing' (pp. 8–36) and 'The First Book Printed in Oxford' (pp. 218–27), to 'Nicholas Love's *Mirror* in Print' (pp. 366–94), 'Wynkyn de Worde and *The book of St Albans*' (pp. 395–409), and 'William Caxton and the Malory Manuscript' (pp. 410–29). There are extensive black and white illustrations throughout (see the 'List of Illustrations', pp. x–xi) and extensive usage of abbreviations (see pp. xii–xiv). There are four indexes: a double-columned curiously arranged 'Subject Index: Text in Printing Houses' (pp. 431–5), containing 'Items in the List of Printer's Copy' (pp. 67–101)— the essay entitled 'List of Printer's Copy Used in the Fifteenth Century'; a double-columned alphabetically arranged by location 'Index of Manuscripts' (pp. 436–7); an 'Index of Books Printed Before 1501' (pp. 438–43), arranged by 'abbreviated short-titles, in ISTC [Incunabula Short-Title Catalogue database recording editions and surviving copies of incunabula world-wide, based at the British Library] order' (pp. 438–43); and a double-columned detailed 'Alphabetical Index' (pp. 444–52). Well printed and bound with an interesting illustrated wrapper, this is a volume replete with learning.

Another learned and informative book is Stephen Orgel's short *The Reader in the Book: A Study of Spaces and Traces*, part of the Oxford Textual Perspective series with Elaine Treharne and Greg Walker as its general editors. Amply accompanied with black and white illustrations of the passages he is discussing, Orgel's work exemplifies his fascination with marginalia. He has 'collected volumes with marks of ownership and annotations for decades' (p. vi). He writes at the opening of the first of his seven chapters, 'Reading in Action' (pp. 1–29), that 'this is a book about individual acts of reading. Writing it has been possible only because reading in early modern culture sometimes left traces, and sometimes these are decipherable.' Drawing upon his own personal collection, Orgel's 'focus ... Is on a particular aspect of this history of the book, and archaeology of the use of margins and other blank spaces, a sociology of reading and writing in relation to ownership' (p. 2). Amongst texts considered in the first chapter are Holinshed's *Chronicles* published in London in 1586 'with heraldic shields added by hand' and 'excised' (pp. 12–13) and Geoffrey Whitney's *Choice of Emblems*, 'the first English emblem book' (p. 16) also published in the same city and year. The second chapter, 'Learning Latin' (pp. 31–49), focuses especially upon schoolboy annotations in copies of the classics such as Virgil's *Bucolica* (Cologne [1507]; pp. 31–5), and Horatius Flaccus' *Opera* (Venice [1490]; pp. 36–8). In the third chapter, 'Writing for the Stage' (pp. 50–83), Orgel turns his attention to theatrical texts. His examples range from the marginalia made by a Scottish reader 'shortly after the publication of the Shakespeare First Folio in 1623' now at Meisei University Japan (p. 50: pp. 50–6), and 'the last quarto of Davenant's version of *Hamlet* (London, 1703), the fourth reprint of the quarto of 1676' (p. 56: pp. 56–9). Orgel observes that 'these two *Hamlet*s are firmly ensconced in the study. Neither reader has any interest in returning the play to the theater, or, indeed, treats it as in any significant way theatrical' Consequently 'a copy of the first edition of the second part of Thomas Heywood's *Iron Age* (1632) provides a contrasting example, uniting the study and the playhouse' (pp. 57–62). Orgel asks 'what is required for the book to become a player again, for the text to become a script?' He responds to this question through a discussion of 'a First Folio in the library of the University of Padua that includes two plays, *Macbeth* and *Measure For Measure*, that have been marked up for performance' (p. 65: pp. 65–73). Correctly Orgel observes that 'plays are by nature unstable, and the history of performance is a history of revision'. He looks 'at a play text in action, a prompt-book for a series of productions over several years. The text is Thomas Otway's *Venice Preserv'd*, the most popular and long-lived of the Restoration tragedies' (p. 75: pp. 75–83) and his text is the 1682 first edition published in London. He concludes that 'the playbook as prompt book is scarcely a book anymore. It is a set of notations for production, and, as such, an archaeological site of evidence about the play's physical, auditory, visual, and spatial requirements and possibilities at a particular moment in theater history.... . The text is endlessly mutable—as the volume testifies, it changed from production to production. Publication, in short, does nothing to fix the text of a play' (p. 83). In his fourth chapter, 'Spenser from the Margins' (pp. 84–113), Orgel turns to a single author, a poet, and to 'the stable texts of literature and a pair of annotated Spensers ... a copy of the 1611/13 folio Works, with an early Puritan marginal commentary on *The Faerie Queene*, a manuscript text in angry dialogue with the printed poem'. The second text is 'the 1609 folio of *The Faerie Queene* alone'. This copy contains 'a more standard set of annotations, which [Orgel] offer[s] not simply as a control text, but as one with its own quite distinctive personality. In both cases—both copies are owned by Orgel—provenance is significant: the owners' marks have deliberately added to both volumes an element of romance, a fictitious history of a sort that is deeply embedded in the history of the book' (p. 84). In his fifth chapter, 'Scherzo: The Insatiate Countess and the Puritan Revolution' (pp. 114–37), Orgel considers Michael Sparke's 1651 *Truth Brought to Light*. 'Sparke (1586–1653) was a prolific printer and publisher ... [who] when the occasion arose ... also dealt in scandal and scurrility' (pp. 114–15). Lady Anne Clifford, countess of Pembroke, and Montgomery's 'copiously annotated' copy 'of the

Elizabethan classic *A Mirror for Magistrates*' (p. 138) preoccupies Orgel in his sixth chapter, 'Reading with the Countess of Pembroke and Montgomery' (pp. 138–57). In a short 'Coda: A Note from the Future' (pp. 158–60), Orgel tantalizingly provides an instance from one of the many letters Edith Wharton sent Bernard Berenson over a twenty-seven-year period, today 'in the archives of Berenson's Villa i Tatti in Fiesole, now a Harvard study center' (p. 158), that Berenson annotated in this instance a 'note, addressed to his wife, Mary, on the back of a letter from Edith Wharton planning a trip to Berlin together in 1913' (p. 160). So that although 'by the twentieth century writings in books had become an egregious form of antisocial behavior. Nevertheless, marginalia remained a potent form of social commentary and interchange' (p. 159). Orgel's fascinating book contains extensive footnote documentation in the text, an alphabetically arranged, largely enumerative bibliography (pp. 161–5), and a double-columned, name-orientated index (pp. 167–71).

Ellen Mazur Thomson, in the preface (pp. ix–xiii) to her *Aesthetic Tracts: Innovation in Late-Nineteenth-Century Book Design*, writes that rather than examining 'the relationship between the text and its physical embodiment, analyzing how a book's material form often unconsciously shapes the sense of the text', she is going to concentrate 'on significant late nineteenth century books designed by writers, artists, and printers who purposely and deliberately sought to create the material housing for specific books that would enhance the text and its meaning.... They designed books to be read with the eye as much as the mind.' Her intention is 'to examine all objects that were *intentionally designed* as aesthetic manifestoes in [Sarah Wyman] Whitman's sense of the term during the period from 1875 to 1900 in France, England, and the United States' (p. x). As Thomson explains, the wealthy Whitman (1842–1904) 'was a successful painter, a stained glass artist, and book cover designer' well known in Boston society (p. ix). Her 1894 lecture on book design to the Boston Art Students' Association is taken as the platform for Thomson's study. There are eight chapters. The first, 'Consequences of Material Abundance' (pp. 1–13), 'considers the technological advances in printing and the reorganization of the book trade that occurred in response to the massive increase in book production' (p. xii). The second, 'Book Covers: A Search for Design Principles' (pp. 14–32), 'focuses on cover design' (p. xii). The third, 'Japonisme in Sarah Wyman Whitman's Book Covers' (pp. 33–50), 'traces the way [Sarah Wyman Whitman] applied Japanese artistic concepts to trade books to engage with the meaning in the text' (p. xii). The fourth explores French examples (pp. 51–66) and the fifth, 'The Text and the Image: Conflict and Compatibility' (pp. 67–82), 'analyzes how the incursion of pictures into literary texts transformed the status of the book and the illustrator and inspired a new kind of book: the *livre d'artiste*' (p. xiii). The sixth chapter, 'The Writer as Book Designer' (pp. 83–101), 'explores ideas about books and their decoration espoused by three contemporary writers: James McNeill Whistler, Stéphane Mallarmé and Oscar Wilde'. The three 'highly self-conscious artists shaped their own books to advance their aesthetics and took great pains to ensure that the material form of these volumes precisely reflected their intentions' (p. xiii); however, 'publishers of their day were also interested in the text, but they designed books for the reader rather than as a form of authorial self-expression' (p. 101). A penultimate chapter, 'Privileging the Text: The Writer and the Reader' (pp. 102–21), develops the observation that 'not all designers wished to create books as objects of material beauty. Instead they insisted on the preeminence of the text'. Such responses are explored 'in the work and ideas of three printer-publishers: Édouard Pelletan, Walter Biggar Balikie, and Theodore Low De Vinne' (p. xii). The final chapter, 'Changes in the Lesson of Things' (pp. 122–32), in addition to exploring important book exhibitions, 'concludes with an account of the changing status of books as objects, the issues of nationalism that affected the critical response to book design, and the evolution of new ideas in book design as revealed in these international events' (p. xiii). An appendix, 'Gillotage' (pp. 133–5), attempts to explain the idea of gillotage developed by the French printer Charles Gillot (whose dates of birth and death the present reviewer looked in vain for in Thomson's work) in his 'attempts to print text and images together by mounting them on relief blocks of the same height' (p. 133). Extensive notes (pp. 19–65) follow the text. There is an enumerative, alphabetically arranged 'Selected Bibliography' (pp. 166–77) and an extensive double-columned index (pp. 174–7) that omits material in the endnotes. A notable feature of this well-designed and -produced book is its illustrations. As may be seen in their itemization (pp. vi–viii) there are sixteen full-page colour plates (between pp. 66 and 67), fifty-one black and white figures scattered throughout, and an attractive front jacket; however, full advantage isn't taken of the back of the jacket. According to Sebastian Carter writing in the TLS 'some of Thomson's matters of detail need to be treated with caution', the reason being that 'the detail of the book is so dense, it's coverage so wide, and the amount of quotations so great that the art slip is inevitable'. However, there are 'more serious flaws of the difficulty of finding what you need in the inadequately signposted end notes' (TLS [8 April 2016] 28).

The Printing History Society and the Vanbrugh Press based in Woodstock, Oxfordshire, have published the History of the Monotype Corporation by three distinguished contributors: the business historian Judy Slinn, the type designer and printer Sebastian Carter, and the typesetter and designer Richard Southall. Edited by Andrew Boag and Christopher Burke, there are three central sections to this volume containing 256 illustrations, twenty-two of which are in colour. In the first, Judy Slinn writes on 'The Business History of the Monotype Corporation' (pp. 13–176). This is followed by Sebastian Carter's 'Typeface Design for the Monotype Corporation' (pp. 179–302) and Richard Southall's 'Technical History of Monotype Composing Machines' (pp. 304–413). Andrew Boag's foreword (pp. 7–8) explains the history of the volume and the reasoning behind inviting 'three authors to write three Monotype histories' (p. 7). Christopher Burke, in his prologue (pp. 9–10), explains that 'this book mainly covers the period defined by the lifetime of the Monotype Corporation, which lasted almost a century, from 1897 to 1992', and that 'the relationship between the British and the American monotype companies remains somewhat mysterious; indeed it was not always clear to the parties involved'; however, this history is that of the British Monotype Corporation (p. 10). It should be remembered that Tolbert Lanston (1844–

1913), an American inventor, patented his monotype system of type composition in 1897. Slinn's contribution is divided into twelve sections: 'The Origin's and Early Development of the Monotype Machine' (pp. 13–23); 'The Establishment and Early Struggles of the Corporation' (pp. 24–41); 'Consolidation and the First World War' (pp. 42–58); 'The 1920s: Depression, Departures, and Developments' (pp. 59–72); 'The Golden Age: Monotype in the 1930s' (pp. 73–87); 'From Keyboards and Casters to Guns and Munitions: 1939–45' (pp. 88–103); 'Reconstruction and Growth: 1945–54' (pp. 104–19); 'Before the Storm: "A More Agreeable Stride," 1955–71' (pp. 120–32); 'The Problems of the 1970s: Attracting "The Take-Over Boys"' (pp. 133–47); 'The Long Road to Survival and Recovery' (pp. 148–50); 'The Corporation's Last Decade: 1982–92' (pp. 160–9); and 'Endings and Beginnings: The Legacy of the Monotype Corporation' (pp. 170–6). Sebastian Carter's section is divided into ten sections. In the first, 'Designing and Making Type before Monotype' (pp. 179–84), Carter writes, 'The second half of the twentieth century brought enormous changes in the technology of type manufacture and composition.' Carter adds that 'this revolution has been so astounding that we need to make an effort of the imagination to appreciate the typesetting revolution of the end of the previous century' (p. 179). His description of this and historical type development in his first section is a model of succinctness and clear exposition. Other sections are also clear. In 'Establishment of the Monotype Type Drawing Office, and the First Typeface Designs' (pp. 185–99), Carter notes that 'by one of the ironies of design history, many of the changes to come were prefigured by a man who was backward looking in almost all respects ... William Morris'. At the Kelmscott Press Morris drew upon type designs that went back to 'the Roman of the Venetian printer Nicholas Jenson (1404–80)'. Also Morris 'drew over enlarged photographs'. Carter adds that 'the use of photography to make working drawings of historical fonts, as well as the selection of the Jenson model, were to prove highly influential' (pp. 186–7). The third section is devoted to 'Imprint, Plantin, and Caslon' (pp. 200–4); the fourth to 'The Early [Stanley] Morison Years' (pp. 205–41). Morison (1889–1967) 'wrote a large number of books, and was a highly influential figure in typographical scholarship and promotion' and his 'influence on the Corporation was immense [although] he never gave it his undivided attention' (p. 210). Illustrations from this period include 'the (1923) title page of the Nonesuch Press edition of *Love poems of John Donne* showing Monotype fleurons in use' (p. 217). Section 5 focuses on 'Display Types, and Americans Abroad' (pp. 242–54). This section includes discussion of Berthold Wolpe (1905–89), who 'from 1941 ... was the designer responsible for book-jackets and bindings at ... Faber & Faber' (p. 244) and the great American book designer 'Bruce Rogers (1870–1957), the supreme master of allusive typography' (p. 248). 'A "Typographical Reformation"' (pp. 255–67), the sixth section, describes types developed by Morrison. The seventh section concerns 'The Second World War: Intermezzo' (pp. 268–72), and the eighth describes the impact of two typographers in the post-Second World War years, 'Jan van Krimpen (1892–1958) and Giovanni Mardersteig (1892–1977)' (pp. 273–83). The final two sections are concerned with 'John Dreyfus (1928–2002), Type

Adaptation, and the First Fonts for the Film Era' (pp. 284–92) and 'Into the Digital Era' (pp. 293–302).

In the final part of the *History of the Monotype Corporation*, Richard Southall writes on the 'Technical History of Monotype Composing Machines' (pp. 305–413). This has seven sections, beginning with the 'Background' (pp. 305–10). Southall explains that 'the growth in the demand for printed text in the latter half of the nineteenth century, fuelled in Europe by the expansion of universal education and in the United States of America by an increasing population of literate and enterprising immigrants, was matched by the development of systems for composing printer's type that were faster than the traditional technique of hand composition' (p. 305). The second section, 'Lanston and Bancroft (1843–1919): The Caster from Prototype to Production' (pp. 311–31), discusses the work of those typographical designers and machine engineers, in these two instances American, who responded to the developing needs and situation. The third section focuses on 'Keyboarding' (pp. 332–49); the fourth on the American-born creator of fonts F. H 'Pierpont (1860–1937) and Punchcutting' (pp. 350–70); the fifth section focuses on 'Photocomposition' (pp. 371–92); the sixth on 'The Monophoto 600 Filmsetter' (pp. 393–9); and the seventh on 'The Monotype Lasercomp' (pp. 400–13). In 'Epilogue: The Continuing Legacy' (pp. 415–19), Andrew Boag and Sue Shaw write firstly on the continuous focus 'on high quality and type technology' and secondly on 'the rescue and continuance of the Monotype hot-metal business, purchase by the Science Museum, with a National Heritage Memorial Fund (MHMF) grant, and dedicated to the care of the Type Museum Trust' (p. 415). The *History of the Monotype Corporation* is case-bound with a monotype set dust-jacket printed by Phil Abel at the Hand & Eye Letterpress, and the book is 'designed, typeset, and made into pages by Christopher Burke, Devizes' and 'Printed by Henry Ling Ltd, Dorchester' (p. 4). There is an appendix, 'List of Directors of the Monotype Corporation, 1897–1990' (p. 420), a double-columned, alphabetical enumerative 'References & Bibliography' (pp. 421–4), followed by an extensive index (pp. 425–32), printed in four columns using 'Monotype Classic Grotesque' which is also used 'for captions [and] footnote numbers'. The typeface used for the main text and footnotes for this fascinating volume is 'Monotype Dante' (p. 424). To learn about the history of printing, specifically nineteenth- and twentieth-century developments in it, and to become familiar with its technology, the *History of the Monotype Corporation* is indispensable. Brief mention too should be made of Tony Seddon's well-illustrated *The Evolution of Type: A Graphic Guide to 100 Landmark Typefaces: Examining Letters from Metal Type to Open Type*. Replete with diagrams and chronologically arranged, Seddon's book supplies the background for 100 eminent typefaces. Seddon has selected what he considers the most important typefaces over the previous two decades, although these no doubt will be subject to subsequent revision. His selective history has a useful double-columned index.

Robert Darnton's *Censors at Work: How States Shaped Literature* is based upon his Panizzi lectures at the British Library given in January 2014 'and dedicated to the memory of the first Panizzi lecturer, D.F. McKenzie' (p. 245). Darnton believes that 'a history of censorship' confronts an issue and that 'we face two conflicting views, one normative, one relative'. He argues that 'they can be reconciled by embracing both and elevating them to another level of analysis, one that' he refers to as 'anthropological'. Consequently Darnton presents a description 'of how censorship actually operated in three very different political systems' (p. 19): 'Bourbon France: Privilege and Repression' (pp. 23–86); 'British India: Liberalism and Imperialism' (pp. 89–143); and 'Communist East Germany: Planning and Persecution' (pp. 147–227). These three states acted in different ways, using different forms of censorship. For instance, 'under the pressure of circumstances, trials in the British Raj return the expected verdicts, yet they adopted elaborate ceremonies to act out the rule of British law and affirm the fiction of freedom of the press' (p. 230). For Darnton, 'the British had the ultimate answer: force. Not that they impounded and imprisoned on a great scale. For the most part, they remained true to form, clinging to common sense and muddling through contradictions.' Consequently 'Liberal Imperialism was the greatest contradiction of them all; so the agents of the Raj summoned up as much ceremony as they could, in order to prevent themselves from seeing it' (p. 143). Danton shows just how complex a notion censorship is and how its operations differ. There are ten black and white illustrations accompanying the text, and extensive notes (pp. 247–93) following the text, revealing the primary sources Darnton has drawn upon. The double-columned index (pp. 295–316) is comprehensive. Mention should be made too of William J. Maxwell's very well documented *H.B. Eyes: How J. Edgar Hoover's Ghostreaders Framed African American Literature*. Maxwell's title 'is inspired by Richard Wright's poem "The FB Eye Blues"' with lines such as 'Everywhere I look, Lord | I see FB eyes', and its concluding line 'I'm getting sick and tired of government spies' (pp. vi–vii). Maxwell's introduction (pp. 1–24), consists of three self-explanatory sections: 'The FBI against and for African American Literature' (pp. 1–6); 'The Files and the FOIA [US Freedom of Information Act]' (pp. 7–14); 'Five Theses and the Way Forward' (pp. 15–24). 'Part One/Thesis One: The Birth of the Bureau, Coupled with the Birth of J. Edgar Hoover, Ensured the FBI's Attention to African American Literature' (pp. 25–58) contains sections on: 'The Bureau before Hoover' (pp. 29–35); 'Hoover before the Bureau' (pp. 35–42); and 'Bureau of Letters: Lit.-Cop Federalism, the Hoover Raids, and the Harlem Renaissance' (pp. 42–58). There are six sections to 'Part Two/Thesis Two: The FBI's Aggressive Filing and Long Study of African American Writers Was Tightly Bound to the Agency's Successful Evolution under Hoover' (pp. 59–125): 'Flatfoot Montage: The Genre of the Counterliterary FBI File' (pp. 63–8); 'The Counterliterary State and the Charismatic Bureaucracy: Trimming the First Amendment, Fencing the Harlem Renaissance' (pp. 68–75); '*Persons* to *Racial Conditions*: Literary G-Men and FBI Counterliterature from the New Deal to the Second World War' (pp. 76–85); 'Afro-Loyalty and Custodial Detention: Files of World War II' (pp. 85–94); 'Total Literary Awareness: Files of the Cold War' (pp. 94–107); and 'COINTELPRO Minstrelsy: Files of Black Power' (pp. 107–25). Part Three/Thesis Three: The FBI Is Perhaps the Most Dedicated and Influential Forgotten Critic of African American Literature' (pp. 127–74) has four sections: 'Reading Like a CIA Agent' (pp. 131–41), which contains an interesting discussion of 'the British

Intelligence Service (SIS)' and its officers, such as Ian Fleming, and the 'vicious clash between enemy espionage outfits: the embryonic war between the FBI and CIA' (pp. 132–3); 'Reading Like an FBI Agent' (pp. 141–50); 'Critics behind the Bureau Curtain: Meet Robert Adger Bowen and William C. Sullivan' (pp. 150–65); and 'Ask Dr. Hoover: Model Citizen Criticism and the FBI's Interpretive Oracle' (pp. 165–74). 'Part Four/Thesis Four: The FBI Helped to Define the Twentieth-Century Black Atlantic, Both Blocking and Forcing Its Flows' (pp. 175–214) has five sections: 'The State in the Nation-State: The State of the Transnational Turn' (pp. 180–6); 'The State of Black Transnationalism: The State in the Black Atlantic' (pp. 186–95); 'Checking Diasporan ID: Hostile Translation and the Passport Office' (pp. 195–205); 'State-Sponsored Transnationalism: The Stop Notice and the Travel Bureau' (pp. 205–12); and 'Jazz Ambassadors versus Literary Escapees' (pp. 212–14). The final section, 'Part Five/Thesis Five: Consciousness of FBI Ghostreading Fills a Deep and Characteristic Vein of African American Literature' (pp. 215–75), also has five sections: 'Reading Ghostreading in the Harlem Renaissance: New Negro Journalists and Claude McKay' (pp. 225–32); 'Invisible G-Men En Route to the Cold War: George Schuyler, Langston Hughes, and Ralph Ellison' (pp. 232–43); 'Mysteries and Antifiles of Black Paris: Richard Wright, William Gardner Smith, and Chester Himes' (pp. 243–59); 'Black Arts Antifiles and the "Hoover Poem": John A. Williams, James Baldwin, Sam Greenlee, Melvin Van Peebles, Ishmael Reed, Amiri Baraka, Nikki Giovanni, and Sonia Sanchez' (pp. 259–69); and 'Bureau Writing after Hoover: Dudley Randall, Ai, Audre Lorde, Danzy Senna, and Gloria Naylor' (pp. 269–75). An appendix is entitled 'FOIA Requests for FBI Files on African American Authors Active from 1919 to 1972' (pp. 277–84). The notes (pp. 285–313) are extensive and informative. They are followed by a partially descriptive, alphabetically arranged listing of works cited (pp. 315–41) and an extensive double-columned index (pp. 343–67). Maxwell's volume is accompanied by revealing black and white figures, for instance 'A once-secret FBI request to place "stop notices" at "all east coast ports of entry" to guard against the re-Americanization of William Gardner Smith. (Courtesy of the FBI.)' (p. 208). As Henry Louis Gates, Jr. observes in an endorsement printed on the back dust-jacket: 'anyone who spies William J. Maxwell's latest book is sure to have her or his eyes pop. *F.B. Eyes* is a fascinating study of the FBI's decades-long surveillance program targeting the who's who of the African American cultural scene. What we read as art, Hoover's G-men coded as threats.' Gates continues: 'in poring over black writers' output across the long arc of the civil rights struggle, the FBI's "ghost readers," as diabolical as they were paranoid, added layers of weight to—and in some cases informed—the African American literary canon, which Maxwell reveals in an irresistible narrative steeped in investigative research.'

Another area of FBI concern was 'the Marxist-Leninist canon' (p. 96). So it is not inappropriate to consider two works that consider this perspective. Tony McKenna writes in his introduction (pp. 1–8) to his *Art, Literature and Culture from a Marxist Perspective* that 'one must try to identify within the work of art the crystallization of a broader historical necessity: the reason why the work has arisen at this moment, at this particular juncture, and how its greatness lies in its ability to preserve in a moment of eternity the historical contradiction and mood of the epoch more generally' (p. 7). Amongst other work considered by McKenna from a Marxist perspective are the rap music of Tupac Shakur, the painting of Van Gogh, HBO's *Breaking Bad*, Balzac's *Cousin Bette*, the magical realm of Harry Potter, the apocalyptic landscape of *The Walking Dead, The Hunger Games*, the *Game of Thrones, Wuthering Heights*, Iris Murdoch's *The Sea, the Sea* and John Williams's novel *Stoner*. Brief footnote documentation is found throughout the text. There is too a brief enumerative, alphabetically arranged bibliography (pp. 210–11) followed by an equally brief author-based double-columned index (pp. 213–15). A more extensive study is John A. Ming Chen and Yuhua Ji's *Marxism and 20th-Century English-Canadian Novels: A New Approach to Social Realism*. Unfortunately this is a volume not easy to use as it lacks an index. In their preface (pp. vii–xx) the authors explain that their work 'examines the effects of realism as a literary theory on a freshly established "canon" of English-Canadian works from the mid-1920s to the end of the 1970s' (p. xii). Further, their book transverses 'discursive or disciplinary boundaries and recommends socialism as a sociopolitical discourse into the account of a "school" of writing—social realism and in some exceptional cases, socialist realism' (p. xiv). The introduction, 'Reality, Realism and (Neo-)Marxist Definitions and Paradigms' (pp. 3–37), draws 'on the aesthetic views of Karl Marx and his followers, ventures a brief historical review of the mimetic/realist discourse since Plato, places the Marxist legacy in the tradition of Western culture, establishes a Marxist(-feminist) critical paradigm and identifies the deficiencies of English-Canadian literary criticism on social realism' (p. xvii). The book is divided into three parts. Chapter headings sufficiently indicate content and style. The second chapter focuses on 'Reinterpreting History from a (Neo-) Marxist Perspective: Social, Intellectual and Literary Background' (pp. 35–68). The third is on 'Early Beginnings of "Violent Duality": From Prairie Realism to Urban Social Realism in Durkin's *The Magpie*' (pp. 69–98). Part II, 'Theory, Urban Alienation, Sex, Politics: Socialism and Canadian Social Realist Novels' (pp. 99–135), apart from an introduction (pp. 99–100) has three chapters: the fourth, 'Theorizing English-Canadian Social Realism' (pp. 101–33); the fifth, 'Metropolis in Contrast with Cabbagetown: Callaghan's *They Shall Inherit the Earth* and Garner's *Cabbagetown*' (pp. 135–69); and the sixth, 'Revolution or Reform: Baird's *Waste Heritage* Versus Birney's *Down the Long Table*' (pp. 171–202). The penultimate part, 'Industrialization, Class Struggle, and Decolonization' (pp. 201–48), following a brief introduction (pp. 201–2), has two chapters: 'From Vision and Ideal to Strategy and Reality: Grove's *The Master of the Mill* and Carter's *Fatherless Sons*' (pp. 203–34) and 'Class, Capital, and the Case of CanLit Par Excellence: A (Neo-)Marxist Study of Margaret Laurence's *The Diviners*' (pp. 235–48). The fourth, concluding, part (pp. 251–61) has a brief introduction (pp. 251–3) and a single chapter, 'Out of the Ivory Tower: Sociopolitical Solution and Criticism?' (pp. 251–61), in which the authors write of Canada escaping 'the American new McCarthyism' (p. 261). The volume concludes with a rather superficial appendix, 'Canadian Chronology of Important Events and Works (1910–2014)' (pp. 263–7). There is a more useful 'Glossary of Key Non-

Literary (Neo-)Marxist Terms', beginning with 'Alienation' (p. 269) and concluding with 'Utopianism' (pp. 278–9). The volume concludes with an enumerative, alphabetically arranged listing of works cited (pp. 281–96).

G. Thomas Tanselle's *Portraits & Reviews* follows hard on the heels of his *Essays in Bibliography* [2013] the fifth collection of his previously published essays (see *YWES* 94[2015] 1300–1). The sixth collection, *Portraits & Reviews*, reprints twenty-seven previously published 'accounts of, or tributes to [book and or manuscript] collectors ... booksellers ... librarians ... scholarly editors ... bibliographical scholars ... historical scholars ... and authors'. Tanselle adds that 'some of these pieces are obituaries, and others focus on a single episode or aspect of a life, but they will attempt to capture a personality': some are very brief. The second section of this collection of essays, 'the "Reviews" section consists primarily of thirty-one book reviews, chosen from the approximately seventy formal reviews, covering about a hundred titles, that [he has] written (not a large number for writing career of fifty-five years)'. The reviews in *Portraits & Reviews* are 'selected only from the ones on bibliographical subjects' (pp. xi–xii). The majority of the essays included here are also found in well-known sources such as the *TLS*, *The Library*, *PBSA*, and elsewhere. The notable exception is the opening essay in the collection (pp. 3–12) on Floyd Dell (1887–1969), the American newspaper and magazine editor, dramatist, writer of fiction, and poet, 'written (with the title "a visit with Floyd Dell") in the summer of 1959 but never submitted for publication. Published here for the first time.' Dell's papers were at the Newberry Library in Chicago. Tanselle 'was gathering material for [his] dissertation' and went to visit Dell in his home 'in the Mount Pleasant section of northwest Washington' (p. 3). The essays chronologically range from 1959 to 2014. There is an extensive index (pp. 459–85) that reveals that Tanselle doesn't belong exclusively to the pre-electronic age of bibliographical endeavour–see for instance the entries under 'Electronic Texts' (p. 467). *Portraits & Reviews* is printed in computer-generated type not too small for ageing eyes, and is nicely bound. The front jacket contains photographic portraits of some of the biographical subjects included in the volume, the inside back jacket has a photograph of Tanselle, and the back jacket a listing of 'Selected Books in Print from the Bibliographical Society of the University of Virginia'.

## 4. Histories and Companions

M. Keith Booker's edited *Literature and Politics Today: The Political Nature of Modern Fiction, Poetry and Drama* 'brings together in a conveniently accessible encyclopedia format a wide variety of information on the relationship between literature and politics. International in scope, it covers authors and literary phenomena from the beginning of the 20th century forward, with a special emphasis on literature written in English'. Furthermore, it 'also includes a secondary emphasis on other world literatures that are particularly relevant to English-language readers, either because the issues addressed in these literatures are of particular importance, or because the authors themselves have been influential in the English-speaking world' (p. xiii). The first entry is on 'Abrahams, Peter (1919–)' by Jean-Philippe Wade (pp. 1–2) and the last on 'Zamyatin, Evgeny (1884–1937)' by Yvonne Howell (pp. 357–8). At the conclusion of each entry is a short list of further reading, limited on the whole to four or five items at the most. Following the main entries is an alphabetically arranged enumerative 'Selected Bibliography' (pp. 359–60), 'About the Editor and Contributors' (pp. 361–8), and a double-columned alphabetically arranged index (pp. 369–77). Apart from author entries, there are ones on topics too, including for instance 'African Literature (Anglophone)' (pp. 12–14), 'American Literature' (pp. 17–20), 'Jewish American Literature' (pp. 156–60)—nothing on British or other Jewish literature in English—'Postmodernism' (pp. 247–56), and 'Proletarian Fiction, American' (pp. 261–7). The length reflects the selective, uneven quality of the volume, clearly aimed at high school and undergraduate audiences.

The Cambridge Encyclopedia of Stage Actors and Acting, edited by Simon Williams, is a single-volume A–Z encyclopedia that aims to offer readers biographical, historical, geographical, and technical information about stage acting. At its core, drawing on the expertise of its eclectic set of contributors, are nearly 1,000 entries that focus on actors of the stage (rather than film or other media) who have earned a national and sometimes international reputation practising their craft. Information on directors and theatrical companies is included as well (e.g. Stanislavsky and the Stanislavsky system are separately covered). The entries are compact, clearly written, and followed by recommended further readings. There is also an enumerative, alphabetically arranged bibliography (pp. 672–5). Inevitably there will be omissions in any selection like this. Although the double-columned 'Index of Actors, Directors, Teachers, and Theorists of Acting' (pp. 676–94) includes mentions of the major mid-twentieth-century director George Devine, he does not warrant an entry of his own. There is no separate entry for the 'Restoration Theatre' but there is one for 'Thomas Betterton', penned by Judith Milhous (pp. 64–5). Worldwide in scope, the encyclopedia also inevitably takes on too much. Following the main entries, there is an appendix offering a 'Chronology of Actors by Year of Birth' that begins with Quintus Roscius Gallus (126–62 BCE) and concludes with Quim Fasano (born 1981 in Angola) (pp. 645–71). This relatively expensive book is sturdily bound and produced with sixteen black and white illustrations and aesthetically pleasing computer-generated sans serif typeface.

Jeffrey Gray, Mary McAleer Balkun, and James McCorkle, edited the two-volume American Poets and Poetry from the Colonial Era to the Present. It 'is a common compendium of full-length informative essays on the most important poets, genres, movements, and trends in American poetry from its virtual beginnings to the twenty-first century'. Additionally there are 'many entries on particular topics, whether those are periods, movements, practices, sub genres, or key terms in poetry'. Amongst topics are, for instance, 'the Harlem Renaissance, Native American poetry, Beat Poetry, Confessional Poetry, Modernism, the San Francisco Renaissance, and many more'. Furthermore, 'short bibliographies appear after each entry, and a long selected bibliography of sources on American poetry appears at the end of volume 2' (p. xi). These bibliographies, arranged by topics such as 'Critical Studies' (vol. 2, pp. 673–5) and 'Reference Works' (vol. 2, p. 675), are enumerative and alphabetically arranged. Following an introduction (pp. xiii–xxiv) and a 'Chronology' (pp. xxv–xxix), the main entries begin with 'African American Poetry' (pp. 1–9) followed by one on 'Ammons, A.R. (1926–2001)' (pp. 9–14). The first volume concludes with an entry on 'Lyric Poetry' (pp. 363–8). The second volume repeats in its opening pages the same materials as the first volume. The entries open with one on 'Masters, Edgar Lee (1868–1950)' (pp. 369–71) and conclude with 'Zukofsky, Louis (1904–78)' (pp. 667–72) that opens with the sentence: 'One of the foremost poets of the twentieth century, Louis Zukofsky was an objectivist who formulated a poetic ethos based on structure and form' (p. 667). Following the 'Selected Bibliography', which includes websites (pp. 673–5), there is information 'About the Editors and Contributors' (pp. 676–92), followed by an extensive, alphabetically arranged index (pp. 693–723). Firmly bound in quarto format with a clear computer-generated typeface, aimed at the high school and undergraduate market, the volumes somewhat surprisingly lack accompanying illustrations. There are exclusions too and missed opportunities, including for instance Julia Alvarez, who receives a short paragraph (vol. 1, p. 334), as opposed to a separate entry in the entry on 'Latino Poetry in the United States' (pp. 330–5), ignoring the fact that she is a fine novelist as well as a poet.

In his introduction (pp. xi–xiii) to *The Oxford Companion to Children's Literature* second edition, Daniel Hahn, indicates the differences from Humphrey Carpenter and Mari Prichard's first incarnation, published in 1984. 'Every entry has been trimmed back ... a process necessary to make space for the new.' In response to the question 'So what's new?' Hahn responds: 'Well, in addition to the edited and updated versions of the old material, there are more than 900 new headwords, with additions stretching from Douglas Adams (British writer [1952–2001], 50 words (p. 3) to Lisbeth Zwerger (Austrian illustrator [1954–], 46 words)'. The lengthiest entry and 'the most substantial newcomer not surprisingly, goes to Harry Potter [1997–2007]. 1,584 words)' (pp. xii, 264–6). There is no separate entry for Harry Potter's creator, J.K. Rowling. Each entry contains titles and publication dates. Hahn's second edition contains a brief foreword (pp. vii–viii) by Michael Morpurgo (1943–), 'English author who was Children's Laureate from 2003 to 2005 in acknowledgement of his position as one of the most popular and critically acclaimed of all contemporary children's writers' (p. 398). Organized alphabetically, the entries are followed by an appendix, 'Award Winners', arranged under different awards such as the 'Astrid Lindgren Memorial Award', the 'Hans Christian Andersen Awards' (p. 653) and concluding with the 'Guardian Children's Fiction Prize' (pp. 662–3).

A reference book missed in the 2014 coverage is Greg Garrard's *The Oxford Handbook of Ecocriticism*. In her preface (pp. ix–xii) Cheryll Glotfelty notes that the thirty-four essays in the volume 'together offer a critical overview of major historical periods, theoretical approaches, topics, genres, and geographies' (p. xi). Divided into four parts, following Garrad's introduction (pp. 1–24) explaining the organization and content, the first part has seven essays on 'History' (pp. 27–151): 'Being Green in Late Medieval English Literature' by

Gillian Rudd (pp. 27–39); 'Shadows of the Renaissance' by Robert N. Watson (pp. 40–59); 'Romanticism and Ecocriticism' by Kate Rigby (pp. 60–79); 'Cholera, Kipling and Tropical India' by Pablo Mukherjee (pp. 80–97); 'Ecocriticism and Modernism' by Anne Raine (pp. 98–117); 'W.E.B. Du Bois at the Grand Canyon: Nature, History, and Race in *Darkwater*' [1919] by John Claborn (pp. 118–31); and 'Pataphysics ['the science of imaginary solutions' that 'studies the particulars and exceptions that ultimately inhabit and subvert the generalizing assumptions of traditional scientific systems' (p. 133)] and Postmodern Ecocriticism: A Prospectus' by Adam Dickinson (pp. 132–51). The second part contains twelve contributions on 'Theory' (pp. 155–357): 'Ecocriticism and the Politics of Representation' by Cheryl Lousley (pp. 155–71); 'Cosmovisions: Environmental Justice, Transnational American Studies, and Indigenous Literature' by Joni Adamson (pp. 172–87); 'Feminist Science Studies and Ecocriticism: Aesthetics and Entanglement in the Deep Sea' by Stacy Alaimo (pp. 188–204); 'Mediating Climate Change: Ecocriticism, Science Studies, and the Hungry Tide' by Adam Trexler (pp. 204–24); 'Ecocriticism, Posthumanism, and the Biological Idea of Culture' by Helena Feder (pp. 225–40); 'Ferality Tales' by Greg Garrard (pp. 241–59); 'Biosemiotics Criticism' ('a discipline that examines sign processes, meanings and communication in and between living organisms', p. 262) by Timo Maran (pp. 262–75); 'Phenomenology' by Timothy Clark (pp. 276–90); 'Deconstruction and/as Ecology' by Timothy Morton (pp. 291–304); 'Queer Life? Ecocriticism After the Fire' by Catriona Sandilands (pp. 305–19); 'Postcolonialism' by Elizabeth DeLoughrey (pp. 320–40); and 'Extinctions: Chronicles of Vanishing Fauna in the Colonial and Post-Colonial Caribbean' by Lizabeth Paravisini-Gebert (pp. 341–57). The third part contains ten contributions on 'Genre' (pp. 361–516): 'Ecocritical Approaches to Literary Form and Genre: Urgency, Depth, Provisionality, Temporality' by Richard Kerridge (pp. 361–76); 'Are You Serious? A Modest Proposal for Environmental Humor' by Michael P. Branch (pp. 377–90); 'Is American Nature Writing Dead?' by Daniel J. Philippon (pp. 391–407); 'Environmental Writing for Children: A Selected Reconnaissance of Heritages, Emphases, Horizons' by Lawrence Buell (pp. 408–22); 'The Contemporary English Novel and Its Challenges to Ecocriticism' by Astrid Bracke (pp. 423–39); ' "A music numerous as space": Cognitive Environment and the House that Lyric Builds' by Sharon Lattig (pp. 440–58); 'Rethinking Eco-Film Studies' by David Ingram (pp. 459–74); 'Green Banjo: The Ecoformalism of Old-Time Music' by Scott Knickerbocker (pp. 475–86); 'Media Moralia: Reflections on Damaged Environments and Digital Life' by Andrew McMurry (pp. 487–501); and 'Talking About Climate Change: The Ecological Crisis and Narrative' by Ursula Kluwick (pp. 502–16). The remaining five contributions to this eclectic collection are geographically orientated and follow the title 'The Views from Here' (pp. 519–65): 'Ecocriticism in Japan' by Yuki Masami (pp. 519–26); 'Engaging with *Prakriti*: A Survey of Ecocritical Praxis in India' by Swarnalatha Rangarajan (pp. 527–36); 'Chinese Ecocriticism in the Last Ten Years' by Qingqi Wei (pp. 537–46); 'German Ecocriticism: An Overview' by Axel Goodbody (pp. 547–59); and 'Barrier Beach' by Rob Nixon (pp. 560–5). The volume has a detailed double-columned index (pp. 567–77). Each contribution is followed by notes and alphabetically arranged enumerative listings of references or works cited. Sturdily bound, Greg Garrad's *The Oxford Handbook of Ecocriticism* is a challenging volume treating an important subject from multiple perspectives on which much has been written in the last few decades. No doubt a second edition will be needed sooner rather than later.

In their introduction, 'Modern Jewish Fiction' (pp. 1–15), to *The Edinburgh Companion to Modern Jewish Fiction* its editors, David Brauner and Axel Stähler, write 'this collection of essays ... Is the first volume to bring together essays on American, British, South African, Canadian and Australian Jewish fiction with such a wide range of reference' (p. 1). Their introduction follows Mark Shechner's preface, 'Jews Have Legs' (pp. ix–xviii), outlining the parameters of the volume. Shechner writes that 'rejecting, exclusionary and cruel as they sometimes might have been, the Anglophone *Abendland* never developed mature cultures of pogrom and massacre towards Jews', adding 'towards others, yes, but the Jews never felt the full brunt of their savagery' (p. ix). Let us hope, given recent events in France and the UK, that this remains so! Above all for Shechner 'The Shoah'—the Holocaust—'is now a vast shadow over the work of all Jewish writers of all nations and probably will remain so many generations from now' (p. xv). Largely but not exclusively focusing on anglophone (written in English) post-Second World War fiction, there are three parts to *The Companion*: twelve essays on 'American Jewish Fiction' (pp. 19–171); nine on 'British Jewish Fiction' (pp. 175–288); and seven on 'International and Transnational Anglophone Jewish Fiction' (pp. 291–377). The first part begins with Lori Harrison-Kahan's 'Pioneering Women Writers and the De-Ghettoisation of Early American Jewish Fiction' (pp. 19–32), beginning with late nineteenth-century fiction. Other contributions to this first part of the volume include Victoria Aarons 'The Making of American Jewish Identities in Postwar American Fiction' (pp. 43–52), Sacha Senderovich, 'Soviet Jews, Re-imagined: Anglophone Émigré Jewish Writers from the USSR' (pp. 90–104), David Brauner's 'History on a Personal Note: Postwar American Jewish Short Stories' (pp. 105–18), reflecting the comprehensive nature of this *Edinburgh Companion*, and, to give one other instance, Deborah Shostak's 'Marginal Writers; or, Jews Who Aren't' (pp. 161–71). A curious omission, however, in this part is the two perfunctory references to the best-selling Herman Wouk, who celebrated his 100th birthday in 2016. In Part II, 'British Jewish Fiction' (pp. 175–288), one of the volume's two editors, Axel Stähler, contributes two chapters. He perceives the first Israeli Lebanese war of 1982 as a turning point in his ' "Almost too good to be true": Israel in British Jewish Fiction, Pre-Lebanon' (pp. 237–52) and 'The Writing on the Wall: Israel in British Jewish Fiction, Post-Lebanon' (pp. 263–6). There are seven other contributors writing on topics ranging from Efraim Sicher's 'The Postwar "New Wave" of British Jewish Writing' (pp. 175–87), David Herman's 'Jewish Émigré and Refugee Writers in Britain' (pp. 188–98), to Beate Neumeier's 'Reading Matters: "Marginal" British Jewish Writers' (pp. 280–8). The essays do not focus upon individual authors: a notable exception is Phyllis Lassner's 'Jewish Exile in Englishness: Eva Tucker and Natasha Solomons' (pp. 199–209)'. Part III, 'International and Transnational

Anglophone Jewish Fiction' (pp. 291–377), consists of seven essays. These include Ira B. Nadel's 'Jewish Writing in Canada' (pp. 291–302), Linda Weinhouse's 'South African Jewish Writers' (pp. 303–17), Emily Robins Sharpe's 'Jewish Novels of the Spanish Civil War' (pp. 355–66), and conclude with Shaul Bassi's thoughtful 'Mooristan and Palimpstine: Jews, Moors and Christians in Amitav Ghosh and Salman Rushdie' (pp. 367–77). Bassi's essay focuses upon perceptions of Jews by the two Indian novelists, both of whom stage 'liminal Jewish identities in a trans-civilizational perspective' and concludes with a paraphrase of lines from the great 'Bombay Jewish poet Nissim Ezekiel [that] if we treasure the "absolute" of the culture we belong to, let us not forget all its relatives' (p. 377). *The Edinburgh Companion to Modern Jewish Fiction* constructs a critical vocabulary appropriate to anglophone Jewish fiction. There are helpful notes at the end of most of the contributions and information on 'Contributors' (pp. 378–82). An extensive, alphabetically arranged enumerative listing of works cited (pp. 383–414) includes primary as well as secondary texts and unpublished materials. Nine black and white illustrations are included in the text. The triple-columned index contains three sections: 'Names' (pp. 415–20); 'Subject' (pp. 420–31); 'Title' (pp. 431–8). This most comprehensive volume is replete with fascinating material creating much food for thought. Sturdily bound, with a typeface not difficult on ageing eyes and an attractive jacket—regrettably the cover image from David Bomberg's 'Ghetto Theatre' [1920] will be removed once the volume reaches libraries— *The Edinburgh Companion to Modern Jewish Fiction* is highly recommended.

Victoria Aarons, Avinoam J. Patt, and Mark Shechner, have edited *The New Diaspora: The Changing Landscape of American Jewish Fiction*, on fiction that has been considered for the annual Edward Lewis Wallant Award, for which all three editors have served as judges, awarded to an American writer, preferably early in his or her career, whose fiction is considered significant for American Jews. There are two sections to this anthology. The first part consists of 'Selections by Edward Lewes Wallant Award-Winning Authors' (pp. 21–309) from 1977 to 2012 and the second 'The New Diaspora' (pp. 313–553) reflecting the landscape of American Jewish fiction during the period 1989 to 2013. An appendix is devoted to the 'History of the Edward Lewis Wallant Award' (pp. 555–8), the first winner being Norman Fruchter with *Coat Upon a Stick* in 1963. This is followed by contributors' details (pp. 559–74) reflecting the tremendous diversity of American Jewish fiction and its exponents. The anthology opens with a comprehensive, useful introduction (pp. 1–18).

David Hopkins and Charles Martindale, the general editors, observe that '*The Oxford History of Classical Reception* (*OHCREL*) is designed to offer a comprehensive investigation of the numerous and diverse ways in which literary texts of the classical world have stimulated responses and refashioning by English writers. Covering the full range of English literature from the early Middle Ages to the present day, *OHCREL* both synthesizes existing scholarship and presents cutting-edge new research, employing an international team of expert contributors for each of the five volumes' (p. ii). In their preface (pp. xi–xiii) to the second volume, covering the period from 1558 to 1660, its editors Patrick Cheney and Philip Hardie write that the '*OHCREL* conceives of "reception" as a complex process of dialogic exchange between two bodies of writing, rather than a one-way "transmission" of fixed and known entities' so their volume 'explores the ways in which classical texts have been remade and refashioned by English writers in ways that might cast (now, as well as then) as much light on the originals as on their English "derivatives"' (p. xii). Furthermore, their introduction (pp. 1–26) explains the three-part division adopted in the volume. The first part, 'Institutions and Contexts' (pp. 29–198), contains eight separate chapters, with the final one, on 'Cultural Contexts', having four separate sections (pp. 147–98). In the initial part the topics are: 'The Classics in Humanism, Education, and Scholarship' by Peter Mack, replete with 111 notes following the text (pp. 29–55); 'The Availability of the Classics: Readers, Writers, Translation, Performance' by Stuart Gillespie (pp. 57–74); 'Classical Rhetoric in English' by Peter Mack (pp. 75–86); 'The Classics in Literary Criticism' by Gavin Alexander (pp. 87–101); 'Classicism and Christianity' by Mark Vessey (pp. 103–28); and 'Women Writers and the Classics' by Jane Stevenson (pp. 129–46). There are four separate sections to the 'Cultural Contexts' chapter: 'a. Politics and Nationalism' by Curtis Perry (pp. 147–58); 'b. Sexuality and Desire' by Cora Fox (pp. 159–71); 'c. Literary Careers' by Patrick Cheney (pp. 172–86); and 'd. Fame and Immortality' by Philip Hardie (pp. 187–98). The second part contains twelve contributions on 'Genres' (pp. 201–483): 'Pastoral and Georgic' by Helen Cooper (pp. 201–24); 'Epic Poetry' by Philip Hardie (pp. 225–51)—an entry that is accompanied by 109 notes (pp. 245–51); 'Elizabethan Minor Epic' by Lynn Enterline (pp. 253–71); 'The Epistolary Tradition' by William Fitzgerald (pp. 273–89); 'Prose Romance' by Helen Moore (pp. 291–310); 'Elegy, Hymn, Epithalamium, Ode: Some Renaissance Reinterpretations' by Roland Greene (pp. 311–43); 'Complaint, Epigram, and Satire' by Susanna Braund (pp. 345–72); 'Tragedy' by Gordon Braden (pp. 373–94); 'Comedy' by Bruce R. Smith (pp. 395–417); 'Tragicomedy' by Tanya Pollard (pp. 419–32); 'Historiography and Biography' by Bart Van Es (pp. 433–59); and 'Discursive and Speculative Writing' by Reid Barbour and Claire Preston (pp. 461–83). The third and final part concentrates on 'Authors' (pp. 487–655) and contains nine contributions on: 'Homer' by Jessica Wolfe (pp. 487–502); 'Plato' by Elizabeth Jane Bellamy (pp. 503–15); 'Virgil and Ovid' by Maggie Kilgour (pp. 517–38); 'Horace' by Victoria Moul (with a contribution by Charles Martindale) (pp. 539–56); 'Spenser' by Richard McCabe (pp. 557–78); 'Marlowe' by Charles Martindale (pp. 579–97); 'Shakespeare' by Colin Burrow (pp. 599–620); 'Jonson' by Sean Keilen (pp. 621–40); and 'Early Milton' by Thomas H. Luxon (pp. 641–55). These contributions are followed by the partially descriptive 'Classical Reception in English Literature, 1558–1660: An Annotated Bibliography' by Craig Kallendorf, divided into 'Key Themes' (pp. 657–76), 'Forms and Genres (in Alphabetical Order)' (pp. 677–98), 'The Reception of Particular Authors: Classical Authors' (pp. 698–732), and 'Classical Reception in Several Key English Authors' (pp. 732–41). A most detailed index (pp. 743–88) concludes this most comprehensive volume.

Norman Vance and Jennifer Wallace, the editors of *The Oxford History of Classical Reception in English Literature*, volume 4: *1790–1880*, remark in their introduction (pp. 1–27), 'the study, influence and conceptualization of the classics were at least as complex, nebulous, and yet culturally important in the period 1790–1880 as at any other time'. The reasons for this were 'partly due to the fact that the century witnessed a huge widening of the potential reading (and viewing) audience, with a greater diversity of gender and class represented than in previous eras, and yet also with a greater stake in the Classics as inherited cultural capital than was evident in the century to come' (p. 1). Accompanied by fifteen black and white illustrations, the volume is divided into two sections. In the first, 'Contexts and Genres' there are eleven contributions: 'Classical Authors 1790–1880' by Norman Vance (pp. 29–55); ' "The principle of the daguerreotype": Translation from the Classics' by John Talbot (pp. 57–78); 'Education and Reading' by Christopher Stray (pp. 79–102); 'Political Writing and Class' by Edmund Richardson (pp. 103–29)— accompanied by 155 notes (pp. 125–9) following the text; 'Barbarism and Civilization: Political Writing, History, and Empire' by Phiroze Vasunia (pp. 131–58); 'American Literature and Classical Consciousness' by Paul Giles (pp. 159–83); 'Myth and Religion' by Norman Vance (pp. 185–202); 'Art, Aesthetics, and Archaeological Poetics' by Jonah Siegel (pp. 203–41); ' "Greek under the Trees": Classical Reception and Gender' by Jennifer Wallace (pp. 243–78); 'The Novel' by Norman Vance (pp. 279–98); and 'Shakespearean Sophocles: (Re)-discovering and Performing Greek Tragedy in the Nineteenth Century' by Fiona Macintosh (pp. 299–323). The second section, on 'Authors' (pp. 325–668), with its fifteen contributions, follows directly without a separate section being indicated in the volume. The subjects are: 'William Wordsworth' by James Castell (pp. 325–46); 'Coleridge' by J.C.C. Mays (pp. 347–64); 'Walter Savage Landor and the Classics' by Adam Roberts (pp. 365–84); 'The Unexpected Latinist: Byron and the Roman Muse' by Timothy Webb (pp. 385–412); 'The Younger Romantics: Leigh Hunt, Keats and Shelley' by Jennifer Wallace (pp. 413–48); 'Elizabeth Barrett Browning' by Isobel Hurst (pp. 449–70); 'Matthew Arnold' by Nicholas Shrimpton (pp. 471–94); 'Arthur Hugh Clough' by Isobel Hurst; 'Translating Tragedy: Robert Browning's Greek Decade' by Yopie Prins (pp. 509–38; a contribution that misses William Baker and Stephen Glass's 'Robert Browning's *Iliad*: An Unnoted Copy' *Studies in Browning and His Circle* 12 [1984] 148–59); 'Tennyson' by A.A. Markley (pp. 539–57); 'William Morris' by Stephen Harrison (pp. 559–78); 'George Eliot' by Shanyn Fiske (pp. 579–99; a contribution that surprisingly omits reference to details concerning its subject's classical reading found in her notebooks, or Vernon Rendall's important 'George Eliot and the Classics', *N&Q* 192[1947] 544–6, 564–5); 'Thomas Hardy' by Ralph Pite (pp. 601–18); 'Swinburne' by Charlotte Ribeyrol (pp. 619–42); and 'Towards the *Fin de Siècle*: Walter Pater and John Addington Symonds' by Stefano Evangelista (pp. 643–68). The volume concludes with Norman Vance's 'Classical Reception in English Literature, 1790–1880: An Annotated Bibliography' (pp. 669–701) divided by the two parts of his and Jennifer Wallace's volume. The volume concludes with an extensive index (pp. 703–46).

   This is the appropriate place to draw attention to a fascinating reference/ critical work edited by Brett M. Rogers and Benjamin Eldon Stevens, *Classical Traditions in Science Fiction*. In their introduction, 'The Past Is an

Undiscovered Country' (pp. 1–24), Rogers and Stevens, referring 'to the divine figure in Roman mythology', write that their 'main purpose . . . is to suggest some of the ways in which serious discussion of the Janus—like character of Modern S[cience]F[iction] might proceed'. The editors also 'hope that this volume's chapters [will] demonstrate the relevance of a wide range of Greek and Roman Classics for modern SF' (p. 6). Rogers and Stevens indicate a 'significant theme common to the following chapters . . . namely, the possible deep epistemological similarities between (studying) the ancient past and (speculating about) the future. These chapters range widely in subject matter, treating some relatively lesser-known classics as well as works of long standing "canonical" status, and likewise covering SF both well known and less mainstream' (p. 20). There are four parts to their work. In the first, 'SF's Rosy-Fingered Dawn' (pp. 27–120), there are four contributions: 'The Lunar Setting of Johannes Kepler's *Somnium*, Science Fiction's Missing Link' by Dean Swinford (pp. 27–45); 'Lucretius, Lucan, and Mary Shelley's *Frankenstein*' by Jesse Weiner (pp. 46–74); 'Virgil in Jules Verne's *Journey to the Center of the Earth*' by Benjamin Eldon Stevens (pp. 75–104); and 'Mr. Lucian in Suburbia: Links between *The True History* and *The First Men in The Moon*' by Antony Keen (pp. 105–20). The second part is on 'SF "Classics"' (pp. 123–96). There are contributions on: 'A Complex Oedipus: The Tragedy of Edward Morbius' by Gregory S. Bucher (pp. 123–44); 'Walter M. Miller, Jr.'s *A Canticle for Leibowitz*, *The Great Year*, and *The Ages of Man*' by Erik Grayson (pp. 145–60); 'Time and Self-Referentiality in the *Iliad* and Frank Herbert's *Dune*' by Joel Christensen (pp. 161–75); and 'Disability as Rhetorical Trope in Classical Myth and *Blade Runner*' by Rebecca Raphael (pp. 176–96). The third part focuses on 'Classics in Space' (pp. 199–259). There are essays on 'Moral and Mortal in *Star Trek: The Original Series*' by George Kovacs (pp. 199–216); 'Hybrids and Homecomings in the *Odyssey* and *Alien Resurrection*' by Brett M. Rogers (pp. 217–42); and 'Classical Antiquity and Western Identity in *Battlestar Galactica*' by Vincent Tomasso (pp. 243–59). The fourth and final part responds to the question 'Ancient Classics for a Future Generation?' (pp. 263–325). It consists of: 'Revised Iliadic Epiphanies in Dan Simmons' *Ilium*' by Gaël Grobéty (pp. 263–79); 'Refiguring the Roman Empire in *The Hunger Games* Trilogy' by Marian Makins (pp. 280–306); and 'Jonathan Hickman's *Pax Romana* and the End of Antiquity' by C.W. Marshall (pp. 307–25). An appendix, 'Suggestions for Further Reading and Viewing' by Robert W. Cape, Jr. (pp. 327–38), is descriptive and divided by subjects chronologically arranged within them, such as 'Stories and Novels' (pp. 327–34), 'Juvenile/Young Adult Literature' (pp. 334–5), and concluding with 'Movies' (pp. 336–8). This is followed by an alphabetically arranged enumerative listing of works cited (pp. 339–70) in the notes found at the foot of pages of individual contributors to the volume. It concludes with a detailed double-columned index (pp. 371–80).

Ulka Anjaria has edited *A History of the Indian Novel in English*. This work 'traces the development of the Indian novel from its beginnings in the late nineteenth century to the present day. Starting with' Anjaria's 'extensive introduction ['Literary Pasts, Presents, and Futures' (pp. 1–30)] that charts important theoretical contributions to the field, this *History* includes twenty-five chapters that shed light on the legacy of English in Indian writing'. Utilizing a thematic organization, the 'chapters examine how English was "made Indian" by writers who used the language to address specifically Indian concerns. These included the question of what it means to be modern as well as how the novel could be used for anticolonial activism.' Furthermore, 'by the 1980s, the Indian novel in English was a global phenomenon, and India is now the third largest publisher of English-language books'. In addition 'this *History* invites readers to question conventional accounts of India's literary history' (p. i). The chapters encompass: 'Beginnings: *Rajmohan's Wife* [1864] and the Novel in India' by Supriya Chaudhuri (pp. 31–44); 'The Epistemic Work of Literary Realism: Two Novels from Colonial India' by Satya P. Mohanty (pp. 45–58); '"Because novels are true, and histories are false": Indian Women Writing Fiction in English, 1860–1918' by Barnita Bagchi (pp. 59–72); 'When the Pen Was a Sword: The Radical Career of the Progressive Novel in India' by Snehal Shingavi (pp. 73–87); 'The Road Less Traveled: Modernity and Gandhianism in the Indian English Novel' by Rumina Sethi (pp. 88–102); 'The Modernist Novel in India: Paradigms and Practices' by Vinay Dharwadker (pp. 103–18); '"Handcuffed to history": Partition and the Indian Novel in English' by Ananya Jahanara Kabir (pp. 119–32); 'Women, Reform, and Nationalism in Three Novels of Muslim Life' by Suvir Kaul (pp. 133–46); 'Found in Translation: Self, Caste, and Other in Three Modern Texts' by Rashmi Sadana (pp. 147–61); 'Emergency Fictions' by Ayelet Ben-Yishai and Eitan Bar-Yosef (pp. 162–76), an essay by two Israeli critics that perceptively focuses upon fictions responding to 'the State of Emergency imposed by Prime Minister Indira Gandhi from June 1975 to March 1977' (p. 162); 'Cosmopolitanism and the Sonic Imaginary in Salman Rushdie' by Vijay Mishra (pp. 177–92); 'Postcolonial Realism in the Novels of Rohinton Mistry' by Eli Park Sorensen (pp. 193–206); 'Far from the Nation, Closer to Home: Privacy, Domesticity, and Regionalism in Indian English Fiction' by Saikat Majumdar (pp. 207–20); 'Ecologies of Intimacy: Gender, Sexuality, and Environment in Indian Fiction' by Kavita Daiya (pp. 221–36); 'Some Uses of History: Historiography, Politics, and the Indian Novel' by Alex Tickell (pp. 237–50). Tickell, in a footnote following his essay, writes that 'the designation of the "Indian" novel is notoriously fraught'. He adds that 'many successful contemporary novels are written by authors who, although they have a comptroller family connection with the subcontinent, live elsewhere. For the purposes of this chapter, "Indian novels" describes works set in India, or with an imaginative investment in Indian cultures, rather than texts written by authors resident in India' (p. 250). Other essays in *A History of the Indian Novel in English* are: 'Virtue, Virtuosity, and the Virtual: Experiments in the Contemporary Indian English Novel' by Rukmini Bhaya Nair (pp. 251–66); 'Of Dystopias and Deliriums: The Millennial Novel in India' by Mrinalini Chakravorty (pp. 267–81); '"Which Colony? Which Block?" Violence, (Post-)Colonial Urban Planning, and the Indian Novel' by Upamanyu Pablo Mukherjee (pp. 282–95); 'Post-Humanitarianism and the Indian Novel in English' by Shameem Black (pp. 296–309), which explores 'the ambivalences that mark Indian novels' engagement with human rights discourse at the turn of the millennium. While these novels draw on this discourse, they also chart changing roles for fiction in the twenty-first century' (p. 297). The concluding chapters include: 'Chetan Bhagat [b.1974]: Remaking the Novel in India' by Priya Joshi (pp. 310–23); '"New India/n Woman": Agency and Identity in Post-Millennial Chick Lit' by E. Dawson Varughese (pp. 324–36); 'The Politics and Art of Indian English Fantasy Fiction' by Tabish Khair and Sébastien Doubinsky (pp. 337–47); 'The Indian Graphic Novel' by Corey K. Creekmur (pp. 348–58); '"Coming to a multiplex near you": Indian Fiction in English and New Bollywood Cinema' by Sangita Gopal (pp. 359–72); and finally 'Caste, Complicity, and the Contemporary' by Toral Jatin Gajarawala. The enumerative and alphabetically arranged list of works cited is divided into 'Primary Sources' (pp. 389–99) and 'Secondary Sources' (pp. 399–423). The double-columned index (pp. 425–30) is printed in a smaller font than the rest of the work. Although if it is reliable there is no mention in Anjaria's *A History of the Indian Novel in English* of an obsession of the Indian subcontinent: cricket. Clearly in a volume containing so many contributors some essays are going to be clearer and more helpful than others although the 'Notes on Contributors' (pp. ix–xvi) reveals that most are eminently qualified to write on a complex subject that encompasses some difficult and sensitive terrain.

Before discussing other literary histories, this seems an appropriate place to draw attention to Suman Gupta's *Consumable Texts in Contemporary India: Uncultured Books and Bibliographical Sociology* published as an addition to the Palgrave Macmillan New Directions in Book History that has Jonathan Rose and Shafquat Towheed as the series editors. It is to be hoped that in future such an interesting series that 'will publish monographs in English that employ advanced methods and open up new frontiers in research, written by younger, mid-career and senior scholars' will be more reasonably priced than Gupta's, which has 179 pages of actual text and costs $95! The series 'scope is global, extending to the Western and non-Western worlds and to all historical periods from antiquity to the 21st century, including studies of script, print and post-print cultures' (p. 1). In his opening section, 'Keywords and Preliminaries' (pp. 1–17), Gupta explains that his study analyses 'the social significance of five kinds of English-language books which are produced, circulated and received in India with varying but marked degrees of market success' (p. 1). The second chapter (pp. 18–38), focuses upon '"commercial fiction" in English' (p. 1). The third chapter (pp. 39–60) concentrates upon 'English translations of vernacular pulp fiction' (p. 1) and the fourth (pp. 61–79) upon 'Hitler's *Mein Kampf*, which sustains a not insubstantial publishing industry and commands a considerable market in India and indeed globally' (p. 1). The fourth kind, 'Group Discussion guidebooks' (p. 1) is the subject of Gupta's fifth chapter (pp. 80–99) and sixth chapter (pp. 100–28). Chapter 7, 'Approaching Public Sector "Value Education"' (pp. 129–44), and chapter 8, 'Mapping Public Sector "Value Education" Publications' (pp. 145–71), focus upon 'probably the most prolifically produced and consumed' of Gupta's 'five kinds of English-language books' (p. 1). His final chapter focuses upon 'Rules of Bibliographical Sociology's Method' (pp. 172–9). Following an 'Eliotian quip' Gupta writes in his concluding sentence that 'the argument of this book doesn't actually have clear beginnings and endings, and certainly doesn't go around a hermeneutic circle; it is merely a moment in a perpetually unfolding conversation' (p. 179). An extensive, largely enumerative, alphabetically arranged bibliography (pp. 180–200) follows Gupta's text that contains four accompanying tables. The alphabetically arranged double-columned index (pp. 201–4) is inadequate.

Gregory Castle has edited *A History of the Modernist Novel*, a volume not limited to the novel in English but one in which the contributions are of considerable interest. In his introduction, 'Matters in Motion in the Modernist Novel' (pp. 1–34), Castle observes that 'a multi-voiced approach to literary history suits well a genre characterized by pluralism and a degree of aesthetic experimentation that frequently entailed collaboration, interdisciplinary borrowings and hybrid literary forms' (p. 1). He concludes that there is 'a false divide between of Modernism and realism, between the world of artistic expression and the world of representation, between ideal beauty and its downfall'. Consequently '*A History of the Modernist Novel* shows how innovation emerges continuously on both sides of a divide that is not really a divide at all, but the banks of one stream—*modernism in motion*' (p. 28). The fivefold division of his volume reflects the multi-voiced dimensions of the modernist novel. The first part, 'Modernism and the Challenge to the Real' (pp. 37–133), contains: 'The Aesthetic Novel, from Ouida to Firbank' by Joseph Bristow (pp. 37–65); 'What Is It Like To Be Conscious? Impressionism and the Problem of Qualia' by Paul Armstrong—'the problem of "qualia," the dilemma of how to explain the first-person, the experience of a sensation such as "seeing red"' (p. 66); 'Modernism and the French Novel: A Genealogy (1888–1913)' by Jean-Michel Rabaté (pp. 86–109); and 'Russian Modernism and the Novel' by Leonid Livak (pp. 110–33). The second part, 'Realism in Tradition' (pp. 137–208), contains: 'Bootmakers and Watchmakers: Wells, Bennett, Galsworthy, Woolf, and Modernist Fiction' by David Bradshaw (pp. 137–52); '"A call and an answer": E.M. Forster, D.H. Lawrence, and English Modernism' by Howard J. Booth (pp. 153–69); 'American Literary Realism: Popularity and Politics in a Modernist Frame' by Janet G. Casey (pp. 170–89); 'Modernist Domesticity: Reconciling the Paradox in Edith Wharton, Willa Cather, and Nella Larsen' by Deborah Clarke (pp. 190–208). The third part, 'The Matter of Modernism' (pp. 211–89), contains: 'Energy, Stress, and Modernist Style' by Enda Duffy (pp. 211–30); 'Modernist Materialism: War, Gender, and Representation in Woolf, West, and H.D.' by Anne Fernihough (pp. 231–53); 'Serial Modernism' by Sean Latham (pp. 254–69); 'Translation and the Modernist Novel' by Emily O. Wittman (pp. 270–89). The fourth part, 'Modernism, Genre, and Form' (pp. 293–385), contains: 'Modernist Style and the "Inward Turn" in German-Language Fiction' by Ritchie Robertson (pp. 293–310); 'Mann's Modernism' by Todd Kontje (pp. 311–26); 'Democratic Form and Narrative Proportion in Joyce and Dos Passos' by Sam Alexander (pp. 327–44); 'The Modernist Genre Novel' by David Earle (pp. 345–68); 'Modernism and Historical Fiction: The Case of H. D.' by Lara Vetter (pp. 369–85). The fifth and final part, 'Modernism in Transit' (pp. 389–507), contains: 'The Modernist Novel in Its Contemporaneity' by Pamela L. Caughie (pp. 389–407); 'The Modernist Novel in the World-System' by Lara Winkiel (pp. 408–28); 'Modernist

Cosmopolitanism' by Jessica Berman (pp. 429–48); 'Modernism and the Big House' by Nicholas Allen (pp. 449–63); 'In the Wake of Joyce: Beckett, O'Brien, and the Late Modernist Novel' by Patrick Bixby (pp. 464–82); and finally and appropriately 'Destinies of *Bildung*: Belatedness and the Modernist Novel' by Gregory Castle (pp. 483–507). Notes follow each individual contribution, which might explain but doesn't justify the absence of a cumulative bibliography: there is, however, a double-columned index (pp. 509–32) using a smaller, computer-generated type font than the rest of the text. There are ten references to 'Postmodernism' in the index (p. 526) but no real distinction between the concepts of 'Modernism' and 'Postmodernism'. In a volume containing so many different contributors inevitably some of the chapters are going to be better written and more acute than others.

Kevin J. Hayes has edited a volume, *A History of Virginia Literature*, that encompasses a more specific geographical location, has a longer historical time-span and transverses the literary genres than the volume edited by Gregory Castle. There are twenty-four contributors. In his introduction (pp. 1–10) Hayes explains that 'supplementing the scholarship of the past with a considerable amount of new information *A History of Virginia Literature* constitutes a comprehensive history. The first of its kind in four hundred years, it is designed to be the standard work in the field for decades to come' (pp. 5–6). Organized chronologically, there are four parts. The first, on 'Colonial Virginia' (pp. 13–108), consists of: 'The Literary Culture of Jamestown' by Karen Schramm (pp. 13–26); 'Colonial Historians' by Jon Kukla (pp. 27–40); 'William Byrd of Westover' by Stephen C. Ausband (pp. 41–53); 'The Poetry of Colonial Virginia' by Nanette C. Tamer (pp. 54–68); 'The Establishment of the Printing Press' by A. Franklin Parks (pp. 69–81); 'The Literature of the Revolution' by Brian Steele (pp. 82–95); 'Letter Writing in Eighteenth-Century Virginia' by Elizabeth Hewitt (pp. 96–108). The second part concerns 'Jeffersonian Virginia' (pp. 111–91) and contains: 'Thomas Jefferson' by Jason Robles (pp. 111–23); 'Notes on the State of Virginia' (pp. 124–36), followed by two more contributions by Kevin J. Hayes, on 'John Page and His Circle' (pp. 137–51) and 'Travels, History, and Biography' (pp. 152–65); 'Romantic Verse' by Russell Brickey (pp. 166–79); and 'Edgar Allan Poe and the Art of Fiction' by Paul Christian Jones (pp. 180–91), who opens his account by observing that 'Edgar Allen Poe became a Virginian only because of the accident of personal tragedy' (p. 180). He closes, 'it seems clear that in the last days of his life, Poe, the perpetual wanderer, did consider Virginia to be his home' (p. 190). Part III of *A History of Virginia Literature*, entitled 'The Civil War Era' (pp. 195–293), contains reflections on: 'The Virginia Novel I' by John L. Hare (pp. 195–207); '*The Southern Literary Messenger*' by Christine Modey (pp. 208–22); 'The Literature of Slavery' by Robyn McGee (pp. 223–36); 'Civil War Diaries and Reminiscences' by David Anderson (pp. 237–51); 'Post-Romantic Poetry' by Lauren Rule Maxwell (pp. 252–65); 'Virginia Folklore' by Ted Olson (pp. 266–79); and 'The Virginia Novel II' by Gwendolyn Jones Harold (pp. 280–93). The final part has contributions on 'Modern Virginia' (pp. 297–375) and has six essays: 'Ellen Glasgow' by Susan Goodman (pp. 297–308); 'The Virginia Writers' Project' by Tom Barden (pp. 309–21); 'Science Fiction and Fantasy' by John D. Miles (pp. 322–34);

'William Styron' by James L.W. West III (pp. 335–47); 'Virginians at a Distance: Willa Cather and Tom Wolfe' by Adam N. Jabbur (pp. 348–61); and the final essay in the section is on 'Modern Poetry' by Chris Beyers (pp. 362–75). In the 'Conclusion' (pp. 376–83), presumably by the editor Kevin J. Hayes although no author attribution is stated, he writes, 'new writers do not have to use the literature of the past for purposes of nostalgia'. On the contrary 'Virginia literary history' can be used to 'advance' its history and 'to experiment with new forms of writing and new modes of expression. The literature of its past projects a new and exciting future for the written word in Virginia' (p. 383). There are notes to individual chapters that give information on 'biographies and critical studies of individual authors' (p. 385) and a welcome alphabetically arranged, enumerative bibliography (pp. 385–8) that 'consists of more general works, presenting a list of anthologies, bibliographies, biographical dictionaries, collections of essays, critical studies, exhibition catalogues, intellectual histories, and literary histories' (p. 385). The very useful double-columned index (pp. 389–420) 'has been designed not only as a guide to the present work but also as a mini-biographical dictionary', consequently 'after each name in the index, the subject's birth and death years appear in parenthesis. In addition, people are identified by the roles for which they are best known to literary history' (p. 389).

In his introduction (pp. 1–13) to *A History of California Literature*, Blake Allmendinger writes that 'most writers portray California as a land of contestation and strife' (p. 4). He concludes his introduction with these words: 'California has attracted more pilgrims and dissidents than any other place in' the history of America. 'Perhaps literature is the medium in which it finds its most apt expression. California is a fanciful conceit, an elusive dream, a celluloid confection—a land where the greatest dreams and darkest disasters come true' (p. 13). As editor Allmendinger divides his collection of essays into seven parts. The first, 'Beginnings' (pp. 17–58), contains three contributions: 'Tales of Native California' by Paul Apodaca (pp. 17–29); 'Indigenous Peoples under Colonial Rule' by Lisbeth Haas (pp. 30–42); and 'Spanish and Mexican Literature' by Vincent Pérez (pp. 43–58). The second part, 'The American Presence' (pp. 61–102), has three contributions: 'White Explorers and Travelers' by David Wyatt (pp. 61–74); 'The Gold Rush' by Nicolas S. Witschi (pp. 75–87); and 'California Nature Writers' by Steven Pavlos Holmes (pp. 88–102). The third part, 'Contested Spaces' (pp. 105–54), also has three contributions: 'The Black Frontier' by Aparajita Nanda (pp. 105–22); 'California as Political Topography: Asian American Literature before 1980' by Catherine Fung (pp. 123–38); and 'Mexican American Literature' by Manuel M. Martin-Rodriguez (pp. 139–54). The fourth part, 'Social Change and Literary Experimentation' (pp. 157–211), has four contributions: 'The Protest Fiction of Frank Norris, Upton Sinclair, Jack London, and John Steinbeck' by Susan Shillinglaw (pp. 157–70); 'Dreams, Denial, and Depression-Era Fictions' by Jan Goggans (pp. 171–81); 'Modernism in the Early Twentieth Century' by Geneva M. Gano (pp. 182–98); and 'The Hard-Boiled California Novel' (pp. 199–211), in which William Marling focuses upon Dashiel Hammett, James M. Cain, Raymond Carver, and, amongst others, Horace McCoy, W.T. Ballard, Erle Stanley Gardner, Ross Macdonald, and subsequent exponents of 'the hard-boiled genre'. Marling observes that 'it is a long way from Hammett's waterfront to Kem Nunn's Imperial Beach where his surfer-detective smells something foul in the waters of the Tijuana Slough. However, the stink remains the same' (p. 211): unfortunately a listing of hard-boiled California novels isn't included after the notes that conclude this and other contributions in the volume. The fifth part, 'Alternative Voices' (pp. 215–79), also has four contributions. The first is 'Writing the Hidden California' by Phillip Round (pp. 215–30). For Round, 'between 1940 and 1963, California literature underwent a major transformation. Where earlier writers aspired to sell the state as "the land of sunshine," authors during this mid-century were more interested in producing literary works that drew power from the increasingly visible disjunction between rich and poor, arid and irrigated, Anglo-Saxon and ethnic other' (p. 215). Round concludes that 'the hidden California is no longer unknown the way it was when writers in the forties and fifties turned to its natural beauty, its social ironies and contradictions, for inspiration in shaping a new literary culture. However, it still beckons' (p. 230). The other contributions are: 'The Beats' by Kurt Hemmer (pp. 231–45); 'Bay Area Poetics, 1944–1981' by Kaplan Page Harris (pp. 246–59); and 'Los Angeles Poetry from the McCarthy to the Punk Eras' by Brian Stefans (pp. 260–79). Part VI is on 'Creating Communities' (pp. 283–323) and has three contributions: 'African American Uprising' by Charles Toombs (pp. 283–94); 'Of Carnales and Coyotes: Chicanalo Literature of California' by Anne Goldman (pp. 295–307)—followed by notes (pp. 307–8) but not by a listing of that literature. The third contribution is 'Interracial Encounters: Face and Place in Post-1980 Asian American Literature' by King-Kok Cheung (pp. 309–23)—like the previous essay accompanied by notes (p. 323) but no listing of the literature. The final Part VII is on 'The Search for Utopia' (pp. 327–84) and has four contributions: 'California and the Queer Utopian Imagination: 1981–2014' by Cael Keegan (pp. 327–42); 'Modern California Nature Writing' by Michael Kowalewski (pp. 343–57); 'Making California's Towns and Small Cities Visible in the Twenty-First Century' by Nancy Cook (pp. 358–70), and finally 'Science Fiction and Mysterious Worlds' by Lynn Mie Itagaki (pp. 371–84). In his succinct 'Conclusion' (pp. 385–9) Blake Allmendinger, the editor, observes that 'early works represent California from a singular perspective'. However, 'more recently, writers have attempted to achieve a balance, refusing to privilege one perspective over another, focusing on the tensions among California's inhabitants'. Moreover, 'this theme appears in the protest fiction of early twentieth-century white male writers such as John Steinbeck, as well as in literature that chronicles the modern urban underclass; in the stories that contrast experiences are first-and second-generation immigrants; and fiction that documents the intersecting lives of the state's multiracial, straight, gay, and bisexual residents'. Allmendinger's final sentence reads 'in a state known for its diversity, this seems like a positive trend' (p. 389). The enumerative, alphabetically arranged bibliography is divided between 'Primary Sources' (pp. 391–400) and 'Secondary Sources' (pp. 400–11). There is an extensive index (pp. 413–31) in a smaller font than the text itself to this comprehensive volume, that appropriately reflects the diverse nature of its subject.

Seven additions to the Cambridge Companions reference series published in 2015 have been drawn to our attention: Julie Bruckner Armstrong edited *The Cambridge Companion to American Civil Rights Literature*; Crystal Parikh and Daniel Y. Kim edited *The Cambridge Companion to Asian American Literature*; David Hillman and Ulrika Maude edited *The Cambridge Companion to the Body in Literature*; Maria Tatar edited *The Cambridge Companion to Fairy Tales*; Celia Marshik edited *The Cambridge Companion to Modernist Culture*; Devoney Looser edited *The Cambridge Companion to Women's Writing in the Romantic Period*; and Peter Sabor edited *The Cambridge Companion to 'Emma'*. Published both in hardback and paperback format, largely they follow a similar formula: 'Notes on Contributors' (pp. ix–xi) are followed by a 'Chronology' (pp. xiii–xxii), then 'Acknowledgments' (p. xxiii), an introduction (pp. 1–16), essays by various hands, an enumerative 'Guide to Further Reading' (pp. 193–200), and a name-orientated index (pp. 201–9; page references are to Bruckner Armstrong's *Companion to American Civil Rights Literature*). Clearly the quality and usefulness of individual contributions vary from volume to volume: some are not without their opaque quality. Parikh and Kim's volume updates King-Kok Cheung's excellent *An Interethnic Companion to Asian American Literature* published by Cambridge University Press (New York) in 1997. Sabor's *The Cambridge Companion to 'Emma'* is devoted to a single novel by Jane Austen and contains twelve essays on its various aspects, including Ruth Perry's contribution on 'Music' in the novel (pp. 135–49) and Deidre Shauna Lynch on 'Screen Versions' (pp. 186–203), accompanied by black and white illustrative stills from various versions. There is too an enumerative, alphabetically arranged 'Guide to Further Reading' divided into 'Primary Editions', writings on 'On the Text', on the 'Context', and an all too brief 'Filmography' (pp. 204–10). The double-columned index (pp. 211–19) is useful. Mention should be made to three additions to the Cambridge Introductions reference works recently published and produced both in hardback and paperback: Anthony J. Cascardi, *The Cambridge Introduction to Literature and Philosophy*, Jean-Michel Rabaté, *The Cambridge Introduction to Literature and Psychoanalysis* and Michael Y. Bennett's *The Cambridge Introduction to Theatre and Literature of the Absurd*. In addition to evaluative narrative, Cascardi concludes with a most useful 'Glossary of Keywords', notes, and index (pp. 189–223). His 'Suggestions for Further Reading' conclude individual chapters in his narrative (see for instance, p. 58); Rabaté concludes with a most useful 'Keywords and Index of Authors', an alphabetically arranged enumerative bibliography, and an index (pp. 215–55). Bennett's chapters encompass an 'Overview of the Absurd' (pp. 1–23) including a discussion of Martin Esslin's important work *The Theatre of the Absurd* (*YWES* [1961] 3–9), a chapter on 'The Emergence of a "Movement": The Historical and Intellectual Contexts' (pp. 35–46), chapters on Beckett (pp. 47–66) and his 'notable contemporaries' such as Harold Pinter (pp. 67–91), and 'Absurd Criticism' (pp. 128–32). There are, following the text, notes (pp. 133–47), enumerative alphabetically arranged further reading lists (pp. 150–9), and an index (pp. 160–3). All three Cambridge Introductions are on the whole clearly written—not an easy task as the subjects treated are complex.

Carla Sassi has edited *The International Companion to Scottish Poetry*. Thomas Owen Clancy acts as the Gaelic adviser. In her introduction (pp. 1–5) Sassi writes that 'the *Companion*' draws attention to 'the objectively extraordinary richness and diversity of Scotland's poetic heritage and contemporary scene'. Further, it draws attention to 'the existence of a relevant number of specific features—cultural, formal, thematic—that create important lines of continuity across regions, languages and centuries, and that allow us (specialists in Scottish studies as well as occasional visitors) to deem the macro-category "Scottish poetry" as a highly meaningful and productive one' (p. 5). The *Companion* is divided into three parts. The first, 'Languages and Chronologies' (pp. 6–93), has nine contributions: 'Early Celtic Poetry (to 1500)' by Thomas Owen Clancy (pp. 6–14); 'Scots Poetry in the Fourteenth and Fifteenth Centuries' by R.D.S. Jack (pp. 15–22); 'Poetry in Latin' by Roger Green (pp. 23–30); 'Poetry in the Languages and Dialects of Northern Scotland' by Roberta Frank and Brian Smith (pp. 31–43); 'The Sixteenth and Seventeenth Centuries' by Sim Innes and Alessandra Petrina (pp. 44–53); 'The Eighteenth Century' by Ronald Black and Gerard Carruthers (pp. 54–63); 'The Nineteenth Century' by Ian Duncan and Sheila Kidd (pp. 64–73); 'The Poetry of Modernity (1870–1950)' by Emma Dymock and Scott Lyall (pp. 74–82); and 'Contemporary Poetry (1950–)' by Attila Dósa and Michelle Macleod (pp. 83–93). The second part is concerned with 'Poetic Forms' (pp. 94–131) and has three contributions: 'The Form of Scottish Gaelic Poetry' by William Gillies (pp. 94–108); 'Scots Poetic Forms' by Derrick McClure (pp. 109–20); and 'The Ballad in Scots and English' by Suzanne Gilbert (pp. 121–31). The third and by far the lengthiest section is centred around essays on 'Topics and Themes' (pp. 132–212). The seven essays include: 'Nature, Landscape and Rural Life' by Louisa Gairn (pp. 132–43); 'Nation and Home' by Carla Sassi and Silke Stroh (pp. 144–55); 'Protest and Politics' by Wilson McLeod and Alan Riach (pp. 156–68); 'Love and Erotic Poetry' by Peter Mackay (pp. 169–78); 'Faith and Religion' by Meg Bateman and James McGonigal (pp. 179–89); 'Scottish Poetry as World Poetry' by Paul Barnaby (pp. 190–201); and finally 'The Literary Environment' by Robyn Marsack (pp. 202–12). Extensive endnotes (pp. 213–60) follow the essays, and there is a further reading listing arranged under subjects such as 'Bibliographical Sources' and 'General' (pp. 261–7). 'Notes on Contributors' (pp. 269–73) are followed by a double-columned, extensive, alphabetically arranged index (pp. 275–300).

Christine Berberich has edited eighteen essays in *The Bloomsbury Introduction to Popular Fiction* that 'highlight and celebrate the multifaceted diversity of popular fiction' (p. 5). In her introduction, 'The Popular/ Literature versus Literature' (pp. 1–8), Berberich explains what is meant by the term 'popular fiction' (pp. 2–5), observing that 'the study of popular fiction is ... the study of an ever-changing, ever-involving and ever-dynamic field that can be ... difficult to pin down' (p. 6). Some clarification of the term is attempted in the two essays in the first of the three parts of this collection, 'History' (pp. 11–49). Christopher Pittard writes on 'The Victorian Context: Serialization, Circulation, Genres' (pp. 11–29) and Christine Berberich on 'Twentieth-Century Popular: History, Theory, and Context' (pp. 30–49). There are seven contributions to the second part, 'Genres' (pp. 53–181), that consists of: Maryan Wherry on 'More than a Love Story: The Complexities of the Popular Romance' (pp. 53–69); Alice Ferrebe on '"The Lads' Own Paper": Male Confessional Literature and the Legacy of Adventure' (pp. 70–86); Andy Sawyer on 'Science Fiction: The Sense of Wonder' (pp. 87–107); Stefania Ciocia on 'Rules are Meant To Be Broken: Twentieth- and Twenty-First-Century Crime Writing' (pp. 108–28); Gina Wisker on 'Disturbance, Disorder, Destruction, Disease: Horror Fiction Today' (pp. 129–46); Lena Steveker on 'Alternative Worlds: Popular Fiction (not only) for Children' (pp. 147–62); and Monica Germanà on 'The Coming of Age of Graphic Narratives' (pp. 163–81). The third part focuses upon specific 'Case Studies' (pp. 185–99) with nine contributions: Ben Clarke on 'H.G. Wells, Élitism, and Popular Fiction' (pp. 185–99); Patrick Parrinder on 'John Buchan and the Spy Thriller' (pp. 200–12); Juan F. Elices on 'Manipulating Popularity: A Case Study of Ian Fleming's James Bond Series' (pp. 213–26); Joanne Bishton on 'Subverting the Romance: The Fiction of Sarah Waters' (pp. 227–40); Bran Nicol on 'The Hard-Boiled Detective: Dashiell Hammett' (pp. 241–53); Petra Rau on 'Violent Pleasures: War as Entertainment' (pp. 254–67); Neil Campbell on 'Popular Vampires: The Twilight Effect' (pp. 268–81); Ben Dew on 'Rewriting Popular Classics as Popular Fiction: Jane Austen, Zombies, Sex and Vampires' (pp. 282–95); and Carl Tighe, 'Edu-Biz: The Worlds of Learning and Writing—A Writer's Perspective' (pp. 296–308). Christine Berberich, in her 'Afterword: The Future of the Popular' (pp. 309–16), concludes that 'popular fiction will continue to constantly reinvent itself and be re-invigorated, and will always serve as an important social and cultural document of its time' (p. 315). Each contribution in her collection is followed by an alphabetically arranged, enumerative listing of works cited (see for instance pp. 197–9), and the beginning of each contribution has a useful 'Chapter Outline' (see for instance p. 200). There is a double-columned, name-orientated index (pp. 317–26) that concludes this interesting *Bloomsbury Introduction to Popular Fiction*. Inevitably some essays will be of better quality than others and less opaque. Some of the contributors should be congratulated, however, for tackling fresh author and subject terrain.

*The 1990s: A Decade of Contemporary British Fiction* belongs to The Decades series. Its editors, Nick Hubble, Philip Tew, and Leigh Wilson, explain in their 'Series Editors' Preface' 'that the aim of these volumes, which include timelines and biographical information on the writers covered, is to provide the contextual framework that is now necessary for the study of the British fiction of these four decades' that is of 'contemporary British fiction published from 1970 to the present' (p. xii). The editors observe on the back outside cover: 'How did social, cultural and political events in Britain during the 1990s shape contemporary British fiction?' They add that 'From the fall of the Berlin Wall to the turn of the millennium, the 1990s witnessed a realignment of global politics. Against the changing international scene, this volume uses events abroad and in Britain to examine and explain the changes taking place in British fiction, including: the celebration of national identities, fuelled by the move toward political devolution in Northern Ireland, Scotland and Wales; the literary optimism in urban ethnic fictions written by a new generation of authors, born and raised in Britain; the popularity of neo-Victorian fiction.' Furthermore, in the volume 'Critical surveys are balanced by in-depth readings of work by the authors who defined the decade, including A.S. Byatt, Hanif Kureishi, Will Self, Caryl Phillips and Irvine Welsh: an approach that illustrates exactly how their key themes and concerns fit within the social and political circumstances of the decade.' Following the editors' 'Critical Introduction: Recovering the 1990s' (pp. 1–35), there are eight chapters: the 'Literary History of the Decade: The Emergence of Post-Industrial British Fiction' by Martyn Colebrook (pp. 37–65); 'Special Topic 1: Re-Writing National Identities in 1990s British Fiction' by Nick Bentley (pp. 67–94); 'Special Topic 2: Satirical Apocalypse: Endism and the 1990's Fictions of Will Self' (pp. 95–122); 'Postcolonial and Diasporic Voices— Bringing Black to the Union Jack: Ethnic Fictions and the Politics of Possibility' by Sara Upstone (pp. 123–48); 'Historical Representations Between the Short and Long Twentieth Centuries: Temporal Displacement in the Historical Fiction of the 1990s' by Nick Hubble (pp. 149–79); 'Generic Discontinuities and Variations: Experimental Enunciations in 1990s British Fiction' by Mark P. Williams (pp. 181–212); 'International Contexts 1: Whatever Do the Germans Want? 1990s British Fiction and the Condition of Germany' by Anja Müller-Wood (pp. 213–37); 'International Contexts 2: National Identity and the Immigrant' by Paoi Hwang (pp. 239–62). At the conclusion of each chapter are alphabetically arranged listings of works cited in them. The narrative chapters are followed by a 'Timeline of Works' from 1990 to 1999 (pp. 263–5), a 'Timeline of National Events' (pp. 266–71), and covering the same period of time a 'Timeline of International Events' (pp. 272–7). A very useful detailed 'Biographies of Writers' beginning with 'Diran Adebayo' and concluding with 'Irvine Welsh' follows (pp. 278–89). The double-columned index (pp. 290–303) is comprehensive. The companion volume in The Decades series follows a similar pattern. The outside back cover of *The 2000s: A Decade of Contemporary British Fiction*, edited by Nick Bentley, Nick Hubble, and Leigh Wilson, conveys the flavour of the volume, asking the question 'How did social, cultural and political events in Britain during the 2000s shape contemporary British fiction?' In addition it explains that 'the means of publishing, buying and reading fiction changed dramatically between 2000 and 2010'. Consequently the 'volume explores how the socio-political and economic turns of the decade, bookended by the beginning of a millennium and an economic crisis, transformed the act of writing and reading'. In addition, 'through consideration of, among other things, the treatment of neuroscience, violence, the historical and youth subcultures in recent fiction, the essays ... explore the complex and still powerful relation between the novel and the world in which it is written, published and read'. Bentley, Hubble, and Wilson's edited collection contains an 'assessment of the fiction of the 2000s'. It 'covers the work of newer voices such as Monica Ali, Mark Haddon, Tom McCarthy, David Peace and Zadie Smith as well as those more established, such as Salman Rushdie, Hilary Mantel and Ian McEwan' making it a 'contribution to reading, defining and understanding the decade'. The 'Series Editors' Preface' (pp. ix–xi) and 'Acknowledgements' (p. xii) are followed by an introduction, 'Fiction of the 2000s: Political Contexts, Seeing the Contemporary, and the End(s) of Postmodernism' by Nick Bentley, Nick

Hubble, and Leigh Wilson (pp. 1–26). Eight essays follow: 'Literary History of the Decade: Fiction from the Borderlands' by Martyn Colebrook (pp. 27–51); 'Special Topic 1: Subcultural Fictions: Youth Subcultures in Twenty-First-Century British Fiction' by Nick Bentley (pp. 53–81; 'Special Topic 2: Translating Neuroscience: Fictions of the Brain in the 2000s' by Laura Salisbury (pp. 83–113); 'Postcolonial and Diasporic Voices: Contemporary British Fiction in an Age of Transnational Terror' by Lucienne Loh (pp. 115–44); 'Historical Representations, Reality Effects: The Historical Novel and the Crisis of Fictionality in the First Decade of the Twenty-First Century' by Leigh Wilson (pp. 145–71); 'Generic Discontinuities and Variations' by Daniel Weston (pp. 173–98); 'International Contexts 1: The American Reception of British Fiction in the 2000s' by Anne Marie Adams (pp. 199–221); and 'International Contexts 2: From Multicultural Enthusiasm to the "Failure of Multiculturalism": British Multi-Ethnic Fiction in an International Frame' by Ulrike Tancke (pp. 223–44). At the conclusion of each chapter are alphabetically arranged listings of works cited in them. The narrative chapters are followed by a 'Timeline of Works' from 2000 to 2009 (pp. 245–51), a 'Timeline of National Events' (pp. 253–60), and covering the same period of time a 'Timeline of International Events' (pp. 261–7). The very useful detailed 'Biographies of Writers', beginning with 'Leila Aboulela' and concluding with 'Alex Wheatle', follows (pp. 269–80). The double-columned index (pp. 281–97) is comprehensive. In addition to critical assessments of authors and their work, *The 1990s: A Decade of Contemporary British Fiction* and *The 2000s: A Decade of Contemporary British Fiction*—not least in the often extensive listing of works cited following individual chapters (see for instance the alphabetically arranged listing following Bentley, Hubble, and Wilson's introduction to *The 2000s*, pp. 23–6) and in the data in the concluding timelines (for instance see Bentley, Hubble, and Wilson, pp. 245–67)—are both highly useful reference tools. Inevitably of course time will change perspectives and the authors they emphasize may well prove to be ephemeral or out of fashion and those ignored or mentioned in passing may well prove to stand the test of time or be in fashion. A caveat is that a few of the essays are uneven in quality, characterized by the use of inflated terminology, and sometimes create the appearance of being written for effect. Such an observation does not apply to most of the contents in what is clearly an interesting and valuable series. An item omitted from the 2014 review was Jonathan Bastable and Hannah McGill's edited *The 21st-Century Novel: Notes from the Edinburgh World Writers' Conference*. This book is an anthology of the best accounts from a year-long discussion that occurred during 2012–13 between writers who participated in seventeen literary festivals worldwide, from Berlin to Melbourne, some of whom participated in a five-day conference in Edinburgh in August 2012—writers such as Irvine Welsh, Ali Smith, Ahdaf Soueif, and Kirstie Gunn, to mention but four from many who considered various aspects of the state of literature today—the challenges literature faces and the directions they see it taking. The anthology is divided into five sections: 'The Future of the Novel' (pp. 29–97); 'Should Literature be Political?' (pp. 99–163); 'Censorship Today' (pp. 165–213); 'A National Literature' (pp. 215–83); and 'Style Versus Content' (pp. 285–323). As Hannah

McGill points out in her 'Afterword' (pp. 325–33) some recurrent concerns ranged from the decline of demand for physical books, the 'dissemination of a work of literature [as] a mere matter of an internet connection' (p. 325), the relationship of the author to a publishing house, the ramifications of Twitter, the issue of self-publishing, and 'the existence or otherwise of objective standards of "good" and "bad" writing, and whether the publishing industry could be trusted to protect the former' (p. 330). There are detailed, alphabetically arranged 'Biographies of Keynote Speakers' (pp. 334–41), followed by a detailed, triple-columned index (pp. 342–52).

Alan Bewell, Neil ten Kortenaar, and Germaine Warkentin have edited *Educating the Imagination: Northrop Frye, Past, Present, and Future*, which pays homage to the work and influence of eminent literary critic and scholar Northrop Frye (1912–91). The thirteen essays have their foundation in the centenary celebrations of Frye's birth which, according to the editors' introduction (pp. 3–15), was 'an ideal moment for reassessment. To establish whether Frye's reputation needs to be refurbished, to assess what needs to be retrieved from his critical insights today, and to take the measure of where literary and cultural scholarship currently stands by gauging our distance from and our dependence on him' (p. 4). Bewell, ten Kortenaar, and Warkentin write that 'at the heart of Frye's work is a recognition of both the extraordinary diversity of literary forms and the degree to which they can nevertheless tell a similar story and speak to enduring aspects of human life' (p. 15). The essays that follow are: 'Reading between the Books: Northrop Frye and the Cartography of Literature' by Robert Bringhurst (pp. 16–35); 'Northrop Frye beyond Belief' by Ian Balfour (pp. 36–47); 'Prophecy Meets History: Frye's Blake and Frye's Milton' by Gordon Teskey (pp. 48–64); 'From the Defeated: Northrop Frye and the Literary Symbol' by Michael Dolzani (pp. 65–82); 'Power to the Educated Imagination! Northrop Frye and the Utopian Impulse' by Robert T. Tally Jr. (pp. 83–95); '*Verum Factum*: Frye, Jameson, Nancy, and the Myth of Myth' by Garry Sherbert (pp. 96–113); 'Frye, Derrida, and the University (to Come)' by Alexander Dick (pp. 114–31); 'Frye's Principles of Literary Symbolism: From the Classroom to the Critical Classics' by Thomas Willard (pp. 132–46); 'Romanticism and the Beyond of Language: Northrop Frye and the Wordsworthian Imitation of the Point of Epiphany' by Mark Ittensohn (pp. 147–63); 'Correspondences: Frye, De Man, Romanticism' by Adam Carter (pp. 164–84); '"Our Lady of Pain": Prolegomena to the Study of She-Tragedy' by Troni Y. Grande (pp. 185–205); and 'Chanting Down Babylon: Innocence and Experience in the Contemporary Humanities' by J. Edward Chamberlin (pp. 206–26). Extensive notes (pp. 227–48) follow each contribution. The bibliography (pp. 249–65) is alphabetically arranged and in places annotated. It is followed by notes on 'Contributors' (pp. 267–70). The double-columned index (pp. 271–8) is name-orientated. In the introduction, Bewell, ten Kortenaar, and Warkentin write: 'No one can read Frye without recognizing what an extraordinary writer he was. He was the master of a witty, elegant, demotic style, one that emerged and developed in the classroom and was published in hundreds of reviews and public lectures.' Furthermore, 'he may be the only literary critic of his time who can be read for sheer pleasure, which may account for his continuing popularity among the non-professional readership'. They add that 'Frye may actually have suffered from the clarity, the grace, and the unbounded self-confidence with which he wrote, but these are qualities that will endure' (p. 5).

Edward Jones writes, in the introduction to *A Concise Companion to the Study of Manuscripts, Printed Books, and the Production of Early Modern Texts: A Festschrift for Gordon Campbell*, that the volume depends upon 'examples to illuminate how manuscripts and published books reflect concerns with literacy, social class, the world of scholarship and scholars, theatrical performances, economic success, and perhaps most of all, literary art'. Containing interesting black and white illustrative figures, *A Concise Companion* has a tripartite division: 'Manuscript Studies' with six essays (pp. 3–128); 'Printed Books' with four essays (pp. 131–205); and 'Production, Dissemination, Appropriation' with six contributions (pp. 209–345). There is a poetic 'Afterword' by Andrew McNeillie, 'By Ferry, Foot, and Fate: A Tour in the Hebrides' (pp. 346–53), followed by a double-columned name-orientated index (pp. 354–66). In addition to its function as *A Concise Companion* this collection serves 'as a tribute to Gordon Campbell—a scholar whose work has influenced all contributors in different ways'. A distinguished scholar and critic, Campbell's 'scholarship insists upon a familiarity with historical details, and ability to read and write in at least a half dozen languages ... and a willingness to explore how discrete disciplines (music, sculpture, architecture, literature, and painting) unite rather than remain apart'. The chronological focus of the volume, the late sixteenth and early to mid-seventeenth centuries, reflects Campbell's own areas of interest that encompass 'multi-volume [award-winning] reference works on art and architecture, editions of poetry and plays, dictionaries on Renaissance art, monographs on Milton's *De Doctrina Christiana*, the King James Bible, and the figure of the garden Hermit; all 'capture his interests in the colossal figures of an age and the minutiae of everyday and scholarly life' (p. xvi). He is an active scholar, the one disappointment in the present volume being that it doesn't include a Campbell bibliography reflecting his tremendous and important productivity. Neither is there a biographical note on his distinguished career and honorary degrees. The volume is a tribute to his friendship, collegiality, and influence. In the first part, focusing on 'Manuscript Studies', there are essays on: 'Stanford University's Cavendish Manuscript: Wolsey, Elizabeth I, Shakespeare, and Milton' by Elaine Treharne (pp. 3–20); 'Texts Presented to Elizabeth I on the University Progresses' by Sarah Knight (pp. 21–40); 'Analysing a Private Library, with a Shelflist Attributable to John Hales of Eton, c.1624' by William Poole (pp. 41–65); 'Young Milton in His Letters' by John K. Hale (pp. 66–86); 'The Itinerant Sibling: Christopher Milton in London and Suffolk' by Edward Jones (pp. 87–105); and 'Milton, the Attentive Mr. Skinner, and the Acts and Discourses of Friendship' by Cedric C. Brown (pp. 106–28). In the second part, 'Printed Books', there are essays on: 'Printing the Gospels in Arabic in Rome in 1590' by Neil Harris (pp. 131–49); 'Tyranny and Tragicomedy in Milton's Reading of *The Tempest*' by Karen L. Edwards (pp. 150–70); 'The Earliest Miltonists: Patrick Hume and John Toland' by Thomas N. Corns (pp. 171–87); and 'The Ghost of

Rhetoric: Milton's *Logic* and the Renaissance Trivium' by Jameela Lares (pp. 188–205). The third part focuses on 'Production, Dissemination, Appropriation' and has essays on: 'Misprinting *Bartholomew Fair*: Jonson and "The Absolute Knave"' by John Creaser (pp. 209–28); '*Reliquiae Baxterianae* and the Shaping of the Seventeenth Century' by N.H. Keeble (pp. 229–48); 'Marvell and the Dutch in 1665' by Martin Dzelzainis (pp. 249–65); 'Did Milton Read Selden?' by Sharon Achinstein (pp. 266–93); 'Hands On' by Neil Forsyth (pp. 294–321); and 'Shakespeare with a Difference: Dismembering and Remembering *Titus Andronicus* in Heiner Müller's and Brigitte Maria Mayer's *Anatomie Titus*' by Pascale Aebischer. There is a curious occurrence in the final two sentences of Edward Jones's acknowledgements, where the last two sentences of the third paragraph are repeated almost verbatim in the two-sentence final paragraph (p. xiv)—something the eagle-eyed Gordon Campbell would spot immediately!

The doyen of Blake scholarship G.E. Bentley Jr. has turned his attention to *The Edwardses of Halifax: The Making and Selling of Beautiful Books in London and Halifax, 1749–1826*. For upwards of seventy-five years the Edwards family of Halifax in Yorkshire was one of the most important bookbinders, publishers, and antiquarian booksellers in Britain. Bentley has produced the definitive record of the family business that was begun in Halifax by William Edwards (1722–1808) and subsequently expanded in London by his sons James (1756–1816) and Richard (1768–1827). James was also an eminent book collector on the European continent, and was active during the Napoleonic Wars looking for volumes and acting as a secret intelligence agent for his friend the aristocratic book collector, George John Spencer, the third earl Spencer and First Lord of the Admiralty. Richard in 1797 published Edward Young's *Night Thoughts*. Its prints were designed and engraved by William Blake, and constitute the most ambitious commercial work ever undertaken by Blake. In his introduction (pp. 3–11) Bentley writes that 'the Edwardses of Halifax and London were important actors in a series of remarkable changes in the book trade in the last twenty years of the eighteenth century' chiefly 'in three areas: quality of materials, skill of craftsmen, and aesthetic ambition' (p. 1). He also traces Richard's connection with William Blake and the poet Edward Young (pp. 9–11) and provides a 'Genealogy: Edwards of Halifax' (pp. 12–13) and 'Genealogy: Edwards of Northowram' (p. 12). The first part of Bentley's book is devoted to 'William Edwards, Paterfamilias' (pp. 1–40). The second part focuses upon 'James Edwards, the Medicean Bookseller' (pp. 43–149) with sections on: 'The Medicean Bookshop and James Edwards's Shop Catalogues 1784–1800' (pp. 43–72); 'Buying on the Continent and Selling at Auction 1786–1799' (pp. 73–86); 'James Edwards as a Publisher 1785–1800' (pp. 87–125); 'The Bookseller as Diplomat: James Edwards, Lord Grenville, and Earl Spencer in 1800' (pp. 126–38); and 'Last Years' (pp. 139–49). The third part is devoted to 'Richard Edwards, Publisher of Church-and-King Pamphlets and of William Blake' (pp. 153–92) and the fourth part to 'Thomas Edwards, an Important Provincial Bookseller' (pp. 195–200), with whose death in 1834 'the dynasty of Edwards of Halifax as makers and sellers of beautiful books came to an end' (p. 200). Extensive notes (pp. 201–42) then follow. There is a detailed index (pp. 243–83) that 'contains references both to *The Edwardses of Halifax* and to additional material found in *The Edwardses of Halifax* online appendices': there are nine of these—an idea of their content is given at the start of the printed version (pp. xi–xii) at http://www.utpublishing.com/pdf/Bentley_EdwarsesofHalifax Vol2.pdf. A 'Note on References' found throughout the book is found in its front pages (pp. xvii–xviii). There are eight colour plates (between pp. 72 and 73), and thirteen black and white ones found in the printed text. According to the list of illustrations (pp. xiii–xv) the appendices contain eight too. To sum up, G.E. Bentley Jr. has produced yet another definitive work.

Innes M. Keighren, Charles W.J. Withers, and Bill Bell's *Travels into Print: Exploration, Writing, and Publishing with John Murray, 1773–1859* contains fifteen colour plates (between pp. 210 and 211), and twenty-five half-tone illustrations. As its triple authors—although it is unclear which of them wrote what in the work—state at the beginning of their 'Preface and Acknowledgements' (pp. ix–xiii)—theirs 'is a book about books—books of travel and of exploration that sought to describe, examine, and explain the different parts of the world, between the late eighteenth century and the mid-nineteenth century'. Keighren, Withers, and Bell's 'focus is on the works of non-European exploration and travel published by the house of Murray, Britain's leading publisher of travel accounts and exploration narratives in this period, between their first venture in this respect', that is, Sydney Parkinson's *A Journal of a Voyage to the South Seas*, published in 1773, and their 1859 publication of Leopold McClintock's *The Voyage of the 'Fox' in the Arctic Seas*. Additionally the three authors are concerned 'with the activities of John Murray I (1737–93), John Murray II (1778–1843), and John Murray III (1808–92) in turning authors' words into print. This book is also about the world of bookmaking'. Further, '*Travels into Print* is a study of the relationships between the facts of travel and of geographical exploration and how the published versions of those travels came to appear in print'. *Travels into Print* well utilizes the 2006 acquisition by the National Library of Scotland of the John Murray Archive and especially 'its rich manuscript materials, the correspondence files of letters into and out from the several John Murrays, and of the production and financial records and the ledger volumes, as well as of the printed books themselves' (pp. ix–x). There are seven chapters: 'Exploration and Narrative: Travel, Writing, Publishing, and the House of Murray' (pp. 1–33); 'Undertaking Travel and Exploration: Motives and Practicalities' (pp. 34–67); 'Writing the Truth: Claims to Credibility in Exploration and Narrative' (pp. 68–99); 'Explorers Become Authors: Authorship and Authorization' (pp. 100–32); 'Making the Printed Work: Paratextual Material, Visual Images, and Book Production' (pp. 133–74); 'Travel Writing in the Marketplace' (pp. 175–208); and 'Assembling Words and Worlds' (pp. 209–26). An appendix contains a partially descriptive chronologically arranged listing of 239 'Books of Non-European Travel and Exploration Published by John Murray between 1773 and 1859: By Date of First Imprint, with Notes on Edition History before 1901' (pp. 227–85). This is followed by extensive notes (pp. 287–323) that are produced in a smaller, computer-generated type font than the main text and an appendix, consequently somewhat distracting from their utilization. In a similar smaller font is the bibliography organized by 'Primary Sources' (pp. 325–6) in alphabetical location order and an alphabetically listed 'Secondary Sources' (pp. 326–45). The double-columned index is author- and title-orientated.

Remaining with the subject of travel, a collection of essays of interest is edited by Julia Kuehn and Paul Smethurst. *New Directions in Travel Writing Studies* is divided into six parts. In the first part, on 'Textuality' (pp. 17–68), contributions include: '"A study rather than a rapture": Isabella Bird on Japan' by Steve Clark (pp. 17–34); 'Top of the World: Tourist's Spectacular Self-Locations as Multimodal Travel Writing' by Crispin Thurlow and Adam Jaworski (pp. 35–53); 'The Garden of Forking Paths: Paratexts in Travel Literature' by Alex Watson (pp. 54–68). The second part relates to 'Topography' (pp. 71–110) and contains: 'Metaphor, Travel, and the (Un)making of the Steppe' by Joseph Gualtieri (pp. 71–82); ' "That mighty Wall, not fabulous / China's stupendous mound!" Romantic Period Accounts of China's "Great Wall" ' by Peter J. Kitson (pp. 83–96)—a fascinating account especially for those fortunate to have visited the area; and ' "Habits of a landscape": The Geocritical Imagination in Robert Macfarlane's *The Wild Places* and *The Old Ways*' by Paul Smethurst (pp. 97–110). The third part is on the topic of 'Mobility' (pp. 113–60) and contains: 'Travel Writing, Disability, Blindness: Venturing Beyond Visual Geographies' by Charles Forsdick (pp. 113–28); 'Travel Literature and the Infrastructural Unconscious' by Caitlin Vandertop (pp. 129–44); and ' "Take out your machine": Narratives of Early Motorcycle Travel' by Tim Youngs (pp. 145–60). Part IV, 'Mapping' (pp. 163–212), consists of: ' "The thing which is not": Mapping the Fantastic History of the Great Southern Continent' by Vanessa Collingridge (pp. 163–79); 'Locating Guam: the Cartography of the Pacific and Craig Santos Perez's Remapping of Unincorporated Territory' by Otto Heim (pp. 180–98); and 'Map Reading in Travel Writing: the "Explorers' Maps" of *Mexico, This Month*' by Claire Lindsay (pp. 199–212). The fifth part contains reflections on the subject of 'Alterity' (pp. 215–46), or 'the representation of otherness in one form or another [that] has always been a central concern of travel writing' (p. 10). There are two essays in this section: 'The Traveller's Eye: Reading European Travel Writing, 1750–1850' by Wendy Bracewell (pp. 215–27); and 'Anthropology / Travel / Writing: Strange Encounters with James Clifford and Nicolas Rothwell' by Graham Huggan (pp. 228–46). The final part, 'Globality' (pp. 249–312), contains: 'Travel and Utopia' by Bill Ashcroft (pp. 249–62); 'Colonial Cosmopolitanism: Constance Cumming and Isabella Bird in Hong Kong, 1878' by Julia Kuehn (pp. 263–80); 'Afropolitan Travels: "Discovering Home" and the World in Africa' by Maureen Moynagh (pp. 281–96); and 'Revising the "Contact Zone": William Adams, Reception History and the Opening of Japan, 1600–1860' by Laurence Williams (pp. 297–312). Each contribution is followed by extensive documentation. There is a detailed double-columned index (pp. 313–25). In a clearly written introduction (pp. 1–13), Julia Kuen and Paul Smethurst place the history of the study of the genre of travel writing in its historical context and explain each of the divisions in the collection and summarize each essay. 'Notes on Contributors' (pp. ix–xiii) reveals that four of the contributors have connections with the School of English at the University of Hong Kong, which appears to be a beehive of activity on the study of travel writing as a genre.

In his introduction (pp. 1–24) to his *London and the Making of Provincial Literature: Aesthetics and the Transatlantic Book Trade, 1800–1850* Joseph Rezek writes that 'The most influential Irish, Scottish, and American fictions of the early nineteenth century were routed through the great metropolis of the English-speaking world. This book argues that the centripetal pull of London created a provincial literary formation that shaped the history of modern aesthetics.' Writers such as Maria Edgeworth, Sydney Owenson, Walter Scott, Washington Irving, and James Fenimore Cooper, in order to succeed in London, 'developed a range of literary strategies'. These included writing 'authenticating prefaces, footnotes, and glossaries', claiming 'exclusive local knowledge grounded in personal experience'; investing 'transnational marriage plots with allegories of cross-cultural communion'; and reworking their 'texts for London republication'. The 'strategies coalesce around a paradox about artistic production: that literature both transcends nationality and indelibly expresses it. This seeming contradiction preoccupied many writers of the Romantic period who offered competing ideological claims for literature's universality and its embodiment of a particular nation's spirit.' Rezek's monograph traces 'a new genealogy of this paradox to the fiction of provincial authors who navigated a subordinate position within the London-centered marketplace for books.' Rezek argues, moreover, that 'the effects of such navigation helped define the distinctly modern idea that literature inhabits an autonomous sphere in society' (pp. 2–3). *London and the Making of Provincial Literature* 'uses a wide range of textual and material evidence gleaned from rare books archives, manuscript collections, digital archives, and primary and secondary sources'. These range from 'data about the distribution of books around the Anglophone Atlantic; the business correspondence of provincial publishers ... angry marginalia American readers scribbled in London printed travel narratives; and numerous trans-provincial borrowings and appropri-ations' (p. 8). Accompanied by eleven illustrations, there are six chapters: 'London and the Transatlantic Book Trade' (pp. 25–39); 'Furious Booksellers and the "American Copy" of the Waverley Novels' (pp. 40–61); 'The Irish National Tale and the Aesthetics of Union' (pp. 62–84); 'Washington Irving's Transatlantic Revisions' (pp. 85–112); and 'The Effects of Provinciality in Cooper and Scott' (pp. 113–48); 'Rivalry with England in the Age of Nationalism' (pp. 149–84). An 'Epilogue. *The Scarlet Letter* and the Decline of London' (pp. 185–98) contains a detailed 'reading of *The Scarlet Letter* [1850] as an allegory for changes in the structure of the transatlantic book trade at mid-century' (p. 9). In tabulated form there is an appendix on 'The London Republication of American Fiction, 1797–1832' (pp. 200–6) followed by extensive notes (pp. 207–49) to the text. The bibliography is divided into an enumerative alphabetical listing of 'Archives Consulted', 'Periodicals', and 'Published Sources' (pp. 251–71), and there is a detailed double-columned index (pp. 273–84). Somewhat curiously this engaging work concludes with a listing of 'Acknowledgments' (pp. 285–6).

Jennifer Orr's *Literary Networks and Dissenting Print Culture in Romantic-Period Ireland* discusses amongst others the work of the 'Northern Irish

Romantic poet Sir Samuel Ferguson (1810–86)' and 'Dissenting republicans Samuel Thomson (1766–1816), James Orr (1770–1816) and Thomas Beggs (1789–1847), as well as the politically conservative coterie of antiquarian Bishop Thomas Percy (1729–1811) author of *Reliques of Ancient English Poetry* (1765)'. Orr is 'one of the first to stretch across [the] historical period [*c.* 1780–1820], mapping the activity of a northern poetic circle in a way that has not been common in Irish studies'. Particular focus is given to Samuel Thomson, who 'from 1790 onwards ... fostered and maintained a circle of correspondents which connected rural and metropolitan radicals, who were actively involved with the Volunteer Movement, Freemason and United Irishman ... the circles' beginnings were inseparably connected with the radical Belfast press' (pp. xi–xii). Orr's introduction, 'Irish Poetic Networks, 1790–1815' (pp. 1–12), is followed by six chapters: 'Sentiment, Sociability and the Construction of a Poetic Circle' (pp. 13–48); 'The Creation of Ulster Labouring-Class Poetry, 1790–3' (pp. 49–82); 'Revolutionary and Radical Dissenting Poetry, 1791–8' (pp. 83–121); '"Here no treason lurks": Post-Union Bardic Regeneration' (pp. 122–61); 'Dissenting Romanticism in the Early Union Period' (pp. 162–95); and 'Metropolitan Print Culture and the Creation of Literary Ulster' (pp. 196–233). Orr's brief 'Conclusion' (pp. 234–7) suggests the after-life of Thomson's circle and activities and is followed by extensive notes to Orr's text (pp. 238–47). The enumerative bibliography is alphabetically arranged and organized by 'Primary Texts' (curiously these, such as the Ulster poet and broadcaster's John Hewitt's 'MA Thesis notes', do not indicate dates), 'Newspapers and Journals', 'Printed Sources', 'Theses (unpublished)', and 'Online Sources for Literary and Linguistic Background' (pp. 248–60). There is a double-columned index (pp. 261–79).

Extensively illustrated in black and white, Katherine D. Harris's pioneering *Forget Me Not: The Rise of the British Literary Annual, 1823–1835* through the study of literary annual's including *Forget Me Not* attempts to 'demonstrate the wealth of scholarly potential in studying the literary annual' (p. 26). The wealth of information and scholarship in her book is reflected in her introduction, 'The Sociology of the Literary Annual' (pp. 1–26) and its seven chapters: 'British Ingenuity from German Invention: The Legacy of Rudolf Ackermann' (pp. 27–60); 'A Family History of Albums, Anthologies, Almanacs, and Emblems' (pp. 61–113); 'The First Generation's Success: *Forget Me Not*, *Friendship's Offering*, and *The Literary Souvenir*' (pp. 113–46); 'Second-Generation Annuals: A Ballroom Filled with Debutants and Comedians, *The Keepsake* and *The Comic Annual*' (pp. 147–69); 'The Artistic Influence of the Annual's Engraving "Copyists"' (pp. 170–87); 'Accumulating Profits or Constructing Taste: Editorial Control of the Literary Annuals' (pp. 188–225); and 'Feminizing the Textual Body: Women and Their Literary Annuals in Nineteenth-Century Britain' (pp. 226–60). Harris's 'Conclusion: The Literary Annual's Evolution from Nineteenth-Century Gothic to Twentieth-Century Homage' (pp. 261–79) opens with sentences reflecting her own excellent scholarly common sense that hers is not the definitive word upon the subject that her innovative monograph has opened up: 'I began this publishing, textual, and bibliographical history of the early literary annuals to highlight their influence and that of their creator Rudolf

Ackermann. After years of research, I finally concluded that a definitive and conclusive history of the annuals was impossible. The genre subsumed literary forms and created others' such as 'Gothic short stories' (p. 261). There are four appendices: a 'Chronological Index of British and American Literary Annual Titles' beginning in 1823 and concluding in 1857 (pp. 280–5); 'Prominent Contributors to British Literary Annuals' alphabetically arranged beginning with 'Baillie, Joanna (1762–1851)' and concluding with 'Wordsworth, William (1770–1850)' (pp. 286–320); an alphabetically arranged listing of 'Editors and Publishers of British Literary Annuals, 1823–31' (pp. 321–6); and the 'Full Text of Nineteenth-Century Writings from Chapters 3 and 4' (pp. 327–33)— the chapters on '*Forget Me Not, Friendship's Offering*, and *The Literary Souvenir*' and '*The Keepsake* and *The Comic Annual*'. The notes to Harris's text that follow are extensive (pp. 335–53), as is her alphabetical, enumerative bibliography organized by 'Substantial Library Collections of British Literary Annuals', 'Online Resources for British Literary Annuals', 'Primary Materials' and 'Secondary Texts' (pp. 355–86). The double-columned index is detailed too (pp. 387–95).

Caroline Davis and David Johnson, eds., *The Book in Africa: Critical Debates*, following an extensive introduction (pp. 1–17) by the editors, is divided into three parts. The first part, 'From Script to Print' (pp. 21–102), 'considers the complex transitions between oral, manuscript and print cultures, challenging what constitutes a "book" and a "reader"' (p. 6). It contains: Archie L. Dick on 'Copying and Circulation in South Africa's Reading Cultures, 1780–1840' (pp. 21–4); Fawzi Abdulrazuk on 'Printing as an Agent of Change in Morocco, 1864–1912' (pp. 44–64)—the printing press was introduced into the country in 1864; in 1912 it 'came under French protection and management, and the direction of the country turned towards an abandonment of the Islamic educational system and the application of Islamic law' (p. 45); Alessandro Gori on 'Between Manuscripts and Books: Islamic Printing in Ethiopia' (pp. 65–82); and Shamil Jeppie on 'Making Book History in Timbuktu' (pp. 83–102). The second part, 'Politics and Profit in African Print Cultures' (pp. 105–97), 'foregrounds the relationship of the book to African politics and economics, contributing to debates about the function of the book (broadly conceived) in colonial and neo-colonial profiteering, in constituting political communities, and in mediating relationships between economic and cultural capital' (p. 6). There are four chapters: David Johnson on 'Print Culture and Imagining the Union of South Africa' (pp. 105–27); Caroline Davis on 'Creating a Book Empire: Longman's in Africa' (pp. 128–52); Jack Hogan and Giacomo Macola on 'From Royalism to E-secessionism: Lozi Histories and Ethnic Politics in Zambia' (pp. 153–75); and Elizabeth le Roux on 'Between the Cathedral and the Market: A Study of Wits University Press' (pp. 176–97). The third and final part, 'The Making of African Literature' (pp. 201–66), 'intervenes in debates about the relationship between African literature and its multiple book-historical, print-cultural and online/e-book contexts' (p. 6). There are three chapters: Ruth Bush and Claire Ducournau on 'Francophone African Literary Prizes and the "Empire of the French Language"' (pp. 201–22); Nourdin Bejjit on 'Heinemann's African Writers Series and the Rise of James Ngugi' (pp. 223–44)—'Ngugi was

Heinemann's first East African author' (p. 11); and Joyce B. Ashuntantang on 'The Publishing and Digital Dissemination of Creative Writing in Cameroon' (pp. 245–66). Each contribution contains extensive end notation followed by detailed, enumerative, alphabetically arranged references. To take one instance, Caroline Davis's chapter's references, following her 97 notes (pp. 144–8), are divided into 'Primary Sources' (pp. 148–9), 'Archival Sources' (pp. 149–50), 'Oral Sources' (p. 150), 'Secondary Sources: Published' (pp. 150–2) and 'Unpublished Sources' (p. 152). *The Book in Africa* has a detailed, double-columned index (pp. 267–80).

Ian Morris and Joanne Diaz in *The Little Magazine in Contemporary America* have collected the thoughts of twenty-three eminent editors whose small magazines have on the whole flourished over the last thirty-five years. Emphasizing both creativity and innovation, the editors provide insights into the ways in which their magazines were a success or folded and how mostly they developed and continued. There is also discussion of the way in which the magazines develop the efforts and concerns of minority and women writers, the role of universities in their support for little magazines, and the future, offline and online, for the little magazine. There are six half-tone illustrations, mainly of front covers. The editors' preface (pp. vii–xvii) is followed by Jeffrey Lependorf's introduction, 'A Decade or So of Little Magazines: One Reader's Perspective' (pp. 1–15), and five parts written by the magazine editors. Each part contains four essays. The first, on 'The Editor as Visionary' (pp. 19–48), contains: Betsy Sussler on 'This History of BOMB' (pp. 19–27); Greg Johnson on 'The Life of *Ontario Review* (1947–2008)' (pp. 28–34); Dave Eggers, editor of *McSweeney's*, on 'The Word *Sacred* Is Not Misplaced' (pp. 35–7); and Keith Gessen on 'On $n + 1$' (pp. 38–48). The second part, 'Politics, Culture, and the Little Magazine' (pp. 51–94), contains: Charles Henry Rowell on '*Callaloo*: A Journal of Necessity' (pp. 51–64); the *Women's Review of Books* is the focus for Amy Hoffman's 'Critical Thinking from Women' (pp. 65–9); Lisa Jervis and Andi Zeisler, interviewed by Joanne Diaz in 'The *Bitch* Interview' (pp. 70–82)—the initial 1996 print run was 300, in 1998 the circulation was 5,000 and in 2010 had risen to 'approximately 47,000' (p. 73); Gerald Maa and Lawrence-Minh Bùi Davis's 'The World Doesn't Stop for Derek Walcott, or, An Exchange between Coeditors', a conversation between the joint editors of the *Asian American Literary Review* (pp. 83–94). Part III focuses upon 'Innovation and Experimentation: The Literary Avant-Garde' (pp. 97–139). Andrei Codrescu writes on '*Exquisite Corpse*' (pp. 97–105), founded in January 1984. 'In 1998 tired of mountains of paper, but also fearful of inevitable institutionalization, ossification, poetry fatigue, and literary institutionalization, and literary ennui', Codrescu observes, 'we suspended publication of the paper *Corpse*, taking it into cyberspace'. He adds 'the cyber *Corpse* is still the *Corpse*, but is more fluid, subject to instant change and, above all, not so labor- and time-intensive for us. And the trees are ecstatic' (p. 105). Bruce Andrews writes on '$L=A=N=G=U=A=G=E$' (pp. 106–23) 'the name of the journal of Poetics that Charles Bernstein and I co-edited & co-produced in New York City, from its first modest issue in February 1978 to its fourth "volume" co-published with Toronto's *Open Letter* in 1981' (p. 106). Rebecca Wolff, in 'Publishing is Personal' (pp. 124–9), in addition confesses that 'over the years [she] has been given a lot of money by some very rich people in support of [her] publishing activities' (p. 125) and her journal *Fence* also observes that it 'is a tax shelter' (p. 129). Andre Monson, in 'This Being 2015' (pp. 130–9), wonders if he 'should be writing' his contribution 'in Macromedia's (now Adobe's) Dreamweaver, the software used for composition and design for the magazine DIAGRAM (The Diagram. com) that [he] founded in 2000 and continue[s] to edit and design' (p. 130). The fourth part has also four contributions on the subject of 'The University Magazine' (pp. 143–85). Lee Gutkind, in his 'War of the Words: Fighting for a Journal and a Genre' (pp. 143–54), writes about the founding of *Creative Nonfiction*. In 'Decent Company between the Covers' (pp. 155–65) a long established journal, *Southern Review* (the initial issue, edited by Robert Penn Warren and Cleanth Brooks, was in 1935), engages Cara Blue Adams, who joined its 'editorial staff in 2008' (p. 155): she now edits the journal. Ronald Spatz discusses '*Alaska Quarterly Review* and the Literary Tonic' (pp. 166–74). This is followed by Carolyn Kuebler's in 'Making a Living and a Life in Little Magazines' (pp. 175–85) on *Rain Taxi* and the *New England Review*. The final part contains four reflections on 'Today's Magazines and the Future' (pp. 189–224). Jonathan Framer writes 'About *At Length*' (pp. 189–97), a primarily poetry magazine that he killed off and then revived. Framer confesses that he is 'just old enough to be uncomfortable reading online, and a hurry I feel in front of screens seeming compatible with reading valuable long work' (p. 191). He also admits that 'this poem or that essay or that interview regenerates in the transmission between the server and the screen, neither of which I have ever seen or really understand' (p. 196). Rebecca Morgan Frank's contribution is on 'Summoning the Bard: The Twenty-First-Century Literary Magazine on the Web' (pp. 198–208), an account of the founding of *Memorious* late in 2004. For Morgan 'one of the most curious misconceptions is the belief that digital magazines are ephemeral'. She believes that 'the reality is that some magazines live and some die, regardless of the medium' (pp. 199–200). Also, 'unlike the editor working on a university publication, my work as an editor is unpaid, and like most editors, I do the work on top of my paying job. It is a labor of love, the tradition of indie literary magazines who maintain the mission of keeping an art with a small audience alive, of creating and sustaining community, of contributing to shaping the history of our art' (p. 204). Jane Friedman 'served as web editor of the *Virginia Quarterly Review* and is also the cofounder and editor of *Scratch*, a digital magazine that focuses on the intersection of writing and money' (p. 226). She writes on 'The Future of the Gatekeepers' (pp. 209–17). She concludes that 'it's time for the magazine [community] to work much harder, and much more transparently in partnership with their community, for the values they believe in, instead of focusing on the fading reputation and the place of print' (p. 217). *The Little Magazine in Contemporary America* is a diverse, interesting collection of essays. The final contribution is, not inappropriately, Don Share's '*Poetry Magazine*: On Making It New' (pp. 218–24). Harriet Munroe's *Poetry Magazine* first appeared in October 1912 and 'the way we do our reading and writing has changed dramatically since Harriet Munroe published her first issue'. Share observes that 'most of the poems we publish [now] are born digital, and presumably will live long lives that way'. Share keeps Ezra Pound's portrait hanging 'right across from [his] desk now' as he works. Share adds that 'serving as Harriet Munroe's successor, the key to keeping the magazine "durable" remains what Pound always said it was'—in his 'Small Magazines' in *English Journal* 19, No. 9 (November 1930)—to 'maintain a species of open-mindedness toward the possible and the plausible' (p. 224). Biographical details of contributors to *The Little Magazine in Contemporary America* (pp. 225–30) are followed by a detailed index (pp. 231–6).

A different facet of magazine studies is reflected in Faye Hammill and Michelle Smith's *Magazines, Travel, and Middlebrow Culture: Canadian Periodicals in English and French, 1925–1960*. Focusing on Canada, the study begins in the 1920s. This was a period that witnessed 'the golden age of the ocean liner, the early development of passenger aviation and the expansion of tourism by rail'. In their introduction (pp. 1–21), Hamill and Smith add that the 1920s were too 'the decade when commercial Canadian magazines began to flourish, in the context of a rapid expansion of periodical publishing on both sides of the Atlantic'. In this study the authors argue 'that magazines, by circulating fantasies of travel, were instrumental in forging a link between geographic mobility and upward mobility'. They focus upon six magazines that 'were the most widely read in Canada in an era when print was the dominant form of mass media'. Furthermore, 'they maintained their leading positions well into the 1950s, and [a handful] have survived into the present'. The six magazines, three catering for French Canadian readers, and three for English Canadian readers, are *Mayfair*, *Chatelaine*, *MacLean's*, *La Revue Moderne*, the *Canadian Home Journal*, and *La Revue Populaire*, all of which began publishing in the opening two decades of the last century (pp. 1–2). There are four chapters. The first, 'Marketplace' (pp. 23–64), 'delineates the mainstream magazine marketplace in Canada over the period from the 1920s until the 1950s'. These magazines have received very little if any scholarly attention. Topics examined include 'pricing, circulation, and the important role of advertising, which increasingly finance the magazines as well as enabling them to shape and address the target audiences'. Another topic addressed is 'the nationalist orientation of the magazines, and the ways in which they differentiated themselves from one another and from their foreign competitors'. There is also analysis of formats, editors, contributors, and the nature of the travel material they published (p. 20). The second chapter, 'Pages' (pp. 65–108), 'examines the relationship between the physical charac-teristics of the magazines and the type of material they published' through analysis of 'an annual volume and of a full run' (pp. 20–1). The third chapter, 'Fashions' (pp. 109–45), 'considers not only the magazines' association of fashionable clothes with mobility and the exotic, but also their presentation of travel itself as a fashionable practice' and the chapter includes 'close readings of different types of fashion report[age]' (p. 21). The final chapter, 'Consumers' (pp. 146–79), 'focuses on the magazines' construction of travel as an opportunity for consumption, a chance to experience luxury as well as to accumulate social and cultural capital' (p. 21). In their 'Conclusion' (pp. 180–4) the joint authors note that 'foreign travel features often focused on destinations which could enhance many white Canadians' sense of connection with their ancestry (holidays in France, England, and Scotland) or with the "British world" (for instance, articles on Jamaica and Bermuda)' (p. 182). The journals that survive such as *Mclean's*, *Chatelaine* or *Châtelaine*, in its renamed title, 'have been and remain, extremely influential, and the cultural work they perform includes mediating ideas of nationhood in relation to gender and class, and constructing Canada's relationship to foreign cultures' (p. 184). *Travel, and Middlebrow Culture* concludes with an alphabetically arranged, enumerative bibliography (pp. 185–203), a name-orientated double-columned index (pp. 205–12), and, inserted at the end, twenty-nine full-page colour figures from the texts discussed.

Finally in this section mention should be made of a collection of essays largely overlooked elsewhere in this volume, contributions to Jim Pearce, Ward J. Risvold, Nathan Dixon, eds., *Renaissance Papers*, the annual volume of the best essays judged to have been submitted to the yearly Southeastern Renaissance Conference in 2014 the seventy-first annual meeting held in this instance at the University of North Carolina, Greensboro, on 3 and 4 October 2014. The opening and concluding contributions to the volume focus on historically based explorations of identity. The first, by Emily Stockard 'Who Was Jane Scope?' (pp. 1–15), discusses the circle of Jane Scroop in John Skelton's *Philip Sparrow* poem. In the final essay, Joanna J. Kucinski's 'English Dogs and Barbary Horses: Horses, Dogs, and Identity in Renaissance England' (pp. 123–35), treats dogs and horses as symbols of national identity in early modern England. There are three essays on Marlowe. Philip Goldfarb's 'The Devil, Not the Pope: Anti-Catholicism and Textual Difference in *Doctor Faustus*' (pp. 47–58) concentrates on the role of anti-Catholicism in the creation of Marlowe's *Dr. Faustus*. Barry Shelton's '"Straunge Motion": Puppetry, Faust, and the Mechanics of Idolatry' (pp. 59–72) reflects on the relationship between puppetry and the Faust legend. Marlowe's non-dramatic work engages Pamela Royston Macfie in her 'The Ovidian *Recusatio* in Marlowe's *Hero and Leander*' (pp. 73–82) and is concerned with Ovidian resonances in Marlowe's *Hero and Leander*. Ben Jonson's work is the subject of three contributions. Emma Annette Wilson writes on Puritan logic in Jonson's *Bartholomew Fair* in her '"All is but Hinnying Sophistry": The Role of Puritan Logic in *Bartholomew Fair*' (pp. 17–28). Sarah Mayo draws attention to grotesque sex in Jonson's *Volpone* in her 'Grotesque Sex: Hermaphroditism and Castration in Jonson's *Volpone*' (pp. 29–45) and William Coulter's '"To catchen hold of that long chaine": Spenserian Echoes in Jonson's "Epode"' (pp. 83–94), as its title suggests, is a reflection on Spenserian echoes in Jonson's *Epode*. Imaginative resources in the Martin Marprelate pamphlets are the subject of Christopher A. Hill's 'Dost thou see a Martin who is Wise in his own Conceit? There is more hope in a fool than in him' (pp. 109–22).

## 5. Shakespeare, History of Libraries, and Collections

The large-format second edition of *The Oxford Companion to Shakespeare* can be treated under the section devoted to 'Companions' or under the 'Shakespeare History of Libraries and Collections' section, where it is placed. The first edition of this excellent reference work appeared in 2001 edited by Michael Dobson and Stanley Wells. Published online two years later and two years subsequently as a paperback, three years later in 2008 it was reprinted with corrections and in 2012 updated on line with over 200 updated entries and sixteen new ones plus an additional 35,000 words. In 2015 a second edition was published with Will Sharpe and Erin Sullivan as the revising editors. This second edition contains these additional materials and more than eighty new entries that include performers, directors, and scholars such as Lucy Bailey (p. 24), Samuel West (p. 554), and Alfredo Michel Modenessi the Mexican professor of English and translator (pp. 396–7). Additions to topics include the ubiquity of plants in his work (pp. 434–5) and entries on interpretation of Shakespeare throughout the world (see for instance 'Israel' and 'Italy', pp. 179–82). Will Sharpe and Erin Sullivan write in their 'Preface to the Second Edition' that 'guides to further reading have been updated, as have entries exploring Shakespeare's digital presence, and play by play analyses are now collated together in the middle of the volume for greater ease of reference' (p. ix). This may be seen as disconcerting. The alphabetical arrangement of entries is halted at the conclusion of the letter 'L' with a sentence on 'Lysimachus' that reads 'Lysimachus is overcome with shame when he meets the virtuous Marina in a brothel, *Pericles* 19' (p. 220), and entries on plays and poems then begin with '*All Is True (Henry VIII)*' (pp. 221–3) and conclude with '*The Winter's Tale*' (pp. 379–82). The alphabetical sequence starting with 'M' then begins again (p. 383), concluding with the final entry on 'Zuccaro, Federico (1543–1609), Italian painter' (p. 561). Instead of an index, at the start of the volume, in addition to a listing of contributors by their initials (pp. xii–xiii), there is a useful 'Thematic Listing of Entries' (pp. xiv–xxix). In a 'Note to the Reader' the alphabetical arrangement, names of plays and characters, cross references, thematic listing of entries, and contributors' initials (p. xxx) are clearly explained. Entries are in three columns on the page; the main body of entries is followed by 'The British Isles and France in the English Histories' and the Scottish play (pp. 562–3), a diagrammatic 'The Royal Family in Shakespeare's English Histories' (p. 564), and 'Shakespeare's Life, Works, and Reception: A Partial Chronology, 1564–2015' (pp. 565–8). The 'Further Reading' listing (pp. 569–71) 'is intended primarily to supplement the bibliographies appended to entries in the body of this Companion' (p. 569). This invaluable reference work concludes with 'Picture Acknowledgements' (pp. 573–4) ,identifying the innumerable black and white illustrations found throughout.

Another excellent—well illustrated in colour and black and white—reference work is Peter Whitfield's *Mapping Shakespeare's World*. Whitfield writes 'that Shakespeare never wrote a play that was explicitly set in the world in which he lived, Elizabethan London. All his plays are located in settings remote in space or time from the England which he and his audiences inhabited, faraway places where the imagination could be set free, where anything could happen' (p. 1). Whitfield 'sets out to survey the settings of Shakespeare's plays, to us how familiar they were, what they might have meant to Shakespeare himself and his contemporaries'. He also maps 'Shakespeare's visual world in a more general sense, looking at historical events, historical figures and cultural stereotypes associated with those places' (p. 4). Whitfield argues that Shakespeare's settings may well have associations that his contemporary audience would have picked up and understood and that the geographical and historical backgrounds of his dramas were of considerable significance. There are three central chapters: 'Greece, Rome & the Mediterranean' (pp. 19–67); 'The Dramas of European Cities & Courts' (pp. 71–123); 'British Plays, Ancient, Medieval & Modern' (pp. 127–85). Each of the three chapters has separate sections. The first chapter: 'The Greek Plays' (pp. 19–37); 'The Roman Plays' (pp. 39–51); 'The Mediterranean Plays' (pp. 53–67). The second: 'The Idea of Europe' (pp. 71–6); 'Italy: The Setting' (pp. 77–90); 'Italy: The Plays' (pp. 91–105); 'The Non-Italian Plays' (pp. 107–23). The third: 'Shakespeare's England: A Sense of Place' (pp. 127–31); 'The Ancient & Medieval Plays' (pp. 133–46); 'The Plays of Dynastic Conflict' (pp. 147–65); 'The Wars of the Roses' (pp. 167–75); 'Two Isolated Plays' (pp. 177–85)—these are *Henry VIII* and *The Merry Wives of Windsor*. The book concludes with notes (pp. 189–91), a brief, alphabetically arranged bibliography (p. 192), a listing of 'Picture Credits' (pp. 193–5)—there are 102 of these—and a brief, rather inadequate, index (pp. 196–8). Whitfield's is a beautiful volume 'designed and typeset in 11½ on 16 Garamond' (p. vi).

Two challenging biblio/textual studies concerning Shakespeare were published in 2015: Zachary Lesser's *'Hamlet' After Q1: An Uncanny History of the Shakespearean Text* and Emma Smith's *The Making of Shakespeare's First Folio*. Lesser, in his introduction (pp. 1–23), relates the story of the momentous discovery by Sir Henry Bunbury in 1823 of 'a small quarto, barbarously cropped, and very ill—bound ... in a closet of the manor house of Great Barton, Suffolk'. In the nineteenth century in the collection of the duke of Devonshire the 'small quarto' containing twelve Shakespeare first editions was disbound. Amongst the editions 'was a copy of the first quarto of *Hamlet* (Q1), published a year prior to the earliest text of the play then known and, at the time, the unique example of the edition' (pp. 1–2). Lesser writes that 'the central argument of this book is that Bunbury's discovery, itself a historical accident, has had profound effects on our understanding of *Hamlet*, of Shakespeare as an author, and of the nature of the Shakespearean text'. Lesser continues, 'the uncanny nature of Q1 challenges both traditional bibliographic scholarship and the historicism criticism that has recently dominated Shakespeare and early modern studies'. Lesser argues that 'we cannot fully understand Q1 without treating it as a text existing simultaneously in two very different historical moments' (pp. 10–12). Lesser's first chapter, 'As Originally Written by Shakespeare: Textual Bibliography and Textual Biography' (pp. 25–71), examines the complicated relations between the three stationers who funded and printed the initial two editions of the play, Nicholas Ling, Valentine Simmes, and James Roberts, and revisits their title pages,. The second chapter, 'Contrary Matters: The Power of the Glass and the History of an Obscenity' (pp. 72–113), focuses upon the phrase 'country matters' used by Hamlet to Ophelia during the mousetrap scene and found in Q2/F but which in Q1 is worded 'contrary matters' (pp. 72–3). In his third chapter, 'Enter the Ghost in his Night Gowne behind Gertrude's Bed' (pp. 114–56), Lesser focuses upon the assumed apparel and location of the closet scene between Hamlet and his mother when Polonius is murdered. Q1 includes the additional stage direction that the Ghost is 'in his night gowne' (p. 122) as opposed to wearing the armour he was dressed in on the battlements: the consequences of this on interpretations of this scene and the play as a whole are considered (pp. 122–56). The fourth chapter, 'Conscience Makes Cowards: The Disintegration and Reintegration of Shakespeare' (pp. 157–206), performs a similar operation on the word 'conscience' in the famous 'To be, or not to be' speech. Lesser writes: 'in all three texts of *Hamlet* ... *conscience* is decidedly unlikely to carry any meaning other than a religious one. Yet in its familiar version, "To be, or not to be" includes no religious language aside from this word, leaving *conscience* curiously unanchored' (p. 195). In Q1 the line in Hamlet's soliloquy reads 'O, this conscience makes cowards of us all' (p. 158). This differs from Q2 and F's 'conscience does make cowards of us all' (p. 197). The implications preoccupy Lesser's fourth chapter. In the concluding chapter, 'Conclusion Q1 in the Library at Babel' (pp. 207–21), Lesser considers the problems for 'New Textualism'—whose advocates 'have generally been more interested in "unediting" than in producing critical editions that purported to recover the lost authorial manuscript' (p. 209)—created by the three versions of *Hamlet*: however, 'if we are interested in *Hamlet*, rather than the metaphysical possibility of infinite *Hamlet*s, then the issue of textual origins can be productively deferred, but it will not ultimately be evaded' (p. 219). Extremely detailed at times lengthy notes follow Lesser's chapters (pp. 223–8). The bibliography is divided into a chronologically arranged 'Frequently Cited Shakespeare Editions' (pp. 259–60) and an alphabetical enumerative listing of 'Other Works' (pp. 261–78). An index (pp. 279–289) followed by 'Acknowledgments' (pp. 291–2) conclude Lesser's deeply engaging, thought-provoking work very well grounded in bibliographical and textual knowledge.

Emma Smith's *The Making of Shakespeare's First Folio*, published by the Bodleian Library, has eight black and white figures, mainly of title pages, and thirty-two colour plates. Most are from the Bodleian Library, but somewhat curiously none from the Folger Library, which has the largest collection of Shakespeare First Folios in the world. Smith comments in the final paragraph of her introduction that she has attempted 'to recover the world into which Shakespeare's collected plays first emerged, and reveal a sampling of the immediate responses of its earliest readers' (p. 4). Her first chapter, 'The Plays & Their Presentation' (pp. 5–52), moves from the Droeshout engraving and the dedications to a discussion of Shakespeare's canon, a genre, the ways in which the plays are ordered, and textual concerns. Smith illuminates for instance the servants' speeches in *King Lear*, writing that 'the servant dialogue may have been unnecessary in the theatre for which F [the First Folio] was prepared, and indoor theatre which had act breaks for the trimming of candle wicks. The servants' role may be more about the practical business of theatre than about the empathetic business of the story' (p. 47). The second chapter,

'Shakespeare's Reputation' (pp. 53–84), relegates bibliographical details, and Smith's focus is much more on the initial reception of the First Folio in the literary and cultural world of 1623. Smith writes that when the Folio was published 'the autumn weather was unremittingly wet, and the London streets were thick with mud' (p. 80). But we learn little about the eighteen months or so that it took to produce the First Folio at the printer's. There is a section too on ' "Buy it first": The Book's Buyers' (pp. 83–4). Seamlessly this leads into the third chapter 'Team Shakespeare: The Backers' (pp. 85–138), containing sections on: 'The Dedicatory Poets: Shakespeare's "Friends" ' (pp. 87–94); ' "The Principal Actors in All These Plays": Shakespeare's Fellow Players' (pp. 94–107); 'The "incomparable pair of brethren": The Book's Patrons' (pp. 107–10); 'Printers and Publishers' (pp. 110–24)—in which we learn that the main publisher, Edward Blount, was 'associated with the import of art objects as well as seeds and exotic foodstuffs' (p. 116), information perhaps covering up the paucity of other data; 'Invisible Hands' (pp. 124–6); and 'Other Playwrights' (pp. 126–38). The fourth and final chapter, 'Printing & Publishing' (pp. 139–59), deals with bibliographical concerns such as 'The Rights to the Plays' (pp. 140–1), 'The Case of *Troilus and Cressida*' (pp. 141–3)—'The catalogue of the plays included in the Folio does not mention *Troilus and Cressida*' (p. 141)—'Putting the Book Together' (pp. 143–6), 'Compositorial Work' (pp. 146–8), 'Paper' (pp. 149–51), 'Printing' (pp. 151–2), 'Corrections' (pp. 153–7), and 'Binding' (pp. 158–9). Smith's explanation of the details is very clear but would have been assisted by the use of diagrams. One can quibble with a few of her observations, for instance that 'a few copies [of the Folio] exist with a cancelled sheet following *Romeo and Juliet* printing only the first two pages of *Troilus*' (p. 143), or, to take another instance, issues relating to the Folio printing of *The Winter's Tale* that are passed over. Smith includes a 'Coda: Early Readers' (pp. 160–6) that focuses upon the annotations in the Cary copy at Glasgow University Library (pp. 161–4) and a copy at the Meisei University Library in Tokyo containing the name 'William Johnstoone' (pp. 164–6). As Smith states in her final sentence: her 'book has traced the processes and the individuals behind Shakespeare's First Folio: we are now at the point when the great variety of readers begin their own most creative, idiosyncratic and diverse engagements with this great book' (p. 166). Notes arranged by chapter follow the text (pp. 167–72). Instead of a formal bibliography there are recommendations for 'Further Reading' (pp. 173–6) organized by topic such as 'Folio Facsimiles' and 'On the First Folio' (pp. 173–4). Smith's interesting account has a name-orientated 'double-columned index (pp. 177–80).

David Vaisey's *Bodleian Library Treasures* has 180 colour plates. Included amongst these are 'the copy of … *Venus and Adonis*, the first of Shakespeare's works to be published -in 1593 - and the only copy known to exist'. This 'came to the Bodleian Library as part of the collection made by the Shakespearean editor Edmund Malone in 1821'. Also illustrated are examples from the Bodleian's First Folio (pp. 132–5), the copy used by Emma Smith. Vaisey has made 'a selection of a hundred or so notable items from the Bodleian Library for inclusion in a book under the general heading' and he has 'chosen some which are undoubtedly treasures and are well known for being so'. On the other hand, 'other chosen items would strain to fit into the category: for example sets of notes kept by civil servants in the seventeenth century ... or a playbill for a performance of little-known plays at the Drury Lane theatre in 1800, a Lancashire schoolboy's writing exercise in 1813 or a battered and damaged copy of a Russian translation of Charles Dickens's *Pickwick Papers'*. Vaisey adds that 'all the items included, however, are noteworthy either for the tales they have to tell, the hands through which they have passed, their beauty or their extraordinary provenance' (p. 4). The colour plates do serve to convey a flavour of the treasures to be found at the Bodleian. Although Vaisey's selection is by no means confined to treasures in English, he does include 'a poem in John Donne's hand' (pp. 140–1), a picture of 'an eighteenth-century book auction' (pp. 178–9), Jane Austen's manuscript for *The Watsons* (pp. 192–3), and, to give to other instances from many, J.R.R. Tolkien's drawings (pp. 212–13) and 'C.S. Lewis's map of Narnia' (pp. 214–15).

Other well-illustrated not unreasonably priced books published by the Bodleian Library imprint include Katharine Duncan-Jones's *Portraits of Shakespeare*. Duncan-Jones provides a critique of the 'three images of William Shakespeare that were tacitly acknowledged as authentic likenesses by people who had been familiar with his appearance. These are the Stratford bust.... The so-called 'Droeshout engraving'.... And the painting known as the "Chandos portrait" painted in oil on canvas and dating from about 1610' (p. vi). These 'earliest surviving images of the great poet-playwright ... have ... prompted recurring questions'. It is these questions that Duncan-Jones examines. They include re-examining the assumption that 'none of the surviving images of Shakespeare originates within his lifetime'. Furthermore, 'do the author portraits made of his contemporaries, such as Ben Jonson, shed any light on this mysterious absence' of portraits from Shakespeare's lifetime? Duncan-Jones also asks 'are there any useful clues to be found in places other than Stratford, such as Oxford and London? And can these three portraits together with the many imitations, commemorative effigies and memorials, tell us anything at all about Shakespeare's life?' (p. ix). Replete with forty colour plates, Duncan-Jones's five chapters concern: 'Shakespeare and the "Author Portrait"' (pp. 1–25); 'The Stratford Bust' (pp. 27–51); 'The Droeshout Engraving' (pp. 53–71); 'The Chandos Portrait' (pp. 73–91); and 'Commemorative, Disputed & Other Portraits' (pp. 93–114). Duncan-Jones concludes that 'the Chandos portrait ... continues to hold its own'. In addition, 'this painting, uniquely, hints at Shakespeare's own voice and presence' (p. 114). Notes (pp. 115–18) follow the text, as does an alphabetically arranged, enumerative bibliography (pp. 119–20) and a listing of the 'Image Sources' (pp. 121–2). There is a useful double-columned, alphabetically arranged index (pp. 124–6) that concludes Duncan-Jones's interesting account of *Portraits of Shakespeare*.

Mary Clapinson's *A Brief History of the Bodleian Library* has eighteen colour plates and twelve black and white figures. Clapinson's account is divided into six chapters: 'The Early Years, 1602–1652' (pp. 1–37); 'Consolidation, 1652–1700' (pp. 38–59); 'The Eighteenth Century' (pp. 60–84); 'The Nineteenth Century' (pp. 85–123); 'A New Century and a New

Bodleian, 1912–1945' (pp. 124–48); and 'Expansion and Modernization, 1945–2002' (pp. 149–82). There is an all too brief 'Postscript: Since 2002' (pp. 180–2) followed by notes (pp. 183–8), an alphabetically arranged, enumerative 'Further Reading' listing (pp. 189–90), and a detailed, double-columned index. Clapinson's book is a succinct 'attempt to explain what enabled' the Bodleian Library 'to develop from a fifteenth-century library room, beautifully restored at one man's expense, into a national and international research centre, ranking among the foremost university libraries in the world. No single factor can account for its longevity, but there can be no doubt that Sir Thomas Bodley's vision and generosity, combined with his sound business acumen, were crucial in laying the foundations on which it grew' (p. 177).

Merton College Oxford houses the archive of the legendary Oxford booksellers and publishers, B.H. Blackwell. Rita Ricketts draws heavily upon this archive and material in the Bodleian Blackwell collections in her fascinating *Scholars, Poets, and Radicals: Discovering Forgotten Lives in the Blackwell Collections*. Accompanied by forty-eight colour, full-page illustrations (between pp. 142 and 143), and black and white illustrations throughout, Ricketts's text relates the history of Blackwell's as a bookshop and as an imprint and draws upon the diaries and papers of its founding family and those they employed, such as Rex King. He kept a diary. His 'life, struggling to make ends meet as a bookseller's assistant, was "ordinary", but his writing was extraordinary it was prolific, despite a twelve-hour day, six days a week, and, very unusually much has survived'. King was 'rescued from bitter poverty when Benjamin Henry Blackwell employed him'. Rex King 'proved to be more scholarly than the shops customers' and his 'diary entries ... incorporate mordant dissections of the text he studied' (pp. 1–2). Ricketts's book is an account of the innumerable 'famous or obscure ... characters' associated with and educated by the Oxford bookshop. Their 'stories provide a tableau of nineteenth- and twentieth-century history ranging far beyond Oxford' (p. 9). The opening chapter, 'An Oxford Education' (pp. 7–35), relates the nineteenth-century history of the bookshop, focusing upon its founder, Benjamin Harris Blackwell. The second chapter, 'A Dreadful Radical', follows the history of the Blackwell family into the twentieth century and examines its political affiliations (pp. 36–55). The third chapter, 'Women Warriors' (pp. 56–80), focuses on the family wives and daughters, and the women who came to work for the firm. There is also discussion (pp. 72–80) of Vera Brittain, who edited Basil Blackwell's *Oxford Poetry*, Dorothy L. Sayers, and Muriel Jaeger, amongst others who came within 'the Blackwell ambit' (p. 74). Ricketts quotes from diaries and journals in her chapter on 'Scholar Apprentices' (pp. 81–109) and shop assistants; Rex King (1886–1950), 'A Baker's Son', is the focus of the next chapter (pp. 110–26): he 'joined Blackwell's in 1916 and was to spend the rest of his life there'; 'working long hours in the shop, and burning the midnight oil compiling catalogues, it is astonishing that Rex found time to write anything. As far as we know, he wrote two diaries, a series of articles, poems, book reviews and memoir fragments' (pp. 113–14). According to Hugo Dyson, at Merton, they reflect 'both how an important but often inarticulate section of our society lived and felt: its governing ideals, its sources of inspiration, its faith and its strength'.

For Dyson the King diaries constitute 'indispensable material' (p. 115). Material from King forms the foundation for Ricketts's sixth chapter, 'A Moral Witness' (pp. 127–51), and seventh chapter, 'The Good Reader' (pp. 152–76). A moving chapter, 'The Patriots' (pp. 177–201), contains the reminiscences of a German Jewish refugee employed by the firm (see for instance pp. 198–9), and chapter 9, 'War on Many Fronts' (pp. 202–29), gives an account of some of the disputes the firm entered into and the causes it espoused. 'Profligate Printers & a Spellbound Princess' (pp. 230–56), in addition to material on Basil Blackwell, A.H. Bullen's Shakespeare Head Press, and fine printing and printers (pp. 230–45), slightly digresses into an account of the last years of May Morris, with a lengthy extract from a meeting with May Morris in June/July 1925 (pp. 248–51). The 'Conclusion' (pp. 257–62) focuses upon Basil Blackwell. In a 'Postscript' called 'Vertex' (pp. 263–5), Sir Martin Taylor, a mathematician and current Warden of Merton College, observes that 'many of the real-life characters that appear in this book were intent on finding the truth' and that 'the autodidact Rex King, whose diary is an important addition to the Merton Blackwell collection, wrote about *his* search' (p. 263). He adds that 'they were no more successful in uncovering any ultimate truth, but they may have encouraged us to try out a few solutions of our own, or at least to write about them' (p. 265). Extensive notes (pp. 266–87) are found at the end of *Scholars Poets and Radicals*. There is an extensive descriptive 'Select Bibliography' (pp. 288–91), detailed 'Acknowledgements' (pp. 292–5), and a useful double-columned, name-orientated index (pp. 296–302) to this fascinating, well-documented, well-designed volume 'typeset in 11½ on 14 Monotype Bembo Book' (p. iv).

Stuart Kells, *Penguin and the Lane Brothers: The Untold Story of a Publishing Revolution*, tells the story of the forgotten Lane brothers who founded the Penguin imprint. Kells, in his preface, writes that 'with unprecedented access to Richard [Lane's, 1905–82] diaries and other family papers (many of them never before studied), the present volume is the first serious biographical treatment of the lives of Richard and John Lane'. Their brother Allen (1902–70) has been well studied, for instance in Steve Hare's *Penguin Portrait: Allen Lane and the Penguin Editors 1935–1970* [1995]; however, Kells's book 'seeks to shed new light on Allen's life and impact and to describe and understand the multifaceted and changing relationship between the brothers, so crucial as a driver and influence of Penguin spirit and success'. He adds that 'for most of Allen's life, Richard and John were his only true peers, and Richard was his conscience, his chief collaborator and his best friend. Although John's part in the Penguin story was cut short, he would continue to be a potent presence at the firm long after his passing' (p. xi). John, born in 1908, died in action in 1942 participating in the Allied North African landings. Kells is an Australian and his book is published in Australia. There is an Australian connection with the Lane family: 'before starting Penguin with his brothers, Richard Lane spent a formative part of his youth in rural South Australia and New South Wales. His experiences there, and how they influence the character and price of the first Penguins, are explored here for the first time' (p. xi). The subsequent history of the firm provides also 'a rich and fascinating story'. The Penguin imprint became highly successful following 'the 1961 share float in which, after spectacular sales of *Lady Chatterley's Lover*, demand for Penguin shares exceeded supply by 15,000 per cent... . Allen made a fortune but his surviving brother was left feeling cheated and betrayed' (pp. x–xi). Kells's examination of 'the brothers and their relationship ... seeks to offer insights into the history of Penguin as an enterprise, a publishing innovation and a pioneering media company' (p. xii). Following the notes (pp. 305–28), there is a detailed index (pp. 329–36), and Kells draws upon Lane family archives to provide black and white and one colour illustration of the main participants in his story (between pp. 180–1).

A memoir that sheds light on a publishing era, a publisher, and publishing survival, is George Braziller's *Encounters: My Life in Publishing* completed when he was 99 years of age. In 1955 he began his own independent publishing house, one still in existence in 2016, noted for publishing poetry, art, fiction, literary criticism, and non-American literary work. His authors include Orhan Pamuk the Nobel Prize-winner Nathalie Sarraute, the eminent New Zealand novelist Janet Frame, Alasdair Gray, and Beryl Bainbridge, amongst others. In a series of short chapters accompanied by illustrations illuminating his content, Braziller, born in 1916, has 'tried to write my thoughts, memories, emotions, and observations simply and honestly'. He confesses in his preface that 'writing' in his nineties 'helps me get through my solitude' (p. 10). There are three parts to *Encounters*. The first 'The Early Years' (pp. 13–36), reveals that his parents emigrated from Minsk to New York in 1900. He was the youngest of seven, his father died two months before he was born, and 'my siblings and I spoke Yiddish before any of us learned to speak English'. He recalls the world of Brooklyn and East New York, 'a place that is now long gone'. His mother, 'from her pushcart ... sold pants and old shoes' (p. 13). When he was 8 his mother remarried and they moved to 'Huntington Station on the north shore of Long Island' (p. 19), where he lived for seven years; he gradually learned to read English and became aware of sex. When he was 15 his stepfather died and the family returned to Brooklyn: 'In Huntington I learned to miss a father' (p. 22). The Depression years 'were among the most difficult years of my life' (p. 25). He worked as a fur coat salesman and as a shipping clerk, became politically engaged on the far left, met Marsha, the dedicatee of *Encounters* whom he married and neglected. She died of cancer aged 51. His start in the world of books was in the creation of a book club, in the mail order business. He bought ten copies of John Hyde Preston's *Seeds of Liberation* 'from the Remainder Book Company for twenty-five cents each and sold them to my subscribers for fifty cents each. Suddenly I was in business' (p. 33). His early titles included Norman Mailer's *The Naked and the Dead*, Upton Sinclair's *Wide Is the Gate*, and Arthur Miller. Membership of the Book Club dropped considerably during the McCarthy era, but subsequently revived. After twenty years he sold the club to Time-Life 'for a considerable sum of money' (p. 35) and in 1955 started his own publishing house. The second part of *Encounters*, 'The War' (pp. 38–47), is the shortest; clearly much is omitted, and serves as an ironic interlude before the longest part, 'Publishing' (pp. 51–145). Called up in 1943, he took part in the D-Day landings, entered liberated Paris, and at the end of the war in Europe found himself in a gun battalion in Austria where he produced a book *The 133d AAA*

*Gun Battalion* 'a tribute to our Battalion ... The story of our basic training in the States, a landing in Cherbourg, our march across Germany, and our occupation duties in Austria ... a tribute to the courage and heroic effort of our men' (p. 45). The third part relates, again in short chapters, his publishing experiences, but omits practical details such as dealing with printers, paper, packing, and so on. There is a focus on contacts, meeting the right people, and individuals whom he met and published such as Chagall, Arthur Miller, Marilyn Munroe, and others. There are some revelations concerning what his house decides to publish: 'twenty percent of our books came from agents and other sources. Nearly eighty percent of our publications grew out of suggestions from our editorial staff' not from 'unsolicited manuscripts', most of which 'remain unopened and are dumped into what is called a slush pile' (p. 85). He does, in six paragraphs entitled 'Albert Einstein', recall 'a major loss', but doesn't say why *Einstein's 1912 Manuscript on the Special Theory of Relativity* was a publishing disaster (p. 95). There is no index or listing of books published by George Braziller, Inc. Mention too should be made of Ken Hyland's *Academic Publishing: Issues and Challenges in the Construction of Knowledge.* Hyland writes in his preface (pp. ix–xi) that he explores 'academic publishing from [his] perspective as an author, editor, and applied linguist, examining how the changes brought about by the globalization of knowledge and the steadily increasing power publishing affect the lives of academics and the work of the academy'. His book has 'been written at a time of massive expansion and change in academic publishing. Not only are more scholars publishing now than ever before, but there are more journals, more scholarly papers, more publishers and crucially, more authors writing in a language which is not their native tongue'. The themes of his book are 'issues of community, competition, corporatization, assessment, authorship, and genre'. Hyland's focus is on applied linguistics. In his chapter 8, 'Gatekeepers: Evaluation and Regulation' (pp. 161–83), a 'corpus of peer-reviewed material was analyzed using frequency counts and concordance techniques to identify recovered words and features in this discipline and how they were used' (pp. ix–x). His book is one of the few to examine the peer review process. In addition to the light it throws upon the academic publishing world and its current hive of activity, his book has much from which *YWES* readers can benefit. It concludes with an alphabetically arranged enumerative listing of references (pp. 207–30), followed by a useful double-columned index (pp. 231–9).

*Word & Image: Art, Books and Design from the National Art Library* edited by curators and librarians Rowan Watson, Elizabeth James, and Julius Bryant, reveals that the much later foundation than the Bodleian, housed within the mid-nineteenth-century creation the V&A, has its own treasures. One hundred and fifty special objects from the National Art Library's literature, print, drawings and photography collections are showcased in *Word & Image*. Edmund De Waal's 'A Reader's Foreword' (p. 9) is followed by Julius Bryant's ' "Word and Image": The Evolution of the Victoria and Albert Museum's Library' (pp. 11–25), Rowan Watson's 'The Growth of the Library Collection 1837–1909' (pp. 27–43), and Elizabeth James's 'Collecting the Art and Design of the Book after 1909' (pp. 45–64). The second section of *Word &*

*Image*—throughout lavishly furnished with colour illustrations—concerns specific instances of 'Art, Books and Design from the National Art Library'. A brief introduction (pp. 66–71) is followed by sections on 'Resources for Art and Design Education' (pp. 72–85), 'Making Images: The Illustrator at Work' (pp. 86–97), 'Designers, Aesthetes and the "Book Beautiful"' (pp. 98–111), 'The Impact of Photography: Extending the Encyclopedia' (pp. 112–28), 'Promoting Commercial Art: The Initiative of 1936' (pp. 128–37), 'The Fashion Archive' (pp. 138–49), and 'Modern Artists and the Book' (pp. 150–65). These are followed by 'National Art Library at the V&A: Timeline', beginning in 1837 and concluding in 2015 (p. 166), an alphabetically arranged listing of further reading, 'Acknowledgements' (p. 167), and notes (pp. 168–72). As the five-column-per-page, alphabetically arranged, extensive index (pp. 174–6), followed by a 'Concordance' (containing 'museum inventory numbers or to library bar codes ... the date of acquisition'), and 'Picture Credits' (p. 176), reveal, the literary treasures at the National Art Library are not confined to William Morris, Charles Dickens, or his biographer John Forster.

The Grolier Club in New York hosted, between 9 December 2015 and 6 February 2015, an exhibition of items drawn from its members' collections. Eric J. Holzenberg and Arthur L. Schwarz explain, in their introduction (pp. 9–11) to *The Grolier Club Collects II: Books, Manuscripts & Works on Paper from the Collections of Grolier Club*, in December 2002 a similar display 'conceived by the club's bibliophilic membership FOR its membership, a purely homegrown celebration of book collecting' (p. 9). This resulted in *The Grolier Club Collects: Books, Manuscripts & Works on Paper from the Collections of Grolier Club* published by the club in 2005. Curated by Eric J. Holzenberg and Arthur L. Schwarz, the subsequent catalogue, compiled and edited by George Ong, contains numerous colour and duotone illustrations and has Aldus and Michelangelo types designed by Hermann Zapf Limited to 1,000 copies, measuring 12 × 9 inches, printed on Cougar Opaque Paper the volume is designed by Jerry Kelly (see p. 184). Of especial pertinence are the sections on 'Association Copies' (pp. 73–92), 'Literature' (pp. 95–106), and 'Bibliography & Book History' (pp. 145–52). 'Association Copies' include Elizabeth Gaskell's *Wives and Daughters*, being the first volume of Smith Elder's *Novels and Tales of Mrs Gaskell* [1880]. A 'note on the pastedown by Margaret Keynes (Darwin's niece) [which] reads: this book was a great favorite of Charles Darwin's and the last book to be read aloud to. He died on April 18th, 1882' is clearly illustrated as is the provenance 'Margaret Keynes; presentation inscription from Charles Darwin's wife, Emma, to their son Leonard' (p. 75). William Zachs describes how he came to acquire 'J.K. Rowling's *Harry Potter and the Philosopher's Stone* published by Bloomsbury in 1997, annotated and illustrated by the author'. This contains Rowling's annotations, and the title page with her illustrations is reproduced. Zachs writes that 'to over 1,000 words of text she added more than twenty illustrations. These skilfully drawn images depict the author's personal vision of her story' (p. 86). 'Literature' includes the unpublished 'Robert Frost High School Senior Year Physics Notebook' with Frost's inscribed front page of his school exercise book and a page with his notes illustrated (p. 100). Illustrated too are letters from the Poet Laureate, the now largely forgotten Alfred Austin, that began when he was 55, written to Violet Maxe when she was 18. As the owner David N. Redden observes, these form 'an astonishing and somewhat inappropriate correspondence' (p. 96). Choosing from the rich illustrated assortment of 'Bibliography & Book History' is also difficult. Two examples will suffice to convey the treasures in *The Grolier Club Collects II*. Marie Korey contributes 'Frances Mary Richardson Currer (1785–1861). Catalogue of the Library at Eshton Hall' published by Robert Triphook in London in 1820. Currer's library 'placed her, in Dibdin's words "at *the head* of all female collectors in Europe"' (p. 146). Finally, G. Thomas Tanselle's contribution is 'Sir Thomas Browne. Bound page proofs for *Urne Buriall and the Garden of Cyrus*. Edited with an introduction by John Carter. Printed by the Curwen Press. London: Cassell and Co.,1932'. The provenance is 'John Carter, with his manuscript corrections and revisions; then John Sparrow, with his signature'. Carter's revisions and page xviii, with his marginal corrections and additions, are illustrated (p. 151). This fascinating, nicely bound volume concludes with a double-columned 'Index of Lenders' (pp. 179–80), a double-columned, alphabetically arranged 'Index of Entries' (pp. 181–3), and a colophon (p. 184).

Donald Jackson Kerr's *Hocken: Prince of Collectors* is the first 'systematic and specific work ... on Hocken as a collector' (p. 17). Dr Thomas Morland Hocken (1836–1910), born in Stamford, Lincolnshire, studied medicine in Dublin, became a surgeon, and arrived in Dunedin, New Zealand, in February 1862, where he became coroner. Obsessed with book and manuscript collecting, he is one of the first eminent New Zealand book collectors: 'throughout his busy life as a medical practitioner in Dunedin he collected books, manuscripts, sketches, maps and photographs pertinent to the history and development of early New Zealand'. Kerr adds that 'much of the driving force for his collecting was based around James Cook and early discovery narratives ... Maori, and early settlement and colonisation, especially in the south' of New Zealand. 'In March 1910 his extensive collection was gifted' to the country 'and eventually passed over to the University of Otago for full stewardship' (p. 17). Kerr's twenty chapters trace his subject from 'Childhood and Schooling' (pp. 24–33), his 'early Beginnings in Dunedin' (pp. 52–65), to his 'Bibliographical Connections' (pp. 157–74), 'The Pinnacle' (pp. 237–57)— his *A Bibliography of the Literature Relating to New Zealand* published a year before his death. In the final chapter, 'The Hocken Legacy' (pp. 279–98), Kerr writes that New Zealand 'as a nation ... would be much poorer without his having collected, and thus preserved, some of [its] earliest records. For his industry and his vision, future generations of New Zealanders will be forever in his debt. This is justly so' (p. 298) . There are three appendices: the first is a letter dated just before his May 1910 death from cancer to his friend George Fenwick written on the occasion of the opening of Hocken's library (pp. 301–3). The second prints Hocken's 'Last Will and Testament' (pp. 304–8), and the third appendix contains 'Selected Book-Collecting Letters' (pp. 309–18). Notes to Kerr's text are extensive (pp. 319–73): they are followed by an extensive enumerative bibliography divided into Hocken's publications arranged in chronological order of appearance, by his books, 'Periodical and Secondary

Publications', 'Introductions', 'Hocken's Own Library', and 'Hocken Collections' (pp. 374–7). There are then 'Archives and Institutions' arranged by country, beginning with 'New Zealand' then moving to 'Australia' and then 'Britain', and within the countries by the names of collection locations (pp. 377–80). The bibliography concludes with an alphabetically arranged enumerative listing of 'Books and Articles' (pp. 380–92) followed by a listing of 'Newspapers', 'Unpublished' materials consulted, 'Web Sources' and f 'Email Correspondence' (pp. 392–3). The double-columned index is extensive (pp. 394–424). Donald Kerr's superb *Hocken: Prince of Collectors* is accompanied by forty black and white and colour photographic illustrations (see between pp. 96 and 97 and pp. 288 and 289). Well designed with computer-generated clear print, the dust-jacket contains a photograph of Hocken on the deck of the steamer he sailed on with his family 'from Sydney on 9 August 1901 on a long overseas trip to England via Japan and the East'. The back jacket contains a photograph of Hocken's 'personalized book label c.1900' (p. 4).

Alice Crawford's collection of essays, *The Meaning of the Library: A Cultural History*, has as a frontispiece a black white illustration of the 'King James Library, University of St. Andrews' (p. ii), five additional black and white illustrations and twenty-six colour plates (between pp. 158 and 159). Crawford writes in her introduction (pp. xiii–xxix) that 'all the essays in this collection tell the story of how, from the earliest times, human beings have with "bewildering optimism" amassed collections of books and created buildings to put them in'. Furthermore, 'each essay enacts in its own way the paradox of ... the confrontation between the drive to build the all-embracing überlibrary and the acceptance that the endeavor will fail'. The immediate context for the essays was the period 'between 2009 and 2013, against a backdrop of economic stringency that has seen many public libraries throughout the United Kingdom close'. The 'essays were written, too, at a time when technological change has created the popular perception that there is no longer any need for libraries or librarians since, with a good search engine and the ever-increasing proficiency of the keyboard-tapping digital native, "everyone's a librarian now"' (pp. xiii–xiv). The first part of the collection contains six essays under the heading 'The Library through Time' (pp. 1–150). The essays are: 'Adventures in Ancient Greek and Roman Libraries' by Edith Hall (pp. 1–30); 'The Image of the Medieval Library' by Richard Gameson (pp. 31–71), accompanied by 92 notes following the text (pp. 56–71); 'The Renaissance Library and the Challenge of Print' by Andrew Pettegree (pp. 72–90); 'From Printing Shop to Bookshelves: How Books Began the Journey to Enlightenment Libraries' by Robert Darnton (pp. 91–102); ' "The Advantages of Literature": The Subscription Library in Georgian Britain' by David Allan (pp. 103–23); and 'Literature and the Library in the Nineteenth Century' by John Sutherland (pp. 124–50) that includes, as well as reflections on 'Libraries: Metropolitan, National, Institutional, and Affiliational' (pp. 128–39), a fascinating discourse on 'Personal Libraries' (pp. 139–45). His accompanying notes too are replete with information, at times of a humorous nature. For instance a note on the London Library reads: 'to insert a personal note, I picked up a copy of one of my books the other day, and my eye was caught by the marginal comment "Sutherland can surely right better than this. Is he a member?"' (p. 148). The second part of Alice Crawford's collection changes course to consider 'The Library in the Imagination' (pp. 153–219) and includes three essays: 'The Library in Fiction' by Marina Warner (pp. 153–75); 'The Library in Poetry' by Robert Crawford (pp. 176–98); and 'The Library in Film: Order and Mystery' by Laura Marcus (pp. 199–219). The third and final part has three contributions on 'The Library Now and in the Future' (pp. 223–66): '"Casting and Gathering": Libraries, Archives, and the Modern Writer' by Stephen Enniss (pp. 223–35), who observes that 'we will not catch and hold onto everything. An archive is also a record of absences at the very brink of oblivion' (p. 234); 'Meanings of the Library Today' by John P. Wilkin (pp. 236–53)—it is reassuring to read Wilkin the 'Dean of Libraries and University Librarian at the University of Illinois at Urbana-Champaign' (p. 283) writing that 'curating, producing, and facilitating the use of the cultural record in all its myriad forms, the library is today a heart of intellectual life, as it has been in the past and will be in the future'. Furthermore, 'the introduction of digital technologies has not changed the essential nature of the library but has created a path for increased vitality and long-term viability' (p. 249). The final contribution is on 'The Modern Library and Global Democracy' by James H. Billington (pp. 254–66). A detailed, alphabetically arranged, enumerative 'Selected Bibliography' (pp. 267–80) is followed by information on the thirteen contributors and the volume's editor (pp. 281–4). The alphabetically arranged index (pp. 285–300) appropriately concludes a most worthwhile well-produced volume.

Frank Felsenstein and James J. Connolly's *What Middletown Read: Print Culture in an American Small City. A Revealing Portrait of Reading in the Quintessential American Town* draws upon the 2003 finding of the circulation records 'covering the years 1891 to 1902, with one two-and-a-half-year gap, from late May 1892 to early November 1894' from the Muncie, Indiana, Public Library. The 'logs recording each circulation transaction, corresponding to numbered lists of patrons and books' allowed Felsenstein and Connolly 'to determine who borrowed what during those years' and afforded unprecedented detail about mid-American reading behaviour during this period. By utilizing this data, the authors 'seek to describe the evolving culture of print in a single, emblematic American community around the turn of the twentieth century'. They also 'explain the origins and demonstrate the value of a digital resource such as the What Middletown Read database' that they have helped create. This data can 'provide clues about why borrowers chose the books they did, about the relationship between readers in one community and their public library, about the nature of the public library as an institution of reading, and about the culture of print in a rapidly industrializing community' (pp. 3–4). Accompanied by fifteen black and white illustrative figures *What Middletown Read*, following an introduction (pp. 1–13), is divided into two parts. The first part, 'A City and Its Library' (pp. 17–96), 'traces the development of the city, it's print culture, and its Library' (p. 13) in three chapters: '"Now we are a city": Portrait of a Boomtown' (pp. 17–36); '"A magnificent array of books": The Origins and Development of the Muncie Public Library' (pp. 37–72); and 'Cosmopolitan Trends: Print Culture and the Public Library in 1890s Muncie' (pp. 73–96). In the second part, 'Reading Experiences' (pp. 99–248), Felsenstein and Connolly 'approach the experience of reading in turn-of the-century Muncie from several angles' (p. 13) in four chapters: 'Borrowing Patterns: The Muncie Public Library and Its Patrons' (pp. 99–135); ' "Bread sweet as honey": Reading, Education, and the Public' (pp. 136–65); 'Reading and Reform: The Role of Fiction in the Civic Imagination of Muncie's Activist Women' (pp. 166–98); and 'Schoolboys and Social Butterflies: Profiling Middletown Readers' (pp. 199–48). An 'Epilogue: Looking Backward, Looking Forward' (pp. 249–60) places the 2013 rediscovery of the Muncie archival record in the context of recent thought on approaches to the history of reading. An appendix, 'The What Middletown Read Database' (pp. 261–8), describes the actual physical condition of 'the three interrelated sets of handwritten ledgers [that] form the bedrock of the database' (p. 261). Extensive notes (pp. 269–96) follow the text, and the double-columned index (pp. 297–304) is comprehensive.

H.J. Jackson's *Those Who Write for Immortality: Romantic Reputations and the Dream of Lasting Fame* is a reception study, 'a book about writing—specifically, about the relationship between seeking lasting fame as an author and getting it' (p. ix). Jackson considers the literary fame of writers from the Romantic period and their afterlife, although what she says could be applied to writers from other periods too. Jackson writes: 'between the introductory first chapter and the conclusion, four chapters highlight different aspects of the process of becoming famous in the nineteenth and twentieth centuries: first concepts of authorship and audience; then the problem of popularity; then the small question of merit; and finally mechanisms of recovery' (p. xiii). The opening chapter, 'The Fame Tradition' (pp. 1–23), examines the 'desire for fame ... among writers' (p. 1), from classical writers such as Cicero, Marcus Aurelius, Horace, to others. She then moves to England in the eighteenth century with especial attention to Samuel Johnson (pp. 15–23). 'Whereas Horace celebrated the divine powers of the true poet, Johnson in a pragmatic, modern way emphasized the continuing role of other human agents in the process of transmission and evaluation. His was the homegrown version of the dream of literary fame that British writers of the Romantic period grew up with and, in some cases, reacted against' (p. 23). In her second chapter, 'A Heroic Model of Authorship' (pp. 24–62), she focuses upon three poets: Wordsworth (pp. 24–43), George Crabbe (pp. 43–51), and Robert Southey (pp. 51–9). There are comparisons between the three throughout the chapter. Wordsworth continues to be read, 'his name is as widely known as that of any of his literary contemporaries.... His works derived accidental benefits from their variety and from the size of the corpus; from their visualizability, or susceptibility to pictorial illustration; from their supposed suitability for children; from discoveries about the author's early life that his descendants would have preferred to conceal; and from his association with the popular Lakes ... and the rise of literary tourism' (p. 40). Crabbe's name did not help him, he wrote few lyric poems, his work 'seems never to have been thought suitable for young children', and 'Suffolk was never as popular a tourist destination as the Lake District'. Furthermore, 'when the label Romantic finally took hold in histories and textbooks at the very end of the nineteenth century, whatever it was taken to mean—anticlassical, anti-Enlightenment, neomedieval, sublime, nature-worshipping, idealistic or individualistic— Crabbe did not fit in. He was not radical enough, not innovative enough, not complicated enough, not Wordsworthian enough' (pp. 47–9). The third poet, Robert Southey, 'unlike Crabbe, *is* an extreme case, a byword for posthumous failure that seems all the more pathetic—or ironic, or ludicrous— in light of his aggressive pursuit of success'. In common with Wordsworth he was from the Lake District, his contemporaries highly praised their early work, both rejected the radicalism of their youth, and 'Wordsworth followed Southey as poet laureate' (p. 51) Southey's poems sold more than Wordsworth's. 'No one could have done more than Southey did, in a practical way, to ensure that his name would not perish' (p. 53); however, there were few translations, and after he became laureate he made enemies, including such powerful figures as Francis Jeffrey, Byron, and Hazlitt. Additionally, there was only 'lukewarm support from his friends and fellow poets'. However, like Crabbe his was an 'almost exclusive commitment to long poems, a form that lost ground to prose fiction steadily and seemingly irreversibly, during and after the Victorian period'. He too 'could not be remade as a lyric poet; his body of work did not readily lend itself to anthology isolation; and so he lost his popular audience'. His 'fantastic tales' did not appeal to the academy, and while the star of Wordsworth became more ascendant, Southey's rapidly diminished (pp. 56–7).

Jackson's third chapter, 'The Stigma of Popularity' (pp. 63–106), focuses upon fiction rather than poetry and 'considers the careers and afterlives of Walter Scott, Jane Austen, and Mary Brunton in conjunction with their ideas about literary fame' (p. 63). Individual discussions of Scott (pp. 64–84), Mary Brunton (pp. 84–94), and Jane Austen (pp. 94–104) are followed by a concluding section, 'Rising to Fame' (pp. 104–6). Jackson observes that they were 'writers of great gifts and great integrity'. However, 'Brunton's success was shortest-lived and most conventional: after a flurry of public interest when her novels were new, they settled into a pattern of more or less respectable reliability'. However, 'after fifty years they ceased to be viable and dropped out of sight' and in spite 'of a feminist recovery project' her novels became 'historical curiosities for specialists, mainly academics'. Scott's work, on the other hand, was enormously popular and influential 'during the nineteenth century. Thereafter, without ever falling into oblivion like Brunton's, Scott's name and work ceased to be of current value'. However, academic editions and 'their historical importance ensured a toehold in the world of learning'. In short, 'Scott's fortunes have risen and fallen and could well rise again.... . Unlike Scott and Brunton who now rely on niche appeal (their Scottishness) and intellectual interest (the universities)' Jane Austen, 'and the characters she created', 'is widely beloved'. Interestingly Jackson has reservations, pointing out that Scott once was widely beloved too. Consequently, 'it seems more than likely that Austen will eventually lose her special status, brought down as he was by overexposure and too much respectability, the price of unusually sustained popularity'. Of course whether this happens or not remains to be determined or influenced by 'the energy and effectiveness of agents acting on' Jane Austen's 'behalf; the buzz generated by the co-existence of multiple audiences; and successful remediation, or transfer into the medium of the day, like the Scott operas of the nineteenth century and the Austen movies of today' (pp. 104–6). It could be added, just like Shakespeare!

Jackson's fascinating work then has an 'Interlude' (pp. 107–12) in which she reflects upon the patterns she has found emerging in her previous chapters. She presents a 'Checklist', approximately chronologically based, of 'a list of categories that appear to be necessary or desirable to produce lasting fame for the cohort of Romantic writers under investigation' (pp. 108–9) and also 'a ranking of categories by importance'. At the top of her list is the 'threshold quality' (p. 112), by which is meant 'outstanding literary merit', recognized as such over a lengthy period of time (p. 109). Last in the list at number twenty-two is 'authorial adjective: positive/negative' (p. 112), i.e. name association. Her fourth chapter, 'What about Merit?' (pp. 113–66), examines the cases of three poets: John Keats (pp. 114–34), who is described as 'the acid test of merit' (p. 114); Leigh Hunt (pp. 134–46), who 'the cynic would say . . . lived too long and wrote too much' (p. 138); and 'Barry Cornwall' (pp. 146–61), whose 'contemporary readers and reviewers and early anthologizers bore witness to [his] outstanding achievement as a poet', and 'it is still possible to find positive value in the body of his early work' (p. 161). Jackson insufficiently explains why Barry Cornwall's star waned rapidly given the very positive qualities that she, in common with the Brownings and Swinburne, admires so much (p. 160). Keats's early death, it seems, guaranteed him literary immortality! In the fifth chapter, 'Raising the Unread' (pp. 167–216), Jackson considers William Blake (pp. 168–89), who 'may be the most extreme case of rescue from oblivion in literary history, and for that reason it is especially instructive' (p. 168). She then considers 'John Clare' (pp. 189–204). The cases of both Clare and Blake are 'proof that the perception of merit is and always has been complicated by other values and other considerations'. Another 'potential candidate for recovery from long-term neglect in the twenty-first century is Robert Bloomfield' (p. 204), discussed by Jackson (pp. 204–15). Presently 'the case for Bloomfield can only be made on extraliterary grounds, highlighting his class, his regional analogy, his status as a self-educated writer, or his influence on one other rising star, John Clare' (p. 214). In her 'Conclusion' (pp. 215–16) to her fifth chapter Jackson argues that, given Blake's resurrection, 'there seems to be no limit to what further efforts of recovery might achieve' (p. 216). In her 'Conclusion' (pp. 217–28), practical suggestions are made as to how this may be achieved in the case of other authors now lost but once recognized and admired. In her final paragraph Jackson observes that 'it is no use striving for immortality—there is nothing a writer, publisher, or publicist can do to guarantee it', and this applies 'to writers today just as much as those of the past'. Furthermore, those 'writers who care about being read for generations to come should aim to please themselves first, their publishers next; and not attempt to restrict the way their work is to be understood' (p. 228) An appendix provides annotated 'accompaniments for chapters 2, 4 and 5' (p. 229)—'Recommended Supplementary Readings' (pp. 229–30). This is followed by detailed notes to the main text (pp. 231–68), an alphabetically arranged, enumerative bibliography (pp. 269–86), and a pertinent index (pp. 287–94). The book's front jacket has in colour 'detail from a watercolor design by William Blake for Edward Young's *Night Thoughts*', and there are twenty black and white figures scattered throughout the text of this deeply engaging and thought-provoking book, one based upon book history. Reprint details are high on Jackson's documentation list for assessing a poet's afterlife, hence so much attention to detail and direct citation from Jackson's book. The study raises of course other cases, such as that of Charles Reade, the novelist, dramatist, and journalist, much admired and well read by his contemporaries, whose reputations have plummeted; similarly Sir Edward Bulwer-Lytton—might they be resurrected? What about the case of D.H. Lawrence, whose early novels and poetry were widely read in post-Second World War Britain, compulsory set texts for schoolchildren but towards the end of the twentieth century no longer so? In contemporary America and academia elsewhere his reputation has suffered largely because of sustained feminist attack. Might he too be revived, or how long will his reputation remain in the shallows? Jackson's book has led one to consider the reputation of contemporary poets such as Heaney, Larkin, and Ted Hughes, who are currently in Britain leading the pack whereas poets such as C.H. Sisson, Edwin Muir, and, to instance one other, Elizabeth Jennings, are not. Will Larkin's and Hughes's stars shine so brightly in the firmament in half a century or is there some poetic voice that few of us have heard of, living and writing today, who will outshine them all? Helen Vendler, an eminent Harvard-based academic critic, after all, persuaded academic and other readers that Seamus Heaney and Derek Walcott are important poets. F.R. Leavis, in his *The Great Tradition* published in 1948, revived George Eliot's fortunes and subsequently in his *D.H. Lawrence: Novelist* [1955] used all his critical acumen and influence to make the case that his subject was a great novelist, indeed a genius. There are two mentions of Leavis in Jackson's book (pp. 4, 103), but no mention of his attempt to determine which poets are important and which not in his *Revaluation: Tradition and Development in English Poetry* [1936]. Which raises the questions, who reads Leavis today, where is he read, and why? If it comes to that, why is literary criticism perhaps the most ephemeral of literary forms? All questions raised by H.J. Jackson's *Those Who Write for Immortality: Romantic Reputations and the Dream of Lasting Fame.*

A work that attempts to make a reputation or reinforce one is Helen Vendler's *The Ocean, the Bird and the Scholar.* In a biographically revealing introduction (pp. 1–14) she writes that, following her discovery when 23 of the poetry of Wallace Stevens, 'it was through him that I understood style as personality, style as the actual material body of inner being'. She confesses that 'all my later work has stemmed from the compulsion to explain the direct power of idiosyncratic style in conveying the import of poetry' (pp. 1–2). She refers to herself not as 'formalist', as that has pejorative connotations, but as an 'aesthetic critic' who 'is naturally concerned with the generic and formal aspects of an artwork, its implicit politics, its internal structures of relation, its intellectual argument, and its expressive means, but such a critic wants also to deduce and describe the internal factors motivating the invention of such idiosyncratic forms'. She adds that 'form is content as deployed. Content is form as imagined.' If Jackson attempts to influence reception history through methods associated with the study of book history, then Vendler attempts to do so as an 'aesthetic critic' (p. 11). Of the twenty-seven chapters in her book, all but the last has appeared elsewhere, and the final chapter, on John Berryman (pp. 399–420), a reassessment of his achievement, was published after her book, in the influential *New York Review of Books* where many of her other essays appeared. For Vendler, Berryman's *Dream Songs* 'flawed as they are, remain infinitely quotable—the witty lament of a singular man with the courage to exhibit himself and shame, indignity, and exuberance speech. Nothing else in Berryman equals them' (p. 420). There are three essays, written at different periods, extolling the virtues of John Ashbery's poems, and there are essays too on favourites such as Wallace Stevens, her first love, A.R. Ammons, Elizabeth Bishop, Jorrie Graham, and Langston Hughes, among others. She also advocates the virtues of Mark Ford (pp. 389–98) and Lucie Brock-Broido (pp. 399–409) to be included in her poetic pantheon. At times her own prose is poetic. For instance at the conclusion of the essay on the English poet Mark Ford she turns to his *Selected Poems* [2014] and his Latin translations. Vendler writes, 'all are worth reading for Ford's vigorous and idiomatic staging as he keeps ancient "spots of time" alive in our Latinless age' (p. 398)—the last eleven words of her sentence have the quality of purple passages. Whether, however, they will have the power to ensure that Ford will be ready fifty years hence is unknown, as unknown as Jackson's advocacy, for instance, of Robert Bloomfield and others. Vendler's collection is well designed and produced, there is an appealing dust-jacket with, on the front, a photograph of birds soaring over the ocean. The index (pp. 437–44) reveals the catholic nature of her reading for one who in her introductory essay reveals her strict Catholic upbringing. This collection of essays further attests to Vendler's eminent stature as a superb reader of poetry, attested also in her other important work such as her studies of *The Art of Shakespeare's Sonnets* (*YWES* [1997]) and *Our Secret Disciple: Yeats and the Lyric Form* (*YWES* [2007]).

In her *Words on Screen: The Fate of Reading in a Digital World* Naomi S. Baron 'asks if digital reading is reshaping our understanding of what it means to read'. She argues 'that digital reading is fine for many short pieces or for light content we don't intend to analyze or reread'; however it is less suitable 'for longer works or even for short ones requiring serious thought'. If this is the case, 'what happens to reading if we shift from print to screens? Will some of the uses of reading (and, for that matter, writing) fall by the wayside? If so, with what implications for education, culture, and ourselves?' (p. xii). Baron's book explores such questions. At the end of her penultimate chapter she comments: 'what the world of reading will look at a decade from now is impossible to know. What we can do is weigh the pros and cons of different possibilities. We can also offer suggestions on how to shape that future' (p. 206). Clearly Baron is hedging her bets. Her study concludes with extensive notes (pp. 239–75) and an alphabetically arranged enumerative list of references (pp. 277–94) that 'includes books and academic articles. References to other sources cited appear in the notes' (p. 277). The double-columned index (pp. 295–304) is comprehensive. The relationship of the digital to writing is explored too by Daniel Punday in his *Computing As Writing*. The 'link between writing and computing' pervades Punday's book, in which he writes on: 'the nature of research'; 'the tensions within professions'; 'the job of the programmer'; 'the idea of the library'; 'invention and the technology patent'; 'the idea of audience' (p. xii). Detailed notes (pp. 155–73) follow the text. There is a largely name-orientated, double-columned index (pp. 175–9). Pertinent is Punday's fourth chapter, 'E-Books, Libraries, and Feelies' (pp. 76–97). He writes, 'although physical books may have a role for the collector in a future where every book is available electronically, it is not clear that gathering up these kinds of physical objects will have the same cultural significance'. Furthermore, 'once libraries lose a connection to these physical objects [books] and [their] accidental life history ... It may be that the idea of the library itself may cease to have it same cultural meaning' (p. 97): a depressing but realistic thought.

Before drawing attention to work that should be mentioned published in 2015 but not easily fitted into other *YWES* sections, mention should be made of two works, each of which represents the eclectic nature of modern literary study. Dino Franco Felluga's *Critical Theory: The Key Concepts*, is an addition to the Routledge Key Concepts series. Felluga, in his 'A Note on the Use of this Key Concepts Guide' (pp. vii–ix), observes that 'one thing that theory has done for scholars is to free them from the exclusive exploration of literary texts or "high" historical documents, opening their sights outward to the entire social world'. What distinguishes his work from other guides to critical concepts such as the late M.H. Abrams and Geoffrey Harpham's *A Glossary of Literary Terms*, now in its tenth edition, is Felluga's attempt 'to represent how critical theory has developed over the last decade' (p. viii). His introduction, 'An Archaeology of the Western Subject' (pp. x–xxv), contains a succinct history of theory and is followed by an alphabetically arranged 'List of Key Concepts' beginning with 'Abject (abjection)' and concluding with 'Wrong' (pp. xxvi–xxxviii) that he explicates (pp. 3–326). Cross-references within entries are usefully indicated by the use of bold letters. Entries vary in length and contain at their conclusion guides for additional reading, and citations from critical theorists. There is a useful, extensive alphabetically arranged bibliography (pp. 327–52) and a detailed double-columned alphabetical index (pp. 353–62) to this highly recommended reference tool. A critical biographical study published in 2013 but previously unmentioned in *YWES* is Simon Berry's *Applauding Thunder: Life, Work, and Critics of Alexander Smith*. Smith, who is known to Victorian scholars for his Spasmodic poem *A Life Drama* (in *Poems* [1853]), his essay collection *Dreamthorp* [1863], and his prose idyll *A Summer in Skye* [1865], now gets into Scottish anthologies chiefly for his poem 'Glasgow' (from his *City Poems* [1857]). His edition of Burns [1865] was still being reprinted in Macmillan's Globe series into the 1930s. Berry's book is sometimes patchy in its account, and use, of earlier Smith criticism and research, and is in need in places of some copy-editing. There is a single-column index (pp. 235–40), no endnotes, and the bibliography (pp. 229–33) omits a primary Smith bibliography. However, Berry's is the only modern book substantially on Smith and as such is a landmark study of a once influential Scottish writer.

Books that should be mentioned, even though briefly, and considered in alphabetical order by the author's name, include the late Daniel Albright's

*Putting Modernism Together: Literature, Music, and Painting 1872–1927* that may be regarded as a guide, a handbook to modernism, examining the question 'What is Modernism?' (p. 3). Accompanied by many black and white illustrations, in addition to illuminating 'Isms' (pp. 49–310) such as 'Impressionism', (pp. 49–73), 'Expressionism' (pp. 74–97), and, to mention others, 'Communism, Fascism, and Later Modernism' (pp. 291–310), Albright's study has deep insights into the work of D.H. Lawrence (see for instance, pp. 134–5), James Joyce (for instance pp. 269–88) and Ezra Pound (for instance pp. 254–68) amongst others. Notes (pp. 313–28) follow the text, but there is no index.

Frank Barrett's *Treasured Island* with an attractive cover design and pleasantly typeset in 'Bembo Regular 11pt' (p. 4), is the record of the writer's travelling around the UK 'visiting literary places' (p. 18). He wanders from 'Bristol to Georgeham' (pp. 19–42), from 'Fowey to East Coker' (pp. 43–63) and elsewhere, to 'London' (pp. 123–53), then north, and finally to 'Burns Cottage Flugga' with its Robert Louis Stevenson connections (pp. 234–55). Notes follow his text (pp. 259–61), there is a 'Select Bibliography' alphabetically arranged (pp. 261–2) followed by an alphabetically arranged, double-columned 'Selected Reading' listing (pp. 263–4). There is too a triple-columned, extensive index (pp. 268–72).

Sibylle Baumbach, in her *Literature and Fascination*, is concerned with the concept of ' "fascination" as aesthetic reaction' (p. 7). Her initial chapter, 'Literature and Fascination' (pp. 11–70), 'provides an overview of the concept and its history, tracing its travels across different eras and disciplines and distinguishing fascination from companion concepts' (p. 7). She then focuses in her second chapter, 'The Power of Magic and the Fear of Contamination: Fascination in Early (Modern) Literature' (pp. 71–113), 'on literary case studies, which exemplify (meta-)fascination as theme and narrative strategy in chosen literary texts' (p. 7): works discussed include various Shakespeare dramas (see pp. 89–113). In her third chapter, 'Facing the *Femme Fatale*: The Poetics of Seduction and the Fascination with Storytelling' (pp. 114–46), attention moves to 'the poetics of fascination in the poetry of' Shelley, Dante Gabriel Rossetti, Coleridge and Keats. In 'The Spark of Inspiration: Mesmerism, Electrifying Fiction and Gothic Fascination' (pp. 147–89), her fourth chapter, she 'turns to the novel and the Gothic tradition' playing especial attention to Mary Shelley's *Frankenstein* and Bram Stoker's *Dracula* 'as key examples' (pp. 8–9). The fifth chapter, 'The Anxiety of Influence: Fascination with the Self and Others' (pp. 190–218), focuses upon three texts: Oscar Wilde's *The Picture of Dorian Gray*, and 'his one-act play *Salome* and Joseph Conrad's *Heart of Darkness*' (p. 9). Chapter 6, 'The Gorgon Gazed Back: Contemporary Fascination' (pp. 219–51), concentrates on contemporary texts such as Sylvia Plath's 'Medusa' poem, Tony Harrison's 'poem/film script *The Gaze of the Gorgon*', Don DeLillo's *Falling Man*, 'and Jonathan Safran Foer's *Extremely Loud and Incredibly Close*' (pp. 9–10). There is a brief 'Conclusion: The Journey Ahead' (pp. 252–4), in which, somewhat predictably, Baumbach observes that 'the complex interplay of literature and fascination prevents a sense of an ending, a conclusion' (p. 253). Notes follow the text (pp. 255–79). The alphabetically arranged, enumerative bibliography is arranged by 'Primary Sources' (pp. 280–5)—largely of texts discussed or referred to—and 'Further References' (pp. 285–308), and includes critical material in German that might otherwise have evaded scrutiny. The double-columned index (pp. 309–18) provides a useful guide to a complex work.

Michael Benton's *Towards a Poetics of Literary Biography* explores areas insufficiently treated in his *Literary Biography: An Introduction* [2009]: 'the question of whether biography had, or needed, a theoretical basis'; 'the unique character of biography as a form of non-fiction narrative'; 'examining how biographical writing works'; 'developing a poetics of biography' (pp. ix). Benton's introduction, 'Lives Without Theories' (pp. 1–10), examines such issues as 'Against Theory' (pp. 1–4), asks 'Why Poetics?' (pp. 4–6) and 'Pragmatisms and Principles' (pp. 6–10) and 'argues the case for seeking an understanding of biography through poetics and practice rather than looking for a set of abstract theoretical principles' (p. x). His first chapter, 'Art and Artifice in Biography' (pp. 11–31), 'considers the nature of the genre, in particular, how biographers reconcile the substantive body of factual data with the relative freedoms of biographical narrative' (p. x). The second chapter, 'Plotting a Life' (pp. 32–48), 'focuses on a single example', Michael Holroyd's *A Strange Eventful History: The Dramatic Lives of Ellen Terry, Henry Irving and Their Remarkable Families* (*YWES* 90[2008] 758–9), 'in order to investigate how biographical writing operates in the space between writing history and writing fiction' (p. x). The third chapter, 'The Author's Work (1): Signs of Life?' (pp. 49–73), 'looks at the problems encountered in relating the works to the subject's life' (p. x), and chapter 4, 'The Author's Work (2): Open to Criticism?' (pp. 74–90) 'asks whether criticism has a role and argues that there are distinctive qualities in "biographical criticism" that can elucidate the creative character and trace the literary development of an author' (p. x). The fifth chapter, 'Their Times and Ours' (pp. 91–117), 'places the narratives of authors' lives and works in the double context of "their times and ours"' (p. x). In chapter 6, 'Framing a Poetics of Literary Biography' (pp. 118–40), Benton writes, 'the anecdote, the image, the semi-dramatised scene, the telling phrase carry their own figurative truth which complements the verifiable information on which a biography is based. In a well-written biography, poetic truth and literal truth are interdependent' (p. 140). 'Notes and References' (pp. 141–58) follow the text. There is an alphabetically arranged, brief, enumerative 'Select Bibliography' (p. 159) and a double-columned, useful index (pp. 160–5).

John Brannigan's *Archipelagic Modernism: Literature in the Irish and British Isles, 1890–1970* begins with a discussion of Richard Jefferies's *After London* in which 'Richard Jefferies imagined a future in which the geography of England has been dramatically altered by an environmental catastrophe' (p. 1). Brannigan uses 'the term "archipelago" to denote a group of islands, and to stress in neutral and plural terms the relationship between those islands'. Consequently, a 'key focus for [his] book is literary representations of the seas and the islands within them as material spaces' (p. 9). His first chapter, 'Folk Revivals and Island Utopias' (pp. 21–67), argues 'that the Atlantic islands which attracted the fascination of some of the key writers of the Celtic Revivals of the 1890s were not peripheral to the sciences of metropolitan modernity' (p. 14). His second chapter, 'James Joyce and the Irish Sea' (pp. 68–106), explores 'the lure of the western islands to James Joyce's preoccupation with the sea which forms the natural centre of the archipelago, the Irish Sea' (p. 15). Chapter 3, 'Virginia Woolf and the Geographical Subject' (pp. 107–43), 'addresses the fraught question of why Virginia Woolf deploys inexactitude in her geographical settings' (p. 15). Brannigan's fourth chapter, 'Literary Topographies of a Northern Archipelago' (pp. 144–206), 'explores how' various twentieth-century writers ranging from Auden and MacNeice to Hugh MacDiarmid and Michael McLaverty 'were concerned with a northern archipelago on the peripheries of Britain and Ireland' (p. 16). His fifth chapter, 'Social Bonds and Gendered Borders in Late Modernism' (pp. 207–48), is primarily concerned 'with the recognition of how seas, coasts, and islands are already invested with particularly gendered meanings, as well as those of race, class, sexuality, and nation' (p. 16). In his 'Epilogue: Coasting', Brannigan in his far-ranging study writes, 'Only when we can articulate the local distinctiveness and plurality of these islands as a geography of inclusion, connection, and openness, can we truly begin to imagine an archipelago "so various, so beautiful, so new"' (p. 255). Brannigan's notes are at the conclusion of each of his chapters. His bibliography (pp. 257–78) is alphabetically arranged and enumerative, and his index (pp. 279–88) largely author-orientated.

In their introduction to *Fictional Objects*, Stuart Brock and Anthony Everett observe that 'fictional objects are the individuals we refer to when we use names (and descriptions) from fiction'. They distinguish 'three kinds of fictional object. First there are real world individuals who appear in fiction. . . . Second, there are individuals that aren't real but are *modelled* on individuals from the actual world... . Third, there are the *merely* fictional objects, individuals that don't reside in the concrete real world and are not based on individuals that do' (p. 2). Eleven essays by academic philosophers explore such issues: 'A Reconsidered Defense of Haecceitism Regarding Fictional Individuals' by William G. Lycan (pp. 24–40); 'Objects of Fiction and Objects of Thought' by Robert Howell (pp. 41–70); 'Wondering about Witches' by David Braun (pp. 71–113); 'The Philosopher's Stone and Other Mythical Objects' by Nathan Salmon (pp. 114–28); 'A Suitable Metaphysics for Fictional Entities: Why One Has To Run Syncretistically' by Alberto Voltolini (pp. 129–46); 'Creationism and the Problem of Indiscernible Fictional Objects' by Frederick Kroon (pp. 147–73); 'Brutal Identity' by Ben Caplan and Cathleen Muller (pp. 174–207); 'The Importance of Fictional Properties' by Sarah Sawyer (pp. 208–29); 'Fictionalism, Fictional Characters, and Fictionalist Inference' by Stuart Brock (pp. 230–54); 'Fictional Discourse and Fictionalisms' by Amie L. Thomasson (pp. 255–74); and 'Ideas for Stories' by Anthony Everett and Timothy Schroeder (pp. 275–93). Each chapter is followed by a listing of references. There is an extensive, subject-based, double-columned index (pp. 295–9).

Frederick Burwick and Manushag N. Powell's illustrated *British Pirates in Print and Performance* explores in its opening chapter, 'A Nation of Pirates' (pp. 15–32), 'what it means for a British audience in the seventeenth, eighteenth, and nineteenth centuries to call someone a "pirate"' (p. 12).

Subsequent chapters (pp. 33–99) 'trace a wide variety of examples of how piratical performance is realized onstage and how it moves between literary and theatrical incarnations' (p. 12). The sixth chapter, 'Pirate Sex' (pp. 101–18), is an 'exploration of fraught pirate masculinity' (p. 14), whereas the following chapter, 'She-Pirates' (pp. 119–38), 'considers the obvious converse question: can a woman play the pirate?' (p. 14). The concluding chapter, 'Pirate Clichés' (pp. 139–59), contains 'a retrospective tour of the origins and dramatic developments of some of the additional signifiers that audiences have learned to attach to piracy' (p. 14). There is an extremely useful appendix, 'Chronology of Pirate Plays in Britain' (pp. 161–6), followed by notes (pp. 167–94) to the text. There is an alphabetically arranged, enumerative bibliography (pp. 195–211), followed by a helpful double-columned index (pp. 213–31).

Conor Carville and Mark Nixon edit sixteen essays written by Beckett scholars and critics in *'Beginnings of the murmur': Archival Pre-texts and Other Sources*, the title for the 2015 annual bilingual review, *Samuel Beckett Today/Aujourd'hui*. Some of the essays reflect 'archival work' using 'Beckett's own manuscripts' (p. 10). For example, John Piling, in his 'Six Notebooks in Search of a Novel: A "First Aperçu" of Beckett's *Murphy* in Embryo' (pp. 13–28), 'provides a fascinating first insight into the "Murphy" Notebooks, acquired in 2013 by the University of Reading' (p. 11): the cover image to Carville and Nixon's volume is taken from one of these notebooks. Pim Verhulst's '"Just howls from time to time": Dating *Pochade radiophonique*' (pp. 143–58) draws upon 'related archival material, such as the Barbara Bray letters', at Trinity College, Dublin, 'the papers of Robert Pinget' in Paris, 'and the BBC Written Archives' in order to posit 'a late 1958 dating' for the radio drama (p. 143). Maria José Carrera's '"And then the Mexican": Samuel Beckett's Notes toward *An Anthology of Mexican Poetry*' (pp. 159–70) 'presents a comparative study of four sets of Beckett's manuscript notes', now at the Harry Ransom Humanities Research Center, University of Texas at Austin, 'made in preparation for his translation of *Antologia de la poesia Mexicana* in 1959' (p. 159). The BBC Written Archives at Caversham Park near Reading are utilized by Jonathan Bignell in his 'Performing Right(s): Legal Constraints and Beckett's Plays on BBC Television' (pp. 129–41). His article 'outlines how BBC television versions of Beckett's plays were affected by copyright' (p. 129). Tim Lawrence in his 'Samuel Beckett's Critical Abstractions: Kandinsky, Duthuit and Visual Form' (pp. 57–71) draws upon letters in 'the Fondation Matisse in Paris archive' and 'Lawrence's work moves out from the archive into the broader culture in search of sources'. Other essays in the collection do so too and in addition to contributions drawing upon 'archival and historical work ... there is also a strong showing for theoretical analysis' in the volume. Notes and works cited follow the individual contributions, and the collection concludes with details of 'Contributors' (pp. 241–44); there is no index.

The comprehensive canvas of Jonathan Culler's the *Theory of the Lyric* makes it an important reference tool as well as an invaluable critical addition to the understanding of a key genre—the lyric. Culler's aim is an 'attempt to work out a general framework, a theory of the lyric' (p. viii). In his introduction (pp. 1–9), Culler observes that 'one of the most important functions of a theory of the lyric or a general model of lyric ... is to highlight aspects of lyric poetry that current conceptions have neglected, underlining connections between lyric practices of the past and lyrics of recent centuries' (p. 9). Beginning with Greek and Roman lyrics, to Petrarch and Goethe and others, for which texts in the original languages and English translations are provided, Culler moves to Lorca, Marianne Moore, and a host of other poets writing in diverse languages. In his 'Conclusion' (pp. 349–53) Culler sagely writes that he has 'not attempted to determine what is or is not a lyric but [I] have been asking what is the best model of the lyric for encouraging a capacious appreciation of' the poems he has been discussing: 'the range of lyrics examined ... makes it clear that there is no simple model that fits them all'. The sheer diversity of 'examples considered ... illustrates the existence of a variety of lyrics and lyric forms at any given time, and whatever one sees them doing in one era—praising the world, bemoaning unhappy love, staging an epiphany, urging the universe to comply with one's desires—can also be discovered elsewhere' (p. 349). Culler is a highly sophisticated thinker and expositor who stresses 'the fundamentally hyperbolic character of lyric' (p. 351). His text is followed by extensive notes (pp. 355–84) and a comprehensive double-columned index (pp. 385–91) that provides a guide to his eclectic and thought-provoking study.

To continue with this alphabetical approach by author's name to studies that may remain ignored, Rodney Stenning Edgecombe's *A Reader's Guide to the Narrative and Lyric Poetry of Thomas Lovell Beddoes* provides a definitive New Critical and intertextual approach to 'an extremely good poet who, had things turned out differently, might have functioned as a missing link between Keats and Tennyson'. Beddoes unfortunately 'fatally divided his attention between verse and medicine, a discipline that by his own admission (made in [his] poem composed for Zoë King) served to wither his creative gift. In this he resembles Alexander Borodin, who could have achieved greater heights as a composer had he not been distracted by his duties as a professor of chemistry' (p. 1). Additionally Beddoes 'wasted so much valuable time' on his *Death's Jest-Book* (p. 8) to the detriment of his other poetry. However, 'many of his lyric poems are fragmentary, and yet, for all their imperfections, much to be preferred to the "laboured masterpieces" of a Southey, say, or a Procter' (p. 9). Each of Edgecombe's chapters focuses on different Beddoes work: his 'Juvenilia' (pp. 10–45); ' "The Improvisatore" ' (pp. 45–105); 'Miscellaneous Poems' (pp. 106–43), 'all the lyric make-weights that appeared alongside "The Improvisatore" in Beddoes' first collection, from the (possibly) lamentable "Comet" to the excellent "Bunch of Grapes" ' (p. 106). Three chapters are devoted to his three-part collection of poems published under the title *Outidana* (pp. 145–245) that has 'the most disciplined and focused ... of Beddoes' narrative poems' (p. 254). There are chapters too on 'Letters in Verse' (pp. 255–86); 'Poems Chiefly from *Death's Jest-Book* (Composed 1825–1829)' (pp. 287–321); 'Poems from the Later Versions of *Death's Jest-Book* and Other Poems, 1829–44' (pp. 322–50); the collection *The Ivory Gate* (pp. 351–92); and Beddoes's 'Last Poems (Composed 1844–8)' (pp. 393–418). Edgecombe's 'survey of Beddoes lyric verse—verse partly defaced by sorrow and neglect, but noble and vivid even so' (p. 418), concludes with notes (pp. 419—63), an extensive enumerative, alphabetically arranged bibliography arranged by 'Primary Texts' (p. 464) and 'Secondary Texts' (pp. 464–89), and a double-columned. name-orientated index (pp. 490–3).

Monika M. Elbert and Lesley Ginsberg edit a collection of sixteen essays in *Romantic Education in Nineteenth-Century American Literature: National and Transatlantic Contexts*. The essays explore 'the mutually constitutive relationships among Romantic conceptions of education, childhood, and American literature across the long nineteenth century' (p. 1). The collection, according to its editors' introduction (pp. 1–12), 'offers timely readings that look at the history of education from the perspective of the "other" or the child left behind—whether that be the unruly child ... the child with physical disabilities, the urban child, the immigrant child, or the racialized child' (p. 7). The contributions ae grouped into four parts: 'Transcendental Education' (pp. 15–71); 'Romantic Education: Origins and Legacies' (pp. 75–135); 'Race and Romantic Pedagogies' (pp. 139–207); and 'Romantic Pedagogies and the Resistant Child' (pp. 211–74). The text of each contribution is followed by notation and an alphabetical listing of works cited. Contributors' details (pp. 275–8) are followed by a double-columned, largely author-orientated index (pp. 279–90).

To return to studies of poetry, Michael Golston, in his *Poetic Machinations: Allegory, Surrealism, and Postmodern Forms*, 'sets out to describe a line ... a practice of postmodern American poetry that [he maintains] is fundamentally allegorical and that early on finds its inspiration in certain aspects of Surrealism, to which it later maintains varying degrees of affiliation' (p. ix). Five chapters in addition to a 'Polemical Preface' (pp. ix–xiv) reflect the range of Golston's analysis: introduction, 'Etymologies, 1980—the Allegorical Moment' (pp. 1–42); 'Entomologies: Louis Zukofsky and Lorine Niedecker' (pp. 43–66); 'Epistemologies: Clark Coolidge' (pp. 67–100); 'A=L=L=E=G=O=R=I=E=S: Peter Inman, Myung Mi Kim, Lyn Hejinian' (pp. 101–44); 'Semiologies: Susan Howe' (pp. 145–84); and 'Fictocritical Postlude: The Melancholy of Conceptualism' (pp. 185–96). Following extensive notes (pp. 197–229) after the text, and there is an enumerative, alphabetically arranged listing of works cited (pp. 231–43). A brief, name-orientated index (pp. 245–7) concludes this challenging study.

Mention too should be made of the second edition of Geoff Hall's *Literature in Language Education*, the first edition of which was published in 2005. Part of the Research and Practice in Applied Linguistics series published by Palgrave Macmillan, as Hall states in his 'Preface to the Second Edition' (pp. x–xi), 'the book has been updated throughout. Every chapter has been revised in detail and substantial new sections have been added. More than 100 new references have been added, mostly relevant publications since 2005. Resources references have been updated as the Internet has become ever more of the daily resource, which it was not for many ten years ago' (p. x). Of particular interest are Hall's descriptive 'Guide to Resources for Research in LLE' (pp. 293–301), 'Glossary' (pp. 302–9), extensive, alphabetically arranged, enumerative listing of references (pp. 310–35), and 'Name Index' (pp. 336–8), followed by his 'Subject Index' (pp. 339–40).

In the 'Preface and Acknowledgments' (pp. ix–xv) to his fascinating *The Poetics of Otherness: War, Trauma, and Literature*, Jonathan Hart writes that his 'book discusses violence, trauma, and war in poetry among ancients and moderns and across cultures. It begins with otherness and difference in prose and poetry and then concentrates most on poetry. In the end, the war texts that receive the most attention are those that represent the First World War and the Second World War' (p. x). His eleven chapters encompass his introduction (pp. 1–12); 'Trauma' (pp. 13–26); 'The Literary and the Other' (pp. 27–54); 'Trauma in Shakespeare and His Contemporaries' (pp. 55–65); 'Travel, Alterity, and Culture' (pp. 67–81); 'War, Violence, Poetry' (pp. 83–121); 'Representing the Great War' (pp. 123–59); 'Poetry and the First World War' (pp. 161–76); 'Representing the Second World War' (pp. 177–91); and 'Voices of the Holocaust' (pp. 193–213). In his 'Conclusion' (pp. 215–23) Hart observes that his concern has been with 'how words in fiction and nonfiction, poetry, and prose represent otherness, violence, and trauma' (p. 215). The text is followed by notes (pp. 225–53), and there is a detailed, double-columned index (pp. 255–63).

Ben Hewitt's *Byron, Shelley, and Goethe's 'Faust': An Epic Connection* 'focuses on an exciting moment in the history of Anglo-German literary exchange in the Romantic period, the moment of Byron's and Percy Shelley's interrelated encounters with Goethe's seminal dramatic poem, *Faust*' (p. 1) According to Hewitt in his introduction, 'An Epic Connection' (pp. 1–6), 'a study of this type has not appeared before' (p. 1). His work has two parts: 'Perspectives on Goethe's *Faust*' (pp. 8–75) and 'Byron, Shelley, and *Faust*' (pp. 79–173). Each part has two chapters. The first: ' "Eine Tragödie"? Goethe's *Faust* in Theory' (pp. 8–38); '*Faust I* in Romantic-Period Britain' (pp. 39–75). The second: 'Infernal Irony: *Faust, Cain*, and Byron's Later Poetry' (pp. 79–121); 'The Un-Faustian Epic: *Faust* and Shelley's *Prometheus Unbound*' (pp. 122–73). In his 'Conclusion: Between Two Worlds' (pp. 175–8), Hewitt modestly hopes that his 'comparative reading of Byron, Shelley, and Goethe has proved suggestive, but not final. Triangulating them has shed some light on aspects of the exchanges and intersections between British and German literature and thought of the Romantic period, which is always valuable, but the comparisons advanced have also tried to do more than this, to show how fundamental elements of the dialogue between our three poets remain alive for contemporary culture' (p. 177). Each of the chapters is followed by extensive notes, the enumerative bibliography (pp. 179–87) is alphabetically arranged, and there is a useful double-columned index (pp. 189–96) in a smaller font than the text in order to be more comprehensive.

Mike Hill and Warren Montag's *The Other Adam Smith* pays attention to Adam Smith's well-known texts and 'sets out to read him as the conflicted interlocutor and sometimes the initiator of a far-reaching set of discourses concerning the production of knowledge, affect, freedom, and markets, as well as social and economic justice, and to consider certain facets of his legacy in a way that is focused on a wider set of texts than is typical in more conventional studies' (p. 9). A detailed introduction, ' "A tendency to absence"; Which *Other* Adam Smith?' (pp. 1–29), is followed by four chapters: ' "The pleasing wonder of ignorance": Adam Smith's Divisions of Knowledge' (pp. 27–104);

' "Tumultuous combinations": The Transindividual from Adam Smith to Spinoza' (pp. 105–46); ' "Numbers, noise, and power": Insurrection as a Problem of Historical Method' (pp. 147–234); and ' "Immunity, the necessary complement of liberty": the Birth of Necro-Economics' (pp. 235–342). The text is followed by extensive notes (pp. 343–83) and by an extensive, double-columned index (pp. 385–97) revealing the cross-disciplinary nature of this book and its relevance for literary study.

Early modernist novels by Oscar Wilde (*The Picture of Dorian Gray*), E.M. Forster (*A Room with a View*), James Joyce (*Stephen Hero* and *A Portrait of the Artist as a Young Man*), and Ford Madox Ford (*The Good Soldier*) receive formalist and contextual reading in Lynne W. Hinojosa's *Puritanism and Modernist Novels: From Moral Character to the Ethical Self*. In her 'Conclusion' (pp. 191–201) Hinojosa observes that 'Modernism in large part to his reaction against Puritanism' (p. 191) and that 'this study is a call for new novels, ones that can incorporate more fully the dialectic of the moral and the ethical' (p. 200). Notes are to be found at the foot of her pages. An alphabetically arranged enumerative list of works cited (pp. 203–10) is followed by a double-columned index (pp. 211–18).

Jacob Sider Jost's *Prose Immortality 1711–1819* traces 'the emergence of the paradigm of prose immortality and cognate changes in the conception of the Christian afterlife over the course of the eighteenth century' (p. 15) There are three parts to Jost's study: 'Daily Time and Horizontal Futurity' (pp. 21–55); 'Theology and the Novel' (pp. 59–11); and 'Afterlife Writing' (pp. 115–73). Texts and authors examined include the *Spectator*, Andrew Young's *Night Thoughts*, Joseph Butler's *Analogy of Religions*, Richardson's *Sir Charles Grandison*, Laetitia Pilkington's *Memoirs*, and various works by Samuel Johnson and James Boswell. In his 'Epilogue: Keats Imagines the Life of Shakespeare' (pp. 175–80), Jost writes: 'Precisely because it is so great, Shakespeare's surviving corpus is inadequate; Malone, as Keats was to do of him, longs for a Shakespeare who lives on after death in the paradigm of prose immortality' (p. 180). Jost writes lucidly; extensive notes (pp. 181–209) follow the text. His bibliography is alphabetically arranged and enumerative; the double-columned index (pp. 225–39) is detailed.

John Leigh's *Touché: The Duel in Literature* covers a wide historical and literary canvas beginning in the reign of Louis XIV of France and Corneille and concluding in the early twentieth century with Joseph Conrad's short story 'A Duel' and Pirandello's drama. Leigh's 'Epilogue: 1918' (pp. 282–99) takes the analysis further thematically and chronologically. He writes that 'life may take the form of a duel in which the younger self is always challenging its older version. In choosing our path through life, and in order to become ourselves, we each need to kill off potential versions of ourselves, the persons we might have become' (pp. 296–7). Extensive notes (pp. 301–26), follow the text of this informative, clearly written work that has an author-orientated, double-columned index (pp. 329–34).

A much later historical period is the focus of Philipp Löffler's *Pluralist Desires: Contemporary Historical Fiction and the End of the Cold War*. Highly priced for less than 150 pages of text, in his introduction, '*Saving Private Ryan*, the End of the Cold War, and the Value of Historical Experience' (pp. 1–19),

Löffler writes that 'all of the novels featured in this book are conjoined by the idea that people write about history not to establish true accounts of particular historical events but to express the particularity of an individual life or individual culture. This impulse to privatize history in the name of a specific community of people is inspired by a looming "pluralist desire"' (p. 5). Authors discussed include Don DeLillo, Toni Morrison, Philip Roth, and Richard Powers. Extensive notes (pp. 145–63) follow the text, and there is an enumerative, alphabetically arranged bibliography (pp. 165–76); the double-columned index (pp. 177–82) is name-orientated.

Another highly priced monograph is Caroline Maclean's *The Vogue for Russia: Modernism and the Unseen in Britain 1900–1930*, which 'concentrates on the exchange and interchange of ideas about arts and the unseen circulating between Russia and England during the period from about 1900 until about 1930'. British writers discussed include Mary Butts, Roger Frye, Annie Besant, Charles Leadbeater, the 'mathematician and philosopher Charles Howard Hinton' (p. 3), Virginia Woolf. and the American H.D. (Hilda Doolittle). Maclean 'offer[s] another fibre for the fabric of modernist studies, a double thread that brings together mainstream British Modernism and alternative Russian-inflected aesthetics of the unseen' (p. 21). Notes follow individual chapters, and in her 'Epilogue' (pp. 168–71) Maclean somewhat provocatively observes that her 'research has challenged formalist readings of modernist aesthetics. In other words, handpicking the forms has dismantled the formalism.' Moreover, 'Modernism, mysticism and materiality should be examined in relation, not in opposition, to each other' (pp. 169–70). An alphabetically arranged listing of archives (showing abbreviations) (p. 172) is followed by an alphabetically arranged, enumerative bibliography (pp. 172–96); the double-columned index (pp. 197–205) provides a useful entrance ticket into Maclean's fascinating comparative study.

Peter Marks comments, in the introduction (pp. 1–11) to his highly priced *Imagining Surveillance: Eutopian and Dystopian Literature and Film*, that his 'study has no pretensions to be comprehensive. The sheer number and astounding variety of utopian novels and films that depict and dissect surveillance regimes, processes, threats and promises makes that impossible' (p. 11). Texts discussed include Margaret Atwood's *The Handmaid's Tale*, Anthony Burgess's *A Clockwork Orange*, Philip K. Dick's *A Scanner Darkly*, Dave Eggers's *The Circle*, Aldous Huxley's *Brave New World*, George Orwell's *Nineteen Eighty-Four*, Peter Weir's *The Truman Show*, and various H.G. Wells novels, amongst others. There is an alphabetically arranged, enumerative bibliography (pp. 172–6) and a name- and novel-orientated index (pp. 177–80).

Steve Mentz's *Shipwreck Modernity: Ecologies of Globalization, 1550–1719* is a 'book about disaster' (p. ix): 'shipwreck stories largely but not exclusively in early modern Europe, with its historical focus ranging between roughly 1550 and the publication of Daniel Defoe's *Robinson Crusoe* in 1719'. For Mentz, 'shipwreck stories represent the human experience of natural hostility, narrating humankind's failed attempts to navigate an uncertain world. By using the shipwreck to examine the ecological crises occasioned by the early stages of globalization, this book aims to reconsider the cultural changes associated with early modernity' (p. xxv). Texts considered include those by

Shakespeare, Jeremy Roch, Edward Barlow, Phineas Fletcher, Defoe, and others. In addition to two detailed and theoretically orientated prefaces (pp. ix–xxiii, xxiii–xxxiv), there are thirteen black and white illustrations accompanying the text of this challenging monograph. Extensive notes (pp. 185–213) follow the text, and there is a largely name-orientated, double-columned index (pp. 215–25). Mentz 'offer[s] a shipwrecked vision of English literary culture that brings together literary invention, ecological crisis, and the human experience of disruptive historical change' (p. xxxi).

A study working with a literary genre and film is Terence Patrick Murphy's *From Fairy Tale to Film Screenplay: Working with Plot Genotypes*. Replete with various black and white illustrative figures and tables, this overpriced monograph is concerned with a 'theory of plot structure' conducted through 'a detailed study of four Hollywood screenplays'—*Pretty Woman*, *Wrong Turn*, *The Mask*, and *Psycho*, 'that will 'thoroughly' verse its readers in 'plot genotype theory' (p. 8). Before examining these four screenplays Murphy has chapters entitled 'From the Hollywood Paradigm to the Proppian Plot Genotype' (pp. 1–8); 'Vladimir Propp's Functional Analysis of the Fairy Tale' (pp. 9–15); 'A Functional Analysis of Charles Perrault's *Cinderella*' (pp. 16–26); a short chapter on 'Formulating the Concept of the Plot Genotype' (pp. 27–30); and 'The Robber Bridegroom Genotype' (pp. 31–45). Notes (pp. 182–7) follow the text, and the alphabetical enumerative bibliography is arranged by 'Fairy Tales' (p. 188), 'Films' (pp. 188–9), and 'General Works' (pp. 189–91). The index (pp. 192–7) provides something of a guide to a highly sophisticated book. The same author's *The Fairytale and Plot Structure* is arranged upon similar lines with many illustrative explanatory diagrams, and is similarly engaged with the work of 'the early twentieth century Russian scholar Vladimir Propp [who] made a substantial contribution to plot analysis when he wrote his ground breaking study on the plot composition of the Russian fairytale . . . *Morphology of the Folktale* (1928)' (p. xiii). The first six of Murphy's thirteen short chapters concern theoretical approaches to plot analysis, and in the remaining seven chapters texts discussed range from the Brothers Grimm's *The Robber Bridegroom* to the *Fitcher's Bird*, *Puss-in-Boots*, *Jack and the Beanstalk*, *Little Red Riding Hood*, and 'the very short plot genotype contained in the English fairytale of *The Story of the Three Bears* or *Goldilocks*'. Murphy's 'Conclusion' (pp. 161–76) 'offer[s] a synthesis of [his] major agreements and disagreements with the work of Vladimir Propp, before concluding with a discussion of some areas of possible future research within plot genotype theory' (p. xv). An Aesop fable is the subject of an 'Appendix . . . The Formal Representation of *The Fox and the Crow*' (pp. 177–80). Extensive notes (pp. 181–92) follow the text; the bibliography (pp. 193–8) is enumerative and alphabetically arranged; the index (pp. 199–204) is helpful.

An interesting collection of essays, *The Persistence of Beauty: Victorians to Moderns*, is edited by Michael O'Neill, Mark Sandy, and Sarah Wootton. In the introduction (pp. 1–14), the editors write that the collection 'articulates a range of nuanced attitudes towards its central topic "beauty" and its representation in literary, as well as other cultural, forms. It would be incorrect to contend that the contributors take a single view of the subject' (p. 1). Contributions include: 'Female Beauty and Portraits of Self-Effacement in Charlotte Brontë's *Jane Eyre*' by Sarah Wootton (pp. 15–30); 'Dickens and *The Line of Beauty*' by Robert Douglas-Fairhurst (pp. 31–43); '"Ugly meanings in beautiful things": Reading the First Wilde Trial" by Simon J. James (pp. 45–58); 'The Beauties of T.S. Eliot' by Seamus Perry (pp. 59–70); '"The enigmatical beauty of each beautiful enigma": The Persistence of Beauty and Death in the Poetics of Walt Whitman and Wallace Stevens' by Mark Sandy (pp. 71–85); 'W.H. Auden: The Loveliness That Is the Case' by Tony Sharpe (pp. 87–102); 'Something in the Works: Frost, Bishop, and the Idea of Beauty' by Angela Leighton (pp. 103–16); 'The Difficulty of Beauty: Hopkins, Yeats, Hart Crane, Spender' by Michael O'Neill (pp. 117–33); '"Beauty in trouble": Robert Graves and Louis MacNeice' by Fran Brearton; and finally 'Beauty is Death' (pp. 151–62) by Timothy Morton, based on 'Kant's "Analytic of the Beautiful," the first part of his *Critique of Judgment*' (p. 151). Notes (pp. 167–90) follow the text, and there is a double-columned, name-orientated index (pp. 191–5).

*Utopian Literature and Science: From the Scientific Revolution to 'Brave New World' and Beyond* is another interesting book by the eminent scholar and critic of H.G. Wells, and 'the so-called transitional of British literature between 1880 and 1920' (pp. vii–viii), Patrick Parrinder. 'The emphasis in this book is on utopia as a literary genre—very often, the "utopian romance"— and its relations with neighboring genres such as science fiction and scientific romance' (p. vi). Clearly written, authors and texts discussed by Parrinder include amongst many, *Frankenstein*, Fitzjames O'Brien's story 'The Diamond Lens' [1858], Hawthorne's 'The Birthmark' [1843], and *The Blithedale Romance*, Stevenson's *Dr Jekyll and Mr. Hyde*, various works by H.G. Wells, J.B.S. Haldane's *Daedalus; or, Science and the Future*, Huxley's *Brave New World*, Bulwer Lytton's *The Coming Race*, Samuel Butler's *Erewhon*, W.H. Hudson's *A Crystal Age*, and Robert Graves. Notes (pp. 189–208) follow Parrinder's text. There is an alphabetically arranged enumerative 'Bibliography of Secondary Sources' (pp. 209–14) followed by an author-orientated index (pp. 215–22).

*Cosmopolitanism and the Literary Imagination* is the title and subject of Cyrus R.K. Patell's book. His 'goal is to take two fields of academic inquiry— theories of cosmopolitanism and contemporary literary studies—and put them together, to see what light each might shed on the other' (p. 4). Both concepts are explained at some length, drawing upon various theories and texts. There is detailed discussion of, for instance, Wilfred Thesiger's 'personal narrative *Arabian Sands* to investigate how even the most worldly traveler can fall short of a truly cosmopolitan perspective'. Other texts include Conrad's *Heart of Darkness*, and 'a reading of Zoroastrian motifs in Herman Melville's novel *Moby-Dick* to take a closer look at the ways in which religious belief can pose significant challenges to a cosmopolitan conception of cultural exchange' (p. 24). There are readings too of Washington Irving's *A History of New York*, and E.L. Doctorow's *Ragtime*, 'two texts that ... challenge our conventional notions of what constitutes historical fiction' (p. 73). Patell's fourth chapter, 'Speculative Fiction' (pp. 87–110), 'explore[s] the ways in which speculative fiction asks us to adopt a cosmopolitan perspective in which we confront otherness and thereby learn more about ourselves', and Patell 'take[s] as [his] anchor point Octavia Butler's trilogy *Lilith's Brood* (p. 88). The fifth chapter, 'Animal Studies' (pp. 111–35), examines Orwell's *Animal Farm* and Philip K. Dick's *Do Androids Dream of Electric Sheep?* In his 'Conclusion' Patell observes that 'a cosmopolitan reading practice requires us to cultivate cosmopolitan irony by attuning ourselves constantly to the interplay of sameness and difference, of comfort and discomfort, in the acts of writing, reading, and performing texts' (p. 149). Notes (pp. 151–65) follow the text; there is an alphabetically arranged enumerative bibliography (pp. 167–74) and a detailed double-columned index (pp. 175–87) to this interesting but highly priced study.

A monograph that shouldn't be ignored is Ged Pope's *Reading London's Suburbs: From Charles Dickens to Zadie Smith*. Accompanied by some startling black and white photographs by Salim Hafejee, largely of the front of suburban houses, Pope's 'book is a readings of London suburban fiction. More exactly it is also a study of the complex connections between fiction and the human need to belong to a particular known habitat, that is, to make a home' (p. 1). Pope's time span ranges from the early Victorians to the contemporary. His first chapter focuses on ' "Houseless-homeless-hopeless!": Suburbs, Slums and Ghosts, 1830–1870' (pp. 20–52) and includes 'a detailed discussion of how Charles Dickens underscores the anxious need to illuminate, categorize and place ... new metropolitan sites and identities' (p. 14) with a special attention to his *Sketches by Boz*. The second chapter concerns ' "A world of mud and fog": The High Victorian and Edwardian Suburb, 1880–1914' (pp. 53–89). Authors discussed range from H.G. Wells, Arnold Bennett, George Gissing, the Grossmiths and E.M. Forster, and William Morris (*News from Nowhere*) to Jerome K. Jerome. The third chapter, ' "The Third England": Suburban Fiction and Modernity, 1918–1939' (pp. 90–124), treats Virginia Woolf, and 'how "middlebrow" fiction, the likes of Pamela Hansford Johnson and Elizabeth Bowen, approach[es] everyday suburban life, and how the suburbs are presented as "Modern" in the sense of being rootless and uncentred' (p. 16): other authors considered in this chapter are Stevie Smith and George Orwell. In the fourth chapter, ' "Your environment makes as little sense as your life": Post-War Suburbia 1945–1980' (pp. 125–60), texts and authors include J.G. Ballard's *The Unlimited Dream Company* [1974], John Wyndham's *The Day of the Triffids* [1951], work by V.S. Naipaul, and Hanif Kureishi's *The Buddha of Suburbia*. In chapter 5, ' "I tried to work out where I was": Contemporary Suburbia' (pp. 161–202), authors drawn upon range from Tim Lott, Zadie Smith, J.G. Ballard, Ian Sinclair, and Nigel Williams to Graham Swift, John Lanchester, Helen Simpson, and Rachel Cusk. In the 'Conclusion: "All stories are spatial stories" ' (pp. 203–10), to this most challenging study, Pope writes: 'suburban fiction actually addresses a key experience over the last century and a half: the profound sense of placelessness' (p. 210). Notes (pp. 211–15) follow his text, as does an extensive, alphabetically arranged enumerative bibliography (pp. 216–31). The double-columned index (pp. 232–9) is largely author-based with compounded subcategories under the index term 'suburb' (pp. 237–8).

To continue with the alphabetically arranged listing by author's name of this account of work that might otherwise be overlooked, brief mention should be made of Melissa Sodeman's *Sentimental Memorials: Women and the Novel in Literary History*. Sodeman writes that 'in the final decades of the eighteenth century, women novelists like [Elizabeth Sophia] Tomlins turned the sentimental novel to new purposes, recording and meta-critically reflecting on the transformations then reshaping literature'. Sodeman's 'book is about those transformations': she argues 'that novels by Sophia Lee, Ann Radcliffe, Charlotte Smith and Mary Robinson memorialize the literary-historical conditions of their writing' (pp. 2–3). Her text is followed by extensive notes (pp. 151–81) and a helpful double-columned index (pp. 183–6).

An interesting topic is treated by Anne Toner in her *Ellipsis in English Literature: Signs of Omission*. An introduction, 'Observing the Ellipsis' (pp. 1–24), is followed by five chapters: 'Ellipsis Marks in Early Printed Drama' (pp. 25–53); 'Chasms and the Eighteenth-Century Novel' (pp. 54–86); 'Ellipsis and the Ends of Novels' (pp. 87–117); 'Nineteenth-Century "Explorations in Dot-and-Dashland"' (pp. 118–50); 'Ellipsis and Modernity' (pp. 151–70). The chapters are followed by discursive notes (pp. 171–217), an alphabetically arranged enumerative bibliography in which 'Primary Sources' (pp. 218–36) are more extensive than 'Secondary Sources' (pp. 236–50). There is a helpful index (pp. 251–5) too, although in smaller font than the rest of the book. A strength of Toner's study is her discussions, although in places these are rather perfunctory, of authorial manuscripts rather than printed texts: in the instance of George Eliot's 'Janet's Repentance', more could be said on the fact that the extant manuscript evidence is from a 'fair' copy and 'drafts' seem to have disappeared (see Toner, pp. 126–31 and 207–9). However, as Toner observes: 'for most of the history covered in this book, authors were encouraged to leave punctuation to printers because of their expertise in pointing or, in the nineteenth and early twentieth centuries, so that they could implement house style'. Toner adds that 'while some authors were willing to concede some control to the printing house, there were others who resisted, and probably many authors did both' (p. 15). A useful 'List of Illustrations'—there are twenty-four of them, ranging from Livy to George Meredith—is provided (pp. vi–viii) in this most interesting, widely ranging, clearly written, thoughtful study.

Different kinds of reading, genre, and text engage Iain Twiddy in his study of *Cancer Poetry*. Twiddy notes that 'although it is addressed indirectly, the most startling early mention of cancer in 20th-century poetry comes in Wilfred Owen's "Dulce Et Decorum Est" (1971), with a description of a man who has been gassed'. However, 'Since 1917, poets have found different ways of speaking about cancer, and speaking to cancer, beyond the horrifying or the obscene' (pp. 3–4). These poems, especially those written in the post-1960 period, are the subject of some very fine detailed new critical analysis. Poets considered range from Rae Armantrout, Ciaran Carson, Douglas Dunn, Donald Hall, Philip Hodgins, Paul Muldoon, Sharon Olds, and Alicia Ostriker to Christopher Reid, Anne Sexton, Jo Shapcott, and Christian Wiman. Although Twiddy is hampered in the extent of his direct citation from poems by copyright issues, a notable absentee voice is Harold Pinter: there is no mention of Pinter's powerful poem 'Cancer Cells' dated March 2002, written in response to his operation at the Royal Marsden Hospital. Following

Twiddy's text are detailed 'Notes and References' (pp. 199–221), an alphabetically arranged enumerative bibliography (pp. 222–7), combining primary and secondary texts, and a name-orientated, double-columned index (pp. 228–32).

To move to another genre, historical period, and topic, only the second chapter of Jobst Welge's *Genealogical Fictions: Cultural Periphery and Historical Change in the Modern Novel* is of direct relevance to *YWES* readers. They might miss Welge's discourse on 'Periphery and Genealogical Discontinuity: The Historical Novel of the Celtic Fringe (Maria Edgeworth and Walter Scott)' (pp. 16–37). For Welge, 'novels by Edgeworth and Scott establish a pattern whereby the narration of private genealogy is connected to the constitution of the British nation, a modern nation-state that is symbolically unified out of its constituent parts' (p. 36): Welge's focus is Scott's *Waverley* and Edgeworth's *Castle Rackrent*. The remainder of the texts he treats in his book are Sicilian, Spanish, Portuguese, and Brazilian. Notes (pp. 205–31) follow his text, his alphabetically arranged enumerative bibliography is divided into 'Primary Sources' (pp. 233–4) and 'Secondary Sources' (pp. 234–48); the index (pp. 249–54) is author-orientated.

Six additional books should be surveyed. Guy Woodward's *Culture, Northern Ireland,& the Second World War* draws upon previously unpublished archival material 'with the aim of recovering forgotten ways of describing the place of Northern Ireland in relation to the Second World War, by examining the impact of that war on literature and culture in the province' (p. 7). In addition to examining work in 'the influential Dublin magazine *The Bell* during the war years' (p. 11), creative artists discussed range from the painters William Conor, Gerard Dillon, and Colin Middleton to writers Robert Greacen, John Hewitt, Benedict Kiely, Roy McFadden, the more well-known Louis MacNeice, Seán Ó Faoláin, and W.R. Rodgers. In addition to a detailed introduction (pp. 1–42), there are chapters accompanied by footnotes on: '"His story was confirmed by others": Autobiographical Fiction and Memoir' (pp. 43–78); '"An angry wind strumming the wires": Poetry' (pp. 79–130); '"Strange Openings": Visual Art' (pp. 131–77), accompanied by black and white illustrations especially from the paintings of Colin Middleton and Gerard Dillon; the ironically titled 'Ulster Quislings and Drapery Romances: Political Writing' (pp. 178–235); and an 'Afterword: "We had met people very different from ourselves"' (pp. 236–42). Woodward's fascinating study concludes with an extensive, alphabetically arranged, enumerative bibliography (pp. 243–56) followed by details of an unpublished doctoral thesis on 'Irish Art, 1943–1960', a 'Reference Work', and holdings in 'Special Collections' (p. 256): there is also a most useful double-columned index (pp. 257–66).

To turn to another work, Chantal Zabus's edited *The Future of Postcolonial Studies*, an addition to the Routledge Research in Postcolonial Literatures series, is not restricted to writing in English. Zabus's collection also contains essays on French, Italian, African, and Arabic literatures. Our attention will be on its writings in English. These include the editor's introduction, 'The Future of Postcolonial Studies' (pp. 1–16), in which Zabus writes that '*The Future of Postcolonial Studies* celebrates the twenty-fifth anniversary of the publication of *The Empire Writes Back* by the now famous troika—Bill Ashcroft, Gareth Griffiths, and Helen Tiffin. When *The Empire Writes Back* first appeared in 1989, it put postcolonial cultures and their post-invasion narratives on the map' (p. 1). The highly priced volume is divided into five parts:' Comparing' (pp. 19–66); 'Converting' (pp. 69–113); 'Greening' (pp. 117–53); 'Queering' (pp. 157–98); and 'Utopia' (pp. 201–53). Pertinent are: 'Conversion, Identity and Resistance in Colonial and Postcolonial Space: The Writings of Tiyo Soga 1829–1871' by Gareth Griffiths (pp. 69–84); 'Fundamentalism and Postcoloniality: Beyond "Westoxification"?' by Klaus Stierstorfer (pp. 101–13); 'Notes on the Postcolonial Arctic' by Graham Huggan (pp. 130–41); 'Animals, Environment and Post-Colonial Futures' by Helen Tiffin (pp. 144–53); 'Postcolonially Queer: Sexual Dissidence as Cultural Struggle in Emergent Democracies in Africa' by William J. Spurlin (pp. 157–71); 'Writing Queer in South Africa: Poetry versus Identity—A Creative Response' by Joan Hambidge (pp. 172–83); 'The Queer Writes Back: Australia' by David Coad (pp. 184–98); 'The Transgendered Nation: Intersexions between the Nation-State and the Transsexual Subject' by Chantal Zabus (pp. 201–16); 'Imperial Diversity: War, Post-humanism, and the Futures of Postcolonial Studies' by Mike Hill (pp. 217–34); and 'Future Thinking: Postcolonial Utopianism' by Bill Ashcroft (pp. 235–53). Each contribution is followed by notes and a listing of works cited, and following detailed information on 'Contributors' (pp. 255–9) there is a double-columned, name-orientated index (pp. 261–5).

Finally, highly recommended is Theodore Ziolkowski's *The Alchemist in Literature: From Dante to the Present*. In his 'Introduction, or *Materia Prima*' (pp. 1–15), Ziolkowski writes that his concern is 'not with ... primary alchemistic texts but with literary works in which alchemists play a role. They constitute a significantly more restricted group than [the] large, diffuse body of literary texts that exploit alchemical imagery' (p. 15). Chronologically organized, authors writing in English discussed range from Chaucer, Gower, Ben Jonson, Donne, Vaughan and Milton, to William Godwin, Shelley, Scott, and, interestingly among the Romantics and Victorians, Henry Hart Milman's *Fazio: A Tragedy* [1818] (see pp. 81–3). Washington Irving, Poe, Hawthorne, and H.P. Lovecraft are amongst the American writers discussed, as are later poets such as Pound and H.D., and Dan Brown's fictional *The Da Vinci Code*. Other writers and their work include Conan Doyle's *Micah Clarke*, Lindsay Clarke's *The Chymical Wedding*, and Peter Ackroyd's *The House of Doctor Dee* amongst others. In his concluding paragraph Ziolkowski asks 'Why has alchemy, apart from the general lure of the occult and regardless of the particular historical circumstances over the centuries, exerted its special appeal ... alchemy pledges to change the present reality: to transmute base metals into gold and bring wealth; or to produce elixirs that restore health and youthful vigor. It is this hope for change ... that for centuries has lured otherwise reasonable people to the often unrealistic promises of the alchemists' (p. 232). Note documentation is provided at the foot of the page of text; there is an author-based, double-columned index (pp. 233–7).

Mention should be made of a sumptuous volume. *Riches of the Rylands: The Special Collections of the University of Manchester Library*, with a foreword by

Jan Wilkinson, is edited by Rachel Beckett and three others, and is replete with full-colour plates. In large format, 11.2 inches in height and 8¾ inches in width, typeset in Adobe Arno Pro with reproductions of feathered front and endpapers including in the front the John Rylands Library 1894 armorial book plate, as Jan Wilkinson explains in her foreword, the volume 'explores and celebrates the remarkable Special Collections of rare books, manuscripts, archives and visual materials to be found within the University of Manchester Library'. These have their genesis in 'the superlative collections purchased by Enriqueta Rylands for the magnificent library she founded as a memorial to her husband John' (p. vii) in the late nineteenth century and merged with the University of Manchester in 1972. *Riches of the Rylands* encompasses more than 150 major 'items described in each chapter ... selected in order to illustrate the strength and variety of the books, manuscripts, archives, maps and visual materials held in this great library' (p. ix). John R. Hodgson's detailed introduction (pp. 1–19) discusses the Cuban-born Enriqueta Rylands' (1843–1908) collections and the development of the library following her death and her 'generous endowment' (p. 6) to the library she had created. A taste of this is reflected in the individual chapters, each fully illustrated. Regrettably, in including this record there isn't space to mention each of the eighty or so individual contributor to sections, but only the name/s of the person/s who appears in the 'Contents' listing (pp. v–vi): 'Beyond Books: From Papyrus to Pixels' by Stella K. Halkyard (pp. 20–43), including the 'Grafton Portrait' of Shakespeare (pp. 28–9) and 'objects with associational value' such as 'Walt Whitman's metal pen nib' (p. 36); 'Through Painted Windows: The Art of Illumination' by John R. Hodgson (pp. 44–67); 'First Impressions: The Early Years of European Printing' by Julianne Simpson (pp. 68–87); 'Master Binders and Their Craft' by Caroline Checkley-Scott and John R. Hodgson (pp. 88–107), concluding with a fascinating decorative illustrated 'Prize binding' by Enid Marx entitled 'Some Birds and Beasts and Their Feasts: An Alphabet of Wood Engravings' produced at Oldham, a place not usually associated with prize bindings, by the Incline Press in 1997 and bound by Dominic Riley in 2007 (pp. 106–7); '"A definite claim to beauty": The Private Presses' by John R. Hodgson (pp. 108–23), beginning with a sample from Thomas James Cobden Sanderson's (1840–1922) Doves Press (1903–5) of *The English Bible* (pp. 116–17); and 'Envisioning Space: Maps and Atlases' by Donna M. Sherman (pp. 124–47), which 'reveals the fascination that many of us have with these objects' (p. 125). There are two contributions introduced by Elizabeth Gow: '"Lively oracles of God": The Bible from Antiquity to Modernity' (pp. 148–67) and '"So many paths": Religious Traditions across the World' (pp. 168–85); '"On the shoulders of giants": Science, Technology and Medicine' has three named contributors, James N. Peters, Julianne Simpson, and Janet L. Wallwork (pp. 186–205); '"Between the covers": A Literary Miscellany' by Fran Baker (pp. 206–19) contains her description of the 1609 copy of 'Shakespeare's sonnets in print' (pp. 214–15), and concludes with Michael Schmidt's 'Carcanet Nobel Laureates and the work of Stephen Raw' (pp. 228–9)—this section also contains descriptions of 'Johnson and Shakespeare' by William Hutchings (pp. 216–17), Alan Shelston writes on Elizabeth Gaskell (pp. 218–19), Fran Baker on Wilfred Owen and Edmund

Blunden (pp. 220–1), Grevel Lindop on Norman Nicholson (pp. 222–3), Robyn Marsack on Edwin Morgan (pp. 224–5), and Elaine Feinstein—also with accompanying illustration—on 'Translation in Practice: Elaine Feinstein and Marina Tsvetaeva' (pp. 226–7). The final three contributions concern the areas of 'Illustrated Imaginative Children's Literature' by Ian Rogerson (pp. 230–45); 'Power, Politics and Propaganda: The Story of Britain from 1215' by Dorothy J. Clayton (pp. 246–65); and 'Manchester: Local Connections' by Julie Ramwell (pp. 266–85). 'Notes on Contributors' (pp. 287–92) are followed by 'Further Reading' (pp. 293–300) arranged by chapter and enumerative. This fascinating, informative, well-produced collection concludes with a detailed double-columned index (pp. 301–8).

Robert Appelbaum's *Terrorism Before the Letter: Mythography and Political Violence in England, Scotland, and France 1559–1642* 'is a book not so much about the violent struggles themselves as those ideas and mythical musings that intersected with them. It is about the literature of terrorism before the letter, fiction and none—fiction, legendary and contemporary, proactive and reflective, amusing or didactic, in favor or against the violence, or somewhere in between', and historically the book is focused on 'the sixteenth and seventeenth centuries in England, Scotland and France'. An appendix to the end of the first chapter, 'A Chronology of Major Events and Literary Works' (pp. 66–70), reveals that English and Scottish authors and works discussed from the period include, in chronological order, Thomas Norton and Thomas Sackville, *Gorboduc* (pp. 140–2), George Buchanan (pp. 169–71), Thomas Lodge (pp. 55, 119), Christopher Marlowe (pp. 80–2, 149–50, 225–6), Shakespeare, especially *Julius Caesar* (pp. 74–7, 88–9, and *passim*), George Chapman (pp. 201–4), Thomas Middleton (pp. 5–6, 194–201), Thomas Dekker (pp. 54, 119–20), Ben Jonson (pp. 25, 29, 56, and *passim*), John Milton (pp. 95–101, and *passim*), James Shirley (pp. 117–18), and Francis Quarles (pp. 214–18), amongst others. Following a lengthy explanatory introduction (pp. 1–38), chapters in Appelbaum's challenging text are headed 'Terrorism Before the Letter' (pp. 39–70), 'The Act' (pp. 71–99), 'Agents' (pp. 100–32), 'Scene' (pp. 133–63), 'Agency' (pp. 164–92), and 'Purpose' (pp. 193–222), followed by 'A Brief Conclusion' (pp. 223–7). Notation is at the foot of Appelbaum's page. There is an enumerative, alphabetically arranged bibliography divided into 'Primary Texts' (pp. 229–41) and 'Secondary Texts' (pp. 241–62), and a double-columned index (pp. 263–70) that curiously truncates entries under the letter 'K', which concludes with the Hegelian interpreter 'Kojève, Alexandre' (p. 266).

Mention should be made too of a monograph whose compass extends over eighty-five years and two centuries. David Deutsch, in his introduction 'Approaches to Classical Music in British Literature, 1870–1945: Theory and Practice' (pp. 1–15) to his *British Literature and Classical Music: Cultural Contexts 1870–1945*, writes that his aim is 'to demonstrate the pervasive and even the popular reformist associations of classical music within British literature and society during' the period from 1870 to 1945 (p. 13). In his first chapter, 'The Liberalization of Music in Aesthetic Literature: Pater and Oxford' (pp. 17–53), he argues that 'authors, particularly those working in Oxford, a nerve-centre for Britain's scholastic and literary production, employed music as an elevated trope for forming an educated, tolerant, and morally harmonious society'. In chapter 2, 'Modernism's Distinctive Musical Rhetoric: Eliot, Huxley, and Woolf', Deutsch demonstrates 'how early-twentieth-century middle-class literati intensify the intellectual connotations of classical music, but appropriate tropes of attaining gentility and social advancement through music for their own benefit'. However, 'a counter-perspective to this exclusivist rhetoric' is provided in his third chapter, 'The Musical Refinement of the Lower-Middle and Working Classes: Bennett, Lawrence, and Their Contemporaries', in which he explores 'how Britain's expanding musical culture offered popular, at times consciously anti-modern-ist authors aesthetic opportunities to assert the intelligence and the refinement of more marginalized musical amateurs'. His fourth chapter, 'Distinguishing a Musical Homoeroticism: Pater, Forster, and Their Aesthetic Descendants', examines 'how myriad British writers capitalized upon Britain's increasingly musical society and worked to legitimize and to validate same-sex-desiring individuals by portraying them as particularly musical'. In these chapters Deutsch explains the ways in which 'British society and British writers frequently used German music to characterize British cultural identities'. In his fifth chapter, 'Classical Music, Cosmopolitanism, and War: From Authors to Audiences', he considers 'how, in the midst of increasing commercial rivalries, political tensions, and military hostilities, Britain's cosmopolitan musical culture offered authors a non-incendiary trope for discussing the complex relationship between Britain and Germany'. In his 'Conclusion: A Literary Coda: Classical Music in British Literature' he 'recapitulates the liberal humanistic legacy embodied in Britain's musical culture that extends from Pater's neo-Platonic ideals presented in the 1870s to W.H. Auden's cautiously optimistic revitalization of these ideals in his "New Year," letter written in 1941' (p. 14). Footnote documentation is at the end of each chapter. There is an extensive enumerative listing of works cited (pp. 251–62) and a detailed, most helpful index (pp. 253–62) to this important, fascinating work.

Finally, *Victorian Literature and Culture* may not be the most obvious journal in which to find material on bibliography and textual studies. However, attention should be drawn to David C. Hanson's 'Sentiment and Materiality in Late Victorian Book Collecting' (*VLC* 43[2015] 758–820), whose 'aim is to demonstrate, first, the complexity of the fin-de-siècle collector's sentiment in grappling with materiality, a complexity that is scuttled in indictments of the sentimental element in Victorian collecting by modernists and New Bibliographers. Next, stepping back to the 1870s' Hanson traces 'how this sentiment was nourished especially by collectors' interest in nineteenth-century authors' juvenilia' (p. 786).

**Books Reviewed**

Aarons, Victoria, Avinoam J. Patt, and Mark Shechner, eds. *The New Diaspora: The Changing Landscape of American Jewish Fiction*. WSUP. [2015] pp. xiv + 578. $35.99 ISBN 9 7808 1434 0554.

Albright, Daniel. *Putting Modernism Together: Literature, Music, and Painting 1872–1927*. JHUP. [2015] pp. xii + 332. $29.95 ISBN 9 7814 2141 6441.

Allmendinger, Blake, ed. *A History of California Literature*. CUP. [2015] pp. xii + 434. $120 ISBN 9 7811 0705 2093.

Anjaria, Ulka, ed. *A History of the Indian Novel in English*. CUP. [2015] pp. xviii + 430. $120 ISBN 9 7811 0707 9960.

Appelbaum, Robert. *Terrorism Before the Letter: Mythography and Political Violence in England, Scotland, and France 1559–1642*. OUP. [2015] pp. xii + 276. $100 ISBN 9 7801 9874 5761.

Armstrong, Julie Buckner, ed. *The Cambridge Companion to American Civil Rights Literature*. CUP. [2015] pp. xiv + 216. $29.99 ISBN 9 7811 0763 5647.

Baron, Naomi S. *Words on Screen: The Fate of Reading in a Digital World*. OUPAm. [2015] pp. xvi + 304. $24.95 ISBN 9 7801 9931 5765.

Barrett, Frank. *Treasured Island*. AAPublishing. [2105] pp. 272. $27.95 ISBN 9 7807 4957 7070.

Bastable, Jonathan, and Hannah McGill, eds. *The 21st-Century Novel: Notes from the Edinburgh World Writers' Conference*. EdinUP. [2014] pp. 352. $32 ISBN 9 7807 4869 8349.

Baumbach, Sibylle. *Literature and Fascination*. PalMac. [2015] pp. viii + 320. $90 ISBN 9 781 3753 8000.

Beckett, Rachel, ., eds. *Riches of the Rylands: The Special Collections of the University of Manchester Library*. Foreword Jan Wilkinson. ManUP. [2015] pp. x + 310. £25 ISBN 9 7807 1909 6358.

Bennett, Michael Y. *The Cambridge Introduction to Theatre and Literature of the Absurd*. CUP. [2015] pp. x + 164. $27.99 ISBN 9 7811 0763 5517.

Bentley, G.E. Jr. *The Edwardses of Halifax: The Making and Selling of Beautiful Books in London and Halifax, 1749–1826*. UTorP. [2015] pp. xxiv + 284. $48.75 ISBN 9 7814 4264 5189.

Bentley, Nick, Nick Hubble, and Leigh Wilson, eds. *The 2000s: A Decade of Contemporary British Fiction*. Bloomsbury. [2015] pp. xii + 298. $140 ISBN 9 7814 4111 2156.

Benton, Michael. *Towards a Poetics of Literary Biography*. PalMac. [2015] pp. xii + 168. $90 ISBN 9 7811 3754 9570.

Berberich, Christine, ed. *The Bloomsbury Introduction to Popular Fiction*. Bloomsbury. [2015] pp. xvi + 328. £19.99 ISBN 9 7814 4113 4318.

Berry, Simon. *Applauding Thunder: Life, Work, and Critics of Alexander Smith*. For the Right Reasons Press. [2013] pp. 240. £12.99 ISBN 9 7819 0578 7593.

Bewell, Alan, N.T. Kortenaar, and G. Warkentin, eds. *Educating the Imagination: Northrop Frye, Past, Present, and Future*. McG–QUP. [2015] pp. x + 278. $37.95 ISBN 9 7807 7354 5724.

Booker, M. Keith, ed. *Literature and Politics Today: The Political Nature of Modern Fiction, Poetry and Drama*. ABC-CLIO. [2015] pp. 377. $89 ISBN 9 7816 1069 9358.

Brannigan, John. *Archipelagic Modernism: Literature in the Irish and British Isles, 1890–1970*. EdinUP. [2015] pp. viii + 288. $35 ISBN 9 7807 4864 3356.

Brauner, David, and Axel Stähler, eds. *The Edinburgh Companion to Modern Jewish Fiction*. EdinUP. [2015] pp. xviii + 446. £150 ISBN 9 7807 4864 6159.

Braziller, George. *Encounters: My Life in Publishing*. George Braziller. [2015] pp. 152. $19.95 ISBN 9 7808 0760 0160.

Brock, Stuart, and Anthony Everett, eds. *Fictional Objects*. OUP. [2015] pp. viii + 312. $75 ISBN 9 7801 9873 5595.

Burwick, Frederick, and Manushag N. Powell. *British Pirates in Print and Performance*. PalMac. [2015] pp. x + 234. $74.99 ISBN 9 7811 3733 9911.

Carville, Conor, and Mark Nixon, eds. *'Beginning of the Murmur': Archival Pre-texts and Other Sources [Samuel Beckett Today/Aujourd'hui]*. Brill/Rodopi. [2015] pp. 244. $95 ISBN 9 7890 0430 9913.

Cascardi, Anthony J. *The Cambridge Introduction to Literature and Philosophy*. CUP. [2014] pp. viii + 262. $29.99 ISBN 9 7805 2128 1232.

Castle, Gregory, ed. *A History of the Modernist Novel*. CUP. [2015] pp. xvi + 536. $115 ISBN 9 7811 0703 4952.

Chen, John A. Ming, and Yuhua Ji. *Marxism and 20th-Century English-Canadian Novels: A New Approach to Social Realism*. Springer.[2015] pp. xxviii + 302. $129 ISBN 9 7836 6246 3499.

Cheney, Patrick, and Philip Hardie, eds. *The Oxford History of Classical Reception in English Literature, vol. 2: 1558–1660*. OUP. [2015] pp. xiv + 798. $215 ISBN 9 7801 9954 7555.

Cheung, King-Kok, ed. *An Interethnic Companion to Asian American Literature*. CUP. [1997] pp. xii + 414. $64.99 ISBN 9 7805 2144 7909.

Clapinson, Mary. *A Brief History of the Bodleian Library*. Bodleian. [2015] pp. vi + 202. £12.99 ISBN 9 7818 5124 2733.

Cochran, Peter. *Manfred: An Edition of Byron's Manuscripts and a Collection of Essays*. CambridgeSP. [2015] pp. x + 264. £47.99 ISBN 9 7814 4387 2072.

Cooke, Stewart, ed. *The Additional Journals and Letters of Frances Burney, vol. 1: 1784–1786*. OUP. [2015] pp. xliv + 488. $200 ISBN 9 7801 9965 8114.

Crawford, Alice, ed. *The Meaning of the Library: A Cultural History*. PrincetonUP. [2015] pp. xxxii + 302. $35 ISBN 9 7806 9116 6391.

Culler, Jonathan. *Theory of the Lyric*. HarvardUP. [2015] pp. xii + 400. $39.95 ISBN 9 7806 7474 4264.

Darnton, Robert. *Censors at Work: How States Shaped Literature*. BL. [2014] pp. 318. £25 ISBN 9 7807 1235 7616.

Davis, Caroline, and David Johnson, eds. *The Book in Africa: Critical Debates*. PalMac. [2015] pp. xii + 282. $95 ISBN 9 7811 3740 1618.

Deutsch, David. *British Literature and Classical Music: Cultural Contents 1870–1945*. Bloomsbury. [2015] pp. x + 262. $104 ISBN 9 7814 7423 5815.

Duncan-Jones, Katherine. *Portraits of Shakespeare*. Bodleian. [2015] pp. x + 126. £14.99 ISBN 9 7818 5124 4058.

Dussinger, John A., ed. *Samuel Richardson: Correspondence with Sarah Wescomb, Frances Grainger and Laetitia Pilkington*. CUP. [2015] pp. lxx + 398. $130 ISBN 9 7805 2183 0348.

Earhart, Amy E. *Traces of the Old Uses of the New: The Emergence of Digital Literary Studies*. UMichP. [2015] pp. x + 162. $34.95 ISBN 9 7804 7205 2783.

Edgecombe, Rodney Stenning. *A Reader's Guide to the Narrative and Lyric Poetry of Thomas Lovell Beddoes*. CambridgeSP. [2015] pp. viii + 494. £57.95 ISBN 9 7814 4388 2569.

Elbert, Monika M., and Lesley Ginsberg. *Romantic Education in Nineteenth-Century American Literature: National and Transatlantic Contexts.* Routledge. [2015] pp. xii + 292. $98.84 ISBN 9 7811 3878 1122.

Errington, Philip W. J.K. *Rowling: A Bibliography 1997–2013.* Bloomsbury. [2015] pp. xxviii + 516. $128 ISBN 9 7818 4966 9740.

Felluga, Dino Franco. *Critical Theory: The Key Concepts.* Routledge. [2015] pp. xxxviii + 368. $27.55 ISBN 9 7804 1569 5657.

Felsenstein, Frank, and James J. Connolly. *What Middletown Read: Print Culture in an American Small City. A Revealing Portrait of Reading in the Quintessential American Town.* UMassP. [2015] pp. xvi + 304. $28.95 ISBN 9 7816 2534 1419.

Fernald, Anne E., ed. *Mrs Dalloway*, by Virginia Woolf. CUP. [2015] pp. civ + 392. $150 ISBN 9 7811 0702 8784.

Fredeman. William E., ed. *The Correspondence of Dante Gabriel Rossetti, vol. 10: Index, Undated Letters and Bibliography.* Brewer. [2015] pp. xxviii + 368. $220 ISBN 9 7818 4384 3956.

Gailey, Amanda. *Proofs of Genius: Collected Editions from the American Revolution to the Digital Age.* UMichP. [2015] pp. ix + 162. $29.95 ISBN 9 7804 7205 2752.

Garrard, Greg, ed. *The Oxford Handbook of Ecocriticism.* OUPAm. [2014] pp. xx + 578. $160 ISBN 9 7801 9974 2929.

Gifford, James, ed. *From the Elephant's Back: Collected Essays & Travel Writings*, by Lawrence Durrell. UAlbertaP. [2015] pp. xxxii + 408. $39.95 ISBN 9 7817 7212 0516.

Goldsby, Jacqueline, ed. *The Autobiography of an Ex-Colored Man*, by James Weldon Johnson. Authoritative Text; Contexts; Criticism. Norton. [2015] pp. lx + 446. $13.12 ISBN 9 7803 9397 2863.

Golston, Michael. *Poetic Machinations: Allegory, Surrealism, and Postmodern Forms.* ColUP. [2015] pp. xviii + 254. $60 ISBN 9 7802 3116 4306.

Gray, Jeffrey, Mary McAleer Balkun, and James McCorkle, eds. *American Poets and Poetry from the Colonial Era to the Present.* 2 vols. Greenwood/ABC-CLIO. [2015] pp. xxx + 724. $189 ISBN 9 7816 1069 8313.

Gupta, Suman. *Consumable Texts in Contemporary India: Uncultured Books and Bibliographical Sociology.* PalMac. [2015] pp. x + 204. $95 ISBN 9 7811 3748 9289.

Hahn, Daniel. *The Oxford Companion to Children's Literature.* . OUP. [2015] pp. xiv + 674. £30 ISBN 9 7801 9969 5140.

Hall, Geoff. *Literature in Language Education* PalMac. [2015] pp. xii + 342. $39.99 ISBN 9 7811 3733 1830.

Hammill, Faye, and Michelle Smith. *Magazines, Travel, and Middlebrow Culture: Canadian Periodicals in English and French, 1925–1960.* UAlbertaP. [2015] pp. xii + 212 + illust. $49.95 ISBN 9 7817 7212 0837.

Harris, Katherine D. *Forget Me Not: The Rise of the British Literary Annual 1832-1835.* OhioUP. [2015] pp. 410. $72 ISBN 9 7808 2142 1369.

Hart, Jonathan. *The Poetics of Otherness: War, Trauma, and Literature.* PalMac. [2015] pp. xvi + 264. $90 ISBN 9 7811 3748 2631.

Hayes, Kevin J., ed. *A History of Virginia Literature.* CUP. [2015] pp. xvi + 420. $120 ISBN 9 7811 0705 7777.

Hellinga, Lotte. *Texts in Transit: Manuscript to Proof and Print in the Fifteenth Century*. Brill. [2014] pp. xiv + 452. $193 ISBN 9 7890 0427 7168.

Hewitt, Ben. *Byron, Shelley, and Goethe's 'Faust': An Epic Connection*. Legenda. [2015] pp. xii + 196. $99 ISBN 9 7819 0966 2414.

Higgins, Lesley, ed. *The Collected Works of Gerard Manley Hopkins: Diaries, Journals and Notebooks*, vol. 3. OUP. [2015] pp. i + 726. $150 ISBN 9 7801 9953 4005.

Hill, Mike, and Warren Montag. *The Other Adam Smith*. StanfordUP. [2015] pp. xii + 402. $29.95 ISBN 9 7808 0479 2943.

Hillman, David, and Ulrika Maude, eds. *The Cambridge Companion to the Body in Literature*. CUP. [2015] pp. xiv + 282. $27.99 ISBN 9 7811 0764 4397.

Hinojosa, Lynne W. *Puritanism and Modernist Novels: From Moral Character to the Ethical Self*. OSUP. [2015] pp. x + 220. $59.95 ISBN 9 7808 1421 2738.

Holzenberg, Eric J., and Arthur L. Schwarz, curators. *The Grolier Club Collects II: Books, Manuscripts & Works on Paper from the Collections of Grolier Club*. GroC. [2015] pp. 184. $75 ISBN 9 7816 0583 0636.

Hubble, Nick, Philip Tew, and Leigh Wilson, eds. *The 1990s: A Decade of Contemporary British Fiction*. Bloomsbury. [2015] pp. xvi + 304. $140 ISBN 9 7814 4117 2587.

Hyland, Ken. *Academic Publishing: Issues and Challenges in the Construction of Knowledge*. OUP. [2015] pp. xiv + 242. $40.73 ISBN 9 7801 9442 3953.

Jackson, H.J. *Those Who Write for Immortality: Romantic Reputations and the Dream of Lasting Fame*. YaleUP. [2015] pp. xiv + 298. $35 ISBN 9 7803 0017 4793.

Jones, Edward, ed. *A Concise Companion to the Study of Manuscripts, Printed Books, and the Production of Early Modern Texts. A Festschrift for Gordon Campbell*. Wiley-Blackwell. [2015] pp. xvi + 368. $130 ISBN 9 7811 1863 5292.

Jost, Jacob Sider. *Prose Immortality 1711–1819*. UPVirginia. [2015] pp. x + 246. $45 ISBN 9 7808 1393 6802.

Keighren, Innes M., Charles W.J. Withers, and Bill Bell. *Travels into Print: Exploration, Writing, and Publishing with John Murray, 1773–1859*. UChicP. [2015] pp. xiv + 370. £31.50 ISBN 9 7802 2642 9533.

Kells, Stuart. *Penguin and the Lane Brothers: The Untold Story of a Publishing Revolution*. Black. [2015] pp. xii + 340. $39.99 ISBN 9 7818 6395 7571.

Kerr, Donald Jackson. *Hocken: Prince of Collectors*. UOtagoP. [2015] pp. 424. $47.95 ISBN 9 7818 7757 8663.

Kuen, Julia, and Paul Smethurst, eds. *New Directions in Travel Writing Studies*. PalMac. [2015] pp. xiv + 328. $90 ISBN 9 7811 3745 7578.

Leask, Nigel, ed. *The Oxford Edition of the Works of Robert Burns, vol. 1: Commonplace Books, Tour Journals, and Miscellaneous Prose*. OUP. [2014] pp. xvi + 432. $200 ISBN 9 7801 9960 3716.

Leigh, John. *Touché: The Duel in Literature*. HarvardUP. [2015] pp. x + 340. $35 ISBN 9 7806 7450 4387.

Lesser, Zachary. *'Hamlet' After Q1: An Uncanny History of the Shakespearean Text*. UPennP. [2015] pp. x + 292. £39 ISBN 9 7808 1224 6612.

Löffler, Philipp. *Pluralist Desires: Contemporary Historical Fiction and the End of the Cold War*. CamdenH. [2015] pp. viii + 182. $85 ISBN 9 7815 7113 9528.

Looser, Devoney, ed. *The Cambridge Companion to Women's Writing in the Romantic Period*. CUP. [2015] pp. xxx + 246. $29.99 ISBN 9 7811 0760 2557.

Loxley James, Anna Groundwater, and Julie Sanders, eds. *Ben Jonson's Walk to Scotland: An Annotated Edition of the 'Foot Voyage'*. CUP. [2015] pp. xviii + 238. $99 ISBN 9 7811 0700 3330.

Maclean, Caroline. *The Vogue for Russia: Modernism and the Unseen in Britain 1900–1930*. EdinUP. [2015] pp. viii + 206. $120 ISBN 9 7807 4864 7293.

Malory, Sir Thomas. *Whole Book of King Arthur and of His Noble Knights of the Round Table. Condensed and Modernized*, introd. Joseph Glaser. Hackett. [2015] pp. xviii + 348. $16 ISBN 9 7816 2466 3598.

Marks, Peter. *Imagining Surveillance: Eutopian and Dystopian Literature and Film*. EdinUP. [2015] pp. iv + 180. $120 ISBN 9 7814 7440 0190.

Marshik, Celia, ed. *The Cambridge Companion to Modernist Culture*. CUP. [2015] pp. xxii + 258. $80 ISBN 9 7811 0704 9260.

Maxwell, William J. *F.B. Eyes: How J. Edgar Hoover's Ghostreaders Framed African American Literature*. PrincetonUP. [2015] pp. xvi + 368. $29.95 ISBN 9 7806 9113 0200.

McKenna, Tony. *Art, Literature and Culture from a Marxist Perspective*. PalMac. [2015] pp. x + 216. $95 ISBN 9 7811 3752 6601.

Mentz, Steve. *Shipwreck Modernity: Ecologies of Globalization, 1550–1719*. UMinnP. [2015] pp. xxxiv + 230. $30 ISBN 9 7808 1669 1067.

Milhous, Judith, and Robert D. Hume. *The Publication of Plays in London 1660–1800: Playwrights, Publishers and the Market*. BL. [2015] pp. xxvi + 484. £50 ISBN 9 7807 1235 7739.

Morris, Ian, and Joanne Diaz, eds. *The Little Magazine in Contemporary America*. UChicP. [2015] pp. xx + 236. $27.50 ISBN 9 7802 2612 0492.

Murphy, Terence Patrick. *From Fairy Tale to Film Screenplay: Working with Plot Genotypes*. PalMac. [2015] pp. xii + 198. $95 ISBN 9 7811 3755 2020.

Murphy, Terence Patrick. *The Fairytale and Plot Structure*. PalMac. [2015] pp. xx + 208. $90 ISBN 9 7811 3754 7071.

Neill, Michael, ed. *The Duchess of Malfi*, by John Webster. Authoritative Text; Contexts; Criticism. Norton. [2015] pp. xlii + 406. $13.75 ISBN 9 7803 9392 3254.

O'Brien, Sharon, ed. *My Ántonia*, by Willa Cather. Authoritative Text; Contexts; Criticism. Norton. [2015] pp. xxvi + 512. $15 ISBN 9 7803 9396 7906.

O'Neill, Michael, Mark Sandy, and Sarah Wootton, eds. *The Persistence of Beauty: Victorians to Moderns*. P&C. [2015] pp. xii + 196. $99 ISBN 9 7818 4893 5112.

Orgel, Stephen. *The Reader in the Book: A Study of Spaces and Traces*. OUP. [2015] pp. xiv + 178. £25 ISBN 9 7801 9873 7568.

Orr, Jennifer. *Literary Networks and Dissenting Print Culture in Romantic-Period Ireland*. PalMac. [2015] pp. xviii + 282. $90 ISBN 9 7811 3747 1529.

Parikh, Crystal, and Daniel Y. Kim, eds. *The Cambridge Companion to Asian American Literature*. CUP. [2015] pp. xxiv + 248. $89.99 ISBN 9 7811 0709 5175.

Parrinder, Patrick. *Utopian Literature and Science: From the Scientific Revolution to 'Brave New World' and Beyond*. PalMac. [2015] pp. x + 224. $90 ISBN 9 7811 3745 6779.

Patell, Cyrus R.K. *Cosmopolitanism and the Literary Imagination*. PalMac. [2015] pp. xii + 192. $90 ISBN 9 7803 1223 3877.

Pearce, Jim, Ward J. Risvold, and Nathan Dixon, eds. *Renaissance Papers 2014*. Southeastern Renaissance Conference. CamdenH. [2015] pp. viii + 140. $55 ISBN 9 7815 7113 9283.

Peters, John G., ed. *The Secret Sharer and Other Stories* by Joseph Conrad. Authoritative Text; Contexts; Criticism. Norton. [2015] pp. xx + 600. $15.62 ISBN 9 7803 9393 6339.

Pope, Ged. *Reading London's Suburbs: From Charles Dickens to Zadie Smith*. PalMac. [2015] pp. xvi + 246. $90 ISBN 9 7811 3734 2454.

Punday, Daniel. *Computing As Writing*. UMinnP. [2015] pp. xvi + 184. $27 ISBN 9 7808 1669 7021.

Rabaté, Jean-Michel. *The Cambridge Introduction to Literature and Psychoanalysis*. CUP. [2014] pp. viii + 264. $27.99 ISBN 9 7811 0742 3916.

Rezek, Joseph. *London and the Making of Provincial Literature: Aesthetics and the Transatlantic Book Trade, 1800–1850*. UPennP. [2015] pp. viii + 288. $59.95 ISBN 9 7808 1224 7343.

Ricketts, Rita. *Scholars, Poets, and Radicals: Discovering Forgotten Lives in the Blackwell Collections*. Bodleian. [2015] pp. xviii + 302. £30 ISBN 9 7818 5124 4256.

Ricks, Christopher, and Jim McCue, eds. *The Poems of T.S. Eliot, vol. 1: Collected and Uncollected Poems*. JHUP. [2015] pp. xxvi + 1,318. $44.95 ISBN 9 7814 2142 0172.

Ricks, Christopher, and Jim McCue, eds. *The Poems of T.S. Eliot, vol. 2: Practical Cats and Further Verses*. JHUP. [2015] pp. xx + 668. $39.95 ISBN 9 7814 2142 0189.

Rogers, Brett M., and Benjamin Eldon Stevens, eds. *Classical Traditions in Science Fiction*. OUP. [2015] pp. xvi + 380. $35 ISBN 9 7801 9022 8330.

Sabor, Peter, ed. *The Cambridge Companion to 'Emma'*. CUP .[2015] pp. xx + 228. $25.99 ISBN 9 7811 0744 2993.

Sassi, Carla, ed. *The International Companion to Scottish Poetry*. ScotLitInt. [2015] pp. xii + 306. £14.95 ISBN 9 7819 0898 0151.

Schellenberg, Betty A., ed. *Samuel Richardson Correspondence Primarily on 'Sir Charles Grandison' (1750–1754)*. CUP. [2015] pp. xlviii + 288. $130 ISBN 9 7805 2183 2182.

Schneider, Thomas E., ed. *Selected Writings of James Fitzjames Stephen: On Society, Religion, and Government*. OUP. [2015] pp. xxviii + 316. £110 ISBN 9 7801 9958 5717.

Seddon, Tony. *The Evolution of Type: A Graphic Guide to 100 Landmark Typefaces: Examining Letters From Metal Type to Open Type*. Firefly Books. [2015] pp. 256. $29.95 ISBN 9 7817 7085 5045.

Sharpe, Will, and Erin Sullivan, eds. *The Oxford Companion to Shakespeare*, general editors Michael Dobson and Stanley Wells. . OUP. [2015] pp. xxx + 574. £32.40 ISBN 9 7801 9870 8735.

Slinn, Judy, Sebastian Carter, and Richard Southall, with Andrew Boag and Christopher Burke, eds. *History of the Monotype Corporation*. Printing Historical Society and Vanbrugh Press. [2014] pp. 432. £50 ISBN 9 7809 9305 1005.

Smith, Emma. *The Making of Shakespeare's First Folio*. Bodleian. [2015] pp. x + 182. £20 ISBN 9 7818 5124 4423.

Sodeman, Melissa. *Sentimental Memorials: Women and the Novel in Literary History*. StanfordUP. [2015] pp. xii + 188. $50 ISBN 9 7808 0479 1328.

Tanselle, G. Thomas. *Portraits & Reviews*. UVirginiaP. [2015] pp. xiv + 488. $55 ISBN 9 7818 8363 1161.

Tatar, Maria, ed. *The Cambridge Companion to Fairy Tales*. CUP. [2015] pp. xiv + 258. $29.99 ISBN 9 7811 0763 4879.

Thomson, Ellen Mazur. *Aesthetic Tracts: Innovation in Late-Nineteenth-Century Book Design*. OakK. [2015] pp. xiv + 178. $55 ISBN 9 7815 8456 3365.

Toner, Anne. *Ellipsis in English Literature: Signs of Omission*. CUP. [2015] pp. x + 262. $95 ISBN 9 7811 0707 3012.

Twiddy, Iain. *Cancer Poetry*. PalMac. [2015] pp. xii + 236. $90 ISBN 9 7811 3736 1998.

Vaisey, David. *Bodleian Library Treasures*. Bodleian. [2015] pp. 232. £20 ISBN 9 7818 5124 4089.

Vance, Norman, and Jennifer Wallace, eds. *The Oxford History of Classical Reception in English Literature, vol. 4: 1790–1880*. OUP. [2015] pp. xiv + 752. $225 ISBN 9 7801 9959 4603.

Vendler, Helen. *The Ocean, the Bird and the Scholar: Essays on Poets and Poetry*. HarvardUP. [2015] pp. x + 452. £25.95 ISBN 9 7806 7473 6566.

Watson, Rowan, Elizabeth James, and Julius Bryant, eds. *Word & Image: Art, Books and Design from the National Art Library*. V&A. [2015] pp. 176. £25 ISBN 9 7818 5177 8089.

Welge, Jobst. *Genealogical Fictions: Cultural Periphery and Historical Change in the Modern Novel*. JHUP. [2015] pp. xii + 260. $54.95 ISBN 9 7814 2141 4355.

Whitfield, Peter. *Mapping Shakespeare's World*. Bodleian. [2015] pp. viii + 200. £25 ISBN 9 7818 5124 2573.

Wiggins, Martin, with Richardson Catherine. British Drama 1533–1642: A Catalogue, vol. 6: 1609–1616. OUP. [2015] pp. xiv + 594. $150 ISBN 9 7801 9873 9111.

Williams, Simon, ed. *The Cambridge Encyclopedia of Stage Actors and Acting*. CUP. [2015] pp. xiv + 698. $190 ISBN 9 7805 2176 9549.

Woodward, Guy. *Culture, Northern Ireland, & the Second World War*. OUP. [2015] pp. xiv + 274. $85 ISBN 9 7801 9871 6853.

Zabus, Chantal, ed., *The Future of Postcolonial Studies*. Routledge. [2015] pp. xii + 268. $145 ISBN 9 7804 1571 4266.

Ziolkowski, Theodore. *The Alchemist in Literature: From Dante to the Present*. OUP. [2015] pp. xiv + 238. $95 ISBN 9 7801 9874 6836.

# YWES Index of Critics

# YWES Authors and Subjects index

## Notes

(1) Material which has not been seen by contributors is not indexed.
(2) Authors such as John Sutherland, who are both authors of criticism and subjects of discussion, are listed in whichever index is appropriate for each reference.
(3) Author entries have subdivisions listed in the following order:
    (a) author's relationship with other authors
    (b) author's relationship with other subjects
    (c) author's characteristics
    (d) author's works (listed alphabetically)

(4) A page reference in **bold** represents a main entry for that particular subject.

*The Year's Work in English Studies, Volume 96 (2017)* © *The Author 2017. Published by Oxford University Press on behalf of the English Association. All rights reserved.*
*For Permissions, please email: journals.permissions@oup.com*
doi:10.1093/ywes/max023